Warman's®

D0580474

38th Edition

Antiques & Collectibles Price Guide

Edited by

Ellen T. Schroy

© 2004
by Krause Publications
All rights reserved.

No part of this publication may be reproduced or transmitted in any form or by any means, electronic or mechanical, including photocopy, recording, or any information storage and retrieval system, without permission in writing from the author, except by a reviewer who may quote brief passages in a critical article or review to be printed in a magazine or newspaper, or electronically transmitted on radio or television.

Published by

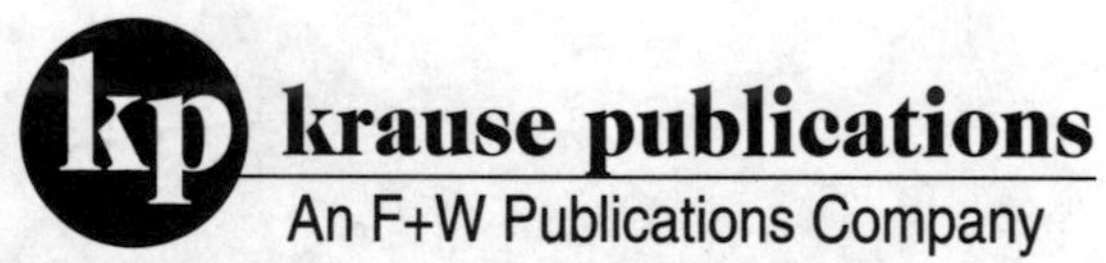

700 East State Street • Iola, WI 54990-0001
715-445-2214 • 888-457-2873
www.krause.com

Please call or write for our free catalog of publications.
Our toll-free number to place an order or obtain a free catalog is 800-258-0929
or please use our regular business telephone 715-445-2214.

Library of Congress Catalog Number: 1076-1985
ISBN: 0-87349-782-1

Printed in the United States of America

Introduction

Warman's: Serving the trade for more than 50 years

In 1994, *Warman's Antiques and Their Prices became Warman's Antiques and Collectibles Price Guide*. The latest edition is bigger than ever—physically, that is. Longtime ***Warman's*** users will find several new changes to this edition. Hopefully you will agree that they are improvements. The first big change is the three-column format, continued from the last edition. The second, and probably the most noticeable, is the dramatic increase in the number of photographs presented. This edition features close to 2,000 photos. The third change is enhanced introductions to several categories. These new introductions try to help the reader establish what historical period their object was created in through the use of clues, photographs, and line drawings.

In true *Warman's* spirit, we've strived to show different items in each category and include detailed descriptions to help explain what the object is, when it was made, and what it is worth. You can always expect more, never less, from *Warman's*.

Individuals in the trade refer to this book simply as *Warman's*, a fitting tribute to E. G. Warman and the product he created. *Warman's* has been around for more than 50 years. We are proud as peacocks that *Warman's* continues to establish the standards for general antiques and collectibles price guides in 2004, just as it did in 1972 when its first rival appeared on the scene.

Warman's, the antiques and collectibles "bible," covers objects made between 1700 and the present. Because it reflects market trends, *Warman's* has added more and more 20th-century material to each edition. Remember, 1900 was more than 100 years ago—the distant past to the new generation of 20-something and 30-something collectors. The general "antiques" market consists of antiques (for the purposes of this book, objects made before 1945), collectibles (objects of the post-World War II era that enjoy an established secondary market), and desirables (contemporary objects that are collected, but speculative in price). Although *Warman's* contains information on all three market segments, its greatest emphasis is on antiques and collectibles. In fact, this book is the essential field guide to the antiques and collectibles marketplace, which indicates that ***Warman's*** is much more than a list of object descriptions and prices. It is a basic guide to the field as a whole, providing you with the key information you need every time you encounter a new object or collecting category.

'Warman's is the Key'

Warman's provides the keys needed by auctioneers, collectors, dealers, and others to understand and deal with the complexities of the antiques and collectibles market. A price list is only one of many keys needed today. *Warman's* 38th edition contains many additional keys including histories, marks, and reproductions. Useful buying and collecting hints also are provided. Used properly, there are few doors these keys will not open. *Warman's* is designed to be your first key to the exciting world of antiques and collectibles. As you use the keys this book provides to advance further in your specialized collecting areas, *Warman's* hopes you will remember with fondness where you received your start. When you encounter items outside your area of specialty, remember *Warman's* remains your key to unlocking the information you need, just as it has in the past.

Organization

Listings: Objects are listed alphabetically by category, beginning with ABC Plates and ending with Zsolnay Pottery. If you have trouble identifying the category to which your object belongs, think about what the object is made of, or who made it, what marks are visible, and use the extensive index in the back of the book. It will guide you to the proper category. We have made the listings descriptive enough so that specific objects can be identified. We also emphasize items that are actively being sold in the marketplace. Some harder-to-find objects are included to demonstrate market spread—useful information worth considering when you have not traded actively in a category recently. Each year as the market changes, we carefully review our categories—adding, dropping, and combining to provide the most comprehensive coverage possible. *Warman's* quick response to developing trends in the marketplace is one of the prime reasons for its continued leadership in the field.

History: Collectors and dealers enhance their appreciation of objects by knowing something about their history. We present a capsule history for each category. In many cases, this history contains collecting hints or other useful information.

References: Krause Publications also publishes other *Warman's* titles. Each concentrates on a specific collecting group, e.g., American pottery and porcelain, Americana and collectibles, glass, and jewelry. Several are second or subsequent editions. Their expanded coverage compliments the information found in *Warman's Antiques and Collectibles Price Guide*. Many categories in the 38th edition feature the cover of a *Warman's* book where you can find more information and in-depth coverage on the subject. These books include *Warman's Advertising; Warman's American Furniture; Warman's American Pottery and Porcelain*, 2nd edition; *Warman's American Records; Warman's Civil War Collectibles, Warman's Coins and Paper Money; Warman's Depression Glass; Warman's English and Continental Pottery and Porcelain*, 3rd edition; *Warman's Glass*, 4th edition; *Warman's Jewelry*, 3rd edition; *Warman's Native American Collectibles*; and *Warman's Pattern Glass*, 2nd edition; *Warman's Sterling Silver Flatware*; and *Warman's Tobacco Collectibles*.

There are also several good publications collectors and dealers should be aware of to be knowledgeable about antiques and collectibles in general:

- *Antique & The Arts Weekly*, Bee Publishing Company, 5 Church Hill Road, Newton, CT 06470; http://www.thebee.com/aweb
- *Antique Review*, P.O. Box 538, Worthington, OH 43085
- *Antique Trader Weekly*, P.O. Box 1050, Dubuque, IA 52001; http://www.csmonline.com
- *AntiqueWeek*, P.O. Box 90, Knightstown, IN 46148; http://www.antiqueweek.com
- *Antiques* (The Magazine Antiques), 551 Fifth Ave., New York, NY 10017
- *Antiques & Collecting*, 1006 South Michigan Ave., Chicago, IL 60605
- *Maine Antique Digest*, P.O. Box 358, Waldoboro, ME 04572; http://www.maineantiquedigest.com
- *New England Antiques Journal*, 4 Church St., Ware, MA 01082
- *New York-Pennsylvania Collector*, Drawer C, Fishers, NY 14453

Space does not permit listing all the national and regional publications in the antiques and collectibles field. The above is a sampling.

Reproductions: Reproductions are a major concern to all collectors and dealers. Throughout this edition, boxes will alert you to known reproductions and keys to recognizing them. Most reproductions are unmarked; the newness of their appearance is often the best clue to uncovering them. Specific objects known to be reproduced are marked within the listings with an (*). The information is designed to serve as a reminder of past reproductions and prevent you from buying them, believing them to be period. We strongly recommend subscribing to *Antique & Collectors Reproduction News*, a monthly newsletter that reports on past and present reproductions, copycats, fantasies, and fakes. Send $32 for 12 issues to: ACRN, Box 12130, Des Moines, IA 50312-9403; (www.repronews.com). This newsletter has been published for several years. Consider buying all available back issues. The information they contain will be of service long into the future.

Index: A great deal of effort has been expended to make our index useful. Always begin by looking for the most specific reference. For example, if you have a piece of china, look first for the maker's name and second for the type. Remember, many objects can be classified in three or more categories. If at first you don't succeed, try, try again.

Black-and-white photographs: You may encounter a piece you cannot identify well enough to use the index. Consult the photographs and marks. If you own several editions of *Warman's*, you have available a valuable photographic reference to the antiques and collectibles field.

Price notes

In assigning prices, we assume the object is in very good condition; if otherwise, we note this in our description. It would be ideal to suggest that mint, or unused, examples of all objects exist. The reality is that objects from the past were used, whether they are glass, china, dolls, or toys. Because of this, some normal wear must be expected. In fact, if an object such as a piece of furniture does not show wear, its origins may be more suspect than if it does show wear. Whenever possible, we have tried to provide a broad listing of prices within a category so you have a "feel" for the market. We emphasize the middle range of prices within a category, while also listing some objects of high and low value to show market spread. We do not use ranges because they tend to confuse, rather than help, the collector and dealer. How do you determine if your object is at the high or low end of the range? There is a high degree of flexibility in pricing in the antiques field. If you want to set ranges, add or subtract 10 percent from our prices.

Price research

Everyone asks, "Where do you get your prices?"

They come from many sources. First, we rely on auctions. Auction houses and auctioneers do not always command the highest prices. If they did, why do so many dealers buy from them? The key to understanding auction prices is to know when a price is high or low in the range. We think we do this and do it well. The 38th edition represents a concentrated effort to contact more regional auction houses, both large and small. The cooperation has been outstanding and has resulted in an ever-growing pool of auction prices and trends to help us determine the most up-to-date auction prices.

Second, we work closely with dealers. We screen our contacts to make certain they have full knowledge of the market. Dealers make their living from selling antiques; they cannot afford to have a price guide that is not in touch with the market. More than 50 antiques and collectibles magazines, newspapers, and journals come into our office regularly. They are excellent barometers of what is moving and what is not. We don't hesitate to call an advertiser and ask if his listed merchandise sold. When the editorial staff is doing fieldwork, we identify ourselves. Our conversations with dealers and collectors around the country have enhanced this book. Teams from *Warman's* are in the field at antiques shows, malls, flea markets, and auctions recording prices and taking photographs. Collectors work closely with us. They are specialists whose devotion to research and accurate information is inspiring. Generally, they are not dealers. Whenever we have asked them for help, they have responded willingly and admirably.

Board of advisers

Our board of advisers is made up of specialists, both dealers and collectors, who feel a commitment to accurate information. You'll find their names listed in the front of the book. Several have authored a major reference work on their subject. Our esteemed board of advisers has increased in number and scope. Participants have all provided detailed information regarding the history and reference section of their particular area of expertise, as well as preparing price listings. Many furnished excellent photographs and even shared with us their thoughts on the state of the market. We are delighted to include those who are valuable members, officers, and founders of collectors' clubs. They are authors of books and articles, and many frequently lecture to groups about their specialties. Most of our advisers have been involved with antiques and collectibles for more than 20 years. Several are retired, and the antiques and collectibles business is a hobby that encompasses most of their free time. Others are a bit younger and either work full time or part time in the antiques and collectibles profession. One thing they all have in common is their enthusiasm for the antiques and collectibles marketplace. They are eager to share their knowledge with collectors. Many have developed wonderful friendships through their efforts and are enriched by them. If you wish to buy or sell an object in the field of expertise of any of our advisers, drop them a note along with a SASE. If time permits, they will respond.

Buyer's guide, not seller's guide

Warman's is designed to be a buyer's guide, suggesting what you would have to pay to purchase an object on the open market from a dealer or collector. It is not a seller's guide to prices. People frequently make this mistake. In doing so, they deceive themselves. If you have an object listed in this book and wish to sell it to a dealer, you should expect to receive approximately 50 percent of the listed value. If the object will not resell quickly, expect to receive even less. Private collectors may pay more, perhaps 70 to 80 percent of our listed price, if your object is something needed for their collection. If you have an extremely rare object or an object of exceptionally high value, these guidelines do not apply. Examine your piece as objectively as possible. As an antiques and collectibles appraiser, I spend a great deal of time telling people their treasures are not "rare" at all, but items readily available in the marketplace. In respect to buying and selling, a simple philosophy is that a good purchase occurs when the buyer and seller are happy with the price. Don't look back. Hindsight has little value in the antiques and collectibles field. Given time, things tend to balance out.

Always improving

Warman's is always trying to improve. Space is freely given to long price descriptions, to help you understand what the piece looks like, perhaps what's special about it. With this edition, we've arranged some old formats, using more bold words to help you find what you're looking for. Some categories have been arranged so that if the only thing you know is how high, you can start there. Many times, identifying what you've got is the hardest part. Well, the first place to start is how big—grab that ruler and see what you can find that's a comparable size. You are still going to have to make a determination about what the object is made of, be it china, glass, porcelain, wood, or other materials. Use all your senses to discover what you've got. Ask questions about your object, who made it, and why, how was it used, where, and when. As you find answers to these questions, you'll be helping yourself figure out just what the treasure is all about. Now take that information and you'll be able to look it up and discover the value.

Eager to hear from readers

At *Warman's* and Krause Publications, we're always eager to hear what you think about this book and how we can improve it. Write to either Ellen Schroy, *Warman's* editor, 135 S. Main St., Quakertown, PA 18951-1119 or e-mail at schroy@voicenet.com. The fine staff at Krause Publications can be reached at 700 E. State St., Iola, WI 54990. It's our goal to continue in the *Warman's* tradition and make it the best price guide available.

STATE OF THE MARKET
SPELLBOUND

Hanging high above the hall, a banner that was originally used to promote the Hitchcock movie "Spellbound" certainly set the mood for a dazzling March 2003 Atlantique City show in Atlantic City, New Jersey. Despite the fact that we were suffering through just the third day of the Iraqi conflict, the hall was bustling with collectors, accumulators, and dealers.

Before the show opened, I walked out through the eager pre-admission ticket-holder crowd waiting to get into the show. My arms were full of show programs. In a matter of minutes, the programs were gone and the anxious show attendees eagerly paged through them in search of information about where a particular dealer was located, or they immediately started scouting out the general layout of the huge show. Inside the hall, the dealers were busy putting the last touches on their booths, making sure everything was ready. As soon as the doors opened up, the anticipation-electricity that had been hanging in the outer halls spread through the whole antiques show as the dedicated early shoppers spread through the aisles. Each one had a mission of their own that morning, as did all the other shoppers who joined them during the day. Each was searching for something wonderful to add to their collection and with a show as big as Atlantique City, almost everyone could find something that soothed their collector's soul. The buzz that soon enveloped the whole hall lasted for the entire weekend: the sounds of dealers chatting with potential customers, of shoppers excitedly chattering about something they found, of old friends greeting one another, of information being freely exchanged.

A huge banner for Spellbound captured all theme of the March Atlantique Show.

Much ado about Nutting

I happened to spy Michael Ivankovich, *Warman's* Wallace Nutting adviser, a few minutes after the doors had opened. He yelled back a greeting and kept on almost racing down the wide aisles, searching for Nutting and other interesting pictures. A few hours later, he slowed down enough to chat a few minutes, and I could see a few parcels tucked under his arm. All during the weekend, I found dealers, collectors, and acquaintances who felt the energy of the show. For many of us, it was truly a wonderful escape to be held "spellbound" by the magic of the antiques show, rather than dealing with the reality of what was happening in the outside world. Most seemed to convey the thoughts that they cared deeply for those in harm's way, but they also felt it was important to keep going on with their lives, doing what they would normally do, supporting a factor of the economy that had been hit as hard as many other segments.

A few months after this experience, I had an opportunity to again visit with Michael Ivankovich. This time he was having an auction of Wallace Nutting and related artists. I decided it was time to expand my personal knowledge of this subject and went to preview the auction. Here I found not only folks who wanted to bid on the pictures and furniture offered, but also wonderful collectors who were eager to teach me about Nutting, why his works are important to them, what makes some more appealing than others, etc. For hours I was held spellbound by their enthusiasm and knowledge of this interesting American icon.

Some of the higher prices achieved that day were for rare photographs and furniture. An 8" x 10" hand-colored photograph titled "Hollyhocks" which featured Nutting's original copyright label on the back and showed bright red, pink, and yellow hollyhocks on the front, brought $1,100. An unusual 12" x 16" hand-colored photograph titled "Delaware Water Gap" sported a scene of a blue river winding between green mountains, and went home with a new owner for $900. A stunning 13" x 16" hand-colored photograph titled "The Eames House" sold for $1,250. Believed to possibly be one-of-a-kind, this architectural view of the Eames House in Farmington, Massachusetts, was eagerly examined by many during the auction preview. A Windsor child's chair, #211, which had a branded block signature, was sold for $2,700.

Perhaps it is the times or the way collectors and dealers are reacting to what is happening around the world, but many seem more eager to share the wealth of information they've gathered through the years with those willing to ask and listen. This spirit of giving was apparent at many of the auctions, antiques shows, flea markets, and shops that I find myself visiting all year long. Many times I happened upon folks eagerly chatting about why a certain piece was so important, whether it was a piece of furniture with a fine provenance or a Hot Wheels car that was made for only a short period of time. Taking the time to listen about what makes something more collectible is always important, and listening to why collectors think they are sure of their treasure chest of knowledge is just as important.

Glimmerglass Antiques, booth 2128, offered fine Victorian colored glassware.

Classic Ford Fairline, 1957, 312 rebuilt engine, new exhaust, brakes, top, **$28,500**.

Save the original boxes

One auctioneer got quite red faced while beginning his auction of Hummels by commenting that one lady had been there earlier in the week to preview the Hummels offered and then promptly went home and had planned to tell her husband to start burning years worth of original Hummel packing boxes she had stored. She told the auctioneer it really didn't matter to her if the Hummels were more valuable with their original boxes since she'd be long gone when her family sold them. The auctioneer quipped that he hoped she knew what she was doing and that the collection they were selling that night was especially wonderful since it had so many of the original boxes. Well, the gal who was the subject of the auctioneer's story was sitting right next to me—she laughed and told us all that her theory was she would have more room for interesting examples for her collection if she could get rid of the boxes. She bought several new pieces that evening and carefully packed them away in the original boxes. Her husband winked at me and said, "No boxes lost their lives" in her clean-out-to-make-more-room flurry.

Hearty laughs were exchanged when fellow collectors kidded him about having a big bon-fire soon. He said he'd invite them all over to warm their toes if he ever got around to building that fire. Watching him carefully carry his wife's new purchases out was a delight. The auction hall was packed that night and if he carried the boxes out, she was able to keep on bidding without missing anything. I later saw this elderly couple telling younger collectors why figurines they had just purchased were good ones to start a collection with, how to display them, and "keep the boxes."

Buck's Antiques display with life-size mannequins captured the eye of many show attendees.

Hot buys at Atlantique City

As America's economy floundered this past year, the antiques and collectibles marketplace also experienced some fluctuation. Many dealers and collectors found themselves able to buy interesting examples at auction for reasonable prices. When dealers buy well, they tend to pass that good fortune on to their favorite buyers, keeping the momentum going. This season saw good buys in many segments, including silver, jewelry, and artwork. Folks disillusioned with the stock markets' poor performance soon found they could invest in antiques and collectibles and enjoy their objects more than they enjoyed their losing stock portfolios. It's much more enjoyable to gaze at a terrific painting than to look at that declining mutual fund balance.

The artwork available for purchase at Atlantique City ranged from wonderful primitives, from $300 to multi-thousands of dollars; and large portraits in exquisite gold frames, ranging from several thousand to tens of thousands. Examples of works by well-known artists were priced to sell, and depending on the artist and size of the work, prices ranged from affordable to investment quality.

Furniture dealers who displayed their wares in well-dressed booths at both Atlantique City shows saw many folks stopping to check prices, and measure to see if the piece they loved would fit. Because furniture dealers offer free delivery, many found themselves writing "sold" tickets. Some large Victorian-era bedroom suites, with elaborate carving, were priced at $20,000. Stacking bookcases with glass fronts were available at several booths and ranged in price from $500 to $1,000, depending on the size and configuration. One dealer exhibited a stunning oak dining room table, with all the leaves in place and all ready to serve dinner on, for a tidy sum of $5,000. If you wanted to add an c1890 Austrian doré bronze and cut glass centerpiece to that table, a lovely example could be had for $14,000. And the service for eight of c1885 Theodore Haviland china with delicate pink flowers would have cost $2,900. Other dealers offered more affordable pieces of furniture and the show always offers shoppers, decorators, and collectors many examples to choose from. One particular Jacobean-style hall bench that caught my attention was absolutely stunning, as it towered at least 15 feet high. The price tag reflected the age of the piece, the time and energy it took to move it from its original mansion location, and restoration, and although it was priced below what it would have cost to build it today, it was a princely sum. It was stunning, although too high for the ceilings at my house.

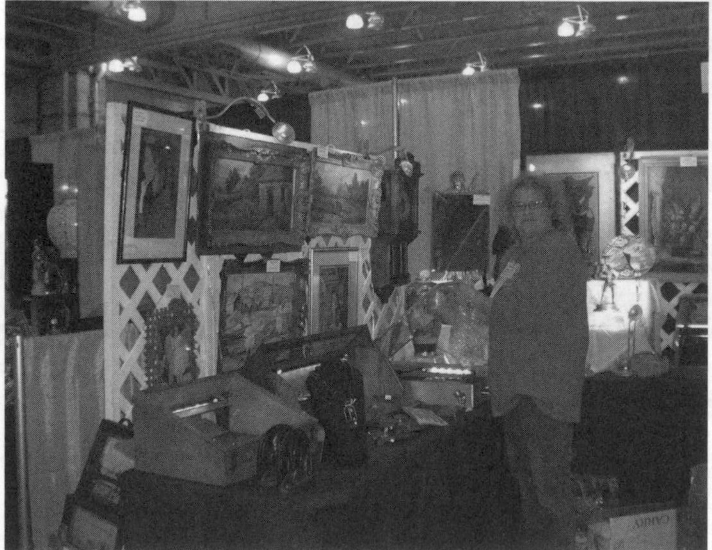

Ella, of Ella Diamond Antiques & Fine Art, busily setting up her booth at the October Atlantique City show.

The jewelry found at Atlantique City is always dazzling, from fine gems that the dealers put back into their safes at night to costume jewelry that is not only affordable but fun to wear. Costume jewelry pins ranged from $5 to several hundred, depending on the maker, style, and desirability of a piece. Cameo brooches were also present with many dealers, ranging in price from $500 to several thousand for delicate landscape scenes. If tastes and checkbook balances could afford precious stones, several dealers were able to show prospective buyers examples ranging from hundreds to several thousands.

Flea markets found new sellers displaying their wares, as new dealers enter that part of the hobby. Many times collectors become dealers as they seek to thin out their collections. Most of these new dealers find themselves re-investing their profits into new pieces for their own shelves. Learning about what new reproductions are coming into the marketplace also helps prevent collectors from buying new copies of McCoy pottery at the same price a vintage piece might command. By reading price guides, such as *Warman's*, today's collectors are better informed and can make more intelligent decisions. Getting out to antiques shows, shops, malls, and flea markets offers opportunities to find interesting treasures and supporting the economy at the same time.

The October Atlantique City Show was a great place to shop at Buck and Barb's Oak Cupboard booth as they showed off fine country furniture with fall accessories.

Fall show just as successful

By the time the October Atlantique City show again spread through the Convention Hall at the New Jersey shore, the leaves were turning, but the atmosphere and the enthusiasm of the antiquers were as revved up as the wonderful exhibits of transportation memorabilia that was this fall's theme. Celebrating the 100th anniversary of Ford Motors, Harley Davidson, and the Wright Brothers meant that many dealers incorporated transportation-related items into their show inventory. Everything from artwork to autographs to neat old duster coats, hats, anything a memorabilia collector might be looking for could be found at Atlantique City. An added bonus was classic cars brought in to further extend the spirit of transportation memorabilia.

I enjoyed one conversation with Atlantique City promoter Ted Jones as he laughingly asked if I thought we could put a few of these beauties on our expense accounts. At the time, we were both in makeup for a television appearance on Comcast's CN8 Your Morning show where Ted told the viewers what they could expect to find at the antiques show, how to get there, etc. I did a segment on how we do appraisals at the show and then talked about the value of some things the staff had brought in for me to look at. Doing verbal appraisals is always an interesting exercise and this was a great warm-up for the two days of appraisals that Kyle Husfloen, Ray Mansfield, and I would be doing at Atlantique City. There we saw everything from books to toys to exquisite Oriental bronzes. The smile on Ray's face as he appeared on the cover of the *Atlantic City Weekly* astride a vintage Harley also helped to set the tone of the show.

Show attendees were treated again to a wide range of quality antiques and collectibles. The exhibitors were eager to display and sell their wares, and to chat about why their wares were special. The hall hummed all day with the chatter of excited participants. Sales were brisk, exhibitors were smiling, and buyers left feeling they had gotten good value, as well as something exciting to add to their collections.

That spellbinding hum makes most of us happy to keep collecting, and to keep treasuring objects made well before we were born an important part of our every day fabric.

Sport and Spool Antiques, offered vintage sporting goods, as well as thread and sewing related items.

Chevrolet Camaro, Official Pace Car, 53rd Annual Indianapolis 500 Mile Race, May 30, 1969, red and white, exhibited at the October 2003, Atlantique City antiques show.

Board of Advisers

John and Alice Ahlfeld
2634 Royal Road
Lancaster, PA 17603
(717) 397-7313
e-mail: AHFELDS@aol.com
Pattern Glass

Bob Armstrong
15 Monadnock Road
Worcester, MA 01609
(508) 799-0644
Puzzles

Al Bagdade
The Country Peasants
1325 N. State Parkway, Apt 15A
Chicago, IL 60610
(312) 397-1321
Quimper

Craig Dinner
P.O. Box 4399
Sunnyside, NY 11104
(718) 729-3850
Doorstops

Roselyn Gerson
P.O. Box 100
Malverne, NY 11565
(516) 593-6746
Compacts

Ted Hake
Hake's Americana & Collectibles Auctions
P.O. Box 1444
York, PA 17405
(717) 848-1333
e-mail: auction@hakes.com
Disneyana, Political

Mary Harris
221 Scarborough Lane
Millersville, PA 17551
(717) 872-8288
e-mail: marymaj@dejazzd.com
Majolica

Tom Hoepf
P.O. Box 90, 27 Jefferson St.
Knightstown, IN 46148
(800) 876-5135
e-mail: antiqueth@aol.com
Cameras

Joan Hull
1376 Nevada
Huron, SD 57350
(605) 352-1685
Hull Pottery

David Irons
Irons Antiques
223 Covered Bridge Road
Northampton, PA 18067
(610) 262-9335
e-mail: Dave@ironsantiques.com
Irons

Michael Ivankovich
P.O. Box 2458
Doylestown, PA 18901
(215) 345-6094
e-mail: Wnutting@comcat.com
Wallace Nutting, Wallace Nutting Look-Alikes

Dorothy Kamm
P.O. Box 7460
Port St. Lucie, FL 34985-7470
(561) 465-4008
e-mail: dorothy.kamm@usa.net
American Hand-Painted Porcelain, American Hand-Painted Jewelry

W.D. and M. J. Keagy
P.O. Box 106
Bloomfield, IN 47424
(812) 384-3471
Yard-Long Prints

Ellen G. King
King's Antiques
102 N. Main St.
Butler, PA 16001
(724) 894-2596
e-mail: egking@attglobal.net
Flow Blue, Mulberry China

Michael Krumme
P.O. Box 48225
Los Angeles, CA 90048-0225
Paden City

Robert Levy
The Unique One
2802 Centre St.
Pennsauken, NJ 08109
(856) 663-2554
e-mail: theuniqueone@worldnet.att.net
Coin-Operated Items

Clarence and Betty Maier
The Burmese Cruet
P.O. Box 432
Montgomeryville, PA 18936
(215) 855-5388
e-mail: burmesecruet@erols.com
Burmese Glass, Crown Milano, Royal Flemish

James S. Maxwell, Jr.
P.O. Box 367
Lampeter, PA 17537
(717) 464-5573
Banks, Mechanical

Bob Perzel
505 Rt. 579
Ringoes, NJ 08551
(908) 782-9361
Stangl Birds

Evalene Pulati
National Valentine Collectors Assoc.
P.O. Box 1404
Santa Ana, CA 92702
Valentines

John D. Querry
RD 2, Box 137B
Martinsburg, PA 16662
(814) 793-3185
Gaudy Dutch

David Rago
David Rago Auctions, Inc.
333 N. Main St.
Lambertville, NJ 8530
(609) 397-9374
e-mail: http://www.ragoarts.com
Art Pottery, Arts & Crafts, Fulper Grueby, Newcomb

Charles and Joan Rhoden
8693 N. 1950 East Road
Georgetown, IL 61846-6254
(217) 662-8046
e-mail: rhoden@soltec.net
Yard-Long Prints

Julie P. Robinson
P.O. Box 117
Upper Jay, NY 12987
(518) 946-7753
Celluloid
Mourning Jewelry

Jerry Rosen
15 Hampden St.
Swampscott, MA 01907
Piano Babies

Kenneth E. Schneringer
271 Sabrina Ct.
Woodstock, GA 30188
(707) 926-9083
e-mail: trademan68@aol.com
Catalogs

Susan Scott
882 Queen St. West
Toronto, Ontario Canada M6K 1Q3
e-mail: Susan@collecting20th century.com
Chintz

Judy Smith
1702 Lamont St. NW
Washington, DC 20010-2602
(202) 332-3020
e-mail: judy@bauble-and-bibebs.com, judy@quilt.net
Lea Stein Jewelry

George Sparacio
P.O. Box 791
Malaga, NJ 08328-0791
(856) 694-4167
e-mail: mrvesta1@aol.com
Match Safes

Henry A. Taron
Tradewinds Antiques
P.O. Box 249
Manchester By-The-Sea, MA 01944-0249
(978) 526-4085
e-mail: taron@tradewinds antiques.com
Canes

Lewis S. Walters
143 Lincoln Lane
Berlin, NJ 08009
(856) 719-1513
e-mail: lew69@erols.com
Phonographs, Radios

AUCTION HOUSES

The following auction houses cooperate with *Warman's* by providing catalogs of their auctions and price lists. This information is used to prepare *Warman's Antiques and Collectibles Price Guide*, volumes in the Warman's Encyclopedia of Antiques and Collectibles. This support is truly appreciated.

Sanford Alderfer Auction Company
501 Fairgrounds Road
Hatfield, PA 19440
(215) 393-3000
Web site: http:/www.alderfer company.com

American Bottle Auctions
1507 21st St.
Suite 203
Sacramento, CA 95814
(800) 806-7722
Web site: www.americanbottle.com

Andre Ammelounx
The Stein Auction Company
P.O. Box 136
Palantine, IL 60078
(847) 991-5927

Arthur Auctioneering
RD 2, P.O. Box 155
Hughesville, PA 17737
(717) 584-3697

Auction Team Köln
Jane Herz
6731 Ashley Court
Sarasota, FL 34241
(941) 925-0385

Auction Team Köln
Postfach 501168 D 5000
Köln 50, W. Germany

Robert F. Batchelder
1 W. Butler Ave.
Ambler, PA 19002
(610) 643-1430

Bear Pen Antiques
2318 Bear Pen Hollow Road
Lock Haven, PA 17745
(717) 769-6655

Bertoia Auctions
2141-F Demarco Dr.
Vineland, NJ 08360
(856) 692-1881

Biders Antiques Inc.
241 S. Union St.
Lawrence, MA 01843
(508) 688-4347

Buffalo Bay Auction Co.
5244 Quam Circle
Rogers, MN 55374
(612) 428-8440
Web site: www.buffalobay auction.com

Butterfield, Butterfield & Dunning
755 Church Road
Elgin, IL 60123
(847) 741-3483
Web site: http://www.butterfields.com

Butterfield, Butterfield & Dunning
7601 Sunset Blvd
Los Angeles, CA 90046
(213) 850-7500
Web site: http://www.butterfields.com

Butterfield, Butterfield & Dunning
220 San Bruno Ave.
San Francisco, CA 94103
(415) 861-7500
Web site: http://www.butterfields.com

Cerebro
P. O. Box 327
East Prospect, PA 17317
(717) 252-3685

W. E. Channing & Co., Inc.
53 Old Santa Fe Trail
Santa Fe, NM 87501
(505) 988-1078

Chicago Art Galleries
5039 Oakton St.
Skokie, IL 60077
(847) 677-6080

Christie's
502 Park Ave.
New York, NY 10022
(212) 546-1000
Web site: http://www.christies.com

Cincinnati Art Galleries
635 Main St.
Cincinnati, OH 45202
(513) 381-2128
Web site: http://www.cincinnati artgalleries.com

Mike Clum, Inc.
P.O. Box 2
Rushville, OH 43150
(614) 536-9220

Cohasco Inc.
Postal 821
Yonkers, NY 10702
(914) 476-8500

Collection Liquidators Auction Service
341 Lafayette St.
New York, NY 10012
(212) 505-2455
Web site: http://www.rtam.com/ coliq/bid.html
e-mail: coliq@erols.com

C. Wesley Cowan Historic Americana
673 Wilmer Ave.
Cincinnati, OH 45226
(513)-871-1670
Fax: (513) 871-8670
e-mail: info@HistoricAmericana.com; wescowan@fuse.net

Decoys Unlimited, Inc.
P.O. Box 206
West Barnstable, MA 02608
(508) 362-2766
Web site: http://www.decoysun limited.inc.com

DeWolfe & Wood
P.O. Box 425
Alfred, ME 04002
(207) 490-5572

Marlin G. Denlinger
RR3, Box 3775
Morrisville, VT 05661
(802) 888-2775

Dixie Sporting Collectibles
1206 Rama Road
Charlotte, NC 28211
(704) 364-2900
Web site: http://www.sport auction.com

Dorothy Dous, Inc.
1261 University Drive
Yardley, PA 19067-2857
(888) 548-6635

Dotta Auction Company, Inc.
330 W. Moorestown Road
Nazareth, PA 18064
(610) 759-7389
Web site: www.dottaauction.com

William Doyle Galleries, Inc.
175 E. 87th St.
New York, NY 10128
(212) 427-2730
Web site: http://www.doyle galleries.com

Early Auction Co.
123 Main St.
Milford, OH 45150
(513) 831-4833

Fain & Co.
P.O. Box 1330
Grants Pass, OR 97526
(888) 324-6726

Ken Farmer Realty & Auction Co.
105A Harrison St.
Radford, VA 24141
(703) 639-0939
Web site: http://kenfarmer.com

Fine Tool Journal
27 Fickett Road
Pownal, ME 04069
(207) 688-4962
Web site: http://www.wowpages. com/FTJ/

Steve Finer Rare Books
P.O. Box 758
Greenfield, MA 01302
(413) 773-5811

Flomaton Antique Auction
P.O. Box 1017
320 Palafox St.
Flomaton, AL 36441
(334) 296-3059

Fontaine's Auction Gallery
1485 W. Housatonic St.
Pittsfield, MA 01201
(413) 488-8922

Freeman\Fine Arts Co. of Philadelphia, Inc.
1808 Chestnut St.
Philadelphia, PA 19103
(215) 563-9275

Garth's Auction, Inc.
2690 Stratford Road
P.O. Box 369
Delaware, OH 43015
(740) 362-4771

Greenberg Auctions
7566 Main St.
Skysville, MD 21784
(410) 795-7447

Green Valley Auction Inc.
Route 2, Box 434
Mt. Crawford, VA 22841
(540) 434-4260

Hake's Americana & Collectibles
P.O. Box 1444
York, PA 17405
(717) 848-1333

Gene Harris Antique Auction Center, Inc.
203 South 18th Ave.
P.O. Box 476
Marshalltown, IA 50158
(515) 752-0600
Web site: www.harrisantique auction.com

Norman C. Heckler & Company
Bradford Corner Road
Woodstock Valley, CT 06282
(203) 974-1634

High Noon
9929 Venice Blvd
Los Angeles, CA 90034
(310) 202-9010
Web site: www.High Noon.com

Historical Collectibles Auctions
24 NW Court Square #201
Graham, NC 27253
(336) 570-2803
Web site: hcaauctions.com

Randy Inman Auctions, Inc.
P.O. Box 726
Waterville, ME 04903
(207) 872-6900
Web site: www.inmanauctions.com

Michael Ivankovich Auction Co.
P.O. Box 2458
Doylestown, PA 18901
(215) 345-6094
Web site: http://www.nutting.com

Jackson's Auctioneers & Appraisers
2229 Lincoln St.
Cedar Falls, IA 50613
(319) 277-2256
Web site: http://www.jackson auction.com

James D. Julia Inc.
Rt 201 Skowhegan Road
P.O. Box 830
Fairfield, ME 04937
(207) 453-7125
Web site: www.juliaauctions.com

Gary Kirsner Auctions
P.O. Box 8807
Coral Springs, FL 33075
(954) 344-9856
Web site: www.garykirsner auctions.com

Lang's Sporting Collectables, Inc.
31 R Turthle Cove
Raymond, ME 04071
(207) 655-4265

Joy Luke
The Gallery
300 E. Grove St.
Bloomington, IL 61701
(309) 828-5533
Web site: http://www.joyluke.com

Mapes Auctioneers & Appraisers
1729 Vestal Pkwy
Vestal, NY 13850
(607) 754-9193

Martin Auctioneers Inc.
P.O. Box 477
Intercourse, PA 17534
(717) 768-8108

McMasters Harris Doll Auctions
P.O. Box 1755
Cambridge, OH 43725
(614) 432-4419

Gary Metz's Muddy River Trading Company
P.O. Box 1430
Salem, VA 24135
(540) 387-5070

William Frost Mobley
P.O. Box 10
Schoharie, NY 12157
(518) 295-7978

William Morford
RD #2
Cazenovia, NY 13035
(315) 662-7625

Neal Auction Company
4038 Magazine St.
New Orleans, LA 7015
(504) 899-5329
Web site: http://www.neal auction.com

New Orleans Auction St. Charles Auction Gallery, Inc.
1330 St. Charles Ave.
New Orleans, LA 70130
(504) 586-8733
Web site: http://www.neworleans auction.com

New Hampshire Book Auctions
P.O. Box 460
92 Woodbury Road
Weare, NH 03281
(603) 529-7432

Norton Auctioneers of Michigan Inc.
50 West Pearl at Monroe
Coldwater, MI 49036
(517) 279-9063

Old Barn Auction
10040 St. Rt. 224 West
Findlay, OH 45840
(419) 422-8531
Web site: http://www.oldbarn.com

Richard Opfer Auctioneering Inc.
1919 Greenspring Drive
Timonium, MD 21093
(410) 252-5035
Web site: www.opferauction.com

Past Tyme Pleasures
PMB #204, 2491 San Ramon Valley Blvd, #1
San Ramon, CA 94583
(925) 484-6442
Fax: (925) 484-2551
Web site: http://www.pastyme.com
e-mail: Pasttyme@excite.com

Pook and Pook
463 East Lancaster Ave.
P.O. Box 268
Downington, PA 19335
(610) 269-4040
Web site: www.pookandpookinc.com

Postcards International
2321 Whitney Ave., Suite 102
P.O. Box 5398
Hamden, CT 06518
(203) 248-6621
Web site: http://www.csmonline.com/postcardsint/

Poster Auctions International
601 W. 26th St.
New York, NY 10001
(212) 787-4000
Web site: www.posterauction.com

Profitt Auction Company
684 Middlebrook Road
Staunton, VA 24401
(540) 885-7369

David Rago Auctions, Inc.
333 S. Main St.
Lambertville, NJ 08530
(609) 397-9374
Web site: http://www.ragoarts.com

Lloyd Ralston Toy Auction
350 Long Beach Blvd
Stratford, CT 06615
(203) 375-9399
Web site: www.lloydralstontoys.com

James J. Reeves
P.O. Box 219
Huntingdon, PA 16652-0219
(814) 643-5497
Web site: www.JamesJReeves.com

Mickey Reichel Auctioneer
1440 Ashley Road
Boonville, MO 65233
(816) 882-5292

Sandy Rosnick Auctions
15 Front St.
Salem, MA 01970
(508) 741-1130

Seeck Auctions
P.O. Box 377
Mason City, IA 50402
(515) 424-1116
Web site: www.willowtree.com/~seeckauctions

L. H. Selman Ltd
761 Chestnut St.
Santa Cruz, CA 95060
(408) 427-1177
Web site: http://www.selman.com

Skinner Inc.
Bolton Gallery
357 Main St.
Bolton, MA 01740
(978) 779-6241
Web site: http://www.skinnerinc.com

Skinner, Inc.
The Heritage on the Garden
63 Park Plaza
Boston, MA 02116
(978) 350-5429
Web site: http://www.skinnerinc.com

Sky Hawk Auctions
P.O. Box 55
Sellersville, PA 18960
(215) 257-6986
Web site: skyhawkauctions.com

Sloans & Kenyon
4605 Bradley Blvd
Bethseda, MD 20815
(301) 634-2330
Web site: www.sloansandkenyon.com

Joseph P. Smalley Jr.
2400 Old Bethlehem Pike
Quartertown, PA 18951
(215) 529-9834

Smith & Jones, Inc., Auctions
12 Clark Lane
Sudbury, MA 01776
(508) 443-5517

Sotheby's
1334 York Ave.
New York, NY 10021
(212) 606-7000
Web site: http://www.sothebys.com

Southern Folk Pottery Collectors Society
220 Washington St.
Bennett, NC 27208
(336) 581-4246

Stanton's Auctioneers
P.O. Box 146
144 South Main St.
Vermontville, MI 49096
(517) 726-0181

Michael Strawser
200 N. Main St., P.O. Box 332
Wolcottville, IN 46795
(219) 854-2859
Web site: www.majolicaauctions.com

Swann Galleries Inc.
104 E. 25th St.
New York, NY 10010
(212) 254-4710
Web site: www.swanngalleries.com

Swartz Auction Services
2404 N. Mattis Ave.
Champaign, IL 61826-7166
(217) 357-0197
Web site: http://www/Swartz Auction.com

The House In The Woods
S91 W37851 Antique Lane
Eagle, WI 53119
(414) 594-2334

Theriault's
P.O. Box 151
Annapolis, MD 21401
(301) 224-3655
Web site: http://www.theriaults.com

Tradewind Antiques & Auctions
P.O. Box 249
Manchester-by-the-Sea, MA 01944-0249
(987) 526-4085
Web site: www.tradewindsantiques.com

Treadway Gallery, Inc.
2029 Madison Road
Cincinnati, OH 45208
(513) 321-6742
Web site: http://www.a3c2net.com/treadwaygallery

Victorian Images
P.O. Box 284
Marlton, NJ 08053
(609) 985-7711
Web site: www.tradecards.com/vi

Bruce and Vicki Waasdorp
P.O. Box 434
10931 Main St.
Clarence, NY 14031
(716) 759-2361
Web site: http://www.antiques-stoneware.com

Wiederseim Associates, Inc.
P.O. Box 470
Chester Springs, PA 19425
(610) 827-1910
Web site: www.wiederseim.com

Woody Auction
Douglass, KS 67039
(316) 746-2694

Jim Wroda Auction Co.
5239 St. Rt. 49 South
Greenville, OH 45331
(937) 548-2640
Web site: www.jimwrodaauction.com

York Town Auction, Inc.
1625 Haviland Road
York, PA 17404
(717) 751-0211
e-mail: yorktownauction@cyberia.com

ABBREVIATIONS

The following are standard abbreviations, which we have used throughout this edition of *Warman's.*

ABP = American Brilliant Period
ADS = Autograph Document Signed
adv = advertising
ah = applied handle
ALS = Autograph Letter Signed
AQS = Autograph Quotation Signed
C = century
c = circa
Cal. = caliber
circ = circular
cyl. = cylinder
cov = cover
CS = Card Signed
d = diameter or depth
dec = decorated
dj = dust jacket
DQ = Diamond Quilted
DS = Document Signed
ed = edition
emb = embossed
ext. = exterior
eyep. = eyepiece
Folio = 12" x 16"
ftd = footed
ga = gauge
gal = gallon
ground = background
h = height
horiz. = horizontal
hp = hand painted
hs = high standard
illus = illustrated, illustration
imp = impressed
int. = interior
irid = iridescent
IVT = inverted thumbprint
j = jewels
K = karat
l = length
lb = pound
litho = lithograph
ll = lower left
lr = lower right
ls = low standard
LS = Letter Signed
mfg = manufactured
MIB = mint in box
MOP = mother-of-pearl
n/c = no closure
ND = no date
NE = New England
No. = number
NRFB = never removed from box
ns = no stopper
r/c = reproduction closure
o/c = original closure
opal = opalescent
orig = original
os = orig stopper
oz = ounce
pcs = pieces
pgs = pages
PUG = printed under the glaze
pr = pair
PS = Photograph Signed
pt = pint
qt = quart
RM = red mark
rect = rectangular
sgd = signed
S. N. = Serial Number
SP = silver plated
SS = Sterling silver
sq = square
TLS = Typed Letter Signed
unp = unpaged
vert. = vertical
vol = volume
w = width
yg = yellow gold
# = numbered

Grading Condition

The following numbers represent the standard grading system used by dealers, collectors, and auctioneers:

C.10 = Mint
C. 9 = Near mint
C.8.5 = Outstanding
C.8 = Excellent
C.7.5 = Fine +
C.7 = Fine
C. 6.5 = Fine – (good)
C. 6 = Poor

ABC Plates

History: The majority of early ABC plates were manufactured in England and imported into the United States. They achieved their greatest popularity from 1780 to 1860. Since a formal education was uncommon in the early 19th century, the ABC plate was a method of educating the poor for a few pennies.

ABC plates were made of glass, pewter, porcelain, pottery, or tin. Porcelain plates range in diameter from 4-3/8 inches to slightly more than 9-1/2 inches. The rim usually contains the alphabet and/or numbers; the center features animals, great men, maxims, or nursery rhymes.

For more information, see *Warman's Glass*, 4th edition, and *Warman's English & Continental Pottery & Porcelain*, 3rd Edition.

Glass

Christmas Eve, Santa on chimney, colorless, 6" d **75.00**

Clock face center, Arabic and Roman numerals, alphabet center, colorless and frosted, 7" d **75.00**

Elephant with howdah, three waving Brownies, Ripley & Co., colorless, 6" d **135.00**

Little Bo Peep, center scene, raised alphabet border, colorless, 6" d **50.00**

Plain center, white scalloped edge, colorless, 6" d **65.00**

Young Girl, portrait, colorless, 6" d **65.00**

Brown transfer print of two men chopping down large trees, verse "Constant Dropping Wears Stones Away, and Little Strokes Fall aGreat Oaks" embossed alphabet on rim, **$200**.

Clock face, two rows of alphabets, row of numbers, Roman numerals on as clock, "Dinner" at top of center dec, "To Bed" at bottom, pink luster rim, marked "Patented School Plate, LS&S," with English registry mark, **$95**.

Pottery or porcelain

Aesop's Fables the Leopard and the Fox, black transfer print, pearlware, England, 19th C **175.00**

Crusoe Finding the Foot Prints, color-enhanced brown transfer, pearlware, England, 19th C, minor discoloration **125.00**

Eye of the master will do no more than his hands, multicolored transfer........ **145.00**

Federal Generals, black transfer print, pearlware, England, 19th C......... **175.00**

Franklin's Provbs, (sic) black transfer print, pearlware, England, 19th C **175.00**

Hunting scenes, molded alphabet rim, hand painted transfer center, 6-3/4" d, repairs, hairline **80.00**

Old Mother Hubbard, brown transfer, polychrome enamel trim, alphabet border, marked "Tunstall," 7-1/2" d **200.00**

Swiss shepherd, molded alphabet rim, hand-painted transfer center, 5" d **115.00**

Take Your Time Miss Lucy, black transfer of money and cat, polychrome enamel, titled, molded hops rim, red trim, ironstone, imp "Meakin," 6" d **125.00**

Teach thy dog to be polite, multicolored transfer **125.00**

The Guardian, molded alphabet rim, hand-painted transfer center with dog, marked "Elsmore & Son," 7" d..... **125.00**

Tin

George Washington profile, rust spot, minor wear, 6-1/8" d................ **200.00**

Girl on swing, lithographed center, printed alphabet border, 3-1/2" d **60.00**

Two kittens playing with basket of wood, 4-1/2" d **80.00**

Who Killed Cock Robin, 7-3/4" d **120.00**

Multicolored transfer print, verse "That Girl Wants the Pup Away, But It's Mother Looks Say Nay," two boys and girl holding puppy, mother dog and second pup in foreground, embossed alphabet rim, **$225**.

Multicolored transfer print, Little Bo Peep verse, blue letters on raised rim, marked "Germany," **$200**.

Advertising

History: Before the days of mass media, advertisers relied on colorful product labels and advertising giveaways to promote their products. Containers were made to appeal to the buyer through the use of stylish lithographs and bright colors. Many of the illustrations used the product in the advertisement so that even an illiterate buyer could identify a product.

Advertisements were put on almost every household object imaginable and constant reminders to use the product or visit a certain establishment.

For more information, see *Warman's Advertising* and *Warman's Glass*, 4th edition.

Grading Condition. The following numbers represent the standard grading system used by dealers, collectors, and auctioneers:

C.10 = Mint
C. 9 = Near mint
C.8.5 = Outstanding
C.8 = Excellent
C.7.5 = Fine +
C.7 = Fine
C. 6.5 = Fine – (good)
C. 6 = Poor

Additional Listings: See *Warman's Americana & Collectibles* for more examples.

Automaton display, Bear Brand Honey, honey bees buzzing in and out of papier-mâché hive, brown bear popping up out of hive clutching jar of Bear Brand Honey, orig rear marquee with two paper Bear Brand Honey labels, orig shipping crate, top of shipping crate missing, 24" w, 18" d, 22" h **200.00**

Back bar light, Blatz, metal figural beer bottle waiter, light socket replacing beer mug he previously held, Plasto Mfg., Chicago, 17" h, no shade **550.00**

Badge, Union Stockyards Co., 2-3/4" h, diecut silvered brass, bar at top, raised images of seated old timer wearing hat, holding large newspaper, raised lettering "I Know Their Records Show," early 1900s **65.00**

Ashtray, tire, green glass insert, embossed "Kelly Springfield," **$12**.

Blotter, unused

Eppens, Smith Co., NY, Coffee and Tea Importer, 1900 seasonal greetings, full-color celluloid, slight use **15.00**

Fairbanks Portable Pumping Outfit, graphics of metal vehicle, road paving machinery, 7-1/4" x 9-1/2" **10.00**

Bookmark

Elastica Floor Finish, 5-3/4" h, diecut celluloid, young boy in Buster Brown-type outfit riding large rocking horse, early 1900s **60.00**

Shredded Whole Wheat, 5" h, celluloid, black on cream, color illus at top of wheat biscuit on plate, C. B. Tappan, Philadelphia, dealer, reverse with offer of recipe booklet from Natural Food Co., Niagara Falls, NY, made by Whitehead & Hoag, early 1900s **45.00**

Cabinet, store type

Diamond Dyes, Court Jester, carved maple, Eastlake style dec and lithographed display, two back panel doors with pigeonhole shelves, c1890, 27" x 19" x 10" **925.00**

Dr. Daniels' Veterinary Medicines, wood, tin litho door front.... **3,700.00**

Lorillard, oak, glass doors **1,500.00**

Peters' Fine Footwear, glass and wood, 36" sq, 72" h **1,050.00**

Calendar, Red Goose Shoes, 1924, colorful print of mountain goat hunter titled "Getting His Goat," H. C. Edwards, artist, ads for Red Goose Shoes, Friedman-Shelby Shoe Col, Atlantic Shoes, Pacific Shoes, 8" x 19" wall type **25.00**

Candy pail, Novia Kiddie Pops, pail shape, image of pops and children and dog on both sides, 3-3/4" d, 3-1/4" h, C.7.5+ **675.00**

Canister, Tiger Rolled Oats, cardboard, Quaker Oats, multicolored image on front and back of snarling tiger, red and black text, 1930s, 5-1/2" d, 10" h, **$115**. Photo courtesy of Hake's Americana & Collectibles.

Canister, Blanke's Coffee, tin, litho paper label **150.00**

Charm, Bull Durham, 1-1/8" l diecut brass company logo, early 1900s **40.00**

Chest cooler, Moxie, on wheels **200.00**

Cigar display, Benson & Hedges, tin, "Three New Cigars," porthole top "Lily," two glass doors "Panatella" and "Oxford," gold letters on black, 24-1/2"....... **550.00**

Cigar tin

Camel brand cigars, 5 cents, 1920s **85.00**

Oricico Cigar Co., Bethesda, OH, Native American illus, copyright 1919, tin litho by Meekim Can Co., 6-1/4" w, 4" d, 5-1/2" h **2,130.00**

Chair, folding, blue and white enamel plaque on back, "Smoke Piedmont, The Cigarette of Quality," **$250**. Photo courtesy of Alderfer Auction Co.

Clicker

Empire Cream Separator, 1-1/4", white text on dark blue rim, black and white equipment image, rim reads "I Chirp For The Empire Because It Makes The Most Dollars For Me" **25.00**

Peters Weatherbird Shoes, 1-7/8" h, litho tin, trademark bird, light green ground, 1930s **30.00**

Twinkie Shoes, litho tin, full-color art of elf character standing on mushroom, dark green background, tiny inscription for "Hamilton-Brown Shoes Co.," 1930s................. **30.00**

Coffee bin, Jos. Strong & Co. Old Dominion Coffee **900.00**

Clock, Blatz Brewing Co., oak, figural half beer keg, three-legged stand, applied brass numerals, name in script, orig key and pendulum, 17-1/2" w, 10" d, 23" h **300.00**

Counter dispenser, Boye Needles and Shuttles, litho tin display, circular dispenser containing numerous orig machine needle wooden boxes, 16" d, 3-3/4" h **225.00**

Coaster, Goodrich Silvertowns, green glass, **$18**.

Counter display

Claytons Dog Remedies, papier-mâché bulldog **1,165.00**

Haines Merrichild Sleepers, small boy and puppy, composition base, 13" d, 21-1/2" h **575.00**

Coffee tin, Bouquet Roasted Coffee, tin, red and white image on front and back of steaming cup of coffee, O.V. Tracy & Co., Syracuse, N.Y., 1 lb, some oxidation on lid, c1900, 4-1/4" d, 5-1/2" h, **$45**. Photo courtesy of Hake's Americana & Collectibles.

Pall Mall and Tareyton brand cigarettes, wood, adv on side panels, 5-1/2" w, 7-1/2" d, 10" h **3,115.00**

West Hairnets, tin, colorful paper label on inside lid, illus of Roaring '20s attired model, her touring car on tropical beach, copyright 1918, two rear storage drawers, 6" w, 6" d, 5-1/2" h, some fading to gilt lettering **520.00**

Counter display, Brown's Jumbo Bread, elephant shape, framed, 19" w, 17" h, **$300**. Photo courtesy of Joy Luke Auctions.

Counter display case

California's Fruit & Pepsin Chewing Gum, J. P. Priwley's, curved glass front **700.00**

Chandler's Laxatives, orig 21 trial-size packages **170.00**

Diamond Die, oak case, tin litho front panel illus of jester in king's court, two rear-hinged doors with multiple die storage compartments, Wells' Richardson & Co., c1890, 20-3/4" w, 10" d, 27" h, missing some int. dividers **500.00**

Kellogg's Toasted Corn Flakes, cardboard, lithographed cardboard model T automobile, two characters, "First Aid to the Hungry," orig product box, 11-1/2" x 17-1/2" **195.00**

O. G. Java, tin, roll-top door enameled "Teas and Coffee," gold stenciled detail, tole-black ground, diamond-shaped mirror panel on front, some scratches, 18" x 13" x 13" **300.00**

Rit Dye, six wooden drawers in tin painted display, orig contents, 16-1/2" h **175.00**

Sprague Warner Co. Spices, roll top door, rotating display, stenciled gold design on black, orange panel depicting children, minor dents, 12" h **175.00**

Display stand, Wise Potato Chips, thin cardboard, image on front of boy and girl at store counter, boy holding up two fingers and smiling as retailer reaches for bags of potato chips from counter display, titled "A Wise Guy," door with logo "Eat Wise Potato Chips," easel back, copyright 1940 Wise Delicatessen Co., Burwick, Va. unused, 17" x 20-1/4", **$50**. Photo courtesy of Hake's Americana & Collectibles

Counter jar, glass

National Biscuit, bulbous **90.00**

Planter's Peanuts, green tin lid depicting Mr. Peanut **100.00**

Crate, Vernor's Ginger Ale, flavor mellowed four years in wood......... **70.00**

Display stand, tin

Canada Dry, The Champagne of Ginger Ales, triangular, enameled green and yellow, 34" h **165.00**

Sunshine Biscuits, tin, graduated shelves, enameled yellow with blue letters, 52" h........................ **275.00**

Door pull, Ex-Lax, metal **45.00**

Egg crate, Humpty Dumpty, tin egg carrier with interior sleeves for two dozen eggs **120.00**

Fan

Bradley Knit Wear, 7" x 8" cardboard mounted on wooden 5-1/2" l handle, colorful art pictures for swimsuits for young adult female and male bathers, reverse with customer service text by merchant, late 1920s **30.00**

Qualtop Beverage, 7-1/2" x 10" diecut cardboard photo image of young lady in sepia, flesh tone tint on face and body, orange tint on headband, reverse "Tell The Boy To Serve You A Cold Bottle Of Qualtop-Any Flavor Has Real Food Value-Refreshing-Nourishing-A Rochester Product," back with publisher Geiger Bros., Newark, NY, 1920s....... **35.00**

The Valley of Fair Play, 9-1/2" x 10-1/2" w diecut cardboard, red on white, half-circle aerial black and white photo view of shoe manuf company, center flesh tone portrait of young man "The Smiling Worker and a cast of 17,000 people," black and white text on back for shoe tanneries and factories, Feb. 1923 patent date **20.00**

Lapel stud

Harley-Davidson Motorcycles, 5/8", copper lustered metal, diecut logo, threaded post, screw cap, 1920s.................................... **80.00**

Smoke Joe Wright Cigars-Equal to Imported, 7/8" d, red, white, and blue company initials and text, c1896 .... **30.00**

Letter opener, Seeley's Hard Rubber Trusses, Philadelphia, 8-3/4" l, cream celluloid handles, Whitehead and Hoag, c1910.. **30.00**

Lunch box, tin litho

US Marine Cut Plug Tobacco, porthole illus of sailor promoting package, end panel lithos of White Fleet battleships, 7-1/2" w, 4-1/2" d, 5" h **4,600.00**

Winner Cut Plug Tobacco, early motorcar racing illus, 7-3/4" w, 5" d, 4-1/2" h, clear coated........ **1,500.00**

Match holder

Buster Brown Bread, tin litho, children at table **290.00**

Universal Stove Co., tin litho .. **85.00**

Match safe, "Cy's Café-Casino-Pool and Bowling Alleys-Best Cigars And Cigarettes, Westminister, Md," 1-1/4" x 1-7/8" x 5", back pack design, hinged lid, black text on tanned paper label, lid reads "Bryant & May Ltd," early 1900s **25.00**

Neon sign

Champagne Velvet Beer ... **1,400.00**

Furs, standing bear braced against tree stump, "Repaired and Remodeled" printed on base of sign, from St Louis store, 9' h..... **4,250.00**

Leisy's Beer, Cleveland, in orig wood crate **375.00**

Paperweight mirror, 3-1/2" celluloid on weighted metal, underside mirror insert C.P.A. Services, brown rim inscribed in white for Indianapolis firm, two officers pictured by inset sepia photos with names, tinted sepia real downtown photo in center, 1920s **30.00**

D. M. Distillery, tinted celluloid, crisp real photo of "Warehouses and Straight American in Yard at D. M. Distillery Juarez, Mexico," names of two distillery officials, ring of whiskey barrels on front, 1920s **40.00**

Rossite, can of drain pipe cleansing compound, 1930s **35.00**

Whitewater Flour Mills, tinted sepia scene of Niagara Falls, brown rim lettered in white "Whitewaters, Kansas," 1920s **35.00**

Pencil clip

Ardee Flour, red, yellow, blue logo, celluloid on brass wire clip, Hubbard Milling Co., Mankato, Minn, sponsor, early 1900s............................ **25.00**

Red Man Cigar Leaf, multicolored, tobacco pack mounted on brass wire spring clip, early 1900s **55.00**

The Metropolitan, black, white, and red celluloid, mounted on brass wire spring clip, sponsor store designates "Hats" and "Furnishings" **20.00**

Display cabinet, Shaeffer Fineline, pencils, semi-circular, 27" w, 14" h, **$250**. Photo courtesy of Joy Luke Auctions.

Pinback button

Babcock's the Safe Milk for the Baby, 1-1/4" d, dark blue on white, Bastian, 1930s..................................... **18.00**

Buy Check Bread Just Right, 1-1/4" d, red, yellow, and blue, circle of red and blue check marks in small panels, center text, 1930s, back paper..................................... **12.00**

Cameo Baking Powder, 1-1/4" d, black, white, red, and cream, bright gold accents, c1900, Pin-Lock Buttons, Chicago, back paper **48.00**

Crown Flour, 1-1/4" d, white text, full color king's crown, dark blue ground, early 1900s, Irwin-Hudson, Portland back paper............................. **35.00**

Du Pont Smokeless Powder, 13/16" d, full color quail, black rim, white lettering, 1897 copyright, back paper missing **48.00**

Display card, pocket watch shape diecut cardboard, Quality Watches, original attached lady's and gent's watches, **$95**.

E. C. Simmons Keen Kutter, 7/8" d, red logo, yellow and white lettering, covered tin back, horizontal bar pin **24.00**

St Charles Evaporated Cream, 1-1/4" d, multicolored, Unsweetened" printed under cow, 1900s **24.00**

Towle's Log Cabin Maple Syrup, 7/8" d, colorful log cabin logo, 1896, Whitehead & Hoag back paper **24.00**

Yale Coffee, 7/8", blue pennant on cream, c1901, Whitehead & Hoag back paper............................ **12.00**

Zaring's Patent, 1-1/4", red, white, and blue, litho of sack, reading "This is the Best That's Made," c1900, Whitehead & Hoag back paper **48.00**

Pocket mirror

ABC Power Washer, color art of lady doing laundry by elaborate washing machine, wringer, tub, woven basket, white lettering on dark rim...... **95.00**

Aetna Life Insurance, red seal logo, inscriptions in red and green lettering on white, issued by St. Louis branch................................. **40.00**

Bar-Keeper's Friend, color art of standing nude lacy, gold and black lettering on rim "George Wm Hoffman Co., Indianapolis, Indiana" **185.00**

Cascarets, 2-1/8", colorful image of lady resting on crescent in night sky, yellow lettering, red slogan "They Work While You Sleep," other health related inscriptions................ **75.00**

Drink Puck Rye, 1-3/4" h, red, blue, and cream on silver ground, center image of youth in black hat and tails, extending bottle of whiskey "At Leading Dealers" **65.00**

Dutch Java Coffee, 2-1/16" h, wharf scene of young Dutch girl kissing boy, large product package, black title "Secret of Happiness" **75.00**

Farmer's Mill Flour, white flour sack silhouette on bright red background, white and pale turquoise letters, miniature sepia on sack, "Longmont Farmers Milling & Elevator Co., Pride of the Rockies" **85.00**

Montezuma Rye Whiskey, 2-3/4" h, large bottle with black and white label, gold accents, swirls of brown and tan background, text "On The Market Over 50 Years," made by Jams McGuire Co., Philadelphia **95.00**

New Century Flour, 2-3/4" h, black on cream, text "You Can See For Yourself That New Century Flour Is Good Enough For The Person Whose Picture Is On The Other Side-Ask Your Dealer" **40.00**

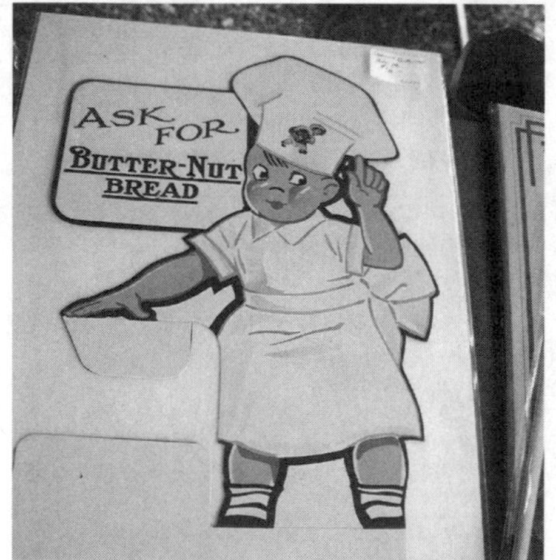

Display stand, Ask For Butter-Nut Bread, child dressed as chef, diecut, **$16**.

New King Snuff, 2-3/4" h, celluloid rect, red and black lettered inscription "Good Snuff Packed Tight Keeps Right," sand colored background........................... **80.00**

Oxford Chocolates, 2-3/4" h, multicolored young lady in graduation garb, deep green blending to lighter green background, "Hazen Confectionary Co. Boston" on rim curl **95.00**

Red Cross Stoves, Ranges, & Furnaces, 2" h, dark blue on white, red center logo...................... **30.00**

Poster, Peerless Rubber Co., litho, harbor scene with steam ships and barges carrying various Peerless products in front of old New York skyline, rainbow spans top stating "Rainbow Packing," 25" w, 16-1/2" h, creases, tears.. **60.00**

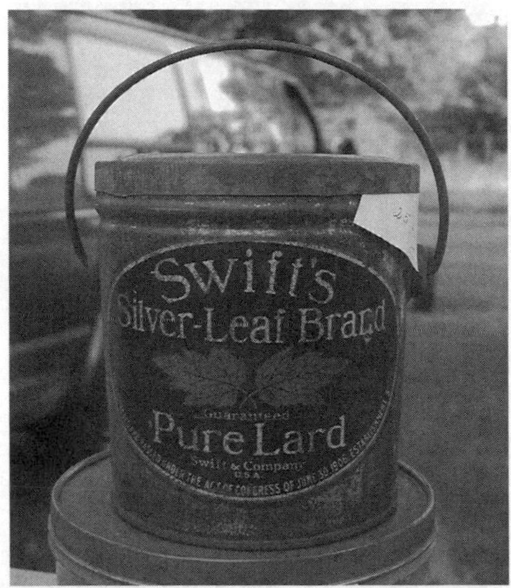

Lard pail, Swift's Silver-Leaf Pure Lard Kettle, red, black, and gold label, original handle and lid, some rust, **$25**.

Sign

Barber shop, metal, double-sided, enameled red, white, and blue, 12" x 24-1/4" **300.00**

Beacon Feeds, "Farm Fresh Eggs," tin, emb folded edge, Scioto Sign, Kenton, OH, 19-1/2" w, 13-1/2" h **250.00**

Cherry Blossom Soda, oval, porcelain **365.00**

Cleo Cola, c1935 .... **400.00**

Coryell 70, porcelain, 1930s, 36" x 48" **1,500.00**

Druggists Straight Five Cigars, metal, wood frame, 13" x 49" **25.00**

Dutch Boy Paints, Dutch Boy trademark lithographed on textured paper captioned "The Dutch Boy Painter," top metal hanger, later frame, 13-1/2" w, 26-1/2" h ... **920.00**

F. R. Knowlton, West Action, Mass, Concord 5 cent cigars, linen backed, 36" x 50" **350.00**

Humphrey's Specifics, tin, Wells Hope Co., Phil., c1893, 16" w, 22" h **360.00**

Interlux Marine Paint Sign, men working on boats, tin, 1940s, 24" x 36" **2,000.00**

Invader Motor Oil, Perfected Lubrication, metal **1,660.00**

Jersey Ice Cream, A. B. Henry, Sandwich, IL, yellow and black, 20" w, 28" h **185.00**

Liner Brand Package Foods, John Blaul's Sons Co., Burlington, Iowa-Cedar Rapids, Iowa, celluloid on cardboard, 1920s **300.00**

Oilzium Motor Oil, tin **1,400.00**

Pan-American Orangeade, metal, 28" x 19-3/4" **435.00**

Player's Please Navy Cut, metal, 29" x 19-1/2" **230.00**

Plow Boy Tobacco, painted canvas **425.00**

Prince Albert, tin, Indian portrait **700.00**

Rexall, orange **175.00**

San Antonio Brewing Association, paper, wood frame, lovely girl in center oval **575.00**

Squires Arlington Hams, Bacon, Sausages, pig in center surrounded by corncob wreath, tin, c1905 .... **4,800.00**

Van Dam Cigars, Java Wrapped, Dutch gentleman **185.00**

Waverly House, Boats to Let, painted wood **850.00**

Wayne Dairy, plastic, light-up, double sided, adv milk and ice cream **225.00**

Spinner top

Hurd Shoes, black and white celluloid, wooden red spinner dowel, Parisian Novelty Co., maker name on rim curl, 1930s **20.00**

Poll-Parrot Shoes, litho tin, wooden spinner dowel, red and yellow parrot striding between black shoes, yellow background, red rim, red star logo, 1930s **25.00**

Spool cabinet

Clark, two drawers, name printed on front **275.00**

J. P. Coats, six drawers **900.00**

Merricks, oval, curved glass, int. compartments missing...... **1,200.00**

Suitcase, Samsonite, streamlite finishes, demonstrator case of seven different colors **225.00**

Syrup dispenser

Cherry Smash, George Washington dec **225.00**

Ginger Mint Julep **375.00**

Lemon Crush **225.00**

Plate, 1972-Doster's Food Market, Kleinfeltersville, PA, multicolored transfer scene of two couples riding in open carriage, **$15**.

Tape measure

Fox's Guernsey Dairy, black lettering on yellow ground, red rim, four red carnations on black ground on reverse **25.00**

Sears, Roebuck & Co., white lettering, black ground, lightning bolt-style lettering for "WLS" (World's Largest Store,) red, white, blue, and green stylized floral design on back **15.00**

Thermometer

Chew Mail Pouch Tobacco, 72" h **725.00**

Mason's Root Beer, round **160.00**

Winchester, shotgun shell shape **100.00**

Tile, 4-1/4" x 5-1/2", Northwestern Terra Cotta Comp., Chicago, Ill, beige unglazed clay, two putti holding swag of cloth over company name **210.00**

Tin, miscellaneous, tin litho

Donald Duck Pop Corn, Disney cartoon characters on both sides, unopened, 2-7/8" w, 4-7/8" h, C.7.5+ **300.00**

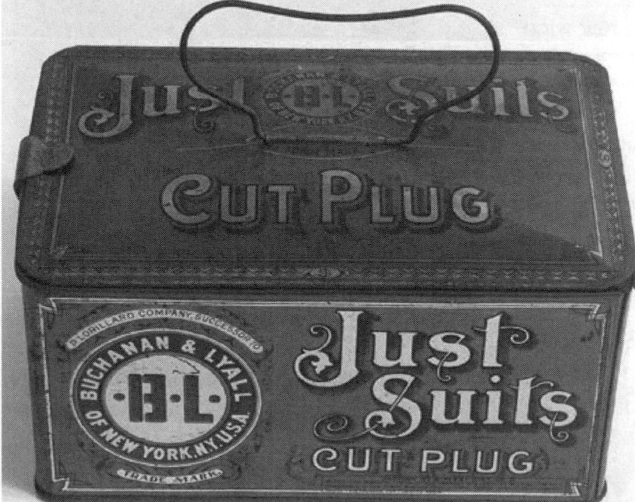

Lunch pail, Just Suits Tobacco, P. Lorillard Co., tin, red, gold text accented in black, lid hinged at right, clasp on left, wire handle on top, designed to be reused as lunch pail, bright glossy finish, gold luster, c1900, 7-3/4" l, 5-1/4" w, 4" h, **$90**. Photo courtesy of Hake's Americana & Collectibles.

Family Tea, New York and China Tea Co., red slip-fit tin, orange black litho illus on four sides, Ginna & Co., 5" w, 5" d, 9-1/2" h **1,560.00**
Imperial Shaving Stick, Talcum Puff Co., New York, image of man lathering face, 3-3/8" l, C.8+ **325.00**
Professor Searele's Veterinary Blood Purifier Medicinal, Sommers Bros., litho of barnyard animals, 3-1/4" x 2-7/8" x 1-3/4", C.8.5+ **450.00**
Spencerian Pen Points, litho tin, sliding lid, steel pen tips, yellow printed in red and black on lid with tiger head logo, ad text on underside, early 1900s **20.00**
Velvet Tread Foot Powder, green, black, and brown, winged foot and giant winged insect, 4-3/4" x 2-1/4" x 1-3/8", C.8 .... **400.00**

Poster, Ault & Wiborg Co, Manufs of Lithographic and letter press printing ink, Cincinnati, New York, Chicago, St Louis, William H Bradley, identified in the matrix, color lithograph, (possibly posthumous printing), sight size 10-1/2" x 8," matted, **$265**. Photo courtesy of Skinner, Inc.

Tobacco bin, Game Cut Tobacco, Jon Babley Co., held forty-eight 5 cent packs of tobacco, litho on tin, 11-1/2" w, 7-3/4" d, 7" h **850.00**
Tobacco humidor, Colt's Tobac-a-dor, Coltrock, table top, lazy susan revolving mechanism, cigarette compartments in base, mfg by Colt's Firearms Mfg Co., Hartford, CT, 8-1/2" d, 7" h **500.00**
Tobacco plug cutter, emb "Joannes Bros. Company-Wholesale Grocers-Greenbay, Wis.," cast iron, 16" l, 7-1/2" h **450.00**
Tobacco tin, pocket, tin litho
Charm of the West, Spaulding & Merrick, horizontal, graphics on both sides, 2-3/8" x 3-3/4" x 5/8" **300.00**
Ensign Perfection Cut Tobacco, vertical, Missouri flag on back, 4-1/2" x 3" x 7/8", C.8+, minor wear, litho chip on back **900.00**

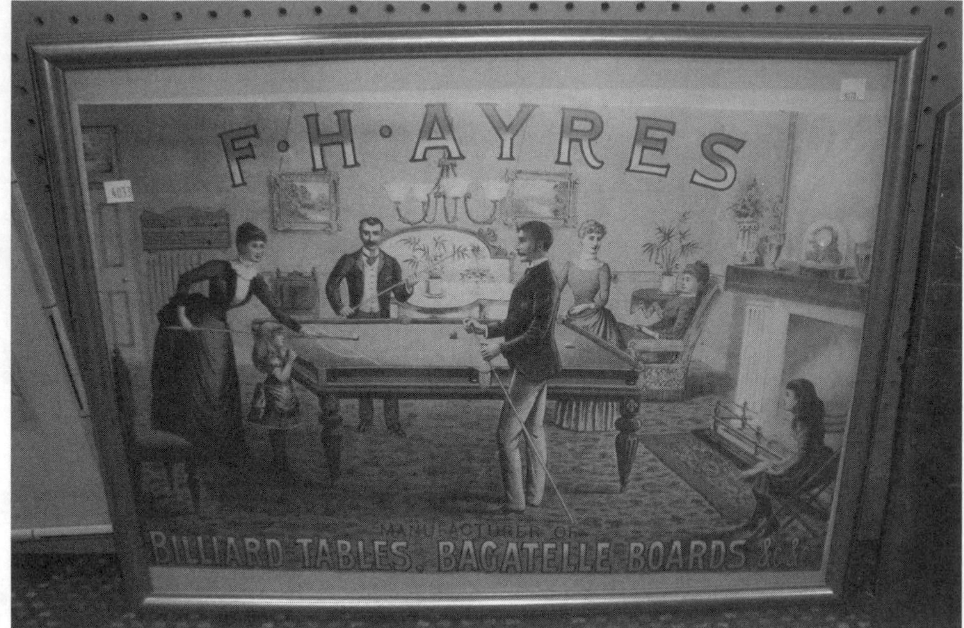

Poster, F. H. Ayres Billiard Tables, Bagatelle Boards, scene of family playing billiards, framed, **$145**.

Forest and Stream, Canadian, vertical, 4-1/4" x 3" x 7/8", C.8+ **425.00**
Lord Kenyon, vertical, dark blue and white, 3" x 3-1/2" x 1", C.8..... **375.00**
Old Glory, Spaulding & Merrick, horizontal, red ground, detailed graphics on both sides, 2-3/8" x 3-3/4" x 5/8", C.8.5 .... **325.00**
Paul Jones Clean Cut Tobacco, vertical, teal ground, multicolored image of Jones on front, sea battle on back, 4-1/2" x 3" x 7/8", C.8.5+ **2,900.00**
Tiger Bright Sweet Chewing Tobacco, P. Lorillard Co., vertical pocket size, 3" w, 7/8" d, 2-7/8" h **275.00**

Sign, Buster Brown Bread – Branch of Golden Sheaf Bakery, featuring Buster Brown & Tige, self-framed tin, 30" x 22", **$1,500**. Photo courtesy of Joy Luke Auctions.

Trout-Line Smoking Tobacco, vertical, dark green ground, image of trout fisherman on both sides, 3-3/4" x 3-1/4" x 1-1/8", C.8+ **775.00**
Uniform Cut Plug, 1 lb, hinged lid, sailor within laurel wreath on front and back, Larus & Bro. Co., Richmond, VA, 6" w, 3-1/4" d, 3-1/4" h **920.00**

Toy
Heathcote Fule Co., coal-coke metal truck **100.00**
Spearmint Gum delivery truck, Buddy L, two wheels missing **150.00**
Speedo, tin windup boat **150.00**

Tray, tin litho
Anheuser-Busch, Bevo wagon, team of horses, c1910, 13" x 10-1/2" **115.00**
Buckeye Root Beer, boy and girl with large mug, 12-1/2" sq........ **1,300.00**
Cunningham Ice Cream, image of early factory and delivery trucks, 15-1/4" x 18-1/2", C.8............ **450.00**
Raleigh Bicycle, oblong, turquoise, 1940s bathing beauty lounging seaside with Raleigh bicycle in front, logo, marked "Sole distributors, Seng Guan Hong & Co., Bangkok, Made in England," 16" l, 12-1/2" h, some surface crazing **480.00**
Velvet Beer, Terre Haute Brewing CO., round, festive banquet scene of men and women in 18th C dress **325.00**

Trolley card sign
Fairbank's Gold Dust, illus of glass baby bottles, captioned "Kept Clean and Safe with Gold Dust," copyright 1921, 20-1/2" w, 10-1/4" h, surface soiling, water stains.............. **480.00**
Fairy Soap, bar of soap and trademark fairy, 24-1/2" w, 15" h **90.00**

Sign, Moehn Brewing Company, Malto-Dextrine Tonic, lady, tin, 15" d, **$500**. Photo courtesy of Joy Luke Auctions.

Watch fob

Allis Chalmers, 1-3/4", silvered white meal, shield design on front "Bullock Electric Apparatus," reverse with diamond shape surrounding center with text "Allis Chalmers Company 1860-1904" **50.00**

Glad Hand Soap, 1-3/8", metal, black finish, bright silver luster on raised elements of wreath design surrounding color celluloid center insert of male hand gently grasping female hand, text on reverse "Glad Hand Soap-A Blessing To All Hands-Martin & Martin, Chicago," orig strap **90.00**

Tin, Wood's Improved Lollacapop, yellow tin, black text and striking art image showing mosquito, "One Of The Greatest Knows Antidotes In The World For Mosquitoes, Black Flies And Knats," 1920s or earlier, original contents, 1-3/4" x 3-1/4" x 3/4", **$70**. Photo courtesy of Hake's Americana & Collectibles.

Tray, Satin Cigarettes, pretty girl in large hat, adv on front and rim, **$195**.

Huber Road Roller, 1-1/2" h, brass, high relief front image of road construction machine, reverse with name in oval below "Rollers, Maintainers, Graders" **55.00**

Tray, New Home Sewing Machine, Cuban dealer imprint, aluminum. Gray accent art of smiling mother at sewing machine mending pants of boy doing handstand on base of machine, c1905, 3-1/2" x 5-1/2", **$35**. Photo courtesy of Hake's Americana & Collectibles.

Savage Arms, emb metal, pointing Indian chief, painted headband, orig patina, 1-5/8" d **325.00**

ADVERTISING TRADE CARDS

History: Advertising trade cards are small, thin cardboard cards made to advertise the merits of a product. They usually bear the name and address of a merchant.

With the invention of lithography, colorful trade cards became a popular way to advertise in the late 19th and early 20th centuries. They were made to appeal especially to children. Young and old alike collected and treasured them in albums and scrapbooks. Few are dated; the prime years for trade card production were 1880 to 1893; cards made between 1810 and 1850 can be found, but rarely. By 1900, trade cards were rapidly losing their popularity, and by 1910, they had all but vanished.

Beverages

Ayer's Sarsaparilla, "Ayer's Sarsaparilla Makes the Weak Strong," two gentlemen **18.00**

Hires' Root Beer, 5" x 6-1/2", full-color portrait of young lady holding package of powdered Hires Improved Root Beer, reverse with brown and white design and text, including medical claims "Best Blood Purifier in the World," late 1800s **18.00**

Gibson's Pure Rye Whiskey **35.00**

Mayer Brewing, Palest Brewery, New York, diecut...................................... **65.00**

Union Pacific Tea, young lad sailors with American flag, includes Easter greeting **8.00**

Clothing

A. S. Shaw Footwear, floral chromo, c1885, 4-1/2" x 7"............................. **12.00**

Child's & Staples, Gilbertsville, ME, young girl chasing butterfly, 2-3/4" x 4-1/2" **12.00**

Honest Abe Work Shirts-Overalls, black and white, Abe Lincoln type with text, sgd by Abe N. Cohen, diecut hole for hanging, c1910, 2-1/2" x 4-1/2" **12.00**

Solar Tip Shoes, Girard College, Philadelphia, Where Boys Wear Our Solar Tip Shoes.. **20.00**

Thompson's Glove Fitting Corsets, lady and cupids.............................. **35.00**

Farm machinery and supplies

Gale Mfg. Co., Daisy Sulky Hay Rake, folder type, four panels, field scene **75.00**

Keystone Agricultural Implements, Uncle Sam talking to world representatives, metamorphic......... **75.00**

New Essay Lawn Mower, scene of Statue of Liberty, New York harbor **35.00**

Reid's Flower Seeds, two high wheeled bicyclers admiring flowers held by three ladies **15.00**

Sheridan's, To Make Hens Lay, Use Sheridan's Condition Powder, before and after views of farmer in chicken house **25.00**

Food

Batsford, W. A., Dealer in Milk in Orange Co., NY, floral motif, c1880, 2" x 3-1/2" **7.50**

Clark's O.N.T., set of four, multicolored image of pretty blond girl on front in various activities, light green border, blue promo text on back, 1883, each 3-3/4" x 6-1/2", **$30**. Photo courtesy of Hake's Americana & Collectibles.

Jumbo the Elephant, colorful image on front of elephant, thread wrapped around his front feet attached to spools being pulled by horses and elephants, text "Jumbo Must Go, Because Drawn By Willimantic Thread!" back with black and white text including "All The Honors America Ahead Atlanta, 1881," 3-3/8" x 5-3/4", **$20**. Photo courtesy of Hake's Americana & Collectibles.

Czar Baking Powder, black woman and boy with giant biscuit......................**25.00**
Heinz Apple Butter, diecut, pickle shape..**48.00**
Pearl Baking Powder, light blue and sepia, reverse with order blank, c1890 ....**35.00**
Royal Hams, Chief Joseph & His Tribe examining barrel of hams............... **48.00**
Tunison, E., Grocer, elf standing next to pansies..**15.00**
Woolson Spice, Lion Coffee, young children portraying Cinderella.........**25.00**

Health and beauty

Ayer's Hair Vigor, four mermaids, ship in background **7.50**
Golf Queen Perfume, Ricksecker Co., c1895, blotter type **12.00**
Hoyt's German Cologne, E. M. Hoyt & Co., mother cat and kittens **25.00**

Laundry and soaps

Empire Wringer Co., Auburn, NY, child helping "I Can Help Mama"...........**35.00**
Fort Wayne Improved Western Washer, Horton Manufacturing Co., Fort Wayne, Ind., one lady watching as other works new machine **35.00**

Left: 4-1/2" fan diecut, multicolored image of pretty blond holding binoculars, red text around border "Morris' Indian Root Pills & Comstocks Dead Shot Worm Pellets Morristown, N.Y."; right: trade card, 3" x 5-1/4", multicolored image on front of children and dog reading large book titled "Indian Cough Cure," back cover text "Dr. Kilmer's Indian Cough Cure Consumption Oil," back with black and white reverse art and text promoting product, 1880s, each, **$10**. Photo courtesy of Hake's Americana & Collectibles.

Wolverine Double Sink Faucets, Ray A. Brosious, Pine Grove, PA, **$4**.

Ivorine Cleanser, lettering on side of elephant, other animals..................**15.00**
Mrs. Potts' Sad Irons, sign painters **35.00**
Soapine, Kendall Mfg. Co., Providence, RI, street scene **12.50**

Medicine

Dr. Kilmer & Co., Binghamton, NY, 36" x 60", Standard Herbal Remedies, detailed graphics **395.00**
King of the Blood Medicine, Automation Musical Band, Barnum's Traveling Museum... **45.00**
Perry Davis, Pain Killer for Wounds, armored man of war ships battle scene **25.00**
Quaker Bitters, Standard Family Medicine, child in barrel.................**17.50**
Scott's Emulsion of Cod Liver Oil, man with large fish over back, vertical format **20.00**

Miscellaneous

Agate Iron Ware, Father Time at stove, 3-7/8" x 2-3/4" **45.00**
American Machine Co., Manufacturers of Hardware Specialties, three women ironing, vertical format....................**40.00**
Emerson Piano Co., black and white illus **40.00**
Forbes, C. P., Jewelry, Greenfield, MA, Santa in front of fireplace, toys on table **15.00**
Granite Iron Ware, three ladies gossiping over tea......................... **25.00**
Landis's Wallpaper, Quakertown, PA, multicolored.................................... **5.00**
Read McCraney, Sonora, Tuolumne Co., CA, Diamonds and Watches, Jewelry & Optical Goods, 1890s, 2-1/2" x 4" **10.00**
Wells Portrait & Landscape Photographer, Sonora, CA, adv on front, ship motif, gold and silver trim, 4-1/4" x 6" **35.00**

Stoves and ranges

Andes Stove, black children **15.00**
Dixon's Stove Polish, Brownies illus **20.00**
Enamieline Stove Polish, paper-doll type, distributed by J. L. Prescott & Co., 11 Jay St., 1900s, Rose, 5" h...........**30.00**
Florence Oil Stove, colorful illus of two women and two children **40.00**
Rising Sun Stove Polish, folder type, "The Modern Cinderella"................**50.00**
Rutland Stove Lining, child talking to parrot..**115.00**

Thread and sewing

Brooks' Spool Cotto, three kittens playing instruments made from spools **25.00**
Corticelli Spool Silks, Nonotuck Silk Co., diecut leaf shape with silkworm, green and white, c1888, 2"............. **10.00**
J. & P. Coats, Best Silk Thread, "We Never Fade," black youngster and spool of thread **12.00**
Singer Manufacturing Co., choir of children singing as birds listen **20.00**
White Sewing Machine Co., elves working at sewing machine............**15.00**

Tobacco

Capadura Cigar, two baseball players, "Judgment, Judgment is always decided in favor of the Capadura Cigar" **30.00**
49 Cut Plug, miners' scene **225.00**

AGATA GLASS

History: Agata glass was invented in 1887 by Joseph Locke of the New England Glass Company, Cambridge, Massachusetts.

Agata glass was produced by coating a piece of peachblow glass with metallic stain, spattering the surface with alcohol, and firing. The resulting high-gloss, mottled finish looked like oil droplets floating on a watery surface. Shading usually ranged from opaque pink to dark rose, although pieces in a pastel opaque green also exist. A few pieces have been found in a satin finish.

Tumblers, rich color, nice shading, 3-3/4" h, price for pair, **$350**.

Bowl, 8" d, 4" h, green opaque body, staining and gold trim............... **1,150.00**

Celery vase, 7" h, sq, fluted top **685.00**

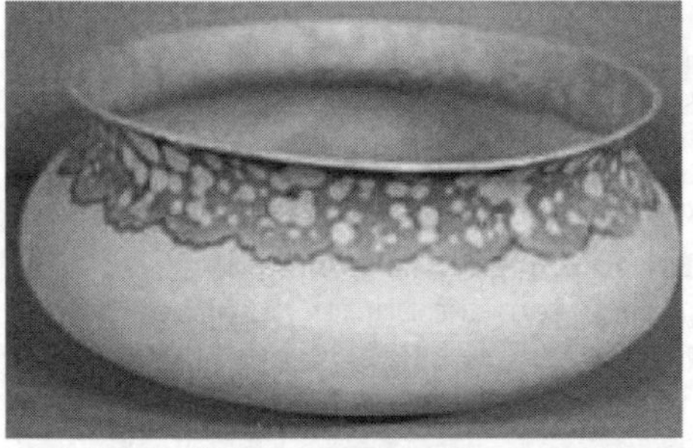

Bowl, thin walled, opaque green, blue watered rim, trimmed with worn gilding, 8-3/4" d, 3-3/4" h, **$3,000**. Photo courtesy of Garth's Auctions, Inc.

Finger bowl and underplate, 5-1/2" d, 2-1/2" h bowl, ruby, golden tracery, flecks of dark mottling, matching 6-1/2" d underplate with piecrust crimped border..................................... **1,250.00**

Pitcher, 6-3/8" h, crimped rim **1,750.00**

Spooner, 4-1/2" h, 2-1/2" w, sq top, wild rose peachblow ground, small areas of wear... **400.00**

Toothpick holder, 2-3/8" h, green opaque, pale mottling **875.00**

Tumbler, 3-3/4" h, rich color, moderate staining, pr................................. **300.00**

Vase

- 4-1/2" h, square scalloped top, gold tracery, crimson peachblow ground **695.00**
- 8" h, lily, shiny surface, crimson peachblow ground, large black splotches.......................... **1,100.00**

AMBERINA GLASS

History: Joseph Locke developed Amberina glass in 1883 for the New England Glass Works. "Amberina," a trade name, describes a transparent glass that shades from deep ruby to amber. It was made by adding powdered gold to the ingredients for an amber-glass batch. A portion of the glass was reheated later to produce the shading effect. Usually it was the bottom that was reheated to form the deep red; however, reverse examples have been found.

1883

Most early Amberina is flint-quality glass, blown or pattern molded. Patterns include Diamond Quilted, Daisy and Button, Venetian Diamond, Diamond and Star, and Thumbprint.

In addition to the New England Glass Works, the Mount Washington Glass Company of New Bedford, Massachusetts, copied the glass in the 1880s and sold it at first under the Amberina trade name and later as "Rose Amber." It is difficult to distinguish pieces from these two New England factories. Boston and Sandwich Glass Works never produced the glass.

Amberina glass also was made in the 1890s by several Midwest factories, among which was Hobbs, Brockunier & Co. Trade names included "Ruby Amber Ware" and "Watermelon." The Midwest glass shaded from cranberry to amber, and the color resulted from the application of a thin flashing of cranberry to the reheated portion. This created a sharp demarcation between the two colors. This less-expensive version was the death knell for the New England variety.

In 1884, Edward D. Libbey was given the use of the trade name "Amberina" by the New England Glass Works. Production took place during 1900, but ceased shortly thereafter. In the 1920s, Edward Libbey renewed production at his Toledo, Ohio, plant for a short period. The glass was of high quality.

Marks: Amberina made by Edward Libbey in the 1920s is marked "Libbey" in script on the pontil.

Reproduction Alert: Reproductions abound.

Additional Listings: Libbey, Mount Washington.

For more information, see *Warman's Glass*, 4th edition.

Basket, 5" d base, 13-1/2" h, shape #3033, fold-in mouth, optic panels, arching handle, 1917, sgd "Amberina Libbey" in circle........................ **2,950.00**

Bowl

- 4-1/4" d, 1-1/2" h, Diamond Quilted.................................... **90.00**
- 4-1/2" d, 3" h, deep coloring **125.00**
- 5-1/2" d, 2-1/2" h, ruffled top, deep coloring **150.00**

Celery vase, 3-1/2" d, 6-1/2" h, sq scalloped top, fuchsia shading to amber base... **350.00**

Cordial, 4-1/2" h, lily form, fuchsia shading to amber, pr **300.00**

Creamer, 4-1/2" h, Thumbprint pattern, polished pontil, Victorian **85.00**

Cruet

- 5-1/2" h, Inverted Thumbprint pattern, fuchsia trefoil spout, neck, and shoulder, Mt. Washington **435.00**
- 6" h, Inverted Thumbprint pattern, gilt dec, replaced stopper, wear to gilt.. **90.00**
- 6" h, Thumbprint pattern, replaced stopper, Victorian **95.00**

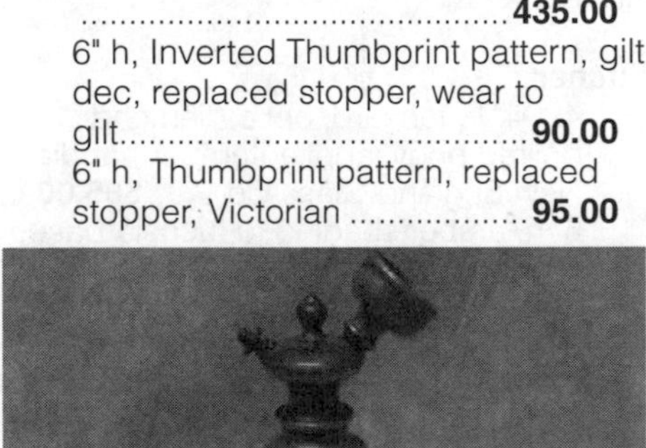

Atomizer, cylindrical bottle, patterned amberina glass, pewter top for atomizer, 7-1/4" h, missing bulb, **$250**. Photo courtesy of Alderfer Auction Co.

Decanter, 12" h, Optic Diamond Quilted pattern, solid amber faceted stopper **475.00**

Finger bowl, 5" d, 2-1/2" h, inverted scalloped rim, deep coloring **175.00**

Lady's cuspidor, 5-1/4" d, 2-1/2" h, fuchsia flaring top shading to amber base... **250.00**

Lemonade glass, 4" h, ribbed, applied reeded amber handles, pr **350.00**

Nappy, 6" l, handle, enameled dec, polished pontil, Victorian **140.00**

Pear, 5-1/2" h, deep red shading to amber, applied stem **520.00**

Cologne bottle, original round blown stopper, Midwest, **$125**.

Pitcher

4-1/4" h, tankard, optic diamond quilted body, applied amber handle, New England Glass Co. **685.00**

6" h, amber shading to fuchsia base, Inverted Thumbprint pattern, applied ribbed colorless handle **265.00**

7" h, fuchsia shading to amber base, sq top, Inverted Thumbprint pattern, applied reeded amber handle, scratches around center, tool marks **150.00**

7-1/2" d, amber shading to fuchsia base, squared-off top with four pinched sides, applied reeded amber handle, several tool marks on top edge............................ **150.00**

8" h, fuchsia shading to amber base, ribbed, applied reeded amber handle **210.00**

Punch cup

2-1/4" h, squatty, applied ribbed amber ring handle................ **150.00**

2-3/8" h, plated amberina, deep mahogany shading to fuchsia to butter cream, twelve ribs, amber curlicue handle, off-white lining **3,750.00**

Sherbet, 4-1/4" h, Inverted Thumbprint amberina bowl, amber stem, pr **200.00**

Sweetmeat, 6" d, Baby Thumbprint pattern, applied colorless florals, feet, and rim, polished pontil................ **320.00**

Syrup pitcher, 5-3/4" h, optic inverted thumbprint, silverplate fitting, sgd "1954" under lid, New England Glass Co. **1,500.00**

Toothpick holder, 2-3/8" h, molded DQ design on ext., Mt. Washington..... **375.00**

Tumbler

3-3/4" h, Inverted Thumbprint pattern.................................. **70.00**

4-1/4" h, fuchsia shading to amber, ribbed, cylindrical shape **115.00**

Vase

4" d, 4" h, sq form, ruffled corners, deep coloring....................... **250.00**

7" h, lily, vertical ribbed body, applied amber foot............... **520.00**

9" h, lily, tri-corn top, ribbed stem, applied amber foot............... **520.00**

10-3/4" h, lily, petaled mouth, honey amber shading to pale yellow, nine optic ribbed body, Libbey, No. 3006, 1917 .... **715.00**

Water set, 7" h pitcher, six 4" h tumblers, Thumbprint pattern, applied reeded colorless handle, 1-1/4" l crack in pitcher at handle, chips on tumblers......... **420.00**

American Hand-Painted China

History: The American china painting movement began in 1876 and remained popular over the next 50 years. Thousands of artisans-professionals and amateur-decorated tableware, desk accessories, dresser sets, and many other items with floral, fruits, and conventional geometric designs and occasionally with portraits, birds, and landscapes. Some American firms, such as Lenox and Willetts Manufacturing Co. of Trenton, New Jersey, produced Belleek, a special type of porcelain that china painters decorated, but a majority of porcelain was imported from France, Germany, Austria, Czechoslovakia, and Japan.

Marks: American-painted porcelains bear foreign factory marks. However, the American style was distinctive, whether naturalistic or conventional (geometric). Some pieces were signed and dated by the artist.

Notes: The quality of the artwork, the amount of detail, and technical excellence—not the amount of gilding or the manufacturer of the porcelain itself—are key pricing factors. Unusual subjects and uncommon forms also influence value.

Adviser: Dorothy Kamm.

Bonbon bowl, double-handles, footed, band of polychrome flowers on interior and exterior, burnished gold handles, ball feet, rim, and border bands, signed "W Wilson," 1900-1915, 5-1/2" d, **$75**. All photos courtesy of Adviser Dorothy Kamm.

Bonbon bowl, 5-1/2" d, double-handles, ftd, band of polychrome flowers on int. and ext., burnished gold handles, ball feet, rim, and border bands, sgd "W Wilson," 1900-1915 .... **75.00**

Bowl, 9-1/2" d, 3" h, polychrome geometric design, burnished gold rim, marked "T & V, Limoges, France," 1892-1907... **50.00**

Salad plate, crescent shaped, pink peonies and leaves, burnished gold stippled in spots on background, burnished gold rim, signed "JHK," marked "T & V, Limoges," 1890s, 9" w, **$50**.

Bread plate, 6-3/4" d, rimmed, pale green geometric border, burnished gold, marked "GDA, Limoges, France," 1900-1930... **25.00**

Chalice, pomegranates and grapes on ivory ground, burnished gold rim, foot, borders, dotted background on cup, marked with crown and two shields, Vienna, Austria, 1890-1908, 9-3/4" h, **$300**.

Chalice, 9-3/4" h, pomegranates and grapes on ivory ground, burnished gold rim, foot, borders, dotted background on

cup, marked with crown and two shields, Vienna, Austria, 1890-1908 .... **300.00**

Chocolate pot, 9-1/2" h, band of conventional florals framed by burnished gold bands, dark blue band, burnished gold handles, marked "Limoges, France," 1900-1915 .... **300.00**

Cracker jar, cov, 9-1/2" d, 5-1/2" h, sweet pea border, ivory ground, burnished gold handles and rims, marked "Rosenthal, Selb-Bavaria," 1900-1915 .... **150.00**

Creamer and covered sugar, conventional florals, opal luster int., burnished gold rims and handles, sgd "Müller-Foster Studio," marked "B & Co., France," 1900-1915 .... **50.00**

Cup and saucer

Decorated with conventional Celtic border design in celadon, light blue border, ivory center, cup bottom and interiors, burnished gold rims and handle, sgd "L.E.S.," marked with crown in double circle, "Victoria, Austria," 1900-1920 .... **30.00**

Decorated with conventional swag design of blue flowers, burnished gold rims and handle, sgd "Jane Bent Telin," marked "Favorite Bavaria," 1910-1925 .... **45.00**

Dessert set, 7" d plate, cup and saucer, border of forget-me-nots and gold scrolls on light blue band, white enamel accents, burnished gold rim, sgd "LUKEN," various marks, 1900-1925 .... **45.00**

Jam jar, 4-3/8" h, 6-3/4" d plate, border design of grapes and leaves, variegated blue enamels, burnished gold ground, yellow luster border band and knob, sgd "L. Vance-Phillips, 1917," Belleek palette mark, "Lenox" **350.00**

Milk pitcher, cov, matching plate, yellow and yellow red flowers on ivory ground, burnished gold rims and trim on handles, sgd "Gertrude Clark, Xmas 1914," marked Rosenthal, Selb-Bavaria" **75.00**

Perfume bottle, stopper, 4-3/4" h, daisies and greenery, ivory ground, burnished gold lip and stopper, marked "O. & E. G. Austria," 1896-1918 .... **45.00**

Pin tray, 5-3/4" l, 4" w, border design of blue and burnished gold moths, connected by burnished gold and black band, ivory ground, burnished gold rim, sgd "E. ARRINDELL, 1-2-18," marked "MZ, Austria" **45.00**

Plate

6-5/8" d, band of conventional style roses and leaves, ivory ground, pale green center, burnished gold rim, sgd "P. M. T.," marked "Bavaria," c1892-1914 .... **20.00**

8-1/2" d, birds, burnished gold rim, sgd "C.S.W., Feb. 26, 1886," marked "D & Co." **65.00**

12" d, conventional border of berries and leaves, sgd "C Goodman, 1918," marked "JHR" **80.00**

Salad plate, 9" w, crescent-shaped, pink peonies and leaves, burnished gold stippled in spots on background, burnished gold rim, sgd "JHK," marked "T & V, Limoges," 1890s **50.00**

Salt and pepper shakers

3" h, conventional blue-winged insects, burnished gold tops, 1905-1920, price for pr.................... **35.00**

4-3/4" w, 2-1/2" h, two-in-one shaker, raised paste garlands cov with burnished gold, accented with turquoise enamel ivory ground, burnished gold tops, handle and foot rim, marked "Germany," c1891-1914 .... **45.00**

Tea set, 5-1/2" h teapot, 3-1/4" h creamer, 4-1/2" h sugar, conventional floral design, various manufacturers, 1900-1920 .... **300.00**

Vase

9-1/2" h, 3-1/8" d, conventional floral border and panels, framed and rimmed with burnished gold, marked "Limoges," 1900-1920.......... **125.00**

17-1/2" h, conventional birds and flowers on top half, bottom divided into eight ivory panels, burnished gold borders and rim, marked "T & V, Limoges, France," 1900-15 .... **850.00**

American Hand-Painted China Jewelry And Buttons

History: The American china painting movement began in 1876, about the time the mass production of jewelry also occurred. Porcelain manufacturers and distributors offered a variety of porcelain shapes and settings for brooches, pendants, cuff links, and shirtwaist buttons. Thousands of artisans painted flowers, people, landscapes, and conventions (geometric) motifs. The category of hand-painted porcelain jewelry comprises a unique category, separate from costume and fine jewelry. While the materials were inexpensive to produce, the painted decoration was a work of fine art.

Marks: American painted porcelain jewelry bears no factory marks, and is usually unsigned.

Notes: The quality of the artwork, the amount of detail, and technical excellence—not the amount of gilding—are the key pricing factors. Uncommon shapes also influence value.

Adviser: Dorothy Kamm.

Brooch, 1-1/2" w, 2" l, oval, violets, ivory ground, burnished gold border superimposed with black line border design of violets and vines, gold-plated bezel, **$75**. All photos courtesy of Adviser Dorothy Kamm.

Bar pin, 1-3/4" wide by 3/8", dark pink roses and leaves, pale blue ground, burnished gold tips and rim, gold-plated bezel, c1880-1915......................... **50.00**

Shirt waist button, 1" d, with shank, conventional design in raised paste, pastel-colored enamel, cobalt blue ground, burnished gold rim, **$20**.

Belt buckle brooch

1-5/8" wide by 2-1/8" oval, stylized tiger lily, buds, and greenery, outlined in gold, burnished gold border, gold-plated bezel, 1900-1917 .... **225.00**

2-1/16" d, forget-me-nots and greenery, polychrome ground, white enamel highlights on petals and flower centers, burnished gold border, 1900-1917................. **95.00**

Set of four buttons, two 1-1/16" d, two 5/8" d cuff buttons, with shanks, various birds, pastel polychrome grounds, each button framed with dots of raised paste covered with burnished gold, burnished gold rims, **$60.**

Brooch

7/8" sq, diamond shape, waterscape with water lilies, white enamel highlights, burnished with gold border, brass bezel, c1920-40 .... **35.00**

7/8" w, 1" l, heart shape, violets and leaves, polychrome ground, white enamel highlights on flower petals and centers, burnished gold rim, gold plated bezel, c1890-1910 .... **40.00**

1" x 1", cross-shape, pink and ruby roses, polychrome ground, tips dec with raised paste dots, burnished gold gold-plated bezel with tubular hinge **80.00**

1" x 3/4" rect, white Florida landscape, platinum ground, sterling silver bezel, c1920-1940 .... **75.00**

1-1/4" x 1-4/8" oval, woman's portrait surrounded by forget-me-nots, ivory ground, white enamel highlights, framed by burnished gold raised paste scrolls and dots, gold-plated bezel **80.00**

1-1/4" w, 1-9/16" l, horseshoe shape, pink and ruby roses and greenery, polychrome ground, white enamel highlights on petals, burnished gold tips, gold-plated bezel, c1890-1915 .... **75.00**

1-1/2" w by 2" l, oval, violets, ivory ground, burnished gold border superimposed with black line border design of violets and vines, gold-plated bezel **75.00**

1-7/16" x 1-7/8" oval, pink roses, burnished gold border, sgd "Albrecht," brass bezel **65.00**

1-1/2" x 2", oval, Art Nouveau-style woman's head and neck, poppies in her hair, gold-plated bezel **90.00**

1-1/2" x 2" oval, stained glass-like conventional design in polychrome colors and burnished gold, gold-plated bezel, 1905-1915 .... **65.00**

1-7/8" w, crescent shape, dec with dark pink roses, burnished gold tips, brass bezel, 1900-1920 .... **45.00**

1-13/16" x 2-3/16" oval, dec with columbine and greenery, polychrome ground, burnished gold trim, gold-plated bezel **75.00**

1-11/16" x 2-1/8" oval, dec with a tropical landscape, burnished gold rim, sgd "OC" (Olive Commons, St. John's Island, FL, 1908-1920), gold-plated bezel **105.00**

2" w, crescent shape, purple pansy and leaves, ivory ground, burnished gold tip, gold-plated bezel, c1890-1915 .... **60.00**

2" x 1-5/8" oval, Art Nouveau-style poppies, burnished gold border, brass bezel, 1856-1915 .... **75.00**

2" x 1-1/2" oval, pink and ruby roses, solid dark blue ground, white enamel highlights, burnished gold border, brass bezel, c1940 .... **65.00**

2-1/16" d, violets, burnished gold rim, brass bezel, 1900-1920 .... **65.00**

Cuff buttons, pr, 3/4" x 1" ovals, lavender flowers, border of burnished gold dots and apple green jewels, burnished gold rims, c1890-1920 .... **40.00**

Dress set

Five pieces: 2" x 2-5/8" belt buckle brooch, oval brass bezel, pr 1" d shirt waist buttons with shanks, pr 1" d shirt waist buttons with sew-through backs, dec with forget-me-nots, black green scalloped borders rimmed in burnished gold, c1900-1917 .... **400.00**

Four pieces: 3/4" d shirt waist collar button, three 5/8" d shirt waist buttons, pink roses, white enamel highlights, burnished gold rims, shank backs **60.00**

Flapper pin, 1-5/8" x 2-1/8" oval, stylized woman, burnished gold border, brass bezel, 1924-1928 .... **75.00**

Hat pin

3/4" w by 1" oval medallion, 6" l shaft, four-leaf clover on burnished gold ground, brass bezel, 1900-1920 .... **115.00**

2" d, 10-1/2" l shaft, circular head, conventional design, polychrome colors and burnished gold, burnished gold rim **200.00**

Pendant

1-5/8" x 2-1/8" oval, violets, burnished bold border, brass bezel, c1880-1914 .... **60.00**

1-3/4" x 1-3/4" oval, forget-me-nots, white enamel highlights, burnished gold rim, brass bezel, c1900-1920 .... **50.00**

Shirt waist button

1" d, with shank, conventional design in raised paste and pastel-colored enamel, cobalt blue ground, burnished gold rim **20.00**

1-3/16" d, with eye, single daisy, burnished gold ground **20.00**

AMPHORA

History: The Amphora Porcelain Works was one of several pottery companies located in the Teplitz-Turn region of Bohemia in the late 19th and early 20th centuries. It is best known for art pottery, especially Art Nouveau and Art-Deco pieces.

Marks: Several markings were used, including the name and location of the pottery and the Imperial mark, which included a crown. Prior to World War I, Bohemia was part of the Austro-Hungarian Empire, so the word "Austria" may appear as part of the mark. After World War I, the word "Czechoslovakia" may be part of the mark.

Additional Listings: Teplitz.

Center bowl, 2-1/8" h, incised dec outlined in black, enameled blue-green and pink cabochons, mottled tan matte ground, four legs, circular base **200.00**

Ewer, 14-1/2" h, pink, gold, and green floral dec, gold accents, salamander entwined handle, c1900 .... **575.00**

Figure, 10-3/4" h, nude boy fetching water, carrying an urn, standing by tree stump, Austria, early 20th C **300.00**

Rose bowl, 12-1/2" h, orange bowl, two colorful medallions, base with four upward flowing arms dec in mottled blue and pink on cream ground, cobalt blue base band, marked **450.00**

Sugar bowl, cov, 6-1/4" d, 4-1/2" h, Art Deco enamel dec, polychrome birds and leaves, stamped mark "15449/30" **280.00**

Urn, stopper, 12" h, painted gold trees, enameled branch of berries, marked, chip, nick to stopper **175.00**

Vase

5-1/4" h, three buttressed handles dec with naturalistic leafy rose vines, rose hip clusters, matte green rose on mottled brown round, gilt highlights, imp mark and stamp on base **250.00**

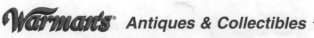

6" h, flattened spherical form, shoulder dec with alternating large and small moths in shades of blue, pink, and yellow, raised gilt outline, relief spider webs and enameled disk centers, gilt highlights on green and blue ground, imp "Amphora" in oval, printed "R. S. & K. Turn-Teplitz Bohemia" with maker's device on base **900.00**

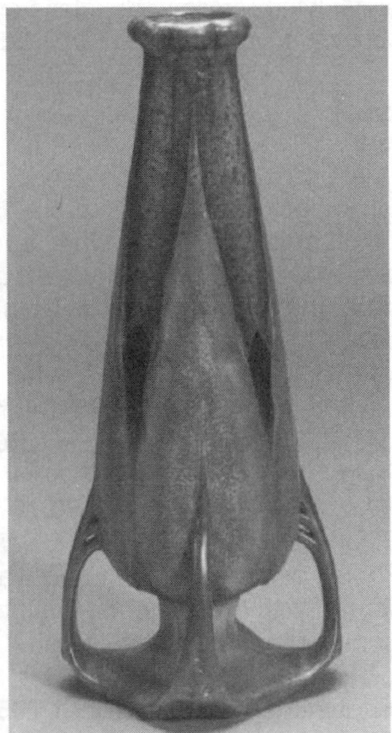

Vase, Art Nouveau, body inverted amphora, molded with stylized pointed leaves, base spreading out and curling upward into gilt tendrils attached to the body, glazed in greens and pinks, Austria, early 20th C, 16" h, **$500**. Photo courtesy of Skinner, Inc.

11" x 7-1/2", cobalt blue enameled basket handle, two ring handles, body incised with embracing couple and stylized polychrome flowers, texture magenta ground, stamped mark, minor nicks **360.00**

Vase, gourd shape, embossed pink cyclamen blossoms on swirling stems, heart-shaped gilded leaves, hammered lustered ground, stamped "Amphora Austria," 8" x 7," **$2,185**. Photo courtesy of David Rago Auctions, Inc.

19" x 12-1/2", bulbous, incised, polychrome enamel vulture and olive branches, Amphora paper label................................. **1,150.00**

Wall plaque, 18-1/2" d, Moorish man and woman in relief, red ground, gilt molded frames, marked "Amphora," price for pr **900.00**

Vessel, covered, squatty, Art Deco-style enamel polychrome decoration with birds and leaves, stamped mark "15449/30," 4-1/2" x 6-1/4", **$300**. Photo courtesy of David Rago Auctions, Inc.

Water jug, 14-1/2" h, crossed handles, polychrome enamel Egyptian motifs, stamped numbers **630.00**

Animal Collectibles

History: The representation of animals in fine arts, decorative arts, and on utilitarian products dates back to antiquity. Some religions endowed certain animals with mystical properties. Authors throughout written history used human characteristics when portraying animals.

The formation of collectors' clubs and marketing crazes, e.g., flamingos, pigs, and penguins, during the 1970s, increased the popularity of this collecting field.

For more information, see *Warman's Glass*, 4th edition.

Additional Listings: See specific animal collectible categories in *Warman's Americana & Collectibles*.

Barnyard

Cane, 37-1/4" l, 5" l x 1-1/2" d x 2" h carved duck, elephant ivory handle, dark brown glass eyes, detailed feathering, 1-1/2" dec silver collar, thick Malacca shaft, 1" replaced brass ferrule, attributed to America, c1870, professional repair to duck's beak **2,400.00**

Carving, folk art, wood

7" l, peep, painted, c1900, with stand **9,545.00**

9-1/2" l, 2-1/2" w, 8" h, rooster, polychrome red, mustard yellow, and brown, base with indistinct pencil inscription, PA, c1840 .... **4,320.00**

17" l, 15" h, rooster, old cream-colored paint, 3/4 flat body, stand **460.00**

Chopper, 12" l, 7-1/2" d, 7-1/4" h, rooster, iron, fanciful silhouette, incised feather detail, mounted on wooden fragment, with stand, late 18th/early 19th C, lacks wooden handle.......................... **1,035.00**

Pill box, shell, silver hinged lid, 2-1/2" h; porcelain hinged lidded trinket box, hen with chicks, 2-1/2" h; trinket box, hinged lid, Halcyon Days, enamel decorated cockerel "First Century BC Mosaic of a Cockerel," 2-1/2" d, **$200**. Photo courtesy of Joy Luke Auctions.

Figure, 21" l, 14-1/2" h, carved walnut, realistically modeled bull, standing on ovoid naturalistic base with grasses and timbers, possibly indistinctly signed to end of one timber, mounted to ovoid mahogany plinth, Black Forest, late 19th C **2,000.00**

Jar, cov, 6" d, 6-1/2" h, stoneware, figure of pig eating from trough on lid, German, some damage to base **115.00**

Painting, 40" w, 32-1/4" h, oil on canvas, big horn sheep on hillside overlooking small fog shrouded lake, sgd "C. O. Williams," back of canvas with preparer's label "Reeves & Sons, London," ornate gilt frame with painted gold highlights **4,100.00**

Stuffed toy, 12-1/2" h, duck with orig straw bonnet, yellow ribbon, orig box, Gund.. **60.00**

Musical picture, tin figures of adult cat playing fiddle, kittens dancing, tin figures move in conjunction with music box attached to back, German, 8-3/4" x 12," missing key, losses to frame, **$10,450**. Photo courtesy of Alderfer Auction Co.

Tin, Dr. Daniels' Cow Invigorator, 18 oz pry lid tin litho, image of cow on each side, C-8+ **275.00**

Toy, stuffed

Cow, 11-1/2" l, 8-1/2" h, brown, felt covering, glass eyes, black painted nostrils and mouth, fur tip of tail, tin wheels attached to wooden hooves, early 20th C, some soil and wear, break to top of leg **230.00**

Goat, 4-3/4" h, black mohair legs and face, long white mohair body, felt horns, green glass eyes **60.00**

Dog collar, leather, decorated with brass French boxer dog heads, early 20th C, 15" l, **$225**. Photo courtesy of Wiederseim Associates, Inc.

Birds

Architectural element, 18-1/2" h, owl, pottery, unglazed, traces of old silver paint, base imp "Owens and Howard, St. Louis, MO," minor hairlines **550.00**

Eagle, cast iron, painted, black with white spots, America, late 19th C, 11" l, 5-1/2" d, 3-1/2" h **250.00**

Figure, sewer tile, 10-1/2" h, horned owl, perched on round pedestal base, orange glaze **450.00**

Lamp base, 16" h, owl perched on stump, sewer pipe, hollow body, good detail, dark brown glaze, shallow edge chips **385.00**

Plaque, 7" x 4" sight, 11-1/2" x 8-1/2" ebonized frame, pietra dura, colorful parrot on perch, Italian, early 20th C **250.00**

Sculpture, 15-1/2" wingspan, 20" h, eagle, carved wood, standing, spread wings **395.00**

Tobacco container, Bob White Tobacco, paper label on cloth pouch, multicolored Bob White on both sides, 1910 tax stamp, 2-3/4" w, 1-1/4" d, 4" h **400.00**

Trivet, parrot, pastel central figure with intricate flower and vine pattern, eight triangular feet, Rookwood marks, 1929, 5-3/4" sq **325.00**

Wall shelf, 16-1/2" w, eagle, carved wood, shaped shelf supported by eagle with spread wings, loss to gilt **475.00**

Cats

Andirons, pr, 17" h, cast iron, seated black cats set with glass eyes, bifurcate scroll base support, 20th C, Wayne makers **375.00**

Cane, 33" l, 1-1/2" x 4" h solid mother-of-pearl handle, carved furry cat, yellow glass eyes, 1/4" silver collar, stepped partridge wood shaft, 1-1/4" brass and iron ferrule, possibly Continental, c1890 .... **2,200.00**

Carnival target, kitten, pr **950.00**

Figure

2-5/8" h, carved marble or alabaster, sitting, glass eyes, America, 19th C, chip on base corner **1,035.00**

7" h, Barum Ware, green, brown, and blue glossy glaze, marked, restoration to ears and tail **115.00**

9" l, sewer tile, reclining, hand-tooled eyelashes, white glazed eyes **360.00**

9-1/2" w, 7" d, 17-1/4" h, carved pine, fat cat, incised "E. Sweet," 20th C, cracks **435.00**

13-1/4" h, sewer tile, elongated form, head cocked to one side, curious look, hand tooled eyelashes, metallic glaze, Ohio **660.00**

Figure, Pointer, bronze, **$250**. Photo courtesy of Wiederseim Associates, Inc.

Miniature vase, 3" h, Pillin, woman with black cat, blended lavender, teal, gray, and black ground **660.00**

Painting

Brown Tabby Kitten with a Rose Bow, John Henry Dolph, sgd "JHDolph" lower left, oil on board, 12" x 9", framed, scattered retouch **4,700.00**

Gray Tiger Cat with a Blue Bow, sgd "MABrown" lower right, American School, 19th C, oil on canvas, 17" x 21", framed, minor scattered retouch, varnish inconsistencies **2,000.00**

Kittens Playing, sgd indistinctly lower right, titled in pencil on reverse, American School, 19th C, oil on panel, 6-1/4" x 8-1/2", framed, minor retouch upper right **530.00**

Sleepy Tabby, Franklin W. Rogers, sgd "F.W. Roger" lower right, label on reverse, oil on canvas, 21" x 17", framed, scattered retouch, varnish inconsistencies, craquelure **1,175.00**

The Sleeping Tabby, monogrammed and dated "JLC 1881" lower left, American School, 19th C, oil on canvas, 9" x 12", framed, scattered retouch, craquelure **3,300.00**

Tiger Cat, unsigned, American School, 19th C, oil on canvas, 19-1/2" x 15-1/2", large tiger cat, yellow eyes, framed, minor retouch **5,875.00**

Stamp box, 4-3/4" l, carved fruitwood, figural cat lying inside shoe, glass eyes, hinged lid, early 20th C **225.00**

Dogs

Artwork

Chalk, *Sporting Dogs*, Thomas Blinks, pr **5,975.00**

Oil on artist board, two white and gray puppies chewing lady's black shoe, mother dog looks on from seat covered in burgundy and blue throw, sgd "G. Johnson," 20th C, gold painted liner, 22-1/4" w, 18-1/4" h **150.00**

Oil on canvas, *A Good Day in the Field,* Arthur Wardle **50,787.00**

Oil on canvas, *Portrait of a Muzzled Puppy*, seated puppy at doorway spread with grass stems, unsigned, Continental School, late 19th C, gilt frame, sight size 19" x 13-1/4", craquelure **1,765.00**

Oil on canvas, *The Harvester's Companions*, Philip Eustace Stretton **29,875.00**

Oil on canvas, *Wake Up England,* Lilian Cheviot **26,290.00**

Painting, portrait of English setter, signed "H De S.R., 09," oil on canvas, replaced frame, **$350**. Photo courtesy of Wiederseim Associates, Inc.

Ashtray, Scottish Terrier, sq, porcelain, center black terrier, images of hounds and rabbits, green and white ground, Hermes **50.00**

Bronze, *Chasing his Tail* and *Standing Scottie*, by Edith Barretto Stevens Parsons, pr **1,135.00**

Cane

35" l, 3-1/2" l x 1-1/2" h carved elephant ivory handle, pug family consisting of father, mother, three pups in line, 1" gold filled collar dec in "C" scrolls, orig owner's elaborate initials, ebony shaft carved with simulated thorns, 1-1/8" burnished brass and iron ferrule, English, c1890 .... **1,570.00**

35-1/4" l, 1-3/4" d x 4-3/4" h carved ivory handle, performing poodle,

wearing toy soldier's cap, holding toy gun, 3/4" silver collar, tan Malacca shaft, 1" replaced brass ferrule, England, c1890 .... **1,120.00**

36-1/2" l, 2-1/2" w x 2" h purple quartz handle carved as French bulldog, upright ears, dec gold-plated collar, ebony shaft, 1" brass and iron ferrule, Continental, c1890 .... **950.00**

Display figure, bulldog, papier-mâché, adv for Claytons Dog Remedies **1,165.00**

Figure, clay

7-1/4" h, white, seated, dark brown shiny glaze, edge flakes, some seam separation **95.00**

8-1/8" h, Ohio white clay, seated, short ears and tail, long jowls, grown glaze, chip on back of base, small flake on ear **110.00**

10" h, Newcomerstown, Ohio, pottery, seated, unglazed clay, good detail, shallow front chip **3,750.00**

Figure, pearlware, 2-7/8" l, 3-1/4" h, long hair seated dog, white, brown and gold spots, minor flakes on base, short hairline **520.00**

Figure, sewer tile

7-1/2" h, seated, hand modeled, tooled fur and facial features, mat glaze with metallic speckles, traces of white paint **110.00**

10-1/2" l, 5-1/2" w, 11-1/2" h, Collie, standing, reddish brown glaze, rect molded base, firing separations, small chips on ears **935.00**

11" h, seated, molded with hand tooled details on ears and face, long eye lashes, glaze varies from light tan to dark reddish brown, Ohio, minor flakes on base **660.00**

Figure, stoneware, 13-1/2" h, Spaniels, tan and brown speckled matte glaze, glass eyes, oval bases, England, c1875, repair to base of one, glaze flakes, price for pr **6,465.00**

Jewelry, brooch

Micromosaic, recumbent King Charles spaniel, gold ropetwist frame, minor lead solder on verso **900.00**

Platinum and diamond, terrier, pavé setting, green stone eyes .. **1,725.00**

Reverse painted crystal, standing boxer, oval 14kt gold frame, sgd "W. F. Marcus" **920.00**

Pepper pot, silver, bulldog, Edwardian **1,020.00**

Pull toy, 10" h mohair dog, metal wheels **725.00**

Sign, 20-1/4" x 21-5/8" w, Toy Manchester Terriers, cutout silhouette of terrier in center, alligatored brown and black paint, stenciled white letters, additional removable sign with name below .. **95.00**

Terra cotta figure, French school, c1870

Recumbent Mastiff **2,700.00**

Seated Bulldog **2,400.00**

Stuffed ride-on toy, 25" l, 24" h, St. Bernard, straw-stuffed mohair, white rubber tires, orig glass eyes, stitched nose, and mouth, pull ring growler not working, some loss to mohair on face **175.00**

Vase, 10" h, Lenox, marked "Hunter Arms Co., First Prize, Class A," image of pointer in clearing, sgd "Delan," stamped Lenox logo **3,665.00**

Weathervane, molded copper, dog-form **7,170.00**

Place setting of Tally Ho pattern, Johnson Bros, service for 12 plus serving pieces, including punch bowl, **$950**.

Horses

Blanket, 68" sq, needlework design of horse, red ground, diamond design in field, black border with cross-stitched multicolored floral design, red yarn fringe, wool backing, reverse stitched with owner's name "Jacob Weber 1871," minor restoration, moth damage in backing **175.00**

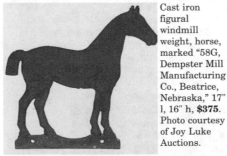

Cast iron figural windmill weight, horse, marked "58G, Dempster Mill Manufacturing Co., Beatrice, Nebraska," 17" l, 16" h, **$375**. Photo courtesy of Joy Luke Auctions.

Book, *Rodeo, A Collection of Tales & Sketches by R. B. Cunningham Graham,* selected by A. F. Tschiffeley, Literary Guild, 1936 .... **10.00**

Cane, 35-3/4" l, 4" l x 2-1/4" h elephant ivory handle carved as two riding horse heads, carved simulated leather tack, 1/2" sterling collar marked "Brigg," London hallmarks for 1897, ebony shaft, 7/8" brass and iron ferrule **1,350.00**

Condiment set, 5" l, 3-5/8" h, electroplate, base formed as horseshoe, spur-form handle, toothpick holder flanked by boot form castor, mustard pot with whip-form spoon, central jockey cap open salt, Elkington & Co., England, late 19th C **175.00**

Figure, carved and painted wood

7-1/2" h, laminated, stylized form, grommet eyes, orig glossy black paint, America, late 19th C, losses to tail **1,610.00**

10-1/2" l, 14-1/2" h, articulated circus figure with red textile shoulder girth, riding horse with glass bead eyes, attributed to Connecticut, c1900-10, stand, minor wear, paint imperfections **2,530.00**

Figure, porcelain

18" l, 20" h, man in colonial dress riding white horse **290.00**

18" l, 20" h, woman in colonial dress riding dappled browhn horse **660.00**

Pull toy, 11-1/4" l, painted and laminated carved pine, full stride, horsehair tail, wheeled platform base, America, early 20th C **635.00**

Trade sign, head, zinc, orig from French meat market **2,400.00**

Weathervane, 26-1/2" l, 16-1/2" h, full-bodied trotting horse, copper, verdigris surface, black metal stand, America, late 19th C, minor dents **4,325.00**

Wild animals

Bookends, pr, fox head, 4-3/8" w, 6-5/8" h, carved wood, mahogany backplate mounted with realistically carved and painted head, stepped base, early 20th C **320.00**

Cane

35-1/2" l, 1-1/3" d x 2-1/4" h figural silver fox head handle, upright eyes, pointed nose, collar with chain dec, marked "800," Continental hallmarks, ebony shaft, 2/3" brass ferrule, c1885 .... **1,000.00**

36-3/4" l, 2" w x 4" l carved wood handle, brown bear with glass eyes, black nose, red tongue, 1-1/2" silver collar marked "sterling," orig owner's initials, thick malacca shaft, 1" replaced brass ferrule, Black Forest, Germany, c1910 .... **1,400.00**

37" l, 1-3/4" w x 5-2/3" h carved elephant ivory handle of two male and one female lions, rocks, and foliage, 3/4" initialed gold collar, ebony shaft, 1" replaced brass ferrule, possibly Continental, c1880 .... **1,400.00**

Figure

Carved alabaster, reclining rabbit, full relief, rect base, 9" l, 5" d, 6" h **2,185.00**

Carved bone, elephant, carved bone, carved wooden armature overlaid with bone tiles in contrasting patterns, India, c1900, 24" l **1,610.00**

Ceramic, white elephant figures, gray and pink enamel detailing, sq bronze bases with gilt rocaille scrollwork to sides, early 20th C, 10" w, 5-3/4" d, 10-1/2" h, price for pr **2,760.00**

Polychromed carved wood, deer, worn brown paint, white accents on nose and underbelly, green ground stand, America, 19th C, missing one antler and part of right foreleg, 18" l, 3-1/4" d, 17-3/4" h.............. **3,450.00**

Sewer tile, molded lion, hand done details, oval base with green felt glued underneath, 13-1/2" l, 9" w, 7-1/2" h, in-the-making separations **615.00**

Terra cotta, lion, some hand tooling, pinkish gray, black, and white overcolors, 10-1/4" l, 4-1/2" w, 5-1/4" h **90.00**

White clay, lion, molded lion reclining on scalloped edge base, darkened to ivory patina, OH, 10-1/2" l, 5" w, 7" h, hairlines to base, some edge damage **250.00**

Mechanical bank, 8-1/2" l, 2-1/2" w, 5-1/2" h, white elephant, trunk flies up to deposit coin into howdah, Hubley **210.00**

Paperweight, 4-3/4" h, rabbit, lead, made from candy container mold of stippled rabbit sitting on grassy mound, front panel marked "V.G. Co., Jeannette, PA, Avor. Oz," plain panel on reverse, c1920.. **980.00**

Silkwork picture, lion lying next to sleeping lioness, Asian, late 19th/early 20th C, sight 8-3/4" x 6", frame 14-1/2" x 11-3/4" oak frame **265.00**

Stirrup cup, 5" l, hand painted

Red fox head, white and black muzzle, Staffordshire............ **550.00**

White fox head, gilt ears, facial features, and trim, marked "Tally Ho" **1,100.00**

Tin, litho

Jumbo Peanut Butter, Frank Tea & Spice Co., one-lb size, 3-3/8" x 3-7/8" **775.00**

Red Wolf Coffee, Ridenour-Baker Co., Kansas City, one-lb size, vacuum pack, trademark wolf, 5" d, 4" h **575.00**

Architectural Elements

History: Architectural elements, many of which are handcrafted, are those items that have been removed or salvaged from buildings, ships, or gardens. Part of their desirability is due to the fact that it would be extremely costly to duplicate them today.

Pair of cast iron garden cherubs, **$250**.

Beginning about 1840, decorative building styles began to feature carved wood and stone, stained glass, and ornate ironwork. At the same time, builders and manufacturers also began to use fancy doorknobs, doorplates, hinges, bells, window locks, shutter pulls, and other decorative hardware as finishing touches to elaborate new homes and commercial buildings.

Hardware was primarily produced from bronze, brass, and iron, and doorknobs also were made from clear, colored, and cut glass. Highly ornate hardware began appearing in the late 1860s and remained popular through the early 1900s. Figural pieces that featured animals, birds, and heroic and mythological images were popular, as were ornate and graphic designs that complimented the many architectural styles that emerged in the late 19th century.

For more information, see *Warman's Glass*, 4th edition.

Fraternal groups, government and educational institutions, and individual businesses all ordered special hardware for their buildings. Catalogs from the era show hundreds of patterns, often with a dozen different pieces available in each design.

The current trend of preserving and recycling architectural elements has led to the establishment and growth of organized salvage operations that specialize in removal and resale of elements. Special auctions are now held to sell architectural elements from churches, mansions, office buildings, etc. Today's decorators often design an entire room around one architectural element, such as a Victorian marble bar or mural, or use several as key accent pieces.

Architectural fan, Federal, painted pine, rect panel with carved quarter fans flanking molded beaded leaf arch centering keystone above conforming panel with molded muntins converging on central fan, probably America, c1800-10, 103" l, 19-3/4" h, **$1,200**. Photo courtesy of Skinner, Inc.

Barber pole

32-1/2" h, wall-mounted, bronze, leaded glass panels, hand-shaped pointer at top **4,250.00**

48" h, painted wood **200.00**

Bird bath, 19" d, 33-1/2" h, cast iron, shallow basin, gadrooned rim mounted by two doves, fluted baluster form standard on circular base cast with pierced rose design **300.00**

Bird cage, 21" x 19-1/2" x 18", house form, grand entrance, front porch, bay windows, dormers, cupola, painted

green, trimmed with red painted wooden buttons, knobs, and perches, some paint loss **230.00**

Bracket, 19-3/4" h, 10-1/2" d, carved wood, mermaids, gilded, bifurcated scrolled tails, America, 19th C, some loss, pr **4,230.00**

Downspouts, molded tin, lower front panels with relief spread-wing eagle and shield motifs, America, 19th C, corrosion, 14" w, 7-5/8" w, 19-3/4" h, price for pair, **$1,410**. Photo courtesy of Skinner, Inc.

Catalog

Hudson Equipment Co., Chicago, IL, 1940, 256 pgs, 6-1/2" x 9-3/4", Hudson Barn Equipment Catalog No. B-31, stalls, stanchions, bull stall, etc. **30.00**

Little Tree Farm, Framingham Center, MA, 1927, 48 pgs, 8-1/2" x 11-1/2", Section II Year Book, No. 37, Complete Catalog of Evergreens, Shrubs, Trees, Vines, Annuals, Perennials, Landscaping Accessories, etc.................... **15.00**

Morgan Sash & Door Co., Chicago, IL, c1953, 180 pgs, 8-1/2" x 11", Catalog & Price List No. 553, Morgan-Anderson Woodwork **35.00**

Chimney pot, terra cotta, tulip top, 48" h **275.00**

Corbels, pr, 5-3/4" x 2-3/4" x 2-3/4", tile, light green glazed abstract design, blue-gray matte ground, sgd "Batchelder Los Angeles," two glaze flakes to corners of one.............. **100.00**

Curtain tiebacks, mercury glass, grape dec, pewter collars, price for set of six, some chips, minor wear **175.00**

Door

27-1/4" w, 69-1/2" h, raised panel, pegged construction, orig red paint, wrought iron thumb latch, old corner chip **580.00**

31-1/2" w, 78-1/2" h, two molded recessed panels, grain painted to resemble exotic wood, attributed to Maine, early 19th C, minor surface imperfections **920.00**

Door knocker, 4" w, 11-1/4" h, wrought and hammered copper, tulip shape, monogrammed "IGW," orig dark patina **175.00**

Fountain, bronze, mermaid and dolphin, wave-form base encrusted with turtle, crab, and shells, 38" d, 85" h, **$3,315**. Photo courtesy of Sloans & Kenyon Auctions.

Door panels, Oriental, carved wood, dark surface, raised framework around each panel, relief carved flying birds in blossoming branches, steel ring hangers, 18" w, 53" h **250.00**

Door pull, 8" d, brass, Arts & Crafts, round, grimacing figure wearing head covering, holding ring in its mouth **270.00**

Eagle

12-3/4" w, 5" h, carved mahogany, bas-relief carving, perched on arrow, gilt highlights, America......... **530.00**

26" w, 31" l, 25" h, carved giltwood, perched on carved rockery, Pilot House type, America, c1875, old regilding, minor wear **2,415.00**

32-3/4" w, 19-1/4" h, gilded tin, outstretched wings, perched on rockery weighted base, holds scales in beak, metal manufacturer M. F. Frand Co., Camden, NJ, tag on lower base, late 19th C, imperfections **1,880.00**

Finial, 18-1/4" h, granite, gray, urn shape, price for pr................................ **225.00**

Fountain, 34" x 35-1/2" x 23", upper part emb pair of peacocks perched on grape vines, below heralding angels, basin with vines, both with blue on beige glaze, stamped "Batchelder Los Angeles," chips, nicks, hairlines **5,350.00**

Fragment, 11-1/2" w, 13" h, lion's head, copper, old verdigris, soldered seams, seven small holes drilled around edges for mounting, larger hold in mouth **350.00**

Safe, cast iron, "Stevens & March, marked "York Safe & Lock Co., York, PA" polychrome scenic decoration, gold trim, original keys and combination, on casters, wear to original paint, **$350**.

Garden bench, cast iron

36" w, 13-1/2" d, 28" h, openwork vintage design, scrolled seat, worn white paint, price for pr **350.00**

43-1/2" w, 15" d, 31" h, openwork fern design on back and legs, geometric cast designs on seat, old white repaint, two hairlines, chip near front corner **325.00**

Garden ornament

10" l, 11-5/8" h, rabbit, cast iron, seated figure, traces of white, green, and red paint, late 19th C, wear **345.00**

16-1/2" l, 29-1/2" h, carved and painted wood and gesso, urn with flame, painted tan, putty, and white, traces of gilt, 19th C **2,185.00**

Garden set, bench and chair, cast iron ends with finely detailed griffins, foliage, and scrolling, old replaced beaded mahogany boards, 57" w, 29-1/2" d, 30-1/2" h bench, 27" w, 28" d, 32" h chair **700.00**

Garden statue, 32" h, cast concrete, cherub, chips **125.00**

Garden urn, cast iron, American

Classical figures, grape and cable handles, orig bases, painted white, c1880, 61" h, pr **9,800.00**

Gadrooned rim and bowl, sq base, 18" d, 12-1/4" h, rusty surface, pr **950.00**

Vault door, center plaque reads "Herring Hall Marvin Safe Co., Hamilton, OH," **$195**. Photo courtesy of Alderfer Auction Co.

Griffins, winged, stone-cut, English, pr **4,200.00**

Hitching post, 24" h above ground, 47-5/8" h total, cast iron, painted black, horse head over fluted column mounted with pendant rings, ending in acanthus leaves, one flute molded with "22 Congress Street," late 19th C **715.00**

Latch, heart shape, wrought iron, 18th C **750.00**

Lock, 8-1/2" w, 11" h, iron, rect plate with male and female silhouettes, key with quatrefoil terminal, 19th C, stand, minor surface corrosion **650.00**

Newel post, 17-3/4" h, carved walnut, figural owl with outstretched wings, perched on pile of books, over quadripartite volutes, black painted step-turned base, early 20th C **940.00**

Obelisk, 22" h, marble, gilt incised band of faux hieroglyphics, horizontally fluted base offset with black slate moldings, foot with further incised dec, Egyptian Revival, late 19th/early 20th C, price for pr **950.00**

Pedestal

Birch, poplar, and pine, 48" h carved angel statue with wings on back, 42" sq paneled wood pedestal with Arts & Crafts designs, minor loss to wing **2,950.00**

Marble, 42" h, white, 11" octagonal top, slightly tapered column with relief stop fluting, round stepped base, lobed urn near bottom, minor edge wear and chips **675.00**

Marble, 44" h, white, 12" octagonal top, spiral column with beaded center ring, octagonal base with stepped rings and round lobed urn near bottom of column, small edge chips **600.00**

Onyx, 38-1/4" h, cream colored, brown striations, 11" octagonal top, ring turned column, sq block base, small edge chips **450.00**

Planter, stump type, sewer tile

10-1/2" l, 15" w, 12" h, textured surface, stamped medallion "Cambria-Co., C. e. Blackfork, Ohio," few chips **385.00**

18" h, three branches, hand tooled bark, carved "Gram" plaque, crack **110.00**

Pump cover, 74" h, poplar, old red and white scrolling paint on green ground, evidence of earlier salmon paint underneath, sgd "Consolidated Pump Co., Toledo, O," cast iron spout and bands, top cap and finial replaced, wear **275.00**

Roof finial, 46-1/2" h, zinc, light gray and white oxidized surface, top column tapering down to point, flower petals at center, square to round formed base, removable flag and scrolled wire arrow, 19th C, soldered restorations, late enameled steel stand **1,320.00**

Safe, 9-1/2" w, 8-1/2" d, 14-1/4" h, cast iron, on rollers, polychrome pinstripe dec, front door dec with oval landscape, gilt lettering, "Deposit Vault," orig key **550.00**

Sink, 19-3/4" x 29-1/2", carved granite, rounded corners, drain holes **1,210.00**

Sphinx, 16" l, 10" h, carved wood, worn surface, good detail on face, carved initials "SV" on base **800.00**

Sundial, 17" d, 34" h, lead, circular, alpha numerics, terra cotta base shaped like three gargoyles, shaped plinth **850.00**

Topiary form, 13-1/2" w, 24" h, lyre-shape, wire, conical base, painted green, America, late 19th/early 20th C **150.00**

Wall brackets, pr, 11-1/2" l, Rococo Revival, mahogany, carved openwork rocaille and C-scrolls supporting small demilune shelf, early 20th C **1,650.00**

Window frame, 35-1/2" w, 35" h, arched, mullions in gothic pattern, five small panes remaining, 20th C green paint **55.00**

Art Deco

History: The Art-Deco period was named after an exhibition, "l'Exposition Internationale des Arts Decoratifs et Industriels Modernes," held in Paris in 1925. Its beginnings succeed those of the Art-Nouveau period, but the two overlap in time, as well as in style.

Art-Deco designs are angular with simple lines. This was the period of skyscrapers, movie idols, and the Cubist works of Picasso and Legras. Art Deco motifs were used for every conceivable object being produced in the 1920s and 1930s (ceramics, furniture, glass, and metals) not only in Europe but in America as well.

Additional Listings: Furniture and Jewelry. Also check glass, pottery, and metal categories.

Aquarium, 41-1/2" h, 18" h stepped and paneled molded translucent yellow glass bowl, dec with six panels of stylized flowers, set in bronzed metal tripod stand, three enameled green handles, legs terminating in stylized dolphins, central light fixture, tri-part base, dark patina, c1925, chips, wear **2,415.00**

Chess set, aluminum, designed by Victor F. Von Lossberg, manuf by Edward F. Caldwell and Co. Inc., New York, c1934, 32 pcs, silver and red finishes, figural player 1-3/4" to 3-7/8" h, original box, paperwork providing provenance as set was exhibited at the Architectural League's 49th Annual Exhibition, held in New York from May 15 to June 2, 1934, **$2,585**. Photo courtesy of Skinner, Inc.

Cane

36" l, 1-3/4" w x 8" l carved elephant ivory handle, flat on one side, carved with slight bend, opposite side with smooth cartouche and long rose and foliage garland, carved hardwood shaft, 3/4" diamond-shaped horn ferrule, English c1920 .... **650.00**

Evening purse, black suede pouch, black enamel 18k gold and platinum frame, opening on six bezel and pave-set rose-cut diamond cylinder hinges, silk satin int., pave-set rose-cut diamond fleur-de-lis clasp, int. frame and pouch signed "Cartier" and "Made in France," small chip to enamel, **$6,500**. Photo courtesy of Skinner, Inc.

36-1/2" l, 4" l x 1-1/2" h squared hard stone handle, inlaid in Italian pietra dura manner with colored hard stones as flowers and foliage, 1" silver collar with worn London hallmarks, ebony shaft, 7/8" replaced brass ferrule, c1920 .... **1,900.00**

Chair, 31" h, 19-1/2" w, 21-1/2" d, Robert Venturi for Knoll, molded plywood, silk-screen print in polychrome on gray ground, unmarked **630.00**

Chandelier

25" l drop, 13-3/4" d, pod and leaf-form patinated metal ceiling mount and three paperclip chains supporting shade with molded floral and geometric devices **575.00**

26-1/2" l, 30" d, cast bronze ceiling mount and lower shade mount, border of stylized bowl of flowers, geometric, and lapped leaves, four conical frosted glass shades with molded geometric floral designs **2,300.00**

28" l drop, 26-1/2" d, paneled wrought iron framework suspending round, paneled, etched colorless glass shade with raised center rosette and geometric elements, four matching shades, center shade sgd "Muller Frères Luneville," smaller shades also sgd, c1928 .... **2,400.00**

Clock garniture, 7" h green onyx Sessions clock with rounded shoulders on onyx plinth, pr 11-1/2" h green onyx urns with ormolu pedestals, bases and finials, **$490**. Photo courtesy of Alderfer Auction Co.

Clock, 16" l, mantle, circular geometric form, green variegated onyx, Whithal electric movement, c1925, some repair, minor loss **100.00**

Coffee set, silver plated, Wilcox, design attributed to Gene Theobald, faceted 10-1/2" h coffeepot, and sugar container with Bakelite finials, matching creamer, 20" l oblong tray, all marked "Wilcox S.P. Co/E.P.N.S./International S.Co./W. M. Wounts/1981N." **1,150.00**

Jars, covered, pottery, stylized angular male and female busts, white glossy glaze, c1935, imperfections, 13-1/2" h, and 14-1/2" h, **$500**. Photo courtesy of Skinner, Inc.

Desk

30" x 44" x 22-1/2", Plycraft, double pedestal, four drawers on each side, single center drawer, stenciled #331 .... **350.00**

66-1/8" l, 36-1/8" d, 29" h, Leopold Corp, Burlington, IA, walnut veneered, semi-oval top over center drawer flanked by pull-out writing surface and two drawers, bronze handles, light brown finish, "Charles S. Nathan Office Equipment New York" distributor's metal tag in drawer, veneer loss, wear **900.00**

Drawings, 13-1/2" x 17", by Alexander Bronson, pencil drawings of two beds by Paul Frankl, other with pedestal table, sgd, mounted in natural wood frames, price for three-pc set **750.00**

End table, 16-1/2" w, 14" d, 29" h, mahogany and burlwood, orig marble tops over single drawers, one with two lower shelves, other with shelf and cabinet, raised rosettes on metal hardware, France, c1930, price for pr **1,400.00**

Evening purse, black suede pouch, black enamel 18k gold and platinum frame, opening on six bezel and pavé-set rose-cut diamond cylinder hinges, silk satin int., pavé-set rose-cut diamond fleur-de-lis clasp, int. frame and pouch sgd "Cartier" and "Made in France" **6,500.00**

Figure, 25-1/4" l, 27" l base, bronze, Man Struggling with a Winch, semi-nude male figure winding a rope around a large turnbuckle, green marble base, Marcel Bouraine (French, c1918-1935) **1,750.00**

Fruit bowl, 12-1/2" d, Christofle silver plate, from the cruise ship *L'Atlantique*, c1930, flattened handles and stepped rim.. **350.00**

Jewelry, 16" l necklace, 7" bracelet, rock crystal, sterling silver................... **470.00**

Lamp, boudoir, Danse De Lumiere, 11" h, molded glass figure of woman with outstretched arms, bearing stylized feather drapery, oval platform base with internal light fixture, molded title and patent mark, c1930, mold imperfections **400.00**

Lamp, floor, 64" h, 16" d amber-colored cameo shade with cast in forms of oak leafs, acorns, birds resting atop three extending tree limbs. Cast metal tree trunk stem base cov with climbing ivy, hand-hammered domed foot, shade sgd "DAUM NANCY FRANCE".......... **9,200.00**

Lamp, table

15-1/4" h, cast metal tropical-colored painted parrot holding cage in mouth, light bulb in the cage, lamp stem with glass ball in center, fluted foot, some paint loss on the foot and some minor bending to cage **635.00**

22-1/2" h, 16" d six-sided shade with alternating silhouettes of man and woman in boat, geese in water against green background, shade sgd "Jefferson" on metal fitter ring, three light base with frosted crackle glass finish, pewter-colored metal fittings................................ **1,725.00**

Night stand, 28-1/4" l, 12-1/2" w, 26-3/4" h, walnut, curvilinear design, walnut and cherry veneers, small drawer with burlwood veneer, chrome and resin handle, flanked by small open shelf over three open shelves, aluminum trim around base, imperfections, price for pr **700.00**

Nutcracker, 9-1/2" l, 4-3/4" h, figural elephant, cast iron, orig orange/red paint, black and white details, twine tail **275.00**

Punch bowl and cordial set, eight-sided finial on paneled cov, 7-1/2" h, 8-1/2" d bowl dec with silver and red geometric design, six 2-1/2" d paneled cordials with similar dec, 14" d round glass tray with multiple star cuts on base, chrome sides, chrome ladle, imperfections.......... **290.00**

Room divider, four panels, black lacquered arched frames inset with canvas, painted abstract gold and black

pattern, each panel 24" w, 71-1/2" h, slight damage to hinges............ **1,725.00**
Salon chair, 28-1/2" w, 26-1/2" d, 24-1/2" h, U-shaped low chair, beige velvet and burlwood, metal tag on bases, "Hotel Le Malandre Modele Depose," c1945, price for pr..................... **2,185.00**
Server, 10-1/2" l, 10-1/2" w, 13" h, Wiener Werkstatte, Austria, second quarter 20th C, scalloped rim on shallow sq light yellow-tinted transparent glass bowl, repeating linear and circle cut glass border, raised on base composed of round silver pan on four colorless glass rod legs over sq platform with four oval bezel-mounted green, pink, purple, and black stones, imp marks, few rim chips and scratches............................ **2,185.00**

Match safe, silvered metal, top and bottom are pale blue plastic material, textured for use as striker, top lip marked "Brevete S.G.," monogrammed, **$215**. Photo courtesy of Alderfer Auction Co.

Sideboard, 54-5/8" w, 16-1/2" d, 43" h, attributed to Jacques-Emile Ruhlmann, France, 1879-1933, inlaid Macassar ebony, elongated rect top with ebony and ivory inlaid trim, three center shelves flanked by cupboards, one fitted with drawer, one with shelf, doors with rect ebony inlay with ivory stringing, applied half-round molding around base, swollen shaped legs, imperfections......... **920.00**
Table, 18-1/2" sq tile top, bright polychrome leaping gazelle and flowers, 15" h mahogany veneer frame, unmarked, CA **535.00**
Tea and coffee service, silver plated, coffeepot, teapot, creamer, cov sugar, serving tray, etched linear dec, rosewood handles, Continental, imp maker's marks with cross flanked by two Ls within octagon, wear............................. **500.00**
Tiles, 6" sq, set of five, two emb with white birds and flowers, three with branches of flowers, matte and glossy glazes, various Grueby artists' marks, glaze flake to one corner of two tiles **2,070.00**
Vase
9-1/4" h, four buttressed handles, emb woven pattern under cream and brown crystalline flambé vase, stamped "Denbac".............. **490.00**
11-3/8" h, ceramic, Boch Frères, extended rim, oval form, stylized light green blossoms, stems, and foliage, gold accents, turquoise ground, glossy glaze, painted "BFK/340," imp "708," minor crazing, minor light scratches, price for pr.......... **920.00**
12-1/4" h, 5-1/2" d, Wiener Werkstatte, bulbous, flaring neck, painted white and black geometric pattern, brown ground, stamped "WWW/Made in Austria/HB" **125.00**
12-1/2" h, molded opalescent glass, Art Deco stylized scene of centaur and panther hunting gazelles, foliage background with blue patina, unmarked, attributed to Sabino **635.00**

Mirror, rectangular, simple etched floral motifs border, c1935, 58-1/2" l, 40-3/4" h, **$600**. Photo courtesy of Skinner, Inc.

Wall sconce
7" h, 3" d, nickeled brass plate and curved arm, frosted glass shade with raised geometric design, rim chips to shade, minor dents to sconce **90.00**
12" h, 5-1/2" w, Art Deco etched colorless glass fanned shades on "V"-shaped silvered metal wall mounts, France, 1928, price for pr **1,150.00**
14-1/2" h, 5-1/4" w, diamond shaped frosted glass inserts, raised geometric design, V-shaped nickeled bronze mounts, France, c1930, minor wear to slip, price for pr **875.00**
Wine cooler, 9" h, Christofle silver plate, from the cruise ship *L'Atlantique*, c1930, angular handles.......................... **400.00**
Wristwatch, lady's, 6-7/8" l, Audemars Piguet & Co., rect silvertone dial with Arabic numeral indicators, bezel and flexible geometric platinum link bracelet bead-set with 105 full and 48 single-cut, five square step-cut, and two half-moon-cut diamonds, approx. total wt. 4.96 cts., 17-jewel two-position Audemars Piguet movement............................... **3,645.00**

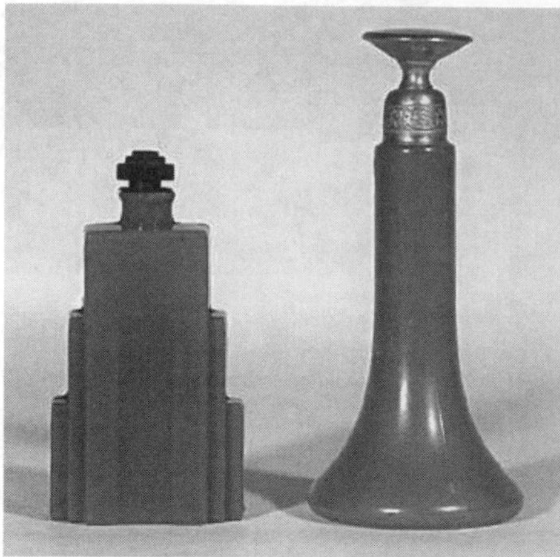

Perfume bottles, left: red skyscraper shape, black stepped stopper; right: slender green satin baluster, gold toned top, each **$125**. Photo courtesy of Joy Luke Auctions.

Vase, cast metal, flaring, buttressed sides, brass patina, 8-1/2" w, 14-1/2" h, **$115**. Photo courtesy of David Rago Auctions, Inc.

Art Nouveau

History: Art Nouveau is the French term for the "new art," which had its beginning in the early 1890s and continued for the next 40 years. The flowing and sensuous female forms used in this period were popular in Europe and America. Among the most recognized artists of this period were Gallé, Lalique, and Tiffany.

Flowing, sensuous lines, florals, insects, and the feminine form can identify the Art-Nouveau style. These designs were incorporated into almost everything produced during the period, from art glass to furniture, silver, and personal objects. Later wares demonstrate some of the characteristics of the evolving Art-Deco style.

Additional Listings: Furniture and Jewelry. Also check glass, pottery, and metal categories.

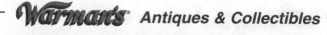

Candelabra, pr, 13" h, .800 silver, two flowering iris stems, sconces within center of flower, removable incised nozzles, realistically styled stems and leaves, base formed as overlapping water lily leaves, 50 troy oz, maker's mark A. Freitag, German, early 20th C, drilled 6,000.00

Vase, designed by Charles Catteau, Belgium, c1923-24, design 1132, graduated stepped shape, patterned black and tan squares, largest band interspersed with stylized floral tan, rust, and soft green dec on cream-colored ground, stamped "Ch. Catteau," wolf over "Boch Freres Keramis Made in Belgium, D 1132," 5-3/4" h, **$400**. Photo courtesy of Skinner, Inc.

Cane

35" l, 2" w x 3" h silver pistol grip with flowing lines with marsh foliage, two clumps of cattails, two flowers above smooth collar, French hallmarks, lignum vitae shaft, 1-1/8" white metal and iron ferrule, French, c1900 .... **650.00**

36" l, 1-2/3" d x 4-1/2" h gilded handle, 3-1/2" x 1-1/4" area dec with naked god, flowers, and scrolls, ebonized hardwood shaft, 1-1/4" horn ferrule, Continental, c1900 .... **350.00**

37" l, 1-1/4" d x 6-7/8" l sterling silver Unger Bros chased handle with three maidens, orig owner's initials, marked "sterling" with double Unger Bros mark, light chestnut shaft, 1-1/3" white metal and iron ferrule, c1900 .... **2,100.00**

Clock

Desk, 3-3/4" w, 4-3/8" h, bronze, Chelsea Clock movement, gilt-metal and glass mount, red enamel dec devices, ftd base, circular face with Arabic chapters, imp "Chelsea Clock Co., Boston, USA, 155252" on inside clock works, worn patina **460.00**

Figural, 12-1/2" h, enameled cast white metal, relief of woman's head, flowing hair, leaves, thistles, Seth Thomas movement, circular dial with Roman numerals, c1900, minor wear **300.00**

Wall, 24-1/2" w, 10" d, 38" h, carved walnut, two-train movement, floral etched gilt metal dial sgd "Trilla, Barcelona," case topped by bust of young beauty on rocaille shell above iris flower, flanked by poppy roundels, case further carved with stylized florets, writing flower buds at corners, Spanish, early 20th C **490.00**

Door pulls, 3" w, 15" h, bronze, whiplash handles, orig patina, Belgian, price for pr **1,150.00**

Doorstop, 8" w, 9" h, bronze, woman with outstretched arms holding her dress edges **520.00**

Garniture, centerpiece with bronze patina, female spelter figure of "L. Historie," flanked by spelter plinth with clock, enameled dial with painted Arabic numbers, sgd "L. Satre-A Pont. Aven," rect molded marble base with center bronze gilt neoclassical mounting, bronze gilded bun feet, pr of bronze patina spelter Louis XVI style urns, ribbons and swags centering figural medallion, sq marble base, bronze gilded feet **950.00**

Inkwell, 7" x 13", bronze, double inkwells flanking shaped pen tray, raised leaf and berry motif, sgd "C.H. Louchet" **460.00**

Bowl, diamond shaped, green glass, white, yellow, and pink enameled orchids, gold tracery foliage, gold border trim, **$95**. Photo courtesy of Dotta Auction Co., Inc.

Jar, cut and etched jar, silver-plated lid, two-handled frame, 8-1/4" h, **$125**. Photo courtesy of Joy Luke Auctions.

Lamp, table

19-1/2" h, cypriot-type glass shades with irid swirled tops, bronze patinated bases with beaded trim, attributed to Austrian, one with concealed chip at fitter ring, pr **2,200.00**

Thermometer, ornate scrolling Art Nouveau scrolls and flowers, brass, **$125**. Photo courtesy of Dotta Auction Co., Inc.

40" h, figural, bronze patina spelter, woman sitting on tree stump with brass cattails around her, cattails house the light sockets and bulbs, plaque on front of foot "PECHEUSE PAR FERRAND RECOMPENSE AU SALON," one cattail leaf missing **1,350.00**

Framed tile backsplash, made up of 15 tiles, three of which are decorated in cuenca, European, three tiles cracked, 10" x 18", **$215**. Photo courtesy of David Rago Auctions, Inc.

Perfume bottle, 4-1/4" h, paneled slender baluster form bottle painted with blue and gold flowers, gilt-metal hinged lid enclosing glass stopper, lid with short chain **520.00**

Picture frame

4-7/8" h, sterling silver, oval, emb flowers and maiden, Unger Bros., Newark **175.00**

8-1/2" w, 11-3/8" h, wood, penwork and colored stained dec of stylized fruiting flowers, easel back **100.00**

Pitcher, 11-3/4" h, relief wheat dec, mottled blue, brown, and green, imp "Gres Mougin Nancy," by Joseph Victor Xavier, Nancy, France, c1900 .... **865.00**

Stove, coal-burning, 32" x 46" x 28", three top elements, six drawers, cov in Talisman majolica tiles with red poppies and green leaves on yellow trellis, Talisman V. L-Maubeuge metal tag, French, completely restored **2,870.00**

Table, side, 24" w, 17" d, 30" h, scallop-edge rect top inlaid with poppies in exotic woods, fluted legs, cabriole feet, lower shelf with variation of poppy motif, orig finish, inlaid "Galle" signature **2,100.00**

Table gong, 21-1/4" x 23", copper and brass whiplash frame and feet, unmarked, attributed to Liberty & Co., some breaks and bends to frame **360.00**

Tea kettle, 11" h, sterling silver, floral repousse dec, curved handle, marked "J. E. Caldwell & Co., 925, Sterling, 1000, Philadelphia," 47 troy oz.............. **550.00**

Tile panel, 42" x 28", 28 tiles, polychrome squeezebag painted hunter and hair, unmarked, framed, hairline across four tiles **1,725.00**

Tray

6-1/2" x 18" Johann Von Schwarz tile, cuenca dec, lady in profile in front of landscape with ruins, her head hand painted, stamped "R5084," rect metal base, restoration to two small tears in metal..................... **2,100.00**

7-1/2" h, pewter, nude woman with arms spread, butterfly-type wings, front sgd "H.P." **460.00**

Vase

3-1/2" d, 6-1/2" h, ovoid, molded celadon beetle on oak branch, textured blue, gold, and purple lustered ground, German or Austrian, c1900 .... **460.00**

Left: tapering 10-1/2" h vessel , right: 6-1/2" h pitcher, pink, yellow, and shades of green flowers and leaves, deep crimson ground, Austrian, stamped numbers, vessel: **$110**; pitcher with small chips, **$75**. Photo courtesy of David Rago Auctions, Inc.

7-3/4" d, 10-3/4" h, two-handles, emb stylized leaves and berries under gold glaze, over-textured matte green body, stamped "Austria," a few glaze flakes **750.00**

Wine cabinet, 46" w, 18" d, 68-1/2" h, carved walnut, panels elaborately carved with nymphs and grapevines, fitted with two pairs of doors and drawer, early 20th C **5,550.00**

Art Pottery (General)

History: America's interest in art pottery can be traced to the Centennial Exposition in Philadelphia, Pennsylvania, in 1877, where Europe's finest producers of decorative art displayed an impressive selection of their wares. Our young artists rose to the challenge immediately, and by 1900, native artisans were winning gold medals for decorative ceramics here and abroad.

The Art Pottery "Movement" in America lasted from about 1880 until the first World War. During this time, more than 200 companies, in most states, produced decorative ceramics ranging from borderline production ware to intricately decorated, labor-intensive artware, establishing America as a decorative art powerhouse.

For more information, see *Warman's American Pottery & Porcelain*, 2nd edition.

Below is a listing of the work by various factories and studios, with pricing, from a number of these companies. The location of these outlets are included to give the reader a sense of how nationally based the industry was.

Additional Listings: See Clewell, Clifton, Cowan, Dedham, Fulper, Grueby, Jugtown, Marblehead, Moorcroft, Newcomb, North Dakota School of Mines, Ohr, Paul Revere, Peters and Reed, Rookwood, Roseville, Van Briggle, Weller, and Zanesville.

Notes: Condition, design, size, execution, and glaze quality are the key considerations when buying art pottery. This category includes only companies not found elsewhere in this book.

Adviser: David Rago.

Arequipa

Bowl, 6-1/2" d, 2-1/4" h, closed-in, emb eucalyptus branches, matte green and dark blue glaze, stamped mark, incised "KH/11" **800.00**

Vase, 3-3/4" d, 5-1/4" h, bulbous, carved eucalyptus leaves, covered in seafoam green matte glaze, brown clay showing through, stamped "AREQUIPA/10?/136," incised B.L. **4,315.00**

Avon, Vance, vase, 5" d, 5-1/2" h, designed by Frederick Rhead, squeezebag stylized trees, orange and green ground, incised "Avon/WPTS. CO./174-1241"............................ **920.00**

Bachelder, O. L., vase, 5" h, 3-3/4" d, bulbous, cobalt blue and teal sheer glossy glaze, incised "OLB/R," ink cipher **500.00**

Bennett, John

Charger

14-1/2" d, dec with polychrome butterfly amidst white azaleas, green leaves, indigo and violet ground, sgd "J. Bennett/412/ E24/NY," few kiln kisses around rim **5,350.00**

Markham, vase, ovoid, two low buttressed handles, green and orange dead matte glaze, incised "Markham 2923," few minor nicks. 7-1/4" x 7-1/2", **$700**. Photo courtesy of David Rago Auctions, Inc.

14-1/2" d, dec with polychrome daisies and poppies enc within hearts, cobalt blue ground, black scroll design, sgd "J. Bennett/412 E24/NY/Oct 9/79," added inscription "Wed last 100 degs in shade" **4,600.00**

Vase, 3-3/4" d, 7-1/2" h, bulbous, painted burgundy phlox and honeybee, ivory ground, minute rim fleck, marked "BENNETT/W2E24/NJ/ artist's cipher" **2,870.00**

Brouwer

Vase

5-1/4" x 5", tear shape, flame-painted in greens and ambers, Incised Flame 81, paper label, restored line running halfway around base **690.00**

12" x 7-1/2", bands of dark brown glaze dripping over flame-painted yellow and orange lustered ground, Ceramic Flame Co. paper label over signature, drilled hole in bottom, several rim flakes **4,025.00**

Chelsea Keramic Art Works

Vase

6" x 3-3/4", ovoid, deep red oxblood glaze, lemon-peel texture, stamped CKAW, 1/2" kiln kiss to shoulder **2,100.00**

6-1/2" x 6", bulbous, satin and glossy amber glaze, stamped CKAW/5/83 .... **2,300.00**

7-1/4" x 3-3/4", bottle shape, oxblood glaze, lemon-peel texture, stamped CKAW **4,025.00**

Cole, A. R., **urn**, 18-1/2" h, 9-1/2" d, hand-thrown, three fanciful twisted handles, mirror black glaze, unmarked, shallow scratches **400.00**

Chicago Cruicible, Chicago, IL, vase, 10-1/2" x 6", bottle shape, scalloped rim, emb grapevines, smooth matte green glaze, stamped "CHICAGO CRUCIBLE, CHICAGO, ILL" **1,100.00**

Denver

Vase

5-1/4" x 3-1/2", baluster, green, blue, and sand marbleized clays, incised "Denver W" **460.00**

5-1/2" x 3-1/2", bulbous, cameo dec, white trees, blue-gray clay, incised "Denver W," firing line to inner rim **490.00**

Frackelton, Susan, **vase**, 3-3/4" d, 6-3/4" h, gourd shape, salt-glaze stoneware, dec with abutilon blossoms alternating with stylized leaves and vines in indigo on ivory ground, sgd "SF/1X/984," chip, nick to rim **20,700.00**

Kenton Hills, **vase**, 4-3/4" d, 7-1/4" h, cylindrical, white prunts cov in mirrored umber glaze, incised "Hentschel" for William Hentschel, imp "KH/124" **775.00**

Markham, **vase**, 7-1/4" x 7-1/2", two low buttressed handles, green and orange dead matte glaze, incised Markham 2923, few minor nicks **700.00**

Merrimac, urn, two handles, feathered matte green glaze, stamped "Merrimac" with fish, 6-3/4" x 6", **$815**. Photo courtesy of David Rago Auctions, Inc.

McLoughlin, Marie Louise

Trivet, 6" d, Losanti Ware, circular, emb with floral motif, celadon glaze, incised cipher, marked "Losanti," clay particles struck to glaze, firing lines, base chips **550.00**

Vase, 3-3/4" d, 4-1/4" h, Losanti ware, incised swirling peacock feathers, beige and oxblood crackled glaze, incised cipher/Losanti/97, short, heavy crazing line to rim **2,615.00**

Merrimac

Urn, 6-3/4" x 6", two handles, fine, feathered matte green glaze, stamped "Merrimac" with fish **815.00**

Vessel, 4-1/2" x 7-1/2", squat, flaring rim, two handles, thick curdled matte green glaze, paper label, stamped MERRIMAC with sturgeon **2,100.00**

Ouachita, Arkansas

Vase

3-1/2" x 3-3/4", bulbous, green and blue speckled matte glaze, stamped "OUACHITA POTTERY SAINT LOUIS," few minor rim nicks **920.00**

9-3/4" x 4", cylindrical, emb and incised butterfly over wild flowers, matte green glaze, stamped "OUACHITA HOT SPRINGS ARK S.E.S.," few glaze flakes **1,955.00**

Pewabic, vase, bulbous, applied blossoms on swirling stems, smooth matte green glaze, mark obscured by glaze. 6-1/4" x 4-1/2", **$4,320**. Photo courtesy of David Rago Auctions, Inc.

Pewabic

Bookends, pr, 4" w, 4-3/4" h, emb animal, lustered blue and green glaze, stamped "Pewabic," repair to small edge chip **415.00**

Miniature, vase, 2" h, crackled turquoise glaze, blue plumes, sgd "Pewabic/Detroit/PP" **265.00**

Plate, 9-1/4" d, white crackleware, rim dec with squeezebag yellow and red roosters on green field, stamped "Pewabic," some loss of glaze, chips on back **920.00**

Vase

4" x 3", baluster, cobalt blue over lustered gold glaze, stamped "PEWABIC DETROIT" **630.00**

5-1/2" x 4-1/4", bulbous, blue, green, and indigo lustered glaze, spherical stamp mark **630.00**

8-1/2" x 5-1/2", sloped shoulder, celadon, indigo, and purple lustered glaze, no visible mark **1,100.00**

Teco, vase, gourd shape, four buttressed handles, #287, veined matte green glaze, stamped "TECO," 6-1/2" x 5-1/2", **$3,450**. Photo courtesy of David Rago Auctions, Inc.

Pisgah Forest

Tea set, Cameo Ware, wagon and landscape dec, dark matte green ground, raised mark and date 1943, 5-1/4" h teapot **950.00**

Vase, 9" x 5", baluster, ivory and blue crystals, celadon ground, 1946, potters mark with date and Stephen **860.00**

Vessel, 5" h, 5-3/4" d, spherical, amber glaze, white and blue crystals, raised potter's mark and date 1947 .... **350.00**

Poillon, Clara, pitcher, 5" d, 4-1/2" h, bulbous, medium green glaze, incised CPI monogram **365.00**

W. J. Walley, vase, baluster, mirrored black glaze, stamped "W.J.W.," 7-1/2" x 3-1/2", **$500**. Photo courtesy of David Rago Auctions, Inc.

Robertson, Frederick, Los Angeles, pitcher, 6" x 5-1/2", emb geese in flight, blue-green matte glaze, unmarked, minor rim flecks **410.00**

Rose Valley, vase, 7-1/2" x 5-1/4", bottle shape, incised hearts and spades, flowing matte green glaze, incised "Rose Valley," rim chip restored **2,415.00**

Ruskin, vase, 4-1/2" h, bulbous, celadon, amber, and indigo flambé crystalline glaze, 1931, stamped **380.00**

Stockton, bud vase, 8" x 4-1/4", ruffled rim, under-glaze painted with orchid branch, brown and green flambe glaze, circular stamp mark **635.00**

Teco

Dish, 4-1/4" d, frog figurine, emb, blue-green mottled glossy glaze, stamped **435.00**

Vase

3-3/4" h, bulbous, matte green glaze, stamped **490.00**

4" h, bulbous, small opening, matte green glaze, marked **750.00**

4-1/2" h, bulbous, smooth matte green glaze, marked **815.00**

13-1/2" x 7-1/4", four sided, imp panels on top, four handles at base, charcoaled matte green glaze, stamped "Teco 258," rim nick, tight cracks to two buttresses **13,800.00**

Wall pocket, 17" x 6-1/2", emb full-height leaves, smooth charcoaled matte green glaze, stamped "Teco," minute fleck to one hole **2,300.00**

Vance Faience, pitcher, 12" h, 9" d, matte green, emb branches of grapes, trees, and dogs, modeled greyhound handle, 12" x 9" **625.00**

Volkmar, pitcher, 4" d, 4-1/2" h, bulbous, collared neck, cucumber green matte glaze, incised illegible inscription **265.00**

Walley, W. J.

Vase

4-3/4" x 3-1/2", bottle shape, dark green, yellow, and ivory glaze over terra cotta ground, stamped WJW **810.00**

7" x 3-1/2", bottle shape, frothy light green glaze dripping over a caramel flambé ground, mark obscured by glaze, opposing rim lines **810.00**

7-1/2" x 3-1/2", baluster, mirrored black glaze, stamped "W.J.W." **500.00**

9" x 5-3/4", green and brown flambé microcrystalline glaze dripping over matte brown ground, stamped "WJW" **2,415.00**

Walrath

Chamberstick, 4" x 4-1/4", emb pinecones, speckled brown glaze, stamped mark, repair to spout **90.00**

Cider pitcher, 7" d, 5" h, matte, yellow fruit, green leaves, brown ground, marked "Walrath Pottery/MI" **1,495.00**

Sculpture, 4" h, 6" l, kneeling nude picking rose, sheer matte green glaze, yellow details, incised "Walrath" **300.00**

Vase, 6-1/4" h, 4" d, painted stylized purple and dark green flowers, light gray-green ground, incised "Walrath Pottery" **4,000.00**

Wheatley

Lamp base, 14" d, 23" h, emb poppy pods, frothy matte green glaze, new hammered copper fittings, Japanese split-bamboo shade lined with new coral silk, stamped mark ... **1,380.00**

Low bowl, 9-3/4" d, emb ridged leaves, brown-speckled matte glaze, stamped WP **1,050.00**

Sand jar, 15" d, 24" h, high relief sculpted grape leaves and vines from rim, feathered medium green matte glaze, incised mark/722, several glaze nicks restored **2,415.00**

Vase, 6-3/4" d, 12-1/4" h, bulbous, three climbing lizards, feathered medium matte green glaze, remnant of paper label, restoration to drill hole on side **1,380.00**

Zark

Low bowl, 10-1/4" d, 5" h, Egyptian, figural handles of crouching scribes, incised bands under smooth matte green glaze, incised OZARK, three small chips **860.00**

Vessel, 7" d, 3" h, squat, two handles, speckled dark green glaze, stamped ZARK **630.00**

ARTS AND CRAFTS MOVEMENT

History: The Arts and Crafts Movement in American decorative arts took place between 1895 and 1920. Leading proponents of the movement were Elbert Hubbard and his Roycrofters, the brothers Stickley, Frank Lloyd Wright, Charles and Henry Greene, George Niedecken, and Lucia and Arthur Mathews.

The movement was marked by individualistic design (although the movement was national in scope) and re-emphasis on handcraftsmanship and appearance. A reform of industrial Society was part of the long-range goal. Most pieces of furniture favored a rectilinear approach and were made of oak.

The Arts and Crafts Movement embraced all aspects of the decorative arts, including metalwork, ceramics, embroidery, woodblock printing, and the crafting of jewelry.

Adviser: David Rago.

Andirons, pr

18" x 11", rectilinear form, faux rivets, stamped 1900, some rust **150.00**

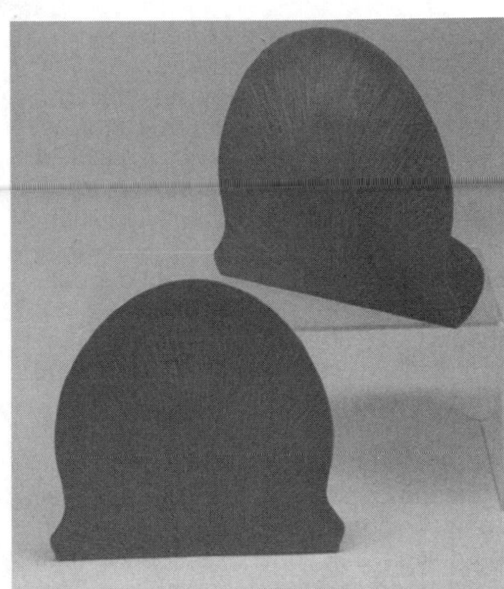

Bookends, pair, Dirk Van Erp, hammered copper, shield-shaped with pine needle texture, medium patina, open box windmill mark, 6" x 5", **$350**. Photo courtesy of David Rago Auctions, Inc.

18-1/2" x 11-3/4", hammered cube over four-sided shaft, unmarked, some rust **535.00**

Bookends, pr, 6" x 7", Karl Kipp, emb quatrefoils and wood grain bands on square ground, medium patina, stamped "KK" **575.00**

Bowl, hammered copper

7" d, applied silver initial "M," good medium patina, stamped "Kalo" **435.00**

9-1/2" d, medium patina, stamped Dirk Van Erp mark **815.00**

10" d, 5" h, hand-wrought, flaring, fluted, medium patina, touch mark with tinsmith's hammer **415.00**

Box, covered, Boston School, hammered copper, square head rivets, lid enameled with bunches of purple grapes and chartreuse leaves on green bricks, original patina, unmarked, 4-1/4" d, 2" h, **$2,620**. Photo courtesy of David Rago Auctions, Inc.

Box, cov

4-1/4" l, 2" h, hammered copper, square-head rivets, enameled bunches of purple grapes and chartreuse leaves on green bricks on lid, orig patina, unmarked Boston School **2,620.00**

8-1/4" x 15" x 12", oak, hinged, two handles, riveted strap hardware, skinned finish **380.00**

Candlestick, 11" h, brass, Alpha, Jarvie, ovoid holder, flat circular base, incised "Jarvie," short shallow base scratches **265.00**

Chair, dining room, Limbert, side, single broad vertical back slat, tacked-on brown leather, orig finish with heavy overcoat, branded mark, 17" w, 37" h, price for set of four **1,610.00**

Coal bucket, Dirk Van Erp, hammered copper, riveted brass bands, flame shaped brass finial, original dark patina, stamped open box mark, normal wear around rim, 10" d, 17" h, **$4,600**. Photo courtesy of David Rago Auctions, Inc.

Chamberstick

4-1/4" h, copper, three sided, enamel green leaves within blue lines, marked "Buffalo Art Craft Shop," orig dark patina, some touch-ups to enamel **750.00**

12" h, 5" l, triangular, Charles Rohlfs, sheet copper top, carved ftd base, 1902, orig ebonized finish, carved "R 1902" **1,840.00**

Chandelier, 16" x 24", leaded glass, band of green and blue grape leaves, red fruit, red and green slag glass ground, unmarked, several breaks, folds, and a couple of missing grape pieces at bottom edge **815.00**

Chest, 27-1/2" l, 14-1/2" w, 13-3/4" h, incised daffodil front panel, Batchelder **8,050.00**

Cigarette box, 2-1/4" x 5" x 4", hammered copper, riveted trim, emb circular medallions, cedar lining, natural patina, unmarked, attributed to England **260.00**

Clock, 14" w, 4-3/4" d, 21-3/4" h, New Haven, Japanese-style, brass hands, keyed through-tenon sides, amber ripple glass, orig ebonized finish, paper label **490.00**

Coal scuttle, 15" x 22", hammered copper, repousse floral motif, riveted seams, rolled rim, new patina, some dents to body, some replaced rivets **575.00**

Coffee and tea service, coffeepot, teapot, creamer, sugar, and tray, pewter, wicker handles, by Archibald Knox, stamped "Liberty/Tudric," price for five-pc set **3,115.00**

Compote, 8" d, 6-3/4" h, pewter, cluthra green glass liner with opalescent and gold swirls, Liberty Tudric, Archibald Knox **3,115.00**

Inkwell, 5-1/4" sq, 3-1/2" h, faceted copper, curled, riveted feet, enameled green, red, and black, spade pattern, orig patina, unmarked Arts & Crafts Shop, couple of nicks to dec **250.00**

Jardiniere

11-1/2" d, 9-3/4" h, fluted hammered copper, classical style, orig verdigris patina, stamped "Jauchens Art Copper Shop San Francisco" **815.00**

14-1/2" d, 8-1/2" h, hammered copper, spherical, two riveted ring handles, orig reddish-brown patina, stamped Turchin Co., some dents **415.00**

Lamp, ceramic, bulbous base, four arms, turtle shade inset with several green slag glass panes, matte green glaze, unmarked, Chicago, restored cracks to arms, 16-1/2" x 11", **$3,335**. Photo courtesy of David Rago Auctions, Inc.

Lamp, ceiling, 8-1/2" d, 11" h, polished hammered brass, four arms, flame-shaped opalescent glass shade with green pulled feather pattern, English **1,355.00**

Lamp, student, 16" h, 13" d, Roycroft brass washed hammered copper base, Stickley Bros. copper and mica shades with silhouetted trees, orig finish, replaced mica, orb and cross mark **1,840.00**

Lantern, hanging, Gustav Stickley, four sided, overhanging vented cap, pierced sides, hammered amber glass, die stamp compass mark, few scratches to original patina, 9" d x 4" h lantern, 21" l chain, **$3,400**. Photo courtesy of David Rago Auctions, Inc.

Lamp, table

20" x 24", attributed to Dirk Van Erp, hammered copper, flaring riveted shade with four mica panels, four-socket bulbous base, orig mica and medium patina, replaced sockets with orig acorn pull chains, unmarked, provenance photographs of orig home **19,550.00**

23-1/2" x 13" sq, hammered copper, four-sided single-socket base converted from an oil font, emb panels, riveted with four flaring legs topped by four-panel flaring shade with trellis bands over caramel hammered slag glass, orig dark patina, unmarked, some dents to curls at top of shade **1,725.00**

30" x 18", Benedict, hammered copper, conical four-panel copper and mica shade, three-socket banded base, medium patina, unmarked **2,300.00**

Lantern, 11-1/2" h, black painted hammered metal, six caramel slag-glass panes, later ceiling cap.............. **265.00**

Library table

47-1/2" l, 36-1/4" w, 28-1/2" h, double oval, flaring legs, cut-out stretchers, orig finish, branded Limbert mark, 1" cut off legs........................ **7,475.00**

52" l, 24" w, 29-1/2" h, two arched drawers, corbels, one shelf, orig finish, Lifetime Paine Furniture Co. metal tag **2,300.00**

Magazine stand

18-1/4" w, 14" d, 50-1/2" h, gallery top, vertical slats all around, five tiers, fine orig dark finish, branded "CPM" **2,415.00**

24" w, 12" d, 41-1/2" h, three shelf, two short drawers, arched side rails over slatted sides, light finish, loose joints **630.00**

Mantel, custom-designed, oak, carved tree of life flanked by stylized floral stained glass cupboard doors, original finish, unmarked, 59" w, 14" d, 82-1/2" h, **$4,100**. Photo courtesy of David Rago Auctions, Inc.

Mantel, 59" w, 14" d, 82-1/2" h, oak, carved Tree of Life flanked by stylized floral stained-glass cupboard doors, original finish, unmarked **4,025.00**

Mirror, 25-1/2" x 21-1/4", frame clad in hand-hammered copper, repousse pattern of joined circles, orig patina **380.00**

Music cabinet, 21-1/2" w, 17" d, 42" h, attributed to G. M. Ellwood for J. S. Henry, c1900, English, mahogany, beveled top, paneled door inlaid with fruitwoods and mother-of-pearl, two drawers, brass hardware, good new finish **2,870.00**

Nut set, hammered copper, 8-1/2" d master bowl, six 3" d serving bowls, Benedict, some wear to patina, unmarked **290.00**

Occasional table, 30" d, 29-1/2" h, circular top over flaring legs joined by cut-out stretchers, orig finish, branded Limbert mark, wear and stains to top **2,070.00**

Pagoda table, Limbert, corbels under sq top, flaring sides, arched apron, lower shelf, cut-out base, orig finish, heavy overcoat, paper label under top, 34" sq, 30-1/2" h **13,800.00**

Photograph, 7-1/4" x 59-1/2", black and white, San Francisco devastated after the earthquake and fires of 1906, unmarked, orig Arts & Crafts frame, some rippling and tears to paper...................... **690.00**

Picture frame

7" x 10", hammered copper, double, in the style of Carence Crafters, emb branches of stylized flowers, unmarked, few minor dents and scratches............................ **265.00**

24" x 28", oak, orig glass, applied ebonized floral motif trim, some loss to dec **230.00**

Pillow, 16" x 25", embroidered stylized orange and green poppies, beige linen ground **490.00**

Planter, 13" d, 6" h, hammered copper, riveted curled legs ending in spade-shaped feet, fitted with plain copper liner, orig medium patina, unmarked ... **460.00**

Print, color linocut, 9" x 7", Tod Lindenmuth, "Moonlight on Cape Cod," houses and tree in moonlight, c1917, matted and mounted in new Arts & Crafts frame, unsigned, some foxing, mainly in margins...................................... **630.00**

Window, leaded polychrome slag glass, arched top, windmill on hill in front of large puffy clouds, unmarked, wooden frame, from a Michigan home, few minor breaks, 41" w, 78-1/2" h, **$4,025**. Photo courtesy of David Rago Auctions, Inc.

Print, color woodblock, matted and framed, pencil sgd

4-1/2" x 6", Jane Berry Judson, "North Main Street, Castile N.Y.," brown ink tree-lined street.... **460.00**

4-1/2" x 6", Jane Berry Judson, "Red Pine Grove Latchworth Park," dark brown ink of mother and children walking through the woods .. **815.00**

5" x 7", Charles H. Richert, coastline with cliffs, unsigned, new Arts & Crafts frame.......................... **750.00**

5" x 7", Charles H. Richert, covered bridge in autumn, unsigned, new Arts & Crafts frame.............. **750.00**

5" x 7", Charles H. Richert, "Maine Fishing Village," birch trees and boats by water, titled and sgd, new Arts & Crafts frame.............. **630.00**

5" x 7", Charles H. Richert, tall trees in autumnal landscape, unsigned, new Arts & Crafts frame **750.00**

6" x 4-1/2", Frances Gearhart, snowy mountainous landscape, pencil-signed, new Arts & Crafts frame **2,185.00**

6-1/4" sq, Gustave Baumann, "Eagle Ceremony at Tesque Pueblo," 1932, chop mark, new Arts & Crafts frame **750.00**

7-1/4" x 9-3/4", Eliza Draper Gardiner, "Passaconaway," lake shore scene with distant mountain, new Arts & Crafts frame, some foxing **1,485.00**

9-1/2" x 12-3/4", Norma Bassett Hall, "Tourrettes-Sur-Loup," 34 out of 75, medieval hilltop town at dusk, new Arts & Crafts frame, light foxing outside of image.................. **865.00**

9-3/4" x 7", Margaret Patterson, purple morning glories in green vase.................................. **2,900.00**

10" x 7", Margaret Patterson, branches of pink, blue, and white foxglove in green vase **2,900.00**

Room divider, 68" h, oak, grid-like top, three-panel, each panel cut out with fern design, replaced linen panels, orig finish, unmarked, some minor chipping to edges **1,200.00**

Sewing table, 18" l, 18" w closed, 29" h, drop leaf, two drawers with wooden pulls, tapering legs, orig finish, two splits to top **350.00**

String holder, 3-1/2", metal, emb Glasgow roses, int. lid etched MK, crossed sword mark/CDE **215.00**

Tablecloth, 39" d, circular, linen, embroidered red poppies, green leaves **860.00**

Table, dining, Limbert, circular, extension, four-sided pedestal base, orig finish with heavy overcoat, 54" d, 27-1/4" h... **2,300.00**

Tabouret, Limbert, sq top, box construction, sq cut outs, top refinished, orig finish on base, branded mark, 16-1/2" sq, 18" h **2,615.00**

Vase

5-1/4" x 7", Dirk Van Erp, hammered copper, spherical, orig patina, open box mark remnant of D'Arcy Gaw.................................. **3,115.00**

8" x 5-1/2", Dirk Van Erp, hammered copper, tapering base, closed-in rim, good orig dark patina. stamped open box mark **2,870.00**

11-1/2" h, 7-1/4" d, flaring hammered copper floriform, fine new patina, stamped "Marie Zimmerman Maker" **1,335.00**

Wall sconce, 9" w, 15" l, Jarvie, brass, double, tooled back plate, two riveted candleholders, each with scrolled braces and flaring bobeche, orig patina, stamped "Made By The Jarvie Shop" **5,750.00**

AUSTRIAN WARE

History: More than 100 potteries were located in the Austro-Hungarian Empire in the late 19th and early 20th centuries. Although Carlsbad was the center of the industry, the factories spread as far as the modern-day Czech Republic.

Many of the factories were either owned or supported by Americans; hence, their wares were produced mainly for export to the United States.

Marks: Many wares do not have a factory mark but only the word "Austrian" in response to the 1891 law specifying that the country of origin had to be marked on imported products.

Additional Listings: Amphora, Carlsbad, Royal Dux, and Royal Vienna.

Bowl, 4-1/2" sq, 3-3/4" h, art glass, sq, pinched-in top, irid blue surface, enameled flowers and leaves **520.00**

Celery tray, 12" l, scalloped border, pink roses, green leaves, gold trim....... **75.00**

Creamer, 3-1/4" w, 3-3/4" h, handleless, art glass, swirled pink, yellow, blue, and white, cased pink int., two bands of enamel dec **460.00**

Ewer, 11-3/4" h, 6" d, rococo gold scroll, hp pink and yellow wild roses, gold outlines, four ftd.......................... **125.00**

Figure

9" h, children in colonial dress, painted, sgd "Tunr-Lepltiz," 19th C, pr... **300.00**

9-1/4" h, 11-1/2" h, pair of white Lipizzaner rearing horses, riders wearing red coats, red saddle blankets.............................. **800.00**

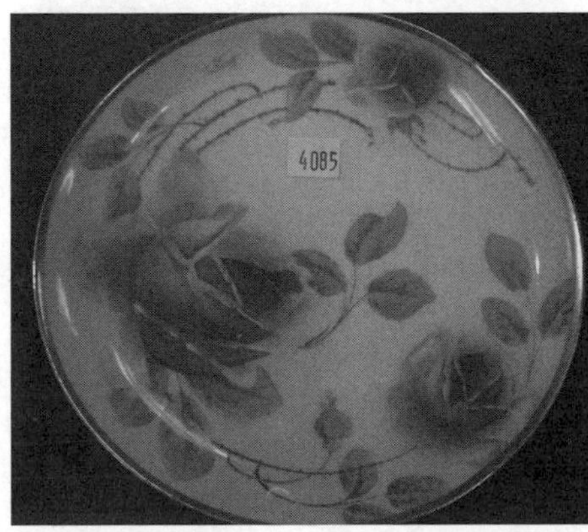

Plate, white, red rose dec, green leaves, gold trim, artist signed "Deligne," marked "Imperial Austria (crown) Peinture Lamain," **$30**.

9-1/2" h, 11-1/2" h, pair of white Lipizzaner horses, one rearing at gate, other jumping, riders in dark brown coats, white pants, black boots standing by, blue Wein mark **900.00**

Oyster plate, 9-7/8" d, porcelain, shell-shaped wells to center, scalloped rim, blue and gilt enamel flowers, fish, and birds dec, 19th C......................... **175.00**

Vase, double gourd shape, arched handles, four tiny openings at rim, leathery blue-green matte glaze, stamped numbers on base, possibly Teplitz, 7" d, 10" h, **$120**. Photo courtesy of David Rago Auctions, Inc.

Perfume set, orange cut glass finials, angular opaque black glass vessels, metal mounts, enameled fan motif, all imp "Austria" on metal, two acid-etched "Austria," 6-1/8" h atomizer, 5-3/8" h perfume, 5" h cov box, imperfections **500.00**

Pokal, glass

17-1/2" h, green, detailed enameled cavalier holding empty stein, c1890 .... **400.00**

18-1/2" h, green, detailed enameled scene of knight on horseback, colorful scrolled acanthus dec, c1890 .... **400.00**

Urn, 12" h, transfer printed roses, marked "Victoria," **$85**; pair of 13" h vases with transfer printed flowers, one genre painting, marked "Royal Wettina," **$115**. Photo courtesy of David Rago Auctions, Inc.

Table lamp, attributed to Wiener Werkstatte, in the manner of Susi Singer, ceramic, ovoid, flanked by two mermaid figures in high relief, fish, octopus, and starfish in relief, glossy aqua, orange, white, and irid glazes, textured mottled green and brown ground, gilt highlights, four patinated metal dolphins on stepped metal base, 22-1/4" h.................. **375.00**

Trinket box, cov, 4-1/4" l, oval, the gilt metal box stamped with continuous bands of anthemion and torches, porcelain set lid with printed scene of two classical beauties on cobalt blue ground, velveteen lining, early 20th C **450.00**

Vase, art glass

- 9" h, folded down tricorn top, irid drag loop, green ground, two open bubbles **230.00**
- 11" h, ruffled top, irid crackle finish, red ground, polished pontil, unsigned **360.00**
- 12" h, three dimpled sides, irid pink swirls, ground top, unsigned **120.00**
- 13" h, four pinched in sides, ruffled top, irid rippled finish, purple and blue highlights, unsigned..... **260.00**

Vase, porcelain, 19" x 12-1/2", bulbous, incised, polychrome enamel vulture and olive branches, stamped "Amphora Austria" with crown.................. **1,150.00**

AUTOGRAPHS

History: Autographs appear on a wide variety of formats—letters, documents, photographs, books, cards, etc. Most collectors focus on a particular person, country, or category, e.g., signers of the Declaration of Independence.

Abbreviations: The following are used to describe autograph materials.

Materials:

ADS	Autograph Document Signed
ALS	Autograph Letter Signed
AQS	Autograph Quotation Signed
CS	Card Signed
DS	Document Signed
FDC	First Day Cover
LS	Letter Signed
PS	Photograph Signed
TLS	Typed Letter Signed

For more information, see *Warman's Americana & Collectibles*, 10th edition.

Colonial America

Duane, James, ALS, member of Continental Congress, Nov. 17, 1782, Philadelphia, to Peter Curtenius, one pg, folded large 8vo sheet with integral blank **300.00**

Floyd, William, DS, Oct. 25, 1781, Poughkeepsie, NY, acknowledging State of NY indebted to Daniel Conkling, also sgd by Isaac Roosevelt, endorsed by Conkling on verso, one pg, single 4to, minor toning................................ **700.00**

Hancock, John, partially printed DS, April 1, 1791, Boston, as Gov of MA, appointing John Thomas as Adjutant of the first regiment in first brigade of 5th div of MA militia, countersigned by John Avery, one pg, 11" x 15", paper seal intact, minor browning along vertical centerfold **2,760.00**

Hooper, William, ALS, Aug. 6, 1776, Philadelphia, sgd to Robert Smith, re: impending conflict between Washington and Howes, blessing America's cause, predicting Britain's ruin, one pg, folded small folio sheet with integral address leaf, minor age toning............ **64,100.00**

Lafayette, Marquis De, ALS, written in French to Countess, accepting party invitation, half pg, folded 8vo sheet with integral address leaf, tissue back closing hole and minor separations, lightly toned overall **815.00**

Morris, Robert, DS, partially printed promissory note, Nov. 10, 1795, Philadelphia, endorsed by Morris, payable to him from John Nicholson, also inscribed on verso "Exhibited to us under the Commission against Robert Morris Philad Sept. 12 AD 1801 John Hallowell and Tho. Cumpson," 4" x 6-1/2" **500.00**

ALS, Connie Mack, "...Felt that I had been in the game along time, am now going back to the game of Golf and am taking long walks which I did before giving up the management of the Athletics. You no [sic] I had given up Golf for a long time will have so much time on my hand...," trimmed, identified in another hand, one page, 5-1/4" x 3", **$290**. Photo courtesy of Historical Collectibles Auctions.

Washington, Lund, letter written to George Washington by his cousin, Lund Washington with postscript by Martha Washington, March 30, 1767 .... **83,650.00**

Foreign

Eiffel, Gustave, TLS, Paris, April 19, 1889, sgd "G. Eissel" to E. Hippeau, in French, one page, single 8" x 10" sheet, business stationary, folds **375.00**

Freud, Sigmund, ANS, sgd "Freud" to Dr. Nunberg, in German, referring case from Dr. Glanz for patient with schizophrenic attack, 1-1/4 pgs, 3-1/4" x 4-1/2" sheet torn from larger one, in pencil, toned, folds.................. **2,760.00**

Peron, Eva, PS, Buenos Aires, Oct. 10, 1950, bust portrait, sgd on mount beneath calligraphic inscription, 9" x 6-1/2" photo on 13-1/2" x 9-1/2" mount, signature light, framed **620.00**

General

Ben Gurion, David, pen and ink and wash cartoon portrait of Ben Gurion by Jack Rosen, sgd by Ben Gurion, 1970, 10-3/4"x 8", framed **350.00**

Byrd, Richard E., Alone, 8vo, publisher's dyed morocco gilt, orig box, NY, 1938, one of 225 numbered copies **460.00**

Edison, Thomas A., PS, inscribed "To Victor Young Thos A. Edison," silver print, seated portrait, sgd on mount above image, 12" x 9-1/2".................... **1,380.00**

Einstein, Albert, TLS, June 14, 1939, Princeton, to S. Hirsenhorn, Jr., thanking for his work with refugees, one page, single 4to sheet, personal stationery, folds.. **4,600.00**

Fulton, Robert, clipped ALS, sgd "Your civilities to him or assistance while he continues in France...," three lines plus signature, 2-1/2" x 7-3/4" sheet **550.00**

Lindbergh, Charles A., TLS, Nov. 17, 1930, NY, sgd to C. B. Whittelsey, declining invitation to banquet, one pg, single 4to sheet, personal stationery, folds... **675.00**

Mack, Connie, TLS, Jan. 26, 1942, to W. A. Davenport, replying to fan's request, one pg, single 4to sheet, American Baseball Club of Philadelphia stationery, minor uneven toning at edges..... **350.00**

Wright, Orville, sgd on selvage of block of 9 two cent International Civil Aeronautics Conference commemoratives, c1928 .... **2,530.00**

Literature

Anderson, Sherwood, TLS, Oct. 14, 1939, to Ralph Hartman, regarding autographing books, one pg, oblong 7" sheet, folds, framed with photograph **220.00**

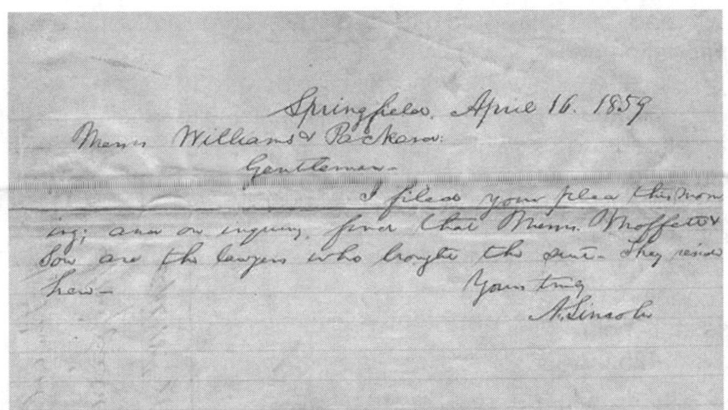

ANS, hand written, written and signed by Abraham Lincoln, dated April 16, 1859, with card supporting authenticity, **$6,800**. Photo courtesy of Joy Luke Auctions.

Emerson, Ralph Waldo, ALS, Concord, Sept. 22, 1846, sgd "R. W. Emerson" to Elliot Cowdin, President of Merchantile Library Assoc., agreeing to give lecture, one page, folded 8" x 10" sheet with integral address leaf, usual folds **575.00**

Hemingway, Ernest, book signed, *The Old Man and the Sea,* Scribner's, NY, 1952, inscribed, orig dj, documentation authenticating signature **25,000.00**

Sinclair, Upton, book signed, *The Jungle,* Sustainer's Edition, inscribed to Edward Everett Hale, 1906 ...... **3,250.00**

Verne, Jules, ALS, collection of 12 handwritten letters, dated between 1894 and 1905 ...... **6,900.00**

Military

Farragut, David G., LS, New York, Dec. 14, 1863, sgd "D. G. Farragut" to Elliot Cowden, regarding department for station, one page, folded sheet, integral blank, blue-ruled paper, folds **350.00**

Marshall, John, ANS, Sept. 28, 1813, to cashier of Bank of Columbia, 3" x 7-1/2", writing on verso slightly visible recto, framed **2,990.00**

Mussolini, Benito, PS, close-up bust portrait, looking downward, sgd on sheet below image, red wax seal affixed to lower left corner, 11" x 7-1/2", minor creases in image, emb stamp on lower right corner of image, framed **520.00**

Sherman, William T, PS, sgd "W. T. Sherman, General, New York, Feb. 8, 1889," standing 3/4 portrait, in uniform, 11-1/2" x 7" image size, matted, framed **2,300.00**

Thomas, Lorenzo, PS, "Brig Genl I. Thomas, Adj. Genl U.S.A.," bust portrait carte-de-visite by Frederick Gutekunst, orig photographer's mount, sgd on recto at bottom of image, bit yellowed and soiled, revenue stamp affixed on verso **260.00**

Music

Caruso, Enrico, souvenir illus menu for dinner in his honor, sgd by Caruso and other attendees, including Otto Kahn, Victor Herbert, Winston O. Lord, David Bispham, and Melville E. Stone, New York, Feb. 5, 1916 ...... **290.00**

Jolson, Al, PS, inscribed to society bandleader Meyer Davis, 3/4 length seated portrait, cigarette in hand, 9" x 7", mounted on board **300.00**

Paganini, Niccolo, ALS, London, July 1, 1831, in Italian, agreeing to take part in benefit for poor musicians, one page 7-1/2" x 7-1/4" sheet, trimmed, minor browning **2,300.00**

Presidents

Adams, John Quincy, partially printed vellum DS, Aug. 4, 1827, Washington, granting 80 acres of land in MI to David Wiley, countersigned by George Graham, one pg, 9" x 14", folds, foxed, minor loss to seal **350.00**

Arthur, Chester, ALS, March 18, (1881-85), Washington, to George W. Pratt, one pg, folded 8vo sheet with integral blank, horizontal fold, remnants of prior mounting on verso of blank **480.00**

Coolidge, Calvin, bust portrait engraving sgd, inscribed, to Gov William Sproul, inscribed in image, 15" x 12", foxed, soiled, framed **200.00**

Eisenhower, Dwight D., typescript of speech, sgd, "Peace is a blessing and, like most blessings, it must be earned," sgd at bottom of first page, printed signature at bottom of 2nd page, each page illus with printed photograph of Eisenhower, two pgs, two single 8vo sheets, folds **415.00**

Fillmore, Millard, inscription sgd, April 20, 1864, Buffalo, "For Miss Annie C. Draper with the Respects of Millard Fillmore," one pg, single 8vo sheet, mounted to larger sheet **230.00**

Hayes, Rutherford B., ALS, Dec. 23, 1885, Fremont, giving permission to publish letter, one pg, singlc 8vo sheet **350.00**

Hoover, Herbert, PS, silver print by Bachrach, inscribed to Wm V. Alexander, 13-1/2" x 9-1/2", orig White House envelope postmarked Feb. 16, 1933 ...... **260.00**

Jefferson, Thomas, DS, land grant, also sgd by James Madison as Secretary of State, dated Oct. 14, 1801, for 2,045 acres between the Little Miami and Scioto rivers (Ohio) to Captain Nathaniel Lucas, makes reference to survey by George Washington, orig applied eagle seal, fold lines, stains, 14-1/4" x 11-3/4" **3,300.00**

Kennedy, Jacqueline, PS, inscribed to Herbert Mayes, family portrait showing First Lady posing with her children, inscribed in image, 10" x 8" **2,100.00**

Lincoln, Abraham, DS, Gen George G. Meade's commission to brigadier general, July 3, 1863, orig tin document tube **44,000.00**

Madison, James, DS, land grant, dated April 12, 1813, fold lines, printed and hand written text on parchment, stamped paper seal for "United States General Land Office," for land sold to Joshua Horner of Scioto County, Ohio, also sgd by Land Office Commissioner Edward Tiffin, 9" x 14" **110.00**

Roosevelt, Franklin D., TLS, June 27, 1936, Washington, to Congressman James Claiborne, discussing highway bill, one pg, single 4to sheet, White House stationery **865.00**

Posters, framed under glass: The Monkees, autographed by Davie Jones, Mickey Dolenz, Peter Tork and Michael Nesmith, 14-1/2" x 18-1/2", **$125**; Batman movie poster, autographed by Adam West, Burt Ward, Lee Merriweather and Frank Gorshin, 20" x 24", **$125**. Photo courtesy of Joy Luke Auctions.

Taylor, Zachary, ALS, March 19, 1825, Louisville, sgd "Z. Taylor" as Lieutenant Colonel in the 1st Regiment of U.S. Infantry, to Brigadier General T. S. Jesup, one pg, folded 4to sheet with integral address leaf, tissued backed closing separations at folds **1,035.00**

Washington, George, ALS, Mount Vernon, as president, April 13, 1793, demonstrating his loyalty to troops as he seeks to collect French and Indian War claims for deceased comrade **19,550.00**

Show business

Crawford, Joan, PS, inscribed "To Maria from Joan Crawford," 14" x 11" portrait by Hurrell, his emb stamp in lower right corner, minor damage at edges, framed **320.00**

Fonteyn, Margot, PS, inscribed "Margot Fonteyn Arias," full-length pose in ballerina costume, 7-1/2" x 6", diagonal crease in upper right corner........ **250.00**

Holiday, Billie, PS, inscribed "To Norman Stay Happy," souvenir group photo taken in Chicago, showing "Lady Day" with five other people, sgd on mat above image, 5" x 7", presentation folder of Garrick Stage Bar, also inscribed by another, inscriptions in pencil.................... **980.00**

Wayne, John, black and white, sgd "Good Luck Tony, John Wayne, 5/27/40," 9" x 7-1/4"................................ **1,035.00**

Statesmen

Boone, Daniel, family, DS, 123-page archive of Daniel Boone family, sgd by Squire Boone, Daniel M. Boone, and Enoch Boone............................ **8,050.00**

Mellon, Andrew W., ALS, Feb. 4, 1921, Pittsburgh, sgd "A. W. Mellon" to Governor Wm. Sproul, thanking him for efforts to appoint Mellon to Pres Harding's cabinet, admitting he has no desire for job, two pgs, folded 8vo, personal stationery................................... **450.00**

Seward, William Henry, ALS, as Secretary of State, Dept. of State letterhead, Nov. 14, 1866, letter to David Hoadley, Pres of Panama Railroad Co., regarding dealings with Columbian government, 10" x 7-3/4" **90.00**

Webster, Daniel, ALS, May 12, 1846, Washington, to Colonel Thomas Aspinwall, thanking him for letters and that "The President has always read your letters to me with commendation-he thinks highly of you," 2-1/2" pgs, folded 8vo.. **320.00**

Young, Brigham, clipped signature, Aug. 11, 1903, Salt Lake City, mounted to ALS sgd by Richard Young to Miss Whiting, sending her the signature and assuring her that "the following signature of my distinguished grandfather is genuine," one pg, oblong 8vo, business stationery **425.00**

Automobiles

History: Automobiles are generally classified into two categories: prewar, those manufactured before World War II; and those manufactured after the conflict. The Antique Automobile Club of America, the world's oldest and largest automobile historical society, considers motor vehicles, including cars, buses, motorcycles, and trucks, manufactured prior to 1930 "antique." The Contemporary Historical Vehicle Society, however, accepts automobiles that are at least twenty-five years old. There are also specific clubs dedicated to specific marques, like the Wills/Kaiser/AMC Jeep Club, and the Edsel Owners Club.

Some states, such as Pennsylvania, have devised a dual registration system for older cars—antique and classic. Models from the 1960s and 1970s, especially convertibles and limited-production models, fall into the "classic" designation if they are not used as daily transportation. Many states have also allowed collectible vehicles to sport "year of issue" license plates, thus allowing an owner of a 1964-1/2 Mustang to register a 1964 license plate from their home state.

Notes: The prices below are for cars in running condition, with a high proportion of original parts and somewhere between 60 percent and 80 percent restoration. Prices can vary by as much as 30 percent in either direction. Prices of unrestored automobiles, or those not running or missing original parts can be 50 percent to 75 percent below prices listed.

Many older cars, especially if restored, are now worth more than $15,000. Their limited availability makes them difficult to price. Auctions, more than any other source, are the true determinant of value at this level.

Prices of high-powered 1964 to 1972 "muscle cars" will continue to escalate, while the value of pre-war cars will remain steady for all but unique custom-built roadsters and limousines.

Two 1950s Ford promotional cars: one black, marked on top "EBY Auto Sales, Inc., Wakarusa, IN," one brown with key wind, **$150**. Photo courtesy of Joy Luke Auctions.

AMC, 1968 AMX Fastback coupe **8,500.00**

Amphicar, 1962 conv **19,500.00**

Jaguar, XK140 Roadster, 1955, manual, white exterior, burgundy interior, odometer reads 20,060 miles, some restoration needed, **$25,850**. Photo courtesy of Skinner, Inc.

Auburn, 1935, Model 6-653, four-door sedan, 6 cyl......................... **23,000.00**

Bricklin, 1975, Model SV-1, gullwing coupe **12,500.00**

Buick, 1941 Roadmaster, four-door sedan, 8 cyl.......................... **17,500.00**

Checker, 1963, Aerobus.......... **6,500.00**

Chevrolet, 1953, pick-up, 6-cylinder, yellow, standard shift............... **1,200.00**

Chrysler, 1932 Imperial Sedan, 6 cyl **18,000.00**

Crosley, 1950 "Hot Shot" Roadster **8,900.00**

Dodge, 1948 Power Wagon..... **9,500.00**

Essex, 1929 Challenger Series, four-door Town Sedan **9,500.00**

Edsel, 1958 Ranger two-door HT **11,000.00**

Ford

- 1924 Model T coupe **8,500.00**
- 1963, Falcon Futura, convertible, red, automatic, replaced V-8 engine **8,500.00**

Honda, 1985, 250SX all terrain **1,600.00**

Hudson, 1951 Hudson Hornet **18,000.00**

International Scout, 4x4, 1966 .... **6,500.00**

Jeep, 1966 Wagoneer, four-door, 4x4 .... **8,500.00**

Julian, 1922 Model 60 coupe, 6 cyl **9,500.00**

Kaiser, 1953 Manhattan, four-door sedan.................................... **12,000.00**

Lambert, 1909, roadster, 6 cyl **12,500.00**

Mercury, 1969 Cougar XR-7 HT **7,500.00**

Nash, Metropolitan, 1956, conv **8,500.00**

Oakland, 1930 sedan **7,500.00**
Oldsmobile, 1967 Toronado **9,500.00**
Packard, 1946 Clipper, sedan **12,000.00**
Plymouth, 1951, Cambridge Club coupe, light gray, 6-cylinder, standard shift **4,500.00**
Pontiac, 1934 two-door sedan **9,500.00**
Rolls Royce, 1951 Silver Wraith **49,000.00**
Studebaker, 1962 Lark **4,500.00**
Volkswagen, 1949 sedan **10,500.00**
Willys, 1954, Eagle **8,500.00**

AUTOMOBILIA

History: Automobilia is a wide-ranging category. It includes just about anything that represents a vehicle, from cookie jars to toys. Car parts are not usually considered automobilia, although there are a few exceptions, like the Lalique radiator ornaments. Most sought after is automobile advertising, especially signs and deal promotional models. The number of items related to the automobile is endless. Even collectors who do not own an antique car are interested in automobile, bus, truck, and motorcycle advertising memorabilia. Many people collect only items from a certain marque, like Hupmobiles or Mustangs, while others may collect all advertising, like matchbooks or color brochures, showing the new models for a certain year. Most material changes hands at automobile swap meets and specialty auctions held throughout the year.

Advertising button

Auto dealership, Butzer Bros, purple on white, early touring car, early 1900s **25.00**

Best Buick Yet, litho of blue night sky studded by tiny white stars, slogan in white outlined in red, late 1930s **35.00**

Buick Fireball 8, graphic red, white, and blue design, for introduction of high-power engine, 1940s **45.00**

Church Brigade Motor Car, black and white, touring car, associated to "Central Church of Christ Bible School," early 1900s **25.00**

Colburn Automobiles, silver on blue, inscribed "Denver Made" **30.00**

Exxon, Conserve Energy, red, white, and blue, early 1970s **5.00**

Fisk Tires, black, white, and yellow, symbolic youngster is ready for bed holding candle and automobile tire, slogan "Time to Re-tire, Get a Fisk," 1930s **20.00**

Flying Red Horse, red on white, symbol for Socony-Vacuum, 1940s **15.00**

Radiator cap, Rolls Royce, chrome plate, figure "Spirit of Ecstasy," mounted on round chrome dish, 8" d, 6-1/2" h, **$500**. Photo courtesy of Joy Luke Auctions.

Nash Airflytes, black inscription on gold, Nash's 50th anniversary year, 1952 .... **28.00**

Pyro-Action Spark Plugs, multicolored image of warrior in armor, orange rim inscribed "Crusade Against Spark Plug Paralysis-Sponsored by Robert Bosch," 1930s **10.00**

Advertising pocket mirror

2-3/4" h, Automobile "R" Invincible Oil, figural brown wooden barrel bounded by dark brown staves, black and gray logo of A. D. Miller's Sons, Co., Pittsburg **55.00**

2-3/4" h, Studebaker Vehicle Works, multicolored, detailed scene of factory complex, titled "Largest in the World, South Bend, Ind." **95.00**

Advertising tab, 1-1/4" x 2-1/2", Ford Motors Merry Christmas, diecut thin metal tab, two gold lusters, red and green image of Santa in sleigh, red lettering, 1950s **50.00**

Banner, Sunoco Gasoline, 1930s, 48" l **400.00**

Calendar, 1926, Shell Oil, full pad **55.00**

Compression tester, Hasting's Piston Ring advertising on dial, orig metal storage box **45.00**

Cooler, Coca-cola, two-wheeled trailer motorcycle hitch **3,600.00**

Decanter, figural race car, Lionstone, Al Unser's Johnny Lightning Special, 1970 and 1972 Indianapolis 500 Winner **75.00**

Display cabinet

Auto Lite Spark Plug, 18-1/2" h, 13" w, painted metal cabinet, glass front **125.00**

Schrader tire gauge cabinet, figural tire gauge, opens to reveal parts **350.00**

Emblem, Studebaker, red on white litho, late 1930s **20.00**

Gas globe

Mobilgas **200.00**

Mobilgas, Pegasus illus **300.00**

Sinclair H-C **475.00**

Gas pump

Bennett, clock-face style, unrestored **1,300.00**

Bennett Dino Sinclair, restored **2,100.00**

Bennett Dino Sinclair, unrestored, globe missing **375.00**

Bowser, clock-face style, modern replacement Richfield Ethyl globe **2,600.00**

Mobilgas Special, ad glass, unrestored **1,300.00**

Texaco Tokheim, clock-face style, restored **2,700.00**

Folder, Chrysler Motors Five Star Show, New York World's Fair, 1940, red, white, and blue cover, rocket taking off from stylized rocket port, diagram of exhibit, products, bottom half with diecut stars denoting attractions, 3-3/4" w, 8-3/4" h, opens to 11-1/4" x 16-3/4", **$30**. Photo courtesy of Hake's Americana & Collectibles.

Grill badge, Sports Car Club of America, black and red wire wheel logo, cloisonné, early 1960s' era **50.00**

Keychain fob

Ford Tractors, dark gold plastic, showing key mechanism for "New Ford Select-O-Speed Tractors," reverse with "Greatest tractor advantage since hydraulics" and Ford logo, late 1940s **12.00**

Shell Oil, silvered metal emblem, painted on reverse with instructions for return if lost, c1930 .... **10.00**

Key ring holder, 3-1/2" h, silvered metal, double ring holder, centered by applied miniature metal 7/8" h figure of smiling and saluting Esso Happy Oil Drop figure finished in porcelain white enamel, copper luster face, Esso logo on chest in red on silver, blue oval logo, 1960s **25.00**

Lapel stud

1/2", Buick, diecut logo, white and dark blue enamel, diecut brass stud fastener, c1930 .... **45.00**

11/16", Chauffeurs Federation of America, dark blue enamel, bright brass luster, threaded post and cap, c1910-20 .... **30.00**

Lunch box, litho tin, Winner Cut Plug Tobacco, early motorcar racing illus, 7-3/4" w, 5" d, 4-1/2" h, clear coated **1,500.00**

Motor oil jar, Sohio, bulbous, metal spout... **295.00**

Name badge, 2-3/4" oval, dark blue and cream, clear cello center window, slots on reverse for card, text "Authorized Chevrolet Service, Genuine Chevrolet Parts," 1930-40............................. **60.00**

Oil can

Esso Handy Oil, 1" x 2-1/4" w x 4" h, tin, 1-1/2" capped spout, blue and white litho design, red, white, and blue Esso logo, small yellow accent on Happy Oil Drop, listing of recommended uses on back, 1960s **15.00**

Red Giant, Council Bluffs, Iowa, one quart, 1960s **110.00**

Oil dispenser, Berne Model 307, restored, 36" h **300.00**

Pail, 11-3/4" h, porcelain, green, black rim, image of early Oldsmobile Horch 8 open air car on either side, 1911, small rim chips.. **420.00**

Paperweight, Atlantic Richfield, 3" x 3" trapezoid, clear Lucite, small dark amber vial holding liquid "Crude Oil-Prudhoe Bay-North Slope, Alaska," and "Atlantic Richfield Co." with logo in internal blue lettering.. **15.00**

Pedal car, Packard, Gendron, orig leather seats, 1931 .... **8,800.00**

Pennant, 9" x 23", The People's Choice, Exxon, orange felt, black printing, smiling tiger head, black felt trim band, 1970s... **20.00**

Pin, 1-1/16" l, Harley-Davidson, replica of gasoline tank, silvered brass, name stamped in red, 1941 .... **145.00**

Pinback button

7/8" d, Studebaker, white name, large gold star, dark blue ground, Bastian back paper, c1907 .... **30.00**

1-1/4" d, Boost the Meek Co., Trans-Continental 1908 Automobile Tour, black and white, green text.... **35.00**

1-1/4", Ford, red text, red airplane flying over globe, dark blue and white, text "Ford-Found The World Sweepstakes," early 1950s **48.00**

1-1/4" d, I Want A Maxwell, dark red lettering on cream, Whitehead & Hoag back paper, 1910 .... **30.00**

Radiator emblem, 2" d, Star Six Durant Motors, bright white enamel circle surround dark blue enamel background, white enamel dragon, 3" raised metal rim on back, c1910.......................... **110.00**

Road map, New York, Shell Oil, 1934... **12.00**

Sign

Chevron Gasoline, porcelain and neon, 1950s, 36" x 60"....... **3,800.00**

Conoco Gasoline, round, porcelain, 1920s, 26" d **2,500.00**

McClanahan Gasoline, two sided, porcelain, gold seal logo, 48" d **1,250.00**

Texaco No Smoking, porcelain, 22" l, 3" h, 1950s.......................... **225.00**

Stickpin

Oldsmobile, 2" pin, diecut silvered brass replica of early Oldsmobile with tiller steering, "Old Motor Works, Detroit, Mich, U.S.A" **25.00**

Polarine Oil, 2-1/4" brass pin, diecut dark red, blue, and white celluloid pennant, black text "Continental Oil Co.," Whitehead & Hoag, 1905 patent **35.00**

Tire inflator, Eco TireFlator, glass globe on top, restored, 60" h **3,995.00**

Tray, Atlantic Richfield, 6-1/4" w, 8-1/4" l, oval, dark glass, gray lettering extending inward from left edge "Atlantic Richfield Company," small logo symbol **15.00**

Baccarat Glass

History: The Sainte-Anne glassworks at Baccarat in Voges, France, was founded in 1764 and produced utilitarian soda glass. In 1816, Aime-Gabriel d'Artiques purchased the glassworks, and a Royal Warrant was issued in 1817 for the opening of Verrerie de Vonâoche éa Baccarat. The firm concentrated on lead-crystal glass products. In 1824, a limited company was created.

From 1823 to 1857, Baccarat and Saint-Louis glassworks had a commercial agreement and used the same outlets. No merger occurred. Baccarat began the production of paperweights in 1846. In the late 19th century, the firm achieved an international reputation for cut glass table services, chandeliers, display vases, centerpieces, and sculptures. Products eventually included all forms of glassware. The firm still is active today.

For more information, see *Warman's Glass*, 4th edition.

Additional Listings: Paperweights.

Paperweight, concentric multi-colored millefiori mushroom, green and white striped stem, light blue-over-white double overlay, multi-faceted top, six-faceted sides, flower-cut bottom, acid-etched insignia and date 1970 on base, 3-1/4" d, **$520**. Photo courtesy of Alderfer Auction Co.

Box, 9-1/2" h, molded black glass, pineapple shape, hinged at the center, leaf tip rim, top gilt metal fronds, gilt bronze scrolled feather base, early 20th C **775.00**

Candelabra, pr, crystal, 32" h, four light, diamond-cut baluster standard, four scrolling candle arms terminating urn-form sockets, etched glass globes hung with prisms **2,000.00**

Decanter, 11-5/8" h, flattened ovoid, scalloped edge, etched flat sides with hunter on horseback, forest animals, scrolling vine, neck with vine etching, similarly shaped and etched stopper, 20th C, price for pr **550.00**

Finger bowl, 4-3/4" d, 6-3/4" d underplate, ruby ground, gold medallions and flowers dec **350.00**

Lamp, 19-1/2" l, 24-1/2" h, central cut glass urn on short brass stem, two horizontal reeded candle arms, fan cut drip pans suspending cut prisms, ovoid glass knop stem, paneled trumpet foot cut with roundels, brass flat leaf base, one with collar at urn for further prisms, other with collars for two etched-glass shades, electrified, early 20th C, price for pr **2,875.00**

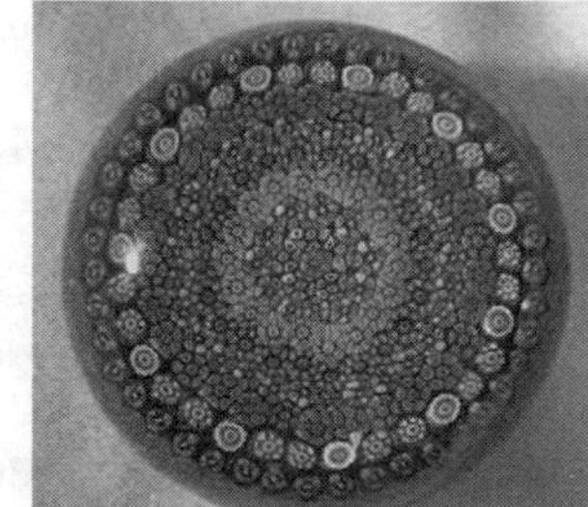

Paperweight, concentric millefiori, central pink cane, encircled by eight close packed rings of canes in yellow, pink, green, blue, and purple, outer-most ring extends in radiating canes on bottom of weight, acid-etched insignia on base, 3" d, **$350**. Photo courtesy of Alderfer Auction Co.

Toothpick holder, 2-1/2" h, Rose Tiente **110.00**

Vase, 9-3/4" h, colorless, tapered cylindrical, slightly everted rim, vertical tapered flutes on body, press-cut, 20th C **165.00**

BANKS, MECHANICAL

History: Banks which display some form of action while accepting a coin are considered mechanical banks. Mechanical banks date back to ancient Greece and Rome, but the majority of collectors are interested in those made between 1867 and 1928 in Germany, England, and the United States.

Initial research suggested that approximately 250 to 300 different or variant designs of banks were made in the early period. Today that number has been revised to 2,000-3,000 types and varieties. The field remains ripe for discovery and research.

More than 80 percent of all cast-iron mechanical banks produced between 1869 and 1928 were made by J. E. Stevens Co., Cromwell, Connecticut. Tin banks are usually of German origin.

Reproduction Alert: Reproductions, fakes, and forgeries exist for many banks. Forgeries of some mechanical banks were made as early as 1937, so age alone is not a guarantee of authenticity. In the following price listing, two asterisks indicate banks for which serious forgeries exist, and one asterisk indicates banks for which casual reproductions have been made.

Notes: While rarity is a factor in value, appeal of design, action, quality of manufacture, country of origin, and history of collector interest also are important. Radical price fluctuations may occur when there is an imbalance in these factors. Rare banks may sell for a few hundred dollars, while one of more common design with greater appeal will sell in the thousands.

The mechanical bank market is being greatly affected by the on-line auctions found on the Internet. This past year has seen more examples of banks being offered for sale than has been seen in decades. Many of these previously unavailable examples are readily purchased by collectors. Because of large numbers of more common banks also coming into the market, this past year represents a drop in the price of many banks, especially those in the under $3,500 range, but recently the market appears to have stabilized on banks under $3,500. It looks like the market is now poised for potential movement upward on these lower priced banks. Additionally, there have been large sums of investment money coming onto the mechanical bank market, as of late, specifically directed at purchasing banks in the $20,000 to $100,000 and up levels per bank, causing an upward trend in these higher priced banks. It is my theory that much of this money has been moved into mechanical banks by non-collecting investors who have become fed up with the performance of the stock market and are searching for other directions of investment to protect their capital. I strongly suspect that this trend will continue.

The values in the list here accurately represent the selling prices of mechanical banks in the specialized collectors' market. As some banks are hard to find, and the market is quite volatile both up and down in price structure, consultation of a competent specialist in mechanical banks, with up-to-the-moment information, is advised prior to selling any mechanical bank.

The prices listed are for original old mechanical banks with no repairs, in sound operating condition, and with at least 90 percent of the original paint intact.

Adviser: James S. Maxwell Jr.

Price note: Prices quoted are for 100 percent original examples with no repairs, no repaint, and which have at least 90 percent bright original paint. An asterisk indicates casual reproductions; † denotes examples where casual reproductions and serious fakes exist.

†Acrobat **1,050.00**

African Bank, black bust, back emb "African Bank" **450.00**

American Bank, sewing machine **850.00**

***Artillery** **900.00**

Automatic Fortune Bank, tin **3,700.00**

Automatic Savings Bank, tin, soldier **270.00**

Automatic Savings Bank, tin, sailor **250.00**

Always Did "Spise a Mule," boy seated on bench, missing trap door, 10" l, 6" h, **$990**. Photo courtesy of Joy Luke Auctions.

†Baby Elephant X-O'clock, lead and wood **1,200.00**

***Bad Accident** **1,650.00**

Bear, tin **280.00**

†Bear and Tree Stump **1,000.00**

†Bear, slot in chest **320.00**

†Bill E. Grin **500.00**

†Billy Goat Bank **230.00**

Bow-ery Bank, iron, paper, wood **1,850.00**

Bowing Man in Cupola **1,700.00**

†Bowling Alley **4,500.00**

†Boy and bull dog **4,500.00**

†Boys stealing watermelons **850.00**

British Clown, tin **12,000.00**

***Bull Dog,** place coin on nose **1,800.00**

†Bull and Bear **75,000.00**

†Bull Dog, standing **950.00**

Bureau, Lewando's, wood **28,000.00**

Burnett Postman, tin man with tray **3,500.00**

†Butting Buffalo **850.00**

†Butting Goat **1,200.00**

***Cabin,** black man flips **575.00**

Caller Vending, tin **2,800.00**

†Calamity **2,800.00**

†Called Out **1,500.00**

Calumet, tin and cardboard, with sailor **18,000.00**

Calumet, tin and Cardboard, with soldier **20,000.00**

†Camera **850.00**

***Cat and Mouse** **775.00**

†Cat and Mouse, giant cat standing on top **45,000.00**

***Chief Big Moon** **1,080.00**

Child's Bank, wood **450.00**

Chocolate Menier, tin **950.00**

†Chrysler Pig **950.00**

Cigarette Vending, tin **420.00**

Cigarette Vending, lead **1,200.00**

Creedmoor, hunter with gun firing into tree, 10" l, 6-3/4" h, **$675**. Photo courtesy of Joy Luke Auctions.

†Circus, ticket collector **300.00**

†Clown on Bar, tin and iron **1,200.00**

***Clown on Globe** **1,800.00**

Clown with arched top, tin **150.00**

Clown with black face, tin **675.00**

Clown with white face, tin **125.00**

Clown with white face, round, tin **3,700.00**

Columbian Magic Savings, wood and paper **12,000.00**

Cowboy with tray, tin **250.00**

Crescent Cash Register **3,100.00**

Crowing Rooster, circular base, tin **6,500.00**

†Cupola **750.00**

***Darktown Battery** **2,200.00**

†Darky Watermelon, man kicks football at watermelon **7,500.00**

Dinah, iron **300.00**

Dinah, aluminum 200.00
†**Dog with tray** 300.00
***Eagle and Eaglettes** 750.00
Electric Safe, steel 1,200.00
***Elephant and Three Clowns** 850.00
***Elephant**, locked howdah 260.00
Elephant, man pops out, wood, cloth, iron 330.00
†**Elephant**, no stars 3,700.00
***Elephant**, pull tail 70.00
†**Elephant with tusks**, on wheels 300.00
English Bulldog, tin 220.00
5 cents Adding 200.00
Football, English football 1,200.00
Fortune Teller, Savings, safe 1,320.00
†**Freedman's Bank**, wood, lead, brass, tin, paper, etc. 55,000.00
Frog on rock 575.00
†**Frogs**, two frogs 450.00
***Gem**, dog with building 1,700.00
German Vending, tin 1,200.00
†**Giant in Tower** 850.00
Girl Feeding Geese, tin, paper, lead 24,000.00
†**Girl in Victorian chair** 1,200.00
Guessing, woman's figure, iron 1,320.00
Guessing, woman's figure, lead 900.00
Hall's Liliput, with tray 200.00
Hartwig and Vogel, vending, tin 750.00
Highwayman, tin 400.00
***Hindu**, bust 450.00
†**Hold the Fort**, two varieties, each 650.00
Hoop-La 2,600.00
***Horse Race**, two varieties, each 1,200.00
†**Humpty Dumpty**, bust of clown with name on back, iron 1,680.00
***I Always Did 'spise a Mule**, black man on mule 750.00
***Indian and Bear** 950.00
†**Indian Chief**, black man bust with Indian feathered headdress, aluminum 575.00
†**Initiating Bank**, first degree 650.00
Initiating Bank, second degree 720.00
John R. Jennings Trick Drawer Money Box, wood 16,500.00
***Jolly Nigger**, American 390.00
Jolly Nigger, lettering in Greek 225.00
Jolly Nigger, lettering in Arabic 1,200.00
***Jolly Nigger**, raises hat, lead 800.00
***Jolly Nigger**, raises hat, iron 1,320.00
***Jolly Nigger**, with fez, aluminum 450.00
***Jonah and the Whale Bank**, large rectangular base 1,200.00
†**Jonah and the Whale Bank**, stands on two ornate legs with rect coin box at center 5,500.00
†**Jumbo**, elephant on wheels 300.00
Kick Inn Bank, wood 1,500.00
†**Leap Frog** 1,320.00
Lehmann Berlin Tower, tin 280.00
Lehmann, London Tower, tin 270.00
†**Light of Asia** 320.00
Lion, tin 345.00
†**Lion and Two Monkeys** 1,110.00
***Little Joe Bank** 570.00
Little Moe Bank 280.00

Man in rustic cabin, flips coin into roof, Pat'd June 30, 1885, 4-1/4" l, 3-3/4" h, **$750**. Photo courtesy of Joy Luke Auctions.

***Magic Bank**, iron house 400.00
Magic Bank, tin 200.00
†**Magician** 950.00
†**Mama Katzenjammer** 1,050.00
†**Mammy and Child** 1,050.00
***Mason** 1,500.00
***Merry-Go-Round**, mechanical, coin activates 1,400.00
†**Merry-Go-Round**, semi-mechanical, spin by hand 510.00
Mikado Bank 5,500.00
†**Milking Cow** 1,600.00
Model Railroad Drink Dispenser, tin 15,500.00
***Monkey and Coconut** 950.00
†**Monkey Bank** 500.00
Monkey, chimpanzee in ornate circular bldg, iron 575.00
†**Monkey**, slot in stomach 300.00
Monkey, tin, tips hat 270.00
Mule Entering Barn 775.00
Musical Church, wood 345.00
Musical Savings, tin 195.00
Musical Savings, velvet-covered easel 270.00
Musical Savings, wood house 570.00
National, Your Savings, cash register 1,680.00
***New Bank**, lever at center 280.00
***New Bank**, lever at left 220.00
†**North Pole Bank** 1,200.00
Old Mother Hubbard, tin 400.00
***Organ Bank**, boy and girl 570.00
***Organ Bank**, medium, only monkey figure 270.00
Organ Grinder and Dancing Bear 875.00
Owl, slot in head 220.00
***Owl**, turns head 280.00
***Paddy and the Pig** 950.00
Pascal Chocolate Cigarettes, vending, tin 1,080.00
Pay Phone Bank, iron 1,680.00
Pay Phone Bank, tin 450.00
***Pelican**, Arab head pops out 345.00
***Pelican**, man thumbs nose 300.00
†**Perfection Registering**, girl and dog at blackboard 900.00
***Picture Gallery** 1,400.00
Pinball Vending, tin 1,320.00
Pistol Bank, iron 250.00
Policeman, tin 300.00
Post Office Savings, steel 1,200.00
†**Presto**, iron building 570.00
***Presto**, penny changes optically to quarter 575.00
Pump and Bucket 1,200.00
***Punch and Judy**, iron 1,400.00
Punch and Judy, iron front, tin back 450.00
†**Queen Victoria**, bust, brass 1,500.00
†**Queen Victoria**, bust, iron 2,500.00
†**Rabbit Standing**, large 410.00
†**Rabbit Standing**, small 225.00
†**Red Riding Hood**, iron 1,650.00
Red Riding Hood, tin, vending 700.00
†**Rival Bank** 1,950.00
Robot Bank, aluminum 390.00
Robot Bank, iron 620.00
Royal Trick Elephant, tin 2,200.00
Safe Deposit Bank, tin, elephant 800.00

Rex Rooster, some wear to original paint, 6-1/4" l, 6-1/4" h, **$550**. Photo courtesy of Joy Luke Auctions.

Sailor Face, tin, pointed top 1,920.00
Sam Segal's Aim to Save, iron 1,080.00
***Santa Claus** 750.00
†**Schley Bottling Up Cevera** 585.00
School Teacher, tin and wood, American 750.00
Seek Him Frisk 2,000.00
†**Shoot That Hat Bank** 1,600.00
†**Shoot the Chute Bank** 1,200.00
†**Smith X-ray Bank** 675.00

***Snap-It Bank** 840.00
Snow White, tin and lead 475.00
***Speaking Dog** 1,125.00
Spring Jawed Cat, pot metal 120.00
Spring Jawed Chinaman, pot metal 550.00
Spring Jawed Felix the Cat, pot metal 3,700.00
Spring Jawed Mickey Mouse, pot metal 13,500.00
Spring Jawed Penguin, pot metal 120.00
Springing Cat 2,820.00
†Squirrel and Tree Stump 410.00
Starkies Aeroplane, aluminum, cardboard 9,500.00
Starkies Aeroplane, aluminum, steel 14,000.00
Stollwerk Bros., two penny, vending, tin 840.00
Stollwerk Bros., Victoria, spar-automat, tin 570.00
***Stump Speaker Bank** 1,200.00
Symphonium Musical Savings, wood 1,200.00
†Tabby 250.00
***Tammany Bank** 225.00
Tank and Cannon, aluminum 1,200.00
Tank and Cannon, iron 1,680.00
†Target Bank 252.00
†Target In Vestibule 570.00
***Teddy and The Bear** 990.00
Tiger, tin 270.00
Time Lock Savings 345.00
***Toad on Stump** 400.00
***Trick Dog**, six-part base 875.00
***Trick Dog**, solid base 400.00
***Trick Pony Bank** 750.00

Uncle Sam, worn original paint, 5" w, 11-1/2" h, **$1,650**. Photo courtesy of Joy Luke Auctions.

Trick Savings, wood, end drawer 400.00
Try Your Weight, tin, mechanical 1,560.00
†Turtle Bank 1,200.00
Two Ducks Bank, lead 2,000.00
†U.S. and Spain 720.00
†Uncle Remus Bank 950.00
†Uncle Sam Bank, standing figure with satchel 1,125.00
†Uncle Sam, bust 280.00
†Uncle Tom, no lapels, with star 255.00
†Uncle Tom, lapels, with star 240.00
†Uncle Tom, no star 230.00
Viennese soldier 750.00
Watch Bank, blank face, tin 120.00
Watch Bank, stamped face, tin 90.00
Weeden's Plantation, tin, wood 510.00
Whale Bank, pot metal 300.00
***William Tell**, iron 775.00
William Tell, crossbow, Australian, sheet steel, aluminum 875.00
Woodpecker Bank, large, tin, c1910 450.00
Woodpecker Bank, small, tin, c1930-1960 50.00
***World's Fair Bank** 720.00
Zentral Sparkasse, steel 750.00
Zig Zag Bank, iron, tin, papier-mâché 4,120.00
***Zoo** 900.00

Banks, Still

History: Banks with no mechanical action are known as still banks. The first still banks were made of wood or pottery or from gourds. Redware and stoneware banks, made by America's early potters, are prized possessions of today's collectors.

Still banks reached a golden age with the arrival of the cast-iron bank. Leading manufacturing companies include Arcade Mfg. Co., J. Chein & Co., Hubley, J. & E. Stevens, and A. C. Williams. The banks often were ornately painted to enhance their appeal. During the cast-iron era, banks and other businesses used the still bank as a form of advertising.

The tin lithograph bank, again frequently a tool for advertising, reached its zenith from 1930 to 1955. The tin bank was an important premium, whether a Pabst Blue Ribbon beer can bank or a Gerber's Orange Juice bank. Most tin advertising banks resembled the packaging of the product.

Almost every substance has been used to make a still bank—die-cast white metal, aluminum, brass, plastic, glass, etc. Many of the early glass candy containers also converted to a bank after the candy was eaten. Thousands of varieties of still banks were made, and hundreds of new varieties appear on the market each year.

Cast-iron banks, both mechanical and still, were originally made as sculptural works of art with excellent detail and casting. Reproductions are rampant. Copies are generally of lesser quality. A cast-iron still bank was usually manufactured in two parts held together by a screw, so it could be separated to remove the coins. Generally, old banks are joined neatly and tightly. Today they are found to have naturally worn, chipped, and faded paint—this effect is difficult to fabricate. Be suspicious of rough, granular finishes, too much rust, and brownish hues which are often meant to deceive by creating artificial aging. Reproduction still banks tend to be heavier, thicker, and smaller than originals.

Brass, beehive, 4" h, 4-1/2" d, EOS, well detailed, base marked "A. B. Dalames Bank" 385.00

Cast iron, cash register, drawer marked "Cash," 4-1/2" w, 5" h, **$35**. Photo courtesy of Joy Luke Auctions.

Cast iron

- Bankers Life Headquarters, Des Moines 115.00
- Buster Brown and Tige, 5" h, orig gold finish 115.00
- Cab, Arcade, 7-3/4" l, Yellow Cab, painted orange and black, stenciling on doors, seated driver, rubber tires, painted metal wheels, coin slot in roof 935.00
- Camel, Hubley, 4-3/4" h 65.00
- Cat with ball, 2-1/2" x 5-11/16", A. C. Williams, painted gray, gold ball 190.00
- Circus elephant, 3-7/8" h, Hubley, colorfully painted, seated position 180.00
- Duck, 4-3/4" h, Hubley, colorfully painted, outstretched wings, slot on back 165.00
- Dutch boy and girl, 5-1/4" and 5-1/8" h, Hubley, colorfully painted, boy on barrel, girl holding flowers, c1930, price for pr 260.00
- Egyptian tomb, 6-1/4" x 5-1/4", green finish, pharaoh's tomb entrance, hieroglyphics on front panel 275.00
- Elk, 9-1/2" h, painted gold, full antlers 155.00
- Globe safe, 5" h, Kenton, round sphere, claw feet, nickeled

combination lock on front hinged door **80.00**

Cast iron, dime register dime, well pump & bucket, partial label "No. 127 Pump Registering...," 5-3/4" w, 6-1/2" h, **$2,500**. Photo courtesy of Joy Luke Auctions.

Good Year Zeppelin **425.00**
Hall clock, 5-3/4" h, swinging pendulum visible through panel **110.00**
Horseshoe, 4-1/4" x 4-3/4", Arcade, Buster Brown and Tige with horse, painted black and gold......... **125.00**
Husky, 5" h, Grey Iron Casting Co., painted brown, black eyes, yellow box, repaired......................... **365.00**
Kodak, 4-1/4" x 5" w, J & E Stevens, nickeled, highly detailed casting, intricate pattern, emb "Kodak Bank" on front opening panel, c1905 .... **225.00**
North Pole, 4-1/4" h, nickeled, Grey Iron Casting Co., depicts wooden pole with handle, emb lettering **415.00**
Mailbox, 5-1/2" h, Hubley, painted green, emb "Air Mail," with eagle, standing type **220.00**
Maine, 4-5/8" l, Grey Iron Casting Co., japanned, gold highlights, c1900 .... **660.00**
Mammy, 5-1/4" h, Hubley, hands on hips, colorfully painted.......... **300.00**
Pagoda, 5" x 3" x 3", England, gold trim, c1889 .... **240.00**
Pershing, General, 7-3/4" h, Grey Iron Casting Co., full bust, detailed casting.................................... **65.00**
Pig, 2-1/2" h, 5-1/4" l, Hubley, laughing, painted brown, trap on bottom **120.00**
Professor Pug Frog, 3-1/4" h, A.C. Williams, painted gold, blue jacket, new twist pin......................... **195.00**
Radio, Kenton, 4-1/2" h, metal sides and back, painted green, nickeled front panel in Art-Deco style **445.00**
Reindeer, 9-1/2" h, 5-1/4" l, A. C. Williams, painted gold, full rack of antlers, replaced screw........... **55.00**
Rumplestiltskin, 6" h, painted gold, long red hat, base and feet, marked "Do You Know Me," c1910 .... **210.00**
Safe, 4-3/8" h, Kyser & Rex, Young America, japanned, intricate casting, emb at top, c1882................. **275.00**
Sharecropper, 5-1/2" h, A. C. Williams, painted black, gold, and red, toes visible on one foot.. **240.00**
Steamboat, 7-1/2" l, Arcade, painted gold **190.00**
Stove, 4-3/4" h, Gem, Abendroth Bros., traces of bronzing, back marked "Gem Heaters Save Money" **275.00**

Cast iron, penny, Dolly Dimple, girl in bonnet with parasol, 4" w, 7-1/2" h, **$125**. Photo courtesy of Joy Luke Auctions.

Tank, 9-1/2" l, 4" w, Ferrosteel, side mounted guns, rear spoke wheels, emb on sides, c1919............. **385.00**
U.S. Mail, 5-1/8" h, Kenton, painted silver, gold painted emb eagle, red lettering large trap on back panel **180.00**
World Time, 4-1/8" x 2-5/8", Arcade, paper time-tables of various cities around the world **315.00**

Celluloid

Keene National Bank, canister, printed in blue, mellowed ivory white ground, one side shows bank building in Keene, NH, other side with dime savings text............ **65.00**
Western Savings Fund Society of Philadelphia, 2-1/2" h, black and light green celluloid, 1930s...........**115.00**

Chalk

Cat, 11" h, seated, stripes, red bow **200.00**
Winston Churchill, 5-1/4" h, bust, painted green, back etched "Save for Victory," wood base **55.00**

Glass

Charles Chaplin, 3-3/4" h, Geo Borgfeldt & Co., painted figure standing next to barrel slotted on lid, name emb on base **220.00**
Liberty Bell, amber, no closure **65.00**

Glass, Bank of Independence Hall 1776 – 1876, 7-1/2" h, **$160**. Photo courtesy of Joy Luke Auctions.

Lead

Boxer, 2-5/8" h, Germany, head, painted brown, black facial details, lock on collar, bent in back ... **130.00**
Burro, 3-1/2" x 3-1/2", Japan, lock on saddle marked "Plymouth, VT" **125.00**
Ocean liner, 2-3/4" x 7-5/8" l, bronze electroplated, three smoking stacks, hinged trap on deck, small hole **180.00**
Pug, 2-3/4" h, Germany, painted, stenciled "Hershey Park" on side, lock on collar......................... **300.00**

Pottery

Acorn, 3-1/2" d, 4" h, redware, paper label reads "Tithing Day/At The/First Methodist Episcopal Church/Sunday January 2nd 1916/In the Interest of the Improvement Fund"......... **220.00**

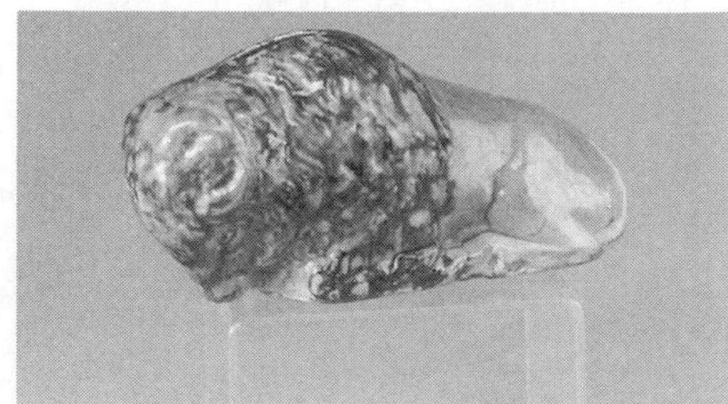

Pottery, buffalo, unmarked Roseville, flecks to ears and tail, several burst bubbles, 3" x 6", **$460**. Photo courtesy of David Rago Auctions, Inc.

Bulbous, 3-1/4" h, redware, marked with initials "C.R.S.," 3-1/4" h, flakes on base **220.00**
Dresser, 6-1/2" w, 4" d, 4-1/2" h, redware, Empire chest of drawers

shape, Philadelphia, PA, loss to feet, roughness on edges **220.00**
Hanging persimmon, 5" x 3", redware, yellow and red paint **90.00**
House, 7-1/2" h, redware, Georgian style house, brown glazed accents, good detail on windows and doorways, central chimney, Jim Seagreaves, sgd "JCS"......... **425.00**
Jug, 7-1/2" h, redware, bulbous, bird atop mouth, green and yellow sgraffito dev, Jim Seagreaves, sgd "JCS"............ **515.00**
Pig, 9-1/2" h, sewer tile, sitting, brown colored glazed with molded detail on snout and around eyes, shallow chip on tail............ **440.00**

Steel

Life boat, 14" l, pressed, painted yellow and blue, boat length decal marked "Contributions for Royal National Life Boat Institution," deck lifts for coin removal, over painted **360.00**
Postal savings, 4-5/8" h, 5-3/8" w, copper finish, glass view front panel, paper registering strips, emb "U.S. Mail" on sides, top lifts to reveal four coin slots, patent 1902........... **95.00**

Pottery, pig, blue and brown dripping glazes, unmarked, possibly Roseville, 2-1/2" x 4", **$50**. Photo courtesy of David Rago Auctions, Inc.

Stoneware

Dog's head, white clay, yellow glaze, two-tone brown sponging, 4" h, shallow flakes............ **175.00**
Ovoid, brushed cobalt blue flowers, leaves, and finial, minor flakes at coin slot, 6" h............ **6,875.00**

Tin litho

Astronaut, dime register........ **250.00**
Monkey, J Chein............ **300.00**
Vacation, little girl and ducks, dime register **75.00**
Wagner Ford Simsbury, 2-1/2", dime register, glossy silver luster front, black text, dark red back, c1950 .... **70.00**

White metal

Cat with bow, 4-1/8" h, painted white, blue bow............ **155.00**
Gorilla, colorfully painted in brown hues, seated position, trap on bottom **165.00**
Spaniel, seated, 4-1/2" h, painted white, black highlights.......... **470.00**
Uncle Sam Hat, 3-1/2" h, painted red, white, and blue, stars on brim, slot on top, trap on bottom.......... **135.00**

Metal, Security Safe Deposit, combination safe, original silver paint, **$45**.

Wood, burlwood inlaid with exotic woods, top dec with geometric banding, front with sailing vessels, end panels with flags, Prisoner of War, late 19th C, 5" x 8" x 5-1/4", imperfections............... **1,150.00**

Barber Bottles

For more information, see *Warman's Glass*, 4th edition.

History: Barber bottles, colorful glass bottles found on shelves and counters in barber shops, held the liquids barbers used daily. A specific liquid was kept in a specific bottle, which the barber knew by color, design, or lettering. The bulk liquids were kept in utilitarian containers under the counter or in a storage room.

Barber bottles are found in many types of glass—art glass with various decorations, pattern glass, and commercially prepared and labeled bottles.

Note: Prices are for bottles without original stoppers, unless otherwise noted.

Advertising

Koken's Quinine Tonic for the Hair, 7-1/2" h, clear, label under glass............ **195.00**
Lucky tiger, red, green, yellow, black, and gilt label under glass, emb on reverse **95.00**

Blue, rounded octagonal form, narrow neck, robin's egg blue with hand-painted floral and leaf decoration, ceramic and cork stopper, pontil scar, 10-3/8" h, **$140**. Photo courtesy of Alderfer Auction Co.

Amber, Hobb's Hobnail **250.00**
Amethyst, Mary Gregory type dec, white enameled child and flowers, 8" h **200.00**
Cobalt blue, cylindrical, bulbous body, long neck, white enamel, traces of gold dec, tooled mouth, pontil scar, 7-1/4" h **100.00**
Emerald green, cylindrical bell form, long neck, orange and white enameled floral dec, sheared mouth, pontil scar, some int. haze, 8-1/2" h............ **210.00**
Latticino, cylindrical, bulbous, long neck, clear frosted glass, white, red, and pale green vertical stripes, tooled mouth, pontil scar, 8-1/4" h............ **200.00**

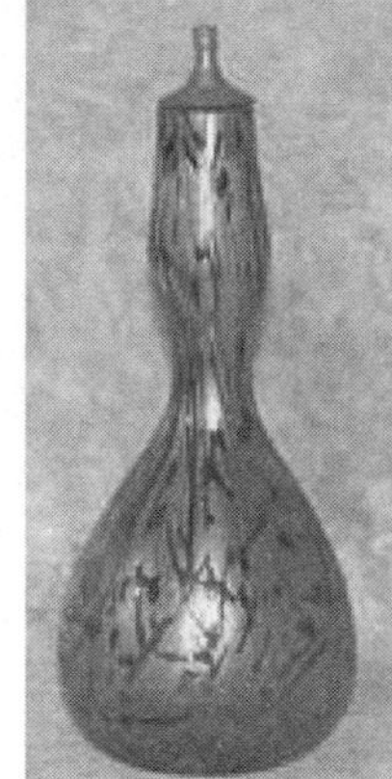

Iridescent glass, gourd form, narrow neck, purple and irid gold glass in seaweed motif, metal and cork stopper, 8-1/4" h, **$435**. Photo courtesy of Alderfer Auction Co.

Milk glass, Witch Hazel, painted letters and flowers, 9" h............ **115.00**

Opalescent

Coin Spot, blue............ **300.00**
Seaweed, cranberry, bulbous **465.00**
Spanish Lace, electric blue ground, sq, long neck, tooled mouth, smooth base, 7-7/8" h, pr............ **250.00**
Stars and Stripes, cranberry, pale blue, tooled mouth, smooth base, 7-1/4" h, pr............ **575.00**

Sapphire blue, enameled white and yellow daisies, green leaves, 8-5/8" h **125.00**

Milk glass, ring turned and maroon-banded necks and shoulders, hand-painted bird and branch decoration, one labeled, "Bay Rum," other labeled "Emil Pehlert Tonic," pewter screw-on tops, embossed mark "W.T. & Co.," scratch on front of tonic bottle, 10-1/2" h, price for pair, **$635**. Photo courtesy of Alderfer Auction Co.

BARBIE

History: In 1945, Harold Matson (MATT) and Ruth and Elliott (EL) Handler founded Mattel. Initially the company made picture frames but became involved in the toy market when Elliott Handler began to make doll furniture from scrap material. When Harold Matson left the firm, Elliott Handler became chief designer and Ruth Handler principal marketer. In 1955, Mattel advertised its products on "The Mickey Mouse Club," and the company prospered.

In 1958, Mattel patented a fashion doll. The doll was named "Barbie" and reached the toy shelves in 1959. By 1960, Barbie's popularity was assured.

Development of a boyfriend for Barbie, named Ken after the Handlers' son, began in 1960. Over the years, many other dolls were added. Clothing, vehicles, room settings, and other accessories became an integral part of the line.

From September 1961 through July 1972, Mattel published a Barbie magazine. At its peak, the Barbie Fan Club was second only to the Girl Scouts as the largest girls' organization in the United States.

Always remember that a large quantity of Barbie dolls and related material has been manufactured. Because of this easy availability, only objects in excellent to mint condition with original packaging (also in very good or better condition) have significant value. If items show signs of heavy use, their value is probably minimal.

Collectors prefer items from the first decade of production. Learn how to distinguish a Barbie #1 doll from its successors. The Barbie market is one of subtleties.

Recently many collectors have shifted their focus from the dolls themselves to the accessories. There have been rapid price increases in early clothing and accessories.

Barbie is now a billion-dollar baby, the first toy in history to reach this prestigious mark—that's a billion dollars per year, just in case you're wondering.

Accessories

Alarm clock, 2-3/4" d, plastic, gold numbers, Ponytail Barbie graphic, dated 1964, non-working, age discolored, scuffed **85.00**

Ballet box, black vinyl, graphics, dated 1966, G, scuffed **65.00**

Barbie and Midge Brunch Bag, oval black vinyl, graphics, black plastic handle, zipper, Thermos paper label on top, dated 1963, VG, scuffed, two small tears on back **105.00**

Barbie Café Today, dated 1970, NRFB, age discoloration to box, fading, slightly scuffed **475.00**

Barbie Goes Travelin' Carrying Case, pink vinyl, see-through windows, plane and car graphics, black plastic handle, dated 1965, VG, age discolored, slightly scuffed **180.00**

Barbie Teen Dream Bedroom, dated 1970, MIB, discoloration to orig box **65.00**

Bedspread, twin size, light weight cotton, red, blue, and gold, red fabric edging, VG, some age discoloration **295.00**

Compact, two-pc, brass, "B" inscription, mirror inside, age discolored, dented **240.00**

Costume trunk, Barbie & Ken, white hard plastic, metal trim, white plastic handle, graphics, dated 1964, NM, age discolored, scuffed **140.00**

Diary, blue vinyl, Barbie graphics, metal closure, dated 1964, G, age discolored, scuffed, few pages missing, some written on **100.00**

Doll jewelry, Barbie & Midge, #7001, gold metal necklace, drop earrings with light blue rhinestones, heart-shaped plastic cover, cardboard backing, dated 1964, Cleinman & Sons, Inc., some age discoloration to cardboard **120.00**

Lunch box and thermos, Ponytail Barbie, black vinyl, graphics, snap closure, black thermos, red cup lid, both dated 1962, VG, name on lunch box, scuffs **150.00**

Paper doll book, Whitman, uncut Barbie and Ken Cut-Outs, #1976, dated 1962, NM **100.00**

- Barbie and Ken Cut-Outs, #1986, dated 1970, NM **35.00**
- Barbie's Boutique, #1954, dated 1973, NM **85.00**
- Francie with Growing Pretty Hair, #1982, dated 1973, NM **35.00**
- Malibu Skipper, #1952, dated 1973, NM **20.00**
- Midge, #1962, dated 1963, NM **145.00**

Pedestal stand, #1, black plastic, two metal prongs, Barbie logo **1,300.00**

Record tote, blue vinyl, Barbie Graphics, intaglio music symbols, black plastic handles, paper record sleeves, VG, age discolored **145.00**

Tutti ice cream stand, vinyl case, hard plastic sides with ice cream cone shapes, clear vinyl window, white plastic handle, F, age discolored, scuff, small tears, creases **160.00**

Wrist watch, gold colored watch, Barbie graphic, blue denim look vinyl band, pink band, white band, red case with cardboard lid liner, plastic liner to hold watch, dated 1971, paper label on end, non-working, face scuffed, metal tarnished **90.00**

No. 3 Barbie, 1960, blond ponytail, pearl earrings, black shoes, stand, plastic box, #850, **$690**. Barbie photos courtesy of Joy Luke Auctions.

Barbie Dolls

American Girl Barbie

- Ash blonde, beige lips, fingernails painted, bendable legs, orig striped turquoise swimsuit, turquoise open toe shoes, VG **270.00**
- Brunette, beige lips, fingernails painted, bendable legs, #1655 Under Fashions, pale pink corselet with ribbon straps, ruffled waistline, attached pink plastic supporters, pink nylon bra, beige textured stockings, pink nylon panties and half slip with lace trim, no box, VG **375.00**
- Brunette, gold lips, fingernails painted, bendable legs, #1658 Garden Wedding, pink satin sheath, white lacy overdress with ribbon waist bow, rose pointed toe shoes, box, VG **350.00**
- Brunette, peach lips outlined in gold, fingernails painted, bendable legs, nude, no box, VG **325.00**
- Brunette, tan lips, fingernails painted, bendable legs, orig one-pc swimsuit, turquoise open toe shoes, gold stand, clear plastic head cover, box, G, box age discolored and worn **500.00**
- Golden blond, beige lips, nostril paint, fingernails painted, orange one-pc swimsuit, no box, VG **350.00**

Light blond hair, orange lips with beige tint, nostril paint, fingernails painted, bendable legs, nude, no box, VG **325.00**

Titian hair, gold lips, fingernails painted, bendable legs, #1665 Here Comes the Bride outfit, white satin sleeveless gown, white tulle long veil, lace trim on gown and veil, ribbon bow accents, white nylon long gloves, blue nylon garter, white pointed toe shoes, box, VG **350.00**

Billions of Dreams Barbie, marked one billionth Barbie sold since 1959, #17641, box dated 1997, serial #00305, orig shipping box, NRFB, box slightly scuffed **225.00**

Bob Mackie design series

Moon Goddess, 9th in series, #14105, box dated 1996, NRFB, box scuffed **90.00**

Neptune Fantasy, 4th in series, #4248, box dated 1992, orig shipping box, MIB, booklet missing **300.00**

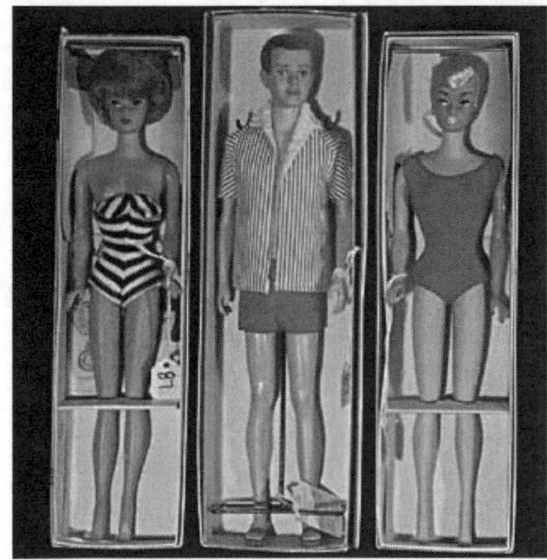

Bubble Cut Barbie, brunette; #850; Ponytail Barbie, platinum, #850; Ken, brown flocked hair, #750; eight dolls for **$5,175**.

Bubblecut Barbie

Blond, coral lips, nostril paint, fingernails and toenails painted, straight legs, #1610 Golden Evening outfit, gold knit shirt, matching long skirt with gold glitter, gold belt with buckle, mustard open toe shoes, three-charm bracelet, no box, VG, loss to glitter **90.00**

Blond, white lips with pink tint, white nostril paint, fingernails painted, toenails with faint paint, straight legs, one-pc red nylon swimsuit, red open toe shoes, orig box with gold wire stand, no box, VG **225.00**

Brunette hair, red lips, fingernails painted, light toenails painted, straight legs, nude, no box, VG **115.00**

Brunette, red lips, fingernails and toenails painted lightly, straight legs, Pak outfit, red and white striped knit shirt, blue shorts, no box, VG/G, frayed tag **135.00**

Dark blond, coral lips, fingernails and toenails painted, straight legs, nude, no box, VG **120.00**

Titian hair, coral lips, nostril paint, fingernails and toenails painted, straight legs, black and white striped one-pc swimsuit, pearl earrings, black open toe shoes, white rimmed glasses with blue lenses, black white stand, booklet, orig box, VG **200.00**

Color Magic Barbie

Lemon yellow hair, blue metal hair barrette, pink lips, cheek blush, fingernails painted, bendable legs, #1692 Patio Party, floral print nylon jumpsuit, blue and green satin overdress, blue pointed toe shoes, no box, NM........................... **550.00**

Midnight/ruby red hair, blue metal barrette, dark pink lips, cheek blush, fingernails painted, bendable legs, orig diamond pattern nylon swimsuit, pink ribbon belt, matching headband, aqua open toe shoes, purple plastic closet, cardboard form, orig accessories, NRFB, age discoloration...................... **1,600.00**

Red hair, green metal hair barrette, pink lips, fingernails painted, bendable legs, nude, no box, VG **550.00**

Red hair, pink lips, cheek blush, fingernails painted, toenails with faint paint, bendable legs, nude, no box, NM/VG................................. **525.00**

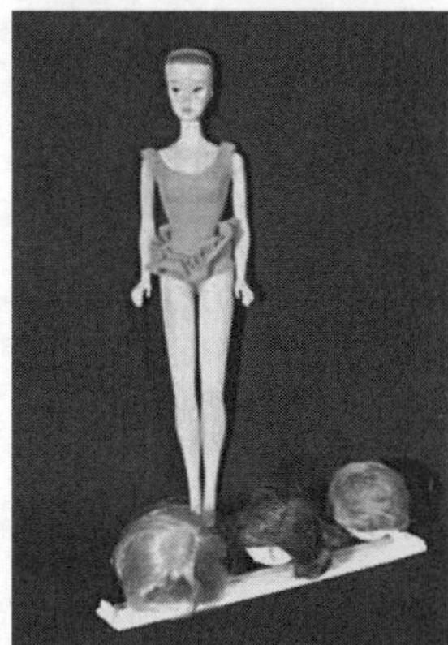

Miss Barbie Sleepeye, 1964, hat, six wigs, wig stand, pink outfit, plastic box, #1060, **$415**. Photo courtesy of Joy Luke Auctions.

Enchanted Seasons Collection, limited edition

Snow Princess, box dated 1994, NRFB, box slightly scuffed...... **75.00**

Spring Bouquet, box dated 1994, NRFB, box slightly scuffed...... **30.00**

Summer Splendor, box dated 1996, NRFB **35.00**

Fashion Queen, painted brunette hair, blue vinyl headband, pink lips, fingernails and toenails painted, straight legs, gold and white striped swimsuit, matching turban cap, pearl earrings in box with white plastic wig stand with brunette pageboy, blond bubblecut, and titian side-part wigs, black wire stand, MIB, orig box **400.00**

Growin' Pretty Hair, blond, peach lips, cheek blush, rooted eyelashes, bendable legs, pink satin dress, wrist tag, orig box with hair accessories, pink high tongue shoes, orig box, NRFB **475.00**

Hair Happenin's, titian hair, pink lips, cheek blush, rooted eyelashes, fingernails painted, bendable legs, nude, titan long hair piece braided with pink ribbon, no box, VG **225.00**

Happy Holidays, orig box

1988, #1, NRFB **230.00**

1989, NRFB, plastic window and box scuffed **70.00**

1990, NRFB, plastic window and box slightly scuffed **75.00**

1991, NRFB, box slightly scuffed and discolored **45.00**

1992, NRFB, box slightly scuffed and worn **35.00**

1993, NRFB, box slightly scuffed, edges worn and creased........ **25.00**

1994, NRFB, box slightly scuffed, sticker residue on plastic window **35.00**

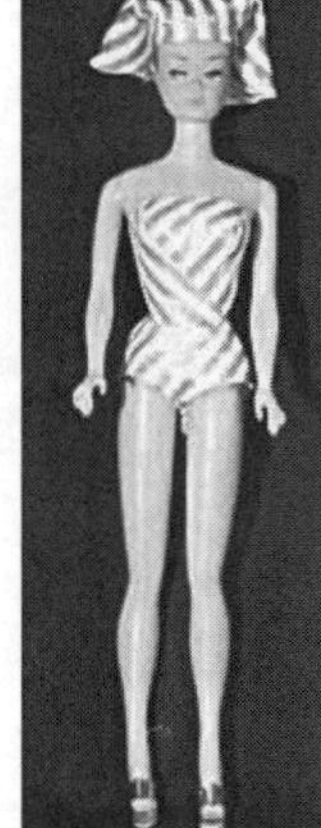

Fashion Queen Barbie, 1963-64, gold and white outfit, #870 and bendable leg Barbie, with shoes, in box, #1070, **$1,725**.

Living Barbie, brunette, pink lips, cheek blush, rooted eyelashes, bendable arms, bendable legs, rotating wrists, orig silver and gold one-pc swimsuit, orange net cover-up with gold trim, booklet, no box, NM...**75.00**

Millenium Bride, box dated 1999, orig shipping box, NRFB **160.00**

Ponytail

#1 ponytail

Blond, red lips, fingernails and toenails painted, straight legs, black and white striped one-pc swimsuit, silver loop earrings, black #1 open-toe shoes with holes, pink cover booklet, VG, orig top knot, feet stained from shoes, booklet worn, box age discolored and worn **2,200.00**

Blond, reset in ponytail, red lips, nostril paint, fingernails painted, TL, straight legs, black and white striped one-pc swimsuit, gold hoop earrings, one black #1 open toe shoe with hole (unmarked), white rimmed glasses with blue lenses, pink cov booklet, VG, orig box with partial Marshall Field's sticker..................... **3,200.00**

#3 ponytail, brunette, red lips, nostril paint, brown eyeliner, fingernails painted, straight legs, #976 Sweater Girl outfit, orange knit sweater, matching shell, gray skirt, black open toe shoes, pearl earrings, wooden bowl with orange, green and yellow yarn with two needles, metal scissors, *How to Knit* book, black pedestal with plastic base, pink cover booklet, white rimmed glasses with blue lenses, no box, VG/G **475.00**

#4 ponytail, blond, red lips, eye shadow, fingernails and toenails painted, straight legs, black and white striped swimsuit, black open toe shoes, white rimmed glasses with blue lenses, VG **225.00**

#5 ponytail, brunette, orig set, red lips, nostril paint, fingernails and toenails painted, straight legs, Khaki car coat, striped slacks, beige sweater, straw hat with attached red chiffon scarf, cork wedgies, road map, wire stand, no box, NM/VG **225.00**

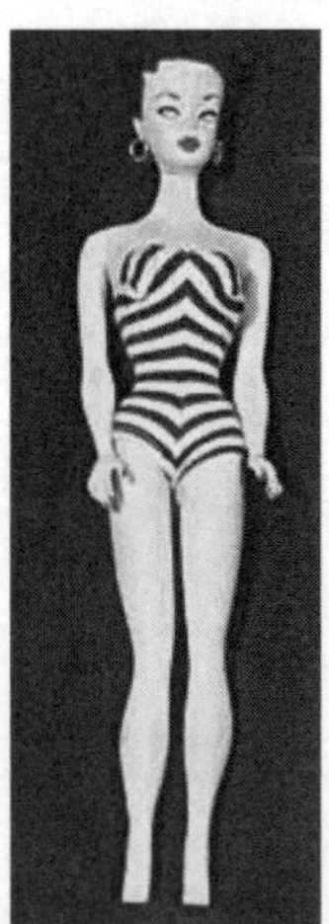

No. 2 Barbie, brunette ponytail, hoop earrings, black and white swimsuit, plastic box, #850, repainted, **$1,800**.

#6 ponytail

Blond, repainted pink lips, fingernails and toenails painted, straight legs, red nylon one-pc swimsuit, red open toe shoes, orig box with cardboard liner, black wire stand, light blue cover booklet, VG................. **215.00**

Titian hair, orig top knot, beige lips, fingernails and toenails painted, straight legs, blue two-pc pajamas with lace trim, button accents, no box, VG **325.00**

Official Barbie Collector's Club, Embassy Waltz, 1999, box dated 1998, NRFB, box insert flaps worn........... **40.00**

Society Style Collection, limited edition

Emerald Enchantment, 3rd ed, box dated 1996, NRFB, box slightly scuffed **40.00**

Radiant Rose, 2nd ed, box dated 1996, NRFB, plastic window slightly scuffed **40.00**

Sapphire Dream, 1st ed., box dated 1995, NRFB, box scuffed........ **35.00**

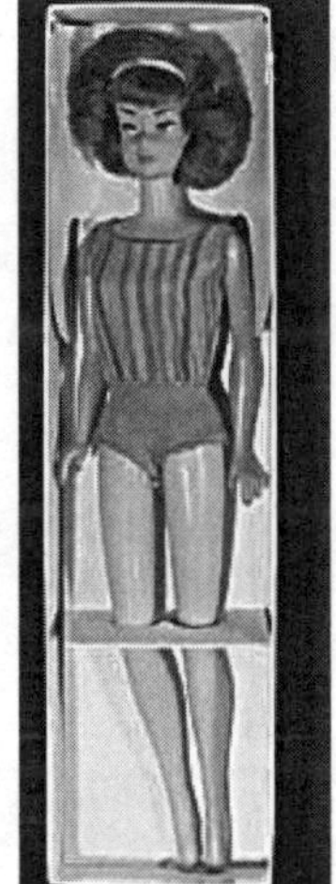

Bendable leg Barbie, brunette hair, side part flip, striped outfit, box, #1070, **$2,990**.

Standard

Brunette, pink lips, cheek blush, fingernails painted, toenails with faint paint, straight legs, orig pink nylon swimsuit bottoms with plastic flower accent, #1804 Knit Hit blue and pink knit dress, pale blue high tongue shows, no box, VG **150.00**

Light brunette, pink lips, cheek blush, fingernails and toenails painted, straight legs, nude, no box, VG, replaced rubber band.... **190.00**

Swirl ponytail

Brunette hair, beige lips, fingernails painted, toenails with faint paint, straight legs, nude, no box, VG **300.00**

Brunette hair in orig set, yellow ribbon, metal hair pin, coral lips, fingernails and toenails painted, straight legs, red nylon one-pc swimsuit, red open toe shoes, pearl earrings, wrist tag, box with gold metal stand, NM **675.00**

Platinum hair in orig set, yellow ribbon, metal hair pin, white lips, fingernails painted, straight legs, nude, no box, NM-VG **475.00**

Talking, brunette, ribbon bow ties, pink lips, cheek blush, rooted eyelashes, bendable legs, red nylon two-pc swimsuit with metal accent on bottoms, white and silver net cover-up with red trim, no box, VG, possible repairs to talker, working condition....................................... **275.00**

Twist 'n' Turn

Blond, pink lips, cheek blush, fingernails and toenails painted, bendable legs, multicolored one-pc knit swimsuit, wrist tag, clear plastic stand, booklet, NRFB **425.00**

Blond, pink lips, cheek blush, rooted eyelashes, fingernails painted, bendable legs, nude, no box, VG **95.00**

Brunette, pink lips, cheek blush, fingernails painted, bendable legs, #1485 Gypsy Spirits outfit, pink nylon blouse, aqua suede skirt, matching vest, no box, VG.................... **125.00**

Pale blond, pink lips, cheek blush, rooted eyelashes, fingernails painted, bendable legs, two-pc orange vinyl swimsuit, white net cover-up with orange trim, trade-in program doll, no box, VG...... **475.00**

Friends and family dolls

Allan, painted red hair, peach lips, straight legs, striped jacket, blue swim trunks, wrist tag, booklet, cork sandals with blue straps in cellophane bag, cardboard leg and arm inserts, black wire stand, MIB, orig box **145.00**

Casey, blond hair, clear plastic headband, peach lips, cheek blush, two-pc hot pink nylon swimsuit, orig clear plastic bag, cardboard hanger, NRFP, orig price sticker........................... **295.00**

Chris, Color Magic-type titian hair, green metal hair barrette, pink lips, cheek blush, bendable arms and legs, #3617 Birthday Beauties outfit, pink floral dress, white slip, white fishnet tights, white shoes with molded straps, gold wrapped present with white ribbon and pink flower accents, one pink crepe paper party favor with gold glitter, white paper invitation, orig box, VG **105.00**

Christie

Talking, red hair, pink lips, cheek blush, rooted eyelashes, bendable legs, wrist tag, clear plastic stand, NRFM, nonworking, box age discolored, scuffed, and worn **250.00**

Twist 'n' Turn, red hair, pink lips, cheek blush, rooted eyelashes, bendable legs, #1841 Night Clouds, yellow, orange and pink nylon ruffled

night gown with ribbon straps, matching yellow nylon robe with ribbon ties and flower accents, no box, VG **115.00**

Francie

Brunette, clear plastic headband, peach lips, cheek blush, two-pc yellow nylon swimsuit, orig clear plastic bag, cardboard hanger, NRFP, orig price sticker......... **250.00**

Brunette, pink lips, cheek blush, straight legs, nude, no box, NM/VG **115.00**

Growin' Pretty Hair, blonde, clear plastic head wrap, pink lips, cheek blush, rooted eyelashes, straight legs, orig pink lame and satin dress, net overskirt, silver braid trim, wrist tag, pink shoes in cellophane bag, instruction pamphlet, box insert, MIB **175.00**

Black Magic Barbie, blond hair, black dress, purse, shoes, book, original box, #1609, **$1,350**.

Malibu, The Sun Set, blond, pink plastic sunglasses, plastic head cover, peach lips, painted teeth, bendable legs, pink and red nylon swimsuit, yellow vinyl waistband, orange terrycloth towel, box dated 1970, NRFB......................... **235.00**

Twist 'n' Turn, blond, pink lips, cheek blush, rooted eyelashes, bendable legs, orig floral print outfit with lace trim, pink nylon bottoms, no box, VG **165.00**

Jamie, walking, Furry Friends Gift Set, Sears Exclusive, titian hair, pink lips, cheek blush, rooted eyelashes, bendable legs, green, pink, and orange knit dress, orange belt with buckle, orange furry coat with pink vinyl trim, orange boots, gray dot with felt features, pink vinyl dog collar with silver accents, leash, no box, VG... **150.00**

Julia, talking, red hair, pink lips, cheek blush, rooted eyelashes, bendable legs, gold and silver jumpsuit with belt, wrist tag, clear plastic stand, NRFB, nonworking, box age discolored, scuffed, and worn **225.00**

Ken

Blonde flocked hair, beige lips, straight legs, red swim trucks, pink cover booklet in cellophane bag, yellow towel, black wire stand, orig box, VG, dark spot in flocking **95.00**

Brown flocked hair, peach lips, straight legs, red swim trucks, cork sandals with red straps, yellow towel, VG **75.00**

Brunette flocked hair, beige lips, straight legs, red swim trunks with white stripe, wrist tag, booklet, yellow terrycloth towel, cork sandals in cellophane bag, black white stand, orig box, VG, oily face, worn wrist tag **155.00**

Brunette flocked hair, beige lips, straight legs, #797 Army and Air Force outfit, beige jacket with button accents, arm decal, matching pants, beige belt with buckle, beige socks and cap, brown necktie and shoes, no box, VG **85.00**

Brunette painted hair, beige lips, straight legs, #1426 Here Comes the Groom outfit, gray jacket with tails, white flower, gray felt vest, white shirt, both with button accents, gray satin ascot with pearl accent, gray and white striped pants, black socks, black shoes, gray flocked plastic gloves, gray plastic top hat, box, VG **500.00**

Painted blond hair, peach lips, straight legs, #789 The Yachtsman outfit, blue denim jacket with zipper closure, matching pants, red and white striped knit shirt, white socks, black shoes, *How to Sail a Boat* book, no box, VG **75.00**

Painted brunette, peach lips, straight legs, #790 Time for Tennis outfit, white knit shirt, white sweater with blue and red trim, white shorts, socks, and shoes, tennis racquet and ball, no box, VG **55.00**

Talking, painted brown hair, peach lips, painted teeth, bendable legs, #1435 Shore Lines outfit, blue nylon jacket with zipper closure, blue shorts, vinyl side stripes, multi-print pants with zipper closure, yellow plastic face mask with elastic head strap, swim fins, no box, NM, nonworking, stretched elastic on mask....................................... **75.00**

Midge

Brown hair, blue ribbon hair band, pink lips, fingernails painted, bendable legs, orig one-pc striped knit swimsuit, white open toe shoes, VG, hair band age discolored **185.00**

Titian hair, ribbon hair band, pink lips, fingernails painted, bendable legs, orig one-pc striped knit swimsuit, aqua open toe shoes, gold wire stand, orig box, VG........ **560.00**

PJ, talking, blond, beaded tie on left pigtail, replaced rubber-band on right pigtail, attached lavender plastic glasses, pink lips, cheek blush, rooted eyelashes, bendable legs, #1796 Fur Sighted outfit, orange jacket with fur trim, metallic gold tab and button closures, matching pants, zigzag print knit sweater, orange hat with fur trim, metallic gold chin strap, yellow high tongue shoes, no box, NM/VG, non-working... **155.00**

Two Bob Mackie Barbie dolls: #5405-9992, Bob Mackie Barbie and #14056-9993, Goddess of the Sun Barbie, both in original boxes, **$535**.

Ricky, painted red hair, peach lips, cheek blush, straight legs, striped jacket, blue shorts, cork sandals in bag, black wire stand, orig box with insert, NM, wrist tag torn **155.00**

Skipper

Blond, pink lips, straight legs, /#1915 Outdoor Casuals, turquoise knit sweater, matching dickey with button closure, pants, white nylon short gloves, white socks, white flat shoes, red wooden yo-yo, no box, VG **55.00**

Color Magic-type dark red hair, pink lips, straight legs, #1902 Silk 'n' Fancy dress, red velvet bodice, white skirt, red lace underskirt, gold braid waistband, white nylon socks, black flat shoes, NM................ **90.00**

Color Magic-type titian hair, pink lips, straight legs, #1926 Chill Chasers, white fur coat, red cap with blue pompon, red flat shoes, no box, NM **120.00**

Dramatic New Living Skipper, blond, pink ribbon ties, dark pink lips, rooted eyelashes, cheek blush, green, blue, pink swimsuit, booklet in cellophane bag, box insert, box, NMIB, box insert creased, hair curls stiff, stand missing **65.00**

Pose'n Play, blond, blue ribbon ties, clear plastic headband, pink lips, cheek blush, bendable arms and legs, blue and white outfit with button

accents, wrist tag, orig clear plastic bag, cardboard hanger, NRFP 85.00
Quick Curl, blond hair, blue ribbon bow, pink lips, cheek blush, straight legs, blue and white long dress, orig clear plastic bag, NRFP 150.00

Skooter

Blond, red ribbon bows, beige lips with tint of pink, cheek blush, straight legs, #1921 School Girl outfit, red jacket with pocket insignia, red and white pleated skirt, white shirt, red felt hat with red and white band and feather accent, white nylon socks, red flat shoes, brown rimmed glasses, arithmetic, geography, and English books, black book strap, red and natural wooden pencils, orig box, VG 90.00
Brunette, hair in orig set with ribbons, pale pink lips, right cheek blush, straight legs, two-pc red swimsuit, red flat shoes, gold wire stand, pink plastic comb and brush, orig box, NM/VG 155.00

Nighty Barbie, brunette hair, pink nighty, slippers, dog, book, original box, #86, **$1,200**.

Brunette, retied with red cord, beige lips, cheek blush, straight legs, wearing Best Buy Fashions #9122, red plaid coat, black belt, matching cap with black ribbon accent, #9122 dress with red plaid skirt, black velveteen top, white nylon shirt, no box, VG 70.00

Tutti, Me and My Dog, brunette, red ribbon bow, pink lips, bendable arms and legs, red felt coat, fur trim, white fur hat with ribbon ties, red tights, white flat shoes, white dog with felt features, attached red leash, no box, VG, leash worn and knotted 75.00

Outfits

Barbie

#872 Cinderella, G 100.00
#951 Senior Prom, NM 85.00
#972 Wedding Day Set, white satin gown with glitter and floral print tulle overdress, white tulle veil, pearl headband, white nylon short gloves, white #1 open toe shoes with holes, pearl necklace and earrings, blue garter, flower bouquet with lace and ribbon accents, VG 115.00
#982 Solo in the Spotlight, VG 45.00
#985 Open Road, G 95.00
#993 Sophisticated Lady, G 55.00
#1456 Dreamy Blues, blue satin mini dress, yellow and blue ruffled organza skirt, blue velvet waistband, blue shoes, blue hanger, booklet, paper label, box age discovered 95.00

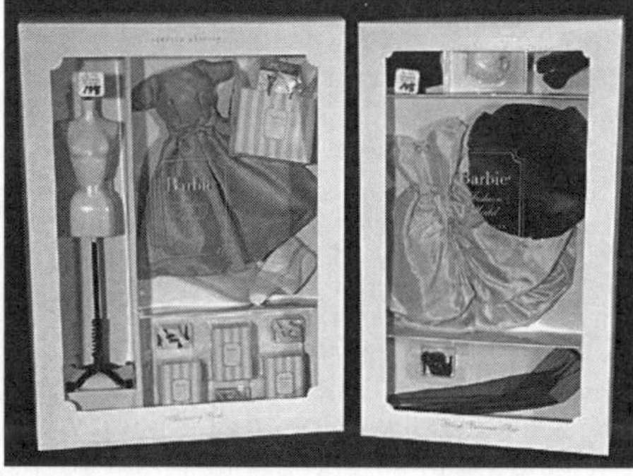

Eight Fashion Model Barbie clothing sets: #29653, FM Boulevard Fashion; #26932, FM Lunch at the Club Fashion; #29652, FM Blush Becomes Her Fashion; #26933, FM Garden Party Fashion; #55499, FM Country Bound Fashion; #55500, FM Black Enchantment Fashion; #56119, FM Accessory Pack; #1646, Classique Collection, Fifth Avenue Style Fashion, all in original boxes, **$100** for all.

#1457 City Sparkler, green lame shirt dress bodice, chartreuse chiffon skirt, pearl button accents, chartreuse shoes and hanger, box, booklet, paper label, box age discolored 85.00
#1470 Intrigue, metallic gold cot, pink lining, dress with gold skirt, white bodice with gold net, M 295.00
#1593 Golden Groove, Sears Exclusive Gift Set, pink and gold lame jacket, matching short skirt, gold thigh-high boots, NM 145.00
#1612 Theatre Date, NRFB 285.00
#1615 Saturday Matinee, NM/VG 310.00
#1617, Midnight Blue, NM-VG 150.00
#1620 Junior Designer, turquoise dress with green design, green pointed toe shoes, metal iron with black handle, *How to Design Your Own Fashion* book, VG 55.00
#1622 Student Teacher, red and white dress, white bodice inset with button accents, red vinyl belt, red pointed toe shoes, black rimmed glasses with clear lenses, plastic globe, wooden pointer stick, geography book, VG/G 175.00
#1629 Skater's Waltz, pink nylon skating suit, pink felt skirt, sheer nylon hose, white skates, pink fur muff, matching mittens, VG 45.00
#1632 Invitation to Tea, pink chiffon jumpsuit, pink and silver lame sleeveless vest, silver belt with buckle, clear open toe shoes with silver glitter, silver colored teapot with "B" monogram and lid, two pale pink plastic teacups and saucers, VG 105.00
#1640 Matinee Fashion, red sheath with braid trim, matching jacket, plush print trim, red pillbox hat, attached chiffon scarf, red pointed toe shoes, VG 135.00
#1644 On the Avenue, white and gold sheath with textured skirt, gold lame bodice, matching jacket, white nylon short gloves, cream colored pointed toe shoes, gold clutch purse, NM/VG, jacket tag frayed, P condition belt 100.00
#1645 Golden Glory, gold floral lame long dress, green chiffon waist scarf, matching gold lame long coat with fur trim, white nylon short gloves, green satin clutch purse, VG 120.00
#1649 Lunch on the Terrace, green and white checkered dress with polka dot bodice, matching hat with white net cover, VG 115.00
#1650 Outdoor Art Show, VG 145.00
#1652, Pretty as a Picture, VG 115.00
#1656 Fashion Luncheon, VG/G 225.00
#1661, London Tour, VG 105.00
#1663, Music Center Matinee, NM-VG 200.00
#1666 Debutante Ball, aqua satin gown with chiffon skirt panels, flower accents, white fur stole with aqua chiffon ties, clear open toe shoes with gold glitter, white nylon long gloves, single pearl necklace, VG 225.00
#1670 Coffee's On, butterfly print dress, orange pointed toe shoes, white casserole dish with lid, blue and white coffeepot with lid, NM 75.00
#1695 Evening Enchantment, red taffeta and chiffon long dress, marabou trim, matching chiffon cape, red pointed toe shoes, VG 135.00

#1783 Ruffles 'n Swirls, turquoise and pink swirled dress, ruffle trim, pink plastic belt with buckle, turquoise shoes, hanger, orig box, booklet, paper label, NRFB, box age discolored **75.00**
#1792 Mood Matchers, paisley print nylon sleeveless blouse, matching pants, aqua nylon shirt, hot pink high tongue shoes, M..................... **65.00**
#1814 Sparkle Squares, checkerboard pattern coat with ruffle trim, rhinestone buttons, matching dress with pleated white nylon skirt, white sheet stockings, NM **105.00**
#1848 All That Jazz, satin striped coat, matching dress with pleated skirt, beige sheer stockings, pink shoes with molded bows, VG **140.00**
#1849 Wedding Wonder, white satin gown, sheer white dress with white flocking, flocked headpiece with metal hair barrette, white tulle veil, white pointed-toe shoes, *World of Barbie Fashions* booklet, VG... **75.00**
#3401 Fringe Benefits, fuchsia knit dress, orange suede neckline, attached belt with fringe, matching orange suede boots with fringe, M **65.00**
#4041 Color Magic Fashion Fun, NM/VG................................ **145.00**
Dressed Up, Barbie Pak, dress with pale blue satin skirt, gold and white striped bodice, attached belt and buckle accents, pale blue pointed toe shoes, NM/VG **105.00**
Gala Abend, foreign market, white brocade gown, matching long coat with pale blue satin lining and fur collar, white nylon long gloves, white pointed toe shoes, VG.......... **700.00**
Midnight Pink, foreign market, pink satin gown, pink and silver lame bodice, matching long coat with fur cape and collar, one pink open toe shoe, pink pearl necklace, white nylon long gloves, G/P **650.00**
Twinkle Togs, green satin dress, blue lame bodice, clear overskirt with lame stripes, green sheer stockings on cardboard forms, blue pointed-toe shoes, hanger, paper label, NRFB, lower right cellophane corner torn, booklet missing............ **285.00**

Francie

#1216 The Lace Pace, gold lame and pink coat cov with white lace, satin bow, matching dress with satin straps, pink shoes with molded bows, VG **105.00**
#1227 Long on Looks, white blouse with lace trim, green pearl buttons, hot pink textured skirt, chartreuse waistband and bow, hot pink nylon slip with white box, pink fishnet hose, hot pink shoes, hanger, box, booklet, NRFB.................................... **115.00**
#1232 Two for the Ball, pink chiffon long coat, black velvet waistband, long dress with pink satin skirt, pink lace overskirt, black velvet bodice, pink soft pumps, VG/G, coat tag frayed **45.00**
#3367 Right for Stripes, blue vest, blue and white striped pants, matching midriff top, floral print shoulder bag, aqua sneakers, VG **65.00**
Pancho Bravo, Francie Pak, blue, pink, green, and white poncho, blue ankle boots, lavender plastic glasses, label, NRFP, some age discoloration to cardboard backing, orig 99 cent price sticker **40.00**
The Bridge Bit, white knit sweater, green and blue stitching, royal blue stretch pants with metal accent, pink pillow with flower design, NM **65.00**

Twelve miscellaneous vintage Ken Fashions and two vintage Ricky Fashions, all in original boxes, **$1,200**.

Ken

#788 Rally Day, NRFB **60.00**
#797 Army and Air Force, NRFB **155.00**
#799 Touchdown, NRFB, box in F/P condition............................... **115.00**
#0770 Campus Hero, NRFB **130.00**
#0772 The Prince, green and gold lamé coat, lace trim, rhinestone buttons, green velvet cape with gold lining, green nylon tights, green velvet shoes with gold trim, gold velvet hat with emerald, pearl, and feather accents, white collar with lace trim, velvet pillow with gold trim and tassels, paper program, VG **150.00**
#0777 Ken in Holland, NRFB **125.00**
#0778 Ken in Mexico, NRFB **155.00**
#1400 Country Clubbin', black and white hounds tooth jacket, black slacks, yellow cov booklet, paper label, NRFB **125.00**
#1404 Ken in Hawaii, VG **25.00**
#1416 College Student, VG..... **65.00**
#1417 Rovin' Reporter, red jacket, navy blue pants, white shirt, black socks and shoes, plastic camera, NM/VG.................................... **75.00**
#1419 TV's Good Tonight, red robe, blue trim, pocket insignia, cork sandals with red straps, brown plastic TV with metal antenna, VG, no tag on robe............................. **50.00**
#1425 Best Man, VG-G **105.00**

Ricky, #1502 Saturday Show, NRFB **75.00**

Skipper

#1738 Fancy Pants, VG........... **50.00**
#1901 Red Sensation, NRFB **135.00**
#1905 Ballet Class, NRFB..... **100.00**
#1910 Sunny Pastels, NRFB ..**115.00**
#1935 Twice as Nice, orange gold felt coat, matching dress, cap with pompon, VG **50.00**
#1972 Drizzle Sizzle, pink and Kelly green knit dress, orange vinyl appliqué flowers, clear plastic raincoat, cap, and boots, VG **35.00**
#3478 Long 'n Short of It, red nylon print mini dress, matching fringed scarf, rd maxi coat, red and white tam with red pompom, red boots, box, booklet, paper label, NRFB, box age discolored **75.00**

Barometers

History: A barometer is an instrument that measures atmospheric pressure, which, in turn, aids weather forecasting. Low pressure indicates the coming of rain, snow, or storm; high pressure signifies fair weather.

Most barometers use an evacuated and graduated glass tube that contains a column of mercury. These are classified by the shape of the case. An aneroid barometer has no liquid and works by a needle connected to the top of a metal box in which a partial vacuum is maintained. The movement of the top moves the needle.

4-1/2" h, aneroid, Taylor, circular mahogany frame **75.00**
21-1/2" l, wheel, Aneroid, Swedish, late 19th C, part ebonized, arch top

with acorn finials, painted milk glass thermometer between turned uprights, open dial with printed enamel bezel signed "C.L. Malmsjo, Guteborg," within turned frame, acorn pendant finial **300.00**

Banjo form, English, mahogany case, bullseye mirror, ivory finial on broken arch, ivory dial, 38" h, loss to ivory change dial, repairs to spandrel around mirror, **$375**. Photo courtesy of Alderfer Auction Co.

26-1/2" h, wheel, Georgian, mahogany, dial sgd "Dolland, London," rounded pediment over thermometer, urn inlaid central roundel line inlay throughout, early 19th C **1,840.00**

33" d, wheel, carved oak, foliage and C-scrolls, English, late 19th C **230.00**

34" l, stick, sgd E. Kendall, N. Lebanon, mahogany, etched steel face, mirrored well cov **550.00**

34-5/8" l, French, Empire-style, late 19th C, giltwood, aneroid topped by lyre centered by thermometer, hexagonal frame with verre eglomise dial accented with black and navy blue foiling **300.00**

36-1/2" l, wheel, English, Georgian, early 19th C, mahogany, dial signed "Dolland, London," rounded pediment over thermometer, urn inlaid central roundel, line inlay throughout **1,840.00**

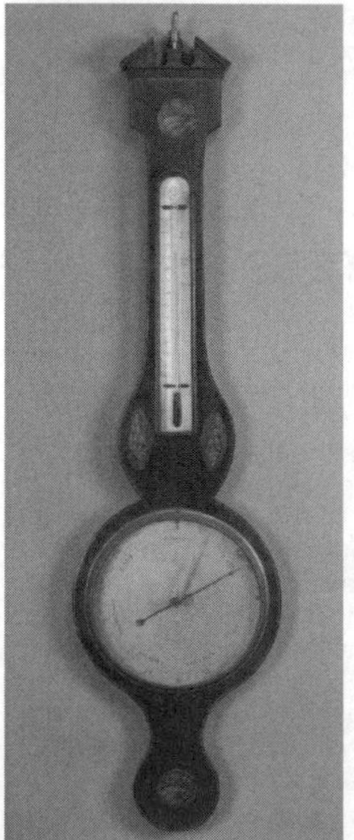

Wheel form, English, George III, inlaid mahogany, baluster case inset with shell paterae, silvered thermometer and dial signed "J. Steele, Liverpool," 39" h, **$830**. Photo courtesy of Sloans & Kenyon Auctions.

37-3/8" l, French, Louis XV/XVI-style, late 19th C, giltwood, frame topped by flower-filled basket over pen and inked barometer dial signed for Carcano, maker, with Frippiere au Phenix retailer's mark, dial flanked by stylized quivers suspending drapery, over thermometer, ending in reeded base **2,650.00**

38-1/4" l, wheel, Hepplewhite-style, English, 19th C, Chester, A. Rivolta, maker, broken pediment centered by brass urn finial, thermometer planked by pair of shell inlays, silvered dial with maker's name, ending in inlaid patera **600.00**

38-3/4" h, banjo, mahogany, dial engraved "P. Nossi & Co. Boston," broken pediment cresting above shaped case with thermometer, circular barometer dial flanked by inlaid patera **690.00**

39" l, wheel, English, early 20th C, mahogany, broken pediment centered by finial, round hygrometer dial over vertical thermometer, convex mirror over barometer dial, ending in dial for level **815.00**

39-3/4" h, banjo, shell inlaid, painted black, Kirner Bros., Oxford, Victorian, mid-19th C **460.00**

40" l, wheel, rosewood veneer, onion top cornice with hygrometer dial over thermometer over convex mirror, large barometric dial, small level at base, English, mid-19th C **350.00**

42" h, 4" w, stick, French, first half 19th C, inlaid mahogany, slender straight case, inlaid to frieze with symmetrical leafage spray above light wood reserves, readings and three gauges, illegibly signed, gauge replaced **600.00**

50" h, barometer and wall clock, G. V. Mooney, NY, walnut, shaped backboard with molded wood and brass bezel framing paper dial and brass lever movement above printed paper dial "G.V. Mooney's Barometer Patented May 30th 1865—Sold by Arnaboldi & Co. 53 Fulton St. New York," mercury tube extending to the base with a molded wooden boss **1,880.00**

Baskets

History: Baskets were invented when man first required containers to gather, store, and transport goods. Today's collectors, influenced by the country look, focus on baskets made of splint, rye straw, or willow. Emphasis is placed on handmade examples. Nails or staples, wide splints that are thin and evenly cut, or a wire bail handle denote factory construction which can date back to the mid-19th century. Decorated painted or woven baskets rarely are handmade, unless they are American Indian in origin.

Baskets are collected by (a) type—berry, egg, or field; (b) region—Nantucket or Shaker; and (c) composition—splint, rye, or willow.

Reproduction Alert: Modern reproductions abound, made by diverse groups ranging from craft revivalists to foreign manufacturers.

Cane and oak splint, round form, raised interior, banded top and base, bentwood handle, 10" d, 12" h, **$220**. Photo courtesy of Alderfer Auction Co.

Coil, rye straw, some splint breaks
- 6-3/4" d, 3-1/4" h **75.00**
- 16" d, 4" h, single edge handle **95.00**

Covered
- 10-1/2" h, woven, ovoid, flared foot, small lid, bale handle, Oriental **220.00**
- 14" w, 10" d, 9-1/4" h, Oneida, red potato stamp dec, inked black dot borders, green leaves, rect shape, wide woven splints, minor split on one bottom corner **450.00**
- 18-1/2" d, 16" h, rye, slightly ovoid, some edge damage **220.00**

Half buttocks, woven splint, thick brown paint, bentwood handle, 8" w, 5" h **200.00**

Melon, 8-1/4" h, 10" w, finely woven brown and tan splint, 22 ribs, arched handle, two minor splint breaks **125.00**

Miniature
- Bushel, painted cream-white over red, America, 19th C, 5-3/4" d, 3-1/4" h **760.00**
- Woven splint, single handle, painted blue, 1-3/4" d, 2" h **550.00**

Nantucket Light Ship, America
- 7-5/8" d, 5-1/8" h plus bentwood swivel handle, band of darker splint around middle, wooden disk base, faint penciled inscription "Nantucket basket presented by Capt...," purportedly by Capt Thomas James of first Nantucket lightship, minor wear **2,530.00**

8-1/8" d, 10" h, brown patina, round, wooden base, high sides, arched swing handle **2,450.00**
9-1/2" d, 6" h plus bentwood swivel handle, turned disk base, varnish finish with some wear **2,420.00**

Laundry basket, woven splint sides, wooden handles, **$50**. Photo courtesy of Dotta Auction Co., Inc.

Native American
Covered, woven splint, attributed to New England Algonkian or Iroquois, early 19th C, round domed lid, round to square form, red and green flowering vine motif, side handles, 15-1/2" h, minor wear, fading **2,000.00**
Covered, woven splint, attributed to New England Algonkian or Iroquois, early 19th C, round domed lid, round to square form, alternating sides painted with baskets of flowers and flowers, shades of salmon green and black, 19-1/2" d, minor wear, fading **2,250.00**
Splint, Schaticoke Tribe, CT, 19th C, rect, two carved handles, decorative bands, polychrome blue, orange, green, and brown splints, 13" l, 10-1/4" w, 7" h..................... **1,725.00**
Oak
Peach basket shape, initials "CMT," 11-1/2" h, 14" d top............... **235.00**
Sewing, rect, compartments woven into one end, 21" l, 12" d, 6" h, minor cracking **250.00**
Painted
Miniature, tapering cylindrical form, loop handles, old taupe paint, America, 19th C, 5" d, 3" h **1,150.00**
Splint, round shape, sq bottom, old dark red paint over white, New England, mid-19th C, minor paint wear, 12" d, 3-3/4" h **200.00**
Vertical-shaped wooden slats joined by twisted wire banding, wooden circular base, old painted surface, America, early 19th C, 12-1/2" d, 18" h **865.00**
Rye straw
23" d, dough rising, shallow, hickory splint binding, PA, late 19th C **125.00**

Nantucket, oval, carved swing handle, oval wood base, 14-1/2" d, 7" h from base to rim, **$1,530**. Photo courtesy of Skinner, Inc.

24" d, domed lid, wear, edge damage, one bentwood rim handle missing **300.00**
Square, 13" w, 6" h, woven splint, light brown, double handles................. **125.00**
Stave construction, vertical wood staves taper down at base, fixed with wire, dark orig finish over varnish, 13" d, 17" h... **250.00**
Storage, cov, splint, painted blue, attributed to New England, late 19th C, 17" d, 24" h **1,380.00**

Splint oak, kettle form, fixed handle, 12" d, 12" h, **$150**. Photo courtesy of Alderfer Auction Co.

Wall
8" w, 6" d, 6-1/4" h, half buttocks shape, woven splint, bentwood handle, remnants of old ivory paint **200.00**
13-1/2" w, 6" d, 14" h, blue-green paint over earlier red, oblong, deep compartment, high crest, minor chips.................................... **450.00**
Woven splint
Buttocks, 16 ribs, 10" l, 8-3/4" h **125.00**
Buttocks, 28 ribs, dark patina, bentwood handle, 10-1/4" l, 5-1/4" h **200.00**
Round, bentwood handle, old gray weathered surface, 13-3/4" d, 8-3/4" h **115.00**
Round, bentwood handle, rim, and foot, alternating salmon colored ribs, 12-1/4" d, 7-1/2" h, minor split on foot **150.00**

Bavarian China

History: Bavaria, Germany, was an important porcelain production center, similar to the Staffordshire district in England. The phrase "Bavarian China" refers to the products of companies operating in Bavaria, among which were Hutschenreuther, Thomas, and Zeh, Scherzer & Co. (Z. S. & Co.). Little of the production from this area was imported into the United States prior to 1870.

Dinner plates, green borders flanked by tooled gilt borders, set of nine 10-3/4" d by Hutschenreuther, and set of six 11" d by Heinrich & Co., **$355**. Photo courtesy of Sloans & Kenyon Auctions.

Bowl, 7-3/8" l, 6" w, ovoid, reticulated sides, beaded rim, center and sides painted with scenic roundels en grisaille, blue ribbon cartouches with gilt detailing, scenes titled on underside "Badenburg," "Apolloscumpeil," and "Schloss Nymphenburg," late 19th C.......... **325.00**
Celery tray, 11" l, center with basket of fruit, luster edge, c1900 .... **45.00**
Chocolate set, cov chocolate pot, six cups and saucers, shaded blue and white, large white leaves, pink, red, and white roses, crown mark................ **295.00**
Creamer and sugar, purple and white pansy dec, marked "Meschendorf, Bavaria" **65.00**

Tea set, gold floral pattern, gold trimmed rims, teapot, creamer, sugar, four cups and saucers, **$90**. Photo courtesy of Dotta Auction Co., Inc.

Cup and saucer, roses and foliage, gold handle **30.00**
Dinner plate, 10-1/4" d, gold emb, stippled bands, "A" monogram, marked "Hutshcenreuther selb Bavaria," price for set of 12 .... **320.00**
Fish set, platter, six plates **200.00**
Pitcher, 9" h, bulbous, blackberry dec, shaded ground, burnished gold lizard handle, sgd "D. Churchill" **125.00**
Portrait vase, 10" h, gold enameled flowers and leaves, hp portrait of Naomi, blue beehive mark and "TG Bavaria" mark **520.00**
Ramekin, underplate, ruffled, small red roses with green foliage, gold rim ... **45.00**
Salt and pepper shakers, pr, pink apple blossom sprays, white ground, reticulated gold tops, pr **35.00**
Vase, 12" h, hp, red poppies, gold enamel dec, marked "Classic Bavaria" **260.00**

Belleek

History: Belleek, a thin, ivory-colored, almost-iridescent porcelain, was first made in 1857 in county Fermanagh, Ireland. Production continued until World War I, was discontinued for a period of time, and then resumed. The Shamrock pattern is most familiar, but many patterns were made, including Limpet, Tridacna, and Grasses.

For more information, see *Warman's English & Continental Pottery & Porcelain*, 3rd edition.

There is an Irish saying: If a newly married couple receives a gift of Belleek, their marriage will be blessed with lasting happiness.

Several American firms made a Belleek-type porcelain. The first was Ott and Brewer Co. of Trenton, New Jersey, in 1884, followed by Willets. Other firms producing this ware included The Ceramic Art Co. (1889), American Art China Works (1892), Columbian Art Co. (1893), and Lenox, Inc. (1904).

Marks: The European Belleek company used specific marks during given time periods, which makes it relatively easy to date a piece of Irish Belleek. Variations in mark color are important, as well as the symbols and words.

First mark	Black	Harp, Hound, and Castle 1863-1890
Second mark	Black	Harp, Hound, and Castle and the words "Co. Fermanagh, Ireland" 1891-1826
Third mark	Black	"Deanta in Eirinn" added 1926-1946
Fourth mark	Green	same as third mark except for color 1946-1955
Fifth mark	Green	"R" inside a circle added 1955-1965
Sixth mark	Green	"Co. Fermanagh" omitted 1965- March 1980
Seventh mark	Gold	"Deanta in Eirinn" omitted April 1980-Dec. 1992
Eighth mark	Blue	Blue version of the second mark with "R" inside a circle added Jan. 1993-present

Additional Listings: Lenox.

Plate, scalloped rim, gold trim, two handpainted pheasants, brown, black, and green garland of leaves, purple ink "O & B, Belleek" (Ott & Brewer), 9" d, **$275**. Photo courtesy of David Rago Auctions, Inc.

American

Bowl

7" d, 4-1/4" h, double handles, ruffled rim, gilt trim and handles, gilt and rose-colored flowers dec, brown Willets mark **275.00**
7-1/2" d, green ext., wide gilt textured border, int. with hp floral design, artist sgd "MS" on base, brown Willets mark **100.00**

Candy dish, 8" x 6", shell form, ivory ground, hp floral dec, ruffled gilt rim, marked "Columbia Art Co., Trenton, NJ" **80.00**
Chocolate pot, 10-1/4" h, ivory ground, Art Deco rose design, pale green and yellow wide borders, gilt accents, green Lenox pallet mark **135.00**
Cup and saucer, 2" cup, 5-3/4" d saucer, hp, pale pink and green beaded dec, gilt borders, brown Willets mark **60.00**

Tea set, partial, Tridacna Tea Set, covered teapot, (shallow chip to spout); creamer; three cups and saucers, (hairline to one cup); and 8" d three plates; 4-1/4" h Neptune tea ware cream jug, c1935, all with printed third black marks, **$300**. Photo courtesy of Skinner, Inc.

Dish, 10-1/2" d, hp, lily dec, gold trim, gilt banding and design on ext., sgd "FML," green Lenox pallet mark **145.00**
Jug, 5-1/2" h, hp, pale yellow ground, floral dec, gilt rim and handle, green CAC pallet mark **110.00**
Pitcher, 7" h, hp, white ground, geometric blue floral design, gilt trim, artist sgd "G. L. Urban," green Willets mark **85.00**
Plate, 7-1/4" d, gilt foliate rim, blue enamel beads, red Willets mark, price for pr **45.00**

Salt, 1-1/2" d

Gilt, ruffled edge, marked "CAC," price for set of six **45.00**
Pale green, hp pink enamel dec, artist sgd "E.S.M.," Lenox pallet mark, price for set of six **135.00**

Swan, 8-1/2" h, ivory, open back, green Lenox wreath mark **90.00**
Tankard, 5-3/4" h, hand painted, multicolored ground, foliage dec, sgd "B.M.A.," brown Willets mark **125.00**
Teapot, 6" h, blue glazed ground, gilt dec, brown Willets mark **135.00**
Vase, 15" h, baluster, hp pine cone dec, artist sgd "A.E.G.," green Lenox pallet mark **450.00**

Urn, spherical, two upright handles, four reticulated feet, red Oriental poppies dec, light wear to gilting around rim, red O&B crown stamp, 8" x 6", **$1,725**. Photo courtesy of David Rago Auctions, Inc.

Irish

Basket, 6-1/2" x 4-1/2", four strand, applied flowers, Belleek Co. Fermangh Ireland pad mark, some repairs, petal missing **80.00**
Bread plate, 10-1/2" l, 9-1/4" w, Shamrock pattern, double handle, third green mark **80.00**
Butter dish, cov, 6-1/2" d top, 8-1/2" d base, Limpet pattern, first black mark **475.00**
Cake plate, 10-1/2" d, mask with grape leaves pattern, four looped handles, pale yellow edge, third black mark **155.00**
Creamer
- 3-1/4" h, Lifford pattern, third green mark **60.00**
- 3-1/2" h, Cleary pattern, first green mark **50.00**
- 4" h, Rathmore pattern, third green mark **40.00**

Cream jug, 5-1/4" h, blue glazed handle and coral relief, first black mark, c1880, footrim chip **520.00**
Cup and saucer, 5-3/8" d saucer, Tea Ware, hexagon, pink tint, second black mark, early 20th C, price for pr **460.00**
Figure
- 2-1/2" h, pig, third green mark **90.00**
- 6" h, harp, third green mark **70.00**

Font, 7" h, Sacred Heart, cross form, shaped font, second green mark **50.00**
Mint tray, 8-1/2" l, shell form, pink highlights on rim, brown mark **70.00**
Mustache cup and saucer, 2-1/2" h cup, 6" d saucer, Tridacna, pink rim, first black mark **495.00**
Pitcher
- 5-1/2" h, Vine and Grape pattern, lavender and green, ivory ground, brown mark **60.00**
- 6-1/2" h, Limpet pattern, third black mark **90.00**

Plate, 10-1/2" d, scalloped edge, woven, three strands, pad mark **200.00**
Spill vase
- 5" h, Shamrock, second green mark **50.00**
- 8" h, owl, second green mark **55.00**

Sugar bowl, 4" h, Shell, pink tinted edge and coral, first black mark, c1880, footrim chips **575.00**
Swan, 4" h, open back, yellow wings and head, brown mark **55.00**
Tea cup and saucer, 5-3/4" d saucer, gilt trimmed relief of horns, orange peel ground, first black and registry marks, c1870, gilt wear, repaired rim chip on saucer **175.00**
Tea kettle, cov, 6" h, Grass Tea Ware, enamel dec relief, first black mark, c1880, spout lips restored **230.00**

Vase, applied flowers & leaves; black mark, 8" h, bowl, green mark, 4-3/4" d; vase, tree trunk shape, 6-1/4" h, **$150**. Photo courtesy of Joy Luke Auctions.

Teapot, cov
- 5" h, Shamrock pattern, brown mark **90.00**
- 6" h, Limpet pattern, third black mark **165.00**

Tea set
- Neptune Tea Ware, 5-1/8" h cov teapot, creamer, sugar, six 6-1/8" d plates, six cups and saucers, each pink tinted, third black marks, 20th C **1,150.00**
- Tridacna Tea Ware, 4-1/8" h cov teapot, creamer, sugar, 6-3/4" d plate, six cups and saucers, each pink tinted, second black marks, early 20th C **460.00**

Vase
- 4-3/4" h, 5-3/4" d, Cardium, shell form, coral and shell base, second black mark **80.00**
- 8" h, coral, pink tinted coral and shell int., first black mark, c1880 .... **1,150.00**
- 8" h, Ribbon, applied flowers, ruffled rim, third black mark, minor flakes on flowers **110.00**
- 9" h, two scrolled and pierced handles, delicate applied bouquet of flowers, 1891 mark, price for pr **690.00**

Bells

History: Bells have been used for centuries for many different purposes. They have been traced as far back as 2697 B.C., though at that time they did not have any true tone. One of the oldest bells is the "crotal," a tiny sphere with small holes, a ball, and a stone or metal interior. This type now appears as sleigh bells.

True bell making began when bronze, a mixture of tin and copper, was invented. Bells are now made out of many types of materials—almost as many materials as there are uses for them.

Bells of the late 19th century show a high degree of workmanship and artistic style. Glass bells from this period are examples of the glassblower's talent and the glass manufacturer's product.

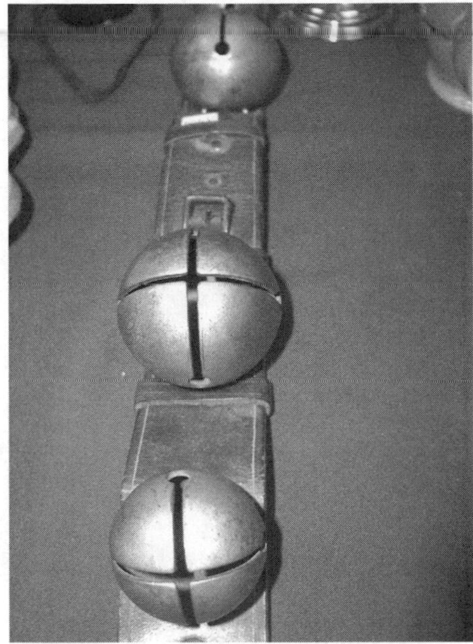

Sleigh bells, large bells on leather strap with buckle, **$60**.

Brass, hand held, Jacobean, head handle, cast figures on sides, emb inscription, 3-1/4" d, 4" h **95.00**
Ceramic, figural
- Anniversary, Florence Ceramics, applied pink Dresden-style flowers, white ground, gold trim, 4-1/2" h **80.00**
- Sovereign Bonnet Lady, Gonder, Mold No. 800, 3-1/2" h **60.00**

Desk type, 4-3/8" h, bell enclosed in five polished mother-of-pearl shells, gilt metal surrounds, small mother-of-pearl mounted striker, round alabaster base, late 19th C **185.00**
Dinner, china
- Figural, Chinaman, Noritake, 3-1/2" h **210.00**
- Rose Tapestry, Royal Bayreuth, three color roses, gold handle, 3-1/4" h **400.00**

Glass
- Cranberry, applied clear handle, English, late 19th C, 11" h **95.00**
- Fostoria, Chintz pattern, orig label **135.00**
- Imperial, Candlewick pattern, No. 400/108, 5" h **95.00**
- Mount Washington, white satin, pink floral dec, gold trim, 5" h **150.00**

Nickel-plated, railroad engine, arched yoke with U-shaped support, pedestal base, 25" h **2,145.00**
School, 10-1/4" h, turned curly maple handle **385.00**

Sleigh, 55" l, 15 graduated brass bells on leather strap, wear **200.00**

Garden bell, bronze, hanging, fern like top, hanging sheet copper pendant, raised square mark for Arcostanti, 10" d, 38" h, **$995**. Photo courtesy of David Rago Auctions, Inc.

Sterling silver, 4-5/8" h, cupid blowing horn, figural handle, foliate strap work border, frosted finish, Gorham, c1870 .... **750.00**

Bennington and Bennington-Type Pottery

History: In 1845, Christopher Webber Fenton joined Julius Norton, his brother-in-law, in the manufacturing of stoneware pottery in Bennington, Vermont. Fenton sought to expand the company's products and glazes; Norton wanted to concentrate solely on stoneware. In 1847, Fenton broke away and established his own factory.

Fenton introduced to America the famous Rockingham glaze, developed in England and named after the Marquis of Rockingham. In 1849, he patented a flint enamel glaze, "Fenton's Enamel," which added flecks, spots, or streaks of color (usually blues, greens, yellows, and oranges) to the brown Rockingham glaze. Forms included candlesticks, coachman bottles, cow creamers, poodles, sugar bowls, and toby pitchers.

Fenton produced the little-known scroddled ware, commonly called lava or agate ware. Scroddled ware is composed of differently colored clays, which are mixed with cream-colored clay, molded, turned on a potter's wheel, coated with feldspar and flint, and fired. It was not produced in quantity, as there was little demand for it.

Fenton also introduced Parian ware to America. Parian was developed in England in 1842 and known as "Statuary ware." Parian is translucent porcelain that has no glaze and resembles marble. Bennington made the blue and white variety in the form of vases, cologne bottles, and trinkets.

The hound-handled pitcher is probably the best-known Bennington piece. Hound-handled pitchers were made by about 30 different potteries in more than 55 variations. Rockingham glaze was used by more than 150 potteries in 11 states, mainly in the Midwest, between 1830 and 1900.

Marks: Five different marks were used, with many variations. Only about twenty percent of the pieces carried any mark; some forms were almost always marked, others never. Marks include:

- 1849 mark (four variations) for flint enamel and Rockingham
- E. Fenton's Works, 1845-1847, on Parian and occasionally on scroddled ware
- U. S. Pottery Co., ribbon mark, 1852-1858, on Parian and blue and white porcelain
- U. S. Pottery Co., lozenge mark, 1852-1858, on Parian
- U. S. Pottery, oval mark, 1853-1858, mainly on scroddled ware

Additional Listings: Stoneware.

Book flask, spine impressed "DEPARTED SPIRITS," spout with circle of raised dots, mottled brown Rockingham glaze, 5-5/8" h, **$350**. Photo courtesy of Skinner, Inc.

Book flask, flint enamel glaze, title on spine

5-1/8" h, *Ladies Companion,* brown with gold **660.00**

5-3/4" h, *Departed Spirits G,* dark brown with some blue and yellow, tiny flake, repaired corner **385.00**

6" h, *Bennington Battle,* brown, blue, and some yellow **635.00**

6" h, *Indians Lament,* light brown, blue, and yellow, minor flake on pages **495.00**

6" h, *Kossuths Life & Suffering,* brown, blue, and light yellow, marked "Fenton's Patented Enamel 1849" minor flake, repaired corners **715.00**

6" h, *Ned Buntline's Bible,* olive tan, gold, and blue, marked "Fenton's Patented Enamel 1849"...... **2,200.00**

6" h, *Ned Buntline's Own,* brown, blue, and light gold, marked "Fenton's Patented Enamel 1849" **2,310.00**

6" h, *Traveler's Companion,* light olive tan, blue, and gold........ **615.00**

Bowl, 7-1/8" d, shallow, brown and yellow Rockingham glaze, Fenton's 1849 mark **775.00**

Candlestick, 8-1/4" h, flint enamel glaze **875.00**

Curtain tiebacks, pr, 4-1/2" l, 1849-58, Barrett plate 200, one chipped **185.00**

Figure, 8-1/2" h, 9" l, poodle, standing, basket in mouth, Barrett plate 367, repairs to tail and hind quarters **2,500.00**

Figural bottle, Coachman, imp Fenton 1849 mark on base, firing cracks in glaze, 10-1/2" h, **$235**. Photo courtesy of Skinner, Inc.

Jug, 11-1/2" h, stoneware, imp signature "L. Norton & Son," ovoid, applied strap handle, brown floral dec, two pot stones **770.00**

Marble, 1-1/2" d, blue, some wear **90.00**

Paperweight, 3" h, 4-1/2" h, spaniel, 1849-58, Barrett plate 407............ **815.00**

Picture frame, 9-1/2" h, oval, 1948-58, Barrett plate VIII, chips and repairs, pr **230.00**

Pitcher

8-1/2" h, parian, white relief scene of woman petting bird on parch, light blue ground, gilt trim, glazed foliage, scroll sides and base **200.00**

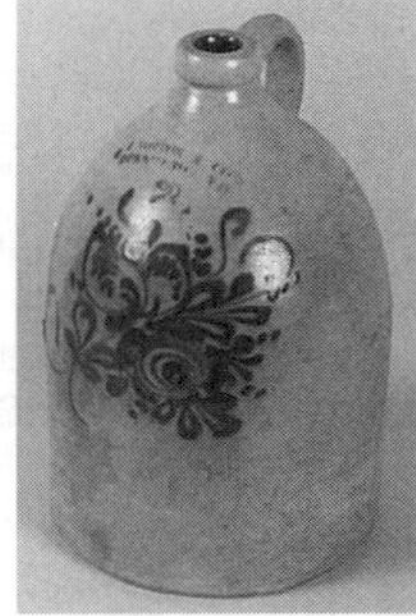
Jug, stoneware, two gals, ovoid, applied strap handle, ornate cobalt blue floral sprig decoration, impressed maker's marks, "J.NORTON & CO BENNINGTON VT," 1839-43, 14" h, **$600**. Photo courtesy of Skinner, Inc.

9" d, 9" h, modeled greyhound handle, emb hunting scene of game hanging from trees, unmarked, 1" bruise with small nick at rim, few minor abrasions......................115.00

10-1/4" h, parian, vining roses, branch handle, molded label "Fenton's Works, Bennington, Vermont," glazed int............. 300.00

Spittoon, 9-1/2" d, flint enamel glaze, rare 1849 mark 450.00

Sugar bowl, cov, 3-3/4" h, Parian, blue and white, Repeated Oak Leaves pattern, raised grapevine dec on lid 150.00

Teapot, cov, flint enamel, Alternate Rib pattern, pierced pouring spout 425.00

Toby, Rockingham glaze, restoration 75.00

Bennington-Type

Bank, 3-1/4" h, 3-3/4" h, chest of drawers shape, Rockingham glaze, Barrett plate 428, small chip to front top edge 150.00

Pitcher, Bennington-type, mottled brown and yellow glaze, 8-1/2" h, **$100**. Photo courtesy of Alderfer Auction Co.

Creamer, 5-1/2" h, 6-3/4" l, figural, cow, Rockingham glaze, Barrett plate 378, chipped cov, repairs 115.00

Flask, book, 7" h, titled "Spiritual Manifestations By" imp on spine, Rockingham glaze, mid-19th C, crack 260.00

Spittoon, 8-1/2" d, scallop shell form, Rockingham glaze, 19th C...........175.00

Biscuit Jars

History: The biscuit or cracker jar was the forerunner of the cookie jar. Biscuit jars were made of various materials by leading glassworks and potteries of the late 19th and early 20th centuries.

For more information, see *Warman's Glass*, 4th edition.

Note: All items listed have silver-plated (SP) mountings unless otherwise noted.

Glass, cobalt blue cut to clear, gold tone top, **$195**. Photo courtesy of Wiederseim Associates, Inc.

Bristol glass, 6-1/2" h, all-over enameled pink, blue, white and yellow floral dec, green leaves, SP top, rim, and handle 125.00

Cranberry glass, 9" h, 6-1/4" d, two applied clear ring handles, applied clear feet and flower prunt pontil, ribbed finial knob...195.00

Nippon China, 7-1/2" h, 4-1/2" w, sq, white, multicolored floral bands, gold outlines and trim 110.00

Opal glass

8" h, sq jar with molded bumpy exterior of white opal glass, dec with pink and green enameled clover blossoms, silver-plated cover and rim mount with floral and scroll repousse motifs, attributed to Mt Washington Glass Co, New Bedford, MA, late 19th C, minor enamel wear 290.00

10" h, white opal glass jar, enameled blue, yellow, pink, and green florals, SP mount, handle, and cov, trefoil finial, attributed to Mt Washington Glass Co., New Bedford, MA, late 19th C.................................. 230.00

Royal Bayreuth, Poppy, blue mark 650.00

Satin glass, 7-1/4" h, pink, molded shell base, enameled floral dec, SP lid and handle...315.00

Turquoise-green glass, 10-1/2" h, different enameled floral motif on each panel, four with butterflies, one dragonfly, and honeybee, electro plated nickel silver fittings, English, some wear to enamel dotted edges 1,500.00

Wave Crest, 9" h, yellow roses, molded multicolored swirl ground, incised floral and leaf dec on lid, marked "Quadruple Plate" 410.00

Satin glass, flowers and leaves dec, non-matching silver-plated lid, **$125**. Photo courtesy of Joy Luke Auctions.

Carlton Ware, Peony pattern, flowers decoration, silver-plated lid, **$295**. Photo courtesy of Joy Luke Auctions.

Wedgwood, jasper

5" h, green dip ground, applied white classical figure groups above acanthus leafs, SP rim, handle and cover, imp Wedgwood mark, late 19th C, footrim nick 400.00

5-3/4" h, central dark blue ground bordered in light blue, applied white Muses in relief, banded laurel border, SP rim, handle and cover, imp mark, c1900, slight relief loss.......... 650.00

5-3/4" h, yellow ground, applied black relief of Muses below fruiting grapevine festoons terminating in lion masks with rings, grapevine border to foot, SP rim, handle and cover, imp mark, c1930......... 800.00

6-3/8" h, light blue ground, applied white relief of Muses within scrolled foliate frames, silver-plated stand, rim and hinged cover, imp mark, mid-19th C............................ 425.00

Bisque

History: Bisque or biscuit china is the name given to wares that have been fired once and have not been glazed.

Bisque figurines and busts, which were popular during the Victorian era, were used on fireplace mantels, dining room buffets, and end tables. Manufacturing was centered in the United States and Europe. By the mid-20th century, Japan was the principal source of bisque items, especially character-related items.

For more information, see *Warman's English & Continental Pottery & Porcelain*, 3rd edition.

Figure, semi-nude child seated on a stone plinth, mold incised "H. Dopping," German, early 20th C, 17-5/8" h, **$250**. Photo courtesy of Skinner, Inc.

Bust, 16-1/2" h, young girl, hand-painted details and gilding, Victorian......... **200.00**
Dish, cov, 9" x 6-1/2" x 5-1/2", dog, brown, and white, green blanket, white and gilt basketweave base **500.00**
Figure, boy playing mandolin, marked "Heubach" **75.00**

Napkin rings, figural clowns holding ring, multicolored, unmarked, **$10** each.

Match holder, figural, Dutch girl, copper and gold trim **45.00**
Planter, carriage, four wheels, pale blue and pink, white ground, gold dots, royal markings...................................... **165.00**
Salt, 3" d, figural, walnut, cream, branch base, matching spoon..................... **75.00**
Wall plaque, 10-1/4" d, light green, scrolled and pierced scallop, white relief figures in center, man playing mandolin, lady wearing hat, c1900, pr........... **275.00**

Bitters Bottles

History: Bitters, a "remedy" made from natural herbs and other mixtures with an alcohol base, often was viewed as the universal cure-all. The names given to various bitter mixtures were imaginative, though the bitters seldom cured what their makers claimed.

The manufacturers of bitters needed a way to sell and advertise their products. They designed bottles in many shapes, sizes, and colors to attract the buyer. Many forms of advertising, including trade cards, billboards, signs, almanacs, and novelties, proclaimed the virtues of a specific bitter.

During the Civil War, a tax was levied on alcoholic beverages. Since bitters were identified as medicines, they were exempt from this tax. The alcoholic content was never mentioned. In 1907, when the Pure Foods Regulations went into effect, "an honest statement of content on every label" put most of the manufacturers out of business.

Solomon's Strengthening & Invigorating Bitters, Savannah, Georgia, applied top, medium vibrant blue, 9-3/4" h, uncleaned condition, almost mint, **$1,500**. Photo courtesy of American Bottle Auctions.

Alpine Herb Bitters, T&T & Co in monogram, tooled top, c1859....... **300.00**
Baker's Orange Grove Bitters, roped corners, applied top, smooth base, slug plate on front and side panels, light yellow pinkish coloration, minor flake off bottom of collar on back............... **850.00**
Bell's Cocktail Bitters, Jas. M. Bell & Co., New York, amber, applied ring, smooth base, 10-1/2" h.................. **450.00**
Browns Celebrated Indian Herb Bitters/ Patented Feb. 11, 1868, figural, emb, golden amber, ground lip, smooth base, 12-1/4" h **350.00**
Bryant's Stomach Bitters, dark green, sticky ball pontil........................... **3,600.00**
Caldwell's Herb Bitters/The Great Tonic, triangular, beveled and lattice work panels, yellowish-amber, applied tapered lip, iron pontil **395.00**
Drakes 1860 Plantation X Bitters, reverse emb PATENTED 1862, four logs **210.00**
Greenley's Bourbon Bitters, moss green, applied top, smooth base **4,000.00**

The Great Tonic Caldwells Herbbitters, applied top, metallic pontil, 13" h, **$230**. Photo courtesy of American Bottle Auctions.

John Moffat Price $1.00 Phoenix Bitters New York, applied top, open pontil, light to medium olive lime, heavily whittled, loaded with crudity **750.00**
Kelly's Old Cabin Bitters, cabin shape, amber, sloping collar lip, smooth base, 9" h.. **725.00**
McKeever's Army Bitters, amber, sloping collared lip, smooth base, 10-5/8" h **1,700.00**
National Bitters, corn-cob shape, puce amber, applied ring lip, smooth base, 12-5/8" h **350.00**
Old Homestead Wild Cherry Bitters, Patent, cabin shape, shaped shingles resemble thatched roof, 9-1/2", hint of int. stain **400.00**
Red Jacket Bitters, Monheimer & Co., sq, amber, tooled lip, smooth base, 9-1/2" h **100.00**
Simon's Centennial, George Washington bust... **3,200.00**
Tippecanoe, Warner & Co., amber, applied mushroom lip, 9" h............. **95.00**
Warner's Safe Bitters, amber, applied mouth, smooth base, 8-1/2" h........ **265.00**

Whitell's Temperance Bitters, Boston, applied tapered top, open pontil, light to medium bluish green, whittle and lots of other crudity **350.00**

I & L M Hellman, St. Louis, applied top, fancy design around sunken panels, very whittled and crude, 9", 1/4" radiating potstone near the bottom part of unembossed panel, **$425**. Photo courtesy of American Bottle Auctions.

Zingan Bitters, amber, applied mouth, smooth base, 11-7/8" h................. **150.00**

Black Memorabilia

History: The term "Black memorabilia" refers to a broad range of collectibles that often overlap other collecting fields, e.g., toys and postcards. It also encompasses African artifacts, items created by slaves or related to the slavery era, modern Black cultural contributions to literature, art, etc., and material associated with the Civil Rights Movement and the Black experience throughout history.

The earliest known examples of Black memorabilia include primitive African designs and tribal artifacts. Black Americana dates back to the arrival of African natives upon American shores.

The advent of the 1900s saw an incredible amount and variety of material depicting Blacks, most often in a derogatory and dehumanizing manner that clearly reflected the stereotypical attitude held toward the Black race during this period. The popularity of Black portrayals in this unflattering fashion flourished as the century wore on.

As the growth of the Civil Rights Movement escalated and aroused public awareness to the Black plight, attitudes changed. Public outrage and pressure during the early 1950s eventually put a halt to these offensive stereotypes.

Black representations are still being produced in many forms, but no longer in the demoralizing designs of the past. These modern objects, while not as historically significant as earlier examples, will become the Black memorabilia of tomorrow.

Reproduction Alert: Reproductions are becoming an increasing problem, from advertising signs (Bull Durham tobacco) to mechanical banks (Jolly Nigger). If the object looks new to you, chances are that it is new.

Advertising box, Aunt Jemima Pancake Flour.. **160.00**

Advertising sign

- Aunt Jemima Pancake Flour, paper, Aunt Jemima seated on swing, string sides................................. **4,700.00**
- Carbo Magnetic Razor, emb tin **3,700.00**
- DuPont Polish, litho cardboard **400.00**

Advertising figure, life-size, polychrome papier-mâché, figure posed in seated position, hands poised as if holding newspaper, white hat with red band, dark blue jacket, white shirt, vest, pants, and shoes, red necktie, America, late 19th/early 20th C, 20" w, 33" d, 48-1/2" h, minor paint wear, separations, **$5,900**. Photo courtesy of Skinner, Inc.

Alarm clock, German, paper face **550.00**

Alms box, 5-1/2" l, 3-1/2" w, 8-1/2" h, composition black youth sitting on wood tree stump box base, when money is deposited, his head nods back and forth, stamped "Germany," c1920 .... **425.00**

Autograph, Martin Luther King, Jr., 11" x 14" photograph, sgd "with best wishes Martin Luther King" **3,220.00**

Bank, 4-3/4" l, 3-1/4" w, 10" h, Thrifty Tom's Jigger, litho tin windup, Strauss Corp, orig box **4,025.00**

Bell, 8-1/4" h, Majolica, figural, small black girl, finger to her chin, pink dress, blue handkerchief cap **1,150.00**

Book

- *George Washington Carver, An American Biography,* Rackham Colt, 1943, ex-library copy **5.00**
- *Who's Who in Colored America,* Volume I, J. Joseph Boris, ed., New York, 1927, first edition, portrait plates, small 4to, orig cloth **375.00**
- *Women of Achievement,* Benjamin Brawley, Woman's American Baptist Home Mission Society, 1919, portrait plates, small 8vo, orig cloth .. **375.00**

Broadside, 1837, in English and French, adv sale of slaves and other Louisiana property..................................... **2,875.00**

Butler, 33-3/4" h, wooden silhouette of gentleman holding ashtray, white shirt, bow tie, red vest, black tails, yellow pants, white spats, silver on copper ash tray with Heintz Art Metal touch mark **360.00**

Alarm clock, advertising Louisiana Molasses, D. B. Scully Co. Syrup Co., Chicago, Ill, Pickaninny with green "moving eyes," yellow and red bow tie, copyright 1938, **$125**. Photo courtesy of Sky Hawk Auctions.

Chalkboard, Black Nancy Coal **260.00**

Cloth doll, uncut, Aunt Jemima...... **80.00**

Coffee can, Luzianne..................... **75.00**

Cookie jar

- Mammy, Brayton Laguna **325.00**
- Mammy, Japan **700.00**
- Mammy, Weller, holding watermelon **2,700.00**
- Watermelon choir girl, Pearl China **700.00**

Creamer and sugar, Mammy, Weller.. **850.00**

Doll

- 18" h, Mammy, stuffed cloth, hand-embroidered features, red trimmed dress, blue and white cap, wear, damage **220.00**
- 20" h, Golliwog, velveteen face, hands, and feet, applied felt eyes and mouth, inked nose, yellow checked shirt, golden crepe pants, red braid trim, removable gray and white checked wool jacket, c1930, some wear and soil **460.00**

Doorstop, Little Black Sambo, cast iron **550.00**

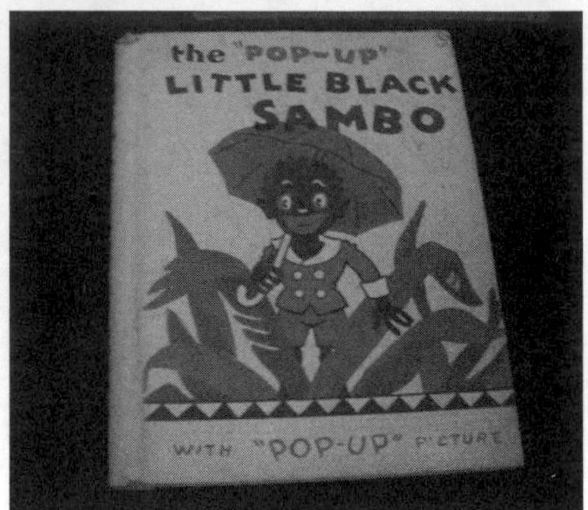

Children's book, Little Black Sambo, pop-up type, yellow cover, **$45**.

Ephemera

Certificate of Freedom, for Thomas Chambers, resident of New York City, September 1814, partly printed document, sgd, small folio, docketed on verso.......... **950.00**

Depositions concerning slave trade by sloop *Fanny* between Africa and North America, Oct 8, 1801, 17 pgs, 9-1/2" x 7-1/2".......... **550.00**

Notice, *The Charleston Daily Courier*, Jan. 5, 1858, regarding issuing of slave badges, giving prices for various trades.......... **1,380.00**

Receipt, "Negro Apprenticeship 2/6," printed, "Bought of the Anti-Slavery Society, Office, No. 18, Aldermanbury," (England) signed and dated by Francis Wedgwood, Society seal, dated 1838.......... **490.00**

Flour sack, Daddy Dollar **75.00**

Game, Shasteen Hot Dog **425.00**

Little Golden Book, *Little Black Sambo* **25.00**

Match and cigarette holder, wall mounted

Adv, Green's August Flower, Boschee's German Syrup, diecut cardboard, unused, 7-1/2" w, 4-1/2" w.......... **825.00**

Realistic features on sculpted man's face, cigarette compartment, raised ridged striking surface, imp "Chelsea Keramics/Robertson & Sons," 6" l **1,210.00**

Perfume bottle, 4-3/4" to 6" h, Golliwogg, stylized faces, black and brown hair covering stoppers, bulbous frosted glass body, painted white collar, black round feet, raised maker's mark for DeVigny, one with partial paper label, c1919, price for three-pc set.......... **575.00**

Pinback button, 7/8" d, Aunt Jemima, "I'se In Town Honey!" 1896, orig backpaper with maker's name "Duryea & Co.".......... **85.00**

Print

10" x 13", N. Currier, NY, lithograph, titled "Washington at Mount Vernon-1797," shows Washington on horseback conversing with two black field hands, framed **295.00**

13-1/4" x 9-3/4", litho, *I'm Not to Blame for Being White Sir,* young white child holding out her hand for coins while passing stranger places coins in hands of black child, c1850, heavily toned.......... **290.00**

A rare grouping of Aunt Jemima paper dolls saw active bidding and brought **$1,495** at Jackson's International July 23-24, 2003 Postcard & Ephemera Auction in Cedar Falls, Iowa.

Sculpture, 15" l, 7" w, 12" h, chalkware, hp, three Black Boys peering over fence into watermelon patch, copyright Jan 1898 by J. Mardi, Boston, MA.......... **460.00**

Slave tag, copper, 1824, made by John J LaFar, Charleston, SC, silversmith **2,415.00**

Souvenir Spoon

Dallas, enameled scene in bowl with three black boys and cotton bales **1,100.00**

Tennessee, 1906, three blacks on watermelon background, 5-3/4" l **230.00**

Spice set, F & F, Aunt Jemima.......... **650.00**

Syrup pitcher, Mammy, Weller **425.00**

Puzzle, Amos and Andy, Pepsodent premium, **$90**. Photo courtesy of Sky Hawk Auctions.

Textile, printed, 32-1/2" x 42", showing Little Black Sambo and tiger, earth tones of red, green, and dark brown, tan linen ground, folded, sewn seam with red ink label "WPA Handicraft Project #10235, Milwaukee, Wisconsin, Sponsored by Milwaukee County and Milwaukee State Teachers College, c1935-43 .... **1,350.00**

Tin, Mazawattee Tea **900.00**

Tobacco jar, German.......... **275.00**

Toy

Folk art type, 3-1/2" h, turn knob and fully animated hand carved figure cuts watermelon, tips head, opens mouth and brings watermelon slice forward, Kobee.......... **260.00**

Jazzbo Jim, litho tin wind-up, Lehmann **1,350.00**

Blown Three Mold

History: The Jamestown colony in Virginia introduced glassmaking into America. The artisans used a "free-blown" method.

For more information, see *Warman's Glass*, 4th edition.

Blowing molten glass into molds was not introduced into America until the early 1800s. Blown three-mold glass used a pre-designed mold that consisted of two, three, or more hinged parts. The glassmaker placed a quantity of molten glass on the tip of a rod or tube, inserted it into the mold, blew air into the tube, waited until the glass cooled, and removed the finished product. The three-part mold is the most common and lends its name to this entire category.

The impressed decorations on blown-mold glass usually are reversed, i.e., what is raised or convex on the outside will be concave on the inside. This is useful in identifying the blown form.

By 1850, American-made glassware was relatively common. Increased demand led to large factories and the creation of a technology, which eliminated the smaller companies.

Bowls, colorless, one Diamond Diaper and Sunburst-in-Square patterns with rayed base, other with Diamond Diaper pattern and base with diamond and ray designs, both with folded rims, eastern US, early 19th C, minor scratches, 8-1/8" d, 8-3/4" d, **$450**. Photo courtesy of Skinner, Inc.

Bowl, 5-1/2" d, 2" h, ftd, amber, shallow bowl, thick foot, folded rim **3,740.00**
Celery vase, colorless, Pittsburgh, McKearin GV-21 .... **650.00**
Condiment bottle
- 3-3/4" h, colorless, wide mouth, McKearin GIII-4 .... **95.00**
- 4-3/4" h, colorless, flat waffle stopper, McKearin GIII-27 .... **115.00**

Creamer, 4-1/4" h, colorless, faint bluish tint, applied handle with rigaree, McKearin GIII-26 .... **600.00**
Decanter
- 7-1/4" h, olive with trace of amber, McKearin GIII-16, minor wear, tiny open blisters.......................... **525.00**
- 9" h, colorless, slightly undersize wheel stopper, McKearin GIII-16 .... **150.00**
- 10-1/2" h, colorless, faint bluish tint, wheel stopper, McKearin GIII-19 .... **95.00**
- 11" h, colorless, Baroque, hollow stopper, McKearin GV-8.......... **95.00**
- 11-1/4" h, colorless, Baroque, oversize wheel stopper, McKearin GIV-7 .... **125.00**

Dish, 5" d, 1-1/4" h, colorless, folded rim, McKearin GIII-20 .... **175.00**
Flip glass, colorless, 6" h, McKearin GII-18.. **125.00**
Hat
- 2" h, colorless, McKearin GIII-7 .... **115.00**
- 2-1/8" h, colorless with faint amethyst tint, McKearin GIII-8 .... **115.00**

Ink, 2-1/4" d, 1-1/2" h, olive amber, McKearin GIII-29, minor wear **145.00**

Three tumblers, colorless, each tumbler with molded patterns including Diamond Diaper, Sunburst, and Sunburst-in-square designs, eastern US, early 19th C, one with rim chips, 3-1/4" to 3-3/8", **$360**. Photo courtesy of Skinner, Inc.

Pan
- 4-5/8" d, 1-1/2" h, light yellow, folded rim, sloped sides, attributed to Kent, OH, two pot stones................ **700.00**
- 7" d, colorless, folded rim, McKearin GII-16 .... **145.00**
- 10" d, 2-1/2" h, light golden amber, swirled ribs, folded rim, attributed to Kent, OH, few pot stones, small broken blisters....................... **110.00**

Salt, basket shape, colorless........ **120.00**
Tumbler, 2-7/8" h, colorless, McKearin GIII-8.. **200.00**
Vinegar bottle, cobalt blue, ribbed, orig stopper, McKearin GI-7 .... **285.00**
Whiskey glass, 2-3/8" h, colorless, applied handle, McKearin GII-18.. **285.00**

Bohemian Glass

History: The once independent country of Bohemia, now a part of the Czech Republic, produced a variety of fine glassware: etched, cut, overlay, and colored. Its glassware, which first appeared in America in the early 1820s, continues to be exported to the U.S. today.

For more information, see *Warman's Glass*, 4th edition.

Bohemia is known for its "flashed" glass that was produced in the familiar ruby color, as well as in amber, green, blue, and black. Common patterns include Deer and Castle, Deer and Pine Tree, and Vintage.

Most of the Bohemian glass encountered in today's market is from 1875 to 1900. Bohemian-type glass also was made in England, Switzerland, and Germany.

Reproduction Alert.

Atomizer bottle, 7" h, cylindrical, ruby flashed, white cased, three roundels, two enamel dec with florals, and one with two girls in Bohemian costumes, in cut surrounds, guilloche and leaf tip gilt metal neck mounted with round stopper, late 19th C, hairline, lacking bulb.. **195.00**
Bowl, 6" d, green ground, random ruby threading, c1910 .... **175.00**
Claret jug, 13" h, cranberry glass body and stopper, cast pewter base, frame, and handle as serpent with maidenhead on back, Northwind below, lion's heads with rings in mouth at waist **1,800.00**
Compote, 3-1/2" h, Pallme Konig, green irid ground, random crimson threading, set in three-ftd metal frame **325.00**
Decanters, pr
- 7-1/4" h, cranberry flashed, cut-to-clear panels, gilt enamel dec with rocaille scrolls, mushroom stoppers, star cut base, late 19th/early 20th C **350.00**
- 14" h, yellow flashed overlay on clear, engraved oriental scenic deco, sterling silver tops, matching overlay stoppers, pr, both ground at base, int. staining **300.00**

Goblet, 6-3/4" h, white and cranberry overlay, thistle form bowl, six teardrop panels alternately enameled with floral bouquets and cut with blocks of diamonds, faceted knob and spreading scalloped foot, gilt trim **600.00**

Cordial set, decanter with four matching wines, ruby flashed, grape and foliage etched decoration, matching tray, **$375**.

Lamp base, 20-1/4" h, cranberry flashed and white cased, ovoid font over bowl-form neck, on flared slender baluster stem and spreading foot, cut with circles throughout, and enamel dec with floral sprays, gilt metal base, electrified, late 19th/early 20th C **100.00**
Lamp shade, 7-3/4" h, 3-1/4" d, dimpled conical shape, irid green, several minor chips around fitter rims, price for pr **425.00**
Miniature, mantel luster, 3-1/2" h, cobalt blue, enameled florals on gilt ground, four cut crystal pendants...................... **150.00**
Rose bowl, 4" h, topaz, enameled figure of man drinking, c1900................. **115.00**

Decanter, amber panels, etched baskets of flowers and scrolls, 800 silver band at rim and collar, matching glass stopper, 8" h, **$225**. Photo courtesy of Joy Luke Auctions.

Urn, cov, 15-3/4" h, colorless, paneled bell-shaped body, tapered octagonal lid with stepped octagonal finial, short baluster stem on octagonal foot, star cut base, late 19th C, price for pr **750.00**

Vase

3-1/2" h, pink opalescent, irid finish, c1910 .... **90.00**

3-3/4" h, Pallme Konig, gray ground, light irid finish, dec with heavy random crimson threading, c1910 .... **290.00**

5" d, green ground, irid finish, c1900 .... **75.00**

5" h, irid textured amber ground, Art Nouveau stemmed flowers, c1920, some loss to silver dec........... **115.00**

5-3/4" h, sculptured drape pattern, gray ground, green oil spot dec, irid finish, c1920......................... **225.00**

6-1/2" h, green oil spot irid finish, c1900 .... **175.00**

8" h, Art Nouveau baluster form, slender neck, enamel dec, stylized wildflowers, gilt details, marked "Turin-Teplitz, Amphora Work Reissner," early 20th C.......... **460.00**

8" h, enameled satin glass, sgd "Fritz Hocker," c1900...................... **400.00**

8" h, Pohl, green translucent body, light irid finish, polychrome enameled daffodil with distant village dec, c1895 .... **575.00**

8-5/8" h, flared rim, double bulbed body, irid red glass, blue-gold irid pulled wavy band dec, polished pontil, few minor scratches **1,150.00**

Four ruby flashed cut and etched glass decanters: three decorated with grapes and leaves, one cut back to clear, four stemmed cordials, **$375**. Photo courtesy of Joy Luke Auctions.

9-1/2" h, inverted rim, tapering body, flaring at base, green irid glass **275.00**

10" h, Prussian blue, applied amber stemmed flowers, amber rigaree at rim, amber scrolled feet **175.00**

10-1/2" h, ruffled rim, tapering body, bulbed ftd base, applied green irid trailing prunts at center **300.00**

13-1/2" h, tricorn rim, hexagonal body, irid translucent amber glass, green irid pulled wavy band dec, large polished pontil.............. **260.00**

Books

History: Collecting books is a popular segment of the antiques marketplace. Collectors of books are rewarded with interesting titles, exquisite illustrations, as well as fascinating information and stories. The author, printer, and publisher, as well as the date of the printing, can increase the value of almost any book. Watch for interesting paintings on the fore-edge of early books.

Adams, Adam, *Why the Chisholm Trail Forks & Other Tales of the Cattle Country*, ed by Wilson Hudson, illus Malcom Thurgood, autographed by Adams, Austin Univ Press, 1965 .... **25.00**

Alexander, William, Earl of Stirling, *Recreation with the Muses,* Tho. Harper, London, 1637, title within woodcut architectonic border, 326 pgs, folio, mid-19th C gilt paneled calf with arabesque centerpiece on covers by Francis Bedford, worn.............................. **260.00**

Audubon, John James, *Viviparous Quadrupeds of North America,* New York, 1854... **10,000.00**

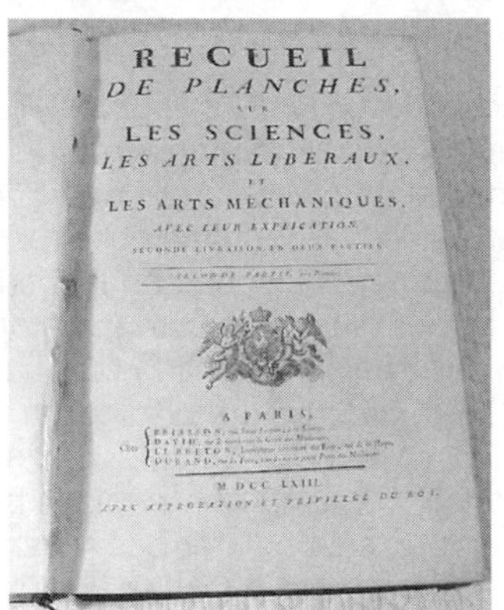

Recueil de Planches Sur Les Sciences et Les Arts, 1763, leather bound, **$1,300**. Photo courtesy of Wiederseim Associates, Inc.

Baskerville, John, *The Book of Common Prayer,* with *Psalter* **or** *Psalms of David,* for B. Dod, 1760, large 8vo, contemporary dark green morocco handsomely gilt with floral border around center lozenge composed of ornamental tools on covers, urn and ornamental tools on spine....................................... **920.00**

Calton, Izaak, *The Complete Angler,* Charles Cotton, London and New York, 1897... **550.00**

Cooper, J. C., *The Long Arm of Lee: The History of the Artillery of the Army of Northern Virginia,* 1915, Oxford Univ Press, dj... **65.00**

Crabbe, George, *The News-Paper: A Poem,* J. Dodsley, London, 1785, 29 pgs, 19th C boards, full length roan lettering piece, contents toned, FE **230.00**

Crane, Walter, *Walter Crane Toy Books,* illus, Routledge, Shilling series, 5 volumes, c1870-90 .... **425.00**

Defoe, Daniel, *The Dyet of Poland, A Satyr,* printed at Dantzick, first edition, 1705, 60 pgs, small 4to, 18th C marbled boards, modern morocco back, contents browned, outer margins trimmed **350.00**

Dodsley, Robert, editor, *A Collection of Poems by Several Hands,* London, J. Hughes, 1748-58, six volumes, 8vo, contemporary calf gilt with red morocco lettering pieces, spine ends chipped, joints reinforced but cracked or starting **100.00**

Fenelon, Francois de Salignac de la Mothe, *Treatise on the Education of Daughters,* Albany, 1806................. **30.00**

Fielding, Henry, *Amelia,* London, A. Millar, 1752, first edition, integral ad leaf at end of Volume 2, four volumes, 12 mo, modern beige calf gilt with morocco lettering pieces............................. **490.00**

Finch, C., The Gamut and Time-Table in Verse For the Instruction of Children, C. Finch, first half 19th C...................... **35.00**

Finley, Anthony, A New General Atlas, Philadelphia, 1824, first edition **6,000.00**

Gay, John, *The Shepherd's Week, In Six Pastorals,* London, Ferd. Burleigh, 1714, first edition, seven full-page etched illus by Louis Du Guernier, 8vo, modern 1/2 calf... **865.00**

Godwin, William, *Things as They Are; or The Adventures of Caleb Williams,* London, B. Crosby, 1794, first edition, three volumes, 12mo, contemporary marbled boards with red morocco lettering, spines darkened, occasional light browning, armorial bookplates and signatures of SC rice planter Charles Izard Manigault (1795-1874)...... **1,840.00**

Goldsmith, Oliver, *The Good Natur'd Man: A Comedy,* W. Griffin, London, 1768, 8vo, olive morocco gilt by Riviere & Son, FE, two-page epilogue, prologue by Samuel Johnson, half title missing, spine slightly faded, front joint cracked, contents washed **320.00**

Howell, William, *An Institution of General History; or The History of the World,* second edition with large additions, London, Thomas Bassett, 1680-80, four volumes in three, folio, modern 1/4 morocco **435.00**

Hoyle, Edmond, *Mr. Hoyle's Games of Whist, Quadrille, Piquet, Chess, and Back-Gammon, Complete,* Thomas Osborne, London, 1757, 11th ed, 208

pgs, 12 mo, half tan calf gilt by Ramage, sgd by Hoyle and Osborne, extremities rubbed....... **250.00**

Hume, David, *The History of England,* London, A. Millar, 1754-59-62, six volumes, 4to, contemporary calf gilt with morocco lettering pieces, few joints cracked....... **980.00**

Johnson, Samuel, *Irene, A Tragedy,* London, R. Dodsley and M. Cooper, 1749, first edition, 8vo, joints rubbed **865.00**

Milton, John, *Paradise Lost, Paradise Regain'd*, Birmingham, John Baskerville for J. and R. Tonson, London, 1760, together, two volumes, large 8vo, contemporary mottled calf, rebacked **575.00**

Nabbes, Thomas, *The Bride, A Comedie,* R. H. for Laurence Blaikenlocke, London, 1640, late 19th/early 20th C navy morocco with gilt floral corner pieces on covers, contents washed with residual darkening, margins trimmed, lacks initial blank and final license leaf, 34 of 36 leaves....... **375.00**

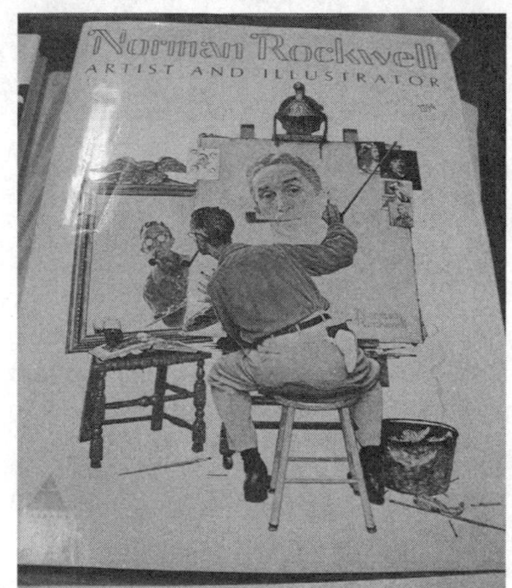

Norman Rockwell, Artist and Illustrator, white cover with classic self portrait illustration, Harry N. Abrams, 1970, original dustjacket, **$20**.

Parker, Richard and Sam. Briscoe, *The Marriage-Hater Match'd: A Comedy,* Sir Thomas D'Urfey, London, 1692, later 19th C mottled sheep gilt, spine ends worn, joints cracked, margins trimmed, FE, bookplates....... **175.00**

Platt, Ward, *The Frontier, A Frontier Town Three Months Old*, Jennings & Graham, Young People's Missionary Movement, 1908, color fold-out maps, illus **18.00**

Prior, Matthew, *When the Cat's Away, the Mice May Play: A Fable*, Humbly inscribed to Dr. Sw—t, attributed to, A. Baldin, London, 1712, FE, folio, unbound, paper toned, cloth folding case, bookplate....... **460.00**

Raffald, Elizabeth, A. Millar, W. Law, and R. Cater, *The Experienced English Housekeeper, for the Use and Ease of Ladies, Housekeepers, Cooks, etc., New Edition,* London, 1793, engraved frontispiece portrait, three folding engraved plates of table settings, 397 pgs, 8vo, spine worn, ends chipped, covers detached, scattered minor foxing **140.00**

Sack, Albert, *Fine Points of Furniture,* Crown Publishers, 1950, hard cover, minor edge wear **140.00**

Salmon, Thomas, *A Critical Essay concerning Marriage...*to which is added, *An Historical Account of the Marriage Rites and Ceremonies of the Greeks and Romans, and Our Saxon Ancestors, and of Most Nations of the World of this Day*, London, Charles Rovington, 1724, first edition, 8vo, early 19th C 1/2 calf, binding broken, bookplates....... **320.00**

Shakespeare, William, *The Famous History of the Life of King Henry the Eight(h)*, extracted from the second folio, London, 1632, modern cloth, calf lettering piece, some foxing and minor stains, 18th C owner's signature on last page **460.00**

Swift, Jonathan, *A Tale of a Tub...*to which is added *An Account of a Battle between the Ancient and Modern Books in St. James's Library,* fifth edition with author's apology and explanatory notes, London, John Nutt, 1710, first illus edition, eight engraved plates, 344 pgs, 8vo, modern 1/2 calf with morocco lettering piece, spine faded **375.00**

Toland, John, *A New Edition of Toland's History of the Druids: with An Abstract of His Life and Writings,* Montrose, 1814, 8vo contemporary cloth, rebacked, repaired, bookplates **260.00**

Ward, John, *The Lives of the Professors of Gresham College,* to which is prefixed, *The Life of the Founder, Sir Thomas Gresham,* London, John Moore for the author, 1740, first edition, five engraved plates, 156 pgs, folio, late 18th C/early 19th C, 1/2 calf, morocco lettering piece, rebacked, orig backstamp **230.00**

Bottles, General

History: Cosmetic bottles held special creams, oils, and cosmetics designed to enhance the beauty of the user. Some also claimed, especially on their colorful labels, to cure or provide relief from common ailments.

A number of household items, e.g., cleaning fluids and polishes, required glass storage containers. Many are collected for their fine lithographed labels.

Mineral water bottles contained water from a natural spring. Spring water was favored by health-conscious people between the 1850s and 1900s.

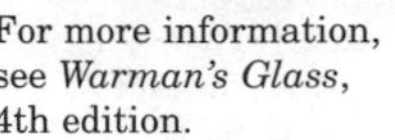

For more information, see *Warman's Glass*, 4th edition.

For more information, see *Warman's Americana & Collectibles*, 10th edition.

Nursing bottles, used to feed the young and sickly, were a great help to the housewife because of their graduated measure markings, replaceable nipples, and the ease with which they could be cleaned, sterilized, and reused.

Beverage

Arny & Shinn, Georgetown, D. C., "This Bottle Is Never Sold," soda water, squat cylindrical, yellow ground, applied heavy collared mouth, smooth base, half pink, professionally cleaned **150.00**

Booth & Co., Sacramento, emb anchor, pint, 1890-1903, swirled haze **900.00**

From Wine House Liquours & Cigars, Reno, Nev, wheat tint, half-pint, 1905-18 .... **1,100.00**

Jesse Moore & Co, Louisville, KY, G. H. Moore Old Bourbon Rye Moore Hunt & Co. Sole agents, emb antlers, pint, banded, double roll collar, 1878-82, 7-3/8" with double roll collar **5,500.00**

Ludlow, 8-1/4" h, amber, faint olive tone, applied lip....... **330.00**

Rum, unidentified maker

- 10-1/2" h, olive amber, globular, crude rolled lip, attributed to New England, 19th C, minor imperfections **650.00**
- 16-3/4" h, amber, one flattened side, eastern US, 19th C, minor imperfections **550.00**

Sarimento, M. R., soda, Union Glass Works, Phila, teal....... **2,200.00**

Squarza, V, soda, blue, c1863, crude top, lots of whittle, bubbles **8,500.00**

Thos Taylor & Co., Virginia, Nevada, medium to deep reddish-chocolate color, c1874-80, few scratches....... **4,400.00**

Whiskey

- Flora Temple, amber, pint, racehorse, faint double impression, small broken blisters, 8-1/2" h....... **400.00**
- W A Gaines & Co's. H.P. Hynds The Capitol Old Crow Whiskey Cheyenne, WY, screw top, ground lip, half-pint, known as Defender shape **210.00**

Wharton's Whiskey 1850, Whitney Glass Works, NY, honey amber, quart, applied handle, 10" h 450.00

Olive-amber, quart, blown, two applied rings on neck, side etched "BEST No 2," America, early 19th C, surface scratches, 10-7/8" h, **$950**. Photo courtesy of Skinner, Inc.

Blown

7-1/2" h, olive green, globular, six lengths of applied rigaree, applied lip, minor surface wear, open blister **1,875.00**
9" h, deep olive green, globular, white and pale blue spatter on neck and shoulders, applied seal with horse "1830" and "DC" with backwards D, applied lip, several broken blisters on white spots **3,300.00**
9" h, olive green club, high kick up, painted portrait of "Michiel de Ruiter Luit Admiral van Holland," yellow shield, red rampant lion, applied lip, minor flaking to paint **1,100.00**
10" h, olive green, elongated club, some white spatter around shoulders, four lengths of applied rigaree, some roughness, few open blisters at white spots **1,815.00**
10" h, olive green, ovoid globular, four lengths of applied rigaree, seal with swordsman and "D McC 1825" with backwards D, applied lip, minor surface wear, open blister **3,450.00**
13" h, grass green, rolled lip, smooth pontil on bottom, broken bubbles **200.00**

Demijohn

16-1/2" h, amber, applied lip, pot stones, blisters, attributed to Zanesville **440.00**
17-1/2" h, 18" l, olive green, watermelon shape, raised spout, applied rim, whittled mold **385.00**

Household

Hair balsam, Henley's Royal Hair Balsam, applied top, light aqua, 1870s, 7" **475.00**
Ink, Waterman's, paper label with bottle of ink, wooden bullet shaped case, orig paper label, 4-1/4" h **10.00**
Sewing Machine Oil, Sperm Brand, clear, 5-1/2" h **5.00**
Shoe Polish, Everett & Barron Co., oval, clear, 4-3/4" **5.00**

A.M. Bininger & Co. 19 Broad St. N.Y. Distilled In 1848, Old Kentucky Bourbon 1849 Reserve, barrel shape, applied top, tubular open pontil, **$240**. Photo courtesy of American Bottle Auctions.

Mineral or spring water

Alburgh A. Spring, VT, cylindrical, golden yellow, applied sloping collared mouth with ring, smooth base, quart **800.00**
Caladonia Spring Wheelock VT, cylindrical, golden amber, applied sloping collared mouth with ring, smooth base, quart **130.00**
Gettysburgh Katalysine Water, yellow olive, applied sloping collared mouth with ring, smooth base, quart **200.00**
Middletown Healing Springs, Grays & Clark, Middletown, VT, cylindrical, yellow apricot amber, applied sloping collared mouth with ring, smooth base, quart **1,200.00**
Saratoga (star) Springs, cylindrical, dark olive green, applied sloping collared mouth with ring, smooth base, quart **300.00**
Vermont Spring, Saxe & Co., Sheldon, VT, cylindrical, citron, applied sloping collared mouth with ring, smooth base, quart **600.00**

Nursing

Acme, clear, lay-down, emb **65.00**
Cala Nurser, oval, clear, emb, ring on neck, 7-1/8" h **10.00**
Empire Nursing Bottle, bent neck, 6-1/2" h **50.00**
Mother's Comfort, clear, turtle type **25.00**

Brass

History: Brass is a durable, malleable, and ductile metal alloy consisting mainly of copper and zinc. The height of its popularity for utilitarian and decorative art items occurred in the 18th and 19th centuries.

Reproduction Alert: Many modern reproductions are being made of earlier brass forms, especially such items as buckets, fireplace equipment, and kettles.

Additional Listings: Bells, Candlesticks, Fireplace Equipment, and Scientific Instruments.

Foot warmer, hexagonal, wedding presentation type, pierced and embossed body, hearts, flowers, and busts of man and woman, Dutch, 18th C, 8-1/2" d, 7" h, **$2,530**. Photo courtesy of Pook & Pook.

Andirons, pr
18" h, ring-turned columns, scalloped cabriole legs, ball feet **360.00**
26-1/2" h, small urn tops over scrolled capitals, tapered urn shaped columns, lobed bases, cabriole legs, 20th C **220.00**
Astral lamp, 23" h, Corinthian column supports font marked "Cornelius & Co. Philad, Patent April 18th 1843," ring of cut glass prisms, no shade, electrified **440.00**
Bed warmer
43" l, floral engraved lid, well turned birch handle with areas of orig red paint **275.00**
45-1/2" l, engraved scrolling and flowers on lid, spun pan, turned cherry handle with chips and replaced pin **250.00**
Candle sconce
23" h, 17-1/2" d, detailed casting, eight medallions with figures divided by faces, round beveled glass mirror, three branches with single candle sockets **200.00**
23-1/4" h, 8" w, cast, beveled mirror backing with openwork floral medallions, urn crest flanked by two dolphins, two scrolled candle arms below **110.00**

Candlestick

4" x 4" base, 4-3/4" h, finely turned column, recessed circle on sq base **200.00**

5" h, short acorn shaped stem, octagonal base with split **220.00**

7" h, sq faceted bases, orig patina, unmarked Prairie School, bobeches missing **115.00**

12" h, faceted and beaded detail on stems, push-ups, octagonal base, pr, one leans slightly **215.00**

Capstan candlestick, 4-3/4" h, flared socket, raised rim, extractor holes, tooled base edge **750.00**

Carriage lamp, 18-1/2" h, two beveled panes of glass, one with vertical lines, removable tin candle socket, traces of red and black paint on tin sections, battered **110.00**

Chandelier, 25" d, 20" h, cast, eight scrolled arms with torch shaped ends, each with small electric socket, simulated candle coverings, 20th C **250.00**

Chestnut roaster, 18-3/4" l, oval, pierced hinged lid, long handle **120.00**

Pipe mold, American, 18th C, 10" l, **$575**. Photo courtesy of Pook & Pook.

Chimes, 18-1/2" w, 27-1/2" h, mahogany and rosewood frame, eight brass chimes, turned pilasters on either side, striker missing, 20th C............ **220.00**

Coal grate, 19-1/2" l, 10-1/4" d, 27" h, Neoclassical-style, late 19th C, back plate cast with scene of figures in revelry, grate with central horizontal bar over guillouche band, uprights with brass urn finials, rear plinth base, front tapered legs **175.00**

Coal hood, 21" l, 15-1/2" h, sheet brass, swing handle, additional support handle, matching scoop with old black paint on turned wooden handle, dents **200.00**

Compote, 10-3/4" d, 6" h, Champlevé, gilt brass, blue, red, yellow, green, and white enameling, pale cream colored onyx base with small stem with relief cast acanthus leaves, scalloped dish with pierced handles, stamped "France" on base............ **250.00**

Curio cabinet, 17-1/2" w, 9" d, 54" h, old patina, pedestal base with intricate shell and acanthus leaf designs, canted sides on case with three glass panels, padded burgundy cloth liner with button back, open top with 10 scalloped acanthus leaves around edge **550.00**

Plant stand, ornate tripod base, 33" h, **$200**. Photo courtesy of Joy Luke Auctions.

Dresser mirror, 11" w, 18" h, French, gilt brass, mirrored glass, scrolls, floral pots, and garlands dec, cracks, loss to silvering **525.00**

Figure, 31-1/2" h, Bodhisattva, dark patina, 10 arms, eight faces, single body, walnut block base **450.00**

Fireplace fender, 54-3/4" l, Rococo-style, 19th C, pierced center with tree flanked by rocaille follies, cartouches engraved with helmets on diapered ground, flanked by leaf scrolls **4,600.00**

Kettle stand, 16-1/2" w, 9" d, 7-1/2" h, pierced top, engraved peacocks, detailed cabriole legs, bird's claw feet, slightly bowed **250.00**

Snuff box, oval, three dials having Roman numerals and arrows for combination, hinged lid, 3-1/2" x 2-1/2", denting, brass button for opening detached, **$175**. Photo courtesy of Alderfer Auction Co.

Letter sealer, 2" l brass tube, 23 double-sided brass discs with various sentimental seals for wax, 19th C **100.00**

Mantle lamp, 16" h, double arms, brands of raised detail around urn tops, columns, bases, shell designs on either side of fonts, old patina, burner and shades missing, one font loose, price for pr **660.00**

Pan set, set of 10 graduated from 4-1/2" d, 10" l to 9-1/2" d, 20" l, spun brass, tubular wrought iron handles attached with copper rivets............ **660.00**

Plant stand, 14-1/2" d, 35-1/2" h, old gilding, round top with leaf drops and three scrolls, scrolled supports, leaves, and large flowers, eagle talon feet, lacquered **450.00**

Steam whistle, 2-1/2" d, 12" h, single chime, lever control **150.00**

Thermometer, ornate frame with mercury tube, bird in nest at top, fancy scrollwork at sides and base, Bradley & Hubbard, #3590, **$250**. Photo courtesy of Joy Luke Auctions.

Umbrella stand, 22-3/8" h, upright formed as tree trunk supporting rifle, bagged hare, and brace of pheasants, base formed as grassy glade with reclining hunting dog, early 20th C **300.00**

Wick trimmers, 5-1/4" l **125.00**

Bread Plates

History: Beginning in the mid-1880s, special trays or platters were made for serving bread and rolls. Designated "bread plates" by collectors, these small trays or platters can be found in porcelain, glass (especially pattern glass), and metals.

Bread plates often were part of a china or glass set. However, many glass companies made special plates that honored national heroes, commemorated historical or special events, offered a moral maxim, or supported a religious attitude. The subject matter appears either horizontally or vertically. Most of these plates are oval and ten inches in length.

Additional Listings: Pattern Glass.

Majolica

Apple and Pear, brown ground, minor wear rim............ **385.00**

Bamboo and Fern, cobalt blue, Wardles **395.00**

Give Us This Day Our Daily Bread, cobalt border and basket center, wheat handles **360.00**

Pineapple, cobalt blue center **440.00**

Milk glass, Wheat & Barley............ **70.00**

Mottos, pressed glass, clear

Be Industrious, handles, oval.. **50.00**

Rock of Ages, 12-7/8" l.......... **175.00**

Pattern glass: "Rock of Ages," oval, "The Last Supper," rectangular, **$70**. Photo courtesy of Joy Luke Auctions.

Waste Not Want Not **35.00**

Pattern glass, clear unless otherwise noted

Actress, Miss Nielson **80.00**
Beaded Grape, sq **35.00**
Cupid and Venus, amber **85.00**
Deer and Pine Tree, amber **110.00**
Good Luck **45.00**
Tennessee, colored jewels **75.00**

Silver

12-3/4" l, 8-1/4" w, oval, molded scroll rim and openwork scroll sides, molded foliate swags, Graff, Washbourne & Dunn, NY, early 20th C, approx 18 troy oz **635.00**
15" x 10-1/2", repousse, cartouches of courtship scene, imp German hallmarks and 800, c1920 ..... **920.00**

Souvenir and Commemorative

Old State House, sapphire blue **185.00**
Three Presidents, frosted center **95.00**
William J. Bryan, milk glass..... **65.00**

Bride's Baskets

History: A ruffled-edge glass bowl in a metal holder was a popular wedding gift between 1880 and 1910, hence the name "bride's basket." These bowls can be found in most glass types of the period. The metal holder was generally silver-plated with a bail handle, thus enhancing the basket image.

Over the years, bowls and bases became separated and married pieces resulted. If the base has been lost, the bowl should be sold separately.

For more information, see *Warman's Glass*, 4th edition.

Reproduction Alert: The glass bowls have been reproduced.

Note: Items listed below have a silver-plated (SP) holder unless otherwise noted.

Cased glass, pink, ruffled rim, silver-plated pedestal stand with handle, 9-1/2" d, 11-1/2" h, **$225**. Photo courtesy of Joy Luke Auctions.

8-1/4" w, sq, cased, deep rose and white ext., whit int., dragon, floral, and leaf dec, ruffled edge, Mt. Washington **675.00**

8-1/2" d, 12" h, amber, enameled berries and buds, SP holder.................. **1,195.00**

9" d bowl, 11-1/4" h silver plated holder, Crown Milano bowl, ruffled yellow top, int. leaf dec, holder with carved feet, two in-flight carved birds rests on handles, one bird needs reattaching **575.00**

9-1/2" d, 12" h, satin, deep pink ruffled bowl, white ext., marked "Nemasket Silver Co." SP holder **275.00**

9-3/4" h, opaline cased in pink, ruffled amber rim, married SP holder **150.00**

9-7/8" d, 3" h, 3-3/4" base, bowl only, peachblow, glossy finish, deep pink shading to pale............................. **250.00**

10" d, 11" h, Vasa Murrhina, outer amber layer, center layer with hundreds of cream-colored spots, random toffee-colored spots, dark veins, gold mica flakes, mulberry pink lining, crossed rod thorn handles **635.00**

10" w, sq, custard, melon ribbed, enameled daisies, applied Rubena crystal rim, twisted and beaded handle, ftd, emb SP frame, marked "Wilcox" **450.00**

10-1/2" h, peachblow, cased rose shading to pink ground, applied amber stem, green leaves, amber handle, four applied feet, some losses **200.00**

10-1/2" d, 12-1/2" h, sculptured Rubena verde vaseline shading to pink, yellow and green enameled flowers, Benedict SP holder **460.00**

10-3/4" d, 3-1/2" h, bowl only, overlay, heavenly blue, enameled white flowers, green leaves, white underside, ruffled **215.00**

Opalescent glass, pink, ruffled rim, lattice design, silver-plated basket stand, 10-1/2" d, 11" h, **$395**. Photo courtesy of Joy Luke Auctions.

11" d, 7-1/2" h, satin, light beige shading to orange ruffled bowl, hp pink, purple and yellow flowers, green leaves, raised gold outlines, blue int., sgd "Simpson, Hall, Miller Co. Quad Plate" holder **895.00**

11-1/8" d, 3-3/4" h, bowl only, satin, brown shaded to cream overlay, raised dots, dainty gold and silver flowers and leaves dec, ruffled **250.00**

11-1/4" h, opalescent Rubena verde, applied lime stepped flower feet, thorny twist handle, Victorian **425.00**

12" d, 7-1/2" h, white opaline, cased in pink, overall colorful enameled dec, emb Middletown plated holder, applied fruit handles, Victorian, minor losses **525.00**

12" d, 12" h, tricorn, blue fading to white shiny int., shiny white ext., SP holder **175.00**

13" w, 12-1/2" h, unfired Mt. Washington Burmese bowl, ruffled top, gold leaves, flower blossoms, stems, and pink tracery, purple crown mark, sgd SP holder with bird figural, some wear to gold on bowl int. **2,100.00**

Bristol Glass

History: Bristol glass is a designation given to a semi-opaque glass, usually decorated with enamel and cased with another color.

Initially, the term referred only to glass

For more information, see *Warman's Glass*, 4th edition.

made in Bristol, England, in the 17th and 18th centuries. By the Victorian era, firms on the Continent and in America were copying the glass and its forms.

Bowl, light blue, Cupid playing mandolin, gold trim **45.00**
Box, cov, 4-1/8" l, 2-3/4" d, 3-1/2" h, oblong, blue, gilt-metal mounts and escutcheon **550.00**
Cake stand, celadon green, enameled herons in flight, gold trim **135.00**
Candlesticks, pr, 7" h, soft green, gold band **75.00**
Decanter, 11-1/2" h, ruffled stopper, enameled flowers and butterfly **75.00**
Dresser set, two cologne bottles, cov powder jar, white, gilt butterflies dec, clear stoppers **75.00**

Vase, white body, blue accents at ruffles, gold, black, and pink floral decoration, 9" h, **$35.**

Ewer, 6-3/8" h, 2-5/8" d, pink ground, fancy gold designs, bands, and leaves, applied handle with gold trim **135.00**
Finger bowl, 4-3/8" d, blue, faceted sides, early 20th C, eight-pc set ... **500.00**
Hatpin holder, 6-1/8" h, ftd, blue, enameled jewels, gold dec **100.00**
Perfume bottle, 3-1/4" h, squatty, blue, gold band, white enameled flowers and leaves, matching stopper **100.00**
Puff box, cov, round, blue, gold dec **40.00**
Sweetmeat jar, 3" x 5-1/2", deep pink, enameled flying duck, leaves, blue flower dec, white lining, SP rim, lid, and bail handle.. **110.00**
Urn, 18" h, pink, boy and girl with lamp **550.00**
Vase, 10" h, frosted ruffled rim shading to brown base, hp and gold floral dec **130.00**

British Royalty Commemoratives

History: British commemorative china, souvenirs to commemorate coronations and other royal events, dates from the 1600s, with the early pieces being rather crude in design and form. With the development of transfer printing, c1780, the images on the wares more closely resembled the monarchs.

For more information, see *Warman's Glass*, 4th edition.

Few commemorative pieces predating Queen Victoria's reign are found today at popular prices. Items associated with Queen Elizabeth II and her children, e.g., the wedding of HRH Prince Andrew and Miss Sarah Ferguson and the subsequent birth of their daughter HRH Princess Beatrice, are common.

Some British Royalty commemoratives are easily recognized by their portraits of past or present monarchs. Some may be in silhouette profile. Royal symbols include crowns, dragons, royal coats of arms, national flowers, swords, scepters, dates, messages, and monograms.

Loving cup, 1952-1977, Elizabeth II Silver Jubilee, two handles, multicolored, majolica type, **$85.** Photo courtesy of Wiederseim Associates, Inc.

Autograph

George II, letter, sgd as Prince of Wales, in French, two pages, 4to, Leicester House, Jan. 11/22, 1723, to Madame Marygrove, sympathies over loss of relation **1,200.00**
William IV, document, sgd as king, one page 4to, Bushby House, Sept. 18, 1827, appoints David Davis as his personal surgeon, red wax seal next to signature.................... **350.00**

Bank, Coronation, 6-5/8" h, Syndeham & McOustra, England, ornately detained, emb busts in center, England, c1911 .... **200.00**
Bottle opener, King Edward, brass, coronation souvenir **8.50**
Box, cov, Elizabeth the Queen Mother, 1980, 80th Birthday, color portrait, Crown Staffordshire, 4" d **90.00**
Cup and saucer, Elizabeth II, portrait flanked by flags, coronation, pairs of flags inside cup and on saucer, marked "Alfred Meakin England," 3" h x 3-1/4" d cup, 6" d saucer **55.00**
Drinking glass, 3-3/4" h, clear, red and blue illus of George VI and Elizabeth I, 1939 Canadian visit......................... **24.00**
Ephemera, 6-1/2" x 9-3/4" folded sheet, text of Queen Victoria's message to Mrs. Garfield as Pres Garfield's Memorial, white sheet, black memoriam graphics including cross and stack of stones, each representing a state of the Union, brief condolence message from Queen, eulogy verse by Wellesley Bradshaw, dated Sept. 1881............................. **25.00**
Figure, 5-1/4" h, Elizabeth I, carved ivory, lower section of skirt hinged to reveal triptych of Queen and Sir Walter Raleigh, Continental, 19th C, hairlines **550.00**
Jug, Victoria, Jubilee, 1887, Doulton **185.00**
Lithophane, cup, crown, and cypher, 2-3/4" h, Alexandra, 1902 .... **195.00**
Loving cup, Elizabeth II and Philip, 1972 Silver Wedding Anniversary, Paragon, 3" h.. **175.00**

Mug, Prince of Wales, gold and black decoration, "To Commemorate the Investiture of His Royal Highness Prince Charles as Prince of Wales, at Caernarnon on 1st July 1969," designed by Richard Guyatt, Wedgwood of Etruria & Barlston, Made in England, **$65.** Photo courtesy of Wiederseim Associates, Inc.

Mug

Edward VIII, Coronation, 1937, sepia portrait of king flanked by multicolored flags, reverse

with Union Jack and Flag of commonwealth, flanking names of some of the nations, topped by crown, gold trim, 2-1/2" h, 2-1/2" d, crest mark and "Empire England" **50.00**

Elizabeth II, Coronation, portrait of Queen facing left, "Coronation of Her Majesty Queen Elizabeth" on reverse, gold trim, 3" h, 3" d, crown and "Radfords Bone China Made in England" mark........ **55.00**

Pinback button

King George VI and Queen Elizabeth I, black and white photos, tiny green maple leaf border, red inscription "Welcome to Canada," orig back paper label, 1939........ **20.00**

Queen Elizabeth and Prince Philip, red, white, and blue cello, center black and white portraits, 1951 visit to Canada, waxed fabric red, white, and blue ribbons........ **20.00**

Paperweight, large central cane marked "ER II 1953," surrounded by concentric red, white, and blue millefiori, 3" d, **$175**. Photo courtesy of Alderfer Auction Co.

Pitcher, 8-3/4" h, marriage of Princess Charlotte and Prince Leopold, c1816, relief dec, double scroll handle, Pratt ware, minor enamel loss........ **1,265.00**

Plate

Edward VII and Alexandra, 1902 Coronation, blue and white, Royal Copenhagen, 7" d........ **200.00**

George VI and Elizabeth, Canadian visit, 1939, word "Canada" in relief under portraits in center, "King George IV, Queen Elizabeth, 1939" in relief on rim........ **95.00**

Postcard, Royal Visit to New Zealand, 1953-54, 39" x 29", creased on folds, small tears........ **20.00**

Program, Prince of Wales Royal Investiture, July 1, 1969, glossy paper, 6-1/2" x 9"........ **12.00**

Snuffbox, 3" d, round, bronze, round, dark patina, angel riding lion with "Regent," reverse emb inscription "In record of the reign of George III" covered by sunburst and cross, visible on int., engraved paper bust and "H.R.H. George Augustus Frederick Prince Regent...Feb 1811"........ **2,100.00**

Teapot

Charlotte, 1817 In Memoriam, black and white dec, 6" h........ **275.00**

Victoria, 1897 Diamond Jubilee, color coat of arms, Aynsley... **225.00**

Trivet, brass, **$45**. Photo courtesy of Wiederseim Associates, Inc.

Tea set, 8-3/4" l cov teapot, creamer, cov sugar, manufactured for the coronation of Elizabeth II, 1953, applied white relief, solid royal blue ground, Wedgwood imp marks, chip on teapot finial........ **250.00**

Tin

Queen Elizabeth II, coronation, sq, Queen Elizabeth II on horseback, full view, marked "Sharp Assorted Toffee," stamped "Made In England by Edward Sharp & Sons Ltd. Of Maidstone Kent," 7" x 6" x 2", minor scratches and edge rubbing **40.00**

Prince of Wales, Yardley Invisible Talc for Men, Prince of Wales crest, "By Appointment to HM Queen Elizabeth II Purveyors of Soap Yardley and Co. Ltd.," 5" h...... **15.00**

View master reel set, Queen Elizabeth II coronation, 4-1/2" sq envelope, set of three color stereo view reels, orig fact leaflet for June 2, 1953 coronation **25.00**

Bronze

History: Bronze is an alloy of copper, tin, and traces of other metals. It has been used since Biblical times not only for art objects, but also for utilitarian wares. After a slump in the Middle Ages, the use of bronze was revived in the 17th century and continued to be popular until the early 20th century.

Notes: Do not confuse a "bronzed" object with a true bronze. A bronzed item usually is made of white metal and then coated with a reddish-brown material to give it a bronze appearance. A magnet will stick to it but not to anything made of true bronze.

A signed bronze commands a higher market price than an unsigned one. There also are "signed" reproductions on the market. It is important to know the history of the mold and the background of the foundry.

Bird sculpture, resting on clamshell, signed "Arson," converted to table lamp, 11" h, **$1,450**. Photo courtesy of Wiederseim Associates, Inc.

Basket, 10-1/4", trompe l'oeil, folded linen form, woven handle, applied florals and insects, Japanese, 19th C...... **350.00**

Bookends, pr, 9" h, daffodil silhouette, imp mark of G. Thew, 1928........ **225.00**

Box, chaise lounge form, topped with monkey on pillows, lid lifts to reveal erotic scene of man and woman with carved ivory features, gilt and polychrome dec, marble base, 20th C........ **1,495.00**

Bust, woman, sgd "E. Villanis," 19" h **800.00**

Candlesticks, pr, 13-1/2" h, simple form, slender stem leading to bulbous candle, slight bulb at the plain foot, sgd "JARVIE" **1,100.00**

Bookends, pair, terriers, marked "Copyr. 1929, PAL," 6" h, **$135**. Photo courtesy of Joy Luke Auctions.

Cannon, 17" l, well done scale replica, leaves, cast dolphins, armorial device with "1785," stamped "Franche" near touch hole, 6-3/4" h wooden carriage with wooden wheels and counterweight **330.00**

Charger, 12" d, doré, deeply cast geometric designs on rim, stamped "Tiffany Studios New York #1746," area of discoloration, minor edge dent..... **330.00**

Figure

4" h, Arabian Merchant, modeled as turbanned man crouching on straw mat, displaying rabbit, bird, fish, pineapples, and other produce, Viennese, cold painted, early 20th C **1,100.00**

4-3/8" l, sleeping chipmunk, tightly curled with tail over head, incised signature and impressed "Paul King Foundry" mark........ **590.00**

8-3/4" l, 6-5/8" h, Arabian Rug Seller, modeled as bearded man displaying carpet, Bergman Viennese maker's mark to underside, pseudonym "Namgreb," cold painted, early 20th C........ **600.00**

Incense burner, 22" h, Oriental, circular base with relief birds and foliage, center medallions, applied handles, old clock set into one side which has a loose hand, some damage, soldered restorations **525.00**

Censor, foo dog, standing, three-dimensional features, open mouth, removable section in back, 20" l, 21" h, loss to tip of mane, **$715**. Photo courtesy of Alderfer Auction Co.

Lamp, table, 27-3/4" h, Sinumbra, frosted glass shade with cut cherry and floral design, bronze standard with brown paint, electrified, minor chips to shade fitter rim........ **1,765.00**

Low bowl, 4" d, shape no. 537, sterling applied geometric designs, imp Heintz logo and "Sterling," c1915 .... **45.00**

Mirror, 5-3/8" d, Chinese, round, cast animals and birds in concentric circles, central animal with hole for hanging, worn back, polished surface........ **200.00**

Mortar, 5-3/4" h, cast, cylindrical, short animal head handles, molded with horizontal bands of scrolls over continuous band of medieval-style peasants and pilgrims, rim molded with "Petrus Uardenchein me fecit," Continental, 19th C........ **425.00**

Parade helmet, cast

15-3/8" l, 11-1/4" h, 19th C, depicting Hercules battling the hydra with cityscape in background, borders of military motifs and emperors **460.00**

Powder jar, figural bronze cold painted woman in bonnet, marble base, **$70**.

18" l, gladiator's, Continental-style, China, early 20th C, four-part hinged visor comprising two-piece pierced eye guard, over two-piece face guard cast as figures before prison gates, helmet with high relief battle scene, further Roman-style figures **690.00**

Pen vase, 3-1/2" h, gilt, cylindrical vessel, flared base, ribbed swirled design, unsigned, attributed to Tiffany Studios, NY........ **175.00**

Plaque, 10" h, two Satyrs and enamored nude in relief, gilt, 19th C **690.00**

Figure, standing peacock with long tail, cold painted, Bergmann, Austrian, 12" l, loss to comb, **$150**. Photo courtesy of Alderfer Auction Co.

Sculpture

A Startled Finch on a Perch, Ferdinand Pautrot, gold-green patina, sgd on base "F. Pautrot," 5" h **260.00**

Mounted Falconer, P. J. Mene, c1876, 29-1/4" h **3,200.00**

Pan feeding bear cubs, sgd "E. Fremiet," patinated, 21-1/2" l **2,100.00**

Slave girl, seated on bench, shackles on her wrists, skirt separate piece, sgd "E. Villanis," 10-1/2" h **350.00**

Smoking tray, 6-1/4" d, Doré finish, applied scrolling on ash bowl, cigar rests, matchbox holder, unmarked, c1910 .... **70.00**

Stable post finial, 15" h, cast, head of purebred horse, saddle, later polychrome over nickeled finish, early 20th C **520.00**

Standish, 16" l, retriever flanked by pair of foliate molded inkwells, oval verte antico marble base, French, early 20th C **445.00**

Statue, 8-1/2" l, 5-1/2" h, reclining lab, alert face, sgd "Doris Lindner"........ **700.00**

Weather station, barometer, clock, and mercury thermometer, ornate, 26" h, **$300**. Photo courtesy of Joy Luke Auctions.

Thermometer, 4-1/8" w, 8-1/4" h, Zodiac pattern, rich brown patina, glass thermometer, back sgd "Tiffany Studios New York 1014" **1,320.00**

Toothpick holder, 3-1/2" d, 3-3/4" h, top hat, dog head handled cane laying on tasseled footstool, round green marble base with black striations........ **150.00**

Tray, 9" d, band of hammered designs, marked "Apollo Studios, New York" c1910 .... **45.00**

Urn, 11-3/8" h, cast, black patinated, everted reeded rim, central band of classical figures, two short handles with male masks, fluted foot, sq black marble base, Classical-style, late 19th/early 20th C, price for pr **2,530.00**

Wall plaque, 21-1/4" d, shield-form, Classical Revival, raised and pointed center section, continuous battle scene, Continental, late 19th C........ **500.00**

BUFFALO POTTERY

History: Buffalo Pottery Co., Buffalo, New York, was chartered in 1901. The first kiln was fired in October 1903. Larkin Soap Company established Buffalo Pottery to produce premiums for its extensive mail-order business. Wares also were sold to the public by better department and jewelry stores. Elbert Hubbard and Frank Lloyd Wright, who designed the Larkin Administration Building in Buffalo in 1904, were two prominent names associated with the Larkin Company.

Early Buffalo Pottery production consisted mainly of semi-vitreous china dinner sets. Buffalo was the first pottery in the United States to successfully produce the Blue Willow pattern. Buffalo also made a line of hand-decorated, multicolored willow ware, called Gaudy Willow. Other early items include a series of game, fowl, and fish sets, pitchers, jugs, and a line of commemorative, historical, and advertising plates and mugs.

From 1908 to 1909 and again from 1921 to 1923, Buffalo Pottery produced the line for which it is most famous—Deldare Ware. The earliest of this olive green, semi-vitreous china displays hand-decorated scenes from English artist Cecil Aldin's *Fallowfield Hunt*. Hunt scenes were done only from 1908 to 1909. English village scenes also were characteristic of the ware and were used during both periods. Most pieces are artist signed.

In 1911, Buffalo Pottery produced Emerald Deldare, which used scenes from Goldsmith's *The Three Tours of Dr. Syntax* and an Art Nouveau-type border. Completely decorated Art Nouveau pieces also were made.

Abino, which was introduced in 1912, had a Deldare body and displayed scenes of sailboats, windmills, or the sea. Rust was the main color used, and all pieces were signed by the artist and numbered.

In 1915, the manufacturing process was modernized, giving the company the ability to produce vitrified china. Consequently, hotel and institutional ware became the main production items, with hand-decorated ware de-emphasized. The Buffalo firm became a leader in producing and designing the most-famous railroad, hotel, and restaurant patterns. These wares, especially railroad items, are eagerly sought by collectors.

In the early 1920s, fine china was made for home use. Bluebird is one of the patterns from this era. In 1950, Buffalo made its first Christmas plate. These were given away to customers and employees primarily from 1950 to 1960. However, it is known that Hample Equipment Co. ordered some as late as 1962. The Christmas plates are scarce in today's resale market.

The Buffalo China Company made "Buffalo Pottery" and "Buffalo China"—the difference being that one is semi-vitreous ware and the other vitrified. In 1956, the company was reorganized, and Buffalo China became the corporate name. Buffalo China was acquired by Oneida Ltd., Oneida, NY, in 1983. They had hoped to expand the china manufacturing facilities, but reports late in August of 2003 indicate that the current down turn in the economy may preclude that.

Marks: Blue Willow pattern is marked "First Old Willow Ware Mfg. in America."

Ewer, covered, green shaded ground, pink roses, blue flowers, green leaves, embossed scrolls, gold trim, **$115**.

Abino Ware

Candlestick, 9" h, sailing ships, 1913 .... **475.00**
Pitcher, 7" h, Portland Head Light **700.00**
Tankard, 10-1/2" h, sailing scene **900.00**

Advertising Ware

Jug, 6-1/4" h, blue and green transfer print, inscribed "The Whaling City Souvenir of New Bedford, Mass," whaling motifs, staining **355.00**
Mug, 4-1/2" h, Calumet Club **110.00**
Plate, 9-3/4" d, Indian Head Pontiac **55.00**
Platter, 13-1/2" l, US Army Medical Dept., 1943 .... **65.00**

Deldare

Bowl, 12" l, Ye Olden Days, c1908, small professionally repaired chip under rim **200.00**
Calling card tray, street scene **395.00**
Cereal bowl, 6" d, Fallowfield Hunt **295.00**
Chop plate, 14" d, Fallowfield Hunt **795.00**
Cup and saucer, street scene **225.00**
Hair receiver, street scene **495.00**
Jardinière, street scene **995.00**
Mug
Fallowfield Hunt, 3-1/2" h **395.00**
Street Scene, 4-1/2" h **395.00**
Three Pigeons, 4-1/2" h **350.00**
Mustard jar, dome cov, Scenes of Village Life in Ye Olden Days, ink mark "A. D.," 1910, 3-1/2" h **2,090.00**

Jug, blue marine motif transfer, black banding at rim and base, bottom mark, dated 1906, 9-1/8" h, crazing, **$350**. Photo courtesy of Alderfer Auction Co.

Pitcher, 12" h, 7" w, The Great Controversy, sgd "W. Fozter," stamped mark **320.00**
Powder jar, street scene **395.00**
Punch cup, Fallowfield Hunt **375.00**
Soup plate, 9" d, street scene **425.00**
Tankard, Three Pigeons **1,175.00**
Tea tile, Fallowfield Hunt **395.00**
Tea tray, street scene **650.00**
Vase, 7-3/4" h, 6-1/2" d, King Fisher, green and white dec, olive ground, stamped mark, artist signature **1,380.00**

Pitcher, George Washington on horseback, blue and white decoration, 7-1/2" h, some staining and crazing, **$160**. Photo courtesy of Joy Luke Auctions.

Emerald Deldare

Creamer **450.00**
Fruit bowl **1,450.00**
Mug, 4-1/2" h **475.00**
Vase, 8-1/2" h, 6-1/2" h, stylized foliate motif, shades of green and white, olive ground, stamp mark **810.00**
Wall plaque, 13-1/4" d, titled "Lost," group of sheep huddled together during storm, artist Ralph Stuart, 1911, ink mark "R. Stuart" **3,575.00**

Miscellaneous

Jug
Chrysanthemum **495.00**
Robin Hood **550.00**
Plate, aqua ground, one "Wild Ducks," other "Gunner", price for pr **65.00**

BURMESE GLASS

History: Burmese glass is a translucent art glass originated by Frederick Shirley and manufactured by the Mt. Washington Glass Co., New Bedford, Massachusetts, from 1885 to c1891.

Burmese glass colors shade from a soft lemon to a salmon pink. Uranium was used to attain the yellow color, and gold was added to the batch so that on reheating, one end turned pink. Upon reheating again, the edges would revert to the yellow coloring. The blending of the colors was so gradual that it is difficult to determine where one color ends and the other begins.

Although some of the glass has a glossy surface, most pieces were acid finished. The majority of the items were free blown, but some were blown molded in a ribbed, hobnail, or diamond-quilted design.

American-made Burmese is quite thin and, therefore, is fragile, and brittle. English Burmese was made by Thos. Webb & Sons. Out of deference to Queen Victoria, they called their wares "Queen's Burmese Ware."

Reproduction Alert: Reproductions abound in almost every form. Since uranium can no longer be used, some of the reproductions are easy to spot. In the 1950s, Gundersen produced many pieces in imitation of Burmese.

Advisers: Clarence and Betty Maier.

Bonbon, 6-1/2" l, 4-3/4" w, 2-3/8" h at handle, Mt. Washington, shiny finish, three applied lemon-yellow prunts, applied handle, re-fired heart shaped rim **835.00**

Bowl

2-3/4" d top, 2-1/2" d base, 2-1/4" h, pedestal foot, satin finish, gold stripes, hp prunus dec, Mt. Washington **635.00**

4-1/4" w, 2-1/2" h, tricorn, shiny finish, refired yellow rim, Mt. Washington **550.00**

5" l, 4-1/2" w, 2" h, oblong, shiny finish, translucent thin walls, buttery yellow base, Mt. Washington **550.00**

Console set, 8-3/4" h vase, 9-1/2" w, 8" d, three 4" d, 3-3/4" h bowls, satin finish, each pc dec with prunus blossom dec, Thomas Webb & Son, slight loss of gilt on metal holder........ **6,750.00**

Cream pitcher, 3-3/4" h, satin finish, applied yellow handle, Mt. Washington **485.00**

Creamer, 3-1/2" h, applied handle **350.00**

Cruet, 7" h, applied handle, mushroom stopper, 30 ribs on body, each with hint of pink, color intensifies at neck and spout, shiny finish........ **1,250.00**

Demitasse cup and saucer, 2" d x 2-1/4" h cup, 4" d saucer, satin finish, Mt. Washington........ **665.00**

Epergne, 14" h, 8" center floriform vase, Webb, satin finish, pastel yellow stripes, unique pink blush borders, undecorated, shallow bowl-shaped base with muted Burmese color, cone-shaped center rising to support brass fittings that hold three petite Burmese bud vases **1,950.00**

Fairy lamp, Webb

5-1/2" h, Cricklite, satin, dome Burmese shade, 6" sq base with fold-in sides, impressed signature "Thos. Webb & Sons Queens Burmeseware Patented," clear glass candle cup signed, "S Clarke Fairy Trade Mark Patent" **985.00**

6" h, 7-1/2" d spreading, skirt-like, pleated base, two acid etched signatures, "Thos Webb & Sons Queen's Burmeseware Patented" and "S. Clarke's Fairy Patent Trade Mark," clear glass candle cup signed, "Clarke's Criklite Trade Mark" **950.00**

Milk pitcher, 5-1/2" w, 4-3/8" h, satin finish, squatty, applied lemon yellow handle, Mt. Washington........ **850.00**

Nappy, 6-1/2" l, 4-3/4" w, 2-3/8" h, re-fired heart-shaped rim, three applied lemon yellow prunts, applied handle, shiny finish, Mt. Washington **1,250.00**

Pitcher, 5-1/4" h, satin finish, ivy shaped, tiny spout, three clear yellow applied feet and handle, sgd "Queen's Burmeseware Patent Tho Webb & Sons" **835.00**

Plate, 8" d, shiny pink to yellow shading **115.00**

Punch cup, 2-3/4" h, satin finish, refired yellow rim, lemon yellow applied handle, Mt. Washington........ **385.00**

Salt shaker, 4-1/4" h, Mt. Washington, lemon-yellow lower half, intense color on upper half, two-part metal top........ **265.00**

Toothpick holder

2-1/2" h, molded-in ribs and rococo scrolls at rim and ftd base, two swags of raised delicate blue and yellow blossoms, Mt. Washington **975.00**

2-5/8" h, sq top, coral rim, tiny blue and pink blossoms dangling from undulating green garland, Mt. Washington **735.00**

Vase

3-1/2" h, shiny finish, applied unfired lemon yellow dec, incised registry number "Rd 80167," c1888-1913, 3/8" chip **285.00**

6-1/2" h, satin finish, urn shape, applied yellow handles, Webb **885.00**

7" h, lily, four-petaled top, satin finish, sepia vine, leaf, and blossoms, intertwined with mature black vine, laden with ripened raised yellow berries, red rose with blooming morning glory vine on wafer base, Jules Barbe dec, Webb **685.00**

7-1/2" h, 5-3/4" d, flared flower form, brown-yellow stem, wafer base, shiny, Thomas Webb & Sons **1,000.00**

8" h, satin finish, prunus blossom dec, shape #145, Mt. Washington **1,000.00**

10-1/2" h, satin finish, daisy like blossoms, buds, and leaves, two thin gold tendrils wrap around bulbous body, one branch climbs up long neck, Mt. Washington........ **1,500.00**

10-1/2" h, satin finish, petticoat, multihued gold dec, rose branch with single petaled roses, buds, and leaves, thorny swag across base continues up neck to trefoil mouth, Mt. Washington **1,975.00**

11-1/2" h, satin, rim band of coral colored lacework, forget-me-not dec, Jules Barbe's 1888 Pattern #3211, Webb........ **935.00**

Busts

History: The portrait bust has its origins in pagan and Christian traditions. Greek and Roman heroes dominate the earliest examples. Later, images of Christian saints were used. Busts of the "ordinary man" first appeared during the Renaissance.

During the 18th and 19th centuries, nobility, poets, and other notable people were the most frequent subjects, especially on those busts designed for use in a home library. Because of the large number of these library busts, excellent examples can be found at reasonable prices, depending on artist, subject, and material.

Additional Listings: Ivory, Parian Ware, and Wedgwood.

African woman, stylized, rect base, bronze, Hagenauer, Austria, impressed maker's marks, 9-3/4" h, **$900**. Photo courtesy of Skinner, Inc.

7-1/2" h, bronze, Nubian Princess, Edrmann Encke, Gladenbeck foundry mark, short socle, marble base..... **415.00**

8-1/4" h, lady, carved facial features, ears, and hair style, stepped base with dentil carving, stamped dec, old surface, America, early 20th C........ **650.00**

9" h, bronze, winged cherub, seated on broken column, playing hornpipe, pair of doves perched opposite, after Mathurin

Moreau, dark brown patination, green marble socle 250.00
9-3/4" h, bronze, Virgin, dark brown patina, Leon Pilet, French, 1836-1916, sgd 575.00
10-1/2" h, John Wesley, green and red speckled self socle, Staffordshire, England, 19th C 265.00
10-7/8" h, bronze, Watteau-style woman, tricorn hat, low décolletage, George (Joris) Van Der Straeten, Paris Bronze Society foundry mark, fluted marble socle, reddish brown and black patination 460.00
11-1/4" h, bronze and marble, medieval woman, after Patricia by Roger Hart, young woman, sheer headdress, marked "Mino di Tiesole" on ovoid white marble base, 20th C 575.00

Dante, bronze, back inscribed "Dante Original. Neapel Akt Ges: Gladenbeck Berlin," mounted on green and black marble base, 18" w, 12" h bronze, 16" total h, **$535**. Photo courtesy of Alderfer Auction Co.

11-1/2" h, bronze, Mercury, chocolate brown and parcel-gilt patina, short socle, sq base, after the antique, 20th C 410.00
12-1/2" h, bronze, child, modeled as the head of a young child with curly hair, on cylindrical stone base, 20th C 635.00
13-3/4" w, 9-3/4" d, 26" h, carved marble, Pharaoh's Daughter, John Adams-Acton, snake headdress, beaded necklace, tapered sq section base, carved on front with scene of the discovery of Moses and title, 13-3/8" w, 10-3/4" d, 39" h breche d'alep marble tapered sq section pedestal, England, late 19th C 16,100.00
15-1/4" w, 6-3/4" d, 15" h, carved marble, Jeanne D'Arc, white marble face and base, pink marble bodice, incised title on front, early 20th C 700.00
16-1/2" h, young girl, hand-painted details and gilding, bisque, Victorian 200.00
17-1/4" h, alabaster, woman in lace headdress and bodice, tapered alabaster socle, early 20th C 450.00

Lord Byron, parian, mounted on waisted circular socle, Copeland, England, c1870, impressed mark, 24" h, **$1,775**. Photo courtesy of Skinner, Inc.

19" h, Majolica, young boy, French colonial dress, marked "BU 677" .. 900.00
20" h, marble, lady with rose, incised "A. Testi," associated partial alabaster pedestal with spiral fluted stem 2,645.00
20-1/2" h, bronze, Rembrandt, Albert-Ernest Carrier-Belleuse, silvered patination, bronze socle, marble plinth 2,300.00
22" h, bronze, gentleman, Leo F. Nock, brown-green patina, sgd on base "Leo Nock Sc," dated 1919, stamped "Roman Bronze Works, NY" 320.00
24" h, bronze, cold painted, Bianca Capello, woman wearing classical clothing, Renaissance Revival motifs, sgd "C. Ceribelli," marble plinth 2,100.00
25-1/4" h, George Washington, by William W. Story, dated 1873, Rome, carved marble 31,900.00
26" h, marble, young pious woman, lace and flower bodice, hair in long braid, matching 6" h marble socle, Italian, late 19th C 7,475.00

BUTTER PRINTS

History: There are two types of butter prints: butter molds and butter stamps. Butter molds are generally of three-piece construction—the design, the screw-in handle, and the case. Molds both shape and stamp the butter at the same time. Butter stamps are generally of one-piece construction, but can be of two-piece construction if the handle is from a separate piece of wood. Stamps decorate the top of butter after it is molded.

The earliest prints are one piece and were hand carved, often heavily and deeply. Later prints were factory made with the design forced into the wood by a metal die.

Some of the most common designs are sheaves of wheat, leaves, flowers, and pineapples. Animal designs and Germanic tulips are difficult to find. Prints with designs on both sides are rare, as are those in unusual shapes, such as half-rounded or lollipop.

Reproduction Alert: Reproductions of butter prints were made as early as the 1940s.

Butter stamp back showing center handle, carved wood, age crack, **$65**. Photo courtesy of Wiederseim Associates, Inc.

Butter mold

2" l, oval, warbonnet with feathers, vine border, good patina, handle with age crack, some edge damage to case 200.00
3-1/2" d, sunflower, carved wood 125.00
4-3/8" d, pineapple, carved wood 325.00
5" x 8", roses, carved maple, serrated edges 165.00

Butter stamp

2-7/8" l, one-pc handle, sheep 990.00
3-1/8" d, one-pc tab handle, six-petal flower with dots, minor age cracks 110.00
3-1/4" d, cased, beaver, rope twist border 110.00
3-1/4" d, cased, cow with fence and tree, traces of black ink 110.00
3-1/4" d, cased, strawberry, scrubbed finish 110.00
3-1/4" w, 6" l, rect, two deeply carved hearts and leaves, threaded handle 770.00
3-3/8" d, one-pc handle, calling blue jay 1,265.00

Pineapple carved butter print, round, single handle, age crack, **$85**. Photo courtesy of Wiederseim Associates, Inc.

3-3/8" d, one-pc handle, tulip and flowers, scrubbed finish **165.00**
3-1/2" d, one-pc handle, basket of flowers, natural finish, some edge damage to top of handle **880.00**
3-1/2" d, one-pc handle, eagle with shield, age crack **110.00**
3-3/4" d, cased, shallow carved rooster and tree, dark patina, age cracks **220.00**
3-3/4" d, one-pc handle, deeply carved rose, scrubbed finish, short age cracks **330.00**
3-3/4" d, one-pc handle, deeply carved tulip with star, natural finish **220.00**
4" d, short threaded handle, intricately carved thistles with double border, minor surface wear **110.00**
4" d, threaded handle, deeply carved, cow and fence, old refinishing **990.00**
4" d, threaded handle, strawberries, short age crack **220.00**

Leaf and vine design, round, single handle, **$65**.

4-1/8" d, one-pc handle, pineapple, old refinishing **220.00**
4-1/8" d, threaded handle, deeply carved rose with two buds, some worm holes **55.00**
4-1/4" d, one-pc handle, cow with thick coat, double border, deeply carved, minor surface wear, age crack **660.00**
4-1/4" d, one-pc handle, eagle with star, refinished, ghost image of stars and feathers on backside, minor age crack **615.00**
4-1/4" d, swan with detailed feathers, short age crack **175.00**
4-1/4" l, heart shape, pine tree on one side, person, fish, and ladder on other side **495.00**
4-1/2" d, one-pc handle, sheaf of wheat design **315.00**
4-7/8" d, one-pc handle, pineapple with long leaves, worn natural finish **90.00**
5" d, replaced handle, deeply carved flowers and buds, rope twist borders, worm holes **70.00**
5-1/4" d, one-pc handle, tulip with flowers, surrounded by fern fronts border, old refinishing, age cracks **175.00**
8" l, lollipop shape, daisy, zigzag border, minor old edge flake **85.00**
8-1/4" l, lollipop shape, double sided, heart and star, soft scrubbed finish **495.00**
8-1/2" l, one-pc handle, oval, tulip, flowers, and leaves, lightly scrubbed surface **60.00**
9" l, lollipop shape, carved border, star center, metal cov handle with metal insert, stamped patent mark on back, edge wear, worm holes **275.00**

Carved rooster, chip carved border, round, single handle, **$95**.

Calendar Plates

History: Calendar plates were first made in England in the late 1880s. They became popular in the United States after 1900, the peak years being 1909 to 1915. The majority of the advertising plates were made of porcelain or pottery and the design included a calendar, the name of a store or business, and either a scene, portrait, animal, or flowers. Some also were made of glass or tin.

Additional Listings: See *Warman's Americana & Collectibles* for more examples.

1906, Compliments of A. K. Clemmer, Kulpsville, PA, scattered florals and calendar pages, crazing, stains, **$25**.

1907, Santa and holly, 9-1/2" d **80.00**
1909, woman and man in patio garden, 9" d **35.00**
1911, Souvenir of Detroit, MI, months in center, hen and yellow chicks, gold edge **30.00**
1912, Martha Washington **40.00**

1909, Compliments of John U. Francis, Jr., Fancy and Staple Groceries, Oaks, PA, multicolored transfer of roses and grapes, calendar pages around rim with holly leaves and berries, worn gold trim, marked "Iron Stone China, lion and shield mark, Extra Quality," **$35**

1913, roses and holly **30.00**
1914, Point Arena, CA, 6-3/4" d **30.00**
1915, black boy eating watermelon, 9" d **60.00**
1916, eagle with shield, American flag, 8-1/4" d **45.00**
1917, cat center **35.00**
1920, The Great War, MO **30.00**
1921, bluebirds and fruit, 9" d **35.00**
1922, dog watching rabbit **35.00**
1969, Royal China, Currier & Ives, green, 10" d **40.00**

1912, Winchester, rifle with gouse, autumn scene, **$75**.

Calling Card Cases and Receivers

History: Calling cards, usually carried in specially designed cases, played an important social role in the United States from the Civil War until the end of World

War I. When making formal visits, callers left their card in a receiver (card dish) in the front hall. Strict rules of etiquette developed. For example, the lady in a family was expected to make calls of congratulations and condolence and visits to the ill.

The cards themselves were small, embossed or engraved with the caller's name, and often decorated with a floral design. Many handmade examples, especially in Spencerian script, can be found. The cards themselves are considered collectible and range in price from a few cents to several dollars.

Note: Don't confuse a calling card case with a match safe.

Ivory, Chinese, Qing dynasty, carved garden scene, 4-1/2" h, **$475**. Photo courtesy of Sloans & Kenyon Auctions.

Case

Ivory, 4" l, rect, wood inlay, block rows, center framed with diamond design rim band **175.00**

Silver, repoussè pagodas, trees, and Asian figures, no hallmarks, lid monogrammed, handwritten provenance contained within, 2-1/4" w, 1/2" d, 3-1/2" h, **$260**. Photo courtesy of Alderfer Auction Co.

Leather, sterling silver plaque depicting young woman in Renaissance costume, seed pearl accents, Art Nouveau, French hallmarks **300.00**

Mother-of-pearl, 3" w x 4", Victorian **180.00**

Silver, American, mid to late 19th C
- Coin silver, Albert Coles, engraved dec, monogram **350.00**
- Coin silver, pointed arched base, engraved dec, monogram **325.00**
- Quadruple silver plate, 3-1/2" x 3-3/4", orig chain, Victorian **125.00**
- Sterling silver, goldwashed, fitted leather case, engine turned dec, monogram **250.00**
- Sterling silver, Gorham, engraved dec, monogram **325.00**

Silver, Chinese-Export, 3" x 4-1/2", rect, obverse with emb genre scenes and central cartouche, reverse with emb bamboo shoots, maker's mark "SM," late 19th/early 20th C, approx two troy oz **300.00**

Tile, 5-1/4" x 6-1/2", emb monks, gun-metal glaze, raised AETCo medallion for American Encaustic Tiling Co., few edge nicks **95.00**

Tortoiseshell, 4" x 3", stylized floral plique, hinged metal lid, 19th C **110.00**

White-metal, 3-3/8" x 3", enamel dec of harem girl disrobing in exotic int., late 19th/early 20th C, giltwood frame **800.00**

Receiver

Bronze
- 7" l, figural, monkey, Victorian **135.00**
- 9-1/2" l, 6" w, hammered, ovoid, emb comedy and tragedy masks, orig dark patina, crisp details, Gorham stamp mark **650.00**

Silver plate, 7-1/4" l, 5-1/2" h, silver plate, marked "Meriden," wear to plating **60.00**

Porcelain, 10" l, hand painted, roses, foliage, gold handles **45.00**

CAMBRIDGE GLASS

For more information, see *Warman's Glass*, 4th edition.

History: Cambridge Glass Company, Cambridge, Ohio, was incorporated in 1901. Initially, the company made clear tableware, later expanding into colored, etched, and engraved glass. More than 40 different hues were produced in blown and pressed glass.

The plant closed in 1954 and some of the molds were later sold to the Imperial Glass Company, Bellaire, Ohio.

Marks: Five different marks were employed during the production years, but not every piece was marked.

Vase, shell shape, Crown Tuscan, Charlton dec with roses, leaves, gold trim, **$175**.

Basket, Apple Blossom, crystal, 7" **475.00**

Bonbon, Chantilly, crystal, Martha blank, two handles, 6" **35.00**

Bowl, Wildflower, flared rim, three-ftd, 9-3/8" d **85.00**

Butter dish, cov, Gadroon, crystal **45.00**

Candlestick
- Caprice, blue, Alpine, #70, prisms, 7" h **195.00**
- Chantilly, crystal, 5" h, pr **75.00**
- Doric, black, 9-1/2" h, pr **160.00**
- Lucia, #647, crystal, two-lite **85.00**
- Rose Point, crystal, two-lite, keyhole, pr **95.00**

Candy jar, cov, Rose, green rose-shaped finial, 8" h **250.00**

Celery, Gloria, five-part, 12-1/2" l **70.00**

Champagne, Chantilly, crystal **30.00**

Cocktail
- Caprice, blue **45.00**
- Stradivary **50.00**

Cocktail shaker, Chantilly, crystal, glass lid **250.00**

Comport
Honeycomb, rubena, 9" d, 4-3/4" h, ftd **150.00**
Shell line, Crown Tuscan **55.00**

Console bowl
Cleo, green, 12" flared, gold trim **70.00**
#3900, crystal, oval, ruffled...... **50.00**

Cordial
Caprice, blue.......................... **120.00**
Chantilly, crystal **75.00**
Rose Point, #3121 .... **78.00**

Cornucopia vase, Chantilly, 9-1/8" h **195.00**

Creamer
Chantilly, crystal, individual size **22.50**
Tempo, #1029.......................... **15.00**

Creamer and sugar, tray, Caprice, crystal **40.00**

Cream soup, orig liner, Decagon, green **35.00**

Cup and saucer
Caprice, crystal........................ **14.00**
Decagon, pink.......................... **10.00**
Mt. Vernon, crystal **15.00**

Vase, opaline, classic baluster shape original paper label, 16" h, **$90**.

Decanter, stopper, Mt. Vernon, crystal **75.00**

Dressing bowl, Wildflower, two parts, #1402-95 .... **55.00**

Flower frog
Draped Lady, dark pink, 8-1/2" h **185.00**
Eagle, pink **365.00**
Jay, green............................... **365.00**
Nude, 6-1/2" h, 3-1/4" d, clear **145.00**
Rose Lady, amber, 8-1/2" h **350.00**
Seagull **85.00**
Two Kids, clear....................... **155.00**

Fruit bowl, Decagon, pink, 5-1/2".... **5.50**

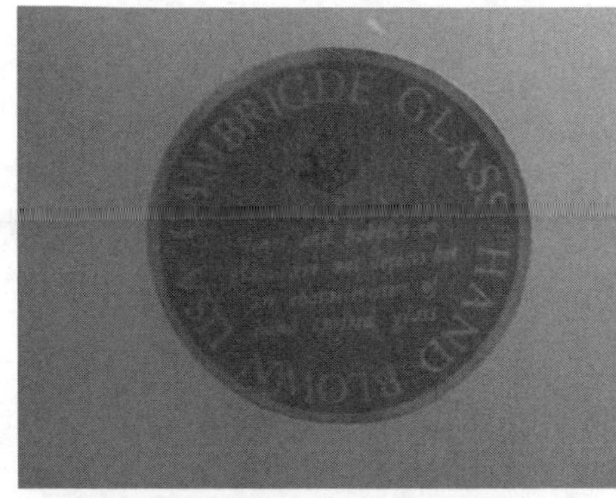

Original Cambridge Glass label: "Lines and bubbles in glass are not defects but are characteristics of hand crafted glass – Cambridge Glass Hand Blown USA" – brown paper label, white lettering, gold logo.

Goblet
Chantilly, crystal, #3625 .... **35.00**
Diane, crystal, #3122 .... **45.00**
Rose Point, #3121 .... **50.00**
Wildflower, gold trim, #3121..... **45.00**

Ice bucket
Blossom Time, crystal **125.00**
Chrysanthemum, pink, silver handle **85.00**
Wildflower, #3400/851 .... **225.00**

Ivy ball, Nude Stem, Statuesque #3011/2, 9-1/2" h, 4-1/4" h d ruby ball, 4" d base **500.00**

Jug, Gloria, ftd, 9-3/4" h **325.00**

Juice tumbler, ftd, Candlelight etch, 5 oz, #3114..................................... **35.00**

Lemon plate, Caprice, blue, 5" d .. **15.00**

Martini pitcher, Rose Point, crystal **700.00**

Mayonnaise set
Diane, divided bowl, liner, two ladles, #3900/111 .... **115.00**
Rose Point, #3900/129, 3 pcs **120.00**

Nut bowl, Diane, crystal, tab handle, 2-3/4" **58.00**

Oyster cocktail, Portia, crystal...... **40.00**

Pitcher, Mt. Vernon, forest green **300.00**

Plate
Apple Blossom, pink, 8-1/2" d.. **20.00**
Chantilly, #3900/22, 8" d........... **18.00**
Crown Tuscan, 7" d **45.00**
Rose Point, crystal, 8" d, ftd **70.00**

Relish
Caprice, club, #170, blue....... **115.00**
Mt. Vernon, crystal, five parts... **35.00**
Wildflower, 8", three parts, three handles................................... **45.00**

Salt and pepper shakers, pr
Rose Point, ball-shaped, silver base, marked "Wallace Sterling 100" **550.00**
Wildflower, chrome tops, one slightly cloudy.................................... **40.00**

Seafood cocktail, Seashell, #110, Crown Tuscan, 4-1/2" oz **95.00**

Server, center handle, Apple Blossom, amber **30.00**

Sherbet
Daffodil, crystal, low **27.50**
Tempo, #1029.......................... **12.50**

Sherry, Portia, gold encrusted **60.00**

Sugar, Tempo, #1029..................... **15.00**

Tea cup, Martha, crystal **6.50**

Torte plate, Rose Point, crystal, 13" d, three ftd **95.00**

Tray, Gloria, four part, center handle, 8-3/4" d **70.00**

Tumbler
Adam, yellow, ftd...................... **25.00**
Diane, crystal, panel optic, 2 oz **110.00**
Rose Point, 10 oz, #3500 .... **35.00**

Vase
Diane, crystal, keyhole, 12" h **110.00**
Rose Point, 3-1/4" d, 10" h, black amethyst.............................. **665.00**
Shell, #131, Crown Tuscan..... **175.00**
Wildflower, #3400, 10-3/4" h **175.00**

Whiskey, Caprice, blue, 2-1/2 oz **225.00**

Wine
Caprice, crystal........................ **24.00**
Diane, crystal, 2-1/2 oz **30.00**

Cameo Glass

History: Cameo glass is a form of cased glass. A shell of glass was prepared, and then one or more layers of glass of a different color(s) was faced to the first. A design was then cut through the outer layer(s), leaving the inner layer(s) exposed.

This type of art glass originated in Alexandria, Egypt, between 100 and 200 A.D The oldest and most famous example of cameo glass is the Barberini or Portland vase found near Rome in 1582. It contained the ashes of Emperor Alexander Serverus, who was assassinated in 235 A.D.

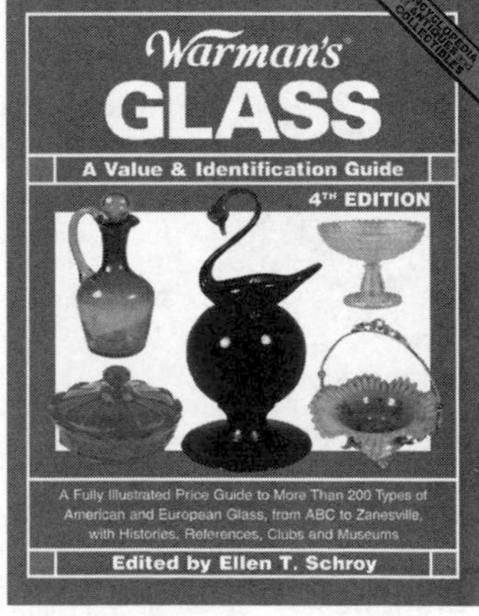

For more information, see *Warman's Glass*, 4th edition.

Emile Gallé is probably one of the best-known cameo-glass artists. He established a factory at Nancy, France, in 1884. Although much of the glass bears his signature, he was primarily the designer. Assistants did the actual work on many pieces, even signing Gallé's name. Other makers of French-cameo glass include D'Argental, Daum Nancy, LeGras, and Delatte.

English-cameo pieces do not have as many layers of glass (colors) and cuttings as do French pieces. The outer layer is usually white, and cuttings are very fine and delicate. Most pieces are not signed. The best-known makers are Thomas Webb & Sons and Stevens and Williams.

Marks: A star before the name Gallé on a piece by that company indicates that it was made after Gallé's death in 1904.

Reproduction Alert.

American

Handel, vase

8" h, frosted body overlaid in transparent yellow, acid-etched thistle and foliage motif, nicks to base edge **800.00**

10" h, cylindrical, colorless body overlaid in yellow, acid-etched palm trees and foliage, raised "Handel 4254" on base, sgd "Pamle" on side for Joseph Palme, Meriden, CT **500.00**

Mount Washington

Bowl, 8" d, 4" h, sq, ruffled edge, two winged Griffins holding up scroll and spray of flowers design, blue over white ground **1,475.00**

Lamp, 17" h, 10" d shade, fluid font and shade composed of opal white opaque glass overlaid in bright rose pink, acid-etched butterflies, ribbons, and bouquets centering cameo-portrait medallions in classical manner, mounted on silver-plated metal fittings, imp "Pairpoint Mfg. Co. 3013," electrified **3,200.00**

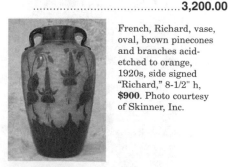

French, Richard, vase, oval, brown pinecones and branches acid-etched to orange, 1920s, side signed "Richard," 8-1/2" h, **$900**. Photo courtesy of Skinner, Inc.

English

Florentine Art, cruet, 6-1/2" h, ruby-red body, textured white enamel meadowland scene, Meadowlark on tall plant stalk, smaller scene on reverse, white rim, trefoil spout, clear frosted handle, teardrop shaped stopper, pontil mark sgd "59" **750.00**

Stevens and Williams, vase, 5-1/2" h, buttercup yellow body shading to cherry blossom-pink, cameo carved twisted Japanese twisted, gnarled, cherry tree branch, pink borders, butterfly on reverse **1,450.00**

Unknown maker, vase, 4-1/2" h, conical rim, round body, overlaid in white on blue ground, cameo-cut rose blossom, leafy stems, borders, rim chips, 20th C **920.00**

Webb

Perfume bottle, 9" l, lay-down type, three-dimensional swan head cameo carved in white over cranberry, orig metal top, orig presentation box marked "MAPPIN & WEBB SILVERSMITH TO THE QUEEN" **14,950.00**

Scent bottle, 3-1/2" d, 4-1/2" h, creamy-yellow ground, pastel pink apple blossom branches, each flower and leaf outlined in gold, tiny gold dots, gold veining on stems and leaves, collar with four stamp marks, sgd "FRM," screw-on cap also sgd "FMR," three shallow dents on cap **1,750.00**

Vase, 5-1/4" h, ivory cameo carved flowers and leaves, base sgd "THOMAS WEBB & SONS" **1,450.00**

French

Arsall, vase

11-3/4" h, cameo carved green and pink flower blossoms, leaves and stem, clear frosted ground, sgd "ARSALL" within design **575.00**

11-3/4" h, cameo carved green leaves, vines, and buds, clear frosted ground, side sgd "ARSALL" **575.00**

Burgen, Schverer, and Cie, Alsace-Lorraine, vase, ftd broad ovoid, frosted colorless glass, amethyst overlay etched and engraved trailing nasturtium blossom, gilt highlights, elaborate gold enamel trademark on base, c1900, enamel wear **2,760.00**

Charder, vase, 5" h, gray ground internally dec with lavender and yellow mottling, overlaid in amethyst, cameo cut lattice and floral design, sgd "Charder" in cameo, c1925.............................. **815.00**

D'Argental, vase

6" h, cameo carved blue blossoms, leaves, and stems on yellow, side sgd "D'ARGENTAL" **700.00**

7" h, cameo carved amethyst morning glories and leaves on frosted yellow ground, sgd on side **575.00**

14" h, rust colored cameo carved floral blossoms and leaves, amber ground, base sgd "D'ARGENTAL" **2,300.00**

D'Argyl, vase, 9" h, cameo carved maroon flowers, branches, and leaves, orange ground, side sgd "D'ARGYL" **460.00**

Daum Nancy

Bowl, low, 7-3/4" d, 2-1/2" h, flaring, etched blue columbines and green leaves, hammered tortoise shell ground, etched "Daum Nancy France" **1,380.00**

Ewer, 7-1/2" h, cranberry ground, highlighted in gold, overlaid in deep purple, cameo cut grapevine motif, metal mount flip lid and handle, emb with matching grape dec, sgd in gold "Daum Nancy," c1895 .... **1,380.00**

Flask, 5-5/8" h, tapered cylindrical bottle, translucent colorless body cameo cut with violet blossoms, enameled purple, yellow, orange and white, gilt highlights, inscribed "Daum (cross) Nancy," mounted with bulbed silver cap with emb flower blossoms, engraved "Lola," small cup with raised leaf blade design, emb "SH" in diamond, cap loose **375.00**

Lamp, floor, 64" h, 16" d Art Deco amber colored cameo shade with cast in forms of oak leafs, acorns, birds resting atop three extending tree limbs. Cast metal tree trunk stem base cov with climbing ivy, hand hammered domed foot, shade sgd "DAUM NANCY FRANCE" .. **9,200.00**

Miniature pitcher, 2-3/4" h, cameo and enamel flower blossoms and vines, applied crystal handle, base sgd "DAUM NANCY" in gold lettering **1,400.00**

Vase

4" h, cameo carved green leaves and stems, two purple padded and wheel-carved Gentian flower blossoms, side sgd "DAUM NANCY" **3,600.00**

4-1/2" h, 7" w, pillow shape, sq top, scenic cameo carved brown, orange and yellow trees and boats, side sgd "DAUM NANCY," roughage to lip **1,100.00**

7-1/2" h, 5" d, gourd shape, etched green branches of chestnuts, orange mottled ground, marked "Daum Nancy A La Marquise De Sevigne, Paris," small base nick **1,380.00**

9-1/4" h, cameo carved green iris blossoms and leaves, frosted chipped ice ground, cameo green spider rests on gold enamel spider web, orig emb silver holder base, base sgd in gold "DAUM NANCY" **5,550.00**

10" h, blown out blossom, leaf, and stem, cameo carved leaf and vines, green and brown on frosted clear background, side sgd "DAUM NANCY" **12,100.00**

15" h, blue and yellow, carved and hand-cut daisies, sgd "Daum Nancy" with cross of Lorraine **13,225.00**

20-1/4" h, cameo carved and enameled lake scene, trees, pink blossoms, green leaves on mottled pink ground, foot sgd "DAUM NANCY" **8,650.00**

Whiskey jug, 10-1/2" h, textured translucent ground, cameo cut and enameled grapevine and leaves, metal lid and handle in form of knight's helmet, lion finial on flip lid, unsigned, c1895 .... **815.00**

French, Le Verre Francais, vase, urn form base, orange and cobalt blue mottled fuschia flowers on ground that gradates from mottled yellow to mottled pale blue, cobalt blue leaves at base, applied black loop handles, bottom signed "Le Verre Francais France," early 20th C, 15-1/2" h, **$2,875**. Photo courtesy of Alderfer Auction Co.

Degue, vase

11-1/4" x 4-1/4", chalice shape, etched cobalt blue leaves, mottled pink ground, etched "Degue" **1,100.00**

19" h, rich royal blue carved cameo stylized design against frosted ground, side engraved "DEGUE," polished pontil engraved "MADE IN FRANCE" **2,050.00**

De Vez, vase

7-1/2" h, cameo carved blue and cranberry tropical palm trees and mountains design, amber ground, sgd "DE VEZ" **815.00**

8" h, cameo carved blue and yellow man and gondola floating past city in the distance, framed by four arched columns, sgd on side **1,380.00**

Fernandez, vase, 5-1/4" h, scenic cameo and enamel trees and fields on mottled orange ground, sgd "FERNANDEZ within design, base numbered "927/684" **815.00**

Galle

Box, cov, 7" h, cameo carved green ferns, cov with green butterflies on frosted green and white ground, side sgd "GALLE" with star, large crack in cov, chip on box rim **575.00**

Centerpiece bowl, 12" l, 6-3/4" w, 4-1/4" h, cameo carved amethyst blossoms, leaves, and stems, frosted ground, side sgd "GALLE" with star **1,100.00**

Perfume bottle, 6" h, cameo carved amethyst and blue flower blossoms, leaves, and vines, amethyst stopper, sgd in design on side of base **1,220.00**

Pin dish, 4-1/4" d, cameo carved amethyst flower blossoms over green and clear frosted ground, side sgd "GALLE" **350.00**

Scent bottle, 5-1/2" h, cameo cut stars, flower basket, and geometric designs, gold enamel trim, base sgd in red enamel "E GALLE NANCY" **1,035.00**

Vase

4-1/4" h, butterscotch yellow cameo carved leaves and berries, applied red and purple cabochons, side sgd "GALLE" **1,495.00**

6-1/2" h, red berries and leaves, clear and yellow background, side sgd "GALLE" with star **1,380.00**

7" h, cameo carved green, orange, and brown leaves and berries, sgd on side, base ground down **660.00**

8-3/4" h, cameo carved green leaves and berries, pink frosted ground, side sgd "Galle" with star **1,650.00**

9-1/2" h, cameo carved green and brown scenic dec, sgd on side **1,440.00**

10-1/4" h, cameo carved flower blossoms and leaves in green, amethyst, and white, side sgd "GALLE" **1,620.00**

10-3/4" h, red flower blossoms and leaves, yellow ground, side sgd "GALLE" **4,400.00**

12" h, cameo carved green pods and leaves, mottled green ground, side sgd "Galle" **2,185.00**

13-3/4" h, 10" d, amethyst and blue over clear and amber, known as Lake Como, shows trees, mountains, castle, and peacock, sgd "Galle" in design **28,750.00**

14-1/4" h, cameo carved green berries, leaves, and branches, amber ground, side sgd "GALLE," foot repaired **2,300.00**

14-1/2" h, 4-1/2" d, bullet-shaped, etched branches of purple sweet peas, chartreuse and yellow ground, etched "Galle," some rim scaling **1,485.00**

14-3/4" h, cameo carved amethyst and green iris blossoms, leaves and ferns on mottled blue, yellow, and orange ground, side sgd "GALLE" **4,500.00**

15" h, cameo carved pink irises, green ground, glossy finish, base sgd "CRISTALLERIE DE GALLE" and "Modeleet Decor Depose" **25,300.00**

25-1/2" h, 9-1/2" w, tapering, etched branch of olive green eucalyptus, pearl gray ground, etched "Galle" **3,115.00**

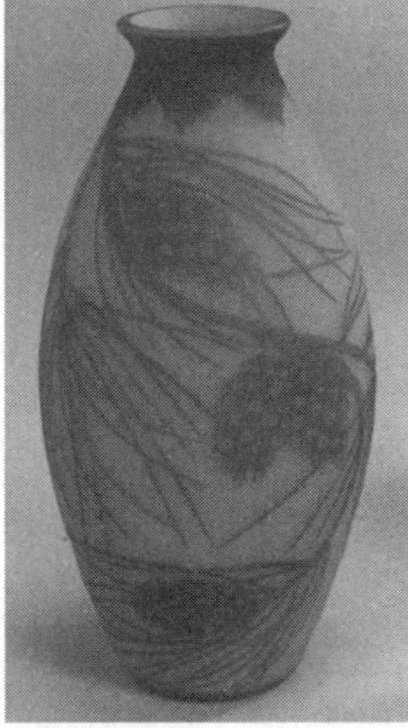

French, Richard, vase, oval, brown pinecones and branches acid-etched to orange, 1920s, side signed "Richard," 8-1/2" h, **$900**. Photo courtesy of Skinner, Inc.

Lamartine

Box, 3" h, triangular form sloping from round opening, cameo cut and etched mountain landscape in blues and greens, sterling silver lid, cameo-etched "Lamartine" on side, int. rim nicks **360.00**

Vase, 6-1/4" h, mottled blue and green ground, cameo cut and enameled birch trees towering over country stream, etched sgd "Lamartine," c1910 .... **1,215.00**

Legras

Bowl, 10" d, 3-3/4" h, olive-green body, heavily etched and engraved Art-Deco swag and drapery design, fire polished, acid-etched "Legras" near base **825.00**

Vase

7-3/4" h, textured gray ground with pink hues, overlaid and cameo cut with green enameled mountainous lake scene, sgd "Legras" in enamel, c1915 .... **490.00**

10-1/4" h, flared rim, elongated neck, bulbed base, light lustrous caramel colored glass, cameo cut branches and leaves, brown and green enameled highlights, cameo-etched "Legras" signature on side, minor rim chips................................**350.00**

11" h, textured translucent shading to crimson ground, cameo cut Art Deco motif, sgd "Legras" in cameo, c1920 ....**550.00**

13-1/2" h, stick, gray shading to mauve ground, cameo cut and enameled underwater foliaged scene, sgd "Legras" in cameo, c1915 ....**650.00**

14" h, gray shading to mauve ground, cameo cut underwater scene, sgd "Legras" in cameo, c1915 ....**825.00**

22" h, underwater scene with cameo carved underwater vegetation and seashells against an apricot ground, enameled in browns, greens and yellows, sgd in cameo and enameled "LEGRAS," two minor foot chips....................................**1,035.00**

Le Verre Francais

Floor vase, 12-1/2" h, Décor Rubanier, gray ground with opalescent mottling, overlaid in variegated orange and amethyst, cameo cut with stylized band of spiral design, base inscribed "Le Verre Francais," c1926...........**850.00**

Lamp, hanging, 11" d, mushroom form, gray ground with yellow mottling, overlaid in orange and brown, cameo cut poppies, hand wrought iron from and suspension chain, c1925........................**2,300.00**

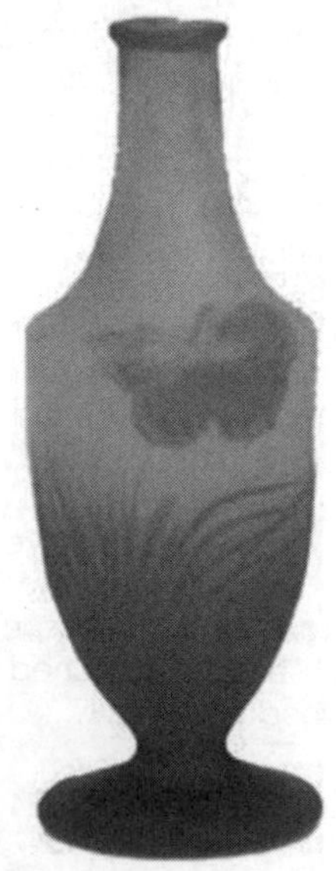

French, unknown maker, vase, cameo carved butterflies and leaves, pink and frosted ground, 5-3/4" h, **$100**. Photo courtesy of Joy Luke Auctions.

Vase

4" h, 5" d, cameo carved mottled brown, orange, and red berries against yellow ground, inscribed signature "LE VERRE FRANCAIS FRANCE," base etched "OVINGTON NEW YORK," small base flake **460.00**

7-3/4" h, mottled brown and white glass over amber, acid cut cameo leaves and vines, sgd in script near base **1,250.00**

13-3/4" h, cameo carved amethyst and blue geese in flight on mottled chartreuse ground, foot script sgd "LEVERRE FRANCAIS" **4,350.00**

19" h, 6" d, etched orange foxglove, pink mottled ground, etched "Le Verre Francais"...................**1,850.00**

Michel, E., vase, 5-1/2" h, cameo carved roses and leaves, green over pink over clear hammered ground............ **6,325.00**

Muller

Biscuit jar, 5-1/4" d, 7" h, cameo and enamel flower blossoms, leaves, and stems on chipped ice ground, orig metal hardware, base sgd "MULLER CROISMARE" **575.00**

Lamp, 20-1/4" h, scenic design with mountains and trees, amethyst, blue, and orange on pale yellow ground, shade sgd "MULLER FRES LUNEVILLE," matching design on base sgd "MULLER FRES LUNEVILLE" **8,625.00**

Vase

4-1/4" h, cameo carved amethyst, orange, and yellow scenic design, sgd "MULLER FRES LUNEVILLE" **600.00**

5-1/2" h, 7-1/4" l, 3-1/2" w, Spanish moss green colored glass, figure of African native and elephant, sgd "MULLER FRES LUNEVILLE" **470.00**

Pantin

Vase, 6" h, cameo carved fuchsia flowers and leaves, turquoise over amber ground, base sgd "CRISTALLERIE DE PANTIN" **700.00**

Violet vase, 5" h, quatrefoil rim on spherical vase, frosted glass overlaid in lavender, acid-etched violet blossoms, inscribed "Christallerie de Pantin" surrounding "STV & Co" monogram on base **520.00**

Richard

Atomizer, 7" h, amethyst over pink glass, cameo carved flower blossoms, stems, and leaves, side sgd **500.00**

Vase

14-1/4" h, cameo carved brown farm scene with farm buildings, two maidens, trees, lake, and mountains, yellow shading to orange ground, side sgd cameo "RICHARD" **1,495.00**

21-1/2", gray ground, overlaid with amethyst, cameo cut mountainous lake scene and medieval castle, sgd "Richard" in cameo, c1915, drilled **650.00**

22-1/2" h, gray and rose mottled ground, overlaid in amethyst, cameo cut shoreline castle between towering trees, distant mountains, sgd "Richard" in cameo, c1915 ....**1,495.00**

Schneider, vase, 4-1/2" h, mottled orange ground, cameo cut with blue Art Deco design, candy-cane signature, c1920.. **490.00**

CAMERAS

History: Photography became a viable enterprise in the 1840s, but few early cameras have survived. Cameras made before the 1880s are seldom available on the market, and when found, their prices are prohibitive for most collectors.

George Eastman's introduction of the Kodak camera in 1888, the first commercially marketed roll-film camera, put photography in the hands of the public.

Most collectors start with a general interest that becomes more defined. After collecting a broad range of Kodak cameras, a collector may decide to specialize in Retina models. Camera collectors tend to prefer unusual and scarce cameras to the most common models, which were mass-produced by the millions.

Because a surplus exists for many common cameras, such as most Kodak box and folding models, collectors are wise to acquire only examples in excellent condition. Shutters should function properly. Minimal wear is generally acceptable. Avoid cameras that have missing parts, damaged bellows, and major cosmetic problems.

Additional Listings: See *Warman's Americana & Collectibles* for more examples.

Adviser: Tom Hoepf.

Argus Inc., Ann Arbor, MI, Argus A, late 1930s, 35mm camera, Argus Anastigmat f4.5/50mm lens, collapsible lens mount, olive drab bakelite body................. **30.00**

Balda-Werk, Dresden, Germany, Balda Poka, 1930s box camera, 6 by 9cm on 120 film, meniscus lens with simple shutter, embossed sunburst design emanating from lens opening......... **15.00**

Bell & Howell, Chicago, IL, Two-fifty-two 8mm movie camera, 1954, two-tone brown die-case aluminum body, eye-level finder, spring motor, Super Comat f2.3/

10mm fixed focus lens, color-coded "Sun Dial" diaphragm settings, leather case **20.00**

Kodak, No. 2 Brownie, original graphic box shows turn of Brownie Character, original instruction book included, and original price tag of **$2.50**, 6" l box, **$90**. Photo courtesy of James D. Julia, Inc.

Bolsey Corp. of America, New York, NY
Bolsey B2, 1949-56, small 35mm camera with coupled rangefinder, f3.2/44mm Wollensak coated lens, double exposure prevention, leather carrying case **25.00**
Bolsey C, 35mm twin lens reflex with coupled rangefinder, f3.2/44mm Wollensak lens, Wollensak 10-200 shutter, $120.00 retail price in 1953 .... **50.00**

Conley Camera Co., Rochester, MN, Conley folding plate camera, c1910, 5" x 7", red bellows, polished cherry interior, leather-covered wooden body **75.00**

Otto Berning & Co., Dusseldorf, Germany. Robot Star II, late 1950s-60s 35mm camera, Primotar f3.5/5.3cm lens, spring motor automatic film advance **80.00**

Eastman Kodak, Rochester, NY
Boy Scout Kodak, c1930, folding vest-pocket camera in drab olive color, Boy Scout emblem engraved on outside of bed, with instructions and case, replaced black bellows in place of original green **150.00**
Kodak Pin-Hole Camera, late 1920s, manual shutter, tan cardboard, given to school children to assemble and used to teach photography principles, orig instructions, assembled **75.00**
Kodak Recomar Model 18, 1930s German-made compact folding view camera, Kodak Anastigmat f4.5/105mm lens with Compur shutter **65.00**
Kodak Retina IIIc, mid-1950s German-made 35mm folding camera, Xenon f2/50mm lens **110.00**
Vanity Kodak Camera, Vest Pocket Kodak Series III camera in color, blue, brown, gray and red, matching satin-lined case, replaced black bellows **125.00**

Expo Camera Co., New York, NY
Expo Watch Camera, introduced 1905, detective camera disguised as railroad pocket watch, lens mounted in "winding stem," cartridge loading with lens cap/knob, lacking its viewfinder, nickel finish **150.00**
Expo Police Camera, c1915, metal box camera, pack of cigarettes size, 12 exposures on special cassettes, achromatic lens, fixed focus, two apertures **275.00**

Franke & Heidecke, Braunschweig, Germany
Baby Rolleiflex, downsized version of classic twin lens reflex camera, 4 x 4cm exposures on 127 film, circa 1958, gray body, Xenar f3.5 lens, ever-ready case **80.00**
Rollei 35, compact 35mm camera, original German version, 1967-75, Tessar f3.5/40mm, heavy wear **150.00**

W. Kenngott, Stuttgart, Germany, Kenngott 10 x 15cm plate camera, triple extension red bellows, polished hardwood interior, leather-covered wooden body, Kenngott Paris Double Anastigmat f6.8/180mm lens with Koilos 1-300 shutter **75.00**

Kochmann, Dresden, Germany, Reflex-Korelle, circa 1946, single lens reflex camera, 12 exposures on 120 film, Xenar f2.8/7.5cm lens, marketed in United States by Burke & James **65.00**

Ernst Leitz, Wetzlar, Germany
Leica IIIc, 1940-46, 35mm camera, with 50mm f3.5 Elmar lens, heavy wear to body's chrome top and bottom **170.00**
Leica IIf, 1951-56, 35mm camera, with 50mm f3.5 Elmar lens, moderate wear **300.00**
Leica IIIg, 1956-60, 35mm camera, with 35mm f3.5 Summaron lens, red case **900.00**

Plaubel & Co., Frankfort, Germany, Veriwide 100, circa 1960, 100-degree wide angle camera, seven 2-1/4" x 3-1/2" exposures on 120 film, Schneider Super Angulon f8/47mm lens, Synchro Compur 1-500 shutter **450.00**

Q.R.S. – DeVry Corp., Chicago, IL, mottled brown brick-shaped bakelite body, c1928, f7.7 Graf Anastigmat lens, metal film advance crank usually missing **40.00**

Universal Camera Corp., New York, NY, C-8 Univex movie camera, c1939, World's Fair model, die-cast metal, bronze finish, interchangeable Ilex Univar f4.5 or f5.6 lenses, orig box **60.00**

Zeiss Ikon, Stuttgart, Germany
Contax III, 35mm rangefinder camera, 1936-42, 50mm 1.5 Sonnar lens, built-in light meter on top **125.00**
Nettar 517/516 folding camera, Novar-Anastigmat f6.3 f75mm lens, Vario 25-200 shutter **25.00**

CANDLESTICKS

History: The domestic use of candlesticks is traced to the 14th century. The earliest was a picket type, named for the sharp point used to hold the candle. The socket type was established by the mid-1660s.

From 1700 to the present, candlestick design mirrored furniture design. By the late 17th century, a baluster stem was introduced, replacing the earlier Doric or clustered column stem. After 1730, candlesticks reflected rococo ornateness. Neoclassic styles followed in the 1760s. Each new era produced a new style of candlesticks; however, some styles became universal and remained in production for centuries. Therefore, when attempting to date a candlestick, it is important to try to determine the techniques used to manufacture the piece.

Candelabras are included in this edition to show examples of the many interesting candelabras available in today's antiques marketplace. Check for completeness when purchasing candelabras, since most are sold in pairs.

Candelabra

12-3/4" h, bronze, two-arm candleholder with green glass inserts, large green glass insert in base, base is signed "TIFFANY STUDIOS NEW YORK" **2,760.00**

15" h, porcelain, hand painted, blond shepherdess and sheep beneath tree cover in pink and orange roses, yellow and pink striped dress, palette and card in hand, underglaze blue double "T" mark, edge damage, two side sockets missing **100.00**

15" h, 13" w, glass, seven-light, hand blown, light amber, hollow stem and arms supporting candle cups, some discoloration to stem inside **250.00**

Brass, Queen Anne, c1750, price for pair, **$750**. Photo courtesy of Wiederseim Associates, Inc.

15-5/8" h, sterling silver, five-light, hand chased, convertible, central thistle sconce with C-scroll candelarms, all with removable floral chased drip pans, 11-1/2" h baluster candlestick with thistle sconce, trumpet foot, chased and embossed with leaves and C-scrolls, approx. 150 troy oz, early 20th C, pr **3,535.00**

16" h, brass, turned top finial, spiral detailed on columns, crosspieces with two candle sockets and drip pans, tripod base, paw feet, thumb screw adjustments, stamped "England," pr **350.00**

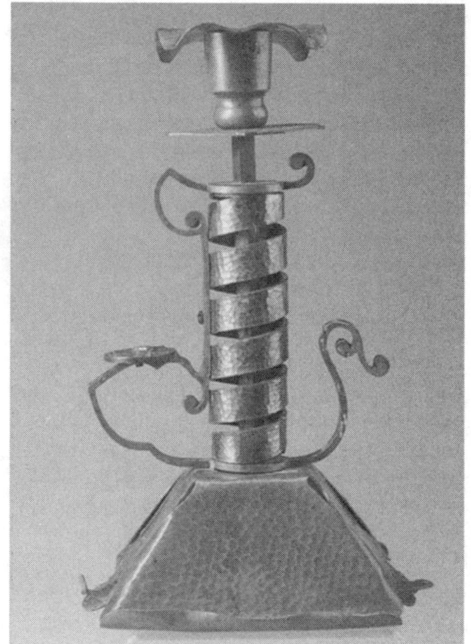

Brass, whimsical, decorated with flying owl, bumblebee, and beetle, stamped "BRADLEY & HUBBARD MFG CO. 767," 8-1/2" h, **$200**. Photo courtesy of David Rago Auctions, Inc.

16-3/4" h, white marble with burgundy striations and ormolu, stepped bases with molded detail, tapered columns, four scrolled branches, turned center column, each with candle socket, small feet below base removed, price for pr **385.00**

20" h, 14-1/2" w, pressed colorless glass, two-light, center faceted prism above drip pan hung with faceted prisms, suspending two chains of prisms to a pair of spiral twisted scrolled arms, flanked by two scrolled candlearms, drip pans hung with further prisms, single knob stem, stepped sq base, late 19th C, bases drilled, price for pr **350.00**

26-1/2" h, bronze, lady holding urn on her shoulder with five branches and sockets, heron finials, brown patina, black onyx pedestal bases with inset panels with relief figures, sgd "J. Salmson (Jules Jean Salmson) France," minor base chips, pr **1,450.00**

30-1/2" h, bronze, five candle sockets near top, crane finial, Minera heads wearing halo of pine cones below tapering columns, three paw feet and griffins divided by large scrolled leaves around base, engraved signatures "F. Barbedienne," design first exhibited at L'Exposition Universelle in 1867, price for pr **3,100.00**

41" h, gilt bronze, ftd base supporting altar from which a column of clouds mounted with winged angels looking up toward five-arm candelabra, French, 19th C **865.00**

Glass, crucifix, marigold carnival iridescent, pair, **$1,400**. Photo courtesy of Seeck Auctions.

Candlesticks

3-1/2" h, 7" w, bronze, woman lying on large leaf holding large bulb/vessel, sgd "Bradley & Hubbard" **415.00**

4-3/4" h, 4-5/8" d, brass, capstan, incised rings, deep socket, two extractor holes, minor wear and dents **715.00**

5-1/8" h, brass, capstan, urn shaped stems, two holes in each socket, pr **935.00**

6-3/4" d, brass, Queen Ann, seamed, sq scalloped base, minor wear, tiny casting imperfection **275.00**

7" h, brass, sq faceted bases, orig patina, unmarked Prairie School, bobeches missing **115.00**

7-1/2" h, brass, deep candle sockets with raised rings top and bottom, baluster turned stems with incised line detail around centers, domed bases with molded edges, soldered splits on columns **1,155.00**

7-7/8" h, brass, saucer base, threaded base, push-ups on columns, dents, pr **330.00**

9-1/2" h, bronze, ovoid sconce over fluted baluster stem ending in flattened knop, fluted foot and ogee shaped base, French Regency, late 18th/early 19th C **470.00**

Candelabra, gilt bronze, urn form supporting five arms with single candle sockets, one central arm with single candle socket, floral foliage, garlands, figural details, 25" h, **$1,760**. Photo courtesy of Alderfer Auction Co.

9-3/4" h, glass, colorless, late, similar to Pittsburgh, columnar, hexagonal paneled sides, round base, pewter bobeches, one with rim chip **200.00**

10" h, hammered copper, tall cylindrical shaft, faceted bottom, squat base, orig dark patina, stamped #135, Stickley Brothers, pr **1,380.00**

11" h, brass, Alpha, Jarvie, ovoid holder, flat circular base, incised "Jarvie," short shallow base scratches **265.00**

11" h, brass, Queen of Diamonds, emb, Victorian, stamp on bases, pr **250.00**

11" h, tin, drop pans, spiral ribs on columns, rings, sloping bases, brown patina, spot soldered **375.00**

12-1/4" h, brass, flared sockets, drop hands, twisted stems, domed bases, hand threaded posts, pr **400.00**

Candy Containers

History: In 1876, Croft, Wilbur, and Co. filled small glass Liberty Bells with candy and sold them at the Centennial Exposition in Philadelphia. From that date until the 1960s, glass candy containers remained popular. They reflect historical changes, particularly in transportation.

Jeannette, Pennsylvania, a center for the packaging of candy in containers, was home for J. C. Crosetti, J. H. Millstein, T. H. Stough, and Victory Glass. Other early manufacturers included: George Borgfeldt, New York, New York; Cambridge Glass, Cambridge, Ohio; Eagle Glass, Wheeling, West Virginia; L. E. Smith, Mt. Pleasant, Pennsylvania; and West Brothers, Grapeville, Pennsylvania.

Additional Listings: See *Warman's Americana & Collectibles* for more examples.

Notes: Candy containers with original paint, candy, and closures command a high premium, but beware of reproduced parts and repainting. The closure is a critical part of each container; if it is missing, the value of the container drops considerably. Small figural perfumes and other miniatures often are sold as candy containers.

Sweet collection

James Julia Auction sold an interesting collection of candy containers recently. Included with the candy containers were several original production molds. One example was the cast iron Dolly Sweeper mold. It is 8-1/2" d, 8" h, and descended from the founder of the Westmoreland Specialty Co. Despite some surface rust, the inside was in excellent condition. It brought $2,415.

Airplane

Liberty Motor, orig tin parts and closure, clear glass **2,100.00**

Passenger, 4-3/4" wingspan, 5" l, all glass fuselage and landing gear, traces of original yellow paint on wings and tin screw-on nose cap with propeller, three windows emb on either side, tail rudder is chipped, nose cap corroded **635.00**

Baseball player, red and white uniform, marked "P" on hat and shirt, holds bat while standing next to ribbed barrel with slotted orange closure, c1920, 4" w, 3-1/4" h, small base chip **865.00**

Bear on circus tub, bear holds fan as he stands atop flared tub with hole in top and side for rubber tube, tin snap-on closure with four tabs, T. G. Stough, c1916, 4-1/4" h, ears repaired, fan and rubber tube possible replacements **600.00**

Bird on mount, pewter whistle, 100% orig paint, orig closure, 1" h **1,100.00**

Birds on egg, composition **350.00**

Black cat, flat bodied black cat atop simulated wood crate with recessed top, marked "Black Cat for Luck" across front and "Pat" below cat, back marked "Pat. Apl'd for," gold tin slide-on closure, 2-3/4" w, 1-3/4" d, 4-1/4" h, small tight hairlines on base **350.00**

Bureau, clear, emb gilt scrollwork front, black painted back mirror, stippled sides, gold slide-on closure, c1915, 2-3/4" w, 1-1/2" d, 4" h, possibly repainted . **130.00**

Camera on tripod, orig box labeled "Chid's Cam-ra," 90% orig paint, orig tin parts, 5" h **880.00**

Cannon

Four wheel mount, 6-1/2" l, orig tin wheels, movable glass barrel **3,740.00**

Two wheel mount #1, gold tone tin screw-on cap at breech, closed at muzzle, two knobs on side of barrel fit into holes on replacement red tin carriage, c1930, 5-1/4" l **765.00**

Two wheel mount #3, orig condition **615.00**

U.S. Defense field gun, tin cylindrical barrel on stippled triangular base emb with gears, barrel rigged with spring to shoot candy projectiles, small screw-on cap at rear marked "Stough," 1940s, 5" l **895.00**

Cat, stretch neck, Victory Glass Co., c1925, black, emb gold painted bow, orig closure, 90% orig paint, 5" h **5,500.00**

Glass, seated rabbit, **$60**; hen, **$20**. Photo courtesy of Joy Luke Auctions.

Chaplin, Charlie

Curved barrel, black coat, brown paints, holding cane next to curved hoop barrel, slotted wood grained litho closure, marked "Charlie Chaplin" on front of base, bottom of barrel marked "Geo Borgfeldt & Co., New York, sold licensees," bottom of figure marked "Serial No. 2862/Net/Wt," c1915, 3" w, 3-3/4" h **195.00**

Straight barrel, standing next to straight sided wide paneled barrel, LE Smith Co., c1920, 4" w, 4" h **175.00**

Clock

Alarm clock, orig closure **315.00**

Round top, replaced paper face, orig closure, 2-5/8" h **1,760.00**

Clown, bobbling nose, composition **450.00**

Coogan, Jackie, emb "Jackie Coogan" on pedestal, orig tin closure marked "Copyright 1925, Jackie Coogan Productions Inc.," Westmoreland Specialty Co., 5" h, slight roughness under closure, 1/4" hole................ **300.00**

Country club bus, metal top, tin wheels, 4" l.. **2,255.00**

Dolly Carpet Sweeper, top center panel marked "Dolly Sweeper," glass painted burgundy, clear panels on top, burgundy tin closure, black tin wheels, twisted wire handle, back edge marked "Net wt. 1-1/2 oz. Serial No. 2862," 2-3/4" w, 2" d, 7-1/4" h, minor paint chips......... **2,100.00**

Eagle watch, emb front reading 8: 22, beads around edge, tin screw-on closure, winder on top has wire with attached fob emb with eagle, wood and wire display stand **300.00**

Elephant

Genteel Elephant, standing with hands in pockets, emb checkered suit, black screw-on hat closure **200.00**

G.O.P., emb "G.O.P." on left, "U.S.A." between feet, "V. G. Co." on bottom, tin slide-on closure, base chipped **150.00**

Felix, smiling comic cat standing next to wide paneled barrel marked "Felix," bottom marked "Copyright 1922-24 by Pat. Sullivan/Pat. applied for," 3-1/2" w, 3-1/2" h, barrel notched to accommodate (missing) snap-on-closure, no paint **1,955.00**

Flossie Fisher's Furniture, yellow tin, black silhouettes of children and animals

Chair, 3" h **1,550.00**

Table, round, 3-5/8" w, replaced pedestal base **2,530.00**

Goblin head, dome shaped, emb features, 80% orig orange paint, 4" h **1,220.00**

Google, Barney

Ball in hands, standing atop vertically lined pedestal, front marked "Barney Google," back "Copyright 1923/King Feature Syndicate, Inc.," tin screw-on closure, 3-3/4" h **150.00**

Facing right, with left foot on step attached to barrel emb diagonally

"Barney Google," midnight blue threaded closure, slotted for bank, underside marked "Copyright 1923, King Feature Syndicate, Inc," 4" w, 3" h, minor scratching on closure, paint loss **1,325.00**

Happifats, 4-3/4" h, portly lad, short jacket, ribbed pants atop emb drum, red tin slotted closure marked "Geo Borgfeldt & Co. NY Sole Licensee Happy Fat-U.S. Des Pat" around edge, c1915, no paint, minor chips **575.00**

Independence Hall, 5" l, 3-1/2" w, 7-1/2" h, clear glass, building form, highly detailed and emb, punched with coin slot on left side of roof, marked "Bank of Independence Hall 1776-1876," lacking clip-on closure, slight chipping to base and coin slot **200.00**

Kaleidoscope, tin construction, glass horizontal cylinder revolves when crank is turned, red and cream decal reading "Moving Pictures," directions for use "By West Bros. & Co., Grapeville, PA," patent by Turney G. Stough, 2-3/4" w, 6-3/4" h **22,245.00**

Lamp, George Washington paper shade, orig closure, 5" h.......................... **715.00**

Lawn swing, glass swing suspended by wire bales below 5-1/2" x 2-3/4" red and white striped canopy, red tin slide-on closure, center emb "West Bro's. Co./ Grapeville, PA/Serial No. 2862/Net Wt. 1 Oz," c1915, 2-1/2" x 1-1/2" **450.00**

Papier-mâché, four rabbits, two with exaggerated ears, other pair dressed as man and lady, German, **$175**. Photo courtesy of Joy Luke Auctions.

Motorcycle and sidecar, yellow-faced rider astride Indian motorcycle with sidecar, hints of red flash on wheels, emb spokes and engine, red tin snap-on closure, Victory Glass Co., left marked "USA," right marked "1/4 Oz. Avor. V.G. Co. Jenet. PA," 5" l x 3-1/4" h........ **460.00**

Phonograph

Glass horn, c1920, gold painted, gold tin slide-on closure, c1920, 2-1/2" sq, 3-3/4" h, break at one corner **950.00**

Unpainted tin horn, emb handle, glass arm, gold tin clip-on closure, c1920, 3" sq, 4-3/4" h, horn loose **850.00**

Piano, upright, gilt painted, black and white emb keys, clear front panel, tin slide-on back closure with coin slot, c1920, 3" l, 1-3/4" d, 2-3/4" h **300.00**

Policeman, mounted, riding pumpkin, 70% orig paint, orig closure **2,100.00**

Pocket watch, Victor, crisscross pattern around edge, ribbed pattern on back, tin clock face shows 11:00, hinged at bottom, serves as closure, knob at top is indented to hold metal ring (possibly replaced), c1913, 2" d, closure is slightly rusted **2,100.00**

Porch swing, all tin, green swing on red A-frame stand, c1933, 4-1/4" w, 2-1/4" d, 4-1/4" h, possibly repainted, repair to base **120.00**

Rabbit

Family, stippled mother, father, and baby rabbit, gilt paint, grassy outcropping, tin snap-on closure, front panel marked "V.G. Co. Jeanette, PA, Avor. Oz," plain panel on back, c1920, 3-3/4" l, 4-3/4" h **2,200.00**

Mother and daughter, hollow mother, hands on hips, gilded stippled fur, red checkered apron, daughter clings to her side, marked "V" over "G" logo above apron strings, "USA Avor" at bottom of dress, tin screw-on closure, 5-1/4" h, right ear chipped **1,150.00**

Papa, short-eared, wearing fedora and scarf, hands in pockets, tin screw-on closure, 5-1/2" h, traces of orig paint, base chipped........ **610.00**

Rabbits running on log, gilt rabbit, log ridged for snap-on closure (missing), marked "1/2 Avor USA," 4-1/4" x 3" h **200.00**

Rabbit with feet together, round nose, tin screw-on closure, c1925, marked "1 oz Avor, USA" **90.00**

Rabbit with forepaws next to body, Victory Glass Co., tin screw-on closure, gilt upper body, blue base, marked "1 oz Avor.U.S.A." **115.00**

Rabbit with wheelbarrow, hollow orange rabbit, green wheelbarrow with white eggs, scrollwork on sides of base, tin slide-n closures, 3-3/4" l x 4" h **185.00**

Stough rabbit, c1948, heavily lined, seated on grassy base, no closure **120.00**

Swan boat, rabbit and yellow chick in boat, gilt painted swan's body, Victory Glass Co., marked "V.G. Co. Jnet, Pa., Avor 7/8 Oz," no closure, chips....................................... **95.00**

Refrigerator, Victory Glass Co, late 1920s, 3-1/2" l, 50% orig paint, no closure, short legs, coil on top **6,050.00**

Rocking settee, clear glass, ruby flashed front panel, marked "Souvenir of Pen Mar, MD," gilt painted arms, emb cushions, curved snap-on closure, c1914, 2-3/4" w, 2-1/4" d, 2-1/2" h **210.00**

Safety First, blue-eyed baby in diaper with large safety pin, bottle at chest, base marked "Safety First" in gold, barrel threaded for lid, West Bros. Co., 3" w, 3-3/4" h... **410.00**

Glass, Santa at chimney, **$75**. Photo courtesy of Joy Luke Auctions.

Santa, sq emb brick chimney, green coat and hood flashing, black boots, yellow tin slide-in closure, LE Smith Co., 1920s, 4" w, 3-3/4" h, some orig paint...... **500.00**

Soldier

Standing by tent, 95% orig paint, orig closure, slight damage........ **1,980.00**

Uniformed, mustache, sword at shoulder atop three-tier stepped base, c1920, 5-3/4" h, missing closure, traces of paint remain, minor base chips............................. **210.00**

Spark Plug, comic horse with shabby patched orange blanket marked "Spark Plug" on left side, "U.S.A." on left between hooves and four dots on right between hooves, bottom marked "Copyright 1923. King Feature Syndicate Inc.," red snap-on closure, c1923, 4-1/4" l, 3" h, tight hairlines **200.00**

Statue of Liberty, 5-3/4" h, clear figural glass base, gold painted lead figure, slotted tin closure, broken and reglued crown point, small base flake.... **7,975.00**

Stop and Go, variation A, unmarked clear bulbous glass, tin blue handle, green post, tin screw-on closure, red traffic paddles, 4-1/4" h, typical roughness under closure **425.00**

Taxi

Yellow, metal roof, tin wheels, Westmoreland Glass Co., 4-1/4" l **1,320.00**

White, Westmoreland Glass Co., 4-1/4" l **990.00**

Telephone

Desk phone, c1950, replaced receiver, 4" l, no closure **1,100.00**

Lynne type, sunken dial, orig closure **60.00**

Redlich's cork top, orig condition **635.00**

Redlich's screw top, replaced receiver **150.00**

Toonerville Trolley, comic trolley manned by conductor, red tin slide-on closure, c1922, traces of paint after the popular tin windup toy. Only remain, marked "Toonerville" on both sides and "7 Depot Line" below windows, copyright symbol and "1922 by Fontaine Fox" on bottom **6,100.00**

Uncle Sam, connected to barrel, slotted top to his right, c1918, 3-3/4" w, 4" h **665.00**

US Express Wagon, 4" l, 1-3/4" w, 6-1/2" h, rect glass bed, red pierced wheels mounted on flanges attached to green tin slide-on closure, twisted wire handle, emb "U.S. Express" on each side, "Net wt. 1-1/4 oz." upside-down on back, c1913, minor chip at one corner at bottom, small flake at top, wheels possibly repainted, one wheel replaced **420.00**

Village building, West Bros, c1914, tin litho ext., marked ftd glass inserts held in by wire retainer clips, some fading to lithography, shallow roof dents

Five-and-Ten Cents Store, orig glass insert, replaced wire clip **2,310.00**

Tudor, 2-1/4" sq, 3" h **450.00**

Village Bungalow, 2-1/4" sq, 2-1/2" h **2,100.00**

Village City Garage, 2-3/4" x 1-3/4" base, 3" h **1,250.00**

Village Drug Store, 2-3/4" x 1-3/4" base, 3" h **1,200.00**

Village Engine Co., No. 23, 2-3/4" x 1-3/4" base, 3" h **1,450.00**

Village Toys & Confectionery, 2-3/4" x 1-3/4" base, 3" h **1,150.00**

Whip, Westmoreland, cloth-covered wire, candy-filled glass handle, 31" l **3,400.00**

Windmill

Candy Guaranteed Windmill, 4" h, orig closure **715.00**

Five windows, souvenir of Tischmills, Wis, ruby flashed glass, orig closure, replaced blades **440.00**

Teddy, 4" h, orig condition **635.00**

World globe, spinning clear glass globe, emb continents, latitude, and longitude lines, mounted in pewter stand, small screw-on closure, marked "Our Country" on North America, stand marked "Pat. Appl'd For," 4-1/4" h **335.00**

Canes

History: Canes or walking sticks have existed through the ages, first as staffs or symbols of authority, and then to items like religious ceremonial pieces. They eventually evolved to the fashion accessory that is the highly desirable antique prized by today's collector for its beauty and lasting qualities. The best were created with rare materials such as carved ivory, precious metals, jewels, porcelain, and enamel, with many being very high-quality works of art. They were also fashioned of more mundane materials, with some displaying the skill of individual folk artists. Another category of interest to collectors is the gadget cane that contained a myriad of hidden utilitarian objects, from weapons to drinking flasks, telescopes, compasses, and even musical instruments, to cite just some.

Adviser: Henry A. Taron.

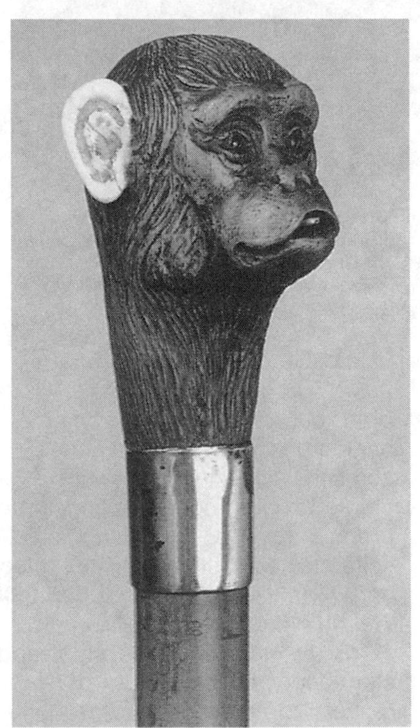

Automation, 3" h x 2" w wood handle carved as monkey, large ivory ears, brown glass eyes, when ivory button on back of head is pushed, long red tongue springs out, 1" plain silver collar, honey toned Malacca shaft, 1-1-2" burnished brass ferrule, English, c1890, 34-3/4" l, **$900**. All cane photographs courtesy of Adviser Henry A. Taron.

Automata, English, c1880, wood, 2" d x 3" h well-carved Turk wearing turban handle, eyes change from clear to red, bright red tongue protrudes, 1/2" ringed silver collar, thick malacca shaft, 1" replaced brass ferrule, 35-3/4" l **1,900.00**

Baleen, America, c1850, carved dog head, shepherd's crook 1/3" thick by 6" l handle, 34-1/2" l......................... **1,400.00**

Bloodstone, Anglo/Indian, custom made for English nobleman, c1890, 3/4" d x 2" h green bloodstone handle with red flecks, gold English coat of arms on top, 1/2" gold collar with rubies and diamonds, carved angular twisted segmented ivory shaft, 38-1/2" l........................... **3,900.00**

Brass, Confederate cannon, c1875, 1-1/8" w x 5-3/4" h cannon handle faces downward, 1/2" brass collar, ebony shaft, brass shield below handle reads "Captain Carter Day N.C. Infty," 1-1/2" white metal and iron ferrule, 35-3/4" l **1,800.00**

Cameo glass, English, c1895, Webb, 1-1/3" d ball handle, white leaves, branches, and foliage, pale blue background, matte finish, 1/2" w cup collar, marked "925," maccassar ebony shaft, 1" replaced brass ferrule, 34-1/2" l **2,400.00**

Enamel, French, c1900, oval 1" d x 2-78" h handle with engine turned guillouche, pale peach tone, oval vermeil ring on top, painted swag of roses, sides with chain and rose wreaths, blue ribbons tied in bows on sides, oval light toned hardwood shaft, 1-1/8" horn ferrule, 35-3/4" l.................................... **1,300.00**

Folk Art, America

Craddock, straight hickory, relief carved animals and leaves, text: "Thos. Jefferson of VA, Born April 13, 1743, was President U.S.A. 1801-1809. Wrote Declaration of Independence May 1773. Independence Day, July 4, 1776. This cane was cut near Jefferson's tomb," carved name "Ed. Ritter, Philadelphia, PA," possibly custom made for Ritter by Thomas Jefferson Craddock, 1-1/4" white metal and iron ferrule, 34" l **800.00**

Schnider, c1910, carved from single piece of hardwood, tight crook handle, starts as boxer head, collar carved "Schnider," large snake and alligator trying to swallow dog, twisted shaft carved with tasseled ropes, two more alligators, 10 ducks, two perched owls, pug dog, crane eating fish, ends with two turtles, 1-1/2" brass ferrule, 36" l **4,500.00**

Gadget

Cigar, English, c1890, 1-1/3" d x 2-1/8" l silver knob handle, gilded silver receptacle, two match holders, underside of lid inscribed with maker's initials and "Patent No. 2048," natural beech shaft, 1-1/8" white metal and iron ferrule, 36-1/4" l **2,000.00**

Cigarette, French, c1895, 7-1/2" l crook handle, Malacca shaft, shoulder silver fitting with flip-open lid, thumb wheel operates string pulley that raises cigarette

for removal, emb "B'vte France, Etranger," and "S.G.D.G.," 1" horn ferrule, 35-3/4" l **1,000.00**

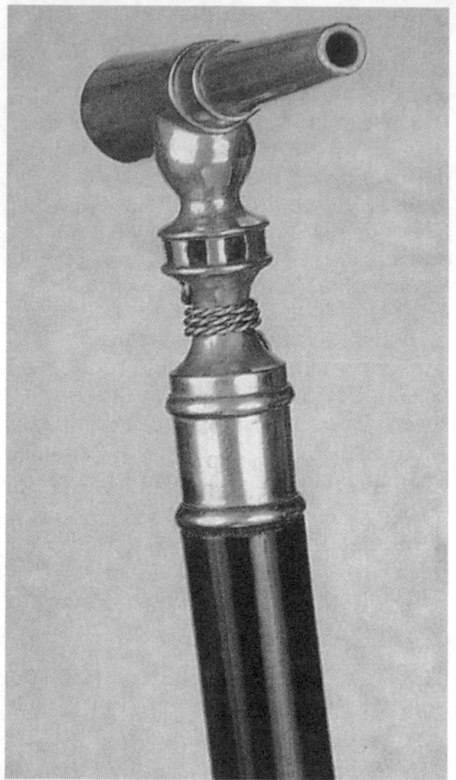

Cheroot, brass, 3" h x 4" l handle fashioned as early naval cannon atop capstan with encircling rope, ebony shaft, 1" brass ferrule, American, c1880, 34-1/2" l, **$1,200**.

Flag, American, 1890, 1-1/8" d x 1" h painted knob handle, wooden dowel shaft with woven linen 20" x 12" 38-star flag with metal stripe, stamped "From B. H. Grubb, The Fishing Rod Co., Post Mills, Vt," 37" l **1,050.00**

Gun, American, c1870, Remington, 2-1/2" l x 1-3/4" h gutta percha doghead, 1/4" nickel collar on gutta percha veneer shaft, 22 caliber, 1-1/3" orig removable ferrule, 35-3/4" l **8,000.00**

Horse trader's, English, 1912, bamboo, sterling, and boxwood, 9" bamboo crook handle, natural root knob at end, sterling push-fitting at shoulder with London hallmarks, long brass and boxwood measure calibrated in inches and hands, hidden brass swing-out arm as working red spirit level, 1-1/2" white metal and iron ferrule, 37-1/2" l **500.00**

Music stand, America, 1877, 1-1/8" d x 1" h ebony handle, unscrews to brass fitting that unscrews so three metal feet can be removed, cane inverts and is attached as base, angled slot in 1-3/4" l brass ferrule holds platform for sheet music, marked "Pat. Aug 28, 1877," black hardwood shaft, 33-1/3" l **1,900.00**

Ocarina, French, c1890, 4" l x 1-3/4" h molded white metal bird-shaped handle, combined with transverse flute, inscribed maker's name "Mathieu," "S.G.D.G.," hardwood shaft, 1" brass and iron ferrule, 34" l **1,300.00**

Pencil, English, 1901, Brigg, 2/3" x 5" l crook gilded sterling silver handle, push-up fitting at shoulder allows pencil to be removed, marked "Brigg," hallmarks, dark bamboo shaft, 1" brass and iron ferrule, 36-3/4" l **700.00**

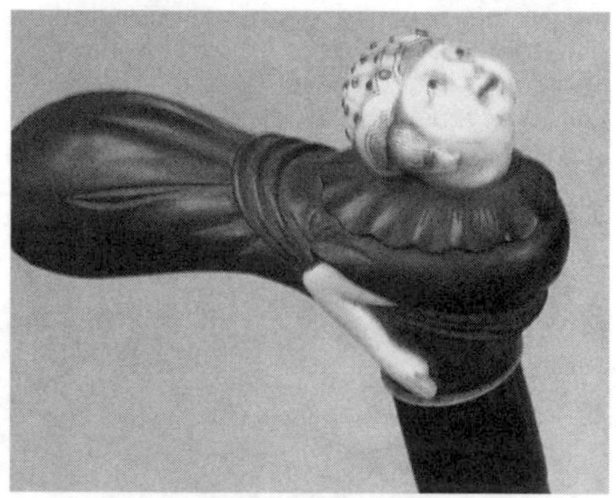

Webb cameo glass, 1-1/3" d ball handle, white leaves, branches, and foliage, pale blue ground, matte finished, 1/2" w cup collar, marked "925," maccassar ebony shaft, 1" replaced brass ferrule, English, c1895, 34-1/2" l, **$4,000**.

Picnic, German, c1885, 5-1/2" l x 2-1/2" h hardwood tau handle, 1/2" brass collar, dark bamboo shaft, handle unscrews to reveal wine corkscrews, next sections with pointed cheese scoop, spoon, three-pronged fork, eating fork, and steel knife marked "Solingen," 1-1/4" black horn ferrule, 34" l **1,600.00**

Watch, French, c1890, silver, 1-1/2" d x 1-1/4" h handle, sides and stem dec, smooth lid flips open to reveal white enameled watch marked "Brevete," snakewood shaft, 1-1/4" horn ferrule, 33-1/3" l **1,800.00**

Gold

America, 1841, pallbearer's, 18kt 1" d x 1-1/4" h octagonal handle, top inscribed "In Memory of Wm B. H. Prindall, died Feb 9th, 1841," elaborately dec side panels alternating with smooth panels, chestnut shaft, gold eyelets, 7/8" brass ferrule, 35-3/4" l **1,900.00**

Chinese, c1840, 1" d x 1-2/3" h, 24kt, Emperor riding dragon on top, trees, animals, and Chinese figures around temple on sides, two floral dec gold eyelets, Malacca shaft, 2-1/4" l brass and iron ferrule, 35-1/2" l **1,100.00**

Carved ivory, 7-1/2" l elephant ivory handle, 1-1/4" d at top, dated 1878 on top and "Wein, Preisveiren," sides carved in high relief as two horse heads and eight dogs, rope rings and shield cartouche, 1/3" silver collar, mahogany shaft, 1-1/8" brass and iron ferrule, Austrian, 39-1/4" l, **$2,200**.

English, c1860, 1-1/3" d x 1-3/4" h knob, inlaid oval mount on top with painted miniature of young Victorian girl, blue dress, flowers in hand, hair, and on bodice, sides engraved with flowers and shells, inscribed "G. T. to Y.T.L., 1860," brown hardwood shaft, 1" horn ferrule, 35-3/4" l, marked 14k, but testing shows it is made of very thick layer of rolled gold......... **620.00**

Ivory, carved, figural handle

American, c1870, elephant ivory 2" w x 4-2/3" h handle, carved skull perched on branch with long snake twisted around branch, head and forked tongue facing skull's chin, worn gold filled collar inscribed "Dr. Alfred Springer, Norwood O (Ohio)," ebony shaft, 1-1/8" brass and iron ferrule, 34-1/8" shaft **4,500.00**

American, c1870, elephant ivory 5-1/2" l x 1-3/4" h handle, carved jockey in full racing tack and racing horse with yellow glass eyes, 1/2" silver collar, full bark malacca shaft, 1-1/2" metal and iron ferrule, 33-7/8" l **4,500.00**

American, c1880, elephant ivory "L" 4-1/2" l x 2" h handle, relief carved full bodied lobster, 3/4" gold gilt collar, stepped partridgewood shaft, 7/8" replaced brass ferrule, 34-1/2" l **800.00**

Austrian, 1-1/4" d x 7-1/2" elephant ivory handle, dated 1878 on top and "Wein, Preisveiren," carved high relief of two horse heads and eight dogs, rope rings, shield cartrouche, 1/3" silver collar, mahogany shaft, 1-1/8" brass and iron ferrule, 39-1/4" l **2,200.00**

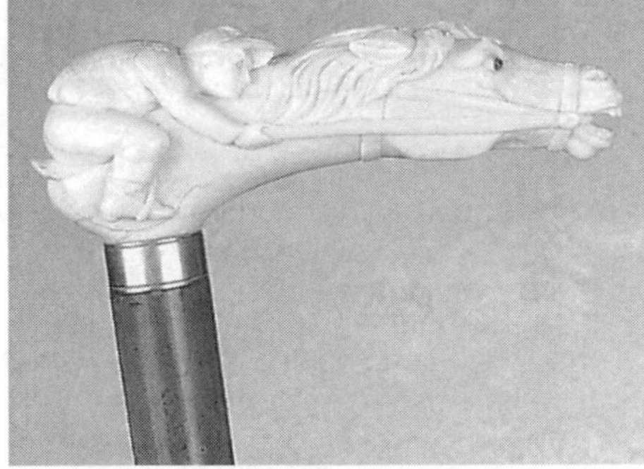

Carved ivory, jockey in full racing tack astride racing horse, 1-3/4" h x 5-1/2" l elephant ivory handle, yellow glass eyes, 1/2" silver collar, full bark Malacca shaft, 1-1/2" metal and iron ferrule, American, c1870, 33-7/8" l, **$4,500.**

Continental, c1895, bulldogs, 3-1/2" l x 3" h elephant ivory, two heads, mouths open, fangs barred, amber eyes, 1" plated gold collar, smooth cartouche and diagonal lines, full bark Malacca shaft, replacement 3/4" grass ferrule, 35-3/4" l... **1,120.00**

English, c1880, 2" w x 1-3/4" h elephant handle, two carved Dickens Oliver Twist faces, one craggy Fagin, other Mr. Bumble, 1/2" gold gilt collar, ebonized hardwood shaft, 1-1/2" horn ferrule, 37" l **1,100.00**

English, c1890, 4-1/2" l x 1-1/2" h elephant ivory carved donkey handle, brown glass eyes, long ears, 1/8" thin silver collar, ebony shaft, 1-1/4" horn ferrule, 36-1/3" l **850.00**

English, c1895, 1-3/4" w x 1-3/4" h elephant ivory handle of Dutch girl, smiling, wearing bonnet, snakewood shaft, 1-1/3" burnished brass ferrule, 36-7/8" l **400.00**

French, c1895, boy with rabbit, 1" w x 2-1/3" h elephant ivory handle, finely carved nude child, sitting on plinth, petting rabbit, 1/4" gold collar marked "18 ct" and "Asprey," tan bamboo shaft, 1" brass and iron ferrule, 34-3/4" l **1,680.00**

German, c1880, falconer, 1-1/2" w x 3-1/2" h elephant ivory handle, 18th C nobleman standing under tree holding falcon, dogs at feet staring up at bird, 1/3" gold gilt collar marked "Briggs London," black hardwood shaft, 7/8" horn ferrule, 36" l, handle possibly German, cane fashioned in London........... **6,385.00**

Japanese, c1890, 1-1/2" w x 4" elephant ivory handle, old man holding cane in one hand, back over shoulder, two small toads crawling out of bag, sgd by carver, 1/3" gold gilt collar, stepped partridgewood shaft, 1-1/2" white metal and iron ferrule, 34-1/3" l **4,000.00**

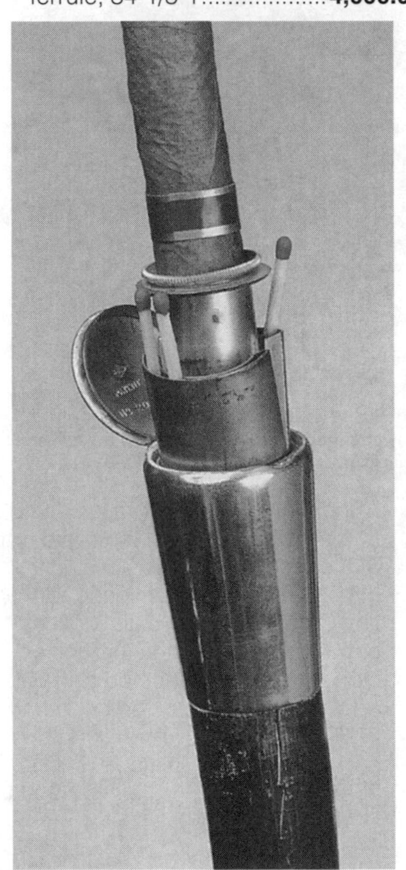

Cigar case, 2-1/8" h x 1-1/3" d silver knob handle, when lid lifted, gilded silver receptacle can be raised, causing two match holders to spread contents, center hollow to store cigars, underside of lid inscribed with maker's initials and "Patent No. 2048," stout beech shaft, 1-1/8" white metal and iron ferrule, English, c1890, 36-1/4" l, **$2,000.**

Ivory, silver inlay, American, c1870, 1-1/2" d x 6-1/2" h elephant ivory ball handle, spiral overlaid silver panels with foliate engraving, one inscribed "F. T. Newman" (orig owner), inlay continues down ivory stem with fancy "C" scrolls and bars, 1-1/8" smooth silver collar, ebony shaft, 1-1/8" brass ferrule, 35-1/2" l.................................... **1,800.00**

Lapis, English, c1900, 1-3/4" d lapis lazuli ball handle, 1" beaded silver cup collar, black hardwood shaft, 7/8" horn ferrule, 36" l.................................. **400.00**

Porcelain

English, c1860, phrenology head, 1-1/3" w x 2-2/3" h, white, black lettering, gold highlighting, man's head delineated with numbers for different areas, decoder indicating character traits assigned to numbers, rosewood shaft, 7/8" horn ferrule, 36" l **3,250.00**

French, possibly Serves, c1895, cobalt blue 5" l x 2-1/4" d tau handle, gold highlights, hp scene on top, black hardwood shaft, 3/4" horn ferrule, 36" l **1,800.00**

Quartz, 1863, 1-1/2" d x 2-1/4" h silver handle, 7/8" faceted and polished gold quart with veins of raw gold on white background, octagon shaped, eight long oval panels, four dec with flowers, leaves, and scrolls, other four inscribed "Presented by H. S. Allen to his mother, 1863," heavy lignum vitae shade, 2" silver and iron ferrule, 35-3/4" l **8,500.00**

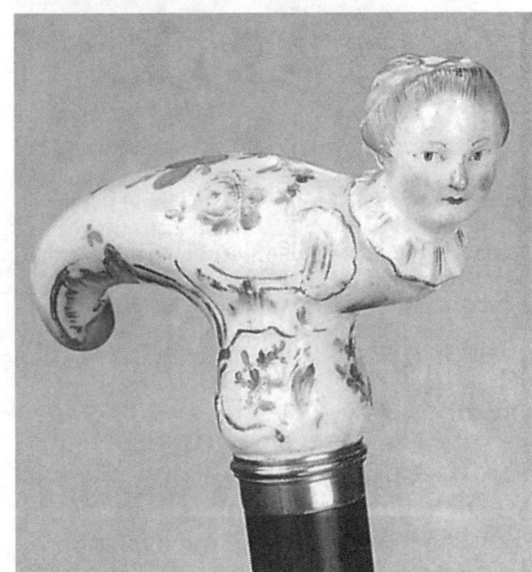

Porcelain, KPM, 2" h x 4-1/4" l tau handle, lady wearing bonnet, lace collar, handpainted floral motif, gold highlights, 1/3" gold collar, ebony shaft, 1-1/2" horn ferrule, Berlin, c1890, 38-1/2" l, **$1,600.**

Rock crystal

English, c1900, 1-1/2" d x 2" h egg-shaped crystal handle, etched with four leaf clovers with Essex crystals with painted objects of mushrooms, four leaf clovers, ladybugs, pig, chimney sweep, and bird mounted in gold as centers, 3/4" green enamel collar, engine turned guillouche, black enameled hardward shaft, 7/8" horn ferrule, 36" l **3,750.00**

French, c1900, 7/8" d x 3" h frosted rock crystal handle with hammered texture, 1/4" silver band with tiny blue faceted sapphires, ring of laurel leaves above band of deep blue enamel at base of handle, French hallmarks, maker's initials, maccassar ebony shaft, 7/8" replaced brass ferrule, 36" l, light surface cracks in enamel **1,700.00**

Russian silver and enamel, 1907-17, 4-1/2" l x 2" h tau handle, blue, green, red, and white enamel, alpha hallmark for St. Petersburg, figured snakewood shaft, 1-3/4" horn ferrule, 36-1/2" l **2,300.00**

Rose quartz, 3" h x 1-1/3" w oval handle, top decorated with silver rope frame around floral enamel work, four rubies, central pearl, three enameled tulips down one side, highlighted with two rubies and pearl, 1/3" oval band of enameled flowers on white background with eight more rubies, oval black hardwood shaft, 7/8" oval horn ferrule, Continental, c1910, 35-3/4" l, **$3,000.**

Silver

American, c1890, 3-1/4" l x 2" h "L" alligator stretched out on log as handle, bright red glass eyes, zebra wood shaft, 1" white metal and iron ferrule, 34-1/2" l **1,000.00**

England, attributed to, c1890, 2-1/2" w x 3-3/4" h figural handle, bulging red glass eyes, front legs tucked under, rear legs extending down black shaft, 1" horn ferrule, 34" l **950.00**

French, c1895, 1" d x 3-1/4" h silver handle, 3/4" polished amethyst cabochon on top, 1/2" band of purple enamel with festoons of silver floral roping above 2" area of engine turned guilloche silver, ring of tiny seed pearls between two rings of silver laurel leaves, tiny hallmarks and maker's initials, ebony shaft, 1" replaced brass ferrule, 36-1/3" l **1,500.00**

Gorham, Rhode Island, c1900, 1-1/8" d x 6-1/2" l sterling handle, 3/4" faceted amethyst stone inlaid on knob top, stem elaborately chased with fancy dec, Gorham hallmarks, sterling stamp, tightly stepped partridge-wood shaft, 3/4" burnished copper ferrule, 36-1/2" l **1,460.00**

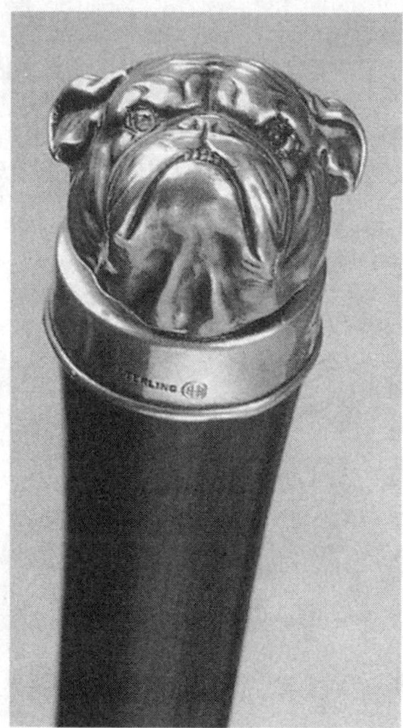

Silver, Unger Bros, 1-1/4" h x 1-1/4" w bulldog handle, cabochon ruby eyes, faux leather collar and buckle, round hallmark, marked "sterling," dense lignum vitae shaft, 1/2" worn brass ferrule, American, c1900, 36-3/4" l, **$2,000.**

Hungarian, c1900, gilt silver, 7/8" d x 5" h handle, small ball top inlaid with 3/8" cabochon garnet, remainder of textured handle fashioned with tiny raised gilt silver balls, dozens of pale blue cabochon turquoise stones, dozens of faceted garnets and amethysts, black enamel shaft, 2-1/8" gilt silver ferrule that matches handle with same inlaid jewels, 35-3/4" l **900.00**

Unger Bros, c1900, 1-1/4" w x 1-1/4" h bulldog, cabochon ruby eyes, faux leather collar and buckle, marked "sterling," round "UB" mark, dense lignum vitae shaft, 1/2" worn brass ferrule, 36-3/4" l **2,000.00**

Tiffany, American, c1895, 3-3/4" l x 2-2/3" h sterling silver handle, Thomas Nast eagle, initialed for orig owner, marked "Tiffany and Co. Maker, Sterling" on lower rim, shaft portion of handle dec with flowing leafy stems and prickly burrs, Malacca shaft, threaded mount, 2-1/4" horn ferrule, 35" l **7,000.00**

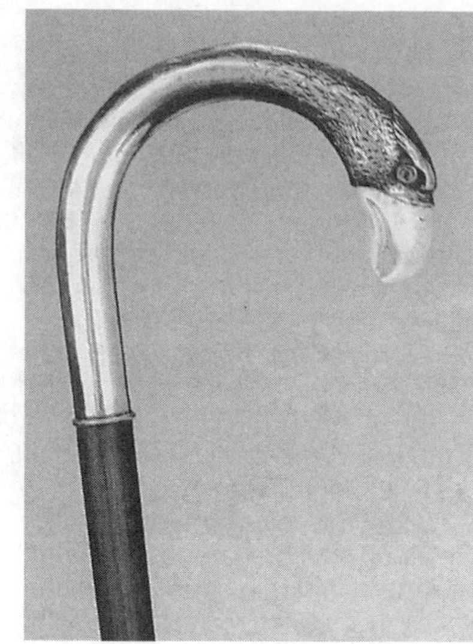

Silver and ivory eagle, 7-1/2" l crook handle ending as eagle's head, 1-1/4" elephant ivory beak, yellow glass eyes, detailed feathering, marked "925," snakewood shaft, 1" brass and iron ferrule, Continental, c1890, 35-1/4" l, **$950.**

Wood

American, 1900, 1-1/2" d x 1" h dec knob handle, inscribed "John Bindley to H. J. Heinz, Nov. 1900," birch, entire shaft etched, titled "Heroes of the U.S. Navy," pictures Spanish-American War Admirals George Dewey, W. S. Schindley, William Sampson, Robley Evans, C. B. Clark, etchings of US flag, Lady Liberty, sailors, flowers, 3/4" white metal ferrule, 34-3/4" l **3,000.00**

American, University of New Hampshire senior cane, 2-1/2" w x 3-3/4" h carved wood handle, two profiles of "Old Man in the Mountain," thin white metal collar, dark stained hardwood shaft carved with initials "N.H. 25" for year it was presented, owner's first name and classmates carved down length of shaft, 1-1/2" white metal and iron ferrule, 36" l **325.00**

English, 1910, carved 2-3/4" w x 3-1/3" hardwood handle, mouse perched on stump with long tail, yellow glass eyes, 1-1/4" silver collar with London hallmarks, birch shaft, 1-1/3" white metal and iron ferrule, 35-1/4" l **1,000.00**

CANTON CHINA

History: Canton china is a type of Oriental porcelain made in the Canton region of China from the late 18th century to the present. It was produced largely for export. Canton china has a hand-decorated light- to dark-blue underglaze-on-white ground. Design motifs include houses, mountains,

trees, boats, and bridges. A design similar to willow pattern is the most common.

Borders on early Canton feature a rain-and-cloud motif (a thick band of diagonal lines with a scalloped bottom). Later pieces usually have a straight-line border.

Early, c1790-1840, plates are very heavy and often have an unfinished bottom, while serving pieces have an overall "orange-peel" bottom. Early covered pieces, such as tureens, vegetable dishes, and sugars, have strawberry finials and twisted handles. Later ones have round finials and a straight, single handle.

Marks: The markings "Made in China" and "China" indicate wares that date after 1891.

Reproduction Alert: Several museum gift shops and private manufacturers are issuing reproductions of Canton china.

Basket, reticulated, oval, blue decorated rim and base, scene of pagodas and junks, 19th C, 9-3/4" l, 3-3/4" h, **$375**. Photo courtesy of Alderfer Auction Co.

Bowl

8-3/4" d, 1-1/2" h, scalloped edges, central design, three blue flowers on outside, orange peel glaze **440.00**

9-1/2" x 9-1/2" x 4-1/4" h, medium blue on white, pagodas, trees, river, mountains, band of blue around rim with broad crosshatching, sq top, scalloped rim, round table ring with small chips **1,100.00**

Bowl and underplate, 8-1/2" l, 3-1/2" h reticulated bowl, matching borders, center design different on 9" l plate... **1,045.00**

Candlesticks, pr, 7-1/2" h, lighthouse shape, sailboat above bridge, incised lines, tiny rim flakes on both...... **1,100.00**

Creamer, 3-1/2" h, bull nose, applied handle... **440.00**

Demitasse cup and saucer, feather-like trees dec **175.00**

Ginger jar, cov, pr, 8-1/2" h, 9" h, blue and white design, some surface wear **500.00**

Mug, 4" h, applied intertwined handle, molded berry ends...................... **550.00**

Pitcher, 7" h, applied handle with molded end **715.00**

Pitcher, cov, 9" h, dark and medium blue dec with good detail, ovoid, double overlapping strap handles, slightly domed lid with foo dog finial **2,100.00**

Bowl, covered, snail finial, blue and white decoration, **$295**. Photo courtesy of Wiederseim Associates, Inc.

Plate

5-7/8" d, slightly scalloped edge **115.00**

7-1/2" d................................ **125.00**

10-1/8" d, pinched rim, set of six **990.00**

Platter, octagonal, blue and white, scenes of pagodas and junks, 15-3/4" l, 12-1/2" w, **$375**. Photo courtesy of Alderfer Auction Co.

Platter

10-1/2" x 13-3/4", dark and medium blue dec, orange peel glaze, unglazed base **495.00**

16" x 20", dark and medium blue dec, orange peel glaze, boat, pagoda, and trees design...... **770.00**

Platter, reticulated, 9-1/4" x 10-3/4", orange peel glaze, some edge roughness **825.00**

Vegetable dish, covered, square, chips, **$195**. Photo courtesy of Wiederseim Associates, Inc.

Posset pot, cov, 3-1/4" h, fruit finial, intertwined handles, molded leaf ends **150.00**

Shrimp dish, acorn shape, medium blue dec, two large shrimp on flange handle **615.00**

Spoon, 5-1/4" l **125.00**

Soup bowl, 9-7/8" d, shallow **125.00**

Sugar, cov, 6-1/4" h, two intertwined handles with molded berry ends, berry finial on lid, lid close match.......... **250.00**

Teapot, cov

4-3/4" h, individual size, fruit finial, intertwined handles **300.00**

6" h, straight sides, applied intertwined handle, molded berry ends, berry finial, minor glazed over rim flake................................ **625.00**

9-3/4" h, dark and medium blue dec, pagodas, boats, sides taper sharply from shoulders to flared foot, scroll ear handle, domed lid, professional restoration to spout, in-the-making imperfection on foot **330.00**

Tureen, cov, 13" w, 9-1/2" d, 7-1/2" h, detailed dark and medium blue dec, flared sides, ftd oval base, applied animal head handles, domed lid with incised feather designs, slight orange peel glaze................................ **1,870.00**

Vegetable bowl, cov, underplate, 6-1/2" l, 3-1/2" h bowl with scalloped corners, boar head handles, molded finial, 7-1/2" l underplate, orange peel glaze, minor roughness, hairline on underplate **525.00**

Capo-Di-Monte

History: In 1743, King Charles of Naples established a soft-paste porcelain factory near Naples. The firm made figurines and dinnerware. In 1760, many of the workmen and most of the molds were moved to Buen Retiro, near Madrid, Spain. A new factory, which also made hard-paste porcelains, opened in Naples in 1771. In 1834, the Doccia factory in Florence purchased the molds and continued production in Italy.

Capo-di-Monte was copied heavily by other factories in Hungary, Germany, France, and Italy.

Reproduction Alert: Many of the pieces in today's market are of recent vintage. Do not be fooled by the crown over the "N" mark; it also was copied.

Basket, yellow, pink, and white roses, green foliage, tan basketweave base, marked with crown and "Capo-di-Monte, Made in Italy," **$75**.

Box, cov, 8" d, 4-1/4" h, round, domed lid molded with low relief figures of cherubs with flower baskets, sides similarly molded with cherubs at various artistic pursuits, gilt-metal rim mounts, int. painted with floral sprigs, late 19th C **475.00**

Creamer and sugar, mythological raised scene, dragon handles, claw feet, lion finial, 5-1/2" x 6" creamer, 6-1/4" x 6" cov sugar **250.00**

Dresser set, mythological raised scene, pair of 4" d, 7" h perfume bottles with figural stoppers, 5" d, 4" h cov powder jar, 30" l x 15" w tray **500.00**

Lamp, green jasper ware type base with white relief, **$150**.

Ferner, 11" l, oval, relief molded and enameled allegorical figures, full relief female mask at each end **120.00**

Figure, sgd "G. Armani," 7-1/2" l, 6-1/2" h, mare and foal **210.00**

Lamp, table, 25" h, figural Bacchus, female, and grapes **1,300.00**

Plate, 8-3/8" d, each with Capo-di-Monte crest at top, pair of swans, pair of cranes, crimson, blue, yellow, and burnt-orange flowers on border, gold trim, minor wear, price for eight-pc set **1,100.00**

Plate, pedestal base, gilt decoration around foot, three mermaid figures supporting plate, gilding and raised allegorical figures around rim, center of plate dec with coat of arms featuring cloak descending from crown with two rampant lions holding crest, surrounded by gilt scrollwork accented with black, marks on bottom of pedestal include under-glaze mark of N below crown in blue, bumblebee painted over glaze in gold, and words, "Napoleon and Josephine," 10-1/4" d, 5" h, **$115**. Photo courtesy of Alderfer Auction Co.

Urn, cov, 21-1/8" h, ovoid, central-molded frieze of Nerieds and putti, molded floral garlands, gadroon upper section, acanthus-molded lower section, socle foot with putti, sq plinth base, applied ram's-head handles, domed cov, acorn finial, underglaze crowned "N" mark, minor chips and losses, pr **1,650.00**

Carlsbad China

History: Because of changing European boundaries during the last 100 years, German-speaking Carlsbad has found itself located first in the Austro-Hungarian Empire, then in Germany, and currently in the Czech Republic. Carlsbad was one of the leading pottery manufacturing centers in Bohemia.

Wares from the numerous Carlsbad potteries are lumped together under the term "Carlsbad China." Most pieces on the market are post-1891, although several potteries date to the early 19th century.

Bowl, 14" d, handles, marked "Imperial H&C Carlsbad Austria," numbers "2552" and "18," wear to gold edge, repaired chip **50.00**

Butter dish, cov, 7-1/4" d, pink flowers, green leaves, wavy gold lines, white ground **65.00**

Chocolate pot, cov, 10" h, blue, scenic portrait, marked "Carlsbad Victoria" **115.00**

Creamer and sugar, Bluebird pattern, marked "Victoria Carlsbad" **70.00**

Cake plates, cherubs decoration, 11" d, **$60**. Photo courtesy of Joy Luke Auctions.

Ewer, 14" h, handles, light green, floral dec, gold trim, marked "Carlsbad Victoria" **85.00**

Game plates, 8" sq, each hand painted with gold trim, light and dark gray corners, center with game birds, gold outlines, mauve circular mark "Carlsbad Mark & Gutherz," price for 11-pc set **700.00**

Demitasse cups and saucers, one pink and one blue, each decorated with scenic panel with figures, gilded interior and banding, **$120**. Photo courtesy of Joy Luke Auctions.

Oyster plate, 8-1/4" d, five wells plus center well, stylized pink-and-blue peonies, green leaves, gold accents, marked "Marx & Gutherz" **120.00**

Pin tray, 8-1/2" l, irregular scalloped shape, roses, green leaves, white ground, marked "Victoria Carlsbad Austria" **40.00**

Sugar shaker, 5-1/2" h, egg shape, floral dec **70.00**

Urn, 14-1/2" h, rose bouquet, shaded ivory ground, marked "Carlsbad Austria" **155.00**

Carnival Glass

History: Carnival glass, an American invention, is colored-pressed glass with a fired-on iridescent finish. It was first manufactured about 1905 and was immensely popular both in America and abroad. More than 1,000 different patterns have been identified. Production of old carnival-glass patterns ended in 1930.

For more information, see *Warman's Glass,* 4th edition.

Most of the popular patterns of carnival glass were produced by five companies: Dugan, Fenton, Imperial, Millersburg, and Northwood.

Marks: Northwood patterns frequently are found with the "N" trademark. Dugan used a diamond trademark on several patterns.

Notes: Color is the most important factor in pricing carnival glass. The color of a piece is determined by holding it to the light and looking through it.

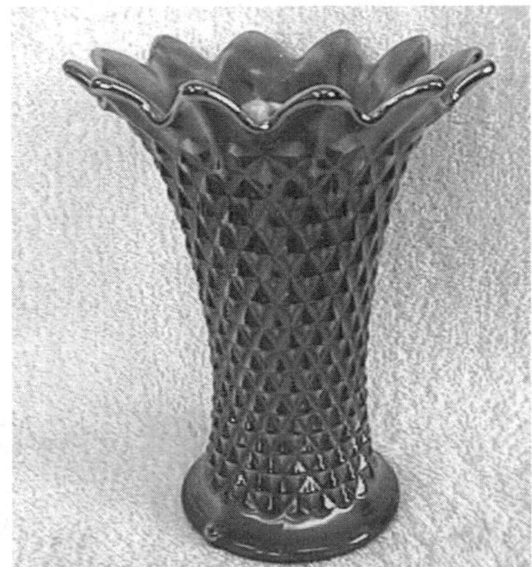

Diamond Points, Northwood, vase, 7" h, squatty, green, **$75**. Photo courtesy of Seeck Auctions.

Acorn Burrs, Northwood, bowl, 4-3/4" d, marigold **30.00**
Acorns, Millersburg, compote, six ruffles, marigold and Vaseline **3,750.00**
Apple Blossom Twigs, Dugan, plate, low, ruffled, purple, electric purple-and-blue highlights **225.00**
Basket of Roses, Northwood, bonbon, stippled, amethyst **475.00**
Beaded Cable, Northwood, candy dish, ftd, amethyst **70.00**
Big Fish, Millersburg, bowl, 7" d, marigold **650.00**
Blackberry Spray, Fenton, hat, 6-1/2" h, Vaseline, sq, four sides up **40.00**
Blackberry Wreath, Millersburg
Bowl, 7-1/2" d, six ruffles, green **65.00**
Ice cream sauce, 5-1/2" d, dark marigold **110.00**
Sauce, 6-1/4" d, six ruffles, green, satiny finish **65.00**
Blossomtime, Northwood, compote, marigold **200.00**
Bouquet, Fenton, water pitcher, marigold **150.00**
Bull's Eye & Beads, Imperial, vase, 7" h, flared, dark marigold **40.00**
Bushel Basket, Northwood, round, sapphire **1,350.00**
Butterfly & Fern, Fenton, tumbler, green **55.00**
Cherries, Dugan, banana boat, electric blue, purple highlights, three ftd .. **275.00**
Chrysanthemum, Nu-Art, chop plate, marigold **450.00**

Fenton #649, Fenton, candlesticks, wisteria, **$450**. Photo courtesy of Seeck Auctions.

Concave Diamond, Northwood
Tumble-up, russet green **900.00**
Vase, 6" h, celeste blue **175.00**
Colonial Lady, Imperial, vase **2,300.00**
Dancing Lady, vase, jade green . **650.00**
Diamond Points, Northwood, vase, 11" h, sapphire **1,700.00**
Diamond Rib, Fenton, vase, 9" h, purple **40.00**
Double Dutch, Imperial, bowl...... **725.00**
Dragon and Lotus, Fenton, bowl, red **750.00**
Drapery, Northwood, rose bowl, aqua opalescent , light butterscotch overlay **250.00**
Embossed Scroll, bowl, 7" d, Hobstar & Tassel exterior, electric purple...... **400.00**
Embroidered Mums, Northwood, Plate, 9" d, ice green **1,100.00**
Enameled Grape, Northwood, water set, six pcs, blue, enamel dec **800.00**
Fanciful, Dugan, bowl, low, ruffled, frosty white, pink, blue, and green highlights **115.00**
Fashion, Imperial
Punch cup, marigold **28.00**
Water set, marigold, seven-pc matched set **150.00**

Fine Rib, Northwood, vase, marigold, 9" h, **$65**.

Field Flower, water pitcher, purple **475.00**

Fine Rib, Fenton, vase
10" h, powder blue **60.00**
11-3/4" h, vaseline, marigold overlay **70.00**
Fishscale & Beads, Dugan
Plate, 7" d, electric purple...... **575.00**
Plate, 7" d, marigold, satin irid . **45.00**
Flowers, Fenton, rose bowl, blue, multicolored irid **110.00**
Flute, Imperial, toothpick holder, blue **925.00**
Frosted Block, Imperial, rose bowl, deep marigold **30.00**
Fruits & Flowers, Northwood, bonbon, handled, lavender **200.00**
Good Luck, Northwood, bowl, 9" d, ruffled, ribbed ext., marigold........ **175.00**
Grape, Imperial
Decanter, electric purple, stopper missing **85.00**
Water carafe, emerald green **4,300.00**
Grape & Cable, Fenton, bowl, 6-1/2" d, smoky blue **40.00**
Grape and Cable, Northwood
Banana boat, purple **195.00**
Cracker jar, cov, handles, amethyst **275.00**
Hatpin holder, amethyst **265.00**
Humidor, amethyst **325.00**
Pin tray, blue **400.00**
Plate, ruffled, stippled, sapphire **2,000.00**
Punch set, 13-1/2" d bowl, base, 10 cups, white **3,500.00**

Heavy Paneled Grape, nappy, purple, **$40**. Photo courtesy of Seeck Auctions.

Grape & Gothic Arches, Northwood, tumbler, electric blue **45.00**
Grape Arbor, Northwood, tankard pitcher, white **575.00**
Grapevine & Lattice, Dugan, tumbler, white **225.00**
Grape Wreath, Millersburg
Bowl, 8-1/2" d, three-in-one-edge, green, radium finish **135.00**
Ice cream bowl, 8" d, amethyst, radium finish **155.00**
Greek Key, Northwood, plate, blue **400.00**
Hanging Cherries, Millersburg, water pitcher, dark **1,700.00**

Heavy Grape, Imperial
Chop plate, 11" d, electric purple **400.00**
Nappy, 5" d, electric purple ... **110.00**
Heavy Iris, Dugan, tumbler, amethyst **75.00**
Heavy Pineapple, Fenton, bowl, ftd, 10" d, amber, satiny iridescence .. **500.00**
Hobnail, Millersburg, spittoon, marigold **700.00**
Hobnail Swirl, Millersburg, vase, 11" h, amethyst, radium iridescence...... **250.00**
Hobstar & Feather, Millersburg
Compote, round, clear **75.00**
Punch cup, crystal **25.00**
Rose bowl, large **3,200.00**

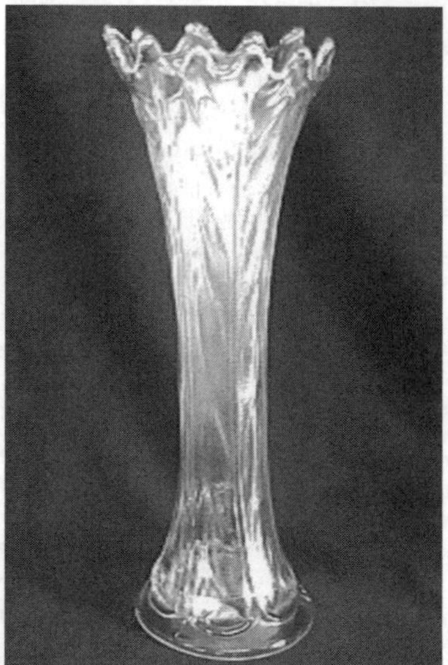

Leaf Columns, Northwood, vase, 10" h, white, **$300**. Photo courtesy of Seeck Auctions.

Holly, Fenton
Bowl, ice cream shape, marigold **150.00**
Jack-in-the-pulpit hat, crimped edge, marigold **50.00**
Holly Sprig, Millersburg, nappy, tri-corn, handle, green **160.00**
Holly Whirl, Millersburg
Bonbon, Issac Benesch 54th Anniversary adv, marigold **150.00**
Bowl, 9-1/2" d, ruffled, marigold, radium finish....... **85.00**
Homestead, Imperial, chop plate, purple **2,700.00**
Horse Head Medallion, Fenton, jack-in-the-pulpit bowl, ftd, marigold **75.00**
Inverted Strawberry, Cambridge, sauce dish, 5" d, marigold **25.00**
Kittens, Fenton
Cup and saucer, marigold **245.00**
Toothpick holder, ruffled, marigold, radium finish....... **115.00**
Leaf and Little Flowers, Millersburg
Compote, flared, deep, green, radium finish with bright blue highlights....... **500.00**
Compote, six ruffles, dark marigold **300.00**
Leaf Columns, Northwood, vase, 10-1/2" h, radium green, multicolored irid, slightly flared top **135.00**
Leaf Tiers, Fenton, tumbler, ftd, marigold **80.00**
Many Stars, Millersburg, bowl, adv, Bernheimer Bros, blue....... **3,000.00**

Open Rose, Imperial, rose bowl, amber, **$25**. Photo courtesy of Seeck Auctions.

Morning Glory, Imperial, funeral vase, 16-1/2" h, 4-3/4" d base, purple.... **250.00**
Nesting Swan, Millersburg, bowl, 9-1/2" d, green **1,000.00**
Night Stars, Millersburg, bonbon, two handles, two sides, olive green, blue radium finish **800.00**
Ohio Star, Millersburg
Cider pitcher, 11" h tankard, crystal **250.00**
Cider set, six pcs, 10" h tankard, crystal, chip on one tumbler **625.00**
Toothpick holder, crystal **115.00**
Open Rose, Imperial
Plate, 9" d, marigold **45.00**
Rose bowl, electric purple int. and ext....... **625.00**

Persian Medallion, Fenton, bowl, blue, 8" d, **$45**; Peacock Tail, Fenton, bowl, blue, 7" d, **$40**. Photo courtesy of Joy Luke Auctions.

Optic & Buttons, Imperial, rose bowl, marigold **30.00**
Orange Tree, Fenton
Bowl, 9" d, ruffled, Tree Trunk center, white, blue irid....... **90.00**
Mug, standard size, amber, weak impression....... **55.00**
Plate, 9-1/2" d, Tree Trunk center, white, frosty irid **185.00**
Punch set, punch bowl, stand, 12 cups, marigold **395.00**
Wine, blue **60.00**
Peacock, Millersburg
Berry bowl, individual, 5" d, purple, radium finish....... **115.00**
Ice cream bowl, 5" d, marigold, satiny irid **200.00**
Peacock at Fountain, Dugan, tumbler, blue....... **35.00**
Peacock at Fountain, Northwood
Tumbler, amethyst **25.00**
Water pitcher, amethyst....... **250.00**
Peacock at Urn, Fenton, compote, stemmed, celeste blue, marigold overlay **150.00**
Peacock at Urn, Millersburg
Berry bowl, master, 9" d, flared, marigold, radium irid with blue highlights....... **275.00**
Bowl, 8" d, blue **2,100.00**
Compote, stemmed, ruffled, large, green **1,500.00**
Ice cream bowl, 9-3/4" d, amethyst, radium finish, bee, no beading **225.00**
Sauce, 6" d, ruffled, blue, no bee, no beading....... **1,050.00**
Peacock Garden, Fenton, vase
Blue **210.00**
Red....... **225.00**
White **185.00**
Peacocks on Fence (Northwood Peacocks), Northwood
Bowl, aqua opalescent....... **1,100.00**
Plate, blue **400.00**
Persian Garden, Dugan, plate, 6-1/2" d, marigold **40.00**
Persian Medallion, Fenton
Bonbon, two handles, vaseline, marigold overlay....... **140.00**
Chop plate, blue....... **195.00**
Hair receiver, frosty white....... **130.00**

Persian Medallion, Fenton, bon bon, aqua, **$160**. Photo courtesy of Seeck Auctions.

Petals, Northwood, compote, 7", marigold **30.00**
Peter Rabbit, Fenton, bowl, ruffled **1,800.00**

Pinecone, Fenton, plate, 6" d, marigold **40.00**

Plume Panels, Fenton, vase, 11" h, green **95.00**

Pond Lily, Fenton, calling card tray, two handles, white, weak irid **25.00**

Poppy, Millersburg, compote, flared, dark marigold **475.00**

Poppy Show, Northwood
- Bowl, electric blue **2,300.00**
- Plate, amethyst **750.00**
- Plate, ice blue **1,800.00**

Rays & Ribbons, Millersburg, bowl, 9-1/2" d, ruffled, crimped edge, Cactus exterior, purple, blue radium irid .. **175.00**

Ribbon Tie, Fenton, bowl, three-in-one edge, low, blue **160.00**

Ripple, Imperial, funeral vase, 17" h, marigold **115.00**

Rosalind, Millersburg
- Bowl, 10-1/2" d, six ruffles, amethyst **225.00**
- Jelly, stemmed, flared, deep, 8-1/2" h, amethyst **3,500.00**

Rose Show, Northwood
- Bowl, ruffled, aqua opalescent **2,000.00**
- Plate, ice blue **2,100.00**

Rose Spray, Fenton, goblet, marigold **30.00**

Round-Up, Dugan, plate, 9" d, blue **385.00**

Rustic, Fenton, swung vase, 15" h, 4-1/4" d base, green, radium multicolored irid **110.00**

Seacoast, Millersburg, pin tray, amethyst **550.00**

Seaweed, Millersburg
- Plate, 9" d, flared, marigold . **1,600.00**
- Sauce, 5-1/2" d, ice cream shape, dark marigold **850.00**

Stag & Holly, Fenton
- Bowl, 10" d, ruffled, ftd, powder blue, marigold overlay **200.00**
- Bowl, 11-1/4" d, ruffled, ftd, light-blue aqua base, marigold overlay **200.00**

Stippled Petals, Dugan, plate, purple, dome ftd, tightly crimped edge **750.00**

Stippled Rays, Fenton
- Ice cream bowl, 6" d, cherry red **450.00**
- Plate, red **750.00**

Strawberry, Northwood
- Bowl, 8" d, pie crust edge, purple **90.00**
- Plate, 9-1/4" d, basketweave back, green **235.00**

Strawberry Wreath, Millersburg
- Bowl, 9" d, low-crimped ruffled, purple **185.00**
- Compote, six ruffles, green **400.00**
- Sauce, 5" sq, crimped edge, green **650.00**

Singing Birds, Northwood, mug, stippled, blue, **$850**. Photo courtesy of Seeck Auctions.

Swirl Hobnail, Millersburg, rose bowl, purple **275.00**

Ten Mums, Fenton, bowl, 9" d, three-in-one edge, green **100.00**

Three Fruits, Northwood
- Bowl, eight ruffles, stippled, green **300.00**
- Plate, stippled, amethyst **300.00**
- Plate, stippled, aqua opalescent **3,400.00**

Tiger Lily, Imperial, tumbler, marigold **75.00**

Tree Trunk, Northwood
- Funeral vase, 10-1/2" h, aqua opalescent, butterscotch overlay, opalescence extending to base **950.00**
- Vase, squatty, ice blue **1,500.00**

Trout and Fly, Millersburg
- Bowl, 9" d, three-in-one edge, light amethyst **700.00**
- Ice cream bowl, 8-1/2" l, green, satiny finish, bruise on base **625.00**

Ski Star, Dugan, bowl, large, ruffled, peach opal, **$265**. Photo courtesy of Seeck Auctions.

Wild Flower, Northwood, compote, stemmed, light marigold **65.00**

Wild Rose, Northwood, rose bowl, ftd, stippled rays int., electric purple.. **650.00**

Wild Strawberry, Northwood, plate, 8" d, hand grip, basketweave back, electric purple **325.00**

Windmill, Imperial
- Pitcher, marigold **65.00**
- Tumbler, purple **75.00**

Wide Panel, Northwood, epergne, ice green **7,000.00**

Wishbone & Spades, Dugan, chop plate, 10-3/4" d, plain back, purple, with electric purple and blue highlights **900.00**

Wreath of Roses, Fenton, punch cups, Vintage interior, blue **40.00**

Zig-Zag, Millersburg
- Bowl, 10" d, three-in-one edge, amethyst **400.00**
- Bowl, tri-corn, crimped edge, amethyst **1,050.00**

Carousel Figures

History: By the late 17th century, carousels were found in most capital cities of Europe. In 1867, Gustav Dentzel carved America's first carousel. Other leading American firms include Charles I. D. Looff, Allan Herschell, Charles Parker, and William F. Mangels.

Notes: Since carousel figures were repainted annually, original paint is not a critical factor to collectors. "Park paint" indicates layers of accumulated paint; "stripped" means paint has been removed to show carving; "restored" involves stripping and repainting in the original colors.

Horse, standing, Philadelphia-style, Gustav A. Dentzel, Germantown, PA, 1890-1906, flowing mane, red-painted flat saddle with carved eagle head cantle; body with green-painted interwoven straps; replaced horsehair tail; tapered hooves with carved horseshoes, 59-1/4" h, **$17,700**. Photo courtesy of Sloans & Kenyon Auctions.

Camel
- European, 1890 .... **2,400.00**
- Loeff **7,000.00**
- Morris, E. Joy **8,000.00**

Chariot bench
- Loeff, gilded **625.00**
- Parker, C. W. **12,500.00**
- Spillman, with flowers **300.00**

Cow, Bayol, France **5,000.00**
Elephant, fiberglass **600.00**
Giraffe, old mottled painted surface, carved mane, attributed to Ohio, c1880-90, some losses, saddle and tail missing, 39" l, 10" d, 53" h **6,325.00**
Goat, Loeff **7,500.00**
Horse, jumper
- Anderson, J. R. **5,000.00**
- Carmel **3,700.00**
- Dentzel, top knot **5,000.00**
- Herschell, Allen, all wood, 1920 .... **2,000.00**
- Herschell-Spillman, North Tonawanda, NY, orange, green, and blue, 60" x 56" x 12" cast iron stand **2,750.00**
- Illions, from Willow Grove Amusement Park, Willow Grove, PA **4,750.00**
- Ortega, jumper **300.00**
- Parker, C. W., inside jumper, carved, sgd on shoes "C. W. Parker, Leavenworth, Kansas," early worn paint, brown body, black mane and tail, relief-carved saddle blanket, green, yellow, and red saddle, incised stars, red-and-yellow bridle, glass eyes, black-enameled steel base with pole with brass-spiral casing, 62" w, 36" h horse, 101" h pole **5,500.00**
- Spillman, restored **3,300.00**
- Stein & Goldstein **2,750.00**

Horse, prancer
- Dentzel, orig paint **8,000.00**
- Hubner, fully restored **4,250.00**
- Loeff, Charles, attributed to, outside prancer, carved, repainted in white, carved black mane, horsehair tail, blue-and-gray relief-carved straps and saddle, plaid saddle blanket, red-and-gold detailing, cobalt-blue faceted jewel on outside, glass eyes, 57" w, 55-1/2" h, enameled steel base and pole with brass-spiral casing, 90" h pole **2,750.00**

Horse, stander
- Dentzel, Gustav, Germantown, PA, c1900-10, flowing mane, double eagle back saddle, outside row, white, green, yellow, and gray over earlier pink paint, 57" l, 12" w, 58" h **10,350.00**
- Looff, Charles, c1905-10, cantle carving behind saddle, flowing mane, second row figure, gray and pink over old pale blue paint, 65" l, 13" w, 48" h **3,750.00**
- Morris, E. J. **10,500.00**
- Spillman, animal pelt **4,600.00**
- Stein & Goldstein **10,500.00**

Indian Pony
- Parker, C. W., pelt saddle **9,000.00**
- Spillman **4,500.00**

Panel, carved wood
- 37-1/2" x 45", cowboy on bucking bronco in panoramic view **200.00**
- 63" x 13", cherub at top, carved leaves overall **450.00**

Pig
- Dentzel, restored **12,000.00**
- Spillman, with pear **5,000.00**

√Castor Sets

History: A castor set consists of matched condiment bottles held within a frame or holder. The bottles are for condiments such as salt, pepper, oil, vinegar, and mustard. The most commonly found castor sets consist of three, four, or five glass bottles in a silver-plated frame.

Although castor sets were made as early as the 1700s, most of the sets encountered today date from 1870 to 1915, the period when they enjoyed their greatest popularity.

2-bottle, English, two cut-glass condiment jars, rect oak caddy mounted with silver-plate frame, upright handle, decorative strapwork and plain central shield, four ball feet, late 19th C, 7-7/8" l, 4-3/8" d, 10-5/8" h **500.00**
3-bottle, salt and pepper shakers, cov mustard pot, silver plated stand emb with fly, Meriden and Longwy, 8" h **490.00**

Two bottles, salt and pepper shapers, covered mustard, glass bases shaped so fit into base around looped handle, silver-plated mounts and round base, **$150**. Photo courtesy of Joseph P. Smalley, Jr., Auctioneer.

4-bottle, clear, mold blown, pewter lids and frame, domed based, loop handle, marked "I. Trask," early 19th C, 8" h **320.00**
4-bottle, cranberry bottles and jars, clear pressed-glass frame, silver-plated look handle, two brass caps, one pewter, 9-1/2" h **275.00**
4-bottle, ruby stained, Ruby-Thumbprint pattern, glass frame **360.00**
5-bottle, clear, Bellflower pattern, pressed stoppers, pewter frame with pedestal **295.00**
5-bottle, clear, all-over cut linear and geometric design, SS mounts and frame, shell-shaped foot, English hallmarks, c1750, 8-1/2" h **625.00**
5-bottle, William Gale & Sons, 1862-66, sterling silver base with foliate molded and looped handle, five holders each with vitruvian scroll and beaded borders, gadrooned circular foot, five cut glass bottles with faceting and trelliswork, monogrammed AMG, approx. 26 oz weighable silver. 12-1/2" h **1,175.00**
6-bottle, cut, diamond-point panels, rotating sterling-silver frame, all-over flowers, paw feet, loop handle, Gorham Mfg. Co., c1880, 11-1/2" h **2,500.00**

Seven-bottle, George III, c1800, Anglo-Irish cut glass shakers, ewers, etc. with silver mounts, fitted oval tray with four feet, 11" h, 8-1/2" l, **$1,675**. Photo courtesy of Pook & Pook.

Catalogs

History: The first American mail-order catalog was issued by Benjamin Franklin in 1744. This popular advertising tool helped to spread inventions, innovations, fashions, and necessities of life to rural America. Catalogs were profusely illustrated and are studied today to date an object, identify its manufacturer, study its distribution, and determine its historical importance.

Additional Listings: See *Warman's Americana & Collectibles* for more examples.

Adviser: Kenneth Schneringer.

American Brass & Copper, New York, NY, 1913, 272 pgs, 6-1/2" x 9-1/2", gas and electric fixtures **150.00**
American Car & Foundry Motor, New York, NY, c1927, eight pgs, 9" x 12", brown tinted cuts of 40 seated

passengers, 40 comfortable standees, specifications for coach **30.00**

Bakers Supply & Equipment, St. Paul, MN, c1929, 116 pgs, 7-3/4" x 10-1/2", bakery and restaurant equipment **34.00**

Dent Hardware Co., Fullerton, PA, c1930, 32 pgs, 6" x 9", Vol. 2, marble and slate stall fittings and trimmings, wardrobe hooks, towel hooks, etc. **18.00**

Ford Motor Co., Detroit, MI, c1920, 16 pgs, 5-1/2" x 8-1/2", *Ford Economy Truck for 1941* **26.00**

G. F. Quinn Refrigertor, Portland, ME, 1896, 32 pgs, 6-3/4" x 8-3/4", combination refrigerators and freezers for home and hotels **45.00**

G. I. Sellers & Sons, Co., Elwood, IN, 1930, 16 pgs, 8-1/2" x 11", *Sellers Catalog of Kitchen Furniture & Sales Manual,* two pgs price list laid-in, colored cuts of kitchen ensembles and “klearfront” kitchen cabinets, utility closets, base units, dinettes, buffets, etc. **50.00**

Haynes Automobile Co., Kokomo, IN, 1918, 20 pgs, 8" x 10-3/4", *America's Greatest Light Six and Light Twelve,* cuts of cars **100.00**

Hendee Manufacturing Co., Springfield, MA, c1916-20, 24 pgs, 7-3/4" x 9-3/4", *Indian Motorcycle,* claiming “The fastest time ever made was an Indian in 35 seconds, 1 mile,” introducing Indian Scout, illus of several models....... **500.00**

Hopkins & Allen Arms, Norwich, CT, 1906, 24 pgs, 5-1/4" x 7-3/4", *Cat. No. 3 for 1906,* cuts of new hammerless double barreled gun **65.00**

International Tailoring, New York, NY, c1925, 12 pgs, 4" x 8", *What You Need for Winter,* fashions and fabrics on display at W. R. Hale & Co. **20.00**

Collection of Old Town Canoe catalogs, 1925 through 2000, sold for **$5,280**. Photo courtesy of Lang's Sporting Collectables, Inc.

Joseph Dixon Crucible Co., Jersey City, NJ, c1927, 56 pgs, 6" x 9", *Dixon Graphite Productions,* tears at binding **24.00**

J. R. Clancy, Inc., Syracuse, NY, 1928, 64 pgs, 6" x 9", *Cat. No. 36,* theatrical stage hardware, cuts of steel stage screws, extension braces, curtain rigging, etc. **18.00**

Koken Companies, US, 1930, 124 pgs, 10-1/4" x 13", barber shop supplies **325.00**

Maxwell Motor Co., Inc., Detroit, MI, 1916, 36 pgs, 6" x 8", cuts of touring cars **110.00**

National Cloak & Suit Co., New York, NY, 1915, 162 pgs, 7-1/4" x 10", *Fall & Winter New York Fashions for Women,* includes some men styles **45.00**

NY Yacht, Launch & Engine, New York, NY, early 1900, 32 pgs, 6" x 9-1/2", 20th C motors, yachts, launches, boat parts **195.00**

Optical Sign Service Co., New York, NY, c1928, four pgs, 8-1/2" x 11", Practo canteen-shaped adv Monax glass globes, five color illus **45.00**

Oswego Tool Co., Oswego, NY, 1929, 43 pgs, 6" x 9-1/4", tools for boilermakers, machinists and pipeworkers, wraps loose **35.00**

Rainbo Paper Favor Works, Chicago, IL, c1933, 64 pgs, 5-1/2" x 8-1/4", mail-out envelope, Cat. No. 57, Dance & Party Favors, holiday decs, eight pgs of Halloween dec, party assortments, paper hats, supplies, decorations, flags, bunting, patriotic novelties **35.00**

Roger & Gallet, New York, NY, 1914, 45 pgs, 5-1/2" x 8", *Wholesale Price List of Paris Perfumes,* description and prices on one page, illus of perfume bottles on opposite sheet, toilet waters, colognes, bath salts, hair tonic, etc. **125.00**

Royal Manufacturing Co., Detroit, MI, 1896, 60 pgs, 9-1/2" x 12", *Illustrated Cat. & Price List of Silverware, Book of Rare Bargains,* dishes, cake baskets, pitchers, teapots, casters, butter dishes, carving sets, etc., light tears at edges, shows some use, folded in vertical center **175.00**

Standard Gas Equip Corp., New York, NY, 1926, 70 pgs, 5-1/4" x 8-1/2", hotel section catalog, 49 cuts of ranges, hotel and restaurant layouts, equipment **45.00**

Syracuse Rubber Co., Syracuse, NY, 1897, 98 pgs, 4-3/4" x 7-3/4", *Rubber & Oil Clothing,* Mackintoches, horse and wagon covers, hats, clothing, nursery and hospital goods, hunting coats, furniture tips, bicycle tires, foot balls, baby items, wraps faded, chips at edges **65.00**

Thwing Instrument Co., Philadelphia, PA, c1916, 46 pgs, 8" x 11", *General Cat. No. 8,* pyrometers for measuring temperatures, graphic records of temperatures, cuts of thermoelectric, galvanometers, indicators, polarity, thermocouplers, etc. **24.00**

W. H. Frear & Co., Troy, NY, 1903, 152 pgs, 8" x 10-1/4", *Fall & Winter Catalog of Clothing for Women and Girls,* illus of clothing, hand fans, embroideries, bird cages, buttons, toiletries, handkerchiefs, collars, cuffs, trunks, furniture, etc., some roughness to binding **48.00**

Ward-Stilson Co., Anderson, IN, 1920, 112 pgs, 9-1/4" x 12-1/4", *Cat. No. 80, Masonic Lodge Supplies,* cuts of costumes, aprons, jewelry, stereopticans, candlesticks, wigs, beards, tools and gauges, etc. **85.00**

White, Van Glahn & Co., New York, NY, 1911, 584 pgs, 8-1/4" x 11", *Cat. No. 99, Merchandise, Clothing & Shoes for the Family,* illus of weather vanes, tools, farm implements, jewelry, silver ware, hollow ware, etc. **100.00**

White Sewing Machine Co., Cleveland, OH, 1897, 32 pgs, 7-3/4" x 7-3/4", very colorful wraps, seven brightly colored farmable pictures, White bicycles, illus **365.00**

Willys-Overland Co., Toledo, OH, 1918, 16 pgs, 8-1/2" x 11", *The Overland Fours,* cuts of cars, oversized, tear at spine **95.00**

Yale & Towne Mfg. Co., Stamford, CT, 1905, 207 pgs, 6" x 9", *Cat. of Locks & Hardware, No. 18, Handy Edition,* padlocks, rim and mortise night latches, dead locks, sets, keys, cabinet and trunk locks, etc., 12 pgs laid-in, hard cover, light dampening at rear of spine .. **125.00**

CELADON

History: The term “celadon,” meaning a pale grayish-green color, is derived from the theatrical character Celadon, who wore costumes of varying shades of grayish green in Honore d'Urfe's 17th-century pastoral romance, *L'Astree*. French Jesuits living in China used the name to refer to a specific type of Chinese porcelain.

Celadon divides into two types. Northern celadon, made during the Sung Dynasty up to the 1120s, has a gray-to-brownish body, relief decoration, and monochromatic olive-green glaze. Southern (Lung-ch'uan) celadon, made during the Sung Dynasty and much later, is paint-decorated with floral and other scenic designs and is found in forms that appeal to the European- and American-export market. Many of the southern pieces date from 1825 to 1885. A blue square with Chinese or pseudo-Chinese characters appears on pieces after 1850. Later pieces also have a larger and sparser decorative patterning.

Reproduction Alert.

Bowl

5-3/4" d, wide flaring form, dark gray-green color, traces of three spurs on base, surface entirely glazed, Korea, Koryo period, 12th C **600.00**

7-1/2" d, sea green color, inlaid in Sangam technique with branches and sprigs of flowers, Korea, Koryo period, 12th/13th C **475.00**

9-1/2" d, 4-1/2" h, cut corner shape, Rose Canton dec, hardwood stand, repaired **385.00**

10-1/2" d, scalloped rim, dec with exotic birds, butterflies, and flowers, repairs and gilt losses to edge **245.00**

Brush box, cov, 7-1/2" w, 3-1/4" d, 2-1/2" h, dec in Rose Medallion palette **400.00**

Center dish, 11-1/4" l, diamond shape, conforming foot, court scenes, central scene contained in vasiform device, Rose Canton pattern, China, 19th C, gilt wear **530.00**

Charger

10" d, Mandarin warrior, One Hundred Antiques border, China, 19th C.................................. **210.00**

13-1/2" d, Rose Medallion, court scene within medallion, Famille Rose border, minor glaze wear **725.00**

Dish, carved stoneware, flower center and foliate border under dark celadon glaze, Chinese, Ming Dynasty, 14th-15th C, 10" d, **$1,100**. Photo courtesy of Alderfer Auction Co.

Ice cream tray, 7" x 13-1/4", rect, flange handles, Rose Canton motif, China, 19th C, minor gilt wear **600.00**

Incense burner, lid surmounted by Buddhist, lion base with lion mask feet, sea-green color, Korea, 12th C **8,000.00**

Plate

5-1/4" d, Rose Canton dec, China, 19th C....................................... **90.00**

10-1/4" d, river scene, butterfly and floral border, minor gilt and glaze wear.. **150.00**

10-1/4" d, whimsical dogs, butterfly and floral border, minor gilt and glaze wear **150.00**

Platter, 13-1/4" x 15-3/4", oval, Rose Canton dec **650.00**

Rice bowl, cov, underplate, 7-1/2" d, 5-3/4" h, dec with various animals, figures, and flowers **390.00**

Sauce tureen, cov, undertray, gilt floriform finial, gilt handles, bird, butterfly, and floral motifs, China, 19th C, minor edge wear **600.00**

Serving dish, cov, 10" d, 6-1/2" h, domed lid, single handle, Rose Canton dec, imperfections **300.00**

Shrimp dish, 10-1/4" x 9-3/4", bird, butterfly, and floral motif, China, 19th C, minor glaze wear **650.00**

Soap dish, three parts, 4-1/8" l, 5-1/4" w, 2-1/2" h, figures in garden on lid, Rose Medallion border, minor edge wear **265.00**

Vase

10-3/4" h, Maebyong form, carved floral sprigs on body and lotus petals at base, deep sea-green color, Korea, Koryo period, 12th/13th C, old repair to mouth **1,800.00**

12-3/4" h, hexagonal paneled form, two handles, bird and floral dec, handle chip, gilt wear **385.00**

Celluloid Items

History: In 1869, an Albany, NY, printer named John W. Hyatt developed and patented the world's first commercially successful semi-synthetic thermoplastic. The moldable material was made from a combination of camphor, the crystalline resin from the heart of a particular evergreen tree, and collodion, a type of nitrated-cellulose substance (also called Pyroxylin), which was extremely flammable. Hyatt and his brother, Isaiah, called their invention Celluloid, a name they made up by combining the words cellulose and colloid.

By 1873, the Hyatts were successfully producing raw pyroxylin plastic material at the Celluloid Manufacturing Company of Newark, NJ. In the early days of its commercial development, Celluloid was produced exclusively in two colors: flesh tone, for the manufacture of denture-base material, and off white, which was primarily used for utilitarian applications like harness trimmings and knife handles.

However, during the late 1870s, advances in plastics technology brought about a shift in the ways Celluloid could be used. Beautiful imitations of amber, ivory, tortoise shell, jet, and coral were being produced and used in the fabrication of jewelry, fashion accessories, and hair ornaments. Because the faux-luxury materials were so realistic and affordable, Celluloid quickly advanced to the forefront of consumerism by the working and middle classes.

By the early 20th century, there were four major American manufacturers firmly established as producers of quality pyroxylin plastics. In addition to the Celluloid Company of Newark, NJ, there was the Arlington Manufacturing Company of Arlington, NJ, which produced Pyralin; Fiberloid Corporation of Indian Orchard, MA, makers of Fiberloid; and the Viscoloid Company of Leominster, MA. Even though these companies branded their plastic products with their registered trade names, today the word "celluloid" is used in a general sense for all forms of this early plastic.

Celluloid-type plastic became increasingly popular as an alternative for costly and elusive natural substances. Within the fashion industry alone, it gained acceptance as a beautiful and affordable substitute for increasingly dwindling supplies of ivory and tortoise shell. However, it should be noted that celluloid's most successful application during the late 19th century was realized in the clothing industry; sheet stock in imitation of fine-grade linen was fashioned into stylish waterproof cuffs and collars.

In sheet form, celluloid found other successful applications as well. Printed political and advertising premiums, pinback buttons, pocket mirrors, and keepsake items from 1890-1920 were turned out by the thousands. In addition, transparent-sheet celluloid was ornately decorated by embossing, reverse painting, and lamination, and then used in the production of decorative boxes, booklets, and albums. The toy industry also capitalized on the used of thin-celluloid sheet for the production of blow-molded dolls, animal toys, and figural novelties.

The development of the motion-picture industry helped celluloid fulfill a unique identity all its own; it was used for reels of camera film, as well as in sheet form by animation artists who drew cartoons. Known as animation cels, these are still readily available to the collector for a costly sum, but because of the degradation of old celluloid, many early movies and cels have been lost forever.

By 1930, and the advent of the modern-plastics age, the use of celluloid began to decline dramatically. The introduction of cellulose-acetate plastic replaced the flammable pyroxylin plastic in jewelry and toys, and the development of non-flammable safety film eventually put an end to its use in movies. By 1950, the major manufacturers of celluloid in the United States had ceased production; however, many foreign companies continued manufacture. Today, Japan, France, Italy, and Korea continue to manufacture cellulose-nitrate plastics in small amounts for specialty items such as musical-instrument inlay, ping-pong balls, and designer fountain pens.

Beware of celluloid items that show signs of deterioration: oily residue, cracking, discoloration, and crystallization. Take care when cleaning celluloid items; it is best to use mild soap and water, avoiding alcohol-

or acetone-based cleansers. Keep celluloid from excessive heat or flame and avoid direct sunlight.

Marks: Viscoloid Co. manufactured a large variety of small hollow animals that ranged in size from two to eight inches. Most of these toys are embossed with one of three trademarks: "Made in USA," an intertwined "VCO," or an eagle with a shield.

Adviser: Julie P. Robinson.

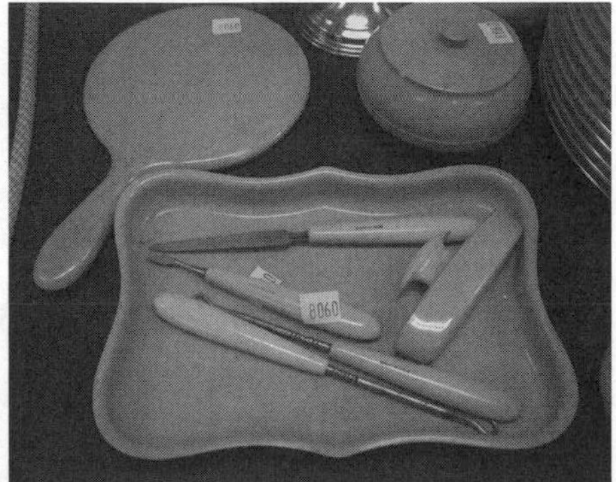

Dresser set, tray, mirror, powder jar, nail accessories, unmarked, **$115**.

Advertising and souvenir-keepsake items

Bookmark, 3 1/4" l, 1/4" w, folded top for slipping over a page, violets dec, "Greetings" on the long flat surface **20.00**

Compact, 1-3/4" d, imitation ivory-grained celluloid with gold Elk motif and "Third Annual Ball, BPOE, Leominster Lodge No. 1237, Jan. 26, 1917," produced by the Viscoloid Co. of Leominster, MA................................ **65.00**

Fan, 4" tall when closed, mottled turquoise-and-cream celluloid Brise fan, light-blue ribbon, shows the Washington Monument and words, "Washington D.C." in gold-tone paint **40.00**

Game counter, 2-3/4" x 1" ivory-grained celluloid, disks turn to keep baseball score, "Peter Doelger Bottled Beer—Expressly for the Home"................ **55.00**

Ink blotter, 4 1/8" x 2 7/8" ivory-grained celluloid, front and back covers w/ blotters inside, engraved scene of Black Diamond File Works, Philadelphia, PA, 1890 calendar, Baldwin & Gleason Co. **45.00**

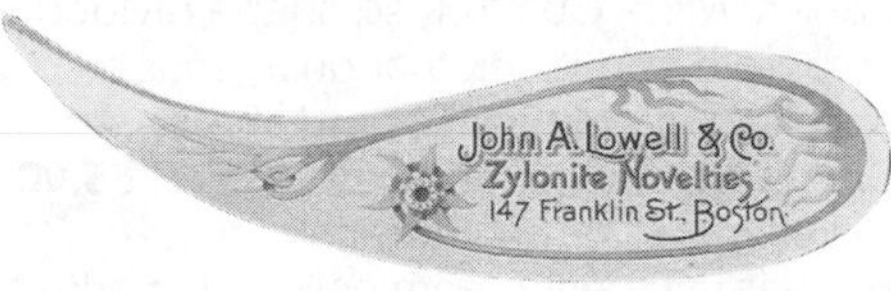

Advertising letter opener, ivory grained, sickle-shaped, advertising for Zylonite Novelties **$85**. Photo courtesy of Julie Robinson.

Pinback button, 3/4" d, red celluloid, white lettering "I'm the Guy that put the oysters in Oyster Bay"................... **18.00**

Pin holder, 1-3/4" d, celluloid disc, metal framework, "F Krupps Steel Works, Thomas Prosser & Son, NY," front shows advertising, back shows small child, engraved ivory-grained celluloid **40.00**

Pocket mirror, 2-1/4" d, beautiful woman with long red hair, wearing teal-blue dress and cloche, holding a bouquet of roses **55.00**

Postcard, 5-1/2" x 3-1/2", emb-fan motif with applied fabric and metal-script words, "Many Happy Returns," applied over fabric, circa 1908 .... **30.00**

Advertising, pocket mirrors for Mennen's, left: violets and image of Mennen, **$65**; right: image of powder tin, pink roses, gold accents, **$60**. Photo courtesy of Julie Robinson.

Tape measure, 1-1/4" d, pull-out tape, colorful pretty girl with flowers, adv for "The First National Bank of Boswell, The Same Old Bank in its New Home," printed by P.N. Co. (Parisian Novelty Co. of Chicago), Patent 7-10-17, emb in the side.. **65.00**

Toy, Easter, duck, chick, and big chick, **$85**. Photo courtesy of Julie Robinson.

Animals

Viscoloid Co. of Leominster, MA, manufactured a variety of small hollow toy animals, birds, and marine creatures, most of which are embossed with one of these three trade marks: "Made In USA," an intertwined "VCO," or an eagle with shield. A host of foreign countries also mass-produced celluloid toys for export into the United States. Among the most prolific manufacturers were Ando Togoro of Japan, whose toys bear the crossed-circle trademark, and Sekiguchi Co., which used a three-petal flower motif as its logo. Paul Haneaus of Germany used an intertwined PH trademark, and Petticolin of France branded its toys with an eagle head. Japanese- and American-made toys are plentiful, while those manufactured in Germany, England, and France, are more difficult to find.

Alligator, 3", green, white-tail tip, VCO/USA... **20.00**

Bear, 5" w, cream bear, pink and gray highlights, VCO/USA **20.00**

Bison, 3-1/4" l, dark brown, eagle-and-shield trademark............................. **22.00**

Camel, 3-1/2" x 2-1/2", peach celluloid, pink and black highlights, marked with crossed circle and "Made in Japan" **20.00**

Cat, 5-1/4", cream, pink and black highlights, molded collar and bell, Made in USA trademark **65.00**

Chick, 7/8", yellow, black eyes and beak, no trademark **12.00**

Chicken, 3" h, standing in grass, cream, gray, yellow feet, VCO/USA trademark **25.00**

Cow, 4-1/2", cream-and-orange cow; intertwined VCO/USA **25.00**

Dog

- Bulldog, 4-3/4" l, 2-1/2" h, spiked neck collar, translucent-green color, rhinestone eyes, intertwined VCO/USA.. **35.00**
- Hound, 5", long tail, peach celluloid, gray highlights, crossed-circle Japan **20.00**
- Scottie, 3-1/4" l, plaster-filled cream-colored celluloid, no detailing, marked JAPAN **20.00**
- St. Bernard, 3-1/4", tan, black highlights, intertwined VCO/USA **18.00**

Donkey, 4" l, 3-3/4" h, molded harnesses, saddles and blankets, grayish brown, red, and orange highlights, intertwined VCO/USA....................................... **35.00**

Swan, cobalt blue, magenta, and teal feathers, red feet and beak, marked "USA," 4" l, 3-1/2" h, **$18**.

Duck, 2-1/4", standing, cream-colored celluloid, hand-painted eyes and bills, original paper label, Made In Japan **20.00**
Elephant, 6-3/4" x 4-3/4", gray elephant, tusks, Made In USA **35.00**
Fish, 2-7/8", yellow, brown highlights, molded scales, intertwined VCO, circle **12.00**
Giraffe, 10" h, cream, beaded neck alternating brown and cream, brown and yellow painted highlights, detailed face, crossed-circle mark of Ando Togoro, Made In Japan **150.00**
Goat, 3", white, curled horns, flower, "N" in circle, Japan **25.00**
Hippopotamus, 3-3/4", pink, closed mouth, crossed circle, Japan **18.00**
Horse, 7", cream, purple and pink highlights, Made in USA **24.00**
Leopard, 4-1/2", white, orange highlights, black spots, Made in Occupied Japan **25.00**

Autograph album, celluloid cover, ocean scene with seagulls, c1907, 5-1/2" x 4", **$75** Photo courtesy of Julie Robinson.

Lion, 3-3/4", tan, brown highlights, TS Made in Japan **22.00**
Pig, 4-1/2", pink, painted eyes, Made in USA **35.00**
Polar Bear, 2-1/4" l, white, USA **18.00**
Ram, 4-1/2", cream, gray highlights, Made in USA **20.00**
Rhino, 5", gray, fine detail, PH trademark, Paul Haneaus **75.00**
Seal, 4-1/2", gray, balancing red ball, VCO/USA **70.00**
Squirrel, 2-7/8", brown celluloid, holding a nut, Made in USA **50.00**
Stork, 6-3/4", standing, white, pink legs, flower mark and Japan **22.00**
Swan, 3-3/8", multicolored purple, pink, yellow, crossed circle **15.00**
Turtle, 1-3/8", two-tone, brown top, yellow bottom, USA on foot **18.00**

Decorative albums and boxes

Autograph album, 6" x 4", silver and violet clear celluloid-coated paper, central emb oval with beautiful lady in wide-brimmed hat, white dress and fur, maroon-velvet back and binding ... **95.00**

Photograph album, celluloid cover decorated with cupids and photographs, **$110**. Photo courtesy of Joy Luke Auctions.

Dresser-set box, 8" x 6-1/4" x 3-1/2" d, emb-white celluloid, cornflower motif in two strips across top, blue-satin lining, fitted with brush, mirror, salve box, file and nail cleaner, all original, pieces individually marked "Celluloid" **250.00**
Hankie box, 7" sq, 3" h, center vignette of pretty girl in hat and gown picking pink flowers, emb Greek-key design on sides, overall pale yellow, green, and blue grapevine with leaf design **165.00**
Necktie box, 12-1/2" x 4", emb script "Neckties," cream-colored celluloid, emb-circular design on sides **145.00**
Photograph album, 8" x 11", Gibson girl, lavender dress, hat with lavender plumes, emb corners, applied-gilt paint.... **195.00**

Doll, Uncle Sam, c1915, some age fading, 7" h, **$60**. Photo courtesy of James D. Julia, Inc.

Dolls and toys

Baby rattle, 2-1/4", peach horse on cream-colored 4-1/2" d ring, two pink and white balls attached to ring, "Japan" on horse **45.00**
Doll

- 3-1/4" black baby, strung arms and legs, unidentified lantern trademark, Made in Japan **50.00**
- 5-3/4" Dutch girl, green, pink, yellow, and black details, butterfly trademark—Made In JAPAN, mfg. by Yoshino Sangyo Co. **35.00**
- 7", molded, moving arms, molded bracelet on right wrist, mermaid in shield trademark on back, DRP Germany, mfg. by Cellba, Celluloidwarenfabrik Co. **95.00**

Roly Poly

- 2-1/2", duckling, peach hat trimmed in flowers, jacket, necktie, green trim, cream celluloid, VCO trademark **85.00**
- 3-1/2", gray man, spectacles; black and white highlights on pink base, emb "Palitoy, Made In England" **95.00**

Toy, 5", steamer, gray and red, flag, intertwined PH **65.00**
Whistle, 3-1/4" l, 2-1/4" h, Nightingale bird, yellow celluloid, green and red highlights, VCO/USA **25.00**

Fashion accessories

Bar pin, 2-1/2" l, ivory-grained rect shape, orange-brown swirled-pearlescent laminate, center hp florals **28.00**
Belt, 22" l, 3/4" x 1-1/2" rect mottled-green celluloid slabs linked by chain, applied silver-tone filigree dec **35.00**
Bracelet, bangle

- Ivory colored, embedded with center row of red rhinestones and flanked by outside rows of clear rhinestones **75.00**
- Molded imitation coral, imitation ivory, or imitation jade, all-over floral dec, blue-ink stamp "Made in Japan," 3" d, each **40.00**

Bracelet, link, 3" d, four oblong two-tone cream and ivory links, attached by smaller round cream links **65.00**
Brooch, 1-1/4" d thin gold-tint metal frame, blue and white enamel floral embellishment, clear celluloid, designed to hold photo, safety clasp **25.00**
Comb and case, 2-1/4" l, folding molded case, emb-rose motif, imitation ivory **30.00**
Cuff links, pr, Separable "Kum-a-part" Baer & Wilde Co., 1/4" sq shape divided by purple and black triangular shapes of celluloid, center diamond shape, Art Deco, mid-1920s, orig card **55.00**
Dress clips, pr, molded-floral motif, semi-translucent cream celluloid, marked "Japan" **35.00**
Eyeglasses, Harold-Lloyd type, black frames **20.00**

Fan, Brise style, diecut and emb-imitation ivory, silk ribbon, mirrored heart on end stick, pink-floral motif, tassel **65.00**

Hair comb, 4" x 5-1/4", imitation tortoiseshell, 24 teeth, applied-metal trim studded with rhinestones and brad-fastened Egyptian-Revival pink and gold metal floral and beetle dec........... **145.00**

Hat pin, 4" l elephant head, tusks, black-glass eyes, imitation ivory **95.00**

Hat ornament, 3-1/2" h, Art Deco, pearlized red and cream half circles, rhinestone trim.............................. **65.00**

Necklace, 2" elegant Art Nouveau-filigree pendant, cream celluloid, oval cameo, profile of a beautiful woman, suspended from 20" cream celluloid-beaded necklace.......................................**110.00**

Purse frame, 6" l, imitation tortoiseshell, crescent shape, molded filigree and center cameo, celluloid push-button latch and linked chain..........................**110.00**

Purse, 4-1/2" x 4-1/2", basketweave, link-celluloid chain, mottled grain ivory and green **185.00**

Holiday items

Angels, 1-1/2" h, set of three, one holding cross, star, or lantern, Japan, Mt. Fuji trademark **35.00**

Christmas decoration, roly poly-type house, opening in back for a small bulb, shows Santa approaching door, red and white, intertwined VCO/USA trademark **125.00**

Christmas ornament, 3-3/4" little boy on swing, all celluloid, dark-green highlights, holding onto string "ropes" for hanging on tree **155.00**

Figure, 5-1/4", Uncle Sam, white celluloid, painted red, white, and blue patriotic clothing......................... **175.00**

Halloween favor, 4" l, orange horn, black witch and trim, intertwined VCO/USA **160.00**

Rattle, 3-3/4" l, standing black cat, orange bow, intertwined VCO/USA **185.00**

Reindeer, 3-1/2", white deer, gold glitter, red eyes and mouth, molded ears and antlers, USA.................................. **20.00**

Roly poly, 3-1/2", black cat on orange pumpkin, intertwined VCO/USA **235.00**

Santa, 4", yellow or mint-green translucent celluloid, holding lantern and sack, Japanese, Mt. in circle trademark **55.00**

Novelty items

Letter opener, 7 3/8" l, ivory grained, magnifying glass in top, coiled-metal snake, red-glass eyes around the handle **85.00**

Pin cushion, 2" h, rabbit with pin cushion baskets, marked "Germany" **130.00**

Tape measure, 2-1/2" h, Billiken, cream celluloid, applied-brown highlights, marked "Japan"........................... **185.00**

Toy, wind-up, Wimpy, blue striped pants, red neck tie, black lapelled jacket and bowler hat, Japan, 1930s, cane missing, 7" h, **$230**. Photo courtesy of James D. Julia, Inc.

Utilitarian and household items

Bookends, pr, 4-1/4" h, 3-1/4" w, 2-1/4" d, mottled-pink celluloid, emb ornamental gold neoclassic drape, plaster weighted, no trademark, c1930 .... **35.00**

Candle holders, pr, 5-1/4" h, cylindrical, round flared-weighted bases, unmarked **60.00**

Clock, 3" sq, New Haven Clock Co., alarm, folding travel case, pearlescent pink laminated over amber celluloid **30.00**

Crumb tray set, two dust pan-shaped trays, ivory celluloid, dark-blue dec border, monogrammed "T" in center of each tray....................................... **50.00**

Cutlery, solid imitation ivory grained-handle utensils, eight forks, eight knives in orig box, Standard Mfg. Co. **30.00**

Frame, 5-1/2" x 7", pearlized-amber celluloid, diecut floral motif, attached over wood frame, celluloid butterflies in each corner **35.00**

Napkin ring, 1" w, basketweave strips of celluloid **15.00**

String holder, round sphere on a weighted base, twist apart, center hole in top for string, imitation-ivory grain, no trademark **65.00**

Vase, 7" h, yellow, bulbous bottom, narrow opening, fluted top, painted pink and blue floral motif, no trademark **30.00**

Watch holder, 6-1/2" l, pearlescent blue, green, and amber, wall-hanging banjo-clock style, Wilcox trademark, late 1920s **25.00**

Vanity items

Dresser boxes, pr, oval-shaped pearlized peach boxes, dec-shaped lids, marked "Amerith," Lotus Pattern, c1929 .... **30.00**

Dresser set, eight piece, pearlized yellow-laminated amber celluloid, black trim, mirror, brush, shoe horn, button hook, soap box, nail buffer, toothbrush holder, hair-pin holder, marked "Arch Amereth, Windsor," c1928, orig box **65.00**

Dresser tray, 7-1/2" l, 5" w, oval, pearlized cream color and amber framework, Normandy lace inserted between double-glass bottom, c1925 .... **30.00**

Hair receiver and powder box set, 3-1/2" d, pearlized-gray containers, octagonal lids, no trademark.......... **25.00**

Hatpin holder, weighted base, 5" h center post, round circular disc on top, circular base, cream celluloid, cranberry-colored velvet cushion **90.00**

Manicure set, rolled-up leather pouch fitted with six imitation-tortoiseshell celluloid manicure tools, gold trim, pink-velvet lining.................................... **30.00**

Trinket box, 5" l, 2" h, oval, amber, butterfly, grass and milkweed silk under clear-celluloid lid **35.00**

Vanity set, amber, teal-green pearlescent laminate surface, dresser tray, octagonal amber hair-receiver box with pearlized lid, nail buffer, scissors, and button hook, hp-rose motif on all pcs, unmarked, c1930... **45.00**

CHALKWARE

History: William Hutchinson, an Englishman, invented chalkware in 1848. It was a substance used by sculptors to imitate marble and also was used to harden plaster of paris, creating confusion between the two products.

Chalkware pieces, which often copied many of the popular Staffordshire items made between 1820 and 1870, was cheap, gaily decorated, and sold by vendors. The Pennsylvania German folk-art pieces are from this period.

Carnivals, circuses, fairs, and amusement parks gave away chalkware prizes during the late 19th and 20th centuries. These pieces often were poorly made and gaudy.

Additional Listings: See Carnival Chalkware in *Warman's Americana & Collectibles*.

Notes: Don't confuse the carnival-chalkware giveaways with the earlier pieces.

Bust of American Indian with headdress, painted, minor damage, 21" h, **$175**. Photo courtesy of Joy Luke Auctions.

Animal

Cat, 5-1/4" h, seated, gray, black spots, ears, and tail, yellow eyes and base, red collar, repaired, some wear, base chips **330.00**

Deer, 5-1/2" h, red, black, and yellow, old worn paint, pr **935.00**

Dog, 5-1/2" h, molded detail, painted brown, black spots, red collar, PA, 19th C, pr **375.00**

Hen and rooster, 15" h hen, 20" h rooster, full bodied, comb, wattle, and feather detail, inset glass eyes, quatrefoil base, scrolled acanthus support, repairs, pr **1,495.00**

Lion, 7" l, 4-3/4" h.................... **315.00**

Poodle, 7" h, white, molded fur, black tail, green base with black dec, wear **315.00**

Squirrel, worn red and green, base flakes **250.00**

Seated cat, 19th C, wear to original paint, 5" h, **$550**. Photo courtesy of Wiederseim Associates, Inc.

Bank, 11" h, seated cat, wearing red bow, minor loss............................ **200.00**

Bust, 10" h, lady, elegant green and gold costume, red beads, raised-letters "Maria" on her shoulders, early 19th C, paint loss **1,495.00**

Mantel ornament

12-1/2" h, fruit and foliage design, American, 19th C, restoration, paint wear, pr **460.00**

16" l, 15-1/2" h, reclining stag, polychrome dec, minor paint loss **300.00**

Match holder, 6" h, figural, man with long nose and beard, Northwestern National Insurance Co. adv, c1890 .... **110.00**

Wall plaque, 9-1/4" h, figural white horse head, black and red painted details, early 20th C, one repaired, price for pr **265.00**

Statue, Faust and Marguerite, Rogers type, marked "Copyr. 1885," some damage, 20-1/2" h, **$120**. Photo courtesy of Joy Luke Auctions.

Character and Personality Items

History: In many cases, toys and other products using the images of fictional comic, movie, and radio characters occur simultaneously with the origin of the character. The first Dick Tracy toy was manufactured within less than a year after the strip first appeared.

The golden age of character material is the TV era of the mid-1950s through the late 1960s; however, some radio-premium collectors might argue this point. Today, television and movie producers often have their product licensing arranged well in advance of the initial release.

Do not overlook characters created by advertising agencies, e.g., Tony the Tiger. They represent a major collecting subcategory.

Additional Listings: See *Warman's Americana & Collectibles.*

Character

Betty Boop

Marble, 11/16", Peltier Glass Co., black and white swirl, black transfer of Betty, c1932 .... **175.00**

Pinback button, 1-1/4" d, celluloid on tin, black and white Betty in front of yellow curtains, copyright Fleischer Studios, c1941 .... **850.00**

String holder, 6-1/2" w, 7-1/2" h, chalk, head and shoulders, orig paint **625.00**

Brownies, Palmer Cox

Book, *The Brownies, Their Book,* Palmer Cox, NY, 1887, first edition, second issue, illus by Cox, 4to, pictorial glazed boards **230.00**

Child's fork and spoon, emb Brownies on handles............... **18.00**

Pinback button, 1-1/4" d, blue on white, eight Brownies around board fence imprinted with calendar page for January, 1897, Whitehead & Hoag...................................... **22.00**

Plate, 7" d, octagonal, china, full-color illus of three Brownies, dressed as Uncle Sam, Scotsman, and golfer, soft-blue ground, gold trim, sgd "La Francaise Porcelain" **95.00**

Buster Brown, adv try, Buster Brown Shoes, brown grain painting, gold lettering, some wear, 13-3/8" d, **$65**. Photo courtesy of Joy Luke Auctions.

Buster Brown

Ashtray, glazed china, figural hat, Buster gesturing towards Tige balancing steaming teapot on nose, 4-7/8" l, 1" h **165.00**

Bank, 5" h, figural cast iron, Buster Brown and Tige, orig gold finish **115.00**

Button, 1/2" d, two pieces, metal, loop shank, price for pr **15.00**

Children's feeding dish, Buster and Tige, wear to gold trim **115.00**

Pencil case, 10-1/2" l, Buster Brown Powers Mercantile Co., Minneapolis, MN, wood, cardboard, and tin, orig label....................................... **85.00**

Sign, neon, outdoor type, head and shoulders of Buster Brown and Tige, Buster Brown Shoes spelled out below, 48"........................... **4,250.00**

Sunday comics, 1914, *St. Paul Daily News*, full section **20.00**

Campbell's Kids

Children's dishes, "Campbell's Lunch Time," 4" x 14" x 17-1/2" unopened display carton, service for six, child's hard-plastic soup bowls and coaster plates, cups, saucers, spoons, and forks, prominent Campbell's marking, sealed in orig clear shrink wrap, six miniature placements on back, ©1984 .... **45.00**

Doll, 16" h, boy, orig clothing, 1970 .... **35.00**
Menu book, 5-1/2" x 7-1/2", softcover, ©1910, 48 pgs, menus for 30 days of the month, full-color Campbell's Kids art on cov **20.00**
Salt and pepper shakers, pr, 4-1/2" h, painted hard plastic, red and white outfits, yellow-molded hair, ©Campbell Soup **40.00**
String holder, 6-3/4" h, chalk, incised "Copyright Campbell" **395.00**

Charlie the Tuna
Animation cel, 10-1/2" x 12" clear acetate sheet, centered smiling full-figured 4" image of Charlie gesturing toward 4" image of goldfish holding scissors, 10-1/2" x 12-1/2" white paper sheet with matching blue/lead pencil, 4" tall image of Charlie, c1960 .... **150.00**
Figure, 7-1/2" h, soft vinyl, blue, dark pink-opened mouth, black-rimmed eyeglasses, orange cap inscribed "Charlie," ©1973 .... **30.00**
Wristwatch, 1-1/2" d bright gold luster bezel, full-color image of Charlie on silver background, ©1971 Star-Kist Foods, grained purple leather band **60.00**

Dutch Boy, string holder, 14-1/2" x 30", diecut tin, Dutch Boy sitting on swing painting the sign for this product, White Lead Paint Bucket houses ball of string **300.00**

Elsie the Cow, Borden
Display, mechanical milk carton, cardboard and papier-mâché, figural milk carton rocks back and forth, eyes and mouth move from side to side, made for MN state-fair circuit, 1940s.................................... **500.00**
Lamp, 4" x 4" x 10", Elsie and Baby, hollow ceramic figure base, Elsie reading to baby nestled on her lap, brass socket, c1950.............. **125.00**
Mug, 3-1/4" h, white china, full-color image of Elmer, gold-accent line, orig sq box with image of child's alphabet block including panels "E for Elsie" and "B for Borden," Elmer pictured on one side panel, ©1950........ **95.00**

Felix the Cat
Figure, 1" h, dark copper-colored plastic, loop at top, 1950s........ **10.00**
Pinback button, 1" d, Herald and Examiner, c1930s.................... **45.00**
Place-card holder, 1-3/4" h celluloid Felix, arched-back black cat, base, glossy black holder, Japanese, 1930s...................................... **85.00**
Valentine, diecut, jointed cardboard, full color, "Purr Around If You Want To Be My Valentine" inscription, ©Pat Sullivan, c1920 .... **20.00**

Happifats, candy container, 4-3/4" h, glass, portly lad, short jacket, ribbed pants atop emb drum, red tin slotted closure marked "Geo Borgfeldt & Co. NY Sole Licensee Happy Fat-U.S. Des Pat" around edge, c1915, no paint, minor chips.. **575.00**

Happy Hooligan
Pin-back button, 11-16" d, brown and cream, profile, inscribed, "Son of Rest," initials below "G.T.A.T.," c1910 .... **30.00**
Stickpin, 2-1/4" l, brass............ **25.00**

Howdy Doody
Belt, suede, emb face **35.00**
Cake-decorating set, unused **40.00**
Clock-A-Doodle, key-wind **2,800.00**
Peter Puppet Playhouse, mid-1950s, three marionettes **1,999.00**

Jiggs and Maggie
Pinback button, 3/4" d, *The Knoxville Sentinel*, black and white image of Jiggs, red bow tie, c1920......... **15.00**
Salt and pepper shakers, pr, ceramic **48.00**

Katzenjammer Kids
Christmas card, 4-1/4" x 4-1/2", 1951, copyright King Features Syndicate **18.00**
Comic strip, Ovaltine ad on back **15.00**

Andy, litho tin wind-up, yellow derby, light blue jacket, red and tan striped trousers, Louis Marx & Co., **$320**. Photo courtesy of Pook & Pook.

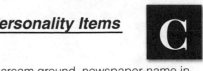

Li'l Abner
Bank, Schmoo, blue plastic **50.00**
Magazine Tear Sheet, Cream of Wheat Breakfast Food, Rastus on front of box illus, 5" w, 11" h...... **20.00**
Pinback button, 13/16", Li'l Abner, *Saturday Daily News*, black litho, cream ground, newspaper name in red **20.00**

Little Annie Rooney, pinback button, 1-1/4" d, comic-strip contest button, serial-number type, c1930 .... **25.00**

Little Orphan Annie
Big Little Book, *Little Orphan Annie Secret of the Well*, No. 1417..... **85.00**
Nodder, bisque, marked "Little Orphan Annie" and "Germany" **150.00**
Toothbrush holder, 4" h, bisque, back inscribed "Orphan Annie & Sandy, © F.A.S., #1565," bottom stamped "Japan," some wear to paint.. **165.00**

Mr. Peanut
Ashtray, Golden Jubilee, 50th Anniversary, gold-plated metal, figural, orig attached booklet, orig box, 5" h, 5-3/4" h **130.00**
Booklet, *Mr. Peanuts Guide to Tennis,* 6" x 9", ©1960, 24 illus pgs **20.00**
Box, Planters Chocolate Covered Nut Assortment, silver-alligator texture, two early Mr. Peanut figures, 8-1/4" sq **350.00**
Paint book, *Planter's Paint Book No. 2,* 7-1/4" x 10-1/2", © 1929, 32 pgs **35.00**
Salad set, ceramic tops, wooden fork and spoon, rhinestone monocle, 10" h **170.00**
Toy, trailer truck, red cab, yellow and blue plastic trailer, 5-1/2" l **275.00**

Mutt & Jeff
Bank, 4-7/8" h, cast iron, orig paint **125.00**
Book, *The Mutt & Jeff Cartoon Book*, Bud Fisher, black and white illus by author, Ball Pub. Co., 1911 .... **100.00**
Sheet music, *Moonlight,* 1911.. **15.00**

Popeye
Cereal bowl, plastic, white ground, red, blue, and black illus of Popeye and Olive Oyl............................. **5.00**
Charm, 1" h, bright copper-luster plastic figure of Olive Oyl, 1930s **10.00**
Figure, 14" h, chalkware **150.00**
Mug, 4" h, Olive Oyl, figural...... **20.00**
Pencil sharpener, figural, Catalin plastic, dark yellow, multicolored decal, 1930s............................ **60.00**

Reddy Kilowatt
Hot pad, 6" d, laminated heat-resistant cardboard, textured top surface with art and verse inscription, "My name is Reddy Kilowatt-I keep things cold. I make things hot. I'm your cheap electric servant. Always ready on the spot," c1940 .... **40.00**
Pinback button, "Please Don't Litter," blue and white, 1950s **15.00**

Pocketknife, metal cast, red-figure image and title on one side, single-knife blade, Zippo, c1950 .... **60.00**
Stickpin, red enamel and silvered-metal miniature diecut figure, c1950 .... **30.00**

Smokey Bear
Doll, 22" h, stuffed, Knickerbocker **75.00**
Little Golden Book, *Smokey Bear and the Campers*, 1971 .... **5.00**
Neck scarf, 22" sq, official Forest Service logo **65.00**
Tab, 2" d, metal, Smokey in center, marked "Green Duck Co., Chicago," unused **15.00**

Three Pigs, toothbrush holder, bisque, figural, marked "Made in Japan, Walt Disney," 1930s, some paint loss, 4" h **85.00**

Yellow Kid
Cap bomb, 1-1/2" h, cast iron, c1898 .... **185.00**
Cigar box, 3-1/2" x 4-1/4" x 9", wood, illus and name inscription in bright gold, brass hinges, label inside says, "Smoke Yellow Kid Cigars/Manuf'd by B. R. Fleming, Curwesville, Pa," tax label strips on back, c1896 .... **225.00**
Pinback button, #2, 1894, orig paper label **60.00**

Amos and Andy, framed black and white facsimile signed photograph and brochure, **$95**. Photo courtesy of Dotta Auction Co., Inc.

Personality

Amos and Andy
Candy container, 4-1/4" l, Amos in gray, Andy in red with brown derby, open air taxi with emb yellow spoked wheels, marked "Avor. 1 Oz." And "Victory Glass Co., Jeannette, PA," c1928, closure missing, traces of orig paint **210.00**
Poster, 13" x 29", multicolored, Campbell's Soup ad, radio show listings, framed **145.00**
Toy, Fresh Air Taxi, litho tin wind-up, Marx, 1929 .... **425.00**

Autry, Gene
Badge, 1-1/4" d, Gene Autry Official Club Badge, black and white, bright orange top rim, c1940 .... **50.00**
Child's book, *Gene Autry Makes a New Friend,* Elizabeth Beecher, color illus by Richard Case, Whitman Tell A Tale, 1952 .... **12.00**
Watch, orig band **145.00**

Ball, Lucille
Magazine, *Life*, April 6, 1953, five-pg article, full-color cover of Lucy, Desi Arnaz, Desi IV, and Lucy Desiree **30.00**
Movie-lobby card, 11" x 14", full color, 1949 Columbia Picture "Miss Grant Takes Richmond" **40.00**

Cassidy, Hopalong
Coloring book, 1950, large size **30.00**
Tablet, 8" x 10", color-photo cov, facsimile signature, unused **24.00**
Wallet, leather, metal fringe, multicolored cover, made by Top Secret **35.00**

Chaplin, Charlie
Candy container, 3-3/4" h, glass, Charlie and barrel, small chip **100.00**
Magazine, *Life*, April 1, 1966, Chaplin and Sophia Loren **10.00**

Dionne Quintuplets, booklet, All Aboard for Shut-Eye Time, Dr. Dufoe and Quints on cover, **$25**. Photo courtesy of Sky Hawk Auctions.

Dionne Quintuplets
Advertisement, 5" x 7", Quintuplet Bread, Schultz Baking Co., diecut cardboard, loaf of bread, brown crust, bright red and blue letters, named silhouette portraits, text on reverse **70.00**
Fan, 8-1/4" x 8-3/4", diecut cardboard, titled, "Sweethearts of the World," full-color-tinted portraits, light-blue ground, ©1936, funeral director name on reverse **35.00**

Earnhardt, Dale, Rookie Sun Drop bottle, 1979, full **8.00**

Garland, Judy
Pinback button, 1" h, "Judy Garland Doll," black and white photo, used on c1930 Ideal doll, name appears on curl, also "Metro-Goldwyn-Mayer Star" in tiny letters **125.00**
Sheet music, "On the Atchison, Topeka, and the Sante Fe," 1945 MGM movie, "The Harvey Girls," sepia photo, purple, light pink, and brown cov **35.00**

Gleason, Jackie
Magazine, *TV Guide*, May 21, 1955, Philadelphia edition, three-pg article on the Honeymooners **18.00**
Pinback button, 1-5/8" d, "Jackie Gleason Fan Club/And Awa-a-ay We Go!," blue on cream litho, checkered suit, 1950s **65.00**

Henie, Sonja, pinback button, 1-3/4" d, "Sonja Henie Ice Review," orange on blue, illus of skater, c1940s **20.00**

Laurel & Hardy, movie poster, When Comedy Was King, 20th C Fox, Laurel and Hardy in center, **$25**.

Laurel & Hardy
Movie poster, "Laurel and Hardy in the Big Noise," Fox, 1944, Tooker Litho **300.00**
Salt and pepper shakers, pr .. **230.00**

Lone Ranger
Coloring book, unused **50.00**
Game board, target bull's eye **185.00**

Mix, Tom
Big Little Book, Whitman, *Tom Mix and The Stranger from the Sea*, Pete Daryll, 1936, #1183 .... **75.00**
Premium, Tom Mix Ralston Telegraph Set, 1940 .... **95.00**
Ring, magnet, 1946 .... **145.00**
Scarf, Tom Mix Ralston Straight Shooters **195.00**

Rogers, Roy
Bank, Roy on Trigger, porcelain, sgd "Roy Rogers" and "Trigger" ... **200.00**
Charm, 1" h, blue plastic frame, black and white glossy paper photo **35.00**
Guitar, orig box, 1950s **140.00**
Ring, litho tin, Post's Raisin Bran premium, Dale Evans, ©1942 .... **45.00**
Watch, Roy and Dale **120.00**

Temple, Shirley
Child's book, *Shirley Temple's Birthday Book*, Dell Publishing Co., c1934, soft cover, 24 pgs **100.00**
Doll, 22" h, composition head, hazel sleep eyes, open mouth with six upper teeth, orig mohair wig, five-pc composition body, dressed in Curly Top outfit, yellow taffeta dress, black

velvet jacket with embroidery, black velvet tam, marked "Shirley Temple" on back of head and back **650.00**

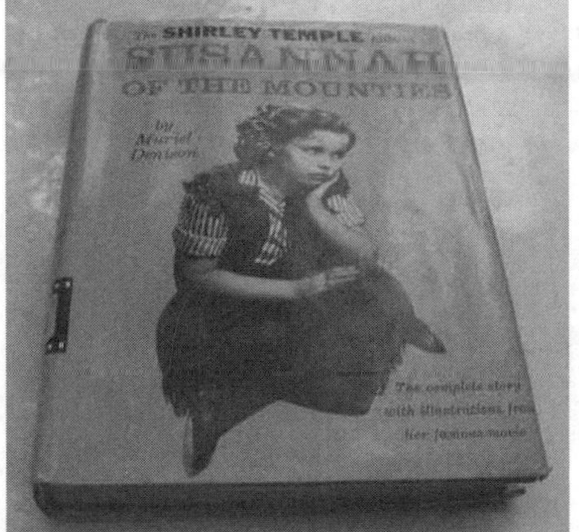

Shirley Temple, book, *The Shirley Temple Edition of Susannah of the Mounties*, by Muriel Denison, Random House, New York, 1936, reprint orange cover with red and black lettering on front and end cover, original dust jacket, **$20**.

Figure, 6-1/2" h, salt-glazed **85.00**
Magazine tear sheet, Lane Hope Chests adv, 1945 ..... **8.00**
Pinback button, 1-1/4" d, brown-tone photo, light-pink rim, Ideal Dolls, 1930s **75.00**

Three Stooges

Autograph, letter, 4-1/2" x 5-1/2" mailing envelope, two folded 6" x 8" sheets of "Three Stooges" letterhead, personally inked response to fan, sgd "Moe Howard," March 10, 1964 Los Angeles postmark **200.00**
Badge, 4" d, cello, black and white upper face image of Curly-Joe on purple background, Clark Oil employee type **20.00**
Photo, 4" x 5" glossy black and white, facsimile signatures of Curly-Joe, Larry, and Moe, plus personal inscription in blue ink by Moe **95.00**

Wayne, John

Magazine tear sheet, 10" x 13", "Back to Bataan," black and white, 1945 ..... **15.00**
Movie poster, "McLintock," 1963 ..... **250.00**

Children's Books

History: Because there is a bit of the child in all of us, collectors always have been attracted to children's books. In the 19th century, books were popular gifts for children, with many of the children's classics written and published during this time. These books were treasured and often kept throughout a lifetime.

Developments in printing made it possible to include more attractive black and white illustrations and color plates. The work of artists and illustrators has added value beyond the text itself.

Additional Listings: See *Warman's Americana & Collectibles* for more examples.

The Wonder Book of Clowns, Little Golden Book, **$10**.

A Child's Garden of Verses, Florence Storer illus, 1st ed, Schriner, 1909.. **45.00**
A Dixie Doll, Katheryn Verdery, Bowen Merill, 1929, six full-page illus, dwgs by W Bromhall **28.00**
Adventures of Danny Meadow Mouse, The, Thornton Burgess, color illus by Harrison Cady, Bedtime Story Books, Little Brown & Co., 1946 ..... **30.00**
Alice's Adventure in Wonderland, Lewis Carroll, MacMillian, 1891, John Tenniel illus **25.00**
Animal Crackers, Harriet Boyd, illus by Fern Bisel Peat, Saalfield, 1929, some stains on cov **45.00**
Becky's Christmas, Tasha Tudor, The Viking Press, 1961 ..... **225.00**
Best Loved Poems of James Whitcomb Riley, The, pen and ink dwgs by Ethel Franklin Betts, Blue Ribbon Pub., 1920 ..... **17.50**
Biggity Bantam, Tasha Tudor, Ariel Books, 1954, sgd by Tudor **450.00**
Burgess Seashore Book, The, Thornton Burgess, b/w illus, Little Brown & Co. **25.00**
Cheery Scarecrow, The, Johnny Gruelle, color and b/w illus by author, M. A. Donohue, 1930s, pc missing from bottom corner **60.00**
Christmas Cat, The, Tasha Tudor, Thomas V. Crowell Co., 1976, sgd by Tudor **325.00**
Count the Kittens, Dorothy King, color illus by Joseph Sica, 1949 ..... **25.00**
Did You Ever, Elizabeth Honness and Pelagie Doane, color illus, Oxford Univ Press, 1940, inscribed by Pealgie Doane **50.00**

Cherry Ames Senior Nurse, Helen Wells, 1944, red cover, original dust jacket, #1 in series, **$15**.

Edgar Allen Crow, Tasha Tudor, illus by author, Oxford Univ Press, 1953, front hinge loose **125.00**
Fairy Tales From Hans Christian Anderson, illus by Tasha Tudor, Oxford Univ Press, 1949 ..... **350.00**
First Delight, A Book About the Five Senses, Tasha Tudor, Platt & Munk, 1966, sgd by Tudor, sketch of dog **550.00**
Glob, The, John O'Reilly, b/w illus by Walt Kelly, Viking Press, 1952, dj **35.00**
Happy Chaps, The, Carolyn Wells, b/w illus by Harrison Cady, The Century Co., 1907, front hinge cracked **50.00**
Hawthorne's Wonder Book, Nathanial Hawthorne, color illus by Arthur Rackham, Doubleday Doran & Co., 1928, 15 full-page color plates **85.00**
Jackanapes, Juliana Horatia Ewing, color and b/w illus by Tasha Tudor, Oxford Univ Press, 1948, dj **85.00**
Lil Hannibal, Carolyn Sherman Bailey, color illus, Platt & Munk Co., 1938, binding loose **50.00**
Mardo's Animal Rhymes, Walter DeWolfill, color and b/w illus by Milo Winter... **45.00**
Mother and Child, Tasha Tudor, The Spiral Press, 1954, sgd **500.00**
My Very Own Fairy Stories, Johnny Grulle, P. F. Volland Co., 1917, 30th ed, color illus **65.00**
Nights with Uncle Remus, Joel Chandler Harris, Houghton Mifflin, b/w illus, 1915 ..... **50.00**
Pinocchio in Africa, Angelo Patri, b/w illus by Charles Copeland, Ginn & Co... **25.00**
Raggedy Ann in Cookie Land, Johnny Gruelle, written by and illus, Volland, 1931, 1st ed **55.00**
Raggedy Ann's Lucky Pennies, Johnny Gruelle, written by and illus, Volland, 1932, 1st ed **48.00**
Riley Farm Rhymes, James Whitcomb Riley, Bowen & Merrill, 1901, illus by Will Wawler **22.50**

A Book of Christmas, Tasha Tudor, Philomel Books, copyright 1979, third Impression, three-dimensional pop-up book, with Advent calendar, signed by Tasha Tudor with greeting and drawing of mouse looking at Christmas ornament, signed, **$110**. Photo courtesy of Alderfer Auction Co.

Robert Louis Stevenson Reader, A Child's Garden of Verses, Schriner, 1906, seven full-page color illus, color drawings, emb picture on cover of boy and girl, school stamp inside front cover **25.00**
Runaway Boy, James Whitcomb Riley, color illus by Ethel Franklin Betts, Bobbs Merrill Co., 1905, binding loose **45.00**
Some Poems of Childhood, Eugene Field, color and b/w illus by Getrude Kay, Charles Scribner Sons, 1937.......... **15.00**
Three Little Kittens, A Little Golden Book, Simon Schuster, 1942, cov illus by Masha Fine... **5.75**
Turnover Book Little Black Sambo/Peter Rabbit, John R. Neill illus, Reilly & Britton Co., 1910, cover wear **65.00**
Uncle Remus and His Friends, Joel Chandler Harris, AB Frost b/w illus, Houghton Mifflin, 1917 .... **50.00**
Uncle Wiggliy's Puzzle Book, Howard Garis, color frontis and b/w drawings by Lang Campbell, 31 puzzles by Cleo Garis, A. L. Burt Co., 1928 .... **45.00**
Wings From the Wind, An Anthology of Poems, selected and illus by Tasha Tudor, J. B. Lippincott Co., 1964, sgd, small drawing of a dog................ **450.00**
Wonderful Wizard of Oz, The, Frank L. Baum, New York, George M. Mill Co., 1900, first edition, first state **7,500.00**

Children's Feeding Dishes

History: Unlike toy dishes meant for play, children's feeding dishes are the items literally used to feed a child. Their colorful designs of animals, nursery rhymes, and children's activities are meant to appeal to the child and make meal times fun. Many plates have a unit to hold hot water, thus keeping the food warm.

Although glass and porcelain examples from the late 19th and early 20th centuries are most popular, collectors are beginning to seek some of the plastic examples from the 1920s to 1940s, especially those with Disney designs on them.

Plate, There Was An Old Woman who Lived Under a Hill verse, multicolored design, white ground, blue exterior, **$60**.

Bowl, Sunbonnet girls dec, pale orange band, cream colored ground, marked "Roseville," slight wear, inner rim chip **200.00**
Butter pat, 3-1/4" d, "A Present For Ann," blue transfer medallion................ **125.00**
Cereal set, Nursery Rhyme, amber, divided plate, Humpty Dumpty on mug and bowl, Tiara............................ **125.00**
Creamer, three yellow ducks, yellow band with black outline, cream-colored ground, marked "R12"................. **125.00**
Cup, Raggedy Ann, Johnny Gruelle, 1941, Crooksville China................. **65.00**

Feeding dish, rocking horse, teddy, and ball center motif, blocks with letters, pale cream ground, marked Mason's (crown) Ironstone, Made in England, Tiffany Toys, Tiffany & Co., (small dog), **$75**.

Cup plate, 4-5/8" d, "Constant dropping wears away stones and little strokes fell great oaks," green transfer, polychrome enamel dec.................................... **90.00**
Feeding dish
- Kiddieware, pink, Stangl **125.00**
- Little Bo Peep, glass, divided, white, red trim **65.00**
- Nursery Rhyme, green enamelware, marked "Made in Germany" **40.00**
- Raggedy Ann, Johnny Gruelle, 1941, Crooksville China, 8-3/4" d **85.00**
- Sunbonnet babies, sweeping, 7-1/4" d **400.00**

Mug
- 1-3/4" h, "A Rabbit for William," yellow glazed, transfer print, England, c1850, glaze and transfer wear...................................... **225.00**
- 2-1/8" h, "Keep thy shop and thy shop will keep thee," yellow glazed, transfer print, England, c1850, luster rim, minor chip **195.00**
- 2-3/8" h, "A new doll for Margaret," yellow glazed, transfer print, England, c1850, glaze and transfer wear, very minor chips **490.00**

Plate
- 5-3/4" d, octagonal, molded flower border, traces of pink luster trim, hand painted transfer scene of girls and pets, one titled "The Pretty Doves," other "The Pet Lamb," staining, one with rim flake..... **225.00**
- 8" d, "Where Are You Going My Pretty Maid, See Saw Margery Daw," three parts, transparent-green Depression-era glass................................. **45.00**

Children's Nursery Items

History: The nursery is a place where children live in a miniature world. Things come in two sizes: Child scale designates items actually used for the care, housing, and feeding of the child; toy or doll scale denotes items used by the child in play and for creating a fantasy environment which copies that of an adult or his own.

Cheap labor and building costs during the Victorian era encouraged the popularity of the nursery. Most collectors focus on items from 1880 to 1930.

Additional Listings: Children's Books, Children's Feeding Dishes, Children's Toy Dishes, Dolls, Games, Miniatures, and Toys.

Baby carriage, 55" w, 22" d, 45" h, for twins, two pivoting canopies, lined and quilted int., stenciled carriage framing and handles, orig stenciled paint on outside, stenciled wooden wheels, some roughness to int. padding, small tears in canopy.. **500.00**
Blocks, boxed set, ABCs, animals, litho of Noah and ark on cov, Victorian **185.00**
Buckboard wagon, 48" l, 35" l handle, 25" d, 26" h, old dark green, red, and black dec, yellow and white line detail, primitive landscape panels on either side, wooden spoked wheels, long handle orig removable seat, minor wear...... **1,760.00**
Chair, child size
- English, yew wood, old dark finish, one board sides, wing back, and

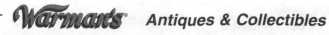

seat, shaped arms, rose-head nail construction, pierced handle at top, warped sides with insect damage and restoration, 7" h seat, 20-1/2" h back **350.00**

Rocking horse, carved and painted, base inscribed "E.F. Eggleston & Co. of 3 Fulton St. N.Y.," original red, blue and pumpkin swirl decoration, 46" w, 23-3/4" h, **$1,840**. Photo courtesy of Pook & Pook.

Windsor, birdcage, orange paint over earlier green, shield-shaped seat, bamboo turned base, late 19th/early 20th C, wear on one seat, 10-1/4" h seat, 20-3/4" h, price for pr..... **650.00**

Chest of drawers, child-size, Hepplewhite-style, curly maple, pine secondary wood, banded inlay around two-board top and base, four graduated dovetailed drawers with dark line inlay, and fans at corners, well-scalloped base, French feet, diamond-shaped escutcheons, emb brasses with cornucopia designs, 27" w, 17" d, 28" h **1,320.00**

Lawn chair, red, yellow, green, gray, and white stripes, wood frame, **$55**; print of boy in red suit, **$6**; Ready Cut Village, original contents, **$28**.

Crib, 38-3/4" d, 69-1/2" h, orig 48" l rails, refinished bird, tapered high posts with incised line beading along edges, urn-shaped supports on all sides, narrow vertical slats added for stability ... **220.00**

Cupboard, child-size, step-back

24" w, 11" d, 37-1/4" h, middle Atlantic States, mid-19th C, cherry, flat-molded cornice above cock-beaded case, two cupboard doors with raised panels, two shelves int., arched opening over projecting case with two short drawers with applied molding, two raised-panel cupboard doors, old red-stained surface **1,725.00**

24-1/2" w, 8-1/8" d, 33" h, New England, early 19th C, stained, molded top overhangs case of two drawers opening to two-shelved int., stepped out board overhangs two drawers on legs, side shaping, orig surface **1,265.00**

Desk, 22-3/4" w, 14-1/4" d, 27" h, Queen Anne, southeastern New England, 18th C, cherry and poplar, slant lid, int. with four compartments over drawers, sliding panel revealing well, case with single thumb molded drawers, bracket feet, replaced brasses, old refinish, restorations............................... **4,120.00**

Child's rocker, Arts & Crafts, Gustav Stickley, New York, 1912-16, model No. 341, two horizontal back slats over reupholstered seat with offset front, back, and side stretchers, branded decal, 14" w, 23" h, **$360**. Photo courtesy of Skinner, Inc.

Doll carriage

30" l, 28" h, Heywood Wakefield, woven wicker, natural finish, diamond patternweave, steel wheels, rubber tires, clamshell hood, maker's label on underside, early 20th C..... **150.00**

30" l, 28" h, natural wicker wooden spoked wheels, original button-upholstered back, red cotton parasol on wire hook, late 19th C........ **230.00**

Doll cradle, 18-1/2" l, 9-1/4" d, 10" h, pine, paint dec in brown over mustard, pale yellow painted int., well-shaped rockers, exaggerated scalloped sides, head, and footboards.................. **500.00**

Game, ring toss, 16" d, green painted wood backplate set with small hooks, each with gold transfer printed number, four leather tossing rings, England, first quarter 20th C **175.00**

Highboy, Queen Anne-style, figured mahogany veneer, band inlay over pine secondary wood, molded cornice, five dovetailed drawers in top, molded waist, three dovetailed drawers in base, scalloped aprons around lower case, two acorn drops, cabriole legs, pad feet, stamped foliage on brasses, early 20th C, 30" w, 18-1/2" d, 56" h................ **2,000.00**

High chair, 22" h seat, 33" h back, pillow-back crest rail, rect splat flanked by raked stiles, scrolled arms, turned supports, rush seat, turned legs joined by stretchers, old beige paint, floral polychrome dec **1,000.00**

Pull-toy, horse, leather hide, Germany, 12" h, **$200**. Photo courtesy of Wiederseim Associates, Inc.

Needlework picture, silk threads and watercolor on silk, titled "The Mother's Hope," young girl in landscape setting, MA, early 19th C, framed in oval format, minor scattered staining, small areas of fabric loss, replaced tablet........ **1,725.00**

Noah's Ark, 18-1/2" l, 5" d, 11-1/2" h, painted red, blue, orange, white, and green wood, roof and one side of base open to inner compartments, six carved and painted animals, Noah, two ladies, one glued leg, some edge wear .. **750.00**

Painting, color, by Tasha Tudor

For book *Kitchen Gardens,* dog and three children holding vegetables **3,750.00**

For book *Pumpkin Moonshine,* boy and girl with big, sgd "T. Tudor," 4" x 3" **11,000.00**

Play house, 60" l, 34-1/2" d, 58-1/2" h, poplar and pine, burgundy, gray, and white paint, peaked roof with chimney painted to simulate brick, single hinged windows on either end, double doors on one side flanked by hinged windows, old print on int. of girl in long dress, wear, edge damage, later red paint on two window frames **600.00**

Portrait, 6" w, 7-1/4" h, pencil and watercolor portraits of two children, one in white dress on green ground, other in blue striped dress on gray ground, matching grained frames with gilt liners, pr **295.00**

Pull-toy, horse, leather hide, Germany, 8" h, **$150**. Photo courtesy of Wiederseim Associates, Inc.

Quilt, 53" x 66", pieced, 20 dark burgundy diamonds, navy blue pinwheels on medium blue ground, meandering line borders divided by blocks and flowers, Mennonite, minor stain **220.00**
Rattle, 4" l, sterling silver, pink coral handle below knopped body with emb dec, five silver bells, whistle, maker's mark "E.S.B.," Birmingham, England, 19th C **475.00**
Rocker, child size, Bliss, wood frame, paper lithographed back and seat with alphabets and decorative bands, c1890 .... **695.00**
Rocking Horse, 40-1/2" l, 14-1/2" w, 21-1/2" h, painted and carved, leather and green velvet saddle, America, mid-19th C, ears, bridle, one stirrup and stirrup leather missing **1,150.00**

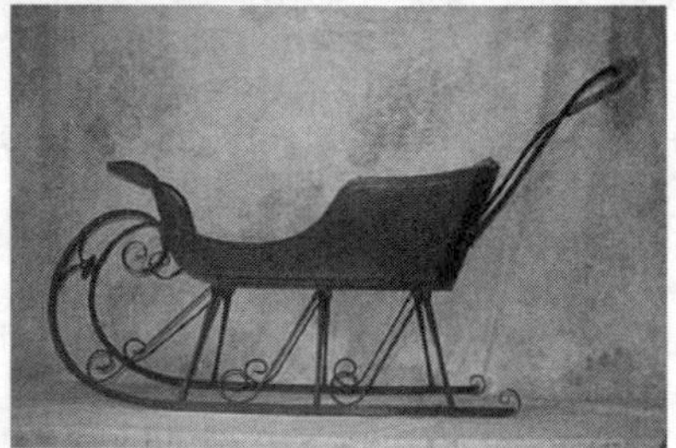

Child's sleigh, hand forged iron work featuring bird's head motif, black painted finish with red band on body, red painted finish on runners, Montgomery County, PA, c1850, 56" l, 14" w, 34" h at handle, **$805**. Photo courtesy of Alderfer Auction Co.

Sled

39" l, 18" d, 8" h, red runners and sides, white and gray line detail, large black horse within landscape panel with blue green and mustard on either side, name "Romaine," areas of wear, split at tail end **935.00**

39-1/2" l, 16" d, 17-1/2" h, orig mauve and yellow roses, green leaves surrounding small angled center panel, dark green ground with black edging, red runners, fine white line borders, cast iron swan head finials on front, red repaint on one runner and on areas of undercarriage **1,155.00**

Sleigh, child's

Dutch, attributed to Friesland area, ice skating scenes, horse-drawn sleighs with buildings, panels on front and back with swans, date "1723," relief carved borders with later dark red and gold paint, old replaced seats **1,650.00**

High serpentine front, bentwood runners, red line edging with flourish dec on front, back, and sides, stained brown upholstery, minor wear, 33" l, 14" d, 26-1/2" h **800.00**

Tricycle horse, 39" l, 22-1/2" w, 33" h, painted wood horse model, glass eyes, suede saddle, velvet saddle blanket, single front wheel, two rear wheels, chain-driven mechanism, by Jugnet, Lyon, repainted **850.00**
Wheelbarrow, painted red, hand painted scenes with American eagle and flags **2,700.00**

Children's Toy Dishes

History: Dishes made for children often served a dual purpose—playthings and a means of learning social graces. Dish sets came in two sizes. The first was for actual use by the child when entertaining friends. The second, a smaller size, was for use with dolls.

For more information, see *Warman's Glass*, 4th edition.

Children's dish sets often were made as a sideline to a major manufacturing line, either as a complement to the family service or as a way to use up the last of the day's batch of materials. The artwork of famous illustrators, such as Palmer Cox, Kate Greenaway, and Rose O'Neill, can be found on porcelain children's sets.

Akro Agate

Tea set, octagonal, large, green and white, Little American Maid, orig box, 17 pcs **225.00**

Water set, Play Time, pink and blue, orig box, seven pcs................ **125.00**

China

Cheese dish, cov, hunting scene, Royal Bayreuth **85.00**

Chocolate pot, Model-T car with passengers **90.00**

Creamer, Phoenix Bird **20.00**

Cup and saucer, Phoenix Bird **15.00**

Dinner set, Willow Ware, blue and white, Japanese **200.00**

Tea set, partial, porcelain, Buster Brown and girl having tea dec, mug and two plates shown from 16-piece set, wear, some damage, **$395**. Photo courtesy of Joy Luke Auctions.

Tea set, children playing, cov teapot, creamer, cov sugar, six cups, saucers, and tea plates, German, Victorian **285.00**

Tureen, cov, Blue Willow, 3-1/2" w, marked "Made in China" **60.00**

Depression glass, 14-pc set

Cherry Blossom, pink **390.00**

Laurel, McKee, red trim.......... **355.00**

Moderntone, turquoise, gold.. **210.00**

Milk glass

Cheese dish, blue opaque, McKee **65.00**

Creamer, Wild Rose................. **65.00**

Cup, Nursery Rhyme............... **24.00**

Tea set, original box, white ground, multicolored floral decoration, service for six, Japan, **$90**.

Pattern glass

Berry set, Wheat Sheaf, seven pcs **85.00**

Butter, cov, Hobnail with Thumbprint base, blue **95.00**

Cake stand, Palm Leaf Fan...... **35.00**

Creamer, Lamb....................... **75.00**

Cup and saucer, Lion **50.00**

Pitcher, Oval Star, clear **20.00**

Punch set, Wheat Sheaf, seven pcs **75.00**

Spooner, Tulip and Honeycomb **24.00**

Sugar, cov, Beaded Swirl **40.00**

Water set, Nursery Rhyme, pitcher, six tumblers **225.00**

Chinese and Japanese Ceramics

History: The Chinese pottery tradition has existed for thousands of years. By the 16th century, Chinese ceramic wares were being exported to India, Persia, and Egypt. During the Ming dynasty (1368-1643), earthenwares became more highly developed. The Ch'ien Lung period (1736-1795) of the Ch'ing dynasty marked the golden age of interchange with the West.

Trade between China and the West began in the 16th century, when the Portuguese established Macao. The Dutch entered the trade early in the 17th century. With the establishment of the English East India Company, all of Europe sought Chinese-made pottery and porcelain. Styles, shapes, and colors were developed to suit Western tastes, a tradition which continued until the late 19th century.

Fine Oriental ceramics continued to be made into the 20th century, and modern artists enjoy equal fame with older counterparts.

Additional Listings: Canton, Fitzhugh, Imari, Kutani, Nanking, Orientalia, Rose Medallion, and Satsuma.

Chinese, Guanyin, Blanc-de-Chine, seated, holding child with ruji scepter, high chignon, loose robes and beaded necklace, c1900, 8-1/2" h, **$450**. Photo courtesy of Sloans & Kenyon Auctions.

Chinese

Bowl, 7" d, carved cloud dec, Qingbai, Song dynasty, 1127-1279............ **300.00**

Brush washer, 4-3/4" d, compressed circular form, splayed base, incurved rim, thick bluish-gray crackle glaze **175.00**

Charger, 13-1/2" d, iron and white, two dragons chasing pearl of wisdom, Guangzu mark and period **500.00**

Cup

3-1/2" d, porcelain, turquoise, enamel stylized lotus and bats with gilt, Kuang Hsu mark in gold, 1874-1908 .... **2,000.00**

4-1/2" x 3", blue and white, rhinoceros horn-form, molded to resemble Buddha's hand, citron, and foliage, Ch'ien Lung period, 1736-95, five spur marks on the base **3,450.00**

9" l, Blanc de Chine, Te Hua ware, rhinoceros horn-form, carved hardwood stand **825.00**

Dish, 9-1/4" d, blue and white porcelain, scalloped, central figural scene surrounded by shaped panels alternating with figures and flowering prunus branches, price for pr................... **450.00**

Figure

9" l, 8" h, mythical animals, porcelain with robin's-egg blue glaze, 19th C **500.00**

16" h, horse, standing, draped trappings and saddle, green, chestnut, and honey glaze, Tang style.. **650.00**

Garden seat, 18" h, porcelain, hexagonal form, blue and white dec, 19th C **900.00**

Ginger jar, cov, 3-1/2" h, blue and white porcelain, figural procession dec, wood cover... **300.00**

Chinese export, creamer, hp over-glaze decoration of man in Western garb riding spotted pony between two fortresses, trees and clouds, gilt decoration on rim, 19th C, 4-1/4" h, **$520**. Photo courtesy of Alderfer Auction Co.

Incense burner, 15" h, pottery, San Tsai glaze, impressed six-character K'ang Hsi mark on the base, 19th C............. **425.00**

Jar, cov, baluster

26" h, blue ground with roses, surround reserves of flowers and butterflies, lotus finial, China, 20th C, hairline.................................. **950.00**

32" h, blue and white dec of Buddhist lion dogs on cloud strewn ground, lion-mask handles, lion finials, 19th C, minor loss **3,200.00**

Jardinière, 14" d, iron red and white, dragon chasing flaming pearl of wisdom dec **150.00**

Lamp base, 16" h vase, celadon and blue ovoid form, warriors in landscape dec **150.00**

Moon flask, 8-1/4" h, blue and white porcelain, two central bird- and flower-filled panels, all-over scrolling floral and foliate dec, c1830............................ **425.00**

Plate, 9-3/8" d, Cabbage Leaf and Butterfly, 19th C, minor chips, gilt and enamel wear, cracks, nine-pc set **375.00**

Soup plate, 9-5/8" d, Cabbage Leaf and Butterfly, 19th C, minor chips, gilt and enamel wear, four-pc set............. **175.00**

Teapot, cov, porcelain, Batavia ware, brown glazed ground, enamel flowers and gilt, 18th C............................ **270.00**

Urn, 17" h, baluster, blue and white, scrolling foliate, floral dec, pr....... **450.00**

Vase, 20-1/2" h, Tsun-shape, Wu Tsai ware, birds and flowers dec, China, Transitional period, c1640......... **2,000.00**

Water pot, 3" d, copper red floral dec, Kangxi mark, 19th C................. **1,200.00**

Chinese export, teapot, squat cylindrical form, hp iron-red floral decoration, berry form finial, twisted branch handle, straight spout, flakes, 5" d, 5-1/2" h, **$125**. Photo courtesy of Alderfer Auction Co.

Chinese export

Basin, 16" d, 5" h, extended rim dec with figures in garden, alternating with reserve of bird on branch surrounded by a border of overlapping blue fans, int. with figures in a garden, 19th C...................... **750.00**

Bough pot, 8-1/2" h, 8-1/4" w, 5-1/4" w base, 7-7/8" d, octagonal, applied dec of squirrels among grapes on canted corners which flank shaped lanes, central floral sprays, gilt-dec base, Famille Rose palette, gilt rope-twist handles, inserts with five circular apertures, gilt edges, Chinese Export for European market, c1775-85, gilt wear, three insert handles missing, pr............................. **13,800.00**

Charger, 13" d, aqua colored ground, polychrome floral design, Greek key border, six character mark, wear.. **120.00**

Plate, 9-3/4" d, gilt and blue, calligraphy center, foliate border, made for Persian market, c1800............................ **250.00**

Tea and coffee service, gilt shields and monograms "AGM" and "RC," gilt borders, fruit finials, coffeepot, teapot, cov sugar bowl, two mugs, two tea bowls, saucer, small bowl, dessert plate, luncheon plate, minor chips and gilt wear, price for 11-pc set **1,265.00**

Tea set, child's, partial, gilt rims, wavy line and dot borders, monogram "CRHL" in oval, teapot, tea caddy, creamer, round tray, three small tea bowls and saucers, larger tea bowl and saucer, 19th C, minor gilt wear, price for 12-pc set......... **865.00**

Tureen, cov, tray, 13" l, 8-1/2" w, 8-1/2" h tureen, short rabbit head handles, cobalt blue underglaze dec, 14-1/2" x 11-1/2" matching tray, late 18th C **2,100.00**

Warming dish, domed cov, 14-1/4" d, 5-1/2" h, fruit finial, Rose Canton dec, repairs, enamel losses **765.00**

Warming plate, 9-1/2" d, Mandarin figures in Famille Rose palette, lattice border **765.00**

Chinese export, flower holder, blue and white, foo dog handles, reticulated lid, late 19th C, 11-1/2" w, 9" h, **$425**. Photo courtesy of Pook & Pook.

Japanese

Bowl, 9-1/2" d, stoneware, gray crackle ware with various fish in polychrome enamels, Japan, Meiji period, 1868-1911 .... **550.00**

Brush washer, 4-3/4" d, compressed circular form, splayed base, incurved rim, thick bluish-gray crackle glaze **175.00**

Censer, 3-1/2" h, compressed globular form, splayed raised foot, everted rim, countersunk band dec, two scroll handles, white glaze, 19th C **395.00**

Charger, 15-1/4" d, Arita ware, blue and white, scholars in garden vignettes, Japan, late 17th/early 18th C **1,500.00**

Dish

4-1/2" sq, Arita, blue and white, floral dec, Edo period, set of four ... **150.00**

7-3/4" l, fan shape, Hizanware, blue and white, Edo period, set of five **700.00**

Garden lantern, 10-1/2" h, Bizen ware, stoneware, rustic form with floral piercings, Japan, 19th C **200.00**

Plate, 8-1/4" d, Kakiemon, lobed form, straw rope edge, relief dec of three friends, pine, bamboo, and prunus, center with pair of pheasants and flowers, red, yellow, blue, turquoise, and black enamel, gilt accents, three spur marks on base, late 19th/early 19th C, small chip and hairline.................................. **520.00**

Vase, 7-1/2" h, celadon glaze with band of peach blooms across boy and mouth, sgd in underglaze blue "Tai Nihon Kozan Sei" within square for Makuzu Kozan, c1900.. **575.00**

Wine Ewer, 7-1/2" h, porcelain with underglaze blue and red decoration of an abstract flowering branch, greenish glaze with crackle, Korea, Yi period, 17th C **1,880.00**

Korean

Bottle, 10" h, stoneware, Punchong ware, globular form with decorative slip swirls on a celadon ground, Yi period, 15th/16th C, repair to mouth......................... **500.00**

Jar, 9" d, 8" h, globular, porcelain, four Bok characters at the sides in underglaze blue, very rare two-character mark on base evidently reading "minister of the right," 18th C, minor rim fretting **9,500.00**

Oil jar, 3" h, stoneware, underglaze iron decoration, celadon ground, Koryo period, 12th C.............................. **650.00**

Vase, 8-3/4" h, porcelain, underglaze blue and red, decoration of landscapes of the sun, mountains, and trees, Maebyong shape with a wide flaring mouth, Yi period, 17th C........... **1,880.00**

CHINTZ CHINA

History: Chintz china has been produced since the 17th century. The brightly colored exotic patterns produced on fabric imported from India to England were then recreated on ceramics. Early chintz patterns were hand painted and featured large flowers, fantastical birds, and widely spaced patterns. The advent of transfer printing resulted in the development of chintz dishes, which could be produced cheaply enough to sell to the masses. By the 1830s, a number of Staffordshire potteries were producing chintzware for everyday use. These early patterns have not yet attracted the interest of most chintz collectors.

Collectors typically want the patterns dating from roughly 1920 until the 1950s although some of the earlier un-named Royal Winton patterns are starting to become popular with longtime collectors. In 1920, A.G. Richardson "Crown Ducal" produced a range of all-over-transfer chintz patterns that proved to be very popular in North America, particularly the East Coast. Florida was the most popular of the Crown Ducal patterns in North America for collectors, but Pink Chintz and Peony have become increasingly popular in the past year or two.

From the late 1920s until the mid-1950s, Royal Winton produced more than 80 chintz patterns. In some cases, the background color was varied and the name changed: Hazel, Spring, and Welbeck is the same pattern in different colorways. After World War II, Royal Winton created more than fifteen new patterns, many of which were more modern looking with large flowers and rich dark burgundy, blue, or black backgrounds—patterns such as May Festival, Spring Glory, and Peony. These patterns have not been as popular with collectors as 1930s patterns, although other 1950s patterns such as Florence and Stratford have become almost as popular as Julia and Welbeck. Some of the more widely spaced patterns, like Victorian Rose and Cotswold, are now attracting collectors.

The 1930s were hard times in the potteries and factories struggled to survive. They copied any successful patterns from any other factories. James Kent Ltd. produced chintzes such as DuBarry, Apple Blossom, and Rosalynde. The most popular pattern for collectors is the white Hydrangea, although Apple Blossom seems to be more and more sought after. Elijah Cotton "Lord Nelson" was another factory that produced large amounts of chintz. The workers at Elijah Cotton were never as skilled as the Grimwades' workers, and usually the handles and spouts of teapots and coffeepots were left undecorated. Collectors love the Nelson Ware stacking teapots, especially in Black Beauty and Green Tulip.

Although a number of factories produced bone china after World War II, only Shelley Pottery seems to be highly desired by today's collector.

By the late 1950s, young brides didn't want the dishes of their mothers and grandmothers, but preferred the clean lines of modern Scandinavian furniture and dishes. Chintz gradually died out by the early 1960s, and it was not until the 1990s that collectors began to search for the dishes their mothers had scorned.

Reproduction Alert: Both Royal Winton and James Kent reproduced some of their more popular patterns. Royal Winton is reproducing Welbeck, Florence, Summertime, and Julia; in 1999 it added Joyce-Lynn, Marion, Majestic, Royalty, and Richmond, Old Cottage Chintz, and Stratford. The company added several new chintz patterns such as Blue Cottage and Christmas Chintz. James Kent reproduced Du Barry, Hydrangea, and Rosalynde, as well as created several new color ways of old patterns. James Kent has discontinued the production of chintz ware. The Elijah Cotton backstamp was purchased and new issue Lord Nelson is now on the market and has confused a number of collectors. Wade is now producing three chintz patterns—Butterfly, Thistle, and Sweet Pea. Two's Company and Godinger have copied some of the Royal Winton patterns. The market for both new and vintage chintz has shrunk dramatically in the last year. Prices for ordinary pieces of vintage chintz have continued to fall, but collectors are still willing to pay for rare shapes in popular patterns especially Royal Winton and Shelley.

Warning: Before you buy chintz, ask whether it is new or vintage. Ask to see a photograph of the backstamps. The "1995" on the RW backstamp refers to the year the company was bought, and not the year the chintz was made. Compare old and new backstamps on www.chintz.net.com or in Susan Scott's *Charlton Standard Catalogue of Chintz*, 3rd edition, *New Chintz Section*. Contact the factories directly for current production lists to avoid confusing old and new chintz.

Adviser: Susan Scott.

Teapots, left: Royal Winton, Welbeck pattern, Lily shape, **$600**; right: Royal Winton, Ascot, two-cup, Summertime pattern, **$325**. All Chintz photos courtesy of Adviser Susan Scott.

Elijah Cotton "Lord Nelson"

Bud vase, 5" h, Rosetime pattern .. **65.00**
Cup and saucer, Black Beauty pattern **60.00**
Jam pot and underplate, Heather pattern **75.00**
Cake plate, 11" handles, Marina pattern **75.00**
Salt and pepper shakers, tray, Rosetime pattern **85.00**
Teapot, stacking, totally patterned Royal Brocade **195.00**

Grimwades "Royal Winton"

Basket, Rowsley shape, Summertime pattern **165.00**
Breakfast set, Summertime pattern **500.00**
Bud vase, 5" h, Old Cottage Chintz pattern **85.00**
Butter dish, Ascot rectangular shape, Julia pattern **175.00**
Cake plate, 11", Sweet Pea pattern **150.00**
Cake stand, 2 Tier Old Cottage Chintz pattern **95.00**
Coffeepot, Norman Shape, Spring pattern **395.00**
Cup and saucer, demi-tasse, Esther pattern **79.00**
Eggcup, footed, Hazel pattern **100.00**
Jug, 5" h, Globe shape, Sweet Pea pattern **225.00**
Salt and pepper shakers, Florence pattern **95.00**

Triple dish, Royal Winton, Summertime pattern, Gem shape, **$195**.

Teapot, stacking
Esther pattern **575.00**
Welbeck pattern, Ajax shape **750.00**
Vase, Gem Shape, Bedale pattern **125.00**

James Kent Ltd.

Biscuit barrel, Du Barry pattern .. **375.00**
Bowl, 7" d, ruffled, Du Barry pattern **75.00**
Coffeepot, Granville shape, Du Barry pattern **300.00**
Creamer and sugar, tray, Rapture pattern **70.00**
Cup and saucer, Rosalynde pattern **75.00**

Stacking teapot, Royal Winton, Summertime pattern, Delamere shape, **$450**.

Jug, 4" h, Hydrangea pattern **145.00**
Nut dish, 3" sq, Rosalynde pattern **35.00**
Plate, 10" round, Rosalynde pattern **75.00**
Salt and pepper shakers, tray, Du Barry pattern **95.00**
Vase, 4-1/2" h, Du Barry pattern **75.00**

A. G. Richardson "Crown Ducal"

Bowl, 12" d, lily shape, flower frog, Ascot pattern **195.00**
Butter dish, Pink Chintz pattern .. **125.00**
Condiment set, Blue Chintz pattern **185.00**

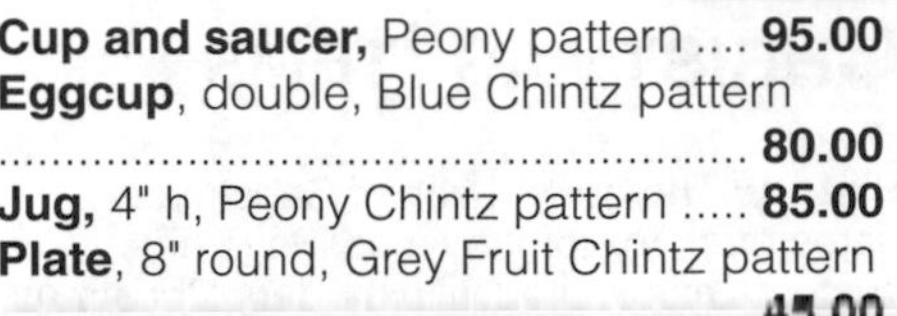

Cup and saucer, Peony pattern **95.00**
Eggcup, double, Blue Chintz pattern **80.00**
Jug, 4" h, Peony Chintz pattern **85.00**
Plate, 8" round, Grey Fruit Chintz pattern **45.00**

Basket, Royal Winton, Somerset pattern, Rowsley shape, **$185**.

Salt and pepper shakers, pr, Pink Chintz pattern **65.00**
Vase
7" h, Marigold pattern **75.00**
9" h, Ivory Chintz pattern **95.00**

Shelley Potteries Ltd.

Cheese dish, round, Melody pattern **275.00**
Coffeepot, Rock Garden pattern **500.00**
Cake plate, Primrose pattern **150.00**
Cup and saucer
Countryside pattern, Oleander shape **275.00**
Maytime pattern **95.00**
Tapestry Rose pattern, Oleander shape **145.00**
Pin dish, 4-1/2" l, Melody pattern **45.00**
Teapot, six cup, Summer Glory pattern **475.00**
Toast rack, 5 bar Melody pattern **125.00**

Eggcup, James Kent, double, Rosalynde pattern, **$80**.

Christmas Items

History: The celebration of Christmas dates back to Roman times. Several customs associated with modern Christmas celebrations are traced back to early pagan rituals.

Father Christmas, believed to have evolved in Europe in the 7th century, was a combination of the pagan god Thor, who judged and punished the good and bad, and St. Nicholas, the generous Bishop of Myra. Kris Kringle originated in Germany and was brought to America by the Germans and Swiss who settled in Pennsylvania in the late 18th century.

In 1822, Clement C. Moore wrote "A Visit From St. Nicholas" and developed the character of Santa Claus into the one we know today. Thomas Nast did a series of drawings for *Harper's Weekly* from 1863 until 1886 and further solidified the character and appearance of Santa Claus.

Reproduction Alert: Almost all holiday decorations, including Christmas, are now being skillfully reproduced. Only by knowing the source of a possible purchase, trusting the dealer, and careful observation can you be sure you are obtaining an antique.

Additional Listings: See *Warman's Americana & Collectibles* for more examples.

Adv trade card, child holding snowballs, "The White is King of all Sewing Machines, 80,000 now in use," reverse reads "J. Saltzer, Pianos, Organs, and Sewing Machines, Bloomsburg, Pa." **10.00**

Banner, advertising "Interwoven Socks for Girls and Boys," scene of Pilgrims in snow, slogan, "The Christmas Ship in Old New York," multicolored, red borders, **$125**.

Candy box, cardboard

- 6" x 5", pocketbook style, tuck-in flap, Merry Christmas, Santa in store window with children outside, marked "USA" **15.00**
- 8" h, four-sided cornucopia, Merry Christmas, Santa, sleigh, and reindeer over village rooftops, string bail, USA **35.00**

Candy container, Christmas lamp, 6" h, clear glass base cov with red brick paper, one side with Santa's face in oval, other with cutout oval to view candy, top and base repainted gray, tin screw-on closure, replaced four-sided tin shade, West Bros, c1913 .... **400.00**

Children's books

- *Becky's Christmas,* Tasha Tudor, Viking Press, 1961 .... **225.00**
- *The Littlest Snowman*, Charles Tazewell, Grosset Dunlap, NY, 1958 .... **18.00**

Christmas card album, Tasha Tudor, personalized cards, samples of cards, order blank, c1956 .... **3,250.00**

Display, mechanical, Santa

- 34" h, red and white overcoat, black pants and boots, glass eyes, long cotton beard, head on pendulum-like device orig hooked up to clockwork mechanism in belly, causing head to "bob," early 20th C, slight soiling to costume, wear on boots, key missing **500.00**
- 72" h, life-size, mechanical, turns at waist, raises and lowers arms, 1940s **1,000.00**

Feather tree

- 6" h, red wooden base **35.00**
- 12" h, green wooden base **95.00**
- 26" h, red and green wooden base **225.00**

Carolers on sled, original boxes, marked "Japan," lot of three, **$30**.

Figures

- Belsnickle, 5-1/8" h, chalk, green-hooded coat with clear mica flecks, painted black base, feather tree missing, minor damage to base **275.00**
- Father Christmas, 7" h, composition, pink face, red-cloth coat, painted blue pants, black boots, mounted on mica-covered cardboard base, marked "Japan" **90.00**
- Reindeer, 1" h, pot metal, marked "Germany" **20.00**
- Santa Claus, 10" h, pressed cardboard, red hat and jacket, black boots **90.00**

Greeting cards

- 1892, "Sincere Good Wishes," purple pansy with green leaves, greeting inside, Raphael Tuck & Sons **12.00**
- 1933, "Merry Christmas," series of six envelopes, decreasing in size, small card in last envelope, American Greeting Publishers, Cleveland, USA **12.00**

House, cardboard, 2" x 2", mica covered, wire loop on top, marked "Czechoslovakia" **12.00**

Child's book, *The Night Before Christmas*, McLaughlin Bros., copyright 1896, **$75**. Photo courtesy of Joy Luke Auctions.

Lantern, 8" h, four sided, peaked top, wire bail, metal candleholder in base, black cardboard, colored tissue paper scenes, 1940s **25.00**

Magazine, *St. Nicholas*, bound edition of 1915 and 1916, color covers, ads, illus, story **15.00**

Ornaments

- Angel, 4" h, wax over composition, human-hair wig, spun-glass wings, cloth dress, Germany **60.00**
- Ball, 2" d, silvered glass, any color **4.00**
- Beads, 72" l, glass, half-inch multicolored beads, paper label marked "Japan" **8.00**
- Bulldog, 3" h, Dresden, three-dimensional, marked "Germany" **250.00**
- Cross, 4" h, beaded, two-sided, silvered, wire hanger, paper label marked "Czechoslovakia" **20.00**
- Father Christmas on Donkey, 10" h, chromolithograph, blue robe, tinsel trim **25.00**

Kugel, 4-1/2" d, round, deep sapphire blue, brass hanger.. **120.00**
Parakeet, 5" h, multicolored glass, spun glass tail, mounted on metal clip.. **20.00**
Santa Claus in chimney, 4" h, glass, Germany **75.00**
Swan, 5" x 6", Dresden, flat, gold with silver, green, and red highlights **150.00**
Tree top, 11" h, three spheres stacked with small clear glass balls, silvered, lametta and tinsel trim, attached to blown glass hooks **90.00**

Christmas Card, 1951, slightly textured white paper, full-color Christmas caroling scene of Mickey, Minnie, and Donald standing in front of The Little House, two of Donald's nephews watching them while holding snowballs behind their backs, card opens to reveal two-panel scene of Susie the Little Blue Coupe pulling wheeled wagons containing many Disney characters such as Seven Dwarfs, Gus and Jaq, Bambi, Pinocchio, etc., each wagon has monthly calendar for 1952, back cover with illustrations of Robin Hood and Peter Pan, title "Coming Soon," 7" x 8", **$75**. Photo courtesy of Hake's Americana & Collectibles.

Pinback button

American Red Cross Health Crusader, red, green, and white celluloid, snow laden pine tree with Red Cross symbol, flanked by red double barred cross symbol for National Tuberculosis Assn, 1917-18 .... **35.00**
Compliments of the Boston Store, multicolored Santa on village rooftop under full moon, early 1900s.... **45.00**
Eagle Tribune, 1991 Santa Fund, red, white, and blue portrait, two green holly sprigs.............................. **25.00**
Joske Bros Santason is Here, litho, color design on yellow ground, Santa and child **60.00**
Macy's Santa Knows, red and white, 1950s...................................... **35.00**
McCurdy's Santa, 1-1/2" d, multicolored Santa surrounded by children in winter outfits, holly leaves and berries in background, Bastian paper backing, c1910........... **125.00**

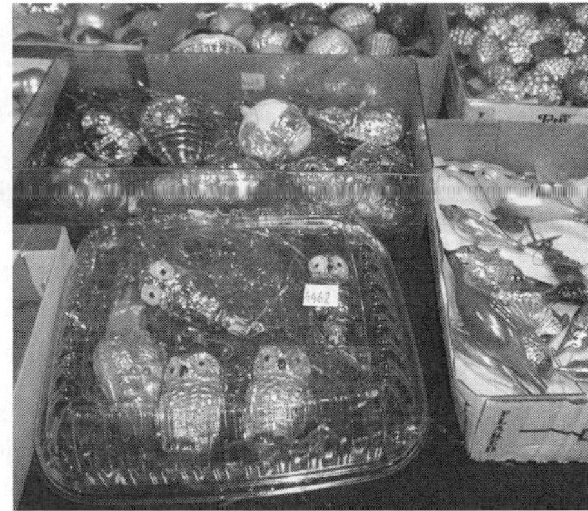

Boxes of ornaments often sell at auction. Look for unusual ornaments and bid accordingly.

National Tuberculosis Assn, Health for All, multicolored litho, Santa, 1936 .... **15.00**
Philadelphia Bulletin, multicolored portrait of Santa, accented by holly sprigs, upper pale blue background blending into tan, 1930s........... **40.00**
Santa Claus at Schipper & Blocks, multicolored, Santa wearing holly leaf and berry crown, nestled by blond child, pale blue blending to white background, early 1900s **85.00**
Spiegel Toyland Santa, multicolored litho, black lettering, 1930s **50.00**

Postcards, Germany, Christmas bells and snow scene, marked "Made in Germany," used, one cent stamp, 1911 .... **24.00**

Record, Little Drummer Boy, Abbey Choir, Diplomat, **$5**.

Putz, Christmas-tree fence, wood, folding red and green sections, 48" l, USA **35.00**

Stickpin, diecut thin cello multicolored portrait of Santa on short hanger stickpin, back inscribed, "Meet Me At Bowman's," c1920.. **48.00**

Toys

Jack-in-the-box, 9-1/2" h, "Santa Pops," hard plastic, red-felt hat, orig box, Tigrette Industries, 1956 .. **30.00**
Merry-go-round, wind-up, celluloid, green and red base, four white reindeer heads, Santa sitting under umbrella, Santa spins around, stars hanging from umbrella bounce of bobbing deer heads, orig box, Japan **65.00**
Pull toy, paper on wood, blue dressed Santa riding in ornate sleigh filled with period toys, possibly by Bliss, 19th C, 12" l **1,275.00**
Santa, riding reindeer, windup **130.00**
Santa, sleigh, cast iron, galloping reindeer pull ornate sleigh with replaced Santa, Hubley, 16" l **750.00**

Tree stand, 9-3/4" sq, 4" h, cast iron, old worn green, gold, white, and red paint, relief tree trunk, foliage, and stairway design.. **110.00**

CLEWELL POTTERY

History: Charles Walter Clewell was first a metal worker and secondarily a potter. In the early 1900s, he opened a small shop in Canton, Ohio, to produce metal-overlay pottery.

Metal on pottery was not a new idea, but Clewell was perhaps the first to completely mask the ceramic body with copper, brass, or "silvered" or "bronzed" metals. One result was a product whose patina added to the character of the piece over time.

Since Clewell operated on a small scale with little outside assistance, only a limited quantity of his artwork exists. He retired at the age of 79 in 1955, choosing not to reveal his technique to anyone else.

Marks: Most of the wares are marked with a simple incised "Clewell," along with a code number. Because Clewell used pottery blanks from other firms, the names "Owens" or "Weller" are sometimes found.

Vase, copper-clad, bulbous, verdigris and bronze patina, etched "Clewell 461-29," 7" x 6", **$990**. Photo courtesy of David Rago Auctions, Inc.

Bud vase, 6-1/4" h, bronze and verdigris patina, incised mark and number **435.00**

Candlesticks, pr, 7" h, 3-1/2" d, copper clad, four sided, dark bronzed patina, unmarked **1,300.00**

Jardinière, 14" h, ovoid, matte finish **150.00**

Mug, 4-1/2" h, copper clad, riveted design, applied monogram, relief signature........ **65.00**

Pitcher, 5-3/4" x 4-3/4", copper-clad, incised Arts & Crafts floral motif, unmarked **535.00**

Other side of Clewell 461-29 vase from pg. 113, showing more striation in the patina. Photo courtesy of David Rago Auctions, Inc.

Vase

3-1/2" d, 8-1/2" h, copper-clad, classical shape, bronze and verdigris patina, marked "Clewell 288-256," some surface scarring **800.00**

4" x 4-1/2", copper-clad over Weller Burntwood blank, unmarked, several tight cracks from rim **375.00**

5" d, 11" h, copper-clad, baluster, verdigris patina, incised "Clewell 315-2-6," surface scratches... **980.00**

7-1/2" h, 4" d, ovoid, copper clad, verdigris to bronze patina, incised "Clewell/351-25"........ **1,000.00**

11" h, 5" d, bulbous, copper clad, bronzed finish, incised "Clewell/357-5," cleaned some time ago.... **500.00**

Vessel, 7-1/2" w, 11" h, copper-clad, verdigris patina, incised "Clewell 72-26" **1,725.00**

Clifton Pottery

History: The Clifton Art Pottery, Newark, New Jersey, was established by William A. Long, once associated with Lonhuda Pottery, and Fred Tschirner, a chemist.

Production consisted of two major lines: Crystal Patina, which resembled true porcelain with a subdued crystal-like glaze, and Indian Ware or Western Influence, an adaptation of the American Indians' unglazed and decorated pottery with a high-glazed black interior. Other lines included Robin's-Egg Blue and Tirrube. Robin's-Egg Blue is a variation of the crystal patina line, but in blue-green instead of straw-colored hues and with a less-prominent crushed-crystal effect in the glaze. Tirrube, which is often artist signed, features brightly colored, slip-decorated flowers on a terra-cotta ground.

Marks: Marks are incised or impressed. Early pieces may be dated and impressed with a shape number. Indian wares are identified by tribes.

Vase, Indian Ware, bulbous, tan, brown and terra cotta rounded panel design, incised "Clifton/231" and "Middle Mississippi Valley" around base, several glaze nicks around rim, 12-1/4" x 8-1/2", **$445**. Clifton photos courtesy of David Rago Auctions, Inc.

Biscuit jar, cov, 7" h, 4-1/4" d, gray-brown ground, enameled running ostrich and stork, florals, bail handle **300.00**

Bowl, 9" d, Indian cooking ware, black glazed dec, marked, minor rim flake **150.00**

Cabinet vase, 3-1/4" h, bulbous, matte green, 1905, marked **200.00**

Creamer, Crystal Patina, incised "Clifton," dated **225.00**

Decanter, 11-1/2" h, rose shading to deep rose, purple flowers, gilt butterfly on neck, applied handle, marbleized rose and white stopper........ **150.00**

Jardinière, 8-1/2" h, 11" d, Four Mile Ruin, Arizona, incised and painted motif, buff and black on brown ground, imp mark and incised inscription, hairline to rim........ **400.00**

Pedestal, 20" h, Indian, unmarked, small chip to top and glaze **690.00**

Sweetmeat jar, 4" h, hp ducks and cranes, robin's egg blue ground, cow finial **375.00**

Teapot, 6" h, brown and black geometric design........ **200.00**

Vessel, Crystal Patina, squat, two-handles, 1906, incised "Clifton/1906/106," 3" x 4-1/2", **$215**.

Vase

6-1/2" d, 5-1/2" h, spherical, Crystal Patina, green and mirrored caramel glaze, sgd and dated 1906.... **575.00**

9-1/2" h, 4-1/2" d, bottle shape, Crystal Patina, incised "Clifton/158" **350.00**

10" h, 7" d, angular handles, Crystal Patina, incised "Clifton"........ **450.00**

Vessel

5-1/4", gourd shape, Indian, swirl pattern, Arkansas, #216, marked **380.00**

7-1/2" x 10", bulbous, Indian, collared rim, geometric chain pattern, "Homolobi, #233," marked, few shallow scratches........ **925.00**

8" x 9", bulbous, Indian, dark birds in flight, "Homolobi, #235," marked **975.00**

Clocks

History: The sundial was the first man-made device for measuring time. Its basic disadvantage is well expressed by the saying: "Do like the sundial, count only the sunny days."

Needing greater dependability, man developed the water clock, oil clock, and sand clock, respectively. All these clocks worked on the same principle—time was measured by the amount of material passing from one container to another.

The wheel clock was the next major step. These clocks can be traced back to the 13th century. Many improvements on the basic wheel clock were made and continue to be made. In 1934, the quartz-crystal movement was introduced.

The first carriage clock was made about 1800 by Abraham Louis Breguet as he tried to develop a clock that would keep accurate time for Napoleon's officers. One special feature of a carriage clock was a device that allowed it to withstand the bumpy ride of a stagecoach. These small clocks usually are easy to carry with their own handle built into a rectangular case.

The recently invented atomic clock, which measures time by radiation frequency, only varies one second in a thousand years.

Notes: Identifying the proper model name for a clock is critical in establishing price. Condition of the works also is a critical factor. Examine the works to see how many original parts remain. If repairs are needed, try to include this in your estimate of purchase price. Few clocks are purchased purely for decorative value.

Advertising

Chew Friendship Cub Plug, face of man with moving mouth chewing Friendship Tobacco to the tic of the clock, pat'd Mar 2, 1886, 4" h.................................. **900.00**

Gruen Watch, Williams Jewelry Co. on marquee at bottom, blue neon around perimeter, 15" x 15"...................... **600.00**

Hire's Root Beer, "Drink Hires Root Beer with Root Barks, Herbs," 15" d..... **250.00**

Longine's Watches, "The World's Most Honored Watch," brass, 18-1/2" d **300.00**

Alarm

Attleboro, 36 hours, nickel-plated case, owl dec, 9" h................................ **75.00**

Bradley, brass, double bells, Germany **40.00**

New Haven, c1900, 30 hours, SP case, perfume-bottle shape, beveled-glass mirror, removable cut-glass scent bottle, beaded handle........................... **185.00**

Advertising, Goulding's Manures are the Best for all Crops, Cork-Dublin, Baird Clock Co., Plattsburgh, New York, painted pressed wood, regulator, **$1,645**. Photo courtesy of Skinner, Inc.

Bracket

Parke, Solomon, Federal case, mahogany veneer, old finish, brass feet, brass hands, brass fusee works, painted steel face with "Strike" and "Silent," labeled "Solomon Parke, Philadelphia," some veneer damage, old veneer repair, pendulum and keys, 17-3/4" h plus top handle...................................... **9,350.00**

Tiffany & Co., bronze, stepped rect-shaped top, four acorn finials, cast foliate frieze, four capitals with reeded columns, shaped and foliate cast base, beveled glass door and panels, circular face dial with Roman numerals, marked "Famiel Marti Medaille...Paris 1900, Tiffany & Co.", 13" h.................................... **600.00**

Carriage

French, late 19th/early 20th C, movement with alarm, date, and push repeater, engraved bronze gorge case with glass to three sides, and engraved backplate with exposed winding pegs, handle emerging from lion's masks, 6-1/4" h **650.00**

Garniture, three-piece marble and gilt bronze clock set, 22" w, 22" h clock with ormolu mountings and bronze figures of robed women and putti, surmounted by footed, lidded bowl with putto finial, two claw and two pedestal feet, conforming 20" h urns with female heads on handles and finials, back of clock missing, some ormolu loose, **$1,725**. Photo courtesy of Alderfer Auction Co.

Lantern, English, c1670, brass, inscribed "Framitten Chichester," hanging shelf with carved face of floral and child's portrait, 15-1/2" clock, **$1,500**. Photo courtesy of Pook & Pook.

French, Maquet, Paris, early 20th C, bronze, navette shaped, angular handle over compass dial, four sides set with time dial, aneroid barometer dial, Fahrenheit thermometer, and centigrade thermometer, 4-7/8" l, set into fitted, monogrammed leathered case.... **825.00**

New Haven Clock Co., gilded brass case, beveled glass, gold repaint to case, orig pendulum and key, 11-1/2" h **315.00**

Carriage clock, LaCoultre Atmos, brass and glass, one panel cracked, 9" h, **$225**. Photo courtesy of Wiederseim Associates, Inc.

China

Ansonia, Crystal Regulator, pink and blue china case, flowers dec, beveled glass panels, mercury pendulum, open escapement, time and strike, 18-1/2" h **3,100.00**

Ansonia, Royal Bonn case, cobalt blue, floral panels, gilding................. **2,900.00**

French, bisque, three-pc garniture, 15" h ovoid clock topped by seated figures of lady, gentleman and dog observing lobster, body enamel dec with panels of floral bouquets, strapwork enclosing urns, paterae, and beading, pair of figures of lady and gentleman in 18th C dress, both with impressed mark "Chantilly," early 20th C, retailed by Ball, Black & Co., NY........................... **950.00**

Royal Bonn, 14" h, floral dec, gilt details, Ansonia Clock Co. (NY) key-wind mechanism, hinged crystal face, marked **825.00**

Victorian, dec china case, ornate brass dial with black Roman numerals, bisque figure of woman sitting on pillow cradling bird to her breast on top, small brass inset plaque: "PRADIER," 9-1/2" w, 15-1/2" h, brass back may be replacement **980.00**

Desk

American, shaped rect, brass case, white enamel bordering cobalt blue, stylized applied monogram, decorative brass corners, central dial with Arabic numerals, 4-3/4" h........................ **150.00**

British United Clock Co., Ltd., Birmingham, England, 20th C, brass, bracket cut-out edges on diamond-shaped brass clock frame, four pierced diamond patterns, floral, bowknot, and fleur-de-lis punch dec, wire easel stand, printed and imp maker's marks, spotty corrosion, 6" w, 4-1/2" h **260.00**

Desk, Retro, Armillary, gilt metal, rotating openwork sphere set with barometer dial, thermometer dial in Celsius and Fahrenheit, and timepiece marked "Imexal," 15-jewel movement, central adjustable world map with names of cities, circular base, mid-20th C, 8-1/4" h, **$250**. Photo courtesy of Skinner, Inc.

Mantel

Aesthetic Movement, probably designed by Lewis Day for Howell and James, Queen Anne style, c1880, ebonized case, turned columns, gilded etched details, porcelain face painted with stylized blue and indigo sunflower, face painted Elkington Liverpool, wear to molding corners, burn mark to side of top, 19" x 13-1/2" x 8-1/2" **1,380.00**

Birge Mallory & Co., Bristol, CT, triple decker, refinished mahogany case, turned ball front, tapered rear feet, center door fitted with mirror, lower door fitted with later reverse painted eagle, turned pilasters on front with basket of fruit and acanthus leaf crest, weights, key, and pendulum bob, restorations, replacements, face chipped, 6" d, 18" w **420.00**

French, marble

Empire-style, white marble temple-form, ormolu-mounted pediment, gilt metal engine turned dial set between four columns, rect ormolu mounted base, early 20th C, 19-3/8" h **600.00**

Mougin chiming movement, temple form case with domed pediment set with gilt metal anthmion, gilt metal dial centered by stars, dial flanked by scroll and husk gilt metal pendants, rect base, late 19th C, 10-3/4" h **500.00**

Low, J & J G, emb dragonflies, deep sea-green glazed tile panels with dragonfly and wasp border, brass frame with relief swirl design, imp "J & JG Low/ Chelsea, Ma," 12" h **5,775.00**

Miller, Howard, 20th C, mahogany, three train, quarter striking movement with strike/silent and three chimes backed by mirrored panel, top with single lifting handle, glass to three sides, front door with burlwood veneer detailing and with fluted pilaster, enclosing gilt and silvered dial, tapered plinth base, set with engraved presentation plaque to A. Wimpfheimer & Bro. Inc. celebrating a 60-year business relationship **250.00**

Mantel, Ansonia, steeple, wood case, time, strike and alarm, **$150**. Photo courtesy of Joy Luke Auctions.

Novelty, figural

Ansonia, Fortuna, swing arm, gold painted spelter, 280-1/2" h **4,800.00**

Homing pigeon, German, key-wound brass works, paper print roller, machine dovetailed oak case, leather strap handle, sgd "Benzing, Made in Germany," key missing, 8" w, 6-1/2" d, 5-1/4" h **325.00**

Unidentified maker, carved European walnut, old dark finish, molded base with high relief carved pheasants, chicks, and oak leaves, two elk at top, brass works, white enameled dial, pendulum, key, removable antlers with some glued points **4,550.00**

Pillar and scroll

Downes, Ephraim, Bristol, CT, 1825, mahogany, 30-hour wooden-weight movement, old finish, imperfections, 31" h **950.00**

Leavenworth and Son, Mark, Waterbury, CT, c1825, mahogany, 30-hour wooden movement, imperfections, 16-1/2" w, 4-1/2" d, 29-3/4" h **950.00**

Thomas, Seth, c1825, Federal, mahogany, scrolled cresting joining three brass urn finials above glazed door, 30-hour wooden weight-driven movement, polychrome and gilt dec dial, landscape tablet, flanked by freestanding columns on cut bracket feet, old refinish, minor imperfections, 17-1/4" w, 4-1/2" d, 32" h **2,185.00**

Shelf

Atkins and Downs, eight-day triple, reverse-painted glass with buildings, pendulum window, and split columns, middle section with mirror and full columns, top section with dec dial, split columns, top crest with spread eagle, most of orig label remains, 38" h, 17" w, 6" d **450.00**

Mantel, French, bronze and marble, ormolu-mounts, pediment having two full-figure putti, one holding bow, swag and scroll mounts, four rocaille feet, 17-1/2" l, 14" h, back of clock missing, **$2,300**. Photo courtesy of Alderfer Auction Co.

Brewster and Ingrahams, Bristol, CT, c1845, Gothic twin steeple, mahogany, peaked cornice, glazed door, stenciled gilt-green on white table showing love birds, enclosing painted zinc dial, double fusee brass movement, flanked by two turned finials and columns, flat base, 19" h, dial replaced, minor veneer loss **1,100.00**

North, Norris, Torrington, CT, c1825, Classical, mahogany, flat cornice above glazed door, eglomise tablet of young woman flanked by engaged black paint stenciled columns, polychrome and gilt white painted dial, 30-hour wooden weight-driven movement, 23-3/4" h, 13-1/2" w, 5-1/4" d...................... **4,900.00**

Mantel, French, bronze, urn finial topping case with architectural details, ormolu mounted, paw feet, Roman numerals on dial, works marked "15725 E.B.," no key or pendulum, 21-1/2" h, **$1,540**. Photo courtesy of Alderfer Auction Co.

Parker, Gardner, Westborough, MA, c1810, Federal, kidney-shaped iron dial sgd "Warranted by G. Parker" in gilt surround, brass eight-day weight driven movement, mahogany case, box base with inlay, curving skirt and feet, 35" h, old refinish, imperfections **26,450.00**

Terry, Eli and Sons, Plymouth, CT, c1810-15, Federal, paper label "Eli Terry and Sons," mahogany, scrolled pediment, wooden painted dial with gilt spandrels, wooden 30-hour movement, eglomise glass, curving case skirt, French feet, 31-1/4" h, restoration **1,955.00**

Thomas, Seth, Plymouth, CT, c1820, Federal, paper label "Seth Thomas," mahogany, wood 30-hour movement, reverse painted glass panels above cyma curved front skirt, thin French feet, 30" h, restoration........................ **1,725.00**

Willard, Aaron, Jr., Boston, MA, c1815, Federal, kidney dial sgd "Aaron Willard Boston," pierced crest, eight-day timepiece with recoil escapement, veneered mahogany case with shaped skirt, flaring feet, 37-1/2" h, old refinish, minor imperfections................ **32,200.00**

Mantel, Gilbert, oak case, bird decoration on glass door, time and strike, **$175**. Photo courtesy of Joy Luke Auctions.

Wood, David, Newburyport, MA, c1815, Federal, mahogany inlaid, dial sgd "David Wood Newburyport," solid crest with star inlays above painted dial, red and gold spandrels, female neoclassical figure encloses brass 60-hour weight-driven movement, seconds dial aperture, engaged quarter-columns flank satinwood inlaid door, curving skirt, flaring French feet, 33-3/4" h, restoration to case.................................... **12,650.00**

Table

French, gilt bronze and enamel, case finely molded gilt bronze with hooved feet, translucent maroon panel enameled with cherubs and floral sprays, maroon enameled dial with circular florals, gilt numerals, surmounted by matching enameled dome, gilt acorn finial, works stamped "Etienne Maxant, Brevete, Paris made in France," c1900, 14" h **2,590.00**

French, gilt bronze and guilloche enamel, round clock, Swiss movement, enameled in translucent azure blue on engraved radiating ground, enameled and gilt chapter ring, gilt bronze case surmounted by petal forms, 19th C, 4" d **600.00**

Wendell, "Mr. Clock," sq ribbon-mahogany box, tall verdigris-patinated copper legs, sgd and dated 1988, 24" x 6".. **1,380.00**

Mantel, Gilbert, ornate cast metal case, finial with basket of flowers, four support pillars, porcelain face, open escapement, mercury pendulum, time and strike, 16-1/2" h, **$750**. Photo courtesy of Joy Luke Auctions.

Tall case

Brokaw, Isaac, Federal, mahogany inlaid, dial marked "Isaac Brokaw Bridge Town" (New Jersey), 1800-10, shaped hood with inlaid patera and book-end inlays above glazed door, painted dial, eight-day weight-driven movement, seconds hand, calendar aperture, waist door with serpentine top and elliptical inlay, oval and quarter-fan inlays on lower case, similar embellishments above the bracket feet, refinished, restored, 94-1/2" h **10,575.00**

Caldwell, J. E., late 19th/early 20th C, Georgian-Revival, mahogany, dial sgd "Caldwell," subsidiary seconds dial, cast scroll and cherub detailing, phases of the moon, two train chiming movement, hood with swan's neck cresting centered by urn, carved scroll detailing, glass front door flanked by tapering and partially reeded circular section columns, case with beveled glass front door flanked by engaged partially reeded columns, paneled plinth base centered by carved shell, front paw feet, rear ogee feet, 24" w, 15" d, 95" h........................... **2,895.00**

Dutch, Baroque, 18th C, marquetry inlaid and parcel gilt, walnut, three figural finials, arched door, three train movement with phases of moon and other apertures, long door with portal, on a bombe shaped base, 90" h **6,000.00**

Mantel, New Haven, kitchen type, oak case, glass door, time and strike, **$100**. Photo courtesy of Joy Luke Auctions.

English Regency, 19th C, mahogany, scrolled cresting above sq door, brass face etched with country scene, two-train movement, date and seconds dials, cross-banded case with tombstone pilasters, bracket fee, 84" h....... **1,200.00**

Farquharson, Alexander, George III, mahogany, gilt bronze mounts, dial signed "Alexander Farquharson, Edinburgh," etched steel face with date aperture and seconds dial, case with broken pediment cresting, dentil molding, two columnar supports with gilt capitals, shaped long door and bracket feet, 89" h **2,760.00**

French, Provincial Renaissance style, quarter strike mobilier, 19th C, serpentine cresting above glass door, brass face depicting courting couple, single train movement with quarter chiming on two bells, hour strike on one bell, case carved with strapwork and mask, 94" h **1,400.00**

Hoadley, Silas, Plymouth, CT, c1820-30, grain painted, hood, three plinths, joined by pierced fretwork, flanking urn finials above arched cove-molded cornice, glazed tombstone door flanked by freestanding columns, polychrome and gilt Masonic dial marked "S. Hoadley, Plymouth," floral spandrels and second hand, wooden movement, waist with thumb molded door above molded base, cut-out feet, orig red-under grain paint, simulated stringing on door and base, 89" h.. **8,820.00**

McDougall, Alexander, inlaid eagle, engraved tag on dial **8,000.00**

Mulliken, Joseph, Concord, MA, c1800-10, Federal, cherry, hood with pierced fretwork joining sq plinths and brass ball finials above arched cornice molding, iron painted tombstone dial with bird and floral designs inscribed "J. Mulliken Concord," eight-day weight-driven movement, flanked by free-standing reeded columns, waist with molded rect door flanked by reeded quarter columns on base with inlaid stringing joining corner quarter fans on flat molding, 88-3/4" h, imperfections, lacks hood door and feet **4,700.00**

Mulliken, Nathaniel, Lexington, MA, c1760, cherry, hood with molded stepped cornice above arched molding, glazed thumb-molded door with flanking engaged columns, brass engraved silvered dial with cast brass spandrels, boss in arch engraved "Nathaniel Mulliken Lexington" above silvered chapter ring, second hand, calendar aperture, thumb-molded tombstone door, base with molded bracket feet, refinished, restoration, loss of height, 89-1/2" h **12,955.00**

Mantel, pink marble case, bronze figural mounts and feet, pair of matching garnitures, chips, **$295**. Photo courtesy of Joy Luke Auctions.

Mulliken II, Nathaniel, Lexington, MA, c1770-75, attributed to, mahogany and cherry, hood with broken arched cornice molding, three sq plinths, tombstone glazed door with flanking engaged columns, brass dial with cast spandrels, silvered banner in arch engraved "Nath. Mulliken + Lexington," above the boss with engraved eagle on branch, silvered chapter ring, seconds indicator, calendar aperture, eight-day weight-driven movement, waist with thumb-molded door, molded base, 88" h, refinished, loss of height, restored **7,650.00**

Munroe, Daniel, Concord, MA, Federal, mahogany

c1800, hood with pierced fretwork joining reeded plinths with brass finials above arched cornice molding, glazed string inlaid tombstone door, floral polychrome and gilt iron dial, seconds and calendar aperture sgd "Daniel Munroe + Co.," brass eight-day weight-driven movement, flanking reeded brass stop-fluted columns, rect molded and inlaid door flanked by reeded brass stop-fluted quarter columns, inlaid base, ogee bracket feet, refinished.................. **25,850.00**

c1810, hood with pierced fretwork joining reeded plinths with brass ball finials above arched cornice molding, glazed tombstone door, white painted iron dial inscribed "warranted by Nath. Munroe Concord," eight-day weight-driven movement, flanked by standing reeded columns, double-beaded crossbanded waist door on base, double-beaded panel above cut-out feet, 93" h, loss of height, dial repainted, other restoration **5,300.00**

Nash, William, Bridge, England, George III, works signed, brass and steel face with date aperture and seconds dial, inlaid mahogany case with swan's neck cresting, columnar supports, cross-banded door inlaid with shell, bracket feet, 85" h.................................. **6,900.00**

Mantel, Welch, elaborate mixed wood case, arched top with three finials, glass door, turned column supports, time and strike, ornate pendulum, glass side panels, 12-1/2" w, 19" h, **$725**. Photo courtesy of Joy Luke Auctions.

Parke, Soloman, late 18th/early 19th C, Phila, cherry, replaced dial........ **7,700.00**

Roberts, Hugh, Llangefni, Welsh, oak with mellow finish, bonnet top, inset panels in door, waist, and base, bracket feet, turned pilasters on case and hood, orig paint on dial with children on the arch, areas of flaking, 88-1/2" h **1,790.00**

Rule, James, Portsmouth, Regency, early 19th C, mahogany, weighted movement with engraved silvered dial with day aperture and strike/silent dial, arched hood with crennelated crest, glass to three sides, door flanked by columns topped by ormolu Corinthian capitals, case with long arch top door with walnut line inlay, door flanked by fluted engaged gilt-metal topped columns, plinth base with applied molding to front panel, 83-1/2" h **6,500.00**

Smith, Benjamin, Provincial, works signed by Benjamin Smith, Leeds, brass face, steel chapter ring, two-train movement, lunar arch, date dial and subsidiary seconds hand, pierced spandrels, inlaid oak case with broken arch cresting, checkered banding, inlaid with shell and fans, bracket feet, 96" h **7,495.00**

Shelf, Ansonia, eight-day movement, time and strike, lion heads on side panels, **$260**. Photo courtesy of Joy Luke Auctions.

Taber, Elnathan, Roxbury, MA c1815, Federal, dial sgd "E. Taber, Roxbury," painted iron dial with calendar aperture, seconds hand, gilt spandrels, two ships, one flying American flag in the arch of dial, eight-day movement, mahogany veneer inlaid case with pierced fretwork, fluted plinths, brass stop fluted free-standing columns flanking bonnet above waist door with applied moldings, flanked by engaged brass stop fluted quarter columns with brass capitols and bases, waist door opens to reveal early 19th C label "Directions for Setting Up a Clock" above box base with inlay in outline, curving skirt, French feet, 92" h, refinished, imperfections **48,875.00**

Unknown maker

Birch and butternut, old refinishing, wooden face retains orig basket of flowers in the arch, relief gold scrolls in spandrels, tombstone shaped windows on either side of hood, reeding on top corners, and at center of hood with scrolled goosenecks, wooden works, narrow tombstone door flanked by reeded edges, molded waist, bracket feet, scalloped aprons, age splints on sides of case, 87-1/2" h....... **2,200.00**

Cherry, poplar secondary wood, old mellow refinishing, dovetailed hood with freestanding turned pilasters, broken arch top with carved rosettes, overhanging door flanked by chamfered corners, molded waist, scalloped aprons, bracket feet, brass works, old floral painted dec on face, brass urn finial, weights and pendulum, no key, repaint on back of face, restoration to goosenecks, orig side finials missing, 92-1/2" h **1,650.00**

Whittaker, Samuel, English, finely engraved brass face, detailed castings of cherubs and crowns in spandrels, pierced steel hour hand, oak, old dark finish, hood with half turned pilasters, scrolled carving below cornice, molded waist with beading around door, bracket feet, shaped aprons, brass works, pendulum, door key, weights and minute hand missing, pieced restorations, slight at waist molding, 75-1/4" h **1,265.00**

Wall, Arts & Crafts, square face, brass pendulum, skinned original finish, remnant of paper label on reverse. 26" x 13", **$150**. Photo courtesy of David Rago Auctions, Inc.

Willard, Benjamin, Lexington, MA, c1771, cherry, brass dial inscribed "Benjamin Willard Lexington," boss inscribed "Tempus fugit," cast brass spandrels, silvered chapter ring, second hand, calendar aperture, eight-day time and strike movement, pagoda style bonnet, fluted plinths above scalloped waist door, molded box base, 82" h, refinished case, restoration to bonnet **12,650.00**

Willard, Ephraim, Hepplewhite, mahogany with inlay, bonnet with freestanding front columns with brass stop fluting, molded curved cornice with fretwork and brass finials on fluted plinths, fluted quarter columns with brass fittings and brass stop fluting and molded edge door in base, molding between sections, base molding, ogee feet, stringing inlay with invected corners, brass works with second hand and calendar movements, painted steel face with polychrome flowers and birds, labeled "Warranted by Em. Willard," weights, pendulum, and key, repairs to feet, pierced repair where lock was removed on waist door, minor repairs to bonnet, 93-3/4" h **33,000.00**

Willard, Simon, Chippendale case, mahogany, old finish, fan and stringing inlay, bonnet with fluted quarter columns, molded arch cornice, fretwork with fluted plinths, moldings between sections, molded edge door, fluted quarter columns, base molding, ogee feet, brass trim with stop fluting and eagle finials, brass works with calendar movement, second hand, painted steel face, rocking ship in arch flying American flag, face labeled "S. Willard," center plinth and fretwork restored, minor restorations to feet, age splits in base, pine secondary wood, weights and pendulum **55,000.00**

Wismer, Henry, Plumstead, Bucks County, PA, c1820, cherry, hood with molded broken-arch resting, carved floral rosettes, three plinths with turned finials, glazed tombstone door, polychrome iron dial, basket of fruit in arch, seashell spandrels, calendar aperture signed "Henry Wismer B.C.," brass weight-driven striking pull-up movement, flanked by turned columns, waist with door flanked by four ring-turned columns, base with canted corners, flaring French feet, old surface, 95-1/2" h **5,875.00**

Wall, gilt bronze, center panel mounted with shell flanked by two ebonized columns over round clock face, Roman numerals on dial, engraved Arabic numeral minute markers, ornamented by winged embossed ro heads and scrolled leaf decoration, figural winged angel ornament at base, conforming scroll and leaf decoration, 14" w, 33" h, **$1,540**. Photo courtesy of Alderfer Auction Co.

Wood, David, Newburyport, MA, c1800-15, Federal, cherry and maple, hood with three reeded plinths above arched molding, glazed tombstone door, polychrome and gilt dial with fruit designs, seconds indicator, calendar aperture inscribed "D. Wood," brass weight-driven movement, flanked by reeded columns, cockbeaded waist door flanked by reeded quarter columns, cove molding, base with reeded band and cut-out feet, engraved label affixed to back of door "David Wood, watch and clockmaker," 89" h, refinished, imperfections............................ **8,820.00**

Travel

Cartier, ivory tone dial, blue enamel Roman numeral indicators, Swiss made quartz movement, gold tone metal mount **300.00**

Van Cleef & Arpels, Pendulette Domino, small wood case with sliding top, integral stand, iridescent blue face with Arabic and abstract numeral indicators, number 433 of an edition of 2001, orig leather pouch and box **180.00**

Wall, French, rect brass case with raised musical instrument and floral decoration, circular dial with Roman numerals and central raised floral decoration, name on dial is worn but appears to be Courvoisier Freres, 6" x 4-1/2", **$1,150**. Photo courtesy of Alderfer Auction Co.

Wall

Banjo

Abbott, Samuel, Boston, MA, c1815-25, attributed to, Federal, mahogany, painted dial, "A"-shaped brass weight-driven eight-day movement, reverse painted throat glass flanked by gilded rope twist and brass side arms, lower eglomise glass depicting in polychrome "Lafayette the Friend of Liberty," 33-1/2" h, restoration **1,955.00**

Ansonia, girandole, etched glass panels, time and strike movement, eagle finial, 40" h **3,600.00**

Cummens, William, Boston, MA, c1820, Federal, dial sgd "warranted by Wm. Cummens," convex painted iron dial enclosed by convex glass and bezel topped by acorn finial, molded mahogany veneer case, T-bridge eight-day weight-driven movement, reverse painted throat glass, flanked by side arms, eglomise tablet marked "Patent" in

box base, 34" l, restoration **6,325.00**

Curtis and Dunning, Concord, MA, c1815, Federal, dial sgd "warranted by Curtis and Dunning," eight-day weight-driven movement, mahogany case with brass bezel and convex glass, tapering throat with reverse painted glass flanked by brass side arms, box base with eglomise panel, rope twist giltwood in outline, 33-1/2" l, period throat glass broken **5,175.00**

Wall, Ithaca, calendar, oak case, carved pediment (replaced), upper dial with Roman numerals, lower calendar dial with date, date and month, marked "H.B. Horton's Patents April 18, 1865 and August 28, 1866, Ithaca Calendar Clock Company, Ithaca, New York," 10-1/2" w, 4-1/4" d, 24" h, **$550**. Photo courtesy of Alderfer Auction Co.

Curtis, Lemuel, Concord, MA, c1815, Federal, brass eagle finials, mahogany and gilt gesso case, brass bezel, painted and gilt iron dial inscribed "warranted by L. Curtis," eight-day weight-driven movement, throat glass enclosing thermometer, inscribed "L. Curtis Patent," lower tablet showing figures in farm landscape, both framed by gilt spiral moldings, flanked by brass side arms, 33-1/4" h, restoration, imperfections **7,650.00**

Dyar, J., Concord, MA, c1815, Federal, mahogany, brass eagle finial above bras bezel, painted metal dial, reading "Warranted by J. Dyar," eight-day eight-drive movement, foliate throat glass reading "Patent," flanked by rope twist dec, brass side arms, lower tablet with eglomise naval battle framed by applied rope twist moldings, 32-3/4" h, lower tablet replaced, other imperfections **2,820.00**

Munroe, Concord, MA, c1820, Federal, gilt mahogany, brass ball finial over dial, eight-day weight-driven movement, throat glass flanked by brass side arms, lower tablet reading "Munroe's Patent Suspension," classical and foliate devices framed by applied rope twist dec, 33-1/2" h, repainted dial, replaced tablets, other imperfections **1,530.00**

Tall case, German, cherry, three finials, moon dial, chimes, three weights, plays seven German folk tones, signed "I. A. MOLLINGER WITTIB.NEUSTADT," 8'7", **$37,500**. Photo courtesy of Dotta Auction Co., Inc.

Munroe and Whiting, Concord, MA, c1808-17, Federal, gilt mahogany, acorn-form finial, iron painted dial enclosing eight-day weight-driven movement, foliate throat glass flanked by side arms, lower panel depicting ship battle, both within rope twist dec frames, 33" h, lower tablet replaced, other imperfections **1,880.00**

Noyes, L. W., Nashua, NH, c1825, Federal, mahogany, brass belted ball finial, brass bezel, printed dial, eight-day weight-drive movement, throat glass flanked by brass side arms and tablet with foliate and eagle devices framed by half round moldings, 34" h, restoration including tablets................................ **1,765.00**

Sawin, John and John W. Dyer, Boston, MA, c1825, Federal, giltwood and mahogany, dial sgd "Sawin and Dyer, Boston," acorn finial above convex glass and brass bezel, brass eight-day weight-driven movement, glass throat panel reads "Patent" flanked by brass side arms over lower glass eglomise tablet which depicts seaside hotel, reads "Nahant," 33" h, minor restoration **4,025.00**

Tall case, New Jersey, Federal, c1800, mahogany, broken arch bonnet with line and oval inlays, white painted face, signed "Joakim Hill, Flemington," case with arched door flanked by fluted quarter columns over rectangular base, scrolled skirt and bracket feet in overall line, oval, and circular inlays, 93" h, **$14,950**. Photo courtesy of Pook & Pook.

Taber, Elnathan, Roxbury, MA, c1810, Federal, dial reads "Warranted by E. Taber," acorn finial above mahogany and cross-banded veneer case, signed, painted dial enclosing brass eight-day weight-driven movement, weight pan inscribed "made by E. Taber, Roxbury, Mafachusetts" (sic), reverse painted throat glass includes "Patent," flanked by brass side arms above lower tablet depicting naval battle, reads "Hornet and Peacock," 33" h, imperfections, note accompanying clock dated June 1961 indicates it was "gift to John May Secretary of State from George Washington" **65,200.00**

Unidentified Concord Massachusetts maker, c1815, Federal, gilt and mahogany Brass ball finial above brass bezel and dial, eight-day weight-driven movement, foliate throat glass reading "PATENT" flanked by brass side arms, lower tablet depicting battle between the *Constitution* and the *Guerriere,* both framed by applied rope twist dec, 35" h, imperfections **2,475.00**

Unsigned painted dial, Concord-type eight-day brass weight drive movement, carved wooden eagle finial, throat glass panel reading "Patent," flanked by brass side arms over reverse painted glass panel in box base, 33-1/2" h, restoration **2,875.00**

Unidentified Massachusetts maker, Federal

c1815, mahogany, unsigned dial, eight-day brass weight drive movement, reverse painted glass panels surrounded by rope gilt, lower tablet with eglomise ship portrait labeled "President Plantagenet," 32" h, restoration **2,615.00**

c1825, giltwood and mahogany, eagle and shield finial above mahogany and giltwood case, brass bezel, convex painted dial, eight-day weight-driven movement, glass throat panel with gilt scroll, lower panel showing sea battle, both framed by gilt spiral moldings, flanked by brass side arms, 33-3/4" h, restorations **1,550.00**

Tall case, Pennsylvania, cherry wood case, flat bonnet, brass dial with Arabic and Roman numerals, central sunburst, inscribed, "Jacob Gottschalk, Towamencin," original works, original lead weight, c1750 to 1780, 19" w, 11" d, 88" h, spandrels missing, top molding and base replaced, repairs to case, **$9,200**. Photo courtesy of Alderfer Auction Co.

Willard, Aaron, Jr., Boston, MA, Federal, c1820-25, mahogany, acorn form finial, brass bezel and painted dial, eight-day weight-driven movement stamped "A. Willard Jr. Boston," throat glass with scrolling devices, reading "Patent," flanked by brass side arms and lower tablet depicting lakeside church, both framed by applied rope twist dec, applied spherules and carved bracket with pendant, 42-3/4" h, imperfections **3,420.00**

Willard, Simon, Roxbury, MA, Federal, c1805, mahogany, unmarked dial, eight-day weight driven T-bridge movement with stepped train, escapement in case with cross-banded veneer, brass side arms, reverse painted throat glass above lower eglomise tablet which reads "S. Willard's Patent," 33-1/2" h, restoration **10,350.00**

Lyre

Chandler, Abiel, Concord, NH, c1825, Classical, dial sgd "A. Chandler," striking brass eight-day weight-driven movement, leaf carved mahogany veneer case with bracket, 43" h, refinished, imperfections **17,250.00**

Sawin, John and John W. Dyer, Boston, MA, mid 1820s, Classical, dial sgd "Sawin and Dyer Boston," eight-day brass weight-driven movement, mahogany case with reverse painted throat and lower eglomise tablets with gilded rope twist surrounds, gilded bracket, 40" l, imperfections **13,800.00**

Tall case, Philadelphia, c1765, Chippendale, walnut, bonnet top, original flame finials, eight-day brass works inscribed "Owen Biddle Philadelphia" beneath an arch inscribed "The man is yet unborn who duly weighs every hour," waist with highly figured arched door, flanked by quarter columns, base with applied scalloped panel, supported by straight bracket feet, 100-1/2" h, **$92,000**. Photo courtesy of Pook & Pook.

Mirror

Chadwick, Joseph, Boscawen, NH, c1825, late Federal, painted dial sgd "Joseph Chadwick Boscawen," surrounded by eglomise glass panel that conceals brass eight-day weight-drive movement above mirror glass, flanked by painted and gilded split balusters punctuated by rosettes, 31-1/2" h, case refinished, some re-gilding to case, imperfections **3,335.00**

Morrill, Benjamin, Boscawen, NH, c1825, late Federal, paper label, dark stained pine case with unsigned dial, eight-day movement, surrounded by eglomise tablet above mirror glass, flanked by split baluster columns punctuated by rosettes at corners, 30" h, imperfections **10,350.00**

Wag on wall

English, sq metal face with orig painting of landscape panel, gold and red flowers in spandrels, illegible signature with calendar dial, engraved copper hands, 12" w, 12" h **295.00**

Unknown maker, orig painted dec on face of yellow and black basket of flowers in arch, red, yellow, and green pillars on either side, small circular panels on either side of base with man standing in canoe, mountains in background, well-executed restoration to lower face, weights, pendulum, no key, 19" x 13-1/2" **880.00**

Watchman

Morrill, Benjamin, Boscawen, NH, 1860s, rect birch box case, painted iron dial marked "B. Morrill Boscawen, eight-day weight-driven brass movement, 54-1/2" h, imperfections **2,875.00**

CLOISONNÉ

History: Cloisonné is the art of enameling on metal. The design is drawn on the metal body, then wires, which follow the design, are glued or soldered on. The cells thus created are packed with enamel and fired; this step is repeated several times until the level of enamel is higher than the wires. A buffing and polishing process brings the level of enamels flush to the surface of the wires.

This art form has been practiced in various countries since 1300 B.C. and in the Orient since the early 15th century. Most cloisonné found today is from the late Victorian era, 1870-1900, and was made in China or Japan.

Box, cov, 4-3/4" d, 2-3/4" h, rounded form, butterflies among flowering branches, turquoise ground, Chinese, 19th C **345.00**

Charger, one with two phoenix on black ground, other with flowers on blue ground, Japanese, Meiji Period, **$560**. Photo courtesy of Sloans & Kenyon Auctions.

Candlesticks, pr, 7-1/8" h, figural, brass, blue mythical animals seated on round dark red base with open work sides, three feet, each animal holds flower in mouth, red candle socket on back **200.00**

Cane, 36" l, 1-1/3" d x 9-1/2" l Japanese cloisonné handle, dark blue ground, long scaly three-toed Japanese dragon in shades of white, pale blue, black, and brown, 1/3" gold gilt collar, black hardwood shaft, 7/8" horn ferrule, fashioned in England, c1890..... **1,460.00**

Cup, 4" h, ftd, butterflies and flowers, lappet borders, Chinese, 19th C **100.00**

Desk set, brush pot, pen, pen tray, blotter, and paper holder, Japanese, price for set **130.00**

Figure, 21" h, Tang-style horse, all-over phoenix and scrolled florals, turquoise ground, removable saddle exposes int. storage compartment, gilt bronze, 20th C **415.00**

Incense burner, 19-3/4" h, globular, three dragon-head feet, high curving handles, scrolling lotus and ancient bronzes motif, openwork lid, dragon finial, raised Quinlong six-character mark, damage **815.00**

Jar, cov, 6" h, ovoid, even green over central band of scrolling flowers, dome lid, ovoid finial, marked "Ando Jubei," 20th C **230.00**

Jardinière, 13" d, 10" h, bronze, bands of cloisonné designs, golden yellow and blue triangles, polychrome geometric designs on dark blue, chrysanthemums on light blue, cast relief scene of water lily, turtle, and flowering branches on int., soldered repair at foot **220.00**

Planter, 11" l, quatralobe, classical symbol and scroll dec, blue ground, Chinese, pr **200.00**

Ship, 54" w, 17-1/2" d, 49" h, copper, blue, green, white, red, and pink enameling, dragon-shaped hull with cast head at one end, fish scale and waves cloisonné on body, pagoda on top with detailed floral panels, matching carved wooden base with relief waves, short bracket feet with scrolling, reputedly made for one of Japanese World's Fair pavilions **6,875.00**

Vase, baluster form body with everted rims, three cranes with navy blue background, silver and copper wire on copper, copper mounts, Japanese, 3" h, bottom missing, **$230**. Photo courtesy of Alderfer Auction Co.

Tea kettle, 10-1/2" h, multicolored scrolling lotus, medium-blue ground, lappets border, waisted neck with band of raised auspicious symbols between key-fret borders, floral form finial, double handles, Chinese, 19th C **690.00**

Teapot, 4-3/4" d, 3-1/4" h, central band of flowering chrysanthemums on pink ground, shoulder with shaped cartouches of phoenix and dragon on floral and patterned ground, lower border with chrysanthemum blossom on swirling ground, flat base with three small raised feet, single chrysanthemum design, spout and handle with floral design, lid with two writhing dragons on peach-colored ground, Japanese, late 19th/early 20th C **4,025.00**

Urn, 23-3/4" h, ovoid, slightly waisted neck, peony dec, black ground, base plaque marked "Takeuchi Chubei," Japanese, late-19th C, Shichi Ho Company, Owari **690.00**

Vase

3 5/8" h, shouldered form, long slender neck flaring at rim, colored enamels, spider chrysanthemums and songbirds, midnight-blue ground, Japanese, Meiji period, pr **550.00**

4-3/4" h, ovoid, continual scene of geese on riverbank, flowering bushes and mountains in distance, Japanese **2,875.00**

6" h, six sided, each side with shield below floral band, alternating dragon and phoenix motif, flecked-blue ground, Japanese, early 20th C **460.00**

8 7/8" h, flattened ovoid, large cartouches of dragon with serpent and phoenix flying among vines, surrounded by flowering vines, black ground, Japanese, Meiji period **8,350.00**

Vase, white cranes on all-over floral blue ground, 15-1/4" h, **$275**. Photo courtesy of Joy Luke Auctions.

9 1/8" h, angled shoulder, ovoid, waisted neck, multicolored flowering chrysanthemum, bright blue ground, Meiji period, Ota, minor crazing **1,380.00**

12-1/4" h, ovoid, waisted neck, inverted rim, two songbirds among prunus and bamboo, colored enamels with silver wire, dark-blue ground, stamped silver rim, wire Ando Jubei mark on base, Meiji period, orig fitted box **4,975.00**

Clothing and Clothing Accessories

History: While museums and a few private individuals have collected clothing for decades, it is only recently that collecting clothing has achieved a widespread popularity. Clothing reflects the social attitudes of a historical period.

Christening and wedding gowns abound and, hence, are not in large demand. Among the hardest items to find is men's clothing from the 19th and early 20th centuries. The most sought after clothing is by designers, such as Fortuny, Poirret, and Vionnet.

Additional Listings: See *Warman's Americana & Collectibles* for more examples.

Note: Condition, size, age, and completeness are critical factors in purchasing clothing. Collectors divide into two groups: those collecting for aesthetic and historic value and those desiring to wear the garment. Prices are higher on the West Coast; major auction houses focus on designer clothes and high-fashion items.

Apron, black and white calico, ruffle at hem, c1910 .... **40.00**

Blouse

Bobbin lace over net, cream, Battenberg lace yoke, stand-up collar, elbow length sleeves, c1900 .... **90.00**

Crepe, peach, glass beading, rhinestones, and pearls, short sleeves, buttons on back, c1935 .... **125.00**

Lawn, white, hand made net darned lace in leaf and vine motif at cuffs, around collar, on front, drawn work, hand done eyelet work with white embroidery, c1910 .... **45.00**

Linen, white, long full sleeves, small MOP buttons up back, hand embroidered on front and cuffs with white cotton thread in flowers and vine pattern, c1900 .... **45.00**

Linen, white, short sleeves, cut work, white floral embroidery, unworn, orig paper hang tag "Fin De Sigio, Habana, Hecho en Cuba," mid-20th C **45.00**

Organdy, cream, embroidered, horizontal bands of lace, crocheted buttons up back, c1935 .... **65.00**

Boater (skimmer), woven natural straw, black grosgrain ribbon band, labeled "Cavalier, Fifth Ave, New York," early 20th C **65.00**

Bonnet, baby's

Lawn, white, ruffles, embroidery, c1840, hand written note about maker **50.00**

Silk, cream, plain, mid-20th C **15.00**

Silk, white, pin tucks, pink silk ties, mid-20th C **20.00**

Afternoon dress, two-piece rust silk, train, fitted bodice trimmed with tan silk knotted fringe, silk covered buttons, c1880, some discoloration, **$450.** Photo courtesy of Alderfer Auction Co.

Bonnet, lady's

Horsehair, straw, lace, and velvet, tan, c1870 .... **50.00**

Silk chiffon and horsehair, black, black sequin trim, black silk rose and ribbons, black silk lining, black grosgrain ties, c1890 .... **75.00**

Silk faille, light tan, brown silk velvet trim, ruched around brim, cream gauze lining, c1890 .... **50.00**

Straw, black, black glass beading, green velvet under lining **60.00**

Straw, natural, elaborate woven detailing on brim, c1870 .... **75.00**

Camisole, cream silk, lace, pin tucks, labeled "Franklin Simon & Co., Fifth Ave, NY" **25.00**

Cape

Velvet, black, tangerine, reversible, full length, hood, tie at neckline, c1935 .... **185.00**

Velveteen, black and tan leopard print, black satin lining, c1960, needs minor repairs **30.00**

Christening dress, white lawn, white embroidery, ruffles, lace trim, late 19th C **95.00**

Coat

Silk velvet, black, appliquéd with black silk, cream silk lining, labels with black soutache, red wool appliqué, gold embroidery, labeled "Lazarus Bros, Wilkes Barre, PA, c1910 .... **225.00**

Vicuna, soft black, long sleeves, three fabric cov buttons, fully lined, labeled "Bernhard Altmann 100% imported Vicuna, Styled by Regency 52349," c1955 .... **85.00**

Wool/cashmere, black, long sleeves, black satin lining, deep cape of black fur, labeled "Kraeler, Jeannette, Reading, Harrisburg," c1940 .... **65.00**

Dress, child's

Cotton, brown and white stripes, lace, tucks **20.00**

Cotton, calico, green and yellow on red ground, linen lined bodice, c1890 .... **40.00**

Cotton, gray, rose, and white stripes, ruffles at hem, cuffs, and collar, c1900 .... **30.00**

Lawn, white, pin tucks, lace, ruffles **35.00**

Dress, lady's

Cotton, floral printed, burgundy, rose, green, and tan, hand stitched, c1860, some damage **70.00**

Dotted Swiss, white, afternoon type, white embroidered dots, lace insertion, tucks, and lace trim at neckline and sleeves, c1910 .... **75.00**

Lawn, white, pin tucks, lace insertion, c1905 .... **125.00**

Raw silk, tan, drawn work, lace insertion on bodice, hem, and cuffs, c1915 .... **75.00**

Sheer cotton, two-pc style, blue dots printed on tan ground, lace and ribbon appliqué, ruffles at hem, c1900 .... **70.00**

Silk chiffon, black roses on cream ground, capelet, deep V-neckline, tie at waistline, uneven hem, c1930 .... **395.00**

Silk chiffon, navy blue and white circular design print, smocking at waistline, short sleeves, deep V-neckline, c1935 .... **75.00**

Silk chiffon, red poppy print on white ground, capelet effect, dropped waistline, labeled "Lucille Chayt," early 1980s **65.00**

Silk crepe, black, panel of beige lace on bodice, long sleeves, belt, black satin slip with ruffle at hem, c1920 .... **40.00**

Silk crepe, violet, rose, and green floral print on navy blue, short sleeves, neck smocking, fabric belt, c1935 .... **50.00**

Silk, gray, black stripes, fabric covered buttons detailing on skirt, satin embroidery in shades or rose and burgundy with lace on sleeves and front of bodice, rose embroidered net and lace, c1910, underarm damage, several stains on skirt **65.00**

Silk, irid mauve/green, hand stitched, full skirt gathered at waistline with smocking, pagoda sleeves, rose silk braid and fringe, lace under-sleeves, hidden inside pocket, c1850, some damage **85.00**

Silk satin, cream, long sleeves, scoop neckline, dropped waistline, bow detail, c1925 .... **45.00**

Taffeta, black, ruched black velvet bodice, spaghetti straps, silver glass bead detailing, c1940 .... **80.00**

Velvet, brown, elbow length sleeves, ruching at shoulders, belt, c1940 .... **85.00**

Viole, sheer, pattern of leaves and flowers in shades of green, white, and tangerine, dropped waistline, tie at neckline, long sleeves, c1925 .... **65.00**

Viole, white, pale link line, pin tucks, Irish crochet insertion, decorative MOP buttons on front, c1925 .... **85.00**

Evening coat, full length, black

Velvet, double-breasted style, long sleeves, black taffeta lining, black faux jewel buttons, c1960 .... **75.00**

Velvet, elaborate metallic lilac, aqua, gold, rose, and pale blue embroidery on long sleeves in leaf motif, ivory

taffeta lining, labeled "Hess Brothers, Allentown, London, Paris," c1940 .... **125.00**

Wool, long full sleeves, varied black soutache on large cuffs, yoke, back, collar, fully lined with taupe silk, labeled "Eisenberg & Sons Original," c1905, some seams in lining open **265.00**

Evening jacket, bolero style, embroidered all over with deep burgundy glass bugle beads, purple satin lining, c1940............ **100.00**

Man's derby-style hat, original Cavanagh's New York, box, **$45.**

Fashion hat

Horsehair and lace, black, wire frame, velvet and silk flower trim, c1920, orig box **70.00**

Horsehair, black, wire frame, trimmed with black glass beads, straw, and flowers, black silk lining, labeled "Anthony N. Campbell, Bradford, PA," c1920, orig box **125.00**

Marabou, white, cream faille lining, labeled "Fleur de Lis, Chapeau," c1960 .... **30.00**

Straw, black, black grosgrain ribbon band, blue silk flowers, green leaves, labeled "Avedon, Fifth Avenue, New York, Paris, London," size 22-1/2", c1925 .... **125.00**

Straw, tan, tan velvet ribbon trim, glass beads, multicolored velvet flowers, orig Dobbs Fifth Avenue, NY, hatbox, c1910 .... **165.00**

Velvet and silk, brown, ruched circle design, MOP centers, black satin lining, c1920, orig hatbox....... **150.00**

Gloves

Kid, cream, rose pattern satin embroidery at cuffs, c1935 ...... **20.00**

Silk, peach, peach satin floral embroidery, labeled "Niagara 6-1/2," c1910, 22" l............ **45.00**

Gown

Crepe, black, full skirt with pin tucks, criss-cross effect at bustline, black illusion sleeves, yoke with deep V neckline, c1940 .... **125.00**

Raw silk skirt, alternating with beige needle lace, short sleeved beige needed lace bodice, ruching on sleeves, scoop neck, c1940 .... **65.00**

Rayon, floral print, red, yellow, green, and blue, beige cotton camisole-type bodice, full skirt, matching short sleeved jacket, c1935 .... **60.00**

Rayon, white, ruching on bodice, elaborately embroidered straps with amber glass beads, gold metallic threads, c1940 .... **150.00**

Silk chiffon, pale blue, pale pink detailing on bodice, ruffles on straps, labeled "Carol, NY, Adorta, Hand Made," c1935 .... **350.00**

Silk, pale gold, cream silk lace bodice, lace tiers on front of skirt, elaborate gold and silver glass beading on bodice, blush silk chiffon overlay............ **185.00**

Silk taffeta, black, sleeveless, ruffles, slight train, scoop neckline, V-back, ruched and embroidered on bodice and on sashes in back in rose motif in shades of blue and rose, rhinestone trim, c1935............ **350.00**

Velvet, purple, rope effect at neckline, ruching on bodice, short sleeves, slightly flared skirt, c1935 .... **135.00**

Velvet, red, rhinestone dec straps and belt buckle, ruffles at hips and back, c1935 .... **45.00**

Wool/cashmere, black, low cut, narrow flat straps, fabric covered buttons on back, large velvet floral appliqué on bodice and waistline in deep red, cream centers, green leaves............ **50.00**

Beaded bag, white band with pink and blue flowers in cornucopia motif, mauve top and bottom bands, green leaves and gold accents, some wear, **$75.** Photo courtesy of Sky Hawk Auctions.

Handbag

Alligator, brown, brass clasp and detailing, tan lining, orig "Dewees" hang tag inside, c1955, 12" x 9" **115.00**

Alligator, brown, yellow leather lining, small mirror, alligator change purse, brass clip, braided brown leather handle, c1900, 8" x 6"............ **75.00**

Bakelite, shaped box-style, caramel striped, brass hinge, Bakelite handles, c1950, 4" sq, 4" h..... **175.00**

Beaded, gold and silver steel beads in geometric design, brass frame, chain handle, gold steel beads fringe, labeled "Made in France," poor condition ivory silk lining, c1915, 5-1/2" x 7" **150.00**

Beaded, silver and white glass beads, dec silver frame, clasp, small chain handle, ivory taffeta lining, c1925, 6-1/4" x 6" **85.00**

Brocade, clutch, tangerine, gold, and pale green, hinged clasp, labeled "Bags by Josef," c1950, 9" x 6-3/4" **25.00**

Crochet, tan, irid copper glass beading, dec brass frame with chain handle, brown silk lining, c1910, 8" x 6" **125.00**

Enameled mesh, bird and branch motif, burgundy and black, cream ground, pierced and dec frame, chain handle, black stone on clasp, rose stones on frame, gray silk lining, c1920, 5-1/2" x 7-3/4" **375.00**

Enameled mesh, rose design, burgundy, rose, and green on yellow ground, elaborately dec and pierced frame, chain handle, rose silk lining, c1920, 4-1/2" x 7-1/2" **275.00**

Reticule, Irish crochet, floral design, ball fringe, drawstring top, c1900, 7" x 6" **75.00**

Top left: blouse, white lawn, handmade lace of net darning in leaf and vine motif, further detailed with drawn work, hand done eyelet work, white embossed roidery, c1910, **$60**; lower left: blouse, white linen, full sleeves, small mother-of-pearl buttons on back, hand embossed roidered on front and cuffs in white in pattern of flowers and vines, c1900, **$60**; right: petticoat, hand made, white lawn, fine pin tucks, eyelet lace, embossed roidery, red silk ribbons insertion, initials, c1900, unworn, possibly trousseau item, **$95**. Photo courtesy of Alderfer Auction Co.

Reticule, white lawn, sgd and dated "Susan B. Arnold, Dec 1, 1813," intricate black pen drawings of flowers and poem script, beehive and buzzing bees **315.00**

Silk, fabric, leather, Louis Vuitton, rect black bag, appliqué landscape, removable leather strap, silvertone fittings, satin interior with one pocket, orig dust bag **365.00**

Tapestry, floral, lilac, green, blue, tan, and rose on cream ground, black edging, brass frame and chain handle, peach moiré silk lining, c1935, 7-1/4" x 6" **75.00**

Velvet, black, clutch, evening type, pierced brass frame in floral design, beaded on one side in clear and green stones, rose cut crystal and pearls, black silk crepe lining, c1935, 9-1/2" x 8" **200.00**

Velvet, black, long braided strap, embroidered with gold metallic threads, blues, and greens peacock and floral design, c1960, 8" x 6" **60.00**

Jacket, tweed, avocado, elaborate button detailing, patch pockets, lined with rust satin, labeled "The Blum Store," c1940 .... **65.00**

Left: nursing mother's dress and capelet, tan floral cotton print, rose and green florals, long sleeves with ruching, ruffles at shoulders, bodice gathered with drawstring to expose slits for nursing of infant, hand stitched, tan linen linen, c1840, **$995**; two capes at right: top: black silk damask, trimmed with black Chantilly lace, black glass beading, black silk ribbon, c1890, **$85**; lower: black wool twill, lined with black silk, rows of black glass beads as trim, c1900, **$65**. Photo courtesy of Alderfer Auction Co.

Jacket, lace

Black Battenberg lace over sheer black silk, c1920, some damage to lace and lining **65.00**

Cream cotton Irish crochet, elbow-length sleeves, peplum, belt, c1910 .... **350.00**

Cream cotton Irish crochet, Irish crochet elaborate borders in shamrock motif, V-neckline, four tan crocheted buttons, c1910 ...... **365.00**

Lederhosen, blue felt belt with floral satin embroidery, dec silver metal buckle, tan cotton velour shorts, bone button detailing, tan leather straps, dec floral satin oval, Austria or Germany, mid-20th C **65.00**

Lingerie dress, white lawn, elaborate embroidery and lace insertion with elbow-length sleeves, slight train, white lawn underpinnings, c1900 .... **175.00**

Nightgown

Cotton, white, embroidered yoke, buttons up front, c1910 .... **60.00**

Cotton, white, lace yoke with cutwork and embroidery, matching lace cuffs, c1910 .... **70.00**

Rayon, peach, purple floral print, cut on bias, c1935 .... **140.00**

Rayon satin, white, full length, lace straps, pink tucks, lace on bodice, slightly flared skirt, c1940 .... **70.00**

Pajamas

Satin brocade, cream, multicolored floral design, diagonal frog closure, black satin Capri pants trimmed with matching brocade, c1945 .... **75.00**

Silk damask, pale green, frog closures, wide legged pants, green and lilac stain embroidered butterflies and flowers motif on front and back of long sleeved jacket and at cuffs, Chinese, c1930 .... **150.00**

Pants suit, wool flannel, charcoal gray, long sleeved tunic with high collar, straight legged pants, fully lined, entirely cov with prong-set rhinestones, labeled "Made in the British Crown Colony of Hong Kong, Best & Co., Fifth Ave, NY," c1960, several rhinestones loose ... **65.00**

Parasol, folding

Avocado green silk overlapping veined leaves, lined with black silk with pinked edge, ivory handle trimmed with green malachite, brass fitting, ivory finial, c1890, 24-1/2" l **175.00**

Black chantilly lace over ivory silk, pinked edge, black intricately carved wooden handle, c1890, 27" l **200.00**

Petticoat, cotton, white

Eyelet lace at hem **30.00**

Eyelet lace, embroidery, deep hem of pin tucks, c1900 .... **35.00**

Pin tucks, ruffles, c1910 .... **40.00**

Robe

Cotton print, aqua, green, blue, yellow, and white water lilies design, full length, wrap style, short sleeves, tie at waistline, patch pocket, c1940 .... **65.00**

Silk satin, cream, long sleeves, tie at waistline, buckle closure at neckline, glass beads, sequins, hand painted pale blue Pegasus motif with rose wings, beaded feet, rhinestone eyes, lined with rose silk chiffon, rose silk garment bag, labeled "Cloud Swept by Madelyn Whiting," c1940 .... **80.00**

Scarf, silk, Hermès, Les Oiseaux Du Roy, hooded falcons on perches and liveried handler, cobalt blue and red ground **235.00**

Shawl

Net, irid gold and brown, embroidered with pale green, rose, and black threads, stylized floral design, c1910, 18" x 88" **200.00**

Silk chiffon, ombre dyed, etched silk velvet, shades of lilac, blue, gold, and rose, early 20th C, 25-1/2" x 83" **315.00**

Silk, cream, printed, embroidered ivory floral pattern, drawn work at ends, possibly Indian, early 20th C, 37" x 74" **300.00**

Silk crepe, satin floral embroidery in shades of rose, lilac, and green, long knotted fringe, Spanish, c1930, 32" sq **125.00**

Shell, white net, embroidered all over with silver sequins, c1950 .... **95.00**

Shoes, lady's

Cotton, dainty boot style, plain weave, brown, black patent leather, straight soles, leather stacked heels, side lacing, c1840, never worn **125.00**

High button boots, brown leather lace-ups, stacked heels, brown leather soles, c1910 .... **60.00**

Lace-up style, white kid, French hells, tan leather soles, c1910 .... **75.00**

Pumps, black silk, rhinestone studded heels, labeled "I. Miller," c1950, some loss to rhinestones **20.00**

Sandals, cork platform, tan leather, brown leather insoles, marked "Made in Italy," c1970 .... **50.00**

Left: skirt, white linen with white soutache up front and round hem, in stylized pattern of flowers, and leaves, c1915, **$85**; right: lingerie dress, white lawn with lace insertion, white embossed roidery, Irish crochet yoke, c1910, **$110**. Photo courtesy of Alderfer Auction Co.

Slip

Crepe, black, drawn work, scalloping, c1930 .... **35.00**
Nylon, red, lace trim, c1950 ..... **25.00**
Satin, ivory, scalloped edging, Formula label **45.00**
Silk, ivory, lace net darning in floral design, camisole top lace straps, ivory satin embroidery, c1910 .... **65.00**

Skirt

Silk, blue, deep pleated hem, c1900 .... **50.00**
Silk brocade, black, deep black lace hem, c1900 .... **60.00**
Wool, black, pleated, faint bands of purple, red, blue, green, and white stripes, crotched red yarn edging, blue cloth band, 31" l **55.00**

Smoking jacket, man's, silver and black floral design brocade, black silk faille labels, black silk lining, c1950 .... **25.00**

Sport coat, man's, black wool tweed with flecks of blue, red, and white, partially lined with black satin, labeled "Prestique Clothes, Reg U. S. Pat Off, Philadelphia," mid-1950s...................................... **40.00**

Special occasion dress

Silk satin, burgundy, deep V-neckline and back, chocker-style closure, sash at waistline, fully lined, labeled "Victor Costa Boutique for Nahdree 6," early 1980s **145.00**
Wool challis, black, appliquéd and embroidered bodice, brocade butterflies, colorful sequins, stones, and glass beads, V-neckline, fabric covered buttons, slightly flared skirt, jacket with appliquéd and embroidered waistline, padded shoulders, long sleeves, shocking pink wool cuffs, shocking pink wool and silk crepe lining, labeled "Bonwit Teller, Philadelphia," c1940 .... **200.00**
Wool/silk blend, cream, two pcs, lace trim at cuffs, cream satin band and lace on bodice, accompanied by framed photo of graduate wearing gown for graduation from West Chester State College, c1890 .... **265.00**

Suit, velveteen

Blue, fitted jacket, trapunto work, fabric covered buttons, slightly flared skirt, c1940.............................. **50.00**
Green, fabric covered buttons edged with brass, slightly flared skirt, stitching on lapel, pockets, labeled "Original Deign, US Patent Office, Pat. Pend.," c1945 .... **40.00**

Sweater

Cashmere, beige, double lining of beige lace and nylon, long sleeves, rhinestone buttons, rhinestone clasp at waistline, tan mink snap-on collar, c1955, some rhinestones missing **45.00**
Cashmere, black, labeled "Made in Scotland for Liberty of London" **35.00**
Cashmere, ivory, yellow roses, green leaves, MOP buttons, labeled "Ballantyne of Peebles, 100% Pure Cashmere, Made in Scotland," c1960 .... **75.00**
Cashmere blend, navy blue, elaborate white glass beading and irid sequin trim, fully lined in navy blue silk, labeled "Made in Hong Kong," c1955 .... **65.00**

Swimsuit, wool, gold and black stripes, labeled "Knicker Knit, All Wool," c1930, snap closure, some small holes **50.00**

Vest, man's

Cotton, floral print, MOP buttons, early 20th C **35.00**
Satin, ivory, cream cotton back, sgd and dated "J. R. Spony, Aug 1845," hand stitching and buttonhole edging **65.00**

Walking suit

Wool twill, navy blue, two pcs, fabric cov button detailing, elaborate embroidery with diminutive navy blue glass beads in floral design on jacket, at hem, and in two panels up front of skirt which has panels of navy blue silk as well, beading on waistband, lined with navy blue silk, labeled "Thurn, New York, Paris," c1910 .... **250.00**
Wool/silk faille, chestnut brown, trimmed with brown silk velvet, pleats at hem, fabric covered buttons, lace collar, tan and rust silk apron with silk fringe, c1880 .... **350.00**

COALPORT

History: In the mid-1750s, Ambrose Gallimore established a pottery at Caughley in the Severn Gorge, Shropshire, England. Several other potteries, including Jackfield, developed in the area.

About 1795, John Rose and Edward Blakeway built a pottery at Coalport, a new town founded along the right-of-way of the Shropshire Canal. Other potteries located adjacent to the canal were those of Walter Bradley and Anstice, Horton, and Rose. In 1799, Rose and Blakeway bought the Royal Salopian China Manufactory at Caughley. In 1814, this operation was moved to Coalport.

A bankruptcy in 1803 led to refinancing and a new name—John Rose and Company. In 1814, Anstice, Horton, and Rose was acquired. The South Wales potteries at Swansea and Nantgarw were added. The expanded firm made fine quality, highly decorated ware. The plant enjoyed a renaissance from 1888 to 1900.

World War I, decline in trade, and shift of the pottery industry away from the Severn Gorge brought hard times to Coalport. In 1926, the firm, now owned by Cauldon Potteries, moved from Coalport to Shelton. Later owners included Crescent Potteries, Brain & Co., Ltd., and finally, in 1967, Wedgwood. The former Coalport China Works factory has been converted to a museum and exhibition space for Caughley and Coalport.

For more information, see *Warman's English & Continental Pottery & Porcelain,* 3rd edition.

Perfume bottle, bulbous, gilt ground, turquoise beaded dec, central band of maroon enameled flowers, crown mark, 4" h, **$770**. Photo courtesy of Alderfer Auction Co.

Creamer, Athione, blue................ **375.00**

Cream soup bowl, two handles, Athione, blue... **330.00**

Demitasse cup and saucer, quatrefoil shape, 2-1/4" x 1-1/2" cup with ring handle, 3-1/8" d saucer, pink, gilt trim **350.00**

Dessert plate, 9-3/8" d, central gilt flowerhead in holly vine roundel, molded rim with further flowerheads and rocaille, late 19th/early 20th C, set of 12, one damaged **920.00**

Fish plates, 9" d, each center painted with different ichthyological specimen, titled on reverse, cobalt blue glazed border, gilt enamel scrollwork, gilt rim, early 20th C, set of four **825.00**

Gravy boat with underplate, Indian Tree **480.00**

Place setting, five pcs

Athione, blue **360.00**
Indian Tree............................. **450.00**

Platter

Athione, blue, 15-3/8" l **750.00**
Hazelton, white, round **360.00**
Indian Tree, small **450.00**

Sugar bowl, cov, Athione, blue ... **385.00**

Set of 12 plates, apple green and gilt borders, green and white enameling, pink rose design on white ground, made for J.E. Caldwell & Co., Philadelphia, 8-3/4" d, one with hairline, **$250**. Photo courtesy of Alderfer Auction Co.

Syrup, 5-1/2" h, raised swirl dec, gold painted florals, applied gold handle, sgd "COALPORT CHINA" under lid, base chip **60.00**

Vegetable dish, cov, Rosalinda **435.00**

Coca-Cola Items

History: The originator of Coca-Cola was John Pemberton, a pharmacist from Atlanta, Georgia. In 1886, Dr. Pemberton introduced a patent medicine to relieve headaches, stomach disorders, and other minor maladies. Unfortunately, his failing health and meager finances forced him to sell his interest.

In 1888, Asa G. Candler became the sole owner of Coca-Cola. Candler improved the formula, increased the advertising budget, and widened the distribution. A "patient" was accidentally given a dose of the syrup mixed with carbonated water instead of still water. The result was a tastier, more refreshing drink.

As sales increased in the 1890s, Candler recognized that the product was more suitable for the soft-drink market and began advertising it as such. From these beginnings, a myriad of advertising items have been issued to invite all to "Drink Coca-Cola."

Notes: Dates of interest: "Coke" was first used in advertising in 1941. The distinctively shaped bottle was registered as a trademark on April 12, 1960.

Grading Condition. The following numbers represent the standard grading system used by dealers, collectors, and auctioneers:

C.10 = Mint
C. 9 = Near mint
C.8.5 = Outstanding
C.8 = Excellent
C.7.5 = Fine +
C.7 = Fine
C. 6.5 = Fine – (good)
C. 6 = Poor

Advertising display, diecut, Santa holding bottle of Coke, wreath in hand with blank for message, **$115**.

Binder, 13" x 15-1/2", rigid cardboard, red oilcloth cover, four-ring metal binder to hold advertising sales sheets, c1950, no contents **48.00**

Bookmark, Romance of Coca-Cola, 1916... **30.00**

Bottle

Amber, marked "Lewisburg" **30.00**

Christmas, Williamstown, WV ... **15.00**

Commemorative, Nascar Series, Bill Elliott, Dale Earnhardt, or Bobby Labonte **5.00**

Bowl, 10" w, Vernon Ware, green, artificial ice, 1930s, C-9.8 .... **600.00**

Calendar, 1913, 13-1/2" x 22-1/2", Hamilton King illus........................ **900.00**

Ceiling globe, 14" d, milk glass, four logos, 1930s, C-9.5 .... **990.00**

Change tray

1914, Betty **150.00**

1941, girl with skates............... **48.00**

1970, Santa Claus **85.00**

Clock, 18" octagonal, neon, silhouette girl, 1939, C-8.5........................ **1,800.00**

Cooler, floor standing, 34-1/2" x 25-1/2" x 30", enameled red and white, two hinged lift doors, bottle opener **445.00**

Bingo cards, diecut, lot of three, each 8-1/2" x 9" cardboard card printed on front in red and black, each has 25 diecut windows which reveal different numbers for use in calling Bingo game, text across bottom "Compliments Coca-Cola Bottling Co," issued by Kemper-Thomas, Cincinnati, OH. Some surface dust soil, bit of light wear around edges, right side of bottom of each has original owner's initials in blue ballpoint pen, 1940s, **$25**. Photo courtesy of Hake's Americana & Collectibles.

Door kick plate, litho tin, 11-1/2" x 35", scrolling logo

Drink Coca-Cola, 1942 couple on right, C-9.9 .... **2,600.00**

Drink Coca-Cola, 1923 bottle on left, C-9.9.................................. **1,765.00**

Door pull, 8" h, plastic and metal, bottle shape, orig instructions and screws, C-9.3-9.5 .... **275.00**

Game board, 11-1/4" x 26-1/2", Steps to Health, prepared and distributed by Coca-Cola Co. of Canada, Ltd., copyright 1938, orig unmarked brown paper envelope.. **60.00**

Mileage meter, 10" x 7", originating in Statesville, NC, C-8.4 .... **1,675.00**

Pin, Hi-Fi Club, gold luster finish, detailed plastic, short metal stickpin, miniature Coke bottle about name in red lettering, phonograph record background inscribed "Sponsored By Your Coca-Cola Bottler," Australian issue, c1950..... **40.00**

Pocket mirror, 1-3/4" w, 2-3/4" h oval, celluloid, 1914, pretty girl, dark green ground, white and red lettering **400.00**

Coca Cola advertising cooler, **$700**. Photo courtesy of Joy Luke Auctions.

Poster, 1943, two farm girls taking a break, caption "Work Refreshed" **2,750.00**

Prize chance card, 4-1/4" x 5-1/4", printed in red and black on white, c1940, unused... **12.00**

Radio

Bottle shape, 24" h, 1930s, C-8.2 .... **8,500.00**

Cooler shape, red, 1950s **2,250.00**

Salesman sample, cooler

By Kay Displays, orig leatherette carrying case, orig cardboard box, 1939, C-9.8....................... **10,000.00**

Glasscock Junior, orig carrying case, six small Coke bottles with nickel-plated hardware, 1929, C-8.5 .... **33,000.00**

Sandwich plate, 7-1/4" d, white ground, script slogan, bottle and glass in center, Knowles, C-9.8 .... **750.00**

Tray, Springboard Girl, 1939, American Art Works, Coshocton, OH, 13-1/2" x 10-1/2", $425. Photo courtesy of Joy Luke Auctions.

Shirt, deliveryman, matching tie, 1950s **255.00**

Sign

6" x 18", porcelain, diecut, two-color, script, orig box, attaching instructions, screws, C-10 .... **1,100.00**

13" x 11", six-pack with two-tone green bottle, color litho metal, some fading **75.00**

23" x 26", porcelain, diagonal slash, fountain service, 1934, C-9.7 .... **4,700.00**

24" d, porcelain, single bottle in center, no slogan, 1950, C-9.2 .... **1,800.00**

26" x 25", double-sided, sidewalk, dispenser, 1939, C-9.5 .... **6,750.00**

60" x 42", porcelain, curb-side service, two-sided, green, red, and white, 1933, C-9.6 .... **3,000.00**

Tray, Roadster, 1942, American Art Works, Coshocton, OH, 13-1/4" x 10-1/2", $450. Photo courtesy of Joy Luke Auctions.

String holder, two-sided, showing six-lace and logo "Take Home in Cartons," 1940s, C-9.5 .... **4,000.00**

Thermometer

5" x 17" diecut emb tin, figural Pat'd Dec 25, 1923 bottle, 1930s **150.00**

12" d, Things Go Better with Coke, 1963, C-9.8 .... **650.00**

29-1/4" h, 8-1/2" h, metal, bottle shape **150.00**

Tip tray, 4-1/2" w, 6" l, oval, "Betty" illus, 1914 .... **200.00**

Toy, 11" l, delivery truck, Metalcraft, Goodrich tires, orig 10 glass Coke bottles **300.00**

Trash can, 37" h, bullet shape, galvanized steel int. receptacle, applied decals, 36" h **2,600.00**

Tray

1906, oval, figure skater seated on log, holding bottle **1,400.00**

1930, bathing beauty, C-8 .... **195.00**

1935, Madge Evans, C-7.5 .... **165.00**

1942, girl in convertible being waited on by another girl, C-9.5 .... **450.00**

Vending machine, 54" h, Westinghouse Model WC-42, pre-1955 version, words "Ice Cold" emb across lower front door, 10-cent mechanism, unrestored condition **1,400.00**

Coffee Mills

History: Coffee mills or grinders are utilitarian objects designed to grind fresh coffee beans. Before the advent of stay-fresh packaging, coffee mills were a necessity.

The first home-size coffee grinders were introduced about 1890. The large commercial grinders designed for use in stores, restaurants, and hotels often bear an earlier patent date.

Arcade, 17" h, wall type, crystal jar, emb design, marked "Crystal" and "Arcade" orig lid rusted **185.00**

Crown Coffee Mill, cast iron, mounted on wood base, decal "Crown Coffee Mill Made By Landers, Frary, & Clark, New Britain, Conn, U.S.A.," number 11 emb on top lid **525.00**

Enterprise

No. 7, cast iron, twin wheels, "Enterprise Mfg. Co. Philadelphia, USA" emb on wheel castings, 13-1/2" w, 16-3/4" d, 24" h, repainted red and blue; replacement wooden drawer; copper hopper missing lid and finial **480.00**

No. 9, 20" wheels **1,650.00**

No. 12, 25" wheels **1,320.00**

Hotel, 8-1/2" w, 8-1/4" d, 13-1/4" h, brass hopper with wrought iron crank, turned wood finial, dovetailed poplar, old dark finish, drawer restoration **200.00**

Parker

No. 200, cast iron, wheels emb "The Cha's Parker Co. Meriden, Conn, USA," orig cast iron drawer emb "Pat'd No. 200 March 9 1897," 9" w, 9" d, 12-1/2" h, repainted **300.00**

Enterprise Mfg. Co. Philadelphia, USA, painted salmon, applied floral and gilt decals, late 19th C, 24-1/2" h, wear, hole drilled for electric fixture, **$500**. Photo courtesy of Skinner, Inc.

No. 502 202, cast iron, twin wheels, emb "The Cha's Parker Co. Meriden, Conn, USA" on wheel castings, 9" w, 10-3/4" d, 16" h, repainted red and blue, drawer missing **1,380.00**

Sun Manufacturing, Greenfield, Ohio, worn orig label, round wooden sides, cast iron hardware, directions for use, 12" h **300.00**

Swift Mill, cast iron, one-wheel, red, blue, and gold paint, orig catch and swivel top lid, wheel marked "Lane Bros., Poughkeepsie, NY.," 14" h, repainted **250.00**

Tin, tole dec of tulip and stars, 12" h **250.00**

Troemner, Henry

24" h, single wheel, funnel top, emb drawer compartment, 1870 patent, missing catch drawer **750.00**

35" h, red enameled cast iron body, blue enameled wheels emb "Star Mill Philadelphia," polished chrome hopper, maker's label, patent marks, c1884, orig condition **1,400.00**

Woodruff Edwards, Elgin, IL, 66" h, store type, 28" d wheels, eagle finial, repainted **1,800.00**

Coin-Operated Items

History: Coin-operated items include amusement games, pinball machines, jukeboxes, slot machines, vending machines, cash registers, and other items operated by coins.

The first jukebox was developed about 1934 and played 78-RPM records. Jukeboxes were important to teen-agers before the advent of portable radios and television.

The first pinball machine was introduced in 1931 by Gottlieb. Pinball machines continued to be popular until the advent of solid-state games in 1977 and advanced electronic video games after that.

The first three-reel slot machine, the Liberty Bell, was invented in 1905 by Charles Fey in San Francisco. In 1910, Mills Novelty Company copyrighted the classic fruit symbols. Improvements and advancements have led to the sophisticated machines of today.

Vending machines for candy, gum, and peanuts were popular from 1910 until 1940 and can be found in a wide range of sizes and shapes.

Additional Listings: See *Warman's Americana & Collectibles* for separate categories for Jukeboxes, Pinball Machines, Slot Machines, and Vending Machines.

Adviser: Bob Levy.

Notes: Because of the heavy usage these coin-operated items received, many are restored or, at the very least, have been repainted by either the operator or manufacturer. Using reproduced mechanisms to restore pieces is acceptable in many cases, especially when the restored piece will then perform as originally intended.

Arcade

Bowling Alley, United, Imperial, c1950 .... **500.00**
Photo Viewing, Amer Mutoscope, c1905 .... **2,000.00**
Toy Digger, Exhibit Sply, 1 Cent Monarch, c1940 .... **2,500.00**

Gum

Atlas Bantam, c1947, tray bulk vendor **150.00**
Automatic Clerk, Mansfield, c1902, stick gum package **900.00**
Columbus, c1915, round globe gum ball **225.00**
Ford, c1950, round globe, chrome, large, organizational use **75.00**
Oak Mfg, c1950, hot nuts........ **100.00**
Pulver, c1940, red porcelain, stick gum, animated clown figure **800.00**

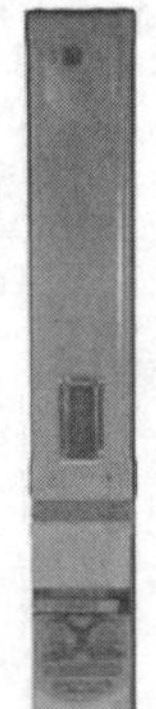

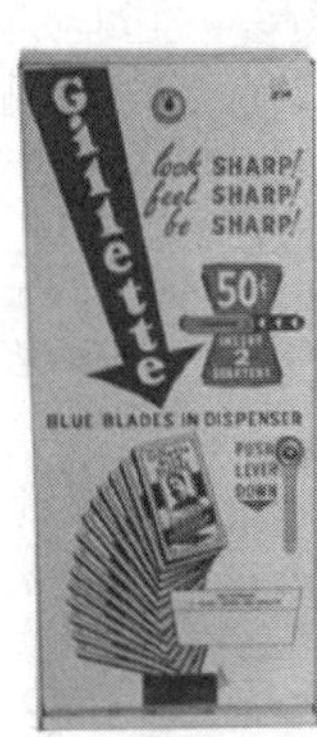

Left: Condom vending machine, with original packets and key, patent July 6, '20, 25" h, **$250**; right: Gillette painted tin razor blade dispensing machine, 18" h, **$275.** Photo courtesy of Joy Luke Auctions.

Jukeboxes

Rockola, Model 1426, c1947, beautiful **4,500.00**
Seeburg, Model 100c, c1952, classic **2,500.00**
Wurlitzer, Model 1100, c1947, colorful **4,000.00**

Slot Machines

Caille, Superior Jackpot, c1930 .... **1,600.00**
Groetchen, Columbia, c1936 .... **500.00**

Jennings Bronze Chief, **$2,800**. Photograph courtesy of Adviser Robert Levy.

Jennings
- Dutchboy, c1929 .... **1,500.00**
- Silver Moon Chief, c1940 .... **1,800.00**
- Standard Chief, c1946 .... **2,000.00**

Mills
- Black Cherry, c1946........ **1,500.00**
- Blue Hightop, c1950 .... **1,500.00**
- Chevron Q T, c1936 .... **1,800.00**
- Silent F.O.K., c1932........ **2,000.00**

Pace
- All Star Comet, c1936 .... **1,600.00**
- Club Special, c1962........ **1,300.00**

Watling
- Blue Seal, c1928 .... **1,200.00**
- Coin Rolatop, c1938........ **4,000.00**

Miscellaneous

Aspirin, Reeds, c1940........ **200.00**
Card vend, Exhibit Sply, c1940 ... **200.00**
Cigarettes, Rowe, c1935........ **450.00**
Cigars, Automatic, c1910 .... **1,500.00**
Cups, Dixie, c1930........ **250.00**
Lighter fluid, Van Light, c1933.... **600.00**
Matches, Diamond, c1930........ **300.00**
Perfume, Perfumatic 4, c1950..... **350.00**
Scale, Watling, c1920 .... **200.00**
Stamps, National Postage, c1940 .... **100.00**

Mills, Bursting Cherry, 1938, **$2,000**. Photograph courtesy of Adviser Robert Levy.

Toilet seat cover, Curnett, c1926 .... **100.00**

COINS

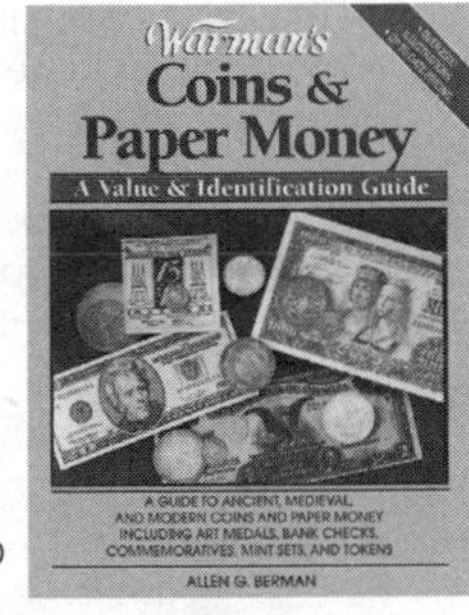

For more information, see *Warman's Coin & Paper Money.*

History: Coin collecting has long been one of the most respected and honored aspects of the collecting world. Today it still holds its fascination as new collectors come onto the scene every day. And just like the old-time collectors, they should be ready to spend time reading and learning more about this fascinating hobby. The States Quarter Series has spurred many of us to save quarters again and that has encouraged all types of coin collecting.

After the Declaration of Independence, America realized it needed its own coinage. Before that time, foreign coins were used in addition to paper currency. The first real coin of the young America was a copper coin, known as the Fugio Cent. Many of the early states created their own coins until the federal mint was constructed in Philadelphia after 1792. By 1837, the purity of silver was increased from 89.24 to 90 percent with minor adjustments to this weight occurring until 1873. Early dominations included a silver 3-cent piece, a gold $3-piece (1854) $1, and $20 (1849). The coinage law of 1857 eliminated the half-cent, changed the size of some coins, and forbid the use of foreign coins as legal tender. By the time of the Civil War, the two-cent and nickel three-cent pieces and the five-cent nickel

were created. The phrase "In God We Trust" was added at this time. From the late 1870s, coins were plentiful. From 1873 to 1918, several laws were passed to force the government to buy silver and strike an abundance of silver dollars. President Theodore Roosevelt is credited with having the Mercury dime, the Walking Liberty half-dollar and the St. Gauden's double eagle, and the buffalo nickel created. Commemorative coins were also becoming very popular at this time. Designs on coins continue to change to reflect events, such as the Bicentennial.

It would be impossible to list values for all types of coins in a general price guide such as *Warman's,* so the following is included to give a general idea of coins. More information about specific coins is available in the various publications, including the *2003 Standard Catalog of World Coins*, published by Krause Publications.

Grading: The value placed on a coin is highly dependent on its "grade" or condition. The general accepted grades are as follows:

Uncirculated (Unc) (Mint State)(Ms) is known as "Very Good." These coins will show no wear at all, and should appear as though they just came from the mint.

Almost Uncirculated (AU) is known as "Good." An *Almost Uncirculated* coin describes coins with slight signs of wear.

Extremely Fine (EX) (Extra Fine) (XF) is known as "Fair." Extremely Fine coins exhibit wear that is readily seen, but still has clear details.

Very Fine (VF) is known as "Poor." A "Very Fine" coin will show obvious signs of wear, but still be clear of defects.

Fine (F) is the lowest grade most people would consider collectible. In this grade, about half the design details will show. The wear should be so slight that the viewer requires a magnifying glass to see it. There are several sub-categories in all these grades.

Very Good (VG). Coins graded at this level will show heavy wear, outlines will be clear.

Good (G). Coins at this grade are considered uncollectible except for novelty purposes.

About Good (AG) and Fair (Fr). These grades are for coins with much wear, often the rims are worn down and the outlines of the design are disappearing.

Poor (Pr) is the lowest grade possible; sometimes the coin will barely be identifiable.

Proof (PF) refers not to a grade, but rather a special way of making coins, usually as presentation pieces. A *Proof* will usually be double struck with highly polished coins on polished blanks.

Reproduction Alert: Counterfeit coins of all denominations exist.

Barber Half Dollar, 1892-1915, designed by Charles E. Barber.
- 1892, VG **23.00**
- 1897S, VF **400.00**
- 1905, VG **19.00**
- 1913, VG **25.00**
- 1915, VF **190.00**

Buffalo Nickel, 1913 to 1938
- 1913, mound, Unc **32.00**
- 1918S, VG **32.50**
- 1936D, VG **25.00**

Eisenhower Dollar, 1971-1978
- 1791D, PF **3.00**
- 1973S, silver, Ms **8.00**
- 1976S, silver, block letters, PF **12.00**
- 1978D, PR **3.50**

Franklin Half Dollar, 1948 to 1963
- 1948, Ms **13.75**
- 1950, XF **6.00**
- 1952, XF **3.00**
- 1961, Ms **4.25**

Half Cent. Production ended in 1859.
- Braided hair, proof, 1849 .... **3,200.00**
- Classic head type, 1810, VG **140.00**
- Draped bust type, 1804, spiked chin version, VG **45.00**
- Liberty cap type, 1793, VG **2,000.00**

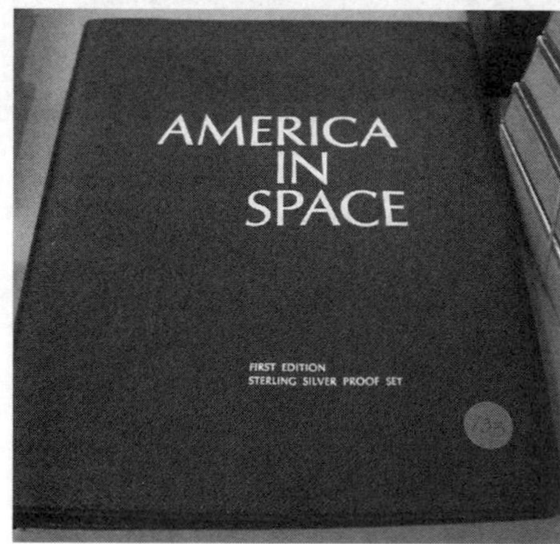

American in Space, proof set, first edition, sterling silver, **$15**. Coin photos courtesy of Dotta Auction Co., Inc.

Kennedy Half Dollar, 1964-2001. Obverse designed by Gilroy Roberts.
- 1964, XF **2.00**
- 1965, silver clad, BU **1.35**
- 1965-70, XF **1.00**
- 1970S, Proof **7.75**
- 1971-date .... **.50**
- 1976, Bicentennial reverse, BU **1.25**
- 1979, filled "S," Proof **2.50**
- 1981S, Proof **2.00**
- 1989D, BU **1.50**
- 1996P, BU **2.00**

Indian Head Cent, 1859-1909
- 1860, copper-nickel allow, F **37.00**
- 1867, bronze, XF **155.00**
- 1909S, F **300.00**

Jefferson Nickel, 1938 to present
- 1938, VG .... **.05**
- 1942-1945, silver, VG .... **.50**
- 1971S, proof **1.60**

Large Cents
- Classic head type, 1808-1814, 1810, VG **600.00**
- Coronet type, 1816-1857
- 1817, 13 stars, VG **15.00**
- 1838, VG **14.00**
- 1847, VG **19.50**
- Draped bust type, 1796 to 1807
- 1800, VG **350.00**
- 1804, restrike, Unc **450.00**
- Flowing hair type, 1793, wreath, VG **1,200.00**
- Liberty cap type, 1793-1796, 1794, VG **250.00**

$10 gold coin, 1899 coronet head, **$150**.

Liberty Nickel, 1883 to 1913
- 1883, no cents, G **3.75**
- 1883-1913, Ms **60.00**

Lincoln Cent, 1909-present
- 1909 to 1958, VG .... **.05**
- 1943, VG .... **.15**
- 1959-82, Ms .... **.15**
- 1982-present .... **.011**

Mercury Dime, 1916-1945, designed by Adolph Weinman.
- 1916, VF **6.00**
- 1929, D, Ms **25.00**
- 1940, VG **1.10**
- 1944D, Ms **5.50**

Morgan Dollar, 1878-1921, designed by George T. Morgan.
- 1878, eight tail feathers, VG **20.00**
- 1881S, VG **15.00**
- 1887, Ms **24.00**
- 1889CC, VF **500.00**
- 1899, Ms **100.00**
- 1921S, Ms **26.00**

Roosevelt Dime, 1946-2001, designed by John R. Sinnock.
- 1946, BU **1.05**
- 1950S, XF **1.25**
- 1953S, XF .... **.65**
- 1964D, BU .... **.90**
- 1970S, proof .... **.80**
- 1980P, BU .... **.40**
- 1995D, BU .... **.35**

Seated Liberty Dime, 1837-1891
- 1837-1838, no stars, G **30.00**
- 1838-1860, Ms **250.00**
- 1860-1891, G **8.75**

$10 gold coin, 1915 Indian head, **$275.**

Seated Liberty Dollar, 1840-1873
1840, G **100.00**
1846, F **175.00**
1853, EF **575.00**
1866, G **100.00**

Seated Liberty Half Dollar, 1839-1891, designed by Christian Gobrecht, several variations.
1839-1886, G **16.00**
1840, small reverse letters, VG **60.00**
1853, arrows and rays, G **16.50**
1854-55, arrows, G **16.00**
1857, arrows removed, VF **45.00**
1873-74, arrows, G **16.50**
1866-1891, G **15.00**

Seated Liberty Quarter, 1838-1891, designed by Christian Gobrecht, several variations.
1840O, VG **25.00**
1852, VG **145.00**
1853, arrows at date, VG **20.00**
1856, arrows removed, VG **20.00**
1860S, arrows removed, VG **50.00**
1866, motto above eagle, VG **450.00**
1873, arrows at date, VG **23.00**
1876, arrows removed, VG **17.00**

Silver Three Cent
1851-1853, G **18.50**
1854-1858, Ms **240.00**
1859-1873, G **17.50**

Walking Liberty Half Dollar, 1916-1947. Designed by Adolph Weinman.
1918, F **12.00**
1935, XF **6.00**
1939, XF **10.00**

Washington Quarter, 1932-1998. Designed by John Flanagan.
1932, VG **7.50**
1941, VG **1.75**
1946, BU **3.75**
1957D, BU **2.50**
1972, BU .... **.75**

Comic Books

History: Shortly after comics first appeared in newspapers of the 1890s, they were reprinted in book format and often used as promotional giveaways by manufacturers, movie theaters, and candy and stationery stores. The first modern-format comic was issued in 1933.

The magic date in comic collecting is June 1938, when DC issued Action Comics No. 1, marking the first appearance of Superman. Thus began the Golden Age of comics, which lasted until the mid-1950s and witnessed the birth of the major comic-book publishers, titles, and characters.

In 1954, Fredric Wertham authored *Seduction of the Innocent*, a book that pointed a guilt-laden finger at the comics industry for corrupting youth, causing juvenile delinquency, and undermining American values. Many publishers were forced out of business, while others established a "comics code" to assure parents that their comics were compliant with morality and decency standards upheld by the code authority.

The silver age of comics, mid-1950s through the end of the 1960s, witnessed the revival of many of the characters from the Golden Age in new comic formats. The era began with Showcase No. 4 in October 1956, which marked the origin and first appearance of the Silver-Age Flash.

While comics survived into the 1970s, it was a low point for the genre; but in the early 1980s, a revival occurred. In 1983, comic-book publishers, other than Marvel and DC, issued more titles than had existed in total during the previous 40 years. The mid- and late-1980s were a boom time, a trend that appears to be continuing.

Reproduction Alert: Publishers frequently reprint popular stories, even complete books, so the buyer must pay strict attention to the title, not just the portion printed in oversized letters on the front cover. If there is any doubt, look inside at the fine print on the bottom of the inside cover or first page. The correct title will be printed there in capital letters.

Also pay attention to the dimensions of the comic book. Reprints often differ in size from the original.

Note: The comics listed here are in near-mint condition, meaning they have a flat, clean, shiny cover that has no wear other than tiny corner creases; no subscription creases, writing, yellowing at margins, or tape repairs; staples are straight and rust free; pages are supple and like new; generally just-off-the-shelf quality.

Aaron Strips, #3, 1997 .... **1.50**
ABC Warriors, #1 .... **2.00**
Accident Man, #1, Dark Horse **3.00**
Adventures of Rex the Wonder Dog, #5 .... **500.00**
Amazing Tales, #2 .... **275.00**
Amazing Spider-Man, #22 .... **325.00**
A-Team, 1984 .... **2.50**
Avengers, #24 .... **200.00**
Daredevil, #9 .... **340.00**
DC Super Spectacular, #20 .... **84.00**

Fantastic Four, Marvel, November 56, Klaw the Murderous Master of Sound, **$65.**

Fantastic Four, #20 .... **200.00**
Fighting Americans, #1, 1996 .... **110.00**
Flame, #5 .... **400.00**

X-Men, If Iceman Should Fail, 18 March, Marvel, **$45.**

Flash Gordon, #16 .... **20.00**
Forbidden Love, #2 .... **325.00**
Forbidden Worlds, #8 .... **450.00**
GI Joe I Battle, #1 .... **64.00**
Green Lantern, #27 .... **125.00**
Justice League of America, #14 ... **150.00**
Leave It To Beaver, #1285 .... **310.00**
Little Orphan Annie, #1 .... **90.00**
Marvel Premiere, #1 .... **160.00**
Modern Comics, #98 .... **200.00**
Mystery in Space, #66 .... **410.00**
Our Army At War, #21 .... **135.00**
Rawhide Kid, #49 .... **100.00**
Sea Devils, #54 .... **125.00**
Six Gun Heroes, #81 .... **12.00**

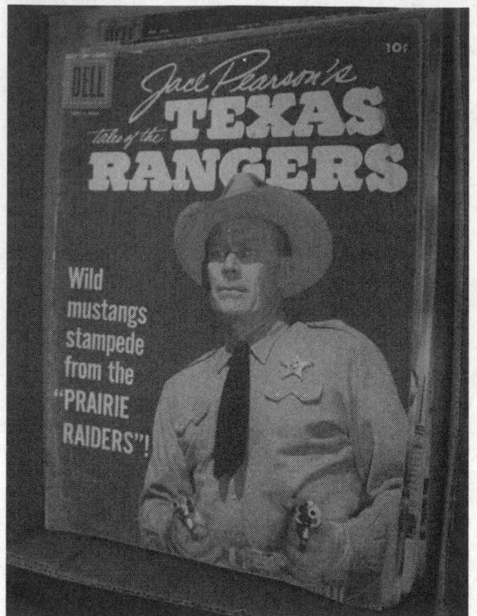

Jace Pearson's Tales of the Texas Rangers, Dell, Sept-November, **$40.**

Strange Tales, #57 .... **265.00**
Superman, #109 .... **420.00**
Tarzan, Lord of the Jungle, 1995 .... **35.00**
Teen Confessions **130.00**
Tip Top Comics, 1938 .... **150.00**
Transformers, 1991 .... **42.00**

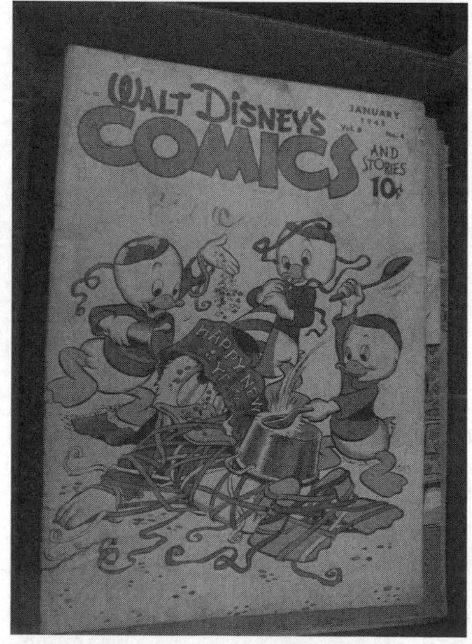

Walt Disney Comics, Donald and Nephews, Happy New Year, January 1948, Vol. 8, No. 4, No. 88, **$75.**

X-Men-14, #18 .... **560.00**
X-Men-24, #60 .... **75.00**
Zane Grey Stories of the West **10.00**
Zoo Funnies, 1946 .... **48.00**
Zorro, 1960 .... **36.00**

COMPACTS

History: In the first quarter of the 20th century, attitudes regarding cosmetics changed drastically. The use of make-up during the day was no longer looked upon with disdain. As women became "liberated," and as more and more of them entered the business world, the use of cosmetics became a routine and necessary part of a woman's grooming. Portable containers for cosmetics became a necessity.

Compacts were made in myriad shapes, styles, combinations and motifs, all reflecting the mood of the times. Every conceivable natural or man-made material was used in the manufacture of compacts. Commemorative, premium, souvenir, patriotic, figural, Art Deco, and enamel compacts are a few examples of the types of compacts that were made in the United States and abroad. Compacts combined with other forms, such as cigarette cases, music boxes, watches, hatpins, canes, and lighters, also were very popular.

Compacts were made and used until the late 1950s, when women opted for the "au naturel" look. The term "vintage" is used to describe the compacts from the first half of the 20th century as distinguished from contemporary examples.

Additional Listings: See *Warman's Americana & Collectibles* for more examples.

Adviser: Roselyn Gerson.

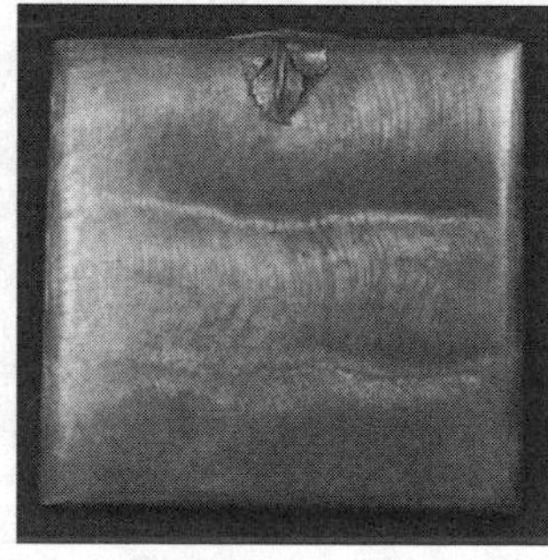

Compact, Gucci, 18k brushed gold, applied leaf accent, mirrored interior, signed "Gucci," 72.1 dwt, **$650**. Photo courtesy of Skinner, Inc.

Art Deco, 14kt yg, linear engine turned design, black onyx edge dec, mirror and powder puff, matching lipstick case, European hallmarks **1,000.00**

BOAC, British Overseas Airways Corp, 3" d, gold, black leatherette, gold metal logo, framed mirror, BOAC puff, royal blue felt cover **70.00**

Cartier, 1-7/8" x 2-5/8", 9kt yg, rect form, ribbed case with diamond-set thumbpiece, powder compact with fitted mirror, 61.5 dwt (including mirror), English hallmarks, sgd "Cartier London" .. **420.00**

Celluloid, unknown maker

2" sq, metal compact, celluloid top showing pastoral scene with lovers, c1940 .... **45.00**

3" d, orange compact studded with floral rhinestone motif **45.00**

5" celluloid diamond shaped purse, 2" tassel and silk cord, mottled cream, green and brown with oval cameo attached to center top, mirror, powder puff and chrome scent vial **275.00**

Coty, #405, envelope box **65.00**

Djer Kiss, with fairy **95.00**

European, 14kt gold compact, rect, linear, engine-turned design, channel-set red stone thumbpiece, European hallmarks **500.00**

Compact, French enamel, enameled lid with heraldic crest featuring a dragon beneath crown surrounded by flames on blue ground, reverse engraved, "Chambord," 1-7/8" d, **$115**. Photo courtesy of Alderfer Auction Co.

Evans, goldtone, heart shape, black twisted carrying cord, lipstick concealed in black tassel suspended from bottom **250.00**

Fifth Avenue, vanity case "Cosmetist," aquamarine enamel, powder, rouge, lipstick, cleansing cream, and mascara, England **175.00**

Foster & Bailey, Providence, vanity case, sterling silver and enamel, 3-1/2" x 2", rect, canted corners, lid enameled in center over diamond-shaped starburst ground, vase of roses on white ground, bordered by turquoise enamel cornered by roses, green cabochon thumb piece open to hinged mirror, off-center hinged double compartment each with cabochon thumb piece, braided wrist chain, c1880 .... **800.00**

German, 3-1/4" l, silver and enameled, ovoid, shaped edge, hinged lid with enameled scene of two ladies reading letter in garden, scrolled border, underside engraved with scrolls, int. of lid set with mirror, .800 silver, 4 troy oz, late 19th/early 20th C **500.00**

Gucci, 18kt yg, brushed gold, an applied leaf accent opening to mirrored interior, 72.1 dwt, sgd "Gucci" **650.00**

Italian, hand-mirror shape, sterling silver, stylized floral engraving, lipstick concealed in handle, coral cabochon thumb piece **325.00**

Jensen, Georg, sterling silver, polished oval case accented with pine cone and leaf motif, hinged cover opens to reveal fitted mirror and powder compact, sgd "Georg Jensen, Inc." **165.00**

Kigu, lady swinging **45.00**

Max Factor, 2-1/4" d, solid perfume, round faux jade pendant, goldtone twisted braided wire disk, orig Khara fragrance **35.00**

Rex Fifth Avenue, vanity-pochette, navy blue, gold polka dots, taffeta drawstring, mirror on outside base **90.00**

Sterling silver

- 2-3/4" l, rect, marked for Tiffany & Co., engine turned sunburst .. **250.00**
- 2-1/2" l, Birks, leaf engraved lid set with roundel formed with small gold nuggets **150.00**
- 3-1/2" l, purse style, James E. Blake Co. engine turned linework, and link chain **225.00**

Tiffany & Co., Art Deco, sterling silver, gold, and sapphire, sq engraved lineal design, surmounted by gold and sapphire crescent, mirror and powder compartment, sgd **450.00**

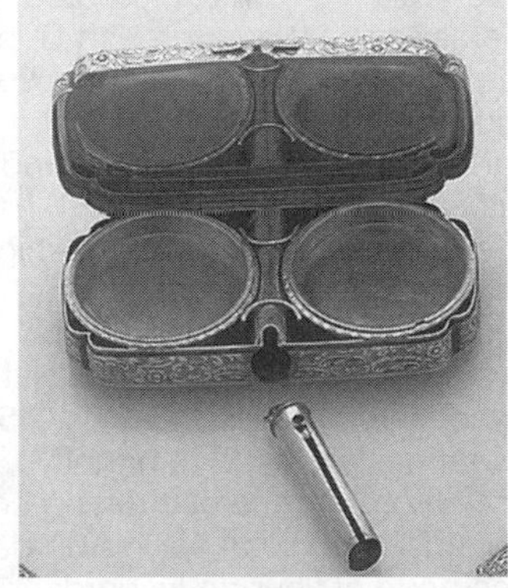

Compact, Austrian, for Houbigant, c1924, 14k yg, channel edged rectangular form, overall flower and scroll chased pattern, interior fitted with pair of rouge pots, mirror and lipstick case, marked "Houbigant," hallmarks and maker mark for F. Mesmer, 1-1/2" x 3", **$635**. Photo courtesy of David Rago Auctions, Inc.

Unknown maker, compact

- Castanets shape, ebony wood, metal Paris insignia centered on lid, orange tasseled carrying cord **220.00**
- Sterling, 2" x 3", enamel panel on one side with landscape and palm trees, rect engraved sterling silver case, chain handle, int. fitted for make-up with mirror, marked "Sterling," minor wear **215.00**
- Telephone-dial shape, red, white, and blue, slogan "I Like Ike" imprinted on lid, red map of USA on lid center **225.00**

Unknown maker, compact, English, Birmingham, sterling silver and enamel

- 2-1/2" sq, canted corners, green enamel over "L"-shaped engine-turning, scalloped sunray issuing from scrolls, c1940 .... **225.00**
- 2-7/8" sq, canted corners, blue enamel over spiraling engine-turning, central nautical flag with crown **250.00**

Unknown maker, compact, Europe, early 20th C, silver, 800 silver

- 2-3/8" l, 1-1/2" w, oval, enameled violet on lid, int. mounted with mirrors, losses to int. **290.00**
- 3" l, quadrangular with shaped edges, engraved lid with polychrome enamel genre scene, underside with engraved foliates, gilt interior with mirror mounted to lid **300.00**

Unknown maker, vanity bag, SS mesh, hallmarked, octagonal, goldtone int. and finger ring carrying chain **500.00**

Van Cleef & Arpels, 2-3/4" x 3-1/2", Retro, silver gilt, rect form, thumbpiece set with single-cut diamonds and calibre-cut sapphires in stylized bow motif, fitted mirror, two powder compartments, and lipstick holder inscribed with name and NY address, brown leather Van Cleef & Arpels slip case **750.00**

Consolidated Glass Company

History: The Consolidated Lamp and Glass Company was formed as a result of the 1893 merger of the Wallace and McAfee Company, glass and lamp jobbers of Pittsburgh, and the Fostoria Shade & Lamp Company of Fostoria, Ohio. When the Fostoria, Ohio, plant burned down in 1895, Corapolis, Pennsylvania, donated a seven-acre tract of land near the center of town for a new factory. In 1911, the company was the largest lamp, globe, and shade works in the United States, employing more than 400 workers.

For more information, see *Warman's Glass,* 4th edition.

In 1925, Reuben Haley, owner of an independent-design firm, convinced John Lewis, president of Consolidated, to enter the giftware field utilizing a series of designs inspired by the 1925 Paris Exposition (l'Exposition Internationale des Arts Décorative et Industriels Modernes) and the work of René Lalique. Initially, the glass was marketed by Howard Selden through his showroom at 225 Fifth Avenue in New York City. The first two lines were Catalonian and Martele.

Additional patterns were added in the late 1920s: Florentine (January 1927), Chintz (January 1927), Ruba Rombic (January 1928), and Line 700 (January 1929). On April 2, 1932, Consolidated closed it doors. Kenneth Harley moved about 40 molds to Phoenix. In March 1936, Consolidated reopened under new management, and the "Harley" molds were returned. During this period, the famous Dancing Nymph line, based on an eight-inch salad plate in the 1926 Martele series, was introduced.

In August 1962, Consolidated was sold to Dietz Brothers. A major fire damaged the plant during a 1963 labor dispute and in 1964, the company permanently closed its doors.

Bonbon, cov, 8" d, Ruba Rhombic, faceted, smoky topaz, catalog #832, c1931 .... **325.00**

Bowl, 5-1/2" d, Coronation, Martelé, flared, blue **75.00**

Box, cov, 7" l, 5" w, Martelé line, Fruit and Leaf pattern, scalloped edge......... **85.00**

Cocktail, Dancing Nymph, French Crystal **90.00**

Cookie jar, 6-1/2" h, Regent Line, #3758, Florette, rose pink over white opal casing **370.00**

Cup and saucer, Dancing Nymph, ruby flashed... **265.00**

Goblet, Dancing Nymph, French Crystal **90.00**

Humidor, Florette, pink satin **225.00**

Jar, cov, Con-Cora, #3758-9, pine cone dec, irid **165.00**

Sugar shaker, Cone pattern, tall, pink blushed milk glass, 2" d base, 5-1/4" h, **$150**.

Lamp, flower basket, 8" h, bouquet of roses and poppies, yellows, pinks, green leaves, brown basketweave, black glass base.. **300.00**

Mayonnaise comport, Martelé Iris, green wash 55.00
Miniature lamp, 10" h, opalescent blue 380.00
Night light, Santa Maria, block base 450.00
Perfume bottle, 5-1/2" h, Ruba Rombic, gray frosted body, nick on stopper 1,420.00
Plate
- 8-1/4" d, Bird of Paradise, amber wash 40.00
- 8-1/4" d, Five Fruits, green 40.00
- 10-1/4" d, Catalonian, yellow 45.00
- 12" d, Martelé, Orchid, pink, birds and flowers 115.00

Puff box, cov, Lovebirds, blue 95.00
Salt and pepper shakers, pr
- Cone, pink 75.00
- Cosmos 115.00
- Guttate, green 85.00

Sherbet, underplate, Five Fruits, amber 75.00

Vase, Catalonian pattern, introduced 1927, bright green, 6-1/2" h, 3" d, **$450**.

Snack set, Martelé Fruits, pink 45.00
Sugar bowl, cov, Guttate, cased pink 120.00
Sugar shaker, 3-1/2" d, puff quilted body, pink, brass lid 150.00
Sundae, Martelé Russet Yellow Fruits 35.00
Syrup, Cone, squatty, pink 295.00
Toothpick holder, Florette, cased pink 75.00
Tumbler
- Catalonian, ftd, green, 5-1/4" h 30.00
- Dancing Nymph, frosted pink, 6" h 175.00
- Guttate, pink satin 65.00
- Ruba Rhombic, faceted, ftd, silver gray, 6" h 210.00

Umbrella vase, Blackberry 550.00
Vase
- Chickadee, crystal 95.00
- Katydid, blue wash, fan-shaped top, 8-1/2" h 300.00
- Love Bird pattern, golden birds, custard ground, 10-1/2" h 600.00

Vase, Ruba Rombic, smokey quartz, interior rim chip, 6-1/2" h, 4-3/4" d, **$575**. Photo courtesy of David Rago Auctions, Inc.

- Regent Line, #3758, cased blue stretch over white opal, pinched, 6" h 175.00

Whiskey glass, 2-5/8" h, Ruba Rhombic, faceted, transparent jungle green, catalog #823 .... 265.00

√Continental China and Porcelain (General)

History: By 1700, porcelain factories existed in large numbers throughout Europe. In the mid-18th century, the German factories at Meissen and Nymphenburg were dominant. As the century ended, French potteries assumed the leadership role. The 1740s to the 1840s were the golden age of Continental china and porcelains.

Americans living in the last half of the 19th century eagerly sought the masterpieces of the European porcelain factories. In the early 20th century, antiques collectors considered this style of china and porcelain "blue chip."

For more information, see *Warman's English & Continental Pottery & Porcelain,* 3rd edition.

Additional Listings: French—Haviland, Limoges, Old Paris, Sarreguemines, and Sevres; German—Austrian Ware, Bavarian China, Carlsbad China, Dresden/ Meissen, Rosenthal, Royal Bayreuth, Royal Bonn, Royal Rudolstadt, Royal Vienna, Schlegelmilch, and Villeroy and Boch; Italian—Capo-di-Monte.

French, Paris, urns, pair with scene of Arabian figures and ruins on green ground with gold highlights, c1850, 8-1/2" h, sold together with smaller example with sailing ship, **$500**. Photo courtesy of Pook & Pook.

French

Choisy, plate, 8-1/4" d, earthenware transfer printed and hand enameled, each with different numbered scene relating to story of soldier's courtship and military life, naïve enamel accenting, mid-19th C, price for set of 12 .... 500.00
Faience
- Bulb pot, 3-1/8" d, sq, molded acanthus-capped scroll feet, conforming handles, front with scene of courting couple, verso landscape, each side with floral sprays, sq form insert, gilt highlights, attributed to Marseilles, last quarter 18th C, pr 900.00
- Inkstand, 13-1/2" l, figural, cartouche-shaped base molded with scrolls, front painted with harbor scene flanked by tower and knight-shaped inkpots, back sections support large figure of lion with raised paw resting on shield with armorial 650.00
- Sugar caster, 8-1/2" h, brightly polychrome scene of courting couple in landscape, floral sprays borders, dec band of fleur-de-lis border, pierced cov with conforming dec, early 19th C 450.00

Lessore, Emile, platter, 14-1/4" l, oval, earthenware, polychrome figural landscape with putti, artist signed, printed factory mark for Hautin and Boulenger, France, c1855, rim chip 450.00

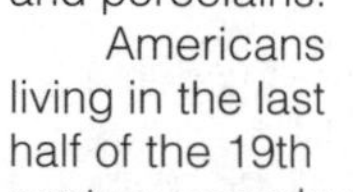
French, unknown maker, sauce tureen, covered, decorated with butterflies and flowers, applied ornate fruit finial and handles, attached underplate matching ladle, **$175**. Photo courtesy of Joy Luke Auctions.

Paris

Cache pot, 6" h, ovoid, apple-green ground, floral roundels in leaf surround, two gilt lion's head masks on sides, narrow undertray, late 19th C **115.00**

Candlesticks, pr, 9" h, everted sconce, column-form standard, shaped base with man and woman among rocaille leaves **200.00**

Dessert plate, 9-1/8" d, hand painted, four with flower centers, two with fruit centers, all with peach borders, gilt scrolls, maroon band at molded rim, late 19th C **750.00**

Vase, 10-1/4" h, narrow neck and short handles, silver enameled porcelain body further enamel dec with two Dionysian putti verso, flower draped Dionysius bust recto, fluted trumpet foot, late 19th C **500.00**

Veilleuse, 4-1/2" h pot, 9" h overall, hand painted, small pot with black and pink bands, over enameled with gilt scrolls, short gilt spout, angular handle, octagonal pagoda-form stand hp with scenes titled "acqueduque de Buc," showing elevated aqueduct, and "a Bonnebose (Calvados)," showing village, 20th C, base missing **475.00**

Samson & Co.

Figure, 12-1/4" h, Neptune, upraised hands standing on scallop shell, dolphin at feet, rocaille base encrusted with shells and seaweed, gilt accents, late 19th C **230.00**

Perfume bottle, 2-7/8" l, figural, boy with vessel seated on dolphin, enamel detailing, boy's head as stopper, late 19th C **230.00**

German, Hochst, figure of young woman wearing white dress, hunting coat, lined in pink, trimmed with turquoise, white hat with turquoise trim, carrying gun, hunting dog and game bird on ground beside her, gilt highlights, six-spoke wagon wheel mark on bottom, mark used 1750 to 1765, 7" h, minor cracking, **$575**. Photo courtesy of Alderfer Auction Co.

Germany

Hutschenreuther

Plaque, 5-1/8" x 6-7/8", oval, Madonna and Child, giltwood frame, late 19th C **600.00**

Service plate, 10-7/8" d, central dec, summer flowers within heavily gilt cavetto, rim worked with scrolling acanthus, textured ground, underglaze green factory marks, minor rubbing, 12-pc set **1,600.00**

Nymphenburg, vase, 10-1/2" d, wide baluster form, enamel dec, continuous landscape scene, titled on underside "Vorfrohling in Oberbayorn," signed "R. Sieck," 20th C **750.00**

Tirschenreuth, service plate, 10-3/4" d, gold inner band of Egyptian Revival lotus and roundel, dark apple green edge, gilt rim, price for set of eight **225.00**

Unknown maker

Cup and saucer, bucket-shaped 3-5/8" h cup, cerulean blue band over horizontal gilt beaded band above landscape scene, short gilt acanthus scroll handle, three gilt paw feet, similarly beaded and gilded saucer **1,035.00**

Plaque, 5" l, girl with candle, titled "Guten Nahct," oval, reeded giltwood frame, late 19th/early 20th C **1,035.00**

Cookie Jars

History: Cookie jars, colorful and often whimsical, are popular with collectors. They were made by almost every manufacturer, in all types of materials. Figural character cookie jars are the most popular with collectors.

Cookie jars often were redesigned to reflect newer tastes. Hence, the same jar may be found in several different variations and these variations can affect the price.

Marks: Many cookie-jar shapes were manufactured by more than one company and, as a result, can be found with different marks. This often happened because of mergers or separations, e.g., Brush-McCoy, which became Nelson McCoy. Molds also were traded and sold among companies.

Watt Pottery, Apple design, **$400**.

Abingdon Pottery

Bo Peep, No. 694D, 12" h **425.00**

Choo Choo, No. 561D, 7-1/2" h **120.00**

Mother Goose, No. 695D, 12" h **550.00**

Pumpkin, No. 674D, 8" h **550.00**

Three Bears, No. 696D, 8-3/4" h **245.00**

Windmill, No. 678, 10-1/2" h **500.00**

Witch, No. 692, 11-1/2" h **1,000.00**

Brayton Laguna Pottery

Mammy, turquoise bandanna, burgundy base **1,300.00**

Partridges, Model No. V-12, 7-1/4" h **200.00**

Swedish Maid, 1941, incised mark, 11" h **600.00**

Hull Pottery

Barefoot Boy **320.00**

Duck **60.00**

Gingerbread Boy, blue and white trim **400.00**

Gingerbread Man, 12" h **550.00**

Little Red Riding Hood, open basket, gold stars on apron **375.00**

Clown, yellow body, remnants of blue trim, unmarked, **$65**.

Metlox Pottery

Bear, blue sweater **100.00**

Chef Pierre **100.00**

Pine Cone, gray squirrel finial, Model No. 509, 11" h **115.00**

Rex Dinosaur, white **120.00**

Tulip, yellow and green **425.00**

Red Wing Pottery

French Chef, blue glaze **250.00**

Grapes, yellow, marked "Red Wing USA," 10" h **125.00**

Rooster, green glaze **165.00**

Shawnee Pottery

Cinderella, unmarked **125.00**

Cottage, marked "USA 6," 7" h **900.00**

Dutch Boy, striped pants, marked "USA," 11" h **190.00**

Dutch Girl, marked "USA," 11-1/2" h **175.00**

Great Northern Boy, marked "Great Northern USA 1025," 9-3/4" h **425.00**

Muggsy Dog, blue bow, gold trim and decals, marked "Patented Muggsy U.S.A.," 11-3/4" h **850.00**

Owl, eyes repainted **95.00**

Smiley Pig, clover blossom dec, marked "Patented Smiley USA," 11-1/2" h **550.00**

Winnie Pig, clover blossom dec, marked "Patented Winnie USA," 12" h **575.00**

Fenton glass, macaroon jar, Big Cookies pattern, ebony, #1681, c1933, 7" h, **$125**. Photo courtesy of Rick Hirte, Sparkle Plenty Glassware.

Stoneware, cobalt blue dec, unknown maker

Basketweave and Morning Glory, marked "Put Your Fist In," 7-1/2" h **625.00**

Flying Bird, 9" h **1,250.00**

Watt Pottery

Apple, No. 21, 7-1/2" h **400.00**

Cookie Barrel, wood grain, 10-1/2" h **50.00**

Morning Glory, No. 95, 10" h **600.00**

Policeman, 10-1/2" h **1,150.00**

Starflower, No. 503, 8" h **350.00**

Copeland and Spode

History: In 1749, Josiah Spode was apprenticed to Thomas Whieldon and in 1754 worked for William Banks in Stoke-on-Trent. In the early 1760s, Spode started his own pottery, making cream-colored earthenware and blue-printed whiteware. In 1770, he returned to Banks' factory as master, purchasing it in 1776.

Spode pioneered the use of steam-powered pottery-making machinery and mastered the art of transfer printing from copper plates. Spode opened a London shop in 1778 and sent William Copeland there about 1784. A number of larger London locations followed. At the turn of the century, Spode introduced bone china. In 1805, Josiah Spode II and William Copeland entered into a partnership for the London business. A series of partnerships between Josiah Spode II, Josiah Spode III, and William Taylor Copeland resulted.

For more information, see *Warman's English & Continental Pottery & Porcelain*, 3rd edition.

In 1833, Copeland acquired Spode's London operations and seven years later, the Stoke plants. William Taylor Copeland managed the business until his death in 1868. The firm remained in the hands of Copeland heirs. In 1923, the plant was electrified; other modernization followed.

In 1976, Spode merged with Worcester Royal Porcelain to become Royal Worcester Spode, Ltd. Royal Worcester Spode was purchased by Derby International in 1988. The two firms split in 1989.

Cup and saucer, Gainsborough pattern, **$65**. Photo courtesy of Joy Luke Auctions.

Bust

15" h, Alexandra, parian, mounted on waisted circular socle, raised title, imp mark, published date, sculptor Mary Thornycroft and Art Union of London, c1868 .... **450.00**

24" h, Lord Byron, parian, mounted on waisted circular socle, c1870, imp mark **1,775.00**

Cabinet plate, 9-1/2" d, artist sgd "Samuel Alcock," 1-3/4" jeweled border, intricate gold, beading, pearl and turquoise jeweling, c1889 .... **750.00**

Coffee cup and saucer, 2-1/4" h cylindrical cup with all-over maroon and gilt scrolled dec, 5" d saucer, retained by Tiffany & Co., late 19th C, price for set of 12... **325.00**

Dinner plate, 9-1/4" d, mint green border with gilt design, labeled "Spaulding & Co., Chicago & Paris, Spode Copeland's China, England," wear, price for 12-pc set... **350.00**

Figure, parian

22" h, Reaper and The Flowers, winged female figure modeled holding baby in her arms, imp title, L.A. Malempre SC, Ceramic and Crystal Palace Art Union, publish date, Copeland factory mark, c1875, finger missing, chip to side of base **1,175.00**

24-1/2" h, Chastity, standing figure, circular base, imp title, J. Durham SC, published date 1865, Copeland factory mark, shallow footrim chip **885.00**

Pitcher, tavern scenes, grape vine trim in relief on green ground, ivory applications, beige borders, branch form handle, marked "Copeland Late Spode," 7" h, **$185**. Photo courtesy of Alderfer Auction Co.

Fish plate, 9-3/4" d, artist sgd "H. C. Lea," four-part gold-swirled design, hp fly in each section, c1891 .... **175.00**

Jug, orange, teal green, and gold dec, matte cream ground, ornate handle with two mythological characters, c1847 .... **450.00**

Platter, 24" l, cobalt blue and iron tree Indian Tree-type pattern, well and tree indentation, c1860....................... **520.00**

Service plate, 10-1/4" d, Brompton pattern, floral border, central design of birds and foliage, retailed by Wright, Tyndale & Van Roden, Inc., Philadelphia, marked "Rd. No. 608584," price for set of 10.. **335.00**

Spill vase, 4-3/4" h, flared rim, pale lilac, gilt octagonal panels with portrait of bearded man, band of pearls on rims and bases, Spode, c1920 .... **425.00**

Platter, flow blue and white, decorated with large turkey, scrolls at border, 26" x 21", **$950**. Photo courtesy of Joy Luke Auctions.

Tea set, teapot, creamer, cov sugar, blue ground, white relief hunt scene, brown label "Copeland Spode England," 3-5/8" h **250.00**

Tray, 8-1/2" l, black transfer, passion flowers, grape vines border, emb grapes, vines, and leaves on tab handles, c1900 .... **200.00**

Tureen, cov, 13" w, 11" h, white, gold and blue accents, marked "Spode New Stone" **1,470.00**
Urn, cov, 15" h, Louis XVI style, cobalt blue ground, medallions on each side with bouquet of roses, majolica, repair to one handle, nick to one lid, pr...... **900.00**
Water pitcher, 8-1/4" h, bulbous, tan acanthus leaf handle and spout, green field dec with white relief classical figures of dancing women, white relief banded floral garland dec at neck, marked "Rd. No. 180288"................................. **250.00**

Copper

History: Copper objects, such as kettles, teakettles, warming pans, and measures, played an important part in the 19th-century household. Outdoors, the apple-butter kettle and still were the two principal copper items. Copper culinary objects were lined with a thin protective coating of tin to prevent poisoning. They were relined as needed.

Reproduction Alert: Many modern reproductions exist.

Additional Listings: Arts and Crafts Movement and Roycroft.

Notes: Collectors place great emphasis on signed pieces, especially those by American craftsmen. Since copper objects were made abroad as well, it is hard to identify unsigned examples.

Candy kettle, iron handles, 18-1/2" d, interior worn, **$150**. Photo courtesy of Joy Luke Auctions.

Bed warmer, 42-1/2" h, faint floral engraving on lid, turned handle with age splints, small chips **110.00**
Bowl, hammered
- 3" d, emb acanthus leaves over arches, medium patina, incised WEHDE.................................. **265.00**
- 8" d, 2-1/8" h, pierced panels of stylized leaves along the rim, orig medium patina, stamped "HANDICRAFT GUILD MINNEAPOLIS".................. **1,380.00**
- 10" d, floriform, ext. with medium copper patina, verdigris rutile int., stamped JJB for John J. Brennan **360.00**

Candlesticks, pr, 10" h, hammered copper, tall cylindrical shaft, faceted bottom, squat base, orig dark patina, stamped #135, Stickley Brothers **1,380.00**
Carpenter's pot, 11" l, 8" h, globular, dovetailed body, raised on three plain strap work iron legs, conforming handle **70.00**
Chamberstick, 4-1/4" h, three sided, enamel green leaves within blue lines, marked "Buffalo Art Craft Shop," orig dark patina, some touch-ups to enamel **750.00**
Cigarette box, 1-3/4" x 4-1/4" x 3-1/2", rect, hinged, cedar lining, lid with large oval medallion polychrome enameled tall ship, orig patina, unmarked, Boston School, small dent to one bottom corner **535.00**
Desk set, hammered blotter, letter holder, bookends, stamp box, each with bone carved cabochon, branch and berry motif, Potter Studio, fine orig patina, die-stamp mark................................... **750.00**
Fish poacher, cov, 20-1/2" l, oval, rolled rim, iron swing ball handle, 19th C **350.00**

Firescreen, hammered copper, three panels, cutout stylized floral motif and riveted corners, unmarked, few scratches to new patina. 28-1/2" x 29" x 14", **$2,300**. Photo courtesy of David Rago Auctions, Inc.

Inkwell, 5" x 4-1/4", hinged, hammered copper, mother-of-pearl panels on top, pierced copper sides four riveted feet, medium cleaned patina, unmarked, liner missing **460.00**
Mirror, wall, 30-1/2" x 40", frame covered in hammered and riveted sheet copper, emb acanthus leaves, set around Ruskin ceramic cabochon, unmarked Liberty & Co., tears and folds to metal, few missing rivets.. **750.00**
Pot, cov, 19-1/2" l, 12" w, 16" h, twin handles, oval, raised on four strap work legs, fitted with tubular end handles, shallow domed cov stamped with shield design, center stationary handle, English, 19th C... **215.00**
Screen, 24" w, 38-1/4" h, Arts & Crafts, ruffled edges, repousse design of oak tree, acorns, sun behind it, iron supports with copper coils wrapped around on front **495.00**
Tankard, 9-1/2" x 6-1/2", hammered copper, rim emb "Midlothian Championship Solace 1907" over stylized pattern, riveted bone handle, cleaned patina, marked "Made by the Jarvie Shop Chicago/Won by Frederick W. Clark/ September 7" **1,725.00**
Tea kettle, 11-1/2" h, curved spout, upright swing handle, brass lid knob, imp "G. Tyron" on handle, dents, wear, PA, 19th C.. **690.00**
Tray, 19" d, hammered, four-sided, four pierced handles, repousse pattern, unmarked Gustav Stickley, new patina **1,725.00**
Umbrella stand, 9-1/2" d, 26-1/2" h, hammered copper, cupped rim, emb dots on body, riveted band on flaring base, new patina, Stickley Bros, stamped 181.. **1,840.00**

Shovel, hand made, rivets at handle, **$75**. Photo courtesy of Wiederseim Associates, Inc.

Vase
- 5-1/4" x 7", Dirk Van Erp, hammered copper, spherical, orig patina, open box mark remnant of D'Arcy Gaw **3,115.00**
- 8" x 5-1/2", Dirk Van Erp, hammered copper, tapering base, closed-in rim, good orig dark patina, stamped open box mark **2,870.00**

Vessel, 10-1/4" d, squat, gold abstract flowers and leaves, bronzed patina, stamped Tiffany & Co.................. **490.00**
Wall sconce, 4-1/2" w, 11" h, hammered, flame head, riveted Arts & Crafts details, attributed to Dirk Van Erp, cleaned patina **425.00**
Water urn, 14" h, copper body, int. with capped warming tube, applied brass ram's head handles, urn finial,

brass spout, sq base with four ball feet, unmarked, repairs to lid **125.00**

Cowan Pottery

History: R. Guy Cowan founded the Cowan Pottery in 1913 in Cleveland, Ohio. The establishment remained in almost continuous operation until 1931, when financial difficulties forced closure.

Early production was redware pottery. Later a porcelain-like finish was perfected with special emphasis placed on glazes, with lusterware being one of the most common types. Commercial wares marked "Lakeware" were produced from 1927 to 1931.

Marks: Early marks include an incised "Cowan Pottery" on the redware (1913-1917), an impressed "Cowan," and an impressed "Lakewood." The imprinted stylized semicircle, with or without the initials "R. G.," came later.

Bookends, pr
- 6-1/4" h, 4" d, boy and girl, Special ivory glaze, stamped "Cowan" **350.00**
- 8-1/2" h, 6" d, flying fish, antique-green glaze, stamped "Cowan" **700.00**

Candleholders, pr, 8-1/2" h, Ming Green glaze, c1928 .... **80.00**

Demitasse cup and saucer, 2-1/2" h cup, 4" saucer, block letter logo **35.00**

Figure
- 9" x 7", Morning, by Walter Sinz, ivory crackle glaze, inscribed in ink "Walter A. Sinz Sc./Mrs. R. A. Dyer Ceramist," minor nick to top, small flat chip on bottom **1,100.00**
- 9" x 7", Nocturne, attributed to Walter Sinz, Special ivory glaze, hp black details, stamped circular mark, 1929 .... **2,300.00**

Flower frog, Swirl Dancer, ivory glaze, stamped "Cowan," 10-3/4" x 4", **$920**. Photo courtesy of David Rago Auctions, Inc.

Flower frog
- 7-3/4" h, 6-1/4" d, Duet, orig ivory glaze, stamped "Cowan" **550.00**
- 10" h, 5-1/4" d, Pan, Special ivory glaze, stamped "Cowan" **350.00**
- 10-3/4" h, 4" d, Swirl Dancer, orig ivory glaze, stamped "Cowan" **850.00**

Lamp base, 11-1/2" h, 9-1/2" d, bulbous, Oriental-red glaze, stamp mark, drilled at side and bottom **300.00**

Match holder, 3-1/2" h, cream color **65.00**

Paperweight, 4-1/2" h, 3-1/4" l, elephant, Special ivory glaze, stamped "Cowan" **300.00**

Snack set, hexagon-shaped plate, solid light blue **115.00**

Trivet, 6-1/2" d, woman's head and flowers, blue, cream, yellow, and pink, die-stamped mark, minor scratches **450.00**

Vase
- 5" d, 7-1/4" h, classical shape, dripping brown crystalline glaze, mirrored orange glaze, ink mark **300.00**
- 5" d, 8-1/2" h, blue, emb flowers and leaves **225.00**

Cranberry Glass

History: Cranberry glass is transparent and named for its color, achieved by adding powdered gold to a molten batch of amber glass and reheating at a low temperature to develop the cranberry or ruby color. The glass color first appeared in the last half of the 17th century, but was not made in American glass factories until the last half of the 19th century.

For more information, see *Warman's Glass*, 4th edition.

Cranberry glass was blown, mold blown, or pressed. Examples often are decorated with gold or enamel. Less-expensive cranberry glass, made by substituting copper for gold, can be identified by its bluish-purple tint.

Reproduction Alert: Reproductions abound. These pieces are heavier, off-color, and lack the quality of older examples.

Basket, 7" h, 5" w, ruffled edge, petticoat shape, crystal loop handle, c1890 .... **250.00**

Bride's basket, 5" h, 3-1/2" d bowl, German silver-filigree frame, plain cranberry bowl **115.00**

Biscuit jar, silver-plated lid, **$175**. Photo courtesy of Joy Luke Auctions.

Centerpiece, 19-1/2" h, central trumpet-form vase, shallow dish, pedestal foot, gilt Greek-key dec, Victorian **300.00**

Condiment set, 1" h x 2" d open salt, 3" h pepper shaker, 3" h mustard pot, lids and frame marked "EPSN" (Electro Plated Nickel Silver), imp maker's mark "J. B. C & S Ltd." on base **385.00**

Creamer, 5" h, 2-3/4" d, Optic pattern, fluted to, applied clear handle **95.00**

Decanter, 8" h, 3" d, gold mid-band, white-enameled trim, clear-faceted stopper **150.00**

Dresser box, 5" d, blown out melon ribs, enameled scrolling on bronze feet, French, late 19th C **175.00**

Epergne, 19" h, 11" d, five pcs, large ruffled bowl, tall center lily, three jack-in-the-pulpit vases **1,200.00**

Finger bowl, Inverted Thumbprint pattern, deep color **200.00**

Epergne, central trumpet form vase and two side vases, all having applied colorless glass decoration, two colorless glass swirled inserts, ruffled edge base, 21" h, **$550**. Photo courtesy of Alderfer Auction Co.

Fruit bowl, frosted cranberry bowl, crystal frosted dolphin stem **200.00**

Garniture, 14" d bowl, pr 11" h candlesticks, cranberry overlay cut to clear, faceted cut dec, Continental **450.00**

Lamp

Kerosene, 22-1/2" h, frosted clear to cranberry ruffled shade, clear sunflower designs, swirl cranberry font, brass stem, black glass base, Victorian, font loose, old repairs **220.00**

Parlor, cranberry hobnail shade with crystal prisms, emb brass frame, orig smoke bell, Victorian **700.00**

Miniature, pitcher, elaborate gold trim and handle **75.00**

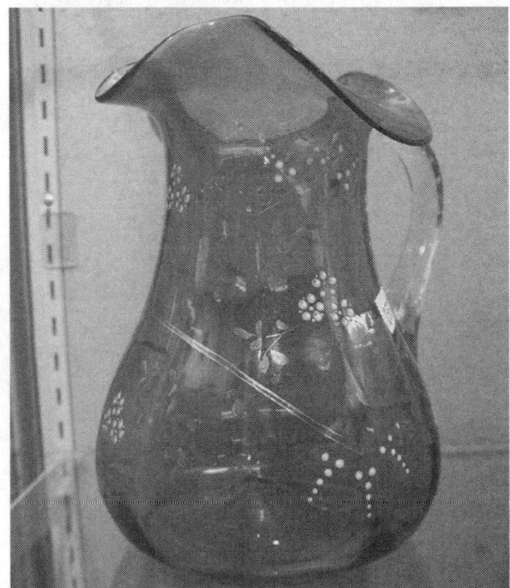

Pitcher, enameled yellow flowers with white centers, white dot enamel trim, worn gold striped design, applied colorless smooth handle, **$250**.

Pickle caster, enameled pink dogwood dec on cranberry glass cylindrical caster **1,150.00**

Pipe, 18" l, hand blown, tapering-bent neck, bulbous bowl, three bulbs at base, white-enamel dec at outer rim of bowl **250.00**

Pitcher

6-1/2" h, 4-1/8" d, Ripple and Thumbprint pattern, bulbous, round mouth, applied clear handle **175.00**

Left: Sugar shaker, pierced silver top, paneled sides, **$125**; mustard, silver top with spoon spot, diamond quilted body, **$145**.

10" h, 5" d, bulbous, ice bladder int., applied clear handle **250.00**

11-3/8" h, 9" w, bulbous, internal vertical ribs, white and blue enameled floral dec, applied clear loop handle, c1895 .... **300.00**

Salt, master, ftd, enameled floral dec **200.00**

Tumble-up, Inverted Thumbprint pattern **195.00**

Tumbler, Inverted Thumbprint pattern **65.00**

Vase

7-1/2" h, emb ribs, applied clear feet, three swirled applied clear leaves around base **120.00**

8-7/8" h, bulbous, white-enameled lilies of the valley dec, cylindrical neck...................................... **150.00**

Crown Milano

For more information, see *Warman's Glass,* 4th edition.

History: Crown Milano is an American art glass produced by the Mt. Washington Glass Works, New Bedford, Massachusetts. The original patent was issued in 1886 to Frederick Shirley and Albert Steffin.

Normally, it is an opaque-white satin glass finished with light-beige or ivory-colored ground embellished with fancy florals, decorations, and elaborate and thick raised gold. The same glass in shiny finish is Colonial Ware.

Marks: Marked pieces have a purple enamel entwined "CM" with a crown on the base. Sometimes paper labels were used. Since both Mount Washington and Pairpoint supplied mountings, the silver-plated mounts often have "MW" impressed or a Pairpoint mark.

Advisers: Clarence and Betty Maier.

Biscuit jar, cov

7" d, 7" h, squatty, pale green ground, pink and cream roses, naturalistically colored foliage, outlined in gold, replaced lid, base with logo and "520" **975.00**

7" d, 8-1/4" h, burnt-orange melon-ribbed body shading to chocolate colored shoulders, raised gold bramble tendrils winding around body, gold colored leaves with raised veins and insect-eaten holes, gold and silver blossoms and berries, fancy elongated chocolate-colored rococo scrolls on three ribs, oxidized metal fittings, emb crab on lid, twig finial, sgd "MW 4415," logo and "522" on base, few in-the-making scratches on two ribs **1,250.00**

Creamer and sugar, melon-ribbed bodies which shade from pale pink to natural white to pale green at base, blue cornflowers and green foliage, silver-plated fittings, sgd "3905/201" **1,500.00**

Demitasse cup and saucer, 3" d x 2-1/4" h cup, 5" d saucer, Scottish thistle dec, name "Felisa" in gold, pastel mauve leaves, pale blue raised veins and borders, gray background grasses, sgd with Crown Milano logo and "602" **1,500.00**

Dresser jar, cov, 4" d, 6" h, snow-white body, nosegays of pastel spring blossoms, two scroll handles with gold trim.. **1,250.00**

Ewer, 7-1/2" d, 6-1/2" h, Colonial Ware, shiny white body, two reserves of colorful blossoms framed by rococo borders of raised gold scrolls, gold cross-hatching across cream-colored shoulder, some loss to wash of color around rope handle, sgd "0100"................................ **1,250.00**

Lamp, banquet, 23" h, 9" d, Colonial Ware, shiny ground, base and globe-shaped shade dec with sprays of golden roes and blossoms, touches of gold accent molded-in dec of florals, swags, and geometric designs, opaque white chimney, brass burner sgd "Made in United States of America" **2,950.00**

Mustard pot, 3" d, 4" h, petaled gold roses, pink highlights, white body, lid hinge broken **285.00**

Plate, 7" d, Colonial Ware, glistening white finish, garden of spring flowers that surround centered lush pink cabbage rose, sprays of blue forget-me-nots, yellow daisies, purple chrysanthemums, dark red tulips, coral nasturtiums, white apple blossoms and white begonias, five elaborate raised gold rococo embellishments, sgd **550.00**

Syrup pitcher, Colonial Ware, 15 sprays of Dresden floral bouquets strewn on white melon-ribbed body, fancy gold scrollwork on body, ornate pewter-like collar and lid................................ **950.00**

Sweetmeat, cov, 5-1/2" d, 6" h, Colonial Ware, blossoms and scrolls on two tendrils encircle glistening bridal-white body, brilliant gold highlights, gold wash collar, lid and bail, red crown and wreath logo, lid marked "MW Pat. Apld. For 2040" **485.00**

Tumbler, Colonial Ware, shiny body, shades of raised gold, swags of finely detailed roses and daisies descend from free-flowing ribbon, numbered "1026" **585.00**

Vanity jar, 3-1/2" d, 5" h, opaque white body, forget-me-not dec, seven pink tourmaline faceted gemstones inset into repousse design of sterling silver flip-up lid, jar sgd "Pat'd," lid sgd "Sterling S3196" with rampant lion, anchor, and English letter "G" hallmarks for Gorham Manuf Co., Smithfield, RI, prior to 1906 .... **1,750.00**

Vase

- 4-1/2" h, white satin body with tint of lilac at neck, three fully opened chrysanthemum blossoms, two partially opened buds, raised gold borders, rich gold rim, raised DQ design, sgd **685.00**
- 7-1/2" h, sand-colored body, 24 swirling molded-in ribs, rare desert tableau, two cactus in full bloom, with five pink, white, and coral blossoms and one bud, outlined in raised gold, gold thorns on branches **2,450.00**
- 9" h, Scottish thistle dec, raised gold outlines, sgd "1526/1234" **785.00**
- 13-1/4" h, melon ribbed, long neck, folded down tricorn top, tulips dec, gold enameled scrolls and leaves, purple "CM" crown mark **4,600.00**

Cruets

History: Cruets are small glass bottles used on the table holding condiments such as oil, vinegar, and wine. The pinnacle of cruet use occurred during the Victorian era, when a myriad of glass manufacturers made cruets in a wide assortment of patterns, colors, and sizes. All cruets had stoppers; most had handles.

For more information, see *Warman's Glass*, 4th edition.

Bluerina, 7-1/4" h, deep royal blue neck fades to clear at shoulder, optic inverted thumbprint design in body, applied clear glass handle, teardrop-shaped air trap stopper, in-the-making thin elongated bubble in neck **500.00**

Bohemian, amber cut to clear, floral arrangement intaglio carved on ruby flashed ground of three oval panels with carved frames of floral swags, five cut-to-clear panels at neck, three embellished with gold scrolls, all edged in brilliant gold, 16 decorative panels edged in gold, base and stopper both sgd "4" **750.00**

Burmese, 7" h, Mt. Washington, shiny finish, butter-yellow ribbed, body, applied handle, and mushroom stopper **1,250.00**

Cranberry opalescent, Hobnail, Hobbs, Brockunier & Co., Wheeling, WV, 7-1/2" h **485.00**

Custard glass, Wild Bouquet pattern, fired-on dec **500.00**

Moser, 6" h, eight raised cabochon-like ruby gems, deep cut edges of burnished gold, mounted on colorless body, eight alternating panels of brilliant gold squiggles and stylized leaves, handle cut in three sharp edges, six gold dec panels on stopper, each set with ruby cabochon, inside of mouth and base of stopper sgd "4," some loss to gold squiggles **585.00**

Pattern glass, orig stopper

- Amazon, bar-in-hand stopper, 8-1/2" h **185.00**
- Beveled Star, green **225.00**
- Croesus, large, green, gold trim **395.00**
- Delaware, cranberry, gold trim **295.00**
- Esther, green, gold trim **465.00**
- Fluted Scrolls, blue dec **265.00**
- Millard, amber stain **350.00**
- Riverside's Ransom, vaseline **225.00**
- Tiny Optic, green, dec **150.00**

Peachblow, New England, shiny finish, Wild Rose, pink-white handle, orig white stopper **1,500.00**

Rainbow, **7**" h, pastel blue, pink, and yellow swirls from base to trefoil spout, molded-in bulging ribs, polished pontil mark, ribbed applied handle, cut glass stopper **975.00**

Sapphire blue, 7-1/4" h, Hobnail, faceted stopper, applied blue handle, damage to three hobs 385.00

Satin, 6-1/2" h, satin, pink shading to silvery white, DQ, MOP, gold on spout, twin rings on neck, multicolored floral dec, sgd in gold "22," replaced stopper incised "190," two in-the-making inclusions **495.00**

Cup Plates

History: Many early cups were handleless and came with deep saucers. The hot liquid was poured into the saucer and sipped from it. This necessitated another plate for the cup, hence the "cup plate."

The first cup plates made of pottery were of the Staffordshire variety. From the mid-1830s to 1840s, glass cup plates were favored. The Boston and Sandwich Glass Company was one of the main manufacturers of the lacy-glass type.

For more information, see *Warman's Glass*, 4th Edition.

Notes: It is extremely difficult to find glass cup plates in outstanding (mint) condition. Collectors expect some signs of use, such as slight rim roughness, minor chipping (best if under the rim), and, in rarer patterns, portions of scallops missing.

The numbers used are from the Lee-Rose book in which all plates are illustrated.

Prices are based on plates in average condition.

Lacy, cobalt blue, left: Hearts and Lyres, Neal 440, 3-1/2" d, flakes, **$125**; right: Neal 262, flakes, **$125**. Photo courtesy of Garth's Auctions, Inc.

Glass

LR 26, 3-9/16" d, colorless, attributed to Sandwich or New England Glass Co. **175.00**

LR 37, 3-1/4" d, opalescent, attributed to Sandwich or New England Glass Co. **200.00**

LR 75-A, 3-13/16" d, colorless, attributed to New England Glass Co. **120.00**

LR 81, 3-3/4" d, fiery-red opalescent, New England origin **350.00**

LR 100, 3-1/4" d, colorless, attributed to Philadelphia area, normal mold roughness **115.00**

Advertising, colorless, lacy, retail importer "E.A. & S.R. Filley Importers of China, Glass & Queensware, Saint Louis, "Rose/Lee No. 315, tiny pinpoint flakes at scalloped edges, **$330**.

LR 121, colorless, lacy, Midwestern **150.00**

LR 242-A, 3-1/2" d, black amethyst, lacy, Eastern origin, mold underfill and overfill **600.00**

LR 476, 3-5/16" d, colorless, hearts, 12 plain sides, attributed to Sandwich **75.00**

American, colorless, lacy, comic Irish "Before & After Marriage" reversible scene, Rose/Lee No. 697, and 20th C reproduction of Rose/Lee No. 698, both with small rim chips, price for pair, **$70**.

Glass, historical

LR 568, 3-7/16" d, colorless, attributed to Sandwich **175.00**

American, cobalt blue, lacy, shield breasted American eagle, star and rayed surround, scalloped edge, Rose/Lee No. 670-A, large rim chip, few nicks, **$150**.

LR 586-B, colorless, Ringgold, Palo Alto, stippled ground, small letters, attributed to Philadelphia area, 1847-48 ...... **665.00**
LR695, 3" d, colorless, Midwestern origin, normal mold roughness........ **135.00**

Pottery or porcelain

Gaudy Dutch, Butterfly pattern ... **750.00**
Leeds, 3-3/4" d, soft paste, gaudy blue and white floral dec, very minor pinpoint edge flakes........ **250.00**
Majolica, leaf motif........ **250.00**
Mulberry, cabbage roses, wheat border **175.00**
Staffordshire, historical views
3-1/8" d, Woodlands near Philadelphia, slightly scalloped edge, partial border, medium blue, unmarked, Stubbs........ **330.00**
3-1/2" d, America and Independence, partial States border, slightly scalloped rim, center with three-story mansion, dark blue, imp "Clews…," tiny rim flakes **550.00**
3-1/2" d, Customs House, Philadelphia, floral border, medium blue, unmarked, one of Ridgway's Beauties of America series **2,100.00**

Nautical, sapphire blue, American frigate under sail, star and floral scroll surround, Rose/Lee No. 610, numerous rim chips, 3-1/2" d, **$60**.

3-1/2" d, Holliday Street Theatre, Baltimore, full fruit and flower border, medium blue, unmarked, attributed to Stubbs, tiny pinpoint rim flakes **880.00**
3-1/2" d, Landing of Gen La Fayette in central oval, floral border, scalloped edge, medium blue, imp "Clews…" **1,430.00**
3-5/8" d, arched stone bridge from French View series, dark blue, imp "Enoch Wood & Sons," minor enamel wear at rim........ **220.00**
3-5/8" d, Cadmus (so-called), trefoil border, dark blue, unmarked, Enoch Wood & Sons........ **330.00**
3-5/8" d, scene of two sailing vessels, partial shell border, slightly scalloped rim, medium blue, transfer "3" on back........ **770.00**
3-3/4" d, Arms of the United States, eagle and shield, partial floral border, scalloped rim, medium blue, unmarked **2,860.00**
3-3/4" d, Boston State House, slightly scalloped edge with beaded border, medium blue, imp "Enoch Wood & Sons" **1,100.00**
3-3/4" d, Castle Garden Battery, NY, full shell border, dark blue, imp "Enoch Wood & Sons"........ **400.00**
3-3/4" d, The Landing of the Pilgrims, Plymouth Rock, scalloped edge, partial border, light blue, imp "Enoch Wood and Sons" **770.00**
3-3/4" d, Woodlands Near Philadelphia, full floral border, slightly scalloped rim, medium blue, unmarked Stubbs, minor flake under rim **465.00**
3-7/8" d, America and Independence, partial States border, three-story mansion in center, dark blue, imp "Clews…" **495.00**
3-7/8" d, Quebec (so-called), ship near shore line, full floral border, medium blue, unmarked, attributed to Clews........ **550.00**
4-1/8" d, Octagon Church, untitled, full acorn and oak leaf border, white molded rim, medium blue, imp "Stevenson"........ **1,650.00**
4-3/8" d, Landing of Gen La Fayette, full floral border, slightly scalloped rim, dark blue, imp "Clews…" **550.00**
4-1/2" d, Peach and Plenty, full floral border, scalloped rim, dark blue, imp "Clews…" **1,650.00**
4-5/8" d, Castle Garden Battery, NY, full sea shell border, slightly scalloped rim, very dark blue, imp "Enoch Wood & Sons," slight in-the-making imperfection **1,375.00**
4-5/8" d, Landing of the Pilgrims, full bird and scroll border, slightly scalloped rim, medium blue, imp "Enoch Wood & Sons"........ **440.00**
4-3/4" d, Boston State House, untitled, full floral border, slightly scalloped rim, light blue, Enoch Woods, stabilized hairline **770.00**
4-3/4" d, Welcome Lafayette the Nation's Guest, white leaf molded border, beaded edge, medium blue medallion portrait of Lafayette, imp "Clews…" **1,980.00**

Custard Glass

History: Custard glass was developed in England in the early 1880s. Harry Northwood made the first American custard glass at his Indiana, Pennsylvania, factory in 1898.

From 1898 until 1915, many manufacturers produced custard-glass patterns, e.g., Dugan Glass, Fenton, A. H. Heisey Glass Co., Jefferson Glass, Northwood, Tarentum Glass, and U.S. Glass. Cambridge and McKee continued the production of custard glass into the Depression.

For more information, see *Warman's Glass*, 4th edition.

The ivory or creamy yellow-custard color is achieved by adding uranium salts to the molten hot glass. The chemical content makes the glass glow when held under a black light. The more uranium, the more luminous the color. Northwood's custard glass has the smallest amount of uranium,

creating an ivory color; Heisey used more, creating a deep yellow color.

Custard glass was made in patterned tableware pieces. It also was made as souvenir items and novelty pieces. Souvenir pieces include a place name or hand-painted decorations, e.g., flowers. Patterns of custard glass often were highlighted in gold, enameled colors, and stains.

Reproduction Alert: L. G. Wright Glass Co. has reproduced pieces in the Argonaut Shell and Grape and Cable patterns. It also introduced new patterns, such as Floral and Grape and Vintage Band. Mosser reproduced toothpicks in Argonaut Shell, Chrysanthemum Sprig, and Inverted Fan & Feather.

Banana stand, Grape and Cable, Northwood, nutmeg stain **315.00**
Berry bowl, individual, Chrysanthemum Sprig, blue, Northwood signature, 5" l, 3-3/4" w, 2-5/8" h **165.00**
Berry bowl, master
- Chrysanthemum Sprig, blue, Northwood signature, 10-1/2" l, 8" w, 4-7/8" h, some gold missing from scalloped top **385.00**
- Diamond with Peg **225.00**

Bonbon, Fruits and Flowers, Northwood, nutmeg stain **225.00**
Butter dish, cov
- Chrysanthemum Sprig, bright gold flowers, vines, and finial, tinted green scrollwork, pink fans, Northwood signature, 7-1/2" d, 6" h **465.00**
- Everglades **375.00**
- Grape and Cable, Northwood, nutmeg stain **450.00**
- Tiny Thumbprint, Tarentum, dec **300.00**
- Victoria **300.00**

Compote, Geneva **65.00**
Creamer, Heart with Thumbprint ... **85.00**
Cruet
- Argonaut Shell, orig stopper, 6-1/2" h **985.00**
- Beaded Circle, 6-1/2" h, gold dec, Northwood **1,250.00**

Goblet, Grape and Gothic Arches, nutmeg stain **80.00**
Hair receiver, Winged Scroll **125.00**
Nappy, Northwood Grape **60.00**
Pitcher, Argonaut Shell **325.00**
Plate, Grape and Cable, Northwood **45.00**
Punch cup
- Diamond with Peg **40.00**
- Louis XV **35.00**

Salt and pepper shakers, pr, Chrysanthemum Sprig **165.00**
Sauce, Intaglio **35.00**
Spooner, Wild Bouquet, 4-1/2" h, loss to floral dec **285.00**
Sugar, cov
- Diamond with Peg **175.00**
- Georgia Gem, pink floral dec **185.00**
- Tiny Thumbprint, rose dec **185.00**

Tankard pitcher, Diamond with Peg **275.00**
Toothpick holder, Louis XV **200.00**
Tumbler
- Argonaut Shell, 3-3/4" h **185.00**
- Cherry Scale **50.00**
- Inverted Fan and Feather **80.00**
- Vermont **90.00**

Cut Glass, American

History: Glass is cut by grinding decorations into the glass by means of abrasive-carrying metal or stone wheels. A very ancient craft, it was revived in 1600 by Bohemians and spread through Europe to Great Britain and America.

American cut glass came of age at the Centennial Exposition in 1876 and the World Columbian Exposition in 1893. The American public recognized American cut glass to be exceptional in quality and workmanship. America's most significant output of this high-quality glass occurred from 1880 to 1917, a period now known as the Brilliant Period.

For more information, see *Warman's Glass*, 4th edition.

Marks: Around 1890, some companies began adding an acid-etched "signature" to their glass. This signature may be the actual company name, its logo, or a chosen symbol. Today, signed pieces command a premium over unsigned pieces since the signature clearly establishes the origin. However, signatures should be carefully verified for authenticity since objects with forged signatures have been in existence for some time. One way to check is to run a fingertip or fingernail lightly over the signature area. As a general rule, a genuine signature cannot be felt; a forged signature has a raised surface.

Many companies never used the acid-etched signature on their glass and may or may not have affixed paper labels to the items originally. Dorflinger Glass and the Meriden Glass Co. made cut glass of the highest quality, yet never used an acid-etched signature. Furthermore, cut glass made before the 1890s was not signed. Many of these wood-polished items, cut on blown blanks, were of excellent quality and often won awards at exhibitions.

Bowl, petals and cane motif, **$100**. Photo courtesy of Wiederseim Associates, Inc.

Banana bowl, 11" d, 6-1/2" d, Harvard pattern, hobstar bottom **220.00**
Basket, 7-1/2" h, 8-1/2" d, four large hobstars, two fans applied crystal rope-twisted handle **350.00**
Bonbon, 8" d, 2" h, Broadway pattern, Huntly, minor flakes **135.00**
Bowl
- 8" d, 4" h, three brilliant cut thistles surround bowl, flower in center, scalloped edge, etched "Libbey" label, price for pr **400.00**
- 12" l, 8" w, 7" h, cranberry cut to clear, Hobb Star dec, scalloped edge, minor rim roughage **2,600.00**
- 12" d, 4-1/2" h, rolled-down edge, cut and engraved flowers, leaves, and center thistle, notched-serrated edge **275.00**

Box, cov, 5" d, 2-3/4" h, cut-paneled base, cover cut with large eight-pointed star with hobstar center surrounded by fans, C. F. Monroe **275.00**
Bread tray, 8" x 12", Anita, Libbey in circle mark **535.00**
Butter dish, cov, Hobstar **250.00**
Candlesticks, pr
- 9-1/2" h, hobstars, teardrop stem, hobstar base **250.00**
- 12" h, Adelaide pattern, amber, Pairpoint **250.00**

Centerpiece, 10-3/4" d, wheel cut and etched, molded, fruiting foliage, chips **490.00**
Champagne, Kalana Lily, pattern, Dorflinger **75.00**
Champagne bucket, 7" h, 7" d, sgd "Hoare" **400.00**

Champagne pitcher, 11" h, Prism pattern, triple notch handle, monogram sterling silver top **425.00**

Cheese dish, cov, 6" h dome, 9" d, plate, cobalt blue cut to clear, bull's eye and panel, large miter splints on bottom of plate.. **250.00**

Cider pitcher, 7" h, hobstars, zippers, fine diamonds, honeycomb-cut handle, 7" h.. **225.00**

Bowl, signed "J. Hoare," 8-1/4" d, 3-3/4" h, $150. Photo courtesy of Joy Luke Auctions.

Cologne bottle, 6" h, Hob and Lace pattern, green cased to clear, pattern-cut stopper, Dorflinger........................ **625.00**

Compote

6-3/4" d, 5-1/2" h, deep bowl with trefoil, curved edge, three hobstars, and panels with diamond point, fan, and zipper patterns, short pedestal, round base, etched maple leaf mark of T. B. Clark & Co., Honesdale, PA, minor grinding to sawtooth edge **395.00**

8-1/4" d, 8-3/4" h, Russian cut, scalloped rim and foot, zipper cut faceted stem teardrop center, minor pinpoints and grinding........... **500.00**

9-1/8" d, 6-1/4" h, hobstars on scalloped edge bowl, straight paneled stem with zipper cut edges, minor flakes............................ **400.00**

Creamer and sugar, pr

3-1/4" h, 3-3/4" h, hobstar designs, handles with oval cutting, minor roughness on spout **250.00**

5-1/2" h, pedestal, Carolyn variation, notched handles **895.00**

Cruet, 6-7/8" h, round, stars on body, paneled neck with zipper cut edges, scallop cut handle, rayed base, faceted stopper, handle sgd "Tuthill" **250.00**

Decanter, orig stopper, 9" h, flowing pattern of green cut to cranberry, applied clear handle, sterling silver collar and stopper, attributed to Stevens & Williams, collar stamped "STERLING 925-1000 FINE" **6,400.00**

Dish, 5" d, hobstar, pineapple, palm leaf 45.00

Compotes, covered, pair, diamond-cut vessel, scalloped rim and foot, dome covers with paneled ovoid finial, late 19th/early 20th C, 11-3/4" h, **$6,550**. Photo courtesy of Sloans & Kenyon Auctions.

Dresser box, cov, 7" h, 7" w, Harvard pattern variation, three-ftd, silver-plated fittings, orig beveled mirror on swivel hinge under lid, cut by Bergen Glass Co., couple of minute flakes **750.00**

Fern dish, 3-3/4" h, 8" w, round, silver-plate rim, C. F. Monroe, minor roughness to cut pattern, normal wear on base, no liner... **200.00**

Flower center, 5" h, 6" d, hobstars, flashed fans, hobstar chain and base **325.00**

Goblet, 8-1/2" h, intaglio vintage cut, 8-1/2" h, sgd "Sinclaire"..................... **80.00**

Humidor, cov, 7-1/2" d, Middlesex, hollow stopper, sponge holder in lid, Dorflinger.. **490.00**

Ice bucket, 6-5/8" h, colorless, body cut with vertical flutes, beaded silver-mounted rim with sterling silver swing handle marked for Wilcox Silver Plate Co., early 20th C.......................... **320.00**

Dresser box, covered, brass rim and lock, 5-1/2" x 3-1/2", 4-1/2" h, **$275**. Photo courtesy of Joy Luke Auctions.

Ice cream set, Russian pattern, eight 7" d dishes, 8-1/2" d serving bowl, 11" d cake plate, some chips to edges , price for 10-pc set **500.00**

Jar, cov, 10" h, diamond cut finial on stepped lid, ftd ovoid vessel, four Oriental influenced cut medallions, cane and star-cut ground, 20th C, several nicks **260.00**

Knife rest, 4" l **90.00**

Lamp, 24" h, cut glass shade with butterfly and foliage design, inverted compote form base, cut star and geometric design base, ring of cut glass prisms.. **550.00**

Loving cup, three handles, sterling top **350.00**

Nappy, two handles, 6" d, hobstar center, intaglio floral, strawberry diamond button border, 6" d **45.00**

Orange bowl, 9-3/4" x 6-3/4" x 3-3/4" h, hobstars and strawberry diamond **200.00**

Perfume bottle, 6-1/2" h, bulbous, all-over cutting, orig stopper **220.00**

Perfume flask, 4-3/4" l, pistol-form, etched silver-gilt mounts, short chain, spring-action trigger opens lid set with maker's medallion, French, late 19th/early 20th C **1,380.00**

Pickle tray, 7" x 3", checkerboard, hobstar **45.00**

Pitcher, 12-1/2" h, tapered body with quatrefoil flowers, tiny diamond point surface, surrounded by fans and hobstars, paneled neck with zipper cuts, spout with diamonds, cut ridges on applied handle, spout has been reworked on underside **475.00**

Plate, cut and etched, red and clear glass plate, peacock and flowers dec, 12-1/2" d, **$100**. Photo courtesy of Joy Luke Auctions.

Plate, 10" d, Carolyn pattern, J. Hoare **525.00**

Potpourri jar, 6" h, baluster shaped cut glass base, silver lid with portrait medallion and floral banding **200.00**

Punch bowl

11" h, 10" w, two pcs, Elgin pattern, Quaker City **600.00**

14-3/8" d, 13-1/4" h, round, set into base, cut rim, miter star cut pattern, acid-etched maker's mark for T. G. Hawkes & Co., Corning, NY, on base **1,880.00**

Relish, 13" l, leaf shape, Clear Button Russian pattern **375.00**

Salt, open, Russian pattern, master size **45.00**

Serving dish, 11" d, two layers, apple and pear branches, grape vine dec, Gravic **395.00**

Tankard pitcher, 10-1/4" h, Harvard cut sides, pinwheel top, mini hobnails, thumbprint notched handle **200.00**

Tray, 12" d, round, Monarch, sgd "Hoare" **975.00**

Tumbler, Harvard, rayed base **45.00**

Urn, cov, Russian pattern **175.00**

Punch bowl, footed, star design, 14"d, 6-1/2" h, 23 cut-glass punch cups, **$225**. Photo courtesy of Joy Luke Auctions.

Vase

- 8" h, 11" d, squatty body, short flaring neck, scalloped rim **550.00**
- 12-1/2" h, 6-1/2" d, floral and diamond point engraving, sgd "Hawkes" **250.00**
- 14" h, ruffled edge, cut iris dec, Gravic **295.00**
- 16" h, corset shape, well-cut hobstar, strawberry diamond, prism, flashed star and fan **300.00**
- 19-1/2" h, lobed rim, alternating vertical cut patterns, star-cut disk base, 20th C **750.00**
- 23-1/4" h, two pcs, trumpet shape, hobstars and paneled ring design, base and top joined with metal post covered with diamond faceted ball **1,350.00**

Water carafe, Pinwheel and Fan cutting, notched neck, 8" h, 4" w **125.00**

Water pitcher, 10" h, Keystone Rose pattern **190.00**

Whiskey jug, 6-1/4" h, bulbous, thistle and grape cutting, orig stopper, sgd "Sinclaire" **295.00**

Wine, 4" h, flint, cut panels, strawberry diamonds, and fans, Pittsburgh **60.00**

Wine cooler, Russian pattern **145.00**

DAVENPORT

History: John Davenport opened a pottery in Longport, Staffordshire, England, in 1793. His high-quality lightweight wares are cream colored with a beautiful velvety texture.

The firm's output included soft-paste (Old Blue) products, luster-trimmed pieces, and pink luster wares with black transfer. Pieces of Gaudy Dutch and Spatterware also have been found with the Davenport mark. Davenport later became a leading maker of ironstone and early flow blue. His famous Cyprus pattern in mulberry became very popular. His heirs continued the business until the factory closed in 1886.

Charger, 17-1/2" l, oval, Venetian harbor scene, light-blue transfer................ **90.00**

Cup plate, Teaberry pattern, pink luster **40.00**

Dish, ftd, tricorn, Belvoir Castle dec **90.00**

Ewer, 9" h, floral dec, multicolored, c1930.. **190.00**

Jug, 5-1/2" h, Jardiniere pattern, blue, orange, green, peach, and gold, peach luster rim, c1805-20..................... **450.00**

Plate

- 7" d, Chinese River Scene, reticulated, medium to dark blue **310.00**
- 9-1/2" d, Flying Bird, blue, orange, pink, yellow, and green **250.00**

Platter, well and tree, cobalt blue and iron red decoration, green and purple painted accents in floral design, gilt trim, marked "Davenport" with anchor, 20" x 15-1/2", **$750**. Photo courtesy of Alderfer Auction Co.

Platter

- 18-1/4", stone china, polychrome dec blue transfer print bird and floral pattern, printed mark, c1810, glaze wear....................................... **230.00**
- 19-1/8" l, purple transfer, idyllic scene, boat and church, marked "Davenport"........................... **440.00**

Sauce tureen, cov, ladle, creamware, molded leaves, lime green veining, early **450.00**

Serving bowl, cov, 7" w, 9-3/4" l, Chinoiserie Bridgeless pattern, internal bowl with steam holes, c1810 ...... **700.00**

Soup tureen, matching stand, 13-1/4" l, stone china, polychrome dec blue transfer printed bird and floral patter, gilded lion mask handles, printed marks, c1810, large hairline on stand, glaze wear.. **1,610.00**

Tea service, Imari pattern, 18" l tray, teapot, creamer, cov sugar, four cups and saucers................................. **850.00**

DECOYS

History: During the past several years, carved wooden decoys, used to lure ducks and geese to the hunter, have become widely recognized as an indigenous American folk-art form. Many decoys are from 1880 to 1930, when commercial gunners commonly hunted and used rigs of several hundred decoys. Many fine carvers also worked through the 1930s and 1940s. Individuals and commercial decoy makers also carved fish decoys.

Because decoys were both hand made and machine made, and many examples exist, firm pricing is difficult to establish. The skill of the carver, rarity, type of bird, and age all affect the value.

Reproduction Alert.

Notes: A decoy's value is based on several factors: (1) fame of the carver, (2) quality of the carving, (3) species of wild fowl—the most desirable are herons, swans, mergansers, and shorebirds—and (4) condition of the original paint.

The inexperienced collector should be aware of several facts. The age of a decoy, per se, is usually of no importance in determining value. However, age does have some influence when it comes to a rare or important example. Since very few decoys were ever signed, it is quite difficult to attribute most decoys to known carvers. Anyone who has not examined a known carver's work will be hard pressed to determine if the paint on one of his decoys is indeed original. Repainting severely decreases a decoy's value. In addition, there are many fakes and reproductions on the market and even experienced collectors are occasionally fooled. Decoys represent a subject where dealing with a reputable dealer or auction house is important, especially those who offer a guarantee as to authenticity.

Decoys listed here are of average wear, unless otherwise noted.

Decoy sets record

On Jan. 18, 2003, Christie's Rockfeller Center salesroom was the site of a new world record price. A preening pintail drake, c1915, by renowned master carver Elmer Crowell (1864-1954) realized $801,500, topping the preview record of $684,500 for a sleeping Canadian goose by the same carver at a January 2000 auction. When sold at auction in 1996, the same decoy brought a then-record price of $319,000. This decoy was the highlight of the Russell B. Aitken's collection of wildfowl decoys, when the collection was sold for $2,853,568. Christies conducted the auction in association with the decoy auction firm of Guyette & Schmidt, Inc., Farmington, MA.

Atlantic Brant, Mason, Challenge grade, c1910, from the famous Barron rig (Virginia), nearly mint condition, age shrinkage neck crack repair, tight filled factory back crack **4,500.00**

Baldgate Wigeon Drake, miniature, A. Elmer, Crowell, East Harwich, MA, identified in ink, rect stamp on base, 2-1/2" x 4"...................................... **635.00**

Black Bellied Bustard, miniature, H. Gills, initialed "H. G. 1957," identified in pencil, natural wood base, 3-1/2" x 4" **230.00**

Black Bellied Plover, unknown American 20th C maker, orig paint, glass eyes, mounted on stick on lead base, 12-1/2" h, minor paint loss, small chips to beak **2,530.00**

Black Breasted Plover, Harry C. Shourds, orig paint.................... **2,650.00**

Black Duck

- A. Elmer Crowell, East Harwich, MA, orig paint, glass eyes, stamped mark in oval on base, sleeping, wear, crack, 5-1/4" h **525.00**
- Ira Hudson, preening, raised wings, outstretched neck, scratch feather paint **8,500.00**
- Mason, Challenge, c1910, hollow, fine orig paint, some neck filler replaced **3,500.00**
- Mason, Premier, c1905, Atlantic Coast, oversized, solid-bodied special order, most desirable snaky head, excellent orig condition, some professional restoration, filled in-the-making back crack, tail chip on one side of crack, neck filler replacement **4,500.00**
- Mason, Standard, c1910, painted eye, dry original paint, all of its original neck filler, invisible professional dry rot repair in the base **750.00**

Black Drake, miniature, A. Elmer Crowell, East Harwich, MA, identified in ink, rect stamp on base, break at neck, reglued, minor paint loss, 3-1/2" x 4-3/4".... **635.00**

Bluebill Drake, Rozell Bliss, Stratford, CT, c1910, **$290**.

Bluebill Drake, Jim Kelson, Mt. Clemens, MI, carved wing detail, feather stamping, glass eyes, orig paint, orig keep and weight, 13-1/2" l, c1930 .... **295.00**

Bluebill Hen, Mason Challenge, c1910, hollow, orig paint **3,450.00**

Blue-Winged Teal Drake and Hen Pair, Davey W. Nichol, Smiths Falls, Ontario, Canada, 1960, matched pair, raised wings, scratch feather patterns, sgd on bottom **1,650.00**

Brant, Ward Brothers, MD, carved, hollow body, head turned left, sgd "Lem and Steve," dated 1917............ **1,650.00**

Broadbill Drake and Hen Pair, Mason, c1910, painted eyes, rare gunning rigmates, untouched original condition, neck filler missing, some shot evidence, hen has small, superficial chip on one side... **1,450.00**

Bufflehead Drake

- Bob Kerr, carved detail, glass eyes, orig paint, scratch carved signature, 10-1/2" l, c1980 .... **250.00**
- James Lagham, Dennisport, MA, identified in ink, oval stamp on base, 3" x 4-1/2" **345.00**
- Harry M. Shrouds, carved, hollow body, painted eyes............ **1,800.00**

Canada Goose, H. Gibbs, identified and initialed "HG 1957" on natural wood base, 2-1/2" x 4-1/2" **290.00**

Canvasback drake, Charles Bean, c1980, orig red, white, black, and gray paint, red glass eyes, minor crazing and chips, 15" l.................................... **110.00**

Canvasback hen, unsigned, by Charles Bean, c1980, brown, black, and gray paint, glass eyes, 14-1/2" l, 6-1/4" h **110.00**

Canvasback pair, Mason, Premier, Seneca Lake, c1910, matched pair, very fine orig paint with strong patterns, drake is excellent with hairline crack in base; hen has filled factory crack on left side of its back, hairline crack part way through neck.. **2,950.00**

Curlew, Dan Leeds, Pleasantville, NJ, 1880-1900, carved and painted brown, stand, 13" l.................................. **2,415.00**

Curlew Oyster Eater, Samuel Jester, Tennessee, c1920, carved and painted, slight paint wear, age crack in body, stand, 16" l, 9" h....................... **1,035.00**

Duck drake, old black, burgundy, and white paint, dark green detail, glass eyes, age split at breast, 16-1/4" l, 7-1/4" h **615.00**

Top: golden Eye or Whistler, Joe wooster, signed "good Hunting, Josef Wooster, '70," original paint, glass eyes, very good detail, 14-1/2" l, **$360**; middle: Merganser Hen, Joe Wooster, signed "Good Hunting Joseph 'Buckeye Joe' Wooster," original paint, glass eyes, very good detail, minor paint separation, 21-1/2" l, **$200**; bottom: Merganser Drake, Joe Wooster, mate to one above, signed the same, minor wear edge, **$385**. Photo courtesy of Garth's Auctions.

Eider Duck, polychrome-carved wood, America, early 19th C, cracks, 15" l **400.00**

Fish, 13-1/4" l, orig mustard paint, black stripes, tin fins, red faceted bead eyes, 13-1/4" l.. **360.00**

Flying Duck, glass-bead eyes, old natural surface, carved pine, attributed to Maine, c1930, 16" l, 11" h......... **2,300.00**

Goldeneye Duck, New England, c1900, minor paint wear, 12" l **2,300.00**

Great Northern Pike, attributed to Menominee Indian, WI, c1900, painted green, glass eyes, ribbed sheet metal fin, tall stand, 36" l, 9" h **3,450.00**

Green Wing Teal Duck, miniature, A. Elmer Crowell, East Harwich, MA, identified in ink, rect stamp on base, 2-1/2" x 4"..................................... **865.00**

Heron, unknown maker, carved wig and tail, wrought iron legs **900.00**

Herring Gull, attributed to Gus Wilson, c1910-20, used as weathervane, traces of old paint, metal feet, weathered and worn, 18-3/4" l............................**3,110.00**

Hooded Merganser Drake, William Clarke, Oakville, Ontario, Canada, c1900, transitional plumage, excellent orig condition, minor in-use wear **2,450.00**

Loon, carved and painted, wooden rudder, America, 19th C, stand, paint wear, 27" l **9,200.00**

Mallard drake

Delaware River, PA, c1920, flocked, old dark gray and green paint, blue green head, green bill, carved eyes, lead keel weight, slightly raised carved wings, some wear, 15-3/4" l **200.00**

Schmidt, Frank, attributed to, gray, brown, black, and white paint, raised carved feathers on back, green head, glass eyes, yellow bill, 16" l **1,210.00**

Mallard drake and hen, unsigned, Frank Schmidt, incised carved detail, glass eyes, brown, tan, white, black, and blue paint, one missing keel, 16-1/2" l, 15-1/2" l **2,585.00**

Mallard Hen, Robert Elliston, carved, hollow body, orig paint **1,800.00**

Merganser Drake, Mason Challenge, Detroit, MI, c1910, strong orig paint with no cracks, some shot holes have been filled on one side, branded "C. Simpson" **7,500.00**

Perch, Heddon, ice-type............. **800.00**

Shore bird, tin, two-piece hollow form, some paint remaining. 11" l x 6" h, mounted on pewter chamberstick, minor loss of tail, rust on surface, **$80**. Photo courtesy of Alderfer Auction Co.

Pintail Duck, Drake and hen, John H. Baker, Bristol, PA, 20th C, painted in naturalistic tones, glass eyes, sgd, imp maker's signature, lead ingot affixed to bases stamped "John Baker Bristol, PA," paint flakes on hen **1,100.00**

Plover, Joe Lincoln, winter plumage, feather painting, orig paint **800.00**

Red Breasted Merganser Drake, George Boyd, NH, carved, orig paint **8,000.00**

Redhead Drake, Dan Bartlett, Prince Edward County, Ontario, Canada, c1920, hollow, fine orig paint.................. **950.00**

Robin Snipe, Obediah Verity, carved wings and eyes, orig paint **4,400.00**

Ruddy Duck, miniature, maker unknown, identified in ink on base, paint loss to bill, 2" x 2-3/4".................................. **690.00**

Ruddy Duck Drake, Len Carmeghi, Mt. Clemens, MI, hollow body, glass eyes, orig paint, sgd and dated, 10-3/4" l **250.00**

Ruffled Grouse, miniature, A. Elmer Crowell, East Harwich, MA, rect stamp, mounted on natural wood base, 3-1/2" x 4-1/2" **865.00**

Sea Gull, 14" l, weathered surface, used as weathervane, attributed to WI, late 19th/early 20th C **1,840.00**

Shorebird, Willard C. Baldwin (1890-1979), CT, 1964, carved wing, mounted on mahogany base branded "WCB" and "TBL", inscribed "Baldwin 1964," minor wear to tail **620.00**

Swan, unknown Chesapeake Bay, MD, maker, carved wood, braced neck, white paint, 30" l.................................. **900.00**

Widgeon hen, NJ, c1890, orig brown and tan paint, olive colored bill, orange glass eyes, wear and putty filled splits, sinker weights and cord, 15" l **495.00**

Wood Duck Drake, miniature, A. Elmer Crowell, East Harwich, MA, identified in ink, rect stamp on base, 3" x 4-1/2" **1,150.00**

Yellowlegs, carved and painted, New Jersey, c1890, stand, 11" l **2,185.00**

DEDHAM POTTERY

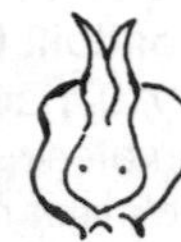

History: Alexander W. Robertson established a pottery in Chelsea, Massachusetts, about 1866. After his brother, Hugh Cornwall Robertson, joined him in 1868, the firm was called A. W. & H. C. Robertson. Their father, James Robertson, joined his sons in 1872, and the name Chelsea Keramic Art Works Robertson and Sons was used.

The pottery's initial products were simple flower and bean pots, but the firm quickly expanded its output to include a wide variety of artistic pottery. It produced a very fine redware body used in classical forms, some with black backgrounds imitating ancient Greek and Apulian works. It experimented with underglaze slip decoration on vases. The Chelsea Keramic Art Works Pottery also produced high-glazed vases, pitchers, and plaques with a buff clay body, with either sculpted or molded applied decoration.

James Robertson died in 1880 and Alexander moved to California in 1884, leaving Hugh C. Robertson alone in Chelsea, where his tireless experiments eventually yielded a stunning imitation of the prized Chinese Ming-era blood-red glaze. Hugh's vases with that glaze were marked with an impressed "CKAW." Creating these red-glazed vases was very expensive, and even though they received great critical acclaim, the company declared bankruptcy in 1889.

Recapitalized by a circle of Boston art patrons in 1891, Hugh started the Chelsea Pottery U.S., which produced gray crackle-glazed dinnerware with cobalt-blue decorations, the rabbit pattern being the most popular.

The business moved to new facilities in Dedham, Massachusetts, and began production in 1896 under the name Dedham Pottery. Hugh's son and grandson operated the business until it closed in 1943, by which time between 50 and 80 patterns had been produced, some very briefly.

Marks: The following marks help determine the approximate age of items:

- "Chelsea Keramic Art Works Robertson and Sons," impressed, 1874-1880
- "CKAW," impressed, 1875-1889
- "CPUS," impressed in a cloverleaf, 1891-1895
- Foreshortened rabbit only, impressed, 1894-1896
- Conventional rabbit with "Dedham Pottery" in square blue stamped mark along with one impressed foreshortened rabbit, 1896-1928
- Blue rabbit stamped mark with "registered" beneath, along with two impressed foreshortened rabbit marks, 1929-1943

Reproduction Alert: Two companies make Dedham-like reproductions primarily utilizing the rabbit pattern, but always mark their work very differently from the original.

Adviser: James D. Kaufman.

Paperweight, frog, signed "Dedham Pottery," artist's initials "C. D.," nick to web, 2-1/8" l, **$715**. Photo courtesy of Skinner, Inc.

Bowl, 5-3/4" d, four painted poppy designs, hand-cut reticulated edge formed peaks and arches around perimeter **1,100.00**

Bowl, 8-1/2" sq

Rabbit pattern, reg. stamp **600.00**

Swan pattern, reg. stamp...... **725.00**

Bowl, 9-3/8" d, 3-3/4" h, Poppy pattern, cut edge rim, Oriental-type, sloping poppies, registered blue ink stamp, "D" in red, minor glaze miss near base edge **1,035.00**

Breakfast plate, 8-3/4" d

Crab pattern, blue ink stamp, glaze imperfections **375.00**

Rabbit pattern, assembled set, marks include blue registered stamp, imp foreshortened rabbit, and 1931 stamp, set of six, one with rim chip **635.00**

Butter plate, 4-3/8" d, Swan pattern, registered blue ink stamp............ **260.00**

Candlesticks, pr

Elephant pattern, reg. blue stamp **525.00**

Rabbit pattern, reg. blue stamp 325.00

Creamer and sugar, 3-1/4" and 4", Rabbit pattern, blue stamp and "1931" on creamer, blue registered stamp on sugar 350.00

Cup and saucer, elephant and baby patterned border, deep blue, stamped, registration mark 880.00

Knife rest, Rabbit form, blue reg. stamp 575.00

Paperweight, Rabbit form, blue reg. stamp 495.00

Pickle dish, 10-1/2" l, Elephant pattern, blue reg. stamp 750.00

Plate, Horse Chestnut pattern, blue ink stamp, early 20th C, 8-1/2" d, **$150**. Photo courtesy of Skinner, Inc.

Pitcher

3-1/4" h, Rabbit pattern 175.00

5-1/8" h, Chickens pattern, blue stamp 2,300.00

7" h, Turkey pattern, blue stamp 585.00

9" h, Rabbit pattern, blue stamp 700.00

Style of 1850, blue reg. stamp 975.00

Plate, 6" d

Clover pattern, reg. stamp 625.00

Iris pattern, blue stamp, Maude Davenport's "O" rebus 280.00

Rabbit pattern, registered blue ink stamp, set of four, foot chips on two 290.00

Plate, 6-1/8" d

Horse Chestnut pattern, one impressed rabbit mark 150.00

Magnolia pattern, blue ink stamp mark 115.00

Plate, 7-1/2" d, Lobster pattern, registered blue ink stamp, two imp rabbits 290.00

Plate, 8" d, Iris pattern, reg. stamp 230.00

Sugar bowl, covered, Rabbit (two ear) pattern, square blue pottery stamp, 4-1/2" h; salt shaker, Rabbit (two ear) pattern, 3-1/2" h, **$300**. Photo courtesy of Alderfer Auction Co.

Plate, 8-1/2" d

Crab pattern, blue stamp 550.00

Elephant pattern, blue reg. stamp 650.00

Orange Tree pattern, stamped rabbit mark, tight lines, price for pr 350.00

Rabbit pattern, blue stamp 175.00

Rabbit pattern, blue stamp, Maude Davenport's "O" rebus 235.00

Snow Tree pattern, blue stamp 210.00

Upside down dolphin, CPUS 900.00

Plate, 9-3/4" d, Owl & Moon pattern, deep blue, stamp and imp rabbit logo 4,950.00

Plate, 10" d

Dolphin pattern, blue reg. stamp 875.00

Elephant pattern, blue reg. stamp 900.00

Pine Apple pattern, CPUS 775.00

Turkey pattern, blue stamp, Maude Davenport's "O" rebus 475.00

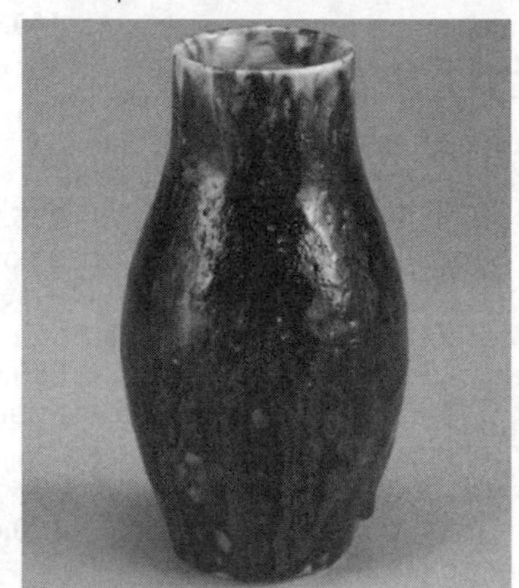

Vase, volcanic, bulbous, frothy chocolate, indigo, and green glaze, incised "Dedham BW Pottery/ DP32A 048646751P," 3-3/4" d, 7" h, 1/2" rim bruise to rim, minor grinding chips, and base lines, **$920**. Photo courtesy of David Rago Auctions, Inc.

Plate, 10-1/4" d, Rabbit pattern, registered blue ink stamp, one imp rabbit 150.00

Platter, 9-7/8" l, 6-3/8" w, Rabbit pattern, rect, blue ink stamp, two imp rabbits 260.00

Salt and pepper shakers, pr, Rabbit pattern, 3-1/2" h, glaze miss 200.00

Sherbet, two handles, Rabbit pattern, blue stamp 350.00

Tea cup and saucer

Azalea pattern, reg. stamp 130.00

Butterfly pattern, blue stamp 345.00

Duck pattern, reg. stamp 190.00

Turtle pattern, reg. stamp 680.00

Water Lily pattern, reg. stamp 130.00

Teapot, 6-1/8" h, Rabbit pattern, blue stamp 875.00

Vase, 5-3/4" d, 7" h, experimental, by Hugh Robertson, bulbous, rich lustered oxblood glaze, incised "DEDHAM POTTERY/HCR," 2-1/2" h hairline from rim 1,355.00

DELFTWARE

History: Delftware is pottery with a soft, red-clay body and tin-enamel glaze. The white, dense, opaque color came from adding tin ash to lead glaze. The first examples had blue designs on a white ground. Polychrome examples followed.

The name originally applied to pottery made in the region around Delft, Holland, beginning in the 16th century and ending in the late 18th century. The tin used came from the Cornish mines in England. By the 17th and 18th centuries, English potters in London, Bristol, and Liverpool were copying the glaze and designs. Some designs unique to English potters also developed.

In Germany and France, the ware is known as Faience, and in Italy as Majolica.

Reproduction Alert: Since the late 19th century, much Delft-type souvenir material has been produced to appeal to the foreign traveler. Don't confuse these modern pieces with the older examples.

Bowl, tin enamel glaze, scalloped edge

8" d, 1-1/4" h, blue on white, fruit, butterfly, and grapevine, flakes, hairlines 350.00

13-1/4" d, 2-1/2" h, blue/gray, violet blue Oriental type design of person sitting in landscape, flakes, old stapled repair 450.00

Charger

13" d, floral design, building scene, manganese and blue, edge chips 615.00

13-1/8" d, blue and white, foliate devices, Dutch, 19th C, chips, glaze wear 410.00

Plate, Dutch, scallop edge, central circular panel featuring crested bird amid flowers, surrounded by concentric bands of floral motifs, concentric blue lines on back of rim, bottom marked with blue under-glaze "hatchet," mark used c1759, 10" d, rim chips, **$350**. Photo courtesy of Alderfer Auction Co.

13-5/8" d, blue and white, foliate devices, 19th C, chips, glass wear, restoration **320.00**
14" d, blue on white tin glaze, flowers in lobed medallions, "X" mark on base, English, rim chips **650.00**

Dish
8-1/4" d, molded rim, blue and white, stylized landscape and floral design, edge chips **315.00**
12-3/8" l, fluted oval, blue and white floral design, attributed to Lambeth, chips **440.00**

Figure, 9" l, recumbent cow, blue and white, enamel dec floral spray on its back, and floral circlet around neck, tapered sq base, early 20th C **250.00**

Flower brick, 4-5/8" l, 2-1/2" h, blue and white, Chinese figures in landscape, Dutch, 18th C, chips, cracks **375.00**

Tile frieze, Dutch landscape with windmills, signed "Delft Blauw/Handpainted/Made in Holland," framed, splintering to two edges of frame, 11-1/2" x 17-1/4" **$245**. Photo courtesy of David Rago Auctions, Inc.

Garniture, three bulbous 17-1/4" h cov urns, two octagonal tapered 12-3/4" h vases, polychrome dec foliage surrounding central blue figural panels, Dutch, late 18th/early 19th C **8,625.00**

Inkwell, 4-1/2" h, heart shape, blue and white floral dec, wear and edge chips **495.00**

Jar, 5" h, blue and white, chips, pr **715.00**

Lamp base, octagonal bottle form with continuous blue and white Oriental figural landscape design, England, 18th C, foot rim chips, drilled **690.00**

Mug, 6-3/8" h, blue and white, armorial surrounded by exotic landscape, palm trees, marked on base, Dutch, 19th C, minor chips, glaze wear **490.00**

Quintal flower vase, 8-1/2" h, underglaze blue dec, leaves, birds and flowers, Holland, late 18th C, rim and footrim chips and flakes **530.00**

Plaque, 19" x 14", emb scrolled acanthus in cartouche form framing hp scene of Dutch windmill and canal, imp "1" and underglaze "A" on verso, c1900 .. **550.00**

Plate
8-3/4" d, manganese, iron red, yellow, and underglaze blue floral design, chips **200.00**
9" d, tin glaze, flowering branch behind fence, blue, yellow, green, and pale purple, English, rim chips **550.00**
10-1/4" d, blue and white Bible illustration, small over reserve with bible reference and date "MAT 2: IV.00, 1752," small edge chips **770.00**
13-3/4" d, Oriental-style hand painted floral dec, shades of red, blue, green, and yellow, black outlining, white ground, England, 19th C, rim chips **775.00**

Posset pot, 4-3/4" h, blue and white, birds among foliage, England, 19th C, minor chips and cracks **920.00**

Sauce boat, 8-1/4" l, applied scrolled handles, fluted flaring lip, blue and white Oriental design, edge chips and hairline, later added yellow enamel rim **440.00**

Spice box, cov, 6" h, sq, spreading branchwork feet and Chinaman knop, lozenge shaped panels with blue maritime scenes, Dutch, mid-18th C **995.00**

Tea caddy, 5-7/8" h, blue and white floral dec, scalloped bottom edge, marked "MVS 1750," cork closure, wear, edge flakes, old filled in chip on lid **550.00**

Tile, 5" sq, Fazackerly, polychrome dec of floral bouquets, c1760, price for pr, one with edge nicks, other with edge flaking and chips **350.00**

Tobacco jar, 10" h, blue and white, Indians and "Siville," older brass stepped lid, chips **1,870.00**

Vase, 19" h, tapering octagonal, molded lobes, blue, green, and red polychromed continuous band of birds of paradise within foliage, marked "J.V.D.H.," late 19th C, pr **1,200.00**

Vase, bulbous, blue and gray floral motif, 7" h, crazing, rim and bottom chips, **$850**. Photo courtesy of Alderfer Auction Co.

Vase, cov, 23" h, Delft blue and white, oval paneled sides with Chinese style dec alternating with female figures in courtyard setting, flowers, and fence design, hexagonal form rim, foot, and cov, cat finial, unidentified mark, Holland, 18th C, rim damage, footrim chips, chips to cat's ears, typical edge flaking of tin glaze **815.00**

Wall pocket, 6-1/4" w, 4-1/2" d, 7" h, vasiform, ogee backplate, pierced grillwork, blue and white scenes of figures at harbor, scrollwork borders, applied flower buds on sides, 20th C, price for pr **350.00**

Depression Glass

For more information, see *Warman's Glass*, 4th edition, *Warman's Depression Glass*, 3rd edition, and *Warman's Depression Glass Field Guide*.

History: Depression glass was made from 1920 to 1940. It was an inexpensive machine-made glass and produced by several companies in various patterns and colors. The number of forms made in different patterns also varied.

Depression glass was sold through variety stores, given away as premiums, or packaged with certain products. Movie houses gave it away from 1935 until well into the 1940s.

Like pattern glass, knowing the proper name of a pattern is the key to collecting. Collectors should be prepared to do research.

Reproduction Alert: The number of Depression glass patterns that have been reproduced continues to grow. Reproductions exist in many patterns, forms, and colors. Beware of colors and forms that were not made in the original production of the pattern. Carefully examine every piece that seems questionable and look for loss of details, poor impressions, and slight differences in sizes.

American Pioneer

Manufactured by Liberty Works, Egg Harbor, NJ, from 1931 to 1934.Made in amber, crystal, green, and pink.

American Pioneer green plate, cup and saucer, **$19.00.**

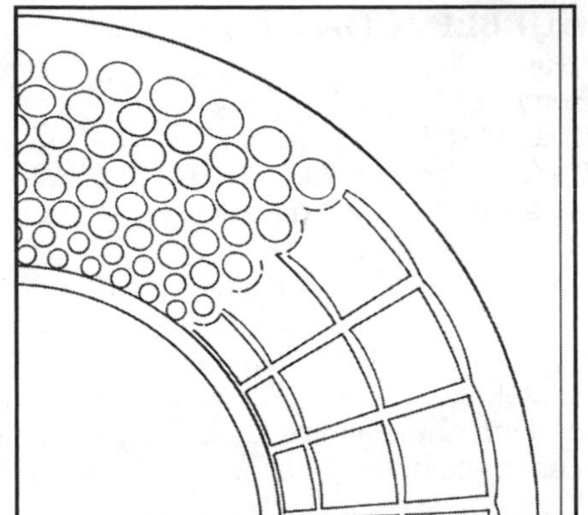

Item	Amber	Crystal	Green	Pink
Bowl				
5" d, handle	45.00	24.00	27.50	24.00
8-3/4" d, cov	—	85.00	125.00	85.00
9" d, handle	—	24.00	30.00	24.00
10" d	—	50.00	70.00	50.00
Candlesticks, pr, 6-1/2" h	—	75.00	95.00	75.00
Candy jar, cov				
1 pound	—	100.00	115.00	110.00
1-1/2 pound	—	70.00	125.00	95.00
Cheese and cracker set	—	50.00	65.00	55.00
Coaster, 3-1/2" d	—	20.00	32.00	30.00
Cocktail	45.00	—	—	—
Console bowl, 10-3/4" d	—	50.00	75.00	60.00
Creamer, 3-1/2" h	60.00	30.00	32.00	30.00
Cup	24.00	10.00	12.00	12.00
Dresser set, two colognes, powder jar, tray	—	300.00	345.00	365.00
Goblet, 8 oz	—	40.00	45.00	40.00
Ice bucket, 6" h	—	50.00	80.00	65.00
Juice tumbler, 5 oz	—	32.00	37.50	35.00
Lamp, 8-1/2" h	—	90.00	115.00	110.00
Mayonnaise, 4-1/4"	—	60.00	90.00	60.00
Pilsner, 5-3/4" h, 11 oz	—	100.00	110.00	100.00
Pitcher, cov 7" h	300.00	175.00	250.00	195.00
Plate				
6" d	—	12.50	17.50	12.50
8" d	28.00	10.00	13.00	14.00
11-1/2" d, handle	40.00	20.00	24.00	20.00
Rose bowl	—	40.00	50.00	45.00
Saucer, 6" sq	11.00	4.00	5.00	5.50
Sherbet, 3-1/2" h	—	18.00	22.00	20.00
Sugar, 2-3/4" h	—	20.00	27.50	25.00
Tumbler, 8 oz, 4" h	—	32.00	55.00	35.00
Vase, 7" h, 4 styles	—	85.00	110.00	90.00
Whiskey, 2 oz, 2-1/4" h	—	48.00	—	48.00

Bubble

Bullseye, Provincial

Manufactured originally by Hocking Glass Co., and followed by Anchor Hocking Glass Corp., Lancaster, OH, from 1937 to 1965. Made in crystal (1937), forest green (1937), pink (limited), Royal Ruby (1963), and sapphire blue (1937).

Bubble blue grill plate, **$8.**

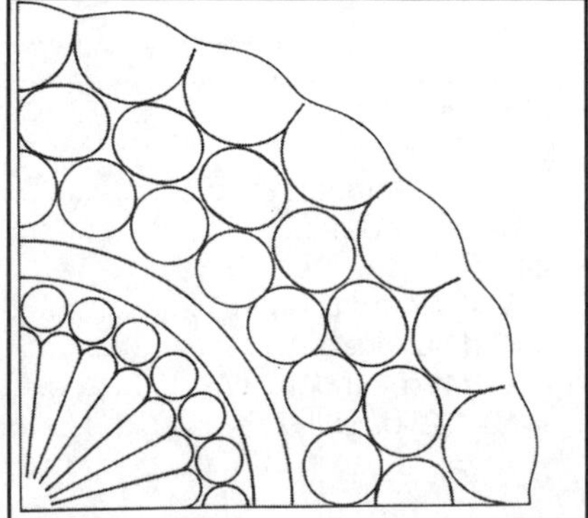

Bubble (cont.)

Item	Crystal	Forest Green	Royal Ruby	Sapphire Blue
Berry bowl, 4" d	5.00	—	6.50	18.00
Bowl, 9" d, fanged	8.00	—	—	335.00
Candlesticks, pr	24.00	40.00	—	—
Cereal bowl, 5-1/4" d	8.00	17.00	—	17.50
Cocktail, 4-1/2 oz	4.50	12.50	12.50	—
Creamer	7.50	15.00	18.00	45.00
Cup	4.50	8.75	12.50	15.00
Fruit bowl, 4-1/2" d	5.00	11.00	9.00	12.00
Goblet, 9 oz	7.50	15.00	15.00	—
Iced tea goblet, 14 oz	8.00	17.50	—	—
Iced tea tumbler, 12 oz	12.50	—	19.50	—
Juice goblet, 4 oz	3.00	8.00	—	—
Juice tumbler, 6 oz, ftd	4.00	12.00	10.00	—
Lemonade tumbler	16.00	—	16.00	—
Old fashioned tumbler	6.50	16.00	16.00	—
Pitcher, 64 oz, ice lip	60.00	—	65.00	—
Plate				
6-3/4" d, bread and butter	3.50	4.50	—	3.75
9-3/8" d, dinner	7.50	28.00	27.50	8.00
Platter, 12" l, oval	10.00	—	—	18.00
Sandwich plate, 9-1/2" d	7.50	25.00	22.00	8.00
Saucer	1.50	5.00	5.00	1.50
Sherbet, 6 oz	4.50	9.50	12.00	—
Soup bowl, flat, 7-3/4" d	10.00	—	—	16.00
Sugar	8.00	13.00	—	28.00
Tidbit, two-tier	—	—	35.00	—
Tumbler, 9 oz, water	6.00	—	16.00	—

Dogwood

Apple Blossom, Wild Rose

Manufactured by Mac Beth Evans Co., Charleroi, PA, from 1929 to 1932. Made in Cremax, crystal, green, Monax, pink, and yellow (rare). Crystal valued at 50 percent of green.

Dogwood pink sugar, **$24.50**; creamer, **$22.50**; and dinner plate, **$42**.

Item	Cremax or Monax	Green	Pink
Berry bowl, 8-1/2" d	40.00	100.00	65.00
Cake plate, 13" d	185.00	130.00	165.00
Cereal bowl, 5-1/2" d	6.00	32.00	35.00
Coaster, 3-1/4" d	—	—	500.00
Creamer, 2-1/2" h, thin	—	48.00	22.50
Cup			
thin	—	32.00	18.00
thick	36.00	40.00	25.00
Fruit bowl, 10-1/4" d	100.00	250.00	435.00
Pitcher, 8" h			
Am Sweetheart style	—	—	420.00
decorated	—	500.00	265.00
Plate			
6" d, bread & butter	22.00	10.00	9.50
8" d, luncheon	—	9.00	9.00
9-1/4" d, dinner	—	—	42.00
10-1/2" d, grill	—	22.00	25.00

Dogwood (cont.)

Item	Cremax or Monax	Green	Pink
Platter, 12" d, oval	—	—	500.00
Salver, 12"d	20.00	—	35.00
Saucer	20.00	10.00	8.50
Sherbet, low, ftd	—	95.00	40.00
Sugar, 3-1/4" h, thick, ftd	—	—	24.50
Tidbit, two-tier	—	—	90.00
Tumbler, 10 oz	—	85.00	53.00
Tumbler, molded band	—	—	25.00

Hobnail

Manufactured by Hocking Glass Co., Lancaster, OH, from 1934 to 1936. Made in crystal, crystal with red trim, and pink.

Hobnail pink sherbert, **$5.**

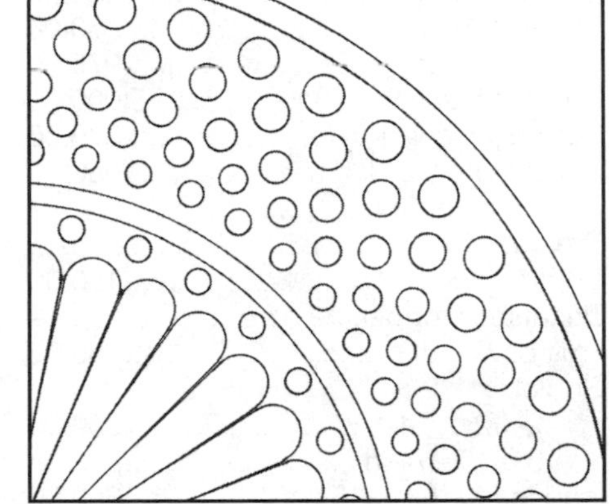

Item	Crystal	Crystal, red trim	Pink
Cereal bowl, 5-1/2" d	4.25	4.25	—
Cordial, 5 oz, ftd	6.00	6.00	—
Creamer, ftd	4.00	4.00	—
Cup	5.00	5.00	6.00
Decanter and stopper	27.50	27.50	—
Goblet, 10 oz	7.50	7.50	—
Iced tea goblet, 13 oz	8.50	8.50	—
Iced tea tumbler, 15 oz	8.50	8.50	—
Juice tumbler, 5 oz	4.00	4.00	—
Milk pitcher, 18 oz	22.00	22.00	—
Pitcher, 67 oz	25.00	25.00	—
Plate			
6" d, sherbet	2.50	2.50	3.50
8-1/2" d, luncheon	5.50	5.50	7.50
Salad bowl, 7" d	5.00	5.00	—
Saucer	2.00	2.00	3.00
Sherbet	4.00	4.00	5.00
Sugar, ftd	4.00	4.00	—
Tumbler, 9 oz	5.00	5.00	—
Whiskey, 1-1/2 oz	5.00	5.00	—
Wine, 3 oz, ftd	6.50	6.50	—

Mayfair

Open Rose

Manufactured by Hocking Glass Co., Lancaster, OH, from 1931 to 1937. Made in crystal (limited production), green, ice blue, pink, and yellow.

Reproductions: † This pattern has been plagued with reproductions since 1977. Items reproduced include cookie jars, salt and pepper shakers, juice pitchers and whiskey glasses. Reproductions are found in amethyst, blue, cobalt blue, green, pink, and red.

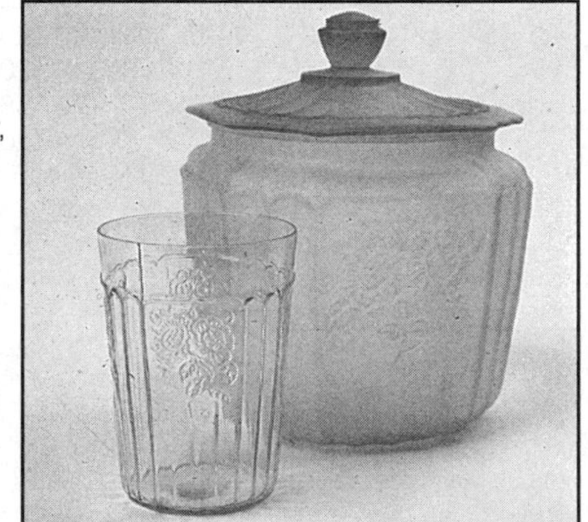

Mayfair Open Rose pink tumbler, **$65** and pink satin-finish covered cookie jar, **$37**.

Mayfair (cont.)

Item	Green	Ice Blue	Pink	Pink Satin	Yellow
Bowl, 11-3/4" l, flat	35.00	75.00	65.00	70.00	195.00
Butter dish, cov	1,295.00	325.00	80.00	95.00	1,295.00
Cake plate					
10" d, ftd	115.00	75.00	40.00	45.00	—
12" d, handles	40.00	70.00	48.00	50.00	—
Candy dish					
cov	575.00	325.00	70.00	85.00	475.00
9" l, divided	155.00	60.00	—	—	150.00
Celery dish, 10" l, undivided	115.00	80.00	45.00	50.00	115.00
Cereal bowl, 5-1/2" d	24.00	48.00	30.00	35.00	75.00
Claret, 4-1/2 oz	950.00	—	1,150.00	—	—
Cocktail, 3 oz, 4" h	975.00	—	75.00	—	—
Console bowl, 9" d, 3 legs	5,000.00	—	5,000.00	—	—
Cookie jar, cov †	575.00	295.00	47.00	37.00	860.00
Cordial, 1 oz, 3-3/4" h	950.00	—	1,100.00	—	—
Cream soup, 5" d	—	—	65.00	68.00	—
Creamer, ftd			35.00	30.00	
Cup	150.00	55.00	24.00	27.50	150.00
Decanter, stopper, 32 oz	—	—	225.00	—	—
Fruit bowl, 12" d	50.00	100.00	65.00	75.00	215.00
Goblet					
2-1/2 oz, 4-1/8"	950.00	—	950.00	—	—
9 oz, 7-1/4" h	—	225.00	250.00	—	—
Iced tea tumbler, 15 oz	250.00	285.00	65.00	65.00	—
Juice pitcher, 6" h †	525.00	150.00	70.00	65.00	525.00
Juice tumbler, 5 oz	—	120.00	45.00	—	—
Pitcher, 60 oz	475.00	175.00	95.00	100.00	425.00
Plate					
5-3/4" d	90.00	25.00	15.00	15.00	90.00
6-1/2" d, indent	115.00	35.00	30.00	35.00	—
6-1/2" d, sherbet	—	24.00	14.50	—	—
8-1/2" d, luncheon	85.00	55.00	40.00	35.00	80.00
9-1/2" d, dinner	150.00	90.00	65.00	62.00	150.00
11-1/2" d, grill	—	—	—	—	100.00
Platter, 12" l, oval	175.00	60.00	40.00	35.00	115.00
Relish, 8-3/8" d					
undivided	275.00	—	200.00	—	275.00
four parts	160.00	65.00	37.50	37.50	160.00
Salt and pepper shakers, pr†	1,000.00	295.00	65.00	70.00	800.00
Sandwich server	48.00	85.00	65.00	50.00	130.00
Saucer	90.00	30.00	45.00	35.00	140.00
Sherbet, 4-3/4"	150.00	75.00	75.00	75.00	150.00
Sugar, ftd	195.00	85.00	35.00	40.00	185.00
Sweet pea vase	285.00	125.00	140.00	145.00	—
Tumbler, 10 oz	—	145.00	65.00	—	185.00
Vegetable bowl					
7" d	33.00	75.00	65.00	70.00	195.00
9-1/2" l	110.00	70.00	40.00	30.00	125.00
10" d cov	—	120.00	120.00	120.00	900.00
10" d open	—	75.00	20.00	19.00	200.00
Whiskey, 1-1/2 oz †	—	—	58.00	—	—
Wine, 3 oz, 4-1/2" h	450.00	—	120.00	—	—

Newport

Hairpin

Manufactured by Hazel Atlas Glass Co., Clarksburg, WV, and Zanesville, OH, from 1936 to the early 1950s. Made in amethyst, cobalt blue, pink (from 1936 to 1940), Platonite white and fired-on colors, from the 1940s to early 1950s.

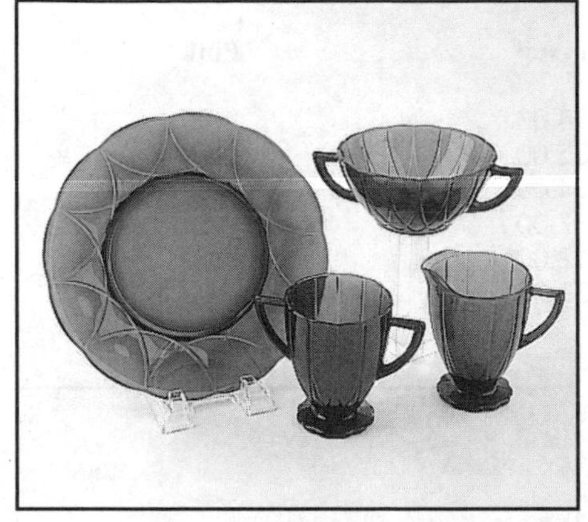

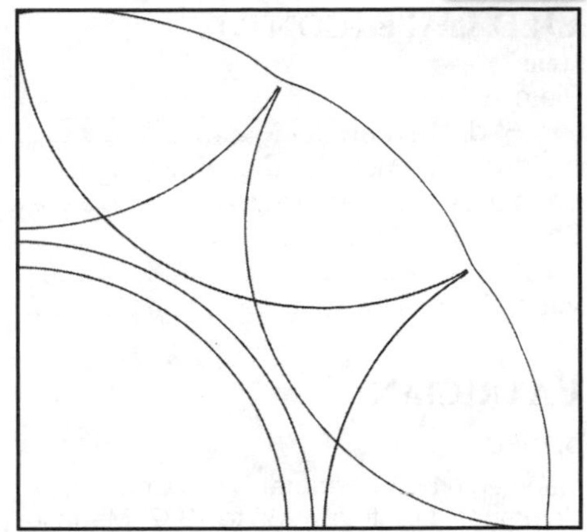

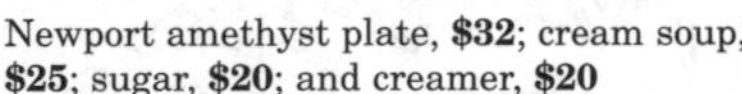

Newport amethyst plate, **$32**; cream soup, **$25**; sugar, **$20**; and creamer, **$20**

Item	Amethyst	Cobalt Blue	Fired-On Color	Pink	Platonite
Berry bowl, 8-1/4" d	50.00	50.00	16.00	25.00	10.00
Cereal bowl, 5-1/4" d	42.00	42.00	—	20.00	—
Cream soup, 4-3/4" d	25.00	25.00	10.00	17.50	8.50
Creamer	20.00	22.00	8.50	10.00	3.00
Cup	12.00	15.00	9.00	6.00	4.50
Plate					
6" d, sherbet	7.50	10.00	5.00	3.50	2.00
8-1/2" d, luncheon	15.00	22.00	9.00	8.00	4.50
8-13/16" d, dinner	32.00	35.00	15.00	15.00	12.00
Platter, 11-3/4" l, oval	42.00	48.00	18.00	20.00	12.00
Salt and pepper shakers, pr	60.00	65.00	32.00	30.00	18.00
Sandwich plate, 11-1/2" d	48.00	50.00	15.00	24.00	10.00
Saucer	5.25	6.00	3.00	2.50	2.00
Sherbet	15.00	18.50	10.00	8.00	4.00
Sugar	20.00	22.00	9.50	10.00	5.00
Tumbler, 9 oz, 4-1/2" h	40.00	48.00	15.00	20.00	—

Old Café

Manufactured by Hocking Glass Co., Lancaster, OH, from 1936 to 1940. Made in crystal, pink, and royal ruby.

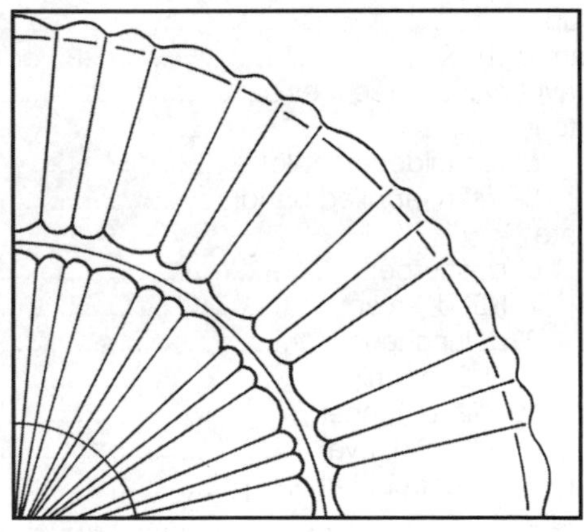

Old Café cereal bowl, ruby, **$12**.

Item	Crystal	Pink	Royal Ruby
Berry bowl, 3-3/4" d	4.50	5.00	6.00
Bowl			
5" d	5.00	6.00	—
9" d, closed handles	10.00	10.00	15.00
Candy dish, 8" d, low	8.00	12.00	16.00
Candy jar, crystal, ruby lid	—	—	20.00
Cereal bowl, 5-1/2" d	9.00	9.00	12.00
Cup	6.00	6.00	10.00
Juice tumbler, 3" h	10.00	10.00	12.00
Lamp	24.00	24.00	35.00
Olive dish, 6" l, oblong	7.50	8.50	—
Pitcher			
36 oz, 6" h	85.00	85.00	—
80 oz	120.00	120.00	—

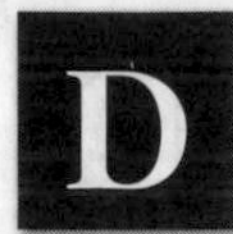

OLD CAFÉ (CONT.)

Item	Crystal	Pink	Royal Ruby
Plate			
6" d, sherbet	4.00	4.00	—
10" d, dinner	35.00	35.00	—
Saucer	4.00	4.00	—
Sherbet, low, ftd	7.00	7.00	12.00
Tumbler, 4" h	12.00	12.00	18.00
Vase, 7-1/4" h	35.00	40.00	45.00

PATRICIAN

Spoke

Manufactured by Federal Glass Co., Columbus, OH, from 1933 to 1937. Made in amber (also called Golden Glo), crystal, green, and pink.

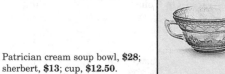

Patrician cream soup bowl, **$28**; sherbert, **$13**; cup, **$12.50**.

Item	Amber	Crystal	Green	Pink
Berry bowl, 8-1/2" d	50.00	15.00	37.50	35.00
Butter dish, cov	95.00	100.00	215.00	225.00
Cereal bowl, 6" d	32.00	27.50	27.50	25.00
Cookie jar, cov	90.00	80.00	500.00	—
Cream soup, 4-3/4" d	28.00	25.00	24.50	22.00
Creamer, ftd	12.50	9.00	12.50	12.50
Cup	12.50	10.00	12.50	12.50
Jam dish	30.00	25.00	35.00	30.00
Mayonnaise, three toes	—	—	—	165.00
Pitcher				
8" h, molded handle	120.00	125.00	125.00	115.00
8-1/4" h, applied handle	150.00	140.00	150.00	145.00
Plate				
6" d, sherbet	10.00	8.50	10.00	10.00
7-1/2" d, salad	17.50	15.00	12.50	15.00
9" d, luncheon	14.00	12.50	12.00	12.50
10-1/2" d, grill	15.00	13.50	20.00	20.00
10-1/2" d, dinner	10.00	12.75	32.00	36.00
Platter, 11-1/2" l, oval	32.50	30.00	30.00	28.00
Salt and pepper shakers, pr	65.00	65.00	65.00	85.00
Saucer	10.00	9.25	9.50	9.50
Sherbet	13.00	10.00	14.00	16.00
Sugar	12.50	9.00	12.50	12.50
Sugar lid	55.00	50.00	75.00	60.00
Tumbler				
5 oz	30.00	28.50	30.00	32.00
8 oz, ftd	50.00	42.00	50.00	—
12 oz	45.00	—	—	—
Vegetable bowl, 10" l, oval	38.00	30.00	38.50	30.00

Queen Mary

Prismatic Line, Vertical Ribbed

Manufactured by Hocking Glass Co., Lancaster, OH, from 1936 to 1948. Made in crystal, pink, and royal ruby.

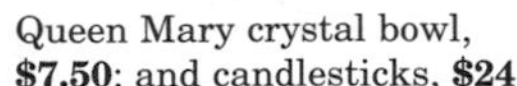
Queen Mary crystal bowl, **$7.50**; and candlesticks, **$24**.

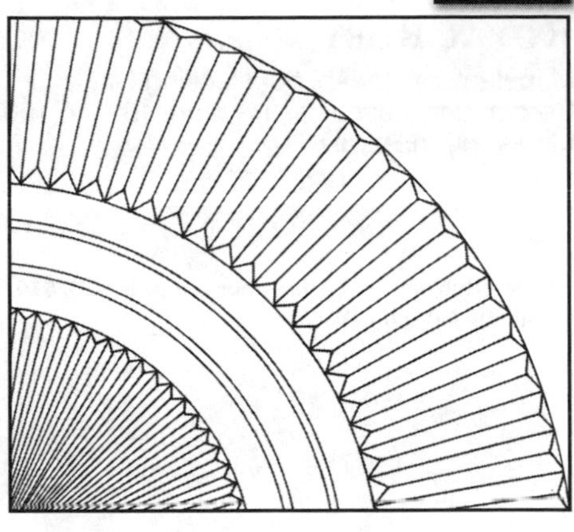

Item	Crystal	Pink	Royal Ruby
Ashtray			
3-3/4" l, oval	4.00	5.50	5.00
3-1/2" d, round	4.00	—	—
Berry bowl, 5" d	5.00	10.00	—
Bowl			
4" d, one handle	4.00	12.50	—
5-1/2" d, two handles	6.00	15.00	—
7" d	7.50	35.00	—
Butter dish, cov	42.00	125.00	—
Candlesticks, pr, two lite, 4-1/2" h	24.00	—	70.00
Candy dish, cov	30.00	42.00	—
Celery tray, 5" x 10"	10.00	24.00	—
Cereal bowl, 6" d	8.00	24.00	—
Cigarette jar, 2" x 3" oval	6.50	7.50	—
Coaster, 3-1/2" d	4.00	5.00	—
Coaster/ashtray, 4-1/4" sq	4.00	6.00	—
Comport, 5-3/4"	9.00	14.00	—
Creamer			
ftd	6.00	40.00	—
oval	6.00	12.00	—
Cup			
large	6.50	10.00	—
small	8.50	12.50	—
Juice tumbler, 5 oz, 3-1/2" h	9.50	15.00	—
Pickle dish, 5" x 10"	10.00	24.00	—
Plate			
6" d, sherbet	4.00	5.00	—
6-1/2" d, bread and butter	6.00	—	—
8-1/4" d, salad	6.00	—	—
9-1/2" d, dinner	15.00	60.00	—
Preserve, cov	30.00	125.00	—
Relish			
Clover-shape	15.00	17.50	—
12" d, three part	10.00	15.00	—
14" d, four part	15.00	17.50	—
Salt and pepper shakers, pr	25.00	—	—
Sandwich plate, 12" d	20.00	17.50	—
Saucer	2.00	5.00	—
Serving tray, 14" d	15.00	9.00	—
Sherbet, ftd	6.50	10.00	—
Sugar			
ftd	—	40.00	—
oval	6.00	12.00	—
Tumbler			
9 oz, 4" h	6.00	19.50	—
10 oz, 5" h, ftd	35.00	70.00	—

Royal Ruby

Manufactured by Anchor Hocking Glass Corporation, Lancaster, PA, from 1938 to 1967. Made only in Royal Ruby.

Royal Ruby sugar, **$8**; creamer (on pedestal), **$10**; cup and saucer, **$12.50**.

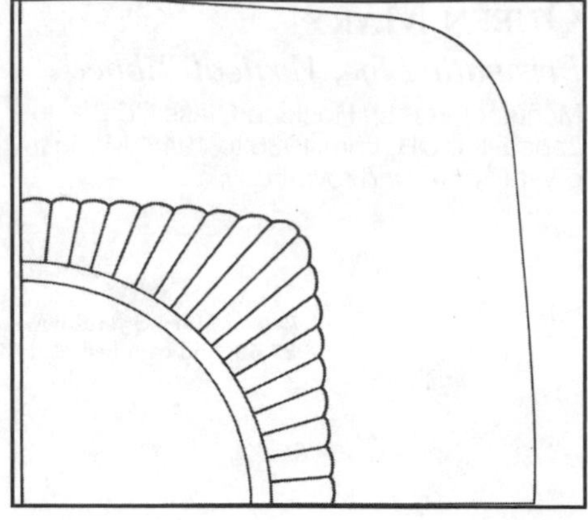

Item	Royal Ruby
Apothecary jar, 8-1/2" h	22.00
Ashtray	
4-1/2", leaf	5.00
5-7/8", sq	9.00
7-3/4"	32.00
Beer bottle	
7 oz	30.00
16 oz	35.00
32 oz	40.00
Berry	
4-5/8" d, sq	9.50
8-1/2" d, round	25.00
Bonbon, 6-1/2" d	20.00
Bowl	
7-3/8" w, sq	18.50
12" l, oval, Rachael	50.00
Cereal bowl, 5-1/4" d	12.00
Cigarette box	90.00
Cocktail	
3-1/2 oz, Boopie	8.50
3-1/2 oz, tumbler	10.00
Cordial, ftd	15.00
Creamer	
flat	10.00
ftd	10.00
Cup	
round	6.00
square	7.50
Dessert bowl, 4-3/4" w, sq	9.00
Fruit bowl, 4-1/4" d	6.50
Goblet	
9-1/2 oz	14.00
ball stem	12.00
Ice bucket	55.00
Iced tea goblet, 14 oz, Boopie	20.00
Iced tea tumbler, 13 oz, 6" h, ftd	10.00
Ivy ball, 4" h, Wilson	12.00
Juice tumbler	
4 oz	7.00
5 oz, flat or ftd	12.00
Juice pitcher	39.00
Lamp	35.00
Marmalade, ruby top, crystal base	22.00
Pitcher	
3 qt, tilted	45.00
3 qt, upright	38.00
42 oz, tilted	35.00
42 oz, upright	40.00
Pitcher, 86 oz, 8-1/2"	35.00
Plate	
6-1/4" d, sherbet	4.50
7" d, salad	5.50
8-3/8" w, sq, luncheon	12.00
9-1/8" d, dinner	14.00
13-3/4" d	35.00
Popcorn bowl	
5-1/4" d	12.50
10" d, deep	40.00
Puff box, crystal base, ruby lid	28.00
Punch bowl and stand	75.00
Punch set, 14 pieces	200.00
Punch cup	3.50
Relish, 3-3/4" x 8-3/4", tab handle	16.00
Salad bowl, 8-1/2" d	19.00
Saucer	
5-3/8" w, sq	4.00
round	4.00
Set, 50 pcs, orig labels, orig box	350.00
Sherbet	
6-1/2 oz, stemmed	7.50
6 oz, Boopie	8.50
Shot glass	4.50
Soup bowl, 7-1/2" d	15.00
Sugar	
flat	8.00
footed	8.00
Sugar lid, notched	11.00
Tray, center handle, ruffled	16.50
Tumbler	
5 oz, 3-1/2" h	6.00
9 oz, Windsor	8.50
10 oz, 5" h, ftd	7.00
14 oz, 5" h	9.00
15 oz, long boy	15.00
Vase	
3-3/4" h, Roosevelt	7.50
4" h, Wilson, fancy edge	12.00
6-3/8" h, Harding	15.00
6-5/8" h, Coolidge	20.00
9" h, Hoover, plain	20.00
9" h, Hoover, white birds on branch dec	25.00
10" h, fluted, star base	35.00
10" h, ftd, Rachael	50.00
Vegetable bowl, 8" l, oval	45.00
Wine, 2-1/2 oz, ftd	12.50

Swirl

Petal Swirl

Manufactured by Jeannette Glass Co., Jeannette, PA, from 1937 to 1938. Made in amber, Delphite, ice blue, pink, and Ultramarine. Production was limited in amber and ice blue.

Swirl ultramarine sugar and creamer, **$18** each

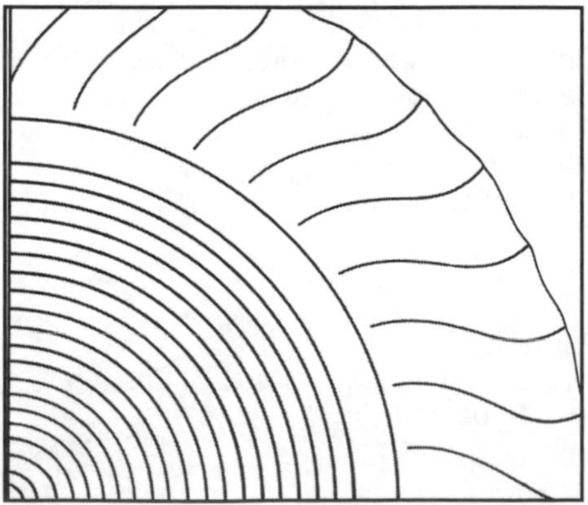

Swirl (cont.)

Item	Delphite	Pink	Ultramarine
Berry bowl	—	—	18.00
Bowl, 10" d, ftd, closed handles	—	25.00	30.00
Butter dish, cov	—	175.00	245.00
Candleholders, pr			
2-lite	—	40.00	45.00
1-lite	115.00	—	—
Candy dish			
cov	—	130.00	150.00
open, three legs	—	20.00	29.50
Cereal bowl, 5-1/4" d	14.00	10.00	15.00
Coaster, 1" x 3-1/4"	—	15.00	14.00
Console bwl, 10-1/2" d, ftd	—	20.00	35.00
Creamer	12.00	9.50	18.00
Cup and saucer	17.50	14.00	22.50
Plate			
6-1/2" d, sherbet	6.50	5.00	8.00
7-1/4" d, luncheon	—	6.50	12.00
8" d, salad	9.00	8.50	12.00
9-1/4" d, dinner	12.00	13.00	22.50
10-1/2" d, dinner	18.00	—	30.00
Platter, 12" l, oval	35.00	—	—
Salad bowl			
9" d	30.00	18.00	35.00
9" d, rimmed	—	20.00	30.00
Salt and pepper shakers, pr	—	—	50.00
Sandwich plate, 12-1/2" d	—	20.00	27.50
Sherbet, low, ftd	—	13.00	23.00
Soup, tab handles, lug	—	25.00	35.00
Sugar, ftd	—	12.00	18.00
Tray, 10-1/2" l, two handles	25.00	—	—
Tumbler			
9 oz, 4" h	—	18.00	42.00
13 oz, 5-1/8" h	—	45.00	90.00
Vase			
6-1/2" h, ftd, ruffled	—	22.00	—
8-1/2" h, ftd	—	—	36.00

Windsor

Windsor Diamond

Manufactured by Jeannette Glass Co., Jeannette, PA, from 1936 to 1946. Made in crystal, green, and pink with limited production in amberina red, Delphite and ice blue.

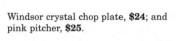

Windsor crystal chop plate, **$24**; and pink pitcher, **$25**.

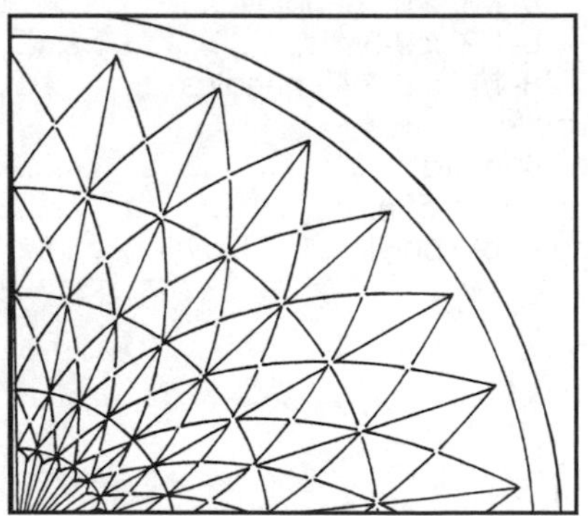

Item	Crystal	Green	Pink
Ashtray, 5-3/4" d	15.00	45.00	45.00
Berry bowl, 8-1/2" d	7.50	18.50	22.00
Bowl			
5" l	10.00	—	25.00
7" x 11-3/4", boat shape	18.00	35.00	32.00
7-1/2" d, three legs	8.00	—	24.00
8" d, two handles	9.00	24.00	20.00
8" l, pointed edge	10.00	—	48.00
10-1/2" l, pointed edge	25.00	—	32.00

Windsor (cont.)

Item	Crystal	Green	Pink
Butter dish, cov	27.50	95.00	60.00
Cake plate, 10-3/4" d, ftd	12.00	22.00	20.00
Candlesticks, pr, 3" h	22.00	—	85.00
Candy jar, cov	18.00	—	—
Cereal bowl, 5-3/8" d	10.00	32.50	25.00
Chop plate, 13-5/8" d	24.00	42.00	50.00
Coaster, 3-1/4" d	8.50	18.00	25.00
Comport	9.00	—	—
Cream soup, 5" d	6.00	30.00	25.00
Creamer	5.00	15.00	20.00
Creamer, holiday shape	7.50	—	—
Cup	7.00	22.00	12.00
Fruit console, 12-1/2" d	45.00	—	115.00
Pitcher			
16 oz, 4-1/2" h	25.00	—	115.00
52 oz, 6-3/4" h	20.00	55.00	35.00
Plate			
6" d, sherbet	3.75	8.00	5.00
7" d, salad	4.50	20.00	18.00
9" d, dinner	9.00	25.00	25.00
Platter, 11-1/2" l, oval	7.00	25.00	25.00
Powder jar	15.00	—	55.00
Relish platter, 11-1/2" l, divided	10.00	—	200.00
Salad bowl, 10-1/2" d	12.00	—	—
Salt and pepper shakers, pr	20.00	48.00	42.00
Sandwich plate			
closed handles	10.00	—	24.00
open handles	12.50	18.00	20.00
Saucer	2.50	5.00	4.50
Sherbet, ftd	3.50	15.00	13.00
Sugar			
cov	10.00	40.00	30.00
cov, holiday shape	12.00	—	100.00
Tray			
4" sq	5.00	12.00	10.00
4" sq, handles	6.00	—	40.00
4-1/8" x 9"	5.00	16.00	10.00
4-1/8" x 9", handles	9.00	—	50.00
8-1/2" x 9-3/4"	7.00	35.00	25.00
8-1/2" x 9-3/4", handles	14.00	45.00	85.00
Tumbler			
4" h, ftd	7.00	—	—
12 oz, 5" h	11.00	55.00	32.50
Vegetable bowl, 9-1/2" l, oval	7.50	29.00	25.00

Disneyana

History: Walt Disney and the creations of the famous Disney Studios hold a place of fondness and enchantment in the hearts of people throughout the world. The 1928 release of "Steamboat Willie," featuring Mickey Mouse, heralded an entertainment empire.

Walt and his brother, Roy, were shrewd businessmen. From the beginning, they licensed the reproduction of Disney characters on products ranging from wristwatches to clothing.

In 1984, Donald Duck celebrated his 50th birthday, and collectors took a renewed interest in material related to him.

Additional Listings: See *Warman's Americana & Collectibles* for more examples.

Adviser: Theodore L. Hake.

Book, *The Art of Walt Disney,* Christopher Finch, copyright Walt Disney Productions, 1973, white cover, black, red, and yellow Mickey on cover, **$20**.

Bambi

Book, *Bambi,* 7" x 8-1/4", hardcover, Grosset & Dunlap, copyright 1942 .... **32.00**

Charm bracelet, 6" l gold luster metal link bracelet, five figural gold luster charms of red/brown Bambi and Faline, blue Thumper, black and white Flower, yellow/green Friend Owl, 1950s **20.00**

Studio fan card, 7" x 9", stiff buff paper, brown design, Walt Disney facsimile signature, small copyright, 1940s **35.00**

Cinderella

Costume, 8-1/4" x 11" x 2-3/4" orig box, two pcs, Ben Copper, copyright Walt Disney Productions, late 1960s, box illus include Spider-Man, Hulk, Thor, and Wonder Woman, wear to box, costume bright **30.00**

Soaky, 10-1/2" h, soft plastic body, hard plastic head, blue dress, movable arms **20.00**

Disneyland

Book, *A Visit to Disneyland,* Whitman Big Tell-A-Tale, copyright 1965, 6" x 8-1/2", 28 pgs, color photos **20.00**

Game, Disneyland Riverboat Game, 8" x 16" x 1-3/4" deep box, Parker Bros, copyright 1960, 14-3/4" sq board, 6-3/4" full-color cardboard movable tack, four different colored metal boat playing pcs **50.00**

Keychain, 1-1/4" d 3/8" thick transparent plastic disc embedded with Mickey head and black text, brass chain, c1960 .... **22.00**

Disney World

Convention badge, 4" d, black printing, gold background, "110 Club '79/Disney World" **10.00**

Flicker, I Like Walt Disney World, red metal case, text on reverse including "Vari-Vue" and Walt Disney World logo, black, white, and red image of Mickey wearing blue bow tie, changes to slogan in white on red background **15.00**

Christmas card, 1943, white card stock, illustration of newborn duck holding card that reads "1944," interior with monthly calendar for 1944 surrounded by choice color illustrations of Disney characters depicting events and holidays, including Mickey, Minnie, Pluto, Goofy, Three Pigs, Donald and his nephews, Joe Carioca and Panchito, small text "A Hallmark Card" on back, 7-3/4" x 10", 3" l vertical crease line, **$95**. Photo courtesy of Hake's Americana & Collectibles.

Donald Duck

Book, *Donald's Penguin,* 8-1/2" x 9-1/2", hard cover, Garden City Publishing, copyright 1940, 24 pgs **70.00**

Button, 13/16", Birthday Club, black and white, inscribed "Member," issued by "Astor Theater, Burwood," (Australia), late 1930s or early 1940s **115.00**

Calendar, 8" x 11" thin cardboard, full-color center scene titled "Bedtime," Donald making sure nephews are getting ready for bed, blue and white border with Mickey, Minnie, Pluto, Dumbo, Timothy, Bambi, and Thumper with stars, American Bedding Co., Portland, OR, only Dec calendar remains **145.00**

Egg cup, 2-1/4" x 4" x 3-1/2" h, color image of Donald pushing wheelbarrow, brown/iridescent tan, unmarked, 1950s **145.00**

Little Golden Book, *Donald Duck in Disneyland,* Golden Press, copyright 1960, 4th printing, 24 pgs **18.00**

Pencil sharpener, 1-11/16", figural, dark red catalin, full-color decal on front **45.00**

Dumbo

Figure, 2" x 2-1/2" x 3-1/2" h, painted and glazed ceramic of newborn Dumbo, red, blue, and silver foil stick on back, Disney copyright and "Modern Ceramic Products Pty Ltd. Sidney," 1940s **185.00**

Premium button, 1-1/4", black, white, bright red, and gray, issued by D-X gasoline, 1941 .... **24.00**

Toothbrush holder, 3-1/2" x 5-1/2" x 3-3/4", painted ceramic, matte finish, three openings for toothbrushes, incised 1942 copyright **150.00**

Serigraph, Cinderella and Prince Charming, color laser background of castle, acetate sheet with 8" x 8" image, blue 16" x 20" mat, attached certificate of authenticity noting series of 9500, Disney Co. seal on one corner of serigraph, bottom margin also signed in black by Marc Davis, **$150**. Photo courtesy of Hake's Americana & Collectibles.

Fantasia

Plate, 9-1/2" d, Flower Ballet, Vernon Kilns, dark maroon, yellow, green, and blue, copyright 1940 .... **75.00**

Souvenir movie program, 9-1/2" x 12-1/2", soft cover, from orig 1940 release, Western Printing Co., black and white photos of Walt Disney and other contributors, full-color plates of scenes from film **50.00**

Goofy

Bank, 5" x 9" x 10-1/2" h, molded hard vinyl head, Play Pal Plastics, Inc., copyright 1971, red shirt collar, bright yellow hat, trap missing **25.00**

Blotter, 4" x 7", Sunoco Oil, Goofy and angry polar bear, broken-down car, copyright 1939, unused **40.00**

Cel, 10-1/2" x 12-1/2" acetate sheet, 4" x 5-1/2" cel image of Sport Goofy, color laser background of stadium, #A-76 from numbered sequence, from 1980s Disney TV show **150.00**

Figure, 2-1/2" h, Hagen-Renaker, painted and glazed ceramic, green shirt and hat, tan vest, blue pants, brown shoes, foil sticker missing, 1950s.................................... **135.00**

Mickey Mouse

Big little book, *Mickey Mouse Sails for Treasure Island,* Whitman, 1935, soft cover premium for Kolynos Dental Cream **40.00**

Book

Mickey Mouse Waddle, 7-3/4" x 10-1/4", hard cover, Blue Ribbon Books, copyright 1934, perforated Waddle pages removed **175.00**

The Adventures of Mickey Mouse, 5-1/2" x 7-3/4", hard cover, 32 pgs, David McCay Co., copyright 1931 .... **85.00**

Candle night light holder, 2-1/2" x 5-1/2" x 4-1/2", ceramic, figural Mickey asleep in chair, 1-1/2" recessed area on front to hold candle, unmarked Crown Devon, 1930s............ **215.00**

Composition book, 6-3/4" x 8-1/4", Mickey Mouse Composition Book, by Powers Paper Co., brown, black and red illus of Mickey and Minnie walking, carrying school books, multiplication tables on back, some penciled school work on pages, dated 1934 .... **60.00**

Doll, 10-1/2" h, Knickerbocker, stuffed cloth, polished cotton face with printed details, separate fabric pants, felt ears, hands, and shoes **410.00**

Magazine, *Mickey Mouse Magazine,* Vol 1, #7, April, 1937, 36 pgs, newsprint, Mickey and W. C. Fields dot-to-dot puzzle neatly done in pencil, near mint................... **475.00**

Marionette, painted composition head, 3-1/2" x 5" x 7" animal fur-covered body, wood pegs hands and feet, 7-1/2" l tail, 1930s **165.00**

Pen clip, 1-1/4" h, silvered metal, 9/16" domed metal attachment with colorful Mickey, tiny copyright initials below WDP, Bastian, early 1950s **35.00**

Pin, 1", diecut brass, enamel, in boxing gloves, 1940s............. **85.00**

Sand pail, 5-3/4" h, 5-3/4" d at top, tin litho, attached carrying handle, Ohio Art, copyright 1938, golf theme, wrap-around illus with Mickey, Donald, Goofy, and black cat, play wear..................................... **300.00**

Watch fob, 1-1/8", silvered brass, loop at top, black accents, reverse "Ingersoll Mickey Mouse Watches & Clocks Copyright Walt Disney," English, 1930s...................... **265.00**

Wristwatch, Ingersoll, 1-1/4" d chromed metal case, dial with large black, white, and yellow Mickey, hands point to numerals, second wheel with three tiny Mickey images, vintage replacement strap, 1933, working order and clean dial **325.00**

Mickey Mouse Club

Button, 1" d, dark blue lettering, "New Lyric Theater Mickey Mouse Club" **145.00**

Scrapbook, 10-3/4" x 14-3/4", Whitman, copyright 1957, but actually 1970s printing, 64 unused pgs, full-color cover of Mouseketeers with art supplies **20.00**

Child's book, *Donald's Penguin,* hardcover, Garden City Publishing Co. Inc., copyright 1940, based on 1939 short of same name, 24 pages, art on every page, either black and white illustrations or choice full-color film scenes, end papers have same design in black and white/green featuring illustration of Donald and penguin, color cover features different penguin illus on front and back, 8-1/2" x 9-1/2", some penciling to inside front cover, moderate scattered wear, surface paper rubs along all edges, front and back covers have small surface paper rubs and scratches, **$65**. Photo courtesy of Hake's Americana & Collectibles.

Minnie Mouse

Child's feeding dish, divided, 8" d, 1-3/4" h, color images of Minnie, Mickey, and Salem China Co., 1930s **125.00**

Pull toy, 3-1/4" h, celluloid figure attached to 4" long freewheeling wood scooter, 19" l string, wood knob on end, marked "Made in Japan," small copyright symbol, 1930s.................................. **320.00**

Salt and pepper shakers, 2" x 2" x 5-1/4" h, painted and glazed ceramic, 1950s, Dan Brechner Exclusive foil sticker, ink stamp copyright, WD-52, standing on top of wood crates which house noisemakers, names on front of base, orig stoppers **75.00**

Teapot, 3-1/2" x 6" x 3-1/2" h, glazed yellow ceramic, full-color image of Minnie, Mickey, and Donald hand-in-hand, text "Ring-A-Ring of Roses," names in blue, roses, unmarked, possibly Wade, 1930s............ **90.00**

Pinocchio

Book, *Pinocchio Linen-Like, #1061,* Whitman, copyright 1940, 7" x 7-3/4", 12 pgs, full-color art on each page **45.00**

Candy bar wrapper, 3-1/4" x 8-1/4", Schutter Candy Co., copyright 1940, black, white, yellow, and red image of Jiminy and premium "Official Conscience Medal"................. **50.00**

Figure, 4-3/4" h, wood, black, white, red, blue, and yellow, separate light blue wood bail hands attached by elastic string, paper label "Pinocchio," copyright, Geo Borgfeldt Corp., 1940............. **95.00**

Game, 10" x 15" x 1-3/4" h, Pinocchio Race Game, Chad Valley, c1940, scene of Pinocchio and Jiminy Cricket encountering Foulfellow and Gideon leaving Geppetto's workshop on box lid, some fading to box, 14-1/2" sq board, game pcs....... **140.00**

Planter, 3" x 5-1/2" x 4-1/2", painted and glazed ceramic, Figaro dipping paw into aquarium planter, raised image of fish on front, c1940 .... **35.00**

Soaky, 9-3/4" h, soft plastic body, hard plastic head, Pinocchio sitting on top of tree stump, holding school slate, 1960s **20.00**

Whitman Big Little Book #717, copyright 1933, first Mickey BLB, original cover version, Mickey on front cover, Walt Disney signature at lower left, illustration on back cover of Mickey and Minnie embossed racing repeated on spine, Floyd Gottfredson story and art, name and address penciled on inside front cover, inked on inside back cover, minor tears, some spine edge repairs with tiny color touchups, **$420**. Photo courtesy of Hake's Americana & Collectibles.

Pluto

Drinking glass, 4-3/4" h, glass, small W.D. Ent. Copyright, Pluto with eyes closed, mouth wide open belting out song, music stand in front of him, music notes scattered around front and back **320.00**

Pin, 1-1/4", brass, rich yellow enamel, black, white, and red accents, WD copyright, 1930s **85.00**

Push puppet, 2-1/2" h hard plastic, Kohner, c1960, green base, foil sticker with orange text **25.00**

Sleeping Beauty

Book, *Sleeping Beauty,* 7-1/2" x 8-1/4", Whitman, Story Hour series, copyright 1959, 32 pgs **18.00**

Box proof, 11-1/4" x 16-1/4", "Sleeping Beauty Colorforms Dress Designer Kit," full-color glossy paper, copyright 1959 .... **65.00**

Figure, 2-3/8" h, Queen, Hagen-Renaker, painted and glazed ceramic, foil sticker, 1950s.... **250.00**

Pencil drawing, Sneezy from Snow White, #157 of numbered sequence, 2-1/2" x 4-3/4" image in lead pencil, full figure image of him about to sneeze on 10" x 12" sheet of animation paper, 1937, **$100.** Photo courtesy of Hake's Americana & Collectibles.

Snow White

Birthday card, 4-1/4" x 5-1/2", White & Wyckoff, copyright 1938, black, white, red, blue, and green design, front with Doc and Sleepy in front of doorway, opens to Snow White dancing with Doc as others play instruments **30.00**

Book, *Edgar Bergen's Charlie McCarthy Meets Walt Disney's Snow White,* 9-1/2" x 11-1/2", Whitman Publishing, soft cover, copyright 1938, 24 pgs **110.00**

Comic book, 5" x 7", 16 pgs, full color, copyright 1958 by Western Printing Co., issued as premium by Reynolds Wrap **22.00**

Pencil sharpener, 1-11/16", figural, dark red catalin, full-color decal on front **65.00**

Pitcher, 3-3/4" h, Sneezy, painted and glazed, relief and dimensional shape, marked "Wadeheath by Permission Walt Disney England," c1938 .... **175.00**

Song folio, *Snow White and the Seven Dwarfs,* 9" x 12", 52 pgs, Bourne Inc. Music Publishers, copyright 1938, 1950s printing **25.00**

Umbrella, 19" l, 24" d open, red, white, and blue wood handle and shaft, metal frame, white silk like synthetic fabric cover, full color images of Snow White and the Seven Dwarfs, names in black letters, c1938, copyright **85.00**

Three Little Pigs

Game board, 16-3/4" sq board, Marks Brothers Co., c1934, ominous image of Wolf towering over dancing Fiddler and Fifer Pigs, Practical Pig putting fishing touches on brick house **40.00**

Plate, 7-1/2" d, white china, full-color center scene of Three Pigs, Little Red Riding Hood, and Grandmother knitting in rocking chair, blue rim trim, marked "Salem China Co./ Patriot China," 1930s **75.00**

Postcard set, set of 12 numbered 3-1/2" x 5-1/5" cards, marked "Paris," French text, backs also marked "Disney," each with full color art telling story, sent by soldier to daughter in US, each with typed or handwritten note, sent on consecutive days in April, 1945 .... **150.00**

Match covers, each flattened, matches neatly removed, red, white, and blue, Pepsi logo plus insignia design on front of each, reverse includes same Pepsi text on each in red, insignia designs feature animal characters as well as Disney characters including Dumbo, Donald Duck, Baby Pegasus, Thumper, Little Hiawatha, Centaurette, etc., #1, 2, 7-29, 32-37, 39, 40, 42 from numbered set of 48, 1940s, 1-1/2" x 4-1/4", scattered general light wear, **$165.** Photo courtesy of Hake's Americana & Collectibles.

Zorro

Costume, 16" x 37", unused, attached to orig diecut cardboard hanger display, Lindsay, late 1950s, black diecut leatherette mask, black fabric cloak/sash, silver image of Zorro on rearing Toronado, 3-1/4" d Member Lindsay Ranch Club badge **50.00**

Figure, 3" x 4" x 7" h, painted and glazed ceramic, Enesco, orig foil sticker, copyright, "WDE.140," attached foil-covered cardboard string tag, replaced metal sword **125.00**

Game, 8" x 15-1/2" x 1-1/2" deep box, Whitman, copyright 1965, 15-1/2" sq board, complete set of picture letter cards, one generic plastic marker missing **75.00**

4" x 4" centered image in lead pencil, 1937, #54 of numbered sequence **100.00**

Puzzle, frame tray, 11-1/2" x 14-1/2", Whitman, copyright 1957, full-color Zorro and Captain Ramone sword fighting **25.00**

Dollhouses

History: Dollhouses date from the 18th century to modern times. Early dollhouses often were handmade, sometimes with only one room. The most common type was made for a young girl to fill with replicas of furniture scaled especially to fit into a dollhouse. Specially sized dolls also were made for dollhouses. All types of accessories in all types of styles were available, and dollhouses could portray any historical period.

Keystone, Fire Department, litho tin, white, green, and gold, **$650.**

American

21-1/4" l, 28-3/4" h, Victorian, last quarter 19th C, two-story house, modified Federal style, mansard roof with widow's walk, fenced-in front garden, simulated grass and fountains, polychrome details **400.00**

28-1/4" w, 17-1/4" d, 32-1/2" h, gambrel roof, painted off-white, red paste board scalloped shingles, front opening half doors, six rooms, original paper wall and floor coverings, hinged door in rear roof, front steps, orig furniture, bisque dolls, accessories, and rugs, some paint and paper wear **920.00**

Bliss, chromolithograph paper on wood

14" h, two-story, blue litho paper on roof, blue wood on back, red wood chimney and base, two open lower windows and two upper windows, house opens in front, litho wall and floor coverings inside, marked "R. Bliss" on door, some wear, one wall slightly warped **575.00**

14" h, two-story, stable, red shingle roof, painted green roof and red spire on cupola, painted red base and side poles of stable, single opening door on second floor, brown papier-mâché horse, marked "R. Bliss" **900.00**

16-1/2" h, two-story, front porch with turned columns, working front door, overhanging roof with lattice-work balcony, blue-gray roof with dormer windows, hinged front, int. with two rooms, printed carpeting and wallpaper, celluloid windows with later lace curtains, electric lights, two scratch-built chairs............ **1,725.00**

Elastolin, Germany, 29" w, farmyard, house, barn, fencing, trees, and various figures..................................... **1,150.00**

German, 35" w, 11-1/4" d, 17" h, Nuremberg Kitchen, dark yellow walls with deep red trim, red and black checkerboard floor, cream stove hood, green furniture, tin stove, tin and copper pots, set of scales, wash boiler, baking pans, utensils, pottery, porcelain, and pewter tableware, late 19th C, some paint wear and imperfections............ **2,300.00**

Marklin, Central Bahnhof train station, 1905, tinplate, O-gauge **4,500.00**

McLoughlin, 12" x 17" x 16", folding house, two rooms, dec int., orig box **950.00**

Schoenhut, 20" x 26" x 30", mansion, two-story, eight rooms, attic, tan brick design, red roof, large dormer, 20 glass windows, orig decal, 1923 .... **1,750.00**

Tootsietoy, 21" w, 10-1/8" d, 16" h, house, furniture, and accessories, printed Masonite, half-timbered style, two rooms down, two up, removable roof, open back, orchid and pink bedroom sets, orchid bathroom, brown dining room set, flocked sofa and chairs, green and white kitchen pcs, piano, bench, lamps, telephone, cane-back sofa, rocker, some damage and wear to 3/4 scale furniture **525.00**

Dolls

History: Dolls have been children's play toys for centuries. Dolls also have served other functions. From the 14th through 18th centuries, doll making was centered in Europe, mainly in Germany and France. The French dolls produced in this era were representations of adults and dressed in the latest couturier designs. They were not children's toys.

During the mid-19th century, child and baby dolls, made in wax, cloth, bisque, and porcelain, were introduced. Facial features were hand painted, wigs were made of mohair and human hair, and the dolls were dressed in the current fashions for babies or children.

Doll making in the United States began to flourish in the 1900s with companies such as Effanbee, Madame Alexander, and Ideal.

Marks: Marks of the various manufacturers are found on the back of the head or neck or on the doll's back. These marks are very important in identifying a doll and its date of manufacture.

Additional Listings: See *Warman's Americana & Collectibles* for more examples.

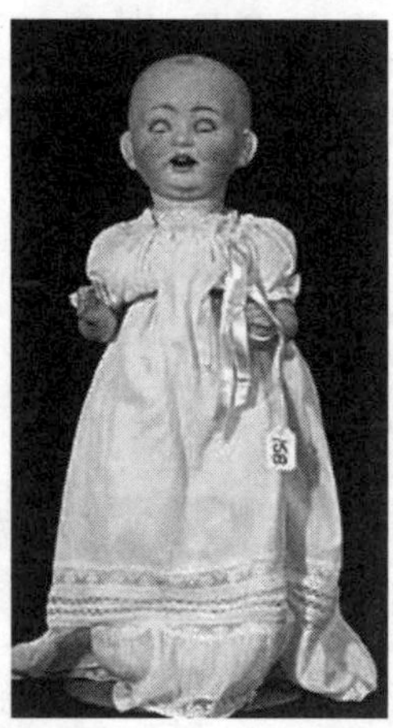

Alt, Beck & Gottschalk, baby character, bisque head, molded hair, blue sleep eyes, open mouth, cloth body, composition arms and legs, 14" h, marked "A.B. & G. 1528-36," **$185**. Doll photos courtesy of Joy Luke Auctions and McMaster Harris Auction Co.

Alt, Beck & Gottschalk, 34" h, #1362, blue glass sleep eyes, ball jointed composition body, rear of torso with panel containing wiring for leg activation, head turning and voice box, redressed **600.00**

Amberg, 12-1/2" h, Bottle Babe Twins, solid-dome bisque heads, light blue sleep eyes, softly blues brows, painted upper and lower lashes, open mouths, molded tongues, lightly molded and painted hair, cloth bodies with non-working criers, composition arms, right arms molded to hold celluloid bottles, orig white lace-trimmed baby dresses, slips, crocheted bonnets, diapers, and socks, hold orig celluloid baby bottle, blue and white celluloid rattle, marked "A.M./Germany/341/3" on back of heads, "Amberg's/Bottle Babe/Pat. Pending/ Amberg Dolls/The World Standard" on dress, both dolls have light rubs on cheeks or hair, cloth bodies are aged, some flaking on arms, paint flaked off right arm of one, price for pr **500.00**

Armand Marseille

6-1/2" h, Googly, bisque socket head, large slide glancing blue sleep eyes, single strike brows, closed smiling mouth, dark mohair wig, crude composition 5-pc toddler body, lace-trimmed organdy baby dress, matching bonnet, slip, diaper, stockings, crocheted booties, marked "G. 253 B Germany A. 11/0 M" on back of head, repainted body **675.00**

10" l, 9" d head circumference, Dream Baby, brown bisque socket head, brown sleep eyes, closed mouth, black painted hair, brown bent limb composition baby body, fine lawn christening gown with tucks, ruffles, and lace trim, c1920 .... **300.00**

23" h, 990 baby, bisque socket head, brown sleep eyes, feathered brows, painted upper and lower lashes, open mouth, well-accented lips, two upper teeth, antique human hair wig, composition bent-limb baby body, antique baby dress, slip, diaper, new crocheted sweater, cap and booties, marked "Armand Marseille/Germany/ 990/A 12 M" on back of head, heavy French-style body, arms repainted and have rough finish, right big toe missing, other toes repaired and repainted, normal wear at joints **275.00**

30" h, Queen Louise, bisque, blue sleep eyes, replaced blond wig, jointed composition body, older cotton print dress **460.00**

Arranbee

17" h, Nancy Lee, composition head, brown sleep eyes with real lashes, painted lower lashes, single stroke brows, closed mouth, orig human-hair wig in orig set, five-pc composition body, orig brown-flannel belted dress, white ruffle trim, orig underwear combination, orig socks and brown-suede shoes with fringe tongue, marked "R & B" on back of head, unplayed with condition **300.00**

18-1/2" h, Debu-Teen, composition socket head, composition shoulder plate, sleep eyes, real lashes, closed mouth, orig human hair wig, cloth torso, composition arms and legs, old pc teddy, orig socks and shoes, blue silk hat, orig box with handmade dress, marked "R & B" on head, under arms, back of legs, Debu'Teen label on end of orig box, eyes cloudy **500.00**

Averill, Georgene, 17" h, Bonnie Babe, bisque flange head, blue sleep eyes, softly brushed brows, painted upper and lower lashes, open mouth, two lower teeth, cloth body with non-working crier, composition lower arms and legs, old white baby dress, marked "Copr by Georgene Averill 1005 3652 4 Germany" on back of head, right foot cracked **425.00**

Bahr & Proschild, 23" h, 585 baby, bisque socket head, blue sleep eyes, feathered brows, painted upper and lower lashes, open mouth with accented lips, two upper teeth, paper tongue, orig human hair wig, composition baby body, long white baby dress, lace-trimmed bonnet, marked "BP (in heart) 585 M 14 I Germany" on back of head, eyes reset, body shows wear **450.00**

Barrois, E., 17-1/2" h, Poupee, pale bisque swivel head on shoulder plate, set blue eyes with threaded detail, fine multi-stroke brows, painted upper and lower lashes, closed mouth with accented lips, orig blond mohair wig with orig tortoiseshell comb, kid body with kid over wood upper arms, mortise-and-tenon type knee joints, white dotted Swiss dress, possibly orig underclothing, socks, and shoes, marked "E 4 B," at rear edge of bisque shoulder plate, lower bisque arms replaced **1,200.00**

Bergman, Carl, 15" h, bisque, three-face, sleeping, crying, and awake expressions, knob on top of head, all orig, antique clothing **900.00**

Bisque

4-1/2" h, Oriental pair, olive-tone bisque socket heads, dark brown pupil-less set eyes, single stroke brows, painted upper and lower lashes, closed mouth, orig black mohair wigs, male with orig queue, five-pc olive-tone bisque bodies jointed at shoulders and hips, Oriental embroidered silk clothing, unmarked, price for pr **825.00**

10" h, Just Me, painted bisque socket head, blue side-glancing sleep eyes, single stroke brows, closed mouth, orig mohair wig, five-pc composition body jointed at shoulders and hips, orig white dress with orange and green felt trim, orig white cotton socks and white paper shoes with buckles, marked "Just Me/Registered/Germany/A 310/6/0 M" on back of head, needs to be restrung **900.00**

18" h, Miss Liberty, bisque shoulder head, painted blue eyes with molded lids, multi-stroke brows, tiny painted upper and lower lashes, closed mouth, molded earrings, molded and painted blond hair with copper molded earrings, molded and painted blond hair with copper tiara, two black ribbons across top of head and lay against left side of neck, molded bun with waterfall effect, cloth body, leather lower arms, red leather boots as part of lower leg, antique ecru wool dress with lace trim, antique underclothing, small holes in dress........... **1,650.00**

C.M. Bergmann II, bisque head, brown eyes, open mouth, jointed composition body, marked "Made In Germany," 24" h, $200.

Bruckner, 12" h, Topsy-Turvey, all cloth, two heads, two sets of arms with mitten hands, one black, one white, one at each end, mask faces, molded and painted features, black face with open-closed mouth, mohair bangs showing under red scarf, white face with closed mouth, painted hair showing under bonnet, orig clothing, marked "Pat'd July 8th, 1901" along bottom of front of mask face **400.00**

Bru Bete Teteur, 15" h, bisque socket head, brown paperweight eyes, feathered brows, round open mouth, rubber ball in head with metal key on back of head to operated mechanism to drink liquid from bottle, caracul wig, crude late S.F.B.J. type wood and composition body, white antique baby dress, lace trimmed bonnet, antique pans and slip, new socks, old shoes, marked "Bru Jne/16" on head, "3" imp on left side of torso **2,000.00**

Bru Jne, 19" h, bisque socket head on bisque shoulder plate with molded breasts, blue paperweight eyes, two-toned feathered brows, painted upper and lower lashes, closed mouth with tip of tongue showing, pierced ears, replaced mohair wig, kid body with bisque lower arms, wooden lower legs, dressed in outfit made from antique fabric and trims, marked "Bru Jne/6" on back of head, "Bru Jne" on back of left shoulder, "No. 6" on back of right shoulder, partial paper label on chest, "6/Bru Jne/Paris" on sole of one shoe... **12,700.00**

Century Doll Co., Kestner, Character Baby, c1920, 17" l, 12-1/2" d bisque head, brown sleep eyes, open/closed smiling mouth with two upper molded teeth and tongue, deep modeling across bridge of nose, light dimples, flange neck on cloth body with side-swivel cloth legs, non-working squeaker, mechanism in body waves composition hands, long white lawn baby gown, imp mark "Century Doll Co Kestner Germany" **550.00**

Madame Alexander, Scarlet, Gone with the Wind, white dress, original box, 12" h, minor stains on dress, $60.

Chase, Martha

16" h, baby, blond painted sculpted hair, brown eyes, mint sateen body with stamp at hip, orig paper label sewn to rear of body **700.00**

24" h, baby, blond painted sculpted hair, brown eyes, mint sateen body, orig box with label **750.00**

China, unmarked

11-1/2" h, Frozen Charlie, pink tint, painted blue eyes with blue accent line, single-stroke brows, closed mouth, accent line between lips, painted blond hair with brush strokes around face, un-jointed body with arms extended, hands held with fingers curled, finger nails and toe nails outlined, color flaw on right side of forehead at edge of hair, couple spots of inherent roughness on right back of head and right shoulder, light color wear on edges of feet and hands, small flake off right finger **450.00**

18" h, open mouth, low brow, china shoulder head with turned head, painted blue eyes, red accent line, single-stroke brows, open mouth, molded teeth, molded and painted wavy hair, cloth body, china lower arms and lower legs, painted garters, molded and painted brown shoes with heels, possibly orig beige print dress, underclothing **850.00**

Cloth, unmarked, 18" h, black cloth head, stiff neck, embroidered features, black curly yarn wig, cloth body with black upper torso, brown twill-type lower torso and legs, arms cov with black fabric, grain stuffing, five stitched fingers, orig multicolored plaid dress, orig eyelet-edged teddy, lace-trimmed half slip, red socks stitched to legs.................... **700.00**

Cuno & Otto Dressel, 14" h, bisque head, blue sleep eyes with lashes, open mouth, two upper teeth, replaced auburn mohair wig, fully articulated composition body, blue dress, imp "Cuno & Otto Dressel," early 20th C, some repair to body **200.00**

Demalcol, 9" h, bisque socket head, blue googly eyes set to side, single stroke brows, closed smiling mouth, curly synthetic wig, crude five-pc composition body, molded and painted socks and shoes, new frilly yellow dress, matching bonnet, orig gauze underclothing, marked "Demalcol/5/0/Germany" on back of head **850.00**

Eden Bebe, 16-1/2" h, bisque socket head, blue paperweight eyes, feathered brows, painted upper and lower lashes, open mouth, six upper teeth, pierced ears, replaced mohair wig, jointed wood and composition French body, redressed, pale blue and ecru outfit, blue and beige jacket, antique underclothing, new stockings, and old shoes, marked "Eden Bebe/Paris/7/Depose" on back of neck, "7" on front of neck, light kiln dust on left cheek, flaking at neck socket of body and on both lower legs, normal wear at joints and on hands **1,200.00**

Effanbee

12" h, Candy Kid, composition head, blue sleep eyes, real lashes, single stroke brows, closed mouth, molded and painted hair, five-pc composition toddler body, orig red and white gingham sunsuit and bonnet, orig socks, red leatherette tie shoes, marked "Effanbee" on back of head and on back, "An Effanbere Durable Doll, The Doll with Satin-Smooth Skin" in heart on end of box, unplayed with condition, orig box **375.00**

19" h, Patsy Ann, composition head, green sleep eyes with real lashes, single stroke brows, painted lower lashes, closed rosebud mouth, molded and painted hair, five-pc composition body with bent right arm, orig mint green silk dress with smocking, matching teddy, green hair ribbon, cotton socks with pink trim, leatherette shoes with button strap, marked "Effanbee/Patsy-Ann/©/Pat #1283558" on back of head, "Effanbee/Durable/Doll" on metal heart bracelet, unplayed with condition, wooden steamer trunk with wardrobe, two McCall's clothing patterns for Patsy Ann, Patsy Ann book **1,500.00**

Revalo, bisque head, blue sleep eyes, open mouth, jointed composition body, marked "Revalo Germany," 15" h, **$245.**

Floradora, 12" h, bisque socket head, blue sleep eyes, open mouth, four upper teeth, orig mohair wig in coiled braids, jointed wood and composition body, jointed wrists, orig Scottish outfit, pants, socks, black leather shoes, matching cap, marked "Made in Germany/ Florodora/A. 5/0 M" on head **200.00**

Gaultier, Francois, 20" h, Bebe, bisque socket head with coiled spring attachment, blue paperweight eyes, painted upper and lower lashes, open-closed mouth, pierced ears, cork pate, orig blond mohair wig, jointed wood and composition body with straight wrists, antique white pique outfit, lacy stockings, antique leather shoes with pompons, marked "F.9 G." incised on on back of head near crown, crossed hammers and "TD" in shield on flat bottom of torso, 3" old hairline from center front edge of crown to left brow **1,300.00**

Halbig, Simon

8" h, bisque head, blue sleep eyes, open mouth, four molded teeth, pierced ears, blond mohair wig, chunky straight wrist articulated composition body, orig finish and stringing, new red faille dress, imp "1079 DEP," c1900, tiny chip to right ear hole **550.00**

17" h, #1329, Oriental, bisque, brown glass sleep eyes, ball jointed composition body, redressed **1,350.00**

33" h, #1079, child, bisque, brown glass sleep eyes, open mouth, ball jointed composition body with orig finish, re-dressed, new wig **1,035.00**

34" h, #1079, child, very fine bisque, blue glass sleep eyes, orig blond human hair wig, jointed composition body, antique white dress, old baby shoes................................ **1,565.00**

40", #1906,18, bisque, brown glass eyes, brown human hair wig, open mouth, ball jointed composition body, marked "SH" and "PB" with star, "1906, 18," redressed **2,100.00**

Hamburger & Co., 22-1/2" h, Viola, bisque socket head, blue sleep eyes, feathered brows, painted upper and lower lashes, open mouth, four upper teeth, synthetic wig, jointed wood and composition body, antique dress with lace trim, underclothing, new socks and leather shoes, marked "Made in/ Germany/Viola/H & Co./7" on back of head, several wig pulls on right side of forehead, light rub on nose, small inherent cut on H in back of head, repairs at neck socket of body, bottom of torso and left upper arm, normal wear at joints, finish of legs slightly different color than rest of body **300.00**

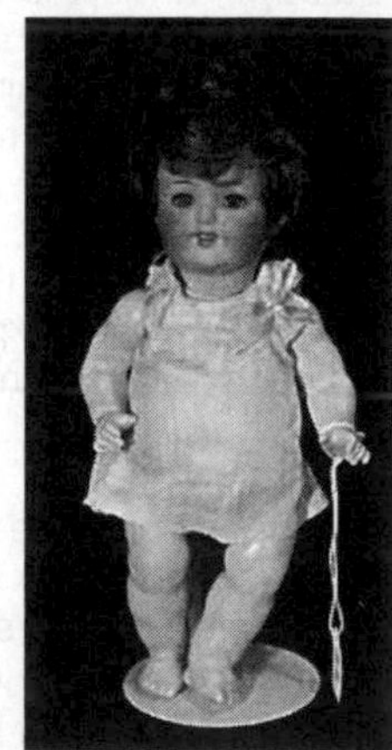

Simon & Halbig, Matthes Berlin, 156/2-1/2, bisque, blue sleep eyes, open mouth, jointed composition body, 9" h, **$365**.

Handwerck, Heinrich, 28" h, #99, bisque, brown sleep eyes, composition ball jointed body, marked "99," antique clothing, replaced wig and shoes **660.00**

Handwerck, Max, 21" h, bisque head**,** blue sleep eyes, open mouth, inset teeth, pierced ears, jointed-composition

body, orig finish, newly made pink linen dress and hat, imp "421 10 Germany M HANDWERCK 2-1/2", bisque speckling, small chin pit **320.00**

Harmann, Kurt, 26" h, bisque head, brown sleep eyes, open mouth, replaced blond mohair wig, fully articulated composition body, new blue satin and lace dress, worn period blue leather shoes, imp mark "30 5 K (over script H) 4," early 20th C, white scratch line each cheek **230.00**

Hertel, Schwab & Co.

9" l, 7" d head circumference, twin character babies, blue sleep eyes, open mouths, two upper teeth, wispy blond tufts of hair, composition bent-limb bodies, matching period long white baby gown, one with pink, one blue ribbon trim, imp marks "152/2/0," early 20th C, price for pair **635.00**

20" h, bisque socket head, blue paperweight eyes, feathered brows, painted upper and lower lashes, open mouth with accented lips and six upper teeth, pierced ears, replaced human-hair wig, jointed composition body with straight wrists, separate balls at shoulders, elbows, hips and knees, nicely redressed in pale pink French-style dress, new underclothing, socks and shoes, marks "8/0" on back of head and "Jumeau Medaille d'Or Paris" stamped in blue on lower back, replaced antique paperweight eyes, tiny flake at each earring hole, tiny fleck on upper rim at inside corner of right eye, body has good orig finish with wear at all joints, on toes and heels **1,100.00**

Tete Jumeau, bisque socket head, large blue paperweight eyes, original mohair wig, jointed wood and compositiong body with jointed wrists, redressed, marked "Depose Tete Jumeau Bte S.G.D.G. 6," red and black artist marks on back of head, "Jumeau Medaille d'Or Paris" stamped on lower back, 15" h, **$3,000.**

Heubach, Ernest, 12-1/2" h, 399 baby, solid dome painted bisque socket head, brown sleep eyes, single stroke brows, painted upper and lower lashes, closed mouth, lightly molded and painted hair, composition bent-limb baby body, orig multicolored "grass" skirt, marked "Heu bach*Koppelsdorf/399*9/0/Germany" on back of head **350.00**

Heubach, Gebruder, 17" h character, bisque head and shoulder plate, blue intaglio eyes, single stroke brows, open-closed mouth with accent colors, two painted lower teeth, molded and lightly painted hair, kid body with gussets at hips and knees, bisque lower arms, cloth lower legs, antique two-pc boy's outfit with belt, new socks and shoes, marked "5/Germany" on back of shoulder plate, arms replaced, repairs on upper legs **475.00**

Heubach, Koppelsdorf, , 24" h, bisque head, blue sleep eyes with lashes, open mouth, brown human-hair wig, fully jointed wood and composition body, period underwear, new print cotton dress, imp mark "312," early 20th C, rub on cheek.. **220.00**

Horsman, 15" h, toddler, composition socket head, brown sleep eyes, single stroke brows, painted upper and lower lashes, mohair wig, jointed composition toddler body, straight wrists, diagonal hip joints, old white organdy dress with lace trim, underclothing, socks, high button boots, marked "E.I.H./Co." on back **650.00**

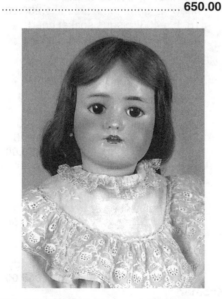

Heinrich Handwerck, bisque socket head, set brown eyes with real lashes, open mouth, four upper teeth, replaced human hair wig, jointed wood and composition body, well dressed in wool dress, marked "Germany Heinrich Handwerck Simon & Halbig 6" on back of head "Heinrich Handwerck Germany" stamped in red on right hip, 29" h, **$600.**

Ideal

13" h, Shirley Temple, composition head, hazel sleep eyes with real lashes, painted lower lashes, feathered brows, open mouth, six upper teeth, orig mohair wig in orig set, five-pc composition body, orig plaid "Bright Eyes" dress, underwear combination, replaced socks, orig shoes, marked "13/Shirley Temple" on head, "Shirley Temple/13" on back **700.00**

28" h, Lori Martin, vinyl socket head, blue sleep eyes with real lashes, painted lower lashes, feathered brows, closed smiling mouth, rooted hair vinyl body jointed at waist, shoulders, hips, and ankles, orig tagged clothing, plaid shirt, jeans, vinyl boots with horses, marked "© Metro Goldwyn Mayer Inc./Mfg by/Ideal Toy Corp/80" on back of head, "© Ideal Toy Corp./6-30-5" on back, "National Velvet's/Lori Martin/© Metro Goldwyn Mayer, Inc./All Rights Reserved" on shirt tag **550.00**

Tete Jumeau, bisque socket head, blue sleep eyes, open mouth, four upper teeth, original human hair wig, jointed wood and composition French body, jointed wrists, non-working crier, original blue organdy dress, underclothing, marked shoes, and kid gloves, marked "30/27" in red, partial label on back of head, stamped inside wig cap, 20" h, **$1,100.**

Jumeau

9" h, Great Ladies series, bisque socket head, blue paperweight eyes, single stroke brows, painted upper and lower lashes, closed

mouth, orig mohair wig, five-pc composition body, painted flat black shoes, orig white brocade gown with gold "diamond" jewelry, orig underclothing, marked "221/3/0" on back of head, "fabrication/Jumeau/ Paris/Made in France" on front of paper tag, "Marie-Louise/2, Femme de/Napoleon Ier/Epogue 1810" hand written on back of paper tag **475.00**

14-1/2" h, 1st series portrait, almond-shaped eye sockets, hazel eyes, mauve eye shadow, orig eight ball jointed repainted body, back of head marked "2/0," redressed, new wig, slight nose rub, slight scuff to cheek **8,625.00**

15", Tete, bisque socket head, blue paperweight eyes, feathered brows, closed mouth with outlined lips, pierced ears, cork pate with orig mohair wig, jointed wood and composition body, jointed wrists, pink silk lace trimmed outfit, matching bonnet, marked "Depose/ Tete Jumeau/Btd S.G.D.G./16," red and black artist marks on back of head, "Jumeau/Medaille d'Or/Paris" stamped on lower back, finish worn on right hand **3,000.00**

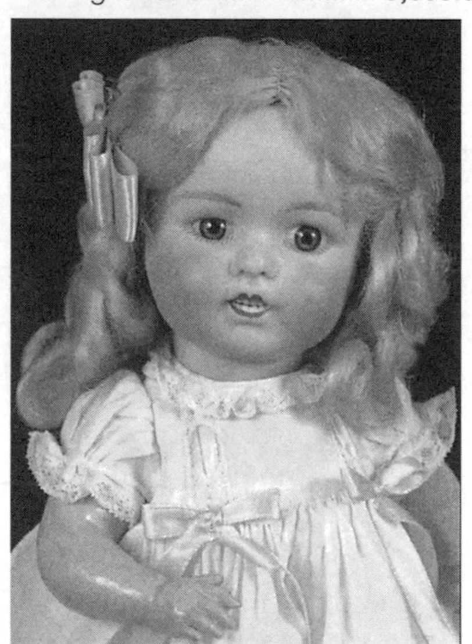

Toto Character, bisque socket head, blue paperweight eyes, open mouth with six upper and four lower replaced teeth, original blond mohair wig, five-piece composition toddler body, redressed, crier missing, unmarked, 13" h, **$400**.

20" h, bisque socket head, large blue paperweight eyes, painted upper and lower lashes, feathered brows, closed mouth, accented lips, pierced ears, replaced human-hair wig, jointed wood and composition Jumeau adult body with jointed wrists, antique ecru and blue dress with lace overlay, new underclothing, black stockings, orig Jumeau shows, " Depose Tete Jumeau Bte. S.G.D.G. 7" on back of head, "Bebe Jumeau/ Diplome d'Honneur" on oval label on back, "9/Paris/(bee)/Depose" on soles of shoes **3,100.00**

26" h, flawless pale bisque, amber eyes, replaced French mohair wig, marked composition Jumeau body with touch up and repairs, antique dress and shoes **3,360.00**

Kamkins, 19" h, girl, cloth, molded face with painted features, blue eyes, orig brown mohair wig, cloth body and limbs, blue cotton dress, orig undergarments, purple Kamkins stamp mark on back of head, early 20th C, some soil and wear on face **1,150.00**

Kammer & Reinhardt

7-1/2" h, 126, toddler, bisque socket head, blue sleep eyes, single stroke brows, painted upper and lower lashes, open mouth with two teeth, replaced synthetic wig, five-pc chubby toddler body, starfish hands, old hand made embroidered teddy, matching orange dress and bonnet, marked "K*R/Simon & Halbig/ Germany/126-19" on back of head **500.00**

8" h, 101, bisque socket head, painted blue eyes, single stroke brows, painted upper and lower lashes, closed pouty mouth, mohair wig with coiled braids, fully jointed composition body, redressed, marked "K*R/101/21" on back of head **1,200.00**

18" h, #403, bisque socket head, blue sleep eyes, feathered brows, open mouth, four upper teeth, pierced ears, orig mohair wig in short bob, jointed wood and composition body, redressed, orig socks and shoes with ribbon ties, orig garter at left knee, marked "K * R/Simon & Halbig/403/Germany/46" on head **650.00**

29" h, #192, pale bisque, brown glass sleep eyes, ball jointed composition body with straight wrists, pull strings say "Mama" and "Papa" **1,495.00**

32" h, baby/toddler, bisque head, brown glass sleep eyes, wobbly tongue, K*R child composition body, redressed, new wig **865.00**

Kestner

10" h, 150, bisque head with stiff neck, brown sleep eyes, feathered brows, painted upper and lower lashes, open mouth with four upper teeth, orig blond mohair wig, all bisque body jointed at shoulders and hips, mold and painted blue shirred socks and black one-strap shoes, antique white dress, imp "150.5" in back of head and inside upper arms **575.00**

14-1/2" h, 257 baby, bisque socket head, blue sleep eyes, feathered brows, painted upper and lower lashes, open mouth, accented lips, two upper teeth, spring tongue, synthetic wig, composition Kestner baby body, antique-style long baby dress and bonnet, slip, diaper and new booties, marked "Made in/ Germany/J.D.K./257/Germany/35" on back of head, "Made in Germany" stamped in red on upper back, real lashes missing, worn body finish, moisture damage on lower right near torso and back of right arm ... **600.00**

23" h, Hilda, solid dome bisque socket head, blue sleep eyes, feathered brows, painted upper and lower lashes, open mouth, accented lips, two upper teeth, lightly molded and painted blond hair composition bent-limb Kestner baby body, antique white baby dress, matching slip, diaper, new pink knit booties, antique baby bonnet, marked "Hilda/ C/J.D.K. Jr. 1914/ges.gesch.N. 1070/ made in 18 Germany" on back of head **4,000.00**

31", #18, pale brown set eyes, closed mouth, replaced human hair wig, orig plaster pate, early chunky composition body, rear of head marked "18" and "103," antique white clothing **2,645.00**

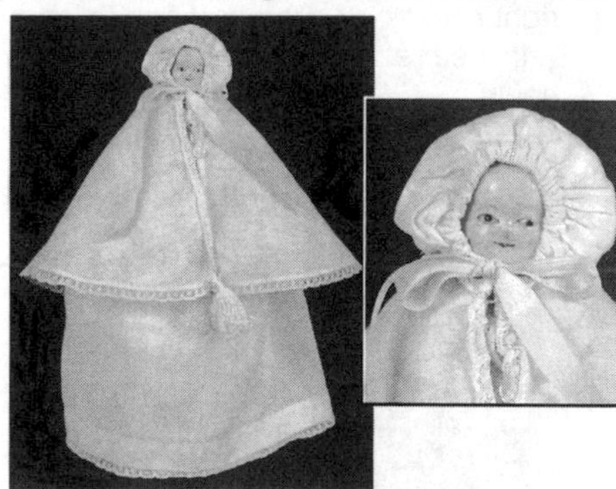

Sonneberg Taufling, papier mâché swivel head, set pupiless dark eyes, closed smiling mouth, painted curls for hair, so-called Motschmann style body, elaborate original clothing, unmarked, 6" h, **$400**.

Kley & Hahn, 11-1/2" h, 525Baby, solid dome bisque socket head, blue sleep eyes, feathered brows, painted upper and lower lashes, open-closed mouth, lightly molded and brush stroked hair, composition baby body, antique baby dress, marked "4/Germany/K&H (in banner)/525" on back of head, repainted **275.00**

Knickerbocker, 11" h, Mickey Mouse, cloth swivel head, white facial, black oilcloth pie eyes, large black nose, painted open/closed smiling mouth with accent lines, black felt ears, un-jointed black cloth body, orange hands with three fingers and a thumb, red oversized composition feet, black rubber tail, orig shorts with two buttons on front and back, some fading................................ **650.00**

Konig & Wernicke, Germany, early 20th C, 17" h, character toddler, bisque head, brown sleep eyes, open mouth, two upper teeth, tongue, orig dark brown mohair wig, fully articulated side hip-joint composition toddler body marked "Made in Germany," period cotton sailor outfit, blue pants, white overblouse, white fabric shoes, imp "Made in Germany 99/7," some wear to finish of limbs, repaint to hands.. **750.00**

Kruse, Kathe, 13" h, Schlenkerchen, all-stockinette, pressed and oil-painted double-seam head, painted features, brown hair, shaded brown painted eyes with eyeliner, light upper lashes, closed mouth in smiling expression, cloth neck ring, stockinette covered, padded armature frame body, mitten hands, rounded feet, period clothing, soles stamped "Kathe Kruse, Germany," c1922 .... **7,475.00**

Lenci

12" h, girl, pressed felt swivel head, painted brown side-glancing eyes, painted upper lashes, closed mouth with two-tone lips, orig mohair wig, cloth torso, felt limbs, orig pink felt dress with blue trim, blue felt coat with matching hat, orig underclothing, socks, blue felt shoes, marked "2" on bottom of right foot, "Lenci/Made in Italy" on cloth label inside coat............................ **400.00**

28" h, lady, "Mary Pickford" felt face, light gray-blue painted eyes to right, long nose, closed mouth, long bare felt arms, classic Lenci fingers, white and green organdy summer frock, felt wide-brimmed bonnet, all trimmed with felt flowers and ruffles, silk stockings, pale green felt shoes with felt flowers, orig Lenci tag sewn to dress, c1930, small stain back of skirt.................................... **1,840.00**

Limbach, 23" h, character, bisque socket head, blue sleep eyes with real lashes, painted upper and lower lashes, open mouth, accented lips, six upper teeth, human-hair wig, jointed wood and composition body, new white lacy dress, underclothing, new socks and shoes, marked "W/crown/17 72 in shamrock/ Limbach" on back of head, two right fingers and three left fingers repaired, finish flaking around neck socket of body, cracks in finish on side seams of torso, wear at all sockets on torso.......... **625.00**

Jumeau, portrait, bisque socket head, light blue threaded paperweight eyes, cork pate with hand tied antique mohair wig, jointed wood and composition body with straight wrists, possibly original factory chemise, white leather marked French shoes, marked "Jumeau Medaille d'Or Paris" stamped on lower back, 13" h, **$3,800.**

Madame Alexander

14" h, Marme from the *Little Women* Series, hard plastic head and body, gray sleep eyes, closed mouth, dark brown wig in snood, gray and pink print dress with orig tags, organdy shawl, shoes and socks, c1955 .... **200.00**

18" h, Sweet Violet, hard plastic head, blue sleep eyes with real lashes, painted lower lashes, feathered brows, closed mouth, orig synthetic wig, hard plastic body jointed at shoulders, elbows, wrists, hips, and knees, walking mechanism, orig tagged blue cotton dress, underclothing, flowered bonnet, white gloves, black side-snap shoes, carrying orig pink Alexander hat box, marked "Alexander" on back of head, "Madame Alexander/All Rights Reserved/New York, U.S.A.," c1954, unplayed-with condition comb and curlers missing.................. **1,700.00**

21" h, Cissy, #2099, hard plastic, blue sleep eyes, closed mouth, orig synthetic wig, hard plastic body jointed at hips and knees, vinyl arms jointed at elbows, orig tagged brocade gown with pale blue sash, jeweled tiara, earrings, long gloves, and, jeweled bracelets, marked "Alexander" on back of head "Cissy by Madame Alexander" on dress tag, c1955 .... **600.00**

Menjou, Adolph, 32" h, composition shoulder head, painted brown eyes with accent line, molded monocle on right eye, feathered brows, molded and painted mustache, open-closed mouth, seven upper teeth, molded white shirt collar with hole, presumably for a tie, molded and painted hair, excelsior-stuffed cloth body with long limbs, composition white hands as gloves, composition lower legs as socks and shoes, orig black two-pc suit with satin lapels.. **725.00**

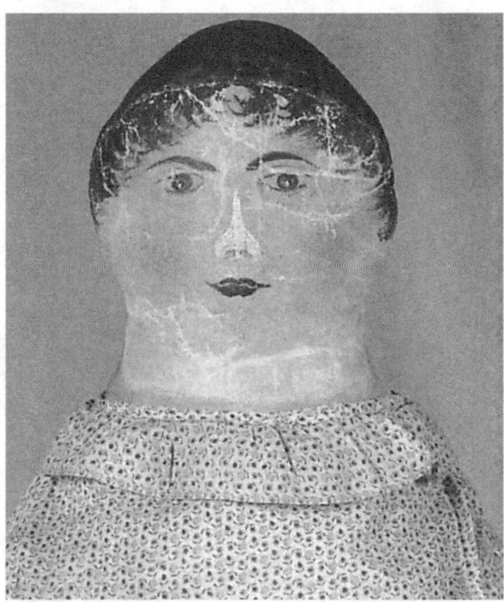

Cloth, primitive, stiff neck, oil painted face and hair, painted features, cloth body jointed at shoulders, hips, and knees, mitten hands, original red print dress, matching chemise, blue and white striped wool socks, black leather high button shoes, unmarked, 31" h, **$2,200.**

Parian, 24" h, untinted bisque shoulder head, painted blue eyes with red accent line, single stroke brows, closed mouth, pierced ears, molded and painted café au lait hair, molded blue tiara trimmed with gold, molded braid across top, on lower sides, and down middle of back of head, old cloth body with red leather boots as part of leg, new arms by Emma Clear, white dotted Swiss and lace dress, antique underclothing, unmarked, old repair to tiara, body aged.......... **1,900.00**

Petzold, Dora, 16-1/2" h, composition head, painted blue eyes with eye shadow, single-stroke brows, accented nostrils, closed mouth, orig mohair wig, stockinette body stitch-jointed at shoulders and hips, mitten-type hands with stitched fingers, possibly orig white velvet dress with embroidery and lace trim, white teddy, orig socks and marked shoes, marked with girl in circle, "D P/7/7/0" on back of head, girl in circle with "D P" on bottom of shoes **275.00**

Poupee Bois, 17-1/2" h, bisque socket head, bisque shoulder plate, pale blue threaded paperweight eyes, feathered brows, painted upper and lower lashes, closed mouth, pierced ears, orig human hair wig, wooden fashion body articulated at shoulders, elbows, wrists, hips, and knees, swivel joint on upper arms and upper legs, nicely redressed with antique fabric and lace, possibly orig stockings and high button boots, marked "4" on back of head **4,400.00**

Poupee Raynal, 19" h, pressed felt swivel head, painted blue eyes, single-stroke brows, painted upper lashes, closed mouth with three-tone lips, orig mohair wig in orig set, five-pc cloth body with stitched fingers, orig light blue organdy dress with pink flower appliqués, matching hat, orig teddy, blue organdy slip, socks, white leather shoes, "Paris" typed on piece of paper pinned to back, unplayed with condition **725.00**

Simon & Halbig 1078, bisque socket head, brown skin tone, brown sleep eyes, open mouth with four upper teeth, original mohair wig, jointed brown wood and composition body, redressed, marked "1078 Simon & Halbig, S & H, Germany, 9" on back of head, 20-1/2" h, **$600**.

Putnam, Grace

8" h, Bye-Lo Baby, solid dome bisque swivel head, tiny blue sleep eyes, softly blushed brows, painted upper and lower lashes, closed mouth, lightly molded and painted hair, all bisque baby body jointed at shoulders and hips, orig knit pink and white two-pc baby outfit with matching cap, marked "Bye-Lo Baby/©/Germany/G.S. Putnam" on label on chest, "6-20/Copr. By/Grace S. Putnam/Germany" incised on back, "6-20" on hips and right arms, "20" on left arm, chip on right back of neck edge of head, minor firing line behind left ear................. **525.00**

21" h, 17" d head circumference, Bye-Lo Baby, solid dome bisque head, blue sleep eyes, softly blushed brows, painted upper and lower lashes, closed mouth, lightly molded and painted hair, cloth body with "frog" legs, celluloid hands, orig white Bye-Lo dress, slip, and flannel diaper, marked "Copr. By/Grace S. Putnam/Made in Germany" on back of head, turtle mark on wrists of celluloid hands, light bur on right cheek, body lightly soiled and aged **600.00**

Kathe Kruse, boy and girl, celluloid, socket head, set eyes, human hair wig, jointed shoulders and hips, girl in original white blouse, print skirt, green pinafore, boy wearing original white shirt, gray felt leiderhosen, green felt hat, marked with turtle in diamond, round hang tag on girl, original boxes, 15-1/2" h, **$425**.

Recknagel, 9" h, character, bisque socket head, tiny painted blue squinty eyes, single-stroke brows, open-closed mouth, five painted upper teeth, four lower teeth, molded tongue, molded and painted short hair with molded pink bow, five-pc chubby composition body, crude unpainted torso, molded and painted socks and shoes, redressed in pink lace-trimmed dress, matching hair ribbon, lace pants, marked "R 57 A/8/0" on back of head, light dust in bisque, light wear on orig body finish....................... **675.00**

S & Q, 28" h, 201 baby, bisque socket head, set brown eyes, feathered brows, painted upper and lower lashes, open mouth, two upper teeth, molded tongue, mohair wig, composition baby body, navy blue velvet boy's shorts, jacket, and matching hat, white shirt, stockings, white baby shoes, marked "+ 201 SQ" (superimposed) "Germany 14" on back of head **700.00**

Schmidt, Bruno, 31", blue sleep eyes, blond wig, open mouth, jointed composition body. Marked "BS W" in heart below "Made in Germany," repainted, redressed **600.00**

Schmidt, Franz, 33-1/2" h, child, bisque head, open mouth, brown glass eyes set stationary, pierced ears, replaced long blond human-hair wig, chunky fully jointed composition body, period undergarments, strong blue silk twill dress, imp "S & C 7 1/2 85," late 19th/early 20th C, light soil, repairs, some repaint **1,035.00**

Schoenau & Hoffmeister, 13-1/2" h, Masquerade set, bisque socket head, set brown eyes, single stroke brows, painted upper and lower lashes, open mouth, four upper teeth, antique mohair wig, five-pc composition body, walking mechanism, orig pastel dress with pale green ribbon trim, orig gauze-type underclothing, socks, leather shoes with black pompons, marked "4000 5/0/S PB (in star) H 10" on back of head, "F" on back of legs, "Germany" stamped on bottom of shoes, tied in red cardboard box with two lace-trimmed compartments, blue pierrot costume brimmed with black, white, and ruffled collar, matching cone-shaped hat, black face mask with lace trim, light rub on nose....................................... **525.00**

Cloth, primitive, stiff neck, oil painted face and features, stripes of hide stitched to head for wig, long mohair braid in back, cloth body jointed at shoulders and hips, kid lower arms, individually stitched fingers, original pink and tan dress, matching bonnet, blue and tan chemise, brown leather boots, unmarked, 13-1/2" h, **$325**.

Schoenhut

12" h, composition head, painted blue eyes, lightly molded and single-stroke brows, closed mouth, molded and painted hair, five-pc composition body with bent right arm, pale pink dotted Swiss dress, panties, replaced socks and shoes, marked "Schoenhut/Toys/Made in/U.S.A." on label on back, light wear on fingers, chipped left first finger **1,300.00**

19" h, 19/308 girl, wooden socket head, brown intaglio eyes, feathered brows, closed pouty mouth, orig mohair wig with orig ribbon, spring-jointed wooden body, holes in feet for orig stand, orig white lace trimmed dress, slip, cotton socks and leather shoes with holes for stand, marked "Schoenhut Doll/Pat. Jan 17th 1911/U.S.A. & Foreign Countries" incised label on back, Schoenhut label in inside and outside of orig box lid, orig Schoenhut booklet **3,100.00**

Schoenhut & Hoffmeister, 20" h, 13-1/2" d head circumference, character baby, bisque head, blue sleep eyes with lashes, hint of smile, open mouth, two upper teeth, pointy chin, orig dark brown mohair wig, bent-limb composition baby body, white cotton slip, imp "SHPB" in a star, "5, Germany," early 20th C, white spot back of head at rim **325.00**

S.F.B.J.

11" h, 301, bisque socket head, blue sleep eyes with real lashes, open mouth, four painted upper teeth, pierced ears, human-hair wig, jointed wood and composition body, jointed wrists, antique white lace dress and bonnet, marked "S.F.B.J./301/Paris/1" on back of head, "2" incised between shoulders, "2" on bottom of feet, good original body finish.................................... **600.00**

17" h, 226, solid dome bisque socket head, blue "jewel" eyes, single-stroke brows, painted upper and lower lashes, open-closed mouth, molded and painted hair, orig finish wood and composition French toddler body with diagonal hip joints, old white top, sweater, maroon velvet pants, new black socks and shoes, marked "S.F.B.J./226/Paris/6" on back of head, flaking, normal wear at joints............................. **1,100.00**

Sonnberg Taufling, 6" h, papier-mâché swivel head, set pupil-less dark eyes, single stroke brows, closed smiling mouth, painted curls for hair, so-called Motschmann-style body with composition shoulder plate, hips, lower arms and lower legs, cloth connecting composition parts, orig clothing, full slip, half slip, blouse, skirt, net cape, full cape trimmed with lace and tassels, unmarked, body aged, light wear on composition **400.00**

Francoise Gaultier Bebe, bisque socket head, brown paperweight eyes, closed mouth, wood and composition body, wooden arms and legs, jointed wrists, two pc outfit made from antique fabrics, matching hat, marked "F. G. 8" on back of head, 20" h, **$2,100.**

Steiner

17-1/2" h, Gigoteur, bisque head, blue threaded paperweight eyes with blush over eyes, delicate feathered brows, painted upper and lower lashes, open mouth and accented lips, four upper and three lower teeth, orig blond mohair wig, papier-mâché torso with walking and crying mechanism, kid covering on lower torso, replaced composition arms, kid-covered upper legs, wax-over composition lower legs, possibly orig white openwork and lace dress, antique underclothing, socks and white leather shoes, unmarked, worn torso, seams taped, kid covering on lower torso and upper legs is deteriorating on left leg, arms replaced, limited movement in legs **1,050.00**

21" h, Figure A, bisque socket head, blue paperweight eyes, feathered brows, painted upper and lower lashes, closed mouth, pierced ears, orig cardboard pate, orig mohair wig, jointed composition body, straight wrists, pale pink dress made of antique fabric, matching bonnet, marked "Steiner/Paris/Fre A 13" on back of head, "Le Petit Parisien/Bebe Steiner" stamped on left hip **4,000.00**

24" h, Figure C, bisque socket head, blue paperweight eyes, blush over eyes, feathered brows, painted upper and lower lashes, closed mouth with accented lips, pierced ears, antique human hair wig, jointed wood and composition French body, jointed wrists, pink silk dress made of antique fabric, underclothing, and straw bonnet with flower trim, new socks and shoes, marked "Figure C No. 3/J. Steiner Bte SGDG/Paris" on back of head, rub on nose, few small flakes at each earring hole, couple small flakes edge of left ear, small flake at edge of cut for eye mechanism, replaced antique paperweight eyes............... **1,600.00**

German Fashion, pale bisque shoulder head, cobalt blue eyes, closed mouth, original skin wig with tiny curls, shapely fashion type cloth body, bisque lower arms, stitch jointed at hips and knees, antique white dress with ruffle at hem, silk bonnet, marked "3" on back of shoulder plate, 11-1/2" h, **$600.**

Terri Lee

16" h, bride, hard plastic head, painted brown eyes, single-stroke brows, painted upper and lower lashes, closed mouth, orig brunette wig, five-pc hard plastic body, orig tagged bride dress, matching veil, panties, satin shoes, marked "Terri Lee" on back and dress tag, accompanied by nine orig outfits in a trunk, including yellow Southern Belle with black shoes, Girl Scout uniform with brown and white shoes, nurse uniform with white shoes, tagged pants outfit with shirt, tagged pajamas with rabbit slippers, sweater, beret, shirt, blouse; school dress with pinafore, cowgirl costume with gauntlets and boots, hat missing, also booklets and papers, as well as extra accessories, unplayed with condition..... **2,400.00**

16" h, Terri Lee, hard plastic head, oversized painted brown eyes, single-stroke brows, long painted upper and lower lashes, closed mouth, synthetic wig, five-pc hard plastic body jointed at shoulders and hips, orig yellow Evening Formal, #3570D orig socks and shoes, long white coat, #3690A, matching hat, 1954, marked "Terri Lee" on back, Terri Lee tag on coat **475.00**

18" Connie Lynn, hard plastic head, blue sleep eyes with real lashes, single-stroke brows, painted lower lashes at corners of eyes, closed mouth, orig skin wig, hard plastic baby body, orig two-pc pink baby outfit, plastic panties, orig socks and white baby shoes, Terri Lee Nursery Registration Form and three Admission Cards to Terri Lee Hospital, Connie Lynn tag on clothing, orig box, unplayed with condition.............................. **625.00**

Thullier, A., 30" h, bisque, large blue paperweight eyes, molded features, closed mouth with protruding upper lip, blond human hair wig, orig jointed repainted composition body, rear of head marked "A. 14 T," antique blue mariner's outfit, antique shoes marked "Bebe Jumeau 12" **21,175.00**

Unis France, 9-1/2" h, 60, bisque socket head, light blue sleep eyes, single stroke brows, open mouth with four upper teeth, orig mohair wig, crude five-pc composition body, dressed in orig ethnic costume of Pont-l'Abbe in Brittany, France, marked "Unis/France/71 60 140/ 11/0" on back of head **175.00**

Kammer and Reinhardt, 121, bisque socket head, blue sleep eyes, open mouth with two upper teeth, spring tongue, original mohair wig, composition baby body with working crier, embossed roidered ribboned baby dress, lace and ribbon trimmed bonnet, marked "K * R, Simon & Halbig, 121 36" on back of head, 15" h, **$450.**

Venus, 16", pressed felt swivel head, well molded and painted features, orig mohair wig, cloth body, celluloid hands, jointed at shoulders and hips, navy blue felt uniform, matching beret, gold buttons, imitation leather belt, blue cloth leg wraps, brown leather boots, marked "Les Poupees/Venus/Paris/Made in France" on gold paper tag on jacket, "Venus/Paris/ Depose" on soles of shoes........... **475.00**

Vogue, Ginny, Red Riding Hood, hard plastic, elastic strung, painted lashes, blue eyes in downcast position, strong cheek color, side-part blond hair, red polka dot dress, red suede-like cape and hat, red straw basket, red shoes, white socks, orig hinged lid pink box #52, illegible Gilchrest's price tag, c1952 .... **490.00**

Walker, Izannah, 18" h, oil cloth, painted features, brown eyes with highlights, pink mouth and cheek coloring, brown hair, two long curls in front of applied ears, four curls down her back onto shoulders, cloth body, oil-painted hands, stockings stitched on, gray-green plaid silk taffeta dress, blue leather shoes, carries period red leather strap slip-on ice skates, Rhode Island, c1870, some paint wear, rubs **24,150.00**

Wax over, unmarked, 32" h, Alice-style, wax shoulder head, brown pupil-less sleep eyes, cloth body, period cotton dress, minor craze lines to wax.... **225.00**

Doorstops

History: Doorstops became popular in the late 19th century. They are either flat or three-dimensional and made out of a variety of different materials, such as cast iron, bronze, or wood. Hubley, a leading toy manufacturer, made many examples.

All prices listed are for excellent original paint unless otherwise noted. Original paint and condition greatly influence the price of a doorstop. To get top money, the original paint on a piece must be close to mint condition. Chipping of paint, paint loss, and wear reduce the value. Repainting severely reduces value and eliminates a good deal of the piece's market value, thereby reducing its value. A broken piece has little value to none.

Adviser: Craig Dinner.

Reproduction Alert: Reproductions are proliferating as prices on genuine doorstops continue to rise. A reproduced piece generally is slightly smaller than the original unless an original mold is used. The overall casting of reproductions is not as smooth as on the originals. Reproductions also lack the detail apparent in originals, including the appearance of the painted areas. Any bright orange rusting is strongly indicative of a new piece. Beware. If it looks too good to be true, it usually is.

Notes: Pieces described here contain at least 80 percent or more of the original paint and are in very good condition. Repainting drastically reduces price and desirability. Poor original paint is preferred over repaint.

All listings are cast-iron and flat-back castings unless otherwise noted.

Doorstops marked with an asterisk are currently being reproduced.

Cat, seated, black and white, marked "15," 11-1/2" h, 6-1/2" w, **$225.** Photo courtesy of Joy Luke Auctions.

Bear, 15" h, holding and looking at honey pot, brown fur, black highlights **1,500.00**

Bellhop, 8-7/8" h, blue uniform, with orange markings, brown base, hands at side... **300.00**

Bowl, 7" x 7", green-blue, natural colored fruit, sgd "Hubley 456" **125.00**

Boy, 10-5/8" h, wearing diapers, directing traffic, police hat, red scarf, brown dog at side... **665.00**

***Caddie**, 8" h, carrying brown and tan bag, white, brown, knickers, red jacket **800.00**

Dog, bulldog, late 19th/early 20th C, wear, 15-7/8" h, **$500.** Photo courtesy of Skinner, Inc.

Cat

*8" h, black, red ribbon and bow around neck, on pillow.......... **175.00**

10-3/4" h, licking paw, white cat with black markings, marked "Sculpture Metal Studios" **475.00**

13-5/8" h, reaching, full figure, two-piece hollow casting, green eyes, off-white body........................ **750.00**

Child, 17" h, reaching, naked, short brown curly hair, flesh color....... **1,450.00**

Clipper ship, 5-1/4" h, full sails, American flag on top mast, wave base, two rubber stoppers, sgd "CJO".... **65.00**

Cosmos flower basket, 17-3/4" h, blue and pink flowers, white vase, black base, Hubley **1,150.00**

Cottage, 8-5/8" l, 5-3/4" h, Cape type, blue roof, flowers, fenced garden, bath, sgd "Eastern Specialty Mfg Co. 14" **165.00**

Dancer, 8-7/8" h, Art Deco couple doing Charleston, pink dress, black tux, red and black base, "FISH" on front, sgd "Hubley 270" **1,250.00**

Dog

7" h, three puppies in basket, natural colors, sgd "Copyright 1932 M. Rosenstein, Lancaster, PA, USA" **350.00**

8" x 7-1/2", Beagle pup, full figure, cream with darker markings **685.00**

9" h, Boston Bull, full figure, facing left, black, tan markings........ **175.00**

10-1/2" x 3-1/2", St. Bernard, lying down, full figure, cream with brown markings, Hubley **650.00**

14" x 9", Sealyham, full figure, Hubley, cream and tan dog, red collar..................................... **675.00**

Dolly, 9-1/2" h, pink bow in blond hair, holding doll in blue dress, white apron, yellow dress, Hubley **365.00**

Doorman in Livery, 12" h, twin men, worn orig paint, marked "Fish," Hubley **1,650.00**

Dog, terrier, painted black and white, red trim, some paint flakes. **$140**. Photo courtesy of Joy Luke Auctions.

Drum major, 12-5/8" h, full figure, ivory pants, red hat with feather, yellow baton in right hand, left hand on waist, sq base **225.00**

Duck, 7-1/2" h, white, green bush and grass.. **335.00**

Elephant, 14" h, palm trees, early 20th C, very minor paint wear.................. **335.00**

Fisherman, 6-1/4" h, standing at wheel, hand over eyes, rain gear **185.00**

Frog, 3" h, full figure, sitting, yellow and green **50.00**

Giraffe, 20-1/4" h, tan, brown spots, squared off lines to casting **2,850.00**

***Golfer**, 10" h, overhand swing, hat and ball on ground, Hubley................ **450.00**

***Halloween Girl**, 13-3/4" h, 9-3/4" l, white hat, flowing cape, holding orange jack-o-lantern with red cutout eyes, nose, and mouth.. **2,000.00**

Indian chief, 9-3/4" h, orange and tan headdress, yellow pants, and blue stripes, red patches at ankles, green grass, sgd "A. A. Richardson," copyright 1928.. **295.00**

Irises, purple, white, and green flowers, marked "469," 11" h, 6-1/2" w, **$250**. Photo courtesy of Joy Luke Auctions.

Lighthouse, 14" h, green rocks, black path, white lighthouse, red window and door trim **385.00**

Mammy

8-1/2" h, full figure, Hubley, red dress, white apron, polka-dot bandanna on head................ **225.00**

*10" h, full figure, one piece hollow casting, white scarf and apron, dark blue dress, red kerchief on head **400.00**

Monkey

8-1/2" h, 4 5/8" w wrap-around tail, full figure, brown and tan **250.00**

14-3/8" h, hand reaching up, brown, tan, and white....................... **650.00**

Old Mill, 6-1/4" h, brown log mill, tan roof, white patch, green shrubs............ **500.00**

Owl, 9-1/2" h, sits on books, sgd "Eastern Spec Co" **335.00**

Pan, 7" h, with flute, sitting on mushroom, green outfit, red hat and sleeves, green grass base.................................. **165.00**

Peasant woman, 8-3/4" h, blue dress, black hair, fruit basket on head **250.00**

Penguin, 10" h, full figure, facing sideways, black, white chest, top hat and bow tie, yellow feet and beak, unsgd Hubley **435.00**

Policeman, 9-1/2" h, leaning on red fire hydrant, blue uniform and titled hat, comic character face, tan base, "Safety First" on front **725.00**

Prancing horse, 11" h, scrolled and molded base, "Greenlees Glasgow" imp on base, cast iron........................ **175.00**

***Quail**, 7-1/4" h, two brown, tan, and yellow birds, green, white, and yellow grass, "Fred Everett" on front, sgd "Hubley 459" **365.00**

Punch, later gold paint, **$115**. Photo courtesy of Pook & Pook.

Rabbit, 8-1/8" h, eating carrot, red sweater, brown pants **375.00**

Rooster, 13" h, red comb, black and brown tail **360.00**

Squirrel, 9" h, sitting on stump eating nut, brown and tan **275.00**

Storybook

4-1/2" h, Humpty Dumpty, full figure, sgd "661" **325.00**

7-3/4" h, Little Miss Muffett, sitting on mushroom, blue dress, blond hair **175.00**

9-1/2" h, Little Red Riding Hood, basket at side, red cape, tan dress with blue pattern, blond hair, sgd "Hubley" **475.00**

12-1/2" h, Huckleberry Finn, floppy hat, pail, stick, Littco Products label **450.00**

Sunbonnet Girl, 9" h, pink dress **185.00**

Whistler, 20-1/4" h, boy, hands in tan knickers, yellow striped baggy shirt, sgd "B & H" **2,750.00**

***Windmill**, 6-3/4" h, ivory, red roof, house at side, green base **115.00**

***Woman**, 11" h, flowers and shawl **315.00**

Zinnias, 11-5/8" h, multicolored flowers, blue and black vase, sgd "B & H" **265.00**

DRESDEN/MEISSEN

History: Augustus II, Elector of Saxony and King of Poland, founded the Royal Saxon Porcelain Manufactory in the Albrechtsburg, Meissen, in 1710. Johann Frederick Boettger, an alchemist, and Tschirnhaus, a nobleman, experimented with kaolin from the Dresden area to produce porcelain. By 1720, the factory produced a whiter hard-paste porcelain than that from the Far East. The factory experienced its golden age from the 1730s to the 1750s under the leadership of Samuel Stolzel, kiln master, and Johann Gregor Herold, enameler.

The Meissen factory was destroyed and looted by forces of Frederick the Great during the Seven Years' War (1756-1763). It was reopened, but never achieved its former greatness.

In the 19th century, the factory reissued some of its earlier forms. These later wares are called "Dresden" to differentiate them from the earlier examples. Further, there were several other porcelain factories in the Dresden region and their products also are grouped under the "Dresden" designation.

Marks: Many marks were used by the Meissen factory. The first was a pseudo-Oriental mark in a square. The famous crossed swords mark was adopted in 1724. A small dot between the hilts was used from 1763 to 1774, and a star between the hilts from 1774 to 1814. Two modern marks are swords with a hammer and sickle and swords with a crown.

For more information, see *Warman's English & Continental Pottery & Porcelain*, 3rd edition.

Dresden

Compote, 14-1/4" h, figural, shaped pierced oval bowl with applied florets, support stems mounted with two figures of children, printed marks, late 19th/early 20th C, pr **350.00**

Bowl, floral form, hand-painted floral decoration, hand-painted gilt design on border, impressed "D" mark, 10" d, 4" h, **$135**. Photo courtesy of Alderfer Auction Co.

Cup and saucer, hp medallion, marked "GLC Dresden" **150.00**

Dessert plate in frame, 8" d printed and tinted plate, scenes of courting couples, insets, and floral sprigs, gilt details, 15-3/4" sq giltwood shadowbox frame, early 20th C, set of four **175.00**

Figure

- 5-3/4" h, 5-1/2" w, Putti charting the heavens, putto seated at table, peering through telescope, another putto studying celestial globe, ovoid base, late 19th/early 20th C, loss, crazing **375.00**
- 8-1/4" h, Spaniel, seated, scratching chin with back leg **525.00**
- 9-1/4" h, foo dog, stylized, seated, curly fur, 20th C **425.00**

Plate, wide reticulated border with polychrome decorated flowers, center with hand-painted courting scene on cobalt blue ground, crossed swords Meissen mark, 9-1/2" d, **$1,650**. Photo courtesy of Alderfer Auction Co.

Loving cup, 6-1/2" h, three handles, woodland scene with nymph, gold trim **475.00**

Perfume bottle, 3-3/8" l, cylindrical, enamel dec with scene of courting couple, floral sprays, gilt-metal lid enclosing cut glass stopper, early 20th C **115.00**

Portrait vase, 6" h, front with oval roundel printed with portrait bust of 18th C lady, gilt floral surround, central band of beaded landscape cartouches and foliate scrolls, faux jeweled diapered ground, two short gilt flying-loop handles **635.00**

Urn, cov, 14-1/2" h, domed lid with fruit finial, body with two gilt flying-loop handles, trumpet foot on sq base, rose Pompadour ground, painted scenes of courting couples and floral bouquets, late 19th/early 20th C, price for pr, one damaged **700.00**

Vase, 13-1/4" h, alternating panels of figures and yellow floral bouquets, Thieme factory, late 19th C........... **115.00**

Vase, cov, 14" h, alternating panels of lowers and turquoise ground floral bouquets, c1900, minor damage, pr **375.00**

Whatnot shelf, 13-1/2" w, 13-1/3" h, figural and foliate porcelain posts, mirrored back, shaped ebonized wood tiers, 20th C **200.00**

Meissen

Basket, 9-3/4" d, oval, everted reticulated sides accented outside with blue flowerheads, short crabstock handles, scattered bocage, enamel dec center with floral bouquet, early 20th C **400.00**

Bowl, 9" d, 5" h, double handled form, reticulated sides, ftd base, polychrome floral dec, gilt accents, wear and damage **295.00**

Cabinet plate, 9-5/8" d, enameled center with cupid and female in wooded landscape, gilt dec pink and burgundy border, titled on reverse "Lei Wiedergut" **490.00**

Cane, c1885, hand painted, 4-3/4" l x 2" h handle, top painted with scene of lady holding fan, and her hand-maiden, talking to seated gentleman with sword at side, pointing to distant manor, 18th C attire, colorful floral sprays, gold highlights, 1-1/4" gold collar marked by maker, Malacca shaft, 1-1/2" horn ferrule, 34-1/8" h **1,180.00**

Center bowl, 15" l, reticulated, ram's head handles, animal feet, center panel of sheep. blue crossed swords mark, c1880, minor losses **920.00**

Chandelier, 23" h, baluster-form shaft with hand-painted flower and leaf motifs, similar applied motifs on white ground, six S-scroll arms with conforming applied floral dec, candle cups, suspending tassels with applied floral bouquets 900.00

Sugar bowl, covered, all-over polychrome floral decoration, applied handles in the form of green stems ending in raised applied flowers and leaves, strawberry finial with raised applied leaf and blossom, gold rim, Meissen, 18th C, 5-1/2" d, 5-1/2" h, very minor loss to petals of one side flower and top strawberry blossom, **$460**. Photo courtesy of Alderfer Auction Co.

Clock, 18-3/4" h, Rococo style, clock face surrounded by applied floral dec, four fully molded figures representing four seasons **3,400.00**

Cup and saucer, flower-filled basket dec **90.00**

Dessert service, partial, pink floral dec, gilt trim, five 8" d plates with pierced rims, two 11-1/2" h compotes with figures of boy and girl flower sellers in center of dish, pierced rims, 20th C **1,850.00**

Dinner service, partial, Deutsche Blumen, molded New Dulong border, gilt highlights, two oval serving platters, circular platter, fish platter, 8-1/2" cov tureen with figural finial, two sauce boats with attached underplates, two serving spoons, sq serving dish, two small oval dishes, cov jam pot with attached underplate and spoon, 20 dinner plates, 11 teacups and saucers, nine salad plates, 10 bread plates, 10 soups, 74-pc set **8,500.00**

Dish, cov, 6-5/8" h, female blackamoor, beside covered dish with molded basketweave and rope edge, modeled on freeform oval base with applied florets, incised #328, 20th C **575.00**

Figure

- 3-1/4" h, 6-1/4" l, seated child feeding small dog from plate, 20th C **1,100.00**
- 5-1/4" h, Motto, modeled as figure of Eros seated on cloud, three-sided base with central cartouche inscribed "Le prends menesser," late 19th/early 20th C **980.00**
- 6-1/4" h, Commedia Dell'Arte, man with red robe and pointed beard, on flower-strewn base, Germany, late 19th C **1,150.00**
- 14-1/4" h, cockatoo, perched on tree stump, flower and leaves at base, early 20th C **2,300.00**

Fruit knives, set of 12, Onion pattern, blue and white **265.00**

Fruit plate, 8-3/4" d, each center printed and painted with fruit sprig, one with grapes, other plums, foliate garland border, entwined monogram in gilt roundel, cobalt blue rim, 20th C, pr **715.00**

Mirror, 9-1/2" l, oval, heavily applied with leaves and flowers, top adorned with two cherubs supporting floral garland, Germany, c1900 .... **1,380.00**

Vase, urn form, bifurcate coiled snake handles ending in acanthus, cobalt blue glazed body painted with floral cartouche in gilt surround, fluted trumpet foot with leaftip base, Meissen, early 20th C, 15-1/4" h, **$1,175**. Photo courtesy of Skinner, Inc.

Plate, 9" d, molded with four cartouches of bunches of fruit, shaped edge with C-scroll and wings, gilt dec, late 19th C, price for pr **250.00**

Serving bowl, 8-5/8" d, oblong, shaped rim with clipped corners, floral bouquet enamel dec center, landscape scenes on two sides, two other sides with foliates on black ground, gilt rim, factory seconds mark, early 20th C **175.00**

Soup tureen, cov, stand, Onion pattern, blue and white **265.00**

Tea set, partial, 4-3/4" h ovoid teapot with dragon head spout, lid with flower blossom finial, 6-5/8" d waste bowl, six teacups, six saucers, all with gilt enamel floral dec, late 19th C, 14 pcs **715.00**

Tray, 17-3/8" l, oval, enameled floral sprays, gilt trim, 20th C **400.00**

Urn on pedestal, 21" h, figural cartouches, scattered floral dec, two handles in form of pair of entwined snakes, mounted as lamps, pr **4,000.00**

Vase

- 10-1/2" h, floral dec, bands of molded gilt dec, each handle molded as two entwined snakes, gilt highlights **475.00**
- 15-1/2" h, scrolled snake handles, cobalt blue ground, gold and silver floral dec, 19th C, new gold trim to handles **2,300.00**

Vegetable tureen, cov, stand, Onion pattern, blue and white **195.00**

Wall garniture, 12-5/8" w, 19" l two-light girandole in rococo-style frame topped by putto figure, two figures of children among flowers on sides, brackets for two serpentine candle arms, two 15-1/2" w, 15-3/4" h scenic plaques with center painted scenes of bustling harbor, similar styled frames, sockets for candle arms, two 15-3/4" w, 15-3/4" h rococo-style three-light wall sconces, framed as rocaille scroll with three floral-encrusted serpentine candle arms, 19th C **3,100.00**

DUNCAN AND MILLER

For more information, see *Warman's Glass*, 4th edition.

History: George Duncan, and Harry B. and James B., his sons, and Augustus Heisey, his son-in-law, formed George Duncan & Sons in Pittsburgh, Pennsylvania, in 1865. The factory was located just two blocks from the Monongahela River, providing easy and inexpensive access by barge for materials needed to produce glass. The men, from Pittsburgh's south side, were descendants of generations of skilled glassmakers.

The plant burned to the ground in 1892. James E. Duncan Sr. selected a site for a new factory in Washington, Pennsylvania, where operations began on February 9, 1893. The plant prospered, producing fine glassware and table services for many years.

John E. Miller, one of the stockholders, was responsible for designing many fine patterns, the most famous being Three Face. The firm incorporated and used the name The Duncan and Miller Glass Company until the plant closed in 1955. The company's slogan was, "The Loveliest Glassware in America." The U.S. Glass Co. purchased the molds, equipment, and machinery in 1956.

Additional Listing: Pattern Glass.

Animal

- Heron, crystal **125.00**
- Swan, 6-1/2" h, opal pink **115.00**

Bowl, Viking Ship, crystal **175.00**

Cake plate, Teardrop, crystal, two handles **45.00**

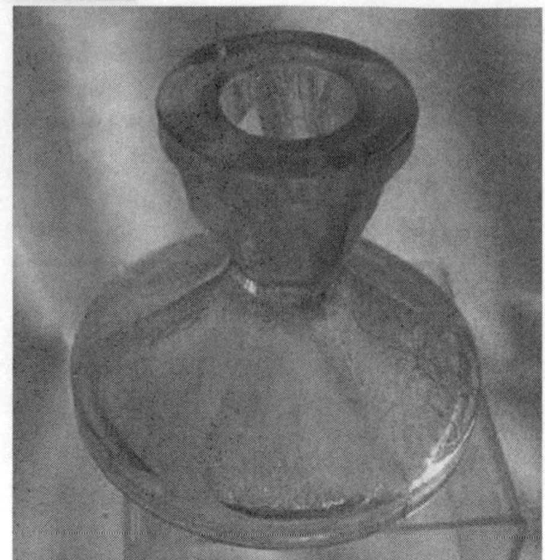
Candlestick, Tree of Life pattern, 4" d base, 3-1/2" h, **$20**.

Candleholder, Canterbury, #115-121, price for pr **55.50**
Candy box, cov, Canterbury, crystal, three parts, 6" d **70.00**
Champagne
- Canterbury, chartreuse **11.50**
- Indian Tree, crystal **30.00**

Cocktail, Caribbean, blue, 3-3/4 oz **45.00**

Compote, Clear Ribbon pattern, c1880, 14" h, **$60**.

Compote, Spiral Flutes, amber, 6" d **20.00**
Console bowl, 11" d, Rose etch, crystal **37.50**
Cornucopia, #121, Swirl, blue opalescent, shape #2, upswept tail **75.00**
Creamer and sugar, individual size, Canterbury, crystal, matching tray **35.00**
Creamer and sugar, table size, Passion Flower, crystal **42.00**
Cup and saucer
- Charmaine Rose, crystal **20.00**
- Teardrop, crystal **15.00**

Finger bowl, Astaire, red **65.00**
Goblet, water
- Canterbury, chartreuse **11.50**
- Caribbean, blue **55.00**
- First Love, crystal, 10 oz **35.00**
- Indian Tree, crystal **35.00**
- Plaza, cobalt blue **40.00**

Iced tea tumbler, ftd, Indian Tree, crystal **30.00**
Juice tumbler, Canterbury, chartreuse **9.50**
Mint tray, Sylvan, 7-1/2" l, crystal, ruby handle **35.00**
Nappy, Sandwich, crystal, two parts, divided, handle **14.00**
Oyster cocktail, Canterbury, citrone **18.00**

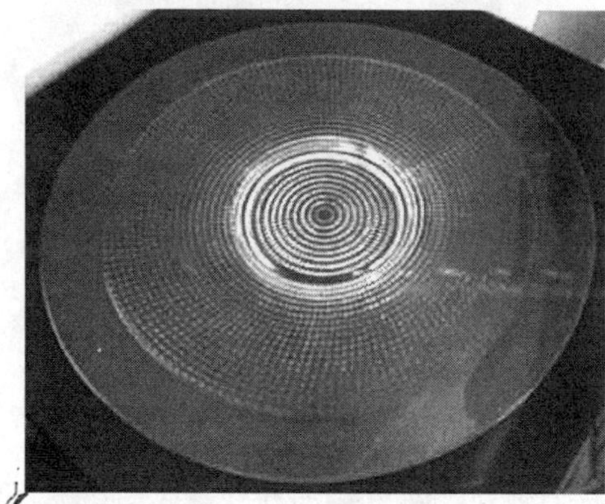
Punch bowl underplate, Teardrop pattern, 23" d, **$200**. Photo courtesy of Matt Freier.

Plate
- Canterbury, 8" d, crystal **8.00**
- First Love, 8-1/2" d **25.00**
- Radiance, light blue, 8-1/2" d **17.50**
- Spiral Flute, crystal, 10-3/8" d **15.00**
- Terrace, cobalt blue, 7-1/2" d **30.00**

Punch cup, Caribbean, crystal **10.00**
Relish
- First Love, three parts, #115, two handles, 10-1/2" x 1-1/4", minor wear **60.00**
- Language of Flowers, three parts, three handles, #115 .... **37.50**
- Terrace, four parts, 9" d, crystal **55.00**
- Tear Drop, three parts, applied handle, crystal **24.00**

Sherbet
- Canterbury, chartreuse **15.00**
- Spiral Flutes, green **13.50**

Sugar
- Caribbean, crystal **12.00**
- Tear Drop, crystal, 8 oz **10.00**

Punch bowl, Teardrop pattern, 13-3/4" across top, 8-1/2" h, **$350**. Photo courtesy of Matt Freier.

Sugar shaker, Duncan Block, crystal **42.00**
Tray, Sandwich, crystal, 8" l, two handles **18.50**
Tumbler
- Canterbury, chartreuse **13.50**
- Spiral Flutes, crystal, amber flashed rim, stem, and foot **20.00**

Whiskey, sea horse, etch #502, red and crystal **48.00**
Wine, Sandwich, crystal, 3 oz **20.00**

DURAND

History: Victor Durand (1870-1931), born in Baccarat, France, apprenticed at the Baccarat glassworks, where several generations of his family had worked. In 1884, Victor came to America to join his father at Whitall-Tatum & Co. in New Jersey. In 1897, father and son leased the Vineland Glass Manufacturing Company in Vineland, New Jersey. Products included inexpensive bottles, jars, and glass for scientific and medical purposes. By 1920, four separate companies existed.

For more information, see *Warman's Glass*, 4th edition.

When Quezal Art Glass and Decorating Company failed, Victor Durand recruited Martin Bach Jr., Emil J. Larsen, William Wiedebine, and other Quezal men and opened an art-glass shop at Vineland in December 1924. Quezal-style iridescent pieces were made. New innovations included cameo and intaglio designs, geometric Art-Deco shapes, Venetian Lace, and Oriental-style pieces. In 1928, crackled glass, called Moorish Crackle and Egyptian Crackle, was made.

Durand died in 1931. The Vineland Flint Glass Works was merged with Kimble Glass Company a year later, and the art glass line was discontinued.

Marks: Many Durand glass pieces are not marked. Some have a sticker with the words "Durand Art Glass," others have the name "Durand" scratched on the pontil or "Durand" inside a large V. Etched numbers may be part of the marking.

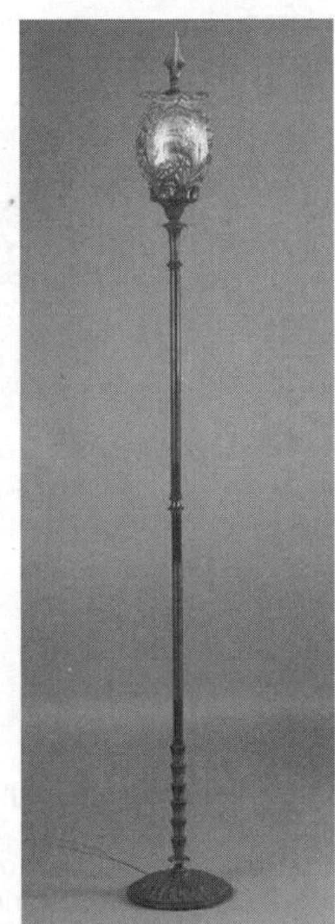

Torchere, blue and white Moorish crackle over ambergris shade with ruffled rim, standard torchere with dome base, unsigned, 3-1/4" shade aperture, 67-1/2" h, fitter rim chip, **$600**. Photos courtesy of Skinner, Inc.

Bowl, 9-3/4" d, butterscotch, partial silver sgd **345.00**
Candlesticks, pr, mushroom, red, opal pulled florals, pale yellow base **725.00**
Compote, 7-1/2" d, 4-1/2" h, irid gold, white pulled feather and blue dot dec, applied blue edge, translucent amber foot, unsigned............ **1,610.00**
Decanter, 12" h, blue cut to clear, mushroom shaped stopper, unsigned **600.00**
Jar, cov, 7-1/4" h, ginger jar form, King Tut, green, irid gold dec, applied amber glass dec on cov............ **3,100.00**
Lamp, 18-1/2" h, 3-1/2" d irid shades with gold applied threading and surface decorated hearts, gold finish int., metal bases appear to be contemporary, pr **575.00**
Lamp shade, 6-3/4" h, spherical, blue and white craquelle, replacement single brass hanging fixture............ **625.00**
Plate, 8" d, green, white pulled feather dec, rim surrounded by garland of cut roses and leaves **980.00**
Sherbet, 3-1/2" h, ambergris, gold luster finish, unsigned **150.00**
Table torchieres, pr, 15-1/2" h, Egyptian crackle, trumpet form, green and white striated glass with irid gold crackle dec, bronze acanthus leaf electrified bases, c1926, pr **1,725.00**

Vase, shape no. 1723, flared ruffle rim tapering to waist and rounding at base, opal heart and vine dec on blue irid glass, polished pontil, unsigned, 4-7/8" h, **$940**.

Vase

4-1/2" h, pinched sides, inverted ruffled top, Cypriot, irid blue and lavender **250.00**
6-3/4" h, flaring top, irid blue, white heart and vine dec, unsigned **1,150.00**
7" h, irid blue shoulder, all over white vine dec, base sgd "DURAND 1721," some int. stains **1,100.00**
7" h, irid gold, applied gold threading, gold int., sgd "DURAND 17107," major threading loss **115.00**
7-1/4" h, shouldered, irid green and gold pulled feather dec, applied gold threading, gold int., base sgd "DURAND 1812-7," some threading missing............ **635.00**
8" h, cranberry, red and white pulled feather dec, five wheel-cut rosettes and leaves, unsigned, int. staining, top ground............ **415.00**
8-1/2" h, King Tut, irid blue finish, white and yellow vine dec, irid blue int., polished pontil with script sgd "DURAND" **2,300.00**
8-3/4" h, cobalt blue, blue and white pulled feather dec, unsigned **1,100.00**
9-1/4" h, irid blue, applied threading, base sgd "DURAND 1707," some threading missing............ **575.00**
9-1/4" h, Moorish crackle, blue and white crackle panels over ambergris lustered body, c1920............ **2,300.00**
10" h, King Tut, irid gold surface finish, all over vine dec, irid gold int., unsigned **1,560.00**
12-1/4" h, ftd, opal, blue pulled feather dec tipped in gold, irid gold overall threading, foot and int. sgd in silver "V Durand 20 120-12," c1920 .... **2,185.00**
12-1/2" h, beehive form, ambergris, reddish gold luster finish, c1915 .... **2,300.00**

Early American Glass

History: The term "Early American glass" covers glass made in America from the colonial period through the mid-19th century. As such, it includes the early pressed glass and lacy glass made between 1827 and 1840.

For more information, see *Warman's Glass*, 4th edition.

Major glass-producing centers prior to 1850 were Massachusetts (New England Glass Company and the Boston and Sandwich Glass Company), South Jersey, Pennsylvania (Stiegel's Manheim factory and many Pittsburgh-area firms), and Ohio (several different companies in Kent, Mantua, and Zanesville).

Early American glass was popular with collectors from 1920 to 1950. It has now regained some of its earlier prominence. Leading auction sources for early American glass include American Bottle Auctions, Garth's, Heckler & Company, Green Valley, James D. Julia, and Skinner, Inc.

Additional Listings: Blown Three Mold; Cup Plates; Flasks; Sandwich Glass; Stiegel-Type Glass.

Bowl, Pittsburgh, 19th C, colorless, round bowl with outfolded rim, alternating cut diamond with fan and printies with blaze cutting, knopped stem on circular base, 11-1/2" d, 9-1/2" h, **$775**. Photos courtesy of Skinner, Inc.

Blown

Bottle, globular

3-1/8" h, Zanesville, light aqua **325.00**
5" h, Midwestern, aqua, 22 swirled ribs, pontil, flared lip............ **550.00**
6" h, Kent/Mantua, aqua, 16 slightly swirled ribs, flattened lip, tiny pot stones............ **200.00**
7-3/8" h, Zanesville, olive green, applied lip, few pot stones **385.00**
7-1/2" h, Zanesville, aqua, 24 swirled ribs, pot stones and scratches **330.00**

7-1/2" h, Zanesville, citron, 24 tightly swirled ribs, one pot stone **4,500.00**

8" h, Kent, brilliant aqua, three-mold, applied collar lip................ **3,200.00**

8" h, Zanesville, dark amber, 24 swirled ribs, tiny pot stones, broken blister.................................... **770.00**

8-1/2" h, Zanesville, olive green, tiny pot stones, overall wear........ **825.00**

Bowl

4-1/4" d, 2-7/8" h, brilliant amethyst, 16 ribs, flared rim with folded lip, applied foot.......................... **550.00**

12-5/8" d, 14-1/2" h, colorless, cylindrical shaped bowl, outward turned rim, raised on flared trumpet base with hollow knop, under-folded rim, light scratches............ **2,000.00**

Candlesticks, pr, 9-1/2" h, Pittsburgh, tulip sockets, round, domed bases with paneled stems with egg shaped int. drop, some roughness at socket attachments **295.00**

Compote, cov, 6-1/4" d, 10-1/4" h, Pittsburgh, clear, prominent swirled ribs on bowl and lid, applied foot and wafer finial, McKearin Plate 55-2....... **10,175.00**

Compote, open, 8-1/4" d, 8-1/2" h, Ribbon, brilliant amethyst, sawtooth edge, reticulated flared sides, hexagonal base with rayed bottom, straw marks, Lee 153.. **22,000.00**

Creamer

4" h, brilliant cobalt blue, 21 slightly swirled ribs, applied handle.. **450.00**

4-1/2" h, Zanesville, brilliant violet blue, applied handle.......... **2,650.00**

4-3/4" h, brilliant peacock blue, applied foot and handle........ **450.00**

Flask, pattern molded, citron green, vertical ribs, sheared lip pontil, Midwestern, 4-3/4" h, **$1,400**. Photo courtesy of Pacific Glass Auctions.

Cruet, 7-1/4" h, cobalt blue, 16 vertical ribs, Pittsburgh stopper, applied handle, tiny pot stone...... **800.00**

Fish bowl, 9-3/4" h, colorless, rolled outward rim, trumpet form foot with under-folded rim.......................... **215.00**

Flask

3" h, chestnut, cobalt blue, 18 swirled ribs, pontil, sheared and fire polished lip........................... **425.00**

3-3/8" h, Mantua, sea green, 16 swirled ribs, few pot stones and residue **500.00**

5" h, Zanesville, deep amber, chestnut, 10 diamond **3,960.00**

5-3/4" h, amber, pint, scroll.... **635.00**

5-3/4" h, Midwestern, light green, chestnut, 16 vertical melon ribs, flared lip, minor scratches, trace of residue **275.00**

Flip glass, 6" h, applied handle, deeply etched basket of flowers............. **550.00**

Ink, 2-1/4" d, 1-1/2" h, olive amber, McKearin GIII-29, minor wear **145.00**

Mug, 4" h, brilliant cobalt blue, applied handle...................................... **1,155.00**

Pan

5-3/8" d, 2" h, Zanesville, aqua, 10 diamond, flared sides, folded-in rim **8,470.00**

5-3/4" d, 2" h, Pittsburgh, amethyst, 12 ribbed-panel bowl, applied foot, folded rim **4,400.00**

8-7/8" d, 2-1/8" h, Zanesville, golden, flared sides, fold-out rim, pot stone **1,045.00**

10-3/8" d, 2" h, Pittsburgh, pale amethyst, eight panels, folded out lip, in-the-making imperfection in one panel **1,750.00**

Pitcher, 6" h, Zanesville, pale green, 24 swirled ribs, applied ribbed handle **21,725.00**

Salt, master, 2-1/2" d, 3" h, dark cobalt blue, diamond quilted pattern...... **250.00**

Sugar, cov, 4-1/4" d, 6-1/2" h, dark cobalt blue, diamond quilted, applied foot, cone-shaped finial.................... **1,925.00**

Wine glass, 7-1/4" h, clear, cotton stem, early 19th C, price for pr **1,380.00**

Lacy

Bowl

8" d, 1-3/4" h, Thistle pattern, octagonal, alternating panels of thistle and flowers, colorless, minor roughness under rim............ **350.00**

10-1/2" d, Oak Leaf pattern, colorless **325.00**

Candlesticks, pr, 6" h, reeded and ribbed socket attached with wafer, reeded stem, sq stepped base, chips, checks in socket.......................... **450.00**

Compote, cov, 9-1/2" h, 8-1/4" d, Sawtooth, flint, chips **155.00**

Dish

4-3/4" x 3/4" h, scalloped border, inner border of scroll and diamonds, starburst and stippled rim center, vaseline-green...................... **215.00**

5" d, 3/4" h, pressed, border with two rows of scroll design, center star with scrolls, stippled background, amethyst, one tooth missing, small chips, and roughness **115.00**

8-1/4" x 6-1/4" x 1-1/2" h, Gothic pattern, Gothic arch and leaf design, minor edge roughness.......... **375.00**

10-3/4" x 9" x 1-1/2" h, Fan and Scroll pattern, diamond center enclosing flower, edge chips................ **395.00**

Miniature lamp, 4" h, lacy cup-plate base, blown spherical font, knob stem, chips on base............................. **385.00**

Pitcher, South Jersey, early 19th C, blown, pale aqua, circular base, applied scrolled handle, 7" h, **$1,000**.

Plate

5-1/2" d, Heart, circle waffle design on rim, three stippled hearts in center, colorless, rim roughness **295.00**

5-1/2" d, Roman Rosette pattern, colorless.............................. **320.00**

6" d, Peacock eye-type pattern, oak leaf and flower border, colorless, rim roughness **225.00**

6-1/4" d, Diamond Waffle border, star center, colorless, edge roughness **200.00**

9" d, 1-1/4" h, Oak leaf pattern, colorless, rim roughness....... **275.00**

Salt, open

3" l, 2" w, 2" h, Wagon, four molded wheels, star and diamond pattern on stippled background sides, colorless, pressed, old corner repair **230.00**

3-3/4" l, 2" w, 1-1/2" h, Steamboat, *Pittsburgh* on end, colorless, very minor edge roughness.......... **520.00**

Toddy, 5-3/8" d, brilliant dark amethyst, lacy, Roman Rosette, Sandwich, edge chips... **330.00**

Pillar mold

Candlestick, 7-5/8" h, teal green, hexagonal, center wafer, small flake on socket, base flakes, chipped corner **1,925.00**

Cologne bottle, 5-5/8" h, cobalt blue, eight ribs, two applied rings, flared lip, mushroom stopper, stopper base shipped **400.00**

Cuspidor, 6-1/2" h, clear, tulip form, ruffled rim, polished pontil, attributed to Pittsburgh **220.00**

Decanter, 9-3/4" h, cobalt blue, applied handle and collar, pewter jigger cap **7,950.00**

Jigger, attributed to Pittsburgh
2-1/4" h, cobalt blue, Loop pattern **115.00**
2-1/2" h, cobalt blue, Arch pattern **125.00**
2-1/2" h, cobalt blue, Broken Arch pattern **110.00**

Lamp, finger, 2-5/8" h plus burner, cornstarch blue, applied handle, brass collar, burning fluid burner with snuffer cap **615.00**

Pitcher, 5-5/8" h, colorless, applied handle, Pittsburgh, bottom ground flat, minor wear **275.00**

Tumbler, attributed to Pittsburgh
3-1/4" h, cobalt blue, Arch pattern **175.00**
3-1/2" h, cobalt blue, Broken Arch pattern **145.00**

Wine, 4-1/4" h, canary, paneled, knop stem **215.00**

English China and Porcelain (General)

History: By the 19th century, more than 1,000 china and porcelain manufacturers were scattered throughout England, with the majority of the factories located in the Staffordshire district.

For more information, see *Warman's English & Continental Pottery & Porcelain*, 4th edition.

By the 19th century, English china and porcelain had achieved a worldwide reputation for excellence. American stores imported large quantities for their customers. The special-production English pieces of the 18th and early 19th centuries held a position of great importance among early American antiques collectors.

Caughley, jug, molded cabbage leaves, mask spout, transfer-printed blue floral decoration, underglaze blue crescent mark, c1785, 8-1/2" h, **$800**. Photo courtesy of Sloans & Kenyon Auctions.

Bow

Candlesticks, pr, two birds on flowering branches, dog and sheep on grassy base, wood stand, c1755.......... **1,200.00**

Egg cup, 2-1/2" h, two half-flower panels, powder blue ground, pseudo Oriental mark, c1760................................ **900.00**

Plate, 9" d, Turk's Cap Lily, dragonfly and moths, c1755.............................. **850.00**

Chelsea

Bowl, 8-3/4" d, swirled ribs, scalloped, foliage and floral dec..................... **75.00**

Candlesticks, pr, 7-1/2" h, figural, draped putti, sitting on tree stump holding flower, scroll-molded base, encircled in puce, gilt, wax pan **850.00**

Cup and saucer, multicolored exotic birds, white ground, gold anchor mark, c1765.. **750.00**

Plate, 8-1/2" d, multicolored floral design, scalloped rim, gold anchor mark **475.00**

Derby

Beaker, 3-1/8" h, two short shell-shaped handles, two painted landscape roundels in gilt borders, scenes titled "Near Spondon" and "Near Breadshall," both Derbyshire scenes, pale yellow ground, late 18th/early 19th C **1,265.00**

Figure, 8" h, 8-1/2" h, pastoral, boy resting against tree stump playing bagpipe, black hat, bleu-do-roi jacket, gilt trim, yellow breeches, girl with green hat, bleu-du-roi bodice, pink skirt, white apron with iron-red flowerheads, gilt centers, leaves, scroll molded mound base, crown and incised iron-red D mark, pr **2,200.00**

Jar, cov, 22" h, octagonal, iron-red, bottle green and leaf green, alternating cobalt blue and white grounds, gilding, grotesque sea-serpent handles, now fitted as lamp with carved base, 19th C, pr **10,000.00**

Plate, 10-1/8" d, enamel dec, stylized Imari-type designs of birds in three, shaped molded rim, Bloor mark, second quarter 19th C, price for set of seven **300.00**

New Hall, 3-3/8" d handleless cup, 5-5/8" d, 2-1/8" h deep saucer, hand-painted queen's rose, rim bands of alternating panels of pink scales and rose decoration, rust accents, unmarked, late 18th/early 19th C, minor crazing, **$135**. Photo courtesy of Alderfer Auction Co.

Flight, Barr & Barr

Crocus pot, 9" w, 4" d, 6-1/4" h, D-form, molded columns and architrave, peach-ground panels, ruined abbey landscape reserve, gilding......................... **2,400.00**

Pastille burner, 3-1/2" h, cottage, four open chimneys, marked, c1815... **425.00**

Tea service, gilt foliate, orange ground banded border, 9-1/2" h cov teapot (finial restoration), 7" l teapot stand, 4-3/4" h creamer, 4-1/2" h sugar bowl, 6-5/8" d waste bowl, two 8" deep dishes, 10 coffee cans, 11 tea cups, 11 saucers, minor chips to cups and saucers, incised "B" mark, c1792-1804, light wear to gilt at rim throughout **1,320.00**

Herculaneum

Jug, 10" h, creamware, black transfer printed, obverse "Washington," oval design with medallion portrait on monument surmounted by wreath, birth, and death dates below, flanked by eagle and grieving woman, upper ribbon inscribed "Washington in Glory," lower ribbon "America In Tears," reverse transfer of American sailing vessel, American eagle beneath spout, inscription "Herculaneum Pottery Liverpool," incised mark on base, imperfections............................ **1,100.00**

Jackfield

Creamer, stippled and rose bands, eagle handle.. **150.00**

Pitcher, 6-1/2" h, applied handle, black, traces of enameling, bird, initials and "1763," wear, small flakes **125.00**

Sugar bowl, cov, 4-1/2" h, 3-3/4" d, scalloped SS rims, SS-mounted cov and ornate pierced finial...................... **250.00**

Teapot, 6-3/4" h, molded roses and thistles, ram's horn mask on handle **250.00**

Masons

Creamer, 4" h, Oriental-style shape, marked "Mason's Patent Ironstone" **85.00**

Jug, 8" h, octagonal, Hydra pattern, waisted straight neck, green-enameled handle, lion-head terminal, underglaze blue and iron-red flowers and vase, two imp marks and printed rounded crown mark, c1813-30 .... **320.00**

Platter, 13-1/2" x 10-3/4", Double-Landscape pattern, Oriental motif, deep green and brick red, c1883.......... **265.00**

Potpourri vase, cov, 25-1/4" h, hexagonal body, cobalt blue, large gold stylized peony blossom, chrysanthemums, prunus, and butterflies, gold and blue dragon handles, and knobs, trellis diaper-rim border, c1820-25 .... **1,750.00**

Creamware, miniature, tea and coffee service, 5" h teapot on stand, 4-3/4" h domed lid coffee pot, canister, four handleless cups and saucers, fluted bodies, green highlights, late 18th/early 19th C, **$8,625**. Photo courtesy of Pook & Pook.

New Hall

Creamer, Chinese figure on terrace, c1790 .... **190.00**

Dessert set, two oval dishes, eight plates, printed and colored named views, lavender-blue borders, light-blue ground, c1815 .... **450.00**

Tea set, interwoven ribbon and leaf trails, blue and gilt oval-medallion border, c1790, minor repairs, 44 pcs **1,500.00**

Salopian

Tea set, 4-1/4" h teapot, 5-1/4" h teapot, creamer, cov sugar with ram's head handles, waste bowl, six handleless cups and saucers, floral borders, oriental designs with boats and pagoda with porch, shallow flakes, repaired spout on creamer **2,200.00**

Swansea

Tea set, floral pattern, underglaze blue, black transfer, gilt trim, 12 8" d plates; 11 each teacups, coffee cups, saucers; teapot; creamer; three trays; 7-1/2" d bowl, some professional repair, worn gilt, several pcs with chips and hairlines **590.00**

Woods

Cup and saucer, handleless, Woods Rose **65.00**

Dish, 8" l, 6" w, dark blue transfer of castle, imp "Wood" **165.00**

Jug, 5-3/4" h, ovoid, cameos of Queen Caroline, pink luster ground, beaded edge, molded and painted floral border, c1820 .... **425.00**

Plate, 9" d, Woods Rose, scalloped edge **125.00**

Stirrup cup, 5-1/2" l, modeled hound's head, translucent shades of brown, c1760 .... **2,200.00**

Whistle, 3-7/8" h, modeled as seated sphinx, blue accents, oval green base, c1770 .... **600.00**

Worcester

Cream jug, cov, 5" h, floral finial, underglaze blue floral and insect dec, shaded crescent mark, 18th C, cover possibly married, slight finial chips, shallow flake to cover **175.00**

Deep dish, 9-1/2" l, oval, underglaze blue Chantilly sprig pattern, shaded crescent mark, 18th C, foot-rim chips **320.00**

Miniature, cup and saucer, handleless, blue and white three-flower and butterfly design, Dr. Wall underglaze blue crescent mark **150.00**

Sauce boat, 5-1/4" l, molded body, panels of underglaze blue flowers, cell border, open crescent mark, 18th C **300.00**

Sweetmeat dish, 9" d, formed as three scallop shells centered by cluster of shells and seaweed, naturalistic base encrusted with further shells and seaweed, 18th C **800.00**

Teapot, cov, globular, 5-5/8" h, underglaze blue dec of Waiting Chinaman, floral finial, open crescent mark, 18th C, slight spout nick, chips to finial **865.00**

Tureen, cov, 10-1/2" l, oval, underglaze blue pine cone pattern, artichoke finial, shell handles, shaded crescent mark, 18th C, one handle restored, int. rim flake **800.00**

English Soft Paste

History: Between 1820 and 1860, a large number of potteries in England's Staffordshire district produced decorative wares with a soft earthenware (creamware) base and a plain white or yellow glazed ground.

Design or "stick" spatterware was created by a cut sponge (stamp), hand painting, or transfers. Blue was the predominant color. The earliest patterns were carefully arranged geometrics that generally covered the entire piece. Later pieces had a decorative border with a central motif, usually a tulip. In the 1850s, Elsmore and Foster developed the Holly Leaf pattern

King's Rose features a large, cabbage-type rose in red, pale red, or pink. The pink rose often is called "Queen's Rose." Secondary colors are pastels—yellow, pink, and, occasionally, green. The borders vary: a solid band, vined, lined, or sectional. The King's Rose exists in an oyster motif.

Strawberry China ware comes in three types: strawberries and strawberry leaves (often called strawberry luster), green featherlike leaves with pink flowers (often called cut-strawberry, primrose, or old strawberry), and relief decoration. The first two types are characterized by rust-red moldings. Most pieces have a cream ground. Davenport was only one of the many potteries that made this ware.

Yellow-glazed earthenware (canary luster) has a canary yellow ground, a transfer design that is usually in black, and occasional luster decoration. The earliest pieces date from the 1780s and have a fine creamware base. A few hand-painted pieces are known. Not every piece has luster decoration.

Because the base material is soft paste, the ware is subject to cracking and chipping. Enamel colors and other types of decoration do not hold well. It is not unusual to see a piece with the decoration worn off.

Marks: Marked pieces are uncommon.

Additional Listings: Gaudy Dutch, Salopian Ware, Staffordshire Items.

Pearlware, figure, crying boy in white smock, sq base, late 18th/early 19th C, 8" h, chips, restoration to hands, **$350**. Photo courtesy of Sloans & Kenyon Auctions.

Creamware

Coffeepot, cov, 10" h, pear shape, polychrome dec black transfer of Tea Party and Shepherd prints, leaf-molded spout, chips, restoration to body, attributed to Wedgwood, c1775 .... **350.00**

Jug, 5-1/8" h, reeded lapped handle, emb floral applications, sides dec with red and green floral sprays, 19th C, glaze wear, small rim nicks **260.00**

Mug, 3-1/3" h, Orange Institution, red transfer printed symbols with verse above "Holiness to the Lord" and verse below "May the Orange Institution stand as firm as the Oak and the Enemies fall off like the leaves in October," England, early 19th C **300.00**

Pitcher, 6-1/4" h, two oval reserves with black transfer printed scenes of naval engagements, "The Wasp Boarding the Frolic," sgd "Bentley, Wear, and Bourne Engravers and Printers Shelton, Staffordshire," reverse depicting "The Constitution taking the Cyane and Livant," light green ground, luster embellishments, imperfections **2,760.00**

Plate, 9-1/2" d, shaped edge, cutout floral design, unmarked, flakes on rim, price for pr **715.00**

Platter, 18" l, 14-1/2" w, oval, scallop dec rim, chips, restorations **300.00**
Sugar bowl, 5-1/8" d, 2-3/4" h, int. with red and green enamel floral dec, purple luster and underglaze blue, ext. marked "Be Canny with the Sugar" flanked by small flowers **385.00**
Teapot, 4-3/4" h, molded acanthus spout, ribbed handle, small flakes **385.00**

Design Spatterware

Bowl, 7-1/2" d, 4" h, polychrome stripes **95.00**
Creamer, 4-3/8" h, gaudy floral dec, red, green, blue, and black, marked "Baker & Co., England" **75.00**
Cup, oversize, gaudy floral dec, red, blue, and green, 6-1/8" d............. **200.00**
Jug, 7" h, barrel shape, blue, rosettes and fern prongs.......................... **185.00**
Miniature, cup and saucer, green and black, polychrome center flower **85.00**
Plate, 8-5/8" d, red, blue, green, and black, imp "Elsmore & Foster," minor wear and scratches, price for set of six **385.00**
Sugar bowl, cov, 5" h, white, blue, and red flowers, green leaves, closed ring and shell handles **120.00**

King's Rose

Bowl, 7-3/4" d, Rose, broken solid border, flakes................................. **55.00**
Cup and saucer, handleless, Oyster pattern, hairline cracks.................. **40.00**
Plate, 7-3/8" d, some flaking **90.00**
Pitcher, 5-5/8" h, dark red rose, blue and yellow flowers, green leaves, some wear **220.00**
Soup plate, 9-1/2" d, broken solid border, scalloped edges, some flakes, three pcs **360.00**
Teapot, 5-3/4" h, broken solid border, some flakes **140.00**

Mug, transfer decoration with Masonic theme, pink luster banding, quote: "The world's a city with many a crooked street. And death's a market place were all men meet. If life was merchandise which men could buy, the rich would live, the poor alone would die," 3-3/4" d, 4" h, wear, **$220**. Photo courtesy of Alderfer Auction Co.

Pearlware

Bowl, 4-3/4" d, black and brown slip-filled rouletted band at rim, field of rust with blue, black, and white scroddled dots, early 19th C, repaired......... **940.00**
Coffeepot, cov, 13" h, baluster form, dome lid, ochre, green, brown, and blue floral dec, early 19th C, imperfections **200.00**
Creamer, cup shape, straight sides, applied handle, light brown stripes, yellow band, gilt and light brown foliage band, slight bubbles to yellow, minor spout rim flake **125.00**
Cup and saucer, handleless, 3-1/2" d cup, 5" d saucer, black transfer scene of horse-drawn chariot, flying putti set of six **525.00**
Figure, 3-1/4" h, squirrel, nut and collar with ring, polychrome, orange coat, attributed to Derby, minor wear and small flakes on base **635.00**
Jar, 12" h, cobalt blue underglaze design of wave formed by diamonds and scrolls, animal form handles, hp red and green flowers **250.00**
Jug, 4-3/4" h, barrel-form, orange, blue, green, white, medium brown, and dark brown marble slip dec, extruded handle, early 19th C, repaired............... **1,175.00**
Mug, 5" h, hp floral bunches, bands of brown and yellow, craquelure, hairline, chip... **200.00**
Pitcher, 6-3/4" h, black transfer printed with polychrome enamel and luster dec, oval reserve depicting "a West View of the Cast Iron Bridge over the River Wear built by R. Burdon Esq.," Sailor's Farewell on reserve, sailor's verse beneath spout, rim dec with floral border, minor rim chips, staining **550.00**
Plate, 6-1/2" d, early depiction of Seal of US, central whimsical eagle in blue, gold, and brown, two brown rim lines **1,410.00**
Punch bowl, 9-5/8" d, 4-3/8" h, stylized floral bands on int., floral bands and central medallion on ext., polychrome enamel dec, late 19th C **1,265.00**
Salt, open, 2-3/4" d, rounded form, dark brown banding, dark brown dendritic dec on rust field, narrow green glazed reeded band, early 19th C, cracked, rim chip **590.00**
Teapot, 5-3/4" h, octagonal, molded designs, swan finial, Oriental transfer, polychrome enamel, attributed to T. Harley, some edge flakes and professional repair....................... **425.00**
Vase, 7" h, five-finger type, underglaze blue, enameled birds and foliage, yellow ochre, brown, and green, silver-luster highlights, chips and crazing, pr **500.00**
Wall plaque, 8-1/2" w, 12-1/4" l, oval, molded, polychrome dec, female Harvest figure, late 18th C, minor chip...... **435.00**

Queen's Rose

Cream pitcher and sugar, cov, vine border, some flakes..................... **250.00**
Cup and saucer, handleless, broken solid border **495.00**
Plate, 7-1/2" d, solid border **75.00**
Tea set, assembled, Strawberry and Queen's Rose, 7" h teapot, creamer, cov sugar, handleless cup and saucer, waste bowl, professional repairs **550.00**

Strawberry China

Bowl, 4" d.................................... **165.00**
Cup and saucer, pink border, scalloped edge **225.00**
Platter, large **450.00**
Soup bowl, 8-1/4" d, red, green, pink, and yellow flower and strawberry border, basket of strawberries and roses in center **880.00**
Sugar bowl, cov, raised strawberries, strawberry knob **175.00**
Tea bowl and saucer, vine border **250.00**
Teapot, 5" h, tall flaring rim, hand-painted red and green strawberries on lid and shoulder, minor wear, short hairline, filled in spout flake **315.00**

Yellow Glazed

Child's mug, 2-1/8" h, silver resist, large florets on field of leaves, rim lines **200.00**
Pitcher, 4-3/4" h, transfer dec of foliate devices, reserve of shepherd with milk maid, hand-painted dec, c1850... **635.00**
Plate, 8-1/4" d, brown transfer print, Wild Rose pattern, imp "Montread"...... **250.00**
Sugar bowl, cov, 5-1/2" h, printed transfer of The Tea Party, fishing scene, iron-red painted rims **1,250.00**
Teapot, 5-1/2" h, printed transfer of The Party, iron-red painted rims, minor hairline, spout damage................. **850.00**

Fairy Lamps

History: Fairy lamps, which originated in England in the 1840s, are candle-burning night lamps. They were used in nurseries, hallways, and dim corners of the home.

Two leading candle manufacturers, the Price Candle Company and the Samuel Clarke Company, promoted fairy lamps as a means to sell candles. Both contracted with glass, porcelain, and metal manufacturers to produce the needed shades and cups. For example, Clarke used Worcester Royal Porcelain Company, Stuart & Sons, and Red House Glass Works in England, plus firms in France and Germany.

Fittings were produced in a wide variety of styles. Shades ranged from pressed to cut glass, from Burmese to Nailsea. Cups are found in glass, porcelain, brass, nickel, and silver plate.

American firms selling fairy lamps included Diamond Candle Company of Brooklyn, Blue Cross Safety Candle Co., and Hobbs-Brockunier of Wheeling, West Virginia.

Two-piece (cup and shade) and three-piece (cup with matching shade and saucer) fairy lamps can be found. Married pieces are common.

For more information, see *Warman's Glass*, 4th edition.

Marks: Clarke's trademark was a small fairy with a wand surrounded by the words "Clarke Fairy Pyramid, Trade Mark."

Reproduction Alert: Reproductions abound.

3-3/4" h, blue satin mother-of-pearl shade, clear Clarke Fairy pyramid insert 225.00

Rare Clarke pyramid light, holder and mug, frosted shade, finger loop signed base, signed pyramid food warmer with white porcelain mug, Clarke advertise slogans, 8-1/2" h, **$125**. Photo courtesy of Woody Auctions.

4" h, blue hobnail shade, blue satin ruffled base, married 30.00
4" h, Burmese, dec shade, clear Clark's Cricklite base 900.00
4" h, yellow satin swirl shade, clear S. Clark's Fairy pyramid base 150.00
4-1/2 h", figural green glass shade in shape of monk, set on frosted shoulders base 110.00
4-1/2" h, 4" d, ruby red, domed Cricklite shade, piecrust crimped base, inclusion in shade 585.00
5" h, blue satin swirl shade, matching base, ruffled top and edge 325.00
5" h, green glass molded leaves, clear emb angel head's base 60.00
5-1/2" h, green Nailsea shade, porcelain Doulton Lamplih dec base, sgd "S. Clarke's Fairy" in center 1,300.00

Fairy lamps, left: satin, pink ruffled top, frosted pedestal base, marked "Desmarais & Robitaille Limitee," 10-1/2" h, **$125**; right: Burmese shade, white opaque base signed "S. Clarke's Fairy," 6-1/2" h, **$425**.

5-1/2" h, lavender and frosted white shade, matching ruffled base, zigzag design 150.00
5-3/4" h, ruby red, profuse white loopings, bowl shaped base with eight turned up scallops, clear glass candle cup holder marked "S. Clarke Patent Trade Mark Fairy" 1,250.00
6" h, white and yellow striped shade, clear S. Clarke Fairy insert, nestled on matching white and yellow ruffled base 500.00
6" h, 8-1/2" w, Nailsea, blue, white loopings, domed shaped shade, bowl shaped base, clear glass candle cup sgd "S. Clarke Patent Trade Mark Fairy" 985.00
6-1/4" h, yellow satin shade, matching ftd base, clear sgd "S. Clarke Fairy" insert 650.00
6-1/2" h, Webb, blue shade dec with bird and branch, clear Clarke's Cricklite insert, sq blue satin base 1,500.00
7" h, 8" w, Nailsea, ruby red, white loopings, dome shaped shade, tricorn base, clear glass candle cup sgd "S. Clarke Patent Trade Mark Fairy" 1,250.00
7-3/4" h, pink, ruffled shade, applied gold monogram, 7-3/4" h 180.00
8-3/4" h, green opaque shade, gold and blue enamel dec, clear pressed glass pedestal base 275.00

Famille Rose

History: Famille Rose is Chinese export enameled porcelain on which the pink color predominates. It was made primarily in the 18th and 19th centuries. Other porcelains in the same group are Famille Jaune (yellow), Famille Noire (black), and Famille Verte (green).

Decorations include courtyard and home scenes, birds, and insects. Secondary colors are yellow, green, blue, aubergine, and black.

Rose Canton, Rose Mandarin, and Rose Medallion are mid- to late- 19th century Chinese-export wares, which are similar to Famille Rose.

Meiping, Famille Rose, painted peaches, flowers, scrolling foliage, and calligraphy, yellow ground, Chinese Jiaqing mark, Republic period, 9-1/2" h, **$3,500**. Photo courtesy of Sloans & Kenyon Auctions.

Bowl, 8" d, shallow, polychrome birds and butterflies, pink flowers, fruit, and vegetables, gilt rims, few rim chips, price for set of six 395.00
Bride's lamp, 14" h, hexagonal form, reticulated panels, electrified 345.00
Cache pot, stand, 11" l, 7-1/4" w, 6" h, clusters of flowers on plain ground, 10-1/2" l, 7-1/2" w, 1-1/2" h stand, repaired, reglued foot 1,100.00
Charger, 12" d, central figural dec, brocade border 265.00
Dish, cov, 11" d, figural dec, Qing dynasty 200.00
Figure
- 13" h, peacocks, pr 275.00
- 16" h, cockerels, pr 550.00

Garden set, 18-1/2" h, hexagonal, pictorial double panels, flanked and bordered by floral devices, blue ground, 19th C, minor glaze loss 1,100.00
Ginger jar, cov, 10-1/2" h, ovoid, foo dog beside sea reserve, floral and butterfly patterned ground, Famille Verte, Kangxi 420.00
Jar, cov, 19" h, baluster form, domed lid, ovoid finial, birds on rocky outcrop, flowering branches dec, early 20th C, price for pr 500.00

Jardinierè, 9-3/4" h, flowering branches dec, Jiaqing.................................700.00
Lamp base, 17" h, figural and crane dec, molded fu-dog mask and ring handles 175.00
Mug, 5" h, Mandarin palette, Qianlong, 1790..425.00

Urns, pair, Famille Verte, cartouches of coastal scenes, Chinese Export, c1900, 17" h urn, 35" h overall, converted to electric lamps, **$615**. Photo courtesy of Pook & Pook.

Plate, 10" d, floral dec, ribbed body, Tongzhi mark, pr..........................275.00
Tea caddy, 5-1/2" h, Mandarin palette, arched rect form, painted front, figures and pavilion reserve, c1780..........550.00
Teapot, figures on a terrace, painted butterflies border, c1835............2,775.00
Tray, 8" l, oval, multicolored center armorial crest, underglaze blue diaper and trefoil borders, reticulated rim, late 18th C..550.00
Urn, cov, pr, 16-1/2" h, painted figural scenes, figural knops on covers, c1840, one cov restored.....................23,000.00
Vase, 17-1/2" h, Rouleau form, molded fu-dog handles, scene of figures picking fruit from large vines, verso with butterflies, traditional borders, late 19th C 250.00

Fenton Glass

History: The Fenton Art Glass Company began as a cutting shop in Martins Ferry, Ohio, in 1905. In 1906, Frank L. Fenton started to build a plant in Williamstown, West Virginia, and produced the first piece of glass there in 1907. Early production included carnival, chocolate, custard, and pressed glass, plus mold-blown opalescent glass. In the 1920s, stretch glass, Fenton dolphins, jade green, ruby, and art glass were added.

In the 1930s, boudoir lamps, Dancing Ladies, and slag glass in various colors were produced. The 1940s saw crests of different colors being added to each piece by hand. Hobnail, opalescent, and two-color overlay pieces were popular items. Handles were added to different shapes, making the baskets they created as popular then as they are today.

For more information, see *Warman's Glass*, 4th edition.

Through the years, Fenton has beautified its glass by decorating it with hand painting, acid etching, and copper-wheel cutting.

Marks: Several different paper labels have been used. In 1970, an oval-raised trademark also was adopted.

Additional Listing: Carnival Glass.

Candy dish, #9519, heart shape, Provincial Blue Opalescent, ribbed, 1987-88, **$18**.

Ashtray, #8482 ruby, three feet 20.00
Basket
- #3839MI, milk glass, 12" oval 60.00
- #7237SC Silvercrest, 7"..........50.00

Bonbon
- #643 Stretch, cov, Celeste Blue 55.00
- #3937MI, milk glass, handle 17.50
- #8230 Rosalene Butterfly, two handles.................................35.00

Bowl
- Rose Crest, 10-1/2" d.............85.00
- #846 Pekin Blue, cupped........40.00
- #848 8 Petal, Chinese Yellow 45.00
- #1562 Satin etched Silvertone, oblong bowl............................55.00
- #7423 Milk glass bowl, hp yellow roses....................................65.00

Loving Cup, Orange Tree pattern, white carnival irid, **$475**. Photo courtesy of Seeck Auctions.

Bride's basket, Cranberry Opalescent Hobnail, 10-1/2" d bowl, 11-1/2" h SP frame 300.00
Candlestick, single
- #318 Pekin Blue, 3" h.............40.00
- #951 Silvercrest Cornucopia 37.50

Candy box, cov
- #1980CG Daisy and Button 45.00
- #7380 Custard hp pink daffodils, Louise Piper, dated March 1975 ....160.00

Compote, #8422 Waterlily ftd, Rosalene 30.00
Cocktail shaker, #6120 Plymouth, crystal 55.00
Cracker jar, Lilac Big Cookies, no lid, handle..250.00

Plate, Bicentennial, Patrick Henry, Give Me Liberty or Give Me Death, opaque blue, **$20**.

Creamer
- #1502 Diamond Optic, black 35.00
- #6464 RG Aventurine Green w/Pink, Vasa Murrhina........................45.00

Creatures (animals and birds)
- #5174 Springtime green iridized blown rabbit..........................45.00
- 5193 RE Rosalene fish, paperweight 25.00
- #5197 Happiness Bird, cardinals in winter.....................................32.50

Cruet, #7701 QJ, 7" Burmese, Petite Floral **175.00**
Cup and saucer, #7208 Aqua Crest **35.00**
Epergne
#3801 Hobnail, milk glass, three horns **60.00**
#3902 Petite Blue Opal, 4" h **125.00**
Fairy light
#3380 CR Hobnail, three pcs, Cranberry Opal **75.00**
#3680 RU Hobnail, three pcs.. **55.00**
#8406 WT Heart, Wisteria **65.00**
#8408 VR Persian Medallion, three pcs, Velva Rose-75th Anniv..... **75.00**
Flower pot, attached dish base, Emerald Crest **75.00**
Ginger jar, #893 Persian Pearl w/base and top **150.00**
Goblet, #1942 Flower Windows Blue **55.00**
Hat, #1922 Swirl Optic, French Opal **110.00**
Jack-in-the-pulpit, Black Rose, irid, ruffled top, 12-1/2" h **375.00**
Jug, #6068 Cased Lilac, handled, 6-1/2" **50.00**

Vase, Egyptian Mosaic, shape No. 3024, urn form, blue disk base, inlaid multicolored mosaic pattern, blue threading, original paper label "2024, vase mosaic inlaid," 1925, 8-1/2" h, **$2,000**. Photo courtesy of Skinner, Inc.

Lamp, Blue Coin Dot, Gone with the Wind, 31" h **300.00**
Liquor set, #1934 Flower Stopper, floral silver overlay, eight-pc set **250.00**
Mayonnaise bowl, liner, Aquacrest, #7203 .... **50.00**
Miniature lamp, Cranberry Coin Spot, 4-5/8" d, 11" h **600.00**
Perfume, French Opalescent, melon ribbed base, coinspot opalescent and white stopper **55.00**
Pitcher
Amber Crest **115.00**
Plum Opal, Hobnail, water, 80 oz. **190.00**

Powder box, #6080, Wave Crest, blue overlay **95.00**
Plate
#107 Ming Rose, 8" **30.00**
#1621 dolphin handled, Fenton Rose, 6" **25.00**
Rose bowl, #8954TH hanging heart **95.00**
Salt and pepper shakers, pr, #3806 Cranberry Opal, Hobnail, flat **47.50**
Sauce, Pinecone, 5" d, red **35.00**
Sherbet
#1942 Flower Windows, crystal **35.00**
#4443 Thumbprint, Colonial Blue **20.00**
Sugar and creamer, #9103 Fine Cut & Block (OVG) **20.00**
Temple jar, #7488 Chocolate Roses on cameo satin **25.00**
Tumbler
#1611 Georgian, Royal Blue, 5-1/2", ftd, 9 oz **18.00**
#3700, Grecian Gold, grape cut **15.00**
Tumble-up, Blue Swirl, 8" h, 5-1/2" w, applied handle, c1939 .... **900.00**

Vase, Rose Overlay, #192A, tri-crimp, c1948, 8-1/2" h, **$30**.

Vase
#847 Periwinkle Blue, fan **62.50**
#3759 Plum Opal, Hobnail, swung **150.00**
#5858 Wild Rose, wheat........ **85.00**
#6457 GA Vasa Murrhina, fan **85.00**
#7460 Amberina Overlay crimped, 6-1/2" h **80.00**
Violet vase
Blackberry Spray, #1216, custard **50.00**
Flowering Dill, #1605, Persian blue, double ruffle **35.00**
Water pitcher, 8-1/2" h, custard, hand-painted fall scene with red barn, chickens, rooster, birds flying, sgd "Jan Curtis," applied ribbed handle **395.00**

FIESTA

History: The Homer Laughlin China Company introduced Fiesta dinnerware in January 1936 at the Pottery and Glass Show in Pittsburgh, Pennsylvania. Frederick Rhead designed the pattern; Arthur Kraft and Bill Bensford molded it. Dr. A. V. Bleininger and H. W. Thiemecke developed the glazes.

The original five colors were red, dark blue, light green (with a trace of blue), brilliant yellow, and ivory. A vigorous marketing campaign took place between 1939 and 1943. In mid-1937, turquoise was added. Red was removed in 1943 because some of the chemicals used to produce it were essential to the war effort; it did not reappear until 1959. In 1951, light green, dark blue, and ivory were retired and forest green, rose, chartreuse, and gray were added to the line. Other color changes took place in the late 1950s, including the addition of a medium green.

Fiesta ware was redesigned in 1969 and discontinued about 1972. In 1986, Homer Laughlin China Company reintroduced Fiesta. The new china body shrinks more than the old semi-vitreous and ironstone pieces, thus making the new pieces slightly smaller than the earlier pieces. The modern colors are also different in tone or hue, e.g., the cobalt blue is darker than the old blue. Other modern colors are black, white, apricot, and rose.

For more information, see *Warman's American Pottery & Porcelain*, 2nd edition.

Reproduction Alert.

Ashtray
Cobalt blue **58.00**
Ivory **55.00**
Red **62.00**
Turquoise **50.00**
Yellow **48.00**
Bowl, 5-1/2" d, green **60.00**
Candlesticks, pr, bulb
Cobalt blue **125.00**
Ivory **125.00**
Red **120.00**
Turquoise **110.00**
Yellow **105.00**
Candlesticks, pr, tripod, yellow ... **550.00**
Carafe
Cobalt blue **495.00**
Ivory **385.00**
Casserole, cov, two handles, 10" d
Ivory **195.00**
Red **200.00**
Turquoise **145.00**

Yellow 160.00
Chop plate, 13" d, gray 95.00
Coffeepot
Cobalt blue 235.00
Ivory 400.00
Red 250.00
Turquoise 250.00
Yellow 185.00
Compote, 12" d, low, ftd
Cobalt blue 175.00
Ivory 165.00
Red 185.00
Turquoise 160.00
Yellow 165.00

Cereal bowl, orange, **$35**. Photo courtesy of Sky Hawk Auctions.

Creamer
Cobalt blue 35.00
Ivory 30.00
Red 65.00
Turquoise 24.00
Yellow 30.00
Creamer and sugar, figure-eight server, yellow creamer and sugar, cobalt blue tray 315.00
Cream soup bowl
Cobalt blue 60.00
Ivory 55.00
Red 65.00
Turquoise 50.00
Yellow 45.00
Cup, ring handle
Cobalt blue 35.00
Ivory 30.00
Red 30.00
Turquoise 25.00
Yellow 25.00
Demitasse cup, stick handle
Cobalt blue 75.00
Ivory 80.00
Red 85.00
Turquoise 75.00
Yellow 65.00
Demitasse pot, cov, stick handle
Cobalt blue 650.00
Ivory 535.00
Red 575.00
Turquoise 650.00
Yellow 465.00
Dessert bowl, 6" d
Cobalt blue 50.00
Ivory 45.00
Turquoise 40.00
Yellow 40.00
Egg cup
Cobalt blue 75.00
Ivory 72.00
Red 80.00
Turquoise 55.00
Yellow 70.00
Fruit bowl, 5-1/2" d
Ivory 33.00
Turquoise 25.00
Yellow 25.00
Fruit bowl, 11-3/4" d, cobalt blue
.... 485.00
Gravy boat
Cobalt blue 75.00
Ivory 65.00
Red 85.00
Turquoise 45.00
Yellow 50.00
Juice tumbler
Cobalt blue 40.00
Rose 65.00
Yellow 40.00

Soup bowl, turquoise, **$30**.

Marmalade jar, cov
Cobalt blue 335.00
Ivory 325.00
Red 345.00
Turquoise 325.00
Yellow 250.00
Mixing bowl
1, 5" d
Cobalt blue 325.00
Ivory 350.00
Red 375.00
#2, cobalt blue 195.00
#2, yellow 140.00
#4, green 195.00
#5, ivory 275.00
#7, ivory 580.00
Mixing bowl lid, #1, red 1,100.00
Mug
Dark green 90.00
Ivory, marked 125.00
Rose 95.00
Mustard, cov
Cobalt blue 325.00
Turquoise 275.00
Nappy, 8-1/2" d
Cobalt blue 55.00
Ivory 55.00
Turquoise 42.00
Red 55.00
Yellow 45.00
Nappy, 9-1/2" d
Cobalt blue 65.00
Ivory 65.00
Red 70.00
Turquoise 55.00
Yellow 60.00
Onion soup, cov, turquoise
.... 8,000.00
Pitcher, disk
Chartreuse 275.00
Turquoise 110.00
Pitcher, ice lip
Green 135.00
Turquoise 195.00
Plate, deep
Gray 42.00
Rose 42.00
Plate, 6" d
Dark green 15.00
Ivory 7.00
Light green 9.00
Turquoise 8.00
Yellow 5.00
Plate, 7" d
Chartreuse 12.00
Ivory 10.00
Light green 8.50
Medium green 30.00
Rose 14.00
Turquoise 8.50
Plate, 9" d
Cobalt blue 15.00
Ivory 14.00
Medium green 75.00
Red 15.00
Yellow 13.00
Plate, 10" d, dinner
Gray 42.00
Light green 28.00
Medium green 125.00
Red 35.00
Turquoise 30.00
Platter, oval
Gray 35.00
Ivory 25.00
Red 45.00
Yellow 22.00
Relish
Ivory base and center, turquoise inserts 285.00
Red, base and inserts 425.00
Salad bowl, large, ftd
Cobalt blue 375.00
Red 460.00
Turquoise 335.00
Yellow 400.00
Salt and pepper shakers, pr
Red 24.00
Turquoise 135.00

Saucer
- Light green **5.00**
- Turquoise **5.00**

Soup plate
- Ivory **36.00**
- Turquoise **29.00**

Sugar bowl, cov
- Chartreuse **65.00**
- Gray **75.00**
- Rose **75.00**

Syrup
- Green **450.00**
- Ivory **600.00**
- Red **695.00**

Sweetmeat compote, high standard
- Cobalt blue **95.00**
- Ivory **85.00**
- Red **100.00**
- Turquoise **125.00**
- Yellow **400.00**

Tea cup, flat bottom, cobalt blue **100.00**

Teapot, cov
- Cobalt blue, large **335.00**
- Red, large **245.00**
- Rose, medium **350.00**

Tumbler, cobalt blue **75.00**

Vase
- 8" h, green **825.00**
- 8" h, ivory, c1936-42 .... **550.00**
- 12" h, cobalt blue, c1936-42 .... **1,275.00**
- 12" h, light green, c1937-42 .... **1,195.00**

FIGURAL BOTTLES

History: Porcelain figural bottles, which have an average height of three to eight inches and were made either in a glazed or bisque finish, achieved popularity in the late 1800s and remained popular into the 1930s. The majority of figural bottles were made in Germany, with Austria and Japan accounting for the balance.

Empty figural bottles were shipped to the United States and filled upon arrival. They were then given away to customers by brothels, dance halls, hotels, liquor stores, and taverns. Some were lettered with the names and addresses of the establishment, while others had paper labels. Many were used for holidays, e.g., Christmas and New Year's.

Figural bottles also were made in glass and other materials. The glass bottles held perfumes, food, or beverages.

Bisque

Cowboy, 7-1/2" h, little black boy dressed in cowboy hat, vest, chaps, marked "Made in Japan" **125.00**

Man, 4-1/" h, toasting, "Your Health," flask style, tree bark back **85.00**

Old Scotch, Little Scotch, 5-1/2" h, 1910-20 .... **275.00**

Sailor, 6-1/2" h, white pants, blue blouse, hat, high-gloss front, marked "Made in Germany" **115.00**

Glass

Ballet dancer, 12" h, milk glass, pink and brown paint dec highlights, sheared mouth, removable head as closure, pontil scar, attributed to America, 1860-90 .... **525.00**

Barrel, 4-7/8" h, yellow olive green, fancy rigaree trailing around body, two sleigh runner feet serve as base, each emb with repeating sunburst motif, tooled mouth, pontil scar, Europe, 18th C **450.00**

Bear, 10-5/8" h, dense yellow amber, sheared mouth, applied face, Russia, 1860-80, flat chip on back **400.00**

Big Stick, Teddy Roosevelt's, 7-1/2" h, golden amber, sheared mouth, smooth base, flat flake at mouth **170.00**

Cherub, holding medallion, 11-1/8" h, blue opaque milk glass, sq collared mouth, ground pontil scar, attributed to America, 1860-90 .... **120.00**

Left: Rooster-shaped bottle, 10-1/2" h, **$35**; right: Venetian glass rooster figure, 11" h, **$25**. Photo courtesy of Joy Luke Auctions.

Fish, 11-1/2" h, Doctor Fisch's Bitters, golden amber, applied small round collared mouth, smooth base, America, 1860-80, some ext. high point wear, burst bubble on base **160.00**

Indian maiden, 12-1/4" h, Brown's Celebrated Indian Herb Bitters, yellow amber, inward rolled mouth, smooth base, America, 1860-80 .... **600.00**

Pig, 10-3/8" l, Berkshire Bitters, golden amber **1,200.00**

Queen Mary, ocean liner, c1936 .. **155.00**

Shoe, dark amethyst, ground mouth, smooth base **125.00**

Washington, George, 10" h, Simon's Centennial Bitters, aquamarine, applied double-collared mouth, smooth base, America, 1860-80 .... **650.00**

Pineapple shape, bitters, golden amber, applied mouth, smooth base, 9" h, **$250**. Photo courtesy of American Bottle Auctions.

Pottery and porcelain

Camel, 4" h, mother of pearl glaze, os **45.00**

Canteen, painted bust of Lincoln, Garfield, and McKinley, half pint **375.00**

Cucumber, 11-3/4" l, stoneware, green and cream mottled glaze **100.00**

Fox, reading book, beige, brown mottled dec **95.00**

Pretzel, brown **85.00**

FINDLAY ONYX GLASS

History: Findlay onyx glass, produced by Dalzell, Gilmore & Leighton Company, Findlay, Ohio, was patented for the firm in 1889 by George W. Leighton. Due to high production costs resulting from a complex manufacturing process, the glass was made only for a short time.

Warman's GLASS

For more information, see *Warman's Glass*, 4th edition.

Layers of glass were plated to a bulb of opalescent glass through repeated dippings into a glass pot. Each layer was cooled and reheated to develop opalescent qualities. A pattern mold then was used to produce raised decorations of flowers and leaves. A second mold gave the glass bulb its full shape and form.

A platinum luster paint, producing pieces identified as silver or platinum onyx, was applied to the raised decorations. The color was fixed in a muffle kiln. Other colors such as cinnamon, cranberry, cream, raspberry, and rose were achieved by using an outer glass plating, which reacted strongly to reheating. For example, a purple or orchid color came from the addition of manganese and cobalt to the glass mixture.

Celery vase, 6-3/4" h, creamy-white ground, silver dec, edge flakes **485.00**

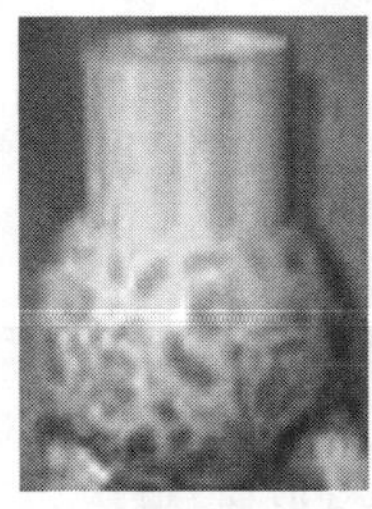

Celery vase, Onyx, bright silver decoration, slight rim chips, 6-3/4" h, **$485.** Findlay photos courtesy of Clarence and Betty Maier.

Creamer, 5" h, creamy-white ground, applied colorless handle, damage to rim and spout **90.00**
Dresser box, cov, 5" d, creamy-white ground **675.00**
Pitcher, creamy-white ground, platinum blossoms, opalescent glass handle **435.00**
Spooner, 4-1/2" h, creamy-white ground, silver dec, shaped top **200.00**
Sugar, cov, 6" h, creamy-white ground, platinum blossoms, silver medallion on base of bowl, rim chip and roughness to cover **485.00**
Sugar shaker, 5-1/2" h, creamy-white ground, silver dec, brass lid **335.00**
Syrup, creamy-white ground, silver dec, applied opalescent handle, hinge missing, thumb-hold repaired **635.00**
Toothpick holder, raspberry **395.00**
Tumbler, 3-3/4" h, straight sided, creamy-white ground, bright silver flowers, slight rim roughness **1,000.00**
Vase, 9" h, creamy-white ground, raised silver dec, rim chips, crack in base **815.00**

Fine Arts

History: Before the invention of cameras and other ways to mechanically capture an image, paintings, known as portraits, served to capture the likeness of an individual. Paintings have been done in a variety of mediums and on varying canvases, boards, etc. Often it was what was available in a particular area or time that influenced the materials. Having one's portrait painted was often a sign of wealth and many artists found themselves in demand once their reputations became established. Today art historians, curators, dealers, and collectors study portraits to determine the age of the painting and often use clues found in the backgrounds or clothing of the sitter to determine age, if no identification is available. Many portraits have a detailed provenance that allows the sitters, and often the artists, to be identified.

In any calendar year, tens, if not hundreds of thousands, of paintings are sold. Prices range from a few dollars to millions. Since each painting is essentially a unique creation, it is difficult to compare prices.

Charles Chaplin, French, 1825-1891, attributed, seated young lady wearing white dress, pink ribbons, blowing bubbles, oil on canvas, 16" x 12-1/2", **$1,610.** Photo courtesy of Pook & Pook.

American School, late 18th C, portrait of man holding sheet of music, believed to be Francis Hopkinson (1737-1791), signer of the Declaration of Independence, unsigned, oil on canvas, 30" x 25", framed **3,750.00**
American School, 19th C
- Barclay, Henry, unsigned, oil on canvas, 30" x 25-1/2", framed, craquelure, scratch in upper right **1,610.00**
- Little girl with her cat, unsigned, pastel on paper, 23-1/4" x 18-1/4", framed, repaired tears, losses, staining **765.00**
- Young boy holding scroll, watercolor on paper, unsigned, 5-3/4" x 4", framed **980.00**

American School, 20th C
- Young girl in pink dress, holding doll, unsigned, oil on canvas, 36" x 28", hand-carved gilt frame **1,650.00**
- Young woman identified as "Mary Key Somervil, mother of James Bunting," unsigned, oil on canvas, 24" x 20", framed **475.00**

Anglo/American School, 18th C style, portrait of a woman as an angel, unsigned, oil on canvas, 29" x 23", framed, lined, retouched, abrasions, surface grime, craquelure **2,715.00**
August, (Augati), F., portrait of a young man, ruffled collar, wide-brimmed hat, sgd lower left, oil on canvas, 30" x 25", framed, paint cracking on forehead **1,700.00**
Barzaghi-Cattaneo, Antonio, (Swiss, 1831-1922), girl with a red scarf, monogram signature "ABARZAGHI," lower left, oil on canvas, 19" x 15", framed, surface grime, craquelure with some alligatoring **1,300.00**
Birch, Thomas, attributed to, portrait of Mrs. Thomas Birch, unsigned, oil on canvas, 30" x 25", framed, restored, relined **1,300.00**
Bouve, Rosamond Lombard Smith, (American, 1876-1948), young woman with flowers, inscribed or initialed "RLS" lower right, inscribed "1923" on reverse, oil on canvasboard, 8-1/4" x 6", framed, damage to upper right corner, retouch, surface grime **1,530.00**

Charles Chase Emerson, American, 1874-1922, portrait of Ludwig Frank, signed "Chase Emerson" lower left, identified on reverse, oil on canvasboard, 22" x 16-1/4", framed, varnish inconsistencies, **$360.** Photo courtesy of Skinner, Inc.

Bredin, Sloan, portrait of Miss Guerie Scott, sgd "R. S. Bredin" lower right, oil on canvas, 30" x 25", framed, exhibited at Sesqui-Centennial International Exposition, Philadelphia, 1926, photograph included in illus catalog of Dept of Fine Arts Exposition **20,900.00**
Continental School, portrait of cavalier, illegible signature upper left, oil on canvas, 32" x 25-3/4", framed, relined **450.00**
English School, 19th C
- Children, full-length portrait of two girls wearing pink dresses, one holding cat, other holding blue bonnet, beside little boy on blue suit with hoop and stick, picturesque landscape, watercolor on paper, 11-3/8" x 9" **920.00**
- English gentleman with horse, unsigned, oil on canvas, 25" x 30", carved wood frame **5,500.00**

European School, early 19th C
- Full-length portrait of standing woman, wearing elaborate dress, chair, unsigned, oil on canvas, 39" x 29", framed **475.00**
- Half-length portrait of woman wearing dark dress, cross, earrings, holding fan, unsigned, oil on canvas, 40" x 30", framed **250.00**

Folinsbee, John, (American), portrait of lady wearing pearls, open neckline, sgd "John Folinsbee" lower right, oil on canvas, 24" x 20", framed, craquelure **900.00**

French School, portrait of woman in blue dress, white shawl, dark hair pinned up, unsigned, oil on canvas, 22-1/2" x 17-1/4", framed, craquelure........ **1,380.00**

Emil Fuchs, American, 1866-1929, portrait of Mrs. E. J. Nolan, signed and dated "EMIL FUCHS 1916" lower left, oil on panel, framed, under glass, 23-1/4" x 15-3/4", split to panel upper left, deaccessioned from collection of Brooklyn Museum of Art, **$2,585**. Photo courtesy of Skinner, Inc.

Fuchs, Emil, (American, 1866-1929)

Portrait of Miss Clements, unsigned, identified on label and label from Brooklyn Museum of Art on reverse, oil on canvas, 50" x 40", unframed, abrasions, retouch, varnish inconsistencies, surface grime, craquelure, deaccessioned from collection of Brooklyn Museum of Art **1,645.00**

Portrait of young woman, unsigned, label from Brooklyn Museum of Art on reverse, oil on canvas, 30-1/4" x 24", unframed, abrasions, bloom, retouch, deaccessioned from Brooklyn Museum of Art..... **1,490.00**

Gassner, George, attributed, (Massachusetts, 1811-1861)

Half-length portrait of Mr. and Mrs. Colbey sitting on sofa, man holding book, woman holding flower, oil on canvas, 28" x 35", framed **29,900.00**

Pair of full-length portraits of children; young girl wearing red dress, holding flowers, standing in landscape with river, inscribed lower left "Arvillannah Colbey Died July 18, 1844 Aged One Year 10 mos & 2 days Painted by Geo. Gassner," 35" x 28-1/4", framed; young boy wearing blue coat and white pants, holding crop, standing in river landscape with horse in background, 35" x 28 1/2", framed **80,500.00**

Hughes, Edward H., (British, 1851-1914), portrait of lady, sgd "Edward Hughes 1906," lower left, oil on canvas, 67-1/4" x 42-1/4", framed, repairs, tears, patches, punctures, scuffing......... **450.00**

Imhof, Joseph A., portrait of "Iron Tail Sioux," Native American man wearing feather headdress, sgd "Imhof" lower right, oil on board, 37" x 31-1/2", framed **4,750.00**

Muller, G., 19th C, portrait of nun wearing habit, rosary and cross, sgd "Muller" upper left, oil on canvas, 26" x 20", framed, relined **475.00**

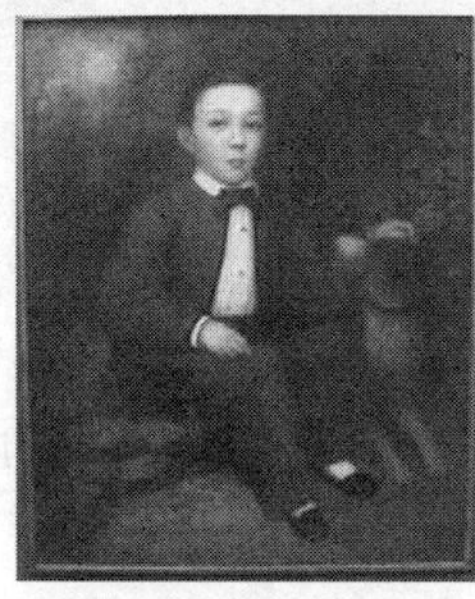

Primitive, illegibly signed, portrait of young boy in garden setting with dog, oil on canvas on board, 36" x 29", loss, inpaint, restoration, **$2,000**. Photo courtesy of Alderfer Auction Co.

Muller-Ury, Adolf Felix (German/ American, 1862-1947), portrait of a woman in profile, sgd "A.Muller-Ury" lower right, oil on canvas board, 13" x 9", framed **1,300.00**

Neagle, John, portrait of Rev. Thomas Sargent, painted from life, Nov. 24, 1824, sgd "J. Neagle 1824" upper left, oil on canvas on board, 17" x 14", framed, restored, relined **1,700.00**

Pennsylvania School, c1840, portrait of lady, wearing white dress, sitting in painted chair, oil on poplar panel, 21-1/2" x 20", framed **600.00**

Perkins, Mary Smyth, (Pennsylvania, 1875-1931), portrait of young girl holding doll, sgd on reverse "Mary Smyth Perkins, 1906," oil on canvas, 30-1/2" x 25-1/2", framed, relined, craquelure **400.00**

Phillips, S. George, (American), portrait of young girl wearing blue dress, holding bouquet of roses, seated on marble bench in garden setting, sgd "S. George Phillips" lower center, oil on canvas, 24-1/2" x 20", framed **700.00**

Pomeroy, Florence W. (American), portrait of man wearing hat and coat, holding cigarette, sgd "F.W. Pomeroy" lower left, oil on canvas, 24" x 20", framed **750.00**

Prior, William Matthew (American, 1806-1873), half-length portrait of young woman, wearing blue dress, seated in red armchair, sgd lower left "Wm. Prior 18__," red label verso "Mrs. Saunders, Baltimore," oil on canvas, 10" x 8", framed **1,725.00**

Ricciardi, Caesar A., (American), Modernist portrait of woman, sgd "C. Ricciardi" lower left, oil on canvas, 30" x 24", unframed **250.00**

Spencer, Frederick R., (American), attributed to, portrait of young girl in burgundy dress, unsigned, oil on board, 24-1/2" x 21", framed **980.00**

Street, Robert, bust portrait of gentleman holding spectacles, sgd "R. Street 1838" lower center, oil on canvas on board, 30" x 25", framed **650.00**

Von Sales, **Carl**, (German, 1797-1870), man and woman, each sgd and dated "C. Sales pinx: 1817," oil on canvas, 27-1/2" x 22", framed, lined, retouched, craquelure **3,175.00**

Walter, Martha, (American, 1875-1976), half length portrait of seated woman holding book, sgd "M. Walter" lower right, oil on canvas, 32" x 17-3/4", framed **3,450.00**

Firearm Accessories

History: Muzzle-loading weapons of the 18th and early 19th centuries varied in caliber and required the owner to carry a variety of equipment, including a powder horn or flask, patches, flints or percussion caps, bullets, and bullet molds. In addition, military personnel were responsible for bayonets, slings, and miscellaneous cleaning equipment and spare parts.

During the French and Indian War, soldiers began to personalize their powder horns with intricate engraving, in addition to the usual name or initial used for identification. Sometimes professional horn smiths were employed to customize these objects, which have been elevated to a form of folk art by some collectors.

In the mid-19th century, cartridge weapons replaced their black-powder ancestors. Collectors seek anything associated with early ammunition—from the cartridges themselves to advertising material. Handling old ammunition can be extremely dangerous because of decomposition of compounds. Seek advice from an experienced collector before becoming involved in this area.

Reproduction Alert: There are a large number of reproduction and fake powder horns. Be very cautious!

Notes: Military-related firearm accessories generally are worth more than their civilian counterparts.

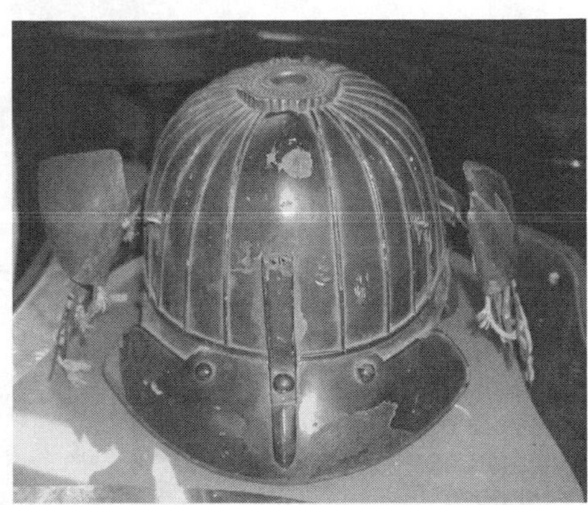

Helmet, Japanese type, leather, laced construction, wear, losses, **$115**.

Belt plate, 2-1/2" d, eagle cross, Civil War era, dug at Manassas Battlefield near Douglas House in 1955, lead back **440.00**

Bullet board, 55-3/4" x 40", Union Metallic Cartridge Co., Bridgeport, CT, 1907, canvasback ducks in snowstorm, litho on cardboard, orig oak frame **9,500.00**

Calendar, 1918, Marble Arms & Mfg Co., artwork by Philip R. Goodwin, top image of two hunters, one with gun raised at animal across river, bottom image with man by campfire, docked canoe **5,230.00**

Canteen, 7" d, 2-5/8" deep, painted, cheese-box style, dark red paint overall, one side painted gold with a large primitive eagle with shield breast, the top of the shield red with cream lettering "No. 37," other side painted in gold letters, "Lt. Rufus Cook," pewter nozzle, sq nail construction, strap loops missing **1,650.00**

Cartridge bag

- 9" w, 7-1/2" h, English, leather, webbed shoulder strap, int. cloth label "Bryant," brass buckles, unused **530.00**
- 15-1/2" w, 8" d, 10" h, Holland Sport (Dunn's), canvas body, leather bottom, handles, brass buckle with leather strap **300.00**

Cartridge box, Civil War era

- 4-1/2" w, 2-1/2" d, 3-7/8" h, Naval, black leather, stamped beneath flap "US NY Boston," star shaped stampings........ **200.00**
- 8-1/2" l, 4-1/2" h, leather, emb maker's mark beneath flap "W. H. Wilkinson, Springfield, Mass," missing two small buckles from bottom and liner **315.00**

Cartridge box plate, 2-1/4" x 3-1/2", US, oval, brass, old patina, minor dents, lead filled back with two loops, dug at Manassas Battlefield near Douglas House **110.00**

Cartridge case, 16" w, 8" d, 9" h, Hollard Sport (Dunn's), belt leather, shoulder strap, brass buckle, large center compartment with two smaller compartments on ends **165.00**

Miniature powder horn, silver metal, panels of hp hunting scenes, hinged lid painted with stag in wooded setting, stylized fish finial, fitted with two metal loops, some loss to paint, chain or cord missing, 5-1/2" l, **$980**. Photo courtesy of Alderfer Auction Co.

Catalog

- *Colt's-The Arm of Law and Order*, 5-3/4" x 7-3/4", 42 pgs, black and white illus and specifications of 16 models of Colt revolvers and automatic pistols **25.00**
- Savage Arms Corp., Chicopee Falls, MA, 1951, 52 pgs, 8-1/2" x 11", No. 51, *Component Parts Price List for Savage, Stevens, Fox Shotguns & Rifles*........ **35.00**
- Winchester Repeating Arms, New Haven, CT, 1918, 215 pgs, 5-1/2" x 8-1/2", Cat No. 81, illus of repeating and single-shot rifles, repeating shotguns, cartridges, shells, primers, percussions caps, shot **250.00**

Flask, 8" l, brass, dead game, emb, stamped "Am. Flask & Cap Co." **200.00**

Dirk, US, enameled handle with incised dec, abalone shell inlays, 4-3/4" blade, 8-1/4" l leather sheath emb "US," nickel silver band on one end, tip of sheath missing **250.00**

Duffel bag, 28" l, Holland Sport, light green canvas, leather trim and straps **120.00**

Handcuffs, wrought iron, dark brown patina, marked "Pat'd June 17 '65, July 17 '66" on each side........ **110.00**

Kit bag, 12-1/2" w, 11" h, Holland Sport, light green canvas, leather sides and strap **75.00**

Knapsack, 13-5/8" x 13-1/4", painted canvas, flap having American eagle with shield among stars and surrounded by oval cloud border, scrolled banner inscribed "RIFLE CADET," painted in red, white, blue, and gold on black ground, two leather strap and iron buckles, reverse with ink inscription, "Benjamin Pope Bridgewater July 4th 1820," minor paint losses, wooden hanger and twine attached to the back **31,725.00**

Signal morter, bronze, marked "J.S." on tapered body, 18th C, 3-3/8", **$200**. Photo courtesy of Pook & Pook.

Poster, store type, 41-1/2" x 32", Winchester Rifles, Shotguns and Ammunition For Sale Here, two bear dogs in foreground, bloodhounds in back **6,300.00**

Powder horn

- 11" l, engraved town surrounding upper part of horn, harbor and ships around plug, sgd "Benjamin Hills Horn, c1760 .... **1,760.00**
- 12" l, engraved coat of arms above house with hunter, deer, and dog, unengraved banner at top **1,550.00**
- 13" l, engraved Adam and Eve with village and lion dec, initialed "G. S. M."........ **1,760.00**
- 18" l, engraved, initialed "Wm M. 1799," also "J. M. 1814," surrounded by series of inscribed circles, flat pine plug **1,200.00**
- 18" l, engraved, "stil not this horn for fear of shame for hear doth stand the oner name jacob lewis 1785, (sic)" two rows of geometric devices round bottom, carved and incised lines at spout, dome-shaped wooden plug, America, late 18th C, small age crack, wear........ **1,610.00**

Product leaflet

- Western Silvertip Ammunition, 3-1/2" x 6" closed, glossy paper, color printing, diecut upper corner, one side shows 18 variations of brass cartridges in differing gauges for large game hunting, one panel devoted to three Winchester hunting rifles, 1956........ **25.00**
- Western-Winchester, 3-1/4" x 6-1/2" closed, full-color printing, illus and describes western Super-X and Xpert shotgun shells and cartridges, 1957 .... **15.00**

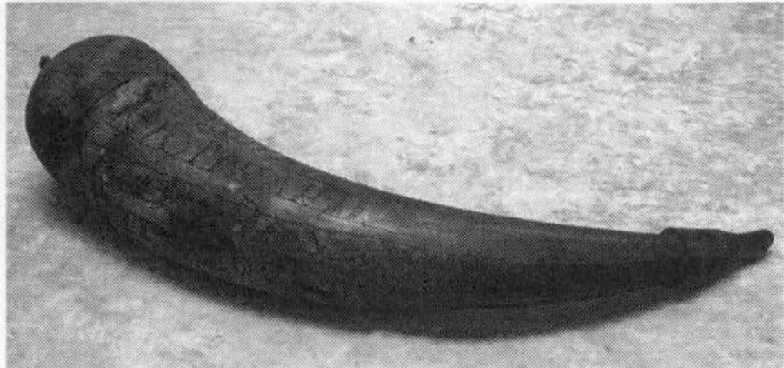

Powder horn, marked "Richard John Banister, Ship Cove, His Horn April 1878," depiction of ship, 10" l, **$350**. Photo courtesy of Alderfer Auction Co.

Shotgun box, empty

Austin Cartridge Co., Crack-Shot, 16 gauge, full-color scene of three hunting dogs on front **2,310.00**

Chamberlin Cartridge Co., 12 gauge, Blue Rocks **1,100.00**

J. F. Schmelzer & Sons Arms Co., 12 gauge carver cartridges, illus of hunter and pointed on front **1,750.00**

Peters Quick Shot, 12 gauge shotgun shells **5,835.00**

Robin Hood Eclipse Cartridge, 12 gauge, near smokeless powder shells **2,550.00**

Tin, Oriental Smokeless Gunpowder, half pound, four litho labels with full-color ducks **1,810.00**

Tinder box, 4-3/8" d, tin, candle socket, inside damper, flint, and steel **330.00**

Tinder lighter, flintlock

5-1/2" l, rosewood pistol grip, tooled brass fittings **750.00**

6-1/2" l, compartment for extra flint, taper holder **550.00**

Water keg, 9" x 7-1/2" x 9", wooden, American, late 18th/early 19th C, oval, flattened bottom, two Shaker-style wide-tongued wooden straps, large hand-forged nail on each end for carrying cord, orig wood stopper **400.00**

Firearms

History: The 15th-century Matchlock Arquebus was the forerunner of the modern firearm. The Germans refined the wheelock firing mechanism during the 16th and 17th centuries. English settlers arrived in America with the smoothbore musket; German settlers had rifled arms. Both used the new flintlock firing mechanism.

A major advance was achieved when Whitney introduced interchangeable parts into the manufacturing of rifles. Refinements in firearms continued in the 19th century. The percussion ignition system was developed by the 1840s. Minie, a French military officer, produced a viable projectile. By the end of the 19th century, cartridge weapons dominated the field.

Notes: Two factors control the pricing of firearms—condition and rarity. Variations in these factors can cause a wide range in the value of antique firearms. For instance, a Colt 1849 pocket-model revolver with a five-inch barrel can be priced from $100 to $700, depending on whether all the component parts are original, some are missing, how much of the original finish (bluing) remains on the barrel and frame, how much silver plating remains on the brass trigger guard and back strap, and the condition and finish of the walnut grips.

Be careful to note a weapon's negative qualities. A Colt Peterson belt revolver in fair condition will command a much higher price than the Colt pocket model in very fine condition. Know the production run of a firearm before buying it.

Laws regarding the sale of firearms have gotten stricter. Be sure to sell and buy firearms through auction houses and dealers properly licensed to transact business in this highly regulated area.

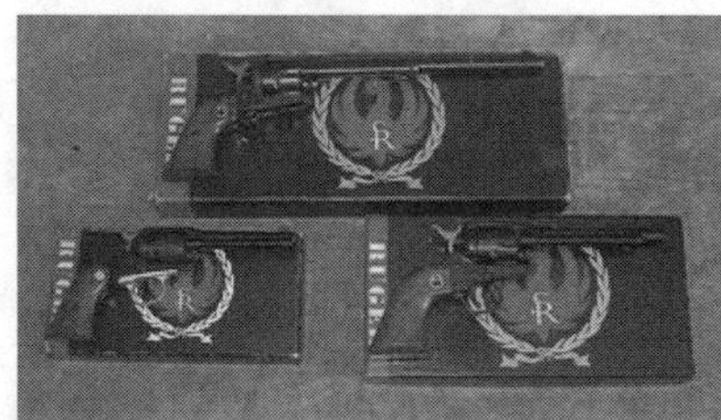

Revolver, Ruger "Single-Six" single action revolver, cal. 22, 9-1/2" bbl, original box, manual, spare target grips, **$385**; Ruger "Single-Six" single action revolver, cal. 22, 5-1/2" bbl, original box, spare cylinder, **$250**; Ruger "Bearcat" single-action revolver, cal. 22, 4" bbl, original box, **$330**. Photos courtesy of Alderfer Auction Co.

Cannon

Unmarked, two-wheeled ammunition trailer, 45" l barrel **1,200.00**

Carbine

Burnside Precision, 21" round barrel, orig dark finish, bold inspectors' marks and signatures, 39-1/2" l, as found condition **1,320.00**

Hall-North, Model 1843,percussion, .52 caliber, rifled 21" barrel, bold metal stampings, signature and 1849 on receiver, traces of old brown finish, walnut stock with old split between trigger guard and barrel, small repairs near breech, 40" l **935.00**

Joslyn Model 1862, .52 caliber, 22" round barrel, walnut stock, clear inspector's markings, brass buttplate, trigger guard and barrel band, stamped signatures on lock and breech block, 38-5/8" l **650.00**

C. S. Richmond, .58 caliber, 25" barrel, all-steel hardware, brass nose cap, butt plate stamped "U.S.," Type 3, humpback lock, "C. S. Richmond, 1864" mark, no sling swivels, 43" l **3,300.00**

Sharp's New Model 1863, breech loading, walnut stock and forearm, double inspectors markings, 22" blued barrel, areas of very light case coloring on lock, butt plate, hammer, barrel band, and receiver, clear stampings on lock, 34" l **1,980.00**

Spencer, Civil War Model, .52 caliber rimfire, 22" round barrel, overall brown finish on all metal surfaces, worn walnut stick, faint inspector's mark, forearm with additional coat of varnish, 39" l .. **2,100.00**

Springfield, Model 1884 Trapdoor, saddle ring, mint bore, Buffington sight, stamped "C. Proper," range with inspector's cartouche **825.00**

Wesson, Frank, 28" octagonal barrel, folding rear peep sight, walnut stock with orig dark finish, rear open sight missing, 43" l overall **275.00**

Dueling pistols, percussion lock

English, London, second quarter 19th C, dolphin hammer, belt clip, engraved scrollwork on frame, checkered burl-wood grip, barrel engraved "London," 8-1/2" l, price for pr **650.00**

English, Queen-Anne style, London, for J. Wilson, late 18th C, scrolled mask butt, grip set with small monogrammed cartouche, plain stylized dolphin hammer, cannon barrel engraved with cartouches, and maker's mark on underside, 8" l, price for pr **500.00**

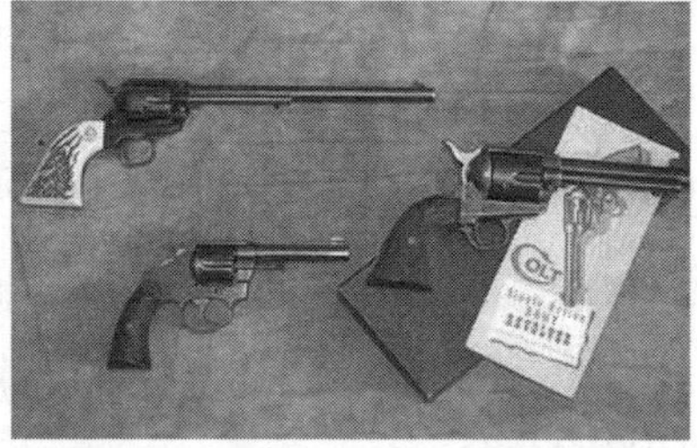

Revolver, Colt Second Generation single-action Army revolver, cal. 45, 5-1/2" bbl, original box, **$2,200**; Colt "Frontier Scout Buntline 62" single-action revolver, cal. 22, 9 1/2" bbl, imitation stag grips, leather holster and belt, **$305**; Colt "Police Positive" double-action revolver, cal. 38, 4" bbl, **$135**.

Flintlock long arms

French, Model 1766 Charlesville Musket, 44-3/4" l orig barrel length, lock plate only partially legible, matching ramrod, top jaw and top screw period replacements **1,250.00**

Kentucky, R. E. Leman, cal. 38, 37-3/8" oct. bbl with small brass front sight and fixed rear sight, top flat in front of chamber area is marked "R.E. LEMAN/LANCASTER PA/WARRANTED," unmarked flat lock plate, applied grain tiger striped stock, simple brass trigger guard, two-pc patch box with crescent butt plate and dbl. set triggers, ovoid forestock with integral ramrod groove

and two small brass guides, dark heavy patina on iron and wood **920.00**

Pennsylvania, attributed to Jacob Stoudenour, "J. S." engraved on lock, curly maple stock with old patina, raised carved detail behind cheek piece and around lock and side plate, engraved brass patch box, stock restoration below lock, ended out ahead of entry pipe, 55" l **1,320.00**

U. S. Model 1819, Hall, breech loading, second-production type, Harpers Ferry Armory, John Hall's patents, .52 caliber, single shot, 32-5/8" round barrel, three barrel bands, breechblock deeply stamped **1,200.00**

Virginia, curly-maple stock with good figure, relief carving, old mellow varnished finish, brass hardware, engraved and pierced patch box, Ketland lock reconverted back to flint, silver thumb piece inlay, 41-1/2" l barrel and fore-end shortened slightly, small pierced repair at breech area, top flat engraved "H. B." **3,300.00**

Flintlock pistols-single shot

English, Tower, .60 caliber, 12" round barrel, full-length military stock, brass trigger guard, butt cap and sidelined, lock plate marked "Tower" behind hammer and crown over "GR" forward of hammer, proofed on left side of barrel at breech, crown on tang behind tang screw, good condition, re-browned and cleaned, replaced front sight, working order **700.00**

French, military, 16" overall length, 9" round iron barrel, flat beveled lock plate with faceted pan fitted with flat beveled reinforced hammer, brass furniture, unmarked **800.00**

Halsbach & Sons, Baltimore, MD, holster pistol, c1785 to early 1800s, 9" brass part round, part octagon barrel, .65 caliber, lock marked "Halsbach & Sons," large brass butt cap with massive spread wing eagle (primitive) in high relief surrounded by cluster of 13 stars, large relief shell carving around tang of barrel, full walnut stock, pin-fastened.................... **1,750.00**

Kentucky, T. B. Cherington, 12-1/2" octagonal smoothbore barrel, stamped "T. P. Cherington" on barrel and lock plate, .45 caliber, brightly polished iron parts, walnut stock **2,500.00**

U. S. Model 1805, 10" round iron barrel with iron rib underneath holding ramrod pipe, lockplate marked with spread eagle and shield over "US" and vertically at rear "Harper's Ferry" over "1808," .54 caliber, walnut half stock with brass butt plate and trigger guard, Flayderman 6A-008 .... **3,000.00**

Revolver, Smith & Wesson Model 629-1 double-action revolver, cal. 44 Mag, 8-1/4" bbl, stainless steel, wood case, **$440**; Smith & Wesson Model 19-4 PA State Police 75th Anniversary Commemorative double-action revolver, cal. 357 Mag, 4" bbl, woodcase with accessories, **$550**.

Musket

Colt, Model 1861, .58 caliber, 39" barrel, "17th N.Y.V." beneath stock, good signature, date, and stampings on metal, inspector's cartouche on stock, bright gray metal, areas of pitting around bolster and lock......................... **1,375.00**

Harper's Ferry, Model 1816, 69 caliber, 42" round barrel, walnut stock with old dark brown patina, stamped "Ohio," inspector's mark opposite lock, lock stamped with eagle, name and "1821," 57-1/2" l.................................... **1,760.00**

Pottsdam, percussion, approx 75 caliber, 41" round barrel, three brass bands with butt plate, stock with old patina, inspector's marking, hammer screw missing, 56-3/4" l................ **450.00**

Richmond Armory, percussion, type I, 58 caliber, 40" round barrel, lock with partial Richmond mark at front and 1861 at tail, walnut stock with good color, milled for Maynard primer system beneath lock, steel bands, brass butt plate, guard, and nose cap, "A. D." initials carved in buttstock, old restored split through wrist, later leather sling with good patina, 56" l **3,630.00**

Springfield, Model 1816, flintlock, 69 caliber, 36" barrel, eagle stamp with "U.S.," maker, and "1832" on lock, walnut stock with dark brown patina, inspector's markings, three bands, bayonet lug, barrel shortened, restored split, 51-1/2" l **550.00**

U.S. Moro, large bore, 31-1/2" round barrel, single shot, center fire, may have been made to shoot shot shells, pulls apart at center for loading, walnut stock with fine figure, 45" l **250.00**

Percussion pistol

English, folding bayonet, simple engraving on frame, stands of flags and "Lenning," old hairlines in grip, 4" l barrel, 8-1/2" l.. **250.00**

U. S. Springfield, lock stamped with signature and 1856, eagle on Maynard primer door, 12" barrel dated 1855, brass hardware with iron back strap, walnut shoulder stock, brass hardware, few hairlines, pierced repair on hammer, 28-1/2" l...................................... **1,750.00**

Target pistol, High-Standard "Supermatic Trophy" semi-automatic target pistol, cal. 22 L.R. 7-1/4" bbl, soft carrying case, **$470**; Hi-Standard "Supermatic Trophy" semi-automatic pistol, cal. 22 long rifle, 7" bbl, original box, spare clip, weights, **$665**.

Waters, 8-1/2" round barrel, bright metal, stamped address and "1838" on lock, double inspector markings on stock, 14" l **660.00**

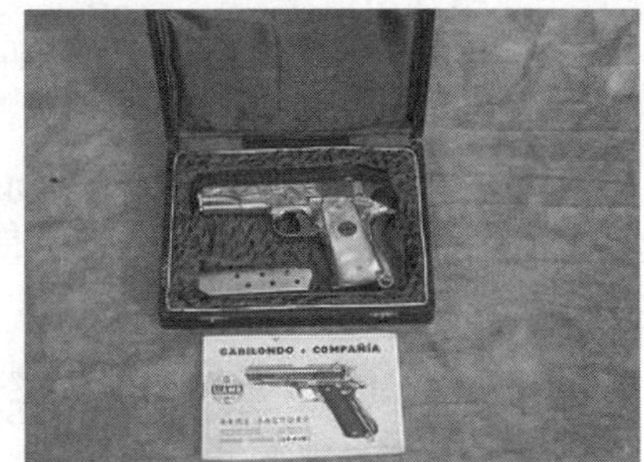

Pistol, Llama semi-automatic, Cal. 32, 3-3/4" bbl, mother of pearl grips, ornately engraved nickel finish, case with spare clip and manual, **$475**.

Pistol

Colt Model 1911 Army, .45 caliber auto, orig blued finish, checkered walnut grips, good signature and other stampings, 8-1/2" l.. **825.00**

Percussion, Southern, sgd "W. S. Spratley, Norfolk, VA" on lock, checkered walnut stock, engraved brass butt cap, cast iron trigger guard with pineapple finial, London swamped barrel approx 58 caliber, missing sliding safety for hammer, 16-1/2" l..................................... **2,145.00**

Sharps Pepperbox, c1859-74, price for pr **575.00**

Winchester Volcanic, lever action, 1855 .... **350.00**

Revolver

Baby Dragoon, cal. 31, standard 5" oct. bbl without rammer, cylinder has round stop holes, brass grip frame with one-pc wood grips, top flat of bbl is devoid of orig Colt markings, very faintly visible word "Orleans," presumably stamp of New Orleans retailer, medium gray-brown

patina on iron, repaired and refinished grip, shoulder repairs on back strap, accompanied by hand-written letter stating that this revolver was owned and used by Confederate Col. Henry C. Kellogg 4,025.00

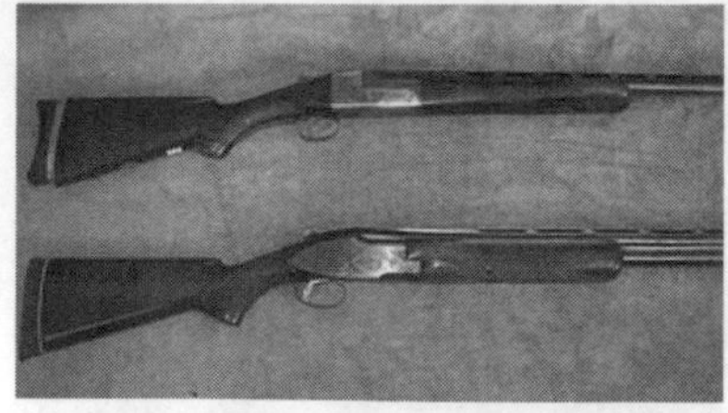
Shotgun, Ithaca single-barrel trap shotgun, Grade 4, 12 ga. 32" bbl, raised ventilated rib, engraved receiver, fancy checkered wood stock with beaver-tailed fore end and pistol grip engraved with name "Ted Rhoden," gold oval disk under butt engraved with initials "T.R.," **$660**; Browning Arms Co., Belgium, "Lightning" Broadway Trap double-barrel over/under shotgun, 12 ga. 32" bbls, raised ventilated rib, fancy checkered wood stock and pistol grip, single trigger, **$1,210**.

Colt

Model 1849, 31 caliber, 5" octagonal barrel with NY address, light overall cleaning, faint cylinder scene remaining, all serial numbers matching 660.00

Model 1851 Navy, engraved by L. D. Nimschke, gold and silver plating, ivory grips with eagle on left side, orig case with accessories, possibly never fired 201,600.00

Model 1860 Army, 44 caliber, 8" barrel, mottled brown surface on metal, areas of light pitting, good amount of engraved cylinder scene remains, inspector's marks on grips, 14" l..................................... 825.00

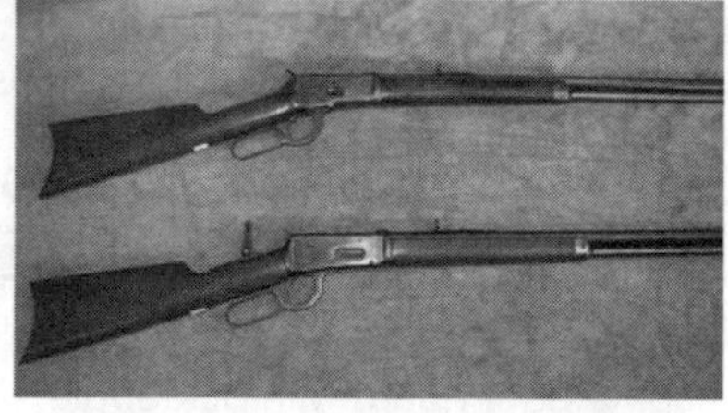
Rifle, Winchester Model 1892 lever action rifle, cal. 38 WCF, 24" octagonal bbl, metal and wood refinished, **$475**; Winchester Model 1894 lever action rifle, cal. 30 WCF, 26" bbl, adjustable rear peep sight, metal and wood refinished, **$550**.

Model 1862 Police, 36 caliber, 4-1/2" barrel with NY address, partially fluted cylinder with areas of orig blue, faint case coloring remains on frame, some silver plating on trigger guard and back strap, 9-1/2" l 615.00

Presentation, Army, Model 1880, matched pair, inscribed to Col. C. A. from Colt, unfired condition 246,500.00

Single action army, presented to Robert A Pinkerton, 1879 .... 414,400.00

Remington, new model Army, gold filled engraving on top barrel flat for "Dr. J. W. Ramsay," remnants of silver plating in some areas, 44 caliber, 8" octagon barrel, ivory grips with split on one side, light overall pitting, 14" l 715.00

Smith & Wesson

Frontier model, designed by Tiffany & Co., provenance included, owned by Walter Winans, target shooter and big game hunter............ 302,400.00

Model 1-1/2, presented by company to Pres Ulysses S. Grant, 1870, orig rosewood case, burgundy velvet lining, .32-caliber, gold inlay, engraving, MOP grips.... 548,800.00

Whitney .36 caliber, holster, identified to Captain William Worrell, 14th Regiment Mississippi Infantry, sold with military records 12,785.00

Whitneyville Armory, 22 caliber, 3-1/4" octagon barrel, brass frame, bird's head rosewood grips, 6-3/4" l.................200.00

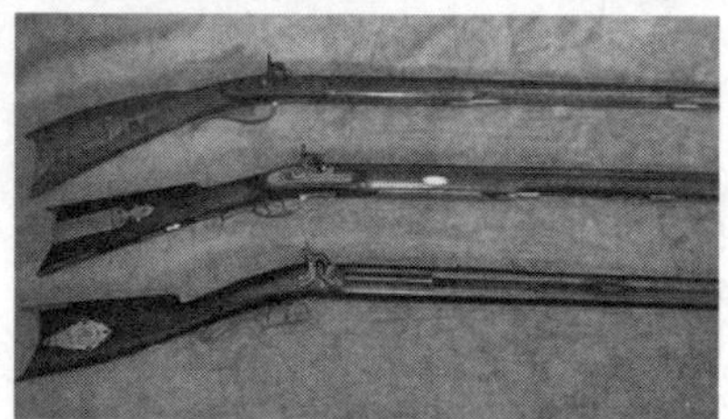
Rifle, American percussion target rifle, lock marked "Henry Parker Warranted," cal. approx. 40, 33-1/2" bbl, brass mounted, brass patch box, double set triggers, **$660**. Percussion rifle stamped " Edwin Hunt" on lock, cal. 60, 40" bbl, brass mounted, brass patch box, appears to be a modern restock, with powder horn, **$360**; double-barrel fixed breech over and under rifle/shotgun combination, top barrel flat stamped "W & C Ogden Owego, New York," cal. approx. 44. 12 ga. 28" bbls, German silver mounted with patch box, **$475**.

Rifle

Colt

Burgess, lever action, 44-40 caliber, 25-1/2" octagon barrel, full-length magazine, fine condition, strong stampings on barrel and receiver, honest wear from use to lever, butt plate, and nose cap, 42-3/4" l, includes two photos of orig owner, one from 1902, other 1906 .... 4,675.00

Lightning, slide auction, 44-40 caliber, 26" octagon barrel, full-length magazine, fine to excellent condition, 43" l, sold with photo of orig owner on hunting camping trip with rifle 2,750.00

Percussion, engraved "T.S." on barrel for Tobias Snyder, Bedford County, fine curly maple stock, engraved patch box, two part cheek piece inlays, five nickel silver inlays, 45-1/4" octagon barrel stamped "H. W. Deeds, Reading, PA," (possible barrel maker), well executed restored split at wrist, 60-1/2" l.................1,100.00

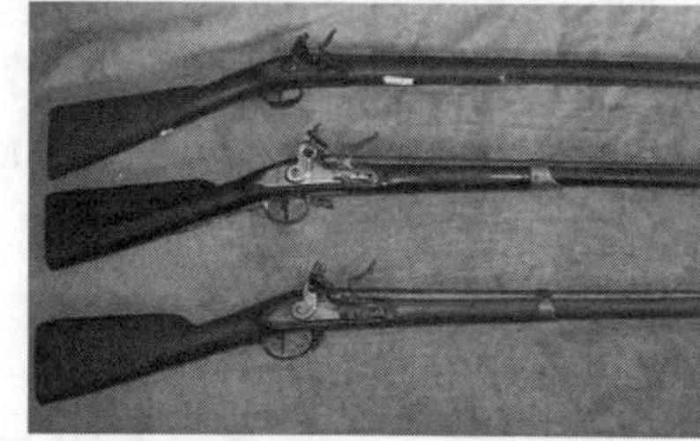
Musket, unmarked flintlock musket, cal. approx. 70, 44-1/2" bbl, scalloped cheek piece, initials "J D" carved in left butt and "D L/R" on right butt, **$715**; Nippes & Co., Phila. Contract flintlock musket, cal. 69, 44" bbl, barrel engraved "No. 507?," side plate engraved "E.J. 1844", **$500**; New England flintlock militia musket, cal. approx. 70, 39" bbl, barrel dated 1836, brass mounted, **$500**.

Remington, rolling block, Fieldmaster Model 121, pump action, 22 caliber, 26" barrel, excellent condition, 41-3/4" l 275.00

Spencer Repeating, 30" round barrel with three bands, walnut stock, old refinish, traces of inspector's stamp, brass inlay added to top of comb, few chips, 47" l 2,310.00

Springfield, Model 1873 Trapdoor, 45-70 caliber, cadet model, 29-1/2" round blued barrel, three click tumbler, eagle mark and signature on lock with eagle's head and "V. P." on breech area, minor dents on stock, ramrod, 48-3/4" l 450.00

Winchester, Model 1873, unfired, c1879, referred to as "One of One Thousand" 683,200.00

Flintlock pistol, English, marked "Tirebuck" on lock and "London" on top barrel flap. Cal. approx. 45, 4" bbl, engraved iron mountings and checkered stock, **$880**.

Shotgun

Browning

Citori Grade VI, over and under, lightning field model, fine engraving, gold overlay on receiver and guard, including pheasants, dog, ducks, and grouse, select grade checkered walnut stock, 12 gauge, 28" barrels, chromed for steel shot, 14-1/4" trigger pull, 45" l overall, leather take down case.......................... 1,870.00

Light 12, 12 gauge, single 30" full choke barrel, extra 30" chrome barrel with invector chokes, walnut stock fitted with pacymayr recoil pad **600.00**

European, double barrel, 12 gauge, 30-1/2" Damascus barrels, silver band overlay, sgd "R. Baumgarter in Bernburg" on barrel, engraved stag on tang, "Hubertus Geweher," figured walnut stock, horn trigger guard, 47" l...... **275.00**

Fox Sterlingworth, 16 gauge, double barrel, 26" barrel, top lever break-open, hammerless, double trigger, blued, checkered walnut pistol grip stock and forearm **400.00**

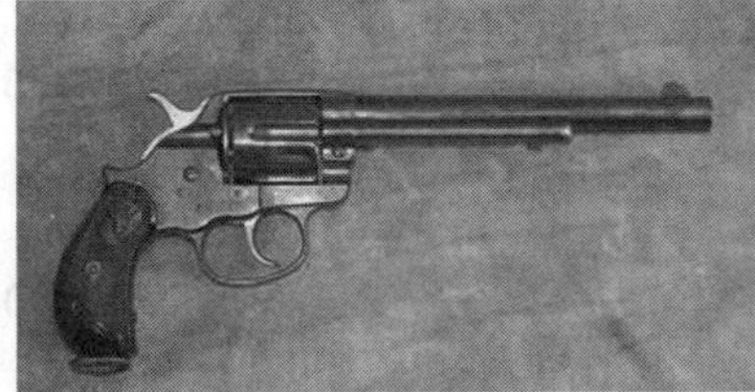

Revolver, Colt Model 1878 Frontier double-action revolver, cal. approx 44, 7-1/2" bbl, **$6,325**.

Percussion, double barrel, attributed to Ohio, sgd "C. Mills" on both of locks, 8 gauge, 40" browned barrels, checkered walnut stock with old patina, some wear, 57" l............ **330.00**

Stevens, Model 970, 12 gauge, single shot, 32" l round barrel with octagonal breech, top lever break-open, hammerless, automatic shell ejector, automatic safety, blued, case hardened frame, checkered walnut pistol grip stock and forearm **95.00**

Firehouse Collectibles

History: The volunteer fire company has played a vital role in the protection and social growth of many towns and rural areas. Paid professional firemen usually are found only in large metropolitan areas. Each fire company prided itself on equipment and uniforms. Conventions and parades gave the fire companies a chance to show off their equipment. These events produced a wealth of firehouse-related memorabilia.

Additional Listings: See *Warman's Americana & Collectibles* for more examples.

Advertising button

Rescue scene, multicolored, firemen rescuing infant from burning building, pre-1920s **20.00**

Sidewalk Fire Chiefs, Holley, NY, red on white, 1940s **15.00**

Automatic alarm indicator gong, 16" d gong, 18-1/2" w, 32" h case, master unit stationed in firehouse, used to receive telegraph signal from call boxes, Gamewell Fire Alarm Telegraph Co., NY, late Victorian oak case with carved crest and half columns, three beveled glass windows with three roll number indicator, cobalt blue cabinet, polished brass mechanism, patent info on brass plate, large brass key **600.00**

Badge

Allentown Fire Dept. 15, silvered brass, engraved serial number, 1930s............ **35.00**

Fleming Fire Dept., silvered metal, fire hydrant on left, hook and ladder on right, 1930s **25.00**

New Hampshire State Firemen's Assn, delegate, 1925 convention, black and white celluloid attachment with Sunapee Lake lighthouse, fabric ribbon............ **20.00**

Wilmington, DE, 1907, fabric with celluloid pin............ **15.00**

Bell, 11", brass, iron back **125.00**

Belt, red, black, and white, 43" l, marked "Hampden"............ **85.00**

Fire bucket, leather, Haverhill, Massachusetts, dated 1768, foliate design over name "David Marsh, born 1731," 11-3/4" h, handle missing, **$2,100**. Photo courtesy of Pook & Pook.

Fire bucket, leather, paint dec

10-3/4" h, "Boston Street Fire Club W. Poor Salem 1826" in diamond and oval, handle replaced, paint loss **2,415.00**

11" h, 9-1/4" d, "Jesse Smith active, 1806" in oval, surrounding winged Goddess with trumpet, handle unattached, damaged, paint losses **1,880.00**

12" h, "Mechanic Fire Society Ezra Young," reverse "No. 2 1811," eagle and shield depicting symbols of boot maker, probably Portsmouth, NH, broken handle, minor paint wear **54,625.00**

12" h, "Warren Fire Club J. Shove Danvers 1829" in oval cartouche surrounded by foliate scrolls and drapery, broken handle, paint loss **4,415.00**

12-1/2" h, green leather, gilt stencil "C. H. Reed," replaced handle, wear, crack **150.00**

13" h, "Leonidas H. Titcomb Jr. 1820 Bid Vulcan Yield to Neptunes Powr" in oval, wreath and drapery, handle replaced, paint loss............ **3,220.00**

Fire extinguisher

Babcock, American La France Fire Engine Co., Elmire, NY, grenade, amber glass **500.00**

Hayward's Hand Fire Grenade, yellow, ground mouth, smooth base, 6-1/4" h, c1870 .... **85.00**

Red Comet, red metal canister, red glass bulb............ **50.00**

Fire mark, cast iron, oval

8" x 11-1/2", relief molded design, pumper framed by "Fire Department Insurance," polychrome paint **495.00**

8" x 12", black, gold eagle and banner dec, marked "Eagle Ins. Co. Cin O"............ **950.00**

Helmet, leather, partial original litho label, **$175**

Helmet, leather, white, silvered front plate embossed "Rescue, AFD," crossed ladders motif, brass eagle, original liner, long back, **$225**.

Helmet

Leather, 9" x 14-1/4" x 11", Anderson + Jones, Broad St., NY, emb and ribbed leather, brass trumpetered holder, painted tin front piece lettered "cataract hose 2 j.g.," manufacturer's stamp on underside of brim, repaint, leather losses **635.00**

Stamped aluminum, black enameling, leather front panel marked "Chopmist, F.D.," interior makers label for Cairns & Brothers, Clifton, N.J." **200.00**

Ink blotter, Fireman's Fund 75th Year, Allendale, CA, fireman with little child, 1938, 4" x 9" **7.50**

Ledger marker, Caisse General Fire Insurance, statue of Liberty illus, multicolored, tin litho, 12-1/4" l, 3" w **275.00**

Medal, Jacksonville Fire Co., silvered brass, firefighting symbols circled by "I.A.F.E.-1917-Jaconsville, Fla.," reverse "Compliments of N. Snellenburg & Co. Uniforms, Philadelphia, Pa," looped ring **15.00**

Nozzle, hose, 16" l, brass, double handle, marked "Akron Brass Mfg. Co., Inc." **165.00**

Photograph, sepia print of uniformed fireman with medal, #4 on helmet, plate, framed, **$25**.

Parade hat, 6-1/2" h, painted leather, polychrome dec, green ground, front with eagle and harp, banner above "Hibernia," back inscribed "1752" in gilt, "1" on top, red brim underside, some age cracks, small losses to brim edge **3,335.00**

Print, 23" w, 28-1/2" h, American Fireman, C#152, fireman at the ready, hand pulled wagon, sgd on stone "L. Maurer," Currier & Ives, hand colored lithograph, overall darkening, few stains, glued down, matted and framed 23" w, 28-1/2" h **660.00**

Sales sheet, 8-1/2" x 11" glossy paper, Iron Horse Metal Ware Products, Rochester Can Co., NY, pictures five galvanized red fire pails **20.00**

Sign, 73-1/2" l, 21" w, Key City Hose Co., Sturgis, SD, late 19th C, repose stylized sheet metal skeleton key, orig painted lettering **500.00**

Stickpin, 7/8" celluloid button on 1-3/4" stickpin, Honor To Our Brave, fireman portrait, red shirt, blue helmet, 1900s **15.00**

Toy, pumper, three horses, painted cast iron, 13-3/4" l, **$375**. Photo courtesy of Joy Luke Auctions.

Toy

Arcade, fire pumper, 1941 Ford, cast iron, painted red, emb sides, cast fireman, hose reel on bed, rubber tires, repaired fender, 13" l **440.00**

Hubley, Ahrens Fox fire engine, cast iron, rubber tires, 7-1/2" l....... **475.00**

Kenton, fire pumper, cast iron, painted red, gold highlights on boiler, and ball, emb sides, disc wheels with spoke centers **615.00**

Kingsbury, horse-drawn ladder wagon, sheet metal, pained red, wire supports, holding yellow wooden ladders, two seated drivers, pulled by two black horses, yellow spoke wheels, bell on frame rings as toy is pulled, 26" l **2,150.00**

Snoopy Gus Fireman, litho tin wind-up **1,250.00**

Williams, A. C., fire pumper, cast iron, painted red, gold highlights, cast driver, bell, and boiler, rear platform with railing, rubber tires, 7-1/2" l **315.00**

Fireplace Equipment

History: In the colonial home, the fireplace was the gathering point for heat, meals, and social interaction. It maintained its dominant position until the introduction of central heating in the mid-19th century.

Because of the continued popularity of the fireplace, accessories still are manufactured, usually in an early-American motif.

Reproduction Alert: Modern blacksmiths are reproducing many old iron implements.

√**Andirons**, pr

19-1/8" h, 9" w, 17-1/4" d, brass and iron, double lemon-top, baluster form shaft, spurred cabriole legs, ball feet, America, 19th C, 19-1/8" h, minor pitting **885.00**

Andirons, pair, cast iron, in form of dachshunds with open mouths, curled tails, 8" h, 21" l, **$350**. Photo courtesy of Alderfer Auction Co.

19-1/4" h, 12" w, 22-1/2" d, brass and iron, faceted acorn finials, acorn finials surmounting faceted acorn, column, ring-turned shaft, spurred cabriole legs, slipper feet, conforming log stops, minor wear, America, late 18th/early 19th C **1,175.00**

20" h, knife blade, seamed brass double lemon top finials, arched bases, penny feet, one log rest bent **350.00**

21" h, 9-3/4" w, 16-1/2" d, brass and iron, double lemon-top, baluster form shaft, spurred cabriole legs and ball feet, minor pitting **410.00**

32" h, 35" d, detailed bronze castings of deco peacocks, old verdigris and areas of alter silver and blue painted, molded octagonal bases with paneled columns, ball-shaped perch on each, iron log rests, later combs **5,650.00**

Andirons and matching tools, Federal, 24" h brass ring-turned shaft andirons with spurred legs, ball feet, similarly turned fireplace 32" h tongs and 33" h shovel **1,100.00**

Bellows, turtleback

17-1/4" l, orig yellow paint, green edging, red, green, and copper colored fruit, brass nozzle, leather has wear, some damage, minor wear to paint **615.00**

18-1/4" l, orig black over cream smoke dec on both sides, fruit and foliage on front, gold and black stenciled border, touch-up on green leaves and handle, expertly restored leather **385.00**

45" l, carved wood "Green Man" grotesque face on each side, long carved vine scroll handle, English, tears to leather in bellows **120.00**

Coal grate, 26" w, 9-1/2" d, 16" h, George II, brass-mounted iron, bowed central section of four rails over grate, ash drawer between bowfront side panels, applied brass starbursts, surmounted with brass urn finials, English, last quarter 19th C **200.00**

Fire back, 36" x 37", cast iron, relief of crossed swords in architectural panel and dates 1746/1756 .... **2,100.00**

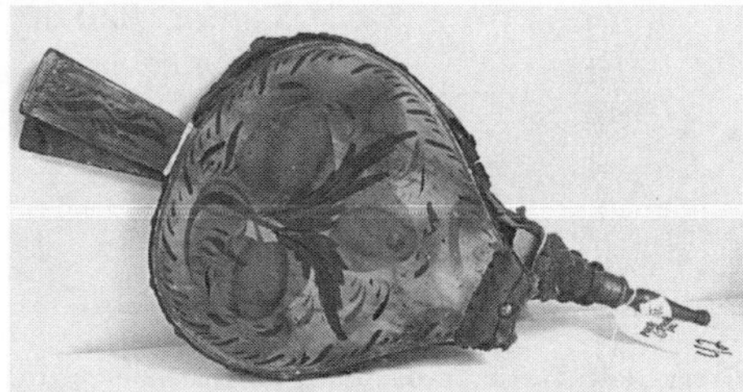

Bellows, painted gold fruit, green leaves, red and black decoration, 19th C, front panel detached at nozzle, wear, **$90**. Photo courtesy of Pook & Pook.

Fireboard, 36" x 44-3/8", wide central raised panel, paint dec to depict seaside village, ships, and houses, surround painted to depict tiles with numerous ships, houses, and trees, America, early 19th C, wear, fading **7,650.00**

Fire dogs, pr

7-1/2" w, 6-1/2" h, brass, central horizontal reeded orb raised on three reeded legs, reeded horizontal bar on top, Aesthetic Movement, English, third quarter 19th C **150.00**

15" h, cast iron, rampant lion bearing twisted horizontal bars, seated on rope twist rounded and octagonal base, late 19th/early 20th C **700.00**

Fire fender, brass and wire, America or England, late 18th/early 19th C

45-1/2" l, 18" h, D-shaped, brass rim, vertical wirework dec with brass swag and scroll work **2,235.00**

49" l, 14" d, 24" h, D-form brass top rail over conforming wirework screen, swag and scroll work, minor wear.................................... **2,350.00**

49-5/8" l, 11-3/8" h, brass rim, entwined wirework, minor pitting **560.00**

Fire place screen, brass, English, **$75**. Photo courtesy of Wiederseim Associates, Inc.

Fire screen

23" w, 36" h, brass, lifting handle and foliate repousse frieze above stained glass trelliswork panel depicting foliage about central panel with bird, trestle support with spindles, Aesthetic Movement, c1875-80 .... **4,000.00**

24" w, 39" h, walnut frame, Persian embroidered panel in center, c1930 .... **225.00**

25-1/2" h, 21-1/4" w, Arts & Crafts style, wrought iron frame, ornate vining and scrolled feet, shield shaped hammered copper center plate with fleur-de-lis **200.00**

53" h, Chippendale-style, English, mahogany, turned urn-shaped column, relief rococo scrolling on knees, cabriole legs, carved scrolls at feet, old dark surface, large petit point panel with white urn of flowers on brown and red ground, restored splits, pieced restoration on corners, 19th C.................................... **500.00**

Fire tools, 30-7/8" and 31-3/8" l, brass and iron, ball finial on belted ball top, shovel and tongs, minor dents, scattered pitting.. **420.00**

Footman, 18" w, 15" d, 12" h, brass, Georgian-style, rect top, turned side handles, pierced apron, cabriole front legs, straight round rear legs, English **365.00**

Hearth broom, 27" l, orig black over yellow smoke dec, turned handle, wear, some bristles missing.................... **110.00**

Fire grate, cast iron and brass, George III, early 19th C, serpentine railed basket above pierced brass frieze centering spread-wing eagle on scrolled supports, vasiform finials, ball feet, 22-1/4" x 21" x 13", **$700**. Photo courtesy of Sloans & Kenyon Auctions.

Kettle stand, 16-1/2" w, 9" d, 7-1/2" h, brass, pierced top, engraved peacocks, cabriole legs, bird's claw feet, slightly bowed at center **265.00**

Mantle, 61-3/4" w, 10" d, 51-3/4" h, 32" w x 34" h opening, pine, old brown over tan graining, raised pilasters and facing, shaped top with rounded edges, sq nail construction, few small sections of molding missing **200.00**

Pole screen

53-1/2" h, Irish, Chippendale, inlaid walnut and fruitwood veneers, oblong panel with scalloped edges, orig silk needlework of a dragon, saber legs with line border inlay graduate into triangular block with three turned supports, tripod base, short turned feet below applied blocks, some stains on fabric, few veneer chips missing **475.00**

54" h, English, Chippendale-style, mahogany, early petit point panel of urn with flowers, urn turned column, high tripod base with cabriole legs, scroll feet, relief rococo carving at knees, late 19th or early 20th C **450.00**

Fragment, cast iron, "MURDOCK AND PARLOR GRATE CO. BOSTON COPYRIGHT FEB. 1885," rect side piece with elongated stylized angel figure holding hourglass aloft in one hand, beaded and relief flame borders, raised maker's marks on reverse, 9-1/2" w, 31" h, **$120**. Photo courtesy of Skinner, Inc.

Tinder lighter, pistol shape, flintlock striker

5-1/8" l, mahogany, brass tinderbox, lyre-shaped front support, small candle socket with drop pan, etched scrollwork on the side **1,430.00**

8" l, walnut, steel tinder box, candle socket, simple curved support, front end with compartment for tinder/ candles, inscribed "Laurent Gille" **935.00**

Fishing Collectibles

History: Early man caught fish with crude spears and hooks made of bone, horn, or flint. By the mid-1800s, metal lures with attached hooks were produced in New York State. Later, the metal was curved and glass beads added to make them more

attractive. Spinners with painted-wood bodies and glass eyes appeared around 1890. Soon after, many different makers were producing wood plugs with glass eyes. Patents, which were issued in large numbers around this time, covered the development of hook hangers, body styles, and devices to add movement to the plug as it was drawn through the water. The wood plug era lasted up to the mid-1930s when plugs constructed of plastic were introduced.

With the development of casting plugs, it became necessary to produce fishing reels capable of accomplishing the task with ease. Reels first appeared as a simple device to hold a fishing line. Improvements included multiplying gears, retrieving line levelers, drags, clicks, and a variety of construction materials. The range of quality in reel manufacture varied considerably. Collectors are mainly interested in reels made with high-quality materials and workmanship, or those exhibiting unusual features.

Early fishing rods, which were made of solid wood, were heavy and prone to breakage. By gluing together tapered strips of split bamboo, a rod was fashioned which was light in weight and had greatly improved strength. The early split-bamboo rods were round and wrapped with silk to hold them together. As glue improved, fewer wrappings were needed, and rods became slim and lightweight. Rods were built in various lengths and thicknesses, depending upon the type of fishing and bait used. Rod makers' names and models can usually be found on the metal parts of the handle or on the rod near the handle.

Reproduction Alert: Lures and fish decoys.

Badge, 1-1/2", Special Fish Warden Board of Fish Commissioners, heavy brass, PA state seal in center, horizontal bar pin on back, stamped "718 Penna" **85.00**

Bait bucket, painted blue, stenciled "Falls City-Magic-Minnow Bucket" **1,980.00**

Bait trap, Katch-N-Karry, Glassman Mfg. Co., Jackson, TN, patented 1941, wood, 4" d wire mesh circle, litho of bluegill and roach **375.00**

Bobber, hand painted, 12" l, pike float, yellow, green, and red stripes **24.00**

Book

- *Lures: The Guide to Sport Fishing,* Keith C. Schuyler, Stackpole Co., 1955, dj **20.00**
- *McClaine's Standard Fishing Encyclopedia and International Angling Guide,* A. J. McClaine, Holt, Rinehart, Winston, 1965, 2nd printing, 1,057 pgs, color and black and white illus by R. Younger, dj **22.00**
- *The Complete Angler: or Contemplative Man's Recreation: A Discourse on Rivers, Fish-Ponds, Fish & Fishing in 2 Parts,* Issac Walton and Charles Cotton, supplementary and explanatory Sir John Hawkins **125.00**

Creel, bamboo and leather, **$85**. Photo courtesy of Alderfer Auction Co.

Cane, 37" l, gaff, with pouch, 1-1/8" d x 1" h silver knob handle, oak shaft, brass fitting 2/3" way down, when button is depressed, cane can be folded, 2-3/4" ferrule machined with threads to accept 3" pointed steel gaff which is carried in separate leather pouch, English, c1890 .... **1,120.00**

Canoe, Old Town Sponson, 16' **1,430.00**

Catalog

- Creek Chub Bait Co., Garrett, IN, 1934 .... **330.00**
- Evinrude Motors, Milwaukee, WI, 1961, Catalog of Outboard Motors **32.00**
- Hardy Brothers, 1910 .... **495.00**
- Martin Bradford, Boston, 1847, tackle **2,415.00**
- Orvis, c1900 .... **330.00**
- Penn Fishing Tackle Mfg., Philadelphia, PA, 1952, Catalog No. 17 of Penn Reels **32.00**
- Shakespeare Co., Kalamazoo, Catalog No. 27, 1927, some pages uncut **175.00**
- Wallsten Tackle Co., Chicago, IL, 1940s, Fishing Tips, Courtesy of Cisco Kid Lures **21.00**
- Weber Lifelike Fly Co., Stevens Point, WI, 1941, Catalog No. 22, Flies & Fly Tackle **70.00**
- White, E. M. & Co., Old Town, ME, c1922, E. M. White Builders of White Canoes **40.00**

Cigarette card, King of England deep-sea fishing, New Zealand, 1937 .... **12.00**

Clock, mechanical, fish punching hole in side of boat with moving hammer, Hero Clock Co., wind-up, marked "Made in China" **40.00**

Creel

- 12" w, 6" d, 8-1/2" h, painted splint, carved wooden wire-hinged top, forest green, America, early 19th C **920.00**

Creels, left: Turtle Trade Mark, wicker, **$260**; right: splint with leather, **$550**. Fishing photos courtesy of Lang's Sporting Collectables, Inc.

- 32" w, 6" h, wicker, leather latch with netted fish head, silver tail on other end, late 1940s **275.00**
- Size 15, Tillamook Model, George Lawrence, Portland, OR, split willow, leather trim, half leather lid, leather pocket on front, c1950, with orig catalog, unused **9,020.00**

Dealer display, Swimmy Bait Co., 12 boxed lures **175.00**

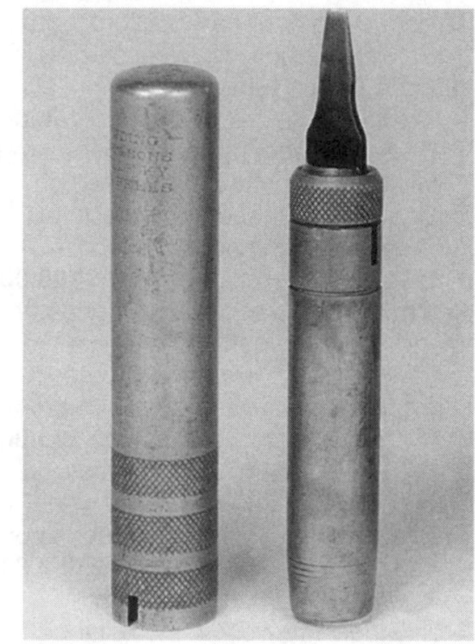

Pocket reel oiler and screwdriver, B. F. Meek & Sons, Louisville, KY, c1910, **$825**.

Fishing license

- California 1934 Resident Citizens Angling License, 1-3/4", dark red, pink, and white, compartment on back for paper license **115.00**
- State of Rhode Island Lobster License, 1-3/4" d, silvered brass, vertical bar pin and lock on reverse, c1930 .... **95.00**

Flask, pewter, emb on both sides, one side with fisherman landing trout, other side with fisherman netting catch, marked "Alchemy Pewter, Sheffield, England" **175.00**

Float, Ideal **200.00**

Fly, Carrie Stevens **440.00**

Fly fishing display, c1910, C. J. Frost, Stevens Point, WI, 9' l **3,080.00**

Folk art, 25" h, 40-1/4" l, wood carving, titled "Two Fish and a Frog," sgd "L.

A. Plummer, 1904" in lower right, polychrome dec, minor cracks **17,250.00**

Knife, Marbles Woodcraft **385.00**

License holder, paper envelope, Florida Game and Fresh Water Commission, stamped with County Judge's name **22.00**

Reel, Lenard Atwood, Farmington Mills, Maine, 1907 patent, original box, **$1,400**.

Lure

- Al Foss Dixie Wiggler, #13, 1928, metal box, extra hook, pocket catalog, 3-1/2" l **100.00**
- Blee, Charles, submarine bait, all metal **2,000.00**
- Carters Bestever, red and white, pressed eyes, 3" l **10.00**
- Creek Chubb Bait Co., fintail shiner **990.00**
- Creek Chubb Bait Co., jigger 4100, red side **140.00**
- Creek Chubb Bait Co., mouse **470.00**
- Creek Chubb Bait Co., plunking dinger, all black **100.00**
- Creek Chubb Bait Co., red beetle **315.00**
- Detroit Glass, minnow tube, fish form, four treble hooks, orig box, c1914 ..... **3,500.00**
- DeWitt, Bil, minnow, orig box with papers **90.00**
- Dunk's Double Header, black plug, c1931 ..... **125.00**
- Four Brothers, Neverfail Minnow, orig box **615.00**
- Hanson, GE pull-me-slow, two hooks **90.00**
- H. Comstock, 1883, Flying Helgramite **4,400.00**
- Heddon, baby lunny frog, c1928 ..... **90.00**
- Heddon, black sucker **3,300.00**
- Heddon, swimming minnow, 1910 ..... **800.00**
- Jamison, W. J.,Chicago, IL, Musky Coaxer Bair, orig box **1,045.00**
- Meadow Brook, rainbow, 1-1/4" l, orig box, flyrod type **120.00**
- Musky, crazy crawler 2510 mouse **250.00**
- Musky, giant vamp 7350, jointed, natural scales, c1930 ..... **130.00**
- Musky Minnow **900.00**
- Paw-Paw, sucker, perch finish, tack eyes **30.00**
- Pfleuger, metal, May-Bug spoon **3,190.00**
- Pfleuger, Never Fail Minnow, five-hook, orig box marked "Neptune Wooden Minnow" **495.00**
- Pflueger for Sears, No. 9007 new winner wood minnow, five-hook, wine colored box **325.00**
- Sam-Bo, 4" l, bass, pike, pickerel, orig box **215.00**
- Shakespeare, mouse white and red, thin body, glass eyes, 3-5/8" l **30.00**
- Shakespeare, underwater minnow, five-hook, c1907 ..... **150.00**
- Smith Bait Co., Wiggle Tail Bait, (aka Smith Minnow), mechanical, hinged tail, early 1900s, orig wood box **11,150.00**
- South Bend Tackle Co., Truck-Oreno, red and white wood **2.970.00**
- Souvenir, Lucky Lure, Souv of Indian Lake, OH, 3-1/2" l, nude black female, MOC **130.00**
- Strike-It-Lure, green, yellow, and red spots, glass eyes **40.00**
- W. D. Chapman, Theresa, NY, metal minnow and propeller **2,200.00**
- Winchester, 9011, three-hook **500.00**

Miniature, canoe, Old Town **10,500.00**

Minnow bucket, green collapsible canvas, wire bail, orig black painted wooden handle, stamped "No. 08 Mfg for the Planet Co. Patent" **155.00**

Pinback button, Johnsburg Fish & Game Club, red and white, forest safety theme, 1930s **10.00**

Poacher's gig, hand forged five pronged rake-type device, long worn wooden handle, from Eastern Shore, MD or VA, 63" l **145.00**

Bait reel, Meek & Milam, Frankfort, KY, #1 size, brass, buffalo horn handle, **$3,850**.

Reel

- Abraham Coates, Watertown, NY, 1888 patent **2,200.00**
- Ambassador 5500C Silver, counter balance, handle, high-speed gear rates **120.00**
- Anson Hatch, New Haven, CT, side-mount, brass, c1866 ..... **7,150.00**
- B. C. Milam, Frankford, KY, #2, casting **1,760.00**
- B. C. Milam & Sons, #3, casting **1,430.00**
- B. F. Meek & Sons, #2, casting **935.00**
- William Billinghurst, Rochester, NY, brass, patent 1859, birdcage-style, fixed handle **2,750.00**
- Bogdan, large trout **1,100.00**
- Charles M. Clinton, Ithaca, NY, German Silver, c1900 ..... **6,820.00**
- Dr. Allonzo H. Fowler, Ithaca, NY, hard rubber, Fowler's Improved Gem Fly Reel **6,600.00**
- Hardy, Hercules, c1890, trout **1,430.00**
- Hendryx Safety Reel, trout **995.00**
- H. L. Leonard, Model 50B, wide spool, fly **1,760.00**
- Horton Mfg., #7 Blueglass **880.00**

Edw. Vom Hofe

- Model 621, size 4/0 ..... **250.00**
- Salmon, Cascapedia **4,290.00**

Julius Vom Hofe

- Fly, plain, early size 3 ..... **880.00**
- German silver and hard rubber, size 3 ..... **550.00**

J. T. Baker, 1871, German silver **1,925.00**

Morgan James, side mount, pillbox style, brass, c1860 ..... **9,350.00**

Trout reel, Edw. Vom Hofe, NY, German silver, c1870, tiny size, **$7,810**.

Niangua, casting **660.00**

Orvis 1874 prototype, fly **1,870.00**

Otto Zward, 2/0 size **1,540.00**

Penn-Jic Master No. 500, 3" d **65.00**

Pflueger

- #1993L, Summit, casting, 1940-50 ..... **100.00**
- 1429-3/4 templar, number engraved on side **125.00**

Restigouche

- 1896 patent **1,540.00**
- 1902 patent **1,540.00**

Shakespeare

- Standard **150.00**
- Tournament **110.00**

South Bend, #1131A, casting, shiny finish, orig box **18.00**
Talbot Star **385.00**
Thos. J. Conroy, NY, Wells model, c1889, trout **3,300.00**
Union Hardware Co., raised pillar type, nickel and brass **25.00**
Unmarked, wood, brass fittings, c1880-1920, 6" d **85.00**
Walker, TR-4, fly **1,210.00**
Wilkerson Quadruple, 1900 .... **95.00**
Winchester, Model #1135, fly, black finish **65.00**
Wm. H. Talbot Eli, casting **880.00**

Trout reel, Morgan James (1815-78), Utica, NY, c1860 brass pillbox style side mount reel, **$9,350.**

Rod

Bamboo, fly fishing, orig reel, wear **125.00**
Clarence Carlson, split bamboo, early 7' **4,400.00**
Everett Garrison, 8' **4,180.00**
F. E. Thomas, three piece fly rod, extra tip, metal case, marked "Special, Bangor, Maine," 8-1/2' **275.00**
George Halstead, Danbury, CT, split bamboo, 7-1/2', trout **3,410.00**
Goodwin Granger, split bamboo, 7' **1,100.00**
Hardy Brothers, Marvel, split bamboo, 7-1/2' **715.00**
Hardy's of England Salmon Deluxe Rod, extra tip, aluminum case, 9' **175.00**
Harold Gillum, Ridgefield, CT, split bamboo, 6-1/2' and 7-1/2', sold as pr **7,700.00**

H. L. Leonard
Fly, 6-1/2" **1,450.00**
Red wrap, 7-1/2' **1,925.00**
Split bamboo, model 50DF, 8' **880.00**
#37ACM-6' **3,025.00**

Horrocks & Illotson, 9' 3", two tips, split-bamboo fly, maroon wraps **50.00**

Jim Payne
#94-7' **2,530.00**
#97-7' **5,500.00**

Kingfisher, brown and red, orig wraps, red agate eyes, paper label **125.00**

Lyle Dickerson
7' **5,225.00**
8' **4,180.00**

Montaque, bamboo, two tips, orig case **135.00**
Orvis, Wes Jordan, 8-1/2' **550.00**
Paul H. Young, 6' 3" Midge **2,470.00**
Payne, salmon **1,320.00**
Shakespeare Springbrook, fly fishing, orig bag **100.00**
S. J. Small, split bamboo, three-rod set **2,640.00**
Superlight, 5' spinning rod **660.00**
Thomas & Thomas, Fountainhead **3,300.00**
Union Hardware Co., 7-1/2', Kingfisher, saltwater boat rod, split-bamboo fly, dark brown wraps **35.00**

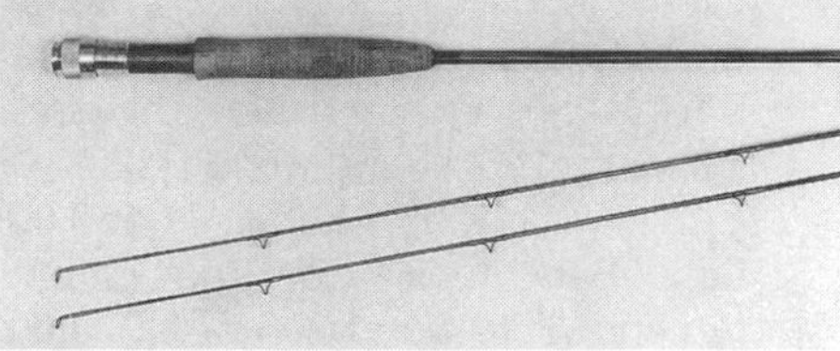

Trout rod, Harold "Pinky" Gillum, Ridgefield, CT, 6-1/2 feet, cane, **$13,200.**

Sign, The Flatfish, World's largest selling fishing plug," Helen Tackle Co., Detroit, metal framed glass, 8" x 16" **350.00**
Tackle box, leather **450.00**
Tobacco tin, Forest & Stream, pocket size, 4-1/4" x 3" x 7/8" **600.00**
Tray, aluminum, lady fishing, catches skirt with hook and lifts it up in the back, red and black dec, scalloped edge **165.00**
Trout net, 22-3/4", nice wood, orig net **100.00**
Vise, fly tying, 7" l, 2-1/2" w, steel and brass, bolts to table **210.00**
Wall plaque, 13" x 9", large mouth bass **115.00**

FITZHUGH

History: Fitzhugh, one of the most-recognized Chinese Export porcelain patterns, was named for the Fitzhugh family for whom the first dinner service was made. The peak years of production were 1780 to 1850.

Fitzhugh features an oval center medallion or monogram surrounded by four groups of flowers or emblems. The border is similar to that on Nanking china. Occasional border variations are found. Butterfly and honeycomb are among the rarest.

Reproduction Alert: Spode Porcelain Company, England, and Vista Alegre, Portugal, currently are producing copies of the Fitzhugh pattern. Oriental copies also are available.

Notes: Color is a key factor in pricing. Blue is the most common color; rarer colors are ranked in the following ascending order: orange, green, sepia, mulberry, yellow, black, and gold. Combinations of colors are scarce.

Dish, two saucers, rectangular tray, riverscape decoration, blue and white, Chinese, Qing dynasty, **$800**. Photo courtesy of Sloans & Kenyon Auctions.

Cider jug, cov, 11 1/2" h, underglaze blue, 19th C **2,650.00**
Hot water dish, 10 5/8" d, underglaze blue, center pine cone and beast medallion, four clusters of flowers and precious objects in trellis diaper border, spearhead and dumbbell border, blue spouts, c1840 .... **450.00**

Plate
9-5/8" d, green butterfly and floral garland outer border, sepia brown center with quatrefoil design, symbols of Chinese scholarship, central chrysanthemum, minor wear to gilt rim, well done professional repair **1,980.00**
9-3/4" d, green butterfly border, quatrefoil center with scholar symbols, qilin beasts **550.00**
9-3/4" d, orange butterfly border, quatrefoil center with scholar symbols, qilin beasts **550.00**
9-3/4" d, rose/pink butterfly border, quatrefoil center with Chinese scholar symbols, mythological qilin beasts **5,500.00**
9-3/4" d, underglaze blue diamond pattern border, quatrefoil center with scholar symbols and qilin beasts, few repaired flakes **330.00**

Platter, oval, orange and white, Chinese, 19th C, 17" l, **$2,585.** Photo courtesy of Skinner, Inc.

Platter, 18" l, oval, 19th C, rim chip **865.00**
Punch bowl, 11" d, white underglaze blue, Fitzhugh border, famille rose floral sprays and shield shaped cartouche,

monogram, scalloped rim, restoration **500.00**

Salt, 4" l, oval, underglaze blue, center pine cone and beast medallion, four clusters of flowers and precious objects spearhead and dumbbell border, ruffled rim, Mared pattern border, feathered edge, fluted sides, c1820, price for pr **1,450.00**

Sauce, 5" d, brown pattern, armorial device in center with motto, monogram, and American Indian, made for Gabriel Henry Manigault, (1788-1834), Charleston, SC, flake and hairline **3,750.00**

Serving dish, ogee-shaped, crest of the Manigault family of Charleston, SC **7,765.00**

Tureen, cov, 14" l, underglaze blue dec, braided handles, restored pineapple knop finial **1,400.00**

Flasks

History: A flask, which usually has a narrow neck, is a container for liquids. Early American glass companies frequently formed them in molds that left a relief design on the front and/or back. Historical flasks with a portrait, building, scene, or name are the most desirable.

For more information, see *Warman's Glass*, 4th edition.

A chestnut is hand-blown, small, and has a flattened bulbous body. The pitkin has a blown globular body with a spiral rib overlay on vertical ribs. Teardrop flasks are generally fiddle shaped and have a scroll or geometric design.

Notes: Dimensions can differ for the same flask because of variations in the molding process. Color is important in determining value—aqua and amber are the most common colors; scarcer colors demand more money. Bottles with "sickness," an opalescent scaling that eliminates clarity, are worth much less.

Calabash, deep amber, sheaf of wheat and star, applied handle, iron pontil, GXIII-45, minor surface wear **1,045.00**

Chestnut, 4-3/4" h, Zanesville, OH, blown, 24 vertical ribs, amber, half pint, minor wear **250.00**

Historical

Clasped Hands/Union-Eagle, Cl & Sons, applied band, smooth base, aqua, McKearin GXI-23, recently cleaned **100.00**

Columbia, Liberty cap, eagle, Kensington and Union on reverse, pale aqua, bubbles **800.00**

Cornucopia/urn, emerald green, pint, pontil, McKearin GIII-17, **$450**. Photo courtesy of American Bottle Auctions.

Double Eagle, sheared lip, pontil, average strike, yellowish amber tone bordering on golden, pint, McKearin GII-83 .... **150.00**

Eagle/Cornucopia, sheared lip, open pontil, pint, tobacco amber, McKearin GII-72, little interior stain **140.00**

Eagle-Willington/Glass Co., Willington glass Works, West Willington, CT, 1860-72, bright medium yellowish-olive, applied double-collared mouth, smooth base, half pint, McKearin GII-63 .... **210.00**

Horse putting cart/eagle, olive green, pint, pontil, McKearin GV-7a, **$700**. Photo courtesy of American Bottle Auctions.

For Pike's Peak Prospector-Hunter Shooting Deer, attributed to Ravenna Glass Works, Ravenna, OH, 1860-80, aquamarine, applied mouth with ring, smooth base, quart, McKearin GXI-47, 1/4" shallow flake **325.00**

Masonic-Eagle, Zanesville, emb "Zanesville, J. Sheppard & Co.," golden amber, pint, McKearin GIV-32 .... **2,975.00**

Success to the Railroad, Keene Marlboro Street Glassworks, Keene, NH, 1830-50, light yellow amber with olive tone, sheared mouth, pontil scar, pint, McKearin GV-3 ..... **250.00**

Pattern molded

4-5/8" l, Midwest, 1800-30, 24 ribs swirled to the right, golden amber, sheared mouth, pontil scar **190.00**

7-3/8" l, Emil Larson, NJ, c1930, swirled to the right, amethyst, sheared mouth, pontil scar, some exterior high point wear....... **250.00**

Hunter-fisher, attributed to Whitney Glass Works, NJ, aqua, 9-1/2" h; aqua glass flask with tree of life and sheaf of wheat designs, 9-1/4" h; aqua ribbed jug form flask, 8-3/4" h, **$415**. Photo courtesy of Pook & Pook.

Pictorial

Cornucopia, eagle, emerald green, pint, applied top, pontil, made by Lancaster, NY, int. stain....... **850.00**

Eye Opener, screw cap, ground lip, natural purple from sun coloring, 5-1/2" **170.00**

Monument-Sloop, Baltimore Glass Works, Baltimore, MD, 1840-60, medium variegated yellow green, sheared mouth, pontil scar, half pint, McKearin GVI-2, some exterior high point wear, overall dullness **1,100.00**

Sunburst, light amethyst, 1810-25 .... **1,200.00**

Pitkin

Golden amber, 36 broken swirl ribs, half post neck, 5-3/4" h, few broken narrow blisters....... **715.00**

Olive green, 36 broken swirl ribs, half post neck, 5" h....... **715.00**

Olive green, 36 broken swirl ribs, half post neck, 7" h, minor wear, two tiny broken blisters....... **715.00**

Pittsburgh or Zanesville, swirled, light green, c1835, 6-3/4" h, **$460**. Photo courtesy of Pook & Pook.

Portrait

Adams-Jefferson, New England, 1830-50, yellow amber, sheared mouth, pontil scar, half pint, McKearin GI-114 .... **325.00**

General Jackson, Pittsburgh district, 1820-40, bluish-aquamarine, sheared mouth, pontil scar, pint, McKearin GI-68 .... **1,500.00**

Lafayette-DeWitt Clinton, Coventry Glass Works, Coventry, CT, 1824-25, yellowish-olive, sheared mouth, pontil scar, half pint, 1/2" vertical crack, weakened impression, McKearin GI-82 .... **2,100.00**

Jenny Lind, medium yellow olive, 1855-60 .... **2,400.00**

Rough and Ready Taylor-Eagle, Midwest, 1830-40, aquamarine, sheared mouth, pontil scar, pint, McKearin GI-77 .... **1,200.00**

Zachary Taylor, corn for the world, portrait **400.00**

Washington-Sheaf of Wheat, Dyottville Glass Works, Philadelphia, PA 1840-60, medium yellow-olive, inward rolled mouth, pontil scar, half pint, McKearin GI-59 .... **9,000.00**

Washington-Taylor, Dyottville Glass Works, Philadelphia, PA 1840-60, bright bluish-green, applied double collared mouth, pontil scar, quart, McKearin GI-42 .... **400.00**

Swirled ribbed body, green, half pint, American early 18th C, 5" h, green glass quart flask, c1830, 9" h, rim chip, **$350**. Photo courtesy of Pook & Pook.

Majolica, 4-1/2" h, polychrome dec bulldog, landscape, and crest design, Italy, 19th C.................................. **200.00**

Pewter, 14" h, Pilgrim, shaped figural handles, moon-shaped body, molded foliage, pierced base, losses, 16th C **345.00**

Scroll

Light apple green, 1845-55... **250.00**

Medium yellow, 1945-55 .... **600.00**

Sunburst, GVIII-29, pint, bluish-green, teardrop shape, **$325**. Photo courtesy of Pacific Glass Auctions.

Silver, sterling

4-1/4" l, America, late 19th/early 20th C, ovoid, emb foliates on textured ground, domed lid with attached chain, approx two troy oz **175.00**

9" h, Clarence Vanderbilt, New York, c1909-35, rect, overall textured finish, reeded circular screw cap, approx 10 troy oz **260.00**

Whiskey, AAA Old Valley Whiskey, medium red amber, 1870-80 .... **800.00**

Flow Blue

For more information, see *Warman's Glass*, 4th edition.

History: Flow blue, or flown blue, is the name applied to china of cobalt blue and white, whose color, when fired in a kiln, produced a flowing or blurred effect. The blue varies from dark royal cobalt blue to navy or steel blue. The flow may be very slight to a heavy blur, where the pattern cannot be easily recognized. The blue color does not permeate through the body of the china. The amount of flow on the back of a piece is determined by the position of the item in the sagger during firing.

Known patterns of flow blue were first produced around 1830 in the Staffordshire area of England. Credit is generally given to Josiah Wedgwood, who worked in that area. Many other potters followed, including Alcock, Davenport, Grindley, Johnson Brothers, Meakin, Meigh, and New Wharf. They were attempting to imitate the blue and white wares brought back by the ship captains of the tea trade. Early flow blue, 1830s to 1870s, was usually of the pearl ware or ironstone variety. The later patterns, 1880s to 1900s, and the modern patterns after 1910, were of the more delicate semi-porcelains. Most flow blue was made in England but it was made in many other countries as well. Germany, Holland, France, Spain, Wales, and Scotland are also known locations. Many patterns were made in the United States by several companies, Mercer, Warwick, Sterling, and the Wheeling Pottery to name a few.

Adviser: Ellen G. King.

Educational Alert: The Flow Blue International Collectors' Club Inc. has been studying and discussing new versus reproduction flow blue and mulberry. There are still areas of personal judgment as yet undetermined. The general rule accepted has been "*new*" indicates recent or contemporary manufacture and "*reproduction*" is a copy of an older pattern. Problems arise when either of these fields is sold at "*old*" flow blue prices.

In an effort to help educate its membership, the Club continues to inform of all known changes through its conventions, newsletters, and the Web site: www.flowblue.com.

Warman's is working to those ends also. The following is a listing of "*new*" flow blue, produced since the 1960s:

Blossom, Ashworth Bros, 1962, wash bowl and pitcher.

Blossom: Ashworth Bros., Hanley, 1962. Wash bowl and pitcher made for many years now, in several items.

Vinranka: Upsala-Ekeby, Sweden, 1967-1968. Now discontinued and highly collectible, a full dinnerware set.

Romantic Flow Blue: Blakeney Pottery, 1970s. Resembles Watteau, but not exact. The old patterns never had the words "flow blue" written on them.

Victoria Ware: mark is of lion and uniform, but has paper label "Made in China," 1990s. Made in various patterns and design, but the give-away is the roughness on the bottoms, and much of it has a pea green background. Some of this line is also being made in Mulberry.

Floral pitchers (jugs) and teapots bearing a copied "T. Rathbone England" swan mark.

Williams-Sonoma and Cracker Barrel are also each releasing a vivid blue and white line. Both are made in China. One line is a simplified dahlia flower on white; the other has summer bouquets. Both are well made and readily available, just not old.

The reproductions are more of a threat to collectors.

Waldorf by New Wharf cups and saucers are out, but missing "England" from their mark and are made in China.

Cracker Barrel, pitcher, made in Chiina.

Iris by Dunn, Bennett, Burslem, has been reproduced in a full chamber set.

Touraine, Stanley, teapot, made in China.

Touraine by Stanley, by far the most prolific reproduction made recently, in 2002. Again, the "England" is missing from the mark, and it is made in China. Nearly the entire dinnerware set has been made and is being sold on the market.

In all cases, regarding new pieces and reproductions, be aware of unglazed areas on the bottoms. The footpads are rough and just too white. The reproductions, particularly the Touraine, are heavier in weight, having a distinctive thick feel. The embossing isn't as crisp and the pieces are frequently slightly smaller in over-all size than the originals.

Check the Flow Blue International Collectors' Club Inc.

Web site at www.flowblue.org and www.flowblue.com and also this repro site: www.repronews.com. Join the Flow Blue International Collectors' Club, 9412 High Drive, Leawood, KS 66206, study the books available, and always, always, *know* your dealer! Good dealers guarantee their merchandise and protect their customers.

Abbey, Jones, relish dish, handled, three pcs.......... **165.00**

Amoy, Davenport

Cake plate, square, tab handle **450.00**

Child's creamer, restoration to rim **550.00**

Child's cup and saucer, cup restoration **500.00**

Child's teapot, restoration to rim **3,000.00**

Plate, 10-1/2" d **175.00**

Platter, 13" l, restoration.......... **225.00**

Albany, Grindley

Soap dish, lid, and drainer.... **220.00**

Soup, tureen, four pcs.......... **550.00**

Alton, Grindley, Sauce tureen, three pcs **250.00**

Arabesque, Mayer

Platter, 17-1/2", chip **350.00**

Teacup and saucer **195.00**

Teapot, restored spout **350.00**

Arcadia, Wilkenson, creamer and cov sugar **195.00**

Argyle, Grindley

Platter, 17" **385.00**

Teapot, cov, restoration to spout **500.00**

Asiatic Pheasant, Hughes, vegetable tureen, cov.......... **225.00**

Astor and Grapeshot, unknown maker, plate, 10" d **185.00**

Atlanta, Regout, Teacupand saucer **110.00**

Athens, Adams, punch cup.......... **200.00**

Azalia, Longton, syrup pitcher, small spider mark **300.00**

Beauties of China, Mellor & Venables, creamer **250.00**

Bluebell, unknown maker, hot water pitcher **350.00**

Atlanta, Regout, teacup and saucer, **$110.** Photos courtesy of adviser Ellen G. King.

Blue Danube, Johnson Bros., platter, 14" l.......... **295.00**

Boston, Possil Pottery, Scotland, bowl, 10" round, handled 275.00
Brushstroke, unknown maker, Platter, 16" l 375.00
Buccleuch, Ridgway, fruit compote, reticulated 475.00
Byzanthium, BWM, child's cup & saucer 50.00
California, Wedgwood, butter dish base 100.00
Candia, Cauldon, syrup pitcher 275.00
Carlton, Alcock, plate, 9" d 65.00
Cashmere, Ridgway, Morley
- Bowl, oval, 8-1/2" 200.00
- Pitcher 700.00
- Plate, 6-1/4" d 100.00
- Plate, 10-1/2" d 250.00
- Sauce dish 100.00
- Soup bowl 145.00
- Teacup and saucer 200.00
- Vegetable tureen cov 975.00

Cavendish, Keeling, vase, 13" h... 150.00

Boston, Possil Pottery, bowl, 10" d, **$275.**

Chapoo, Wedgwood
- Pitcher, 6-1/2" h 300.00
- Plate, 9-1/2" d 150.00
- Platter, 12-1/2", under rim chip 250.00
- Soup bowl 125.00
- Tureen, vegetable, cov, hairline in base 350.00

Chen-Si, Maddock, sugar, cov 225.00
Chen-Si, Meir
- Cup and saucer, handle less 120.00
- Soup bowl, 10-1/2" d 110.00

Chinese, Dimmock, potpourri jar, cov, restoration 1,800.00
Chinese Bells, Meigh, toy undertray 250.00
Chusan, Clementson
- Platter, 13" l 325.00
- Sugar bowl, cov 250.00
- Vegetable tureen, cov, hexagonal, ftd 325.00

Clayton, Johnson Bros., platter, 16" l 350.00
Colburg, Edwards, oyster bowl 100.00
Colonial, Meakin, gravy boat, undertray 125.00
Copper Luster, unknown pattern and maker, pitcher, 6" h, hexagonal 100.00
Conway, New Wharf, platter, 14" x 10" 225.00
Cora, G & S, toothbrush holder..... 275.00
Countess, Grindley, teapot, cov... 350.00

Morrison, Doulton, pitcher, 7" h, **$275.**

Country Scenes, unknown maker
- Gravy, tray 125.00
- Plate, 9" d 60.00

Cracked Ice, Warwick, ferner, restoration 175.00
Dainty, Maddock
- Creamer 185.00
- Platter, 12-1/2" l 200.00

Delft, Minton, pitcher, 5-1/2" h....... 115.00
Delhi, Dimmock, child's wash basin and pitcher set 550.00
Dove, unknown maker, platter, 20" well and tree 450.00
Equestrian, Doulton, mug 195.00
Excelsior, Fell
- Soup tureen, cov 550.00
- Waste bowl 120.00

Fairy Villas, Adams, butter dish, cov, drainer 325.00
Figural, unknown pattern and maker, jug, large relief, w/figural handles 1,850.00
Florida, Ford
- Plate, 9-1/2" d 85.00
- Soup bowl 65.00

Formosa, Mayer
- Plate, 9-3/4" d 110.00
- Teapot, cov 575.00

Gaudy Strawberry, unknown maker, cup and saucer, handleless 175.00
Gironde, Grindley, platter, 21-3/4" l 495.00
Glorie De Duci, Doulton, biscuit jar, cov 325.00
Gothic, Furnival, plate, 10-1/2" d 85.00
Grace, Grindley
- Gravy boat, undertray 225.00
- Vegetable tureen, cov 350.00

Harley, Grindley
- Shaving mug 150.00
- Toothbrush holder 175.00

Harvest, Hancock, chamber pot .. 250.00
Hawthorne, Mercer, jardinière 355.00
Heaths Flower, Heath, teapot, cov 475.00
Hindustan, Maddock, butter dish, cov 275.00
Hindustan, Wood & Brownsfield
- Soup tureen, cov 500.00
- Soup tureen ladle 455.00

Hong Kong, Edge, Malkin, loving cup 155.00
Hong Kong, Meigh
- Child's creamer 300.00
- Platter, 16" l 450.00
- Potato bowl, 10" d 450.00
- Sugar bowl, cov 300.00
- Teapot, cov, restoration to pot edge 475.00

India, Villeroy and Boch, plate, pierced 100.00
Indian, Pratt
- Creamer, large...................... 350.00
- Soup bowl, 10-1/2" d 100.00

Indian Jar, Furnival
- Plate, 9-1/2" d 80.00
- Soap dish, cov, drainer 275.00

Iris, Royal, soup tureen, cov 300.00

Poppy, unknown maker, teapot, covered, removable strainer, **$365.**

Ivanhoe, Wedgwood, platter, 10" l 125.00
Kezle, Grindley, gravy boat, undertray 200.00
Knox, New Wharf
- Butter pat............................... 45.00
- Platter, 11-1/2" l 150.00

La Belle, Wheeling
- Bread tray............................. 150.00
- Cake plate 175.00
- Celery dish 280.00
- Charger, 11" 275.00
- Punch cup 365.00
- Slaw dish 225.00
- Sugar bowl, cov 250.00
- Teacup and saucer 175.00

Ladas, Ridgways, gravy boat 160.00
Lahore, Phillips, teapot, cov, inverted heart 375.00
Lakewood, Wood & Son, vegetable tureen, cov 350.00
Leaf and Swag, unknown maker
- Relish, 10" l 100.00
- Wash basin 475.00

Lonsdale, Ford, vegetable tureen, cov 225.00
Lorne, Grindley
Creamer, small 135.00
Platter, 16" l 275.00
Lugano, Ridgway
Bowl, 9-1/2" d, round, open ... 150.00
Platter, 11-1/2" l 250.00
Luzerne, Mercer
Platter, 13-1/4" l 395.00
Relish dish, 12" l 175.00
Madras, Upper Hanley
Child's teapot, cov 225.00
Vegetable tureen, cov, oval ... 275.00
Mandarin, Maddock
Creamer 150.00
Soup tureen, cov, ladle, undertray, large 1,400.00
Manilla, Podmore Walker
Syllabub cup 150.00
Teacup and saucer 110.00
Teapot, cov 575.00
Margot, Grindley, mug 200.00
Marble, Copeland, razor/toothbrush box, cov 275.00
Meissen, unknown maker, demitasse cup and saucer 65.00
Melrose, Gibson, teapot, cov 225.00
Messina, Cauldon, demitasse cup and saucer 75.00
Mongolia, Johnson Bros., platter, 16-1/2" l 450.00
Morning Glory, Ridgway
Platter, 12" l 275.00
Teacup and saucer 135.00
Morrison, Doulton, pitcher, 7" h 275.00
Nankin, Fell, platter, 11" 100.00
Neopolitan, Johnson Bros., vegetable tureen, cov 245.00

Unknown pattern and maker, jug, figural, **$1,850.**

Ning Po, Hall
Plate, 10-1/2" d 125.00
Teapot, cov 450.00
Non Pariel, Burgess & Leigh
Cake plate, tab handles 265.00
Demitasse cup and saucer ... 150.00
Pitcher, 8" h 220.00

Normandy, Johnson Bros.
Bacon platter, 10", oval 225.00
Punch cup and saucer, ftd 275.00
Vegetable bowl, 10", oval 150.00
Oregan, Mayer
Creamer 250.00
Plate, 8" d 100.00
Wash basin and pitcher 950.00
Oregon, Johnson Bros., platter, 12-1/4" l 250.00
Oriential, Alcock
Teacup and saucer 125.00
Wash basin and pitcher 1,100.00
Osaka, Kent, biscuit jar, cov 250.00
Pansy, Warwick
Bean pot, cov 550.00
Cake plate, 11" d 150.00
Chocolate pot, cov 550.00
Plate, 9" d 100.00
Pears, unknown maker, creamer 200.00
Pekin, Wood & Son, milk jug, large 180.00
Pelew, Challinor, cup and saucer, handle less 175.00
Persia, Allertons, child's tea set, 16 pcs 300.00
Polychrome patterns, unknown maker
Barber bottle, oranges, reds 325.00
Biscuit jar, cov, turquoise 450.00
Milk pitcher, 7-1/2" h, florals, pinks 175.00
Tazza, ftd, handled, greens, pinks 375.00
Urn, cov, ashes, vivid reds 325.00
Poppy, unknown maker, teapot, cov, removable strainer 365.00
Princess, Wood & Son, soap dish, cov 200.00
Regalia, Hughes, vegetable tureen, cov 175.00
Romance, Meigh
Child's cup and saucer 100.00
Toy undertray 100.00
Rosebud, unknown maker, razor/ toothbrush box, cov 225.00
Roseville, Maddock
Gravy boat, w/undertray 165.00
Vegetable tureen, cov 250.00
Ross, Meadin, chamber pot, cov and mug 450.00
Rhoda Gardens, Hackwood, teapot, cov 400.00
Scinde, Alcock
Child's tea bowl 800.00
Creamer, gothic shape 450.00
Plate, 9-1/2" d 125.00
Platter, 20" l 850.00
Soup bowl, 9-1/2" d, flanged 150.00
Sugar bowl, cov 350.00
Teacup and saucer, pumpkin shape 225.00
Teapot, cov 650.00

Unknown pattern and maker, tea caddy, polychrome, **$450.**

Undertray for rosebud finial sauce tureen 600.00
Vegetable tureen, cov, ftd 550.00
Wash pitcher 500.00
Waste bowl 250.00
Shanghai, Grindley
Creamer 195.00
Gravy boat, attached tray 200.00
Plate, 10" d 100.00
Platter, 14" l 325.00
Soup bowl, 9" d 55.00
Sugar bowl, cov 225.00
Vegetable tureen, cov 350.00
Shanghai, Kensington & Co., pitcher, 7" h, floral, polychrome 255.00
Shapoo, Hughes, plate, 9-1/4" d .. 100.00
Shell, Challinor, relish dish, shell shape 275.00
Shusan, Pratt, teapot, cov 250.00
Simla, Elsmore, Forester, platter, 13-3/4" l 225.00
Sloe Blossom, unknown maker, child's cup and saucer 250.00
Sobraon, Alcock
Chamber pot 250.00
Punch cup 150.00
Shaving mug 225.00
Sugar, cov, pumpkin shape... 350.00
Temple, Podmore Walker
Plate, 9-3/4" d 120.00
Platter, 20" l 395.00
Teacup and saucer, handle less 125.00
The Holland, Meakin, vegetable tureen, cov 250.00
The Trieste, Johnson Bros., cake stand, stemmed 350.00
Touraine, Alcock
Butter pat 125.00
Plate, 10" d 125.00
Teacup and saucer 95.00

Teapot, cov **675.00**
Vegetable tureen, cov **350.00**

Touraine, Stanley, soup tureen, cov **1,850.00**

Tonquin, Adams
Gravy boat **150.00**
Plate, 10-1/4" d, paneled **145.00**

Tonquin, Heath
Creamer **375.00**
Plate, 10-3/4" d **150.00**

Trilby, Wood & Son, cake plate, advertising **225.00**

Troy, Meigh, teapot, cov **550.00**

Unknown pattern, unknown maker, vase, 10-1/2" h, serpent handles **245.00**

Virginia, Maddock, butter dish, cov **225.00**

Waldorf, New Wharf
Creamer **220.00**
Plate, 9" d **80.00**
Platter, 11" x 9" **150.00**
Teacup and saucer **110.00**
Vegetable tureen, cov **350.00**
Waste bowl, 5-1/2" d **100.00**

Water Lily, A.N., pitcher, 10" h, hot water or milk **465.00**

Waverly, Maddock
Butter dish, cov **275.00**
Teacup and saucer **115.00**

Whampoa, Mellor & Venables
Butter tub, cov and drainer **315.00**
Teapot, cov **425.00**

Wild Rose, Warwick
Cake plate, 12" d, handled **195.00**
Pitcher, 7" h **250.00**

Willow, Doulton
Cheese dish, cov, slant top **375.00**
Pitcher, 5-1/2" h **200.00**
Vegetable bowl, 8" d, round, open **130.00**

York, unknown maker, dresser jar, cov **175.00**

FOLK ART

History: Exactly what constitutes folk art is a question still being vigorously debated among collectors, dealers, museum curators, and scholars. Some want to confine folk art to non-academic, handmade objects. Others are willing to include manufactured material. In truth, the term is used to cover vintage items ranging from simple objects, drawings, handmade sculpture, etc., to academically trained artists' paintings of "common" people or scenery, as well as quality handmade crafts.

Bank, 3-1/4" h, gourd form, paint decorated with face **115.00**

Biplane, orig dark mustard paint, red propeller, blue, red, and white stripes on tail, wood, tin wings, contemporary steel stand, 15-1/2" l, 10-3/4" h **470.00**

Blanket chest, painted pine, attributed to David Ellinger (American, 1913-2003), lid with two central stylized hearts over case with two arched panels with potted tulips and birds, flanked by sides with similar hearts and tulips, straight bracket feet, 41-1/2" w, 28-1/2" h, **$14,950**. Photo courtesy of Pook & Pook.

Bird tree, carved and painted wood, 9" h, America, c1900, mother robin with nest, two chicks perched on tree branch, imperfections **1,380.00**

Box, cov, 6" w, 3-1/2" d, 4-1/2" h, carved oak, America, late 19th/early 20th C, figure of man wearing cap with visor, sitting cross-legged on large dog, both have tails, border of turned finials joined by spiral rails, dovetailed box, leaf-carved drawer, paneled sides, old variegated varnish finish **1,265.00**

Candle stand, make-do, 18-3/4" w, 18" d, 26" h, New England, early 19th C, sq top, pedestal fashioned from parts of a yarn winder, tripod cabriole leg base on pads, old cream-colored paint, minor surface imperfections **1,150.00**

Figure, man, carved and painted, wearing top hat and tails, jointed arms, underside base signed "W.H. Stephens Uniondale PA 1938," 15" h, **$1,265**. Photo courtesy of Pook & Pook.

Cane
6" l, carved snake swallowing person, alligatored black paint with black stripes on snake body, minor wear **475.00**
36" l, carved Indian head handle, metal ferule and cap, "Darmouth, FX Heep, Tommy Rae" carved, as well as armorial shield with "Delta Delta, 1928," minor edge wear **385.00**

Carving
Angel, 41" l, 9" h, pine plank naively carved with face of angel, outstretched wings, radiating layered feathers, remnants of orig polychrome dec, light weathering to gray patina, possibly PA, 19th C **900.00**
Bulls heads, life-size, real horns, glass eyes, old weathered paint, carved by Noah Weiss (1842-1907, Northampton County, PA), dated 1870, price for pr **38,500.00**

Family record, watercolor
17" x 22", for family of Abraham Brunson and Laura Aries, c1840, dec with watercolor floral and column design, tears, staining **335.00**
20" x 15", for family of Joshua Washburn and Sylvia Mosman, written and drawn by Martha Ann Washburn, March 1841, marriage date and names of their children, birth and death dates, dec with floral and foliage designs in green, blue, and white, some stains **295.00**

Figure
4-3/4" h, carved burlwood, lady, carved facial features, hair styled in bun, ruffled collar, old dark stained surface, America, late 19th/early 20th C **425.00**
13" l, 2-1/4" w, 10-1/4" h, carved and polychrome, horse and groom, leather Western saddle, America, early 20th C **5,175.00**
19-3/4" l, 3-1/2" w, 14" h, trotting horse, polychrome-molded copper over wood, attributed to Louis Jobin (1870-90, Quebec City,) twilled mane and tail, worn red paint, black hooves, stand, losses **11,500.00**
26" h, root, glass eyes, applied shell and minerals dec, attributed to Moses Ogden (1844-1919, Angelica, NY,) stand **1,495.00**
36-1/2" h, carved and painted wood, figural waiter, standing black man in white coat, green jacket and hat, bearing salver, turned wood base, 20th C **765.00**

Frame, 19-1/4" x 23-1/4", cross corner, applied leaves, rosettes, and fish, chip carved edges, alligatored black paint **200.00**

Garniture, 8" x 13-1/2" x 4-1/2" h, carved wooden tray of fruit with banana, grapes, pears, and apples, two metal and wood handles, orig polychrome paint, age crack **550.00**

Scherenschnitte, valentine for Amy DuBois, circular form originally folded into eight sections, each with different handwritten verse, cutwork design accented with watercolor, 19th C, 13" d, foxing, loss to edges, **$550**. Photo courtesy of Alderfer Auction Co.

Grotesque face jug, stoneware, 5-1/2" h, brown-speckled glaze, found in Ohio, 19th C, imperfections **14,950.00**

Hammer, 13" l, oak and iron, figural, handle surmounted by carved man's head and upper torso, found in PA, 19th C **1,955.00**

Theorem, basket of fruit, blue grapes, green leaves, wheat, red cherries, 20th century example, 16" x 20", **$150**. Photo courtesy of Wiederseim Associates, Inc.

Memorial, 31" x 23" x 6-1/2", incised gilt and ebonized deep recessed shadow box frame, white painted cast iron profile of Lincoln surrounded by wreath of wire stemmed wax silk flowers, grouped with ribbon tied and waxed silk roses and calla lilies, surmounted by white dove with wings spread in flight, c1875 .... **700.00**

Plaque, 14" d, sun face, carved polychrome, molded edge, America, early 19th C, minor imperfections, stand **16,100.00**

Scherenschnitte, 11-1/2" x 14-1/2", birth certificate, dated Sept. 5, 1780, for Anna Elizabeth Lauerin, Berks County, PA, Tolpehaden Tow ship, cut-work and painted dec border of flowers, tulips, and hearts attached with vine-work, black ink text, glued down, staining, loss..... **925.00**

Sandstone carving, 58" h, Native American woman with baby in cradle board, two other children, carrying jar in front of her, partial signature "carved by E. Reed, O.B...," head needs to be reattached **16,500.00**

Still life, watercolor on paper, American School, 19th C, framed

- 10-3/4" x 9-1/2", fruit and foliage in gray bowl, shades of red, green, and blue, pinprick dec, general toning, tiny scattered stains **1,150.00**
- 15" x 13", *Bouquet of Spring Flowers in a Vase,* sgd "Frances Thompson, 1841," tulips, narcissus, and other spring flowers, white handled urn-form vase dec with sea shells, very minor toning **2,715.00**

Theorem

- 6" x 6-1/2", watercolor on velvet, American School, early 19th C, unsigned, flowers, shades of blue, gold, green, and brown, ivory ground, period gilt frame, toning, losses to frame **440.00**
- 13-1/2" x 11", on ivory velvet, freehand peaches, grapes, and cherries, gilt frame, minor surface wear and stains **450.00**
- 16" x 20", on paper, colorful basket of fruit, blue and green grapes, red cherries, green and brown pears, green grape leaves, small blue and burgundy flowers, minor light staining from separations in orig backboards, 19th C molded 19-1/2" x 23-1/4" molded frame with old gold paint **1,450.00**
- 21-1/8" x 20", on velvet, basket of strawberries, yellow and black bird perched on top, small vine border with strawberries, dec frame with red over brown sponging, raised corner blocks, by W. Rank, David Ellinger pupil **825.00**

Theorem, rooster, David Y. Ellinger, (American, 1913-2003), oil on velvet, signed lower left "D. Ellinger," 13" x 12-3/4", **$2,875**. Photo courtesy of Pook & Pook.

Tinsel picture, 22" x 17", flower arrangement, reverse-painted glass backed with foil and paper, American School, late 19th C, Victorian frame, repaired **180.00**

Watercolor drawing on paper

- 6-1/4" w, 7" h, yellow, red, blue, and green birds on branches, sgd in blue ink "Catharine E. Habecker 1844," molded frames with minor wear, price for pr............................ **990.00**
- 6-1/4" w, 7-3/4" h, orange and blue naïve painting of a woman, long striped dress, blue gloves, holding tulip and flower, bird above her head, wood frame **470.00**
- 7-1/2" w, 7-1/2" h, green, red, and yellow bird, flower and star, painted on lined paper, beveled frame **550.00**
- 12" w, 10" h, Jemima Harlin was born April 27th, 1901, crescent border, geometric corners with poppies, house, and fence in middle, reds and blues, stains and edge damage, mortise and peg walnut frame **2,420.00**

Food Molds

History: Food molds were used both commercially and in the home. Generally, pewter ice-cream molds and candy molds were used commercially; pottery and copper molds were used in homes. Today, both types are collected largely for decorative purposes.

The majority of pewter ice-cream molds are individual-serving molds. One quart of ice cream would make eight to 10 pieces. Scarcer, but still available, are banquet molds which used two to four pints of ice cream. European-made pewter molds are available.

Marks: Pewter ice-cream molds were made primarily by two American companies: Eppelsheimer & Co. (molds marked "E & Co., N.Y.") and Schall & Co. (marked "S & Co."). Both companies used a numbering system for their molds. The Krauss Co. bought out Schall & Co., removed the "S & Co." from some, but not all, of the molds, and added more designs (pieces marked "K" or "Krauss"). "CC" is a French mold mark.

Manufacturers of chocolate molds are more difficult to determine. Unlike the pewter ice-cream molds, makers' marks were not always used or were covered by frames. Eppelsheimer & Co. of New York marked many of their molds, either with their name or with a design resembling a child's toy top and the words "Trade Mark" and "NY." Many chocolate molds were imported from Germany and Holland and

were marked with the country of origin and, in some cases, the mold-maker's name.

Additional Listing: Butter Prints.

Tin, fish mold, **$45**. Photo courtesy of Dotta Auction Co., Inc.

Chocolate mold

Basket, 3-1/2" x 6", one cavity **50.00**
Chick and egg, 3-1/2" h, two parts, folding, marked "Allemagne," Germany **65.00**
Easter Rabbit, 18-1/2" h, standing, two-part mold, separate two-part molds for ears and front legs, "Anton Reiche, Dresden, Germany" **220.00**
Elephant, tin, three cavities **95.00**
Heart, 6-1/2" x 6", two cavities..........**70.00**
Hen on basket, two pcs, clamp type, marked "E. & Co./Toy" **60.00**
Pig **95.00**
Skeleton, 5-1/2" h, pressed tin **60.00**
Witch, 4-1/2" x 2", four cavities **75.00**

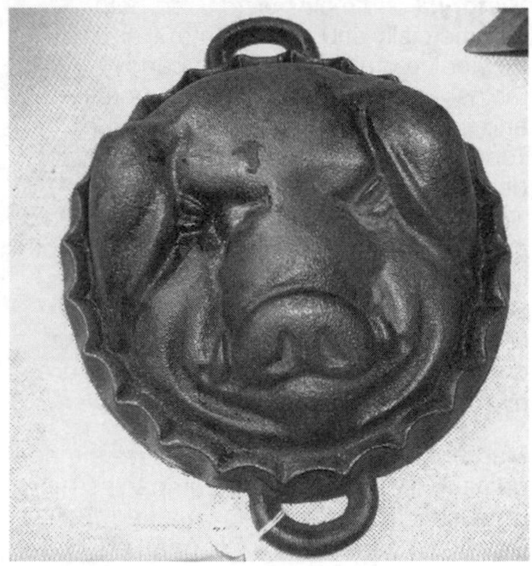

Cast metal, figural pig's face with snout, two handles, **$55**.

Food mold

Cake mold, 9-3/4" l, 11-1/2" h, cast iron, two-part full-figure seated rabbit, Griswold, Erie, PA, late 19th C **260.00**
Cheese, 5" x 13", wood, relief-carved design and "Bid," pinned, branded "Los," carved scratch date 1893 ....**60.00**
Cookie, 6-5/8" x 7", carved fruitwood, floral and foliate carved design in heart shape, 19th C, minor wear **355.00**
Pudding, tin and copper
- 4-1/2" d, round, star, ribbed sides **175.00**

Candy molds, six-rabbit mold, lamb-shaped mold, **$150**. Photo courtesy of David Rago Auctions, Inc.

- 6-1/2" d, round, fruit design... **125.00**
- 8" l, oval, lion **220.00**
- 9" l, rect, oval sheaf **175.00**

Pudding, white ironstone, corn, marked "Made in USA," chips, hairline **35.00**

Yellow ware pudding mold, embossed ear of corn, **$115**. Photo courtesy of Wiederseim Associates, Inc.

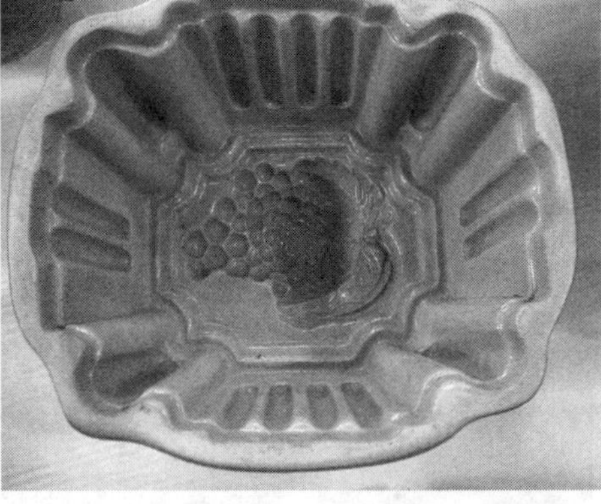

Yellow ware pudding mold, embossed bunch of grapes, **$125**. Photo courtesy of Wiederseim Associates, Inc.

Ice cream mold, pewter

Camel, pewter, marked "E & Co. NY, #681" **75.00**
Cherub riding Easter Bunny, 4" h....**45.00**
Easter Lily, three parts **75.00**
Egg, 2-3/4" d, marked "E & Co. NY" **35.00**
Flag, 13 stars **125.00**
Man in the Moon, 5-1/2" h, marked "E & Co. copyright 1888" **95.00**
Pear, banquet size, marked "S & Co. 17" **325.00**
Rose, two parts, 3-1/2" d **125.00**
Ship, banquet size, two quarts **265.00**
Steamboat **115.00**
Tulip, 4-1/8" h, marked "E. & Co. NY" **45.00**

Fostoria Glass

History: Fostoria Glass Co. began operations at Fostoria, Ohio, in 1887, and moved to Moundsville, West Virginia, its present location, in 1891. By 1925, Fostoria had five furnaces and a variety of special shops. In 1924, a line of colored tableware was introduced. Lancaster Colony purchased Fostoria in 1983.

For more information, see *Warman's Glass*, 4th edition.

Note: Prices are for crystal (clear) pieces except as noted.

Ashtray
- American, 2-7/8" sq **7.50**
- Fairfax, blue, small **15.00**

Bell, Chintz, orig label..........**130.00**
Berry bowl, June, blue, 5" d..........**50.00**
Bouillon, Versailles, topaz..........**30.00**
Bowl
- Corsage etch, Baroque, 12" d flared **110.00**
- Grape Leaf etch, green, 12" d **175.00**
- Trojan etch, topaz, 12" d.......... **125.00**

Bud vase, American, 6" **30.00**
Cake salver
- Century.......... **60.00**
- Corsage, 10-1/2" d **32.00**
- Navarre, handles, 10" d.......... **60.00**

Candleholders, pr
- Baroque, 4" h, one-lite, silver deposit Vintage dec on base, #2496... **75.00**
- Buttercup, 8" h, 8" w **150.00**
- Meadow Rose **185.00**

Candy dish, cov
- Coin, amber.......... **30.00**
- Navarre, three parts **175.00**
- Versailles, blue, three parts... **345.00**

Card tray, Brocaded Daffodil, two handles, pink, gold trim..........**40.00**
Celery tray
- Raleigh **18.00**
- Trojan etch, topaz.......... **95.00**

Champagne
- Buttercup etch.......... **40.00**
- Camelia **24.00**
- Georgian **18.00**
- June, saucer, petal stem **27.00**
- Versailles, pink **40.00**

Nappy, Coin pattern, orange, frosted coins, ring handle, large, $15.

Cheese and cracker
- Chintz **70.00**
- Colony **55.00**

Cigarette box, cov
- Morning Glory etching **65.00**
- Oriental **170.00**

Claret
- Heather **40.00**
- Navarre **80.00**
- Wilma, pink bowl, crystal stem and foot **42.00**

Cocktail
- Buttercup **22.50**
- Christina **20.00**
- Trojan etch, topaz **48.00**

Pickle castor insert, clear, pattern stateside copy of Baccarat's famous Bambou Torque pattern, 2-5/8" d at top, 3-1/8" d at ground base, 4-1/4" h, $90.

Compote, Century, 4-1/2" **20.00**

Condiment set, Baroque, azure, shakers, cov mustard, spoon, tray **450.00**

Console set, Lido, 10-1/2" d #2545 bowl, pr 4" #2496 candlesticks **200.00**

Cosmetic box, cov, American, 2-1/2" d, flake on bottom **900.00**

Courting lamp, Coin, amber **150.00**

Creamer, individual size
- Century **9.00**
- Lido **18.00**
- Raleigh **8.00**

Creamer, table size
- Baroque, azure **95.00**
- Raleigh **10.00**
- Trojan, topaz **22.00**

Creamer, sugar, tray, individual size
- Camelia **45.00**
- Century **30.00**

Cream soup
- Versailles, pink **65.00**
- Vesper, amber **30.00**

Cruet, June, yellow **700.00**

Cup and saucer
- Buttercup **21.00**
- Camelia **20.00**
- Rose **25.00**
- Vesper, amber **28.00**

Demitasse cup and saucer, Mayfair, pink **35.00**

Dinner plate
- Versailles, pink, slight use **75.00**
- Vesper, amber **30.00**

Figure
- Lute and Lotus, ebony, gold highlights, 12-1/2" h, price for pr **975.00**
- Mermaid, 10-3/8" h **225.00**

Goblet, water
- Baroque, azure **45.00**
- Buttercup etch, low **40.00**
- Camelia **32.00**
- Chintz **40.00**
- Woodland **15.00**

Grapefruit, Coronet **9.00**

Gravy boat, liner, Fairfax, green **100.00**

Ice bucket, Versailles, pink **155.00**

Vase, yellow, Celestrial, marked, $75.

Iced-tea tumbler
- American, flared **30.00**
- Bouquet etch **35.00**
- Fostoria Wheat **28.00**
- Heraldry **26.00**
- Jamestown, pink **35.00**
- Rhapsody, turquoise **24.00**

Jelly, cov, Baroque, topaz **150.00**

Jug
- Manor 4020 etch, wisteria foot **1,500.00**
- Meadow Rose, #5000 .... **450.00**

Juice tumbler, June, topaz, ftd **30.00**

Lily pond, Buttercup, 12" d **55.00**

Marmalade, cov, American **125.00**

Mayonnaise, liner, Navarre **90.00**

Milk pitcher, Century **60.00**

Mint dish, Fairfax, blue, three ftd **30.00**

Nappy, handle, Century, 4-1/2" d **12.00**

Nut cup, Fairfax, amber **15.00**

Oil cruet, Versailles, yellow **550.00**

Old-fashioned tumbler
- Coin **30.00**
- Hermitage, topaz **24.00**

Oyster cocktail
- Hermitage, amber **18.00**
- Shirley **17.50**

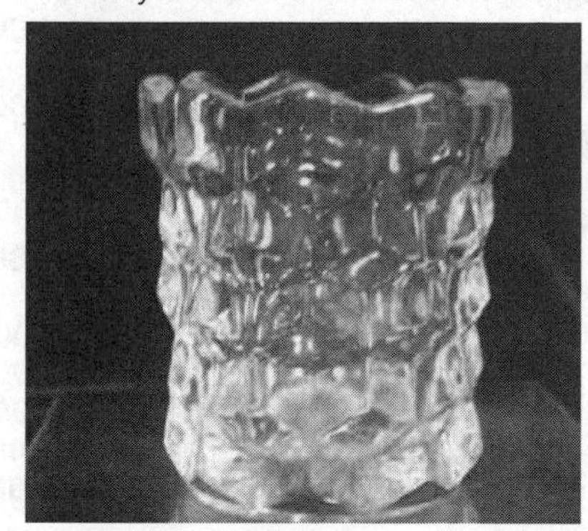

Toothpick holder, American pattern, $25.

Parfait, Woodland **15.00**

Pickle tray, Century, 8-3/4" **15.00**

Pitcher, Lido, ftd **225.00**

Plate
- Holly, 8-1/2" d **25.00**
- Midnight Rose, 7" d **9.50**

Platter
- Fairfax, green, 10-1/2" **75.00**
- June, topaz, 12" l, oval **145.00**
- Trojan, topaz, 12" l, oval **80.00**

Punch bowl, ftd, Baroque, orig label **425.00**

Relish
- Corsage etch, Baroque, three parts **75.00**
- June, topaz, two parts, 8-1/4" l **40.00**

Ring holder, American, 4-1/2" l, 3" h **800.00**

Rose bowl, American, small **18.00**

Salad plate, Buttercup **12.00**

Salt and pepper shakers, pr
- Coin, red **60.00**
- Coronet **15.00**
- Versailles, topaz, ftd **200.00**

Sauce boat, Versailles, pink, matching liner **300.00**

Sherbet
- Baroque, azure **45.00**
- Fern, etching #305 .... **25.00**
- Hermitage, low, green **22.00**

Snack plate, Century, 8" d **25.00**

Bud vase, **$45**; jug, **$65**; tall covered urn, **$65**; Coin pattern, olive green.

Sugar, individual size, Baroque, blue **4.00**
Sugar, cov, table size, Trojan, topaz **22.00**
Syrup, American, Bakelite handle **200.00**
Torte plate, Baroque, azure, 14" d **125.00**
Tray, center handle
- Fairfax, pink........ **55.00**
- Sonata, 11-1/4"........ **35.00**
- Trojan etch, topaz........ **135.00**

Tumbler, water, Woodland, ftd........ **15.00**
Urn, cov, Coin, amber, 12-3/4" h........ **68.00**
Vase
- American, pedestal foot, 10" h **100.00**
- Baroque, azure, 7"........ **195.00**

Wedding bowl, Coin, amber........ **70.00**
Whipped-cream bowl, June........ **50.00**
Whiskey, June, yellow........ **85.00**
Wine
- Hermitage, amber........ **20.00**
- Jamestown, amethyst........ **25.00**

FRAKTUR

History: Fraktur, the calligraphy associated with the Pennsylvania Germans, is named for the elaborate first letter found in many of the hand-drawn examples. Throughout its history, printed, partially printed/partially hand-drawn, and fully hand-drawn works existed side by side. Schoolteachers or ministers living in rural areas of Pennsylvania, Maryland, and Virginia often made frakturs. Many artists are unknown.

Fraktur exists in several forms—geburts and taufschein (birth and baptismal certificates), vorschrift (writing examples, often with alphabet), haus sagen (house blessings), bookplates and bookmarks, rewards of merit, illuminated religious texts, valentines, and drawings. Although collected for decoration, the key element in fraktur is the text.

Notes: Fraktur prices rise and fall along with the American folk-art market. The key marketplaces are Pennsylvania and the Middle Atlantic states.

Framed manuscript, musical score, tulips decoration, **$215**. Photo courtesy of Wiederseim Associates, Inc.

Birth certificate (Geburts and Taufschein)
- 11-3/4" w, 7-3/4" h, attributed to Fredrich Krebs, scalloped heart, flowers, and two long necked birds, shades of brown, red, yellow/tan, records birth of Anna Barbara Huinelsin, Bethlehem Tow ship, PA, 1805, fold lines, stains, damage **1,155.00**
- 12" h, 15" w, hand-colored printed form, Frederick Krebs, watercolor elements, red and green parrots, tulips, sun faces and crown, for Henrich Ott, Bucks County, Bedminster Township, PA, dated Oct. 29, 1800........ **990.00**
- 12-1/4" h, 15-1/2" w, watercolor, pen, and ink on paper, Berks County artist, winged angels, paired birds, and mermaids, for Frederick Heverling, dated 1784........ **2,100.00**
- 12-3/4" h, 15-1/2" w, watercolor, pen, and ink on paper, Flat Parrot artist, for Susana Gensemer, dated 1811 .... **1,265.00**
- 13" h, 15-7/8" w, hand-colored printed form, printed by Gottleib Jungmann, Reading, 1795, Friedrich Krebs imprint, paired parrots, blossoms, and sun faces, for Johannes Ries, Paxton Township, Dauphin County, PA, dated Aug. 28, 1799........ **2,185.00**
- 15" x 11-5/8", printed and hand colored, printed by D. P. Lange, Hanover, PA in 1822, records 1823 Adams County, PA, birth, eagle, angels cherub, and birds, margin damage and stains, 17-1/4" x 14" **450.00**
- 16" x 13", printed and hand colored, John Ritter, Reading, dated 1816, "Died Jan 9, 1884" added in pencil below, angels, birds, cherub colored blue, red, and yellow, tear at top and bottom, minor edge damage, 20" x 17-1/4" cherry frame........ **250.00**
- 16" x 13", printed, "Reading, By Gebbrudt und zu haben ben Ritter und Comp," angels with birds, cherub, and bible, bright blue, red, yellow, and green details, dated 1838, taped margin repairs, 20-1/4" x 17-1/4" cherry frame........ **200.00**
- 16-1/2" x 12-1/2", printed and hand colored, printed by Lutz & Scheffer, Harrisburg, PA, recording birth of Charles Henry, Oct. 9, 1844, in Warren Township, Trumbull County, Ohio, matted and framed........ **100.00**
- 19-3/8" w, 16-5/8" h, printed, some hand coloring, angels cherubs, and fruit in red and pale gold, dated 1814, Huntingdon, PA, glued down, foxing and tears, beveled curly maple frame with gunstock finish **660.00**

Bookplate
- 2-1/4" w, 4-1/2" h, red and green watercolor German verse, crown, heart, and red, green, and yellow bird with flower, German New Testament, published 1796, gold tooling on cover "J. G. St. 1807," loose from book, few stains **220.00**
- 3-7/8" w, 6-3/4" h, for Jacob Hekler, calligraphy, verse, and pot of flowers, red, yellow, blue, shades of green watercolor, brown ink, leather bound German New Testament book, published in Philadelphia, 1813, stains, some damage to both bookplate and book........ **110.00**
- 4-1/4" w, 3-3/4" h, pen and ink inscription, "Catharina Barbara Heinlenin," watercolor floral garland below in red and yellow, black ink, light foxing, 5-7/8" w x 5-1/2" h burl frame........ **360.00**
- 4-3/8" w, 5-7/8" h, watercolor red, yellow, and dark green flower, paid paper, date appears to be 1800, stains, light wear, taped split in middle, black painted frame with minor wear........ **615.00**

Child's Book of Moral Instruction (Metamorphis), watercolor, pen and ink on paper
- 6" x 7", printed form on paper, hand-colored elements, The Great American Metamorphosis, Philadelphia, printed by Benjamin Sands, 1805-06, printed on both sides of four leaves, each with upper

and lower flaps, engraved collar illus by Poupard **420.00**
6-1/4" x 7", dec on both sides of four leaves, when folded reveals different versus and full-page color illus, executed by Sarah Ann Siger, Nazareth, PA, orig string hinges **575.00**

Song book, watercolor and ink on paper, colorful fraktur of birds and floral vines flanking inscription "Jacob Gerberich...1806," Bucks County, PA, early 19th C, 3-5/8" x 6-1/4", losses, **$1,955**. Photo courtesy of Pook & Pook.

Confirmation certificate, 6" x 7-3/4", watercolor, pen and ink on paper, David Schumacher, paired tulips and hearts, for Maria Magdalena Spengler, dated 1780 .... **4,600.00**
Copybook, Vorschrift, 8" w, 5-5/8" h, pen and ink, red watercolor, laid paper, German text with ornate Gothic letters in heading, blocked cut area in lower left unfinished, minor edge damage, 11-3/8" w, 9-1/2" h yellow and red leather covered frame **250.00**
Drawing, watercolor, pen and ink
4" h, 2-3/4" w, red, yellow, and blue rooster with bushy tail, American School, 19th C **865.00**
15-3/8" w, 12-1/2" h, central heart bordered in blue, orange, and light brown, flowering tulip plant with four buds in blue, red, black, and light brown, compass star flowers, brown and white foliate at upper corners, six pointed starts in lower corners, colors similar to those found on Shenandoah Valley, VA, examples, foxing, stains, and tears, contemporary frame **495.00**
Family register, 19-3/4" w, 16" h, hand drawn, blue-green and red border with stars and flowers in corners, hearts, cherubs, and cross hatch work at center, German names, written in old brown ink, dates from 1814 to 1870, heart and hand medallion with inscription "Orphans Home and Ft. Wayne Hospital, Allen Co., Ind," sgd "John Cornelius Martin," old taped tear near top margin, small piece of corner missing **1,100.00**
House blessing (Haus Segen), 15-1/2" h, 11-3/4" w, printed by Johann Ritter, Reading, hand colored, orange, green, blue, yellow, brown, and black, professionally repaired and rebacked on cloth, 18-1/4" h, 14-3/8" w old stenciled dec frame **500.00**
Marriage certificate, 8" x 12-1/2", watercolor, pen and ink on paper, Daniel Schumacher, paired red, yellow and green birds flanking an arch with crown, for Johannes Haber and Elisabeth Stimmess, Windsor Township, Berks County, PA, dated 1777 .... **1,035.00**
Reward of merit, American School, early 19th C, watercolor, pen, and ink on paper
3-5/8" x 3-1/8", red, yellow, and blue-tailed bird perched on flowering branch **1,092.00**
4-1/8" x 3-1/4", red and yellow birds, green and yellow pinwheel flower **345.00**

Fraternal Organizations

History: Benevolent and secret societies played an important part in America from the late 18th to the mid-20th centuries. Initially, the societies were organized to aid members and their families in times of distress. They evolved from this purpose into important social clubs by the late 19th century.

In the 1950s, with the arrival of the civil rights movement, an attack occurred on the secretiveness and often-discriminatory practices of these societies. Membership in fraternal organizations, with the exception of the Masonic group, dropped significantly. Many local chapters closed and sold their lodge halls. This resulted in the appearance of many fraternal items in the antiques market.

Benevolent & Protective Order of the Elks, (BPOE)

Beaker, 5" h, cream, black elk head, marked "Mettlach, Villeroy & Boch" **110.00**
Book, *National Memorial*, 1931, color illus **35.00**
Bookends, pr, bronzed cast iron, elk in high relief **75.00**
Pinback button, 1-1/2" d, McKenny, "Welcomes The Elks," multicolored pair of elks, gold background, scene set within oyster shell design, including crab, turtle, and flying duck, early 1900s **18.00**
Shaving mug, pink and white, gold elk head, crossed American flags and floral dec, marked "Germany" on bottom **90.00**
Tip tray, Philadelphia, 21st Annual Reunion, July 1907, rect, 4-7/8" x 3-1/4" **135.00**

Eastern Star

Demitasse cup and saucer, porcelain **25.00**
Pendant, SP, rhinestones and rubies **45.00**
Ring, gold, Past Matron, star-shape stone with diamond in center **150.00**

Lions International, sign, round, metal and enamel, 30" d, **$50**. Photo courtesy of Joy Luke Auctions.

Independent Order of Odd Fellows (I.O.O.F)

Ceremonial staff, 3" w, 1-1/2" d, 64" h, polychrome carved wood, reverse tapering staff surmounted by carved open hand in cuffed sleeve holding heart in palm, old red, gold, and black painted surface, mounted on iron base, minor surface imperfections **2,300.00**
Gameboard, reverse painted black and gold metallic squares bordered by "I.O.O.F" chain links and other symbols, areas of flaking, 20-1/2" x 20-1/2" black oak frame **350.00**
Shaving mug, 3-3/4" h, B. F. Smith, insignia, gold trim, wear **165.00**
Vignette, 7-3/4" x 14-1/2", oil on board, hand beneath three links holding heart and card bearing archery scene, molded gilt gesso frame, flaking, subtle surface grime **920.00**
Watch fob, 94th Anniversary, April 12, 1913 .... **30.00**

Knights Templar

Business card, Reynolds, J. P., Columbia Commandery No. 18 (K of P) Sturgis, MI, color logo, c1890 .... **6.00**
Loving cup, china, three handles, green and white, gold tracery, Knights Templer insignia and Pittsburgh, 1907, marked "American China Co." **75.00**
Shot glass, bowl supported by three golden swords, dated 1903, Pittsburgh **25.00**
Tumbler, emb Indian head, dated 1903, Pittsburgh **45.00**

Masonic

Advertising button, Illinois Masonic Hospital, black and white litho, c1920 .... **10.00**

Apron, 14" x 12", leather, white, blue silk trim, white embroidery, silver fringe **35.00**

Book, *Morals & Dogma of the Ancient & Accepted Scottish Rite of Freemasonry*, Albert Pike, L. H. Jenkins, 1949, 861 pgs **20.00**

Bookends, pr, patinated metal, "appl'd for" on back **200.00**

Box, cov, 5" x 16-1/4" x 12-1/2", Chinese Export black lacquer, molded top with mother-of-pearl and lacquer Masonic devices, sides with floral dec, top loose, lock mechanism missing, minor lacquer loss **920.00**

Ceremonial cane, 33-1/2" l, carved lizards, rounded top knop with emblem and eagle, metal top, several age cracks **350.00**

Fob, silvered brass, June 14-15, 1927 event, inscription for "Grand Lodge, F & A.M. Wisconson," blank reverse **18.00**

Goblet, St. Paul, 1908 .... **70.00**

Jug, 5-5/8" h, lusterware, transfer printed and painted polychrome enamels, horseman, inscribed "James Hardman 1823," Masonic dec, royal coat of arms, minor wear **410.00**

Match holder, 11" h, wall type, walnut, pierce carved symbols **75.00**

Pendant, 1" l, 14k rose gold, enameled blue and white **110.00**

Ring, 14k rose gold, enameled cross on one side, enameled 32 degrees on other, double eagle head set with 10-point diamond, hand engraved 1900-20 .... **175.00**

Sign, 28-3/4" w, 34" h, shield shape, polychrome wood, several applied wood Masonic symbols, including All-Seeing Eye, sun, moon, stars, large central "G," pillars, etc., gilt highlights, blue field, red and white stripes below, molded gilt frame, wear and losses **3,055.00**

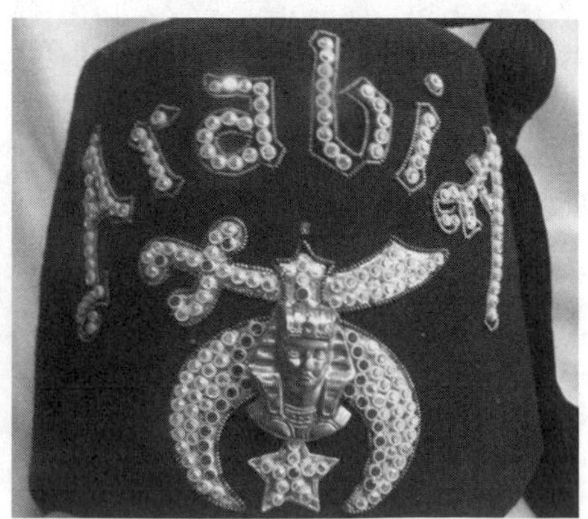

Shriners, fez, Arabia Shrine Temple, Houston, 7-1/8", **$35**.

Shriner

Cup and saucer, Los Angeles, 1906 .... **70.00**

Dinnerware, Rajah, partial set, various marks, 52 pcs **150.00**

Goblet, St. Paul, 1908, ruby stained, pedestal foot **70.00**

Mug, Syria Temple, Pittsburgh, 1895, Nantasket Beach, gold figures **125.00**

Shot glass, cranberry and clear, symbols and officers' names, St. Louis, 1909 .... **300.00**

Woodmen of the World

Spinner top, blue lettering on white celluloid, wooden red spinner dowel, Parisian Novelty Co., maker name on rim curl, 1930s **18.00**

Fruit Jars

History: Fruit jars are canning jars used to preserve food. Thomas W. Dyott, one of Philadelphia's earliest and most innovative glassmakers, was promoting his glass canning jars in 1829. John Landis Mason patented his screw-type canning jar on November 30, 1858. This date refers to the patent date, not the age of the jar. There are thousands of different jars and a variety of colors, types of closures, sizes, and embossings.

Additional Listings: See *Warman's Americana & Collectibles* for more examples.

Flaccus Bros., steer's head, amber, reproduction lid, **$220**. Photo courtesy of American Bottle Auctions.

Atlas Mason's Patent, medium yellow green, ABM lip, qt **50.00**

Ball, Ideal, colorless, bottom emb "Pat'd July 14, 1908," wire closure **7.50**

Ball, Mason, yellow green, amber striations, qt **75.00**

Canton Domestic, Patent 1889, clear **85.00**

Crystal Jar, Patd Dec. 17, 1878, clear, ground lip **70.00**

Dillion G. Co., Fairmont, IN, green, quart, wax seal, long crack **12.50**

Dodge Sweeney & Co.'s California, aqua, ground lip, glass insert, zinc band, 1-1/2 qt **425.00**

Excelsior, aqua, ground lip, insert, zinc band, qt **575.00**

Fahnestock Albree & Co., aqua, applied mouth, qt **35.00**

Flaccus Bros., steer's head, amber, reproduction lid **220.00**

Franklin Fruit Jar, aqua, ground lip, zinc lid, qt **225.00**

Good Luck, Hazel Atlas, four-leaf clover on front, glass lid, half gal **50.00**

Helmen's Railroad Mills, amber, ground lip, insert, zinc band, pt **70.00**

High Grade, aqua, ground lip, zinc lid, qt **150.00**

Johnson & Johnson, New York, cobalt blue, ground lip, orig insert, screw band, qt **325.00**

Star and crescent, self-sealing jar, embossed star and crescent moon, pint, ground lip, **$450**. Photo courtesy of American Bottle Auctions.

Keystone Mason, Patent Nov. 3, 1858, quart, aqua **50.00**

Lafayette, aqua, tooled lip, orig three-pc glass and metal stopper, qt **200.00**

Mason Crystal Jar, clear, ground lip, zinc lid **65.00**

Mason's Patent Nov. 30th, 1858, light green, profuse amber striations, machined mouth, zinc lid, smooth base, half gallon, some int. stain, L#1787 .... **325.00**

Peerless, aqua, applied mouth, iron yoke, half gallon **85.00**

Pet, aqua, applied mouth, qt **55.00**

Protector, aquamarine, ground mouth, unmarked tin lid, smooth base, qt, L #2420 .... **70.00**

Star, aqua, emb star, ground lip, zinc insert and screw band, qt **300.00**

Sun, aquamarine, ground mouth, glass lid, iron clamp, smooth base, qt **130.00**

The Pearl, aqua, ground lip, screw band, qt **40.00**

Union N1, Beaver Falls Glass Co., Beaver Falls, PA, aqua, applied wax seal ring, half gallon **45.00**

Woodbury Improved (monogram), aquamarine, ground mouth, quart, L #3029 .... **40.00**

FULPER POTTERY

History: The Fulper Pottery Company of Flemington, New Jersey, made stoneware pottery and utilitarian ware beginning in the early 1800s. It switched to the production of art pottery in 1909 and continued until about 1935.

The company's earliest artware was called the Vasekraft line (1910-1915), featuring intense glazine and rectilinear, Germanic forms. Its middle period (1915-1925) included some of the earlier shapes, but they also incorporated Oriental forms. Their glazing at this time was less consistent but more diverse. The last period (1925-1935) was characterized by water-down Art-Deco forms with relatively weak glazing.

Pieces were almost always molded, though careful hand glazing distinguished this pottery as one of the premier semi-commercial producers. Pieces from all periods are almost always marked.

Marks: A rectangular mark, FULPER, in a rectangle is known as the "ink mark" and dates from 1910-1915. The second mark, as shown, dates from 1915-1925; it was incised or in black ink. The final mark, FULPER, die-stamped, dates from about 1925 to 1935.

For more information, see *Warman's American Pottery & Porcelain*, 2nd edition.

Adviser: David Rago.

Low bowl, collar rim, covered in fine, frothy blue mirror glaze dripping over Famille Rose ground, vertical mark, 3-3/4" x 10", **$490**. Photo courtesy of David Rago Auctions, Inc.

Bowl

- 8" d, 3-1/2" h, floriform, sheer turquoise glaze, vertical stamp mark **85.00**
- 10" d, 4-1/2" h, ftd, flaring, frothy blue and white glaze dripping over Famille Rose ground, vertical stamp mark **150.00**

Bud vase

- 5-1/4" h, squat base, Flemington Green flambé glaze, vertical mark **365.00**
- 5-1/2" h, bullet shape, Flemington Green flambé glaze, illegible mark **380.00**
- 6-1/2" h, baluster, amber and celadon flambé glaze, vertical mark **200.00**
- 8-1/2" h, tall narrow neck, Chinese Blue flambé glaze dripping over speckled matte green ground, vertical mark **360.00**

Candlestick, 8" d, twisted, Chinese blue flambé glaze, vertical ink mark **95.00**

Chamber sconce, 7-1/2" h, dark brown matte crystalline glaze, vertical mark, 1" shallow chip on bottom ring **250.00**

Urn, embossed upright handles, covered in frothy blue-green mirrored glaze, vertical mark, 11-1/2" x 9", **$2,530**. Fulper photos courtesy of David Rago Auctions, Inc.

Cider set, 13" h tankard, five 4" h mugs, emb monogram "S," mottled Leopard Skin Crystalline glaze, vertical marks, chip on one mug **980.00**

Console set, 7-3/4" d floriform bowl, pr 4-1/4" h candlesticks, cov in turquoise and clear crystalline flambé glaze, ink racetrack mark, touch-up on one candlestick rim **100.00**

Effigy bowl, 10" d, 8" h, blue, ivory, and green flambé int., matte blue glaze base, rect ink mark **8,050.00**

Ibis bowl, 10-1/2" d, 5-1/2" h, green and blue flambé over Copperdust Crystalline, ink racetrack mark **815.00**

Lamp, table, 14-1/2" x 10", mushroom-shaped, helmet-shade inset with pieces of yellow, pink, and green slag glass, over trumpet base, covered in Leopard Skin Crystalline glaze, single socket, orig pull switch, vertical mark, restoration to several hairlines on shade, tiny base chip **18,400.00**

Low bowl

- 9-1/2" d, dripping mahogany over speckled mustard glaze, vertical ink stamp **115.00**
- 13" d, lobed, fine green and blue mottled glaze ext., caramel int., vertical ink stamp **290.00**

Vase, baluster, covered in glossy amber glaze dripping over rare Mirror Brown base, vertical mark, few scratches, 13" x 6-1/2", **$2,300**.

Mug, 4-3/4" h, mahogany and caramel mottled glaze, horizontal marks, pr **150.00**

Plate, 9" d, lotus blossoms, sheer turquoise glaze, vertical marks, pr **250.00**

Urn

- 7-1/2" h, squat, ridged, Leopard Skin Crystalline glaze, horizontal mark **290.00**
- 11-3/4" d, 11-3/4" h, hammered, frothy indigo and light blue glaze, incised racetrack mark, stilt-pull bruise **865.00**

Vase, flat shoulder, covered in fine Leopard Skin Crystalline glaze, vertical mark, 7-1/4" x 8", **$1,150**.

Vase

4-1/4" h, three handles, purple microcrystalline glaze, marked **250.00**

6-1/2" h, baluster, Chinese Blue flambé glaze, vertical mark **230.00**

6-1/2" h, bullet shape, three buttressed handles, Cat's Eye flambé glaze, vertical mark **435.00**

6-3/4" h, three handles, turquoise crackled glaze, horizontal mark **148.00**

7" h, flat shoulder, unusual green and blue crystalline flambé glaze, vertical mark **460.00**

7" h, two handles, bulbous, Moss-to-Wisteria flambé glaze, vertical mark **415.00**

8" h, three sides, corseted, Cat's Eye flambé glaze, vertical mark **360.00**

8" h, two handles, fan, purple and amber flambé glaze, vertical mark **435.00**

8" h, 6-1/4" d, corseted, buttressed handles, frothy matte amber glaze, horizontal mark **200.00**

8-1/2" h, tapered, four buttresses, glossy amber and turquoise glaze, vertical mark, short tight line to rim **175.00**

11-1/2" h, 6" d, bulbous, Famille Rose matte glaze, vertical stamp mark, deep rim crazing lines **360.00**

Vessel

5-1/2" h, spherical, closed-in rim, Leopard Skin Crystalline glaze, vertical mark **290.00**

7-1/2" x 9-1/2", two ring handles, ftd, rich matte green, cobalt blue, and turquoise glossy glaze dripping over matte ultramarine ground, vertical mark **920.00**

11-1/2" d, 13-1/4" h, bulbous, four short handles, covered in Leopard Skin Crystalline glaze, incised racetrack mark, restoration to drill hole in bottom **2,990.00**

FURNITURE

History: Two major currents dominate the American furniture marketplace—furniture made in Great Britain and furniture made in the United States. American buyers continue to show a strong prejudice for objects manufactured in the United States. They will pay a premium for such pieces and accept them above technically superior and more aesthetically appealing English examples.

For more information, see *Warman's American Furniture*.

Until the last half of the 19th century, English examples and design books dictated formal American styles. Regional furniture, such as the Hudson River Valley (Dutch) and the Pennsylvania German styles, did develop. Less-formal furniture, often designated as "country" or vernacular style, developed throughout the 19th and early 20th centuries. These country pieces deviated from the accepted formal styles and have a charm that many collectors find irresistible.

America did contribute a number of unique decorative elements to English styles. The American Federal period is a reaction to the English Hepplewhite period. American designers created furniture that influenced, rather than reacted to, world taste in the Gothic-Revival style and Arts and Crafts, Art Deco, and Modern International movements.

Furniture Styles

Furniture styles can be determined by careful study and remembering what design elements each one embraces. To help understand what defines each period, here are some of the major design elements for each period.

Chair, arm, William and Mary, well-carved shaped crest rail, three-slat banister back, turned legs. Bold stretcher to front legs, replaced rush seat, seat height 18" h seat, 47-1/2" h back, **$1,150**. Photo courtesy of James D. Julia, Inc.

William and Mary, 1690-1730. The style is named for the English King William of Orange and his consort, Mary. New colonists in America brought their English furniture traditions with them and tried to translate these styles using native woods. Their furniture was practical and sturdy. Lines of this furniture style tend to be crisp, while facades might be decorated with bold grains of walnut or maple veneers, framed by inlaid bands. Moldings and turnings are exaggerated in size. Turnings are baluster-shaped and the use of C-scrolls was quite common, giving some look of moment to a piece of furniture. Feet found in this period generally are round or oval. One exception to this is known as the Spanish foot, which flares to a scroll. Woods tend to be maple, walnut, white pine, or Southern yellow pine. One type of decoration that begins in the William and Mary period and extends through to Queen Anne and Chippendale styles is known as japanning, referring to an imitation lacquering process.

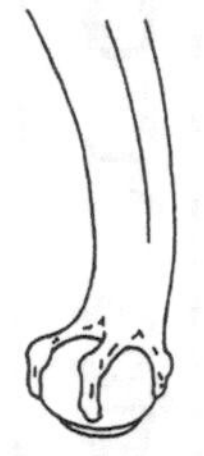

Claw and Ball

Triffid

Pad

Chair, side, Queen Anne, eastern MA, walnut, carved crest rail, curved vasiform back, replaced balloon seat, block and turned stretcher, good carved Queen Anne legs, some repairs, 40" h, seat height 17" h seat, 40" h back, price for pair, **$4,025**. Photo courtesy of James D. Julia, Inc.

Queen Anne, 1720-1760. Evolution of this design style is from Queen Anne's court, 1702 to 1714, and lasted until the Revolution. This style of furniture is much more delicate than its predecessor. It was one way for the young Colonists to show their own unique style, with each regional area initiating special design elements. Forms tend to be attenuated in New England. Chair rails were more often mortised through the back legs when made in Philadelphia. New England furniture makers preferred pad feet, while the makers in Philadelphia used triffid feet. Makers in Connecticut and New York often preferred slipper and claw and ball feet. The most popular woods were walnut, poplar, cherry, and maple. Japanned decoration tends to

be in red, green and gilt, often on a blue-green field. A new furniture form of this period was the tilting tea table.

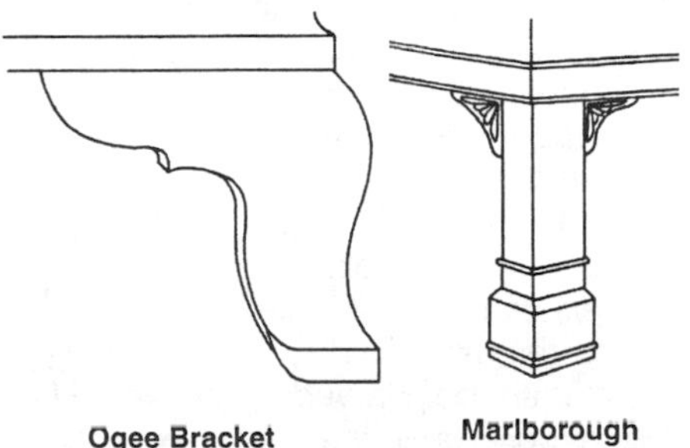

Candlestand, Chippendale, American, mahogany, serpent feet, 18" d, 27-1/2" h, **$1,850.**

Chippendale, 1755-1790. This period is named for the famous English cabinetmaker, Thomas Chippendale, who wrote a book of furniture designs, *Gentlemen and Cabinet-Makers Director*, published in 1754, 1755, and 1762. This book gave cabinetmakers real direction and they soon eagerly copied the styles presented. Chippendale was influenced by ancient cultures, such as the Romans, and Gothic influences. Look for Gothic arches, Chinese fretwork, columns, capitals, C-scrolls, S-scrolls, ribbons, flowers, leaves, scallop shells, gadrooning, and acanthus. The most popular wood used in this period was mahogany, with walnut, maple, and cherry also present. Legs become straight and regional differences still exist in design elements, such as feet. Claw and ball feet become even larger and more decorative. Pennsylvania cabinetmakers used Marlborough feet, while other regions favored ogee bracket feet. The center of furniture manufacturing gradually shifts from New England and Mid-Atlantic city centers to Charleston. One of the most popular forms of this period was a card table that sported five legs instead of the four of Queen Anne designs.

Sideboard, Hepplewhite, inlaid mahogany, bowfront center section with central door having inset panel and center inlay, flanked by two bottle drawers, top of center section has center drawer flanked by two smaller drawers, side sections have large door and drawer above, shaped backsplash, line inlay, tapered short square legs, L.N. Arnall Richmond, VA, label on reverse, refinished, some restoration, 71" l, 21-1/2" d. 53" h, **$2,550.**

Federal (Hepplewhite), 1790-1815. This period reflects the growing patriotism felt in the young American states. Their desire to develop their own distinctive furniture style was apparent. Stylistically it also reflects the architectural style known as Federal, where balance and symmetry were extremely important. Woods used during this period were first and foremost mahogany and mahogany veneer, but other native woods, such as maple, birch, or satinwood, were used. Reflecting the architectural ornamentation of the period, inlays were popular, as was carving, and even painted highlights. Some of the motifs used for inlay include bellflowers, urns, festoons, acanthus leaves, and pilasters. Inlaid bands and lines were also popular and often used in combination with other inlay. Legs of this period tend to be straight or tapered to the foot. The foot might be a simple extension of the leg or bulbous, or spade shaped. Two new furniture forms were created in this period. They are the sideboard and the worktable, reflecting forms that came into favor as they served a very functional use. Expect to find a little more comfort in chairs and sofas, but not very thick cushions or seats.

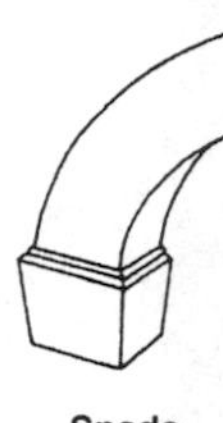

When a piece of furniture is made in England, or styled after an English example, it may be known as Hepplewhite. The time frame is the same. Robert Adam is credited with creating the style known as Hepplewhite during the 1760s and leading the form. Another English book heavily influenced the designers of the day. This one was by Alice Hepplewhite, and titled *The Cabinet Maker and Upholsterer's Guide,* with publisher dates of 1788, 1789, and 1794.

Chair, arm, Sheraton, lyre back, balloon seat, tiger maple arms and crest, 17-1/2" h seat, 34" h back, **$425.** Photo courtesy of James D. Julia, Inc.

Sheraton, 1790-1810. The style known as Sheraton closely resembles Federal. The lines are somewhat straighter and the designs plainer than Federal. Sheraton pieces are more closely associated with rural cabinetmakers. Woods would include mahogany, mahogany veneer, maple, and pine, as well as other native woods. This period was heavily influenced by the work of Thomas Sheraton and his series of books, *The Cabinet Maker and Upholster's Drawing Book*, from 1791-1794, and his *The Cabinet Directory*, 1803, and *The Cabinet-Maker, Upholsterer, and General Artist's Encyclopedia* of 1804.

Empire (Classical), 1805-1830. By the beginning of the 19th Century, a new design style was emerging. Known as Empire, it had an emphasis on the classical world of Greece, Egypt, and other ancient European influences. The American craftsmen began to incorporate more flowing patriotic motifs, such as eagles with spread wings. The basic wood used in the Empire period was mahogany. However, during this period, dark woods were so favored that often mahogany was painted black. Inlays were popular when made of ebony or maple veneer. The dark woods offset gilt highlights, as were the brass ormolu mountings often found in this period. The legs of this period are substantial and more flowing than those found in the Federal or Sheraton periods. Feet can be highly ornamental as when they are carved to look like lion feet, or plain when they extend to the floor with a swept leg. Regional differences in this style are very apparent, with New York City being the center of the design style as it was also the center of fashion at the time.

Desk, Empire, French, flame grain mahogany veneer, black marble top, thin long drawer, fall front, interior fitted with bird's eye maple veneer, leather writing surface, valanced shelf over eight drawers with line inlay, two-door base with three interior shelves, 32-1/2" w, 16" d, 57-1/2" h, **$1,800**. Photo courtesy of Sanford Alderfer Auction Co.

New furniture forms of this period include a bed known as a sleigh bed, with the headboard and footboard forming a graceful arch, similar to that found on a sleigh, hence the name. Several new forms of tables also came into being, especially the sofa table. Because the architectural style of the Empire period used big open rooms, the sofa was now allowed to be in the center of the room, with a table behind it. Former architectural periods found most furniture placed against the outside perimeter of the walls and brought forward to be used.

Victorian, 1830-1890. The Victorian period as it relates to furniture styles can be divided into several distinct styles. However, not every piece of furniture can be dated or definitely identified, so the generic term "Victorian" will apply to those pieces. Queen Victoria's reign affected the design styles of furniture, clothing, and all sorts of items used in daily living. Her love of ornate styles is well known. When thinking of the general term, Victorian, it is best to think of a cluttered environment, full of heavy furniture, and surrounded by plants, heavy fabrics, and lots of china and glassware.

Sub-categories of the Victorian era:

French Restauration, 1830-1850. This is the first sub-category of the Victoria era. This style is best simplified as the plainest of the Victorian styles. Lines tend to be sweeping, undulating curves. It is named for the style that was popular in France as the Bourbons tried to restore their claim to the French throne, from 1814 to 1848. The Empire (Classical) period influence is felt, but French Restauration lacks some of the ornamentation and fussiness of that period. Design motifs continue to reflect an interest in the classics of Greece and Egypt. Chair backs are styled with curved and concave crest rails, making them a little more comfortable than earlier straight back chairs. The use of bolster pillows and more upholstery is starting to emerge. The style was only popular in clusters, but did entice makers from larger metropolitan areas, such as Boston, and New Orleans, to embrace the style.

Stand, étagére, Victorian, walnut, beveled, arched top, central mirror, five shelves on each side, white marble top, cupboard in base, 43" w, 85" h, **$880**. Photo courtesy of Joy Luke Auctions.

The Gothic Revival period, 1840-1860. This is one relatively easy period to identify for collectors. It is one of the few styles that celebrates elements found in the corresponding architectural style: turrets, pointed arches, and quatrefoils—things found in 12th and 16th centuries that were adapted to this interesting mid-century furniture style. The furniture shelving form known as an étagère is born in this period, allowing Victorians to have more room to display their treasured collections. Furniture that had mechanical parts also was embraced by the Victorians of this era. The woods preferred by makers of this period were walnut and oak, with some use of mahogany and rosewood. The scale used ranged from large and grand to small and petite. Carved details gave dimension and interest.

Rococo Revival, 1845-1870. This design style features the use of scrolls, either in a "C" shape or the more fluid "S" shape. Carved decoration in the form of scallop shells, leaves, and flowers, particularly roses, and acanthus further add to the ornamentation of this style of furniture. Legs and feet of this form are cabriole or scrolling. Other than what might be needed structurally, it is often difficult to find a straight element in Rococo Revival furniture. The use of marble for tabletops was quite popular, but expect to find the corners shaped to conform to the overall scrolling form. To accomplish all this carving, walnut, rosewood, and mahogany were common choices. When lesser woods were used, they were often painted to reflect these more expensive woods. Some cast iron elements can be found on furniture from this period, especially if it was cast as scrolls. The style began in France and England, but eventually migrated to America where it evolved into two other furniture styles, Naturalistic and Renaissance Revival.

Cabriole

Elizabethan, 1850-1915. This sub-category of the Victorian era is probably the most feminine-influenced style. It also makes use of the new machine turned spools and spiral turnings that were fast becoming popular with furniture makers. New technology advancements allowed more machined parts to be generated. By adding flowers, either carved, or painted, the furniture pieces of this era had a softness to them that made them highly suitable. Chair backs tend to be high and narrow, having a slight back tilt. Legs vary from straight to baluster turned types to spindle turned. This period

of furniture design saw more usage of needlework upholstery and decoratively painted surfaces.

Sideboard, late Victorian, Elizabethan, c1910, mahogany, full-length beveled glass mirror, gallery supported by fluted columns, molded cornice, resting on four drawer cabinet base with two carved panel doors with stylized florals, original hammered bronze fittings, original finish, rich patina, 77" l, 24" w, 72" h, **$1,610**. Photo courtesy of Jackson's International Auctioneers & Appraisers.

Louis XVI, 1850-1914. One period of the Victorian era that flies away with straight lines is Louis XVI. However, this furniture style is not austere; it is adorned with ovals, arches, applied medallions, wreaths, garlands, urns, and other Victorian flourishes. As the period aged, more ornamentation became present on the finished furniture styles. Furniture of this time was made from more expensive woods, such as ebonized woods or rosewood. Walnut was popular around the 1890s. Other dark woods were featured, often to contrast the lighter ornaments. Expect to find straight legs or fluted and slightly tapered legs.

Chair, Fauteuils, Louis XV, satin-type rose upholstery, carved frame, cream and rust colored re-paint, 34" h. Photo courtesy of James D. Julia, Inc.

Naturalistic, 1850-1914. This furniture period takes the scrolling effects of the Rococo Revival designs and adds more flowers and fruits to the styles. More detail is spent on the leaves—so much that one can tell if they are to represent grape, rose, or oak leaves. Technology advances enhanced this design style as manufacturers developed a way of laminating woods together. This layered effect was achieved by gluing thin layers together, with the grains running at right angles on each new layer. The thick panels created were then steamed in molds to created the illusion of carving. The woods used as a basis for the heavy ornamentation were mahogany, walnut, and some rosewood. Upholstery of this period is often tufted, eliminating any large flat surface, as the tufting creates curved peaks and valleys. The name of John Henry Belter is often connected with this period, for it was when he did some of this best design work. John and Joseph W. Meeks also enjoyed success with laminated furniture. Original labels bearing these names are sometimes found on furniture pieces from this period, giving further provenance.

Hall bench, Naturalistic, Black Forest, c1880, two full standing glass eyed bears supporting detailed curved seat, 55" w, 18" d, 32" h, **$8,960**.

Renaissance Revival, 1850-1880. Furniture made in this style period reflects how cabinetmakers interpreted 16th and 17th century French designs. Their designs range from curvilinear and florid early in the period to angular and almost severe by the end of the period. Dark woods, such as mahogany and walnut, were primary with some use of rosewood and ebony. Walnut veneer panels were a real favorite in the 1870s designs. Upholstery, usually of a more generous nature, was also often incorporated into this design style. Ornamentation and high relief carving included flowers, fruits, game, classical busts, acanthus scrolls, strapwork, tassels, and masks. Architectural motifs, such as pilasters, columns, pediments, balusters, and brackets are another prominent design feature. Legs are usually cabriole or pretty substantial turned legs.

Renaissance Revival, c1875, walnut step-back, three doors, arched center door, buried trim, 79" w, 20" d, 85" h, **$6,720**. Photo courtesy of Fontaine's Auction Gallery

Néo-Greek, 1855-1885. This design style easily merges with both the Louis XVI and Renaissance Revival styles. It is characterized by elements reminiscent of Greek architecture, such as pilasters, flutes, column, acanthus, foliate scrolls, Greek key motifs, and anthemion high relief carving. This style originated with the French, but was embraced by American furniture manufacturers. Woods are dark and often ebonized. Ornamentation may be gilded or bronzed. Legs tend to be curved to scrolled or cloven hoof feet.

Side table, Eastlake, walnut, white marble top, ornate base, 29" l, 21" d, 31" h, **$350**. Photo courtesy of Joy Luke Auctions.

Eastlake, 1870-1890. This design style is named for Charles Locke Eastlake who wrote a very popular book in 1872 called, *Hints on Household Taste*. It was originally published in London. One of his principles was the relationship between function, form, and craftsmanship. Shapes of furniture from this style tend to be more rectangular. Ornamentation was created through the use of brackets, grooves, chamfers, and geometric designs. American furniture manufacturers were enthusiastic about this style since it was so easy to adapt for mass production. Woods used were again dark, but more native woods, such as maple and pine were incorporated. Legs and chair backs are straighter, often with incised decoration.

Art Furniture, 1880-1914. This design period represents furniture designs gone mad, almost an "anything goes" school of thought. The style embraces both straight and angular with some pieces that are much more fluid, reflecting several earlier design periods. This period sees the wide usage of turned moldings and dark woods, but this time stained to imitate ebony and lacquer. The growing Oriental influence is seen in furniture from this period, including the use of bamboo, which was imported and included in the designs. Legs tend to be straight; feet tend to be small.

Straight

Arts and Crafts, 1895-1915. The Arts and Crafts period furniture represents one of the strongest periods for current collectors. Quality period Arts and Crafts furniture is available through most of the major auction houses. And, for those desiring the look, good quality modern furniture is also made in this style. The Arts and Crafts period furniture is generally rectilinear and a definite correlation is seen between form and function. The primary designers of this period were George Stickley, Leopold Stickley, J. George Stickley, George Niedeken, Elbert Hubbard, Frank Lloyd Wright, and the Englishman William Morris. Their furniture designs often overlapped into architectural and interior design including rugs, textiles, and other accessories. Woods used for Arts and Crafts furniture is primarily oak. Finishes were natural, fumed, or painted. Upholstery is leather or of a fabric design also created by the same hand. Hardware was often made in copper. Legs are straight and feet are small, if present at all, as they were often a simple extension of the leg. Some inlay of natural materials was used, such as silver, copper, and abalone shells.

Cabinet, vice, Arts & Crafts, Limbert, pull-out bar shelf inset with hammered glass, single drawer, two cabinet doors, and square brass pulls, branded mark, leaned finish and hardware, 36" x 31" x 19", **$2,300**. Photo courtesy of David Rago Auctions.

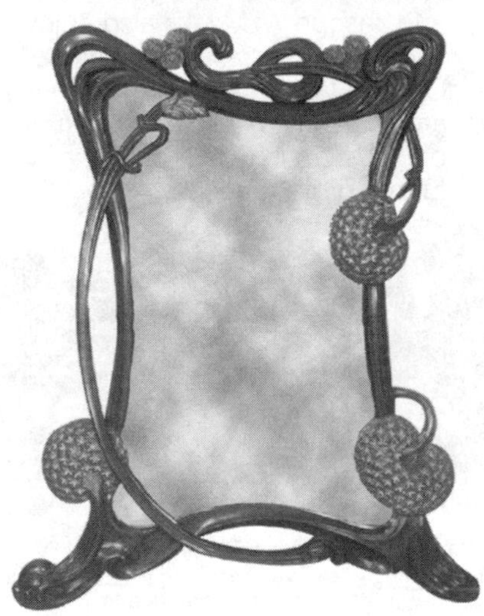

Art-Nouveau style mirror, mahogany, old finish and gilding, age cracks, 47-1/2" h, 38" w, **$175**. Photo courtesy of Garth's Auctions, Inc.

Art Nouveau, 1896-1914. Just as the Art Nouveau period is known for women with long hair, flowers, and curves, so is Art Nouveau furniture. The Paris Exposition of 1900 introduced furniture styles reflecting what was happening in the rest of the design world, such as jewelry and silver. This style of furniture was not warmly embraced, as the sweeping lines were not very conducive to mass production. The few manufacturers that did interpret it for their factories found interest to be slight in America. The French held it in higher esteem. Woods used were dark, stylized lilies, poppies, and other more fluid designs were included. Legs tend to be sweeping or cabriole. Upholstery becomes slimmer.

Art Deco, 1920-1945. Furniture of the Art Deco period reflects the general feel of the period. The Paris *"I Exposition International des Arts Décorative et Industriels Modernes"* became the mantra for designs of everything in this period. Lines are crisp, with some use of controlled curves. The Chrysler Building in New York City remains the finest example of Art Deco architecture and those same straight lines and gentle curves are found in furniture. Furniture makers used expensive materials, such as veneers, lacquered woods, glass, and steel. The cocktail table first enters the furniture scene during this period. Upholstery can be vinyl or smooth fabrics. Legs are straight or slightly tapered; chair backs tend to be either low or extremely high.

Straight

International Movement, Dux sofa, fully-upholstered in orange fabric, four loose seat and back cushions, bright chrome base, 88" l, 34" w, 29-1/2" h, **$865**. Photo courtesy of David Rago Auctions.

International Movement, 1940-present. Furniture designed and produced during this period is distinctive as it represents the usage of some new materials, like plastic, aluminum, and molded laminates. The Bauhaus and also the Museum of Modern Art heavily influenced some designers. In 1940, the museum organized competitions for domestic furnishings. Designers Eero Saarien and Charles Eames won first prize for their designs. A new chair design combined the back, seat, and arms together as one unit. Tables were designed that incorporated the top, pedestal, and base as one. Shelf units were also designed in this manner. These styles could easily be mass-produced in plastic, plywood, or metal.

Different types of feet found on furniture

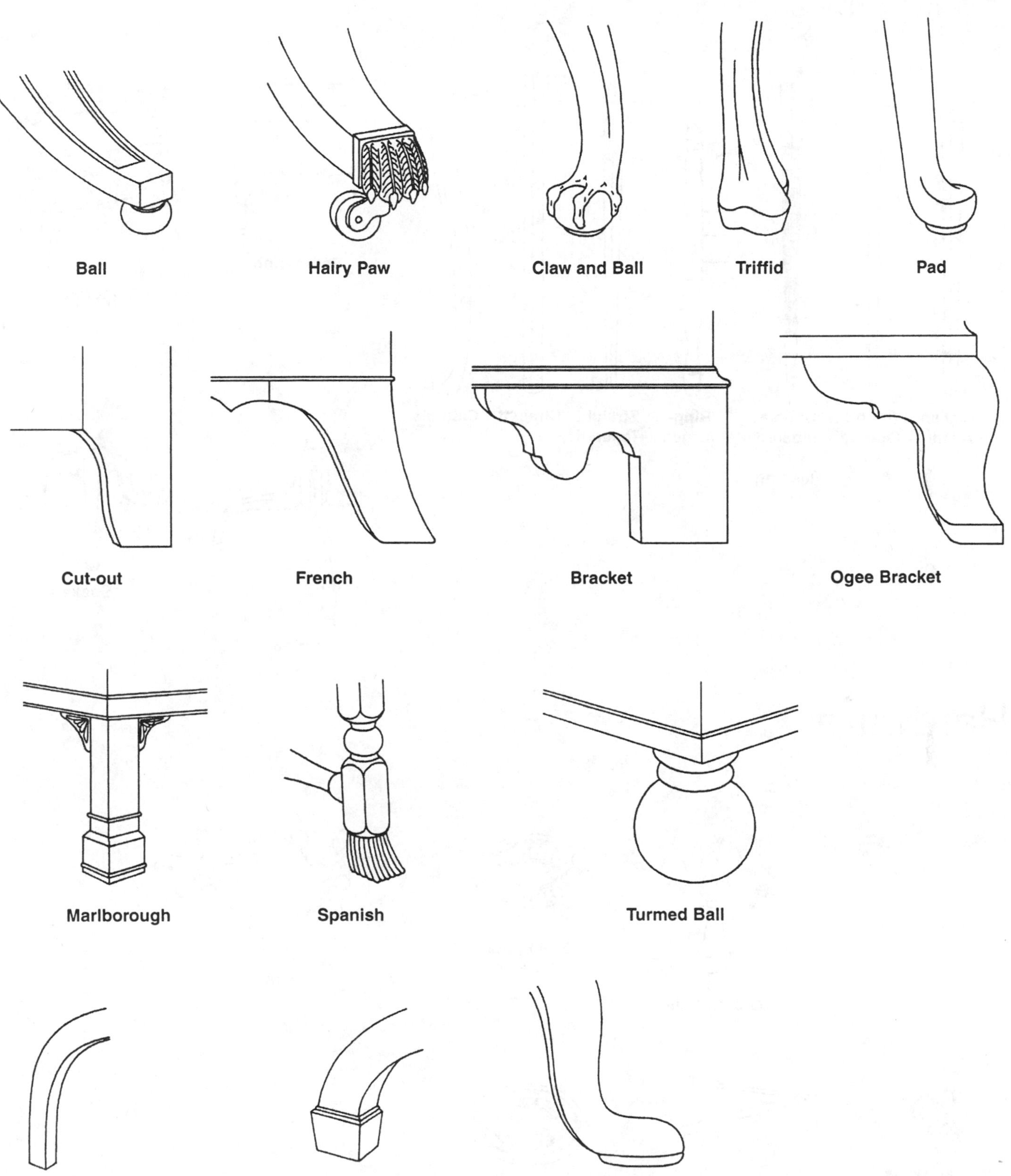

Different types of legs and hardware found on furniture

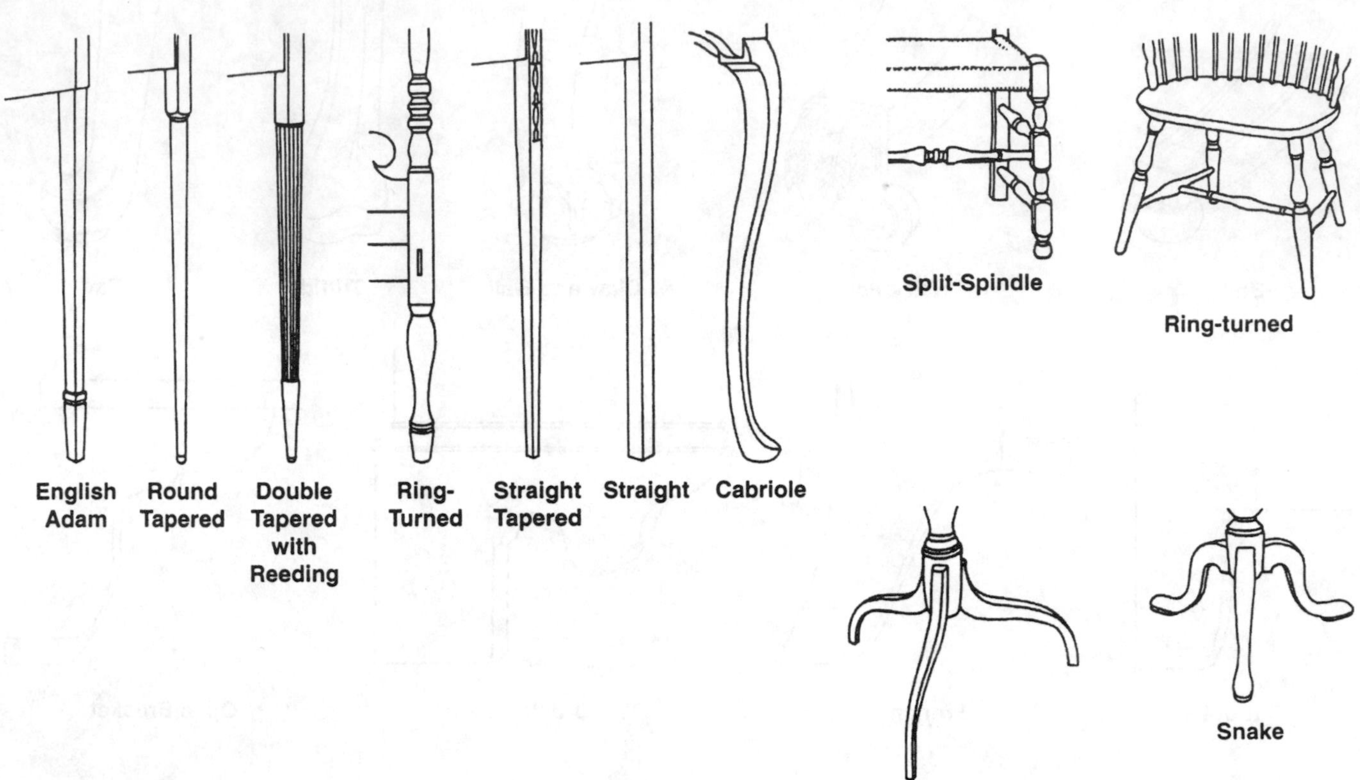

Hardware

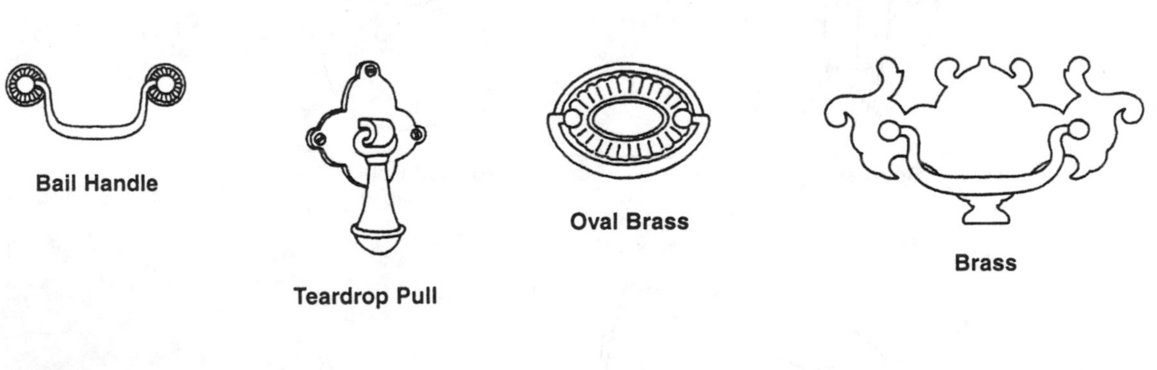

Pressed Glass

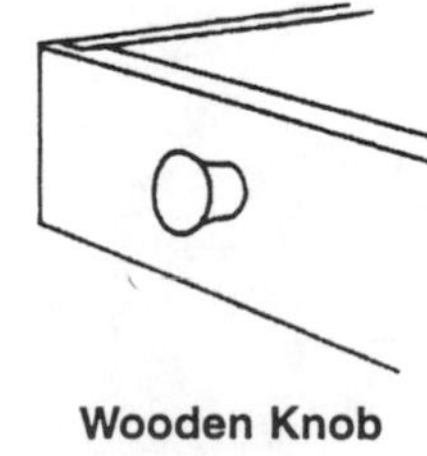
Wooden Knob

Eagle Brass

Construction details

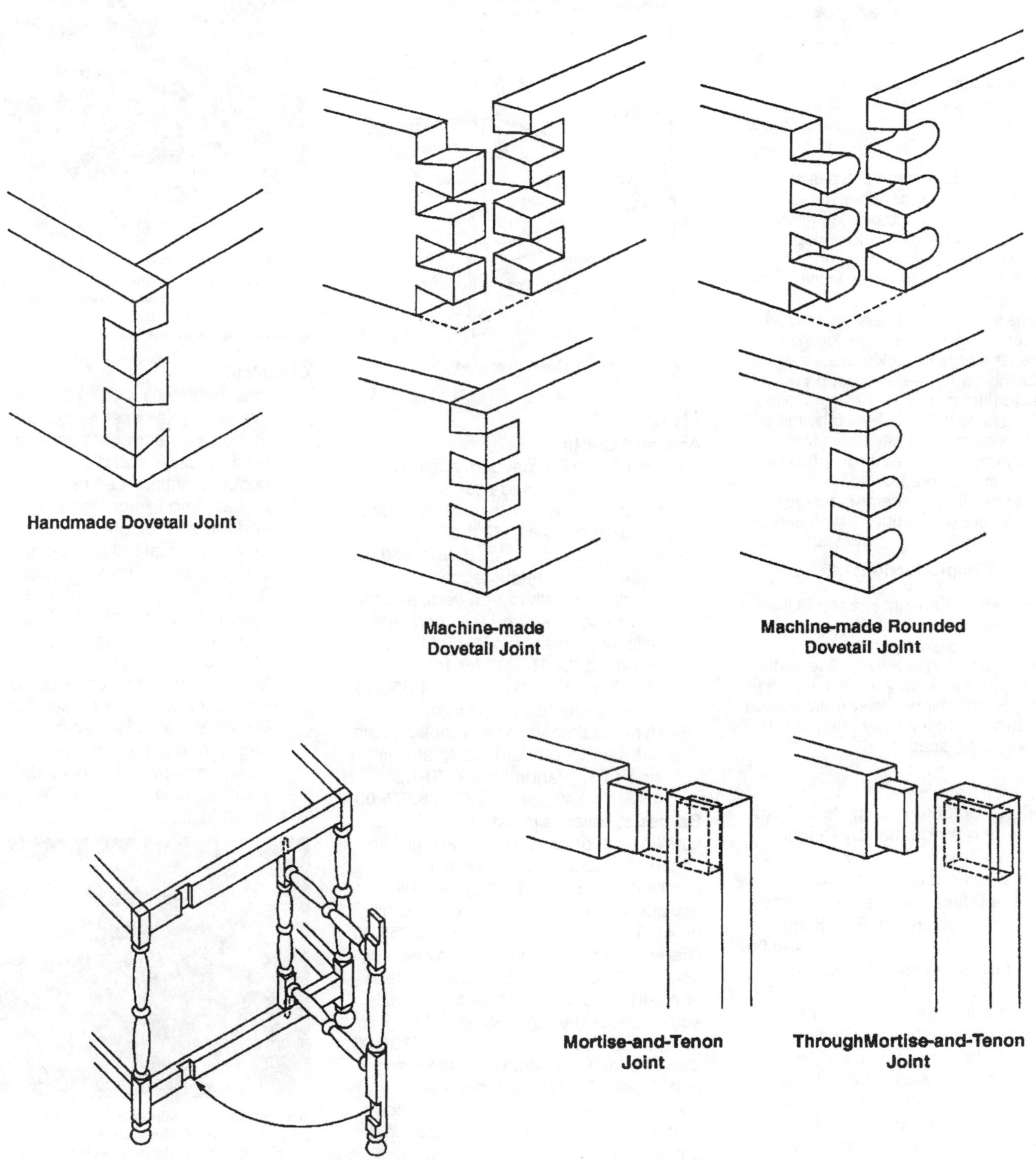

Reproduction Alert: Beware of the large number of reproductions. During the 25 years following the American Centennial of 1876, there was a great revival in copying furniture styles and manufacturing techniques of earlier eras. These centennial pieces now are more than 100 years old. They confuse many dealers, as well as collectors.

Additional Listings: Arts and Craft Movement, Art Deco, Art Nouveau, Children's Nursery Items, Orientalia, Shaker Items, and Stickley.

Notes: Furniture is one of the types of antiques for which regional preferences are a factor in pricing. Victorian furniture is popular in New Orleans and unpopular in New England. Oak is in demand in the Northwest, but not as much so in the Middle Atlantic States.

Prices vary considerably on furniture. Shop around. Furniture is plentiful unless you are after a truly rare example. Examine all pieces thoroughly—avoid buying on impulse. Turn items upside down; take them apart. Price is heavily influenced by the amount of repairs and restoration. Make certain you know if any such work has been done to a piece before buying it.

The prices listed here are "average" prices—they are only a guide. High and low prices are given to show market range.

Reproductions

Reproduction furniture is a fact of life in the antiques world. Today, modern reproductions are extremely well made and are starting to achieve respectable prices on the secondary market. Here's a sampling of what high-quality reproduction furniture brought at auction during the 2003 season:

Bed, tester, pencil post, Henry Ford Museum reproduction by Century Furniture Co., mahogany, sq legs, scalloped headboard, flat test with small peg finials, edge split on one post, 76" l rails, 83" h, 57-5/8" h headboard **440.00**

Chest of drawers, Chippendale-style, block front, "Museum reproduction authorized by the Edison Institute from Colonial Mfg," mahogany, oak secondary wood, molded edges on top, four dovetailed drawers with batwing brasses, beaded edges around drawer openings, molded base, bracket feet with scalloped returns, 35-1/4" w, 21" d, 31-1/2" h .. **1,100.00**

Desk, child size, crafted by Bernard Harter, NC, Ohio, sgd underneath drawer, Chippendale, walnut, poplar and oak secondary wood, four graduated dovetailed drawers, five int. drawers, one with star inlay, four pigeon holes, dovetailed bracket feet, batwing brasses, 20-1/4" w, 10-1/4" d, 25-1/4" h............ **1,100.00**

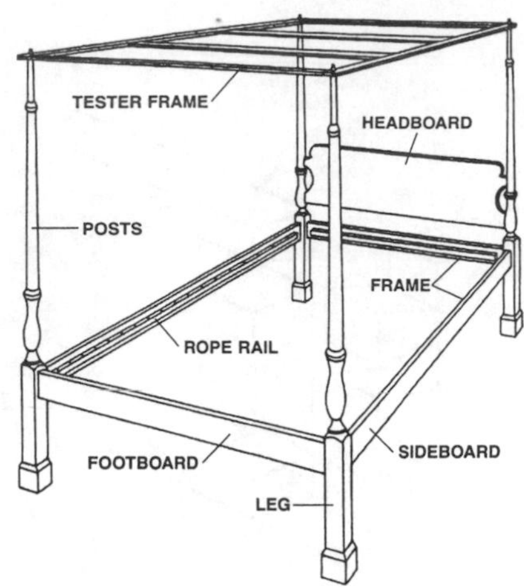

Typical Parts of a Bed

Beds

Arts and Crafts

Limbert, #651, daybed, angled headrest with spade cut-out, orig finish, recovered cushions, branded, numbered, 74" w, 25" d, 23" h **650.00**

Stickley Bros, attributed to, headboard with narrow vertical slats and panels, tapered feet, orig side rails, orig finish, minor scratches, stenciled "9001-1/2," 80-1/2" l, 56-1/2" w, 30" h.................. **1,355.00**

Stickley, Gustav, single size, pyramidal posts, nine spindles to the head and footboard, complete with side rails, branded mark, 79-1/2" l, 43-3/4" w, 49-1/4" h............ **8,575.00**

Baroque, Italian, simulated marble high scrolling headboard dec in patiglia with vacant cartouches and foliage, carved scrolling feet, painted, green and blue marbleized dec, losses to paint and gilt, pr, 45-3/4" w, 84" h..................... **3,750.00**

Biedermeier, figured mahogany veneer, octagonal posts, turned feet and finials, paneled head and footboards, orig rails, some veneer damage, 38" w, 72" l, 45" h, pr **750.00**

Centennial, Federal-style, in the manner of A. Quervelle, Philadelphia, solid mahogany, canopy, sq and turned posts with acanthus leaf, pineapple and rosette carvings, matching elaborately carved headboard, queen size, 94" h **7,975.00**

Chippendale, tall post, curly maple, turned posts, scrolled headboard with poplar panel, orig side rails, old mellow refinishing, minor repairs to posts, 60" w, 72" l, 80" h.................................. **3,000.00**

Bed, Arts & Crafts, Gustav Stickley, pyramidal posts, nine spindles to the head- and footboard, original side rails, branded "Stickley," single size, 49-1/4" x 43-3/4" x 79-1/2", **$8,575**. Photo courtesy of David Rago Auctions.

Classical

Massachusetts, c1825-35, carved mahogany, tall post, scrolled mahogany headboard flanked by reeded, carved, and ring-turned posts, acanthus leaf, beading, gothic arches, and foliage carving, reeded and turned feet, orig rails later fitted for angle irons and bed bolts, orig surface, central finial missing, 59" w, 81" d, 98" h **6,900.00**

Middle Atlantic States, 1835-45, carved mahogany veneer, low post, scrolled and paneled headboard, leaf-carved finials flanked by posts with pineapple finials, acanthus leaves above spiral carved and ring-turned posts, orig rails, bed bolts, and covers, refinished, imperfections, 58-1/2" w, 78" d, 56-1/2" h **1,100.00**

Bed, cottage type, painted decoration, gold-green background, blue panels with florals, gold flourishes, high headboard, conforming footboard and decorated sides, sold with matching chest of drawers and wash stand, **$950**. Photo courtesy of Alderfer Auction Co.

New England, c1820, painted, turned tall post, turned and tapering head posts flanking shaped

headboard, spiral-carved foot post joined by rails fitted for roping, accompanying tester, old red paint, restored, 54" w, 79" l, 60-1/2" h **1,400.00**

Country, American, trundle, southwestern PA, walnut, mortised joints, turned posts, and finials, shaped corners along top edge of head, foot, and sideboards, refinished, 71-1/2" l, 44" d **125.00**

Empire, American

Single, fitted as daybed or sofa, mahogany and mahogany figured veneer, turned and acanthus carved posts, upholstered cushion, 31-1/2" x 80" x 43-3/4" h **825.00**

Tall post, curly maple posts, poplar scrolled headboard with old soft finish, turned detail, acorn finials, rails and headboard replaced, 57-1/4" w, 72-1/2" l rails, 89" h **1,650.00**

Empire-style, sleigh, red painted, scrolled ends, bronze mounted foliate and mask mounts, 20th C, price for pr **1,650.00**

Federal

American, first half 19th C, cherry, tester, three-quarter, rect headboard with concave side edges, footboard lower, baluster-turned posts continuing to turned legs, rails with rope pegs, 81-1/2" l, 53-1/2" w, 78-1/4" h **500.00**

New England, c1810, tester, maple, vase and ring-turned foot posts continuing to tapering sq legs and molded spade feet joined to sq tapering head posts continuing to sq legs, arched headboard, later arched canopy, refinished, 51" w, 83-3/4" h **815.00**

New England, c1810-15, mahogany, turned and carved, tall post tester, arched canopy frame on vase and ring-turned spiral carved fluted tapering foot posts, joined to the turned tapering head posts with shaped headboard, ring-turned tapering feet, 45-1/2" w, 72" d, 61" h **1,775.00**

Salem, MA, c1810, mahogany, tall post, vase and ring-turned swelled fluted foot post with leaf carving on fluted plinths continuing to vase and ring-turned legs joined to ring-turned tapering head posts, shaped headboard, old surface, 51" w, 71" d, 650" h **3,175.00**

George III, four poster, carved walnut, brass mounted, circular tapered head posts, shaped mahogany headboard, reeded and acanthus-carved foot posts, ring-turned feet, casters, 9-1/2" h **10,000.00**

Bed, Federal, Pennsylvania, c1810, cherry, tester, pencil post, original finish, **$700**. Photo courtesy of Pook & Pook.

Gothic Revival, American, c1850, carved mahogany, tall headboard with three Gothic arch panels, leaf-carved crest rail, flanked by heavy round ribbed posts topped by ring-turned finials, arched and paneled footboard flanked by lower foot posts, heavy bun feet **4,750.00**

Hepplewhite-style, Philadelphia, c1943, mahogany, four tall posts each with reeded slender vasiform section over short vasiform turned carved with continuous swag designs, upholstered tester, 82" l, 62" w, 93" h............. **1,550.00**

Modern, George Nelson for Howard Miller, Thin Edge, caned headboard, 34" x 76" x 35"................................ **1,610.00**

Queen Anne, Pennsylvania, early 19th C, low poster, turned and painted pine, head and foot posts with flattened ball finials, shaped head and footboards, tapered feet, orig rope rails, orig green paint, 48-1/2" w, 74-3/4" h........... **3,600.00**

Bed, hired man's, soft wood, high poster headboard, folding bed frame, red wash, 78" l, 51" w, 77" h, **$300**. Photo courtesy of Alderfer Auction Co.

Renaissance Revival, walnut, double bed with high pediment, columned back, burled panels incised with birds, bees, and pyramids, carved figural bird heads on either side, matching dresser and washstand with marble tops, brass handles, and escutcheons....... **12,650.00**

Rope, country

Cherry, urn and ball finials, scalloped head and footboards, ring turned legs, tapered feet, mellow brown finish, poplar secondary wood, later framework and 78-1/2" l rails, 52" w, 42-1/4" h **250.00**

Curly maple with good figure, arched headboard with scalloped ends, footboard with arched and turned cross pieces, turned posts with mushroom shaped finials and tapered feet, golden refinishing, headboard is old replacement, orig rails extended to 74" l, 51-1/2" w, 55" h **1,450.00**

Bed, poster, c1850, poplar and birdseye maple poster, turned posts, 3/4 size, 54" w, 76-1/2" h, **$1,850**. Photo courtesy of Alderfer Auction Co.

Sheraton, canopy

Carved mahogany, headboard posts simple turned with ring and block turnings, simple headboard, heavily carved footboard posts with spiral turnings and acanthus leaf bell, sq tester with curtains, 58" w, 73-1/2" l, 88" without finials............... **3,200.00**

Painted, headboard with D-type cut outs on side, footboard with reeded and turned posts, canopy frame, painted red, 52" w, 76" l, 68" h **750.00**

Bed, tester, c1860, mahogany, massive turned posts, with tester, full size, 96" h, veneer chips, **$3,450**. Photo courtesy of Alderfer Auction Co.

Victorian

American, refinished walnut, paneled head and footboards with applied scroll and fruit detail, matching crest, orig 73" l side rails, 54" w, 71-1/2" h **450.00**

Brass, c1900, straight top rail, curved corners, ring-shaped capitals, cast iron side rails, 55" w, 61" h 1,200.00

Half Tester, attributed to Prudent Mallard, New Orleans, LA, c1850, carved rosewood, tall arched headboard, shell carved crest, fruit and nuts, scroll carved borders, shaped bordered panels flanked by tall tapering turned head posts supporting upholstered half tester, scroll carved crest, turned finials, paneled sideboards and footboard, turned and carved details, scroll carved corner braces **15,000.00**

Bedroom suite, International Movement, Norman Bel Geddes for Simmons, black lacquered metal, pair of twin beds, two chests of drawers with horizontal pulls, free-standing mirror, single desk chair upholstered in orange corduroy, 45" x 31" x 19" highboy, **$2,100**. Photo courtesy of David Rago Auctions, Inc.

Benches

Arts & Crafts, settle

Stickley Bros, cube, vertical slats, orig drop-in seat covered in new green leather, excellent orig finish, stenciled number, 50" l, 22-1/2" d, 33" h **2,530.00**

Stickley, Gustav, No. 208, even arm, vertical slats all around, top rail mortised through legs, drop-in spring seat covered in new green leather, red Gustav decal, 76-1/2" l, 32" d, 29-1/4" h, light standing, some color added to orig finish **6,900.00**

Stickley, Gustav, No. 222, tapering posts, tightly spaced canted slats to back and sides, leather upholstered drop-in seat, fine orig finish, red decal, minor veneer chips, 36" x 80" x 32".................................. **11,500.00**

Stickley, Gustav, No. 225, single board horizontal back panel, vertical side slats, recovered brown leather drop-in seat, over-coated orig finish, unmarked, 59-3/4" l, 31" d, 29-1/4" h **7,475.00**

Stickley, L. & J. G., cube, border vertical panels on back and under each arm, brown leather cushion, orig condition and finish, orig upholstery, "The Work of L. and J. G. Stickley" label, 72" l, 27" w, 28" h **3,450.00**

Stickley, L. & J. G., open arm, cloud lift top rail, horizontal backslat and corbels, new tan leather upholstered seat cushion, new finish, The Work of L & J. G. Stickley label, 53" l, 26" w, 36" h, some looseness **1,650.00**

Young, J. M., cube, capped top rail, vertical slats all around, fabric cov drop-in spring seat, refinished, unmarked, 78" l, 29-1/2" h, 34" h **2,870.00**

Bucket, country, poplar, evidence of old red wash, two paneled doors in base with cast iron sliding latches, three wide backboards, 5" d, 7-1/2" and 16" d shelf, canted sides, shaped bracket feet, refinished, 41" w, 16-1/2" d, 45" h **1,550.00**

Chippendale-style, late 19th or early 20th C, mahogany, scalloped crests, double back splats with Gothic pierced designs, serpentine shaped arms, six sq legs, stretcher base, beading on front corners and seat frame, refinished, slip seat upholstered in pink and cream-colored silk with floral motif, 47" w, 19" d, 36-1/2" h **1,500.00**

Bench, International Movement, George Nelson for Herman Miller, two blond wood slatted benches on ebonized round edged legs, early, unmarked, some finish wear, 48-1/4" l, 18-3/4" w, 14" h, **$1,400**. Photo courtesy of David Rago Auctions, Inc.

Classical, window

Boston, 1835-45, carved mahogany veneer, upholstered seat, veneered rail, leaf-carved cyma curved ends, joined by ring-turned medial stretcher, 48" w, 16-1/4" d, 17-1/2" h **2,185.00**

New York, 1815-25, mahogany veneer, curving upholstered seat flanked by scrolled ends, scrolled base, old refinish, some veneer cracking and loss, 20th C olive green velvet upholstery, 39-1/2" w, 14" d, 23-5/8" h **3,500.00**

Classical Revival, mahogany, carved paw feet and lion's heads, maroon velvet cushion, old finish, 16-1/2" l, 29-1/4" w, 23" h.. **600.00**

Country

96" l, 18-1/4" w, 13" h, pine, orig red paint, PA, early 19th C........... **750.00**

104" l, 13-1/2" w, pine, old worn and weathered green repaint, one board top with rounded front corners, beaded edge apron, cut-out feet mortised through top, age crack in one end of top **325.00**

Decorated, orig dark green with reddish brown paint, yellow line dec, mortised construction, some sq nails, arched end panels, replaced shoe feet, some later nails added, 33" w, 14" d, 23-1/4" h **275.00**

Federal

New England, c1810, window, mahogany, upholstered seat and rolled arms, sq tapering legs, H-form stretchers, refinished, minor repair to one leg, 39-1/2" l, 16" d, 29" h **900.00**

New York, c1825, window, figured mahogany, each end with rect crotch-figured crest centering removable slip seat, matching seat rail, saber legs, 40-1/2" l..... **3,500.00**

George III, English, mid-18th C, window, mahogany, rect seat, scrolling arms, later velvet cov, straight legs, blind fret craved, H-form stretcher, pr, 38" l............ **4,750.00**

Bucket bench, softwood, original blue-green paint, three tiers, 54" w, 50" h, **$2,250**. Photo courtesy of Wiederseim Associates, Inc.

Gothic Revival, American, c1820-40, carved mahogany, angled over-upholstered seat, carved seat rails centering quatrefoil, facet lancet-carved legs, molded faceted feet, 65" l, 20" d, 15-1/2" h **1,750.00**

Harness-maker's, pine, hand hewn seat and post legs, 41" x 24" x 15"........ **100.00**

Louis XVI-style, window, carved cherry, overstuffed seat, channeled rails, flanked by molded, overscroll arms carved with be-ribboned foliate sprays, turned, tapered, and leaf-capped legs **200.00**

Piano, Arts & Crafts, L. & J. G. Stickley, No. 211, overhanging top, slatted sides, broad cross stretchers, orig label, orig finish, wear to top, 40" l, 15-1/2" w, 22-1/2" h **2,100.00**

Settle

Country, curly maple, back divided into three sections with scalloped crests and slats, caned seat with meandering serpentine front, scrolled arms, eight saber legs,

narrow front stretcher, turned rungs, refinished, 71" w, 19" d, 33-1/3" h 1,100.00

Settle bench, pine, two-board top over two drawers, mortised through, cutout feet, c1840-1850, refinished, 56" l, 18" w, 49" h, **$2,600**. Photo courtesy of Alderfer Auction Co.

Queen Anne, English, oak, pegged construction, molded crest, reeded detail along front edge of seat, shaped arms and turned supports, five tombstone panels across back with relief fan and rosette carvings, cabriole front and tapered rear legs with turned end rungs, pad feet, old dark finish, old replacement seat boards, two returns replaced, 73" l, 27-1/2" d, 38-1/4" h................ 600.00

William and Mary, English, oak, mortised construction, six inset back panels, shaped arms, stretcher base with turned leg and arm supports, plank seat, old dark finish, age splits, edge damage, 57" w, 18" d, 52" h 500.00

Victorian-style, chaise lounge, Chesterfield, early 20th C, tufted brown leather, adjustable backrest, casters, 62" l 3,000.00

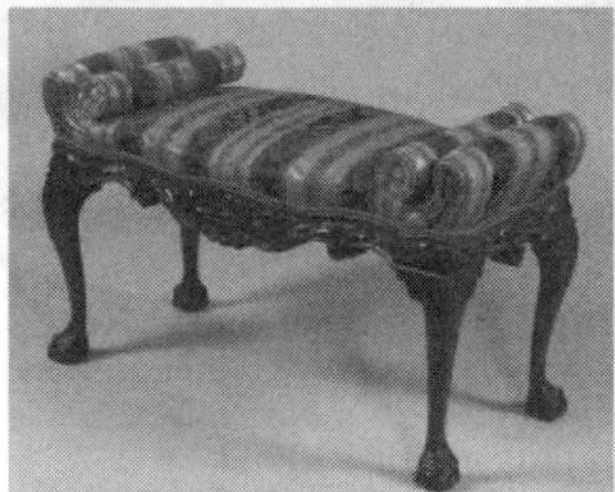

Window bench, Victorian-style, carved mahogany, raised and upholstered ends, foliate carved apron, cabriole legs, silk upholstery, 40" l, **$450**. Photo courtesy of Skinner, Inc.

Wagon seat, New England, late 18th C, painted, two pairs of arched slats joining three turned stiles, double rush seat flanked by turned arms ending in turned hand-holds, tapering legs, old brown paint over earlier gray, 15" h seat, 30" h 1,200.00

Wicker, painted white, hooped crest rail flanked by rows of dec curlicues, spiral wrapped posts and six spindles, pressed-in oval seat, dec curlicue apron, wrapped cabriole legs, X-form stretcher, 35" w, 31" h.................................. 500.00

Windsor, settle, 20th C green paint, yellow in turnings, 29 spindles with bamboo turnings across back with turned arms, well-shaped seat with incised rain gutter around back, eight splayed legs joined by cross stretchers, splits in seat, old iron braces added underneath for support, 77-1/2" w, 22" d, 36-3/4" h 2,100.00

Bentwood

In 1856, Michael Thonet of Vienna perfected the process of bending wood using steam. Shortly afterward, Bentwood furniture became popular. Other manufacturers of Bentwood furniture were Jacob and Joseph Kohn, Philip Strobel and Son, Sheboygan Chair Co., and Tidoute Chair Co. Bentwood furniture is still being produced today by the Thonet firm and others.

Bar stool, Thonet, black suede upholstery, ebonized frame with circular stretchers, two have Thonet factory tags, 14-1/4" d, 30-1/4" h, **$525**. Photo courtesy of David Rago Auctions, Inc.

Box

8" d, 7" h, round, worn orig paint resembles wallpaper, yellow and black foliage scrolls on blue ground, some edge damage to lid..... 750.00

17-1/4" l, band, pine, orig blue paint, unusual decoupage paper scene of black man, woman, and child, foreign inscription, wear and loose bottom board........................ 550.00

Lounge chair, Thonet, rocking, cane paneled back and seat. 40" x 26" x 38", **$175**. Photo courtesy of David Rago Auctions, Inc.

Chair, Austrian, Vienna Secession-style, c1910, side, back splat with three circular perforations, three slender spindles, painted black, set of eight.......... 5,500.00

Cradle, 41" l, 39" h, ivory fittings ... 440.00

Hall tree, Thonet, c1910, bentwood frame, contrasting striped wood inlay, coat hooks with central beveled mirror above one door, metal drip pan, orig label, 57" w, 13" d, 76" h 2,750.00

Arm chair, adjustable-position, laminated bentwood frame, detachable brown vinyl seat/back cushion with headrest, and padded arms, unmarked, 41-1/4" x 30" x 37", **$500**. Photo courtesy of David Rago Auctions, Inc.

Plant stand, Thonet, Austria, late 19th C, round top with black printed classical urn and flower motif, bentwood tripod base, imp "Thonet," paper label, wear, couple of breaks on feet, 18-5/8" d, 30-5/8" h 210.00

Rocker, Thonet, arched twined top rail, cut-velvet fabric fitted back, armrests, and seat, elaborate scrolling frame, curved runners, 53" l 750.00

Stool, Thonet, attributed to Marcel Kammerer, Austria, 1901, beech, sq seat, four legs, U-shaped braces forming spandrels, shaped bronze sabot feet, 14-1/4" sq, 18-1/2" h 1,500.00

Table, Josef Hoffman, c1905, circular top, wooden spheres dec below rim, 21-1/4" h.. 500.00

Side table, Austria, late 19th C, circular top in black stain, three curvilinear bentwood legs joined to center ring, crack to ring, 19-1/4" d, 31-1/2" h, **$200**. Photo courtesy of Skinner, Inc.

Blanket chests

Chippendale, country, poplar, dovetailed case, three dovetailed drawers across lower front with molded overlapping edges, replaced molded base, replaced scalloped bracket feet, int. till with wrought iron strap hinges, refinished, traces of old salmon paint, replaced brasses, 51-1/2" w, 23" d, 28-1/2" h **450.00**

Country, curly maple with strong figure, reconstructed single drawer, scalloped base, bracket feet, int. fitted with till with replaced cover, golden refinishing, 37-1/2" w, 19-3/4" d, 24-3/4" h **1,100.00**

Blanket chest, Lancaster, Pennsylvania, painted dower chest by Embroidery Artist, dated 1788, molded lift lid decorated with central cartouche in black, red, and white with tulip and geometric border, stylized stars in corners, over case with central heart inscribed "Maria Stohlern 1788," flanked by tombstone panels with tulips and stars, over midmolding above two short drawers with stars, straight bracket feet, blue ground, illus in *The Pennsylvania -German Decorated Chest* by Fabian, 52" l, 23" d, 27" h, **$55,200**. Photo courtesy of Pook & Pook.

Decorated

America, birch, poplar, and basswood, unusual orig red grained dec, beveled molding around lid, inset side panels, tapered legs, turned button feet, interior cut for till, glued restorations long hinge rail, 33-1/2" w, 16-1/2" d, 21" h **3,000.00**

America, poplar, old dec, three cream-colored tombstone-shaped panels across top with black unicorns, red, black, and yellow urns of tulips, yellow and gray birds, date "1817," one board top, dovetailed case and bracket feet, beaded edging around base, replaced hinges, pieced restoration on one rear foot, age splits in base, 37" w, 15-1/2" d, 17-3/4" h............ **1,100.00**

America, poplar, orig brown sponged vinegar dec, two-board top with molded edge, dovetailed case with int. covered till, base molding and turned feet with later black paint, wrought iron strap hinges (one restored), 47-1/2" w, 23" d, 27" h **1,100.00**

America, tiger maple, dovetailed, short turned legs **1,500.00**

America, walnut, poplar secondary wood, old dark red paint, molded edge around lid fastened with wooden pegs, dovetailed case and bracket feet with finely scalloped aprons, two dovetailed drawers with beaded edges, old oval brasses, int. till with lid, 49-1/2" w, 20-3/4" d, 27-1/2" h **1,100.00**

Ohio, c1820-40, pine and poplar, six-board construction, eagle dec, cover with considerable paint wear, restoration, 49-1/2" w, 21" d, 23-3/4" h **2,300.00**

Ohio, attributed to Knox County, dovetailed poplar, orig sponged circles and meandering borders, two board top with molding, scalloped base painted black, beveled aprons, fitted int. with covered till, early iron casters, 39" w, 29-1/2" d....... **825.00**

Pennsylvania, attributed to Somerset County, poplar, green stenciled signature for "Hiram Gardner, 1852," salmon, light and dark green, stenciled foliage and scroll detail, freehand heart just below keyhole, green trim on lid and base, dovetailed case and feet, molded apron and scrolling, int. till, replaced hinges, restorations, split in lid, corner chips, 43-1/2" w, 18" d **825.00**

Pennsylvania, Mahatonga Valley, early 19th C, pine and poplar, molded lift top painted with American flag, lattice and banded border above recessed paneled sides with banded borders, joined by stiles continuing to feet, dec attributed to third quarter 19th C, 33" w, 19" d, 21" h **17,250.00**

Blanket chest, Lehigh Valley, Pennsylvania, painted poplar, dower chest, dated 1786, lift lid over case, cartouche inscribed "Elisabeth Schonlisi 1786" above three panels with potted flowers, sides with similar panels over mid molding above two short drawers, straight bracket feet, 47" w, 27-1/2" h, **$4,000.** Photo courtesy of Pook & Pook.

Dowry, Mahantango Valley, Pennsylvania, "Samuel Grebiel 1799," orig paint dec, red, blue, mustard, black, and white, two shaped polygons painted in blue grain painting, identical polygons on each side, two in front with banner above with name and date, int. lidded till, black painted dovetailed bracket base, off-set strap hinges, orig lock, 48-1/2" w, 21" d, 23-1/2" h **3,000.00**

Federal, PA, early 18th C, pine and cherry, molded lift top, well with till, case with two thumb-molded graduated drawers, dovetailed bracket feet, old refinish, minor imperfections, 40" w, 20-1/2" d, 43" h **1,880.00**

Grain painted, New York state, c1830, molded hinged lift top, lidded till, molded bracket black painted base, orig fanciful ochre and raw umber graining, 48" w, 22" d, 29" h **1,265.00**

Jacobean, oak, paneled construction with relief carving, drawer and feet replaced, repairs to lid and molding, old dark finish, 44-1/2" w, 19-1/2" d, 31-3/4" h **825.00**

Miniature, England, early 19th C, mahogany, molded lift-top with wire hinges, dovetail constructed box base, mid molding trim, heavy molded bracket base, worm holes, wear, 14-1/4" l, 6-3/4" h **1,035.00**

Mule, America, pine, thumb-molded top, two overlapping dovetailed drawers, bracket feet, old dark finishing, int. lined with 1875 Boston newspaper, pierced repairs to feet and drawer fronts, 40" w, 18" d, 34-3/4" h **700.00**

Blanket chest, grain painted, Pennsylvania, c1840-50, original green on yellow ground graining, red trim, dovetailed case, turned feet mortised through bottom, int. till with lid, 51" l, 22-1/4" w, 27" h, **$1,695**. Photo courtesy of Cowan's Historic Americana Auctions.

Painted

Massachusetts, first quarter 19th C, molded hinged top, case of two drawers, tall cut-out feet with valanced skirt, orig red-brown grain paint with contrasting beige grained drawers, orig pulls, 36-3/4" w, 17-1/4" d, 37-3/4" h........ **11,750.00**

New England, early 19th C, hinged top, well with till, case with singe drawer, cut-out base, orig mustard-brown graining resembling wood, minor imperfections, 39-1/4" w, 18-1/4" d, 40" h **850.00**

New England, early 19th C, six-board, rect top, case with two drawer, cut-out feet joined by straight skirt, all-over orig reddish brown and yellow grain paint resembling exotic wood, old brass pulls, minor imperfections, minor paint wear, 41-1/4" w, 18-1/2" d, 32-1/4" h **2,115.00**
Ohio, wide poplar boards, orig red paint, traces of silvery white star designs on lid and front, dovetailed case, molded top edge, bracket feet, small scalloped returns, molded base, int. till with lid, hinges and narrow hinge rail old replacements, minor edge wear, 49-1/4" w, 21" d, 26" h **650.00**
Pennsylvania, Bucks County, dated 1770, red moldings and base, mottled reddish-brown ground, large triple banded hearts on front and sides, corners with half-hearts, over lozenges with names and date, two lower drawers, molded skirt with central drop, cut-out bracket feet, int. till, secret drawers, orig paint, minor losses, one side foot and back braces replaced, 49" l, 24" d, 29-1/2" h **18,750.00**

Blanket chest, paint grained to resemble striped wood, bun feet, **$250**. Photo courtesy of Wiederseim Associates, Inc.

Queen Anne, New England, c1750, marriage chest, pine, hinged rect lift lid, upper half faced with faux drawer fronts, brown paint, 35".........................**4,000.00**
Sheraton, country, pine and poplar, orig red paint, molded edge top, paneled front and ends, sq corner posts, mortised and pinned frame, scalloped apron, turned feet, 44" w, 19-1/2" d, 25-1/2" h **900.00**
William and Mary, New England, c1700, oak and yellow pine, joined, drawer base, old finish, minor imperfections, 48-1/2" w, 22" d, 32-3/4" h **4,500.00**

Bookcases

Arts & Crafts

English, double door, corbelled overhanging top, inlaid pewter, ebony, and fruitwood tulips, leaded glass panels with green tear-shaped inserts, curvilinear backsplash, emb strap handles, orig finish, unmarked, some corbels loose, 46" w, 12-1/2" d, 52-1/2" h **2,615.00**
Limbert, Grand Rapids, MI, early 20th C, oak, two elongated glass panels on each of two doors, three adjustable shelves on each side, round copper pulls, medium brown finish, branded mark on reverse, imperfections, 40-1/2" l, 14" d, 57-1/2" h **2,775.00**
Stickley Bros, quarter-sawn oak, double door, slatted gallery top, single panes of glass, orig medium finish, brass tag, 35-1/2" w, 12" d, 50" h **4,875.00**
Stickley, Gustav, quarter sawn oak, double door, eight glass panes to each door, gallery top, hammered copper V-pulls, three int. shelves, top and bottom mortised thru sides, red decal and paper Craftsman label, refinished, 42-3/4" w, 13" d, 56-1/4" h **5,175.00**
Stickley, Gustav, quarter sawn oak, double door, 12 panes per door, gallery top, brass V-pulls, mortised top, paper label, 54" w, 13" d, 55" h, refinished, warp in right door, stripped hardware.............. **5,175.00**
Stickley, L. & J. G., No. 641, quarter sawn oak, single door, gallery top and keyed through-tenons, unsgd, refinished, 30" w, 12" d, 54-1/2" h **4,600.00**

Bookcases, stacking, Victorian, glass fronts, **$425**. Photo courtesy of Dotta Auction Co., Inc.

Biedermeier-style, inlaid cherry, outset molded cornice with ebonized bead, front with two recessed glazed doors, four shelves, outset molded base raised on black feet, burr poplar panels, ebonized stringing, 53-1/2" w, 21" d, 72" h.... **700.00**
Chippendale, New England, southern, late 18th C, mahogany and maple, scroll top, top section with molded scrolled cresting, carved pinwheel terminals centering carved fan and bordered with punchwork flanked by flame urn-turned finials, two thumb-molded recessed panel doors opening to compartmented shelved int., lower section with fall front desk opening to stepped multi-drawer compartmented int. above case of four graduated scratchbeaded drawers, bracket feet, replaced brasses, refinished, imperfections, 39" w, 21" d, 84-3/4" h **7,100.00**
Chippendale-style, New England, mahogany, broken arch pedestal over two arched-paneled doors, fitted secretary int. with pigeonholes, six small drawers, lower section with fall front, stepped fitted int., straight front, two small and two wide drawers, brass bail handle, escutcheons, lock plates, straight bracket feet, 42" w, 24" d, 93-3/4" h **3,200.00**

Bookcase, Arts & Crafts, Gustav Stickley, c1908, No. 715, fumed oak, gallery top over single door with 12 panes, V-pull, original paper label, 36" w, 13" d, 56" h, **$6,170**. Photo courtesy of Skinner, Inc.

Classical, Boston, 1830s, carved mahogany veneer, cove molded cornice above two glazed doors flanked by columns with leaf carved tops and turned bases, fold-out felt lined writing surface, sectioned for writing implements, two small cock-beaded drawers over two long drawers, flanked by similar columns with carved tops, four reeded and carved bulbous feet, glazed doors open to bird's eye maple veneered int. with two adjustable shelves, valanced open compartments, five small drawers, brasses and wooden pulls appear to be orig, old refinish, imperfections, 44-3/4" w, 22-1/4" d, 88" h **11,500.00**
Eastlake, America, c1880, cherry, rect top, flaring bead-trimmed cornice, pair of single-pan glazed cupboard doors, carved oval paterae and scrolls across

top, adjustable shelved int., stepped base with line-incised drawers, bail handles, 47-1/2" w, 15-1/4" d, 69-1/4" h 1,200.00

Empire, crotch mahogany veneers, top section: large architectural type cornice, two large glass doors with cathedral top muttons, three adjustable shelves; base: 11 drawers, oval brass knobs, applied base molding, two panes of glass cracked, 66" w, 83" h 5,500.00

Empire-style, mahogany, two-door bookcase top with cathedral-type door, base with one top drawer over two doors, three smaller drawers under doors, shelved int., 43-1/2" w, 83-1/2" h 1,700.00

Federal, Southern States, attributed to, 1790-1810, mahogany, veneered pediment embellished with inlaid floral vines and leaves above mullioned glazed doors, int. adjustable beaded shelves, lower case as hinged butler's desk with int. of valanced compartments and small drawers outlined with stringing, case of three graduated string inlaid drawers, skirt with inlaid vines and leaves, French feet, old refinish, replaced brasses, restored, 40-1/2" w, 21-1/2" d, 93-1/2" h 4,700.00

French Empire-style, 19th C, brass mounted mahogany, rect cornice, two grill inset doors, shelved int. and mirrored back, bracket feet, 63" w, 9" d, 78" h 2,000.00

Bookcase, George III-style, mahogany, shaped cornice, two mullioned and glazed doors opening to shelves, lower section fitted with two small glazed doors, ball feet, 43" w, 17-1/2" d, 80" h, **$1,550**. Photo courtesy of Skinner, Inc.

George III, third quarter 18th C, inlaid mahogany, dentil-molded cornice above two paneled doors, shelved interior, two candle slides, slant front enclosing fitted interior, two short and three graduated drawers, bracket feet, 37" w, 22" d, 85-1/2" h 4,600.00

George III-style, with 18th century elements, mahogany, later swan's neck cresting above pair of paneled doors opening to shelves, fitted with candle rests, lower section with slant lid enclosing a fitted int., all above three long drawers, ogee bracket feet, 35" w, 20" d, 95" h 2,650.00

Louis XV-style, mid-18th C, walnut, shaped top, pr glazed center doors over five drawers, scalloped skirt with center ornament, cabriole legs 4,000.00

Modern

Baker, George III-style, bookcase/breakfront, mahogany, c1950 .... 4,510.00

Beacon Hill, bookcase/breakfront, mahogany, Gothic-arch accents, c1950 .... 5,170.00

Bookcase, breakfront, by Union National, Inc., Jamestown, New York, 20th C, mahogany, rect stepped molded top above four beveled glass doors enclosing shelved interiors, long drawer flanked by two short drawers; base with four paneled cupboard doors enclosing single shelf interiors, plinth base, 83" x 90", **$2,700**. Photo courtesy of Sloans & Kenyon Auctions.

Queen Anne-style, late 19th C, walnut, double-dome top above two doors opening to shelves, fitted with candle-slides, lower section fitted with slant lid desk and seven drawers, bracket feet, 38" w, 19" d, 82" h 2,600.00

Regency, late, early 19th C, mahogany, bookcase/breakfront, concave fronted cornice, frieze carved with anthemion, upper section fitted with four arched and glazed doors; lower section fitted with fall front writing surface and fitted int., all above two pedestals fitted with shelves and drawers, 84" w, 26" d, 93" h 7,475.00

Renaissance Revival, c1870, figured and solid walnut, four doors, egg and ribbon carved mullions, 80" w, 98" h 9,350.00

Revolving, American, second half 19th C, oak, molded rect top, five compartmentalized shelves with slatted ends, quadruped base with casters, stamped "Danners Revolving Book Case…Ohio," 24" w, 24" d, 68-1/4" h 1,200.00

Bookcase, Victorian, revolving, square, oak, four shelves, **$400**. Photo courtesy of Joy Luke Auctions.

Stacking

Corner unit, four stacks, fully leaded doors, separated by a paneled oak center section 3,100.00

Globe-Wernicke, oak, five stacks, fully leaded doors 2,000.00

Victorian, two parts, walnut, pair glazed doors over drawers, **$5,000**. Photo courtesy of Wiederseim Associates, Inc.

Victorian

Walnut, four doors, three drawers below, pierced carving above 6,000.00

Walnut, three sections, center desk with drop front writing surface over four graduated drawers, fitted int., carved frieze panel and gallery, end sections with open shelving over side-by-side drawers, 10' l 5,775.00

Boxes

Band

Oblong, wallpaper covered

11-1/8" l, 9" w, 6-3/8" h, cov in various floral patterns, lid centered with figures by manor **250.00**

15" l, 11-3/4" w, 10-1/4" h, oblong, printed "Sandy Hook" lighthouse, ships motif, shades of red, green, white, and brown, blue ground, America, mid-19th C, fading, tears, sewn repairs to lid and base **1,410.00**

Document box, hand made, lined with green wool fabric, "Levina, Scotland 1862" cross-stitched in lid, **$100**. Photo courtesy of Dotta Auction Co., Inc.

Oval, wallpaper covered

11-1/2" l, 9-3/8" w, 6-1/4" h, beaver pattern, black, brown, and green, blue ground, wear **765.00**

14-3/4" h, floral drapery motif, blues, greens, and browns, tears, separations, fading **940.00**

17" l, 14" w, 12" h, large eagle motif, trees in background, green, white, and brown on blue field, wear, losses, fading **355.00**

19-1/4" l, 14" w, 12-1/4" h, fire brigade motif, green, brown, and tan, yellow ground, losses, wear, fading **1,880.00**

19-1/4" l, 17" w, 13-1/2" h, Castle Garden pattern, brown, yellow and green, blue field, cover missing, wear, fading.......................... **470.00**

Band box, oval, blue wall paper, yellow and brown floral design, interior lined with newspaper in German, 8-1/4" l, 5-1/2" d, 5" h, minor losses to paper, **$3,850**. Photo courtesy of Alderfer Auction Co.

Bible

Contemporary, oak, lift lid with inset panel and applied medallion with Adam and Eve in a tree, two rows of columns on three sides, rosehead nails, iron staple hinges, 10-1/4" x 11-1/2" x 6-1/2" h **250.00**

English, oak, two-board top, well executed raised floral carving on front, molded base with "T" head nail construction, iron lock, old dark finish, replaced top and hinges, 23" w, 15-3/4" d, 9" h............. **425.00**

English, oak, two-board top, carved three fan-shaped leaves, scrolled rosettes across front, wrought iron strap hinges, front escutcheon plate with detailed castings of lion and bird heads, old dark brown finish, base boards, hinges, and lock replaced, 29" w, 21" d, 10" h **200.00**

Book, Maine, carved spruce gum, sliding lids, carved rosette and triangle motifs, chip-carved embellishments, gilt highlights, minor wear, late 19th/early 20th C, 4-3/4" w, 6" h **420.00**

Bride's, oval, bentwood, overlapping laced scenes, orig painted dec, couple in colonial dress, white, red, brown, and black on brown stained ground, German inscription and 1796 in white, edge damage, 15-7/8" l, 10" w, 6-1/2" h **495.00**

Book form, hinged lid, brown grain painted decoration, original lock and key, 12" l, 10" w, 3" h, paint worn, **$110**. Photo courtesy of Alderfer Auction Co.

Candle

Country, hanging, pine, keyhole-shaped crest, rect shaped box, wooden pegs, rosehead nails, refinished, small pierced restoration on lower corner, 13-1/4" w, 5-1/4" d, 11-1/4" h **315.00**

PA, carved curly maple, inlay, dark stain, sgd "J. N. Mattheslee, Bedford County, Gunsmith," 12" l, 3-1/4" w, 2-1/4" h **19,800.00**

Casket, Italian Renaissance Revival, 19th C, paint dec wood rect, hinged lid with lappet carving, sides with panels painted with grotesques bearing swags, chip carved borders, front corners with foliate carving, paw feet, 13-1/2" w, 9-1/2" h **560.00**

Cheese, 6-1/2" h, 12-1/8" d, pine, circular, incised "E. Temple" on lid, painted blue, America, 19th C, cracks, paint wear, minor losses **175.00**

Bride's box, late 18th/early 19th C, cylindrical-form wood box, laced, lapped panel construction, painted polychrome red and black with yellow highlights, one panel stylized scale with floral embellishments, 14" d, 9-5/8" h, **$500**. Photo courtesy of Skinner, Inc.

Collar, 13" l, 5" h, wallpaper covering, oval, marked "E. Stone no. 116 1/2 William Street, New York" **575.00**

Cutlery, Victorian, 19th C, mahogany, brass lifting handle, three divisions, later sq tapered legs, 11" w, 14" d, 23" h **260.00**

Decorated, dovetailed, pine, orig grain painting, rect, dovetailed, conforming hinged lid, ochre ground paint with red putty or vinegar painted seaweed-like designs, orig lock, wallpaper lined int., New England, 1820s, missing top bail handle, later waxing of surface, 14-5/8" w, 7-1/8" d, 6-3/4" h........................... **690.00**

Document

America, mid to late 19th C, walnut, dovetailed, rect, hinged lid, side till, turned feet, 14" w, 8" d, 10-1/2" h **385.00**

America, 19th C, hinged lid with central diamond motif, rect, bird's-eye maple, mahogany, and satinwood veneers, minor wear, a couple of small edge losses, 7-1/2" l, 4-3/8" d, 3-1/8" h.................... **500.00**

America, 19th C, paint dec pine, rect, hinged lid decorated with a stenciled basket of fruit in green, yellow, and white with gilt highlights on a green ground, yellow and green borders, heart-shaped brass escutcheon, minor wear, 12-1/4" l, 7-7/8" d, 4-3/4" h.................... **600.00**

Dome top

America, 19th C, grain painted, pine, wire hinges, iron handles and latch, dovetailed joinery, minor cracks, 19-3/4" l, 11" d, 8-7/8" h **990.00**

Box, Bucher-type, Pennsylvania, 19th C, sliding lid, pine, painted floral decoration, salmon bands, 6-3/4" l, 3-1/2" h, **$1,265**. Photo courtesy of Pook & Pook.

Vermont, Shaftsbury, 1820s, attributed to Matteson family, whitewood, green and yellow vinegar painted central dec surrounded by simulated inlaid quarter round fans, cross banded tiger maple veneers and circles, repeated on four areas of six-board form, orig surface, varnished, imperfections, 24" w, 12-1/2" d, 12" h **5,465.00**

Pennsylvania, Lancaster County, decorated, orig blue paint, incised compass start designs painted red and white, orig punched tin latch, tin and wire hinges, some damage, few holes where hinges attach, 5-1/2" w, 3-7/8" d, 4-3/4" h **11,550.00**

Document box, English, late 19th/early 20th C, Pollard oak, rect, inlaid with specimen wood bands, hinged lid with central monogrammed silver metal roundel, crenellated trim to sides, cedar lined, **$275**. Photo courtesy of Skinner, Inc.

Dough, pine and poplar, rect removable top, tapering well, splayed ring-turned legs, ball feet, Pennsylvania, 19th C, 38" w, 19-3/4" w, 29-1/2" h **500.00**

Dressing, early 19th C, dovetail, orig black paint, patriotic dec of eagle, *Mayflower, USS Constitution,* one board domed lid, fitted int. with mirror and drawer, bun feet, 17" w, 12" d, 8" h **5,225.00**

Glove, late 19th C, lacewood and inlay, rect, canted corners, hinged lid with featherbanding to perimeter, 13-1/2" l **360.00**

Grain painted, America, 19th C, pine, rect, brass ring pull on lid, minor wear, small loss on one corner, 10-1/2" l, 6-1/2" d, 3-1/8" h **250.00**

Knife

9" w, 10" d, 15-3/4" h, English, inlaid flame mahogany veneer over pine, bowfront, scalloped corners with banded inlay, brass handles on both sides, star inlay on int. of lid, old refinish, contemporary, dovetailed int. lifts out, slotted for letters, hidden compartment below, some sections of inlay missing, age splits in veneer **550.00**

14-1/2" h, mahogany veneer with inlay, edge veneer damage, int. incomplete, inlaid oval on inside of lid... **225.00**

16" h, 9-3/4" w, 14-1/2" d, Federal, flamed grained mahogany, serpentine and block front, reeded front columns, fitted int., orig keys, pr **2,500.00**

Lap desk, quarter-sawn oak, felt writing surface, letter file, inkwell **825.00**

Letter, Gothic Revival, English, late 19th/early 20th C, oak, sloped lid with brass trefoil strapwork, two handles on sides, front doors opening to fitted int., single drawer in base, maker's tag for "Lechars," London and Paris, 16" w, 12-1/4" d, 15-1/4" h **635.00**

Pantry, circular, nailed construction, swing handle

7-1/2" d, 3-1/2" h, green, two-finger construction, orig paint **250.00**

12" d, 6-3/4" h, orig green painted surface, 19th C, minor surface abrasion **550.00**

Dresser box, inlaid, geometric designs in mixed woods on sarcophagus form box, fitted interior, 14" w, 7" d, 5-1/2" h, **$250**. Photo courtesy of Alderfer Auction Co.

Pencil, 10-1/2" l, swivel lid, carved from one piece of pine, old red paint **175.00**

Pipe

16-3/4" h, pine, red stain, molded bottom edge, one dovetailed drawer, two compartments with later, but finely cut, scalloped edges, three cut-out hearts and elaborately scrolled crest, back of drawer with scratch carved inscription "January 13, 1813, John _," minor repairs and small hole added for hanging **1,320.00**

19-1/2" h, 8-3/8" w, 5-1/4" d, carved cherry, painted red, metal lined int., old finish, CT River Valley, late 18th/early 19th C **6,000.00**

21-1/4" h, 6" w, 4-1/4" d, yellow pine, traces of red paint, old finish, southern New England, early 19th C, very minor losses, crack, minor insect damage to base **2,650.00**

Salt, 11-1/2" w, 7-1/4" d, 9" h, oak, dovetailed, lift lid, crest, divided int., old finish **120.00**

Dressing, Regency, English, c1800, ebony inlaid ebony, rectangular top, brass carrying handle, three small drawers over two deep drawers, ivory pulls, brass paw feet, 19" l, 8-1/2" w, 9" h, **$750**. Photo courtesy of Sloans & Kenyon Auctions.

Sewing

America, 19th C, mahogany inlaid, hinged lid, center inlaid oval reserve with shell motif, ext. with inlaid borders and corners, int. lid centered with diamond motif, lift-out tray with several compartments, minor imperfections, 12-1/4" w, 7-1/4" d, 5-5/8" h **1,000.00**

Chinese Export, 19th C, lacquered, Chinoiserie dec, scenic panels surrounded by mosaic patterns, Greek key border, brass bail handles on each end, int. with mirrored lid and fitted compartments, single fitted drawer, containing various sewing implements, minor wear and crackling, 17-1/4" w, 11-1/2" d, 5-3/4" h **475.00**

Spice, America, 19th C, pine, six drawers, turned wooden knobs, old surface, wear, 15" l, 7-1/2" d, 13" h **940.00**

Hat box, American, early 19th C, wallpaper, 14-1/4" w, 10 1/2" h, **$350**. Photo courtesy of Pook & Pook.

Storage

8-1/2" l, 6-1/2" w, 3-1/2" h, America, late 19th C, pine, painted red, floral and linear dec, int. paper lined **635.00**

18-7/8" l, 8-3/4" h, Massachusetts, early 19th C, ochre-painted pine, six board, dovetailed, thumb molded lid dec with flags, shield, and banner inscribed "Mass. Militia 2nd Regt. 1st B. 2nd D," partial paper tag tacked to lid inscribed "...K Rogers Boston," minor imperfections **1,150.00**

Tea bin, 24-1/8" h, 17-1/2" w, 25" d, dec of gentleman toasting lady, dec by Ralph Cahoon, oil on wood, with certificate of authenticity from Cahoon Museum of American Art **2,530.00**

Wall

7-7/8" w, 3-1/4" d, 15" h, attributed to New York State, early 19th C, painted, shaped top, open rect compartment with worn dark gray patina **2,760.00**

14" x 11-1/2" x 6-3/4", New England, mid-19th C, red stained chestnut, rect open box, two compartments, extended back board, round hanging loop, stamped initials "J. M." and several other scribed circles, wear...................................... **250.00**

Work, 12" w, 10-1/2" d, 7-1/4" h, European, marquetry inlaid mahogany veneer, pine secondary wood, slant top lid with pincushion covered in old burgundy velvet, paper lined int., till with lid, engraved strap hinges, old finish, repairs **275.00**

Salt box, Pennsylvania, early 19th C, walnut, hanging, scalloped lift lid, 11" w, 15-1/2" h, **$530**. Photo courtesy of Pook & Pook.

Spice box, Chester county, Pennsylvania, c1780, walnut, molded cornice, single paneled door, fitted interior with 12 drawers, 16-1/4" w, 20" h, losses and repairs, **$1,495**. Photo courtesy of Pook & Pook.

Cabinets

Apothecary, pine, yellow grain dec, 29 drawers over two open shelves, cut-out base and sides, bracket feet, open back, 62" l, 12" d, 54" h........................ **1,550.00**

Bar, Art Deco, walnut, sarcophagus form, two doors, sq top with drop-front cabinet on left, mirrored bar, small drawer on right between two open bays, 48" w, 21" d, 54-1/2" d **600.00**

Cellarette

English, mahogany veneer, dovetailed, rounded front lid, old refinishing, divided lined velvet int., six blown decanters (chips, stoppers missing), two wines, 10-3/8" w, 7-1/4" d, 8-3/4" h.................... **250.00**

Georgian, early 19th C, mahogany, inlaid boxwood, rect case and int., sq tapered legs, 14" w, 14" d, 24" h **950.00**

China, Victorian, late 19th C, oak, curved glass door and side panels, turned supports with vasiform elements, four shelves, 50" w, 67" h, **$1,800**. Photo courtesy of Joy Luke Auctions.

China

Art Moderne, mahogany, double doors, floral-carved relief panels, int. shelves, two drawers below, 45" w, 17" d, 62" h **2,000.00**

Arts & Crafts, Limbert, #428, trapezoidal form, two doors, each with four windows at top over one large window, orig copper pulls, sides with two windows over one, refinished, branded, 40" w, 19" d, 63" h **4,250.00**

Edwardian-style, curved glass sides, single flat glazed door, illuminated int., mirrored back, 42" w, 16" d, 64" h, pr **1,675.00**

International Movement, Gilbert Rhode, manufactured by Herman Miller, glass-sided china cabinet top over two doors with burled fronts, brushed steel pulls, refinished, glass doors and shelves missing, 36" w, 17" d, 58" h **800.00**

Victorian, American, c1900, shaped crest with lion's head and carved foliage, curved central door flanked by curved glass to either side, four ball and claw feet, 48" w, 16" d, 72" h **1,500.00**

Chinoiserie, two drawers, double doors, two adjustable int. shelves, walnut veneer with inlay and black lacquer, gilded detail, attached base with turned legs, 20th C, 43" w, 15-1/2" d, 63" h **625.00**

Corner, display, Georgian-style, c1880, mahogany and inlay, swan's crest, pair of glazed mullioned doors, int. shelves, pair of cabinet doors with marquetry, bracket feet... **2,415.00**

Curio, French

Bombé-shaped base, ornate, old gold repaint, carved rococo dec and gesso, beveled glass front, glass side panels, high scrolled feet, scalloped base aprons, 35" w, 15" d, 71-1/2" h **950.00**

Serpentine front, flowers around case, courting scene on lower case and door, metallic gold ground, ormolu dec around edges and arched crest, two removable glass shelves, worn red velvet covering bottom shelf, mirrored back, 33-1/2" w, 17" d, 74" h............ **850.00**

Corner, country, walnut and cherry, molded cornice, two glazed doors over two drawers over two paneled doors, wooden knobs, 56" w, 81-1/2" h, **$1,800**. Photo courtesy of Joy Luke Auctions.

Display

Biedermeier-style, poplar and burr-poplar, single door, outset molded cornice, three-pane glazed door flanked by similar stiles and sides, three mirror-backed shelves supporting shaped half shelves, block feet, 41" w, 16" d, 68" h **800.00**

Edwardian, late 19th C, rosewood, dentil molded cornice, two glazed doors and projecting lower section fitted with three drawers, sq tapered legs joined by shelf stretcher, 25" w, 15" d, 56" h **2,415.00**

Empire-style, gilt metal mounted mahogany, rect case fitted with arched glass door, stemmed bun feet, foliate cast mounts, 33" w, 16" d, 68" h **1,975.00**

Rococo, South Germany, 18th C, walnut, scrolling heavily molded open pediment, center gilt-bronze cartouche plate, two arched doors of fielded panels, mahogany figures of court ladies, basal-molded and conforming stand, shaped apron, cabriole legs, 46" w, 19-1/2" d, 71-1/2" h **4,750.00**

Corner, George III, late 18th C, mahogany, hanging, bowfront, hinged doors, green painted interior with four shelves, 40" x 27" x 18", **$850**. Photo courtesy of Sloans & Kenyon Auctions.

Filing, Arts & Crafts

American, c1910, golden oak, plain vertical stack, five drawers, orig brass nameplates and pulls **650.00**

Stickley, L. & J. G., Manlius, NY, re-issue, two-drawer, rect, hammered copper hardware, branded "Stickley," round yellow and red decal in int. drawer, wear to top finish, 21-3/8" w, 28" l, 31" h... **360.00**

Ledger, American, 19th C, walnut and mixed hardwoods, poplar secondary wood, dovetailed case, single paneled door, int. with divided compartments, later salmon paint, pr, 15-1/2" w, 12" d, 24" h.. **600.00**

Music, two door, full relief figures carved into front, 1920s, 48" h.................. **950.00**

Corner, Victorian, late 19th C, walnut, three graduated shelves supported on openwork scrolls, accented with split spindles, base with central cupboard door set with carved fruit, enclosing drawer, short bracket feet, 75-1/2" h, **$1,175**. Photo courtesy of Skinner, Inc.

Side

Arts & Crafts, oak, single door, orig sq copper pull, notched toe-board, refinished, 22" w, 22" d, 38" h **700.00**

Baroque, Dutch, oak, rect case fitted with three paneled doors, borders carved in shallow relief with scrolling tulip vines, stemmed bun feet, 82" w, 20" d, 53" h **1,380.00**

Biedermeier, late 19th C, fruitwood parquetry, rect top, canted corners, pr of cabinet doors enclosing shelves, bracket feet, 55-1/4" w, 24-3/4" d, 40-1/2" h............ **1,725.00**

Empire-style, late 19th/early 20th C, gilt bronze mounted mahogany, rect marble top, conforming case fitted with cabinet door, pull-out shelves, plinth base, 20-3/4" w, 16-1/4" d, 52-1/4" h **750.00**

Gothic-style, late 19th/early 20th C, oak, rect case fitted with two doors, upper door carved with gothic tracery, lower with linen-fold paneling, sides with linen-fold paneling, block feet, 22" w, 19" d, 52" h **450.00**

Louis XVI, Provincial, late 18th/early 19th C, oak, paneled door carved with urns, 41" w, 18-1/2" d, 73" h **1,380.00**

Oriental, black lacquer, hand-painted Chinoiserie dec on front, traces of dec on top, two doors, stepped arrow shaped feet, scalloped returns on three-drawer base, top 19th C, base 20th C, 32-1/2" w, 20-3/4" d, 31-1/2" h **425.00**

Regency-style, 19th C, cross-banded satinwood, serpentine top, case fitted with three small drawers, two cabinet doors, inlaid with stringing and ovals, 25" w, 12" d, 20" h **1,750.00**

Renaissance Revival, attributed to New York, c1865-75, ebonized, marquetry, and parcel-gilt, central elevated cupboard flanked by two similar cupboards, 75" w, 15" d, 64" h **4,900.00**

Display, Aesthetic Movement, America, late 19th C, carved mahogany, pair of glass doors, two drawers fitted in plinth base, 61" w, 23" d, 72" h, **$2,850**. Photo courtesy of Skinner, Inc.

Spice

Counter-type, poplar, old brown sponge dec, vertical stack with four sq nailed drawers with beveled edges, turned wooden pulls, chamfered side moldings, tongue and groove boards on sides of case, one drawer front split, 8-3/8" w, 17-1/2" d, 19-5/8" h................ **495.00**

Hanging, second half 20th C, rope twist top molding over geometric border flanking eight drawers, inlaid star and heart dec, porcelain knobs, inlaid with ivory and mixed woods, minor losses, 15" w, 8" d, 18" h **475.00**

Table, Continental, late 19th C, ebonized fruitwood, paneled rect, lifting handles to sides, hinged lid opening to mirror flanked by floral needlepoint, pair of front doors opening to int. fitted with series of small drawers, each fronted by silk

and metallic needlepoint and stumpwork panel of bird within metallic surround, drawers arranged around central compartment opening to further smaller drawers with foliate needlework panels, molded base, 18-1/4" w, 17" h.... **9,990.00**

Medallion display cabinet, 19th C, mahogany, fitted with shallow drawers, single paneled solid door mounted with a portrait cameo, 10-1/2" w, 10-1/4" d, 14" h, **$500**. Photo courtesy of Skinner, Inc.

Medicine, New England, early 19th C, hanging, flat cornice molding above hinged raised panel door, shelved interior, original brown-painted surface, imperfections, 21" w, 6-1/2" d, 31-1/2" h, **$500**. Photo courtesy of Skinner, Inc.

Vitrine

Edwardian, c1900, corner, inlaid mahogany, D-shape, two bow-fronted glass doors, sq legs joined by shelf stretcher, inlaid with checker banding throughout, 22" w, 51-1/2" h **800.00**

English, late 19th or early 20th C, mahogany, pine secondary wood, lift lid top, oval inlaid shell medallion, single pane door lower front, sq legs with chamfered backs, "X"-shaped cross stretcher, turned shelf, band inlay around apron, old refinishing, restored splint on lower shelf, chips to band inlay, 14-1/4" w, 14-1/4" d, 31-1/2" h **475.00**

Louis XV-style, late 19th/early 20th C, giltwood, boxed glass on each side, cabriole legs, 19" w, 17" d, 38" h **800.00**

Louis XVI-style, c1850, giltwood, outset molded rect top, frieze with beribboned floral garlands, front with glazed door with inset corners, flanked by fluted stiles, opening to two shelves, glazed sides, paneled skirt with swags, turned, tapered, and fluted legs with paterae, 27-1/4" w, 16" d, 61-1/2" h.............. **1,200.00**

Spice, eight small drawers, each with stenciled spice name, 11" w, 17" h, **$325**. Photo courtesy of Joy Luke Auctions.

Wall, hanging, Arts & Crafts, Liberty, softwood, overhanging top, side shelves, door stenciled with panel titled "Spring," pre-Raphaelite maiden with irises, refinished, some breaks to back panel, ivorine Liberty tag, 22" w, 8" d, 23" h **1,610.00**

Spool, Victorian, late 19th C, walnut, three long over six short drawers, 29" w, 22-1/2" h, **$460**. Photo courtesy of Pook & Pook.

Storage, Art Deco, Chinese, c1930, hardwood, rectangular, two doors opening on two sections, one with two shelves, 49" x 15-1/2" x 38-3/4", **$750**. Photo courtesy of Sloans & Kenyon Auctions.

Candlestands

Chippendale

Boston or Salem, MA, late 18th C, mahogany, carved oval tilt top, vase and ring-turned post, tripod cabriole leg base ending in arris pad feet on platforms, refinished, one leg repaired, 16-1/2" w, 22-3/4" d, 27-1/2" h **1,535.00**

Connecticut River Valley, late 18th C, cherry, old refinish, minor imperfections, 17" w, 16-1/2" d, 25-1/2" h **16,100.00**

Country, curly maple with bold striping, round one board top, ring turned column, well-shaped cabriole legs, pad feet, mellow golden refinishing, professional restoration to one foot, later bracing, 14" d, 25" h **825.00**

New England, late 18th C, tilt-top, walnut, circular molded top, vase and ring-turned post and tripod cabriole leg base, arris pad feet, old refinish, imperfections, minor repair, 17" d, 28" h **2,500.00**

New Hampshire, attributed to Lt. Samuel Dunlap, old refinish, birch, painted red, imperfections, 16-1/2" w, 16-1/8" d, 26-1/2" h............. **2,950.00**

Pennsylvania, late 18th C, walnut, circular molded top, turned birdcage support, vase and ring-turned post, tripod cabriole leg base, pad feet on platforms, old refinish, 20-1/2" d, 29" h **3,450.00**

Chippendale, attributed to England, 18th C, walnut, circular molded top, vase and ring turned support, tripod cabriole leg base, arris pad feet on platforms, possible height loss, 20-3/4" d, 22-1/2" h, **$450**. Photo courtesy of Skinner, Inc.

Chippendale-style, America, early 20th C, inlaid mahogany, round tilt top with small raised edge, circular inlaid center fan, reeded urn shaped column, tripod base, well carved claw and ball feet, orig dark finish, 23-3/4" d top, 28-1/2" h **225.00**

Country, cherry and maple, southeastern New England, late 18th C, circular top, vase and ring turned post and tripod

base, three tapering legs, remnants of old dark green paint, imperfections, 12" d, 25" h **1,150.00**

Chippendale, probably Massachusetts, late 18th C, carved mahogany, tilt-top, square molded diagonally hinged top on tapering vase and ring post, tripod cabriole leg base ending in elongated claw and ball feet, refinished, minor imperfections, 17-3/4" l, 17-1/4" w, 27-1/2" h, **$1,650**. Photo courtesy of Skinner, Inc.

Federal

Connecticut River Valley, attributed to, c1800-15, cherry, octagonal top with beaded edge, tilts on vase and ring turned post and tripod shaped leg base, old refinish, minor imperfections, 15-3/4" w, 25" d, 27-1/2" h **1,100.00**

Dunlap School, Antrim, New Hampshire area, late 18th century, painted, octagonal top with shaped underside, turned tapering pedestal ending in turned cap flanked by cabriole leg base ending in pad feet, Victorian polychrome dec with gilt highlight, minor imperfections, 13-5/8" x 13-1/2" top, 26-1/2" h **25,850.00**

New England, attributed to, c1810-20, stained cherry, octagonal top tilting over vase and ring-turned post, tripod base, curved legs, ball feet, worn stain, 21-1/2" x 17" top, 27-1/4" h **475.00**

Federal, New England, c1825, maple, octagonal top, vase and ring turned support, tripod base of shaped legs, old green paint with unfinished top, repairs, 14-1/2" w, 22" d, 28" h, **$3,820**. Photo courtesy of Skinner, Inc.

New Hampshire, early 19th C, birch, painted, sq top with rounded corners, urn shaped turned pedestal, high arched cabriole tripod base, pad feet, old red paint, imperfections, 13-3/4" w, 13-1/4" d, 26-1/4" h **7,475.00**

Rhode Island, late 18th century, cherry, circular top with scratch-beaded edge, ring-turned tapering column, tripod cabriole leg base ending in arris pad feet, old finish, minor imperfections, 17-1/2" d, 27-3/4" h **1,100.00**

Hepplewhite, America, tilt-top, mahogany, single board top with line border inlay, small arrow shaped inlays at corners, ring turned column with old black paint on every other ring, ball feet, lines of inlay down each saber leg of tripod base, ball feet, block replaced, two legs with restored breaks, 25-1/2" w, 21" d, 27-3/4" h **350.00**

Painted and decorated, Connecticut, late 19th C, cherry, octagonal top with molded edge, turned pedestal with urn shaping over high-arched cabriole leg base ending in pad feet, early black paint with 19th C yellow striping on pedestal and legs, minor imperfections, 15-1/4" w, 15-3/4" d, 29-1/2" h **4,025.00**

Primitive, 40" h, wooden, adjustable candle arm, dark brown patina, early 19th C **715.00**

Queen Anne-style, beveled edge square top, vasiform turned pedestal, three cabriole legs, 14" square, 26" h, repairs, **$350**. Photo courtesy of Alderfer Auction Co.

Queen Anne, attributed to Vermont, 18th C, cherry, circular top, vase and ring turned post, tripod cabriole leg base ending in arris pad feet on platforms, old refinish, 15-1/4" d top, 25-3/4" h **1,150.00**

Regency, English, mahogany, tilt-top, scalloped one board top, boldly turned column, tripod base, saber legs with beaded edges, old refinish, repairs and restoration to top, label underneath "From the summer home (1890-1929) Goshen, NY of Charlotte Beardsley (1852-1914) and George Van Riper (1845-1925), 24" w, 17-1/2" d, 28" h................... **595.00**

Windsor, pine, one board top with old patina and traces of finish on underside, circular platform at center, tapered column, old gold and dark brown repaint on tripod base, 16" x 16-3/4" top, 27-1/2" h **725.00**

Chairs

Arm

Adirondack-style, rustic twig construction, including small arms, green paint, roped seat, c1910 .... **2,300.00**

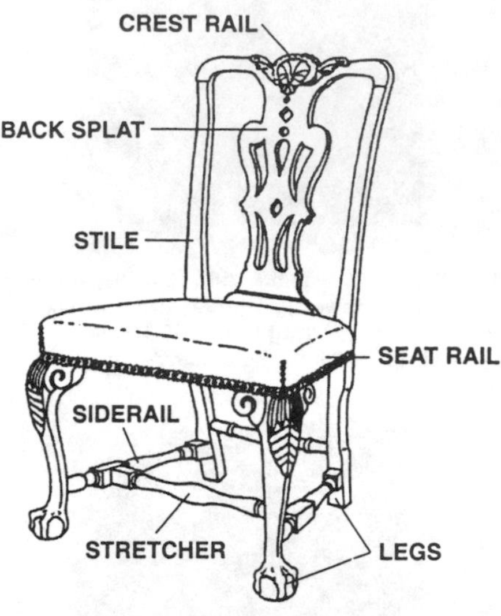

Typical Parts of a Chair

Aesthetic Movement, after Philip Webb's Sussex chair for Morris & Co., c1885, new natural rush seat, turned spindles, orig black paint, unmarked, 21-1/4" w, 19" d, 36-1/4" h **1,045.00**

Art Deco, France, c1925, giltwood, sloping U-form back rail ending in gently swollen reeded arm supports, D-shaped seat upholstered seat cushion, pr **15,750.00**

Chair, arm, Adams-style, c1900, pierced splat with swag motif, square tapering legs, painted black, all-over painted floral decoration, yellow striped silk cushion, **$750**. Photo courtesy of Sloans & Kenyon Auctions.

Art Nouveau, L. Majorelle, France, c1900, carved mahogany, horseshoe-shaped back rail, upholstered back, front of arm supports carved with pine cones and needles, continuing to form molded front legs with similar carving, dark green leather upholstery....................... **7,000.00**

Arts & Crafts

Indiana Hickory, twig construction, orig hickory splint seat, weathered finish, branded signature, 26" w, 17" d, 37" h **50.00**

Olbrich, Joseph Marie, Jugendstil, mahogany, small back panel inlaid with fruitwood floral pattern, inset upholstered seat, unmarked, good old refinish, 23-1/2" w, 19" d, 41-1/2" h **1,840.00**

Stickley, Charles, four back slats, recovered spring cushion seat, orig finish, remnant of decal, 26" w, 22" d, 41" h **230.00**

Stickley, Gustav, Model no. 2604, oak, arched crest rail over three horizontal back slats, shaped flat open arms, prominent front leg posts, offset front, back, and side stretchers, dark brown finish, red decal under arm, c1902, wear, 26-3/4" w, 26" d, 37" h......... **1,840.00**

Stickley, Gustav, Thornden, two horizontal back slats, narrow arms, 1902-04 red decal, replaced seat, orig finish, minor edge wear, 37" x 21" x 21-1/2" **3,105.00**

Chair, arm, Arts & Crafts, Limbert, Grand Rapids and Holland, Michigan, early 20th C, oak, four curved horizontal back slats, shaped arms with corbel supports, medium brown finish, marked with indistinct number, 31-1/2" w, 35" d, 32" h, **$1,880**. Photo courtesy of Skinner, Inc.

Stickley, Gustav, V-back, vertical back slats, replaced leather seat, orig faceted tacks, good orig finish, red decal, 27" w, 20-1/2" d, 37" h **1,045.00**

Stickley, L. & J. G., fixed back, drop arm, slats to seat, corbels, replaced drop-in green leather spring seat and back cushion, waxed finish, L & J. G. Stickley Handcraft label, 32-1/2" w, 33" d, 41" h......... **5,750.00**

Stickley, L. & J. G., spindled back, open arms, corbels, seat recovered in leather, refinished, unmarked, 24-1/2" w, 21" d, 38-1/2" h **690.00**

Banister-back, New England, 1760-80, painted, shaped crest flanked by turned finials over banisters and serpentine arms, over-upholstered seat, boldly turned front legs and stretchers, old black paint with gold trim, red velvet seat, imperfections, 17" h seat, 46" h.. **1,175.00**

Centennial, Colonial Revival, Queen-Anne Style, wing back, hardwood cabriole legs, turned stretcher, upholstery removed, old dark finish, 46" h...... **900.00**

Chippendale, Hartford, CT, area, late 18th C, painted, scrolling crest above pierced splat with center urn, old black paint with traces of yellow striping, 14-3/4" h seat, 40" h, minor paint wear **2,100.00**

Chippendale-style, English, 19th C, oak, mortise and peg construction, detailed pierced backsplat, shaped arms with scrolled handholds, slip seat with contemporary brown velvet upholstery, sq legs with chamfered backs, scalloped seat aprons, mellow refinishing, 19" h seat, 42" h.................................... **400.00**

Chair, arm, New England, c1740, banister back, carved yoke crest, **$575**. Photo courtesy of Pook & Pook.

Egyptian Revival, American, c1865, ebonized and parcel-gilt, upholstered scrolling back and seat, matching upholstered arm pads, sphinx head arm supports, claw feet, 39-1/2" h..... **8,050.00**

Empire-style, mahogany, rect padded back, padded arms, ormolu-mounted classical busts, bowed padded seat, sq tapering legs with brass caps, white striped upholstery **850.00**

Flemish-style, carved walnut, scrolled arm supports and front legs, turned stretcher base, large relief scroll front stretcher with pierced rococo leaves, burgundy velvet upholstery, refinished, glued split at back of arm, 18" h seat, 53" h... **550.00**

Chair, arm, Chippendale, English, c1760, shaped crest rail, upholstered arms with scrolled wood fronts, Chinese Chippendale legs, H stretcher, upholstered in green textured fabric, 19" h seat, 34-1/2" h, repair to both arms, **$800**. Photo courtesy of Alderfer Auction Co.

George III, late 18th C, in the French taste, giltwood, beaded oval backrest carved with anthemion, scrolled arms similarly beaded, serpentine seat raised on circular reeded legs **8,100.00**

Gothic Revival, America, walnut, old finish, reupholstered in damask, age cracks, 52-1/2" h............................ **200.00**

Louis XIV, early 18th C, fauteuil, giltwood, serpentine cresting, scrolled and reeded arms, over upholstered seat, scrolled legs joined by stretchers **2,990.00**

Louis XIV-style, Baroque, late 19th C, walnut, rect backrest, foliate carved arms and legs, X-form stretcher, price for pr **2,650.00**

Modern, Verner Panton, heart chair, by Plus-Linji, orig red fabric upholstery over metal frame, swivel chrome base, 40" w, 24" d, 36" h **10,350.00**

Chair, arm, Jacobean-style, caned back, 20th C, **$150**. Photo courtesy of Wiederseim Associates, Inc.

Neoclassical, Italian, late 18th/early 19th C, walnut, urn and wheat carved splat, down-swept arms, raised sq tapering legs, 34-1/4" h............................ **1,100.00**

Queen Anne

Middle Atlantic states, last half 18th C, arched crest with square corners, raked stiles, scrolled arms on vasiform supports, trapezoidal seat, frontal cabriole legs ending in pad feet, raked rear legs, imperfections, 16-1/2" h seat, 49" h **21,150.00**

New Hampshire, hardwood with old black repaint, molded and curved back posts with vase splat and carved crest, turned posts support molded and scrolled arms, turned legs, Spanish feet, turned rungs with bulbous front stretcher, old rush seat, some loss of paint to feet, 15-3/8" seat, 41" h......................... **4,125.00**

Renaissance Revival, attributed to Pottier & Stymus, New York, 1865, walnut, scrolled arms, upholstered back and seed, spherules on seat rail, 38" h **1,100.00**

Chairs, arm, International Movement, pair of Norman Cherner for Plycraft, molded plywood, walnut veneer, bentwood legs, one has Plycraft label, 24-1/4" w, 17" d, 30-3/4" h, **$1,150**. Photo courtesy of David Rago Auctions, Inc.

Rococo Revival, attributed to J and J Meeks, laminated rosewood, Stanton Hall pattern variant, high relief fruit carving and gadrooning on crest, fine pierced carvings around back, green silk upholstery, refinished, professional restorations to rear legs, 17" h seat, 42" h **3,500.00**

Rococo-style, Italian, late 19th/early 20th C, grotto, scallop shell seat, dolphin-shaped arms, rusticated legs **1,725.00**

Shaker, attributed to Canterbury, NH, c1835, birch and pine, concave rect back rail, turned stiles, four spindles, shaped seat, splayed turned tapering legs joined by stretchers, old refinish, traces of red stain, minor imperfections, 17" h seat, 24-1/2" h **600.00**

Victorian, George Huntzinger, NY, patent March 30, 1869, walnut, pierce carved crest, rect upholstered back panel flanked by turned and curved slats and stiles, low upholstered barrel-back, arm frame carved with classical heads, upholstered seat, pierced and scroll-carved front drop under seat connected to turned rung joining carved and turned front legs, ball feet, front leg stamped **2,100.00**

Chair, arm, Womb Chair, International Movement, early Eero Saarinen for Knoll, 1948, newly upholstered in Knoll red wool fabric on rare bronze frame, unmarked, this piece is from first year of production and pre-dates design of Womb ottoman by three years, 40-1/2" x 31-1/2" d x 36-1/2" h, **$2,600**. Photo courtesy of David Rago Auctions, Inc.

Windsor

Bowed back, New England, attributed to, c1790, bowed incised crest rail continuing to scroll-carved handholds, nine spindles and swelled incised arm supports, shaped saddle seat, splayed and incised turned legs joined by conforming turned stretchers, old refinish, minor imperfections, 18" h seat, 40" h.......................... **1,300.00**

Braced fan back, Pennsylvania, late 18th C, serpentine crest rail with carved terminals, five spindles vase and ring-turned stiles flanked by shaped incised arms with scrolled hand-holds, vase and ring-turned supports, shaped circular seat, splayed vase and ring-turned legs joined by swelled stretchers, 19th C rosewood grained paint with gilt striping, 17" h seat, 43" h **3,415.00**

Comb back, attributed to Philadelphia, PA, mixed woods, areas of old dark green paint, arched top with finely scrolled ears, nine back spindles, bentwood arm rain ending in shaped hand rests, D-shaped seat with incised line borders around edges, baluster and ring turned legs, blunt arrow feet, stretcher base, old pegged restoration on arm rail, 23-1/2" w, 17-1/2" h seat, 42" h **11,275.00**

Continuous arm, New England, c1815, nine-spindle back, saddle seat, stamped "J Ash," 36" h **1,100.00**

Continuous arm, Pennsylvania, early 19th C, nine-spindle back, bamboo turnings, 38" h **275.00**

Double bow-back, New England, c1800-15, maple, ash, and pine, incised crest rail above seven spindles, applied scrolled arm, writing surface to right, both with bamboo-turned supports on shaped seat, centering drawer mounted on underside, splayed bamboo-turned feet joined by stretchers, orig red-brown stained surface, imperfections, 16" h, 45-1/2" h **3,525.00**

Chair, arm, Naturalistic, America, early 20th C, rustic burlwood framework, cushion seat, brown weathered patina, 34-1/2" w, 25-1/2" d, 34" h, **$950**. Photo courtesy of Skinner, Inc.

Fan back, maple with some curl, hickory, shaped crest with flared ears, seven spindles, shield-shaped pine seat with incised rain gutter, baluster and ring turned legs, "H"-shaped stretcher, refinished, split in one rear post, 17" h seat, 35" h **450.00**

Sack back, America, painted, bowed crest over six spindles joining shaped arms with vase and ring-turned supports, incised seat, four splayed vase and ring-turned legs joined by H-form bulbous stretchers, old dark brown over red paint, minor imperfections, 17" h seat, 37-3/4" h **4,995.00**

Chair, arm, Renaissance Revival, elaborately carved mahogany, carved top rail with crest and finials, carved arm rests and supports decorated with figures and wings, embroidered tapestry upholstery, **$850**. Photo courtesy of Joy Luke Auctions.

Sack back, Lancaster County, PA, c1745-55 .... **14,500.00**
Sack back, New England, c1790, bowed crest rail above seven spindles and arms, vine and ring-turned supports, saddle seat, splayed legs joined by stretchers, painted yellow, later coat of salmon paint and green, 17-1/2" h seat, 40-1/2" h, price for pr **72,900.00**
Slough-back, English, George III, late 18th C, yew and elm, back with turned spindles, center vasiform splat framed by pair of flattened stoles surmounting serpentine crest rail, shaped arm rail on plain spindles, saddle shaped seat, cabriole legs, pad feet, repairs, refinished, 29" w, 15-1/2" d, 46" h **500.00**

Chair, side, dining, Queen Anne, Pennsylvania, c1765, walnut, serpentine crest rail, shaped splat, cabriole legs terminating in trifid stocking feet, **$2,185**. Photo courtesy of Pook & Pook.

Corner

Chippendale

America, walnut, rolled back rest with stepped detail, pierced harp shape splats, serpentine arm supports, scrolled handholds, molded seal frame, slip seat covered in worn upholstery, scalloped aprons, cabriole legs with relief carved shells on knees, claw and ball feet, old dark surface, restorations and replacements **1,870.00**
English, fruitwood, rolled crest, pierced back and turned supports with shaped handrail, sq legs with beaded edges, chamfered backs, "X" stretcher, slip seat with old rush covering, old refinishing, restorations at back rail and slip seat, 17-1/2" h seat, 32" h............................. **400.00**

Chippendale-style, 20th C, mahogany, shaped arms, openwork splats, rush slip seat raised on cabriole legs, claw and ball feet....................................... **575.00**
Country, New England, late 18th/early 19th C, maple, arms with scrolled terminals, shaped crest, scrolled horizontal splats attached to swelled and turned baluster forms continuing to turned legs, joined to similar stretchers, old surface, replaced rush seat, minor imperfections, 16-3/8" h seat, 30-1/2" h back.. **1,610.00**
Queen Anne, New England, walnut, shaped seat rail with turned stiles, vasiform splats inlaid with cartouche of Roman warriors, deep shaped skirt, sq legs, sq slip seat with needlepoint upholstery, replaced inlay, 33" h **550.00**
William and Mary, New England, 18th C, shaped backrest and chamfered crest, scrolled handholds, three vase and ring-turned stiles continuing to turned legs, joined to front leg by turned double stretchers, old dark brown paint, replaced wood seat, 30" h.......... **1,380.00**

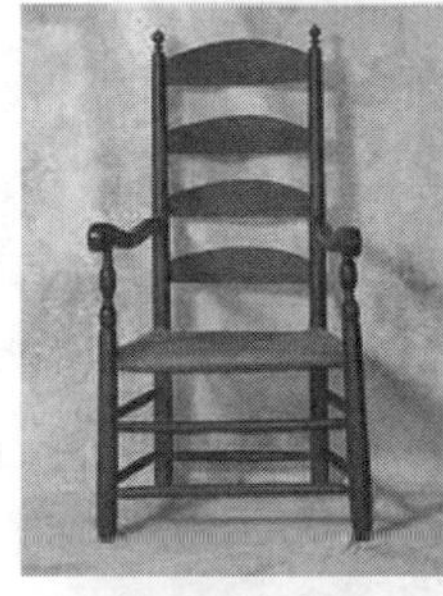

Chair, arm, Pennsylvania, c1770-90, four-slat ladder back, acorn turnings, splay legs, plain stretchers, remnants of black, green and red paint, 16" h seat, 42-1/2" h, **$450**. Photo courtesy of Alderfer Auction Co.

Chair, arm, William and Mary, c1710, walnut, straight back, baluster turned arm supports, block and turned legs joined by turned front stretcher, **$3,220**. Photo courtesy of Pook & Pook.

Dining

Arts & Crafts

Stickley, Gustav, ladder-back, four slats, cloud-lift aprons, drop-in seats recovered in leather, 37" h, overcoat finish, roughness to edges, some with red Gustav decal, set of eight **6,300.00**
Stickley, L. & J. G., arched vertical back slats, drop-in spring seat, covered in new green leather, good new finish, orig labels, 37-1/2" h, 17" w, price for set of four... **3,335.00**

Assembled set, English, c1800-60, turned ash and alder, open spindle back with two or three tiers of short turnings between flattened stiles, rush seat, tapered round legs, pad feet, bulbous turned front stretcher, plain turned side and rear stretchers, two-arm chairs, 10 side chairs, some with feet ended out, 19" w, 16" d, 38" h, price for set of 12 .... **1,875.00**
Biedermeier, fruitwood and part ebonized, black faux-leather upholstery, 36" h, restorations, set of four..... **2,500.00**
Centennial, Colonial Revival, Sheraton-style, mahogany, two arms, eight sides, shield back, reeded front legs, corner posts with carving of urns, needlepoint slip seats, 19-1/2" w, 17-1/4" d, 37-1/2" h **3,000.00**
Chippendale, two arm chairs, six sides, mahogany, four pierced ribbons on back, each with raised carved acanthus leaves, back, sq molded legs, stretcher bases, mauve velvet upholstery seats, 19" h seat, 39" h, price for eight-pc set **2,500.00**

Chair, arm, Windsor, continuous arm, nine spindles, saddle seat, reduced height, 15" h seat, **$550**. Photo courtesy of Wiederseim Associates, Inc.

Classical, New England, c1830-40, figured maple, concave crests above vasiform splats and rails, scrolled and raked stiles, caned seats with serpentine fronts, saber legs joined by stretchers, old refinish, 17-1/4" h seat, 32" h, set of six **950.00**
Eastlake, American, c1870, mahogany, one armchair, six side chairs, fan-carved crest rail, reeded stiles and stretchers, block-carved front legs, 35" h, minor damage, set of seven.................... **850.00**

Federal, Rhode Island or Salem, MA, c1795, mahogany carved, set of four side and matching arm chair, shield back with molded crest and stiles above carved kylix with festoons draped from flanking carved rosettes, pierced splat terminating in carved lunette at base above molded rear seat rail, seat with serpentine front rail, sq tapering legs joined by stretchers, over-upholstered seats covered in old black horsehair with scalloped trim, old surface, 16-1/2" h seat, 37-3/4" h **23,000.00**

George III, c1800, carved mahogany, yoke back, upswept reeded terminals, carved openwork vasiform splat with center pendant tassels over three flowerheads, green leather over upholstered seat, nailhead trim, fluted, molded, and chamfered front supports, H-form stretchers, swept rear supports, set of six **5,500.00**

George III-style, late 19th C, mahogany, anthemion pierced backrest, over upholstered seat, cabriole legs, claw and ball feet, set of six side chairs, associated arm chair **2,100.00**

Queen Anne-style, Southwood, c1985, mahogany, serpentine front and crest, acanthus carving at knees and returns, claw and ball feet, red silk damask upholstery with floral design, one leg with restored break, 17" h seats, 41" h, price for pr **995.00**

Regency, c1830, walnut, curved cresting, slip-seat and saber legs, set of eight **4,500.00**

Renaissance Revival, America, c1870, oak, two arm and eight side chairs, each with foliate and beast-carved cresting, paneled seat rail and turned legs, set of 10... **3,105.00**

Sheraton, Hitchcock type, two arm chairs, six side chairs, old red and black repaint, yellow striping, stenciled and freehand dec, replaced rush seats, 18" h seat, 33-1/2" h............................ **2,500.00**

William IV, c1835, mahogany, two arm and six side chairs, shaped slat, slip seat, paneled seat rail, reeded circular legs, set of eight **1,550.00**

Folding, Austrian, Thonet, late 19th C, bentwood, oval backrest and seat, scrolling arms and legs **600.00**

Highchair, child's

Ladderback, early dark green paint with traces of earlier green beneath, well-defined turnings on arms, three slat back, turned legs with blunt arrow feet on front, tapered rear feet, old worn woven tape seat, 20-1/2" h seat, 38-1/2" h..... **3,850.00**

Windsor, New England, 1825-40, rect crest above three spindles and outward flaring stiles, turned hand-holds on shaped seat, splayed turned tapering legs joined by stretchers, vestiges of stippled red and black paint, "M.H. Spencer, N.Y." in script on bottom of seat, 22-1/2" h seat, 31-1/2" h **775.00**

Dining chairs, Aesthetic Movement, American, late 19th C, carved mahogany, one armchair and nine side chairs, each with foliate carved cresting, overupholstered seat, molded square legs, **$4,150**. Photo courtesy of Skinner, Inc.

Ladderback, five-splat, attributed to Delaware Valley region, c1760, orig red painted surface **25,300.00**

Library, George III, c1800, mahogany and caned, pink upholstered loose cushion, 33-1/2" h...................... **2,070.00**

Chair, high, Windsor-style, bow back, Ohio, late 19th C, original red paint, black pin striping, underside of plank seat marked "J.R. MacCormick Mt Vernon, Ohio," 25 percent paint loss, foot rail missing, 24-1/2" h seat, 36-1/2" h overall, **$125**. Photo courtesy of Cowan's Historic Americana Auctions.

Lolling, Federal

Massachusetts, 1790-1800, mahogany, serpentine crest above half serpentine molded shaped arms, concave supports, over-upholstered serpentine seat on sq tapering frontal legs, raked rear legs, casters missing, minor imperfections, 16-1/2" h seat, 42" h **4,700.00**

New England, c1790, mahogany, reverse serpentine crest over upholstered back joining shaped arms and molded concave supports on four tapering sq legs, joined by sq stretchers, old refinish, imperfections, 17" h seat, 43-1/4" h **6,900.00**

Morris chair, Arts & Crafts

Stickley, Gustav, no. 332, slats to the floor under flat arms, orig brown leather cushions, orig finish, red decal, arms re-pegged and re-glued, 31-1/2" w, 36" d, 37" h......... **6,275.00**

Stickley, L. & J. G. paddle arm, long corbels, drop-in upholstered seat, orig finish, Handcraft decal, tops of arms overcoated, some looseness, 35" w, 38" d, 43" h.............. **4,315.00**

Potty, Queen Anne, country, corner, maple and pine, old red repaint, shaped crest and arms, three turned posts, heart-shaped pierced splats, slip seat with base recovered in green leather upholstery, turned legs, button feet, deep aprons, 16" h, 31" h **770.00**

Fauteuil a la Reine, Louis XV Provincial, c1760, beechwood, foliate carved backrest, voluted arms, serpentine seat, cabriole legs, **$1,500**. Photo courtesy of Skinner, Inc.

Savanarola, Renaissance Revival, Italian, late 19th C, folding, walnut, backrest carved with putti, armorial, masks and foliage; seat and arms carved with scale work, guilloche and foliage, X-form legs **480.00**

Wing, (Great Chair)

Chippendale, mahogany, serpentine wings, molded legs, stretcher base, old refinishing, restored splits in legs, upholstery partially removed, 16" h seat, 43-1/2" h **2,200.00**

Georgian-style, late 19th C, mahogany, padded backrest and scrolled arms, over-upholstered seat, foliate and shell carved cabriole legs, later red velvet upholstery, 47" l **800.00**

Writing, Wallace Nutting, comb-back, left-handed writing arm, branded signature beneath seat, 43-1/2" h 2,750.00

High chair, Louis XV, c1800, fruitwood, crest rail with flower carved cartouche, pierced splat with potted flower, square tapering legs with H stretcher, **$300**. Photo courtesy of Pook & Pook.

Side

Arrowback, 19th C mustard paint, tan, brown, red, and black dec of cornucopias on crest, leaves on back and front stretcher, incising around seat, brushed detain between, evidence of earlier green, bamboo-turned base, 15-3/4" h, 32" h **935.00**

Art Deco, Europe, wooden gondola backs, ivory sabots on front legs, cream striped fabric upholstery, pr, 25" h **2,000.00**

Arts & Crafts

Stickley, Gustav, three horizontal back slats, tacked-on leather upholstered seats, red decal inside back stretchers, partially refinished, 17" w, 36" h, set of five........ **2,990.00**

Stickley, L. & J. G., Fayetteville, NY, model no. 350, c1910, oak, three horizontal back slats, orig leather seat, wide front stretcher, double side stretchers, red handcraft decal, imperfections, 16-5/8" w, 18-3/4" d, 35" h **300.00**

Banister back

New England, mid- to late-18th C, painted black, shaped crest flanked by vase and ring-turned stiles, urn-form finials over three split banisters, trapezoidal cane seat, ring-turned frontal legs joined by double turned stretchers, minor imperfections, 16-3/4" h seat, 41-1/4" h........ **360.00**

High chair, Victorian, fold-down type, walnut, caned seat and back, **$225**. Photo courtesy of Dotta Auction Co., Inc.

New England, last half 18th C, painted black, shaped crest above four split banisters flanked by urn finials, vase and ring-turned stiles, trapezoidal rush seat, turned legs joined by double sausage-turned stretchers, imperfections, 17" h seat, 47" h **1,300.00**

New Hampshire, coastal, mid-to late-8th C, painted black, flaring fishtail carved crest over three split banisters flanked by vase and ring-turned stiles with ball finials, trapezoidal rush seat over ring-turned frontal legs joined by double turned stretchers, rear legs with old piecing, 17" h seat, 43" h.... **1,425.00**

Baroque Revival, ornate, applied carvings on scalloped aprons, pierce carved legs and stretchers, gold repaint, worn burgundy velvet upholstery, glued restorations, foot chips, 19" h seat, 39-1/4" h, set of six **1,300.00**

Chair, wing, Chippendale-style, molded legs connected by H-stretcher, cream trellis-pattern upholstery, **$750**. Photo courtesy of Sloans & Kenyon Auctions.

Biedermeier, fruitwood, lyre back, incurvate seat rail with rosettes, carved lyre splats, sq tapered legs, upholstered slip seats, repairs, replacements, 35" h, price for set of three **350.00**

Centennial, Colonial Revival, Chippendale-style, walnut, pierced ribbon back, molded seat frame, legs, orig dark finish, slip seat is period replacement with old rush covering, restorations to mortise joints of stretcher base, 17-1/2" h seat, 37-1/2" h **200.00**

Chippendale

Boston or North Shore, c1760-80, carved mahogany, leaf-carved lunettes and C-scrolls centered in shaped crests, raked molded terminals above pierced splats and over-upholstered seats, cabriole front legs terminating in scratch carved high pad feet, old refinish, 18" h seat, 37-1/4" h, price for pair..... **13,800.00**

Boston or Salem, MA, 1760-80, carved walnut, raked terminals of crest above pierced splat with C-scrolls, compass slip seat, cabriole legs, high pad feet, old refinish, restoration to stiles, 16-1/2" h seat, 38-1/2" h **2,185.00**

Chair, side, Arts & Crafts, early 20th C, oak, curved crest rail over eight spindles, leather seat with original tacks, cross and side stretchers, seat torn, 17-3/4" w, 16-1/2" d, 41-1/2" h, **$600**. Photo courtesy of Skinner, Inc.

Country, cherry, mortise and peg construction, serpentine crest with small raised ears at corners, two beads on either side of center, Gothic pierced back splat with tapered rear stiles, side seat rails tenoned through rear stiles, beaded edges on outer seat frame and down leg fronts, stretcher base, old refinishing, old pine slip seat covered in linen and later floral crewelwork, 16-1/4" h seat, 36" h **990.00**

English, walnut, molded crest, three scalloped back slats, sq legs with faint molding on corners, stretcher base, contemporary burgundy, light blue, dark blue, and teal upholstered seat, old refinishing, pegged construction, 19-1/2" h seat, 36-1/2" h back **200.00**

English, yew wood, pierced back splat with overlapping scrolls, relief carving around crest, sq legs with chamfered backs, stretcher base, light brown refinishing, contemporary flame stitch upholstery, glued restoration to stretcher, 19" h seat, 37-1/2" h **495.00**

Chair, side, Chippendale, America, possibly eastern Massachusetts or Concord area, birchwood, each with serpentine crest centering carved fan with flared ears, vasiform pierced splat, trapezoidal padded seat, sq legs joined by stretchers, remnants of faux graining remain, price for pair, **$2,500**. Photo courtesy of Sloans & Kenyon Auctions.

Massachusetts, Boston or Salem, c1760-80, mahogany, serpentine crest with molded and beaded terminals, scrolling pierced splat flanked by slightly raked stiles, trapezoidal slip seat with 19th C needlework cover in molded frame, frontal arris cabriole legs ending in claw and ball feet, joined to chamfered rear legs by H-form block, vase, and ring-turned stretchers, old surface, minor imperfections, 16-1/2" h seat, 37" h **4,700.00**

New York, 1755-65, carved mahogany, carved crest ending in raked molded terminals above pierced splat with C-scrolls, slip seat, molded seat frame, front carved cabriole legs ending in ball and claw feet, rear raked legs, old surface, imperfections, 18" h seat, 39-1/2" h **2,990.00**

Pennsylvania, 1760-80, carved walnut, serpentine crest with center shell, scrolled-back terminals, pierced splat, molded and shaped seat rail, front cabriole legs with shell carving, through tenons, rear rounded legs, ball and claw feet, old surface, red velvet slip seat, minor imperfections, 17-1/4" h seat, 40" h **6,465.00**

Rhode Island, c1765-95, mahogany, shaped and carved crest rail, pierced splat, raked stiles, trapezoidal slip seat, molded front legs joined to raked rear legs by sq stretchers, old finish, imperfections, 18" h seat, 38" h.................. **1,100.00**

Chair, side, Eastlake, each with carved back depicting bell and flowers, turned legs, green velvet pholstery, 16-1/2" h seat, 34" h, repair to side rail of one chair, price for set of four, **$300**. Photo courtesy of Alderfer Auction Co.

Chippendale-style, late 19th C, carved mahogany, foliate and C-scroll carved baluster splat, over upholstered seat, cabriole legs ending in scrolled toes, price for set of six **2,990.00**

Classical

Baltimore, painted and dec, scrolled crest above inverted vase-shaped splat, cane seat, dec front legs joined by medial stretcher, stencil dec, orig gilt classical motifs on black ground, 34-1/2" h......... **750.00**

Connecticut, 1830-50, tiger maple, curving shaped crests, curving front rail, Grecian legs, branded "A. G. Case," refinished, seats missing caning, other imperfections, 17-3/4" h seat, 33-1/2" h, set of six **3,200.00**

Middle Atlantic States, 1830s, mahogany veneer, curving veneered crests, similar horizontal splats, upholstered seats, Klismos-type legs, old refinish, 17-3/4" h seat, 33-1/2" h, set of seven........ **1,850.00**

New York, 1810-20, carved mahogany veneer, scroll back, beaded edges, horizontal splats carved with leafage and other classical motifs, slip seat, curving legs, old surface, 16-1/2" h, 32" h, set of six **5,200.00**

Decorated, Pennsylvania, worn orig tan paint, yellow, white, and red floral dec, green leaves, black line borders, scrolled crests, lyre shaped back splats, plank seats, turned and tapered legs, front stretcher, age splits, wear, 17-1/2" h seat, 33" h, price for set of four **550.00**

Chair, side, Edwardian, c1905, mother-of-pearl and brass inlaid rosewood, shaped backrest inlaid with foliage, serpentine seat, cabriole legs, **$235**. Photo courtesy of Skinner, Inc.

Federal

Massachusetts, early 19th C, carved mahogany, shaped crests and stiles above stay rails, beaded edges, seat with serpentine front, sq tapering molded legs, beaded edges, joined by sq stretchers, old surface, over-upholstered needlepoint seats, 17" h seat, 36" h, set of three....... **1,150.00**

Massachusetts or Rhode Island, c1780, mahogany inlaid, shield back, arched molded crest above five molded spindles and inlaid quarter fan, over-upholstered seats with serpentine fronts, molded tapering legs joined by stretchers, 17-1/2" h seat, 37" h, pr...... **5,475.00**

New England, attributed to, maple, rush seat, dec with polychrome flowers on yellow ground, 18" w, 16" d, 35" h, price for pr **500.00**

Chair, side, Federal-style, late 19th C, mahogany, pressed backs, French feet, seats upholstered in yellow striped fabric, price for set of six, **$2,300**. Photo courtesy of Alderfer Auction Co.

New Hampshire, Portsmouth, attributed to Langley Boardman, 1774-1833, mahogany, sq back, reeded on rest rail, stiles, and stay rail, over upholstered serpentine seat, molded sq tapering front legs, sq stretchers and rakes rear legs, refinish, minor imperfections, 18" h seat, 36" h.......................... **1,035.00**

George III, English, mahogany, ladder back, swelled crest rail over three graduated ribbon form pierced slats, broad over-upholstered seat in blue fabric, sq legs joined by H-stretcher, 23" w, 19" d, 36" h **500.00**

Gothic Revival, New York City, 1850s, mahogany veneer, trefoil pierced splats, curved stay rails, veneered seal rails, curving rococo legs, old refinish, 20th C upholstery, 16-1/2" h seat, 33-1/2" h, set of eight.................................. **6,900.00**

Hepplewhite, American, mahogany, shield back, rush seat **325.00**

Chair, side, Gothic Revival, attributed to New York, c1840, stained maple, each with shaped crest above four turned spindles, cane seat, serpentine front seat rails on sabre legs connected by concave stretcher, price for pair, **$750**. Photo courtesy of Sloans & Kenyon Auctions.

Hitchcock, old black repaint, gold stenciling of baskets of fruit on back slats, sgd on back of seat rails, ring turned front legs and stretchers, button feet, paper rush seats with some breaks, 16-1/2" h seat, 33-1/4" h, price for set of four **300.00**

Ladderback

Attributed to Shakers, South Union, KY, maple, hickory rungs, old worn woven splint seat, refinished, age splits, 15" h seat, 37" h **315.00**

Country, curly maple, three half turned slats on back, short turned finials on rear posts, orig work splint seat with some restoration, old mellow finish, 14-3/4" h seat, 32-1/4" h **250.00**

Neoclassical, Russian, c1810, brass inlaid mahogany, sloping backrest, three slats and over-upholstered seat, saber legs, set of four.......................... **1,200.00**

Plank, northern New England, 1830s, side, arrow-back, yellow ground, stencil dec with dark green and blue leafage and fruit, gold accents, shaped plank seat, splayed bamboo turned legs, paint loss, minor imperfections, 17-3/4" h seat, 35" h, set of five **1,725.00**

Chair, side, Renaissance Revival, attributed to John Belter, c1855, rosewood laminated, floral crests, intricate pierced curved backs, 40" h, price for pair, **$5,040**. Photo courtesy of Fontaine's Auction Gallery.

Queen Anne

American, early 18th C, burl walnut, shaped cresting, serpentine slat, slip-seat raised on shell carved cabriole legs, hoof feet, price for pr **1,650.00**

Country, maple and hickory, baluster and ring turned stiles, vase-shaped back splat, old woven splint seat, sausage turned legs, well-turned front stretchers, old refinishing, corner damage to edge of seat, 14" h seat, 39-1/2" h **275.00**

English, stamped "IF" on back, mahogany, urn shaped back splat, pierced top, cabriole legs, pad feet, block and turned stretcher base, tapered rear stiles, refinished, restorations, later paper rush seat, 18" h seat.............................. **350.00**

Chair, side, Queen Anne, Boston, c1740-60, carved walnut, shaped crest rail centering carved shell above vasiform splat, shaped stiles, compass slip seat, frontal cabriole legs with shell and bellflower carved knees ending in claw and ball feet joined to rear raking chamfered legs by block vase and ring-turned stretchers, refinished, repaired, 17" h seat, 35-1/2" h, **$2,115**. Photo courtesy of Skinner, Inc.

Massachusetts, attributed to, mid- to late-18th C, red stained maple, yoke back, craved beaded crest continuing to beaded stiles flanking vasiform splat on beaded stay rail over trapezoidal rush seat, block, ball, and ring-turned frontal legs joined by bulbous stretchers, old red stain with varnish, minor repairs and imperfections, 17" h seat, 41" h **425.00**

Newport, RI, 1750-75, black walnut, curving crest above vase-shaped pierced splat, compass seat, front and side rail shaping, cabriole front legs joined to rear sq tapering legs by block and vase-swelled side stretchers, swelled and turned medial stretchers, rear feet without chamfering, old refinish, minor repairs, affixed brass plaque reads "Ebenezer Storer 1730-1807," 17" h seat, 38-1/4" h **2,990.00**

Pennsylvania, Philadelphia, c1760-80, walnut, bow shaped crest rail, solid vasiform splat, scrolled ears, trapezoidal slip seat, plain cabriole legs, pad feet, patch repair, 22" w, 18" d, 40" h **2,750.00**

Rococo Revival, attributed to J & J Meeks, Stanton Hall pattern variant, laminated rosewood, high relief carved rose and shell crests, pierced carved back frames, button backs, urn medallions, round seats, finger carved front legs, green silk upholstery, refinishing, 17" h, seat, 40-1/2" h, price for pr **3,600.00**

Chair, side, dining, Centennial Revival, late, walnut, shaped crests with scroll and acanthus leaf, pierced splat, shell carved frieze, cabriole legs, acanthus leaf carved knees, claw foot, 19" h seat, 42" h, married set, five chairs are near matching with slight variations in carvings, four with straight front, two with oxbow front frieze, two with arms, repairs, **$1,265**. Photo courtesy of Alderfer Auction Co.

William IV, England, carved rosewood, foliate carved backrest with central diamond shaped upholstered panel, slip seat, leaf carved circular legs, c1835, price for pr.................................... **700.00**

Windsor

Birdcage, attributed to MA, c1810-15, red painted, birdcage, concave crest above seven spindles on incised shaped seats, bamboo-turned swelled and splayed legs

joined by stretchers, old worn red paint, minor imperfections, 17-1/2" h, 34-1/2" h **1,100.00**

Birdcage, small ink signature on bottoms of seat for "Fitch," one has later painted name, seven-spindle back, bamboo turnings, shield shaped seat with incised detail, refinished, small corner chip on one crest, edge of seat chip on other, 17" h, 33-1/2" h, price for pr **750.00**

Bow back, New England, late 18th/early 19th C, bowed crest over nine spindles, incised shape seat, splayed swelled legs joined by swelled stretchers, green over older black paint, surface and other minor imperfections, 19" h, 39" h **600.00**

Bow back, reproduction, well executed by L. E. Partridge, nine spindles, incised molding around bow, deeply scooped sets, boldly turned legs and stretchers, mellow light brown finish, surface wear, 18" h seat, 39-1/4" h, price for pr **550.00**

Chair, side, Windsor, bow back, America, early 19th C, mixed wood, one with added rockers, both refinished, price for pair, **$250**. Photo courtesy of Cowan's Historic Americana Auctions.

Brace back, nine spindles bow back, well shaped seat with incised detail around spindles, vase and ring turned legs, turned "H" stretcher, old mellow refinish, restorations, 17-1/2" h, seat, 36-3/4" h **385.00**

Butterfly, Pennsylvania, seven-spindle back, bamboo turnings, poplar seats, hickory legs and spindles, refinished, price for pr, one with crack in top rail **285.00**

Clerk's, attributed to New England, c1790, ash, shaped concave crest above seven spindles, vase and ring-turned stiles, shaped saddle seat, splayed vase and ring-turned legs joined by turned, swelled stretchers, old refinish, imperfections, 26" h, 41-1/2" h **1,430.00**

Comb back, mixed woods, arched crest with flared ears, seven-spindle back, turned arms, bentwood arm rail, shield shaped seat, vase and ring turned legs, stretcher base, light refinish, 17" h seat, 38-1/4" h **800.00**

Fan back, America, mixed hardwoods, arched crest with flared ears, seven spindles, shield shaped seat, baluster and ring turned legs, "H" stretcher base, old refinishing, 15-1/2" h seat, 32-1/2" h **440.00**

Fan back, New England, c1780-90, concave serpentine crest rail above seven spindles, vase and ring-turned stiles, shaped seat, splayed vase and ring-turned legs joined by swelled stretchers, old dark finish, 18" h seat, 37" h................. **1,530.00**

Chair, side, dining, Queen Anne-style, c1900, cherrywood, each with vasiform splat, compass seat frame enclosing upholstered slip seat, cabriole legs connected by shaped stretcher, two of shown from set of six, **$2,100**, Photo courtesy of Sloans & Kenyon Auctions.

Rod back, New England, early 19th C, bamboo carved crest and stiles flanking seven spindles over rounded seats, four swelled bamboo-turned legs joined by H-form swelled stretchers, dark brown stain, very minor imperfections, price for pr...................................... **600.00**

Slipper

Arts & Crafts, Gustav Stickley, spindled back, drop-in spring seat recovered in brown leather, orig finish, black decal, 17-3/4" w, 16" d, 37" h................ **1,150.00**

Victorian, c1875, rosewood, angular foliate carved backrest with urn form splat, over upholstered seat and circular turned legs **300.00**

Victorian, late, c1880, ebonized and bobbin turned needlepoint upholstery, foliate dec seat............................ **175.00**

Chair, side, Windsor, New England, late 18th C, fan-back, serpentine concave crest above vase and ring turned stiles, seven spindles, shaped saddle seat, splayed vase and ring turned legs joined by swelled stretchers, old black painted surface, 17" h seat, 37" h, **$940**. Photo courtesy of Skinner, Inc.

Wingback

Chippendale, country, birch base, old dark finish, sq slightly tapered legs with molded corners, H stretcher, reupholstered, glued split on one foot, 47-1/2" h **1,650.00**

Louis XV-style, late 19th C, old dark gold painted surface, butterfly wing, finely carved acanthus leaves and ribbon designs around frame, later velvet upholstery, 19" h seat, 47" h **700.00**

Modern, upholstered in athletic award letters mounted on Amish wool **4,200.00**

Vintage, red, white, and blue flag fabric covering.. **950.00**

Chests of drawers

Art Deco, Quigley, France, c1925, parchment covered, rect top, three tapering drawers, pyramid mirrored stiles, bracket feet, back branded, 44-1/2" x 35" **2,750.00**

Arts & Crafts, English, dresser, orig pivoting mirror with chamberstick shelves, glove boxes, copper repoussé panels, two drawers over one long drawer, orig medium-dark finish, unmarked, split to side, 42-3/4" w, 21-1/2" d, 64" h **1,725.00**

Biedermeier, c1820, maple, rect case fitted with two drawers, splayed sq legs, 36" w, 19" d, 31" h **1,725.00**

Charles II, oak, walnut, and snakewood **5,000.00**

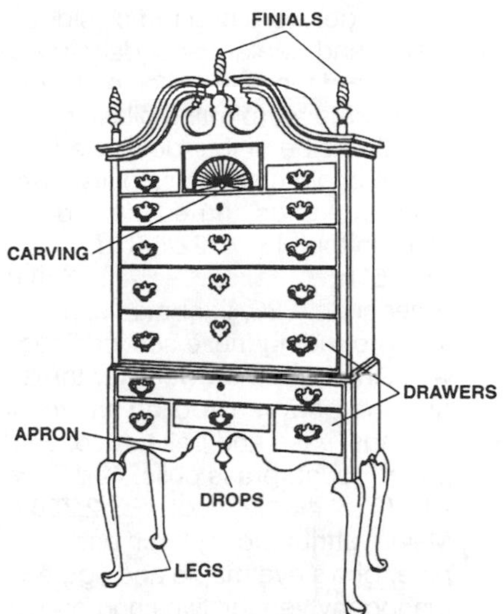

Typical Parts of a Highboy

Chippendale

America, cherry and cherry veneer, oval medallion "M. L. 1813" on front center of top, double line inlay around top and base, four graduated dovetailed drawers with overlapping edges, bracket feet, shaped returns, refinished, poplar secondary wood, late oval brasses, restoration, replacements, 40-1/2" w, 21" d, 38-3/4" h **1,200.00**

America, cherry, top with molded edge, four dovetailed drawers with beaded edges flanked by fluted corners, molded base, ogee feet with scalloped aprons, mellow brown refinishing, replaced batwing brasses and escutcheons, restorations, 41" w, 20" d, 37-1/2" h **2,200.00**

America, curly maple, solid maple boards with bold figure, pine secondary wood, cove molded cornice, six graduated dovetailed drawers with beaded edges, molded base, case dovetailed at bottom, high ogee feet with scalloped returns, old mellow brown refinishing, old replaced brasses, 39-1/4" w, 19-3/4" d, 55-3/4" h **10,450.00**

Boston, 1750-90, mahogany, block front, thumb-molded shaped top, conforming case, four graduated drawers, molded base, bracket feet, old refinish, replaced brass, rear foot missing, backboard inscribed "G. Russell" (George Russell, 1800-1866, born in Providence, RI, married Sarah Shaw, and died in Manchester, MA,) 33" w, 19-1/4" w, 29-1/4" h **46,000.00**

Connecticut, Calchester, cherry, two-board top with thin molding around edges, dovetailed case, four dovetailed drawers with overlapping beaded edges and restorations, double molding around base, dovetailed ogee feet with scalloped returns, mellow refinishing, replaced batwing brasses, pine secondary wood, 41-1/2" w, 18-1/4" d, 38-1/2" h **2,750.00**

Chest of drawers, Arts & Crafts, Gustav Stickley, designed by Harvey Ellis, gallery top, nine drawers, tapered trapezoidal legs, mushroom pulls, arched apron, original finish, red decal inside top right drawer, 36" w, 20" d, 50-1/2" h, **$8,100**. Photo courtesy of David Rago Auctions, Inc.

Connecticut, Litchfield, 1760-80, cherry, overhanging top, three scratch-beaded drawers, flanked by reeded quarter-engaged columns with lambs' tongues, ball and claw feet with shaped brackets, old refinish and color, probably original brasses, 38-1/2" w, 19" d, 35" h **7,050.00**

Country, curly maple, four dovetailed drawers, bracket feet, refinished, bottom backboard and feet replaced, brasses replaced, 41-1/4" w, 19-1/2" d, 37-1/2" h **2,450.00**

Massachusetts, Boston, 1770-95, serpentine, carved mahogany, overhanging molded serpentine top with blocked ends, conforming case of four graduated drawers separated by cock-beaded dividers, heavy molded base, intricately shaped bracket ending in ball and claw feet, some original brasses, old refinish, repairs, imperfections, 36-3/4" w, 20-3/4" d, 32-3/4" h.......... **116,000.00**

Massachusetts, Salem, late 18th C, serpentine, inlaid mahogany, overhanging serpentine top with end-blocking and string inlaid edges, case of four drawers with cock-beaded surrounds and quarter-fan inlays, molded base with fan inlaid drop pendant and front feet, old replaced brass, old refinish, imperfections, 38-3/4" w, 22-3/4" d, 33-1/4" h **21,150.00**

Chest of drawers, Chippendale, attributed to Connecticut, late 18th C, cherry, rectangular molded top, four graduated drawers, fluted quarter corner columns, bracket feet, 35" x 45-1/2" x 21", **$2,250**. Photo courtesy of Sloans & Kenyon Auctions.

Massachusetts, late 18th C, cherry, oblong top with serpentine front, case with four graduated scratch-beaded drawers, bracket feet, old brasses, refinished, minor imperfections, 35-1/4" w, 20" d, 32-1/2" h **4,115.00**

New England, southern, 1780-1800, maple, flaring molded cornice, case of six thumb-molded graduated drawers, molded base with shaped bracket feet, old replaced brasses, minor imperfections, 40-3/8" w, 18-1/2" d, 50-5/8" h............ **9,990.00**

New Hampshire, birch, orig reddish brown surface, pine secondary wood, deep cove molding around top, thin beaded edges around dovetailed case and drawer openings, five beaded graduated dovetailed drawers with orig batwing brasses, molded base, high bracket feet with finely scalloped returns, 37-3/8" w, 19-3/4" d, 42-3/4" h **4,950.00**

Pennsylvania, c1760-80, walnut, rect overhanging top with applied molded edge, case of four thumb-molded graduated drawers flanked by reeded quarter columns, ogee bracket feet on platforms, possibly orig brasses, refinished, 37-5/8" w, 22" d, 34-1/2" h **30,550.00**

Rhode Island, late 18th C, carved tiger maple, tall, cornice with dentil molding, case of seven graduated thumb-molded drawers, molded tall bracket base with central drop, top drawer with fan-carving, orig brasses, early surface, 38" w, 18-3/4" d, 63-3/4" h.......... **27,600.00**

Chest of drawers, Chippendale, middle-Atlantic states, attributed to Charleston, c1790, mahogany, rect top with thumb molded serpentine front and sides, conforming case with four serpentine drawers flanked by chamfered satinwood inlaid stiles, straight bracket feet with line inlays, brasses appear to be originalinal, 46" w, 36-3/4" h, **$23,000.** Photo courtesy of Pook & Pook.

Chippendale to Hepplewhite Transitional, attributed to the Chapius family, CT, cherry, bowfront, line inlay around two-board top, four dovetailed drawers with beaded edging, reeded quarter columns, ogee feet with boldly scalloped returns, molded base, orig oval emb brasses, drawer glides fitted through the backboards and pegged, restorations to feet.................. **17,160.00**

Chippendale-style, Eldred Wheeler, Hingham, MA, curly maple, dovetailed case, deep cove molding around top, five dovetailed drawers with beaded edges, batwing brasses, molded base, bracket feet with scalloped returns, labeled reproduction, 36-1/2" w, 19" d, 48-1/2" h **1,350.00**

Classical

New England, 1825-30, bird's eye maple, rect top, case with projecting cock-beaded bird's-eye maple veneered drawers, above three graduated drawers with flanking engaged vase and ring-turned spiral carved columns continuing to turned feet, opalescent pattern glass pulls, refinished, 41" w, 20" d, 47-1/2" h **1,530.00**

Chest of drawers, Chippendale, New England, c1770-90, original red painted finish, cove molded dovetailed top, five graduated overlapping thumb molded drawers, high scroll cut bracket base, original brass bale handles, oval keyhole escutcheons, faint chalk signature on rear boards of top drawer "? Alexander," 38-1/4" w, 18" d, 45" h, **$9,100.** Photo courtesy of Cowan's Historic Americana Auctions

Ohio, attributed to, 1830s, tiger and bird's-eye maple, backsplash above overhanging top, case with recessed panel sides, cock-beaded graduated drawers flanked by spiral carved columns and colonettes above dies, turned tapering legs and feet, shaped skirt, refinished, replaced glass pulls, imperfections, 46" w, 19-3/4" d, 57-1/4" h............ **2,000.00**

Eastlake, curly walnut, burl veneer, carved detail, scrolled crest, four dovetailed drawers, two handkerchief drawers, well detailed molded panel fronts, refinished, 39" w, 17-1/2" d, 46" h **750.00**

Chest of drawers, Chippendale, Philadelphia, c1770, small size, mahogany, thumbmolded top over case with four graduated drawers retaining original bail and rosette brasses, flanked by fluted quarter columns, spurred ogee bracket feet, retains an old dry surface, 33" w, 33" h, **$11,500.** Photo courtesy of Pook & Pook.

Empire

America, c1830, cherry, orig dark red flame graining over salmon ground on façade, worn orig red on sides, maple and poplar secondary woods, two-board top with old chip along back edge, serpentine pilasters on either side of four dovetailed drawers, old clear glass pulls, inset panels on ends, turned feet, age splits in top, 43" w, 22-5/8" d, 46-3/5" h **500.00**

America, c1830, tiger maple, rect top, protruding frieze section fitted with single wide drawer over three drawers between applied half-round turnings, vase and ball turned feet, period round brass pulls, 42-1/2" w, 21-1/2" d, 44-1/2" h............ **2,750.00**

Maine, attributed to, birch and pine, bird's eye maple and figured mahogany veneer, two short drawers over four long drawers, shaped back, ball feet..................... **1,760.00**

Chest of drawers, Empire, attributed to western PA or OH, butler's, cherry, curly maple and pine, mahogany veneering, high scrolled broken crest, interior of top drawer with three solid curly maple drawers, five pigeon holes, two flat paper slots, paneled ends, with half turned and carved pilasters on either side of lower dovetailed drawers, carved hairy paw front feet, turned rear feet, original dark surface, 45-3/4" w, 22-3/4" d, 57-3/4" h, **$1,100.** Photo courtesy of Garth's Auctions, Inc.

Federal

America, bowfront, mahogany, flame mahogany veneer, pine secondary wood, old replaced top with biscuit corners, four dovetailed drawers with applied beading, replaced brass pulls, rope twist carvings on front pilasters, high boldly turned feet, refinished, pierced restorations, one rear foot replaced, 40-1/2" w, 19" d, 36-3/4" h **770.00**

Baltimore, MD, c1810, mahogany veneered and inlaid, serpentine, top with veneered edge overhangs conforming case of four graduated drawers outlined in narrow banding and stringing with ovolo corners, shaped skirt, flaring French feet connected to shaped sides, replaced brasses, old refinish, imperfections, 45-3/4" w, 22-1/4" d, 38" h **5,585.00**

Connecticut, attributed to, c1790-1810, cherry, rect overhanging top with string inlaid edge, case with four scratch-beaded graduated drawers, bracket base, replaced brasses, refinished, minor imperfections, 37-3/4" w, 19-1/2" d, 35" h........ **4,415.00**

Massachusetts, Boston area, early 19th C, bowfront, mahogany veneer, figured mahogany top with lunette inlaid edge overhangs case of four cock-beaded veneered graduated drawers, serpentine veneered skirt flanked by flaring French feet, drawers include cross banded mahogany veneer bone inlaid escutcheons, orig brasses, old refinish, veneer losses, 41-1/2" w, 22-1/2" d, 35-3/4" h........... **24,150.00**

Massachusetts or New Hampshire, late 18th/early 19th C, mahogany and mahogany veneer, bowfront top with ovolo corners above engaged columns which have colonettes and reeding, flank cock-beaded drawers embellished with quarter-fan inlays, turned, swelled, tapering legs and feet, old refinish, imperfections, 43-3/4" w, 24" d, 41" h......... **4,420.00**

Chest of drawers, Classical, attributed to New England, c1825, grain painted, backboard with simulated tiger maple panels above case of deep drawer and painted panels above three recessed drawers flanked by half engaged polychrome decorated columns continuing to turned feet, sides with recessed panels simulating tiger maple, opalescent and clear glass pulls, 45" w, 19" d, 62" h, **$1,880**. Photo courtesy of Skinner, Inc.

Middle Atlantic states, 1815-25, mahogany, mahogany veneer, and cherry, rect, top above case of four graduated, cock-beaded drawers, upper drawer with cross banded mahogany inlay, shaped veneered skirt, slightly flaring French feet, refinished, replaced brasses, restored, 44-1/4" w, 19-7/8" d, 45-1/2" h **2,115.00**

New England, southern, c1820, maple, bird's eye maple, and birch, rect top with scratch-beaded edge, rounded front corners, four scratch-beaded graduated drawers flanked by rounded reeded stiles, vase and ring-turned legs, refinished, replaced brasses, minor imperfections, 41" w, 20" d, 36-3/4" h **1,200.00**

New England, c1820-25, mahogany, birch, and bird's eye maple inlaid, rect top with ovolo corners, case with four drawers with bird's eye maple panels bordered by mahogany cross banding with flanking quarter engaged vase and ring-turned, spiral carved columns continuing to vase and ring-turned feet, replaced brasses, refinished, minor imperfections, 37" w, 19" d, 42" h **3,300.00**

Chest of drawers, Federal, cherry, bird's eye maple veneer, six dovetailed drawers, one with mahogany crossbanding, paneled ends, turned legs, refinished, top and turned pulls replaced, 43" w, 19-3/4" d, 46" h, **$800**. Also shown aer pewter candlesticks, tumblers, teapot, and charger, Photo courtesy of Garth's Auctions, Inc.

New England, c1820-25, wavy birch, bird's eye maple, and mahogany veneer, overhanging rect top with scrolled backboard, case with four graduated drawers flanked by fluted pilasters, vase and ring-turned legs, replaced pulls, refinished, imperfections, 41-1/2" w, 20" d, 40-1/2" h **1,775.00**

New Hampshire, c1790-1810, mahogany veneer inlaid and birch, overhanging top with swelled front, inlaid edge, conforming case of four cock-beaded and string inlaid graduated drawers on base of flaring French feet joined by shaped inlaid skirt centering contrasting rect drop panel bordered by inlay, old oval eagle brass pulls, old refinish, restoration, imperfections, 39" w, 21-1/4" d, 37-1/2" h..............**4,115.00**

Portsmouth or Greenland, New Hampshire, 1810-14, bowfront, mahogany and flame birch veneer, bowfront mahogany top with inlaid edge overhanging conforming case, four cock-beaded three-paneled drawers, divisions outlined with mahogany cross-banded veneer and stringing above skirt, central veneered rect drop panel, high bracket feet joined by shaped side skirts, similar rear feet, turned pulls appear to be orig, old refinish, minor repairs, 40-1/4" w, 21-1/4" d, 39" h **28,750.00**

Rhode Island, c1800-10, maple, rect top, molded edge, case of four thumb-molded graduated drawers, valanced skirt joining shaped French feet, orig oval brasses, old refinish, imperfections, 42" w, 18-1/4" d, 38-3/4" h **1,765.00**

Chest of drawers, Federal, mid-Atlantic, c1820, figured maple, rect top, four graduated drawers, bracket feet, 37" x 41-1/4" x 19-1/2", **$2,500**. Photo courtesy of Sloans & Kenyon Auctions.

George III, 19th C, cross banded mahogany, serpentine, four graduated drawers, bracket feet, 36" w, 22-1/2" d, 31-1/2" h **3750.00**

George III-style, 19th C, mahogany, serpentine-front, thumb-molded top above four graduated and cock-beaded drawers, channel-carved bracket feet, 43" w, 24" d, 43" h **4,415.00**

Hepplewhite, America

Cherry, cove molded cornice, nine dovetailed drawers with beaded edges, orig brasses with areas of gilding remaining, marked "H.J." under bale, lock escutcheons, row of top three smaller drawers have wooden spring latches underneath, French feet with scalloped returns, strip of beading around base of lower case, old mellow refinishing, pine secondary wood, 42-1/4" w, 21" d, 63" h **7,500.00**

Chest of drawers, International Movement, George Nelson for Herman Miller, "Thin-Edge" rosewood veneer, five graduated drawers next to cabinet door of rare book-matched veneer, all with conical white pulls on brushed chrome tapering legs, Herman Miller foil label, 55-3/4" l, 18-1/2" d, 40-3/4" h, **$5,500**. Photo courtesy of David Rago Auctions.

Cherry, variegated band inlay around two-board top, five dovetailed drawers with beaded edges, and line border inlay around fronts, chevron band inlay around base, French feet, scalloped front apron, old refinishing, replaced eagle brasses, old repairs, 40" w, 20-1/4" d, 43-1/2" h **2,000.00**

Mahogany and figured mahogany veneer, bowfront, poplar and pine secondary woods, four dovetailed drawers with beaded edges, orig emb eagle brasses, high tapered legs, veneer restorations, minor chips, 45-1/2" w, 22-3/4" d, 39-1/2" h **700.00**

Chest of drawers, George III, c1800, inlaid mahogany, bowfront crossbanded top, conforming case fitted with two short over three long drawers, high bracket feet, 40" w, 19" d, 39" h, **$1,300**. Photo courtesy of Skinner, Inc.

Queen Anne, Southeastern New England, c1700, painted oak, cedar, and yellow pine, rect top with applied edge, case of four drawers each with molded fronts, chamfered mitered borders, separated by applied horizontal moldings, sides with two recessed vertical molded panels above single horizontal panel, base with applied molding, four turned ball feet, old red paint, minor imperfections, 37-3/4" w, 20-1/2" w, 35" h **26,450.00**

Renaissance Revival, c1870, rosewood, marble top, carved lion heads and leaf scrolls, three graduated drawers, 88" h, price for pr **17,600.00**

Sheraton, cherry, one board top, three dovetailed drawers with beaded edges, burled veneer fronts, inset panels around sides of case, finely turned legs, small ball feet, old pressed glass pulls, old mellow varnished finish, poplar and pine secondary woods, 18-5/8" w, 15-1/4" d, 29" h.. **1,890.00**

Sheraton to Empire, transitional, cherry, simple arched back splash, four dovetailed drawers with beaded edges and orig turned wood pulls, thin applied molding around base, boldly turned feet, old dark varnished finish, pieced restoration to one drawer lip, 42-3/4" w, 20-1/2" d, 45-3/4" h **700.00**

Victorian, American, poplar, mahogany veneer facade, serpentine top drawer, two serpentine stepback drawers, five dovetailed drawers, applied beading, worn finish, 40" w, 19-3/4" d, 47" h **330.00**

Chest of drawers, Italian, ornately inlaid, three full drawers, all-over flowers, leaves, and scrolls, inlaid banding, oval panel on top and center drawer fronts, one panel decorated with inlaid and painted landscape with figures, chariot, and buildings, one with landscape of musicians and dancers, two round side panels decorated with inlaid and painted landscape with figures, square tapered legs, 47" w, 22-1/2" d, 39" h, **$2,200**. Photo courtesy of Joy Luke Auctions.

William and Mary

American, burl veneer, bachelor's, five dovetailed drawers, pull-out shelf, worn finish, veneer damage, replaced base molding, turned feet, and backboards, orig brasses, 30" w, 19" d, 35" h **1,980.00**

Chest of drawers, Sheraton, Massachusetts, c1825, mahogany, bowfront, arched backsplash with applied brass rosettes above four drawers flanked by rope carved three-quarter columns, scalloped skirt resting on turned feet, 41-1/4" w, 44-1/2" h, **$1,610**. Photo courtesy of Pook & Pook.

Southern Massachusetts or Rhode Island, tiger maple, graduated drawer construction, two over four drawers, applied moldings to top and bottom, turned turnip feet, old grunge finish, three escutcheon plates present, rest of hardware missing, some repair, 36-1/4" w, 18-1/4" d, 48" h **2,950.00**

William IV-style, mahogany, canted rect top, open int., bulbous turned legs, 20" w, 13-1/2" d, 22" h **1,200.00**

Chests of drawers, other

Apothecary, painted blue, 32 drawers, 96" l.. **2,900.00**

Bachelor, late George III, English, early 19th C, mahogany, rect top with molded edge, slide, four graduated cock-beaded drawers, bracket feet, veneer damage, restoration to feet, 37" l, 33-1/2" h **2,750.00**

Campaign, mahogany, pine secondary wood, brass trim, dovetailed case, int. with lift-out tray, one dovetailed drawer, some shrinkage to lid, 30-3/4" w, 18-1/4" d, 19" h **385.00**

Chamber, Federal, attributed to the Seymour Workshop, Boston, c1915, mahogany inlaid, rect top with inlaid edge overhangs case with single tripartite drawer above six smaller drawers flanking central cabinet on arched inlaid skirt, four turned reeded and tapering legs, similar arched side skirts, upper drawer with oval central stringing reserve, all drawers are outlined in ebonized inlay, missing dressing mirror from int. drawer,

minor imperfections, 44-3/4" w, 19-1/2" d, 34-1/4" h **42,550.00**

Chest on Chest

Chippendale, Dunlap School, NH, c1770-80, cove molded cornice over case of four thumb-molded long drawers, upper with five short drawer façade centrally carved with pinwheel and fan motif, three graduated drawers below, lower case of four graduated long drawers, four short cabriole legs ending in ball and claw feet, centering central fan-carved drop, refinished, some orig red staining, possibly orig brasses, minor imperfections **18,800.00**

George III, c1790, mahogany, upper section with dentil-molded cornice, fitted with three short over three long drawers, lower section fitted with three graduated long drawers, bracket feet, 43" w, 21" d, 67" h **7,000.00**

Queen Anne

Salem, MA, attributed to, c1740-60, tiger maple, upper case with molded cornice, five graduated thumb-molded drawers, lower case with one long drawer with two drawer façade, and one long drawer with three short drawer façade, centrally caved fan, four arris cabriole legs with high pad feet on platforms, joined by cyma-curved skirt centering scrolled drops, old brasses, old refinish, minor imperfections, 38-3/4" w, 19-1/2" d, 73-3/4" h........... **16,450.00**

Chest of drawers, other, bonnet cupboard, oak, back splash, scalloped top, two half drawers, three full drawers, some applied dec, 34" w, 54" h, **$325.** Photo courtesy of Joy Luke Auctions.

Southern NH, late 19th C, maple, upper case with cove molded cornice, five graduated thumb-molded drawers, lower case with three graduated drawers, valanced frame joining four short cabriole legs on high pad on platform feet, old refinish, replaced brasses, drawers with chalk and pencil inscriptions, vestiges of old red paint, minor imperfections, 40-1/2" w, 20" d, 80" h **11,750.00**

Chest on Frame

Georgian, 18th C, oak, rect case, two short and three long drawers, base with three short drawers, cabriole legs ending in pointed pad feet, 40" w, 18" d, 51-1/2" h **2,500.00**

Queen Anne, Connecticut, 1740-70, painted, flaring cornice with cove molding, case of thumb-molded drawers, arranged in two over four graduating pattern, frame with vigorously scrolling front and side skirts joined to cabriole legs with arris knees, arris disc feet, old red repaint, imperfections, 40" w, 23-1/4" d, 63-1/2" h............ **9,200.00**

Queen Anne-style, English, walnut and burl veneer, mahogany secondary wood, case with four dovetailed drawers, brass teardrop pulls, cabriole legs, duck feet, 20th C, 19-1/4" x 33-1/2" base, 38-1/2" h **825.00**

Coffer, oak

Chip carved, three panels across front with incised dates and initials "1648, I C," two inset panels on ends, old dark finish, hinges added to early ones for strength, 50-1/2" w, 22" d, 25-1/2" h.................. **2,200.00**

Inlaid, three panels on front, two with arched tombstone tops, other sq, all with variegated flowering plant inlay, divided by relief carved floral moldings, dark refinishing, top hinged at middle at later date, drawer and some base boards replaced, panel moldings incomplete, 63" w, 23" d, 29-1/2" h **700.00**

Commode

Biedermeier, north Germany or Scandinavia, c1840, pearwood, stepped rect top, three drawers, shaped apron, 35" w, 20" d, 31" h **2,000.00**

Directorie, c1800, fruitwood, rect to, two long drawers, sq tapered legs, restored, 36-1/2" w, 32" h **2,500.00**

French Provincial, Neoclassical, early 19th C, gray and white mottled marble top, conforming case fitted with three drawers, sq tapered legs, 44" w, 21" d, 34-1/2" h......... **2,300.00**

Louis XV-style, 19th C, marquetry, gilt bronze mounts, bombe, serpentine molded edge marble top, exotic wood floral marquetry on rosewood panels, mahogany cross banding, two drawers, legs ending in scroll and cabochon cast sabots, 53" w, 22" d, 33" h.............. **1,350.00**

Victorian, walnut, carved pilasters, open scrolling and leaves, three graduated drawers with fruit carved pulls, light refinishing, back splash missing, 36" w, 19" d, 32" h ... **400.00**

Credenza

Chippendale-style, Kittinger, mahogany and mahogany veneer, oak secondary wood, four dovetailed drawers down left, smaller center drawer with cabinet below, longer drawer over open compartment flanking on right with adjustable shelf, molded edge and base trip, branded label, emb metallic emblem in drawer, 81-1/2" l, 19-1/2" d, 30" h **900.00**

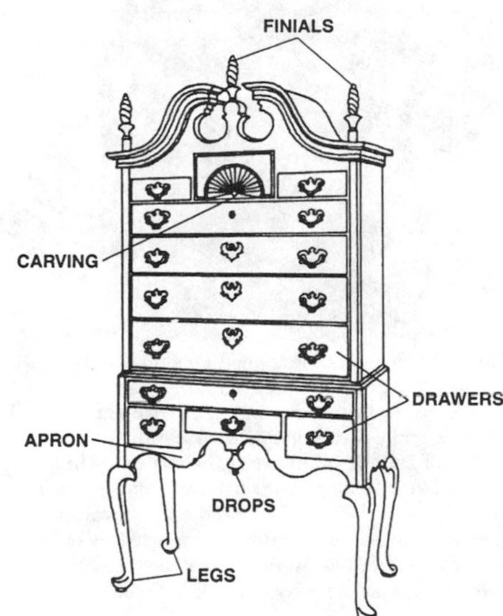

Typical Parts of a Highboy

Highboy

Chippendale, associated with John Goddard and Job Townsend, Newport, RI, 1760-80, carved mahogany, enclosed scrolled pediment centering fluted plinth surrounded by urns and flame finials above two applied plaques over two short and three long graduated thumb molded drawers, set into lower case of one long and three short drawers above cyma curved skirt, centered carved shell, frontal cabriole legs ending in ball and claw feet, similar rear legs ending in pad feet, old replaced brasses, refinished, repairs, 39" w, 20-1/2" d, 84" h **36,550.00**

Chippendale-style, America, late 19th/early 20th C, mahogany, broken arch pediment, flame finials, reeded quarter columns at corners, inset panels on either end of top, eight dovetailed drawers with brass pulls, gadrooning around base and edges of base and lower section, cabriole legs with scrolled returns, raised acanthus leaf carvings, claw and ball feet, old reddish brown finish, 48-1/2" w, 24-1/4" d, 81" h.............. **1,200.00**

Chest of drawers, other, chest on chest, Chippendale, Philadelphia, c1770, figured mahogany, broken arch pediment with carved rosettes and c-scroll lattice work centering basket of fruit finial above two short over three long drawers, bottom one with fall front enclosing fitted interior, flanked by fluted quarter columns, base with three long drawers supported by ogee bracket feet, 41-3/4" w, 93" h, feet restored, **$16,100**. Photo courtesy of Pook & Pook.

Queen Anne

America, maple, curly maple, and walnut, eight drawer fronts and façade have relief scrolled foliage, deeply scalloped aprons, cabriole legs with claw and ball feet, dark refinishing, replaced batwing brasses, restorations, base is old replacement, 46" w, 23-1/2" d, 85" h **4,400.00**

Connecticut, attributed to, c1760-80, cherry and maple, broken arch pediment with three flame finials on fluted plinths, upper case with fan carved thumb-molded short drawer flanked by two shaped short drawers, four graduated long drawers, lower case with long drawer over two short drawers flanking fan carved drawer, carved scrolling skirt joining four cabriole legs, pad feet, replaced brasses and finials, old refinish, repairs and imperfections, 38-1/4" w, 19" d, 86" h....... **24,675.00**

Dunlap School, NH, c1770-80, carved maple, cove-molded cornice over upper case of five graduated long drawers, lower case of three graduated thumb-molded long drawers, upper and lowermost drawers each fan carved, cyma-curved skirt centering scrolling drops, joining four cabriole legs with shaped returns, pad feet on platforms, dark stained surface, possibly orig brasses, minor imperfections, chalk inscriptions on drawer backs, 39-1/4" w, 21-1/2" d, 78-3/4" h **14,100.00**

Massachusetts or southern New Hampshire, 1760-80, tiger maple, flaring cornice above four thumb-molded drawers on lower case of one long drawer and three small drawers, the central one with fan carving above three flat-headed arches, cabriole legs, high pad feet, replaced brasses, refinished, minor imperfections, 37-3/4" w at mid molding, 19-5/8" d at mid-molding, 72" h **16,450.00**

North Shore, MA, 18th C, maple, flaring cove-molded cornice with concealed drawer above four thumb-molded graduated drawers in upper case over mid-molding, two long drawers, lower case visually divided into three drawers centering by carved fan over cyma-curved side skirts, cabriole legs and high pad feet, old surface, old brasses, imperfections, 35-1/2" w, 17-5/8" d, 71" h **31,050.00**

Rhode Island, c1730-60, attributed to Abram Utter, tiger maple and cherry, top section with flat molded cornice, case of two thumb-molded short drawers, three long drawers, lower section with projecting molding above case of central thumb-molded short drawer flanked by deeper drawers, four arris cabriole legs, pad feet, all joined to deeply valanced skirt with applied cock beading and two turned drop pendants, replaced brasses, old refinish, minor imperfections, 37" w, 19-1/4" d, 63-3/4" h **29,375.00**

William and Mary-style, 18th C, cross banded walnut, upper section with two short over three long drawers, base with three drawers on trumpet turned legs, 40" w, 21" d, 69" h **1,850.00**

Chest of drawers, other, high chest, Chippendale, Pennsylvania, c1775, ogee cornice above Greek key molding, nine drawers flanked by fluted quarter columns, spurred ogee bracket feet, 39" w, 63-3/4" h, **$12,650**. Photo courtesy of Pook & Pook.

Linen

Modern, George Nakashima, cherry, fabric behind sliding doors, hutch top with two sliding doors, base with two doors, small feet, 85" w, 80" h **11,750.00**

Chest of drawers, other, high boy, Queen Anne, two pieces, flat top, birch and pine, mortise and peg and rosehead nail construction, cove molded cornice, 11 dovetailed drawers, one hidden inside cornice, beaded edges, double-waist mouldings, scalloped aprons with small acorn shaped drops, cabriole legs, pad feet, old batwing brasses, old deep red wash, 40" w, 19-1/2" d, 71" h, **$33,000**. Photo courtesy of Garth's Auctions, Inc.

Liquor chest

Early 19th century, mahogany veneer, chest with brass swing handles opens to reveal compartmented int., 12 blown molded wine and spirit bottles, each with inscribed paper labels and dec with gilt flowers, bowknots, and borders about the neck and shoulders, lift out tray fitted with tumblers, funnel and stemware with similar gilt decoration, one tumbler cracked, some veneer loss, 17" w, 12-1/2" d, 11-1/2" h **1,410.00**

Lowboy

Chippendale-style, English, 19th C, mahogany, oak secondary wood, molded one-board top, three dovetailed drawers with beaded edges, scalloped aprons, sq molded legs with chamfered backs, refinished, replaced batwing brasses, 30-1/4" w, 18-1/4" d, 28-3/4" h **800.00**

William and Mary, walnut and pine, early reddish brown finish, one board top with figured veneer, replaced drops **5,225.00**

Chest of drawers, other, linen press, New Jersey, c1790, applewood, upper section with two raised panel doors flanked by fluted pilasters, base with two short and two long drawers resting on straight bracket feet, repairs to cornice, 45-1/2" w, 76-1/2" h, **$7,475**. Photo courtesy of Pook & Pook.

Mule

Chippendale, country, attributed to New England, pine, cove molding around lid and base, two overlapping dovetailed drawers below two false drawer fronts, high dovetailed bracket feet with stylish scroll returns, old reddish brown finish, old replaced batwing brasses and escutcheons, wrought iron staple hinges, restorations to lid and feet, hand painted inscription on back "R. Hathaway, Hudson, Mich," later railway express labels from 1950s, 40-3/4" w, 18-1/2" d, 42-1/4" h **1,350.00**

Queen Anne, poplar, mellow old red paint, one board top with thin cove molded trim, two dovetailed drawers, molded base, high bracket feet with scalloped returns, replaced batwing brasses and escutcheon plates, wrought "T" head nails, 41" w, 18-1/4" d, 41-1/2" h **3,850.00**

Spice

Ohio, walnut, poplar secondary wood, mortised and paneled front door, small brass pull, three drawers with orig turned walnut pulls, turned feet, 14-1/2" w, 12-1/4" d, 18-3/4" h **2,400.00**

Pennsylvania, 1780-1800, walnut, dovetailed, cove-molded cornice, raised panel hinged door, opens to int. of 11 small drawers, brass pulls, molded base, old surface, 15-1/2" w, 11" d, 18-1/4" h **14,950.00**

Chest of drawers, other, tall chest, Federal, attributed to New Hampshire, c1800, birch, pine top with cove-molded cornice, six graduated drawers, shaped apron, sides extend to form bracket feet, originally painted red, 52" x 40" x 19-3/4", **$2,500**. Photo courtesy of Sloans & Kenyon Auctions.

Tall

Federal, New England, late 18th C, tiger maple, cove molded top, case with six thumb-molded drawers, central fan carved drop pendant flanked by high bracket feet, orig brasses, old refinish, repairs, 41" w, 54-5/8" h **8,625.00**

Chest of drawers, other, tall chest, Queen Anne, Chester County, Pennsylvania, c1740, "Octorara," walnut, ogee cornice, three over two short drawers over four long drawers, removable Spanish feet with incised C-scroll returns, old dry surface, original plate brasses, 37-1/2" w, 61-1/2" h, **$21,850**. Photo courtesy of Pook & Pook.

Wardrobe

Classical, Mid Atlantic States, 1840, mahogany veneer, two recessed panel doors, similar sides, int. with veneered drawers, base with platform feet, small int. drawers added, 65" w, 26" d, 79-1/2" h **3,200.00**

Cradle, Victorian, stained pine, 30" x 41" x 20", **$175**. Photo courtesy of David Rago Auctions, Inc.

Cradles

Chippendale-style, birch, canted sides, scalloped headboard, turned posts and rails, refinished, 37-1/2" l **400.00**

Country

America, Tiger maple, dovetailed, heart cut-outs, large rockers, 36" l, 26" w, 16" h **675.00**

Pennsylvania, late 18th C, dovetailed, refinished curly maple,

cutout hearts, age cracks and shrinkage, 41" l...................... **550.00**
Eastlake, 1875, walnut, paneled headboard, footboard, and sides, scrolling crest above short turned spindles, platform support, orig finish, dated........................... **495.00**
Rustic, twig construction, rocker base, unsigned, 33" l, 22" d, 22" h **120.00**
Victorian, cast iron, painted black, wooden slat bottom, finial missing, 37" l, 21" d, 36" h **200.00**
Windsor, New England, c1800-20, bamboo turned spindles, worn finish **850.00**

Decorated, old brown over yellow comb graining, black trim, two white porcelain pulls on either side, cutout handles in ends, initialed "J. H." underneath, high canted sides with step down corners, remnants of leather bands beneath runners, chips on molding, 35-1/4" l, 17-1/4" d, 30-1/2" d x 20" h rockers **275.00**

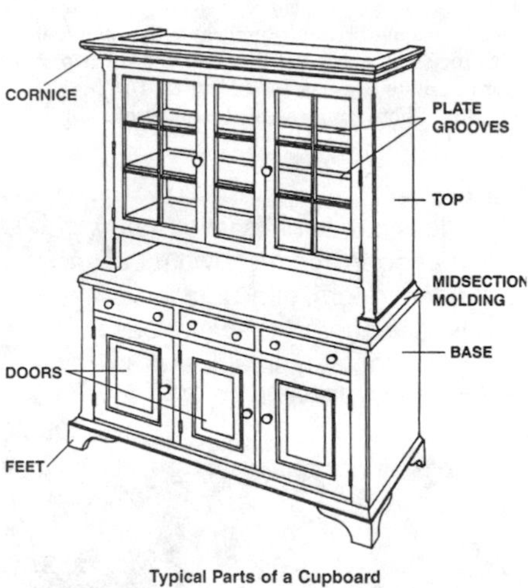

Typical Parts of a Cupboard

Cupboards

Armoire

Arts & Crafts, English, single-door, overhanging top supported by corbels, mirror, emb copper panels of stylized flowers, unmarked, refinished, new back and shelves, one corbel missing, 40" w, 18" d, 75" h **1,050.00**
Classical, New York, c1835, mahogany, bold projecting molded Roman arch cornice, two paneled doors flanked by tapered veneered columns, ogee bracket feet, 74" w, 31" d, 94" h **3,200.00**
Empire-style, Continental, early 19th C, mahogany, shaped cornice above two paneled doors opening to shelves, ribbed lunette-shaped feet, 42" w, 17" d, 74" h............... **1,610.00**
Louis XV-style, oak, molded cornice above pair of foliate carved doors, bun feet, 69" w, 27" d, 82" h... **900.00**
Restoration, New York, c1830, mahogany, flat top with cornice molding, two doors, birds' eye maple lined int., concealed drawer below, ribbed blocked feet, 56" w, 19-1/2" d, 90" h **2,800.00**
Victorian, American, c1840, walnut, bold double ogee molded cornice, two arched paneled doors, shelved int., plinth base, ogee bracket feet, 62" w, 24" d, 89" h.............. **1,400.00**

Bee keeper's hutch, Canadian, pine, orig red and black painted top panel, paneled door on lower front, door on either end, drop front covers interior workshelf, hinged lid, pegged construction, lid marked "Patent Union, Bee Hive, W. Phelps Pat." 47" w, 19" d, 43-1/4" h **750.00**

Chifforobe, Art Deco, 1935, herringbone design waterfall veneer, arched center mirror, dropped center section, four deep drawers flanked by tall cupboard doors, shaped apron **450.00**

Chimney, decorated, poplar, pine shelves, ash backboards, orig dark red over lighter red dec, one door with four panes of glass at top over two raised panels, white mullions, white porcelain knob, surface wear, doors have restoration at hinges, price for pr **2,365.00**

Cupboard, corner, one piece, Federal, Pennsylvania, c1810, cherry, convex molded and paneled cornice over conforming case, 12-pane glazed door, flanked by half turned and reeded columns, central short drawer flanked by two faux drawers, two paneled cupboard doors, applied ogee bracket feet, 48" w, 87" h, **$21,850**. Photo courtesy of Pook & Pook.

Corner, hanging, English, mahogany, pine secondary wood, cove molded cornice, paneled door with early brass escutcheon, single drawer on lower apron, smaller false fronts on either side, three scalloped shelves, old finish, replaced brass pulls, late mustard painted interior, pieced restorations, section of trim molding missing from door, 27" w, 14" d, 42-3/4" h.................... **300.00**

Corner, wall

Biedermeier, c1820, fruitwood and part ebonized, two parts, upper section fitted with glass door and shelved int., projecting lower section fitted with paneled door, shaped block feet, 35" w, 19" d, 80" h **2,600.00**
Blind door, painted, c1830, pine, blind door, bird's eye maple paint dec, two paneled doors, base with two paneled doors, bracket feet, 29" w, 83" h **2,750.00**
One piece, Chippendale, Southern states, 1760s, pine, heavy projecting cornice molding above arched molded surround, flanking similarly shaped raised panel doors opening to two shelves above two additional fielded panel doors, flanked by fluted pilasters, opening to single serpentine shelf, refinished, hardware replaced, repairs, 64" w, 30" d, 93-3/4" h.................. **7,475.00**
One piece, country, decorated, poplar, stepped and cove molded cornice, two paneled doors with mortise and peg construction, thin picture frame molding around case, scalloped front apron, molded base, bracket feet, four shaped int. shelves, well-executed 20th C red over burnt orange grained dec, blue-green int., sections of foot facings and back foot are replaced, some insect damage to back of base, 33-3/4" w, 18-1/4" d, 78" h .. **2,750.00**
Two pieces, Lancaster County, PA, cherry, documented to Jacob Kintz family, East Stroudsburg, PA, c1810-20, broken arch, molded cornice terminating in rosettes, center plinth with flame finial, fluted quarter columns, arched doors with molded mullions, orig glass, yellow int. with shaped shelves, spoon slots, double plat rails, 39" w, 90" h **14,800.00**
Two pieces, painted, c1790, green, architectural design, fluted pilasters, arched doors, 52" w, 93" h **19,500.00**

Court, English, carved oak

Overall stylized line and scroll motif carving, two doors with inset panels, boldly carved pilasters, two drawers

in base with diamond panels, flat top, dark finish, several backboard missing, 66" w, 22-1/2" d, 65" h **1,000.00**

Seven inset base panels, three on each side, all relief carved scrolling, "1649" on lower case, acorn finials, two doors on top, center base door, old replaced feet, old dark finish, replaced hinges, 56" w, 23" d, 56-1/2" h **1,200.00**

Jelly, pine, mortise and peg construction, sq nails, red wash with areas of wear from use, beaded edges along edges of case, around both doors, along sides of door panels, angled bracket feet, four int. shelves, restorations at hinges, one foot chipped, replacement brass pull, 38-1/2" w, 14" d, 67-1/2" h........... **1,650.00**

Kas, Long Island, NY, c1730-80, cherry, pine, and polar, architectural cornice molding, two raised panel thumb-molded doors flanked by reeded pilasters, applied moldings, single drawer, painted detachable disc and stretcher feet, replaced hardware, refinished, restored, 65-1/2" w, 26-1/4" d, 77-1/4" h **4,500.00**

Kitchen, orig blue paint, six center drawers with porcelain pulls, two side bins, one bin lid sgd "Ezra Woodside Montare, April 20, 1905," cutting board, continuous scalloped face board covering lower front and feet, back shaped like picket fence, 72" l, 21" d, 54" h... **7,200.00**

Cupboard, corner, one piece, New England, c1750, pine, molded cornice over open arch, three scalloped shelves over single double raised panel door, flat molded base, 57" w, 91" h, **$4,400**. Photo courtesy of Pook & Pook.

Linen press, attributed to Union Village Shakers, OH, walnut, one piece, 45-1/2" w, 21" d, 89" h................ **3,850.00**

Pedestal, Biedermeier, c1830, walnut, inset white marble top, fluted sides, fitted with door, octagonal plinth base, 16" d, 30" h.. **1,575.00**

Pewter, two parts, top: cornice molding, two six-glass pane doors, two shelves, open pie shelf; base: two drawers over raised panel doors, one shelf int., short turned feet, 56" w, 20" d, 87" h **2,250.00**

Pie safe

Paint decorated, attributed to Shenandoah Valley, poplar, old worn blue pain on front, reddish-brown on sides, areas of earlier mustard paint, 12 punched tins, well-executed pots of flowers with scrolled handles, diagonal line punched borders, double doors, one drawer in base, high sq legs, few tins damaged, 38" w, 16-3/4" d, 54-1/2" h .. **2,300.00**

Poplar, 12 punched tins, three tins in each side, matching doors on front, punched stars surrounded by circles, three-line borders with corner fans, dovetailed drawer in base, turned wooden pulls, areas of pitting on some of the tins, old finish, front lightly cleaned, 41-1/2" w, 17-1/2" d, 57-1/4" h **1,000.00**

Southeastern United States, early 19th C, walnut, rect top above along drawer, two hinged cupboard doors each with two pierced tin panels with designs of hearts and initials "J.B." flanked by leafy branches, ends with three conforming decorated panels, sq tapering legs, refinished, minor imperfections, 39-1/2" w, 17" d, 49-1/2" h **5,300.00**

Cupboard, corner, two pieces, cherry, architectural domed door with 15 original panes, burled mahogany panels on lower doors, Sandwich glass knobs, ivory inlay, **$8,500**. Photo courtesy of Dotta Auction Co., Inc.

Slant back, New England, late 18th C, pine, flat molded cornice above beaded canted front flanking shelves, projecting base with single raised panel door, old refinish, doors missing from top, imperfections, 37-1/2" w, 18" d, 73" h **2,300.00**

Spice, northern Europe, last half 18th C, wall-type, painted, flat molded cornice, hinged cupboard door, molded recessed panel opening, compartmentalized int., molded base, old dark green paint bordered by red, int. drawers missing, imperfections, 16" w, 8" d, 17" h **1,500.00**

Step-back, one piece, country

Pine, cove molded cornice, paneled doors, double doors in top, single door in base, high pie shelf, scalloped apron, cutout feet, old mellow refinishing, top dovetailed, 28-1/4" w, 81-1/2" h............ **1,925.00**

Poplar, open top with three shelves and pie shelf, one paneled base door, refinished, reconstruction using old boards, 28" w, 18-1/2" d, 69-3/4" h **615.00**

Step-back, two pieces, Sandusky County, OH, c1830-50, tiger maple, narrow strip of wavy black walnut trim which outlined the bottom door panels, traced bottom edge of wide cornice, two glazed doors with two horizontal mullions, three drawers, two paneled doors in base, shaped apron, 56" w, 89" h **29,000.00**

Vitrine, Edwardian, c1900, inlaid mahogany, corner-style, d-shape, fitted with two bow-fronted glass doors, sq legs joined by shelf stretcher, inlaid with checker banding throughout, 22" w, 51-1/2" h **800.00**

Cupboard, kas, Hudson Valley, c1740, gumwood, two pieces, upper section with boldly molded cornice over two paneled cupboard doors flanked by stiles with molded panels, lower section with single long drawer, bun feet, losses, 59-3/4" w, 81-1/2" h, **$34,500**. Photo courtesy of Pook & Pook.

Wall

America, two pieces, pine and walnut, old mustard paint and faint brown grain dec, traces of earlier red in some areas, brown sponging to three curved front drawers and on raised panels of lower doors, cove molded cornice, two-door top with six panes of glass in each door, vertical central panel with three panels, all top panes are tombstone shaped, chamfered corners, turned feet with applied half turned pilasters, blue painted int. with cut-outs for spoons, 61" w, 21" d, 85-3/4" h **5,500.00**

American, one door, old brown over mustard paint, comb graining, molded top and base, molded mullions and openings for six panes of glass on door, later light brown paint on int., three shelves, some repairs, 27-1/2" w, 12" d, 40" h **1,100.00**

American, Chippendale, country, two pcs, curly maple, poplar secondary wood, molded cornice, top pair of doors with double beaded frames, nine panes of old wavy glass each, dovetailed case and bracket feet, three dovetailed drawers with edge beading, two raised paneled doors in base, top and bottom shelves feature plate bars, center shelf cut out for spoons, secret drawers in base, old replaced thumb latches, redware drawer pulls with dark sponging, old refinishing, evidence of orig red wash, 65-1/2" w, 19-3/4" d, 84" h **13,750.00**

American, two pcs, grain dec, step-back, pine and poplar, old mustard and brown paint, top of doors with arched glazed panels, 54" w, 88" h **6,600.00**

Canadian, Hepplewhite, two pieces, pine, beveled and cove molded cornice, two doors in top section with two panes of glass each, two int. shelves with red and white paint, molded waist, five drawers in base with incised beading, turned wooden pulls, well scalloped base, high bracket feet, refinished, evidence of earlier red paint, edge chips, couple of glued splits to feet, 48" w, 23-1/2" d, 78-1/2" h............... **935.00**

Jacobean, oak and part painted, two parts, upper section with pegs and shelves, projecting lower section with two doors, each with geometric and floral carving, 64" w, 20" d, 80" h **3,000.00**

New England, early 19th C, painted pine and cherry, rect case, single door with four recessed panels, scratch-beaded left edge, int. of 21 scratch-beaded drawers, seven compartments of assorted sizes, sides of case continuing to shaped cut-out feet, early red paint, minor imperfections, 27-3/4" w, 11-1/4" d, 59" h **4,370.00**

New York, upstate, early 19th C, painted, flat cornice, case with two hinged doors each with two recessed vertical panels, shelved int., old gray paint, imperfections, 43" w, 18" d, 78" h.............. **1,000.00**

Wardrobe, Renaissance Revival, c1875, burled walnut, three arched doors, step out center, 84" w, 28" d, 100" h, **$3,080**. Photo courtesy of Fontaine's Auction Gallery.

Wardrobe

Decorated, one pc, pine, wooden peg construction, removable cornice, large white panels with bright flowering plants on blue ground, dated 1805, one dovetailed base drawer, two added int. shelves, 48-1/4" w, 21" d, 69-1/2" h **950.00**

French, figured walnut veneers, graining applied on diagonal, crest with raised rococo carving and medallion, large floral swag and ribbons, reeded pilasters on front, two doors with beveled mirrors, turned legs, base with dovetailed drawer, 45-1/2" w, 16-1/2" d, 98-1/2" h **950.00**

Victorian, burled walnut, ornate top, two paneled doors, base with two drawers **2,400.00**

Desks

Aesthetic Movement, late 19th C, solid and burl walnut, cylinder roll, fitted int., drawer over two doors, top with two glass doors between full turned columns, carved crest **2,420.00**

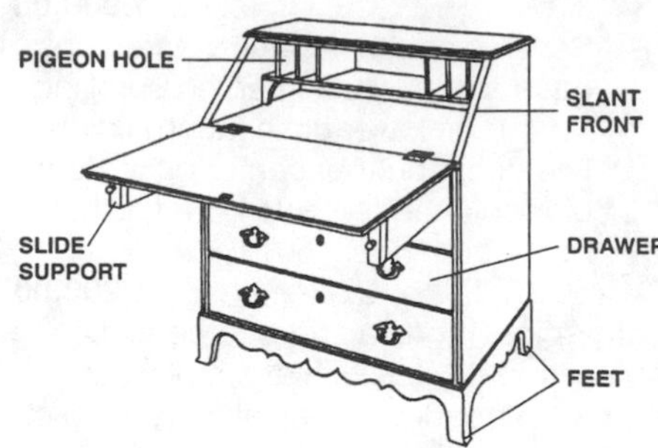

Typical Parts of a Desk

Art Deco, Leopold Corp, Burlington, IA, walnut veneered, semi-oval top over center drawer flanked by pull-out writing surface and two drawers, bronze handles, light brown finish, "Charles S. Nathan Office Equipment New York" distributor's metal tag in drawer, veneer loss, wear, 66-1/8" l, 36-1/8" d, 29" h **900.00**

Arts & Crafts, Stickley, Gustav, Syracuse, NY, lady's, c1912, model no. 720, cabinet with four vertical shelves, two small drawers, three horizontal shelves, rect top, two short drawers, paper Craftsman label, 38" w, 23" d, 37" h **1,725.00**

Desk, Art Nouveau, made for Boys Lyman St. School, Westborough, MA, mahogany, cast iron mounts, drop front, fitted interior, open shelves, weighted pulleys working sliding panel which opens to reveal drawers and shelves, three drawers, open shelf, paw feet, 33-1/2" w, 17" d, 83-1/2" h, **$3,525**. Photo courtesy of Skinner, Inc.

Chippendale

America, oxbow, mahogany, dovetailed case, four graduated dovetailed drawers with old red stained interiors, seven interior drawers, eight pigeon holes, blocked fan on center drawer, large fan on lid, relief carved drop, molded base, ogee feet with shaped returns, refinished, restorations, replacements, replaced brasses,

large brass pulls on sides, 42-1/2" w, 21-1/2" d, 44-1/2" h **2,000.00**
America, slant lid, cherry, pine secondary wood, dovetailed case, four dovetailed drawers, stepped int. with seven large pigeon holes across top, seven small drawers across center, three drawers at bottom, stepped molding around base, ogee feet, refinished, replaced batwing brasses, pieced restorations, 37-1/2" w, 19-1/2" d, 39-1/4" h **1,650.00**
America, slant lid, maple, refinished, pine secondary wood, dovetailed case, four dovetailed drawers with beaded overlapping edges, molded base, semicircular drop on front apron, bracket feet, scalloped returns, six int. drawers below nine pigeon holes, large replaced batwing brasses, restorations, 37-1/2" w, 18-1/2" d, 41-1/4" h **1,550.00**
Connecticut, late 18th C, mahogany, block front, slant front lid, fitted tiered int. with nine dovetailed drawers, pigeonholes, two pull-out letter drawers with fluted columns, flame-carved finials and door with blocking and fan carving, dovetailed case, four dovetailed drawers, conforming apron, bracket feet, replaced brasses, old refinishing, feet replaced, repairs to case, 41-3/4" w, 21-1/2" d, 42-3/4" h **3,850.00**
Massachusetts, c1770-80, slant lid, mahogany, lid opens to int. of central fan, concave caved drawer, two conforming drawers flanked by document drawers with half-baluster fronts, four valanced compartments, two drawers, cock-beaded case of four graduated drawers, ogee bracket feet, center drop pendant, old brass bail pulls, refinished, imperfections, 40" w, 20" d, 43" h **9,400.00**
Massachusetts, Salem, 1780-1800, oxbow, carved mahogany, slant lid opens to int. of small drawers and valanced compartments flanking central fan-carved drawer with two others below, all with end-blocking, above case of reverse serpentine drawers with cock-beaded surrounds, heavy molded base with central fan carved pendant, shaped ogee bracket feet ending in platforms, original brasses, minor imperfections, 41-1/2" w, 22-1/2" d, 44" h **17,625.00**
New England, 18th C, slant lid, maple, pine secondary wood, dovetailed case, stepped interior with six drawers, blocked fronts, fan carving on top three, four pigeon holes, two dovetailed drawers on lower tier, four dovetailed drawers with molded trim, replaced batwing brasses and lock escutcheons, bracket feet with scalloped returns, molded base, refinished, some restorations, 36" w, 20" d, 41-1/4" h **3,575.00**
PA, attributed to Lancaster County, PA, slant lid, walnut, poplar and pine secondary wood, dovetailed case with chamfered corners with line inlay, four overlapping drawers with beaded edges, cove molded base, ogee feet with scalloped returns, replaced wooden pulls, int. with seven small dovetailed drawers plus secret drawer, brass pulls, eight pigeon holes, center door, 33" h writing surface, 39-1/4" w, 19-1/4" d, 43-3/4" h **4,000.00**
Rhode Island, late 18th C, cherry, slant front, stepped int. of small drawers, central one with shaping, case of beaded graduated drawers, ogee bracket feet, orig brasses, old refinish, restoration, 39" w, 20" d, 43" h **3,800.00**

Desk, Arts & Crafts, retail label "Geo. C. Flint Co., West 23rd St. New York," c1908, oak, drop front, gallery top, exposed tenons, V-groove sides, brass wash strap hinges and escutcheon, fitted interior compartment, lower open shelf, imperfections, 25-3/4" w, 10-3/4" d, 49" h, **$2,500**. Photo courtesy of Skinner, Inc.

Chippendale-style, fall-front, pyrography dec of drawings and scrollwork on entire surface, c1890 .... **1,300.00**
Eastlake, lady's, walnut, two parts, top section sits on pegs, top: mirror with two columns supported shelves, fancy carving, pressed dec; base section: double hinged writing surface with dec floral carving, writing surface with two panels of green felt, lifts to reveal compartment desk int. with two drawers, one side fitted with two long drawers, gallery shelf in base, dec applied pieces, shoe foot base, metal asters, 31-1/2" w, 19" d, 57" h **1,150.00**

Desk, Arts & Crafts, Gustav Stickley, postcard desk, letterholder backsplash, two drawers, paneled back and sides, recessed bookshelf below, original finish, early red decal, 39-1/2" l, 22" d, 36" h, **$1,610**. Photo courtesy of David Rago Auctions, Inc.

Edwardian, c1900, kneehole, mahogany, rect cross banded top with central oval medallion, front canted corners, long frieze drawer, two banks of three drawers, center cupboard door, foliate marquetry dec, 37-1/2" w, 31" h...................... **600.00**
Edwardian-style, 20th C, marquetry inlaid mahogany, U-shaped superstructure fitted with drawers and doors, serpentine case fitted with drawers, sq tapered legs, 35" w, 24" d, 37" h.. **2,645.00**
Empire, butler's, cherry and curly maple, poplar secondary wood, scrolled crest with turned rosettes, pull-out desk drawer with arched pigeon holes and three dovetailed drawers, three dovetailed drawers with applied edge beading, turned and carved pilasters, paneled ends, paw feet, old finish, some edge damage, 44-1/2" w, 23" d, 57-3/4" h **1,925.00**
Federal
Massachusetts, North Shore, 1795-1815, mahogany, inlaid, reverse serpentine, the slant lid opens to int. of small drawers, valanced compartments which flank the inlaid prospect door with cross banded inlay opening to three small drawers, case of four graduated cock-beaded drawers, top one arched, shaped bracket feet, original brasses, old surface, repairs and losses, 41-3/4" w, 23-5/8" d, 43" h .. **5,300.00**
New Hampshire, early 19th C, slant lid, wavy birch, lid opens to two-stepped int. case of drawers with four cock-beaded surrounds, serpentine skirt, tall arched feet, orig brasses, old refinish, repairs, 37-1/2" w, 18-1/4" d, 45" h .. **2,760.00**

New York State, early 19th C, mahogany veneer inlaid, slant lid and three graduated drawers outlined in stringing with ovolo corners, int. of veneer and outline stringing on drawers, valanced compartments, prospect door opening to inner compartments and drawers, flanking document drawers, orig brasses, old surface, veneer cracking loss and patching, other surface imperfections, 41-1/2" w, 21-1/2" d, 44" h **2,550.00**

Pennsylvania, early 19th C, walnut inlaid, slant front, lid and cock-beaded drawers outlined in stringing, base with band of contrasting veneers, int. of small drawers above valanced compartments, scrolled dividers flanking prospect door which opens to two small drawers, three drawers, old refinish, repairs, 40" w, 20" d, 44-1/2" h......... **3,550.00**

Desk, English, partner's, mahogany, one long drawer flanked by two small drawers on left, one drawer on right, tapered legs with brass terminations, leather top embossed ossed with gold, worminess on legs, 58" w, 29" d, 29" h, **$3,175**. Photo courtesy of Alderfer Auction Co.

George III, c1810, butler's, mahogany, rect case fitted with secretary's drawer having satinwood-fronted small drawers; case fitted with two doors opening to shelves and two drawers, bracket feet, 43" w, 20" d, 40" h....................... **2,000.00**

George III-style, partner's, third quarter, 19th C, burl elm, rect top, gold tooled green leather writing surface, molded edge, four cross banded cock-beaded frieze drawers, two banks of three cross banded cock-beaded and opposing cupboard doors, plinth base, 72" w, 31" h **2,875.00**

Hepplewhite, slant lid, cherry, dovetailed case, chamfered pilasters with four lines of inlay, four dovetailed drawers with beaded edges, thin band inlay above bracket feet with scalloped returns, single board ends, eight int. drawers, center door, eight pigeon holes, refinished, poplar secondary wood, replaced brasses, restorations, replacements, 39-1/2" w, 19-3/4" d, 43-3/4" h **2,000.00**

Queen Anne

America, early 18th C, cross banded walnut, slat front, fitted int. of wells and drawers, three frieze drawers, cabriole legs, pad feet **5,750.00**

Northern Maine, 19th C, maple, slant front, int. with valanced compartments above small drawers, end drawers separated by scrolled dividers, case of three thumb-molded drawers, molded bracket base with central drop pendant, old darkened surface, 35-1/2" w, 17-1/2" d, 40-1/4" h............ **5,175.00**

Vermont, c1750, tiger maple and cherry, slant front, int. with central fan-carved drawer, two valanced compartments flanked by molded document drawers, four valanced compartments, three drawers, case with four thumb-molded graduated drawers, bracket feet, replaced brasses, old refinish, imperfections, and repairs, 36" w, 18" d, 41-1/2" h **3,220.00**

Regency, English, c1850, lady's, cylinder, mahogany, tambour top, fitted int., slide-out writing surface, over two drawers, lyre base, 30" h writing surface, 35-1/2" w, 20" d, 38" h................... **3,000.00**

Renaissance Revival, English, partner's, carved oak, rect top with rounded corners, molded edge, front and back each carved with three frieze drawers, one pedestal with three drawers, other with paneled door opening int. with drawers and shelves, canted corners with figural pilasters, conforming molded plinth base, compressed bun feet, profusely carved with fruiting swags, grotesque masks, and heraldic devices, 72" w, 39-1/2" d, 30" h................. **5,500.00**

Roll top, quarter sawn oak, orig finish, 34 int. drawers, orig inkwells, two orig keys, two pedestals with four drawers each, center drawer **4,250.00**

Desk, International Movement, partner's, Tommi Parzinger for Charak Modern, ebonized, top, sides, and single drawer covered in tooled tan leather with Greek key pattern, four adjustable refinished shelves to one side, eight drawers with circular brass pulls to other, stenciled mark, 48" l, 27 3/4" w, 28-1/2" h, **$2,990**. Photo courtesy of David Rago Auctions, Inc.

Sheraton

American, stand-up, walnut, slant front, four graduated drawers, turned feet, ivory escutcheons, Sandwich glass pulls, flanked by paint dec columns, simply fitted int. with secret drawers, one pull replaced, repair to lid, hinges replaced, int. refitted, 35" h writing surface, 35" w, 43" h **1,200.00**

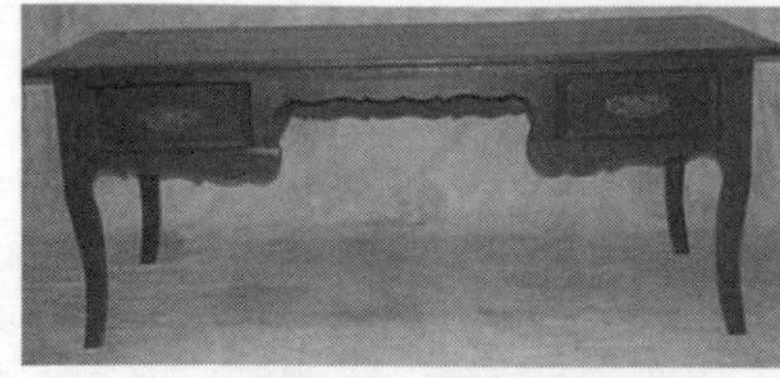

Desk, Louis XV-style, French, country, walnut, three board top, two drawer base, scalloped frieze, paneled sides, 75" l, 32" d, 30" h, **$3,750**. Photo courtesy of Alderfer Auction Co.

Country, slant lid, cherry, pine and poplar secondary wood, two dovetailed drawers behind slant lid, two large compartments, three dovetailed drawers in base, turned feet, orig oval brasses with emb pineapple in basket design, refinished, alternations, restored break on one back leg, 37" w, 19-1/4" d, 38-1/2" h............... **990.00**

Victorian, early, mahogany**,** base labeled, upper section with slant lid writing surface, flanked by two pedestals each fitted with four drawers, lower pedestal desk fitted with three frieze drawers, two pedestals each having three drawers, U-shaped plinth, 58" w, 32" d, 47" h **1,200.00**

William and Mary, New England, walnut, eight-point mariner's compass inlaid in drop front, ball foot **8,350.00**

William and Mary-style, American, 20th C, oak, seven dovetailed drawers, applied moldings, molded edge top, brass tear drop pulls, old finish, turned legs and stretchers, one piece of molding missing from drawer, 27-3/4" x 59" x 31" h **500.00**

Dry sinks

Curly maple, rect well, work surface on right with small drawer, two poplar wood cupboard doors, short bracket feet, hardwood edge stripes, minor repairs, refinished, 55" w, 34-1/2" h **2,400.00**

Grain painted, c1840, mustard colored, dovetailed well, two drawers over two paneled doors, orig knobs **1,950.00**

Painted, attributed to PA, early 19th C, rect overhanging top, well, cut-out ends with exposed tenons, joined by medial shield fitted with later copper insert, painted red, 44-3/4" w, 18-1/2" d, 32" h **2,645.00**

Pine, three drawers on high back, sink with back-curved sides, paneled doors opening to self, stile feet, c1900, 43" w, 18-1/2" d, 33-1/2" h....................... **900.00**

Dry sink, attributed to Shakers, Union Village, Ohio, walnut, poplar, and pine, two raised panel doors, cast iron latch, wide single board ends slightly arched at base, refinished, later red paint on interior and sink, restorations, 38-1/4" w, 20-3/4" d, 32" h, **$950**; country tilt top curly maple candlestand to left, **$450**; decorated box with sliding top, **$250**; hooked rug with polychrome oval center and stripes, **$350**; carved horse handle smooth board in well of dry sink, **$185**. Photo courtesy of Garth's Auctions, Inc.

Pine and poplar, galleried well, one small dovetailed drawer, two paneled doors, cut-out feet, 46" w, 18-1/4" d, 37-3/4" h **600.00**

Poplar, country

Square nail construction, pr mortise and pegged doors, single board ends, angled bracket feet, old mellow scrubbed finish, old replaced turned wood pulls, 63-1/2" w, 21" d, 34-3/4" h **950.00**

Two pieces, old brown and tan combed graining, top: cove molded cornice, two paneled doors, three int. shelves, orig cast iron latches; base: zinc-lined well, two dovetailed drawers, two doors, two int. shelves, bracket feet with scalloped end aprons, double panels on either end, white porcelain drawer pulls, 40-1/2" w, 21" d, 78-3/4" h .. **2,750.00**

Hall trees and hat racks

Bench

Gothic Revival, oak, composed of some antique elements, tall backrest inset with foliate and figural panels, lift seat and foliate carved lower panels, 34" w, 73" h **690.00**

Gothic-style, late 19th C, oak, tall backrest fitted with three figural, foliate, and seraph carved panels, lift seat, chip-carved sq legs, 60" w, 66-1/2" h **1,855.00**

Victorian, oak, twist spindles on sides, man's face carved into applied carving, four orig hooks, large oval beveled mirror, lift seat storage **1,300.00**

Chair

Arts & Crafts, Limbert, #79, hall chair, unique "bicycle" shape, orig leather back and shaped seat over slab leg with keyed construction, orig finish, branded and numbered, orig leather has been reinforced, 19" w, 20" d, 42" h **1,100.00**

Cast iron, Union Army motif, patch boxes on base, belt with buckle carved for cane holder, swords and rifles forming back, topped with Union shield, piece found in PA GAR hall.................................. **10,500.00**

Hall mirror, Aesthetic Movement, late 19th C, carved walnut, molded rect frame carved with border of vines, accented with quatrefoil flowerheads, set with seven angular brass coat hooks, 52-1/2" x 40-3/4".. **950.00**

Magazine stand, Arts & Crafts, Gustav Stickley, No. 514, oak, tongue-and-groove paneled sides, square posts, leather strips tacked to shelf ends, original finish, early red decal under top shelf, wear to top, 35-1/2" x 14-1/4" x 14-1/2", **$8,100**. Photo courtesy of David Rago Auctions, Inc.

Hall rack

Art Nouveau, France, early 20th C, mahogany, flaring mahogany panel, five brass curved coat hooks centered by mirror, umbrella stand below, 47" w, 85" h............. **1,200.00**

Arts & Crafts, attributed to Charles Rohls, early 20th C, oak, tall sq shaft, two tiers of four wooden hooks, each near the top, half buttresses running up from the cross base on all four sides, sq wafer feet, 64" h **1,100.00**

Colonial Revival, Baroque-style, American, 1910, cherry, shell carved crest over cartouche and griffin carved panel back, lift seat, high arms, mask carved base, paw feet, 39-1/2" w, 21-1/2" d, 51" h **700.00**

Oak, carved cornice, carved lions heads, oval beveled mirror, orig hooks, lift-up seat storage, orig finish, 36" w **2,800.00**

Oak, keyhole shaped mirror, carved crest, throne-like shape, rolled arms extending to sides, round feet **1,700.00**

Magazine stand, Eastlake, c1880, ebonized and parcel gilt, two adjustable hinged racks, turned supports, shaped legs, folding easel support, 19" w, 45" h, **$850**. Photo courtesy of Skinner, Inc.

Hat rack

Arts & Crafts, wrought steel, hat and coat style, our sided, double hooks and spindles, unmarked, 21" w, 21" d, 75" h **865.00**

International Movement, Charles Eames, "Hang-It-All," manufactured by Tigrett Enterprises, c1953, white enameled metal frame, multicolored wooden balls, 20" w, 6" d, 16" h **800.00**

Windsor, American, pine, bamboo turned, six knob-like hooks, orig yellow varnish, black striping, 33-3/4" w............................... **200.00**

Stand, Arts & Crafts, coat and umbrella type, wrought steel, cut-out apron, spindles, brass hooks, unmarked, 27" w, 10-1/2" d, 73" h **850.00**

Umbrella stand, Black Forest, Germany, early 20th C, carved walnut, figural bear, fierce expression, loose chain around neck, holding tray in raised paw, porcelain base liner, 48" h **5,750.00**

Mirrors

Aesthetic Movement, late 19th C, over mantel, ebonized, rect frame carved with olive branches, patera to four corners, mirror plate with beveled edge, bead-board backing, 61-1/4" x 55-1/4"... **800.00**

Art Deco, French, c1930, giltwood, frame closed at bottom and sides, carved chevrons, stylized sundials and Chinese scrolls, hung by gilt thread rope, tapered rect beveled mirror plate, 27" w, 37" h 1,500.00

Mirror, Chippendale, American, c1775, mahogany, scrolled crest, ears, and base, 21-1/2" w, 41-1/2" h, **$1,265**. Photo courtesy of Pook & Pook.

Arts & Crafts

Boston Society of Arts and Crafts, 1910, carved wood, rect, carved and gilded frame, ink mark, initials, orig paper label, 11-1/4" w, 18-1/2" h **700.00**

Limbert, oak, frame with geometric inlaid design over rect cane panel shoe-foot base, recoated orig frame, orig glass, 20" w, 8" d, 22" h **600.00**

Baroque, Continental, second quarter 18th C, giltwood, fruit filled cartouche form resting, mirrored borders with grapevines and scrolls, foliate carved pendant, 63" h **5,750.00**

Mirror, Classical style, Continental, 19th C, gilded and gessoed, octagonal, della robia style frame carved with fruit, nuts, and foliage, 34" x 33-1/4", **$1,900**. Photo courtesy of Sloans & Kenyon Auctions.

Biedermeier, c1830, walnut, ogee molded cresting, paneled sides, 26" w, 37" h.. **350.00**

Centennial, Queen Anne-style, American, late 19th C, mahogany faced, scalloped, shell pendant, 32" h..... **250.00**

Cheval, German, ebonized, swivel rect mirror, rounded ends, low sq mount, artist sgd, 70" h **425.00**

Mirror, George III, England, late 18th C, hall, giltwood and verre eglomise, bearing paper label for "J. & W. Vokins, Looking Glass and Picture Frame Manufacturers," London, rectangular mirror plate flanked by fluted columns, topped by row of spherules, peaked pediment topped by pineapple finial hung with pair of spherules on chains, centered by verre eglomise panel of musical instrument vignette on green ground, losses, 45" h, **$1,175**. Photo courtesy of Skinner, Inc.

Chippendale

America, late 18th C, mahogany, scroll cut crest with eagle, old gold on eagle and liner, refinished, writing on backboards states earlier owner's name, base board and sections of lower ears replaced, 11-1/4" w, 17" h **400.00**

America, early 19th C, pine, figured mahogany veneer, arched crest, tightly scrolled ears, molded frame around glass, gilt inner liner, minor ear damage, 17-3/4" w, 33-3/4" h **1,775.00**

England, mid-18th C, walnut and parcel-gilt, gilt-gessoed carved phoenix on leafy branch above scrolled frame with applied gilt leafy floral and fruit devices, gilt incised liner framing beveled glass, restoration, 20-1/2" w, 44" h **6,465.00**

New England, late 18th C, mahogany and gilt gesso, scrolled frame centering gilt gesso eagle in crest above gilt incised molded liner, imperfections, 18-1/2" w, 40" h **500.00**

Pennsylvania, label for retailer John Elliott, Jr., 1739-1810, Philadelphia, mahogany, domed crest, shallow apron both jig sawed with symmetrical leafy scrolls, molded upright rect frame, rounded upper corners, enclosing early mirror plate, refinished, 21-1/2" w, 40-1/2" h **1,100.00**

Chippendale-style, cheval, late 19th C, carved mahogany, oval plate, four-legged base carved with foliage, claw and ball feet, 75" h.. **635.00**

Mirror, George IV, 19th C, triptych, over mantel, inlaid mahogany, cove molded crest above three satinwood inlaid panels, three-part mirror plate flanked by reeded colonettes headed by square corner blocks with gilt-bronze wheat sheaf mounts, 29" x 56-1/2" **$1,200**. Photo courtesy of Sloans & Kenyon Auctions.

Classical

Dressing, America or England, 1810-20, carved mahogany and mahogany veneer, cylinder top opens to reveal four drawers, centering one door, ivory pulls, above single divided long drawer, restoration, 19" w, 10-5/8" d, 32" h **1,610.00**

Girandole, America or England, 1810-20 gilt gesso, crest with eagle flanked by acanthus leaves, convex glass, ebonized molded liner with affixed candle branches, foliate and floral pendant, imperfections, 23" w, 35" h **5,175.00**

Overmantel, New England, c1820-40, painted and giltwood, rect mirror frame with sq corner blocks, applied floral bosses joined by vase and ring turned split baluster columns, molded black liner, old gilt surface, replaced mirror glass, surface imperfections, 46" w, 23" h **920.00**

Wall, New York, 1830s, carved and eglomise, entablature overhangs veneered frieze, reverse painted land and waterscape flanked by leaf carved split balusters, orig eglomise and mirror glass, old refinish, minor losses and crazing, 38" h...... **460.00**

Courting, wooden frame, reverse painted glass inserts and crest with bird and flowers, orig mirror glass with worn silvering, penciled inscription on back with "restored 1914," touch-up to reverse painting, brass back corner braces, 10-7/8" w, 16-1/2" h 935.00

Mirror, Louis XIV style, carved giltwood and gesso, sunburst, tiers of rays centering circular 12" d mirror plate, 59" d, **$4,200**. Photo courtesy of Sloans & Kenyon Auctions.

Edwardian, late 19th C, overmantel, boxwood marquetry inlaid, arched cresting inlaid with musical still life and scrolling vines, shaped mirror plate flanked by cross banded stiles, 60" w, 68" h 900.00

Empire, flame mahogany veneer over pine, scalloped crest with scrolled ends, inset oval panel at top, applied half turned pilasters, ogee base, worn silvering, glue repairs at ends of crest, old alligatored varnish finish, 21" w, 51" h 770.00

Mirror, Queen Anne, Philadelphia, late 18th C, mahogany, bearing paper label inscribed in both English and German, "John Elliott," losses, 21" x 10", **$2,185**. Photo courtesy of Pook & Pook.

Federal

Architectural, two parts, pine, old alligatored white paint over orig gilding, stepped cornice with applied ball dec, molded pilasters on sides, applied corner blocks at bottom, reverse dec with ribbons, silver, and black leaves on white ground, edge damage, 15-1/4" w, 24-1/4" h 450.00

America, over mantel, classical frieze, paterae, anthemion, garlands, and bows, three sections, 35" h 4,990.00

New England, c1800, mahogany inlaid, scrolled frame, rect mitered string-inlaid liner, 18" w, 31" h 1,530.00

New York City, c1780-1800, mahogany, swan's neck crest, carved urn, bouquet-type finial with carved florets on wires, veneered frame flanked by wire-bound wood vine work pendants, scrolled apron, heavily reworked, refinished, gold paint, 21-1/2" w, 53" h 675.00

Tabernacle, attributed to New York or Albany, 1795-1810, gilt gesso, molded cornice with pendant spherules over frieze with applied sunflower and wheat sheaf device, flanked by checkered panels over two-part looking glass, flanked by applied double half columns, gilt surface, replaced glass tablet, 14" w, 30-1/2" h 865.00

Wall, giltwood, labeled "Parker and Clover Looking Glass and Picture Frame Makers 180 Fulton St. New York," molded cornice with applied spherules above eglomise table of girl in pasture landscape holding dove, mirror flanked by spiral carved pilasters, 13-3/4" w, 29-1/8" h 2,875.00

Mirror, Queen Anne style, early 20th C, black painted Chinoiserie decoration, domed crest painted with two figures, foliates, pagoda, and pair of hoho birds, similarly painted raised frame, hinged backing, 34" h, **$825**. Photo courtesy of Skinner, Inc.

Federal, late, attributed to New England, c1820-30, gilt gesso, molded cornice with acorn form drops over frieze centering carved leaf motif flanked by vine and leaf applied devices, two-part mirror glass with grape and leaf designs, flanked by vase, ring, and spiral turned split balusters, old gilt surface, minor imperfections, including replaced mirror glass, 19" w, 37" 700.00

Federal-style, America, c1900, mahogany, swan's neck crest, carved urn-form finial with carved wood flowers on wires atop mirror, flanked by wired wood vine work drop, eglomise panel above mirror, elaborately jig sawed domical scrollwork apron, replaced gold work, restoration, damage, 23" w, 52" h 900.00

Folk Art, America, 1902, possibly prisoner made, pine, carved hearts, stars, and various numerals and patterns, year "1902," minor wear, 29-1/2" x 29-7/8" 1,410.00

Mirror, Regency style, giltwood, circular convex mirror plate within conforming concave frame, carved bands of beading, ribbon tied reeding, applied gilt balls, 35-1/4" d, **$1,000**. Photo courtesy of Sloans & Kenyon Auctions.

George II-style, English, 19th C, carved gesso and giltwood, C-scroll and shell carved arched crest, serpentine and rect mirror plate, scrolled foliate corner pendants, C-scroll, shell, and acanthus carved shaped apron, 29" w, 65-1/2" h 1,800.00

Louis XV-style, pier, 19th C, carved giltwood, large rect mirror topped by crest carved with leafy scrolls and rocaille, marble-topped ovolo 19-1/4" h shelf, flat leaf edge, gilt metal brackets, reeded scrolls with anthemion and female mask terminals, 33" w, 73" h 1,725.00

Louis XVI-style, French, early 20th C, giltwood, openwork crest topped by flower-filled basket over scrolls and husk garlands, rect mirror frame with beaded surround, ending in fluted stiles, 43" h 2,250.00

Neoclassical, English, c1810-15, giltwood, flat molded cornice above eglomise tablet with center sailing vessel within a black oval, red and silver lattice panel bordered by black and white, mirror below flanked by reeded columns on sq plinths with rosettes, 18-1/8" w, 36" h.......... **1,725.00**

Mirror, Renaissance Revival, late 19th C, ebonized and parcel gilt, walnut, molded frame with incised geometric and scrolling decoration, each corner with ebony roundel, gilt framed rect mirror plate, 34" x 30-1/4", **$800**. Photo courtesy of Sloans & Kenyon Auctions.

Queen Anne, English
- Rectangular, walnut and parcel gilt, scrolled crest set with giltwood rocaille, rect frame with beaded surround, ending in small further giltwood accent, 31" l.......... **500.00**
- Scroll, mahogany, old finish, molded frame, detailed scrolled crest, minor split in bottom edge of frame, 9" w, 16-1/4" h.......... **550.00**
- Two-part, walnut and parcel gilt, fretted crest centered by gilt shell, mirror plated with ogee molded surround, 48-3/8" l.......... **600.00**
- Walnut, scrolled crest above molded rect frame enclosing beveled mirror glass, backboard inscribed "Capt S Cobb," refinished, glass resilvered, 10-1/2" w, 22-1/2" h.......... **1,175.00**

Regency-style, late 19th C, bull's eyes, giltwood, eagle cresting, spherule-mounted slip, pendant carved with foliage and shell, 34" h.......... **1,530.00**

Renaissance Revival, c1870, ebonized and parcel-gilt, elaborate pediment carved with cornucopia, dentil molding and foliage, arched mirror plate and anthemion carved borders, 50" w, 79" h.......... **2,695.00**

Reverse painted, two part
- 16-1/4" w, 31-3/4" h, gilt half turned pilasters with rosette corner blocks, applied acanthus leaves, orig green, white, yellow, and red painting of cottage in woods, white border with green and red spatter, gilt shells and grapes, wear to gilt, some flaking to painting, mirror may be old replacement.......... **495.00**

Mirror, Victorian, over mantel, gilt gesso, carved floral garland decoration, surmounted by seated putti, losses to carvings, 63" w, 59" h, **$2,875**. Photo courtesy of Alderfer Auction Co.

- 18" w, 39" h, orig gilt and black paint on applied half turnings on framework, raised corner blocks with gesso rosettes orig painting of girl wearing red and white dress, seated on yellow and red footstool, swags across top with lions heads.......... **1,155.00**

Rococo, Continental, third quarter 18th C, giltwood, shaped mirror plate, arched top, frame carved with foliage and C-scrolls, 28" w, 54" h.......... **4,025.00**

Mirror, Victorian, walnut, arched top, carved crest, 26" w, 63" h, **$1,150**. Photo courtesy of Joy Luke Auctions.

Shaving, mahogany, pine secondary wood, shell crest, incised acanthus leaves and scrolls on pilasters and mirror frame, serpentine base with trim moldings, dovetailed drawer with applied carvings, brass candlesticks with scissor brackets, old dark finish, glued split on crest, 28" w, 35-1/2" h.......... **850.00**

Sheraton, mahogany, spiral turned split columns and bottom rail, inlaid panels of mahogany, rosewood, and cherry, architectural top cornice, split mirror, 24-1/2" w, 47" h.......... **300.00**

Victorian, over mantel, 1880s, gilt, leaves, roses, shells, and fruit, 59" w, 66" h.......... **2,475.00**

Rocker, Arts & Crafts, L. & J. G. Stickley, Fayetteville, New York, c1912, No. 803, three horizontal back slats, flat shaped arms, spring cushion seat, signed with white decal under arm, 21-3/4", 32-1/2" h, **$400**. Photo courtesy of Skinner, Inc.

Rockers

Art Nouveau, American, c1900, oak, fumed finish, carved arms, saddle seat, three splats with floral-type capitals.......... **400.00**

Arts & Crafts
- American, oak, four vertical back slats, corbel supports under arms, recovered orig spring cushion, orig finish, 29" w, 34" d, 36" h.......... **200.00**
- Limbert, #580, oak, T-back design, orig recovered drop-in cushion, recent finish, branded, 24" w, 29" d, 34" h.......... **150.00**
- Stickley Brothers, oak, six vertical back slats, recovered orig spring cushion, worn orig finish, branded, 25" w, 27" d, 35" h.......... **220.00**

Boston, American, 19th C, maple, spindle back.......... **200.00**

Colonial Revival, Windsor-style, Colonial Furniture Co., Grand Rapids, MI, comb back, birch, mahogany finish, turned legs, 21" w, 17" d, 27-1/2" h.......... **200.00**

Decorated
- America, orig black over red dec, gold stenciled urn of fruit and flowers on crest, shaped seat, scrolled arms, well turned legs, repaired damage to arms, 15" h seat, 40" h.......... **220.00**
- Pennsylvania, dark green, gold foliate on crest, slats, and seat, traces of red border with yellow line detail, turned legs, shaped medallion stretcher, scrolled arms, repaired break in one arm, 17" h seat, 42" h.......... **220.00**

International Movement, Charles Eames, manufactured by Herman Miller, salmon fiberglass zenith shell, rope edge, black wire struts, birch runners, c1950, 25" w, 27" d, 27" h.......... **1,400.00**

Ladderback, Portsmouth, NH area, late 18th C, turned finials above arched slats joined to down turned natural arms with carved Indian faces on terminals, old dark brown paint, imperfections, 16" h seat, 46-1/2" h.............................**4,600.00**

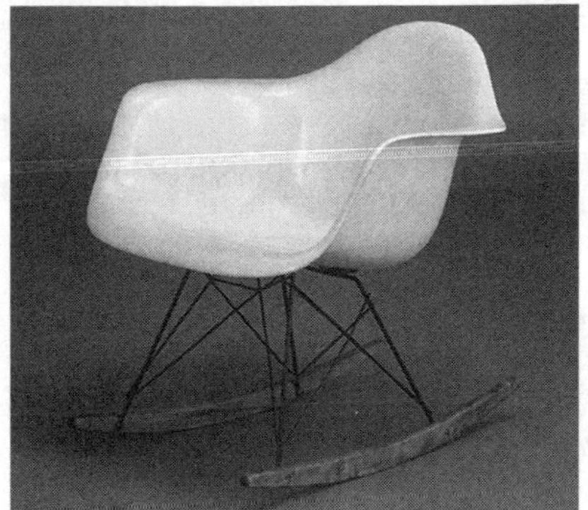

Rocker, International Movement, Charles Eames for Zenith, yellow fiberglass, rope edge, black wire cat's cradle base, birch runners, Zenith label, one re-glued shock mount, some staining to seat, 27-1/4" x 25" x 27", **$865**. Photo courtesy of David Rago Auctions, Inc.

Wicker, painted white, sq back, basket weave pattern over openwork back, rect armrests with wrapped braces, openwork sides, braided edge on basketweave seat and skirt, X-form stretcher, 32" w, 33" h...**200.00**

Rocker, wicker, Cape Cod weave, painted white, new floral seat, **$50**. Photo courtesy of Dotta Auction Co., Inc.

Windsor, arrowback, step down comb crest, deep "D" shaped seat with incised detail around six spindles, scrolled arms, bamboo turned legs and rungs, shaped rockers, mellow brown refinishing, 14" h seat, 39-1/2" h...............................**350.00**

Secretaries

Biedermeier-style, inlaid walnut, molded rect top, four drawers, top drawer with fall front, fitted int. with ebonized writing-surface, molded block feet, 50-1/4" w, 23-3/4" d, 35-1/2" h....................**1,000.00**

Butler's, c1820, flame and solid mahogany, molded and flared Gothic arched one pane doors in top, paneled doors in base, acanthus carvings, classical columns, bun feet, 90" h **6,325.00**

Centennial, inlay mahogany, two parts: top with four drawers over six cubbyholes center, line inlay door opening to reveal two cubbyholes and large drawer, sliding tambour doors flanked by inlay panels with simulated columns; lower: fold-over line inlay lid, two drawers with line inlay, diamond inlay on legs, some lifting to veneer, replaced cloth writing surface, 37-1/4" w, 19-3/4" d, 46" h.............**800.00**

Chippendale

Massachusetts, c1770-90, carved mahogany, scrolled and molded pediment above tympanum with projecting shell and arched raised panel doors flanked by fluted pilasters, candle slides, raised panel slant lid with blocked facade, molded conforming base, bracket feet, int. of upper bookcase divided into nine open compartments above four small drawers, int. of lower case with two fan-carved blocked drawers, similar prospect door, small blocked and plain drawers, scrolled compartment dividers, replaced brasses, old finish, restored, 39" w, 22" d, 93-1/2" h................ **19,550.00**

New England, late 18th C, block front, two pieces, upper section: flame finial, two blind doors, cyma-carved panels, various-sized open compartments on int., lower section with fur front drawers, plain slant front, fitted int., some later replacements, 91" h **38,180.00**

Rhode Island, Providence area, 1765-85, carved cherry, scrolled molded pediment flanks central plinth and finial above applied shell carving atop central fluted and stop-fluted column flanked by raised panel doors, shelved int. enclosed by quarter-engaged fluted and stop-fluted columns, lower case of two stepped int, of serpentine end-blocked drawers with serpentine dividers, valanced compartments, central document drawers with applied columns, above four graduated thumb-molded drawers flanked by fluted and stop-fluted engaged quarter-columns, shaped bracket feet ending in platforms, old surface, some original brasses, presumed owners' names scratched on underside of case: "Abner Lampson, 1743-1797 and Ward Lampson, 1773-1850, Washington N.H." imperfections, 38-1/4" w, 21" d, 80" h **55,815.00**

Classical, Boston, 1820-25, secretaire a'abattant, carved mahogany and mahogany veneer, marble top above cove molding, mahogany veneer facade flanked by veneered columns topped by Corinthian capitals, terminating in ebonized ball feet, recessed panel sides, fall front opens to desk int. over two cupboard doors, old refinish, 35" w, 17-1/2" d, 57-1/2" h..................**16,100.00**

Colonial Revival, Colonial Desk Co., Rockford, IL, c1930, mahogany, broken arch pediment, center finial, two glazed mullioned doors, fluted columns, center prospect with acanthus carving flanked by columns, four graduated drawers, brass eagle, carved claw and ball feet, 41" w, 21" d, 87" h......................**1,000.00**

Eastlake, American, burl walnut and mahogany, shaped cornice, pair of glazed cabinet doors, cylinder front, writing surface, two doors in base, shaped apron, 27" w, 22" d, 66" h **1,500.00**

Empire, America, c1840, mahogany veneer, fall-front, dovetailed construction, two sections, top with two four-light cathedral glass doors, base with fall-front deck, five-drawer int., over three drawers flanked by curved columns, turned feet, 41-1/2" w, 20" d, 7' 4" h..............**1,425.00**

Empire-style, late 19th C, gilt bronze mounted mahogany, rect top, fall front with fitted int., over pr of recessed cupboard doors, flanked by columns, paw feet, 44-1/4" w, 23-1/2" d, 49-1/4" h **1,955.00**

Secretary, Edwardian, two sections, upper section: fan-pierced broken pediment above ribbon-tied foliate spray, two glazed doors with gothic arch mullions, adjustable shelved interior; base with cylinder front, fitted interior of small drawers and pigeon holes, adjustable tooled-leather writing slope, cylinder front inlaid with tassel-and-bead draped urn suspended from ribbon-tied chain within satinwood inlaid oval reserve flanked by foliate-inlaid spandrels, two small drawers inlaid with laurel swags, lion's head circular pulls, square tapering bellflower inlay base, **$7,500**. Photo courtesy of Sloans & Kenyon Auctions.

Federal

Massachusetts, coastal southern, c1816, inscribed "Wood" in chalk, mahogany, three pcs, molded cornice with inlaid dentiling above diamond inlaid frieze over two paneled cupboard doors with quarter-fan inlays opening to eight-compartment int., center case with tambour doors centering oval veneered prospect door, flanked by inlaid and reeded applied pilasters, valanced compartments, prospect door opens to single valanced compartment with drawer below, lower case with string inlaid fold-out writing surface, similarly inlaid drawers flanked by stiles, panel inlays, skirt, inlaid dentiling above legs with inlaid bellflowers, line inlay and inlaid cuffs, early surface, replaced pulls, minor veneer loss, 40" w, 20-1/2" d, 81-3/4" h **34,500.00**

New Hampshire, paint decoration, two pieces, pine, old alligatored reddish-brown and yellow dec over earlier red, chamfered corners on dovetailed cases, molded cove cornice, tree dec on two paneled doors, slant front with tree dec, int. with 13 dovetailed drawers with central prospect door, four dovetailed drawers in base with applied beading, slightly shaped bracket feet with applied base molding, replaced wooden pulls, replaced H hinges, touch-up to top doors **7,425.00**

George III, English, early 19th C, japanned, swan neck pediment, rosette carved terminals, two glazed cupboard doors, fitted int. of compartments and small drawers, fall front writing surface with cubbyholes and drawers, four graduated drawers, shaped apron, bracket feet, gilt and polychrome warrior and figural landscape scenes, birds, and flowering trees, green ground, over painting and minor reconstruction, 40-1/4" w, 21-1/2" d, 96-1/2" h **5,000.00**

George III/Early Federal, America, third quarter 18th C, mahogany, two sections, upper: shaped architectural pediment with gilt-metal ball and spike finials, cavetto cornice over cross banded frieze, checker-banding, front with pair of 13-pane astragal doors, two adjustable shelves; base: outset fall-front opening, fitted int., four graduated cock-beaded oxbow-fronted drawers, conforming molded plinth base, molded and spurred bracket feet, 44-1/4" w, 24-1/4" d, 93-1/2" h **17,000.00**

Hepplewhite, North Shore, MA, mahogany, bookcase upper section, slant front desk **6,250.00**

International Movement, Gilbert Rhode, manufactured by Herman Miller, upper bookcase with drop front desk over four doors, carved wooden pulls in burl and paldio veneers, refinished, c1940, 66" w, 15" d, 72" h **2,600.00**

Renaissance Revival, American, c1865, walnut, two sections, upper: bookcase section, S-curved pediment with center applied grapes and foliage carving, two arched and molded glazed doors, shelved int., three small drawers with applied grapes and foliage carved pulls; lower: fold-out writing surface, two short drawers over two long drawers with oval molding and applied grapes and foliage carved pulls, matching ornamentation on skirt, 48" w, 21" d, 95" h **5,000.00**

Secretary, Louis XVI style, Provincial, slant front, arched ogee cornice above paneled cupboard doors, fitted interior, two cupboard doors, short scroll legs, 44" w, 19" d, 103-1/2" h, **$3,200.** Photo courtesy of Sloans & Kenyon Auctions.

Sheraton, New England, mahogany and mahogany flame veneer, cove molded cornice, three drawers across top with oval brasses, two paneled doors in top with fine flame veneer, three interior drawers, four pigeon holes with adjustable shelf, three dovetailed drawers with applied beading, figured book page veneer, reeded legs with ring turnings and molded surround at base of case, refinished, few repaired veneer splits, pierced repairs, stains in bottom, replaced brasses, 42" w, 20" d, 50-1/2" h **1,760.00**

Victorian, Gothic-style, c1870-80, walnut, carved, detailed cornice, two small bookcases flank center fold-down desk section, four drawers over two additional bookcase sections which flank double paneled doors **17,000.00**

William III, English, c1700-10, burl walnut veneer, two sections, recessed upper with double-domical crest, pair of domically crested doors mounted with beveled glass mirror panels of conforming upper outline, plain int. of three adjustable wood shelves above pr of candle slides; lower section with canted front, hinged fall-front writing board, shaped desk int. with valanced central cubby hole between two pairs of valanced narrow cubby holes over two shaped drawers each, horizontal sliding door, flanked by two-tier side units with single-drawer bases, straight front of two graduated narrow drawers over two graduated wide drawers, highly figured burl on drawers match writing board and doors, engraved period brasses, later short straight bracket feet, minor veneer damage, 40" w, 23-1/2" d, 84" h **18,750.00**

Settee, Federal, Baltimore, c1800, attributed to Renshaw, triple chairback, downward sloping arms with urn turned supports, bowfront seat supported by turned legs, original overall gilt decoration on black painted ground, 48" l, 18-1/2" w, 34" h, **$5,750.** Photo courtesy of Pook & Pook.

Settees

Adams-style, late 19th or early 20th C, mahogany, relief carved double medallion back with pierced urn finials, relief carving of graduated bellflowers down front legs, fan medallions on aprons, arms, white stripe silk upholstery seat, refinished, restoration to back of seat and one arm, 39" w, 18-1/2" d, 38-1/2" h **1,100.00**

Art Deco, attributed to Warren McArthur, c1930, tubular aluminum frame, sheet aluminum seat and back supports, removable vinyl cushions, 68" l .. **5,750.00**

Arts & Crafts

Limbert, #939, oak, 11 back slats, corbels under arm, recovered orig

drop-in cushion, branded, refinished, 75" w, 27" d, 40" h.................. **800.00**

Stickley, Gustav, No. 165, with tapering pyramidal posts, arched vertical backslats and cloud lift stretcher, leather cushion, refinished, 59-1/2" l, 28" d, 40-1/2" h.... **6,275.00**

Stickley, L. & J. G., No. 232, even arm, horizontal backslats, broad vertical side slats, drop-in cushion, replaced leather, orig finish, unsgd, 72" l, 24" d, 32-1/2" h.......... **3,220.00**

Unknown America maker, 20th C, even arm, oak, crest rail over nine wide vertical slats, three on each side, joined by sq vertical posts, medium brown finish, replaced seat, joint separation, 65" w, 25-3/4" d, 32" h.................................. **2,650.00**

Biedermeier-style, beechwood, curved open back, three vasiform splats, out-curved arms, caned seat raised on six sq-section sabre legs.................... **650.00**

Classical, American, c1850, mahogany, serpentine front, carved crest, transitional rococo design elements, 82" l....... **600.00**

Colonial Revival, William and Mary style, American, c1930, loose cushions, turned baluster legs and stretcher, 48" l... **750.00**

Settee, Federal style, carved mahogany, downcurving reeded arms, reeded tapering legs ending in peg feet, 60-1/2" l, **$850+**. Photo courtesy of Sloans & Kenyon Auctions.

Empire-style, late 19th/early 20th C

Gilt bronze mounted mahogany, settee, pair of side chairs, each with foliate and figural mounts, 80" l settee, price for three pieces **1,725.00**

Mahogany, two seats, curved backs, each armrest ending on ram's head, hoof-foot feet...................... **2,100.00**

French Restauration, New York City, c1840, rosewood, arched upholstered back, scrolled arms outlined in satinwood terminating in volutes, rect seat frame with similar inlay, bracket feet, 80" l, 27" d, 33-1/2" h.................................... **1,200.00**

George III, early 19th C, black lacquer and faux bamboo, settee, pair of arm chairs, price for three pieces **1,265.00**

Gothic Revival, American, c1850, carved walnut, shaped crest rail surmounted by center carved finial, stiles with arched recessed panel and similarly carved finials, upholstered back and seat, open arms with padded armrests and scrolled handholds, carved seat rail, ring turned legs, ball feet, 67-1/2" w, 23-1/2" d, 49-3/4" h............................ **800.00**

Hepplewhite, English, shield back, mahogany, three molded shields across back, pierced urn splats in each, molded arms with relief scrolls, serpentine arm supports, two slip seats with rush coverings, molded detail around seat frame, tapered legs, old finish, repairs, 17-1/4" h seat, 57-1/2" w, 20" d, 36-1/2" h **600.00**

Louis XVI-style, third quarter 19th C, gilt bronze mounted ebonized maple, Leon Marcotte, New York City, c1860, 55-1/2" l, 25" d, 41-1/2" h........................... **2,185.00**

Renaissance Revival, America, c1875, carved walnut, triple back, each having carved crest and ebonized plaque inlaid with musical instruments, red floral damask upholstery..................... **1,200.00**

Rococo Revival

Attributed to John Henry Belter, c1885, 65" l settee, pair of lady's chairs, pair of side chairs, each with laminated rose and foliate carved cresting, grapevine openwork sides, cabriole legs, price for three pieces **14,375.00**

Attributed to J. & J. Meeks, rosewood, laminated curved backs, Stanton Hall pattern, rose crest in scrolled foliage and vintage, tufted gold velvet brocade reupholstery, age cracks and some edge damage, 65-1/2" l............................ **5,500.00**

Settee, Victorian, oval medallion back with button trim, olive brocade upholstery, 58" l, **$600**. Photo courtesy of Joy Luke Auctions.

Victorian, carved rosewood, c1870, shaped and padded back, two arched end sections joined by dipped section, each with pierced foliate crest, over upholstered serpentine front seat, flanked by scroll arms, conforming rail continue to cabriole legs, frame leaf carved **850.00**

Wicker, tightly woven rect back, inverted triangle-dec, tightly woven arms, rect seat with woven diamond herringbone pattern, continuous braided edging from crest to front legs, turned spindle apron, 43" w, 36" h.................................. **500.00**

Windsor, New England, early 19th C, birdcage, maple, ash, and hickory, bamboo turned birdcage crest over 27 turned spindles flanked by stiles joining bamboo-turned arms and supports over bench seat, eight bamboo-turned legs joined by stretchers, old refinish, imperfections, 72" l, 14-1/2" h seat, 31-1/2" h.................................... **2,415.00**

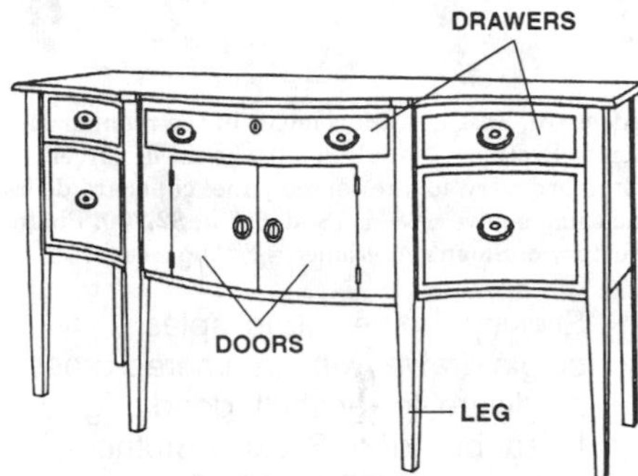

Typical Parts of a Sideboard

Sideboards

Art Deco, attributed to Jacques-Emile Ruhlmann, France, 1879-1933, inlaid Macassar ebony, elongated rect top with ebony and ivory inlaid trim, three center shelves flanked by cupboards, one fitted with drawer, one with shelf, doors with rect ebony inlay with ivory stringing, applied half-round molding around base, swollen shaped legs, imperfections, 54-5/8" w, 16-1/2" d, 43" h............. **920.00**

Art Nouveau, Louis Majorelle, 1900, oak and mahogany, rect, bowed front, inset marble top, tow long drawers, undulating brass pulls cast with sheaves of wheat, tow cupboard doors with large applied brass sheaves of wheat and undulating leaves, molded apron, four lug feet, 65" w, 39-1/8" h.......................... **6,000.00**

Arts & Crafts

English, attributed to, with two "V" backsplashes, two drawers with ring pulls, bottom shelf, casters, orig finish, marked "S79FUM90," 42" l, 20" d, 45-1/4" h................... **1,150.00**

Limbert, Charles P., Grand Rapids, MI, c1910, oak, oblong top, mirrored back above case, three short drawers flanked by paneled cupboard doors over long drawer, cooper pulls and strap hinges, sq legs, chamfered tenons, branded mark, 49-1/2" w, 53-1/2" h...... **900.00**

Sideboard, Aesthetic Movement, in the manner of Herter Brothers, NY, c1880-90, ebonized, parcel gilt, marquetry, foliate carved panel cupboard doors enclosing shelves, 68" l, 18" d, 69" h, **$2,700**. Photo courtesy of Sloan's Auctioneers & Appraisers.

Stickley Brothers, backsplash, single drawer with hammered brass hardware, lower shelf, good orig finish, branded "Stickley Brothers," stenciled "B735," light edge wear, 36" l, 19" d, 37" h **2,185.00**

Stickley Brothers, paneled plate rack, four drawers, three panel doors with hammered brass hardware, good orig finish, branded "Stickley Brothers," stenciled "8833," wear to copper patina on iron hardware **4,025.00**

Stickley, Gustav, designed by Harvey Ellis, backsplash, plate rest, six drawers, hammered copper pulls, arched apron, lower shelf, orig finish, red decal, replaced back paneling, minor nicks to legs, 42" x 54" x 21" **11,500.00**

Stickley, Gustav, model no. 967, gallery top over two short drawers and long drawer, two cupboard doors below, iron strap hinges and door pulls, red decal, 1902, imperfections, 59-3/4" w, 23-3/4" w, 43-3/4" h **32,300.00**

Centennial, Chippendale-style, America, late 19th C, mahogany, block front with shell carving, four drawers, front cabinet doors, gadrooned apron, cabriole legs, claw and ball feet, 68" w, 24" d, 40" h **950.00**

Classical

Mid Atlantic States, 1840-45, carved mahogany and cherry veneer, rect top over mahogany veneered drawer, two recessed panel doors opening to one shelf int., flanked by veneered scrolled supports, veneered base, old refinish, hardware changes, splashboard missing, 40" w, 18-3/4" d, 40-1/8" h **2,550.00**

Sideboard, Arts & Crafts, Gustav Stickley, plate rail, two cabinets and three drawers over linen drawer, all with hammered copper hardware, Craftsman paper label, refinished, veneer damage on left side, some edge roughness, 66" l, 23-3/4" d, 47-1/2" h, **$4,600**. Photo courtesy of David Rago Auctions.

New York, 1830s, carved mahogany veneer, splashboard with molded edge and four spiral carved and turned columns, topped by urn-shaped finials, rect top overhands recessed paneled case, cock-beaded drawers and cupboards outlined with crass banded mahogany veneer, two top drawers with dividers above short drawers, bottle drawers flanked by end recessed panel doors, left one with single shelf int., right one with two-shelf int., flanked by columnar leaf carved supports over frontal carved paw feet, rear feet are heavily turned and tapering, old refinish, imperfections, 60-1/4" w, 23-5/8" d, 56-3/4" h **2,760.00**

Eastlake, oak, shelf, mirror on high back, spoon carving.............................. **800.00**

Sideboard, Federal, attributed to Albany, New York, early 19th C, mahogany, bowed rectangular top, one long drawer, two cupboard doors flanked by cupboard and bottle drawer, all-over lightwood crossbanding and string inlay, tapering square legs, 70-3/4" l, 26-3/4" d, 35-3/4" h, **$6,800**. Photo courtesy of Sloans & Kenyon Auctions.

Empire, c1830, solid and mottled mahogany, deep ogee skirt, three drawers, deep triple-serpentine front with paneled doors and Gothic arches, side stenciled "Journeyman Cabinet Makers, Baltimore," restored orig finish, 72" w, 48" h... **11,550.00**

Federal

America, c1830, flame and solid mahogany, pineapple carving between three beveled, paneled doors, four full-standing classical columns, scalloped arches with fern carving, concave skirt, folded acanthus leaf and paw feet **6,050.00**

Massachusetts, Boston, 1810-20, mahogany, maple, and rosewood veneer, two-tiered case, demilune superstructure, maple inlaid panels surrounded by cross banded rosewood veneer above cock-beaded end drawers, small central drawer flanked by end cupboards, six ring turned tapering legs, case with concentric turnings, reeding, cock beading, and scenic landscape jointed on underside of arched opening, old surface, replaced pulls, replaced leg, veneer loss, later landscape painting, 74-1/2" l, 24-1/2" d, 44-3/4" h............ **9,200.00**

Sideboard, Hepplewhite, Pennsylvania, c1810, cherry, bowfront top over frieze drawer flanked by two short drawers above two cupboard doors flanked by bottle doors, all with line inlaid edges, square tapering legs with bellflower inlay and banded cuffs, 67" w, 41" h, **$7,475**. Photo courtesy of Pook & Pook.

Middle Atlantic States, c1790, attributed to, mahogany and cherry inlaid, overhanging top with canted corners and serpentine front, central cock-beaded door inlaid with cherry panel with quarter fan inlays and mahogany mitered border, cock-beaded wine drawer with three-drawer facade at one end, three cock-beaded graduated drawers on other, ends with cherry veneered panels, 4 sq inlaid tapering legs ending in molded spade feet, lower edge of case with molding, old finish, minor imperfections, 48-1/2" w, 21-5/8" d, 37" h................ **19,950.00**

New England, c1790, mahogany and mahogany veneer, overhanging top with shaped front, conforming case, central pullout surface, bowed

cock-beaded drawers, two cupboard doors flanked by concave drawers and cupboard doors, six sq tapering legs, replaced brasses, old refinish, imperfections, 64" w, 20-1/8" d, 37-1/2" h **5,500.00**
Virginia, 1790-1810, walnut and yellow pine, molded rect top, cock-beaded case with end drawers, right drawer visually divided into two drawers, left with two working drawers, central cupboard cock-beaded door, four square tapering legs, old brass pulls, old refinish, repairs, inscription on drawer reads "Virginia Hunt Board, early 19th cent. from family of Admiral Todd, Naval Commander prior to and during the Civil War, Virginia," 56" w, 22" d, 39" h **5,520.00**

Federal-style, Southern States, huntboard, yellow pine, overhanging rect top, case with three drawers, skirt with central shaping, four sq tapering legs, orig brasses, refinished, 21" w, 19-1/2" h **1,840.00**

Sideboard, International Movement, Heywood-Wakefield, champagne finish, drawers over three cabinet doors, two interior drawers and single shelf, branded mark, 59-3/4" l, 19" d, 32-1/2" h, **$500**. Photo courtesy of David Rago Auctions, Inc.

George III-style, late 19th C, mahogany, bowed front, three central drawers, flanked by short drawer over cupboard door on sq legs, 71" w, 24" d, 42" h **2,185.00**

George III/Hepplewhite, mahogany, flame grain mahogany, satinwood, and oak, paterae and shell inlay, 36" h **11,160.00**

Gothic, Kimbel & Cabus, New York, c1875, design no. 377, walnut, galleried top over two cupboard doors over open self over slant front over central drawer over open well flanked by twocupboard doors, galleried base shelf, bracket feet, 39-1/4" w, 17-3/4" d, 73" h........... **9,775.00**

Hepplewhite, mahogany and mahogany veneer with inlay, bowed center section with conforming doors and dovetailed drawer, two flat side doors, sq tapered legs, banding and stringing with bell flowers on legs, corner fans on doors and drawers, reworked, repairs, replaced brasses, 58-1/4" w, 18-1/2" d, 37-3/4" h **2,200.00**

Sideboard, International Movement, George Nelson for Herman Miller, walnut veneer, three drawers, wooden cupcake pulls, ebonized plank leg base, foil label, 34" l, 20" d, 29-3/4" h, **$575**. Photo courtesy of David Rago Auctions, Inc.

Neoclassical, Boston, 1820-25, mahogany veneer, corner style, paneled and scrolled splashboard over top with veneered molded edge, curving front which overhangs conforming case of three veneered drawers over two recessed paneled doors, single shelved int., similar recessed panel sides above flattened ball feet with brass banding, replaced brass pulls, old surface with some imperfections, 60" w, 35" d, 42" h **55,200.00**

Regency-style, 19th C, inlaid mahogany, two pedestals, central drawer, silver drawer, 58" w, 24" d, 36" h **1,610.00**

Renaissance Revival, America, cherry, curled mahogany drawer fronts, burled arched panel doors **900.00**

Sideboard, Victorian, c1870, English, oak and Pollard oak, upper section with architectural splashboard and long shelf, lower section with two drawers and two doors each having angular geometric raised panels, 73" l, 21" d, 81" h, **$1,750**. Photo courtesy of Skinner, Inc.

Sheraton, country, walnut and curly maple, beaded edge top, four dovetailed drawers, scalloped aprons, turned legs, line inlay around apron and drawer fronts, old varnish finish, replaced glass pulls, wear and edge damage, one heart inlay missing, large water stain on top, 69-1/2" w, 21-1/2" d, 43-1/2" h **5,500.00**

Victorian, American, late 19th C, pine, serpentine crest, rect top, four small drawers over two banks of four drawers, center cupboard, 65" w, 19" d, 51-1/2" h **750.00**

Sofas

Art Nouveau, Carlo Bugatti, 1900, ebonzied wood, rect back, mechanical seat, slightly scrolling rect arms, parchment upholstery, painted swallows and leafy branches, hammered brass trim, four block form feet, 68-3/8" l **1,900.00**

Biedermeier, recamier
c1820, maple, high and low scrolled ends, angular stepped backrest, sq tapered legs, 64" l **1,175.00**
c1830, fruitwood, high C-shaped end, low end with cylindrical turned cresting, canted seat rails, turned feet, 31" w, 80" l **3,200.00**

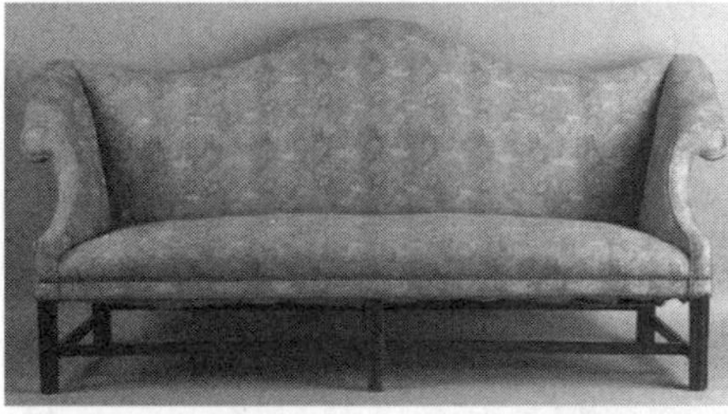

Sofa, Chippendale, Philadelphia, c1785, mahogany, serpentine back over raking outward scrolling arms supported by square Marlborough legs joined by stretchers, 89" w, 42" h, **$27,600**. Photo courtesy of Pook & Pook.

Centennial, Chippendale-style, American, late 19th C, mahogany, shaped back, rolled arms, yellow velvet upholstered seat, gadrooned apron, cabriole legs with carved knees, claw and ball feet, 62" l **1,500.00**

Chinese Chippendale-style, 20th C, mahogany frame, relief geometric designs on legs, piercings on stretchers, white upholstery with colorful flowers, pagodas, and birds, 74" w, 20" d, 34-1/2" h **700.00**

Chippendale, country, step down back with step down arms, bowed front with large down filled cushions, eight molded carved legs, cup caster feet, reupholstered, 76" w, 32" d, 36" h **3,000.00**

Classical
Mid Atlantic States, 1805-20, carved mahogany and bird's eye-maple veneer, Grecian style, scrolled and reeded arm and foot, punctuated with brass rosettes, continuing to similar reeded seat rail with inlaid dies, reeded saber legs flanked by brass flowerettes, brass paw feet on casters, old surface, 75" l, 14-1/2" h seat, 35" h.......................... **3,680.00**
New England, 1820-40, carved mahogany veneer, cylindrical

crest ends, leaf carved volutes, upholstered seat and rolled veneer seat rail, leaf carved supports, carved paw feet, 92" w, 16-1/2" h seat, 34-3/4" h **1,650.00**

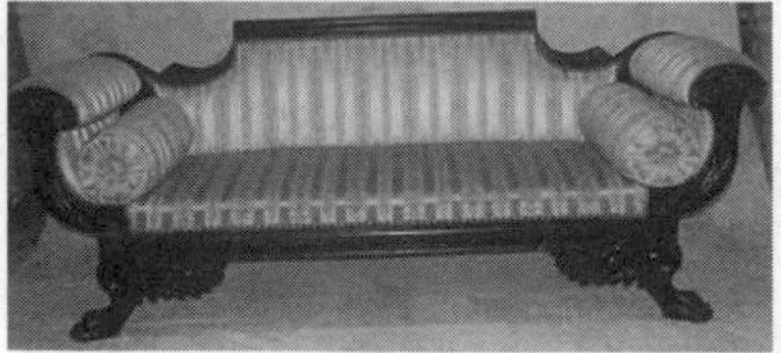

Sofa, Empire, c1870, walnut and mahogany, flower carving, checkering and leaf carvings on rolled arms, round cushions, claw feet, gold silk fabric upholstery, 84" l, 33-1/2" h, **$3,750**. Photo courtesy of Alderfer Auction Co.

Empire, mahogany and figured mahogany veneer frame, well-detailed carving with sea serpent front legs, turned back legs, lyre arms with relief carved flowers and cornucopia, rope turned crest rail, refinished, reupholstered in floral tapestry on ivory ground, bolster pillows, 107" l............................. **3,850.00**

Federal

America, carved mahogany, mahogany veer paneled top crest with scrolled sides, front carved with rosette and leaf dec, carved paw feet with front stylized wings, red flower dec upholstery, 96" w, 19-1/2" d, 32" h **1,000.00**

Massachusetts or New Hampshire, c1810, mahogany and bird's eye-maple veneer, raked veneered crest divided into three panels by cross banded mahogany inlay, flanked by reeded arms, similar supports terminating in down-scrolling terminals, ring turned baluster forms, slip seat, bird's eye maple veneered seat rail, four frontal reeded turned legs ending in casters, old refinish, minor re-veneering, 75-1/2" l, 32-1/2" h **6,900.00**

Sofa, Georgian, c1800, mahogany, molded arms over square tapering legs joined by stretchers, 66-1/2" w, 35" h, **$2,760**. Photo courtesy of Pook & Pook.

New Hampshire, c1815, carved mahogany, upholstered, straight crest continuing to shaped sides with carved arms on vase and ring reeded and swelled posts and cock-beaded panels, bowed seat rail, vase and ring-turned legs with cock-beaded rect inlaid dies, old finish, minor imperfections, 78" w, 24" d, 17" h seat, 34" h back......... **2,415.00**

George III-style, English, carved oak, double arched upholstered high backrest, scrolled arms, loose cushion seat, acanthus carved legs, claw and ball feet, 58" l................................... **1,200.00**

Louis XVI-style, late 19th or early 20th C, upholstered arms with ornate carved cornucopia filled with fruit and flowers, turned and tapered legs with reeding, floral band beneath scrolled tops, raised floral carved borders around framework, old dark finish, dark gold painted detail, contemporary golden brocade upholstery, 44" h **2,950.00**

Neoclassical, Baltic, c1825, carved mahogany, paneled cresting, padded arms with lions heads and anthemia, upholstered seat and back, shaped feet, 68" l.. **2,185.00**

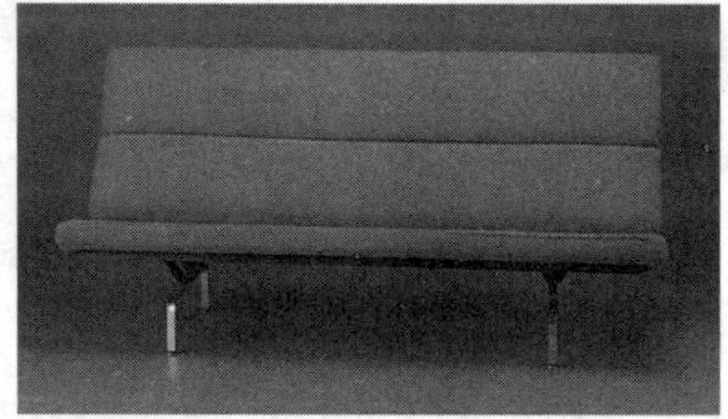

Sofa, International Movement, Charles Eames for Herman Miller, upholstered in original orange and red Alexander Girard fabric, chromed and black enameled flat steel frame, unmarked, 72-1/4" l, 28-1/2" d, 35-3/4" h, **$1,400**. Photo courtesy of David Rago Auctions, Inc.

Renaissance Revival, Jeliff, suite, rosewood, sofa, two side chairs **3,500.00**

Rococo Revival

Belter, John Henry, meridienne, Tuthill King variant pattern, laminated rosewood.......................... **9,350.00**

Meeks, J. J., attributed to, Stanton Hall variant, laminated rosewood, high raised floral crest, elaborate pierced grapevine along top edges, finger carved arms and frame with three relief carved leaves on serpentine front, contemporary burgundy silk upholstery with button back, refinished, old repairs, 76" w, 32" d, 49" h **6,100.00**

Meeks, J. J., attributed to, Stanton Hall variant, laminated rosewood, high relief roses and shell crest, finely pierced detailed scrolled foliage and vintage, green silk upholstery, restoration to crest and one rear foot, 63" w, 37" d, 36-1/2" h **9,350.00**

Unknown maker, suite, rosewood, fruit carved, tufted back sofa, four side chairs......................... **3,600.00**

Sofa, Victorian, mahogany, rolled arms, raised center back with carved crest, mahogany front with carved swan decoration to front of rolled arms, recently professionally upholstered, 78" w, 37" h to top of back crest, **$920**. Photo courtesy of James D. Julia, Inc.

Sheraton, mahogany, narrow crest with figured veneer, acanthus leaf relief carved scrolled arms and pineapple shaped supports with brass rosettes, ring turned legs with applied ormolu urns on corners, blue brocade upholstery, old dark refinishing, maple secondary wood **6,500.00**

Victorian, late, American, c1890, camel back, reupholstered, turned legs, 60" l **750.00**

Stands

Baker, wrought iron, 48" h, 14-1/2" d, 84" h.. **500.00**

Basin, Federal, attributed to Seymour Workshop, Boston, c1810-15, mahogany and bird's eye-maple veneer, small round table with concentric incised circles around basin opening above three veneered and cock-beaded drawers, two of which are hinged, turned and reeded legs joined to the round incised platform, ending in brass paw feet, orig brasses, old refinish, 18-1/8" d, 28-1/4" h **36,800.00**

Bird cage, wicker, painted white, tightly woven quarter moon-shaped cage holder, wrapped pole standard, tightly woven conical base, 74" h............. **225.00**

Book, Gothic Revival, manufactured by Betjamann's, retailed by Tiffany & Co., Union Square, late 19th C, burlwood veneer, pointed arch uprights pierced with trefoils, beveled rect base, 13-1/2" l, 5-3/4" w... **350.00**

Canterbury, Regency, early 19th C, mahogany, drawer with paper label for "G. Ibison Furniture Broker & Appraiser, Cumberland Place, Near the Elephant & Castle," restoration, 19-1/4" l, 14" d, 22-1/2" h **1,380.00**

Drink stand, Arts & Crafts, L. & J.G. Stickley, circular copper-covered overhanging top, circular apron, cross stretchers, branded mark, original finish, replaced z-clamps under top, drill holes to underside, finishing nails to bottom of skirt into legs, 18" d, 28" h, **$2,300**. Photo courtesy of David Rago Auctions.

Cellarette

Arts & Crafts

Stickley, Gustav, flush top, pull-out copper shelf, single drawer, cabinet door, copper pulls, orig finish, large red decal, veneer lifting on sides and back, 22" w, 16" d, 39-1/2" h **4,315.00**

Stickley, L. & J. G., arched backsplash, pull-out copper shelf, two-door cabinet, hammered copper strap hinges, ring pulls, top refinished, orig finish on base, "The Work of..." decal, 35-1/2" x 32" x 16" **13,800.00**

Federal, attributed to Middle Atlantic states, c1790-1800, mahogany inlaid, octagonal top, conforming case, both inlaid with contrasting stringing, interior well with removable lead liner, four sq tapering legs inlaid with bellflowers and stringing, brasses appear to be orig, old refinish, sun faded top, imperfections, 22-1/4" w, 17-1/4" w, 25-1/4" h **28,200.00**

George III, English, mid-19th C, mahogany, lozenge form, brass bands, twin loop carry handles, racked chamfered tapering legs, 24" w, 17-1/2" d, 27-1/2" h .. **7,500.00**

Chamber, Federal

New England, early 19th C, painted and dec, dec splashboard above wash stand top with round cut-out for basin, medial shelf with drawer below, orig yellow paint with green and gold stenciling and striping, paint wear, imperfections, 18-1/4" h, 1" d, 39-1/4" h **350.00**

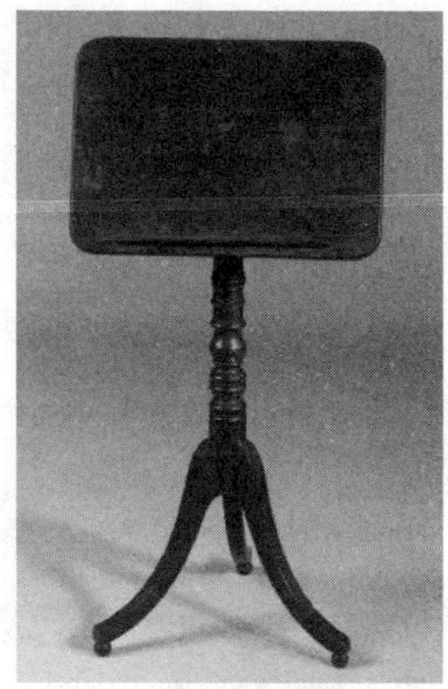

Bookstand, Victorian, c1860, mahogany, tilting top with bookrest, turned standard, tripod base, 19" w, 13-1/2" d, 31" h, **$360**. Photo courtesy of Skinner, Inc.

North Shore, MA, c1815-25, carved mahogany, shaped splashboard, veneered cabinet door flanked by ovolu corners, carved columns of leaves and grapes on punch-work ground, ring turned tapering legs, brass casters, old replaced brasses, old refinish, minor restoration, 21-1/2" w, 16" d, 35-5/8" h .. **2,300.00**

Portsmouth, NH, c1800, mahogany inlaid, shaped splashboard with center quarter round shelf, pierced top with bowfront, square string inlaid supports continue to outward flaring legs with patterned inlays, medial shelf, satinwood skirt, small center drawer with patterned inlaid lower edge, shaped stretchers with inlaid paterae, old finish, minor imperfections, 23" w, 16-1/2" d, 41" h **5,750.00**

Dumbwaiter

George III style, 19th C, mahogany, three-tier, typical form, graduated dished tiers, baluster turned supports, tripod base, 43" h **985.00**

Queen-Anne style, walnut, three circular shelves, splayed legs, pad feet, 21" d, 39" h **300.00**

Easel

Aesthetic Movement, attributed to Cincinnati furniture maker, cherry, intricate carved sunflowers and oak leaves, orig finish, 23" w, 36" d, 75" h **2,500.00**

Louis XVI-style, mahogany and parcel-gilt, picture support hung with berried laurel swags, trestle-end frame carved with acanthus, imbrications, and dolphins, 25" w, 23-1/2" d, 82" h **950.00**

Ètagére, Victorian, rosewood, ornate carved crest, mirrored back, three shelves on each side, bow fronted base section with mirrored back, 54" w, 9'7", **$4,400**. Photo courtesy of Joy Luke Auctions.

Étagère

Classical, New England, 1860s, mahogany and mahogany veneer, spool turned gallery, ball finials, three shelves with similar supports, two recessed panel cupboard doors, single shelf int., ball turned feet, old refinish, imperfections, 35-1/4" w, 15-3/4" d, 66" h **990.00**

Regency, late, English, early 19th C, six tiers, corner, columnar supports, basal drawer, brass casters, 18" w, 14" d, 62" h **3,000.00**

Victorian, late, English, bamboo and Japanese lacquer, three tiers, corner, scalloped form shelves, raised, colored and gilt Chinoiseries, 16-1/2" w, 45" h...................... **800.00**

Music stand, George II, c1750, mahogany, adjustable tab with ratchet support, 18-3/4" w, 28-1/2" h, **$6,325**. Photo courtesy of Pook & Pook.

Folding, Chippendale

New York State or Pennsylvania, 1755-775, cherry, dished top rotates and titles, birdcage support, swelled and turned pedestal, cabriole tripod base, pad feet, old refinish, imperfections, 17-1/2" d, 26" h **3,220.00**

Pennsylvania, 1760-80, walnut, molded dish top, inscribed edge tilts, tapering pedestal with suppressed ball, cabriole legs ending in pad feet, imperfections, 22" d, 29" h **4,600.00**

Nightstand, Heywood-Wakefield, Sculptura, single drawer, original Wheat finish, branded mark, finish wear, 20" w, 16" d, 23-3/4" h, **$300**. Photo courtesy of David Rago Auctions, Inc.

Magazine

Arts & Crafts

Stickley, Gustav, paneled sides, four shelves under arched apron, refinished, tacks missing, 15" w, 14-1/4" d, 35-1/4" h............ **2,415.00**

Stickley, Gustav, Tree of Life, carved sides, four shelves, orig finish and tacks, unmarked, minor edge wear, 14" sq, 43-1/2" h **1,610.00**

Stickley, L. & J. G., No. 46, slat sided, four shelves, arched top rails and apron, Handcraft decal, orig finish, 20" w, 12" d, 42-1/4" h **3,450.00**

Renaissance Revival, third quarter 19th C, mahogany, walnut, parcel-gilt, and ebonized gilt-metal, hanging, back plate with acanthus crest flanked by fleur-de-lis and bellflowers, uprights mounted on top with gilt-metal bust roundels, central hinged magazine folio set with gilt composition oval bust of Mercury, gilt incised detailing, 19-3/4" w, 21-1/2" h **300.00**

Music

New England, c1840, painted ash and pine, adjustable, two canted sides, vertical slats on cylindrical shaft, chamfered rect post, chamfered cross legs, painted blue-green, 15-1/2" w, 14" w, 78" h **635.00**

Plant stand, attributed to George Hunzinger, New York, c1860, walnut, nine circular platforms on central baluster-turned support, joined by vertical and horizontal turned spindles, all resting on reeded sphere, four vase and ring-turned splayed legs centering turned drop pendant, old white and gold repaint, 38-1/2" w, 38-1/2" d, 55-1/2" h, **$1,175**. Photo courtesy of Skinner, Inc.

Plant

Arts & Crafts

Limbert, ebon-oak line, overhanging top, four caned panels on each side, recent finish, branded signature, 14" w, 14" d, 34" h.................... **2,100.00**

Stickley, Gustav, sq top flush with cloud-lift apron, narrow board mortised through corseted stretchers with tenon and key, orig finish, 1902-04 red decal, crack in one stretcher, 14" sq, 27" h **3,450.00**

Empire-style, French, late 19th C, ebonized walnut, inverted pear shaped body set with rim of porcelain enamel dec with black and green Greek key on pink ground, gilt metal openwork rim, set with Minerva masks, three legs topped by ormolu griffin masks conjoined by suspended chains, round open base with ball feet, set with further chains, 31-1/2" h **400.00**

Victorian, wirework, painted, late 19th C, demilune, three-tier, each tier with ornately curled rim, fout slender legs heading by scrolled wire design, joined by single stretchers, X-bracing at back, casters, 45" l, 40" h **750.00**

Portfolio, William IV, English, c1830, carved rosewood, folding mechanism **3,500.00**

Reading, Federal, Albany, NY, early 19th C, mahogany, reading stand above ring-turned tapering post on rect shaped canterbury, turned tapering spindles, casters, 22-1/4" w, 14" d, 47-1/2" h **3,200.00**

Sewing, Sheraton, country, cherry and walnut, curly maple veneer, figured cherry veneer top, two dovetailed drawers with beaded edges, old pressed glass pulls, bowed compartments for cloth scraps or supplies at either end with hinged lids, reeded panels on top of ring turned legs, ball feet, old dark brown finish, poplar and pine secondary woods, areas of veneer loss, restorations, 30" w, 17-3/4" d, 29" h.......................... **1,375.00**

Sewing stand, Victorian, c1850-60, walnut, octagonal, hourglass form, hinged lid, compartmented interior, single door in base, 17-1/2" d, 29" h, **$415**. Photo courtesy of Alderfer Auction Co.

Shaving, quarter-sawn oak, shaped beveled mirror on lyre shaped back, two drawers in swelled case, four tall saber legs, two small shelves.............. **1,500.00**

Stand, Federal, attributed to New England, early 19th C, rectangular top with gallery, single drawer, square tapering legs, painted gray with smoke decoration, opalescent glass pull, imperfections, 20-1/4" w, 19-3/4" d, 32-1/4" h, **$650**. Photo courtesy of Skinner, Inc.

Side

Classical, southern New England, c1825, tiger maple, sq overhanging top over base having single beaded drawer, four swelled and tapering ring-turned legs joined by beaded skirt, opalescent glass pull, refinished, 19-3/4" x 20" top, 29" h **2,115.00**

Empire, mixed hardwoods, flame mahogany veneer, one board top with drop leaves, two dovetailed drawers with pressed-glass pulls, flanked by half turned columns, apron with gadrooning at bottom, carved pineapple column, platform base with scrolled leaf returns to carved paw feet, 15-1/5" w, 16-3/4" d, 28" h **450.00**

Federal

New England, c1820-30, sq slightly overhanging top, base with single drawer, four sq tapering legs, all-over yellow grain paint, drawer with red and green floral and foliate device flanked by dies painted with trailing vines continuing to simulate stringing, possibly orig brass pulls, very minor imperfections, 16" x 18" top, 28-1/2" h **27,025.00**

Northern New England, c1800, birch and bird's eye maple veneer, sq top, conforming base, single drawer, four tapering sq legs joined by straight skirt, replaced brass pull, refinished, 16" w, 15-1/2" d, 27" h......... **1,175.00**

Hepplewhite, curly maple, one board top, sq legs taper from 1-1/2" below top to 3/4" at feet, golden refinishing, 18" x 18" top, 27-7/8" h **660.00**

Sheraton, two drawers

Cherry with burl veneer trim around drawer fronts, one board top, two dovetailed drawers with clear pressed lacy type pulls and newer bolts, ring turned legs ending with ball feet, old mellow brown surface, poplar secondary wood, 18-1/2" w, 18-1/2" d, 31" h **550.00**

Curly maple, bold figure on case and legs, mahogany veneer drawer fronts, one board top, two dovetailed drawers with beaded edges and unusual orig brasses, turned legs, orig brass casters, 20-3/4" w, 17-1/2" d, 26-1/2" h............. **1,760.00**

Stand, Federal, attributed to Vermont, c1820, tiger maple, rectangular overhanging top, single drawer, straight skirt, ring-turned tapering legs, tapering peg feet, original brass turned pull, original surface, 22" w, 17-3/4" d, 28-3/4" h, **$2,000**. Photo courtesy of Skinner, Inc.

Tabouret, Arts & Crafts, L. & J. G. Stickley

No. 558, octagonal, cross-stretchers, branded mark, orig finish, overcoated, 15" d, 17" h........ **875.00**

No. 559, octagonal, cross-stretchers, Handcraft decal, top refinished, restoration to base, 18" d, 20-1/4" h **1,380.00**

Umbrella, Arts & Crafts, early 20th C, oak, sq form, four posts, top and bottom stretchers with mortise and tenon joinery, one dark brown finish, other medium brown finish, marked "Cedric S. Sweeter Jan. 23, 1920," 12" w, one 28-3/4" h, other 29" h, price for pr.......................... **230.00**

Vitrine, Mahogany, line border inlay, satinwood panels, top with drop front, molded edges, tapered sq legs, brass casters, joined by stretcher base, 21-1/2" w, 16-1/2" d, 28" h............. **600.00**

Tabouret stand, Arts & Crafts, Stickley, dark finish, 29" h, **$300**. Photo courtesy of Wiederseim Associates, Inc.

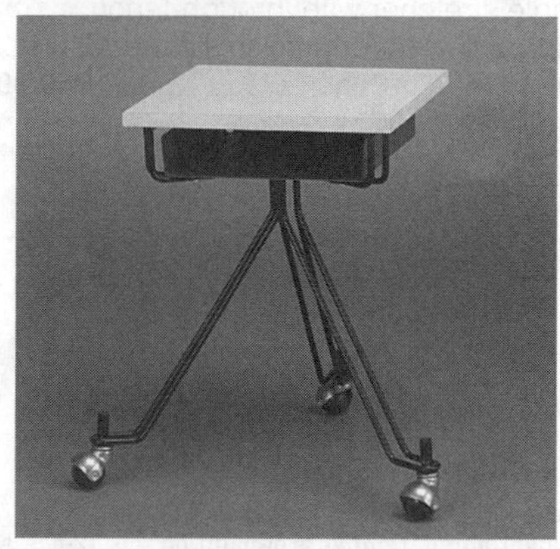

Telephone stand, International Movement, Elliot Noyes for Knoll, IBM, rectangular white laminate top over gray enameled metal compartment, tubular black metal tripod base with ball casters, unmarked, 21-1/2" w, 18-1/2" d, 22-1/4" h, **$540**. Photo courtesy of David Rago Auctions, Inc.

Wash

Empire, figured mahogany veneer, poplar secondary wood, dovetailed gallery fitted with narrow shelf, bowed top with cut-outs for wash bowl and two jars, serpentine front supports, turned rear posts, dovetailed drawer in base with brass pulls, high well turned legs, refinished, edge chips, 18" w, 16" d, 37-3/4 h **385.00**

Federal, Rhode Island, c1790, mahogany veneer, top with four shaped corners, canted corners, engaged ring-turned columns ending in reeded legs flanking cock-beaded drawers outlined in cross banded veneer, top two drawers with sections, replaced brasses, old refinish, imperfections, 20-3/4" w, 15-1/2" d, 28-1/2" h............ **4,025.00**

Hepplewhite, country, pine, worn brown paint over earlier red, dovetailed gallery on top, narrow shelf along back, sq legs, shaped two-board base shelf, 26-3/4" w, 18-1/2" d, 39-1/4" h................ **800.00**

Sheraton, mahogany, cutout top, shaped gallery, high scrolled crest, one dovetailed drawer in base, shelf, delicate turned legs and supports, refinished, old replaced brass pull, 17-1/2" w, 14-3/4" d, 38-3/4" h **600.00**

What-not, Regency, 19th C, mahogany, three shelf tiers, bottom tier fitted with drawer, circular turned legs, 45" h **1,410.00**

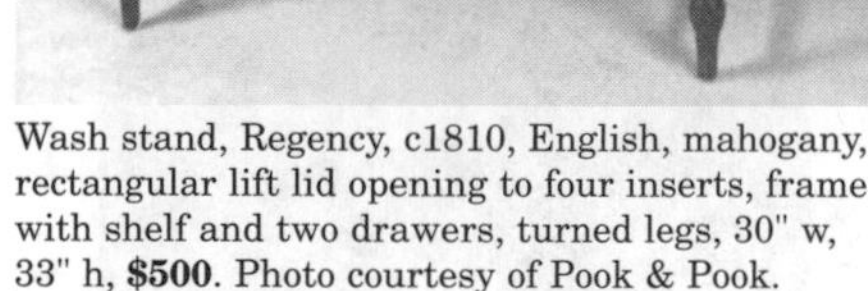

Wash stand, Regency, c1810, English, mahogany, rectangular lift lid opening to four inserts, frame with shelf and two drawers, turned legs, 30" w, 33" h, **$500**. Photo courtesy of Pook & Pook.

Work stand, Federal, New York, 1825, mahogany, two lyre form supports, ormolu mounts, 22-1/2" w, 31" h, **$1,380**. Photo courtesy of Pook & Pook.

Work

Classical, early 19th C, carved maple and rosewood veneer, top outlined with rosewood veneer banding above sectional veneered drawer, lower drawer flanked by short columns, tapering pedestal joining four leaf carved legs ending in carved hairy paw feet on castors, old refinish, 20-3/4" w, 18-1/2" d, 28-3/4" h **500.00**

Hepplewhite, New England, c1810, cherry inlaid, sq top, outline stringing and quarter fan inlays on ovolo corners, line inlaid drawer and skirt, line inlaid sq tapering legs, cross banded cuffs, brass drawer pull, refinished, 19" w, 19" d, 27" h **2,650.00**

Renaissance Revival, American, c1860, lift top opening to real satinwood interior fitted with compartments, narrow drawer above semi-circular bag drawer, pair of stylized lyre form ends jointed by arched stretcher surmounted by turned finial **875.00**

Sheraton, country, drop leaves, orig red and black grained dec on top and D-shaped drop leaves, areas of figured mahogany veneer on base and drawer fronts, well turned legs with raised center blocks, ball feet, two drawers pegged at corners, old turned wooden pulls, veneer chips, 16" w, 24" d, 28-1/2" h........... **275.00**

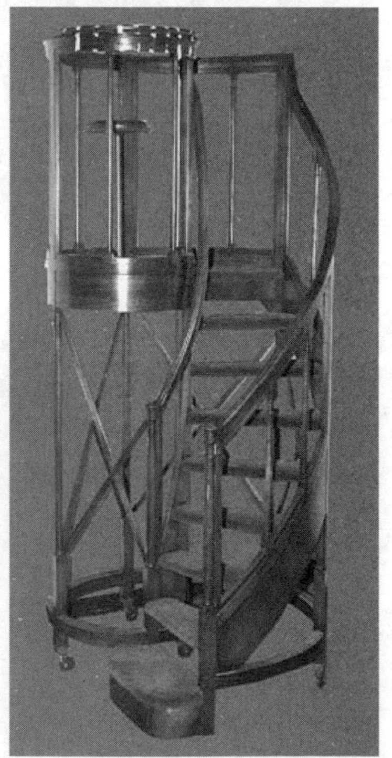

Library steps, English, 20th C, spiral, mahogany, upper platform with leather upholstered stool and hinged reading surface, 52-1/2" w, 106" h, **$4,000**. Photo courtesy of Sloans & Kenyon Auctions.

Steps

Bed, New England, early 19th C, pine and tulipwood, two steps, thumb-molded drawer below bottom one, flanked by shaped sides, demilune base, old color, repaired, 15-1/2" w, 10" d, 17-1/2" h **575.00**

Circus, America, early 20th C, painted white stringers, red, yellow, and blue treads, 25" w, 90" d, 27" h............. **435.00**

Library

George III, English, late 18th C, mahogany, rect molded hinged top, eight steps, 49-1/2" w, 53-1/2" h **2,500.00**

Regency, English, early 19th C, mahogany, three steps, inset green leather treads, scrolling banister, sq balusters, feet with brass casters, 46" w, 27" w, 56" h.............. **2,400.00**

Stools

Cricket, Arts & Crafts, Limbert, #205-1/2", rect top covered with new leather, splayed sides, inverted heart cut-out, single stretcher with through-tenon, replaced keys, orig finish, branded, 20" w, 15" d, 18" h......................... **950.00**

Footstool, wood, splayed legs, bootjack ends, straight apron, remnants of paint on top, 12-5/8" w, 7-1/2" d, 7-1/2" h, **$80**. Photo courtesy of Alderfer Auction Co.

Joint stool, William and Mary, English, c1690, oak, molded rect top, scalloped edge frame supported by turned legs joined by box stretchers, 18" l, 19-1/2" h, **$1,150**. Photo courtesy of Pook & Pook.

Foot

Arts & Crafts, oak

Barber Brothers, oak, nicely replaced leather seat, some color added to orig finish, paper label, 13" w, 13" d, 11" h **110.00**

Limbert, cricket, #205-1/2, rect orig leather top and tacks, splayed sides with inverted heart cut-out having single stretcher with through-tenon construction, orig finish, branded and numbered, 20" w, 15" d, 19" h **2,000.00**

Orig leather and tacks, slightly arched rails, orig finish, 12" sq, 8" h **90.00**

Worn orig drop-in leather cushion with 4 vertical slats to side, orig finish, 16" w, 14" d, 14" h **260.00**

English, yew wood and walnut, splayed thick turned legs with turned rungs, oval seat, old dark finish, 13-1/4" w, 9-1/4" d, 17-1/2" h **200.00**

Sheraton, curly and bird's eye maple, old finish, cane top, minor damage to top, 7-3/4" w, 13" l, 6-1/2" h **440.00**

Victorian, flame grain mahogany veneer, ogee base, scalloped bracket feet, lift top with yarn needlework of blue, red, and yellow bird, gray ground, polychrome scrolled border, int. lined with yellow emb paper, replaced hinges and hinge rail, 13-3/4" x 10" x 8" h **350.00**

Windsor, attributed to Maine, early 19th C, rect top, four swelled legs joined by X-form stretchers, orig dark brown grain paint which resembles exotic wood, yellow line accents, paint imperfections, 12" 2, 8" d, 7" h **625.00**

Gout, Empire, mahogany, turned and tapered legs, ogee base molding, serpentine ends with raised rosettes, contemporary green upholstery, old refinishing, 13-1/2" w, 13" d, 8" h ... **350.00**

Joint

Early, oak, old finish, wear and age cracks, 11" w, 16-1/2" l, 17-3/4" h **990.00**

Jacobean-style, oak, rect plank top, shaped skirt, block and ring-turned legs joined by box stretcher, 18" w, 11-1/4" d, 21" h **700.00**

Ottoman, Classical, attributed to Boston, MA, c1830, mahogany veneer, overstuffed cushions rest inside mitred frame atop molded base, ogee bracket feet, wooden casters, refinished, minor imperfections, 20" w, 18" d, 17-1/2" h, price for pr................................ **2,235.00**

Piano

Louis XVI-style, late 19th C, carved beech, circular, adjustable, close-nailed over stuffed top, petal-carved frieze, leaf-capped turned, tapered, and fluted legs, wavy cross-stretcher **850.00**

Renaissance Revival, American, 1870, walnut, sq upholstered seat, acanthus carved baluster supports, four outswept legs, hoof feet **350.00**

Ottoman, Empire, c1830, figured mahogany, serpentine form, shaped supports, wooden casters, green and gold velvet upholstery, 17" w, 13" h, **$480**. Photo courtesy of Sloans & Kenyon Auctions.

Seat-type

Country, folk art, attributed to Fredericksburg, PA, late 19th/early 20th C, painted and dec, octagonal seat, chamfered edge, trimmed with border band of carved hearts, tall splayed and chamfered legs also trimmed with carved hearts and joined by slender rungs, overall polychrome **1,850.00**

Piano stool, mixed wood, spindle splats, claw and ball feet, 36" h, **$100**. Photo courtesy of Joy Luke Auctions.

George III, late 19th C, mahogany, gold floral satin upholstered rest seat, sq tapering supports, molded H-form stretchers, pr, 19-1/2" l, 17" h **1,650.00**

International Movement

Eames, Charles, manufactured by Herman Miller, Time-Life, walnut, concave seat, 13" d, 15" h **1,000.00**

Platner, Warren, manufactured by Knoll, bronze wire base, peach fabric upholstered seat, 17" d, 21" h **325.00**

Windsor, American, 19th C, oblong plant seat raised on three tall, turned and slightly swelled legs joined by T-stretcher, traces of old green paint, 15" w, 24-1/2" h **200.00**

Vanity, Portuguese Colonial, 18th C, ebonized walnut, slip-seat, shaped serpentine apron, cabriole legs, claw and ball feet, 22" w, 21" d, 20" h **400.00**

Work, Biedermeier, c1825, fruitwood, ebonized and parcel-gilt, tufted cushion lifting to well, case with foliate gilt bronze frieze, ebonized splayed feet and elongated gilded leaf tips with flower-head pendant, 19" h **3,000.00**

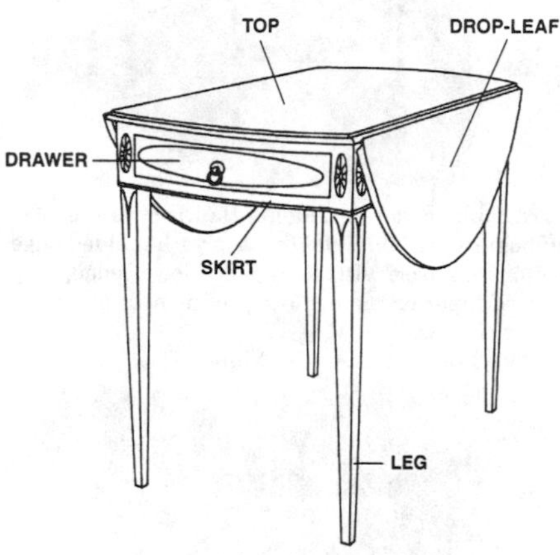

Typical Parts of a Table

Tables

Architect's, drafting, early 19th C, solid rosewood **4,125.00**

Banquet, Empire, c1830, solid and flame mahogany, octagonal pedestal, pull ends with turned, drop-down legs, restored orig finish, extended to 18' **11,550.00**

Breakfast

Chippendale to Hepplewhite, transitional, walnut, one board top, beaded edge apron, sq legs with slight taper, molded corner, and inside chamfer, H stretcher, old finish, stains on top, 19" w, 29-1/4" l, 28-1/4" h **8,250.00**

Classical, New York, 1820-30, carved mahogany inlaid, top with brass inlay in outline, stamped brass on edge of shaped leaves, one working and one faux drawers, flanked by drop pendants, foot pillar curved platform support, leafage carved legs, carved paw feet, casters, replaced pulls, old finish, repairs, losses, 39" w, 24" d, 28" h **2,450.00**

Federal

Massachusetts, central, c1810, inlaid cherry, rect hinged top with ovolo corners, base with straight skirt, edged with lunette inlay, flanked by sq tapering legs outlined in stringing, topped with icicle inlay, old refinish, 36" w, 17" d, 29" h **1,150.00**

Massachusetts or New England, 1815, mahogany oval top, hinged leaves, flanking two drawers, one working, one faux, both outlined in stringing and have central panel of figured mahogany veneer above chevron-style inlaid banding, reeded, turned, tapering legs, turned feet, old refinish, surface imperfections, 35-3/8" w, 20-1/4" d, 29-3/4" h **8,225.00**

New York City, c1815, carved mahogany veneer, rect top, shaped leaves, one working and one faux end drawers, cross banded mahogany veneer, turned acanthus leaf carved pedestal, four acanthus leaf carved legs, brass hairy paw feet, old refinish, repairs, 25" w closed, 38-1/2" l, 30-1/4" h **1,725.00**

Regency, 1820, rosewood, brass inlaid **2,200.00**

Book table, Arts & Crafts, America, early 20th C, oak rectangular top over two shelves with backstop, double side supports with keyed and beveled tenons joined to shoe foot, unsigned, 26" w, 14" d, 26-1/2" h, **$825**. Photo courtesy of Skinner, Inc.

Card

Biedermeier, c1810, fruitwood, part ebonized, rect top, swivel felt playing surface, sq tapered legs, 36" w, 18" d, 30" h **1,550.00**

Classical, New York, 1820-30, carved mahogany, mahogany veneer rect swivel top with rounded front carved corners, leaf carved and shaped shaft, curving platform which joins four scrolling leaf caved legs ending in carved paw feet, refinished, minor imperfections, 36" w, 17-1/2" d, 30" h **1,495.00**

Empire, mahogany and figured mahogany veneer, hinged two board top slightly warped, ogee aprons with moldings, scrolled uprights, stepped platform base with delicate molding, bracket feet, old worn

finish, pine secondary wood, 34-1/2" w, 17" d, 27-1/4" h **375.00**

Card table, Federal, Boston, Massachusetts, c1810, mahogany serpentine top with lunette inlayed edge, conforming case with three tiger maple panels over lunette inlay, resting on turned and reeded legs, 6-1/2" w, 17-1/2" d, 30" h, **$6,900**. Photo courtesy of Pook & Pook.

Federal

Massachusetts, c1790-1800, mahogany inlaid, rect folding top with ovolo corners, string inlaid edge, conforming skirt, central oval panel and rect panels on corners and ends defined by stringing, four sq tapered legs with string inlaid panels and borders, refinished, minor restoration, 34-1/4" w, 17" d, 30" h **2,600.00**

Massachusetts, c1810-15, mahogany and mahogany veneer, folding top with serpentine front, half serpentine ends, corners and scratch-beaded edge, conforming cock-beaded skirt joining half-engaged vase and ring-turned legs, ball feet, old refinish, 36-3/4" w, 18-1/2" d, 29-3/4" h............ **1,120.00**

New England, early 19th C, painted rect, rect slightly overhanging folding top, conforming base, four sq tapering legs joined by straight skirt, old red-painted surface, minor surface imperfections, 35-3/4" w, 17-1/2" d, 30-1/4" h............ **1,300.00**

Newburyport, MA, c1800, mahogany veneer, elliptic shaped top with inlaid edge, overhangs divided skirt with panels of stringing and figured maple dies at top of sq tapering legs, outline stringing on legs with cuff inlays, old surface, veneer losses, 36" w, 17-5/8" d, 30" h **3,335.00**

New York, c1810, mahogany and mahogany veneer, folding rect top with canted corners, conforming base, single long cock-beaded drawer, dies inlaid with fiddle back mahogany veneered panels, five reeded tapering legs ending in brass ball feet joined by straight cock-beaded skirt, repairs, 36" w, 18-1/4" d, 30-1/2" h............ **1,955.00**

Providence, RI, c1790-1800, mahogany inlaid, demilune, folding top with string inlaid edge above conforming skirt joining five sq tapering legs with bookend, icicle, diamond, and string inlay continuing to inlaid cuffs, old refinish, imperfections, 35" w, 17-1/4" d, 28-1/2" h **1,880.00**

Card table, Federal, middle Atlantic states, c1800, mahogany, demilune folding top with molded edge, conforming base with cockbeaded lower edge, four sq tapering molded legs, refinished, minor imperfections, 35-1/4" w, 17-1/2" d, 28-1/2" h, **$2,250**. Photo courtesy of Skinner, Inc.

Card table, Queen Anne, walnut, crossbanded, concertina-action, rectangular top with outset rounded corners and interior felt surface, cabriole legs, pad feet, 33-1/2" w, 16-1/2" d, 20-3/4" h, **$2,235**. Photo courtesy of Skinner, Inc.

Georgian-style, late 19th C, carved mahogany, foliate carved top, polished playing surface, foliate carved circular legs, pad feet, 27-1/2" w, 13" d, 29" h......... **1,495.00**

Hepplewhite, figured mahogany, mahogany veneer, ovolo-cut corners on top and aprons, line border inlay on edges of top, aprons, and tapered legs, old dark finish, few age splits, minor veneer chip on apron, slight warp in top, 34-1/4" w, 17" d, 30-1/2" h **3,300.00**

Neoclassical, New York City, c1825, carved mahogany veneer, shaped swivel top with cross banded veneer in outline above inlaid edges and veneered skirt, central raised plaque above scrolled and waterleaf carved supports, fluted curving platform, similarly carved legs, carved paw feet on casters, old refinish, imperfections **4,600.00**

Sheraton-style, early 20th C, demilune folding two-part top, mahogany, variegated band inlay around aprons and top, oval and diamond inlaid panels with floral dec, ring turned legs, tapered feet, refinished, 36" w, 18" d, 30" h **350.00**

Center

Biedermeier, inlaid walnut, shaped rect top, molded frieze with drawer, canted, sq-section cabriole legs, 25" w, 37" l, 27-3/4" h......... **1,100.00**

Classical

Boston, attributed to, c1825, carved mahogany and mahogany veneer, circular top with inset leather surface, cross banded border, conforming base with four drawers, gilt brass lion's head ring pulls, vase and ring-turned spiral carved center support, gadrooned circular platform, four scrolled reeded and paneled legs, gilt brass hairy paw feet and casters, refinished, minor imperfections, 27-3/4" d, 28" h **12,925.00**

Philadelphia, c1827, carved mahogany veneer, rect top with molded edge, cock-beaded frieze with single central working drawer flanked by faux drawers, turned and carved pedestal ending in gadrooning above stepped, curved pedestal, 4 belted ball feet, old surface, minor imperfections, carving similar to work of Anthony G. Quervelle (1789-1856), Philadelphia, 45-1/4" w, 20" d, 34-3/4" h .. **2,550.00**

Gothic Revival, attributed to New York State, 1935-45, mahogany veneer, hexagonal top with molded edge overhangs shaped frieze, three faceted columns atop flat base with concave sides on scrolled feet, old refinish, restored, 34-1/4" d, 31" h **1,120.00**

International Movement, Wienerwerkstatte, c1930, mahogany and brass, circular top with cross banded edge, conforming frieze, sq-section support flanked by four further cylindrical supports, raised on truncated pyramidal base, 25-1/4" d, 30-1/2" h................ **550.00**

Neoclassical-style, Maitlin Smith, 20th C, pietra-dura marble and bronze, circular top inlaid with vitruvian scrolls, full gallery, drapery covered urn standard on three-sided base, gadrooned ball feet, 30" d, 31-1/2" h **2,000.00**

Renaissance Revival, American, c1875-80, burl walnut, top with rounded ends, turned pendants, trestle supports, carved stylized foliage and urns, 55" w, 31" d, 30" h **1,610.00**

Coffee table, International Movement, Paul Evans, 1970, sculpted bronze base comprised of multi-level vertical panels, rectangular glass top with beveled edge, base marked "PE/70," 72" l, 36" w, 16-1/4" h, **$860**. Photo courtesy of David Rago Auctions, Inc.

Conference table, International Movement, Florence Knoll for Knoll, elliptical rosewood veneer top, chrome-plated steel pedestal base, Knoll Associates label, 96" l, 54" w, 28-1/2" h, provenance: from o ffice of John Wanamaker, Philadelphia, PA, **$2,300**. Photo courtesy of David Rago Auctions, Inc.

Console table, Arts & Crafts, Limbert, trestle legs, three central slats over one long stretcher, branded under top, refinished, 72" l, 22" d, 29" h, **$5,200**. Photo courtesy of David Rago Auctions, Inc.

Chair

American, late 18th C, cherry, three-board top, hinged seat lid, scalloped edge sides, apron, shoe feet, black paint on underside of top, old refinishing on base, minor repairs, 45-1/2" d top, 28-1/2" h....... **9,350.00**

New England, late 18th C, pine and birch, top tilts above plant seat flanked by sq tapering arm supports which continue to chamfered legs, four sq stretchers, old refinish, 40-1/2" w, 42" d, 28-3/4" h **1,100.00**

New England, early 19th C, pine, maple, and walnut, three-board top tilts above plank seat, walnut arms with turned tapering supports, similar legs terminate in ball and pad feet, old stained red brown surface, repairs, 48-1/4" w, 46-3/4" d, 27-3/4" h **3,300.00**

Coffee, Chippendale-style, Kittinger, mahogany, large tray top, folding sides with cut-out handles, molded legs, stretcher base, branded label, 40" w, 20-1/4" d, 25" h **660.00**

Console

Arts & Crafts, Limbert, trestle legs and three central slats over one long stretcher, branded under top, refinished, 72" l, 22" d, 29" h **5,175.00**

George III, c1790, japanned pine, serpentine top dec with black japanned scenes of Chinese landscapes, fluted frieze on fluted sq legs, 34" w, 20" d, 32" h, price for pr **3,105.00**

Regency, painted and parcel gilt-rect marble top with outset corners, frieze carved with foliage, legs headed by masks and ending in hoof feet, plinth base, 44" w, 21" d, 31" h..... **1,955.00**

Second Empire, French, second quarter 19th C, marble-top mahogany, rect speckled black marble top, frieze drawer, applied with wreaths, sq tapered legs headed by herm busts, plinth base, 37-1/2" w, 17" d, 34" h......... **2,300.00**

Dining

Arts & Crafts

Limbert, #403, cut-corner top over intricate base, slab supports with three spindles in an oval cut-out keyed stretchers connecting to a center leg, one leaf, orig finish, numbered, 50" w, 50" d, 30" h **2,500.00**

Stickley, Gustav, No. 656, split-pedestal, five leaves, shadow of decal on pedestal, refinished, veneer chips to skirt and base, 60" d, 29" h **5,175.00**

Empire-style, Continental, 19th C, walnut, quarter-veneered top with cross banded border, conforming frieze, four canted scroll supports, rect platform stretcher with concave sides, gilt lion-paw feet, octagonal center support, one leaf, 46-1/4" w, 94-3/4" l extended, 31-1/4" h **2,300.00**

Federal, New England, c1820-25, cherry and bird's eye maple, two parts, two rect ends each with hinged drop-leaf, ring-turned tapering legs ending in ball feet, orig surface, minor surface mars, 82" w, 44-1/2" d, 28-3/4" h............ **1,725.00**

Federal-style, 20th C, mahogany, rect cross banded top, two pedestal bases each with foliate carved posts on four downswept leaf carved legs, casters, three leaves, 72" l without leaves, 48" w, 29" h............ **3,220.00**

George III-style, mahogany, D-shaped top with rounded corners and reeded edge, twin pedestal bases of column raised on tripod base, down-swept legs, brass toe caps and casters, 120" l, 44" w, 29-1/4" h **2,100.00**

International Movement, Paul Evans, manufactured by Directional, sculptured bronzed metal abstract design base, plate-glass top, 72" w, 37" d, 29" h **2,300.00**

Regency, Late, early 19th C, inlaid mahogany, three parts, D-shaped ends, rect center section, all cross banded in satinwood, checker cross banded frieze and sq tapered legs ending in spade feet, four leaves, 155" l, 54" w, 29" h **5,175.00**

Sheraton-style, early 20th C, mahogany, light band inlay around tilt top, turned urn shape columns, two end pedestals with three reeded legs each, center pedestal with four matching legs, cast paw feet and casters, 138-1/2" l total, 29" h **1,500.00**

Console table, Victorian, Gothic Revival, c1850, carved mahogany, rectangular, Gothic apron and faceted posts joined by turned stretcher, 39" x 40" x 18-1/2", **$535**. Photo courtesy of David Rago Auctions, Inc.

Dressing

Chippendale, walnut, pine and poplar secondary woods, pegged construction, cove molded edged two board top, four dovetailed drawers, shaped aprons, cabriole legs, Spanish feet, old refinishing, newer felt drawer liners, brass bale pulls, possibly orig high boy base with alterations, 42" w, 23-1/4" d, 34-1/2" h **800.00**

Classical, New England, c1820-40, grain painted and dec, scrolling crest over two short drawers, projecting top with rounded corners on conforming base, single drawer, ring-turned and incised tapering legs, all-over grain paint resembling rosewood, highlighted by stencils of fruit bowls and scrolling leaves and flowers, gold, green, and black line dec, minor imperfections, 30" w, 15-1/4" d, 39" h **1,550.00**

Empire, mahogany, small case top with drawer, dovetailed drawer in center, thin molding around lower apron, figured mahogany veneer over pine, high ring turned legs with relief rope twist carvings, small pieced restorations, 35-1/2" w, 17-3/4" d, 36-1/2" h............ **1,650.00**

Federal, New England, c1825, mahogany and mahogany veneer, scrolled backboard, two cock-beaded short drawers, projecting rect top, cock-beaded long drawer, straight beaded skirt joining fout vase and ring-turned tapering legs, refinished, 32" w, 17-1/4" d, 37-1/4" h **1,175.00**

George I/II, English, c1725, walnut veneer, banded rect top with rounded front corners overhanging shallow straight front fitted with five shallow drawers of banded treatment, plain cabriole legs, pad feet, veneer losses, worm damage, 32" w, 17" d, 30" h.............. **1,875.00**

Mid-Georgian, English, c1760, mahogany, rect case fitted with one long drawer, seven short drawers and recessed kneehole fitted with door, bracket feet, 35" w, 19" d, 30" h **1,110.00**

Painted, New England, c1830, scrolled backboard, two short drawers, projecting top, long drawer, straight skirt joining four ring-turned and swelled tapering legs, old yellow paint with mustard and green pin striping and floral dec, minor imperfections, 36" w, 17-1/2" d, 38" h **1,765.00**

Queen Anne, cherry, pine secondary wood, four dovetailed drawers with beaded edges, carved shell on lower center drawer, cabriole legs, pad feet, shaped aprons, turned drops, old refinishing, pressed glass swirl knobs, possibly orig high boy base with later added top, alterations to apron, 44-1/2" w, 22" d, 35-1/2" h **1,100.00**

Drop leaf

Chippendale

America, walnut, two board top, deeply scalloped aprons, finely shaped cabriole legs, ball and claw feet, refinished with mellow brown color, pine secondary wood, 42" w, 19" d, 20" leaves with notched corners (one with glued splits), 27-3/4" h **1,550.00**

Dining table, Hepplewhite, Pennsylvania, c1810, inlaid mahogany, two parts, each with demilune end and single drop leaf, decorated with line inlays and banded cuffs, one later leaf, 118" l open, 47-1/2" w, 29" h, **$3,910**. Photo courtesy of Pook & Pook.

Dining table, Queen Anne, attributed to Pennsylvania, last half 18th C, walnut, rectangular dropleaf overhanging top, four cabriole legs ending in pad feet joined by straight apron with shaped edge, refinished, minor imperfections, 54-1/2" l, 43-3/4" w, 27-1/2" h, **$2,250**. Photo courtesy of Skinner, Inc.

Dining table, Sheraton, Pennsylvania, c1815, tiger maple and cherry, two parts, top with rounded corners, conforming skirt supported by turned and reeded legs, 76" l, 40-1/2" w, 29" h, **$5,300**. Photo courtesy of Pook & Pook.

New England, southern, c1760-80, cherry, oval overhanging drop leaf top, cut-out apron, scrolled returns, four cabriole legs ending in claw and ball feet, imperfections, 44-1/2" l open, 15-1/2" w, 27" h......... **4,410.00**

Pennsylvania, late 18th C, walnut, shaped skirt, molded Marlborough legs, old surface, minor imperfections, 15-1/2" w, 46-3/4" l, 29" h **550.00**

Rhode Island, c1780, carved mahogany, rect drop leaf top, four sq molded stop fluted legs joined by cut-out apron, repairs, 47-3/4" w, 38-1/4" d, 29" h.................. **2,100.00**

Classical, attributed to NY, c1820, carved mahogany and mahogany veneer, rect top, overhanging shaped leaves, conforming base with single drawer, beaded skirt, suspending four circular drops on leaf carved pedestal, four curved scrolling acanthus leaf carved and molded legs, brass paw feet on casters, possibly orig glass drawer pull, old refinish, very minor imperfections **1,650.00**

Federal, in the manner of M. Allison, NY, c1820, solid and flame mahogany, spiraled acanthus leaf pedestal, acanthus leaf and hairy paw legs, paw feet............ **3,135.00**

Hepplewhite, cherry, one board top, finely tapered legs, old mellow finish, pieced restorations at rule joints, replaced hinges, 48-3/4" l, 15-1/4" d, 28" h **1,100.00**

Queen Anne

Country, cherry, one board top, mortise and peg joints with dovetailed corner joints on int. aprons, cabriole legs, pad feet, old refinishing, maple and pine secondary woods, some age splits, 36" l, 11" d, 11" leaves, 28-1/2" h **5,775.00**

Country, maple, 14" D-shaped leaves, dovetailed aprons, scalloped moldings on end aprons, swing cabriole legs, pad feet, pegged joints, refinished, pine secondary wood, restoration, replacements, 42-1/2" w, 13-1/2" d, 28" h .. **1,760.00**

English, mahogany, oak secondary wood, one board top with molded edges, tapered legs, pad feet, old refinishing, top old replacement, added braces, restorations at rule joints, 43" w, 17" d, 17-3/4" D-shaped leaves, 27-1/2" h.................... **400.00**

New England, c1750-70, maple, overhanging circular drop leaf top, four cabriole legs, pad feet on platforms, shaped apron, refinished, imperfections, 47-1/2" w, 46-1/4" d, 27-3/4" h **7,675.00**

Sheraton, Country

Birch, old red on one board top and leaves, later black on base, crisply turned legs pegged at aprons, crack in top of one leg, 36-1/4" w, 14" d, 10-7/8" l leaves, 28-3/4" h...... **495.00**

Cherry, one board top, beaded edge aprons, well turned legs, old mellow refinish, walnut secondary wood, 37" l, 19" d, 28-3/4" h **450.00**

Curly maple with good figure, one board top and leaves, single dovetailed drawer with orig maple pull, ring turned legs, bold tapered feet, old mellow refinishing, poplar secondary wood, age split in top, 40-1/4" l, 18-3/4" d, 27-3/4" h **1,760.00**

Walnut, 20-1/2" d x 48" l one board top, 20-3/4" d leaves, six turned legs, one foot chipped, refinished **300.00**

William and Mary-style, oak, deep d-shaped leaves, block and ring-turned legs joined by box stretcher, 54" w, 23" d, 29" h.............. **2,750.00**

Dressing table, New England, c1830, paint decoration, scrolled backboard centering gold stenciled design of flowers and fruit flanked by houses, projecting rectangular top with canted corners and chamfered edge, four ring-turned tapering legs joined by straight skirt with drawer, gold stenciled floral sprays flanking turned wooden knob, painted white accented by brown pinstriping and blue banding, very minor imperfections, 21-1/2" w, 16" d, 29" h, **$2,350**. Photo courtesy of Skinner, Inc.

Games table, Chippendale, Philadelphia-style, late 19th C, mahogany, flip-to, shaped top, molded legs, 30" h, **$2,250**. Photo courtesy of Wiederseim Associates, Inc.

Extension

Country, curly maple, striking broad stripes, mortise and peg construction, top divided into six different sections with boards surrounding each one and alternating curl, leaves divided into two sections each and surrounded by narrow boards, leaf hidden beneath each end of top, turned legs with inset panels on aprons, pierced spacers fill part of the mortise joints on each leg just below aprons, golden refinishing, 51-1/4" l, 32-3/4" d plus 23" leaves, 97-3/4" l total, 30" h **3,100.00**

Game

Arts & Crafts, Miller Furniture Co., removable circular top, four plank legs inlaid with stylized floral design, paper label, felted gaming surface missing, overcoated top, 36" d, 31" h **1,150.00**

Empire, tilt-top, mahogany and mahogany flame veneer, top with ogee aprons on sides, turned drops, carved pineapple column, platform base with scrolled leaf returns to carved paw feet, one drawer on side, old dark finish, 40-1/2" w, 20" d, 30" h **450.00**

George III, English

c1790, cross banded mahogany, D-shaped, plain frieze, sq tapered and molded legs, 35" w, 17" d, 28" h **1,150.00**

18th C, mahogany, concertina-action, rect top, suede int., blind fret carved legs, 36" w, 17-1/2" d, 29" h **1,495.00**

Hepplewhite, American, 19th C, inlaid cherry, hinged demilune to, conforming apron, sq tapering legs **400.00**

Phyfe, Duncan, c1820, mahogany, top with band of line inlay on edge, urn pedestal, saber legs, top loose, minor veneer loss, 39" w top open, 29" h **1,875.00**

Queen Anne, English, mahogany, hinged two-board top with molded edge, dovetailed drawer, shaped returns, relief carved detail at knees, well shaped cabriole legs, pad feet, rear swing legs, old dark finish, old replaced brass pulls, minor restoration, side returns missing, old splits in top, 35-1/2" w, 16" d, 28-3/4" h **1,550.00**

Regency, c1810, mahogany, drop-leaf, pedestal, sliding reversible top opening to backgammon board, chess board on reverse of top, turned standard with leaf carved and reeded legs, brass cap casters, 21" w, 21" d, 29" h.................. **650.00**

Renaissance Revival, A. Cutler & Son, Buffalo, NY, c1874, ebonized and parcel-gilt, drop leaf, orig paper label, wear to baise surface, 36" w, 13-3/4" d, 28-3/4" h................ **700.00**

Sheraton, mahogany, shaped top, cookie corners, shaped frieze, turned reeded legs, replaced supports under top, 36" w, 30-1/2" h **1,225.00**

William and Mary-style, with antique elements, seaweed marquetry inlaid walnut, D-shaped top with concave front, frieze similar shaped, frieze drawer, turned legs joined by stretchers, 32" w, 14" d, 30" h **2,875.00**

Games table, Hepplewhite style, English, mahogany, D-front, line inlay on legs and top edges, tapered legs, 35" w, 18" d closed, 28-1/2" h, **$2,300**. Photo courtesy of Alderfer Auction Co.

Games table, International Movement, Edward Wormley for Dunbar, top inset with green-tooled leather panel, circular recesses in each corner, dark stained wood frame. Green Dunbar tag, some scratches to top, small nicks along edges, 36" square, 28" h, **$750**. Photo courtesy of David Rago Auctions, Inc.

Harvest

English, early, yew and oak, dark finish, old replaced thick five-board top with breadboard ends, beaded aprons, large turned legs, stretcher base, mortise and peg construction, age splits and alterations, 71-1/2" w, 28" d, 29" h **1,500.00**

New England, early 19th C, drop-leaf, pine, scrubbed top, hinged leaves, olive green painted base, ring turned tapering legs, early surface, 102-34" l, 18-1/4" d, 39-3/4" extended, 20-1/2" h........... **11,500.00**

New England, mid-19th C, drop-leaf, painted pine, rect hinged leaves with rounded corners flanking single drawer at each end, ring turned bulbous legs, orig olive-yellow surface, turned pulls, legs pierced,

72-1/2" l, 26-1/2" w, 26" w extended, 29-1/2" h **19,550.00**

Lamp, Arts & Crafts

Brooks, attributed to, four-sided top, flaring legs, floriform lower shelf, new finish, unmarked, seam separation on side, 20" w, 19-3/4" d, 29-3/4" h **2,300.00**

Stickley, Gustav, No. 644, circular top, arched cross-stretchers topped by finial, mortised legs, good new finish, replaced finial, Als Ik Kan brand, 29-1/2" d, 28-3/4" h **2,300.00**

Library

Arts & Crafts

English, overhanging top, arched apron, legs carved with stylized tulips, unmarked, refinished, seam separation to top, minor nicks and edge roughness at feet, 46" w, 27" d, 30" h **1,955.00**

Robertson Co., H. P., Jamestown, NJ, early 20th C, oak, oval top over single drawer, flanked by side shelves, lower median shelf, imperfections, 48" w, 29-1/4" d, 29-1/4" h **950.00**

Stickley, Gustav, three drawers, hammered copper pulls, sq posts, broad lower shelf, red decal, refinished, 66" l, 36" w, 30-1/2" h **3,775.00**

Stickley, L. & J. G., Fayetteville, NY, similar to model no. 520, oak, rect top, single drawer, corbel supports, low median shelf with through tenons, red and yellow decal "The Work of L. & J. G. Stickley" on int. drawer, imperfections, 42" w, 28-1/8" d, 29-1/4" h........... **1,265.00**

Eastlake, Hunzinger, oak, rope-twist molding on frieze and stretchers, winged griffins supports on legs **3,500.00**

Georgian-style, Morris and Co., late 19th/early 20th C, mahogany, tooled red leather top and gadrooned edge, two end drawers, boldly carved cabriole legs, claw and ball feet, 90" l, 53" d, 30" h **3,450.00**

Renaissance Revival, third quarter 19th C, carved oak, rect top, two frieze drawers with mask form pulls, griffin form legs, shaped plinth, 54" w, 28" d, 30" h.............. **3,910.00**

Occasional

Arts & Crafts, Gustav Stickley, circular overhanging top, faceted finial over arched cross-stretchers, very good orig finish, red decal, 24" d, 29" h **2,185.00**

Biedermeier, early 19th C, birchwood, solid gallery top, inset petit point needlework panel, plain frieze, turned legs joined by stretchers, casters, inscription underneath reading "J. J. Werner, Paris," 21-1/2" w, 18-1/2" d, 29-3/4" h **2,760.00**

Gate leg table, William and Mary, English, c1730, rectangular top, frame with single drawer, ring and baluster turned legs, **$800**. Photo courtesy of Pook & Pook.

Lamp table, Arts & Crafts, Gustav Stickley, No. 436, legs mortised through top, stacked cross stretchers topped by finial, original finish, early red decal, 23-1/2" d, 28" h, **$9,200**. Photo courtesy of David Rago Auctions, Inc.

Parlor

Gothic Revival, walnut, rosewood veneer apron, replaced top, 20" x 36" x 29-1/4" h **500.00**

Victorian, walnut, molded detail, white marble turtle top, carved dog on base shelf, old dark finish, old repairs, top cracked, 23" x 3" x 29" h **770.00**

Pedestal

Aesthetic Movement, French, c1875-80, brass and pottery, sq top with recessed tile, dec with foliage, pedestal with pottery cylinder, four angular legs, foliate dec, 14" w, 34" h **8,100.00**

Biedermeier-style, cherry and burr poplar, circular top with cross banded edge, conforming apron, hexagonal support rising from triangular platform base with concave sides, three scroll supports, 29-1/2" d, 27-1/2" h.................. **600.00**

Second Empire-style, walnut, marquetry, and parcel-gilt, quarter-veneered circular top, polychrome floral marquetry, gilt-metal gadrooned edge, sq section tapered pedestal with concave sides and canted corners, gilt hairy-paw feet, 33-1/2" d, 28-1/4" h............ **1,000.00**

Pembroke

Chippendale, New England, late 18th C, mahogany, figured one board top and leaves, old finish **7,975.00**

Federal

New England, 1795-1810, inlaid mahogany, oval top with outline stringing, conforming base with string inlaid drawer flanked by inlaid paterae in the dies, four sq tapering legs with stringing, pendant bellflowers, and inlaid cuffs, old refinish, minor imperfections, 32" w, 18-1/2" d, 27-1/2" h........... **10,925.00**

New York, c1810-15, mahogany, rect overhanging drop leaf top with canted corners, conforming base, single drawer, paneled dies on four tapering reeded legs ending in casters joined by cock-beaded skirt, refinished, 36" l, 20-3/4" w, 28-1/4" h **850.00**

George III, c1785, mahogany, diminutive drop leaves, frieze drawer, sq fluted and tapered legs, casters, 28" l, 34" w, 28" h **1,175.00**

Hepplewhite, English, mahogany, figured veneers, dovetailed drawer in one end, tapered sq legs, line border inlay, oval medallions at tops, brass casters, old refinishing, 29-1/4" l, 18-1/2" d, 9-1/2" l leaves, 27-1/2" h **1,595.00**

Sheraton, New York, mahogany, double drop shaped leaves, single end drawer, well proportioned tapering turned elongated legs fitted with brass ferrules and casters, inlaid mahogany tombstone panels beside drawer, fine reeding to legs, 43" w open, 21" closed, 35-1/2" d, 29" h **6,500.00**

Pier, Classical, Boston, 1835-40, mahogany veneer, replaced carrara marble top, straight paneled veneered frieze above scrolled and carved frontal supports with flattened veneered columns flanking pier glass, old refinish, feet missing, some veneer loss, 41" w, 17-3/4" d, 36" h, price for matched pair **10,925.00**

Refectory, late 19th or early 20th C, oak, 1-1/2" thick three-board top, two

large turned and carved supports, stretcher base, shoe feet, old dark finish, 71-1/2" l, 27-1/2" d, 30-1/2" h **1,550.00**

Rent, George III-style, Kittinger, mahogany and figured veneer, oak secondary wood, circular drum top with four drawers alternating with false fronts, leather inset top, single pedestal cabinet base with door, applied trim on sides, metallic label inside drawer, minor burns on top, old pieced veneer restorations, 48" d, 30-1/2" d.................. **1,775.00**

Occasional table, Arts & Crafts, early 20th C, oak, round top over smaller round low median shelf on cross-stretchers, dark brown finish, unsigned, 24-1/2" d, 29-1/4" h, **$800**. Photo courtesy of Skinner, Inc.

Serving

Empire, c1830, "mint julep" type, flame mahogany, white marble top, ogee skirt with panels and leafy carvings, narrow waist, unusual tapered columns flanking mirror, side compartment, ogee base with scroll carved apron and feet........ **6,660.00**

Parlor, Renaissance Revival, American, c1860-70, incised carved top over single drawer, carved frieze, turned tapered legs and shaped stretcher, ormolu trim, loss to veneer on top, repair to stretcher, 52" w, **$600**. Photo courtesy of Alderfer Auction Co.

Federal, New England, c1800, inlaid mahogany, band inlay around top and leaves, large satinwood oval on top, single dovetailed drawer with satinwood band inlay, bow-front top with end-blocking and serpentine sides with string-inlaid edge above conforming base, single drawer outlined in veneer banding flanked by rect dies above similar banding and string inlaid legs, brasses appear original, old refinish, imperfections, 34-1/2" w, 17" d, 32" h **16,450.00**

George III, c1800

Mahogany, slightly bowed top, pair of drawers, sq tapering legs **1,725.00**

Satinwood and marquetry, demilune, later fitted with spring action drawers, restoration, 62-1/4" w, 23-1/2" d, 32-3/4" h.......... **19,550.00**

Sewing

Federal

Boston, MA, c1805, mahogany veneer, mahogany top with outset corners above two veneered cock-beaded drawers, sliding bag frame, flanked by legs with colonettes above reeding, ending in turned tapering feet, old brass, old finish, 20-3/4" w, 15-3/4" d, 28-1/4" h **1,610.00**

New England, mahogany veneer, mahogany top with hinged drop leaves, reeded edge, flanking three veneered drawers, top fitted for writing, bottom with sliding sewing bag frame, ring-turned and spiral carved legs, casters, old refinish, replaced brasses, 18-1/2" w, 18-1/8" d, 29-1/4" h............ **1,150.00**

French-style, early 20th C, inlaid mahogany, hinged scalloped top finely inlaid with flowers and scrolled leaves, scalloped aprons, delicate cabriole legs with beaded edging, applied ormolu on apron, knees, and feet, shallow int. compartment, old refinish, some alterations, 25" w, 18-1/2" d, 30-1/2" h................ **600.00**

Sheraton, mahogany, drop leaf, two drawers over one drawer, ring and spiral turned legs, brass cup and caster feet, 20-1/2" closed, 27-3/4" open, 18" d, 28-1/2" h......... **1,200.00**

Pembroke, Hepplewhite, Pennsylvania, c1805, walnut, single drawer, line inlay, 35-1/4" w, 28-1/2" h, **$990**. Photo courtesy of Pook & Pook.

Sewing table, mahogany, drop leaf, two drawers, bulbous pedestal, curled foot, 27-1/2" h, **$175**. Photo courtesy of Joy Luke Auctions.

Side

Classical, New York, 1835-45, mahogany, rect marble top with rounded corners, conforming ogee molded skirt, pierced and scrolled supports, pillar and scroll bases, applied ripple molding joining scrolled medial shelf, casters, old finish, minor imperfections, 31" w, 18-1/2" d, 31" h................... **3,750.00**

Federal, attributed to southern New England, c1800-10, mahogany and tiger maple veneer inlay, serpentine top with elliptic ends, conforming base, frieze drawer, inlaid tiger maple veneer panels outlined with crossbanding and stringing, four sq tapering legs with conforming inlay continuing to inlaid cuffs, restored, 23-1/4" w, 17" d, 28-1/4" h **10,575.00**

Louis XV/XVI-style, late 19th C, tulipwood, kidney-shaped, breche d'alep marble top above galleried medial shelf, trestle supports, 25" w, 12" d, 26" h **425.00**

Louis XVI-style, third quarter 19th C, tulipwood parquetry, gilt bronze mounted, trelliswork inlaid top and sides, frieze fitted with two drawers, sq tapered legs, foliate cast mounts, 43-1/2" w, 26" d, 31" h......... **3,820.00**

Renaissance Revival, America, c1870, walnut, inset marble top, maidenhead carved frieze raised on angular legs, X-stretcher, 35" l, 22" d, 30-1/2" h **1,495.00**

Silver, George III, c1765, carved mahogany, galleried tray top, low relief carved everted lip, repeating border of C-scrolls and foliage, swirling scroll bordered apron, molded sq cabriole supports with trailing acanthus carving at knees, Spanish feet, alternations to top, repairs, 31-3/4" l 28-3/4" h.. **2,000.00**

Sofa, Edwardian, c1895, painted satinwood, rounded drop leaves, two frieze drawers, trestle supports ending in brass paw casters, 36" w closed, 26-1/2" d, 28-1/2" h **8,100.00**

Tavern

Chippendale, Massachusetts or New Hampshire, late 18th/early 19th C, cherry top, thumb molded edge overhangs maple base with straight molded skirt, sq tiger maple legs with beaded front edges, chamfered rear ones, early surface, minor surface stains, 34" w, 25" d, 27-5/8" h **4,600.00**

Hepplewhite, two-board breadboard top, large overhang, one drawer base, tapered sq legs, grungy finish, 42-1/2" w, 29-3/4" d, 28" h **750.00**

Queen Anne, birch and pine, one board top with breadboard ends, single drawer with worn overlapping beaded edges with orig turned wooden pull, mortised and pegged joints, turned and tapered legs ending in pad feet, old refinishing, restorations, 53-1/4" w, 30-1/2" d, 26-3/4" h **1,775.00**

William and Mary, New England, 18th C, maple and pine, rect overhanging top, straight skirt with drawer, joining block base and ring turned legs, feet joined by square stretchers, old refinish, minor imperfections, 33" w, 21" d, 27" h **1,610.00**

William and Mary-style, oak, rect thumb-molded top, frieze drawer, turned legs joined by box stretcher, 33" w, 24" d, 29" h.................. **575.00**

Windsor, New England, early 19th C, black painted, oval overhanging top, four vase and ring-turned splayed legs, turned feet, joined by stretchers, old paint, imperfections, 26-3/4" l, 21-3/4" d, 22-1/4" h **1,100.00**

Tea

Chippendale

America, possibly Philadelphia, piecrust tilt top, figured mahogany one-piece circular top, ogee and crescent form carving, birdcage support, fluted column, compressed ball knop, three legs with plain knees, ball and claw feet, 28-1/2" h **10,575.00**

Pennsylvania, c1760-80, cherry, circular tilt top with molded edge, birdcage mechanism, ball and ring-turned post, tripod cabriole legs, arris pad feet, old refinish, very minor restorations, 27-1/4" d, 28-3/4" h **3,820.00**

Sofa table, English, c1820-30, mahogany, banded inlay on top edges, one working drawer, five false drawers on each side, lyre feet with line inlay, 19-1/2" l, 33" w open, 28" h, **$1,725**. Photo courtesy of Alderfer Auction Co.

Philadelphia, 1760-80, cherry, molded and carved bird cage, round top with molded rim, tilts and rotates above pillar, suppressed belted ball over knees carved with C-scrolls and leafage on cabriole legs, pad feet, early surface, minor imperfections, provenance: bought from Mary Ball Washington, 21" d, 28-1/4" h **409,500.00**

Philadelphia, c1760-80, mahogany and walnut, circular tilt top with pie crust edge, bird cage support, carved pedestal with fluted cylindrical section over bun–shaped section carved with leafage to upper half above billet and beat perimeter, plain bottom half, fillet molding above collar of guilloche, cabriole legs carved with scrolling leaves, each with rococo cartouche on upper knee surface, slender claw and ball feet, top replaced, refinished, 33" d, 28" h **..... 19,800.00**

Chippendale-style, early 20th C, mahogany, pie crust tilt top with large inland panel of roses and geometric marquetry, finely carved detail on knees and column, claw and ball feet, old finish, split along pie crust molding, two small burns on top, 31-3/4" d, 29-1/2" h.................... **500.00**

Georgian

Mid-period, third quarter 18th C, carved mahogany, piecrust tilt top, bird cage support, fluted standard, foliate carved cabriole legs ending in claw and ball feet, 22-1/2" d, 29" h **1,645.00**

Third quarter 18th C, carved mahogany, circular top tilting above standard carved with twist reeding and leaf carved cabriole legs ending in claw and ball feet, 29" d, 28-1/2" h **2,750.00**

Hepplewhite, tilt top, poplar one board top with cut corners, birch tripod base with spider legs, turned column, old refinishing with painted foliage border designs in shades of gold and black, top replaced, repairs, 15-1/2" w, 23-1/2" l, 28-3/4" h **440.00**

Queen Anne, New England, c1760-80, cherry, circular tilt top, vase and ring-turned post and tripod cabriole leg base, pad feet, refinished, minor imperfections, 34-1/4" d, 27-1/2" h **1,175.00**

Shaker, attributed to Mt. Lebanon, NY, c1830, birch, circular tilt top with bull-nose edge, tilts on platform, tapering turned pedestal, tripod cabriole legs, pad feet, old refinish, 34-1/4" d, 26-3/4" h............ **6,465.00**

Tea table, English, c1860, mahogany, candle slides on each side, two drawers, reeded legs with brass tips and caps, marble insert, brass gallery and banding, **$1,380**. Photo courtesy of Alderfer Auction Co.

Trestle table, Arts & Crafts, L. & J.G. Stickley, overhanging top, double-column sides and broad lower shelf keyed-through the sides, unmarked, original finish to base, cleaned finish with color added to top, seam seperations to ends, dets and chipping around stretcher, 72" l, 45" d, 29" h, **$4,890**. Photo courtesy of David Rago Auctions.

Tilt-Top

Chippendale, cherry sq three-board top with hand plane marks underneath, mahogany base, urn-shaped column, cabriole legs mortised and pegged into column, padded snake feet, old dark finish, minor edge splits at knees, 30-1/2" d, 31-1/2" h **550.00**

Federal, New England, mahogany inlaid, octagonal top with string inlay in outline, urn shaped pedestal, cabriole legs, arris pad feet on platforms, orig surface, very minor imperfections, 22" w, 14-3/4" d, 29-1/2" h **3,750.00**

Georgian, late 18th C, mahogany, plain circular top over turned

baluster standard, three cabriole legs ending in shaped pad feet, 32" d, 27-3/8" h **1,100.00**

Tray, Edwardian, c1900, satinwood and inlay, two oval tiers, removable wood and glass tray, slightly splayed sq tapering legs joined by stretcher, 36" w, 20-1/4" d, 32" h.. **1,150.00**

Vitrine, Louis XVI-style, c1880, gilt bronze mounted mahogany, beveled glass panels and turned legs joined by stretchers, foliate cast bronze mounts, 26" w, 16" d, 30" h **3,450.00**

Work

Biedermeier, c1825, fruitwood, part gilded and ebonized, circular lift top opening to wells, inlaid with angular foliage, hemispherical base, three legs headed by rams' heads and ending in hoof feet, 20" d, 30" h **2,820.00**

Classical, Boston, 1830, mahogany veneer, solid top, hinged rounded drop leaves with beaded edges, flank two convex veneered drawers, top one fitted for writing, lower with replaced fabric sewing fabric bag, turned tapering legs which flank shaped veneered platform, ebonized bun feet, orig stamped brass pulls, imperfections, minor warp in leaf, 19" w, 19" d, 28-3/4" h........... **980.00**

Federal, New England, first quarter 19th C, cherry, rect top overhangs two drawers, swelled and ring-turned legs, pegged feet, old refinish, one glass knob missing, 19-7/8" w, 14-1/2" d, 28-1/4" h............... **500.00**

Federal, late, MA, c1825, carved mahogany and mahogany veneer, rect top with molded edge, rounded drop leaves, two working drawers and false drawer, four vase and ring-turned spiral carved legs ending in turned feet on casters, old refinish, replaced brass pulls, imperfections, bottom drawer missing, 18" w, 18" d, 28-1/4" h **900.00**

George III, early 19th C, mahogany, rect top, canted corners, fitted int., sq tapered and slightly splayed legs joined by stretchers........... **2,380.00**

Hepplewhite, country

Walnut and pine, wooden peg construction, one board top, tapered and splayed legs, later blue paint, thin coat of varnish, minor hairlines, split, minor insect damage on legs, 25" x 33" top, 29-1/2" h **650.00**

Walnut, pegged construction, three-board top, dovetailed drawer, turned wooden pull, tapered legs, old dark mellow finish, evidence of earlier blue paint, restoration and replacements, 55-3/4" w, 35-3/8" d, 27" h **450.00**

Queen Anne

Black walnut and pine, painted, PA, c1760-1800, removable blank three-board pine top, supported by cleats and four dowels, two thumb-molded drawers, straight skirt with breaded edge above straight cabriole legs ending in pad feet, orig apple green paint, old replaced wooden pulls, surface imperfections, cracked foot, 48-1/2" w, 32" d, 27" h......... **2,500.00**

Maple and pine, New England, late 18th C, scrubbed top, straight skirt with beaded edge, turned tapering legs ending in turned button feet, old surface, remnants of red on base, 28" w, 28-1/2" l, 27" h......... **2,530.00**

Walnut, removable three-board top, two dovetailed overlapping drawers, mortised and pinned apron with edge beading, turned legs, weathered duck feet, old refinishing, period replaced brasses, pieced repairs to top, age cracks, 32" w, 49-1/2" l, 28" h **2,750.00**

Sheraton, country, pine and poplar, old pumpkin colored paint, traces of earlier red underneath, old replacement one-board top with good overhang, two dovetailed drawers with old replaced pulls, well-turned legs with ball turnings above tapered feet, age splits, 34-1/2" w, 21" d **1,550.00**

William and Mary-style, walnut, ebonized trim, two-board top, one dovetailed drawer, turned stretchers and legs, repairs and old replacements, 22-3/4" w, 34" d, 27-1/4" h **935.00**

Vitrine, Edwardian, early 20th C, inlaid mahogany, typical form, hinged glass top and sides, square tapered legs, casters, 24" w, 17" d, 29" h, **$450**. Photo courtesy of Skinner, Inc.

Game Boards

History: Wooden game boards have a long history and were some of the first toys early Americans enjoyed. Games such as checkers, chess, and others were easy to play and required only simple markers or playing pieces. Most were handmade, but some machine-made examples exist. Game boards can be found in interesting color combinations. Some include small drawers to hold the playing pieces. Others have an interesting molding or frame. Look for signs of use from long hours of enjoyment. Today, game boards are popular with game collectors, folk art collectors, and decorators because of their interesting forms.

Reproduction Alert.

Checkerboard, America, 19th C, inlaid wood, rectangle, alternating light and dark wood inlaid squares, contrasting rayed corners and borders, ebony pegged frame with inlaid triangle decoration, age crack, 18-1/2" x 24", **$300**. Photo courtesy of Skinner, Inc.

Checkerboard

10-1/2" w, 19-1/2" h, painted green and yellow, late 19th C, paint imperfections **1,955.00**

12-1/2" w, 12-3/4" h, painted black and white, tan colored ground, sgd "F. Smith," PA, c1870 .... **1,955.00**

13-7/8" w, 13-3/4" h, painted hunter green and iron red, black frame, yellow grain paint on reverse, America, 19th C, minor paint wear.................................. **1,380.00**

14" w, 20-1/4" h, oak and mahogany squares, galleried edge with two reserves on sides with sliding lid compartments to hold checkers, two sets of checkers, one round, one square, minor wear, light alligatoring to old black paint on lids and gallery.. **330.00**

14-1/4" x 14-1/2", painted pine, orig black paint border, inner yellow band around red and black squares, applied gallery **1,600.00**

15-1/4" sq, painted black and salmon, New England, 19th C **2,300.00**

16" sq, blue and white, yellowed varnish, New England, 19th C **3,335.00**
16-1/2" x 16-1/4", pine, applied trim pcs, black and red blocks around edges, dark stained squares opposing red in central ground, age splits, two sections of trim replaced **195.00**
17" w, 16" h, painted green and white, unfinished, inscribed on reverse, late 19th/early 20th C **460.00**
17-3/4" w, 17-5/8" h, painted salmon red with ochre and black checkerboard, indistinct pencil inscription on reverse, America, 19th C, scratches and minor paint wear.................................... **800.00**
18-1/2" sq, painted yellow and black, green detailing, c1880 .... **5,465.00**
19-1/2" sq, painted slate, incised geometric design, hand painted to resemble hardstones, shades of marbleized green and red, solid dark red checks, shaded yellow ground, mottled black border, New England, late 19th C, minor paint wear at margins...... **1,645.00**
21-1/2" x 17-1/2", incised checkerboard under glass, red, lime green, yellow, and black, reverse painted in red, white, and blue, framed, America, 20th C, minor paint wear.................................... **650.00**
25" w, 19" h, painted red and black, gilt trim, second half 19th C **2,300.00**

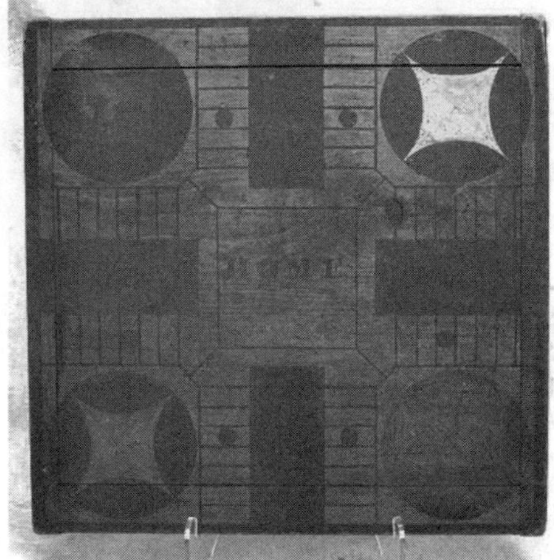

Double sided, one side with checkerboard design, other with Parcheesi, wood, hand-painted wood, minor loss and wear, 20" square, **$535**. Photo courtesy of Alderfer Auction Co.

Double-sided

7-1/4" w, 7" h, painted pine, brown and black checkerboard on one side, painted brown Old Mill game inscribed on reverse, two sliding panel compartments, New York State, early 19th C..... **1,150.00**
12-1/4" w, 12" h, painted apple green, brown, and black, obverse with checkerboard, reverse with snake-motif game, America, mid-19th C **36,800.00**
14" sq, painted salmon, green, and yellow, New England, 19th C, loss to frame **3,740.00**
14-1/4" sq, painted black and red, obverse with checkerboard, reverse with Old Mill, applied molded edge, New England, c1850-70 .... **4,890.00**
14-7/8" w, 15-7/8" h, painted deep blue-green, red and black, checkerboard on obverse, backgammon on reverse, America, 19th C........................ **2,530.00**
15" w, 16" h, painted mustard, red, and green, checkerboard on obverse, backgammon on reverse, America, 19th C **3,335.00**
17" sq, obverse with Parcheesi, painted red, teal, orange, and green, checkerboard on reverse with orange, black, and yellow paint, c1900, paint wear to obverse at edges......... **2,530.00**
18-1/2" w, 20" h, New Hampshire, Parcheesi game scribed and painted in eight colors, checkerboard on reverse, New Hampshire, 19th C, minor wear, crack....................................... **21,850.00**
20-1/8" x 20-1/2", painted wood, sq board with applied frame, one side checkerboard painted yellow, black, green, and red, other side backgammon game in the same colors, America, 19th C, wear **1,645.00**
22" x 28-3/4", painted wood, rect, polychrome Parcheesi game on one side, red and black checkerboard on reverse, wear... **1,880.00**
23" w, 17-1/4" h, painted apple green, black, and red, checkerboard on obverse, backgammon on reverse, game piece compartments, America, c1870-80 .... **3,750.000**

Marbles, 19th C, mahogany, 10" d turned round game board with 33 indentations in a cruciform shape, 33 mostly vintage handmade marbles, several with latticinio cores, onion skins, and mica flecked, marbles 3/4" to 7/8" d, **$600**. Photo courtesy of Skinner, Inc.

Hinged

8" x 8-1/4", checkers, Parcheesi, two-part backgammon board, orig orange paint with red and white on two games, black and white for checkers, light blue trim, six wooden checkers, age split in one side, darker patina on ext. **3,100.00**

Numbered

14-1/2" w, 16-1/2" h, painted red and black, gold striping and numbers 1 through 32, New York, c1870 .... **4,350.00**

Parcheesi

18" w, 17-3/4" h, folding, patriotic red, white, and blue stars and dec, New England, late 19th C................. **4,350.00**
19-1/2" sq, folding, painted green, white, black, and yellow, varied geometric designs on game corners, America, 19th C.. **2,875.00**
25" w, 24-1/2" h, painted, center rosette, bull's eye corners, attributed to Maine, 19th C, wear **4,600.00**
27-1/2" w, 27" h, painted red, yellow, and green, New England, 1870-80 .. **5,750.00**

Three-panel board

33" x 36", painted pine, red, green, and yellow playing field, light blue ground **825.00**

Games

History: Board games have been commercially produced in this country since at least 1822, and card games since the 1780s. However, it was not until the 1840s that large numbers of games were produced that survive to this day. The W. & S. B. Ives Company produced many board and card games in the 1840s and 1950s. Milton Bradley and McLoughlin Brothers became major producers of games starting in the 1860s, followed by Parker Brothers in the 1880s. Other major producers of games in this period were Bliss, Chaffee and Selchow, Selchow and Righter, and Singer.

Today, most games from the 19th century are rare and highly collectible, primarily because of their spectacular lithography. McLoughlin and Bliss command a premium because of the rarity, quality of materials, and the extraordinary art that was created to grace the covers and boards of their games.

In the 20th century, Milton Bradley, Selchow and Righter, and Parker Brothers became the primary manufacturers of boxed games. They have all now been absorbed by toy giant Hasbro Corporation. Other noteworthy producers were All-Fair, Pressman, and Transogram, all of which are no longer in business. Parker Brothers and All-Fair games from the 1920s to 1940s also have some excellent lithography and are highly collectible.

Additional Listings: See *Warman's Americana & Collectibles.*

Notes: While people collect games for many reasons, it is strong graphic images that bring the highest prices. Games collected because they are fun to play or for nostalgic reasons are still collectible, but will not bring high prices. Also, game collectors are not interested in common and "public domain" games such as checkers, tiddlywinks, Authors, Anagrams, Jackstraws, Rook, Pit, Flinch, and Peter

Coodles. The game market today is characterized by fairly stable prices for ordinary items, increasing discrimination for grades of condition, and continually rising prices for rare material in excellent condition. Whether you are a dealer or collector, be careful to buy games in good condition. Avoid games with taped or split corners or other box damage. Games made after about 1950 are difficult to sell unless they are complete and in excellent condition. As games get older, there is a forgiveness factor for condition and completeness that increases with age.

These listings are for games that are complete and in excellent condition. Be sure the game you're looking to price is the same as the one described in the listing. The 19th century makers routinely published the same title on several different versions of the game, varying in size and graphics.

Elsie and Her Family, Selchow & Righter, N.Y. #204, copyright 1941, 12-1/2" x 14" x 1-1/2" deep colorful red box with Elsie, Elmer and Beulah on lid, **$65**. Photo courtesy of Hake's Americana & Collectibles.

American Revolution, Nora Norwood, c1850 .... **750.00**
Authors Improved, Milton Bradley, 1872 .... **150.00**
Auto Racing, Milton Bradley **200.00**
Bull in a China Shop, Milton Bradley, 1937 .... **100.00**
Chiromagia Game, McLoughlin, 1879 .... **450.00**
Clue, Parker Brothers, c1949, separate board and pieces box **25.00**
Dixie Pollyana, Parker Brothers, c1952, 8" x 18" **100.00**
Elsie and Her Family, Selcrow & Righter Co., 1941 .... **250.00**
Fish Pond, McLoughlin Bros., c1898, 8" x 18" **125.00**
Flying the United States Air Mail Game, Parker Bros, 1929 copyright, 17" x 27-1/2" playing board **55.00**
Game of Battles or Fun For Boys, McLoughlin Bros., c1900, 23" x 23" **2,500.00**
Game of Billy Possum, c1910, 8" x 15" **600.00**
Game of Bo Peep, J. H. Singer, 8-1/2" x 14" **275.00**
Game of Pinafore, Fuller, Upham & Co., 1879 .... **350.00**
Game of Pope and Pagen, W. & S. B. Ives, 1844 .... **2,100.00**
Game of Railway Traffic, Fisher & Denison, 1870 .... **500.00**
Game of the Wizard of Oz, The, Whitman, c1939, 7" x 13-1/2" **300.00**
Hi Ho Silhouette Game, 1932 .... **30.00**
Jolly Darkie Target Game, Milton Bradley, c1900, 10-1/2" x 19" **750.00**
Limited Mail and Express Game, **The**, Parker Brothers, c1894, 14" x 21" **250.00**
Lone Ranger Hi Yo Silver Game, Parker Brothers, 1938 .... **200.00**
Mansion of Happiness, **The**, W. & S. B. Ives, c1843 .... **950.00**
Mickey Mantle's Big League Baseball Game, Gardner Games **195.00**

Junior Combination Board, Milton Bradley, c1905, 16-1/2" sqare two-sided board, **$85**. Photo courtesy of Vicki and Bruce Waasdorp.

Monopoly, Parker Brothers, c1935, white box edition #9, metal playing pieces and embossed hotels **150.00**
Monopoly, Parker Brothers, 1946 Popular Edition, separate board and pieces box **25.00**
Motorcycle Game, Milton Bradley, c1905, 9" x 9" **250.00**
Peter Coddles Trip to New York, Milton Bradley, 6" x 8-1/2" **65.00**
Radio Amateur Hour Game, 10" x 13" **145.00**
Razzle Dazzle Football Game, Texantics, 1954, 10" x 17" **225.00**
Strange Game of Forbidden Fruit, Parker Brothers, c1900, 4" x 5-1/2". **35.00**
Uncle Sam's Mail, Milton Bradley, 16-1/4" x 15", some pcs of flap missing **95.00**
Whirlpool, McLoughlin Brothers, 1899, #408, 7-1/4" sq, instructions on cover **40.00**
Yacht Race, Franklin and Great Republic, A. N. Jordan, S. W. Chandler, 1853 .... **2,475.00**

Gaudy Dutch

History: Gaudy Dutch is an opaque, soft-paste ware made between 1790 and 1825 in England's Staffordshire district.

The wares first were hand decorated in an underglaze blue and fired; then additional decorations were added over the glaze. The over-glaze decoration is extensively worn on many of the antique pieces. Gaudy Dutch found a ready market in the Pennsylvania German community because it was inexpensive and extremely colorful. It had little appeal in England.

For more information, see *Warman's English & Continental Pottery & Porcelain*, 3rd edition.

Marks: Marks of various potters, including the impressed marks of Riley and Wood, have been found on some pieces, although most are unmarked.

Reproduction Alert: Cup plates, bearing the impressed mark "CYBRIS," have been reproduced and are collectible in their own right. The Henry Ford Museum has issued pieces in the Single Rose pattern, although they are porcelain rather than soft paste.

Adviser: John D. Querry.

Butterfly
Coffeepot, 11" h **9,500.00**
Cup and saucer, handleless, minor enamel flakes, chips on table ring **950.00**
Plate, 7-1/4" d **645.00**
Sugar bowl, cov **900.00**
Teapot, 5" h, squat baluster form **2,400.00**

Carnation
Bowl, 6-1/4" d **925.00**
Creamer, 4-3/4" h **700.00**
Pitcher, 6" h **675.00**
Plate, 9-3/4" d **1,265.00**
Saucer, cobalt blue, orange, green, and yellow, stains, hairline, minor flake on table ring, 5-1/2" d **115.00**
Teapot, cov **2,200.00**
Waste bowl **675.00**

Dahlia
Bowl, 6-1/4" d **1,800.00**
Cup plate, green, gold, blue, and brown, deep green scalloped edge, molded feather and fish scale design, 4-1/4" d **1,210.00**
Plate, 8" d **2,800.00**
Tea bowl and saucer **8,000.00**

Double Rose
Bowl, 6-1/4" d **545.00**
Creamer **650.00**
Cup plate, 3-5/8" d, orange, two shades of blue, pink, and green, minor scratch **1,320.00**
Gravy boat **950.00**
Plate, 8-1/4" d **675.00**
Sugar bowl, cov **750.00**
Tea bowl and saucer **675.00**

Toddy plate, 4-1/2" d **675.00**
Waste bowl, 6-1/2" d, 3" h **850.00**

Dove
Creamer **675.00**
Plate, 8-1/8" d, very worn, scratches, stains **245.00**
Plate, 8-1/2" d **770.00**
Tea bowl and saucer **500.00**
Waste bowl, 6-1/4" d, 3" h, orange, cobalt blue, yellow, and green, hairlines, light stains, crow's foot **360.00**

Flower Basket, plate, 6-1/2" d..... **375.00**

Cup and saucer, War Bonnet pattern, **$520**. Photo courtesy of Pook & Pook.

Grape
Bowl, 6-1/2" d, lustered rim **475.00**
Cup plate, 3-1/2" d, orange, cobalt blue, yellow, and pale green **990.00**
Plate, 7-1/8" d, deep blue, yellow, green, and orange, stains, crazing **450.00**
Plate, 8-1/4" d, cobalt blue, orange, green, and yellow, minor stains **450.00**
Sugar bowl, cov **675.00**
Tea bowl and saucer **475.00**
Toddy plate, 5" d **475.00**

Leaf, bowl, 11-1/2" d, shallow ... **4,800.00**

No Name
Plate, 8-3/4" d **17,000.00**
Teapot, cov **16,000.00**

Oyster
Bowl, 5-1/2" d **675.00**
Coffeepot, cov, 12" h **10,000.00**
Plate, 10" d **1,550.00**
Soup plate, 8-1/2" d............... **550.00**
Tea bowl and saucer **1,275.00**
Toddy plate, 5-1/2" d **475.00**

Single Rose
Coffeepot, cov **8,500.00**
Cup and saucer, handleless, minor wear and stains **330.00**
Cup plate, 4" d, orange, cobalt blue, yellow, and pale green **990.00**
Plate, 7-1/4" d, cobalt blue, yellow, green and orange, wear, knife scratches............................... **470.00**
Plate, 10" d **975.00**
Quill holder, cov **2,500.00**
Sugar bowl, cov **700.00**
Teapot, cov **1,200.00**

Toddy plate, 5-1/4" d **250.00**

Sunflower
Bowl, 6-1/2" d **900.00**
Coffeepot, cov, 9-1/2" h **6,500.00**
Cup and saucer, handleless, wear, chips....................................... **575.00**
Plate, 9-3/4" d **825.00**

Plate, Urn pattern, c1810, some loss to glaze, 9-7/8" d, **$920**. Photo courtesy of Pook & Pook.

Urn
Creamer **475.00**
Cup and saucer, handleless **550.00**
Cup plate, 3-3/4" d, orange, cobalt blue, pink, yellow, and green **2,200.00**
Plate, 8-1/4" d **910.00**
Plate, 9-7/8" d, very worn, scratches, stains, rim, chips **225.00**
Sugar bowl, cov, 6-1/2" h, round, tip and base restored................ **295.00**
Teapot.................................... **895.00**

War Bonnet
Bowl, cov **225.00**
Coffeepot, cov..................... **9,500.00**
Cup plate, 3-1/2" d, orange, cobalt blue, green, and gold, minor surface wear.................................. **1,375.00**
Plate, 8-1/8" d, pinpoint rim flake, minor wear............................ **880.00**
Teapot, cov......................... **4,400.00**
Toddy plate, 4-1/2" d **975.00**

Zinna, soup plate, 10" d, impressed "Riley" **4,675.00**

GAUDY IRONSTONE

History: Gaudy Ironstone was made in England around 1850. Ironstone is an opaque, heavy-bodied earthenware that contains large proportions of flint and slag. Gaudy Ironstone is decorated in patterns and colors similar to those of Gaudy Welsh.

Marks: Most pieces are impressed "Ironstone" and bear a registry mark.

Bread plate, 10-1/4" l, 5-1/4" w, marked "Tunstall, England, by Enoch Wedgwood" **65.00**

Pitcher, large red rose, blue cornflowers, green leaves, embossed scrolls around top and handle, **$225**.

Platter, octagonal, Morning Glory pattern, deep cobalt blue, green, pink, **$500**. Photo courtesy of Joseph P. Smalley, Jr., Auctioneer.

Chop plate, 12-1/2" d, brick red and green over glaze dec of florals with pagoda and foot bridge with figures, crown mark with "Ashworth Bros. Hanley" and "England" **125.00**

Coffeepot, cov, 10" h, Strawberry pattern **650.00**

Creamer and sugar, 6-3/4" h, fruit finial, Blackberry pattern, underglaze blue, yellow, and orange enamel and luster, wear, small flakes, int. chip on sugar **990.00**

Cup and saucer, Blackberry pattern, handleless, underglaze blue, yellow, and orange enamel and luster, imp label or registry mark with "E. Walley," price for set of 10....................................... **1,375.00**

Jug, 7-1/2" h, yellow, red, white, and blue tulips on sides, light blue pebble ground, luster trim, rim outlined **350.00**

Pitcher, 11" h, six-color floral dec, blue, green, burgundy, mauve, black, and yellow, molded serpent handle, dec has been enhanced, then reglazed, spider **320.00**

Plate

6-1/4" d, Morning Glories and Strawberries pattern, underglaze blue, polychrome enamel and luster trim 80.00

9-1/2" d, Blackberry pattern, underglaze blue, yellow, and orange enamel and luster, some wear, set of seven.................................... 1,320.00

Platter, 13-1/2" x 16-3/4", cobalt blue, tomato red, and violet floral dec, gold highlights, light green and gray over glaze dec with wear, sgd "Davenport" 250.00

Soup plate, 9-7/8" d, Blackberry pattern, underglaze blue, yellow, and orange enamel and luster, one imp "Elsmore & Forster, Tunstall," price for set of three 650.00

Sugar bowl, cov, 8-1/2" h, Strawberry pattern 425.00

Teapot, 9-3/4" h, domed cov, floral finial, paneled body, blue flower, red and green strawberries, gilt highlights, c1850 .... 2,300.00

Platter, oval, floral motif in Imari colors with gilt accents, blue under glaze, red and gilt painted over glaze, mark on bottom denotes Mason's Ironstone, after 1891, 17-1/4" l, 14" w, 1-1/2" h, **$175**. Photo courtesy of Alderfer Auction Co.

Vegetable, open, 8-3/4" d, Blackberry pattern, underglaze blue, yellow, and orange enamel and luster 350.00

Wash basin and pitcher, 14" d bowl, 13" h pitcher, hexagonal, blue morning glories and leaves, copper accents, hp red, green, and yellow berries, hairlines 1,225.00

Gaudy Welsh

For more information, see *Warman's English & Continental Pottery & Porcelain*, 3rd edition.

History: Gaudy Welsh is a translucent porcelain that was originally made in the Swansea area of England from 1830 to 1845. Although the designs resemble Gaudy Dutch, the body texture and weight differ. One of the characteristics is the gold luster on top of the glaze. In 1890, Allerton made a similar ware from heavier opaque porcelain.

Marks: Allerton pieces usually bear an export mark.

Carnation, 6-1/4" h...................... 550.00

Chinoiserie, teapot, c1830-40..... 750.00

Columbine

Bowl, 10" d, 5-1/2" h, ftd, underglaze blue and polychrome enamel floral dec 400.00

Plate, 5-1/2" d 85.00

Tea set, c1810, 17-pc set....... 625.00

Conwys, jug, 9" h....................... 750.00

Daisy and Chain

Creamer 175.00

Cup and saucer 95.00

Sugar, cov 195.00

Teapot, cov........................... 225.00

Flower Basket

Bowl, 10-1/2" d 190.00

Mug, 4" h 90.00

Plate 75.00

Sugar, cov, luster trim............ 195.00

Grape

Bowl, 5-1/4" d 55.00

Cup and saucer 75.00

Mug, 2-1/2" h......................... 70.00

Plate, 5-1/4" d 65.00

Grapevine Variant, miniature pitcher and bowl, 4-1/4" h pitcher, 4-1/2" d bowl, cobalt blue, orange, green, and luster, scalloped edges......................... 250.00

Oyster

Bowl, 6" d 80.00

Creamer, 3" h......................... 100.00

Jug, 5-3/4" h, c1820 .... 85.00

Soup plate, 10" d, flange rim.... 95.00

Pitcher, green mark "Allertons, Est. 1831, Made in England," **$125**. Photo courtesy of Dotta Auction Co., Inc.

Primrose, plate 8-1/4" d.............. 350.00

Strawberry

Cup and saucer 75.00

Mug, 4 1/8" h 125.00

Plate, 8-1/4" d 150.00

Tulip

Bowl, 6-1/4" d 60.00

Cake plate, 10" d, molded handles 120.00

Creamer, 5-1/4" h.................... 125.00

Plate, tea size 95.00

Tea cup and saucer, slight crazing in cup 115.00

Teapot, 7-1/4" h 225.00

Wagon Wheel

Cup and saucer 75.00

Mug, 2-1/2" h......................... 95.00

Pitcher, 8-1/2" h 195.00

Plate, 8-3/4" d 85.00

Platter 125.00

Girandoles and Mantel Lustres

History: A girandole is a very elaborate branched candleholder, often featuring cut glass prisms surrounding the mountings. A mantel lustre is a glass vase with attached cut glass prisms.

Girandoles and mantel lustres usually are found in pairs. It is not uncommon for girandoles to be part of a large garniture set. Girandoles and mantel lustres achieved their greatest popularity in the last half of the 19th century both in the United States and Europe.

Mantel lusters, ruby glass bowl featuring scalloped gilded rim, hand-painted floral and heart decoration, baluster form standard on circular foot with conforming painted decoration, gilt accents, nine cut crystal glass pendants, wear to gilding, minor chipping to both bases and to pendants, 6" d, 14" h, **$325**. Photo courtesy of Alderfer Auction Co.

Girandoles

9-7/8" w, 17" h, Longwy, Aesthetic Movement, third quarter 19th C, two-light, rect, central beveled mirror plate, surrounded by Islamic-inspired tiles in brass frame, scrolled candle arm with two acorn-shaped nozzles, removable bobeches 750.00

Mantel lusters, pink cased glass, hand-painted floral panel, gilt accents, large hanging prisms, gilt wear, flakes on rim, 14-1/4" h, **$650**. Photo courtesy of Alderfer Auction Co.

16-3/4" h, Louis XIV-style, late 19th/early 20th C, three-light candelabra style, brass wirework lyre form standard, scrolled arms hung with colorless and amethyst glass drops, three short serpentine candle arms with tulip-shaped nozzles, offset with further drops, tripartite wirework base, price for pr **875.00**

18" h, 15" w, cast brass, high relief rococo scrolling and vintage detail, applied flowers on base, columns shaped like large leaves about to burst into blossom, three sockets each with clear cut glass prisms, orig gilding and bobeches, soldered restorations on branches, price for pr........ **990.00**

Hurricane girandoles, colorless glass, Anglo-Irish, c1820, prisms, 23" h, pair, **$1,725**. Photo courtesy of Pook & Pook.

Mantel garnitures

10-1/4" h, urn form, two short scroll handles, incised on side with Japonesque florals in silver and gold coloration, trumpet foot further dec with Japonesque patterning and insects, sq section marble base, inset to front with mixed metal-style patinated plaque depicting drummer and dancer, Aesthetic Movement, third quarter 19th C, price for pr **690.00**

14" h, 12" h, three cov baluster jars and two vases, Hundred Antiques dec, in famille rosé enamels, China, 19th C, price for five-pc set........ **2,185.00**

20-5/8" h, bronze and crystal, three-light candelabra, stylized lyre form garniture hung with cut and pressed glass prisms, above three scrolled candle arms, trefoil base, price for pr........ **980.00**

Mantel lusters

9" h, overlay glass, white cut to pink, enamel flowers, gilt accents, cut glass prisms, Bohemian, price for pr..... **425.00**

12" h, ruby glass, overlay and enameled plaques, fluted, heavy gilt, cut glass prisms, France, 19th C, price for pr **2,645.00**

13-5/8" h, Continental, late 19th C, green glass, trumpet shaped body with crenellated rim hung with faceted colorless lustres, stem tapering to annulated knop, wound by stylized snake, spreading foot, traces of gilt enameling, one cracked, price for pr **200.00**

Goofus Glass

History: Goofus glass, also known as Mexican ware, hooligan glass, and pickle glass, is a pressed glass with relief designs that were painted either on the back or front. The designs are usually in red and green with a metallic gold ground. It was popular from 1890 to 1920 and was used as a premium at carnivals.

It was produced by several companies: Crescent Glass Company, Wellsburg, West Virginia; Imperial Glass Corporation, Bellaire, Ohio; LaBelle Glass Works, Bridgeport, Ohio; and Northwood Glass Co., Indiana, Pennsylvania, Wheeling, West Virginia, and Bridgeport, Ohio.

Goofus glass lost its popularity when people found that the paint tarnished or scaled off after repeated washings and wear. No record of its manufacture has been found after 1920.

Marks: Goofus glass made by Northwood includes one of the following marks: "N," "N" in one circle, "N" in two circles, or one or two circles without the "N."

Bowl, Leaf and Beads, Northwood, c1906-08, opalescent ruffled ring around center design of leafs, center cold painted gold and red, N mark, 9" d, **$55**.

Ashtray, red rose dec, emb adv ... **20.00**

Basket, 5" h, strawberry dec **55.00**

Bonbon, 4" d, Strawberry pattern, gold, red, and green dec **40.00**

Bowl

- 6-1/2" d, Grape and Lattice pattern, red grapes, gold ground, ruffled rim **45.00**
- 7" d, thistle and scrolling leaves, red dec, gold ground, ruffled rim ... **35.00**
- 10-1/2" d, 2-1/2" h, Cherries, gold leaves, red cherries........ **38.00**

Bread plate, 7" w, 11" l, Last Supper pattern, red and gold, grapes and foliage border........ **65.00**

Candy dish, 8-1/2" d, figure-eight design, serrated rim, dome foot........ **60.00**

Charger, grape and leaves center **125.00**

Coaster, 3" d, red floral dec, gold ground **12.00**

Compote

- 4" d, Grape and Cable pattern **35.00**
- 6" d, Strawberry pattern, red and green strawberries and foliage, ruffled **40.00**
- 6-1/2" d, Poppy pattern, red flowers, gold foliage, green ground, sgd "Northwood"........ **40.00**

Decanter, orig stopper, La Belle Rose **55.00**

Dresser tray, 6" l, Cabbage Rose pattern, red roses dec, gold foliage, clear ground........ **35.00**

Jar, cov, butterflies, red and gold .. **35.00**

Jewel box, 4" d, 2" h, basketweave, rose dec **50.00**

Mug, Cabbage Rose pattern, gold ground........ **35.00**

Nappy, 6-1/2" d, Cherries pattern, red cherries, gold foliage, clear ground **35.00**

Perfume bottle, 3-1/2" h, pink tulips dec **20.00**

Pickle jar, aqua, molded, gold, blue, and red painted floral design **50.00**

Pin dish, 6-1/2" l, oval, red and black florals **20.00**

Cake plate, roses decoration, painted red roses, gold background, **$65**.

Plate

6" d, Sunflower pattern, red dec center, relief molded................. **40.00**

11" d, Cherries, some paint worn off **35.00**

Platter, 18" l, red rose dec, gold ground **65.00**

Powder jar, cov, 3" d, puffy, rose dec, red and gold................................ **40.00**

Salt and pepper shakers, pr, Grape and Leaf pattern **45.00**

Syrup, relief molded, red roses dec, lattice work ground, orig top **85.00**

Toothpick holder, red rose and foliage dec, gold ground........................... **40.00**

Tray, 8-1/4" d, 11" d, red chrysanthemum dec, gold ground........................... **45.00**

Tumbler, 6" h, red rose dec, gold ground **35.00**

Vase

6" h, Cabbage Rose pattern, red dec, gold ground **45.00**

9" h, Poppies pattern, blue and red dec, gold ground **55.00**

Gouda Pottery

History: Gouda and the surrounding areas of Holland have been principal Dutch pottery centers for centuries. Originally, the potteries produced a simple utilitarian tin-glazed Delft-type earthenware and the famous clay smoker's pipes.

When pipe making declined in the early 1900s, the Gouda potteries turned to art pottery. Influenced by the Art Nouveau and Art Deco movements, artists expressed themselves with free-form and stylized designs in bold colors.

Reproduction Alert: With the Art Nouveau and Art Deco revivals of recent years, modern reproductions of Gouda pottery currently are on the market. They are difficult to distinguish from the originals.

Bowl

7" h, Art Nouveau scrolled floral and foliage dec, shades of green, brown, and blue, cracked white semi-matte glazed ground, black rooster mark on base, Arnhem factory, c1910, repairs to rim **100.00**

10-1/4" d, 2-1/2" h, dec with three clusters of flowers in symmetrical pattern, matte glaze, shades of orange, yellow, and blue, black ground, blue painted maker's mark, c1927 .... **225.00**

11-3/4" d, 2-3/4" h, stylized floral design, matte glaze, yellow, orange, green, and blue, black ground, black painted Regina marks, c1927, rim repair **185.00**

Candlesticks and vase set, pr 9-1/2" h candlesticks, 10-3/4" h vase, Art Nouveau style dec, matte glaze blue, orange, turquoise, brown, and yellow, painted "Westland (house) Gouda Holland," date and artist's initials **400.00**

Candlesticks, pr, 18" h, bulbed cup, ruffled rim drop pan, tall ribbed flared standard, Art Nouveau-style motif, high glaze, shades of blue, green, yellow, and black, underglaze mark "Gouda Blauw (house)," date mark, artist's initials, and "Made in Holland, 872, 893," dec attributed to Franciscus Ijsselstein, c1926, base chip on one............. **435.00**

Clock garniture, 20-1/2" h clock, 16-3/4" h pr candlesticks, circular clock mouth with painted ceramic face supported by four ceramic arms on baluster-shaped body and flared base, candlesticks of similar form, all dec with Art Nouveau-style flowers, glossy glaze pink, purple, blue, green, and tan, sgd "Zuid Holland" and imp house and "R" on base, repairs to candlesticks **2,875.00**

Charger, 12" d, multicolored flowers, rope border, black trim **150.00**

Compote, 7-5/8", black ground, geometric design, multicolored scroll int **175.00**

Ewer

7" h, handle, floral and foliage design, high glaze, shades of purple, mauve, green, blue, and taupe, base painted "Made in Zuid Holland (house)," and artist's initials **325.00**

7-5/8" h, handle, stylized floral and foliage design, high glazes, shades of green, pink, and purple on tan and brown ground, painted "Made in Zuid, Holland" **350.00**

Incense burner, 8" h, Roba, flowers and geometric designs, green ground **120.00**

Jug, 5-3/4" d, Rosalie, cream ground, green handle, turquoise interior, marked "Rosalie, #5155," and "Zuid-Holland, Gouda," c1930 .... **195.00**

Lamp base, 11-3/4" h, flared rim, tapered oval form, butterfly design, matte glaze, shades of green, blue, gold, red and cream, base painted "380 Butterfly (tree, house) AJK Holland," c1920 .... **290.00**

Tray, scalloped, painted yellow flowers and cobalt blue medallions, stamped "Fanny Gouda," 10" x 13", **$195**. Photo courtesy of David Rago Auctions, Inc.

Miniature, vase, 2-1/4" h, floral and foliate design, high glaze, shades of green, purple, red, brown, and black **125.00**

Pitcher, 10-1/2" h, angled handle, flared form, stylized flower design, semi-matte soft green, rust, and blue tones, cream colored ground, maker's mark "Marantha" and artist's initials on base, Arnhem factory, c1910, minor crazing....... **250.00**

Plate, 10" d, ivory, pink and yellow border, pink fuchsia flowers, marked "Fuehsia Goededwaagen-Gouda, Made in Holland" **45.00**

Shoe, 4-7/8" h, floral and foliate design, high glaze, shades of green, purple, red, brown, and black......................... **125.00**

Tray, 10" x 13", scalloped, painted yellow flowers and cobalt blue medallions, stamped "Fanny Gouda"............. **175.00**

Urn, 7-3/8" h, two handles, stylized flowers and leaves, high glaze, blue, brown, pink, and green, painted "Distel 27/24," and artist's initials............. **325.00**

Vase

4-1/2" h, raised rim, squatty form, flower blossoms dec, semi-matte glaze, yellow, brown, blue, and cream, black ground, painted and paper labels **200.00**

6" h, ivory, cobalt blue, rust, green, and yellow, black base, paper and handwritten label "Serma Royal Zuid-Holland, Gouda"....................... **95.00**

6-3/4" x 3-1/2", corseted, geometric polychromatic design, marked 2073/ Futurist/8/TNT/MH/Italiano 175.00
7-1/4" h, two handles, ftd, bulbous, brown, blue, and green butterflies dec, crackled white matte ground, black stamped rooster mark on base, Arnhem factory, c1910 .... 150.00
7-3/4" h, two handles, bulbed neck flanked by arched handles on squatty body, tulip and foliate designs, high glaze gray, green, yellow, and brown tones, painted "Distel," Distel factory, early 20th C 520.00
8-3/4" h, waisted, floral and foliage design, high glaze, shades of purple, mauve, green, blue, and taupe, base painted "Made in Zuid Holland (house)," and artist's initials 325.00
10" h, two handles, ovoid, ftd, floral and foliage design, high glaze, shades of purple, mauve, green, blue, and taupe, base painted "Made in Zuid Holland (house)," and artist's initials 350.00
10-1/2" h, tapered oval, flowers and leaves, semi-matte glaze, gold, brown, turquoise, cream, and black, painted maker's marks 200.00
10-3/4" h, flared rim, ovoid form, stylized flowers and foliage, matte glaze, shades of yellow, green, blue, orange, and brown, painted mark "Del Breetvelt (house) Zuid Holland Gouda" 420.00
13-1/4" h, elongated neck on bulbous body, Art Nouveau stylized lilies, foliage, high glaze purple, green, yellow, and black, base painted with wooden shoe "NB Faience du (illegible) Holland 504 Dec A" 865.00
19" h, tall tapered vessel, Impressionist country scene with figures, trees, and flowers, glossy glaze, naturalistic tones, underglaze painted "Made in Z Holland" with house mark, c1906-17 .... 1,265.00

GRANITEWARE

History: Graniteware is the name commonly given to enamel-coated iron or steel kitchenware. The first graniteware was made in Germany in the 1830s. Graniteware was not produced in the United States until the 1860s. At the start of World War I, when European companies turned to manufacturing war weapons, American producers took over the market.

Gray and white were the most common graniteware colors, although each company made its own special color in shades of blue, green, brown, violet, cream, or red. Older graniteware is heavier than the new. Pieces with cast-iron handles date between 1870 to 1890; wood handles between 1900 to 1910. Other dating clues are seams, wooden knobs, and tin lids.

Reproduction Alert: Graniteware still is manufactured in many of the traditional forms and colors.

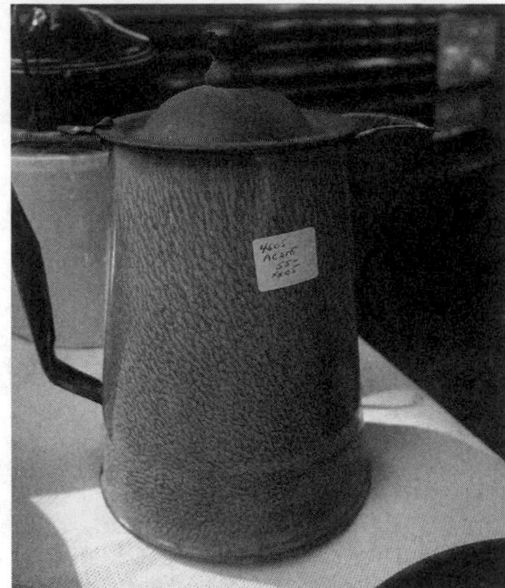

Coffeepot, gray, wooden finial, wear on lid, **$55.**

Batter jug, 6" h, gray mottled, tin lid, tin spout cover, seamed body, wire handle with wood carrying grip 425.00
Berry pail, cov, 7" d, 4-3/4" h, gray and black mottled 50.00
Bowl, 11-3/4" d, 3-3/4" h, green and white 50.00
Cake pan, 7-1/2" d, robin's egg blue and white marbleized 45.00
Canister, small, gray.................. 550.00
Coffeepot, 10" h, gray, tin handle, spout, and lid... 525.00
Colander, 12" d, gray, pedestal base 30.00
Cup, 2-3/4" h, blue and white medium swirl, black trim and handle 50.00
Frying pan, 10-1/4" d, blue and white mottled, white int. 135.00
Funnel, cobalt blue and white marbleized, large 50.00
Grater, medium blue.................... 115.00
Hotplate, two burners, white graniteware, Hotpoint...................................... 165.00
Kettle, cobalt blue swirl, bail handle 260.00
Measure, one cup, gray................ 45.00
Mixing bowls, red and white, nested set of four, 1930s.............................. 155.00
Muffin pan, blue and white mottled, eight cups.. 250.00
Pie pan, 6" d, cobalt blue and white marbleized.................................... 25.00
Pitcher, 11" h, gray, ice lip............ 110.00

Coffeepot, shaded blue, white shamrocks and flowers, gold dec, minor wear, **$45.**

These graniteware coffee grinders were cleverly displayed at the October 2003 Atlantique City Antiques show.

Refrigerator bowls, red swirl, four-pc set 585.00
Roaster, emerald green swirl, large 250.00
Skimmer, 10" l, gray mottled 25.00
Sugar devil, dated 1876............. 170.00
Teapot, 9-1/2" w, 5" h, enameled dec, small chips 525.00
Tube pan, octagonal, gray mottled 45.00
Utensil rack, 14-1/2" w, 22" h, shaded orange, gray bowls, matching ladle, skimmer, and tasting spoon 400.00
Wash basin, 11-3/4" d, blue and white swirl, Blue Diamond Ware 150.00

Greenaway, Kate

History: Kate Greenaway, or "K.G.," as she initialed her famous drawings, was born in 1846 in London. Her father was a prominent wood engraver. Kate's natural talent for drawing soon was evident, and she began art classes at the age of 12. In 1868, she had her first public exhibition.

Her talents were used primarily in illustrating. The cards she decorated for Marcus Ward are largely unsigned. China and pottery companies soon had her drawings of children appearing on many of their wares. By the 1880s, she was one of the foremost children's book illustrators in England.

Reproduction Alert: Some Greenaway buttons have been reproduced in Europe and sold in the United States.

Advertisement, 5" x 10" print, black and white, for Kate Greenaway fashions, two little girls dressed in Spanish Plaids **12.00**
Butter pat, transfer print of boy and girl **35.00**
Button, 3/4" d, girl with kitten on fence **12.00**
Child's book, Mother Goose or The Old Nursery Rhymes, Warne, c1900, 44 rhymes, Kate Greenaway illus, pictures on both front and back cov **45.00**
Figure, 5-3/4" h Emma, pink and white, Royal Doulton **375.00**

Toothpick holder and stand, Kate Greenaway figures, cut glass bowl, Meriden silver plate, **$700**. Photo courtesy of Joy Luke Auctions.

Handkerchief, 11-1/2" sq, sunbonnet girl, "Love's gentle touch means so much," lace trim **5.00**
Inkwell, bronze, emb, two children **200.00**
Match safe, SP, emb children **50.00**
Napkin ring, SS, girl feeding yearling **160.00**
Picture frame, 10-7/8" w, 13-1/2" h, wood frame applied with stamped sheet of pewter, shepherdess and sheep, birds and flowering tree, easel back, England or America, early 20th C **150.00**
Salt and pepper shakers, pr, 2-3/4" h, incised "5103," wear to gold trim ... **95.00**
Tape measure, figural, girl holding muff **45.00**
Tile, each 6-3/8" d, transfer print, four seasons, one spacer, brown and white dec, blue border, stamped mark, produced by T & R Boote, 1881, framed, five-pc set **325.00**
Toothpick holder, 3-3/8" h, silver plated, girl with low-cut ball gown standing beside barrel holder, marked "2302/ Derby Silver Co." **125.00**

Grueby Pottery

GRUEBY·POTTERY·BOSTON·U·S·A

History: William Grueby was active in the ceramic industry for several years before he developed his own method of producing matte-glazed pottery and founded the Grueby Faience Company in Boston, Massachusetts, in 1897.

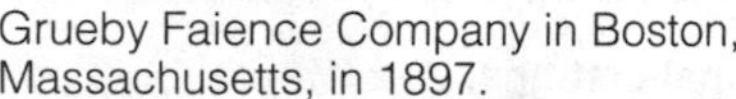

The art pottery was hand thrown in natural shapes, hand molded, and hand tooled. A variety of colored glazes, singly or in combinations, was produced, but green was the most popular. In 1908, the firm was divided into the Grueby Pottery Company and the Grueby Faience and Tile Co. The Grueby Faience and Tile Company made art tile until 1917, although its pottery production was phased out about 1910. Minor damage is acceptable to most collectors of Grueby Pottery.

Adviser: David Rago.

Floor vase, tooled and applied yellow buds alternating with full height leaves, covered pulled and feathered matte green glaze, GRUEBY FAIENCE circular stamp, drilled hole to bottom, restored 8" line around body, 8-1/2" d, 23" h, **$14,850**. Photo courtesy of David Rago Auctions, Inc.

Jardinière, 7-1/2" x 9", two-color three rows of curled leaves below nine light blue five-petaled flowers, oatmeal matte green glaze, stamped "Grueby Faience/ 174" and "EG," couple of minor flecks **575.00**
Lamp base, gourd shape, by Wilhemina Post, organic matte blue glaze, orig converted three-socket fixture, hemispherical leaded glass shade with band of green leaves on blue slag glass ground, original patina and wiring to fixture, base stamped with pottery mark/W.P./228, paper label remnant: "(Electri)city three lights glass shade 14 IN. Rush," break to one piece and two inner lead strips on shade **9,200.00**
Low bowl
- 4-1/4" d, squat, matte ochre glaze, circular stamp, paper label **535.00**
- 7-3/4" d, leathery matte green glaze, circular pottery mark, rim hairline, grinding loss **380.00**
- 9" d, swirled interior, thick curdled matte green glaze, pottery mark **815.00**

Paperweight, 3-3/4" x 2-3/4", scarab, matte green glaze, circular faience mark, minute base fleck **1,380.00**
Tile, cuenca dec
- 6" sq, large oak tree against blue sky, puffy white clouds, #28 on reverse **1,150.00**
- 6" sq, "The Pines," polychrome cuenca, marked "FH" **1,485.00**

Humidor, cylindrical, decorated by Wilhemina Post, band of ivory and yellow five-petaled tobacco blossoms, thick curdled matte green ground, stamped pottery mark, WP, paper label, three hairlines from rim, restoration to lid, 4-1/2" d, 7-1/2" h, **$4,600**. Photo courtesy of David Rago Auctions, Inc.

Vase
- 3-3/4" x 3", flat shoulder, oatmeal matte indigo glaze, stamped pottery mark, two minor under rim flakes **1,100.00**
- 4-1/2" x 5", by Wilhemina Post, squatty, bulbous shoulder with

tooled and applied broad light green leaves, bright yellow four-petal blossoms at corseted neck, frothy dark matte green glaze, stamped pottery mark/MWP **8,600.00**

Vessel, spherical vessel, broad leaves, covered in leathery matte green glaze, stamped pottery mark, initials "ERF," partial paper label, few minor edge nicks to edges, 4-3/4" d, 4" h, **$5,750**. Photo courtesy of David Rago Auctions, Inc.

4-3/4" h, bulbous, vertical ribs, curdled matte green glaze, circular stamp **1,355.00**

7-3/4" x 4-1/4", six-sided opening, full-height tooled and applied leaves alternating with bright yellow buds and covered in matte green glaze, faint circular stamp, restoration to rim chip **8,100.00**

8-3/4" h, ribbed, tapering, leathery matte green glaze, pottery stamp **1,355.00**

9" x 3-3/4", cylindrical, vertical ridges, thick curdled matte indigo glaze, by Ruth Ericson, stamped pottery mark RE **2,530.00**

11" x 5-1/4", bulbous, floriform rim, three tooled and applied ivory, lemon yellow, and burgundy jonquils in amidst tall and narrow medium green leaves, feathered matte green glaze, stamped Pottery mark/JE, green glaze drips over yellow blossom, professional restoration to several small rim chips **13,550.00**

11-1/2" x 6", by Wilhemina Post, tooled and applied full-height leaves alternating with yellow buds, curdled organic matte green glaze, circular pottery stamp 5-19 WP **11,150.00**

Vessel, 4" x 4-1/2", by Ruth Ericson, squat, small opening, tooled and applied leaves all around its protruding shoulder creating star effect, matte ivory glaze, stamped pottery mark, some peppering **2,100.00**

Hall China Company

History: Robert Hall founded the Hall China Company in 1903 in East Liverpool, Ohio. He died in 1904 and was succeeded by his son, Robert Taggart Hall. After years of experimentation, Robert T. Hall developed a leadless glaze in 1911, opening the way for production of glazed household products.

For more information, see *American Pottery & Porcelain*, 2nd edition.

The Hall China Company made many types of kitchenware, refrigerator sets, and dinnerware in a wide variety of patterns. Some patterns were made exclusively for a particular retailer, such as Heather Rose for Sears.

One of the most popular patterns was Autumn Leaf, a premium designed by Arden Richards in 1933 for the exclusive use by the Jewel Tea Company. Still a Jewel Tea property, Autumn Leaf has not been listed in catalogs since 1978, but is produced on a replacement basis with the date stamped on the back.

Additional Listings: See *Warman's Americana & Collectibles* for more examples.

Cookie jar, cov

Autumn Leaf, Tootsie **275.00**
Blue Blossom, Five-Band shape .. **300.00**
Meadow Flower, Five-Band shape **260.00**
Owl, brown glaze.......................... **120.00**
Red Poppy..................................... **60.00**

Kitchen ware

Bean pot, New England, #1, Orange Poppy **100.00**
Butter dish, cov, Hercules, Westinghouse, yellow.. **42.00**
Casserole, cov, Chinese Red, Sundial, #4, 8" w.. **125.00**
Jug, Primrose, rayed **20.00**
Leftover, General Electric, gray and yellow.. **18.00**
Water server, Hotpoint, blue........... **90.00**

Patterns

Autumn Leaf
Bean pot, cov **700.00**
Bowl, 5-1/2" d **7.50**
Bud vase, 5-3/4" h.................. **300.00**
Coffeepot, electric.................. **500.00**
Cup and saucer **18.00**
Juice reamer **300.00**
Plate, 8" d **15.00**
Teapot, cov, automobile shape, 1993 .... **500.00**
Tidbit tray, three tiers............. **125.00**
Utensil holder, 7-1/4" h, marked "Utensils" **275.00**

Blue Bouquet
Creamer, Boston........................ **25.00**
Cup and saucer **28.00**
French baker, round **35.00**
Spoon **100.00**
Teapot, Aladdin infuser **200.00**

Cameo Rose
Bowl, 5-1/4" d **3.00**
Butter dish, 3/4 lb. **30.00**
Casserole **25.00**
Creamer **12.00**
Cup and saucer **9.00**
Platter, 11-1/2" l **25.00**
Sugar... **12.00**
Teapot, cov, six cup **35.00**
Tidbit, three tiers **40.00**

Teapot, globe shape, bright turquoise, gold mark, **$45**.

Mount Vernon
Berry bowl, 5" d........................... **7.50**
Coffeepot.................................. **125.00**
Creamer **12.00**
Cup and saucer **12.00**
Gravy boat................................. **20.00**
Plate, 10" d **12.00**
Sugar... **12.00**
Vegetable bowl, 9-1/4" l, oval ... **20.00**

Red Poppy
Bowl, 5-1/2" d **5.00**
Cake plate **17.50**
Casserole, cov **25.00**
Coffeepot, cov............................ **50.00**
Creamer **15.00**
Cup and saucer **8.00**
French baker, fluted **15.00**
Jug, Daniel, Radiance................ **28.00**
Plate, 9" d **6.50**
Sugar... **15.00**

Silhouette
Bean pot..................................... **50.00**
Bowl, 7-7/8" d **50.00**
Coffeepot, cov............................ **30.00**
Fruit bowl................................... **12.00**
Mug **35.00**
Pretzel jar **75.00**
Trivet.. **125.00**

Tulip
Bowl, 10-1/4" l, oval.................. **36.00**
Casserole, cov **65.00**

Coffee maker, drip, Kadota, all china 115.00
Condiment jar 165.00
Fruit bowl, 5-1/2" d 10.00
Mixing bowl, 6" d 27.00
Plate, 9" d, luncheon 16.00
Platter, 13-1/4" l, oval 42.00
Sugar, cov 25.00

Teapots

Aladdin, black, gold trim 95.00
Cadet, Radiance 350.00
Donut
Chinese Red, donut, 9-1/2" w, 7-1/2" h 600.00
Orange Poppy, donut 395.00
Cleveland, turquoise and gold 165.00
Target shape, red and black Dutch windmill decal, marked "The Enterprise Aluminum Company, Massillon, Ohio" 95.00
Windshield, Camelia, gold dots 85.00

HAMPSHIRE POTTERY

History: In 1871, James S. Taft founded the Hampshire Pottery Company in Keene, New Hampshire. Production began with redwares and stonewares, followed by majolica in 1879. A semi-porcelain, with the recognizable matte glazes plus the Royal Worcester glaze, was introduced in 1883.

For more information, see *Warman's American Pottery & Porcelain*, 2nd edition.

Until World War I, the factory made an extensive line of utilitarian and art wares including souvenir items. After the war, the firm resumed operations, but made only hotel dinnerware and tiles. The company was dissolved in 1923.

Lamp base, squatty, embossed ossed tulips, matte green glaze, stamped "HAMPSHIRE POTTERY," 11-1/2" d, 6" h, **$1,100**. Photo courtesy of David Rago Auctions, Inc.

Bowl, 5-1/2" d, 2-1/2" h, matte green glaze over foliate-forms, imp "Hampshire, M.O." 320.00

Umbrella stand, embossed with branches of ivy on bamboo ground, matte green glaze, unmarked, glaze flake and several lines to bottom, 8" d, 17-1/2" h, **$1,955**. Photo courtesy of David Rago Auctions, Inc.

Chocolate pot, 9-1/2" h, cream, holly dec 275.00
Compote, 13-1/4" d, ftd, two handles, Ivory pattern, light green highlights, cream ground, red decal mark..... 175.00
Inkwell, 4-1/8" d, 2-3/4" h, round, large center well, three pen holes 125.00
Lamp base, 15" h, 9" d, tall cylindrical form, vertical leaves, stems, and flowers, matte green glaze 2,185.00
Low bowl, 5-1/2" d, 2-1/2" h, squat, emb geometric pattern, matte green glaze, marked 350.00
Pitcher, 6" h, ftd, matte green glaze, Keene mark 150.00
Tankard, 7" h, band of stylized dec, green matte glaze, imp "Hampshire" 120.00
Urn, 14-1/2" h, leathery matte green glaze, Keene stamp 1,485.00
Vase
6-3/4" h, emb leaves and buds, green and brown frothy matte glaze, marked, tight inner line........ 750.00

Vessel, squatty, covered in green frothy glazes, incised "Hampshire Pottery," 3-1/4" d, 3-1/2" h, **$415**. Photo courtesy of David Rago Auctions, Inc.

7" h, bulbous, lotus leaves and buds, smooth matte green glaze, marked 1,100.00
7" h, emb full height leaves, fine matte blue-green feathered glaze, marked 1,100.00
7" h, full height leaves, mottled and veined cafe-au-lait glaze against a darker brown ground, marked, hairline to rim 365.00
8-1/2" h, bulbous, emb tulips, smooth matte green glaze, marked, 1/4" kiln kiss to leaf 630.00
Vessel, 5-1/2" d, emb trees under veined matte green glaze, marked, dark crazing lines 250.00

HATPINS AND HATPIN HOLDERS

History: When oversized hats were in vogue, around 1850, hatpins became popular. Designers used a variety of materials to decorate the pin ends, including china, crystal, enamel, gem stones, precious metals, and shells. Decorative subjects ranged from commemorative designs to insects.

Hatpin holders, generally placed on a dresser, are porcelain containers that were designed specifically to hold these pins. The holders were produced by major manufacturers, among which were Meissen, Nippon, R. S. Germany, R. S. Prussia, and Wedgwood.

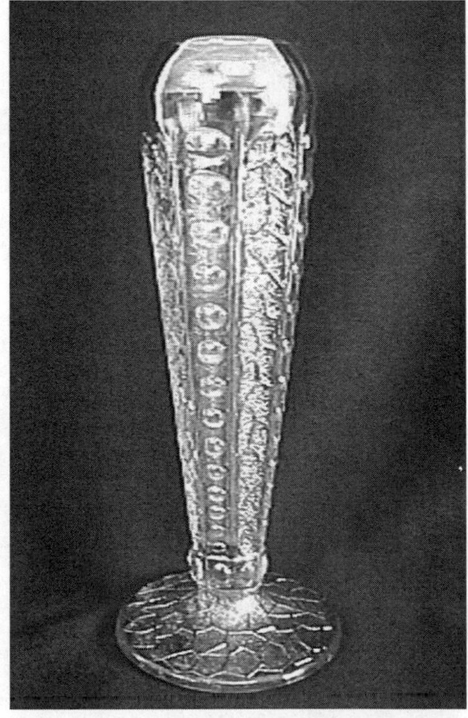

Hatpin holder, carnival glass, Formal pattern, marigold iridescent, **$350**. Photo courtesy of Seeck Auctions.

Hatpin

Brass

- 1-1/4" d, 9" l pin, Victorian Lady, cameo type profile, round, Victorian, orig finish **110.00**
- 1-1/2" x 1-3/4", 9" l pin, child with flowing hair, flanked by sunflowers, Victorian, orig finish **125.00**
- 2" d, 9-1/2" l pin, military button **125.00**
- 2-1/4" l, oxidized, four citrine-colored stones in each of four panels, citrine-colored stones on 1/2" bezel **315.00**
- 2" l, 12" l shaft, Art Nouveau teardrop shape, small diamond mounted on each side **200.00**

Enamel, black tracery, surmounted by small pearl, 14k yg, pr **150.00**
Hand-painted china, roses, gold trim **35.00**
Glass, 2" l faceted amber glass bead, 13-1/4" l japanned shaft **125.00**
Ivory, ball shape, carved design ... **65.00**
Jet, 1-1/4" elongated oval knobby bead, 8" l pin **200.00**
Metal, 9-1/4" l, round disk, Art-Nouveau style lady with flowing hair **125.00**

Sterling silver

- 1-1/4" d, 11" l pin, Arts & Crafts motif of ivy leaf in circle, Charles Horner, hallmarks for Chester, England, 1911 .... **195.00**
- 6-1/2" l, elongated tear shape, marked "Horner" **95.00**

Hatpin holder, porcelain, flowers and hatpins decoration, German, **$120**. Photo courtesy of Joy Luke Auctions.

Hatpin holder

Belleek, 5-1/4" h, relief pink and maroon floral dec, green leaves, gold top, marked "Willets Belleek," dated 1911 .... **125.00**
Limoges, grapes, pink roses, matte finish, artist sgd **60.00**
Nippon, 4-7/8" d, hp blue daisy flowers, marked "E. O. China" **185.00**
Royal Bayreuth, tapestry, portrait of lady wearing hat, blue mark **575.00**
R. S. Germany, 4-1/2" d, pink roses, green foliage, pink luster trim **315.00**
R. S. Prussia, 7" h, 3" d, peach flowers, green foliage **180.00**

Haviland China

H&C° L   H &C° L FRANCE

History: In 1842, American china importer David Haviland moved to Limoges, France, where he began manufacturing and decorating china specifically for the U.S. market. Haviland is synonymous with fine, white, translucent porcelain, although early hand-painted patterns were generally larger and darker colored on heavier whiteware blanks than were later ones.

David revolutionized French china factories by both manufacturing the whiteware blank and decorating it at the same site. In addition, Haviland and Company pioneered the use of decals in decorating china.

David's sons, Charles Edward and Theodore, split the company in 1892. In 1936, Theodore opened an American division, which still operates today. In 1941, Theodore bought out Charles Edward's heirs and recombined both companies under the original name of H. and Co. The Haviland family sold the firm in 1981.

For more information, see *Warman's American Pottery & Porcelain*, 2nd edition.

Charles Field Haviland, cousin of Charles Edward and Theodore, worked for and then, after his marriage in 1857, ran the Casseaux Works until 1882. Items continued to carry his name as decorator until 1941.

Thousands of Haviland patterns were made, but not consistently named until after 1926. The similarities in many of the patterns makes identification difficult. Numbers assigned by Arlene Schleiger and illustrated in her books have become the identification standard.

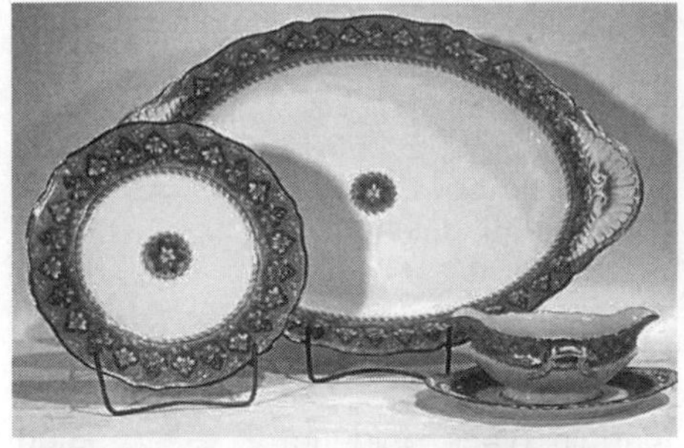

Dinner plate, 21" l platter, gravy, pink flowers on green gilded border, marked "Theodore Haviland," plate, **$20**; platter, **$45**; gravy, **$40**. Photo courtesy of Joy Luke Auctions.

Bone dish, 8-1/4" l, hp, turtle dec.. **65.00**
Bouillon, underplate, Rajah pattern, marked "Theo Haviland" **25.00**
Bowl, 8" d, hp, yellow roses **35.00**
Butter dish, cov, Gold Band, marked "Theo Haviland" **45.00**
Butter pat, sq, rounded corners, gold trim **12.00**
Cake plate, 10" d, gold handles and border **35.00**
Celery dish, scalloped edge, green flowers, pale pink scroll **45.00**
Chocolate pot, cov, 10-1/2" l, Countess pattern, green mark, c1893 .... **475.00**
Cream soup, underplate, cranberry and blue scroll border **30.00**
Creamer and sugar, small pink flowers, scalloped, gold trim **65.00**
Cup and saucer, Etoile **470.00**
Game plate, 9-1/4" d, hp, center scene of shore birds in natural setting, apple green edge, printed gold scrolled rim dec, artist sgd "B. Albert," Theodore Haviland & Co. blanks, early 20th C, price for set of 12 .... **865.00**

Gravy boat, attached underplate

- Chantilly **270.00**
- Monteray **315.00**

Hair receiver, cov, squatty, three gold feet, blue and green hp flowers, gold trim, Charles Field Haviland mark **150.00**
Milk pitcher, 8" h, 4-3/4" d, pink flowers, green branches, underglaze green Haviland mark, red "Haviland & Co., Limoges for PDG, Indianapolis, Ind." **450.00**

Oyster plate, five wells

- Forget-me-not dec, white ground, brushed gold trim **250.00**
- Mussels, brushed gold trim.... **800.00**
- Seascape, shellfish and aquatic plants dec **975.00**
- Wave design, mauve, brushed gold trim **325.00**

Pitcher, 7-1/2" h, Rosalinde **280.00**

Plate, dinner

- Baltimore Rose **295.00**
- Etoile **400.00**
- Golden Quail **275.00**

Dinner service, white, delicate pink florals, green leaves, gold trim, 86 pieces, marked "Theodore Haviland, Limoges China," **$200**. Photo courtesy of Dotta Auction Co., Inc.

Platter, Chantilly.......................... **275.00**
Sandwich plate, 11-1/2" d, Drop Rose pattern **275.00**
Sugar bowl, cov, Golden Quail ... **435.00**
Tankard pitcher, 9" h, Ranson blank, floral band around top, gold handle, trim bands, factory decorated............ **225.00**
Teacup and saucer, small blue flowers, green leaves.................................. **30.00**
Tea set, 8-1/2" d, 8" h teapot, rope and anchor pattern, transfer-printed, hand-tinted blossoms, stamped "Haviland-Limoges" mark, restoration to lids, price for three-pc set **200.00**
Tureen, cov, pink roses, green ivy, 12" l, 6-1/2" h **360.00**
Vase, 5-1/2" h, 3-5/8" d, tan, brown, pink, and rose, two oval scenes of lady in large hat, baskets and flower garlands, Charles Field Haviland and GDA Limoges mark **275.00**

HEISEY GLASS

History: The A. H. Heisey Glass Co. began producing glasswares in April 1896, in Newark, Ohio. Heisey, the firm's founder, was not a newcomer to the field, having been associated with the craft since his youth.

Many blown and molded patterns were produced in crystal, colored, milk (opalescent), and Ivorina Verde (custard) glass. Decorative techniques of cutting, etching, and silver deposit were employed. Glass figurines were introduced in 1933 and continued in production until 1957 when the factory closed. All Heisey glass is notable for its clarity.

For more information, see *Warman's Glass*, 4th edition.

Marks: Not all pieces have the familiar H-within-a-diamond mark.

Reproduction Alert: Some Heisey molds were sold to Imperial Glass of Bellaire, Ohio, and certain items were reissued. These pieces may be mistaken for the original Heisey. Some of the reproductions were produced in colors never made by Heisey and have become collectible in their own right. Examples include: the Colt family in Crystal, Caramel Slag, Ultra Blue, and Horizon Blue; the mallard with wings up in Caramel Slag; Whirlpool (Provincial) in crystal and colors; and Waverly, a 7-inch, oval, footed compote in Caramel Slag.

Animal
- Gazelle **1,450.00**
- Plug horse, Oscar **115.00**
- Sealyham terrier **145.00**
- Sparrow **150.00**

Ashtray, Old Sandwich, #1404, moongleam, individual size............ **67.50**
Bitters bottle, #5003, tube **165.00**
Bowl, Queen Anne, 8" d, light use . **25.00**
Buffet plate, Lariat, #1540, 21"...... **70.00**
Butter dish, cov, Rose................ **200.00**
Cake plate, Rose, 15" d, pedestal **325.00**
Camellia bowl, Lariat, #1540, 9-1/2" d **40.00**
Candelabra, crystal, 10" w, 16-1/2" h, price for pr.................................. **695.00**
Candlesticks, pr
- Cascade, triple, #142............ **110.00**
- Crystolite, triple **115.00**
- Trophy, #126, flamingo........... **275.00**
- Windsor, #22, 7-1/2" h **140.00**

Candle vase, Ipswich, orig candle cup **185.00**
Celery, Empress, Sahara, 10" l **45.00**

Sherbert, Victorian pattern, footed, signed, **$20**.

Centerpiece bowl, Ridgeleigh, #1469, 11" d **225.00**
Champagne, Fairacre, crystal bowl, diamond optic, flamingo stem and foot **25.00**

Cheese dish, cov, Lariat, #1540, ftd **40.00**
Cheese plate, Twist, #1252, Kraft, moongleam.................................... **62.50**
Cigarette holder, Crystolite........... **25.00**
Claret, Orchid, Tyrolean line, 4-1/2 oz **150.00**
Coaster, Colonial **10.00**
Cocktail, New Era......................... **20.00**
Cocktail shaker, Orchid Etch, sterling foot... **200.00**
Compote, Rose, #1519, low, ftd, 6-1/2" **65.00**
Cordial, 5th Avenue-Mitchell, #829 .... **45.00**
Creamer, Ridgeleigh, #1469.......... **20.00**
Creamer and sugar, Twist, #1252, oval, Sahara **165.00**
Cream soup, Queen Anne, etching **20.00**
Cruet, Plantation, crystal, #1567.. **155.00**
Cup and saucer
- Crystolite **32.50**
- Yeoman, pink.............................. **28.50**

Custard cup, Queen Anne **15.00**

Orchid pattern, large sandwich plate, 14" d, **$80**. Photo courtesy of Sanford Alderfer Auction Company.

Orchid pattern, tall water pitcher, **$500**. Photo courtesy of Sanford Alderfer Auction Company.

Finger bowl, 4-1/4" d, 6-1/2" d underplate, Colonial **25.00**
Gardenia bowl, Orchid, Waverly, 13" d **90.00**
Goblet
Everglade, cutting #913, Duquesne blank...................... **55.00**
Fairacre, crystal bowl, diamond optic, flamingo stem and foot... **40.00**
Pied Piper...................... **55.00**
Plantation...................... **55.00**
Rose **50.00**
Honey, Plantation, #1567, ivy etch, 6-1/2" **80.00**
Hurricane lamp base, Lariat, #1540, pr **85.00**
Iced-tea tumbler, ftd, Orchid, #5025, Tyrolean line **70.00**
Jug, Old Sandwich, #1404, Sahara, half gallon...................... **225.00**
Mayonnaise bowl, Orchid, two-part, Queen Anne **65.00**
Mayonnaise ladle, #6, Alexandrite **245.00**
Muffin plate, Octagon #1229, 12" d, moongleam...................... **47.50**
Mustard, cov, Crystolite **55.00**
Nut dish, Narrow Flute, #393, moongleam...................... **15.00**
Oyster cocktail, Pied Piper **15.00**
Paperweight, rabbit...................... **225.00**
Parfait glass, Orchid, 5-1/2" h, 2-7/8" d, price for set of eight **480.00**
Pitcher, Orchid, tankard **625.00**
Plate, Everglade, cutting #913, 7-1/2" d **55.00**
Punch bowl set, Crystolite, punch bowl, 12 cups, ladle...................... **400.00**
Relish
Crystolite, three parts...................... **40.00**
Empress, pink, three parts...... **45.00**

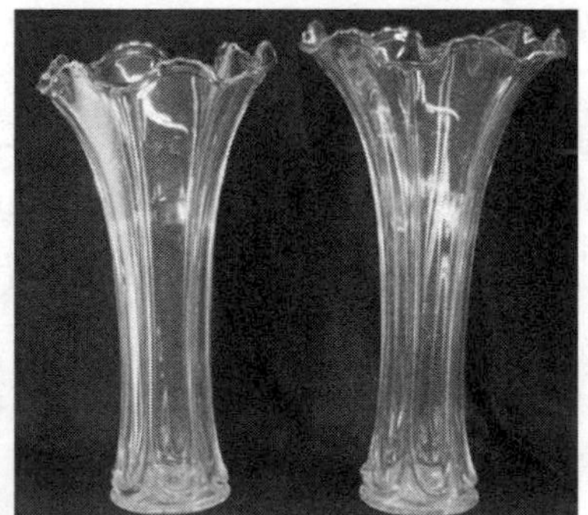

Vase, 12" d, 23-1/2" h, 12" d, **$315**. Photo courtesy of Joy Luke Auctions.

Rose bowl, Plateau, #3369, flamingo **65.00**
Salt shaker, Old Sandwich, #1404 **30.00**
Sandwich plate, Rose **220.00**
Serving tray, center handle, Orchid Etch **150.00**
Sherbet
Lariet **12.50**
Old Dominion, Sahara...................... **35.00**
Soda
Coronation, #4054, 10 oz...................... **9.50**
Newton, #2351, 8 oz, Fronetnac etch **20.00**
Stanhope, #4083, 8 oz, ftd, zircon bowl and foot...................... **155.00**
Strawberry dip plate, Narrow Flute, #393, with rim **195.00**
Sugar, Crystolite, individual...................... **17.50**
Tankard, Orchid, ice lip, 9-1/2" h, 7" w **480.00**
Toothpick holder, Fancy Loop, emerald, small base flake, wear to gold trim **120.00**
Tumbler, Ipswich, ftd **45.00**
Vase, Prison Stripe, #357, cupped, 5" **55.00**
Water bottle, Banded Flute, #150 .... **125.00**
Wine, Orchid etch, 3 oz **75.00**

HOLT-HOWARD COLLECTIBLES

History: Three young entrepreneurs, Grant Holt and brothers John and Robert Howard, started Holt-Howard from their apartment in Manhattan, in 1949. All three of the partners were great salesmen, but Robert handled product development, while John managed sales; Grant was in charge of financial affairs and office management. By 1955, operations were large enough to move the company to Connecticut, but they still maintained their New York showroom and later added their final showroom in Los Angeles. Production facilities eventually expanded to Holt-Howard Canada; Holt-Howard West, Holt-Howard International.

The company's first successful product was the Angel-Abra, followed closely by its Christmas line. This early success spurred the partners to expand their wares. Their line of Christmas and kitchen-related giftware was popular with 1950s consumers. Probably the most famous line was Pixieware, which began production in 1958. Production of these whimsical pieces continued until 1962. Other lines, such as Cozy Kittens and Merry Mouse brought even more smiles as they invaded homes in many forms. Three things that remained constant with all Holt-Howard products were a high quality of materials and workmanship, innovation, and good design.

The founders of this unique company sold their interests to General Housewares Corp. in 1968, where it became part of the giftware group. By 1974, the three original partners had left the firm. By 1990, what remained of Holt-Howard was sold to Kay Dee Designs of Rhode Island.

Holt-Howard pieces were marked with an ink-stamp. Many were also copyright dated. Some pieces were marked only with a foil sticker, especially the small pieces, where a stamp mark was too difficult. Four types of foil stickers have been identified.

Adviser: Walter Dworkin.

Pitcher and mug set, Cloud Santa, **$85**.

Christmas

Air freshener, Girl Christmas Tree **65.00**
Ashtray, Snow Baby...................... **35.00**
Bells, Elf Girls, pr **55.00**
Bottle opener, wooden
Santa **28.00**
Snowman...................... **28.00**
Candle climbers, Ole Snowy, snowman, set...................... **48.00**
Candleholders
Carolers trio...................... **30.00**
Green Holly Elf, pr **35.00**
Madonna and Child...................... **25.00**
Naughty Choir Boy, set of two **30.00**
Santa driving car candleholers, traffic light candle rings, pr **55.00**
Santa riding stage coach, pr.... **38.00**
Santas, NOEL, set of four......... **90.00**
Snow Babies, igloo, set of two **55.00**
Three Choir Boys...................... **60.00**
Three Snowmen **50.00**
Cigarette holder with ashtrays, Santa King, stackable...................... **70.00**
Coffee mug, Green Holly Elf.......... **23.00**
Cookie jar, pop-up, Santa **150.00**
Cookie jar/candy jar combination, Santa **155.00**
Creamer and sugar
Reindeers...................... **48.00**
Winking Santas...................... **55.00**
Decanter and glasses, Santa King **100.00**
Dish, divided, Green Holly Elf........ **50.00**
Floral ring, Green Holly Elf **48.00**
Letter and pen holder, Santa........ **55.00**
Napkin holder, Santa, 4" **25.00**
Nutmeg shaker, Winking Santa..... **55.00**
Pitcher and mug set, Winking Santa **75.00**
Place card holders, Green Holly Elf, set of four **40.00**
Planter, Green Holly Elf, pr **75.00**
Punch bowl set, punch bowl and eight mugs, Santa **145.00**
Salt & pepper shakers, pr
Holly Girls, pr...................... **23.00**

Santa and Rudolph sleeping in bed 105.00
Santa and snowman in NOEL candleholder 95.00
Server, divided tray, Santa King 60.00
Wall pocket, Green Holly Elf 65.00

Cozy Kittens

Bud vase, pr 105.00
Butter dish, cov 105.00
Condiment jar, Cat
Instant Coffee 190.00
Jam 'n' Jelly 180.00
Ketchup 180.00
Mustard 180.00
Cookie jar, pop-up 250.00
Cottage cheese crock 60.00
Match dandy 75.00
Memo minder 90.00
Meow oil and vinegar 175.00
Salt & pepper shakers, pr 20.00
Spice set of four, with rack 110.00
Sugar pour 85.00
Totem pole stacking seasons 65.00

Cows

Creamer and sugar 75.00
Milk glass, moo cow 32.00
Salt & pepper shakers, pr
Heads 40.00
Moveable tongues 50.00

Merry Mouse

Cocktail kibitzers, mice, set of six 120.00
Coaster, ashtray, corner 55.00
Crock, "Stinky Cheese" 50.00
Desk pen pal 85.00
Match mouse 70.00
Salt & pepper shakers, pr 35.00

Minnie & Moby Mermaids

Ashtray, Moby 55.00
Cotton ball dispenser, Minnie 75.00
Matchbox holder, Moby 65.00
Pill box, Minnie & Moby 50.00
Planter, seahorse, Minnie & Moby, pr 85.00
Powder jar, Minnie & Moby 50.00

Miscellaneous

Ashtray
Golfer Image 110.00
Li'l Old Lace 50.00
Bank, bobbing, Dandy Lion 135.00
Bud vase, Daisy Dorable 70.00
Candelabra, Li'l Old Lace, spiral ... 50.00
Candle climbers, Honey Bunnies, with bases, set 85.00
Candle holder, Market Piggy 28.00
Candle rings, Ballerina, with bases, set 58.00
Cookie jar, pop-up, Clown 225.00
Desk organizer, Market Piggy 78.00
Planter, Doe & Fawn 35.00
Salt & pepper shakers, with napkin holder, Winking Wabbits 60.00
Peepin' Tom & Tweetie Birds
Butter dish, cov 65.00
Candle holder/floral holder 38.00
Candle food-warmer set, three pcs 65.00
Creamer, sugar, and saccharin holder, 4-1/2" 75.00
Egg cups, thermal salt & pepper tops, 4" h 60.00
Salt & pepper shakers, set 35.00
Stackable condiment bowls, set of three 40.00

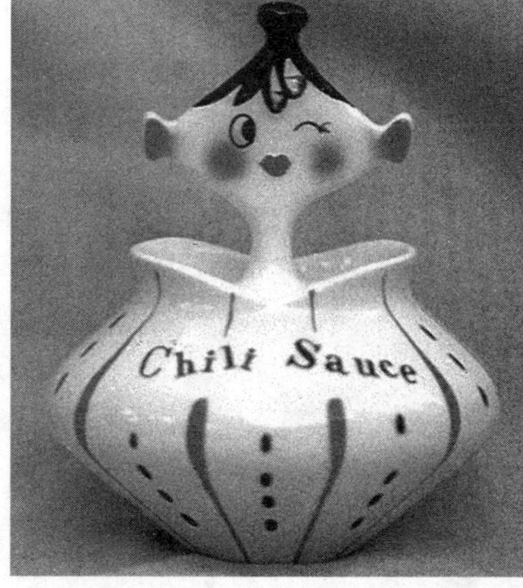

Pixieware, condiment jar, chili sauce, 1959, **$365**. Photo courtesy of Walter Dworkin.

Pixiewares, 1958

Bottle bracelets, Bourbon, Gin, Scotch, or Whiskey 100.00
Child's Pixie spoon
Carrot nose, flesh-colored Pixie 135.00
Green head Pixie 135.00
Orange head Pixie 135.00
Yellow chicken beak Pixie 135.00
Condiment jar
Cherries 120.00
Cocktail Olives 130.00
Instant Coffee 255.00
Jam 'N' Jelly 75.00
Ketchup 75.00
Mustard 75.00
Onions 145.00
L'il sugar and cream crock 155.00
Liquor decanter, "Devil Brew" 580.00
Oil cruet, Sally 185.00
Stacking seasons, shakers, set of four 85.00

Pixiewares, 1959

Ashtray Pixie, blue stripe, green stripe, pink stripe, or red stripe 160.00
Condiment jar
Chili Sauce 365.00
Honey 725.00
Mayonnaise 185.00
Relish 225.00
Hanging planter, rare 450.00
Party Pixies hors d'oeuvre dish
Green stripe boy pixie 200.00
Pink stripe girl pixie 200.00
Salad dressing jar
Flat head, French Pixie, Italian Pixie, or Russian Pixie 140.00
Round head, French Pixie, Italian Pixie, or Russian Pixie 125.00
Salty & Peppy shakers 350.00
Snack Pixie bowl
Berries 685.00
Goo 1,000.00
Ketchup Katie 675.00
Mustard Max 675.00
Nuts 600.00
Onion Annie 685.00
Oscar Olives 575.00
Peanut Butter Pat 675.00
Pickle Pete 675.00
Tartar Tom 850.00
Teapot candleholder hurricane vase, complete with glass globe
Blue stripe boy 285.00
Pink stripe girl 285.00

Red Rooster, "Coq Rouge"

Butter dish, cov 65.00
Candleholders, pr 30.00
Coffee mug 14.00
Coffee server, 36 oz 65.00
Cookie jar 100.00
Creamer and sugar 55.00
Dinner plate 18.00
Electric coffee pot, six cups 70.00
Mustard condiment jar 55.00
Pitcher
12 oz 45.00
32 oz 60.00
48 oz 75.00
Salt & pepper shakers, pr, 4-1/2" 25.00
Snack tray 18.00
Spoon rest 25.00
Wooden
Canister set, four pcs 85.00
Cigarette carton holder 45.00
Recipe box 70.00
Salt & pepper shakers, pr 23.00

HORN

History: For centuries, horns from animals have been used for various items, e.g., drinking cups, spoons, powder horns, and small dishes. Some pieces of horn have designs scratched in them. Around 1880, furniture made from the horns of Texas longhorn steers was popular in Texas and the southwestern United States.

Netsuke, tablet form, carving depicting man and woman in garden setting, outlined by carved geometric design border, 1-3/4" w, 2-3/4" h, **$230**. Photo courtesy of Alderfer Auction Co.

Ale set, silver plate-mounted cov 9-3/4" h jug, two 5-1/2" h beakers, fitted 17-3/4" l x 15" h plated frame with twisted gallery and upright handle, tripartite circular base with Greek Key border, raised on stepped block feet, English, early 20th C\ **850.00**

Arm chair, steer horn, leather upholstered seat, four pairs of matched horns form base, American, 20th C **575.00**

Cane, 35" l, 1-3/4" w, 4" h dark horn handle, carved as perched eagle, clear and black glass eyes, lighter horn beak, 2/3" woven silver thread collar, blond Malacca shaft, 1-1/2" horn ferrule, Continental, c1895 .... **490.00**

Cup, 5" h, rhinoceros, carved as magnolia flower, base of branch and leaves, carved wood stand, 18th C or earlier, losses **1,100.00**

Foot stool, eight black buffalo horns form feet, light blue, red, burgundy, gray, and dark brown upholstered top, 22" w, 20-1/2" d, 11" h **665.00**

Plaque, wall mounted, water buffalo horns, brass caps on ends, engraved dec, 33" l...................................... **275.00**

Snuff box, 2" l, 2-3/4" w, 3/4" h, rect, carved PA motifs, floral dec, red paint on hinged lid, birds carved on sides, star on bottom **450.00**

Tea caddy, cov, 14-1/2" w, 9" d, 7-1/2" h, Ango-Indian, Vishapatnam, early 19th C, antler veneer, steer horn, ivory, int. cov compartments, etched scrolling vines, restorations.............................. **1,850.00**

Vinaigrette, Victorian, late 19th C, staghorn, 2-1/2" l rough-textured horn mounted with thistle-cast lid, quatrefoil neck band, horn with guilloche strapping, short link chain **350.00**

HULL POTTERY

History: In 1905, Addis E. Hull purchased the Acme Pottery Company, Crooksville, Ohio. In 1917, the A. E. Hull Pottery Company began making art pottery, novelties, stoneware, and kitchenware, later including the famous Little Red Riding Hood line. Most items had a matte finish, with shades of pink and blue or brown predominating.

After a disastrous flood and fire in 1950, J. Brandon Hull reopened the factory in 1952 as the Hull Pottery Company. New, more-modern-style pieces, mostly with glossy finish, were produced. The company added dinnerware patterns, and glossy finished pottery. The company closed its doors in 1986.

Marks: Hull pottery molds and patterns are easily identified. Pre-1950 vases are marked "Hull USA" or "Hull Art USA" on the bottom. Many also retain their paper labels. Post-1950 pieces are marked "Hull" in large script or "HULL" in block letters.

Each pattern has a distinctive letter or number, e.g., Wildflower has a "W" and a number; Waterlily, "L" and number; Poppy, numbers in the 600s; Orchid, in the 300s. Early stoneware pieces are marked with an "H."

Additional Listings: See *Warman's Americana & Collectibles* for more examples.

Adviser: Joan Hull.

Pre-1950 Matte

Bowknot
- B-4 6-1/2" h vase **250.00**
- B-7 cornucopia **325.00**
- B-12, 10-1/2" h basket........... **750.00**
- Teapot and creamer, pink and blue **450.00**

Calla Lily, 500-32 bowl **200.00**

Dogwood (Wild Rose), 508 10-1/2" window box **195.00**

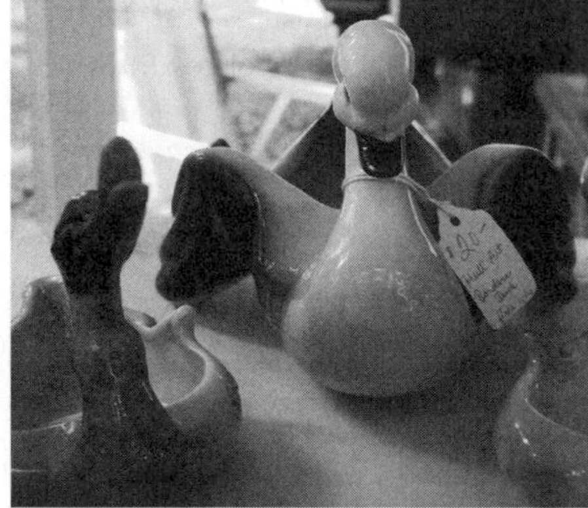
Bandana Duck, green and yellow, black beak, marked "Hull Art," **$35**.

Little Red Riding Hood
- Creamer and sugar, side pour **400.00**
- Dresser or cracker jar **800.00**
- Teapot, cov............................ **395.00**

Magnolia
- 3 8-1/2" h vase....................... **125.00**
- 14 4-3/4" h pitcher.................... **75.00**
- 20 15" floor vase...................... **500.00**

Open Rose/Camellia
- 106 13-1/2" h pitcher **650.00**
- 127 4-3/4" h vase...................... **75.00**

Orchid
- 302 6" h vase......................... **175.00**
- 310 9-1/2" jardinière **450.00**

Poppy
- 601 9" h basket........................ **800.00**
- 610 13" pitcher **900.00**

Rosella
- R-2 5" h vase **35.00**
- R-15 8-1/2" h vase **75.00**

Tulip
- 101-33 9" h vase..................... **245.00**
- 109-33-8" pitcher.................... **235.00**

Waterlily, L-14, 10-1/2" basket **350.00**

Wild Flower, No. Series
- 53 8-1/2" h vase...................... **295.00**
- 66 10-1/4" h basket **2,000.00**
- 71 12" h vase.......................... **450.00**

Woodland
- W9 8-3/4" h basket **245.00**
- W11 5-1/2" flower pot and saucer **175.00**
- W14 10-1/2" window box........ **200.00**

Hull Ware pottery "Little Red Riding Hood" lidded cracker jar, 13" h and two salt shakers, 5-1/2" h, **$325**. Photo courtesy of Joy Luke Auctions.

Post 1950

Blossom Flite, T4 8-1/2" h basket **125.00**

Butterfly
- B9 9" h vase **55.00**
- B15 13-1/2" h pitcher............. **200.00**

Continental
- C55 12-1/2" basket................. **150.00**
- C62 8-1/4" candy dish.............. **45.00**

Ebb Tide
- E-8 ashtray with mermaid **225.00**
- E-10 13" h pitcher................... **275.00**

Parchment and Pine
- S-11 and S-12 tea set............ **250.00**
- S-15 8" h coffeepot................ **175.00**

Serenade
- S-15 11-1/2" d fruit bowl, ftd... **125.00**
- S17 teapot, creamer and sugar **275.00**

Sunglow

53 grease jar **60.00**
82 wall pocket, whisk broom **75.00**

Tokay/Tuscany

3 8" h pitcher **95.00**
10 11" l cornucopia **65.00**

Tropicana

T53 8-1/2" h vase **550.00**
T55, 12-3/4" h basket **750.00**

Woodland (glossy)

W1 5-1/2" h vase **45.00**
W19 14" d console bowl **100.00**

Hummel Items

History: Hummel items are the original creations of Berta Hummel, who was born in 1909 in Massing, Bavaria, Germany. At age 18, she was enrolled in the Academy of Fine Arts in Munich to further her mastery of drawing and the palette. Berta entered the Convent of Siessen and became Sister Maria Innocentia in 1934. In this Franciscan cloister, she continued drawing and painting images of her childhood friends.

In 1935, W. Goebel Co. in Rodental, Germany, began producing Sister Maria Innocentia's sketches as three-dimensional bisque figurines. The Schmid Brothers of Randolph, Massachusetts, introduced the figurines to America and became Goebel's U.S. distributor.

In 1967, Goebel began distributing Hummel items in the U.S. A controversy developed between the two companies, the Hummel family, and the convent. Law suits and counter-suits ensued. The German courts finally effected a compromise: the convent held legal rights to all works produced by Sister Maria Innocentia from 1934 until her death in 1946 and licensed Goebel to reproduce these works; Schmid was to deal directly with the Hummel family for permission to reproduce any pre-convent art.

Marks: All authentic Hummel pieces bear both the signature "M. I. Hummel" and a Goebel trademark. Various trademarks were used to identify the year of production:

Crown Mark (trademark 1)	1935-1949
Full Bee (trademark 2)	1950-1959
Stylized Bee (trademark 3)	1957-1972
Three Line Mark (trademark 4)	1964-1972
Last Bee Mark (trademark 5)	1972-1979
Missing Bee Mark (trademark 6)	1979-1990
Current Mark or New Crown Mark (trademark 7)	1991 to the present

Additional Listings: See *Warman's Americana & Collectibles* for more examples.

Angel, Festival Harmony, #172/II, with mandolin, **$140**. Photo courtesy of Dotta Auction Co., Inc.

Ashtray, Happy Pastime, #62, mark #3, **$20**. Photo courtesy of Dotta Auction Co., Inc.

Bookends, pr, Chick Girl, #618, full bee, trademark-2 .... **320.00**

Candleholder, Watchful angel, #194, trademark 2 .... **400.00**

Candy box, cov, Happy Pastime, #III/169, trademark 4 .... **125.00**

Christmas Angel, Girl, #116, fir tree, 3" h, trademark 3 .... **40.00**

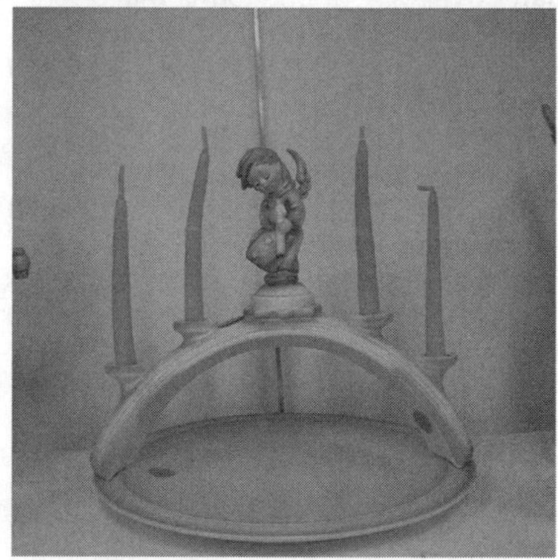

Candleholder, Angel Lights, plate, original beeswax candles, #241, mark 5, **$150**, Photo courtesy of Dotta Auction Co., Inc.

Figure

Puppy Love, trademark 1 .... **850.00**
School Boys, trademark 3 ... **2,100.00**
Sister, trademark 1 .... **650.00**
Telling Her Secret, trademark 2 .... **625.00**
Wayside Harmony, #111/3/0, trademark 4 .... **100.00**

Font

Child Jesus, #26/0, MK 4 .... **35.00**
Seated Angel, #10/1, trademark 3 .... **420.00**

Lamp, table, Culprits, #44, 9-1/2" h, c1930 .... **475.00**

Plate, Christmas, 1971, Heavenly Angel, #264, first edition, **$700**.

Nativity set, Virgin Mary, Carpenter, Wisemen, Shepherd and lamb, Baby Jesus in manger, stable, Robson, bee in V mark, 4-1/2" h figures, c1959-61 .... **795.00**

Plaque, Madonna, #48/0, trademark 7 .... **250.00**

Waiter, 6" h, and Little Fiddler, 5" h, both mark 5, each, **$160**. Photo courtesy of Joy Luke Auctions.

Wash Day, 5-1/2" h, and Kiss Me, 6" h, both mark 5, each **$200**. Photo courtesy of Joy Luke Auctions.

Imari

History: Imari derives its name from a Japanese port city. Although Imari ware was manufactured in the 17th century, the pieces most commonly encountered are those made between 1770 and 1900.

Early Imari was decorated simply, quite unlike the later heavily decorated brocade pattern commonly associated with Imari. Most of the decorative patterns are an underglaze blue and overglaze "seal wax" red complimented by turquoise and yellow.

The Chinese copied Imari ware. The Japanese examples can be identified by grayer clay, thicker glaze, runny and darker blue, and deep red opaque hues.

The pattern and colors of Imari inspired many English and European potteries, such as Derby and Meissen, to adopt a similar style of decoration for their wares.

Reproduction Alert: Reproductions abound, and many manufacturers continue to produce pieces in the traditional style.

Bowl, ribbed, flared scalloped rim, phoenix bird and cactus dec, rim flake, 9-1/2" d, 3-1/2" h, **$210**. Photo courtesy of Alderfer Auction Co.

Bottle vases, 11" h, lobated form, underglaze blue with red, green, aubergine enamels and gilt, Japan, late 19th C, price for pr **775.00**

Bowl

8-1/2" d, 3-1/4" h, red, blue, white, and gold dec **425.00**

13-1/2" d, 5-1/2" h, blue and white, edge chips **715.00**

16" d, 8-1/2" h, scalloped edge, int. dec with fish and water plants, ext. with dragons and phoenixes, Japan, late 19th C **1,200.00**

Charger

20-1/4" d, 4-3/4" h, hp, cinnabar red, underglaze dark blue, green, and gilt, dragons in clouds circle border, leaves and clouds below, two phoenixes in center, ext. cov with blossoming vines, center base with cinnabar and gilt flower, glued repair to edge, gilt imperfections **715.00**

22" d, fans with warriors and dragons dec, sgd "Koransha," late 19th C **1,645.00**

Creamer and sugar, 5-1/2" h creamer, 5-7/8" cov sugar, ovoid, dragon form handles, gilt and bright enamels, shaped reserves, dragon-like beasts, stylized animal medallions, brocade ground, high dome lid, knob, cipher mark of Mount Fuji, Fukagama Studio marks, Meiji period **500.00**

Dish, 8-3/8" d, central scene with fence and flowering tree dec, shaped cartouches enclosing flowers and hares on crackle blue ground at rim, gilt highlights, Meiji period, price for pr **650.00**

Vase, baluster form, paneled floral design, rim chip, 9-1/2" h, **$175**. Photo courtesy of Alderfer Auction Co.

Charger, blue tree and moths design, red and gold geometric design on border, four character mark on base, 18-1/4", **$660**. Photo courtesy of Alderfer Auction Co.

Food box, 6" h, three section, ext. and lid with phoenix and floral design, underglaze blue, iron-red, and gilt enamels, 19th C **400.00**

Jar, cov, 26" h, ribbed forms with shishi finials, Japan, late 19th C, price for pr **2,000.00**

Jardinière, 10" h, hexagonal, bulbous, short flared foot, alternating bijin figures and immortal symbols, stylized ground **250.00**

Planter and stand, 17" d, 43" h, lobed form, floral dec, brocade patterns, Japan, late 19th C **460.00**

Plate

8-1/2" d, scalloped edge, rib banding, polychrome dec, floral panels, surrounding floral medallions, bats on reverse, character mark, gilt loss.......... **55.00**

10-1/4" d, scalloped edge, rib banding, polychrome gilt dec, floral panels, surrounding floral medallion, bats on reverse, rim chip **65.00**

Platter, 18" d, alternating panels of figures and foliage, trellis work ground, Japanese, late 19th C **475.00**

Punch bowl, 12" d, rubbed, c1870 .... **1,650.00**

Teabowl and saucer, 5" d, floriform, floral spray dec, gilt highlights on saucer **200.00**

Umbrella stand

23" h, ribbed form, Imari underglaze blue with red dec, gilt, Japan, late 19th C **775.00**

25" h, all-over hexagonal panels with gold pheasants and orange drawings, flowers, and plant, orange, tomato red, yellow, green, and cobalt blue, old shield shaped "U.S. Customs" label underneath **550.00**

Urn, 36-1/2" h, tomato red, light green, mauve, and cobalt blue, dark gold details, floral panels on sides with pheasants and cranes, geometric band of dec around base, minor roughness around rim **2,100.00**

Vase, 14-1/2" h, baluster, late Meiji period, c1900 .... **775.00**

Imperial Glass

History: Imperial Glass Co., Bellaire, Ohio, was organized in 1901. Its primary product was pattern (pressed) glass. Soon other lines were added, including carnival glass, Nuart, Nucut, and Near Cut. In 1916, the company introduced Free-Hand, a lustered art glass line, and Imperial Jewels, an iridescent stretch glass that carried the Imperial cross trademark. In the 1930s, the company was reorganized into the Imperial Glass Corporation. The firm was sold to Lenox, in 1976, and ceased all operations by 1984.

IMPERIAL NUCUT NUART

For more information, see *Warman's Glass*, 4th edition.

Imperial acquired the molds and equipment of several other glass companies—Central, Cambridge, and Heisey. Many of the retired molds of these companies once again in use for a short period of time before Imperial closed.

Marks: The Imperial reissues were marked to distinguish them from the originals.

Engraved or hand cut

Bowl, 6-1/2" d, flower and leaf, molded star base **25.00**
Candlesticks, pr, 7" h, Amelia **35.00**
Celery vase, three-side stars, cut star base **25.00**
Pitcher, tankard, Design No. 110, flowers, foliage, and butterfly cutting **60.00**
Plate, 5-1/2" d, Design No. 12 .... **15.00**

Egg tray, Candlewick pattern, center handle, **$85**. Photo courtesy of Dotta Auction Co., Inc.

Jewels

Bowl, 6-1/2" d, purple Pearl Green luster, marked **75.00**
Compote, 7-1/2" d, irid teal blue **65.00**
Rose bowl, amethyst, green irid **75.00**
Vase
- 5" h, stretch, amber shading to light irid finish, early 20th C **150.00**
- 7-3/4" h, classic baluster, white body, mirror bright tray-blue surface, deep orange irid int. rim **320.00**

Lustered (freehand)

Candlestick, 10" h, slender baluster, cushion foot, clear, white heart and vine dec, tall cylindrical irid dark blue socket, orig paper label **440.00**
Hat, 9" w, ruffled rim, cobalt blue, embedded irid white vines and leaves **120.00**
Ivy ball, 4" h, Spun, red, crystal foot **90.00**
Vase
- 6" h, opal glass, glossy orig irid finish, c1920 .... **150.00**
- 8-1/2" h, cylindrical, irid green heart and vine design, white ground, marigold lining, some wear ... **385.00**
- 9-1/2" h, green drag loops on iridized surface finish, three pull-down handles, applied foot, unsigned **1,050.00**

Nuart

Ashtray **20.00**
Lamp shade, marigold **50.00**
Vase, 7" h, bulbous, irid green **125.00**

Goblet, Chroma pattern, 1950s, **$20**.

Pressed

Ashtray, Candlewick, 6", cranberry **30.00**
Baked apple, Cape Cod, 6" **9.00**
Bar bottle, Cape Cod **150.00**
Basket, Cape Cod, No. 160/73/0 .... **350.00**
Birthday cake plate, Cape Cod **325.00**
Bowl, Windmill, amethyst, fluted, 8" d, 3" h **45.00**
Bread and butter plate, Cape Cod .. **7.00**
Butter dish, cov, Cape Cod **50.00**
Candy box, cov, Candlewick, #400/110, three sections **195.00**
Center bowl, Cape Cod, No. 160/751, ruffled edge **65.00**
Champagne, Cape Cod, azalea **22.00**
Coaster, Cape Cod, No. 160/76 .... **10.00**
Creamer, #400/30 .... **9.00**
Cruet, orig stopper, Cape Cod, No. 160/119, amber **28.00**
Cup and saucer, Candlewick, #400/37 .... **15.00**
Decanter, orig stopper, Cape Cod, No. 160/163 .... **75.00**
Fruit bowl, Cape Cod, 4-1/2" **12.00**
Goblet
- Candlewick, Starlight cutting **40.00**
- Cape Cod, No. 1602, Verde green **20.00**
- Skanda, azalea **15.00**

Gravy boat, liner, Candlewick **200.00**
Iced tea tumbler, Cape Cod, ftd **25.00**
Juice tumbler, Cape Cod, 6 oz **10.00**
Mug, Cape Cod **58.00**
Nappy, Quilted Diamond, marigold, ring handle **35.00**
Pitcher, Cape Cod, No. 160/19, ice lip **85.00**
Plate, Windmill, glossy, green slag, IG mark **45.00**
Relish
- Candlewick, two parts, 6-1/2" **25.00**
- Cape Cod, three parts **35.00**

Rose bowl, Molly pattern, pink, short foot, four wide toes, eight scalloped top, light ribbed body, 4-1/2" h, 5-1/2" w, **$25**.

Rose bowl, Molly, black, silver deposit floral dec, 5" h **45.00**
Salad set, Cape Cod, 11" salad bowl, 14" cupped plate **110.00**
Sherbet
- Cape Cod **10.00**
- Tradition, red **18.00**

Sugar, #400/30 .... **9.00**
Tea cup, #400/35 .... **8.00**
Toothpick holder, 2-1/2" h, carnival or milk white, IG mark **30.00**
Tumbler, Georgian, red **18.00**
Wine
- Cape Cod **14.00**
- Skanda, azalea **20.00**

Indian Artifacts, American

History: During the historic period, there were approximately 350 Indian tribes grouped into the following regions: Eskimo, Northeast and Woodland, Northwest Coast, Plains, and West and Southwest.

American Indian artifacts are quite popular. Currently, the market is stable following a rapid increase in prices during the 1970s.

For more information, see *Warman's Native American Collectibles*.

Awl case, 17" l with fringe, Southern Plains, Mescalero Apache, c1900, tapered hide body and cap beaded with bold zigzag pattern in amber, dark blue, yellow, and light blue seed beads, red stained buckskin fringe with tin crimps hang from bottom **765.00**

Bag

5-1/2" l, Great Lakes, Ojibwa, polychrome wool, finger-woven rect form with red and dark brown geometric devices on tan ground, old yellow tag reads in part "Ojibway Yarn bag from Tom Stone (sow-cug-ifish) 89 years old of Danbury Wisconsin on St. Croix River coll. 1935" **825.00**

7" h, Northwest, c1900, U-shaped hide bag partially beaded on front in unusual abstract floral devices using multicolored glass and metallic seed beads, pink ribbon edging.... **200.00**

14" l, Plains, Ute, c1870, rect buffalo hide, beaded on both sides, flap with unusual Ute style linear geometric devices, bottom fringe **2,875.00**

16" x 9-1/2", Plateau, c1900, hide, rect form, beaded on front with warrior in profile, wearing feather headdress and necklace with heart-shaped medallion, various colored beads on light blue ground, contour overlay stitch, fringe at bottom, framed, not examined out of frame **1,725.00**

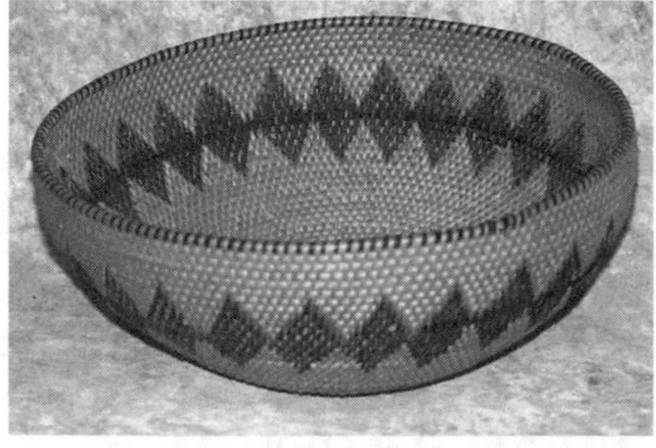

Basket, coiled basket, diamond design, 8-3/4" d, 4" h, **$275**. Photo courtesy of Alderfer Auction Co.

Basket, 7" l, Northwest Coast, Tlingit, twined polychrome rattle top, lidded jar form, woven with bold false embroidered geometric devices using five colors **2,415.00**

Basketry bowl, coiled, 7" d, Western, Washo, c1900, slightly flared, simple stacked wedge devices **375.00**

Belt, child's, 26" l, Plains, 19th C, commercial leather belt with roller buckle and 18 remaining German silver discs **185.00**

Blanket, 2' 10" x 2' 10", Chimayo, hand woven, red, black, and white stripes and crillo design elements, gray ground, small holes..................................... **90.00**

Blanket strip, 58" l, Central Plains, Lakota, late 19th C, beaded hide, repeated cross roundel devices separated by barred zigzag devices, green, royal blue, white-center red, and metallic beads, white ground, water damage, bead loss **1,035.00**

Bottle, twined basketry cover, 9-1/4" h, Northwest Coast, Tlingit, c1900, bands of repeated birds, simple fretz, openwork, glass decanter, minor fading......... **750.00**

Bow, 47-1/2" l, Central Plains, last quarter 19th C, ash, tapered hand grip, double notch, twisted sinew string........... **750.00**

Bow case and quiver, 44" l, Southwest, Plains Apache, last quarter 19th C, hide bow case, red and yellow details, orig sinew-backed bow, well-worn quiver with 11 steel-tipped arrows, hide loss, stiffness to leather **2,415.00**

Bowl, pottery, Southwestern, Hopi, polychrome, red and dark brown slip, cream-colored ground, 12" d, high rounded form, highly abstract avian devices, cross-hatching, two encircled stylized butterflies, corn logo at bottom **1,955.00**

Cane, 31" l, Central Plains, probably Lakota, late 19th C, polychrome wood, carved as twined diamond-form snakes, traces of black and green pigments **320.00**

Belt, Plateau, late 19th C, beaded, commercial leather panel, white center red, bottle green, yellow, and white geometric devices, medium blue panels between, hide tie, 32" l, **$450**. Photo courtesy of Skinner, Inc.

Charm bag, 2-1/2" x 2-1/2", Western Great Lakes, late 19th C, small sq bag, two thunderbirds beaded on one side and diagonal sawtooth pattern on reverse, multicolored glass seed beads on white ground, beaded neck strap and tassels **1,300.00**

Club, Skull Cracker, 26-1/2" l, Central Plains, last quarter 19th C, stone-headed club with rawhide covered wood handle, handle wrapped with plaited polychrome quillwork, quilled strap holding pointed stone head in place with remnant white bead edging, minor bead and quill loss, includes metal stand **2,950.00**

Cradle, 31" l, Plains, probably Cheyenne, c1880, buffalo hide form beaded with classic Cheyenne pattern, white-center red, green, and dark blue beads, white ground, hide board attachments remaining on back, orig tag reads "Crow Indian Baby cov from 'Spotted Tail' Crow Agency Montana, Ter. May 30th, 1888," collected on Crow Reservation **1,500.00**

Cradleboard, 27" l, Central Plains, probably Cheyenne, beaded buffalo hide form attached to later boards, large stepped diamond devices, bottle green, greasy yellow, translucent rose, black, and white seed beads, bead loss **18,400.00**

Doll, 8" h, Southern Plains, Comanche, c1900, hide, male form wearing partially beaded fringed buckskin shirt and leggings, yarn hair wrapped in calico cloth, red pigment **2,000.00**

Dress, woman's, 52" l, Central Plains, Lakota, late 19th C, blue trade cloth, ribbon work above selvage edging on sleeves and bottom, large metal sequins sewn to ribbon, yoke dec with rows of cowry shells, cloth belt beaded in "salt and pepper" beadwork **950.00**

Effigy ladle, 9-1/4" l, Western Great Lakes or Prairie, carved wood, shallow shovel-shaped scoop with handle terminating in stylized bear's head, heart shape is carved on back of head, small brass eyes, medium brown patina **4,115.00**

Fetish figure, carved stone, Southwest, 10" h, 19th C, volcanic stone, possibly representing snake, eyes inlaid with old turquoise beds, smaller stone piece tied to back with buckskin, traces of red pigment **520.00**

Handbag, 8-3/4" l, Plateau, late 19th C, beaded cloth and hide, rect canvas form, beaded on both sides, bold simple geometric devices, different color backgrounds, edged at opening, red trade cloth and buckskin.............. **210.00**

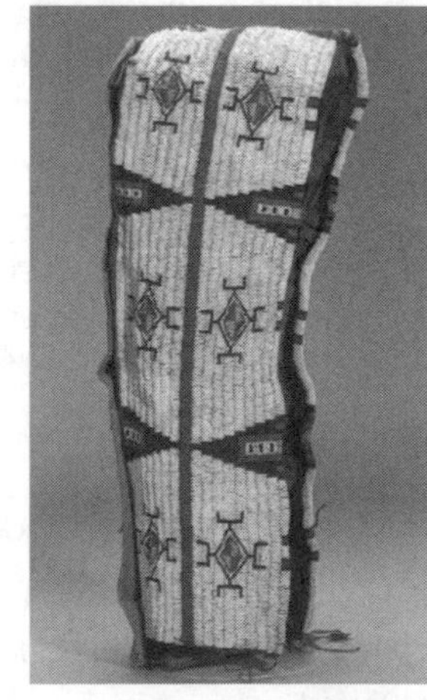

Cradle, Plains, Cheyenne, 1880s, beaded hide and cloth, buffalo hide form, continuous red stripe bisecting stepped triangles, floating forked diamond devices, rawhide and canvas backing, bead colors: white center red, medium green, yellow, light blue, and translucent dark blue on white ground, fragments of hide ties to secure missing boards, some stiffness to hide, 26-1/2" l, **$8,850**. Photo courtesy of Skinner, Inc.

Jar, pottery, 8" h, Southwest, possibly Tesuque, bulbous form, black curvilinear devices, cream-colored slip, red bands painted on inside rim and below cream-colored slip **1,380.00**

Kachina, Southwest, polychrome carved wood and cloth, 10-1/4" l, Hopi, first quarter 20th C, painted kilt, red and yellow body paint, large white case mask with protruding ears, snout, and Popeyes, black and red stepped devices connecting eyes and ears **2,070.00**

Knife sheath, beaded hide, 9" l without tab, Northern Plains, Cree, third quarter 19th C, tapered hide sheath with commercial leather liner, partially beaded on front in deep transparent red, off white, black, and white, unusual abstract floral beaded tabs hang from side and bottom, tin cone danglers and fringe details, bead loss **4,200.00**

Leggings, man's, 34" l, Northern Plains or Plateau, c1900, made from old faded trade blanket with red cloth panels at ankles, partially beaded in linear devices, red and green trade cloth sewn up sides **360.00**

Leggings, woman's, 17" l, Central Plains, Arapaho, last quarter 19th C, hide, yellow and blue stained leggings beaded along bottom with stacked crosses and box and border devices using black, greasy blue, and white center red devices on white ground, roll beaded short flap along the side **1,200.00**

Mask, wood, painted, 6-1/4" h, Inuit, northern Alaska, last half 19th C, hollow oval form, brow line in form of stylized whale fin, small round pierced eyes, pierced smiling mouth, traces of red pigment on upper lip, two small holes for attachment, minor wood loss **5,465.00**

Moccasins, pr, infant's, Woodlands, probably Micmac, mid-19th C, puckered tow soft hide, red cloth cuffs and vamps, beaded geometric and floral devices, multicolored small seed beads, silk ribbon ties................................. **1,265.00**

Frock coat, infant's, Southern Plains, Cheyenne, last quarter 19th C, beaded hide, unusual tailored buckskin coat with yellow stain overall, fringed cape collar and fringed details, small polychrome seed bead trim, red silk ribbon trim, evidence of sequin trim, 21" l, **$4,700**. Photo courtesy of Skinner, Inc.

Moccasins, pr, child's, 5-1/2" l, Northern Plains, possibly Crow, c1880, soft sole side-seamed, beaded on vamps and along seam, multicolored linear devices, medium blue ground **1,100.00**

Moccasins, man's, beaded hide

9-1/2" l, Western Great Lakes, Ojibwa, late 19th C, soft sole forms partially beaded with multicolored floral devices, hide loss......... **400.00**

10" l, Central Plains, Lakota, last quarter 19th C, beaded with hexagons and stepped pyramids in cobalt blue, greasy yellow, and white center red on white ground, apple green "buffalo tracks," beaded bifurcated tongues with tin cone danglers **4,700.00**

10" l, Southwest, Apache, c1900, hard sole form with soft uppers stained in two shades of ochre pigment, simple red and green cross beaded on vamp.................. **650.00**

10-1/2" l, Eastern Plains, Dakota, c1860, hard sole buffalo hide forms partially beaded with bilateral floral devices of multicolored small seed beads, remnant silk ankle trim **1,800.00**

Moccasins, pr, woman's, 24" l, high-top, Southwest, Apache, first quarter 20th C, yellow stained tops and bottoms, rawhide soles with Cactus Kicker toes, beaded Maltese crosses on vamps, dark red, dark blue, and white seed beads **920.00**

Necklace, 26" l, Plains, late 19th C, stacked shell discs interspersed with large medium-blue trade beads strung on hide and cord, traces of red-orange pigment **265.00**

Olla, pottery, Southwest, 10-1/2" h, Acoma, late 19th C, high rounded sides, tapering neck and concave base, orange, red, and dark brown slip, cream-colored ground, four large Acoma parrots, foliate, and rainbow devices, repaired neck section................ **8,625.00**

Parfleche envelope, polychrome

19" l, Plains, c1900, front flaps painted with hourglass and diamond devices using green, red, and blue pigments **2,350.00**

25" l, Plains or Plateau, late 19th C, front flaps painted with bordered hourglass devices using red, green, blue, and yellow pigments **900.00**

28-1/2" l, Plains or Plateau, last quarter 19th C, polychrome, front flaps painted with bold geometric devices using red, green, blue, and yellow pigments **1,880.00**

Pipe bag, beaded hide

18" l, Plains, Cheyenne, c1870, four-tab top edge beaded in white and white-center red seed beads, buckskin bag sinew sewn with three feather devices on each side, typical bar design pattern, white, dark bottle green, pumpkin, and Kiowa red, traces of yellow pigment on fringe and bag............................. **6,900.00**

31" l, Northern Plains, Cree, c1880, six-tab top edge beaded in pink, panel beaded on both sides with multicolored bilateral floral devices, white ground, fringe with dark bugle bead attachments on top ... **1,725.00**

35" l, Central Plains, Lakota, last quarter 19th C, yellow stained buckskin bag, row of beadwork at top, three rows of lazy-stitch beadwork descending to a lower beaded panel, both sides beaded with typical Lakota dark blue, white centered, and green designs on white ground, below beaded panel are quill wrapped rawhide slats and long yellow stained fringe, "C. E. Dallin" printed on upper part **3,220.00**

Pipe, 20" l, Plains, late 19th C, file-branded ash stem, red pipestone elbow-type bowl **825.00**

Olla, pottery, Southwest, Acoma, c1900, high rounded sides, tapering neck, concave base, black geometric and floral devices, cream colored ground, red painted bottom and inner rim, broken and reassembossed led, 12-1/2" d, 10-1/2" h, **$940**. Photo courtesy of Skinner, Inc.

Pipe tomahawk, 18-1/2" l, Northeast, hand-forged head, possibly ash, stem pierced for smoking, four pierced holes along stem for attachments, missing gasket... **950.00**

Pouch, beaded hide

4-1/2" l, Northern Plain, Crow, c1880, rect commercial hide, beaded on front in geometric devices, white-center red, dark and light blue, greasy yellow seed beads, tin cone danglers along bottom, orig tag "From the Crow Indian 'Alligator' Crow Agency Montana Ty April 27th 1888," collected on Crow Reservation **2,760.00**

6" l, Southern Plains, third quarter 19th C, "Strike-a-lite," trapezoid leather form, beaded stepped geometric devices in Kiowa red and blue on white ground, tin cone danglers hanging from flap and bottom, remains of old paper label on flap **3,100.00**

7-3/4" l, Plains, Ute, late 19th C, trapezoid form with pointed top, four triangular tabs off bottom, beaded on one side with multicolored glass seed beads in classic Ute-Crow geometric devices, beaded danglers from tabs **650.00**

Rug, Navaho

3' 9" x 4' 8", Ganado, stepped motif of two interlocking diamonds, deep red, dark brown, and cream, red ground, cream and brown stepped borders, c1930, minor stains **1,610.00**

4' 6" x 7' 4", crystal regional weaving, spun and hand-carded wool, shaded gray/tan and natural white, minor wear, light stains, one end rebound................................ **965.00**

Saddle blanket, Navaho, red and orange stripes, corner blocks centered by geometric stylized butterflies, 2' 6" x 2' 6" **150.00**

Pipe bowl, Great Lakes, Ojibwa, 19th C, black pipestone form, slightly flared round bowl, square shaft, red pipestone, round-topped tapered prow, lead inlay, bold checkered and linear devices, 7-1/4" l, **$1,175**. Photo courtesy of Skinner, Inc.

Scepter, 33" l, Northeast, 19th C, carved wood, tapered form, profusely carved spiral, linear, and geometric devices, knobbed end carved with myriad devices, including snake, turtle, heart, and human face, dark patina **425.00**

Shirt, man's, 35" l, Great Lakes, Winnebago, c1900, cotton shirt with loom beaded strips on shoulders and bib, beaded tabs and yarn tassels, medium and dark blue glass seed beads on white ground, silk ribbon detailing, silk loss **2,235.00**

Skirt, Northern California, probably Yurok, 19th C, back skirt an entire deerskin folded laterally, dec with thin strips wrapped with three colored maiden hair fern fibers, fringe dec with small white clam shells, large abalone plaques, and glass grade beads, smaller front apron of long buckskin fringe wrapped and braided with vegetal fibers, trimmed white olivella shells, minor damage to buckskin **36,800.00**

Snow snake, 92" l, Northwest, Iroquois, late 19th C, wood and metal, long rounded form, flattened belly, pointed end with pewter cap...................... **435.00**

Totem pole, Northwest Coast, carved wood

24" h, flat backed, bears and eagles, commercial paint details, first half 20th C.................................. **575.00**

113", hollowed stem, raven, shaman eating frog, tribal chief eating frog, painted commercial pigments, collected in 1953, southeastern Alaska................................. **5,750.00**

War club, Central Plains, probably Lakota, last quarter 19th C, rawhide wrapped wood handle stained dark blue, ax-shaped white quartz head, quilled horsehair adornment attached to handle, 29-1/2" h **420.00**

Watch case, 7" l, Northern Plains, Crow, c1880, beaded cloth and hide, teardrop form, beaded front with multicolored geometric devices, back cov in calico, orig tag "Watch case made by Crow Indian half breed Martha Rumpard, Crow Agency, Mont., ty 1888," collected from Crow Reservation **1,265.00**

Ink Bottles

History: Ink was sold in glass or pottery bottles in the early 1700s in England. Retailers mixed their own formula and bottled it. The commercial production of ink did not begin in England until the late 18th century and in America until the early 19th century.

Initially, ink was supplied in often poorly manufactured pint or quart bottles from which smaller bottles could be filled. By the mid-19th century, when writing implements had been improved, emphasis was placed on making an "untippable" bottle. Shapes ranging from umbrellas to turtles were tried. Since ink bottles were usually displayed, shaped or molded bottles were popular.

The advent of the fountain pen relegated the ink bottle to the back drawer. Bottles lost their decorative design and became merely functional items.

Carter's, Cathedral, cobalt blue, emb lettering, orig cap, 3" d, 9" h.......... **250.00**

Cylindrical, 5-5/8" h, America, 1840-60, "Harrison's Columbia Ink," cobalt blue, applied flared mouth, pontil scar, 3" crack, mouth roughness, C #764 .... **140.00**

Figural, America, 1860-90

2" h, house, domed offset neck for, emb architectural features of front door and four windows, colorless, sheared mouth, smooth base, Carter's Ink, some remaining int. ink residue, C #614..................... **650.00**

2-5/8" h, house, 1-1/2-story cottage form, full label on reverse "Bank of Writing Fluid, Manuf by the Senate Ink Co Philadelphia," aquamarine, tooled sq collared mouth, smooth base, small area of label slightly faded, C# 682 .... **300.00**

Hexagonal, 9-7/8" h, America, 1900-20, "Carter," cathedral panels, colorless with pale yellow cast, machined mouth, smooth base, similar to C #820..... **700.00**

Boot shape, pale green glass, **$25**. Photo courtesy of Joy Luke Auctions.

Inverted concial

2-3/8" h, Stoddard, NH, 1846-1860, deep yellow-olive, sheared mouth, pontil scar, pinhead flake on mouth edge, C #15 .... **170.00**

2-1/2" h, America, 1840-60, medium cobalt blue, tooled mouth, tubular pontil scar, C #23 .... **800.00**

Octagonal

G. H. Gilbert Co., West Brookfield, MA, orig label....................... **150.00**

Harrison's Colombian Ink, light green **60.00**

Laughlin's And Bushfield Wheeling Va., 2-7/8" h, aquamarine, inward rolled mouth, pontil scar........ **300.00**

Sanford's, 2-1/4" h, 3-3/4" l, sterling silver stopper with flag and star dec **125.00**

Sawyer's Crystal Blue Ink, 6-1/4" h **10.00**

Umbrella, America, 1840-60

2-1/4" h, New England, 1840-60, octagonal, golden amber, sheared mouth, C #145....................... **160.00**

2-5/8" h, octagonal, lime green, labeled "Williams/Black/Empire/Ink/ New York," tooled mouth, smooth base, label 95 percent intact, C #173 .... **160.00**

2-5/8" h, octagonal, sapphire blue, inward rolled mouth, pontil, scar, C #129 .... **950.00**

Inkwells

History: Most of the commonly found inkwells were produced in the United States

or Europe between the early 1800s and the 1930s. The most popular materials were glass and pottery because these substances resisted the corrosive effects of ink.

Inkwells were a sign of the office or wealth of an individual. The common man tended to dip his ink directly from the bottle. The years between 1870 and 1920 represent the golden age of inkwells when elaborate designs were produced.

Ceramic, French, pelican standing on rectangular base, green crystalline glaze on yellow ground, painted "8115/56/ FRANCE," base glaze chip, 7-1/2" h, **$500**. Photo courtesy of Skinner, Inc.

Brass

Embossed, double, two porcelain inserts, late 19th/early 20th C, 10-1/2" l, 6-1/2" w.................. **150.00**

Engraved peaked cornice-form backplate cut with central trefoil and flowers, cabochon bloodstone surrounded by four cabochon red stones, rect base with engraved border, central cut glass well flanked by turned pen supports, Gothic Revival style, England, third quarter 19th C, 9-1/4 l, 5-7/8" h.......... **250.00**

Raised birds, cattails, flowers, sq base, ball feet, hinged lid with serpent finial, shell handles **500.00**

Bronze

6-1/2" d, gold doré finish, orig divided glass insert, flower design on hinged cover, three protruding legs end in paw feet, bottom of one foot sgd "TIFFANY STUDIOS NEW YORK 1086" **1,610.00**

6-3/4" d, 3-3/4" h, six-sided, removable clear glass insert, hinged top with doré finish, Zodiac pattern, imp "Tiffany Studios New York 1072" **420.00**

8" d, 5-1/2" h, central lidded baluster form inkwell, round dish raised on quadripartite leaf-form bronze base, dark green enamel ground, stylized foliate bands with gilt accents, faux jewelling, French, late 19th C **435.00**

12" l, cast, Victorian, figural, greyhound dog changed to fencepost, two orig glass wells with covers.................................. **815.00**

Glass, crystal, square, four molded rococo feet, 3-1/4" w, 3-1/2" h........ **175.00**

Gilt metal, 14" l, bronze, French, rococo style, lion's head supporting pen rest above tray with two cov wells, dolphin feet... **460.00**

Cut glass, round cut inkwell with etched design, rayed base, silver lid, mounted on black base with grooves to hold pens, **$500**. Photo courtesy of Wiederseim Associates, Inc.

Horse's hoof, 5-1/2" l, English silver lid, horseshoe, and pastern with detailed hair, London hallmarks for 1890, glass insert with chips **400.00**

Paperweight, 6-1/4" h, 4-1/2" d, multicolored concentric millefiore, base with 1848 date canes, Whitefriars **175.00**

Pearlware, 5-1/2" h, gilt highlights, imp "By F. Bridges, Phrenologist," and "EM" on base, England, 19th C, very minor chips, gilt wear **520.00**

Sterling silver, two bottles, matching pen tray, center sander, Victorian, hallmarked................................. **1,800.00**

Stoneware

Brushed cobalt blue on top, imp "C. Crolius.Manhattan-Wells, New York," 3-1/8" d, 1-5/8" h, few chips on base **3,200.00**

Incised oval stamp "C. Crolius Stone Ware Manufacturer Manhatten Wells, New York," flat cylindrical form, incised edges, upper one enhanced with cobalt blue slip, center well surrounded by three pen holders, 3-1/2" d, 1-1/4" h, three lower edge chips.................................. **2,990.00**

Bronze, late 19th/early 20th C, child emerging from dog house, true occupant waiting alongside, roof of dog house hinged, ovoid base with tree stump pen holder, barrel with hinged lid, black slate socle, 6" h, **$500**. Photo courtesy of Skinner, Inc.

Tile, 2-3/4" x 3-1/2" sq, Enfield, each side carved with primitive scene with four people facing each other, matte green glaze, rare paper label "Registered Enfield Trade Mark/Hand Made Pottery & Tile/Enfield, P.O., Penna," original glass liner, minor rim nicks, missing lid **460.00**

Wood, Matthew Bolton, Birmingham, c1795, rect, emb silver mounts, gadroon and shell edge, two silver mounted cut glass inkwells in gardrooned holders, four scroll legs, paw feet, 14" l, 10" w **1,725.00**

IRONS

History: Ironing devices have been used for many centuries, with the earliest references dating from 1100. Irons from the medieval, Renaissance, and early industrial eras can be found in Europe, but are rare. Fine engraved brass irons and hand-wrought irons predominated prior to 1850. After 1850, the iron underwent a series of rapid evolutionary changes. Between 1850 and 1910, irons were heated in four ways: 1) a hot metal slug was inserted into the body, 2) a burning solid, e.g., coal or charcoal, was placed in the body, 3) a liquid or gas, e.g., alcohol, gasoline, or natural gas, was fed from an external tank and burned in the body, or 4) conduction heat, usually drawing heat from a stove top. Electric irons are just beginning to find favor among iron collectors.

When trying to identify and date irons, collectors are well advised to reference some excellent books by Adviser David Irons, *Irons by Irons, More Irons by Irons,* and *Even More Irons by Irons.*

Additional Listings: See *Warman's Americana & Collectibles* for more examples.

Advisers: David and Sue Irons.

> **Reproduction Alert**: Several of the highly prized European irons are being reproduced. Workmanship on these in many cases is very good. Look for lack of wear and metal pattern to determine if the piece is original. Reproductions include the German Prometheus Revolving Iron, Scottish box, and even special hand-made slug irons in iron or brass. Also old irons are being enhanced with engraving, inlay, or brass.

Charcoal

Brass

Large box iron, India **60.00**

Openwork on sides, Dutch.... **200.00**

Turned tall chimney, brass heat shield, European **120.00**

Double chimney, NePlus Ultra, 1902 .... **200.00**

Junior, 1911................................. **160.00**

Pan, Oriental, ivory handle........... **160.00**
The EverReady............................ **125.00**

Children's

Brass box, European, 3-1/2" **160.00**
Cast iron, swan, 5"...................... **450.00**
Cast sleeve, rope handle, 4-1/4" **50.00**
Cross rib handle, 3" **35.00**
Enterprise, #115, cold handle, holes in handle, 3-7/8"............................. **120.00**
Ober, Chagrin Falls, sleeve, 4-1/2" **180.00**
Sensible, No. 0, 4" **120.00**
The Gem, 3-7/8"........................... **160.00**
Wire handle, 3-1/4"........................ **35.00**

Charcoal, German 3, Muster Schutz, griffin latch, late 1800, IBI 60(R), 8-1/2" l, **$250**. All iron photographs courtesy of adviser Dave Irons.

Flat iron

All cast, anchor design.................. **35.00**
Dover sad iron, detachable **50.00**
Enterprise, #55, detachable.......... **35.00**
French, La Caiffa **50.00**
German, twist latch, detachable... **175.00**
Harper, detachable, 1906............ **130.00**
Hood's, 1867, soapstone base..... **200.00**
Monitor, all cast, double pointed **200.00**
Ober, detachable, 1895................. **80.00**
Slant handle, detachable............ **150.00**
Universal Thermo Cell, detachable, 1911.. **140.00**
Wrought, bell in handle **140.00**

Fluter, combination

Charcoal iron, side fluter, fluter rocker in handle.. **200.00**
Flutes inside, marked "Pat'd Aug 2 '70" **170.00**
Ladies Friend, slug iron, side fluter, revolves **800.00**

Fluter, machine type

Companion, clamp-on type, good paint **400.00**
Dudley, 1876, good paint **500.00**
Eagle, American Machine Co., Phila **160.00**

Saverbier & Son........................... **165.00**

Fluter, rocker type

Geneva Hand Fluter, most common type **125.00**
The Best, Hope Mfg Co................. **90.00**
The Globe.................................... **150.00**

Fluter, roller type

Indicator, temperature indicator **450.00**
J. Johnson, cross-wise roller **275.00**
Shephard Hardware, 1879.......... **120.00**

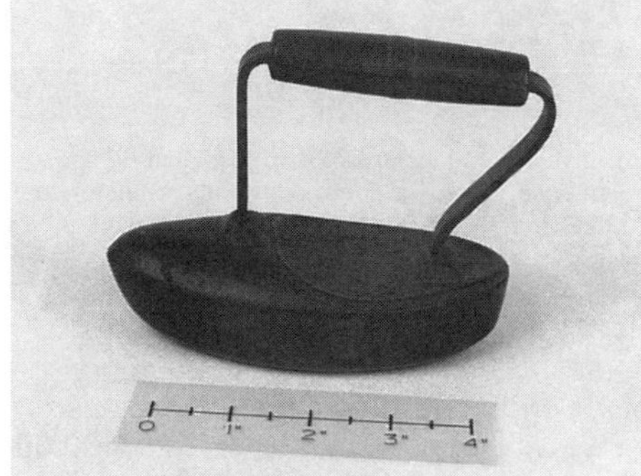

Polisher, MAB COOKS, Patd Dec. 5, 1848, IBI 271(M), 5" l, **$135**.

Goffering iron

Double barrel, all brass, paw feet **650.00**
Single
- Brass, Queen Anne tripod base **350.00**
- "S" wire, round base, most common **75.00**
- Wrought, spiral monkey tail... **600.00**

Liquid fuel, gasoline, kerosene, alcohol

Coleman #5, green **225.00**
Comfort Iron............................... **100.00**
Jubilee Iron **180.00**
Omega, German, alcohol............. **200.00**
The Monitor, 1903 .... **100.00**

Liquid fuel, natural gas

Bless & Drake, hinge at front **225.00**
English, Beetall, turned chimney **300.00**
Uneedit Gas Iron......................... **130.00**
Wright, 1911 .... **120.00**

Mangle board

Double headed horse handle, highly carved **1,500.00**
Plain handle, minor carvings **150.00**

Miscellaneous items

Advertising tip tray, Dover Mfg Co. **125.00**
Advertising trade card, Mrs. Pons **35.00**

Candy mold, cast iron, cap iron style **200.00**
Stove top heater, pyramid type, holds three irons.................................. **150.00**
Suitcase iron, Iron Case, iron is the handle... **350.00**

Slug iron

Belgium, round back, drop-in-the-back slug, with trivet............................. **600.00**
English
- Iron box, very common **90.00**
- Ox tongue, brass, "L" handle **175.00**

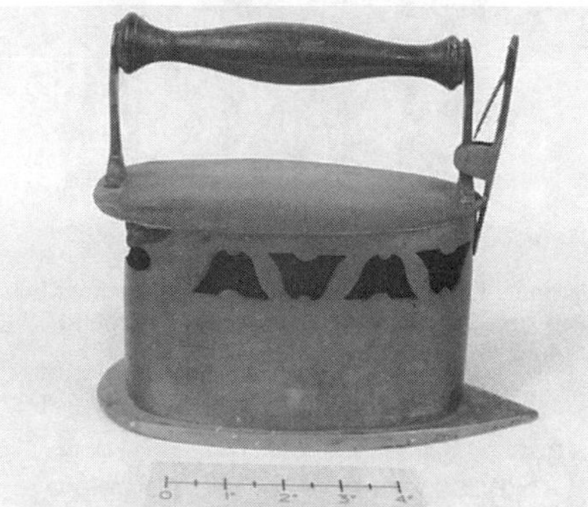

Charcoal, Dutch brass, mid-1800, IBI 65, 8" l, **$425**.

French, hand made, lift gate, "S" posts **600.00**
Magic No. 1, top lifts off **200.00**
Scottish, "S" posts, top lifts off **1,000.00**

Special purpose

Billiard table, London.................. **300.00**
Egg iron, standing, French, tripod base **200.00**
Hat iron
- Cutler Hammer Mfg Co., slug iron **160.00**
- McCoy's.............................. **140.00**
- Revolving, English, natural gas heated **180.00**

Hot water iron, English, curved bottom **350.00**
Polisher
- Enterprise Star, round bottom **140.00**
- French, round bottom........... **100.00**
- MAB Cooks, 1848 .... **120.00**
- Sweeney Iron....................... **200.00**

Seam iron, Ames, all cast............ **400.00**
Sleeve iron
- Sensible #1, detachable handle **60.00**
- Sherman's Improved **80.00**

IRONWARE

History: Iron, a metallic element that occurs abundantly in combined forms,

has been known for centuries. Items made from iron range from the utilitarian to the decorative. Early hand-forged ironwares are of considerable interest to Americana collectors.

Reproduction Alert: Use the following checklist to determine if a metal object is a period piece or modern reproduction. This checklist applies to all cast-metal items, from mechanical banks to trivets.

Period cast-iron pieces feature well-defined details, carefully fitted pieces, and carefully finished and smooth castings. Reproductions, especially those produced by making a new mold from a period piece, often lack detail in the casting (lines not well defined, surface details blurred) and parts have gaps at the seams and a rough surface. Reproductions from period pieces tend to be slightly smaller in size than the period piece from which they were copied. Period paint mellows, i.e., softens in tone. Colors look flat. Beware of any cast-iron object whose paint is bright and fresh. Painted period pieces should show wear. Make certain the wear is in places it is supposed to be.

Period cast-iron pieces develop a surface patina that prevents rust. When rust is encountered on a period piece, it generally has a greasy feel and is dark in color. The rust on artificially aged reproductions is flaky and orange.

Additional Listings: Banks, Doorstops, Fireplace Equipment, Food Molds, Irons, Kitchen Collectibles, Lamps, and Tools.

Andirons, pr, 20" h, cast, faceted ball finials, knife blade, arched bases, penny feet, rusted surface **325.00**

Ashtray, wrought iron stand, Celtic repoussè pattern on base, copper liner, match holder, triangular Bradley & Hubbard mark, 8-1/2" d, 27" h, **$150**. Photo courtesy of David Rago Auctions, Inc.

Apple roaster, 34-1/4" l, wrought, hinged apple support, pierced heat end on slightly twisted projecting handle, late 18th C **1,650.00**

Baker's lamp, 4-1/4" h, 8-1/2" l, cast iron, attached pan, hinged lid, bottom marked "No. 2 B. L.," pitted **250.00**

Bill holder, Atlantic Coast Line, cast, c1915, 4" h **50.00**

Boot scraper, 11-1/2" l, 18-1/2" h, cast, Scottie Dog, figural side profile, America, early 20th C, minor surface rust **590.00**

Calipers, pr, wrought

- 18-1/2" l, double, two arms meeting at "Y"-shaped central piece, ring handle with old split **125.00**
- 18-1/2" l, ending in delicate ladies legs, stamped "WTI 1863" **115.00**

Candleholders, pr, 14" h, small spring twist finials, scrolled columns, spring holders for candles, pan bases, three scrolled feet **90.00**

Cannon, cast

- 16" l, 7-1/8" h, heavy cast cannon with touchhole, wooden carriage with cast iron wheels, wrought iron axle and tongue **200.00**
- 16-3/4" l, Winchester, worn black paint, stamped signature on barrel, 10 gauge **425.00**

Carriage fenders, cast, shaped like horse leg, sgd "Fiske, New York," c1880, price for pr **4,800.00**

Cleaver, 11-1/2" l, 4-1/2" h, figural-shaped blade with eagle's head, handle terminating in brass boot, 20th C, stand, minor surface corrosion **490.00**

Compote, 10" w, 7" h, cast, flower form bowl, shaped and molded star base, America, late 19th C, old rust surface **200.00**

Cookie mold, 5-1/4" l, oval, bird on branch, cast iron **335.00**

Door knocker, 5-1/2" l, cast, fox head, ring hangs from mouth **85.00**

Embossing wheel, 4" l, 1-3/4" w, 9-1/4" h, cast iron and bronze, scrolled foliate motif on wheel edge, imp maker's marks for M. W. Baldwin, Philadelphia, handle missing **460.00**

Figure, 24-1/4" w, 39" h, cast, Lady Liberty, Mott Foundry, New York, c1850, holding goblet and torch with octagonal marble base, later white wood plinth **7,425.00**

Fireback, 21-1/2" w, 33" h, cast, late Regency-style, arch top flanked by dolphins, central polychrome scene of shepherd with his flock by fountain, beaded surround, scrolling leaf border **300.00**

Herb grinder, 16-1/2" l, 4-1/2" w, 4" h, cast, footed trough form, 6" d round disk-shaped crusher with wooden handle through center, late 18th/early 19th C **980.00**

Doorknocker, wrought iron serpent form, 19th C, 11" l, **$460**. Photo courtesy of Pook & Pook.

Hitching post, 31" h, cast, jockey, yellow, red, green, black, and white painted detail, wired for lantern **275.00**

Jousting helmet, 18" h, wrought, 12th C style, 19th C, cylindrical, tapering vertically at front, narrow eye slits, pierced circular and cruciform breaths **1,495.00**

Kitchen utensils, 17-3/4" l, spatula, 19" l two-tined fork with diamond shaped handle and ring hanger, 18-1/2" l two-tined fork with stamped triangles and sunbursts **220.00**

Lamp, floor, arrow-shaped finial on shaft, two sockets, scrolled wrought iron tripod feet, woven striped paneled shades, scattered corrosion, price for pr **815.00**

Letter sealer, 1" d, coat of arms, European, late 18th/early 19th C **40.00**

Mold, 7-1/4" w, 8" d, 8" h, figural pumpkin, smiling man face, invented by John Czeszczicki, Ohio, 1930, used to grow pumpkins in human forms, surface corrosion, later stand **635.00**

Mortar and pestle, 10-1/2" d, 8-1/4" h, urn shape, cast iron, pitted **50.00**

Ornament, 11" w, 4-1/2" d, 8" h, cast, figural lions, full bodied, nickel plated lions, rect plinths with cast and applied dec, open backs, price for pr **615.00**

Peel, 46-1/4" l, ram's horn finial **100.00**

Pipe tongs, 17-1/4" l, wrought iron, 18th C **1,150.00**

Rush light holder, 15-3/4" h, wrought, twisted detail on stem and arm of counterweight, high tripod feet riveted to disk, traces of black paint **330.00**

Nutcracker, cast iron, repainted, **$75**. Photo courtesy of Joy Luke Auctions.

Safe, 9-1/2" w, 8-1/2" d, 14-1/4" h, on rollers, polychrome pinstripe dec, front door dec with oval landscape, gilt lettering, "Deposit Vault," orig key **550.00**

Spittoon, cast iron, top hat, Standard Manuf Co., Pittsburgh, PA, painted black, glazed porcelain int. **415.00**

Sugar nippers, 10" l, tooled flower at pivot points **600.00**
Trivet, 7-3/4" d, round, marked "The Griswold Mfg. Co., Eire, PA, USA/8/Trivet/ 206" **35.00**

Toy, horse and buggy, cast iron, some original paint, 11" l, **$250**. Photo courtesy of Joy Luke Auctions.

Umbrella stand, 14-1/2" w, 8" d, 24-1/2" h, seated terrier on back, crossed canes with horse and dog head handles, short scrolled feet, old dark brown matte surface, raised signature in base "J. W. Fiske, NY" **880.00**
Utensil rack, 10-3/4" l, wrought iron, scrolled crest, five hooks with acorn terminals, minor brazed repair **770.00**
Wafer iron, 5-1/4" d, 24" l, imp with seal of U.S., c1800, minor imperfections **550.00**
Wall frame, 8-1/2" h, 6" d, cast iron, gilt eagle crest, elaborately dec frame, C-scrolls and foliate devices, 19th C **575.00**

IVORY

History: Ivory, a yellowish white organic material, comes from the teeth or tusks of animals and lends itself to carving. Many cultures have used it for centuries to make artistic and utilitarian items. A cross section of elephant ivory will have a reticulated crisscross pattern. Hippopotamus teeth, walrus tusks, whale teeth, narwhal tusks, and boar tusks also are forms of ivory. Vegetable ivory, bone, stag horn, and plastic are ivory substitutes, which often confuse collectors. Vegetable ivory is a term used to describe the nut of a South American palm, which is often carved. Look for a grain that is circular and dull in this softer-than-bone material.

Note: Dealers and collectors should be familiar with The Endangered Species Act of 1973, amended in 1978, which limits the importation and sale of antique ivory and tortoiseshell items.

Box, 2-5/8" d, lid painted with profile busts of man and woman in 18th C dress, blue ground, gilt-metal mounts on lid and base, French, late 19th................. **450.00**
Bridge, 12" l, carved from hippopotamus tusk, various figures in palace setting **175.00**

Cribbage board, Inuit, 20th C, top depicting hunter in kayak, walrus, dwelling, and various fish; bottom depicting Alaskan coast with place names, seal on block of ice, bone end cap, 25-1/2" l, **$800**. Photo courtesy of Skinner, Inc.

Bust, 2-7/8" h, gentleman, wavy hair, low curly beard, round ivory plinth **225.00**
Cane
35" l, 4" l x 1-1/2" h "L"-shaped elephant ivory handle carved three-toed Japanese mythological dragon twisted among rocks and foliage, inlaid mother-of-pearl eyes, sgd by Japanese maker, 1-1/4" silver collar initialed for orig owner, dec with "C" scrolls, dark bamboo shaft, 7/8" replaced brass ferrule, England, c1890 .... **1,680.00**
36-1/4" l, 5-1/4" l x 1-1/2" elephant ivory handle carved as cannon, 1/4" dec silver collar, black shaft, 7/8" horn ferrule, English, c1890 .... **1,235.00**
Carving
6-3/4" h, allegorical scene, two men and large urn beneath tree, mountain and clouds, urn broken and has water and another figure spilling from it, red signatures on base and back **450.00**
8-1/2" h, heavily carved tube, open, four-ftd base, flowers and birds, pierced ground, duck finial ... **360.00**
9" h, openwork, 3-D phoenix with tree and roses, age split in back, attached to wooden base **330.00**
Chess set
2-1/2" to 5" h, 16 crimson stained pieces, 15 natural pieces, detailed Chinese figures, lacquered case, gilt dec scenes and mother-of-pearl inlay, Oriental, 20th C **1,100.00**
3-1/2" to 7" h, each piece carved in form of Chinese figures, 16 natural color, 16 tea stained, fitted wood case with playing field, Oriental, 20th C.. **920.00**

Letter seal, form of elaborate floral and swag carved knob descending into hand holding fluted handle of sterling silver seal with crosshatch and scrolling decoration, two Old English initials, "DE," hallmarked, repair to joint between ivory and silver, 4-1/2" l, **$450**. Photo courtesy of Alderfer Auction Co.

Cup, cov, foliate finial, oval body, carved frieze of putti with hound, mask and acanthus baluster stem, round foot, Continental, early 18th C............ **1,200.00**
Fan, 11" l, sword form, anthemion-shaped fan, handle of fan with spiral reeding, kidskin case shaped as scabbard, ivory link chain and shield shaped belt clip with carved monogram, Continental, late 19th C **920.00**
Figure
Laughing monk, carrying turtle, staff with palm frond, bat on head, dark yellow stain, sgd, 6-1/4" h **200.00**
Man and woman wearing matching ornate costumes, carrying swords, riding horses with matching tack, dangles, and chain link reins, faux jewels, sgd on base, wooden bases, 9" h, 6" l, one rein broken, pr **700.00**
Man, elaborate dragon carved robe, sword, elephant headdress, holding dragon box, faux jewels, signature on base, wooden base, 14-1/4" h **525.00**
Jewelry, bracelet, ring, and pr earpendants, ivory plaques engraved with traditional scenes of mountains, lakes, and figures, silver filigree mounts, orig box, China............................ **360.00**
Letter opener, 9-3/4" l, oblong blade carved to end with writhing dragon, Chinese, early 20th C **115.00**
Measure, 14-7/8" l, whalebone, ivory, and exotic wood, American shield inlay, inscribed "WH," 19th C, minor imperfections................................ **195.00**

Figure, female warrior, standing, holding sword, Chinese, late Qing dynasty, early Republic period, 12" h, **$1,775**. Photo courtesy of Sloans & Kenyon Auctions.

Figure, man with monkey on leash, man smoking pipe, wearing mask lifted to top of head, carrying bag, colored carved detail on clothing and features of man and monkey, red inlaid signature cartouche on bottom, 6-1/2" h, **$550**. Photo courtesy of Alderfer Auction Co.

Miniature furniture, 4-1/2" h dressing table with two foliate pierced velvet-lined drawers, upright mirror, table with applied carved bottles, boxes, and basin, two miniature brushes and pen, glass dome, 5" l Regency-style scrolled settee with pierced outward scrolled arms, Continental, late 19th C **525.00**

Okimono, man giving grapes to child, Japanese, early 20th C **350.00**

Patch box, 3-3/8" l, oval, hinged lid set with rose gold metal vignette of plinth topped by plique urn, plique and line inlay stylized willow tree, int. velvet lined, mirror inset in lid, England/France, late 18th C **300.00**

Puzzle ball, 14" h, carved and pierced with dragons and flowers, China... **320.00**

Rolling pin, 19th C, minor insect damage, 13-5/8" l, exotic wood, baleen spacers, 19th C, cracks **225.00**

Seal, 3-7/8" l, intaglio, handle, 19th C, cracks.. **400.00**

Sewing bird, 4-1/8" l, four side-mounted spools, geometric and heart exotic wood inlay, 19th C, inlay loss and replacements **1,150.00**

Stand, 7" h, pierced relief, pink and cream flowers, peony and lotus flowers, green stones................................ **425.00**

Tusk, 59" l, matched pair, full sized, polished satin finish, warm patina, fitted ivory end caps, 20th C **5,175.00**

Vase, 10-3/4" h, gourd shape, acanthus leaves around neck, two bands of dragons chasing pearls through clouds, carved in high relief, incised signature, few age cracks **375.00**

Wrist rest, 10-1/4" h, carved in high relief with numerous figures in palace garden, China, 19th C............................ **1,265.00**

JADE

History: Jade is the generic name for two distinct minerals: nephrite and jadeite. Nephrite, an amphibole mineral from Central Asia that was used in pre-18th-century pieces, has a waxy surface and hues that range from white to an almost-black green. Jadeite, a pyroxene mineral found in Burma and used from 1700 to the present, has a glassy appearance and comes in various shades of white, green, yellow-brown, and violet.

Jade cannot be carved because of its hardness. Sawing and grinding with wet abrasives such as quartz, crushed garnets, and carborundum achieve shapes.

Prior to 1800, few items were signed or dated. Stylistic considerations are used to date pieces. The Ch'ien Lung period (1736-1795) is considered the golden age of jade.

Oriental lady, detailed carving, **$125**. Photo courtesy of Wiederseim Associates, Inc.

Box, 3-3/8" l, rect, silver mounted, early 20th C **320.00**

Bowl, 5-1/2" d, highly translucent stone with lavender tone, deeply infused with apple green, well-formed foot ring, China, 19th C............................ **2,650.00**

Brush pot, 4-1/4" h, scrolling cloud pattern, Chinese, 19th C **320.00**

Candlesticks, pr, 12-7/8" h, dark green, carved low relief goose with out-spread wings, stands on tortoise, head supports three-tiered pricket, tripod bowl with int. carving, reticulated wood base with carved key scroll motifs and floral scrolls **550.00**

Cane, 33-1/2" l, 1-1/2" d jade ball handle, seven inlaid cabochon sapphires set in gold, 1/3" 18kt yg collar, French, c1900 .... **1,570.00**

Jar, covered, carved elephant finial, dragon's mouth with rings handles, paw feet, **$95**.

Carving, 4" l, pair of crabs, celadon color, broad areas of russet **475.00**

Dish, 5-3/4" d, brownish-celadon, carved in Mughal style, open chrysanthemum flower, China, 19th C **475.00**

Ruyi scepter, jade and wood, each plaque carved to depict a dragon chasing the flaming pearl of wisdom, Chinese, late Qing dynasty-early Republic period, 21-1/2" l, **$1,000**. Photo courtesy of Sloans & Kenyon Auctions.

Figure

12" h, pair of phoenixes standing on curved rockery, polished finish, nephrite jade, Oriental, 20th C **690.00**

16" h, pair of phoenixes, mottled dark green, carved rosewood bases, Oriental, 20th C, price for pr **520.00**

16" h, three Chinese Gods, garden setting, white, lavender, and green colored jadeite, polished finish, fitted wood base, Oriental, 20th C **1,035.00**

18" h, wise man with scroll, white, lavender, and green, polish finish, Oriental, 20th C **1,495.00**

21" l, three Chinese Gods, dark green mottled jadeite, polished finish, fitted wood base, Oriental, 20th C **460.00**

24" h, Chinese princess and royal attendants, garden setting, fitted wood base, Oriental, 20th C, some repairs **1,150.00**

Inkstone, 3-5/8" l, oval, depression to one side, black and white mottling, incised rim band **200.00**

Letter opener, 10-3/4" l, carved interlocking C scrolls between keyfret bands handle, SS knife **250.00**

Libation cup, 5" l, celadon jade, incised dec, dragon head handles, Chinese, Qing dynasty, price for pr **425.00**

Seal, white jade with brown mottled coloring, irregular ovoid shape, cat finial, cat running down one end, Chinese, 19th C, 1-5/8" l, 3/4" w, 1-5/8" h, **$300**. Photo courtesy of Alderfer Auction Co.

Palace figure, 76" h, carved herons, more than 200 pieces of dark green mottled jadeite feathers applied over wooden form, mahogany stained wooden plinth, 20th C, minor losses, price for pr **1,150.00**

Plaque, 5-1/2" x 8", spinach-green, carved and pierced lattice pattern, squirrel with grapes, China, 20th C, price for pr **300.00**

Snuff bottle, Grayish-white, mottled russet skin on one side, rose quartz stopper **550.00**

Urn, cov, 11" h, Buddhist figure, open work foliage, lavender and green jadeite, polished finish, Oriental, 20th C **1,100.00**

JEWEL BOXES

History: The evolution of jewelry was paralleled by the development of boxes in which to store it. Jewel-box design followed the fashion trends dictated by furniture styles. Many jewel boxes are lined.

3-1/2" l, silver gilt, shell shaped, hinged lid engraved with scrolled and lozenge patterned lobes, set with scrolls, central acanthus leaf with tendrils, mounted with crimped collet-set red and green cabochon and faceted hardstones, seed pearls, accented with small putto figure, body accented with beading, raised on leaf tip base, single patera-topped scroll foot, 6 troy oz, European Rococo Revival, possibly Turkey, French import mark, late 19th/early 20th C **850.00**

4-3/4" l, silver gilt, ovoid, body engraved with navettes, set with raised openwork leaves and scrolls, centered by four cabochon amethysts, accented with seed pearls, lid set with similar raised scrolls accented with two further amethysts and seed pearls, central amethyst on purple enameled ground, four scroll feet, 10 troy oz, European, possibly Turkey, bearing French import mark, late 19th/early 20th C **950.00**

Cranberry glass, elaborate enamel and gold tracery, gilt foliate mounts, **$295**.

4-3/4" x 8-3/4", Russian Silver, rect, sky blue, deep red, and white enameled diapering patter, stylized flower heads, raised studded bands, swing handles on lid and sides, pale blue padded satin lining, four bun feet **2,500.00**

5-1/8" w, 4" d, 4-3/8" h, Bohemian glass, white overlay cut to cranberry, oblong, gilt-metal hinge mount, cut with roundels and leaves, roundels enamel dec with floral bouquets, gilt details, late 19th C **1,035.00**

5-1/4" l, 2-5/8" d, 3-3/4" h, cranberry flashed glass, dome top box with scroll-engraved brass mounts, two round pendant handles, open C-scroll feet, Continental, late 19th C **750.00**

6" h, 10" w, 6-3/4" d, engraved whalebone, top polychrome dec of elegant ladies and child flanked by birds among trees, sides with reserves of birds among foliage, top lists to reveal a removable tray, four cov compartments and door, dec with snakes, fish, and foliate devices, shaped bracket feet, minor imperfections **5,660.00**

6-1/2" l, German Silver, heavily molded and bellied sides, winged dolphin form feet, early 19th C, 13 oz **850.00**

Ruby glass, brass mounted, ornamented with gilded and painted flowers and leaves in turquoise and white, twisted wire and beading legs, ball feet, twisted wire and beading swing handles on each end, Moser, wear to gilding on edges, 5" l, 3"d, 5-1/4" h, **$700**. Photo courtesy of Alderfer Auction Co.

7" x 6-1/2", Wave Crest, puffy egg crate mold, hp lid, child with bow and arrow, satin finish, ftd, orig lining **1,200.00**

7-1/4" l, 4" w, 4-1/4" h, silver plate, cov on all sides and domed lid with Art Nouveau flowers in relief, lock and bale handle, int. lined with red velvet, underside stamped "G. G. Lelykauf Nururnbert" **125.00**

8-1/8" l, 5-3/8" w, 2-7/8" h, mother-of-pearl and paper, rect box, mother-of-pearl plaques with floral etched banding on top and three sides, ormolu mounts cast with florals, husks, and beading throughout, sloped hinged lid set with painted paper floral spray under glass dome, four ball feet, faille-lined interior, French, Second Empire, c1870-80 .... **2,415.00**

9-1/2" h, 16" w, gilt bronze, elaborate Moorish design, semi precious stones, enamel dec **900.00**

9-5/8" w, faux tortoise shell, Louis XV/XVI-style, bombe form, flat hinged lid with lifting handle, set with ormolu mounted Minerva masks at corners, rocaille escutcheon, and pad feet, int. with damask lining, French, early 20th C **950.00**

10" h, 11-1/2" w, 10-1/2" d, Victorian, painted and decoupage, lift top, pr of doors opening to small drawers, Chinese scenes on mustard yellow ground **815.00**

11-1/4" l, porcelain and ormolu mounted, Renaissance Revival, late 19th/early 20th C, walnut, rect, hinged lid with center porcelain roundel enamel dec with Cupid and amorous friend, raised surround accented with gilt metal anthemia, front set with ormolu and giltwood columns and escutcheon, incised linework all over, int. with remnants of moire lining, 11-1/4" l **500.00**

Pietra Dura, Italian, late 19th/early 20th C, oblong, hinged lid and four sides set with foliate pietra dura roundels in beaded surrounds, gilt metal, velvet-lined interior, ball feet, 3-3/8" h, **$650**. Photo courtesy of Skinner, Inc.

11-1/2" w, 9-5/8" d, 15-1/2" h, satinwood and inlay, molded top opening to fitted int., faux front drawer with shield shaped ivory escutcheon, over two glass fronted doors with ivory escutcheons, three drawers with turned ivory pulls, four pointed feet, English, mid-19th C **1,100.00**

12" h, 10" w, 10" d, painted papier-mâché, lit top, fitted int., two doors enclosing small drawers, Victorian, mid-19th, minor restorations **520.00**

JEWELRY

For more information see *Warman's Jewelry*, 3rd edition.

History: Jewelry has been a part of every culture. It is a way of displaying wealth, power, or love of beauty. In the current antiques marketplace, it is easiest to find jewelry dating after 1830.

Jewelry items were treasured and handed down as heirlooms from generation to generation. In the United States, antique jewelry is any jewelry at least 100 years old, a definition linked to U.S. Customs law. Pieces that do not meet the antique criteria but are at least 25 years old are called "period" or "heirloom/estate" jewelry.

The names of historical periods are commonly used when describing jewelry. Styles found in antique jewelry reflect several different design styles. These styles usually mirror what is found in the same period in other mediums, whether it is fine art, furniture, clothing, or silver. Each style has some distinctive characteristics that help to determine what style it is. However, it is also important to remember that design styles may overlap as popular designs were copied and/or modified slightly from one designer and decade to another. Fashions often dictated what kind of jewelry was worn.

Georgian, 1714-1830. Fine jewelry from this period is very desirable, but few very good quality pieces have found their way to auction in the last few years. More frequently found are memorial pieces and sentimental jewelry. Memorial pieces were made or worn to commemorate a loved one. Sentimental jewelry was often worn to express emotions that were not proper to express during those times. Often these sentimental jewelry pieces had flowers and other items, with each flower having a different sentiment attached to it. Diamonds were set open backed. Colored gemstones were set with closed-back settings lined with colored foil that enhanced their natural color. A popular motif was the bow, along with floral sprays and feathers. These designs tend to be rather stylized and flat. Paste (a high lead content glass) stones were popular and when set with foil backs they sparkled. Sadly, much jewelry from this period has been lost, as it was melted down to fund war efforts. During this time period, many folks would not wear expensive looking jewelry, as it was not wise to show one's wealth in such a manner. Gold was in short supply, so other metals were used to make fittings and chains.

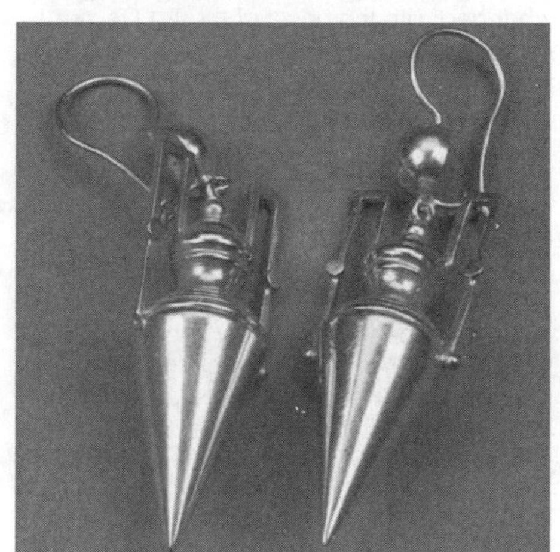

Earrings, Victorian, 15k yg, architectural design, **$250**. Photo courtesy of Sloan's Auctioneers & Appraisers.

Victorian, 1837-1901. The life of Queen Victoria set this whole period of design style. While Prince Albert lived, romantic themes in jewelry prevailed. One design element identified from the early part of the Victorian period is the snake, then thought of as a symbol of eternity or everlasting love. Victoria's engagement ring was a snake with a tail in its mouth. Snake necklaces, bracelets, and rings were also very popular. Floral designs of this period become more three-dimensional and truer in form to nature. The term "en tremblant," where the piece is designed to move with the motion of the wearer, reflects on the design as well as the French influence. Another popular symbol is a hand. Again, symbolic means were taken from whether the hand was clasped or open, holding flowers, or gemstones. Hair jewelry made from a loved one's hair was often given as a token of love. The fashion of long-sleeved bodices with high necks caused throat pins to be popular. The practice of wearing ribbons around the neck and pinned with a brooch was also popular when necklines were lower. Earrings were not very popular in the early Victorian period because of the popular hairstyles. Bracelets were usually worn in multiples and on both arms. When Prince Albert suddenly died in 1861, the gaiety of English life subsided. Add to this the many widows created by the Civil War and one can understand why black mourning jewelry became such a fashion statement. Entirely black jewelry was popular, as was jewelry with black trim or backgrounds, such as black onyx. Positive influences of this period included interest in revivals of ancient cultures, such as Egypt. By this period, manufacturers were learning how to mass-produce jewelry. By the end of the Victorian period, smaller and lighter pieces of jewelry became fashionable. Gold was still in short supply, but the newly developed electro-plating techniques allowed more gold-colored jewelry to be made. Seed pearls were plentiful. Cameos and mosaics also became popular. Diamonds move from closed and foil settings to open-backed settings during this period. New cuttings shaped diamonds and other gemstones in ways that allowed more facets. The discovery of diamonds in South Africa helped lower prices in the 1880s, but they were always expensive. Other gemstones, like garnets, are found as both facet cut and cabochon. Natural stones like turquoise and agates were popular, too.

Necklace, Edwardian, 18kt white gold, negligee design featuring two diamond set drops surmoounted by bead set diamond plaque suspending diamond pendulum, approx. 0.75 cts., **$800**. Photo courtesy of Sloan's Auctioneers & Appraisers.

Edwardian, 1890-1920. The Edwardian period also takes its name from an English Monarch, King Edward VII. This style emphasized the use of diamonds, pearls, and platinum in more monochromatic designs. The development of platinum led to strong, but lacy looking, filigree designs. Up until the Edwardian period, platinum used in jewelry making was usually plated with other metals as it was considered a lesser material. Diamond-cutting techniques continued to improve and new cuttings, such as marquise, baguette, and emerald cuts, became popular. Gemstones such as amethysts and peridots, blue sapphires, demantoid garnets, alexandrites, and rubies are also cut in these styles. Turquoise and opals are used as highlights. Jewelry for men was very popular in this period. The style is also known as Belle Époque.

Pin, Art Nouveau, attributed to Freys, figural bat, blue opalescent enamel work on spread wings, body is paved with approx. 41 full-cut diamonds, one red stone eye, unmarked, 2-1/2" w, 1-1/4" h. Photo courtesy of James D. Julia, Inc.

Arts and Crafts, 1890-1920. This period of jewelry is dominated by hand made creations, often inspired by medieval and renaissance designs. Known for the high level of craftsmanship evident in metals, jewelry reflected the natural elements so loved in this period. Guilds of artisans banded together. Some jewelry was mass-produced, but the most highly prized examples of this period are handmade and signed by their makers. The materials used reflect what was being used in other crafts: silver, copper, and some gold. Enamel highlights added colors. Cabochons, leaves, and naturally shaped pearls predominate the style.

Brooch/pin, sterling, C. 1935, round rectangular plaque, chased and repoussé cornucopia motif, marked "PEER SMED STERLING HAND CHASED," safety clasp, 2-1/2" w x 2", **$750**. Photo courtesy Janet Zapata.

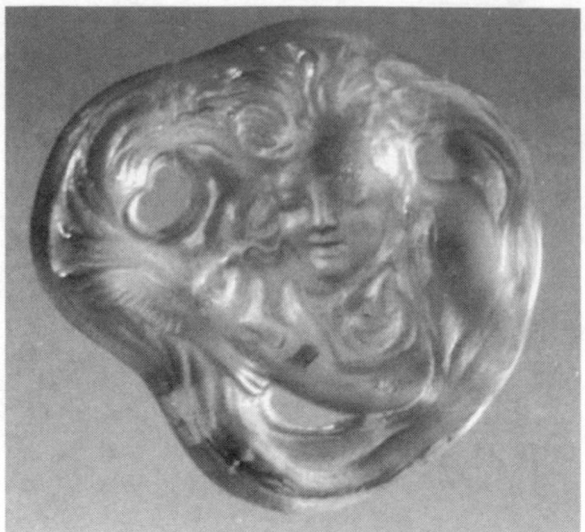

Pendant, Art Nouveau, Lalique, c1920, Ange et Colombe, clear and frosted glass with gilt backing, sepia patina, engraved "R. Lalique," 1-3/4" d, **$650**. Photo courtesy of David Rago Auctions.

Art Nouveau, 1895-1910. The free-flowing designs associated with the Art Nouveau period are what are found in jewelry from that time. Borders and backgrounds undulate and often include vines, flowers, and leaves. Enamel decoration is one of the more distinctive elements of this style. Gemstones also enhanced the wide palette of colors available. Jewelry from this period is again mass-produced, but quickly went the way of fashion when clothing styles changed with the onset of the Art Deco period.

Art Deco, 1920-1935. The flappers and their love of straight lines dominate this period. When examining Art Deco jewelry, look for a skyscraper or fireworks motif, as both symbolize this striking period. French designers were the most influential. Many pieces from this period are large and were used as accents to the new lighter clothing styles. In 1924, Coco Chanel declared, "It does not matter if they are real, as long as they look like junk," setting the stage for an explosion of costume jewelry. Rhinestones, pastes, and cut glass became important parts of molded designs of silver or pot metal.

Retro-Modern 18kt yg cocktail ring, large emerald-cut aquamarine flanked three rows of 3.00 carats. Circular-cut diamonds, **$2,200**. Photo courtesy of Sloan's Auctioneers & Appraisers.

Beads, Post-War Modern, three strands of graduated faceted amethyst beads, Indian style adjustable clasp. **$1,500**. Photo courtesy of Sloan's Auctioneers & Appraisers.

Retro Modern, 1935-1945. A resurgence of romanticism overtook the design world at the start of this period. Colored gemstones were back, along with the now popular costume jewelry. The style embraces some aspects of former periods, such as the streamlined look of the 1920s, but also the softness and natural aspects of the Victorian period. Color spilled over to settings with bi-color, rose, and yellow gold being popular. Machine-made pieces incorporate bold designs and colors with most motifs rather massive.

Post-War Modern, 1945-1965. Designer jewelry is the most collected of this jewelry period. Names such as Harry Bertoia, Sam Kramer, and Ed Wiener are just a few of the top designers from this period. These designs were executed in various mediums, including brass, silver, Lucite, and plastics, as well as traditional materials. To be collectible, jewelry from this period should be signed or somehow identifiable. Designs tend to be sleek and innovative.

Notes: The value of a piece of old jewelry is derived from several criteria, including craftsmanship, scarcity, and the current value of precious metals and gemstones. Note that antique and period pieces should be set with stones that were cut in the manner in use at the time the piece was made. Antique jewelry is not comparable to contemporary pieces set with modern-cut stones and should not be appraised with the same standards. Nor should old-mine, old-European, or rose-cut stones be replaced with modern brilliant cuts. The pieces listed here are antique or period and represent fine jewelry (i.e., made from gemstones and/or precious metals). The list contains no new reproduction pieces. Inexpensive and mass-produced costume jewelry is covered in *Warman's Americana & Collectibles*.

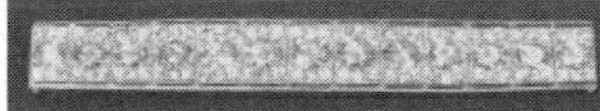

Bar pin, Art Deco, platinum, bead-set with 13 old European and transitional-cut diamonds weighing approx 13.99 cts., flanked by 78 full-cut diamond melee, approx. total wt. 17.63 cts., detachable pinstem, former center section of a bracelet, **$35,250**. Photo courtesy of Skinner, Inc.

Bar pin

Art Deco

Bezel and bead-set throughout with 66 old European, French, baguette, and single-cut diamonds, approx. total weight 1.98 cts, rect and triangular-cut sapphire accents, millegrain accents and pierced platinum gallery.................. **3,055.00**

Channel-set with 21 French-cut sapphires, engraved 14k white gold mount, hallmark for Wordley, Allsop & Bliss..................................... **600.00**

Platinum, bead-set with 13 old European and traditional-cut diamonds weighing approx 13.99 cts, flanked by 78 full-cut diamond melee, approx. total wt. 17.63 cts, detachable pinstem, former center section of bracelet............ **35,250.00**

Edwardian, platinum, set with line of 13 old mine-cut 5.25 ct diamonds, framed by 28 dematoid garnets in scalloped design, millegrain accents......... **6,800.00**

Stickpins, 14k yg, ribbon swags suspending five antique and Art Nouveau full-cut diamond-set stickpin heads, diamond flowerhead surmount, stickpins with hallmarks for Carter, Howe & Co. and Dieges & Clust............................. **650.00**

Victorian, center coral cabochon, 10k yg **275.00**

Beads

Gold, 14k yg, 50 9.00 mm beads, monoxide sgd "Tiffany & Co.," orig suede sleeve, 31.0 dwt, 18" l................ **1,300.00**

Onyx beads accented by turquoise and gold disks, conforming spherical 14k yg clasp, 37" l.................................. **215.00**

Bracelet, bangle

Art Nouveau

14k yg, bezel-set round coral cabochon flanked by scrolling leaf motifs, interior inscribed "F.O.H. 1907," worn hallmark for Riker Brothers............................... **885.00**

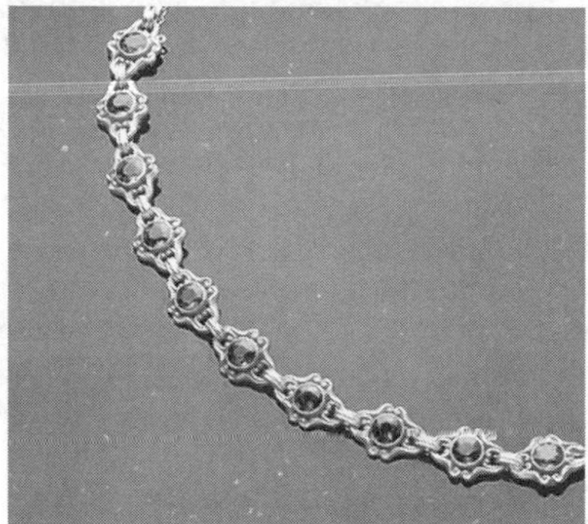

Bracelet, Art Nouveau, 14k yellow gold, 10 undulated scroll links, each with collet-set circular 7mm amethyst joined by reeded links, mark for Photo courtesy of Sloans & Kenyon Auctions, 7-1/2" l, **$1,850**. Photo courtesy of David Rago Auctions, Inc.

14k yg, hinged, bear clutching old European-cut diamond in its teeth, diamond melee eyes, 16.4 dwt, hallmark for Alling & Co...... **2,235.00**

Etruscan Revival, 14k yg, bead, and wiretwist dec, 46.1 dwt, minor discoloration to gold, surface scratches, price for pr................................ **2,550.00**

Garnet, hinged, flower head surmount, bead and bezel-set throughout with oval and circular-cut garnets, gilt mount **275.00**

Lucite, tapering, amber and green, interior leopard design **200.00**

Post-War Modern, cuff, 14k yg, wave design, section of pavé set diamonds, 5.50 cts.................................... **1,800.00**

Victorian, 14k yg, hinged, four-leaf clover mount and seed pearl stem, interlocking loop design, three green stone accents............................... **265.00**

Bracelet, cuff, Modern, Georg Jensen, Denmark, c1940, sterling silver, cuff, marked "55," original box, **$875**. Photo courtesy of David Rago Auctions, Inc.

Bracelet, charm

14k yg, fancy-link chain suspending engraved cylindrical locket charm star set with ruby and sapphire melee unfolding to display six oval photo compartments, 22.dwt, 7" l............ **470.00**

Bracelet, coin

18k yg, fancy link bracelet suspending seven bezel-set coins from various countries, 80.5 dwt, 7-1/2" l........ **1,100.00**

Bracelet, link

Art Deco

Articulated geometric-form links bezel and bead-set with 186 full-cut, 36 baguette, six trapezoidal, and three sq step-cut diamonds, approx. total wt. 6.75 cts., millegrain accents, pierced gallery with swags, platinum mount, 7-1/4" l **10,575.00**

Articulated geometric-form plaques set with three marquise, four half-moon, 90 baguette, and 394 full and single-cut diamonds, approx. total wt. 11.00 cts., 7-1/4" l....... **22,915.00**

Articulated links, channel-set calibre and square step-cut sapphires and bead-set old European, rose, and single-cut diamonds, approx. total wt. 3.34 cts., 7-1/4" l.......... **11,165.00**

Platinum, 38 box-set old European-cut diamonds, approx. total weight 5.97 cts, millegrain accents, engraved gallery, 7-1/4" l ... **5,525.00**

Bracelet, Retro, platinum, 18k yellow gold, stylized design of ruby circular links, platinum and diamond spacers, gold modified V-shaped links, approximately 0.80 cts, 7-1/2" l, 26.8 dwt, **$1,950**. Photo courtesy of Sloans & Kenyon Auctions.

Arts and Crafts, 18k yg, five flexible foliate and beaded links each bezel-set with oval faceted citrine flanked by silver pearls with rose overtones, joined by floral links, floral box clasp, 7-1/4" l **1,530.00**

Retro Modern, interlocking hexagon-shaped 18k yg links, clasp with radiating

elements in white and yellow gold bead-set with single-cut diamond highlights, 33.0 dwt, 7" l 715.00
Revival-style, 22k yg, flexibly-set diminutive florets, beadwork accents, Asian hallmarks, 56.4 dwt, 6-1/4" l 885.00

Victorian

Carved coral plaques, engraved "Ida W. Roth 1865," gilt mounts 290.00

14k yg, center 17.3 x 15.9 x 11.4 mm almandine carbuncle, within ornate engraved frame with scrolling accents, engraved tapering links, later clasp and chain extender, 17.6 dwt, 7-1/2" l 940.00

Bracelet, Victorian, 14k yellow gold, wide woven band completed by fringed buckle closure with bezel-set turquoise cabochons, 31.8 dwt, missing two turquoise cabochons, 7-1/2" l, **$900**. Photo courtesy of Skinner, Inc.

Bracelet, Victorian, 18k yellow gold, garter, fine 22 mm wide mesh ribbon, adjustable ogee slide, refined taille d'epargne tracery, foxtail fringe with losses, **$635**. Photo courtesy of David Rago Auctions, Inc.

Bracelet, woven

Victorian, 14k yg, turquoise, wide woven band, fringed buckle closure with bezel-set cabochons, 31.8 dwt, 7-1/2" l, missing two turquoise cabochons 890.00

Brooch

Art Deco

Platinum, bead-set with 110 old European and single-cut diamonds, channel-set French-cut onyx and millegrain accents, pierced gallery 4,230.00

Platinum, bezel and bead-set throughout with 41 old European and single-cut diamonds, approx. total weight 3.11 cts, millegrain accents, pierced gallery 3,415.00

Three concentric circles bead-set with 73 old European-cut diamonds, approx. 2.92 cts, center bezel-set emerald-cut emerald, moveable platinum mount, later 14k white gold pinstem, evidence of solder 2,470.00

Art Nouveau

Sterling silver, black opal-in-matrix scarab framed by lotus flowers with green enamel accents, minor enamel loss, worn gilt surface 450.00

Sterling silver, stylized woman with flowing hair surrounded by four lotus flowers, foliage, and buds, hallmark for Unger Brothers 470.00

Arts & Crafts, sterling silver, sq form, center orange stone cabochon, hallmarked for R. Blackinton & Company 200.00

Brooch, Art Nouveau, Chinese, enamel, grapevine motif with carnelians, vermeil, some enamel loss, 2-1/2" x 3-1/2", **$375**. Photo courtesy of David Rago Auctions, Inc.

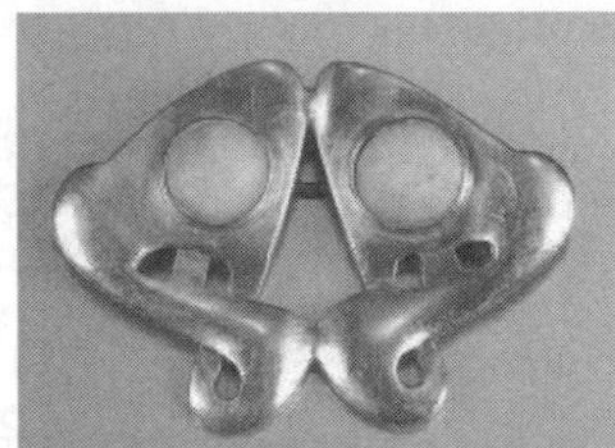

Brooch, Arts & Crafts, Carence Crafters, Chicago, early 20th C, sterling silver, mirrored abstract design with two cabochon corals inset, imp "CC" mark and "STERLING," 1-3/8" l, **$650**. Photo courtesy of Skinner, Inc.

Cameo, 18k yg, carnelian agate hardstone, young bejeweled lady, gold beads frame, four prong-set split seed pearl accents, French import stamp 650.00

Edwardian

Feather, bead-set throughout with old European-cut diamonds, approx. total weight 1.72 cts, platinum topped 14k yg mount 1,200.00

Oval opal framed by seed pearls and old European-cut diamonds, 14k yg mount, hallmark for Krementz & Co., orig Tiffany & Co. box 1,300.00

Platinum, 76 rose, single, and full-cut diamonds, bead and prong-set throughout, approx. total weight 1.70 cts, French hallmark 2,350.00

Etruscan Revival, 18k yg, double ram's head bosses surmounted by owl, suspending three drops, wirework accents, 22.3 dwt 1,410.00
Memorial, swiveling oval form, initial "S" and floral spray executed in blond hair on mother-of-pearl ground, black enamel mount with C-scroll and leaf accents, 14k gold mount 265.00

Pearl

18k yg, leaf flexibly set with circular white cultured pearl, full-cut diamond links suspended from bar pin, approx. total diamond wt. 2.50 cts 1,645.00

Brooch, Edwardian, platinum, bead and prong-set throughout with 76 rose, single, and full-cut diamonds, approximate total weight 1.70 cts, French hallmark, **$2,350**. Photo courtesy of Skinner, Inc.

Platinum, camelia formed of freshwater pearl petals centering three semi-baroque silver pearls with rose overtones, eight bezel-set full-cut diamond melee accents, sgd "KY" for Kai Yin Lo 2,235.00
Post-War Modern, Georg Jensen, sterling silver

Bezel-set cabochon green chalcedony accent, sgd "Georg Jensen," No. 138 .... 450.00

Circle, bird among leaves, sgd "Georg Jensen," No. 123 ...... 300.00

Moonstone, sgd "Georg Jensen," No. 159 .... 765.00

Retro Modern, 18k yg, fist holding carved light green beryl engraved with foliate motifs, 8.2 dwt 350.00
Scottish Agate, sterling silver

Garter buckle design, bloodstone, carnelian agate, and sardonyx, engraved mount 680.00

Star, center circular-cut citrine, engraved mount 715.00

Brooch, Victorian, gold, Rococo relief centering an emerald-cut citrine, approximately 18 cts, old marks for 800 gold, possibly Portuguese, **$810**. Photo courtesy of David Rago Auctions, Inc.

Victorian

Bicolor gold, shield form, hardstone cameo, applied flowering branch,

enamel accents, 10k yg mount 175.00
Bombe form, applied bead and wirework, suspended tassel, 14k yg 750.00
Coral, carved as classical nude reclining among roses and scrolling leaves, 9k gold mount with partial hallmarks 1,645.00
Cross form, claw set with pearls, black enamel accents, 14k gold mount 530.00
Flower with blossom set en tremblant, claw and bead-set throughout with old mine-cut pastes, silver mount 650.00
Ivory, floral motif 90.00
Onyx leaves, seed pearl accent, 14k yg mounts............................. 195.00
Spaniel, red stone eyes, on tasseled pillow, 14k yg........................ 650.00
Venetian glass, oblong form bezel-set with Venetian glass intaglio of draped classical figure, white cultured pearl terminals, cabochon onyx accents, 18k yg, hallmark for Elizabeth Locke.................... 765.00

Chain

Fob, 14k yg, rect fancy links, 43" l, 18.1 dwt... 360.00

Platinum open fancy links, bezel-set old mine-cut diamonds, seed pearls joined by trace-link chain, 27-1/2" l 1,550.00

Cigarette case

14k yg, c1930, leaf engraved edges, 179.2 dwt, inscribed initials ABL, American hallmark..................... 1,410.00

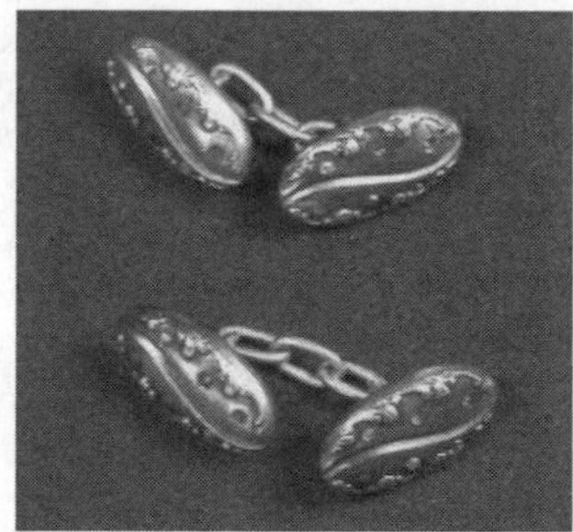

Cufflinks, pair, Art Nouveau, 18k yellow gold, edges with leaf motifs, diamond emerald and ruby accents, French guarantee stamps, **$215**. Photo courtesy of Skinner, Inc.

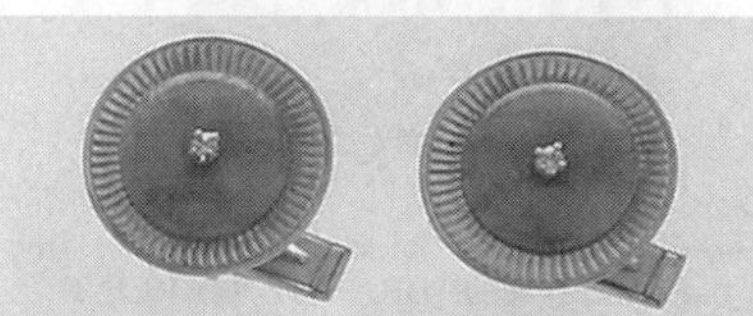

Cufflinks, pair, Retro, 14k yellow gold, 18mm disks with radial-cut detail surmounted by abright green jade "wheel of life" centered by aprong-set diamond, Tiffany & Co., **$575**. Photo courtesy of David Rago Auctions, Inc.

Cufflinks, pr

Art Nouveau, 18k yg, edges with leaf motifs, diamond emerald and ruby accents, French guarantee stamps 215.00

Post-War Modern

14k yg, baseball and bat joined by single link, engraved "8-23-20," 4.2 dwt.. 765.00
18k yg, malachite, double cabochon link within gold foliate mount, 10.9 dwt, sgd "Schlumberger" and "Tiffany & Co." 950.00
Platinum, double oval link with engraved border of geometric and foliate motifs, 12.4 dwt 500.00

Demi-parure

Post-War Modern, brooch composed of 14 prong-set sapphire cabochons interspersed with six full-cut diamond highlights, earclips each with four sapphire cabochons framing white gold leaf set with single-cut diamonds, diamond and cultured pearl drop, 14k white gold mounts, all sgd "Seaman Schepps," brooch formerly a clasp 3,415.00

Victorian

14k bi-color gold, brooch designed as scroll-handled scissors snipping bunches of angel skin coral grapes from leafy vine, earpendants ensuite 1,880.00
Pendant brooch with pastel enamel portrait of 18th C lady wearing rose-cut diamond diadem and collier de chien, in 18k yg scrolling frame with flexible pendant beads, earpendants (with later fittings) ensuite, orig fitted box 1,880.00

Dress clips, pair, Art Deco, bead-set with 72 full- and single-cut diamonds, channel-set square step and calibre-cut sapphire highlights, millegrain accents, platinum mount, with brooch conversion, **$3,200**. Photo courtesy of Skinner, Inc.

Dress Clips, pr

Art Deco, bead-set with 72 full and single-cut diamonds, channel-set square step and calibre-cut highlights, millegrain accents, platinum mount, with brooch conversion 3,200.00

Post-War Modern, Georg Jensen, sterling silver, sgd "GJ" for Georg Jensen, No. 57 .... 650.00

Earrings, pr

Art Nouveau, 18k yg, catkin composed of flexibly set rose-cut diamonds, freshwater pearl accents, sgd "Vever," (Henri Vever, 1854-1942), fitted box, three small rose-cut diamonds missing 4,115.00

Egyptian Revival, 14k yg, each with three ancient Egyptian amulet drops 590.00

Georgian, day/night, florets suspending elongated drops with stippled surface, applied flower and wirework lyre motifs, together with second pr of spiral-engraved drops with applied wirework florets, later findings, dents........... 825.00

Pearl

Cultured, bezel-set full-cut diamond suspending cultured 9.20 pearl, approx. total diamond wt. 0.54 cts, 14k white gold mounts 530.00
Cultured, curving pavé-diamond and black enamel elements, white cultured pearl center, 18k yg 715.00
South Sea, stud, 11.90 mm white pearl, 18k white gold mounts 850.00
Tahitian, 13.20 x 11.70 gray pearl suspended from 18k white gold and diamond melee ear wire..... 1,410.00

Earstuds, pair, Retro, 14k bi-color gold, designed as a cluster of yellow and rose gold blossoms, full-cut diamond and garnet accents, 7.4 dwt., **$560**. Photo courtesy of Skinner, Inc.

Post-War Modern

Butterflies, inlaid onyx and opal wings, 18k yg, 8.7 dwt, sgd "Tiffany & Co.," designed by Angela Cummings............................ 765.00
Center pyramidal blue topaz cabochon, 18k bi-color gold, sgd "Bulgari" 2,235.00
Textured leaf in white and yellow 18 k gold, 6.5 dwt, sgd "M. Buccellati" 950.00

Retro Modern

Aquamarine, stylized knot suspending rect step-cut aquamarine, platinum-topped 18k rose gold mounts 390.00
Cluster of yellow and rose gold blossoms, full-cut diamond and garnet accents, 7.4 dwt. 560.00
Diamond and shell, white shell flower, bead-set diamond melee center, 18k yg, 22.1 dwt, sgd "Trio" 890.00

Platinum, bead-set and bezel-set, single-cut and full-cut diamonds, approx. total weight 1.10 cts 1,250.00

Victorian

Carved coral, rose blossoms and leaves cascade 125.00

Coral and onyx, center carved coral flower surrounded by faceted onyx ring, 14k yg mount, later findings 470.00

14k yg, center claw-set 10.6 x 10.3 x 4.9 mm amethyst in openwork scrolling mount, applied beads, ropetwist dec, later earwires 7.5 dwt 445.00

14k yg, each designed as hemisphere and sphere suspending bow and hanging tassel, bezel and gypsy-set throughout with turquoise cabochons, applied wirework accents, 10.5 dwt, evidence of solder, small dents, missing elements

14 k yg, two domes with pavé-set turquoise cabochons, centering bead-set single and old European-cut diamond highlights, wirework frame 2,000.00

Grape clusters with coral beads 250.00

Hip flask

Edwardian, c1910, 18k gold, curved form, engraved with four-leaf clover, capacity of two gills, 252 dwt, sgd "Tiffany & Co.," #19579, maker's #7322, and "M" 3,200.00

Lavaliere, Art Deco, 14k white gold, filigree link, rectangular stamped links with three octagonal frosted crystal panels, each set with diamond suspending similar rect panel with filigree decoration and diamond, 15" l chain, 2-3/4" l pendant, **$750**. Photo courtesy of David Rago Auctions, Inc.

Lavaliere

Edwardian, platinum, 18k yg, delicate trace link chain suspending old European and old mine-cut diamond floral pendant, channel-set emerald scrolls, bezel-set diamond and seed pearl accents, brooch fittings, 15" l, orig German court jeweler fitted box 3,200.00

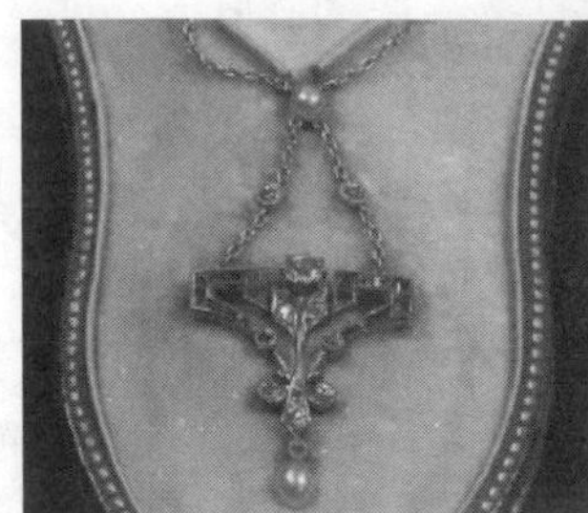

Lavaliere, Edwardian, platinum, 18k yellow gold, delicate trace link chain suspending old European and old mine-cut diamond floral pendant with channel-set emerald scrolls, bezel-set diamond and seed pearl accents, brooch fittings, original German court jeweler fitted box, 15" l, **$3,200**. Photo courtesy of Skinner, Inc.

Locket

Art Nouveau, 14k yg, high relief image of young lady, floral and rose-cut diamond hair ornaments and choker, locket sgd Frainier, fancy link chain with hallmarks for Ste. EE, French guarantee stamps, 22.1 dwt, 24-1/2" l 2,115.00

Edwardian, center is exotic bird in flight, bead-set single-cut diamond body and ruby eye, black enamel ground with delicate white enamel border, opens to reveal two interior compartments, 14k yg, platinum bail, 15.5 dwt. 2,350.00

Locket, Victorian, designed as micromosaic Roman temple set in malachite ground, surrounded by decorated leaves, beadwork, and wiretwist frame, attached to 15k yellow gold Victorian chain, **$715**. Photo courtesy of Sloans & Kenyon Auctions.

Victorian, bloomed

14k yg, star-form oval faceted ruby and rose-cut diamond mount, 15.8 dwt 1,000.00

Tri-color, mounted with flower on leafy stem, seed pearl accent, applied bead and ropetwist decoration, verso with locket compartment, suspended from short fancy link chain 360.00

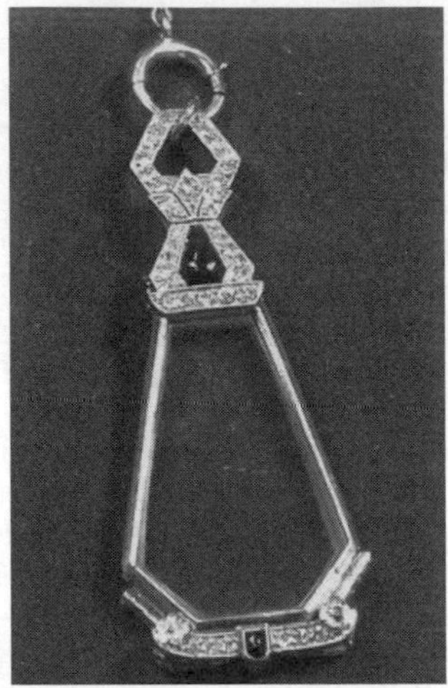

Lorgnette, Art Deco, platinum, set with 39 full- and single-cut diamonds, two calibre-cut onyx cabochons, millegrain accents, suspended from added sterling silver paper clip chain with black enamel baton links, 24-1/4" l, **$1,650**. Photo courtesy of Skinner, Inc.

Lorgnette

Art Deco, platinum, set with 39 full and single-cut diamonds and two calibré-cut onyx cabochons, millegrain accents, suspended from later sterling silver paper clip chain with black enamel baton links, 24-1/4" l 1,650.00

Edwardian, 18k yg, engraved dec handle and eye piece, handle set with three bands of rose-cut diamonds, French assay marks 750.00

Necklace, Art Nouveau style, sterling silver, floral motif around green and black scarab beetle, link chain, back impressed "BRANDT/STERLING," 12-1/2" l, **$470**. Photo courtesy of Skinner, Inc.

Necklace

Art Deco, 14k yg, two carved coral plaques depicting flowers and leaves

suspended from fancy-link chain with rocaille motifs, c1930, hallmark for Krementz & Co., 17-1/4" l **500.00**

Art Nouveau, articulated chased C-scrolls, 15 boulder opal drops, suspended from chain composed of hammered 14k yg links in various abstract shapes, additional length of later chain, later clasp, 13" l **4,820.00**

Arts & Crafts, Silver delicate trace link chain, bezel-set oval faceted citrine framed by florets and leaves, 20" l, slight break at bail.................................. **300.00**

Edwardian, fringe, 18k yg, ruby and seed pearl florets joined by seed pearl links suspending graduating circular and square-cut ruby fringe from knife edge bars, center pendant hook, 16" l **1,765.00**

Etruscan Revival, ivy leaf and berry motif, barrel clasp, 18k yg, 15-3/8" l **2,850.00**

Fringe necklace, Edwardian, 18k yellow gold, composed of ruby and seed pearl florets joined by seed pearl links suspending graduating circular and square-cut ruby fringe from knife edge bars, center pendant hook, 16" l, **$1,765**. Photo courtesy of Skinner, Inc.

Pearl Necklace

Cultured, 46 white 8.05 to 8.20 mm pearls with rose overtones, 18k gold ribbed X-form clasp, sgd "T & Co." for Tiffany & Co., orig suede pouch, 16-1/4" l **2,235.00**

Cultured, 101 white pearls graduating in size from 3.75 to 7.01 mm completed by an openwork 18k white gold barrel clasp with diamond accents, Continental hallmark, 22" l **385.00**

South Sea, 37 graduated 10.10 to 13.50 white pearls, 18k yg spherical ropetwist clasp, 18-1/4" l **8,000.00**

Tahitian, 35 pearls graduating in size from 11.20 to 13.10mm, 14k yg pavé-set diamond boule, 18-1/4" l **3,290.00**

Tahitian, 37 graduated gray pearls measuring approx. 11.00 to 13.90 mm, 18k yg spherical ropetwist clasp, 19-1/4" l................... **9,990.00**

Necklace, dog collar, composed of eight rows of cultured pearls centering sapphire and diamond plaque of open-work filigree design, further accented with diamond set bars, approx 1.00 cts, **$4,150**. Photo courtesy of Sloans & Kenyon Auctions.

Festoon necklace, Art Nouveau, 14k yellow gold, paper clip chain suspending five pear-shape faceted amethysts, delicate trace link festoons accented by seed pearls, 15-1/4" l, **$1,410**. Photo courtesy of Skinner, Inc.

Post-War Modern

Galalith, geometric black and white plastic links, sgd "Guillemette l'Hoir, Paris," 1970s, 18" l **350.00**

Open abstract form 18k yg links each bezel-set with full-cut diamonds, approx. total wt 0.82 ct., 15" l, sgd "C. Deneuve" for Catherine Deneuve **1,410.00**

Revival-style 18k yg, Asian hallmark, 62.5 dwt, 15" l............................ **1,300.00**

Victorian

Coral, bezel-set coral links joined to wirework flowers by trace link chain, 15-1/2" l **325.00**

14k bi-color gold, reeded trace-link chain suspending three foxtail tassel pendants and medallion with enamel cherubs, all joined by swags, black tracery enamel accents, 16-1/2" l **765.00**

14k yg, fancy link chain suspending oval pendant with bezel and pavé-set turquoise cabochons, applied bead and wirework accents, locket compartment, 19.2 dwt, 19-1/4" l, two turquoise cabochons missing **450.00**

Necklet

Edwardian, delicate trace link chain suspending pendant with two bezel-set harlequin black opals, 31 bead and bezel-set single-cut diamonds, millegrain accents and pierced gallery, platinum topped 18k gold mount, platinum chain, 16-1/2" l...................................... **3,525.00**

Pendant

Art Deco, center is carved serpentine Buddha, carved lapis lotus blossom base, four cultured pearl highlights, rose-cut diamond and millegrain accents, platinum and 18k yg mount, French hallmarks **2,585.00**

Art Nouveau, large freshwater pearl, scalloped bail, gypsy-set with three demantoid garnets, 14k gold mount **180.00**

Enamel, green basse taille enamel serpent coiled around a blue enamel egg, diamond melee eyes, freshwater pearl drop, 18k gold mount, probably Continental hallmarks **765.00**

Pate de Verre, Poissons, Lalique design introduced in1928, Marcilhac No. 1664, rounded triangular form with school of blue fish against frosted background, sgd "R. Lalique" **470.00**

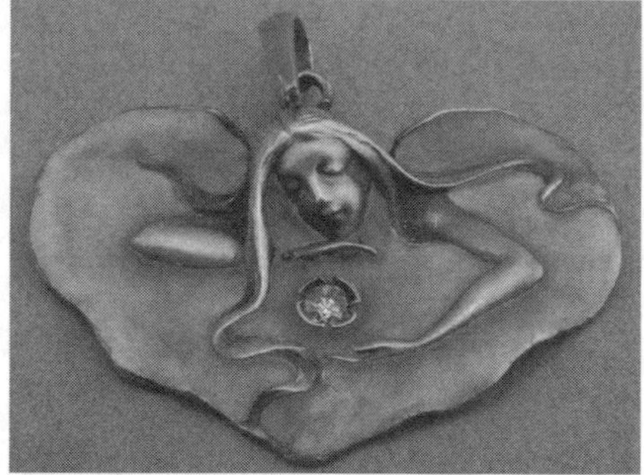

Pendant, Art Nouveau, 14k yellow gold, enameled, designed as undulating heart with woman's face, flowing hair in shaded pink and white enamel, accented with old European-cut diamond, **$695**. Photo courtesy of Sloans & Kenyon Auctions.

Pendant brooch

Art Deco, platinum, oblong openwork form bead-set with 57 old European and full-cut diamonds, approx. total wt. 2.20 cts, detachable bail.................... **2,470.00**

Cameo, 18k yg, hardstone cameo, Roman maiden in profile framed by seed pearls, suspended from later trace link chain interspersed with seed pearls, bail with green enamel and bead-set diamond accent, 23" **1,300.00**

Edwardian, center 6.15 mm cultured pearl framed by circular design of seed pearls and 72 old European, single, and rose-cut diamonds, approx. total weight 1.13 cts. **1,750.00**

Habille, shell cameo, young lady with floral corsage, diamond melee necklace and ear pendant, 14k white gold filigree frame **200.00**

Victorian

Amethysts, 25 graduating collet-set oval faceted amethysts joined by seed pearl and twisted wire florets, 14k gold mount, 16-3/4" l, orig fitted box **2,350.00**

Athena wearing pale blue dolphin helmet, orange and green bodice depicted in painted Limoges enamel, rose-cut diamond accents, seed pearl and rose-cut diamond frame, 18k yg, reverse with evidence of solder at frame **715.00**

Shell cameo, young woman in profile with flowers, 14k yg mount.... **300.00**

Shield form claw-set with hardstone cameo of lady, applied leaf and scroll devices, 14k yg, one leaf missing **365.00**

Pin, Arts & Crafts, James Woolley, Boston, early 20th C, sterling silver, rectangular pin with Art Nouveau flowers on each end, linear pattern in center, impressed cipher and "STERLING," 2-5/8" l, **$450**. Photo courtesy of Skinner, Inc.

Pin

Art Deco

Black, green, and yellow enamel pagoda framing pierced jadeite plaque with bird among flowers, 14k yg mount, hallmark for Sloan & Co **3,055.00**

Circle, platinum, five bezel-set round sapphires, 20 bezel-set old European-cut and transitional-cut diamonds, approx. total weight 0.80 ct, millegrain accents **2,000.00**

Art Nouveau

Black enamel dogwood blossoms, seed pearl accents, 14k gold mounts, hallmark for Whiteside & Blank, pr **650.00**

Dark pink enameled poppy blossom with two buds, framed by sinuous vines, prong-set old European-cut diamond highlight, 14k yg 2.6 dwt **300.00**

Griffin clutching old European-cut diamond, rose-cut diamond accents, 18k yg, maker's mark "GC" **2,350.00**

Pin/pendant, Art Nouveau, enameled, designed as flower with freshwater pearl stamen resting upon leaf with bezel-set diamond highlight, hallmark for Krementz & Co., **$530**. Photo courtesy of Skinner, Inc.

Edwardian

Circle, diamond melee leaves accented by seed pearls, platinum-topped 18k yg mount **450.00**

Crescent bead-set with five pale blue, three yellow, one brown, and two near-colorless old-mine and old European-cut diamond melee, approx. total wt. 0.66 ct., platinum topped 14k gold mount...... **1,765.00**

Lapel, scrolling green enamel, 14k yg mount, suspending enamel flower basket with rose-cut diamond bird, old mine-cut diamond and seed pearl accents, 18k yg mount, lapel pin with hallmark for Krementz & Co **1,650.00**

Micromosaic, dove flanked by scrolls, white and sky blue tesserae, scrolling wirework and beads accents,18k yg, partial Continental hallmark.................. **1,000.00**

Victorian, classical lady in painted Limoges enamel, floral rose-cut diamond hair ornament, red orange basse taille enamel ground, ropetwist and seed pearl 18k yg frame.................. **1,300.00**

Ring, Art Deco, platinum, approximately 1 ct mine-cut and Holland-cut diamonds, calibre-cut sapphires, **$635**. Photo courtesy of David Rago Auctions, Inc.

Rings

Gentleman's, Gothic Revival, 14k yg, bezel-set rect cut-corner color-change synthetic sapphire, bezel and shank incised with Gothic arches and trefoil motifs, hallmark for Larter & Sons **500.00**

Lady's

Art Deco, platinum

Center bead-set circular-cut sapphire within openwork mount with diamond melee, millegrain accents and engraved shank **1,000.00**

Center pinkish-purple star sapphire measuring approx. 12.45 x 6.25 mm, flanked by bead-set single-cut diamond split shoulders, channel-set French-cut rubies, millegrain accents **1,880.00**

Center sq step-cut emerald framed by six old European-cut diamonds weighing approx. 0.57 ct., openwork mount with millegrain accents, engraved shoulders **1,000.00**

Navette-shape onyx tablet bezel-set with old European-cut diamond weighing approx. 2.89 cts., platinum and 18k gold mount, evidence of solder **6,200.00**

Openwork square set throughout with single-cut diamonds, millegrain accents, openwork gallery and engraved shank **530.00**

Prong-set cushion-cut sapphire weighing 3.01 cts. flanked by old mine-cut diamonds, approx. total diamond wt. 1.00 ct., open gallery **4,415.00**

Art Nouveau, 18k yg, shaped rect plaque etched with initials "HP," flanked by stylized flowers within open and ribbed shank, inscribed "Vitaline a Hubert, 2 Janv, 1910" **375.00**

Edwardian, platinum on 14k gold, 6 x 6mm sq cut emerald, two old mine-cut diamonds, 20 single-cut diamonds **800.00**

Ring, Art Nouveau, Egyptian style, 14k yellow gold, designed as bypass of two scarabs with collet-set star sapphires, **$435**. Photo courtesy of David Rago Auctions, Inc.

Post-War Modern

Cat's Eye Chrysoberyl, center 15.10 x 14.10 x 6.60 mm cat's eye chrysoberyl surrounded by 18 round brilliant-cut diamonds, approx. total weight 1.26 cts, 14k gold mount **3,100.00**

Pavé-set full-cut pink diamond panther, curling tail, cabochon onyx spots, marquise-cut emerald eyes, 18k gold mount **1,375.00**

Turquoise, asymmetrical design centering a prong-set turquoise cabochon, offset by 19 baguette and full-cut diamonds, approx. total weight 1.87 cts, three circular-cut sapphire highlights, 14k yg, 4.8 dwt **490.00**

Retro Modern, set, platinum, three interlocking rings, middle ring centering round full-cut within a curving mount bead-set throughout with single-cut diamonds, approx. total weight 0.75 cts, millegrain accents **750.00**

Victorian, hardstone cameo of maiden in classical dress, framed by six seed pearl accents, engraved band, 10k yg mount **200.00**

Suite

Archaeological Revival, 18k yg, fringe necklace composed of 25 coral cameos of bacchante maidens suspended from tubular links interspersed with disc-shaped gold beads, bead and wirework accents, "S" clasp mounted with cameo, pr earpendants ensuite, made by Giacinto Melillo, orig fitted box, descended in one family **42,300.00**

Arts and Crafts, 14k yg, lapis and silver bracelet, ring: floral carved and pierced oval lapis plaque, shoulders with floral and leaf motifs, matching earpendants with gilt mounts, 7-1/2" l Bigelow and Kennard box **450.00**

Post-War Modern, "Connections," 18k yg, 16-1/2" l necklace and 7-1/2" l bracelet designed as interlocking circles, sgd "Paloma Picasso" and "Tiffany & Co.," orig suede sleeve **2,235.00**

Torsade

Ten strands of white freshwater pearls, ribbed hook-form 18k gold clasp, sgd "Paloma Picasso" and "Tiffany & Co.," orig suede sleeve, 16" l **650.00**

Watch chains, Victorian, one heavy gold filled rope chain with fob and watch key with micromosaic scene, other heavy link chain with abalone and onyx fob, **$175**. Photo courtesy of Joy Luke Auctions.

Watch pin

Art Nouveau, profile of young woman with flowing hair encircled by enameled buds, foliage, and emerald-set blossoms, 14k yg mount **1,775.00**

Judaica

History: Throughout history, Jews have expressed themselves artistically in both the religious and secular spheres. Most Jewish art objects were created as part of the concept of Hiddur Mitzva, i.e., adornment of implements used in performing rituals both in the synagogue and home.

For almost 2,000 years, since the destruction of the Jerusalem Temple in 70 A.D., Jews have lived in many lands. The widely differing environments gave traditional Jewish life and art a multifaceted character. Unlike Greek, Byzantine, and Roman art, which have definite territorial and historical boundaries, Jewish art is found throughout Europe, the Middle East, North Africa, and other areas.

Ceremonial objects incorporated not only liturgical appurtenances, but also ethnographic artifacts such as amulets and ritual costumes. The style of each ceremonial object responded to the artistic and cultural milieu in which it was created. Although diverse stylistically, ceremonial objects, whether for Sabbath, holidays, or the life cycle, still possess a unity of purpose.

Notes: Judaica has been crafted in all media, though silver is the most collectible.

Amulet, 2-3/4" h, Italian, 18th/19th C, silver and silver filigree, irregular outline, inscribed "Shadai," with pendant chain and fitted leather box **520.00**

Autograph, letter, four pages, hand written by Solomon Nunes Carvalho, 1852, regarding the rise of American reformed Judaiasm in Charleston, SC **3,165.00**

Breast plate, 14" h, Damascene, 20th C, cartouche form, surmounted by crown and dec with tablet, candleabrum, foliate motifs **550.00**

Candelabra, 15" h, brass, Polish, late 19/20th C, three-branch, lions and Star of David device supporting disks of candlesockets **365.00**

Candlesticks, pr, 4" d, 8-3/4" h, sterling silver, raised letters, one with "Shabbat," other with "Kadosh," slightly flaring bobeche, European hallmarks **300.00**

Ceremonial ring, 3-1/4" h, sterling silver, top applied with pavilion, side pierced with door and windows, three semi-precious stones, chased Hebrew words **425.00**

Chalice, 13" h, Continental silver, Herman Lang, Augsburg, 17th C, 29 oz **2,400.00**

Charity container, 3-3/4" h, silver, inverted-pear form, body engraved banding, and molding hinged lid with money slot and hasp, scroll handle, front inscribed "Zeduke für Arme kinder," German, late 19th/20th C **920.00**

Circumcision cup, 5" h, double, silver gilt, marked "Johanna Becker, Augsburg," 1855-57 .... **13,500.00**

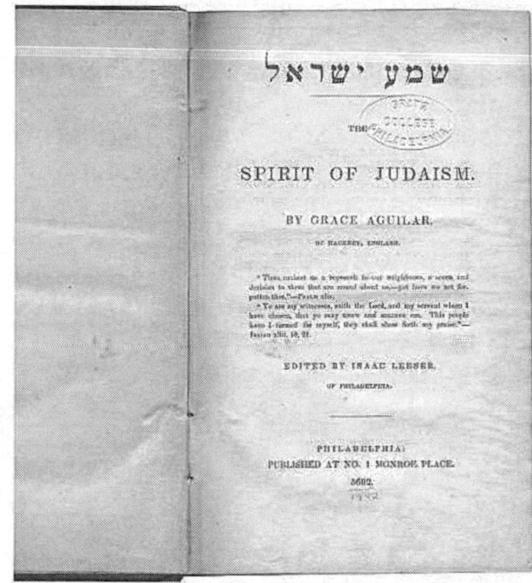

Book, *The Spirit of Judiasm,* by Grace Aguilar, edited by Issac Lesser, Philadelphia, 1842, Sherman & Co., printers, original cloth hard covers, some fading, 255 pgs, **$750**. Photo courtesy of Historical Collectibles Auctions.

Coffee pot, 10-1/2" h, silver, American, mid-19th C, maker illegible, overall foliate and scroll repousse dec, scrolled handle, spreading circular foot, inscribed "Presented by the --smouth Hebrew Congregation to Mr. Lewis Nathan, for his valuable services as Honorary Secretary, November 30th 5617-1856," small repair to cartouche **700.00**

Esther scroll, cased, 9" l, parcel-gilt and filigree, Continental, 19th C, applied jewels, hand-form thumb pc, nicely written ink on vellum scroll, fitted box **9,200.00**

Haggadah, Haggadah Shel Pesach, Offenbach, Zvi Hirsch Segal and his son Abraham, (1800), 40 leaves, 8vo, marbleized paper boards, new edition with German translation printed in Hebrew script beneath original woodblock illus, discoloration, shaken **815.00**

Hanukah lamp

4-5/8" h, bronze, Italian, 17th C, arched backplate with pierced geometric motifs, fronted by bank of oil fonts, old repair................ **665.00**

9-1/2" h, silver, Russian/Polish, late 19th C, hallmarked, shaped backplate with lions, foliage, and candelabrum, servant lamp and oil jug, fronted by rect base with candleholders, cast feet........ **600.00**

14-3/4" h, Damascene, 20th C, arched backplate with central servant lamp, with scrolling foliage, lions, and tablets, fronted by eight deep oil fonts..................... **1,450.00**

Hanukah menorah, 11-1/2" h, silver plated, Polish, Warsaw, late 19th C, cartouche-shaped backplate with crown, palm trees, and lions, fronted by serpentine bank of candleholders, raised on cast feet, rosing **500.00**

Kiddish cup, sterling silver, 3" h, George III, double barrel form, Charles Aldridge, London, 1791-92, inscribed with the seven benedictions of wedlock, pr **7,200.00**

Light bulb, 3-3/4" l, Star of David **100.00**

Menorah, 20" h, gilt bronze, after Salvador Dali, c1980, set on Jerusalem stone base **2,415.00**

Mezuzah, 5-1/2" h, 14k yg, after Ilha Schor, emb and cut-out with figure of Moses, "shin" finial **920.00**

Pamphlet, Charter and Bye-Laws of Kaal Kadosh Micheve Israel of the City of Philadelphia Incorporated 5584, sgd by Hyman Gratz, 1824 .... **2,645.00**

Document signed, letter from D. C. Levy, Philadelphia, to T. I. Tobias, N. Y., Dec. 6, 1848, "...The gentlemen of whom you inquire arrived yesterday...will leave this day for Washington and then proceed by the mail route to his residence in Mississippi...likely he may go to New Orleans as he lives not far from there...," **$100.** Photo courtesy Historical Collectibles Auctions.

Passover plate, 15" l, pewter, 19th C, rim dec with figures amidst foliage, Hebrew text, center with lions, crown **775.00**

Passover table cloth, 76" x 56", linen, rect with shaped edges, white background, multicolored embroidered Passover implements, some staining **920.00**

Prayer book, miniature, Seder U-Velechtekha Ba-derekh, Feival Monk, Warsaw, 1884, Ashkenazi rite, gilt-stamped calf, faux jewel insets, 60 x 40 mm **490.00**

Print, hand tinted, Foul Play or Humphreys and Johnson A Match for Mendoza, 18th C, championship boxer illus **1,610.00**

Rosewater bottle, 12" h, silver, South East Asian, late 19th/early 20th C, shaped as water bird swallowing fish swallowing acanthus bouquet, stepped pedestal base, emb and engraved dec, domed top pierced, approx 8 troy oz **225.00**

Sabbath candlesticks, pr, 12-1/2" h, silver plated, B.R. Henneberg, Warsaw, dated 1909, molded bobeche, baluster-form body, spreading circular foot on sq base, cast overall with foliage and Star of David, wear **500.00**

Sabbath platter, 10-1/2" l, tin washed copper, marked "Israel Made, Hakushut" orig sticker, die struck imprinted mark **150.00**

Shabbat candelabrum, 20" h, brass, Continental, early 20th C, five-light, supported by deer amidst branches, baluster turned support, domed circular foot, cast Hebrew inscription for Shabbat **500.00**

Spice box, silver, windmill form, 5-1/2" h, applied with floral baskets and birds, sq base, four scroll and foliate feet, 7 oz, 4 dwt.. **875.00**

Spice container, 7-1/4" l, German silver, articulated fish form, red glass eyes, mouth opens, scales with etched detail marked "835" and "Handarbeit".... **700.00**

Spice tower, 7-3/4" h, silver, second half 20th C, indistinctly marked, Nuremberg-type, steep roof, pendant flags, square body with door, spreading circular foot **650.00**

Torah breastplate, silver and silver filigree, Russian hallmarks, 20th C, cartouche-shape with crown finial, Decalogue, temple columns, festival plaques, etc................................ **900.00**

Torah crown, miniature, 5" h, silver-gilt filigree, Continental, probably Eastern Europe, early 19th C, unmarked, acorn finial, with bells, stepped form, inset paste stone details, cross support with apertures to base, lacking two stones **2,200.00**

Torah finials (Tik), 14" h, silver, Near Eastern, late 19th/20th C, unmarked, book-form, overall heavily repoussé decoration of grape leaves and vines, fronted by temple columns, Decalogue, and candelabra, fitted with 11-1/2" h handwritten ink on parchment torah scroll **3,500.00**

Torah pointer (Yad), 8" l, silver, North African, early 20th C, unmarked, slender form, turned and leaf-tip dec, Hebrew text, terminating in pointed hand, suspension loop **350.00**

Traveling menorah, 3-1/2" x 2-1/2", sterling silver, book form, pierced flowers, animals, center anukah lamp, int. fitted with dividers to form eight oil receptacles, 11 oz, 6 dwt **1,200.00**

Watch, 2-1/2" d, Near Eastern, 19th C, silver-gilt, enamel, and rock crystal, six-sided star, floral enamel work, Hebrew numbers, rock crystal bezel and backplate, minor damage, enamel losses **2,415.00**

JUGTOWN POTTERY

History: In 1920, Jacques and Julianna Busbee left their cosmopolitan environs and returned to North Carolina to revive the state's dying pottery-making craft. Jugtown Pottery, a colorful and somewhat off-beat operation, was located in Moore County, miles away from any large city and accessible only "if mud permits."

Ben Owens, a talented young potter, turned the wares. Jacques Busbee did most of the designing and glazing. Julianna handled promotion.

Utilitarian and decorative items were produced. Although many colorful glazes were used, orange predominated. A Chinese blue glaze that ranged from light blue to deep turquoise was a prized glaze reserved for the very finest pieces.

Jacques Busbee died in 1947. Julianna, with the help of Owens, ran the pottery until 1958 when it was closed. After long legal battles, the pottery was reopened in 1960. It now is owned by Country Roads, Inc., a nonprofit organization. Vernon Owens purchased the pottery in 1982.

Candleholders, pair, flaring base, covered in amber crystalline glaze, stamped "Jugtown Ware," 3-3/4" d, 3" h, **$175.** Photo courtesy of David Rago Auctions, Inc.

Bowl, 2" h, 4-1/4" d, Chinese blue glaze, imp mark, pr **425.00**

Candlesticks, pr, 3" h, Chinese Translation, Chinese blue and red, marked **125.00**

Vessel, shouldered, four pinched handles, covered in textured gray semi-matte glaze, stamped Pewabic/Detroit, 5" d, 5-1/2" h, **$265**. Photo courtesy of David Rago Auctions, Inc.

Charger, 15" d, orange glaze, marked, abrasion and flakes to surface **230.00**
Lamp base, 9-1/2" x 5", bulbous, flowing white semi-matte glaze over dark body, circular stamp **360.00**
Vase
3-3/4" h, 2-1/2" d, Chinese blue flambé glaze, imp mark......... **325.00**
6" x 5", pear shape, Chinese blue glaze with red flashes, circular stamp mark **1,150.00**
8-3/4" h, 6-1/2" d, stoneware, two small handles, top cov with matte mustard glaze, bottom with clear coating, imp mark **850.00**
Vessel
7-1/4" h, 5" d, ovoid, white satin glaze, hairline to rim, stamped "Jugtown Ware"..................... **300.00**
9" h, 6-1/4" d, four small handles, brown speckled luster glaze, red clay body, glaze flakes in making, imp mark **650.00**

KPM

History: The "KPM" mark has been used separately and in conjunction with other symbols by many German porcelain manufacturers, among which are the Königliche Porzellan Manufactur in Meissen, 1720s; Königliche Porzellan Manufactur in Berlin, 1832-1847; and Krister Porzellan Manufactur in Waldenburg, mid-19th century. Collectors now use the term KPM to refer to the high-quality porcelain produced in the Berlin area in the 18th and 19th centuries.

Cane, 38-1/2" l, 4-1/4" l x 2" h porcelain handle of lady wearing bonnet and lace collar, hp floral motif, gold highlights, ebony shaft, 1/3" gold collar, 1-1/2" horn ferrule, c1890 .... **1,600.00**

Chocolate cup, ovoid form, slightly everted rim, patera loop handle, raised on three gilt-paw feet, painted portrait of brunette beauty reclining in her boudoir, gilt rim, Berlin, mid to late 19th C, 5-1/8" h, **$470**. Photo courtesy of Skinner, Inc.

Cup and saucer, hunting scene, filigree, 19th C... **65.00**
Dinner service, partial, basketweave molded rim, enamel painted sepia-toned floral sprays, 10 6-3/4" d side plates, nine 9-1/2" d dinner plates, eight 8-3/8" d salad plates, 12" l oval platter, 13-5/8" l oval platter, 8" oblong dish, late 19th/early 20th C, price for 30-pc set **520.00**
Figure, 8-1/2" h, 3-1/2" d, young man with cocked hat, long coat, trousers, and boots, young lady in Empire-style dress, fancy hat and fan, white ground, brown details, gold trim, round base, blue underglaze KPM mark, price for pr **350.00**
Perfume bottle, 3-5/8" l, rococo-cartouche form, sepia enamel dec of cherub in flight, floral bouquet, gilt detailing, gilt-metal and coral mounted stopper, late 19th C **230.00**

Portrait plaque, oval, young woman wearing locket and open blouse, impressed KPM mark on back, 10-1/4" x 8-1/2", **$2,200**. Photo courtesy of Alderfer Auction Co.

Plaque
6" d, German officer, round, painted with central rectangular portrait of gentleman in uniform, gilt frame with laurel and helmet, in gilt-metal surround, paper label identifying it as loan from the Fogg Art Museum, early 19th C **4,320.00**
9-3/4" l, 5-1/4" w, Aurora by Bierschneider, hp in very fine detail, beehive mark...................... **3,500.00**
12-1/2" x 10", portrait of elegant lady, imp KPM **7,150.00**
13-3/4" d, titled "Entflohen," two young beauties seated in windswept wood, diaphanous gowns, floral headbands, anthemion and quatrefoil border, irid teal ground, 22-1/4" d giltwood and gesso frame **10,925.00**

Tea bottle, ovoid, molded and gilt enamel decoration with rocaille vines, domed lid with gilt flower finial, late 19th C, 4-1/4" h, **$150**. Photo courtesy of Skinner, Inc.

Punch bowl, cov, 12" d, 14-1/2" h, domed lid, Dionysian putto figural finial, enamel dec on one side with 18th C wigged gentleman at a drunken meeting of punch society, similar scene of gentleman at table to one side, vignette of couple outside village on other, floral bouquets and sprigs, imp basketweave rim, gilt edging, underglaze blue mark, late 19th C **2,775.00**
Vase, 8-1/2" h, baluster, two handles, hp multicolored florals, celery green ground **200.00**

Kauffman, Angelica

History: Marie Angelique Catherine Kauffmann was a Swiss artist who lived from 1741 until 1807. Many artists who hand-decorated porcelain during the 19th century copied her paintings. The majority of the paintings are neoclassical in style.

Box, cov, 2-3/4" x 4-1/2", lilac, two maidens and child in woods on cov, brass hinges.................................. **70.00**
Cake plate, 10" d, ftd, classical scene, two maidens and cupid, beehive mark **90.00**

Charger, Austrian porcelain, central panel decorated with figures, signed Kaufmann, 12" d, **$100**. Photo courtesy of Joy Luke Auctions.

Compote, 8" d, classical scene, beehive mark, sgd **85.00**
Cup and saucer, classical scene, heavy gold trim, ftd **90.00**

Plaque of Vestal, 5-1/2" x 3-1/2", reverse titled "Vestalin" after Angelica Kaufmann, seated figure in white classical garb, holding oil lamp, painted porcelain, Dresden, late 19th/early 20th C, gilt-metal and green lined ribbon-topped, **$2,585**. Photo courtesy of Skinner, Inc.

Demitasse set, 8" h demitasse pot, creamer, sugar, three cups and saucers, extra saucers, all with country scene, marked "Conaty, Germany," sgd "Kauffmann" on scene, price for 13-pc set **190.00**
Dresser tray, 11-1/2" x 7-1/2", cherub center, marked "Carlsbad, Austria" **75.00**
Pitcher, 8-1/2" h, garden scene, ladies, children, and flowers, sgd **100.00**
Plate, 8" d, cobalt blue border, reticulated rim, classical scene with two figures **65.00**
Portrait plate, portrait with cherubs, dark green and cream ground, gold trim, sgd "Carlsbad, Austria, Kaufmann," four-pc set **495.00**
Tobacco jar, classical ladies and cupid, green ground, SP top, pipe as finial **415.00**
Vase, 10" h, baluster, small wing handles, cobalt blue ground, roundel with semi-nude painting, sgd "K," c1870, price for pr, damage to one handle **225.00**

Kitchen Collectibles

For more information, see *Warman's Glass*, 4th edition.

History: The kitchen was the focal point in a family's environment until the 1960s. Many early kitchen utensils were handmade and prized by their owners. Next came a period of utilitarian products made of tin and other metals. When the housewife no longer wished to work in a sterile environment, enamel and plastic products added color, and their unique design served both aesthetic and functional purposes.

The advent of home electricity changed the type and style of kitchen products. Fads affected many items. High technology already has made inroads into the kitchen, and another revolution seems at hand.

Additional Listings: Baskets, Brass, Butter Prints, Copper, Fruit Jars, Food Molds, Graniteware, Ironware, Tinware, and Woodenware. See *Warman's Americana & Collectibles* for more examples, including electrical appliances. See *Warman's Flea Market Price Guide* also.

Butter paddles, left with wide blade, right with long handle, **each $65.**

Apple butter kettle, 25" d, 29-1/4" h, copper, dovetailed construction, wrought iron handle, dents........................ **350.00**
Apple peeler, cast iron, Reading Hardware Co. **90.00**
Bean pot, cov, 6-1/2" h, Bristol glaze, handle, c1900................................ 25.00
Broom holder, Little Polly Brooms, tin litho, image of little girl sweeping floor, 2-1/2" w, 6-1/4" h.......................... **425.00**
Butter churn, on stand, 25-3/4" w, 20-3/4" d, 35" h, churn with four interlocking staves, wrought steel hardware on removable lid, serpentine crank with wood handle, orig dasher, pegged saw buck base, some edge damage, nailed split in one leg **120.00**
Butter paddle, 10" l, bird's eye maple, carved hook handle, patina.......... **175.00**
Cheese sieve, 10" d, 7" h, plus handle, hand-molded yellow clay, Albany glaze **320.00**
Churn, Dazey, one quart, clear glass **1,300.00**
Colander, 13" h, stoneware, brown Albany glaze, handled, attributed to Midwest, c1870 .... **75.00**

Cookbook

- Cook It Outdoors, James Beard, 1941, 1st ed **10.00**
- Mastering the Art of French Cooking, Julia Child, volumes one and two, Knopf, 1971-76, dj....................**25.00**
- The Good Housekeeping Illustrated Book of Desserts, Step-by-Step Photographs, Hearst Books, 1991, 5th printing, dj **12.00**

Cookie mold

- 2-1/2" to 3-3/4" l, yellow clay, detailed, squirrel, iris, burro, knot, kneeling man, woman, soldier on horseback, wolf in boots, traces of stenciled labels on backs, minor edge flakes............................**350.00**
- 2-5/8" x 11", wood, kangaroo, bear, and crested duck, good patina, minor age splits.....................**165.00**
- 4-3/8" x 3-1/8", wood, ear of corn, deep carving **225.00**
- 4-3/8" x 3-1/8", wood, snail on leaf, ash, deep carving **585.00**
- 4-1/2" x 3", wood, bouquet of roses, deep carving **250.00**
- 12" l, 4-1/4" w, wood, swaddle baby, ruffled bonnet, raised tin edge on carving, worm holes, age crack **300.00**

Dough box, pine and turned poplar, PA, 19th C, rect removable top, tapering well, splayed ring-turned legs, ball feet, 38" w, 19-1/4" d, 29-1/2" h **425.00**
Egg beater, 10-1/2" l, Jacquette Scissor, marked "Jacquette, Phila, PA, Patented No. 3".. **550.00**
Flatware, four 8-7/8" l knives and four forks, wooden handles, knife blades marked "J. Ward & Co., Riverside, Mass.," wear and some damage to orig box... **90.00**

Flour sifter, 14" h, 12" w, Tilden's Universal, wood, partial intact paper label 335.00
Food chopper, 7" w, wrought iron, scalloped edge blade, turned wood handle........ 270.00

Left: griddle, Griswold, #9, Erie, PA, cast iron, **$35**; right: camp-type shovel, metal, soldered, loop hanging handle, **$15**.

Griddle, cast iron, Griswold, No. 10 .... 70.00
Ice bucket, Frigidaire, frosted green glass........ 35.00
Kettle, cast iron, Griswold No. 4.... 85.00
Kraut cutter, 24-1/2" l, 7-1/2" w, walnut, round crest with hanging hole, old patina, two sides attached by screws........ 95.00
Ladle, 15" l, wood, pothook handle 50.00
Lemon squeezer, iron, glass insert, marked "Williams" 50.00
Meat tenderizer, 9-1/2" h, stoneware, orig wood handle, marked "Pat'd Dec. 25, 1877" in relief on bottom, diamond point extensions with some use wear...... 90.00
Nutmeg grater, 7" l, Champion, brass and wood........ 635.00
Pantry box, cov, 11-1/2" d, 6-1/2" h, oak, bail handle........ 175.00
Pastry board, wood, three sided... 32.00
Pie crimper, 7" l, carved bone, unicorn with carved fish tail, ball-shaped hooves, front let glued, late replacement crimper, medium brown stain........ 220.00
Pie safe, hanging, 31" w, 19" d, 31" h, mortised pine case, old thin red wash, door, sides, and back with punched tins with geometric circles and stars, white porcelain door pull, two int. shelves, edge damage........ 990.00
Potato masher, 9" l, turned maple 40.00

Popcorn popper, embossed "Wilson Mfg Co.'s Family Corn Popper, Miles, O," some discoloration and rust, **$30**.

Pot scraper, Sharples Tubular Separator, tin litho, graphic advertising on both sides, 3-1/8" x 2-1/4"........ 275.00
Rack, 20" l, rect backplate with arched top, red and white enameled checkerboard pattern, narrow well, single rod suspending two strainer spoons 250.00
Reamer, Orange, Sunkist, blocked pattern, white milk glass, Walker #331b 125.00
Rolling pin
- Stoneware, marked "Compliments of W. M. Holbert," chip on end 315.00
- Wood, curly maple, good figure, patina, deep ridges, 19" l....... 275.00

Sausage stuffer, 17-1/2" l, turned wood plunger........ 30.00
Skillet, cast iron, Griswold, No. 14 .... 165.00
Spatula, 17-3/4" l, brass and wrought iron, polished........ 175.00
Spice set, Griffiths, set of 16 glass jars with yellow tops, each with spice name, orig rack........ 160.00
Stove, cast iron, chrome, nickel, colorful ceramic tile back........ 6,000.00
Sugar shaker, Dutch boy and girl, Tipp City........ 22.00
Syrup jug, 8" h, adv, clay inscribed "W. D. Streeter, Richland, NY," Albany glaze, c1890, tight hairline on side........ 35.00
Taster, 7" l, brass and wrought iron, polished........ 150.00

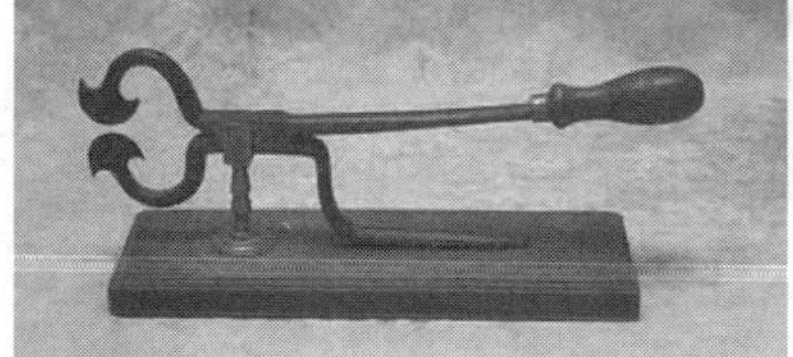

Sugar nipper, forged iron, mounted to mahogany board, turned wooden handle, turned brass support. 14" l, **$385**. Photo courtesy of Alderfer Auction Co.

Utensil, tin, two graters, crimper, and cookie cutters all in one cylindrical form, 2-3/4" d, 4-1/2" h, **$315**. Photo courtesy Alderfer Auction Co.

Tin
- Egg-O Brand Baking Powder, paper label, 2-3/4" h, 1-1/4" d........ 110.00
- Kavanaugh's Tea, 1 lb, little girl on porch in dress, talking to doll, mother sipping tea in window, cardboard sides, tin top and bottom, 6" h, 4-1/2" w, 4-1/2" d........ 500.00
- Miller's Gold Medal Breakfast Cocoa, red and black, c1890, 2" h, 1-5/8" w, 1-1/8" d........ 250.00
- Parrot and Monkey Baking Powder, 4 oz, full, 3-1/4" h, 2-1/8" d........ 375.00
- Sunshine-Oxford Fruit Cake, early 1900s, sq corners........ 20.00

Trivet, 12" l, lyre form, wrought iron frame and turned handle, brass top, replaced foot, stamped maker's mark........ 45.00
Wafer iron, cast iron, octagonal, church with steeple and trees dec on one side, pinwheel with plants and star flowers on reverse, wrought iron handles...... 400.00
Water filter, Allen, Toledo, OH, "Germ Proof"........ 300.00

KUTANI

History: Kutani originated in the mid-1600s in the Kaga province of Japan. Kutani comes in a variety of color patterns, one of the most popular being Ao Kutani, a green glaze with colors such as green, yellow, and purple enclosed in a black outline. Export wares made since the 1870s are enameled in a wide variety of colors and styles.

Beaker, 4-1/2" h, hp flowers and birds, red, orange, and gold, white ground, marked "Ao-Kutani" **95.00**
Biscuit jar, cov, Geisha Girl, c1890 .... **190.00**
Bowl, 6-3/8" d, gilt and bright enamel design, figural, animal, and floral reserves, kinrande ground, base inscribed "Kutani-sei," set of 10 ... **400.00**
Charger, 18-3/8" d, pomegranate tree, chrysanthemums, and two birds on int., birds and flowers between scrolling foliate bands, irregular floral and brocade border, 11-character inscription ... **600.00**
Chawan (tea bowl), 5" d, 3" h, sunflower design, orange and green, imp mark "RIJU" **100.00**

Vaes, paneled, Foo dog mounts, two handles. Chinese, late 19th C, 24-1/2" h, **$500**. Photo courtesy of James D. Julia, Inc.

Creamer and sugar, summer scene, two court ladies, red, blue, gray, and gold, red handle, spout, and feet with gold overlay, c1910 .... **95.00**
Dessert service, country life dec, gold cloud borders, eight plates, two compotes, 20th C **435.00**
Figure, 7" l, duck, gilt figure, purple, blue, green, and yellow feathers, Japan, late 19th C **1,100.00**
Jar, cov, 20-1/2" h, ovoid, fan-shaped reserves of warriors, molded ribbon tied tasseled ring handles, shippo-tsunagi ground, multicolored brocade patterned dome lid, pr **1,400.00**
Sake cup, 2-3/16" h, 1-1/8" w, crane in red center, gold lacquer trim **35.00**
Tea caddy, 6" h, bulbous, hexagonal, Nishikide diapering, figural raised gold reserves of children, red script mark **195.00**
Teapot, cov, 8" h, white, trees and flowers, gold trim, marked "Hand Painted Craftsman China, Kutani 391 Japan" **45.00**
Tray, 14" l, polychrome and gilt dec, figural scene, red, orange, and gold border **350.00**
Vase
10" h, double-gourd, red and gold roundels of auspicious animals on flowered ground, Japan, 19th C **300.00**
14" h, pear shape, Satsuma type dec of traveling scholar, Japan, late 19th/ early 20th C **200.00**

LALIQUE

LALIQUE

R.LALIQUE

History: René Lalique (1860-1945) first gained prominence as a jewelry designer. Around 1900, he began experimenting with molded-glass brooches and pendants, often embellishing them with semiprecious stones. By 1905, he was devoting himself exclusively to the manufacture of glass articles.

In 1908, Lalique began designing packaging for the French cosmetic houses. He also produced many objects, especially vases, bowls, and figurines, in the Art Nouveau and Art Deco styles. The full scope of Lalique's genius was seen at the 1925 Paris l'Exposition Internationale des Arts Décorative et Industriels Modernes.

For more information, see *Warman's Glass*, 4th edition.

Marks: The mark "R. LALIQUE FRANCE" in block letters is found on pressed articles, tableware, vases, paperweights, and automobile mascots. The script signature, with or without "France," is found on hand-blown objects. Occasionally, a design number is included. The word "France" in any form indicates a piece made after 1926.

The post-1945 mark is generally "Lalique France" without the "R," but there are exceptions.

Reproduction Alert: The Lalique signature has often been forged; the most common fake includes an "R" with the post-1945 mark.

Animal, 3" h, toad, Gregoire, sitting, polished crystal, inscribed "Lalique France," 20th C, minor nicks to one leg **290.00**
Ashtray
Alice, clear and frosted, gray patina, c1924, molded "R.LALIQUE," stenciled "R. LALIQUE FRANCE" **535.00**
Martinique, deep amber, c1928, wheel-cut "R. LALIQUE FRANCE" **1,100.00**

Automobile hood ornament, Sainte-Christophe, clear and frosted, c1928, molded "R. LALIQUE FRANCE," **$1,150.** Photo courtesy of David Rago Auctions, Inc.

Automobile hood ornament
Coq Nain, clear and frosted, c1928, molded "R. LALIQUE FRANCE" **1,045.00**
Hirondelle, clear and frosted, c1928, molded "R. LALIQUE FRANCE" **1,955.00**
Sainte-Christophe, clear and frosted, c1928, molded "R. LALIQUE FRANCE" **1,150.00**
Bookends, pr, 5-1/2" l, 3-1/8" w, 8-3/4" h, kneeling nude female figures, press-molded, acid finished, polished colorless glass, paper label, late 20th C **635.00**

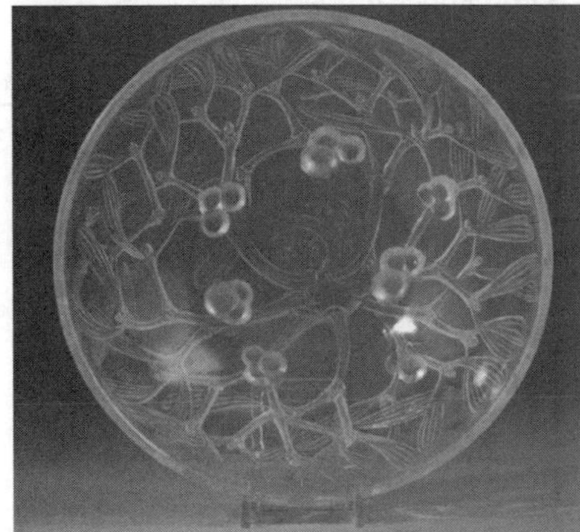

Bowl, Gui, opalescent, c1921, stenciled "R. LALIQUE FRANCE," **$520**. Photo courtesy of David Rago Auctions, Inc.

Box, cov
Cerises, red celluloid box, rare, c1923, molded "R. LALIQUE" **1,100.00**

Eglantines, clear and frosted glass, green patina, c1926, engraved "R. Lalique France" 750.00
Fontainebleau, clear and frosted glass, gray patina, c1921, molded "R. LALIQUE" 630.00
Mesanges, opalescent amber glass, c1921, molded "R.LALIQUE" 1,150.00

Bowl

Bulbes, opalescent, c1935, stenciled "R. LALIQUE FRANCE" 520.00
Fleurons, opalescent, c1935, stenciled "R. LALIQUE FRANCE" 630.00

Clock frame, Inseparables, clear and frosted, c1926, molded "R. LALIQUE" 750.00
Cocktail glass, William, clear and frosted, blue enameled details, c1925, engraved "R. Lalique France" 380.00
Decanter set, 11" h decanter with donut stopper, Highlands, four matching glasses, #13301 and #1333412 ... 800.00
Drawing, for jewelry design, drawn by Rene Lalique, c1898, ink and watercolor, BFK Rives parchment paper, 7-3/4" x 5-3/4", Pendentif Feuilles a Baies, swirl of leaves and berries, one berry with notation "Diamant" 5,350.00

Figure, cat, 9-1/4" l, $550. Photo courtesy of Joy Luke Auctions.

Figure, 10-1/4" h, Two Dancers, sgd in script, c1960 .... 1,475.00
Ice bucket, 8-7/8" h, cylindrical, press-molded dec of two nude dancing women with foliage background, acid finished and polished colorless glass, paper label, base inscribed "Lalique France," late 20th C 550.00

Jewelry, pendant

Muguet, lozenge-shape, opalescent glass, orig green silk cord, c1921, molded "R. LALIQUE" 1,100.00
Trefles, yellow glass, c1920, molded "LALIQUE" 575.00

Knife rest, Nippon, Art Deco, clear, set of six, stenciled "R. LALIQUE" 575.00

Letter seal

Hirondelles, clear and frosted, c1919, engraved "R. Lalique" 575.00

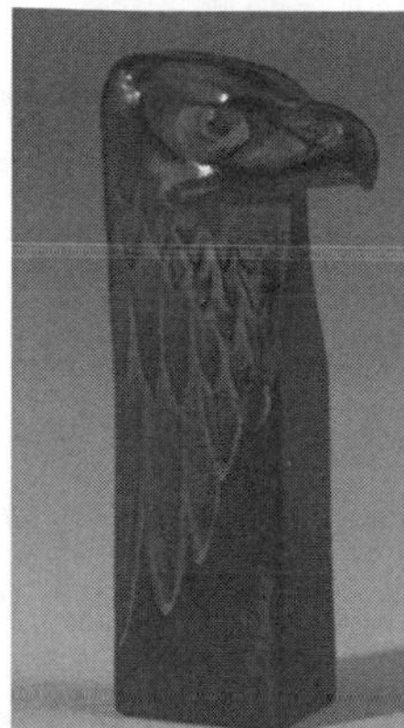

Letter seal, Tete D'Aigle, black, whitish patina, c1911, engraved "Lalique," $1,725. Photo courtesy of David Rago Auctions, Inc.

Lapin, topaz, c1925, engraved "R. Lalique France" 630.00
Tete D'Aigle, black, whitish patina, c1911, engraved "Lalique" 1,725.00
Victoire, clear and frosted, sepia patina, engraved with intaglio monogram YS, c1920, molded "LALIQUE" 1,380.00

Paperweight

Moineau Moqueur, clear and frosted, c1930, stenciled "R. LALIQUE" 435.00
Toby, clear and frosted, c1931, stenciled "R. LALIQUE FRANCE" 2,070.00

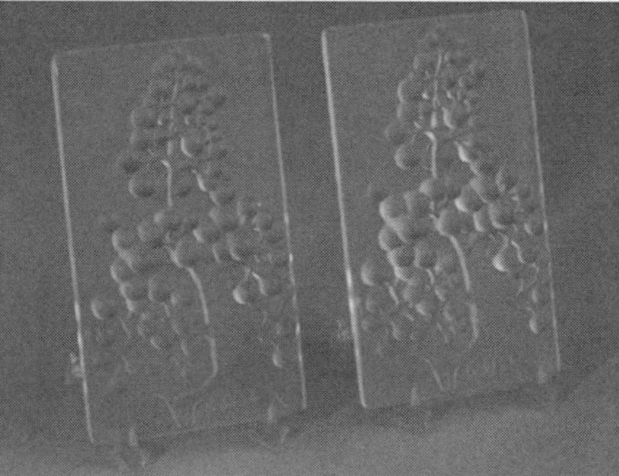

Menu plaques, pair, Raisin Muscat, clear and frosted, c1924, engraved "R. Lalique France No. 3475," $815. Photo courtesy of David Rago Auctions, Inc.

Paperweight, Moineau Moqueur, clear and frosted, c1930, stenciled "R. LALIQUE," $435. Photo courtesy of David Rago Auctions, Inc.

Perfume bottle, 3-7/8" h, finial of roses, roses and column on bottle, peach patina, engraved "R. Lalique France," M 719 .... 575.00
Plate, 7-1/4" d, black crystal, Algues, sgd "Catalogue Number 10421," price for set of eight 2,500.00
Powder box, cov, Le Lys, clear and frosted, sepia patina, for D'ORSAY, c1922, molded "R. LALIQUE FRANCE" 365.00
Retail sign, Lalique Cristallerie France, c1950 .... 920.00
Rocker blotter, Faune et Nymphe, clear and frosted, sepia patina, orig metal, c1920, molded "R. LALIQUE," engraved "France" 2,100.00

Vase

Avalon, clear and frosted, c1927, wheel-cut "R. LALIQUE FRANCE" 1,485.00
Grenade, deep amber, c1930, engraved "R. Lalique France" 1,840.00
Le Mans, amber, white patina, c1931, stenciled "R. LALIQUE FRANCE" 2,000.00
Rampillon, topaz, c1927, wheel-cut "R. LALIQUE FRANCE" 1,380.00
Violettes, clear and frosted, blue patina. c1921, engraved "R. Lalique" 1,485.00

Perfume, atomizer, Epines, clear and frosted, metal mount, c1920, stenciled "R. LALIQUE FRANCE," $230. Photo courtesy of David Rago Auctions, Inc.

Wine cooler, Epernay, clear and frosted, c1938, stenciled "R. LALIQUE FRANCE" 1,485.00
Wine rinse, Malaga, clear and frosted, designed 1937, this example c1950, engraved "Lalique France" 350.00

Lamp Shades

History: Lamp shades were made to diffuse the harsh light produced by early gas lighting fixtures. These early shades were made by popular Art Nouveau manufacturers including Durand, Quezal, Steuben, and Tiffany. Many shades are not marked.

For more information, see *Warman's Glass*, 4th edition.

Leaded glass shade, muted slag glass panels, red cherries, purple grapes, shaded apples and pears, green leaves, crown like top, **$250**. Photo courtesy of Dotta Auction Co., Inc.

Aladdin, satin, white, dogwood dec **65.00**

Cased art glass, 5" h, 2-1/4" d fitter, green and gold pulled feather dec, irid surface finish, unsigned, pr, one with rim chips at fitter, other with minor surface scratches **320.00**

Durand, 9-1/2" l, gold Egyptian crackle, blue and white overlay, bulbous, ruffed rim, sgd **225.00**

Fenton, 4" d, white opal hobnails, blue ground **90.00**

Fostoria, 5-1/2" d, Zipper pattern, green pulled dec, opal ground, gold lining **225.00**

Handel, 10" d, tam o'shanter, hand-painted green silhouette village scene with windmill and harbor, sgd "Handel 2862" **325.00**

Imperial, NuArt, marigold **65.00**

Leaded glass, 17-1/2" d, 3" d opening, narrow topped umbrella-shape, dropped apron, four bright red starburst blossoms with yellow disks on green stems, green slag background segments, conforming motif on apron, some restoration to inside leading **635.00**

Red fabric, beaded fringe, 10″ d, **$200**. Photo courtesy of Joy Luke Auctions.

Loetz, 8-1/2" d, irid green oil spotting, ribbon work, white glass int., c1900 .... **250.00**

Lustre Art, 4-1/2" h, lily, opal, descent gold pulled feathers, sgd "Lustre Art" **260.00**

Muller Freres, 6" h, frosted satin, white top, cobalt blue base, yellow highlights, three-pc set **400.00**

Pairpoint, 7" h, puffy, flower basket, reverse painted pink and yellow poppies and roses **425.00**

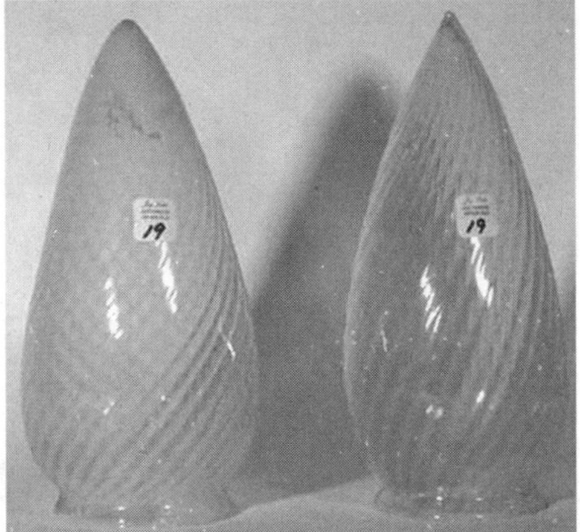

Vaseline glass, swirl, cone shaped, price for pair, **$350**. Photo courtesy of Joy Luke Auctions.

Quezal, 5-1/2" d, dark green, platinum feathers, gold lining **650.00**

Rubena, 7-1/4" d, 3-7/8" d fitter ring, cranberry shading to clear, frosted and clear etched flowers and leaves, ruffled **460.00**

Steuben, aurene, 4-1/4" h, 4-1/4" d, 2-1/4" fitter, irid gold, blue and purple highlights, fleur-de-lis mark **360.00**

Tiffany, attributed to, 6" h, translucent glass, green tipped irid gold pulled feather dec, early 20th C **560.00**

Lamps and Lighting

History: Lighting devices have evolved from simple stone-age oil lamps to the popular electrified models of today. Aimé Argand patented the first oil lamp in 1784. Around 1850, kerosene became a popular lamp-burning fluid, replacing whale oil and other fluids. In 1879, Thomas A. Edison invented the electric light, causing fluid lamps to lose favor and creating a new field for lamp manufacturers. Companies like Tiffany and Handel became skillful at manufacturing electric lamps, and their decorators produced beautiful bases and shades.

Reproduction Alert.

Astral

21-1/2" h, brass, heavy marble base, topped with frosted and cut shade with flowers and foliage surrounding waist, glass prisms at shade ring, some wear to finish, drilled to electrify **210.00**

22" h, finely cut period shade with scrolls and flowers, marble base with fire gilded finish, unusual foliage dec within remaining gilt, two different types of prisms around side, shade ring and burner adapted to fit lamp **660.00**

22-1/2" h, frosted glass shade with cut vintage designs, gilded brass reeded column, scrolled top, sq base, oval signature plate for "Cornelius & Co. Philadelphia" on font, prisms incomplete, light wear, base drilled for electricity, burner missing **880.00**

Astral, frosted clear leaded glass shade with vintage copper wheel engraved design, 12 hanging three-part cut glass prisms, cast gilt bronze baluster form column with waist-length portrait of George Washington on each side, floral scrollwork surround, surmounted by spread-winged eagle, mounted on stepped white marble base with bronze acanthus scroll dividers, attributed to Sandwich, wear to gilt, electrified, 28" h, **$975**. Photo courtesy of Cowan's Historic Americana Auctions.

Banquet

33" h, 4" d x 6-1/2" h cranberry to clear ruffled shade with ribbed swirls, cut glass with ruby highlights font, brass base with three raised nude figures of hunter with game and faces on handles, minor dent in bass, one ruffled chipped **360.00**

Boudoir

Aladdin, 14-1/2" h, 8" d, reverse painted bell shade, pine border, floral molded polychromed metal base.............. **225.00**

American, early 20th C, 18-1/2" h, reverse painted conical shade with house, bridge, and tree-filled landscape, orange ground, metal base with raised foliate and geometric motif, raised "F. M." and partially visible marks on base **290.00**

Handel, 14" h, 7" d, gilt-finished spelter base, reverse painted etched glass shade with umber harbor scene, orange sky, shade stamped "Handel 6450," Handel Lamps cloth tag on base, chips to patina.................................... **1,150.00**

Heintz Art Metal Shop, Buffalo, NY, 10-1/2" x 8", single socket, sterling on bronze, helmet shade, overlaid with geometric bands on orig bronzed patina, felted bottom, some scratches from chain **630.00**

Pairpoint, 16" h, 7" d reverse painted parrots against yellow shading to orange ground, ribbed ext. with slightly blown-out figures and perch, inside of shade sgd "THE PAIRPOINT CORP," sgd "PAIRPOINT" base, some bottom edge roughness to shade, wear and discoloration on base **900.00**

Pittsburgh Lamp, Brass & Co., 14" h, 7" d shade, reverse painted ribbed shade, winter landscape of black barren trees on snowy ground, blue shading to yellow and orange ground, metal base with raised foliage dec, raised "P.I.B. & Co." 2080" on base **635.00**

Chandelier, Victorian, basket form, gilt metal basket weave, crystals in interstices, large glass finial rising from center of basket, eight scrolling arms with acanthus leaf terminations, crystal swirl glass bobeches, four ascending scrolls ending in acanthus leaves and berries, crystal drops throughout, 24" h, 27" d, **$1,955.** Photo courtesy of Alderfer Auction Co.

Chandelier

Arts & Crafts, 27" h, 32" d six panel, red brass, replaced mica panels, three-light cluster, orig dark patina, period chain and ceiling cap......................... **2,300.00**

Empire-style, 31" l, 20th C, gilt metal and cut glass, six light, top with six outscrolled flat leaves hung with crystals, slender reeded standard with central cut glass orb, flat leaf ring supporting six short serpentine scrolled candle arms offset by pierced ribbon-tied laurel wreaths, strung throughout with crystal strands, end of standard with further crystals **1,100.00**

French, 32" w, hand wrought iron frame supporting four arms with lavender mottled art glass shades, matching central planfonier, c1925............. **850.00**

Morreau, 20" h, 20" d, gilt and emb iron frame suspending four leaded glass domed shades, central matching spherical shade, frame emb "The Morreau Co." **1,100.00**

Desk

Handel, Arts & Crafts style, hand-painted shade....................................... **1,495.00**

Steuben, 20" h, 7" d, bronze, adjustable, irid hammered glass shade, orig patina, shade sgd "Steuben" **860.00**

Student, 23-1/2" h, brass frame and adjustable arm, white glass shade, early 20th C.. **260.00**

Tiffany, 13-1/2" h, 7" d swirl dec irid green ribbed dome Damascene shade cased to white, marked "L.C.T" on rim, swivel-socket bronze harp frame, rubbed cushion platform, five ball feet, imp "Tiffany Studios New York 419" **3,740.00**

Early American

Betty lamp, 3-1/2" h wrought iron lamp, stamped "M," 4-1/4" h redware stand with incised wavy lines, minor rim chips **440.00**

Blown, colorless, 10" h, drop burners, pressed stepped base, chips on base, pr **385.00**

Cage lamp, 6" d, wrought iron, spherical, self righting gyroscope font, two repaired spout burners **500.00**

Candle holder, 19" h, wrought iron, hanging type, primitive twisted arms and conical socket **385.00**

Candle stand, 57-1/4" h, 24-1/2" w, wrought iron, double arms, brass candleholders and drip pans, attributed to PA, 18th C, pitting, losses to drip pans **8,100.00**

Dietz dainty, 12-1/2" h, brass, orig glass in doors, ring handles, slot for mounting bracket on either side, ruby glass inserts in backs, price for pr **225.00**

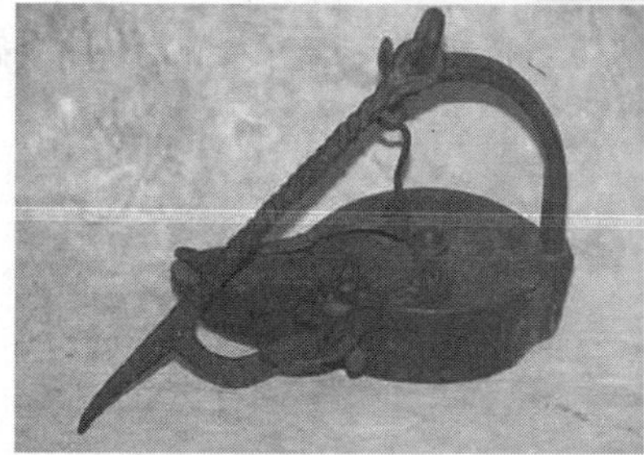

Early, Betty lamp, iron, hinged lid, chain, circular finial, iron hook with spiral twist dec, 4-1/4" l, 4" h, **$145.** Photo courtesy of Alderfer Auction Co.

Fluid

Pattern glass, 9-1/2" h, Moon and Star font, baluster stem, hexagonal base, brass collar, Sandwich **200.00**

Presentation, 14-1/2" h, attributed to Sandwich Glass, blown opaque white glass font with hand painted gold scrolling, tapered and fluted column, sq milk glass base, minor broken blister on base **250.00**

Vesuvius, 42" h, 10" d base, four burners complete with tools and emb cut-out reflector with butterflies design, entire lamp is emb with leaf and flower designs, silver colored finish, some wear and pitting to finish **300.00**

Grease, 7" h, tin, conical base, hollow stem, semicircular lidded font with wick support, scrolled finial, wick pick, hanging hole................................ **275.00**

Hour glass, 7" h, clear blown glass, pine and oak frame, whittled baluster posts, old brown finish, glued break in bottom plate.. **275.00**

Loom light, 14-3/4" h, wrought iron, candle socket, trammel **500.00**

Miner's lamp, 7-3/8" h, cast and wrought iron, chicken finial, replaced hanger **110.00**

Peg, 2" d, 4-1/2" l, overlay glass, pink cut to white cut to clear, frosted peg attached with clear wafer, brass collar **450.00**

Petticoat, 9" h, tin, round pan base, large ring handle applied to one side of column, small pick and chain attached to handle... **260.00**

Rush light holder

21" h, wrought iron, spring clamp, attached to wooden pole and base **275.00**

23-1/2" h, wrought iron, spring clamp, attached to wooden pole and base **470.00**

Skater's lamp, 6-3/4" h, brass, clear glass globe marked "Perko Wonder Junior," polished, small splint in top of brass cap **160.00**

Splint holder, 9-1/2" h, wrought iron, candle socket counter weight, tripod base, diamond-shaped feet......... **415.00**

Taper jack, 5" h, Sheffield silver on copper, old repairs **195.00**

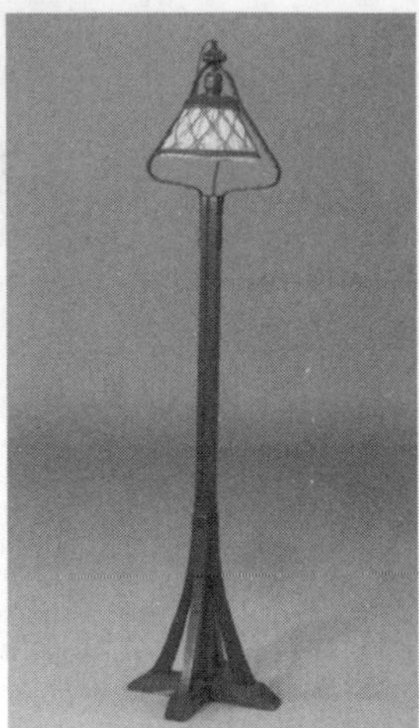

Floor, Gustav Stickley, mahogany, silk-lined wicker shade, wrought iron hardware, buttressed base, original finish, branded on bottom, drilled hole on side, some breaks in shade, socket shaft broken. 58" h, **$2,990**. Photo courtesy of David Rago Auctions, Inc.

Floor, wicker, curved watermelon-style shade, painted red, **$195**. Photo courtesy of Dotta Auction Co., Inc.

Floor

Bradley and Hubbard, 56" h, 7" d, small domed leaded glass shade, green slag glass, gold key border, open framework adjustable standard, domed circular foot **400.00**

Cameo glass, wrought metal, 64" h, 16" d Art Deco amber-colored cameo shade with cast in forms of oak leafs, acorns, birds resting atop three extending tree limbs, cast metal tree trunk stem base cov with climbing ivy, hand hammered domed foot, shade sgd "DAUM NANCY FRANCE"......... **9,200.00**

Faries Mfg. Co., Decatur, IL, 65-1/4" h, 12" d, bright chrome torchere, flaring trumpet shade, diecast mark **150.00**

Handel, 64" h, 24" d yellow and amber opalescent bent glass paneled shade with faux lead came, green diamond details, five-light, patinated copper columnar base, scrolling feet, marked "HANDEL" on base **9,780.00**

Rayo, 69" h, 26" d bent panel shade with caramel slag glass at top, green slag glass border, ruby border at crown and base, overlay metal design, heavy cast bottom with garland and acanthus leaves, kerosene font sgd "RAYO," minor wear to shade........................... **1,850.00**

Tiffany/Aladdin, 50" h, 10" d spun bronze shade, reflective white int., marked "Tiffany Studios New York," adjustable bridge lamp base with Arabian Nights motif, orig dark bronze patina, elaborate platform base, stamped "Tiffany Studios New York 576" **2,990.00**

Unknown maker, Brass, 56-1/4" h, brass, hammered surfaces, electric sockets above oval rosettes, reeded columns, curved legs, quatrefoil bases, base stamped "L.C.T. NY 810," price for pr **750.00**

Hanging

American, 19th C, 18" h, patinated metal and cut glass, hall type, candle socket, Gothic arches, diamonds and flowerheads dec........................ **1,380.00**

Arts and Crafts, 17" drop, 22-1/2" d, four massive iron cross bars, hand hammered and bronzed surface, support chocolate slag glass shades with brass fleur-de-lis guards, electrified **950.00**

Handel, 10" d, hall type, spherical form, acid cut, translucent white, brown, vase and foliate dec, ornate orig hardware **4,200.00**

Morgan, John, and Sons, NY, attributed to, 39-1/2" h drop, 25-1/4" d, 11-1/2" h leaded shade, verdigris bronze leaves surrounding ceiling hook suspending four chains supporting six-socket domed shade, similar bronze leaf dec, dropped apron, shade with striated green, amber, and white slag glass segments, round transparent purple "jewels" form grape-type clusters, few cracked segments **6,325.00**

Perzel, 40-1/4" d, chrome, metal, and glass.. **1,225.00**

Tiffany, 18" l, 15" d, attributed to Tiffany Glass and Decorating Co., late 19th C, square green and opalescent diamond-shaped glass jewels arranged as central pendant chandelier drop, twisted wire frame **2,990.00**

Unknown maker, 22" l, 9-3/4" d, cast iron, open work fixture with fleur-de-lys, three graduated levels of faceted prisms, electrified with reflective surface above light socket **315.00**

Victorian, 28" h, 8" d ribbed ruby glass globe in brass frame, six vertical brass bands on lower half of shade sport four multi-colored jewels each, electrified **1,700.00**

Hanging, opaline glass shade dec with applied cranberry glass prunts, **$200**. Photo courtesy of Joy Luke Auctions.

Piano

Handel

17" l, gilt leaded lavender and opalescent yellow leaded shade suspended from bronze base, scrolled arm, unmarked, attributed to, c1915 .... **750.00**

Tiffany, 6-3/4" h, 19" l tripartite gold amber glass turtleback shade, framed in bronze, three center gold irid turtleback tiles, single-socket swiveling "dog leg" shaft, shade and weighted base imp "Tiffany Studios New York" **4,025.00**

Student

Handel, 20" h, 7" d shades, double, bronze finish, two high sweeping arms that support contemporary damascene replacement shades, base sgd on bottom with cloth tag "HANDEL LAMPS," some minor blistering to finish of base **1,440.00**

Table

American, early 20th C, 19-1/4" h, 15-1/2" d, 20 radiating caramel and white slag glass panels on domed shade, medial geometric green glass border, alternating green and caramel slag glass border, undulating dropped apron, two-socket fixture, ribbed trefoil base with brown/green patina, minor corrosion, some cracked segments........................ **920.00**

Table, figural, spelter, female figure holding lyre and basket of flowers, etched glass shade, **$75**. Photo courtesy of Joy Luke Auctions.

Arts & Crafts, 22" h, 18" d leaded glass shade of variegated caramel and green panels, bronzed base with hammered design **980.00**

Bigelow Kennard, Boston, 26" h, 18" d domed leaded shade, opalescent white segments in geometric progression border, brilliant green leaf forms repeating motif, edge imp "Bigelow Kennard Boston/Bigelow Studios," three socket over Oriental-style bronze base cast with foo dog handles, Japonesque devices **2,875.00**

Table, figural, ceramic, woman in gold drape, multicolored flowers, three floral gilt sockets, Italian, 30" h, price for pair, **$375**. Photo courtesy of Wiederseim Associates, Inc.

Boston Glass Works, early 20th C, 22" h, 18-1/2" d bent panel slag glass shade, floral and foliate overlay, bronze patina over six radiating striated caramel and white bent slag glass panels, two-socket fixture with similar illuminated base, minor patina wear, few dents **750.00**

Bradley & Hubbard, Meriden, CT, early 20th C, 29" h, 20" d 10-panel shade with extensive metal overlay work of flower baskets and garlands, caramel slag glass background, cast base with new four-socket cluster, finish wear **1,380.00**

Degue, 7-3/4" x 4", French bronzed metal base, cobalt blue, orange, and yellow shade set within hammered rose blossom and leaves mount, shade sgd "Degue," orig patina **1,100.00**

Duffner & Kimberly, New York, 21" h, 16" d leaded glass Roman pattern shade with rich greens, browns, and ambers florals, bronze colored base with four paw feet, pad double step base **8,100.00**

Durand, 29-1/2" h, brass, blue glass standard, opaque white and clear feather pattern **300.00**

Table, Bigelow and Kennard, leaded glass shade, gothic geometric pattern in white and light green slag glass, three-socket bronze-patinated base, unmarked, 21-1/2" h, 16" d, **$4,025**. Photo courtesy of David Rago Auctions, Inc.

Handel, Meriden, CT, early 20th

- 18" h, reverse painted lakeside scene with trees, orig bronzed base **7,700.00**
- 21-1/2" h, 17-3/4" d, leaded shade of green slag ground glass, irregular border of orange and red flowers, green leaves and stems, sgd "HANDEL" base emb at foot and narrow stem, three-socket cluster, fitter rim replaced **1,400.00**
- 22-1/2" h, 18" d obverse dec shade, browns and greens, oak leaves and acorns against beige chipped ice ground, inside of shade sgd "HANDEL," shade ring sgd "HANDEL PAT'D NO. 979664," slender base with three socket cluster, acorn pulls, some minor roughness to shade edge, wear to base finish **3,335.00**
- 23-1/2" h, 18" d reverse painted shade, orange background with scenic view of trees, water, fields, and birds in sky, metal shade ring sgd "HANDEL LAMPS PAT'D NO. 979664," also numbered "HANDEL 7104," bulbous Handel base with three-socket cluster, some wear to finish, rewired **5,100.00**
- 24" h, 18" d reverse painted shade with full moon, cloud streaking across front, scenic view of woods and fields around body of water, int. sgd "7107 HANDEL COM," textured and painted base with double sockets and acorn pulls **5,750.00**

Table, Handel, Meriden, CT, early 20th C, cylindrical textured Teroma shade with stylized border painted brown, signed "HANDEL 7766 1/2," rectangular metal base with scroll motif at posts, brown patina, 11" h, 15-1/2" l, **$1,880**. Photo courtesy of Skinner, Inc.

Heintz, 11" x 8", single socket, sterling on bronze, goldenrod overlay on verdigris-patinated ground, small dent in shade **815.00**

Jefferson, 17" h, 12" d, reverse painted scenic shade with winter scene on textured satin shade, brass candlestick base, unsigned, c1915 .... **460.00**

La Verre Francais, 19" h, cased glass, frosted ext. over swirled orange, yellow, and cobalt blue, sgd on both shade and base, electrified, replaced shade holder **1,350.00**

Moe Bridges, 22-1/2" h, 18" d reverse painted shade depicts scenic view of trees, water, and hill, edge of shade sgd "MOE BRIDGES-CO-18-2," also sgd on inside with artist's initials "H. H.," copper-colored base with double sockets, green enamel highlights to imp designs **3,500.00**

Muller Frères, 19-1/4" h, 9-1/2" d round, paneled, etched colorless glass shade with rosette and geometric skyscraper influenced design, wrought iron base, shade sgd "Muller Frères Luneville," France, c1930, several minute rim nicks **1,100.00**

Pairpoint

- 22" h, 13" d open top puffy shade on 10" d ring, well-painted red roses on green ground, yellow buds and leaves, well painted, rim marked "PAT. APPLIED FOR," tree trunk base sgd "PAIRPOINT MFG. CO. 3091" plus "P" in diamond mark, chips, very worn patina **2,650.00**
- 22" h, 18" d reverse painted scene of castles, fields, trees and rivers, people in foreground, shade is sgd

"THE PAIRPOINT CORP'N," sgd "PAIRPOINT" base, minor wear to base finish **4,025.00**

Table, Handel, Meriden, CT, early 20th C, faceted shade, each panel pierced with repeated tropical landscape against polychromatic slag glass, faceted three-socket base with original bronzed patina, base and shade stamped "HANDEL," 25" h, 20" d, **$6,275.** Photo courtesy of David Rago Auctions, Inc.

Pittsburgh Lamp, Brass and Glass Co., Pittsburgh**,** 19-1/2" x 14", bell-shape "hammered" glass shade, reverse-painted with red poppies and green leaves on shaded yellow ground, urn-shaped bronzed base with single socket, base marked PLB&G Co./2049, few rim chips on shade, some wear to patina on base **575.00**

Suess Ornamental Glass Co., Chicago, 23" h, 22" d leaded glass shade with stylized yellow, orange, green, and white slag flowers and leaves, brass-washed base, unmarked **5,350.00**

Tattorino, figural, alabaster, snake charmer, sgd "Prof. E. Tattorino" **1,925.00**

Tiffany Studios, 22-1/2" h, 16" d dome shade, layered and striated leaded glass segments designed as tulip blossoms and leaves, red, orange, amber, blue, and green, metal rim tag imp "Tiffany Studios New York 1456," three-socket bronze base with three pronged crutch supporting oval shaft, sq base with mottled brown and green patina, round disk on base imp "Tiffany Studios New York 444" **32,220.00**

Unknown maker, figural

15-1/2" h, 5-3/4" sq base, woman playing croquet, open tree trunk match holder, two emb cigar holders attached to lamp stem, hammered brass dome shade set with multi-colored faceted glass jewels, glass bead fringe, Victorian, some wear **980.00**

Table, Pittsburgh Lamp Co., Pittsburgh, PA, 1890-1930, large domical reverse-painted "Call of the Wild" shade with partial paper label, unsigned owl base, 22" h, 18" d, **$2,820.** Photo courtesy of Skinner, Inc.

20" h, cold metal base shaped as peacock's body, glass cabochons as eye accents on enameled dec plumage, 9" d chipped ice shade dec with enameled feathers **9,900.00**

Unknown maker, leaded

22" h, 18" d shade with translucent green ground panels, irregular border of pink flowers and green leaves, base with slender stem, dished foot, three-socket cluster, acorn pulls, unsigned, heat cap soldered to shade **4,025.00**

28" h, 20" d shade with caramel colored ground, green stylized oak leaves, green and purple acorns, brass base with acanthus leaves at top and foot, four-socket cluster, unsigned, several panels cracked but all intact, some wear to base finish **2,185.00**

Van Erp, Dirk, 17-1/2" h, 13" d, hammered copper classical base, four paneled mica shade with vented cap, single socket, fine orig patina and mica, open box mark/San Francisco .. **9,200.00**

Wilkinson, 18-1/2" d leaded shade, water lily and cattail design, several hairlines **3,000.00**

LANTERNS

History: A lantern is an enclosed, portable light source, hand carried or attached to a bracket or pole to illuminate an area. Many lanterns have a protected flame and can be used both indoors and outdoors. Light-producing materials used in early lanterns included candles, kerosene, whale oil, and coal oil, and, later, gasoline, natural gas, and batteries.

Barn, 14" h, dark red repaint, visible hand plane marks on top and bottom, old wavy glass with horizontal cracks in two panes, circular vent in top, arched tin shield, replaced turn buckle, door pane has later putty along edges **385.00**

Brass, cast, Arts & Crafts, faceted, rustic branch pattern, original white frosted seedy glass panels, original patina, original chains, replaced ceiling plate unmarked, 7" w, 9-1/2" h, price for pair, **$630.** Photo courtesy of David Rago Auctions.

Campaign torch, 56" h, tin font, brass top, old cloth wick, "U"-shaped bracket mounted to wooden pole **55.00**

Candle, 10-1/4" w, 9-3/4" l, 16-1/2" h, old red painted pine, rect, pierced top, bentwood handle, four sides with three rect glazed and pierced panels, door with leather hinges opening to candle socket, New England, 19th C, door appears to be replacement, imperfections **2,415.00**

Dark room, 17" h, orig black paint, white striping, tin kerosene font and burner "Carbutt's Dry Plate lantern, PA April 25th 1882" label **75.00**

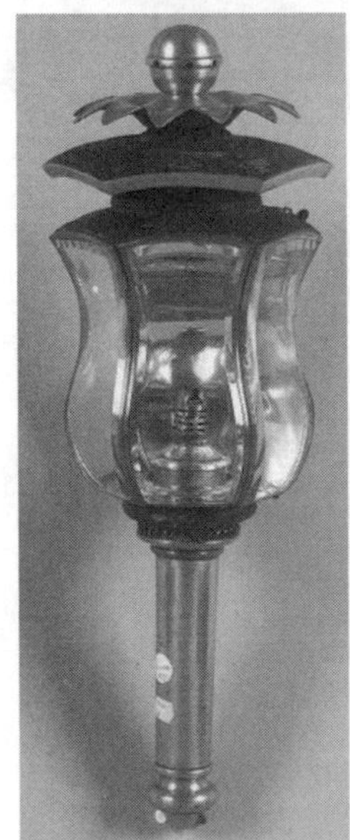

Coach, E. Miller & Co., America, late 19th/20th C, kerosene, hourglass-shaped beveled glass walls, black painted sheet iron components with nickel-plated brass trim, maker's mark on burner, wear, 22-3/4" h, **$450.** Photo courtesy of Skinner, Inc.

Folding, 10" h, tin, glass sides, emb "Stonebridge 1908" **75.00**

Globe, 17-1/2" h, fixed pear-shaped globe, pierced tin frame, ring handle, traces of black paint, America, mid-19th C **215.00**

Hanging

10" x 6", Handel, faceted, pierced top, trellis panels, red flower wreaths, green and caramel slag glass, single socket, faceted sq plates, unmarked, pr **2,615.00**

37 h, emb brass-finished metal font, conical black shade, glass chimney, enameled black hanging armature **175.00**

Japanese, Patterson Bros., Lansing, MI, adv, panes with General U. S. Grant, puppies, young girl, and wilderness scene **195.00**

Jeweled, 11-1/2" h, sheet brass, punched designs radiating out from faceted blue, red, green, and pale gold glass jewels, bottom marked "NH Car Trimming Co. New Haven, Conn," ring hanger **250.00**

Miner, 9-3/4" h, heavy duty iron and brass, threaded brass font and hasp, iron top with brass label "Thomas & Williams, Cambria Type...Aberdare," minor dents **115.00**

Nautical, 23" h, 11" d, masthead, copper and brass, oil fired, orig burner, label reads "Ellerman, Wilson Line, Hull," mid-19th C **265.00**

Hanging, Bradley and Hubbard, Meriden, CT, c1910, pagoda style, octagonal paneled metal roof over eight caramel slag glass panels with metal overlay, B&H mark, 8" d, 18" l lantern, drop including ceiling plate 30" l, **$1,300**. Photo courtesy of Skinner, Inc.

Painted tin, 15-3/4" l, 12" d, 19-3/4" h, triangular black painted tin frame with glass panels, int. mirror paneled reflector, small tin kerosene lamp, glass chimney, America, late 19th C, seam separations **175.00**

Punched tin, 14" h, three protruding glass panes, single candle socket, conical top, ring handle, thick layer of later black paint, electrified **220.00**

Railroad, Pennsylvania Railroad, 5" h red globe, marked "Keystone Lantern Co., Philadelphia," wire ring base **445.00**

Skater, 13-1/2" h, cast iron, lacy base, bulbous clear globe, pierced tin top and wire bail handle **245.00**

Station, 18" h, Dietz No. 1, glass panel door, enameled black, orig oil font and chimney **265.00**

Wood, 9-1/2" h, pine, old black over red paint, four sides glass, candle access from top, socket pulled by wire bale handle **690.00**

LEEDS CHINA

LEEDS POTTERY
LEEDS ✱ POTTERY

History: The Leeds Pottery in Yorkshire, England, began production about 1758. Among its products was creamware that was competitive with that of Wedgwood. The original factory closed in 1820, but various subsequent owners continued until 1880. They made exceptional cream-colored wares, either plain, salt glazed, or painted with colored enamels, and glazed and unglazed redware.

Marks: Early wares are unmarked. Later pieces are marked "Leeds Pottery," sometimes followed by "Hartley-Green and Co." or the letters "LP."

Reproduction Alert: Reproductions have the same marks as the antique pieces.

Miniature, dinner service, early 19th C, blue and yellow floral and green vine decoration on cream reserve, 25 3-1/4" d plates, five soup bowls, 10 lunch plates, four 4" to 5-1/4" l platters, three open vegetables, covered vegetable, two tureens, undertray, ladle, **$5,750**. Photo courtesy of Pook & Pook.

Bowl, 8" d, 3-1/4" h, blue and white Oriental design, wear, light stains, flakes on table ring **275.00**

Charger, 14-3/8" d, yellow urn with double handles and brown swag design holds cobalt blue, brown, and yellow flowers, green foliage, blue line detail surrounding dec, scalloped blue father edge, in-the-making separation along inner edge, minor glaze flakes **1,870.00**

Chop plate, 11-1/4" d, blue and yellow brown polychrome flowers, green foliage, white ground, blue scalloped feather edge, wear, old chip beneath rim **825.00**

Creamer, yellow, brown, and green tulip, umber and green sprig design on sides, dark brown stripe on rim and applied handle, flakes on table ring **800.00**

Cup and saucer, handleless, Brown rim stripes, blue, green, shades of gold, and yellow floral swag, flakes, chips on saucer table ring, stains on cup **170.00**

Cup plate

4" d, orange, gold, and blue peafowl, brown and green tree branch, brown feather edge, minor edge wear **990.00**

4-1/4" d, scalloped, blue feather edge, molded fish scales **850.00**

4-3/8" d, brown eagle, blue and green American shield, green branch, scalloped, blue feather edge, small flake under rim **1,980.00**

Pitcher, trailing orange, blue and green floral vines, 5-1/4" h, **$1,035**. Photo courtesy of Pook & Pook.

Dish, 5-3/4" l, leaf form, green feathered edge, imp "Rogers" **225.00**

Egg cup, 2-3/4", creamware, reticulated **150.00**

Miniature

Cup and saucer, handleless, pearlware, gold flower, green and brown leaves **275.00**

Teapot, cov, 4" h, yellow bands with green, orange, blue, and brown sprigs, flakes **450.00**

Mug, 5" h, multicolored polychrome floral dec **250.00**

Plate, green scalloped edge, blue and yellow flowers, brown and green leaves, 8-3/4" d, **$575**. Photo courtesy of Pook & Pook.

Pepper pot, 4-1/2" h, green feathered edge, roughness, loss on rim and near holes **200.00**
Plate, 8" d, blue scalloped edge, American eagle dec **450.00**
Platter, 9-1/4" x 12", green edge with molded leaves and fish scales, gold, brown, blue, and sage green Gaudy floral center, glued repair **550.00**
Sauce boat, underplate, 7-1/2" l, 3-3/4" h, 6-1/2" x 5-1/4" underplate, green feathered edge, small crack on base, minor edge roughness **335.00**
Sugar, cov, 4-1/2" d, 4-1/2" h, blue vine, green leaves accented by brown and gold, flake and short hairline **175.00**
Teapot
- 3-1/2" h, hand-painted portrait of Prince and Princess of Orange, ribbed, intertwined handle, some damage, no lid **275.00**
- 6-1/2" h, brown stripes, blue and yellow figure "8" flowers, green leaves, small edge chips **250.00**

Tureen, cov, 8-1/2" h, cov with pierced rim, melon finial, enamel dec, feather edge trim, floral sprays and wreaths, urn designs, late 18th C, slight edge nicks and enamel flaking **980.00**
Waste bowl, 5-1/4" d, 2-1/2" h, gold and green leaves, blue sprigs, hairlines **150.00**

Lefton China

History: China, porcelain, and ceramic with that now familiar "Lefton" mark has been around since the early 1940s and is highly sought by collectors in the secondary marketplace today. George Zoltan Lefton, a Hungarian immigrant who arrived in the United States in 1939, founded the company. In the 1930s, he was a sportswear designer and manufacturer, but his hobby of collecting fine china and porcelain led him to a new business venture.

After the bombing of Pearl Harbor in 1941, Lefton aided a Japanese-American friend by helping him to protect his property from anti-Japanese groups. As a result, Lefton came in contact with and began marketing pieces from a Japanese factory owned by Kowa Toki KK. At this time, he embarked on a new career and began shaping a business that sprang from his passion for collecting fine china and porcelains. Though his funds were very limited, his vision was to develop a source from which to obtain fine porcelains by reviving the postwar Japanese ceramic industry, which dated back to antiquity. As a trailblazer, George Zoltan Lefton soon earned the reputation of "The China King."

Figurines and animals, plus many of the whimsical pieces such as the Bluebirds, Dainty Miss, Miss Priss, Angels, Cabbage Cutie, Elf Head, Mr. Toodles, and the Dutch Girl, are popular with collectors. Collectors eagerly acquire all types of dinnerware and tea-related items. As is true with any antique or collectibles, prices vary, depending on location, condition, and availability.

Marks: Until 1980, wares from the Japanese factory include a "KW."

Anniversary ware, 25th teapot, **$15**; 50th plate, **$10**; 35th cup and saucer, **$12**; 25th ewer, **$12**. Photos courtesy of Joy Luke Auctions.

Animal
- 8-1/2", tiger, black, white with gold **65.00**
- 10", koala bear with club **180.00**

Bank, 7-1/4" h, Kewpie, orig foil label "Lefton Exclusives, Japan," stamped "145" **145.00**
Cake plate, 10" d, server, Hollyberry **45.00**
Coffee set, 8-1/2" h coffeepot, creamer, cov sugar, 4" d coffee cups, 8" d scalloped plates, green and white background, deep pink roses, ornate gilt trim, price for 13-pc set **200.00**
Compote, 8-3/16" d, 3" h, Americana pattern, green mark "940" **125.00**
Cookie jar, cov
- Holly, white, No. 6054 .... **115.00**
- Lady with scarf, 7-1/4" h, pastels, marked "Geo. Z. Lefton, 1957, 040" **325.00**

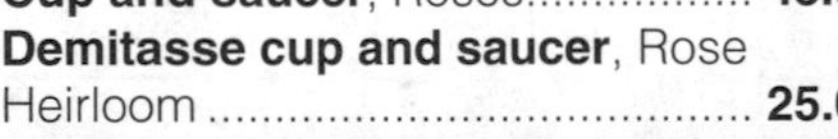

Cup and saucer, Roses **45.00**
Demitasse cup and saucer, Rose Heirloom **25.00**

Plaque, basketweave border and center, rose, yellow, purple, and blue flowers, green leaves, **$6.50**.

Figure
- Flamingo mother watching young, wings wide spread, marked "Lefton's, Occupied Japan" **165.00**
- Rock A Bye Baby in the Treetop, 8" h **100.00**
- Siamese Dancers, pr, 6-1/2" h **120.00**

Head vase, 7" h, Kewpie, orig foil label "Lefton Exclusives, Japan," stamped "3631" **135.00**
Miniature lamp, 3-5/8" d, 7-3/4" h, hp red flowers, green leaves, white ground, three gold dec feet, glass chimney with scalloped top, frosting on lower third, orig wick **15.00**
Mug
- Hollyberry, 4" **10.00**
- Poinsettia, white ground **15.00**

Planter
- Angel, on cloud, with stones **40.00**
- Calico Donkey, 5-1/2" **32.00**

Plate, 9" d, Magnolia **28.00**
Salt and pepper shakers, pr
- Fruit Basket, 2-3/4" **24.00**
- Rustic Daisy, 6-3/4" **24.00**

Teapots, stacking creamers and sugars, decorated with pink flowers, left: roses and gold trim, right: Chintz-type pattern, **$175**.

Sugar, cov, Rose Chintz **175.00**
Tea cup and saucer, ftd, Elegant Rose **45.00**
Teapot
- Grape Line **85.00**
- Honey Bee **125.00**

Wall plaque, boy and girl, oval, bisque, pr **90.00**

Lenox China

History: In 1889, Jonathan Cox and Walter Scott Lenox established The Ceramic Art Co. at Trenton, New Jersey. By 1906, Lenox formed his own company, Lenox, Inc. Using potters lured from Belleek, Lenox began making an American version of the famous Irish ware. The firm is still in business.

Marks: Older Lenox china has one of two marks: a green wreath or a palette. The palette mark appears on blanks supplied to amateurs who hand painted china as a hobby. The Lenox company currently uses a gold stamped mark.

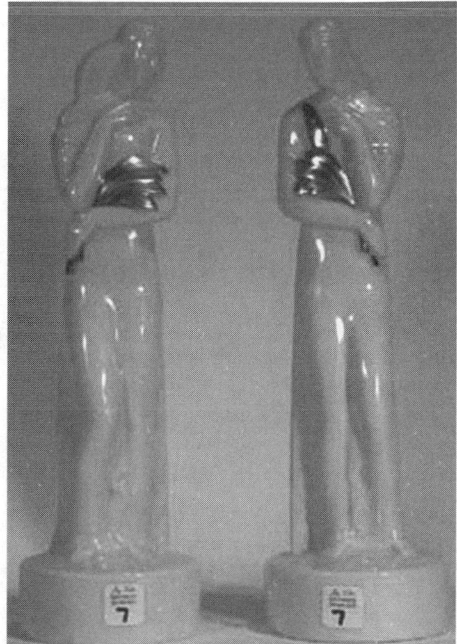

Figures, female, white, gilded flowers, pair, 12" h, **$50**. Photo courtesy of Joy Luke Auctions.

Bouillon cup and saucer, Detroit Yacht Club, palette mark **85.00**
Coffee set, Rhodora pattern, 8-1/8" h coffeepot, creamer, sugar, 17-1/2" l platter **675.00**
Cream soup, Tuxedo, green mark **40.00**
Cup and saucer, Alden **25.00**
Demitasse cups and saucers, 2-5/8" h, Lenox porcelain liners with turquoise jewels on gilt enamel rim, sterling frame with pierced rocaille flower and scroll rim and foot, scrolled handle, similarly styled sterling saucers, sterling marked "Redlich & Co.," late 19th/early 20th C, set of 12, approx. 36 troy oz **1,200.00**
Fish plates, 9-1/8" d, hand painted in pale gray and green depicting various specimens, gilt rims, eleven signed W. H. Marley, made for Tiffany & Co., early 20th C, price for 12 pc set................. **1,300.00**
Jug, 4" h, hp, grapes and leaves, shaded brown ground, sgd "G. Morley" **250.00**
Mug, 6-1/4" h, monk, smiling, holding up glass of whine, shaded brown ground, SS rim.. **160.00**
Perfume lamp, 9" h, figural, Marie Antoinette, bisque finish, dated 1929 .... **650.00**
Salt, 3" d, creamy ivory ground, molded seashells and coral, green wreath mark **35.00**
Shoe, white, bow trim................... **190.00**

Vase, ovoid vase, attributed to William Morley, pre-1932, large pink tea roses, green Lenox stamp, 8" d, 18-3/4" h, **$2,400**.

Tea set, cov teapot, creamer, cov sugar, Hawthorne pattern, silver overlay **225.00**
Tea strainer, hp, small pink roses **70.00**
Vase, 14-3/4" x 9", bulbous, painted by George Morley, pink and white roses, artist sgd, green CAC Lenox stamp, small rim scratch................................. **1,485.00**

Libbey Glass

1896–1906

History: Edward Libbey established the Libbey Glass Company in Toledo, Ohio, in 1888 after the New England Glass Works of W. L. Libbey and Son closed in East Cambridge, Massachusetts. The new Libbey company produced quality cut glass, which today is considered to belong to the brilliant period.

In 1930, Libbey's interest in art-glass production was renewed, and A. Douglas Nash was employed as a designer in 1931.

For more information, see *Warman's Glass*, 4th edition.

Cream pitcher, peachblow, made by Mount Washington Glass Company and sold by Libbey at 1893 Chicago World's Fair — The Columbian Exposition, minor loss to gold signature, 2-5/8" h, **$585**. Photo courtesy of Clarence and Betty Maier.

Art glass

Basket, 5" d base, 13-1/2" h, amberina, shape #3033, fold-in mouth, optic panels, arching handle, 1917, sgd "Amberina Libbey" in circle......................... **2,950.00**
Bud vase, 12" h, amberina, shape 3004, c1917, sgd in polished pontil **1,400.00**
Celery vase
6-1/2" h, Maize, white ground, gold tipped forest-green husks, small rim flake.. **265.00**
6-5/8" h, Maize, clear, slight gold irid to leaves **185.00**
Cologne bottle, 8-3/4" h, 4" l orig dauber, #3041, amberina, quadrate-form top, deep fuchsia shading to pale pink at shoulders shading to pale yellow base, dauber with airtrap, 1917 .... **2,500.00**
Compote, 10-1/2" w, 4" h, colorless, pink Nailsea-type loops, flaring top, sgd "Libbey" **595.00**
Creamer and sugar, 5-3/8" h creamer, 3-1/2" h, 4-3/4" d sugar, crystal, blue-green opaque dot trim, dark blue-green glass feet, polished pontil **475.00**
Jack in the pulpit vase, 16" h, amberina, #3000, 1917, deep fuchsia top shades to honey amber bulbous base **2,450.00**
Spooner, Maize, orig paint, slight rim roughness...................................... **65.00**
Vase, 4-1/4" h, ftd, red, vertical blue-gray dots form lines, swirled vertical ribs, unfinished pontil **775.00**

Cut glass

Banana boat, 13" x 7" x 7", scalloped pedestal base, 24-point hobstar, hobstar, cane, vesica, and fan motifs, sgd **1,500.00**
Bowl, 8" d, 4" h, three brilliant cut thistles surround bowl, flower in center, scalloped edge, etched "Libbey" label, price for pr **400.00**

Dish, shallow, opaque white, Santa Maria, pale blue sky, blue sky, blue sea, sold by Libbey as souvenir of 1893 Colombia Exposition, **$635**. Photo courtesy of Clarence and Betty Maier.

Candy dish, cov, 7", divided, clover shape, hobstar and prism, sgd...... **90.00**
Charger, 14" d, hobstar, cane, and wreath motifs, sgd........................ **300.00**
Miniature lamp, 2" sq base, 10-3/8" h, pinwheel design, sgd.................. **425.00**
Tumble-up, star burst, hobstar, fern, and fan motifs, minor handle check **725.00**
Vase, 18" h, No. 982, Senora pattern, cut glass, ftd, hexed vesicas, deep miter cuts, three 24-point hobstars at top between crossed miter cuts, small stars and trellises, clear knob and stem, scalloped foot cut with extended single star, Libbey over saber mark, c1896-1906, some flaws...................... **2,500.00**
Wine, Harvard pattern, faceted cut knob stems, sgd, 12-pc set.................. **350.00**

Limoges

History: Limoges porcelain has been produced in Limoges, France, for more than a century by numerous factories, in addition to the famed Haviland.

Marks: One of the most frequently encountered marks is "T. & V. Limoges," on the wares made by Tressman and Vought. Other identifiable Limoges marks are "A. L." (A. Lanternier), "J. P. L." (J. Pouyat, Limoges), "M. R." (M. Reddon), "Elite," and "Coronet."

Berry set, 9-1/2" d, master bowl, eight 8" serving bowls, hp, purple berries on ext. white blossoms on int., marked "T & V" **265.00**
Bowl, 4-1/2" h, ftd, hp, wild roses and leaves, sgd "J. E. Dodge, 1892" **85.00**
Box, cov, 4-1/4" sq, cobalt blue and white ground, cupids on lid, pate-sur-pate dec **195.00**
Cache pot, 7-1/2" w, 9" h, male and female pheasants on front, mountain scene on obverse, gold handles and four ball feet....................................... **225.00**

Condensed milk container, currants and foliage decoration in naturalistic colors, gold trim handle, **$165**. Photo courtesy of Dotta Auction Co., Inc.

Cake plate, 11-1/2" d, ivory ground, brushed gold scalloped rim, gold medallion, marked "Limoges T & V" **75.00**
Candy dish, 6-1/2" d, ftd, two handles, silver overlay, white ground, c1920 .... **95.00**
Chocolate pot, 13" h, purple violets and green leaves, cream-colored ground, gold handle, spout, and base, sgd "Kelly JPL/France"................................. **350.00**
Creamer and sugar, cov, 3-1/4" h, purple flowers, white ground, gold handle and trim **100.00**

Creamer and cracker jar, both decorated with roses and gold trim, creamer with blue shaded ground, cracker jar with dark green background, **$200**. Photo courtesy of Joy Luke Auctions.

Cup and saucer, hp, roses, gold trim, artist sgd **75.00**
Dessert plates, 8-1/4" d, Laviolette, gilt scalloped rim, printed green husk trim, center violet and grape sprays, retailed by Lewis Straus & Sons, New York, late 19th/early 20th C, price for 12-pc set **220.00**
Dinner plate, 10-1/2" d, border of gilt stylized chrysanthemums and flower buds, gilt rim, retailed by R. Briggs Co., Boston, early 20th C, price for set of 12 .... **250.00**
Dresser set, pink flowers, pastel blue, green, and yellow ground, large tray, cov powder, cov rouge, pin tray, talc jar, pr candlesticks, seven-pc set........... **425.00**
Figure, 25" h, 13" w, three girls, arms entwined, holding basket of flowers, books, and purse, marked "C & V" and "L & L".. **460.00**
Game plates, 9-5/8" d, each hand painted with a game bird in flight, signed L. Labania, gilt scrolled rim, early 20th C, set of 12....................................... **715.00**
Hair receiver, blue flowers and white butterflies, ivory ground, gold trim, marked "JPL"................................ **80.00**

Plaque, pate-sur-pate, oval, classical lady with harp, blue ground, signed with initials "CP" and "Limoges" lower right, early 20th C, unframed, 10-5/8" l, **$300**. Photo courtesy of Skinner, Inc.

Lemonade pitcher, matching tray, water lily dec, sgd "Vignard Limoges" **350.00**
Mortar and pestle, 3-1/4" x 2" mortar, 3-1/2" l pestle, hp flowers gold trim, deep rose ground, marked "GL, Halga, Decor Main, Paris, France, Limoges" **95.00**
Mug, corn motif, sgd "T & V Limoges France"... **65.00**
Nappy, 6" d, curved gold handle, gold scalloped edges, soft pink blossoms, blue-green ground **35.00**
Oyster plate, 9-1/4" d, molded, scalloped edge, gilt rim, enamel dec of poppy sprays, raised gilt detailing, marked "A. Lanternier & Co., Limoges," early 20th C, price for set of eight **1,500.00**
Panel, 4-1/2" x 3-3/8", enameled, Christ with crown of thorns, framed........ **250.00**
Pitcher, 6" h, 5-1/8" d, platinum handle, platinum mistletoe berries and leaves, gray and pink ground, Art Deco style, marked "J. P. Limoges, Pouyat" ... **155.00**

Plate, set of six, each decorated with scenic central panel with cupid, wide gilded floral borders, 9" d, **$380**. Photo courtesy of Joy Luke Auctions.

Plaque, 7-5/8" x 4-1/2", enameled, cavalier, after Meissonier, multicolored garb and banner, late 19th C **460.00**
Plate, 8" d, transfer scene of peacocks and flowers, hp border **290.00**

Punch bowl, grapes and leaves decoration, separate stand with four lion paw feet, 14-3/4" d, 9-3/4" h, **$700**. Photo courtesy of Joy Luke Auctions.

Punch bowl, 14" d, hand painted grapes, marked "T& V Limoges France Depose," minor repairs **320.00**
Service plate, 8-5/8" d, Pres Harrison, scalloped rim, gilt corn and star borders, central enamel eagle emblem, printed marks, France, c1892.................. **500.00**
Snuff box, cov, hp, wildflowers and gold tracery, pink ground, artist sgd, dated 1800... **200.00**
Tankard set, 14" h tankard, four mugs, hp, grape dec, gold and green ground, five-pc set.................................... **450.00**
Tea set, 9-1/2" h cov teapot, two 3" h cups, two 4-1/2" d saucers, 15" d tray, cream ground, floral dec, gold trim, red stamp "L. S. & S. Limoges France," green stamp "Limoges France" on two saucers, slight wear **500.00**
Vase, 15" h, hand painted, sgd "Florence Sladnick" **350.00**

LITHOPHANES

History: Lithophanes are highly translucent porcelain panels with impressed designs. The designs result from differences in the thickness of the plaque; thin parts transmit an abundance of light, while thicker parts represent shadows.

Lithophanes were first made by the Royal Berlin Porcelain Works in 1828. Other factories in Germany, France, and England later produced them. The majority of lithophanes on the market today were made between 1850 and 1900.

Gas lamp, four scenic removable panels, cube shape, pewter-colored metal holder, 4-1/2" x 5-1/2", **$195**. Photo courtesy of Woody Auctions.

Candle shield, 9" h, panel with scene of two country boys playing with goat, castle in background................... **275.00**
Cup and saucer, gold, brown, and beige dragon dec, Geisha girl in base..... **75.00**
Fairy lamp, 9" h, three panels, lady leaning out of tower, rural romantic scenes..................................... **1,250.00**
Lamp, figural, 23" h, 9" d base, five panel lithophane shade, each panel with different scene, figural Southern gentleman on base, applied plaque on front "Southern as Dundreary," base sgd "Baker Old (?) & Co., Philadelphia," old repair **980.00**
Lamp shade, 6-1/2" h, five panels, each panel with different scene, KPM... **750.00**
Night lamp, 5-1/4" h, sq, four scenes, irid green porcelain base, gold trim, electrified..................................... **650.00**

Panel, bride preparing for wedding, marked "KPM/306/N," 5-7/8" x 4-1/2", **$200**. Photo courtesy of Alderfer Auction Co.

Panel, 7-1/2" x 6" panel, mounted in 16-1/4" h holder, young girl reading scroll on panel, wear to holder finish **460.00**
Pitcher, puzzle type, Victorian scene, nude on bottom **175.00**
Stein, regimental, half liter **200.00**
Tea warmer, 5-7/8" h, one-pc cylindrical panel, four seasonal landscapes with children, copper frame, finger grip and molded base **250.00**

LIVERPOOL CHINA

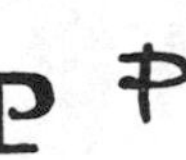

History: Liverpool is the name given to products made at several potteries in Liverpool, England, between 1750 and 1840. Seth and James Pennington and Richard Chaffers were among the early potters who made tin-enameled earthenware.

By the 1780s, tin-glazed earthenware gave way to cream-colored wares decorated with cobalt blue, enameled colors, and blue or black transfers.

Bubbles and frequent clouding under the foot rims characterize the Liverpool glaze. By 1800, about 80 potteries were working in the town producing not only creamware, but soft paste, soapstone, and bone porcelain.

Reproduction Alert: Reproduction Liverpool pieces were documented as early as 1942. One example is a black transfer-decorated jug made in the 1930s. The jugs vary in height from 8-1/2 to 11 inches. On one side is "The Shipwright's Arms"; on the other, the ship Caroline flying the American flag; and under the spout, a wreath with the words "James Leech."

A transfer of the *Caroline* also was used on a Sunderland bowl about 1936 and reproduction mugs were made bearing the name "James Leech" and an eagle. The reproduction pieces have a crackled glaze and often age cracks have been artificially produced. When compared to genuine pieces, reproductions are thicker and heavier and have weaker transfers, grayish color (not as crisp and black), ecru or gray body color instead of cream, and crazing that does not spiral upward.

Bowl, creamware

10-1/2" d, transfer printed and painted polychrome enamel dec, Hope with three-masted ship flying two American flags, six figural reserves on int., three transfer country scenes on ext., red enameled rim, repaired **815.00**

11-3/8" d, black transfer printed, polychrome enamel dec, int. with American sailing vessel Apollo, border of military devices, ext. with nautical themes, coat of arms, vignette of lovers holding heart, above inscription "J. & S. Appleton," green, yellow, red, white, and blue enamels, imperfections **5,875.00**

Jug, creamware, black transfer printed, obverse "Washington," oval design with medallion portrait on monument surmounted by wreath, birth and death dates below, flanked by eagle and grieving woman, upper ribbon inscribed "Washington in Glory," lower ribbon "American in Tears"; reverse transfer of American sailing vessel, American eagle beneath spout, imperfections, 10-1/4" h, **$1,295.** Photo courtesy of Skinner's Auctioneers and Appraisers.

Cup and saucer, handleless, black transfer, bust of Washington and other gentleman on cup, "Washington, His Country's Father" on saucer, hairlines in cup **330.00**

Jug, creamware

7-1/4" h, 3-1/2" d, transfer printed, obverse with compass and verse, reverse with The Sailors Adieu, minor imperfections **750.00**

8" h, black transfer printed, obverse American eagle surrounded by ring chain inscribed with names of 15 states, reverse with two-masted American sailing vessel, American eagle beneath spout, minor imperfections **2,465.00**

8-1/8" h, black transfer printed, obverse "O. Liberty thou Goddess!," poem in oval, bordered by wreath of olive leaves surrounded by entwined ribbon containing names of 15 states, reverse with stern view of sailing ship, American eagle beneath spout, imperfections **1,100.00**

8-1/4" h, 4-1/2" d, transfer printed, obverse with eagle and shield, reverse with Independence with "as he tills your rich globe..." stanza, imperfections **1,150.00**

8-5/8" h, 4-3/8" d, transfer printed and painted with polychrome enamels, obverse with Tom Truelove Going to Sea, reverse with three-masted ship with "Success to Trade" banner below, oval reserve of three figures by lake with "Peace to all Nations" below the spout, remnants of gilt lettering reading "John Frank" below that, imperfections.... **1,100.00**

8-3/4" h, black transfer printed and polychrome dec, obverse American Militia, oval scenic reserve with militiaman with flag, ships, and armament, surrounded by inscription, reverse with American sailing vessel above banner inscribed "Success to Trade," American eagle with Jefferson quote, dated 1802 under spout, red, blue, green, and yellow enamels, yellow highlight around rim, minor imperfections **3,525.00**

8-3/4" h, 4-3/4" d, transfer printed, obverse with Commodore Prebels Squadron Attacking the City of Tripoli Aug. 3, 1804, reverse with Salem Shipyard scene and verse, eagle and shield below spout, imperfections **2,300.00**

9-1/8" h, 5" d, transfer printed, obverse with Commodore Preble, reverse with Commodore Prebles Squadron Attacking the City of Tripoli Aug. 3, 1804, imperfections **2,185.00**

9-1/4" h, hand-painted transfer, Brig Adventure of Salem, American flag on one side, other side with uncolored transfer of the East Coast of US with George Washington and Lady Liberty, American eagle and "James Barr" under spout, hairline along spout **4,475.00**

10" h, 5" d, transfer printed and painted with polychrome enamels, obverse with Proscribed Patriots, reverse with "Success to America whose Militia...," eagle and shield with Jefferson quote dated 1802 below spout, repaired **3,220.00**

10-1/4" h, black transfer printed, obverse "Washington," oval design with medallion portrait on monument surmounted by wreath, birth and death dates below, flanked by an eagle and grieving woman, upper ribbon is inscribed "Washington in Glory," lower ribbon "America in Tears"; reverse transfer of American sailing vessel, American eagle beneath spout, imperfections **1,295.00**

10-1/2" h, black transfer printed and polychrome, obverse "Washington," portrait surrounded by three female figures, Justice, Liberty, and Victory, cherub above, scrolling ribbon inscribed with names of 15 states and stars surround oval reserve, reverse with American three-masted sailing vessel dec in red, white, blue, yellow, and green enamels, monogram within wreath above American eagle beneath spout, traces of gilt and black highlights, minor imperfections **3,055.00**

11-3/4" h, 6-5/8" d, transfer printed, obverse with ship Massachusetts, reverse with map of Newburyport Harbor with "Success to the Commerce of Newburyport" on other, gilt embellishments, circular reserve of Columbia, minor imperfections **14,950.00**

14-1/4" h, 6-1/4" d, transfer printed and painted with polychrome enamels, obverse with Hope on one side "Her lefs'ning boat u willing rows to land," reverse with three-masted ship flying American flag, below spout with transfer scenes around rim and base, motto reserve "From Rocks & Sans and ever ill May god preserve The Sailor still" below handle, gilt highlights, imperfections **6,325.00**

Jug, pearlware, 6-1/4" h, black transfer printed, obverse with American eagle

with ribbon in its beak, inscribed "E. Pluribus Unum," 15 scattered stars above it's head, reverse with vignette of embracing couple, fleet of sailing vessels below spout, rim dec with scattered blossoms, black enamel highlights on rim, shoulder, and handle edges, minor imperfections **1,120.00**

Jug and plate, 4-7/8" d, 8" h, creamware, jug transfer printed with Poor Jack on one side, "The Engagement between the Nymph 32 Guns 240 Men and the Cleopatra..." on other, garland and grape design below spout, plate with Poor Jack transfer dec **980.00**

Plate, 10" d, black transfer printed, 10 are dec with sailing vessels, one inscribed "Returning Hopes" with lady waiting for return of her lover's ship, minor imperfections, price for 11-pc set **1,570.00**

Sauce boat, 5-3/4" l, oval, paneled sides, underglaze blue floral dec, attributed to Pennington & Part, c1780 .... **460.00**

Tureen, cov, 12-1/4" d, 9-1/2" h, domed cov with oval handle, round base, black transfer dec on lid, int., and ext. depicting figure flanked by two coat-of-arm shields, two monograms "TF" and "BW" within oval, imperfections **1,100.00**

Loetz

History: Loetz is a type of iridescent art glass that was made in Austria by J. Loetz Witwe in the late 1890s. The Loetz factory at Klostermule produced items with fine cameos on cased glass, good quality glassware for others to decorate, as well as the iridescent glasswares more commonly associated with the Loetz name.

For more information, see *Warman's Glass*, 4th edition.

Marks: Some pieces are signed "Loetz," "Loetz, Austria," or "Austria."

Atomizer, 7" h, cameo, lemon yellow ground overlaid in blue, cameo cut leafy stemmed cockle shell flowers, sgd "Loetz" in cameo, c1910, no stopper **435.00**

Bowl, 3-5/8" x 6", 3-1/2" h, oblong, folded over and pinched rim, irid green threading on irid white body, etched label "Loetz Austria," minor frit specks on int **250.00**

Candlestick, 15-1/2" h, irid finish, base chip...**115.00**

Center bowl, 10" d, Onyx, dec **395.00**

Vase, bulbous, pulled decoration and oil spots, lemon yellow ground, unmarked, 5" h, **$815**. Photo courtesy of David Rago Auctions, Inc.

Compote, 10-5/8" d, 5-1/4" h, bright orange int., deep black ext., white flaring circular rim, three ball feet, c1920 .... **310.00**

Cup, 3-3/4" d, round bowl, gold and polychrome irid, applied handle, incised "Loetz Austria" **290.00**

Inkwell, 3-1/2" h, amethyst, sq, irid, web design, bronze mouth **125.00**

Rose bowl, 6-1/2" d, ruffled purple irid raindrop dec **265.00**

Sweetmeat jar, cov, 5" h, irid silver spider web dec, green ground, sgd **450.00**

Urn, 9-1/4" h, ovoid, irid, blue oil spot dec, inscribed "Loetz, Austria" **1,600.00**

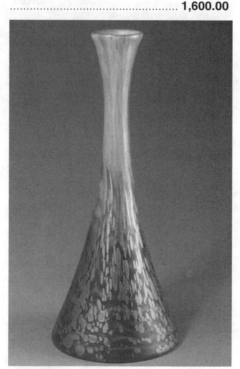

Vase, tapered, oilspots, lemon yellow ground, unmarked, some minor flecks, 7-1/2" d, 18-1/2" h, **$5,350**. Photo courtesy of David Rago Auctions, Inc.

Vase

- 6" h, irid blue swirls, amber ground, base sgd "LOETZ AUSTRIA" **1,600.00**
- 7" h, ruffled top, irid blue swirls and dot dec, irid gold ground with purple highlights, unsigned **2,875.00**
- 7-1/2" h, flaring top, irid blue and gold waves, raisin-colored ground, pontil sgd "LOETZ AUSTRIA" **2,100.00**
- 10-1/4" h, Octopus, swirl and scroll pattern, applied enamel leaves, vines and blossoms, glossy finish, int. white lining, sgd "PATENT 9159," minor surface scratches **2,100.00**
- 10-1/2" h, irid blue pulled feather dec on green ground, unsigned ... **920.00**
- 15-1/4" h, 8-1/2" d, Papillion, lustered gold, purple, and green **750.00**

Wall sconce, three-light, brass, three bulbous opalescent shades with oil-spot pattern, green chain pattern, replaced brass parts, few minor nicks to top rim of one shade.................................... **690.00**

Luster Ware

History: Lustering on a piece of pottery creates a metallic, sometimes iridescent, appearance. Josiah Wedgwood experimented with the technique in the 1790s. Between 1805 and 1840, lustered earthenware pieces were created in England by makers such as Adams, Bailey and Batkin, Copeland and Garrett, Wedgwood, and Enoch Wood.

Luster decorations often were used in conjunction with enamels and transfers. Transfers used for luster decoration covered a wide range of public and domestic subjects. They frequently were accompanied by pious or sentimental doggerel, as well as phrases that reflected on the humors of everyday life.

Copper luster was created by the addition of a copper compound to the glaze. It was very popular in America during the 19th century, and collecting it became a fad from the 1920s to the 1950s. Today it has a limited market.

Using a gold mixture made pink luster. Silver luster pieces were first covered completely with a thin coating of a "steel luster" mixture, containing a small quantity of platinum oxide. An additional coating of platinum, worked in water, was then applied before firing.

Sunderland is a coarse type of cream-colored earthenware with a marbled or spotted pink luster decoration, which shades from pink to purple. A solution of gold compound applied to the white body developed the many shades of pink.

The development of electroplating in 1840 created a sharp decline in the demands for metal-surfaced earthenware.

Reproduction Alert: The market for copper luster has been softened by reproductions, especially creamers and the "polka" jug, which fool many new buyers. Reproductions are heavier in appearance and weight than the earlier pieces.

Creamer, copper luster, applied white, blue, yellow, and green floral decoration on gold band of lower half, scrolled handle, **$45**. Photo courtesy of Dotta Auction Co., Inc.

Canary

Child's mug, 1-3/4" h, "A Present for Charles," pink luster trim, minor wear **625.00**

Miniature, creamer, 2-3/4" h, red and green flowers, pink luster accents and rim, pinpoint flake **850.00**

Pitcher, 6-1/4" l, 6" h, baluster form, low neck and spout, sides printed with scenes titled "Attempt before the guard...," On Guard, Single Stick, Staffordshire, c1810 .... **220.00**

Copper

Goblet, 3" d, 3-3/4" h, mauve and green colored band with floral dec around mid section, c1850 .... **85.00**

Pitcher, 4" h, blue band with molded flower dec on both sides, copper luster bulbous base **50.00**

Planter, 4-1/4" d, 3-3/7" h, three ftd, kettle shape **25.00**

Tea cup and saucer, turquoise blue background, copper luster floral band **65.00**

Vase, 7-1/4" w, 6-1/2" h, two handles, stag scene **70.00**

Pink

Child's mug, 2" h, pink luster band, reddish hunter and dogs transfer, green highlighted foliate transfer **85.00**

Creamer, 4-3/8" h, stylized flower band, pink luster highlights and rim, ftd ... **75.00**

Cup and saucer, magenta transfers, Faith, Hope, and Charity, applied green enamel highlights, pink luster line borders **60.00**

Creamer, copper luster, wide cream-colored band, two panels of rust transfer depicting woman listening to musician, band of magenta and rust leaf garland decoration on cream ground, 6-1/4" w spout to handle, 5-1/2" h, small spout flake, **$80**. Photo courtesy of Alderfer Auction Co.

Figure, 4-1/2" h, dogs, white, luster gilt collar, cobalt blue base with gilt trim, Staffordshire, pr **620.00**

Pitcher, 5-3/4" h, emb ribs, eagle, and flowers in pink and purple luster **150.00**

Plate, 9-3/4" d, painted flowers and leaves, pink, purple, and yellow, green and red overglaze **45.00**

Plaque, 9-3/8" l, 8-3/8" h, rect, "The Great Eastern Steam Ship," black transfer with polychrome, pink luster shaped border **450.00**

Posset cup and saucer, tray, 5" h, wide luster bands flanked by two red bands, 19th C **295.00**

Punch bowl, 10" d, black transfer print, "The Shipwright's Arms" on int., pink luster borders on ext., imperfections **120.00**

Teapot, 12" h, House pattern, Queen-Anne style, repaired finial on lid **285.00**

Toddy plate, 5-1/16" d, pink luster House pattern, emb floral sprigs border **45.00**

Waste bowl, 6" d, House pattern **125.00**

Flower pot, pink luster, pearlware flower pot, undertray raised ring and shell-form handles, stylized floral and foliate pink luster resist designs, England, 19th C, minor base hairlines, 6" h, **$1,000**. Photo courtesy of Skinner, Inc.

Silver

Coffee service, 7-3/8" h cov coffeepot, cov sugar bowl, six coffee cans and saucers, silver luster grape and leaves, rust enamel accents, yellow ground **450.00**

Creamer, 4" h, 5" w, ribbed loop base, incised band near top, shaped handle **85.00**

Cup and saucer, handleless, overall floral band on cup, scattered florals on saucer **45.00**

Figure, 11-7/8" l, standing lion, paw on globe, rect base, early 19th C, repaired **900.00**

Goblet, 4-3/8" h, silver luster grapes and vines, white ground, lustered foot **220.00**

Jug, 6-1/2" h, shell detail, minor wear **100.00**

Pitcher, 5-1/2" h, squatty body, wide lip, overall silver luster, 19th C **95.00**

Spill vase, 4-1/8" h, gray marbleized applied vines and fruits, silver luster accents, white int., pr **95.00**

Teapot, 5-1/4" h, reeded detail **140.00**

Pitcher, copper luster, two embossed figures of dancing ballerinas, blue polychrome scroll decoration, scrolled handle, **$75**. Photo courtesy of Dotta Auction Co., Inc.

Sunderland

Bowl, 8-1/4" d, polychrome highlighted black transfers of ship and verse, pink marble luster, mid-18th C **265.00**

Creamer, 5" h, "The Sailor's Tear," outlined in florals, verse with sailing ship and "May Peace and Plenty...," luster trim **275.00**

Jug, pearlware

8-3/4" h, God Speed the Plow, black and white printed transfer of farmer's coat of arms flanked by farmer and wife, surrounded by various symbols

in agricultural setting, hand colored with polychrome enamels, reverse with inspirational verse, oval reserve beneath spout sgd "Mary Hayward Farmer Sandhurft Kent," embellished with pink luster and floral dec, imperfections **1,150.00**

9-3/8" h, black transfer printed, pink luster and polychrome enamel dec, obverse "The Sailor's Farewell," reverse with sailor's verse, panel under spout inscribed "George Henry Page Born Sept. 7th, 1800, Charlotte Page Born Feb," imperfections **3,290.00**

10-1/8" h, black transfer printed, pink luster dec, obverse "A West View of the Iron Bridge over the Wear under the Patronage of R. Burdon Esq. M. P.," reverse with inspirational verse in floral wreath, pouring handle beneath spout and sailing vessel transfer, inscription "Auther Rutter 1840," minor imperfections **1,650.00**

Plate, copper luster rim and leaf decoration, strawberries decoration, marked "RM Czech," **$45**. Photo courtesy of Wiederseim Associates, Inc.

Mug, 5" h, black transfer of compass on front, "The Sailor's Farewell" on reverse **160.00**

Mustard pot, 4" h, loop handle.... **150.00**

Pitcher, 7-1/4" h, three oval medallions around body in free hand-painted orange, red, and green, black transfer of sailing ship within one below spout, religious verse on one, Captain's verse on one, minor spout roughness **550.00**

Plaque

7-1/2" x 8-1/2", Thou God sees't me, pink and copper luster border **300.00**

7-3/4" x 8-3/4", black transfer romantic scene, marked "Adam Clarke".................................. **275.00**

7-3/4" x 8-3/4", exotic birds and flowers, some hand painting in blue and green.............................. **275.00**

7-3/4" x 9", black transfer, The Revd John Wesley, A.M., Imp "Dixon Co." **245.00**

8-1/2" x 8-3/4", black transfer romantic scene, copper luster trim, "Dixon & Phillips Co." **250.00**

8-1/2" x 9-1/2", black transfer, ship, "May Peace & Plenty...," copper luster trim................................ **225.00**

Plate, 10" d, center transfer print of Pike and "Be always Ready to Die for your Country," pink luster and yellow banded border, c1820 .... **2,650.00**

Maastricht Ware

History: Petrus Regout founded the De Sphinx Pottery in 1836 in Maastricht, Holland. The firm specialized in transfer-printed earthenwares. Other factories also were established in the area, many employing English workmen and adopting their techniques. Maastricht china was exported to the United States in competition with English products.

Two bowls, Oriental scenic decoration, 8" d, **$85**; 6" d, **$50**. Photo courtesy of Joy Luke Auctions.

Ashtray, 4-1/2" d, Victoria Hotel, Amsterdam, Holland, white ground, magenta printing **15.00**

Bowl

5-3/4" d, red, green, and blue agate pattern, "Petrous Regout, Maastricht" and lion mark........................... **45.00**

8-1/4" d, ftd, windmill with people finishing, brown transfer........... **35.00**

8-5/8" d, Blue Willow, marked "Petrus Regout & Co, Maastricht, Holland," c1929 .... **25.00**

Cup and saucer, Oriental pattern, 3-1/4" d, 2" h cup, c1929 .... **25.00**

Pitcher, 5" h, rooster with iris and leaves, red transfer, marked "Regout & Co. Haan"... **75.00**

Plate

7" d, blue, red, purple stick spatter wide border design, green foliage in center, marked "Petrus Regout & Co., Maastricht, Made in Holland" **20.00**

8-1/4" d, Timor pattern **30.00**

8-1/2" d, Canton pattern, Geisha girls and man on walkway, marked "Canton, P. Regout Maastricht," c1836 .... **40.00**

9-1/2" d, rust-colored border, red cherries in center, marked "Petrous Regout & Co., Maastricht, Made in Holland"................................... **40.00**

10" d, Delft, blue and white windmill scene, Royal Sphinx mark........ **50.00**

Platter, 11-1/2" d, gaudy polychrome florals, red, yellow, and green white ground **70.00**

Majolica

History: Majolica, an opaque, tin-glazed pottery, has been produced in many countries for centuries. It was named after the Spanish Island of Majorca, where figuline—a potter's clay—is found. Today, however, the term "majolica" denotes a type of pottery was made during the last half of the 19th century in Europe and America.

Majolica frequently depicts elements of nature: leaves, flowers, birds, and fish. Designs were painted on the soft-clay body using vitreous colors and fired under a clear lead glaze to impart the rich color and brilliance characteristic of majolica.

Victorian decorative art philosophy dictated that the primary function of design was to attract the eye; usefulness was secondary. Majolica was a welcome and colorful change from the familiar blue and white wares, creamwares, and white ironstone of the day.

For more information, see *Warman's English & Continental Pottery & Porcelain*, 3rd edition and *Warman's American Pottery & Porcelain*, 2nd edition.

Marks: Wedgwood, George Jones, Holdcraft, and Minton were a few of the English majolica manufacturers who marked their wares. Most of their pieces can be identified through the English Registry mark and/or the potter-designer's mark. Sarreguemines in France and Villeroy and Boch in Baden, Germany, produced majolica that compared favorably with the finer English majolica. Most Continental pieces had an incised number on the base. Although 600-plus American potteries produced majolica between 1850 and 1900, only a handful chose to identify their wares. Among these manufacturers were George Morely, Edwin Bennett, the Chesapeake Pottery Company, the New Milford Wannoppee Pottery Company, and the firm of Griffen, Smith, and Hill. The others hoped their unmarked pieces would be taken for English examples.

Reproduction Alert: Majolica-style pieces are a favorite of today's interior decorators. Many exact copies of period pieces are being manufactured. In addition, fantasy pieces incorporating late Victorian-era design motifs have entered the market and confused many novice collectors.

Modern majolica reproductions differ from period pieces in these ways: (1) modern reproductions tend to be lighter in weight than their Victorian ancestors; (2) the glaze on newer pieces may not be as rich or deeply colored as on period pieces; (3) new pieces usually have a plain white bottom, period pieces almost always have colored or mottled bases; (4) a bisque finish either inside or on the bottom generally means the piece is new; and (5) if the design prevents the piece from being functional—e.g., a lip of a pitcher that does not allow proper pouring—it is a new piece made primarily for decorative purposes.

Some reproductions bear old marks. Period marks found on modern pieces include (a) "Etruscan Majolica" (the mark of Griffen, Smith and Hill) and (b) a British registry mark.

Adviser: Mary D. Harris.

Note: Prices listed are for pieces in mint condition and with good color. For less-than-perfect pieces, decrease value proportionately according to the degree of damage or restoration.

Asparagus stand, Minton, England, c1868, rectangular tray, attached arched asparagus dish, impressed mark, 10" l, **$1,000**. Photo courtesy of Skinner, Inc.

Asparagus server, French
- 13", two pcs **300.00**
- 15" **200.00**

Basket
- Shell and seaweed, rope handle, 8-3/4" **500.00**
- Tree bark form, 8" **175.00**

Bread tray, Shell and Seaweed, Etruscan GHS mark, 11-1/2" l, firing hairline on back **350.00**

Bud vase, Bamboo, triple, 5-3/4" h **200.00**

Butter pat
- Begonia Leaf, pointed **125.00**
- Chrysanthemum, Wedgwood **110.00**
- Ivy, yellow center **90.00**
- Pansy, Etruscan **135.00**
- Pond Lily, Etruscan **125.00**

Bowl, footed, scallop shell and seaweed, Phoenixville, PA, 8" d, **$110**. Photo courtesy of Wiederseim Associates, Inc.

- Shell and Waves, Wedgwood **200.00**

Cheese keeper, cov
- Argenta Primrose, Wedgwood, 9-1/2" **475.00**
- Begonia leaf, white, 6-1/2" **450.00**
- Birds, cobalt blue, 10-1/2" **700.00**

Cornucopia, figural, 4-3/4" h **150.00**

Cup and saucer
- Bird and Fan, Shorter & Bolton **100.00**
- Pineapple **175.00**
- Tree Bark and Floral **110.00**

Cuspidor, Sunflower, Etruscan, cobalt, unmarked, 6" h **390.00**

Fish plate, Argenta, Wedgwood, dated 1880, three fish and aquatic foliage in naturalistic color, impressed marks, date code, 8-1/4" d, **$150**. Photo courtesy of David Rago Auctions.

Figure, cat on bowl, French, 4-1/2" **300.00**

Game dish, Quail, George Jones, cobalt blue, 11-1/4" **4,250.00**

Humidor, figural
- Indian head, 9" h **100.00**
- Jockey head, 7" h **150.00**
- Man with hat, 7-3/4" **150.00**
- Penguin, 7" h **175.00**

Mug
- Blackberry, Clifton, 3-1/2" h **75.00**
- Sunflower and Butterfly, cobalt blue **225.00**

Oyster plate
- Argenta, Oriental-style, Wedgwood **550.00**

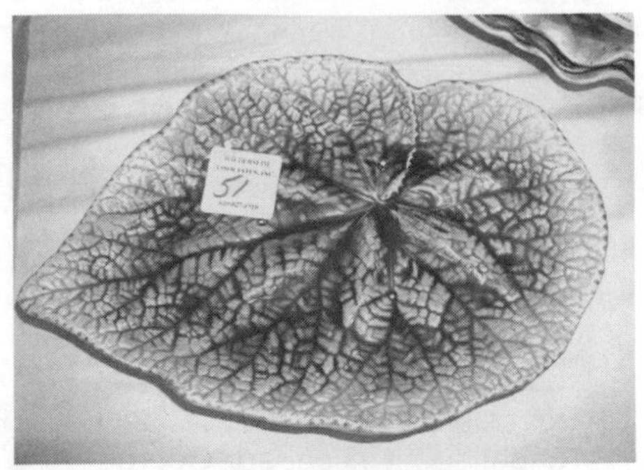

Leaf shaped dish, yellow edge, green, brown, red center, **$85**. Photo courtesy of Wiederseim Associates, Inc.

- Basketweave, French, Longchamp **125.00**
- Crescent shape, five wells **700.00**
- Fish and Seaweed, Shorter & Son **325.00**
- Minton, nine wells **950.00**
- Mottled green-brown **150.00**
- Russian Imperial eagle **750.00**
- St. Clement, pink and green **300.00**

Paperweight, owl, Mayer, figural **75.00**

Dessert plate, Strawberries, George Jones, c1870, pale blue ground, painted design number 3363, 8" d, **$350**. Photo courtesy of David Rago Auctions.

Pitcher
- Acorn and Oak Leaf, yellow top and brown base, 6-3/4" h **200.00**
- Asparagus, French, 8" h **300.00**
- Bird's Nest, begonia leaf spout, 9-1/4" h **250.00**
- Corn, 9-1/2" h **175.00**
- Fan and Scroll Insect, Fielding, lavender and yellow, 7" h **225.00**
- Primose, cobalt blue, 5-1/2" h **200.00**

Planter, boy with goat, figural **75.00**

Plate, Sunflower and Urn, Samuel Lear, English, 11" l **260.00**

Platter
- Oriental Urn and Floral, Wedgwood, cobalt blue, 12" l **275.00**
- Stork in Bull Rushes, French, handles, 13-1/2" l **350.00**

Salt dip, dolphin and shell, figural, 4" 225.00

Sardine box, covered, George Jones, England, c1880, rectangular basketweave molded dish with fish applied to foliate form cover, impressed mark, rim chips, 8" l, **$650**. Photo courtesy of Skinner, Inc.

Sardine box, cov
- Fan and Scroll, yellow **350.00**
- Fish and Seaweed, Minton, cobalt blue **1,800.00**
- Fish on lily pad, Victoria Pottery Co **1,200.00**

Server, shell, three parts, dolphin handles, George Jones, 15" **1,200.00**

Shaving mug
- Wheat Floral Ribbon and Bow, Fielding, 3-1/4" h **150.00**
- Shell and waves, 3-1/2" h **125.00**

Strawberry server, lily flower holders, George Jones **1,600.00**

Table center
- Rabbit under cabbage, Minton, 9-1/2" x 4-1/2" **9,500.00**
- Scenic panels, eagle handles, Eichwold, 20" **375.00**

Teapot, covered, seaweed and colorful shells, pink interior, shell finial, branch form handle and spout, embossed bottom mark indicates manufacture by Griffen, Smith & Hill between 1878 and 1889, impressed mark, "E24," 9-1/2" w from handle to spout, 6-1/2" h, small flakes on rim and spout, hairline crack on inside lip of lid, **$400**. Photo courtesy of Alderfer Auction Co.

Teapot
- Bird and Fan, Wardle **225.00**
- China man, Holdcroft, figural **4,000.00**
- Pineapple, 5-1/2" **300.00**
- Rooster, George Jones, figural, 11" **7,000.00**

Toothpick holder, eagle, 3-1/2" **150.00**

Tray
- Basketweave, George Jones, cobalt blue, yellow border, round, 10" d **450.00**
- Leaf and Floral, Holdcroft, 10-1/2" **225.00**

Vase
- Crane and Fan, oriental, flat sided, 6" h **175.00**
- Happy Hooligan with flower, figural **75.00**
- Man and woman by tree, figural, Continental, 9-3/4" h, pr.......... **100.00**

MAPS

History: Maps provide one of the best ways to study the growth of a country or region. From the 16th to the early 20th century, maps were both informative and decorative. Engravers provided ornamental detailing, such as ornate calligraphy and scrolling, especially on bird's-eye views and city maps. Many maps were hand colored to enhance their beauty.

Maps generally were published as plates in books. Many of the maps available today are simply single sheets from cut-apart books.

In the last quarter of the 19th century, representatives from firms in Philadelphia, Chicago, and elsewhere traveled the United States preparing county atlases, often with a sheet for each township and each major city or town.

Notes: Although mass-produced, county atlases are eagerly sought by collectors. Individual sheets sell for $45 to $95. The atlases themselves can usually be purchased in the $250 to $500 range. Individual sheets should be viewed solely as decorative and not as investment material.

A Map of the British Empire in America, Samuel Dunn, Sayer & Bennett, London, 1776, engraved, folding, hand colored, wide margins, 495 x 320 mm, small stain.......... **1,725.00**

A Map of Florida and Ye Great Lakes of Canada, Robert Morden, London, c1688, engraved, English text on verso, 130 x 125 mm, matted and framed........ **520.00**

A Map of the Most Inhabited Part of Virginia, Joshua Fry and Peter Jefferson, London, 1775, engraved, hand colored in outline, four-sheet map, joined to form two horizontal sheets, tissue backed, 790 x 1235 mm, FE.......... **29,900.00**

A Plan of the Town, Bar, Harbour and Environs, of Charlston in South Carolina, William Faden, London, 1780, double page, engraved, hand colored, 510 x 685 mm.......... **4,370.00**

A New Map of the English Empire in America, John Senex, London, 1719, double page, engraved, hand colored in outline, 510 x 600 mm, matted.. **1,150.00**

A New Discription (sic) of Carolina by Order of the Lord Propietors, John Ogilby and James Moxon, London, c1672, engraved, 465 x 570 mm, tissue backed, matted and framed...... **9,200.00**

A Sketch of the Operations Before Charlestown, South Carolina, 1780/ Sketch of Sr. Peter Parker's Attack on Fort Moultrie, June 28th, 1776, Thomas Conder, London, 1788, engraved folding map, 295 x 170 mm, matted and framed **430.00**

Asia, Giovanni Botero, Rome, c1595, small double page, engraved, trimmed margins, 205 x 245 mm.......... **300.00**

Lehigh County, PA, wall type, published by G.A. Aschbach, 1862, features central map of county, surrounded by 32 vignettes of local businesses, residences, and scenes, canvas backed with wood rod top and bottom, age yellowing, some cracking and damage at upper left affecting single vignette, some breakaway from top wood rod, 61" x 69", **$300**. Photo courtesy of Alderfer Auction Co.

Cabinet Map of the Western States, Rufus Blanchard, Chicago, 1868, lithographed folding pocket map, hand colored, 450 x 565 mm, ex-library **1,035.00**

Canada ou Nouvelle France, Alain M. Mallett, Paris, 1683, single page, engraved, French text on verso, 140 x 100 mm, minor age toning **175.00**

Chapman's Sectional Map of Wisconsin, Silas Chapman, Milwaukee, 1856, hand colored, lithograph, folding pocket, 910 x 840 mm, some separations, ex-library, orig gilt-lettered cloth case **415.00**

Colton's New Mexico and Arizona, G. W. and C. B. Colton, New York, 1881, engraved hand colored, folding pocket, 450 x 650 mm, ex-library, faded inked stamp on verso, gilt lettered cloth case **1,840.00**

Colton's Wyoming, Colorado and Utah, G. W. and C. B. Colton, New York, 1873, engraved hand colored, folding pocket, 445 x 645 mm, ex-library, small inked stamped on verso, orig gilt-lettered cloth case.......... **2,070.00**

Floride, Alain M. Mallett, Frankfu8rt, 1686, single page, engraved, 155 x 115 mm, browned at edges **290.00**

Haemisphaerium Stellatum Astrale Antiquum, Andres Cellarius, Amsterdam, 1660, double page, engraved celestial map, hand colored, wide margins, clear tear at vertical fold at lower margin just extending into image, 440 x 515 mm 2,530.00

Map of the Country Thirty Three Miles around the City of New York, G. W. and C. B. Colton, engraved hand colored folding pocket, ex-library, small inked stamps on verso, orig gilt-lettered cloth case, front cover loose, 610 x 605 mm 825.00

Map of the Southern Parts of the United States of America, Abraham Bradley, Philadelphia, 1797, engraved, folding, 205 x 395 mm.................. 375.00

Map of the Territory of Montana, Walter W DeLacy, G. W. and C. B. Colton, New York, 1870, hand colored folding pocket, 710 x 1040 mm, ex-library, inked stamp on verso, folds into publisher's gilt-lettered cloth case, worn at corners 5,980.00

Mappa Aestivarum Insularum alias Barmudas, John Ogilby, London, 1670, double page, engraved, 295 x 355 mm 920.00

Norman's Plan of New Orleans & Environs, Benjamin Moore Norman, New Orleans, 1857, lithographed, folding, 370 x 510 mm, separations at folds, ex-library, inked stamp on front pastedown, folds into publisher's boards with orig cover label.. 1,035.00

Plan de Port Royal, John Gascogine, Sartine, Paris, 1778, double page engraved, 890 x 605 mm, repaired along fold, bottom edge reinforced with tape 2,760.00

Reynold's New Map of London and its Suburb, divided into quarter-mile sections for measuring distances, James Reynolds, London, 1870, engraved 40 section map, partially hand colored, linen backed, 665 x 1000 mm, folds into orig 8vo format cloth case, accompanying text leaves 415.00

The World on Mercator's Projection, Revised and Improved to 1818, John Melish, Philadelphia, 1818, engraved 32 sections, hand colored, folding, linen backed as issued, 960 x 1280 mm 8,625.00

Township, County, and Railroad Map of Dakota, Rand McNally & Co., Chicago, 1879, color lithographed, folding, pocket, 570 x 485 mm, separations at folds, ex-library, inked stamp on verso, folds into publisher's lettered wrappers, early owner's inscriptions..................... 575.00

Untitled bird's eye view of Butte, Montana, H. Wellge, Milwaukee, 1904, lithograph, 355 x 795 mm, some discoloration at edges, mounted to stiff board.. 210.00

United States of America, W. and D. Lizars, London, c1810, engraved, folding, hand colored, margins trimmed, several folds closed at lower edge with archival tape, 395 x 460 mm..................... 260.00

Virginia and Maryland, Herman Moll, London, c1739, engraved, 285 x 220 mm 635.00

Marblehead Pottery

History: This hand-thrown pottery was first made in 1905 as part of a therapeutic program introduced by Dr. J. Hall for the patients confined to a sanitarium located in Marblehead, Massachusetts. In 1916, production was removed from the hospital to another site. The factory continued under the directorship of Arthur E. Baggs until it closed in 1936.

Most pieces found today are glazed with a smooth, porous, even finish in a single color. The most desirable pieces have a conventional design in one or more subordinate colors.

Bowl, flaring, exterior covered in dark matte smooth glaze, sky blue interior, stamped ship mark, 1-1/2" rim hairline, 9" d, 3" h, **$200**. Marblehead photos courtesy of David Rago Auctions, Inc.

Bookends, pr, 5-1/2" x 5-1/2", emb tall ship in blues and greens on white ground, stamped ship mark and paper label, touch-up to one base 1,100.00

Bud vase

- 3-3/4" h, spherical, smooth matte green glaze, circular stamp mark 435.00
- 4-1/2" h, corseted, smooth matte gray glaze, circular stamp mark 365.00

Bulb bowl, 6" d, slate gray glaze, c1915 .... 160.00

Centerpiece bowl, 3-3/4" h, 8-1/4" d, flaring, incised lotus leaf design on ext., dark blue matte glaze, imp sip mark 425.00

Chamberstick, 4-1/4" h, matte green glaze, imp ship mark.................. 435.00

Humidor, 5" h, 4-1/4" d, lightly modeled stylized dark blue flora, speckled sandy ground, rare large paper label, Arthur Baggs, marked "AEB and MHC/$5.00" 4,100.00

Cabinet vase, cylindrical, covered in matte mauve glaze, stamped ship mark, 2-1/4" d, 3-1/4" h, **$365**.

Low bowl

- 6" d, matte pink glaze, imp ship mark 175.00
- 8-1/2" d, wisteria matte glaze, imp ship mark, shallow scratches 210.00

Cabinet vase, cylindrical, covered in rose and gray matte speckled glaze, stamped ship mark and paper label, 2-1/4" d, 3-1/2" h, **$365**.

Tile, 6" sq, cuerda seca, polychrome trees and house, matte gray ground, mounted in period frame, ship mark, remnant of paper label, restoration to Y-shaped crack 1,725.00

Trivet tile, 5" d, circular, incised sea plant in matte dark brown glaze, speckled matte ochre ground, stamped ship mark, very light surface abrasion........... 690.00

Vase, bulbous, covered in smooth matte green glaze, stamped ship mark and paper label, 3-1/4" d, 3-1/2" h, **$420**.

Vase

4" x 4", barrel shape, matte blue glaze, faint ship mark **535.00**

4-1/4" d, 6-1/4" h, geometric, lightly tooled, stylized light brown trees, matte speckled sand-colored ground, imp ship mark **4,750.00**

5" d, 6" h, beaker shape, brown gooseberry leaves, indigo branches, dark blue ground, imp ship mark **1,955.00**

6" h, curved rim, widening at base, mottled lavender semi-matte glaze, imp mark, c1915-36 .... **650.00**

Vessel, bulbous, covered in smooth matte mauve glaze, stamped ship mark, 4-1/2" d, 3-3/4" h, **$435.**

Vessel, squat, covered in smooth speckled brown glaze, stamped ship mark, 5-1/2" d, 3-3/4" h, **$460.**

Vessel

2-1/2" d, squat two handles, curdled and speckled matte ochre glaze, circular stamp mark **500.00**

3-1/4" d, spherical, dark indigo speckled glaze, mark obscured by glaze.................................... **535.00**

3-1/2" x 4-1/4", bulbous, incised and matte-painted by Hannah Tutt, bouquets of stylized dark brown blossoms, smooth speckled matte green glaze, imp ship mark HT **3,220.00**

3-3/4" x 4-1/2", bulbous, cupped rim, thick curdled blue-gray matte glaze, imp ship mark........................ **865.00**

3-3/4" x 5-1/4", tapered, incised stylized dark brown pattern on speckled matte green ground, imp ship mark/MT...................... **4,600.00**

4" x 5-1/4", bulbous, matte blue glaze, imp ship mark............. **535.00**

4-1/2" x 5", flaring, band of blue stylized trees, speckled gray matte ground, imp ship mark, rim hairline **980.00**

Wall pocket, 5-1/4" x 7", faceted, central panel emb with love birds on branch, speckled green and red, indigo ground, stamped ship mark, few minor scratches and flecks **2,185.00**

Match Holders

History: The friction match achieved popularity after 1850. The early matches were packaged and sold in sliding cardboard boxes. To facilitate storage and to eliminate the clumsiness of using the box, match holders were developed.

The first match holders were cast iron or tin, the latter often displaying advertisements. A patent for a wall-hanging match holder was issued in 1849. By 1880, match holders also were being made from glass and china. Match holders began to lose their popularity in the late 1930s, with the advent of gas and electric heat and ranges.

Grading Condition. The following numbers represent the standard grading system used by dealers, collectors, and auctioneers:

C.10 = Mint
C. 9 = Near mint
C.8.5 = Outstanding
C.8 = Excellent
C.7.5 = Fine +
C.7 = Fine
C. 6.5 = Fine – (good)
C. 6 = Poor

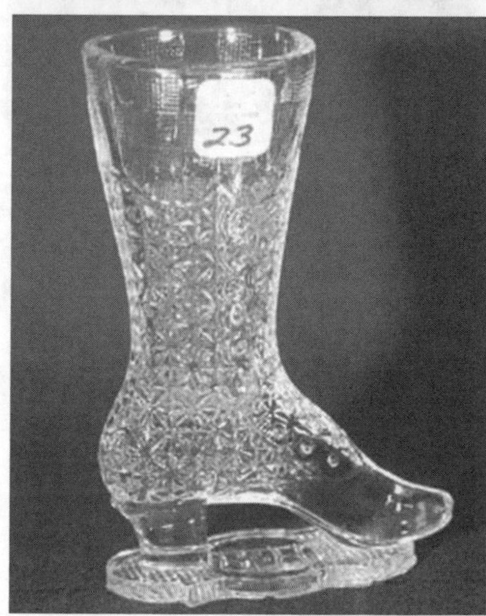

Glass, boot shaped, marked B & H, 5-1/2" h, **$30.** Photo courtesy of Joy Luke Auctions.

Advertising

Dr. Shoop's Health Coffee, tin litho, hanging, 3-1/2" w, 5" l, C.8+... **275.00**

Ferris Seed Co., 6" h **45.00**

New Process Blue Flame Oil Stove, tin litho, hanging, red ground, blue image of stove, 2-1/2" w, 1" d, 3" h, C.8+ **275.00**

Bisque, 4" h, 3-5/8" d, natural-colored rooster with beige basket, two compartments, round base with pink band **135.00**

Brass, 3" h, bear chained to post, cast, orig gilt trim................................. **225.00**

Bronze, 3" h, shoe, mouse in toe. **125.00**

Cast iron, figural, high-button shoe, 5-1/2" h, black paint, c1890........... **50.00**

Glass, 3" h, 3-1/4" d, shaded rose to pink overlay satin, ball-shape, glossy off-white lining, ground pontil..................... **155.00**

Majolica

Dog, striker, Continental......... **195.00**

Monk, striker.......................... **180.00**

Pottery, Newcomb College, painted by unknown artist with poplar trees in green and blue, 1907, marked "NC/AF/BY39/JM," 3" d, 2" h, **$3,450.** Photo courtesy of David Rago Auctions, Inc.

Papier-mâché, 2-3/4" h, black lacquer, Oriental dec **25.00**

Porcelain, seated girl, feeding dog on table, sgd "Elbogen" **125.00**

Sterling silver, 1-3/4" x 2-1/2", hinged lid, diecut striking area, cigar cutter on one corner, lid inscription "H. R." and diamond, inside lid inscribed "Made for Tiffany & Co./Pat 12, 09/Sterling" ... **95.00**

Tin, 2-3/8" h, top hat, hinged lid, orig green paint, black band **65.00**

Torquay pottery, 2" h, 3-1/8" d, ship scene, reads "A match for any Man, Shankin" **70.00**

Match Safes

History: Pocket match safes are small containers used to safely carry matches in one's pocket. They were first used around the 1840s. Match safes can be found in various sizes and shapes, and were made from numerous materials such as sterling, nickel-plated brass, gold, brass, ivory, and vulcanite. Some of the most interesting and sought after ones are figurals in the shapes of people, animals, and anything else imaginable. Match safes were also a very popular advertising means from 1895-1910, and were used by both large and small businesses. Match safes are known as vesta cases in England.

Reproduction Alert: Reproduction, copycat, and fantasy match safes abound. Reproductions include Art Nouveau styles, figural/novelty shapes, nudes, and many others. Fantasy and fakes include Jack Daniel's and Coca-Cola.

A number of sterling reproduction match safes are marked "925" or "Sterling 925." Any match safe so marked requires careful inspection. Many period, American match safes have maker's marks, catalog numbers, 925/1000, or other markings. Period English safes have hallmarks. Beware of English reproduction match safes bearing the "DAB" marking. Always verify the date mark on English safes.

Check enameled safes closely. Today's technology allows for the economic faking of enamel motifs on old match safes. Carefully check condition of enameling for telltale clues.

Note: While not all match safes have a striking surface, this is one test, besides size, to distinguish a match safe from a calling card case or other small period boxes. Values are based on match safes being in excellent condition.

Car, figural, brass, made in Germany, 2" x 2-1/2", **$500**. All photos courtesy of adviser George Sparacio.

AAONMS, Egyptian motif, figural fez, sterling by Simons Bros., 2-5/8" x 1-7/8" **650.00**

Anheuser Busch, beer, mascot type by C. Hauck, patented Aug. 14, 1883, 3" x 1-5/8" **100.00**

Anheuser Busch, refrigerated rail car, "20,000 car loads," nickel plated brass, 3" x 1-1/2" **275.00**

Anvil, figural, brass, 1" x 2-1/4" **250.00**

Arabian man motif, by Aikin Lambert Co., sterling, 2-3/4" x 1-3/4" **350.00**

Auto, speeding down road, sterling by R. Blackinton & Co., catalot #1332, 2-1/2" x 1-7/8" **500.00**

Baden Powell, real photo, book shaped, vulcanite, 2" x 1-1/2" **135.00**

Banded agate, orange/red color, rounded end, flat top, brass trim, 2-3/4" x 1-1/8" **75.00**

Brunswick Colander Co., Mineralite, bowling motif, printed accented in white, slip top, gutta percha, 2-7/8" x 1-1/2" **225.00**

Bryant & May, Sportsman vesta, litho tin, 1-5/8" x 2-3/8" **40.00**

Car, figural, brass, marked "Made in Germany," 2" x 2-1/2" **500.00**

Cat clawing rat, figural, Japanese, nickel plated brass, 2-3/4" x 1-1/2" **250.00**

Cawston Ostrich Farm, multicolored celluloid wrap, nickel plated brass ends, by Whitehead & Hoag, 2-3/4" x 1-1/2" **250.00**

Champagne basket, figural, G. H. Mumm & Cie, brass, 1-3/8" x 1-7/8" **165.00**

Champagne bottle, figural, nickel plated brass, 2-1/4" x 7/8" **80.00**

Cherry motif, silver plated by Wallace & Son, catalog #005, 2-1/2" x 1-3/8" **120.00**

Cherubs, nine faces along edges, by Unger Bros., catalog #7568, sterling, gold wash int., 2-3/4" x 1-3/4" **375.00**

Cigar bundle, 8-10 cigars, figural, LJM maker mark on bezel, sterling, French, 1-7/8" x 1-1/4" **250.00**

Colonial gentleman, reverse with young lady in garden, sterling by Codding Bros & Heilborn, 2-1/4" x 1-3/8", **$350**.

Colonial couple, gentleman and young lady in garden, sterling by Codding Bros. & Heilborn, 2-1/4" x 1-3/8" **350.00**

Columbus, figural, plated brass by Simon Zinn, patented 10/25/92, 2-5/8" x 1-5/8" **200.00**

Conquistador, Spanish damascene, gold inlaid metal, 1-7/8" x 1-3/4" ... **525.00**

Cricket and golf motifs, book shaped, vulcanite, by Hamburg Rubber Co., 2" x 1-1/2" **175.00**

Devil head, hand holding torches, by Gorham Mfg Co., catalog #695, 2-3/4" x 1-5/8" **1,000.00**

Conquistador, Spanish damascene, gold on metal, 1-7/8" x 1-3/4", **$525**.

Egyptian motif, sphinx, pyramids, etc., sterling, 1-3/4" x 2-3/8" **475.00**

Fish motif, by Gorham Mfg Co., catalog #340, sterling, 2-3/4" x 1-1/2" **250.00**

Fishing motif, fisherman holding umbrella, litho tin, by Diamond Match Co., 1-5/8" x 2-3/8" **35.00**

Fraternal Order of Eagles (FOE), applied emblem, sterling by Fairchild & Co., 2-5/8" x 1-5/8" **135.00**

Game counters, silver plated by Gorham Mfg Co., catalog #075, 2-3/4" x 1-1/2" **350.00**

Geisha girl, figural, oriental, patinated brass, 2-1/2" x 1-7/8" **600.00**

Holly and berry motif, by Whiting Mfg Co., sterling, catalog #6209, 2-5/8" x 1-3/8" **225.00**

Hunting dog, duck in mouth, by Pairpoint Mfg Co., catalog #5006, silver plated, 2-5/8" x 1-1/2" **85.00**

Indian tobacco pouch, by Gorham Mfg Co., sterling with gold wash inside, 2-9/16" x 1-5/8" **850.00**

Ironsides Company, logo in shield, multicolored graphics, by J. E. Mergott Co., 2-3/4" x 1-1/2" **150.00**

Jamestown 1907 Exposition, floral motif, G. silver, 2-5/8" x 1-1/2" **85.00**

Japanese mask, figural, flat back, sterling by Lawrence Emanuel, English hallmarks, 2" x 1-3/8" **950.00**

Karlsbad souvenir, inlaid stone top, steel body, 2-1/8" x 3/4" x 3/4" **125.00**

Kidney shaped, sea life motif, by Whiting Mfg., catalog #2337, sterling, 2-3/4" x 1-3/8" **175.00**

Knights of Templar, 25th Conclave, Busch Beer, nickel plated brass, 2-7/8" x 1-5/8" **275.00**

Lady golfer motif, clubhouse in background, G. silver, 2-3/4" x 1-5/8" **325.00**

Lady of the Light, Palace of Machinery, 1904 World's Fair, brass, 2-3/4" x 1-1/2" **125.00**

Leg, leather wrap, figural, plated brass ends, by G. Goliasch & Co., 2-1/4" x 1-1/8" **135.00**

Lion, sterling, saw-tooth striker, 2-3/8" x 1-1/2" **200.00**

Marble's, cylindrical, marked "Recreation Waterproof Matchbox, Pat. Allowed," nickel-plated brass, orig version, 2-5/8" x 1".. **250.00**
McKinley for President, nickel-plated brass, 2-7/8" x 1-1/2" **275.00**

Scientific American newspaper, figural, sterling with enameled stamp, by Enros Richardson & Co., 2-7/8" x 1-1/8", **$600**.

Mermaid in wave, by Wm Kerr, catalog #33, sterling, 2-1/2" x 1-1/2".......... **650.00**
Monkey holding baby monkey, figural, Japanese, patinated brass, 2-1/2" x 1-1/2" **650.00**
Mr. Punch, figural, hand holding vesta socket, brass, 2-3/8" x 1-1/2"........ **150.00**
Oni, with three toes, holding bird, figural, Japanese, patinated brass, 2-1/2" x 1-3/8" **500.00**
Order of Odd Fellows, insert type, nickel plated brass, 2-3/4" x 1-1/2" **75.00**
Penknife, propelling pencil, button hook combo, sterling by Sampson Mordan & Co., 2-7/8" x 3/4".......................... **800.00**
Pickle/gherkin, figural, brass, green paint, 2-1/2" x 3/4"........................ **225.00**
Pillar postal box, bone vesta socket on top, by Bryant & May, Victoria Regina postal rates, litho tin, 2-5/8" x 1-3/4" **65.00**
Pneumatic Tool, figural, silver plated by Barstow & Williams, 3-1/2" x 1-3/4" **275.00**
Queen Victoria, applied bust on purse, hinged longitudinally, aluminum, 2-3/8" x 1-1/2" **95.00**
Rampant lion, paws form vesta socket, figural, nickel plated brass, 2-1/2" x 1-1/2" **250.00**
Royal Arcanum motif, insert type, by Aug. Goertz, nickel-plated brass, 2-3/4" x 1-1/2" **75.00**
Saddle, polo mallet and bridle motif, silver plate, 2-1/2" x 1-7/8"........... **225.00**
Sarah Bernhardt, figural, sterling by Howard Sterling Co., 2-1/2" x 1-7/8" **500.00**
Scientific American newspaper, figural, sterling with enameled stamp, by Enros Richardson & Co., 2-7/8" x 1-1/8" **650.00**
Serpent/snake wrapped around body of safe, red glass eyes, by Carter, Howe & Co., sterling, 2-5/8" x 1-1/2".......... **375.00**
Shoe, cigar cutter attached to lid, figural, nickel plated brass, 2-3/4" x 3/4" **85.00**

Shotgun shell, figural, advertises Joyce's, painted metal, 2-3/4" x 3/4", **$350**.

Shotgun shell, figural, advertises Joyce's, painted metal, 2-3/4" x 3/4" **350.00**
Skull, sunken eyes, push nose to open lid, figural, brass, 1-7/8" x 1-1/2" **175.00**
Stamp combo, front slides up to revel stamp compartment, sterling, by The Sterling Co., catalog #5444, 2-1/2" x 1-1/2" **200.00**
Tartan, Prince Charlie tartan design, oval with bone socket on end, 2-5/8" x 1-1/2" **150.00**
Temptation of St. Anthony, by Wm Kerr Co., sterling, 3" x 1-3/4" **800.00**
Terrier dog, seated with whistle combo, figural, nickel plated brass, 3" x 1" **300.00**
Vice motif, cars, liquor, women, cards, enameled on sterling, 1-3/4" x 1-3/4" **475.00**
White Star Line, Cadbury Chocolate, litho tin, 2-3/4" x 1-3/4".................. **125.00**
Wild boar head, whistle combo, figural, brass, 3-3/4" x 1-1/2" **375.00**

McCoy Pottery

History: The J. W. McCoy Pottery Co. was established in Roseville, Ohio, in September 1899. The early McCoy company produced both stoneware and some art pottery lines, including Rosewood. In October 1911, three potteries merged, creating the Brush-McCoy Pottery Co. This firm continued to produce the original McCoy lines and added several new art lines. Much of the early pottery is not marked.

In 1910, Nelson McCoy and his father, J. W. McCoy, founded the Nelson McCoy Sanitary Stoneware Co. In 1925, the McCoy family sold their interest in the Brush-McCoy Pottery Co. and started to expand and improve the Nelson McCoy Co. The new company produced stoneware, earthenware specialties, and artware.

Marks: The Nelson McCoy Co made Most of the pottery marked "McCoy."

Reproduction Alert: Unfortunately, Nelson McCoy never registered his McCoy trademark, a fact discovered by Roger Jensen of Tennessee. As a result, Jensen began using the McCoy mark on a series of ceramic reproductions made in the early 1990s. While the marks on these recently made pieces copy the original, Jensen made objects that were never produced by the Nelson McCoy Co. The best-known example is the Red Riding Hood cookie jar, originally designed by Hull, and also made by Regal China.

The McCoy fakes are a perfect example of how a mark on a piece can be deceptive. A mark alone is not proof that a piece is period or old. Knowing the proper marks and what was made in respect to forms, shapes, and decorative motifs is critical in authenticating a pattern.

Additional Listings: See *Warman's Americana & Collectibles* for more examples.

Planter, figural turtle, green, yellow flower trim, **$85**. Photo courtesy of Wiederseim Associates, Inc.

Bean pot, cov, Suburbia Ware, brown, blue lid... **48.00**
Cookie jar, cov
- Bugs Bunny, cylinder, 1971-72 .... **185.00**
- Chef, "Cookies" on hat band **85.00**
- Clown, bust, c1943 .... **95.00**
- Dalmations rocking chair **315.00**
- Davy Crocket, 10" h, c1956.... **325.00**
- Engine, black **175.00**
- Jack-O-Lantern, orange and green **600.00**
- Kangaroo with Joey, 12" h...... **525.00**
- Kittens, basketweave base, 10-1/2" h **1,285.00**
- Little Red Riding Hood, 10-1/2" h **650.00**
- Mammy, #17, 1947-58............ **300.00**
- Panda, upside down, Avon label in heart logo on paw **150.00**
- Rooster, shades of brown, light tan head, green highlights **225.00**
- Squirrel **225.00**
- Touring Car, 6-1/2" h, marked "McCoy USA," c1962-64........ **155.00**

Creamer and sugar, Sunburst **120.00**

Decanter set, Jupiter 60 Train, Central Pacific locomotive, c1969 .... **350.00**
Flower pot, saucer, hobnail and leaf **40.00**
Hanging basket, Pine Cone Rustic **45.00**
Jardinière, green, emb fern motif **65.00**

Tea set, ivy decoration, raised mark, minute nick to teapot finial, 9" h, **$40**. Photo courtesy of David Rago Auctions, Inc.

Jardinière pedestal, 16-1/4" h, Onyx glaze, sgd "Cusick," c1909 .... **400.00**
Lamp base, 14" h, cowboy boots, c1956 .... **150.00**
Mug, corn **90.00**
Pitcher, Hobnail, pastel blue, 48 oz **120.00**
Planter, 8" h, three large pink chrysanthemums, marked "McCoy" **155.00**
Scoop, 7-1/4" w, 5" h, Mammy, yellow scoop, black Mammy with white dress, red scarf **225.00**
Soup tureen, cov, 12-1/2" d, 12" h, El Rancho **375.00**
Spoon rest, 8" l, yellow, foliage, 1940s, overall crazing **145.00**
Strawberry jar, 12" h, stoneware **150.00**
Tankard pitcher, 8-1/2" h, Buccaneer, green **135.00**
Tea set, cov teapot, open creamer and sugar, Daisy, 1940s **350.00**

Vase, classic shape vase, stylized band of enamel decorated scarabs and papyrus in polychrome, outlined in black, speckled green semi-matte ground, faint number mark, Brush McCoy, 5-3/4" d, 11-3/4" h, **$8,250**. Photo courtesy of David Rago Auctions, Inc.

Umbrella stand, 11" d, 22" h, maroon, rose, and yellow glaze, c1915...... **795.00**
Valet, eagle **75.00**
Vase, 9-1/2" h, ram's head, chartreuse, 1953 .... **250.00**

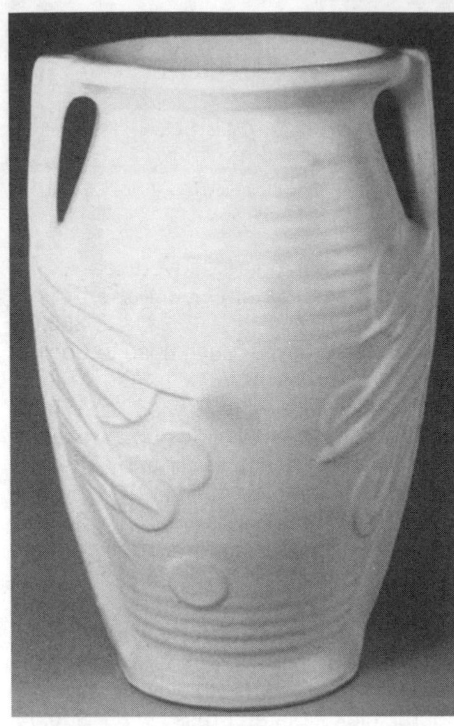

Vase, two handles, embossed stylized leaves and berries, white semi-matte glaze, marked "USA," attributed to Nelson McCoy, very short tight rim line, 8-1/2" d, 14-1/4" h, **$230**. Photo courtesy of David Rago Auctions, Inc.

Wall pocket
- Bellows **60.00**
- Fan, blue **65.00**
- Sunflower, blue **80.00**
- Woman in bonnet, bow, white, red trim **70.00**

Water server, 7-1/2" w, 10-3/4" h, El Rancho, metal spigot, orig S & H Green Stamp sticker on base **360.00**
Window box, Pine Cone Rustic..... **40.00**

McKee Glass

c1852–1950

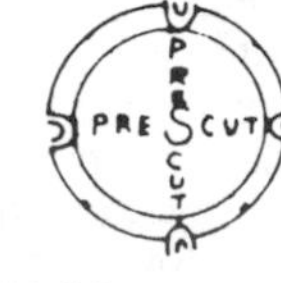

1904–30s

History: The McKee Glass Co. was established in 1843 in Pittsburgh, Pennsylvania. In 1852, it opened a factory to produce pattern glass. In 1888, the factory was relocated to Jeannette, Pennsylvania, and began to produce many types of glass kitchenwares, including several patterns of Depression glass. The factory continued until 1951, when it was sold to the Thatcher Manufacturing Co.

McKee named its colors Chalaine Blue, Custard, Seville Yellow, and Skokie Green. McKee glass may also be found with painted patterns, e.g., dots and ships. A few items were decaled. Many of the canisters and shakers were lettered in black to show the purpose for which they were intended.

For more information, see *Warman's Glass*, 4th edition.

Batter bowl, Skokie Green, spout, c1940 .... **55.00**
Berry set, Hobnail with Fan pattern, blue, master berry and eight sauce dishes **170.00**
Butter dish, cov, Ships, red dec on white **85.00**
Candleholder, 6-3/4" w, 5-1/2" h, Rock Crystal, clear, double light............ **65.00**
Candy dish, cov, Rock Crystal, red, 4-1/2" w, 10-1/2" h............ **400.00**
Canister, cov, 10 oz, custard......... **75.00**
Celery tray, 12" x 5-1/2", cut glass, Innovation line, hobnails, hobstars, and pointed diamond nailheads, sawtooth edge, small self handles with engraved intaglio daisies, c1918............ **220.00**
Cereal canister, cov, Skokie Green, 48 oz **175.00**
Cheese and cracker set, Rock Crystal, red **170.00**
Compote, 6" d, 5-1/2" h, cut glass, Innovation #410, intaglio daisies, c1916
Creamer, Aztec, purple carnival.. **125.00**
Egg beater bowl, spout
- Ships, black dec on white........ **70.00**
- Skokie Green **50.00**

Flour shaker
- Custard **58.00**
- Seville Yellow **65.00**

Kitchen bowl, 7" d, spout, Skokie Green **75.00**

Mustard, Wild Rose & Bowknot, satinized crystal, ornate metal bail handle, lid with slot for spoon, 3" h glass base, 1-7/8" d, **$135**.

Advertising, Campbell's Tomato Soup cardboard store display, **$95**.

Advertising, butter carton, Maple Grove Brand, **$20**.

Advertising, Santa Claus cardboard stand-up, 54" h, mid-1940s, **$400-$450**. The jolly old man was a favorite motif on Coca-Cola advertising, second only, perhaps, to the freshly scrubbed faces of beautiful young women.

Movie poster, "The Life of Buffalo Bill," **$1,950**.

Transportation memorabilia, tobacco tin, Hi-Plane Smooth Cut Tobacco, four-engine plane, red ground, vertical pocket type, **$600**. Photo courtesy of Bear Pen Auction.

Rookwood Pottery, rare and exceptional Carved Black Iris vase by Matthew A. Daly, 1900, with fleshy poppies in burgundy with green leaves and pods in high relief against a jet black background, 13-1/2" x 6", **$50,000**. Photo courtesy David Rago Auctions.

Rookwood, plaque, vellum glaze, landscape, titled "Sunset," by Sara Sax, original wood frame and backing, c1910-15, 4-3/4" x 9", **$4,000**. Photo courtesy of Freeman/Fine Arts of Philadelphia.

Staffordshire, plate, blue-transfer design, "Public Library Boston," 10-1/4" diameter, **$65**.

Bow, sweetmeat dish, 7-1/4" h x 10" w, c1760, **$2,650**.

Vase, 16" h, Hermann August Kahler, "imp DENMARK" mark, c1900, **$4,500**.

Staffordshire, figures, Prince of Wales and Queen Victoria, 16" h, **$880**. Photo courtesy of Jackson's Auctioneers & Appraisers.

Old Sleepy Eye commemorative, 1982 collector's convention, 7" h, **$65**.

Left: chalkware, leopard television light, **$65**.

Right: Roseville, Gardenia vase, 8" h, **$125**.

Right: Jardinière, Doulton Lambeth, 9" w, "imp DOULTON LAMBETH SLATER'S PATENT" mark, **$4,500**.

Swarovski, apple photo stand, small, gold, CRV, **$195**..

Salt and pepper shakers, pair, caramel slag cactus pattern, **$275**. Photo courtesy of Jackson's Auctioneers & Appraisers.

Animal-covered dish, glass, Mule-earred Rabbit on Picket Base, Westmoreland Specialty Co., early 20th century, **$75-$85**.

They don't make souvenirs like they used to. Ruby-stained glass was made in the late 19th century by several glassmakers. The pieces, sold as blanks, were etched with names, places, and dates to commemorate exhibitions or tourist venues. This glass ranges between **$15-$30.**

Amberina, boot toothpick, L.E. Smith Glass, 4" h, **$10**.

Northwood carnival glass fruit bowl, Peacock at the Fountain pattern, amethyst/purple, three feet, **$600-$900.**

Unmarked opaque glass dresser box, 7" l, held in Pairpoint marked feet, **$522**. Photo courtesy of Jackson's Auctioneers & Appraisers.

Lalique perfume bottle, "Quatre Cigales," in clear and frosted glass with sepia patina, c. 1910, 5-1/8" h, **$1,800-$2,000**.

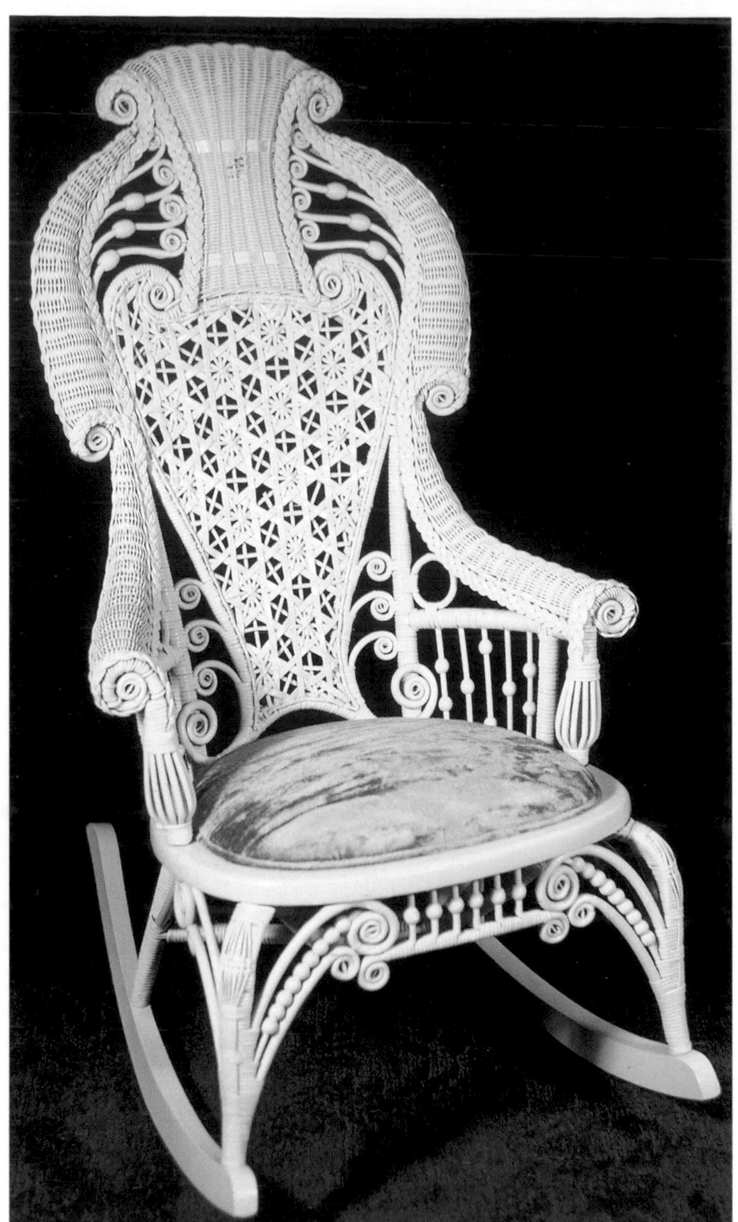

Ornate late Victorian wicker rocker, **$550-$750.**

L. & J.G. Stickley two-door china cabinet with over-hanging top, mullioned panes over a long glass panel on doors and sides, with one fixed interior plate shelf and two adjustable shelves, refinished, unmarked, 62" x 46" x 16", **$4,200-$5,000.**

Victorian Baroque-Style dining room suite, oak, ornately carved with figural griffin legs, late 19th c, the set **$19,500**.

Victorian Rococo-style firescreen, carved walnut with adjustable screen frame originally fitted with fabric, c1860, **$850.**

Classical Revival armchair, carved oak, arms formed by carved winged lions, American, c1880-90, **$5,500.**

Chippendale sofa, mahogany, upholstered camel-back form, England or America, late 18th-early 19th century, **$2,310**.

Miniature early blanket chest, natural wood, **$500-$1,000.**

Left: Rosewood mantel clock, 1860s, made by Gilbert, 8-day model, **$250**.

Porcelain shelf clock, Ansonia "La Charny" Royal Bonn porcelain dial, French sash bezel, 8-day, 11" x 12" h, **$675**.

Left: Parlor clock, walnut, 8-day, early 1900s, British Unified Clock Company, 13-3/4" x 17-1/2" h, **$500**.

Keebler pendulette, molded wood, spread-winged eagle at the top, green leaves, 30-hour, time only, spring driven 4" x 5" h, **$55**.

Right: German clock depicting chalk figure at well and inscription that reads, “Return from Work,” c 1920, 30-hour time only, 10" x 23-1/2" h, **$140**.

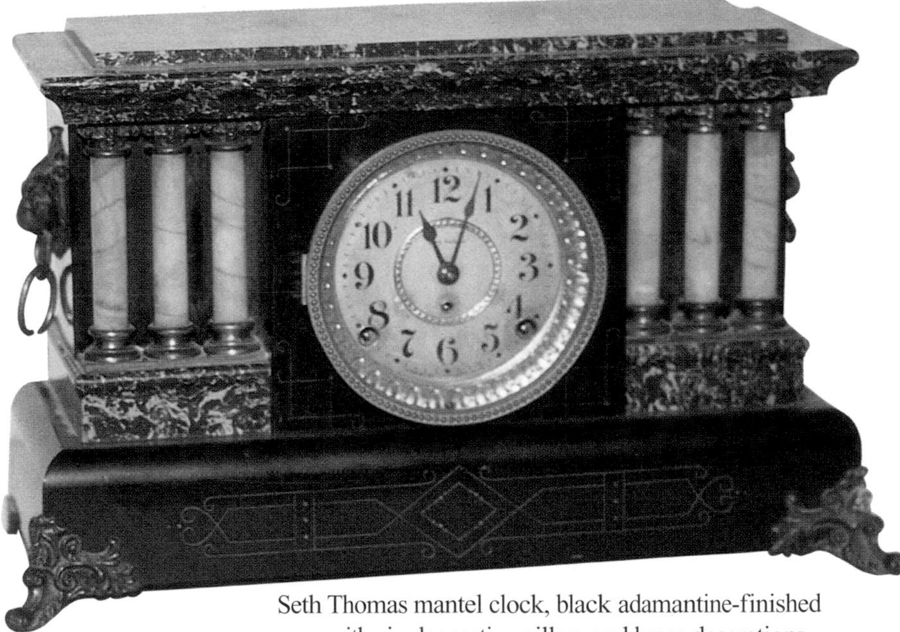

Seth Thomas mantel clock, black adamantine-finished case with six decorative pillars and brass decorations, early 1900s, 8-day time and strike, 18" x 11" h, **$200**.

Left: W.M. Gilbert wooden mantel clock with bell, early 1900s, 8-day time and strike, 17" x 19" h, **$695**.

Waterford mahogany weight clock, c1840s, lantern pinions vs. cut teeth, bottom tablet is a replacement, 15-1/2" x 26" h, **$150**.

Comic book, *The Amazing Spider-Man,* #3, Marvel, **$2,500.**

Children's book, *The Emerald City of Oz*, Reilley & Lee Co., 1910, **$125.**

Tiddledy Winks Game, stork motif, **$15.**

Volkwagen Micro-Bus, 1960s, Bandi, orange with white top, model No. J256, **$200.**

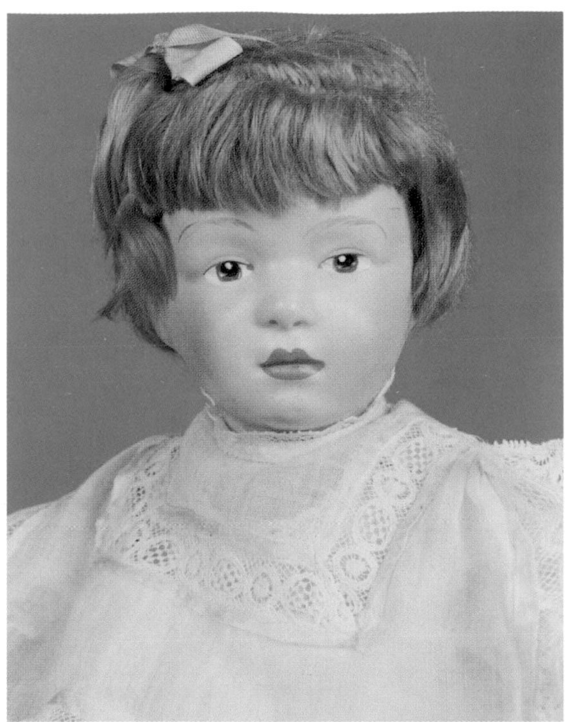

Schoenhut, doll, girl, #16/301, wood head, painted facial features, original wig, 16" h, **$1,900**. Photo courtesy of McMasters.

Teddy bear, mohair, brown, 20" h, **$1,025**; Hertel, Schwab & Co. #152 baby doll, 12" h, **$400**. Photo courtesy of McMasters Auctions.

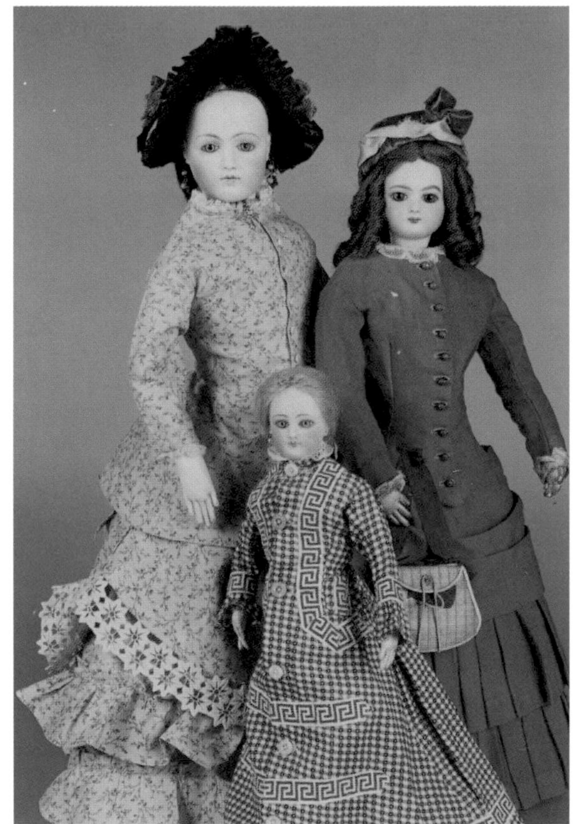

Dolls, from left: Portrait Jumeau Fashion, bisque swivel head on bisque shoulder plate, kid body, dressed in antique clothes, 22" h, **$2,200**; center: F.G. Fashion Lady, bisque swivel head, kid fashion body, antique fashion dress, 14" h, **$1,000**; right: Jumeau Fashion, bisque socket head on bisque shoulder plate, kid body, 19" h, **$1,000**. Photo courtesy of McMasters Doll Auction.

Doll, Kammer & Reinhardt, K*R 114, bisque socket head, original dark mohair wig, original Tryolean outfit, 7-1/2" h, **$1,200**. Photo courtesy of McMasters Doll Auctions.

Sewing items, spool dispenser, counter top, Merrick's, curved glass sides, **$1,980**. Photo courtesy of Jackson's Auctioneers and Appraisers.

Coin-operated slot machine, Little Duke, c1931, **$1,900**. Photo courtesy of Auction Team Breker.

Coffee grinder with cast-iron top and handle, **$150-$250.**

Scientific instruments, replica of first mechanical calculator, by Blaise Pascal, Paris, 1652, **$11,500**. Photo courtesy of Auction Team Breker.

Bracelet, Victorian, 14k, yellow gold, flexible design centering oval locket compartment with engraved floral and blue enamel cover, hinged to nine decorated links, **$450**. Photo courtesy of Sloans & Kenyon Auctions.

Pocket watch, Omega, c1905, 14k multicolored HC fancy dial, 16 size 21J, **$4,000-$5,000**. Photo courtesy of Antiquorum.

Watch fob with clip, 18k yellow gold, four body keyless "bassine," polished, the back set with a large garnet cabochon within a stylized chased foilage frame, hinged gold cuvette, matching gold and garnet clip, with enamel with Arabic numerals and sunk subsidiary seconds, gold hands, 15 jewel, dial and movement signed "Longines," made for L. Peslier à Avalon, Swiss, c1890, **$1,380.**

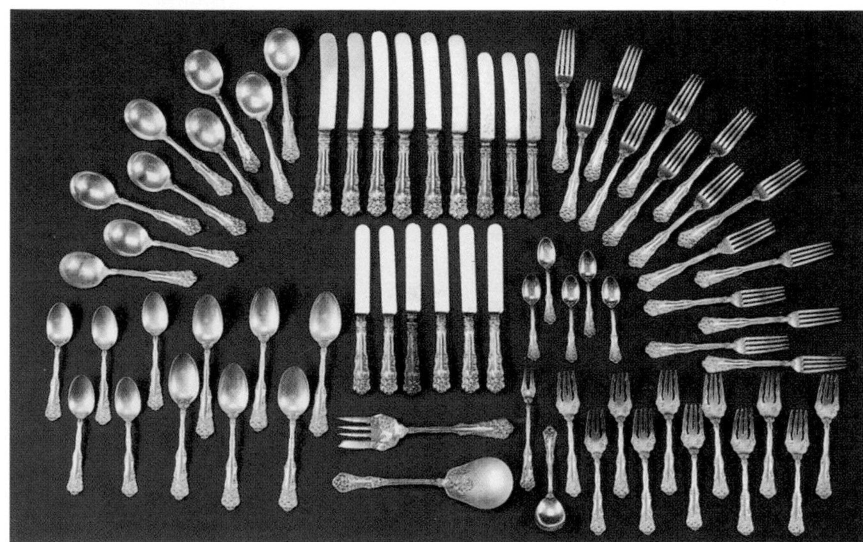

A sixty-five piece Rodger's silver-plated flatware in the Poppy pattern, patent 1904, with assorted serving pieces, and tableware. Excellent overall condition. Some missing pieces, one broken knife, die-stamped mark, **$350**.

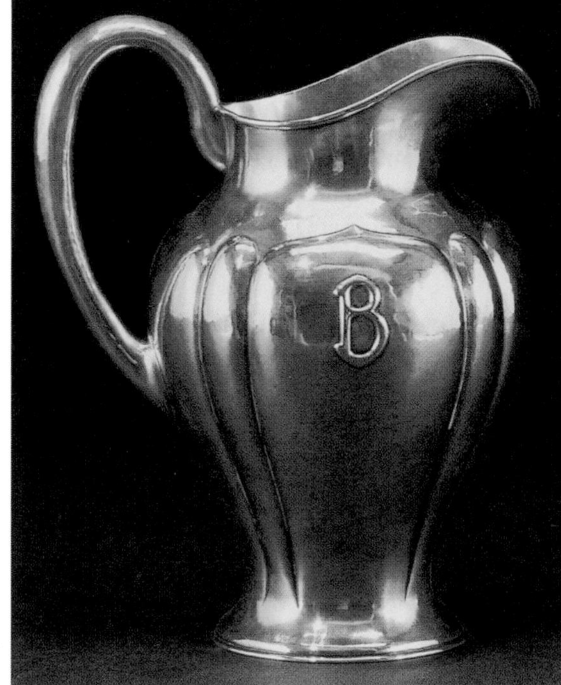

Silver, Arts & Crafts, pitcher, Kalo, hammered sterling silver, embossed sections, monogrammed, stamped mark, 10-1/2" x 8", **$2,600**. Photo courtesy of David Rago Auctions, Inc.

Tin rabbit chocolate mold, **$100-$125.**

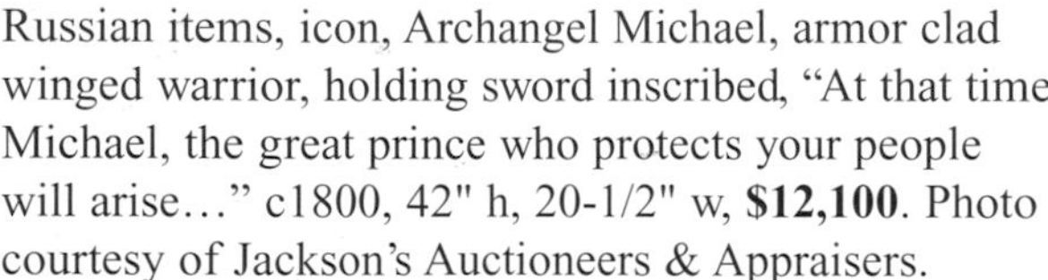

Russian items, icon, Archangel Michael, armor clad winged warrior, holding sword inscribed, "At that time Michael, the great prince who protects your people will arise…" c1800, 42" h, 20-1/2" w, **$12,100**. Photo courtesy of Jackson's Auctioneers & Appraisers.

Religious items, triptych, Russian, micro-mosaic, period of Tsar Nicholas I, removable center pendant of St. Nicholas, gilded silver frame with swivel mosaic of Eye of God, gilded silver sunburst, left and right wings both inset with removable pierced and carved bone crucifixes, left panel finely engraved with St. John Chrysostom, St. Gregory "Dvoeslova," Pope of Rhome, St. Basil the Great and St. Gregory the Theologian, right panel finely engraved with St. John, St. Philip, St. Peter, and St. Alexei, upper left and right wings engraved with continuous prayer, each section hallmarked St. Petersburg, central panel dated 1855, all with maker's mark "C.E.," 7-1/2" w open, 6-3/4" h, **$19,600**. Photo courtesy of Jackson's Auctioneers & Appraisers.

Left: Religious items, crucifix, carved ivory figure mounted to wooden cross, 10" h, **$2,100**. Photo courtesy of Jackson's Auctioneers & Appraisers.

Carved ivory minstrel group, **$3,300**. Photo courtesy of Jackson's Auctioneers & Appraisers.

Fine arts, Prior School, pair, man and woman, oil on academy board, minor edge damage, some touch up, 12" w, 15" h, **$4,400**. Photo courtesy of Garth Auctions, Inc.

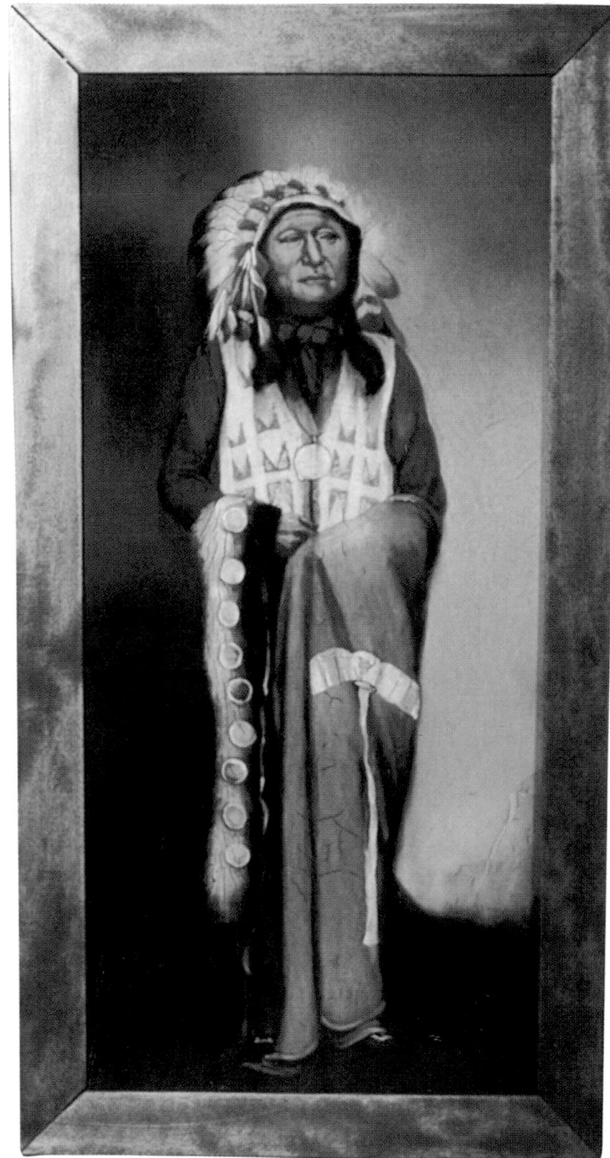

Rookwood Pottery, fine and important Standard-glaze "indian" portrait plaque painted by William P. MacDonald, 1886, depicting a standing Native American chief in headdress, 23-1/4" x 11-1/4", **$47,500**. From the Cincinnati Museum Collection, deaccessioned in 1937. Photo courtesy of David Rago Auctions.

Black memorabilia, painting, oil on board, African American man with basket of cotton, signed "W. A. Walker," 6" w, 12" w, modern frame, **$7,700**. Photo courtesy of Garth's Auction, Inc.

Fine arts painting, Henry Percy Gray, California artist, watercolor landscape, 10" x 14", **$5,880**. Photo courtesy of Jackson's Auctioneers & Appraisers.

Oriental rug, Heriz, unusual design elements, red border and ground, dark blue spandrels, overall pile wear and damage, 10' 10" x 10' 13", **$12,925**. Photo courtesy of Garth's Auction, Inc.

Oriental rug, Sarouk, red rust border, midnight blue spandrels, ivory ground, 4' 3" x 6' 10", **$3,575**. Photo courtesy of Garth's Auctions, Inc.

Quilt, pieced and appliqué, calico and chintz, cotton homespun ground, large central star, chintz border, appliqué chintz birds, butterflies, and flowers, flower and foliage quilted design, wear, age stains, some wear to chintz border, attributed to New York state, 115" x 142", **$4,400**. Photo courtesy of Garth's Auction, Inc.

Quilt, appliqué, album, thirty squares with floral and bird appliqués, red, green, yellow, and gold calico, some blue/green floral chintz, red and green calico border, cotton homespun ground, five squares with quilted initials, descended through Saint Mary's County, Maryland family, 77" x 91", **$4,950**. Photo courtesy of Garth's Auction, Inc.

Measuring cup, 4-cup, Seville Yellow 185.00
Mixing bowls, nested set, Ships, red dec on white, 6", 7", 8", 9" 185.00
Pepper shaker
Roman Arch, black, "P" 40.00
Ships, red dec on white 35.00
Pitcher
7-1/2" h, Rock Crystal, crystal 230.00
9" h, Rock Crystal, emerald green 600.00
Reamer, grapefruit, Seville yellow, 8-1/4" d 45.00
Refrigerator dish, cov
Custard, 4" x 9" 42.00
Ships, clear lid, 4" x 5" 34.00
Rolling pin, 16-3/8" l, custard, shaker lid closure 390.00
Salt shaker, 2-3/8" sq, 5" h, Skokie Green, orig label and top, inside rim chip 75.00
Server, center handle, Rock Crystal, red 140.00
Sugar bowl, Aztec, purple carnival 125.00
Sugar shaker, 2-3/8" sq, 5" h, Skokie Green, orig label and top 115.00
Syrup pitcher, 8-1/2" h, 5" w, ruby 200.00
Tea canister, custard, 48 oz 145.00
Tom and Jerry punch bowl set, 11-1/2" d, 5" h punch bowl, eight 3-1/2" h mugs, white, black lettering and trim, three mugs with chips 125.00
Tray, 13-1/2" l, 6-1/2" w, 2-1/2" h, Rock Crystal, red, rolled rim 150.00
Tumbler, Bottoms Up, caramel, 3-1/8" h, 2-3/4" d 110.00
Water cooler, 21" h, spigot, vaseline, two pcs 325.00
Window box planter, lion, Skokie Green 195.00

Medical and Pharmaceutical Items

History: Modern medicine and medical instruments are well documented. Some instruments are virtually unchanged since their invention; others have changed drastically.

The concept of sterilization phased out decorative handles. Handles on early instruments, which were often carved, were made of materials such as mother-of-pearl, ebony, and ivory. Today's sleek instruments are not as desirable to collectors.

Pharmaceutical items include those things commonly found in a drugstore and used to store or prepare medications.

Apothecary chest, table-top type, old blue painted surface, Pennsylvania, late 19th C, 20-3/4" w, 11-1/4" h, **$3,450**. Photo courtesy of Pook & Pook.

Advertising, button, Cloverine Salve Authorized Agent, celluloid, product described in detail, tiny white clover buds on green stems, blue, red, or white rim inscriptions 45.00
Advertising tin, Dr. White's Cough Drops, tin litho, white ground, red lettering, 3-1/2" l, 2-1/4" w, 5/8" h, C-8+ 550.00
Apothecary storage jar, marked "ESS: Cloves," globular, 13" d, 16" h ... 1,050.00
Bifocal spectacles, by McAllister, Philadelphia, silver frame, horseshoe-shaped lenses, sliding temples 375.00
Book
Diseases of the Blood, Roy R. Kracke, 1941, 2nd ed., 54 color plates, 46 illus, 692 pgs 25.00
Harris' Principles and Practice of Dentistry, Ferdinand Gorges, D.D.S., Philadelphia, 1892, 10th ed., 1,222 pgs, ads and numerous illus 50.00
Infectious Lung Diseases, Med Clinics of N. America, September 1978 .... 7.50
Box, Dr. Kilmer's Headache Cure, cardboard, slide tray, orig contents and flier, 2-1/2" l 325.00

Apothecary chest, wall hanging type, walnut, glass door, reverse painted sign "Family Medicines," 21" w, 37" h, **$395**. Photo courtesy of Joy Luke Auctions.

Broadside, Dr Harding's Vegetable Medicines, top text reads "Dr. Harding's Vegetable Medicines; A Cure For Constipation, and Those Diseases…," text details various medicines, mid-19th C, some folds, light foxing, minor edge chipping, ink notation on bottom border, 18" x 9-3/4" 150.00
Capsule filler, 5" h, Eastman, complete, three extra insert rings 1,050.00
Dental cabinet, 55-3/4" h, 34" w, 12-1/8" h, mahogany, flat top surmounted at rear with long drop-front cabinet raised on stepped base, streamlined main cabinet fitted with tree banks of five stacked short drawers over two banks of two stacked short drawers, over three banks of assorted short drawers above central kneehole franked by two deep short drawers, molded colorless glass drawer pulls, some drawers with porcelain and white glass receptacles and liners, four sq tapering legs, old medium finish, America, early 20th C 1,035.00
Dental chair, portable, 60" h extended, oak, adjustable height, back, and head rest, seat leather replaced, late 19th C 1,150.00
Dental sterilizer, 11-3/4" x 7" x 8", paneled mahogany case, nickeled brass fittings, compartment with alcohol burner, steam boiler fitted in large zinc copper cavity, three removable wood slat racks, 19th C 230.00

Lamp, Vapo-Cresolene, original box, used for whooping cough, **$50**. Photo courtesy of Dotta Auction Co., Inc.

Electro-medical induction coil, 10" h, T. Hall, Boston, silvered coil and switches, mahogany base, pair of later handles 1,150.00
Field surgeon's set, 10-1/2" w, Lentz & Sons, Philadelphia, all metal instruments, including Rust's pattern bone saw, Liston knife, trephine, bone forceps, etc., metal case with canvas cover case, both marked "2nd Reg. N.G.P." 350.00
Forceps tooth key, 7-1/2" l, removable bolster/claw, hatched handles, W & H Hutchinson, Sheffield, England, mid-19th C, restorations 690.00
Hour glass, 9-1/2" h, Tartanware, McDuff pattern, half hour 175.00

Jar, orig stopper, 10-1/2" h, Duff's Colic & Diarrhea Remedy, cylindrical glass, recessed reverse painted on glass label, ground stopper matches pattern at base, some minor staining **250.00**

Medicine chest, 15" w, 15" d, 22" h, on later stand, American, 19th C, mahogany, lift top, fitted int. above base drawer, brass mounts, top with brass plaque inscribed "U.S. Standard Medicine Chest, made by J.N. Hegeman & CO., New York" **650.00**

Optician's trial set, 21" w, Brown, Philadelphia, retailer's label, oak case, partial set.................................... **175.00**

Optometrist's sample case, 20" w, mahogany, containing three trays of 20 spectacles each, chart in lid........ **690.00**

Periodontal set, 16" l, 140 (out of 150) various scalers, fitted cream-colored painted wood case........................ **60.00**

Phrenological bust, 9-1/2" h, plaster, Fowler, Wells & Co., Boston, labeled cranium, label on back, damaged **80.00**

Plugger, 8" l, Goodman & Shurtler's Patent, mechanical gold foil, sprung, hinged mallet on ebonite body, interchangeable head **460.00**

Scarificator, brass, 16 blades, sgd "Kolb," European, early 19th C **215.00**

Show globe, orig matching wall brackets, chains, jars, and lids, 33" h, price for pr............................... **1,150.00**

Microscope, Spencer, orig carrying case, 13" h, **$150**. Photo courtesy of Joy Luke Auctions.

Sign

- Dr. Cox's Barbed Wire Liniment, cardboard, Carlisle, IN, professionally matted and framed, 29" x 25"................................**375.00**
- Scheneck's Pulmonic Syrup Sea Weed Tonic and Mandrake Pills, litho tin, trimmed to 27-3/4" x 22" **1,850.00**
- Scotch Oil for Man or Beast is the Best Liniment, young woman sitting on stone fence, marked "J. H. Burfords Sons Litho," 1887 copyright, canvas, roll-down, wooden frame, 17" w, 30-1/2" w **2,200.00**

Spittoon, brass, Rochester Stamping Co **90.00**

Tooth extractor, 6-3/4" l, W. R. Goulding, New York, marked "Baker & Riley patented 1845," removable claw/bolster, cross-hatched handles............. **1,380.00**

Tooth key

- 5" l, turned horn handle, cranked shaft, adjustable claw **150.00**
- 6-1/2" l, turned and hatched removable rosewood handle, turned cranked shaft, adjustable circular bolster and claw, early 19th C **215.00**
- 7-1/2" l, turned ivory handle, turned shaft, adjustable claw **460.00**

Trade catalog, 4-3/4" x 7-3/8", Van Schaack, Stevenson & Co., Chicago, 1883, 575 pgs, listings, illus, color plates **1,800.00**

Trepan, 10-1/4" l, burnished steel, sgd "Sir Henry a Paris," 18th C, arrowhead perforator, ivory pivot, ebony handle, five elevators **1,725.00**

Veterinary cabinet, 20" w, 10-1/4" d, 27-3/4" h, Humphrey's Remedies, tin front lists remedies, seven different unopened orig remedies in cabinet, some damage **400.00**

Medicine Bottles

History: The local apothecary and his book of formulas played a major role in early America. In 1796, the U.S. Patent Office issued the first patent for a medicine. At that time, anyone could apply for a medicinal patent and as long as the dosage was not poisonous, the patent was granted.

Patent medicines were advertised in newspapers and magazines and sold through the general store and at "medicine" shows. In 1907, the Pure Food and Drug Act, requiring an accurate description of contents on a medicine container's label, put an end to the patent medicine industry. Not all medicines were patented.

Most medicines were sold in distinctive bottles, often with the name of the medicine and location of manufacture in relief. Many early bottles were made in the glass-manufacturing area of southern New Jersey. Later, companies in western Pennsylvania and Ohio manufactured bottles.

American Expectorant, America, 1840-60, octagonal, greenish aquamarine, outward rolled mouth, pontil scar, 5-7/8" h **425.00**

Crockett's Amygdaline, R. Hall & Co., Proprietors, applied top, late 1860s, 7" **200.00**

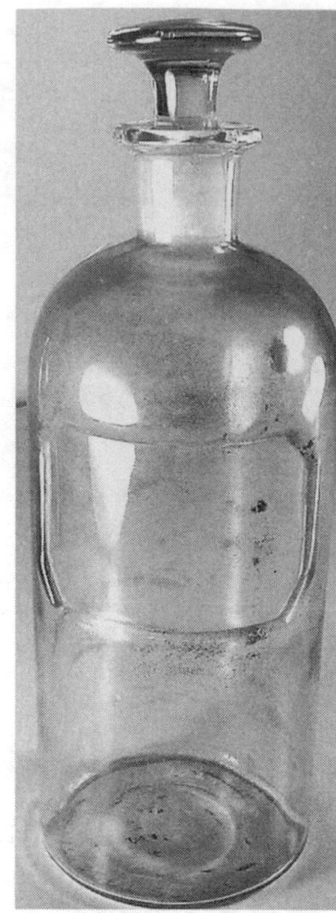

Civil war era, glass stopper, bottom marked "Pat'd Sept 23d 1862/W. N. Walton," 9" h, **$230**. Photo courtesy of Historical Collectibles Auction.

Dr. Chas T. Price-67 William St., New York, Cure for Fits, oval, tooled mouth, smooth base, c1880-95, clear, 8-1/2" h **330.00**

Dr. Ham's Aromatic Invigorating Spirit, cylindrical, applied mouth, smooth base, c1875-85, orange-amber, 8-1/2" h **65.00**

Dr. Lepper's Mountain Tea, tooled top, bluish-aqua, 8-1/2" h **100.00**

Dr. Warren's Botanic Cough Balsam, San Francisco, CA, applied top, deep blue aqua, 8-1/4" **275.00**

E. A. Buckhout's Dutch Liniment, Prepared At Mechanicsville, Saratoga Co. NY, rect, beveled corners, figure of standing Dutch man, tooled mouth, pontil scar, 4-5/8" h................................ **400.00**

From the Laboratory of G. W. Merchant, Chemist, Lockport, N. Y., attributed to Lockport Glass Works, Lockport, NY, 1840-60, rect, chamfered corners, deep yellowish green, applied sloping collard mouth, tubular pontil scar, 5-1/2" h **500.00**

Gleet Seven-Days Gonorrhea, rect, tooled mouth, "M. B.W. Millville" on smooth base, c1890-1910, deep cobalt blue, 5" h, some stains **800.00**

Gogings Wild Cherry Tonic, sq, beveled corners, tooled mouth, smooth base, c1890-1900, medium amber, 8-3/4" h **90.00**

Houcks Vegetable Pancea, Goodlestville, Tenn, rect, beveled corners, applied double-collar mouth, smooth base, c1855-60, deep blue-aqua, 7-1/8" h **700.00**

Fountain Of Youth Hair Restorer, cobalt blue, tooled lip, attributed to Sacramento, 7-1/2" h, **$1,050**. Photo courtesy of Pacific Glass Auctions.

Iceland Balsam for Pulmonary Consumption, Iceland Balsam, America, 1830-50, rect, beveled corners, emb on three sides, yellow olive, short applied sloping collared mouth, pontil scar, 6-1/2" h, professionally cleaned, light emb lettering **5,500.00**
Leving's Hoarhound and Elecampane Syrup, crude applied top, heavy thick writing, 7" h **425.00**
O'Rourke & Hurley Druggist & Pharmacists, 501 Main Street Little Falls, N.Y. in cursive writing, tooled top, brilliant cobalt blue, 4-1/4" h, c1890 .... **50.00**
Shaker Family Pills, Dose 2 to 4, A. J. White, rect, paneled sides, sheared lip, smooth base, c1890-1900, medium amber, 2-1/4" h **95.00**

E.R. SQUIBB embossed on shoulder, clear 2" stopper, smooth base, applied square collar, 7-3/4" h, **$425**. Photo courtesy of American Bottle Auctions.

Swaim's Panacea, Philada, paneled cylinder, applied sloping double collar, open pontil, c1840-50, medium yellow-olive, 7-3/4" h **860.00**
Swift's Syphilitic Specific, flask form, applied mouth, smooth base, c1870-90, deep cobalt blue, 9-1/8" h, some roughness on orig strap edge...... **635.00**
Turner's Balsam, eight sided, aqua, 4-7/8" h.. **65.00**
Warner's Safe Nervine, amber bottle, orig contents and fliers, box 98 percent complete, 9-1/2" h **575.00**

Mercury Glass

History: Mercury glass is a light-bodied, double-walled glass that was "silvered" by applying a solution of silver nitrate to the inside of the object through a hole in its base.

F. Hale Thomas of London patented the method in 1849. In 1855, the New England Glass Co. filed a patent for the same type of process. Other American glassmakers soon followed. The glass reached the height of its popularity in the early 20th century.

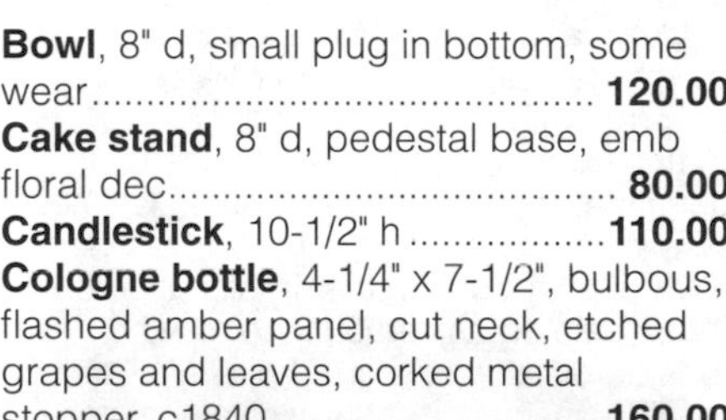

For more information, see *Warman's Glass*, 4th edition.

Bowl, 8" d, small plug in bottom, some wear... **120.00**
Cake stand, 8" d, pedestal base, emb floral dec.. **80.00**
Candlestick, 10-1/2" h **110.00**
Cologne bottle, 4-1/4" x 7-1/2", bulbous, flashed amber panel, cut neck, etched grapes and leaves, corked metal stopper, c1840 .... **160.00**

Butler's ball, glass ball on pedestal base, 10-1/2" h, **$400**. Photo courtesy of Alderfer Auction Co.

Creamer, 6-1/2" h, etched ferns, applied clear handle, attributed to Sandwich **140.00**
Curtain tiebacks, 3-1/8" d, 4-1/2" l, etched grape design, price for pr **140.00**
Door knob set, 2-1/4" d **80.00**
Goblet, 5" d, gold, white lily of the valley dec **40.00**

Pitcher, 5-1/2" x 9-3/4" h, bulbous, panel cut neck, engraved lacy florals and leaves, applied clear handle, c1840 .... **225.00**
Salt, 3" x 3", price for pr **100.00**
Sugar bowl, cov, 4-1/4" x 6-1/4", low foot, enameled white foliage dec, knob finial **65.00**
Vase, 9-3/4" h, cylindrical, raised circular foot, everted rim, bright enameled yellow, orange, and blue floral sprays and insects, pr.................................... **225.00**

Mettlach

History: In 1809, Jean Francis Boch established a pottery at Mettlach in Germany's Moselle Valley. His father had started a pottery at Septfontaines in 1767. Nicholas Villeroy began his pottery career at Wallerfanger in 1789.

In 1841, these three factories merged. They pioneered underglaze printing on earthenware, using transfers from copper plates, and also were among the first companies to use coal-fired kilns. Other factories were developed at Dresden, Wadgassen, and Danischburg. Mettlach decorations include relief and etched designs, prints under the glaze, and cameos.

For more information, see *Warman's English & Continental Pottery & Porcelain*, 3rd edition.

Marks: The castle and Mercury emblems are the two chief marks, although secondary marks are known. The base of each piece also displays a shape mark and usually a decorator's mark.

Additional Listings: Villeroy & Boch.

Note: Prices in this listing are for print-under-glaze pieces, unless otherwise specified.

Coaster, 4-7/8" d, PUG, drinking scene, marked "Mettlach, Villeroy & Boch" **150.00**
Jardinière, 5-1/2" h, 8-3/4" x 10", green ground, off-white cameo figures of Grecian men and women riding in carriage, sitting at table and drinking, base imp "#7000" and "#17"........ **425.00**
Loving cup, 7-3/8" w, 6-3/4" h, three handles, musicians dec **185.00**

Plaques, pair, stoneware, Aesthetic Movement, one depicting springtime lady with watering can and flowering vine, other summer lady gathering produce in basket, both with incised signature "C. Warth," and dated 1882, velvet-edged frames, plaque sight 16" x 10", frame 20-1/2" x 14- 5/8", **$1,100**. Photo courtesy of Skinner, Inc.

Plaque, #2196, castle scene and boats, 17-1/2" d, **$490**. Photo courtesy of James D. Julia, Inc.

Plaque

#1168, Cavalier, threading and glaze, sgd "Warth," chip on rear hanging rim, 16-1/2" d **465.00**

#2196, Stolzensels Castle on the Rhein, 17" d **1,100.00**

#2443, classical scene of women and eight attendants, cameo, white high relief, blue-gray ground, artist sgd "J. Stahl," blue-gray ground, 18-1/4" d **1,550.00**

Stein, #3878, stoneware, 1/2 litre, stoneware lid with pewter rim and thumb rest, **$60**. Photo courtesy of Joy Luke Auctions.

Stein

#1896, 1/4 liter, maiden on one side, cherub face on other, grape dec, pewter lift handle **350.00**

#2028, 1/2 liter, etched, men in Gasthaus, inlaid lid **550.00**

#2057, 1/2 liter, etched, festive dancing scene, inlaid lid **325.00**

#2100, 1/3 liter, etched, Germans meeting Romans, inlaid lid, H. Schlitt **495.00**

#2950, 1/2 liter, cameo, Bavarian crest, pewter lid with relief crest **825.00**

#5001, 4.6 liter, faience type, coat of arms, pewter lid **850.00**

MILITARIA

For more information, see *Warman's Civil War Collectibles*.

History: Wars have occurred throughout recorded history. Until the mid-19th century, soldiers often had to provide for their own needs, including supplying their own weapons. Even in the 20th century, a soldier's uniform and some of his gear are viewed as his personal property, even though issued by a military agency.

At end of World War I, when a soldier was discharged, he was issued a new woolen uniform. Insignia from aviation squadrons, Chemical Corps, Postal Express, and Trench Mortar battalions are the desirable to modern collectors. Uniforms with a solid provenance command premium prices. The better the identification, the higher the price. Helmets were painted by soldiers themselves in WWI, often repeating the divisional patch. Those painted as camouflage may be considered "soldier's art." Fake WWI shoulder insignia exist as well as painted helmets, and collar discs. WWI aviation material is often a favorite target of fakers—assume it's faked until proven otherwise.

Conquering armed forces made a habit of acquiring souvenirs from their vanquished foes. They also brought their own uniforms and accessories home as badges of triumph and service.

Saving militaria may be one of the oldest collecting traditions. Militaria collectors tend to have their own special shows and view themselves outside the normal antiques channels. However, they haunt small indoor shows and flea markets in hopes of finding additional materials.

Reproduction Alert: Pay careful attention to Civil War and Nazi material.

Revolutionary War

Autograph, document sgd, promotion of First Lieutenant, by Benjamin Harrison, 1783, paper seal, 6" x 8" **650.00**

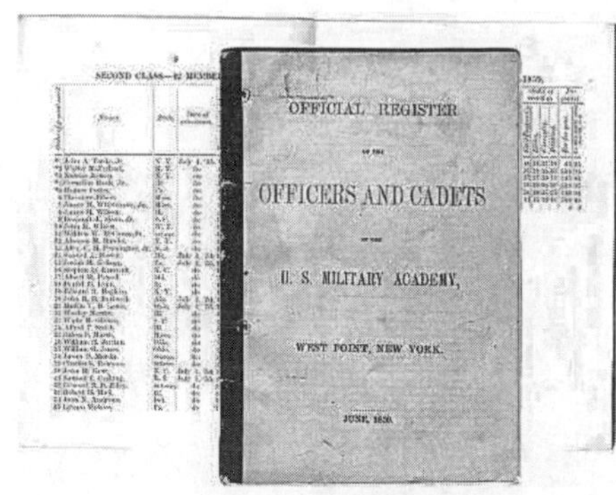

Booklet, *Official Register of the Officers and Cadets of the US Military Academy, West Point, New York*, professors and cadets listed in order of merit, June 1859, 18 pages, 4-1/2" x 6-3/4", **$260**. Photo courtesy of Historical Collectibles Auctions.

Canteen, cooper-made barrel stave, initials AK, JR, and OD, 1778, 1788 .... **4,260.00**

Drum, snare, large red and brown eagle, E Pluribus Unum banner, orig skins, hoops, ropes, and pulls **12,000.00**

Medal, bronze, John Paul Jones **210.00**

Print, Perry's Victory on Lake Erie, Perry in rowboat, eight sailors in midst of battle, steel engraving from painting by Thomas Birch, engraved by A. Lawson, published by William Smith, Philadelphia, Eastlake frame, 24" x 31" **295.00**

Pocket watch, key wound, orig key, inscribed "I Shelby 1802," watch movement by John J Wilmurt of NY, English silver case with paper label from GW Stewart, Lexington, KY watchmaker, hero Issac Shelby was first governor of KY **3,520.00**

Saddle cover, leopard or cheetah skin, holster and valise, framed orig trade card for "Saddles, Chaises, Harnesses, Trunks, Caps & Military Equipment, Made by John Burlington, Corner of Liberty and Vines Streets, Salem, Mass" **4,500.00**

Shoe buckles, pr, silver over iron, embellished with two medallions of Washington in profile, inauguration souvenirs, 1789 .... **20,000.00**

Snuff box, cov, 2-7/8" d, gutta percha, round, relief scene of battle, ships, coastline, buildings, French inscription "Prise d'Yorck 1781 (Taking of Yorktown or Battle of Yorktown)" **750.00**

French and Indian War

Marching order, letter addressed to Captain Josiah Thatcher, Yarmouth, his Majesty's Service, Boston, June 24, 1761, ordering Thatcher to march troops to Springfield to be mustered, sgd by J. Hoar, some fold weakness, 8" x 6-1/4" **185.00**

Uniform button mold, 9" l, brass, American, 18th C, casts six round buttons with central raised letter "I" for infantry, one 25 mm, one 18 mm, four 14.5 mm, each with eyelet, wooden handles missing **625.00**

War of 1812

Broadside, 15-1/2" h, 12-1/4" w, "Citizens to Arms!," New York, Aug 27, 1814, reverse with inscription suggesting it was given to Archibald Robertson by his father-in-law **13,000.00**

Cartridge box, leather, white cloth strap, very worn, missing plate **70.00**

Cannon jack, 24" h, cast iron and brass, stamped "USA Waterviet Arsenal," c1820 .... **6,000.00**

Epaulets, pr, War of 1812, officer's, gilt metal, brass spread-wing eagle **6,000.00**

Flag, 60-1/2" x 110", 13 stars, Naval, hand sewn **1,100.00**

Knapsack, insignia and initials of light artillery, c1812-15 .... **10,000.00**

Military drum, large eagle painted on sides, red, and blue stripes, one drumhead, 22" h, 17" d **750.00**

Ship document, British, articles pertaining to private armed ship Dart and four carriage guns, six nine-pounders, four swivel guns lying in St. John, New Brunswick, designed to cruise against Americas, details prize division, chain of command, other shipboard administration, dated July 1813, right section includes signatures and ratings of 44 seamen and officers as crew, some staining, edge chipping, foxing, and fold splitting, Whatman 1808 watermark, 21" x 29".. **500.00**

Watercolor, British militiaman in full dress uniform, titled "Peter Medicott, 1st Co.," war of 1812............................... **2,250.00**

Book set, *The Soldier in our Civil War,* volumes I and II, copyright 1890, both illustrated, **$200**. Photo courtesy of Joy Luke Auctions.

Civil War

Ammunition pouch, leather, Private John F. Shawmon, Company F, 1st PA Calvary, bull's eye canteen, orig blue cover, lock-blade knife, sold with military records, family history, and rubbing of soldier's Gettysburg tombstone **1,150.00**

Autograph, Robert E Lee

Letter, three pages, hand written, discussed assignment of officers of Louisville's 2nd Calvary..... **13,800.00**

Telegraph, dated June 1864, sent by Maj Gen John C. Breckenridge to Gen G. T. Beauregard, sgd on back **10,925.00**

Autograph album, GAR, 4-1/2" x 7", most pages signed at Milwaukee Reunion, Aug. 29, 1889, maroon velvet cover **110.00**

Civil War, backpack, tarred cotton, large 14" x 13" pouch, 10" x 13" pouch, double leather closure straps, leather shoulder harness, brass and iron hooks and buckles, one strap marked "WM. BUTTE NY, August 13, 1864," tears, leather dry and crackled, **$230**. Photo courtesy of James D. Julia Auctions.

Badge

Delegate, G.A.R., Indiana, metal hanger bar, cello pendant joined by red, white, and blue striped ribbon, inscribed in gold, dark bronze luster hanger with IN state seal, view of "Entrance to Soldier's Home, Marion, Ind.," 36th annual encampment, May, 1915, ribbon worn........... **25.00**

G.A.R. 31st National Encampment-Buffalo, 1897, dark bronze luster finish, diecut link badge, official star symbol, eagles, flags, patriotic shield dated 1897 .... **35.00**

Belt and plate, black leather belt, brass loops, two-piece brass VA state plate, minor wear and splits **2,350.00**

Book

Gettysburg to the Rapidan by General Meade's Chief of Staff, Andrew Humphreys, 1883, 243 pgs, maps **45.00**

The Life of Stonewall Jackson, J. E. Cooke, 1863 .... **45.00**

Bridle bit, officer's, silvered lion eagle **2,000.00**

Cabinet card, 5th Marine Brigade **145.00**

Cavalry guidon, Confederate, 17" x 11" guidon with 11 white four-point stars on blue field, broad red, white, and red stripes, all handsewn, small holes, stitched tear, 107" oak or ash staff with dark patina, 9-1/2" l wrought iron lance tip, early attached tag "Confederate lance, as captured at Richmond 1865," accompanied by letter of provenance from Norm Flayderman **14,300.00**

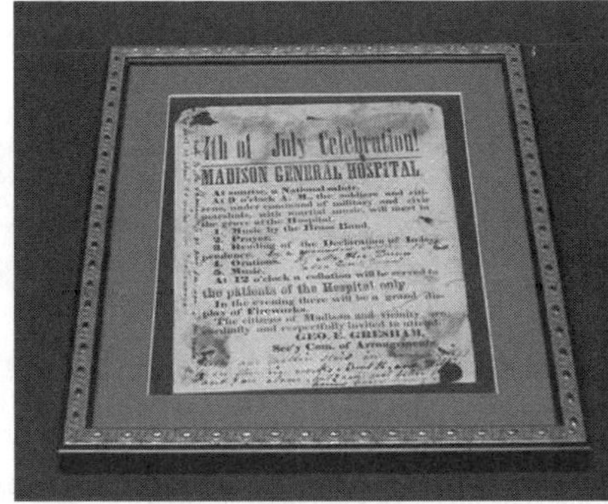

Book set, *The Soldier in our Civil War,* volumes I and II, copyright 1890, both illustrated, **$200**. Photo courtesy of Joy Luke Auctions.

Cane, 35-3/4" l, carved wood, 1-1/2" w x 3" h oval wood knob, relief carved and polychromed shaft with American flag, 24 Union army corps badges, worn red, white, blue, and green polychrome, 1-3/4" brass ferrule, made for veteran, c1880... **350.00**

Canteen

Cedar, old mellow brown finish, flat steel bands and loops around sides, cork stopper with emb tin top sgd "G. H. Mumm & Co." around top, slight warp to sides, 8" d..... **1,650.00**

Cheesebox type, rosehead nail dec, pale turquoise ground, gold spread eagle, calligraphic initials JB **4,500.00**

Wool covered, Model 1858, orig cloth strap, cork stopper with finger loop, tin spout, 10" with spout **360.00**

Carte de visite, with sgd card, John Surratt, Confederate secret agent and associate of John Wilkes Booth, unpublished.............................. **4,888.00**

Cartridge box, cross belt and eagle plate, "Calhoune New York" maker's stamp on inner flap, tin liners, oval U.S. plate.. **900.00**

Collection of textiles and relics, all identified on small cards, fragment of battle flag with star from 91st regt, PA Vol.; section of Rebel flag taken down by Col Ellsworth; piece of Ft. Sumpter flag with presenting officers' names including Doubleday and Cadwalader; fragment of Col. Baker's shirt from CA regiment killed at Balls Bluff; Silk & Grass from Hartford's flag; sliver of wood from George Washington's casket; horsehair from tail of Gen Taylor's charger, 14-1/2" x 36-1/2" frame **4,400.00**

Grouping, Eli Tucker diary, dated 1865, Eli Tucker Union discharge certificate, Confederate State of Georgia complete page of 40 coupon bonds, all framed under glass, **$750**. Photo courtesy of Joy Luke Auctions.

Confederate notes, group of $500, $10, and $5, from Richmond, matted and framed, 21-1/2" x 17" **275.00**

Coat, Confederate Officer's, double breasted, blue-gray wool, low collar, blue piping along front, 12 large VA and NC buttons marked "Scovill Mfg. Waterbury," three small buttons with same markings, two have black velvet coverings, Captain's bars on collar, buttons and insignia removed for previous cleaning, minor moth damage to ext. **39,600.00**

Envelope, 3" x 5-1/2", white, printed in tiny letters on reverse flap for Congressional entry in 1861 by publisher J. Magee, Philadelphia, front left third with blue cachet cartoon of Jefferson Davis noosed for hanging as disenchanted Black man walks away carrying hobo stick, descriptive verse **20.00**

Fife, 17-1/2" l, rosewood, nickel silver ends, eight bands, orig dark finish, faint signature "W. Crosby, Boston" **125.00**

Flag, GAR, Maine, 45 stars, from post of Maj Gen Joshua L. Chamberlain **690.00**

Helmet

Dragoon, c1830-50, New York pattern, lettered to the side "5th Reg't Cavalary H'D Qrt's, New Milford, CT, gilded and emb leather New York state seal **38,000.00**

Dragoon, c1840, brass sunburst hat plate stamped "A," brass comb with horsehair plume **2,500.00**

Newspaper, Cincinnati Gazette, for year of 1863, fold lines and minor damage, group of 19 newspapers **150.00**

Photograph, painted ambrotype, ninth plate photo size, Confederate soldier, red haired, blue uniform, brass buttons, wearing red and black bow tie, 8-3/4" x 6-7/8" carved split baluster frame with cornice moldings, shaped side pieces, painted in black and brown with gold highlights, wear **1,410.00**

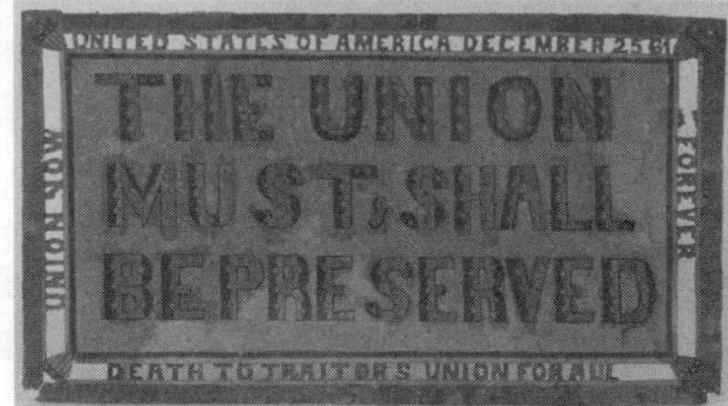

Watercolor on paper, Civil War, dated "Dec. 25, '61," verse "The Union Must and Shall Be Preserved," 13" x 23", **$1,495**. Photo courtesy of Pook & Pook.

Photograph, tintype, cased

Cavalryman, wearing shell jacket with gilt detail on collar and buttons, lightly tinted blue pants, holding cavalry saber, Colt pistol in belt, forage cap with "D2," sixth plate **770.00**

Confederate, checked shirt, butternut colored coat, CDV mount **110.00**

Soldiers in front of tent, very worn quarter plate tintype, gutta-percha case with relief scene of officers standing at table, scrolled border, minor edge chips **470.00**

Pinback button

Battle of Gettysburg 1913 Anniversary, multicolored, blue lettering **25.00**

Col. W. C. Johnson, G.A.R., black and white photo, orange ground, black lettering for sponsor "Snellenburg Stores, Philadelphia, Pa.," and "G.A.R. Encampment 1899" **20.00**

Powder flask, copper, stamped "ADK 1849," 9-3/4" h **500.00**

Print, framed

Emmitsburg Road, by Don Troiani, battlescene............................ **250.00**

Night Conference, by John Paul Strain, shows Gen. Robert E. Lee meeting with two of his generals under large tree...................... **300.00**

Tomorrow We Must Attack, by Dale Galion, showing Confederatel generals **125.00**

Quilt, 84-1/2" x 79", cotton, three central panels, upper with American eagle pieced of yellow and brown, holding red banner in beat, inscribed "The Union Forever," above white dotted blue field with 34 stars arranged in Great Star pattern, above white field containing symbolic broken chain and pieced letters "End of the War," quilted stars and ships on panels, flanked by 13 red and white stripes quilted alternately with guns and swords, backed with white cotton, edged in blue, made by Ladies Auxiliary group of mothers and sisters of boys serving in Union Army from Sandy Creek Co., NY, started in 1861, sent to Gen. Grant in April 1865, who returned it with a note of thanks and asking it be sold to raise funds for local charity, sold at auction at rally to Mr. P. M. Newton of Sandy Creek, then descended in family, imperfections **21,150.00**

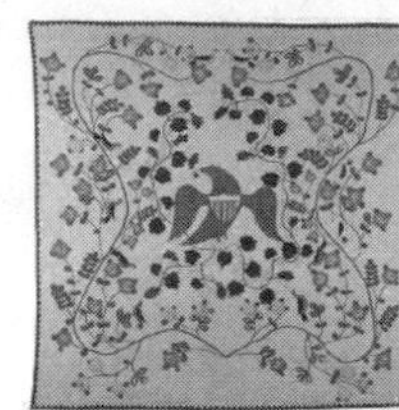

Quilt, Civil War, pieced, made by Mary Bell Shawvan, c1863, solid color and calico printed cotton, central spreadwing eagle with shield surrounded by meandering flowering vines and grapevines with perching birds; leaves, flowers, birds, and fruit stuffed for three-dimensional effect, black silk accenting the birds' wings and tails, yellow-orange floral print ground, dark green scalloped border quilted in a scallop pattern, off-white muslin backing, minor imperfections, 84" x 81-1/2", **$149,000**. Photo courtesy of Skinner, Inc.

Recruiting poster, New York state, "War Meeting, Attend to the Draft!" Aug. 16, 1862, framed **2,185.00**

Ribbon, 2" x 3-1/2", white silk, center red, white and blue US flag with twenty stars, graphic area beneath flag blue on white image of bugle and saber sword crossed over flag pole, blue lettering "Union and Democracy" **70.00**

Civil War, pocket watch, Confederate, gold hunter case, key wind, early wood fired locomotive engraved on cover with surrounding floral and arabesque pattern and engraving, back cover engraved "TGR TO S.W. RABB," inside back cover engraved "John Watt Rabb/Son Of John Glazier Rabb/Was Killed In The Battle Of Gaines/Milles, Va., June 30-1862, Wearing/This Watch, And Carrying The/Colors Of The 6th South Carolinas/ Regiment," size 16, single spring-loaded cover, unmarked dial, watch is accompanied by invoices of sale and letter from Sumpter Military Antiques dated 1-31-96 and two packets of copies of archival muster rolls of the 6th Reg't So. Carolina Infantry giving more information about original owner, **$4,255**. Photo courtesy of James D. Julia, Inc.

Spurs, pr, 4" h, brass, Confederate, Leech & Rigdon style **115.00**

Stereoview daugerreotype, occupational scene **6,038.00**
Sword, belt rig, non-commissioned officer, NCO sword by Ames Mfg, Chicopee MA, marked on blade, also marked "US, GWC, 1864," marked "GKC" on guard, leather scabbard, NCO sword belt ring, eagle buckle, plated wreath, frog for NCO sword and hangers, some leather deterioration to belt and scabbard **900.00**

Indian War

Bayonet, Model 1873, 3-1/2" w blade **80.00**
Belt buckle, Naval officer, brass, stamped "Horstman, Phila" **120.00**
Broadside, Ohio massacre, No. 4, 1791, printed in Boston, 1792, foxed, water stained, modern frame **900.00**
Hat plate, toleware, tombstone shape
- 7-1/4" h, Westbrook Artillery, MA, c1820 .... **8,000.00**
- 8" h, CT, 1819 .... **1800.00**

Spanish American War

Cartridge box, U.S. Army **125.00**
Hat badge, infantry, brass, crossed krag rifles, 2" l **55.00**
Pinback button, "Remember the Maine," battleship scene, patent 1896........ **25.00**
Spy glass, pocket, brass, Naval, round holder, brown leather grip, 16" l..... **110.00**

Star for J. P. Lewis, PA Vol, Company B, 29, photo of Lewis's cemetery marker, daugerrotype case, materials used for pilgrimage by World War I soldier, **$600**. Photo courtesy of Joseph P. Smalley, Jr., Auctioneer.

World War I

American flag, 6-1/4" x 10-1/4" sight, cloth, eight stars and five stripes, made by Prisoner of War, "Arlon Belgium Dec 11th, 1918" written on mat, framed, some losses, discoloration.................... **350.00**
Bayonet, British, MK II, No. 4, spike, scabbard **20.00**
Book, Regimental History of the 316 Infantry **25.00**
Buckle, U.S. Balloon Corps, emb hot air balloon.. **75.00**
Compass, marked "Made in France" **45.00**
Dog tag stamping kit, orig wood box, complete..................................... **250.00**
Flare pistol, Model 1918, French **100.00**
Gun sling, soft leather, 1917, for 03 Springfield **17.50**
Helmet
- 6th Marines, British Brodies, painted **195.00**
- 35th Division 139th Infantry Regiment, camouflaged.......... **85.00**
- German, Pattern, 1916, painted gray/ green **80.00**

Toy, World War I, tin horse-drawn ambulance wagon with two horses, four composition soldiers on horseback, 15 composition figures, **$490**. Photo courtesy of Joy Luke Auctions.

Trench flashlight and note pad, German, black tin container, orig pad and pencil... **65.00**
Tunic and breeches, 5th Division band leader, custom tailored **275.00**
Tunic, triple-patch, 332 Infantry, 83rd Division, 3rd Army **1,450.00**
Trunk group, 28th Division 103rd Ammunition Train, soldier's (things backed in trunk in 1919, such as uniform, dog tags, etc.)............................ **625.00**
Watch fob, Federal Seal, U.S. officer **15.00**

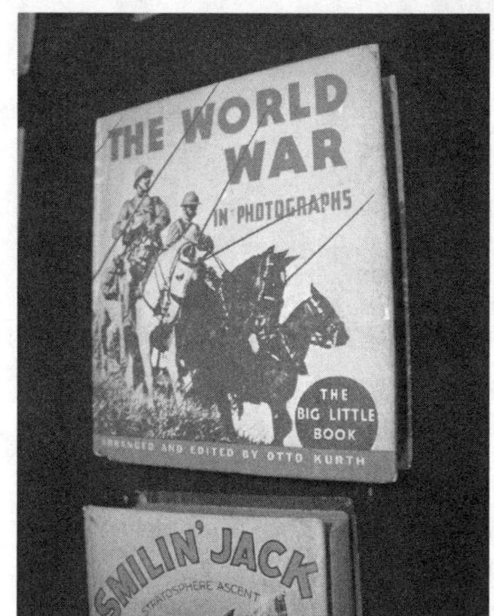

Big Little Book, *The War in Photographs*, Otto Kurth, red, black, and white cover, **$35**.

World War II

Armband, Japan, military police, red lettering, white cotton **48.00**
Cane, 30-3/4" l, Civilian Conservation Corps, fully carved, U-shaped horse-head handle, one piece, carved low relief of trees, bathing beauty, alligator, name of carver's friends, "Middle Creek Camp F34 Co. 997," 1933, finish removed around later added date **125.00**
Cookbook, Meat Reference Manual for Mess Sergeants and Cooks, Prepared for the United States Army by the National Live Stock and Meat Board, March 1943, 36 pgs, soft cover.......................... **18.00**
Flag, New Zealand PT boat, printed on blue cotton................................... **55.00**
Flyers goggles, Japanese, boxed, gray fur lined cups, yellow lenses **35.00**
Gas mask, German, canister style, rubber mask, canvas straps, carrying container....................................... **80.00**
Hat, flat, Navy Destroyer Tender USS Prairie **85.00**

Timepiece, wall, British Royal Airforce, second half 20th C, single fusee movement by Elliot Ltd., round dial with standard and military time, accented with orange, blue, and yellow triangles, RAF embossed lem above the hands, mahogany case, 18-1/2" d, **$450**. Photo courtesy of Skinner, Inc.

Helmet, Italian, steel, leather chip strap **100.00**
ID tag, U.S. Army, oval pattern, instruction envelope, chain **25.00**
Manual, 6-1/4" x 10", War Department, FM30-30, Military Intelligence, Aircraft Recognition Pictorial Manual, Bureau of Aeronautics, Washington, DC, 1943, 179 pgs, illus of US, Great Britain, German, Japanese, Italian, Russian, etc. plans **40.00**
Matchsafe, brass, orig German matches **150.00**
Poster, "This Isn't War...It's Murder," 21-1/8" x 17"....................................... **95.00**
Shell casing, 31st Division, "Diary" **490.00**
Telescope, 14" l, Australian, MK 1, heavy leather case and carrying straps **45.00**

MILK GLASS

History: Opaque white glass attained its greatest popularity at the end of the 19th century. American glass manufacturers made opaque white tablewares as a substitute for costly European china and glass. Other opaque colors, e.g., blue and green, also were made. Production of milk-glass novelties came in with the Edwardian era.

For more information, see *Warman's Glass*, 4th edition.

The surge of popularity in milk glass subsided after World War I. However, milk glass continues to be made in the 20th century. Some modern products are reissues and reproductions of earlier forms. This presents a significant problem for collectors, although it is partially obviated by patent dates or company markings on the originals and by the telltale signs of age.

Collectors favor milk glass from the pre-World War I era, especially animal-covered dishes. The most prolific manufacturers of these animal covers were Atterbury, Challinor-Taylor, Flaccus, and McKee.

Notes: There are many so-called "McKee" animal-covered dishes. Caution must be exercised in evaluating pieces because some authentic covers were not signed. Furthermore, many factories have made, and many still are making, split-rib bases with McKee-like animal covers or with different animal covers. The prices here are for authentic McKee pieces with either the cover or base signed.

Covered dish, Battleship, **$115**. Photo courtesy of Sky Hawk Auctions.

Animal dish, cov
- Cat on hamper, green, V mark **115.00**
- Chick on sleigh, white **115.00**
- Cow **160.00**
- Dewey, chips on base **90.00**
- Dolphin **145.00**
- Duck, white, top **145.00**
- Kitten, ribbed base, Westmoreland, white **130.00**
- Robin on nest, med blue **165.00**
- Setter dog, blue **265.00**
- Swan, closed neck, white **120.00**
- Turkey, amethyst head, white body **220.00**
- Turkey, white head, dark amethyst body **170.00**

Bowl, 8-1/4" d, Daisy, all-over leaves and flower design, open scalloped edge (F165) **85.00**
Bust, 5-1/2" h, Admiral Dewey **300.00**
Butter dish, cov, 4-7/8" l, Roman Cross pattern, sq, ftd base curves outward toward top, cube-shape finial (F240) **75.00**
Calling card receiver, bird, wings extended over fanned tail, head resting on leaf, detailed feather pattern (F669) **150.00**
Centerpiece bowl, 13" l, 11" w, lattice edge, Westmoreland **125.00**
Child's mug, elephant handle **60.00**
Compote, Atlas, lacy edge, blue **185.00**

Plate, Indian chief center, three strands of beads, scalloped edges with embossed decoration, attributed to Westmoreland, 7-1/2" d, **$35**.

Creamer and sugar, Trumpet Vine, fire painted dec, sgd "SV" **130.00**
Egg cup, cov, 4-1/4" h, bird, round, fluted, Atterbury (F130) **135.00**
Hat, Stars and Stripes, black rim **235.00**
Lamp, 11" h, Goddess of Liberty, bust, three stepped hexagonal bases, clear and frosted font, brass screw connector, patent date, Atterbury (F329) **300.00**
Match holder, smiling boy **170.00**
Milk pitcher, 8-3/4" h, Wild Iris, gilt trim, c1825 ..... **125.00**
Mug, 3-1/4", Medallion, c1870 ..... **50.00**

Plate
- Easter, bunny, basket of eggs **35.00**
- Rabbit center, horseshoe and clover border **145.00**
- Three dogs and squirrel **65.00**

Spooner, 5-1/8" h, monkey, scalloped top (F275) **125.00**

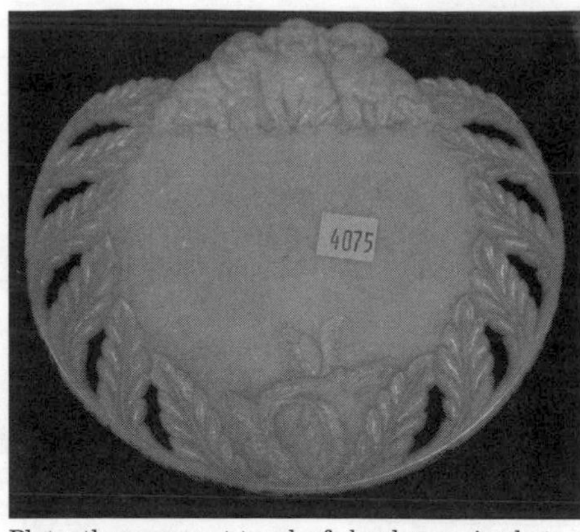
Plate, three pugs at top, leafy border, squirrel at bottom, **$45**.

Sugar shaker, Forget-me-not, green, orig top **50.00**
Tumbler, Royal Oak, orig fired paint, green band **50.00**
Vanity box, cov, 7" l, 2" w, 2" h, hand painted enamel floral dec, gold trim, imp "16" on both lid and base **250.00**
Water pitcher, Guttate, gold trim **175.00**

Miniature Lamps

For more information, see *Warman's Glass*, 4th edition.

History: Miniature oil and kerosene lamps, often called "night lamps," are diminutive replicas of larger lamps. Simple and utilitarian in design, miniature lamps found a place in the parlor (as "courting" lamps), hallway, children's rooms, and sickrooms. Miniature lamps are found in many glass types, from amberina to satin glass.

Miniature lamps measure 2-1/2 to 12 inches in height, with the principle parts being the base, collar, burner, chimney, and shade. In 1877, both L. J. Atwood and L. H. Olmsted patented burners for miniature lamps. Their burners made the lamps into a popular household accessory.

Reproduction Alert: Study a lamp carefully to make certain all parts are original; married pieces are common. Reproductions abound.

Note: The numbers given below refer to the figure numbers found in the Smith books.

Amberina, 3-1/2" w, 9" h, pressed, deep red to yellow, several chips **175.00**
Cosmos, emb pink, yellow, and blue flowers **200.00**
Consolidated, 10-1/4" h, milk glass, raised thumbprints **295.00**

Bull's eye pattern, colorless, ring handle, **$65**. Photo courtesy of Joy Luke Auctions.

Fenton, Cranberry Coin Spot, 11" h, 4-1/2" d globe shade **600.00**
Figural, Log Cabin, blue, handle **1,200.00**
Libbey, cut glass, 10-3/4" h base, 2" sq base, sgd **425.00**

Red satin lamp, embossed shade and base, original burner and chimney, **$125**.

Milk glass

Apple Blossom, light pink band around top of base and shade, white mid-section with floral dec, green band at base, nutmeg burner, 7-1/4" h **225.00**

Moon & Stars, L. G. Wright, white **295.00**

Swan, Smith #327-II **250.00**

Opalescent, cranberry, Spanish Lace **750.00**
Pattern glass, , Sweetheart pattern, Dalzell, Gilmore & Leighton Co., Findlay, OH, emb dotted hearts on green font and base... **250.00**
Satin, pale blue, quilted, pale blue, hairline cracks **450.00**

Back row, left and right: cranberry glass, daisy and button with thumbprint panels, ormolu frames, **$125 each**; painted pink opaque lamp with floral decoration, matching frosted pink shade, **$165**; front: pink satin melon shaped base, original burner, no shade or chimney, **$45**; opaque blue shade and base, no chimney or burner, scrolled decoration, **$35**.

Unknown maker, Grecian Key, emb clear glass base, acorn burner, red cased to white shade, patent date Nov. 14, 1911 in glass around collar.... **135.00**

Miniature Paintings

History: Prior to the advent of the photograph, miniature portraits and silhouettes were the principal way of preserving a person's image. Miniaturists were plentiful, and they often made more than one copy of a drawing. The extras were distributed to family and friends. Miniaturists worked in watercolors and oil and on surfaces such as paper, vellum, porcelain, and ivory. The miniature paintings were often inserted into jewelry or mounted inside or on the lids of snuffboxes. The artists often supplemented commission work by painting popular figures of the times and copying important works of art.

After careful study, miniature paintings have been divided into schools, and numerous artists are now being researched. Many fine examples may be found in today's antiques marketplace.

Gentleman, handpainted on ivory, by repute, attributed to George Patten (English, 1801-1865), man in blue coat, cravat, sitter identified on reverse as William Clark, died 1810, 2-3/8" l painting, 4-5/8" l ebonized square frame, **$560**. Photo courtesy of Skinner, Inc.

1-7/8" x 2-1/4", on ivory, Julia Clarke Brewster (1796-1826), attributed to John Brewster Jr., painted in the Columbia or Hampton, CT area, c1820, orig oval gilded copper locket case within orig red leather hinged case.................. **4,600.00**

2-3/8" x 2-7/8", ivory, woman in white, elaborate white wig, light blue ground, sgd "R.C. 1778" (Richard Cosway, English), brass frame **350.00**

2-1/2" l, on ivory, oval format, dark haired lady in late 18th C dress, Continental School, 19th C, gilt metal easel backed frame topped by foliates **275.00**

2-1/2" x 3-1/2", on ivory, Louis XV style, young girl with dog, shadow box frame **500.00**

2-5/8" x 3-3/8", ivory, woman with brown hair in ringlets, white dress, pink shawl, artist sgd, tortoise shell frame with engraved flowers......................... **350.00**

2-3/4" x 2-1/4", watercolor on ivory, young gentleman, black great coat, white waist coat, pleated shirt with stickpin and black neck cloth, unsigned, Anglo/American School, 19th C, gilt-metal frame, aperture containing lock of braided hair, fitted leather case................................ **950.00**

2-3/4" x 3-1/2" h, ivory, woman in white dress, white wig, sgd "Cosway," (Richard Cosway, English), brass locket with glens lens on back, beaded edge......... **300.00**

2-3/4" w, 3-1/2" h, painted on milk glass, over-varnish, King George IV, England, red military uniform with medals, blue cloth case, varnish darkened, edge flakes **425.00**

3" x 2-1/2", watercolor on ivory, attributed to Frederick Buck, late 18th/early 19th C, young woman with curled hair, wearing coral necklace, oval format.......... **825.00**

3" x 2-1/2", watercolor on ivory, Gustavis Tuckerman Jr., sgd and dated "Sacro Fratelli 1847" lower right, inscribed on paper within opening on reverse "Gustavis Tuckerman (Jr.,) Born Edgbaston, England, May 15th 1824, Died New York, February 12, 1897," painted in Palermo, Italy, 1847 by Sacro Fratelli, oval engine-turned gilt-metal frame within rect papier-mâché frame inlaid with abalone floral dec........ **450.00**

3" x 2-1/2" d, watercolor on ivory, portrait of balding man, American School, 19th C **415.00**

Gentleman, handpainted on ivory, man wearing powdered wig, white high-collared shirt, yellow vest, brown jacket, signed "Von der Tachlen," 2-1/4" d, **$330**. Photo courtesy of Alderfer Auction Co.

3-1/8" x 4-1/4" h, young brunette seated in lush interior, hair dressed with pearls, lace-trimmed gown and blue wrap, signed to left "J. Isabey," Continental, late 19th C, 6" x 4-7/8" gilt-metal frame **1,725.00**

3-1/4" x 2-1/2", watercolor on ivory, Napoleonic portrait, tortoiseshell and brass frame, oval format, signature obscured **725.00**

Mme. De St. Marc, hand-painted on ivory, woman wearing powdered wig, large bonnet with white veil, blue dress with pink bow dec, signed "Saintet," 3" x 2-1/4", **$315**. Photo courtesy of Alderfer Auction Co.

3-1/4" x 3-3/4", enamel on copper, Oliver Cromwell, paper label states after portrait by Cooper, ebonized oval wood frame, split in frame **375.00**

3-1/2" h, ivory, young man, brown hair, blue eyes, dark blue military coat with red collar, white bandolier, gold insignia, silver colored frame **350.00**

3-1/2" x 2-3/4", watercolor on ivory, lady in burgundy, wearing lace bonnet, sgd "G. Harvey" lower right, hinged red leather case with ormolu mat **725.00**

3-1/2" x 3-1/2", watercolor on ivory, young gentleman sitter identified on note as Johannes Josephus Kidder, Medford, Massachusetts, attending "Boy's school preparing for Harvard," seated on classical sofa having red upholstery, matching drapery and column in background, American School, early 19th C, framed in red leather case, heavy gilt liner, velvet int., minor abrasion to center background **1,645.00**

4" x 3-1/4", watercolor and pencil on paper, lady in black, hair comb, reverse inscribed "painted May 12th 1834 by J Sears," oval eglomise mat, framed, scattered small abrasions, toning **470.00**

4" x 4-3/4", ivory, portrait of young soldier, white wig, red coat, black lapels, black lacquered frame, brass fruit hanger **550.00**

4-1/2" x 3-1/2", ink and watercolor on paper, young lady, attributed to Rufus Porter, oval mat, framed, hinged at top, toning **1,170.00**

4-1/2" x 5-1/2", ivory, young child with lace bonnet, elaborate clothing, holding apple, sgd "Smart," brass frame with worn burgundy velvet liner **525.00**

Pair, Martha and George Washington, hand-painted on ivory, piano key ivory frames, George signed "Kahn," 4" x 3-1/4" overall, **$295**. Photo courtesy of Joy Luke Auctions.

4-5/8" x 5-5/8", ivory, young lady with white wig, pale blue dress, pink scarf with gold pendant, initialed "K.Y.," black frame with emb copper liner **360.00**

5" x 4", watercolor on ivory, young girl, unsigned, American School, early 19th C, brass and ebonized wood frame **500.00**

5" x 5-1/2", ivory, octagonal, oval portrait of George Washington, dark blue coat, sgd "Gainsborough," pierced ivory frame with scrimshaw flowers and copper dividers **300.00**

5" x 5-3/4", ivory, oval portrait of Napoleon, military coat and hat, sgd "Jsoby," pieced ivory frame with scrimshaw border, age splits **350.00**

5-3/4" x 4-3/4", watercolor on paper, gentleman, reverse identified as "1825, Eleazar Graves, father of Laura Graves Lincoln," unsigned, attributed to Rufus Porter, America, c1792-1884, grain painted frame, laid down, staining in margins, minor toning **445.00**

6-3/4" x 7-3/4", watercolor, gentleman with black hair, pale blue eyes, black coat, painted on heavy stock, penciled on back "WP 9 Strand," partial inked name on backing "Mr. Peter Van Buck-," wide rosewood veneered frame with gilt liner, minor edge damage **360.00**

Miniatures

History: There are three sizes of miniatures: dollhouse scale (ranging from 1/2 to 1 inch), sample size, and child's size. Since most early material is in museums or extremely expensive, the most common examples in the marketplace today are from the 20th century.

Many mediums were used for miniatures: silver, copper, tin, wood, glass, and ivory. Even books were printed in miniature. Price ranges are broad, influenced by scarcity and quality of workmanship.

The collecting of miniatures dates back to the 18th century. It remains one of the world's leading hobbies.

Chest of drawers, Biedermeyer, six drawers, German cherry, full column front, block feet, brass trim, repairs to two drawer fronts, 14-1/2" w, 7-1/2" d, 20" h, **$1,610**. Photo courtesy of Alderfer Auction Co.

Child or doll size

Bed, 28-5/8" l, 16" w, 15-3/4" h, Arts & Crafts, rect headboard with two cartoon-like images of baby dolls, footboard with two sq-form cut-outs, imperfections **230.00**

Blanket chest

13" w, 7-1/2" d, 6-1/4" h, dovetailed case, old dark green paint, molded base and lid, int. till missing lid, hidden compartment in till, edge chips **495.00**

15-1/4" l, 11-1/4" d, 12-1/8" h, pine, old red paint, sq nail construction, thin molding around lid, beveled molding around base, turned tapered feet with later black paint, orig brass lock escutcheon, initials "DHB" painted on back, old repairs **850.00**

Bookcase, hp, scalloped cornice over four open shelves, base with three drawers, Peter Hunt dec **1,650.00**

Chair, arm, 7" w, 5-3/4" d, 13-1/2" h, New England, mid-19th C, carved maple, ball, vase, and ring turnings on banister back, stiles ending in ball finials, finely turned arms, legs, and stretchers, orig upholstered seat.......................... **470.00**

Chair, side, 10-3/4" seat, 22" h, worn orig light green paint, black striping, gold stenciling, polychrome floral dec, pr **625.00**

Chest of drawers, Chippendale style, four drawers, bird's eye maple drawer fronts, mahogany case, brass knobs, bun feet, **$350**.

Chest of drawers

Country, pine and poplar, oak crest, stain finish, three drawers, faceted wood pulls, cutout feet, stains, 12" w, 7" d, 12-3/4" h........................ **275.00**

Country, walnut, pine secondary wood, refinished, sq and wire nail construction, variegated diamond inlay on top with triangles at each corner, three drawers with inlaid diamonds on fronts, raised molding around base, replaced brass pulls, 14-3/4" w, 8" d, 14" h.............. **550.00**

Hepplewhite, walnut, poplar secondary wood, small cove molding around top, four dovetailed drawers with molded edges, orig brass pulls, French feet with scalloped base, replaced side aprons and facings, minor restorations, 20" w, 13" d, 23-1/2" h **3,420.00**

Sheraton, pine, three mahogany veneer drawers, inset side panels, ball feet, turned wooden pulls, cherry colored stain, nailed construction, 13-1/2" w, 6-1/2" d, 11-1/4" h **425.00**

Mantel luster, 3-1/4" d, 7" h, mint green Bristol glass, hp mauve and pink flowers, blue forget-me-nots, green leaves, ruffled edge, remnants of gold trim, polished pontil, c1890, 2" l crystal prisms **275.00**

Rocker, child's

Empire style, mahogany, vase-shaped splat, rush seat, scrolled arms, 22" h **225.00**

Ladderback, attributed to Shakers, birch and hickory, old bittersweet colored paint, woven splint seat, turned front legs, handholds, two slat back and small egg shaped finials, couple of splint breaks, old make-do tin repair on one runner, 7" h seat, 21-1/2" h overall..................... **250.00**

Ladderback, dec, PA, old dec of black and red cattails and line borders, black, red, and white foliage on crest, brown combed ground, turned legs, arms, arm supports, and stiles, plank seat, 10" h seat, 22" h overall........................... **200.00**

Child's cast iron toy stove with utensils, door embossed "Pet," **$180**; miniature tin bathtub in front, **$75**; miniature pot, **$20**; and coal scuttle, **$15**. Photo courtesy of Joy Luke Auctions.

Settee, 7-5/8" l, 7-5/8" w, 4-1/4" h, carved wood, dark stained finish, serpentine back, openwork spindled flowerheads and chip-carved and stippled stylized floral dec, hinged lid, Normandy, early 20th C **145.00**

Settle bench, 24" l, 6-1/2" w, 6-1/2" h seat, PA, orig gold, copper, and silver fruit dec along crest and back slats, mustard yellow ground with areas of wear and touch-up, scrolled arms, plank seat with incised borders, eight turned legs, restoration.................................... **825.00**

Sideboard, oak, ornate trim, beveled mirror, 36" h.............................. **2,100.00**

Spiral staircase, 17-5/8" w, 8-5/8" d, 22-1/8" h, mahogany, dark rosewood grained finials, rect base with demilune cut out in center, late 19th C **1,500.00**

Steam engine, 25" x 40" platform **2,200.00**

Table, drop leaf, Sheraton, walnut, pine secondary wood, leaves with decoratively cut corners, one dovetailed drawer, turned legs, old finish, minor edge damage, hinges replaced, age crack on top, 23-1/2" l, 12-1/2" w, 10-3/4" l leaves, 19" h.. **1,100.00**

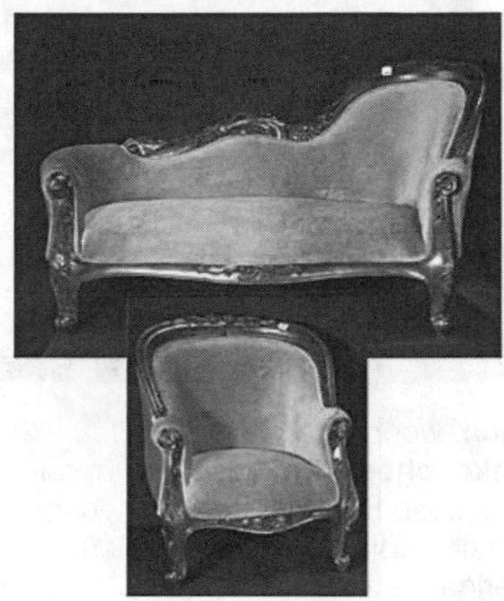

Parlor suite, Victorian, doll sized, mahogany, rose velvet upholstery, 34" l x 18" h sofa with carved backrail, 15" w x 18" h armchair, **$150**. Photo courtesy of Joy Luke Auctions.

Dollhouse accessories

Bird cage, brass, bird, stand, 7" h **65.00**

Carpet sweeper, gilt, Victorian...... **65.00**

Cup and saucer, china, flower design, c1940.. **10.00**

Decanter, two matching tumblers, Venetian, c1920............................ **35.00**

Fireplace, tin, Britannia metal fretwork, draped mantel, carved grate **85.00**

Radio, Strombecker, c1930 .... **35.00**

Refrigerator, Petite Princess......... **75.00**

Silhouettes, Tynietoy, c1930, pr.... **25.00**

Telephone, wall, oak, speaker and bell, German, c1890 .... **40.00**

Towel stand, golden oak, turned post **45.00**

Umbrella stand, brass, ormolu, sq, emb palm fronds **60.00**

Urn, silver, handled, ornate.......... **100.00**

Dollhouse furniture

Armoire, tin litho, purple and black **35.00**

Bathroom, wood, painted white, Strombecker................................. **40.00**

Bedroom, Victorian style, metal, veneer finish, bed, nightstand, commode with faux marble tops, armoire and mirror, cradle, Biedermeier clock, metal washstand **675.00**

Tea set, silverplated, 4" h teapot, covered sugar, creamer, waste bowl, six cups and saucers, and five spoons, fitted box bearing label "Manufactured by James W. Tufts, 33 to 39 Bonker St. Boston," 12-3/8" l, 5" h, 12-3/8" l, **$500**. Photo courtesy of Pook & Pook.

Bench, wood, rush seat **25.00**
Blanket chest, 7-1/8" l, 4-3/4" h, painted wood, six-board, wallpaper lined int., open till, replaced hinges, lock missing, America, 19th C........................ **2,990.00**
Buffet set, stenciled, three shelves, column supports, Biedermeier, 6" h **400.00**
Chair, ormolu, ornate, 3" h, c1900, pr **75.00**
Cradle, cast iron, painted green, 2" l **40.00**
Desk, Chippendale style, slant front, drawers open **60.00**
Kitchen set, litho tin, Modern Kitchen, all parts and pieces, animals, and related items, orig box, Louis Marx **250.00**
Living room, Empire-style, sofa, fainting couch, two side chairs, upholstered tapestry, matching drapery **350.00**
Piano, grand, wood, eight keys, 5" h **35.00**
Rocker, painted tin, lithographed tin seated child holding doll, compartment under seat concealed candy storage, Meier, Germany, 3" l..................... **275.00**
Sewing table, golden oak, drawer, c1880 **100.00**
Table, tin, painted brown, white top, floral design, 1-1/2" x 3/4" h, ornate **30.00**
Tea cart, Petite Princess **25.00**
Vanity, Biedermeier **90.00**

Minton China

History: In 1793, Thomas Minton joined other men to form a partnership and build a small pottery at Stoke-on-Trent, Staffordshire, England. Production began in 1798 with blueprinted earthenware, mostly in the Willow pattern. In 1798, cream-colored earthenware and bone china were introduced.

A wide range of styles and wares was produced. Minton introduced porcelain figures in 1826, Parian wares in 1846, encaustic tiles in the late 1840s, and Majolica wares in 1850. Many famous designers and artists in the English pottery industry worked for Minton.

In 1883, the modern company was formed and called Mintons Limited. The "s" was dropped in 1968.

Marks: Many early pieces are unmarked or have a Sevres-type marking. The "ermine" mark was used in the early 19th century. Date codes can be found on tableware and majolica. The mark used between 1873 and 1911 was a small globe with a crown on top and the word "Minton."

Dinner service, Gold Rose pattern, 116 pieces, 12 each: dinner plates, dessert plates, bread plates, fruit bowls, coffee cups, saucers, demitasse cups, demitasse saucers; six bouillon cups; seven bouillon saucers; covered sugar bowl; creamer; teapot; covered serving dish; gravy boat with attached undertray; round serving plate; square serving plate, printed mark on bottom, mark used from 1912 to 1950, **$600**. Photo courtesy of Alderfer Auction Co.

Bowl, 12" x 10", oval, Palissy style, minor base chip................................ **3,080.00**
Centerpiece, 16" l, elongated parian vessel, molded scroll handles and feet, pierced rim, two brown reserves, white pate-sur-pate amorini, gilding, dec, attributed to Lawrence Birks, marked "Minton," retailer's marks of Thomas Goode & Co., Ltd., London, c1889 .... **1,400.00**
Compote, 10-1/2" l, majolica, figural, lobed oval dish and plinth, brown glaze on agate body, dish supported on backs of two cherubs holding laurel wreaths, center lovebirds, impressed mark, c1863 .... **2,415.00**
Dinner service, bone china, partial
Ancestral pattern, 13 teacups, 12 saucers, 11 dessert plates, 10 side plates, 10 side bowls, eight dinner plates, two open vegetable dishes, oval 15-1/4" l platter, teapot, creamer, and covered sugar, 70 pcs **360.00**
Gold-banded pattern, made for Tiffany & Co., white body with two gilt bands molded with vine and guilloche respectively, 12 each teacups, teacup saucers, side plates, coffee cups, chocolate cup saucers, 11 each soup plates, 9" d luncheon plates, 10 each chocolate cups, coffee cup saucers, 10-1/4" d dinner plates, 8-1/4" l serving bowl, 10-1/4" l serving bowl, 9-3/8" oblong condiment dish, 9-3/4" l condiment dish, 13-3/8" platter, 15-1/2" l platter, chocolate pot, butter dish dome, 119 pcs **3,055.00**

Pilgrim flask, designed by Christopher Dresser, butterflies within Oriental border, sky blue ground, stamped "Minton's" with crown, 6" x 5-1/2", **$2,990**. Photo courtesy of David Rago Auctions, Inc.

Figure, 10-1/2" h, putti, yellow basket and grape vine, 1867, professional repair at rim of basket.......................... **2,750.00**
Floor urn, 35" h, 18" d, majolica, Neo-Classical, turquoise, massive foliage handles.................................. **12,650.00**
Garden set, 17-3/4" h, earthenware, barrel form, central pierced band of entwined rings between blue printed

bands of flowers, scrolled vines, imp mark, 19th C, glaze wear, price for pr **1,100.00**

Jardinière, 7" h, molded wooden plants, white vines, lilac int., majolica, matching stands, pr **475.00**

Nut dish, 9-3/4" l, majolica, leaf molded dish with squirrel handle, imp mark, c1869, restored chips to ears ... **1,840.00**

Oyster plate, majolica

Cobalt blue........ **1,650.00**

Turquoise........ **495.00**

Oyster server, four tiers, majolica, green and brown, white wells, turquoise finial, rim damage to six wells, mechanical turning mechanism missing **3,575.00**

Plaque, 11-1/2" sq, painted scene of Dutch man reading document by row of books, initials "HH" lower right, date mark for 1883, framed **290.00**

Plate, enamel decoration, Oriental medallion of peony and prunus, sky blue ground, faint stamp, 1874, light wear to gild on rim, 9" d, **$700**. Photo courtesy of David Rago Auctions, Inc.

Plate, 10-1/8" d, India Tree-type pattern, underglaze blue and iron red stylized tree, gilt detailing, retailed by Davis Collamore & Co., NY, late 19th C, 12-pc set **500.00**

Portrait plate, 9" d, Duchess de Berri Caroline, Princis Lambelle, Madame Mars, Madame Elizabeth, sgd "A.S.I.," names on reverse, price for set of four **350.00**

Sweetmeat dish, 8" d, majolica, blue titmouse on branch, leaf-shaped dish, imp mark, 1888........ **675.00**

Tile, 7-1/2" w, 10" h, Middle Eastern woman in colorful attire, hands on large vessel, self-standing metal and wooden frame, sgd, scratch **125.00**

Tower pitcher, 12-1/2" h, majolica, castle molded body with relief of dancing villagers in medieval dress, imp marks, c1873, chips to cov thumb rest, spout rim **1,035.00**

Vase, 6-1/4" h, celadon green ground, five-spout, fan form, applied white floral relief, fish head feet, imp mark, c1855, foot rim chip........ **215.00**

Mocha

History: Mocha decoration usually is found on utilitarian creamware and stoneware pieces and was produced through a simple chemical action. A color pigment of brown, blue, green, or black was made acidic by an infusion of tobacco or hops. When the acidic colorant was applied in blobs to an alkaline ground, it reacted by spreading in feathery designs resembling sea plants. This type of decoration usually was supplemented with bands of light-colored slip.

Types of decoration vary greatly, from those done in a combination of motifs, such as Cat's Eye and Earthworm, to a plain pink mug decorated with green ribbed bands. Most forms of mocha are hollow, e.g., mugs, jugs, bowls, and shakers.

English potters made the vast majority of the pieces. Collectors group the wares into three chronological periods: 1780-1820, 1820-1840, and 1840-1880.

Reproduction Alert.

Bowl, white and brown bands, white band with blue seaweed decoration, hairline, 12" d, 5-1/2" h, **$100**. Photo courtesy of Alderfer Auction Co.

Beaker, pearlware, 3" h, dark brown, medium brown, and ochre marble decoration on rust field, thin lines of medium brown at rim and base, England, early 19th C, rim chips and glaze wear **2,475.00**

Bowl

5" d, 2-1/4" h, brown, white, black, and café au lait, tooled green rim, minor int. wear, tiny rim flakes **1,550.00**

5-5/8" d, 3" h, gold and dark brown stripes, dark brown seaweed on brown band **500.00**

6-1/4" d, 3-1/4" h, black rim, white wavy line, tan band with black, pale blue, white, and brown earthwork design, small flake on foot **2,100.00**

10-1/4" d, 5-1/4" h, ftd, two earthworm designs in white, rust, and brown, pale blue bands, black stripes, tooled green rim, edge wear, short hairline........ **3,850.00**

Canister, cov, 4-1/2" h, café au lait, dark brown stripes, seaweed dec, conical lid, minor flakes **2,100.00**

Child's mug, 2-1/2" h, pearlware, green glazed rouletted upper and lower bands flanking rust field with dark brown scroddled dots, with bisecting lines cut through slip to white body, applied handle, England, early 19th C, repaired **825.00**

Coffeepot, baluster-form, footed, pearlware, dark brown bands on buff body, dark brown "tree" designs, extruded ribbed handle, England, 19th century, rim chips on cover, 10-3/4" h, **$1,100**. Photo courtesy of Skinner, Inc.

Creamer, band of decoration in blue and brown on yellow body, hairlines, 4-1/2" h, **$120**. Photo courtesy of Alderfer Auction Co.

Creamer, 4" h, tooled green band, black stripes, light brown band with white, black, and slate blue tri-colored balls, molded leaf handle, some wear on handle and rim **3,000.00**

Cup, 2-7/8" h, imp border above brown and white earthworm design, blue ground, 19th C, imperfections...... **375.00**

Ink sander, 3-1/4" h, pearlware, two rows of dark brown trailed slip "tendrils" on blue field, England, early 19th C, two small chips **1,175.00**

Jug, 7-1/2" h, barrel-form, banded in blue and black, black, white, and blue earthworm dec on ocher field, handles with foliate terminals, England, c1840, 5/8" rim chip, associated crack, 1/2" chip on spout........ **1,880.00**

Measure, 5", 6", and 6-1/4" h, tankard, blue, black and tan seaweed dec, one with applied white label "Imperial Pint," other with resist label "Quart," minor stains, wear, and crazing, three-pc set **440.00**

Milk pitcher, 4-5/8" h, dark bluish-gray band, black stripes, emb band with green and black seaweed, leaf handle, wear and painted over spout flake **440.00**

Mug, band of blue seaweed on cream band on yellow ground, 3" d, 3" h, **$460**. Photo courtesy of Alderfer Auction Co.

Mug

3-1/2" h, black stripes and seaweed dec on brown band, hairline, rim flakes **770.00**

3-1/2" h, tan stripes, tooled green bands, tooled black and white scalloped lines around middle, molded leaf handle, base chip, minor rim wear and flakes **1,540.00**

4-7/8" h, tan, brown, white, and gold marbleized ground, brown edges, molded leaf handle, small edge chips, short hairline, some enamel flaking **2,420.00**

5-1/2" h, orange and brown earthworm dec **3,200.00**

5-3/4" h, tooled blue bands, black stripes, center band of golden orange, slate blue striping, dark brown seaweed, molded leaf handle, minor rim roughness, few flakes, some int. staining **3,100.00**

Mustard pot, cov

2-1/2" h, creamware, blue banded lid with blue reeded band, cylindrical body with matching banding, dark brown, rust, gray, and white earthworm pattern, extruded handle with foliate handles, creamware, England, early 19th C, chips to the lid, small crack to the body, discoloration **1,300.00**

3-1/2" h, pearlware, lid with acorn finial, brown bands with dendritic seaweed on rust field, body decorated in the same manner, extruded handle with foliate terminals, England, early 19th C, finial repair, small rim and base chips **1,645.00**

4" h, black stripes, two brown and golden orange bands, seaweed dec, molded leaf handles, repairs to lid **1,540.00**

Pepper pot

4" h, flat top, light blue and black stripes, minor in-the-making imperfections **800.00**

4" h, tooled green band at shoulder, burnt umber stripes, taupe top, wide band with white, umber, and black feather design, top flaked ... **2,750.00**

4" h, tooled green band, light brown stripes, black checked middle, some staining and flakes **1,320.00**

4-1/2" h, black stripes, tan band and stripe, tooled black circles around middle, minor flake **1,050.00**

4-1/2" h, blue top, tooled band, wide blue band with earthworm and white, tan, and black balls, white and black stripes, repaired ring with minor flaking **3,850.00**

4-1/2" h, green tooled band, black stripes, brown top, wide band, black seaweed dec, minor flakes **935.00**

Cream pitcher, seaweed design on tan stripe with blue stripe at neck, chip on base and handle, 4-1/2" h, **$75**. Photo courtesy of Alderfer Auction Co.

Pitcher

4-3/4" h, marbleized gray and white body, minor spout flake **250.00**

5-5/8" h, brown, tan, and white feathered marbling, tooled green rim, minor wear on spout, edge flakes **3,200.00**

7" h, tooled green bands, dark brown stripes, dark brown seaweed on pale orange, molded leaf handle, make-do tin bottom **1,100.00**

7-1/8" h, double earthworm design on neck, earthworm with balls on body, white, black, and slate blue dec, tan bands, slate blue stripes, molded leaf handle, minor rim flakes **4,125.00**

7-1/4" h, medium blue, white, blue, and dark brown earthworm design, old paper label dated 1914 on base, light stains, flakes, and hairlines **275.00**

8" d, tooled green bands, black stripes, café au lait center band with dark brown seaweed, molded leaf handle with green accents, spout hairline, overall darkening, some staining **4,625.00**

9" h, ovoid, alternating horizontal bands of dark blue, black, and brown, applied ear handle **1,100.00**

Salt, master, 3-1/8" d, 2" h, orangish sand ground, blue, white, and black wavy cat's-eye pattern line, two black stripes, slight rim wear **2,100.00**

Tankard, 5" h, golden orange ground, black stripes, dark brown seaweed dec, molded leaf handle with minor wear, pewter lid with thump latch, rampant lion touch mark, crow's foot in base **1,320.00**

Tea canister, rare slip-marbled creamware tea appliqué marbled in dark brown, ochre, white, and gray with green-glazed reeded bands at foot and shoulder, England, c1780, one rim chip and slip/glaze losses to side, lacking cover, 4-3/4" h, **$2,500**. Photo courtesy of Skinner, Inc.

Tea canister, 4" h, blue, black, and white band on shoulder, white fluted band on bottom, medium blue glaze........ **125.00**

Teapot, 5-7/8" h, oval shape, medium blue, fluted band on bottom, black and white checkered band on top, acorn finial **500.00**

Tumbler, 2-1/2" h, gold, white, brown, and black feathered marbling, tooled gold trim, enamel flaking at rim **3,520.00**

Waste bowl

4-3/4" d, 2-3/4" h, gray, white, dark brown, and tan earthworm design, two hairlines **315.00**

6-1/2" d, 3-1/4" h, dark brown stripes, brown band with white, dark brown, and pale blue earthworm design, two hairlines **330.00**

7" d, 3-1/2" h, light blue stripes, wide orange band with light blue and tan earthworm design, wear, light stains, faint hairlines **225.00**

Mont Joye Glass

History: Mont Joye is a type of glass produced by Saint-Hilaire, Touvier, de Varreaux & Company at its glassworks in Pantin, France. Most pieces were lightly acid etched to give them a frosted appearance and were also decorated with enameled florals.

For more information, see *Warman's Glass*, 4th edition.

Jack in the pulpit vase, 14-1/2" h, amethyst shading to clear, enamel dec, gold sponged dec, polished pontil 995.00

Pitcher, 10" h, amethyst, enameled flowers, aqua, blue, pink, and gold, sgd 350.00

Rose bowl, 4-1/4" h, crimped top, cameo and enamel cyclamen blossoms and leaves 550.00

Vase, bulbous, green frosted glass etched with gold chrysanthemums, stamped, minor flake under rim, 12" h, **$375**. Photo courtesy of David Rago Auctions, Inc.

Vase

4" h, pink enameled poppy and gold leaves, frosted textured ground, marked 275.00

7-1/2" h, cameo carved yellow and gold flower blossoms, green leaves, brown chipped ice ground, sgd on base 675.00

10" h, bulbous, narrow neck, clear to opalescent green, naturalistic thistle dec, gold highlights 375.00

12" h, bulbous, frosted green, etched gold chrysanthemums, stamped, minor under rim flake 375.00

15-1/4" h, cameo, cut with flowering iris, enameled dec, sgd "Mont Joy" in gilt, c1900 .... 500.00

Violet vase, 6" h, frosted etched surface, colorless glass, naturalistic enameled purple violet blossoms, gold highlights, base marked "Dimier Geneve" 260.00

Moorcroft

History: William Moorcroft was first employed as a potter by James Macintyre & Co., Ltd., of Burslem in 1897. He established the Moorcroft pottery in 1913.

The majority of the art pottery wares were hand thrown, resulting in a great variation among similarly styled pieces. Color and marks are keys to determining age.

Walker, William's son, continued the business upon his father's death and made wares in the same style.

For more information, see *Warman's English & Continental Pottery & Porcelain*, 3rd edition.

Marks: The company initially used an impressed mark, "Moorcroft, Burslem"; a signature mark, "W. Moorcroft," followed. Modern pieces are marked simply "Moorcroft," with export pieces also marked "Made in England."

Bowl, covered, round, hibiscus decoration, glossy glaze of pink, purple, and green on blue-green ground, stamped "MOORCROFT/MADE IN ENGLAND," 5-3/4" d, 3-1/2" h, **$215**. Photo courtesy of Skinner, Inc.

Bowl, 3-5/8" d, pansy dec, pale green ground, imp maker's mark 150.00

Box, cov, 4-3/4" l, 1-1/2" w, 1-3/4" h, pansy dec on lid, pale green ground, imp maker's mark, crazing 200.00

Compote, 7-1/4" d, Lily motif, yellow and green ground 150.00

Ginger jar, cov, 11-1/2" h, pomegranate dec 525.00

Jar, cov, Cornflower, ivory ground, coat of arms of Kings College, Oxford, c1911 .... 1,450.00

Lamp base, 6-1/4" d, 11-1/4" h, Anemone 920.00

Loving cup, 6" d, 5-1/2" h, Pomegranate pattern, stamped mark, 1914-16, minor rim fleck 1,150.00

Cabinet vase, orchid design, glossy cobalt blue ground, paper label, 2-1/2" d, 3-3/4" h, **$235**. Photo courtesy of David Rago Auctions, Inc.

Pitcher, 6-1/4" h, Forget-Me-Not, c1902 .... 1,350.00

Plate, 7-1/4" d, toadstool, blue ground, imp "Moorcroft Claremont" 600.00

Urn, 5-5/8" h, anemone design in shades of pink, purple, and cream on green, turquoise, and blue ground, glossy glaze, impressed "Made in England" and "Potter to H. M. the Queen," with facsimile signature and painted Walter Moorcroft signature, 1928-49, pr, crazing 600.00

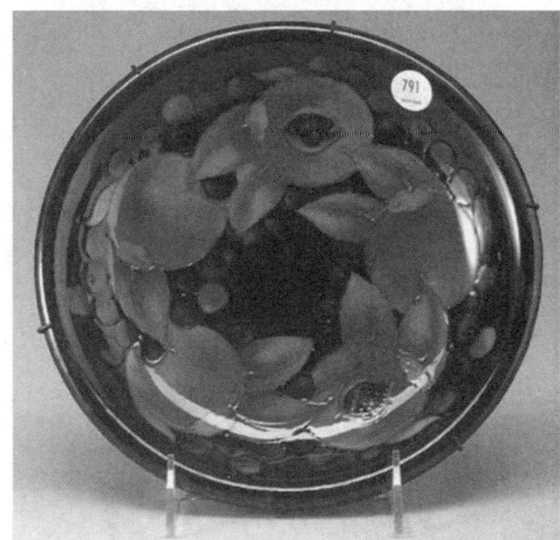

Plate, Pomegranate and Berry pattern, glossy cobalt blue ground, stamped "Made In England," ink signature, mounted in metal plate hange, small plate ring chip, 8-1/2" d, **$175**. Photo courtesy of David Rago Auctions, Inc.

Vase

4-1/2" x 2-1/4", bottle shape, Falling Leaves, paper label 115.00

7" h, ovoid, orange hibiscus, green ground, paper label and stamp mark, minor fleck to base 365.00

8-3/8" h, swollen cylindrical, alternating bands of floral motifs and ovals, red and blue semi-gloss

glaze, imp "Moorcroft, Made in England" 700.00
10" h, Clematis, blue Walter initials, imp mark 1,050.00
12" h, Orchid, flambé, sgd by William in blue, imp "Potter to HM The Queen" 4,350.00

MORGANTOWN GLASS WORKS

For more information, see *Warman's Glass*, 4th edition.

History: The Morgantown Glass Works, Morgantown, West Virginia, was founded in 1899 and began production in 1901. Reorganized in 1903, it operated as the Economy Tumbler Company for 20 years until, in 1923, the word "Tumbler" was dropped from the corporate title. The firm was then known as The Economy Glass Company until reversion to its original name, Morgantown Glass Works, Inc., in 1929, the name it kept until its first closing in 1937. In 1939, the factory was reopened under the aegis of a guild of glassworkers and operated as the Morgantown Glassware Guild from that time until its final closing. Purchased by Fostoria in 1965, the factory operated as a subsidiary of the Moundsville-based parent company until 1971, when Fostoria opted to terminate production of glass at the Morgantown facility. Today, collectors use the generic term, "Morgantown Glass," to include all periods of production from 1901 to 1971.

Morgantown was a 1920s leader in the manufacture of colorful wares for table and ornamental use in American homes. The company pioneered the processes of iridization on glass, as well as gold and platinum encrustation of patterns. It enhanced Crystal offerings with contrasting handle and foot of India Black, Spanish Red (ruby), and Ritz Blue (cobalt blue), and other intense and pastel colors for which it is famous. The company conceived the use of contrasting shades of fired enamel to add color to its etchings. It was the only American company to use a chromatic silk-screen printing process on glass, its two most famous and collectible designs being Queen Louise and Manchester Pheasant.

The company is also known for ornamental "open stems" produced during the late 1920s. Open stems separate to form an open design midway between the bowl and foot, e.g., an open square, a "Y," or two diamond-shaped designs. Many of these open stems were purchased and decorated by Dorothy C. Thorpe in her California studio, and her signed open stems command high prices from today's collectors. Morgantown also produced figural stems for commercial clients such as Koscherak Brothers and Marks & Rosenfeld. Chanticleer (rooster) and Mai Tai (Polynesian bis) cocktails are two of the most popular figurals collected today.

Morgantown is best known for the diversity of design in its stemware patterns, as well as for its four patented optics: Festoon, Palm, Peacock, and Pineapple. These optics were used to embellish stems, jugs, bowls, liquor sets, guest sets, salvers, ivy and witch balls, vases, and smoking items.

Most glass collectors recognize two well-known lines of Morgantown Glass today: #758 Sunrise Medallion and #7643 Golf Ball Stem Line. When Economy introduced #758 in 1928, it was originally identified as "Nymph." By 1931, the Morgantown front office had renamed it Sunrise Medallion. Recent publications erred in labeling it "dancing girl." Upon careful study of the medallion, you can see the figure is poised on one tiptoe, musically saluting the dawn with her horn. The second well-known line, #7643 Golf Ball, was patented in 1928; production commenced immediately and continued until the company closed in 1971. More Golf Ball than any other Morgantown product is found on the market today.

Basket
Patrick, #19-4358, Ritz Blue, applied crystal twisted handle, mint leaf prunts, 5" d, 9-3/4" h 750.00
Trindle, #4357, amethyst, applied crystal twisted reed handle, c1930, 9" 725.00
Berry jug, Palm Optic, #37, pink, 8-1/2" w, 9-1/8" h 235.00
Bowl
Fantassia, Bristol Blue, #67, 5-1/2" d 95.00
Woodsfield, Genova Line, 12-1/2" d, #12-1/2 .... 565.00
Brandy snifter, Golf Ball, #7643, red, crystal base, 4" w, 6-1/4" h 130.00
Candleholders, pr
Golf Ball, #7643, Torch Candle, single, Ritz Blue, 6" h 300.00
Hamilton, #87, Evergreen, 5" h 65.00
Modern, #80, Moss Green, 7-1/2" h 90.00
Candy jar, cov
Mansfield, #200, burgundy matte, 12" h 200.00
Rachael, crystal, Pandora cutting, 6" h 395.00
Cereal bowl, Crinkle, pink 20.00
Champagne
Empress, Spanish Red, crystal stem 45.00
Majestic, #7662, Spanish Red, 6 oz 50.00
Queen Elizabeth, #7664 .... 80.00

Champagne, saucer type, Carola, #7516, #703 Bernadette etch, 6 oz, **$15**. Photo courtesy of Rick Harte, Sparkle Plenty Glassware.

Cocktail
Fernlee, #7695, trumpet, 3 oz 40.00
Golf Ball, #7643, Spanish Red, 4 oz 55.00
Majestic, #7662, Spanish Red 60.00
Plantation, #8445, Spanish Red, crystal stem 95.00
Queen Elizabeth, #7664, crystal 70.00
Rooster, ruby 45.00
Top Hat, Copen Blue, 5-1/4" h, 3-1/8" d 95.00
Venus, #7577, Anna Rose, Palm Optic, 3 oz 40.00
Cocktail set, Deco, black, 7-3/4" h pitcher with weighted base, five 3" w, 3" h cocktail glasses 65.00
Compote, Reverse Twist, #7654, aquamarine, 6-1/2" d, 6-3/4" h 225.00
Console bowl, El Mexicana, #12933, Seaweed, 10" d 425.00
Cordial, 1-1/2 oz
Brilliant, #7617, Spanish Red 140.00
Golf Ball, #7643, Pastels 65.00
Mikado, crystal 30.00
Finger bowl, Art Moderne, #7640, Faun etch, crystal and black, 4-1/2" d, ftd 150.00
Goblet
Art Moderne, #7640, Faun etch, crystal and black, 7-3/4" h 125.00
Courtney, #7637, DC Thorpe satin open stem 195.00
Golf Ball, #7643, Ritz blue 60.00
Laura, #7665, Nasreen etch, topaz 115.00
Manchester Pheasant, #7664, Queen Anne 325.00
Queen Louise, #7664, 3-1/2" d, 7-1/2" h 400.00
Guest set, Trudy, #23, Bristol Blue, 6-3/8" h 145.00
Iced tea tumbler, Crinkle, pink, flat 15.00
Ice tub, El Mexicana, #1933, Seaweed, 6" d 225.00

Jug

Kaufmann, #6, Doric star sand blast, 54 oz....... **295.00**

Melon, #20069, Alabaster, Ritz Blue trim....... **1,450.00**

San Juan, Crinkle, peacock blue....... **115.00**

Vase Electra, #35-1/2, Old Amethyst, Continental Line, applied clear twisted handles, 10" h, **$1,400**. Photo courtesy of Michael Krumme.

Juice tumbler, Crinkle, green, flat....... **10.00**

Measuring cup, 3-1/8" d, 2-7/8" h, adv "Your Credit is Good Pickerings, Furnishings, 10th & Penn, Pittsburgh," clear....... **315.00**

Oyster cup, 2-3/8" d, Sunrise Medallion, blue....... **190.00**

Pilsner, Floret, etch #796, Lando, 12 oz....... **65.00**

Plate

Anna Rose, #734 American Beauty etch, 7" d....... **65.00**

Carlton Madrid, topaz, 6" d....... **35.00**

Country Ladies Violets, 1982, orig box and certificate, 9" d....... **40.00**

Crinkle, pink, 7-1/2" d....... **15.00**

Sherbet

Crinkle, #1962, pink, 6 oz....... **30.00**

Golf Ball, #7643, Ritz blue....... **50.00**

Manchester Pheasant, #7664, Queen Anne....... **250.00**

Sophisticate, #7646, Picardy etch, 5-1/2 oz....... **55.00**

Sherry, Golf Ball, #7643, Spanish Red....... **43.00**

Tumbler, water

Crinkle, peacock blue, flat....... **15.00**

Crinkle, pink, flat....... **15.00**

Majestic, #7662, Spanish Red....... **60.00**

Vase

Catherine, #26, Azure, #758 Sunrise Medallion etch, bud, 10" h....... **265.00**

Daisy, #90, crystal, green and white wash, 9-1/2" w....... **475.00**

Golf Ball, #7643, Kimball, Spanish Red, crystal stem....... **165.00**

Peacock Optic, tangerine, cylinder, c1958, 60-1/2" h....... **35.00**

Raindrop pattern, red/orange, yellow base, hobnail design on inside graduating in size down to base, 4-1/2" d, 10" h....... **35.00**

Wine

Empress, #7680-1/2, Spanish Red, 3 oz....... **90.00**

Monroe, Stiegel green....... **70.00**

Moser Glass

Moser Moser Karlsbad

History: Ludwig Moser (1833-1916) founded his polishing and engraving workshop in 1857 in Karlsbad (Karlovy Vary), Czechoslovakia. He employed many famous glass designers, e.g., Johann Hoffmann, Josef Urban, and Rudolf Miller. In 1900, Moser and his sons, Rudolf and Gustav, incorporated Ludwig Moser & Söhne.

For more information, see *Warman's Glass*, 4th edition.

Moser art glass included clear pieces with inserted blobs of colored glass, cut colored glass with classical scenes, cameo glass, and intaglio cut items. Many inexpensive enameled pieces also were made.

In 1922, Leo and Richard Moser bought Meyr's Neffe, their biggest Bohemian art glass rival. Moser executed many pieces for the Wiener Werkstätte in the 1920s.

Cup and saucer, cobalt blue, brilliant gold decorated background, 43 pink, blue, and coral enamel daisy-type flowers, raised gold stems and tendrils, various shades of green on leaves with painted veins, 2-3/4" h cup, 5-5/8" d saucer, **$395**. Photo courtesy of Clarence and Betty Maier.

Basket, 5-1/2" h, green malachite, molded cherubs dec, pr....... **800.00**

Berry set, 10-1/2" d master bowl, five 6" d bowls, cobalt blue, gilt scalloped edges, cut to clear with stars, circles, and panels, further cut with flowering vines with gilt enamel embellishment, Czechoslovakia, early 20th C....... **600.00**

Bowl, 12-1/4" w, 3" h, cameo, cobalt blue, 18 elephants, nine palm trees, birds, large polished pontil, sgd in four places, minor int. scratching....... **3,000.00**

Cologne bottle, 7-1/2" h, 3-1/2" d, amethyst shaded to clear, deep intaglio cut flowers and leaves, orig stopper, sgd....... **695.00**

Cup and saucer, amber, gold scrolls, multicolored enameled flowers....... **295.00**

Demitasse cup and saucer, amber shading to white, enameled gilt flowers....... **100.00**

Ewer, 10-3/4" h, cranberry, gilt surface, applied acorns and clear jewels....... **2,000.00**

Goblet, 8" h, cranberry, Rhine-style, enameled oak leaves, applied acorns, four-pc set....... **1,800.00**

Jack-in-the-pulpit vase, 16" h, cranberry opalescent to colorless, ruffled tops, hp and gold floral dec, some wear to gold....... **865.00**

Jar, cov, 4" d, 4" h, cranberry, gold and hp enamel dec....... **450.00**

Loving cup, 6-3/4" h, three colorless handles, cranberry, gold enameled dec, polished pontil, marked "2773"....... **1,275.00**

Perfume, 4-3/4" h, pink-lavender alexandrite, faceted panels, matching stopper, sgd in oval....... **275.00**

Tumblers, set of eight, colorless, each hand-painted paneled decoration, varying genre scenes, surrounded by gilt scrolled borders, gilt rim, 2-1/4" d, 4" h, **$990**. Photo courtesy of Alderfer Auction Co.

Pitcher, 6-3/4" h, amberina, IVT, four yellow, red, blue, and green applied glass beaded bunches of grapes, pinched in sides, three-dimensional bird beneath spout, allover enamel and gold leaves, vines, and tendrils....... **3,200.00**

Portrait vase, 8-1/2" h, woman, gold leaves, light wear....... **450.00**

Rose bowl, 3-1/2" h, cranberry ground, enameled florals and butterfly, applied acorns, c1900....... **750.00**

Two modern Moser examples, both decorated with gilded roses and leaves, 8" h vase, **$65**; 8-3/4" d bowl, **$45**. Photo courtesy of Joy Luke Auctions.

Tankard, 12-1/4" h, emerald green shading to colorless ground, finely dec with silvered and gilt scrolled florals, c1910 .... **450.00**
Tray, 7-1/4" w, cranberry, crackle, hand enameled white and blue marsh scene with egret, polished edges **2,500.00**
Tumbler, 3-3/4" h, enameled dec, c1910
- Pale amber **50.00**
- Pale blue **50.00**

Urn, 15-3/4" h, cranberry, two gilt handles, studded with green, blue, clear, and red stones, highly enameled surface, multicolored and gilt Moorish dec **3,500.00**
Vase
- 7" h, paneled amber baluster body, wide gold medial band of women warriors, base inscribed "Made in Czechoslovakia-Moser Karlsbad" **550.00**
- 9" h, cranberry, two gilt handles, medallion with hp roses, sgd **1,050.00**
- 10" h, heavy walled dark amethyst faceted body, etched and gilded medial scene of bear hunt, spear-armed men and dogs pursuing large bear **345.00**
- 15-3/4" h, green ground, enameled dec, c1900 .... **150.00**

Mount Washington Glass Company

History: In 1837, Deming Jarves, founder of the Boston and Sandwich Glass Company, established for George D. Jarves, his son, the Mount Washington Glass Company in Boston, Massachusetts. In the following years, the leadership and the name of the company changed several times as George Jarves formed different associations.

In the 1860s, the company was owned and operated by Timothy Howe and William L. Libbey. In 1869, Libbey bought a new factory in New Bedford, Massachusetts. The Mount Washington Glass Company began operating again there under its original name. Henry Libbey became associated with the company early in 1871. He resigned in 1874 during the Depression, and the glassworks was closed. William Libbey had resigned in 1872, when he went to work for the New England Glass Company.

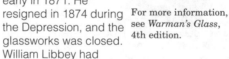

For more information, see *Warman's Glass*, 4th edition.

The Mount Washington Glass Company opened again in the fall of 1874 under the presidency of A. H. Seabury and the management of Frederick S. Shirley. In 1894, the glassworks became a part of the Pairpoint Manufacturing Company.

Throughout its history, the Mount Washington Glass Company made different types of glass including pressed, blown, art, lava, Napoli, cameo, cut, Albertine, and Verona.

Additional Listings: Burmese, Crown Milano, Peachblow, and Royal Flemish.

Beverage set, satin, mother-of-pearl, yellow sea weed coralene dec, glossy finish, 9" h, bulbous water pitcher, three spout top, applied reeded shell handle, three matching 4" h tumblers, two blisters on pitcher, three-pc set **750.00**
Bowl, 4-1/2" d, 2-3/4" h, Rose amber, fuchsia, blue swirl bands, bell tone flint **295.00**
Bride's bowl, 13" w, 12-1/2" h, unfired Burmese bowl, ruffled top, gold leaves, flower blossoms, stems, and pink tracery, purple crown mark, sgd silver plated holder with bird figural, some wear to gold on bowl int. **2,100.00**

Temple jar, blue draping flowers, green leaves and vines, all high-lighted with gold enamel, gold beads at lip, 8" h, **$650**. Photo courtesy of James D. Julia, Inc.

Compote, 6" d, 9-1/2" h, Napoli, clear, 10 hp pink tea roses on ext., outlined in gold on int. **875.00**
Condiment set, 6-1/2" h, opaque white, salt and pepper shakers, mustard pot, silver-plated holder sgd "Wilcox Silverplate Co.," wear to dec, fittings different on salt and pepper **235.00**
Cracker jar, 8" h, opalware, Egyptian motif, several camels at oasis, distant pyramid and mosque, sgd in lid with Pairpoint Diamond P, #3910, corresponding #3910/530 on jar **2,760.00**
Cruet, 7" h, Burmese, shiny finish, butter-yellow body, applied handle, mushroom stopper, each of 30 ribs with hint of pink, color blush intensifies on neck and spout, Mt. Washington **1,250.00**
Flower holder, 5-1/4" d, 3-1/2" h, mushroom shape, white ground, blue dot and oak leaf dec **425.00**
Humidor, 5-1/2" h, 4-1/2" d top, hinged silver-plated metalwork rim and edge, blown-out rococo scroll pattern, brilliant blue Delft windmills, ships, and landscape, Pairpoint **950.00**
Jar, cov, 6" w, 5-1/2" h, peachblow, rim of jar and rim of lid cased in gold metal with raised leaves **400.00**
Jug, 6" h, 4" w, satin, Polka Dot, deep peachblow pink, white air traps, DQ,

unlined, applied frosted loop handle **475.00**

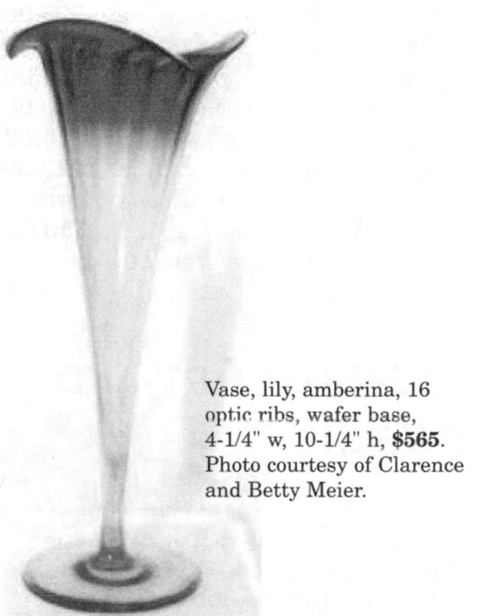
Vase, lily, amberina, 16 optic ribs, wafer base, 4-1/4" w, 10-1/4" h, **$565**. Photo courtesy of Clarence and Betty Meier.

Lamp, parlor, four dec glass oval insert panels, orig dec white opalware ball shade with deep red carnations, sgd "Pairpoint" base, c1890............ **1,750.00**
Lamp shade, 4-1/4" h, 5" d across top, 2" d fitter, rose amber, ruffled, fuschia shading to deep blue, DQ............ **575.00**
Miniature lamp, 17" h, 4-1/2" d shade, banquet style, milk glass, bright blue Delft dec of houses and trees, orig metal fittings, attributed to Frank Guba.. **795.00**
Mustard pot, 4-1/2" h, ribbed, bright yellow and pink background, painted white and magenta wild roses, orig silver-plated hardware **185.00**
Perfume bottle, 5-1/4" h, 3" d, opalware, dark green and brown glossy ground, red and yellow nasturtiums, green leaves, sprinkler top................................ **375.00**
Pickle castor, 10-3/8" h, Colonial Ware, yellow chrysanthemum dec, sp holder and lid, holder sgd "Pairpoint Mfg Co., New Bedford, Mass, B 603," orig tongs **735.00**
Punch cup, 4" w, 2-1/2" h, Napoli, Palmer Cox Brownie holding goose, hound chasing him, second Brownies watching, outlined in gold in ext., twisted handle, sgd "Napoli 6" **2,500.00**
Rose bowl, 3-1/2" h, beige shading to off-white, floral and leaf dec, inverted pinched rim **350.00**
Shaker, 2-1/2" h, fig shake, leaves and flowers dec **230.00**
Sugar shaker, 4-1/4" h, egg shape, white opaque body, holly leaves and raised enameled red berries dec........... **150.00**
Sweet meat, 5-1/2" d, opaque ground, pseudo Burmese enameling, gilt flowers and leaves, accented with jeweled cabochons, emb bail handle, sgd, lid #P4408, one jewel missing........... **815.00**
Tankard pitcher, 9" h, Burmese, green and brown ivy dec, gold tracery, applied gold enameling on rim and handle **4,600.00**
Toothpick holder, 2-1/2" h, Burmese, flared painted blue rim, mold-in ferns motif, scrolls at base, white blossoms with yellow dot centers............. **1,085.00**
Vase
5-3/8" h, 4-1/8" d, Lava, jet black body, chips of blue, jade green, gray, white, rose, and black, tiny broken blister **2,500.00**
13-1/4" h, Crown Milano, melon ribbed, long neck, folded down tricorn top, tulips dec, gold enameled scrolls and leaves, purple "CM" crown mark........... **4,600.00**
15" h, Garden of Allah dec, two saddled camels, two Bedouin Nomads on prayer rugs, sand dunes, pyramids, palm tree, gold enamel borders, orig paper label "Crown Pairpoint French China," sgd "Pairpoint Limoges 2016/70"..... **2,450.00**

Mulberry China

History: Mulberry china was made primarily in the Staffordshire district of England between 1830 and 1860. The ware often has a flowing effect similar to flow blue. It is the color of crushed mulberries, a dark purple, sometimes with a gray tinge or bordering almost on black. The potteries that manufactured flow blue also made Mulberry china, and, in fact, frequently made some patterns in both types of wares. To date, there are no known reproductions.

For more information, see *Warman's English & Continental Pottery & Porcelain*, 3rd edition.

Adviser: Ellen G. King.

Reproduction Alert: For information see the Flow Blue section of this edition.

Arabesque, Wedgwood
Creamer **75.00**
Plate, 10" d **80.00**
Athens, Adams
Cup plate.................................**65.00**
Plate, 9" d **80.00**
Posset cup, 12 panel **90.00**
Avon, Furnivals, teapot, cov, spout restored **450.00**
Beauties of China, Venables, teapot, cov... **550.00**
Berry, Ridgways, plate, 10" d **145.00**
Blackberry Lustre, Mellor Venables, plate, 9" d **95.00**

Berry, Ridgways, plate, 10" d, **$145**. Mulberry photos courtesy of adviser Ellen G. King.

Bluebell and Fern, unknown maker, plate, 10" d **125.00**
Bluebell and Leaf, unknown maker
Plate, 9" d **65.00**
Sugar, cov **125.00**
Teacup and saucer, handleless **95.00**
Wash bowl pitcher..................**250.00**
Bryonia, Utzschneider
Berry bowl, master **120.00**
Cake/dessert plate, 14" d, pedestal base **375.00**
Compote, handles, 10" d........**225.00**
Dessert/individual vegetable dish **30.00**
Demitasse cup and saucer......**65.00**
Plate, 7-1/4" d..........................**45.00**

Bryonia, Utzschneider, demitasse cup and saucer, **$65**.

Corea, Clementson, cake plate, handles **100.00**
Corean, Podmore Walker
Chamber pot **325.00**
Milk pitcher.............................**195.00**
Plate, 10" d **125.00**
Platter, 20" l...........................**495.00**
Sauce tureen, cov, tray (no ladle) **450.00**
Teapot, cov, gothic, eight panels **350.00**
Cyprus, Davenport
Cup plate.................................**85.00**
Shaving mug, 3-1/2"...............**275.00**
Teacup and saucer, handleless **100.00**

Corean, Podmore Walker, teapot, covered, gothic, eight panels, **$350**.

Wash bowl and pitcher set, hairline in pitcher spout **625.00**

Eagle, Podmore Walker, vegetable tureen, cov, undertray **375.00**

Flora, Walker, plate, 9" d, **$90**.

Flora, Walker
- Plate, 9" d **90.00**
- Teacup and saucer, handleless **85.00**

Heaths Flower, Heath, plate, 10-1/2" d **125.00**

Jeddo, Adams
- Plate, 7-1/2" d **40.00**
- Teacup and saucer **75.00**
- Wash bowl and pitcher **450.00**

Keswick, Wood & Son
- Bowl, 9" d, round, open........... **60.00**
- Teacup and saucer **55.00**
- Vegetable tureen, cov **225.00**

Lillium, Davenport, platter, 15" l **275.00**

Loretta, Alcock, platter, 13-1/4" l **200.00**

Marble, Wedgwood
- Plate, 8-1/2" d **45.00**
- Teacup and saucer, handleless **100.00**
- Teapot, cov............................ **325.00**

Medina, J F & Co.
- Plate, 10-1/4" d **65.00**
- Teapot, cov, coxcomb handle **750.00**

Nankin, Davenport
- Creamer **75.00**
- Honey dish **60.00**
- Plate, 9" d **65.00**

Neva, Challinor, plate, 10" d......... **145.00**

Ning Po, Hall
- Butter dish, cov, drainer **225.00**
- Creamer and sugar, set.......... **350.00**
- Cup plate................................ **75.00**
- Milk pitcher, restored spout.... **175.00**
- Plate, 9-1/2" d **50.00**
- Teapot, cov, lid restored **325.00**

Pelew, Challinor
- Gravy boat.............................. **145.00**
- Tea set, cov teapot, creamer, cov sugar **900.00**

Rhone Scenery, Mayer
- Plate, 10" d **70.00**
- Sauce tureen, cov, ladle, undertray **650.00**
- Teacup and saucer, handleless **55.00**

Rose, Challinor, plate, 10" d.......... **110.00**

Rose, Walker, milk pitcher............ **225.00**

Scinde, Walker, soup tureen, cov **2,000.00**

Scrolls, Mayer, milk pitcher, 8" h, burgundy polychrome................. **275.00**

Seaweed, Ridgway, teacup and saucer, handleless, **$125**.

Seaweed, Ridgway
- Platter, 16" l............................ **395.00**
- Teacup and saucer, handleless **125.00**

Strawberry, Walker, plate, 9" d **110.00**

Temple, Podmore Walker
- Cup plate................................ **75.00**
- Plate, 9" d **80.00**
- Sauce tureen stand, on small foot **60.00**
- Wash pitcher **275.00**

Tiger Lily, Furnivals, punch bowl, pedestal, polychromed dec **850.00**

Vincennes, Alcock
- Cup plate................................ **85.00**
- Platter, 15-1/2" l **265.00**
- Punch cup **150.00**
- Relish dish, mitten shape **250.00**
- Vegetable tureen, cov, 8-3/4" **325.00**
- Wash bowl and pitcher set..... **900.00**

Washington vase, Podmore Walker
- Creamer **195.00**
- Pitcher, 8" h, octagonal **325.00**
- Plate, 8-1/2" d **85.00**
- Platter, 17-3/4" l **300.00**
- Relish, mitten shape.............. **150.00**
- Teacup and saucer **95.00**
- Teapot, cov............................ **420.00**

Wisteria, unknown maker, fruit compote, stemmed...................................... **350.00**

Zinna, Bourne & Co., sugar, cov **175.00**

Mourning Art and Jewelry

History: During the mid to late 1800s, proper social etiquette dictated that upon the death of a loved one, a respectable period of mourning be observed. It was Victorian tradition for the bereaved to enter full mourning for two years, followed by six months of half mourning. The catalyst for this somber 19th century ritual was the death of Queen Victoria's husband Prince Albert in 1861, and the practice was perpetuated in America with the outbreak of the Civil War in 1861 and later the assassination of President Abraham Lincoln in 1865. Mourning art includes needlework pictures hand crafted to show the needle worker's devotion to the deceased. Other forms of mourning memorabilia include paper ephemera. Many times these funeral notices, memorial cards, letters of condolences, etc. descend through families, adding in genealogical research as well as preserving an important part of a family's past.

During the full mourning period as dictated by the Victorians, all black clothing was worn and decorative accessories were kept at a minimum. The six month half-mourning period was a time when white lace and dark colors were incorporated slowly back into the wardrobe. Today the symbolic accoutrements of mourning not only reflect the beliefs and practices of the past but also give us insight into the development of a number of substances that were used in order to meet the demand for black mourning jewelry and accessories. In order to supply the need for all black goods, a variety of natural and man-made materials were utilized in their production. The most popular material was jet, a hard lignite coal mined along the Yorkshire coast and carved into brooches, beads, buttons, pendants, and hair ornaments in the village of Whitby. When supplies of natural jet began to dwindle, other materials were sought out, especially bituminous cannel coal from Scotland, which was imported to Whitby and combined with authentic jet.

Eventually other materials needed to be developed as the demand for black was so great on both sides of the Atlantic. French jet, also called Vauxhall, is molded

black glass, which mimics the appearance of authentic jet so well it can fool even the most seasoned collector. Shellac, a black composition material was used, mainly for molding daguerreotype/union cases, but jewelry and fashion accessories were also made from this substance. Hardened black rubber, called vulcanite, was also used extensively to mold pendants, brooches, hair combs, lockets and chains, as well as a host of other items. Dark horn and tortoise shell, materials acceptable for the half mourning period, were also made into a variety of brooches and pendants.

The symbolic images depicted on mourning goods are a somber reminder of grief and sorrow. Floral motifs are often seen with roses symbolizing love, lily and lily of the valley representing eternal life, and forget-me-nots expressing devotion. Draped urns and wreaths represent sorrow, stars are symbolic of heaven, while the cross expresses faith, the anchor represents hope and the heart signifies love. The shamrock, with its three petals, is often seen on Irish pieces and represents the Trinity. Sometimes tiny diamonds—symbolic of devotion and seed pearls, which represented tears—were incorporated into the design of half-mourning jewelry. Lockets were made with compartments for a lock of hair and eventually, with the development of photographic technology, they came to include personal images as well.

It should be noted that since black was in vogue during the last half of the 19th century, not all black jewelry and accessories were worn for mourning. Only those items that have symbolic imagery of grief can be positively identified as authentic mourning jewelry.

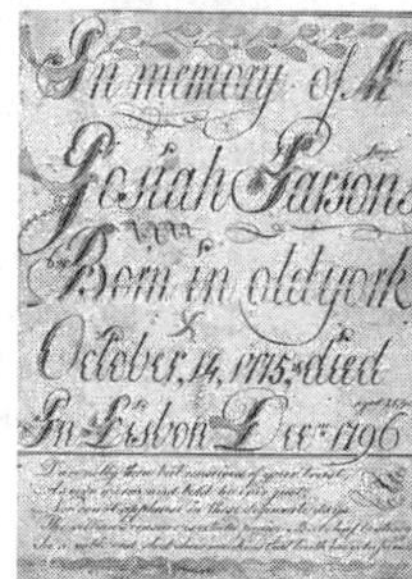

Calligraphic memorial, polychrome and ink on paper, one side with inscription reading "In memory of Mr. Josiah Parsons junr. Born in old york October, 14, 1775, died In Lisbon Dec. in 1796 aged 21 yr.," over poetic verse, embellished with birds, leafy vine, and wavy line borders, reverse with verses and mottos, inscription "Written for Miss Abigail Peasley By Abraham Kimball," paper sandwiched between glass and framed, minor toning, foxing, creases, small tears, 8-1/4" x 5-3/4", **$825**. Photo courtesy of Skinner, Inc.

Clothing and accessories

Blouse, black silk, Victorian, hand-made natural jet appliqué on front, high collar, trimmed in dark green velvet, hook and eye back closure, old well done repair **95.00**

Fan, 13-1/2" l, 25-1/2" w open, painted black wood sticks and guards, black satin front, black cotton backing .. **250.00**

Handkerchief, 12" sq, linen, hand embroidered in black on each corner **24.00**

Mourning veil, black toile open pillbox hat, black grosgrain ribbon edging, 1960s **18.00**

Jewelry

Bracelet, bangle, adjusts from 6" to 7", 1" d jet faceted circle, 3/4" w celluloid band, brass hardware attaches jet front face and other dec elements **250.00**

Brooch

3/4" d, gold filled faceted frame, glass cover over woven hair, C-clasp **450.00**

1-1/4" d, 14 kt yg, black enameling, beveled glass, finely woven blond and brown hair, marked "John Osborne, Aug 8th 1861" **250.00**

1-7/8" x 1-1/2", picture of a gentleman in one side, very tightly woven hair on other side, center rotates, black enamel border on one side, C-clasp **450.00**

2-1/2" l, pressed horn, outstretched hand holding a floral and foliate wreath, dark brownish black, c-clasp **95.00**

2-1/2" l, shield shaped base of pressed horn, circular dec motif of jet including French jet star representing heaven **115.00**

3-3/4" l, pressed horn, anchor, dark brown suitable for half mourning, French jet floral ornament attached to lower left **95.00**

Earrings, pr

2-3/4" l, tortoiseshell, pierced, urn shape, inlaid with gold pique stars and flowers **375.00**

Teardrop shape, carved Whitby jet, porcelain inset with portrait of young lady, c1860 .... **550.00**

Hat pin, 9" l, 1-7/8" d French jet disc molded with three petal stylized floral motif **105.00**

Lace pin

1-1/4" w, French jet, shamrock fashioned from three bezel set faceted petals mounted in machine stamped brass scalloped setting trimmed in stars, C-clasp **65.00**

2" l, combination jet and French jet, "S" shaped flat jet base with saw tooth edge and center jet shamrock attached by French jet bead, shamrock is flanked by faceted French get ovals, C-clasp **85.00**

Locket

1-1/2" l, Vulcanite (hardened rubber), oval, ornate lily of the valley motif in relief on front **325.00**

1-1/2" l, tortoiseshell, plain, dark mottled tortoiseshell, 11" linked tortoiseshell chain suitable for half morning, opens to photo of widow in mourning, set under crystal, gold frame **450.00**

2-1/4" l, Vulcanite (hardened rubber), pointed oval, ornate draped urn and floral motif, four round compartments set with crystal inside for hair or photographs **425.00**

Mourning jewelry, locket, Victorian, cabochon crystal view magnifier for portrait, 14k yellow gold, banded agate cabochon accents surround, reverse is rock crystal covered cache used for personal momento, such as a lock of hair, **$950**.

Pendant

1-1/4" x 1/2", child's, Vulcanite (hardened rubber), oval, scrolled edging, rose in relief, small liked Vulcanite chain **325.00**

2" l, ebony, heart, suspended on 11" hardened rubber linked chain **250.00**

2-7/8" l, Vulcanite (hardened rubber), foliate, palmette, and tear drop shaped trim, central rose motif in relief **275.00**

3" l, shellac, cross with Greek key, palmette and lily motif, suspended from 12" black enamel metal chain **375.00**

3" l, Vulcanite (hardened rubber), cross, filigree lily and urn motif, suspended from 11" linked chain **375.00**

Ring, 1-1/8" l, 3/4" w, gold mounting, sepia on ivory plaque over hair compartment, painting of urn "Sacred to Memory" written on base, delicate weeping willow, branches falling around monument, inscription on reverse tells of woman who died a day of her son, inscribed "Harriet Brown Died 3 July 1787 Ag'd 17 Years, Douglas Brown Died 2 July 1787 Ag'd 19 mo's," surrounded by 35 natural seed pearls.......... **2,100.00**

Stick pin

2-1/2" l, polished black onyx oval, bezel set in chased setting, hallmarked OB10K **55.00**

2-3/4" l, round black onyx circle set in sterling bezel with tiny diamond set in center **75.00**

Watch chain, two ropes of woven hair, 14k rose gold engraved fittings.... **650.00**

Needlework memorial, silk on silk, wrought by Mary Ann Mitchell, student at Bethlehem (PA) Female Seminary (1806-09), floral garland suspending central cartouche of mourning lady beside tomb, inscribed "George Mitchell departed this life the 14th day of June 1793 Aged 5 months and 18 days," beneath willow tree, reverse painted frame, 18-1/8" x 20-1/2", provenance: George Mitchell was first born child of Nathaniel Mitchell (1752-1813), Revolutionary War hero and later Governor of Delaware, **$4,600**. Photo courtesy of Pook & Pook.

Needlework picture

Hair art

11" x 11", traditional willow tree, monument, executed complete in hair, framed **500.00**

Weeping willow tree and lawn with flowers, classical urn with flowers on stepped marble plinth, and sky with stars, oval medallion giving names and dates that reads "Clara gest 15 Dec./Anna - 19 - /E" **200.00**

Textile

Mandell, silk threads and watercolor on silk, urn topped memorials flanking pointed section with verse, kneeling woman to side, willow tree behind monuments, sailing vessels in background, left memorial in memory of Paul Mandell Esq. 1809, right memorial in memory of Mrs. Susannah, consort of Mr. Paul Mandell 1812, MA, c1812, framed, 16-1/2" x 20-5/8" sight size, some foxing and staining, tears, stabilized in middle of monument........... **980.00**

No names, silk threads, silk ground, central weeping willow tree, tombstone, obelisk, church in far left ground, never embroidered with names, framed, 16-1/4" x 22", minor losses, deterioration of silk ground **600.00**

Pike, Zebulon, "In Memory of Genl. Zebulon M. Pike who fell in the arms of glory in the moment of victory at York, UC April 27th, 1813," two mourning women at tomb, weeping willow tree above them, angel flying overhead with banner that reads "Wreaths of laurels over his tomb entwine," 10-3/4" x 6-3/4", foxing, tears, minor loss throughout **700.00**

Richardson family, c1820, two painted urn-topped monuments beneath willow tree, inscribed "Sacred to the Memory of Mrs. Hannah Richardson who died May 31st 1820 Aged 36," other "Sacred to the memory of John Gilson who died April 21st 1816 Ae 7 wks," two painted gravestones in solidly stitched foreground, flowering tree, small church, background with painted hills and blue sky, gilt and eglomise mat, 24" x 24-1/4" **4,700.00**

Spicer, Thayer, Clark, large center monument, surrounded by grieving family, tablet inscribed "Mrs Fanny Spicer Ob't Aug 18th 1795, AE 20 Mrs. Mary Thayer Ob't Sept – 1806, AE 36 Mrs Sarah Clark Ob't Oct 12 1810 AE 24," mourners, landscape, and sky painted in watercolor and gouache, monument, foliate tree, and shrubbery solidly stitched in silk and chenille threads, silk ground, eglomise mat, period frame, splits to silk inscriptions, some paint separation on glass, losses to mat and frame **4,700.00**

Needlework memorial, silk, pencil, paint, and ink on silk, by Sarah E. Sawyer, dated 1833, elaborate landscape of Portland (Maine), memorial to her son William, who was lost at sea, reverse painted mat, tear, losses, mat crack, 21-1/2" x 25-1/4", **$4,370**. Photo courtesy of Pook & Pook.

Paper ephemera

Autographed document, John Evans, document appointing administrator of an estate, March 24, 1704, wax seal, some fold weakness, 9-1/2" x 15"........... **485.00**

Autographed letter

Butcher, John, Alexandria, VA, January 4, 1800, to daughter, giving lengthy comments on last will and testament of George Washington whereby he wills 130 Negroes free after Martha's death, 2 pgs, folio, integral address leaf **1,035.00**

George II, sgd as Prince of Wales, in French, 2 pages 4to, Leicester House, Jan 11/22, 1723, to Madame Marygrove, sending sympathies on loss of her close relation, written completely in the hand of George II **1,000.00**

Ephemera, 6-1/2" x 9-3/4" folded sheet, text of Queen Victoria's message to Mrs. Garfield as Pres Garfield's Memorial, white sheet, black memoriam graphics including cross and stack of stones, each representing a state of the Union, brief condolence message from Queen, eulogy verse by Wellesley Bradshaw, dated Sept 1881............................ **25.00**

Memorial card, black, gold lettering **10.00**

Mourning envelope, very heavy black borders on front and back, hand addressed to Miss C. L. Ransom, Washington, DC by Lucretia Garfield, sgd in full "Lucretia R. Garfield" at top for franking purposes, embossed LRG monogram on back of envelope, postmarked 1885 Washington, DC **265.00**

Scrapbook, neatly filled with newspaper clippings of obituaries, starting with accounts of Lincoln's assassination up to 1930s, leather cover....................... **50.00**

Musical Instruments

History: From the first beat of the prehistoric drum to the very latest in electronic music makers, musical instruments have been popular modes of communication and relaxation.

The most popular antique instruments are violins, flutes, oboes, and other instruments associated with the classical music period of 1650 to 1900. Many of the modern instruments, such as trumpets, guitars, and drums, have value on the "used," rather than antiques market.

Collecting musical instruments is in its infancy. The field is growing very rapidly. Investors and speculators have played a role since the 1930s, especially in early string instruments.

Banjo, Global, with case.............. **225.00**

Cello, with bow and case............. **200.00**

Clarinet, with case, Henry Bouche **675.00**

Coronet, English, silver plated, stamped "F. Besson, Brevetee...," with case **320.00**

Drum set, Gretsch, three pcs, aqua sides **600.00**

Euphonium, double horn, silver-plated, three finger valves with fourth for second horn, mouthpiece like French horn, made by J. W. York & Sons, Grand Rapids, MI, patented 1910, 21" w, 11" d, 26" h, few minor dents.................................. **865.00**

Drum, metal, leather skin, rope binders and wood trims, Uncle Sam, c1914, scribbling on drumheads, puncture in bottom head, dent to side, 10-7/8" d, **$175**. Photo courtesy of James D. Julia, Inc.

Fife, American, Meacham & Co., Albany, maple, brass fittings, case........... **320.00**

Flute, American

Gemeinhardt, with case......... **125.00**

Haynes, William S., Co., Boston, 1911, Grenadilla, open G key **1,100.00**

Peloubet, C., five keys, rosewood, round key covers.................... **550.00**

Flute, English

Cubitt, W. D., & Son, London, 19th C, blackwood, open and nickel covered case, case............................. **690.00**

Rudall Carte & Co., London, silver, multiple stamps, hallmarks, case **750.00**

Wrede, H., London, c1840, four keys, stained boxwood, ivory fittings, silver round cover keys, case.......... **320.00**

Guitar, archtop, Gibson Inc., Model Super 400, irregular curl maple two-piece maple back, medium curl sides, spruce top with medium grain, light medium curl neck, inlaid pearl Gibson logo peghead with split-diamond design, bound fingerboard with split-block pearl inlay, natural finish, labeled "Gibson Super Style 400, Number EA-5309 is hereby guaranteed, Gibson Inc., Kalamazoo, Michigan, USA," 21-7/8" l back, 17-13/16" w lower bout, c1939, with orig hard shell case and cover........................ **14,950.00**

Guitar, classical

Chica, Manuel de la, two-piece Brazilian rosewood back, labeled "Manuel De La Chica, Constructore, De, Violines Y Guitarras, Placeta De La Silleria 8, Granada, Ano De 1966," 19-1/4" l back........... **1,725.00**

Martin, C. F., Style D-35, three-piece Indian rosewood back, similar sides, spruce top of fine to medium grain, mahogany neck with bound ebony fingerboard, inlaid pearl eyes, stamped internally "CF Martin & Co., Nazareth, PA, Made in USA, D-35," 1975 .... **1,475.00**

Fischesser, Leon, narrow curl two-piece back, similar ribs and scroll, fine grain top, red color varnish, labeled "Leon Fischesser Luthier D'Art, No. 47, 28 Faubuorg Poissonniere Paris L'Anno 1907," 14" l back, 356 mm, with case **2,760.00**

Guitar, flat top, Gibson, flat top, orig case.. **900.00**

Hawaiian guitar, National, New Yorker, with case **395.00**

Melodeon, Victorian, labeled "C.W. Fisk and Co., Ansonia Conn. Sold by John Marsh, Philadelphia," rosewood, matching stool, **$300**. Photo courtesy of Pook & Pook.

Mandolin

Gibson, F5, orig case........ **29,000.00**

Washburn, melon base, with case **100.00**

Piano, grand

Chickering, c1885-60.......... **3,410.00**

Mathushek, New Haven, CT, rosewood, c1865-70, medallion carved cabriole legs and lyre, 58" w **5,500.00**

Piano, upright, French Rococo-style, carved, c1867 .... **2,750.00**

Recorder, Moeck......................... **135.00**

Trumpet, valve type, Buescher.... **125.00**

Ukulele, Hawaiian, three mele, Bares inscription, no strings **90.00**

Vibraphone................................. **350.00**

Viola, no inscription, with orig case, orig bow... **475.00**

Violin, **German**, D'Amore, faint curl on one-piece back, irregular curl ribs, later carved scroll of narrow curl, fine grain top, brown color varnish, unlabeled, c 1780, 13-3/8" l back, 339 mm, case, ivory mounted period bow **4,150.00**

Violin, **Hungarian**, medium curl two-piece back, similar ribs, medium curl scroll, fine grain top, red color varnish, labeled "Janos Spiegel, Budapest, 1907," 14-1/16" l back, 358 mm, with case **6,620.00**

Violin, Italian, Bisiach, Leandro, strong medium curl two-piece back, strong narrow curl ribs and scroll, fine grain top, golden brown color varnish, labeled "Leandro Bisiach Da Milano, Fece L'Anno 1942," sgd, 14" l back, 356 mm, with case, undated numbered certificate **18,400.00**

Violin, Mittenwald, Klotz School, medium curl two-piece back, similar ribs and scroll, fine grain top, brown color varnish, unlabeled, c1780, 13-7/8" l back, 353 mm, with case **2,415.00**

Violin bow, gold mounted

Ouchard, Emile, round stick stamped "Emile Ouchard" at butt, ebony frog with Parisian eye, plain gold adjuster, 63 grams **4,025.00**

Unstamped, octagonal stick, later frog engraved "A. Vigneron A Paris 1886," 59 grams.................. **1,485.00**

Violin bow, silver mounted

Hill, W. E., round stick stamped "W. E. Hill & Sons" at butt, ebony eye with Parisian eye, plain silver adjuster, 60 grams, baleen wrap **2,530.00**

Unstamped, French, Francois-Nicolas Voirin, c1860, round stick, ebony frog with pearl eye, later silver and ebony adjuster, 63 grams **4,890.00**

Weichold, Richard, octagonal stick stamped "R. Weichold A. Dresden" and "Imitation De Tourte" at butt, ebony frog with pearl eye, silver and ebony adjuster, 56 grams ... **1,265.00**

Violoncello, America, Settin, Joseph, strong narrow curl two-piece back, similar ribs and scroll, fine to medium grain top, golden brown color varnish, labeled "Joseph Settin Venetus, Fecit Anno Domani 1953," 29-7/16" l back, 748 mm.. **8,100.00**

Violoncello, child's, plain one-piece back, similar ribs and scroll, medium curl top, brown color varnish, possibly Italian, 22-13/16" l back, 581 mm.......... **3,795.00**

Violoncello, Czech, two-piece medium curl back, similar ribs and scroll similar, medium curl top, red color varnish, labeled "CAK Dvorni, A Armadni Dodvatel, Preniceska Tovarna Nastrouju Na Morave, Josefidil V Brne Zelny Irh 11," 30-3/16" l back, 767 mm **3,795.00**

Violoncello, English, James and Henry Banks, narrow curl two-piece back, medium curl ribs, faint curl scroll, fine to medium grain top, red color varnish, sgd internally on table, "James and Henry Banks, Salisbury," c1800, 28-34" l back, 729 mm.................................. **18,400.00**

Organ, high ornate walnut case, red lining, marked "Dyer & Hughes," **$750**. Photo courtesy of Joseph P. Smalley, Jr., Auctioneer.

Violoncello, French, Thibouville-Lamy, Jerome, narrow curl two-piece back, similar ribs, medium curl scroll, medium to wide grain top, orange color varnish, labeled "Jerome Thibouville-Lamy, 70 Rue Reaumur, Paris, 1938," 29-3/4" l back, 756 mm, with case **3,795.00**

Violoncello, German, irregular narrow curl two-piece back, similar ribs, narrow curl scroll, medium to wide grain top, orange color varnish, labeled "Erich Grunert, Penzberg Anno 1976," 29-3/4" l back, 756 mm, with case **1,150.00**

Violoncello bow, nickel plated, round stick stamped "L. Bausch, Leipzig," 81 grams **1,840.00**

Music Boxes

History: Music boxes, invented in Switzerland around 1825, encompass a broad array of forms, from small boxes to huge circus calliopes.

A cylinder box consists of a comb with teeth that vibrate when striking a pin in the cylinder. The music these boxes produce ranges from light tunes to opera and overtures.

The first disc music box was invented by Paul Lochmann of Leipzig, Germany, in 1886. It used an interchangeable steel disc with pierced holes bent to a point that hit the star-wheel as the disc revolved, and thus produced the tune. Discs were easily stamped out of metal, allowing a single music box to play an endless variety of tunes. Disc boxes reached the height of their popularity from 1890 to 1910, when the phonograph replaced them. Music boxes also were incorporated in many items, e.g., clocks, sewing and jewelry boxes, steins, plates, toys, perfume bottles, and furniture.

Swiss, six-tune music box, case with inlaid floral motif in lid and painted grain decorated sides, ebonized interior, one cylinder and one 52-tooth comb, three bells with bird strikers, scratch on front of case, 16-3/4" w, **$1,220**. Photo courtesy of Alderfer Auction Co.

Bremond, 23" w, No. 2630, 13" cylinder with bird strikers, nine bells, plays eight airs, veneered and inlaid case **3,680.00**

Cellesta, 8-1/4" disc, single-comb ratchet-wind mechanism, walnut case with bone inlaid top and color print in lid, 16 discs **980.00**

Chautauqua roller organ, 18" w, 15" d, 12-1/2" h, oak tabletop crank organ, stenciled top, plays 6-3/8" wooden cob/cylinders, 12 included, restored in 1963 .... **9,200.00**

Criterion 3, 16" w, 15" d, 12" h, double comb, 11-5/8" zinc discs, mahogany table model case with egg and dart molding, rope turn molding, replaced paper picture in lid, eight discs, mechanically restored **460.00**

Imperial Symphoniom, 24" w, 21" d, 12" h, double comb, 15-5/8" disc, mahogany case with fancy moldings around base, sides, and lid with orig lithograph, orig celluloid tags, six orig steel discs, orig finish, orig crank, mechanically restored **400.00**

Lecoulture, D., 17" l, 8-1/4" cylinder, plays four airs, plain case **1,100.00**

Nicole Freres, Swiss, 39-1/2" w, 15-1/2" d, 13-1/4" music box, quarter sawn oak case, matching 44" w, 21-1/2" d, 30" h table, carved molding around base and lid, elaborately carved front, coin operated, reproduction tune card listing all 12 tunes, case and table refinished, mechanism restored **4,600.00**

Olympia, No. 6566, 20-1/2" upright disc, twin-comb mechanism, disengaged coin slide, manual control, two-piece mahogany cabinet, side disc storage, 32 discs, sounding boards replaced, 70" h **6,900.00**

Paillard, tune card, 34" l, No. 32378, Excelsior Interchangeable, three 9-1/4" cylinders, plays eight airs each, double-spring motor, tune indicator and zither attachment, grained case, torn tune card, veneered and inlaid front and lid, cylinder drawer in plinth **3,750.00**

Swiss, marquetry inlaid music box on stand by Bremond, lid with inlaid mother-of-pearl butterfly, case marked "BAB," 11" cylinder, stand with single fitted drawer containing five additional cylinders, turned, fluted and blocked legs joined by stretcher with central finial, 19th C, 33" h, 26" w, 22-3/4" d, 33" h, **$4,600**. Photo courtesy of Pook & Pook.

Polyphon, Orpheus, manufactured by Ludwig & Wild, Leipzig-Neuschoenfeld, intro 1897, upright, 13 18-1/2" dia disks, coin operated **5,900.00**

Regina

14-1/2" w, 13-1/2" d, 9" h, 11" single comb, carved oak case with heavily carved cherubs, lattice, and musical instruments on all four sides and lid, orig paper photo in lid, two celluloid instruction tags inside box, five steel discs, replaced crank, mechanically restored **1,725.00**

15" w, 14" d, 10" h, 11" single comb, mahogany table model, four steel discs, pillow lid with orig paper picture, base molding, mechanically restored **1,440.00**

22" w, 20" d, 13-1/2" h, 15-1/2" double comb, oak box with celluloid inlay, pillow top with orig picture in lid, two celluloid tags, six steel discs, refinished case, orig crank, mechanically restored **700.00**

22-1/2" w, 20" d, 13" h, 15-1/2" double comb, oak box, carved molding around base and corners, beaded molding around pillow lid with orig paper inside, two orig celluloid tags, orig finish, orig crank, six steel discs, mechanically restored **865.00**

Singing bird, 3-3/4" w, blue enameled case, ivory beak, moving wings and perch, lid with Alpine scene and floral spray **2,645.00**

The Criterion, tabletop, walnut case, litho paper cupid under lid, five discs, **$1,700**. Photo courtesy of Joy Luke Auctions.

Swiss

Jacots Safety Check, patent 1886, oak case with metal dec, two 14-1/2" d cylinders **2,900.00**

Unidentified maker, 6-1/2" cylinder, quarter-sawn oak case, six tunes **950.00**

Unidentified maker, 13-1/2" cylinder, 28" quarter-sawn oak case, applied carving, 12 tunes................ **1,400.00**

Unknown maker, 5-3/8" w, 4" d, 6-5/8" h, morocco covered case formed as upright piano, plays march and air, hinged lid enclosing ivory and ebonized keys with starting latch, mirrored backplate, fitted with two glass perfume bottles, four-piece cut-steel manicure set, Continental, late 19th C **550.00**

Nanking

History: Nanking is a type of Chinese porcelain made in Canton, China, from the early 1800s into the 20th century. It was made for export to America and England. Four elements help distinguish Nanking from Canton, two similar types of ware. Nanking has a spear-and-post border, as opposed to the scalloped-line style of Canton. Second, in the water's edge or Willow pattern, Canton usually has no figures; Nanking includes a standing figure with open umbrella on the bridge. In addition, the blues tend to be darker on the Nanking ware. Finally, Nanking wares often are embellished with gold, Canton is not. Green and orange variations of Nanking survive, although they are scarce.

Reproduction Alert: Copies of Nanking ware currently are being produced in China. They are of inferior quality and decorated in a lighter, rather than in the darker, blues.

Nanking, covered tureen and undertray, oval, entwined lapped foliate handles, lotus flower finial, China, 19th C, rim chips, 7-3/4" l, 6" h, **$500**. Photo courtesy of Skinner, Inc.

Bowl, 6-1/2" d, 3" h, white glazed int., brushed with blue flowers, brown matte glazed ext., from ship sunk in 1750 .... **825.00**

Candlesticks, pr, 9-1/2" h **775.00**

Cider jug, 10" h, gilt highlights, 19th C, pr **825.00**

Platter, 11-1/2" x 14-1/2", **$345**.

Cup and saucer, handleless, 3-3/4" h cup, 5-3/4" d saucer, pagodas, man on bridge, c1780-1820..................... **235.00**

Ewer, 11" h, small spout, blue and white, mid-19th C................................. **300.00**

Pitcher, cov, 9-1/2" h, blue and white, Liverpool shape.......................... **550.00**

Plate, 9-1/2" d, water's edge scene, c1780-1800 .... **90.00**

Platter, 12-3/4" l, Chinese, 19th C, chips **415.00**

Rice bowl, 19th C **100.00**

Soup bowl, 9-1/2" d, pagodas, man on bridge, islands, and horse, c1840-60 .... **240.00**

Soup tureen, cov, 11-3/4" h, 19th C, imperfections.............................. **475.00**

Teapot, 6-1/2" h, globular, diaper border above watery pagoda landscape reserve **155.00**

Napkin Rings, Figural

History: Gracious home dining during the Victorian era required a personal napkin ring for each household member. Figural napkin rings were first patented in 1869. During the remainder of the 19th century, most plating companies, including Cromwell, Eureka, Meriden, and Reed and Barton, manufactured figural rings, many copying and only slightly varying the designs of other companies.

Notes: Values are determined by the subject matter of the ring, the quality of the workmanship, and the condition.

Central napkin ring supported by two winged figures holding drape, etched decoration, inscribed name "Crane," sterling silver, Gorham anchor mark with #2, 2" h, **$600**. Photo courtesy of Alderfer Auction Co.

Baby, seated, arms extended, Pairpoint #52, resilvered **650.00**
Bird, perched on top, four delicate feet, marked "Sterling," 2-3/4" h **145.00**
Boy, Kate Greenaway, bat and ball, resilvered **1,100.00**
Butterfly, perched on pair of fans **145.00**
Cat, glass eyes, ring on back **275.00**
Cherub, holding reins of detailed stag, marked "Toronto," resilvered **1,500.00**
Cherub, winged, looking into mirror and bud vase, marked "Rockford #178," resilvered **850.00**
Child, crawling, ring on back **300.00**
Conquistador, marked "Toronto #1137," resilvered **1,500.00**
Dachsund, ring on back, silverplate **1,100.00**
Deer, long horns, marked "Toronto #1205," resilvered **850.00**
Double rifles, Meriden B. #235 .... **850.00**
Frog, holding drumstick, pushing drum-like ring **300.00**

Turtle supporting ring napkin holder, footed rectangular base, small vase with Egyptian motifs, silverplate, Derby Co. Quadruple Plate, #342, 3-1/4" h, **$425**. Photo courtesy of Alderfer Auction Co.

Goat, pulling wheeled flower cart **250.00**
Kate Greenaway, girl sitting on branches, marked "211," resilvered **1,250.00**
Mastiff dog, Reed & Barton, #1185, resilvered **1,700.00**
Owl, sitting on leafy base, owls perched on upper limbs **250.00**
Pan, prancing on earthen mound, marked "Pairpoint #82," resilvered **950.00**
Rabbit, sitting alertly next to ring **195.00**
Sailor boy, anchor **250.00**

Two putti supporting an engraved napkin ring, engraved base with four ball feet, silverplate, Wilcox Quadruple Plate, #01536, Meriden, Conn., 3-1/4" x 2-1/4", **$225**. Photo courtesy of Alderfer Auction Co.

Schoolboy with books, feeding begging puppy **235.00**
Turtle, crawling, ornate ring on back **300.00**
Water lily, marked "Meriden and Co.," c1880, silverplate, some wear **170.00**

Nash Glass

History: Nash glass is a type of art glass attributed to Arthur John Nash and his sons, Leslie H. and A. Douglas. Arthur John Nash, originally employed by Webb in Stourbridge, England, came to America and was employed in 1889 by Tiffany Furnaces at its Corona, Long Island, plant.

While managing the plant for Tiffany, Nash designed and produced iridescent glass. In 1928, A. Douglas Nash purchased the facilities of Tiffany Furnaces. The A. Douglas Nash Corporation remained in operation until 1931.

For more information, see *Warman's Glass*, 4th edition.

Bowl, 7-3/4" x 2-1/2", Jewel pattern, gold phantom luster **285.00**
Candlestick, 4" h, Chintz, ruby and gray, sgd **450.00**
Compote, 7-1/2" d, 4-1/2" h, Chintz, transparent aquamarine, wide flat rim of red and gray-green controlled stripe dec, base inscribed "Nash RD89" **865.00**
Cordial, 5-1/2" h, Chintz, green and blue **95.00**

Vase, iridescent gold, cupped rim tapering to footed base, lower half relief-decorated with stylized flowers on tall leafy stems, base inscribed "Nash 549," 5-3/4" h, **$940**. Photo courtesy of Skinner, Inc.

Creamer and sugar, 5-3/8" h creamer, 3-1/2" h sugar, blue-green opaque dots, dark blue-green base, creamer with polished pontil, sugar with waffle pontil **475.00**
Goblet, 6-3/4" h, feathered leaf motif, gilt dec, sgd **295.00**
Lamp, 16" h, 8" d irid gold DQ shade, gold doré base, textured gold irid stem of graduated balls, irid gold glass finial, bottom of base sgd "A. DOUGLAS NASH CORP. 708," top cap hides small rim chip **3,250.00**
Plate, 8" d, Chintz, green and blue **195.00**
Sherbet, bluish-gold texture, ftd, sgd, #417 .... **275.00**
Vase
- 8-1/4" h, Chintz, irid gold stripes, gold and green ground, unsigned **750.00**

9" h, Polka Dot, deep opaque red oval, molded with prominent 16 ribs, dec by spaced white opal dots, base inscribed "Nash GD154"..... **1,100.00**

Nautical Items

History: The seas have fascinated man since time began. The artifacts of sailors have been collected and treasured for years. Because of their environment, merchant and naval items, whether factory or handmade, must be of quality construction and long lasting. Many of these items are aesthetically appealing as well.

Account book, Bark Arab, showing purchases and sales from October 1853 to December 1856, 96 pgs, folio, New Bedford or Hawaii, label reads "purchased of John Kehew at his Navigation Store in New Bedford," Kehew's label mounted on front paste down, two volumes.................... **1,955.00**

Banner, 26" x 8-1/2", carved and polychrome painted pine, "Don't Give Up The Ship!," American eagle, attributed to John Hales Bellamy................ **24,150.00**

Book

Bligh, William, Dangerous Voyage of Captain Bligh, in an Open Boat, over 1200 Leagues of the Ocean, in the Year 1789, Dublin, 1818, five full-page woodcut engraved illus, 180 pgs, small 12mo.................... **345.00**

Dexter, Elisha, Narrative of the Loss of the William and Joseph, of Martha's Vineyard, Boston, 1842, five wood engraved plates, 54 pgs, 8vo **1,370.00**

Box, cov, 4-3/4" h, 12" l, 6-5/9" d, walnut, dovetailed, ropework handle, polyhedron carved terminals, attributed to New England sailor, early 19th C, one terminal missing....................................... **460.00**

Pond model of sloop, red topsides, original sails, 29" l, **$250**. Photo courtesy of Wiederseim Associates, Inc.

Broadside, 415 x 335 mm, issued as circular to mariners at Table Bay, Robben Island, advising of berthing procedures, 1827... **345.00**

Cane, 32-7/8" l, carved from single piece of tooth, 1-3/4" d x 2" h whale ivory handle, carved sailor's Turks-head knot, thin baleen spacer separates whalebone shaft, inlaid at top with four-pointed baleen fingers, white whalebone shaft, tapered with very slight natural bow, American, c1850...................... **2,800.00**

Canoe paddle, 60" l, painted deep red with black crescent moon and star, America, late 19th C, with stand .. **375.00**

Children's book, Adventures of Jack, or a Life on the Wave, The, Charles L. Newhall, Southbridge, 1859, 134 pgs, 12 mo.. **230.00**

Chronometer, 8-1/2" h, 8-1/4" w, 8-1/4" d, "M.F. Dent, 33 Cockspur St. Chronometer Maker to the Queen, London," late 19th C, gimbal mounted in brass fitted mahogany case, brass bezel, silver wash dial, eight days......................... **5,175.00**

Ship's compass, John Bliss & Co., New York, early 20th C, brass, gyroscopic, set in brass collar, spherical removable cover with oval glass viewscreen, two cylindrical siphoning chambers to either side, 13" h, **$235**. Photo courtesy of Skinner, Inc.

Clock, 10-1/2" h, brass, Seth Thomas, one-day lever-striking movement, circular case, domed bell mounted below on wooden backboard, late 19th C **520.00**

Compass, lifeboat, 8" sq, 7-1/4" h, boxed, 20th C.............................. **175.00**

Crew list, partly printed, two languages, Jireh Swift, lists 13 additional Hawaiian crew members, Lahaina, March 29, 1865 .... **2,000.00**

Diorama, 23-1/2" x 36", wooden three-masted black and white ship, white sails, American flag, smaller ship at front, three sea gulls overhead, relief-carved ridges beneath ships, dec frame with gilt liner **1,430.00**

Figurehead, 30" h, carved, Nantucket Island origin, c1830................ **12,000.00**

Fishing license, issued to sloop Kial, April 23, 1808, for cod fishing, issued in Newport, RI, some edge chipping, fold splitting, 16-1/2" x 10-1/2"............ **165.00**

Ship's lamp, wrought iron ball-form gimbaled, 18th C, 4-1/2" d, **$460**. Photo courtesy of Pook & Pook.

Hourglass, 7" h, 19th C **550.00**

Inclinometer, 4-1/2" d, brass, cased, bubble type, Kelvin Bottomley & Baird Ltd. **65.00**

Indenture, document indenturing William McGraa to Isaac Fisher as apprentice mariner for four years, details duties, payment schedule, May 19, 1813, signed by all parties, some foxing, edge chipping, 1810 watermark, 16" x 13-1/2" **100.00**

Log book, Ship Geneva, George M. Tucker, Master, sailed from Boston, March 4, 1852 towards Richmond, later to San Francisco, then to Calcutta, back to Boston where she docked at Central Wharf on Aug. 13, 1853, worn spine, cover... **1,150.00**

Masthead, 16" h, 9-1/2" d, copper and brass, oil fired, complete with burner, 360 degrees, late 19th C..................... **200.00**

Sailor's whimsy, America, 19th C, painted, carved pine, ball finial atop graduated sectional frame with five carved spheres, old salmon-colored painted surface, square canted base, minor wear, 18-1/4" h, **$1,530**. Photo courtesy of Skinner, Inc.

Membership certificate, 12-3/8" x 17-1/2", certifying "...That Capt. Green

Walden was by a majority of votes regularly admitted a member of the Portland Marine Society at a meeting held the 17th day of September 1839...," certificate dec with reserves depicting various marine scenes, toning, foxing, framed **530.00**

Model, carved and painted wood

31" l, 19-1/2" h, three-masted square-rigged ship, metal fittings, black and white painted hull with light blue details, wooden stand, some breaks in rigging **600.00**

31-1/2" l, 22-3/8" h, three-masted ship Corsair, carved wood, ivory, and metal implements and fittings, hull painted green and black, red, yellow, and white details, mounted on wooden stand, some breaks **950.00**

Oar, 57-1/2" l, curly maple, well carved, thin broad end, good figure **420.00**

Quadrant, ebony, cased, marked "D Booth" and "New Zealand" **330.00**

Sail maker's bench, 77" l, 16" w, 15" h, long canvas cov bench, turned splayed legs, one end with compartments and pierced for tools, suspending two canvas pouches, two canvas sacks with sail maker's tools, America, 19th C **1,765.00**

Sailor's valentine, 9-5/8" octagonal segmented case, various exotic shells, "For My Love," 19th C, very minor losses **750.00**

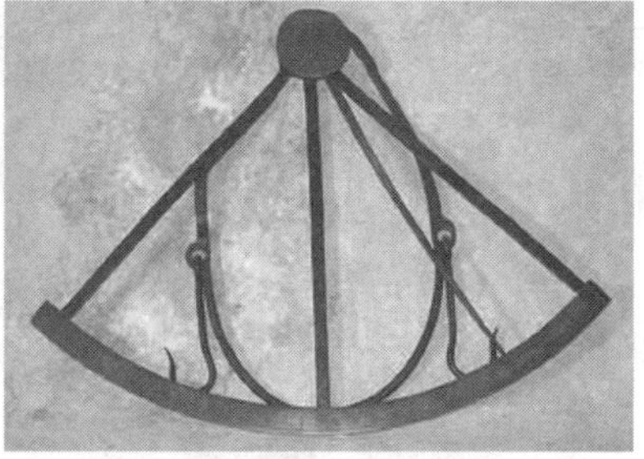

Seaman's scale, wrought iron framework, hooks and needle, brass curved scale with etched numbers, 17-1/2" w, 13" h, **$230**.

Seaman's chest, 44" w, 17-1/2" d, 19" h, old green paint over earlier blue, int. lid with orig painting of sailing ship "Witchcraft built at Chelsea, 1852, William C. Rogers and Co., Boston," flying American flag, canted sides, dovetailed, panel on front with another ship, old rope handles, age splits **1,980.00**

Ship anchor, 54" w, 106" h, cast, iron ring and chain, mounted on later iron brackets, corrosion....................... **825.00**

Ship bell, cast bronze

13" d, 13-1/2" h, weathered surface, raised "J. Warner & Sons, London, 1855" **1,175.00**

14" d, 17" h, raised linear bands **560.00**

Ship billet head, carved wood, 19th C, 27-1/2" l, 5-1/2" w, and 23" l, 7-1/4" w, scrolled foliate design, weathered cracked surface, pr **4,995.00**

Watch hutch, Continental Prisoner of War, carved bone, dated "1807," lion, swags, vases of flowers, birds, hearts, etc. on case with single drawer, 6" w, 4" d, 10-1/2" h, with Irish silver pocket watch marked "Geo. Rycroft Dublin," **$2,530**. Photo courtesy of Pook & Pook.

Ship builder's half model, America, 19th C

30" l, 6" h, alternating laminated mahogany and other wood, mounted on walnut panel **1,995.00**

42" l, 10-5/8" h, natural finished pine, black and gilt trim, loose stem post **9,400.00**

Ship license

Issued for schooner Trafalgar Nelson, issued on the island of Montserrant, dated Nov. 17, 1813, some edge chipping, hinge weakness, minor foxing, 8" x 13" **35.00**

Issued for ship Aurora, 303 tons, armed with 14 guns, two swivel guns, 20 muskets, 20 pistols, 20 cutlasses, 20 pikes, Nov. 4, 1912, minor edge chipping, 12-1/2" x 8" **135.00**

Ship lantern, 17" h, copper and brass, plate sgd "Meteorite," round base, glass lens on one side, vented top, swing handle, burner missing, tin signal shutters remain on inside **110.00**

Ship wheel, 45" d, walnut, old dark varnished finish, eight turned spokes and handles, one spoke with glued restoration **275.00**

Stern board, 7-3/4" h, 66" l, Hesperus, New England, 19th C, rect form, rounded ends, chamfered edges, chiseled carved letters flanked by star, painted white on black ground, imperfections **980.00**

Telescope, brass table top, English, mid-19th C, 35" l, 19" h, **$950**. Photo courtesy of Pook & Pook.

Telescope, 32-3/4" l, silver plated, one draw, Troughton & Simms, London, mid-19th C, orig leather casing, inscription reads "Presented by the British Government, Captain Christopher Crowell, Master of the American Ship 'Highland Light' of Boston, in acknowledgment of his humanity and kindness to the Master and the Crew of the Barque 'Queen of Sheba' when he rescued from their waterlogged vessel, on the 16th, December 1861," damage to leather.. **980.00**

NETSUKES

History: The traditional Japanese kimono has no pockets. Daily necessities, such as money and tobacco supplies, were carried in leather pouches, or inros, which hung from a cord with a netsuke toggle. The word netsuke comes from "ne"—to root—and "tsuke"—to fasten. Netsukes originated in the 14th century and initially were favored by the middle class. By the mid-18th century, all levels of Japanese society used them. Some of the most famous artists, e.g., Shuzan and Yamada Hojitsu, worked in the netsuke form.

Netsukes average from 1 to 2 inches in length and are made from wood, ivory, bone, ceramics, metal, horn, nutshells, etc. The subject matter is broad based, but always portrayed in a lighthearted, humorous manner. A netsuke must have smooth edges and balance in order to hang correctly on the sash.

Reproduction Alert: Recent reproductions are on the market. Look for lack of detailed carvings, lack of patina and gentle wear as signs of newer netsukes

Notes: Value depends on artist, region, material, and skill of craftsmanship. Western collectors favor katabori, pieces which represent an identifiable object.

Boxwood

Ashikaga and Tenaga seated **450.00**

Fisherman holding basket of fish, horn inlay, sgd "Akinide," Japan, 20th C **815.00**

Rice mixer, ivory inlaid eyes, teeth, and rice, carved by Tokoku, 19th C **5,750.00**

Shoki with demon, damage to sword **250.00**

Ivory, carved, man with pipe holding basket, leaning down toward an animal, some etched details, signed on feet, 2" h, **$100**. Photo courtesy of Sanford Alderfer Auction Company.

Horn

Lotus leaf, stag horn, 19th C **100.00**

Shishi form, pressed, 19th C **50.00**

Ivory

Camel, mouse on back, Japanese, 3" h, glued foot **95.00**

Cat and kitten, 1-3/8" h **165.00**

Drummers with mask, 1-3/8" h **165.00**

Eagle on top of tortoise shell, 1-3/4" h **150.00**

Family with horse, 1-3/4" h **200.00**

Figure with cask and hammer, 2" h **200.00**

Fisherman with net, 1-5/8" h **150.00**

Man painting lantern, 1-3/8" h **200.00**

Man painting masks, 1" h **195.00**

Man with basket, 1-1/4" h **175.00**

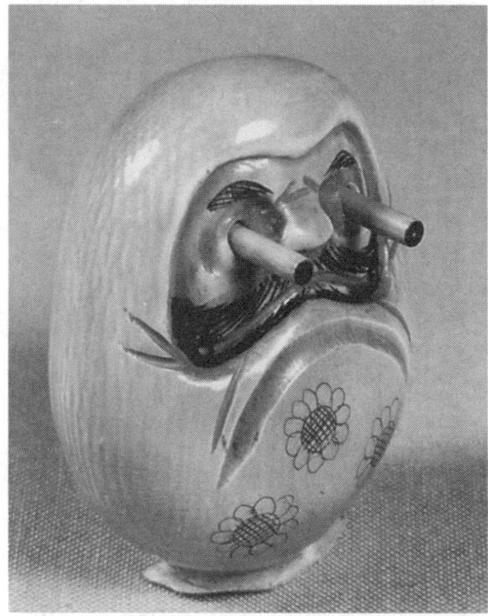

Ivory, carved, creature with popping eyes, **$115**.

Man with box and spoon, 1" h **175.00**

Man with boy, 1-5/8" h **185.00**

Man with hooded robe, 1-3/8" h **135.00**

Man with leaf and turtle, 1-1/2" h **200.00**

Man with rat, 1-1/4" h **150.00**

Mask carver, 1" h **185.00**

Robed figure with hammer, 2-1/4" h **120.00**

Samurai, bowing, stained details, sgd "Meigyokusai" **425.00**

Samuri with child and kite, 1-1/8" h **200.00**

Samurai with kite, brown coloring, 1-1/2" h **200.00**

Carved ivory, ebony, and coral, mounted on carved ivory base of seashells and scrolling waves, 2" x 1-1/4", minor imperfections, **$375**. Photo courtesy of Sanford Alderfer Auction Co.

Scholar with hood and child, 2" h **200.00**

Two figures in wooden bucket, compartment in base, 1-3/4" h **120.00**

Two figures wrestling, 1-1/2" h **175.00**

Woman with basket of fruit, 1-1/4" h **185.00**

Wood worker, 1-1/4" h **150.00**

Ivory and wood, Oni demon in ivory, inside box with horn, coral, and gold inlay, sgd "Meigyokusai" **700.00**

Porcelain

Fruit and leaves, red, brown, and celadon, 19th C **60.00**

Two puppies, 19th C **85.00**

Sandalwood, carved rustic retreat with pavilions, trees, mountains, and figures **635.00**

Wood

Geisha, seated, wearing flowing robe, holding tray, carved by Toshikazu, 19th C **245.00**

Noblewoman, wretched beggar form, dying by roadside, carved by Ichihyo, first half 19th C **300.00**

Persimmon, stippled skin and leaves, unsgd, 19th C **295.00**

Scribe, sitting, holding writing slip and brush, carved by Shinsai, 19th C **275.00**

NEWCOMB POTTERY

History: The Sophie Newcomb Memorial College, an adjunct of Tulane University in New Orleans, LA, was originated as a school to train local women in the decorative arts. While metalworking, painting, and embroidery were among the classes taught, the production of fine, handcrafted art pottery remains its most popular and collectible pursuit. Pottery was made by the Newcomb women for nearly 50 years, with earlier work being the rarest and most valuable. This is characterized by shiny finishes and broad, flat-painted and modeled designs. More common, though still quite valuable, are the matte glaze pieces, often depicting bayou scenes and native flora. All bear the impressed NC mark.

Adviser: David Rago.

Bud vase

6" h, carved by A.R. Urquhart, blue-green leaves on lighter ground, 1905, marked, reglued top **1,485.00**

6-1/4" h, 2-3/4" d, corseted, decorated by A.F. Simpson, white crocuses, 1921, stamped mark, artist's mark **2,300.00**

6-1/2" h, cylindrical, carved by Sadie Irvine, tall pines, full moon, 1931, marked, hairlines and repair to rim **1,485.00**

Charger, painted by Mary Sheerer, medallion of the Newcomb chapel surrounded by trees, border with NEWCOMB COLLEGE N.O., marked "NC/ JM/MS/M," c1900, 10-3/4" d, **$18,400**. Newcomb photos courtesy of David Rago Auctions, Inc.

Lamp base, carved and slip-decorated by Elizabeth Rogers, ivory mums and green leaves on celadon ground, 1895-98, marked "NC/JM/U/EGR," featured in "Newcomb Pottery: An Enterprise for Southern Women, 1895-1940" exhibition, photographed in accompanying catalog, 10-1/2" d, 14-1/4" h, **$1,355**.

Low bowl, 7-1/2" d, 2-1/4" h, carved by Sadie Irvine, rim band of pink trillium, purple ground, 1919, stamped mark "SI" **1,100.00**

Mug, 4-1/2" x 4-1/2", high-glaze, painted by Desiree Roman, band of scarabs, blue-green ground, 1902, NC/D.R./K75+ **2,185.00**

Pitcher, 3-3/4" x 3-3/4", by Sadie Irvine, shoulder excised "You Must Still Be Bright And Quiet," blue-green ground, 1907, NC/SI/JM/Q/CA14............ **2,415.00**

Plate, 9-1/2" d, carved by M. Baker, band of blue fish, indigo and blue ground, 1906, NC/MFB/JM/W/AZ38, tight line to hanging hole............ **5,175.00**

Trivet tile, 6" d, circular, carved by Anna Frances Simpson, paperwhite blossoms on green stems, light blue ground, 1917, NC/JM/AFS455/IN25, rim restoration **1,725.00**

Vase

4-1/4" x 5-1/4", squat, transitional, attributed to Alix Bettison, carved band of blue bell flowers, c1911, NC/ B/JM/?I69 .... **2,990.00**

Vase, bulbous, crisply carved by A.F. Simpson with Spanish moss on live oak trees, full moon in hilly landscape, 1926, marked "NC/AFS/PO81/ JM184," 6-1/2" d, 8-1/4" h, **$11,100**.

Loving cup, Katherine Kopman, 1902, white clover blossoms, green leaves, pale blue and white glossy ground, NC/KK/E18/X, 1" rim chip, 5" d, 4" h, **$7,500**. Photo courtesy of David Rago Auctions.

Vase, transitional, carved by A.F. Simpson, light green crocuses, dark green leaves, indigo ground, 1912, marked "NC/AFS/JM/B/FI30," 3-3/4" d, 8-1/4" h, **$5,350**.

4-3/4" x 4-3/4", bulbous, carved by Henrietta Bailey, white roses on blue ground, 1926, NC/PV35/HB/JM/29 .... **2,100.00**

5" x 5-1/2", bulbous, three-pointed opening, carved by Sadie Irvine, pink and yellow dogwood blossoms on green leaves, 1922, NC/SI/186/ MW95 .... **2,760.00**

5-1/4" x 3-3/4", ovoid, carved by Henrietta Bailey, white blossoms, blue ground, 1930, NC/HB/SR98/35 .... **1,610.00**

6" h, bulbous, carved by Henrietta Bailey, band of white and yellow blossoms, medium blue ground, 1932, marked, 2" hairline to rim **1,355.00**

6" x 3", transitional, "Cypress," carved by A.F. Simpson, tall trees, dripping green Spanish Moss, blue-green ground, c1912, paper label, NC/AFS/19............ **3,775.00**

6" x 6", bulbous, carved by Sadie Irvine, live oak trees, Spanish Moss, full moon, 1930, NC/SI/JH/500/SL47, restoration to two hairlines .. **2,185.00**

6-1/4" x 6", bulbous, carved by Sadie Irvine, Spanish moss on live oak trees under a full moon, 1932, NC/SI/ JH/500/T056 .... **5,750.00**

6-1/2" x 6", bulbous, carved by Sadie Irvine, blue and yellow irises, green leaves, blue ground, 1919, NC/JM/ SI/KG23/292 .... **5,175.00**

7" x 4", transitional, carved by A.F. Simpson, blue and yellow jonquils, green stems, 1915, NC/AFS/JM/ HS87, tight 1" rim hairline.... **2,415.00**

8" x 5", bulbous, carved by A.F. Simpson, pink irises and green leaves, blue ground, 1923, NC/ NO72/AFS/JM/161, paper label **3,775.00**

8-1/4" x 3-3/4", transitional, carved by Sadie Irvine, green Spanish moss on live oak trees and full moon over landscape of green grass and picket fence, 1919, NC/SI/JM/ 250 .... **6,900.00**

8-1/4" x 5", bulbous, painted by M. Ross, green grape leaves and clusters, buff and blue-green ground, c1902, NC/Ross/Q **10,925.00**

8-1/2" x 4", carved by Marie De Hoa LeBlanc, white and yellow trillium on tall green stems, light blue ground, 1906, NC/MHLB/BJ49 .... **10,925.00**

9-1/2" x 7-1/2", painted by Mary Butler, large blue tulips, blue-green leaves, light green ground, 1903, NC/MWB/Y44 .... **28,700.00**

10" x 4-1/2", trumpet shape, carved by Marie De Hoa LeBlanc, yellow freesia blossoms, ivory and celadon ground, 1904, NC/JM/Q/SS57/ MHLeB, opposing hairlines. **5,750.00**

10-1/2" x 4-1/2", ovoid, carved by Sadie Irvine, blue and yellow irises, green stems, blue matte ground, 1925, NC/SI/OM94/150/JM **5,175.00**

Vase, transitional, carved by Sadie Irvine, Spanish moss on live oak trees with full moon, 1908, marked "NC/CF59/SI/JM/236," 4" d, 7" h, **$4,325.**

Vessel, transitional, bulbous, carved by Cynthia Littlejohn, blue and yellow jonquils with green leaves, indigo ground, marked "NC/JM/GI22/49/CL," restoration to opposing hairlines, 8-1/2" d, 6-3/4" h, **$5,750.**

Vessel

- 4" x 4-3/4", squat, two handles, carved by A.F. Simpson, pink crocuses around shoulder, purple-to-blue ground, 1922, NC/AFS/ME87/254/JM, Minor stilt-pull nicks outside foot ring **2,415.00**
- 4-1/4" x 7-1/2", squat, carved by A.F. Simpson, light blue and yellow daisies, 1920, NC/KX98/AFS/JM/257, shallow lines, couple of base flecks **1,100.00**
- 5" x 8-1/2", transitional, squat, carved by Sadie Irvine, light blue and yellow magnolia blossoms, green ground, 1914, NC/GO65/ SI/JM/248, two rim hairlines from rim **1,725.00**

Niloak Pottery, Mission Ware

History: Niloak Pottery was made near Benton, Arkansas. Charles Dean Hyten experimented with native clay, trying to preserve its natural colors. By 1911, he perfected Mission Ware, a marbleized pottery in which the cream and brown colors predominate. The company name is the word "kaolin" spelled backward.

After a devastating fire, the pottery was rebuilt and named Eagle Pottery. This factory included enough space to add a novelty pottery line in 1929. Hyten left the pottery in 1941, and in 1946 operations ceased.

Marks: The early pieces were marked "Niloak." Eagle Pottery products usually were marked "Hywood-Niloak" until 1934, when the "Hywood" was dropped from the mark.

For more information, see *Warman's American Pottery & Porcelain*, 2nd edition.

Note: Prices listed below are for Mission Ware pieces.

Floor urn, Mission Ware, marbleized clay in blue, beige, terra cotta, and gray, stamped "Niloak," factory bubble, 12" d, 23-1/2" h, **$8,050.** Photo courtesy of David Rago Auctions, Inc.

Bowl, 4-1/2" d, marbleized swirls, blue, tan, and brown **68.00**

Candlesticks, pr, 8" h, marbleized swirls, blue, cream, terra cotta, and brown **250.00**

Console set, pr 8-1/2" h candlesticks, 10" d bowl, marbleized swirls, marked **275.00**

Flower pot, ruffled rim, green matte glaze, c1930 .... **155.00**

Toothpick holder, marbleized swirls, tan and blue **100.00**

Urn, 4-1/2" h, marbleized swirls, brown and blue **65.00**

Vase, ovoid, Mission Ware, marbleized clays, stamped "Niloak," spider line to base, 4" d, 8" h, **$115.** Photo courtesy of David Rago Auctions, Inc.

Vase

- 3-1/4" h, early foil label, c1920-30 .... **95.00**
- 6" h, applied twisted handles, Ozark Dawn glaze, c1930 .... **120.00**
- 8-1/2" h, swirled colors, first art mark, c1910-24 .... **230.00**
- 9-1/4" x 4-1/2", corseted, Mission Ware, stamped Niloak **175.00**
- 10-1/2" h, swollen baluster with broad rim, brown, rose, blue, and cream, second art mark **500.00**
- 16" x 7-1/2", Mission Ware, blue-green, terra cotta, brown, and beige marbleized clay, stamped "Niloak" **920.00**

Nippon China, 1891-1921

History: Nippon, Japanese hand-painted porcelain, was made for export between 1891 and 1921. In 1891, when the McKinley Tariff Act proclaimed that all items of foreign manufacture be stamped with their country of origin, Japan chose to use "Nippon." In 1921, the United States decided the word "Nippon" no longer was acceptable and required all Japanese wares to be marked "Japan," ending the Nippon era.

Marks: There are more than 220 recorded Nippon backstamps or marks; the three most popular are the wreath, maple leaf, and rising sun. Wares with variations of all three marks are being reproduced today. A knowledgeable collector can easily spot the reproductions by the mark variances. The majority of the marks are found in three different colors: green, blue, or magenta. Colors indicate the quality of the porcelain used: green for first-grade porcelain, blue for second-grade, and magenta for third-grade. Marks were applied by two methods: decal stickers under glaze and imprinting directly on the porcelain.

Reproduction Alert

Distinguishing old marks from new:

A common old mark consisted of a central wreath open at the top with the letter M in the center. "Hand Painted" flowed around the top of the wreath; "NIPPO Box N" around the bottom. The modern fake mark reverses the wreath (it is open at the bottom) and places an hourglass form, not an "M," in its middle.

An old leaf mark, approximately one-quarter inch wide, has "Hand" with "Painted" below to the left of the stem and "NIPPO Box N" beneath. The newer mark has the identical lettering, but the size is now one-half, rather than one-quarter, inch.

An old mark consisted of "Hand Painted" arched above a solid rising sun logo with "NIPPO Box N" in a straight line beneath. The modern fake mark has the same lettering pattern, but the central logo looks like a mound with a jagged line enclosing a blank space above it.

Cider set, squatty pitcher, six matching mugs, shaded beige top band, white narcissus, green leaves, gold trim, marked "China, -E-ON, Hand Painted, Nippon," **$195**.

Basket, 7-1/4" h, rose dec, pale yellow ground, gilt accents, unmarked, flakes on base **265.00**

Bowl, 10" d, 2-3/4" h, green, pink, and white florals and roses, gold trim **475.00**

Cake plate, 10-1/2" d, lavender coastal scene, green and gilt borders, blue maple leaf mark **195.00**

Cake set, 10-1/4" d cake plate, six 6-1/2" d serving plates, two handles, scenic dec with swans, floral borders with gilt accents, green M in wreath mark **330.00**

Chocolate pot, 7-1/2" h, hp, cottage and lake scene, green wreath mark **260.00**

Chocolate set, 10" h cov pot, four 3" h cups, 5" saucers, gold dec and borders **675.00**

Condensed milk jar, cov, underplate, pink roses, green leaves, gilt accents, unmarked **295.00**

Asparagus set, master serving dish, six individual plates, each decorated with asparagus and radish design, gilt edge on yellow border, self handles, green wreath mark, **$95**.

Ewer, 9" h, moriage, hp roses, gold trim **475.00**
Nut dish, 7-1/4" d, blown-out design, three ftd, green M in wreath mark .. **55.00**
Pitcher, 9-1/4" h, 6-1/4" w, cobalt blue ground, pinks, blues, browns, and greens, gold beaded dec, three small squatty gold feet, slight wear to gold **495.00**

Lemonade mug, pink roses decoration, **$40**. Photo courtesy of Joy Luke Auctions.

Plate
- 7-1/2" d, rose dec, raspberry and gilt border, blue maple leaf mark **220.00**
- 10" d, scalloped edge, rose dec, gilt dec, blue maple leaf mark **250.00**

Punch set, bowl with double handles, claw foot base, six ftd cups, grape dec, green M in wreath mark **990.00**
Stein, 7" h, hp, horses on one side, throne on other, raised fluting....... **995.00**
Tankard, 13" h, hp, gold dec rim and base, applied scrolled handle, blue maple leaf mark, minor gold loss **350.00**
Tea set, hp, powder blue background, swans dec, Paolownia flower mark **325.00**

Platter, round, game birds, heavily gilded border, 11" d, **$150**. Photo courtesy of Joy Luke Auctions.

Tobacco jar, cov
- Bulldog dec........ **1,100.00**
- Horse portrait, 5-3/4" h **495.00**
- Stag dec, green mark, 6" h **2,100.00**

Urn, 13" h, 7" w, hp, scenic **495.00**

Urn, six-sided, hand-painted, scene of trees and lake, marked, some fading of gilt on handles, rim, and base, 14-3/4" h, **$395**. Photo courtesy of David Rago Auctions, Inc.

Vase
- 7" h, hp, moriage dec, four painted floral panels, two handles **430.00**
- 8-1/2" h, hp, lake with swan, green wreath mark........ **400.00**
- 9" h, 8" w, hp roses, gold scrolling, green maple leaf mark **1,650.00**
- 10" h, 6-1/4" d, blown-out, hp scenic dec of three eagles sitting on rocks, green mark........ **3,220.00**
- 11-1/2" h, hp, yellow and gold roses, three gold handles with rings **320.00**
- 12" h, hp, gold ferns, jeweled designs, magenta maple leaf mark **400.00**
- 13" h, two handles, gold dec, lake scene with mountains and trees **415.00**

Whiskey jug, 7-1/4" h, hp, hunt scene, blue maple leaf mark........ **1,150.00**

Noritake China

History: Morimura Brothers founded Noritake China in 1904 in Nagoya, Japan. The company made high-quality chinaware for export to the United States and also produced a line of china blanks for hand painting. In 1910, the company perfected a technique for the production of high-quality dinnerware and introduced streamlined production.

During the 1920s, the Larkin Company of Buffalo, New York, was a prime distributor of Noritake China. Larkin offered Azalea, Briarcliff, Linden, Modjeska, Savory, Sheridan, and Tree in the Meadow patterns as part of its premium line.

The factory was heavily damaged during World War II, and production was reduced. Between 1946 and 1948, the company sold its china under the "Rose China" mark, since the quality of production did not match the earlier Noritake China. Expansion in 1948 brought about the resumption of quality production and the use of the Noritake name once again.

Marks: There are close to 100 different marks for Noritake, the careful study of which can determine the date of production. Most pieces are marked "Noritake" with a wreath, "M," "N," or "Nippon." The use of the letter N was registered in 1953.

Basket, 5-3/8" w, 4-5/8" h, hp blue floral design, luster int., gold handle, brown mark........ **225.00**
Bowl, 7-1/8" w, 3-5/8" h, Azalea, shell shape........ **430.00**
Cake set, 11" d cake plate, six 6-1/4" serving plates, desert scene with tent and man on camel, cobalt blue and gilt border, marked "Noritake/Made in Japan/ Hand Painted" **770.00**
Candlesticks, pr, 8-1/4" h, gold flowers and bird, blue luster ground, wreath with "M" mark........ **125.00**
Child's tea set, Bluebird pattern, 3-1/2" h teapot, 1-7/8" h creamer, 2-3/4" h sugar, six 4-1/4" d plates, six 1-1/4" h cups, six 3-3/4" d saucers **300.00**
Creamer and sugar, Art Deco, pink Japanese lanterns, cobalt blue ground, basket type handle on sugar, wreath with "M" mark........ **50.00**
Cruet set, 6-1/2" w, 3-1/2" h, cottage scene, oil and vinegar, two spouts, gold handle........ **250.00**
Cup and saucer, Florola........ **24.00**
Demitasse set, 6-1/2" h demitasse pot, 2-7/8" h creamer, 3-1/2" h sugar, hp, pink ground........ **275.00**
Dinner set
- Beverly pattern, service for six **550.00**
- Colby pattern, service for eight, serving pcs........ **400.00**
- Princeton, service for six, serving pcs, c1960 .... **430.00**

Figure
- 6-1/2" h, mother crane feeding her young, marked "Nippon Toki Kaiska Noritake"........ **275.00**
- 13-1/2" h, rooster sitting on limb, long flowing feathers **275.00**

Gravy boat, Tree in the Meadow **50.00**
Inkwell, owl, figural **125.00**
Marmalade, underplate, 5-1/2" h, poppy dec, double handled jar........ **185.00**

Serving bowl, gold background, red, blue, and yellow floral decoration, green stems, two self handles, green wreath mark, $45.

Match holder, 4" d, 3" h, attached ashtray, Art Deco design, Oriental lady in suit of hearts, blond Flapper in suit of clubs, card motifs on rim of ashtray **325.00**
Napkin ring, Art Deco man and woman, wreath with "M" mark, pr **60.00**
Place card holder, figural, bluebird with butterfly, gold luster, white stripes, wreath with "M" mark, pr **35.00**
Plate, two 8-1/2" d, seven 6-1/4" d, cranberry and pale blue rose motif dec, gilt borders, blue "RC Noritake Nippon Hand Painted" mark **175.00**
Punch bowl set, 12" h two-part punch bowl with three-ftd base, six 2-3/4" h cups, Cottage landscape at dusk, swans in pond dec, cobalt blue and gilt borders, opalescent melon int. **880.00**
Salt, 3" l, swan, white, orange luster, pr **25.00**
Salt and pepper shakers, pr, Tree in the Meadow, marked "Made in Japan" **35.00**
Soup bowl, Florola **15.00**
Tea tile, Tree in the Meadow, 5" w, green mark **35.00**
Vase, 10" h, cottage and lake scene, gold accents **265.00**
Vegetable bowl, cov, Magnificience, #9736 .... **350.00**
Waffle set, handled serving plate, sugar shaker, Art Deco flowers, wreath with "M" mark **50.00**
Wall pocket, butterfly, wreath with "M" mark **75.00**

North Dakota School Of Mines

History: The North Dakota School of Mines was established in 1890. Earle J. Babcock, a chemistry instructor, was impressed with the high purity level of North Dakota potter's clay. In 1898, Babcock received funds to develop his finds. He tried to interest commercial potteries in the North Dakota clay, but had limited success.

In 1910, Babcock persuaded the school to establish a Ceramics Department. Margaret Cable, who studied under Charles Binns and Frederick H. Rhead, was appointed head. She remained until her retirement in 1949.

Decorative emphasis was placed on native themes, e.g., flowers and animals. Art Nouveau, Art Deco, and fairly plain pieces were made.

Marks: The pottery is marked with a cobalt blue underglaze circle of the words "University of North Dakota/Grand Forks, N.D./Made at School of Mines/N.D. Clay." Some early pieces are marked only "U.N.D." or "U.N.D./Grand Forks, N.D." Most pieces are numbered (they can be dated from University records) and signed by both the instructor and student. Cable-signed pieces are the most desirable.

Bowl

7-1/4" d, flaring, painted circular blue flowers and leaves, circular stamp, glaze flake **350.00**
9" d, flaring, polychrome enamel fruits dec by Tobiason, beige ground, circular stamp and signature, burst glaze bubbles to dec **230.00**

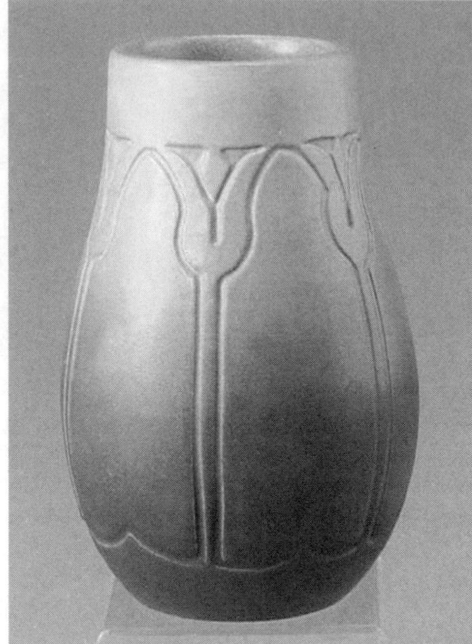
Vase, bulbous, by Margaret Cable, incised tulips, matte gold to brown glaze, signed "M Cable," circular ink stamp, $815. Photo courtesy of David Rago Auctions, Inc.

9-1/2" d, flaring, squeezebag dec by Swenson, pink, red, and purple blossoms, celadon ground. 1951, circular stamp, artist sgd, dated, surface abrasion, glaze flakes **175.00**

Box, cov, 4-1/4", Scottie dog finial lid, carved by Trickey, teepees under light turquoise glaze, 1946, circular stamp, artist's mark **460.00**
Cabinet vase, 2-1/4" h, carved sgraffito, beige clay sheaves of wheat, blue glazed ground, marked **460.00**
Creamer and sugar, 2" x 4", painted by Ruth Schnell, yellow and blue blossoms, lavender ground, 1955, circular stamp, artist's mark **350.00**
Figure, 4-3/4" h, rabbit, by Margaret Cable, green and brown flowers, brown ground, marked MC/105 .... **630.00**
Jardiniére, 6-1/2" x 8", spherical, painted by Eleaner Allen, birds and butterflies, 1955, stamped and sgd **265.00**
Low dish, 6-1/2" d, excised stylized blue blossoms, AC monogram on white ground, circular stamp/AC **690.00**
Mask, 5" w, 7-1/2" h, by Julia Mattson, "Mr. Freckles," painted polychrome, buff clay, incised "J. Mattson, Mr. Freckles, UND," ink stamp **1,100.00**
Planter, 5" x 6", excised by R. Schnell, brown blossoms, full-height leaves, textured darker brown ground, 1945, circular stamp, incised "Ruth R. Schnell For Richard from mother, 2-20-45" **810.00**

Plate

8-1/4" d, painted by Schnell, polychrome flowers, white ground, 1955, marked **360.00**

9-1/2" d, by Margaret Cable, 1949, cuerda seca dec with polychrome floral design, stamped mark/ M.Cable/1949 .... **435.00**

Trivet tile, 6" d, circular, carved indigo and yellow pasque flowers, lavender ground, circular ink stamp **460.00**

Vase, conical, by Flora Huckfield and student, glossy celadon and brown glaze, circular ink stamp, incised "Huck and Le Masurier 2371," 3" x 5", **$235**. Photo courtesy of David Rago Auctions, Inc.

Vase

3-3/4" h, flaring, by F. Huckfield, blue "Pasque Flower," shaded ground, circular stamp, artist's mark ... **520.00**

4-1/2" x 5", bulbous, carved by F. Huckfield, pink blossoms and green leaves, green to pink ground, circular ink stamp "BUSTIN-HUCK" **630.00**

5" h, tapering, by F. Huckfield, blue and orange blossoms, pale pink ground, circular stamp, artist's mark **630.00**

5-3/4" h, cylindrical, painted by M. Cable, decorative polychrome pattern, 1949, circular stamp, artist's mark **690.00**

6" h, flaring, terra cotta speckled semi-matte glaze, ink stamp "WPA Ceramics N DAK" **535.00**

7-3/4" x 5-1/2", baluster, excised butter yellow stylized motif around neck, matte blue-gray ground, stamped WPA CERAMICS/N.DAK **860.00**

9" x 5", carved by F. Cunningham, brown daffodils, darker brown ground, 1950, circular stamp mark, artist sgd **1,380.00**

Vessel

2-3/4" x 5", squat, by P. McLaine, indigo arabesques, red ground, 1949, circular stamp and incised mark **690.00**

3", Bentonite clay, painted by Phyl Darwin, birds and leaves, terra cotta ground, marked...................... **460.00**

3-1/2", bulbous, rose to blue matte glaze, stamped mark **360.00**

Vessel, spherical, closed-in rim, by R. Skyberg, embossed band of stylized charcoal geometric forms, green matte ground, circular ink stamp, incised artist signature, 6-1/4" x 6-3/4", **$860**. Photo courtesy of David Rago Auctions, Inc.

4-1/4" x 5", bentonite clay, bulbous, painted by Armstrong, black and yellow abstracted birds, terra cotta ground, 1948, circular stamp, artist's mark **1,100.00**

4-1/2" x 4-1/2", bulbous, carved by F. Huckfield, white geometric band, black shoulder over red to blue ground, circular stamp, artist's mark, minor rim touch-up **1,100.00**

5" d, squat, carved by M. Cable, band of blue flowers and green leaves, light blue ground, circular stamp, artist mark **980.00**

WALLACE NUTTING

History: Wallace Nutting (1861-1941) was America's most famous photographer of the early 20th century. A retired minister, Nutting took more than 50,000 pictures, keeping 10,000 of his best and destroying the rest. His popular and best-selling scenes included "Exterior Scenes," apple blossoms, country lanes, orchards, calm streams, and rural American countrysides; "Interior Scenes," usually featuring a colonial woman working near a hearth; and "Foreign Scenes," typically thatch-roofed cottages. Those pictures that were least popular in his day have become the rarest and most-highly collectible today and are classified as "Miscellaneous Unusual Scenes." This category encompasses such things as animals, architecturals, children, florals, men, seascapes, and snow scenes.

Nutting sold literally millions of his hand-colored platinotype pictures between 1900 and his death in 1941. Starting first in Southbury, Connecticut, and later moving his business to Framingham, Massachusetts, the peak of Wallace Nutting's picture production was 1915 to 1925. During this period, Nutting employed nearly 200 people, including colorists, darkroom staff, salesmen, and assorted office personnel. Wallace Nutting pictures proved to be a huge commercial success and hardly an American household was without one by 1925.

While attempting to seek out the finest and best early American furniture as props for his colonial Interior Scenes, Nutting became an expert in American antiques. He published nearly 20 books in his lifetime, including his 10-volume State Beautiful series and various other books on furniture, photography, clocks, and his autobiography. He also contributed many photographs published in magazines and books other than his own.

Nutting also became widely known for his reproduction furniture. His furniture shop produced literally hundreds of different furniture forms: clocks, stools, chairs, settles, settees, tables, stands, desks, mirrors, beds, chests of drawers, cabinet pieces, and treenware.

The overall synergy of the Wallace Nutting name, pictures, books, and furniture, has made anything "Wallace Nutting" quite collectible.

Marks: Wallace Nutting furniture is clearly marked with his distinctive paper label, glued directly onto the piece, or with a block or script signature brand, which was literally branded into his furniture.

Note: "Process Prints" are 1930s' machine-produced reprints of 12 of Nutting's most popular pictures. These have minimal value and can be detected by using a magnifying glass.

Adviser: Michael Ivankovich.

As It Was in 1700, Massachusetts scene, long country road winding around long stone wall towards stately distant country house, 10" x 12", **$295**. All Wallace Nutting photographs courtesy of Michael Ivankovich Auctions.

Books

American Windsors **85.00**

England Beautiful, 1st ed. **125.00**

Furniture of the Pilgrim Century, 1st ed **140.00**

Furniture Treasury, Vol. I **125.00**

Furniture Treasury, Vol. II **140.00**

Furniture Treasury, Vol. III **115.00**

Ireland Beautiful, 1st ed. **45.00**

Social Life In Old New England...... **75.00**

At Dixville, NH scene with hilltop view across Echo Lake of NH's Dixville Notch, 12" x 15", **$235**.

State Beautiful Series

- Connecticut Beautiful, 1st ed. .. **75.00**
- Maine Beautiful, 1st ed. **45.00**
- Massachusetts Beautiful, 2nd ed **45.00**
- New Hampshire Beautiful, 1st ed **75.00**
- New York Beautiful, 1st ed. **85.00**
- Pennsylvania Beautiful, 1st ed **48.00**
- Vermont Beautiful, 2nd ed. **40.00**
- Virginia Beautiful, 1st ed. **60.00**

Catalog, Wallace Nutting's Original Studio **1,100.00**

Joy Patch, garden scene with narrow path leading through colorful flower garden towards partially-hidden distant house, original copyright label preserved on back, England, 9" x 11", **$175**.

Furniture

Candle stand, #17, Windsor **495.00**

Chair

- #390, Ladderback, arm, script brand **300.00**
- #440, Windsor, writing arm, Pennsylvania turnings, drawer beneath seat, block brand **2,145.00**

Cupboard, #923, pine, scrolled **4,290.00**

High chair, liftable food tray, New England turnings, orig light maple finish, block branded signature **2,310.00**

Stool, #102, Windsor, script brand **220.00**

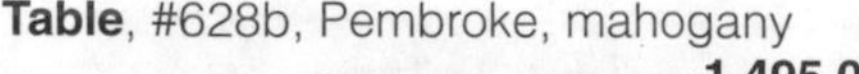

Table, #628b, Pembroke, mahogany **1,495.00**

Larkspur, path winds past girl in flower garden towards quaint thatch-roofed cottage, England, 14" x 17", **$195**.

Pictures

- A Birch Grove, 9" x 11" **175.00**
- A Colonial Kitchen, 14" x 17" **350.00**
- An Annapolis Garden **1,375.00**
- An Old Time Romance, 11" x 14" **295.00**
- As It Was in 1700, 10" x 12" **295.00**
- A Patriarch in Bloom, 10" x 12" **175.00**
- Better than Mowing, 16" x 20" **490.00**
- Blossom Point, 11" x 17" **200.00**
- By the Sea, Capri **605.00**

June Beautiful, country road runs past pink blossoms and apple orchard, Carroll NH, 10" x 12", **$185**.

- Drying Apples, 13" x 16" **695.00**
- Dykeside Blossoms, 10" x 13" **275.00**
- From Pocono Heights **1,815.00**
- Garden Steps **580.00**
- Gloucester Cloister, 16" x 20" **1,100.00**
- Golden Harvest **2,255.00**
- Gorgeous May, 10" x 12" **185.00**
- Honeymoon Cottage, 10" x 12" **175.00**
- In Tenderleaf, 11" x 14" **195.00**
- Jersey Blossoms, 13" x 16" **195.00**
- Joy Path, 9" x 11" **175.00**
- June Beautiful, 10" x 12" **185.00**
- Larkspur, 14" x 17" **195.00**
- Orchard Heights, 11" x 14" **185.00**
- Priscilla's Cottage, 14" x 17" **360.00**
- Russet and Gold, 16" x 20" **315.00**
- Shadowy Orchard Curves, 11" x 14" **85.00**

The Coming Out of Rosa, little Rosa holds Mother's hand while standing on rose-bordered porch, MA, 13" x 15", **$275**.

- The Coming Out of Rosa, 20" x 24" **395.00**

The Quilting Party, quilting scene with three girls working on large quilt in Wentworth-Gardiner House bedroom, Portsmouth NH, 13" x 16", **$375**.

- The Donjon Chenaceau, French Castle **660.00**
- The Home Room, 13" x 16" **325.00**
- The Old Homestead **880.00**
- To Meet the Rector **990.00**
- Tranquility Farm **880.00**
- Watching for Papa, 13" x 16" **420.00**

Untitled exterior, country road winds past pink blossoms, stone wall, and wood rail fence, 8" x 10", **$110**.

Silhouettes

George and Martha Washington, 3" x 4" **90.00**

Girl sniffs flower, 4" x 5" **40.00**
Girl with parasol, 4" x 5" **40.00**
Girl with sewing basket, 4" x 5" **40.00**
Scenes **40.00**

Wallace Nutting-Like Photographers

History: Although Wallace Nutting was widely recognized as the country's leading producer of hand-colored photographs during the early 20th century, he was by no means the only photographer selling this style of picture. Throughout the country, literally hundreds of regional photographers were selling hand-colored photographs from their home regions or travels. The subject matter of these photographers was comparable to Nutting's, including Interior, Exterior, Foreign, and Miscellaneous Unusual scenes.

Several photographers operated large businesses, and, although not as large or well known as Wallace Nutting, they sold a substantial volume of pictures, which can still be readily found today. The vast majority of their work was photographed in their home regions and sold primarily to local residents or visiting tourists. It should come as little surprise that three of the major Wallace Nutting-like photographers—David Davidson, Fred Thompson, and the Sawyer Art Co.—each had ties to Wallace Nutting.

Hundreds of other smaller local and regional photographers attempted to market hand-colored pictures comparable to Wallace Nutting's during the period of 1900 to the 1930s. Although quite attractive, most were not as appealing to the general public as Wallace Nutting pictures. However, as the price of Wallace Nutting pictures has escalated, the work of these lesser-known Wallace Nutting-like photographers has become increasingly collectible.

A partial listing of some of these minor Wallace Nutting-like photographers includes: Babcock; J. C. Bicknell; Blair; Ralph Blood (Portland, Maine); Bragg; Brehmer; Brooks; Burrowes; Busch; Carlock; Pedro Cacciola; Croft; Currier; Depue Brothers; Derek; Dowly; Eddy; May Farini (hand-colored colonial lithographs); George Forest; Gandara; Gardner (Nantucket, Bermuda, Florida); Gibson; Gideon; Gunn; Bessie Pease Gutmann (hand-colored colonial lithographs); Edward Guy; Harris; C. Hazen; Knoffe; Haynes (Yellowstone Park); Margaret Hennesey; Hodges; Homer; Krabel; Kattleman; La Bushe; Lake; Lamson (Portland, Maine); M. Lightstrum; Machering; Rossiler Mackinae; Merrill; Meyers; William Moehring; Moran; Murrey; Lyman Nelson; J. Robinson Neville (New England); Patterson; Owen Perry; Phelps; Phinney; Reynolds; F. Robbins; Royce; Frederick Scheetz (Philadelphia, Pennsylvania); Shelton, Standley (Colorado); Stott; Summers; Esther Svenson; Florence Thompson; Thomas Thompson; M. A. Trott; Sanford Tull; Underhill; Villar; Ward; Wilmot; Edith Wilson; and Wright.

Adviser: Michael Ivankovich.

Notes: The key determinants of value include the collectibility of the particular photographer, subject matter, condition, and size. Exterior Scenes are the most common. Keep in mind that only the rarest pictures, in the best condition, will bring top prices. Discoloration and/or damage to the picture or matting can reduce value significantly.

David Davidson, Snow Basin, Western Canada scene with tall snow-draped Rocky Mountains standing beside large blue lake, 5" x 7", **$135**. All Wallace Nutting Look-A-Likes photographs courtesy of Michael Ivankovich Auctions.

David Davidson

Second to Nutting in overall production, Davidson worked primarily in the Rhode Island and southern Massachusetts areas. While a student at Brown University around 1900, Davidson learned the art of hand-colored photography from Wallace Nutting, who happened to be the minister at Davidson's church. After Nutting moved to Southbury in 1905, Davidson graduated from Brown and started a successful photography business in Providence, Rhode Island, which he operated until his death in 1967.

A Puritan Lady **80.00**
Berkshire Sunset **80.00**
Christmas Day **160.00**
Driving Home the Cows **135.00**
Her House in Order **75.00**
Neighbors **170.00**
Old Ironsides **170.00**
Rosemary Club **40.00**
Snow Basin **135.00**
The Lamb's May Feast **130.00**
Vanity **70.00**

Meta Grimball, Gutmann & Gutmann artist

A Call to Arms **415.00**
Now Don't Tell **410.00**
Pies that Mother Used To Make **1,980.00**
The Grand Finale **465.00**

Bessie Pease Gutmann, Love's Blossoms, sleeping little boy with blue ribboned blanket, 11" x 14", **$110**.

Bessie Pease Gutmann

Daddy's Coming **440.00**
Chums **360.00**
Little Mother **360.00**
Lorelei **1,760.00**
Please Go 'Way **400.00**
Preparing for the Seashore **360.00**
The Great Love **1,155.00**

Sawyer

A father and son team, Charles H. Sawyer and Harold B. Sawyer, operated the very successful Sawyer Art Company from 1903 until the 1970s. Beginning in Maine, the Sawyer Art Company moved to Concord, New Hampshire, in 1920 to be closer to its primary market—New Hampshire's White Mountains. Charles H. Sawyer briefly worked for Nutting from 1902 to 1903 while living in southern Maine. Sawyer's production volume ranks third behind Wallace Nutting and David Davidson.

A February Morning **210.00**
Cypress Point, Monterey **265.00**
Echo Lake, Franconia Notch **50.00**
Lake Willoughby **50.00**
Mt. Washington in October **55.00**
San Juan, Capistrano **195.00**

The Meadow Stream **80.00**

Sawyer, Cypress Point, Monterey, California Seascape with tall tree standing upon rocky shoreline overlooking Pacific Ocean and rocky point, lone cypress tree, original Sawyer title-specific "Monterey, California" label on back, 11" x 14", **$265**.

Fred Thompson, Portland Head, Portland, Maine, scene of white waves crashing against large shoreline rocks near tall white Portland Head Light House, 11" x 17", **$165**.

Fred Thompson

Frederick H. Thompson and Frederick M. Thompson, another father and son team, operated the Thompson Art Company (TACO) from 1908 to 1923, working primarily in the Portland, Maine, area. We know that Thompson and Nutting had collaborated because Thompson widely marketed an interior scene he had taken in Nutting's Southbury home. The production volume of the Thompson Art Company ranks fourth behind Nutting, Davidson, and Sawyer.

Apple Tree Road............................. **45.00**
Brook in Winter **190.00**
Calm of Fall.................................... **50.00**
Fireside Fancy Work..................... **140.00**
High and Dry **45.00**
Knitting for the Boys **160.00**
Lombardy Poplar........................... **100.00**
Nature's Carpet **50.00**
Portland Head **165.00**
Six Master..................................... **100.00**
The Gossips **80.00**

Minor Wallace Nutting-Like Photographers

Generally speaking, prices for works by minor Wallace Nutting-like photographers would break down as follows: smaller pictures (5" x 7" to 10" x 12"), $10-$75; medium pictures (11" x 14" to 14" x 17"), $50-$200; larger pictures (larger than 14" x 17"), $75-$200+.

Baker, Florian A., Rushing Waters **50.00**
Farini, In Her Boudoir **30.00**
Gardiner, H. Marshall, The Rainbow Fleet, Nantucket **635.00**
Haynes, Untitled Waterfalls **20.00**
Higgins, Charles A., A Colonial Stairway **65.00**
Payne, George S., Weekly Letter ... **25.00**

Ohr Pottery

G.E.OHR,
BILOXI.

History: Ohr pottery was produced by George E. Ohr in Biloxi, Mississippi. There is a discrepancy as to when he actually established his pottery; some say 1878, but Ohr's autobiography indicates 1883. In 1884, Ohr exhibited 600 pieces of his work, suggesting that he had been a potter for some time.

Ohr's techniques included twisting, crushing, folding, denting, and crinkling thin-walled clay into odd, grotesque, and, sometimes, graceful forms. His later pieces were often left unglazed.

For more information, see *Warman's American Pottery & Porcelain*, 2nd edition.

In 1906, Ohr closed the pottery and stored more than 6,000 pieces as a legacy to his family. He had hoped the U.S. government would purchase it, but that never happened. The entire collection remained in storage until it was rediscovered in 1972.

Today Ohr is recognized as one of the leaders in the American art-pottery movement. Some greedy individuals have taken the later unglazed pieces and covered them with poor-quality glazes in hopes of making them more valuable. These pieces do not have stilt marks on the bottom.

Marks: Much of Ohr's early work was signed with an impressed stamp including his name and location in block letters. His later work was often marked with the flowing script designation "G. E. Ohr."

Coffeepot, snake spout, mirrored green mottled glaze, stamped "G.E. OHR, Biloxi, Miss." 6-1/4" d, 6" h, **$11,000**. Ohr photo courtesy of David Rago Auctions, Inc.

Bank, 2" d, 4" h, acorn shape, lustered brown and mirror black glaze, int. rattle, stamped "G.E.OHR/Biloxi, Miss" **1,100.00**

Bottle, 4-1/4" x 3-3/4", squat base, tapered neck, covered in exceptional green, gunmetal, and pink mottled glaze, script signature **4,600.00**

Candleholder, 6-1/2" h, 4" d, organic, pinched ribbon handle, in-body twist, ribbed base, yellow, green, and raspberry matte mottled glaze, small chip to base, script mark **3,300.00**

Corner shelf, 5-1/2" x 5-3/4", honeycomb texture under gunmetal-speckled olive green glaze, back incised with sheaves of wheat, marked "GE OHR Biloxi, Miss/ JP," small nick to back edge **865.00**

Milk pitcher, 3" x 4-1/2", cinched waist, brown and light green mottled semi-matte glaze, stamped G.E. OHR/Biloxi, Miss, firing line through base............. **1,840.00**

Mug, 4-1/2" d, 4-1/2" h, ear-shape handle, fine mottled deep rose, green, and blue glaze, 1896, stamped "G.E. OHR, Biloxi, Miss. 3-18-96" **4,315.00**

Pitcher, ribbon handle, incised bird of paradise and framed landscape, mottled brown and amber glaze, handle incised HP, bottom stamped G.E. OHR, BIOLOXI, 7" d, 7-1/2" h, **$6,275**. Photos courtesy of David Rago Auctions.

Pitcher

2-3/4" x 4", pinched and cut-out handle, dimpled spout, olive green glaze with red and indigo flashes, marked "GO.E.OHR, BILOXI, MISS" **3,450.00**

2-3/4" x 4-1/2", pinched and cut-out handle, dimpled spout, black-speckled blue-gray mirrored glaze, marked "GO.E.OHR, BILOXI, MISS," minor spout flecks **5,350.00**

5" x 6-1/2", bisque, marbleized clay, pinched handle, folded rim, script sgd **4,025.00**

Teapot

3-1/2" x 8-1/2", crinkled handle, deep in-body twist, snake spout, covered in amber glaze with gunmetal brown and green sponged pattern, stamped "GEO.E.OHR BILOXI MISS," several rim chips, missing lid **9,800.00**

5-1/4" x 9-1/2", ear-shape handle, snake-shape spout, brown, green, and gunmetal marbled glaze, stamped "G.E. OHR, Biloxi, Miss" **6,275.00**

Puzzle jug, stepped handle, brown semi-gloss glaze, stamped twice "G.E. OHR, BILOXI," 5" d, 6-1/2" h, **$9,200**.

Vase, bulbous, lobed rim, carved band, fine pink, green and cobalt blue mottled glaze, stamped "G.E. OHR, Biloxi, Miss," firing line to shoulder, 4-1/2" d, 5" h, **$9,750**.

Vase

2-3/4" x 4", flaring, closed-in rim, gunmetal brown-speckled light green glaze, stamped G.E.OHR BILOXI, minor glaze flakes to rim **2,070.00**

3" x 4-1/4", squat, gunmetal-speckled matte blue-gray and green glaze, script sgd, rim glaze flake... **1,610.00**

3" x 4-1/2", corseted shoulder, purple, green, and black-speckled matte pink glaze, script sgd, small nicks to shoulder and base **4,900.00**

3-1/4" x 3", bulbous base, folded and pinched rim, covered in mirrored olive green glaze, marked "G.E.OHR, Biloxi, Miss," minor fleck to tip of fold **3,775.00**

3-3/4" x 3", bulbous, deep in-body twist at neck, covered in exceptional red, turquoise, and amber sponged and dripped glaze, stamped "GEO.E.OHR BILOXI, MISS," minute fleck to rim **11,150.00**

3-3/4" x 4", bulbous, folded rim, bisque, red and brown clay, script sgd, short rim firing line **1,380.00**

3-3/4" x 4", bulbous top and base, white clay, chartreuse, green, and gunmetal brown flambé glaze, script sgd **1,840.00**

3-3/4" x 4-1/2", bulbous, folded rim, indigo over green-speckled rose glaze, stamped "G.E.OHR Biloxi, Miss" **7,475.00**

4" x 3-1/2", bulbous, dimpled base, in-body twist, covered in mottled green over green-speckled pink glaze, script signature **13,550.00**

4-1/4" x 3", bulbous, dimpled base, ruffled body, flaring rim, vertical sections of gunmetal, green, and amber mottled glazes, marked "G.E.OHR BILOXI" **4,900.00**

4-1/2" x 2-1/4", corseted, indigo, green, and rose sponged glaze, stamped G.E.OHR Biloxi, Miss, minute rim fleck **3,220.00**

4-3/4" x 3-3/4", bulbous, cupped rim, indigo, green, red, and amber mottled glaze, stamped "G.E.OHR Biloxi, Miss" **8,050.00**

5" x 4-1/2", ovoid, deep in-body twist and torn rim, green and gunmetal-speckled amber glaze, stamped "G.E. OHR/Biloxi, Miss"..... **16,100.00**

6" x 2-1/2", pinched rim, seven-point flower and bulbous base, covered in light green to dark red flambé glaze, stamped "G.E.OHR, Biloxi, Miss," minor rim flecks **4,900.00**

Vessel, squat, speckled brown and green glaze, stamped GEO E. OHR/BILOXI, MISS, repair to rim chip, 5-1/2" d, 3-1/2" h, **$1,100**.

Vessel

2-1/2" x 4-3/4", squat, folded rim, covered in mahogany and gunmetal speckled green glaze, marked "G.E.OHR, Biloxi, Miss" **3,400.00**

3" x 6-1/2", bisque, beige clay, one pinched side, script sgd, nicks and rim chips **2,300.00**

3-1/4" x 4", squat, star-shape folded rim, deep in-body twist, gunmetal glaze, marked "G. E. Ohr" in script, restoration to three tips **2,530.00**

3-1/2" x 3-3/4", red bisque clay, rounded neck, protruding shoulder, stamped G.E. OHR/Biloxi, Miss., rim flecks, base grinding chips **1,355.00**

4" x 3", four-lobed squat, ridged base, speckled dark green glaze, marked "G.E. OHR, Biloxi, Miss" **5,175.00**

4-1/4" x 6-1/2", bisque, marbleized clay, one pinched side, script sgd, restored chips and hairlines **3,335.00**

Water jug, 11" h, unglazed, die-stamped mark, few spout and base chips **2,185.00**

Old Paris China

History: Old Paris china is fine-quality porcelain made by various French factories located in and around Paris during the 18th and 19th centuries. Some pieces were marked, but most were not. In addition to its fine quality, this type of ware is characterized by beautiful decorations and gilding. Favored colors are dark maroon, deep cobalt blue, and a dark green.

Pitcher, paneled body, multicolored floral decoration with tulips, roses, etc., white ground, ornate gold trim, wear to gold, **$195**. Photo courtesy of Wiederseim Associates, Inc.

Cake stand, Honore style, green border, c1845 .... **220.00**

Charger, 13-1/2" d, hp portrait of young girl with feathered hat and ringlet curls, artist sgd "P. Amaury" **150.00**

Cup and saucer, 5-3/4" d saucer, ftd, floral dec **55.00**

Figure, 18-3/4" h, Napoleon, standing, one arm tucked behind back, other tucked into shirt, full military dress, gilt dec, low sq base, inscribed "Roussel-Bardell," late 19th C **700.00**

Luncheon set, light blue ground banding, gilt and iron-red cartouche and monogram, 28 9-1/4" d plates, 18 8-1/4" d plates, 11 6-5/8" d plates, 12 sauce dishes, 11 soup plates, oval 12-1/2" l serving bowl, oval 17-1/2" l platter, two circular cov vegetable tureens, cov sauce tureen, cov oval 12-1/4" tureen with underplate, cov jam jar with attached dish, chips, gilt wear **1,610.00**

Mantel vase, bell-like flowered handles, blue ground, paneled enamel portraits of lowers, gilt trim, minor flower damage, pr **350.00**

Vases, multicolored floral decoration, white ground, ornate gold trim, handles, pair, **$250**. Photo courtesy of Wiederseim Associates, Inc.

Plate, 9-1/2" d, dec by Boyer Feuillet Studio, cobalt blue and gold cobblestone border, hp flower arrangement in center, some wear to gilt, price for pr **250.00**

Tea set, 7" h teapot, creamer, cov sugar, paneled sides, gilt trim, handles, fruit finials, and spout, hp flowers, undersides marked with hp black roses, stamped retailer's mark "A. Schmidt & Son, Washington, DC (and New York)," minor wear to gilt **350.00**

Urn, 15-1/2" h, facing portraits of Napoleon and Josephine, gilt handles, 19th C **900.00**

Vase, 7" w, 9" h, two nude women on sides, one draped with blue fabric, other with pink fabric, hp rose and peach flowers, wear to gilt trim **2,195.00**

Old Sleepy Eye

History: Sleepy Eye, a Sioux Indian chief who reportedly had a droopy eye, gave his name to Sleepy Eye, Minnesota, and one of its leading flour mills. In the early 1900s, Old Sleepy Eye Flour offered four Flemish-gray heavy stoneware premiums decorated in cobalt blue: a straight-sided butter crock, curved salt bowl, stein, and vase. The premiums were made by Weir Pottery Company, later to become Monmouth Pottery Company, and finally to emerge as the present-day Western Stoneware Company of Monmouth, Illinois.

For more information, see *Warman's American Pottery & Porcelain*, 2nd edition.

Additional pottery and stoneware pieces also were issued. Forms included five sizes of pitchers (4, 5-1/2, 6-1/2, 8, and 9 inches), mugs, steins, sugar bowls, and tea tiles (hot plates). Most were cobalt blue on white, but other glaze hues, such as browns, golds, and greens, were used. Old Sleepy Eye also issued many other items, including bakers' caps, lithographed barrel covers, beanies, fans, multicolored pillow tops, postcards, and trade cards. Regular production of Old Sleepy Eye stoneware ended in 1937.

In 1952, Western Stoneware Company made 22- and 40-ounce steins in chestnut brown glaze with a redesigned Indian's head. From 1961 to 1972, gift editions were made for the board of directors and others within the company. Beginning in 1973, Western Stoneware Company issued an annual limited edition stein for collectors.

Marks: The gift editions made in the 1960s and 1970s were dated and signed with a maple leaf mark. The annual limited edition steins are marked and dated.

Reproduction Alert: Blue-and-white pitchers, crazed, weighted, and often with a stamp or the word "Ironstone" are the most common reproductions. The stein and salt bowl also have been made. Many reproductions come from Taiwan.

A line of fantasy items, new items which never existed as Old Sleepy Eye originals, includes an advertising pocket mirror with miniature flour-barrel label, small glass plates, fruit jars, toothpick holders, glass and pottery miniature pitchers, and salt and pepper shakers. One mill item has been made: a sack marked as though it were old, but of a size that could not possibly hold the amount of flour indicated.

Mill items

Cookbook, Sleepy Eye Milling Co., loaf of bread shape, portrait of chief... **150.00**
Label, 9-1/4" x 11-1/2" d, egg crate, Sleepy Eye Brand, A. J. Pietrus & Sons Co., Sleepy Eye, MN, red, blue, and yellow.. **25.00**
Letter opener, bronze, Indian-head handle, marked "Sleepy Eye Milling Co., Sleepy Eye, MN".......................... **750.00**
Pinback button, "Old Sleepy Eye for Me," bust portrait of chief............ **175.00**

Framed advertising print "Sleepy Eye Mills, Sleepy Eye, Minn," 30" x 24" overall, **$75**. Photo courtesy of Joy Luke Auctions.

Pottery and stoneware

Bowl, 4" h, ftd, Bristol glaze, relief profile of Indian on one side, floral design on other, imp "X" on bottom **360.00**
Butter crock, cov, 4-3/4" h, blue and gray salt glaze, relief and blue accented Indian profile on one side, trees and teepee on other side, imp "H" on bottom, surface rim chip **495.00**
Mug, 3-1/2" d, 4-3/4" h, marked "WS Co. Monmouth, Ill"............................. **395.00**
Pitcher, 7-3/4" h, #4 .... **675.00**
Stein, 7-1/2" h, Bristol glaze, relief and blue accented Indian profile on one side, trees and teepee on other side **470.00**
Tile, cobalt blue and white.......... **950.00**
Vase, cylinder, cobalt blue dec.... **250.00**

Onion Meissen

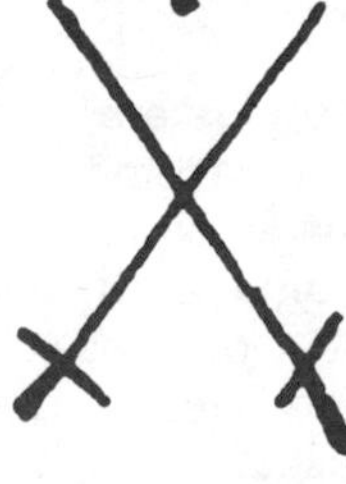

History: The blue onion or bulb pattern is of Chinese origin and depicts peaches and pomegranates, not onions. It was first made in the 18th century by Meissen, hence the name Onion Meissen.

Factories in Europe, Japan, and elsewhere copied the pattern. Many still have the pattern in production, including the Meissen factory in Germany.

Marks: Many pieces are marked with a company's logo; after 1891, the country of origin is indicated on imported pieces.

Note: Prices given are for pieces produced between 1870 and 1930. Early Meissen examples bring a high premium.

Ashtray, 5" d, blue crossed swords mark **75.00**
Bowl, 8-1/2" d, reticulated, blue crossed swords mark, 19th C **395.00**
Box, cov, 4-1/2" d, round, rose finial**80.00**
Bread plate, 6-1/2" d..................... **75.00**
Cake stand, 13-1/2" d, 4-1/2" h.... **220.00**
Compote, 11" d, 9-3/4" h, restoration to edge **950.00**
Creamer and sugar, gold edge, c1900 .... **175.00**
Demitasse cup and saucer, c1890 .... **95.00**

Meissen covered tureen, 10" x 13", matching underplate, Blue Danube ladle, 20th C, **$920**. Photo courtesy of David Rago Auctions, Inc.

Dish, 12" d, circular, divided........ **175.00**
Fruit compote, 9" h, circular, openwork bowl, five oval floral medallions.... **375.00**
Ladle, wooden handle **115.00**
Lamp, 22" h, oil, frosted glass globular form shade **475.00**
Plate, 7-3/4" d, reticulated border with three floral cartouches................. **125.00**
Platter, 12" l................................ **650.00**
Pot de creme............................... **65.00**
Serving dish, 9-1/4" w, 11" l, floral design on handle.................................... **200.00**
Tray, 17" l, cartouche shape, gilt edge **425.00**
Vegetable dish, cov, 10" w, sq **150.00**

Opalescent Glass

History: Opalescent glass, a clear or colored glass with milky white decorations, looks fiery or opalescent when held to light. This effect was achieved by applying bone ash chemicals to designated areas while a piece was still hot and then refiring it at extremely high temperatures.

There are three basic categories of opalescent glass: (1) blown (or mold blown) patterns, e.g., Daisy & Fern and Spanish Lace; (2) novelties, pressed glass patterns made in limited quantity and often in unusual shapes such as corn or a trough; and (3) traditional pattern (pressed) glass forms.

For more information, see *Warman's Glass*, 4th edition.

Opalescent glass was produced in England in the 1870s. Northwood began the American production in 1897 at its Indiana, Pennsylvania, plant. Jefferson, National Glass, Hobbs, and Fenton soon followed.

Additional Listings: Pattern Glass.

Vases, pair, 4" h, ruffled rims, Polka Dot pattern, cranberry ground, Fenton, **$85**. Photo courtesy of Wiederseim Associates, Inc.

Blown

Basket, 7-1/2" h, Stripes, cranberry, four-corner ruffled top, applied twisted handle **180.00**
Barber bottle, Raised Swirl, cranberry **295.00**
Biscuit jar, cov, Spanish Lace, vaseline **275.00**
Bride's basket, Poinsettia, ruffled top **275.00**
Butter dish, cov, Hobbs Hobnail, vaseline **250.00**
Celery vase, Seaweed, cranberry **250.00**
Creamer, Windows Swirl, cranberry **500.00**
Cruet, Ribbed Opal Lattice, white **135.00**
Finger bowl, Hobbs Hobnail, cranberry **65.00**
Lamp, oil, Inverted Thumbprint, white, amber fan base **145.00**

Mustard, cov, Reverse Swirl, vaseline **65.00**
Pickle castor, Daisy and Fern, blue, emb floral jar, DQ, resilvered frame...... **650.00**

Vases, pair, 8" h, ruffled rims, Coin spot pattern, **$115**. Photo courtesy of Wiederseim Associates, Inc.

Pitcher
- Arabian Nights, white............. **450.00**
- Hobbs Hobnail, cranberry **315.00**
- Seaweed, blue **525.00**

Rose bowl, Brocade, Vaseline **140.00**
Salt shaker, orig top
- Consolidated Criss-Cross, cranberry **85.00**
- Ribbed Opal Lattice, cranberry **95.00**

Spooner, Reverse Swirl, cranberry **175.00**
Sugar, cov, Reverse Swirl, cranberry **350.00**
Sugar shaker, Ribbed Opal Lattice, cranberry.................................... **325.00**
Syrup, Coin Spot, cranberry........ **175.00**
Tumbler
- Acanthus, blue **90.00**
- Christmas Snowflake, blue, ribbed **125.00**
- Maze, swirling, green **95.00**
- Reverse Swirl, cranberry.......... **65.00**

Waste bowl, Hobbs Hobnail, vaseline **75.00**

Water pitcher, Hobnail pattern, square top, cranberry, applied clear ribbed handle, **$175**.

Water set
- Buttons & Braids, blue, pitcher, four tumblers **850.00**
- Polka Dot Swirl, white, pitcher, six tumblers **650.00**

Novelties

Barber bottle, 8" h, sq, diamond pattern molded form, light cranberry, white vertical stripes **275.00**
Bowl, Winter Cabbage, white **45.00**
Bushel basket, blue **75.00**
Chalice, Maple Leaf, vaseline........ **45.00**
Hat, Opal Swirl, white, blue edge... **95.00**
Jack-in-the-pulpit vase, 6" h, green swirl, applied red flower, crystal stem **115.00**

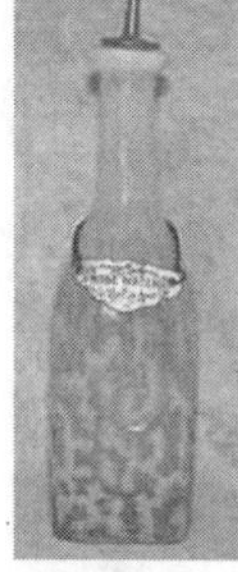
Barber bottle, square body, white opalescent seaweed motif, hanging enameled tag with floral decoration and "Rose Water" label, metal and cork stopper, 9-1/2" h, **$260**. Photo courtesy of Alderfer Auction Co.

Pressed

Biscuit jar, cov, Wreath and Shell, vaseline **750.00**
Compote, Maple Leaf, 4" h.......... **100.00**
Creamer, Inverted Fan and Feather, blue **125.00**
Cruet, Stars and Stripes, cranberry **575.00**
Jelly compote, Intaglio, blue......... **55.00**
Rose bowl
- Klondyke, canary **95.00**
- Pearl and Scale, pedestal base, green, 4-3/4" h........................ **110.00**

Sauce, Drapery, blue, hp dec........ **35.00**
Spooner, Swag with Brackets, blue **70.00**
Toothpick holder, Ribbed Spiral, blue **90.00**
Tumbler, Drapery, blue **90.00**
Vase, Northwood Diamond Point, blue **75.00**

Opaline Glass

History: Opaline glass was a popular mid- to late-19th century European glass. The glass has a certain amount of translucency and often is found decorated with enamel designs and trimmed in gold.

For more information, see *Warman's Glass*, 4th edition.

Basket, 7-1/4" h, opaque white ground, applied amber stemmed pink flowers, amber twist handle........................ **90.00**
Bouquet holder, 7" h, blue opaline cornucopia-shaped gilt dec flower holders issuing from bronze stag heads, Belgian black marble base, English, Victorian, early 19th C, pr............ **725.00**
Box, cov, 5-1/2" w, 3-1/2" d, 4-1/2" h, bright blue, hinged, rect.............. **595.00**
Bride's basket, 12" d, 7-1/2" h, white opaline, cased in pink, overall colorful enameled dec, emb Middletown plated holder, applied fruit handles, Victorian, minor losses **525.00**

Chandelier, French Empire-style, late 19th C, gilt metal, inverted bell-shaped glass orb crowned with pressed metal cartouches, mounted with pressed colorless glass lustres, suspending by chains, blue glass urn-form body hung with further colorless lustres, six serpentine candle arms, one sconce off but present, 36-1/2" l, **$1,765**. Photo courtesy of Skinner, Inc.

Candelabra, Louis XV style, late 19th C, 18-1/2" h, gilt bronze and blue opaline, scrolled candle arms and base, two-light **175.00**
Dresser set, 10" h perfume bottle and 6" h powder jar, pink, encrusted gold dec, orig feathered puff with ivory handle **700.00**
Ewer, 13-1/4" h, white ground, Diamond Point pattern **135.00**
Jardinières, 5-1/4" h, gilt bronze and blue opaline, sq, Empire style, tasseled chains, paw feet, early 20th C, pr **1,610.00**
Mantel lusters, 12-3/4" h, blue, gilt dec, slender faceted prisms, Victorian, c1880, damage, pr................................. **250.00**
Oil lamp, 24" h, dolphin-form stepped base, clear glass oil well, frosted glass shade, late 19th C, converted to electric, chips... **460.00**
Salt, boat shaped, blue dec, white enamel garland and scrolling......... **75.00**

Vases, pair, Fireglow, gilded banding, 13-3/4" h, **$95**. Photo courtesy of Joy Luke Auctions.

Benches, near pair, Chinese, c1850, Zhejang Province, beechwood, rectangular top, apron with openwork, 45-1/2" l, 13" d, 18-1/2" h, **$750**. Photo courtesy of Sloans & Kenyon Auctions.

Vase
- 6-1/4" h, cased pink ground, colorful enameled flower spray **225.00**
- 8-1/8" h, bulbed rim, urn-form, enameled dec of Etruscan figures in beige, gold accent designs, stamped "Richardson's Strourbridge," England, c1845-50 .... **750.00**
- 9-1/2" h, pink cased ground, enameled gold day lilies, three rolled over handled rim, Victorian **125.00**
- 10" h, homogenized gray ground, enameled perched birds, 19th C, price for matched pr **175.00**

Water pitcher, 12-1/4" h, blue, high looped handle, bulbous, early 20th C **240.00**

ORIENTALIA

History: Orientalia is a term applied to objects made in the Orient, an area which encompasses the Far East, Asia, China, and Japan. The diversity of cultures produced a variety of objects and styles.

Additional Listings: Canton, Celadon, Cloisonné, Fitzhugh, Nanking, Netsukes, Rose Medallion, Japanese Prints, and other related categories.

Bronze piece breaks record

A new world-record price was set for a 7th C seated Buddha of the Future, Mitreya, gilt-bronze, when it realized $1,575,500 at Christies' March 24-27 Spring Asian auction. One of the few known Maireya bronzes from the Paekche Kingdom, the other known examples are in the collection of the National Museum of Korea, Seoul. "This exceptional piece was coveted by two buyers in the room and sold for a world auction record for a Korean bronze," said Yamaguchi (Katsura Yamaguchi, Christie's senior specialist in Japanese art)

Altar table, 58-1/2" x 34-1/4" x 16", China, chi chi mu or chicken wing wood, archaic-style spandrels, beaded borders, 18th C **1,955.00**

Architectural element, Capitals, 22" l, carved wood, foo dogs, gold lacquered surface, China, 19th C, price for pr **775.00**

Bell, 19" h, bronze, lid surmounted by two kneeling figures, iron mount with two apsara figures, Burma, 19th C **400.00**

Bottle, 11-1/2" d, porcelain, sq form, blue and white dec of Buddhist lion dogs, China, Transitional period, 1630-50 .... **2,850.00**

Box, cov, 4" h, iron, hexagonal form with mixed metal inlay, sgd "Seijo," Japan, 19th C **1,550.00**

Bowl, Chinese, 7-1/2" d, porcelain, dark blue ext. with gilt dragons, clouds, and pearls, white int., Ch'ien Lung six-character seal mark, 1736-95 ...... **600.00**

Bowl, northern India or central Asia, parcel gilt **209,100.00**

Brush pot, 4-3/4" h, rect, pale green glaze, Ch'ien Lung mark, 1736-1795 .... **900.00**

Buddha, 24" h, Buddha, stucco, Gandhara, 3rd C **276,300.00**

Buddhist bell, 14" d, Japan, hammered brass with a lacquered design of a dragon and thunder meanders, late 19th/ early 20th C **450.00**

Butter dish, cov, 5-1/8" d, silver, domed lid set with dragon's head, chased and embossed with dragon's body amidst cloud work, rim of dish pierced and similarly chased and embossed, 8 troy oz, Chinese Export, maker likely Wing Chun, early 20th C **450.00**

Chair, arm, carved, mortised construction, old reddish brown finish, back splats with solid relief carved floral panel, pierced design on lower panel, rounded legs, stretcher base, applied aprons, 19-1/2" h seat, 40-1/2" h overall, price for pr **300.00**

Charger, 23-1/2" d, Imari dec, tomato red, blue, green, orange, and gold, center scene of family with nine figures at table beneath tree **495.00**

Cup, Chinese, porcelain, engraved dragons under egg yolk yellow color, six-character underglaze blue Kuang Hsu mark, 1874-1908, possibly of the period **200.00**

Embroidery, on silk, 17" x 13", crane by flowering tree, Japanese, Meiji period, 1867-1912 .... **320.00**

Fan, folding, China, 19th C
- Ivory, shaped stays with numerous figures in garden scenes, fan painted with harbor scene, other vignettes of idyllic village scenes, black lacquer box with gilt butterflies and flowers **490.00**
- Wooden stays with black lacquer and gold dec, fan of paper dec with figures in silk and ivory, reverse magenta with three reserves of

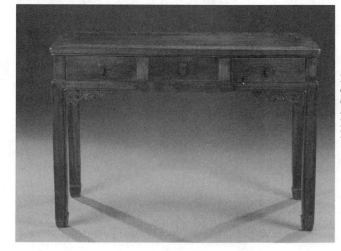

Desk, Chinese, Shuzhou Province, c1850, beechwood, rect top, three drawers, carved apron, 45-1/2" w, 20" d, 32-1/2" h, **$750**. Photo courtesy of Sloans & Kenyon Auctions.

country scenes, gold and black lacquer case 250.00

Fan, folding, Japan, 19th C

All ivory stays dec with shibayama inlay of gold lacquer and semi-precious inlay of birds and flowers, 11-1/2" l, orig box 4,025.00

Carved ivory stays with shibayama inlay, one side dec with landscape, other with children watching fireworks 375.00

Figure, Chinese, 19th C, Goddess Kuan Yin, 20" h, **$2,715**. Photo courtesy of Skinner, Inc.

Figure

5-1/2" h, seated goddess of mercy, Blanc de Chine, Te Hua ware, sgd with illegible mark within double-gourd, carved hardwood stand, ornate glass case, China, 19th C 920.00

8" l, 7-1/4" h, rabbit, bronze, textured surface, sgd, Japan, Meiji period (1868-1911)........................ 3,500.00

12" h, carved ivory, wise man with branch of fruit, young woman with cherry blossoms, etched details, incised chop marks on base, early 20th C.................................... 615.00

40" h, Goddess, carved stone, gray schist image of Kuan Yin, China, 20th C.. 285.00

Foo Dog, 11" l, 10-1/2" h, carved wood, surface lacquered in red and gold, China, 19th C.. 600.00

Garden seat, 18" h, porcelain, hexagonal form, blue and white dec, China, 19th C 900.00

Ginger jar, 8-1/2" h, China, blue and white mythical animals and floral sprays, K'ang His mark on base, 19th C .. 250.00

Hand scroll, 65-1/2" x 3", ink on silk, landscapes, colophons by various members of the Wu family, Tao Kuang period, 1821-48........................... 400.00

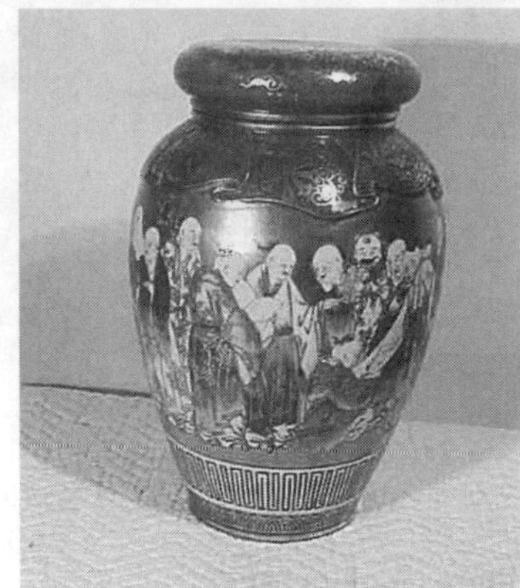

Ginger jar, covered, porcelain, jovial figures, 11" h, **$225**. Photo courtesy of Wiederseim Associates, Inc.

Hanging scroll, 42-1/2" x 22-1/4", ink and color on paper, map of the temples of Wu Tai Shan with a central figure of Manjushri, the Buddha of the future, China, Ching dynasty, probably 18th/19th C.. 950.00

Incense box, 2" x 2", Komei-style, iron inlaid with gold and silver, Japan, Meiji period (1868-1911)...................... 600.00

Incense burner

6-1/2" h, silver, China, 19th C, chalice form, claw feet, cover pierced and engraved with flowers, body engraved with flowers on punch-work ground, three illegible touch marks on the base, China, 19th C 470.00

16" h, bronze, inlay of silver and copper in the manner of Shih So, China, 19th C 775.00

Jacket, Chinese

Blue silk damask, black silk, black silk damask, elaborately embroidered with flowers and butterflies in ivory, pale green, tangerine, and black, lined with blue linen, c1900........................... 300.00

Blue silk damask, lined with pale blue polished cotton, appliquéd at hem and cuffs with border of blue satin embroidery with flowers and butterflies, background for embroidery is black up front and around hem, pale green silk at cuffs, c1900 .... 300.00

Wool/silk blend with blue, red, lilac swirls and flowers on cream ground, ivory silk damask lining, early 20th C 45.00

Jar, cov, baluster, 32" h, blue and white dec of Buddhist lion dogs on cloud strewn ground, lion-mask handles, lion finials, China, 19th C, minor loss 3,200.00

Obi, printed silk, tan, green, cream, and rust leaf pattern, lilac ground, fully lined with lilac silk satin, Chinese, early 20th C, 12" w, 148" l 200.00

Okimono, 3" l, ivory study of group of rats and lantern, horn inlay, 19th C 635.00

Pajamas, pale green silk damask, frog closures, wide-legged pants, green and lilac satin embroidery in butterflies and flowers motif on back and front of long sleeved jacket and at cuffs, Chinese, c1930, three very small holes near hem on front of jacket.......................... 150.00

Palace urn, 24" h, bronze, elaborately dec with scenes of birds, Foo dogs, foliage, large applied dragons, rich chocolate brown patina, Chinese, c1900, price for pr.................................. 750.00

Plaque, 8" x 6", bronze, relief dec of Kuan Yin surrounded by attending deities, extensive inscription on back, China, 19th C.............................. 135.00

Pottery birds, Chinese, 19th C, 8" h, **$115**. Photo courtesy of Wiederseim Associates, Inc.

Robe, Chinese

Aqua gold/silver rayon brocade with long sleeves, mandarin collar, frogs up front, pale green silk/rayon lining, c1955 .... 30.00

Blue silk crepe, printed in mushroom motif in cream and blue, partially lined with red silk, early 20th C, altered at waistline, some damage to lining... 50.00

Blue silk with satin embroidery, braid and cream silk cuffs with embroidery including metallic, fully lined with blue silk damask, labeled "Made in China," c1940........................ 325.00

Ivory silk crepe, lined with ivory silk, rolled hem, elaborate floral satin embroidery of wisteria, flowers, and foliage in pastel colors of rose, gray, lilac, blush, and ivory, further dec with several butterflies in deeper hues, early 20th C 250.00

Ivory silk with trapunto work and floral embroidery, further embroidered with gold metallic threads, brass buttons and silk loops, some damage on ivory silk lining, c1900.......................... 400.00

Woven cotton in shades of blue, geometric patterns with burgundy centers, royal blue in cotton/satin blend with birds, dragons, and flaming pearl motif, early 20th C, some damage on collar **350.00**

Screen, 41" x 27-1/2", two panels, mahogany frame, pierced fretwork across center, worn silk panels on top, small scroll missing from base **55.00**

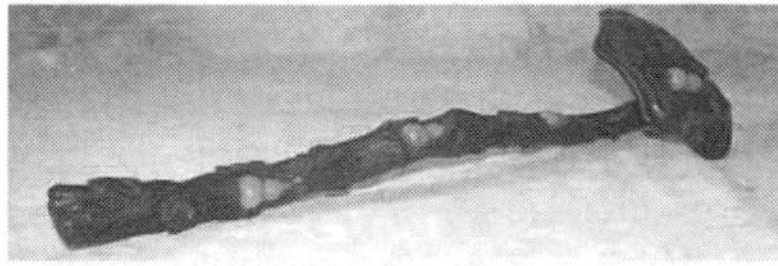

Scepter, Chinese, 19th C, brown wood, carved floral and leaf motif, inlaid with white jade, 14-1/4" l, **$990**. Photo courtesy of Alderfer Auction Co.

Sculpture

Horse, glazed pottery, Tang-dynasty, 33" l.................................. **477,900.00**

Bodhisattva torso, limestone, attributed to Buddhist trinity in Tianlognshan Caves of China's Shanxi Province, 48" h....... **1,183,500**

Skirt, Chinese, late 19th C

Silk damask, tangerine, very elaborate silk satin embroidery of butterflies and flowers in rose, green, purple, lilac, pink, and blue, pleating, borders of blue silk satin floral embroidery on black ground, deep 8" waistband of beige cotton with frogs **600.00**

Wool, red, satin embroidered edging in shades of blue and silver, deep cream linen waistband, blue silk lining, moth holes in red wool... **85.00**

Tankard, 8" h, blue and white, scholar in garden scene, Continental silver mounts with Dutch export hallmarks, China, Transitional period, c1620 .... **3,985.00**

Table, side, teakwood, dark finish, high rect legs with relief edge moldings and scrolling with foliage, pierced aprons with dragons' heads, scrolled returns of raised paneled top match pierced apron, 20th C, 20-1/4" l, 16-3/4" d, 33-1/2" h ... **450.00**

Sewing box, Chinese Export, wood box heavily inlaid overall with ivory, silver, ebony and green onyx, stepped lid, interior fitted with boxes having conforming decoration, ivory spools, thimble, inlay-framed mirror, lift-out tray, brass lock and swing handles, 19th C, losses, splitting, 12-1/2" l, 8-3/4" d, 5-1/2" h, **$650**. Photo courtesy of Alderfer Auction Co.

Tea chest, gold lacquer, teahouse scenes, foliate and floral borders, engraved pewter liner with ivory knob, English lock with hallmarks, cracking, touch-up, **$990**. Photo courtesy of Sanford Alderfer Auction Company.

Vase

8-1/2" h, studio pottery, ovoid form, four lug handles, top covered in blue-brown glaze, bottom engraved with Archaic-style horses and fish, sgd with an impressed seal on bottom, Japan, late 19th/early 20th C **395.00**

15" h, bronze, relief dec of waves with dragon in round holding glass pearl, sgd "great Japan sei don sai," Japan, Meiji period............. **1,650.00**

20-1/2" h, Tsun-shape, Wu Tsai ware, birds and flowers dec, China, Transitional period, c1640 .... **2,000.00**

42" h, bronze, flared rim, paneled shoulder takers to base with flower petals, detailed peacock sits on flowering tree branch, peahen below, dark patina, peacock's crest missing **3,500.00**

Water coupe, 5" d, porcelain, deep crushed-strawberry copper-red color, China, 18th C............................... **275.00**

Wine ewer, 6-1/4" h, Hirado ware, form of Hoi tea, bag of wealth, underglaze blue, yellow, pale green, tan, and black accents, 19th C, cover missing **750.00**

Oriental Rugs

History: Oriental rugs or carpets date back to 3,000 B.C., but it was in the 16th century that they became prevalent. The rugs originated in the regions of Central Asia, Iran (Persia), Caucasus, and Anatolia. Early rugs can be classified into basic categories: Iranian, Caucasian, Turkoman, Turkish, and Chinese. Later India, Pakistan, and Iraq produced rugs in the Oriental style.

The pattern name is derived from the tribe that produced the rug, e.g., Iran is the source for Hamadan, Herez, Sarouk, and Tabriz.

Reproduction Alert: Beware! There are repainted rugs on the market.

Notes: When evaluating an Oriental rug, age, design, color, weave, knots per square inch, and condition determine the final value. Silk rugs and prayer rugs bring higher prices than other types.

Afshar, 5' 2" x 7' 9" dark blue and dark red borders, midnight blue ground, dark red serebend pattern, wear lines, flat woven ends with damage **800.00**

Anatol, prayer, 3' 7" x 5' 8", gray border, light camel ground, red center, minor wear and tiny hole **250.00**

Armenian Karabagh, South Caucasus, dated 1911, 8' 10" x 3' 9", three lightning medallions each inset with quatrefoil floral motifs, navy blue, royal blue, dark red, rose, camel, aubergine, and blue-green on midnight blue field, navy blue rosette border, small replied areas, corner repairs **1,265.00**

Baluch, Northeast Persia, second half 19th C, prayer rug, eight columns of meandering vines in midnight blue, red, brown, and aubergine on ivory field, borders of similar coloration, even wear, brown corrosion........................... **600.00**

Bidjar, Northwest Persia, late 19th C, 8' x 4' 2", overall Herati design in red, royal blue, camel, plum, gold, and dark blue-green on midnight blue field, red spandrels, royal blue border, slight even wear to center, small corner gouge **2,235.00**

Ersari Torba, West Turkestan, late 19th C, 6' x 1' 3", three elongated hexagons surrounded by geometric motifs in rust-red, ivory, gold, and royal blue on variegated midnight blue, dark brown field, multicolored border, small stain, very slight moth damage............. **825.00**

Caucasian, Shiraz, saddle cover, central medallion, dark blue ground, 3' x 4', **$250**.

Ferahan Sarouk, 4' 5" x 6' 4", black border, detailed floral design, camel ground with intricate design of facing pairs of figures, including lions, deer, birds, bulls, and dragons **4,400.00**
Hamadan, 4' 5" x 6' 9", deep colors, blue border, red spandrels, dark blue ground, edge wear, partial border loss **600.00**
Heriz, Northwest Persia, 20' x 10' 4", second quarter 20th C, large multi-gabled medallion surrounded by serrated leaves and flowering vines, midnight, royal, and ice blue, rose, gold, red-brown, and dark green on red field, large ivory spandrels, midnight blue turtle border, small areas of minor wear, some black corrosion......................... **5,875.00**
Jaf Kurd, Northwest Persia, early 20th C, bagface, 2' 7" x 2' 7", diamond lattice of hooked diamonds in midnight and navy blue, red, gold, brown, rust, aubergine, and blue-green, aubergine border, slight brown corrosion.......................... **530.00**

Farchalo Kazak, prayer rug, c1870, rare sea foam green field, red Mihrab within running dog border, 3' 6" x 5' 4", **$3,220**. Photo courtesy of Pook & Pook.

Karaja, runner, 3' x 13", black border, red ground **495.00**
Kazak, Southwest Caucasus, late 19th C, 10' 4" x 3', column of eight square panels each inset with pair of plant motifs in red, royal blue, black, ivory, gold, rose, and blue-green, ivory border, rewoven ends, small repairs **1,200.00**
Kuba, Northeast Caucasus, late 19th/early 20th C, 4' x 5' 1", vibrant colors, blue, red, brown, and goldenrod borders, midnight blue ground, minor wear **550.00**
Kurd, Northwest Persia, late 19th C, bagface, 3' 8" x 2' 2", two square panels each inset with a serrated hexagon in navy blue, sky blue, red, aubergine, ivory, and blue-green on gold field, navy blue border, areas of some wear, rewoven ends... **350.00**
Kurdish, runner, 2' 11" x 8' 8", blue, camel, and light orange borders, red ground **550.00**
Lesghi, Northeast Caucasus, last quarter 19th C, 4' 10" x 3' 9", column of four Lesghi stars in red, sky blue, ivory, tan-gold, and blue-green on navy blue field, two ivory borders, even wear, slight end fraying....................................... **1,300.00**
Malayer, Northwest Persia, second quarter 20th C, 4' 10" x 3' 6", overall design of flowerheads and blossoming vines in red, ice blue, camel, and olive on royal blue field, ivory border, outer guard stripes partially missing from both ends **1,000.00**

Moghan Kazak, runner, c1910, repeating medallions, cobalt blue and ivory borders, 3' 10" x 11' 3", **$2,070**. Photo courtesy of Pook & Pook.

Qashqai, Southwest Persia, late 19th/early 20th C, 6' 9" x 4', large hooked hexagonal medallion inset with blossoming angular vines in red, navy blue, ivory, gold, brown, and blue-green, midnight blue field, brown border, slight wear to center, minor moth damage, small repair **1,100.00**
Senneh, Northwest Persia, late 19th C, 5' 9" x 4' 3", diamond medallion and large matching spandrels with overall Herati design in sky blue, red, rose, gold, and gray-brown on midnight blue field, slate blue border, even wear, slight moth damage, guard stripe missing from both ends.. **890.00**
Shirvan, East Caucasus, late 19th C

5' 6" x 3' 10", prayer rug, serrated diamond lattice of flowering plants in midnight and navy blue, red, gold, and blue-green on ivory field, dark red border, creases, black corrosion, small repairs....................... **1,645.00**

5' 10" x 3' 3", large keyhole medallion inset with four octagons in midnight and royal blue, ivory, gold, and blue-green on red field, ivory border, guard stripe partially missing from both ends, some moth damage, small repairs....................... **1,425.00**

Sarouk mat, reds, tans, white, **$250**. Photo courtesy of Wiederseim Associates, Inc.

Suzani, Central Asia, 19th C

Prayer, 5' 2" x 3' 2", empty ivory field, wide ivory border with blossoming plants in cochineal, rose, sky blue, gold, and blue-green, small repair, slight staining, backed with fabric **600.00**

Rug, 7' 5" x 5' 4", four columns of seven palmettes in navy and sky blue, cochineal, rust, rose, gold, apricot, light aubergine, and blue-green on ivory field, ivory border, some embroidery losses, small repaired area, backed with fabric **900.00**

Tabriz, Northwest Persia, late 19th C, prayer rug, 6' 3" x 4' 4", silk, vase with large blossoming plant in sky blue, aubergine, gold, apricot, olive, and blue-green on tan field, sky blue border, small spots of wear and corrosion, ends backed with fabric.................... **2,500.00**
Yomud Chuval, West Turkestan, last quarter 19th C, 3' 4" x 2' 3", nine Chuval guls in midnight blue, red, ivory, and blue-green on dark aubergine field, ivory border, plain aubergine elem, small spots of slight wear, re-overcast **825.00**
Ziegler Mahal, 7' 5" x 9' 11", Oushak pattern, midnight blue border, ivory and

pink spandrels, brick ground with blue designs, minor wear, areas of rebinding on edge, minor border loss....... **3,550.00**

Shirvan, runner, c1925, overall pattern on rust field, 6' 2" x 8' 7", **$1,955**. Photo courtesy of Pook & Pook.

Owens Pottery

History: J. B. Owens began making pottery in 1885 near Roseville, Ohio. In 1891, he built a plant in Zanesville and in 1897, began producing art pottery. After 1907, most of the firm's production centered on tiles.

Owens Pottery, employing many of the same artists and designs as its two cross-town rivals, Roseville and Weller, can appear very similar to that of its competitors, e.g., Utopian (brown glaze), Lotus (light glaze), and Aqua Verde (green glaze).

There were a few techniques used exclusively at Owens. These included Red Flame ware (slip decoration under a high red glaze) and Mission (over-glaze, slip decorations in mineral colors) depicting Spanish Missions. Other specialties included Opalesce (semi-gloss designs in lustered gold and orange) and Coralene (small beads affixed to the surface of the decorated vases).

Bud vase, 6-1/4" h, 2-1/2" w, standard glaze, yellow roses, marked "#804," initials for Harry Robinson **150.00**

Ewer, 10" h, brown high glaze, cherry design... **200.00**

Jug, 8" w, 4-1/2" w, standard glaze, ear of corn dec, marked and sgd "Tot Steele" **230.00**

Three-tile frieze, decorated in cuenca, rural landscape in matte polychrome, stamped "Owens," one tile missing in sequence, some pitting to glaze, mounted in new rustic frame, 14-1/2" x 30", **$3,775**. Owens photos courtesy of David Rago Auctions, Inc.

Lamp base, 5" d, 11-1/4" h, classic shape, painted yellow daffodils, unmarked, drilled, some glaze bubbles on back.. **365.00**

Mug, 5" x 4-1/4", Utopian, painted berries and leaves, stamped mark, tight 1" line from rim **150.00**

Pitcher, 8-1/2" h, dark brown to green, orange and brown flowers, green leaves, marked "JBO" intertwined, artist sgd "HK," crack in handle.................... **110.00**

Tankard, 7" h, brown high glaze, Indian design, incised signature, restored **325.00**

Vase, bottle shape, Utopian, by A. Haubrich, dec with portrait of spaniel, shaded blue and gray ground, stamped mark, artist sgd on body, tight rim hairline, 6-1/2" d, 16-1/4" h, **$1,355**.

Vase

- 4" h, Lotus, bee flying above green blades of grass, ivory to blue ground, imp mark, artist initials **400.00**
- 6-3/8" h, Utopian Ware, silver overlay, flared rim on tapered oviform, glossy glaze, cream and brown rose blossoms and leaves, shaded brown ground, silver overlay imp "Utopian J. B. Owens 923" and "Phee F.N. Silver Co.," crazing, scratches, nicks **290.00**
- 7-1/2" x 7", squatty, matte green, four sq cut-outs to neck, incised key pattern around shoulder, stamped mark, small rim burst............. **920.00**
- 8" h, 8-1/2" w, ftd pillow, dark to light brown with yellow ground, Indian portrait, cream and red vest, blue in hair, imp mark, repaired top **1,100.00**
- 9-1/4" x 4", tapering, buttressed base, unmarked **290.00**
- 10-1/4" x 5", Utopian, bulbous, painted orange poppies, marked **290.00**
- 11-3/4" h, ovoid, pierced rectangles on shoulder, panels of stylized swans in relief, matte green, imp "Owens 1025," c1905 .... **1,495.00**
- 13" x 6-1/2", Utopian, matte, painted chrysanthemums on bisque ground, imp "Owens," artist's initials TS, abrasion to bottom, minor glaze flecks **275.00**
- 13-1/2", Utopian, matte, painted nasturtiums on bisque ground, imp "Owens," artist's initials FC..... **255.00**

Vessel, 4-1/4" x 5", squat, incised by Pollock with dragonflies, covered in matte green glaze, impressed "OWENS," body incised "Pollock".......................... **920.00**

Paden City Glass

For more information, see *Warman's Glass*, 4th edition.

History: Paden City Glass Manufacturing Co. was founded in 1916 in Paden City, West Virginia. David Fisher, formerly of the New Martinsville Glass Manufacturing Co., operated the company until his death in 1933, at which time his son, Samuel, became president. A management decision in 1949 to expand Paden City's production by acquiring American Glass Company, an automated manufacturer of bottles, ashtrays, and novelties, strained the company's finances, forcing it to close permanently in 1951.

Contrary to popular belief and previously incorrect printed references, the Paden City Glass Manufacturing Company had absolutely no connection with the Paden City Pottery Company, other than its identical locale.

Although Paden City glass is often lumped with mass-produced, machine-made wares into the Depression glass category, Paden City's wares were, until

1948, all handmade. Its products are better classified as "Elegant Glass" of the era, as it ranks in quality with the wares produced by contemporaries such as Fostoria, New Martinsville, and Morgantown.

Paden City kept a low profile, never advertising in consumer magazines of the day. It never marked its glass in any way because a large portion of its business consisted of sales to decorating companies, mounters, and fitters. The firm also supplied bars, restaurants, and soda fountains with glassware, as evidenced by the wide range of tumblers, ice cream dishes, and institutional products available in several Paden City patterns.

Paden City's decorating shop also etched, cut, hand painted, and applied silver overlay and gold encrustation. However, not every decoration found on Paden City shapes will necessarily have come from the factory. Cupid, Peacock and Rose, and several other etchings depicting birds are among the most sought-after decorations, even though they were apparently made in greater quantities than some of the etchings that are less known, but just as beautiful.

Paden City is noted for its colors: Opal (opaque white), Ebony, Mulberry (amethyst), Cheriglo (delicate pink), yellow, Forest (dark green), crystal, amber, several shades of blue ranging from aquamarine to medium blue to a deep rich cobalt blue, and great quantities of Ruby (red). The firm also produced transparent green in numerous shades, ranging from yellowish to a distinctive electric green that always alerts knowledgeable collectors to its Paden City origin.

Rising collector interest in Paden City glass has resulted in a sharp spike in prices on some patterns. Currently, pieces with Orchid etch are bringing the highest prices. Several truly rare items have recently topped the $1,000 mark, and a few have even broke the $2,000 mark. Advanced collectors seek out examples with unusual and/or undocumented etchings. Colored pieces which sport an etching that is not usually found on that particular color are especially sought after and bringing strong prices. In contrast, prices for common items with Peacock and Rose etch remain static, and the prices for dinnerware in Ruby Penny Line and Cheriglo or green Party Line have inched up only slightly, due to its greater availability.

Adviser: Michael Krumme.

Color is crystal (clear) unless otherwise noted.

Bowl, console
- #215 Glades, three-footed, two sides turned up, Ruby **50.00**
- #220 Largo, three-footed, gray cutting **25.00**
- #300 Archaic, oval, Cupid etch, Cheriglo or green **250.00**
- #300 Archaic, 11" d, Cupid etch, Cheriglo **200.00**
- #300 Archaic, oval, Peacock & Rose etch, one panel plain **230.00**
- #300 Archaic, 13" d, Cupid etch, Cheriglo **300.00**
- #412 Crow's Foot Square, Delilah Bird etch, cobalt blue **650.00**
- #412 Crow's Foot Square, Opal **75.00**
- #412 Crow's Foot Square, Orchid etch, yellow **150.00**
- #555, beaded edge, cutting **30.00**
- #890 Crow's Foot Round, three-footed, cupped up, amber **50.00**
- #890 Crow's Foot Round, three-footed, flat rim, Ruby **150.00**
- Unknown #, all-over Frost etch **140.00**

Candy dish, Black Forest pattern, #210 Regina shape, ebony, silver-enhanced Black Forest etching, silvered finial, rim, and foot edge, 6-1/4" d, 6" h, **$250**. Photo courtesy of Michael Krumme.

Bowl, nappy
- #210 Regina, Black Forest etch, Ebony **130.00**
- #211 Spire, Eden Rose etch **38.00**
- #701 Triumph, 6-1/2", Gothic Garden etch, amber **50.00**

Bowl, **serving**, two handles
- #210 Regina, Black Forest etch, Cheriglo **75.00**
- #220 Largo, 9-1/2", Ruby or light blue **50.00**
- #412 Crow's Foot Square, Opal **75.00**
- #440 Nerva, Ruby **75.00**
- #881 Gadroon, Irwin etch, Ruby **145.00**

Bowl, vegetable, oval, #412 Crow's Foot Square, Ruby **25.00**

Cake salver, stemmed
- #191 Party Line, high foot, green **85.00**
- #210 Regina, Black Forest etch, Ebony **75.00**
- #300 Archaic, low, ftd, Cupid etch, Cheriglo **250.00**
- #411 Mrs. B., Ardith, yellow **70.00**
- #412 Crow's Foot Square, 4-1/2" tall, Opal **100.00**
- #890 Crow's Foot Round, cobalt blue **45.00**

Candy box, cov, flat
- #211 Regina, Harvesters etch, amber **80.00**
- #215 Glades, Spring Orchard etch **50.00**
- #411 Mrs. B., Gothic Garden etch, Cheriglo **225.00**
- #412 Crow's Foot Square, square shape, Ruby **80.00**
- #412 Crow's Foot Square, Orchid etch, Ruby **250.00**
- #412-1/2 Crow's Foot Square, cloverleaf shape, cobalt blue **125.00**
- #440 Nerva, Ruby **170.00**
- #555 7" flat with teardrop finial, blue **25.00**
- #555 heart-shaped, Utopia etch **75.00**

Candy dish, covered, Vermillion, Line 555, crystal, three parts, heart-shaped, floral cutting, 7-1/2", **$35**. Photo courtesy of Rick Hirte, Sparkle Plenty Glassware.

Candy dish, cov, footed
- #191 Party Line, gold encrusted band etch, green **30.00**
- #300 Archaic, Cupid etch, Cheriglo **440.00**
- #555, Gazebo etch, light blue **75.00**
- #555, Trumpet Flower etch **100.00**
- #890 Crow's Foot Round, three-footed, Leeuwen etch **50.00**

Candleholders, pr
- #191 Party Line, dome foot, early blue **25.00**
- #300 Archaic, Ardith etch, mushroom style, green **150.00**
- #411 Mrs. B., keyhole style, Ardith etch, Ebony **95.00**
- #412 Crow's Foot Square, keyhole style, Ruby, silver overlay **50.00**
- #412 Crow's Foot Square, keyhole style, Orchid etch, crystal **65.00**
- #440 Nerva, double, Ruby **125.00**

Cheese and cracker set
- #210 Regina, Black Forest etch, green **145.00**
- #215 Glades, Spring Orchard etch **45.00**
- #220 Largo, cutting **40.00**
- #220 Maya, dome lid, light blue **60.00**

Cigarette box and lid, #220 Largo, Ruby **200.00**

Cocktail shaker

#215 Glades, Spring Orchard etch, gold encrusted etch **55.00**

#902, three-part with strainer, Rooster stopper **85.00**

Compote, footed

#191 Party Line, 6" h, green **15.00**

#210 Regina, Black Forest etch, Cheriglo **85.00**

#211 Spire, 7", Trumpet Flower etch **27.00**

#215 Glades, low foot, 11" cobalt blue **165.00**

#300 Archaic, Cheriglo **35.00**

#300 Archaic, Cupid etch, green **250.00**

#411 Mrs. B., 7-1/2" h, Ebony... **20.00**

#411 Mrs. B, 10" w, 5" h, Gothic Garden etch, Cheriglo or yellow **95.00**

#412 Crow's Foot Square, Mulberry **35.00**

#412 Crow's Foot Square, 9" w, 5" h, Delilah Bird etch **128.00**

#444 Nerva 9" wide **125.00**

#890 Crow's Foot Round, Ruby **50.00**

#890 Crow's Food Round, 6-1/2", green **50.00**

#895 Lucy, Oriental Garden etch, amber **115.00**

Creamer and sugar, set

#90 Chevalier, Ruby **40.00**

#191 Party Line, Cheriglo **40.00**

#210 Regina, Harvesters etch, amber **85.00**

#220 Largo, Garden Magic etch **50.00**

#412 Crow's Foot Square, cobalt blue, silver overlay **80.00**

#412 Crow's Foot Square, Paden Pony etch **85.00**

#701 Triumph, Cupid etch, Cheriglo **300.00**

#777 Comet, light blue **90.00**

#881Gadroon, Irwin etch, Ruby **95.00**

#890 Crow's Foot Round, Forest Green **50.00**

Cream soup

#215 Glades, Mulberry **15.00**

#220 Largo, Ruby **20.00**

#412 Crow's Foot Square, cobalt blue **25.00**

Cruet, stopper, #210 Regina, yellow **40.00**

Cup and saucer

#191 Party Line, Cheriglo **15.00**

#412 Crow's Foot Square, Ruby **15.00**

#412 Crow's Foot Square cup, yellow, Delilah Bird **95.00**

#991 Penny Line, Ruby **20.00**

Decanter

#69 Georgian, cobalt blue **85.00**

#191 Party Line, cordial, Cheriglo **140.00**

#215 Glades, bottle shape, Ruby **85.00**

#215-1/2 Glades, handle, tilt-style, cordial, gold encrusted Spring Orchard etch **50.00**

#991 Penny Line, Ruby **65.00**

Horseshoe shape, Spring Orchard etch, etched "Scotch" or "Rye" **40.00**

Epergne, three pieces, #888, Forest Green **150.00**

Hat, 5-1/2", Trumpet Flower etch.... **75.00**

Ice bucket, metal bail

#191 Party Line, green **40.00**

#902, Cupid etch, green **350.00**

Ice tub, tab handles

#210 Regina, Black Forest etch, Ebony **250.00**

#210 Regina, green **25.00**

#300 Archaic, Cupid etch **300.00**

#300 Archaic, Peacock & Rose etch **110.00**

Lamp, Emeraldglo candlelamp, brass base, cut stars on chimney **70.00**

Mayonnaise comport

#221 Maya, Ruby **42.00**

#300 Archaic, Cupid, green, with orig ladle **100.00**

#411 Mrs. B., Orchid etch, green **65.00**

#412 Crow's Foot Square, Delilah Bird etch, Ruby **175.00**

#701 Triumph, Cupid etch variant, green **175.00**

#890 Crow's Foot Round, with orig liner, cobalt blue **100.00**

Napkin holder, #210 Regina, green **150.00**

Pitcher, Penny Line, #991, ruby, 8" h, **$175.**

Pitcher

#191 Party Line, Eden Rose etch, green **125.00**

#991 Penny Line, cobalt blue, orig label **700.00**

Plate

#221 Maya, 9" dinner **45.00**

#412 Crow's Foot Square, 8-1/2", Orchid etch, cobalt blue **150.00**

#890 Crow's Foot Round, 9" dinner **30.00**

Platter, oval

#412 Crow's Foot Square, cobalt blue **50.00**

#412 Crow's Foot Square, Ruby **35.00**

Powder jar, cov

#191 Party Line, flat, Marie cut, Cheriglo **25.00**

Victory Vanity, (military hat,) amber **40.00**

Samovar, three-piece, all glass, amber **155.00**

Syrup pitcher, #180 with glass lid, applied handle, gold encrusted band etch **35.00**

Tray, center handle

#210 Regina, Black Forest etch, green or Cheriglo **75.00**

#215 Glades, Garden Magic etch **40.00**

#220 Largo, Garden Magic etch **50.00**

#220 Largo, Ruby **55.00**

#300 Archaic, Cupid etch **125.00**

#300 Archaic, Cupid etch, cupped, green **200.00**

#411 Mrs. B., Ardith etch, cupped, Cheriglo or Ebony **85.00**

#411 Mrs. B., Gothic Garden etch, cupped, yellow **170.00**

#412 Crow's Foot Square, cobalt blue **50.00**

#412 Crow's Foot Square, Orchid etch **75.00**

#412 Crow's Foot Square, Orchid etch, green **175.00**

#701 Triumph, Black Forest etch, green **120.00**

#881 Gadroon, Irwin etch **45.00**

#881 Gadroon, Irwin etch, Ruby **95.00**

#890 Crow's Foot Round, platinum Cupid & Venus etch, Ruby **50.00**

#1504 swan-shaped handle, Gazebo etch **35.00**

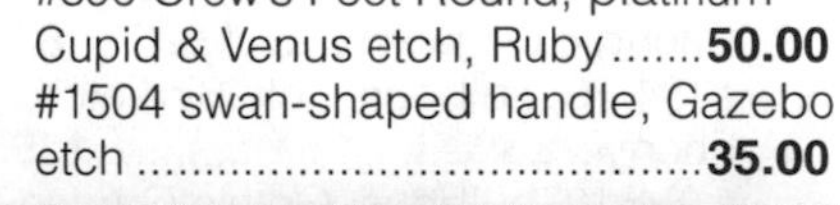

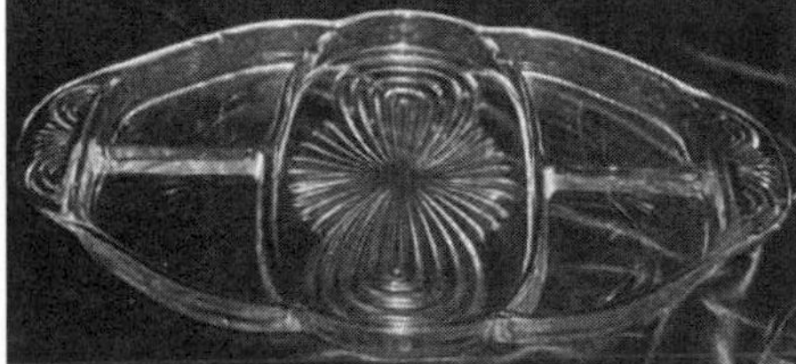

Tray, Largo, #220 line, five parts, crystal, 14" l, 8" w, **$45.**

Tray, two handles

#210 Regina, Black Forest etch, Cheriglo **50.00**

#220 Largo, forest green..........65.00
#221 Maya, Ruby....................95.00
#411 Mrs. B., Ardith Garden, Ebony 65.00
#412 Crow's Foot Square, Opal 75.00
#881 Gadroon, Irwin etch, Ruby 145.00
#890 Crow's Foot Round, cobalt blue 40.00

Tumblers and stemware

#154 Rena tumbler, 9 oz, green 15.00
#191 Party Line, parfait, Cheriglo 20.00
#191 Party Line whiskey, green 6.00
#210 Regina, tumbler, 3-1/2", Black Forest etch, green..........55.00
#215 Glades, water goblet, Ruby 25.00
#890 Crow's Foot Round, tumbler, cobalt blue..........75.00
#991 Penny Line, champagne, cobalt blue..........10.00
#991 Penny Line, whiskey (shot glass), Mulberry..........6.00
#991 Penny Line, low sherbet, Mulberry..........6.00
#994 Popeye & Olive, goblet, Ruby 14.00
Unknown #, 1-1/2 oz whiskey, Black Forest etch, Cheriglo..........110.00

Vases

#180 Butterfly & Zinna, Cheriglo 155.00
#180 Rose Bouquet etch, green 270.00
#182 8" elliptical, Peacock and Rose etch, Cheriglo..........200.00
#182 8" elliptical, Utopia, Ebony 170.00
#182-1/2 5" small elliptical, Ardith etch, Ebony..........185.00
#184 8" bulbous, Ardith etch, Cheriglo..........185.00
#184 10" bulbous, Cupid silver dec, Cheriglo..........250.00
#184 10" bulbous, Daisy etch, Cheriglo or green..........85.00
#184 10" bulbous, Lela Bird etch, Ebony..........125.00
#184 12" bulbous, Gothic Garden etch, Ebony..........200.00
#184 12" bulbous, Lela Bird etch, Ebony, gold encrustation..........235.00
#184 12" bulbous, Peacock & Rose etch, Ruby..........950.00
#184 12" bulbous, Utopia etch, Ebony..........275.00
#191 Party Line, 8" blown, hourglass shape, crimped top, Cheriglo or green..........40.00
#191 Party Line, fan, Cheriglo or green..........35.00
#210 Regina 7" squatty, Ardith etch, Ebony..........175.00
#210 Regina 9" cylinder, Black Forest etch, Ebony..........285.00
#411 9" satin finish, silver overlay lilies and butterfly..........90.00
#412 Crow's Foot Square, 10" cupped rim, Ruby..........110.00
#412 Crow's Foot Square, 12" cupped rim, cobalt blue..........130.00
#503 dome footed, fan, blue satin, Eden Rose etch..........260.00
#881 Gadroon, 12", Trumpet Flower etch with Irwin etch around rim, Ebony..........2,700.00
#994 Popeye & Olive, 7", cobalt blue 80.00
Unknown #, 7-1/2", squat base, slender neck, Delilah Bird etch, Ebony..........365.00
Unknown #, 7-1/2", squat base, slender neck, Orchid etch, Ebony 400.00

Water bottle, #191 Party Line, Cheriglo 60.00

Pairpoint

For more information, see *Warman's Glass*, 4th edition.

History: The Pairpoint Manufacturing Co. was organized in 1880 as a silver-plating firm in New Bedford, Massachusetts. The company merged with Mount Washington Glass Co. in 1894 and became the Pairpoint Corporation. The new company produced specialty glass items, often accented with metal frames.

Pairpoint Corp. was sold in 1939. After becoming manager, Robert Gunderson operated it as the Gunderson Glass Works until his death in 1952. From 1952 until the plant closed in 1956, operations were maintained under the name Gunderson-Pairpoint. Robert Bryden reopened the glass manufacturing business in 1970, with glass production in Sagamore, MA. The Pairpoint Crystal Glass Company is now owned by Robert and June Bancroft, and it continues to produce pressed glass and fine quality blown glasswares.

China

Box, cov, 5" l, 3-1/2" w, 2-1/2" h, raised gold rococo scrolls, reverse on lid with three Palmer Cox Brownies playing cards, Pairpoint-Limoges logo, numbered 750.00

Chocolate pot, 10" h, cream ground, white floral dec, gold trim and scrolls, sgd "Pairpoint Limoges 2500 114" 675.00

Gravy boat and underplate, fancy white china with scrolls, Dresden multicolored flowers, elaborate handle, Limoges, two pcs..........175.00

Plate, 7-3/8" d, hp harbor scene, artist sgd "L. Tripp," fuchsia tinted rim, gold highlights, back sgd "Pairpoint Limoges" 550.00

Lamp, table

12" h, 11" d, mushroom shape, frosted and textured ground, three panels of hp chrysanthemums with yellow outside petals, red inside petals, brown ground, shade marked "PATENTED APRIL 29, 1913," orig brass base with two applied brass handles..........865.00
22" h, 10" d puffy azalea shade, more than 20 pink to pure white azaleas, yellow centers, brown stamens, pale green leaves, dark green ground, four-sided base with raised floral design, four delicate arms dec with vines, green patina, base sgd "Pairpoint Mfg Co., 3049" and "P" in diamond..........16,800.00

Table lamp, 31-1/2" h, 18-3/4" d octagonal shade with basketweave and swag motifs inset with blue, purple and green puffed slag glass panels, base embossed with leaves, base stamped Pairpoint with "P" in diamond/C3066, **$920**. Photo courtesy of David Rago Auctions.

22" h, 13" d open top puffy shade on 10" d ring, well painted red roses on green ground, yellow buds and leaves, well painted, rim marked "PAT. APPLIED FOR," tree trunk base sgd "PAIRPOINT MFG. CO. 3091" plus "P" in diamond mark, chips, very worn patina...2,650.00
22" h, 18" d reverse painted scene of castles, fields, trees and rivers, people in foreground, shade is sgd "THE PAIRPOINT CORP'N," sgd "PAIRPOINT" base, minor wear to base finish 4,025.00
22" h, 18" d reverse painted shade shows marble columns with steps

leading upward to curtain, Roman temple surrounded by water and trees, artist signed "C. DURAND," marked "THE PAIRPOINT CORP'N," three-socket cluster base with bulbous base, sgd "PAIRPOINT," small repaired chip on shade bottom rim, some wear to finish **3,795.00**

31-1/4" h, 18-3/4" d, octagonal shade with basketweave and swag motifs inset with blue, purple, and green puffed slag glass panels, base emb with leaves, base stamped with "P" in diamond/C3066 .... **920.00**

Metal

Castor set, 8" w, 17" h, pr matching cruets, sp holder with birds, flowers and stylized designs, marked "Pairpoint Mgf 1099, x799, Quadruple Plate" **625.00**

Lamp base

12" h, 8" d ring, patinated metal, quatrefoil wirework supporting shade ring, ribbed standard with applied foliate handles and feet, bronze patina on white metal, imp "Pairpoint Mfg Co., "P" in diamond and "30031/2" on base, worn patina.........**400.00**

Pitcher, Alexandrite, blue shading to amber, applied amber handle and foot, rough pontil, 6-3/4" h, **$575**. Photo courtesy of James D. Julia.

15" h, patinated metal, two-socket fixture, four-sided shaft and lobe base, bronze patina on white metal, imp "Pairpoint Mfg Co.," "P" in diamond, and "B3040" on base, patina wear.............................**350.00**

Trophy, 7" d, 8-1/2" h, copper, two fancy handles, feather design, plaque inscribed "New Bedford Yacht Club Ocean Race won by Nutmeg for the fastest time, Aug. 5, 1909," base marked "Pairpoint Mfg Co.," "P" in diamond mark, numbered **400.00**

Glass

Basket, 10-1/2" l, 5-1/2" w, 7-1/4" h, folded-in sides, designed as lotus leaves, striated veins, twisted handle, ext. painted pastel green, raised gold lotus blossoms, cream-colored int........ **385.00**

Box, cov, 7-1/2" x 6-1/4", hinged, white, orig silk lining........................... **1,195.00**

Bride's basket, 8" d ruffled cranberry opalescent bowl, 9" h stand **395.00**

Candlestick

10" h, Auroria, colorless controlled bubble ball connectors, pr **550.00**

10-3/4" h, Auroria, shape 1600 ....**225.00**

11" h, amethyst, shape 1600, very lightly ribbed, polished pontil **130.00**

16" h, light green, shape B1811 ....**525.00**

Compote, cov, 13" h, amethyst, colorless controlled bubble ball connector and finial **525.00**

Compote, open, 4-3/4" h, 7-1/4" d, Auroria, Blackberry pattern bowl, colorless bubble ball connector, foot engraved with vine pattern, shape B-228 .... **345.00**

Cornucopia, 5-1/2" d, 11-1/2" h, red, shape 6991.................................. **185.00**

Cracker jar, cov, 6-3/4" h, 7-1/2" w, Mt. Washington opalware, pistachios green top and bottom, 3-1/2" w band of deep pink and red roses, green leaves, gold trim, fancy silver-plated cov, handle, and bail, cov sgd "Pairpoint -3912," base sgd "3912-268"................................... **725.00**

Dish, fish shape, teal blue, controlled bubbles dec, late **275.00**

Perfume bottle, 6-3/4" h, amethyst, painted butterfly, teardrop stopper, "P" in diamond mark **375.00**

Pitcher, 6-3/4" h, Alexandrite, blue shading to amber, applied amber handle and foot, rough pontil **575.00**

Pokal, cov, 14" h, Chrysopras, dark yellow-green, wheelcut grapes and leaves, finial wheelcut with eight-petaled flower... **625.00**

Top hat, peach blow, hp Queens Lace pattern, sgd, c1950...................... **500.00**

Vase, 10-1/4" h, cobalt blue, swirled body, colorless controlled bubble ball connector **300.00**

PAPER EPHEMERA

History: Maurice Rickards, author of *Collecting Paper Ephemera*, suggests that ephemera are the "minor transient documents of everyday life," material destined for the wastebasket but never quite making it. This definition is more fitting than traditional dictionary definitions that emphasize time, e.g., "lasting a very short time." A driver's license, which is used for a year or longer, is as much a piece of ephemera as is a ticket to a sporting event or music concert. The transient nature of the object is the key.

Collecting ephemera has a long and distinguished history. Among the English pioneers were John Seldon (1584-1654), Samuel Pepys (1633-1703), and John Bagford (1650-1716). Large American collections can be found at historical societies and libraries across the country, and museums, e.g., Wadsworth Athenaeum, Hartford, CT, and the Museum of the City of New York.

When used by collectors, "ephemera" usually means paper objects, e.g., billheads and letterheads, bookplates, documents, labels, stocks and bonds, tickets, and valentines. However, more and more ephemera collectors are recognizing the transient nature of some three-dimensional material, e.g., advertising tins and pinback buttons. Today's specialized paper shows include dealers selling other types of ephemera in both two- and three-dimensional form.

Additional Listings: See Advertising Trade Cards, Catalogs, Comic Books, Photographs, Postcards, and Sports Cards. Also see Calendars, Catalogs, Magazines, Newspapers, Postcards, and Sheet Music in *Warman's Americana & Collectibles*.

Calendar, 1941, K & L Lumber, shows bungalow styles, **$18.**

Bookmarks

Advertising

Bell Pianos, Art Nouveau woman, multicolored...............................**12.00**

Palmer Violets Bloom Perfume, gold trim **15.00**

Youth's Companion, 1902, multicolored, 2-3/4" x 6" **8.00**

Cross-stitch on punched paper, Black Emancipation, black couple dancing, 1860s, 3-7/8" x 1-1/2" **40.00**

Calendars

1886, Middlesex Fire Insurance, Concord, MA, 11" x 5-1/2" **100.00**

1889, Great Lake images, set of 12 postcards, each 5" x 7" **65.00**

1892, diecut, child peering through window surrounded by garlands of flowers, berries, full pad **95.00**

1893, Aetna, scene of sailing ship on lake, volcano in background, full pad **110.00**

1894, Prang, folding **35.00**

1896, folding, four seasons **40.00**

1897, Maude Humphrey, four diecut figures of Japanese girls, each holding fans with calendar pages, 13" x 8" **125.00**

1907, Odds and Ends, Tuck, postcard type **350.00**

1916, Putnam Dyes **40.00**

1913, Lucky Year **60.00**

1918, Jan/Feb/March, Swifts Premium, soldier saying good-bye to his love, "The Girl I Leave Behind," illus by Haskell Coffin, 15" x 8-1/4" **100.00**

1923, Winona, F. A. Rettke, Indian Princess on cliff overlooking body of water, full pad, 6-1/2" w, 21-1/2" l ... **50.00**

1932, Betsy Ross sewing flag, George Washington looking on, full calendar pad, large size **35.00**

1934, Enchanted Garden, Liberty Furniture Co., Peoria, IL **50.00**

1948, Esquire, pin-up, 9" x 12" **135.00**

Calling cards

Acme Card Co., Ivoryton, Conn, Agents' Pocket Sample Book **28.00**

Clara A. Shaw, diecut, one corner appears as if turned down, small bouquet **4.50**

Clara M. Brigmeyer, pansies dec ... **4.00**

Jennie M. Koch, pretty little girl among flowers **3.50**

Madam E. Jordan, human hair goods **12.00**

Rose Drey, Easton, PA, rose motif, green background **4.00**

William Shott, horseshoe and floral motif **5.00**

Wilmer E. Shaw, hand holding dove motif **4.50**

Diecuts

Black

- Child, dressed in colonial garb, holding basket in one hand, bouquet of flowers in other **75.00**

Music folio, including "Lincoln's Funeral March," copyright 1865, $450. Photo courtesy of Joy Luke Auctions.

- Child, in washtub **65.00**
- Musician, playing fiddle, white coat with red polka dots **115.00**

Hurdy Gurdy man, 11" h **70.00**

Pickle, Heintz, child holding product, 5" h, set of 12 .... **415.00**

Santa

- Riding gray horse, 12" h, minor losses **75.00**
- Standing, holding tree, pack of toys over shoulder, 10" h **85.00**
- Standing, red robe, holding tree, pack of toys over shoulder, emb, glued paper remnant on back **145.00**

Yellow Kid, adv New York evening paper **350.00**

Greeting cards

Christmas

- Everybody "knows" I wish you a merry Xmas, black man in scarf pulling nose of black man, mechanical **60.00**
- Prang, c1881, "Prang's American Fourth Prize Christmas Card by Rosina Emmett" printed on back, 9" x 5-1/2" **65.00**

Sample book, Victorian cards, c1900 .... **250.00**

Miscellaneous

Broadside

- Auction! Boot & Shoe Factory, Stable with Stock, Brockton, MA, late 19th C, framed, creases, 13-3/8" w, 19-1/4" h **60.00**
- Ford's Theater, April 14th, 1865, Benefit and Last Night of Miss Laura Keene, partial printers signature "H. Polkinhorn & Son, Washington, DC," black lettering on white, night Lincoln was assassinated, fold lines, tars, glued to backing, 18-1/4" x 5-3/4", contemporary frame **2,420.00**

Fan, adv for New Home Sewing Machines, litho, medallions of young boy and girl wearing elaborate hats, 14" h **65.00**

Mask, diecut, emb litho, half face, young black man with straw hat, 12" l **230.00**

Menu, Collation at Norombega Hall, Bangor, Wednesday, Oct. 18, 1871 to the President of the United States, the Governor-General of Canada...Upon the Formal Opening of the European & North America Railway, four pgs, decorative stick, 8" x 5-1/4" **95.00**

Needle book, The Dirigible Needle Book, shows dirigible flying over New York skyline, Statue of Liberty **15.00**

Package, pyrotechnic toy balloon, showing "War Balloon as used in South Africa," text relating to Lord Roberts, c1900, 6-1/2" h **25.00**

Paper dolls, Aunt Jemima pancake flour, showing Aunt Jemima and family before and after recipe sold, diecut, 12" l **1,495.00**

Program, Richland Library Literary Society, Benefit Musical, opens, lists musical selections, poems to be read, black and white **5.00**

Puzzle, White Rose Tea, orig envelope, 7" x 9" **25.00**

Receipt, 7" x 8-1/2", Lake George House and Steamer Minnehaha, dated July 28, 1859 .... **165.00**

Theater program, Oxford Theater, c1894, tri-fold, 9-1/2" **165.00**

Ticket, Twelfth Annual Ball, Volunteer Engine Co., Ladies Ticket, rose dec, calling card size **5.00**

Program, Ringling Bros & Barnum & Bailey circus, 1955, full-color cover, $15.

Newspaper

1876, June 25, Custer's Massacre, but not reported in newspapers until July 7 and later **260.00**

1909, Dayton Daily News, Wright Brothers Welcome Home, framed **160.00**

1912, April 15, Titantic hits iceberg and sinks **600.00**
1927, May 21, Lindbergh successfully lands in Paris **170.00**
1934, July 13, Babe Ruth hits his 700th homerun **40.00**

Scraps

Album, 49 leaves with cards pasted on each side, over 350 images, 11" x 14" **520.00**
Victorian, friendship token, paper and foil baskets of flowers, shadowbox frame
- 3-1/4" x 2-1/2", "Out of Gratitude," reverse glass painted edges **175.00**
- 4" x 3", "Think of Me," reverse glass painted edge **275.00**
- 4-1/4" x 3-1/2", reverse glass painted edge, wear **220.00**
- 4-1/4" x 5", blue "Think of Me," wear **225.00**
- 4-3/4" x 3-1/2", reverse painted scalloped edges, wear **195.00**
- 4-3/4" x 5", red "As a Remembrance," damage **215.00**
- 5" x 3-3/4", reverse painted scalloped edges, wear **215.00**

PAPERWEIGHTS

History: Although paperweights had their origin in ancient Egypt, it was in the mid-19th century that this art form reached its zenith. The finest paperweights were produced between 1834 and 1855 in France by the Clichy, Baccarat, and Saint Louis factories. Other paperweights made in England, Italy, and Bohemia during this period rarely match the quality of the French paperweights.

For more information, see *Warman's Glass*, 4th edition.

In the early 1850s, the New England Glass Co. in Cambridge, Massachusetts, and the Boston and Sandwich Glass Co. in Sandwich, Massachusetts, became the first American factories to make paperweights.

Popularity peaked during the classic period (1845-1855) and faded toward the end of the 19th century. Paperweight production was rediscovered nearly a century later in the mid-1900s. Baccarat, Saint Louis, Perthshire, and many studio craftsmen in the U.S. and Europe still make contemporary weights.

Antique

Baccarat, France, 19th C
- Pansy, deep purple upper petals, black striped purple and yellow lower petals, stardust and bull's eye center cane, stalk, yellow and purple bud, green leaves, 3-3/16" d **1,100.00**

Antique, Abraham Lincoln portraits, left: black and white marbleized background, black and white etching of Lincoln in center, **$50**; right: cobalt blue background, sulphide bust portrait, **$65**. Photo courtesy of Joy Luke Auctions.

- Stardust carpet ground, six-pointed star, arrow, whorl, cog, shamrock, and trefoil canes, coral, orange, yellow, plum, cadmium green, cobalt blue, ruby, and turquoise, sea of red and white stardust canes, silhouette canes including primrose portrait cane, signature cane "B 1848," 3-1/8" d **11,000.00**
- Wallflower garland, five white petals outlined in ruby, red, white, and blue cog, six-pointed cane center, emerald green leaves, white upset muslin ground inside cobalt blue, emerald green, white, and ruby arrow and six-point cane garland, 2-7/8" d **1,150.00**

Clichy, France, 19th C
- Chequer, complex millefiori canes centered by pink and green Clichy rose, all divided by white latticinio twists, 2-3/4" d, 2" h **1,265.00**
- Garland, pink central rose cane, blue millefiori circlet, pink garlands, 2-3/8" d **375.00**
- Mushroom, close concentric design, large central pink and green rose surrounded by pin, white, cobalt blue, and cadmium green complex millefiori, middle row of canes with 10 green and white roses alternating with pink pastry mold canes, pin and white stems, 2-3/4" d **6,600.00**
- Swirled, alternating cobalt blue and white pinwheels emanating from green and pink rose cane, 2-9/16" d **7,200.00**

Degenhart, John, window, red crystal cube with yellow and orange upright center lily, one to window, four side windows, bubble in center of flower's stamens, 3-3/16" x 2-1/4" x 2-1/4" **1,225.00**
Gillinder, orange turtle with moving appendages in hollow center, pale orange ground, molded dome, 3-1/16" d **500.00**
Millville, umbrella pedestal, red, white, green, blue, and yellow int., bubble in sphere center, 3-1/8" d, 3-3/8" h **800.00**
New England Glass Co.
- Apple, three dimensional, yellow, rose peach blush, yellow stem, green glass stamp on blossom end, 3" d **1,100.00**
- Fruit bouquet, five pears, four cherries, green leaves, white double-swirl latticinio basket, 2-3/4" d **400.00**
- Poinsettia, double tier of pointed petals, swirled matched center, furled ruby bud, spring green leaves, white double swirl latticinio bed, 2-11/16" d **1,100.00**

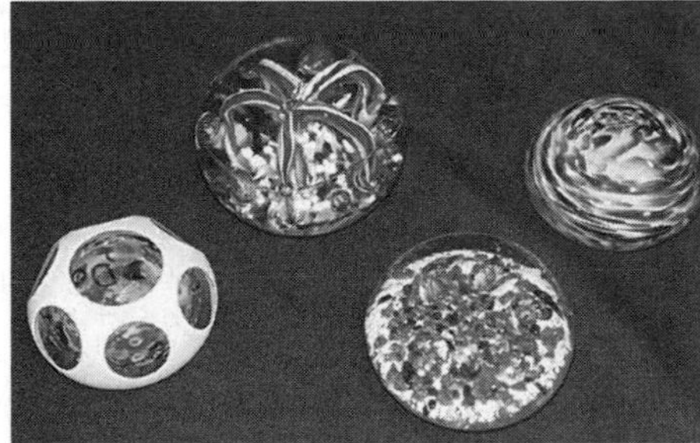

Four glass paperweights with multi-colored internal designs, **$110**. Photo courtesy of Joy Luke Auctions.

Pinchbeck, armed men riding on horseback through woods, young boy leading girl by arm, ftd, 3-1/4" d **650.00**
Sandwich Glass Co.
- Dahlia, c1870, red petaled flower, millefiori cane center, bright green leafy stem, highlighted by trapped bubble dec, white latticino ground, 2-1/2" d, 1-3/4" h **650.00**
- Poinsettia, double, red flower with double tier of petals, green and white Lutz rose, green stem and leaves, bubbles between petals, 3" d **1,200.00**

St. Louis
- Fruit basket, red and green ripening fruits, latticino base basket, central base cane, 3" d, 2-1/2" h **1,150.00**
- Pompon, pink flower, segmented C-shaped petals, millefiori center with tiny ruby figure eight shaped canes, ruby bed, variegated spring green leaves, white double swirled latticinio ground, 3-3/16" d **4,125.00**
- Queen Victoria, c1840, sulfide portrait sgd "Victoria" in blue at base, 3-1/2" d, 2-1/2" h, few small inclusions **750.00**

Val St. Lambert, patterned millefiori, four red, white, blue, pistachio, and turquoise complex canes circlets spaced around central pink, turquoise and cadmium green canes circlet, canes set on stripes of lace encircled by spiraling red and blue torsade, minor blocking crease, 3-1/2" d **950.00**

Modern, Rick Ayotte, two chickadees sitting on holly leaves, berries on ground of fallen snow, signed, dated 1990, 3-1/2" d, **$865**. Photo courtesy of Alderfer Auction Co.

Modern

Ayotte, Rick, Paradisa Butterfly, bouquet of pale pink, yellow, and white roses, dark green leaves and stems, sgd "Rick Ayotte LE-35 '98," 1998, 3-3/4" d **700.00**

Baccarat, Gridel pelican cane surrounded by five concentric rings of yellow, pink, green, and white complex canes, pink canes contain 18 Gridel silhouette canes, lace ground, 1973 date cane, signature cane, sgd and dated, limited ed. of 350, 3-1/16" d **850.00**

Banford, Bob, cornflower, blue flower, yellow center, pink and white twisted torsade, "B" cane at stem, 3" d **550.00**

D'Albret, sulphide cameo of Albert Schweitzer, translucent dark purple ground, diamond cut base, six and one faceting, dated, 1969, 2-7/8" d..... **165.00**

Kaziun, Charles, concentric millefiori, heart, turtle silhouette, shamrocks, six-pointed stars, and floret canes encircled by purple and white torsade, turquoise ground flecked with goldstone, K signature cane, 2-1/16" d **1,200.00**

Labino, free form, white, amber, and irid gold flower center, air bubbles, surrounded by green glass, sgd "Labino 1969," 2-1/2" d.............................. **210.00**

Orient and Flume, red butterfly with blue and white accents, brown and green vines, white millefiori blossoms over dark ground, 3-1/2" d, dated 1977, orig sticker and box **235.00**

Modern, Perthshire, central dark green seaweed, yellow coral and three fish, one facet on top, two rows of facets on sides, signature cane, dated 1998, 3-1/4" d, **$350**.

Parabelle, Five rows of concentrically arranged canes around larger center rose cane, closely packed white millefiori ground, signature/date cane, 2-3/8" d **425.00**

Perthshire, crown, blue and red twisted ribbons alternating with white filigree spokes, complex millefiori center cane, sgd "P1969" in canes on base, 1969, 3" d **660.00**

Rosenfeld, Ken
- Apples and Blossom, three red apples, pink blossoms, two buds, "R" signature cane, 1989, 2-3/4" d **365.00**
- Monarch butterfly, leafy stem, red blossom with three buds, R signature cane, inscribed "KR 2001," 1-7/8" h, 2-5/8" h **350.00**

Stankard, Paul, Flowering Seed Pod with Insects and Berries, red berries, white and yellow flowers, ants, bee, figural roots, word canes "Seeds" and "Fertile," inscribed "Paul J Stankard 2000 M5," 2-1/2" h, 3-1/4" h **3,220.00**

Modern, Saint Louis, spray of flowers lying on white base, yellow, pink, white, light blue, and cobalt blue flowers, green leaves, signed, dated 1988, 3-1/2" d, **$575**. Photo courtesy of Alderfer Auction Co.

St Clair, Joe
- Crocus.................................. **300.00**
- Pedestal rose, etched and faceted **4,250.00**
- Rose, irid **850.00**
- Rose, pink, small **600.00**

St Clair, Maude and Bob
- Apple, pink highlighted art glass **475.00**
- Bumble bee on lily pad, sulphide **250.00**
- Mouse, sulphide, etched and faceted **600.00**
- Pedestal, two pcs, multicolored **500.00**

St Clair, Paul, faceted and controlled bubble, clear, sgd "Paul St. Clair" **500.00**

Tarsitano, Debbie, orange and purple bird of paradise flower on stalk, striped green leaves, star cut ground, DT signature cane, 2-15/16" d **550.00**

Trabucco, Victor, Buffalo, NY, Chinese red rose, four buds, green leaves, sgd cane, 1987, 3" d **635.00**

Whitefrairs, Star of David, five rows of tightly packed blue and white millefiori canes, 3" d.................................... **395.00**

Modern, Paul Ysart, double-tiered pink and green flower, white millefiori center, green leaves, and curved stem, encircled by purple and white complex millefiori garland, translucent dark purple ground, "PY" signature cane in center of flower, 3" d, **$750**. Photo courtesy of Alderfer Auction Co.

Ysart, Paul, green fish, yellow eye, yellow and white jasper ground encircled by pink, green, and white complex cane garland, PY signature cane.......... **550.00**

PAPIER-MÂCHÉ

History: Papier-mâché is a mixture of wood pulp, glue, resin, and fine sand, which is subjected to great pressure and then dried. The finished product is tough, durable, and heat resistant. Various finishing treatments are used, such as enameling, japanning, lacquering, mother-of-pearl inlaying, and painting.

During the Victorian era, papier-mâché articles such as boxes, trays, and tables were in high fashion. Banks, candy containers, masks, toys, and other children's articles were also made of papier-mâché.

Advertising display, figural bulldog, Claytons Dog Remedies............ **1,165.00**

Box, cov, 3" d, round, black lacquer with hand-painted decoupage print of people in boat fishing **50.00**

Candy container, 5-1/2" h, turkey, polychrome dec **45.00**

Cat, 4" h, black, Halloween type, head only **350.00**

Halloween lantern, black cat, **$65**.

Fan, 15-1/2" l, demilune, scalloped border, turned wooden handle, one side painted with variety of ferns on ochre ground, black japanning on other side, Victorian, late 19th C, price for pr **250.00**

Milliner's model, attributed to France, early 19th C

14-3/4" h, green, yellow, and white striped cap, name "Delphine" painted in script in oval on base, crack, some repaint **1,645.00**

16" h, applied lithographed paper eyebrows, eyes, and mouth, wear **1,000.00**

Nodder, 10-1/2" l, elephant, flocked finish, hp details, wooden tusks, felt riding blanket........ **60.00**

Notebook, 11-1/2" x 9-1/2", black lacquered ground, dec with floral arrangement, mother-of-pearl vines, hand painted accents, int. with notebook with some sketches, blank pages **295.00**

Pip-squeak, 4-1/4" h, rooster, orig paint, yellow, orange, and black, recovered wooden bellows, faint squeak....... **85.00**

Numismatist's chest, French, 19th C, rectangular, exterior with black finish, ogee base, lid opening to red painted interior containing 109 blue paper-wrapped deal labeling bars, most inked with titles in French such as "Monnaie de Cuivre," "Francois I (1544-1545)," etc., red painted front of case with 18 small drawers labeled A through T with small twine pulls, decorative roundels of the Vatican, and Colosseum painted on sides, 24-1/2" w, 13" d, 17-1/4" h, **$1,000**. Photo courtesy Skinner, Inc.

Plate, 12" d, painted cat, marked "Patented August 8, 1880"........ **35.00**

Roly-poly, 11-1/2" h, Punch-type clown, hp, German **375.00**

Sign, "Eat-it-all Vanilla" ice cream cone shape, flared top **200.00**

Snuffbox, 3-7/8" d, round, lid painted with interior genre scene of family with baby, interior lid painted with title "Die Tanzpuppen," painted mark "StabwassersFabrik in Braunschweig," German, late 19th/early 20th C **460.00**

Table, 26" w, 21" d, 27" h, oval tilt top, serpentine borders, top inlaid with mother-of-pearl, elaborate painted floral spray, circular stem, shaped circular base, cast iron feet, Victorian, mid-19th C **450.00**

Tray, 12" d, Victorian, English, mid-19th C, round, black ground, large central scene of Master of Hounds seated on bobtail bay in wooded setting, house in background, gold scroll painted rim **980.00**

Tray and stand, 30" l, 24" w tray, 11-1/4" w, oval, black ground, large central scene with two scarlet-coated huntsmen, one standing, other seated on bobtail chestnut with black foal on a hill, border with gilt transfer printed guilloche border, Mark Knowles & Son maker, English Registry mark for 1864, burl hardwood 6-1/4" d, 18-3/4" h stand........ **1,250.00**

Parian Ware

History: Parian ware is a creamy white, translucent porcelain that resembles marble. It originated in England in 1842 and was first called "statuary porcelain." Minton and Copeland have been credited with its development; Wedgwood also made it. In America, parian ware objects were manufactured by Christopher Fenton in Bennington, Vermont.

At first, parian ware was used only for figures and figural groups. By the 1850s, it became so popular that a vast range of items was manufactured.

Figure, Homer, partially draped adult male and youth figures mounted atop oval base, England, c1870, 13-1/2" h, **$1,000**. Photo courtesy of Skinner, Inc.

Bust

15" h, Alexandra, mounted on waisted circular socle, raised title, imp mark, published date, sculptor Mary Thornycroft and Art Union of London, Copeland, c1868 ..... **450.00**

24" h, Lord Byron, mounted on waisted circular socle, Copeland, c1870, imp mark **1,775.00**

Creamer, 5" h, Tulip pattern, relief dec **100.00**

Doll, 18-1/2" h, Countess Dagmar, shoulder head, café au lait molded hair with side-swept wings to comb and curls in back, curls on forehead held by molded band, blue painted eyes, pierced ears, cloth body, brown leather arms, blue plaid wool dress, orig underwear, blue leather shoes, c1870........ **250.00**

Figure, Milton, standing figure, modeled leaning on pedestal topped with stack of books, England, c1870, 14" h, **$600**. Photo courtesy of Skinner, Inc.

Figure

11" h, Dorothea, female modeled seated on rock, from design by John Bell, Minton, c1860........ **450.00**

11-1/2" h, 9" l, Maenad seated on lion skin, staff at feet, child on her lap, wine cup, one foot damaged . **275.00**

13-1/2" h, Clorinda, modeled by John Bell, incised sculptor and imp cipher mark, Minton, c1868, shallow foot-rim chips........ **500.00**

13-1/2" h, Homer, partially draped adult and youth male figures mounted on oval base, unmarked, England, c1860........ **1,000.00**

15-1/4" h, Miranda, by John Bell, female figure seated on rocky base, shell and waves at her feet, impressed Minton ciphers, artist and title, c1857........ **560.00**

17" h, Go to Sleep, young girl with dog on her lap, by J. Durham, imp Art Union of London, sculptor, date and Copeland factory mark, England, c1862, finger and end of dog's tail restored, fitted on brass base **360.00**

18-3/4" h, modeled classical male and female subjects walking arm in arm, England, c1870........ **775.00**

18-3/4" h, Niaid, modeled partially draped female figure seated on rock, one arm supported by V-shaped branch, by Pradier, unmarked, England, c1870, base rim chips **950.00**

19-1/4", Wood Nymph, modeled as seated nude female with deer and fawn, inscribed sculptor C.B. Birch, England, c1865, tip of one hoof repaired........ **1,530.00**

20-1/4" h, classical female, modeled as partially draped female with putti by her feet, England, c1875, hairline, foot restored at ankle **1,880.00**

20-1/4" h, Niobe and Daughter, title incised on base, England, c1870, shallow foot-rim chips **1,000.00**

20-3/4" h, Temperance, standing figure holding pitcher for pouring water into wine ewer by her feet, modeled by Filippo Della Valle, Minton, imp 1874 date cipher, foot-rim chip to backside............... **825.00**
22" h, Reaper and The Flowers, winged female figure modeled holding baby in her arms, imp title, L.A. Malempre SC, Ceramic and Crystal Palace Art Union, publish date, Copeland factory mark, c1875, finger missing, chip to side of base **1,175.00**
24-1/2" h, Chastity, standing figure, circular base, imp title, J. Durham SC, published date 1865, Copeland factory mark, shallow footrim chip **885.00**

Figure, mother and first-born, by A. Carrier-Belleuse, incised artist and impressed mark, Minton, England, c1872, 12-1/4", **$1,775.** Photo courtesy of Skinner, Inc.

Plaque, 6" d, relief, angels, brass frames, orig German labels, Boston retailers label, pr.......................... **275.00**
Urn, cov, 20" h, classical shape, allegorical scene in low relief, three Graces, temples, revelers, and centaur, fish scale pattern on pedestal base, double scrolled handles, fruit finial, base marked with crown with ribbon and "FB" **250.00**
Vase, 10" h, applied white monkey type figures, grape clusters at shoulders, blue ground, c1850, pr........................ **265.00**

Pate-De-Verre

History: The term "pate-de-verre" can be translated simply as "glass paste." It is manufactured by grinding lead glass into a powder or crystal form, making it into a paste by adding a two percent or three percent solution of sodium silicate, molding, firing, and carving. The Egyptians discovered the process as early as 1500 B.C.

For more information, see *Warman's Glass*, 4th edition.

In the late 19th century, the process was rediscovered by a group of French glassmakers. Almaric Walter, Henri Cros, Georges Despret, and the Daum brothers were leading manufacturers.

Contemporary sculptors are creating a second renaissance, led by the technical research of Jacques Daum.

Bookends, pr, 6-1/2" h, Buddha, yellow amber pressed molded design, seated in lotus position, inscribed "A Walter Nancy" **2,450.00**
Bowl, 3-3/8" h, squatty form, mottled brown translucent glass, inscribed "Daum (cross) Nancy" on side..... **300.00**
Clock, 4-1/2" sq, stars within pentagon and tapered sheaves motif, orange and black, molded sgd "G. Argy-Rousseau," clock by J. E. Caldwell **2,750.00**
Compote, 5-1/4" d, 3-1/2" h, lime green, sgd "A. WALTER NANCY" **1,900.00**
Dish, 5" l, leaf shape, salamander, yellow, aqua-green, and violet, inscribed "Daum France" **300.00**

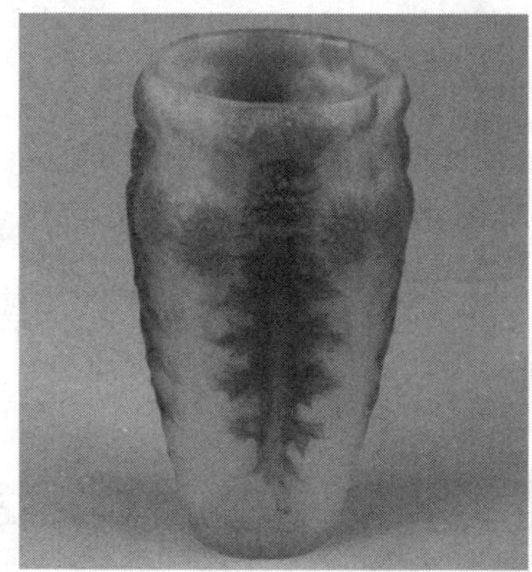
Vase, embossed red thistles and green leaves, stamped "ARGY ROUSSEAU 8442," 3-1/2" d, 6" h, **$4,900**. Photo courtesy of David Rago Auctions, Inc.

Figure, 4-3/4" l, mouse, translucent blue, green, and rust, inscribed "Daum France" **250.00**
Jewelry, earrings, pr, 2-3/4" l, teardrop form, molded violet and rose-shaded tulip blossom, suspended from rose-colored swirl molded circle **2,200.00**
Paperweight, 3/4" w, 1-1/4" h, large beetle, green leaves, mottled blue ground, intaglio "AW" mark **6,800.00**
Sculpture, 9-5/8" l, crab in sea grasses, lemon yellow, chocolate brown, pale mauve, and sea green, sgd "A. Walter/Nancy" and "Berge/SC" **8,500.00**
Tray, 6-3/4" d, lizard on leaves, sgd "A. Walter Nancy"........................... **5,750.00**
Vase, 10" h, 8" w, purple and black wolves, shaded purple, lavender, and green ground, white snow dec, sgd "G. Argy-Rousseau" **48,875.00**
Veilleuse, 8-1/2" h, Gabriel Argy-Rousseau, press molded oval lamp shade, frosted mottled gray glass, elaborate purple arches with three teardrop-shaped windows of yellow, center teal-green stylized blossoms on black swirling stems, imp "G. Arty-Rousseau" at lower edge, wrought iron frame, three ball feet centering internal lamp socket, conforming iron cover **6,900.00**

Pate-Sur-Pate

History: Pate-sur-pate, paste-on-paste, is a 19th-century porcelain-decorating method featuring relief designs achieved by painting layers of thin pottery paste one on top of the other.

For more information, see *Warman's English & Continental Pottery & Porcelain*, 3rd edition.

About 1880, Marc Solon and other Sevres artists, inspired by a Chinese celadon vase in the Ceramic Museum at Sevres, experimented with this process. Solon immigrated to England at the outbreak of the Franco-Prussian War and worked at Minton, where he perfected pate-sur-pate.

Vase, classical shape, polychrome birds on a branch, marked "Doulton/Lambeth/Feb/264/FCMD," 1880s, 7" h, **$575**. Photo courtesy of David Rago Auctions, Inc.

Box, cov, 5-3/4" d, round, white female portrait, blue ground, Limoges, France, late 19th C **690.00**
Bud vase, 4-3/8" h, gourd shape, irid mother-of-pearl ground, raised gilt foliate framed cartouche, central pale mauve roundel featuring white painted female figure blowing bubbles, Germany, 20th C **290.00**
Centerpiece, 16" l, elongated parian vessel, molded scroll handles and feet, pierced rim, two brown reserves, white pate-sur-pate amorini, gilding, dec attributed to Lawrence Birks, marked "Minton," retailer's mark of Thomas Goode & Co., Ltd., London, c1889 .... **1,400.00**
Dresser jar, 3-3/4" d, ovoid, cobalt blue ground, lid with pate-sure-pate profile bust of classical woman, gilt banding, Meissen, Germany, early 20th C **1,955.00**

Lamp base, 10-1/4" h, Chinoiserie-style, black ground moon flask with pate-sur-pate and blue-printed dec of village scenes, mounted on gilt-metal beaded and scroll ftd base, 20th C, price for pr **490.00**

Medallion, 2-3/8" x 3-3/8", oval, blue ground, white relief cherub figure, unidentified factory mark on reverse, France, 19th C, edge ground....... **320.00**

Plaque, rectangle, pale blue ground, white slip decoration of female and putti, France, 19th C, set in modern gilt-wood frame, no visible marks, 5-3/4" x 7-1/2" plaque, **$550**. Photo courtesy of Skinner, Inc.

Plaque

- 7-5/8" d, one with maiden and cupid spinning web, other with maiden seated on bench with whip in one hand, sunflowers stalked with humanistic snail on other, artist sgd "Louis Solin," both marked on back, framed, pr........ **2,500.00**
- 15" l, demi-lune shape, green ground, white slip, central figure of Venus holding mirror in each hand, fending off two groups of putti with their reflections, artist sgd Louis Solin, rosewood frame......... **9,200.00**

Plate, 9-1/8" d, deep brown ground, gilt trim, white dec of nude child behind net supported by two small trees, artist monogram sgd "Henry Saunders," printed and imp Moore Brothers factory marks, c1885........ **750.00**

Tile, 7" l, 5" w, sword wielding warrior on horseback, cobalt blue ground, sgd "Limoges France" in gold script, mounted in antique frame........ **220.00**

Urn, 8" h, double handles, pedestal base, portrait medallion, pale green ground, ivory trim, gilt accents........ **250.00**

Vase

- 6-1/2" h, cov, two handles, deep teal blue ground, gilt framed gray ground panel with white slip dec of reclining maiden, artist sgd Albione Birks, printed Minton factory marks, c1900, shallow restored chip on cov **1,840.00**
- 13-3/4" h, cov, dark brown ground, white slip of partially draped female figure holding flowering branch, shaped tripod base, gilt dec at rim, artist sgd Louis Solon, printed and imp marks, 1898, rim cover damage, minor gilt wear........ **2,300.00**

Pattern Glass

For more information, see *Warman's Pattern Glass* and *Warman's Glass*, 4th edition.

History: Pattern glass is clear or colored glass pressed into one of hundreds of patterns. Deming Jarves of the Boston and Sandwich Glass Co. invented one of the first successful pressing machines in 1828. By the 1860s, glass-pressing machinery had been improved, and mass production of good-quality matched tableware sets began. The idea of a matched glassware table service (including goblets, tumblers, creamers, sugars, compotes, cruets, etc.) quickly caught on in America. Many pattern glass table services had numerous accessory pieces such as banana stands, molasses cans, and water bottles.

Early pattern glass (flint) was made with a lead formula, giving many items a ringing sound when tapped. Lead became too valuable to be used in glass manufacturing during the Civil War, and in 1864, Hobbs, Brockunier & Co., West Virginia, developed a soda lime (non-flint) formula. Pattern glass also was produced in transparent colors, milk glass, opalescent glass, slag glass, and custard glass.

The hundreds of companies that produced pattern glass experienced periods of development, expansions, personnel problems, material and supply demands, fires, and mergers. In 1899, the National Glass Co. was formed as a combine of 19 glass companies in Pennsylvania, Ohio, Indiana, West Virginia, and Maryland. U.S. Glass, another consortium, was founded in 1891. These combines resulted from attempts to save small companies by pooling talents, resources, and patterns. Because of this pooling, the same pattern often can be attributed to several companies.

Reproduction Alert: Pattern glass has been widely reproduced. Items in the listing marked with this symbol—ϕ— are those for which reproductions are known to exist. Care should be exercised when purchasing such pieces.

Additional Listings: Bread Plates, Children's Toy Dishes, Cruets, Custard Glass, Milk Glass, Sugar Shakers, Toothpicks, and specific companies.

Advisers: John and Alice Ahlfeld.

Abbreviations:

ah	applied handle
GUTDODB	Give Us This Day Our Daily Bread
hs	high standard
ind	individual
ls	low standard
os	original stopper

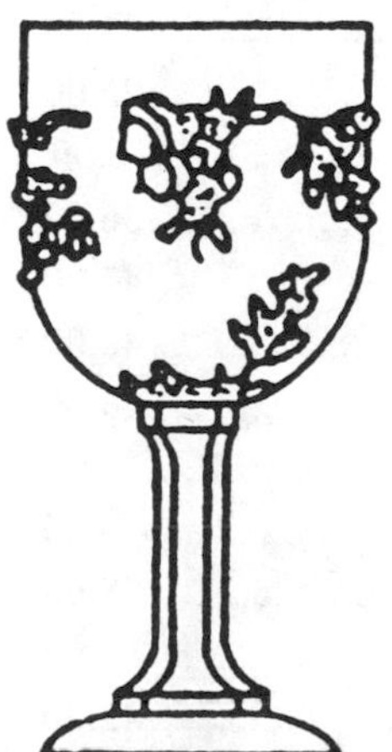

Acorn

Acorn Band, Acorn Band and Loops, Paneled Acorn Band, Beaded Acorn

Acorn and the variant patterns were made in flint and non-flint, 1860s-70s. There are additional acorn variant patterns, but they were not made in table sets. Prices for all the acorn variants are similar.

Reproductions: The *Acorn* goblet is reported to be reproduced in blue. Originally it was only made in clear.

Items	Flint	Non-Flint
Bowl, cov	-	60.00
Bowl, open	-	42.00
Butter dish, cov	65.00	-
Celery	60.00	-
Compote, cov	225.00	90.00
Compote, open	90.00	72.00
Creamer	55.00	42.00
Egg cup	30.00	18.00
Goblet ø	48.00	30.00
Pitcher, water, ah	180.00	90.00
Sauce, flat	-	9.00
Spooner	48.00	36.00
Sugar bowl, cov	90.00	60.00
Sugar, open, buttermilk type	42.00	24.00

Baltimore Pear

Double Pear, Fig, Gipsy, Maryland Pear, Twin Pear

Manufactured originally by Adams & Company, Pittsburgh, PA, in 1874. Reissued by United States Glass Company in the 1890s, at Factory "A." There are eighteen different size compotes. Different manufacturers and organizations gave some forms as premiums. Made in non-flint, clear.

Reproductions: Heavily reproduced in clear and cobalt blue, with the first reproductions documented in the 1930s. Imperial Glass, Jeannette Glass Company, and Westmoreland Glass Company all were making reproductions by the 1950s.

Items	Clear
Bowl, cov, 5" d	42.00
Bowl, cov, 7" d	55.00
Bowl, cov, 8" d	60.00
Bowl, open, 6" d	36.00
Bowl, open, 9" d	42.00
Bread plate, 12-1/2" d	85.00
Butter dish, cov ϕ	75.00
Cake plate, flat	55.00
Cake stand, 9" d ϕ	66.00
Cake stand, 10" d ϕ	66.00
Celery vase ϕ	60.00
Compote, cov, hs, 5" d	55.00
Compote, cov, hs, 7" d	95.00
Compote, cov, hs, 8-1/2" d	95.00
Compote, cov, ls, 6" d	48.00
Compote, cov, ls, 7" d	55.00
Compote, cov, ls, 8-1/2" d	55.00
Compote, open, hs, 5" d	36.00
Compote, open, hs, 8" d	42.00
Compote, open, ls, 6" d	30.00
Compote, open, ls, 7" d	36.00
Compote, open, ls, 8" d	42.00
Creamer ϕ	36.00
Goblet ϕ	42.00
Honey dish, octagonal, 3-1/2" d	18.00
Honey dish, round, 3-1/2" d, flat or footed	12.00
Jelly compote, open	30.00
Pickle	24.00
Pitcher, milk ϕ	95.00
Pitcher, water ϕ	115.00
Plate, 8-1/2" d	36.00
Plate, 9" d ϕ	42.00
Plate, 10" d ϕ	48.00
Relish	24.00
Sauce, flat ϕ	10.00
Sauce, footed	18.00
Spooner	48.00
Sugar bowl, cov ϕ	60.00
Tray, 10-1/2" d ϕ	42.00

Bleeding Heart

King's Floral Ware, New Floral, US Glass Pattern Line No. 85

Manufactured originally by King Son and Company, Pittsburgh, PA, c1875. Reissued by United States Glass in 1898, at Factory "C." Shards have also been found at Boston and Sandwich Glass Company, Sandwich, MA, and the Burlington Glass Works, Hamilton, Ontario, Canada. The Speciality Company, East Liverpool, OH, also made only the goblet and mug in 1888. Made in non-flint, clear and some milk glass.

Goblets found with six variations. A goblet with a tin lid, containing a condiment, such as mustard, jelly, or baking powder, was also made. It is of inferior quality compared to the original goblet.

Items	Clear
Bowl, cov, 6" d	48.00
Bowl, cov, 8-1/4" d	66.00
Bowl, open, oval, 5" l	24.00
Bowl, open, oval, 7" l	30.00
Bowl, open, oval, 9" l	42.00
Bowl, open, round, 5" d	24.00
Bowl, open, round, 7" d	30.00
Bowl, open, round, 8" d	42.00
Butter dish, cov	75.00
Cake stand, 9" d	72.00
Cake stand, 10" d	85.00
Cake stand, 11" d	110.00
Cake stand with dessert slots	130.00
Compote, cov, hs, 7" d	75.00
Compote, cov, hs, 8" d	85.00
Compote, cov, hs, 9" d	115.00
Compote, cov, ls, 7" d	72.00
Compote, cov, ls, 7-1/2" d	72.00
Compote, cov, ls, 8" d	75.00
Compote, open, hs, 8" d	48.00
Compote, open, ls, 8-1/2" d	36.00
Creamer, applied handle, ftd	72.00
Creamer, molded handle, flat	36.00
Dish, cov, 7" d	55.00

Items	Clear
Egg cup	55.00
Egg rack, cov, three eggs	360.00
Goblet, knob stem, barrel bowl	42.00
Goblet, knob stem, straight bowl	42.00
Honey dish, 3-1/2" d	18.00
Mug, 3-1/4" h	48.00
Pickle, 8-3/4" l, 5" w	36.00
Pitcher milk, ah, quart, bulbous	130.00
Pitcher, water, ah, half gallon, bulbous	180.00
Plate	75.00
Platter, oval	85.00
Relish, oval, 5-1/2" x 3-5/8"	42.00
Salt, master, ftd	72.00
Sauce, flat, oval, 3-1/2" d, 4" d, or 5" d	18.00
Sauce, flat, round, 3-1/2" d, 4" d, or 5" d	18.00
Spooner	30.00
Sugar bowl, cov, ftd, short	85.00
Sugar bowl, cov, ftd, tall	85.00
Tumbler, flat	110.00
Tumbler, footed	95.00
Waste bowl	66.00
Wine, hexagonal stem	165.00
Wine, knob stem	190.00

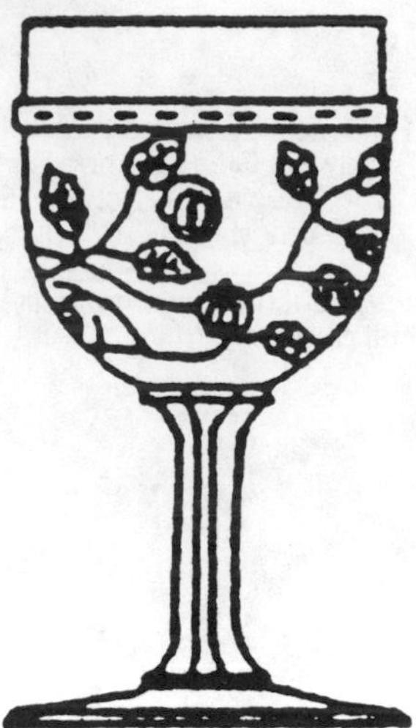

Cabbage Rose
Central's No. 140, Rose

Manufactured by Central Glass Company, Wheeling, WV, c1870. The design was patented by designer John Oesterling (No. 4,263) on July 26, 1870. Made in non-flint, clear.

Reproductions: Mosser Glass Company, Cambridge, OH, made reproductions in clear and colors during the early 1980s.

Item	Clear
Basket, 12" h	130.00
Bitters bottle, 6-1/2" h	130.00
Bowl, cov, round, 6" d	55.00
Bowl, cov, round, 7" d	72.00
Bowl, cov, round, 7-1/2" d	85.00
Bowl, oval, 7-1/2" d	42.00
Bowl, oval, 8-1/2" d	48.00
Bowl, oval, 9-1/2" d	55.00
Bowl, round, 6" d	30.00
Bowl, round, 7-1/2" d	42.00
Butter dish, cov	72.00
Cake plate, sq, flat	65.00
Cake stand, hs, 9" d	42.00
Cake stand, hs, 10" d	48.00
Cake stand, hs, 12-1/2" d	60.00
Celery vase, pedestal	60.00
Champagne	60.00
Compote, cov, hs, deep bowl, 7-1/2" d	135.00
Compote, cov, hs, deep bowl, 8" d	118.00
Compote, cov, hs, deep bowl, 10" d	142.00
Compote, cov, hs, regular bowl, 8" d	110.00
Compote, cov, hs, regular bowl, 9" d	120.00
Compote, cov, hs, regular bowl, 10" d	135.00
Compote, cov, hs, shallow bowl, 6" d	90.00
Compote, cov, hs, shallow bowl, 7" d	95.00
Compote, cov, hs, shallow bowl, 8" d	115.00
Compote, cov, ls, deep bowl, 7" d	120.00
Compote, cov, ls, deep bowl, 8" d	120.00

Item	Clear
Compote, cov, ls, deep bowl, 9" d	124.00
Compote, cov, ls, regular bowl, 8" d	135.00
Compote, cov, ls, regular bowl, 9" d	124.00
Compote, cov, ls, regular bowl, 10" d	135.00
Compote, cov, ls, shallow bowl, 6" d	115.00
Compote, cov, ls, shallow bowl, 7" d	120.00
Compote, cov, ls, shallow bowl, 8" d	135.00
Compote, open, hs, 6-1/2" d	65.00
Compote, open, hs, 7-1/2" d	90.00
Compote, open, hs, 8-1/2" d	85.00
Compote, open, hs, 9-1/2" d	120.00
Cordial	55.00
Creamer, ah, 5-1/2" h	55.00
Egg cup, with or without handle	55.00
Goblet ϕ (two styles)	55.00
Mug	72.00
Pickle dish	42.00
Pitcher, milk, quart	180.00
Pitcher, water, half gallon	130.00
Relish, 8-1/2" l, 5" w, rose filled horn of plenty center	48.00
Salt, master, ftd	30.00
Sauce, flat, 4" d	12.00
Spooner ϕ	30.00
Sugar bowl, cov	55.00
Tumbler	48.00
Wine	55.00

Daisy and Button with Crossbars

Daisy and Thumbprint Crossbar, Daisy and Button with Crossbar and Thumbprint Band, Daisy with Crossbar, Mikado

Manufactured by Richards & Hartley, Tarentum, PA, c1895. Reissued by United States Glass Company, Pittsburgh, PA, after 1891. Shards have been found at Burlington Glass Works, Hamilton, Ontario, Canada. Made in non-flint, amber, blue, clear, and vaseline.

Items	Amber	Blue	Clear	Vaseline
Bowl, oval, 6" l or 8" l	24.00	36.00	18.00	30.00
Bowl, oval, 9" l	48.00	48.00	30.00	42.00
Bread plate	36.00	55.00	30.00	42.00
Butter dish, cov, flat	55.00	55.00	55.00	55.00
Butter dish, cov, footed	-	75.00	30.00	72.00
Celery vase	42.00	48.00	36.00	60.00
Compote, cov, hs, 6" d	55.00	65.00	55.00	55.00
Compote, cov, hs, 8" d	65.00	75.00	55.00	65.00
Compote, cov, ls, 7" d	42.00	42.00	30.00	42.00
Compote, cov, ls, 8" d	48.00	48.00	36.00	48.00
Compote, open, hs, 7" d	48.00	55.00	30.00	48.00
Compote, open, hs, 8" d	55.00	60.00	36.00	55.00
Compote, open, ls, 7" d	36.00	42.00	24.00	55.00
Compote, open, ls, 8" d	36.00	42.00	24.00	55.00
Cordial	36.00	42.00	30.00	36.00
Creamer, individual	30.00	36.00	25.00	36.00
Creamer, regular	30.00	55.00	42.00	48.00
Cruet, os	75.00	85.00	42.00	120.00
Finger bowl	55.00	48.00	36.00	42.00
Goblet	48.00	48.00	30.00	55.00
Ketchup bottle	110.00	135.00	42.00	110.00
Lamp, oil, four sizes	130.00	155.00	110.00	130.00
Mug, large, 3" h	18.00	35.00	15.00	24.00
Mug, small	18.00	35.00	15.00	24.00
Pickle dish	24.00	24.00	12.00	24.00
Pickle jar, cov	36.00	55.00	30.00	48.00
Pitcher, milk	65.00	72.00	55.00	110.00
Pitcher, water	115.00	85.00	65.00	130.00
Salt and pepper shakers, pr	48.00	5000	36.00	55.00
Sauce, flat	18.00	25.00	12.00	18.00
Sauce, footed	25.00	30.00	18.00	30.00
Spooner, ftd	42.00	42.00	30.00	42.00
Sugar bowl, cov, individual	30.00	42.00	12.00	30.00
Sugar bowl, cov, regular	60.00	72.00	30.00	55.00

Daisey and Button with Crossbars (cont.)

Items	Amber	Blue	Clear	Vaseline
Syrup, orig top	120.00	130.00	65.00	130.00
Toothpick holder	48.00	48.00	85.00	42.00
Tumbler, flat	24.00	30.00	25.00	30.00
Wine	36.00	42.00	30.00	36.00

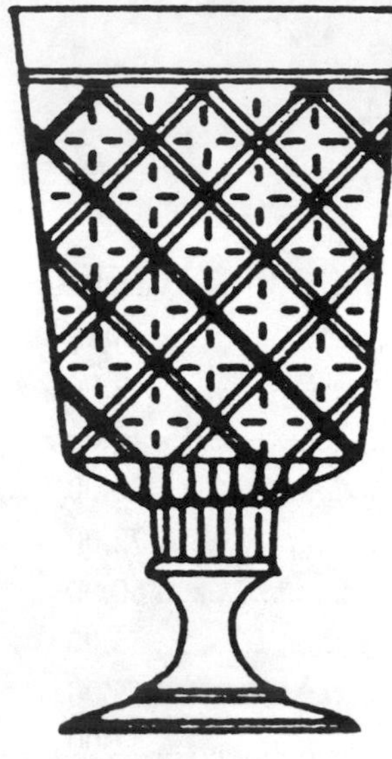

Finecut

Flower in Square, Bryce Pattern Line No. 720

Manufactured by Bryce Brothers, Pittsburgh, PA, c1885, and by United States Glass Company, Pittsburgh, PA, in 1891. Made in non-flint, amber, blue, clear, and vaseline.

Items	Amber	Blue	Clear	Vaseline
Bowl, 8-1/4" d	18.00	24.00	12.00	18.00
Bread plate	60.00	72.00	30.00	60.00
Butter dish, cov	55.00	75.00	55.00	95.00
Cake stand, hs	-	-	42.00	-
Celery tray	-	55.00	-	-
Celery vase, silver plated holder	-	-	-	118.00
Compote, cov, hs	65.00	75.00	55.00	75.00
Creamer	310.00	48.00	42.00	75.00
Goblet	55.00	55.00	40.00	45.00
Pitcher, water	120.00	120.00	72.00	125.00
Plate, 6" d or 6-1/4" d	-	24.00	10.00	-
Plate, 7" d or 7-1/4" d	30.00	48.00	18.00	24.00
Plate, 10" d or 10-1/4" d	36.00	60.00	30.00	55.00
Relish tray	18.00	18.00	12.00	24.00
Sauce, flat	18.00	18.00	12.00	18.00
Spooner	36.00	55.00	40.00	48.00
Sugar bowl, cov	55.00	55.00	42.00	55.00
Tumbler	-	-	40.00	50.00
Vegetable dish, oblong	24.00	30.00	18.00	24.00
Water tray, 10" d	60.00	85.00	30.00	60.00
Wine	-	-	30.00	36.00

Ivy In Snow
Ivy in Snow-Red Leaves, Forest Ware

Manufactured by Co-Operative Flint Glass Company, Beaver Falls, PA, in the 1880s. Phoenix Glass of Monaco, PA, also produced this pattern, from 1937 to 1942, and then it was called "Forest Ware." ***Ivy In Snow-Red Leaves*** is the name used for pieces where the leaves are ruby stained. Made in non-flint, clear, amber stained, and ruby stained. Some pieces have a ruby stained barrel.

Reproductions: This pattern has been widely reproduced with many reproductions in white milk glass. Kemple Glass Works, East Palestine, OH, is credited with most of the milk glass reproductions, which date to the 1940s.

Items	Clear	Ruby Stained
Berry bowl, 7" d	24.00	-
Bowl, 8" x 5-1/2" ϕ	36.00	-
Butter dish, cov	65.00	-
Cake plate, round or square	36.00	80.00
Cake stand, hs, 8" d	55.00	-
Celery vase, pedestal ϕ	36.00	90.00
Champagne	42.00	65.00
Compote, cov, hs, 6" d	55.00	90.00
Compote, cov, hs, 8" d	60.00	-
Cordial	42.00	-
Creamer, regular	36.00	90.00
Creamer, tankard	42.00	142.00
Cup and saucer ϕ	42.00	-
Finger bowl	30.00	-
Goblet ϕ	42.00	80.00
Jelly compote, open	42.00	65.00
Marmalade jar	42.00	-
Mug	30.00	48.00
Pitcher, milk, quart	105.00	240.00
Pitcher, water, half gallon ϕ	65.00	240.00
Plate, 6" d	24.00	-
Plate, 7" d	30.00	-
Plate, 10" d	36.00	-
Relish tray	24.00	36.00
Sauce, flat, 4" d	18.00	24.00
Spooner	42.00	72.00
Sugar bowl, cov ϕ	60.00	90.00
Syrup, orig top	85.00	290.00
Tumbler ϕ	30.00	55.00
Wine	40.00	65.00

Leaf and Dart

Double Leaf and Dart, Pride

Manufactured by Richards & Hartley Flint Glass Company, Pittsburgh, PA, c1875. Reissued by United States Glass Company, Pittsburgh, PA, c1891. Shards have been found at the Boston and Sandwich Glass Works, Sandwich, MA, as well as the Burlington Glass Works, Hamilton, Ontario, Canada. Made in non-flint, clear.

Items	Clear
Bowl, footed, 8-1/4" d	30.00
Butter dish, cov	72.00
Butter pat	24.00
Celery vase, pedestal	36.00
Compote, cov, ls	75.00
Compote, open, hs	42.00
Creamer, ah, pedestal	48.00
Cruet, ah, pedestal, os	120.00
Egg cup	24.00
Goblet	210.00
Honey dish	10.00
Lamp, finger, flat	90.00
Pitcher, milk, bulbous, ah, quart	90.00
Pitcher, water, bulbous, ah, half gallon	95.00
Relish tray	18.00
Salt, master, ftd, cov	75.00
Salt, master, ftd, open	36.00
Sauce, flat, 4" d	8.50
Spooner	36.00
Sugar bowl, cov	55.00
Syrup, orig top	110.00
Tumbler, ftd	30.00
Wine	36.00

Open Rose

Moss Rose

Manufacture attributed to Boston and Sandwich Glass Company, Sandwich, MA, c1870. Made in non-flint, clear.

Reproductions: Reproduced in clear and color.

Items	Clear
Bowl, flat, 5" d	35.00
Bowl, oval, 9" x 6"	30.00
Butter dish, cov	65.00
Cake stand, hs	55.00
Celery vase, pedestal	36.00
Compote, cov, hs, 6" d	75.00
Compote, cov, hs, 7" d	85.00
Compote, cov, hs, 8" d	90.00
Compote, cov, hs, 9" d	110.00
Compote, open, ls, 6" d	30.00
Compote, open, ls, 7" d	36.00
Compote, open, ls, 7-1/2" d	42.00

Open Rose (cont.)

Items	Clear
Compote, open, ls, 8" d	48.00
Compote, open, ls, 9" d	55.00
Cordial	55.00
Creamer, ah	55.00
Dish, flat, 7" d	30.00
Egg cup	30.00
Goblet, lady's	36.00
Goblet, regular ϕ	36.00
Pickle dish, oval	18.00
Pitcher, milk, ah, bulbous	160.00
Pitcher, water, ah, bulbous	175.00
Relish tray	18.00
Salt, master, ftd	36.00
Sauce, flat, 4" d	12.00
Spooner ϕ	48.00
Sugar bowl, cov	60.00
Tumbler	60.00

Paneled Daisy

Brazil, Daisy and Panel

Manufactured by Bryce Bros., Pittsburgh, PA, in the late 1880s. Reissued by United States Glass Company, Pittsburgh, PA, in 1891 at Factory "B." Made in non-flint, clear. Also found in amber (sugar shaker, $130) and blue (sugar shaker, $155). Milk glass pieces include 7" round plate ($48), 9" sq plate ($55), and sugar shaker ($95).

Reproductions: Both the goblet and tumbler have been reproduced by L. G. Wright Glass Company, New Martinsville, WV, c1960, in amber, blue, clear, pink, and ruby. They also reproduced the relish scoop in amber, amethyst, blue, and green. Fenton Art Glass Company, Williamstown, WV, created a high standard covered compote in carnival, clear, and opalescent colors in 1970. A toothpick holder was added in 1973.

Items	Clear
Bowl, flared rim, 6" d or 7" d	18.00
Bowl, shallow, 8" d or 9" d	35.00
Bowl, sq, 8" w	35.00
Bowl, sq, 10-1/2" w	30.00
Butter dish, cov, flat	60.00
Butter dish, cov, footed	60.00
Cake stand, hs, 8" d	36.00
Cake stand, hs, 9" d	48.00
Cake stand, hs, 10-1/4" d	55.00
Cake stand, hs, 11" d	60.00
Celery vase	48.00
Compote, cov, hs, 5" d	48.00
Compote, cov, hs, 7" d	60.00
Compote, cov, hs, 8" d ϕ	60.00
Compote, cov, hs, 10" d	72.00
Compote, open, hs, 7" d	48.00
Compote, open, hs, 9" d	48.00
Compote, open, hs, 10" d	48.00
Compote, open, hs, 11" d	48.00
Creamer	410.00
Dish, oval, 9" l	35.00
Goblet ϕ	30.00
Jelly compote, cov, hs, 6" d	55.00
Mug	36.00
Pickle jar	110.00
Pickle scoop	18.00
Pitcher, water, half gallon	72.00
Plate, round, 7" d	36.00
Plate, round, 9" d	36.00
Plate, sq, 9-1/2" w	36.00
Plate, sq, 10" w	42.00
Relish, 5" x 7", wider at one end ϕ	25.00
Salt shaker	30.00
Sauce, flat, round, 4" d or 4-1/2" d	12.00
Sauce, footed, round, 4" d or 4-1/2" d	12.00
Spooner	30.00
Sugar bowl, cov	48.00
Sugar shaker	55.00
Syrup, orig top	85.00
Tumbler ϕ	30.00
Waste bowl	18.00
Water bottle	72.00
Water tray	55.00

Queen

Daisy and Button with Pointed Panels, Daisy with Depressed Button, Paneled Daisy and Button, Pointed Panel Daisy and Button, Sunk Daisy and Button, McKee's Pattern Line No. 2

Manufactured by McKee Glass Company, Jeannette, PA, c1894. Shards have been found at Burlington Glass Works site, Hamilton, Ontario, Canada. Made in non-flint, original production included amber, apple green, blue, canary yellow, and clear.

Reproductions: Reproductions have been made by Boyd's Crystal Art Glass Company, Cambridge, OH, and include the open low standard bowl, covered butter dish, high standard cake stand, high standard open compote, and goblet in clear, cobalt blue, and vaseline.

Items	Amber	Apple Green	Blue	Canary Yellow	Clear
Basket	130.00	130.00	142.00	118.00	90.00
Berry bowl, 8-1/2" d	55.00	55.00	60.00	55.00	36.00
Bread plate	55.00	60.00	60.00	55.00	42.00
Butter dish, cov ϕ	100.00	100.00	115.00	95.00	65.00
Cake stand, hs, 6-1/2" d ϕ	72.00	72.00	75.00	60.00	36.00
Cheese dish, cov	120.00	120.00	130.00	115.00	90.00
Compote, cov, hs ϕ	90.00	90.00	110.00	85.00	55.00
Compote, open, hs	55.00	55.00	75.00	48.00	30.00
Creamer	42.00	42.00	48.00	42.00	36.00
Goblet ϕ	36.00	36.00	42.00	36.00	30.00
Pickle tray, oval	18.00	35.00	30.00	35.00	12.00
Pitcher, milk	55.00	60.00	65.00	60.00	42.00
Pitcher, water	90.00	90.00	95.00	90.00	65.00
Sauce, flat, 4" d	18.00	18.00	35.00	18.00	12.00
Sauce, footed, 4" d	35.00	35.00	30.00	35.00	18.00
Spooner	36.00	36.00	42.00	36.00	30.00
Sugar bowl, cov	60.00	65.00	65.00	60.00	60.00
Tumbler	36.00	42.00	42.00	36.00	30.00
Wine	42.00	48.00	48.00	42.00	35.00

Roman Rosette

U.S. Glass Pattern Line No. 15,030

Manufactured by Bryce, Walker and Company, Pittsburgh, PA, c1890. Reissued by United States Glass Company, Pittsburgh, PA, in 1892 and 1898. Also attributed to Portland Glass Company, Portland, ME. Also seen with English registry mark. Made in non-flint, clear, ruby stained and amber stained.

Reproductions: Clear goblets were reproduced in the early 1960s.

Items	Clear	Ruby Stained
Bowl, 5" d or 5-1/2" d	12.00	-
Bowl, 6" d	15.00	-
Bowl, 7" d or 8" d	18.00	-
Bowl, 8-1/2" d	18.00	60.00
Bread plate	36.00	90.00
Butter dish, cov	60.00	130.00
Cake stand, hs, 9"	55.00	-

Roman Rosette (cont.)

Items	Clear	Ruby Stained
Cake stand, hs, 10" d	55.00	-
Castor set, two bottles, glass stand	60.00	-
Castor set, three bottles, glass stand	75.00	-
Celery vase	36.00	115.00
Compote, cov, hs, 5" d	60.00	100.00
Compote, cov, hs, 6" d	65.00	110.00
Compote, cov, hs, 7" d	72.00	115.00
Compote, cov, hs, 8" d	75.00	120.00
Condiment set, salt & pepper shakers, tray	48.00	-
Condiment set, salt & pepper shakers, cov mustard, tray	60.00	130.00
Cordial	60.00	135.00
Creamer	40.00	55.00
Egg cup	72.00	-
Goblet ϕ	48.00	75.00
Honey dish, cov, sq	55.00	-
Jelly compote, cov, hs, 4-1/2" d	60.00	100.00
Jug, 5 ounce	55.00	120.00
Jug, 6 ounce	60.00	112.00
Jug, 7 ounce	65.00	135.00
Mug, large	42.00	60.00
Mug, small	36.00	55.00
Mustard Jar, cov	55.00	-
Pickle dish, boat shape	35.00	55.00
Pitcher, milk	55.00	160.00
Pitcher, water	60.00	148.00
Plate, 7" d or 7-1/2" d	42.00	75.00
Platter, oval or round	42.00	90.00
Preserve dish, oval, 7" l, 8" l, 9" l	30.00	48.00
Relish, oval, 9"	35.00	48.00
Salt, master, footed	55.00	-
Salt and pepper shakers, pr	48.00	90.00
Sauce, flat, 4" d or 4-1/2" d	18.00	35.00
Sauce, ftd, 4" d or 4-1/2" d	35.00	30.00
Sherbet	35.00	42.00
Spooner	30.00	55.00
Sugar bowl, cov	48.00	95.00
Syrup, orig top	100.00	130.00
Tumbler	42.00	60.00
Wine	55.00	75.00

Scroll With Flowers

Manufacture attributed to Central Glass Company, Wheeling, WV, in the 1870s and the Canton Glass Company, Canton, OH, c1880. Made in non-flint, clear. Occasionally found in amber, apple green, and blue.

Items	Clear
Butter dish, cov	48.00
Cake plate, handle, 10-1/2" d	30.00
Celery vase	45.00
Compote, cov, ls	55.00
Cordial	45.00
Creamer	48.00
Egg cup, handle	24.00
Goblet	30.00
Mustard jar, cov	60.00
Pickle tray, handle	20.00
Pitcher, water, half gallon	55.00
Plate, double-handles, 10-1/2" d	48.00
Sauce, double-handles	12.00
Spooner	28.50
Sugar bowl, cov	55.00
Syrup, orig top	90.00
Wine	36.00

Tree of Life
Portland's

Manufactured by Portland Glass Company, Portland, ME, c1870. Made in flint, and non-flint, in amber, clear, dark blue, green, light blue, purple, and, yellow. Color is rare. A blue finger bowl in a silver-plated holder is valued at $190.

Reproductions: Reproductions of *Tree of Life* were made by L. G. Wright Glass Company, New Martinsville, WV, 1968. Colors of these reproductions include amber, blue, and clear.

Items	Non-Flint
Bowl, berry, oval	36.00
Butter dish, cov	65.00
Celery vase, silver plated frame	65.00
Cologne bottle, facetted stopper	55.00
Champagne	65.00
Compote, open, hs, 8-1/2" d	130.00
Compote, open, hs, 10" d	112.00
Compote, open, ls, 10" d	60.00
Creamer, applied handle	85.00
Creamer, molded handle	60.00
Creamer, silver plated holder	90.00
Egg cup	36.00
Epergne, sgd "P.G. Company Patd"	130.00
Finger bowl, underplate	72.00
Fruit dish, silver plated holder	110.00
Goblet, clear shield on side	60.00
Goblet, plain ϕ	45.00
Goblet, regular, sgd "P.G. Flint"	75.00
Ice cream tray	60.00
Lemonade	60.00
Mug	60.00
Pitcher, milk, applied handle	115.00
Pitcher, milk, molded handle	75.00
Pitcher, water, applied handle	115.00
Pitcher, water, molded handle	75.00
Plate, 6" d	30.00
Sauce, flat, 3-3/4" d ϕ	15.00
Sauce, leaf shape	18.00
Spooner	45.00
Sugar bowl, cov	85.00
Sugar bowl, silver plated holder	90.00
Toothpick holder, footed, scalloped	60.00
Tumbler, ftd	48.00
Vase	60.00
Water tray	110.00
Wine ϕ	65.00

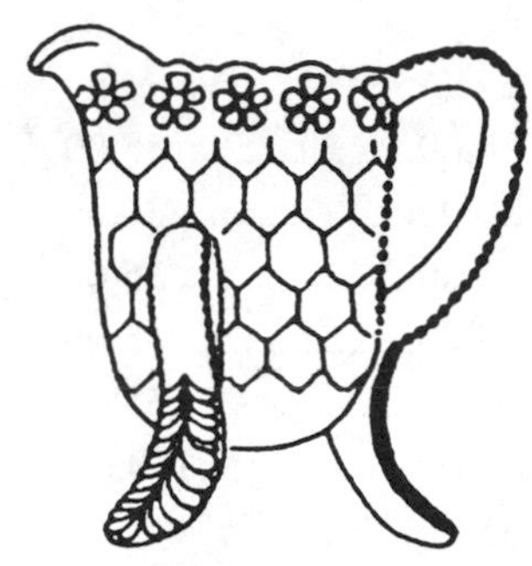

Vermont

Honeycomb with Flower Rim, Inverted Thumbprint with Daisy Band, US Glass Pattern Line No. 15,060

Manufactured by United States Glass Company, Pittsburgh, PA, 1899-1903, as part of its States series. Made in non-flint, clear, and green. Both clear and green are found with gold trim. Rare examples in blue, clear with amber stain, clear with ruby stain, and clear with green stain. Very rare in custard (usually decorated), milk glass, and blue.

Reproductions: Toothpick holder holders have been reproduced by Crystal Art Glass Company, Cambridge, OH, and Mosser Glass Company, Cambridge, OH, and Degenhart Glass Company, Cambridge, OH, who marks its colored line.

Items	Clear w/Gold	Green w/Gold
Basket, handle	42.00	65.00
Berry bowl	35.00	65.00
Butter dish, cov	55.00	110.00
Card tray, large	30.00	45.00
Card tray, medium	30.00	42.00
Card tray, small	25.00	35.00
Celery tray	42.00	45.00
Compote, cov, hs	80.00	135.00
Compote, open, hs	45.00	90.00
Creamer, ph, 4-1/4" h	42.00	80.00
Finger bowl	35.00	65.00
Goblet	55.00	75.00
Pickle tray	30.00	42.00
Pitcher, water	75.00	135.00
Salt shaker	30.00	45.00
Sauce, footed	25.00	30.00
Spooner	35.00	110.00
Sugar bowl, cov	45.00	115.00
Toothpick holder ϕ	42.00	75.00
Tumbler, footed	30.00	55.00
Vase	30.00	65.00

Wildflower

Adams Pattern Line No. 140

Manufactured by Adams & Company, Pittsburgh, PA, c1885, and by United States Glass Company, Pittsburgh, PA, at Factory "A," c1891-1900. Made in non-flint, amber, apple green, blue, clear, and vaseline.

Reproductions: This pattern has been heavily reproduced. Reproductions date as early as 1936. L. G. Wright Glass Company, New Martinsville, WV, and Crystal Art Glass Company, Cambridge, OH, Summit Art Glass Company, Akron, OH, and Mosser Glass Inc., Cambridge, OH, have issued items from new molds and in additional colors. Careful study of the details usually reveals poorly molded vines and flowers on reproductions.

WILDFLOWER (CONT.)

Items	Amber	Apple Green	Blue	Clear	Vaseline
Bowl, round, 6" d	35.00	45.00	45.00	30.00	35.00
Bowl, sq, 6" w, 7" w, or 8" w	35.00	45.00	45.00	30.00	30.00
Bowl, sq, 9" w	42.00	55.00	55.00	35.00	35.00
Butter dish, cov, collar base	55.00	75.00	75.00	45.00	65.00
Butter dish, cov, flat	45.00	65.00	65.00	42.00	55.00
Cake basket, oblong, metal handle1	15.00	110.00	120.00	75.00	110.00
Cake plate, sq, 10" w	42.00	42.00	65.00	35.00	42.00
Cake stand, hs, 10-1/2" d	75.00	115.00	110.00	65.00	75.00
Champagne ϕ	55.00	80.00	75.00	35.00	65.00
Celery vase	80.00	85.00	80.00	45.00	80.00
Compote, cov, hs, oblong, 8" l	115.00	110.00	110.00	75.00	110.00
Compote, cov, hs, round, 8" d ϕ	115.00	110.00	110.00	75.00	110.00
Compote, cov, hs, sq, 8" w	110.00	120.00	125.00	80.00	115.00
Compote, cov, ls, 7" d ϕ	-	-	100.00	-	-
Compote, cov, ls, 8" d ϕ	-	-	110.00	-	-
Creamer ϕ	45.00	75.00	65.00	55.00	60.00
Dish, sq, 6-1/2" w	30.00	42.00	42.00	25.00	30.00
Goblet ϕ	42.00	55.00	55.00	35.00	55.00
Pitcher, water	80.00	120.00	90.00	55.00	100.00
Platter, oblong, 10" l	55.00	65.00	55.00	42.00	42.00
Platter, oblong, 11" l, 8" w	-	-	65.00	-	-
Relish tray	30.00	25.00	30.00	20.00	30.00
Salt, master, turtle shape ϕ	65.00	75.00	75.00	42.00	55.00
Salt shaker	45.00	80.00	55.00	30.00	65.00
Sauce, flat, 3-1/2" d or 4" d	15.00	25.00	25.00	15.00	15.00
Sauce, ftd, 3-1/2" d or 4" d ϕ	20.00	20.00	20.00	20.00	20.00
Spooner	42.00	45.00	42.00	30.00	55.00
Sugar bowl, cov ϕ	65.00	65.00	75.00	42.00	65.00
Syrup, orig top	135.00	175.00	155.00	90.00	175.00
Tumbler ϕ	55.00	45.00	45.00	35.00	45.00
Water tray, oval	75.00	85.00	85.00	55.00	80.00
Wine ϕ	65.00	65.00	65.00	35.00	65.00

PAUL REVERE POTTERY

History: Paul Revere Pottery, Boston, Massachusetts, was an outgrowth of a club known as The Saturday Evening Girls. The S.E.G. was composed of young female immigrants who met on Saturday nights to read and participate in craft projects, such as ceramics.

Regular pottery production began in 1908, and the name "Paul Revere" was adopted because the pottery was located near the Old North Church. In 1915, the firm moved to Brighton, Massachusetts. Known as the "Bowl Shop," the pottery grew steadily. In spite of popular acceptance and technical advancements, the pottery required continual subsidies. It finally closed in January 1942.

Items produced range from plain and decorated vases to tablewares to illustrated tiles. Many decorated wares were incised and glazed either in an Art Nouveau matte finish or an occasional high glaze.

Marks: In addition to an impressed mark, paper "Bowl Shop" labels were used prior to 1915. Pieces also can be found with a date and "P.R.P." or "S.E.G." painted on the base.

Basket, 5-1/2" x 9", ftd, woven bands in swirled design, blue and buff semi-matte crackled glaze, circular stamp, Paul Revere paper label, restoration to foot **175.00**

Bowl, interior decorated with band of white flowers and buds, leafy green stems, yellow and light blue bands, green center, blue exterior, painted "S. E. G. 7-18," Boston, 1918, 8-3/8" d, 2-1/2" h, **$5,000**. Photo courtesy of Skinner, Inc.

Bookends, pr, 4" h, 5" w, night scene of owls, 1921, ink marked "S.E.G./11-21," flat chip to one base **1,300.00**

Bowl

6-1/4" d, 2-3/4" h, squatty, cuerda seca dec, puffy green trees in landscape, dark blue ground, circular stamp/illegible date **1,610.00**

10" d, tree and landscape border, dated 1913 .... **1,725.00**

11-1/2" d, 5" h, hemispherical, cuerda seca dec, geese and tree trunks, green, brown, and white, Paul Revere paper label **575.00**

Candlesticks, pr, 7-1/2" h, 3" d, mustard semi-matte glaze, SEG mark **200.00**

Child's breakfast set, 3-1/2" h mug, 5-5/8" d bowl, and 7-3/4" d plate, dec with running rabbits, white, green, and blue, monogrammed "David His Mug," "His Bowl," "His Plate," potter's mark, two chips on mug **1,380.00**

Dessert plate, 7-3/8" d, experimental speckled glaze, light gray and green, marked "S.E.G. 5310.09," unglazed base, c1909 .... **265.00**

Goblet, 3-3/4" h, band of gray rabbits, yellow and gray ground, SEG mark, hairlines and chip **230.00**

Humidor, cov, 6-1/4" h, 5-3/4" d, spherical, blue matte glaze, pink int., minute int. rim nick, sgd in slip "P.R.P. 3/36" **400.00**

Pitcher, blue-gray matte glaze, frothy white glaze around rim, stamped "PAUL REVERE POTTERY," 4-1/2" d, 4-1/2" h, **$95**. Photo courtesy of David Rago Auctions, Inc.

Lamp base, 18-3/4" h, ovoid, yellow glaze, reticulated wooden base, unmarked **230.00**

Luncheon plate, 7-5/8" d, borders dec with incised lotus blossoms in white on blue ground, green-blue center, marked "S.E.G. 6-14," artist's initials S.G., c1914, one cracked, price for three plates **1,100.00**

Milk pitcher, 4-1/4" h, David His Jug, polychrome medallion of white goose in landscape, yellow ground, circular stamp **815.00**

Pitcher, 7-1/8" h, ovoid, applied handle, green glaze, painted "J.M.D. June 17, 1920 S.E.G. 5-20," by Josephine M. Davis, handle repaired **115.00**

Planter, 3-3/4" h, incised panel with trios of white flowers and green leaves, golden-yellow sun, stele blue base, marked "AM," c1917 .... **2,930.00**

Plate

6-1/2" d, incised white mice, celadon and brown band, ink mark "Dorothy Hopkins/Her Plate," 1911 .... **1,300.00**

8" d, cuerda seca dec, white and blue geese and water lilies, green matte ground, marked "S.E.G./6-17/ AM" **1,380.00**

Ring tray, 4" d, circular, blue-gray and green band of trees, blue-gray ground, marked "S.E.G./J.G." **275.00**

Vase, ovoid, curved rim, matte yellow, impressed circular mark, painted "10-24 J," Boston, 1924, interior crazing, 8-1/2" h, **$1,100**. Photo courtesy of Skinner, Inc.

Serving bowl, 8-1/2" d, yellow, white wax-resist rim, 1922, SEG mark, several hairlines **148.00**

Teapot, 4-1/2" h, 9" d, brown and white wavy band of sailboats, yellow sky, 1918, restored **700.00**

Tile, 3-3/4" sq, Washington Street, blue, white, green, and brown, marked ""H.S. S4 9/1/10," edge chips **420.00**

Trivet, 4-1/4" d, medallion of house against setting sun, blue-gray ground, 1924, imp P.R.P. mark **425.00**

Vase

5-3/4" x 4-1/2", ovoid, closed-in rim, cuerda seca dec, green trees in landscape, 1922, marked "SEG 3-22 EG" **2,185.00**

7" h, 5-1/4" d, baluster shape, band of orange lotus blossoms, frothy green ground, green base, imp P. R. mark **1,300.00**

PEACHBLOW

History: Peachblow, an art glass which derives its name from a fine Chinese glazed porcelain, resembles a peach or crushed strawberries in color. Three American glass manufacturers and two English firms produced peachblow glass in the late 1880s. A fourth American company resumed the process in the 1950s. The glass from each firm has its own identifying characteristics.

For more information, see *Warman's Glass*, 4th edition.

Hobbs, Brockunier & Co., Wheeling peachblow: Opalescent glass, plated or cased with a transparent amber glass; shading from yellow at the base to a deep red at top; glossy or satin finish.

Mt. Washington "Peach Blow": A homogeneous glass, shading from a pale gray-blue to a soft rose color; some pieces enhanced with glass appliqués, enameling, and gilding.

New England Glass Works, New England peachblow (advertised as Wild Rose, but called Peach Blow at the plant): Translucent, shading from rose to white; acid or glossy finish; some pieces enameled and gilded.

Thomas Webb & Sons and Stevens and Williams (English firms): Peachblow-style cased art glass, shading from yellow to red; some pieces with cameo-type relief designs.

Gunderson Glass Co.: Produced peachblow-type art glass to order during the 1950s; shades from an opaque faint tint of pink, which is almost white, to a deep rose.

Marks: Pieces made in England are marked "Peach Blow" or "Peach Bloom."

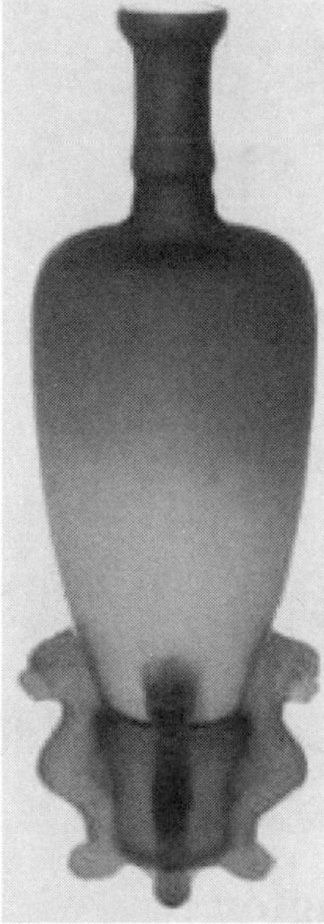

Morgan vase, Hobbs, Brockunier & Co., satin finish, deep blush at neck and shoulders gradually changes to buttery-cream lower half, satin Griffin holer with minor chips, 2" h holder, 8" h vase, **$1,750**. Photo courtesy of Clarence and Betty Maier.

Gundersen

Bottle, 2-1/2" d, 6" h, shaded pink to white **110.00**

Cruet, 8" h, 3-1/2" w, matte finish, ribbed shell handle, matching stopper with good color **875.00**
Cup and saucer **275.00**
Decanter, 10" h, 5" w, Pilgrim Canteen form, acid finish, deep raspberry to white, applied peachblow ribbed handle, deep raspberry stopper **950.00**
Goblet, 7-1/4" h, 4" d top, glossy finish, deep color, applied Burmese glass base **285.00**
Jug, 4-1/2" h, 4" w, bulbous, applied loop handle, acid finish **450.00**
Pitcher, 5-1/2" h, Hobnail, matte finish, white with hint of pink on int., orig label **550.00**
Plate, 8" d, luncheon, deep raspberry to pale pink, matte finish **375.00**
Punch cup, acid finish **275.00**
Tumbler, 3-3/4" h, matte finish **275.00**
Urn, 8-1/2" h, 4-1/2" w, two applied "M" handles, sq cut base, matte finish **550.00**
Vase, 5" h, 6" w, ruffled top, pinched-in base **525.00**
Wine glass, 5" h, glossy finish **175.00**

Harrach

Finger bowl, 5-1/2" d, 2-1/2" h, shiny deep pink shading to off-white, ruffled top **150.00**
Vase
8" h, pink shading to rose glossy cased ground, enameled gold trailing vine, propeller mark **250.00**
12-1/4" h, stick, pink shading to deep rose cased ground, enameled flowers, propeller mark **300.00**

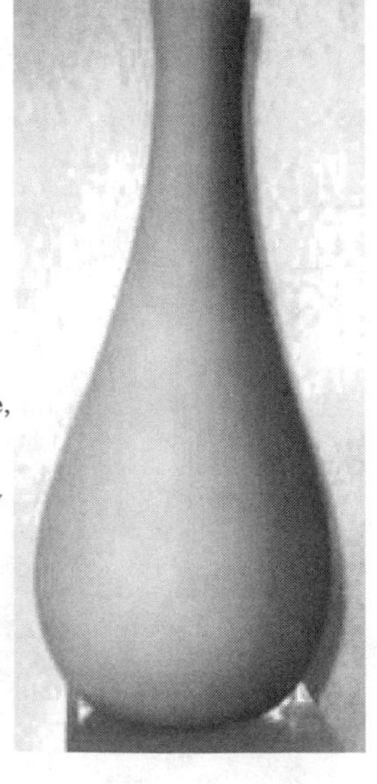

Vase, Mt. Washington, shape #148, satin finish, c1885, pale pink color shading to pale blue-gray base, 8-1/2" h, **$1,975**. Photo courtesy of Clarence and Betty Maier.

Mount Washington

Bowl, 3" w, 2" h, tricorn, pink shading to pale blue color, ground pontil **700.00**
Bride's basket, shades of pink, replated Meriden frame **650.00**
Low bowl, 5" d, 2-12" h, deep rose shading to amber, cased in powder blue, gold enameled trailings **365.00**
Milk pitcher, 7" w handle to spout, 5-3/4" h, thin walls, gray handle **3,950.00**
Vase, 8-1/4" h, lily form, satin finish **1,850.00**

New England

Bowl, 9-1/4" d, 3" h, ruffled top, deep coloring, small chips on rim **300.00**
Celery vase, 7" h, 4" w, sq top, deep raspberry with purple highlights shading to white **785.00**
Creamer and sugar, 2-1/2" h, applied handles, pontil scars, 1893 World's Fair **850.00**
Cruet, 6-3/4" h, 4" d at base, petticoat form, applied white handle and stopper, three lip top, acid finish **1,950.00**
Nut dish, 3-3/4" d, 1-1/4" h, satin, smooth pontil mark **495.00**
Pitcher, 6-3/4" h, 7-1/2" w, 3-1/4" w at top, bulbous, sq top, applied frosted handle, 10 rows of hobs, Sandwich **550.00**
Rose bowl, 5-1/2" d, 4" h, deep pink shading to yellow, folded ruffled rim **150.00**
Spooner, 4-1/2" h, deep pink shading to off-white, sq crimped rim **550.00**
Tumbler, 3-3/4" h, shiny finish, deep color upper third, middle fading to creamy white bottom, thin walls **445.00**
Vase
6-3/4" h, lily, satin, deep crimson upper third shading to pale white stem and wafer base **635.00**
9-3/4" h, lily, shiny, blushed color on top 3" shading to creamy white stem and wafer base **785.00**
10-1/2" h, 5" w at base, bulbous gourd shape, deep raspberry with fuchsia highlights to white, coloring extends two-thirds way down, four dimpled sides **1,450.00**

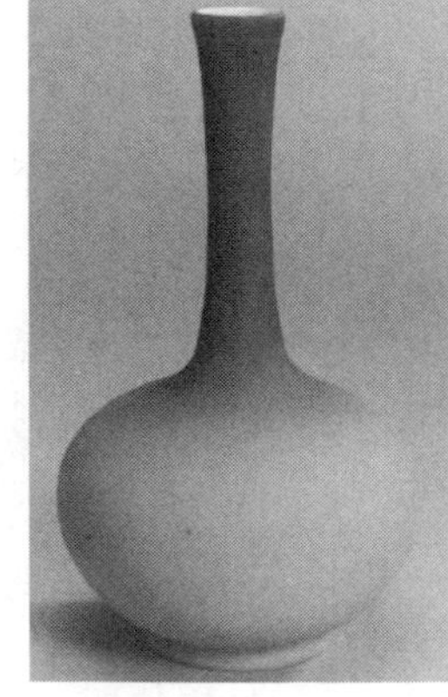

Vase, attributed to Thomas Webb & Sons, England, late 19th/early 20th C, narrow neck over bulbed base, cream-colored glass cased in red shading to pink, polished pontil, unsigned, 10-1/4" h, **$300**. Photo courtesy of Skinner, Inc.

Webb

Creamer, satin finish, coralene dec, rolled rim, flat base **650.00**
Finger bowl, 4-1/2" d, cased **195.00**
Shaker, 2-1/2" h, squatty, deep fuchsia shading to yellow, creamy whit int., small base chips **230.00**
Vase
7-1/2" h, dark rich pink fading to light pink, creamy white int., gold and pink floral dec, insects, and butterfly, minor wear to gold **450.00**
8-1/2" h, glossy cased rose shading to pink, flat-sided, enameled gold ferns and flowers, four applied amber feet **690.00**
10" h, cased deep crimson to pink, cascading green leafy branch, gold highlights **1,265.00**

Vase, Webb, frilly ruffled top, gold and silver butterfly hovering over gold and silver branch and prunus blossoms, smaller branch on reverse, knurled amber handles, signed "10," 4-1/2" h, **$485**. Photo courtesy of Clarence and Betty Maier.

Wheeling

Cruet, 5-1/2" h, bulbous, fuchsia shading to amber, creamy white int., applied reeded amber handle, replaced stopper **920.00**
Ewer, 6-3/4" h, 4" w, glossy finish, duck bill top, applied amber loop handle **3,500.00**
Morgan vase, 8" h, shiny finish, mahogany neck and shoulder, butterscotch on one side, other side with darker butterscotch with red overtones **585.00**
Morgan vase with stand, 10" h, Hobbs, Brockunier & Co., satin finish, deep blush at neck and shoulders shades to buttery cream, satin Griffin holder with small flake **1,750.00**
Mustard pot, 3-1/4" h, metal slotted cov, Hobbs, Brockunier & Co **685.00**
Punch cup, 2-1/2" h, Hobbs, Brockunier **535.00**
Salt and pepper shakers, pr, 4" h, deep pink shading to off-white, bulbous **230.00**
Tumbler, 3-3/4" h, deep red upper body changes sharply to butter yellow, molded pinwheel design in base **385.00**
Vase
7-1/2" h, double gourd, fuchsia

shading to amber, creamy white int. **2,875.00**
9" h, shiny, slender mahogany neck shading cherry red to ovoid butter-cream body **985.00**

Peking Glass

For more information, see *Warman's Glass*, 4th edition.

History: Peking glass is a type of cameo glass of Chinese origin. Its production began in the 1700s and continued well into the 19th century. The background color of Peking glass may be a delicate shade of yellow, green, or white. One style of white background is so transparent that it often is referred to as the "snowflake" ground. The overlay colors include a rich garnet red, deep blue, and emerald green.

Bowl, green overlay, white ground, carved prunus branches, flowers, and butterfly, late Ching dynasty **375.00**

Cup, footed, Ch'ien Lung period (1736-95), carved opaque pale lemon yellow, two dragons form handle, geometric symbols, Chinese seal-type characters on sides, 3" d, 2-1/4" h, **$750**. Photo courtesy of Cowan's Historic Americana Auctions.

Vase, cameo green carved to white, scene of man riding tiger, next to tree-lined mountain stream, Mei-Ping, some wear on base, 10-1/4" h, **$350**. Photo couretesy of Cowan's Historic Americana Auctions.

Cup, 3" d, 2-1/4" h, carved opaque pale lemon yellow, geometric symbols, Chinese seal-type characters on sides, two dragons form handles, ftd, Ch'en Lung period **750.00**
Dish, 11-3/4" l, flattened round form, bright yellow, 19th C **850.00**
Ginger jar, cov, 9-1/4" h, three different scenes on white grounds, coral-colored ground **750.00**
Snuff bottle, flattened ovoid, enameled birds perched on flowering tree, marked "Ku Yeh Hsuan Ancient Moon Terrace," Chinese, Qianlong **550.00**
Vase
8-3/4" h, carved green over white lotus design, small rim chip **900.00**
10-1/4" h, cameo green carved to white, scene of man riding tiger, next to tree-lined mountain stream, Mei-Ping, some wear on base **350.00**
10-1/2" h, turquoise on blue, interior painted landscape, China, early 20th C **500.00**

Vase, China, early 20th C, turquoise blue, an interior painted landscape, 10-1/2" h, **$500**. Photo courtesy of Skinner Auctioneers and Appraisers.

Perfume, Cologne, and Scent Bottles

History: The second half of the 19th century was the golden age for decorative bottles made to hold scents. These bottles were made in a variety of shapes and sizes. An atomizer is a perfume bottle with a spray mechanism. Cologne bottles usually are larger and have stoppers that also may be used as applicators. A perfume bottle has a stopper that often is elongated and designed to be an applicator.

For more information, see *Warman's Glass*, 4th edition.

Scent bottles are small bottles used to hold a scent or smelling salts. A vinaigrette is an ornamental box or bottle that has a perforated top and is used to hold aromatic vinegar or smelling salts. Fashionable women of the late 18th and 19th centuries carried them in purses or slipped them into gloves in case of a sudden fainting spell.

Blue opalescent glass perfume bottle, ruffled sides, gold washed atomizer top, bulb missing, 7" h, **$70**. Photos courtesy of Joy Luke Auctions.

Atomizer

Art glass, iridized gold/green, teardrop shaped body with flaring foot **275.00**
Cambridge, 6-1/4" h, stippled gold, opaque jade, orig silk lined box **140.00**
Cameo, 8-1/4" h, cameo carved scenic dec of trees and pond in greens over clear frosted glass, unsigned, attributed to France **520.00**
Malachite, 4" h, elephant, green **235.00**
Moser, 4-1/2" h, sapphire blue, gold florals, leaves, and swirls, melon ribbed body, orig gold top and bulb **275.00**

Cologne

Art glass, 11" h, transparent green bottle, delicate floral design, colorless pedestal foot, faceted teardrop stopper **175.00**
Baccarat, 5-7/8" h, colorless, panel cut, matching stopper **75.00**
Cut glass, 7" h, cranberry cut to colorless, cane cut, matching stopper **250.00**
Flask, 2-5/8" h, scrolls on each side, blue, uneven ground lip, smooth base, medium cornflower blue, America, c1860, McKearin GIX-40 .... **1,000.00**
Paperweight, 7" h, 5" d, , double overlay, crimson red over white over colorless squatty bottle, five oval facet windows reveal concentric millefiore cane int., matching stopper **460.00**

Vaseline, 4-1/2" h, vaseline, attributed to New England Glass Co., flint, orig stopper 225.00

Perfume

Enamel, Continental, 2-1/8" l, tapered colorless glass bottle encl in rect enamel case with hinged lid, pink ground, green ground roundels with white birds and flowers, crenellated surrounds, late 18th/ early 19th C 115.00

Cut glass perfume bottle, cut and etched glass figural stopper with flapper-style lady, 8-3/4" h, $135.

Glass

- 4" h, French, late 19th/early 20th C, baluster form, blue opaline bottle, gilt metal floral overlay, foot, and neck mounts, hinged lid set with shell cameo of young man in feathered cap 250.00
- 5" h, red and black, frieze of three nudes 2,800.00
- 6" h, clear, twin intaglio nudes 4,200.00
- 7" h, amber, 3-D flower stopper, leaping gazelle on base 3,800.00

Pair blown glass 4-1/4" h perfume bottles with gold metal overlay with floral design; dresser tray with lace doily center, amber glass dish with gilt border, $120.

Glass and silver, Victorian, London, 1885, fish-form flask, 6-1/4" l, green and metallic flecked blown glass body, gilt over enamel detailing of scales and eyes, engraved silver tail, retailed by W.Thornill & Co., fitted velvet lined case.... 1,500.00

Malachite, 5" h, elephant, green 550.00

Porcelain

- 2-1/2" l, Meissen, Germany, late 19th C, courting couple, ivy covered tree trunk, enamel and gilt detailing, orig stopper 635.00
- 3-1/4" l, Continental, late 18th/19th C, swaddled infant shape, enamel detailing, silvertone domed lid, tapered base 325.00
- 3-1/2" l, Brenner & Liebmann, Eduard Liebmann Porcelain Factory, Germany, late 19th C, oblong, Blue Onion style underglaze dec, red overpainted detailing, silver gilt neck and stopper mount 290.00

Silver gilt, 1-3/4" l, shield shaped, collet-set heart-shaped opal applied to front, surrounded by applied ropetwist, green and yellow enamel dec, back engraved with leafy scrolls, conical screw-in stopper, Hungarian, 20th C 115.00

Silver plate, Victorian, London, 1885, 2-3/4" l, bud shape, engraved rim, all over repoussé reeding, glass int. 190.00

Sterling silver, 2-3/4" l, Victorian, London, 1885, bud shape, engraved rim, body with all over repoussé reeding, glass int. 175.00

Sterling silver and champleve enamel, Gorham, everted oblong flask with diapered champleve centered by stars on cobalt blue enamel ground, small silver screw-in lid, late 19th/early 20th C 290.00

Pink glass 5-1/2" h perfume bottle, handpainted scenic panel with castle, matching stopper, $75; Limoges blue porcelain 6-1/2" h perfume bottle decorated with flowers and gilding, $80.

Scent

Agate, 3" h, flattened globe form, silver hinged rim and screw cap, marked "Black, Starr, & Frost" 260.00

Glass, blown

- 2-3/8" l, deep amethyst, shell shape, minor flakes 200.00
- 2-1/2" l, amethyst, orig cap, minor lid damage 145.00
- 2-1/2" l, cobalt blue, orig cap, minor lid damage 145.00
- 2-1/2" l, deep violet, tightly swirled ribs 150.00
- 2-1/2" l, peacock blue, orig cap, minor lid damage 145.00
- 2-1/2" l, violet blue, bulbous neck, vertical ribbing 185.00
- 2-3/4" l, deep violet blue, shield shape with sunburst 215.00
- 2-3/4" l, peacock green, some opalescent swirls, swirled ribs 195.00
- 2-7/8" l, opalescent swirls and clear, scrolled end, applied rigaree... 65.00
- 2-7/8" l, violet blue, slightly swirled ribs 110.00
- 3" l, deep violet blue, swirled ribs, flake 185.00
- 3" l, green, opaque green, cobalt blue, and amber, swirled ribs. 150.00
- 3" l, sapphire blue, swirled ribs 250.00
- 3-3/8" l, deep amethyst, swirled ribs 110.00

Porcelain, 3" h, egg shape, Germany or Russia, late 19th C, dec with scene of pedestrians in front of building and monument, gilt border, reserves of gilt foliate scrolls, corn and brass stopper 1,955.00

Silver, 3-5/8" l, Japanese, late 19th/early 20th C, tear shape, molded dragon dec on stippled ground, attached silver chains, approx 1 troy oz 450.00

Ruby glass 10-faceted double ended perfume bottle having silver plate lids, one lid hinged with glass stopper beneath, other screw top, small chip to one facet corner, chipping to stopper, monogrammed. 5-1/2" l, $190.

Vinaigrette

Cranberry glass, 2-1/4" x 1", rect, all-over cutting, enameled tiny pink roses, green leaves, gold dec, hinged lid, stopper, finger chain 185.00

Cut glass, 3-7/8" l, cobalt blue, yellow flashing, sterling silver overlay, emb sterling silver cap 125.00

English, silver, 7/8" l, tooled purse shape, gilded int., John Turner, Birmingham hallmarks, 1792 .... 250.00

European, silver, late 19th/early 20th C, 3" shaped as three squashes on vine, engine-turned textured dec, threaded bases, largest with pierced grate to interior, 1 troy oz 350.00

Victorian, late 19th C, staghorn, 2-1/2" l rough-textured horn mounted with thistle-cast lid, quatrefoil neck band, horn with guilloche strapping, short link chain 350.00

Peters and Reed Pottery

History: J. D. Peters and Adam Reed founded their pottery company in South Zanesville, Ohio, in 1900. Common flowerpots, jardinieres, and cooking wares comprised the majority of their early output. Occasionally, art pottery was attempted, but it was not until 1912 that their Moss Aztec line was introduced and widely accepted. Other art wares include Chromal, Landsun, Montene, Pereco, and Persian.

Peters retired in 1921 and Reed changed the name of the firm to Zane Pottery Company.

Marks: Marked pieces of Peters and Reed Pottery are unknown.

Vase, Chromal Ware, ovoid, unmarked, 4" d, 9-1/4" h, **$815**. Photo courtesy of David Rago Auctions, Inc.

Vase, Moss Aztec, corseted, stylized flowers and leaves, unmarked, 4-1/4" d, 10-1/2" h, **$235**. Photo courtesy of David Rago Auctions, Inc.

Vase, Moss Aztec, jeweled, unmarked, c1925, few small chips to decoration, 9-1/2" d, 9" h, **$250**. Photo courtesy of David Rago Auctions, Inc.

Bowl, 9" d, 3-1/4" h, closed-in rim, round tapering bowl, raised budding branches and berries in relief, matte green glaze, couple of chips on branch **175.00**
Doorstop, cat, yellow.................. **375.00**
Ewer, 11" h, orange and yellow raised grapes dec, brown ground **50.00**
Jardinière, 9-1/2" d, 9" h, Moss Aztec, c1925, unmarked, few small chips to dec **200.00**
Umbrella stand, 15-3/4", speckled brown matte glaze, indigo and yellow streaked glazes, unmarked, glaze flaking, several nicks **255.00**
Vase
- 6-1/2" x 4-1/2", Landsun, bulbous, unmarked **175.00**
- 6-3/4" x 4", Shadow Ware, baluster, covered in indigo, ochre, and brown dripping glaze, unmarked, few shallow rim scratches............ **150.00**
- 8" x 5-1/2", corseted, covered in striated black, green, and ivory glaze against russet ground, unmarked **75.00**
- 9" x 5", cupped rim, cov in bright green dripping glaze over deep blue-green mottled ground, unmarked **435.00**
- 9-1/4" x 4", Chromal Ware, ovoid, unmarked **815.00**
- 12" h, Landsun, ftd, unmarked **230.00**
- 13" x 7-1/2", Shadow Ware, bulbous, flat shoulder, covered in indigo, ochre, and seafoam dripping glaze, faint Zaneware stamp mark.... **415.00**
- 13-1/2" x 7", Chromal Ware, shades of brown and yellow, unmarked, 1/4" glaze chip, 1" rim bruise......... **920.00**

Vessel, 5-1/4" h, Sprig Dawn, unmarked **95.00**

Pewter

History: Pewter is a metal alloy consisting mostly of tin with small amounts of lead, copper, antimony, and bismuth added to make the shaping of products easier and to increase the hardness of the material. The metal can be cast, formed around a mold, spun, easily cut, and soldered to form a wide variety of utilitarian articles.

Pewter was known to the ancient Chinese, Egyptians, and Romans. England was the primary source of pewter for the American colonies for nearly 150 years until the American Revolution ended the embargo on raw tin, allowing the small American pewter industry to flourish until the Civil War.

Note: The listings concentrate on the American and English pewter forms most often encountered by the collector.

Basin, 10-3/4" d, 2-3/4" h, hammered booge, flattened rim with incised line, partial touch for Townshend and Compton, wear, minor battering... **195.00**
Beaker, 4-3/8" h, unidentified maker, faint touch mark under mid-bands, flaring lip, minor dents.................................... **60.00**
Bowl, 17-3/4" d, illegible portico touchmarks, partial "London" mark, tooled rim, hammered booge, light overall pitting, two small restorations....... **440.00**
Bud vase, 5" d, 10-1/2" h, Secessionist style, orig green glass insert, peacock feather emb, stamped "WMF"...... **865.00**

Basin, American, Parks Boyd, Philadelphia, 1771-1819, touch mark on center interior, 9" d, **$275**. Photo courtesy of Alderfer Auction Co.

Candlesticks, pr, 8-3/4" h, marked "Jacobs," 1822-71........................ **950.00**
Chalice, 7-7/8" h, flower and crown touch with "TG" on base, slightly flared rim, baluster turned stem with large round stepped base, small areas of filing at rim **2,450.00**
Charger, 13-7/8" d, angel touchmarks with "Reutlinger," raised tooled line around rim, minor restoration and dents **360.00**
Coffeepot, cov, 12" h, unmarked America, attributed to Ashbil Griswold or his apprentice Luther Boardman, relief turned rings on body, domed lid with wafer, worn black paint on handle, small holes near bottom......................... **315.00**
Creamer, 5-7/8" h, unmarked American, teapot shape **250.00**
Deep dish
- 8-5/8" d, John Brunstrom, two touch marks on reverse.................... **295.00**

Chamberstick, American, 2nd quarter 19th C, push-up form chamberstick, ring handle, 5-1/8" circular tray base, **$325**. Photo courtesy of Alderfer Auction Co.

11" d, Samuel Kilbourn, Baltimore, Maryland, 1814-30, impressed maker's touchmark on the reverse, minor dents **650.00**
13" d, Thomas Danforth, III, Philadelphia, PA 1717-1818, reverse with eagle touch mark and "T.D.", separate "T. DANFORTH/PHILDA" touch mark **475.00**

Flagon, 14" h, Thomas D. and Sherman Boardman, Hartford, CT, marked "Laughlin," 1810-30.................. **3,750.00**

Inkwell, 8-3/4" d, 3-3/4" h, unmarked, incised rings around base, three raised rings on body, soldered splits on hinge, no insert.. **110.00**

Ladle, 13" l, plain pointed handle, touch mark "WH" in oval, 19th C............. **65.00**

Whale oil lamp, unmarked, egg/acorn shaped font, double burner, stepped round base, 9" h, **$225**. Photo courtesy of James D. Julia, Inc.

Lamp
5-3/4" h plus brass and tin whale oil burner, Putnam touch, James Putnam, Madison, MA, some splits in rim of base **315.00**
8-1/2" h plus burner, Yale and Curtis, NY 1 touch, matching fluid burner missing, snuffers and one brass tube loose...................................... **190.00**

Measure, 2-3/8" to 8" h, assembled set, bellied, English, minor damage.... **550.00**

Mug, quart, 5-7/8" h, Samuel Hamlin, Hartford, Middletown, CT, and Providence RI, dent at base **625.00**

Pitcher, 6" h, Freeman Porter, Westbrook, ME, two quart **225.00**

Plate, 7-3/4" d, Thomas Danforth III, Philadelphia, 1717-1818, reverse with eagle touch mark and "T. D.," separate 'T. DANFORTH/PHILDA" touch mark **350.00**

Plate, double marked "G. Lightner, Baltimore, Md," minor bends, short split in shoulder, shallow knife scratches, 8-1/2" h, **$275**. Photo courtesy of Cowan's Historic Americana Auctions.

Platter, 28-3/4" l, Townsend and Compton, London, pierced insert, marked "Cotterell" **2,400.00**

Porringer, 5-1/4" d, 7-1/8" l, Westtown School, PA, form, possibly by Elisha Kirk, York, PA, plain tab handle with hole for hanging **775.00**

Porringer, Westtown School, PA form, attributed to by Elisha Kirk, York, PA, plain tab handle with hole for hanging, 7-1/8" l, 5-1/4" d, **$700**. Photo courtesy of Alderfer Auction Co.

Soup plate, 8-7/8" d, unmarked Continental, angel touch **75.00**

Sugar bowl, 6" h, Ashril Griswold, Meriden, CT, eagle touch **490.00**

Syrup pitcher, 4-1/2" h, hinged lid, unmarked, American **220.00**

Tablespoon, rattail handle, heart on back of bowl, marked "L. B.," (Luther Boardman, MA and CT). set of six **330.00**

Tea box, 5-1/2" l, 5" h, oblong, leaf dec handle top, four bun feet, marked "Littlejohn," two feet bent............. **150.00**

Teapot
7-1/2" h, sgd "Sellew & Co., Cincinnati, 5," (1830-1860), tooled rings on shoulder and foot, domed lid, scrolled ear handle with later black paint............................. **420.00**
8" h, touchmark of "J. Danforth, No. 14," (Josiah Danforth, Middletown, CT, 1825-1837), domed lid, wafer finial, scrolled ear handle with later black paint, cast scrolling on fittings, soldered restorations **440.00**

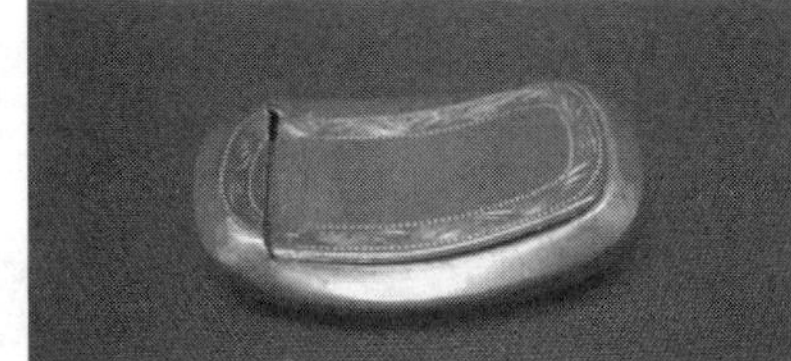
Snuff box, presentation type, American, dated 1785, illegible mark on inside of lid, broken hinge, 2-3/4" l, **$100**. Photo courtesy of Alderfer Auction Co.

Tobacco box, 4-3/8" h, Thomas Stanford, cast eagle feet, engraved label with scroll work "Thomas Stanford, Gospel Hill, 1838," wear, final and one foot soldered **125.00**

Tumbler, 2-3/4" h, Thomas Danforth Boardman, Hartford, CT, partial eagle touch.. **175.00**

Warming platter, 19" l, hot water type, tree and well, marked "Dixon & Sons," English, repairs............................ **250.00**

PHOENIX GLASS

History: Phoenix Glass Company, Beaver, Pennsylvania, was established in 1880. Known primarily for commercial glassware, the firm also produced a molded, sculptured, cameo-type line from the 1930s until the 1950s.

For more information, see *Warman's Glass*, 4th edition.

Ashtray, Phlox, large, white, frosted **80.00**

Bowl, 14" d, nude diving girl, white **495.00**

Compote, Lacy Dewdrop, pink on white **195.00**

Creamer and sugar, Catalonia, light green **45.00**

Lamp shade, ceiling type, 12" d, pale pink, emb floral dec...................... **115.00**

Table lamp, decorated with berries and leaves, **$120**. Photo courtesy of Joy Luke Auctions.

Lamp, table, 22" h, 16" d reverse painted shade, nighttime scene of trees, water and hills with moon, dark blue ground, base with emb leaf and flower design, slight staining to int. edge of shade, minor corrosion and paint loss to base, one socket replaced.................... **300.00**

Umbrella stand, 18" h, Thistle, pearlized blue ground **450.00**

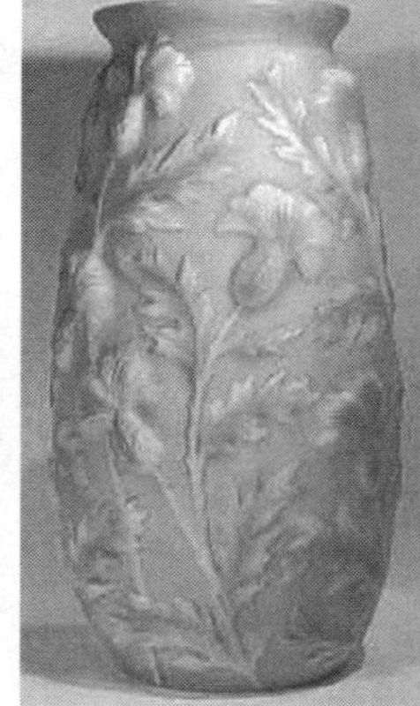

Vase, molded thistle, orig paper label, 18" h, **$450**. Photo courtesy of Joy Luke Auctions.

Vase

6-1/2" w at top, 3-1/2" d base, 7-1/2" h, blue, white floral dec, orig sticker, two chips inside rim ... **190.00**

8" h, Daisy, pearlized daisies, light green ground, orig label **360.00**

9-1/2" h, oval, blue, three raised white geese in-flight dec on each side, orig paper label, two small rim chips...................................... **320.00**

11" h, Wild rose, blown out, pearlized dec, dark rose ground, orig label **275.00**

14" h, Philodendron, blue, ormolu mounts.................................. **400.00**

PHONOGRAPHS

History: Early phonographs were commonly called "talking machines." Thomas A. Edison invented the first successful phonograph in 1877; other manufacturers followed with their variations.

Adviser: Lewis S. Walters.

Columbia Grafonola, oak case, needs restoration, **$75**.

Columbia

Grafonola, A. M. Graphophone Co., Bridgeport, CT, hardwood case, horizontal louvers in front **600.00**

BQ cylinder player **1,200.00**

Decca, Junior, portable, leather case and handle.. **150.00**

Edison

Amberola 30........................... **400.00**

Army-Navy, WWI **1,200.00**

Excelsior, coin op **2,500.00**

Fireside, with original horn **750.00**

Gem, maroon, 2- to 4-minute reproducer **1,200.00**

Standard, Model A, oak case with metal horn **550.00**

Triumph, with cygnet horn, mahogany case.................. **2,500.00**

Edison Fireside, Model A cylinder phonograph, oak case and lid, Model K reproducer, 19-1/2" l, two-piece maroon Fireside horn with front mount crane, 58 assorted cylinder records in original boxes, **$850**. Photo courtesy of Joy Luke Auctions.

Graphone

12.5 oak case, metal horn, retailer's mark, cylinder......................... **375.00**

15.0 oak case with columns on corners, nickel-plated platform, metal horn, stenciled cast-iron parts **725.00**

Home Grand, oak case, nickel-plated works, #6 spring motor **1,300.00**

Harvard, trumpet style horn......... **300.00**

Kalamazoo, Duplex, reproducer, original horns with decals, pat. date 1904 .... **3,300.00**

Odeon Talking Machine Co., table model, crank wind, brass horn, straight tone arm **500.00**

RCA-Victor, "45" Bakelite Record Player **65.00**

Silvertone (Sears), two reproducers **500.00**

Sonora, Gothic Deluxe, walnut case, triple spring, gold-plated parts, automatic stop and storage **400.00**

Talk-O-Phone, Brooke, table model, oak case rope decorations, steel horn **200.00**

Victor, table top, model #VV-IX, mahogany case, **$190**. Photo courtesy of Joy Luke Auctions.

Victor

Credenza, crank **1,100.00**
Monarch, table model, corner columns, brass bell horn **1,500.00**
School House **2,500.00**
Victor I, mahogany case, corner columns, bell horn **1,500.00**
Victor II, oak case, smooth oak horn **5,500.00**
Victor III, papier-mâché horn **1,400.00**
Victor V, oak case, corner columns, no horn **1,500.00**
Victor VI, oak case, no horn **3,000.00**

Photographs

History: A vintage print is a positive image developed from the original negative by the photographer or under the photographer's supervision at the time the negative is made. A non-vintage print is a print made from an original negative at a later date. It is quite common for a photographer to make prints from the same negative over several decades. Changes between the original and subsequent prints usually can be identified. Limited edition prints must be clearly labeled.

Album

Egypt, 31 photographs of people, temples, ruins, and hieroglyphs, 8-1/2" x 11" albumen prints, many with photographer's credit and signature in negative or on mount, oblong folio, gilt lettered 3/4 morocco, edges worn, c1890 .... **2,070.00**
Japan, 58 hand-colored photographs, portraits, landscapes, architecture, 8-1/4" x 10-1/4" and smaller albumen prints, text captions in negative, oblong folio, decorative cloth, ties, front cover detailed and worn, 1880s....................... **1,725.00**

Ambrotype, Southern Cheyenne Chief War Bonnet, c1863, probably taken during the 1863 delegation to Washington DC, wearing his war shirt, German silver pectoral, buffalo robe on his lap, photograph is in half its original leather covered case, 3-1/4" x 2-5/8", **$5,875**. Photo courtesy of Skinner, Inc.

New Zealand, 89 photographs of New Zealand views and Maori portraits by Iles Photo, Burton Brothers, Wheeler & Son, Josiah Martin, Ring Photo, etc., 7-3/4" x 5-1/2" to 7-1/4" x 9" albumen prints, many with photographer's credit and captions in negative, oblong, gilt-stamped leather, corners worn, 1880s.................................. **3,910.00**

Albumen print, Philadelphia, bustling Market Street scene, calligraphic caption on mount reverse, 5-1/2" x 10"...... **460.00**

Ambrotype, William Gannaway Brownlow, known as Parson Brownlow, the fightin' preacher, half plate .. **3,190.00**

CDV, carte-de-visite

Colored Baptist Church, Petersburg, VA, Lazell & McMillin, Petersburg, photographers, 1966, ext. view, men and women sitting on front fence, pencil inscription "Church of Petersburg Negroes burned by rebels, given by Lottie, Feb 9th, 1868," soil, wear, slight crimp **345.00**
Frederick Douglas, full-length portrait, c1860, erased pencil marks on top border **550.00**
Sojourner Truth, 3/4 view, seated at table, knitting, "I Sell the Shadow to Support the Substance," 1864, corners clipped, toning, light browning **660.00**

Carte-de-Visite, George Bancroft, by Brady, red mount border, encased with signature "George Bancroft" on 3" x 1-1/2" paper, **$175**. Photo courtesy of Historical Collectibles Auctions.

Daguerreotype

Afro-American woman, seated, keeps-in chair, patterned dress, white apron and head wrap, sixth-plate image, unknown photographer, orig seal, slight tarnishing at ends of matte opening, full leatherette case, c1850 .... **4,775.00**
Sell, John Todhunter, seated young child, tinted, sixth-plate by M.A. Root, Philadelphia, stamped on matte, orig. seal, some discoloration to mat, damaged leatherette case, c1840 .... **475.00**
Store front, four-story brick building, signage on building, crates pilled in front, man with top hat, unknown photographer, quarter-plate, image not sealed, plate marked "Chapman," leatherette case with some damage, c1850 .... **4,775.00**
Unknown gentleman, sixth-plate image by Robert Cornelius, orig. brass Cornelius frame with repeating diamond pattern, orig. seal, affixed yellow paper label on reverse "Daguerreotype Miniatures by R. Cornelius, Eighth Street, above Chestnut, Philadelphia," minor oxidation to image, slight mineral deposits on glass, c1840 .... **13,200.00**
Unknown gentleman, seated, sixth-plate image by W & F Langenheim, Philadelphia Exchange, re-sealed image, verdigris on mat, heavy tarnish halo at mat opening, leatherette case with photographer's name one pad,c1840 .... **425.00**
Unknown woman, seated, dark taffeta dress, quarter-plate image by unknown photographer, image resealed, paper matte, leatherette case with hinge separation, c1840 .... **395.00**
Unknown woman, seated, sixth-plate image by W & F Langenheim, Philadelphia Exchange, re-sealed image, verdigris on mat, heavy tarnish halo at mat opening, leatherette case with photographer's name on pad, c1840 .... **425.00**
Unknown woman, well dressed in dark taffeta dress, lace collar and cuffs, leather gloves, portrait brooch at neck, slight tint on cheeks, by Collins, 3rd & Chestnut St., Philadelphia, half-plate, orig. seal, Collins paper label, full leatherette case, c1840-50 .... **450.00**

Magic lantern slides, group of 320 photographic images from 1920s and 1930s, Atlantic City views and events, yachting, fireboats, Mohonk (NY), Duluth

(MN), etc. housed in four individual carrying cases, several slides cracked **230.00**

Photogravure, Alfred Stieglitz, A Bit of Venice, blue tone, printed title, Stieglitz's cred on reverse, c1895, 7" x 4-3/4" **2,530.00**

Platinum-palladium print, Edward S. Curtis, Homeward, tipped in orig mount, Curtis' signature, copyright, and date in plate, his blind stamp on reverse, 1898, 5-3/4" x 7-3/4" **1,100.00**

Salted paper print

Baldus, Edouard-Denis, La Ponte de la Sainte, Baldus's signature, title, and number in the negative, c1855, 13-1/2" x 17-1/4" **1,380.00**

Hill, David Octavius and Robert Adamson, Dr. Harris, James Gordon, Mr. Cowan, from calotype negative, pencil notations on mount reverse, c1845, 6-1/4" x 4-1/2" **3,220.00**

Talbot, William Henry Fox, Windsor Chapel, East End of St. George's, from calotype negative, c1845, 6-1/2" x 7-3/4" **8,050.00**

Hand-colored photograph of American Indian with large drum, blankets, and pot, oak frame, 37-1/2" x 27", **$625**. Photo courtesy of Joy Luke Auctions.

Silver print

Abbott, Berenice, James Joyce, sgd, editioned 67/100 in pencil on mount reverse, photographer's hand stamp on back, 1928, printed c1982, 14" x 11" **3,450.00**

Boubat, Edouard, Woman Walking in Field, sgd in ink on back, sgd, dated, and titled in pencil, 1959, printed later, 14" x 9-1/2" **750.00**

Evans, Walker, Farm from Train Window, notations in black and red pencil, titled in blue pencil, two Fortune hand stamps on reverse, 1950, 10-3/4" x 10-1/2" **1,380.00**

Horst, Horst P., Still Life with Greek Statue, sgd in pencil on reverse, photographer's hand stamp, framed, 1930s, 9-1/2" x 7-1/2" **2,070.00**

Mole, Arthur and J. D. Thomas, The Human US Shield, 30,000 Officers and Men, Camp Custer, Michigan, credit, date, and caption in negative, 1918, 13" x 10-1/4" **815.00**

Schulke, Flip, Muhammad Ali Under Water, sgd by Muhammad Ali, dated and inscribed by Schulke in ink on reverse, taken 1961, printed 1977 .... **2,185.00**

Stereograph

Set

Martinique volcanic eruption, French West Indies, 1902, Keystone View Co., 18 views **95.00**

Stereograph Record William McKinley, Beloved by All the People, Underwood & Underwood, 1901 copyright, boxed set of 60 cards **375.00**

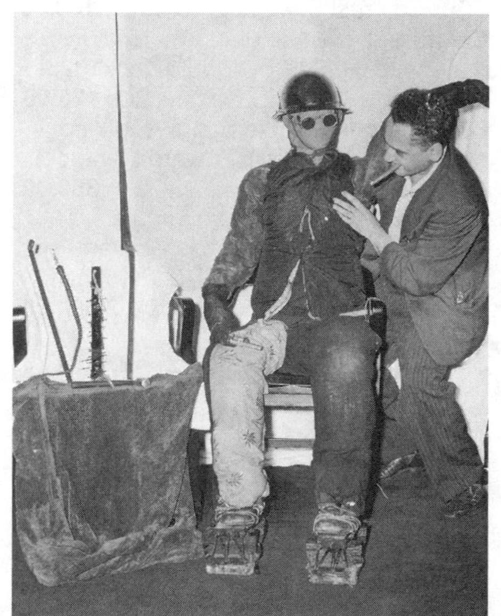

One of a group of three gelatin silver prints by American photographer Arthur Fellig Weegee, with some losses, sold for **$1,610** at Jackson's International July 23-24, 2003 Postcard & Ephemera Auction in Cedar Falls, Iowa.

Single card

Pai Ute mother nursing her baby, John Hillers from Powell Survey, American Indians of the West, northern AZ, 1874 .... **125.00**

The Baltimore & Ohio RR Bridge and Maryland Heights, steam locomotive pulling train across bridge at Harper's Ferry, c1870, photographed by E. Totherick, published by J. F. Jarvis **50.00**

Whittier, John Greenleaf, posed with black woman (possibly Sojourner Truth) and man at poet's Amesbury, MA, home, c1870 .... **225.00**

Tintype

Family, identified on mat "Marshall Kimpton," man wearing military coat, wife wearing elaborate hat, huge bow, daughter stands behind, ninth plate, cased, minor bends, case hinge has old taped repair **150.00**

Unidentified Union soldier with rifle and bayonet, 1/6th plate **360.00**

Piano Babies

History: In the late 1900s, a well decorated home had a parlor equipped with a piano, which usually was covered by a lovely shawl. To hold the shawl in place, piano babies were used. Piano babies are figures of babies, usually made of unglazed bisque. These "Piano Babies" range in size from 3 inches to over 20 inches. They were made in a variety of poses—sitting up, crawling, lying on their tummies, and lying on their backs.

Most piano babies were produced in Germany and France. There were more than 15 factories in Germany that produced this type of bisqueware. Among them Hertwig and Co., Julius Heubach, Royal Rudolstadt, Simon and Halbig, Kling and Co, and Gerbruder Heubach, were the most prolific. Ger. Heubach produced most of his wares for export, between 1914 and 1918. Many of these manufacturers also made dolls and carried the artistry required for fine doll making to their piano baby creations.

Many of the piano babies found today were manufactured by the Heubach Brothers (1820-1945) in Germany, whose rising sun mark is well known. However, many pieces left factories with no mark. The Heubach factory is well known also for creating the same baby but in different sizes. The Heubach babies are well known for their realistic facial features as well as their attention to minute details, such as intaglio eyes, small teeth looking out from lips, blond hair, blue eyes, etc.

Adviser: Jerry Rosen.

2-3/4" h, German, girl, lying down on tummy, looking upright, hands folded, crisp mold, fine details in face and hands **75.00**

4" h, baby, seated, holding rattle, yellow floral trimmed nightgown with large bows and gold beading **250.00**

4" h, 6" l, Hertwig, Pansy, baby girl, intaglio eyes, rosy cheeks, smiling lips, delicately pansy flowers painted around head **250.00**

4-3/8" h, baby, sitting up, legs slightly crossed, rosy cheeks, brown hair, dressed in an old fashioned one piece shorty pajama, white with gold trim, tiny bisque beads **175.00**

4-3/4" h, Heubach, nude, angry looking expression, both hands fisted near face, intaglio blue eyes, rosy complexion, pouting red lips **350.00**

5" h, boy, arms at sides, in Dad's shoes 175.00
5-1/4" h, Heubach, Dutch boy and girl, standing back to back........ 125.00
6" h, Heabach, Flower Child, blue bonnet shaped as flower, sitting, hands folded on lap........ 400.00
6-1/2" h, Heubach, Victorian girl, pleated dress, intaglio blue eyes, blond hair 240.00
7" l, 4-1/2" h, Heubach, crawling, up on two arms, one leg in the air, other bent for crawling, blond molded and painted hair, blue intaglio eyes, rosy cheeks, nice red lips........ 350.00
7-1/4" h, baby, sitting upright, holding sock in right hand, marked "Germany 1182"........ 175.00
8" h, Heubach, intaglio blue eyed molded baby wearing white gown with mint green trim, white raised dots along ruffling at top gown front, detailed dimples in knees, elbows and back, incised mark on back with Heubach sunburst marking, green #37 on bottom........ 600.00
8" l, 4" w, Gebruder Heubach, little boy holding his dog, blond, intaglio eyes, sunburst Heubach mark, model #11160 dep, Germany........ 560.00
9" h, bisque, baby, standing in boots, incised number "6751" on back of gown 175.00
9" h, baby, sitting up, arms raised, feet crossed, beautiful facial expression, dressed in a Victorian white baby gown with pink detailing........ 400.00
9" h, German, all bisque, Heubach character, boy in rabbit suit holding blue bisque egg........ 650.00
10-1/2" h, girl in laced nightee, white bonnet with pink ribbon and bow, green dress, wicker baby walker, right foot protruding out of walker........ 2,000.00
10-7/8" l, 4-1/2" h, lying on tummy with Pug Dog........ 310.00
12" l, baby, blond, blue intaglio eyes, white molded on gown, pale yellow ruffle around top, pink bow on right shoulder, crawling position, arms and hands away from body, circle mark with smaller circle in center, "H" in circle........ 300.00

Pickard China

History: The Pickard China Company was founded by Wilder Pickard in Chicago, Illinois, in 1897. Originally the company imported European china blanks, principally from the Havilands at Limoges, which were then hand painted. The firm presently is located in Antioch, Illinois.

For more information, see *Warman's American Pottery &Porcelain*, 2nd edition.

Bowl
6" d, Autumn Blackberries, sgd "O. Goess" (Otto Goess), 1905-10 mark 200.00
10" d, red and white tulips, gold dec, Limoges blank........ 230.00
Cabinet plate
8-1/2" d, heavy gold enameled border, Limoges blank........ 175.00
9" d, lilies, gold background, artist sgd "Yeschek"........ 100.00
Celery set, two-handled oval dish, five matching salts, all-over gold dec, 1925-30 mark........ 125.00
Chocolate pot, white poppies, gilded band, sgd "Menges" (Edward Mentges), 1905-10 mark........ 350.00
Claret set, claret jug, five tumblers, 11-1/2" d tray, Deserted Garden pattern, sgd "J. Nessy" (John Nessy), 1912-18 mark 2,600.00

Lemonade pitcher, Lilum Ornatum, white lilies, signed Beulet, 1910-1912 mark, 8" h, **$600**. Photo courtesy of Joy Luke Auctions.

Coffee set, Modern Conventional pattern, coffee pot sgd "Hessler" (Robert Hessler), 1910-12 mark, eight cups and saucers sgd "Hess & RH" (Robert Hessler), 1912-18 mark........ 1,450.00
Creamer, 5-1/4" h, Tulip Conventional, sgd "Tomash" (Rudolph Tomascheko), 1903-05 mark........ 400.00
Creamer and sugar
Deserted Garden pattern, sgd "J. Nessy" (John Nessy), 1912-18 mark 200.00
White Poppies & Daisy, sgd, 1912-18 mark........ 250.00
Demitasse cup and saucer
Gold Tracery Rose & Daisy pattern, green band, 1925-30 mark........ 40.00
Poppy pattern, sgd "LOH" (John Loh), 1910-12, price for pr........ 325.00
Lemonade pitcher
Lilum Ornatum pattern, white lilies, sgd "Beulet," 1910-12 mark........ 600.00
Schoner Lemon pattern, sgd "Schoner" (Otto Schoner), 1903-05 mark........ 1,700.00
Match holder, Rose & Daisy pattern, all-over gold, 1925-30........ 40.00
Pin dish, violets dec........ 40.00

Cake plate, pastel scenic view of Yosemite Valley, gold rim, artist signed "E. Challinor," Nippon blank, two handles, original paper label "Pickard Studio Chicago, 3 Cake Tray, Yosemite Valley," maple leaf mark, Pickard mark, 10-1/2" d, **$425**.

Plate
8-1/4" d, gooseberries dec, sgd "P. G." (Paul Gasper), 1912-18 mark 45.00
8-1/2" d, Gibson Narcissus pattern, sgd "E. Gibson" (Edward Gibson), 1903-05 mark........ 300.00
8-3/4" d, Florida Moonlight, sgd "E. Challinor" (Edward Challinor), 1912-18 mark........ 2,300.00
8-3/4" d, orange flowers, sgd "James" (Florence James), 1905-10 mark........ 100.00
9" d, Yeschek Currants in Gold pattern, sgd "Blaha" (Joseph Blaha), 1905-10 mark........ 110.00
Tankard, 16" h, hexagonal, Chrysanthemums, Lustre & Matte Red pattern, sgd "Rean" (Maxwell Rean Klipphahn), 1905-10 mark........ 950.00
Tea set, cov teapot, creamer, cov sugar, Metallic Grape pattern, each sgd "Hessler," (Robert Hessler), 1905-10 marks........ 750.00
Vase
8" h, Golden Pheasant pattern, sgd "E. Challinor" (Edward Challinor), 1919-22 mark........ 500.00
11" h, Calla Lily pattern, sgd "Marker" (Curtis H. Marker), 1905-10 mark........ 550.00
13-3/4" h, two handles, scenic, birch trees, gilding, sgd "E. Challinor" (Edward Challinor), 1912-18 mark 1,900.00

Pickle Castors

History: A pickle castor is a table accessory used to serve pickles. It generally consists of a silver-plated frame fitted with a glass insert, matching silver-plated lid, and matching tongs. Pickle castors were very popular during the Victorian era. Inserts are found in pattern glass and colored art glass.

For more information, see *Warman's Glass*, 4th edition.

Amber, coin spot insert, E.G. Webster Bros. Quadruple purple plate frame with tongs, replaced old silver plate lid, 10-1/2" h, **$410**. Photo courtesy of James D. Julia, Inc.

Amber, 10-1/2" h, Coin spot insert, E. G. Webster Bros. Quadruple plate frame, tongs, replaced SP lid **410.00**

Colorless, 11-3/4" h, acid etched insert, floral dec with bird medallion, octagonal SP frame, marked "Meriden Co. 182" **200.00**

Mount Washington, 10-3/8" h, Colonial Ware, yellow chrysanthemum dec, sp holder and lid, holder sgd "Pairpoint Mfg Co., New Bedford, Mass, B 603," orig tongs.. **735.00**

Opalescent, Daisy & Fern, blue, emb DQ floral jar, resilvered frame **450.00**

Pattern glass, 11" l, 7" h, double, two colorless Valencia Waffle pattern glass inserts, Aurora SP holder.............. **250.00**

Pigeon blood glass, 9-1/2" h, IVT insert, SP frame, orig tongs, minor denting **575.00**

Pipes

History: Pipe making can be traced as far back as 1575. Pipes were made of almost all types of natural and manmade materials, including amber, base metals, clay, cloisonné, glass, horn, ivory, jade, meerschaum, parian, porcelain, pottery, precious metals, precious stones, semiprecious stones, and assorted woods. Some of these materials retain smoke and some do not. Chronologically, the four most popular materials and their generally accepted introduction dates are: clay, c1575; wood, c1700; porcelain, c1710; and meerschaum, c1725.

Pipe styles reflect nationalities all around the world, wherever tobacco smoking is custom or habit. Pipes represent a broad range of themes and messages, e.g., figurals, important personages, commemoration of historical events, mythological characters, erotic and pornographic subjects, the bucolic, the bizarre, the grotesque, and the graceful.

Pipe collecting began in the mid-1880s; William Bragge, F.S.A., Birmingham, England, was an early collector. Although firmly established through the efforts of freelance writers, auction houses, and museums, but not the tobacco industry, the collecting of antique pipes is an amorphous, maligned, and misunderstood hobby. It is amorphous because there are no defined collecting bounds, maligned because it is perceived as an extension of pipe smoking, and now misunderstood because smoking has become socially unacceptable—even though many pipe collectors are avid non-smokers.

Burl, 3-1/2" w, 7-1/4" h, carved tiered archways and staircase, animal and human faces, traces of old dark paint, America, late 19th/early 20th C, minor repair **115.00**

Clay, 6-5/8" l, red clay, 18 incised presentation signatures, unglazed, chips **95.00**

Meerschaum, carved figure, **$125**. Photo courtesy of Dotta Auction Co., Inc.

Glass, large ovoid bowl, long shaped stem, red and ivory dec **90.00**

Meerschaum

Abraham Lincoln, white.......... **520.00**

4" l, bowl carved with figure of nude woman, later faux amber stem, fitted leathered case, Continental, late 19th C.. **275.00**

Porcelain, 19" l, drunken man lying under barrel, small porcelain animal on bowl lid **280.00**

Regimental, 41" l, porcelain bowl, 112 Infantry, Sohlettstadt 1888, named to Res. Huck., two scenes, helmet cover, new spike and hairline in bowl, minor repair on flexible cord **225.00**

Wood, carved

7-1/2" l, hand carved bears crawling on stump, 3-5/8" l celluloid stem **250.00**

8-1/4" l, bearded man's head above deer's head, stem with carved dog's head, America, 19th C, stand **700.00**

Poison Bottles

History: The design of poison bottles was meant to serve as a warning in order to prevent accidental intake or misuse of their poisonous contents. Their unique details were especially helpful in the dark. Poison bottles generally were made of colored glass, embossed with "Poison" or a skull and crossbones, and sometimes were coffin-shaped.

John H. B. Howell of Newton, New Jersey, designed the first safety closure in 1866. The idea did not become popular until the 1930s, when bottle designs became simpler and the user had to read the label to identify the contents.

Owl Drug Co., three-sided, embossed owl, cobalt blue, 9-3/4" h, **$650**. Photo courtesy of American Bottle Auctions.

Bowker's Pyrox Poison, colorless **30.00**

Coffin, 3-1/2" h, cobalt blue, emb, 1890 .... **100.00**

Cylindrical, crosshatch dec, cobalt blue, flared mouth with stopper, smooth base, 6-1/4" h **250.00**

Diamond Antiseptics, 10-3/4" h, triangular shape, golden amber, emb **385.00**

Figural, skull, America, 1880-1900, cobalt blue, tooled mouth, smooth base, 2-7/8" h **500.00**

Imperial Fluid Co. Poison, one gallon, colorless **95.00**

Norwich Coffin, 3-3/8" h, amber, emb, tooled lip **95.00**

Owl Drug Co., 3-3/8" h, cobalt blue, owl sitting on mortar **70.00**

Plumber Drug Co., 7-1/2" h, cobalt blue, lattice and diamond pattern **90.00**

Poison, 3-1/2" h, hexagonal, ribbed, cobalt blue **20.00**

Tinct Iodine, 3" h, amber, skull and crossbones **45.00**

Political Items

History: Since 1800, the American presidency has been a contest between two or more candidates. Initially, souvenirs were issued to celebrate victories. Items issued during a campaign to show support for a candidate were actively being distributed in the William Henry Harrison election of 1840. There is a wide variety of campaign items—buttons, bandannas, tokens, pins, etc. The only limiting factor has been the promoter's imagination. The advent of television campaigning has reduced the quantity of individual items, and modern campaigns do not seem to have the variety of materials that were issued earlier.

Reproduction Alert
Campaign Buttons

The reproduction of campaign buttons is rampant. Many originated as promotional sets from companies such as American Oil, Art Fair/Art Forum, Crackerbarrel, Liberty Mint, Kimberly Clark, and United States Boraxo. Most reproductions began life properly marked on the curl, i.e., the turned-under surface edge.

Look for evidence of disturbance on the curl where someone might try to scratch out the modern mark. Most of the backs of original buttons were bare metal or had a paper label. Beware of any button with a painted back. Finally, pinback buttons were first made in 1896, and nearly all made between 1896 and 1916 were celluloid covered. Any lithographed tin button from the election of 1916 or earlier is very likely a reproduction or fantasy item.

Additional Listings: See *Warman's Americana & Collectibles* for more examples.

Adviser: Theodore L. Hake.

Bookmark, McKinley, Pan-Am Expo, McKinley portrait above image of "Temple Of Music" exhibit, black olive branch beneath portrait, colorful fan-shaped design at bottom tip suspends thread tassel, reverse marked "Copyrighted," 10-1/2" l, 2-1/2" w, **$145**. Photo courtesy of Hake's Americana & Collectibles.

Badge, Eisenhower, 2-3/4" x 2-3/4" cardboard pinback changes image when tilted from black and white smiling Ike portrait to red, white, blue and silver design of crossed US flags and "Welcome Mr President" in black lettering, 1-1/2" x 4-1/2" red fabric ribbon inscribed in gold "Inaugural 1953" **25.00**

Bank, T Roosevelt, 5" h, cast iron, 3-D bust of T Roosevelt, inscribed "Teddy," gold paint, silver eyeglasses, small red accent on his Spanish-American War hat, 75 percent orig paint remains, c1898-1904 .... **195.00**

Bar pin, Hoover, 3/4" l, brass lettering, whit enamel dec **5.00**

Campaign poster, Lyndon Johnson, 11" x 14", red, white, and blue cardboard, for Senate election lost by LBJ to W, Lee O'Daniel, 1941 .... **165.00**

Car attachment, Willkie for President, 3-1/4" x 5", diecut metal, attachment bracket at bottom, Donaldson Art Sign Co., Covington, KY, printed dark blue, red, creamy tan, varnish finish **85.00**

Carte de visite, Lincoln family, 2-1/2" x 4" stiff card, artist re-touched sepia portrait of family gathered around Lincoln, holding book on lap, blank reverse **25.00**

Convention bandanna, GOP, Fort Worth, TX, 1984, 11-1/2" sq folded, opens to 21-1/2" x 22", red, bright white block printing, circle of repeated GOP elephant symbols within 1984 date at each corner, center Lone Star symbol surrounded by text and cowboy boot design **25.00**

Carte-de-visite, Lincoln family, artist re-touched sepia photo of family gathered around Lincoln who holds book on his lap, 1860s image, 2-1/2" x 4", **$20**. Photo courtesy of Hake's Americana & Collectibles.

Convention button

Carter, 3" yellow cello, black lettering, Indiana Labor Coalition, name over outline of state of Indiana, 1976 .... **25.00**

Reagan, 3", green on white cello, sponsored by "The other Washington-Reagan Country," used at Rep. Convention-Dallas Aug 1984 .... **48.00**

Dinner program, Ford, 7-1/2" x 11", slightly textured stiff paper folder, Feb. 15, 1974 annual Republican Douglas County dinner, Omaha Hilton Hotel Ballroom, front cover with black and white photo and id of Ford as Vice President, lists of "Our Republican Family" inside **25.00**

Cello with easel, McKinley, sepia, real photo, reverse covered metal back, small center stamp by "J. Abrahams 229 Bowery New York" plus 1896 patent date, two cutout notches holding replacement easel wire. 3-1/2" d, **$290**. Photo courtesy of Hake's Americana & Collectibles.

Ferrotype pin

Grant, portrait with name on 7/8" brass frame, outer edge of diecut circular designs, vertical pin and clasp on back **295.00**

Lincoln & Hamlin, 5/8", portraits, slogan around front rim, circle of stars, 1860, rim hole **750.00**

Hat, Theodore Roosevelt caricature, 1912, dark blue felt, stenciled large letters on front "Bull-Moose" under image of TR in tan Rough Rider hat, red bandanna, white eyeglasses and teeth, roll up brim 2" high in front, 3" h in back, 12" conical shape **2,025.00**

Jugate button

Bryan-Stevenson, 7/8", black and white photos accented by silver central area, surrounded by red, white, and blue stars and stripes, narrow silver rim **65.00**

Bush, 3-1/2"d cello, small Bush and Dan Quayle black and white portraits on red, white, and blue double flag symbol, black lettering "On His Way To The White House," 1988 ...... **90.00**

McKinley-T Roosevelt, 1-1/4", black and white photos surrounded by gold beaded circles accented by additional gold scrolls at top center and bottom, dark blue background, W&H backpaper **125.00**

Kennedy-Johnson, 4" cello, black and white photos, top third with names in white lettering on red, bottom margin with blue arc inscribed in white "America's Men For The 60s" **90.00**

Reagan-Bush, 1-3/4", 1981 inaugural, white cello pinback, black and white jugate photo accented by five tiny blue stars, 5" l red, white, and blue striped fabric ribbon with gold lettering "Presidential Inauguration Wash DC Jan 20, 1981" **20.00**

Roosevelt, T. and Fairbanks, 1-1/4", black and white portraits against red, white, and blue shield, Pulver, 1904 .... **265.00**

Elephant, cast iron, anti-FDR, 1936, hollow iron figural GOP symbol, dark red molded blanket with gold raised slogan on both sides "Land-on Roosevelt 1936," 90 percent original paint, 90 percent original gold lettering on one side, 50 percent on other side, 2-1/2" x 5" x 3", **$495**. Photo courtesy of Hake's Americana & Collectibles.

Lapel stud

Cleveland, 3/4", horseshoe, dark red fabric, name in white lettering, dark blue horseshoe **30.00**

Harrison, 9/16" diecut top hat, silvered brass, silver luster....... **25.00**

Mechanical pin, 2" h, Taft, Presidential Chair, brass luster back and legs, silver luster seat cover "Who Shall Occupy It," small tab at bottom seat edge pulls and seat flies open to reveal sepia glossy paper real photo of Taft, 1908 ...... **150.00**

Flue cover, US for Ike, red, white, and blue shield with portrait, **$15**.

Medalet, uncirculated

Blaine and Logan, 1" brass, front shows both men, reverse with shield at center "Union" on diagonal, surrounded by "The Republicans Have Ruled Since 1860 And With Blaine & Logan Are Good For Another Term," top rim hole, mint luster....................................... **50.00**

Grant, 1" copper, raised portrait and name on front, designer's name below his shoulder, reverse "Gen US Grant Our Next President May He In Wisdom Rule The Country He Has Saved," 1868, bright copper flashing worn **85.00**

Harrison, 1" brass, portrait, name, and 1841 on front, reverse with eagle with ribbons above and below, slogan "Got It Tip-Come It Tyler" **40.00**

Pennant, inaugural, Eisenhower, 12" x 29", brown felt, white letters, fleshtone portrait, pale turquoise suit jacket, gray necktie, yellow-gold felt trim band and streamers, 1953............................ **30.00**

Hat, Bull Moose, Theodore Roosevelt caricature image, 1912 Progressive Party, dark blue felt, stenciled letters, image of Teddy in tan Rough Rider hat, red bandanna, white eyeglasses and teeth, 13" across base, 12" h, **$2,085**. Photo courtesy of Hake's Americana & Collectibles.

Pinback button

Bryan, 1-1/4", colored portrait, silver background, brown and white shoulder areas, light fleshtone coloring on face, unusual twisted wire orig pin, 1900.................... **70.00**

Goldwater, 3-1/2", Go-Go Goldwater in '64, gold cello, black printing, small image of elephant as hyphen, tiny union printer symbol.......... **24.00**

Kennedy, 1-3/4", All The Way With Kennedy For President, slogan in blue, white background, name in bright red................................ **75.00**

Stevenson, 1" d, Aldai Likes Me, red, white and blue litho **20.00**

Truman, 1-1/4", For President Harry S. Truman, black on cream **60.00**

Press photo, 6-1/2" x 8-1/2", glossy sepiatone, President Harding and young Douglas MacArthur, second unnamed individual in civilian cloths, authorization stamp by International Pres service, early 1920s.. **25.00**

Jugate, Kennedy-Johnson, 1960, cello centered by black and white photos of JFK and LBJ, last names in white lettering on red, blue arc inscribed in white "America's Men For The 60s," **$90**. Photo courtesy of Hake's Americana & Collectibles.

Print, Andrew Jackson, 10-3/4" x 13-1/2" stiff paper centered by 8-3/4" x 11" N Currier hand-colored print, undated, c1840, "Andrew Jackson Seventh President of the United States" **125.00**

Ribbon

Cass, Lewis, 3" x 6-1/2" black on off-white, text above portrait "For President, Lewis Cass, Of Michigan, For Vice President, William O. Butler, Of Kentucky," below portrait "If we are not struck with judicial blindness, we shall cling to this Constitution as the mariner clings to the last plank, when night and the tempest close around him-Lewis Cass," slight folds **10,000.00**

Cleveland, Grover, 3" x 5", 1885 NY inaugural, purple fabric, gold "New York County Democracy March 4, 1885," top overlaid with brocade like band of woven gold brass thread,

stickpin fastener on back, 1" gold luster fringe **65.00**
Eisenhower/Nixon, 2" x 6-1/2", blue fabric, gold lettering "Presidential Campaign Kick-Off-Eisenhower-Nixon-Sept. 19, 1956, Whittier, Calif Campaign Committee" **65.00**
McKinley and Roosevelt Prosperity Parade, 2-1/4" x 7", white fabric, dark blue printing, furled and crossed flags, lunch pail, tiny union printer symbol, issued for Nov. 3, 1900 Cleveland, OH, event **90.00**
Washington, George, 12" l, 1-3/4" w, black on white silk, 2" center inscription, "Washington Association, First In War, First In Peace, First in the Hearts of His Countrymen," oval portrait surrounded by wreath, sword and quill pen, c1832, creases, some missing threads **250.00**

Portrait button, Truman, 1948, cello, centered by black and white portrait circled by gold leafing, dark blue outer rim, crossed red white and blue flags, cardboard insert on back with bar fastener, 3-1/2" d, **$200**. Photo courtesy of Hake's Americana & Collectibles.

Ribbon, George Washington, c1832, black on white silk, "Washington Association," "First In War, First In Peace, First In The Hearts Of His Countrymen," oval portrait surrounded by wreath, burst of black lines, miniature sword and quill pen immediately above portrait, some fold damage, 12" l, 1-3/4" w, 2" h inscription/portrait area, unlisted in Sullivan-Fischer reference, **$150**. Photo courtesy of Hake's Americana & Collectibles.

Stickpin, Harrison Morton, 1-3/4" x 1-3/4" metal eagle, 1-1/2" reverse stickpin, wings open to reveal cardboard photos, July 10, 1888 patent date and number, replaced suspended tassel, images faded **200.00**
Tintype, George Washington, 2-1/2" x 4" card with centered 1-1/4" x 1-3/4" oval center opening over 1-3/4" x 2" tintype with octagonal edges, possibly 1876 Centennial souvenir **150.00**
Watch fob, 1-3/4", brass, Bull Moose, raised moose image, "National Progressive Party New York State Convention, Syracuse, Sept 5 & 6, 1912," Bastian logo **125.00**

Portrait Ware

History: Plates, vases, and other articles with portraits on them were popular in the second half of the 19th century. Although male subjects, such as Napoleon or Louis XVI, were used, the ware usually depicts a beautiful, and often unidentified, woman. A large number of English and Continental china manufacturers made portrait ware. Because most was hand painted, an artist's signature often is found.

Charger, 14" d, Marie Antoinette, sgd "Johner," dark green border, gilt scrolled and leaf dec, blue Austrian beehive mark **275.00**
Dresser box, cov, 4" l, 3-1/4" w, 1-1/2" h, brass heart-shaped box, inlaid lid with hp portrait on ivory of women in formal dress, Florentine designs on box, portrait sgd "Brun" **350.00**
Medallion, 3-1/2" d, Le Pensee, sgd "Wagner," jeweled gilt bronze frame **975.00**

Grouping of five Haviland Limoges portrait plates, each having central hand-painted portrait of French noblewoman, surrounded by concentric gold bands, scalloped rims having floral cartouches and gilt scrollwork, three plates with yellow rims, two blue, all artist signed "A.E. Ring," most identify individual portrayed, green under-glaze mark, "H & Co. L. France," late 1800s, wear, 9-1/2" d, **$550**. Photo courtesy of Alderfer Auction Co.

Plaque
4-7/8" l, 18th C lady in red hat, signed "Hein," reverse titled "Tess of Yarborough, after Gainsborough," Hutschenreuther, Germany, early 20th C, framed **450.00**
5" l, Erbluht, after painting by A. Asti, oval format, seminude woman with flowing brunette tresses, signed lower left, Hutschenreuther, early 20th C, gilt wood frame **950.00**

Plate
9-1/4" d, central portrait of elegant lady with gold circlet, reverse titled "La G de D D'Orleans," bright blue border, three reserves of fruit and floral sprays in gilt borders, top reserve centered by small heraldic crest over monogram, French, late 19th C **425.00**
9-1/2" d, Napoleon I, sgd "Wagner," cobalt blue and pale blue band, cornucopia and urn ornamentation, inscribed "Made for Mrs. John Doyle" verso, minor gilt loss ... **970.00**
9-3/4" d, octagonal shape, hp portrait of Psyche, blue Vienna beehive mark **490.00**
10" h, young woman with wreath of flowers in hair, marked "Royal Munich" **115.00**
12" d, young woman, gilt bronze-colored border, mounted in 15" x 17" walnut frame, German **300.00**

Plaque, German, titled "Odaliske," oval form, woman with long hair, bare breast, back stamped "Heubach Bros.," artist signed, 3-3/8" x 2-5/8" plaque, carved gilt wood frame of scrolled leaves, **$315**. Photo courtesy of Alderfer Auction Co.

Tray, 9-1/2" sq, Napolean I, standing, looking left, left hand behind back exposing dress sword and medals, background of fine furniture and papers, gilt garland border, dark blue-green ground, fitted frame, sgd "Reseh," marked "Vienna, FD, Austria" **1,320.00**
Urn, cov, 15-1/2" h, double handles, "Mme de Montesson," central portrait of French woman wearing white wig, floral

designs, reverse with floral dec, marked "2912, S-2," illegible ring mark, restored lid 275.00

Vase

4-3/4" h, bulbous, titled "Ariadne," sgd "Wagner," maroon ground, gilt floral dec, Austrian beehive mark 850.00

5-3/4" h, gold enamel framed portrait of Ruth, violet luster ground, blue beehive mark with "Germany" in script 435.00

7" h, young beauty in red dress, red roses in hair, finely enameled on bronze, tinted silver foil cartouche against translucent emerald green ground, French, c1900.......... 865.00

Vase, Austrian, late 19th/early 20th C, slender ovoid body, acanthus molded neck, pair of openwork C-scroll handles, trumpet foot, body with central portrait of Ruth, signed "Graf" lower right, gilt surround, horizontal band of birds, strapwork, and stag in landscape, body with overall pattern of raised gilt quatrefoils offset with turquoise beads, 18-3/4" h, **$2,585.** Photo courtesy of Skinner, Inc.

8-1/2" h, Clementine, sgd "N. Kiesel," Art Nouveau form, green-brown mirrored ground, heavily gilt acanthus leaves and vines, bearing mark of Richard Klemm....... 1,690.00

12" h, woman holding yellow roses, opalescent ground in shades of green and purple, gilt floral design, Dresden, wear to gilding..... 1,570.00

13-1/8" h, French, Aesthetic Movement, third quarter 19th C, earthenware, portraits of ladies in exotic costumes, one sgd lower right "Leonard" in gilt border, reverse painted with landscape scenes, sides with royal blue stars outlined in gold on cobalt blue ground, two short gilt handles, ovoid foot, price for pr.................................. 2,300.00

Postcards

History: Postcard collecting is again becoming one of the largest growing areas of antiques. The golden age of postcards dates from 1898 to 1918. Cards printed earlier are collected for their postal history. European publishers, especially in England and Germany, produced the vast majority of cards during the golden age. The major postcard publishers are Raphael Tuck (England), Paul Finkenrath of Berlin (PFB-German), and Whitney, Detroit Publishing Co., and John Winsch (United States). However, many American publishers had their stock produced in Europe.

Postcards fall into two main categories: view cards and topics. View cards are easiest to sell in their local geographic region. View cards that are actual photographs are known as "Real photo" postcards. These were created by itinerant photographers who crossed America, visiting small towns and capturing scenes which range from Main Street to children at play, factories, families, etc. Because these types of photo postcards were created in very small quantities, they are eagerly sought by today's postcard collectors.

Although cards from 1898 to 1918 are the most popular with collectors, the increasing costs of postcards from this era have turned attention to postcards from the 1920s, 1930s, and 1940s. Art Deco cards from the 1920-1930 period are the most desirable. The 1940s "linens," so called because of their textured linen-like paper surface, are the most popular cards of that time period. Cards from the 1950 to 1970 period are called "Chromes" because of their shiny surface.

Note: The following prices are for cards in excellent to mint condition—no sign of edge wear, no creases, untrimmed, no writing on the picture side of the card, no tears, and no dirt. Each defect reduces the price given by 10 percent.

See *Warman's Americana* for more common examples of postcards.

Postcards are popular

An auction of the ephemera and postcard collection of Abe Samuels was held by Jackson's International, in July 2003. The strength of the postcard collecting category was apparent during this auction which attracted bidders from 39 countries and five continents. Holiday postcards were eagerly bid to high amounts. Real photo postcards were well represented, with one of ACLU founder Elizabeth Gurley Flynn, speaking at an Industrial Workers of the World rally in Patterson, MA, selling for $1,265.

Artist signed

Cady, Harrison, Happy Jack Squirrel 300.00

Christy, F. Earl, College Kings and Queens, Tuck series 2766 and 2767, pr... 150.00

Feilig, Hank, Sinner Liqueur, Elves Frog 50.00

Fisher, Harrison, Their New Love, couple with newborn, Charles Schribner Sons, NY, Reinthal and Newman Publisher, NY, glued to backing, framed 50.00

O'Neill, Rose

Babies for Suffrage 635.00

Votes for Women, Klever Kard 115.00

Werkstatte, Wiener, Santa ... 1,150.00

One of a group of three Ellen Clapsaddle Mechanical Halloween postcards, sold for **$1,480.** All postcard photos courtesy of Jackson's International July 23-24, 2003 Postcard & Ephemera Auction in Cedar Falls, Iowa.

Baseball

Palace of Fans Ballpark, Cincinnati, stamped "Sept. 18 1908"....... 125.00

Red Stockings, 1869, real photo of team, Peck & Snyder trading card back 6,038.00

Halloween

Clapsaddle

Mechanical, white child with "O" mouth, looking forward........... 260.00

Series 501 .... 230.00

Series 1301 .... 230.00

Drayton, Grace, #807, for Tuck, girl flying on broom with cat 115.00

Griggs, H., devil in pumpkin 150.00

Schmucker, Samuel L., children in costume, bright moon background 210.00

Schmucker Winsch, 1911

Pretty lady in gray hooded outfit, holding candle 215.00

Pretty lady in green gown, riding broomstick in front of moon.... 150.00

Sleeping lady with fairies floating around head.......................... 195.00

Whitney Publishing, children in costume, bright moon background 195.00

Winsch

Black cat and two children in blue moon **215.00**

Frexius Kid **175.00**

Pumpkins atop corn stalks, spell out Halloween, brown owl in yellow moon, 1913 .... **100.00**

Wiener Werkstatte Santa, **$1,150**.

Hold to light

A Merry Christmas to You, unused **125.00**

Angel, A Merry Christmas, 1907, Belgium, used **100.00**

Black man holding tamborine, Ellem **130.00**

Cinderella, 1900, Belgium, used **85.00**

Girl with Umbrella, used **30.00**

Happy New Year, 1910, windmill **85.00**

Kind Christmas Greetings, 1908, used **50.00**

Santa

Diecut, 1905, cancel on front **115.00**

Mailick **320.00**

Riding in red car **260.00**

Mechanical

Atkins Saw Works, rolling screen **50.00**

Couple, black and white beach scene, pull screen, couple becomes color, screams, some wear **50.00**

Couple, spanking, roles reverse, pr **95.00**

Drinking girls, pr **115.00**

Harold Lloyd, dancing eyes **130.00**

Real photo, known photographer

Beals, Jessie Tarbox, American 1871-1942

Real photo postcard depicting ACLU founder, Elizabeth Gurley Flynn, speaking at an I.W.W. rally, **$1,265**.

Minetta Street **690.00**

The Crumperie, 6th Sheridan Sq, Greenwich Village **575.00**

The Ink Pot **920.00**

Dutcher, H. F., image of Jacob Ruppert Brewer, beer wagon #197, ad on back for G. V. Electric Trucks of Long Island, NY **575.00**

Moyer, Salem C., photo of R.F.D. carrier, New Ringgold, PA, 1907 .... **175.00**

Real photo, unknown photographer

Baker, Josephine, with leopard **140.00**

Belason Theater, Jane Grey billboards **550.00**

Biederwolf Tabernacle Convert's Club, Ohio **750.00**

Boxcar, Santa-Fe, open door shows man sitting on wicker settee with dog **185.00**

Carriages outside French book store **85.00**

Circus views, set of 30 .... **550.00**

Fabric store interior **100.00**

Fireman's parade, Labor Day, 1909, Reading, PA, identified in white lettering on front **130.00**

Golfing, two caddies, Pinehurst, NC, 1910 .... **345.00**

Hot air balloons, National Geographic Society, group of 22 .... **250.00**

Ice Man, "Compliments of Harry the Ice Man" **140.00**

Interior walls, Indian décor, cowboy sitting in upholstered rocking chair, marked "70 Tepee," price for pr **1,065.00**

Jello window display, Cadillac, Michigan, January 1912 .... **140.00**

Male conjoined twins **85.00**

May, Phil, British postcard artist **215.00**

Movie stars, Greta Garbo, Shirley Temple, Clark Cable, Tallulah Bankhead, etc., set of 30 .... **220.00**

Parr, Lulu, bucking horse rider, 1908 .... **320.00**

Peck's Hardware Store, three men standing in front of store **140.00**

Pierrot, set of three, different expressions **60.00**

Riverton, CT, Halloween, image of stuffed horse and person in field, 1911 .... **90.00**

Shakers Women of Mt Lebanon, NY **175.00**

Surveyors building paper mill **150.00**

Titanic, unused **230.00**

West, Mae, commemorating her role in "Catherine Was Great," autographed, c1944, creases, fair condition **85.00**

Zeppelins, set of five **175.00**

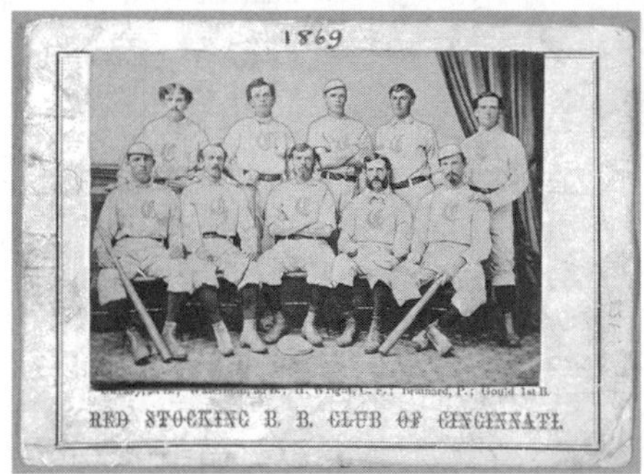

Rare 1869 Red Stockings real photo baseball card, suffering from a myriad of condition problems including losses, folds, creases, and staining, **$6,037.50**.

Santa

Clapsaddle, red suit, white snowflakes **30.00**

Hold to light

Blue and green robes **255.00**

Blue robes, commercial punched hole lower left, printed message on back **200.00**

Purple robes, village scene **175.00**

Salesman's sample, Christmas Joy Fill Your Heart, plain back **230.00**

Horizontal image, Santa holding teddy **50.00**

Humorous, Santa catching trolley **45.00**

Kirchner, Raphael, writing on front, used 1903, small tear in bottom **145.00**

Metamorphic, images of children and cat form eyes, Punch & Judy in beard 210.00

Race gate, Santa in brown fur trimmed blue robes, starry night background 415.00

Silk robe 50.00

Schmucker Whitney 35.00

Wiener Werkstatte, #900, unused 1,150.00

Set

Toy circus, complete set of 50 cards 175.00

Molly and Teddy series, M. Greiner, International Art Publishing, series 791, complete set of six 120.00

Posters

History: Posters were a critical and extremely effective method of mass communication, especially in the period before 1920. Enormous quantities were produced, helped in part by the propaganda role posters played in World War I.

Print runs of two million were not unknown. Posters were not meant to be saved; they usually were destroyed once they had served their purpose. The paradox of high production and low survival is one of the fascinating aspects of poster history.

The posters of the late 19th and early 20th centuries represent the pinnacle of American lithography. The advertising posters of firms such as Strobridge or Courier are true classics. Philadelphia was one center for the poster industry. Europeans pioneered posters with high artistic and aesthetic content, and poster art still plays a key role in Europe. Many major artists of the 20th century designed posters.

Adviser: George Theofiles.

Advertising

E. Dethleffsen & Co., Bern, Ski Fabric, Carl Kunst, Reichhold & Lang, Munich, c1905, male skier 4,370.00

Johnston Harvester, Roberts & Co., Paris, c1900, five vignettes of farmers in their fields with bright red harvesters, green, yellow, brown, and blue, wheat themed red and orange border, dark red lettering on green, 31-3/4" x 23" 750.00

L. Prang & Co.'s Holiday Publications, 1895, 22" x 16" 1,265.00

Pneu Velo Michelin, Hingre, La Lithographic Parisienne, Paris, c1900, young woman in yellow and red riding behind Bibendum as he outdistances pierrot on country road, 37" x 23-3/4" 4,140.00

Prudential Insurance Company of America, Hughson Hawley, Forbes Litho, Boston, new Gothic headquarters in Newark, shades of brown and blue, colorful pedestrians, trolleys, and horses in street, 33-3/4" x 23-1/2" 865.00

Renault, Reunies, Paris, different car models, royal blue ground, yellow lettering, 47-1/2" x 63-1/4", restored, repairs, overprinting 515.00

Uncle John's Syrup, Donaldson Litho, KY, Uncle John in red, yellow, and gray, collecting maple syrump with brown and black oxen, dark blue sky, giant can bearing his likeness, 105-1/2" x 230" 230.00

Campaign, Bryan and Sewell, 1896, full-color chromolithograph, oval black and white bust portraits of candidates, spread winged bald eagle sitting atop U.S. shield and arrows, and "Free Silver Sixteen to One" above laurel wreath and ribbon banner with "Democratic Nominees" and "1896" below, light blue background, red band across center, 20-1/4" x 26-1/4" poster, mounted on acid free backing and framed, light even toning, **$3,100**. Photo courtesy of Cowan Historic Americana Auctions.

Circus Shows, and Acts

Barnum & Bailey Colossal New Free Street Parade, Strobridge, Cincinnati 1,265.00

Miss Juliana & Little Freddy, Adolph Friedlander, Hamburg, 1897, portrait of performers, green background, gold frame, flanked by vignettes of duo in action, red lettering, 26" x 33-3/8" 750.00

Ringling Bros. Barnum & Bailey Liberty Bandwagon, color litho, ornate wagon with Merue Evans portrait, 1943, 30" x 19" 225.00

Tim McCoy's Wild West, circle of riders around red circle, on canvas, 1938, 54" x 41" 900.00

Magic

Buddha and Heartstone, Polish magician performing tricks, English and Polish text, c1914, 14" x 26" 100.00

Carter Beats the Devil, Otis, Cleveland, 1927, window card, Carter in black jacket, multicolored turban, playing cards with Devil in red jacket, yellow, orange, and white lettering, 22" x 14" 500.00

Friedlander Stock Magic, Adolph Friedlander #6966, smiling devil holds card-like vignettes of magic acts in one hand, wand in other, yellow ground, c1919, 14" x 19" 150.00

Kar-Mi Swallows a Loaded gun Barrel, National, "Shoots a cracker from a man's head," Kar-Mi with gun in mouth blasts away at blindfolded assistant, crowd of turbaned Indians, 1914, 42" x 28" 350.00

Movies

"Amazing Transparent Man," Miller Consolidated, D. Kennedy, Marguerite Chapman, sci-fi silhouette against blue, 1959, 27" x 41" 125.00

"Bad Boy," James Dunn and Louise Fazenda, Fox, 1934, 27" x 41" 150.00

"Double Danger," Preston Foster and Whitney Bourne, RKO, 1938, 27" x 41" 110.00

"Goodbye Mr. Chips," Robert Donat and Greer Garson, MGM, 1939, 27" x 41" 450.00

"I'll Be Seeing You," Ginger Rogers, Joseph Cotton, and Shirley Temple, United Artists 1945, 27" x 41" 150.00

"Love Takes Flight," Bruce Cabot and Beatrice Roberts, Grand National, 1937, 22" x 28" 135.00

"Mule Train," Columbia Pictures, Gene Autry, Champion, full-color portraits, 1950, 27" x 41" 150.00

"Smoldering Fires," Pauline Frederick and Laura La Plante, Universal, 1925, 14" x 22" 125.00

"I Want You for US Army," James Montgomery Flagg, American, 1877-1960, colored lithograph of Uncle Sam, c1917, 40" x 29-7/8", **$4,370**. Photo courtesy of Pook & Pook.

Political and patriotic

America Lets Us Worship As We Wish—Attend The Church Of Your Choice, for American Legion sponsored "Americanism Appreciation Month," full-color image of praying Uncle Sam, family at dinner table behind him, c1945, 20" x 26"........ **275.00**

Bridge of Peace, Venette Willard Shearer, anti-war poster from American Friends Service Committee, National Council to Prevent War, in color, children of all nations play beneath text of song of peace, c1936, 16" x 22"........ **125.00**

Confidence, large color portrait of Roosevelt over yacht at sea, "Election Day was our salvation/Franklin Roosevelt is the man/Our ship will reach her destination/Under his command...Bring this depression to an end...," c1933, 18" x 25"........ **250.00**

United Nations Day, blue and white U.N. banner waves over airbrushed stylized brown and yellow globe, minor edge crumple, 1947, 22" x 23"........ **250.00**

Theater

Bringing Up Father, McManus, "Jiggs, Maggie, Dinty Moore-George McManus's cartoon comedy with music," early newspaper cartoon characters against New York skyline, c1915, 41" x 81"........ **425.00**

Claudine Clerice Fr, Collette Willy opera, full color, French, 1910, 26" x 35"........ **275.00**

Uncle Tom's Cabin, Courier, Buffalo, two men in black blazers, green and white striped pants, carrying red umbrellas, passing each other in the woods, riding identical brown horses, text "We are lawyers and our name is Marks, always looking for Business," 82" x 41-3/4"........ **1,100.00**

Transportation

Always in the Sun, Pacific Line, liner beneath large yellow sun, orange map of South America, light blue ground, orange lettering, 39-3/4" x 24-3/4"........ **300.00**

Pan American, Flying Down to Rio, Paul George Lawler, 41" x 27"........ **1,495.00**

Royal Mail Atlantis, Padden, tourists in Royal mail motor launch approaching harbor village, mountains in background, c1923, 25" x 38"........ **675.00**

SS France, Bob Peak, launching of French ocean liner, champagne and confection in front of huge, night-lit bow of ship, 1961, 30" x 46"........ **450.00**

SS Michelangelo **and** ***SS Raffaello***, Astor, detailed cutaway of Italian ocean liners, designed for use in travel office, printed on plasticized stock, metal frame, 1964, 54" x 22"........ **300.00**

WWI, stone litho, "Boys and Girls! You can help your Uncle Sam win the war. Save your quarters. Buy War Savings Stamps," full color, issued by the U.S. Government with Torch of Liberty seal, James Montgomery Flagg artist, c1917, overall light browning of paper, 20" w, 30" h, **$700**. Photo courtesy of James D. Julia, Inc.

Travel

A Sorel Grande Quinzaine de Paris a Port-Aviation, 1909, Societe Generale d'Impression, Paris........ **6,900.00**

Canadian Pacific, Quebec, 1937, resort hotel towering over city, brown, green, and yellow, dark and light blue water, 34-1/2" x 23-1/2"........ **1,100.00**

Documents Decoratifs/Nectar, 1902, Librarie Centrale des Beaux-Arts, 18" x 12"........ **5,175.00**

National Alfred Oppenheim Internationale Lutschiffart Ausstelung, 1909, Wusten & Co., Frankfurt........ **3,450.00**

Plume et Primevere, 1899, F. Champenois, Paris, two decorative panels each 28" x 11"........ **13,800.00**

Sun Valley, Idaho, gouache maquette on illus board, woman skier on chair lift........ **4,830.00**

Sun Valley, Idaho, gouache maquette on illus board, black, white, and gray, standing woman, skis in snow... **5,060.00**

Zodiac, 1896, F. Champenois, Paris, 25" x 19"........ **5,865.00**

World War I

Call to Duty—Join the Army for Home and Country, Cammilli, recruiting image of Army bugler in front of unfurled banner, 1917, 30" x 40"........ **325.00**

Clear the Way!, Howard Chandler Christy, Columbia points the way for Naval gun crew, c1918, 20" x 30"........ **250.00**

Follow the Flag—Enlist in the Navy, James Daugherty, sailor plants flag on shore, 1917, 27" x 41"........ **450.00**

Treat 'Em Rough—Jon The Tanks, A. Hutaf, window card, electric blue-black cat leaping over tanks in fiery battle, white border, c1917, 14" x 22"...... **900.00**

World War II

Loose Talk Can Cost Lives, Keep it under your Stetson, attributed to Frank Godw, two men in white life boat drifing on breen and blue sea, 39" x 29"........ **950.00**

You buy 'em, we'll fly 'em, Wilkinsons, US Government Printing Office, smiling pilot in open cockpit, khaki brown and green flight jacket and helmet, 27-7/8" x 20-1/4"........ **350.00**

Pratt Ware

History: The earliest Pratt earthenware was made in the late 18th century by William Pratt, Lane Delph, Staffordshire, England. From 1810 to 1818, Felix and Robert Pratt, William's sons, ran their own firm, F. & R. Pratt, in Fenton in the Staffordshire district. Potters in Yorkshire, Liverpool, Sunderland, Tyneside, and Scotland copied the products.

The wares consisted of relief-molded jugs, commercial pots and tablewares with transfer decoration, commemorative pieces, and figures and figural groups of both people and animals.

For more information, see *Warman's English & Continental Pottery & Porcelain*, 3rd edition.

Marks: Much of the early ware is unmarked. The mid-19th century wares bear several different marks in conjunction with the name Pratt, including "& Co."

Bank, 5" h, figural, underglaze enamel dec center chimney house, male and female figure to either side, Yorkshire, 19th C, damage to chimney and backside of roof........ **275.00**

Cradle, pearlware
4" l, underglaze polychrome enamels, one molded with baby sleeping, c1800, repairs to hood and side of body........ **100.00**

7-3/4" l, underglaze polychrome enamels, oval form molded as hooded cradle with sleeping child, c1800, restored to lower body and under base, chip and hairline to hood **600.00**

Creamer, 5-1/4" h, cow and milkmaid, yellow and black sponged cow, underglaze enamels, translucent green stepped rect base, horns chipped **450.00**

Cup plate, 3-1/8" d, Dalmatian, white, black spots **95.00**

Jug, ovoid, short shell molded spout, transfer printed with two cartouches, one with washerwomen, other horsemen, black enameled ground, mid-19th C, 5" h, **$150**. Photo courtesy of Skinner, Inc.

Figure, pearlware

8-1/2" h, Autumn, underglaze polychrome enamels, c1800 .... **125.00**

9" h, Summer, underglaze polychrome enamels, c1800, chip on plinth base **115.00**

Flask, 4-1/8" l, pearlware, shell-form, underglaze polychrome enamels, c1800, slight glaze blemishes **765.00**

Jar, cov, polychrome transfer

2-1/2" d, 2-1/4" h, large dog guarding baby in wicker cradle, bulbous base with rim flakes **135.00**

4-1/4" d, 2" h, fishermen at sea, stains, small rim flakes **120.00**

4-1/2" d, 2" h, Shakespeares House Henley St, Stratford on Avon, stains, minor rim flakes **80.00**

Jug, 8" h, molded leaves at neck and base, raised and polychrome painted hunting scene on colored ground, c1800 .... **750.00**

Mug, 4" h, colorful tavern scene transfer **95.00**

Mustard jar, cov, dark blue hunt scene, tan ground **75.00**

Pitcher, 9-3/8" h, yellow, black, red, green, and gray on white ground, relief faces, pig, sheaves of whet, keys, helmet, crossed muskets, and swords, imp around foot "The Reverend Shepherd of His Flock, His Greaze, The Lord Bishop of Shearemclean," also "Gentle Persuasive of Government Religion, Tithe" in banners, minor hairline at rim, minor touch up glaze wear on handle **700.00**

Plate, framed, 9-1/2" d, bittersweet border, polychrome transfer scene with some hand painted details, harbor with came drawn cart in foreground, Sebastopol, black frame with gold repaint **65.00**

Pot lid, framed, polychrome transfer with some hand painting

5-3/4" d, mother and children playing hide and seek **95.00**

6" d, Shakespeares House, Henley St. **85.00**

6-1/2" d, boys fighting, "The Wolf and the Lamb," glued, black frame **50.00**

8" d, "The room in which Shakespeare was born…," oak frame **100.00**

Tea caddy, 6-1/4" h, rect, raised figural panels front and back, fluted and yellow trimmed lid, blue, yellow, orange, and green dec **350.00**

PRINTS

History: Prints serve many purposes. They can be a reproduction of an artist's paintings, drawings, or designs, but often are an original art form. Finally, prints can be developed for mass appeal rather than primarily for aesthetic fulfillment. Much of the production of Currier & Ives fits this latter category. Currier & Ives concentrated on genre, urban, patriotic, and nostalgic scenes.

Reproduction Alert: The reproduction of Maxfield Parrish prints is a continuing process. New reproductions look new, i.e., their surfaces are shiny and the paper crisp and often pure white. The color on older prints develops a mellowing patina. The paper often develops a light brown to dark brown tone, especially if it is acid based or was placed against wooden boards in the back of a frame.

Size is one of the keys to spotting later reproductions. Learn the correct size for the earliest forms. Be alert to earlier examples that have been trimmed to fit into a frame. Check the dimensions before buying any print.

Carefully examine the edges within the print. Any fuzziness indicates a later copy. Also look at the print through a magnifying glass. If the colors separate into dots, this indicates a later version.

Apply the same principles described above for authenticating all prints, especially those attributed to Currier & Ives. Remember, many prints were copied soon after their period introduction. As a result, reproductions can have many of the same aging characteristics as period prints.

Additional Listings: See Wallace Nutting.

Will Barnet, (American, b 1911,) *Persephone,* 1982, edition of 250, published by Associated American Artists, printed by Fine Creations, Inc., New York, sgd and dated "© Will Barnet 1982" in pencil lower right, numbered "71/250" in pencil lower center, titled in pencil lower left, color screenprint on Arches paper, 34" x 16-1/2", unframed, wide margins, handling marks, creases, **$470**. Photo courtesy of Skinner, Inc.

Arms, John Taylor, Rodez/The Tower of Notre Dame, etching on paper, edition of 120 plus six trial proofs, sgd and dated "John Taylor Arms-1927" in pencil lower right, inscribed "Arms 1926" and "Rodez 1926" in the plate, 11-7/8" x 4-7/8", framed **230.00**

Atkins & Nightingale, publisher, J. Cartwright, engraver, Georgetown and Federal City, or City of Washington, 1801, etching with aquatint and hand coloring on paper, 16" x 23-1/4", framed, few minor scattered stains, light toning ... **17,625.00**

Baille, James, publisher, colored lithograph, The Marriage, 1849, 12" x 8-1/2", period frame **115.00**

Benson, Frank Weston, Geese Alighting, drypoint on paper, 1916, second of two published states, sgd "Frank W. Benson" in pencil lower left, dated in the plate lower left, numbered "44" in pencil lower right, 9-3/4" x 8" plate size, framed **1,035.00**

Benton, Thomas Hart

Going West, locomotive, 1934, 11-1/2" x 22-1/2" **36,800.00**

Slow Train Through Arkansas, 1941, Assoc American Artists limited edition of 250, 12-1/2" x 17". **3,500.00**

Threshing, 1941, Assoc American Artists limited edition of 250, 12-1/4" x 17-3/8" **3,700.00**

Wreck of the OL, 97, 1944, Assoc American Artists limited edition of 250, 12-3/4" x 17", slight foxing **7,500.00**

Boydell, John, publisher, image by Benjamin West, engraved by John Hall, William Penn's Treaty with the Indians, When He Founded the Province of Pennsylvania in North America in 1681, hand colored engraving, c1775, 18-1/2" x 23-1/2", minor repairs to border **1,450.00**

Frank Weston Benson (American, 1862-1951), *River Drifters,* 1914, published state, edition of 50, signed "Frank W. Benson" in pencil lower left, numbered "18/50" in pencil lower right, drypoint on paper, plate size 8-7/8" x 7", framed, **$1,880**. Photo courtesy of Skinner, Inc.

Chagall, Marc, The Cello, color litho on wove paper, sgd "Marc Chagall" in pencil lower right, numbered "38/50" in pencil, 13-1/2" x 9-3/4", framed **5,750.00**

Currier, Nathaniel, publisher, after Arthur Fitzwilliam Tait, The Cares of a Family 1856, lithograph with hand coloring heightened by gum Arabic on paper, identified in inscription in the matrix, Conningham, 814, 22" x 28", matted, unframed **2,990.00**

Currier, Nathaniel, publisher, Frances Flora Palmer, lithographer, lithograph with hand coloring on paper, identified in inscription in matrix

- American Farm Series No. One, 1853, Conningham 134, 21-3/8" x 28-1/4", framed.................... **2,185.00**
- American Farm Series No. Two, 1953, Conningham 135, 22" x 29-1/8", matted, unframed, toning, hinged to mat **2,990.00**
- American Farm Series No. Three, 1853, Conningham 133, 20-3/4" x 27-3/4", matted, unframed... **2,415.00**
- American Farm Series No. Four, 1853, Conningham 136, 20-1/8" x 26-3/4", label from Kennedy & Co., New York, framed **5,465.00**
- American Winter Scene, Morning, 1854, Conningham 208, 21-1/4" x 28", framed **19,550.00**
- American Winter Scene, Evening, 1854, Conningham 207, 20-3/4" x 27", unframed **8,625.00**
- The American Clipper Ship, Witch of the Wave, undated, Conningham 115, 13" x 16-1/2", framed, overall toning, scattered staining, fox marks, creases throughout **865.00**
- The Last War Whoop, Conningham 3457, folio colored lithograph, 29-3/4" w, 23-3/4" h, contemporary 36-1/4" w, 30" h frame, restored tear **1,540.00**

Currier & Ives

- A Summer Ramble, Conningham 5874, hand colored, minor foxing, few repairs, title worn but readable, trimmed margins, 13" w, 17" h, 17-1/4" w, 21-1/2" h oak frame **550.00**
- Edward and Swiveller, Conningham 940, sgd "Scott Leighton," printed in oil colors, some hand colored, wide margins, 38-1/2" w, 26" h, cherry 41-1/2" w, 29" h frame.......... **3,245.00**
- Flora Temple, Conningham 891, sgd "L. Mauer" on the stone, hand-colored lithograph, 28" w, 20-5/8" h, carved 35" w, 28" h frame, restoration **1,650.00**
- Life in the Woods, Returning to Camp, Conningham 3513, hand-colored lithograph, margins trimmed, some stains, surface wear, 29-1/4" w, 23" h, matted and framed 37-1/4" w, 27-1/4" h **1,650.00**
- The Celebrated Stallions George Wilkes and Commodore Vandebilt, Conningham 897, hand-colored lithograph, restorations in sky, 20-1/4" x 28-3/4", molded 23" x 31-1/2" oak frame **1,650.00**
- The Fiend of the Road, Conningham 1945, "Printed in Oil Colors," sgd on the stone by "Scott Leighton," some hand coloring, glued down, minor stains and edge damage, 27-3/4" w, 19-1/4" h, 32-1/4" w, 22-1/2" h frame **990.00**

Endicott & Co., NY, publisher, The United States Gunboat Ascutney, hand colored, artist sgd on stone, dated "63," light foxing, stains, small repair to margin, 36" w, 21" h, black painted 37-1/4" w, 24-1/4" h frame....................... **1,100.00**

Greenbough, F. W., Phila, published by, printed and colored by I. T. Bowen, titled Ahyouwaighs, Chief of Six Nations, wearing yellow fringed coat, red sash, holding knife, tomahawk in belt, red and white headdress, peace medal, 18-1/2" x 13", contemporary paint dec frame with red and black graining, marbleized corner blocks............................ **990.00**

Hall, Edith Emma Dorothea, Still Life/ Vegetables, color woodcut on paper, sgd and dated "Emma Hall '54" in pencil lower right, 9-1/4" x 7-1/2", matted **115.00**

Alexander Calder (American, 1898-1976). *Blue Moon*, c1970, edition of 100, published by Associated American Artists, signed "Calder" in pencil lower right, numbered "66/100" in pencil lower left, identified on AAA label affixed to backing, color lithograph on paper, image/sheet size 23" x 30-1/2", framed, deckled edges, cockling, not examined out of frame, **$1,765**. Photo courtesy of Skinner, Inc.

Hyde, Helen, Moon Bridge at Kameido, color woodcut on paper, sgd "Helen Hyde" in pencil lower right, monogram and clover seals lower left, numbered "67" in pencil lower left, inscribed "Copyright, 1914, by Helen Hyde" in the block lower left, 13-1/4" x 8-7/8", framed **460.00**

Icart, oval, hand colored, sleeping woman, blond hair, light green dress, brown and white dog at foot of bed, imp windmill mark at lower margin with signature, glued to matting, 23-1/2" x 27-1/4" **1,320.00**

Kellogg, The Farmer's Pet, girl in pink dress, holding yellow, blue, and red rooster, light stains, margin damage, 12-1/4" w, 16" h, period paint dec frame **415.00**

Kent, Rockwell, Diver, wood engraving on paper, 1931, edition of 150, sgd "Rockwell Kent" in pencil lower right, 7-3/4" x 5-1/4" image size, framed, 3/8" margins or more **1,120.00**

Knight, Dame Laura Knight, Gilding the Lily, etching and aquatint on paper, edition of 35, sgd "Laura Knight" in pencil lower right, 11-1/2" x 7-1/2" plate size, framed, margins over 1" **750.00**

Leighton, Clare, The Lovers, woodcut on paper, 1940, edition of 30, sgd "Clare Leighton" in pencil lower right, numbered and titled "26/30..." in pencil lower left, 7" x 4-7/8" image size, matted, unframed, margins over 1", scattered foxing, annotations to margins **325.00**

Lindenmuth, Tod, Low Tide, color woodcut on paper, sgd "Tod Lindenmuth" in pencil lower right, titled in pencil lower left, 15" x 14" image size, framed **1,600.00**

Lindner, Richard, Man's Best Friend, color lithograph on paper, c1970, edition of 250, sgd "R. Lindner" in pencil lower right, numbered "31/250" in pencil lower left on Arches cream paper with

watermark, 27-3/4" x 21-1/2" sheet size, unmatted, unframed, minor handling marks, nicks, creases **530.00**

Alice Willets Donaldson, *The Old Bay,* sgd lower right, framed under glass, 18" x 24", **$395**. Photo courtesy of David Rago Auctions, Inc.

Marin, John, La Cathedral de Meaux, 1907, etching on Arches wove paper with watermark, sgd "...de J. Marin" in pencil lower center, sgd and dated within the plate, 8-1/2" x 6-1/8" plate size, matted, deckled edges on two sides **350.00**

Marsh, Reginald, Old Paris Night Street with Two Girls, litho on chine collé, sgd "Reginald Marsh" in pencil lower right, sgd and dated within the matrix, inscribed "30 proofs" in pencil lower left, 12-3/4" x 8-7/8" image size, framed **1,150.00**

Matisse, Henri, lithograph on paper

Danseuse au Fauteuil en Boi, from DIX DANSEUSE, 1927, total edition of 150, sgd and numbered "3/15 Henri-Matisse" in pencil lower right, 18" x 10-1/2" image size, framed, approx 1" margins, toning, subtle rippling and soiling............**10,575.00**

Danseuse au Divan Pliee en deux from DIX DANSEUSES, 1927, total edition of 150, sgd and numbered "51/130 Henri-Matisse" in pencil lower right, label from Goodspeed's Book Shop, Boston, on reverse, 18" x 11" image size, framed, deckled edges to three sides, mat staining, subtle soiling, masking tape to upper edge on reverse **14,100.00**

Milton, Peter, Light Sweet Crude, etching and aquatint, 1996, edition of 175, sgd and dated "PMilton 96" in pencil lower right, numbered "71/175" in pencil lower left, titled in pencil lower center, on Somerset cream wove paper with watermark, 18-3/8" x 15-1/4" plate size, unmatted, unframed, margins over 2" with deckled edges, subtle foxing and/or staining **235.00**

Newell, J. P., lithographer and publisher, Newport, R.I., identified in inscription in matrix, lithograph with hand-coloring on paper, framed, tear to margin upper right, toning, stains, foxing **1,175.00**

Picasso, Pablo

Deux Femmes Nues, etching on paper, 1930, edition of 125, sgd and numbered "34/125 Picasso..." in ink beneath image, label from Goodspeed's Book Shop, Boston, on reverse, 12-1/4" x 8-7/8" plate size, framed, scattered pale foxing **5,875.00**

La Guitare Sur la Table, etching with drypoint on paper, 1922, reprinted 1961, total edition of 70, stamped signature "Picasso" lower right, numbered "29/50" in pencil lower left, 3-1/8" x 4-3/4" plate size, framed.............................. **1,100.00**

Andred V. Stevovich, *Morningstar,* 1980, edition of 75, signed and dated "AndrewVStevovich 1980" in pencil lower right, titled in pencil lower center, numbered "65/75" in pencil lower left, color lithograph on paper, image size 10" x 14-1/2", framed, **$325**. Photo courtesy of Skinner, Inc.

Prior, Scott, Provincetown Rooftops, etching on heavy wove paper, 1971, sgd and dated "Scott Prior 1971" in pencil lower right, titled in pencil lower center, inscribed "Artist's Proof" in pencil lower left, 8-7/8" x 11-3/4" plate size, matted, unframed, wide margins, minor staining **230.00**

Ramos, Mel, Phantom Lady, color screenprint on paper, 1963, sgd "Mel Ramos" in pencil lower right, numbered "HC 9/20" in pencil lower left , copyright, printer and publisher noted within matrix, 37" x 30" sheet/image size, unmatted, unframed, minor handling marks and creases **420.00**

Sachse, View of Washington City, Capitol building in foreground, Washington monument in back, colored lithograph, marked "Lith. & Print by E. Sacshe & Co., Baltimore, MD," stains and edge tears, 36" w, 28" h **700.00**

Sloan, John, Washington Arch, etching on paper, sgd "John Sloan" in pencil lower right, sgd and dated within the plate lower right, titled in pencil lower left, 7-3/4" x 4-3/4", framed.............. **1,265.00**

Soyer, Raphael, Bust of a Girl, lithograph in black, red and blue on paper, edition of 300, sgd "Raphael Soyer" in pencil lower right, numbered "86/300" in pencil lower left, image size 18-3/8" x 13-5/8", framed, over 1" margins............................ **210.00**

Spence, R. S., publisher, printed by Wm Robertson, NY, American Hunting Scene, four gentlemen with guns, dogs, and boat hunting waterfowl, hand colored lithograph, 22" x 28", framed, some foxing and waterstains at borders........... **330.00**

Sterner, Albert Edward, The Reveil, etching with drypoint on wove paper with watermark, sgd "Albert Sterner" in pencil lower right, numbered "Ed. 250" in pencil lower left, annotated within lower margin, 8-7/8" x 7" plate size, matted........ **325.00**

Prang & Mayer, publishers, J. F.A. Cole, delineator and lithographer, New Bedford, Massachusetts, identified in inscriptions in the matrix, hand coloring, 16" x 32" image size, framed, repaired tears and punctures, scattered fox marks, staining, light toning **865.00**

Vogt, C H., View of the City of New Bedford, Massachusetts, 1876, identified in inscriptions in the matrix, 22" x 33" image size, framed, tear at left margin, scattered fox marks, overall toning**525.00**

Walker, George H. and Co., publisher, Joe L. Jones, lithographer, Deacon Jones' One Hoss Shay, No. 2, lithograph in blue and black, hand coloring, on paper, identified in inscriptions in matrix, 22-1/2" x 29-5/8" **490.00**

Hutton Webster, Junior (American, 1910-1954), *Cactus Flowers*, signed "Hutton Webster, Jr." in ink lower center, color monotype on paper, image size 9-1/4" x 8-3/8", framed, margins 1/2" or more, soiling and foxing, rubs to sheet below image lower right, **$235**. Photo courtesy of Skinner, Inc.

Welliver, Neil G., Shadow from Zeke's, color screen print on paper, sgd "Welliver" in pencil lower right, numbered "116/144" lower left, identified on label on reverse, 36" x 36-1/4", framed **920.00**

Wengenroth, Stow, Great Horned Owl, litho on paper, 1960, sgd "Stow Wengenroth" in pencil lower right, numbered "Ed./50" in pencil lower left, titled and annotated lower left, 15-1/4" x

11-3/4", matted, deckled edges on two sides, mat and other toning.......... **575.00**

Whistler, James Abbott McNeill

Billingstate, c1859, etching with drypoint on paper, sgd and identified within the plate, 6" x 9" plate size, framed, rippling, minor creases **1,035.00**

Fumette, c1858, etching on paper, sgd and identified within the plate, identified on label from Frederick Keppel, NY, on reverse, 6-1/2" x 4-1/4", framed, rippling........ **1,495.00**

Wood, Grant, published by Associated American Artists

Tree Planting Group, litho on paper, sgd "Grant Wood-1937" in pencil lower right, 8-3/8" x 10-7/8", matted **4,025.00**

Vegetables, 1938, litho with hand coloring on paper, sgd "Grant Wood" in pencil lower right, identified on label from AAA on reverse, 7" x 9-1/2", framed........................ **550.00**

Prints, Japanese

History: Buying Japanese woodblock prints requires attention to detail and abundant knowledge of the subject. The quality of the impression (good, moderate, or weak), the color, and condition are critical. Various states and strikes of the same print cause prices to fluctuate. Knowing the proper publisher's and censor's seals is helpful in identifying an original print.

Most prints were copied and issued in popular versions. These represent the vast majority of the prints found in the marketplace today. These popular versions should be viewed solely as decorative since they have little monetary value.

A novice buyer should seek expert advice before buying. Talk with a specialized dealer, museum curator, or auction division head.

The following terms are used to describe sizes: chuban, 7-1/2 x 10 inches; hosoban, 6 x 12 inches; and oban, 10 x 15 inches. Tat-e is a vertical print; yoko-e a horizontal one.

Note: The listings here include the large amount of detail necessary to determine value. Condition and impression are good, unless indicated otherwise.

Album, Toyokuni III, Kuniyoshi, Hiroshige, mostly from series Ogura Imitations of the One Hundred Poets and Keniyshi Genji **2,645.00**

Chikanobu, framed triptych of women by lake, c1890, good impression, somewhat faded **125.00**

Eishi, four courtesans in elaborate kimonos, 1790s, framed, good impression, somewhat faded **345.00**

Eisan, courtesan with water view in background, fair impression, faded **245.00**

Goyo, Portrait of a Beauty, Dai-oban, excellent impression, toned and matted to within image **1,100.00**

Hasui, Cryptomeria Avenue to Nikko, excellent impression, color, and condition, framed **500.00**

Hiroshige III, c1885, color woodblock, harbor scene, two chop marks, mounted in Arts & Crafts style frame, image size 6-1/4" x 19", **$150**. Photo courtesy of David Rago Auctions, Inc.

Hiroshige, Fireworks, Ryogoku **130,700.00**

Hiroshige II, Mimeguiri Embankment and the Sumida River, from Toto Meisho, 1862, good impression, fine color **350.00**

Hiroshi Yoshida, Fuji san from Yamanka, good impression, juzuri seal, good color, slight soil to margins..................... **375.00**

Hokusai, Flower Arrangement, surimono, early 19th C, good impression and color, some toning and rubbing............ **245.00**

Kawamishi, The Water Lily Season, sgd and titled in pencil, dated, numbered, framed **425.00**

Kiyonaga, Torri, two women wearing kimonos by side of stream, wooden garden trellis in background, red, green, brown, and black, old wooden mat and frame, c1800, 16-1/4" w, 19-3/4" h, split to mat..**110.00**

Kiyotomo, A Samurai with a Courtesan, c1740, hosoban, with hand-coloring (tan-e), toning, creases, holes, and abrasions **230.00**

Koryusai, pair of prints, Young Samurai with Letter Calling on a Lady, c1780 or later, good impression, fair color and condition, faded with stains and creases; and A Courtesan with a Playful Monkey, c1780 or later, good impression and color, slight staining.................. **2,750.00**

Kunisada, courtesan and two kamuro, landscape in background, printed in blue, c1830, good impression and color **215.00**

Kuniyoshi, A Courtesan in Elegant Kimono Holding a Pipe, excellent impression and color with visible wood grain, slight staining and holes **190.00**

Okiie Hashimoto, Village in the Evening, sgd in pencil in margin, dated, Hashi seal, good impression, framed, 17" x 21-1/2" **250.00**

Hausi, winter snow scene, 10-1/4" w, 15-1/2" h, **$200**.

Sekino, Bridge in Snow, sgd in image, seal, good impression, 18" x 12-1/2" **200.00**

Shigenobu, surimono of courtesan in an interior, make-up table and mirror to left, fine impression and color............ **634.00**

Toyokuni, perspective print of busy shopping area and temple grounds, 1790s, framed, good impression, faded **260.00**

Toyokuni II, Two Courtesans, c1800, good impression, faded, trimmed, small hole, stains, and creases **150.00**

Toyokuni III, Pentaptcyh of people in boat feeding goldfish, iris garden, framed, very good impression, missing leaf, somewhat faded.................. **230.00**

Utamaro, Woman Washing Her Hair, good impression, stained, rubbed, and faded, framed............................. **725.00**

Utamaro II, three women in an interior, c1811, good impression, faded, soiled **175.00**

PUZZLES

History: The jigsaw puzzle originated in the mid-18th century in Europe. John Spilsbury, a London mapmaker, was selling dissected-map jigsaw puzzles by the early 1760s. The first jigsaw puzzles in America were English and European imports aimed primarily at children.

Prior to the Civil War, several manufacturers, e.g., Samuel L. Hill, W. and S. B. Ives, and McLoughlin Brothers, included puzzles in their lines. However, it was the post-Civil War period that saw the jigsaw puzzle gain a strong foothold among the children of America.

In the late 1890s, puzzles designed specifically for adults first appeared. Both forms—adult and child—have existed side by side ever since.

Prior to the mid-1920s, the vast majority of jigsaw puzzles were cut out of wood for the adult market and composition material for the children's market. In the 1920s, the die-cut, cardboard jigsaw puzzle evolved and was the dominant medium in the 1930s.

Interest in jigsaw puzzles has cycled between peaks and valleys several times since 1933. Mini-revivals occurred during World War II and in the mid-1960s, when Springbok entered the American market. Internet auction sites are impacting the pricing of puzzles, raising some (Pars, Pastimes, U-Nits, figure pieces), but holding the line or even reducing others (Straus, Victory, strip cut). As with all auctions, final prices tend to vary depending upon the time of year and the activity of at least two interested bidders.

Adviser: Bob Armstrong.

Note: Prices listed here are for puzzles that are complete or restored, and in good condition. Most puzzles found in attics do not meet these standards. If evaluating an old puzzle, a discount of 50 percent should be calculated for moderate damage (one to two missing pieces, three to four broken knobs), with greater discounts for major damage or missing original box.

Cardboard, pre-1950

Consolidated Paper Box, Windward Ho, 1940-50, 19-1/2" x 15-1/2", 375 pcs, orig box **12.00**

Gelco, Weekly Interlocking, The Old Fort, 1933, 11-3/4" x 8-3/4", 150 pcs, orig box, trick corners, one pc replaced **12.00**

Sheahan, M. T., In A Fix, c1909, 13-3/4" x 9-1/2", 84 pcs, orig box, three pcs replaced **20.00**

Tuco Workshops, Picture Puzzles

Double Trouble, Hy Hintermeister artist, 1940s, 11" x 15", 200 pcs, orig box **18.00**

Stratford On Avon, 1930s, 19" x 15", 357 pcs, orig box **16.00**

Dissected map of the United States, Milton Bradley Co., Springfield, MA, c1890, full color litho on paper, mounted on wood, orig. box, 9-3/4" x 14-1/4", **$115**. Photo courtesy of James D. Julia, Inc.

University Dist, Jig-Of-Week, Milady of the Tavern, 1932-33, 13-1/4" x 10", 300 pcs, orig box, five figures, Ser. #17 .... **12.00**

Western/Whitman, Spring Song, 1930-40, 13" x 18-3/4", 375 pcs, orig box **12.00**

Wood and/or Handcut, pre-1930

Ayer, Isabel, Picture Puzzle Exchange, The Presentation, c1909, plywood, 16-1/4" x 15-1/2", 372 pcs, orig box **165.00**

Batterson, Emily, J. L. G. Ferris artist, Picture Puzzle Exchange, Washington's Second Inauguration, 1920s, plywood, 22" x 15-3/4", 543 pcs, orig box ... **220.00**

Geographia, Ltd., Pictorial Map of London, 1920s, plywood, 30" x 20", 600 pcs, orig box, unusual shaped pcs **175.00**

Leisure Hour, The Sung Wong Pavillion, c1909, plywood, 14-1/4" x 22-1/4", 612 pcs, replaced box **250.00**

Milton Bradley, Perfection, Evening in Holland, c1909, solidwood, 17-1/2" x 11-3/4", 500 pcs, orig box, cutter #411, three pcs replaced **200.00**

Noyes, Helen, Swastika, Between Two Fires, 1920s, solidwood, 15-3/4" x 12-1/2", 218 pcs, orig box, one figural pc ... **95.00**

Parker Bros, Jig-Saw Picture Puzzle, Old Homestead, c1909, plywood, 11-3/4" x 7-1/2", 100 pcs, orig box, two pcs replaced **25.00**

Rawson, Clara, Delft, Frank Schoonover artist, Return of the Refugees, c1909, solidwood, 8-3/4" x 12-1/4", 151 pcs, orig box, five pcs replaced **65.00**

Treichel, Katinka, The Village Smithy, 1920s, plywood, 20" x 16", 428 pcs, orig box **185.00**

Tuck, Zag-Zaw, Dick Coach, Mr. Pickwick, His Friends, and Mr. Jingle, 1910s, plywood, 11-1/2" x 6-3/4", 147 pcs, orig box, 24 figures **70.00**

Unknown

Daniel in the Lions' Den, c1909, plywood, 16-1/4" x 15-1/2", 363 pcs, orig box **150.00**

Hiawatha's Wedding Journey, 1910s, plywood, 8-1/4" x 8-3/4", 154 pcs, orig box **65.00**

Morning on the Mohawk, 1910-20, plywood, 22-3/4" x 15-3/4", 826 pcs, replaced box, train image **200.00**

Plymouth Rock $3 Pants, colonial humor, c1909, solidwood, 15-1/2" x 8-3/4", 204 pcs, orig box **75.00**

Wood and/or Handcut, 1930s-40s, plywood

Allen, P. J., Sparetime, Flowers of Holland, Van Freeland artist, 1930s, 9" x 11-3/4", 170 pcs, orig box **35.00**

Apollo, Vera, Marine, G. Seurat artist, 1930-40s, 12" x 8-3/4", 395 pcs, orig box, two pcs replaced **110.00**

Bigelow, Ray, Enjoy-A-Jig, untitled mountain lake scene, 1930s, 7-3/4" x 6", 105 pcs, orig box, two-sided.......... **25.00**

Bliss, R. W., Dance of the Coronade, 1930s, 15-1/2" x 11-1/2", 529 pcs, orig box, five replaced pcs................ **100.00**

Byram Speciality Sales, The Angelus, Millet artist, 1930s, 16" x 12", 320 pcs, orig box, seven figures................ **100.00**

Chad Valley, London Highways, Buckle artist, 1930s, 17-1/2" x 10-3/4", 200 pcs, orig box **50.00**
Hammond, One Leisure Hour, John Paul Jones Flag Party, 1930s, 9" x 7", 150 pcs, orig box **40.00**
Happy Hour Puzzles, Buffeting the Billows, Gourley artist, 1930s, 11-3/4" x 15-3/4", 357 pcs, orig box, eight figures **110.00**
Hayes, J. M., Woodcraft, Where Memory Loves to Linger, 1940s, 16" x 21", 602 pcs, orig box, two pcs replaced **125.00**
Hayter, Victory Artistic, Giselle, Edwards artist, 1930-40s, 35-1/4" x 23-1/2", 1,400 pcs, orig box, 75 figures **210.00**
Jewel Puzzle Co., The Old Windmill, 1930s, 7" x 9-3/4", 100 pcs, orig box, one figure, Jewel sgd pc, one pc replaced **20.00**
Lending Library, An Early Evening Sunset, 1930s, 16-1/4" x 12", 319 pcs, orig box, jagged 1-by-1 cut, one pc replaced **75.00**
Madmar, Interlox, Dawn of Comnmerce, 1930-40s, 12" x 9", 200 pcs, orig box **60.00**
Milton Bradley, Premier, Lincoln's First Nomination, Clyde Deland artist, 1930s, 12-3/4" x 9-3/4", 200 pcs, orig box, 100 figures, glossy finish **75.00**
Parker Brothers/Pastime
- Charge of the Legions, 1932-35, 23" x 15-3/4", 520 pcs, 60 figures, #18R **200.00**
- Day Dreamsm, 1930-40s, 19-3/4" x 14", 405 pcs, orig box, 48 figures, #731 .... **150.00**
- Memories Garden, 1920-30, 21-3/4" x 18-3/4", 500 pcs, replaced box, 60 figures, three replaced **220.00**
- Springtime Apple Blossoms, Hy Whitroy artist, 1930-40s, 9-1/2" x 8", 105 pcs, orig box, 12 figures, #97 .... **45.00**
- Winter Morning, 1930-40s, 12" x 8-3/4", 154 pcs, orig box, 18 figures, #754, repaired silverfish damage **50.00**

Stoughton Stud/Tiz-A-Teezer, Lake Louise Campfire, Thompson artist, 1930s, 11-3/4" x 15-3/4", 400 pcs, orig box, five pcs replaced **90.00**
Straus, Joseph, 1930s
- Autumn Brilliance, 9" x 12", 200 pcs, orig box **25.00**
- Cradled in Rustic Charm, 15-3/4" x 12", 300 pcs, orig box **30.00**
- O'er Hill and Dale, 28" x 21-3/4", 1,000 pcs, orig box, 12 figures, one pc replaced **120.00**
- Paradise Lake, 23-3/4" x 17-3/4", 750 pcs, orig box, two pcs replaced **85.00**

University Dist/Jig Wood, Napolean on the Bellerophon, 1930s, 13-1/2" x 10", 150 pcs, orig box, one pc replaced **30.00**
Unknown
- Henry Rex, 1930s, 21" x 21", 1,010 pcs, replaced box, two pcs replaced **200.00**
- Untitled, confrontation between bear and dog, 1930s, 16" x 12", 350 pcs, replaced box, two pcs replaced **75.00**
- Washington at Valley Forge, Relyea artist, 1930s, 13-3/4" x 11", 300 pcs, replaced box, five figures, minor discoloring **60.00**

Wood and/or Handcut, post 1950, plywood

Browning, James, U-Nit, To The Victor, Frank E Schoonover artist, 11" x 8", 200 pcs, orig box, 16 figural pcs **80.00**
Hayter, Victory/Popular, To the First Cover, 1950-60s, 20" x 14", 500 pcs, orig box **50.00**
Par Co., Let it Blow, 1940-50, 23-1/2" x 13", 650 pgs, orig box, 24 figures, personalized with two monograms **1,000.00**
Pleasure Toys, Tate Gallery, The Derby Day 1856-8, W Frith artist, 1950-70, 29" x 12-3/4", 750 pcs, canister **100.00**
Spear/Hayter, Vict A Gold Box, Romance of the Sail, Frank Vining Smith artist, 1970-80, 27-1/2" x 21-1/2", 1,000 pcs, orig box, 54 figures **150.00**

QUEZAL

History: The Quezal Art Glass Decorating Company, named for the quetzal—a bird with brilliantly colored feathers—was organized in 1901 in Brooklyn, New York, by Martin Bach and Thomas Johnson, two disgruntled Tiffany workers. They soon hired Percy Britton and William Wiedebine, two more Tiffany employees.

For more information, see *Warman's Glass*, 4th edition.

The first products, which are unmarked, were exact Tiffany imitations. Quezal pieces differ from Tiffany pieces in that they are more defined and the decorations are more visible and brighter. No new techniques were developed by Quezal.

Johnson left in 1905. T. Conrad Vahlsing, Bach's son-in-law, joined the firm in 1918, but left with Paul Frank in 1920 to form Lustre Art Glass Company, which copied Quezal pieces. Martin Bach died in 1924 and by 1925, Quezal had ceased operations.

Marks: The "Quezal" trademark was first used in 1902 and placed on the base of vases and bowls and the rims of shades. The acid-etched or engraved letters vary in size and may be found in amber, black, or gold. A printed label that includes an illustration of a quetzal was used briefly in 1907.

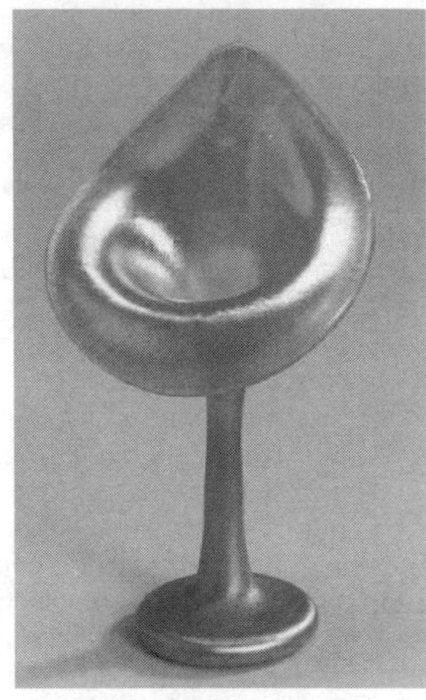

Jack-in-the-pulpit vase, irid gold, stretched rim on narrow vessel widening at base, inscribed "Quezal T 565," 6-3/4" h, **$1,300**. Photo courtesy of Skinner, Inc.

Bowl, 9-1/2" d, irid gold Calcite ground, stretch rim, pedestal foot, sgd "Quezal" **800.00**
Candlesticks, pr, 7-3/4" h, irid blue, sgd **575.00**
Ceiling lamp shade, 13-3/4" d, 21-1/2" l drop, radiating irid gold and green leaf dec, domed irid ivory glass shade supported by brass ring suspended from three ball chains, two-socket fixture, shade inscribed "Quezal," Brooklyn, NY, early 20th C **6,325.00**
Chandelier, gilt metal, 14" h, four elaborated scroll arms, closed teardrop gold, green, and opal shades, inscribed "Quezal" at collet rim, very minor roughness at rim edge **2,000.00**
Cologne bottle, 7-1/2" h, irid gold ground, Art Deco design, sgd "Q" and "Melba" **250.00**
Compote, 6" d, 4-1/2" h, pastel opalescent blue, applied stem and foot, sgd "QUEZAL NO. 1" on underside **815.00**
Jack-in-the-pulpit vase, 8-1/2" d, irid gold, purple highlights, polished pontil sgd "QUEZAL" **2,650.00**
Lamp, desk, 14-1/2" h, irid gold shade with green and white pulled feather dec, inscribed "Quezal" at rim, gilt metal adjustable crook-neck lamp **575.00**

Lamp shade, green damascene dome shade, inscribed "Quezal," fitter rim chips, 7-7/8" d; bronze adjustable socket on harp arms and round base, impressed "TIFFANY STUDIOS NEW YORK 21601 TDCo," early 20th C, 11" h, **$4,700**. Photo courtesy of Skinner, Inc.

Lamp shade

4" h, 5-1/2" d, irid gold, pr **325.00**

5-1/2" h, 2-1/4" fitter, irid gold, slight DQ pattern, ruffled rim, sgd, very minor fitter edge roughness, pr **250.00**

Salt, open, 2-1/2" w, 1-1/4" h, irid, sgd **375.00**

Toothpick holder, 2-1/4" h, melon ribbed, pinched sides, irid blue, green, purple and gold, sgd.................. **200.00**

Lamp shade, feather-pull glass shade, signed, 5-1/4" h, **$175**. Photo courtesy of David Rago Auctions, Inc.

Vase

6" h, gold with green zipper dec, gold pulled feather, creamy white ground, base sgd "QUEZAL," minor wear at neck........................ **1,725.00**

6" h, shouldered, irid blue, purple highlights, polished pontil sgd "QUEZAL," some int. staining **635.00**

6-3/4" h, irid gold, purple highlights, finished pontil sgd "QUEZAL" **420.00**

8-1/2" h, irid gold swirls on creamy ground, irid gold int., sgd "QUEZAL" **2,100.00**

12-5/8" h, flared rim, urn form, bulbed base, irid gold swirl pattern, crack at base **290.00**

Whiskey taster, 2-3/4" h, oval, irid gold, four pinched dimples, sgd "Quezal" on base.. **200.00**

QUILTS

History: Quilts have been passed down as family heirlooms for many generations. Each one is unique. The same pattern may have hundreds of variations in both color and design.

The advent of the sewing machine increased, not decreased, the number of quilts made. Quilts are still being sewn today.

Notes: The key considerations for price are age, condition, aesthetic appeal, and design. Prices are now level, although the very finest examples continue to bring record prices.

Applique, coverlet, tree of life motif on white ground, calico border, some staining, dust ruffle torn and tattered, 74" w, 83" l, 13" dust ruffle, **$1,725**. Photo courtesy of Alderfer Auction Co.

Appliqué

Album, red plaid separates squares with appliquéd polychrome prints, most are floral, some have deer or birds, two have Eastern scenes with camels and elephants, inked signatures, dates in the 1850s, stains, 64" sq **1,870.00**

Carolina Lily, red and green prints, white quilted ground, each plant divided by diamond block with large quilted flowers, meandering line borders with small tulips, no batting, minor stains, areas of pencil marks remaining, 57" x 56"........... **675.00**

Central star, surrounded by American eagles in corners, light pink, pale yellow, each, and green, hand stitched, attributed to PA, minor fading, edge wear, 81" x 87"...................................... **660.00**

Feather pinwheels, four green and red pinwheels, hearts and eighteen point star centers, surrounded by light green, white, and red borders, white ground, some stains, small holes, 82" x 89" **200.00**

Flower medallions, nine red, white, and yellow medallions, green foliage, white diamond quilted ground, green zigzag borders, attached note states quilt was "Made by Mary Magdaline Recher, 1850," along with her birth and death dates, few light fold line stains, 87" x 87" **1,210.00**

Four petal flowers, light pink flowers, green and pink buds, darker pink draped swags, hand stitched, diamond and sunflower quilting, pink binding, light stains, 76" x 92" **200.00**

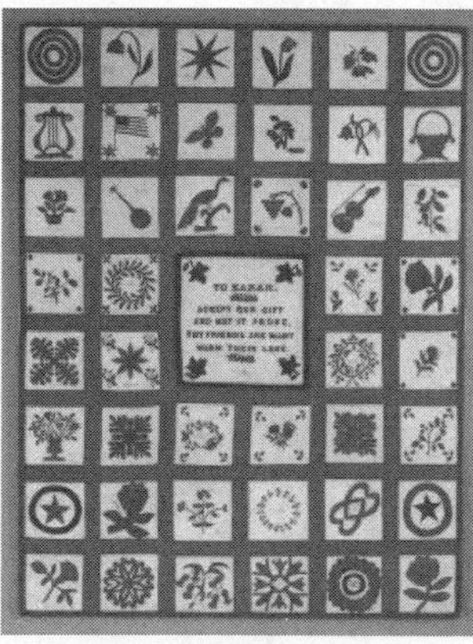

Appliqué, Friendship Album, America, 1858, 48 blocks of red, blue, and green mostly solid color fabrics appliquéd to white ground, separated by red cotton grid, naturalistic, patriotic, geometric, and musical instrument motifs including flowers, fruit, butterfly, peacock, flag, violin, circles, stars, etc., larger central square with appliquéd lettering "TO SARAH ACCEPT OUR GIFT AND MAY IT PROVE THY FRIENDS ARE MANY WARM THEIR LOVE," with embroidered signature "Amanda Birdsell Apr 20th, 1858," many squares with embroidered and pen and ink signatures, mounted on wood frame, minor fading, 86" x 65-1/2", **$4,200**. Photo courtesy of Skinner, Inc.

Nine blocks, each with large red flower, pink and yellow center, blue leaves and vines, red buds, border of blue quarter moons and red stars, white quilted ground, signed with embroidery "Polly Matthias (heart) Lug March 1837," 84" x 84".. **1,750.00**

Nine floral medallions, red, yellow, and green, red and green sawtooth edging, hand quilted, feathering between medallions, scroll work along border, stains, 82" x 83" **1,430.00**

Secession, eagle center, c1860, 108" sq **74,250.00**

Tulip medallions, pale green and red, divided by individual tulips, green foliage, crib size, small hole and stains, 35-1/2" x 36-1/2" **385.00**

Tulips, navy blue calico, white squares with three goldenrod, brown, and green tulips, green border, goldenrod edging, hand sewn, small hole, 67" x 82" **825.00**

Twelve flower baskets, double sawtooth borders, tan and red on white, hand sewn, princess feather medallion quilting, intact pencil marks, few stains, 72" x 90" **525.00**

Appliqué, girl with parasol appliqué, scalloped border, **$165**. Photo courtesy of Dotta Auction Co., Inc.

Chintz

Printed overall design of exotic birds drinking from urns hanging from trees, brown on white, printed gold, blue, green, and reddish-brown, brown floral baking, light stains, 94" x 116"................ **1,450.00**

Crazy

Pieced, many embroideries, including chenille goldenrod, owl at center of pin-wheeled fabrics, 1891 .... **4,500.00**

Pieced, squares in shades of blues, reds, and greens, brick purple bands, black corners, wide dark green border, hand stitched, flowers and feather meandering quilting, Mennonite, contemporary, 91" x 100"..**110.00**

Pieced velvet, black, burgundy, purple, red, gold, gray, green, and brown solid and printed shaped patches, arranged in 16 squares, colorful velvet border, late 19th C, 72" x 74".......................... **885.00**

Hawaiian, pieced, nine pineapple medallions, meandering floral vines, green and orange, white ground, quilted floral rosettes in corners, 64" sq **600.00**

Crazy, silk and velvet, America, c1885, multicolored quilt embellished with variety of embroidery stitched and painted motifs, black satin border, stitched "1885" date, 64" x 64", **$1,300**. Photo courtesy of Skinner, Inc.

Pieced

Bear Paw, light red colored calico, white quilted blocks divided by blue and white lines, small bright red blocks where lines intersect, stains, 87" x 86"............ **400.00**

Birds in Flight, dark multicolored triangles alternating with lighter triangles inside 6-1/8" blocks, red calico blocks, small stains, 65" x 72".................. **470.00**

Blocks, navy blue borders, alternating navy blue and black blocks, tan, brown, or black rectangles in center, black blocks with raised quilted double spade and circle design, blue striped flannel backing, Amish, 62" x 85"............ **350.00**

Broken Star, medium rainbow colors, hand stitched, princess feather medallions, orig pencil lines, blue edging, 75" x 75".. **750.00**

Central red diamond on dark green ground, surrounded by mint green border, wide black outer border, mint green corner blocks with hand quilted tulips, diamond with quilted star and feather medallion, Amish, 20th C, 86" x 86"... **715.00**

Concentric squares, blue, gray, black, ecru, and tan, various fabrics including corduroy, Mennonite, stains, 68" x 86" **110.00**

Diamond Block, white and cobalt blue print fabric, each blocked joined by double lattice of diamond blocks **460.00**

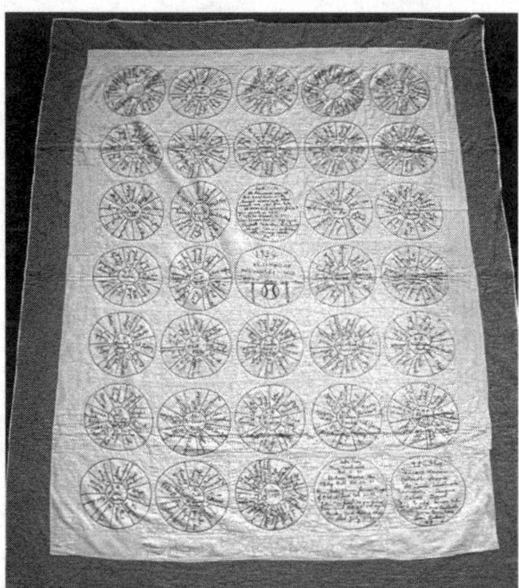

Pieced and embroidered, baseball theme, center dated "1934 Al Simmons, Milwaukee, WI," other panels naming various teams, together with two matching pillowcases, **$350**. Photo courtesy of Pook & Pook.

Four petal flowers in two shades of light yellow and pale green, white ground, border of arches with buds, hand stitched, princess feather medallions, fancy scrolls, and interlacing lines quilting, scalloped edge, light stains, 84" sq.. **495.00**

Irish Chain, green and brick red calico, white ground, finely quilted cross hatching, minor stains, 79" x 81" **615.00**

Log Cabin, polychrome print fabrics **195.00**

Nine Patch, green and pale orange calico, brown backing with floral print design, attached note gives provenance, made by Amish in Harrisburg, PA area, minor small stains, 74" x 83"......... **550.00**

Nine Patch variant, Chintz squares edged with triangles, floral printed border, hand stitched, diamond and floral quilting, orig pencil marks, some stains, 82" x 83".................................... **1,540.00**

Pieced, Basket pattern, blue and white, **$300**. Photo courtesy of Dotta Auction Co., Inc.

Octagonal medallions, pink, red, and navy blue calico on white, hand sewn, machine sewn blue binding, quilted princess feather medallions, light overall stains, 67" x 86" **635.00**

Rainbow stripes, diagonal border, hand stitched with alternating quilting patterns, pencil and chalk lines remain, Amish, 20th C, 78" x 83".......................... **475.00**

Sawtooth, red diamond and border, ivory ground, wide purple border, black binding, hand stitched in red thread, quilted princess feather meandering, grapevine and diamonds, Amish, 20th C, 102" x 102".................................. **475.00**

Squares and diamond chains, red on white, red edging, hand sewn, quilted spoked wheels, wavy lines, 66" x 82" **750.00**

Pieced, Maple Leaf pattern, red and white, **$150**. Photo courtesy of Pook & Pook.

Star, eight-pointed, intricate polychrome pattern fabrics, white ground **520.00**
Stars, twenty navy blue and red stars on white, quilted postage stamp grid, pencil marks, one block with faint ink stamped number, 66-1/2" x 84" **700.00**
Trip Around the World

Dark blue, brown, green, purple, grays, pink, hunter green border, brown corner blocks, black binding, hand stitched with floral quilting, embroidered initials "MS," Amish, 20th C, some fabric has separated, 82" x 84"................................**950.00**

Vibrant polychrome colors, both solid and calico, orange, black, slate gray, and red borders, hand stitched, printed paisley backing, minor staining and fading, 82" x 85" **825.00**

Windmill, yellow, red, green, and blue printed calico patches, wide red calico with swag quilting, PA, late 19th C, 86" x 76"... **690.00**

Pieced, sixteen 8-pointed stars, yellow, red and green calico, white ground, elaborately quilted in foliate and geometric designs, red, green and cream calico border, 103" l, 100" w, **$1,725**. Photo courtesy of Alderfer Auction Co.

Trapunto

Star medallions, softly faded blue calico star medallions, diamond band borders on white, hand sewn, well-done trapunto roses between medallions and borders, minor edge wear, small pieced corner repairs, stains, 76" x 90" **2,475.00**
Striped, broad bands of print fabric, green, pink, and yellow, intricate swirling hand stitched pattern **200.00**

Quimper

History: Quimper faience, dating back to the 17th century, is named for Quimper, a French town where numerous potteries were located. Several mergers resulted in the evolution of two major houses—the Jules Henriot and Hubaudière-Bousquet factories.

The peasant design first appeared in the 1860s, and many variations exist. Florals and geometrics, equally popular, also were produced in large quantities. During the 1920s, the Hubaudière-Bousquet factory introduced the Odetta line, which utilized a stone body and Art Deco decorations.

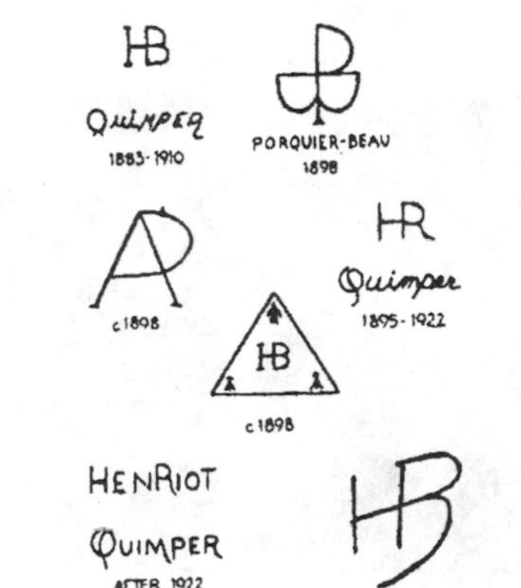

The two major houses merged in 1968, the products retaining the individual characteristics and marks of the originals. The concern suffered from labor problems in the 1980s and was purchased by an American group.

For more information, see *Warman's English & Continental Pottery & Porcelain*, 3rd edition.

Marks: The "HR" and "HR Quimper" marks are found on Henriot pieces prior to 1922. The "Henriot Quimper" mark was used after 1922. The "HB" mark covers a long time span. Numbers or dots and dashes were added for inventory purposes and are found on later pieces. Most marks are in blue or black. Pieces ordered by department stores, such as Macy's and Carson Pirie Scott, carry the store mark along with the factory mark, making them less desirable to collectors. A comprehensive list of marks is found in Bondhus book.

Adviser: Al Bagdade.

Additional Terms:

A la touche border decor—single brush stroke to create floral.

Breton Broderie decor—stylized blue and gold pattern inspired by a popular embroidery pattern often used on Breton costumes, dates from the Art Deco era.

Croisille—criss-cross pattern.

Decor Riche border—acanthus leaves in two colors.

Fleur de lys—the symbol of France.

Ivoire Corbeille pattern—red dots circled in sponged blue with red touches forming half a floral blossom, all over a tan ground.

Quintal—five-fingered vase.

Asparagus plate, 8-3/4" d, figural green and yellow asparagus spear across middle, walking female peasant with basket in upper section, red, green, and blue foliage below, similar sprigs on border separated by four blue dot designs, scalloped rim, marked "HB" **350.00**
Biberon, 5" h, center band of single stroke red, green, and blue florals, blue and yellow concentric bands on base, blue dash spout and handle, unmarked **275.00**
Bookends, pr, 7" h x 7-1/2" l, seated figural male peasant, orange accented black hat, cobalt blue jacket, gray trousers, playing brown bagpipe, seated female peasant, white coif, cobalt blue dress, yellow apron, holding gray goose, cream supports, marked "HB Quimper" **675.00**
Bottle, 13" h, stoneware, overall mottled brown glaze, marked imp "PORQUIER QUIMPER" **285.00**
Breakfast set, cup, 7" l bagpipe shaped plate, female peasant on cup, vertical blue and yellow wavy lines and dots, vertical red interlocked "S" chain, brown pipe handle with blue ribbon wrap, vertical red and green foliage on dish, red "S" chain rim, brown pipe and blue figural ribbon border, marked "HB Quimper" **225.00**

Bowl, covered, Ivoire Corbeille, black hat, cobalt blue jacket with orange stripes, chains of blue or green sponged circlets with red centers, red half flowerheads, blue sponged handles and knob, ivory ground, marked "HenRiot Quimper," 9-3/4" handle to handle, **$325**. Photos courtesy of Al Bagdade.

Candlesticks, pr, 8" h, lighthouse shape, frontal view of male peasant with walking stick, female holding pail, bands of blue circles and dots above green circles, red dots on base, blue sponged base and rim, marked "Lisieux 707" **275.00**
Cider jug, 6" h, male peasant in orange shirt, blue trousers, holding pipe under spout, blue floral sprays and four blue dot designs, blue sponged overhead handle, marked "HB"................................ **150.00**
Dish

6-1/2" sq, indented sides, female peasant, orange blouse, blue shirt, red apron, red, blue, and green border florals, blue dots in corners, marked "HenRiot Quimper France" 150.00

9-1/2" l, figural fish, standing male peasant blowing horn, flanked by green, red, yellow centered blue dot florals, orange and blue accented fish head and tail, marked "HenRiot Quimper France 101" 150.00

Egg cup, 3-3/4" h, male peasant, orange shirt, red trousers, horizontal band of red, green, and blue single stroke flowers and foliage, blue and yellow striped base, blue lined rim, marked "HenRiot Quimper France 272" 75.00

Figure, 10" h, Virgin Mary holding infant Jesus, orange edged cobalt blue cloak, white gown, small orange and blue florals, circular base with blue and yellow stripes and "Ste Viege," marked "HR Quimper" 495.00

Fruit bowl, 12-1/2" d, female peasant, blue vest, olive green blouse, orange skirt, red apron, flanked by red, blue, and green vertical florals, blue and yellow striped border, marked "HR Quimper 118" 160.00

Inkstand, crest of Brittany on backplate, dark blue acanthus borders, yellow continued shells and swirls, blue dotted feet, marked "HenRiot Quimper," 7-1/4" w, 6-1/2" h, **$750**.

Inkstand, 6-1/4" l, dbl wells and pen tray, seated male peasant blowing bagpipe, orange edged dark blue acanthus borders, scattered local florals, four pen holes on top, four small feet, marked "HB Quimper" 800.00

Menu, 5-1/2" h, 3-1/2" w, female peasant holding basket of fish, crest of Britanny in corner, "Menu" in opposite corner, Porquier Beau 550.00

Pitcher

3-3/4" h, female peasant, olive green blouse, blue skirt, red apron, flanked by typical red, green, and blue florals, yellow and blue striped base, blue rim, marked "HenRiot Quimper France 120" 145.00

7" h, figural Breton head, white coif, black collar, orange and yellow base, brown handle, marked "HenRiot Quimper, C. Maillard" 250.00

Platter, female peasant, three blue stripes inner border, yellow scalloped border, pierced for hanging, marked "Henriot Quimper France –6," **$150**.

Plate

6" d, Modern Movement, kneeling male peasant offering plant in pot to female peasant, house and fence in background, orange-gold zigzag and red dot border, blue lined rim, marked "HB Quimper" 85.00

7-3/8" d, large yellow-centered red petaled single stroke flower in center flanked by blue, green, and red foliage, red dash and blue dot border band, red, and blue striped rim, marked "HB" 195.00

8-3/8" d, hp dark red centered yellow flowerheads, large green leaves, orange crenulated rim, marked "Porquier Beau" 1,450.00

Porringer, 8" handle to handle, female peasant in center flanked by vertical florals, blue and yellow striped border, blue sponged handles, marked "HB Quimper France" 115.00

Quintal, 6-1/2" h, frontal view of male peasant leaning on walking stick, typical vertical florals, sprigs and florals on reverse, scattered four blue dot designs, orange and blue lines around five spouts, marked "HenRiot Quimper France" 380.00

Serving bowl, 11" handle to handle, octagonal, crest of Quimper flanked by rampart lions, red, blue and yellow lambrequin border, blue rope twist handles, Porquier Beau 1,000.00

Snuff bottle, 3" l, raised black lined yellow sunflower center, blue striped eight-pointed star on red croisille ground, blue and yellow rim, six-pointed star and blue brush stroke stripes on reverse 460.00

Soup tureen, 5-1/2" h x 6" handle to handle, center body band of red, green, and blue single stroke florals, yellow and blue border and base, male peasant on cov, typical single stroke florals, blue knob, scroll handles, marked "HB" 345.00

Plate, florals, marked "Henriot Quimper, France 92," **$50**.

Syrup jug, cov, 4-7/8" h, male peasant, blue shirt, red trousers, flanked by red, green, and blue single stroke florals, four blue dot designs, blue lined rims, blue dash handle, marked "HB Quimper++" 125.00

Teapot

6" h, lobed, light and dark fleur-de-lys, black ermine tails, blue chains on rims, blue dash handle, marked "HB," restored chip 495.00

8" h, hex shape, bust of male or female peasant on sides, hanging blue sponged chains, red, yellow, and green single stroke sprigs, blue sponged circles on handle, red dash spout, marked "HenRiot Quimper France," chip 525.00

Tobacco jar, 8-5/8" h, male peasant seated on rock, female on reverse, green sponged borders, blue stripes, crest of Quimper on cov with ermine tails, green sponged knob, marked "HB" 295.00

Plate, female peasant, florals, marked "Henriot Quimper, France 96," **$50**.

Vase

4-5/8" h, overlapped horn shape, male or female peasant, flanked by vertical foliage, overlapped blue scales on backplate, yellow lined rect base w/Souvenir de Bretagne, marked "HB", pr **495.00**

12" h, dancing peasant couple on front, scattered sprigs of local flowers, crest of Quimper flanked by lion rampants and crown on reverse, yellow tassel handles, green accents and red dots, green lined flared rim, marked "HenRoit Quimper".... **775.00**

15-1/2" h, bag shape, flared neck, male peasant blowing horn, another with bagpipe, trees in background, crest of Britanny on neck, vertical orange edged dark blue acanthus designs and rim, large yellow or mauve flowers, yellow and green leaves on reverse, marked "HenRoit Quimper 154" **950.00**

Wall pocket

7-1/4" h, figural bagpipe, orange ribbon, blue pipes, male peasant blowing horn of front flanked by red and blue florals, red "S" chain borders, "HR Quimper" on front **155.00**

10-3/4" l, overlapped cone shape, male peasant holding pipe on yellow and green ground, flanked by red, green, and blue single stroke florals and foliage, blue rim, red accented blue flowerhead over hole in backplate, marked "HenRoit Quimper France" **175.00**

RADIOS

History: The radio was invented more than 100 years ago. Marconi was the first to assemble and employ the transmission and reception instruments that permitted the sending of electric messages without the use of direct connections. Between 1905 and the end of World War I, many technical advances affected the "wireless," including the invention of the vacuum tube by DeForest. Technology continued its progress, and radios filled the entertainment needs of the average family in the 1920s.

Changes in design, style, and technology brought the radio from the black boxes of the 1920s to the stylish furniture pieces and console models of the 1930s and 1940s, to midget models of the 1950s, and finally to the high-tech radios of the 1980s.

Additional Listings: See *Warman's Americana & Collectibles* for more examples.

Adviser: Lewis S. Walters.

Admiral

Portable, #33-35-37 .... **30.00**

Y-2127, Imperial 8, c1959 .... **45.00**

Air King, tombstone, Art Deco **2,200.00**

Arvin

Hoppy with lariatenna **585.00**

Mightymite #40 .... **75.00**

Rhythm Baby #417 .... **225.00**

Table, #522A **75.00**

Tombstone, #617 Rhythm Maid **250.00**

Atwater Kent Type TA, 1924, **$1,465**. Photo courtesy of Auction Team Breker.

Atwater Kent

Breadboard style, Model 9A **1,200.00**

Breadboard style, Model 12 .... **1,250.00**

Cathedral, 80, c1931 .... **375.00**

Table, #55 Keil **225.00**

Tombstone, #854 .... **155.00**

Bulova, clock radio, #100 .... **30.00**

Colonial "New World Radio"..... **1,000.00**

Columbia, table radio, oak **125.00**

Crosley

ACE V **170.00**

Bandbox, #600, 1927 .... **70.00**

Dashboard **120.00**

Gemchest, #609 .... **350.00**

Sheraton, cathedral **290.00**

Showbox, #706 .... **100.00**

Super Buddy Boy **100.00**

#4-28 battery operated **130.00**

#10-135 .... **55.00**

Dumont, RA346, table, scrollwork, 1938 .... **110.00**

Emerson

AU-190 Catalin Tombstone **1,200.00**

BT-245 .... **1,100.00**

Patriot **700.00**

#409 Mickey **2,000.00**

#411 Snow White **1,200.00**

#570 Memento **100.00**

#640 Portable **50.00**

#888 Vanguard **80.00**

Fada

#43 .... **275.00**

#53 .... **750.00**

#60W **75.00**

#115 bullet shape **750.00**

#252 .... **575.00**

#1000 red/orange bullet **750.00**

#L56 Maroon and White **1,750.00**

Federal, #58DX **750.00**

General Electric

#81, c1934 .... **200.00**

#400, 410, 411, 414 .... **30.00**

#515, 517 clock radio **25.00**

K-126 .... **150.00**

Tombstone **250.00**

Grebe

CR-8 .... **700.00**

MU-1 .... **250.00**

Service Manual **50.00**

Majestic

Charlie McCarthy **1,100.00**

#381 .... **225.00**

Treasure Chest **200.00**

Metrodyne Super 7, 1925 .... **220.00**

Motorola

#68X11Q Art Deco **75.00**

Jet Plane **55.00**

M logo **25.00**

Pixie **45.00**

Table, plastic **35.00**

Olympic, radio with phonograph **60.00**

Paragon

DA, two table **775.00**

RD, five table **775.00**

Philco, radio and turn table, table model, original condition, **$100**. Photo courtesy of Dotta Auction Co., Inc.

Philco

T-7, 126 transistor **65.00**

T1000 clock radio **80.00**

#17, 20, 38 Cathedral **250.00**

#20 Cathedral **250.00**

#37, 62 table, two tone **100.00**

#40, 180 console wood **150.00**

#52, 544 Transitone **40.00**

#60, Cathedral **125.00**

#551, 1928 .... **175.00**

Radiobar, with glasses and decanters **1,000.00**

Radio Corporation of America–RCA

LaSiesta **550.00**

Radiola

#17 .... **120.00**

#18, with speaker **200.00**

#20 .... **165.00**

#33 .... 60.00
#6X7 table, plastic 25.00
40X56 World's Fair 1,000.00

Silvertone-Sears
#1 table 75.00
#1582 Cathedral, wood 225.00
#9205 plastic transistor 45.00
Clock radio, plastic 15.00

Sony, transistor
TFM-151, 1960 .... 50.00
TR-63, 1958 .... 145.00

Sparton
#506 Blue Bird, Art Deco 3,500.00
#5218 .... 95.00

Stewart-Warner, table, slant 175.00

Stromberg Carlson, # 636A console 125.00

Westinghouse, Model WR-602 .... 50.00

Zenith
#500 transistor, owl eye 75.00
#500D transistor 55.00
Trans-Oceanic 200.00
Zephyr, multiband 95.00

Railroad Items

History: Railroad collectors have existed for decades. The merger of the rail systems and the end of passenger service made many objects available to private collectors. The Pennsylvania Railroad sold its archives at public sale.

Notes: Railroad enthusiasts have organized into regional and local clubs. Join one if you're interested in this collectible field; your local hobby store can probably point you to the right person. The best pieces often pass between collectors and rarely enter the general market.

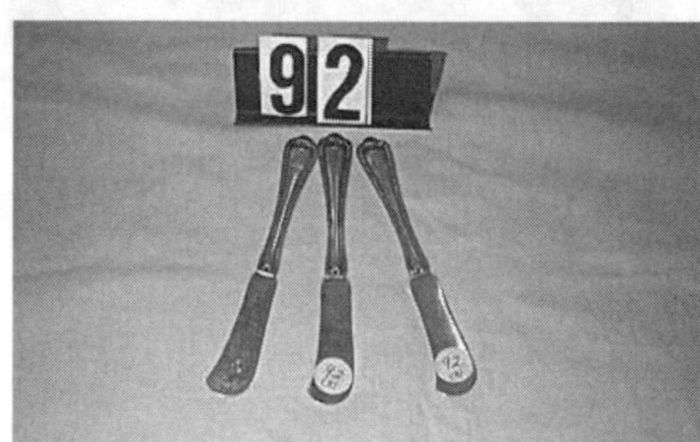

Butter knives, Lehigh Valley Railroad, set of three, **$35**. Photo courtesy of Dotta Auction Co., Inc.

Baggage tag, 1-1/2" x 2-1/2", SOO Line, celluloid, leather strap, "Tag Your Grip, Take a trip, the New Train" 20.00

Book, Confessions of a Railroad Signalman, James Fagan, Boston, 1908 .... 20.00

Builder's plate, Schenectady Locomotive Works, 1899 .... 725.00

Button, uniform, 3/4" d, "Baggage Master," silvertone 8.00

Cabinet, American Railway Express, wood, countertop, front door stenciled "AM R.Y. EX. CO," 33" x 25" x 11-1/2" 80.00

Calendar, framed
1922, New York Central, illustration depicting travel in 1830 and 1920, timetables for various lines in margins, some minor losses, period oak frame, 18" x 30" 265.00
1930, Soo Line, illus, Lake Louise Alberta by R. Atkinson Fox, later oak frame and mat, overall 34" x 29" 230.00

Cap, conductor's, Milwaukee RR, Carlson & Co., Chicago 45.00

China
Butter Pat, PA RR, backstamp . 75.00
Cereal Bowl, Union Pacific, Challenger pattern, no backstamp, Syracuse China 25.00
Cup and Saucer, Chicago Burlington & Quincy, Chuck Wagon pattern, backstamp, Syracuse China 250.00
Ice Cream Dish, B&O, Capitol pattern, ftd 50.00
Plate, dinner, Wabash RR, Banner pattern, Syracuse China, 9-1/2" d 225.00
Sauce Dish, Atchison Topeka & Santa Fe, Mimbreno pattern, backstamp "Made expressly for Santa Fe dining car service," Syracuse China, 5-1/2" d 80.00

Cuspidor, Texas & Pacific Railroad, white porcelain on metal, blue lettering, minor loss, 8" d 260.00

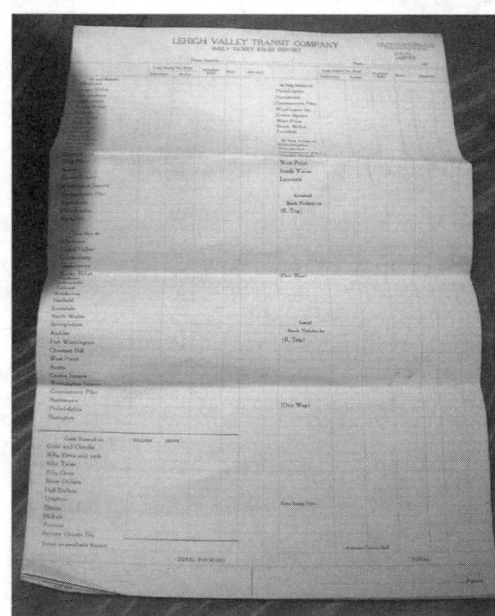
LEHIGH VALLEY TRANSIT COMPANY
DAILY TICKET SALES REPORT

Daily Ticket Sales Report, Lehigh Valley Transit Company, unused, folded, **$15**. Photo courtesy of Sky Hawk Auctions.

Date stamp, Atlantic Coast Line Railroad, c1940, Defiance Stamp Co., 4" h ... 35.00

Depot sign, Rock Island System, reverse painted and mother of pearl, c1905, Chicago, Rock Island & Pacific 4-4-0 locomotive #801 pulling five Pullman cars, against detailed mountain scene, foreground of cattle, cowboy on horseback, orig oak ogee frame, 90" x 26-1/2", some losses 9,775.00

Directory, Soo Line Shippers Directory, Vol. III, 1918-19, soft cover, 644 pgs, gilt, ads, illus, two-pg Soo Line map, four color maps of MI, MN, ND, WI 60.00

Fire bucket, Missouri, Kansas & Texas Railroad, orig red paint, stenciled "Fire," emb "MK&T," 12" h 60.00

Flare and flag box, Gulf Mobile & Ohio, tin, stenciled letters, contains flag and fuses, 30" l 20.00

Hollowware
Coffee pot, silver plate, Chicago & Eastern Illinois, 10-oz size, marked "Reed & Barton 086-H, C&E.I.RY.CO" on base, 7" h 265.00
Sauce tureen, silvered, Chicago Great Western Railway, two handles, lid. backstamped "C.G.W.R.R.–Reed & Barton," 8" l 125.00
Sugar bowl, silvered, New York Central, imp "NYC" on hinged lid, 3-3/4" h 50.00
Tea pot, silvered, Missouri Pacific & Iron Mountain, 10-oz size, front engraved "M.P.I.Mt.RY," backstamped "Missouri Pacific & Iron Mountain R. Wallace 03295," 4-1/2" h 230.00

Kerosene can, Chicago & Northwestern, one gal, oxidized finish, emb "C&NRR," 13" h 25.00

Lantern
5" h, PRR, etched red globe and dome, marked "Keystone Lantern Co., Phila, PA, USA," wire ring bail 445.00
13" h, Boston & Worchester, emb "B&W RR," fixed globe 665.00

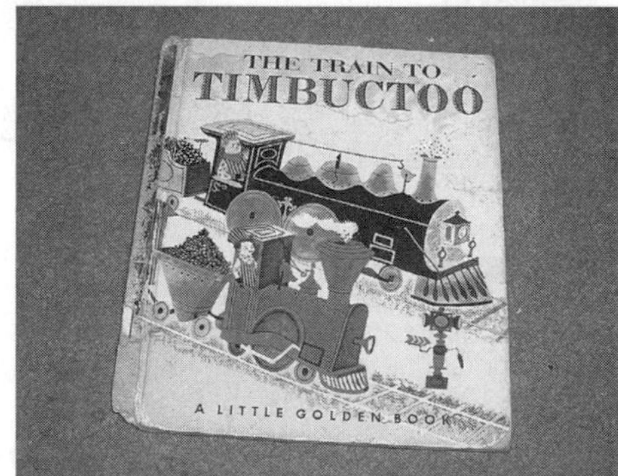

Little Golden Book, *The Train to Timbuctoo*, **$100**.

Lantern globe, clear, emb letters, by CNS, 5-1/2" h
Long Island RR 70.00
Pennsylvania RR, logo 60.00
Pittsburgh & Lake Erie RR 60.00

Letter opener, Southern Pacific, orig case, 7-3/4" l 30.00

Locomotive nose plate, Frisco, black, heavy 1/8" stainless steel, 28" l **1,150.00**

Map

Chicago, Iowa, and Nebraska Railroad, color litho, published by J. Sage & Sons, Buffalo, NY, 1859, some discoloration and losses, mounted on linen, 26" x 23" **450.00**

Williams Telegraph and Railroad Map of the New England States, dated 1852, by Alexander Williams, published by Redding & Co. Boston, printed table of construction costs for area railroads, hand-colored state borders, separated folds with later linen backing, some toning, 32" x 30" **60.00**

Operation manual, 4-1/2" x 7", New York Air Brake Co., 1909 ..... **5.00**

Pass

Reading Company, 1939, issued **12.00**

The Rocky Mountain Parks Transportation Co., 1930, issued **15.00**

Photo

Chicago, Rock Island & Pacific, Rocky Mountains, c1910, orig frame, 7" mat, 53" x 23" **920.00**

Denver & Rio Grande Railroad Depot, Canyon of the Rio Las Animas, Colo, hand colored black and white print, printed logo and title, "Copyright 1900 by Detroit Photographic Co.," orig oak frame, stains in margin, overall 33-1/2" x 27-1/2" **2,645.00**

Sullivan, OH, train wreck, 7" x 10" **50.00**

Puzzle, paper covered wooden blocks, six scenes, **$70**. Photo courtesy of Joy Luke Auctions.

Playing cards, 1" x 2-3/4" x 3-1/2", cardboard slipcase, complete deck, Southern Pacific Lines, back of each card with full color art of Southern Pacific Daylight streamliner passenger train passing through scenic landscape, late 1930s **20.00**

Pocket watch

American Waltham Watch Co., size 16, open face, gold filled case, damascened Vanguard movement, 23 jewels, wind indicator, adjusted for six positions **450.00**

Hamilton Watch Co., model 999, made for the Ball Watch Co., size 18, open face, gold filled case, 21 jewels, damascened plates, inscribed gold lettering, c1895 ..... **300.00**

Postcard, 8-3/4" x 5-1/2", marked "Kodachrome Transparency by James W. Watson," c1974

Milwaukee 419, Fairbanks-Morse H-16-44, Council Bluffs, Iowa **8.00**

Union Pacific #5010, North Platte, Nebraska **9.00**

Poster

Boston—New Haven Railroad, full color, stylized montage of Historic Boston by day and night, faint folio folds, c1938, 28" x 42" **275.00**

Midland Railway, H. Gray, Courmont, Paris, c1899, elegant woman bundled up in red and blue, standing on yellow and red map of French shore, brown luggage, 41" x 49-3/4" **815.00**

Sign, grade crossing, wood, circular, black "RR" and white "X," white ground, worn **15.00**

Steam whistle, brass, 3" d, 8" h, single chime, lever control **200.00**

Step stool, Denver & Rio Grande Western RR, rubber no-skid top, 9" h **260.00**

Switch lamp

13" h, Handlan, single blue lens, marked "UPRR" **125.00**

14" h, Adlake, two light blue and two dark blue lenses, marked "PPR" **125.00**

Ticket cabinet, Soo Line, c1914, oak, locking tambour slant front, divided compartments for tickets, timetables, one drawer, stenciled "M.ST.P. & S.S.M.RY" on back, 21" x 35" x 16" **460.00**

Ticket window, 28" x 33-1/2", Baltimore & Ohio, clear emb glass, B&O logo on diamond point textured field, later walnut frame **600.00**

Timetable

1928, Louisville and Nashville Railroad **32.00**

1946, Charleston and Western Carolina **15.00**

1951, Delaware & Hudson **10.00**

1954, New York-New Haven & Hartford **8.50**

Water bucket, metal, bail handle **25.00**

Wax sealer

Illinois Central Railroad, Agent-Minonk, brass die, wood handle, 4" l **375.00**

S.W. & B.V. RR, Agent-Bryan, Texas, one-piece brass die and handle, 2-1/2" l **550.00**

Razors

History: Razors date back several thousand years. Early man used sharpened stones; the Egyptians, Greeks, and Romans had metal razors.

Razors made prior to 1800 generally were crudely stamped "Warranted" or "Cast Steel," with the maker's mark on the tang. Until 1870, razors were handmade and almost all razors for the American market were manufactured in Sheffield, England. Most blades were wedge shaped; many were etched with slogans or scenes. Handles were made of natural materials: horn, tortoiseshell, bone, ivory, stag, silver, or pearl.

After 1870, razors were machine made with hollow ground blades and synthetic handle materials. Razors of this period usually were manufactured in Germany (Solingen) or in American cutlery factories. Hundreds of molded-celluloid handle patterns were produced.

Cutlery firms produced boxed sets of two, four, and seven razors. Complete and undamaged sets are very desirable. The most popular ones are the seven-day sets in which each razor is etched with a day of the week.

Notes: The fancier the handle or more intricately etched the blade, the higher the price. Rarest handle materials are pearl, stag, sterling silver, pressed horn, and carved ivory. Rarest blades are those with scenes etched across the entire front. Value is increased by the presence of certain manufacturers' names, e.g., H. Boker, Case, M. Price, Joseph Rogers, Simmons Hardware, Will & Finck, Winchester, and George Wostenholm.

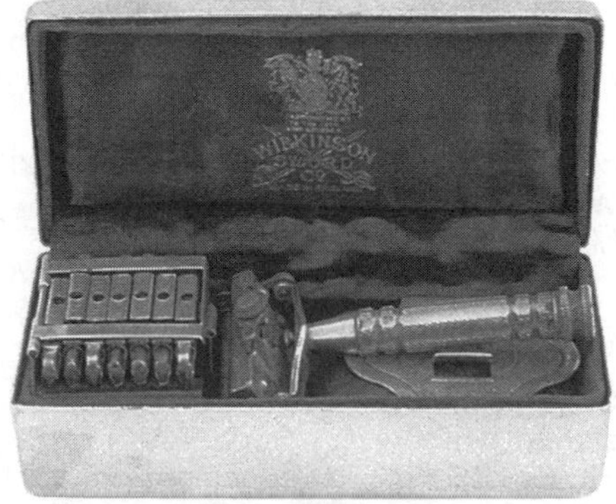

Safety, Wilkinson Sword Co., seven day, 5" l, 2-1/4" d, 1-5/8" h, **$165**.

American blades

Abrams, Blue Bird, dark green translucent plastic handle, rusty thumb rest... **48.00**

Case Bros., Tested XX, Little Valley, NY, hollow point, slick black handles, MOP inlaid tang................................ **400.00**

Cattaraugus Cutlery Co., Little Valley, NY, sq point, blue handles with white liners.. **35.00**

Kinfolk, brown and yellow swirl design celluloid handle, orig box marked "The J.R. Torrey Razor Co., Worchester, Mass" **55.00**

Standard Knife Co., Little Valley, NY, arc mark, round point, yellow mottled handles with beaded borders, 1901-03 .... **150.00**

The Army Razor, marked "Manufactured Expressly for the Army & Navy" on one side, 3" blade, wood handle, plain black finish, rust and wear **50.00**

Universal Safety, marked "Universal, LF&C, New Britain, Conn., USA," patent numbers under handle attachment, blade marked "Universal, Landers Frary & Clark, New Britain, Conn, USA, patent no. 26278," orig case, celluloid handle **150.00**

Wilbert Cutlery, blade engraved "Pearl," mother of pearl with black plastic, orig box, 5" l blade.............................. **85.00**

English blades

Joseph Rodgers & Sons, Sheffield, wedge blade, stag handle with inlaid rect escutcheon plate......................... **125.00**

Rolls Razor, marked "Made in London, England," orig box with razor, strop, and stone.. **85.00**

German blades

Cosmos Mfg. Co., hollow ground blade, ivory handle, raised nude picking purple grapes, green leaves **125.00**

F. A. Koch & Co., ivory handle, colored scene with deer, branches, and oak leaves **50.00**

Imperial Razor, blade etched with U.S. Battleship Oregon scene, dark blue celluloid handle **45.00**

Wadsworth Razor Co., semi-wedge blade, carved bone handle, c1870 .... **60.00**

Sets of razors

Crown & Sword, seven-day set, blades etched "The Crown & Sword Razor Extra Hollow Ground," black handles with raised "Crown and Sword," homemade wood case with felt lining, emb "RAZORS," plaque on top............. **85.00**

Ideal Safety Razor, patented Sept. 21, 1868, June 12, 1900, and March 5, 1906, leather like case, 9-1/2" l, **$20**.

Gift set, Watertown Daily Times, subscription premium, made by Valet Auto Strop Razor, patent April 9, 1912 on razor, orig metal box, some wear ... **50.00**

G. W. Ruff's Peerless, two, hollow ground blade, ivory handles, leather over wood case with "Gentlemen's Companion Containing 2 Razors Special Hollow Ground," red lining **70.00**

Wilkinson Sword, seven days, safety, 5" l, 2-1/2" d, 1-5/8" h orig box......... **125.00**

Records

History: With the advent of the more sophisticated recording materials, such as 33-1/3 RPM long-playing records, 8-track tapes, cassettes, and compact discs, earlier phonograph records became collectors' items. Most have little value. The higher-priced items are rare (limited-production) recordings. Condition is critical.

For more information, see *Warman's American Records*, 1950-2000.

All records start with a master tape of an artist's or groups' performance. To make a record, a mastering agent would play the master tape and feed the sound to a cutting lathe which electronically transcribed the music into the grooves of a circular black lacquer disc, known as an acetate. The acetate was then played to determine if the sound quality was correct, to listen for defects or timing errors, order of presentation, etc. The finished acetate was then sprayed with a metal film. Once the film dried, the acetate was peeled away, creating a new "master" with a raised groove pattern. Another metallic compound was sprayed on the new "master" and after this compound was removed, a "mother" disc is created. The "mother" disc was then coated with another metallic compound, and when that was removed, a "stamper" was made. Pertinent production information was often written on the stamper before it was pressed in the production process. Each two-sided record has two stampers, one for each side. The material used for early 45s and LPs was polyvinyl chloride (PVC), and commonly called "vinyl." To make a record, hot PVC was pressed between the stampers using a compression molding process. Excess vinyl was trimmed away after the pressing process is recycled. When this re-cycled material is reused, it may result in a record that looks grainy or pockmarked. Each stamper was good for about 1,000 pressings, and then the whole process began again. Vinyl is still used for LPs, but polystyrene is now used for 45s. The production process for polystyrene is slightly different in that the base material is more liquid. Application of labels can be made directly to the polystyrene record, eliminating the label stamping process used with vinyl. To tell the difference between vinyl and styrene records, consider the following points:

- Vinyl records are thicker and heavier.
- 7-inch vinyl 45s won't bend.
- A label of one color with information "engraved" or spray painted in the center indicates a styrene record.

As with many types of antiques, a grading scale has been developed.

Mint (M): Perfect condition, no flaws, scratches, or scuffs in the grooves. The cardboard jacket will be crisp.

Near Mint (NM) or Mint-Minus (M-): The record will be close to perfect, with no marks in the grooves. The label will be clean, not marked, or scuffed. There will be no ring wear on the record or album cover.

Very Good Plus (VG+): Used for a record that has been played, but well taken care of. Slight scuffle or warps to the grooves is acceptable as long as it does not affect the sound. A faint ring wear discoloration is acceptable. The jacket may appear slightly worn, especially on the edges.

Very Good (VG): Used to describe a record that has some pronounced defects, as does the cover. The record will still play well. This usually is the lowest grade acceptable to a serious collector. Most records listed in price guides are of this grade.

Good (G): This category of record will be playable, but probably will have loss to the sound quality. Careful inspection of a styrene record in this condition may allow the viewer to see white in the grooves. The cover might be marked or torn.

Poor or Fair (P, F): Record is damaged, may be difficult to play. The cover will be in damaged condition, usually marked, dirty, or torn.

Additional Listings: See *Warman's Americana & Collectibles* for more examples.

Note: Most records, especially popular recordings, have a value of less than $3 per disc. The records listed here are classic recordings of their type and are in demand by collectors.

Frankie Lane, Mercury Wing, **$10.**

Blues, 78 rpm

Armstrong, Shelley, B & O Blues, Champion 50028 .... **15.00**
Blind Blake, Too Tight, Paramount 12431 .... **95.00**
Charles, Ray, Trio, Late in the Evening Blues, Swing Time **8.00**
King, B. B., Mistreated Woman, RPM 304 .... **25.00**
Muddy Waters, My Fault, Chess 1480 .... **15.00**

Elvis Presley "Love Me Tender" on an RCA label design that lasted until 1965, VG, **$7.50.**

Country Western, 78 RPM

Allen, Jules, The Texas Cowboy, Victor V40068 .... **10.00**
Blue Ridge Cornshuckers, Old Time Corn Shuckin', Victor 20835 .... **25.00**
Corn Cob Crushers, Dill Pickle Rag, Champion 16373 .... **50.00**
Girls of the Golden West, The Cowgirl's Dream, Victor 23857 .... **35.00**
Macon, Uncle Dave, Peek-A-Book, Bluebird 7779 .... **15.00**
Strawberry Shortcake, 1980, LP **20.00**
Newman, Roy & His Boys, Birmingham Jail, 03212 .... **8.00**
Rogers, Roy, When the Sun is Setting on the Prairie, Vocalion 04389 .... **10.00**
Tommie & Willie, By My Side, Champion 16240 .... **10.00**

Woodfield, Jake, There's a Mother Old and Gray Who Needs Me Now, Crown 3103 .... **12.50**

Gloria Lynn, Lena Horne, Coronet Records, wear and tape repairs to cover, **$5.**

Jazz, 78s

Alabama Creoile Band, Choo Choo, Claxtonola 40397 .... **15.00**
Armstrong, Louis & His Hot Five, No-One Else But You, Okeh 8669 .... **35.00**
Dixie Jazz Band, Flag that Train, Oriole 424 .... **7.50**
Ellington, Duke, Animal Crackers, Brunswick 8063 .... **150.00**
Goodman, Benny, Music Hall Rag, Columbia 3011-D **20.00**

In the Wee Small Hours by Frank Sinatra was released as a series of EPs, on two 10-inch LPs, and on a single 12-inch LP. This VG price of **$25** is for the 10-inch LP.

Holiday, Billie, Without Your Love, Vocalion 3593 .... **10.00**
Original Tuxedo Jazz Orchestra, Black Rag, Okeh 8198 .... **120.00**

Lounge, LP

Ames, Ed, My Cup Runneth Over, RCA LPM-3774, mono, 1967 .... **2.50**
Astaire, Fred, Another Evening with Fred Astaire, Chrysler 1088 .... **12.00**
Como, Perry, Merry Christmas Music, Pickwick, Camden, CAS-660, black label with rainbow letter "P" in center, 1961 .... **10.00**
Ray Conniff & Johnny Mathis, Something Special, four-album boxed set, Columbia Special Products, C4 10303, red labels **18.00**
Crosby, Bing, Jerome Kern Songs, Decca, 5001 .... **20.00**
Denny, Martin, Hawaii Tattoo, Liberty LST-7394 .... **10.00**
Day, Doris, Wonderful Day, Columbia Records XTV 82022, 1960s **8.00**
Jones, Tom, Tom, Parrot, XPAS 71037, black label with green and yellow parrot **18.00**
Lee, Brenda, 10 Golden Years, Decca, DL 74757, black label with rainbow band through center **22.00**
Mills Brothers, The, Fortuosity, Dot, DLP 25809, black label, c1959 .... **12.00**
Sinatra, Frank, Cycles, Reprise, 1027, gold/orange label with picture of Frank **8.00**

The picture sleeve for the Jan Berry/Brian Wilson collaboration of "Surf City," VG, **$10.**

Torme, Mel, California Suite, Capital P-200 .... **30.00**
Williams, Andy, Honey, Columbia, CS 9662, red label **8.00**

Rock

Animals, The, The Best of the Animals, MGM E-4324, 1966, yellow label promo **20.00**
Asylum Choir, Asylum Choir II, Shelber, SW-8910, LP, orig insert **10.00**
Beatles
- Can't Buy Me Love, You Can't Do That, Capitol 4140, 1964, picture sleeve **200.00**
- Help, I'm Down, Capitol 5476, 1965, with "A Subsidiary of Capitol" in white along perimeter **25.00**
- I Wanna Hold Your Hand, Capitol 5112, 1964 .... **10.00**
- Old Brown Shoe, Apple EPEM-10540, Mexican pcs, 45 rpm ... **18.00**

Bowie, David, Man Who Sang, Mercury SR-61325, LP **18.00**
Lennon, John, Roots, Adam Vii-A-80180, orig, LP **200.00**

Four Beatles LP albums: Capitol T2385 "Beatles VI"; Vee Jay VJP 1085 "The Beatles and Frank Ifield"; Capitol 2835 Mono, "Magical Mystery Tour" and Capitol ST 8-2047 "Meet the Beatles," all in original covers, **$150**. Photo courtesy of Joy Luke Auctions.

Nelson, Ricky, Lonesome Town, Imperial 5545 .... **8.00**

Presley, Elvis, 45

Christmas Album, RCA Victor 1035, LP, mono **80.00**

Elvis' Golden Records, RCA Victor 1707, LP **50.00**

I Got A Woman, RCA Victor, 6637, EP, maroon label **20.00**

Starlites, They Call Me A Dreamer, Ember 1011 .... **25.00**

REDWARE

History: The availability of clay, the same used to make bricks and roof tiles, accounted for the great production of red earthenware pottery in the American colonies. Redware pieces are mainly utilitarian—bowls, crocks, jugs, etc.

Lead-glazed redware retained its reddish color, but a variety of colored glazes were obtained by the addition of metals to the basic glaze. Streaks and mottled splotches in redware items resulted from impurities in the clay and/or uneven firing temperatures.

Slipware is the term used to describe redwares decorated by the application of slip, a semi-liquid paste made of clay. Slipwares were made in England, Germany, and elsewhere in Europe for decades before becoming popular in the Pennsylvania German region and other areas in colonial America.

Bank

5" h, high shoulders, mustard glaze on top, tan glaze on bottom, worn **215.00**

5" h, ovoid, orange glaze on top half, some wear **250.00**

Bowl

4-1/2" d, 1-1/4" h, tooled rim, glazed int., dark brown starflower, old small rim chip and wear **360.00**

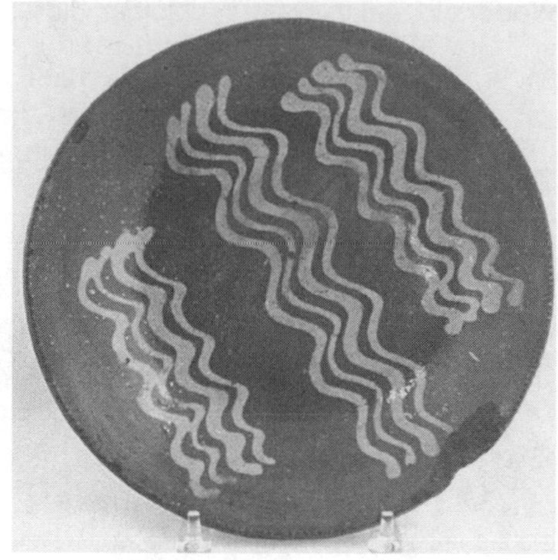

Charger, yellow four-line slip decoration, Pennsylvania, 19th C, chip, 12" d, **$350**. Redware photos courtesy of Pook & Pook.

5-1/2" d, 2-1/4" h, ftd, incised lines at rim, dark brown design of random brush strokes, some edge and int. wear **425.00**

6-3/4" d, 1-1/2" h, glazed int., manganese "X" surrounded by four daubs **475.00**

7" d, 2" h, dark brown glaze resembles tortoiseshell, minor rim flake **330.00**

8-1/8" d, 2-3/4" h, brown glaze, black dot dec, canted sides, raised rim, hairlines, rim chips **95.00**

Cup, handled, pouring lip, incised banding decoration in green glaze with dark blue-green spots, marked "Made by R.R. Stahl, 10/14/48," glaze flake, 4" d, 2" h, **$365**. Photo courtesy of Sanford Alderfer Auction Company.

8-1/2" d, 3-1/2" h, flat rim, incised line, burnt orange glaze with black flecks, wear, hairline **100.00**

11" d, 3-1/2" h, slanted sides, glazed int. with dark brown flecks and streaks, overall gold metallic specks, incised yellow slip lines, use wear **125.00**

Chamberstick, 5-1/4" d, 7" h, tapered column, round base, applied strap handle, in-the-making hole in socket **2,650.00**

Charger

12-1/4" d, coggled rim, large yellow slip script "W" with bow-shaped flourish across center, some glaze wear, small edge chips **2,750.00**

13-1/4" d, applied yellow wavy latticework slip design, coggled rim, some surface center wear, rim chips, hairline **4,290.00**

Chicken feeder, red and brown mottled applied glaze, one quart, c1850, minor surface use wear, 7" h, **$750**. Photo courtesy of Vicki and Bruce Waasdorp.

Doorstop, 6-1/2" d, 6" h, hollow, inverted top shape, orig red and white paint, dark gold stripes, wear, edge chips **360.00**

Figure

6" h, dog, seated, molded, hand detailed face, dark brown glaze **175.00**

6-1/2" h, dog, seated, hand detailed collar and face, semi-matte dark brown glaze, inscribed "FK" **130.00**

Jug, ovoid form, applied handle, mottled green and brown glaze, imperfections, 10-1/2" h, **$935**. Photo courtesy of Sanford Alderfer Auction Company.

Flask

6-3/8" h, ring under lip, dark brown spots, wear at rim **365.00**

9" h, light pumpkin color, dark brown splotches 450.00

Loaf dish, yellow slip decoration, borders of triple wavy lines and central "S" designs, minor rim chipping, 9-1/2" x 13-1/2", **$935**. Photo courtesy of Sanford Alderfer Auction Company.

Flower pot, 5-1/2" d, 5" h, mottled cream, light orange, and brown glaze, attached saucer, attributed to Shenandoah, rim wear, few flakes **275.00**

Harvest jug, 9-1/4" h, applied ribbed strap handle on top, spout, incised lines, medium brown splotches in glaze, some damage to base **550.00**

Egg cup, green and orange manganese decoration, attributed to by Bell Pottery, 19th C, 2-1/2" h, **$2,185**.

Jar, cov

7-1/4" h, tapered at foot, incised lines, black specks in glaze, dark brown daubs around shoulder and neck, lid different color, minor rim wear, few glaze flakes **330.00**

8-1/4" h, 5" d, straight sides, daubs of dark brown around body, some edge damage......................... **330.00**

8-1/2" h, black sponge dec, reddish brown glaze, incised line below shoulder, raised foot, small glaze flakes, shallow chips around foot **770.00**

Jar, open

5-1/2" h, 4-1/2" d, dark glaze with dark mottled brown, incised line, applied ribbed strap handle, minor rim flakes **495.00**

5-7/8" h, raised rim, brown glaze, incised line dec, flakes............ **85.00**

6" h, 4-3/4" d, ovoid, flared rim, applied strap handle, splotches of manganese glaze, few chips, hairline at handle **360.00**

7-3/4" h, ovoid, greenish brown glaze, brown dots, flakes **95.00**

Jug

5-1/4" h, ovoid, applied strap handle, incised line, brushed dark brown lines around shoulder, glaze flakes **990.00**

6" h, squatty, applied handle, dark reddish glaze, three faint dark brown splotches, glaze wear **330.00**

7" h, ovoid, applied strap handle, several daubs of dark brown in glaze, chip on foot, glaze flaked at mouth **550.00**

9-1/4" h, ovoid, sponged and running glaze dec on brown ground, thin raised bead around base, flared spout, applied strap handle, small base chips............................. **330.00**

11-3/4" h, ovoid, reddish brown glaze runs to base, unglazed raised foot, applied strap handle, wear, some glaze flakes **330.00**

Lamp, 23" h with harp, made from jar, reddish brown glaze with black sponging, straight sides, incised lines at shoulder, flared rim, drilled for cord beneath turned wooden base............................... **275.00**

Loaf pan

7-1/2" x 10-1/2", "Martha" in dark brown glaze, overall metallic speckles, coggled rim, old shallow rim flake.............................. **2,100.00**

9" x 14", coggled rim, yellow slip "LaFayette," rim flakes, some wear **3,300.00**

11-1/4" x 15-1/2" x 1-3/4" h, reddish brown glaze, three rows of continuous script "L"s in yellow slip, rect, gently sloping sides, cogged rim, rim chips, back with dark black patina, minor glaze wear..... **3,650.00**

Flower pot, attached undertray, green and brown glaze over cream ground, Shenandoah Valley, 19th C, 7-1/2" d, 8" h, **$2,900**.

11-3/4" x 14-3/4" x 2-3/4" h, oval, brown glaze, yellow slip double line criss-cross dec, wear, flake, two hairlines **825.00**

13-3/4" w, 9-1/4" d, 2-1/2" h, coggled rim with high sloping sides, yellow slip three-line dec, bird claw designs at corners divided by wavy lines top and bottom, narrow braid down center, area of orange peel glaze, old patina on bottom, minor rim chips................................... **1,870.00**

Measure, 5-1/2" d, 2-7/8" h, pitcher shape, applied strap handle, tooled line under spout, dark brown mottled rim, few flakes and glaze wear **525.00**

Turk mold, green mottled alkaline glaze, relief oak leaf interior, minor glaze flake, 9" d, 3-1/2" h, **$80**. Photo courtesy of Vicki and Bruce Waasdorp.

Milk pitcher, 8-3/4" h, reddish brown glaze, white splotches, paneled sides, applied handle, sgd "Henry Swopes Pottery" on octagonal base, edge chips, firing separations in handle....... **1,210.00**

Miniature

Bowl, 3-3/4" d, ftd, pumpkin glaze, dark brown daubs **215.00**

Crock, 3" d, 3" h, yellow, dark green, and orange spotted glaze...... **200.00**

Jardinière, 1-7/8" h, pumpkin glaze, green rim **195.00**

Jug, 2-5/8" h, manganese glaze **175.00**

Pitcher, 2-1/4" h, tooled line.... **250.00**

Tumbler, 2-1/2" h, dark green/brown glaze..................................... **215.00**

Mug, 4-1/4" h, incised lines, applied handle, running yellow glaze inside and out, possibly Shenandoah, some rim wear... **715.00**

Pepper pot, 5" h, orange glaze, band of manganese under top, chips on top **1,100.00**

Pie plate

4" d, coggled rim, yellow slip three-line design, minor surface wear **1,450.00**

4-1/4" d, plain rim, three yellow slip stripes, small flakes, flaked glaze **425.00**

Plate, yellow slip decoration, Pennsylvania, 19th C, chip, 5-3/4" d, **$415**.

6-3/4" d, coggled rim, green and dark brown central double "S" design **2,100.00**
7" d, dark brown and yellow slip intersecting lines, sgd "W. Smith, Womelsdorf," (Willoughby Smith, Berks County, PA), surface wear, minor damage **2,530.00**
7-3/4" d, coggled rim, three yellow slip "W" designs, surface wear **616.00**
8" d, coggled rim, green and brown slip tulip design, attributed to Dryville, Berks County, PA, some surface wear and rim flakes **7,975.00**
8" d, coggled rim, yellow slip wavy lines in three sets, few shallow edge flakes **1,430.00**
8-1/4" d, coggled rim, dark green pinwheel type design, surface wear, few rim flakes **935.00**
8-1/2" d, slightly coggled rim, yellow slip crossed snowshoe and dots design, minor edge flakes... **5,610.00**
9" d, coggled rim, overall yellow slip grid design and wavy lines, six broken out blisters **1,650.00**
9-1/4" d, coggled rim, yellow slip dec "Mary's Dish," crazing, wear, two chips **1,540.00**
9-3/4" d, coggled rim, yellow clip wavy flag type dec, faint knife scratches, possible repair...... **660.00**
10-1/4" d, coggled rim, yellow slip dec "Agness" and flourishes, rim flakes, center wear **1,760.00**
10-1/4" d, coggled rim, yellow slip dec "James," and flourishes, rim flakes, minor wear **3,300.00**
10-1/2" d, coggled rim, yellow slip wavy triple line dec, hairline, minor rim flake **1,540.00**
12-1/4" d, coggled rim, yellow slip large script initials "W S G," paper label on back "apple pie dish was a wedding present to William and Gerta Shiller, 1820-1840, Lancaster County, Penn," areas of minor rim roughness, shallow chip **1,690.00**
13-1/4" d, 2-1/2" h, coggled rim, yellow slip curlicues and dots around central feather, edge chips, hairline **15,125.00**

Pitcher
6" h, incised ring, applied ribbed handle, dark brown graduated splotches around shoulder and on rim, minor edge damage **1,130.00**
6" h, narrow, flared neck, applied ribbed handle, running green and brown glaze over creamy yellow, attributed to Shenandoah Valley, edge roughness, crack stabilized with glue **360.00**

Turk's head, **$200**. Photo courtesy of Wiederseim Associates, Inc.

6-1/4" h, thick walls, applied strap handle, black speckled glaze, dark brown splotches, some edge wear **660.00**
7" h, applied ribbed strap handle, coggled band at neck, sgraffito American eagle with shield below spout, mottled olive, orange, and dark brown glaze, unsigned, attributed to Jacob Medinger, Neiffer, Montgomery County, PA, c1880-1930, well done repair to top of spout **1,760.00**

Pitcher, cov, 7" h, 6-1/4" d, galleried rim with spout, applied strap handle, tooled incised lines, dark brown sponged lines, edge flakes **635.00**
Plate, 9-1/4" d, coggled edge, dark brick red glaze, yellow slip "X" within circle surrounded by wavy line, attributed to Huntington Pottery, Long Island, NY, minor edge and glaze flakes........ **935.00**
Storage jar, 8-1/2" h, ovoid, incised lines along shoulder and base, applied handles, brick red colored glaze, black sponged lines applied at angle around sides, glaze flakes **275.00**

Red Wing Pottery

History: The Red Wing pottery category includes several potteries from Red Wing, Minnesota. In 1868, David Hallem started Red Wing Stoneware Co., the first pottery with stoneware as its primary product. The Minnesota Stoneware Co. started in 1883. The North Star Stoneware Co. was in business from 1892 to 1896.

The Red Wing Stoneware Co. and the Minnesota Stoneware Co. merged in 1892. The new company, the Red Wing Union Stoneware Co., made stoneware until 1920 when it introduced a pottery line that it continued until the 1940s. In 1936, the name was changed to Red Wing Potteries, Inc. During the 1930s, this firm introduced several popular patterns of hand-painted dinnerware, which were distributed through department stores, mail-order catalogs, and gift-stamp centers. Dinnerware production declined in the 1950s and was replaced with hotel and restaurant china in the early 1960s. The plant closed in 1967.

Marks: Red Wing Stoneware Co. was the first firm to mark pieces with a red wing stamped under the glaze. The North Star Stoneware Co. used a raised star and the words "Red Wing" as its mark.

Crock, 15 gallons, lily decoration, **$5,250**. Photo courtesy of Seeck Auctions.

Applesauce jar, three gal, 2" wing, potteries oval **95.00**
Baking dish, spongeware, small, "Holstein Produce and Hatchery" **425.00**
Beanpot
"Compliments of Pennock Cooperative Co. General Merchandise, Pennock, MN" adv **75.00**

"Farmer's Cooperative Grain & Lumber Co., Felco, phone 82, Gowrie, Iowa" adv **105.00**

Beater jar, cov

Blue band, "When Beating Think of Eating Pure Food Groceries From Atkisson & Davis" adv **135.00**

"Fancy Potted Lunch Cheese Guttman Bros. St. Paul, MINN" adv **175.00**

Bowl

6", spongeware, panel, "It Pays to Mix with Lincoln Malt Co., 1037 Windlake Avenue" adv **175.00**

8" d, white, red and blue sponging, "Compliments of Producers Marketing Co., Grain, Feed, Fuel, Cayuga, N. Dak" adv, hairline **125.00**

12" d, blue banded................. **65.00**

Butter churn

Four gal, salt glaze, ribcage .. **275.00**

Five gal, 4" wing, Union oval, lid, dasher **235.00**

Six gal, 4" wing, Union oval.... **185.00**

Butter churn lid, for five or six gal size **115.00**

Butter crock, 20 lb

Pound sign, crow's foot in base **150.00**

20 lb mark in blue square **165.00**

Churn

Three gal, 2" wing, potteries oval, no handles, chip on lid................. **95.00**

Five gal, 2" wing, potteries oval, bail handles.................................. **75.00**

Six gal, oval over 6" wing **550.00**

Convention commemorative

1977, salt glaze crock......... **1,200.00**

1978, brown jug **750.00**

1979, two-gal butter churn..... **800.00**

1980, sponge bowl............. **1,300.00**

1981, mini jug....................... **350.00**

1982, mug, cherry band **375.00**

1983, canning jar **525.00**

1984, salt glaze water cooler **350.00**

1985, ice water cooler........... **325.00**

1986, acid proof measure, orig box **105.00**

1987, wing ashtray................ **125.00**

1988, Pompeii plate **90.00**

1989, pitcher, sponge band... **250.00**

1990, fancy jug....................... **75.00**

Low bowl, exterior incised with band of leaves around rim, apple green glaze interior, circular stamp mark, 9" d, **$40**. Photo courtesy of David Rago Auctions, Inc.

Cookie jar, cov, Carousel, repaired lid **135.00**

Cookie jar, cov, Cattails

Blue, brown shading, bottom marked **165.00**

Green, bottom marked, wooden lid **55.00**

Yellow, bottom marked, chip on bottom of base, hairline in lid... **75.00**

Crock, birchleaf

Three gal, Minnesota Stoneware oval **850.00**

Twenty-five gal, four birchleaf dec, no oval mark, minor chip on handle **145.00**

Thirty gal, four birchleaf dec, Union Stoneware oval...................... **185.00**

Crock, elephant ears, Union oval

Three gal, bottom marked...... **115.00**

Six gal.................................. **215.00**

Crock, 4" wing

Two gal, Union oval................. **50.00**

Three gal, ski oval **65.00**

Six gal, Union oval, bail handles **65.00**

Twenty gal, potteries oval, bail handles, hairline...................... **50.00**

Crock, 6" wing

Eight gal, Union oval **185.00**

Ten gal, Union oval, bail handles **65.00**

Fifteen gal, Union oval, bail handles **105.00**

Crock, salt glaze, butterfly

Ten gal, back stamped........ **1,500.00**

Twenty gal **1,200.00**

Vase, ovoid, raised rim, relief decorated with lions and foliage, sage green and blue semi-glossy glaze, partial circular stamp, 7-5/8" h, **$200**. Photo courtesy of Skinner Auctioneers and Appraisers.

Crock, salt glaze, double P

Two gal, crow's foot on base.... **65.00**

Two gal, bottom marked......... **105.00**

Crock, salt glaze, leaf

Three gal, bottom marked...... **875.00**

Five gal................................. **135.00**

Crock, salt glaze, ribcage

Three gal **155.00**

Five gal, crow's foot, repaired spot on back **75.00**

Crock, salt glaze, single P

Three gal **105.00**

Three gal, single P and target **115.00**

Fruit jar, 1/2 gal, Stone Mason, blue label.. **265.00**

Jar, self draining, 4" wing, Union oval **225.00**

Jug, beehive

Four gal, 4" wing, Union oval **425.00**

Five gal, birch leaves only...... **260.00**

Teapot, butter yellow glaze, stamped "Red Wing," two short hairlines, 8-1/2" w, 6" h, **$85**. Photo courtesy of David Rago Auctions, Inc.

Jug, fancy, one gal, "M.Wollstein & Co. Wholesale Liquor Dealers, Branch Stores in Omaha, So. Omaha, Council Bluffs" adv.. **550.00**

Jug, shoulder

One gal, brown top **165.00**

One qt, "William Steinmeyer Co. Wine Merchants, Milwaukee, WI" adv, nick on handle............... **115.00**

Five gal, brown top, 4" wing, Union oval...................................... **825.00**

Vase, tapered cylinder, straight neck, relief floral design, red matte glaze, stamped "Red Wing/ Union/Stoneware/Co/Red Wing/Minn," 8-1/4" h, **$75**.

Jug, shoulder, dome top, one gallon, salt glaze, bottom marked **75.00**

Koverwate

Five gal **200.00**

Fifteen gal, minor nicks **200.00**

Twenty gallon **350.00**

Miniature, jug, Albany slip, "Minnesota Stoneware Co., Red Wing, MN" paper label on bottom **650.00**

Pitcher, Hamm's Beer, bottom marked **525.00**

Pitcher, mottled, blue, repaired spout **165.00**

Pitcher, Saffronware, "The Farmers Store, Northwood, N Dak" adv, small size **145.00**

Rolling pin, Gray Line **105.00**

Salt shaker, Gray Line **550.00**

Storage jar, Wyoming Territory, sponge dec **55.00**

Vase, classical shape, embossed lions, mottled, dripping green over matte beige glaze, circular stamp mark, 6" d, 7-1/2" h, **$120**. Photo courtesy of David Rago Auctions, Inc.

Vase, 7-1/4" h, bulbous, mottled amber and green crystalline glaze, stamped, tight line to rim **415.00**

Water cooler

Six gal, 4" wing, Union oval **255.00**

Eight gal, 4" wing, Union oval **335.00**

Ten gal, metal stand, lid, 4" wing, oval, ladle chip on lid **525.00**

Wax sealer, Albany slip, bottom marked **30.00**

Religious Items

History: Objects used in worship or as expressions of man's belief in a superhuman power are collected by many people for many reasons.

This category includes icons, since they are religious mementos, usually paintings with a brass encasement. Collecting icons dates from the earliest period of Christianity. Most antique icons in today's market were made in the late 19th century.

Reproduction Alert: Icons are frequently reproduced.

Altar, 16" w, 31" h, intricately carved wood, each figure polychromed, resurrected Christ in center flanked by Virgin on left and Apostle John on right, God the Father at top center, carved tabernacle atop altar rotates to reveal monstrance, crucifix, or covered ciborium, German or Spanish, 18th C, slight scattered loss to paint **2,875.00**

Altar cross, 18" h, bronze cross, crucified Christ below two angels of the Lord, beneath a hollow crystal receptacle containing fine ashes, French, 19th C **400.00**

Angel, Italian, polychrome and gilt carved in the round wood, 18th C, 41" h, **$3,000**. Photo courtesy of Jackson's International Auctioneers & Appraisers.

Angel, wood, fully carved in the round, 18-5/8" w, 15-5/8" l, gessoed, young standing figure, wings outstretched, face set with glass eyes, painted and gilded finish, Continental, mid-19th C **490.00**

Bible

Biblia, Die gantze heil. Schrift, Alten und Neuen Testaments, Durch D. Martin Luther verteutscht, Daniel Tschiffelin, Basel & Bern, 1701, in German, column-width woodcut text illus, folio, worn covers, catches, clasps, binding worn, contents heavily browned **550.00**

Biblia, Johannes Herbort, de Seligenstadt, April 30, 1484, Venice, in Latin, Gothic type, 4to, old vellum, book block loose in binding, marginal dampstaining, some conspicuous worming in blank upper and lower outer corners, Drexel Institute bookplate **3,220.00**

Old Testament, Annotations upon the Third Book of Moses, called Leviticus, Henry Ainsworth, Giles Thorp, Amsterdam, 1618, 4to, contemporary vellum, soiled, recased **400.00**

The Holy Bible, Old Testament, University Printers, Oxford, 1696, contemporary red velvet over pastedown, embroidered with gold thread to simple center, corner design on covers, spine faded, front cover detailed, velvet rubbed, cloth folding case **375.00**

Bible cover, 10-1/2" x 7-1/2", vellum cover, front overlaid with massive gilded bronze and silvered plaque with champlevé enamel, depicting crucifixion with the four Evangelists, back cover with gilded bronze Romanesque-style angel and polished stone feet held in gilded and enamel frames, spine imp "Santa Biblia," matching bronze clasps **1,100.00**

Ecclesiastical vestments, left: burgundy floral silk damask, trimmed with ivory and burgundy silk fringe, fully lined in tan linen, c1900, **$125**; right: rose and tan brocade with bird, urn and flower motif, trimmed with gold metallic lace, lined with yellow and green cotton, c1890, wear, **$115**. Photo courtesy of Alderfer Auction Co.

Book

An Historical Account of the Laws enacted against Catholics, both in England and Ireland...to which is added, A Short Account of the Laws for the Punishment of Heresy in General, James Baldwin Brown, London, 1813, 8vo, contemporary half calf gilt, FE, inscribed by author on half title, spine ends damaged, joints cracked **175.00**

Primitive Christianity, or The Religion of the Ancient Christians in the First Ages of the Gospel, William Cave, 4th edition, J. H. for R. Chiswel, London, 1682, contemporary calf, rebacked **490.00**

Buddha

21" h, Thai, 19th C, gilt bronze, hands clasped in prayer, stepped base **2,300.00**

33" h, Japan, 19th C, carved and gilt wood, standing on lotus throne, scrolled clouds backed by aureole, some losses **3,450.00**

Candlesticks, pr, 25" h, gilt bronze, pricket, ftd bases with open fretwork, enamel medallions inscribed "S. J.," building tools, flowers, and cabochons, French, 19th C **980.00**

Casket, 11" l, 8" w, 8-1/2" h, Pattarino, 22 scenes from Old Testament, each scene hand molded and applied figures, hinged lid, scattered losses **1,380.00**

Chalice and paten, 8-1/4" h, silver gilt, French Gothic style, repousse and finely chased node, stem, and base, cup resting on pierced basket of floral forms, hallmarks, 19th C...................... **1,150.00**

Communion set, bishop's or cardinal's, 13-3/4" h chalice with chased base and three circular reserves of the Passion, separated by winged cherubs, oversized central node with wheat and grapes between three oval medallions depicting Christ, Virgin, and Apostle St John, flared cup resting on intricate pierced basket with winged cherubs, three roundels sculpted with additional scenes from the Passion, 7-1/2" d paten with miniature sculpted depiction of Last Supper, edges engraved with implements of the Passion, 11-1/2" h cruet tray dec with repoussé grapes and cattails, wine cruet chased with grapes, grape finial on lid, water cruet chased with cattails, sea shell finial on lid, gilded silver, ornately dec, A. Renaud, Paris, c1890, each pc clearly marked, custom fitted silk-lined wood case... **9,200.00**

Creche figure, 15-3/4" to 17-3/8" h, carved wood, two young women, old woman, painted detailing, glass eyes, excelsior bodies, and silken garb, mounted to turned wooden socles, young figures with fragmentary labels to bases concerning sale of the figures taken from suppressed Italian convents to benefit Catholic Church, price for three figures **2,415.00**

Figure

20-1/2" h, Madonna and Child, standing Madonna holding the Christ child, both wearing crowns with traces of paint, carved alabaster, Continental, 19th C............. **1,300.00**

Madonna, carved wood, 16" h, **$575**. Photo courtesy of Jackson's Auction.

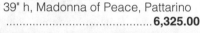

39" h, Madonna of Peace, Pattarino **6,325.00**

41" h, carved and painted, depicting St. James of Santiago di Campostella, seated figure, red robe, satchel, black cap set with seashell, Tyrolean, 15th C, restorations **3,820.00**

Madonna and Child, Italian, gilt and painted carved in the round wood, c1800, 33" h, **$1,610**. Photo courtesy of Jackson's International Auctioneers & Appraisers.

Gospel stand, 14" x 14-1/2", gilt bronze, four massive figural winged griffin feet, front and sides with elaborate fret work, embellished with Austrian crystals, 19th C.. **435.00**

Holy water font, 6-1/4" w, 8-1/2" h, gilded bronze, figural, guardian angel, French, 19th C...................................... **1,265.00**

Communion table, oak, English, 1680-1720, four-board top with breadboard ends, on stretcher base, bold reeded and fluted urn shaped turnings, six legs, 11' 5" l, 34" w, 32" h, **$3,300**. Photo courtesy of Sanford Alderfer Auction Company.

Icon, Greek, 19" x 15", The Mother of God of the Life Bearing Font, tempera on wood panel **1,250.00**

Icon, Italo Cretan, The Mother of God of Consolation, c1500, finely painted in naturalistic manner, haloes tooled with arabesques, 28-1/2" x 19" **5,750.00**

Icon, Russian

8-1/2" x 10-1/2", Three Hierachs, finely painted, St. Gregory the Theologian, St. Basil the Great, and St. John Chrysostom, dressed as Bishops, Christ delivers blessing at center, incised gold leaf, c1890 .... **1,120.00**

12" x 14", John the Forerunner with Life Scenes, winged John the Baptist in center, delivers blessing, holds open scroll, top margin with God the Father, kovcheg intricately dec with scrolling foliate, title inscribed in abbreviated Slavonic near gold leaf halo, attributed to Palekh or Mstera, 19th C **1,700.00**

Retablo, Spanish Colonial School, 19th C, Our Lady of Guadalupe with Juan Diego, paint decoration gesso on wood panel, 11" x 7-1/2", **$800**. Photo courtesy of Skinner, Inc.

Monstrance

30" h, possibly German, 19th C, gilt bronze, oval form ftd domed base heavily repousséd with scrolling foliage, wheat, grapes, cast relief medallion of Nativity of Christ and Adoration of the Shepherds, baluster shaped central stem dec with grapevines, large node with two angels supporting large sunburst set with silvered grapevines surrounding central exposition window, two additional angels at top, intricately cast relief medallion depicting the Wedding of the Virgin, cross finial, further embellished with cabochons and paste stones, decorative luna supported by winged cherub, custom fitted case **900.00**

30-1/2" h, Celtic, c1920, gilt bronze, circular ftd base set with four Celtic crosses, supporting twist stem with large node displaying Celtic designs, ornate sunburst set with large Celtic cross form, exposition window at apex, cross finial **920.00**

Virgin and child, French Gothic-style, carved wood, 19th C, 27" h, **$1,100**. Photo courtesy of Jackon's International Auctioneers & Appraisers.

Painting, oil on canvas

29" x 24", Perseverantia, unsigned, Italian School, 18th C **750.00**

30" x 39", Adoration of the Shepherds, unsigned, European School, 19th C **575.00**

36" x 24", Seated Madonna, 20th C follower of Jan Van Eyck **1,840.00**

39" x 29", The Immaculate Conception, unsigned, Spanish Colonial, 18th C, laid down **1,035.00**

39" x 29", The Visitation, unsigned, Spanish Colonial, 18th C........ **865.00**

Reliquary

8" w, 7-1/2" h, gilt bronze, eye-shaped, displaying relics on both sides and stored below with documents, 19th C **1,150.00**

18-1/4" h, gilt bronze, exposition window containing reliquary with 11 individual relics, 19th C **920.00**

20" h, gilt bronze, arched exposition window containing sealed oval reliquary with relics, verso with wax seal, 19th C **1,035.00**

Retablo, gessoed wood panel, polychrome, New Mexico, 19th C, 9-1/2" x 7-1/4", Arroyo Hondo or José Aragón, San José, verso with hand written label relating work to N Mexican church **4,600.00**

Santos, Philippine, carved and painted wood

13" h, carved winged angel playing lute **200.00**

Virgin, South German, polychrome and carved in the round wood, 19th C, 24-1/2" h, **$1,150**. Photo courtesy of Jackson's International Auctioneers & Appraisers.

14" h, The Christ Child **120.00**

19" h, Mary **150.00**

Santos Shrine, two pcs, top with two front doors revealing fitted int., conforming base with two cupboard doors, sides also have doors, inlaid panels, 40" w, 17" d, 60-1/2" h **200.00**

Santos, two monk form figures, losses, 10-1/2" h, 10-3/4" h, **$150**. Photo courtesy of Alderfer Auction Co.

Reverse Painting On Glass

History: The earliest examples of reverse painting on glass were produced in 13th-century Italy. By the 17th century, the technique had spread to central and eastern Europe. It spread westward as the center of the glassmaking industry moved to Germany in the late 17th century.

The Alsace and Black Forest regions developed a unique portraiture style. The half and three-quarter portraits often were titled below the portrait. Women tend to have generic names, while most males are likenesses of famous men.

The English used a mezzotint, rather than free-style, method to create their reverse paintings. Landscapes and allegorical figures were popular. The Chinese began working in the medium in the 17th century, eventually favoring marine and patriotic scenes.

Most American reverse painting was done by folk artists and is unsigned. Portraits, patriotic and mourning scenes, floral compositions, landscapes, and buildings are the favorite subjects. Known American artists include Benjamin Greenleaf, A. Cranfield, and Rowley Jacobs.

In the late 19th century, commercially produced reverse paintings, often decorated with mother-of-pearl, became popular. Themes included the Statue of Liberty, the capitol in Washington, D.C., and various world's fairs and expositions. Today craftsmen are reviving this art, using some vintage-looking designs, but usually with brighter colors than their antique counterparts.

Church scene, mica highlights, framed, **$65**. Photo courtesy of Dotta Auction Co., Inc.

Portraits

Geisha, holding paint brush, red robe, black and gold trim, gold hair ornaments, partially screened, much hand painting, 15-1/4" w, 21-1/2" h, minor flaking at top, black wooden frame with minor damage on back....................................... **175.00**

Lincoln, Abraham, framed, 21-1/2" h, 18" w.. **425.00**

Military officer, blue coat, red collar, white band with name "Jagson," cracked, black painted frame, 5-3/4" w, 8" h **330.00**

Oriental boy, 16" x 22", young boy holding basket of red flowers, red pants, cloud design blue jacket, fancy gilt embroidered trim, black and salmon ground, double framed with black wooden frames, wide woven mat liner painted gold, 29" h x 35" outer frame **300.00**

Royal Couple, unsigned, Chinese Export School, 19th C, period Chinese frames, 15-1/2" w, 21-1/2" h, portrait of gentleman cracked lower left, price for pr **3,450.00**

Washington, George, silhouette, intricately painted border maple veneer frame, gilded liner with minor damage, 12-3/4" h, 11" w............................ **250.00**

Woman, brown hair and eyes, named "Clara," green dress, blue belt, red trim, brown background, white border, black painted pine frame, 10-1/2" w, 12-1/2" h **690.00**

Young well-dressed lady, inscription "This box belonged to Lydia A Dowell, daughter of Richard and Barbara Dowell, She died in 1834 in the 13th year of her age," 5-1/2" x 7-1/4", probably lid to dresser box, **$110**. Photo courtesy of Cowan's Historic Americana Auctions.

Portrait of Martha Washington, c1830, 23-1/2" x 19-1/2", **$250**. Photo courtesy of Pook & Pook.

Statue of Liberty, mica accents, oval frame **175.00**

Scenes

Country house in winter, gold painted frame, 10-1/2" h, 12-1/2" w **75.00**

Ship, Ohio, side wheeler steamship, poplar frame, 10-1/2" h, 12-1/2" w **175.00**

Silhouette

Coaches, painted and printed dark red, gold, blue, and green, coaches and travelers, eglomise mats and titles "The London and Oxford Coach" and "The Oxford and London Coach," bird's eye maple frames, 18" w, 13" h, price for pr **350.00**

Couple, double reverse painted, seated husband and wife, man with walking stick, lady with book, hand drawn inked background of Queen Anne lowboy with vase of flowers, 10" w, 8-1/4" h, slight flaking, worn gilt frame................. **825.00**

Rockingham and Rockingham Brown-Glazed Wares

History: Rockingham ware can be divided into two categories. The first consists of the fine china and porcelain pieces made between 1826 and 1842 by the Rockingham Company of Swinton, Yorkshire, England, and its predecessor firms: Swinton, Bingley, Don, Leeds, and Brameld. The Bramelds developed the cadogan, a lidless teapot. Between 1826 and 1842, the Bramelds developed a quality soft-paste product with a warm, silky feel. Elaborate specialty pieces were made. By 1830, the company employed 600 workers and listed 400 designs for dessert sets and 1,000 designs for tea and coffee services in its catalog. Unable to meet its payroll, the company closed in 1842.

The second category of Rockingham ware includes pieces produced in the famous Rockingham brown glaze that became an intense and vivid purple-brown when fired. It had a dark, tortoiseshell appearance. The glaze was copied by many English and American potteries. American manufacturers that used Rockingham glaze include D. & J. Henderson of Jersey City, New Jersey; United States Pottery in Bennington, Vermont; potteries in East Liverpool, Ohio; and several potteries in Indiana and Illinois.

Additional Listings: Bennington and Bennington-Type Pottery.

Bedpan, 15" l, Rockingham glaze, chip **40.00**
Bowl, 9-1/2" d, 3-1/4" h **65.00**
Caterer jug, 8-3/4" h, Rockingham glazed Vigornian, tapering form with acid etched geometric design to either side of a floral bouquet, impressed Wedgwood mark, c1880, restored spout **650.00**
Creamer, 6-3/4" h, cow-form, 19th C, minor chips **260.00**
Cuspidor, 6-5/8", 4" h, four sides, molded eagles, dark brown Rockingham glaze **330.00**
Dish, 11-1/2" l, octagonal, spotted Rockingham glaze **170.00**
Figure, 10" h, 7-1/2" l, seated spaniel, good molded detail, freestanding front legs, scrolls and shells on base, few edge chips **225.00**
Flask, 8" h, molded floral dec, band **45.00**
Flower pot, 10-1/4" h, emb acanthus leaves, matching saucer **45.00**
Inkwell, 4-1/8" l, shoe shape **60.00**
Mixing bowl, nested set of three, emb design **95.00**
Pie plate, Rockingham glaze, 10" d **80.00**
Pitcher, Rockingham glaze
- 4-3/8" l, squatty, C scroll handle **75.00**
- 8" h, molded peacocks, rim chips **90.00**

Plate, 9" d, painted center with exotic bird in landscape, raised C-scroll border with gilt and painting, puce griffin and green number marks **650.00**

Pitcher, applied dog handle, overall hunt scene, late 19th C, 11-1/2" h, **$520**. Photo courtesy of Pook & Pook.

Potpourri vase, cov, 11" h, two handles, pink ground borders with central enamel dec floral bouquets, gilt foliage and trim, pierced neck, rim, and cov, printed griffin mark, c1835, slight gilt rim wear to vase, rim chips and hairline to cover **290.00**
Tea service, gilt cell and scroll dec on cobalt blue and yellow ground bands, 8-1/4" h cov teapot; 7-1/2" h cov sugar bowl; 5-3/4" h cream jug, (repaired handle); 7" d waste bowl; 8-3/4" d circular serving dish, (hairline to center); two 10-3/4" square serving dishes, (one with center hairline); 13 coffee cups; nine tea cups, (one with hairline); 10 6" d saucers; light gilt wear, England, c1840 ..... **450.00**
Tea set, rococo-style, each with central pale buff band, enamel decorated landscape cartouche, gilt scrolled foliate trim, 10-1/2" l cov teapot with scrolled foliate handle and serpent-form spout, rim hairline, light gilt wear to spout and handle; 4-3/8" h creamer, slight chip to side of handle; 6" h cov sugar bowl; 7-1/8" d waste bowl, c1820 .... **220.00**
Vase
- 4-3/8" h, flared, painted view of Larington Yorkshire, figures and sheep, wide gilt border, dark blue ground, restored, c1826-30, iron-red griffin and painted title **420.00**
- 6-1/2" h, flared hexagon, painted sprays of colored garden flowers alternating with blue panels, gilt scrolls, c1831-42, puce griffin mark **800.00**

Washboard, 24-1/4" h, 19th C, imperfections **350.00**

Rock 'n' Roll

History: Rock music can be traced back to early rhythm and blues. It progressed until it reached its golden age in the 1950s and 1960s. Most of the memorabilia issued during that period focused on individual singers and groups. The largest quantity of collectible material is connected to Elvis Presley and The Beatles.

It is important to identify memorabilia issued during the lifetime of an artist or performing group, as opposed to material issued after they died or disbanded. Objects of the latter type are identified as "fantasy" items and will never achieve the same degree of collectibility as period counterparts.

Reproduction Alert: Records, picture sleeves, and album jackets, especially for The Beatles, have been counterfeited. When compared to the original, sound may be inferior, as may be the printing on labels and picture jackets. Many pieces of memorabilia also have been reproduced, often with some change in size, color, and design.

Additional Listings: See The Beatles and Rock 'n' Roll in *Warman's Americana & Collectibles* and *Warman's Flea Market Price Guide.*

Autograph, photo signed
- Beatles, Pete Best, drummer, photo of Beatles, photographed by Troy Alders, published by Art Rock, San Francisco, sgd "Pete Best" below photo, certificate of authenticity, clear plexiglass frame, 10-1/2" x 14-1/2" photo, 16" x 20" frame .. **2,500.00**
- Stewart, Rod, 8" x 10", certificate of authenticity, maple frame, 12-1/2" x 10-1/2" **125.00**

Record, Beatles, "Sgt. Pepper's Lonely Hearts Club Band," framed, 11-1/2" d, **$45**. Photo courtesy of Joy Luke Auctions.

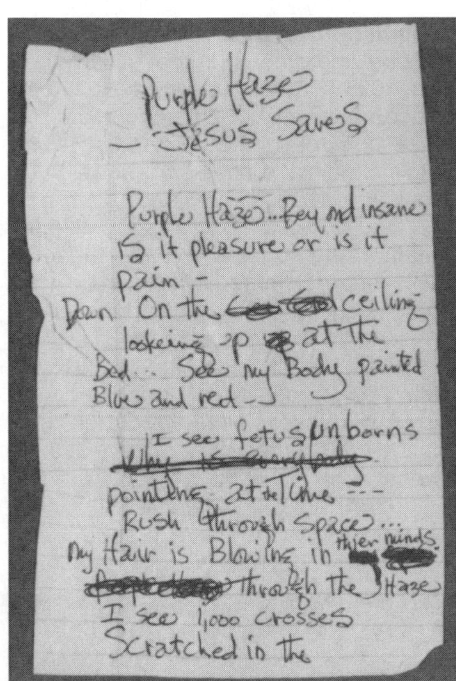

Signed document, Jimi Hendrix, hand-written lyrics, "Purple Haze," **$18,000.**

Book

Beatlebook of Recorded Hits, No. 2, copyright 1964, pullout photo section, official fan club membership application form, slight wear to cover **95.00**

Elvis Presley, 1994, 240 pgs **24.00**

Bracelet, Monkees, pictures of four members, 1967 .... **35.00**

Bubble gum cards, complete set, issued by Boxcar Enterprises, 1978 .... **135.00**

Comic book, *The Monkees*, #9, copyright 1967 .... **35.00**

Doll, 5" h, Beatles George Harrison Doll, 1962, marked "EEGEE" on bottom of foot **45.00**

Drawing, Psychedelic, Jimi Hendrix, 1969, **$6,875.**

Drumsticks

Black Crows, concerned used, logo **20.00**

Randy Castillo, Ozzy Osbourne **35.00**

Iron Maiden, 1985 .... **50.00**

Pinback button, Elvis Presley National Fan Club Member, black and white, c1956, 15/16" d, **$175.** Photo courtesy of Hake's Americana & Collectibles.

Flyer, concert, Aerosmith, 1988, 8" x 6", two sided, Whitesnake and Def Leppard on back **45.00**

Key chain, Rolling Stones, six different photos, orig package, unopened... **12.00**

Miscellaneous vintage Beatles items. Lot contained: five licorice records in original wrappers, four metal Beatles pins on original card and gold-tone pin with photo of Beatles, on original card, **$150.** Photo courtesy of Joy Luke Auctions.

Label sticker, Deep Purple, promo LP label made for Come Taste The Band **25.00**

Magazine

Life, Atlantic ed., Oct. 14, 1968, photo of The Beatles cover; feature inside **45.00**

Rolling Stone, April 2, 1981, Roman Polanski, Elvis Costello, Dan Rather, death of Deborah Harry, orig mailing label on front **6.50**

Microphone, autographed by Rod Stewart, sgd March 2003 in NYC, certificate of authenticity **180.00**

Model kit, MPC Monkees Monkeemobile, #605, 1967, unassembled, orig instructions, orig box **150.00**

Pinback button

Beatles, "I'm an official Beatles fan," photo of each Beatle **25.00**

Elvis Presley National Fan Club Member, black and white, c1956 .... **175.00**

Postcard, The Beatles, wearing gray suits, full color card, marked "Made in Germany" **40.00**

Postcard book, 11" h, John Travolta, licensed by Meryl Corey Enterprises LTD 1978, 23 full-color glossy photograph postcards **25.00**

Poster, movie, Beatles Yellow Submarine, linen, German **600.00**

Press kit, KISS, Casablanca, 1976, custom folder, three-page bio, one-page press clipping, five 8" x 10" black and white photos, orig mailing envelope with no writing or postage **500.00**

Two autographed photos: one Yoko Ono, signed "To Billy, Love Yoko, NYC '89" and one black & white photo of Paul McCartney, **$50.** Photo courtesy of Joy Luke Auctions.

Record award

Billy Joel, "Songs from the Attic," RIAA Platinum Strip plate, orig silver wood frame **450.00**

Eagles, "The Long Run," RIAA Platinum for four million sales. **600.00**

Hootie & the Blowfish, "Fairweather Johnson," RIAA Gold LP **600.00**

Record album

The Beatles "A Hard Days Night," orig motion picture soundtrack, orig owner's name on back **35.00**

The Birds, The Bees and The Monkees, side one: "Dream World," "Auntie's Municipal Court," "We Were Made for Each Other," "Tapioca Tundra," "Daydream Believer," and "Writing Wrongs"; side two: "I'll Be Back Up on My Feet," "The Poster," "P. O. Box 9847," "Magnolia Sims," "Valleri," and "Zor and Zam," copyright 1968, slight damage to cover, record used, several scratches **10.00**

Tour book

Depeche Mode, Devotional Tour 1993/94 .... **10.00**

KISS, 10th anniversary, Vinnie V in makeup **125.00**

Transfers, rub-off, 11" l sheet, Rolling Stones, back with info on joining first official stones fan club, unopened **15.00**

T-shirt

Bob Dylan, XL, True Confession, worn **10.00**

Bon Jovi, L, Slippery When..., never worn **25.00**

Rookwood Pottery

History: Mrs. Marie Longworth Nicholas Storer, Cincinnati, Ohio, founded Rookwood Pottery in 1880. The name of this outstanding American art pottery came from her family estate, "Rookwood," named for the rooks (crows) that inhabited the wooded grounds.

Though the Rookwood pottery filed for bankruptcy in 1941, it was soon reorganized under new management. Efforts at maintaining the pottery proved futile, and it was sold in 1956 and again in 1959. The pottery was moved to Starkville, Mississippi, in conjunction with the Herschede Clock Co. It finally ceased operating in 1967.

Rookwood wares changed with the times. The variety is endless, in part because of the creativity of the many talented artists responsible for great variations in glazes and designs.

Marks: There are five elements to the Rookwood marking system—the clay or body mark, the size mark, the decorator mark, the date mark, and the factory mark. The best way to date Rookwood art pottery is from factory marks.

From 1880 to 1882, the factory mark was the name "Rookwood" incised or painted on the base. Between 1881 and 1886, the firm name, address, and year appeared in an oval frame. Beginning in 1886, the impressed "RP" monogram appeared and a flame mark was added for each year until 1900. After 1900, a Roman numeral, indicating the last two digits of the year of production, was added at the bottom of the "RP" flame mark. This last mark is the one most often seen on Rookwood pieces in the antiques marketplace.

Bowl, Wax Matte, painted by Louise Abel, red blossoms on mustard ground, interior covered in mottled burnt sienna glaze, 1924, flame mark/XXIV/2757/artist's mark, 7-1/4" d, 2-1/4" h, **$750.** Photo courtesy of David Rago Auctions, Inc.

Bowl

6-1/2" d, 2-1/4" h, Production, squat, emb gingko leaves and fruit, purple and green matte glaze, 1913, flame mark/XIII/1680, short tight line to rim **815.00**

7-1/2" l, Standard Glaze, boat shape, attributed to Irene Bishop, hibiscus branch, 1898, flame mark **385.00**

Bud vase, 6-1/2" x 3-1/4", Jewel Porcelain, painted by Charles J. McLaughlin, pink apple blossoms, ivory and indigo ground, 1919, flame mark/XIX/2308/CJM **815.00**

Butter dish, cov, pieced int. tray, 3-1/2" x 5", Cameo, painted by A. Van Briggle, white roses, blue and pink ground, 1884, flame mark/892W/AVB/77 .... **690.00**

Cabinet jug, 4-1/2" h, Limoges-style painted bats and bamboo by Hattie Horton, 1883, marked **385.00**

Plaque, Standard glaze, by Grace Young, 1902, "Study Head after Rembrandt," necessarily original gilded frame, flame mark/II/Study head after Rembrandt/GY, minute, glazed-over clay blemish to nose, **$3,750.** Photo courtesy of David Rago Auctions, Inc.

Cabinet vase, 3-1/4" x 2-1/2", sea green, white snowdrops painted by Sallie Coyne, 1901, flame mark/I/654E/SEC **1,955.00**

Candlestick, 7-3/4" h, Standard Glaze, ruffled base, painted by Jeanette Swing with honeysuckle, 1894, marked **385.00**

Vase, Iris Glaze, by Caroline Steinle, 1906, ovoid, painted indigo iris, green leaves, shaded blue-green, ivory, yellow ground, flame mark/VI/904E/artist's, clipher, overall crazing, 3" d, 6-3/4" h, **$1,610.**

Chambersticks, pr, 5-1/4" h, Waterlily, one pink and green butterfat glaze, other rose, 1925 & 1926, flame mark **230.00**

Chocolate pot, 9" x 6-1/4", Standard Glaze, composed and painted by Caroline Steinle, orange and brown nasturtium, 1899, flame mark/772/CS **920.00**

Creamer and sugar, 5" x 4-1/2" sugar, basket shape, pierced rims, painted Limoges-style by N. Hirschfeld, bats in flight and owl on branch, incised NJH **815.00**

Dish, 7" d, Cameo Ware, ribbed and folded, wild roses painted by Grace Young, 1890, marked **365.00**

Ewer

3-3/4", Standard Glaze, squat, painted by C.A. Baker, orange clover, 1898, marked **350.00**

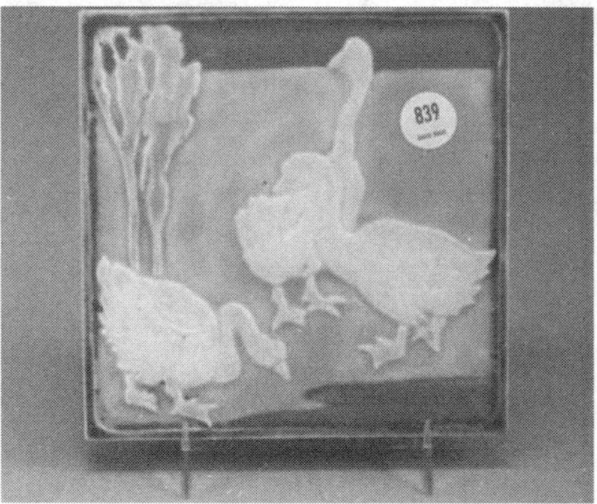

Trivet, three white geese in green and blue landscape. 1925, flame mark/XXV/3207, minor fleck to one edge, 5-3/4" square, **$435.** Photo courtesy of David Rago Auctions, Inc.

8", Standard Glaze Light, bulbous, branches of yellow roses pained by Mary Nourse, 1893 .... **630.00**

12-3/4" x 6-1/2", Standard Glaze Light, painted by Matt Daly, branches of orange and yellow bellflowers, 1892, flame mark/387B/W/MAD/L **1,100.00**

Floor vase, 24-1/2" x 11", production, emb full-height leaves, fine indigo butterfat glaze, 1916, flame mark, 4" line from rim, base scratches **2,185.00**

Jug, 4-1/2" d, Aesthetic Movement enamel dec, celadon and brown flowers, ivory and red ground, incised mark, stamped 1885 date **520.00**

Jug, stopper

7" x 4-1/2", Standard Glaze, corn painted by unidentified artist, silver stopper engraved "JTK," 1896, flame mark **815.00**

14" x 6-1/2", painted white dogwood and star-shaped blossoms, mottled indigo ground, 1885, stamped "ROOKWOOD 1885," chips on stopper **810.00**

Lamp base
- 11-1/2" x 6", Jewel Porcelain, painted by Margaret McDonald, wheat sheaves, ivory ground, single socket and bronzed fittings marked "Crest," body artist sgd **365.00**
- 13" h, Tiger Eye, emb fruit and flowers, mounted in orig bronzed fittings, no visible mark, pr **860.00**

Milk pitcher, 6-1/2" h, Standard Glaze Light, painted by Josephine Zettel, orange clover blossoms, 1893, marked **435.00**

Mug
- 4-1/2", Iris Glaze, painted by A. Bookprinter, yellow blossoms and green leaves, 1904, marked **630.00**
- 5", Iris Glaze, painted by Irene Bishop, celadon grapevine, 1903, marked **1,150.00**

Vase, vellum, painted by Carl Schmidt, blue arrowroot blossoms, green leaves, blue to green ground, 1914, flame mark/XIV/922B/V/CS, minor peppering, 5-3/4" d, 11" h, **$2,425**. Photo courtesy of David Rago Auctions, Inc.

Paperweight
- 3" h, Rook, matte blue glaze, 1921, marked **290.00**
- 4", crouching monkey, matte green glaze, 1930, marked **380.00**

Pitcher
- 4-3/4" h, bulbous, Standard Glaze, maple leaves painted by Leona Van Briggle, 1899, marked........... **535.00**
- 8" x 7-1/2", organically-shaped, Limoges-style, painted attributed to M.L. Nichols, spiders in web amidst bamboo plants, 1883, stamped "ROOKWOOD 1883"........... **1,610.00**
- 11-1/2" x 5", Standard Glaze, painted by Constance Baker, green apple on branch, 1898, lame mark/781B/CAB **750.00**

Plaque, 5" x 8", Scenic Vellum, painted by Lenore Asbury, wind-swept trees by river, 1920, flame mark/LA/XX, orig Arts & Crafts frame.............................. **5,750.00**

Vase, Banded Scenic Vellum, by Ed Diers, 1916, tall, dark elm trees, blue sky with white clouds, flame mark XVI/ED/892C/V, uncrazed, 4-3/4" d, 9-1/4" h, **$3,450**.

Plate, 7-1/4" d, branch of white cherry blossoms painted by Laura Fry in Delft-style, artist cipher **290.00**

Scrapbook, 12-3/4" x 10", Facing the Footlights, compiled by Grace Young and Sara Sax, 1902 .... **360.00**

Tankard, 8" x 6", incised by E.P. Cranch, bar scene, sgd "Last work by E.P. Cranch, Nov, 1892," flame mark/286C/W **2,415.00**

Teapot, 4-3/4", Standard Glaze, painted and incised by Laura Fry, yellow pansies on yellow ground, 1885, marked.. **630.00**

Trivet tile, 6-1/4" d, circular, emb seagulls over green waves, blue-green sky, 1925, flame mark/XXV/2350.. **290.00**

Urn, 7" h, Standard Glaze, painted by unidentified artist, thorny branches of hibiscus, 1891, marked **435.00**

Vase
- 3-1/2" x 3-1/2", carved matte, bulbous, by C.S. Todd, sharply tooled green and blue peacock feathers, red ground, 1915, flame mark/XV/1064/C.S.T............ **1,725.00**

Vase, Jewel Porcelain, cylindrical, finely painted by Arthur Conant, branches of blossoms in pink, caramel, blue, and green, 1928, uncrazed, flame mark/XVIII/1873/P/C, 3-3/4" d, 5-1/4" h, **$2,300**. Photo courtesy of David Rago Auctions, Inc.

Vase, Scenic Vellum, by E.T. Hurley, 1916, ovoid, cluster of birch trees, shaded pink and blue sky with distant mountains, flame mark XVI/V/932CCI/ETH, uncrazed, 4-1/2" d, 11" h, **$3,775**.

- 4-1/2" x 5-1/2", Jewel Porcelain, coupe-shape, painted by Lorinda Epply, Art Deco pink and yellow blossoms, ivory ground, 1931, flame mark/XXXI/2254E/LE **1,100.00**
- 5-1/4" x 3-3/4", Jewel Porcelain, bulbous, painted by K. Van Horn, band and wreath of stylized indigo blossoms and berries, pink ground, 1917, flame mark/XVII/162D/P/KVH **815.00**
- 6" h, Iris Glaze, bulbous, painted by Constance Baker, lavender and purple pansies, 1902, flame mark/II/921/CAB **1,485.00**
- 6" x 4-1/2", Vellum, bulbous, painted by Elizabeth Lincoln, swans in flight, blue and white ground, 1911, flame mark/XI/942D/V/LNL........... **2,415.00**

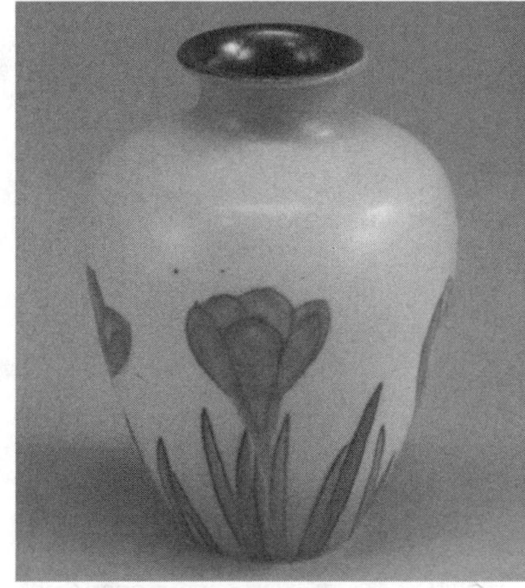

Vase, vellum, bulbous, by Kataro Shirayamadani, brown crocus and green leaves on shaded yellow ground, 1934, flame mark/XXIV/S/X and artist's cipher, seconded mark for small black glaze spots, 4" d, 5-1/2" h, **$1,610**. Photo courtesy of David Rago Auctions, Inc.

Rose Bowls

History: A rose bowl is a decorative open bowl with a crimped, pinched, or petal top which turns in at the top, but does not then turn up or back out again. Rose bowls held fragrant rose petals or potpourri, which served as an air freshener in the late Victorian period. Practically every glass manufacturer made rose bowls in virtually every glass type, pattern, and style, including fine art glass.

For more information, see *Warman's Glass*, 4th edition.

Reproduction Alert: Rose bowls have been widely reproduced. Be especially careful of Italian copies of satin, Mother of Pearl satin, peachblow, and Burmese, and recent Czechoslovakian ones with applied flowers.

Burmese, hand-painted decoration, **$45**. Photo courtesy of Dotta Auction Co., Inc.

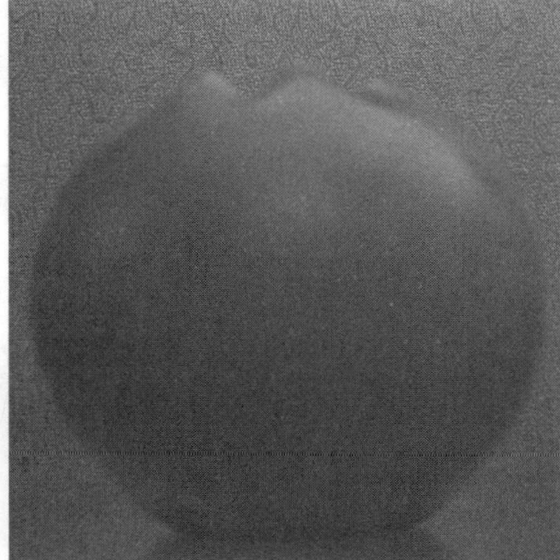

Peachblow, crimped top, white interior, **$125**.

2" h, 2-1/4" w, Bohemian, transparent amethyst with enameled flowers, polished bottom, six crimps ... **225.00**

2-3/4" d, satin, baby blue, mother-of-pearl, ground pontil, attributed to Webb ... **385.00**

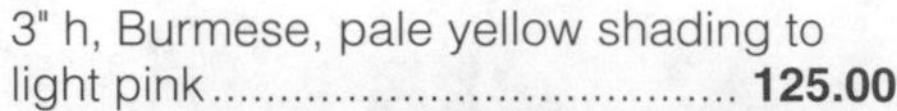

3" h, Burmese, pale yellow shading to light pink ... **125.00**

Cut glass, hobstars, zipper cut rim and feathered fans, minor roughness, 6-1/2" w, 6-1/4" h, **$230**. Photo courtesy of James D. Julia, Inc.

3" h, 3" w, millefiore, glossy white opaque background with individual millefiore scattered throughout the glass, nine uneven crimps, semi-ground bottom, c1960 ... **45.00**

3" h, 3-1/2" w, satin, shaded pink to white, soft white interior, undecorated, eight crimps, ground pontil ... **55.00**

Carnival Glass, Honeycomb pattern, peach opalescent, **$85**. Photo courtesy of Seeck Auctions.

3-1/4" h, Burmese, salmon shading to pale yellow, amethyst flower leafy stem, Webb ... **260.00**

Opalescent, green ribbed, applied pink flowers and clear glass stems, chips to four petals, 6" d, 5" h, **$65**. Photo courtesy of James D. Julia, Inc.

Stevens & Williams, Jewell glass, Zipper pattern, light sapphire blue, six box pleats, polished pontil, Rd. #55693, 4" h, 5" w, **$125**. Photo courtesy of Johanna Billings.

3-1/2" h, 3-1/2" d, DQ MOP, golden brown shading to cream ext., white lining ... **495.00**

3-3/4" h, 4" d, mother-of-pearl satin, rainbow, Diamond Quilted pattern, ground pontil ... **1,100.00**

4" h, spatter, cobalt blue ground, white spatter ... **65.00**

4" h, topaz, enameled figure of man drinking, Bohemian, c1900 ... **115.00**

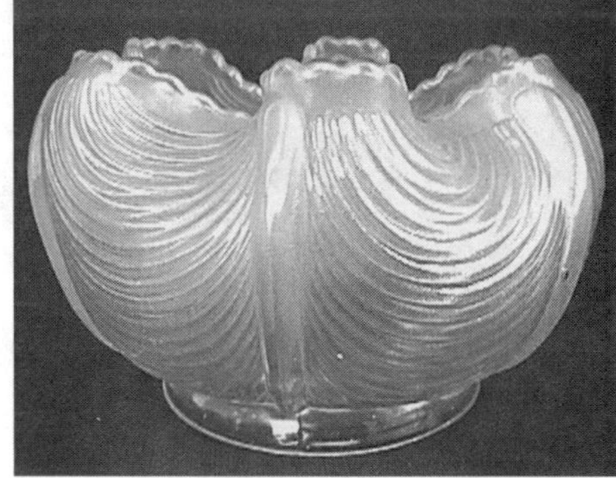

Carnival Glass, Drapery pattern, white iridescent, **$250**. Photo courtesy of Seeck Auctions.

4-1/4" h, crimped top, cameo and enamel cyclamen blossoms and leaves, attributed to Mont Joye ... **550.00**

4-1/2" h, amberina, applied amber petal feet, Lutz-type, price for pr ... **300.00**

Lavender, applied clear glass rigaree flowers and leaves, **$190**. Photo courtesy of Joy Luke Auctions.

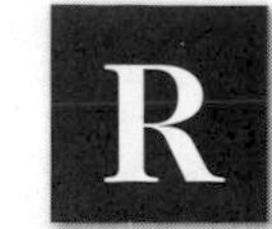

4-3/4" h, 5-3/4" w, Consolidated Lamp & Glass Co., c1894, embossed Shell & Seaweed pattern, shaded purple to lavender, white interior, eight crimps, rough pontil **125.00**

Rose Canton, Rose Mandarin, and Rose Medallion

History: The pink rose color has given its name to three related groups of Chinese export porcelain: Rose Mandarin, Rose Medallion, and Rose Canton.

Rose Mandarin, produced from the late 18th century to approximately 1840, derives its name from the Mandarin figure(s) found in garden scenes with women and children. The women often have gold decorations in their hair. Polychrome enamels and birds separate the scenes.

Rose Medallion, which originated in the early 19th century and was made through the early 20th century, has alternating panels of figures and birds and flowers. The elements are four in number, separated evenly around the center medallion. Peonies and foliage fill voids.

Rose Canton, introduced somewhat later than Rose Mandarin and produced through the first half of the 19th century, is similar to Rose Medallion except flowers replace the figural panels. People are present only if the medallion partitions are absent. Some patterns have been named, e.g., Butterfly and Cabbage and Rooster. Rose Canton actually is a catchall term for any pink enamelware not fitting into the first two groups.

Reproduction Alert: Rose Medallion is still made, although the quality does not match the earlier examples.

Rose Mandarin, vase, famille rose enamels, dragons, and foo dogs, 19th C, 25" h, **$2,470**. Photo courtesy of Skinner, Inc.

Rose Canton

Brush pot, 4-1/2" h, scenic, ladies, reticulated, gilt trim **275.00**
Charger, 12" d, floral panels, 19th C **350.00**

Rose Mandarin, platter, 15" l, 12" w, **$200**. Photo courtesy of Alderfer Auction Company.

Dish, 8" d, round, scalloped edges, 19th C **350.00**
Fruit basket, 8-1/2" x 10" x 4" h, oval, gently flaring reticulated sides, gilt leaf form handles, 19th C **415.00**
Platter, 16-1/2" l, 19th C, enamel and gilt wear **200.00**
Puzzle teapot, 6" h, Cadogan, painted birds and foliage, light blue ground, late 19th C, minor chips **150.00**
Umbrella jar, 24-1/4" h, 19th C, minor chips **805.00**
Urn, cov, 19-1/4" h, minor chips, cracks, gilt wear, pr **2,990.00**
Vase, 14" h, 19th C, chips, minor cracks, pr **1,265.00**

Rose Mandarin

Bowl, 8-3/8" d, shallow, tightly scalloped rim, int. dec with four alternating reserves of figures and florals, 15 figures on ext., orange peel glaze, 19th C **525.00**

Rose Medallion bowl, scalloped rim, decorated with panels of birds and flowers, 10" d, **$475**. Photo courtesy of Joy Luke Auctions.

Cider jug, cov, 9-1/2" h, woven double strap applied handle, foo dog finial, 19th C, wear **2,990.00**
Cup and saucer, scalloped edge rim, chips, price for pr **60.00**
Dish, 10-3/4" l, oblong, lobed, figural center scene, butterflies around rim, orange peel glaze, 19th C **600.00**
Garden seat, 18-1/2" h, barrel shape, court scenes, upper and lower bands of butterflies and floral designs, 19th C **2,650.00**
Plate, 8" d, luncheon, worn gilt, price for set of six **260.00**
Platter, 16-1/4" l, chip **250.00**
Punch bowl, 14-3/4" d, glaze wear **2,650.00**
Rice bowl, 4-5/8" d, scalloped rim, four-pc set..**110.00**
Sauce boat, 8-1/4" l, intertwined handle **110.00**
Serving dish, 9-7/8" d, 19th C, minor chips, enamel wear **460.00**
Soup plate, 9-3/4" d, three with chips, six-pc set **55.00**
Teapot, cov, 8-1/2" h, domed lid .. **660.00**
Tureen, 13-3/4" l, 11-1/4" h, gilded handles and final **1,100.00**
Umbrella stand, 24" h, wrapped bamboo form, 19th C, star cracks, gilt and enamel wear **1,495.00**
Vase, 10" h, beaker, figural cartouche, chicken skin ground, Qianlong, c1775, price for pr **1,900.00**

Rose Medallion

Basket and undertray, 9-3/4" l, 7-1/4" w, 3-3/4" h, two handles, reticulated, China, 19th C, chips **325.00**
Bowl, 9" x 10-1/4", 4" h, reticulated high sides, flared rim, Mandarin scenes, red, blue, pink, and yellow, orange peel glaze, tiny rim flakes................................ **450.00**
Charger, 13" d, celadon, court scene bordered with animals and floral trophies, textured ground, minor gilt wear **360.00**

Rose Medallion, 18" d, charger, 9-3/4" w, lidded tureen, **$295**. Photo courtesy of Joy Luke Auctions.

Dish, 9-1/4" d, scalloped rim, 19th C **275.00**
Platter, 8-1/2" x 11", 19th C, minor glaze wear **175.00**
Punch bowl, 24" d, hp scenes, four with birds, fruits, clouds, and flowers, alternating with panels of village scenes, gilt rim and highlights **3,680.00**

Roseville Pottery

History: In the late 1880s, a group of investors purchased the J. B. Owens Pottery in Roseville, Ohio, and made utilitarian stoneware items. In 1892, the firm was incorporated and joined by George F. Young, who became general manager. Four generations of Youngs controlled Roseville until the early 1950s.

Roseville U.S.A.

A series of acquisitions began: Midland Pottery of Roseville in 1898, Clark Stoneware Plant in Zanesville (formerly used by Peters and Reed), and Muskingum Stoneware (Mosaic Tile Company) in Zanesville. In 1898, the offices also moved from Roseville to Zanesville.

In 1900, Roseville introduced Rozane, an art pottery. Rozane became a trade name to cover a large series of lines. The art lines were made in limited amounts after 1919.

The success of Roseville depended on its commercial lines, first developed by John J. Herald and Frederick Rhead in the first decades of the 1900s. In 1918, Frank Ferrell became art director and developed more than 80 lines of pottery. The economic depression of the 1930s brought more lines, including Pine Cone.

In the 1940s, a series of high-gloss glazes were tried in an attempt to revive certain lines. In 1952, Raymor dinnerware was produced. None of these changes brought economic success and in November 1954, Roseville was bought by the Mosaic Tile Company.

Basket, Columbine, yellow flowers, blue ground, #368-12, 12" h, **$250**. Photo courtesy of Joy Luke Auctions.

Basket, Pine Cone, brown, imp mark, 353-11, some staining to int. **650.00**

Bookends, pr, Apple Blossom, green, raised marks, 359, 5" **265.00**

Bookends, pair, Dawn, impressed mark, 5-1/4" x 4-1/4" x 4-1/2", **$500**.

Bud vase, Pine Cone, 8-1/4", brown, triple, unmarked **365.00**

Bud vase, Vintage, double, RV ink stamp, 4" x 8", **$225**.

Candlesticks, pr, Carnelian II, unmarked, 3-3/4" h **230.00**

Center bowl, Tourmaline, cornucopia, raised USA 2 mark, 5" x 11".......... **175.00**

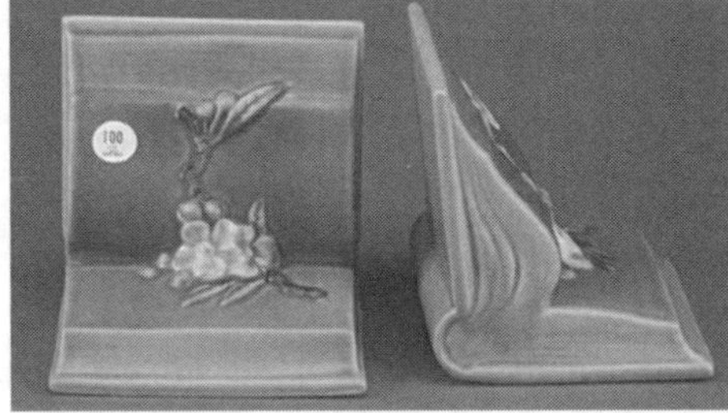

Bookends, pair, Apple Blossom, green, 359, raised marks, 5", **$265**. Unless otherwise noted, Roseville photos are courtesy of David Rago Auctions, Inc.

Candlesticks, pair, Morning Glory, green, foil label, minor bruise to base of one, 5" x 4-1/4", **$475**.

Center bowl, Jonquil, flaring, attached flower frog, black paper label, 10-1/2", **$950**.

Console set

- Fuchsia, brown, imp marks, No. 1133-5 and No. 350-8" **490.00**
- Iris, pink, No. 360-10" oval centerbowl, pair of No. 1135-4-1/2" candlesticks, imp marks **375.00**
- Thorn Apple, pink, low center bowl No. 307-6", pair of No. 1111 candlesticks, imp marks **290.00**

Cookie jar, Freesia, blue, raised 4-8" mark, 1/2" bruise to rim and lid, small glaze nicks to high points, **$400**.

Cookie jar, cov

- Clematis, No. 3-8, green ground **550.00**
- Magnolia, No. 2-8, tan ground **450.00**
- Zephr Lily, No. 5-8, blue ground **360.00**

Cornucopia vase, Pine Cone...... **140.00**

Ewer

- Peony, green, raised mark, 9-15" **435.00**
- Pine Cone, blue, imp mark, 909-10" **690.00**

Floor vase

Iris, blue, imp mark, 929-15" **750.00**

Waterlily, pink, raised mark, 83-15" **460.00**

Console set, Topeo, blue, silver foil label, 12-3/4" d, x 4-1/4" h bowl, pair 4" h candlesticks, **$600**.

Cornucopia, centerbowl, Tourmaline, blue, USA 2, raised mark, 11" d, 5" h, **$175**.

Ewer, Pine Cone, blue, 909-10", impressed mark, **$690**.

Hanging basket

Matte Green, 5-1/4" x 8-1/4", matte green, lobed, emb spade shape forms, unmarked, minor abrasions **375.00**

Moss, blue, unmarked, 5" x 7-1/2", faint spider-line to body, few small flecks **375.00**

Flowerpot and underplate, Cosmos, blue, raised 650-5" mark, **$200**.

Jardinière, Florentine, 12-1/2" **250.00**

Hanging basket, Iris, blue, two handles, unmarked, some abrasion (shown upside down in photo), 5-1/4" x 8-1/2", **$300**.

Jardinière and pedestal set

Clematis, blue, marked, 8-1/2" jardinière, 17" h pedestal, 1" line from rim of jardinière **2,100.00**

Donatello, unmarked, 7-1/2" x 10" jardinière, 15" h pedestal **750.00**

Freesia, blue **1,450.00**

Mostique, unmarked, 13" d jardinière **1,150.00**

Pine Cone, blue, both marked, jardinière (403-10") and pedestal (406-10"), crisp mold, two small inside base rim chips **3,625.00**

Lamp base, Pine Cone, brown, unmarked, 7-3/4" d, 10-14" h, small base chips **1,955.00**

Planter, Sunflower, four-sided, unmarked, 11" l, 3-3/4" h, **$1,200**.

Hanging basket, Fuschsia, green, unmarked, small chip to one hole and fleck to leaf, 7" d, 5" h, **$365**.

Low bowl

Blackberry, unmarked, 7-3/4" d, 3-1/4" h, minor glaze bubbles ... **345.00**

Sunflower, low shoulder, unmarked, 7-1/4" d, 4" h, burst bubble on one leaf **535.00**

Pedestal

Magnolia, 16" h, brown, marked "USA" **175.00**

Tourist, 21-1/2" x 11", unmarked, 3/4" tight line to rim (possibly in making), very minor losses to paint **2,530.00**

Jardinière, Bleeding Heart, orange ground, green leaves, lighter flowers, #651-6, 7" h, **$140**. Photo courtesy of Joy Luke Auctions.

Pitcher

Fuchsia, brown, imp mark, 8-1/2" d, 8" h, peppering to body **400.00**

Pine Cone, no. 415, green glaze, brown, and cream tones, raised "Roseville, U.S.A." mark, c1931, 9-1/4" h **750.00**

Planter

Blackberry, faceted, unmarked, 9-3/4" d, 3-1/2" h **435.00**

Florentine, brown, rect, 11-1/4" l, 5-1/4" h, few base chips **290.00**

Pine Cone, blue, rect, 469-12" **520.00**

Sunflower, four-sided, unmarked, 11" l, 3-3/4" h **1,380.00**

Sand jar, Primrose, blue, 15-3/4" h, base chip and hairline **575.00**

Tea set, cov teapot, creamer, cov sugar

Freesia, blue, raised marks **415.00**

Sconces, pair, Burmese, green, raised 80-B marks, 8" h, **$200**.

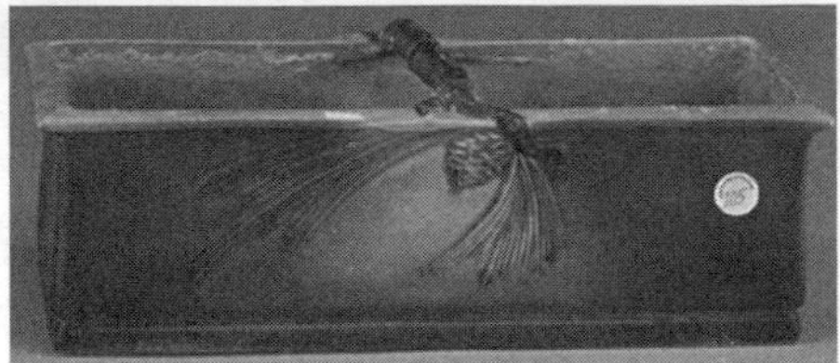
Planter, Pine Cone, blue, rectangle, 469-12", **$520**.

Teapot, Apple Blossom, orange ground, white flowers, green leaves, twig type handle, #371P, 7" h, **$225**. Photo courtesy of Joy Luke Auctions.

Peony, yellow, raised marks **415.00**
Snowberry, blue, raised marks **750.00**
White Rose, pink raised marks **490.00**
Wincraft, brown, raised marks, minor flaws **200.00**

Umbrella stand, Pine Cone, brown, raised mark, No. 777-20", minor scaling area at handle, 1" rim bruise **2,070.00**

Urn, Clemana, brown, 122-7", impressed mark, **$365**.

Urn

Clemana, brown, imp mark, 122-7" **365.00**
Moss, blue, imp mark, 799-8" **380.00**
Teasel, flaring, blue, imp mark, No. 888-12" **435.00**
Thorn Apple, ftd, pink, imp mark, No. 822-10" **290.00**

Urn, Moss, blue, 799-8", impressed mark, **$380**.

Vase

Azurine, 7-1/2" x 4", bottle shape, painted roses, stamped mark **750.00**
Baneda, bulbous, pink, black paper label, 10-1/4" x 8", 1/4" firing line at foot **1,355.00**
Baneda, gourd-shape, pink, foil label, 5-1/4" x 4" **460.00**

Vase, Futura, flaring pillow, fir tree pattern in mottled orange, blue and green matte glazes, unmarked, 6-1/4" x 9", **$400**.

Carnelian III, four buttresses around neck, mottled pink, seafoam, ochre, and lavender glaze, unmarked, 16-1/2" x 11" **6,275.00**
Cherry Blossom, bulbous, brown, unmarked, 7" x 5" **435.00**
Della Robbia, triangular panels with carved tall cypress tree, dark brown ground, taupe dec, designed by Frederick H. Rhead, sgd "B. K.," incised "BK/Rozane," 10-1/2" h **2,860.00**
Earlam, flaring, buttressed base, mottled blue-green glaze, foil label, 9-1/4" x 5-1/2" **445.00**

Vase, Baneda, bulbous, pink, black paper label, 1/4" firing line to foot, 8" d, 10-1/4" h, **$1,355**.

Experimental, Imperial II blank, band of waves under streaked blue, green, and pale yellow glaze, blue crayon experimental marks, 9-1/2" x 5-1/4" **16,100.00**
Ferella, brown, bulbous, buttressed handles, unmarked, 9" x 4-3/4" **750.00**

Vase, Morning Glory, flaring, green, unmarked, restoration to flat chip under foot ring, 10" d, 14-3/4" h, **$2,000**.

Futura, coupe-shape, thistle on pink to purple ground, unmarked, 8" x 6", nick on foot **865.00**
Futura, flaring star shape, pink and green, black paper label, 8" x 3" **520.00**
Hexagon, faceted, green, ink mark, 5-1/4" x 3" **415.00**
Jonquil, spherical, unmarked, 6-1/4" x 5-1/2", several minor nicks to flowers **230.00**
Laurel, russet, foil label, 6" x 3-1/2" **290.00**

Vase, Rozane, tear shape, Rooyal Dark, Turkish man in profile painted by H. Dunlavy, Rozane wafer and artist's signature, opposing tight lines to rim, 5" d, 8" h, **$920**.

Luffa, brown, foil label, 8-1/4" x 6-3/4" **415.00**
Mara, crackled red and beige glaze, faint stamp mark, 8-1/4" x 6-1/2" **1,380.00**
Montacello, bulbous, brown, unmarked, 7-1/2" x 6-1/4" **815.00**
Moss, pillow, blue, imp mark, 781-8" **460.00**

Vase, Cherry Blossom, bulbous, brown, unmarked, 5" d, 7" h, **$435**.

Panel, brown, dandelions, ink mark, 7" x 3-1/4" **380.00**
Pine Cone, bulbous, brown, imp mark, 711-10" **815.00**
Pine Cone, pillow, green, imp mark, 114-8" **460.00**
Silhouette, red, fan vase, raised mark, 783-7" **435.00**
Sunflower, flaring, unmarked, 7-1/4" x 5", pr **1,610.00**
Velmoss, cylindrical, unmarked, 8-1/4" x 2-1/2" **575.00**
White Rose, bulbous, pink, raised mark, 991-12", minute base fleck, peppering **365.00**
Wisteria, gourd shape, brown, foil label, 6-1/4" x 4-1/2" **435.00**
Wisteria, tapering, blue, foil label, 10" x 5-3/4", restored, inner rim chip **920.00**

Vase, experimental, on Imperial II blank, band of waves under streaked blue, green, and pale yellow glaze, experimental marks in blue crayon, 5-1/4" d, 9-1/2" h, **$16,100**.

Vase, Rozane Aztec, gourd shape, flaring rim, squeezebag decoration, blue and yellow stylized motif on peach semi-matte ground, artist signed "R" on bottom, 4-1/2" d, 11-1/4" h, **$815**.

Vessel

Baneda, squat, green, unmarked, 4-1/2" x 5-1/2" **460.00**
Chloron, tapering, two handles, scalloped rim, body emb with cherries, stamped "Chloron/T.R.P. Co.," 7" d, 6-1/2" h **1,380.00**
Imperial II, squat, flat shoulder, fine blue-green mottled glaze, band of geometric design at rim, unmarked, 5" x 6-1/2" **200.00**
Jonquil, squatty, pinched and scalloped rim, unmarked, 7" l, 5" h **975.00**
Savona, covered, yellow, black paper label, 8" l, 4" h **980.00**

Wall pocket

Apple Blossom, blue, marked, 366-8", pr **490.00**
Blackberry, chapel style windows, black paper label **1,650.00**

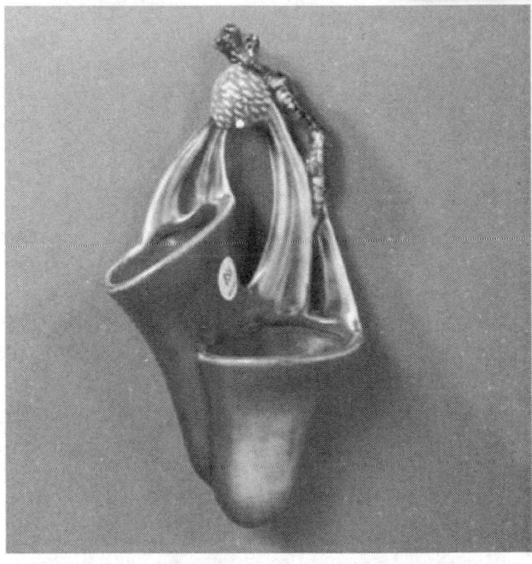
Wall pocket, Pine Cone, double, blue, silver foil label, 8-3/4" x 4-1/2", **$500**.

Bleeding Heart, pink, #1287-8", restoration to top of one, pr **460.00**
Bushberry, brown, marked, 1291-8", pr **415.00**
Cameo II, c1915, hairline **250.00**
Carnelian I, green, ink mark, 8-1/2" l **300.00**

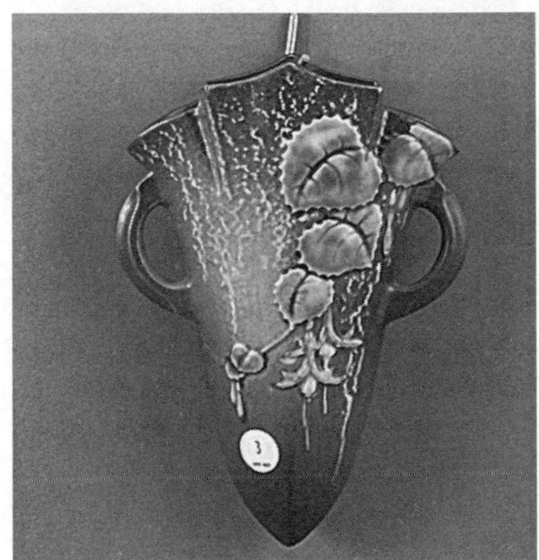
Wall pocket, Fuschia, blue, 1282-8", impressed mark, **$750**.

Cherry Blossom, brown, foil label, 8-1/4" h **920.00**
Columbine, brown, 1290-8" **415.00**
Donatello, unmarked, 10" **230.00**
Ferella, red, foil label, 6-3/4" x 6-1/2", 1/8" fleck to back edge **1,725.00**
Freesia, green, marked, 1276-8", pr, one with fleck **365.00**
Fuchsia, blue, imp mark, 1282-8" **750.00**
Imperial II, triple, russet and green, unmarked, tight line to edge **460.00**
Iris, pr, one pink, one blue, marked, 1284-8", small bruise to tip of blue **535.00**
Jonquil, unmarked, 8-1/4" x 6-1/2" **980.00**

Luffa, green, unmarked, 8-1/2" h **855.00**

Wall pocket, Imperial II, triple, russet and green, unmarked, tight line to edge, **$460**.

Moss, pink, imp mark, 10-1/4" x 5-1/4", professional restoration **290.00**
Nude Panel, ink mark, 7-1/4" x 5", chip on rear of handle **460.00**
Panel, green, orange daisies, ink mark, 9-1/4" h **490.00**
Peony, yellow, marked, 1293-8", restoration to one corner, pr **290.00**

Wall pocket, Panel, green, ink mark, 9" x 5", **$300**.

Pine Cone, triple, green, #366, raised mark, 4" h, restoration to break at joint **350.00**
Poppy, green, triple bullet shape, marked, 1281, 8-1/4" h, joint repaired **460.00**
Rosecraft Vintage, ink mark, 9-1/4"h **435.00**
Snowberry, blue, WP-8" **200.00**
Sunflower, unmarked, 7-1/4" x 6", tight line at handle **1,610.00**
Tuscany, gray, unmarked, 8-1/2" **200.00**

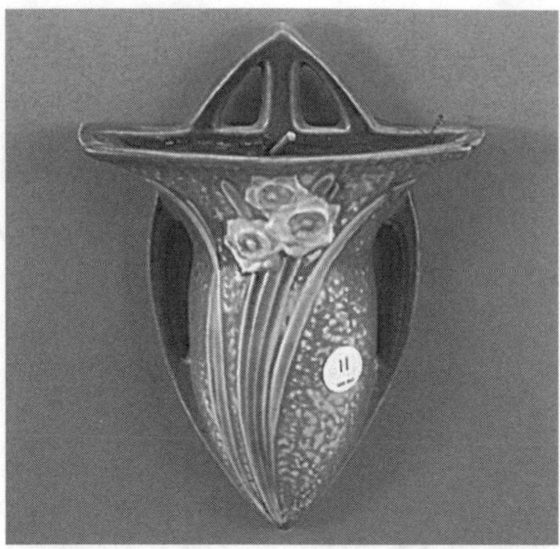
Wall pocket, Jonquil, unmarked, 6-1/2" w, 8-1/4" l, **$975**.

Wisteria, brown, unmarked, 8-1/2" x 7-1/4" **1,150.00**
Wall shelf, Pine Cone, green, unmarked, 5" w, 8" h **490.00**

ROYAL BAYREUTH

History: In 1794, the Royal Bayreuth factory was founded in Tettau, Bavaria. Royal Bayreuth introduced its figural patterns in 1885. Designs of animals, people, fruits, and vegetables decorated a wide array of tablewares and inexpensive souvenir items.

Tapestry wares, in rose and other patterns, were made in the late 19th century. The surface of the piece feels and looks like woven cloth. Tapestry ware was made by covering the porcelain with a piece of fabric tightly stretched over the surface, decorating the fabric, glazing the piece, and firing.

Top row, from left: Chamber-stick with shield, scene of woman in hat with fan, 7-1/2" h, **$175**; pitcher, scene of woman with basket of flowers, 4-1/2" h, **$100**; bottom row, from left: ashtray, belt strap as handle, dogs hunting stag, 5-1/2", repaired, **$80**; toothpick holder, three handles, woman looking out, 3" h, **$90**. Photo courtesy of Woody Auctions.

Royal Bayreuth still manufactures dinnerware. It has not maintained production of earlier wares, particularly the figural items. Since thorough records are unavailable, it is difficult to verify the chronology of production.

For more information, see *Warman's English & Continental Pottery & Porcelain*, 3rd edition.

Marks: The Royal Bayreuth crest used to mark the wares varied in design and color.

Ashtray, elk **225.00**
Bell, Musicians scene, man playing cello and mandolin **300.00**
Candlestick, Dutch girl scene, blue mark, 20th C **70.00**
Charger, 10" d, center portrait, gold trim, blue mark **900.00**
Child's plate, 7-1/2" d, children on beach scene, blue mark **75.00**
Creamer
Black cat, sgd "Washington DC" **350.00**
Butterfly, 6-1/8" w, 3-3/4" h, blue mark **425.00**
Lamplighter, green **250.00**
Pansy, 4" h, blue mark **425.00**
Pear, green handle, brown stem, c1902, 4-1/2" h, raised flower mark **575.00**

Rooster, 4-3/8" h, gray, blue mark 550.00
Rose, light yellow, pink highlights, green branch handle, 3-1/4" h 475.00
Strawberry, c1902 .... 325.00

Cup and saucer, yellow and gold, purple and red flowers, green leaves, white ground, green mark 80.00

Hatpin holder, courting couple, cutout base with gold dec, blue mark 400.00

Inkwell, 5" w, 3-1/2" h, elk, green mark 525.00

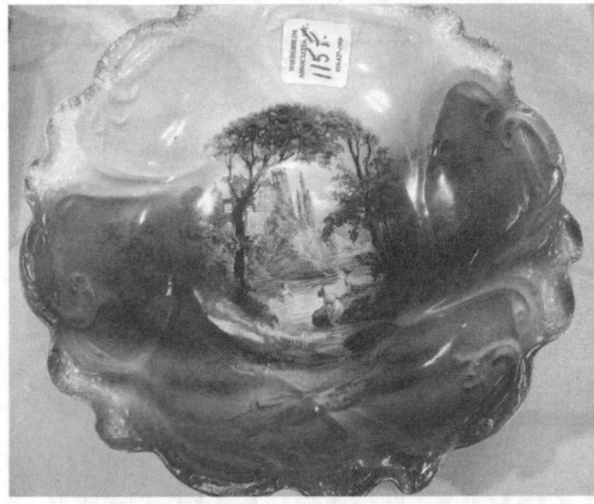

Bowl, green ground, landscape scene, signed "Gi. Johns," **$125**. Photo courtesy of Wiederseim Associates, Inc.

Milk pitcher
Dachsund, c1900, blue mark 725.00
Poodle, 4-1/2" h, blue mark 450.00

Plate, 6-1/4" d, musicians 65.00

Dresser box, covered, tapestry, chrysanthemums decoration, 4-3/4" x 4", **$325**; rose tapestry creamer, 3-1/4" h, **$150**. Photo courtesy of Joy Luke Auctions.

Ring box, cov, pheasant scene, glossy finish 85.00

Salt and pepper shakers, pr, Elk 165.00

Vase, 6-1/2" h, hummingbirds dec 2,900.00

Patterns

Conch Shell
Creamer, green, lobster handles 125.00
Match holder, hanging 225.00
Sugar, cov, small flake 85.00
Water pitcher, 5-1/2" h, green mark 700.00

Devil and Cards
Ashtray 650.00

Bowl, molded with four portraits, central panel decorated with flowers, pearlized finish, 10-1/2" d, **$250**. Photo courtesy of Joy Luke Auctions.

Creamer, 3-3/4" h 195.00
Mug, large 295.00
Pitcher, 7-1/4" h, orange-red devil shaped handle, blue mark 775.00
Salt, master 325.00

Lobster
Ashtray, claw 155.00
Celery tray, 12-1/2" l, figural, blue mark 245.00
Pitcher, 7-3/4" h, figural, orange-red, green handle 175.00
Salt and pepper shakers, pr 150.00

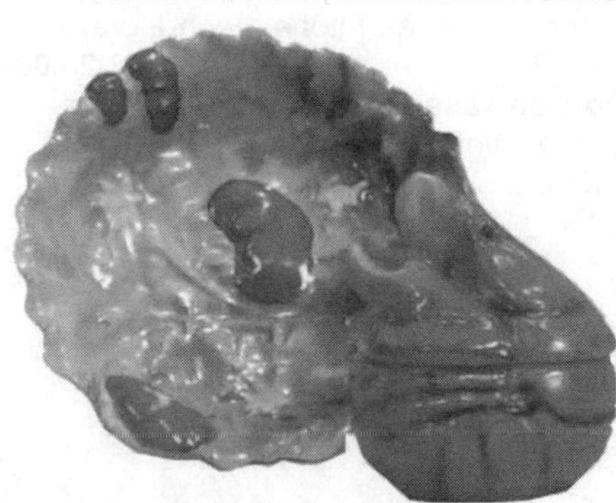

Mustard pot, covered, Lobster pattern, **$150**; 4" h, pair leaf-shaped dishes decorated with tomatoes, 5-1/2" d, **$120**.

Nursery Rhyme
Bell, Jack and the Beanstalk 425.00
Planter, Jack and the Beanstalk, round, orig liner 225.00
Plate, Little Jack Horner 125.00
Plate, Little Miss Muffet 100.00

Snow Babies
Bowl, 6" d 325.00
Creamer, gold trim 110.00
Jewelry box, cov 275.00
Milk pitcher, corset shape 185.00
Tea tile, 6" sq, blue mark 100.00

Sunbonnet Babies
Bell, babies sewing, unmarked 425.00
Cake plate, 10-1/4" d, babies washing 400.00
Cup and saucer, babies fishing 225.00
Dish, 8" d, babies ironing, ruffled edge, blue mark 175.00
Nappy, Sunbonnet Babies, Wash Day, blue mark, 6" l 230.00
Plate, Sunbonnet Girls, pair, one washing, other sweeping 290.00

Tomato
Creamer and sugar, blue mark 190.00
Milk pitcher 165.00
Mustard, cov 125.00
Salt and pepper shakers, pr 85.00

Rose tapestry

Basket, 5" h, reticulated 400.00

Pitcher, tapestry, grazing mountain sheep, gold trim, marked, 5" h, **$285.**

Bell, American Beauty Rose, pink, 3" h 500.00

Bowl, 10-1/2" d, pink and yellow roses 675.00

Cache pot, 2-3/4" h, 3-12/4" d, ruffled top, gold handles 200.00

Chocolate set, chocolate pot, four cups and saucers, pink roses 3,950.00

Creamer, 3-1/4" h, pink, yellow, and white roses, blue mark, some wear to gold rim 425.00

Dresser tray 395.00

Hair receiver, pink and white, blue mark 325.00

Nut dish, 3-1/4" d, 1-3/4" h, three-color roses, gold feet, green mark 175.00

Pin tray, three-color roses 195.00

Plate, 6" d, three-color roses, blue mark 150.00

Salt and pepper shakers, pr, pink roses 375.00

Shoe, roses and figures dec 550.00

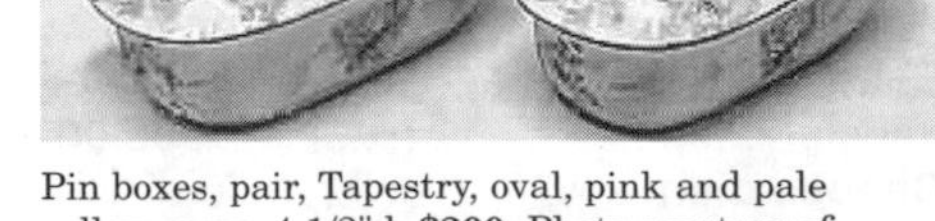

Pin boxes, pair, Tapestry, oval, pink and pale yellow roses, 4-1/2" l, **$200**. Photo courtesy of Alderfer Auction Co.

Tapestry, miscellaneous

Bowl, 9-1/2" d, scenic, wheat, girl, and chickens **395.00**
Box, 3-3/4" l, 2" w, courting couple, multicolored, blue mark **245.00**
Charger, 13" d, scenic, boy and donkeys **300.00**
Hatpin holder, swimming swans and sunset, saucer base, blue mark ... **250.00**
Tumbler, 4" h, barrel shape, gazebo, deer standing in stream, blue mark **200.00**
Vase, 4-5/8" h, 2" w, tavern scene, two small handles **350.00**

ROYAL BONN

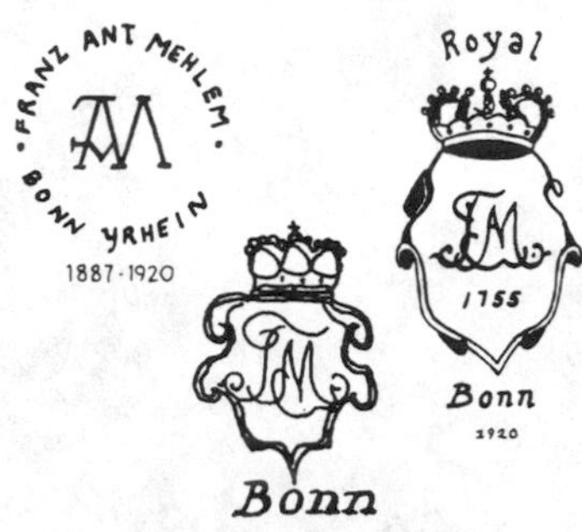

History: In 1836, Franz Anton Mehlem founded a Rhineland factory that produced earthenware and porcelain, including household, decorative, technical, and sanitary items.

The firm reproduced Hochst figures between 1887 and 1903. These figures, in both porcelain and earthenware, were made from the original molds from the defunct Prince-Electoral Mayence Manufactory in Hochst. The factory was purchased by Villeroy and Boch in 1921 and closed in 1931.

Marks: In 1890, the word "Royal" was added to the mark. All items made after 1890 include the "Royal Bonn" mark.

Charger, blue and white transfer decoration of pastoral scene, rose border, rim chip, overall crazing, light staining, 15" d, **$65**. Photo courtesy of Alderfer Auction Co.

Cake plate, 10-1/4" d, dark blue floral transfer **35.00**
Cheese dish, cov, multicolored floral dec, cream ground, gold trim **90.00**

Mantel clock, Rainbow, green floral decoration, gold highlights, 11" x 12-1/2", **$450**. Photo courtesy of Woody Auctions.

Clock
- 14" h, floral dec, gilt details, Ansonia Clock Co. (NY) key-wind mechanism, hinged crystal face, marked **825.00**
- 17" h, cobalt blue case, floral panels, gilding, Ansonia Clock Co. (NY) key-wind mechanism **2,900.00**

Cup and saucer, relief luster bands, marked **40.00**
Ewer, 10-1/8" h, red and pink flowers, raised gold, fancy handle.............. **75.00**
Plate, 8-1/2" d, red and white roses, green leaves, earthtone ground, crazing, c1900 .... **20.00**
Portrait vase, 8-1/4" h, central female portrait, floral landscape, printed mark, c1900 .... **575.00**

Vase, tapered vasiform body, sinuous everted rim with short openwork loops, sinuous spreading base with openwork loops, glazed in maroon and green, body hand-painted with roses, gilt accenting, Franz Anton Mehlem Earthenware Factory, Bonn, Germany, early 20th C, 12-3/8" h, **$300**. Photo courtesy of Skinner, Inc.

Urn, 15-1/2" h, classical form, floral still life, two gold mask-form handles, paw feet, c1900 .... **320.00**
Vase
- 8" h, blue scenic transfer panels, marked "Royal Bonn," c1870, price for pr **195.00**
- 11-1/2" h, ivory ground, gilt and enameled flower garden designs, two scrolled handles, late 19th C **200.00**

Vases, left: double gourd with Art Noouveau design in shades of green, pink, purple, blue and brown, high gloss, painted "Royal-Bonn Old-Duton," crazing, 11" h, **$350**; right: squatty, narrow rim, pink poppies, green foliage, shaded brown ground, high gloss, painted "Royal-Bonn Old Butch," 3-3/4" h, **$2,000**. Photo courtesy of Skinner Auctioneers and Appraisers.

ROYAL COPENHAGEN

History: Franz Mueller established a porcelain factory at Copenhagen in 1775. When bankruptcy threatened in 1779, the Danish king acquired ownership, appointing Mueller manager and selecting the name "Royal Copenhagen." The crown sold its interest in 1867; the company remains privately owned today.

Blue Fluted, Royal Copenhagen's most famous pattern, was created in 1780. It is of Chinese origin and comes in three styles: smooth edge, closed lace edge, and perforated lace edge (full lace). Many other factories copied it.

Flora Danica, named for a famous botanical work, was introduced in 1789 and remained exclusive to Royal Copenhagen. It is identified by its freehand illustrations of plants and its hand-cut edges and perforations.

Marks: Royal Copenhagen porcelain is marked with three wavy lines, which signify ancient waterways, and a crown, added in 1889. Stoneware does not have the crown mark.

Bowl, reticulated blue and white, round **125.00**

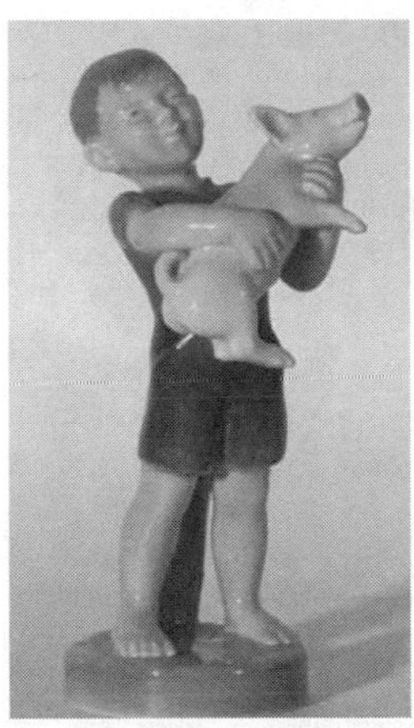

Figure, boy holding pig, 7" h, **$80**. Photo courtesy of Joy Luke Auctions.

Butter pat, Symphony pattern, six-pc set **35.00**

Candlesticks, pr, 9" h, blue floral design, white ground, bisque lion heads, floral garlands **160.00**

Cream soup, #1812....................... **75.00**

Cup and saucer, 2-1/2" h cylindrical cup with angular handle, 5-1/2" d saucer with molded and gilded rim, hp floral specimen, 20th C **575.00**

Dinner plate, Flora Danica pattern, reticulated rim, gilt detailing, hand-painted center floral specimen, reverse titled "Ribes rubrum L.," 20th C, 10-3/4" d, **$775**. Photo courtesy of Skinner Auctioneers and Appraisers.

Demitasse service, Flora pattern, 36 pcs, coffeepot, dessert plates, demitasse cups and saucers, coffee cups and saucers....................................... **850.00**

Dish, reticulated blue and white **175.00**

Figure

- 2" h, 5" l, mouse on ear of corn, #512 .... **65.00**
- 4" h, 9" l, Great Dane, #1679 .... **275.00**
- 4" h, faun on tortoise, #858 .... **175.00**
- 6-1/2" h, February Boy Juggler, #4524 .... **175.00**
- 6-3/4" h, Hans Clodhopper, #1228 .... **300.00**
- 6-3/4" h, Sandman, #1145...... **125.00**

Plaque, oval, beaded rim surmounted by ribbon and bow decoration, depicting Fredensborg Castle, back marked "Prove," 5-3/4" w, 8" h, **$615**. Photo courtesy of Alderfer Auction Co.

- 7" h, toddler and teddy bear, #3468 .... **225.00**

Fish plate, 10" d, different fish swimming among marine plants, molded and gilt border, light green highlights, gilt dentil edge, crown circular mark, 10-pc set **8,250.00**

Inkwell, Blue Fluted pattern, matching tray... **150.00**

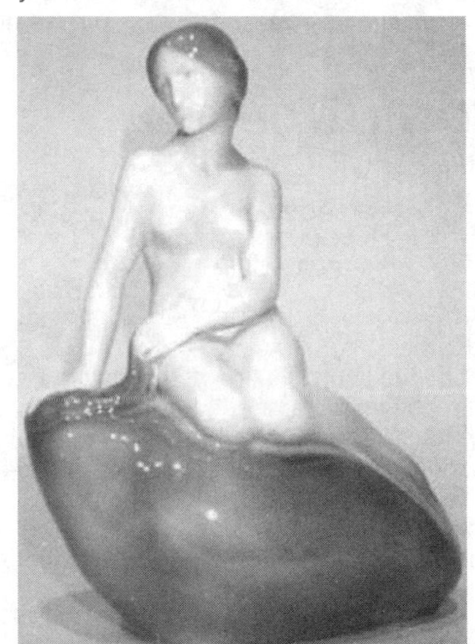

Figure, Little Mermaid, 8-1/2" h, **$100**. Photo courtesy of Joy Luke Auctions.

Pickle tray, 9" l, Half Lace pattern, blue triple wave mark **70.00**

Plates, two 7-5/8" d, six 10" d, each with gilt serrated rim and central hp floral specimen, price for eight-pc set **2,990.00**

Rose bowl, 8" d, spherical, dark blue ground, white painted blossoms, green leaves, #424 .... **200.00**

Salad bowl, 9-7/8" d, Flora Danica, botanical specimen, molded gilt border, dentil edge, pink highlights, blue triple wave and green crown mark........ **825.00**

Teaset, teapot, sugar, and creamer, blue and white, floral decoration, **$395**. Photo courtesy of Joy Luke Auctions.

Soup tureen, cov, stand, 14-1/2" l, Flora Danica, oval, enamel painted botanical specimens, twin handles, finial, factory marks, botanical identification, modern **5,750.00**

Tray, 10" l, Blue Fluted pattern....... **65.00**

Vase, 7" h, sage green and gray crackled glaze... **150.00**

ROYAL CROWN DERBY

History: Derby Crown Porcelain Co., established in 1875 in Derby, England, had no connection with earlier Derby factories which operated in the late 18th and early 19th centuries. In 1890, the company was appointed "Manufacturers of Porcelain to Her Majesty" (Queen Victoria) and since that date has been known as "Royal Crown Derby."

Most of these porcelains, both tableware and figural, were hand decorated. A variety of printing processes were used for additional adornment.

Marks: Derby porcelains from 1878 to 1890 carry only the standard crown printed mark. After 1891, the mark includes the "Royal Crown Derby" wording. In the 20th century, "Made in England" and "English Bone China" were added to the mark.

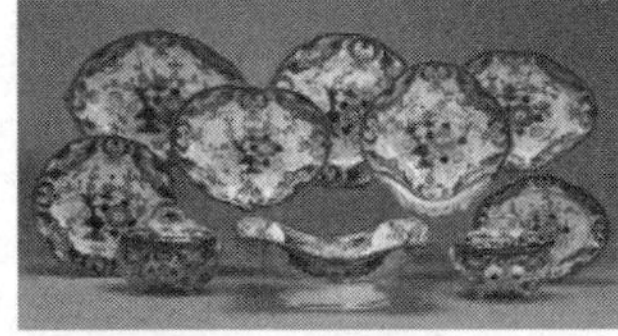

Luncheon Service, England, early 19th C, 45 pieces, Imari pattern in iron red, blue, and gold, including 12 10" d plates; 15 8-3/4" d plates; four 9-3/4" shrimp dishes; two covered oval 6-3/8" l sauce tureens with one stand; 11-3/4" l double-handled rectangular footed bowl; four oval vegetable dishes; two 10-1/4" l kidney-shaped dishes; three associated coffee cans; all with red painted marks; later condiment set in silver-plated stand; several pieces with chips, repairs, stains, **$2,585**. Photo courtesy of Skinner, Inc.

Bottle, 6" h, orig stopper, molded body, two handles, hp flowers, gold accents **150.00**

Compote, 9-1/4" d, geometric dec, black crown monogram mark, early 20th C, price for pr **375.00**
Cup and saucer, 5" d saucer, Imari pattern, 20th C **65.00**
Ewer, 6" h, Oriental-style gold enameled dec, soft coral ground, handle **200.00**

Soup tureen, covered, stand, Kings pattern, oval, c1830, 10" x 17-1/2", **$2,300**.

Jug, Imari palette, pink round, gold trim, c1885, pr **750.00**
Luncheon service, Imari pattern, iron red, blue, and gold, 12 10" d plates; 15 8-3/4" d plates; four 9-3/4" l shrimp dishes; two cov oval 6-3/8" l sauce tureens with one stand; ftd double-handled 11-3/4" rect bowl; two 10-3/8" l oval vegetable dishes; two 11-7/8" l oval vegetable dishes; two 10-1/4" l kidney-shaped dishes; three associated coffee cans; all with red painted marks; later condiment set in silver plated stand, many with damage, 44 pcs, England, early 19th C **2,585.00**
Mug, grapes and vines dec, blue and gold **125.00**
Soup plate, 9-7/8" d, inner band of gold jewelling with wide rim of gilt quatrefoils, grapevine, and leaf sprays, some leaves accented with bronze tone, shaped beaded edge, retailed by Tiffany & Co., early 20th C, price for set of 18 .... **5,750.00**
Urn, 12" h, squatty, double reticulated handles and finials, birds, butterfly, and floral designs, ivory ground, gilt accents, marked "Bailey, Banks, and Biddle," drilled for lamp, finials replaced, restoration to one handle, price for pr **1,325.00**

Vase, covered, England, c1894, globular shape, raised gold foliate decoration, deep cobalt blue ground, printed mark, chips to finial, hairline to cover insert, 15" h, **$2,585**. Photo courtesy of Skinner, Inc.

Vase

5-1/4" h, round, narrow mouth, polychrome dec with chinoiserie style flowering branches, multicolored beading, c1886 .... **275.00**

13" h, ovoid, narrow neck, flared rim, serpent handle, cobalt blue and iron-red Imari type dec, gilt accents, hp floral panels, minor gilt loss, touch-up, price for pr **925.00**

ROYAL DOULTON

DOULTON LAMBETH

History: Doulton pottery began in 1815 under the direction of John Doulton at the Doulton & Watts pottery in Lambeth, England. Early output was limited to salt-glazed industrial stoneware. After John Watts retired in 1854, the firm became Doulton and Company, and production was expanded to include hand-decorated stoneware such as figurines, vases, dinnerware, and flasks.

In 1878, John's son, Sir Henry Doulton, purchased Pinder Bourne & Co. in Burslem. The companies became Doulton & Co., Ltd. in 1882. Decorated porcelain was added to Doulton's earthenware production in 1884.

Most Doulton figurines were produced at the Burslem plants, where they were made continuously from 1890 until 1978. After a short interruption, a new line of Doulton figurines was introduced in 1979.

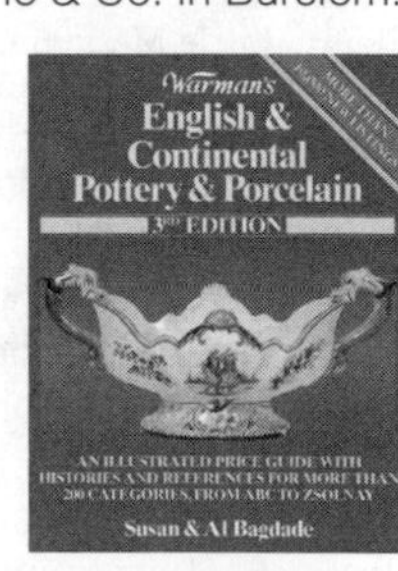

For more information, see *Warman's English & Continental Pottery & Porcelain*, 3rd edition.

Dickens ware, in earthenware and porcelain, was introduced in 1908. The pieces were decorated with characters from Dickens's novels. Most of the line was withdrawn in the 1940s, except for plates, which continued to be made until 1974.

Character jugs, a 20th-century revival of early Toby models, were designed by Charles J. Noke for Doulton in the 1930s. Character jugs are limited to bust portraits, while Royal Doulton toby jugs are full figured. The character jugs come in four sizes and feature fictional characters from Dickens, Shakespeare, and other English and American novelists, as well as historical heroes. Marks on both character and toby jugs must be carefully identified to determine dates and values.

Doulton's Rouge Flambé (Veined Sung) is a high-glazed, strong-colored ware noted primarily for the fine modeling and exquisite colorings, especially in the animal items. The process used to produce the vibrant colors is a Doulton secret.

Production of stoneware at Lambeth ceased in 1956; production of porcelain continues today at Burslem.

Marks: Beginning in 1872, the "Royal Doulton" mark was used on all types of wares produced by the company. Beginning in 1913, an "HN" number was assigned to each new Doulton figurine design. The "HN" numbers, which referred originally to Harry Nixon, a Doulton artist, were chronological until 1940, after which blocks of numbers were assigned to each modeler. From 1928 until 1954, a small number was placed to the right of the crown mark; this number added to 1927 gives the year of manufacture.

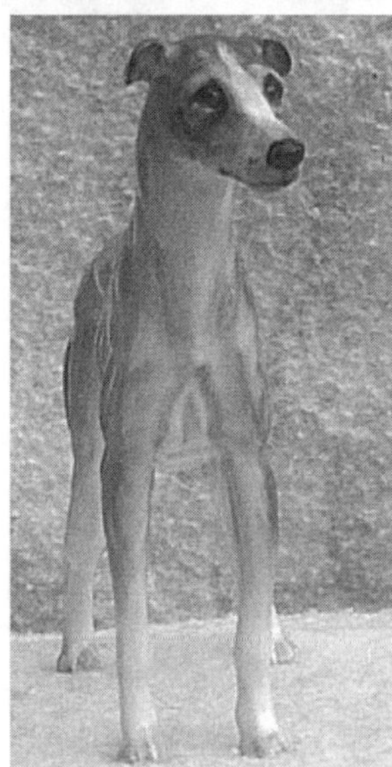

Figure, Greyhound, smallest of series produced in 1931, mark on paw, hand written "1067" on paw, tiny flake on ear, 4-1/2" h, **$285**. Photo courtesy of Forrest D. Poston.

Animal

Dragon, 7-1/2" h, Flambé, red glaze mottled with blue and yellow, late 20th C, printed mark **850.00**

Irish setter, HN1055................ **150.00**

Bottle, figural, Sandeman, King George on base, dark, 1937, marked "Royal Doulton" **75.00**

Cabinet vase, 2-1/2", scalloped rim, squat body encrusted with seashells, amber and celadon glaze, stamped/E.B **175.00**

Candlesticks, pr, 6-1/2" h, Walton Ware, Battle of Hastings, cream-color earthenware ground, stamped mark, c1910, small base chip on one **290.00**

Charger, Coaching Days, decorated with coach and horses, 15-1/4" d, **$180**. Photo courtesy of Joy Luke Auctions.

Chamberstick, 2" h, Walton Ware, fishermen dec, ivory earthenware ground, stamped mark, c1910, one of pair damaged **400.00**

Character jug, large,
- Cardinal **150.00**
- Poacher, D6781 .... **350.00**

Character jug, miniature,
- Blacksmith **50.00**
- Pickwick **65.00**

Character jug, small,
- Pearly King **35.00**
- Toby Philpots **85.00**

Figure, The Ballerina, HN 2116, 7-1/2" h, **$250**. Photo courtesy of Joy Luke Auctions.

Charger, 12-5/8" d, hp, all-over incised leaf, berry, and vine border, central fruits and leaves, attributed to Frank Bragwyn, printed mark, c1930 .... **245.00**

Clock case, King's are, night watchman, c1905 .... **450.00**

Console bowl, 9-1/2" d, Rutland pattern, transfer florals, crown mark, c1900 .... **65.00**

Cracker jar, 5" d, 6" h, Burslem, flowers, silver plated lid **115.00**

Dinner plate, 10-3/8" d, molded gilt inner border of floral plaques, cobalt blue outer border overprinted with gilt swags, 20th C, 12 pc set **765.00**

Dinner plate, set of 12, cobalt blue rim with raised gilt decoration, printed, impressed, and enameled marks, 10" d, **$1,100.** Photo courtesy of Sloan's Auctioneers & Appraisers.

Figure
- Carolyn, HN 2112, 71/4" h, 3-1/2" d **335.00**
- Fair Lady, coral pink, HN2835 .... **225.00**
- Nicola, HN2839 .... **350.00**
- Orange Lady, HN1758 .... **245.00**
- Sandra, HN2275 .... **200.00**
- The Leisure Hour, HN2055 .... **400.00**
- Victorian Lady, HN1208, 1926-38 .... **355.00**

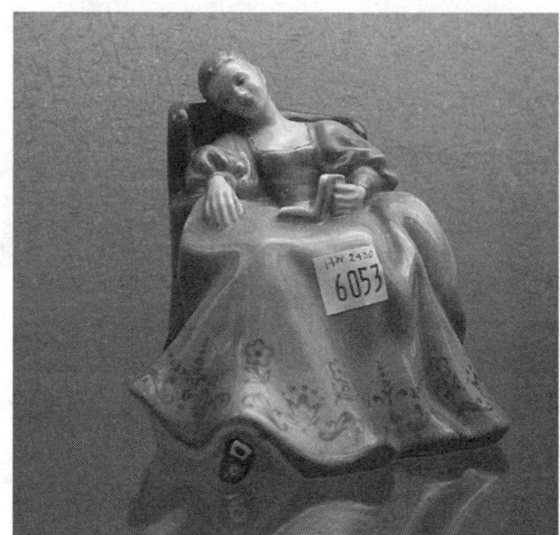

Figure, HN2430, holding book on lap, **$200.**

Fish plate, 9" d, swimming fish centers, pale yellow ground, gold bands and rims, sgd "J. Hallmark," 10-pc set **700.00**

Jardinière, 9-3/4" h, white slip dec on textured ground, stiff leaf borders at top and foot, impressed mark and artist signed by Eliza Simmance, late 19th C **500.00**

Jug
- Kingsware, Mr. Pickwick, yellow, 8-1/2" h, c1932 .... **200.00**
- Kingsware, Sporting Square, full figure, fox handle and spout, 1909 .... **450.00**
- Victoria, commemorating Jubilee, 1887, Doulton **185.00**

Match holder, Dewar's, striker, hairline on base **55.00**

Toby mug, Santa, **$195.**

Mug
- Gladstone, Wm. Stewart, 7-1/4" h, commemorating the death of Gladstone, c1898, Doulton Lambeth **125.00**
- Here's Luck, Ha! Ha!, leather look, Doulton Slater, stoneware **45.00**
- Sayings, small rim flake, Doulton Burslem **15.00**

Pitcher
- 3" h, Lord Nelson, blue stoneware **65.00**
- 7" h, bulbous, carved brown, blue, and green swirls of wheat, mottled amber ground, stamped "Doulton Lambeth, artist sgd "RB" **380.00**

Gibson girl plate, Miss Babbles, The Authoress Calls & Reads Aloud, 10-1/2" d, **$75.**

- 8" h, Good Is Not Good Enough...The Best Is Not Too Good, beige cameo figures, brown ground **120.00**
- 8-1/2" h, incised indigo and amber floral medallions, white and blue

dots, marked "MA," Doulton Lambeth, small hole drilled on bottom **150.00**
12-1/2" h, Walton Ware, fishermen dec, ivory earthenware ground, stamped mark, c1910, price for pr, one with bruise and restoration **400.00**

Puzzle pitcher, The Landlord's Caution, leather look, 7-1/2" h, Doulton Lambeth **150.00**

Vase, tapering, stylized fruit and leaves in yellow and green on shaded blue ground, stamped mark, 4" rim crack, 4" d, 7-1/2" h, **$290**. Photo courtesy of David Rago Auctions.

Service plate, 10-5/8" d, cream-colored ground, interior band of gilt anthemia, rim with gilt scrollwork over cream-colored ground, apple green reserves, gilt-shaped rim, mold date mark 1910, price for 18-pc set **5,465.00**

Spirits barrel, 7" l, King's Ware, double, silver trim rings and cov, oak stand, c1909 ...... **1,200.00**

Tankard, 10-1/2" h, stoneware, tooled leaves on brown and beige ground, hinged pewter lid, marked "Doulton Lambeth" **175.00**

Tile panel

42" x 18", painted by F. Pilter in Oriental style, prophet wearing headdress, Long embroidered robe, holding a snake staff, surface sgd "F. Pilter 1902/Doulton & Co.," hairlines to two tiles **2,300.00**
47" x 71", group of 88 hand-painted tiles titled "The Goose Girl," shepherdess with flock of geese beside her, solid brown tile border, few minor chips to border **10,000.00**

Toby

Cliff Cornell, blue outfit, 9-1/2" h, Royal Doulton **200.00**
Double X, toby on barrel, 10" h, stoneware, Doulton Lambeth, old base repair, c1869-72 ...... **200.00**
Huntsman **300.00**

Toby mug, large, pirate, green and yellow parrot for handle, black hat with white skull and crossbones, brown shirt, **$85**.

Pearly Boy, small size, blue, white buttons, "A" backstamp **1,770.00**

Toothpick holder, Walton Ware, Battle of Hastings, cream-color earthenware ground, stamped mark, c1910, set of six **535.00**

Trivet, 6-1/2" d, Series Ware, "Promise Little and Do Much," c1900...... **165.00**

Umbrella stand, 23-1/2" h, stoneware, enamel dec, applied floral medallions within diamond formed panels, framed by button motifs, imp mark, glaze crazing, c1910 ...... **550.00**

Vase

6-3/4" h, stoneware, baluster form, neck molded with flowerheads, body with lizards eyeing beetles on lotus leaves, body ending in anthemion leaves, spreading foot, Doulton Lambeth, early 20th C **215.00**
6-3/4" x 6", gourd shape, cafe-au-lait crystalline glossy glaze, stamp mark **980.00**
7" h, Flambé, tear shape, cottage by river, stamped "ROYAL DOULTON FLAMBE" **380.00**
9" h, ruffled rim, emb, carved, and imp polychrome floral motifs, no visible mark, drilled hole in base, small nicks **690.00**
11-3/4" h, cylindrical, top half covered in glossy cobalt blue glaze, base in checked pattern under caramel semi-matte glaze, marked **145.00**

Vessel, 6" l, 2" h, squat, deep in-body twists at rim, cobalt blue flambé glaze, circular Doulton stamp JH **460.00**

Water jug, 10-3/4" h, stoneware, "The Old Sarum Kettle," emb symbol under dark and light brown glaze, stamped... **175.00**

Whiskey jug

Alexander and McDonald Whiskey, dark, professional repair to spout **55.00**
Dewar's, Egyptian dancer **95.00**

Vase, mid-scenic band showing mother and two children in classical setting, decorative upper and bottom borders, artist signed "J.P. Hewitt," black Doulton Burslem mark, 10-1/2" h, **$1,380**. Photo courtesy of James D. Julia, Inc.

Dewar's, J.R.D. **145.00**
Dewar's, man with long pipe dec, 1904 ...... **200.00**
Dewar's, The Spirit of Friend-"Ship" **125.00**
Highland Whiskey, emb sailing ship dec with wreath, stoneware, marked "Doulton Lambeth" **150.00**

Royal Dux

ROYAL
DOULTON
FLAMBE

History: Royal Dux porcelain was made in Dux, Bohemia (now the Czech Republic), by E. Eichler at the Duxer Porzellan-Manufaktur, established in 1860. Many items were exported to the United States. By the turn of the century, Royal Dux figurines, vases, and accessories, especially those featuring Art-Nouveau designs, were captivating consumers.

Marks: A raised triangle with an acorn and the letter "E" plus "Dux, Bohemia" was used as a mark between 1900 and 1914.

Figure, bather, nude woman seated on rocky outcrop, drying her foot with gilt enameled cloth, oblong base, Czechoslovakia, early 20th C, 18-1/2" h, **$1,000**. Photo courtesy of Skinner, Inc.

Bust, 14" h, female portrait, raised leaves and berries on base, Czechoslovakia, early 20th C, unmarked, chips **290.00**

Center bowl, 20" l, formed as ovoid shallow bowl, set with figures of happy shepherd family group and sheep, Czechoslovakia, early 20th C....... **450.00**

Compote, figural, 14-1/2" l, modeled as female atop shell-form bowl, another figure within the wave modeled freeform base, imp mark, early 20th C **750.00**

Figure, shepherd and shepherdess, lady standing holding staff, man seated playing an instrument, naturalistic ovoid base, indistinct initials OAP?, man lacking item from hands, Czechoslovakia, early 20th C, 22" h, **$825**. Photo courtesy of Skinner, Inc.

Figure

10" h, young girl holding cat, raised pink triangle mark "Royal Dux Bohemia #421"................... **1,150.00**

19-1/2" h, Gypsy Shepherdess, standing, diaphanous dress and sheepskin, holding staff and tambourine, naturalistic base, Czechoslovakia, early 20th C **560.00**

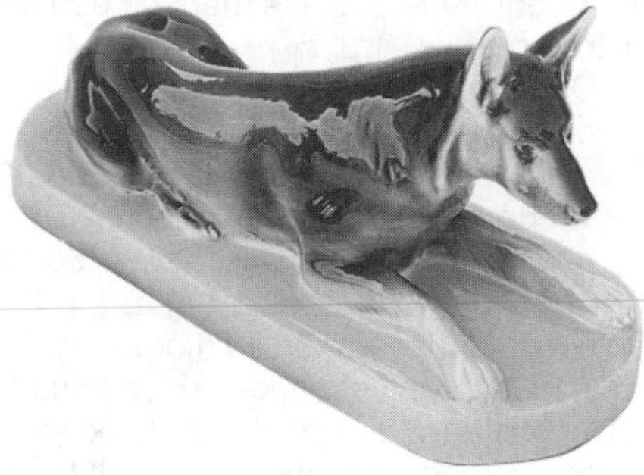

Figure, dog, pink triangle mark, 11-3/4" l, **$290**.

21" h, bathing semi-nude woman, realistically painted, sgd on base, applied pink triangle emb "Royal Dux, Bohemia," early 20th C **3,350.00**

Floor vase, 36-1/2" h, 37-1/4" h, date palm tree form, Middle Eastern woman and water urn on one, her suitor playing lute on other, matte finish flesh toned skin, cobalt blue clothing against white, gilt rims and highlights, ink labels "Royal Dux Bohemia" with acorn in triangle, glued unstable repairs to man, price for pr **5,225.00**

Vase

11" h, Grecian, "E" mark......... **595.00**

Figure, man on camel, boy with baskets, bisque, 18" h, **$250**. Photo courtesy of Joy Luke Auctions.

19-1/4" h, bisque, Art Nouveau-style female to one side of leaf and floral molded body, imp mark, early 20th C **290.00**

ROYAL FLEMISH

History: Royal Flemish was produced by the Mount Washington Glass Co., New Bedford, Massachusetts. Albert Steffin patented the process in 1894.

Royal Flemish is a frosted transparent glass with heavy raised gold enamel lines. These lines form sections—often colored in russet tones—giving the appearance of stained-glass windows with elaborate floral or coin medallions.

RF

1892

For more information, see *Warman's Glass*, 4th edition.

Advisers: Clarence and Betty Maier.

Biscuit jar, cov, 7" h jar, 9-3/4" to top of bail handle, irregular panels divided between clear frosted and very pale tan, raised gold lines frame each panel, two Frank Guba painted ducks in full flight, blazing sun, trace of orig gilt finish on ext. of metal fittings, int. of lid sgd "M. W. 4404/a," sgd with Royal Flemish logo and "253".. **3,750.00**

Box, cov, 5-1/2" d, 3-3/4" h, swirled border, gold outlined swirls, gold tracery blossoms, enameled blossom with jeweled center on lid **1,500.00**

Ewer, 10-1/2" h, 9" w, 5" d, circular semi-transparent panel on front with youth thrusting spear into chest of winged creature, reverse panel shows mythical fish created with tail changed into stylized florals, raised gold dec, outlines, and scrolls, rust, purple, and gold curlicues, twisted rope handle with brushed gold encircles neck, hp minute gold florals on neck, burnished gold stripes on rim spout and panels................................ **4,950.00**

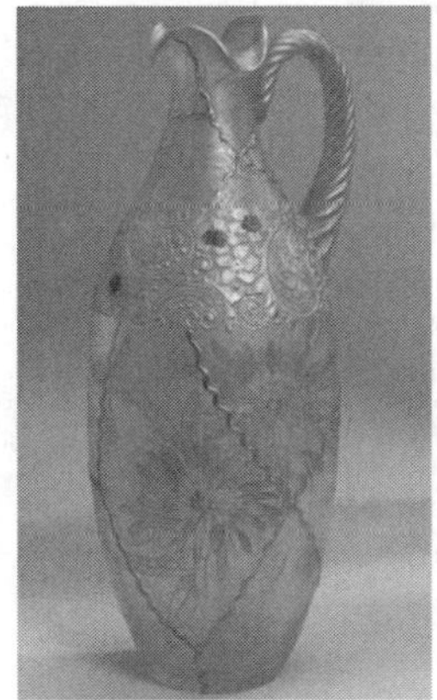

Ewer, oval, rope handle, ruffled spout, decorated with light purple and pink flowers, intricate gold enamel floral motif and lines on frosted glass, signed with red "FR," in diamond and "566," Boston, late 19th C, 13-3/4" h, **$3,290**. Photo courtesy of Skinner, Inc.

Jar, 8" h, classical Roman coin medallion dec, simulated stained glass panels, SP rim, bail, and cov, paper label "Mt. W. G. Co. Royal Flemish" **1,650.00**

Vase, globular, Roman heads in medallions, signed, original paper label, 6" d, **$6,500**.

Vase, 6" d, 6-1/2" h, stylized scrolls of pastel violet sweep down two tiny handles and across body, realistically tinged sprays of violets randomly strewn around frosted clear glass body, gold lines define violet nosegays and frame scrolls, gold accents daubed here and there, sgd with Royal Flemish logo and "0583"....................................... **2,200.00**

Ewer, sepia-colored body with cerise-colored shoulder, eight vertical panels framed in heavy raised gold, four tinted pale mauve, alternating with four smokey-gray panels, raised gold tendril laden with multi-petaled blossoms of encrusted gold and tinted autumn leaves, 16 sky-blue circular medallions, each with frosted clear-glass stylized cross and framed in raised gold. Raised gold stylized floral dec on cerise spout and diminutive frosted clear-glass handle, slight loss of gold on rim and raised lines, 5-1/2" d, 12" h, **$8,500**. Photo courtesy of Clarence and Betty Maier.

Royal Rudolstadt

History: Johann Fredrich von Schwarzburg-Rudolstadt was the patron of a faience factory located in Rudolstadt, Thuringen, Germany, from 1720 to c1790.

In 1854, Ernst Bohne established a factory in Rudolstadt.

The "Royal Rudolstadt" designation originated with wares which Lewis Straus and Sons (later Nathan Straus and Sons) of New York imported from the New York and Rudolstadt Pottery between 1887 and 1918. The factory manufactured several of the Rose O'Neill (Kewpie) items.

Marks: The first mark of the original pottery was a hayfork; later, crossed two-prong hayforks were used in imitation of the Meissen mark.

"EB" was the mark used by Ernst Bohne. A crown over a diamond enclosing the initials "RW" is the mark used by the New York and Rudolstadt Pottery.

Box, cov, 4-1/2" w, 5" d, 5-1/2" h, relief dec panels of nude allegorical garden scene, bronze trim and hinge, mark of crowned N, Ernst Bohne Sons, early 1900s **425.00**

Chocolate set, decorated with white roses, **$195**; R.S. Germany three-footed bowl decorated with flowers, **$95**. Photo courtesy of Joy Luke Auctions.

Figural bowl, bowl formed as stylized chariot drawn by winged lion ridden by cherub, ovoid rocaille C-scroll base, early 20th C, 11-1/2" h, **$360**. Photo courtesy of Skinner, Inc.

Bust, 15" h, classical figure, glazed to simulate marble **165.00**
Cake plate, 12" d, pink, white roses, gold handles and trim **75.00**
Ewer, 10" h, ivory, floral dec, gold handle and trim **125.00**
Figure, 8-1/4", muse Euterpe, wearing classical garb, flowers in hair, lute at her feet, holding scroll of poetry and flute **225.00**
Hatpin holder, lavender and roses **65.00**
Plate, 8-1/2" d, pink, white, and yellow roses, gold molded piecrust rim **35.00**
Teapot, cov, 5-1/2" h, hp, ivory, pink, lavender, and green floral dec **95.00**
Urn, 10" h, mythological scene, Hector and Andro crowning maiden, cobalt blue ground, gold handles, artist sgd, stand **145.00**
Vase, 8" h, hp florals, handle, crown "RW" mark **125.00**

Royal Vienna

History: Production of hard-paste porcelain in Vienna began in 1720 with Claude Innocentius du Paquier, a runaway employee from the Meissen factory. In 1744, Empress Maria Theresa brought the factory under royal patronage; subsequently, the ware became known as Royal Vienna. The firm went through many administrative changes until it closed in 1864, but the quality of its workmanship was always maintained.

Marks: Several other Austrian and German firms copied the Royal Vienna products, including the use of the "Beehive" mark. Many of the pieces on today's market are from these firms.

Cabinet vase, 3-1/2" h, children of four seasons, blue beehive mark **350.00**

Portrait plate, Ayesta, gypsy in green dress, red hat, gold and blue enameling on rim, blue beehive mark, 9-1/2", **$700**. Photo courtesy of James D. Julia, Inc.

Chocolate pot, cov, 10" h, large reserve with artist dec vase, woman looking on, cream ground, gilt handles and trim, Knoeller **350.00**
Cup and saucer, 2-3/4" h, cobalt blue, gold enamel dec, blue beehive mark, titled "Sommer" **200.00**
Ferner, 7-3/4" w, 4" h, portrait of lady one side, portrait of different lady on other, burgundy, green, and gold, beaded, scalloped edges, ftd, marked "Royal Vienna, Austria," artist sgd **425.00**
Perfume bottle, 4" h, 2-3/4" w, dark haired maiden leaning against wall, white gown with purple sash, reverse with topless maid sitting on rocks above water, purple material draped across her waist and legs, holding a sheer scarf blowing in the wind, cobalt blue enamel sides with gold scrolls and flower basket, applied rose and leaves on top of stopper, blue beehive mark, cork loose from stopper, few gold beads missing from portrait **750.00**

Pancake server, covered, rose colored borders, gold decoration, multicolored rose transfers, **$85**.

Plate, 9-1/2" d, hp, scene from Tannhauser, Act II, sgd "Wagner," c1890, blue beehive underglaze mark **990.00**
Portrait plate, 9-1/2" d
- Dark haired mother and child, deep olive green border, gold tracery, marked "Royal Vienna" **265.00**
- Young woman, titled "Andacht," beehive mark **750.00**

Snuffbox, 3" w, 2-1/2" d, 2-1/8" h, quatrefoil, landscape on lid, floral dec sides, blue beehive mark **250.00**
Urn, cov, 11-1/2" h, hp, elaborate scene of man, women, and cherub, cobalt blue ground, gold trim, beehive mark **1,200.00**
Vase, 10-1/2" h, facing female portrait medallions, banded ground of medium green, pale green, and pink, gilt filigree, floral panels, blue beehive mark, gilt wear, price for pr **2,100.00**

Royal Worcester

History: In 1751, the Worcester Porcelain Company, led by Dr. John Wall and William Davis, acquired the Bristol pottery of Benjamin Lund and moved it to Worcester. The first wares were painted blue under the glaze; soon thereafter decorating was

accomplished by painting on the glaze in enamel colors. Among the most-famous 18th-century decorators were James Giles and Jefferys Hamet O'Neale. Transfer-print decoration was developed by the 1760s.

c1876-1891

1891

For more information, see *Warman's English & Continental Pottery & Porcelain*, 3rd edition.

A series of partnerships took place after Davis' death in 1783: Flight (1783-1793); Flight & Barr (1793-1807); Barr, Flight, & Barr (1807-1813); and Flight, Barr, & Barr (1813-1840). In 1840, the factory was moved to Chamberlain & Co. in Diglis. Decorative wares were discontinued. In 1852, W. H. Kerr and R. W. Binns formed a new company and revived the production of ornamental wares.

In 1862, the firm became the Royal Worcester Porcelain Co. Among the key modelers of the late 19th century were James Hadley, his three sons, and George Owen, an expert with pierced clay pieces. Royal Worcester absorbed the Grainger factory in 1889 and the James Hadley factory in 1905. Modern designers include Dorothy Doughty and Doris Lindner.

Basket, 8-1/2" d, flaring pierced sides mounted with floral heads, pinecone and floral cluster int., blue and white transfer dec, first period, mid-18th C **550.00**

Bowl, 10" d, scalloped border, shell molded boy, fruit and floral spray, blue and white transfer dec, first period, mid-18th C **320.00**

Butter tub, cov, 4-1/4" d, 3-1/4" h, cylindrical, fully sculpted finial, painted floral sprays below geometric borders, first period, c1765 .... **450.00**

Bud vase, decorated with flowers, 7-1/4" h, **$265**. Photo courtesy of Joy Luke Auctions.

Ewer, handle, gold stippled background, colorful fern motif, 13-1/2" h, **$175**. Photo courtesy of Woody Auctions.

Candelabrum vase, 7-3/4" h, model no. 1130, squat conical form, crenellated neck, molded with vertical bands of flowers, two candle sconces flanking neck, raised on stylized dolphin herm handles, body dec with two blue and gold flower sprays, early 20th C **825.00**

Chamberstick, 4-5/8" h, model no. 1088, stylized lotus blossom shape, small frog perched on gilt leaf, late 19th/early 20th C **165.00**

Creamer and sugar, 2-1/2" h, hp florals, purple crown mark, c1900 .... **95.00**

Dinner service, Doncaster pattern, 12 five-pc place settings, plus serving pcs, 92 pcs **450.00**

Dish, 8" l, leaf form, molded body, underglaze blue floral sprays, branch handle, first period, c1765 .... **500.00**

Ewer, 12-3/4" h, ivory, basketweave pattern, raised floral scrolls, shaped dragon handle with foliage tail, gilding, purple label "Roehm & Son, Detroit" **250.00**

Dinner service, Evesham Vale, 10 each dinner plates, salad plates, bread plates, bowls, saucers; four lidded jars; cup; two cov casseroles; hors d'oeuvres tray; round tray; two round baking dishes' six ramekins; covered jam pot; covered butter dish; covered sugar; creamer; mug; three salt shakers; slotted spoon; two tab-handled bowls, **$450**. Photo courtesy of Joy Luke Auctions.

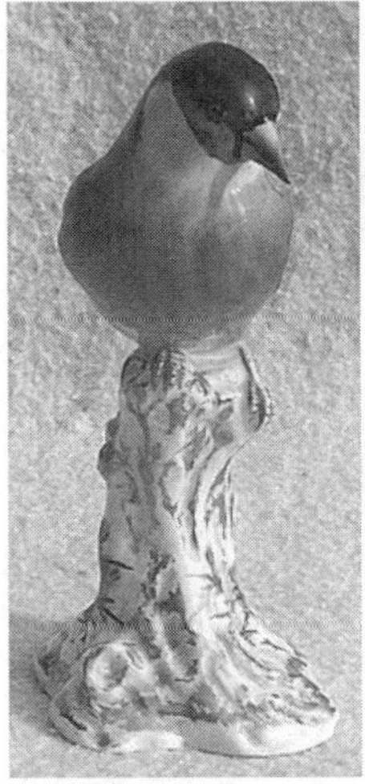

Figure, gold finch, model #2667, tree trunk-shaped base with hand-painted thistle decoration, marked, c1951, 6-1/8" h, **$145**. Photo courtesy of Forrest G. Poston.

Figure

6-1/2" h, Welsh girl, enamel porcelain, sgd "Hadley," late-19th C **690.00**

7-3/4" h and 8-1/4" h, lady and gentleman, George III costumes, sgd "Hadley," pr **1,100.00**

Figures, titled "Crabapple & Butterfly," by Dorthoy Doughty, each 9" w, 9-1/2" h, **$230**. Photo courtesy of James D. Julia, Inc.

8-3/4" h, Cairo water carrier, 1895 .... **635.00**

Fish plates, 9-1/4" d, bone china, hp fish, gilt lattice and foliage border, sgd "Harry Ayrton," printed marks, c1930, 13-pc set **2,300.00**

Fruit cooler, 6-1/4" h, cylindrical, Royal Lily pattern, stylized floral reserve, stepped circular foot, first period, c1800 .... **225.00**

Lamp base, 13-3/4" h, baluster vase form, slender gilt neck, two short Moorish-style gilt handles, hand-painted scene of gilt shipwreck on shore by lighthouse, reverse with small scenic roundel, gilt guilloche foot, electrified **325.00**

Mustard pot, 4" h, cylindrical, blue and white transfer, floral clusters, floral finial, first period, mid-18th C **325.00**

Pitcher

5-3/4" h, Indian elephant head handle **175.00**

6" h, 5" d, floral dec, gold handle **230.00**

Pair of plates, decorated with flowers, gilded borders, 8" d, **$120**. Photo courtesy of Joy Luke Auctions.

Plate

7" w, octagonal, landscape fan form reserves, cobalt blue ground, first period, 18th C, pr **350.00**

7-3/4" d, Blind Earl pattern, raised rose spray, polychrome floral sprays, scalloped border, first period, mid-18th C **1,100.00**

Sauce boat, 4-1/4" h, geometric band above foliate molded body, painted floral sprays, oval foot, first period, c1765, pr **275.00**

Soup set, 17-1/2" l cov tureen with elephant head handle, undertray, 17 soup plates, underglaze blue all-over transfer pattern of flowerheads, and chinoiserie branches, gilt detailing, c1883, price for 19-pc set **750.00**

Vases, pair, squared form, circular necks, applied lion mask and ring handles, footed base, full length carved decoration of Chinese-style work scenes on one side, carved oval cartouche of Chinese men working on other side, chips on one foot, 11" h, **$1,540**. Photo courtesy of Sanford Alderfer Auction Company.

Sweetmeat jar, 6" d, molded swirl base, thistles dec, silverplate lid, bail, and handle, marked "RW" with crown **200.00**

Tankard, 6" h, cylindrical, blue and white transfer dec of parrot among fruit, first period, mid-18th C **325.00**

Tea bowl and saucer, painted chinoisiere vignette, blue border, first period, c1865 .... **185.00**

Pitcher, handpainted polychrome flowers, cream ground with gilded details, purple ink stamp, fully marked. 5-1/4" d, 6-1/2" h, **$150**. Photo courtesy of David Rago Auctions, Inc.

Teapot, cov, 6-1/2" h, globular form body, fully sculpted blossom finial, domed top, painted floral sprays, first period, c1765 .... **375.00**

Salver, round, wide band of underglaze blue transfer printed Middle Eastern-style flowers, inner and outer rim accented with gilt scrolls and linework, 1878, 14-1/2" d, **$300**. Photo courtesy of Skinner, Inc.

Vase

15-3/8" h, Aesthetic Movement, slender baluster form with short loop handles, enamel dec, owl about to fly from Japonesque pine tree branch, against gilt moon and clouds, reverse with pair of sparrows in flight over wheat stems, low beaded foot, c1883 .... **950.00**

17" h, ovoid, slender reticulated neck rim, short scrolled gilt handles, enamel dec, polychrome branches, short gilt foot, 1889 .... **450.00**

Vase, cov, fruit dec, c1910 .... **460.00**

Wall pocket, 8-1/4" h, realistically modeled orchid flower with gilt enameled petals, date marked 1883 .... **450.00**

ROYCROFT

History: Elbert Hubbard founded the Roycrofters in East Aurora, New York, at the turn of the century. Considered a genius in his day, he was an author, lecturer, manufacturer, salesman, and philosopher.

Hubbard established a campus that included a printing plant where he published *The Philistine, The Fra*, and *The Roycrofter*. His most-famous book was *A Message to Garcia*, published in 1899. His "community" also included a furniture manufacturing plant, a metal shop, and a leather shop.

Bed, double, headboard and baseboard with vertical slats, Mackmurdo feet, excellent original finish and condition, orb and cross mark, 80" l, 55" w, 49" h, **$6,900**. Photo courtesy of David Rago Auctions, Inc.

Ali Baba bench, 42-1/2" l, 11" w, 20" h, half-log top, flaring plank legs, keyed through tenon stretcher, carved orb and cross mark, minor loss to bark, orig finish **16,500.00**

Book, Book of Job, 1897, tooled full-leather binding, hand-illumined pages, orig water colors, signed by Elbert Hubbard and numbered 2, 7-3/4" x 5" **3,000.00**

Bookends, pair, brass-washed hammered copper, embossed rope and ship medallion, orb and cross mark, minor wear to original patina, 5" x 5-1/2", **$225**. Photo courtesy of David Rago Auctions.

Bookends, pr

5" x 3-3/4", oval, hammered copper, etched and roped panel, orb and cross mark, some pitting to orig patina **115.00**

5" x 6", hammered copper bookends, emb oval medallion with dogwood blossoms in repousse, orig finish, unmarked **410.00**

5-1/4" x 5", Poppy, brass washed hammered copper, emb and riveted, orig patina, orb and cross mark, light wear to high points **460.00**

Bud vase

7-3/4" x 4-1/4", hammered copper, four buttressed supports, applied nickel silver squares around rim, orb and cross mark, cleaned patina **2,415.00**

7-3/4" x 4-1/2", cylindrical, hammered copper, silver squares alternating with riveted full-height buttressed handles, orig patina, orb and cross mark, few short scratches ... **4,320.00**

Dinner bell, brass-washed hammered copper, orb and cross mark, 1-3/4" d, 3" h, **$350**. Photo courtesy of David Rago Auctions, Inc.

Candlesticks, pr, 7-3/4" x 3", Princess, hammered copper, each with double stems riveted to faceted base, orig patina, orb and cross marks **815.00**

Console set, 11" d bowl, pr 3-1/2" h candlesticks, acid-etched silver finish, orb and cross mark, minor wear to bowl int........ **460.00**

Desk lamp, 14-3/4" h, 7" d Steuben blown glass lustered glass shade, hammered copper, shaft of four curled and riveted bands, stamped orb and cross mark........ **5,750.00**

Dresser, four drawers, integrated mirror, brass pulls, Mackmurdo feet, excellent original finish and condition, orb and cross mark, 43-1/2" l, 25-1/2" w, 61-1/2" h, **$10,450**. Photo courtesy of David Rago Auctions, Inc.

Bowls, pair, hammered copper, crimped rims, orb and cross marks, 4-1/4" d, 2-1/2" h, **$350**. Photo courtesy of David Rago Auctions.

Desk set, hammered copper, paper knife, pen tray, stationery holding, perpetual desk calendar, pr of bookends, flower holder, match holder with nested ashtray, c1915........ **550.00**

Dresser set, two pcs, 2-3/4" h, 2-1/4" x 4", hammered copper, emb quatrefoils, set on brass ball feet, brass quatrefoil finial, orig lacquer over light finish, orb & cross mark with dot, benchmark notation **3,150.00**

Goody box, 23" l, 13" d, 10" h, mahogany, wrought cooper strap hardware, monogrammed "H," orig finish, carved orb and cross on top........ **630.00**

Desk blotter, hammered copper, oversized, two riveted corners, two pentrays flanking an inkwell, orb and cross mark, original patina, missing inkwell liner, new green leather blotter, 18-1/2" x 28", **$2,760**. Photo courtesy of David Rago Auctions.

Humidor, 4-3/4" w, 5-3/4" h, hammered copper, covered in brass wash, Trillium pattern, stamped orb and cross mark, minor wear to patina........ **690.00**

Footstool, mahogany, original tacked-on cordovan leather seat, carved orb and cross mark, refinished, filled-in-tack holes, 10" x 15-1/4" x 9-3/4", **$800**. Photo courtesy of David Rago Auctions.

Letter holder/perpetual calendar, 3-1/2" x 4-3/4" x 2-1/4", copper, acid-etched border, orb and cross mark with "Roycroft," normal wear to patina **150.00**

Two complete sets of Little Journeys; one set of Great Philosophers, Jan.-Dec., 1904, paper-bound, excellent condition; one set of Great Scientists, Jan.-Dec., 1905, tears to some covers, **$100**. Photo courtesy of David Rago Auctions, Inc.

Magazine stand, 17-3/4" w, 15-1/2" d, 37-1/2" h, mahogany, three shelves, canted sides, arched top, orb and cross mark, orig finish........ **2,990.00**

Motto sign, 5" x 19", carved oak, "Be Yourself," orig dark finish, orb and cross mark........ **2,615.00**

Pedestal, oak, square form with stepped base, signed with orb and cross at side, original finish, c1907, minor wear, joint separation, 15" square, 39-1/8" h, **$4,200**. Photo courtesy of Skinner Auctioneers and Appraisers.

Desk blotter, hammered copper, oversized, two riveted corners, two pentrays flanking an inkwell, orb and cross mark, original patina, missing inkwell liner, new green leather blotter, 18-1/2" x 28", **$2,760**. Photo courtesy of David Rago

Nut set, hammered copper, ftd bowl, spoon, six plates, six picks, all but picks marked with orb and cross, orig patina, price for 14-pc set........ **4,890.00**

Occasional table, rectangular shaped slat top, four supports joined to shoe foot base, branded mark on base, top possibly altered, 30" w, 18" d, 26" h, **$825**. Photo courtesy of Skinner, Inc.

Russian Items

History: During the late 19th and early 20th centuries, craftsmen skilled in lacquer, silver, and enamel wares worked in Russia. During the Czarist era (1880-1917), Fabergé, known for his exquisite enamel pieces, led a group of master craftsmen located primarily in Moscow. Fabergé also had an establishment in St. Petersburg and enjoyed the patronage of the Russian Imperial family and royalty and nobility throughout Europe.

ВРАТЬЕВЪ
Baterin's factory
1812-1820

КорНИЛОВЫХЪ
Korniloff's factory
c1835

Almost all enameling was done on silver. The artist and the government assayer both marked pieces.

The Russian Revolution in 1917 brought an abrupt end to the century of Russian craftsmanship. The modern Soviet government has exported some inferior enamel and lacquer work, usually lacking in artistic merit. Modern pieces are not collectible.

Candlesticks, pair, silver, 1838, Chernigov, chased with leaves and scrolls, 9-1/2" h, **$2,500**. Photo courtesy of Sloans & Kenyon Auctions.

Enamels

Blood cup, 4" h, transfer dec with Imperial double headed eagle and Cypher of the Tsar Nicholas II above date 1896 .... **690.00**

Cane, 35" l, 4-1/2" l x 3-1/4" tau handle dec with champleve style raised enamel, light blue, dark blue, green, white, and red, worn Russian hallmarks, heavy ebony shaft, 7/8" replaced brass ferrule, c1900 .... **2,350.00**

Cigarette box, silver-gilt
- Arabesque design **750.00**
- Engraved int. monogram **1,380.00**

Cup, ftd, silver-gilt, base with presentation inscription, c1900 .... **1,380.00**

Group of silver and shaded enamel, top: set of four silver-gilt and cloisonné enamel cups, Antip Kuzmichev, Moscow, dated 1895, maked "Made for Tiffany & Co.," 3" w, 2-1/4" h, **$4,025**; bottom left: Kovsh, Vasliy Agafonov, Moscow, 1896, 4" l, **$865**; bottom right: Kovsh, Moscow, after 1908, Cyrillic maker's mark EC, 4" l, **$900**. Photo courtesy of Jackson's International Auctioneers & Appraisers.

Tray, painted and lacquered metal, Lukutin, 19th C, Troika scene, verso signed in Cyrillic beneath Imperial warrant, 13-1/2" l, 10-1/2" h, **$700**.

Knives, 9-1/2" l, silver-plated blades engraved with monogram, rounded handles with scrolled champleve enameling, three matched, one aqua, and two with various scrolls and patera, Moscow, c1880, marked "Klinger" **1,100.00**

Kovsh, 4-1/4" l, enameled silver and gilt, typical form, flat handle, dec of horse in the well, bands of scrolling floral vines, late 19th C, bearing stamp of Ovchinikov **2,250.00**

Napkin ring, 1-3/4" x 1" x 1-1/2", enameled green, blue, pink, brown, white, light blue and maroon, Maria Semenova, Moscow, c1890 .... **700.00**

Picture, 7-3/4" x 6-3/4", enamel dec, Holy Bishop Tikhon of Voronezh, orig copper frame, chased feather lined inner border, Rostov, c1880 .... **750.00**

Cross, Palekh or Mistera, 19th C, recessed edges, painted in classic 16th style, 19th C, 22" w, 47" h, **$4,600**.

Caviar tub, silver, 1860, faux wood grain, vermeil reeded bands, locking cover, glass liner, 4" d, 10 oz, **$950**. Photo courtesy of Sloans & Kenyon Auctions.

Spoon
- 7-1/4" l, silver-gilt and shaded enamel, back with colorful plumed bird on stippled ground, beaded border, Dmitri Nicholiaev, Moscow, c1900 .... **865.00**
- 7-1/2" d, round bowl, twisted handle ending in crown finial with enamel accents, obverse of bowl dec with hp portrait of woman surrounded by band of blue and green plique-a-jour in geometric design, illegible mark **1,760.00**

Vase, 11-1/2" h, champleve enamel, central cartouche on both sides, one with stylized double headed eagle, other side with roosters, Slavonic inscription at base rim, hallmarked Moscow, dated 1874, Cyrillic "P. Ovchinnikov" under Imperial Warrant **5,750.00**

Icon, St. Nicholas, 1893, Moscow, silver-gilt Oklad, richly enameled halo, 12-1/2" x 10-1/4", **$1,200**. Photo courtesy of Sloans & Kenyon Auctions.

Icon

2" h, The Kazan Mother of God, mother-of-pearl, encased in engraved silver frame, suspension loop, 19th C ... **350.00**

3" h, pendant, double sided, obverse with Virgin in prayer, reverse with Annunciation, entirely encased in silver repousséd and chased riza, inscribed March 25, 1828, hallmarked St. Petersburg, dated 1829 .... **575.00**

5-1/2" x 4-1/2", The Appearance of the Mother of God to the Venerable Sergiy Radonezh, 19th C......................... **320.00**

7" x 5-1/2", The Three-Handed Mother of God, finely painted on gold field, 19th C **400.00**

7" x 5-1/2", The Vladmir Mother of God, fully painted, overpaid with silver repoussé riaza, applied gilded halo, c1850... **500.00**

Figural group, couple being driven in Troika, bronze, deep brown patina, signed on base in Cyrillic, "Tratchev" and "Voerfiel Foundry, St. Petersburg," 1831-1905, 12-1/4" l, 7" w, 7-1/2" h, **$2,875**.

9" x 7", The All-Seeing Eye of God, corners with four Evangelists, upper margin inscribed in Old Church Slavonic "Vsevidyashchee Oko Bozhie," 19th C **750.00**

9" x 7", The Mother of God "It Is Truly Meet," angels carry icon, below Apostle and Evangelist John, Prophetess Anna, Martyr Warrior Saint Theodore, 19th C **375.00**

Figural group, bronze, mounted Imperial soldier, c1890, indistinguishably signed in Cyrillic on base, dark brown patina, 38-1/2" w, 16-1/2" h, **$2,300**.

11" x 13", Saint Nicholas, embroidered, silk thread flesh tones, bullion thread clothing, embellished with seed pearls and beads, 20th C, custom made glazed wood frame................................... **665.00**

12" x 10", The Archangel Michael and the Holy Alexi Metropolitant of Moscow, Christ delivering blessing from above, c1890... **350.00**

13-1/4" x 11-1/2", The Tikvin Mother of God, entire icon overlaid with silver repousse, chased riza hallmarked St. Petersburg, dated 1843, Cyrillic maker's mark "L. M.," borders with Saints Domentiy and Katherine, 19th C **1,150.00**

46" x 17-1/2", The Crucifixion, ornately tooled gold leaf field, center crucified Christ on cross, Mother and Apostle John looking on, c1890....................... **3,115.00**

Kovsh, silver-gilt and enamel, 1895, probably Moscow, typical shape, notched handle and band of trailing flowering branches in colors, 4-1/4" l, **$675**. Photo courtesy of Sloans & Kenyon Auctions.

Metal

Bonbonniere, 3-3/8" d, 2-3/16" h, orchid guilloche enamel on silver, cylindrical, cast silver bas-relief applied dec on cov and back, applied relief, monogram of Nicholas II set with precious stones, Henrik Wigstrom, workmaster, St. Petersburg, 1908-17, slight damage **4,225.00**

Bust, 10" h, Tsar Alexander Mikhailovich, Cyrillic foundry mark "F. Shopeen," dated 1867, bronze **1,250.00**

Cross, 47" x 22", Palekh or Mstera, 19th C, recessed edges (kovcheg), painted in classic 16th C style, top with Holy Napkin and Angels, center crossbeam with Mary and Apostle John, center with crucified Christ with implements of the passion, base with skull of Adam **4,600.00**

Tray, painted and lacquered metal, Lukutin, 19th C, Troika scene, verso signed in Cyrillic beneath Imperial warrant, 13-1/2" l, 10-1/2" h, **$700**.

Sculpture, bronze, 18-1/2" x 16-1/2" h, mounted Imperial soldier, dark brown patina, c1890, indistinguishably signed in Cyrillic on base......................... **2,300.00**

Icon, Saint Nicholas, c1880, kiot with carved and gold leaf inner frame of scrolling foliage and grapes surrounding colorfully painted icon, executed on gold leaf ground, storage drawer for candles, 3'5" x 3'3", **$5,175**.

Tray, 13-1/2" x 10-1/2", painted and lacquered metal, troika scene, verso sgd in Cyrillic "Lukutin," beneath Imperial Warrant, 19th C **690.00**

Icon, New Testament Trinity, Eliya Yakovlev, 1843, lower right corner signed: "This Holy Image was Painted on the 15th day of May by Icongrapher Eliya Yakovlev, St. Petersburg," 23" x 28", **$2,875**.

Salt and Pepper Shakers

For more information, see *Warman's Glass*, 4th edition.

History: Collecting salt and pepper shakers, whether late 19th-century glass forms or the contemporary figural and souvenir types, has always been a mainstay of the antiques and collectibles world. The supply and variety is practically unlimited; the price for most sets is within the budget of cost-conscious collectors. In addition, their size offers an opportunity to display a large collection in a relatively small space.

Specialty collections can be by type, form, or maker. Great glass artisans, such as Joseph Locke and Nicholas Kopp, designed salt and pepper shakers in the normal course of their work.

Additional Listings: See *Warman's Americana & Collectibles* and *Warman's Flea Market* for more examples.

Figural, brown turkey, yellow serving platter, **$6**.

Art glass (priced individually)

Burmese, 4" h, branches and leaves dec, metal top, Mt. Washington **85.00**
Cranberry, Inverted Thumbprint, sphere **175.00**
Fig, enameled pansy dec, satin, orig prong top, Mt. Washington **120.00**
Hobnail, sapphire blue, Hobbs, Brockunier & Co., one orig metal top, 2-3/4" h **95.00**
Wave Crest, egg shape, opaque white ground, yellow and orange hp flowers, 2" h **185.00**

China

Lefton, Rustic Daisy, 6-3/4" h, pr **24.00**
Noritake Nippon, 3" h, hp, poppy and floral design, heavy gilt top, marked "Noritake Nippon," c1906, single **30.00**
Royal Bayreuth, lobsters, pr **175.00**

Figural and souvenir types (priced by set)

Black native in boat, 4" l, 3-1/2" h, boy holding paddle, black canoe, black "Japan" stamp mark, 1950s, orig corks **175.00**

Opaque glass, Muranese pattern, New Martinsville, white, embossed scroll design, 3-1/2" h, **$60**.

Bride and Groom pigs, nodder base, Japan, 1940s **350.00**
Cardinal Tuck, 3-1/4" h, holding books, Goebel, marked "W. Germany" with bee inside "V," paper label on back "Cardinal Tuck," orig closures **195.00**
Gas pumps, 2-3/4" h, Pure Oil, adv on back "Mower County Oil Co. Pure Oil Products PH. He. 3-2089 Austin Minn.," plastic **135.00**
Goofy and Pluto, 4" l, 4-1/4" h, anthropomorphic car, 1930s, orig souvenir label "Souvenir of Burlington Iowa," red "Japan" mark **300.00**

Opaque white ground, yellow and orange flowers, green leaves, St. Paul in gold letters, egg shape, original tops, 2" h, pair, **$215**.

Hen and rooster, nodder base, Japan, 1940s **165.00**
Huggies, 7" w, 6-1/2" h, one says "His," the other says "Hers," Grey R. Bendel, 1958, marked **500.00**
Little Red Riding Hood, 4-1/2" h, made by Regal China for Hull Pottery, poinsettia design, marked "Pat Des. No. 135889," orig corks **750.00**
Mammy, 3-1/2" h, nude, nodder base, Japan, 1940s **300.00**
Matador and bull, nodder base, Japan, 1940s **245.00**
Shmoo, 3-1/2" h, Al Capp character, hp, 1940s **225.00**
Strawberries, flashed amberina glass strawberry-shaped shakers, white metal leaf caps, suspended from emb white metal fancy holder, 2-3/4" h strawberries, 5" h stand, sgd "Japan," c1921-41 ..... **285.00**

Crystal bodies, applied black glass handle and foot, mechanical tops marked "Reiner Products, Inc. Neverklog Pat. Applied For," 2-7/8" h, **$45**. Photo courtesy of Michael Krumme.

Opaque glass (priced individually)

Bulge Bottom, blue **25.00**
Cathedral Panel, white **20.00**
Creased Bale, pink **20.00**
Fleur de Lis Scrolling, custard **20.00**
Heart, blue **25.00**
Little Shrimp, white **20.00**
Muranese, white, emb scroll design, New Martinsville, 3-1/2" h **60.00**
Swirl Wide Diagonal, white **20.00**
Torch Wreath, white **20.00**

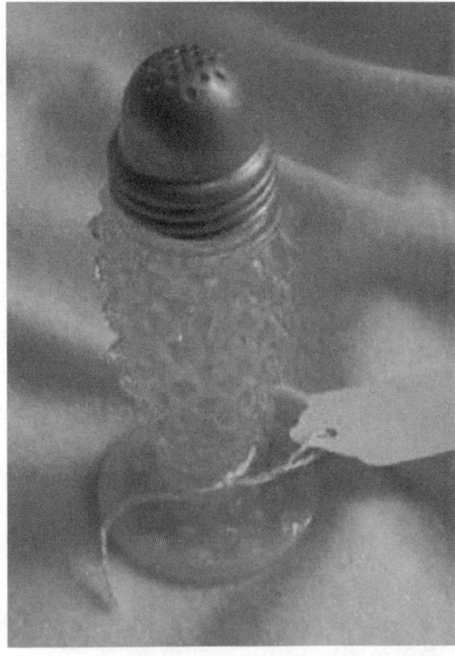

Fenton, Topaz Opalescent Hobnail, #389, 1941-43, **$45**.

Pattern glass, Daisy & Cube, light blue, original top, **$30**.

Pattern glass (priced individually)

Actress, pewter top 45.00
Beautiful Lady, colorless, 1905 .... 25.00
Daisy and Cube, light blue, orig top 30.00
Franesware, Hobbs, Brockunier Co., c1880, hobnail, frosted, amber stained 45.00
Lobe, squatty 120.00
Tulip 100.00

Salt-Glazed Wares

History: Salt-glazed wares have a distinctive pitted surface texture made by throwing salt into the hot kiln during the final firing process. The salt vapors produce sodium oxide and hydrochloric acid, which react on the glaze.

Many Staffordshire potters produced large quantities of this type of ware during the 18th and 19th centuries. A relatively small amount was produced in the United States. Salt-glazed wares still are made today.

For more information, see *Warman's English & Continental Pottery & Porcelain*, 3rd edition.

Miniature jug, brown and white salt glaze, blue stencil on front "Wallace & Gregory Bros., Pure Vinegars, Paducah KY," 2-3/4" h, some age crazing, **$70**. Photo courtesy of Vicki and Bruce Waasdorp.

Bottle, 7-1/2" h, flat form, Albany glaze int., c1810 .... 210.00
Canister, 7-1/4" h, one gallon, relief oak leaf design, blue and navy blue accents, orig matching lid and bale handle, relief diamond pattern all around 220.00
Canteen, 7-1/2" h, relief and blue accented tavern scene on front, relief and blue accented leaf design around rim, orig bale handle 495.00
Cheese jar, 4-1/2" h, blue accent bands, diamond point design, imp and blue accented "Bayle's Cheeses St. Louis, MO," nicely fitted replacement wooden lid, int. surface chip on back 110.00
Cream pitcher, 6-1/4" h, relief daffodil dec on front and back, heavy blue accents at floral designs and on handle 110.00
Figure, 4-1/2" l, 3-1/4" h, seated ram, molded stoneware, blue accents at eyes and end of protruding horns, attributed to mold maker George Hehr, Red Wing Stoneware Co., c1896, piece broken off one horn, museum inventory code number inked on bottom 825.00
Humidor, cov, 6-1/2" h, matching lid, relief and blue accented hunting dog on front, blue accent band at rim, overall diamond relief pattern 250.00

Match safe, incised "Matches" on front, three blue accent bands, rim chip, stained from use, 5" h, **$385**. Photo courtesy of Vicki and Bruce Waasdorp.

Mug

4" h, bulbous, two blue accent bands, imp and blue accented "Granby CT 1896," blue accents at handle, Albany glaze int., short hairline extending from rim..... 440.00

Teapot, globular shape, light blue enamel ground, polychrome cartouches of flowers, Staffordshire, England, c1760, restored chips to cover and spout, 4-1/4" h, **$3,450**. Photo courtesy of Skinner, Inc.

6-1/2" h, hinged pewter lid, two blue incised accent bands, Albany glaze int., attributed to New York state, c1840 .... 210.00

Mustard pot, 4" h, relief and blue accented grape vine design on front, blue accent band at rim and knob of orig lid, turned wooden spoon 220.00
Pilsner glass, 7" h, imp and blue accented tooled lines top and bottom, center imp "Crystal Springs Lager" 330.00

Pitcher, relief bark design, relief and blue accented male portrait on one side, leafy rose on other, mold mark #9, 8" h, age spider, **$70**. Photo courtesy of Vicki and Bruce Waasdorp.

Pitcher, 9-1/4" h, acanthus scrolls around two women reading tea leaves, marked "Edward Walley, Cobridge, Staffordshire," interior glaze, rim flake 150.00
Plate, shaped reticulated rim, 8-1/4" d, emb border 600.00
Platter, 16-3/4" d, molded diaper-work panels, scalloped rim, 18th C 250.00
Salt, helmet shape, latticino star and lion, bird and shell dec, claw feet, c18th C 880.00
Sauce boat, 3-1/8" l, oval, relief-molded diaper, ozier, and scrolling panels, loop handle 425.00
Syrup pitcher, 6-1/2" h, cylinder shape, relief and blue accented grape-vine design 90.00
Tea caddy, 4-1/4" h, pear shape, latticino dec, knob finial, 18th C 375.00
Teapot, cov, 7" h, ball shape, raised branch dec, bird finial on lid, 18th C 2,850.00

Salts, Open

History: When salt was first mined, the supply was limited and expensive. The necessity for a receptacle in which to serve the salt resulted in the first open salt, a crude, hand-carved, wooden trencher.

As time passed, salt receptacles were refined in style and materials. In the

For more information, see *Warman's Glass*, 4th edition.

1500s, both master and individual salts existed. By the 1700s, firms such as Meissen, Waterford, and Wedgwood were making glass, china, and porcelain salts. Leading glass manufacturers in the 1800s included Libbey, Mount Washington, New England, Smith Bros., Vallerysthal, Wave Crest, and Webb. Many outstanding silversmiths in England, France, and Germany also produced this form.

Open salts were the only means of serving salt until the appearance of the shaker in the late 1800s. The ease of procuring salt from a shaker greatly reduced the use of and need for the open salts.

Note: Salt collecting has been guided by several standard references. One is L. W. and D. B. Neal, *Pressed Glass Dishes Of The Lacy Period 1925-1950,* published by author, 1962. Allan B. and Helen B. Smith have authored and published ten books on open salts beginning with *One Thousand Individual Open Salts Illustrated* (1972) and ending with *1,334 Open Salts Illustrated: The Tenth Book* (1984). Daniel Snyder did the master salt sections in volumes 8 and 9. In 1987 Mimi Rudnick compiled a revised price list for the ten Smith Books. The numbers in parentheses refer to plate numbers in the Smiths' books. The abbreviation "Neal" refers to the book by L. W. and D. B. Neal.

Chinese Export, porcelain, master, oval, scalloped rim, blue under-glaze dec, handpainted polychrome bird and foliage motif over the glaze, scalloped base decorated with blue under-glaze tea leaf accented with red over-glaze painting, ground has slight bluish tint, 3-1/2" l, 2-7/8" w, 1-3/16" h, **$920**. Photo courtesy of Alderfer Auction Co.

Condiment sets with open salts

Doulton Lambeth, stoneware, 1-1/2" open salt, 3" pepper shaker with sterling silver top, c1891-1921, repairs to pepper **165.00**

English, Birks, 2-7/8" l, 2-1/4" w, 2-1/2" h salt with cobalt blue glass liner, matching 4" h pepper shaker, orig spoon, repoussé design with sea shells, lion face and claw feet dec, marked "Birks, Regency Plate, F.S.M. England" **225.00**

German silver, two castors, two salts, two salt spoons, Renaissance style with swan supports, c1900, marked ".800 fine" **800.00**

Limoges, double salt and mustard, sgd "J. M. Limoges" (388) **80.00**

Quimper, double salt and mustard, white, blue, and green floral dec, sgd "Quimper" (388) **120.00**

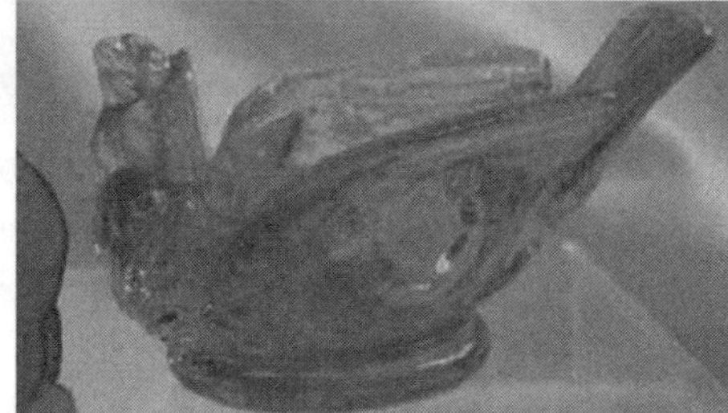

Chicken, Kanawha Glass Co, Dunbar, WV, golden canary yellow, original label, **$12**.

Early American glass

2-5/8" l, colorless, variant, Neal MN3, chips **315.00**

3" x 2" x 2" h, Eagle with shield pattern, colorless, lacy, Sandwich, minor roughness **415.00**

3" l, fiery opaque white, Neal 1, slight roughness **600.00**

3-1/8" l, fiery opalescent, 3-1/8" l, Neal BS2, chips **275.00**

3-1/4" l, fiery opalescent, eagles, Neal EE3b, chips **500.00**

Pearlware, rounded form, medium blue rim band, vertical ribbed dark brown slip dec on white ground, England, early 19th C, 2-1/2" d, **$590.** Photo courtesy of Skinner Auctioneers and Appraisers.

3-3/8" h, cobalt blue, facet cut, fan rim, sq foot, edges ground **125.00**

3-5/8" l, sapphire blue, Neal BT 2, very minor flakes **1,075.00**

Figurals

Basket, 3" h, 2-3/4" d, coral colored glass, SP basket frame, salt with cut polished facets **55.00**

Boat, lacy, colorless, New England, Neal BT-9, slight rim roughness **160.00**

Bucket, 2-1/2" d, 1-5/8" h, Bristol glass, turquoise, white, green, and brown enameled bird, butterfly and trees, SP rim and handle **75.00**

Individual, china, white ground, blue butterfly and floral decoration, red "China" on base, #599, 2-1/4" w, 2" h, **$12**.

Sea horse, Belleek, brilliant turquoise, white base, supports shell salt, first black mark (458) **350.00**

Individual, china, orange basketweave ground, red, and purple flowers, green leaves, marked "Marotomo Ware, Made in Japan," #472, 3" d, **$10**.

Wagon, 3" w, 2" d, 2" h, four molded wheels, star and diamond pattern on stippled background sides, colorless, pressed, old corner repair **230.00**

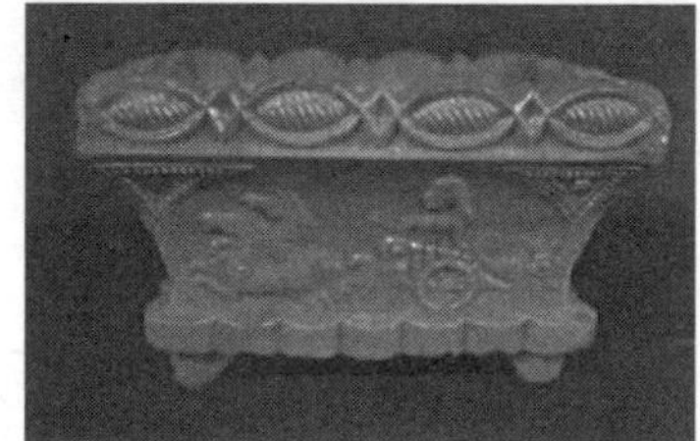

Lacy, Chariot pattern, silvery opaque blue, CT-1, shallow edge damage, 2-7/8" l, **$450**. Photo courtesy of Garth's Auctions, Inc.

Individual

Cambridge, Decagon pattern, amber (468) **42.00**

Cut glass, 2" d, 1-1/2" h, cut ruby ovals, all-over dainty white enameled scrolls, clear ground, gold trim, scalloped top **60.00**

German silver, dolphin feet, 1890-1910 (353) **100.00**

Lead crystal, colorless, English 2-1/4" d, faceted, hallmarked silver rim, orig 2-3/4" l hallmarked salt spoon, Sheffield crown, lion, W&H, letter m for 1904 .... **120.00**

Individual, milk glass, pedestal base, #582, 2-5/8" d, 2" h, **$15**.

3-5/8" l, 2-5/8" w, 1-7/8" h, rect, c1900 .... **60.00**
3-3/4" x 2-3/4" x 1-3/4" h, oval, fluted **90.00**
4-1/2" l, 2-1/2" h, Chippendale style, boat shape, handles, pedestal, c1880-1900 .... **35.00**

Lenox, shell, 1-5/8" w, gold trim, "L" palette mark **25.00**

Mount Washington, blue Johnny Jump-ups, cream ground, raised gold dots on rim **135.00**

Tray lot of colorless individual pattern glass open salts, grouping sold for **$30**.

Pattern glass
Hobnail pattern, vaseline, 3" sq, 1-3/8" h **40.00**
Kenneth, colorless, 4-1/8" l, 2-1/2" h, marked "Krys-tol," c1907-24 .... **15.00**

Purple slag, 3" d, 1-1/4" h, emb shell pattern **50.00**

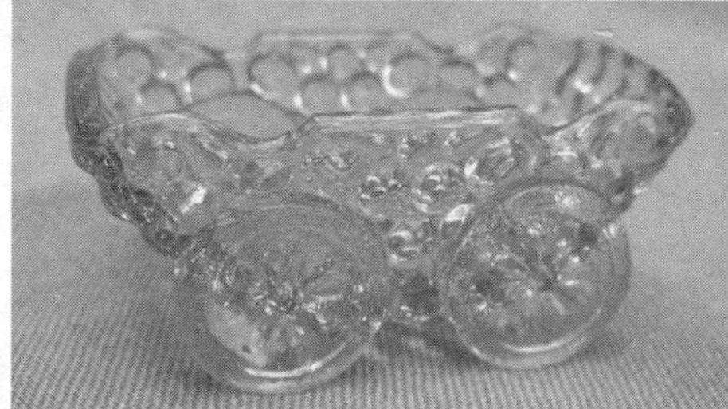
Individual, vaseline glass, carriage shape, #573, 3-1/2" l, 1-7/8" h, **$45.**

Royal Bayreuth, lobster claw (87) **80.00**

Russian, 1-1/4" h, 1-3/4" d, colorless glass liner, gold finished metal, red and white enamel scallop design, Russian hallmarks, c1940 .... **110.00**

Sterling silver, Georg Jensen, Denmark, porringer (238) **200.00**

Intaglios

2-1/2" l, 1-3/4" w, 1" d, aqua blue, octagonal, intaglio of angel sitting on draped column **45.00**
3-1/2" l, 2-3/8" w, 2-5/8" h, rect, colorless, intaglio leaf design **50.00**

China, master salt and six individual oval serving salts, gold floral border and trim, marked "Nippon," **$30**.

Masters

China
Belleek, 4-1/4" l, 3" d, 2" h, boat floating on jelly fish, green mark **60.00**
Lenox, swan, 4" l, 3" h, blue mark **40.00**
Nippon, 3" d, 1-1/2" h, hp, rose motif, jeweled, moriage dec, blue maple leaf mark, c1861 .... **35.00**
Rose Canton, 3-3/4" l, 3-5/8" w, 1-1/16" h, Famille Rose colors, floral, foliage, and bird dec, concave curved sides dec with foliage, flowers, and fruits, gold top rim, green enamel foot rim **490.00**

Cranberry, 3" d, 1-3/4" h, emb ribs, applied crystal ruffed rim, SP holder with emb lions heads **160.00**

Cut glass, 2" d, 2" h, green cut to clear, SP holder **115.00**

Mocha, seaweed band, yellow ware ground, 2" h **250.00**

Master, sterling silver, Faberge, Moscow, c1896-1908, three ball feet, engraved EG monogram, 1-3/4" w, **$900.** Photo courtesy of Sloans & Kenyon Appraisers.

Pattern glass
Basketweave, sleigh (397) **100.00**
Diamond Point, cov **75.00**
Portland, branches handle **110.00**
Snail, ruby stained **75.00**

Pearlware, 2-1/2" d, rounded form, medium blue rim band, vertical ribbed dark brown slip dec on white ground, England, early 19th C **590.00**

Pewter, pedestal, cobalt blue liner (349) **65.00**

Sterling silver, 1-3/4" h, Stieff Co., early 20th C, chased and emb all-over floral pattern, applied floral rim, three scrolled shell feet, pr, 6 troy oz **260.00**

Vaseline, 3" d, 2-1/4" h, applied crystal trim around middle, SP stand **125.00**

Sterling silver, set of 12, porringer shape, by Towle Silversmiths, gold washed interiors, small pierced handle, retailed by Bigelow Kannard & Co., **$175.** Photo courtesy of James D. Julia, Inc.

SAMPLERS

History: Samplers served many purposes. For a young child, they were a practice exercise and permanent reminder of stitches and patterns. For a young woman, they were a means to demonstrate skills in a "gentle" art and a way to record family genealogy. For the mature woman, they were a useful occupation and method of creating gifts or remembrances, e.g., mourning pieces.

Schools for young ladies of the early 19th century prided themselves on the needlework skills they taught. The Westtown School in Chester County, Pennsylvania, and the Young Ladies Seminary in Bethlehem, Pennsylvania, were two institutions. These schools changed their teaching as styles changed. Berlin work was introduced by the mid-19th century.

Examples of samplers date back to the 1700s. The earliest ones were long and narrow, usually done only with the alphabet and numerals. Later examples were square. At the end of the 19th century, the shape tended to be rectangular.

The same motifs were used throughout the country. The name of the person who stitched the piece is a key factor in determining the region.

179-, Sarah Davey, green, ivory, gold, and pink satin and cross-stitch on linen, urns of tulips and other flowers, birds, two story house with fruit trees, strawberry border, verse, and "Sarah Davey 179-," stains and holes, framed, 23-1/2" w, 26-1/2" h **770.00**

Sampler, 1838, silk on linen, wrought by "Mary Mercer…1838 Aged 12 years," alphabet and verse above floral sprays, potted flowers, peacock, turkey, meandering vine border, attributed to Pennsylvania, 19" x 17-1/4", **$1,840.** Photo courtesy of Pook & Pook.

1791, Ann Wilks, green, ivory, gold, blue, and dark blue silk thread, linen, Lord's Prayer, urns of flowers, strawberries, and acorns, "Ann Wilks fecit June 7th, 1791," plain wood frame, few small holes, 14" w, 18-3/4" h **500.00**

1794, M. Gray, alphabets, multicolored floss on tan linen ground, "Done By Me Aged 13, 1794, M. Gray," name "H. Common" with crown, fabric stitched around backing board so some of borders are hidden behind frame, 13-1/3" x 11-1/2".................................... **495.00**

Sampler, silk on linen, wrought by "Susan E. Cutter aged 12," central alphabets within double sawtooth border surmounted by floral vines, New England, 16-1/4" x 15", **$2,300**. Photo courtesy of Pook & Pook.

1795, Lucy Pratt, linen, soft green, tan, and ivory, dark blue, pink, and brown silk thread, vining starflower border with verse, alphabets, man in hat, "Lucy Pratt is my Name, New England is my Station, Mansfield is my Native-Place," finished April 22, 1795, carved maple frame, some running from dark brown, 25-1/4" w, 28-1/2" h **1,100.00**

1796, Susanna Murphy, sgd lower left "Susanna Murphy, Mt Melick Boarding School, 1796," titled within scroll "A Map of England and Wales," black thread on tan silk, red, blue, gold, and yellow outlines, minor thread loss, edge stains, mahogany veneer frame with line border inlay, small chip, 20-1/2" x 18-1/2" **1,200.00**

1843, Margaret Ann McCoy, from "Miss Decker's School," dated January 12, 1843, rose border surrounds alphabet and numbers, over verse "First at ? Shrine devoutly bend/And early make her guardian God thy friend/She'll safely guide thee through the snares of youth/And fix thy weaving steps in paths of truth", peacock in landscape, minor losses, 15" x 17", **$615**. Photo courtesy of Sanford Alderfer Auction Company.

1808, Abigail A Jenney, Plainfield, New Hampshire, three alphabets, trees, various devices, upper and lower borders, silk threads on linen ground, shades of green, yellow, and brown, 4-3/4" x 3-3/4" sight size, 6-3/4" x 5-3/4" frame **2,585.00**

1866, Aeta Frazer, May 31, small embroidered sampler with alphabet and numbers, 7" x 11-1/2", **$120.** Photo courtesy of Joy Luke Auctions.

1809, Elizabeth H. Kay's Work, 1809, PA, family register surrounded by foliate, bird, and geometric motifs, inspirational verses, lower panel of various animals among trees, meandering and geometric floral borders, framed, 21-5/8" x 22-3/4", toning, scattered staining, fading **3,750.00**

1809, Waterford Township School Elizabeth Homer Kay's Work Wrought in the Year 1809, PA, alphabets above inspirational verses, geometric floral borders, framed, 17" x 16-1/4", minor toning, staining......................... **2,990.00**

1814, Ann Broadbent, satin, chain, and tiny cross-stitch on line, shade of blue, pink, ivory, yellow, brown, and green silk thread, multicolored strawberry border with birds, butterflies, trees, angels, verse "The Rose of Sharon," and "Ann Broadbent, hir (sic) work done in the year of our Lord 1814 aged 12 years," minor thread loss, stain, faux tortoise shell shadow box frame, gold repaint, 16" w, 19" h.. **1,320.00**

Sampler, Victorian, wool on linen needlework, wrought by "Rebecca Pursel Age 11," figure and landscape, "We Hope to Meet," 12-1/2" x 12-3/4", **$300.** Photo courtesy of Pook & Pook.

1822, Mary C. Root, silk thread on linen, alphabets in shades of blue and brown, house, hearts, birds, and shepherdess with sheep in greens, pinks, ivory, and brown, "Mary C. Root Royalton born March 14th 1822," gold painted frame, 19-3/4" w, 18" h, light stains, two bird stitched in wool may be later additions **525.00**

1823, Ann Smith, shades of pink, green, brown, black, and soft orange silk thread on linen, alphabet, verse, strawberries, birds, deer, dogs, Adam and Eve near the apple tree, "Ann Smith Aged 11 Norton 1823," stains, black painted frame with gilt liner, wear, 14-1/2" w, 19" h **935.00**

1828, Wilhelmina Nicholas Work, green and brown floss on natural, sgd, verse, meandering floral vine border, four baskets of fruit and flowers, cloth tape edge binding, mahogany veneer frame with edge chips, small holes, minor stains, word "My" added later within verse, 15-3/4" x 20-3/4"................. **550.00**

1843, Doddiscombsleigh, Feb. 23, on linen, religious poem, petit-point floral border, framed, fabric losses **2,400.00**

1849, Sarah Wilshaw, needlepoint, colorful little girl with her dog, seated in garden with poem above that reads "Our days are as the grass, Or like the morning flower; If one sharp blast sweep oer the field, It withers in an hour," colorful chain of flowers border, flame mahogany ogee frame, gold leaf liner, 12-1/2" x 14", **$350.** Photo courtesy of Cowan's Historic Americana Auctions.

1850, O.B., alternating rows of large and small vining and flowers, burgundy, tan, green, black, and blue on white, small girl with cat or dog on leash, bird, monkey, small restorations, few stains, reduced in size along left margin, 13" x 14-1/4", date is later addition........ **440.00**

1851, needlepoint, red house, trees with red birds, domestic scenes, scrolling vine border, wide wood frame, minor discoloration................................ **125.00**

Late 18th C, Cynthia Taft, Uxbridge, MA, pink and green floral vine encloses verse worked in pink linen above pictorial lower half with garden, trees, flowers, birds, and grass, pink, green, and red hues, good coloration and condition, reframed, minor imperfections, 10-5/8" w, 12" h, **$4,115.** Photo courtesy of Skinner Auctioneers and Appraisers.

Undated

Unsigned, green, red, brown, tan, silver, and blue floss, natural linen, six birds within trees surrounding two flowering plants in urns, "On Virtue" verse at top surrounded by thin green border, two crowns, floral zigzag border, fanciful flowers in urn, baskets, central bouquet, 20th C curly maple frame, small moth holes, 19-1/4" x 17-1/4"..................... **990.00**

Weekes, Jane, tiny precise stitches, shades of green, ivory, pale gold, brown, and dark blue silk threads on linen, trees, flowers, vining border, man and woman with dog and bird on either side of urn, verse and "Done by Jane Weekes at E. Mardon's School, Aged 11 years, November 15th," framed, nailed to stretcher, few holes, 10-1/2" w, 14" h **1,210.00**

Sandwich Glass

History: In 1818, Deming Jarves was listed in the Boston Directory as a glass factor. That same year, he was appointed general manager of the newly formed New England Glass Company. In 1824, Jarves toured the glassmaking factories in Pittsburgh, left New England Glass Company, and founded a glass factory in Sandwich.

For more information, see *Warman's Glass*, 4th edition.

Originally called the Sandwich Manufacturing Company, it was incorporated in April 1826 as the Boston & Sandwich Glass Company. From 1826 to 1858, Jarves served as general manager. The Boston & Sandwich Glass Company produced a wide variety of wares in differing levels of quality. The factory used the free-blown, blown three mold, and pressed glass manufacturing techniques. Both clear and colored glass were used.

Competition in the American glass industry in the mid-1850s resulted in lower-quality products. Jarves left the Boston & Sandwich company in 1858, founded the Cape Cod Glass Company, and tried to duplicate the high quality of the earlier glass. Meanwhile, at the Boston & Sandwich Glass Company, emphasis was placed on mass production. The development of a lime glass (non-flint) led to lower costs for pressed glass. Some free-blown and blown-and-molded pieces, mostly in color, were made. Most of this Victorian-era glass was enameled, painted, or acid etched.

By the 1880s, the Boston & Sandwich Glass Company was operating at a loss. Labor difficulties finally resulted in the closing of the factory on January 1, 1888.

Bowl, Gothic paneled arches, hexagonal, clambroth.................................... **150.00**

Butter dish, cov, colorless, flint, Gothic pattern.. **225.00**

Cologne bottle, stopper, blown molded, yellow, Star and Punty pattern, polished pontil, 1841-70, imperfections, 7-3/8" h, **$450.** Photo courtesy of Skinner, Inc.

Candlesticks, pr

8-3/8" h, translucent blue socket, hexagonal clambroth shaft, stepped base, c1840-60, chips on base **765.00**

Candlesticks, pair, flint, amber, hexagonal form, 7-1/2" h, **$400.** Photo courtesy of Cowan's Historic Americana Auctions.

9-3/4" h, canary, petal sockets, dolphin standards, double-step sq bases, c1845-70, minor roughness at underside of one petal and base edge..................................... **825.00**

Champagne, Sandwich Star........ **850.00**

Creamer, blown, translucent clambroth vessel, applied blue handle, green disk base, attributed to end-of-day glassmaker's whimsy, 19th C, 4" h, **$275.** Photo courtesy of Skinner, Inc.

Creamer and sugar, colorless, flint, Gothic pattern **175.00**

Cup plate, lacy, blue, ship **125.00**

Decanter, 6-3/4" h, cobalt blue, ribbed, tam o'shanter stopper................... **195.00**

Decanters, matching stopper, sunburst and waffle design, other scrolls and ribs design, both 9" h, **$250**. Photo courtesy of James D. Julia, Inc.

Dish, 4-1/4" d, 1" h, small scalloped rim, sunburst with nineteen rays on bottom, opalescent, edge rim roughness ... **90.00**
Fluid lamp, 9-1/2" h, mottled blue, Star and Punty pattern font, hexagonal standard and base, brass fitting, 1840-65, very minor base chips, price for pr **7,050.00**
Goblet, colorless, flint, Gothic pattern, 12-pc set **650.00**
Inkwell, 2-9/16", cylindrical-domed form, colorless, pink and white stripes, sheared mouth, applied pewter collar and cap, smooth base **2,300.00**

Decanter, blown three-mold, colorless, quart, Arch and Fern leaf pattern bottle with medallion formed by entwined serpents containing the word "RUM," blown three-mold diagonal ribbed stopper, McKearin GIV-7, 1825-35, 10-5/8" h, **$450.** Photo courtesy of Skinner, Inc.

Pitcher, 10" h, Amberina Verde, fluted top **525.00**
Plate, 6" d, lacy, Shell pattern **175.00**
Pomade, cov, figural, bear, imp retailer's name, 3-3/4" h, clambroth, imp "F. B. Strouse, N.Y.," chips **525.00**
Salt, cov, 3" w, 2" d, 3" h, Beaded Scroll and Basket of Flowers pattern, colorless, lacy, pinecone finial, small chips to cover rim, minor roughness on base...... **815.00**

Miniatures, pair 2" h vaseline candlesticks, 1" clear chamber stick, **$550.** Photo courtesy of James D. Julia, Inc.

Salt, open, 3" x 2" x 2" h, Eagle with shield pattern, colorless, lacy, minor roughness **415.00**
Spooner, colorless, flint, Gothic pattern **85.00**
Sugar, cov, 6-1/4" h, pressed, Loop pattern, canary yellow, seven elongated petals in base, hexagonal top on lid, one rim chip on cov, two chips and top roughness on base **350.00**
Undertray, Heart, lacy, flint.......... **400.00**

Vase, trumpet, amethyst and colorless, gauffered rim, slightly twisted eight-panel vase, pestle stem fluted on inside, square base, 1840-60, McKearin plate 195, couple minor small base cracks, 10-1/8" h, **$5,000.** Photo courtesy of Skinner, Inc.

Vase, 4-3/4" h, pressed, Elongated Loop with Bisecting Lines pattern, fiery opalescent, six flaring petals as rim, hexagonal base, no wafer, very small open bubble with side fleck on base **635.00**
Whiskey taster, cobalt blue, nine panels **175.00**

Sarreguemines China

History: Sarreguemines ware is a faience porcelain, i.e., tin-glazed earthenware. The factory that made it was established in Lorraine, France, in 1770, under the supervision of Utzschneider and Fabry. The factory was regarded as one of the three most prominent manufacturers of French faience. Most of the wares found today were made in the 19th century.

Marks: Later wares are impressed "Sarreguemines" and "Germany" as a result of changes in international boundaries.

Jug, modeled as head of bewigged 18th C, gentlemen, majolica, c1900, printed mark, 6-1/2" h, **$350.** Photo courtesy of David Rago Auctions.

Basket, 9" h, quilted, green, heavy leopard skin crystallization........... **250.00**
Centerpiece, 14-3/4" h, 14-3/4" d, bowl with pierced ringlets to sides, supported by center stem flanked by sea nymphs either side, mounted atop circular base on four scrolled feet, polychrome dec, imp marks, chips, restorations, c1875 .... **900.00**
Cup and saucer, Orange, majolica, crack to one cup, nicks, set of four **200.00**
Face jug, 8" h, majolica, jovial man, green hat, imp "Sarreguemines, France 652" **200.00**

Vase, pair, earthenware, Aesthetic Movement, ovoid, body printed and enamel decoration with morning glories and butterflies on green ground, against vertical brown panels, quatrefoil borders, rim with band of butterflies, gilt accenting, early 20th C, 17" h, **$2,000.** Photo courtesy of Skinner, Inc.

Garniture, Art Nouveau faience, 10-3/4" h pr of vases, shouldered trumpet form, shaped oval centerpiece bowl, each with wide gilt band of foliage within diamond borders centered by decorative medallion, verte ground **350.00**
Humidor, man with top hat, majolica **195.00**

Plate, 7-1/2" d, dec with music and characters from French children's songs, 12-pc set **375.00**

Oyster plate, majolica, six shell-form oyster wells, glazed in pastel colors, printed mark, c1920, 9-1/2" d, **$125.** Photo courtesy of David Rago Auctions.

Tankard, cov, 11" h, stoneware, continuous country scene of dancing and celebrating villagers, branch handle, pewter lid with porcelain medallion and painted polychrome coat of arms, dated 1869... **325.00**

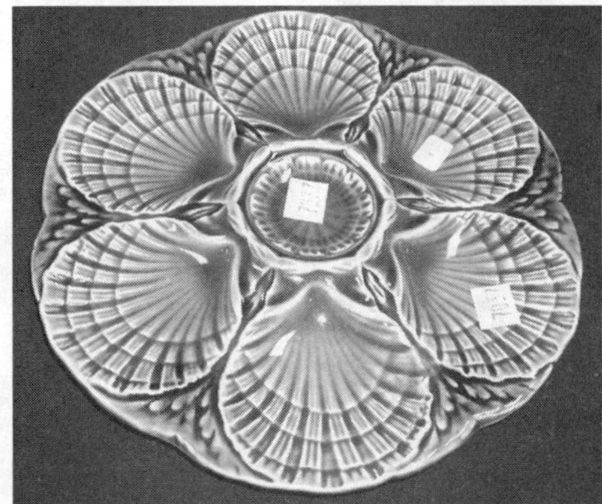

Oyster plate, majolica, six shell-form oyster wells, center well, golds and browns, green seaweed decoration, printed mark, 9-1/2" d, **$150.**

Urn, 31-1/4" h, gilt metal mounted majolica, baluster form, cobalt blue glazed, mounted with the figure of a crowned lion holding sword, lion and mask handled sides, pierced foliate rim, raised on four scrolling foliate cast feet, imp "Majolica Sarreguemines," second half 19th C **1,800.00**

Sarsaparilla Bottles

History: Sarsaparilla refers to the fragrant roots of a number of tropical American, spiny, woody vines of the lily family. An extract was obtained from these dried roots and used for medicinal purposes. The first containers, which date from the 1840s, were stoneware; glass bottles were used later.

Carbonated water often was added to sarsaparilla to make a soft drink or to make consuming it more pleasurable. For this reason, sarsaparilla and soda became synonymous even though they originally were two different concoctions.

Dr. J. Townsend Sarsaparilla New York, applied top, graphite pontil, amber variant 9-1/2" h, cleaned, **$850.** Photo courtesy American Bottle Auctions.

Brown's Sarsaparilla, aqua............. **12.00**
Compound Extract of Sarsaparilla, amber, gallon............................... **140.00**
Dalton's Sarsaparilla and Nerve Tonic, blue label...................................... **40.00**
Dr. Beldings Wild Cherry Sarsaparilla, Dr. Belding Medicine Co, Minneapolis, MN, aqua, complete label, orig contents, orig fancy box (top missing), 9-1/4" h **180.00**
Dr. Guysott's Compound Extract of Yellow Dock and Sarsaparilla, peacock green, sloping lip, iron pontil, 9" h **1,350.00**
Dr. Henry's Sarsaparilla, 9-1/2" h, applied top, deep green, late 1870s.......... **80.00**
Dr. Ira Belding's, Honduras Sarsaparilla, colorless, 10-1/2" h......................... **30.00**
Dr. J. Townsend Sarsaparilla, Albany, NY, crudely whittled
- 9-1/4" h, applied top, smooth base, brilliant green **550.00**
- 9-1/2" h, applied top, graphite pontil, amber variant **3,600.00**
- 9-1/2" h, applied top, sticky ball pontil, olive green with some amber **350.00**

Foley's Sarsaparilla........................ **20.00**
Guysott's Yellow Dock & Sarsaparilla **40.00**
John Bull Extract of Sarsaparilla, Louisville, 9" h, applied top, smooth base, bluish-green, crudely whittled, int. open bubble back mid side......... **375.00**
Lancaster Glassworks, barrel, golden amber **125.00**
Log Cabin, 9" h amber bottle sealed with orig contents, orig box **1,050.00**
Sand's Sarsparilla Genuine, NY, 9-3/4" h, applied top, smooth base, colorless, partial open bubble on left shoulder...................................... **100.00**
Sawyers Eclipse, aqua.................. **35.00**

Satin Glass

History: Satin glass, produced in the late 19th century, is an opaque art glass with a velvety matte (satin) finish achieved through treatment with hydrofluoric acid. A large majority of the pieces were cased or had a white lining.

For more information, see *Warman's Glass*, 4th edition.

While working at the Phoenix Glass Company, Beaver, Pennsylvania, Joseph Webb perfected mother-of-pearl (MOP) satin glass in 1885. Similar to plain satin glass in respect to casing, MOP satin glass has a distinctive surface finish and an integral or indented design, the most well known being diamond quilted (DQ).

The most common colors are yellow, rose, or blue. Rainbow coloring is considered choice.

Additional Listings: Cruets, Fairy Lamps, Miniature Lamps, and Rose Bowls.

Reproduction Alert: Satin glass, in both the plain and mother-of-pearl varieties, has been widely reproduced.

Perfume bottle, Birmingham, England, c1895, narrow neck on bulbed vessel, pulled loop decoration in peach and yellow on white ground, mounted foliate silver lid and ring, struck with lion, anchor, and two maker's touchmarks "CS FS," 6-1/2" h, **$500.** Photo courtesy of Skinner, Inc.

Bowl, 4-1/2" h, 2-3/4" h, MOP, cased, blue shading to white, white int., Coinspot pattern, faint flowering branch dec **75.00**
Bride's basket, 15-1/2" h, deep rose, enamel swan and floral dec, heavy bronze holder with birds perched at top **450.00**
Celery vase, 5" h, MOP, cased blue, Herringbone pattern, waisted squared body **200.00**
Creamer and sugar bowl, 4-1/2" d, 4-1/2" h, MOP, cased pink, DQ, tightly crimped rim, ground pontil........... **350.00**
Cup and saucer, Raindrop MOP, pink to white, 3" h cup, 5" d saucer.......... **385.00**
Epergne, 13-3/4" h, 10" d, pink and white, hobnail bowl, resilvered base and lily vase holder............................. **395.00**

Ewer, 9-1/2" h, cased blue ground, enameled bird, coralene trailing branch with leaves **70.00**

Pink satin glass dresser set: powder jar, covered, cosmetic jar, covered, perfume bottle, with figural crown stopper, gold trim, wear to gold, **$175.** Photo courtesy of Joy Luke Auctions.

Mustard pot, 2-1/2" h, bright yellow, gold prunus dec, SP top, Webb **450.00**

Table lamp, green, molded cupid heads on font and globe shade, 27" h, **$950.** Photo courtesy of Joy Luke Auctions.

Rose bowl, 5-1/2" h, MOP, DQ, shaded purple to white **210.00**

Salt shaker, 3-1/4" h, rose shaded to white, MOP, DQ, tapered barrel, orig two-pc lid **550.00**

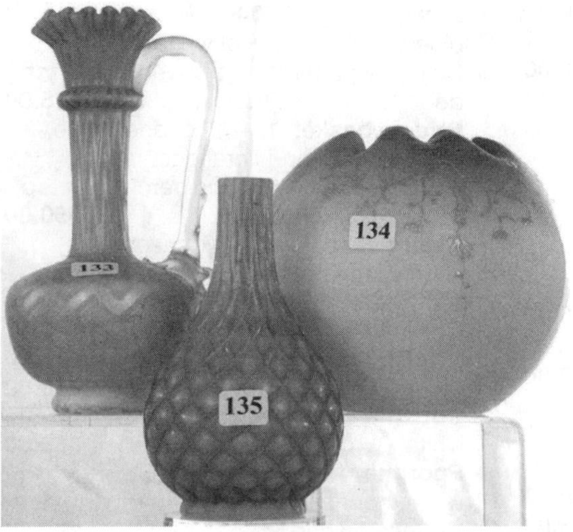

Left, ewer, Zig-zag pattern, blue, frosted handle, 8" h, **$90;** right: rose bowl, blue, yellow floral decoration, 5-1/2" d, **$100;** center: vase, cut-velvet satin, teardrop shape, blue, 6-1/2" h, **$75.** Photo courtesy of Woody Auctions.

Sugar shaker, 6-1/4" h, blue, Raindrop, MOP, SP top **425.00**

Tumbler, 3-3/4" h, rainbow DQ, bands of blue, pink, and yellow swirl over molded in tufts, gold buttons, narrow band of bright raised gold enamel stylized florals at rim **575.00**

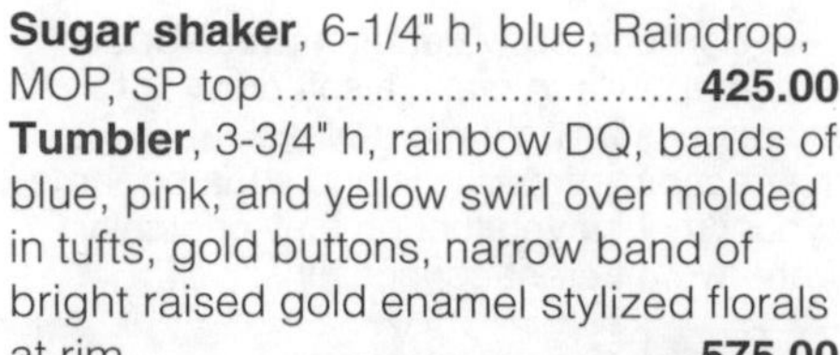

Water pitcher, Coin Spot, red shading to white, ruffled top, applied frosted reeded handle, 8-1/2" h, **$350.** Photo courtesy of James D. Julia, Inc.

Vase

5-1/2" h, Pompeian swirl, pale blue, MOP, soft pale blue int. **500.00**

7-1/2" h, 4 1/2" d, DQ pattern, sq ruffled top, orange shading to opalescent, engraved silver plated holder with flowers, leaves, cherries, and birds **600.00**

8" h, cranberry shading to white, rim possibly ground **40.00**

9" h, Zipper pattern, shading from brown to white, pink int., MOP, English **1,250.00**

12" h, pink shading to gray, applied rigaree handle, ground pontil, Victorian **115.00**

12-1/2" h, DQ, lavender **520.00**

Tumbler, Rainbow, bands of blue, pink, and yellow swirl over molded-in tufts, lace-like narrow band of bright raised gold enamel encircles rim, 3-7/8" h, **$500.** Photo courtesy of Clarence and Betty Maier.

SATSUMA

History: Satsuma, named for a war lord who brought skilled Korean potters to Japan in the early 1600s, is a hand-crafted Japanese faience (tin-glazed) pottery. It is finely crackled, has a cream, yellow-cream, or gray-cream color, and is decorated with raised enamels in floral, geometric, and figural motifs.

Figural satsuma was made specifically for export in the 19th century. Later satsuma, referred to as satsuma-style ware, is a Japanese porcelain also hand decorated in raised enamels. From 1912 to the present, satsuma-style ware has been mass-produced. Much of the ware on today's market is of this later period.

Bowl, Japanese, Showa period, 9-3/4" d, **$300.** Photo courtesy of Sloans & Kenyon Auctions.

Bowl, 4-3/4" d, design of women and children viewing cherry blossoms, sgd, early 20th C **250.00**

Bowl, design of women and children viewing cherry blossoms, early 20th C, signed, 4-3/4" d, **$250.** Photo courtesy of Skinner Auctioneers and Appraisers.

Pair of miniature vases, three sages on one side, priestess surrounded by four sages on other, gilt dragon handles, red and gold royal mark on base, 3-3/4" h, **$165.** Photo courtesy of Cowan's Historic Americana Auctions.

Cache pot, 6-1/2" h, figural and landscape scene.......................... **120.00**

Censor, 10-1/4" h, tapering rect form, lobed base, two squared handles, pierced domed lid, all-over dec or Arhats, Meiji period................................ **635.00**

Censor, earthenware, ovoid, tripod, fu dog head form handles, floral decoration, Japanese, Meiji period, 5" h, **$500.** Photo courtesy of Sloans & Kenyon Auctions.

Cup and saucer, bird and floral motif, cobalt blue border, Kinkozan, Japanese **115.00**

Dish, fan shape, pottery, Japan, 20th C **850.00**

Incense burner, 5" d, two reserves, one with sparrows and flowers, other of Mijo shrine, borders of brocade patterns, butterflies caught in net, and hanging jewels, sgd "Kinkozan," Meiji period, 1868-1911 .... **5,500.00**

Jar, cov, 4" d, 6" h, two cartouche panels, one of Samurai, other with birds, insects, and flowers, one side ring missing**230.00**

Koro, pierced lid, 3" h, hexagonal, six bracket feet, each side with flowers blooming behind garden fences, domed lid, sgd with Shimazu mon **2,185.00**

Saki bottle, 6" h, two cartouches of Samurai, 19th C........................... **115.00**

Vase, ovoid, earthenware, ribbed body, Immortals and geisha decoration, Japanese, Meiji period, 10" h, **$600.** Photo courtesy of Sloan's Auctioneers & Appraisers.

Tea bowl, 4-3/4" d, dec with butterflies, powdered gold ground, sgd "Kinkozan," Japan, Meiji period, 1868-1911.... **350.00**

Tea cup and saucer, 1-3/4" h cup, 4-3/4" d saucer, colorful groups of flowerheads with scrolling gilt vines, minor gilt wear, sgd "Yabu Meizan" **900.00**

Tea set, 6-1/2" h teapot, creamer, sugar, six cups and saucers, 6 7-1/4" d plates, paneled designs of courtesans in courtyard settings, c1900............ **290.00**

Vessel, decorated with allover florals, saucer form on three feet, signed on underside, lid broken, 1-1/2" d top opening, 5" d base, 2" h, **$210.** Photo courtesy of Sanford Alderfer Auction Company.

Tray, 11-1/2" d, rounded form with indented edge, design of scrolls of birds, flowers, and women, cobalt ground with gold bamboo, sgd with imp seal "Kinkozan," Japan, Meiji period, 1868-1911.. **1,650.00**

Urn, 37-1/2" h, dragon handles, geishas in landscape................................ **295.00**

Vase, ovoid form, scene having many figures, reverse with floral decoration, unmarked, crazed, 7" h, **$100.** Photo courtesy of Alderfer Auction Co.

Vase, roundels with children and sages, floral borders, 19th C, 6" h, **$415.** Photo courtesy of Skinner, Inc.

Vase

- 10" h, ovoid, earthenware, ribbed body, immortals and geisha dec, Japan, Meiji period................ **600.00**
- 18-1/2" h, drum-shaped body with trumpet mouth and foot, molded dec of various birds and flowering cherry branches, Japan, Meiji period, 1868-1911, minor loss.................... **950.00**

Scales

History: Prior to 1900, the simple balance scale was commonly used for measuring weights. Since then, scales have become more sophisticated in design and more accurate.

Apothecary, walnut, fitted ivory dec, 19-1/2" l, 15-3/4" h **250.00**

Egg

- Acme Egg Grading, 1924 ....**55.00**
- Sears and Roebuck Farm Master, colorful enameled dial with egg grades, Extra Large, Large..." **85.00**
- Zenith, cast iron, some losses **45.00**

Small brass shop counter scale with wooden stand & drawer, **$175.** Photo courtesy of Joy Luke Auctions.

Gold, emb eagle on top of case, CA, dated 1853 on bottom................. **315.00**

Grain, Fairbanks, Chonodrometer, brass, arm graduated for "lbs per bush," "lb & oz," and "% of lb," sliding weight, bucket, and suspension ring, 11" l **350.00**

Jewelry, Becker & Sons, NY, precision balance beam, mahogany case, glazed panels, 19th C, 15" x 19" **230.00**

Letter scale, 3-1/4" h, bronze, Zodiac pattern, graduated markings on front, marked "CRESCENT PATENTS PENDING," base imp "TIFFANY STUDIOS NEW YORK 874," minor wear to patina and front panel **920.00**

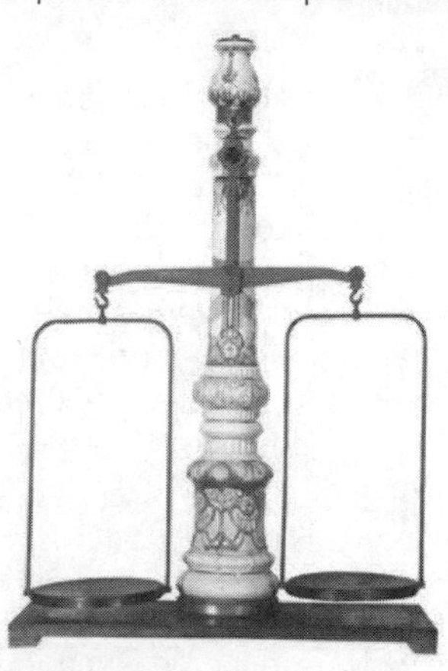

Shop scales, Majolica central support, brass pans and chains, German, 45" h, **$1,450.** Photo courtesy of Joy Luke Auctions.

Miniature, sterling silver, scalloped base, ivory insert with weight indicators, impressed marks for Birmingham, England, 1900-1901, numbers worn off, 3-1/8" h, **$150.** Photo courtesy of Alderfer Auction Co.

Postal

English, for American market, 1840s, candlestick-style, gilt metal, circular pan with scrolled foliate borders, red enameled stem, trellis work and C-scrolls, rate table with eagle dec, circular foot modeled in high relief with locomotive, steam clipper and farm implements interspersed with cornucopia, 7-3/4" h **275.00**

S. Mordan & Co., England, 19th C, plates with blue and white Wedgwood jasper neoclassical roundels in ropetwist surround, rect base with three weights, 4-1/2" h, 6-3/4" l, ... **350.00**

Store type

Dayton, Moneyweight, country store counter, painted cast iron base, glass shelf, beveled glass rear windows, brass trim, patented March 6th, 1917, 19" w, 20" d, 31" h, professional restoration, gilt lettering **635.00**

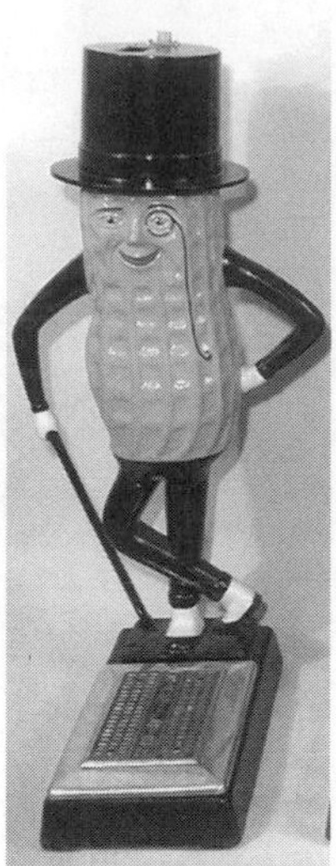

Planter's Peanut, exact duplicate of Mr. Peanut mounted to old Hamilton scale mechanism, c1960, 44" h, **$3,165.** Photo courtesy of James D. Julia, Inc.

Detectomatic, hanging, chrome framed circular scale, glass front, and mounting armature **150.00**

Hanson Weightmaster, cast iron, gold case with ground, black lettering and indicator, 6" x 14" x 10" **45.00**

Harvard, tip balance table top **65.00**

Way Rite, table top **80.00**

SCHLEGELMILCH PORCELAINS

History: Erdmann Schlegelmilch founded his porcelain factory in Suhl in the Thuringia region in 1861. Reinhold, his brother, established a porcelain factory at Tillowitz in Upper Silesia in 1869. In the 1860s, Prussia controlled Thuringia and Upper Silesia, both rich in the natural ingredients needed for porcelain.

By the late 19th century, an active export business was conducted with the United States and Canada due to a large supply of porcelain at reasonable costs achieved through industrialization and cheap labor.

The Suhl factory ceased production in 1920, unable to recover from the effects of World War I. The Tillowitz plant, located in an area of changing international boundaries, finally came under Polish socialist government control in 1956.

For more information, see *Warman's English & Continental Pottery & Porcelain*, 3rd edition.

Marks: Both brothers marked their pieces with the "RSP" mark, a designation honoring Rudolph Schlegelmilch, their father. More than 30 mark variations have been discovered.

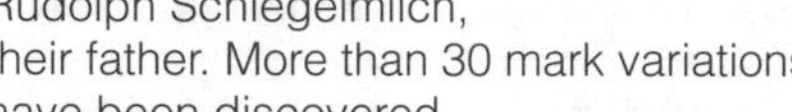

Reproduction Alert: Many "fake" Schlegelmilch pieces are appearing on the market. These reproductions have new decal marks, transfers, or recently hand-painted animals on old, authentic R. S. Prussia pieces.

Reproduction Alert: Dorothy Hammond in her 1979 book, *Confusing Collectibles*, illustrates an R. S. Prussia decal that was available from a china-decorating supply company for $14 a sheet. This was the first of several fake R. S. Prussia reproduction marks that have caused confusion among collectors. Acquaint yourself with some of the subtle distinctions between fake and authentic marks as described in the following.

The period mark consists of a wreath that is open at the top. A five-pointed star sits in the opening. An "R" and an "S" flank a wreath twig in the center. The word "Prussia" is located beneath. In the period mark, the leg of the letter "P" extends down past the letter "r." In the reproduction mark, it does not. In the period mark, the letter "I" is dotted. It is dotted in some fake marks, but not in others.

The "R" and the "S" in the period mark are in a serif face and uniform in width. One fake mark uses a lettering style that utilizes a thin/thick letter body. The period mark has a period after the word "Prussia." Some fake marks fail to include it. Several fake marks do not include the word "Prussia" at all.

The period mark has a fine centerline within each leaf of the wreath. Several fake marks do not.

R.S. Germany

Biscuit jar, cov, 6" h, loop handles, roses dec, satin finish, gold knob **95.00**

Bowl, 5-3/4" d, scenic, bird dec, Prov. Saxe E.S. mark **35.00**

Cake plate, 11" l, lilac dec, floral scrolled mark, unmarked **70.00**

Calling card receiver

5-1/2" l, hp leaf form mold, unmarked **60.00**

5-1/2" l, hp lily form mold, blue R.S. Germany mark 40.00
7" l, red and yellow roses, green mark 35.00

Celery tray, 11" l, 5-3/4" w, lily dec, gold rim, open handles, blue label....... 120.00
Cup and saucer, plain mold, swan, blue water, mountain and brown castle background, RM.......................... 225.00
Demitasse cup and saucer, 3" h, pink roses, gold-stenciled dec, satin finish, blue mark...................................... 90.00
Dresser tray, 11" l, scrolled and emb floral mold, unmarked.................... 85.00
Hatpin holder, floral dec 95.00
Lemon plate, cutout handle shaped as colorful parrot, white ground, gold trim, artist sgd "B. Hunter" 60.00

R. S. Germany, cheese keeper, white and yellow flowers, brown centers, green leaves, peach colored ground, gold trim, marked, **$115**.

Muffineer, 4" h, floral dec, gold steeple mark.. 70.00
Nappy, 8" d, stage coach scene, Prov. Saxe E.S. mark 70.00
Plate, 8-1/2" d, floral dec, emb molds, red RSP mark, pr 140.00
Powder box, cov, 4" l, white roses, Art Deco mold, blue RSG mark........... 35.00

E.S. Germany, double-handled urn mounted on coonforming porcelain squared pillar, pale green to light yellow body, hand-painted gilt accents, oval portrait panels of women, marked "Prov. Saxe E.S. Germany," wear, chip on base of urn, 17-1/2" total height, **$275**. Photo courtesy of Sanford Alderfer Auction Company.

Punch bowl, 17-1/4" d, 8" h, mahogany shading to pink, polychrome enameled flowers with gilt, imp fleur-de-lis mark with "J. S. Germany" 275.00
Sauce dish, underplate, green, yellow roses, blue mark........................... 45.00
Tea tile, peach and tan, greenish white snowballs, RM over faint blue mark 165.00
Vase, 4-1/2" h, purple violets dec, Prov. Saxe E.S. mark, pr......................... 80.00

R. S. Poland

Calling card receiver, 6" l, heart shaped mold 344, handle, red mark 60.00
Creamer and sugar, 8" l, white roses dec, fitted silver plate caddy, red RSP mark... 65.00
Dresser set, glossy, pink roses, pr 6-1/4" h candlesticks, 5" h hatpin holder, 13" x 9" tray.................................. 425.00
Flower holder, pheasants, brass frog insert... 675.00

R.S. Prussia covered biscuit jar, decorated with pink flowers; R.S. Prussia bowl decorated with pink flowers, daisies and stream, molded scalloped rim, damaged at rim, 11" d, **$200**. Photo courtesy of Joy Luke Auctions.

Vase

8-1/2" h, 4-3/4" d, large white and tan roses, shaded brown and green ground.................................. 195.00
12" h, 6-1/4" d, white poppies, cream shaded to brown ground, pr 750.00

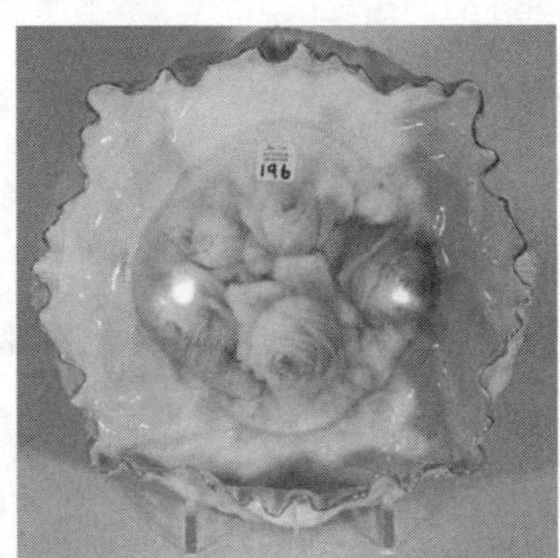

R.S. Prussia, bowl, cabbage leaf design, pink roses, 9-1/2" d, 3-1/2" h, **$200**. Photo courtesy of Joy Luke Auctions.

R. S. Prussia

Berry set, 11" d master bowl, four individual bowls, rose dec, satin finish, mold 279, red mark, one individual bowl repaired 320.00

R.S. Prussia bowl decorated with pink and yellow roses, molded iris border, 10-1/2" d, matching two-handled dish with molded poppy border, 9-1/4" l, **$250**. Photo courtesy of Joy Luke Auctions.

Bowl

9-1/4" d, cranberry colored florals, cranberry ground, Iris mold 25 .... 350.00
10" d, multicolored blossoms, mold 128, red mark 490.00
10" d, multicolored florals, mold 86, unmarked 350.00
10" d, red florals, olive green accents, mold 79, red mark ... 490.00
10" d, red poppies, blue ground, mold 90 .... 175.00
10" d, red roses, satin finish, mold 128, red mark 260.00

Cake plate

10" d, multi-floral dec, mold 91, red mark 435.00
11" d, pink roses, gilt foliage, mold 9 .... 460.00

Celery tray

Hanging basket dec, mold 155, red mark 210.00
Melon Eaters, surrounded by portrait medallions, black accents, gold trim 1,800.00

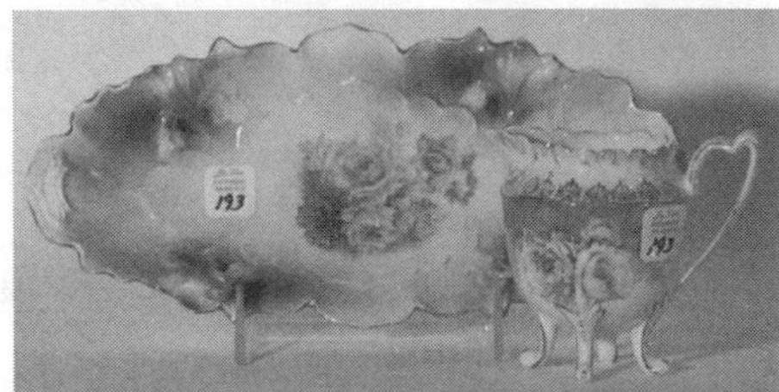

R.S. Prussia, footed creamer; two-handled oval celery dish, both decorated with roses, **$95**. Photo courtesy of Joy Luke Auctions.

Cider pitcher, 9" h, red mark, professional repair....................... 175.00
Cracker jar, 7" h, autumn figural décor, Iris mold 628............................ 1,035.00
Creamer and sugar

5" h, floral spray dec, blue arched panel, unmarked 115.00
5" h, steeple scene, red mark, minor professional repair 230.00

R.S. Prussia, plate, three swimming swans decoration, 9" d, **$250**. Photo courtesy of Joy Luke Auctions.

Dresser tray, 11-1/2" l, red roses, carnation mold 28, red mark **200.00**
Egg box, cov, 4-3/4" l, rose band dec, red mark **115.00**

R.S. Prussia, dresser tray, pink and apricot roses, white daisies, two handles, 7-1/2" w, 11-1/2" l, **$100**. Photo courtesy of Joy Luke Auctions.

Hatpin holder with pin tray, hp **290.00**
Pitcher, 9-3/4" h, four fruits dec, mold 584, c1900, unmarked **375.00**
Plate, 8-1/2" d, Melon Eaters, keyhole medallion **900.00**

R. S. Prussia, chocolate set, chocolate pot, four cups and saucers, white ground, purple violets, green leaves, gold trim, **$295**.

Shaving mug, 3-1/2" h, floral dec, Fleur-de-lis mold 609, red mark **115.00**
Spoon holder, 14" l, pink and white roses **200.00**
Tankard, 11" h, Carnation mold, white, all-over pink poppies, Tiffany carnations, satin finish, RM **1,100.00**
Tea set, floral dec, mold 664, professional repair to teapot lid, unmarked **210.00**
Vase, 6" h, poppies and snowball dec, red mark **265.00**

R. S. Suhl

Coffee set, 9" h, coffeepot, creamer, sugar, six cups and saucers, figural scenes dec, some marked "Angelica Kauffmann" **1,750.00**
Pin tray, 4-1/2" d, round, Nightwatch **375.00**
Plate, 6-3/4" d, cherubs dec **90.00**
Vase, 8" h, four pheasants, green mark **275.00**

R. S. Tillowitz

Bowl, 7-3/4" d, slanted sides, open handles, four leaf-shaped feet, matte finish, pale green ground, roses and violets, gold flowered rim, marked **125.00**
Creamer and sugar, soft yellow and salmon roses **65.00**
Plate, 6-1/2" d, mixed floral spray, gold beading, emb rim, brown wing mark **120.00**
Relish tray, 8" l, oval, hp, shaded green, white roses, green leaves, center handle, blue mark **45.00**
Tea set, stacking teapot, creamer, and sugar, yellow, rust, and blue flowers, gold trim, ivory ground, marked "Royal Silesia," green mark in wreath **95.00**

Schneider Glass

Schneider Schneider

History: Brothers Ernest and Charles Schneider founded a glassworks at Epiney-sur-Seine, France, in 1913. Charles, the artistic designer, previously had worked for Daum and Gallé. Robert, son of Charles, assumed art direction in 1948. Schneider moved to Loris in 1962.

For more information, see *Warman's Glass*, 4th edition.

Although Schneider made tablewares, stained glass, and lighting fixtures, its best-known product is art glass that exhibits simplicity of design and often has bubbles and streaking in larger pieces. Other styles include cameo-cut and hydrofluoric-acid-etched designs.

Marks: Schneider glass was signed with a variety of script and block signatures, "Le Verre Francais," or "Charder."

Compote, purple and orange, circular flaring top, pedestal base, four applied loop handles, c1925, vase mark, 11-1/4" d, **$900**. Photo courtesy of Sloan's Auctioneers & Appraisers.

Bowl, 14" d, shallow, flared rim, pink, frosted ext. design of lines and circles, ftd base, etched "Schneider" on side of base, scratches to base **285.00**
Ewer, 10-3/4" h, elongated spout, mottled purples, pink, yellow, and orange splashes, applied purple handle, bulbed disk foot, acid stamp "France" on base, c1925 .... **450.00**
Finger bowl and underplate, 4-1/2" d bowl, 7-1/4" d underplate, mottled red, burnt umber and clear, stamped mark **350.00**
Tazza, 7-5/8" h, shallow white bowl rising to mottled amethyst and blue inverted rim, amethyst double-bulbed stem, disk foot, sgd "Schneider," c1920 .... **865.00**

Pitcher, Art Deco, ovoid, carved with stylized orange and violet flowers, shaded matte ground, applied handle and foot of violet glass, etched "Le Verre Francais," 5" d, 10" h, **$1,250**. Photo courtesy of David Rago Auctions.

Vase
- 7-1/2" h, cameo carved amethyst Art Deco design, base sgd "SCHNEIDE" in block letters, minor chip in design, bruise on side **460.00**
- 8-1/4" h, 5" d, hourglass, amethyst with yellow swirls, applied amethyst handles, side sgd in script **700.00**

Fish shape, scuttle, green and brown **75.00**

Horses in storm, white and black horses, copied from painting **100.00**

Skull, white, gray, black, and cream, scuttle, marked "Bavaria" **135.00**

Shawnee Pottery

History: The Shawnee Pottery Co. was founded in 1937 in Zanesville, Ohio. The company acquired a 650,000-square-foot plant that had previously housed the American Encaustic Tiling Company. Shawnee produced as many as 100,000 pieces of pottery a day until 1961, when the plant closed.

Shawnee limited its production to kitchenware, decorative art pottery, and dinnerware. Distribution was primarily through jobbers and chain stores.

Marks: Shawnee can be marked "Shawnee," "Shawnee U.S.A.," "USA #—," "Kenwood," or with character names, e.g., "Pat. Smiley" and "Pat. Winnie."

Creamer, Smiley Pig, 1940s, marked, **$165**. Photo courtesy of L & J Antiques & Collectibles.

Basket, 9" l, 5-1/2" h at handle, turquoise glaze, relief flowers and leaves, USA 688 .... **45.00**

Batter pitcher, Fern **65.00**

Casserole, cov, Corn Queen, large **40.00**

Child's feeding dish, pig shape, floral dec, gold trim, marked, 8-1/4" l, 5-1/2" w, 2" h **190.00**

Cookie jar/bank, Smiley, 10-1/4" h **475.00**

Dish, covered, King Corn, oval, 10-3/4" l, **$75**; pitcher, 5" h, **$40**. Photo courtesy of Joy Luke Auctions.

Cookie Jar

- Great Northern Dutch girl, 10-1/4" h, blue and white, brown hair and yes, marked "Shawnee Great Northern U.S.A. 1026" **290.00**
- Jill, yellow skirt, gold decals and trim, marked "USA," 11-1/2" h **375.00**
- King Corn, marked "Shawnee USA #66," 10-1/2" h **265.00**
- Mugsey, 11-3/4" h, blue scarf, marked "Patented, Mugsey, USA" **600.00**
- Puss 'n Boots, 10-1/4" h, marked "Patented Puss 'n Boots USA" **300.00**
- Winking owl, white, gray and peach feathers, marked, c1940, 11-1/2" h **230.00**

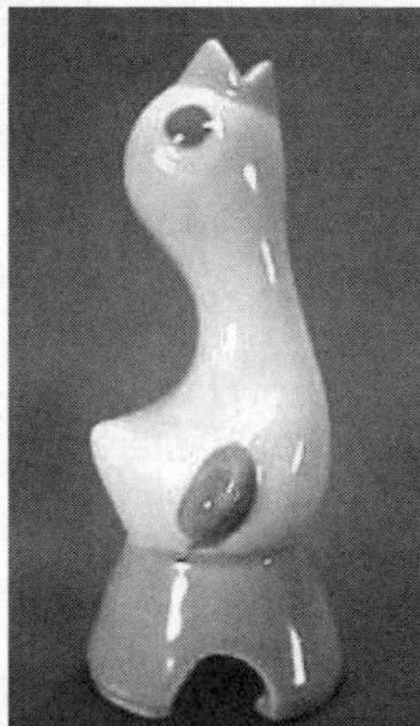

Pie bird, white bird, pink and green accents, made for Pillsbury, late 1940s or early 1950s, 5-1/2" h, **$90**. Photo courtesy of L & J Antiques & Collectibles.

Creamer

- Puss 'n Boots, yellow, green, and burgundy dec, gold trim, marked "Shawnee USA #85," 5" w, 5" h **250.00**
- Smiley Pig, marked "Shawnee USA 86" **165.00**

Figure

- Deer, white, black trim **300.00**
- Puppy **55.00**
- Rabbit **50.00**

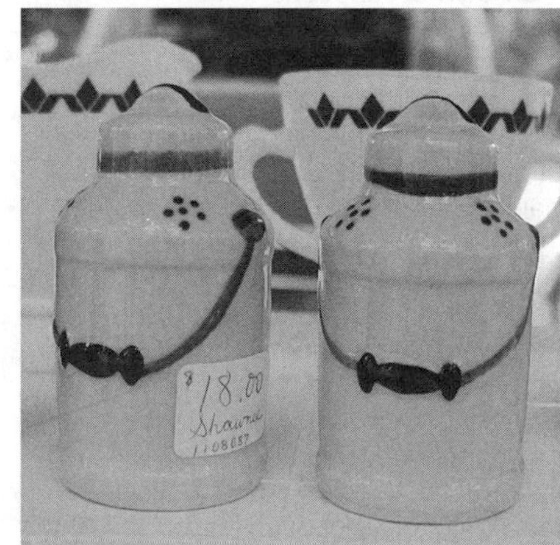

Salt and pepper shakers, pair of milk cans, cream, blue and red decoration, **$18**; owls, cream, red, green, and black decoration, one of pair shown, **$24**.

Fruit bowl, Corn Queen **25.00**

Lamp, 12" h Oriental figure, orig shade, pr **175.00**

Mug, Corn King **35.00**

Pie bird, bird, Pillsbury, white, pastel pink and blue dec, 5-1/2" h **85.00**

Pitcher

- Bo Peep, blue hat, yellow and pink dress, blue staff, marked, #47, 7-1/2" h **185.00**
- Little Boy Blue, 7-1/2" h **250.00**
- Smiley, emb flowers, gold trim, marked "Patented Smiley U.S.A.," 7-3/4" h **225.00**

Plate, King Corn, marked "Shawnee USA Oven-Proof", 10" d, **$50**. Photo courtesy of L & J Antiques & Collectibles.

Planter

- Canopy bed, #734 .... **95.00**
- Locomotive, black **60.00**
- Mouse and cheese, pink and yellow **25.00**
- Rocking horse, blue **30.00**

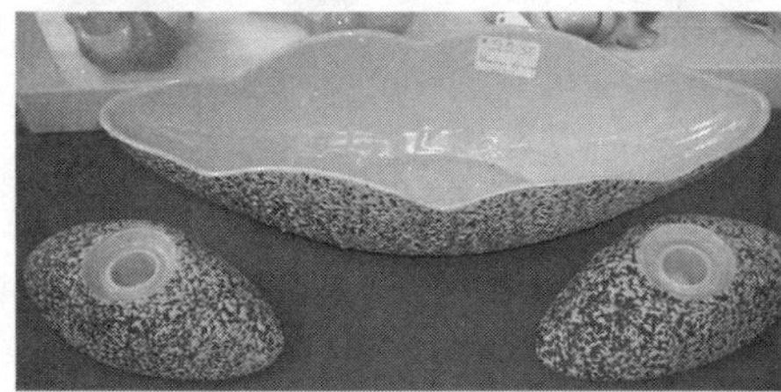

Console set, Kenwood, pink interior black and white pebbled, exterior, low bowl and pair candlesticks, **$25**.

Salt and pepper shakers, pr

- Chanticleer, large, orig label **45.00**
- Dutch boy and girl, blue eyes and trim, brown hair and shows, 5" h **115.00**
- Milk cans, small **18.00**
- Mugsey, range size, 5-1/2" h **225.00**
- Puss n' Boots, small **30.00**
- Smiley Pig, red kerchief, orig size, range size, 5-1/4" h **185.00**

Teapot

- Burgundy floral dec, gold trim, 9-1/2" w, 6-1/2" h **90.00**
- Granny Ann, lavender apron, green trimmed cape, flowered hat, marked, c1940 .... **200.00**
- Tom the Pipers Son, matt colors, marked "Patented U.S.A. 44" **150.00**

Silhouettes

History: Silhouettes (shades) are shadow profiles produced by hollow cutting, mechanical tracing, or painting. They were popular in the 18th and 19th centuries.

The name came from Etienne de Silhouette, a French Minister of Finance, who cut "shades" as a pastime. In America, the Peale family was well known for the silhouettes they made.

Silhouette portraiture lost popularity with the introduction of the daguerreotype prior to the Civil War. In the 1920s and 1930s, a brief revival occurred when tourists to Atlantic City and Paris had their profiles cut as souvenirs.

Marks: An impressed stamp marked "PEALE" or "Peale Museum" identifies pieces made by the Peale family.

Two silhouettes of woman, one with light pencil sketch of face in upper right corner, gilt frames, **$195**. Photo courtesy of Wiederseim Associates, Inc.

4-1/4" h, 3-1/4" w, young man, cutout portrait, worn gilt frame **175.00**

4-1/2" h, 3-1/2" w, woman, hollow cut, delicately worked bonnet, on laid paper, worn gilt frame **225.00**

5" h, 4" w, gentleman, hollow cut portrait, partial "Peales Museum" label with eagle, black painted frame with gilt beading, traces of ghost image of another silhouette, small water stain, wear **175.00**

5-1/4" h, 3-3/4" w, man wearing hat and heavy coat, cutout portrait, black and gold shadow box frame................ **165.00**

5-1/4" h, 4-1/4" w, pair, portraits of husband and wife, cutout and emb details, man with wavy hair, wife with hair up in ringlets, oval black painted frames with worn gilt liners....................... **300.00**

5-1/4" h, 4-1/2" w, pair, hollow cut portraits of man and woman, black ink details to hair and clothing, woman wears tortoiseshell comb, pine frames with emb brass coverings, minor wear and dings **990.00**

5-1/2" h, 4-1/8" w, young woman, hollow cut portrait, emb "Museum" (Peale) stamp, few imp outlines, gilt frame with some gold repaint, wear.............. **220.00**

5-1/2" h, 4-3/4" w, man, hollow cut portrait, scarf and ruffled shirt, penciled hair and chalk details, black frame with gilt liner **275.00**

5-5/8" h, 5-1/8" w, cutout portrait of wife or mother of William or Thomas Seabert, penciled label on back, gold ink details, beveled mahogany veneer frame with edge damage............................. **415.00**

6-1/2" h, 8-1/4" w, cutout family portrait of husband, wife, four children, partial penciled background, few inked details, old black frame with worn gilt liner **660.00**

Husband and wife, profiles, pen and ink and watercolor on paper, c1830, 5-3/8" x 4-1/4", **$920**. Photo courtesy of Pook & Pook.

6-5/8" h, 5-5/8" w, man, hollow cut portrait, emb "Museum" (Peale) stamp, mahogany veneer frame with wear and split **440.00**

7" h, 6" w, inked portraits of husband and wife, refinished pine frames **440.00**

7" h, 10-1/4" w, facing woman and man, emb "Peales Museum" labels with eagles, mahogany beveled frame **440.00**

8-3/4" h, 7-1/4" w, full length cutout portrait of child in long dress and pantaloons, glued on laid paper with some foxing, gilt frame with some wear **825.00**

10-1/4" h, 14" w, family, nine full length silhouettes of Hutton family members and a servant, of Birmingham, by Edouart, individual descriptions written in ink both on backs and below them on front, two pages with images on both sides, stains, foxing, minor edge damage......... **825.00**

12" h, 8-1/2" w, full-length cutout portrait of gentleman, lithograph background of balcony, sgd in ink "Aug. Edouart, fecit 1846 Saratoga," bird's eye maple veneer frame **1,650.00**

14-1/4" h, 11-1/4" w, full-length cutout portrait of Rebecca Smith of Stamsbury, carrying bouquet of flowers, hand-painted background in ink wash on laid paper, sgd "Aug. Edouart-fecit 1841," light foxing, beveled mahogany veneer frame with gilt liner **770.00**

15-1/2" h, 12-1/4" w, full-length cutout portrait of Hon Oliver Hatcher, with hat and cane, hand-painted background in ink wash on laid paper, sgd "Aug. Edouart–fecit 1840," very minor surface scratches, gilt frame with minor wear **990.00**

Girl with sewing basket, girl wearing long lace-trimmed dress sitting beside sewing basket, Wallace Nutting, 1927, 4" x 5", **$40**. Photo courtesy of Michael Ivankovich Auctions.

16" h, 13-3/4" w, full-length cutout portrait, probably from portfolio, identified on back as Geo. Frederick Muntz, Birmingham 23d Jany 1838, paper watermarked "Weatherly 1835," cane and are separate, matted with contemporary wood frame **220.00**

Silver

History: The natural beauty of silver lends itself to the designs of artists and craftsmen. It has been mined and worked into an endless variety of useful and decorative items. Pure silver is too soft to be fashioned into strong, durable, and serviceable utensils. Therefore, a way was found to give silver the required degree of hardness by adding alloys of copper and nickel.

Silversmithing in America goes back to the early 17th century in Boston and New York and the early 18th century in Philadelphia. Boston artisans were influenced by the English styles, New Yorkers by the Dutch.

American, 1790-1840

Mostly coin

Coin silver is slightly less pure than sterling silver. Coin silver has 900 parts silver to 100 parts alloy. Sterling silver has 925 parts silver. American silversmiths followed the coin standards. Coin silver is also called Pure Coin, Dollar, Standard, or Premium.

Butter knives, pr, master, 7-1/4" l, Albert Coles maker, mid-19th C, medallion of classical helmeted man, 2 troy oz **300.00**

Creamer, 4-1/2" h, unmarked, Federal, c1795, wide baluster form, high looped handle, upper band of scrolling ribband

and leaftips above laurel wreath and shield-shaped cartouche, 3 oz **225.00**

Creamer, cov sugar bowl, William Thomson, NY, c1810, large, lobed bodies, foliage molded handles, borders dec with molded shells, 38 troy oz **775.00**

Cream jug

5-3/4" h, Jabez C. Baldwin, Boston, c1800, squat ovoid, horizontal panels, engraved at waist with band of overlapping leaves, short spout, flying loop handle ending in raptor mask, oblong tiered base with leaf tip rim, engraved with monogram and name on one side, 7 troy oz **275.00**

6" h, E. Waton, Boston, c1820, helmet-shape, leaftip molded lip, scrolled handle and circular foot, 10 oz........ **250.00**

6-1/4" h, John W. Forbes, NY, c1805, shaped body molded with a band of fruiting grape vines, thistles and foliage, wide spout, gadrooned lip, leopard headed handle, leaf molded legs, paw and ball feet, 12 troy oz **775.00**

Julep cup, 3-7/8" h, beaded detail, imp "McDannold," small dents, attributed to Winchester County, KY, 19th C **1,210.00**

American, basket, Unger Bros, Art Nouveau style, footed, pierced scrollwork design, flared scrolled rim, double banded swing handle, stamped on bottom with interlaced "UB" for Unger Brothers, surrounded by "Sterling 925 Fine" mark used between late 1800s and 1914, also stamped "02622," monogrammed, 11-1/2" w, 11-1/2" h, **$650**. Photo courtesy of Alderfer Auction Co.

Kettle on stand, 15-1/2" h, Jones, Ball & Poor, Boston, mid-19th C, pear-shaped kettle, scalloped rim engraved with acanthus, domed and reeded lid with further leaves, finial formed as a woman kneeling over cauliflower, scrolled swing handle, crabstock serpentine spout, one side engraved with names, dated 1854, base with acanthus and shell serpentine legs conjoined by floral garlands, unmarked burner and stand, 38 troy oz **1,550.00**

Loving cup, unmarked, early 19th C, urn form, tiered spreading foot, two cast loop handles, bright cut engraved to each side with husk roundel, husk swag above, bow below, one side engraved "Sarah Barnes," other "John Barnes," both dated 1806, gold washed int., 13 troy oz........ **900.00**

Milk jug, 9" h, Charters, Cann & Dunn, NY, c1850, retailed by Robert Rait, baluster form, chased and embossed with florals within C-scroll cartouches, angular handle, short spout, beading to rim, neck, and domed trumpet foot, monogrammed, 14 troy oz **470.00**

Mug

4-1/2" h, mid-19th C, baluster, looped handle, repousse C-scrolls and foliage around central cartouche, monogrammed, 4 troy oz **250.00**

5-1/8" h, unmarked, 18th C, leaftip molded and scrolled handle, baluster body and circular turned foot, monogrammed BS, 12 troy oz **900.00**

Salver, 12-1/4" l, Jones, Ball, & Poor, Boston, mid-19th C, oval, beaded rim, engraved border of leafy scrolls and cornucopia, heraldic device of a boar's head over coronet over monogram R, shell feet, 18 troy oz **775.00**

Sugar urn, 9-1/2" l, R. & H. Farnam, Boston, c1800, ovoid, angular handles, domed lid with urn finial, trumpet foot, bright cut monogram, 14 troy oz **470.00**

Tankard, 6-1/4" h, William A. Williams, Alexandria, early 19th C, balustroid, cast handle, reeding to lip and domed foot, lightly engraved presentation inscription to underside of foot, 18 troy oz **2,250.00**

Tea set, Bailey & Kitchen, Philadelphia, PA, second quarter 19th C, 7-1/4" h squat ovoid teapot, cream jug, cov sugar, tiered spreading foot, bright cut monogram, lids with flowerhead finial, 52 troy oz **1,200.00**

American, bowl, oval, scalloped edge, 15" l, **$250**. Photo courtesy of Wiederseim Associates, Inc.

American, 1840-1920

Mostly sterling

There are two possible sources for the origin of the word *sterling*. The first is that it is a corruption of the name Easterling. Easterlings were German silversmiths who came to England in the Middle Ages. The second is that it is named for the sterling (little star) used to mark much of the early English silver.

Sterling is 92.5 percent per silver. Copper comprises most of the remaining alloy. American manufacturers began to switch to the sterling standard about the time of the Civil War.

Basket, 13" l, Jennings Silver Co., NJ, early 20th C, boat shaped, molded rim, pierced and engraved with foliate panels, swing handle pierced and engraved with floral drops, 20 troy oz........ **775.00**

Bowl, 5" d, Wm. B. Kerr & Co., early 20th C, mounted with cherubs bearing floral swags **200.00**

Bread tray, Frank W. Smith, lobed edges, the base inscribed and dated 1953, 15 oz........ **150.00**

Butter dish, 5-1/2" d, Forbes for Ball, Tompkins and Black, NY, second quarter 19th C, flower molded finial, saucer-shaped cover and under bowl, 15 troy oz **725.00**

Candlesticks, set of four, 9-1/2" h, Gorham, 1911-12, urn-form nozzle, faceted stem, hexagonal foot, weighted **950.00**

American, pitcher by International Silver Co., Lord Saybrook pattern, baluster, leaf-capped scroll handle, 26 oz. two dwt, 8-3/4" h, **$250**. Photo courtesy of Sloans & Kenyon Auctions.

Center bowl

11-3/8" l, 9-3/4" h, Ford & Tupper, NY, 1867-74, ovoid bowl, loop handles, medallion of a male and female classical bust in profile, trumpet foot with cylindrical knop, rim, knop and foot with ovolo trim, gold-washed int., monogrammed, 26 troy oz **2,235.00**

13" l, McAuliffe & Hadley, Boston, first quarter 20th C, ovoid, hammered surface, angular handles embellished to top with pierced and engraved foliates enclosing subtle monograms, engraved "1917" on low foot, 18 troy oz........ **1,000.00**

Cocktail shaker, 8-1/4" h, Meriden Brittannia Co., early 20th C, tapered ovoid, acid etched all over with fruiting grape vine, lid with ovoid cap, internal strainer, central monogrammed roundel, 18 troy oz **900.00**

Cruet, 12-1/2" h, William Gale & Sons, 1862-66, foliate molded and looped handle, five holders each with vitruvian scroll and beaded borders, gadrooned circular foot, five cut glass bottles with faceting and trelliswork, monogrammed AMG, approx. 26 oz weighable silver **1,175.00**

American, compote, Black, Starr & Frost, **$450**. Photo courtesy of Wiederseim Associates, Inc.

Demitasse set, Reed & Barton, 1929-30, 9-1/2" h coffeepot, creamer, open sugar, and tray, pots tapered cylindrical, each stamped with acanthus to base, leaftip rim, acanthus topped angular handle, small tray also with leaftip rim, monogrammed, 56 troy oz **1,175.00**

Dessert spoons, Gorham, retailed by Tiffany & Co., third quarter 19th C, pattern date 1864, 12 5-3/4" dessert spoons, two 9" l serving spoons, sugar spoon, and sugar sifter, all with gold-washed bowls, dessert spoons, sifter, and sugar with medallion of Mars, serving spoons with Minerva, engraved with monogram and heraldic device on reverse, purple velvet and satin lined leathered case.......................... **2,350.00**

American, compote, Kalo, hammered, floriform, monogram "GSH," stamped "STERLING HAND WROUGHT KALO SHOP CHICAGO, U.S.A., CHRISTMAS 1929," 7" x 9", **$1,100**. Photo courtesy of David Rago Auctions, Inc.

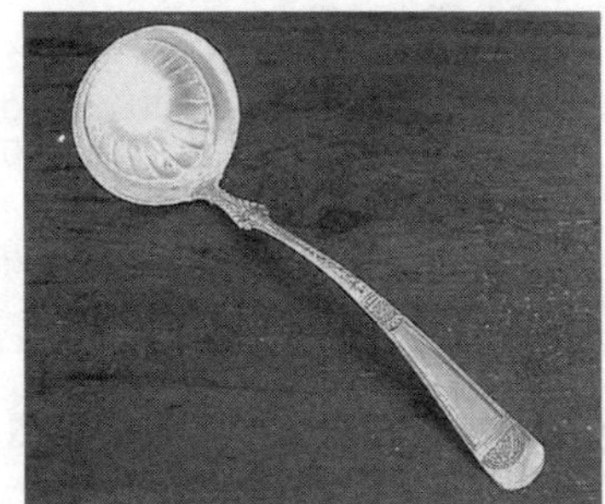

American, ladle, Gorham, no monogram, **$275**. Photo courtesy of Wiederseim Associates, Inc.

Dish, 8" l, Howard & Co., quatrefoil form, filigree sides in fleur-de-pattern, applied ornamentation on rim of "C" and "S" scrolls and shells, marked "Howard & Co., New York, Sterling, 1903," 15 troy oz **300.00**

Fruit bowl

10" d, Unger Bros, flat flared lip above faceted sides, 12 troy oz **225.00**

11-1/2" d, Gorham, early 20th C, wide openwork borders of foliage, int. with etched floral designs, monogrammed, 22 troy oz **600.00**

Grape shears, 6-5/8" l, Tiffany & Co., NY, 1938-47, stylized grape vine handles, 4 troy oz **215.00**

Meat platter, 21-1/8" l, Gorham, c1916, ovoid, shaped, reeded edge, applied monogram "EBW," 60 troy oz **400.00**

Pie server, 9-3/4" l, Shreve & Co., San Francisco, late 19th/early 20th C, handle ending in Arts & Crafts trefoil with studded accents, smaller trefoil at top of pointed blade, with overall hammered texture, 4 troy oz **775.00**

American, punch bowl, retailed by J.E. Caldwell & Co., Philadelphia, molded rim and footed base, approx. 130.6 oz., 13-1/2" d, 7-3/4" h, **$1,850**. Photo courtesy of Pook & Pook.

Platter, Dominick & Haff, oval, border repoussé with flowers and leaves on fine matted ground, monogrammed, 16 oz **475.00**

American, serving bowl, Tiffany & Co., Art Deco, footed, marked "23356," approximately 47.10 oz, 12-1/2" d, 4-1/4" h, **$1,150**. Photo courtesy of Pook & Pook.

Punch bowl, 15-1/4" d, 9" h, Manchester Silver Co., early 20th C, ovoid, slightly everted rim, monogrammed and engraved with dates on two sides, low domed foot, 88 troy oz **1,200.00**

Salt, open, pr, 3-1/4" l, Durgin, early 20th C, oval, floral molded borders, repoussé floral sides, splayed legs, hoof feet and ram's heads, 8 troy oz **300.00**

Salver, 13" d, Tiffany & Co., NY, 1947-56, plain applied rim, 29 troy oz......... **500.00**

Serving dish, 14" l, Gorham, Aesthetic Movement, third quarter 19th C, flared oval shape, applied reeding to rim, short angular handles set on ribbon and stylized palm frond, shields on sides, stylized fan and scroll ground, gold washed int. with leafy vine roundel

Left: Florist, hanging wicker flower arrangement, bold red drapery surround, gilt "S. K. Ellis" below, minor wear to gilt edging, unmarked, **$90**; center: fabric salesman, painted interior of fabric shop with Victorian woman seated at counter while male salesman shows her bolt of fabric, shelving of bolts and gild scrollwork at ends, name "W.A. Bowermaster" in gilt, Vienna mark on base, minor wear to gilt edging, **$850**; left: Mason, black and brown painted crossed mason's trowel and hammer, gilt laurel wreath surrounds "C. G. Bertholet," minor wear to gilt edging, **$275**. Photo courtesy of Cowan's Historic Americana Auctions.

ending in acanthus, low spreading foot, 34 troy oz **1,775.00**

Serving spoon, 10-3/8" l, Franklin Porter, c1925, openwork arts and crafts style handle, three troy oz **450.00**

Tazza, 3-1/4" h, Black, Starr & Frost, NY, early 20th C, ovoid, fluted pierced rim, mounted at edge with S-scrolled and shells, similarly styled domed trumpet base, set of four, 43 troy oz **1,880.00**

Teapot and sugar, cov, 8-1/2" h, William Gale & Sons, NY, 1853, each lobed form with melon finial, scrolled handles, bodies repousse molded with flowers and rocaille, openwork feet with C-scrolls and shells, 51 troy oz **940.00**

American, stamp box, Pottery Studio, round box, oval green chrysophrase among raised foliate design, slit in side for stamps, impressed "POTTER STUDIO STERLING," approximately 2 troy oz., 1-7/8" d, **$415**. Photo courtesy of Skinner, Inc.

American, tea set, Dunkirk Silversmiths, coffeepot, teapot, creamer, double-handled covered sugar, and waste bowl, ovoid form, floral repoussè decoration, marked "Hand Chased/500/Sterling," approximately 72 troy oz, **$900**. Photo courtesy of Alderfer Auction Co.

Tea and coffee service

Roger Williams, 20th C, Colonial revival pattern, coffeepot, teapot, hot water kettle, creamer and cov sugar, 113 troy oz **1,200.00**

Shreve, Crump & Low, early 20th C, 9-1/2" h coffeepot, teapot, kettle on stand, creamer, covered sugar, and waste bowl, all paneled ovoid, reeding at rim and foot, domed lids with urn finials, angular handles, kettle stand with scrolled bifurcate uprights, all engraved with entwined initials within larger scrolled initials, 170 troy oz **1,650.00**

Whiting Mfg, c1916, 10" h coffeepot, teapot, kettle on stand, creamer, cov sugar, open sugar, and 31" l tray, flattened ovoid, waist applied with guilloche band, beaded neck and foot rim, angular handles, urn form lid finials, kettle stand with bifurcate uprights, ovoid tray with shaped edge and beaded rim, monogrammed, 289 troy oz **6,600.00**

Tureen, 13" l, Gorham, early 20th C, ovoid body with bat's wing fluting, beaded rim, pendant reeded handle, peaked lid with further fluting and urn finial, ovoid trumpet foot with fluting and beading, fitted electroplated flower arranging frog liner with urn finial, 45 troy oz **2,000.00**

American, tea set, Gorham, 10" h coffeepot, teapot, creamer, double handled covered sugar, and waste bowl, ovoid form, acanthus leaf and beaded details, engraved with crown over "RR," monogrammed "MGD," wooden handles on tea and coffee pots, marked "2910/Sterling," minor denting, approximately 74 troy oz, **$900**. Photo courtesy of Alderfer Auction Co.

American, Stieff, tea set, teapot, hot water pot, sugar bowl, creamer, and under tray, classical urn form hexagonal bodies, conforming finials on lids, square-topped handles with ivory inserts, pedestal feet, impressed mark on bottom, "Stieff Sterling," monogrammed, minor use wear to tray, approximately 122 troy oz, **$1,500**. Photo courtesy of Alderfer Auction Co.

Vase, 12-3/4" h, Shreve & Co., San Francisco, late 19th/early 20th C, slender trumpet body flaring at rim, pierced and emb with ribbon-tied husk swags, similarly pierced and emb weighted domed foot, shaped molded rim **800.00**

Water pitcher

8-3/4" h, Durgin, early 20th C, retailed by Brand-Chatillon Co., squat baluster form, reeded waist, short spout, serpentine handle, all over hammered texture, monogram "ABW" applied to one side, 28 troy oz **500.00**

10-5/8" h, Frank M. Whiting Co., early 20th C, tapered ovoid, short spout, angular handle, band of patera conjoined by husk swags on fluted ground at waist, flanked by engraved scrolls, raised on trumpet foot, monogrammed **550.00**

American, water pitcher, presentation type, Tiffany & Co., 1875-91 mark, baluster body, repoussè and chased with Bacchanal couple, medallions framed by scrolling grape vines and acanthus leaf tips, centering presentation tablet inscription 'Monmouth Park, July 12th 1879, Three Quarter Dash, Gentlemen Riders Won By Mr. W. C. Sanford's, Brg. Kadi by Lexington, Owner," wrapped anthemion-form handle rising from bacchanal mask, 38 oz 4 dwt., 8-3/4" h, **$5,350**. Photo courtesy of Sloans & Kenyon Auctions.

Continental

Generations have enjoyed silver created by Continental silversmiths. Expect to find well-executed forms with interesting elements. Most Continental silver is well marked.

Continental

Candlestick, 9" h, Neoclassical-style, 20th C, circular nozzle, faceted stem and stepped square foot, decorated with husks and flowerheads, weighted **150.00**

Fruit bowl, 16" w, coin silver, circular form, four shaped openwork handles of birds and foliage, int. inset with coins from realm of Charles III and others, 38 troy oz **950.00**

Muffineer, 6-3/4" h, 18th C, pierced fruit-form cover, baluster body molded with leaftips, circular foot, marked "C.G N," 7 troy oz **265.00**

Mug, 5-1/4" h, baluster form, serpentine handle, later fruit and floral chasing, central rococo cartouche engraved with initials DM, presentation inscription on underside, 19th C, 11 troy oz **195.00**

Salad servers, late 19th C, fork and knife with carved bone tines and bowl, fiddle shaped silver handles with bifurcate scrolled socket, .950

silver, associated case, 10-1/2" l **150.00**

Danish, Georg Jenson

Compote

5-3/8" h, 8" d, Johan Rohde, maker, 1926-32, style number 171, bowl with slightly everted rim, openwork stem formed as budding flower stems enclosing beaded bud, conjoined by scrolls, tiered spreading foot, 20 troy oz....................................... **2,600.00**

Continental, Austria, Argentor, teapot, diamond-shaped, woven rattan handle, impressed hallmark and "N 144," 9" l, 3-3/8" h, **$300**. Photo courtesy of Skinner, Inc.

6-1/2" h, 1926-1932, design number 263B by Jensen, hammered bowl set with stylized fruiting grape vine, spiral fluted stem accented with more grapes, hammered spreading foot, 19 troy oz.................... **2,750.00**

Demitasse set, 6-1/4" h teapot, creamer, cov sugar, Blossom pattern, 1933-44, marked 2A, B, and C, carved ivory handles set at right angle to spout, stylized blossom finials, 21 troy oz **3,200.00**

Napkin rings, pr, 2" l, Cactus pattern, oval, three troy oz.................. **350.00**

Salad servers, pr, 7-1/2" l, each with openwork handle with elongated leaftip and seed pods, hammered bowls, 4.5 troy oz **1,200.00**

Sandwich server, 8-1/4" l, 1933-44, tongs with bladed surface and pointed end, the scrolled handles ending in beads, and with fan decoration at hinge, three troy oz **450.00**

Serving spoon

5" l, looped handle **150.00**

6-1/2" l, heart-shaped handle molded with a flat leaf **215.00**

Sugar tongs, pr, 3-5/8" l, Acorn pattern, stylized acorn handles and small pointed nips, 20th C, 1 troy oz **225.00**

Continental, Austria, Hagenauer, compote, round bowl raised on base with stylized cutout golfing scene, imp "WHW" in circle and "Hagenauer/Wein/Austria," 7-3/4" d, 4-1/4" h, **$950**. Photo courtesy of Skinner, Inc.

Dutch

Bowl, 14-1/4" l, 3" h, 19th C, .833 fine, Dutch export mark, repoussé, lobed, reserves with chased and emb country scenes, two pierced handles with putto to top, central flowers flanked by putto riding dolphins, 15 troy oz................ **460.00**

Box, late 19th C, .833 silver, 2-5/8" w, 5-1/2" l, rect, shaped lid with engraved nativity scene within foliates, base with two biblical scenes, banded sides with engraved foliates, 8 troy oz **960.00**

Chatelaine, c1890, 12-1/8" l, cast brooch with scene of putti with goddess, medallion mounted chains supporting two boxes, cylindrical container, pair of scissors, stylized crown, 9 troy oz...................... **600.00**

Pitcher, 5-1/2" h, late 19th C, .833 line, baluster form, neck with band of fluting, repoussé to lower section of foliage, birds and putti, domed foot with vertical ribbing, spout with putto, beaded serpentine handle, lid with vertical reeding, repoussé and vegetal finial, base engraved "Esther Cleveland," 6 troy oz, descended in family of Grover Cleveland..... **260.00**

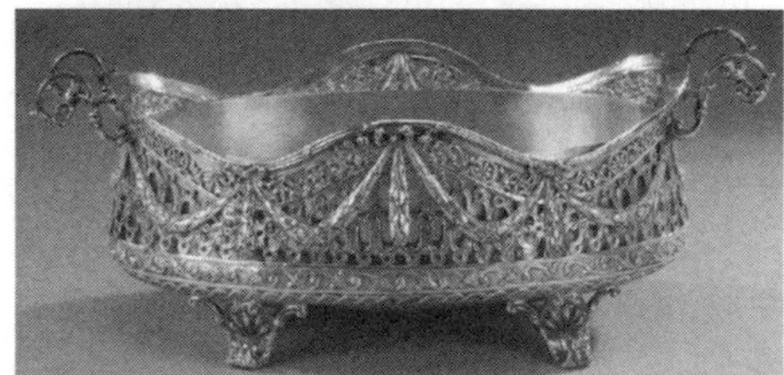

Continental, centerpiece, oval, foliate scroll and shell feet, sides pierced with guilloches, hung with ribbon-tied berried laurel swags between bands of vitruvian scrolls, pierced anthemion, open double scrolls handles, fitted with silver-plated liner, crowned A, crowned P and crowned fleur-de-lis marks, 27 oz, 14" h, **$1,100**. Photo courtesy of Sloans & Kenyon Auctions.

French, .950 fine

Coffeepot, 9-1/4" h, third quarter 19th C, pear-shaped, cast quadripartite scroll embellished serpentine spout and handle, heat stops, domed lid with flower form finial, 22 troy oz **460.00**

Dish, cov, undertray, Paris, 1819-38, "C. P." maker's mark, cylindrical body with acanthus and flat leaf handles, rim with beading and flat leaf band, base with band of flat leaves, foot with band of laurel, lid with beaded edge, removable circular handle formed as cornucopia on leaf and flower base, fitted leather case, 30 troy oz **2,615.00**

Tray, 17-3/8" l, 13" w oval, late 19th C, partially obscured maker's mark, beaded edge, engraved initial in center, 34 troy oz................... **575.00**

Tureen, cov, 12-3/4" l, 10-1/2" h, third/fourth quarter 19th C, sprays of acorns and oak leaves to top, reeded rim, lid with flat leaf rim, stem with reeded shoulder, oval foot, flat leaf band, angular handles with flat leaf to bottom, stylized corn finial about flat leaf and lotus ground **1,840.00**

Wine taster, late 19th C, .950 fine, inset with crest to handle **125.00**

Continental, Denmark, George Jensen, after 1945, No. 80, tea service, teapot, creamer, covered sugar, and oval tray, ivory finials and handles, beaded edges, impressed Jensen mark, "DENMARK/STERLING," and numbered, scratches, 54 troy oz., 14" l tray, **$3,290**. Photo courtesy of Skinner, Inc.

German, .800 fine

Claret Jug, silver and cut glass

11-3/4" h, flattened baluster form colorless glass body etched with flower stems and scrolls, mounted with .800 silver hinged lid, neck mount, pierced handle, and oblong foot, monogrammed, early 20th C **940.00**

14-3/4" h, Renaissance Revival, late 19th C, marked for E. Goldschmidt, long neck with panels of figural strapwork, over scrolled waist rim with putto bacchante masks, short spout with Minerva mask, lid with fancy urn finial, female bacchante herm scroll handle, ovoid body cut with swags of cross hatched diamonds, ovoid beaded foot on four satyr masks foot, .800 silver **1,800.00**

Tea and coffee service, early 20th C, Dutch import mark, tea pot, 12" h coffee pot, kettle on stand, cov sugar, milk jug, and tray, balustroid bodies chased and embossed with vertical foliate panels conjoined by foliate swags, domed lids with rocaille finials, kettle on trefoil scroll stand, 29-1/8" l tray with foliate and swag rim, .800, 275 troy oz. total **4,500.00**

Vase, 14-5/8" h, late 19th/early 20th C, trumpet shape, colorless etched glass liner with band of foliates, tapered cylindrical frame swelling at base, domed foot, pierced and stamped all over with scenes of dancing and courting couples and mischievous putti, with scrolls, masks, fans, and diapered reserved, .800, liner possibly reduced, 11 troy oz **775.00**

Wedding cup, 9" h, figural, beaded figure with chased and emb skirt, cup chased and emb with scrolls and grotesques, 15 troy oz **1,955.00**

Continental, salver, chased floral decoration, early hallmark with heart with P surmounted by crown, zigzag below, 7" d, **$375**. Photo courtesy of Wiederseim Associates, Inc.

Italian

Asparagus tongs, F. Broggi, Milan 20th C, 5-1/4" l, individual, plain, tapered form, set of six, 6 troy oz **115.00**

Portuguese, .833 silver

Chalice, 12-1/2" h, domed lid with applied openwork foliate band, engraved bands and cruciform finial, bowl with engraved band with Latin inscription, applied gothic style openwork mounts, stem with beaded and engraved knop, stepped circular base, int. gilt, 31 troy oz **690.00**

Ewer, maker's mark "S&P," late 19th/ early 20th C, 11-3/4" h, bulbous, molded shaped rim, body with chased stippled dec, emb foliate, scroll, and shell band, cast scroll handle, molded circular foot with emb dec, 33 troy oz **815.00**

Salver, 11-5/8" d, molded openwork scroll and foliate rim, bright cut foliate dec on face, three cast legs with shell feet, 25 troy oz **350.00**

Tea and coffee service, 20th C, Oporto, classical revival style, baluster shaped teapot, 13-1/4" h coffeepot, and milk jug, urn shaped cov sugar, all with fluting to lower portion of bodies, ribbon swag and roundel engraving above, with beaded rims, and domed lids with urn finials, .916 silver, 110 troy oz **1,675.00**

Russian

Candlesticks, pr, 7-1/2" h, Neoclassical, bearing marks for Petrograd, 1828, also stamped Ludvig, gadrooned nozzle, anthemion decorated button knop, circular standard with reeding, circular foot similarly decorated with anthemion, .840 silver, 16 troy oz **1,200.00**

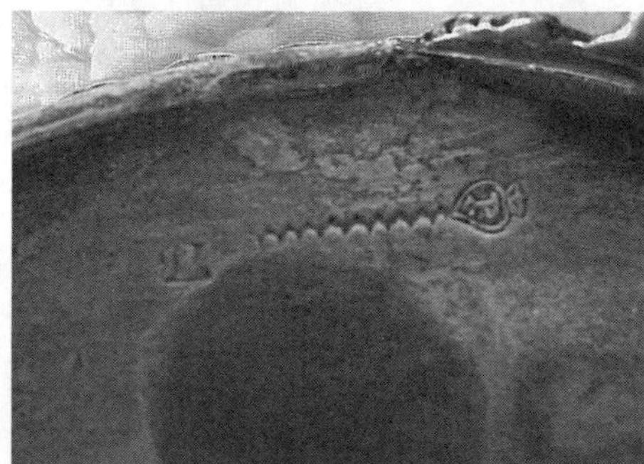

Close-up of hallmark, heart with P surmounted by crown, zigzag below. Photo courtesy of Wiederseim Associates, Inc.

Cream jug, cov, 6" h, maker's marks AA and LIH, 1780-84, molded baluster body, wide spout flower shaped finial, and angular shaped feet, 12 troy oz **200.00**

Salt, open, salt spoon, late 19th C, standard touch marks, polychrome enameled stylized foliate dec, gilt, .840 silver **125.00**

Turkish, Scholar's pen case, 9-1/8" l, 19th C, with tugrah marks, flattened cylindrical, ovoid lidded inkwell mounted to one end, engraved all over with trefoil leaf tip, patera, and stylized vines, 10 troy oz **2,000.00**

English

From the 17th century to the mid-19th century, English silversmiths set the styles which inspired the rest of the world. The work from this period exhibits the highest degree of craftsmanship. English silver is actively collected in the American antiques marketplace.

Castor, attributed to Jabez Daniel, London, 1750, George II, pear shape, pierced domed lid, should banded, spreading circular foot, 2 troy oz, 4" h, restorations **230.00**

Chocolate pot on stand, 10" h, George III, maker Robert Salmon or Robert Sharp, London, 1791, cylindrical body, turned fruitwood handle set at right angle to short spout, reeded rim, flat lid with moveable ball finial, stand raised on three reeded serpentine legs ending in hoof feet, conjoined by stretchers supporting ovoid burner, 25 troy oz **2,450.00**

Coaster, 4-3/8" d, Edward VII, Birmingham, 1904, "W.H.H." maker's mark, round, inset to center with George III Irish 10-pence bank tokens dated 1905, four troy oz, pr **115.00**

Coffeepot

10" h, George II, maker possibly Fuller White, London, 1748, pear-shaped body, serpentine fruitwood handle, tiered lid with berry finial, bat's wing fluted serpentine spout, short serpentine feet ending in shells, engraved heraldic device, 30 troy oz **2,600.00**

English, candlesticks, pair, George II-style, square drip pans above stop-fluted column, stepped square weighted bases with gadrooned rims, spurious marks for London, 1846 and maker's mark ER, also bearing two illegible marks, possibly import marks, 11" h, **$2,125**. Photo courtesy of Sloans & Kenyon Auctions.

12-1/2" h, George III, maker likely William Garrard, London, 1777, baluster form, domed lid with ovoid finial, rocaille serpentine spout and fruitwood handle, beaded rim, beaded trumpet foot, engraved presentation plaque from New York Racing Association's The Wood Memorial (First Division), Aqueduct, won by Bounding Basque, 1983, 32 troy oz **2,500.00**

English, coffeepot and teapot, Georgian, late 18th C, bearing mark of "W.S." (attributed to Wm. Sutton, London), concave paneled bodies, wooden handles, approximately 55 oz, **$1,380**. Photo courtesy of Pook & Pook.

Dish ring, 6-3/4" d, possibly Irish, bearing only maker's mark GH, struck twice on rim, typical flared form, reticulated sides, engraved gentleman playing pipes, bird, rocaille folly, amidst C-scrolls and flowerheads, central roundel engraved with mottoed coat of arms, 13 troy oz........................ **4,460.00**

Egg cup frame, Henry Nutting maker, London, 1800, George III, reeded central handle, four ball feet, six associated Sheffield egg cups, five associated demitasse spoons, 18 troy oz **550.00**

English, fruit compote, cover, strawberry finial, opaque white glass liner, 9" h, **$375**. Photo courtesy of Wiederseim Associates, Inc.

Entree dish, cov, 12-1/8" l, 5-3/4" h, "BS" makers mark, London, 1820, George IV, lid modified with later band of foliate repoussé and engraved with heraldic crest and monograms, base with gadroon and shell rim, removable leaf and shell handle, 67 troy oz..................... **1,725.00**

Hot water urn, 17-1/2" h, George III, maker's mark for Robert Sharp, London, 1792, classical urn form, pine cone finial, lion mask and ring handles, shaped spout and angular legs ending in paw feet, plinth with scrolled feet; dec all over with bright cut stippling, foliage and other motifs, 104 oz........................... **3,350.00**

Inkwell, 6-1/4" h, George V, Crichton Bros., London, 1924, circular, turned cover, four pen receptacles, circular foot, inscribed "Phelps Cup, March 16th, 1925, Won by N.F. Reynal," 13 oz **375.00**

English, page turner, horn handle in twisted motif, ivory blade, sterling silver fitting with raised scroll dec, hallmarks for Birmingham 1893-94, 15-1/2" l, **$265**. Photo courtesy of Alderfer Auction Co.

Muffineer

7" h, Victorian, W. Comyns maker, London, 1891, pierced pear-shaped lid with flame finial, inverted pear shaped body, trumpet foot, lid and body with diagonally curved lobing, seven troy oz......................... **250.00**

8-1/4" h, Edward VII, maker's mark M & Co., Birmingham, 1904, waisted baluster form, fluted base, short spreading foot, lid with stylized flowerhead and foliage piercing, urn finial, eight troy oz **250.00**

Peg tankard, 6-3/4" h, Charles II, Francis Singleton maker, London, 1683, cylindrical, low stepped lid with cast volute thumbpiece, reeded trim to lid and foot, ear handle, fully marked at body and lid, maker's mark at handle, int. set with vertical row of six pegs, engraved with later coat of arms featuring quartered shield topped by two helmets and two supporters, flanked by leafy scrolls, 25 troy oz....................................... **8,200.00**

Platter, 17-3/4" l, George III, Sebastian and James Crespell makers, London, 1769, ovoid, molded edge and gadrooned rim, engraved mottoed coat of arms and crest on edge, 48 troy oz **1,535.00**

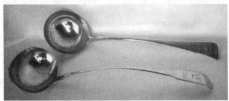

English, punch ladle, bearing marks of William Gibson and John Langman, London, c1899, 13" l; together with English silver punch ladle, c1789, bearing mark of "T.S." (Thos. Shephard), 13-1/2" l, **$500**. Photo courtesy of Pook & Pook.

Presentation ewer, 13" h, Victorian, Martin Hall & Co. makers, Sheffield, 1854, ovoid body, slender neck, short spout, small trumpet foot, loop handle, chased and embossed all over with floral sprays in C-scroll frames, pendant fruit swags and leaves, neck chased and embossed with beaded cartouches, finial missing from hinged lid, central cartouche engraved with inscription from the Officers of the Duke of Lancaster's own Rifle Regiment of Militia, to Sergeant Major James Mills, dated 1st March 1856, 25 troy oz................................ **1,410.00**

Punch ladle, 12-1/4" l, George III, maker's mark rubbed, London, 1809-10, back tipped handle engraved with hound, plain bowl, six troy oz....... **300.00**

Salver

7-5/8" d, George II, William Hunter maker, London, 1755, ovoid, engraved with C-scroll, rocaille, and foliates to border, molded rim applied with rocaille, three hoof feet, scratch weight to underside, 10 troy oz.. **500.00**

12" d, Victorian, Martin Hall & Co. makers, London, 1885, ovoid, shaped rim set with beaded acanthus and shell rim, int. with bead and husk embossed border, engraved guilloche roundels enclosing floral and fruit sprays, three ball and claw feet, 26 troy oz **600.00**

Serving spoons, pr, 8-3/4" l, Victorian, Aesthetic Movement, maker's mark FE, Birmingham, 1877, end of handle with peacock over stylized Moorish-style acanthus, ovoid-shaped bowl engraved with quatrefoils and stylized lotus leaves, six troy oz **300.00**

Serving trowel, 11" l, Victorian, maker's mark TP&S, Birmingham, 1875, trowel-shaped blade engraved with border of scrolls and flowerheads, turned ivory handle with traces of blue stain, fitted boat shaped case, four troy oz **200.00**

Sugar bowl

7-3/4" l, George III, J. McKay maker, Edinburgh, 1802, ovoid, angular handles, bright cut engraved with bands of lappets, over entwined branch and husk swags, seven troy oz.. **650.00**

9" l, George III, maker's mark rubbed, London, 1807, waisted ovoid, angular reeded handles, ball feet, gold-washed interior, 10 troy oz **450.00**

English, tea strainer, shaped handle with shell motif, hallmarked, 4" d, **$500**. Photo courtesy of Alderfer Auction Co.

Tete-a-Tete, 5" h teapot, open sugar, and creamer, George V, W. Hutton & Sons, Ltd. makers, London, 1912, ovoid, base of bodies with reeding, angular handles, teapot with angular fruitwood handle, urn finial, 13 troy oz **250.00**

Teapot

4-1/4" h, George V, Charles & Richard Comyns makers, London, 1921, flattened ball-shaped body, turned wood finial, shaped wood handle, 10 troy oz.................. **365.00**

5-1/4" h, George III, Hester Bateman, London, 1785, oval, straight spout,

fruitwood handle and lid finial, bright cut engraved bands of paterae and navettes to lid, lip and base, body with ribbon topped roundels on each side, one engraved with heraldic device, with associated 6" l oval Sheffield plate tea pot stand with reeded rim and paw feet, 11 troy oz **2,650.00**

6-3/8" h, George IV, John Angell maker, London, 1824, waisted ovoid, reeded girdle, spout topped by acanthus, ribbed ear handle, slightly domed lid, gadrooned finial, four ball feet, 22 troy oz........................ **650.00**

8" h, George III, maker's mark for George Burrows, London, 1798-99, ovoid, ivory mushroom-shaped finial, scrolled spout and lighted fluted body, trelliswork band dec, serpentine oval foot, 18 troy oz **850.00**

11" l, George III, maker possibly John Robins, London, 1800, ovoid, ivory finial, dec with bright-cut designs of scrolling foliate vines, wriggle-work and lines, 15 troy oz **850.00**

Tea set, William IV, Edward, Edward Jr., John and William Barnard makers, London, 1834-35, tea pot, 9-3/8" h coffeepot, milk jug, and open sugar, all melon shaped, chased and embossed at waist with leaves offset with flowerheads, ear handles topped by acanthus leaves suspending berry garlands, lids with melon finial on leafy ground, raised on four acanthus feet joined by openwork scrolls, 80 troy oz **3,355.00**

English, trowel, George IV, engraved floral and foliate decoration around edge of blade, carved ivory handle with sterling silver termination, blade engraved with coat of arms, banner: "Domine dirige nos" (God lead us), hallmarks for London, c1827, certification from P.A. Freeman, Inc., 13-1/2" l, **$400**. Photo courtesy of Alderfer Auction Co.

Wine coaster, 5-3/4" d, 2-3/4" h, Joseph and John Angel makers, London, 1846, Victorian, applied scroll and shell rim, reticulated sides, engraved to base with scrolls, shells, and central heraldic crest, pr **5,465.00**

Irish

Fine examples of Irish silver are becoming popular with collectors.

Candlesticks, pr, George III/IV, Dublin, attributed to John Laughlin, Jr., larger gadrooned knob over gadrooned knob below partially vertically reeded stem with single horizontal beaded band, well with applied stylized wheat or grass fronds, domed gadrooned base, vertically reeded sconce, removable nozzle with gadrooned rim, small heraldic crest engraved on foot and nozzle, 49 troy oz **7,475.00**

Caudle cup, cov, 7-1/4" h, Dublin, mid-18th C, marked for John Hamilton, domed lid topped by ovoid finial, body with single molded band, crabstock handles, lobed spreading foot, no date mark, 37 troy oz, pr **5,175.00**

Cup, 4-7/8" h, mid-18th C, marked for John Letabliere, tapered cylindrical body with leaf cut card work, band of foliate engraving, domed spreading foot, scroll handles topped with flat leaves, engraved on one side with cartouche, no date marks, 44 troy oz, pr **5,465.00**

Salver, 6-1/2" l, George II/III, Dublin, William Townsend maker, shaped molded border, engraved center with heraldic crest in rococo cartouche, three pad feet with scroll legs, eight troy oz **1,100.00**

Snuffer tray, George III, Dublin, 1798, William Doyle maker, octagonal boat shape, base with bright-cut engraved husk drops, heraldic crest within roundel flanked by leaves, sides reticulated with arcading, paterae, four troy oz..... **700.00**

Soup ladle, 13" l, John Power, Dublin, 1791, reeded bowl, engraved lozenge handle, five troy oz **435.00**

Sheffield, English

Sheffield silver, or Old Sheffield Plate, has a fusion method of silver-plating that was used from the mid-18th century until the mid-1880s, when the process of electroplating silver was introduced.

Sheffield plating was discovered in 1743, when Thomas Boulsover of Sheffield, England, accidentally fused silver and copper. The process consisted of sandwiching a heavy sheet of copper between two thin sheets of silver. The result was a plated sheet of silver, which could be pressed or rolled to a desired thickness. All Sheffield articles are worked from these plated sheets.

Most of the silver-plated items found today marked "Sheffield" are not early Sheffield plate. They are later wares made in Sheffield, England.

English, Sheffield, candlesticks, two pairs, one columnar, other baluster, **$765**. Photo courtesy of Skinner, Inc.

Basket, 7-3/4" w, 13-3/4" l, S. Smith & Son, England, second half 19th C, oval, molded foliate rim, emb and reticulated sides, cast foliage handles, oval reticulated and engraved base, cobalt blue glass liner **460.00**

Biscuit box, 7" w, 7-1/2" h, oval, hinged lid, gadrooned trim, lion mask side handles, attached tray base on ball feet, late 19th C **120.00**

Coffee pot, 12" h, English, late 18th/early 19th C, pear shaped, domed lid, pineapple finial, rocaille serpentine spout, fruitwood handle, trumpet foot with beaded edge............................... **600.00**

Cruet, 6-3/4" h stand, Matthew Boulton, late 18th C, ovoid stand with gadrooned rim, central upright with four reeded bottle frames, four shell supports, whole raised on scroll feet, set of four 4-1/8" h colorless mold cut baluster form bottles, fine diamond cut bands across body, diamond orb stoppers................. **400.00**

Epergne, 12-3/8" h base, 19th C, central upright with collar set with rocaille scrolls and raised on four acanthus leaves, four C-scroll arms, upright and arms supporting five colorless mold cut glass bowls (replaced), oblong waisted base with shell and rocaille mounts over scrolled feet.............................. **1,800.00**

Plate, 9-3/4" d, circular, gadrooned rim, engraved Carlill crest, George III, price for pr **175.00**

English, Sheffield, plated, hot water urn, urn form, reeded urn finial, beaded decoration, two swan neck handles, sq base with ball feet, bone knob on spout, engraved crest, 21" h, **$400**. Photo courtesy of Alderfer Auction Co.

Serving dish, cov, England, first half 19th C, rect, gadrooned rim and lid, cast branch and maple leaf handle, engraved coat of arms, 11-1/2" l, 8-5/8" w **230.00**

Tantalus, England, late 19th/early 20th C, central casket with two engraved hinged lids below handle, sides supporting two cut and pressed glass decanters, pedestal base supported by four column legs, 5-3/4" w, 15" l ... **490.00**

Urn, cov, 14-1/2" h, Neoclassical, beaded loop handles, peaked lid with artichoke finial, lid, body and trumpet foot with husk swags, rim with paterae and leaftip, early 19th C, rosing **425.00**

Vegetable dish, cov, 13" l, plated, shaped rect, applied grapevine, scroll, and foliage handle, monogrammed **250.00**

Wine bottle holder, 16" l, wooden base, vintage detail, ivory casters **275.00**

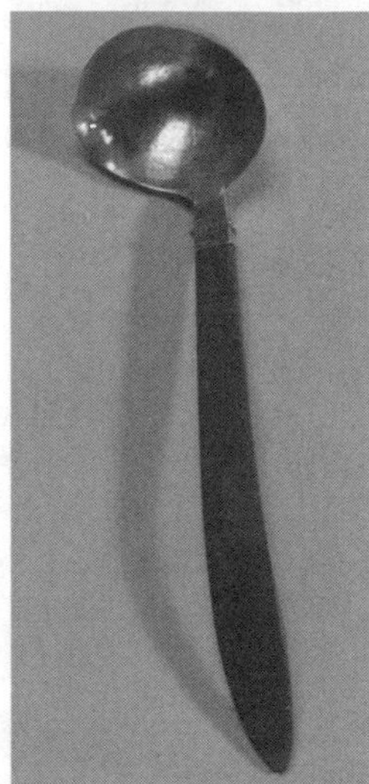

Mexican, ladle, Spratling, 1935-45, hammered, rope finial, rosewood handle, impressed "Spratling Silver" and circular hallmark, 2-1/2" l, **$415**. Photo courtesy of Skinner, Inc.

Mexican, tea set, 16" h, tea kettle on stand, coffeepot, teapot, creamer, double handled covered sugar, open waste bowl, and 30" x 19", tray, ovoid form, scrolled accents, marked "JMS," "Hecho En Mexico/925/Sterling," 345 troy oz, **$1,750**. Photo courtesy of Alderfer Auction Co.

Silver, plated

Englishmen G. R and H. Elkington are given credit for being the first to use the electrolytic method of plating silver in 1838.

An electroplated-silver article is completely shaped and formed from a base metal and then coated with a thin layer of silver. In the late 19th century, the base metal was Britannia, an alloy of tin, copper, and antimony. Other bases are copper and brass. Today, the base is nickel silver.

In 1847, Rogers Bros. of Hartford, Connecticut, introduced the electroplating process in America. By 1855, a number of firms were using the method to produce silver-plated items in large quantities.

The quality of the plating is important. Extensive polishing can cause the base metal to show through. The prices for plated-silver items are low.

Candelabrum, 31-3/4" h, English, late 19th C, maker's mark HE & Co., seven-light, reeded serpentine candelarms set with scrolls and female herms, hexagonal sconces and C-scroll drip pans, paneled three sided stem topped by three figures of female bacchantes, ending in scrolled acanthus leaves, tapered base molded with rocaille cartouches topped by female masks, lappet rim, three scroll feet, with 13-5/8" d associated ovoid mirrored plateau, beaded rim, sides with shells and foliates, shell feet **2,500.00**

Candlesticks, pr, with hurricane shades, 12-1/4" h candlestick, 20-3/4" h total, candlesticks with gadrooning on sconce, top of tapered stem, loaded trumpet foot, colorless glass hurricane shades with applied etched-style foliate dec, 19th C ... **530.00**

Coffee urn, Continental, 19-1/2" h, vase form, body and lid fluted in sections, acanthus-capped handles, reeded spigot, sq pedestal base with ball feet **375.00**

Epergne, 19" h, four 6" d x 6" h baskets, tall trumpet vase with octagonal bowl around center, pierced scroll detail, scroll hangers, stamped signature for "Robert Scott, Glasgow" **450.00**

Silverplated, tea kettle on stand, Barbour Silver Plate Co., engraved floral decoration on round body, monogrammed "WGD," marked "5309/34, BSCEP," base engraved June 24, 1910, **$125**. Photo courtesy of Alderfer Auction Co.

Kettle on stand, 13-1/2" h, English, late 19th C, ovoid pot stamped and engraved with fruit-filled baskets over scrolls and diapering, flat lid, rocaille finial, upright handle, spreading foot, pierced stand, raised on rocaille feet, burner missing **200.00**

Perfume tantalus, English, mid-19th C, marked "Betjemann's Patent," "The Tantulus," 9" h locking frame with top handle, tapered weighted base with rope twist trim, three 5-1/4" h cylindrical-cut colorless glass perfume bottles with faceted round stoppers, blue velvet-lined frame **350.00**

Silver plated, carriage, standing female figure, movable wheels, ornate scrolls and flowers, Simpson, Hall, Miller Co., 16" l, 11" h, **$650**. Photo courtesy of Joy Luke Auctions.

Punch bowl, 14" d, 8-1/2" h, English, ftd, swirled ribs, repoussé floral garlands, marked "Made in England, Hand Chased, LFS Ltd.," and arm holding hammer, minor wear **330.00**

Soup tureen, repoussé floral designs around bowl and lid, sgd "Meriden Silver Plate," engraved initials on bottom "B.C.", 12-1/2" l, 8-1/2" d, 8-1/2" h **220.00**

Toast rack, 7" l, 2-5/8" w, England, late 19th/early 20th C, oval, central ring handle above cast cricket ball, rack formed as crossed cricket bats, four ball feet **90.00**

Tray, 32" l, Victorian, oval, field engraved with floral and diaper medallions flanked by foliage with foliate garlands at intervals, beaded and geometrical design border and handles **350.00**

Silver-plated, tureen, covered, rectangular, vegetable finial, 15" x 11", **$500**. Photo courtesy of Joy Luke Auctions.

Sheffield

Englishmen G. R. Elkington and H. Elkington are given credit for being the first to use the electrolytic method of plating silver in 1838.

Candlesticks, pr, 24" h, ornate columns with composite capitals, pale blue blown glass hurricane shades with cut floral designs **425.00**

Entree dish, 11" x 8", shaped rect, gadrooned rim, detachable handle with gadroon dec **75.00**

Hot water urn, 22-3/4" h, early 19th C, Philip Ashberry & Sons makers, urn-form body with flat leaf engraving at base, wide central band of engraved anthemion, round domed base with beaded rim, trumpet foot with band of guilloche centered by flowerheads and accented with husks, angular handles terminating in flat leaves, anthemion handle on top, domed lid with flat leaf engraving and foliage baluster finial, inner sleeve **750.00**

Sauceboat with underplate, rim applied with grapevines **95.00**

Tankard, 5" h, Hy Wilkinson & Co. makers, tapered cylindrical form, plain ear handle, gold washed int., fitted leather case, 10 troy oz **235.00**

Tea and coffee service, baluster shaped coffeepot, 12-1/4" h kettle-on-stand, teapot, creamer, two handled open sugar, waste bowl, oval with canted corners, angular handles........................... **425.00**

Tray, 15-1/2" x 10-1/4", octagonal, openwork foliage gallery, stepped feet, double handles with Green Man masks, center hand chased, "Henry Hobson & Co., Sheffield"............................... **550.00**

Silver Flatware

History: The silver table service became a hallmark of elegance during the Victorian era. In the homes of the wealthy, sterling silver services made by Gorham, Kirk, Tiffany, and Towle were used. Silver place settings became part of a young girl's hope chest and a staple wedding gift. Sterling silver consists of 925 parts silver and 75 parts copper per 1,000 parts sterling.

When electroplating became popular, silver-plated flatware allowed the common man to imitate the wealthy. Silver-plated flatware has a thin layer of silver, which has been plated onto a base metal by a chemical process known as electrolysis. The base metal is usually britannia (an alloy of tin, antimony, and copper) or white metal (an alloy of tin, copper, and lead or bismuth). Leading silver-plate manufacturers are Alvin, Gorham, International Silver Co. (a modern company created by a merger of many older companies), Oneida, Reed & Barton, William Rogers, and Wallace.

Focus on one pattern by one maker. The same pattern names were sometimes used by several makers for similar pattern designs. Always check the marks carefully; several thousand patterns were manufactured. Popularity of pattern, not necessarily age, is the key to pricing.

A monogram on a piece will reduce its value by at least 50 percent. Monograms on sterling occasionally can be removed. This, however, is not the case with silver plate. A worn piece of silver plate has virtually no market value.

Silver flatware sold in sets often brings less than pieces sold individually. The reason is that many buyers are looking to replace pieces or add place settings to a pattern they already own. Sterling silver sets certainly retain their value better than silver-plated sets. A number of dealers specializing in replacement services have evolved over the past several years. Many advertise in *The Antique Trader Weekly*.

Acanthus, Georg Jensen, sterling
- Fork, 7-1/8" l **65.00**
- Pie server, hollow handle **90.00**
- Teaspoon **48.00**

Acorn, Georg Jensen, sterling, demitasse spoon, set of six.......... **250.00**

Bamboo, Tiffany & Co., sterling, iced tea spoon, 8" l, four in orig Tiffany & Co. box, blue cloth bag **175.00**

Buttercup, Gorham, sterling, 64 pcs, incomplete service for eight, case, 64 troy oz excluding knives **1,320.00**

Chambord, Reed & Barton, sterling, salad serving fork and spoon, monogrammed, 9" l, 5 oz, 6 dwt **200.00**

Chantilly, Gorham, sterling, luncheon set, service for eight, 48 pcs, 39 troy oz **635.00**

Chased Diana, Towle, sterling, partial service, 36 pcs, nine luncheon knives, nine luncheon forks, seven dessert forks, two teaspoons, three coffee spoons, two dessert spoons, butter spreader, jelly server, sauce ladle, sugar spoon, monogrammed, fitted case, 35 oz, four dwt... **250.00**

Chateau Rose, Alvin, sterling, partial service, 95 pcs, some serving pcs, 86 oz, two dwt **600.00**

Chatham, Durgin, sterling, service for 12, early 20th C, applied stylized monogram "EBW," comprising: 12: butter spreaders, bouillion soup spoons, dinner knives, dinner forks, luncheon forks, dessert knives, ramekin forks with gold washed tines, cream soup spoons, fish forks, solid fish knives; 11: dessert forks, luncheon knives, dessert forks; 10: seafood forks, grapefruit spoons; nine teaspoons; eight demitasse spoons; six large tablespoons; three-piece large carving set; two-piece small carving set; two serving forks; two sauce ladles; a pie server; and ice cream slice; a serving spoon; nut cracker; and pair of sugar tongs, the knives with stainless blades, 205 pcs, approx. 214 troy oz. weighable silver **2,115.00**

Chrysanthemum, Durgin, sterling, serving pieces, early 20th C, comprising a serving spoon, an asparagus server, a cold meat fork, and a beef fork, lg. to 9-3/4", approx. 14 troy oz **1,530.00**

Chrysanthemum, Tiffany & Co., sterling
- Tablespoon, 8-1/2" l, price for set of nine.................................... **1,265.00**
- Teaspoon, two troy oz **85.00**

Chippendale, Towle, sterling, service for 12, plus sugar spoon, 73 pcs, 60 troy oz **980.00**

Classic Rose, sterling
- Butter, master, hollow handle ... **25.00**
- Iced tea spoon **30.00**
- Salad fork **30.00**
- Sugar spoon **25.00**

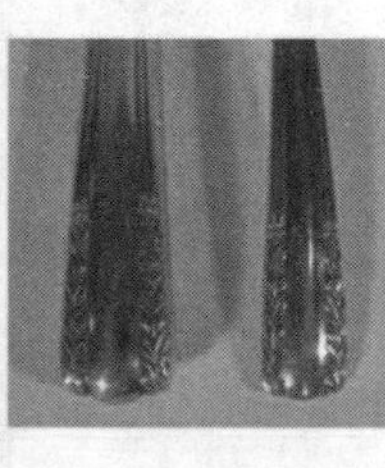

Chapel Bells pattern, Alvin, sterling silver, place setting shown from 196-piece set, **$1,500**. Photo courtesy of Joy Luke Auctions.

Clinton, Tiffany & Co., sterling, 1912, partial service, eight salad forks and breakfast knives, 13 troy oz.......... **400.00**

Colonial Eagle, Gorham, sterling, service for eight plus serving pcs, 59 pcs, 77.85 oz... **1,400.00**

Columbia, 1847 Rogers, silverplate, carving set, three pcs, hollow handle **110.00**

Dresden Scroll, Lunt, sterling
- Place fork **28.00**
- Place knife............................... **24.00**
- Place setting, four pcs **88.00**
- Tablespoon, pierced **45.00**
- Teaspoon................................. **21.00**

Early American, Lunt, sterling
- Cake server **25.00**
- Cocktail fork **20.00**
- Demitasse spoon **15.00**
- Fish set, hollow handle............ **40.00**
- Gravy...................................... **45.00**
- Salad fork **15.00**

Eglantine, Gorham, 1870, sterling
- Ice cream spoon, fruit and leaf dec bowl, set of 10....................... **425.00**
- Server, engraved floral detail on blade **390.00**

English King, Tiffany & Co., silver gilt, 90 pcs... **7,600.00**

Federal Cotillion, Frank Smith, sterling
- Butter knife **24.00**
- Dessert fork............................. **38.00**
- Gravy ladle.............................. **95.00**
- Iced tea spoon **35.00**
- Knife, 9-1/4" l **30.00**
- Serving fork, monogram.......... **75.00**
- Sugar shell **40.00**

Tablespoon.....55.00
Teaspoon.....25.00

Fiddle Thread, Lincoln and Reed, Boston, MA, sterling, 1835-46
Butter knife.....25.00
Cold meat fork.....45.00
Cream soup spoon.....25.00
Fork, 7" l.....35.00
Gravy ladle.....55.00
Master butter, monogram.....25.00
Salad fork.....35.00
Soup ladle, monogram.....150.00
Tablespoon.....50.00

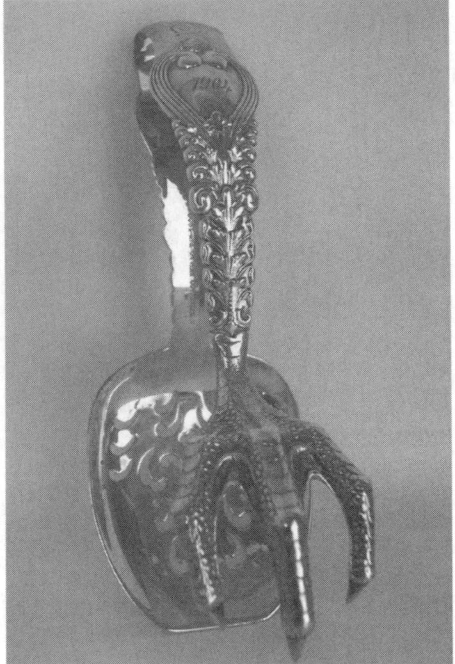

Florentine pattern, Tiffany & Co., sterling silver, oyster tongs, c1900, 3.55 oz, **$865**. Photo courtesy of Pook & Pook.

Francis I, Reed and Barton, 1907, sterling
Partial service, 15 salad forks, 16 teaspoons, 11 butter spreaders, eight bouillon spoons, eight dinner knives, eight luncheon forks, three tablespoons, ladle, cold meat fork, bonbon spoon, carving knife and fork, 87 troy oz.....1,480.00
Stuffing spoon, 14" l.....350.00

French Renaissance, Reed and Barton, sterling
Baked potato server.....45.00
Butter fork.....20.00
Cocktail fork.....25.00
Fork, 7-1/4" l.....35.00
Knife, 8-3/4" l, monogram.....30.00
Teaspoon.....20.00

French Scroll, Alvin, sterling
Citrus spoon.....20.00
Dinner knife, monogram.....28.00
Fork, 7-1/4" l.....28.00
Ice cream soup spoon.....25.00
Knife, 8-7/8" l, monogram.....20.00
Lunch setting, monogram.....80.00
Sugar spoon.....25.00

Gadroon, International, sterling
Butter fork.....15.00
Cream soup spoon.....24.00
Ice cream fork.....20.00
Iced tea spoon.....20.00
Knife, 8-3/4" l, monogram.....18.00

Gadroonette, Manchester, sterling
Baked potato serving fork.....30.00
Bouillon spoon, 6" h.....15.00
Bread knife.....30.00
Butter fork.....8.00
Casserole spoon, long.....60.00
Dessert spoon.....28.00
Dinner knife.....25.00
Dinner setting.....82.00
English server.....28.00
Gumbo spoon.....25.00
Ice cream fork.....20.00
Knife, 8-7/8" l.....18.00
Lunch setting.....70.00
Salad fork.....28.00
Serving spoon.....40.00
Sugar spoon.....28.00
Teaspoon.....18.00

Gainsborough, Alvin, sterling
Cold soup spoon.....18.00
Dinner fork.....24.00
Ice cream fork, monogram.....12.00
Iced tea spoon, monogram.....25.00
Lunch fork.....20.00

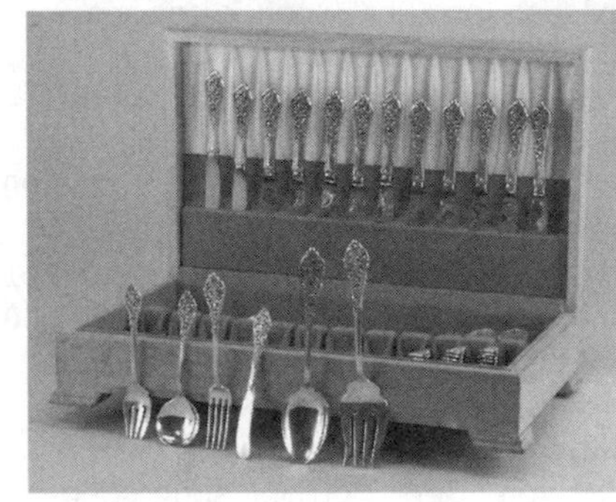

Florentine Lace pattern, Reed & Barton, sterling silver, 1951, service for 12, 87 pieces, **$1,850**. Photo courtesy of David Rago Auctions, Inc.

George and Martha, WML, sterling
Baked potato serving fork.....35.00
Butter, master.....15.00
Cake breaker.....36.00
Carving fork.....38.00
Citrus spoon.....24.00
Cocktail fork.....18.00
Cold meat fork.....48.00
Cream soup spoon.....25.00
Dessert spoon.....32.00
Dinner fork.....38.00
English server.....30.00
Gravy ladle.....36.00
Gumbo spoon.....38.00
Ice cream fork.....24.00
Ice tongs.....20.00
Lunch fork.....24.00
Lunch knife.....15.00
Salad fork.....25.00
Teaspoon.....18.00

George II, Watson, sterling
Butter fork.....24.00
Cold meat fork.....65.00
Cream soup spoon.....38.00
Knife, 9" l.....32.00
Serving spoon.....66.00
Sugar spoon.....35.00

George VI, Frank Smith, sterling
Mustard ladle.....48.00
Sugar spoon.....38.00

Georgian Colonial, Wallace, sterling
Baked potato serving fork.....32.00
Butter fork.....12.00
Butter, master.....15.00
Citrus spoon.....24.00
Cocktail fork.....18.00
English server.....28.00
Jam server.....15.00
Lunch knife.....22.00
Serving spoon.....28.00

Georgian Garland, Frank Smith, sterling
Bouillon spoon.....20.00
Butter fork.....18.00
Pastry fork.....24.00

Harmony House set, silver plated, service for 12, marked "Rogers Bros.," plus a few odd pieces, wood box, **$50**.

Georgian Maid, International, sterling
Bouillon spoon.....16.00
Butter fork.....12.00
Cake breaker.....32.00
Citrus spoon.....15.00
Cocktail fork.....15.00
Cold meat fork.....40.00
Coffee spoon.....15.00
Dinner fork.....28.00
Dinner knife.....24.00
English server.....40.00
Gravy ladle.....35.00
Iced tea spoon.....20.00
Lunch fork.....28.00
Lunch knife.....35.00

Serving spoon **35.00**
Sugar spoon **25.00**
Teaspoon **15.00**
Youth spoon **15.00**

Georgian Rose, Reed and Barton, sterling
Baked potato serving fork **30.00**
Butter fork **18.00**
Cream soup spoon.................. **27.00**
Citrus spoon **20.00**
Dessert spoon **30.00**
English server.......................... **27.00**
Ice cream fork **20.00**
Lunch fork **28.00**
Lunch knife.............................. **28.00**
Salad fork **28.00**
Serving spoon **46.00**
Teaspoon, 6" l **15.00**

Georgian Shell, Whiting, sterling, service for eight plus serving pcs, 86 pcs, fitted box, 90.04 oz **1,200.00**

Hanover, Gorham, sterling, 1895, serving tongs, pierced bowl, claw-form fork, two troy oz **150.00**

Heraldic, sterling silver
Asparagus Fork, monogram .. **475.00**
Dessert spoon, monogram **42.00**
Fork, 6-7/8" l, monogram **32.00**
Fork, 7-1/2" l, monogram **45.00**
Salad set, 12" l, monogram **550.00**

King George, sterling silver
Fork, 7-3/4" l, monogram **30.00**
Knife, 9-5/8" l, monogram **24.00**
Teaspoon, monogram **15.00**

King Richard, Towle, sterling, 18 dinner knives, 10 dinner forks, 11 fish forks, 14 teaspoons, eight butter spreaders, 11 bouillon spoons, one table spoon, 73 pieces, approx. 78 troy oz......... **1,200.00**

La Perle, Reed & Barton, sterling, serving tongs, reticulated bowl, claw terminals **175.00**

Lily, sterling
Fruit knife, cast handle, monogram **85.00**
Ice cream fork, monogram....... **75.00**
Knife, 8-7/8" l **60.00**
Pie server, monogram **80.00**
Salad fork, monogram............. **95.00**
Teaspoon................................. **21.00**

Lily of the Valley, Whiting, 1885, sterling, demitasse spoon, set of six.......... **135.00**

Madame Jumel, sterling
Coffee spoon **10.00**
Fork, 6-3/4" l **20.00**
Salad fork **30.00**
Tablespoon............................... **36.00**
Teaspoon.................................. **10.00**

Magnolia, Watson Silver Co., sterling, punch ladle, monogrammed, 12" l, eight troy oz... **250.00**

Majestic, Reed & Barton, sterling, partial service, 100 pcs, some serving pcs, 82 troy oz... **550.00**

Mary Chilton, Towle, sterling, partial service, 45 pcs, two luncheon forks, three luncheon knives, six salad forks, six teaspoons, eight bouillon spoons, six butter spreaders, three serving spoons, jelly spoon, pierced serving spoon, pickle fork, sugar tongs, sugar spoon, three serving spoons, carving fork and knife, pie server, partly monogrammed, 35 oz, eight dwt..................................... **320.00**

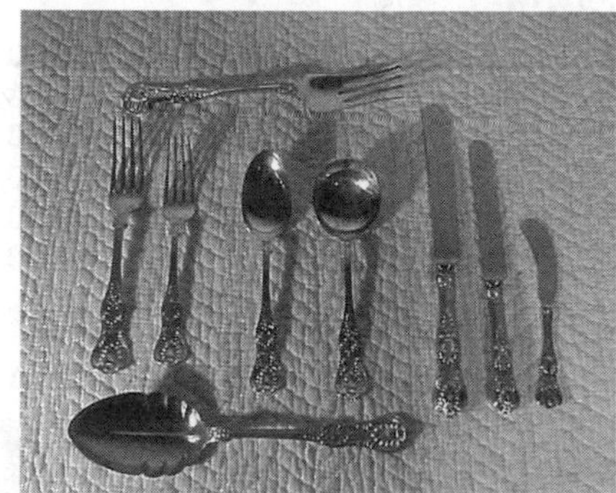

King pattern, Dominic & Haff, sterling silver, partial setting, service for 12 plus serving pieces sold for **$2,250**. Photo courtesy of Wiederseim Associates, Inc.

Mary II, Lunt, sterling, 68 pcs, service for eight, extra teaspoons, four serving pcs, monogrammed, wooden case, 58 troy oz excluding knives.......................... **385.00**

Meadow Rose, Watson, sterling, 108 pcs, incomplete service for 16, carving knife, case, 113 troy oz excluding knives **1,485.00**

Meadow Wreath, Watson, sterling
Butter knife **18.00**
Fork, 7-1/8" l **20.00**
Gravy ladle **46.00**
Iced tea spoon **12.00**
Knife, 8-3/4" l **18.00**
Salad fork **25.00**
Sugar spoon............................. **18.00**
Tablespoon............................... **40.00**

Oak, Frank Smith, sterling
Citrus spoon **18.00**
Gravy ladle **45.00**
Sauce ladle **30.00**
Sugar shell **25.00**
Teaspoon.................................. **12.00**

Orange Blossom, Gorham, sterling, fork, set of eight.................................. **180.00**

Orange Blossom, Rogers, silverplate
Bouillon spoon............................ **8.00**
Butter spreader **6.00**
Cocktail fork **10.00**
Cold meat fork.......................... **22.00**
Cream soup spoon................... **10.00**
Demitasse spoon **10.00**
Dessert knife **10.00**
Fruit knife.................................... **6.00**
Grapefruit spoon **5.00**
Gravy ladle **25.00**
Ice cream fork **20.00**
Iced tea spoon **15.00**

Pie knife.................................... **32.00**
Salad fork **12.00**
Tomato server........................... **48.00**

Palmette, Tiffany & Co., NY, 1947-56, sterling, partial service, 16 teaspoons; and 12 each: tablespoons, butter spreaders, dessert forks, 7-1/4" l luncheon/dinner forks, and 8-5/8" l knives with pointed stainless blades; six demitasse spoons, and a cheese knife, reverse of handle monogrammed, 83 pieces total, approx. 123 troy oz weighable silver......................... **3,450.00**

Persian, Tiffany & Co., sterling, 1872, service for 12, butter knives, dinner forks, dinner knives, dessert forks, dessert knives, dessert spoons, salad forks, tablespoons, teaspoons, 155 troy oz **7,475.00**

Poppy, Rodgers, silverplate, patent 1904, 65 pcs, serving pieces and tableware, die-stamped mark **350.00**

Priscilla, Frank Smith, sterling
Butter pick **45.00**
Gravy ladle **50.00**
Soup spoon **25.00**
Teaspoon.................................. **12.00**

Queen, Imperial, sterling
Asparagus fork, monogram **325.00**
Berry spoon, monogram **125.00**
Ice cream slice, 10-1/2" l, monogram **245.00**
Tablespoon, monogram **40.00**

Queen Anne, J. E. Caldwell, sterling, service for 12, monogrammed, 84 pcs total, sold with orig invoice from J. E. Caldwell, Jewelers and Silversmiths, Phila, 98 troy oz **1,320.00**

Queen Anne, Pierre Platel, London, 1705, silver-gilt, 12 fish forks and 12 spoons, all fully marked, spoons with trefoil tips **6,275.00**

Rapalloi, Lunt, sterling
Place knife................................ **20.00**
Place setting, four pcs **95.00**
Place spoon **25.00**
Salad fork **24.00**
Soup spoon, oval **24.00**
Sugar spoon............................. **24.00**
Teaspoon.................................. **24.00**

Renaissance, Tiffany & Co., sterling, ladle, lobed ovoid bowl, handle monogrammed, 1902-07, 10-1/2" l, 7 troy oz.. **920.00**

Royal Danish, International Silver Co., c1939, sterling
Bonbon..................................... **22.00**
Butter, master **25.00**
Cocktail fork **25.00**
Cold meat fork.......................... **40.00**
Iced tea spoon **30.00**
Lemon fork **22.00**
Partial dinner service, nine: butter knives, dinner forks, luncheon forks;

10 dinner knives; 18 teaspoons, seven soup spoons, five tablespoons, gravy ladle, jelly spoon, wooden case, 79 troy oz **920.00**
Sugar tongs **40.00**

Arthur Stone, executed by Charles Brown, Gardner, MA, 1912-37, sterling silver, salad fork and spoon, impressed Stone touchmark, "STERLING," and "B," scratches, 7 troy oz, 11-1/2" l, **$650**. Photo courtesy of Skinner, Inc.

Sir Christopher, Wallace, sterling, 12 each: dinner knives, luncheon knives, dinner forks, demitasse spoons, and teaspoons; 10 each: luncheon forks, fish forks, butter spreaders, and cream soup spoons; eight bouillon spoons, six grapefruit spoons, carving set, five various serving spoons, pastry knife, cold meat fork, and master butter spreader, approx. 148 troy oz **2,600.00**

Versailles, Gorham, sterling
- Asparagus server, hooded **35.00**
- Berry spoon, large or small **45.00**
- Bouillon spoon, monogram **30.00**
- Cold meat fork **145.00**
- Fork, 6-3/4" l **30.00**
- Fork, 7-5/8" l, monogram **50.00**
- Fruit knife **40.00**
- Gumbo soup, monogram **46.00**
- Jelly spoon, reticulated circular blade **195.00**
- Knife, 8-3/4" l, monogram **48.00**
- Ladle, 12-1/2" l **500.00**
- Partial service, 116 pcs, 114 troy oz **3,220.00**
- Serving pieces, carving knife and fork, pie server, salad serving fork and spoon, two serving spoons, shell-form gold washed serving spoon, sauce ladle, aspic/tomato server, 14 pcs, 25 troy oz **1,725.00**
- Teaspoon, monogram **20.00**

Vintage, 1847 Rogers, silverplate
- Butter spreader, individual **15.00**
- Cocktail fork **15.00**
- Demitasse spoon **12.00**
- Dinner fork **8.00**
- Olive spoon **55.00**
- Salad fork **48.00**
- Youth set, three pcs, orig box **48.00**

Violet, Wallace, sterling, 85-pc set, master butter, eight 6-1/2" hollow handle butter knives, eight 3-3/4" demitasse spoons, eight 6" forks, eight 6" hors d'ouerves, eight 6" ice tea spoons, eight 7" iced tea spoons, 6" jelly spoon, eight 8-3/4" knives, 7" ladle, eight 7" salad forks, eight 6" soup spoons, 16 6" teaspoons, one drawer lift top case with sterling plaque with inscribed name **1,200.00**

Violet, Whiting Div, sterling
- Butter knife, master **60.00**
- Butter pick, monogram **55.00**
- Cold meat fork, monogram **75.00**
- Fork, 6-5/8" l, monogram **25.00**
- Pie server spoon **90.00**
- Teaspoon, monogram **22.00**

Wave Edge, Tiffany & Co., sterling, ladle, 11" l, marked "Tiffany & Co., Sterling Pat. 1884 M," six troy oz **320.00**

Wild Rose, International Silver, sterling, partial service, serving pcs, monogrammed, 145 pcs, 136 troy oz **1,100.00**

Winthrop, Tiffany & Co., silver gilt
- Pastry server, 1909, two troy oz **320.00**
- Service for 12, butter spreaders, coffee spoons, dessert forks, dinner knives, dinner forks, luncheon forks, luncheon knives, seafood forks, soup spoons, teaspoons, plus serving pieces: three-piece large carving set, cheese scoop, gravy ladle, pie server, two serving forks, two-piece steak carving set, sugar tongs, four tablespoons, monogrammed, fitted walnut case, 175 troy oz **8,625.00**

Silver Overlay

History: Silver overlay is silver applied directly to a finished glass or porcelain object. The overlay is cut and decorated, usually by engraving, prior to being molded around the object.

Glass usually is of high quality and is either crystal or colored. Lenox used silver overlay on some porcelain pieces. Most designs are from the Art Nouveau and Art Deco periods.

For more information, see *Warman's Glass*, 4th edition.

Basket, 5-1/2" l, 6" h, deep cranberry body, all-over floral and lattice design, sterling handle **600.00**

Cologne bottle, 5-1/2" h, W. Comyns & Sons makers, London, 1900, pr oblong bottles tapering to neck, mounted with Continental-style chased and embossed silver overlay with cartouches of two ladies being serenaded by man with lute, foliate and C-scroll borders, rounded hinged lid with foliate border, opening to cut glass stopper, fitted red leathered case **2,500.00**

Glass perfume bottle, silver overlay decoration, 4" h, **$100**. Photo courtesy of Joy Luke Auctions.

Decanter, 12-5/8" h, colorless, baluster form, blown glass four-part decanter in pierced and engraved overlay of dense fruiting grapevines, nibbled on by figures of squirrels, each part of decanter centered by shell engraved with name of cordial including "Cointreau," "Dom," "Brandy," and "Freezomint," two neck rings, four narrow stoppers, short spreading foot set with four further squirrels, Chinese Export, early 20th C, maker possibly Luen Hing, Shanghai **750.00**

Two glass perfume bottles, silver overlay decoration, both 2-1/2" h, **$110**. Photo courtesy of Joy Luke Auctions.

Flask, 5" h, clear bottle shaped body, scrolling hallmarked silver, hinged cov **275.00**

Inkwell, 3-3/4" x 3", bright green ground, rose, scroll, and lattice overlay, matching cov, monogram **650.00**

Jug, 9" h, colorless glass, tapered baluster form, star-cut base, silver cased applied draw handle, overlay of twining grapes and grape vines, plain cartouche beneath spout, stylized cobweb overlay

below, Alvin Mfg Co., late 19th/early 20th C 1,380.00

Divided relish dish, mayonnaise bowl with underplate and ladle, small plate, **$100**. Photo courtesy of Joy Luke Auctions.

Perfume bottle, 5" h, baluster, elongated neck, colorless glass, scrolling foliage overlay, central monogrammed cartouche **225.00**

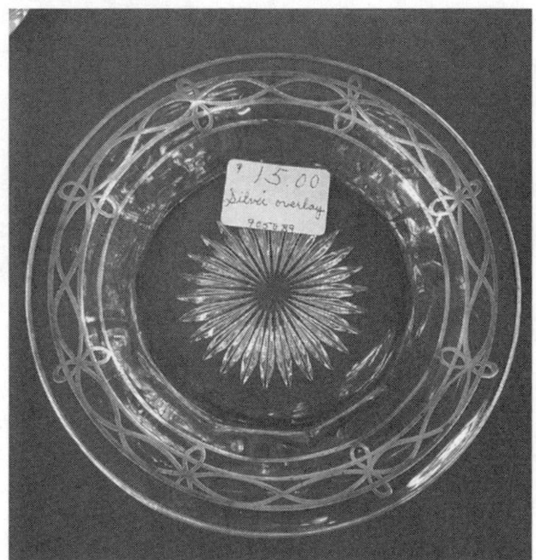

Plate, colorless, looped border silver overlay on broad rim, rayed star center, **$15**.

Tea set, 8-3/4" h, Lenox porcelain body, Reed & Barton silver overlay, three-pc set **325.00**

Apple-green Lenox with Mauser silver overlay, salt and pepper shakers overlaid with violets, c1905; 4" h jam jar overlaid with apples, pre-1932, green stamp marks, **$395**. Photo courtesy of David Rago Auctions.

Vase, 7" h, Art Nouveau free-form irid blue body, applied silver overlay in iris pattern **1,100.00**

Flask, 3/16" pint, monogrammed, dated 1904, heavy overlay grape and leaf decoration, some dents, 5" h, **$200**. Photo courtesy of James D. Julia, Inc.

Vase, Heintz, sterling on bronze, cylindrical, rolled rim, cattail overlay on original verdigris patina, stamped mark and patent, 3" d, 6" h, **$375**. Photo courtesy of David Rago Auctions.

Vase, baluster, satin finished diamond quilted turquoise glass, Art Nouveau floral design silver overlay, marked "L Sterling," imperfections in glass, 10" h, **$550**. Photo courtesy of Sanford Alderfer Auction Company.

Smith Bros. Glass

For more information, see *Warman's Glass*, 4th edition.

History: After establishing a decorating department at the Mount Washington Glass Works in 1871, Alfred and Harry Smith struck out on their own in 1875. Their New Bedford, Massachusetts, firm soon became known worldwide for its fine opalescent decorated wares, similar in style to those of Mount Washington.

Marks: Smith Bros. glass often is marked on the base with a red shield enclosing a rampant lion and the word "Trademark."

Reproduction Alert: Beware of examples marked "Smith Bros."

Atomizer, 7" h, tan shading to cream opaque body, enameled amethyst and pink flowers, painted lion trademark, new hardware **260.00**

Biscuit jar

- 6" d, melon ribbed body shading from white to blue, polychrome enameled flowers **150.00**
- 7" h, opaque cream ground, sculptured diagonal swirl pattern, polychrome flower dec, red lion trademark **300.00**
- 7" d, 8-1/2" h, green and pastel brown tendrils of ivy wind around melon ribbed body, gold plated fittings, sgd "405" **885.00**

Bowl

- 3" d, lobed, pale pink ground, daisies dec, red rampant lion mark **150.00**
- 9" d, 4" h, melon ribbed, beige ground, pink Moss Rose dec, blue flowers, green leaves, white beaded rim **675.00**

Bride's bowl, 9-1/2" d, 3" h bowl, 16" h overall, opal glass bowl, painted ground, 2" band dec with cranes, fans, vases, and flowers, white and gray dec, fancy silver-plated holder sgd and numbered 2117 .... **1,450.00**

Creamer and sugar, 3-3/4" h creamer, 3-1/4" sugar, cream ground, blue pansies dec, tarnished silver plated hardware 250.00

Sugar bowl, covered, melon ribbed, gold enamel blossoms, leaves, and branches, original metal hardware stamped "S.B.," 4-1/4" h, **$230**. Photo courtesy of James D. Julia, Inc.

Humidor, 6-1/2" h, 4" d, cream ground, eight blue pansies, melon-ribbed cov 850.00

Jar, cov, 4" h, melon ribbed cream body, white daisies dec, red lion trademark 150.00

Mustard jar, cov, 2" h, ribbed, gold prunus dec, white ground 300.00

Rose bowl, 2-1/4" h, 3" d, cream ground, jeweled gold prunus dec, gold beaded top, sgd 285.00

Salt and pepper shakers, silverplate napkin ring center on platform base, white shakers with blue floral trim, marked "Rockford #29" 750.00

Salt, open, 2-1/2" d, 1-1/4" h, white ground, amber dec, sgd with trademark and lion shield 225.00

Sugar shaker, 5-3/4" h, pillar ribbed, white ground, pink wild rose and pale blue leaves, blue beaded top, orig cov fair.. 495.00

Sweet meat jar, cov, 5-1/2" h, 5-1/2" d, melon ribbed, faded yellow ground, floral dec, gold highlights, dec silver plated cov, rope twisted handle, sgd 260.00

Toothpick holder, 2-1/4" h, barrel shape, opaque white body, swag of single petaled blossoms 265.00

Vase

- 8" h, beige ground, vibrant hummingbird and flowers, gold trim, minor rim roughness, wear..... 150.00
- 11" h, beige ground, multicolored floral dec, three-legged silver plated stand with three perched birds, small rim flake................................. 425.00
- 11-1/2" h, pink and white shaded bodies, hp birds, flowers, and trees, gold highlights, matching sgd "Pairpoint" silver plated stands with cross-legged winged cherub, pr, minor rim flaking.................. 1,500.00

Vase, melon ribbed body, three enameled clusters of pastel blue raised gold outlined wisteria blossoms clinging to golden vines that meander across shoulder, pendants of old-gold-colored leaves, other pendants of gray shadow-like leaves in the distance, cream background, 6-1/2" d, 8-1/2", **$1,000**. Photo courtesy of Clarence and Betty Maier.

Snuff Bottles

History: Tobacco usage spread from America to Europe to China during the 17th century. Europeans and Chinese preferred to grind the dried leaves into a powder and sniff it into their nostrils. The elegant Europeans carried their boxes and took a pinch with their fingertips. The Chinese upper class, because of their lengthy fingernails, found this inconvenient and devised a bottle with a fitted stopper and attached spoon. These utilitarian objects soon became objets d'art.

Snuff bottles were fashioned from precious and semi-precious stones, glass, porcelain and pottery, wood, metals, and ivory. Glass and transparent-stone bottles often were enhanced further with delicate hand paintings, some done on the interior of the bottle.

Agate, Chinese, Chalcedony, high relief carving of old man riding mule, attendant, people with parasol, 3" h 350.00

Amber, landscape and figures, caramel inclusions, conforming id, Chinese, late 19th C, 4" l 1,265.00

Celadon, flattened ovoid short neck, 2-1/4" h.. 185.00

Chrysoprase, flattened ovoid, light green, conforming stopper, 3" h 215.00

Cinnabar lacquer, ovoid, continual scene of scholars and boys in a pavilion landscape, dark red, conforming stopper, 3-1/4" h 230.00

Agate, Chinese, flattened circular form carved as two men in garden, woman in background on one side, man and woman in garden on reverse, carved lizards on narrow sides, coral stopper, intact ivory spoon, 1-7/8" w, 2-3/8" h, **$1,035**. Photo courtesy of Alderfer Auction Co.

Cloisonné, auspicious symbols among clouds, yellow ground, lappet base border, ruyi head neck border, conforming stopper with chrysanthemum design, Qianlong four-character mark 185.00

Hardstone, hand-carved agate, high-relief flowers and crane, Chinese, mounted on hardwood stand, domed lid glued down, chips, 3" h, **$65**. Photo courtesy of Cowan's Historic Americana Auctions.

Coral, cylindrical, carved kylin, Chinese, 2-1/2" h 175.00

Enameled glass, each side dec with deer beneath flowing trees, seal mark in red on base, 2-3/8" h 920.00

Enameled porcelain, Chinese

- Crane and pine tree dec, metal spoon, c1800, 2 3/4" h 250.00
- Dragon going through clouds above waves and fish design, late 1800s, 3-5/8" h 175.00

Ivory, corn-cob shape, late 1800s 250.00

Jade, black, flattened rect form, relief carved mountains, applied white jade figural grouping on one side, rose quartz stopper, wood base, 2-1/2" h 255.00

Lapis lazuli, ovoid, relief carved, figures beneath tree, Chinese, 4" h **115.00**
Malachite, carved, gourd, Chinese, 3" h **75.00**
Opal, carved sage seated before gourd, Ch'ing Dynasty, 3" h **125.00**

Pudding stone, Chinese, flattened squared form, conforming stopper, intact ivory spoon, 3" h, $550. Photo courtesy of Alderfer Auction Co.

Glass, interior painted, Chinese, flattened squared form, painting of female figures in snow, ivory and coral stopper, red stained ivory spoon intact, signed, 1-3/4" w, 2-3/4" h, **$500**. Photo courtesy of Alderfer Auction Co.

Peking glass, Snowflake, red overlay, flattened ovoid, one side with serpent and tortoise, other with frog sitting under lily pad, 2-1/4" h......................... **1,265.00**

Carved ivory, double, form of a Japanese lady with bouquet and Japanese man with walking stick and fan, colorful ink decoration, each container has its own ivory spoon attatched to the heads of figures, 2-3/4" h, **$275**. Photo courtesy of Alderfer Auction Co.

Rose quartz, flattened ovoid, relief carved leaves and vines, Chinese, 3" h **45.00**

Snuffbox, agate quartz, brass trimmed, lid lined with slate, Inscription on slate reads "N.K. to W.B. Dance," mosiac star design on outside of lid, 1802, 2-1/2" l, **$440**. Photo courtesy of Sanford Alderfer Auction Company.

Silveria, attributed to Kralik, hexagonal, engraved copper neck, attached chain, hinged lid with faceted ruby red stone, orig sp, orig cork stopper, c1900, 2-3/4" h **395.00**

Snuffbox, wood, bellows shape, decorated with brass tack lettering, reads "Forget Me Not," 4-3/4" l, **$225**. Photo courtesy of Sanford Alderfer Auction Company.

Stag horn, flattened ovoid, one side with inset ivory panel with two laughing figures, reserve with inset panel with gold archaic script, 2-1/8" h **175.00**

Soapstone

History: The mineral steatite, known as soapstone because of its greasy feel, has been used for carving figural groups and designs by the Chinese and others. Utilitarian pieces also were made. Soapstone pieces were very popular during the Victorian era.

Vase, four opening, red tones, Chinese, c1900, 9-1/2" l, 6-3/4" h, **$125**.

Bookends, pr, 5" h, carved, block form, fu lion resting on top, Chinese...... **300.00**
Bullet mold, 6" l, inscribed "Don't Tread on Me," locations for Fort Lewis, Goshen, Buffalo Gap, Bull Pasture, Deerfield, Shenandoah Mt. **850.00**
Candlesticks, pr, 5-1/8" h, red tones, flowers and foliage **85.00**
Carving
- 3" h, even white color, servant kneeling before woman holding fan, China, 19th C **115.00**
- 4" w, 4-1/2" d, 3-1/2" h, dog's head, old darkened color, America, 19th C, chips, with stand **420.00**
- 8-1/2" h, man, standing, smiling, holding lotus flower **60.00**
- 9-1/4" h, Buddha, seated, praying, carved stone base **60.00**
- 12" h, woman, standing, wearing robe, restoration **120.00**

Vase, carved peacock and chrysanthemums, stand, 15-1/2" h, $495. Photo courtesy of Joy Luke Auctions.

Hot plate, 16" l, 8-1/2" w................ **75.00**
Plaque, 9-1/2" h, birds, trees, flowers, and rocks.................................... **125.00**
Sculpture, 10-1/4" h, 4-1/2" w, kneeling nude young woman, Canadian **95.00**
Sealing stamp, carved dec, 5" h, 1" d, curved scroll................................. **95.00**
Toothpick holder, two containers with carved birds, animals, and leaves **85.00**

Souvenir and Commemorative China and Glass

History: Souvenir, commemorative, and historical china and glass includes those items produced to celebrate special events, places, and people.

Collectors particularly favor China plates made by Rowland and Marcellus and Wedgwood. Rowland and Marcellus, Staffordshire, England, made a series of blue-and-white historic plates with a wide rolled edge. Scenes from the Philadelphia Centennial in 1876 through the 1939 New York World's Fair are depicted. In 1910, Wedgwood collaborated with Jones, McDuffee, and Stratton to produce a series of historic dessert-sized plates showing scenes of places throughout the United States.

Many localities issued plates, mugs, glasses, etc., for anniversary celebrations or to honor a local historical event. These items seem to have greater value when sold in the region in which they originated.

Commemorative glass includes several patterns of pressed glass that celebrate people or events. Historical glass includes campaign and memorial items.

Ashtray, New York City, blue and white transfer, Empire State Building, Statue of Liberty, Rockefeller Center, harbor scene, marked "Fine Staffordshire Ware, Enco, National, Made in England," **$15**.

Creamer

Oconomowoc, Wis., white-glazed porcelain, hp scene, marked "Produced by the Jonroth Studios, Germany, imported for O. R. Eddy, Oconomowoc," early 1900s, 3-3/4" h **50.00**

Plate, Adriance Memorial Library, Poughkeepsie, New York, reticulated border, marked "Wheelock, Made for J. B. Flagler, Poughkeepsie, New York, Germany," **$45**.

The Alamo, glass, ruby-stained top with silver illus of Alamo, "The Alamo, Built 1718, San Antonia, Tex," Button Arches pattern base, 4" h......... **85.00**

Cup and saucer, Niagara Falls, cobalt blue ground, gold trim, 1-1/4" h x 1-3/4" d, 3-1/2" d saucer, scene of falls on saucer, marked "Made in Japan," matching wooden display stand **20.00**

Demitasse cup and saucer, My Old Kentucky Home, 2" h x 2" w cup, 4" d saucer, marked "Handpainted, Made in Japan, NICO" **15.00**

Dish, cov, Remember the Maine, green opaque glass.............................. **135.00**

Figure, souvenir of Atlantic City, two pigs having picture taken, green ground, marked "Germany"...................... **150.00**

Goblet, Michigan City, Ind., custard glass, Ribbed Drape pattern, red roses, red lettering, 6-1/8" h..................... **90.00**

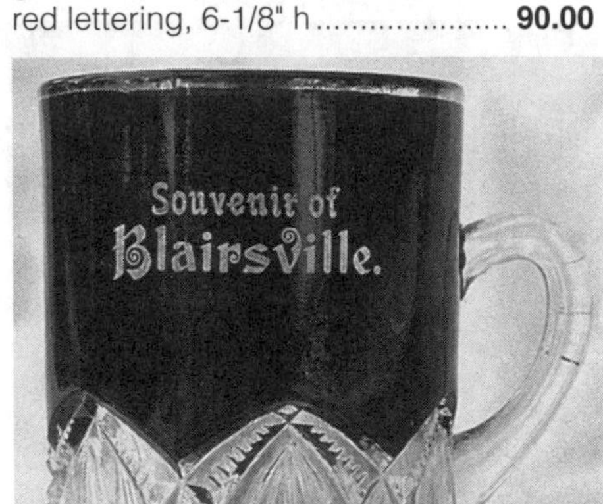

Mug, ruby stained, "Souvenir of Blairsville," applied clear handle, **$25**.

Mug, Market Place and Town Hall, Preston, photos on front and back, pink luster ground, dated 1894, 3-1/2" h **35.00**

Paperweight

Plymouth Rock, clear **95.00**

Ruth the Cleaner, frosted........ **125.00**

Washington, George, round, frosted center **295.00**

Pin dish

Eastbourne, England, 1950s, 4" **10.00**

Isle of Wight, oval, 6" l **15.00**

Pitcher, Souvenir of Rapid City, SD, frosted glass, green wreath with blue and yellow flowers, gold lettering, trim and handle, 5" h.................................. **50.00**

Plate

Canada Centennial, center "The Fathers of Confederation," Canadian seat at top, titled "1867-1967 Centenaire Canada Centennial," Providence seals for Ontario, Quebec, British Columbia, Nova Scotia, Saskatchewan, Prince Edward Island, Newfoundland, Alberta, New Brunswick and Manitoba surround center design, along with maple leaf dec, sepia tone, marked "Alpine White Ironstone Wood & Sons, England," 9-3/4" d **60.00**

Plate, memorial, Garfield center, clear pressed glass, 10" d, **$65**.

Plate, Abraham Lincoln, Lincoln Memorial, Hodgenville, KY, scroll mark with information about Lincoln on back, marked "Old English Staffordshire Ware, Made in Staffordshire, Eng., Imported for Nancy Lincoln Inn, Hodgenville, KY," multicolored transfer, **$20**.

Columbia University, School of Mines, Morningside, center scene, six border scenes, blue and white, marked "Wedgwood, Alumni Federation of Columbia University, Inc.," c1932, 10-7/8" d............. **85.00**

Hermitage, Nashville, TN, Johnroth Studios, Made in Germany, c1920, 4" d **30.00**

Our Union Forever, Centennial, beaded and molded border, brown transfer with hand coloring of American eagle with banner and flag, ironstone, imp "Edge Malkin & Co," 8-3/8" d........................... **220.00**

Souvenir of Chicago, vignettes of State Street, Chicago Univ, New Post Office, Masonic Temple, Public

Library, Union Stock Yards, Board of Trade, blue transfer, Rowland & Marcellus, 10" d **115.00**

Souvenir of Old Albany, vignettes of Fort Frederick, English Church, Albany Academy, State House, The Dutch Church, Van Rensselaer Manor House, Schuyler Mansion, blue transfer, Rowland & Marcellus, 10" d **100.00**

Texas, Southwest Methodist University, Dallas, Vernon Kilns, marked "Made exclusively for Titche-Goettinger Co." **35.00**

Plate, Boston department stores, founders in border, blue transfer, white ground, Wedgewood, 9-3/4" d, **$35**.

Washington, Bellingham, green print, Vernon Kilns **60.00**

Punch cup, From Ida to Momma, 1891, King's Crown pattern, 1/2" w bade of ruby staining, ring handle **50.00**

Shoe, Souvenir of Rochelle, Ill, figural green glass, gold lettering, 4-5/8" l **60.00**

Tumbler, Emma 1910, ruby stained top, Button Arches base, 3-7/8" h.......... **75.00**

Wine glass, Souvenir Waumandee, Wis, custard glass, Thumb print pattern, hp red floral dec, red lettering, gold trim **95.00**

Souvenir and Commemorative Spoons

History: Souvenir and commemorative spoons have been issued for hundreds of years. Early American silversmiths engraved presentation spoons to honor historical personages or mark key events.

In 1881, Myron Kinsley patented a Niagara Falls spoon, and in 1884, Michael Gibney patented a new flatware design. M. W. Galt, Washington, D.C., issued commemorative spoons for George and Martha Washington in 1889. From these beginnings, a collecting craze for souvenir and commemorative spoons developed in the late 19th and early 20th centuries.

Canada, Banff in bowl, maple leaf dec, Canada on handle, marked "Sterling BMCO" on back, 3-3/4" l **15.00**

Graubunden, Switzerland, heraldic figure on front, back hallmarked "PL," silver, 1950s, 4" l **20.00**

Kansas, map marked "Topeka, Kansas City & Wichita," state seal on handle, demitasse, marked "TH. Marthinsen, E.P.N.S., Norway," 4-1/4" l.............. **15.00**

Memorial Arch, Brooklyn, NY, round oak stove **40.00**

Philadelphia, Independence Hall in bowl, SS....................................... **45.00**

Prophet, veiled **135.00**

Richmond, MO, SS....................... **30.00**

Royal Canadian Mounted Police, "Victoria, British Columbia" in bowl, marked "Made in Holland," 4-1/2" l **30.00**

Salem, MA, witch handle **45.00**

Seattle, WA, Indian on handle, etched bowl, sterling **35.00**

SS Momus, Westfield Pattern, Meridan Britannia, 1903, back engraved "L. P. Co.," 6" l **10.00**

St. Paul, The Tower, Houses of Parliament, West Minister, each marked "L. E. P. A1" on back, set of four in orig box.. **42.00**

Washington, DC, marked "Sterling," 5-1/2" l... **15.00**

Spangled Glass

History: Spangled glass is a blown or blown-molded variegated art glass, similar to spatter glass, with the addition of flakes of mica or metallic aventurine. Many pieces are cased with a white or clear layer of glass. Spangled glass was developed in the late 19th century and still is being manufactured.

For more information, see *Warman's Glass*, 4th edition.

Originally, spangled glass was attributed only to the Vasa Murrhina Art Glass Company of Hartford, Connecticut, which distributed the glass for Dr. Flower of the Cape Cod Glassworks, Sandwich, Massachusetts. However, research has shown that many companies in Europe, England, and the United States made spangled glass, and attributing a piece to a specific source is very difficult.

Basket, 7" h, 6" l, ruffled edge, white int., deep apricot with spangled gold, applied crystal loop handle, slight flake.... **225.00**

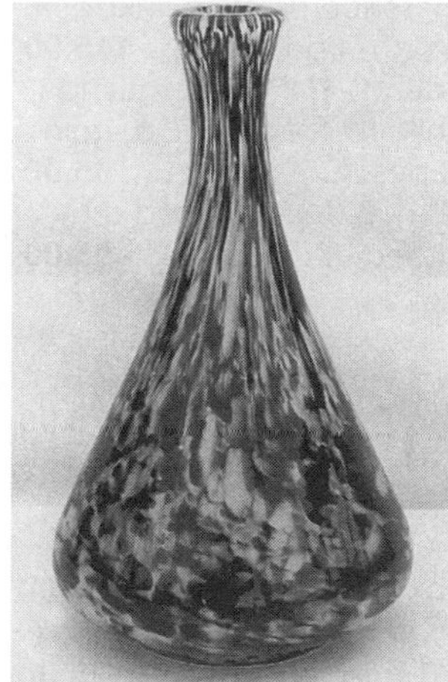

Barber bottle, red and white spatter, mica flecks, no stopper, 8-1/4" h, $195.

Candlesticks, pr, 8-1/8" h, pink and whit spatter, green aventurine flecks, cased white int. **115.00**

Creamer, 3-1/4" d, 4-3/4" h, bulbous, molded swirled ribs, cylindrical neck, pinched spout, blue ground, swirled mica flecks, applied clear reeded handle **225.00**

Cruet, Leaf Mold pattern, cranberry, mica flakes, white casing, Northwood **450.00**

Ewer, 9-1/2" h, raspberry pink ext., white int., mica flecks, twisted applied handle, rough pontil **250.00**

Jack-in-the-pulpit vase, 6-1/4" h, oxblood, green, and white spatter, mica flakes, c1900 .... **125.00**

Basket, pink glass exterior, embedded mica flakes, opaque white interior, applied ribbed coloress glass bent handle with impressed design in ends, 5-1/4" w, 8" h, **$100**. Photo courtesy of Alderfer Auction Co.

Pitcher, 7-1/2" d, 8-3/4" h, cased ruby, white and mica dec, nine ribs, six ruffles, applied clear handle, ground pontil **350.00**

Rose bowl, 4" d, 3-1/4" h, pink cased body, Vasa Murrhina dec **50.00**

Salt shaker, cranberry, cased white int., molded leaf design, Hobbs, c1890 .... **125.00**
Sugar shaker, cranberry, mica flakes, white casing, Northwood.......... **115.00**
Toothpick holder, 2-1/4" h, alternating crimson and white mottled ground, gold mica, lattice stripes **65.00**
Tumbler, 2-3/4" d, 3-3/4" h, cased ruby, white and mica dec.......... **95.00**
Vase
6-3/4" h, glossy pink cased satin, silver mica, two applied crystal handles.......... **75.00**
8-3/4" h, stick, cased satin glass alternating pink and blue panels, overall silver mica, crystal rigaree around neck **75.00**
9-1/4" h, stretched, green, silver-plated rim, bruise on side **120.00**

SPATTER GLASS

History: Spatter glass is a variegated blown or blown-molded art glass. It originally was called "end-of-day"" glass, based on the assumption that it was made from batches of glass leftover at the end of the day. However, spatter glass was found to be a standard production item for many glass factories.

For more information, see *Warman's Glass*, 4th edition.

Spatter glass was developed at the end of the 19th century and is still being produced in the United States and Europe.

Reproduction Alert: Many modern examples come from the area previously called Czechoslovakia.

Basket, tortoiseshell, cream, tan, yellow, white, and brown spatter, white lining, rect, tightly crimped edge, colorless thorn handle.......... **120.00**
Berry set, master bowl and two sauces, Leaf Mold, cranberry vaseline.......... **300.00**
Bowl, 10" d, deep red, white spatter, gold enamel dec, numbered, c1900.......... **375.00**
Candlestick, 7-1/2" h, yellow, red, and white streaks, clear overlay, vertical swirled molding, smooth base, flanged socket.......... **60.00**
Cologne bottle, 5-1/2" h, white spatter, enamel dec, orig stopper applicator, marked "Made in Czechoslovakia," price for pr.......... **115.00**
Creamer, Leaf Mold, cranberry vaseline **250.00**
Darning egg, multicolored, attributed to Sandwich Glass.......... **125.00**

Fairy lamp, orange, red, yellow, and white spatter, clear marked "Clarke's Patent" base, 4-1/2" h, **$145**.

Ewer, yellow ground, white spatter, tri-fold spout, flared applied clear handle, sharp pontil, 8-3/4" h **85.00**

Marble, onionskin, blue, orange, yellow, and pink, white spatter, 2" d, **$200**. Photo courtesy of Joy Luke Auctions.

Finger bowl and underplate, 6" d, 3-1/4" d, tortoiseshell, ruffled.......... **275.00**
Jack-in-the-pulpit, 5" h, 3-1/2" d, Vasa Murrhina, deep pink int., clear ruffled top **115.00**
Lamp, 15-1/2" h, blown egg-shaped font and holder, red and black Vasa Murrhina glass with gold mica flecks, brass and steel base with tripod holder, old double burner sgd "Young's Duplex," possibly Stevens & Williams, minor wear, later frosted shade **400.00**
Pitcher, 6-1/2" d, 8" h, burgundy and white spatter, cased in clear, ground pontil, clear reeded handle.......... **395.00**
Rose bowl, 4-1/2" d, 3-1/2" h, multicolored spatter, white int., seashell scalloped rigaree **165.00**
Salt, 3" l, maroon and pink, white spatter, applied clear feet and handle.......... **125.00**
Sugar shaker, Leaf Umbrella pattern, cranberry.......... **495.00**
Tumbler, 3-3/4"h, emb Swirl pattern, white, maroon, pink, yellow, and green, white int. **65.00**
Vase
7" h, 4-3/4" w at top, trumpet shape, red-orange, white spatter, marked "Made In Czechoslovakia".......... **95.00**

Pitcher, hand blown, multicolored spatter, interior cased in white glass, applied clear reeded handle, 8-1/2" h, **$225**. Photo courtesy of James D. Julia, Inc.

12" h, bright orange, ruffled top, cobalt blue spatter at base, sgd "Czechoslovakia" **200.00**
Watch holder, 3-3/4" x 4-1/4" dish, ruffled rim, blue spatter, 7" h ormolu metal watch holder **175.00**

SPATTERWARE

For more information, see *Warman's English & Continental Pottery & Porcelain*, 3rd edition.

History: Spatterware generally was made of common earthenware, although occasionally creamware was used. The earliest English examples were made about 1780. The peak period of production was from 1810 to 1840. Firms known to have made spatterware are Adams, Barlow, and Harvey and Cotton.

The amount of spatter decoration varies from piece to piece. Some objects simply have decorated borders. These often were decorated with a brush, requiring several hundred touches per square inch to achieve the spatter effect. Other pieces have the entire surface covered with spatter.

Like any soft paste, spatterware is easily broken or chipped.

Marks: Marked pieces are rare.

Reproduction Alert: Cybis spatter is an increasingly collectible ware in its own right. The pieces, made by the Polishman Boleslaw Cybis in the 1940s, have an Adams-type peafowl design. Many contemporary craftsmen also are reproducing spatterware.

Notes: Collectors today focus on the patterns—Cannon, Castle, Fort, Peafowl, Rainbow, Rose, Thistle, Schoolhouse, etc. The decoration on flatware is in the center of the piece; on hollow ware, it occurs on both sides.

Aesthetics and the color of spatter are key to determining value. Blue and red are the most common colors; green, purple, and brown are in a middle group; black and yellow are scarce.

Miniature tea set, partial, green spatter, peafowl decoration, teapot, creamer, two cups, three saucers, **$1,610**. Photo courtesy of Pook & Pook.

Bouillon cup and saucer, blue and red stars, green and black flowers, partial imp name.................................... **175.00**

Cup and saucer, handleless, green and red design, 2-3/4" d, **$120**.

Bowl, 6-3/4" d, 3-1/2" h, rainbow, vertical red, blue, and green stripes, int. blue rim and center spot, minor flake and wear, hairlines **825.00**

Creamer

3-1/2" h, blue spatter, red and blue tulip, green leaves, crazing and minor overall darkening.......... **330.00**

3-3/4" h, purple and blue spatter, red and green Adam's Rose, wear, minor filled in flakes......................... **275.00**

4" h, red spatter, green, red, and dark blue peafowl, green spatter branch, leaf molded handle, rim flake, some edge wear.......... **525.00**

Cup and saucer, handleless

Blue and red rainbow spatter, red and blue dahlia, stains, hairline **290.00**

Blue spatter, red and green rose, stains, hairline **265.00**

Blue spatter, red stars, green and black flowers, partial imp name **150.00**

Blue spatter, red, yellow, and blue peafowl, minor roughness, glazed over flake on saucer............... **330.00**

Medium green borders, red, yellow, and light blue peafowl, light stains and crow's foot on saucer **225.00**

Rainbow spatter, purple and blue stripes, bull's eye centers....... **550.00**

Red spatter, brown, green, and blue peafowl, light staining, hairline in cup **360.00**

Red spatter, yellow bull's eye, minor staining.................................. **880.00**

Cup plate

3-3/8" d, green spatter, red, yellow, and dark blue peafowl **375.00**

3-7/8" d, green spatter, red, gold, and light blue peafowl, some bubbling and flaking in enamel, pinpoint flake under rim **425.00**

4" d, blue spatter, paneled rim, green, light yellow, and red peafowl, imp "Stoneware FW & Co.," minor enamel bubbling **275.00**

4" d, blue spatter, paneled rim, white star center **300.00**

4" d, red spatter, red green, and blue peafowl on green spatter branch, feather molded edge, propeller mark **500.00**

4-1/4" d, blue spatter, twelve sided, Fort pattern, yellow, red, brown, and green, faint crow's foot on back **475.00**

4-1/8" d, blue spatter, red and green rose center **425.00**

4-1/8" d, pale yellow spatter, red and green rose center, small flake on table ring **1,320.00**

4-1/8" d, rainbow spatter, olive green, light red striped border, bull's eye center **385.00**

4-1/8" d, yellow spatter, paneled rim, red and green cockscomb center **1,650.00**

Miniature

Cup and saucer, handleless cup Purple spatter........................ **200.00**

Pitcher, eight-panel earthenware vessel, angled handle, hand-painted tulip designs, blue spatter background, England, early 19th C, hairlines, wear, 8-1/8" h, **$825**. Photo courtesy of Skinner, Inc.

Red spatter, blue, black, and green morning glory design **1,100.00**

Tea set, 4" h teapot, cup, cov sugar, green spatter leaves, red, gold, and blue peafowl, spout repair to teapot, lid missing, flakes on sugar lid **200.00**

Mush cup and saucer, flow blue, red and green stick spatter designs, light stains, in-the-making hairline in saucer **315.00**

Pitcher, 6-1/2" h, rainbow spatter, hexagonal, red and blue vertical stripes, molded fan under spout, edge wear on base, repaired yellow spout **495.00**

Plate, Tulip pattern, yellow rim, wear, knife marks, 8-1/2" d, **$265**.

Plate

6-3/8" d, magenta spatter, red and green thistle center, feather molded edge, few rim chips............... **125.00**

7" d, rainbow spatter, concentric rings of strong red, blue, and green, scalloped rim, minor edge wear, crow's foot **150.00**

7-1/2" d, blue paneled border, blue and yellow open tulip with red and green in center, two flakes **220.00**

8" d, paneled, light blue and red stick spatter leaf borders, red and green rose center **110.00**

8" d, yellow paneled border, red and green tulip center, minor wear, edge flakes, short hairlines **2,420.00**

8-1/8" d, light purple border, blue spatter flowers, red and green rose center, edge damage.............. **90.00**

8-1/4" d, purple border, red and green center rose, light stains, rim flakes.................................... **110.00**

8-1/4" d, rainbow, rayed design, yellow, green, red, light blue, and black, scalloped edge, professional restoration **1,265.00**

8-1/4" d, red and blue rainbow border, red, blue, and green dahlia, damage **195.00**

8-1/2" d, green and blue rainbow, green bull's eye center, damage **800.00**

9-1/4" d, rainbow, rayed design, green, red, blue, black, and yellow, scalloped edge, minor edge flakes, some stains **6,930.00**

9-1/4" d, red spatter, red and green rose center, edge and minor surface wear....................................... **150.00**

9-1/2" d, blue spatter border, light red spatter underneath, red and green center rose with blueberries, imp anchor and "Witte," two hairlines **560.00**

9-1/2" d, dark red, green, and dark blue six-pointed star center, red sunburst border, hairline, flake **365.00**

9-1/2" d, green border, red schoolhouse center, damage **695.00**

9-1/2" d, yellow border, red and green thistle center, molded feather edge **4,300.00**

10-1/4" d, rainbow, red and blue sponged arrow pattern border, red star in center, paneled rim, chips on table ring **275.00**

Plate, paneled, red, green, and blue rainbow spatter, 9-1/4" d, **$1,150**. Photo courtesy of Pook & Pook.

Soup plate, 9-7/8" d, blue spatter border, green and red four-petal flower, wear, rim flake **100.00**

Plates, 7-1/2" d, blue spatterware, green, yellow and red peafowl in center, marked "Stoneware/PW & Co.," 8-1/4" d, red spatterware, blue, yellow and green peafowl in center, **$425**. Photo courtesy of Sanford Alderfer Auction Company.

Sugar, cov

4-1/2" h, blue spatter, gray and brown fort design, molded ring handles, repaired **250.00**

4-3/4" h, green spatter, red, yellow, and blue peafowl, added spoon slot, repaired **200.00**

5" d, 4-3/4" h, blue spatter, light blue, red, and green diagonally striped peafowl, molded shell handles, edge damage, glued flake **420.00**

5" d, 5-1/2" h, blue spatter, red and green roses on each side, minor roughness and in-the-making hairline, lid repaired **275.00**

6-1/2" h, yellow spatter, red and green tulips, paneled body, molded handles, professionally restored **1,100.00**

Sugar bowl, covered, alternating blue and red stripes, England, early 19th C, cover chip, 4-5/8" h, **$300**. Photo courtesy of Skinner, Inc.

Teapot

5-1/2" h, red and blue vertical stripes, matching lid, edge damage to spout **2,420.00**

9-3/4" h medium to dark blue, white ground, paneled sides and lid, scrolled handle, professional restorations **5,775.00**

Tureen lid, 9" x 9", octagonal, light blue spatter as leaves, two dark red, green, and blue gooney birds **250.00**

Waste bowl, 6-1/4" d, 3-1/2" h, brown, red, and black Fort pattern, blue spatter, hairline **200.00**

Spongeware

For more information, see *Warman's Glass*, 4th edition, and *Warman's English & Continental Pottery & Porcelain*, 3rd edition.

History: Spongeware is a specific type of decoration, not a type of pottery or glaze.

Spongeware decoration is found on many kinds of pottery bodies—ironstone, redware, stoneware, yellowware, etc. It was made in both England and the United States. Pieces were marked after 1815, and production extended into the 1880s.

Decoration is varied. On some pieces, the sponging is minimal with the white underglaze dominant. Other pieces appear to be solidly sponged on both sides. Pieces made between 1840 and 1860 have circular or horizontally streaked sponging.

Blue and white are the most common colors, but browns, greens, ochres, and a greenish blue also were used. The greenish blue results from blue sponging with a pale yellow overglaze. A red overglaze produces a black or navy color. Blue and red were used on English creamware and American earthenware of the 1880s. Other spongeware colors include gray, grayish green, red, dark green on stark white, dark green on mellow yellow, and purple.

Bank, 5-1/2" l, figural, piggy, blue and cream, pierced coin slot on top ... **155.00**

Bowl, 7" d, fluted, brown and blue sponge, cream ground **60.00**

Butter crock, 4-5/8" d, 3" h, blue and white, back labeled "Village Farm Dairy," chips, hairlines, crazing **300.00**

Carpet ball, 3-1/2" d, red and green sponged dec **125.00**

Creamer, 3" h, green, blue and cream **100.00**

Cup and saucer, handleless, red and blue sponging, cluster of buds, stains on cup **375.00**

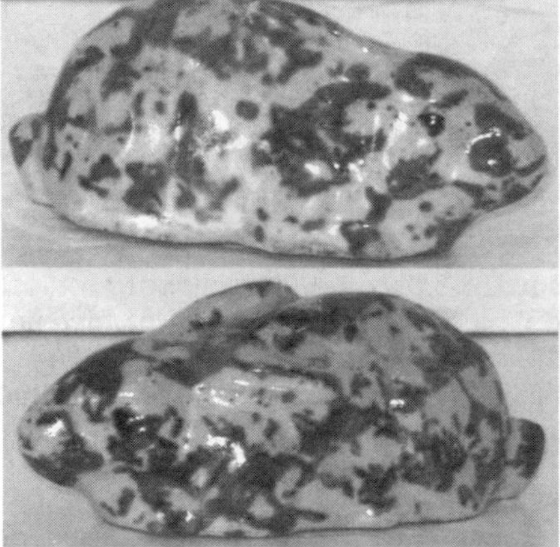

Figure, bunny, two views, dark cobalt blue at eyes, initialed "JC," c1880, 4-1/2" l, glaze flake at one ear and front paw, **$1,760**. Photo courtesy of Vicki and Bruce Waasdorp.

Figure, rabbit, 4-1/2" l, blue and white, dark blue accent at eyes, initialed "JC," c1880, glaze flake at one ear and front paw **1,760.00**

Gravy boat, ftd, rainbow, scrollwork along handle, red, blue, and green spatter, 6-1/2" l, 4" h **415.00**

Marble, 2" d, gray, blue sponge, late 19th C **220.00**

Milk pitcher, 7-1/2" h, black sponge, white ground **185.00**

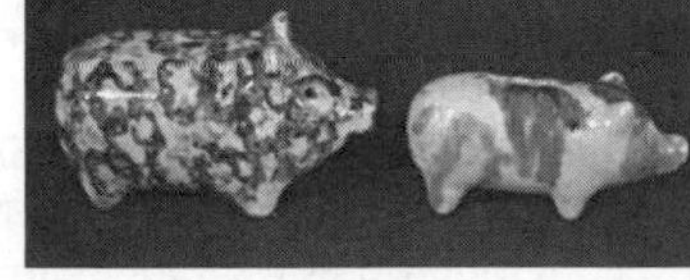

Banks, pigs, probably of Ohio origin, left: blue and brown sponging, cream glaze, 5-1/2" l, flakes, **$85**; right: running brown and green sponging, cream glaze, 5" l, flakes, **$75**. Photo courtesy of Garth's Auctions, Inc.

Mush cup and saucer, 8-1/2" d, blue and white, tight sponge dec, close mismatch **250.00**

Jardiniére, earthenware, blue greenish-brown sponge decoration over cream ground, hairline, imperfections, 10-1/2" d, 9-1/2" h, **$210**. Photo courtesy of Sanford Alderfer Auction Company.

Pitcher

6-1/2" h, blue and white, blue accent around rim, professional restoration to surface chip at spout, two short hairlines **155.00**

7-7/8" h, green and faded purple grapes, blue sponge dec, molded leaf spout, chips, handle glued **615.00**

9" h, navy blue and white, bulbous-shaped base **385.00**

Miniature advertising jug, brown and white Bristol glaze, frame with black stenciling "Compliments of The Phoenix Bar, Los Angeles, CA 1911," back stenciled "Brook Hill None Superior," c1911, 3-3/4" h, **$100**. Photo courtesy of Vicki and Bruce Waasdorp.

Plate

8-3/4" d, blue sponge, centralized tulip motif in burgundy red, forest green leaves **220.00**

9" d, dark blue on cream **195.00**

9-1/2" d, rainbow sponge, paneled, red and blue arrow border, red star center, light stains, crazing on underside **550.00**

9-3/4" d, red and blue sponged border, red and green tulip center, imp "Cotton and Barlow," flake under rim, short hairlines **220.00**

Platter

9-1/4" x 13-1/4", medium mottled blue with darker specks and white, rect, slightly curving sides, scroll molded rim **125.00**

10-1/8" x 13-3/4", blue and white, rect, slightly curving sides, faint sponging on back **250.00**

10-1/4" x 13-3/4", blue and white, rect, slightly curving sides **220.00**

Soup bowl, 9-1/4" d, scalloped, scroll molded edges, dark blue sponging **110.00**

Spittoon, 5" h, blue sponge, linear dec on white glazed ground, late 19th C **90.00**

Sugar bowl, rainbow, emb shell shape handles, blue and red spatter panels, lid missing **310.00**

Teapot, 5-1/2" h, red and green cluster of buds design, few stains, spout flakes **315.00**

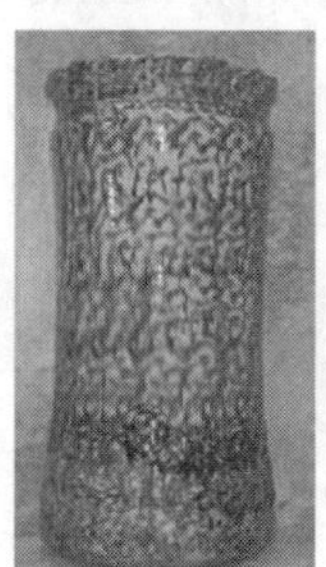
Umbrella stand, cylindrical, flared and scalloped rim, molded scroll motif, brown sponge decoration on rim and base, blue sponging on body, gilt highlights, crazing, rim chip, 11" d, 21-1/2" h, **$250**. Photo courtesy of Alderfer Auction Co.

Tray

6-1/2" x 9-3/4" d, oval, dark blue and white **145.00**

7" x 11", oval, blue and white **115.00**

10" d, round, blue and white, molded scroll rim, gilt spatter, two one-pc handles **115.00**

10" d, round, blue and white, scalloped rim, molded ruffles, two molded wreaths for handles, little white shows **75.00**

Umbrella stand, blue with white, two white accent bands, four blue accent bands, 21" h, glued repair, **$580**. Photo courtesy of Vicki and Bruce Waasdorp.

Umbrella stand, 21" h, blue and white, two white accent bands, four blue accent bands, 6" U-shaped piece at top that was broken and reglued **580.00**

Water cooler, 18" h, blue and white, marked "Fulper Pottery Co. Flemington, NJ, Gate City Natural Stone Filter," stenciled "No. 6," two-pc construction, orig spigot, minor stone pig on front of filter top **385.00**

Sports Cards

For more information, see *Warman's Sports Collectibles*.

History: Baseball cards were first printed in the late 19th century. By 1900, the most common cards, known as "T" cards, were those made by tobacco companies such as American Tobacco Co. The majority of the tobacco-related cards were produced between 1909 and 1915. During the 1920s, American Caramel, National Caramel, and York Caramel candy companies issued cards identified in lists as "E" cards.

During the 1930s, Goudey Gum Co. of Boston (1933 to 1941) and Gum Inc. (in 1939) were prime producers of baseball cards. Following World War II, Bowman Gum of Philadelphia (B.G.H.L.I.), the successor to Gum, Inc., led the way. Topps, Inc. (T.C.G.) of Brooklyn, New York, followed. Topps bought Bowman in 1956 and enjoyed a virtual monopoly in card production until 1981.

In 1981, Fleer of Philadelphia and Donruss of Memphis challenged Topps. All three companies annually produce sets numbering 600 cards or more. In the late 1980, the new-card industry expanded yet again, with Upper Deck, Score, Pacific joining the fray. Ultimately, the market for new cards would change dramatically from what it had been in the past, with about a half-dozen companies each producing dozens of cards sets in all four major sports, reducing the print runs to relatively miniscule numbers and elevating the wholesale and retail prices of the cards in the process.

Football cards have been printed since the 1890s. However, it was not until 1933 that the first bubble gum football card appeared in the Goudey Sport Kings set. In 1935, National Chicle of Cambridge, Massachusetts, produced the first full set of gum cards devoted exclusively to football.

Both Leaf Gum of Chicago and Bowman Gum of Philadelphia produced sets of football cards in 1948. Leaf discontinued production after its 1949 issue; Bowman continued until 1955.

Topps Chewing Gum entered the market in 1950 with its college-stars set.

Topps became a fixture in the football card market with its 1955 All-American set. From 1956 thorough 1963, Topps printed card sets of National Football League players, combining them with the American Football League players in 1961.

Topps produced sets with only American Football League players from 1964 to 1967. The Philadelphia Gum Company made National Football League card sets during this period. Beginning in 1968 and continuing to the present, Topps has produced sets of National Football League cards, the name adopted after the merger of the two leagues.

The expansion of the new-card industry noted above took place in a similar fashion in football, basketball and hockey cards, with many new licensees emerging after 1989.

Note: Prices shown are taken from the 2002 and 2003 editions of Krause Publications' Standard Catalogs of Baseball, Football and Basketball.

Baseball

American Caramel

E90-1, 1909-11, Keeler, throwing, Excellent (EX)....... **850.00**

T206 White Border

1909-11, Cobb, red background, Very Good (VG)....... **1,500.00**

Sporting News

1916 M101-4, No. 87, Jackson, VG-EX....... **2,750.00**

Bowman

1948

No. 1, Elliot, Near-Mint (NM) **125.00**

No. 8, Rizzuto, NM....... **255.00**

No. 14, Reynolds, NM....... **40.00**

1949

No. 36, Reese, NM....... **150.00**

No. 50, Robinson, Near-Mint to Mint (NM-MT)....... **2,000.00**

No. 84, Campanella, NM....... **350.00**

No. 131, Lehner, NM....... **15.00**

1951No. 1, Ford, NM....... **950.00**

No. 3, Roberts, EX....... **35.00**

No. 26, Rizzuto, NM-MT....... **375.00**

No. 253, Mantle rookie, NM **5,500.00**

1953, Color

No. 6, Ginsburg, NM....... **35.00**

No. 18, Fox, EX....... **45.00**

No. 19, Dark, NM....... **30.00**

No. 32, Musial, NM....... **550.00**

No. 33, Reese, EX....... **300.00**

No. 59, Mantle, EX....... **675.00**

Cracker Jack

1914, No. 30, Ty Cobb, 1914, NM **5,000.00**

Diamond Stars

1935, No. 50, Mel Ott, NM....... **300.00**

Fleer, complete sets

1959, Ted Williams set, NM **1,600.00**

1957 Topps, **$190.**

1960, Greats, VG....... **235.00**

1961-62, Greats, EX....... **375.00**

1963, with checklist, NM....... **1,300.00**

1982, MINT....... **45.00**

1984, NM....... **35.00**

1986, NM....... **25.00**

Goudey

1933, No. 75, Kamm, NM....... **260.00**

1933, No. 91, Zachary, NM....... **60.00**

1933, No. 92, Gehrig, NM....... **3,500.00**

1933, No. 144, Ruth, NM....... **4,000.00**

1933 uncut sheet, NM....... **6,995.00**

Leaf

1948-49, No. 1, DiMaggio, EX **1,125.00**

1948-49, No. 4, Musial rookie, NM **1,350.00**

1948-49, No. 76, Williams, NM **825.00**

Play Ball

1939, No. 26, DiMaggio, EX....... **500.00**

1939, No. 92, Williams, VG....... **660.00**

1939, No. 103, Berg, NM....... **190.00**

1940, No. 27, DiMaggio, NM **1,850.00**

1941, No. 14, Williams, NM **1,900.00**

1941, No. 71, DiMaggio, NM **2,600.00**

1953 Bowman color, **$2,100.**

Topps

1951, Red Backs

No. 1, Berra, NM....... **85.00**

1951, Blue Backs

No. 3, Ashburn, NM....... **95.00**

No. 20, Branca, EX....... **20.00**

No. 50, Mize, NM....... **65.00**

1952

No. 29, Kluszewski, PSA 9 (MINT) 8,....... **750.00**

No. 175, Martin, NM....... **375.00**

No. 261, Mays, PSA 8 (NM-MT) 5,....... **108.00**

No. 311, Mantle, PSA 9 (MINT) **88,000.00**

No. 356, Atwell, NM....... **220.00**

No. 384, Crosetti, EX....... **200.00**

No. 392, Wilhelm, PSA 9 .... **7,760.00**

1953

No. 1, Robinson, NM....... **675.00**

No. 4, Wade, NM....... **25.00**

No. 82, Mantle, NM....... **2,000.00**

No. 220, Paige, NM....... **500.00**

1954

No. 1, Williams, NM....... **625.00**

No. 22, Greengrass, NM....... **15.00**

No. 94, Banks rookie, PSA 9 .... **12,500.00**

No. 128, Aaron rookie, PSA 9 .... **30,200.00**

No. 250, Williams, PSA 8 .... **26,500.00**

1955

No. 1, Rhodes, NM....... **290.00**

No. 123, Koufax rookie, PSA 9 .... **25,600.00**

No. 124, Killebrew rookie, PSA 10 (GEM MINT)....... **45,000.00**

No. 220, Snider, NM....... **475.00**

Basketball

Bowman

1948

No. 2, Hamilton, NM....... **50.00**

No. 9, Philip, NM....... **140.00**

No. 32, Holzman, NM....... **425.00**

No. 66, Pollard, NM....... **400.00**

Topps

1957

No. 1, Clifton rookie, NM....... **250.00**

No. 2, Yardley rookie, NM....... **55.00**

No. 13, Schayes rookie, NM **125.00**

No. 17, Cousy rookie, NM....... **525.00**

No. 42, Stokes rookie, NM....... **120.00**

No. 77, Russel rookie, NM **2,000.00**

1974-75

No. 1, Jabbar, NM....... **35.00**

No. 10, Maravich, NM....... **20.00**

No. 39, Walton rookie, NM....... **60.00**

No. 200, Erving, NM....... **55.00**

Football

Bowman, 1950

No. 1, Walker, NM....... **175.00**

No. 45, Graham rookie, NM **450.00**

1986-87 Fleer, **$1,550**.

Fleer, 1961
- No. 30, Unitas, NM **70.00**
- No. 41, Meredith, NM **140.00**
- No. 155, Kemp, NM **155.00**

1963
- No. 6, Long (short print), NM **180.00**
- No. 47, Dawson, NM **250.00**

Topps

1955, All-American
- No. 1, Herman Hickman rookie, NM **90.00**
- No. 12, Graham, NM **175.00**
- No. 16, Rockne, NM **325.00**
- No. 20, Baugh, NM **200.00**
- No. 27, Grange, NM **350.00**
- No. 37, Thorpe, NM **375.00**
- No. 97, Hutson rookie, NM **225.00**
- No. 98, Feathers rookie, NM **75.00**

1959
- No. 10, Brown, NM **125.00**
- No. 44, Johnson, NM **7.00**
- No. 118, Cardinals team, NM **5.00**
- No. 126, Rams Pennant, NM **4.00**

1960
- No. 1, Unitas, NM **80.00**
- No. 4, Berry, NM **8.00**
- No. 74, Gifford, NM **65.00**

1961
- No. 166, Kemp, NM **150.00**

1966
- No. 96, Namath, NM **340.00**

Sports Collectibles

History: People have been saving sports-related equipment since the inception of sports. Some was passed down from generation to generation for reuse; the rest was stored in closets, attics, and basements.

In the 1980s, two key trends brought collectors' attention to sports collectibles. First, decorators began using old sports items, especially in restaurant decor. Second, sports collectors began to discover the thrill of owning the "real" thing. All sport categories are collectible, with baseball items paramount and golf and football running close behind.

For more information, see *Warman's Sports Collectibles*.

Baseball

Advertising sign, diecast, Ted Williams Wilson **4,125.00**

Baseball, autographed, Negro League players, including Josh Gibson, c1933 .... **24,200.00**

Baseball, game used
- 1903 World Series **17,050.00**
- 1905 World Series, last out ball, sgd by John McGraw **27,500.00**

Baseball glove, game used, Brooks Robinson **5,500.00**

Baseballs, unopened, sealed, J Heydler, NL balls **10,450.00**

Bat, gamed used, Max Carey ... **4,950.00**

Book, Casey at the Bat, 1901, first edition **5,500.00**

Cabinet card, New York Giants, 1988, large size **15,400.00**

Archery licenses, PA, 1980s, nine licenses in plastic sleeve, **$90**.

Candy container, 5" h, figural glass, baseball player standing on sq base, mitt on left hand, gold and red painted uniform, c1916, replacement screw-on closure **300.00**

Hat, game used, Homestead Grays, c1940 .... **10,400.00**

Jacket, 1914 Les Mann, Miracle Braves **7,700.00**

Jersey, game used
- Cincinnati Reds, C. Heathcote, 1931 .... **10,450.00**
- Milwaukee Braves, Warren Spahn, home **9,570.00**

Photograph, Babe Ruth, by N. Fein, c1948 .... **6,875.00**

Program, Cleveland Indians, 1948 World Series **120.00**

Stadium seat
- Briggs, figural end seat, painted green **1,925.00**
- Yankee Stadium, row of two, painted blue **1,760.00**

Tea set, presentation, Johnny Evers, 1914 .... **3,190.00**

Telegram, sent to Joe Jackson, 1923 .... **8,250.00**

Ticket stub
- 1909, Shibe Park, first game **1,100.00**
- 1939, American League of NY, last game played by Lou Gherig **3,650.00**

Uniform, Chicago White Sox, Nemo Liebold, 1920 .... **9,350.00**

Photograph, silver print, ladies baseball team wearing numbered uniforms, two hold bats, three with gloves, verso "Ladies baseball team 1900, Photog by Brown Brothers, New York City," 6" x 8", **$350**. Photo courtesy of Historical Collectibles Auctions.

Basketball

Autograph, basketball
- Archibald, Nate **100.00**
- Bird, Larry **200.00**
- Bradley, Bill **150.00**
- O'Brien, Larry **125.00**

Autograph, photograph, 8" x 10"
- McGuire, Dick **20.00**
- Thurmond, Nate **24.00**

Magazine, Sports Illustrated, Feb. 1949, Ralph Beard, Kentucky cover **95.00**

Pin, Chicago Americans Tournament Championship, brass, 1935 .... **75.00**

Program
- Basketball Hall of Fame Commemoration Day Program, orig invitation, 1961 .... **75.00**
- NCAA Final Four Championship, Louisville, KY, 1967 .... **175.00**
- World Series of Basketball, 1951, Harlem Globetrotters and College All-Americans **55.00**

Shoes, pr, game used, autographed
- Drexler, Clyde, Avais **225.00**

Sikma, Jack, Converse.......... **100.00**
Webber, Chris, Nikes............. **550.00**

Souvenir book, Los Angeles Lakers, with two records, Jerry West and Elgin Baylor on action cover............................. **75.00**

Ticket, NBA Finals Boston Celtics at Los Angeles Lakers, 1963.................... **95.00**

Yearbook
1961-62, Boston Celtics......... **150.00**
1965-66, Boston Celtics........... **85.00**
1969-70, Milwaukee Bucks...... **40.00**

Pocket flask, pottery, green glaze, black lettering, Beneagles Scotch Whiskey, Sportsman's Flask, Red Deer, **$5.**

Boxing

Autograph, photo, sgd
Max Baer, 8" x 10" **180.00**
Mike Tyson **60.00**

Badge, 4" d, Larry Holmes, black and white photo, red and black inscriptions, 1979 copyright Don King Productions **25.00**

Boxing gloves, 35 readable autographs **380.00**

Cabinet card, 4" x 6", Corbett, James F., dressed in suit **375.00**

Figure, 8" w, 20-1/4" h, carved fruitwood, fully carved figure throwing right jab, standing on continuation of trunk with tree bark intact, attributed to New Hampshire, c1900....................................... **1,955.00**

Plaque, 6" d, 1920s-30s, boxer, brass **85.00**

Football

Autograph, football
Bergey, Bill **70.00**
Ditka, Mike............................ **125.00**
Long, Howie **75.00**

Autograph, helmet
Dawson, Len, Kansas City Chiefs **250.00**
Elway, John, Denver Broncos **275.00**

Autograph, photograph, 8" x 10"
Bradshaw, Terry **40.00**
Brown, Jim............................... **30.00**
Thomas, Thurman **25.00**

Game, Tom Hamilton's Navy Football Game, 1940s **45.00**

Football, used for championship game, Eagles, 1960............................ **4,510.00**

Pennant, felt, A.F.L.
Boston Patriots, white on red, multicolored Patriot **75.00**
Buffalo Bills, white on blue, pink buffaloes................................. **95.00**
Houston Oilers, white on light blue **75.00**

Playoff guide, 1965 NFL, Green Bay Packers vs. St. Louis Cardinals...... **40.00**

Program
Army vs. Duke, at the Polo Grounds, 1946 .... **40.00**
Green Bay Packers, 1960 .... **30.00**
Heisman Trophy, 1957, John David Crow **30.00**
Rose Bowl, 1974, USC vs. Ohio State **40.00**

Pool table, together with accessories such as cue racks, cues, bridge, two sets of balls, brushes, score keepers, etc., 98" l, 50" w, 32" h, **$900.** Photo courtesy of Sloans & Kenyon Auctions.

Golf

Autograph, photo, sgd, Tiger Woods **60.00**

Book, George Fullerton Carnegie, Golfiana: or Niceties Connected with the Game of Golf, Edinburgh, 1833, 18 pgs of poetry **21,850.00**

Magazine, American Golfer, June 1932 .... **10.00**

Noisemaker, 2-3/4" d, 6-1/2" l, litho tin, full-color image of male golfer, marked "Germany" on handle, 1930s......... **35.00**

Print, Charles Crombie, The Rules of Golf Illustrated, 24 humorous lithographs of golfers in medieval clothes, London, 1905... **1,265.00**

Program, Fort Worth Open Golf Championship, Glen Garden Country Club, Ft. Worth, TX, 1945 .... **100.00**

Toy, 6-1/2" l, 4" w, 6-1/2" h, Jocko, litho tin wind-up, red, green, and yellow outfit, litho base **300.00**

Hockey

Autograph
Orr, Bobby, photograph, 8" x 10" **50.00**
Smith, Clint, photograph, 8" x 10" **12.00**
Thompson, Tiny, puck **50.00**
Watson, Harry, puck **55.00**

Hockey stick, game used, autographed
Beliveau, Jean, 1960s CCM, cracked **700.00**
Cashman, Wayne, Sher-wood, uncracked **175.00**
LeBlanc, J. B., Koho, cracked **50.00**

Jersey, game used, Wayne Gretzky, Rangers, autographed **415.00**

Magazine, Sport Revue, Quebec publication, Feb 1956, Bert Olmstead, Hall of Fame cov.............................. **15.00**

Program, Boston Bruins, Sports News, 1937-38 .... **250.00**

Tobacco tin, Puck Tobacco, Canadian, tin litho, detailed image of two hockey players on both sides, 4" d, 3-1/4" h **190.00**

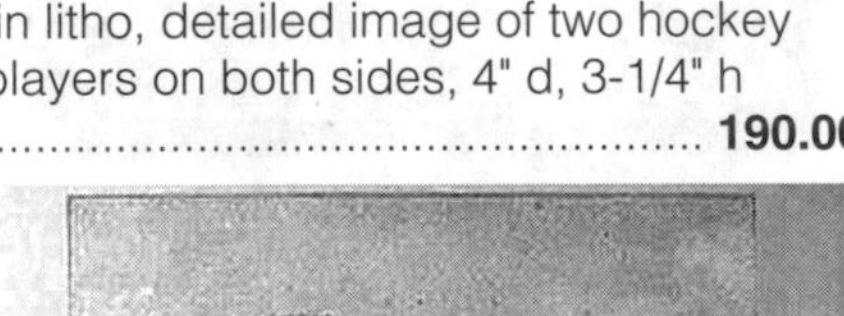

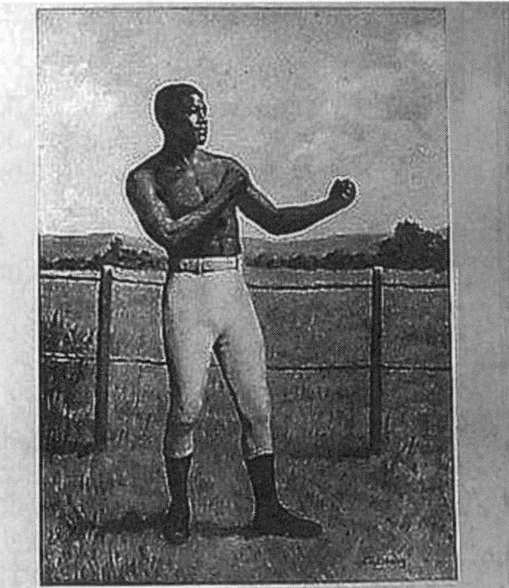

Print, gravure, Peter Jackson by A. D. Baston, published by Cadbury, Jones & Co., London, 1894, black Australian boxer who held heavyweight titles for Australia and Britain, inducted into International Boxing Hall of Fame in 1990, professionally framed, 27-1/2" x 37-1/2", **$230.** Photo courtesy of Historical Collectibles Auctions.

Hunting

Badge, Western Cartridge Co., plant type, emb metal, pin back, 1-3/4" x 1-3/8" **100.00**

Book, The World of the White-Tailed Deer, Leonard Lee Rue III, J. B. Lippencott, 1962, 134 pgs, black and white illus, dj **15.00**

Box, Peters High Velocity, two-pc cardboard shot gun shells, multicolored graphics, 25 16-gauge shells....... **250.00**

License
Arkansas 1939-1940 Resident, 1-3/4", bright red and white, twist-off back for insertion of paper license, celluloid center window.......... **235.00**
Wisconsin 1928 Resident, 1-1/4" d, blue, white, and bright green ... **60.00**

Print, "Life in the Woods-The Hunters Camp," published by Lyon & Co., printed

by J. Rau, NY, five gentlemen in camp, two more fishing in lake, framed, 22" x 28", some foxing, center line burn, water stains in borders **150.00**

Sign

Paul Jones Whiskey, game-hunting scene, orig gold gilt frame, 43" x 57" **750.00**

Winchester, diecut, cardboard, stand-up, Indian Chief with Winchester shotgun in one hand, additional barrels in other hand, 24" x 60" **200.00**

Watch fob, Savage Revolver, figural, metal **110.00**

Olympics

Badge, 1-3/4" x 2-1/4", enamel on brass, Winter Olympics, Albertville, red and blue on white, colored Olympic rings..... **25.00**

Brochure, 9-1/4" x 12-1/2", Official Pictorial Souvenir, 1932, issued by organizing committee, Los Angeles, stiff paper covers, lightly emb soft green cover design with silver and gold accents, 64 black and white pages **40.00**

Cartoon, 8-1/2" x 12-1/2", white art sheet centered by 6-1/4" x 12" orig art cartoon in black ink by Carl Hubenthal, Los Angeles Examiner, 1956, art and caption relate to first ever 7' high jump in Olympic trials by US athlete Charlie Dumas **45.00**

Pinback button, 3" d, Minute Maid sponsor, orange and black cello, 1980 .... **25.00**

Torch, 31-1/2" l, gold plated brass, aluminum, and pecan wood, engraved "Atlanta 1996" **250.00**

Staffordshire, Historical

History: The Staffordshire district of England is the center of the English pottery industry. There were 80 different potteries operating there in 1786, with the number increasing to 179 by 1802. The district includes Burslem, Cobridge, Etruria, Fenton, Foley, Hanley, Lane, Lane End, Longport, Shelton, Stoke, and Tunstall. Among the many famous potters were Adams, Davenport, Spode, Stevenson, Wedgwood, and Wood.

For more information, see *Warman's English & Continental Pottery & Porcelain*, 3rd edition.

Notes: The view is the most critical element when establishing the value of historical Staffordshire; American collectors pay much less for non-American views. Dark blue pieces are favored; light views continue to remain under-priced. Among the forms, soup tureens have shown the largest price increases.

Prices listed here are for mint examples, unless otherwise noted. Reduce prices by 20 percent for a hidden chip, a faint hairline, or an invisible professional repair; by 35 percent for knife marks through the glaze and a visible professional repair; by 50 percent for worn glaze and major repairs.

The numbers in parentheses refer to items in the Armans' books, which constitute the most detailed list of American historical views and their forms.

Adams

W.ADAMS&SONS ADAMS

The Adams family has been associated with ceramics since the mid-17th century. In 1802, William Adams of Stoke-on-Trent produced American views.

In 1819, a fourth William Adams, son of William of Stoke, became a partner with his father and was later joined by his three brothers. The firm became William Adams & Sons. The father died in 1829 and William, the eldest son, became manager.

The company operated four potteries at Stoke and one at Tunstall. American views were produced at Tunstall in black, light blue, sepia, pink, and green in the 1830-40 period. William Adams died in 1865. All operations were moved to Tunstall. The firm continues today under the name of Wm. Adams & Sons, Ltd.

Adams, bowl, dark blue transfer printed decoration, villa at Regent's Park, London, difficult to read impressed mark, crazing, 10" d, **$150**. Photo courtesy of Alderfer Auction Co.

Bowl, 11" d, 2-1/2" h, English scenes with ruins, dark blue transfer, yellowed repair on back **155.00**

Creamer, 5-3/8" d, English scene, imp "Adams," dark blue **175.00**

Pitcher, 5-3/4" h, Eagle, Scroll in Beak, blue and white transfer, illegible imp mark for William Adams, Stoke, 1827-31, glaze scratches **1,320.00**

Plate, 10-1/4" d, Mitchell & Freeman's China and Glass Warehouse, Chatham St, Boston, blue and white transfer, imp marker's mark and printed title on reverse **500.00**

Adams, plate, Mitchell & Freemans China & Glass Warehouse, Chatham Street, Boston, dark blue transfer, c1804-10, marked, 10-1/4" d, **$715**.

Teapot, Log Cabin, medallions of Gen. Harrison on border, pink (458) **450.00**

Clews

CLEWS WARRANTED STAFFORDSHIRE

From sketchy historical accounts that are available, it appears that James Clews took over the closed plant of A. Stevenson in 1819. His brother Ralph entered the business later. The firm continued until about 1836, when James Clews came to America to enter the pottery business at Troy, Indiana. The venture was a failure because of the lack of skilled workmen and the proper type of clay. He returned to England, but did not re-enter the pottery business.

Bowl, Landing of Lafayette, 9" d, ext. floral design, rim repair **410.00**

Clews, plates, left: Landing of General Lafayette, flowered border, dark blue transfer print, impressed Clews mark, 9" d, **$400**; right: View of Trenton Falls, shell border, dark blue transfer print, impressed "E. Wood & Sons," slight wear, light crazing, 7-1/2" d, **$295**. Photo courtesy of Cowan's Historic Americana Auctions.

Cup plate, imp "Clews..."

America and Independence, dark blue, full States border, scalloped rim, three-story mansion in center, 4-1/2" d **600.00**

Landing of Gen La Fayette, medium blue, scalloped edge, no border **525.00**

Pittsfield Elm, dark blue, full floral border including two vignettes, scalloped rim, 4-5/8" d **500.00**

Pitcher

6" h, Welcome Lafayette the Nation's Guest and Our Country's Glory, blue and white transfer, handle repair, int. staining **2,070.00**

6-3/4" h, States Border pattern, scenic country vista with mansion on hill, river in foreground, blue and white transfer dec, minor int. staining **980.00**

James and Ralph Clewes, plate, dark blue transfer printed decoration, Landing of La Fayette at Castle Garden New York 16th August 1824, printed title below image, floral border, impressed maker's mark, Cobridge, England, 1819-36, minor rim nick, 10-1/8" d, **$420**. Photo courtesy of Skinner, Inc.

Plate, 8-3/4" d, Winter View of Pittsfield, Mass, medium blue transfer, imp label "Clews," surface wear, flake, stains visible on reverse **225.00**

Clews, plate, Winter View of Pittsfield, Mass, vignettes of central scene in miniature on border, floral surround, dark blue transfer print, Clews mark, printed pattern mark, 8-1/2" d, **$400**. Photo courtesy of Cowan's Historic Americana Auctions.

Platter, Landing of Gen LaFayette at Castle Garden New York 16 August 1824, 11-3/4" x 15-1/4", blue and white transfer, imp maker's mark, minor glaze scratches **2,200.00**

Soup plate, 10-1/2" d, Picturesque Views, Pittsburgh, PA, imp "Clews," steam ships with "Home, Nile, Larch," black transfer, chips on table ring **330.00**

Saucer, Landing of Gen. Lafayette, dark blue transfer, imp "Clews Warranted Staffordshire" **275.00**

Toddy plate, 5-3/4" d, Winter View of Pittsfield, Mass, scalloped edge, medium blue transfer, imp "Clews Warranted Staffordshire" **400.00**

J. & J. Jackson

J&J. JACKSON

Job and John Jackson began operations at the Churchyard Works, Burslem, about 1830. The works formerly were owned by the Wedgwood family. The firm produced transfer scenes in a variety of colors, such as black, light blue, pink, sepia, green, maroon, and mulberry. More than 40 different American views of Connecticut, Massachusetts, Pennsylvania, New York, and Ohio were issued. The firm is believed to have closed about 1844.

J. & J. Jackson, plate, The Race Bridge, Phila, American Scenery series, light blue transfer, Arman, #485, **$175**.

Deep dish, American Beauty Series, Yale College (493) **125.00**

Plate, 10-3/8" d, The President's House, Washington, purple transfer **275.00**

Platter, American Beauty Series

12" l, Iron Works at Saugerties (478) **275.00**

17-1/2" l, View of Newburgh, black transfer (463) **575.00**

Soup plate, 10" d, American Beauty Series, Hartford, CT, black transfer (476) **150.00**

Thomas Mayer

In 1829, Thomas Mayer and his brothers, John and Joshua, purchased Stubbs' Dale Hall Works of Burslem. They continued to produce a superior grade of ceramics.

Cream pitcher, 4" h, Lafayette at Franklin's Tomb, dark blue **550.00**

Cup plate, Arms of South Carolina, medium blue, unmarked, pinpoint rim flakes, 4-1/4" d **1,155.00**

Gravy tureen, Arms of the American States, CT, dark blue (498) **3,800.00**

Plate, 8-1/2" d, Arms of Rhode Island, blue and white transfer, eagle back stamp, 1829, minor glaze scratches **790.00**

Platter, 19" l, Arms of the American States, NJ, dark blue (503) **7,200.00**

Sugar bowl, cov, Lafayette at Franklin's Tomb, dark blue (510) **850.00**

Mellor, Veneables & Co.

Little information is recorded on Mellor, Veneables & Co., except that it was listed as potters in Burslem in 1843. The company's Scenic Views with the Arms of the States Border does include the arms for New Hampshire. This state is missing from the Mayer series.

Plate, 7-1/2" d, Tomb of Washington, Mt. Vernon, Arms of States border **125.00**

Platter

14-1/2" x 19-3/4", European view, light blue and white transfer, imp and printed maker's mark, c1843, hairline, light wear **365.00**

15" l, Scenic Views, Arms of States border, Albany, light blue (516) **265.00**

Sugar bowl, cov, Arms of States, PA, dark blue **350.00**

Teapot, 9-1/2" h, Windsor pattern, dark blue **200.00**

J. & W. Ridgway and William Ridgway & Co.

John and William Ridgway, sons of Job Ridgway and nephews of George Ridgway, who owned Bell Bank Works and Cauldon Place Works, produced the popular Beauties of America series at the Cauldon plant. The partnership between the two brothers was dissolved in 1830. John remained at Cauldon.

J.W.R.
Stone China

W. RIDGWAY

William managed the Bell Bank Works until 1854. Two additional series were produced based upon the etchings of Bartlett's American Scenery. The first series had various borders including narrow lace. The second series is known as Catskill Moss. Beauties of America is in dark blue. The other series are found in light transfer colors of blue, pink, brown, black, and green.

Plate

6" d, Catskill Moss, Anthony's Nose (925) **85.00**

10" h, Beauties of America, City Hall, NY, dark blue (260) **225.00**

J.W. Ridgway, platter, Beauties of America series, Deaf & Dumb Asylum, Hartford, CT, c1820-40, medium blue transfer, **$925**.

Platter

12-3/4" x 16-1/2", Beauties of America series, Alms House New York, blue and white transfer, printed title, scratches, scattered minor staining **1,265.00**

John & William Ridgeway, soup plate, dark blue transfer printed decoration, Boston Octagon Church, from Beauties of America series, floral medallion border, printed title and maker on the reverse, Hanley, England, 1814-30, 9-3/4" d, **$400**. Photo courtesy of Skinner, Inc.

19" l, Catskill Moss, Boston and Bunker's Hill, imp "William Ridgway Son & Co," medium blue, dated 1844, minor chips, knife marks, edge wear **525.00**

Relish tray, 5-3/8" x 8-1/4", Savannah Bank, Beauties of America Series, blue and white transfer, printed title, c1814-30, minor imperfections **750.00**

Soup plate, 9-7/8" d, Octagon Church Boston, imp "Ridgway," dark medium blue **330.00**

Wash bowl, American Scenery, Albany (279) **325.00**

Rogers

ROGERS

John Rogers and his brother George established a pottery near Longport in 1782. After George's death in 1815, John's son Spencer became a partner, and the firm operated under the name of John Rogers & Sons. John died in 1916. His son continued the use of the name until he dissolved the pottery in 1842.

Basket and undertray, 3" x 6-1/2" x 9-1/4", Boston State House, blue and white transfer, imp marker's mark for John Rogers and Son, Longport, 1815-50, hairline cracks **2,760.00**

Cup and saucer, Boston Harbor, dark blue (441) **650.00**

John Rogers & Son, platter, dark blue transfer printed decoration, oblong, beaded edge, Musketeer pattern from Oriental Scenery series, impressed "ROGERS" on reverse, Longport, England, 1784-1814, old rim chips, 17" d, **$530**. Photo courtesy of Skinner, Inc.

Cup plate, Boston Harbor (441) dark blue, eagle on ocean wave with American shield, 4" d **1,210.00**

Deep dish, 12-3/4" d, Boston State House, blue and white transfer, imp marker's mark for John Rogers and Son, Longport, 1815-42, minor glaze scratches **2,070.00**

Plate, 9-5/8" d, The Canal at Buffalo, lace border, purple transfer, int. hairline **55.00**

Platter, 16-5/8" l, Boston State House, medium dark blue (442) **1,000.00**

Sauce tureen, cov, undertray, Boston State House, blue and white transfer, imp maker's mark for John Rogers and Son, Longport, 1815-42 .... **2,900.00**

Waste bowl, Boston Harbor, dark blue (441) **850.00**

Stevenson

R. S. W.

As early as the 17th century, the name Stevenson has been associated with the pottery industry. Andrew Stevenson of Cobridge introduced American scenes with the flower and scroll border. Ralph Stevenson, also of Cobridge, used a vine and leaf border on his dark blue historical views and a lace border on his series in light transfers.

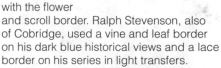

The initials R. S. & W. indicate Ralph Stevenson and Williams are associated with the acorn and leaf border. It has been reported that Williams was Ralph's New York agent and the wares were produced by Ralph alone.

Bowl, 8-3/4" d, Park Theater New York, blue and white transfer, printed mark, Ralph Stevens and Williams, Cobridge, 1815-40, minute scratches **2,530.00**

Cup and saucer, New Orleans, floral and scroll border **95.00**

Cup plate

Boston State House, medium blue, transfer label for R.S.W., scalloped edge, acorn and oak leaf border, 4-1/4" d **990.00**

Octagon Church, Boston, dark blue, labeled incorrectly actually shows Staughton's Church, Philadelphia, imp "Stevenson," white molded scalloped edge, acorn and oak leaf border, 4-1/8" d **1,980.00**

Scudder's American Museum, medium blue, transfer label, scalloped rim, full acorn and oak leaf border, 4-1/4" d **1,430.00**

Pitcher, 10" h, Almshouse, Boston, reverse with Esplanade and Castle Garden New York, blue and white transfer, unmarked **2,300.00**

Stevenson, platter, Alms House, Boston, vine border, dark blue transfer, impressed mark, 12-1/2" w, 16-1/4" l, **$800.**

Plate

6-7/8" d, Battery, NY, vine border (367) **800.00**

7-1/2" d, Columbia College, portrait medallion of President Washington, inset View of the Aqueduct Bridge at Rochester, blue and white transfer, Ralph Stevens and Williams, Cobridge, 1815-40, minor scratches **8,625.00**

9" d, Boston Hospital, blue and white transfer, stamped title, maker's initials, imp maker's mark, minor glaze scratches **350.00**

10-1/4" d, New York from Brooklyn Heights, printed title, imp maker's mark, A. Stevenson, Cobridge, 1808-29 .... **900.00**

Platter

7-1/4" x 9-1/4", Troy from Mount Ida, by W. G. Wallogy, landscape scene, floral border, blue and white transfer, back stamped with American eagle, marked "A. Stevenson Warranted Staffordshire" **1,550.00**

10-1/4" x 13", Battle of Bunker Hill, blue and white transfer, printed title, imp maker's mark, Ralph Stevenson, Cobridge, 1815-40, one scratch **8,625.00**

14-1/2" x 18-1/2", New York Esplanade and Castle Garden, blue and white transfer, printed title, imp maker's mark, Ralph Stevenson, Cobridge, 1815-40, minor glaze scratches............ **5,750.00**

Soup plate

9" d, View on the Road to Lake George, printed title, imp maker's mark, A. Stevenson, Cobridge, 1808-29 .... **1,100.00**

10" d, Erie Canal at Buffalo, lace border (386) **95.00**

Wash bowl, Riceborough, GA, lace border (388) **375.00**

Stubbs

In 1790, Stubbs established a pottery works at Burslem, England. He operated it until 1829, when he retired and sold the pottery to the Mayer brothers. He probably produced his American views about 1825. Many of his scenes were from Boston, New York, New Jersey, and Philadelphia.

Cup plate, Woodlands near Philadelphia, medium blue, unmarked, slightly scalloped edge, partial border, 3-1/8" d **220.00**

Gravy boat, 4-1/4" h, Hoboken in New Jersey, Steven's House, blue and white transfer, printed title, Joseph Stubbs, Burslem, 1790-1829, minor imperfections **550.00**

Pitcher, 6" h, Boston State House, reverse with City Hall New York, blue and white transfer, unmarked, small chip on handle............ **980.00**

Joseph Stubbs, plate, Fairmont near Philadelphia, spread eagle border, dark blue transfer, 10" d, **$195**.

Unknown maker, platter, Vue Du Temple, scene of figures at temple looking across river, dark blue transfer, wear, chip, 13" x 16-1/2", **$550**. Photo courtesy of Sanford Alderfer Auction Company.

Plate

6-1/2" h, City Hall New York, floral and eagle border, medium blue transfer, unmarked, minor wear and small repair............ **225.00**

9" d, Upper Ferry Bridge of the River Schuylkill, blue and white transfer, printed title, Joseph Stubbs, Burslem, 1790-1829, imperfections **950.00**

10-1/4" h, Fair Mount near Philadelphia, floral border with eagles, medium blue transfer, imp "Stubbs" **475.00**

Platter

12" x 14-3/4", State House Boston, blue and white transfer, printed title, marked "Joseph Stubbs, Burslem," 1790-1829, minor scratches and crazing **1,265.00**

15-1/2" x 18-3/4", Upper Ferry Bridge over the River Schuylkill, well and tree, printed title on reverse, hairline **715.00**

Salt shaker, Hoboken in NJ, spread eagle border, dark blue (326)....... **700.00**

Wash bowl and pitcher, Upper Ferry Bridge Over the River Schuylkill, 12-5/8" d bowl, 10" h pitcher, blue and white, printed title, Joseph Stubbs, Burslem, 1790-1829 .... **1,840.00**

Unknown maker, coffeepot, dark blue transfer printed decoration, wide floral and scroll border, English landscape scene with old woman and seated man, rim chip, lid broken, 9" h, **$390**. Photo courtesy of Alderfer Auction Co.

Unknown makers

Bowl, 11-1/8" d, 3-1/4" d, Franklin, scene of Ben flying kite, red transfer, minor wear **495.00**

Coffeepot, Lafayette at Franklin's tomb surrounded by flowers, dark blue transfer, scrolled ear handle, domed lid with beehive shaped finial, restoration to lid and tip of spout, shallow edge chip on lid, 12-3/4" h............ **2,200.00**

Cup, handleless, dark blue transfer, Quadruped series, llama on both sides, floral border, scalloped rim........... **115.00**

Fruit bowl, undertray, 10-1/2" l, 5" h, reticulated, blue and white transfer, figures, cows, and manors in rural landscape, floral borders **765.00**

Jug, 6-3/4" h, pearlware, brown transfer print, commemorating British Admiral Nelson, portrait, ship Victory, various nautical devices, orange enamel highlights on rim and edges of handle, minor imperfections............ **1,650.00**

Pitcher, 5-7/8" h, dark blue transfer, View of the Erie Canal, floral borders, transfer slightly blurred, repairs............ **715.00**

Unknown maker, plate, Fair Mount near Philadelphia, eagle and floral border, dark blue transfer 10-1/4" d, **$225**. Photo courtesy of Sanford Alderfer Auction Company.

Plate

7" d, Junction of the Sacandaga & Hudson River, black transfer, small rim glaze defect **95.00**

7-3/4" d, Near Fishkill, small chip on table ring **100.00**

8-3/4" d, Nahant Hotel near Boston, dark blue transfer, wear, chips on table ring **200.00**

9" d, "The Residence of the late Richard Jordon, New Jersey," brown, minor wear and stains............ **250.00**

10-1/4", Fulton's Steamboat, blue and white transfer, floral border, minor scratches and rim chips......... **890.00**

Platter, 16-5/8" l, Sandusky, dark blue, very minor scratches............ **8,525.00**

Unknown maker, plate, dark blue transfer printed decoration, scalloped rim, centered with words of First Amendment of United States Constitution, border of eagles with American shields and four medallions; two with quotations from Constitution, third with pair of scales, fourth with Justice pardoning a slave, England, 19th C, 9-1/2" d, **$500**. Photo courtesy of Skinner, Inc.

Saucer, 5-7/8" d, scene of early railroad, engine and one car, floral border, dark blue **275.00**

Soup plate, 8-3/4" d, Cuba, two classical columns, Spanish verse, titled "La Capetera Havana, Alnacen de Gamba Y Co.," dark blue transfer, 8-3/4" d **615.00**

Teapot, 8-1/4" h, The Residence of the Late Richard Jordan, New Jersey, brown transfer, small chip, stain and repair to lid **715.00**

Tea service, partial, Mount Vernon the Seat of the Late Gen. Washington, blue and white transfer, floral border, three teapots, creamer, three cov sugar bowls, waste bowl, 13 tea bowls, 12 saucers, some with printed titles, imperfections **8,625.00**

Wood

Enoch Wood, sometimes referred to as the father of English pottery, began operating a pottery at Fountain Place, Burslem, in 1783. A cousin, Ralph Wood, was associated with him. In 1790, James Caldwell became a partner and the firm was known as Wood and Caldwell. In 1819, Wood and his sons took full control.

Enoch died in 1840. His sons continued under the name of Enoch Wood & Sons. The American views were first made in the mid-1820s and continued through the 1840s.

It is reported that the pottery produced more signed historical views than any other Staffordshire firm. Many of the views attributed to unknown makers probably came from the Woods.

Marks vary, although always include the name Wood. The establishment was sold to Messrs. Pinder, Bourne & Hope in 1846.

Creamer, 5-3/4" h, horse drawn sleigh, imp "Wood," dark blue, minor hairline in base.. **550.00**

Cup and saucer, handleless, ship with American flag, Chancellor Livingston, imp "Wood & Sons" **770.00**

Enoch Wood & Sons, plate, dark blue transfer printed decoration, titled The Landing of the Fathers at Plymouth, Dec 22 1620, border with medallions with ships and inscriptions, "America Independent July 4 1776," and "Washington Born 1732 Died 1799," impressed maker's mark, Burslem, England, 1819-46, 10-1/8" d, **$300**. Photo courtesy of Skinner, Inc.

Cup plate, Castle Garden Battery, NY, dark blue, unmarked, trefoil border, 3-5/8" d **425.00**

Gravy boat, 7-1/2" l, Catskill Mountains Hudson River, blue and white transfer, printed title, minor imperfections **650.00**

Pitcher, 6" h, Entrance of the Erie Canal into the Hudson River at Albany, reverse with View of the Aqueduct Bridge at Little Falls, blue and white transfer, printed title, scattered glaze loss to int. **1,725.00**

Wood, plate, Erie Canal Aqueduct Bridge at Rochester, dark blue transfer, 7-5/8" d, **$145**.

Plate

6-1/2" d, Cowes Harbour, blue and white transfer, shell border, imp maker's mark on reverse, light wear **245.00**

7-1/2" d, The Capitol Washington, blue and white transfer, imp maker's mark, 1819-46 .... **450.00**

8-1/2" d, Boston State House, blue and white transfer, imp maker's mark, 1819-46 .... **325.00**

9-1/4" d, The Baltimore & Ohio Railroad, (incline), imp "Enoch Wood," dark blue **770.00**

10-3/8" d, Constitution and Guerriere, imp "Wood," dark blue minor scratches............................ **1,760.00**

10-1/2" d, East Cowes Isle of Wright, shell border, blue and white transfer **765.00**

Platter, 12-3/4" x 16-1/2", Lake George State of New York, blue and white transfer, printed title, partial imp marker's mark, c1819-46, minor glaze imperfections............................ **2,585.00**

Sugar bowl, cov, 7" d, 6" h, Wadsworth Tower, blue and white transfer, scalloped shaped handles, minor imperfections **265.00**

Tea service, partial, Wadsworth Tower, cov teapot, two large teacups, one large saucer, five teacups, six saucers, 15 plates, imperfections **2,645.00**

Toddy plate, 6-1/2" d, dark blue transfer, Catskill House, Hudson, imp "Wood," minor wear and stains **525.00**

Enoch Wood & Sons, plate, dark blue transfer printed decoration, titled View of Trenton Falls, seashell border, impressed mark,"Wood & Sons," 7-1/2" d, **$315**. Photo courtesy of Alderfer Auction Co.

Tureen, cov, 7" h, Passaic Falls, State of New Jersey, blue and white transfer, repairs, glaze wear **200.00**

Undertray, 8-1/8" l, Pass in the Catskill Mountains, blue and white transfer, imp maker's mark, printed title, repair to handle.. **200.00**

Waste bowl, 6-1/4" d, 3-1/4" h, Washington standing at Tomb, scroll in hand, blue and white transfer, unmarked, Enoch Wood & Sons, Burslem, 1819-40, minor imperfections..................... **750.00**

Staffordshire Items

History: A wide variety of ornamental pottery items originated in England's Staffordshire district, beginning in the

17th century and still continuing today. The height of production took place from 1820 to 1890.

Many collectors consider these naive pieces folk art. Most items were not made carefully; some even were made and decorated by children.

The types of objects are varied, e.g., animals, cottages, and figurines (chimney ornaments).

For more information, see *Warman's English & Continental Pottery & Porcelain*, 3rd edition.

Reproduction Alert: Early Staffordshire figurines and hollowware forms were molded. Later examples were made using a slip-casting process. Slip casting leaves telltale signs that are easy to spot. Look in the interior. Hand molding created a smooth interior surface. Slip casting produces indentations that conform to the exterior design. Holes occur where handles meet the body of slip-cast pieces. There is not hole in a hand-molded piece.

A checkpoint on figurines is the firing or vent hole, which is a necessary feature on these forms. Early figurines had small holes; modern reproductions feature large holes often the size of a dime or quarter. Vent holes are found on the sides or hidden among the decoration in early Staffordshire figurines; most modern reproductions have them in the base.

These same tips can be used to spot modern reproductions of Flow Blue, Majolica, Old Sleepy Eye, Stoneware, Willow, and other ceramic pieces.

Note: The key to price is age and condition. As a general rule, the older the piece, the higher the price.

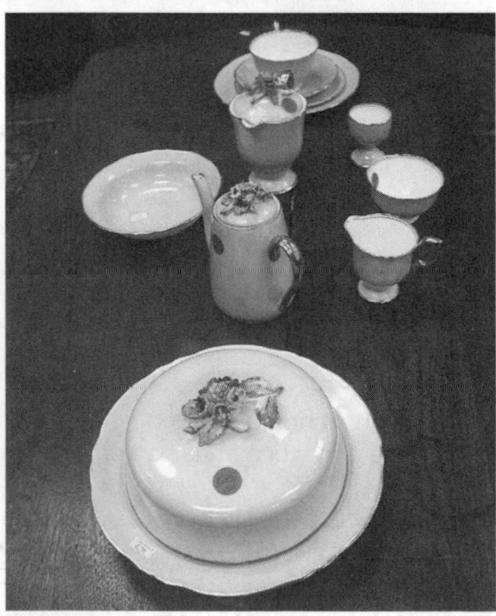

Breakfast set, Crown Staffordshire, turquoise blue ground, applied floral decoration, 11-piece set, **$175**. Photo courtesy of Dotta Auction Co., Inc.

Cabinet plate, 8" d, emb floral border, polychrome scene of woman in ruins **75.00**

Candlestick, 11-1/4" h, lead glazed creamware, underglaze translucent colors, free form tree with leaf molded sconce and applied florets, late 18th C, restorations **1,175.00**

Charger, 13-3/4" d, creamware, lead glaze, octagonal form with reeded rim, mottled brown tortoiseshell ground, surface wear, late 18th C **500.00**

Bust, George Washington, blue jacket, floral patterned vest, black cravat, simulated marble plinth, early 19th C, minor chip, retouch, 8" h, **$500**. Photo courtesy of Skinner, Inc.

Chimney piece

12-3/4" h, man, lady carrying rushes on her head, orange, green, pale violet, black, and yellow, crazing, minor wear **250.00**

13-1/8" h, spaniel, white, yellow and black eyes, black nose, hollow body with vase opening above head, glaze runs on back, minor firing separation on base **470.00**

15" h, Robin Hood, two men in white coats, gold detail, red and blue hat feathers, spaniel lying at their feet **400.00**

Chimney piece, cow and milk maiden, dark brown hair, orange and green trim, 7" l, 6-3/4" h, **$275**.

Chimney vase

6-3/4" h, two red and black spotted dogs chasing red deer through woods, hand painted, coleslaw leaves, some flaking, short hairline **250.00**

7-1/8" h, couple wearing dark blue coats, man with pink breeches, shovel, and potted plant, woman with apron, enamel wear and flake **150.00**

7-3/4" h, Scottish shepherd and shepherdess, black spotted dog, red spotted sheep, dark red, orange, and green, coleslaw vegetation, repaired hairline **110.00**

Coffeepot, cov, 9" h, pear shape, s-scrolled handle, relief fruiting grapevines, three paw feet, chips to cover rim, pot and spout lip, c1775 .... **650.00**

Compote, 9" d, polychrome dec, printed registry mark **75.00**

Cradle, 4-1/2" l, 3-1/2" h, hand painted, dark yellow basketweave cradle, pink rockers, baby in red sprig frock, blue and green bedding, professional restoration **275.00**

Cup, 4-3/4" h, figural satyr's head, grapevine wreath, shell base, polychrome enamel, green frog inside **500.00**

Figure, calico cat, seated on oval scroll decorated base, early 19th C, minor chips, 3-5/8" h, **$1,000**. Photo courtesy of Skinner, Inc.

Figure

6-1/8" h, 5-1/2" l, zebra, black stripes, mane, and bridle, green foliage, some wear, small stain **330.00**

Figural group, older Quaker-type gentleman with little girl at his side, light post on right, shovel and pick-axe resting on lamp post, polychrome enamel decoration, Victorian, professional repair to top of lamp post, 10-1/4" h, **$250**. Photo courtesy of Cowan's Historic Americana Auctions.

7-1/2" h, adventurer, dark blue doublet, pink striped pantaloons, orange cape, telescope, flaking **150.00**

Figural group, Jolly Traveler Group, man with walking stick, mule, dog by their feet, impresed title to lozenge mounted to face to freeform oval base, applied with florets and encrusted grass, c1820, bocage missing, losses to applied leaves on basket and flowers on base, donkey's ears and man's arm with chips restored, 6-1/4" h, **$450**. Photo courtesy of Skinner Auctioneers and Appraisers.

7-1/2" h, bocage, couple in bower, woman with pink shawl, floral sprig dress, man with green coat, orange breeches, green and brown trees, coleslaw leaves, flake **200.00**

7-3/4" h, Scottish couple, feathered caps, man with red and green plaid cape, blue stockings, woman with matching skirt, minor flaking **200.00**

Poodle with seated puppy, cobalt blue base, 7" h, **$190**. Photo courtesy of Cowan's Historic Americana Auctions.

9" h, Scottish couple, man with bagpipe horn, red and green plaid cape, woman with yellow striped floral dress and basket, yellow base **250.00**

9" h, woman standing next to column topped by vase of flowers, white, pink, orange, blue, and green on shawl, hat feathers, and flowers, hairline **150.00**

Jar, cov, 3-1/4" h, melon shape, alternating yellow and green stripes, cov with molded leaf, lead glaze, 18th C, hairline to cover, finial and rim chips **4,315.00**

Plate, 10-1/2" d, Peaceable Kingdom, 10-1/2" d, red transfer, scalloped edge **145.00**

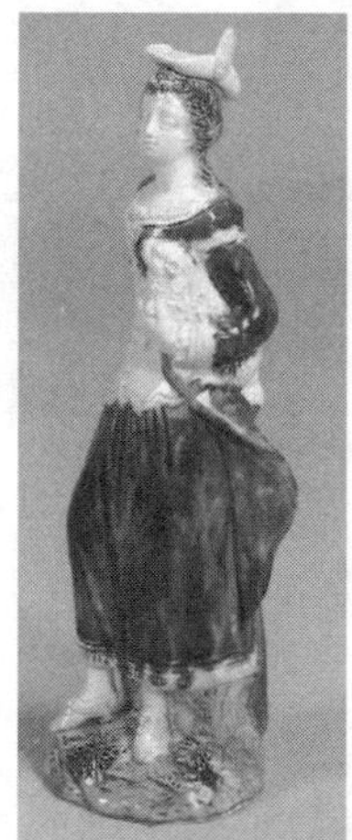

Figure, shepherdess, standing, blue skirt, jacket trimmed in yellow, holding lamb in one arm, early 19th C, 10-1/4" h, **$1,175**. Photo courtesy of Skinner, Inc.

Stirrup cup, hand painted

4-1/2" l, red fox head, yellow eyes and rim, minor paint wear **500.00**

5" l, hound head, tan with black spatter spots **770.00**

5" l, red fox head, white and black muzzle, minor wear **550.00**

5-1/4" l, red fox head, black muzzle, incised whiskers, gilt trim, some grazing, glued ear **500.00**

Sugar, cov, 4-3/8" d, Cauliflower, creamware, scalloped rim, green glazed leaf molding on bowl, cream glazed cov with molded florets, hairline to cover rim, c1775 .... **2,820.00**

Tea canister, rouletted cylindrical melon body, alternating green and yellow stripes, lead glaze, c1770, rim repair, hairline, foot-rim flake, 3-3/4" h, **$2,000**. Photo courtesy of Skinner, Inc.

Pastile burner, cottage shape, applied green bocage, gold trim, white ground, open door and chimney, **$225**.

Tea canister

3-3/8" h, lead glazed creamware, mottled tortoiseshell glazes, straight sided cylindrical form, 18th C, hairline **550.00**

4" h, Cauliflower, creamware, molded body with green leaves below cream glazed florets, shallow rim chip, c1775 .... **775.00**

Teapot, cov

4-3/4" h, black glaze, modeled as tree stump, branch handle and spout, relief fruiting grapevines, slight nicks to cover and spout rim, chips to interior rim of pot, early 19th C **550.00**

5-1/2" h, lead glazed creamware, all-over mottled brown glaze, globular pot, crab-stock handle and spout, three mask and paw feet, bird finial, restored spout tip, bird's beak chip, late 18th C **1,100.00**

5-1/2" h, lead glazed creamware, rouletted globular melon shape body with alternating green and yellow striping, leaf molded spout and double-scrolled handle, applied leaves and florets, c1770, slight nick to cover and spout rim, some glaze missing on lower body **8,225.00**

Waste bowl, 5-5/8" d, Forget Me Not, red transfer, edge roughness **60.00**

Whistle, 3-1/2" h, overglazed enamel dec, modeled as bird perched on tree trunk, applied florets, c1820, tail restored **420.00**

STAFFORDSHIRE, ROMANTIC

For more information, see *Warman's Glass*, 4th edition.

History: In the 1830s, two factors transformed the blue-and-white printed wares of the Staffordshire potters into what is now called "Romantic Staffordshire." Technical innovations expanded the range of transfer-printed colors to light blue, pink, purple, black, green, and brown. There was also a shift from historical to imaginary scenes with less printed detail and more white space, adding to the pastel effect.

Shapes from the 1830s are predominately rococo with rounded forms, scrolled handles, and floral finials. Over time, patterns and shapes became simpler and the earthenware bodies coarser. The late 1840s and 1850s saw angular gothic shapes and pieces with the weight and texture of ironstone.

The most dramatic post-1870 change was the impact of the craze for all things Japanese. Staffordshire designs adopted zigzag border elements and motifs such as bamboo, fans, and cranes. Brown printing dominated this style, sometimes with polychrome enamel highlights.

Marks: Wares are often marked with pattern or potter's names, but marking was inconsistent and many authentic, unmarked examples exist. The addition of "England" as a country of origin mark in 1891 helps to distinguish 20th-century wares made in the romantic style.

Caledonia, Williams Adams, 1830s
- Plate, 9-1/2" d, purple transfer, imp "Adams" **60.00**
- Platter, 17" l **500.00**

Plate, Corintha pattern, E. Challinor, blue and white transfer, blue mark, **$85**. Photo courtesy of Dotta Auction Co., Inc.

- Soup plate, two colors **175.00**

Canova, Thomas Mayer, c1835; G. Phillips, c1840
- Plate, 10-1/2" d **95.00**
- Pudding bowl, two colors **200.00**
- Vegetable, cov **325.00**

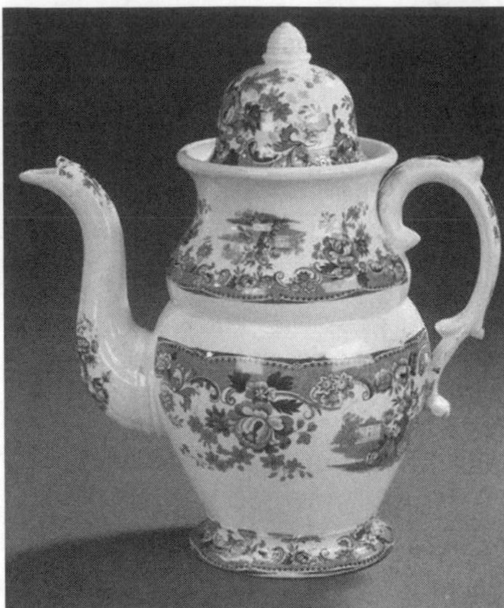

Coffeepot, by Enoch Wood & sons, c1830, printed "HARP" and "EW&s," black transfer of house, urn, and bird in landscape, floral borders, spout printed with harp and sheet music laying by flowering urn, border at shoulder and cover printed upside down, 11" h, **$350**. Photo courtesy of Sloan & Kenyon Auctions.

Columbia, W. Adams & Sons, 1850
- Creamer **115.00**
- Cup and saucer **65.00**
- Plate, 10" d **60.00**
- Relish **65.00**

Pitcher, Tamara, polychrome decoration, purple transfer, **$125**. Photo courtesy of Wiederseim Associates, Inc.

Dr. Syntax, James and Ralph Clews, Cobridge, 1819-36
- Plate, 10" d, blue and white transfer, imp Clews mark with crown, c1818-34 .... **160.00**
- Platter, 14-1/4" x 19", Dr. Syntax Amused with Pat in the Pond, blue and white transfer, glaze scratches, scattered minor staining **1,840.00**

Soup bowl, Italian Villas, marked "J. & H. Co," for J. Heath, 8-3/4" d, **$45**.

- Undertray, 10" x 5-3/4", Death of Punch, Dr. Syntax literary series, blue and white transfer, crazing on reverse **85.00**

Madras, serving tray, 6-1/2" l and 12-1/2" l, Wood & Son, price for pr **275.00**

Marmora, William Ridgway & Co., 1830s
- Platter, 16-1/2" l **325.00**
- Sauce tureen, matching tray **350.00**
- Soup plate **100.00**

Moral Maxims, plate, 10-1/2" d, black transfer, center fishing scene, Clews, hairline **95.00**

Palestine, William Adams, 1836
- Creamer and sugar **265.00**
- Cup and saucer, two colors **135.00**
- Cup plate **75.00**
- Platter, 13" l **325.00**
- Vegetable, open, 12" l **200.00**

Coffeepot, blue transfer decoration, Oriental-type scene, **$350**. Photo courtesy of Dotta Auction Co., Inc.

Persia, pitcher, 10-1/2" h, Wm Adams & Son, light blue transfer, marked "Persia, W.A.& S" **140.00**

Quadrupeds, John Hall, 1814-32
Plate, 10" d, central medallion with lion, printed maker's mark for John Hall, 1814-32, pattern mark in crown, price for pr **865.00**
Platter, 14-3/4" x 19", Quadrupeds pattern, central cartouche of elephant, printed maker's mark for John Hall 1914-32, pattern mark in crown, minor surface imperfections **4,315.00**

Shell pattern, Stubbs and Kent, Longport, 1828-30
Cream jug, 5" h, blue and white transfer, unmarked, imperfections **1,200.00**
Milk pitcher, 7" h, blue and white transfer, unmarked, imperfections **900.00**
Plate, 10" d, blue and white transfer, imp maker's mark, imperfections, price for eight-pc set **2,645.00**
Platter, 18-1/2" l, oval, blue and white transfer, imp maker's mark, repaired rim chip **1,955.00**
Soup plate, 10" d, blue and white transfer, imp maker's mark, wear, price for three **750.00**
Tea bowl and saucer, 2-1/2" h, blue and white transfer, imp maker's mark **450.00**
Vegetable dish, 12-1/4" d, 2-1/2" h, oval, blue and white transfer, imp maker's mark, scratches, wear **1,150.00**

Plate, Andalusia pattern, red and white transfer, name on back, impressed "Adams," **$76**.

Union, William Ridgway Son & Co., 1840s
Plate, 10-1/2" d **70.00**
Platter, 15" l **165.00**

Unknown pattern
Cup and saucer, two dogs, flower and leaf border, imp maker's mark for James & Ralph Clews, Cobridge, 1817-34, 2-1/4" h, 5-3/4" h, minor light wear **150.00**
Sugar, cov, 6-3/4" h, medium blue transfer of mother and child playing in cottage yard with dog, floral borders, molded ring handles, imp "Adams...," lid with repair matches, but does not fit properly, edge flakes, crow's feet **200.00**

Sugar bowl, covered, medium blue transfer, allover floral design with flowers in basket and blossom border, scalloped top rim, scrolled handles, marked "Stevenson Warranted Staffordshire, Stevenson Stone China," chips, rim repair, 6-1/2" w, 6" h, **$250**. Photo courtesy of Sanford Alderfer Auction Company.

Tea set, partial, blue and white transferBird in oval reverse, floral border, two teapots, creamer, small bowl, waste bowl, imperfections **1,265.00**
Three figures in landscape, manor house in distance, teapot, creamer, and two cov sugar bowls **1,610.00**

Venus, Podmore, Walker & Co., 1850s, plate, 7-1/2" d **50.00**

Stained and/or Leaded Glass Panels

History: American architects in the second half of the 19th century and the early 20th century used stained- and leaded-glass panels as a chief decorative element. Skilled glass craftsmen assembled the designs, the best known being Louis C. Tiffany.

The panels are held together with soft lead cames or copper wraps. When purchasing a panel, protect your investment by checking the lead and making any necessary repairs.

Leaded

Firescreen, 48-1/2" w, 32" h, three panels, clear glass top half, hammered white glass lower half, central applied Art Nouveau floral design, green bull's eye highlights **2,750.00**

Panel, 96" h, 20" w, rect, rippled, and opaque glass, turquoise, white, and avocado, clear glass ground, stylized flowering plant motif, c1910, six panels **6,000.00**

Triptych, 34-3/4" h, 17-3/4" w, twining grapevines and grape clusters, green slag, textured purple and brown glass, amber border segments, textured colorless glass background, wood frame, cracks **1,380.00**

Stained glass panel, green and red heart pattern, framed, modern, 25" x 28", **$195**. Photo courtesy of Joy Luke Auctions.

Stained and leaded glass panel, waterlillies, framed, 23-3/4" x 36", **$250**. Photo courtesy of Joy Luke Auctions.

Window
27-1/4" x 22-1/2", Prairie School, stylized pink and green tulips set in pastel tone slag glass panels, mounted in orig oak window frame, frame, two short breaks **435.00**
28-1/2" x 18-1/2", Prairie School, rectilinear pattern in clear and milk glass within orig oak frames, unmarked, pr **860.00**

Stained and leaded glass panel, red flowers, green leaves, jeweled, framed, 18-1/2" x 32", **$175**. Photo courtesy of Joy Luke Auctions.

Window, Henry Belcher, mosaic and chunk jewel, original frame, 93" l, 29" h, **$8,400**. Photo courtesy of Fontaine's Auction Gallery.

Door, bench leaded, clear glass, elongated with ornate part beveled glass inserts, 28" w, 78" h, **$1,450**. Photo courtesy of James D. Julia, Inc.

Stained and leaded glass panel, central panel with French horn, jeweled, framed, 24" x 37", **$150**. Photo courtesy of Joy Luke Auctions.

Stained

Panel

24" x 14", red, white, green, pink, and blue floral design, two layers of striated and fractured glass, green patinated bronze frame, stamped "Tiffany Studios New York" pr **2,400.00**

19-1/4" x 16-1/4", shield shaped, heraldic coat of arms in center, topped by helmet, European, late 19th C.................................... **950.00**

3402D, orioles, artist signed "MW," green "Stangl Pottery Birds" mark, **$380**. Photo courtesy of Joseph P. Smalley, Jr., Auctioneer.

Transom window

59" x 17", arched form, amber, green, and red, later walnut frame, brass plaque "Illinois Traction System Car Number 523" **260.00**

61-1/2" h, 61" l, over entry door type, blue and orange shield and geometric design, c1920 .... **490.00**

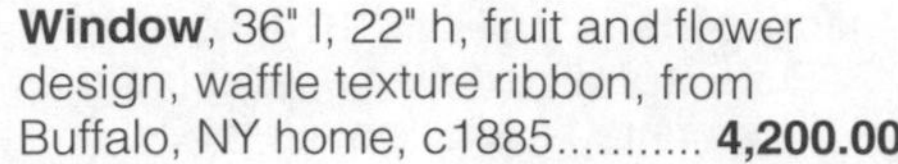

Window, 36" l, 22" h, fruit and flower design, waffle texture ribbon, from Buffalo, NY home, c1885........... **4,200.00**

Stangl Pottery Birds

For more information, see *Warman's American Pottery & Porcelain*, 2nd edition.

History: Stangl ceramic birds were produced from 1940 until the Stangl factory closed in 1978. The birds were produced at Stangl's Trenton plant and either decorated there or shipped to its Flemington, New Jersey, outlet for hand painting.

During World War II, the demand for these birds, and other types of Stangl pottery as well, was so great that 40 to 60 decorators could not keep up with the demand. Orders were contracted out to be decorated by individuals in their own homes. These orders then were returned for firing and finishing. Colors used to decorate these birds varied according to the artist.

Marks: As many as 10 different trademarks were used. Almost every bird is numbered; many are artist signed. However, the signatures are used only for dating purposes and add very little to the value of the birds.

Adviser: Bob Perzel.

Note: Several birds were reissued between 1972 and 1977. These reissues are dated on the bottom and are worth approximately the same as older birds, if well decorated.

3250, preening duck, natural colors **100.00**
3273, rooster, 5-3/4" h................ **1,000.00**
3276, bluebird **80.00**
3400, lovebird, old, wavy base **100.00**
3400, lovebird, revised leaf base **60.00**

Window, stained, fruit and flower design, from west side Buffalo, NY, home, c1885, layered glass in ewer and some in fruit, waffle texture ribbon, 36" l, 22" h, **$4,200**. Photo courtesy of Fontaine's Auction Gallery.

Hummingbirds, #3599, marked, 10-1/2" h, **$325**. Photo courtesy of David Rago Auctions.

3402, pair of orioles, revised **380.00**
3402, pair of orioles, old **400.00**
3405, pair of cockatoos, revised, open base **125.00**
3407, owl **300.00**
3430, duck, 22" **8,000.00**
3431, duck, standing, brown **850.00**
3432, rooster, 16" h **3,500.00**
3443, flying duck, teal **300.00**
3445, rooster, yellow **175.00**
3446, hen, gray **225.00**
3450, passenger pigeon **1,600.00**

3402D, orioles, artist signed "MW," green "Stangl Pottery Birds" mark, **$380**. Photo courtesy of Joseph P. Smalley, Jr., Auctioneer.

3451, William Ptarmigan **3,500.00**
3453, mountain bluebird **2,100.00**
3454, Key West quail dove, single wing up **225.00**
3455, shoveler duck **1,300.00**
3457, walking pheasant **3,000.00**
3459, falcon/fish hawk/osprey ... **8,000.00**
3490, pair of redstarts **175.00**
3492, cock pheasant **175.00**
3518, pair of white-headed pigeons **1,000.00**
3582, pair of green parakeets **270.00**
3582, pair of blue parakeets **200.00**
3584, cockatoo, large **250.00**
3590, chat **190.00**
3595, Bobolink **165.00**
3596, gray cardinal **65.00**
3597, Wilson warbler, yellow **45.00**
3599, pair of hummingbirds **275.00**
3625, Bird of Paradise, large, 13-1/2" h **2,500.00**
3634, Allen hummingbird **125.00**
3635, group of goldfinches **175.00**
3715, blue jay with peanut **920.00**
3717, pair of blue jays **3,000.00**
3746, canary, rose flower **275.00**
3749, scarlet tanager **475.00**

Blue Jay with peanut, #3715, marked, 10-1/4", **$920**. Photo courtesy of David Rago Auctions.

3752, pair of red-headed woodpeckers, red matte **550.00**
3754, pair of white-winged crossbills, pink glossy **450.00**
3755, audubon warbler **400.00**
3756, pair of audubon warblers **600.00**
3758, magpie jay **1,400.00**
3810, blackpoll warber **165.00**
3811, chestnut chickadee **145.00**
3812, chestnut-sided warbler **150.00**
3813, evening grosbeak **150.00**
3814, blackthroated green warbler **165.00**
3815, western bluebird **400.00**
3848, golden crowned kinglet **100.00**
3850, yellow warbler **150.00**
3852, cliff swallow **150.00**
3853, group of golden crowned kingfishers **700.00**
3921, yellow-headed verdin **1,200.00**
3922, European finch **1,200.00**
3924, yellow-throated warbler **650.00**
3925, Magnolia warbler **2,700.00**
Bird sign **1,500.00**

STEIFF

History: Margarete Steiff, GmbH, established in Germany in 1880, is known for very fine-quality stuffed animals and dolls, as well as other beautifully made collectible toys. It is still in business, and its products are highly respected.

The company's first products were wool-felt elephants made by Margaret Steiff. In a few years, the animal line was expanded to include a donkey, horse, pig, and camel.

By 1903, the company also was producing a jointed mohair teddy bear, whose production dramatically increased to more than 970,000 units in 1907. Margarete's nephews took over the company at this point.

Newly designed animals were added: Molly and Bully, the dogs, and Fluffy, the cat. Pull toys and kites also were produced, as well as larger animals on which children could ride or play.

Marks: The bear's-head label became the symbol for the firm in about 1907, and the famous "Button in the Ear" round, metal trademark was added.

Notes: Become familiar with genuine Steiff products before purchasing an antique stuffed animal. Plush in old Steiff animals was mohair; trimmings usually were felt or velvet. Unscrupulous individuals have attached the familiar Steiff metal button to animals that are not Steiff.

Bear, early, jointed, 12" h, **$1,400**. Photo courtesy of McMasters Harris Auction Co.

Bear

5" h, blond mohair, rattle, no button, black shoe button eyes, fully jointed, embroidered nose and mouth, overall wear, stains, rip on arm, working rattle, excelsior stuffing, no pad style, c1910 .... **415.00**

8-1/2" h, golden mohair, shoe button eyes, embroidered nose, mouth, and claws, fully jointed, excelsior stuffing, no pad arms, c1915, moth damage to foot pads **1,380.00**

12-1/2" h, light apricot, ear button, fully jointed, shoe button eyes, embroidered nose, mouth, and claws, excelsior stuffing, felt pads, c1905, fur loss, lower back and back of legs, slight moth damage on pads **1,610.00**

17" h, One Hundredth Anniversary Bear, ear button, gold mohair, fully jointed, plastic eyes, black embroidered nose, mouth, and claws, peach felt pads, excelsior

stuffing, certificate no. 3934, orig box **200.00**
20" h, golden long mohair, shoe button eyes, embroidered nose, mouth and claws, fully jointed, excelsior stuffing, c1905 ..... **8,920.00**
30" h, blond mohair, script ear button, glass eyes, embroidered nose, mouth, claws excelsior stuffed, fully jointed, mid-19th C, felt feet pads have scattered moth holes, break at sides **1,955.00**

Beaver, 6" l, Nagy, mohair, chest tag, post WWII **95.00**

Bison, 9-1/2" l, mohair, ear button, chest tag, post WWII **200.00**

Boxer, 16-1/2" l, 15-1/2" h, beige mohair coat, black trim, glass eyes, leather collar marked "Steiff," head turns, minor wear, straw stuffing **165.00**

Boxer puppy, 4-1/4" h, paper label "Daly" **135.00**

Cat, 14" l, pull toy, white mohair coat, gray stripes, glass eyes, worn pink ribbon with bell, pink felt ear linings, button, cast iron wheels **1,980.00**

Character, Fat Captain, Katzenjammer Kids, 15" h, all felt, swivel head, black shoe button eyes on felt circles, faded single stroke eyebrows, felt shaped nose and ears, closed smiling mouth, fringe beard and tufts of hair, felt cap attached to heat, stuffed felt body, disk jointed arms, red plaid felt shirt, black felt pants, beige felt shoes, unmarked **1,400.00**

Cocker spaniel, 5-3/4" h, sitting, glass eyes, ear button, chest tag, post WWII **125.00**

Dog, 15-1/2" l, 14" h, pull toy, orange and white mohair coat, glass eyes, steel frame, cast iron wheels, one ear missing, button in remaining ear, voice box does not work **280.00**

Frog, 3-3/4" l, velveteen, glass eyes, green, sitting, button and chest tag **125.00**

Goat, 6-1/2" h, ear button **150.00**

Gussy, 6-1/2" l, white and black kitten, glass eyes, ear button, chest tag, post WWII **125.00**

Hobby horse, 40" l, brown felt, button in ear, 1940s **60.00**

Kangaroo and joey, 20-3/4" h mohair mother, 4" h velveteen baby both with glass eyes, embroidered nose, and mouth, ear button and tag, ... **395.00**

Koala, 7-1/2" h, glass eyes, ear button, chest tag, post WWII **135.00**

Lion, 21" l, 18" h, pull toy, worn gold mohair coat, glass eyes, worn streaked mane incomplete, no tail, ring pull voice box, steel frame, sheet metal wheels with white rubber treads marked "Steiff" **500.00**

Lizard, 12" l, Lizzy, velveteen, yellow and green, black steel eyes, chest tag **200.00**

Llama, 10" h, glass eyes, ear button, chest tag, post WWII **125.00**

Monkey, 5" h, Coco, glass eyes, ear button, chest tag, post WWII **125.00**

Owl, 4-1/2" h, Wittie, glass eyes, ear button, chest tag, post WWII **95.00**

Palomino colt, 11" h, ear button, wear **330.00**

Panda, 6" h, black and white mohair, fully jointed, glass eyes, excelsior stuffing, felt open mouth and pads, c1950, some fur loss, moth damage on pads, button and tag missing **260.00**

Parakeet, 6-1/2" h, Hansi, bright lime green and yellow, airbrushed black details, plastic eyes, button tag, chest tag, plastic beak and feet **115.00**

Three Steiff fish, one large, two small, **$75**. Photo courtesy of Joy Luke Auctions.

Penguin, 5-1/2" h, Peggy, glass eyes, ear button, chest tag, post WWII **95.00**

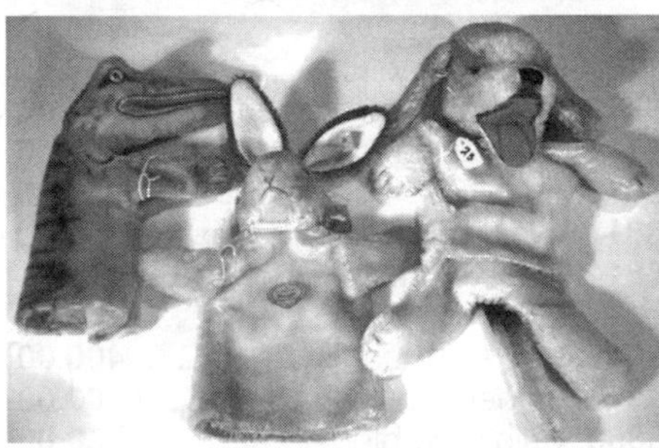

Three Steiff hand puppets: Mimic Biggie dog, rabbit, and Gaty alligator, **$145**. Photo courtesy of Joy Luke Auctions.

Pig, 15" l, pull toy, blonde mohair, button eyes, ear button, cast iron wheels, repairs, very worn mohair **330.00**

Tiger cub, 7" l, fully jointed, orig tag **80.00**

Turtle, 7" l, Slo, plastic shell, glass eyes, ear button, chest tag, post WWII **85.00**

Walrus, 6-1/2" l, Paddy, plastic tusk, glass eyes, ear button, chest tag, post WWII **145.00**

Stein, Lea

History: Lea Stein, a French-trained artist born in Paris in 1931, began making her whimsical pieces of jewelry in 1969, after her husband, Fernand Steinberger, came up with a process of laminating layers of rhodoid (cellulose acetate) sheets with interesting textures and colors. The layers were baked overnight with a secret component of his creation and then cut into shapes for various designs of pins, bracelets, earrings, and shaped decorative objects. From the side, in some pieces, as many as 20 layers of cellulose have been bonded together to make these pieces.

The most easily recognizable Lea Stein pin is the 3-D fox, produced in a myriad of colors and designs. Often, lace or metal layers were incorporated into the celluloid, which produced an astounding number of unique textures. The 3-D fox's tail is looped from one piece of celluloid. Many different styles of cats, dogs, bugs, bunnies, birds, ducks, and other creatures were introduced, as well as Art Deco-styled women, mod-styled children, flowers, cars, hats, purses, gold-encased and rhinestone encrusted designs, and lots of little "things," such as stars, hearts, rainbows, and even pins resembling John Travolta and Elvis Presley. In addition, collectors can find many bangles, rings, cuffs, earrings, barrettes, and rarer boxes, mirrors, and cigarette cases. The designs seem endless and to a Lea Stein collector, the ability to collect one of everything is almost impossible, because so many pieces were one of a kind. One particularly elusive piece is called "Joan Crawford" in the U.S. and "Carmen" in France. This piece was made in limited quantity and always hard to find, but, lo and behold, a new cache has recently hit the market and they are not so difficult to find anymore.

These "vintage" pieces of jewelry were made from 1969 until 1981 and are identified by a V-shaped pin-back that is heat mounted to the back of each piece, as are the pin-backs on her newer pieces. The pin back is always marked "Lea Stein Paris." Some of the later issues have riveted backs, but all of them are marked in the same way. At one time the age of a pin could be determined by the pin back, but because of many newly released pieces in the past few years, that no longer is always the case. Stein's workshop is still producing jewelry. While some of the vintage pieces are rare, it is virtually impossible to tell the difference between old and new releases, except with the knowledge of which designs were created at what time in Stein's career. Whether old or new, Lea Stein's jewelry is quite collectible.

Many different stories about the history of Lea Stein's jewelry have been circulated, but here are the facts, some of which are in direct discrepancy with many of the well-known jewelry collecting books.

In 1957, Lea Stein started her own company, and from 1957 to 1965 was in the textile business. From 1965 to 1967, she made buttons. In 1967, she began making buttons in rhodoid, the cellulose acetate associated with her jewelry. Her skills at making rhodoid buttons were put to use in her first jewelry collection, which she began producing in 1969.

The vintage period of Lea Stein's jewelry was really a short period of 12 years, from 1969 to 1981, when her company, which by that time employed 50 workers and was mass-producing jewelry, failed due to the influx of Asian competition.

Reports in different books describing Stein's jewelry vary the time period of her "golden years" as anywhere from the 1930s to the 1960s. This is untrue, as she would have been but a schoolgirl in the 1930s. Part of this speculation is due to the fact that Lea Stein's work is heavily influenced by the Art-Deco period and that rhodoid strongly resembles Bakelite and some older plastics, such as galalith.

After the failure of her company in 1981, an American dealer in New York bought a big part of her remaining stock and began selling her jewelry in the U.S. It was not until after 1981 that the trademark Lea Stein pieces began to be well known in the U.S. It was somewhat ironic that Stein became known as a famous designer of French jewelry only after the failure of her business.

In the late 1980s, after running a computer business, Lea Stein returned to the profession she liked best—creating and making plastic jewelry. Every year since 1988, she has created a new piece for her collection. These new designs include: Buba (owl), Bacchus (cat's head), Gomina (sleeping cat), Attila (standing cat), the tortoise, and Ric the dog. Her newest designs are the Porcupine and Goupil in 2000 and the Penguin, Cicada and Christmas Tree in 2001. Sacha, a sitting cat, was introduced in 2002. 2003 brought us a new cat design, Quarrelsome, as well as a beautifully layered Maple Tree. Despite what you may have heard, there are no first and second editions of these pieces. These designs did not exist in the 1970s and early 1980s.

Lea Stein's designs are once again being produced in Paris. New releases are still being made, both from the older and newer patterns, and vintage pieces are still being re-released, making it more difficult to differentiate between old and new pieces.

Adviser: Judy Smith.

Pin, black butterfly, white lace body encrusted with clear rhinestones, signed V-shaped clasp, 2-1/8" w, 1-5/8" h, **$80**. Lea Stein photographs courtesy of adviser Judy Smith.

Pin, bowl pin, shades of beige, faux-tortoise, and faux-ivory, V-shaped Lea Stein Paris clasp, 2-5/8" w x 7/8" h, **$75**.

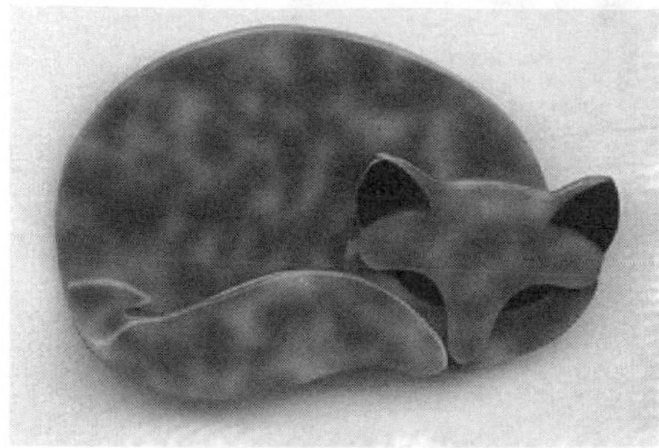

Cat, Gomina, rusty faux-tortoise, shiny black eyes and ears, V-shaped Lea Stein Paris clasp, **$65**.

Bracelet, bangle, dark green and red swirled peppermint stick swirls **95.00**

Earrings, pr, clip, bright green swirls on pearly white, stamped on back, 1-3/8" d **95.00**

Pin, all with signature Lea Stein-Paris V-shaped pin back

Bacchus, cat, pearly silver and black, 2-3/8" w, 1-1/8" h........... **65.00**

Bee, transparent wings with gold edge, faux ivory body and head, topaz colored glass edge eye, 2-3/8" wingspan................................. **80.00**

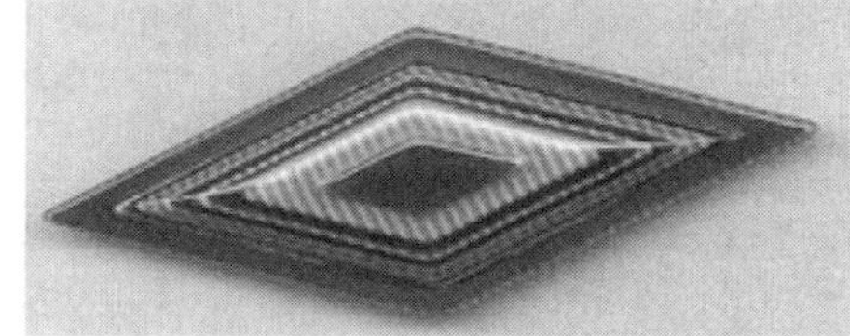

Geometric diamond, red outlined with mauve and gray, signed Lea Stein V-shaped clasp, 3-3/8" w, 1-1/4" h, **$70**.

Blueberries, peach lace, 2-7/8" l **65.00**

Cicada, irid red wings, striped body and head, 3-3/8" l, 1-1/4" w **85.00**

Edelweiss, coral flowers, white and marbled green stem, 3-3/8" h... **75.00**

Limo, crackly pink, highlighted by pearly pink and white moiré bumper, pink and white pearly wheels, small V-shaped Lea Stein signed clasp, 2-3/4" w, **$50**.

Flamingo, pink, 1-7/8" w, 2-3/8" h **55.00**

Flower pot, two flowers, one aqua lacy turquoise, other purple lacy, dark blue leaves, turquoise lacy pot, 1-1/2" w, 2-1/2" h...................... **85.00**

Fox, red tones **100.00**

Goldenberries, shades of plum, gold, and white, 2-3/8" w, 1-5/8" h..... **65.00**

Gomina, cat, shiny black body, accented with waves of silver and blue, dark pearly blue ears and eyes, 3" w, 1-7/8" h............................ **85.00**

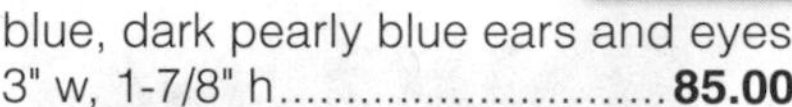

Ric the Terrier, faux ivory, black eye, nose, ears and collar. 2-1/8" w, 3-5/8" h, **$65**.

Joan Crawford........................ **125.00**

Mistigri Kitty, caramel, 4" 2, 3-7/8" h **70.00**

Pin, Joan Crawford, also known as "Carmen" in Europe, gray tinged waved brown lace hair, creamy skin, bead earring, pearly purple dress with striated beige and gray collar, V-shaped Lea Stein Paris clasp, 2-1/8" w, 1-3/4" h, **$125**.

Oriental girl, shades of blue and white, transparent light blue hat, faux-ivory face, transparent light blue eye, 2" w, 2-1/8" h..................... **90.00**

Panther, shades of brown, irid faux tortoiseshell, 4-1/4" l, 1-3/4" h **65.00**

Panther, silvery moiré, 4-1/4" l, 1-3/4" h **65.00**

Fox, swirled red moiré, black eyes, V-shaped signature clasp, 2" w, 4" h, **$65**.

Book, silver glitter spine, pink plaid cover, shiny black pages, 3/8" thick including a faux-turtoise back, signed V-shaped clasp, 1-1/8" w, 1-3/4" h, **$45**. Photo courtesy of Judy Smith.

Penguin, dark red brocade body and head, yellow lace beak, eye, neck, and feet, pearly harlequin lace body, 1-3/4" w, 3-1/8" h....................... **85.00**

Porcupine, irid gold and dark red body with black accents, black face and paws, dark red eye and nose, 3" w.. **80.00**

Pin, Quiet Elephant, faux-ivory, shiny black ear and tusk, V-shaped Lea Stein Paris clasp, 2-5/8" w, 1-3/4" h, **$100**.

Ric, pearly ivory harlequin pattern, shiny black ears, nose, eye and collar.. **65.00**

Sailor, faux ivory face, neck, hands and feet, pearly purple suit and cap, pearly gray collar, 1-5/8" w, 2-3/8" h **80.00**

Swallow, pink and white lace wings, 2-3/4" w, 1-3/8" h...................... **85.00**

Three ducks, orange lace bodies, dark royal blue heads, dark blue wings, 1" w, 2-1/4" h **75.00**

STEINS

History: Steins, mugs especially made to hold beer or ale, range in size from the smaller 3/10 and 1/4 liter to the larger 1, 1-1/2, 2, 3, 4, and 5 liters, and in rare cases to 8 liters. A liter is 1.05 liquid quarts.

Master steins or pouring steins hold 3 to 5 liters and are called krugs. Most steins are fitted with a metal-hinged lid with thumb lift. The earthenware character-type steins usually are German in origin.

For more information, see *Warman's English & Continental Pottery & Porcelain*, 3rd edition.

Copper luster, cream-colored ground, **$120**.

Character

Beethoven, half liter, porcelain, lire on side of body and on porcelain inlaid lid, E. Bohne & Sohn **570.00**

Monk, 1/3 liter, design by Frank Ringer, marked "J. Reinemann, Munchen" on underside of base, inlaid lid, 5" h **580.00**

Salt glazed, White's Utica, mold #45, relief and blue accented tavern scene on one side, framed German verse on other, relief and blue accented gargoyle handle, conical pewter lid, matching thumb lift, small surface chip on base, 9-1/2" h, **$180**. Photo courtesy of Vicki and Bruce Waasdorp.

Pug dog, Mettlach, #2018, 1/2 liter, character, pug dog, inlaid lid **1,100.00**

Skull, 1/3 liter, porcelain, large jaw, inlaid lid, E. Bohne & Sohn, pewter slightly bent **550.00**

Faience

French, 18th C, baluster form with ear handle, enamel dec, figure of woodsman, flattened domed pewter lid with turned ovoid thumbpiece, spreading pewter foot, 10-1/2" **560.00**

German, military scene, pewter mounts, dated 1515, 8-1/2" h.................... **700.00**

Thuringen, 1 liter, 9-1/2" h, hp, floral design on front, purple trees on sides, pewter top rim and lid, pewter base ring, 18th C, tight hairline on side...... **1,155.00**

Mettalach, #2382, 1/2 liter, knight drinking in cellar and riding off into night, conical lid, signed "H. Schlitt," 9" h, **$865**. Photo courtesy of James D. Julia, Inc.

Glass

9-1/2" h, 1 liter, blown, wedding type, hp floral design and verse, pewter lid with earlier date of 1779, pewter brass ring, c1850... **925.00**

15-1/4" h, 6-1/2" d, amber, encased in fancy French pewter frame, ram's heads around stein, hinged top lid **495.00**

Delftware, England or Continental, 18th C, hinged pewter lids with egg-shape finials mounted on rims and handles of cylindrical vessels, one lid engraved "GHW 1752," hallmarks impressed on underside of lid, decorated with building, trees, and flowers; other lid engraved "F.G.R. 1815," polychrome decoration as scene with peasant woman carrying basket an indistinct MI- mark impressed into the base, chips, 10-1/4" h, 9-3/8" h, **$650**. Photo courtesy of Skinner, Inc.

Porcelain and Pottery

Delft, 1/2 liter, elaborate scene of two people playing lawn tennis, porcelain inlaid lid of sail boat, marked "Delft, Germany" **1,390.00**

Meissen, 1 liter, 7" h, hp, scene of three people in forest, floral design around sides, porcelain lid with berry finial and painted flowers, closed hinge, cross swords and "S" mark, c1820, strap repoured **3,100.00**

Mettlach

#1896, 1/4 liter, maiden on one side, cherub face on other, grape dec, pewter lift handle **350.00**

#2007, 1/2 liter, etched, black cat, inlaid lid **660.00**

#2580, 1/2 liter, etched, Die Kannenburg, conical inlay lid, knight in castle **695.00**

Stoneware, German, half liter, decorated with dancing figures, pewter lid with porcelain inset decorated with portrait of lady, **$95**. Photo courtesy of Joy Luke Auctions.

Unknown maker, 1/4 liter, transfer and enameled, color, Ulmer Splatz!, The Bird from the City of Ulm, pewter lid **115.00**

Regimental, 1/2 liter, porcelain

2 Schwer. Reit. Regt. Erzh. Fz, Ferd u. Osterr-Este Esk Landshut 1899-02, named to Friederich Schmidt, two side scenes, lion thumb lift, old tear on lid repaired, minor scruffs, 11-1/2" h **675.00**

120 Infantry, Ulm 1899-01, named to Tambour Wurst, two side scenes, Wurttemberg thumb lift, 10-1/2" h **520.00**

123 Grenadier, Ulm 1908-10, named to Grenadier Schindler, four side scenes, roster, bird thumb lift, open blister on int. base, finial missing **550.00**

Wood and pewter,

Daubenkrug

1/2 liter, 6-1/2" h, pewter scene of deer, vines and leaves on sides, pewter handle and lid, c1820, some separations to pewter **925.00**

Stoneware, Simon Peter Gerz German, three liter, decorated with relief panels of warriors with shields, marked "Saul, Hologernes & Sanherib," **$125**. Photo courtesy of Joy Luke Auctions.

1/3 liter, 5-1/2" h, floral design on sides, oval with crown on front, pewter handle and lid, 18th C, splints in pewter and wood **1,270.00**

STEUBEN GLASS

For more information, see *Warman's Glass*, 4th edition.

History: Frederick Carder, an Englishman, and Thomas G. Hawkes of Corning, New York, established the Steuben Glass Works in 1904. In 1918, the Corning Glass Company purchased the Steuben company. Carder remained with the firm and designed many of the pieces bearing the Steuben mark. Probably the most widely recognized wares are Aurene, Verre De Soie, and Rosaline, but many other types were produced.

Animal, elephant, trunk raised, signed, 7-1/4" h, **$275**. Photo courtesy of Sloan & Kenyon Auctions.

Animals, colorless, NY, 20th C, inscribed "Steuben"

Donkey, standing, 10-1/2" h **950.00**

Dove, on stand, 12-1/8" h, abrasion to side of dove **635.00**

Eagle, 4-3/4" h, imperfections **350.00**

Fish, #8338, design by Paul Schulze, 8-1/4" l **180.00**

Frog, sitting, 4-1/4" l, minor base wear **230.00**

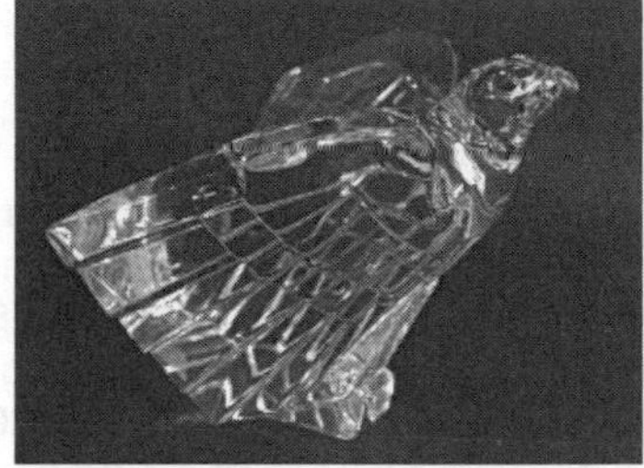

Animal, eagle, crystal, script signature, 4-3/4" h, **$350**. Photo courtesy of Garth's Auctions, Inc.

Seal, resting on flippers, 8-1/2" l **375.00**

Squirrel, 4-1/8" h **350.00**

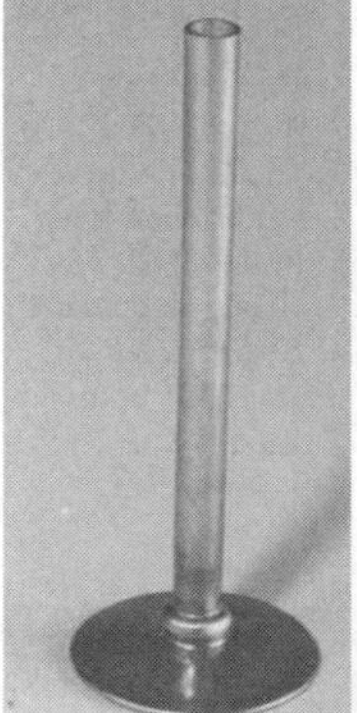

Aurene, bud vase, iridescent gold, acid etched "STEUBEN/AURENE/2556," minor interior rim nicks, 8" h, **$950**. Photo courtesy of David Rago Auctions, Inc.

Aurene, compote, gold, catalog No. 2642, rounded bowl raised on slightly bulbed stem, disk base, inscribed "Aurene 2642," 8" h, **$1,175**. Photo courtesy of Skinner, Inc.

Aurene

Atomizer, 6-3/4" h, irid blue, sgd "De Vilbis," later stopper **460.00**

Bowl, 10" d, amber, gold irid finish, sgd "Aurene 5061," orig triangular paper label, c1910 .... **460.00**

Bud vase, 3" d base, 10" h, blue, gold highlights, sgd "Steuben Aurene 2556" **700.00**

Candlesticks, pr, 10-1/8" h, catalog #686, amber, twist stems on applied disc foot, strong gold luster, sgd "Aurene 686," c1920 .... **1,100.00**

Aurene, perfume bottle, shape #2183, iridescent gold with blue highlights, unsigned, 6" h, **$635**. Photo courtesy of James D. Julia, Inc.

Compote, 6" d, 2-3/4" h, gold aurene on calcite, applied pedestal foot, unsigned **300.00**
Darner, 6-1/2" l, irid blue finish, unsigned, small chip **920.00**
Dome, 8-1/4" d, 8-1/4" h, irid gold, blue highlights, silver plated metal rim, unsigned, minor edge roughness **1,320.00**
Planter, 12" d, blue, inverted rim, three applied prunt feet, engraved "Aurene 2586" **775.00**

Aurene, vase, blue, catalog No. 7447, flared rim, ribbed body, double bulb at waist, inscribed "Steuben," 6" h, **$1,175**. Photo courtesy of Skinner, Inc.

Vase
- 4-1/2" h, four pinched-in sides, flaring four-sided top, irid gold, green swirls, base sgd "AURENE 131B" **2,100.00**
- 6" h, flaring ruffled top, irid blue, base sgd "AURENE 723" **920.00**
- 6-1/4" h, gold Aurene over calcite, ground pontil, unsigned, early 20th C **500.00**

Aurene, vase, gold, catalog No. 2683, flared rim, shouldered bulbous form, inscribed "Steuben," 8" h, **$1,175**. Photo courtesy of Skinner, Inc.

- 12" h, irid gold swirl vases with blue and purple highlights, applied aurene foot, bases sgd "STEUBEN AURENE 6034," pr **3,450.00**
- 16-1/2" h, amber, irid finish shading from red gold at top to blue good foot, double sgd "Steuben Aurene," numbered 3285, c1920 .... **3,165.00**
- 18-1/4" h, trumpet, amber, gold luster irid finish, sgd "Aurene 1213," c1915, wear to neck and foot **990.00**

Calcite, bowl, gold interior, cased calcite exterior, unsigned, 9-3/4" d, 2-1/2" h, **$225**. Photo courtesy of Garth's Auctions, Inc.

Calcite

Bowl, 8" d, ftd, opal, gold Aurene int., c1915 .... **230.00**

Aurene, vase, baluster gold, iridescent finish over blue, magenta shades at neck, signed "Aurene/F. Carder," 8" d, 15-3/4" h, **$110**. Photo courtesy of Sanford Alderfer Auction Company.

Compote, 8" h, amber bowl and foot, red and gold irid finish, irid blue rope twisted stem with gold finish **1,880.00**
Low bowl
- 10" d, gold irid int. **350.00**
- 12" d, rolled rim, irid gold int., c1915 .... **460.00**

Sherbet and underplate, 6" d, 4" h, calcite body, irid gold int., c1920, set of four **575.00**

Celeste Blue

Candlesticks, brilliant blue, applied foliate form bobeche and cups, bulbed shafts, c1920-33, set of four **2,300.00**
Center bowl, 16-1/4" d, 4-1/4" h, catalog #112, swirled optic ribbed broad bowl, rolled rim, applied fluted foot, partially polished pontil, c1925 .... **400.00**
Iced tea goblet, 6-1/2" h, catalog #5192, blue, flared, light ribbon, c1918-32, set of eight **400.00**
Luncheon plate, 8-1/2" d, molded blue body, Kensington pattern variant, engraved border of leaves and dots, c1918-32, set of 12 .... **550.00**

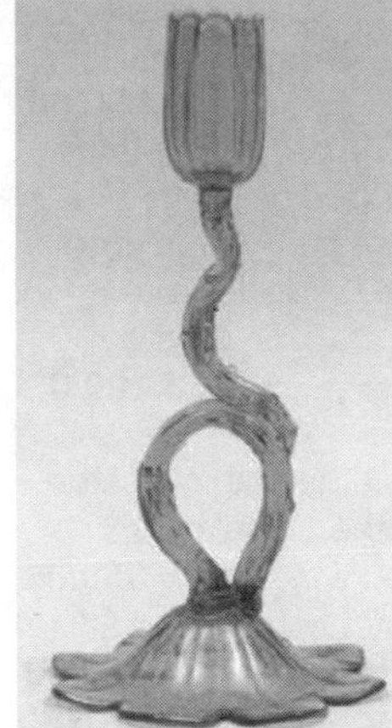
Celeste Blue, candlestick, Celeste blue and amber, tulip candleholder, lily pad foot, 12" h, **$1,495**. Photo courtesy of James D. Julia, Inc.

Cluthra, urn, pink, allover bubbles, ground pontil, 6-1/2" h, **$1,380**. Photo courtesy of James D. Julia, Inc.

Cluthra

Lamp base, 12-1/2" h, ovoid, creamy white cluthra acid-etched Art-Deco flowers, acid-etched fleur-de-lis mark near base, orig gilded foliate bronze lamp fittings, c1925 .... **2,070.00**
Vase, 10-1/4" h, 9" d, bulbous, flaring top, yellow amber, bruise at shoulder and base **1,955.00**
Wall pocket, 15-1/2" w, 8" h, half round flared bowl, black and white cluthra, cut and mounted to foliate gilt metal framework, polished pontil, c1930, slight corrosion to metal **490.00**

Crystal

Bowl, 10-7/8" d, 6-7/8" h, cylindrical hollow body, applied wave motifs on base, inscribed "Steuben" **490.00**
Calyx bowl, 9-1/2" d, 3-3/8" h, floriform oval, solid foot, inscribed "Steuben" **230.00**
Candelabra, two candle cups supported on scrolled shaft, inscribed "Steuben," 7-1/4" and 7-5/8" l, 4-1/4" and 4-3/4" h, base scratches, price for pr **490.00**

Cocktail set, 15" h cocktail shaker, six matching 2-1/2" h glasses, two applied red cherries, wheel-cut leaves, and stems on shaker, ruby stopper, same dec on glasses, some with fleur-de-lis marks, slight damage to stopper **3,700.00**

Goblet, 7-1/16" h, flared cylindrical vessel, knobbed stem, sq base, small "S" inscribed on base, designed by Arthur A. Houghton, Jr., 1938, Madigan catalog #7846, set of six, two with small chips **260.00**

Paperweight, 2-1/2" d, sphere with randomly imp heart motifs, late 20th C **115.00**

Vase, 7-3/8" h, catalog #SP919, flared wing form, pedestal base, inscribed "Steuben" on base **330.00**

Miscellaneous, wine glasses, amethyst cut to clear bowls with lion head decoration, clear stems, signed, identically cut but different sizes, 9" h, 8" h, **$2,130**. Photo courtesy of James D. Julia,

Grotesque

Bowl, 11-1/2" d, 6-1/4" h, amethyst shading to clear, base sgd, int. scratches **360.00**

Vase, 9-1/4" h, amethyst, catalog #7090, pillar molded floriform body, ruffled rim shaded to colorless crystal at applied disk foot, acid script "Steuben" mark in polished pontil, c1930 .... **525.00**

Jade

Bowl, 8" d, 6" h, two-line pillar, ftd, alabaster int., fleur-de-lis acid stamp mark.. **800.00**

Bud vase, 7-3/4" h, green trumpet form vase with ruffled rim, supported on scrolled tripod hammered silver mount over round base, engraved "RAP" monogram, imp "Black Starr & Frost 7050 Sterling" on base **460.00**

Candlesticks, pr, 10" h, No. 2956, jade candle cup and base, alabaster shaft, gold foil labels **550.00**

Compote, 10" h, yellow, ftd....... **1,450.00**

Lamp base, 12" h, catalog #7001, urn form, plum jade, intricately etched in Belgrade pattern, gilt-metal lamp fittings, c1925, chips to rim under mounting **2,415.00**

Parfait, 6" h, applied alabaster foot **350.00**

Rose bowl, 7" d, 7" h, spherical, smooth jade crystal **350.00**

Vase, 8" h, 10" d, plum jade, acid cut back dec, two hairline cracks ... **1,150.00**

Miscellaneous, vase, cranberry, shape #6030, spiral ribbed, polished pontil, faint acid stamp "Steuben" near edge of base, partly lost due to wear, c1925, 6-3/4" h, **$295**. Photo courtesy of Forrest D. Poston.

Miscellaneous

Candlesticks, pr, 11-3/4" h, catalog #2956, amber glass baluster shaped stems, wide disk foot, c1925 .... **690.00**

Center bowl, 14" d, 8" h, ftd, topaz body, celeste blue rims, eight swirl cabochons **375.00**

Compote, 8-1/4" h, cobalt blue, flat bowl **200.00**

Exhibition sculpture, 18" h, Salmon Run, designed by James Houston, engraved by George Thompson, number 14 in series of 20, orig red leather and velvet box.. **13,500.00**

Lamp base, 14" h, Cintra, yellow, acid cut design, unsigned...................... **1,035.00**

Paperweight, Excalibur, designed by James Houston, 1963, catalog #1000, faceted hand-polished solid crystal embedded with removable sterling silver sword, 18kt gold scabbard, base inscribed "Steuben" **1,955.00**

Parfait and underplate, 4-1/2" h, 5-1/4" d underplate, Calcite, gold, partial paper label.. **625.00**

Pitcher, 9" h, catalog #6665, Spanish Green, slightly ribbed oval, flared mouth, applied angled handle, raised disk foot, acid fleur-de-lis mark................... **460.00**

Scent bottle, 4-1/2" h, deep green transparent, shape 1455, small chips to stopper bottom, pr....................... **635.00**

Miscellaneous, pair of vases, green opaque, rectangular vases, applied lion head medallions, unsigned, 7-1/2" h, **$250**. Photo courtesy of Woody Auctions.

Vase

7-1/4" h, 4-1/4" across shoulder, Tyrian, heart and vine dec, purple and blue glass, base sgd "TYRIAN" **9,000.00**

Grotesque, fan vase, ruby shading to clear crystal, applied crystal foot, signed on base with fleur de lis acid insignia, 11-1/4", **$525**. Photo courtesy of James D. Julia, Inc.

8-3/4" h, acid etched, black over alabaster, Stamford pattern, leaping stylized gazelles, unsigned **5,100.00**

Selenium, goblet, red, engraved grapevines, deep ruby red ground, etched "Steuben" in block letters, 5-7/8" h, **$325**. Photo courtesy of Garth's Auctions, Inc.

Rosaline

Bowl, 8" l, 7" w, 3-1/4" h, one end folded in, other pinched spout, inscribed "F. Carder Steuben 723" on edge of polished pontil **350.00**
Compote, 4" h, ruffled, alabaster stem and foot **275.00**
Cornucopia vase, 8" h, Rosaline body, alabaster foot, sgd in block letters, minor int. surface scratches **300.00**
Goblet, crystal foot **90.00**
Perfume, 5-3/8" h, catalog #6412, teardrop shape, cloudy pink, applied alabaster glass foot, c1925, pr **435.00**

Acid cut back, vase, black amethyst, portrait medallions, floral garlands, 8" h, **$3,140**. Photo courtesy of Fontaine's Auction Gallery.

Table setting, 7-1/2" h, four goblets with translucent rose bowl, clambroth foot, four matching 8-1/2" d plates **1,260.00**

Verre De Soie

Bonbon, 6" h, compote form, overall irid surface, swirled celeste blue finial, twisted stem **850.00**
Console set, 9-3/4" d bowl, pr 6" h candlesticks with twist stems, frosted irid glass, unsigned **1,265.00**
Perfume, 4-1/2" h, catalog #1455, ribbed body, celeste blue flame stopper, c1915 .... **400.00**
Vase, 6" h, frosted irid glass, applied cranberry threading, unsigned **200.00**

STEVENGRAPHS

History: Thomas Stevens of Coventry, England, first manufactured woven silk designs in 1854. His first bookmark was produced in 1862, followed by the first Stevengraphs, perhaps in 1874, but definitely by 1879 when they were shown at the York Exhibition. The first portrait Stevengraphs (of Disraeli and Gladstone) were produced in 1886, and the first postcards incorporating the woven silk panels in 1904. Stevens offered many other items with silk panels, including valentines, fans, pincushions, and needle cases.

Stevengraphs are miniature silk pictures, matted in cardboard, and usually having a trade announcement or label affixed to the reverse. Other companies, notably W. H. Grant of Coventry, copied Stevens's technique. Their efforts should not be confused with Stevengraphs.

Collectors in the U.S. favor the Stevengraphs with American-related views, such as "Signing of the Declaration of Independence," "Columbus Leaving Spain," and "Landing of Columbus." Sports-related Stevengraphs such as "The First Innings" (baseball), and "The First Set" (tennis) are also popular, as well as portraits of Buffalo Bill, President and Mrs. Cleveland, George Washington, and President Harrison.

Postcards with very fancy embossing around the aperture in the mount almost always have Stevens' name printed on them. The two most popular embossed postcard series in the U.S. are "Ships" and "Hands across the Sea." The latter set incorporates two crossed flags and two hands shaking. Seventeen flag combinations have been found, but only seven are common. These series generally are not printed with Stevens' name. Stevens also produced silks that were used in cards made by the Alpha Publishing Co.

Stevens' bookmarks are longer than they are wide, have mitered corners at the bottom, and are finished with a tassel. Many times his silks were used as the top or bottom half of regular bookmarks.

Marks: Thomas Stevens' name appears on the mat of the early Stevengraphs, directly under the silk panel. Many of the later portraits and the larger silks (produced initially for calendars) have no identification on the front of the mat other than the phrase "woven in pure silk" and have no label on the back.

Bookmarks originally had Stevens' name woven into the foldover at the top of the silk, but soon the identification was woven into the fold-under mitered corners. Almost every Stevens' bookmark has such identification, except the ones woven at the World's Columbian Exposition in Chicago, 1092 to 1093.

Note: Prices are for pieces in mint or close-to-mint condition.

Bookmarks

Centennial, USA, 1776-1876, General George Washington, The Father of Our Country, The First in Peace, The First in War, The First in the Hearts of Our Countrymen!, few small stains **125.00**
Forget-Me-Not, Godden #441 .... **350.00**
I Wish You a Merry Christmas and a Happy New Year **75.00**
Lord Have Mercy **400.00**

Bookmarks, silk, both with George Washington, left marked "T. Stevens Coventry, England," right marked "Silk City," mounted in small glass display case, light staining, 9" h, **$250**. Photo courtesy of James D. Julia, Inc.

Mother and Child, evening prayers, 10-1/2" l, 2" w, 1-1/2" silk tassel **400.00**
Mourning, Blessed Are They Who Mourn, 9-1/2" l, 2" w, 2" silk tassel **450.00**
My Dear Father, red, green, white, and purple **200.00**
Prayer Book Set, five orig markers attached with small ivory button, cream-colored tape fastened to orig frame, Communion, Collect, Lesson I, Lesson II, Psalms, gold lettering, gold silk tassels, orig mount, c1880-85 .... **3,400.00**
The Old Arm Chair, chair, full text, musical score, four color, 2" w, 11" l **125.00**
The Star Spangled Banner, U.S. flag, full text and musical score of song, red tassel, seven color, no maker's mark, 2-1/2" w, 11" l **185.00**
To One I Love, Love me little, love me long is the burden of my song, Love that is too hot and strong, burneth soon to waste, Still I would not have thee cold, not too backward or too bold; Love that lasteth till this old fadeth not in haste **175.00**

Postcard

RMS Arabic, Hands Across the Sea **465.00**
RMS Elmina **225.00**
USMS Philadelphia **225.00**

Stevengraph

Buffalo Bill, Nate Salsbury, Indian Chief, orig mat and frame, 8" x 7" **500.00**
Coventry, 7-1/4" x 13", framed **100.00**
Death of Nelson, 7-1/4" x 2-1/2" .. **200.00**

Ribbon, Lincoln bust under American eagle, flag, and shield, excerpt from Gettysburg address, red, blue, white, and black, minor edge splits, c1860, 2-3/4" w, 13-1/2" l, **$200**. Photo courtesy of Historical Collectibles Auction.

Declaration of Independence **375.00**
For Life or Death, fire engine rushing to burning house, orig mat and frame **350.00**
Good Ole Days, Royal Mail Coach, orig title, re-matted, framed **485.00**
H. M. Stanley, famous explorer ... **300.00**
Kenilworth Castle, 7-1/4" x 13" framed **120.00**
Landing of Columbus........ **350.00**
President Cleveland........ **365.00**
The Water Jump........ **195.00**
Untitled, life-saving boat........ **175.00**

Stevens and Williams

History: In 1824, Joseph Silvers and Joseph Stevens leased the Moor Lane Glass House at Briar Lea Hill (Brierley Hill), England, from the Honey-Borne family. In 1847, William Stevens and Samuel Cox Williams took over, giving the firm its present name. In 1870, the company moved to its Stourbridge plant.

19th C

In the 1880s, the firm employed such renowned glass artisans as Frederick C. Carder, John Northwood, other Northwood family members, James Hill, and Joshua Hodgetts.

For more information, see Warman's Glass, 4th edition.

Stevens and Williams made cameo glass. Hodgetts developed a more commercial version using thinner-walled blanks, acid etching, and the engraving wheel. Hodgetts, an amateur botanist, was noted for his brilliant floral designs.

Other glass products and designs manufactured by Stevens and Williams include intaglio ware, Peach Bloom (a form of peachblow), moss agate, threaded ware, "jewell" ware, tapestry ware, and Silveria. Stevens and Williams made glass pieces covering the full range of late Victorian fashion.

After World War I, the firm concentrated on refining the production of lead crystal and achieving new glass colors. In 1932, Keith Murray came to Stevens and Williams as a designer. His work stressed the pure nature of the glass form. Murray stayed with Stevens and Williams until World War II and later followed a career in architecture.

Additional Listings: Cameo Glass.

Two bride's bowls, top is pink and white bowl with silver mica highlights, signed Pairpoint base, 11" x 10", **$150**; other is shell-shaped footed bowl with pink interior, white exterior, amber feet, Stevens & Williams, 10-1/2", **$60**. Photo courtesy of Woody Auctions.

Basket, 5-1/2" d, 5" h, rect, translucent amber basket, applied green-stemmed red strawberries, applied amber feet, amber handle **400.00**
Biscuit jar, cov, 7-1/2" h, 5-1/2" d, cream opaque, large amber and green applied ruffled leaves, rich pink int., SP rim, lid, and handle **300.00**
Bowl, 4-1/2" d, 3-1/2" h, MOP satin, turquoise cased to yellow, Zipper pattern, engraved English registry mark, RD 55693........ **700.00**
Box, cov, 4-1/2" l, 3-1/2" w, 2-1/2" h, aventurine spatter, green metallic flecks, white lining, cased, metal fittings and hinge, polished pontil, late 1800s **225.00**
Calling card receiver, 10" l, applied amber handle, rolled edge, translucent opalescent ground, three applied berries, blossoms, and green leaves, three applied amber feet........ **750.00**
Decanter, 10-1/2" h, flowing fan pattern in ruby cut to cranberry, clear glass applied handle, sterling stopper and collar, stamped "STERLING 925-1000 FINE," minor roughness to two corners near the base and a small piece of glass missing on inside, underneath silver collar **4,025.00**
Ewer, 8-1/2" h, 5" w, Pompeiian Swirl, deep rose shading to yellow, off white lining, frosted loop handle, all over gold enameled wild roses, ferns, and butterfly **1,500.00**
Jardinière, 6-1/2" d, 10" h, pink opalescent, cut back, two spatter flowers and sunflowers, three applied opalescent thorn feet, leaves, and stems, minor damage **350.00**
Perfume, 4-3/4" h, spherical, heat reactive dark amber shaded to green satin, spiraled air-trap switch, hallmarked and chased silver cap, c1890...... **635.00**
Pitcher
- 6" d, 8-1/2" h, aventurine, white spatter, applied amber reeded handle, late 19th C........ **550.00**
- 7-1/4" h, Cottage Ware, multicolored spatter, white int., applied colorless ribbed handle........ **200.00**

Vase, reddish-amber clear ground, swirling white Osiris decoration, 5-1/2" h, **$1,350**. Photo courtesy of Clarence and Betty Maier.

Rose bowl
- 4-1/2" h, Matsu No Ke, peachblow, shiny finish, crimped top, applied trailings of crystal twist and turn around perimeter to create knurled branches, seven Matsu No Ke florets, clear glass knobby base, inscribed "Rd 15353"........ **750.00**
- 6-1/4" d, 5-1/2" h, Pompeian Swirl, blue and brown swirls, box pleated top, chartreuse int. **2,185.00**

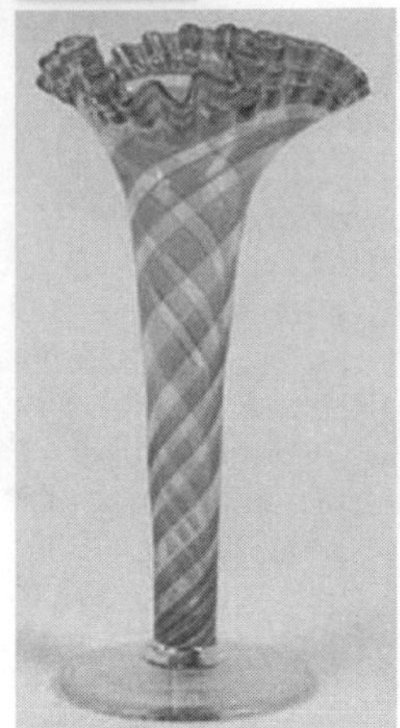

Vase, candy striped in light green and pink, ruffled, 8" h, **$225**. Photo courtesy of James D. Julia, Inc.

Vase

4-1/2" h, 5-1/2" d, amber shading to pink swirls, light blue int., inverted ruffled top **865.00**

5" h, pull-up form, amber and white, applied amber base and dec, minor chipping to applied dec......... **350.00**

5-1/2" h, buttercup yellow body shading to cherry blossom-pink, cameo carved twisted Japanese twisted, gnarled, cherry tree branch, pink borders, butterfly on reverse **1,450.00**

Stiegel-Type Glass

For more information, see Warman's Glass, 4th edition.

History: Baron Henry Stiegel founded America's first flint-glass factory at Manheim, Pennsylvania, in the 1760s. Although clear glass was the most common color made, amethyst, blue (cobalt), and fiery opalescent pieces also are found. Products included bottles, creamers, flasks, flips, perfumes, salts, tumblers, and whiskeys. Prosperity was short-lived; Stiegel's extravagant lifestyle forced the factory to close.

It is very difficult to identify a Stiegel-made item. As a result, the term "Stiegel-type" is used to identify glass made during the time period of Stiegel's firm and in the same shapes and colors as used by that company.

Enamel-decorated ware also is attributed to Stiegel. True Stiegel pieces are rare; an overwhelming majority is of European origin.

Beaker, 5" h, blown peacock blue glass, six panels, enameled birds, dog, tiger, stag, fruit, and florals, loop design around base, polished pontil, c1840, slight lower crizzling **425.00**

Bottle, blown, colorless, enamel dec, Continental, 19th C

4-1/4" h, paneled sides, gentleman raising his glass, inscription on reverse, pewter color, imperfection **325.00**

5-1/2" h, paneled sides, flowers, heart, birds, and inscription on reverse **265.00**

5-7/8" h, paneled sides, floral dec, pewter collar, imperfection..... **200.00**

6" h, paneled sides, flowers and bird dec, pewter collar, imperfection **220.00**

8-3/4" h, flattened side, dec with cross and various symbols, depicting Crucifixion of Christ, inscription on reverse, pewter screw-cap **295.00**

8-7/8" h, flattened round glass stopper, flowers and leave dec, pewter collar, imperfection..... **265.00**

Bottle, half post, colorless, pewter lip, minor enamel flaking

5-3/8" h, polychrome enameled flowers and birds.................... **360.00**

5-1/2" h, polychrome enameled flowers, bird in medallion, some residue, threads incomplete **250.00**

5-7/8" h, polychrome enameled flowers, inscription, fox with birds in basket.................................... **300.00**

6-3/4" h, polychrome enameled flowers, man with yoke, and buckets **175.00**

Mug, enameled, center shield with carpenter's and blacksmith tools, floral decoration on sides, **$325**.

Bride's or cordial bottle, 6-1/8" h, blue, "VIVAT, es leben alle miller 1764," (long live all Miller's) central floral motifs surrounding folklore symbols **3,100.00**

Christmas light, 4" h, yellow-green, expanded diamond pattern, metal fixture **150.00**

Creamer

3-1/8" h, pattern molded, 15 diamond pattern, emerald green, ovoid, applied handle, tooled rim, pour spout, pontil scar................. **2,000.00**

3-7/8" h, deep cobalt blue, 20 diamond mold, applied foot and handle, flake on bottom of handle, pinpoint rim flake.................... **500.00**

4-1/8" h, cobalt blue, 20 expanded diamonds **350.00**

Firing glass, blown, colorless, European, late 19th C

4" h, Masonic engraving, traces of gilding, pontil scar.................. **200.00**

4-1/4" h, copper wheel engraving around rim, hollow stem, pontil scar **175.00**

Flask

4-3/4" h, amethyst diamond and daisy...................................... **495.00**

5" h, blown, flattened oval, enameled Masonic dec, florals and inscription, sheared lip, pontil, scar, mid-18th C **295.00**

5-1/4" h, two hearts and dove in round floral bordered reserve, inscription on reverse, half pint **245.00**

5-1/2" h, flowers, scissors, and inscription on reverse, half pint **275.00**

Flip glass, colorless, sheared rim, pontil scar

3-1/2" h, handle, engraved repeating swag motif around rim, lower body emb with graduated panels, form similar to McKearin plate 22, #2 .... **210.00**

3-7/8" h, band of floral dec, Continental, 18th C................. **215.00**

5-1/4" h, engraved top border frieze of ovals, leaves, and berries beneath loop ribbon design................ **150.00**

6-1/4" h, engraved floral motif and sunflower, form similar to McKearin plate 22, #2 .... **300.00**

7" h, engraved basket and floral motif, form similar to McKearin plate 22, #2 .... **350.00**

7-3/4" h, 6" d, engraved Phoenix bird between two tulips **175.00**

7-7/8" h, engraved pair of birds perched on heart within sunburst motif, form similar to McKearin plate 22, #2 .... **475.00**

8" h, engraved large flower and floral motif, form similar to McKearin plate 22, #2 .... **325.00**

Flip, cov, blown, colorless, sunburst medallion, bird, and floral dec, conical knop, etched spotted border on lid, Continental 18th or 19th C, minor imperfections............................ **2,100.00**

Humpen, 9-1/4" h, blown colorless glass, enameled men smoking pipe, florals, and inscriptions, pontil scar, etched "FH 304/1" on base, European, late 19th C **275.00**
Jar, cov, 10-1/2" h, colorless, engraved sunflower and floral motifs, repeating dot and vine dec on cov, applied finial, sheared rim, pontil scar, form similar to McKearin plate 35, #2 and 3........ **750.00**
Miniature, flip glass, 3" h, colorless, engraved bird within sunburst motif, seared mouth, pontil scar............ **325.00**
Mug, blown, colorless
- 3-3/8" h, enameled polychrome dec of birds, hearts, and flowers, applied strap handle, European, 18th C **395.00**
- 5-1/4" h, engraved floral design, pontil scar, applied strap handle with medial crease, Bohemia, mid-18th C **275.00**
- 6" h, cov, engraved floral motif, strap handle **425.00**
- 6-1/8" h, elaborate frosted engraving, large applied strap handle **265.00**

Perfume bottle, Daisy in Hexagon pattern, flake on neck................ **4,000.00**
Pitcher, 9-3/4" h, blown, aqua, twelve bands of threading around neck, enameled polychrome floral design, c1820-40 .... **2,000.00**
Salt, blown
- 2-5/8" h, blue, checkered diamond pattern **750.00**
- 2-3/4" h, colorless, ogee bowl, 18 vertical ribs, applied petaled foot **225.00**
- 2-7/8" h, 2-1/4" d, pattern molded, cobalt blue, checkered diamond pattern, double ogee bowl with short stem from same gather, plain applied circular foot, sheared rim, pontil scar, attributed to Amelung Glass Works, Frederick, MD, 1785-1797 ..**1,200.00**

Stein, 6" h, opalescent, applied strap handle, flowers and portrait of gentleman in round floral bordered reserve, Continental, 18th C, minor scratches **550.00**
Sugar, cov, deep sapphire blue, 11 expanded diamond pattern **2,650.00**
Tankard, handle, cylindrical, applied solid reeded handle, flared foot, sheared rim, pontil scar, form similar to McKearin plate 22, #4
- 5-3/4" h, colorless, engraved with bird in elaborate sunburst motif **500.00**
- 6-1/4" h, colorless, engraved elaborate bird and tulip dec... **475.00**

Tumbler, blown, colorless
- 2-7/8" h, paneled, polychrome enameled flowers **220.00**
- 3-1/8" h, enameled polychrome dec of bird, heart, and foliage, minor enamel wear **265.00**
- 4-3/8" h, 3-1/2" d, 22 vertical flutes, engraved dec, cross-hatched ovals **50.00**

Whiskey tumbler, blown
- Cobalt blue, pattern mold, 12 oval diamonds over 12 flutes design **500.00**
- Colorless, enameled man on prancing horse **275.00**

STONEWARE

For more information, see *Warman's American Pottery and Porcelain*, 2nd edition.

History: Made from dense kaolin and commonly salt-glazed, stonewares were hand-thrown and high-fired to produce a simple, bold, vitreous pottery. Stoneware crocks, jugs, and jars were made to store products and fill other utilitarian needs. These intended purposes dictated shape and design—solid, thick-walled forms with heavy rims, necks, and handles and with little or no embellishment. Any decorations were simple: brushed cobalt oxide, incised, slip trailed, stamped, or tooled.

Stoneware has been made for centuries. Early American settlers imported stoneware items at first. As English and European potters refined their earthenware, colonists began to produce their own wares. Two major North American traditions emerged based only on location or type of clay. North Jersey and parts of New York comprise the first area; the second was eastern Pennsylvania spreading westward and into Maryland, Virginia, and West Virginia. These two distinct geographical boundaries, style of decoration, and shape are discernible factors in classifying and dating early stoneware.

By the late 18th century, stoneware was manufactured in all sections of the country. This vigorous industry flourished during the 19th century until glass fruit jars appeared and the use of refrigeration became widespread. By 1910, commercial production of salt-glazed stoneware came to an end.

Advertising crock, three gallon, D Atkins and Co., Dealer in Groceries and Queensware, Louisa, KY, cobalt blue stenciled name, further dec at ears, c1860-70 .... **4,100.00**
Advertising jar, 14-1/2" h, unsigned, "Runpoint & McCormick Dry Goods, Groceries and Notions, Meyersville, W Va," elaborate freehand designs above and below adv, c1870, in-the-making overglaze on front left side........... **990.00**

Butter churn, John Burger, Rochester, five gallons, ribbed double flower design, navy blue decoration at name and script gallon designation, original stoneware churn guide, c1865, 19" h, **$7,150.**

Advertising jug, 11" h, G. S. Guy & Co., Fort Edward, NY, one gal, bold blue script across front "Whitehead & Co., Wholesale Liquor Dealer, Amsterdam, NY," c1885, minor surface flakes **330.00**
Advertising rolling pin, rust bands, adv "J. P. Sweeney General Merchandise, Holy Cross, IA," repaired chip...... **225.00**

Crock, E. Norton, late 19th C, five gallons, large cobalt blue stylized flower, impressed "E. Norton & Co., Bennington, VT," 12-1/2" h, **$250**. Photo courtesy of Pook & Pook.

Batter pail, 9" h, unsigned, 1 gal, flower dec under spout, orig handle, c1870, interior chipping at rim, stone ping at shoulder **415.00**

Batter pail, Cowden & Wilcox, Harrisburg, two gallons, large brushed floral design on back, large brushed plume all around pouring spout, original bale handle, minor use stains, c1870, 10" h, **$1,430**. Stoneware photos courtesy of Vicki and Bruce Waasdorp.

Bottle, 9-1/2" h, imp and blue accented "C. F. Washburn," minor crow's foot at shoulder.. **35.00**

Bowl, 11" d, 4" h, dec, ear handles, tight cracks on sides **150.00**

Butter crock, 1-1/2 gal, dec lid and body, blue at ear handles, chips.. **550.00**

Jar, Burger Bro's & Co., Rochester, NY, four gallons, deep blue tulip with "4," also impressed "Rochester, N. Y.," double handles, spider hairlines, good contrast with bubbling in the decoration, 15-1/2" h, **$425**. Photo courtesy of Garth's Auctions, Inc.

Butter churn

12" h, unsigned, two gals, long tailed bird amid fern design, c1870, tight hairlines **1,715.00**

16" h, A. O. Whittemore, Havana, NY, four gals, large stylized swirls and dots, double "4"s, blue accents at name, c1870, professional restoration **500.00**

17" h, T. Harrington, Lyons, four gals, star face, c1850, professional restoration to rim chips........ **6,875.00**

Cake crock, covered, unsigned, one gallon, brushed cobalt blue flowers repeated front and back, cobalt blue accents at handles, matching brushed design on lid, few chips at knob, c1850, 9" d, 6" h, **$1,705**.

Cake crock, 7-3/4" h, Bullard & Scott, Cambridgeport, Mass, two gals, squatty bird dec, partial blue accent at name, c1870, professional restoration **635.00**

Canning jar, wax seal

one gal, Hamilton & Jones, Greensboro, PA, rim chips **80.00**

Two gals, A. Conrad, New Geneva, PA, stencil dec, old repair of decorative brass ring around top **100.00**

Two gals, Hamilton & Jones, chips on top rim, spider line on back **110.00**

Cheese basket, six qt............ **200.00**

Jug, America, 19th C, ovoid form, applied strap handle, stylized cobalt blue floral and leaf decoration, minor rim chips and hairlines, 8" h, **$600**. Photo courtesy of Skinner, Inc.

Churn

13" h, unsigned, two gals, table-top type, fitted carved wooden guide, brushed double plume design repeated front and back, c1870 .... **275.00**

17" h, Hart Bros, Fulton, NY, four gals, floral and plume dec, brush and slip application, c1880, some surface chipping to orig dasher guide **440.00**

19-1/4" h, imp "H. A. White & Son, Utica, NY 8," large dark cobalt blue bird on branch, applied handles, lid with Albany slip and edge chips, hairlines in churn **4,675.00**

Cooler

Three gals, salt glaze, beehive, target, upside "G" stamped in back **195.00**

20-1/2" h, ovoid, three raised lines around foot, combed wavy line round top runs beneath large handles, iron based slip or glaze, incised eagle with flag and shield, cobalt blue on tips of wings, head, tail, flag, and stripes on shield, stamped star designs throughout dec, brown rough textured glaze applied on lower wings, legs, and alternating stripes on shield, three faint initials on back were of applied raised clay, raised rings around spout, attributed to OH, crack on left side of eagle **29,700.00**

Jug, Cowden and Wilcox, Harrisburg, PA, late 19th C, cobalt blue foliate decoration, impressed name, 11-1/2" h, **$375**. Photo courtesy of Pook & Pook.

Cream pot

12" h, N. Clark & Co, Lyons, two gals, trophy filled with flowers, partially hand incised, blue accents, name imp high on rim, c1850, long tight hairline in front.................... **1,075.00**

11" h, E. S. Fox, Athens, two gals, ovoid, brushed blue date 1832, blue accents at handle, name, and gallon designation, few surface flakes **690.00**

1-1/2 gal, A. P. Donagho, Fredericktown, PA, stenciled eagle and banners **850.00**

Crock

9" h, E. W. Farrington & Co., Elmira, NY, two gals, drooping flower dec, blue at name, design attributed to John Young, c1885, front rim chip **615.00**

9" h, G. W. Fulper & Bros, Flemington NJ, two gals, blue slip singing bird, light blue wash at name, c1880, in-the-making clay indentation **770.00**

Crock, Ottman Bros & Co., Fort Edward, NY, four gallons, large signature bird on stump, cobalt blue at name, 1" hairline at rim, c1870, 11-1/2" h, **$1,075.**

9" h, N. A. White & Son, Utica, NY, two gals, heron dec, tall foliage on either side, c1870, professional restoration **7,700.00**

9-1/2" h, Edmands & Co., two gals, ribbed leaf and flower design, c1870, some use staining **250.00**

9-1/2" h, Whites, Utica, two gals, cobalt blue running bird design, c1865, chip at leaf ear, minor rim surface chipping **525.00**

9-3/4" h, T. Harrington, Lyons, three gals, large flower dec, one bud on either side of larger flower, blue at imp maker's mark, c1850, professional restoration, int. wear due to use to Albany glaze **250.00**

10" h, Brady & Ryan, Ellenville, NY, three gals, large detailed two masted sailing ship, ear to ear dec, c1885, minor staining from use..... **10,725.00**

Crock, Ottman Bros & Co., Fort Edward, NY, four gallons, large signature bird on stump, cobalt blue at name, 1" hairline at rim, c1870, 11-1/2" h, **$1,075.**

10" h, Pottery Works Little Wst 12 St, NY, three gals, wedding proposal dec, period gentleman facing woman, c1870, rim chips, very tight hairlines **10,450.00**

10" h, unsigned, possibly NY state, three gals, large bright blue chicken pecking corn dec, c1880, glaze drip at base of design, some use staining **750.00**

10-1/2" h, unsigned, three gals, flying bird chasing butterfly, c1880, surface chipping **500.00**

11" h, 9-3/4" d, three gals, double handles, incised line, free-form brushed cobalt blue flowers with stylized "3" **325.00**

11" h, C. Hart Sherbourne, four gals, dotted triple flower, blue at name, c1870, full-length very tight hairline on back **310.00**

11" h, Burger Bros., Rochester, NY, four gals, large cabbage flower, blue at name, c1869, two stone pings, stain spots, Y-shaped hairlines **330.00**

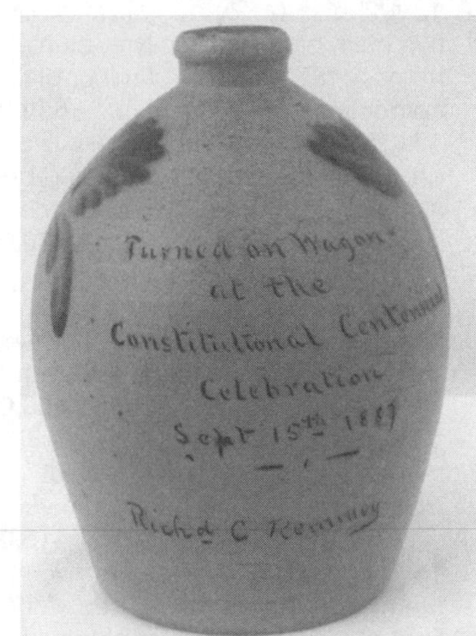

Jug, Remmey Pottery, PA, inscribed "Turned on wagon at the Constitutional Centennial Celebration Sept. 15th 1889, Richard C. Remmey," cobalt blue floral decoration, 7-3/4" h, **$13,800.** Photo courtesy of Pook & Pook.

11-1/2" h, W. Roberts, Binghamton, NY, four gals, ribbed and dotted standing bird perched on long curled vine, c1860, extremely tight spiders on side................................ **1,100.00**

11-1/2" h, unsigned, attributed to Ellenville factory, four gals, large long tailed bird on tree stump, c1870, professional restoration to full length line on back and glaze flakes on front **580.00**

12-3/8" h, 14-1/2" d, lug handles, cobalt blue peafowl perched on floral spray, imp "Whites Utica" near rim, brownish discoloration **2,990.00**

12-1/2" h, A. O. Whittemore Havana, NY, six gals, polka dotted and ribbed partridge, c1870, professional restoration **1,210.00**

13" h, C Crolius Manufacturer Manhattan Wells New York, three gals, ovoid, open handles, blue at name and handles, c1800, base chipping, slight misshapen.... **990.00**

16" h, J. Fisher, Lyons, NY, 10 gals, brushed tulips cover entire front, brushed blue accent under applied ears, cobalt blue gallon designation, c1880, professional restoration to three full-length through lines **470.00**

25-1/4" h, stenciled signature "C. L. Williams and Company, Best Blue Stoneware, New Geneva, PA, 20," some freehand line dec, double handles, flared rim, cracks..... **495.00**

Flask, 8" h, brushed cobalt blue leaf designs around shoulder, repaired lip **500.00**

Pitcher, America, 19th century, spouted ovoid form, applied ribbed strap handle, stylized floral and linear cobalt blue decoration, 16-1/2" h, **$1,000.** Photo courtesy of Skinner, Inc.

Jar

10" h, imp signature for "I. M. Mead & Co.," (Portage County, OH," cobalt blue detail on handles and over name, ovoid, applied handles, flared rim, pot stone on side with spider hairline.................................. **315.00**

Jug, G. Lent Troy, two gallons, ovoid, incised bird perched between double flower, accented by deep cobalt blue wash, repeated at maker's mark and handle, c1820, 14" h, **$10,725.**

11-3/4" h, unsigned, two gals, double heart design, blue at ears, imp "22" at rim, minor stone pine in design, minor base chip **750.00**
12" h, Burger & Lang, Rochester, NY, two gals, wreath design, c1870, some staining from use **310.00**
13" h, unsigned, attributed to NY state, three gals, cobalt blue Christmas tree dec, dots ornaments, star at top, slip blue "3" below tree, c1870, cinnamon clay color in the making, some surface roughness at rim from use **360.00**
15" h, unsigned, attributed to Frederick Carpenter, three gals, light ochre accents at shoulder and handles, deep incised accent lines at shoulder and rim, c1800, some surface chipping and staining from use.. **495.00**

Pitcher, attributed to Remmey Pottery, Pennsylvania, late 19th C, cobalt blue floral decoration, 6-1/2" h, **$1,725**. Photo courtesy of Pook & Pook.

Jug

10" h, W. Roberts, Binghamton, NY, one gal, dark navy blue bird on twig dec, c1860 .... **1,020.00**
10" h, Whites, Utica, NY, one gal, squat bird, c1865, stained from use **635.00**
11" h, G. Heiser, one gal, ovoid, brushed flower design, blue at name, c1838, clay discoloration **550.00**
12" h, delicately brushed cobalt blue bird on leafy branch, 1-1/2 imp label highlighted in blue "Haxston, Ottman & Co., Fort Edwards, NY," damage around lip **525.00**
12" h, unsigned, attributed to Jonathon Fenton Boston, MA, one gal, ovoid, cross-hatched brushed lollipop flower, c1790, some use staining.................................. **865.00**

Jug, A. O. Whittemore, Havana, NY, one gallon, beehive, cobalt blue decoration compote of fruit, c1870, professional restoration to neck hairline, 9" h, **$330**.

13" h, Albany, NY, bull's eye dec over tornado, c1865 .... **275.00**
13-1/2" h, J. M. Pruden Elizatown NJ, two gals, blue slip dec lyre, blue at name, c1870, couple of minor glaze spider lines **550.00**
14-1/2" h, N. Clark Jr., Athens, two gals, blue stylized tornados and bee stingers, lightly imp maker's name, c1850, 4" crow's foot spider ... **470.00**
14-1/2" h, unsigned, attributed to New York, two gals, hand incised holes pierced on every other incised line, wide mouth, c1870, horizontal line at base **800.00**
15" h, Burger & Lang, Rochester, NY, two gals, dancing tulip dec, blue at maker's name, c1870, stack mark **415.00**
15" h, Mantell & Thomas Penn Yan, three gals, double flower dec, very light blue wash at name, blue accent at handle, c1854 .... **1,100.00**
15" h, N. Clark & Co., Lyons, two gals, ovoid, dotted tulip dec, blue at name, c1850 .... **1,100.00**
17" h, F. Stetzenmeyer, Rochester, NY, three gals, large ribbed floral design, c1860, professional restoration to spout chip, tight glaze spider between spout and imp name **2,035.00**

Milk pan, 1-1/2 gals, D. P. Shenfelder, Reading, PA, blue at ear handles, spider line on side **425.00**

Mug, 4-1/2" h, applied strap handle, brushed cobalt blue tulip dec, glazed underside **1,240.00**

Pitcher

7-1/4" h, straight neck, incised lines, applied strap handle, brushed cobalt blue dec of drooping foliage and tulips, Albany slip int., minor roughness, shallow chips.... **1,760.00**

Pitcher, unsigned, one quart, two cobalt blue brushed double flower decorations, cobalt blue accents around rim and at handle, professional restoration to two through lines, c1850, 7" h, **$1,430**.

10-3/4" h, cobalt blue double flowering tulip plant below spout, ovoid base, raised ring around base and rim, applied strap handle, hairlines, edge chips........... **1,100.00**
11" h, F. Stetzenmeyer & G. Goetzman, Rochester, NY, 1-1/2 gals, dotted sunflower, blue tornado design at spout, c1857, some loss of cobalt blue due to over firing, few surface chips at spout **1,265.00**
11" h, Satterlee & Mory, Fort Edward, NY, 1-1/2 gals, bird on stump, blue at name, c1870, professional restoration **1,595.00**
13" h, stenciled and freehand dec, sgd "Williams and Reppert, Greensboro, PA, 2," stenciled scrolling, cracks, spout chip **1,100.00**

Preserve jar

9" h, Penn Yan, one gal, stoneware lid, brushed flower design, blued named, c1860, few stone pings in the making............................. **360.00**
10-1/2" h, Cortland, two gals, fancy double flower, blue at name, tornado design at base of flower, orig lid, c1860, 1" d surface chip on front rim **360.00**
11" h, C. Haidle & Co., Union Pottery, Newark, NJ, 1-1/2 gals, lid, military general in full dress regalia, plumed helmet, detailed uniform, c1871, few very tight hairlines **18,700.00**
11" h, F. Stetzenmeyer & G. Goetzman Rochester, NY, two gals, blue dec ribbed leaf and flower bud

design, c1857, long glaze spider on side....................................990.00

Preserve jar, Hamilton & Jones, Greensboro, PA, two gallons, striped cobalt blue accents above and below stenciled name, stenciled flower design around name and gallon designation, c1870, 11-1/2" h, **$310**.

11" h, Harrington & Burger, Rochester, two gals, bowed wreath design, script blue in canter of wreath, blue at name, c1853, int. short clay separation line at rim occurred in making **330.00**
11-1/2" h, Burger Bros & Co, Rochester, NY, two gals, lid, blue slip flower, blue at name, c1869, repaired back rim chip **330.00**
11-1/2" d, N. Clark & Co., Rochester, NY, two gals, stoneware lid, finely executed floral design, c1850, int. lime staining, couple of surface chips at rim, stone ping on side....**1,760.00**
12" h, Brady & Ryan, Ellenville, NY, two gals, fitted stoneware lid, bushy tailed bird on dotted plume dec in bright blue, c1885, surface chip on lid, mottled clay color in the making **470.00**
14" h, C. W. Braun, Buffalo, NY, four gals, orig lid, rooster with dotted body, elaborate tail feathers, wide eye, c1870, few short hairlines on back **34,100.00**

Spittoon, 8" d, 4-1/2" h, slip cup dec, slight chips **330.00**
Syrup jug, 14" h, Fort Edward Pottery Co., two gals, parrot on plum dec, light blue wash at name, c1860, professional restoration to spout chip............ **1,320.00**
Wash board, The Common Sense Wash Board, Manuf by Western Reserve Pottery Co., Warren OH, crack to stoneware **110.00**

Stretch Glass

History: Stretch glass was produced by many glass manufacturers in the United States between 1916 through the mid 1930s. The most prominent makers were Cambridge, Fenton (which probably manufactured more stretch glass than any of the others), Imperial, Northwood, and Steuben. Stretch Glass is pressed or blown-molded glass, with little or no pattern, that is sprayed with a metallic salt mix while hot, creating a iridescent, onionskin-like effect, that may be velvety or shiny in luster. Look for mold marks. Imported pieces are blown and show a pontil mark.

Basket, 9-1/2" d, Celeste blue, Fenton #1135, Family Signature Series, sgd by Bill Fenton and Frank M. Fenton, coralene floral dec by Martha Reynolds **135.00**
Bowl
8" d, 3" h, Celeste blue, Northwood **55.00**
9-1/2" d, 3-1/4" h, 2-1/2" d collar base, vaseline **75.00**
9-1/2" d, 3-1/2" h, yellow, pink and green irid **75.00**
10" d, 4-3/4" h, flared, crimped, ftd, yellow-green, Fenton, #857 pattern, c1927 ....**125.00**

Bonbon, cov, Celeste blue, Fenton #643 .... **55.00**
Candlestick, 8-1/2" h, Blue Iris, Northwood, c1920.......................... **65.00**
Compote
4" d, 4-1/2" h, blue, black trim at rim and ftd base, paneled bowl **60.00**

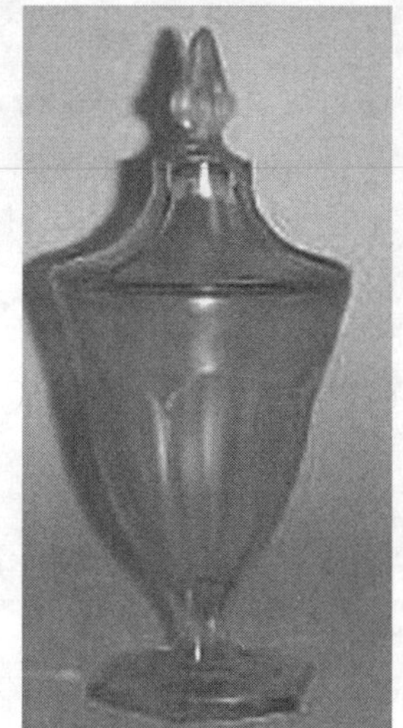
Fenton, candy jar, covered, Florentine Green, #835, 1917-29, 1/2 lb, **$48**. Photo courtesy of Rick Hirte, Sparkle Plenty Glassware.

7-1/4" d, 3-7/8" h, yellow...........**80.00**
7-1/2" d, silver colored, irid finish, early 20th C.............................**45.00**

Console bowl, 10" d, 3-3/4" h, ftd, topaz **65.00**
Epergne, Diamond Lace, Sunset Stretch, Fenton.. **125.00**
Figure, 11" h, Alley Cat, red, rainbow irid, Fenton, marked, orig tag and label **115.00**
Plate
9-1/2" d, Florentine Green, rainbow irid **50.00**
10" d, rose amber, rainbow irid, 1920s.......................................**70.00**

Rose bowl, 5" w, 7" h, ftd, Celeste Blue, Northwood **120.00**
Sherbet plate, 9-3/4" d, topaz, rainbow irid... **65.00**

Vase
8-3/4" h, Imperial Jewel, ruby, irid stretched rim, round pontil, early 20th C **215.00**
9-3/4" h, 6" w, deep red ground, butterscotch int., polished pontil, Kralik **410.00**
10-1/2" h, 3-3/4" d, trumpet shape, red shading to yellow ground, blue, and green highlights **230.00**
22" h, amber, hobnails at base **70.00**

String Holders

History: The string holder developed as a useful tool to assist the merchant or manufacturer who needed tangle-free string or twine to tie packages. The early holders were made of cast iron, with some patents dating to the 1860s.

When the string holder moved into the household, lighter and more attractive forms developed, many made of chalkware. The string holder remained a key kitchen element until the early 1950s.

Reproduction Alert: As a result of the growing collector interest in string holders, some unscrupulous individuals are hollowing out the backs of 1950s figural-head wall plaques, drilling a hole through the mouth, and passing them off as string holders. A chef, Chinese man, Chinese woman, Indian, masked man, masked woman, and Siamese face are altered forms already found on the market.

Figural wall lamps from the 1950s and 1960s also are being altered. When the lamp hardware is removed, the base can be easily altered. Two forms that have been discovered are a pineapple face and an apple face, both lamp-base conversions.

Advertising
Chase & Sanborn's Coffee, tin, 13-3/4" x 10-1/4" sign, 4" d wire basket string holder insert, hanging chain **825.00**
Dutch Boy Paints, diecut tin, Dutch Boy painting door frame, hanging

bucket string holder, American Art Sign Co., 13-3/4" x 30"......... **2,000.00**

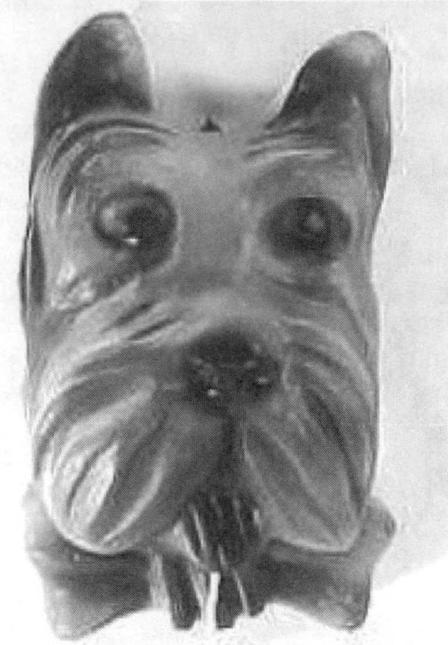

Dog, chalkware, 7" h, **$155**. Photo courtesy of L & J Antiques & Collectibles.

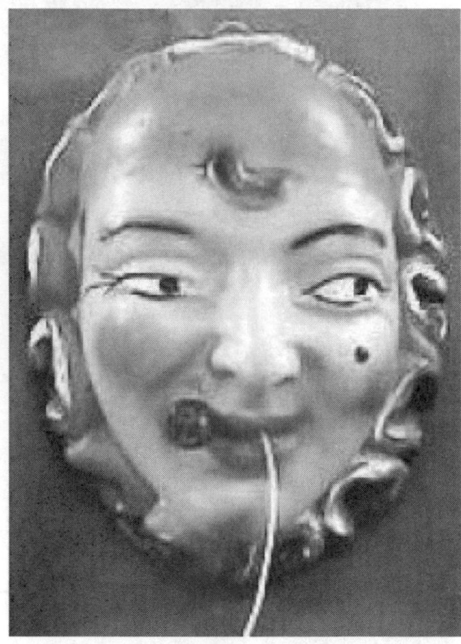

Jester, chalkware, 7-1/4" h, **$195**. Photo courtesy of L & J Antiques & Collectibles.

Es-Ki-Mo Rubbers, tin, cutout center holds string spool, hanging boot moves up and down on sign, 17" x 19-3/4" h **2,500.00**

Heinz, diecut tin, pickle, hanging, "57 Varieties," 17" x 14"....... **1,650.00**

Figural

Ball of string, cast iron, figural, hinged, 6-1/2" x 5" h **100.00**

Bonzo, blue, chalkware, 6-1/2" h **185.00**

Boy, top hat and pipe, chalkware, 9" h **125.00**

Bride, ceramic, marked "Made in Japan," 6-1/4" h...................... **145.00**

Cat face, white, pink and black trim, Holt Howard, **$95**.

Carrots, chalkware, 10" h **225.00**

Cat, red rose on top of face, green bow under chin, chalkware **165.00**

Chef, multicolored, chalkware, 7-1/4" h **165.00**

Chipmunk, ceramic, 5-1/8" h.. **135.00**

Dutch girl, chalkware, 7" h **100.00**

Gourd, green, chalkware, 7-1/2" h **135.00**

Indian, 10-1/4" h, chalkware... **285.00**

Mammy, face, orig paint, inside incised "Glue an old razor blade in my bow, honey for to cut the string, Florence Art Company, San Francisco, California," chalkware, 6-1/2" h **400.00**

Parrot, chalkware, 9-1/4" h **235.00**

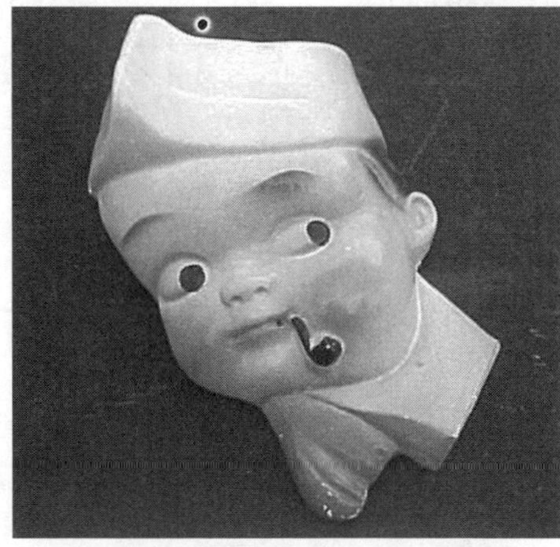

Soldier boy, tan cap, pipe in mouth, chalkware, 5-1/4" w, 8" h, **$85**.

Pineapple, face, chalkware, 7" h **165.00**

Porter, chalkware, 6-1/2" h **220.00**

Rose, red, green leaves, chalkware, 8" h **175.00**

Senorita, chalkware, 8" h........ **275.00**

Shirley Temple, chalkware, 6-1/4" w, 6-3/4" h **395.00**

Strawberry, chalkware, 6-1/2" h **115.00**

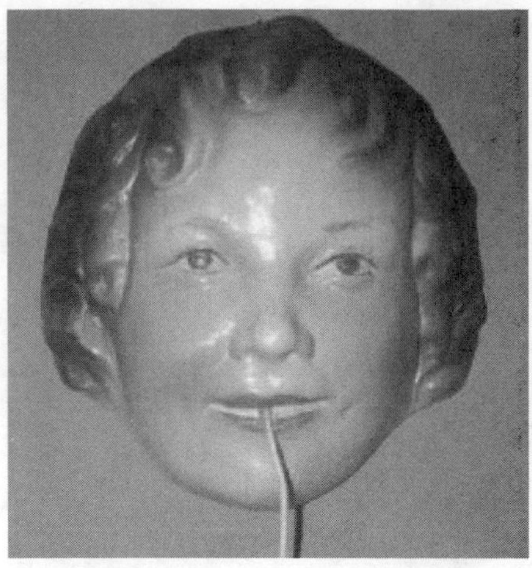

Shirley Temple, chalkware, 6-1/4" w, 6-3/4" h, **$395**. Photo courtesy of L & J Antiques & Collectibles.

Terrier, chalkware, gray and white, 8-1/2" h **195.00**

Woody Woodpecker, chalkware, copyright Walter Lantz, 9-1/2" h **345.00**

Sugar Shakers

History: Sugar shakers, sugar castors, or muffineers all served the same purpose: to "sugar" muffins, scones, or toast. They are larger than salt and pepper shakers, were produced in a variety of materials, and were in vogue in the late Victorian era.

Reproduction Alert. The following examples are all glass. Sugar shakers were also made in other materials, such as porcelain, silver, and pewter.

Amber

Paneled Daisy, Bryce Bros./US Glass Co., 4-1/4" h.......................... **275.00**

Rope and Thumbprint, Central Glass Co., 5-1/4" h........................... **140.00**

Amethyst, nine panel, attributed to Northwood Glass Co., 4-1/2" h **180.00**

Apple green, Inverted Thumbprint, tapered, 5-3/4" h......................... **160.00**

Blue

Inverted Fern, 5" h................. **325.00**

Nine panel, attributed to Northwood Glass Co., 4-1/2" h **220.00**

Bristol, 6-1/4" h, tall tapering cylinder, pink, blue flowers and green leaves dec **75.00**

Cobalt blue, Ridge Swirl, 4-3/4" h **375.00**

Crackle, cranberry, two part brass lid, 4-1/4" h **60.00**

Cranberry

Argus Swirl, attributed to Consolidated Lamp & Glass Co., 3" h, minor wear...................... **350.00**

Consolidated Glass, Quilted Phlox pattern, original lid, cased green body, $95.

Baby Inverted Thumbprint, Fenton Art Glass Co., 4-3/4" h............**210.00**
Inverted Thumbprint, nine-panel mold, 4-3/4" h.........................**250.00**
Twelve exterior cut panels, lid stamped "E.R.N.S.," 6-1/2" h **90.00**

Crown Milano, melon shape, ribbed, dec, Mt. Washington two-pc top **395.00**

Custard, Paneled Teardrop, Tarentum Glass Co., 4-3/4" h........................**110.00**

Cut glass
English, plain, engraved stars, 4-1/4" h **95.00**
Russian pattern alternating with clear panels, orig SS top.................**375.00**

Emerald green
Aster and Leaf, Beaumont Glass Co., 5" h **450.00**
Hobnail, US Glass Co., 4-1/4" h **170.00**
Melligo, Consolidated Lamp & Glass Co., 4-3/4" h.............................**200.00**

Green, four blown molded panels, diamond and cross design, rib between each panel, lid mkd "E. P.," 5-3/4" h, open bubble on surface **100.00**

Light blue, Paneled Daisy, Bryce Bros./ US Glass Co., 4-1/4" h.................. **375.00**

Milk glass
Apple Blossom, Northwood Glass Co., 4-1/2" h.............................**160.00**
Paneled Sprig, fired-on green dec, gilt accents, Northwood Glass Co., 4-3/4" h, wear to dec **65.00**
Quilted Phlox, white, hand painted blue flowers, Northwood Glass Co./ Dugan Glass Co., 4-1/2" h......**100.00**

Opalescent
Blown twist, nine panel, Northwood Glass Co., 4-1/2" h
Blue **275.00**
Green **295.00**
White **100.00**

Milk glass, Waffle pattern, metal top, bottom embossed "Pat'd Appl. For," 7" h, $45.

Bubble Lattice, blue, 4-3/4" h **325.00**
Chrysanthemum Base Swirl, blue, Buckeye Glass Co., 4-3/4" h **275.00**
Coin Spot, bulbous base, blue, Hobbs, Brockunier & Co./Beaumont Glass Co., 4-3/4" h **160.00**
Coin Spot, nine-panel mold, blue, Northwood Glass Co., 4-1/2" h **200.00**
Coin Spot, ring neck, rubena, Hobbs, Brockunier & Co., 4-1/2" h......**220.00**
Coin Spot, wide waisted, white, Northwood Glass Co./Buckeye Glass Co., 4-3/4" h...........................**100.00**
Daisy & Fern, Northwood mold, blue, Northwood Glass Co., 4-1/4" h **210.00**
Daisy & Fern, wide waisted mold, blue, Northwood Glass Co., 4-1/4" h **180.00**
Poinsettia, blue, H. Northwood & Co., 5" h **475.00**
Polka Dot, cranberry, Northwood & Co., 4-1/4" h...........................**800.00**
Reverse Swirl, blue, satin, Buckeye Glass Co./Model Flint Glass Co., 4-3/4" h **300.00**
Ribbed Opal Lattice, tall, blue, 4-1/2" h **170.00**
Spanish Lace, cranberry, Northwood Glass Co., 4-1/2" h **325.00**
Stripe, wide, cranberry, 4" h **600.00**
Swirl, bulbous base, light blue, Hobbs, Brockunier & Co., 4-3/4" h **350.00**
Swirl, cranberry, 5" h, chips....**375.00**
Swirl, tapered, blue, 5-1/2" h **400.00**
Swirled Windows, blue, Hobbs, Brockunier & Co., 5" h **325.00**

Opalware
Blue shaded to cream, hand-painted dainty floral dec, 5" h, wear spot on back **100.00**
Draped Column, skirt with shaded background, hand painted floral dec, Wave Crest, 5" h, some wear to dec, replaced lid **60.00**
Egg shape, soft pink background, hand painted floral dec, two-piece metal lid, Mt. Washington Glass Co., 4-1/4" h **400.00**
Erie Twist, hand-painted pansy dec, Wave Crest, 2-1/2" h, lid missing **110.00**
Gillinder Melon, light blue shading to white, satin finish, hand-painted multicolored floral dec, Gillinder & Sons, 4-1/2" h **180.00**
Ostrich egg, overall light pink, satin finish, hand painted multicolored floral dec, Mt. Washington Glass Co., 3-3/4" h, manufacturing bubble on surface **400.00**

Opaque
Acorn, blue, Beaumont Glass Co., 5" h **230.00**
Acorn, white shading to pink, hand-painted gilt floral dec, Beaumont Glass Co., 5" h, wear to gilt **190.00**
Alba, pink, Dithridge & Co., 4-1/2" h **190.00**
Argus Swirl, white, netted floral transfer dec on shoulder, attributed to Consolidated Lamp & Glass Co., 3" h **100.00**
Challinor's Forget-Me-Not, pink, Challinor, Taylor & Co., 3-3/4" h **190.00**
Cone, blue, Consolidated Lamp & Glass Co., 5-1/4" h **140.00**
Cone, squatty, lemon satin, Consolidated Lamp & Glass Co., 3" h **270.00**
Little Shrimp, ivory, Dithridge & Co., 3" h **100.00**
Owl, full figure, white, plain flat oval on chest, 5" h............................**50.00**
Parian Swirl, green, hand-painted floral dec, Northwood Glass Co., 4-1/2" h **175.00**
Quilted Phlox, light green, cased, Northwood Glass Co./Dugan Glass Co., 4-1/2" h..........................**210.00**
Rings & Ribs, white, hand-painted floral dec, 4-1/2" h **50.00**
Utopia Optic, green, hand-painted floral dec, Buckeye Glass Co./ Northwood Glass Co., 4-1/2" h **300.00**

Ruby Stained, Duncan Late Block, orig top **295.00**

Satin, Leaf Mold, light blue, Northwood Glass Co., 4" h..... **325.00**

Slag, Creased Teardrop, brown shading to green, 4-3/4" h.......................... **275.00**

Spatter

Inverted Thumbprint, ring neck, white, hint of cranberry, 4-3/4" h **60.00**

Leaf Umbrella, cased cranberry, Northwood Glass Co., 4-1/2" h **350.00**

Reverse Swirl, colorless, frosted, Buckeye Glass Co., 4-3/4" h, internal fracture following one rib.......... **70.00**

Ribbed Pillar, pink and white, Northwood Glass Co., 4-3/4" h **160.00**

Royal Ivy, rainbow, cased, Northwood Glass Co., 4" h, splits in lid.. **500.00**

Surveyors' Instruments

History: From the very beginning of civilized cultures, people have wanted to have a way to clearly delineate what lands they owned. Surveying instruments and equipment of all kinds were developed to help in this important task. The ancients learned to use the sun and other astronomical bodies as their guides. Early statesmen like Washington and Jefferson used brass and ebony instruments as they surveyed the young America. A surveyor must know how to measure lines and angles of a piece of land, using the principles of geometry and trigonometry.

To accomplish this often-complicated mathematics, instruments of all types were invented and often patented. Accuracy is important, so many are made with precision components. A surveyor's level is an instrument that consists of a revolving telescope mounted on a tripod and fitted with cross hairs and a spirit level. It is designed to allow surveyors to find points of identical elevation. A transit is used to measure horizontal angles and consists of a telescope mounted at right angles to a horizontal east-west axis. English mathematician, Leonard Digges, invented an instrument called a "theodolite," used to measure vertical and horizontal angles. From a simple compass to high-tech transits, today's collectors are finding these devices interesting. Fine examples of early instruments are coming into the antiques and collectibles marketplace as modern day surveyors now use sophisticated lasers and computers.

Alidade, cased, 11" l, W. & L. E. Gurley, Troy, NY, orig leather covered case, minor spots to lacquered finish.............. **440.00**

Anemometer, six register, eight blades, 2-5/8" d, fan drives 2-1/4" d silvered dial, brass, mounting bracket, softwood case, c1875.. **345.00**

Astronomical Theodolite, 15-1/2" h, 10-1/2" l telescope, 5-1/2" d, two vernier vertical circle, 6", two vernier 20" horiz. circle, telescope and plate vials, microscope vernier readers, detachable alcohol lamp, detachable four-screw leveling base, trough compass on telescope, orig dovetailed mahogany box with accessories, marked "Stanley, Great Turnstile, Holborn, London, 7534," c1890, Heller & Brightly label mahogany ext. leg tripod **2,185.00**

Astronomical Transit, 20" h, 8-1/2" w, 15-3/4" telescope with rt. Angle prism eyepiece with removable strider level, 7" d double frame, two vernier, vertical circle with indexing vial and circle control, 6" d, two vernier, 15", silver horizontal scale, plate vial with ivory scale, tribrach leveling base, bright brass finish, pine case, marked "Blunt, New York," c1860 .... **7,500.00**

Circumferentor, 5-1/4" h, 9" d outside dia., 4-1/8" compass in center, attached to rotating sight vane/vernier arm, inset vial, silvered dial and outer ring, engraved with eight-point star, two outer fixed sight vanes, brass, marked "Dollond London," c1825........................ **1,955.00**

Drawing instruments, French, cased set, brass and steel instruments, wood scale, brass protractor, rosewood veneered case with warped lid **220.00**

Flat plate transit, Edmund Draper, Philadelphia, #259, 13-1/2" h, 7-3/4" w, 10" telescope, 5" d vert. circle, 4-1/2" compass, 6" d single vernier, silver horiz. scale, two plate vials, four4 screw leveling, darkened brass finish, pine case, c1850.............................. **1,725.00**

Nonius compass, 6 Inch, 15-1/8" x 6-7/8" x 7-1/8" h, 5-1/4" l detachable sight vanes, top designed to hold 7/8" d telescope, plate vials, silvered dial and edge engraved outer ring, unique 5' vernier moves the south sight vane by means of worn gear, mahogany case, marked "J. Hanks," Troy, NY, c1825 .... **1,725.00**

Octant, 10-7/8", Riggs & Bro., Philadelphia, ebony, ivory inlaid signature panel, scale with brass trim **550.00**

Pocket compass

1-1/2 inch, 2-1/4" x 2-1/4" mahogany case with hinged cov, 1-1/2" needle floats over engraved finely detailed mariner's star inside 2° increment quadrant outer ring, marked "T. T. Rowe, Lockport, N.Y.," c1825 .... **230.00**

2 inch, 2-5/8" d, brass, worn silvered dial, full circle, 180° cliometer scale, marked "Breiothaupt in Cassel," c1800 .... **565.00**

Reconnaissance transit, Buff & Buff Mfg. Co., Boston, 12007. 10-1/2" h, 5-1/4" w, 8 3/4" l telescope with rt. Angle solar eyep., 3-1/2" vial, 4" d vert. circle, crossed vials, 3" compass 4-1/2" d, two vernier, 1', silver horiz. scale, four-screw leveling, black leather finished brass, mahogany box, c1918.................. **920.00**

Saegmuller solar attachment, Fauth & Co., Washington, DC, Saegmuller's pat May 2, 81, 6-1/2" l, 4" h, brass and aluminum construction, level vial, sun lens, horiz. motion, c1885 .... **920.00**

Solar transit, 17" h, Burt Solar Attachment, hour circle, 6.45" engineer's transit, 11" telescope, 3" rad vert. arc., 5" compass, telescope and plate vials, four-screw leveling, brass construction, rubbed bronze finish, detailed mahogany case, label, brass plummet, accessories, "W. & L. E. Gurley, Troy, NY," c1890 .... **3,335.00**

Replica of world's first working calculating machine for all four basic arithmetical operations, by German Philipp Matthäus, 1774, **$25,100**. Photo courtesy of Auction Team Breker.

Surveying/astronomical theodite, 15-1/2" h, 10-1/2" l telescope, 5-1/2" d, two vernier vertical circle, 6", two vernier 20" horiz. circle, telescope and plate vials, microscope vernier readers, detachable alcohol lamp, detachable four-screw leveling base, trough compass on telescope, orig. dovetailed mahogany box with accessories, Heller & Brightly label, mahogany ext., leg tripod, "Stanley, Great Turnstile, Holborn, London, 7535," c1890... **2,185.00**

Surveyor's compass

Davenport, Wm, Phila, 5" engraved face with tripod mount, plum bob, small magnifying glass, ivory scale, 14" l cherry case stenciled "A. C. Farrington" in gold and white **1,155.00**

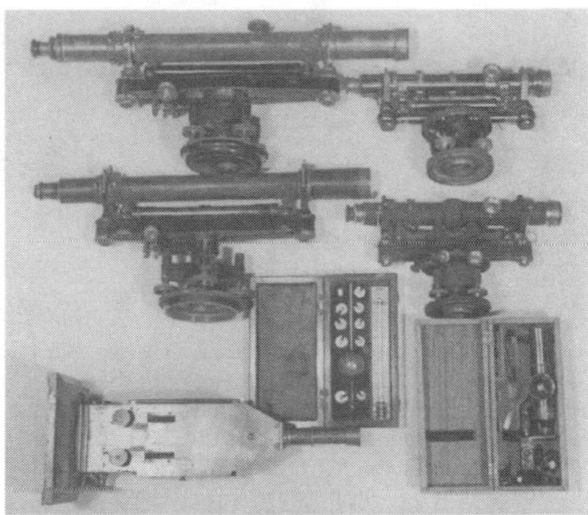

Top left: Bausch, Lomb and Saegmuller level, brass and enameled brass, some wear, rings for tube have engine turnings, mahogany case, 8-3/8" x 21", **$300;** top right: W & L.E. Gurley level, orig carrying case and tripod, 6-3/8" x 11-1/4", **$300**; middle row: left, Wm. Ainsworth & Sons, Denver, CO, level, enameled brass, some wear, dovetailed mahogany case with leather strap, **$300**; middle right: unidentified maker, level, tripod, and carrying case, with wear, 6-3/4" x 11-1/4", **$275**; bottom row: left: (scientific instrument) J. Dubosco & P. Pelin, Paris, colorimeter, brass, steel base, label "Arthur Thomas, Phila," minor surface rust, 15-1/2", **$285**; center: Sikes Hydrometer, inlaid mahogany case with label "Re-adjusted by W.R. Loftu Ltd. London," plate missing from ext. lid, 2" x 8" x 4", **$110**; left: small microscope, mahogany case, 3" x 8-3/4" x 3-1/2", **$140**. Photo courtesy of Garth's Auctions, Inc.

Patten, Richard, NY, 6" compass with engraved face, walnut case with litho label of eagle, ship, and signature, minor age cracks in lid, resoldered rim on brass cover, early tripod **990.00**

Surveyors' and engineers' transit

Buff & Burger, Boston, #2149, 11" telescope wit vial, vert. arc., 6-1/4", 30" horiz. circle with inlaid silver scales, plate vials, four-screw leveling, green leather finish, orig dovetailed mahogany box with labels, c1890 .... **920.00**

Paten, Richard, & Son, 6" d lens, 13-1/2" l, 8-5/8" h, brass, glass lens and level compass labeled "Richard Paten & Son, Baltimore," no tripod base **385.00**

Pike, B. & Sons, 166 Broadway (N.Y.), 10-1/2" h, 8-3/8" w, 9-1/4" l telescope with vertical circle, 5" compass, 6-1/2" d horiz. scale (single vernier), telescope vial, plate vials, lacquered brass, orig mahogany case with Gurley label, dated 11/11/1873 .... **980.00**

Surveyors' vernier transit compass, 13-1/2" h, 11" telescope with vial, 3-1/2" d vert. circle, 5-3/4" compass, 4" rad. Declination vernier, two plate vials, cross sights, four-screw detachable leveling base, staff adaptor, stiff leg tripod, brass plumb bob, orig case with labels, bronzed brass, marked "W. & L. E. Gurley, Troy, NY," c1874 .... **1,840.00**

Theodolite, Tackpole & Brother, New York, 1559, miniature, 8-1/2" h, 4-1/8" w, 7-1/8" l telescope with vial, 3-1/4" d, 1' vert. circle, 2" compass, 3-1/2" d, 2 vernier, 1' vert. circle, 2" compass, 3-1/2" d, two vernier, 1' silver horiz. scale, tribrach leveling base, black and brass finish, orig box, extension leg tripod, c1870 .... **1,495.00**

Theodolite/Level, one-minute type, Wm Wurdemann, Washington, DC, 10" l telescope, 5-1/2" h, labeled "Gr. No. 5," 4" d, 1' vernier, silver metal horiz. scale, bull's eye-level vial, telescope motion screw, three-screw leveling base, telescope reversible in its yokes, c1860 .... **635.00**

Theodolite with compass, Wm Wurdemann, Washington, DC, No. 155, 10-1/2" reversible telescope, 12-3/4" h, 6" d silver metal horiz. scale, two microscope read verniers, 4" compass, single-plate vial, telescope vial, three-screw leveling base and truss frame, c1865 .... **1,725.00**

Vernier compass

Gurley, W. & L. E., Troy, NY, 13-1/4" h, 11" telescope, 6" compass with outside declination vernier, crossed plate vials, detachable four-screw leveling base, leveling adapter, sunshade, orig mahogany box with label, bronzed finish brass, c1865 .... **2,300.00**

Young, Wm. J, Maker 3694 Philadelphia, 13-3/4" l, 6-1/8" w, 9-1/4" h, detachable sight vanes, bull's eye vial (empty), outkeeper, non-reflecting dial and silver ring, 25º 5' vernier, brass cover and 6-1/8" l adapter, darkened brass, case and Jacob staff **1,725.00**

Wye Level, 8-1/4" h, 4" w, 16-1/4" l, 1-3/8" d reversible telescope with 6-3/4" l, 4 screw leveling base, horiz. motion clamp and screw, eyepiece attachment, marked "Kuebler & Seelhorst Makers Philada, 597, Oct. 1, 1867 Patent" **500.00**

Swords

History: The first swords used in America came from Europe. The chief cities for sword manufacturing were Solingen in Germany, Klingenthal in France, and Hounslow and Shotley Bridge in England. Among the American importers of these foreign blades was Horstmann, whose name is found on many military weapons. New England and Philadelphia were the early centers for American sword manufacturing. By the Franco-Prussian War, the Ames Manufacturing Company of Chicopee, Massachusetts, was exporting American swords to Europe.

Sword collectors concentrate on a variety of styles: commissioned vs. non-commissioned officers' swords, presentation swords, naval weapons, and swords from a specific military branch, such as cavalry or infantry. The type of sword helped identify a person's military rank and, depending on how he had it customized, his personality as well.

Following the invention of repeating firearms in the mid-19th century, the sword lost its functional importance as a combat weapon and became a military dress accessory.

Note: Condition is key to determining value.

Japanese, Samurai, black lacquer case, painted gold squid motif, mother of pearl inlay, 43-1/2" l, **$1,150**. Photo courtesy of Alderfer Auction Co.

Sword, presentation, to Gen George H. Thomas from enlisted men of 4th Regiment, Kentucky Volunteer Infantry, one side etched "Mill-Springs, KY, Jan 19, 1862, First Victory Won by the Union Army" **224,000.00**

French, late 19th C, gilt bronze, grip with flowering vines on stippled ground, ending in leopard's mask, short reeded quillions, red morocco sheath hare, scroll engraved endcap, mounted with metallic stitched waist sash, watered steel blade etched and gilded with cartouches of game, scrolls, and military trophies, 24-1/2" l, **$3,000**. Photo courtesy of Skinner, Inc.

Calvary saber

41" l, 35-1/2" l import blade with later date stamp of 1851, brass three branch hilt missing leather and wire wrapping, with scabbard **220.00**

41-1/2" l, Civil War, 35-3/4" blade stamped "Ames Mfg. Chicopee Mas, U.S.J.R. 1857," brass three-branch hilt with good patina, part of wire wrap and most of leather remains, iron scabbard **700.00**

43" l, 1840, stamped "U. S. 1862," brass three branch hilt with leather and wire wrapped handle, steel scabbard **660.00**

Basket hilted, steel basket hilt cast with roundels of Romaine heads, grotesque figures, military trophies, similarly styled pommel over spiral-carved wooden grip, blade marked for Andrea Ferrara, 43-3/4" l, **$1,550**. Photo courtesy of Skinner, Inc.

Infantry officer, Model 1850, Ames, 30-1/4" l etched and engraved blade with "Chicopee, Mass" address, cast hilt wash with open work, leather scabbard with brass bands and drag, engraved "Lt. Geo. Trembley, 174th N.Y.S.I.," 36-1/4" l **1,980.00**

Naval cutlass, 32" l, 26" blade, scroll signature "Ames Chicopee, Mass, 1862," brass hilt with minor dents, leather and wire wrap missing......................... **250.00**

Continental rapier, lobed grip with crosshatched pommel, faceted quillions, cup pierced and engraved with scrolls, long wavy textured blade, 58-1/2" l, **$750**. Photo courtesy of Skinner, Inc.

Officer

Civil War, Confederate, sgd on scabbard "Ames Mfg Chicopee, Mass," sword maker's signature scratched out on lower blade, scrolled etching on blade with raised etched inscription "Col. P. O. Tricou, Qr. Mr. Gen. LA Army" with star, orig sharkskin grip, wire wrap, leather and brass scabbard, 36" l, letter of providence from Norm Flayderman **5,500.00**

Civil War, presentation sword and sash, finely engraved on top band of scabbard "Presented to Lieut Wm P Spaulding, 27th Regiment, Mich, Infantry By The True and Loyal Men, Sault Ste Marie, Lake Superior, Michigan, October 7, 1862," 30-1/4" l blade etched, with engraved signature "Ames Mfg Chicopee, Mass," openwork brass hilt missing leather wrapping, leather and brass scabbard, maroon sash with tassels **3,575.00**

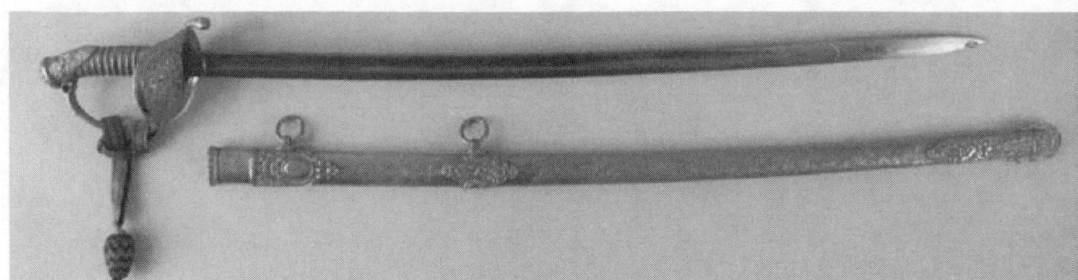

U.S. Model 1851 Staff & Field presentation sword, made by C. Roby to Colonel Harry Harris Davies, NY, slightly curved single edged blade signed "C. Roby & Co./W. Chelmsford, MASS" on ricasso, both faces of blade heavily decorated with etching of eagles, flags, stands of arms, florals, and "U.S.," half basket guard gilded cast brass with sprays of laurel, scrolls, and an inset rococo escutcheon surrounded by stars, all cast in very high relief and gold plated, grip also gold-plated cast brass simulating leather and wire wrap, heavy relief pommel with scroll and floral work overall, regulation black and gilt cloth sword knot attached to knuckle bow, gold-plated brass scabbard with engraved decoration over 80 percent of body, engraved with floral scrolls and flames, spread winged eagle and shield on a cloud with sunburst and arch of stars above, mountings cast in high relief with classical scrolls and floral work, Presented to/Col. Harry Harris Davies/by his numerous friends in New York City, Brooklyn/and Bayonne/U.S. of America, accompanied by notebook filled with information accumulated about Col. Davies, blade faded to gray, numerous dark spots, not affecting the etching, **$6,325**. Photo courtesy of James D. Julia Auctions.

Presentation grade, American, "F. W. Widmann, Phila," eagle head pommel with spiraling leaves and beads around single branch guard, raised cast eagle on langet, 29-1/2" l blade etched with gold overlay and blued panels, brass scabbard fully engraved on one side with eagles, shields, tulips, and stars, stand of flags around signature on other side, possible restoration of brass wire wrapped around "l" section of scabbard **1,925.00**

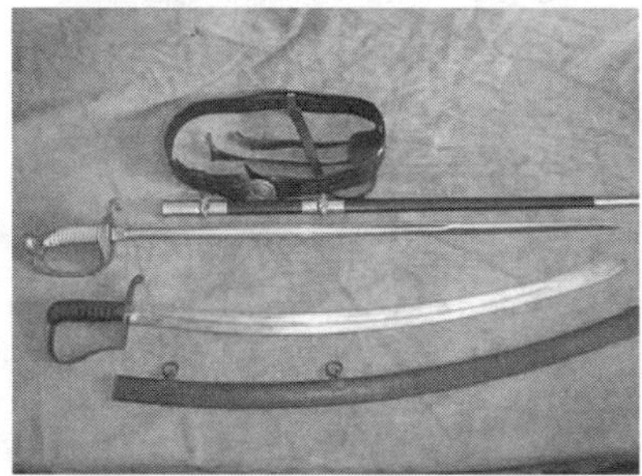

U.S. Model 1818 Cavalry, Nathan Starr contract, with scabbard, **$550**; U.S. Model 1852 Naval Officer's sword, circa 1950 with scabbard and sword belt with hangers, **$275**. Photo courtesy of Alderfer Auctions Co.

US Naval, patriotic etched bland sgd "Ridabock & Co, New York," hilt and scabbard bands with orig gilding, orig sword knot, scabbard, 33-1/2" l **200.00**

Staff and field officer, Model 1850, emb letter within two circles on ricasso "S. H.," etched and engraved 31" blade with stand of flags, eagle, "E. Pluribus Unum," scrolled foliage with "U.S," orig wire wrap with section of orig sword knot, blued steel scabbard with brass bands and drag, descended in family of Col. Edward Scovel, stationed at Johnson Island, some surface rust, 37" l............. **1,265.00**

European Cavalry saber, 19th C, sword with 35" slightly curved blade, wide unstopped fuller with 12" back grind at tip, flat iron, three-branch hand guard with ball quillion and tear-drop pommel cap, two-piece checkered hard rubber handle secured with 5 iron rivets, ricasso marked with crown over "L" over "8," original steel scabbard with two iron rings and drag, unit markings near the throat, blade has been cleaned with light surface pitting and several nicks to the cutting edge, wear to scabbard, **$460**. Photo courtesy of James D. Julia Auctions.

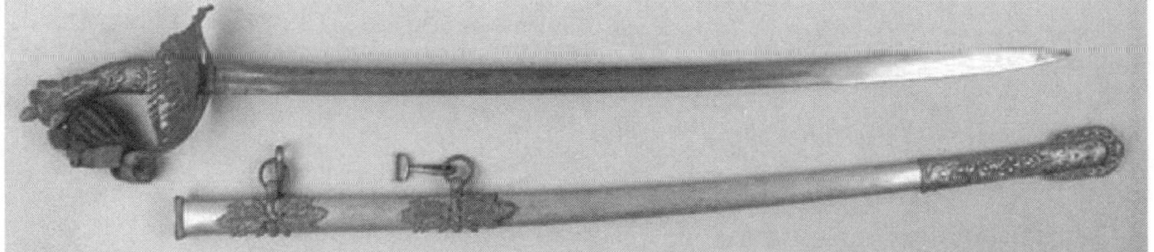

Civil War, Staff and Field Officers presentation, inscribed to Capt. Hitchcock, 153rd Illinois volunteers, unsigned European made non-regulation sword of presentation grade, 31" l single-edged blade with slight curve, faces are heavily etched with American trophies, floral sprays, spread winged eagle, and "U.S.," cast brass gold washed hilt, half basket guard with panalopy of flags, tilted U.S. shield, drums, cannons, Liberty cap above, all resting on bed of oak leaves, edge of guard scalloped, single knuckle bow rising to fancy cast pommel with classical head on back and pineapple cap stain, cast German silver grip with acanthus leaf sprays top and bottom, laurel wrap, original gilt cloth sword knot at knuckle bow, steel scabbard, plated in German silver, brass top and middle mounts in leaf-like design, heavily engraved drag, casting of running flag bearer on face, scabbard is engraved: "Presented to/CAPT. C.H. HITCHCOCK/by Co. K 153 Regt. Ill. Vol. Inf./March 3, 1865," factory finish on blade, scabbard dirty, **$5,175**. Photo courtesy of James D. Julia Auctions.

Tea Caddies

History: Tea once was a precious commodity and stored in special boxes or caddies. These containers were made to accommodate different teas and included a special cup for blending.

Around 1700, silver caddies appeared in England. Other materials, such as Sheffield plate, tin, wood, china, and pottery, also were used. Some tea caddies are very ornate.

Fruitwood, Georgian, late 18th C, apple shaped, realistically turned, small wood stem, small iron escutcheon, traces of foil in interior, 5" h, **$3,525**. Photo courtesy of Skinner, Inc.

Ivory tusk, 4-1/4" w, 5" h, formed as section of tusk, silver-plated mountings, flat hinged top with foliate finial, engraved scrolls, beaded and waved rim bands, 19th C **460.00**

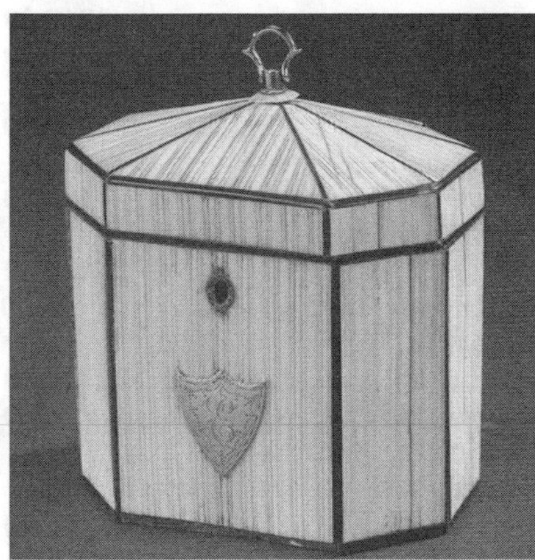

Ivory veneered, English, late 18th/early 19th C, octagonal, carved reeding, tortoise shell stringing, monogrammed shield form reserve, 5" h,, **$1,800**. Photo courtesy of Sloan & Kenyon Auctions.

Papier-mâché, 9-1/4" l, 6-3/4" d, 6" h, Regency Chinoiserie-style, rect case with canted corners, ornately dec with figural reserves within flower blossoms bordered by wide bands of gilding, conforming hinged lid opening to int. fitted with two removable pewter tea canisters with dec chasing....................................... **950.00**

Quillwork, 8-3/8" l, 4-3/4" d, 5-1/4" h, hexagonal, inlaid mahogany frames, blue and gilt quillwork panels covered with glass, floral vintage and leaf designs with crown and "MC 1804," two int. lidded compartments, replaced foil lining, English..................................... **2,750.00**

Lacquered, Chinese Export, 19th C, eight-sided oblong box, hinged lid, brass swing handles, top and sides gilt decorated with reserves, painted figures in courtyard, surrounded by floral and foliate borders and dragons on black ground, interior fitted with two canisters engraved with figures, scroll, and foliate designs, 12" w, 9" d, 5-3/4" h, **$940**. Photo courtesy of Skinner, Inc.

Silver, 7" h, lobed hexagonal form, lobed lid with filigree finial, all-over Eastern style bird and foliate enamel dec, mounted with semi-precious stones, gilt int., approx 17 troy oz, Europe, late 19th/early 20th C.. **500.00**

Rosewood box, inlaid medallions, domed lid, ivory finial, **$200**.

Tortoiseshell, 6-1/2" h, oblong, domed hinged lid with ball finial and silvered fillets, monogrammed silvered cartouche and ovoid escutcheon, int. with two lidded, foil lined wells, four silvered ball feet, late Georgian, 19th C **2,115.00**

Mahogany, George III, late 18th C, octagonal bombe form, mounted brass handle and escutcheon, 7-1/4" w, **$1,900**. Photo courtesy of Sloan's Auctioneers & Appraisers.

Wood

Mahogany and inlay, 4-1/2" h, sarcophagus shape, hinged lid with plain center plaque, line inlay to perimeters, hexagonal escutcheon, ball feet, int. with fragmentary foil lining, Georgian-style, 19th C **300.00**

Satin wood, inlaid borders all around, diamond-shaped mahogany inlaid panels, two on front, one on each end and one large one on top, silver ring pull, inlaid escutcheion, interior with two satin wood ivory handled lids, round center compartment with glass bowl, underside of lid quilted, 6" h x 12" w x 6" d, **$2,200**. Photo courtesy of James D. Julia, Inc.

Mahogany and walnut, 11-3/4" l, rect with canted corners, hinged lid with silvered metal handle, inlaid all over with burl walnut roundels in chequer-banded roundels, husk garlands, int. fitted with two lidded wells, central well for mixing bowl, Hepplewhite-style, late 19th C, later sterling bowl **1,000.00**

Mahogany, oblong octagonal form, veneered body with line inlay and monogrammed cartouche, ebonized accents, minor losses to moldings, 6" l, 4" d, 5" h, **$165**. Photo courtesy of Alderfer Auction Co.

Sterling silver, James T. Woolley, Boston, early 20th C, shouldered footed vessel, monogrammed "VH" on lid, impressed "WOOLLEY STERLING," 7 troy oz, 4-3/4" h, **$500**. Photo courtesy of Skinner, Inc.

Mahogany veneer, 9-1/2" w, 5-1/2" d, 6" h, brass bale handle and keyhole escutcheon, three int. compartments, secret drawer behind sliding panel, professional restorations, lids missing **250.00**

Burl, striped inlay across top and along edges, ivory escutcheon, four brass claw feet, brass ring handles on ends, interior with two burl top hinged lid compartments, open round center compartment with glass bowl, glass bowl inside, 12-1/2" w, 6-1/2" d, 8" h, **$2,400**. Photo courtesy of James D. Julia, Inc.

Rosewood, 12" l, sarcophagus, inlaid ivorine diamond escutcheon, mounted with later gilt metal patera roundels to sides, hinged lid opening to two lidded wells, paper foil-lined interior, brass ball feet, Georgian-style, late 19th C..................... **500.00**

TEA LEAF IRONSTONE CHINA

History: Tea Leaf ironstone flowed into America from England in great quantities from 1860 to 1910 and graced the tables of working-class America. It traveled to California and Texas in wagons and down the Mississippi River by boat to Kentucky and Missouri. It was too plain for the rich homes; its simplicity and durability appealed to wives forced to watch pennies. Tea Leaf found its way into the kitchen of Lincoln's Springfield home; sailors ate from it aboard the *Star of India*, now moored in San Diego and still displaying Tea Leaf.

Contrary to popular belief, Tea Leaf was not manufactured exclusively by English potters in Staffordshire. Although there were more than 35 English potters producing Tea Leaf, at least 26 American potters helped satisfy the demand.

Anthony Shaw (1850-1900) is credited with introducing Tea Leaf. The most prolific Tea Leaf makers were Anthony Shaw and Alfred Meakin (1875-present). Johnson Bros. (1883-present), Henry Burgess (1864-1892), Enoch Wedgwood, and Arthur J. Wilkinson (1897-present), all of whom shipped much of their ware to America.

Although most of the English Tea Leaf is copper luster, Powell and Bishop (1868-1878) and their successors, Bishop and Stonier (1891-1936), worked primarily in gold luster. Beautiful examples of gold luster were also made by H. Burgess; Mellor, Taylor & Co. (1880-1904) used it on children's tea sets. Other English potters also were known to use gold luster, including W. & E. Corn, Thomas Elsmore, and Thomas Hughes, companies which have been recently identified as makers of this type of ware.

J. & E. Mayer, Beaver Falls, Pennsylvania, founded by English potters who immigrated to America, produced a large amount of copper luster Tea Leaf. The majority of the American potters decorated with gold luster that had no brown underglaze beneath the copper luster.

East Liverpool, Ohio, potters such as Cartwright Bros. (1864-1924), East End Pottery (1894-1909) and Knowles, Taylor & Knowles (1870-1934) decorated only in gold luster. This also is true of Trenton, New Jersey, potters, such as Glasgow Pottery, American Crockery Co., and Fell & Thropp Co. Since no underglazing was used with the gold, much of it has been washed away.

By the 1900s, Tea Leaf's popularity had waned. The sturdy ironstone did not disappear; it was stored in barns and relegated to attics and basements. While the manufacture of Tea Leaf did experience a brief resurgence from the late 1950s through the 1970s, copper lustre Tea Leaf didn't recapture the hearts of the American consumer as it had a generation before.

Tea Leaf collectors recognize a number of "variant" decorative motifs as belonging to the Tea Leaf family: Teaberry, Morning Glory, Coral, Cinquefoil, Rose, Pre-Tea Leaf, Tobacco Leaf, Pepper Leaf, Pinwheel, Pomegranate, and Thistle & Berry, as well as white ironstone decorated with copper lustre bands and floral and geometric motifs. Once considered the stepchildren of Tea Leaf, these variants are now prized by collectors and generally bring strong prices.

Today's collectors eagerly seek out Tea Leaf and all of its variant motifs, and copper-lustre decorated white ironstone has once again become prized for its durability, beauty, simplicity, craft, and style.

Advisor: Dale Abrams.

Notes: Tea Leaf values have increased steadily for the last decade, but there are some general rules of thumb for the knowledgeable collector. English Tea Leaf is still more collectible than American, except for rare pieces. The earlier the Tea Leaf production (1850s-1860s), the harder it is to find pieces and, therefore, the more expensive they are. Children's pieces are highly collectible, especially those with copper lustre decorative motifs. Hard-to-find Tea Leaf pieces include mustache cups, eggcups, covered syrup pitchers, ladles, oversized serving pieces, and pieces with significant embossing. Common pieces (plates, platters) of later production (1880-1900) need to be in excellent condition or should be priced accordingly, as they are not that difficult to find.

Bone dish
Meakin, crescent shape.......... **55.00**
Shaw, fluted edge **60.00**

Bowl, Alfred Meakin, 8-1/2" sq, 2-7/8" h **40.00**

Brush vase
Burgess, Pagoda **215.00**
Meakin, Fishhook **200.00**
Shaw, plain round, drain hole **225.00**

Butter dish, three pcs, base, cover, liner
Meakin, Fishhook **185.00**
Wedgwood, simple square **185.00**

Butter dish liner, sq........................**25.00**

Butter pat, Meakin
Square.................................... **15.00**
Round, Chelsea...................... **25.00**

Cake plate
Edwards, Peerless (Feather), sq, handles................................. **185.00**
Meakin, Bamboo, 8-3/4" with handles **85.00**
Wilkinson, Senate shape, oval **150.00**

Chamber pot, Meakin
Bamboo, two pcs **265.00**
Scroll, two pcs....................... **285.00**

Children's dishes
Mug, child's, Shaw **375.00**
Tea set, Knowles, Taylor & Knowles, four cups and saucers, teapot, creamer and sugar................ **850.00**
Tea set, Mellor-Taylor, round bottom, gold luster, six cups and saucers, six plates, teapot, creamer, sugar, waste bowl................................... **1,850.00**

Coffeepot, cov
Furnival, Gentle Square (Rooster) **325.00**

Meakin, Chelsea 300.00
Shaw, Lily-of-the-Valley 475.00

Compote

Mellor Taylor, sq, ridged 325.00
Red Cliff, simple square, 1960s 150.00
Shaw, plain, round 310.00
Unmarked, unusually deep bowl, 8" d, 5" h 435.00

Creamer

Edwards, Peerless (Feather) 285.00
Meakin, Bamboo 185.00
Red Cliff, Chinese shape, 1960s 80.00
Shaw, Cable 250.00

Cup and saucer

Adams, Empress shape, 1950s 30.00
Meakin 65.00
Shaw, Lily-of-the-Valley 125.00

Egg cup

Meakin, Boston Egg Cup, 4" d, 1-3/4" h 395.00
Unmarked, 3-1/2" h 325.00

Gravy boat

Johnson Bros., Acanthus, with stand 160.00
Mayer, American 90.00
Meakin, Bamboo 85.00
Shaw, basketweave, with stand 185.00
Wedgwood, simple square 65.00

Mug

Meakin, Scroll 195.00
Shaw, Lily-of-the-Valley 350.00

Mush bowl, Meakin 85.00

Nappy

Meakin, Fishhook, 4-1/4" sq 20.00
Wedgwood, 4-1/4" sq, scalloped edge 24.00

Pitcher and bowl set

Furnival, Cable 495.00
Meakin, Fishhook 285.00
Shaw, Cable 525.00

Pitcher/jug

Meakin, Chelsea 375.00
Shaw, Chinese shape, 7-1/2" 500.00

Plate

Furnival, plain, round, 8-1/4" 12.00
Johnson Bros., Acanthus, 9" d 22.00
Meakin, plain, round, 8-7/8" d, chip on table rim 15.00
Shaw, plain, round, 10" d 25.00
Wedgwood, 8-5/8" d, some discoloration 15.00

Platter

Meakin, Chelsea, 10" x 14", oval 65.00
Royal Ironstone, W. H. Grindley & Sons, England 70.00
Shaw, Lily-of-the-Valley, 13" 150.00

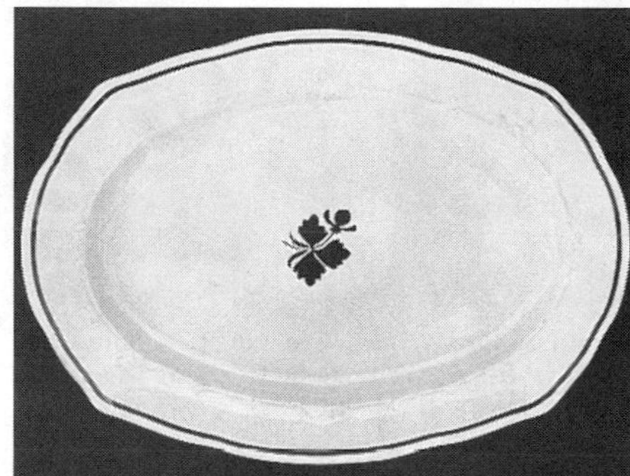

Platter, Alfred Meakin, England, Royal Ironstone China, oval, scalloped edges, single center Tea Leaf, 12-1/2" l, **$55.**

Punch bowl, Shaw, Cable 525.00

Relish dish, Shaw, Chinese shape 265.00

Sauce tureen

Furnival, Cable, three pcs 185.00
Meakin, Bamboo, four pcs, including ladle 425.00
Red Cliff, four pcs, including ladle 175.00

Serving bowl, open

Grindley, round, scalloped edge 135.00
Meakin, sq, scalloped edge, 6" sq 45.00

Soap dish, cov

Grindley, Bamboo, three pcs, liner, rect 225.00
Shaw, Cable, three pcs, liner, oval 300.00

Soup bowl, Meakin, 7" d 18.00

Soup plate, Meakin, plain, round, 10" d 50.00

Soup tureen, Meakin, Bamboo, four pcs with ladle 1,500.00

Sugar bowl, cov

Meakin, fishhook 85.00
Shaw, cable shape 145.00

Vanity box, cov, Furnival, Cable, horizontal 325.00

Vegetable, cov

Meakin, Bamboo 165.00
Powell & Bishop, c1866-78 .... 200.00
Shaw, basketweave 325.00
Wilkinson, Maidenhair Fern 275.00

Waste bowl

Meakin, plain, round 110.00

Shaw, Niagara Fan 120.00

Teapots

History: The origins of the teapot have been traced to China in the late 16th century. Early Yixing teapots were no bigger than the tiny cups previously used for drinking tea. By the 17th century, tea had spread to civilized nations of the world. The first recorded advertisement for tea in London is dated 1658 and called a "China drink…call Tcha, by other Nations Tay, alias Tee…" Although coffee houses were already established, they began to add tea to their selections.

While the Chinese had long been producing teapots and other tea items, the English were receiving these wares along with shipments of tea. By the early 1700s, British china and stoneware producers were manufacturing teapots. It was in 1706 that Thomas Twining bought his own coffee house and thwarted the competition of the many other such establishments by offering a variety of quality tea. Coffee houses were exclusively for males; thus, women would wait outside, sending their footmen inside for purchases. For the majority of the 1700s, teapots were Oriental imports. British factories continued experimenting with the right combination of materials that would make a teapot durable enough to withstand the daily rigors of boiling water. Chinese Export Porcelain was an inspiration to the British and by the end of the 1700s, many companies found the necessary combinations of china clay and stone, fired at high temperature, which could withstand boiling water needed to brew precious pots of tea.

From the very first teapots, figural shapes have always been a favorite with tea drinkers. The Victorian era saw a change from more utilitarian teapots toward beautiful, floral, and Rococo designs, yet figural pots continued to be manufactured.

Early American manufacturers mimicked Oriental and British designs. While the new land demanded sturdy teapots in the unsettled land, potteries were established steadily in the Eastern states. Rockingham teapots were produced by many companies, deriving this term from British companies manufacturing a strong, shiny brown glaze on heavy pottery. The best known is from the Bennington, Vermont, potteries.

By the 1800s and the turn-of-the-century, many pottery companies were well established in the U. S., producing a lighter dinnerware and china including teapots. Figural teapots from this era are highly desired by collectors, while others concentrate on collecting all known patterns produced by a company.

There has seen a renewed interest in

teapots and collectors desire not only older examples, but also high-priced, specialty manufactured teapots or individual artist creations commanding hundreds of dollars.

Reproduction Alert: Teapots and other ware with a blurry mark of a shield and two animals, ironstone, celadon-colored body background, and a design made to look like flow blue, are new products, possibly from China. Yixing teapots have been reproduced or made in similar styles for centuries.

Adviser: Tina M. Carter.

Oriental teapot with original basket, Famillie Rose decoration, **$95**.

Basalt, 9-3/4" l, black, oval form, scalloped rim and classical relief centering columns with floral festoons, banded drapery on shoulder, incised brick banded lower body, unmarked, England, early 19th C, restored spout **360.00**

Cloisonné, panel with butterflies and flowers, Chinese, late 19th C........ **450.00**

Graniteware, large teapot with pewter handle, lid and spout, Manning Bowman & Co. Manufacturers, called Perfection Granite Ironware, West Meriden, Connecticut **325.00**

Lenox, Art Deco, applied sterling silver dec, c1930, three-pc set **400.00**

Majolica, fish, multicolored, Minton, no mark, late 1800s **2,000.00**

Parian ware, Brownfield, Mistletoe pattern **450.00**

Rockingham glaze, 4-3/8" h, brown glaze,tree trunk form body, molded fruiting vines, branch handle, twig finial, imp Wedgwood, England, mark, c1870, chip to cover collar **520.00**

Silver, 5-3/4" h, Hester Bateman, London, 1786, oval, domed lid with beaded rim, engraved bands, body with engraved bands and central cartouche, wood ear handle and finial, approx 13 troy oz **3,450.00**

Staffordshire, creamware

- 3-5/8" h, mottled translucent brown lead glaze, side strap handle and crabstock molded spout, c1770, nicks to spout rim, missing cover **450.00**

Royal Doulton, Walton Ware, c1910, four-piece tea set, 5" h teapot with underplate, covered sugar bowl, creamer, all depicting Battle of Hastings, cream-color earthenware ground, stamped mark, chip to spout, hairline to sugar lid, **$365**. Photo courtesy of David Rago Auctions, Inc.

- 5" h, black glaze, globular shape, crabstock handle and spout, bird finial, traces of gilt floral dec, slight chip to finial and tip of spout, cov rim repaired, hairline to body, England, c1780 .... **350.00**
- 5-1/2" h, lead glaze, rouletted globular melon-shape body with alternating green and yellow striping, leaf molded spout and double-scrolled handle, applied leaves and florets, c1770, slight nick to cover and spout rim, some glaze missing on lower body **8,225.00**

Royal Doulton, Dickensware, Little Nell, **$195**. Photo courtesy of David Joy Luke Auctions.

Yixing, bamboo handle, Chinese "chop mark" or signature, c1880 .... **450.00**

Teddy Bears

History: Originally thought of as "Teddy's Bears," in reference to President Theodore Roosevelt, these stuffed toys are believed to have originated in Germany. The first ones to be made in the United States were produced about 1902.

Most of the earliest teddy bears had humps on their backs, elongated muzzles, and jointed limbs. The fabric used was generally mohair; the eyes were either glass with pin backs or black shoe buttons. The stuffing was usually excelsior. Kapok (for softer bears) and wood-wool (for firmer bears) also were used as stuffing materials.

Quality older bears often have elongated limbs, sometimes with curved arms, oversized feet, and felt paws. Noses and mouths are black and embroidered onto the fabric.

The earliest teddy bears are believed to have been made by the original Ideal Toy Corporation in America and by a German company, Margarete Steiff, GmbH. Bears made in the early 1900s by other companies can be difficult to identify because they were all similar in appearance and most identifying tags or labels were lost during childhood play.

Notes: Teddy bears are rapidly increasing as collectibles and their prices are rising proportionately. As in other fields, desirability should depend upon appeal, quality, uniqueness, and condition.

3-3/8" h, Schuco, c1920, golden mohair perfume bear, black steel eyes, embroidered nose and mouth, jointed at shoulders and hips, overall fur loss, soil **150.00**

10" h

- Ideal, c1905, light yellow short mohair pile, fully jointed, excelsior stuffing, black steel eyes, embroidered nose, mouth, and claws, felt pads, spotty fur and fiber loss, pr **920.00**

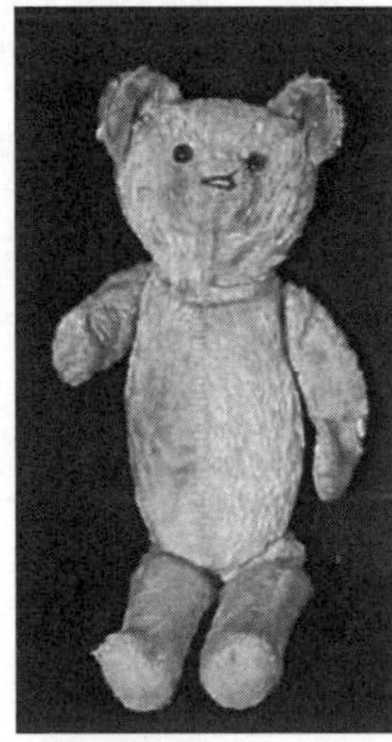

Mohair teddy bear, early, 20" h, **$230**. Photo courtesy of Joy Luke Auctions.

- Steiff, ginger mohair, fully jointed, black steel eyes, black embroidered nose, mouth, and claws, felt pads, blank ear button, spotty fur loss **1,150.00**

11" h, unknown maker, c1908, blond mohair, fully jointed, excelsior stuffing, black steel eyes, open composition mouth with full set of teeth, fiber wear around mouth and nose, some fur wear at seams **750.00**

11-1/2" h, Steiff, gold mohair, fully jointed, glass eyes, excelsior stuffing, button missing, remnants of embroidered nose, mouth, and claws, spotty fur loss, extensive moth damage to pads 200.00

Boyds, Truman S. Bearington, jointed brown mohair, suede paws and feet, original box, 17" h, **$50**. Photo courtesy of Joy Luke Auctions.

12" h, Schuco, early 1920s, yellow mohair, fully jointed, glass eyes, embroidered nose and mouth, excelsior stuffing, felt pads, moth damage, spotty fur loss **350.00**

13-1/2" h, Steiff, dark brown mohair, jointed, restored felt pads **650.00**

14" h, unknown maker, light mohair, excelsior stuffed swivel head, black shoe button eyes, floss nose and horizontal stitching, excelsior stuffed five-pc body jointed at shoulders and hips, three black floss claws on paws and feet, old black velvet ribbon, some mohair missing, old pending **800.00**

16" h

- Bing, c1907, ginger mohair, fully jointed, excelsior stuffing, glass eyes, long arms, shaved muzzle, vertically stitched nose, felt pads, arrow ear button, very slight fur loss, head disk broken through front of neck **2,300.00**
- Burnie Boozle, hand made, jointed, chocolate mohair, stitched claws, glass eyes, birth certificate **40.00**
- Unknown maker, black mohair, gray glass eyes, long nose, swivel head, moveable limbs, gray wool yarn stitched vertically on nose, red yarn lining around mouth frayed, minor wear **525.00**
- Unknown maker, gold mohair, excelsior stuffed swivel head, amber glass eyes, triangle cloth nose, black floss mouth, jointed at shoulders and hips, back hump, felt pads on paws and feet, three black floss claws on paws **800.00**

Mohair jointed monkey perfume bottle, red, 3-1/4" h. $490. Photo courtesy Joy Luke Auctions.

16-1/2" h, American, c1919, ginger mohair, fully jointed, black steel eyes, black embroidered nose, mouth, and claws, beige felt pads, excelsior stuffing, patchy fur loss, felt damage **800.00**

17-1/2" h, Steiff, blond mohair, jointed, button in ear **1,375.00**

Yes/No Bear, gold plush, glass eyes, embroidered muzzle, slight wear to stomach, 5-1/2" h. **$250**. Photo courtesy of James D. Julia, Inc.

19" h, Hermann, 1940s, brown tint gold mohair, fully jointed, glass eyes, shaved muzzle, black embroidered nose and mouth, excelsior stuffing, clipped mohair pads, fur slightly matted in spots **250.00**

20" h, French, 1930s blond plush wool, glass eyes, jointed, non-working growler, repair to one leg, nose missing **350.00**

24" h, unknown maker, 1920s, golden brown mohair, fully jointed, glass eyes, embroidered nose and mouth, kapok and excelsior stuffing, felt pads, wearing dress, bonnet, and glasses, spotty fur loss and felt damage **350.00**

25" h

- Bing, c1915, jointed, orig felt pads **7,000.00**
- Ideal, 1920s, yellow mohair, fully jointed, glass eyes, black embroidered nose, mouth, and claws, felt pads, excelsior stuffing, slight fur loss and matting **635.00**

Teplitz China

History: Around 1900, there were 26 ceramic manufacturers located in Teplitz, a liquor town in the Bohemian province of what was then known as Czechoslovakia. Other potteries were located in the nearby town of Turn. Wares from these factories were molded, cast, and hand decorated. Most are in the Art Nouveau and Art Deco styles.

Marks: The majority of pieces do not carry a specific manufacturer's mark; they are simply marked "Teplitz," "Turn-Teplitz," or "Turn."

Vase, conical, applied large and small cream color and gilt Glasgow roses, accented with swags of beads, blue-gray ground, imp "1198 16," Paul Dachsel, c1904, 6" h, **$2,715**. Photo courtesy of Skinner, Inc.

Amphora

- 5-1/2" h, molded with three lion's head masks above incised foliate swags, Turn-Teplitz, early 20th C **300.00**
- 14-1/2" h, hp lilies, cobalt blue ground, scrolling gold ribbon, marked "Turn Teplitz-Bohemia, Made in Austria," imp "Amphora" **520.00**

Bust, 22-1/2" h, young woman, elaborate dress, fan, flowers, and hat with reticulated border, putto on shoulders, Ernest Wahliss, c1900, repaired **1,700.00**

Candlestick, 13" h, applied flowers, gold trim **125.00**
Creamer, hp, scene of bird in flight, gold trim **195.00**
Ewer, 10-5/8" h, gilt trimmed ivory ground, enameled birds in paneled sides, c1900 .... **300.00**

Pitcher, body decorated with red flower sprigs, molded dragon handle, fish spout, ink stamp mark, restoration, 12" h, **$350**. Photo courtesy of David Rago Auctions.

Figure, 8" h, 8-1/2" l, two children, young boy in hat with pink ribbon, pushing young girl carrying umbrella and basket, soft beige ground, pink and blue highlights, sgd "Teplitz Bohemia," imp "4007" **450.00**
Jar, 8-1/4" w, 6-1/2" h, hp, parcel gilt, molded dragon handles, marked "Alfred Shellmacher Teplitz" **850.00**
Pitcher, 12" h, cylindrical, bulbous base, leaf-shaped handle, reticulated rim, ivory ground, iris and foliate dec, Ernst Wahliss Alexandra Porcelain Works, early 20th C, crown and shield mark on underside, hairline and crack at handle **110.00**

Vase, swollen neck, bulbed vessel, medial band of bees, green, white, and brown on blue ground with gilt highlights, maker's stamp on base, 1892-1904, 6" h, **$415**. Photo courtesy of Skinner, Inc.

Urn, 14" h, ovoid, two delicate handles, textured neck, handles, and base, ivory and pale green, gilding, hp floral center, marked "Turn-Teplitz-Bohemia" in circle around vase mark, also marked "RS + K Made in Austria" **295.00**

Teplitz vase, 13" h, Art Nouveau, two buttressed floriform handles, shaded amber and green matte glaze, marked, post-factory drill hole to bottom, small bruise to rim, **$225**; 6-1/2" d pie-crust dish, Rookwood, by E.P. Cranch, 1885, "Brer Bear and his Family," from Uncle Remus series, marked, **$200**. Photo courtesy of David Rago Auctions.

Vase

6-1/4" h, Art Nouveau sand textured pod-form, scrolled leafage, matte green, tan, and ivory glaze, gilt highlights, printed maker's stamp on base, Paul Dachsel, c1905 .... **260.00**
8" h, Art Nouveau baluster form, slender neck, enamel dec, stylized wildflowers, gilt details, marked "Turin-Teplitz, Amphora Work Reissner," early 20th C **460.00**
11-1/2" h, stylized blue and green scene of sun through trees, lower band with ivory and blue insect and blue floral dec, gold accents, stamped "Turn-Teplitz-Bohemia/ RS+K/Made in Austria" **480.00**

Terra-Cotta Ware

History: Terra-cotta is ware made of hard, semi-fired ceramic. The color of the pottery ranges from a light orange-brown to a deep brownish red. It is usually unglazed, but some pieces are partially glazed and have incised, carved, or slip designs. Utilitarian objects, as well as statuettes and large architectural pieces, were made.

Architectural fragment, 38" l, lintel supports, from Solomon Blumenfield Flats, 1884, pr **550.00**
Bowl, 6" d, 2" h, glazed **30.00**
Figure, 11" h, St. Joseph, wearing long loose robes, black hat, polychrome dec, Spanish, 19th C **600.00**

Bust, Marie Antoinette, France, late 19th C, applied sepia toned finish, gray marble socle, 25-1/2" h, **$1,175**. Photo courtesy of Skinner, Inc.

Pedestal, 7" sq top, 24" h, price for pr **400.00**

Wall relief, three-dimensional head, green and blue matte glazes, incised signature of G. Staindl, 15-1/2" x 10-1/2" x 2-1/2", **$235**. Photo courtesy of David Rago Auctions, Inc.

Planter, 10-1/4" h, garland and mask motif **100.00**
Sculpture, 20" h, 22" w, jumping buffalo, Art Deco raised step designs on base, imp signature for "A. Vozech" (Anthony Vozech, Toledo, OH, 1895-) **400.00**
Tray, 9" x 7", hp, pilgrims resting, gilt dec, 1920 .... **85.00**
Urn, 29-1/2" h, molded putti and foliage dec, green glaze, waisted neck, two handles, circular base **395.00**
Water pitcher, 13" h, c1810, base chip **325.00**

Textiles

History: Textiles is the generic term for cloth or fabric items, especially anything woven or knitted. Antique textiles that have survived are usually those that were considered the "best" by their original owners, since these were the objects that were used and stored carefully by the housewife.

Textiles are collected for many reasons—to study fabrics, to understand the elegance of a historical period, for

decorative purposes, or to use as was originally intended. The renewed interest in antique clothing has sparked a revived interest in period textiles of all forms.

Coverlet, glazed chintz, composed of four panels, printed with exotic birds and flowers, shades of red, blue, and green, mustard yellow ground, quilted with circle and diamond pattern, muslin backing, America, 19th C, minor stains, 84" x 92", **$1,530**. Photo courtesy of Skinner, Inc.

Aubusson-style tapestry panel, 102" x 39", palm fronds on top draping over hanging basket of flowers, over blossoming fuchsia plant and further palm, vine border, fabric backed, early 20th C **1,300.00**

Bandana, printed on silk, Harrison and Morton, 1892 election **1,100.00**

Bedspread, embroidered candlewick, by Eliza Spink, (1807-77), Auburn, NY, white on white embroidered dec, central cartouche with floral urn, medallion above name and date surrounded by grapevine border, further framed by grapevine and tulip border, central floral urn, 108" x 112", small holes, light staining, repairs **1,840.00**

Coverlet, jacquard, two-piece double-weave, blue and white, rows of floral medallions and diamonds, border on three sides with stylized eagles and fruiting trees, signed and dated in lower corner blocks "Selah Lambertson N.Y. 1836," minor scattered stains, 75" x 92", **$360**. Photo courtesy of Skinner, Inc.

Bell pull, 5-1/2" w, 70" l, needlework, white and yellow lilies, brown ground, brass fittings with grapevines **125.00**

Coverlet, jacquard, one pc, double weave, floral medallions with double vining tulip borders, burgundy, medium blue, green, and white, dated "1824" along border, 66" x 90" **295.00**

Coverlet, jacquard, one pc, single weave

Green, navy blue, and red on natural, large oval star, vintage medallion at center flanked by two large baskets, harp, and scrolled foliage borders, sgd across bottom "Made by Peter Seibert, Easton, Pennsyl," minor stains, 88" x 94" **650.00**

Red on white, sgd in corners blocks "Made by J. D. Wieand, Allentown, 1868," center star medallion surrounded by rose wreath and eagles in each corner, vintage side borders with tulip, rose, and urn end borders, minor stains, 80" x 86" **420.00**

Tomato red, navy blue, and green on natural ground, unusual double borders with woodpeckers on stumps, separated by flowering plants, date 1858 in lower corners, 25 large stars, each surrounded by floral wreath and smaller stars, minor moth damage and stains, 75" x 92" **880.00**

Coverlet, jacquard, red, blue and green, eagle border, made for Elisabeth Rischel, 1836, **$350**. Photo courtesy of Pook & Pook.

Coverlet, jacquard, two pcs, Biederwand, green, navy blue, tomato red, and white, circular and rose medallions with borders of double headed eagles, foliage swags, tassels, and Maltese crosses, corner blocks "Peter Lorenz 1841," 78" x 85"... **1,320.00**

Coverlet, jacquard, two pc, double weave

Crisscross bands of tomato red, navy blue, teal blue, and navy, intricate design with floral medallions, diamonds, and foliage, double border with birds, oak leaves, and elaborate building with double towers, corner blocks with four frames with "1859" inside, stains, top edge bound in plaid cloth, 76" x 84" **635.00**

Coverlet, jacquard, woven in two pieces, American indigo blue and white wool, buildings and floral urns at bottom corner, spread=wing eagles, and "Liberty," white and blue side and bottom fringe, slight brown spots, very minor edge wear, 7'2" x 5'10", **$150**. Photo courtesy of Cowan's Historic Americana Auctions.

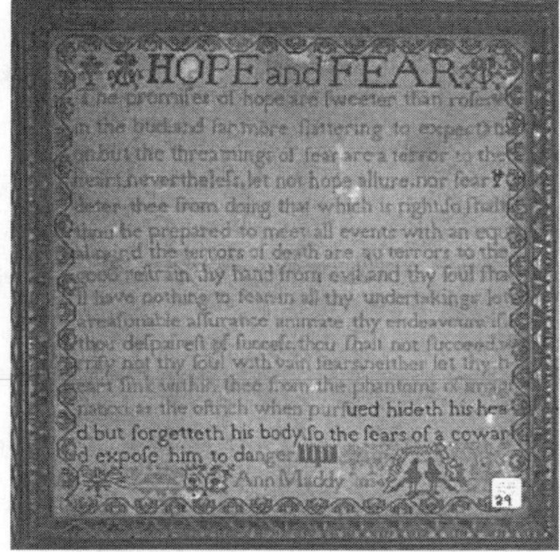

Embroidered verse, "Hope and Fear," made by "Ann Maddy 1834," some wear, framed, 14" square, **$250**. Photo courtesy of Joy Luke Auctions.

Floral and star medallions, borders of stars and birds with urns and buildings, flower corner block for Sarah (1822-1914) and Henry LaTourette, Fountain County, IN, "Year 1850," navy blue, tomato red, and burgundy bands with natural, some edge damage, bleach spots, 72" x 86" **750.00**

Floral medallions, border of acanthus leaves, baskets of flowers, navy blue and natural, some staining, 72" x 86" **440.00**

Geometric design, navy blue and natural, pine tree border, 78" x 90" **275.00**

Medallions with roses and thistles, double borders of roses and leaves, navy blue, tomato red, mustard, and natural, four-part corner blocks with leaves, minor wear, fringe loss, some bleeding of blues, 75" x 84".... **660.00**

Urns of fruit, birds feeding their young, Christian and Heathen border, no corner blocks, dark blue and natural, attributed to Jefferson County, OH, some fringe loss, one end turned over and stitched, 66" x 76" **935.00**

Coverlet, jacquard, two pcs, summer/ winter

Navy blue, tomato red, olive green, and natural, rose and sun medallions in unusual garland swag border with tassels and Maltese crosses, corner blocks sgd "Peter Lorenz 1842," minor fringe loss, 76" x 86"..... **770.00**

Tomato red, navy blue, and olive bands with natural, fruit and floral medallions, corner blocks dated 1855, fringe loss, seams needs to be resewn, 76" x 88" **250.00**

Crewelwork panel, 71" x 41-1/2", stitched with central tree of life motif in flowering vine frame, floral bouquet border, some metallic threads, embellished with fringing, satin backed, Continental, (possibly a bed covering) **1,880.00**

Hooked rug, floral and geometric, red roses, yellow centers, green leaves, cream ground, **$250**. Photo courtesy of Skinner, Inc.

Embroidery panel, 30-1/2" x 30-1/2", linen ground, cutout silk panels, satin stitched silk threads, Lady Liberty with horn and cap on pole, crowning draped bust with laurel wreath, standing on cliff on top of French flag, overlooking town harbor several ships in background, soft faded blue, red, green, gold, brown, and ivory, matted with rope twist detailed gilt frame, slight stains, some damage, wear to frame **250.00**

Hooked rug

23" x 35", two blue and red birds facing black urn, flowering tree, white ground, surrounded by meandering black line, yellow border, olive green outer border with pink and white diamonds, light green leaves, minor repair, small hold in urn **500.00**

Hooked rug, winter landscape with sleigh and figures in village, framed, 26" x 37" sight, **$400**. Photo courtesy of Sanford Alderfer Auction Company.

20" x 40", raised block with shadow design, outlined in brown and tan, shadows fading from light blue to navy blue to black, mounted on stretcher **330.00**

24-3/4" x 40", 10-point star at center, alternating black, blue/brown, green, and burgundy on medium blue ground, black scalloped border, mounted on stretcher, very minor edge damage........................ **600.00**

26" x 48", gray house, black trim, red roof, green bushes, brown path and fence, blue sky, flying birds, burgundy border dated 1940, some black bleeding **150.00**

Needlepoint picture, woolwork, rooster and two chickens in landscape, multi-color floral border, America, 19th C, 24-3/8" x 21-3/8", **$275**.

26" x 52", muted blue-gray, yellow, red, white, and pink, brown ground, large center pinwheel surrounded by six small pinwheels, mounted on stretcher, areas of edge wear, minor restoration **385.00**

26-1/2" x 43-1/2", Edward Sands Frost pattern, beige, brown, and black spaniel lying on green, red, and tan checked floor, black borders, large tan and red oval, small green leaves, few minor thread pulls...................................... **590.00**

37-3/4" x 61-1/2", Grenfell Industries, Newfoundland, Labrador, 1900-25, rescue scene with three figures, supply-laden dog sled, shades of brown, black, gray, green, blue, and yellow, brown border, staining, fading **1,410.00**

46-1/2" x 71", central oval medallion with brightly colored flowers and leaves in tan, salmon, gray, red, and white on black and brown ground with shirring, tan and ivory outer borders with red leaves, wear **350.00**

48" x 74", multiple borders, broken stripe ground in shades of red, brown, tan, gray, green, and ivory, cloth binding, several well done patches **220.00**

53-1/2" x 67", bright multicolored lines across middle ground, five striped borders on both ends, Maine, old cloth binding on two sides..................................... **225.00**

Needlework picture, Continental, 18th C, depicting adoration of Christ child, oval, framed, 7" x 5" sight, **$450**. Photo courtesy of Sloan's Auctioneers & Appraisers.

56-1/4" x 70", red, blue, yellow, and green on gray ground, PA Dutch designs of man and woman in to corners, roosters, hearts, pears, large flowers in lower corners, early style train with mountains on gray center medallion, 20th C, minor areas of color bleeding **550.00**

101" x 53", large leaf medallion, larger oak leaves around borders, brown, blue, red, tan, and black, dark and light brown ground, wear, small restorations, rebound edges **330.00**

Pillow, Arts & Crafts, stylized gold and red floral motif, beige ground, 20" x 20", **$365**. Photo courtesy of David Rago Auctions.

Folk ark, "This man hath reached a sorry plight, strange creatures haunt his dreams at night, a helping hand, a mug of beer, might ease the way to water clear," sleeping man surrounded by lizard, parrot, flying elephant, and snake and stars, designed by James and Mercedes Hutchinson **7,500.00**

Needlework genealogy, silk on linen, wrought by "Eliza Jordan 1828," floral border, American, 15-1/2" x 16-3/4", **$1,100**. Photo courtesy of Pook & Pook.

Pillow, needlework

7" x 17", matching pr, one with red roses, other with lavender roses, tan silk tassels, green velvet backing **150.00**

17" sq, tapestry of hunting falcon on perch, hunting hood beside it, background with potted plants, roses, fence, classical building, gray silk fringe, wear, few tears **150.00**

Presentation panel, 11-1/2" w, 32" h, framed, quilted, pieced diamond design, white and red calico, sgd in ink "Philadelphia 1842 Mary Ann Winner," and "Susannah McGowan," center fish scale quilting, inked picture of American eagle with banner, woman by seaside cliff with ships, well and cornucopia, "Presented to the Rev'd Thomas P. & Anna Hunt by the Ladies Total Abstinence Society of...Philadelphia...," stains, minor damage **800.00**

Table scarf, silk, comprised of silk ribbons for cigar brands, with tassels, 36" square, **$250**.

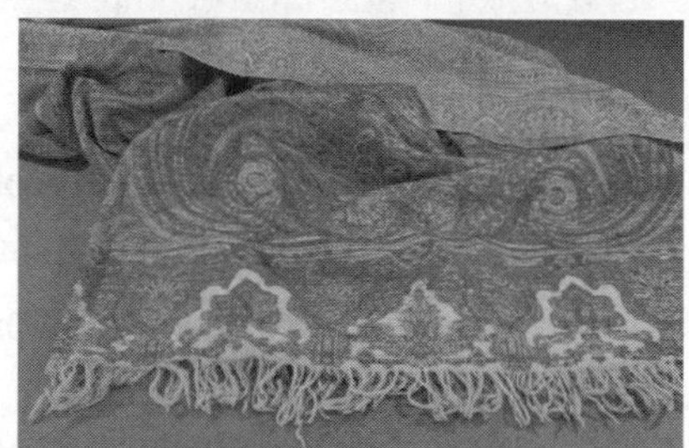

Paisley shawl, woven with cashmire motifs, 126" x 58", **$425**. Photo courtesy of Sloans & Kenyon Auctions.

Shawl, 40" x 44", Victorian era, colorful silk floral, satin stitch flowers, green feather medallions, white ground, long tied multicolored fringe, Persian **275.00**

Silhouttes, lace, two presidents and general, black paper fan, framed, **$45**. Photo courtesy of Dotta Auction Co., Inc.

Table cloth, 58" x 70", overshot linen, hand-tied fringe, some stains **100.00**

Table mat, 41" x 53", pieced, red, green, black, white, and light blue wool, scalloped edges with diamond borders, star in each corner, large red and black checkered blocks within center panel surrounded by another band of diamonds, tacked blocks at each corner, smaller checkerboard blocks surround panel, black cloth backing and stretcher, minor damage and stains **1,155.00**

Show towel, signed "C.K.," dated 1822, geometric border, flowering vines with hearts in white embroidery on white linen, fish net type fringe at end of towel, framed, 17-1/2" w, 24" l sight, **$125**. Photo courtesy of Sanford Alderfer Auction Company.

Table rug

20" w, 42" l, appliqué, penny, mostly orange, blue, light green, and mauve wool, oblong with "tongue" border, round blue cut-outs, light purple background, some stains....... **250.00**

24-1/2" w, 15" h, wool yarn, two flowering plants, pink and beige blossoms, olive ground, New England, early 19th C, some losses **2,875.00**

Threaded Glass

History: Threaded glass is glass decorated with applied threads of glass. Before the English invention of a glass-threading machine in 1876, threads were applied by hand. After this invention, threaded glass was produced in quantity by practically every major glass factory.

Threaded glass was revived by the art glass manufacturers such as Durand and Steuben, and it is still made today.

Basket, 11" h, 12" d, pink opalescent and amber basket, threaded and raised hobnail design, twisted thorn handle, Victorian **125.00**

Bowl

7" d, 3" h, light pink, green threaded swirl design **45.00**

14-1/4" d, 2-1/8" h, pale rose, int. concentric air bubbles, applied threading under wide rim, attributed to Steuben **220.00**

Vase, green threading, colorless body, 5" h, **$65**.

Candlestick, 9-7/8" h, colorless, cut, flared base, bell nozzle with frosted floral and beaded dec, amethyst rim and threading on stem **175.00**
Celery vase, 6-7/8" h, colorless, floral enamel dec.................................... **30.00**
Champagne tumbler, 4" h, colorless, floral enamel dec............................ **30.00**
Cheese dish, cov, 7-1/2" h, colorless, light blue opalescent threading on upper half of bell-shaped dome, faceted knob **140.00**
Claret jug, 11-1/2" h, 3-1/2" d, chartreuse green, emb scrolled French pewter hinged top, handle, and pedestal foot **245.00**
Compote, 4-5/8" h, ruffled rim, gold colored threading on shallow colorless glass bowl, with trapped bubbles, stem with air-trapped bubble, polished pontil **200.00**
Creamer, 4-3/4" h, colorless with slight blue tint, threaded neck and lip, applied ribbed handle, Pittsburgh.............. **170.00**
Epergne, four purple lilies, white threading **375.00**
Finger bowl and underplate, 4-3/4" d, 2-3/4" h bowl, cranberry, light blue opalescent, ruffled rim, 6-3/4" d underplate **110.00**
Goblet, 5-3/4" h, colorless, diamond molded bowl, Pomona blue reeding, applied Bristol yellow disk foot, stamped "Steuben," set of three **225.00**
Honey pot, cov, 5-3/4" h, 6-1/2" w, satin finished crystal ground, pulled and twisted pattern of blue and white threads, twig finial on cov, twig-like metal frame **450.00**
Lemonade mug, 5-3/8" h, colorless ground, cranberry threading, Sandwich **125.00**
Luncheon plate, 8-1/4" d, green threading on flattened rim, colorless ground with trapped bubbles.......... **65.00**
Mayonnaise, underplate, cranberry ground, ground pontil scar............. **90.00**
Perfume bottle, 5-1/2" h, colorless ground, pink threading................. **175.00**
Pitcher, 7" h, Lily Pad, aqua, threaded neck and lip, applied hollow handle **550.00**
Powder jar, 2-1/2" d, 3" h, Palme Koenig, cranberry ground, random irid threading, dec brass lid................................ **175.00**
Rose bowl, 6" h, 5" d, colorless ground, pink threading **60.00**
Salt, 2-3/4" d, cranberry ground, opaque white threads, applied colorless petal feet... **75.00**
Sherbet, 4-3/4" d, 2-3/4" h, colorless bowl, band of ruby threading around rim, ruby machine threading from shoulder to colorless disk base, acid stamp "Steuben" on base **110.00**
Tumbler, 3-1/8" h, opalescent ribbed ground, blue threads, Lutz type **30.00**
Vase
- 4-1/4" h, ruffled rim with green threading, Verre de Soie body, polished pontil....................... **125.00**
- 6" h, pink threaded flared rim, diamond quilted colorless glass body, polished pontil, Carder Steuben, Catalog No. 6817, minor threading loss........................ **195.00**
- 8" h, petal top, cranberry ground, white threading, sgd "Stevens and Williams"................................ **150.00**
- 10-1/4" h, Kralik, green threading, strong blue and fuchsia threads, polished rim........................... **195.00**
- 12" h, 4" w, red ground, green random threadings at top, flat flared rim, Loetz type....................... **250.00**
- 14" h, Palme Koenig, random threading, amber body, gold irid **270.00**

TIFFANY

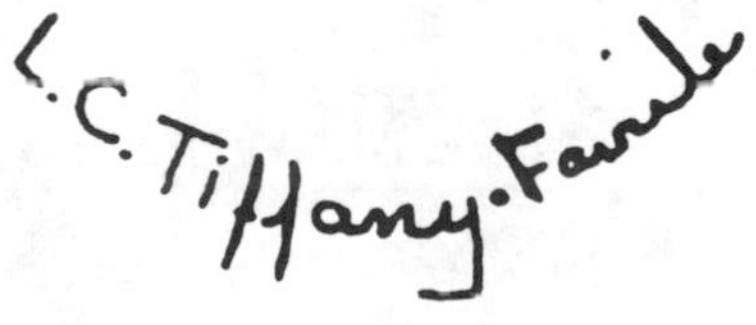

History: Louis Comfort Tiffany (1849-1934) established a glass house in 1878 primarily to make stained glass windows. In 1890, in order to utilize surplus materials at the plant, Tiffany began to design and produce "small glass," such as iridescent glass lampshades, vases, stemware, and tableware in the Art Nouveau manner. Commercial production began in 1896.

Tiffany developed a unique type of colored iridescent glass called Favrile, which differs from other art glass in that it was a composition of colored glass worked together while hot. The essential characteristic is that the ornamentation is found within the glass; Favrile was never further decorated. Different effects were achieved by varying the amount and position of colors.

For more information, see *Warman's Glass*, 4th edition.

Louis Tiffany and the artists in his studio also are well known for their fine work in other areas—bronzes, pottery, jewelry, silver, and enamels.

Marks: Most Tiffany wares are signed with the name "L. C. Tiffany" or the initials "L.C.T." Some pieces also are marked "Favrile," along with a number. A variety of other marks can be found, e.g., "Tiffany Studios" and "Louis C. Tiffany Furnaces."

Reproduction Alert: Tiffany glass can be found with a variety of marks, but the script signature is often faked or added later. When considering a purchase of Tiffany glass, look first to the shape, the depth of the iridescent coloring, then the signature.

Bronze

Bill file, 7-1/2" h, 3-1/2" d, Zodiac pattern, brown patina with some verdigris, base imp "TIFFANY STUDIOS NEW YORK 962" **520.00**

Box, gilt bronze, caramel and white slag glass framed by the Pine Needle pattern reticulated metalwork, imp "TIFFANY STUDIOS NEW YORK 800," crack in corner of base glass, 4-1/4" l, 1-1/2" h, **$450**. Photo courtesy of Skinner, Inc.

Candlesticks, pr, 13-1/2" d, 5-3/4" d foot, slender stems extending to candle cups with green reticulated glass blowouts, imp "TIFFANY STUDIOS NEW YORK 1310," wear and scratches to patina, one broken at stem and repaired, electric socket inserted into candle cup without drilling **2,150.00**
Cigar box, 6-1/2" l, 6" w, 2-1/2" h, Zodiac pattern, good brown patina, wood lined int., imp "TIFFANY STUDIOS NEW YORK 1655" **1,200.00**
Desk clock, 4-1/4" w, 5-1/4" h, cathedral shape, Zodiac pattern, zodiac symbols on sides and front, gold doré finish, brass dial marked "TIFFANY & CO. NEW YORK," black numerals and sweep

second hand, back imp "TIFFANY STUDIOS NEW YORK 1075" 2,100.00

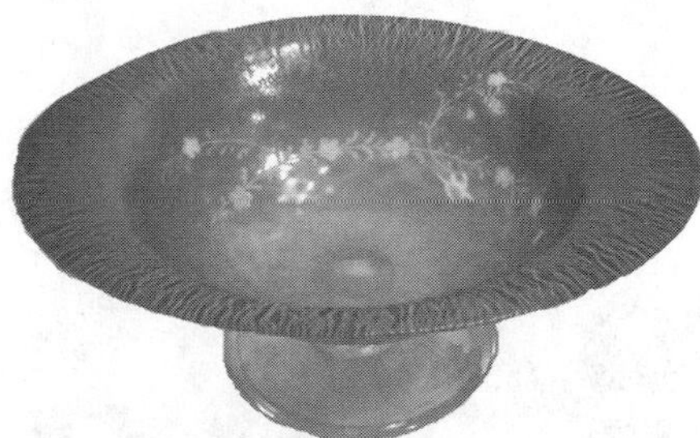

Bowl, oval, footed, blue iridescent, interior with etched vines, flowers, and leaves, base inscribed "L.C. Tiffany-Favrile #1895," 11" w, 4" h, **$4,100**. Photo courtesy of Joy Luke Auctions.

Candlestick, pulled feather shade, snuffer, original patina, signed, hairline crack to shade, **$2,690**. Photo courtesy of Fontaine's Auction Gallery.

Lamp, "Lily," seven amber/violet Favrile glass shades, bronze lilypad base, original patina, shades marked "L.C.T. Favrile" or "L.C.T.," base stamped "TIFFANY STUDIOS NEW YORK, 385," minor chips to flange of two shades, 20-1/2" x 9-3/4", **$10,000**. Photo courtesy of David Rago Auctions.

Desk set

8 pcs, Zodiac pattern, gold doré finish, large blotter ends, pen tray, matchbox holder, inkwell with glass insert, rocker blotter, notepad holder and calendar **1,265.00**

10 pcs, bright gold finish, each inset with abalone shell disks, four blotter corners, pen tray, inkwell, pen brush, rocker blotter and bookends, each impressed "TIFFANY STUDIOS NEW YORK" and numbered **3,650.00**

Inkwell, 6-1/2" w, 3-1/4" h, Zodiac pattern, rich brown-green patina, orig glass inserts, three bottom hinged doors open to compartments, base imp "TIFFANY STUDIOS NEW YORK 1072" **4,950.00**

Letter opener, 9-1/4" l, pine needle handle inset with caramel slag glass, medium brown patina, blade imp "TIFFANY STUDIOS NEW YORK" **540.00**

Letter scale, 3-1/4" h, Zodiac pattern, graduated markings on front, marked "CRESCENT PATENTS PENDING," base imp "TIFFANY STUDIOS NEW YORK 874," minor wear to patina and front panel **920.00**

Glove box, 13-1/2" l, 4-1/2" d, 3-1/8" h, Grapevine pattern, striated green slag glass inserts, ball feet, imp "Tiffany Studios, New York" **980.00**

Planter, squat, conical, low relief bronze arrowhead flowers and leaves, background of inset bands of irid glass tiles in striated yellows, greens, and blues, impressed "TIFFANY STUDIOS, NEW YORK 835," lacking liner, missing some glass tiles on top border, 11-3/4" h, **$27,025**. Photo courtesy of Skinner, Inc.

Magnifying glass, 8-3/4" l, Zodiac pattern, gold doré finish, handle imp "TIFFANY STUDIOS NEW YORK 928" **900.00**

Oil lamp, 3" w, 2-1/2" h, Zodiac pattern, single handle, small dome hinged lid, removable bronze wick holder, brown patina, imp "TIFFANY STUDIOS NEW YORK S880" **2,990.00**

Penholder, 7" l, 4-1/4" w, Zodiac pattern, double Bakelite penholders attached to bronze base with gold doré finish, center zodiac medallion, two Tiffany pine needle pens, imp "TIFFANY STUDIOS NEW YORK 2114" **1,700.00**

Picture frame, 7-1/4" h, 6" w, 3-1/4" h, 2-1/4" w opening, Grapevine pattern, rounded corners, brown, green, and red patina, backed with green slag glass, back imp "TIFFANY STUDIOS NEW YORK" **2,530.00**

Rolodex, 4-1/2" l, 3-1/2" w, Zodiac pattern, gold doré finish, side knob turns roll of paper through open window while pointer at top moves through letters of alphabet, imp "TIFFANY STUDIOS NEW YORK 1074" **2,450.00**

Tray, 11" x 9", braided swirl border, gold doré finish, imp "TIFFANY STUDIOS NEW YORK 1676" **435.00**

Vase, bronze holder

12" h, irid blue stick bud vase, flaring top, sgd "LCT," bronze holder sgd "TIFFANY STUDIOS NEW YORK 717" **1,275.00**

14-1/4" h, irid, green and gold pulled dec, gold irid int. finish with purple highlights, orig bronze holder sgd "TIFFANY STUDIOS NEW YORK 1049," vase signed "LCT FAVRILE," pr, one vase broken near base **2,450.00**

15-3/4" h, irid gold vase with vertical ribs, scalloped top, damage to unsigned brass holder **850.00**

Glass, all Favrile

Bowl

5" d, irid gold, vertical ribbing, scalloped top, sgd "LCT FAVRILE 1253," base crack **210.00**

8-1/4" d, irid gold, vertical ribs, scalloped top, sgd "LC TIFFANY FAVRILE 1284," minor int. scratches **500.00**

Desk lamp, bronze, fluted base, three pendant fixtures, each with flaring white opalescent and green pulled feather art glass shade, base stamped "Tiffany Studios/New York," 17" x 11", **$3,220**. Photo courtesy of David Rago Auctions.

8-1/4" d, 2-3/4" h, opalescent pulled feather dec, green pastel coloring, foot sgd "LC TIFFANY INC FAVRILE 5-1578" **920.00**

9" d, scalloped top, irid gold, blue and purple highlights, base sgd "L.C.T." **550.00**

9-1/2" d, DQ dec, pastel yellow and opalescent irid finish, applied foot, sgd "LC TIFFANY INC FAVRILE 1576-3785" **1,700.00**

10-1/4" d, 3-1/2" h, Favrile, blue, ribbed, flared rim, irid blue and violet, pink and gold highlights, sgd "L. C. T. Favrile" **1,210.00**

Candlesticks, pr

5" h, 4" d, twisted, cupped bobeches, gold lustered finish, marked "LCT" **1,355.00**

12" h, pastel yellow, white opalescence, twisted stem, one stick with orig Tiffany paper label, one with two tiny chips to underside of foot **2,750.00**

Bud vase, floriform, bronze base and Favrile glass insert, ambers with pulled green and amber leaves, original patina, base stamped "TIFFANY STUDIOS, NEW YORK 1043," inset marked "LCT Favrile," 5" d, 12" h, **$1,450**. Photo courtesy of David Rago Auctions.

Compote, 6-1/2" d, 5-1/4" h, irid green and opalescent, scalloped edge, applied stem and foot, sgd "LCT FAVRILE 845T," orig paper label **2,300.00**

Finger bowl, 4-3/4" d, 2-1/2" h, irid gold, ten twists around sides, sgd "LCT FAVRILE" **480.00**

Jack-in-the-pulpit, lustrous amber gold irid body, flared and ruffled rim with stretched irid to edge, pink optic ribbed throat tapering to slender stem supported by bulbous base, inscribed "L. C. T. Y5472," paper label on button pontil, c1905 .... **14,950.00**

Inkwell, bronze, Grapevine pattern, lined in green slag glass, original patina, stamped "TIFFANY STUDIOS NEW YORK 847," 6-1/2" d, 4" h, **$1,100**. Photo courtesy of David Rago Auctions, Inc.

Jam jar, cov, 3" d, 6" h, irid gold finish with blue highlights, sgd "L.C.T.," sterling silver mechanical lid and bale sgd "TIFFANY & CO." **1,840.00**

Lamp shade

6-1/2" d, candle lamp, ruffled, irid green and gold King Tut pattern, unsigned, edge chip **1,035.00**

8" d, green linenfold glass, int. sgd "TIFFANY STUDIOS NEW YORK PATENT APPLIED FOR," several cracks and chips, paint added later **3,450.00**

Plate, 7-1/4" d, irid gold, vertical ribs, scalloped edge, sgd "LCT FAVRILE 3085," minor int. scratches........... **260.00**

Salt, 2-1/4" d, 1" h, bowl shape, round feet, folded rims, gold Aurene, inscribed "L.C.T." **200.00**

Spice dish, 3" d, irid gold Favrille, inscribed "L.C.T.," c1900............. **260.00**

Tankard pitcher, 6-1/2" h, irid gold, green leaf and vine dec, applied irid gold handle, base sgd "L.C. TIFFANY FAVRILE" **3,800.00**

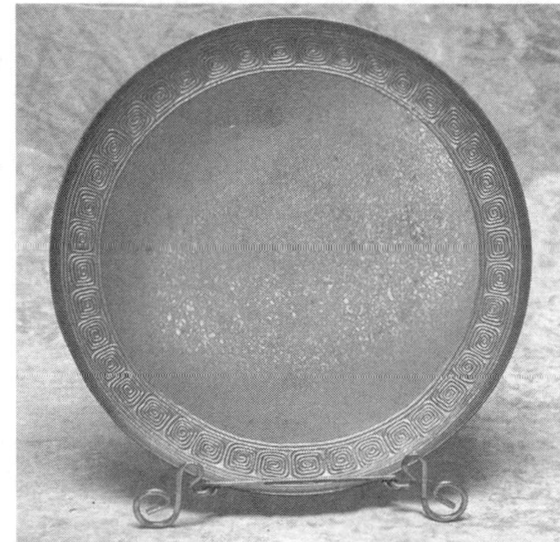

Plate, bronze, gilt wash, Greek Key design border, marked "Tiffany Studios/New York/1743," 8" d, **$220**. Photo courtesy of Alderfer Auction Co.

Vase

3" h, irid gold, blue highlights, base sgd "L.C.T. M1438" **575.00**

Desk set, Pine Needles pattern, green opalescent glass with bronze overlay, 16v l two-handled tray, letter-holder, inkwell with glass insert and hinged lid (#56), bronze match-pot, original patina, each stamped "TIFFANY STUDIOS, NEW YORK," cracks to glass in letter-holder and tray, chip to insert, **$2,400**. Photo courtesy of David Rago Auctions.

3-1/2" h, irid Favrille, pulled double hook pattern, inscribed "L.C.T. 0934," c1901 .... **2,415.00**

4" h, irid gold with blue and amethyst highlights, eight applied rattails, base sgd "L.C.T. M5649," small chip to one rattails **550.00**

4-3/4" h, 5-3/4" d, floriform, ruffled top, green and white pulled feather dec, irid gold int., irid gold applied foot, base sgd "LC TIFFANY INC. FAVRILE 1529-4337M" **2,800.00**

5-1/2" h, green and gold wavy shoulder dec, gold chain mid-section dec, sgd "LCT B772," paper label, int. stains **2,250.00**

5-3/4" h, translucent, applied irid finish, vertical ribbing, flaring top, sgd "L.C.T. V3177" **635.00**

6-1/2" h, double gourd, irid butterscotch color ext., irid gold int., base sgd "LC TIFFANY FAVRILE 46802" **2,185.00**

7" h, irid blue, heart and vine dec, button pontil, base sgd "LC TIFFANY FAVRILE. 244G" **2,875.00**

7-1/2" h, Favrile paperweight type, c1906 .... **18,400.00**

10" h, irid green color shoulder, cream color lining, button pontil sgd "LC TIFFANY FAVRILE 118L" **4,100.00**

11" h, floriform, gold, ribbed body, iridized foot, sgd "1941K LC TIFFANY FAVRILE" **2,760.00**

11-3/4" h, double gourd shape, long neck, irid gold finish, base sgd "LC TIFFANY-FAVRILE 9000G" ... **2,600.00**

12" h, floriform, ftd, slight wear to irid int....................................... **8,920.00**

14" h, floriform, transparent green stem leading to green pulled feather orange irid bowl, opaque cream rim,

gold irid foot, line of in-the-making natural inclusion in opaque rim as well as several dark inclusions on one section of lip **3,000.00**

15-1/2" h, 6-1/2" d, floriform, large ruffled vessel on long stem, gold lustered finish, etched "L.C.T./669A" **4,325.00**

16" h, floriform, irid green pulled feather on creamy white back, irid gold applied foot with blue and purple highlights, irid gold int., sgd "L.C.T." **6,350.00**

Lamps

Candle

9" h gold lustered candlestick base, 5-1/4" d pierced pine needle shade with silver-beaded trim, oil burner, base marked "LCT," shade marked "Tiffany Studios" **1,485.00**

Table lamp, dome shade of green and white leaded glass in floral and geometric pattern over footed converted oil font base with single socket, shade and font stamped "TIFFANY STUDIOS," normal wear to original patina, few small breaks to glass panel, 16" d, 22" h, **$10,925**. Photo courtesy of David Rago Auctions, Inc.

Table lamp, green damascene Favrile dome shade inscribed "L. C. T. Favrile," double-curved arm and ball on stepped base, brown patina, base impressed "Tiffany Studios New York 417," shade 7-1/8" d, 14-3/4" h, **$11,200**. Photo courtesy of Skinner, Inc.

16" h, 22" w, six shades, center finial and pedestal base, each marked "Tiffany Studios, 495," pr... **20,000.00**

Asparagus server, footed square tray, lift-out pierced double handled serving tray, central monograms, marked "15158A Makers 2837" "C 1" and "2," 53 troy oz, 13" w, 10-1/2" d, 2-1/4" h, **$1,450**. Photo courtesy of James D. Julia, Inc.

Desk

13" h, harp-type, 6" d green pulled feather against a cream to orange ground shade, gold doré finish, zodiac symbols around foot, shade sgd "LCT," base imp "TIFFANY STUDIOS NEW YORK 661," minor wear to finish **3,850.00**

15" h, shade with two large turtleback panels in irid blue, green, and gold, surrounded by heavy bronze border emb with zodiac symbols, bronze base features zodiac symbols surrounding foot which extends to heavy harp, patina shows deep browns and reds, base marked "TIFFANY STUDIOS NEW YORK 541" **9,775.00**

Hanging, 28" d shade, nasturtium and trellis pattern, red, amber and lavender flowers, green striated and mottled leaves and stems, mottled blue-gray ground, numerous pieces of fracture glass (confetti glass), orig mounting hardware and bronze beaded trim around base, six-socket cluster, several tight hairline cracks **83,375.00**

Table

16-1/2" h, 11" d leaded shade of mottled green glass in plain geometric panels, zodiac design extending around foot and up stem, rich brown patina, two panels with tight hairlines, one spider crack hidden by cap **8,100.00**

22" h, 16" d daffodil shade, mottled green and cream ground panels with deeper green stems and leaves, yellow daffodils, inside sgd "TIFFANY STUDIOS NEW YORK 1449-2," Handel base fitted with Tiffany hardware, side of base marked "HANDEL," some cracked panels............................... **22,725.00**

26" h, 18" d Poinsettia shade, rich red variegated flowers, centers highlighted in amber, green, and blue, green mottled and variegated leaves and flower stems, mottled light green background panels, tapering base stem impressed with stylized flower buds and stems, wide foot, brown-green patina, sgd "TIFFANY STUDIOS NEW YORK 1558" **51,750.00**

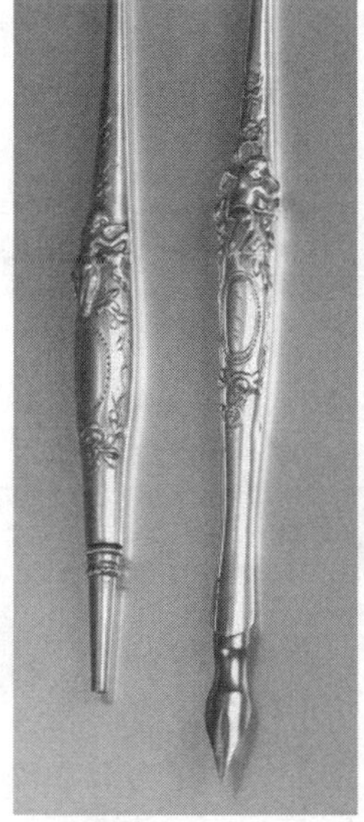

Fountain pen and pencil set, sterling silver, relief decorated with raised putti, floral swags, monogrammed medallion "M. V. P.," impressed "Tiffany & Co. Sterling," minor wear, 7" l, 7-3/4" l, **$265**. Photo courtesy of Skinner, Inc.

Silver

Basket, 9-1/2" d, fixed handle, circular bowl with openwork border and plain int., 17 troy oz, 1907-47...................... **350.00**

Bowl

7-3/4" d, 5-1/2" h, Aesthetic Movement, in the Japonesque style, hammered ovoid bowl on flared foot, rims applied with wave edge, the bowl incised with stylized water ripples, applied silver frog seated upon copper lily pad cluster, bee, two carp, foot applied with one brass carp, one silver carp, foot enclosed at base, marked with pattern number 6919, and order number 3855, approx. 20 troy oz, 1875-91 .... **11,750.00**

9-1/8" d, round, flared sides, tapering at base, monogrammed, 31 troy oz, 1907-38 .... **500.00**

Center bowl, 12" w, shallow ovoid, molded and shaped rim, trumpet foot, with Tiffany & Co. gilt brass reticulated and engraved insert frog, 32 troy oz, 1907-38 .... **1,550.00**

Cigarette box, 6-1/2" w, plain rect, small escutcheon, int. fitted with two-part cedar lining, approx. 25 troy oz, 1902-07 .... **500.00**

Compote, 7-1/2" d, ovoid, scrolling vine rim, beaded trumpet foot, monogrammed, 11 troy oz, 1875-91 .... **400.00**

Demitasse spoons, 4-3/4" l, Iris pattern, handle with two iris stems on stippled ground, fitted Tiffany case, 5 troy oz, 1875-91 .... **800.00**

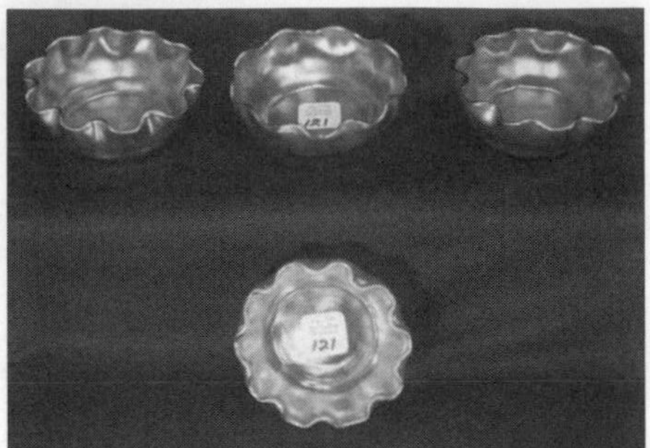

Salt, open, iridescent Favrille glass, set of four, each marked "L.C.T. Favrille 1255," 3" d, **$500**. Photo courtesy of Joy Luke Auctions.

Hot water kettle and stand, 13" h, squat inverted pear shape, set with geometric band at waist, short spout, swing handle with turned wood, emanating from shell terminals, low foot, turned wood handles on stand, ovoid waisted base with geometric border, paw feet flanked by scrolls, silver plated burner, monogrammed and dated 1865, 52 troy oz, 1854-70............................... **1,450.00**

Picture frame, 11" w, 14" h, rect, borders with stylized flowerheads and strapwork, monogrammed "AHG," 1907-47 .... **1,530.00**

Serving bowl, 8-3/4" w, ovoid, shaped sides, rim applied with reeded band, gold washed int., monogrammed, 24 troy oz, 1907-38.................................. **550.00**

Serving dish, 9-1/2" w, sq, flared lip molded with shells, scrolling vines and foliage, sides with open trelliswork and C-scrolls, center with fluted circular design, paw and ball feet, 23 troy oz..... **1,800.00**

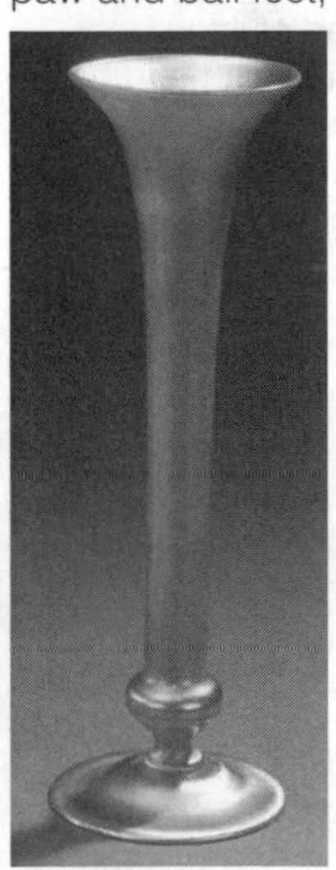

Vase, Favrile, trumpet shape, short knopped stem, domed base, signed "L. C. Tiffany Favrile, 1905-9850L," 9-7/8" h, **$790**. Photo courtesy of Sloans & Kenyon Auctions.

Tea and coffee service

7-3/4" h coffeepot, teapot, kettle on stand, creamer, cov sugar, open sugar, and 26" l tray, style number 17042, paneled ovoid pots, lids with ovoid urn finial, angular handles and serpentine spouts, short scroll feet, kettle stand with bifurcate uprights, ovoid tray with paneled edges, cut out handles, all with Arts and Crafts engraved monogram, 298 troy oz total, 1907-38 .... **9,400.00**

8-5/8" coffeepot, teapot, creamer, cov sugar, and open sugar, coffeepot paneled waisted baluster form, other pieces paneled ovoid, urn lid finials, angular handles, reeded rims, monogrammed, 61 troy oz, 1907-38 .... **4,700.00**

9" h coffeepot, teapot, creamer, covered sugar, and open sugar, ovoid bodies chased and embossed at waist with dense foliate vine, acanthus ear handles, serpentine spouts, flat lids with leafy bud finials, monogrammed and dated 1886, presentation inscription on underside, 107 troy oz **3,525.00**

Teaspoons, set of 12, 6" l, etched with a different Japonesque motif, one spider on a web, one beetle, one songbird on a branch, other nine depicting various flowering branches and floral specimens, monogrammed F on back of handle, 12 troy oz, 1875-91........................ **2,350.00**

Tray, 16" l, oval, beaded and Greek key rim, pointed bracket feet flanked by scrolls, engraved with wide band of fruiting grapevine, two roundels with reveling Dionysian couple, stippled ground, central monogram, 21 troy oz, 1854-70 .... **1,880.00**

Vase, oval, early bicycling design, c1890 .... **1,955.00**

Tiffin Glass

c1960

[Warman's Glass cover image]
For more information, see *Warman's Glass*, 4th edition.

History: A. J. Beatty & Sons built a glass manufacturing plant in Tiffin, Ohio, in 1888. On January 1, 1892, the firm joined the U. S. Glass Co. and was known as factory R. Fine-quality Depression-era items were made at this high-production factory.

From 1923 to 1936, Tiffin produced a line of black glassware called Black Satin. The company discontinued operation in 1980.

Marks: Beginning in 1916, wares were marked with a paper label.

Basket, Black Satin, #8574-6"...... **115.00**

Bonbon, cov, Satin, light green, high standard, #330 .... **65.00**

Bowl

Mystic, #17466, crystal, 4-1/4" d **15.00**

Princess, #13643, crystal, 4-1/4" d **12.00**

Candlesticks, pr, twist stem, black **75.00**

Champagne

Cherry Laurel, crystal, gold trim **22.50**

June Night................................ **25.00**

Killarney Green, #17450, crystal stem and foot **25.00**

Lovelace, crystal **15.00**

Shamrock, #17458, Killarney Green **25.00**

Wisteria, #17507, crystal stem and foot **35.00**

Cocktail

Byzantine, yellow....................... **15.00**

Cerise, crystal **28.00**

Fuchsia, crystal **20.00**

June Night, crystal **20.00**

Compote, Black, twist stem........... **65.00**

Console set, Pumpkin Opaque, 9" d flanged rim floral bowl, black amethyst base, pr #151-9 candleholders.... **295.00**

Tumbler, #517 blown 12-ounce optic, classically influenced Eldorado etching, with griffin-like creature, c1920-29, 5" h, **$24**. Photo courtesy of Michael Krumme.

Cordial

Cordelia, crystal **10.00**

Fuchsia, crystal **40.00**

Persian Pheasant, crystal......... **45.00**

Cornucopia, Copen Blue, 8-1/4" ... **90.00**

Creamer, Flanders, pink, flat **230.00**

Cup and saucer, Flanders, yellow **100.00**

Decanter, Byzantine, crystal........ **600.00**

Goblet

Cherry Laurel, crystal, gold trim **25.00**

Close-up of Eldorado etching.

Cut Rock, #17467-3, crystal..... **15.00**
Killarney Green, #17450, 9 oz, crystal stem and foot................ **35.00**

Iced tea tumbler
Cherry Laurel, crystal, gold trim **27.50**
Killarney Green, #17394, ftd **30.00**
Mystic, #17466, crystal **22.50**

Juice tumbler, ftd, Rose Marie, crystal **18.00**

Martini glass, 4-1/2" d, 3" h, Shawl Dancer, set of four **150.00**

Oyster cocktail, Killarney Green, dolphin stem.. **20.00**

Parfait, Princess, #13643, crystal **22.50**

Luncheon plate, Persian Pheasant etch on #17601 Encanto blank, pink, 8" d, **$25**. Photo courtesy of Rick Hirte, Sparkle Plenty Glassware.

Plate
Byzantine, crystal, 8-1/2" d **12.00**
Cut Rock, #17467-3, crystal..... **10.00**
Killarney Green, 8" d **15.00**

Rose bowl
Copen Blue, Swedish optic, three crystal ball feet....................... **125.00**
Copen Blue, wide vertical optic, 4-1/2".. **45.00**
Copen Blue, wide vertical optic, four large sand carved leaves, stems, and berries.............................. **75.00**
Killarney Green, #17430, applied crystal feet............................ **150.00**

Sherbet
Cut Rock, #17467-3, crystal, high **12.00**
Lovelace, crystal **15.00**

Sweet pea vase, Reflex Green Satin, #151... **65.00**

Salad bowl, June Night, crystal, 1940s-50s, 10-1/4" d, **$65**. Photo courtesy of Rick Hirte, Sparkle Plenty Glassware.

Vase
Copen Blue, Swedish Optic, crystal ball stem, 9-1/4" h.................. **120.00**
Crystal #17350, tub, bubble stem, sand carved flying egret, clouds, bird swimming among rushes **225.00**
Dahlia, Black Satin, 10-1/2" h... **75.00**
Daisy, #17430, Killarney Green, applied crystal foot **170.00**
Twilight, #17430, flared, 7-1/2" h **175.00**

Wine
Byzantine, crystal **18.00**
Cut Rock, #17467-3, crystal..... **15.00**
Fuchsia, crystal **35.00**
Laurel, gold etch and trim **35.00**
Mystic, #17466, crystal **27.50**
Wisteria, #17507, crystal stem and foot **40.00**

TILES

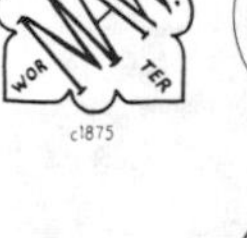

History: The use of decorated tiles peaked during the latter part of the 19th century. More than 100 companies in England alone were producing tiles by 1880. By 1890, companies had opened in Belgium, France, Australia, Germany, and the United States.

Tiles were not used only as fireplace adornments. Many were installed into furniture, such as washstands, hall stands, and folding screens. Since tiles were easily cleaned and, hence, hygienic, they were installed on the floors and walls of entry halls, hospitals, butcher shops, or any place where sanitation was a concern. Many public buildings and subways also employed tiles to add interest and beauty.

Notes: Condition is an important factor in determining price. A cracked, badly scuffed and scratched, or heavily chipped tile has very little value. Slight chipping around the outer edges of a tile is, at times, considered acceptable by collectors, especially if a frame can cover these chips.

It is not uncommon for the highly glazed surface of some tiles to have become crazed. Crazing is not considered detrimental as long as it does not detract from the overall appearance of the tile.

Batchelder, two single landscape tiles, two with tree tops, part of a frieze, stamped "BATCHELDER LOS ANGELES," some minor chips and abrasions, 5-3/4" x 5-3/4", **$300**. Photo courtesy of David Rago Auctions, Inc.

American Encaustic Tiling Co., 30" x 6", pr five-tile friezes, emb planted hollyhocks, brown majolica glaze, unmarked, few edge and high point chips.. **460.00**

Batchelder
5-3/4" sq, emb medieval city behind stone wall, gray, red, and blue engobe, stamped BATCHELDER LOS ANGELES, some abrasion to high points of frame and stone wall **175.00**
9" x 5-3/4", pr, molded peacocks facing each other under grape vines, rubbed with blue engobe, stamped BATCHELDER/PASADENA, period molding frames, restoration to edge of one, corner of other............ **980.00**

California Art Tile, 5-3/4" sq, molded houses in mountainous landscape, road bearing right, dark brown matte glaze, stamped CALIFORNIA ART TILE/ RICHMOND/CALIFORNIA............ **230.00**

California Faience, 5-1/2" d, circular, cuenca dec
Aloe plant in desert landscape, cactus, mountains, and blowing clouds, stamped "California Faience," light abrasion around frame **200.00**
White bell-tower, greens and amber landscape, blue sky, stamped "California Faience" **1,485.00**

De Morgan, William, 6" sq
Designed for William Morris & Co., painted stylized blossoms in Persian blue, eggplant, and green, on an ivory ground, raised circular mark DM/98, two minute corner flecks **270.00**
Three "BBB" tiles, each painted with stylized blossom in Persian blue with purple center, lush green leaves, each stamped with circular mark, edge chips to one, corner chips to another **1,380.00**

Claycraft, 24-tile frieze depicting landscape in low relief, tall trees in shades of brown and green within half-round border, box frame, **$7,475**. Photo courtesy of David Rago Auctions, Inc.

De Porceleyne Fles

4-3/4" x 9", horizontal, cuenca dec, brown leaping hare under branches with red fruit, stamped bottle/TL/Delft, glaze flakes to two corners and one back edge................ **815.00**

13" x 4-3/4", cuenca dec, swan and two young, polychrome crystalline glaze, Stamped bottle/TL/Delft, mounted in new rustic frame **1,100.00**

Empire, from nursery rhymes series, cuerda seca dec, stamped "EMPIRE," mounted in new black frame, each 11-3/4" sq

Daffy Down Dilly, young woman in period dress walking down a cobbled street, few edge chips **2,070.00**

Hush-A-Bye, Baby, toddler in a cradle perched in a tree, few edge chips................................... **1,725.00**

Old Mother Goose, old woman surrounded by children, parrot, dog, and white goose, filled in edge chips **2,070.00**

Grohn, Belgium, 6" sq, cuenca dec, stylized red and amber blossom, indigo ground, stamped numbers, pr **490.00**

Mosaic Faience, 1920s, green and yellow semi-matte ground; one with pink chick; other with pink duck, stamped mark, 4-1/4" x 4-1/4", **$700**. Photo courtesy of David Rago Auctions, Inc.

Grueby

4" sq, cuenca dec, entertwined geese under arc of green trees, blue ground, circular paper label, few small nicks to corner edges **3,775.00**

6" sq, designed by Addison Le Boutillier, cuenca purple tulip and green leaves, lighter green ground, sgd "RE," mounted in period copper trivet frame **4,900.00**

6" sq, designed by Addison Le Boutillier, cuenca yellow tulip and green leaves, darker green ground, sgd "E. S.," mounted in copper trivet frame **4,320.00**

6" sq, designed by Addison Le Boutillier for Dreamwold mansion, Scituate, MA, frieze of white horses against blue sky, green ground, sgd "K.Y.," mounted in copper trivet frame **4,600.00**

6" sq, The Pines, cuenca dec, two trees in a hilly landscape, greens, blues, and brown, sgd "MD," small pock-mark to top of tree, nick to back of corner **6,275.00**

Hemixem, Belgium

6" x 4", four-tile frieze, squeezebag wreath of brightly colored flowers, raised "H MADE IN BELGIUM" **210.00**

12" x 7", two-tile vertical frieze, cuenca dec, green and blue thistle, rich amber ground, marked "H," minute flecks **150.00**

International, 6" sq, "Old Age," old couple and cat, amber glaze, raised I.T.& Co., large chips to two corners, smaller ones along bottom edge, nicks to figures **75.00**

Moravian, "Tempus," depicting Father Time, covered in blue and ivory glaze, red clay showing through, unmarked, small glaze flake to one edge, 10" x 7-1/4", **$1,150**. Photo courtesy of David Rago Auctions, Inc.

Low, J. & J. G., Chelsea, MA

4-1/4" sq, putti carrying grapes, blue, pr **75.00**

6" d, circular, yellow, minor edge nicks and glaze wear **35.00**

6" sq, woman wearing hood, brown **95.00**

Marblehead

4-1/4" sq, matte painted landscape of green trees on hill, sky with indigo clouds, stamped ship mark **1,095.00**

6-1/4" sq, incised sailboat on calm waters, three tones of matte blue-grays, stamped ship mark, mounted in Arts and Crafts frame **4,025.00**

Minton, 8" sq, modeled violin player, after E. Hammond, c1880, amber majolica glaze, velvet and fruitwood frame, light abrasion and surface scratch **260.00**

Oriental framed tile, white heron on blue ground, 11-1/2" x 10", **$150**. Photo courtesy of Joy Luke Auctions.

Newcomb College, 5" sq, carved by E.A. Horner, branches of blue blossoms on green stems, blue-green ground, E.A.H./EW40, 1911, glaze flakes to two corners **2,760.00**

North Dakota School of Mines, 6" sq, four-tile panel, cuerda seca dec Hispano-Moresque pattern, unmarked....... **200.00**

Northwestern Terra Cotta Comp., Chicago, Ill, 4-1/4" x 5-1/2", beige unglazed clay, two putti holding swag of cloth over company name........... **210.00**

Overbeck

5" sq, trivet tile, four pink carved flowers, blue centers, green leaves, matte black ground, incised OBK/EF **2,300.00**

6" sq, surface excised and enamel-decorated with two stylized birds in green and yellow, pink and red wings, within web of Celtic knots, textured beige ground, incised OBK/EH....................................... **8,050.00**

8" d, circular, incised with two young girls in blue-gray frocks, stylized green, red, blue and white landscape, incised OBK/EH, probably made for the Public Works Administration for Central School, Cambridge City, IN, restoration to line...................................... **1,380.00**

Owens

11-3/4" sq each, two-tile frieze, cuenca dec, evergreens in a snowy landscape, stamped OWENS, some surface abrasion, mounted in new rustic frame **6,275.00**

Unmarked, cat motif, light green glaze, **$35**. Photo courtesy of Wiederseim Associates, Inc.

12" x 9", cuenca dec, white and purple geese, dark green ground, stamped OWENS, some abrasion to clay walls, mounted in new rustic frame **1,150.00**

14-1/2" x 30", three-tile frieze, cuenca dec, matte polychrome rural landscape, stamped OWENS, one tile missing in sequence, some pitting to glaze, mounted in new rustic frame **3,775.00**

San Jose, 8" sq, cuerda seca dec, ducks flying near cattails, bright glossy and matte polychrome, unmarked, 2" tight line to one edge, very short one to another **200.00**

Teichert, Ernest, Meissen, 6" sq, emb fleshy red poppies, celadon ground, raised "So. Meissen" **230.00**

Unmarked European, 24" x 8", eight-tile panel, squeezebag laurel wreath, pink, blue, and red primrose, white crackled ground, few minor edge nick **230.00**

Tinware

History: Beginning in the 1700s, many utilitarian household objects were made of tin. Because it is nontoxic, rust resistant, and fairly durable, tin can be used for storing food; and because it was cheap, tinware and tin-plated wares were in the price range of most people. It often was plated to iron to provide strength.

An early center of tinware manufacture in the United States was Berlin, Connecticut, but almost every small town and hamlet had its own tinsmith, tinner, or whitesmith. Tinsmiths used patterns to cut out the pieces, hammered and shaped them, and soldered the parts. If a piece was to be used with heat, a copper bottom was added because of the low melting point of tin. The industrial revolution brought about machine-made, mass-produced tinware pieces. The handmade era had ended by the late 19th century. Today, craftsmen have revived the art and are making interesting copies of period pieces.

Watering can, some rust and corrosion, **$15**.

Anniversary top hat, 11" d, 5-3/4" h, 19th C **1,150.00**

Candle box, 14-1/2" h, cylindrical, hanging, some battering **220.00**

Candle mold

12-1/2" l, 11-1/8" h, 24 tin tubes, double handles **350.00**

17" w, 60 tubes, applied ear handles, minor corner break on base, couple spots resoldered **495.00**

Candle sconces, pr

14" h, round crimped crests, tall ribbed backs, rounded base, hanging holes with small splits **525.00**

14" h, scalloped crest, candle socket, rounded base, label attributes them to tinsmith in Marietta, PA, resoldered, enlarged hanging holes, some rust **220.00**

Chandelier, 29" d, 14-1/2" h, 28" l chain, diamond-shaped body, four arms each with candle socket, old finish, late 19th C, line of small holes on bottom **1,215.00**

Cheese sieve, 6" h, heart shape, resoldered hanging ring **360.00**

Colander, 11" d, 5-3/4" h, conical, two ribbed handles, attributed to Shakers, minor dent in foot......................... **110.00**

Cheese mold, heart shaped, punched circular design in base, applied handle and three feet, 4" w, 4-3/4" d, 2-7/8" h, **$210**. Photo courtesy of Alderfer Auction Co.

Cookie cutter

4-1/8" h, woman, long skirt, punched hole.. **90.00**

Foot warmer, mortised and turned wood frame, punched tin sides with heart and circle design, wire bale handle at top, original tin tray for hot coals on interior, American, slight wear, 9" l, 7-3/4" w, 5-1/2" h, **$200**. Photo courtesy of Cowan's Historic Americana Auctions.

4-3/4" l, tulip, scalloped edge **150.00**

6" h, stylized eagle **200.00**

7-1/4" l, elephant, seams loose **100.00**

9-7/8" h, man with hat............ **195.00**

10" x 14-1/4", rocking horse, with handle **495.00**

12-5/8" h, Uncle Sam, full length, back marked "G.M.T. Co., Germany" **825.00**

Creamer, 4" h, polychrome spray of yellow, green, and red flowers beneath spout, attributed to New York, mid-19th C, minor paint loss........................ **200.00**

Foot warmer

7-3/4" x 9" x 5-3/4" h, punched panels with diamond designs, mortised frame with turned posts, wire bale handle, minor edge damage at post, wire latch missing **110.00**

8-3/4" x 7-3/4" x 6" h, punched panels with heart in circle design, mortised wooden frame with turned posts and incised lines, wire bale handle, refinished.................. **315.00**

9" x 7-1/2" x 5-5/8" h, punched panels with heart in circle design, mortised wooden frame with turned posts, old red stain, wire bale handle, traces of rust, penciled note inside.................................. **200.00**

Lamp, 11" h, orig tin shade attached by wires, oblong font with ring handle, saucer base, brass plaque "SN & HC Ufford...Boston...Kinnear's Patent," old resoldering to base, wear............ **495.00**

Lantern, 17-1/2" h, hanging, old dark green repaint, rococo detail, six panes of glass with reverse painted dec, candle socket in base, attributed to Ohio, one pane with corner missing **420.00**

Squirrel cage, "Lehigh" stamped into side under gable, rotating cage, **$250**. Photo courtesy of Dotta Auction Co., Inc.

Quilt template, 4-5/8" d, star **30.00**

Shore bird, 9" l, 11-3/4" h, outstretched wings, curved tail, orig brown, white and black paint, some flaking, wooden base **295.00**

Snuffbox, oval, marked "Pat'd Jan. 24 1860 G. Parker," American, 3-1/4" l, **$145**. Photo courtesy of Sanford Alderfer Auction Company.

Squirrel cage, 26-1/2" l, 10-1/2" d, 15" h, old patina, house with peaked roof, small cupola with pierced dec on sides, 9" d exercise wheel attached, sliding door missing from one end, flag or weather vane missing **300.00**

Parade flag holder, molded, polychromed, two-part shield with spreadwing gilded eagle in relief above seal of United States shield, tubular tin devices support flag staffs on reverse, America, 19th C, minor wear, dents, 28-5/8" w, 22-1/4" h, **$2,715**. Photo courtesy of Skinner, Inc.

Tea bin, 8-3/4" w, 8" d, 10" h, painted red, litho portrait of pretty young lady, stenciled gold dec, America, 19th C, minor paint loss, price for pr **750.00**

Teapot, 6-1/2" d, spout resoldered **150.00**

Wall pocket, 6-3/4" w, 11-3/4" l, two tiers, extended round top back, punched hanging hole, America, 19th C, minor corrosion..................................... **115.00**

Tinware, Decorated

History: The art of decorating sheet iron, tin, and tin-coated sheet iron dates back to the mid-18th century. The Welsh called the practice pontypool; the French, töle peinte. In America, the center for tin-decorated ware in the late 1700s was Berlin, Connecticut.

Several styles of decorating techniques were used: painting, japanning, and stenciling. Both professionals and itinerants did designs. English and Oriental motifs strongly influenced both form and design.

A special type of decoration was the punch work on unpainted tin practiced by the Pennsylvania tinsmiths. Forms included coffeepots, spice boxes, and grease lamps.

Box, cov, dome top

6-3/4" l, 3-1/8" w, 3-5/8" h, orig dark brown japanning, white band on front panel, green leaves, red cherries, yellow border dec, wire bale handle, tin latch, slight wear **660.00**

11-1/2" l, 5" w, 6-1/4" h, brown japanning, red raped swags, yellow leaves, wavy lines, tin hasp, brass bale handle, int. lined with remnants of glue-on leaves, minor touch-up on front of lid and some edges, some wear....................................... **990.00**

Toleware, basket, Federal, crescent form, reticulated, swing handle, oval base, red paint decoration, hand-painted gilt and black accents, paint loss, splint in handle, 8" l, 5-1/2" d, 8-1/2" h, **$330**. Photo courtesy of Alderfer Auction Co.

13-3/4" l, 8-3/4" d, 9" h, wire and turned wooden handle on lid, yellow scrolled foliate designs, box with red and white swags, yellow leaf embellishments, black ground, America, 19th C **765.00**

Bread tray, 12-1/2" x 8-1/4", red, green, and yellow floral dec, yellow swag border, red edge, black ground, minor paint loss **345.00**

Canister, cylindrical, 6-1/4" h, 6" h, red cherries, green leaves, white border, yellow stylized leaves and swag borders, lid centered with leaf dec, red japanned ground, minor scratches **400.00**

Chandelier, 30" h, yellow and red paint, three circular tiers, 12 candle sockets, tulip-shaped petals, turned wooden column and center finial, 20th C **350.00**

Coal hood, cast iron, brass, and ceramic mounts, S-curved lid, hp fight scene of European red deer, gilt stylized floral surround, top mounted cast white ware ceramic handle with brass mounts, cast iron feet with hidden casters, slot on rear for hand shovel, original hand shovel and interior liner (rusted) present, English, 30 percent gilt missing, painting with minor soil and scratches, 11-1/2" w, 17-1/2" deep, 17-1/2" h, **$375**. Photo courtesy of Cowan's Historic Americana Auctions.

Coal scuttle, 15-1/2" l, 11-3/4" w, rect, sloped hinged lid, painted floral sprays and gold edging to three sides, top handle, coal scoop on back, four cast metal trefoil-paneled feet, removable liner, England/France, late 19th C **245.00**

Coffeepot, cov, goose-neck spout, dome top

10-1/2" h, yellow birds, red pomegranates, yellow stylized leaves, black ground, minor paint loss, lid unattached, repair to finial **1,100.00**

10-5/8" h, flowers and foliage in shades of yellow, green, and red, black ground, America, 19th C, wear **765.00**

Creamer, hinged lid, 4-1/4" h, dark brown japanning, yellow, green, red, and white floral dec, some wear **525.00**

Creamer, blue ground, red flowers, yellow details, wear, **$225**.

Milk can, 8-1/2" h, black japanning, stenciled red and gold stylized floral design **200.00**

Toleware, teapot, Oliver Filley Tinsmiths, yellow bird and fruit decoration, inscribed on underside "H. Case, April 1824," Pennsylvania, paint loss, 11" h, **$1,725**. Photo courtesy Pook & Pook.

Spice box, 7-1/4" d, round, seven int. containers, worn orig brown japanning, gold stenciled labels **175.00**

Sugar bowl, 3-1/2" h, worn orig red paint, brown and yellow comma type foliage, foot slightly battered **190.00**

Tea caddy, 8-1/4" l, dark ground, worn stenciled bronze powder dec, int. lift-out tray fits over two lidded compartments, orig emb brass handle, minor damage **220.00**

Toleware, tray, oval, double handles, hand-painted barroom scene with sailors and dancing woman, paint loss, discoloration, 14-1/2" d, 21-3/4" l, **$450**. Photo courtesy of Alderfer Auction Co.

Tray

- 18-3/4" x 24", scalloped edges, orig orange and tan floral dec on black and gold ground, green leaves, minor wear, bent edge **100.00**
- 28" l, oval, handles cut out to sides, scene of crags beside village painted in center, farmer and livestock in foreground, Europe, mid-19th C **500.00**
- 30" l, 24" w, oval, molded edge, large landscape scene painted in center, fruiting vine surround, faux bois woodgrained ground, mid-19th C **400.00**

Urn, cov

- 13-1/4" h, slender stem, ovoid foot, gilt florals, birds, and butterflies, 19th C, pr **1,725.00**
- Two handles, acorn finials, dec with floral sprays and birds, scalloped floral and repeating gilt leaf borders, weighted base, French, 19th C, some paint loss, minor dents, pr **575.00**

Fruit basket, Regency, japanned decoration, gilt decoration, black ground, English, some scratches, light fading, 12-1/4" l, 6-1/4" w, 3-1/2" h, **$350**. Photo courtesy of Cowan's Historic Americana Auctions.

TOBACCO CUTTERS

History: Before pre-packaging, tobacco was delivered to merchants in bulk form. Tobacco cutters were used to cut the tobacco into desired sizes.

Arrow **35.00**
Brown Mule **40.00**
Climax **50.00**
Drummond's Good Luck Tobacco Cutter, American Machine Co., 16" l **185.00**

Red Tin Tag, Lorillards Chew Climax Plug, brass, made by Penn Hardware Co., Reading, PA, 17-1/4" l, **$115**.

Enterprise Mfg Co., Philadelphia, April 13, 1875 patent **195.00**
Five Brothers Tobacco Co., Louisville, KY **50.00**
Griswold, Erie, PA......................... **70.00**
Little Imp **45.00**

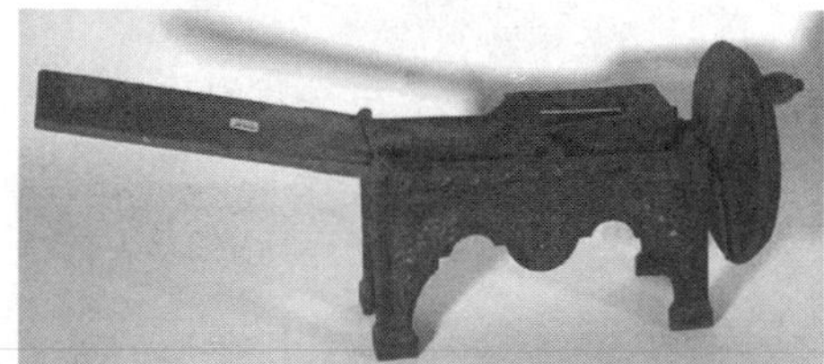

Cast iron, marked "Gesetzl. Geschutzt," **$150**. Photo courtesy of Joy Luke Auctions.

P Lorillard & Co. **95.00**
S A Pace Grocery Co., Corcisana, TX **145.00**
R J R Tobacco Co. **95.00**
Shunhoff Mfg Co., Cincinnati, OH, cast iron **65.00**

TOBACCO JARS

History: A tobacco jar, also known as a tobacco humidor, is a container for storing tobacco. Tobacco humidors were made of various materials and in many shapes, including figurals. The earliest jars date to the early 17th century; however, most examples seen in the antiques market today were made in the late 19th or early 20th centuries.

Boy, kerchief around head and neck, green tea leaf poking out at forehead, red bow tie, eyes glancing to the side, unmarked, **$145**. Photo courtesy of Joseph P. Smalley, Jr., Auctioneer.

Glass and bronze, 6" x 3", Handel, body with painted horse's head, lid with "Cigars," raised scrolled design, marked Handel Ware - 4091H, some minor paint losses **435.00**

Hand painted by Florence Weaver, c1925, Indian bust, multicolored, gold trim and finial, initials on final, blank marked "Favorite, Bavaria," 7-1/4" h, **$250**.

Majolica, figural

- Barrel shape, 6" h, cobalt blue, green, gold, and brown, Doulton, Lambeth, England, #8481, artist's initials **225.00**
- Bear with beehive, 6-1/2" h, Continental **770.00**
- Blackamoor, 6" h, marked "DEP" in circle, c1900, some restoration **330.00**
- Black boy, red hat with tassel, repainted, nicks..................... **275.00**

Indian chief, multi-colored head dress, red head band, red beads at neck, unmarked, **$185**. Photo courtesy of Joseph P. Smalley, Jr., Auctioneer.

- Dog's head, pipe and green hat and collar...................................... **375.00**
- Man with top hat, Sarreguemines **365.00**
- Owl, 11" h, brown, yellow glass eyes **825.00**

Papier-mâché, Mandarin.............. **95.00**

Porcelain, figural

- Bull dog, German.................. **275.00**
- Moose, Austrian **200.00**
- Toby, Shorter and Sons **85.00**

Royal Doulton, Walton Ware, 1910; one depicting Battle of Hastings, 7-1/2" h; other street scene, 5-1/2" h, both cream-color earthenware ground, stamped marks, minor wear, **$365**. Photo courtesy of David Rago Auctions, Inc.

Porcelain, round bowl, metal fittings

- Gray's Pottery, transfer dec of sailing ships, gold luster trim, yellow ship mark "Gray's Pottery, England" **150.00**
- John Marresh, 5" d, 7-1/2" h, wooden barrel shape, dog coming out of the top, dog with open mouth, paws extending over edge of barrel, bottom imp "J M 167", slight char mark on side.......................... **425.00**

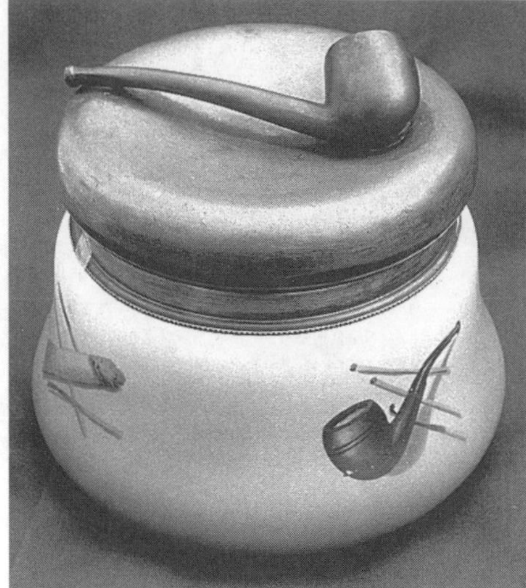

White porcelain base with transfer decoration of pipes, cigarettes, cigars, matches, figural pipe on lid, 6-1/4", **$90**.

- Royal Winton, hp relief scene, marked "Royal Winton, England" **195.00**

Terra cotta, 8" h, dwarf in sack, multicolor dec, marked "JM3478," chips, wear.. **255.00**

Wave Crest, 5" sq, white opaque body, SP fittings.................................... **450.00**

Wood, 7" l, 6-1/2" h, hand-carved walnut, knotty tree trunk, foreground of foliage, rabbit exiting his lair, flowering trumpet fine encircling vase, side inscribed "Viv Le Vin Lamour et le Tabac 1871," fitted lid with carved branch finial **320.00**

TOBY JUGS

History: Toby jugs are drinking vessels that usually depict a full-figured, robust, genial drinking man. They originated in England in the late 18th century. The term "Toby" probably is related to the character Uncle Toby from Tristram Shandy by Laurence Sterne.

Reproduction Alert: During the last 100 years or more, tobies have been copiously reproduced by many potteries in the United States and England.

Bennington type, 9-1/2" h, standing **175.00**

Delft, 11-1/4" h, man seated on barrel, green hat, green and black sponged coat, blue and yellow pants, old cork stopper, c19th C.......................... **365.00**

Kent, James, & Sons, 5-1/2" h, c1900, blue willow dec, yellow vest, brown striped trousers, black shoes....... **495.00**

Luster ware, 6-1/2" h, blue coat, spotted vest, 19th C **175.00**

Majolica, 8-3/4" h, monk **165.00**
Minton, 11-1/4" h, majolica, Quaker man and woman, polychrome dec, imp mark, pr **4,600.00**
Pratt, 10-3/4" h, Hearty Good Fellow, blue jacket, yellow-green vest, blue and yellow striped pants, blue and ochre sponged base and handle, stopper missing, slight glaze wear, c1770-80 .... **1,500.00**

Royal Doulton, gent in black top hat, maroon coat, gold braid trim, **$125**.

Royal Doulton

6-1/2" h, stoneware, blue coat, double XX, Harry Simson **395.00**
8-1/2" h, Falstaff, designed by Charles Noke, D6062, 1939-91 .... **175.00**

Royal Doulton, Neptune, D6652, 1960, 4" h, **$75**.

9" h, Winston Churchill, DT6171 .... **175.00**

Shaker, 5" h, polychrome dec, standing figure, yellow hat, blue coat, and red breeches with pink luster highlights, England, 19th C............................ **150.00**
Shorter Son, Ltd., England, Long John Silver, 9-3/4" h **375.00**
Staffordshire

9-1/2" h, seated, enamel washes, brown coat, blue vest, yellow breeches, blue sponged stockings, green base, colored in flake on rim of hat **220.00**

Staffordshire, seated man, tricorn hat, pitcher of ale on knee, polychrome decoration, indistinct mark, crack in lid, tiny rim flake on hat, 10-1/2" h, **$745**. Photo courtesy of Cowan's Historic.

9-1/2" h, snuff taker, mid-19th C **150.00**

Stoneware, 6-1/2" h, blues, greens, and yellows, seated **75.00**
Unmarked, 11" h, cobalt blue coat, tomato red vest, yellow pants, sitting on corner chair, holding stein, green base, applied strap handle on back, minor hairlines on handle, corner base chip, pipe missing from hand................ **250.00**
Whieldon, 9-1/2" h, pearlware, seated figure, yellow greatcoat, green vest, blue trousers, holding brown jug in left hand, raises foaming glass of ale towards mouth, lid missing, c1770-80 .... **1,600.00**
Wilkinson, 10-3/4" h, Field Marshall Haig, modeled by Sir Francis Carruthers Gould, titled "Push and Go," printed marks, c1917.. **460.00**

Tools

History: Before the advent of the assembly line and mass production, practically everything required for living was handmade at home or by a local tradesman or craftsman. The cooper, the blacksmith, the cabinetmaker, and the carpenter all had their special tools.

Early examples of these hand tools are collected for their workmanship, ingenuity, place of manufacture, or design. Modern-day craftsman often search out and use old hand tools in order to authentically recreate the manufacture of an object.

Anvil, hand forged, 8" **60.00**
Archimedian drill, bit, c1915 .... **50.00**
Awl, bone, 5" l **25.00**
Axe, wrought iron blade, wooden handle old replacement **45.00**

Broad ax, hand forged, early 1900s, 12-1/4" w blade, **$85**.

Bench press, Sherman, solid brass, 12 lbs, 9-1/2" x 6"................................ **65.00**
Blasting machine, 5-3/4" w, 8-1/4" d, 16-1/2" h, early plunger-type detonator, dovetailed mahogany case, brass manufacturer tag "Reliable Blasting Machine No. 3," terminal hardware replaced, overall wear.............. **4,370.00**

Machinist's toolbox, Gerstner, walnut, 11 drawers, 26" w, 9" d, 15-1/2" h, **$390**. Photo courtesy of Joy Luke Auctions.

Clamp, wood, jaws, 13-1/2" l, pr **115.00**
Chisel, blade stamped "E. Connor," 22-1/2" l.. **45.00**

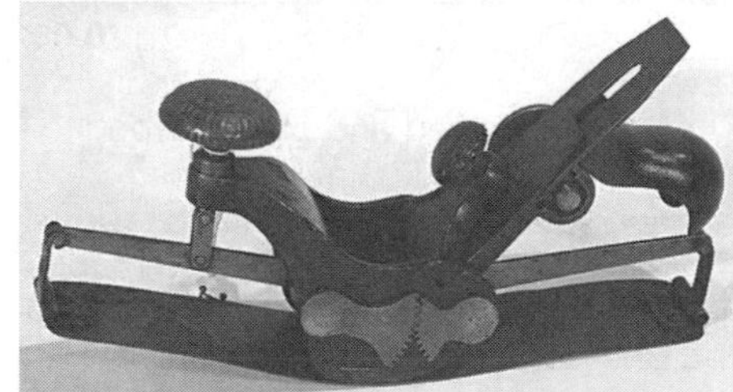

Plane, Stanley, cast iron, type 2, circular, No. 113, 10" l, **$70**. Photo courtesy of Joy Luke Auctions.

Drill, hand, Goodel and Pratt, brass ferrules... **28.00**
File, half round, 20" l **15.00**
Funnel, 9" d, 7-1/2" h, slightly tapered sides, two wooden staves, tapered spout on bottom, cut nails, orig green paint, edge wear, couple of rim chips, attributed to Shakers.................................... **330.00**
Hammer, claw type, Winchester.... **55.00**

Key hole saw, British, 15-1/2" l...... **30.00**
Level, wood and brass, Stanley, rosewood, patent 1896, 30" l........ **150.00**
Mallet, burl, hickory handle, 34" l **200.00**
Mitre box, laminated maple, birch, and oak, graduated quadrant, Stanley **45.00**

Sugar nips, wrought iron, engraved decoration, 9-3/4" l, **$165**. Photo courtesy of Sanford Alderfer Auction Company.

Plane
- Keen Kutter, K110 .... **45.00**
- Ohio Tool Co., walnut, inscribed with carpenter's name, 9-1/2" l **25.00**
- Stanley, #10-1/2...................... **120.00**
- Varvill & Son, York, England, boxed bead molding planes, 9-1/2" l, 10-pc set.. **595.00**
- Winchester Repeating Arms Co. No. 3208, smoothing, metallic, mahogany handles, 9" l.......... **185.00**

Router, Stanley, #71-1/2", patent date 1901.. **40.00**

Planes, wooden, Baldwin, two Sandusky, Mornanell, **each $45**. Photo courtesy of Dotta Auction Co., Inc.

Rule, Stanley, #32, two-fold, 12" l, caliper **120.00**
Saw
- Band, mortised and pinned wood frame, orig red paint with blue and white striping, black and lade guides, laminated cherry and maple top, 76"................................ **300.00**
- Buck, wood, worn varnish finish, marked "W. T. Banres," 30" **45.00**
- Dovetail, Hague, Clegg & Barton, brass back, 9" l........................ **95.00**

Keyhole saw, British, 15-1/2" l, **$30**.

- Turning, W. Johnson, Newark, NJ, Richardson blade, 21" l.......... **165.00**

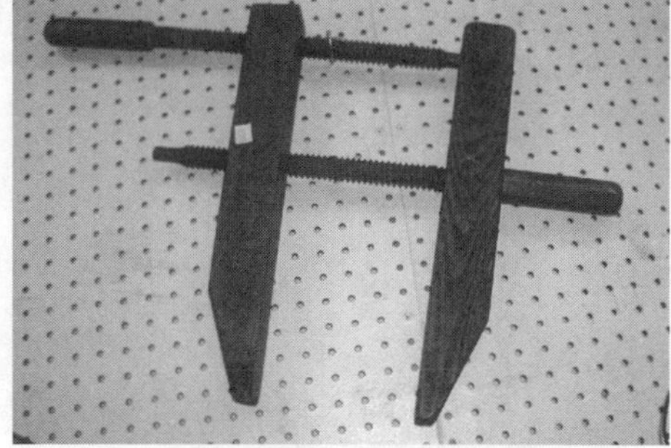

Wood clamp, adjustable, **$45**.

Screwdriver, flat wood handle, round sides, 9" blade.............................. **35.00**
Scribe, curly maple adjustable fence and arm, 21" l **75.00**
Shoot board, Stanley, No. 51/52, orig decal, 14" l................................ **1,295.00**
Tool chest, 36" w, 17-1/2" d, 14-1/2" h, poplar, birch, and ash, orig red paint, old worn white on rect raised panel in center of lid, molded base, paneled ends with steel handles and hasp **250.00**
Wagon wrench............................. **30.00**
Wheel measure, wrought iron, 14-1/2" l **45.00**

Toothpick Holders

History: Toothpick holders, indispensable table accessories of the Victorian era, are small containers made specifically to hold toothpicks.

They were made in a wide range of materials: china (bisque and porcelain), glass (art, blown, cut, opalescent, pattern, etc.), and metals, especially silver plate. Makers include both American and European firms.

By applying a decal or transfer, a toothpick holder became a souvenir item; by changing the decal or transfer, the same blank could become a memento for any number of locations.

For more information, see *Warman's Glass*, 4th edition.

Figural, frog and snail, green glass, **$140**. Photo courtesy of Joy Luke Auctions.

Bisque, skull, blue anchor-shape mark **68.00**

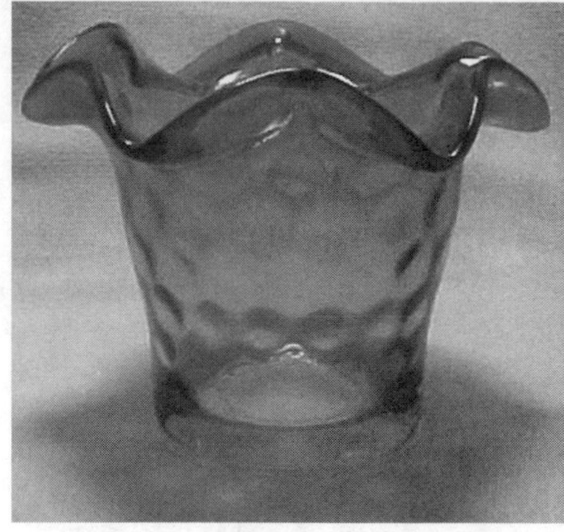

Amberina toothpick holder, inverted thumbprint type optic, made by New England Glass Company, Hobbs Brucknier, or Libbey, late 19th century, hand-crimped ruffled edge, nice shading, ground pontil, and considerable wear on base, 3-1/4" d, 2-1/2" h, **$85**. Photo courtesy of Michael Krumme.

Burmese, Mt. Washington, flared painted blue rim, white blossoms with yellow centers, molded ferns and scrolls at base, 2-1/2" h, **$1,085**. Photo courtesy of Clarence and Betty Maier.

Burmese, 2-1/2" h, shiny, soft peach blush fading to buttery-yellow, eggshell-thin body..................................... **425.00**
China
- Royal Bayreuth, elk **120.00**
- Royal Doulton, Santa scene, green handles.................................... **75.00**
- R. S. Germany, Schlegelmilch, MOP luster.. **40.00**

Glass
- Amberina, DQ, sq top **350.00**
- Cameo, Daum Nancy, winter scene, sgd **750.00**
- Cranberry, coralene beaded flowers **285.00**
- Cut, pedestal, chain of hobstars **145.00**
- Libbey, Little Lobe, hp violets, blue beading around top **250.00**

Opalescent, Reverse Swirl, blue 85.00

Figural, two cupids with barrel on backs, blue glass, footed, **$195**. Photo courtesy of Wiederseim Associates, Inc.

Pattern glass

Arched Fleur-De-Lis **45.00**
Carnation, Northwood **75.00**
Daisy and Button, blue **75.00**
Delaware, rose stain, gold dec **175.00**
Fandango, Heisey **55.00**
Hartford, Fostoria **85.00**
Jewel with Dewdrop **55.00**
Kansas **45.00**
Kentucky, green, gold trim **125.00**
Michigan, clear, yellow stain **175.00**
Paneled 44, Reverse, platinum stain **75.00**

California pattern, aka Beaded Grape, green, beaded edge, worn gold trim, 2-1/2" h, **$65**.

Texas, gold trim **50.00**
Truncated Cube, ruby stained **75.00**
US Coin, colorless, frosted Morgan one dollar coin, c1892 .... **290.00**

Tortoiseshell Items

History: For many years, amber and mottled tortoiseshell has been used in the manufacture of small items such as boxes, combs, dresser sets, and trinkets.

Note: Anyone dealing in the sale of tortoiseshell objects should be familiar with the Endangered Species Act and Amendment in its entirety. As of November 1978, antique tortoiseshell objects can be legally imported and sold with some restrictions.

Also see *Celluloid* for imitation tortoiseshell items.

Bottle from traveling case, mushroom-shaped threaded tortoise shell lid, nickel and cork stopper, 19th C, 5" h, **$170**. Photo courtesy of Cowan's Historic Americana Auctions.

Bellows, 20-1/8" l, 8" w, Continental, late 19th C, coromandel backing, front with premier part Renaissance-style scroll inlay, woven leather panel over brass tip **575.00**

Box, cov, 2-1/2" d, 1" h, enamel insert on lid surrounded by gold band, hp enamel with seated woman in garden looking into mirror held by putti, French, loss to tortoise shell **450.00**

Cane, 35-1/3" l, 2-1/3" w x 3-1/2" h carved handle, crook head of swan preening feathers, 1" gold-plated collar dec with diagonal lines and orig owner's initials, briarwood shaft, 1-1/3" white metal and iron ferrule, American, c1890, minor roughness to beak **700.00**

Cigar case

5-1/2" l, rect, case inlaid with three-color gold, reserve with vacant silver cartouche, hinged, pink silk lined int., fitted, expandable, Victorian, 19th C **450.00**

5-5/8" x 2-7/8", rect, silver inlaid crane and foliate stalks, brass border with clasp, silk lined int., monogrammed, Continental, late 19th C **550.00**

Cigarette case, 4-1/4" l, domed oval, applied central carved monogram, Continental, late 19th/early 20th C **325.00**

Clock, mantel, 4-3/8" w, 3-1/2" d, 9-1/8" h, George III-style, early 20th C, balloon shape, enamel dial with Roman numerals, silver plated banding on front, four plated ball feet **950.00**

Clock, travel, 4-3/8" l, 3-3/4" w case, 3-3/4" l watch, London, c1910, rect black morocco case with tortoiseshell panel on front in silver surround, enclosing nickel-cased watch with eight day movement **290.00**

Comb and hairpin, gold lacquer dec, Japan **230.00**

Diary, 3-3/4" x 2-5/8", silver inlaid floral bouquet and bird, silk lined int. fitted with pencil, monogrammed, French, late 19th C **400.00**

Display case, 21" w, 11-1/2" d, 19-1/2" h, veneer and ebonized, pieced gallery with finials over single door, conforming base, ebonized compressed bun feet, Dutch **1,080.00**

Hair comb, intricately carved 3-1/2" w band, 4" l prongs, **$65**.

Dresser box, 4" l, 3-1/2" w, 2-1/8" h, Birmingham, England, 1901, maker's mark "L. & S.," heart shape, hinged lid with tortoiseshell inlaid with silver harp and ribbon tied husk swags, husk surround, velvet-lined interior, three short ball and claw feet **575.00**

Dressing table mirror, 7" w, 5-1/4" d, 8-1/4" h, Regency-style, mid-19th C, oval mirror plate in ivory surround, round ivory standards on tortoiseshell columns, ormolu finial, breakfronted with tortoiseshell and ivory base, four ormolu female herm supports **1,265.00**

Etui, 1-7/8" w, 1-1/2" d, 3-1/2" h, French, mid-19th C, tapered rect form, hinged lid with sloping sides, scalloped silver mounts at edges, fitted int. with four utensils, glass perfume bottle **550.00**

Hair comb, row of rose-cut diamonds spaced by bezel-set oval rubies, mounted in silver-topped gold,

Edwardian, French hallmarks, price for pr **1,645.00**

Lorgnette, 3-1/2" l closed, silver border with floral details, applied tortoiseshell over engine-turned ground, lever action, maker's mark rubbed, Continental, late 19th C **150.00**

Miniature, mandolin, 5-1/4" l, tortoiseshell, ivory, and mother-of-pearl, Continental **175.00**

Razor box, 7" l, 3" w, 1-3/4" h, rect box set with stylized monogram on lid, gold mountings, ebonized bun feet, William Comyns & Sons, London, c1904-5, sold with four ivorine straight razors (three Wilkinson, one German) **1,150.00**

Scent box, 2-1/4" h, trapezoid, blond tortoiseshell veneer, divided int. compartments, late Regency, c1825, scent bottles missing.................... **375.00**

Snuffbox, dark tortoise shell box, white beaded floral designs covered with glass and gold band edge, inscribed "Belonged to Jedida Dewer in 1784," losses, 3" d, **$275**. Photo courtesy of Sanford Alderfer Auction Company.

Snuff box, 3-3/8" l, 1-7/8" w, 1-1/8" d, book form, realistically modeled, tortoiseshell on front and back, cover set with oval silver plate formal miniature of 18th C boy and girl, sgd lower left "D. Drouris(?)" **350.00**

Tea caddy, two compartments on interior with tortoiseshell lids and ivory surround, pine frame covered with tortoise shell, satinwood bun feet, original foil lining, English, 19th C, 6" l, 3-1/2" d, 4-1/2" h, **$2,600**. Photo courtesy of Cowan's Historic Americana Auctions.

Tea caddy, English, early 19th C, tortoise shell veneered, ivory mounts, silvered-copper ball feet, escutcheon and monogrammed reserve, interior with two covered compartments, 6-3/4" w, **$1,800**. Photo courtesy of Sloan's Auctioneers & Appriasers.

Tea caddy, English, late 18th/early 19th C

4-3/4" w, 3-3/8" d, 4-3/8" h, rect, hinged lid, small brass plate and escutcheon, int. fitted with tortoise shell veneered cover, some small losses **885.00**

6-3/4" w, 3-5/8" d, 4-1/2" h, rect, light matched panels, domed lid with plain silvered plaque, plain sq escutcheon, hinged lid opening to two lidded wells...................**2,185.00**

7-5/8" w, 4" d, 4-1/4" h, rect, dark mottling, serpentine front, silvered escutcheon and lid with monogrammed silvered cartouche, hinged lid opening to two lidded compartments, bands of ivory veneer at perimeter, molded base **2,530.00**

Toys

History: The first cast-iron toys began to appear in America shortly after the Civil War. Leading 19th-century manufacturers include Hubley, Dent, Kenton, and Schoenhut. In the first decades of the 20th century, Arcade, Buddy L, Marx, and Tootsie Toy joined these earlier firms. George Brown and other manufacturers, who did not sign or label their work, made wooden toys.

Nuremberg, Germany, was the European center for the toy industry from the late 18th through the mid-20th centuries. Companies such as Lehman and Marklin produced high-quality toys.

Today's toy collectors have a wonderful assortment to choose from. Many specialize in one company, time period, or type of toy, etc. Whatever their motivation, their collections bring joy. Individual collectors must decide how they feel about the condition of their toys, whether they prefer mint-in-the box or gently played with examples or perhaps even toys that have been played with extensively. Traditionally, the toys in better condition have retained their values more than those in played-with condition. Having the original box, instructions, and/or all the pieces, etc., adds greatly to the collectiblity, and therefore the value.

Toy collectors can find examples to add to their collections at most of the typical antique and collectibles marketplaces, from auctions to flea markets to great antique shows, like Atlantique City, and even shows and auctions that specialize only in toys.

Additional Listings: Characters, Disneyana, and Dolls. Also see *Warman's Americana & Collectibles* and *Warman's Flea Market* for more examples.

Notes: Every toy is collectible; the key is condition. Good working order is important when considering mechanical toys. Examples in this listing are considered to be at least in good condition, if not better, unless otherwise specified.

Arcade, cast iron, Greyhound bus, #385, 7-3/4" l, **$90**. Photo courtesy of Joy Luke Auctions.

Arcade, USA

Auto, cast iron, Model A Landau sport coupe, three-window, green with gold pin striping, opening rumble seat, nickel-plated spoke wheels, orig white rubber tires marked "The Republic Rubber Co.," 6-1/2 Toys, l, driver missing, some paint flaking **175.00**

Bus, open top, white rubber tires, 1930s **3,500.00**

Fire trailer truck, red, blue fireman, detachable trailer, hose reel and ladder turntable, 16" l, ladders missing, paint loss **325.00**

Ice truck, cast iron, Mack, railed open bed body, rear platform, rubber tires, emb sides, painted blue, 6-7/8" l **275.00**

Arcade, Farmall tractor, driver, disc, cast metal, **$740**. Photo courtesy of Joy Luke Auctions.

Milk truck, cast iron, Borden's, painted green, classic milk bottle design, rubber tires **1,430.00**
Pick-up truck, cast iron, "International" decals on door, painted bright yellow, black rubber tires, 9-1/4" l, some rust on left side **330.00**
Racer, Bullet, cast iron, classic bullet-shaped body, painted red, nickeled driver and mechanic, side pipes, and disc wheels, emb "#9" on side **550.00**
Stake truck
Ford Model T, 1927, 9" l **600.00**
Mack, No. 246X, 1929, 12" l **1,400.00**
Tank, cast iron, camouflage painting, large metal wheels, 7-1/4" l **330.00**
Thresher, McCormick-Deering, gray and cream wheels, red lining, chromed chute and stacker, 12" l **320.00**
Tractor, cast iron, McCormick Deering tractor and baler, painted gray, red pin-striping highlights, nickel-plated driver, 17 Toys, ... **350.00**
Trolley, Greyhound, New York World's Fair, blue and orange, nickel driver, decals, three cars with tinplate canopies, black tires, 16" l, some chipping and scratching **635.00**
Wrecker, cast iron, Mack, No. 255, 1930, 12-1/2" l **1,500.00**

Arnold, Germany

Mac motorcycle, complex mechanism allows helmeted rider to mount cycle, accelerate forward, stop and dismount, marked "U.S. Zone, Germany," 7-1/2" l, overall soiling **480.00**

Bandai, Japan

Auto, Rolls Royce, Silver Cloud, tin, 12" l **115.00**

Bing, Gebruder, Germany

Auto, tin, clockwork, center door model, black, seated driver, radiator cap ornament, spare tire on rear, 6-1/4" l **385.00**
Garage, litho tin, double doors, extensive graphics, houses sedan and roadster **550.00**
Limousine, litho tin wind-up, red, maroon and orange striping, orig driver, c1910, 5-1/4" l **690.00**
Open tourer, four seater, litho tinplate, gray-green, black and yellow lining, red button seats, black wings, front steering, orange and gray wheels, twin lamps, windscreen frame, hand-brake operated clockwork motor, c1915, 12-1/2" l, chauffeur missing, lamps detached **2,400.00**
Touring car, driver, tinplate, clockwork motor, front steering, 6-1/2" l **230.00**

Brenco, England

Phaeton, garage, tin touring auto with opening hood, fold down windshield, wind-up action, 12" l litho garage with brick façade, opening doors, orig box hand inscribed "From Father Christmas," copyright 1921 .... **415.00**

Brevete

Autoscooter, bumper car, battery operated, orig box **2,200.00**

Britains, England

Airplane, single wing, military, six cylinder rotary engine, painted mustard color, white rubber tires, c1920, 9" wing span **2,250.00**
Armored car, army green, white rubber tires, swiveling turret gun, orig box, 4-1/2" l **150.00**

Buddy L, steam shovel, pressed steel, **$285.**

Buddy L, USA

Airmail truck, black front, hood fenders, enc cab, red body and chassis, 1930, 24" l **675.00**
Airplane, catapult airplane and hangar, 5000 Monocoupe, olive/gray hangar, 1930, 9-7/8" wingspan **950.00**
Auto, Coupe, rect decal, near mint, 11" l **1,725.00**
Cement mixer truck, red body, white side ladder, water tank, mixing drum, 1965, 15-1/2" l **75.00**
Dump truck
Husky, yellow hood, chrome one-pc wraparound bumper, 1969, 14-1/2" l **75.00**
Hydraulic Construction, medium blue front, large green dumper, 1967, 15-1/4" l **50.00**
Jr Dumper, avocado cab, tiltback dump section, 1969, 7-1/2" l **335.00**
Electric Emergency Unit wrecker, white pressed steel, rear hoist, 16-1/2" l, paint wear and staining **215.00**
Express Line delivery truck, black pressed-steel, front steering and rear doors, 24" l **750.00**
Fire truck
Aerial, 38" l, some loss to nickel on extension ladders **1,380.00**
GMC fire pumper, red, aluminum finish ladders, chrome bar grille, horn, 1958, 15" l **150.00**
Ladder truck, red, bright metal grille and headlights, two white ladders, 1939, 24" l **100.00**
Greyhound bus, pressed steel, clockwork, bright blue and white, "Greyhound Lines" on sides, rubber tires, 16" l **275.00**
Mining train, engine, five work cars, 12 pcs of circular track, 3-1/2" l **1,725.00**
Overhead yard crane, pressed steel, five crank action pulleys, 45" l, 12" w, 33" h **2,760.00**
Set
Fire department set, aerial truck, fire pumper with action hydrant, two plastic hoses, two plastic fireman, fire chief's badge, 1960 .... **250.00**
GMC Highway Maintenance Fleet, orange truck, trailer, sand and stone dump truck, scoop-n-load conveyor, sand hopper, steel scoop shovel, four white steel road barriers, 1957 .... **300.00**
Western Roundup set, turquoise fenders, hood, cab and frame, white flatbed cargo section, six sections of rail fencing, standing horse, cowboys, calf, steer, 1960 .... **175.00**
Telephone maintenance truck, No. 450, two-tone green, ladder, two poles, orig maker's box **350.00**
Tractor, Husky, bright yellow body, large rear fenders, black engine block, 1966, 13" l **50.00**
Truck
Pick up, rag top, rect decal, near mint, 11" l **2,200.00**
US Mail, olive green, orig decals **125.00**

Cast iron, unknown American makers

Dump truck, green Mack style front, C-cab, red bed with spring lever, spoked nickel wheels, 7-3/4" l **490.00**
Gasoline truck, blue, Mack-style front, C-cab, rubber tires, one tire missing, 7" l **200.00**
Milk wagon, black cast-iron horse, gilt harness, yellow wheels, blue steel wagon body, 6-3/4" l **150.00**
Stake truck, Ford Model A, red, 7" l **200.00**

Champion

Auto, cast iron, coupe, painted red, nickeled grill and headlights, rumble seat, rubber tires, spare mounted on trunk, 7" l, repainted **250.00**
Gasoline truck, cast iron, painted red, Mack "C" cab, tanker body, emb on sides, rubber tires, 8-1/8" l **385.00**

Racer, cast iron, painted red, silver trim, wind deflector on rear, separately cast driver painted blue, nickeled disc wheels, 8-1/2" l **1,815.00**
Stake truck, cast iron, painted red, Mack "C" cab, stake side body, nickeled spoke wheels, 7" l **660.00**
Truck, cast iron, "C" Mack cab, blue body, 7-3/4" l, replaced wheels **195.00**
Wrecker, cast iron, red C-cab with crane, nickel plated crank and barrel, rubber tires, 8-1/4" l **330.00**

Chein, Popeye with parrot cages, litho tin windup, walks forward, rolling cages at side, 8-1/2" h, **$230**. Photo courtesy of James D. Julia, Inc.

Chein

Barnacle Bill, tinplate, red hat, clockwork walking mechanism, 6-1/4" h........ **290.00**
Disneyland ferris wheel, clockwork motor, bell, six gondolas, litho Disney characters and fairgrounds scenes, 16-3/4" h, distortion and paint loss **350.00**
Hercules ferris wheel, clockwork motor, bell, six gondolas, litho children and fairground scenes, 16-1/2" l **325.00**
Wagon, horse-drawn, "Fine Groceries," tinplate, 12" l **290.00**

Chromolithograph paper on wood, unknown maker

Bagatelle game, two clowns with cup hats, patent date "March 7, 1895," 15" l **290.00**
Brownie Ten Pins, set of 10 different Palmer Cox Brownie figures, each with printed poem on reverse about their character, © Palmer Cox 1892, two mallets and three balls, wood box **1,150.00**
Noah's Ark, incised and applied dec, hinged roof, four carved humans, 40 animals, 19" l hull.......................... **750.00**
Trinity Chimes, eight chimes, cathedral scenes, upright case, 18" h.......... **150.00**

Citroen, France

Aviation fuel truck, pressed steel, clockwork, painted red, enclosed cab with opening driver's door, tanker body with filler cap and brass drain valve, electric headlights, rear decal "AVIA," 18" l **1,350.00**
5CV, open tourer, two-seat, blue boat tail body, black wings and wheels, gray tires, front steering and clockwork motor, orig maker's box, 12" l **2,070.00**
Fire engine, painted tin, clockwork, red, open bench seats, removable hose reel, ladders mount on rear body, disc wheels, rubber tires, orig box, 18" l **2,900.00**
Race car, pressed steel, clockwork, blue, molded seated figure with hand painted composition head, rubber tires, decal "Petite Rosalie," 12-1/4" l............. **450.00**

CKO

Cabrio Super Coupe, tin friction, MIB **1,000.00**

Converse, USA

Heffield Farms delivery wagon, articulated horse, 21-1/2" l, considerable wear and paint loss **320.00**
Klondike Ice Co. delivery wagon, tinplate on wood, two litho horses, 17" l, paint poor **175.00**
Trolley, open sides, pressed steel, blue and mustard, stenciled dec, marked "City Hall Park 175" on both ends, reversible benches, large clockwork motor, 16" l, paint poor, destination boards missing **260.00**

Corgi

Ambulance, Chevrolet Superior, white body, orange roof, Red Cross decals, 4-3/4" l.. **30.00**
Auto
- Chevrolet Impala, pink body, 4-1/4" l **50.00**
- Datsun 240Z, red body **15.00**
- Ford Mustang Fastback, metallic lilac, metallic dark blue, silver, or light green body **30.00**
- Ford Zephyr Estate Car, light blue, 3-7/8" **30.00**
- Jeep CJ-5, dark metallic green body **10.00**
- Mercedes-Benz 240D, silver, blue, or copper body, working trunk **10.00**
- MGA, red or metallic green body **60.00**
- Porsche Carrera 6, white body, red or blue trim **30.00**
- Renault 16TX, metallic blue body **20.00**
- Volkswagen 1200 Driving School **25.00**

Camera van, Commer Mobile, metallic blue body, black camera on gold tripod, cameraman, 3-1/2" **60.00**
Car transporter, Bedford, black diecast cap, 10-1/4" l **100.00**
Character cars
- Batmobile, glossy black body, gold tow hook **200.00**
- Captain Marvel Porsche, white body, 4-3/4" l **20.00**
- James Bond Aston Martin, metallic silver body, diecast base, red int., two figures, working roof hatch, ejector seat.................................... **100.00**
- Kojak's Buick Regal, metallic bronze brown body **25.00**
- Popeye's Paddy Wagon **195.00**
- Supervan, silver, Superman decals, 4-5/8" l **15.00**

Helicopter, Chopper Squad, blue and white body **20.00**
Set
- Agricultural, No. 55 Fordson Tractor, No. 51 Tipping Trailer, No. 438 Land Rover, No. 101 Flat Trailer, 1962-64 .... **280.00**
- British Racing Cards, No. 152 Lotus, No. 151 PRM, No. 150 Vanwall, 1959 .... **150.00**
- Corporal Missile, No. 112 missile, No. 1113 ramp, No. 1118 army truck **350.00**
- Emergency set, No. 339 Land Rover police car, No. 921 police helicopter **30.00**
- Tarzan, metallic green No. 421 Land Rover, trailer, dinghy, cage, five figures **100.00**

Tractor, Ford 5000, blue body, yellow scoop arm and controls, chrome scoop, 3-1/8" l.. **55.00**
Van, Coca-Cola 5" l diecast metal and plastic replica, copyright 1978, 2-3/4" x 6" x 3-1/2" color box with display window **35.00**

Cor-Cor

Automobile, Graham, 1936, 20" l, pressed steel, brown and beige, full running boards, black rooftop, electric headlights, spare disc wheels, emb "Cor-Cor Toys," chromed grill and rubber tires, restored **935.00**
- Green, electric headlights, switch on side, rubber tires, metal wheels, chromed grill, restored.......... **660.00**

Bus, sheet metal construction, green, orange wheels, "Inter City" decals on side, bench seats diecut from window wells, 23-1/2" l.............................. **990.00**
Dump truck, black body, orange bed and wheels, pressed steel, 23-1/2" l **260.00**
Stake truck, sheet-metal construction, black, brown stake body and rear

platform, rubber tires, emb "Cor-Cor" on sides 770.00
Truck, sheet-metal construction, enclosed black cab, green van body, rear platform, large painted metal wheels, 23" l 825.00

Courtland Toys

G-Man
Gun........ 50.00
Siren 75.00
Log truck, #620, pressed steel, 1936, 13" l........ 175.00

Cragstan, Mechanical Monkey Batter, painted tin windup, 7-1/2" h, original box, **$750**. Photo courtesy of Joy Luke Auctions.

Dent, USA

Auto, sedan, 1930, cast iron, painted blue, partial black paint on roof, nickeled wheels, spare on rear, 7-1/2" l, repainted 330.00
Contractor's truck, cast iron, Mack, painted red, dual dump gondolas, open frame, nickeled disc wheels, painted centers, emb on sides, 7-1/2" l 1,050.00
Dump truck, cast iron, green-gray, Mack-style front, C-cab, driver, red spoked wheels, spring-operated bed, swinging tailgate, 7" l, paint loss 320.00
Fire patrol, cast iron, open-seat truck, rail sided open-bed body, rear platform, disc wheels, 5-3/4" l........ 220.00
Taxi, cast iron, painted orange and black, repainted seated driver, replaced painted disc wheels........ 315.00
Transfer wagon, cast iron, open seat, wagon painted orange, flared sides, seated driver on full width bench set and splash board sides, marked "Transfer," yellow spoked wheels, pulled by three horses, 18" l........ 1,100.00

Dinky

Airplane
Autogyro, gold, blue rotor, 1934-41 .... 90.00
Bristol Beinhem, 1956-63........ 20.00
Douglas DC3, silver, #60t, 1937-41 .... 125.00
Lockheed Constellation, #66b, 1940 .... 70.00
Percival Gull, camouflaged, #66c, 1940 .... 100.00
Ambulance, Range Rover, #268, 1974-78........ 25.00
Auto
Cadillac Eldorado, #131, 1956-62 .... 60.00
DeSota, Diplomat, orange, F545, 1960-63........ 70.00
Ford Fairlane, pale green, #148, 1962-66........ 30.00
Jaguar XK 120, white, #157, 1954-62 .... 120.00
Mustang Fastback, #161, 1965-73 .... 45.00
Studebaker Commander, F24Y, 1951-61........ 65.00
Triumph TR-2, gray, #105, 1957-60 .... 60.00
Volkswagen 1300 sedan, #129, 1965-76........ 20.00
Bulldozer, Blaw Knox, #561........ 45.00
Bus, Routemaster, #289, 1964-80 .... 75.00
Motorcycle, Police Motorcycle Patrol, #42B, 1946-53........ 30.00
Police car, Citroen DS19, #F501, 1967-70........ 75.00
Taxi
Austin, #40H, 1951-52........ 60.00
Ford Vedette, F24XT, 1956-59 .... 80.00
Plymouth Plaza, #266, 1960-67 .... 60.00
Tractor
David Brown, #305........ 35.00
Field Marshall, #37N/301........ 60.00
Massey-Harris, #27A/300........ 50.00
Truck
Austin Van, Nestle's, #471........ 60.00
Foden Mobilgas Tanker, #941 .... 145.00
Leland Tanker, Shell/BP, #944 .... 125.00
Royal Mail Van, #260........ 65.00

Distler, Germany

Toonerville Trolley, litho tin wind-up, trolley rolls forward with rocking action, animated Fontaine Fox character at controls, copyright 1922, 7" h........ 50.00

Fisher Price, USA

Amusement Park, #932, 1963 .... 55.00
Butch the Pup, #333, 1951 .... 65.00
Cotton Tail Cart, #700, 1951........ 165.00
Donald Duck Delivery, #715, 1936 .... 365.00
Donald Duck xylophone
#177, 1946 .... 275.00

Fisher Price, Donald Duck, pull toy #185, copyright 1938 W.D.P., some wear to paint, one wooden wheel split, **$275**. Photo courtesy of James D. Julia, Inc.

#185, 1938 .... 500.00
Fido Zito, #707, 1955 .... 50.00
Gabby Goose, #120, 1936 .... 45.00
Jumbo Jitterbug, #422, 1940 .... 70.00
Kitty Bell, #499, 1950........ 80.00
Pull-A-Tune xylophone, #870, 1957 .... 40.00
Pushy Elephant, #525, 1934........ 350.00
Teddy
Xylophone, #752, 1948 .... 200.00
Zilo, #777, 1950........ 40.00

Gilbert, Uncle Sam, gravity toy, c1920, slight wear, 8" x 7", **$460**. Photo courtesy of James D. Julia, Inc.

Fleischman, Germany

Ocean liner, litho tin wind-up........ 1,300.00

Gibbs, US

Overland covered wagon, animated paper on wood, horses pull canvas cov tin and wood wagon, cast wheels, 19" l, loss to paper covering........ 180.00

Gunthermann

Fire truck, five figures, orig ladders **7,500.00**

Hot Wheels, Mattel, vintage, MIP

Audi Avus, #453, red **4.00**
Big Bertha, #489, Nite Force **2.50**
Blue Angels, pink **100.00**
Boss Hoss, #6406, 1971 .... **75.00**
Buzz Off, #6976, blue, 1974 .... **90.00**
Captain America, #2879, white, 1979 .... **175.00**
Cement Miser, #6452, 1970 .... **60.00**
Circus Cats, #3303, white, 1975 ... **75.00**
Custom Police Cruiser, #6269, 2969 .... **200.00**
Datsun 200XS, #3255, maroon, Canada, 1982 .... **175.00**
Dune Daddy, #6967, light green, 1975 .... **75.00**
Early Times, Tail Dragger **20.00**
El Rey Special, #8273, light blue, 1974 .... **1,200.00**

Hot Wheels, collector's case, blue, holds 24 vehicles, Mattel, played with condition, **$25**.

Emergency Squad, #7650, red, 1975 .... **65.00**
Fire Engine, #6554, red, 1970 ..... **100.00**
Flat Out 442, green, Canada, 1984 .... **150.00**
Fuel Tanker, #6018, 1971 .... **200.00**
Funny Car, Mongoose, red **20.00**
Grand National Roadster Show, 33 Ford Roadster, red **18.00**
Heavy Chevy, #6408, 1970 .... **200.00**
Hot Heap, #6219, 1968 .... **65.00**
Incredible Hulk Van, #2850, white, 1979 .... **125.00**
Jet Threat, #6179, 1976 .... **60.00**
Jurassic Park, helicopter, aqua **45.00**
Letter Getter, #9643, white, redline, 1977 .... **550.00**
Letter Getter, #9643, white, blackwall, 1977 .... **15.00**
Lexmark, Passion, white **20.00**
Lotus Turbine, #6262, 1969 .... **60.00**
Mantis, #6423, 1970 .... **60.00**
Maxi Taxi, #9184, yellow, blackwall, 1977 .... **60.00**
Motorcross Team Van, #2853, red, 1979 .... **125.00**
Neet Streeter, #9510, chrome, 1976 .... **40.00**
Olds 442, #6467, 1971 .... **800.00**
Poison Pinto, #9240, green, blackwall, 1977 .... **30.00**
Police Cruiser, #6963, white, 1973 .... **550.00**

Hot Wheels, rows of MIP cars, sold for various prices. Photo courtesy of Sky Hawk Auctions.

Porsche 911, #6972, orange, 1975 .... **65.00**
Race Ace, #2620, white, 1968 .... **75.00**
Red Baron, #6963, red, blackwall, 1977 .... **25.00**
Rescue Ranger, #45, red **12.00**
Sand Drifter, #7651, green, 1975 .... **375.00**
Silhouette, #6209, 1979 .... **90.00**
Sir Sidney Roadster, #8261, yellow, 1974 .... **90.00**
Six Shooter, #6003, 1971 .... **225.00**
Super Van, #9205, chrome, 1976 .... **40.00**
Sweet 16, #6422, 1970 .... **75.00**
Tow Truck, #6450, 1970 .... **55.00**
T-Totaller, #9648, brown, blackwall, 1977 .... **40.00**
Twinmill II, #8240, orange, 1976... **35.00**
Volkswagen, #7620, orange, bug on roof, 1974 .... **60.00**
Warpath, #7654, white, 1975 .... **110.00**
Whip Creamer, #6457, 1970 .... **50.00**
White's Guide, '56 Flashsider, gold **18.00**
Z Whiz, #9639, gray, redline, 1977 .... **70.00**

Hubley, Lancaster, PA

Airplane, cast iron, Air Group Commander USS Enterprise, plane, name on fuselage, hard rubber tires, orig camouflage paint **75.00**

Hubley, cast iron, pumper with rubber tires, red body, #2167, **$250**. Photo courtesy of Joy Luke Auctions.

Auto, cast iron
- Chrysler Airflow, battery operated lights, 1934 .... **1,250.00**
- Coupe, 1928, 8-1/2" l **600.00**
- Lincoln Zephyr and trailer, painted green, nickeled grill and bumper, 13-1/2" l **825.00**
- Sedan and trailer, painted red sedan, trailer panted silver and red, rubber tires, factory sample tag, 9-1/2" l **715.00**
- Streamlined Racer, 5" l **400.00**

Bell telephone, cast iron, 8-1/4" l, painted green, silver sides, emb company name, Mack "C" cab, nickeled ladders, long handled shovels, pole carrier, spoked wheels, repainted **250.00**
Boat, cast iron, painted red, emb "Static" on sides, sleet form, seated driver, hand on throttle of attached motor, chromed air cleaner, painted orange, three tires, clicker, 9-1/2" l, over painted **1,650.00**
Bus, cast iron, service coach, 5" l **700.00**
Cement mixer truck, cast iron, red and green, nickel tank, rubber wheels, Mack, 8" l, restored **1,760.00**
Delivery truck, Merchants, 1925, 6-1/4" l **400.00**
Fire truck, cast iron
- Fire Engine, 5" l, 1930s **75.00**
- Fire Patrol, 7-men, 1912, 5" l **3,575.00**
- Hook and ladder, 1912, 23" l **1,850.00**
- Ladder truck, 5-1/2" l **40.00**

Log truck
- 12" l, Kiddie Toy Log Truck, pressed steel **90.00**
- 19" l, diecast **145.00**

Merchants delivery truck, cast iron, 6-1/4" l, 1925 .... **400.00**

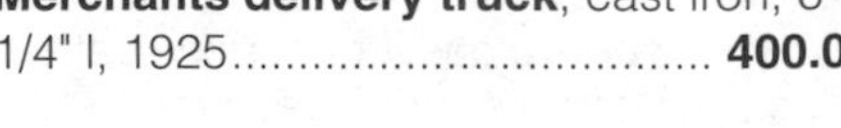

Hubley, racing car, cast metal, moveable cylinders, 1938, **$465**. Photo courtesy of Joy Luke Auctions.

Milk truck, cast iron, painted white, emb "Borden's" on side panel, rear opening door, nickeled grill, headlights, and spoke wheels, 7-1/2" l, repaired headlights **1,980.00**

Motorcycle, cast iron, Crash Car, 1930s, 9" l **900.00**

Overland circus

Bandwagon, two white horses with riders pulling six-pc band on wagon with driver, 14-1/2" l, some chipping to horses **920.00**

Caged bear, two white horses with riders pulling caged bear in elaborate circus wagon, cast iron, orig reins, 14" l **460.00**

Racer, cast iron

Painted blue, painted red articulated pistons, seated driver, black tires, spoked wheels, 10-1/2" l **1,760.00**

Painted red, seated driver, emb "#1" on sides, rubber tires, 7-3/4" l **385.00**

Road roller, Huber, cast iron, painted green, large fancy spoke wheels painted red, figure stands on rear platform, 7-1/2" l **1,320.00**

Santa and sleigh, cast iron, galloping reindeer pull ornate sleigh with replaced Santa, 16" l **750.00**

Stake truck, cast iron, two piece mold, chassis and hood painted red, stake body and cab painted blue, six rubber tires, 6-1/2" l **375.00**

Street sweeper, Elgin, cast iron, uniformed driver, 1930, 7-1/2" l **3,750.00**

Taxi cab, painted orange and black, separate driver chassis and luggage rack, rubber tires, yellow cab stencil on rear doors, 8-1/4" l, professionally restored **470.00**

Tow truck, cast metal, Ford, 1950s, 7" l **50.00**

Wrecker, cast iron, 5" l **60.00**

Ives, Bridgeport, CT

Cuzner trotter, red tinplate carriage marked "Pat'd March 7, 1871," black spoked wheels, white horse with articulated legs, driver with striped trousers, black hat, brass clockwork motor, 11-1/2" l, some chipping **2,590.00**

Steamer, King, clockwork motor, black and red hull, brown superstructure with single funnel, 10-1/2" l, some wear **345.00**

Japanese

Electro, Teddy the Artist, battery operated, with orig damaged box **225.00**

Frankonia, Y-Japan, Happy the Clown Puppet Show, battery operated, MIB **200.00**

Japanese, San, painted tin toy friction operated truck "Children – Truck," truck bed decorated with Christmas items, 8" l, **$115**. Photo courtesy of Joy Luke Auctions.

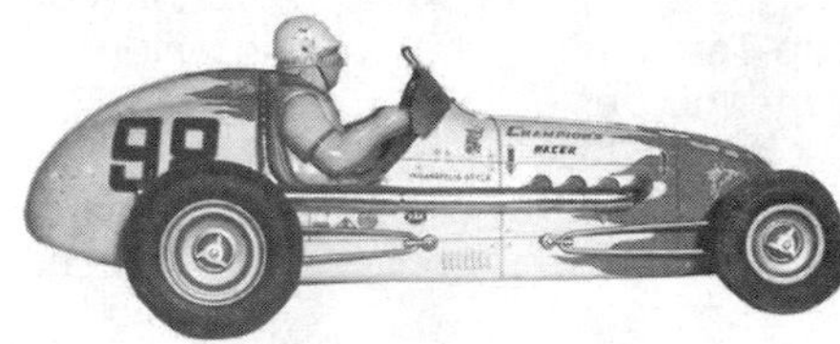

Japanese, E.T. Co., painted tin toy friction operated Indianapolis Style racing car with driver, "Champions Racer 98," 19" l, **$1,750**. Photo courtesy of Joy Luke Auctions.

Tomiyama, Flying Circus, battery operated, orig box **500.00**

TPS, Climbing Linesman, battery operated, orig box **450.00**

Kenton, Kenton, OH

Bus, Nile Coach, cast iron **750.00**

Elephant and clown chariot, remnants of silver paint and red blanket, yellow spoked wheels, detachable clown, 6-1/4" l, considerable paint wear and chips **130.00**

Kenton, road scraper, #151, cast iron, green body, nickel plated blade, rubber tires, **$150**.

Farm wagon, cast iron, orig driver, one upright broken off, good paint, 11-1/2" l **165.00**

Fire pumper, cast iron, painted red, gold boiler top and lamps, driver, white tires, 10-1/4" l, some chipping **230.00**

Kenton, fire pumper, horse drawn, cast iron, two black and one white horse attached to movable triple hitch, metal link reins that attach to driver seated on the top, removable 9" long rubber hoses with brass ends on each side, slight aging, 98 percent original paint, 22" l, 7" w, 8-1/4" h, **$165**. Photo courtesy of Hake's Americana & Collectibles.

Hose reel, cast iron, three white horses, white carriage and reel, driver, hose, and spoked wheels, 13-3/4" l, horses repainted, other paint poor **435.00**

Overland circus, horse drawn wagon, two horses

Band, six musicians, driver, orig white, red, blue, yellow, and gold paint, 16-1/2" l **650.00**

Polar bear in cage, driver, two out riders, orig labeled box, 14-1/2" l **525.00**

Sulky and driver, nickeled cast iron, red spoked wheels, 5" l **115.00**

Tractor trailer set, all cast iron, tractor painted red, orange tanker, two speed stake trailers, nickeled disc wheels, 22" l **1,210.00**

Touring car, cast iron, painted white spoke wheels, cast headlamps and lanterns, 7-3/4" l, replaced figures **250.00**

Yellow cab, cast iron, painted orange and black, white disc wheels, orange centers, 6-1/2" l **495.00**

Keystone, litho tin fire station, red, white, green, and gold, **$650**.

Keystone Mfg. Co., Boston

Air mail plane, olive green, three propellers, 25" **1,600.00**

Ambulance, canvas cover and stretcher, 27-1/2" l **1,000.00**

Bus, Coast to Coast, blue, 31-1/4" l **1,200.00**

Dump truck, open cab, crank dumping mechanism, red hubs, black rubber tires, 27" l **420.00**

Moving van, black cab, red body, rubber tires, 26-1/4" **1,000.00**

Packard ride-on water tower, tower, nozzle, tank, and seat, lg. 32" l **1,035.00**

Police patrol truck, decals, 27-1/2" l **700.00**

Railroad train, engine tender, gondola, and work crane, all with individual steering, 65" l **1,800.00**

Steamroller, red roof, 21" l, minor wear **520.00**

World's Greatest Circus truck, six removable animal cages, 26-1/4" l **2,500.00**

Kilgore, Canada

Airplane, cast iron, Seagull, painted red, nickeled wheels and wing mounted propeller, 7-3/4" l **880.00**
Auto, open roadster, 1928, cast iron, painted blue, nickeled wheels and driver, decal reads "Kilgore, Made in Canada," 6-1/8" l **825.00**
Delivery truck, cast iron, Toy Town, painted red, emb on side panels, gold highlights, silver disc wheels, 6-1/8" l, repainted **360.00**
Dump truck, cast iron, painted blue enclosed cab, red dump body, lever to lift, nickeled disc wheels, 8-1/2" l **330.00**
Ice cream truck, cast iron, enclosed cab painted blue, orange body, emb "Arctic Ice Cream" on sides, disc wheels, 8" l **420.00**

Kingsbury Toys, Keene, NH

Auto, Cadillac sedan, four doors, sliding sun roof, army green, white rubber tires marked "Kingsbury Toys, Keene, N.H.," wind-up, 14-1/2" l, possibly repainted **350.00**
Blue Bird racer, black details, U.S. and U.K. flags, 20" l **4,140.00**
Dump truck **200.00**
Streetcar, orange, black bumpers, No. 781, 9-1/4" l, scratching and chipping **200.00**

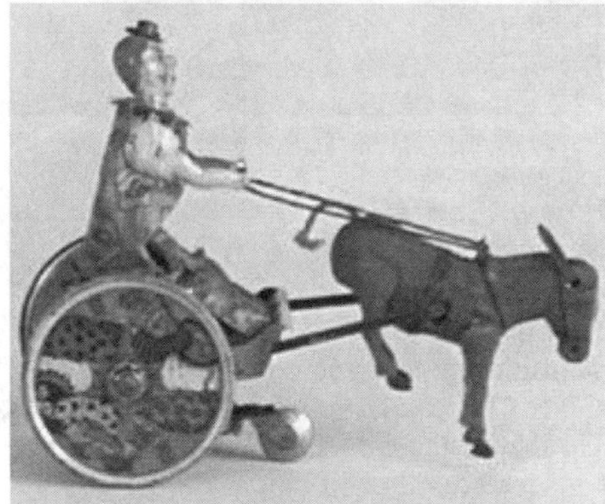

Lehmann, donkey with clown cart, litho tin windup, earlier version with hand-painted tin arms and pants, flocked finish on Donkey, 7-1/2" l, **$115**. Photo courtesy of James D. Julia, Inc.

Lehmann, Germany

Aha, #550, litho tin wind-up, delivery van, open area for driver, 5-1/2" l **460.00**
Hip-Hop, bunny **45.00**
Kadi, litho tin wind-up friction, two walking Chinamen, carrying tea chest marked "Kanton, Peking, Shang Hai," 7" l **480.00**
Naughty Boy, wind-up, father vs son animation, copyright 1903, 5" l **875.00**
New Century Cycle, wind-up, hp Victorian rider tips hat and waves cane as tricycle vehicle rolls forward, back rear passenger holds spinning umbrella, 5" l, refinished blue gilt trim **420.00**
Oho, litho tin wind-up, green, open style vehicle with chauffer, copyright 1903, 4" l **230.00**
Paak-Paak, #645, litho tin wind-up, Mother duck tows basket full of animated ducklings, 7-1/2" l **320.00**
Paddy and the Pig, hp, cloth dressed, copyright 1903, 6" h, clothing shows wear **900.00**
Tap-Tap, wind-up, hp, walking white porter pushes delivery cart, 5-1/2" h **460.00**
Tut-Tut, hp driver, orig working squeak bellows, 7" l **840.00**

Lindstrom

Circus, Greatest Show on Earth, circus wagon being pulled by elephant **625.00**

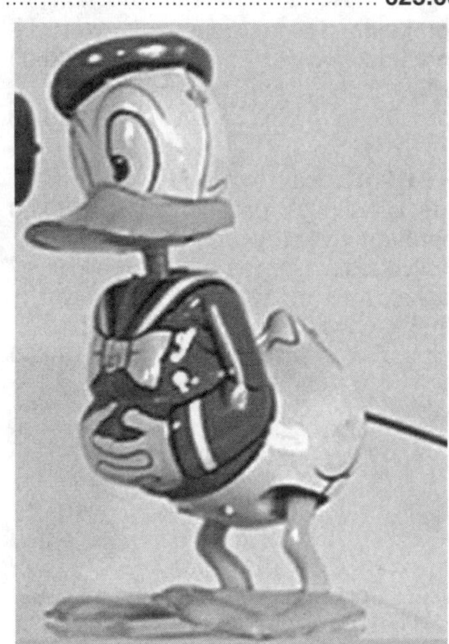

Linemar, Hopping Donald, mechanical, tin, copyright W.D.P. Japan, hopping action with spring action nodding head, 6" h, **$210**. Photo courtesy of James D. Julia, Inc

Linemar, Japan

Donald Duck, Huey, Louey, and Dewey Marching Soldiers, clockwork motor, rubber titles, 11-1/4" l, scratches **375.00**
Mickey Mouse with xylophone, litho, clockwork motor, black, red, and yellow, foliate dec on xylophone, orig box lid, 7" h, chips, tears to lid **750.00**
Popeye, rowboat, battery-operated tinplate, orig controller and maker's box **9,200.00**

Martin, Paris, France

Violin player, well dressed lead footed gentleman plays violin as he vibrates around, hp features, well marked top hat with Martin logo, Paris, France, 8" h **575.00**

Marx, Amos & Andy, lithograph tin wind-up, Fresh Air Taxi, **$600**. Photo courtesy of Skinner, Inc.

Marx, Louis & Co., NY

Airplane

- American Airlines, flagship, pressed steel, wood wheels, 1940, 27" wingspan **200.00**
- Bomber, metal, wind-up, four propellers, 14-1/2" wingspan **100.00**
- Floor Zeppelin, 1931, 9-1/2" l **225.00**
- Hangar with one plane, 1940s **150.00**
- Lucky Stunt Flyer, litho tin wind-up, 1928, 6" l **150.00**
- Pan American, pressed steel, four engines, 1940, 27" wingspan **90.00**
- Sky Flyer, biplane and Zeppelin, 8-1/2" h tower, 1927 .... **225.00**
- Trans-Atlantic Zeppelin, litho tin wind-up, 1930, 10" l **225.00**

Amos 'n' Andy taxi, fresh air taxi rolls forward, black radio and comic characters on board, copyright "Correll & Gosden," 8" l, hand crank missing under radiator and windshield **375.00**

Marx, Merry Makers, litho tin windup, 1930s, four mice playing piano, 9-1/2" h, **$660**. Photo courtesy of James D. Julia, Inc.

Auto

- Army car, battery operated **65.00**
- Dippy Dumper, celluloid Brutus, litho tin wind-up, 1930s, 9" l **350.00**

Marx, Charlie McCarthy Car, litho tin windup, minor touch up to rear wheel, 8" l, **$200**. Photo courtesy of James D. Julia, Inc.

Marx, Popeye the Pilot, litho tin built-in key, copyright 1940 KFS, slight wear, 8" l, 7" w, 5-1/4" h, **$525**. Photo courtesy of Hake's Americana & Collectibles.

Falcon, plastic bubble top, black rubber tires **50.00**
Jalopy, tin driver, friction, 1950s **150.00**
Leaping Lizzie, litho tin wind-up, 1927, 7" l **250.00**
Queen of the Campus, four college students, 1950 .... **250.00**
Rocket Racer, tin litho, 1935 .... **275.00**
Siren police car, 1930s, 15" l **75.00**
Speed racer, 1937, 13" l **250.00**
Streamline Speedway, two litho tin wind-up racing cars, 1936 .... **175.00**

Cycle, helmeted and goggled rider with gun and holster, wind-up action activates siren and circular motion, 8-1/2" l **175.00**

Donald Duck Duet, litho tin wind-up, jointed Goofy does a jig as Donald beats drum, copyright 1946, 10-1/2" h, Goofy missing ears **420.00**

Honeymoon Express, clockwork motor, circular base **100.00**

Joe Penner and his duck, walks forward with tipping hat and moving cigar, litho tin wind-up, 8-1/2" h, soiling and light abrasions **175.00**

Popeye and parrots, tinplate, clockwork motor, 8-1/4" h **350.00**

Ring-A-Ling Circus, litho tin wind-up, ringmaster at center of toy ring, spins with raised cane, directs four circus performers, base with litho circus parade antics, pre-war, 8-1/2" h **700.00**

Set, Circus, 26" l tin litho circus tent, plastic circus animals, trapeze artists, clowns, strong men, etc., tin stages with backdrops of sideshow entertainers **115.00**

Truck
Auto Transport, Mack, dark blue cab, dark green trailer, wind-up, 1932, 11-1/2" l **150.00**
Dump truck, yellow cab, blue bumper, red bed, 1950, 18" l **100.00**
Gravel truck, pressed steel cab, red tin dumper, 1930, 10" l **100.00**
Mack towing truck, dark green cab, wind-up, 1926, 8" l **175.00**
Pet shop truck, plastic, six compartments with vinyl dogs, 11" l **125.00**
RCA television service truck, plastic Ford panel truck, 1948-50, 8-1/2" l **175.00**
Royal Oil Co., Mack, dark red cab, medium green tank, wind-up, 1927, 8-1/4" l **200.00**
Searchlight, toolbox behind cab, 1930s, 10" l **150.00**
Stake bed, pressed steel, wooden wheels, 1936, 7" l **65.00**

U. S. Army division tank, No. 392, green, detailing, recoiling gun barrel, clockwork motor with start/stop action, 9-1/2" l **60.00**

Zippo the climbing monkey, multicolored litho tinplate, pull-string mechanism, 10" l **60.00**

Matchbox

Aston Martin DB2 Saloon, metallic light green, 1958 .... **20.00**
Big Bull, orange, 1975 .... **5.00**
Boat and trailer, white full, blue deck, 1970 .... **3.00**
Case Tractor Bulldozer, red body, yellow base, 1969 .... **5.00**
Chevrolet Impala, taxi, orange, 1965 .... **10.00**
Daimler ambulance, silver trim, red cross on roof, 1958 .... **40.00**
Desert Dawg Jeep, #20 .... **4.00**
Ford GT, yellow or white body, 1965 .... **20.00**
Ford Perfect, #30, 1956 .... **20.00**
Fork lift truck, red body, yellow hoist, 1972 .... **5.00**
Harta tractor shovel, orange, 1965 .... **20.00**
Hi Ho Silver, #15 .... **8.00**
Horse drawn milk flat, orange body, 1954 .... **25.00**
Land Rover Fire Truck, 1966 .... **10.00**
Leyland Royal Tiger Coach, silver-gray, 1961 .... **10.00**
London Bus, red body, 1965 .... **5.00**
Mercedes Benz Coach, white, 1965 .... **30.00**
MGA sports car, white body, 1958 .... **50.00**
Mod Tractor, #25 .... **10.00**
Morris Minor 1000, dark green, 1958 .... **20.00**
Peterbilt Quarry Truck, #30, 1982 .... **2.00**
Plymouth Grand Fury police car, white body, black detailing, 1979 .... **5.00**
Prime Mover, 1957 .... **20.00**
Rolls-Royce Phamton V, 1964 .... **15.00**
Safari Land Rover, 1965 .... **8.00**
Setra Coach, #12, 1970 .... **5.00**
Shunter, #24, 1978 .... **4.00**
Snowtrac Tractor, red body, silver painted grille, 1964 .... **10.00**
Swamp Rat, #30, 1976 .... **2.50**
Thames Wreck, red body, 1961, 2-1/2" **15.00**
Weatherhill Hydraulic Excavator, decal, 1956 .... **20.00**

Nylint, tin, Pepsi Cola truck, scratches to original paint, **$40**. Photo courtesy of Joy Luke Auctions.

Modern Toys

Kitchen set, living set with cupboard, Mickey Mouse and Donald Duck on box, other characters on toy, tin, orig box **550.00**

Pratt & Letchworth

Dray wagon, cast iron, open bed wagon, single slat slides, wooden floor, standing

figure, red spoke wheels, one horse, 10-1/4" l 175.00
Hook and ladder truck, cast iron, horse drawn, one red and one white horse, black frame with red detailing, spoked wheels, seated front driver, seated rear steerer, two wood ladders and bell, 23" l 460.00
Surrey, cast iron, open carriage, low splash board, two full width seams with arm and back rests, emb upholstering mounted on two prs of spoked wheels, pulled by one horse, c1900, 14" l 990.00

Rich Toys, Illinois

Milk wagon, Borden's horse drawn milk wagon, stenciled wood and tin horse pulls well marked milk and cream wagon, tin litho adv graphics, 19-1/2" l, loss of litho to one side 150.00

Schieble

Airplane, single motor, blue body, yellow wings, red and yellow tail, balloon type metal tires, decal of pilot and passengers, all orig, 26-3/4" wing span, 29" l 350.00

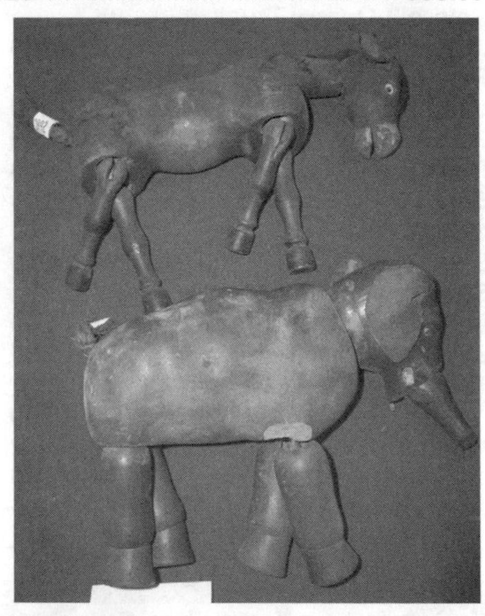

Schoenhut, donkey and elephant, played with condition, **$375**.

Schoenhut, USA

Koko the Clown, orig woven tag with 1920 copyright, orig clothes...... 8,000.00

Schuco, trademark of Schreyer and Co., Germany

Acrobat bear, yellow mohair, glass eyes, embroidered nose and mouth, turns somersaults when wound, orig key, 1950s, 5" h.................................... 575.00
Hopsta dancing monkey, red and yellow, baby mouse, clockwork motor, 4-1/2" h 175.00
Mercedes Simplex, wind-up, 8-1/2" l 125.00
Porsche microracer, No. 1037, red, key missing 55.00
Set, Highway Patrol, squad car, 1958 .... 100.00
Tank, keywind 40.00
Tumbling monkey...................... 100.00
Van, battery operated, 4" l 75.00

Skoglund & Olson, Sweden

Coupe, cast iron, painted gray, spare tire mounted on rear, rubber tires, red disc wheels, 8" l, repainted 550.00
Farm tractor, cast iron, painted blue, red traction wheel, seated nickel driver, replaced steering wheel........... 1,100.00
Pick-up truck, cast iron, painted yellow, enclosed cab, low side body, removable tailgate, rubber tires, red disc wheels, 10-3/4" l, repaired 950.00
Sedan and ramp, cast iron, green touring sedan with spare tire, resting in gray car ramp, 7-1/4" to 14-1/4" l, overpainted 1,870.00
Wrecker, cast iron, painted white, red winch and crane on open body, rubber tires, painted red disc wheels, sides emb "Central-Garage," 11-3/4" l........ 1,540.00

Smith-Miller

Custom Fred Thompson limited editions, 1980s-1990s. Sold by Aumann Auctions, Oct. 20, 2002, Nokomis, IL. Serially numbered limited edition issues, no original Smith-Miller trucks, known as Smitty Toys and made from 1945 until 1954 were reproduced or reissued by Thompson's resurrected Smith-Miller Corp.

Auto transport
- Smith Miller auto transport, cream color, red fenders 925.00
- Smith Miller auto transport, Mack tractor, red 1,000.00
- Smith Miller auto transport, Mack tractor, yellow 950.00

Fire truck, Smith Miller fire department ladder truck 575.00
Moving van
- Lyon Van Lines 575.00
- Mayflower World Wide Movers van 900.00
- Smith Miller "Smitty" Van Lines, red tractor and trailer.................... 900.00

Tanker, Mobilgas tanker 625.00
Truck, Pacific Intermountain Express, truck and trailer 925.00
Wrecker
- Cleveland Coast to Coast Wrecking Co., yellow tractor trimmed in blue, 12-wheel open semi trailer 1,000.00
- Smitty's Garage Union 76 Wrecker 975.00

Strauss, Ham and Sam, litho tin windup, dated 1921, toy in good condition, original box in fair condition, 6-1/2" w, **$635**. Photo courtesy of James D. Julia, Inc.

Strauss, Ferdinard, Corp., New York City

Flying graf zeppelin, aluminum, clockwork mechanism, maker's box, 16" l, some tabs broken........................ 290.00
Jazz Bo Jim, litho tin wind-up, banjo playing jointed black man dances atop roof of cabin with highly graphic with black caricatures lithographed on all sides, 10" h 450.00
Red cap porter, bulldog popping out of trunk, lid missing, uniform faded.. 230.00
Santee Claus, lithograph tinplate with two reindeer and clockwork motor, arms missing 375.00
Tombo, Alabama Coon Jigger, litho tin wind-up, black gentleman in Sunday attired tap dances on stage, copyright 1918, 10" h................................. 550.00

Structo

Bearcat Auto, 16" l, 1919 .... 850.00
Cement mixer truck, 18-1/2" l, 9" h 150.00
Climbing military tank, green, 1929 .... 450.00
Contractor truck, orange dump truck, 1924....................................... 525.00
Fire insurance patrol, 18" l, 1928 .... 250.00
Fire truck, hydraulic hook and ladder, pressed steel, red, 3" l................. 175.00
Log truck, #940, pressed steel ... 150.00
Motor dispatch, blue, decals, 1929, 24" 850.00
Sky King airplane, blue, gray wings, 1929....................................... 900.00

Sturdy Toy

Water tower, two rubber hoses, rubber tip on end of water tower, 33" l, unplayed with condition 5,300.00

Tinplate, unknown makers

Mickey Mouse sweeper, litho tin, Mickey and Minnie making music on piano, 7-1/2" w, 24" l 215.00
Struwelpter/Slovenly Peter from Heinrich Hoffman's story, tinplate wind-up, tuft of straw hair, German 1,850.00

German U.S. Zone, painted tin toy key-wind monkey on tricycle, original box, **$95**. Photo courtesy of Joy Luke Auctions.

Unknown maker, probably Germany, 19th C, Noah's Ark, boat painted green, creamy yellow, and ochre, lift off cover, several carved and painted pairs of animals, 8-5/8" l, 4-5/8" h, **$2,000**. Photo courtesy of Skinner, Inc.

Unknown maker, drum, litho, red sides with parading children, white top, **$50**.

Tonka

Boat transport, 1960, 38" l **250.00**

Construction

- Aerial sand loader, #0922, 1955 .... **275.00**
- Cement Mixer, #0620, 1962 ..... **85.00**
- Road grader, #0600, 1953 .... **75.00**
- Trencher, #0543, 1963 .... **40.00**

Fire truck, Rescue van, 1955 ...... **200.00**

Mini

- Camper, #0070, 1963 .... **75.00**
- Livestock Van, 1964, 16" l **50.00**
- Stake truck, #0056, 1963 .... **35.00**

Truck

- Air Express, #0016, 1959 .... **350.00**
- Car Carrier, #0040, 1960 .... **100.00**
- Carnation Milk delivery van, #0750, 1954 .... **200.00**
- Deluxe Sportsman, #0022, 1961 .... **100.00**
- Farm state truck, 1957 .... **190.00**
- Green Giant Transport semi, 1953 .... **150.00**
- Service truck, #001, 1960 ...... **100.00**
- Wrecker truck, #0018, 1958 .... **100.00**

Tootsietoy

Airplane

- Low wing **20.00**
- Top wing **20.00**

Auto

- Auburn Roadster **15.00**
- Buick Roadster **20.00**
- Cadillac Brougham **40.00**

Bus

- Cross Country **30.00**
- GMC Greyhound, 1948 .... **20.00**

Cannon

- Army tank, six wheels, 1950s... **10.00**
- Long range **8.00**

Construction

- Caterpillar bulldozer **25.00**
- Grader **20.00**
- Steamroller **75.00**

Truck

- Chevrolet delivery van **25.00**
- Ford F6 pickup, 1949 .... **20.00**
- International Sinclair Oil, 6" l **35.00**
- Mack B-line cement truck, 1955 .... **20.00**

Unique Art, Kiddy Cyclist, litho tin windup, bell rings as boy pedals, 9" h, **$150**. Photo courtesy of James D. Julia, Inc.

Unique Art, Newark, NJ

Dog Patch Band, litho tin wind-up, comic characters playing piano, copyright 1945, 7-1/2" h **435.00**

Sky Rangers, litho tin wind-up, 7" single wing plane and blimp circle 8" h lighthouse tower **90.00**

Wilkins

Ladder truck, pressed steel chassis, cast driver and operator, red spoked wheels, clockwork motor and ladder, 13-1/4" l, old repainting **230.00**

Steam pumper, cast iron, two black and one white horse, yellow frame, red wheels, nickeled boiler, 21" l **690.00**

Wolverine Supply & Mfg. Co.

Mystery car, pressed down action propels all tin 3-window coupe forward, 13" l, some dimpling to roof **150.00**

Zilotone, clown like tin figure plays 6 different tunes on xylophone, 8" w **700.00**

Wyandotte Toys, Humphreymobile, litho tin windup, copyright Ham Fisher, original box with tattered end flaps, 7" h, **$420**. Photo courtesy of James D. Julia, Inc.

Wyandotte, USA

Dump truck, pressed steel, white rubber tires marked "Wyandotte Toys," 1930s, 12-1/2" l **150.00**

Engineer Corps truck, 17-1/2" l **75.00**

Land cruiser auto set **50.00**

Lumber truck

- Lumber Supply, 1952, pressed steel, four logs, 10-1/4" l **50.00**
- Lumber truck, 1956-57, pressed steel, three logs, 11-1/2" l **50.00**
- Lumber truck, 1956-57, pressed steel, three logs, 24" l **65.00**
- Timberland Lumber Supply, 1950, pressed steel **70.00**

Sand hopper set, 7" l **20.00**

Zephyr roadster, rubber wheels, 13-3/8" l **400.00**

TRAINS, TOY

History: Railroading has always been an important part of childhood, largely because of the romance associated with the railroad and the prominence of toy trains.

The first toy trains were cast iron and tin; wind-up motors added movement. The golden age of toy trains was 1920 to 1955, when electric-powered units and high-quality rolling stock were available and names such as Ives, American Flyer, and Lionel were household words. The advent of plastic in the late 1950s resulted in considerably lower quality.

Toy trains are designated by a model scale or gauge. The most popular are HO, N, O and standard. Narrow gauge was a response to the modern capacity to miniaturize. Today train layouts in gardens are all the rage and those usually feature larger scale trains.

Notes: Condition of trains is critical when establishing price. Items in fair condition and below (scratched, chipped, dented, rusted, or warped) generally have little value to a collector. Accurate restoration is accepted and may enhance the price by one or two grades. Prices listed below are for trains in very good to mint condition, unless otherwise noted.

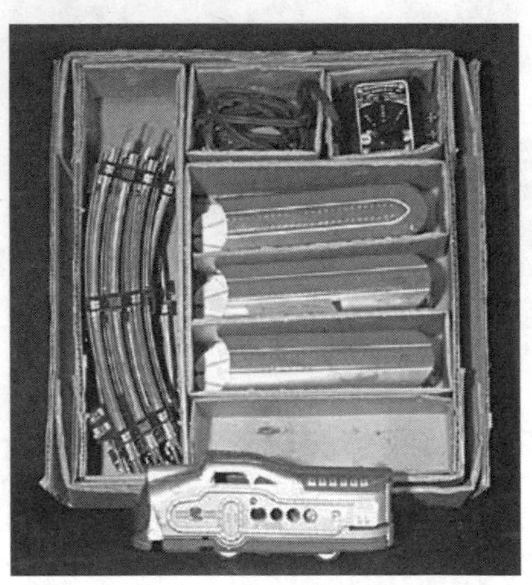

Marx tin toy train set: diesel Union Pacific engine, three passenger cars, track, transformer, original box, **$295**. Photo courtesy of Joy Luke Auctions.

American Flyer

Accessories, S-gauge
- Coal loader............................**140.00**
- Log loader with two flat cars **150.00**

Box car, #988, S gauge.............. **125.00**

Flat car, S gauge, carrying semi-tractor-trailer rig with caged circus animals **170.00**

Locomotive
- New Haven Electric, #499......**325.00**
- Northern Pacific, #377 and 378, diesel............................**350.00**
- Northern Pacific, #470, 471, and 473, diesel............................**310.00**
- Northern Pacific, #490 and 492, diesel............................**350.00**
- Santa Fe, #484, three unit diesel **500.00**
- Steam, #322, 4-6-4................**160.00**
- Union Pacific, #336, steam, 4-8-4, tender............................**480.00**

Passenger, American Flyer's World's Greatest Show circus **80.00**

Refrigerated car, #981 .... **100.00**

Set, S-gauge, circus train, red stem loco #353, tender **250.00**

Set, S-gauge, passenger
- #4340, #4341, two-tone red, brass trim **320.00**
- #4653 electric locomotive, two Bunker Hill coaches, Yorktown observation car, orange, pre-war **865.00**

Tank car, #910, Gilbert............... **175.00**

Tanker, #912, Koppers................. **65.00**

Bing, German

Locomotive, O gauge, pre-war
- Clockwork, cast iron, no tender, headlight missing....................**70.00**
- Live steam, 0-4-0, minor fire damage, no tender................**815.00**

Set, #1 gauge, passenger, litho, dark maroon, lettered "Pennsylvania Lines," combine #1250, coach #1207...... **435.00**

Ives

Baggage car, #50, 1908-09, O gauge, four wheels, red litho frame, striped steps, white/silver body, sides marked "Limited Vestibule Express, United States Mail Baggage Co." and "Express Service No. 50," three doors on both sides, one on each end, black roof with celestory **150.00**

Caboose, #67, 1918, O gauge, eight wheels, red litho body, sliding door on each side, gray painted tin roof with red cupola, "The Ives Railway Lines" ... **45.00**

Gravel car, #63, 1913-14, O gauge, eight wheels, gray litho, rounded truss rods, marked "63" on sides.................... **35.00**

Locomotive
- #11, 1910-13, O gauge, 0-4-0, black boiler and cab, litho plates beneath arched cab windows, cast iron wheels, L. V. E. No. 11 tender **165.00**
- #25, 1906-07, O gauge, 4-4-2, black body, boiler tapers towards front, four separate boiler bands, three square windows on both sides of cab, gold frames and stripes, tin pony wheels, four-wheel L.V.E. No. 25 tender............................**275.00**

Parlor car, #62, 1924-30, O gauge, eight wheels, tin litho steel, red-brown, one-pc roof with clerestory stripe, five windows, two doors on each side, marked "The Ives Railway Lines" above windows **75.00**

Set, O gauge, litho, freight, #3 cast iron stem locomotive, #1 tender, three #54 gravel cars, #56 caboose, c1910-14 .... **700.00**

Tank car, #66, 1921-35, O gauge, eight wheels, gray painted body, black dome **25.00**

Tender, #25, 1928-30, O gauge, diecast body, coal load, two four-wheel trucks **150.00**

Lionel, "O" Gauge locomotive, Santa Fe, #2333-20, 1949, silver and red, yellow trim, mint, original box, 3-1/2" x 13-1/4" l, 3-1/2" h, **$55**. Photo courtesy of David Rago Auctions.

Lionel

Baggage car, #2602, O gauge, 1938, red body and roof **100.00**

Boxcar, #HO-874, HO gauge, 1964, NYC **25.00**

Marklin, steam locomotive, rare green version, 1935, **$3,555**. Photo courtesy of Auction Team Breker.

Lionel, Mickey Mouse/Santa car, composition Santa, Mickey rides behind in Santa's toy sack, 10-1/2" l, **$350**. Photo courtesy of James D. Julia, Inc.

Caboose, #217, Standard gauge, 1926-40, orange and maroon **150.00**
Cattle car, #213, Standard gauge, 1926-40, cream body, maroon roof **450.00**
Hopper car, #216, Standard gauge, 1926-40, silver, Sunoco decal **350.00**
Locomotive, #2333-20, O gauge, Santa Fe, silver and red, yellow trim, orig box, 1949 .... **55.00**
Observation car, #322, Standard gauge, 1924 .... **95.00**
Pullman, #35, S gauge, c1915, orange **65.00**
Set, O gauge, Passenger, Union Pacific, #752E power unit, #753 coach, #754 observation, silver, c1934............ **350.00**
Set, standard gauge, freight, #513, #516, #517, c1926-32 .... **290.00**
Set, standard gauge, passenger, #18, #19, #190, dark olive green, c1906-10 .... **230.00**

Marx, streamline, 9-1/2" l diecast loco marked "666," NY Central coal car, Sante Fe oil tanker, Rock Island container car, "556" red caboose, orig transformer, instructions, track, orig box........... **120.00**

Tramp Art

History: Tramp art was an internationally practiced craft, brought to the United States by European immigrants. Its span of popularity was between the late 1860s to the 1940s. Made with simple tools—usually a pocketknife, and from scrap woods—non-reusable cigar box wood, and crate wood, this folk-art form can be seen in small boxes to large pieces of furniture. Usually identifiable by the composition of thin-layered pieces of wood with chip-carved edges assembled in built-up pyramids, circles, hearts, stars, etc. At times, pieces included velvet, porcelain buttons, brass tacks, glass knobs, shards of china, etc., that the craftsmen used to embellish his work. The pieces were predominantly stained or painted.

Collected as folk art, most of the work was attributed to anonymous makers. A premium is placed on the more whimsical artistic forms, pieces in original painted surfaces, or pieces verified to be from an identified maker.

Bank, 6" h x 4" w x 4" d, secret access to coins **335.00**

Cigar box, early 20th C, three- and four-layer chip carving, sliding lid, **$165**. Photo courtesy of Pook & Pook.

Bird cage, 28" h x 22" w x 13-1/2" d, house with two compartments **775.00**
Box, cov
- 4-1/4" w, 3" d, 1-3/4" h, hinged cover, dove, heart, and anchor dec **200.00**
- 14" l, 7-1/8" d, 8-1/4" h, hinged top, cast brass pull, mounted pincushion on base, two concealed short drawers, painted blue and gold, c1890-1910 .... **815.00**

Cabinet, building shape, two towers, steeple roofline, small shelves **3,600.00**
Chest of drawers, 40" h x 29" w x 20" d, scratch built from crates with four drawers, 10 layers deep............ **2,400.00**
Christmas tree, 25-1/2" h, carved wood, branching sections, painted cross finial, stepped polychrome base, sgd "D. Hafner," c1900 .... **2,070.00**
Clock, mantel, 22" h x 14" w x 7" d, red stain with drawers at base............ **475.00**
Comb case, 27" h x 17" w x 4"d, adorned with horseshoes, hearts, birds, two drawers and mirrors **700.00**

Document box, c1900, five-layer chip carved design and appliqués, 19" w, 8" h, **$150**. Photo courtesy of Pook & Pook.

Crucifix, 16" h x 7" w x 4-1/2" d, wooden pedestal base, wooden carved figure **185.00**
Document box, 14" h x 9-1/2" w x 9" d, diamond designs, sgd and date **375.00**

Box, three layers, green velvet, mirror inside, brass lion head pulls and paw feet, 12-1/2" x 7-1/2" x 8", **$345**

Doll furniture
- Chair, 10" h, 7" w, 12" d, dec with brass tacks **450.00**
- Bureau, 14" h x 12" w x 9" d, drawers and mirror **650.00**

Frame, five layers, diamonds and pyramids, 18-1/2" x 16-1/2", **$275.**

Frame
- 9" h, 6-3/4" w, photograph of maker, signed and dated "1906" **275.00**
- 13" h x 12" w, horseshoe shape, light and dark wood **465.00**
- 14" h x 24" w, double opening frame with oval opening for photos **325.00**
- 16" h x 18" w x 4-3/4" d. crown of thorns, multiple opening frame with minor losses, dark stain **495.00**
- 25" h, 22" w, 13-1/2" x 15-1/2" opening five layers, hearts in each corner, orig gold and red speckled paint, minor wear.................... **715.00**
- 26" h x 24" w, velvet panels and sq corners **350.00**

Grotto, 12" w, 8" d, 29" h, carved and painted, carved cross steep on bell tower above grotto, applied floral, foliate, and geometric motifs, int. fitted with platform and drawer, two standing floral devices, painted red and green, cream-white ground, found in Ohio, late 19th/early 20th C **420.00**

Jewelry box

6" h x 11" w x 6" d, covered with hearts painted silver over gold, velvet lined **595.00**

8" h x 11" w x 7" d, hinged, pedestal, dark stain **175.00**

9" h x 11-1/2" w x 7" d, large, dated "1898," metal lion pulls **300.00**

Lamp

24" h, 10" w, 10" d, table, double socket **550.00**

68" h, 17" w, 17" d, floor, heavy pedestal base, no shade **1,200.00**

Match safe, 9" h x 2" w x 2" d, strike surface, open holder for matches **75.00**

Medicine cabinet, 22" h x 18" w x 10" d, light and dark woods **675.00**

Miniature

Chair, 8" h x 6" w x 5-1/2" d, crown of thorns **245.00**

Chest of drawers, 14" h x 5" w x 4" d, made of cigar boxes **375.00**

Music box, 3" h x 7" w x 6" d, velvet sides **425.00**

Night stand, 37" h x 22" w x 14" d, dark stain, drawer on top and cabinet on bottom, no losses **1,600.00**

Pedestal

14 1-2" h x 12" w x 8" d, multi-level, six draws **675.00**

16" h x 7" w x 4-1/2" d, polychromed in green and black paint **950.00**

Pedestal box

8-1/4" h x 9" w x 6-1/2" d, double, bar connecting top pyramids, velvet lined, precise notching **325.00**

29-1/2" h x 16" w x 15" d, light and dark stained, made from fruit crates **1,850.00**

Pedestal, early 20th, diamond and circle appliqués, 11-1/2" w, 30" h, **$250**. Photo courtesy of Pook & Pook.

Plant stand, 22" h x 11" w x 11" d, painted gold, heavily layered **675.00**

Pocket watch holder, 9" h x 6-1/2" w x 5-1/2" d, ftd **375.00**

Radio cabinet, 50" h x 33" w x 16" d, box type radio encased behind doors, ornate **3,600.00**

Sewing box

8-1/2" h x 11-1/2" w x 8-1/2"d, velvet pin cushion on top **265.00**

9" h x 16-1/2" w x 8" d, painted red, white and blue sewing box, Uncle Sam cigar label under lid **1,600.00**

Sewing cabinet, 27" h x 16" w x 9"d, lift top and three drawers made from crate wood **1,400.00**

Vanity mirror, 26" h, 14" d, 10" d, table top, heart on top and drawer **375.00**

Pin cushion box, seven layers, blue velvet interior, brass lion head pulls, 10-3/4" x 3-1/2" x 6" deep, **$285.**

Wall pocket

8" w, 3-1/2" d, 14" h, three pockets, hearts on crest, diamond and circle dec, trim and dec painted orig medium blue and goldenrod **275.00**

14" h x 11" w x 7"d, painted with hearts and stars, pr **700.00**

TRUNKS

History: Trunks are portable containers that clasp shut and are used for the storage or transportation of personal possessions. Normally "trunk" means the ribbed flat- or domed-top models of the second half of the 19th century.

Early trunks frequently were painted, stenciled, grained, or covered with wallpaper. These are collected for their folk-art qualities and, as such, demand high prices.

Dome top, wood rim, wooden slats, interior shelf, old lining, 20-1/4" x 32" x 25", **$120.**

Chinese, brass bound camphor wood, 19th C, minor imperfections, 16" h, 36" w, 18" d, polychrome foliate dec on top, nailhead trim **1,035.00**

Dome top trunk, wood stays, paper covering with lithographed straps, original hardware, **$165**. Photo courtesy of Sky Hawk Auctions.

Dome top

6" l, 3-1/2" w, 2-5/8" h, paper-covered box green and red sponge dec, blue line and dot patterned paper-lined int., brass ring and iron latch, America, 19th C, wear **265.00**

33-1/4" w, 16-1/4" d, 18-3/4" h, black japanned brass mounts, gilt Chinoisiere dec of figures in garden landscape, side handles, late 18th/ early 19th C, restoration **750.00**

44-1/2" w, 22-3/4" d, 19-1/2" h, hinged top, dovetailed box, white painted vine, floral and leaf dec over black painted ground, int. papered with early 19th C Boston area broadsides, attributed to MA, 19th C, some later paint **1,035.00**

Flat top, 19-1/4" x 29" x 18", black and red lacquered elm, sq outline, two sections int., Chinese, Qing dynasty **200.00**

Louis Vuitton trunk, John Wannamaker label, early 20th C, 20" w, 20" h, **$1,725**. Photo courtesy of Pook & Pook.

Immigrants, Norwegian, dated 1860, dovetailed pine, worn floral dec on top and front, decorative wrought iron straps, areas of blue paint on int., covered till, 49" w, 25" d, 26" h **425.00**

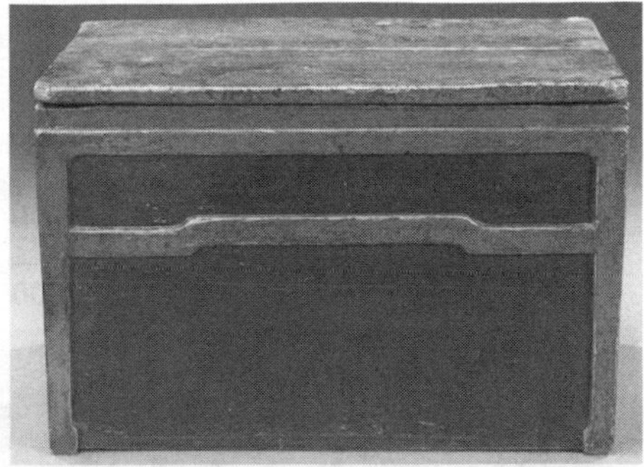

Flat top, black and red lacquered elm, square outline, two sections interior, Chinese, Qing dynast, 19-1/2" x 29" x 18", **$200**. Photo courtesy of Sloan's Auctioneers & Appraisers..

Japanese, 18th C, lacquer, domed top, ext. painted with landscape scenes, base with ball feet, 35-1/2" w, 22" d, 33" h **2,100.00**

Military, 21-3/4" w, 17" d, 12-1/2" h, brass bound camphor wood, hinged rect top, storage well, brass bail handles, English, second half 19th C **200.00**

Vuitton, Louis, early 20th C, wardrobe, rect, wooden strapping, leather handles on ends, brass corners and clasps, int. with hanger bars, eight Vuitton hangers, 21-1/2" d, 15-1/2" d, 40-1/2" h.... **1,100.00**

Val St.-Lambert

History: Val St.-Lambert, a 12th-century Cistercian abbey, was located during different historical periods in France, Netherlands, and Belgium (1930 to present). In 1822, Francois Kemlin and Auguste Lelievre, along with a group of financiers, bought the abbey and opened a glassworks. In 1846, Val St.-Lambert merged with the Socété Anonyme des Manufactures de Glaces, Verres à Vitre, Cristaux et Gobeletaries. The company bought many other glassworks.

Val St.-Lambert developed a reputation for technological progress in the glass industry. In 1879, Val St.-Lambert became an independent company employing 4,000 workers. The firm concentrated on the export market, making table glass, cut, engraved, etched, and molded pieces, and chandeliers. Some pieces were finished in other countries, e.g., silver mounts were added in the United States.

Val St.-Lambert executed many special commissions for the artists of the Art Nouveau and Art Deco periods. The tradition continues. The company also made cameo-etched vases, covered boxes, and bowls. The firm celebrated its 150th anniversary in 1975.

For more information, see *Warman's Glass*, 4th edition.

Console set, pair 12-1/2" d cobalt blue shading to clear candlesticks, 9-1/2" d, 6-1/2" h matching pedestal bowl, signed, **$600**. Photo courtesy of Woody Auctions.

Bottle, 6-7/8" h, cameo-etched, green vines and flowers dec, acid finished ground, green cut to clear overlay edge, sgd "Val/St. Lambert" **120.00**

Bowl, cov, 6-1/2" d, cameo-etched, deep cut purple florals, frosted ground, sgd "Val St Lambert" **750.00**

Bowl, open, 10" d, 4" h, red flashed overlay, sgd **350.00**

Bud vase, 11" h, small flared mouth, elongated neck over bulbous body, opal white glass with brick red powder-pulled dec, mottled blue ground, interlocking VSL monogram within base........... **575.00**

Cologne bottle, 6-1/2" h, cameo-etched, textured colorless ground, cranberry florals, cut fern, partial paper label, replaced cut stopper.................... **220.00**

Compote, 3-1/2" d, amberina, ruby rim, mottled glass bowl, applied amber foot and handles.................................. **175.00**

Finger bowl, 4-1/2" d, crystal, half pentagon, cut edge, sgd................ **45.00**

Goblet, 5-3/8" h, colorless, blown mold, applied foot and stem **50.00**

Pitcher, colorless, paneled, cut diamond design, sgd **95.00**

Presentation vase, 14" h, green ground, cameo cut chrysanthemums, maroon enameling, c1900........................ **500.00**

Tumbler, 3" h, cameo-etched, blue florals, rim ground **40.00**

Tumble-Up, decanter and matching tumbler, amber-crystal, marked **95.00**

Vase

- 6-1/2" h, flared mouth tapering to neck, ovoid body, opal white glass layered in rosy red, cameo-etched flowering branches, sgd "VSL" in cameo near base, c1910 .... **575.00**
- 7-1/2" h, cameo-etched, colorless frosted ground, emerald green floral cutting, base marked "Made in Belgium, Val St. Lambert" **660.00**
- 8-1/2" h, heavy colorless oval, engraved rose in center, base inscribed "VSG C. Graffart/Piece Unique 1949," attributed to Charles Graffart **375.00**
- 10" h, cameo-etched, attributed to Desire and Henri Muller, Belgium, c1906, elongated triangular form, opaque white cased to colorless and chartreuse, fluogravure dec of dragonfly over poppies, rust, ochre, and beige colors, script "VSL" signature near base **3,115.00**
- 11-1/2" h, cobalt blue ground, overlaid in copper, all over emb rosettes, emb "Val St Lambert Belgique," c1910.................... **575.00**
- 11-3/4" h, cameo-etched, frosty textured ground, life size enameled teasel and leaves, long woody stems, natural colors, gold highlights **500.00**

Valentines

History: Early cards were handmade, often containing both handwritten verses and hand-drawn pictures. Many cards also were hand colored and contained cutwork.

Mass production of machine-made cards featuring chromolithography began after 1840. In 1847, Esther Howland of Worcester, Massachusetts, established a company to make valentines that were hand decorated with paper lace and other materials imported from England. They had a small "H" stamped in red in the top left corner. Howland's company eventually became the New England Valentine Company (N.E.V. Co.).

The company George C. Whitney and his brother founded after the Civil War dominated the market from the 1870s through the first decades of the 20th century. They bought out several competitors, one of which was the New England Valentine Company.

Lace paper was invented in 1834. The golden age of lacy cards took place between 1835 and 1860.

Embossed paper was used in England after 1800. Embossed lithographs and woodcuts developed between 1825 and 1840, and early examples were hand colored. There was a big revival in the 1920s by large companies, like R. Tuck in England, which did lots of beautiful cards for its 75th Diamond Jubilee; 1925 saw changes in card production, especially for children with paper toys of all sorts, all very collectible now. Little girls were in short dresses, boys in short pants, which helps date that era of valentines. There was an endless variety of toy types of paper items, many companies created similar items and many stayed in production until World War II paper shortages stopped production both here and abroad.

Adviser: Evalene Pulati.

Animated, large, Felix, half tone, German **25.00**
Bank True Love note, England, 1865 .... **75.00**
Bank of Love Note, Nister, 1914 ... **38.00**
Charm string, Brundage, three pcs **50.00**
Comic, Woodcut, Strong, USA, 1845 .... **35.00**
Diecut foldout
Brundage, flat, cardboard **35.00**

Folk art, scherenschnitte, Pennsylvania, 19th C, circular, heart cutouts, 6-3/4" d, **$575**. Photo courtesy of Pook & Pook.

Cherubs, two pcs **40.00**
Clapsaddle, 1911 .... **50.00**
Documentary, Passport, love, 1910 .... **45.00**
English Fancy, from "Unrequited Love Series," 8" x 10", aquatint, couple, wedding **135.00**
Engraved, 8" x 10" sheet, English, hand colored **55.00**
Handmade
Calligraphy, envelope, 1885 .... **135.00**
Cutwork, hearts, 6" x 6", 1855 .... **250.00**
Fraktur, cutwork, 1800 .... **950.00**
Pen and ink love knot, 1820 .... **275.00**
Puzzle, purse, 14" x 14", 1855 .... **450.00**
Theorem, 9" x 14", c1885 .... **325.00**
Woven heart, hand, 1840 .... **75.00**

American, pull down, World War II, **$25**. Photo courtesy of Evalene Pulati.

Honeycomb
American, kids, tunnel of love **48.00**
American, wide-eyed kids, 9" **40.00**
German, 1914, white and pink, 11" **75.00**
Simple, 1920, Beistle, 8" **18.00**
Lace paper
American, layered, McLoughlin Co., c1880 .... **35.00**
Cobweb center, c1855 .... **250.00**
English, fancy, 8" x 10", 1840 .... **175.00**
Hand layered, scraps, 1855 .... **65.00**
Layered, in orig box, 1875, Howland **75.00**
Orig box, c1890 .... **65.00**
Simple, small pc, 1875 .... **22.50**
Tiny mirror center, 4" x 6" **75.00**
Whitney, 1875, 5" x 7" **35.00**
Novelty, American Fancy, c1900, originally sold in a box
5" x 7-1/2", mat, fancy corners, parchment, orig box **45.00**
7-1/2" x 10", rect, panel with silk, celluloid, orig box **75.00**
10-1/2" x 10", star shape, silk rusching, orig box **85.00**
16" x 10-1/2", oblong, satin, celluloid, orig box **95.00**

Fancy layered pull down, 1914, **$175**. Photo courtesy of Evalene Pulati.

Pulldown, German
Airplane, 1914, 8" x 14" **175.00**
Auto, 1910, 8" x 11" x 4" **150.00**
Car and kids, 1920s **35.00**
Dollhouse, large, 1935 .... **45.00**
Rowboat, small, honeycomb paper puff **65.00**
Seaplane, 1934, 8" x 9" **85.00**
Tall Ship, 8" x 16" **175.00**
Silk fringed
Prang, double sided, 3" x 5" **24.00**
Triple layers, orig box **38.00**
Standup novelty
Cupid, orig box **45.00**
Hands, heart, without orig box **35.00**
Parchment
Banjo, small, with ribbon **85.00**
Violin, large, boxed **125.00**

Vallerysthal Glass

History: Vallerysthal (Lorraine), France, has been a glass-producing center for centuries. In 1872, two major factories, Vallerysthal glassworks and Portieux glassworks, merged and produced art glass until 1898. Later, pressed glass animal-covered dishes were introduced. The factory continues to operate today.

For more information, see *Warman's Glass*, 4th edition.

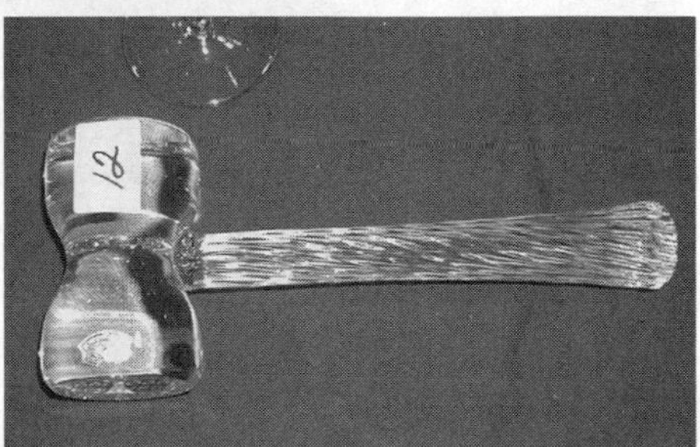

Gavel, crystal, original foil label, **$45**.

Animal dish, cov
- Alligator, opaque white **2,000.00**
- Elephant and rider, opaque blue, 7-1/4" l **195.00**
- Hen, opaque white, 5" h **85.00**
- Swimming duck, opaque white, traces of orig paint, 6-1/2" l, 5-1/2" h **125.00**
- Turtle, opaque white, snail finial **120.00**
- Water buffalo and rider, opaque caramel **2,600.00**

Box, cov, 5" x 3", cameo, dark green, applied and cut dec, sgd **950.00**
Bowl, 8-1/2" l, 4-3/4" w, Ribs & Scallops pattern, opaque turquoise, vertical ribs, rounded edge scallops **70.00**
Candlesticks, pr, Baroque pattern, amber **75.00**
Compote, 6-1/4" sq, blue opaque glass **75.00**

Honey dish, covered, opaque green, detailed thatch roof, embossed door and other details, **$350**.

Goblet, 5-3/4" h, 2-3/4" d, colorless, green grapes and "B" monogram **225.00**
Mustard, cov, swirled ribs, scalloped blue opaque, matching cover with slot for spoon **35.00**
Plate, 6" d, Thistle pattern, green **65.00**
Sugar, cov, 5" h, Strawberry pattern, opaque white, gold trim, salamander finial **85.00**
Toothpick holder, hand holding ribbed vessel, opaque blue **30.00**
Vase, 8" h, flared folded burgundy red rim, oval pale green body, matching red enamel berry bush on front, inscribed "Vallerysthal" on base **490.00**
Wine, 4-1/4" h, 2-1/2" d, translucent rose, set of four **160.00**

VAN BRIGGLE POTTERY

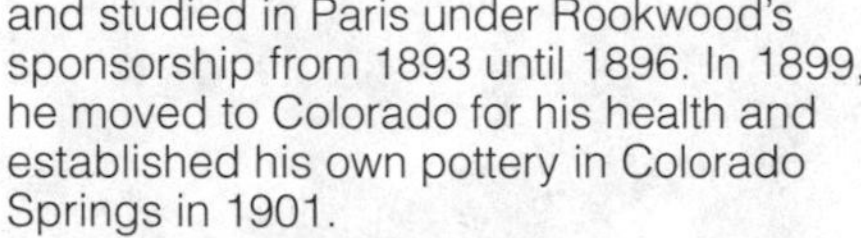

History: Artus Van Briggle, born in 1869, was a talented Ohio artist. He joined Rookwood in 1887 and studied in Paris under Rookwood's sponsorship from 1893 until 1896. In 1899, he moved to Colorado for his health and established his own pottery in Colorado Springs in 1901.

The Art Nouveau schools he had seen in France heavily influenced Van Briggle's work. He produced a great variety of matte-glazed wares in this style. Colors varied.

Artus died in 1904. Anne Van Briggle continued the pottery until 1912.

Marks: The "AA" mark, a date, and "Van Briggle" were incised on all pieces prior to 1907 and on some pieces into the 1920s. After 1920, "Colorado Springs, Colorado" or an abbreviation was added. Dated pieces are the most desirable.

Reproduction Alert: Van Briggle pottery still is made today. These modern pieces often are mistaken for older examples. Among the glazes used are Moonglo (off white), Turquoise Ming, Russet, and Midnight (black).

Advertising plaque, c1930, embossed "VAN BRIGGLE POTTERY/COLORADO CLAY," green and blue matte glaze, small chip to one corner, few smaller edge chips, 5-3/4" x 11-1/2", **$2,300**. Photo courtesy of David Raog Auctions.

Advertising plaque, 11-1/2" l, 5-3/4" h, green and blue matte glaze, emb "VAN BRIGGLE POTTERY/COLORADO CLAY," 1/3" corner chip, few smaller edge chips **2,300.00**

Bookends, pair, owls standing on books, Persian Rose glaze, one incised AA, 5" x 5", **$200**.

Bookends, pr, 4" x 5-1/2", each modeled with bear, brown and green matte glaze, incised AA, one with small base chip, firing line to base of other **415.00**
Bowl, 5-1/4" d, 3-3/4" h, #578, emb leaves, fine feathered grape-purple glaze, 1908-11, marked **815.00**

Pitcher, #452, 1906, matte gray glaze, marked and dated, 4-3/4" h, **$520**. Van Briggle photos courtesy of David Rago Auctions, Inc.

Bud vase, 6" x 3-3/4", cylindrical shaft, squat base, veined beige glaze with chartreuse, marked "AA VAN BRIGGLE 1902 84" **2,300.00**
Cabinet vase
- 2-1/4" x 3-1/2", emb trefoils, ultramarine matte glaze, sgd and dated 1914 .... **360.00**
- 2-1/2" h, emb pasque flowers, ultramarine frothy glaze, 1908-11, marked **360.00**
- 3", emb trefoils under mottled green to purple glaze, 1908-11, marked "AA VAN BRIGGLE COLO SPGS 190" **535.00**
- 3-1/4", #310, incised, emb trefoils in peacock feathers, experimental teal blue frothy sheer glaze, 1930s, AA VanBriggle/Colo.Spgs., ink mark 12 .... **360.00**

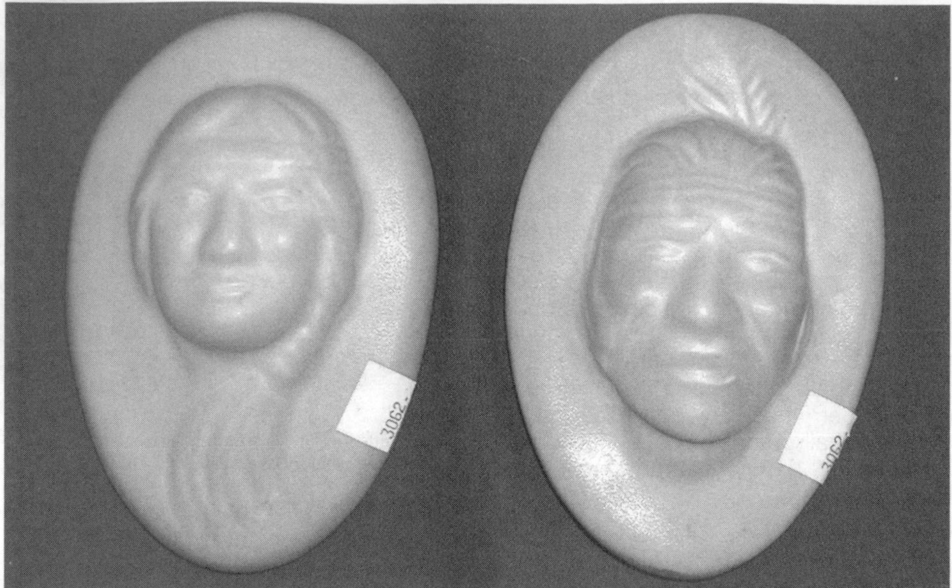
Plaques, Indian heads, pale blue, A-in-box mark, impressed "Van Briggle, Colorado Spgs, Co, CB," **$95**.

4" x 2-1/4", tear shape, emb daisies under a frothy dark blue-green glaze, 1908-11, marked "AA VAN BRIGGLE COLO SPGS 682" **630.00**

Chamberstick, 5-1/2" h, molded-leaf shape, hood over candle socket, green glaze **115.00**

Figure, 7" h, female nude holding shell, matte Persian blue glaze, incised "Van Briggle" **250.00**

Flower bowl, 14" l, Lady of the Lake, turquoise, blue overspray, incised logo, Colorado Springs, USA **525.00**

Incense burner, 4-1/2" h, gnome crouching in crescent, purple and indigo glaze, unmarked........................... **380.00**

Indian vase

11" x 5", three different Indian chief heads emb under deep red and green matte glaze, 1930s, incised AA/Van Briggle/COLO. SPGS, one chin bruised **690.00**

11-1/4" h, three different Native American heads emb under green and brown matte glaze, c1928, marked **750.00**

Lamp base, 9" h, emb stylized florals under maroon glaze with blue over-spray, orig factory fittings, incised varnished bottom with logo, name, and Colo. Sprgs, c1920 .... **115.00**

Low bowl, 6-1/2" h, shape no. "689," emb arrow root design, under matte green glaze, incised with logo, varnished bottom, Colo Sprgs, c1920 .... **260.00**

Mug, 4-1/2", emb coat-of-arms and owl, inscribed "PELing pug 19" in gold, dark indigo glaze, 1916, incised AA/1916, rim crack.. **360.00**

Night light, 5", mountain lion, matte green glaze, 1914, unmarked, wiring missing **690.00**

Plate

6" d, emb stylized wild rose, brown and blue-green feathered glaze, 1908-11, marked.................... **575.00**

Two trays, 1908-1911, both marked, one embossed with floral design in gray and green, 6" d; other covered in pink glaze, 4-1/2" d, **$425**.

8-1/4" d, emb dogwood blossoms, turquoise and brown matte glaze, marked "AA VAN BRIGGLE COLO SPGS 17," 1908-11 .... **690.00**

Tile, 18" x 12", six tile frieze, cuenca with stylized trees against blue sky, framed **250.00**

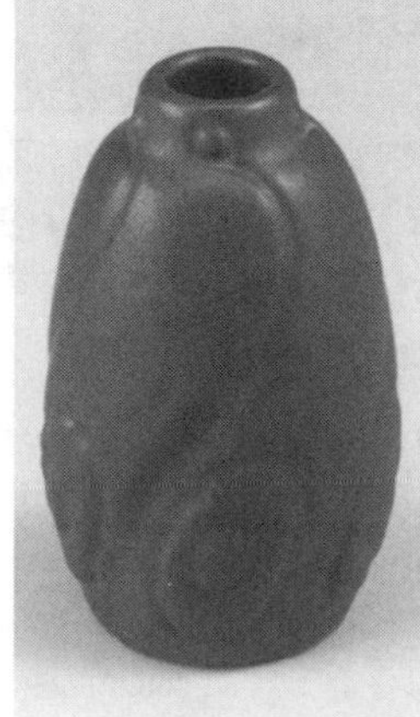
Cabinet vase, 1904, embossed flowers in curved panels, dark teal (possibly experimental) matte glaze, Incised AA/Van Briggle/190?/186, with XXII/IV/33188 in ink, 2-1/2" d, 4-1/4" h, **$1,610**.

Paperweight, scarab, 1915, matte turquoise glaze, stamped VBP CO., 2-3/4" x 2", **$350**.

Urn, 13-1/4" x 6", emb pointed leaves and berries, frothy light green matte glaze, marked "AA VAN BRIGGLE COLO. SPGS.," 1908-11, handle hairline, 1" stilt-pull.. **920.00**

Vase

4-1/2" x 4-1/2", bulbous, emb swirling leaves under frothy pearl-gray glaze, 1908-11, marked "AA VAN BRIGGLE COLO SPGS 357" **630.00**

5-1/4" x 4", gourd shape, smooth speckled green and blue glaze, marked "AA VAN BRIGGLE 1905 319" **1,150.00**

Vase, bulbous, 1907-11, crisply embossed spade-shaped leaves, mottled purple dripping over green matte glaze, incised AA/Van Briggle/Colo. Spgs./804/18/7, 3/4" bruise to rim, 8-1/4" x 2-3/4", **$1,100**.

5-1/2" h, sloping shoulder, #454, emb leaves, matte blue-green glaze, 1908-11, marked **630.00**

6-1/2" x 4", emb daffodils, frothy pink glaze, mark obscured by glaze, c1907, very short tight line to rim, base restoration **750.00**

Vase, 1908-1911, embossed blossoms, unusual lavender to chartreuse matte glaze, marked, 1" line from rim, 3-3/4", **$250**.

7-1/4" x 3-1/4", corseted, emb trillium, chartreuse and turquoise sheer glaze, c1907, dark partially obscured by glaze **860.00**

7-1/2" x 5-1/4", ovoid, matte yellow glaze, 1907-12, incised AA/Van Briggle/Colo. Spgs./269 .... **690.00**

Vessel, flat shoulder, 1908-1911, yellow and light green matte glaze, marked, 4", **$350**.

10-1/2" x 4-1/2", emb bell-shape flowers and swirling leaves, smooth matte green glaze, marked "AA VAN BRIGGLE 1902," opposing rim lines **2,530.00**

11" h, Indian Chief, chocolate brown glaze, green over spray, incised "Van Briggle, Colo. Springs," 1920s, minor shallow flake **550.00**

Vessel

2-1/4" x 6-1/4", squat, emb leaves under active matte mustard glaze, 1905, mark partially obscured by glaze, surface burst glaze bubbles to surface **460.00**

3-12" x 5-1/2", #209, squat, frothy blue-gray matte glaze over red clay, 1906, marked **520.00**

Vase, bulbous, 1915, embossed trefoils, blue-green matte glaze, incised 695/AA/1915, 3-3/4" x 4-1/2", **$400**.

4", bulbous, speckled blue-over-rose matte glaze, 1915, incised AA/1915/414 .... **290.00**

4-3/4" x 4-1/4", squat, stylized floral pattern emb at neck, fine feathered ochre glaze, marked "AA VAN BRIGGLE COLO SPGS 696," 1908-11 .... **750.00**

Vessel, squat, embossed butterflies, Persian Rose glaze, marked, 4", **$125**.

Vessel, squat, embossed leaves, Mountain Craig Brown, 1930s, marked "AA Van Briggle/Colo. Spgs," 5" d, 4-1/4" h, **$175**.

5" d, squat, emb leaves, red, green, and blue feathered matte glaze, 1908-11, mark cov by glaze, tight rim line **350.00**

Venetian Glass

History: Venetian glass has been made on the island of Murano, near Venice, since the 13th century. Most of the wares are thin walled. Many types of decoration have been used: embedded gold dust, lace work, and applied fruits or flowers.

Reproduction Alert: Venetian glass continues to be made today.

Beverage set, 10-1/2" h, pitcher, applied striped handle, eight flared tumblers, six spherical glasses, each striped with opaque orange, transparent yellow-amber, and clear crystal, design attributed to Fulvio Bianconi, 15-pc set **1,950.00**

Bowl, 7-1/2" w, 6-1/8" w, deep quatraform bowl, applied quatraform rim, blue, internal dec, trapped air bubble square, circles, and gold inclusions, c1950 .... **360.00**

Table service, green and gold, applied fish motif, 12 7-1/2" h stems, pair 15-1/2" h candlesticks, 10-1/2" x 16" center bowl, chips, cracks and losses, **$2,415**. Photo courtesy of David Rago Auctions, Inc.

Candlesticks, pr, 8-3/8" h, white and black glass, formed as coat on twisted stem coat rack on tripod base, black domed foot, 20th C **275.00**

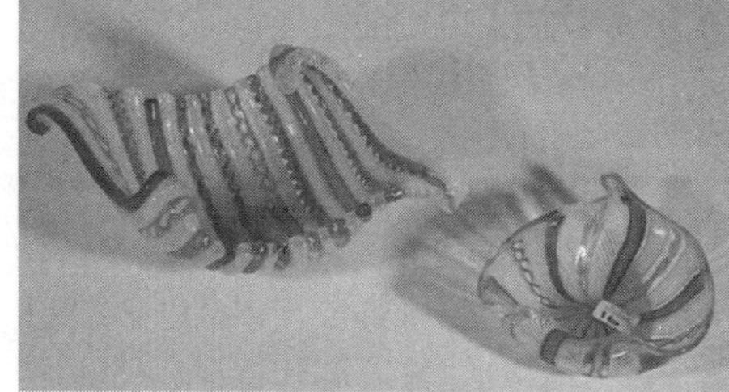

Two dishes, rolled over rims, spiral turned canes, latticework, heart-shaped dish, 4-1/2" w, 9" l, **$120**. Photo courtesy of Joy Luke Auctions.

Centerpiece set, two 8-1/2" baluster ftd ewers, 78-1/2" ftd compote, red and white latticinio stripes with gold flecks, applied clear handles and feet, three-pc set **150.00**

Wine and sherbet from 26 wine glasses, 12 sherbets, white swirl design, **$650**. Photo courtesy of Joy Luke Auctions.

Decanter, 13" h, figural clown, bright red, yellow, black, and white, aventurine swirls, orig stopper 250.00

Goblet, 6-1/2" h, ruby red, baluster stem, applied amberina rigaree, price for nine-pc set.. 250.00

Sherry, amber swirled bowls, blue beaded stems, eight-pc set 495.00

Table garniture, two 14-1/4" h colorless glass dolphins on white diagonally fluted short pedestals, six 5-3/4" h to 7-3/4" h colorless glass turtle, bird, seahorse, dolphin, two bunches of fruit in bowls, figures on similar white pedestals, including 20th C 550.00

Vase, 10-3/4" h, gold trim, white latticinio, clear ground, applied colorless handles 225.00

Villeroy & Boch

History: Pierre Joseph Boch established a pottery near Luxembourg, Germany, in 1767. Jean Francis, his son, introduced the first coal-fired kiln in Europe and perfected a water-power-driven potter's wheel. Pierre's grandson, Eugene Boch, managed a pottery at Mettlach; Nicholas Villeroy also had a pottery nearby.

In 1841, the three potteries merged into the firm of Villeroy & Boch. Early production included a hard-paste earthenware comparable to English ironstone. The factory continues to use this hard-paste formula for its modern tablewares.

Stein, three litre, stoneware, verse, figure of lady holding goblet, pewter lid, **$200**. Photo courtesy of Joy Luke Auctions.

Bowl, 8" d, 3-3/4" h, gaudy floral dec, blue, red, green, purple, and yellow, marked "Villeroy & Boch," minor wear and stains 50.00

Charger, 15-1/2" d, gentleman on horseback, sgd "Stocke"............. 600.00

Dish, cov, triangular, orange and black dec, marked "Villeroy & Boch, Mettlach," and "Made in Saar-Basin," molded "3865," c1880-1900...................... 125.00

Pitcher, stoneware, #1726, panels decorated with stylized design and florets, 1-1/2 liter, **$175**. Photo courtesy of Joy Luke Auctions.

Ewer, 17-3/4" h, central frieze of festive beer hall, band playing white couples dance and drink, neck and foot with formal panels between leaf molded borders, subdued tones, c1884, imp shape number, production number and date codes 900.00

Jardinière, 13" d, 12-1/2" h, maidens in field scene, marked "Villeroy & Boch" and Mettlach castle mark, early 1900s 895.00

Pitcher, 1-1/2 liter, stoneware, panels dec with stylized designs and florets, #1726.. 195.00

Plate, white ground, cobalt blue Delft-style dec, blue mark "Villeroy & Boch, Dresden, Saxony," imp "GR W 5" 45.00

Plate, cobalt blue Delft-style design, back marked in blue "villeroy & boch, Dresden, Saxony," impressed "GR W 5," **$45**. P

Platter, 9-1/4" l, 8" w, white basketweave ground, blue fish and aquatic plants dec, marked "Villeroy & Boch, Delphin, Mettlach, Ceschutzt" 110.00

Stein, half liter, pewter lid, stoneware, barrel shape, relief hops and leaves dec on lid.. 125.00

Stein, 1/2 litre, stoneware, dancing figures, King of Hops, #1909, pewter lid, **$100**. Photo courtesy of Joy Luke Auctions.

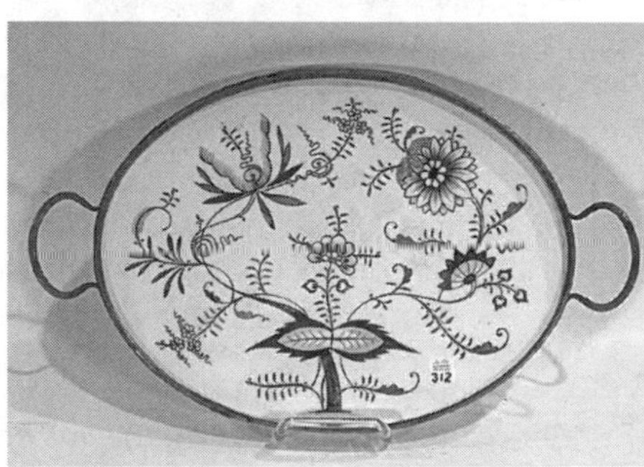

Tray, oval, blue flowers and vines, white ground, metal rim, handles, **$50**. Photo courtesy of Joy Luke Auctions.

Tile frieze, 6" x 12", two tiles, carp swimming amidst white waterlilies, green ground, raised V&B mark, small corner nick.. 490.00

Tray, 11-1/4" d, metal gallery with geometric cut-outs, ceramic base with

border and stylized geometric pattern, white ground, soft gray high gloss glaze, blue accents, base marked **200.00**

Stein, stoneware, barrel shap, half liter, inlaid lid decorated with relief hops and leaves, **$110**. Photo courtesy of Joy Luke Auctions.

Tureen, cov, 11" w, Burgenland, dark pink transfer, white ground, marked "Mettlach, Made by Villeroy & Boch" **195.00**

Vase, 15" h, bulbous, cylindrical, deep cobalt blue glaze, splashes of drizzled white, three handled SP mount cast with leaves, berries, and blossoms, molded, pierced foot, vase imp "V" & "B," "S" monogram, numbered, c1900, price for pr **2,750.00**

Wall plaque, 13-1/4" d, stoneware, wide border with relief dec of fruit garlands, insects, and faces surrounding mythological center on black ground, marked #834, rim separations, minor scratching.................................... **220.00**

Warwick

History: Warwick China Manufacturing Co., Wheeling, West Virginia, was incorporated in 1887 and remained in business until 1951. The company was one of the first manufacturers of vitreous glazed wares in the United States. Production was extensive and included tableware, garden ornaments, and decorative and utilitarian items.

Pieces were hand painted or decorated with decals. Collectors seek portrait items and fraternal pieces from groups such as the Elks, Eagles, and Knights of Pythias.

Some experimental, eggshell-type porcelain was made before 1887. A few examples are found in the antiques market.

Bowl, semi-porcelain, shaped swirled edge, pink, violet, and blue flowers, cream ground, raised gold branches and accents, marked "100" with crossed swords mark **35.00**

Plate, earthenware, marked "Ch. Rodney Stone," 10-1/4" d; mug marked "Ch. Bromley Crib," both decorated with bull dog, **$110**. Warwick photos courtesy of Joy Luke Auctions.

Jardinière, pedestal, ironstone, floral dec, 35" h **725.00**

Luncheon plate, garland of pink roses, gold coin trim, white ground........... **18.00**

Mug

4-1/8" h, B.P.O.E., elk dec, marked "IOGA Warwick" with crossed swords and knights head stamp **95.00**

5" h, Osiris Temple, A.O.N.M.S., Wehhling, W.Va., Atlantic City, July 13 & 14, 1905, Indian dec...... **185.00**

Mustard pot, slotted cov, 3" h, 2-3/4" d

Virginia pattern, black transferware **15.00**

White ground, rust and black stripes, 1947, marked **30.00**

Plate

9" d, multicolored spring flowers, gold trim, white ground, marked **20.00**

9-1/2" d, pink flowers dec, white ground, gold trim, c1930-40 .... **48.00**

Tankard, 12-3/4" h, elk lodge, c1910, professional repair........................ **50.00**

Urn, 11-1/2" h, soft matte finish, hp pine cones and pine branches, two handles, marked "IOGA," old repair to one handle **165.00**

Vases, pair, two handles, decorated with portraits of ladies, 10-1/2" h, **$250**.

Vase

9-3/4" h, 8" w, hp pink and green floral design, black ground, gold trim, two handles................... **250.00**

10-1/8" h, 5-1/2" w, hp floral design, brown ground, gold trim......... **250.00**

11" h, Gypsy girl dec.............. **350.00**

Vegetable dish, 7-1/4" d, 3-1/4" w, purple flowers, green leaves and stems, white ground, gold and gray border, marked "Warwick" **35.00**

Wash pitcher, semi-porcelain, transfer print of blue, yellow, green, and brown flowers, white ground, gold accents, gold emb dec on spout and handle..... **175.00**

Watches, Pocket

History: Pocket watches can be found in many places—from flea markets to the specialized jewelry auctions. Condition of movement is the first priority; design and detailing of the case is second.

Descriptions of pocket watches may include the size (16/0 to 20), number of jewels in the movement, whether the face is open or closed (hunter), and the composition (gold, gold filled, or some other metal). The movement is the critical element, since cases often were switched. However, an elaborate case, especially if gold, adds significantly to value.

Pocket watches designed to railroad specifications are desirable. They are between 16 and 18 in size, have a minimum of 17 jewels, adjust to at least five positions, and conform to many other specifications. All are open faced.

Study the field thoroughly before buying. There is a vast amount of literature, including books and newsletters from clubs and collectors.

Watch, pendant, Edwardian, opalescent enamel dial with blue Arabic numeral indicators, subsidiary seconds dial, pave-set with seed pearl case, case and lever escapement movement no. 1238735 signed Bartens & Rice Co. New York, 14kt gold case with Swiss hallmark and "AW," 0 size, **$850**. Photo courtesy of Skinner, Inc.

Chatelaine, lady's

Edwardian, 18kt yg, brooch bezel-set with oval lapis in ribbed mount with seed pearl highlights framed by openwork bow and bellflowers, circular lapis connector, suspending open face watch, white enameled Roman numeral dial, jeweled movement, 0 size, key, French 18kt gold horology import mark **1,530.00**

Victorian, 14kt yg, white enamel dial, black Roman numerals edged by Arabic second numerals, fancy scrolled hands, textured back case dec with red enamel stars, suspended from 27-1/4" l curb and translucent red enamel baton link chain **235.00**

Lapel, lady's

Starr, Theodore B., NY, triple signed, Edwardian, 18kt yg, white porcelain dial, black Roman numerals, subsidiary seconds dial, jeweled nickel movement, inscribed dust cover, back case dec with pink guilloche and gold foliate motifs, 0 size, suspended from 14kt gold and pink enamel fleur-de-lis pin **715.00**

Unknown maker, 18kt gold and enamel, cream porcelain dial with Roman numerals, gold fancy scroll hands, jeweled gilt movement, cylinder escapement, back cover with cobalt blue enamel and gold fleur-de-lis, woven watch chain with enamel and seed pearl barrel-shape slides, onyx fob and key, back cover detached **450.00**

Watches, pocket, ladies, hunting cases; first designed with decorated circular dial with Roman numerals and "Louis XIV hands," within engraved scenic case set in 18k yelow gold, key, wind and set; second designed with white circular dial with Roman numerals, "spade" hands, set in 14k yellow gold, **$450**. Photo courtesy of Sloans & Kenyon Auctions.

Pendant, lady's

American Waltham, 14kt yg, hunting case, white enamel dial with Roman numeral indicators and subsidiary seconds dial, stem-set gilt lever escapement movement no. 6600607, case no. 4899952, engraved mountain landscape and floral motifs, size 0, 46" l rope-twist watch chain with star-set pearl slide **235.00**

Eterna, 18k yg, rushed gold, rect form, black line indicators, hallmark, 23.10 dwt **230.00**

C.H. Meylan, Brassus, 18kt gold, hunting case, white enamel dial with Arabic numeral indicators, chapter ring and subsidiary seconds dial, engraved case with white and green enamel floral sprays and black tracery enamel C-scrolls, no. 89928, cuvette inscribed and dated 1899, enclosing sgd jeweled lever escapement movement, size 0, wear to enamel **600.00**

Unknown maker

18kt yg, white enamel dial with Arabic numeral indicators, floral chased and engraved case, red-orange guilloche enamel reserve with birds, roses and scrolling vines, case marked H&D, 371, and 635, French import stamp **200.00**

18kt gold, white enamel dial with Roman numeral indicators, case with red, white and blue enamel framing a scene of a couple in the countryside, 16.7 dwt, dial with hairlines **300.00**

Pocket, gentleman's

Agassiz Watch Co., Switzerland, made for Tiffany & Co., 18kt yg, seventeen jewel movement, subsidiary seconds dial, back with blue enameled monogram JDW, fitted Tiffany & Co. box, early 20th C, 1-11/16" d watch case, 2-1/4" l **600.00**

American Waltham

14kt yg, hunting case, white enamel dial with black Roman numeral indicators, subsidiary seconds dial, jeweled nickel movement, no. 5491495, engine-turned case no. 741687, 6 size **215.00**

14kt yg, open face, white enamel dial with Arabic indicators, subsidiary seconds dial, 17-jewel movement, case engraved with large HJ monogram, dust cover engraved "March 22 1907," 16 size, 65.9 dwt **300.00**

Gentleman's, Vacheron & Constantin, c1920, ultra thin platinum case, blue sapphires channel mounted around outside of case stamped 18J, eight adjustments, platinum 16" watch chain, **$1,265**. Photo courtesy of James D. Julia, Inc.

Bautte, Jq Fd. Geneve, 18k yg, white dial, Roman numerals, chased case with bi-color floral bouquet on one side, mixed meal and enamel dec on other, scalloped edges, enamel damage **260.00**

Bijou Watch Co., lady's label, 14k yg, dec dial with ornate hands, subsidiary seconds hand and dial, diamond-set engraved crescent moon and star on case, 14k yg ribbon shaped watch pin, c1900 .... **390.00**

Bourquin, Ami, Locle, #30993, 18 kt yg, key wind, white porcelain dial, black Roman numerals, subsidiary seconds dial, engraved case with black and blue enamel, accented with rose-cut diamonds, fitted wooden box with inlaid dec **1,100.00**

Boutte, #277389, 14k yg, 10 rubies, white dial, black Roman numerals, chased case with red and blue enamel star dec, Russian hallmarks, 29" l ropetwist chain, enamel loss **300.00**

Caldwell, J. E., & Co., openface, 18 kt gold, white enamel dial, black Roman numerals, subsidiary seconds dial, Vacheron and Constantin jeweled movement, cavette dated June 5, 1900, verso monogrammed, 16 size **900.00**

Watch, pocket, American Waltham, tri-color gold hunting case, inner case engraved "Mary E. Baker 1893" with photograph of Mary E. Baker, gold watch chain, **$300**. Photo courtesy of Joy Luke Auctions.

Cartier, 18kt yg, Art Deco, open face, engine-turned dial with black Roman numeral indicators, Breguet hands, and subsidiary seconds dial, 19-jewel eight-adjustment movement, case and movement sgd "European Watch and Clock Company," serial no., model no. 88537, with trademark C-bow, French guarantee stamps, dial with oxidation, plastic crystal **1,410.00**

Champney, S. P., Worcester, MA, 18k yg, openface, gilt movement, #8063, key wind, white dial, Roman numerals, subsidiary seconds dial, hallmarks, orig key, c1850, dial cracked, nicks to crystal **250.00**

Elgin, 14kt gold, hunting case, white porcelain dial, black Arabic numerals, blue-steeled hands, subsidiary seconds dial, 15 jewel nickel movement, monogrammed, 16 size, suspended from 14kt gold curb link watch chain ... **300.00**

Howard, E., & Co., Boston, 18kt gold, hunting case, white enamel dial, black Roman numerals, blue-steeled scroll hands, subsidiary seconds dial, dust cover inscribed and dated June 6, 1872, monogrammed, 16 size................ **980.00**

Jacot, Charles E., 18k yg hunter case, nickel jeweled movement, #9562, numbered on dust cov, case and movement, white porcelain dial, Roman numerals, subsidiary dial for seconds, monogrammed case, orig wood case with extra spring, 14k yg chain **750.00**

Jurgensen, J. Alfred, Copenhagen, #784, 18k yg hunter case, highly jeweled movement, patent 1865, white porcelain dial, subsidiary dial for seconds, fancy hands, elaborate monogram..... **3,300.00**

L'Epine, Paris, openface, white enamel dial, key wind, tri-color gold engraved case, 8 size, hand missing, chips to dial **375.00**

Meylan, C. H., Brassus, openface, 18kt gold, white enamel dial, Arabic numerals, scrolled hands, subsidiary seconds dial, 19 jewel movement, 10 size......... **635.00**

Patek Philippe & Co., Geneve, 18k yg, open face, movement and case No. 161442, white dial, Roman numerals, bail missing **575.00**

Roulet, Georges, 14kt yg hunting case, white enamel dial with Roman numeral indicators and Breguet hands, subsidiary seconds dial, lever set jeweled nickel lever escapement movement by Georges Roulet, no. 80643, polished case with box hinge and engraved edges, 8 size, orig fitted burlwood veneer box........... **500.00**

Tiffany & Co., hunter's case, 18k yg, enamel dial with Roman numerals, subdial second hand, Swiss movement, triple sgd, monogrammed on both covers **450.00**

Unknown maker

18kt, circular goldtone dial with raised Roman numeral indicators and engraved picturesque scene, subsidiary seconds dial, engine turned case no. 14311, gilt fully-jeweled lever escapement movement, dust cover sgd "H. Rosselet," with gold-filled curb link chain and two keys, plastic crystal **425.00**

Metal, coach, triple calendar, white enamel dial with black Roman numeral indicators, subsidiary day, date, and month dials, moonphase aperture, pin-set, stem wound gilt movement no. 38358, d1890, plastic crystal.................................... **360.00**

Pocket, lady's

Meylan, C. H., 18kt gold and enamel, openface, white enamel dial with black Arabic numerals, fancy scrolled hands, gray guilloche enamel bezel, cover enameled with gold flowers set with diamonds, suspended from platinum and purple guilloche enamel baton link chain, crystal replaced, minor enamel loss **850.00**

Unknown maker, retro, pink gold, hinged rect cover surmounted by rubies and diamonds, similarly set scroll and geometric shoulders, snake link bracelet, 6-1/4" l.. **750.00**

Watch, pocket, Tiffany, hunting case, sterling silver, **$250**. Photo courtesy of Joy Luke Auctions.

Vacheron & Constantin, 18kt gold, hunting case, white enamel dial, Roman numerals, gilt bar movement, cylinder escapement, sgd on cuvette, engraved case, 10 size **350.00**

Waltham, 14kt yg, hunting case, white enamel dial, Arabic numeral indicators, subsidiary seconds dial, Lady Waltham jeweled nickel movement by A.W.W. Co., floral engraved case no. 224709, 0 size, gold ropetwist chain..................... **300.00**

Whipperman, A. J., Idaho Falls, Idaho, 14kt yg, hunting case, white enamel dial, black Arabic numeral indicators, subsidiary seconds dial, 15 jewel nickel movement by Rode Watch Co., floral engraved case dec with pale pink guilloche enamel, old mine-cut diamond in center, signed Gruen, dust cover inscribed, "Father to Elsie 1914," 0 size, fancy 14kt yg curb link and pink enamel baton link chain........................... **180.00**

WATCHES, WRIST

History: The definition of a wristwatch is simply "a small watch that is attached to a bracelet or strap and is worn around the wrist." However, a watch on a bracelet is not necessarily a wristwatch. The key is the ability to read the time. A true wristwatch allows you to read the time at a glance, without making any other motions. Early watches on an arm bracelet had the axis of their dials, from 6 to 12, perpendicular to the band. Reading them required some extensive arm movements.

The first true wristwatch appeared about 1850. However, the key date is 1880 when the stylish, decorative wristwatch appeared and almost universal acceptance occurred. The technology to create the wristwatch existed in the early 19th century with Brequet's shock-absorbing "Parachute System" for automatic watches and Ardien Philipe's winding stem.

The wristwatch was a response to the needs of the entrepreneurial age with its emphasis on punctuality and planned free time. Sometime around 1930, the sales of wristwatches surpassed that of pocket watches. American makers quickly joined Swiss and German manufacturers.

The wristwatch has undergone many technical advances during the 20th century including self-winding (automatic), shock-resistance, and electric movements.

Wristwatch, gentleman's, Hamilton, gold-filled shield shape case, 17 jewels, leather band, **$350**. Wristwatch photos courtesy of Joy Luke Auctions.

Gentleman's

Boucheron, dress tank, A250565, white gold, reeded bezel and dial, invisible clasp, black leather Boucheron strap, French hallmarks, orig leather pouch **2,150.00**

Buccellati, Gianmaria, dress, 18k yg, fancy engraved dial, black tracery enamel, black leather strap, 18k yg clasp, Italian hallmarks.............. **6,900.00**

Cartier, Tank Basculante, stainless steel, rect white dial with Roman numeral indicators and blue hands, outer frame opening to vertical position allowing case to swivel, quartz movement, adjustable dark blue leather Cartier band, orig presentation box, cabochon accent missing **1,510.00**

Concord, 14kg, rect gold-tone dial with engraved dot indicators and vertical striations, black leather band, orig box, c1940... **300.00**

Gübelin, stainless steel, silvertone dial with Roman and stick numeral indicators, day, month, and moonphase apertures, inner date ring, stainless steel bezel joining curved 14kt yellow gold lugs, case inscribed and dated "C.H.K. 1952," sgd 25-jewel two adjustment automatic damascened movement sgd "Gübelin," leather band **1,175.00**

Jurgensen, Jules, dress, 14k white gold, Swiss movement, silvertone brushed dial, abstract indicators, diamond-set bevel, black faux alligator strap **290.00**

Le Coultre, Futurematic, goldtone dial, subsidiary seconds dial, power reserve indicator, 10k yg-filled mount, lizard strap, 1950s **425.00**

Wristwatch, gentleman's, Rolex Oyster perpetual date, 14k yellow gold case and band, original fitted box, **$2,500**.

Nardin, Ulysse, 14k yg, chronometer, goldtone dial, luminescent quarter sections, applied abstract and Arabic numeral indicators, subsidiary seconds dial, lugs with scroll accents, leather strap, discoloration and scratches to dial **290.00**

Wristwatch, gentleman's, Raymond Weil double dial, rectangular case, leather band, original fitted case, **$395**.

Omega, 18k yg, round cream dial, goldtone Arabic numeral and abstract indicators, heavy mesh bracelet, mild soil to dial, 44.80 dwt **460.00**

Patek Philippe et Cie

Calatrava, ref. No. 96, 18kt gold, silvered dial with stick numeral indicators, subsidiary seconds dial, dia. 31 mm, 18-jewel five-adjustment damascened movement, dial, case and movement triple-sgd , case no. 319925, movement no. 734009, brown leather strap **3,290.00**

Twenty-4, 18kt white gold, white face with Arabic and diamond numeral indicators and luminescent hands, sapphire crystal, bezel channel-set with lines of princess and single-cut diamonds, approx. total wt. 1.11 cts, Swiss quartz movement, model no. 4910/20G, retailed by Tiffany & Co., orig presentation boxes and leather-bound documentation **10,285.00**

Rolex, Oyster Perpetual, 14k yg, goldtone dial, abstract indicators, sweep second hand, ostrich strap, slight spotting to dial **850.00**

Tiffany & Co., 18k yg, lapis lazuli color dial, stepped bezel, black crocodile strap **635.00**

Universal, Geneve, Uni-Compax, 18k yg, two-dial chronograph, silver-tone dial, sweep seconds hand, black lizard strap **980.00**

Vacheron & Constantin, 18kt gold, white round dial, abstract numeral indicators, 17-jewel nickel movements, 7-1/4" l associated 18kt gold brickwork band **1,495.00**

Hamilton, lady's, 17 jewels, model 750, #72052A, 14K white gold decorated case framed with 17 single cut diamonds, white gold band decorated with 38 single-cut diamonds, replaced clasp, one stone missing, 10.6dwt., **$260**. Photo courtesy of Sanford Alderfer Auction Co.

Lady's

Audemars Piguet & Co., Art Deco, rect silvertone dial with Arabic numeral indicators, bezel and flexible geometric platinum link bracelet bead-set with 105 full and 48 single-cut, five square step-cut, and two half-moon-cut diamonds, approx. total wt. 4.96 cts., 17-jewel two position Audemars Piguet movement, 6-7/8" l **3,645.00**

Bueche Girod, 18k yg, elongated oval goldtone dial, rect bezel with stylized hinge lucks, satin band, c1970 .... **980.00**

Cartier, 18kt gold, Pathere, sq goldtone dial with diamond bezel, quartz movement, case and deployment buckle sgd "Cartier," flat rect link band **4,025.00**

Chopard, Geneva, 18kt gold, oval goldtone dial within larger oval crystal with seven floating collet-set diamonds, diamond-set dial, crystal, and shoulders, 8" l maroon leather band **2,760.00**

Elgin, platinum, Art Deco, rect ivory-tone dial with Arabic numeral indicators, 17 jewel movement, set with old mine and single-cut diamonds, approx. total weight 2.00 cts.. **890.00**

Gruen, Art Deco, platinum, rect silvertone dial, black Arabic numerals, bezel enhanced with 32 circular-cut diamonds, mesh strap edged by box-set single-cut diamonds, highlighted by diamond-set floret shoulders, 6-1/4" l............. **4,225.00**

Gübelin, platinum, silvertone dial with abstract numeral indicators, bezel, lugs, flexible strap set with 88 single-cut diamonds, approx. total wt. 2.12 cts, 6" l **1,300.00**

Hamilton

14kt yg, navette-shaped ivory tone dial with abstract indicators, 17-jewel movement, prong-set with six full-cut diamonds, approx. total weight 1.10 cts, silk cord band................. **390.00**

14kt yg, sq ivory tone dial with Arabic numeral indicators, 17 jewel movement, set with single-cut, baguette, and old European-cut diamonds, 6-3/4" l **650.00**

Hermès Pullman, white metal dial with Arabic numeral indicators and date aperture, gold-tone bezel and arched lugs, adjustable leather strap, water resistant quartz movement, orig box **530.00**

Le Coultre, Jaeger, 14kt gold, Reverso, silvertone dial with black Arabic numeral indicators, blue-steeled hands, case flips to reveal polished gold monogrammed cover, case sgd and numbered, 8" l tan ostrich leather strap.................. **1,380.00**

Lehman, Retro, Uti movement, 18k yg, round goldtone dial with ruby indicators, one half framed in graduated calibre-cut channel-set rubies, snake like bracelet, French hallmarks, slight discoloration to dial... **1,495.00**

Patek Philippe et Cie

18kt yg, Calatrava, silver dial with gold baton numeral indicators and

reeded bezel, 18-jewel manual wind movement, with mesh band and deployant clasp adjustable to three lengths, 5-3/4" to 6" l............ **2,585.00**

18kt yg, white enamel dial with blue Arabic numeral indicators and Louis XV hands, display back enclosing sgd movement no. 107961, blue guilloche enamel case #223710 with scene of pink and yellow roses framed by rose-cut diamonds and scrolling vines, outer case with repousee scene of Hercules, Hebe and Cupid, dial and movement sgd, size 0, c1895, with Art Nouveau lapel pin bezel-set with circular-cut sapphire, pearl accent, dial with hairlines **9,400.00**

Lady's, Movado, 14kt white gold, small square watch accented at top and bottom with two bands containing 14 diamond melees, engraved name on back plate, **$460**. Photo courtesy of James D. Julia, Inc.

Perraux, Retro, 14kt gold, sq white metal dial with gold indicators, lugs set with modified bullet-shaped aquamarines, flanked by diamonds, 17 jewel movement, black cord band with deployment clasp **635.00**

Rolex, Oyster Perpetual, stainless steel, precision, cream dial, abstract indicators with phosphorescent, subsidiary seconds dial, slight discoloration to dial **1,380.00**

Swiss, 18k yg, Swiss movement, manual wind, domed bezel, gold-tone dial, black Roman numerals, hallmark, leather strap **920.00**

Tiffany & Co., 14kt gold, oval white dial with black Roman numerals, diamond-set bezel, 6-3/4" l flexible flat rect link band **1,150.00**

Van Cleef & Arpels, 18kt yg, gold dial with full-cut diamond bezel, tapering woven herringbone and rope-twist gold band, French guarantee stamp, sgd "Van Cleef & Arpels, no. 77976." **4,115.00**

WATERFORD

For more information, see Warman's Glass, 4th edition.

History: Waterford crystal is high-quality flint glass commonly decorated with cuttings. The original factory was established at Waterford, Ireland, in 1729. Glass made before 1830 is darker than the brilliantly clear glass of later production. The factory closed in 1852. One hundred years later it reopened and continues in production today.

Candlesticks, pair, short candle cups, round pedestal base, original green and gold foil label, **$75**.

Bowl, 8" d, large waffle cut pattern, sgd "Waterford," last half 20th C **140.00**

Cake plate, 10" d, 5-1/4" h, sunburst center, geometric design **85.00**

Cake server, cut-glass handle, orig box **80.00**

Champagne flute, 6" h, Coleen pattern, 12-pc set **450.00**

Compote, 5-1/2" h, all-over diamond cutting above double wafer stem, pr **400.00**

Creamer and sugar, 4" h creamer, 3-3/4" d sugar, Tralee pattern **85.00**

Decanter, orig stopper, 10" h, ship's, diamond cutting **200.00**

Honey jar, cov **75.00**

Decanter, Lismore pattern, 10-1/2" h, roughness on stopper, **$110**. Photo courtesy of Sanford Alderfer Auction Company.

Juice pitcher, 6-1/2" h, Glandore pattern, sgd "Waterford," last half 20th C **175.00**

Lamp, 23" h, 13" d umbrella shade, blunt diamond cutting, Pattern L-1122 .... **450.00**

Fruit bowl, turned down rim, pedestal base, 6-3/4" d, 5-3/4", d, 5-3/4", **$295**.

Napkin ring, 2" h, 12-pc set......... **225.00**

Old fashioned tumbler, 3-1/2" h, Comeragh pattern, pr..................... **70.00**

Ring dish, 5" d, colorless, cut glass, price for three-pc set.................... **110.00**

Tumbler, Colleen, set of six, orig box **400.00**

Vase, 6" h, diamond pattern, wreath around center, sgd **225.00**

Mugs, pair, ring handle, footed, original foil label, original box, **$65**.

Wine set, Kenmare pattern, 12-1/2" h stopered decanter, six stemmed wines, sgd "Waterford," last half 20th C **375.00**

WAVE CREST

WAVE CREST WARE

c1892

History: The C. F. Monroe Company of Meriden, Connecticut, produced the opal glassware known as Wave Crest from 1898 until World War I. The company bought the opaque, blown-molded glass blanks from the Pairpoint Manufacturing Co. of New Bedford, Massachusetts, and other glassmakers, including European factories. The Monroe company then decorated the blanks, usually with floral patterns. Trade names used were "Wave Crest Ware," "Kelva," and "Nakara."

For more information, see Warman's Glass, 4th edition.

Biscuit jar, cov, unmarked, 5-1/2" d, 5-1/2" h, pink and white background, melon ribbed, hp flowers........ **250.00**

Dresser box, hinged scenic panel of Niagara Falls on lid, unsigned, 7" l, 4" h, **$800**. Photo courtesy of Joy Luke Auctions.

Bonbon, 7" h, 6" w, Venetian scene, multicolored landscape, dec rim, satin lining missing........ **1,200.00**

Box, cov

- 3" d, Double Shell, molded-in shells on lid and body, aqua blue tin, hp florals, no lining........ **275.00**
- 5-1/2" w, man on bended knee proposing to lady, roses, rococo swirls, orig lining........ **1,300.00**
- 6" d, heart shape, opaque tan glass body, dec with red and yellow mums, Belle Ware, #4625/10........ **460.00**
- 8" d, 3-1/2" h, raised scalloped edging around lid and base, hp floral dec on lid, sgd "Kelva"........ **415.00**

Cigar humidor, 8-3/4" h, blue body, single-petaled pink rose, pink "Cigar" signature, pewter collar, bail, and lid, flame-shaped finial, sgd "Kelva" **685.00**

Cracker jar, Helmschmidt swirl, pink floral decoration, original metal hardware, original Wave Crest label, 10" h, **$350**. Photo courtesy of James D. Julia, Inc.

Cracker jar, 5-1/4" d, 10-1/2" h, blue and white hp florals, green and brown leaves, white Johnny jump-ups, puffy egg crate mold........ **700.00**

Collar jar, opaque white, molded scrolls, hand-painted purple and white chrysanthemums, light beige silk lining, stenciled label on bottom "Wavecrest Trademark," 9" d, 6" h, **$525**. Photo courtesy of Garth's Auctions, Inc.

Dresser jar, hinged, lid decoraated with white daisies, unsigned, 4-3/4" d, **$140**. Photo courtesy of Joy Luke Auctions.

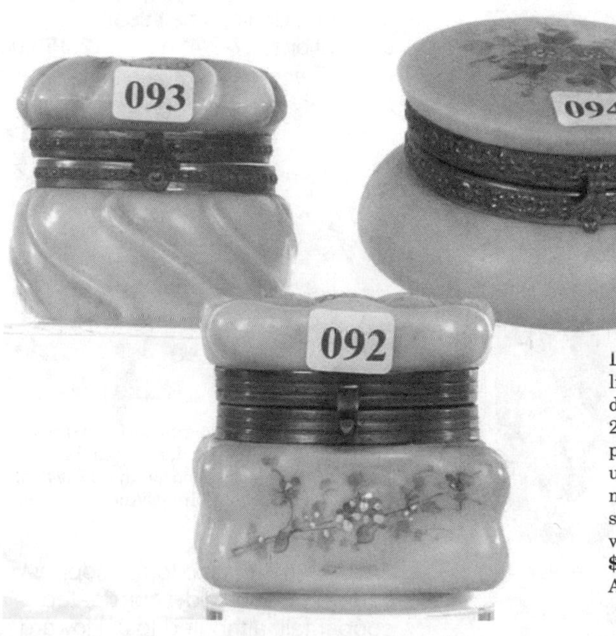

Left: 3" jewel box, swirl mold, light blue, pink blossom decoration, signed, **$200**; center: 2-1/2" x 4-1/4" powder box, pink, blue floral decoration, unsigned, **$75**; right: 3" h puffy mold hinged jewel box, white shading to light blue, pink and white floral branch decoration, **$100**. Photo courtesy of Woody Auctions.

Dresser jar, silver-plated lid, apricot colored ground, white and blue flowers, scrolls, **$190**. Photo courtesy of Joy Luke Auctions.

Dresser box
- 3" d, opaque ground, enameled cherub, married top and base **435.00**
- 4" d, opaque blue body, red enameled flowers, orig lining **345.00**
- 5" d, 5-1/2" h, egg crate mold, alternating turquoise and opal panels, pink stemmed yellow flowers, four ftd emb metal holder **1,265.00**
- 5-1/2" d, mottled red opaque ground, earthtone enameled flowers, red Kelva mark **690.00**
- 6-3/4" d, Helmschmied swirl, blue to white opaque body, burgundy, rose, and yellow enameled violets **500.00**
- 7" d, Baroque shell mold, opaque ground with pink hues, colorful pointillism design **525.00**

Ewer, lavender, figural woman on handle, ornate base **225.00**

Ferner, 7" d, 5" h, opalescent, gold and floral dec, metal rim cap and lion's face feet........ **320.00**

Mustard jar, cov, spoon, green ground, floral dec, unmarked **140.00**

Pin dish, open
- 3-1/2" d, 1-1/2" h, pink and white, swirled, floral dec, unmarked... **35.00**
- 5" d, 1-1/2" h, white, scrolls, pink floral dec, marked **80.00**

Plate, 7" d, reticulated border, pond lily dec, shaded pale blue ground **750.00**

Powder jar, cov, 5" d, 3" h, dec opaque white ground, sgd, hinge broken, lining missing **130.00**

Salt and pepper shakers, pr, Swirled, light yellow ground, floral dec, unmarked **75.00**

Sugar shaker, 3-1/2" d, 5-1/4" h, Helmschmied Swirl, enameled pink florals, gray and brown foliage..... **575.00**

Syrup pitcher, Helmschmied Swirl, ivory-colored body, blue and white floral dec, smoky-gray leafy branches, SP lid and collar........ **485.00**

Left: 4-1/2" x 5" square box, pink and white, floral decoration, egg crate and scroll mold, signed, **$400**; center: 4-1/4" square jewel box, red mottled ground, white floral decoration, signed "Kelva," **$300**; right: 4-1/4" x 6" letter holder, light yellow, pink rose decoration, scroll mold brass rim, signed, **$225**. Photo courtesy of Woody Auctions.

Tobacco jar, opaque white, yellow diagonal bands alternating with white bands, hand-painted pink roses and "Tobacco," brass collar, red label on bottom "Wavecrest" on flag, 5-1/4" h, **$365**. Photo courtesy of Garth's Auctions, Inc.

Trinket dish, 1-1/2" x 5", blue and red flowers **175.00**

Urn, 6-1/2" h, white opal, light pink at neck, raised gold frame on each side surrounding floral bouquet, metal fittings with bright gold patina........ **445.00**

Vase, 10" h, pale pink accents on white, pink and orange chrysanthemums, enameled foliage, beaded white top **600.00**

Weather Vanes

History: A weather vane indicates wind direction. The earliest known examples were found on late 17th-century structures in the Boston area. The vanes were handcrafted of wood, copper, or tin. By the last half of the 19th century, weather vanes adorned farms and houses throughout the nation. Mass-produced vanes of cast iron, copper, and sheet metal were sold through mail-order catalogs or at country stores.

The champion vane is the rooster—in fact, the name weathercock is synonymous with weather vane—but the styles and patterns are endless. Weathering can affect the same vane differently; for this reason, patina is a critical element in collectible vanes.

Whirligigs are a variation of the weather vane. Constructed of wood and metal, often by the unskilled, whirligigs indicate the direction of the wind and its velocity. Watching their unique movements also provides entertainment.

Reproduction Alert: Reproductions of early models exist, are being aged, and then sold as originals.

Banner, attributed to J. Howard & Co., West Bridgewater, Massachusetts, third quarter 19th C, zinc arrow point on cutout sheet copper, scroll and tulip elements, crack on tip, small loss, dents, 33-3/4" l, 7-3/4" h, **$3,175**. Photo courtesy of Skinner, Inc.

Arrow, 36" l, 16" h, gilt copper, ball finial, weathered gilt surface, no stand, dents **360.00**

Banner, 71-1/2" l, 17-3/4" h, pierced scrolled sheet copper, old surface, traces of gilt, no stand, minor dents..... **2,715.00**

Whirligig, faceless family, carved wood, painted green, brown, and white, **$2,900**.

Bird and fish, 18-1/2" w, 19" h, molded metal, full bodied, bird flies with aid of propellers above fish, marble eyes, unpainted weathered gray surface, Illinois, early 20th C, tall stand **1,150.00**

Eagle, America, 19th C, copper, repairs, leaning against table leg, **$950**. Photo courtesy of Wiederseim Associates, Inc.

Eagle, 21" wing span, 18-1/2" h, copper, full bodied, cast zinc feet, wooden base, one foot loose, arrow bent........... **250.00**

Fish

- 12-3/4" l, 3-1/4" h, carved wood, full bodied, tail wrapped with lead sheeting, tacked button eyes, Midwestern U.S., late 19th C, remnant of post, minor losses, with stand **2,645.00**
- 26" l, 6-1/2" h, white painted carved wood and sheet metal, America, mid-20th C, tall stand......... **1,495.00**
- 27" l, 6" h, carved and painted wood, salmon orange, chamfered edge, tin reinforced carved bracket, Wakefield, MA, 19th C, inscribed "this set on a cedar tree near our farm before the Civil War," with stand **1,150.00**

Heart and feather, 76-3/4" l, 13-1/4" h, sheet iron, found in New York, late 18th C, fine rust and overall pitting, with stand **4,900.00**

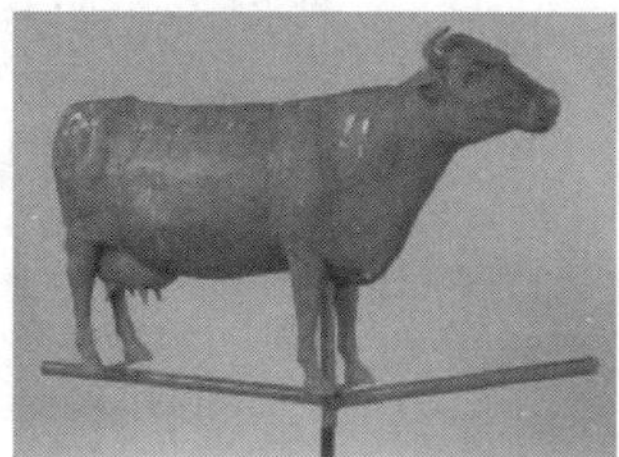

Cow, America, 19th C, cast zinc head on molded copper full-body figure, painted rust color with traces of gilt, raised on iron rod and wood shaft with cast iron directionals, imperfections, figure 42-1/2" l, 25" h, 94-1/2" h shaft, **$14,100**. Photo courtesy of Skinner, Inc.

Horse

- 17-3/4" h, running, copper, verdigris patina, traces of gilt, America, late 19th C, includes copper sphere, no stand, dents, small seam separations, 17-3/4" h **2,350.00**

Running horse, copper, verdigris patina, traces of gilt, copper sphere, no stand, America, late 19th C, dents, small seam separations, 17-3/4" h, **$2,350**. Photo courtesy of Skinner Auctioneers and Appraisers.

- 24" l, 18-1/2" h, zinc torso, copper ears, legs, and body, corrugated copper tail, attributed to J. Howard & Co., West Bridgewater, MA, third quarter 19th C, old surface with vestiges of gilt, no stand, old repair on one leg, wear, minor dents **7,650.00**
- 26-1/4" l, 16" h, running, gilt copper, no stand, couple of small dents **2,470.00**
- 29" l, 14" h, running, molded copper and cast zinc, verdigris surface, attributed to A. L. Jewell & Co., Waltham, MA, 1850-67, no stand, minor dents, seam separation **4,625.00**
- 29-5/8" l, 18" h, running, molded copper, full bodied, verdigris surface, traces of gilt, no stand, wear, hole **3,410.00**
- 30" l, 20" h, running, gilded copper and zinc, full bodied horse, zinc head, stand, repair to tail, minor dents and seam separations **2,715.00**
- 31-1/8" l, 20-5/8" h, running, gilt copper and zinc, copper full bodied horse, zinc head, no stand, later gilt, replaced rod, wear............. **1,175.00**
- 32" l, 17" h, running, painted copper, flattened full bodied, older darkened putty painted surface, traces of gilt, no stand, dents, bullet hole repairs **1,410.00**
- 32" l, 18-3/8" h, running, copper, zinc ears, full-bodied, verdigris, yellow sizing, traces of gilding, body with imp maker's mark "A. J. Harris & Co., Boston," late 19th C, no stand, minor seam separation, repaired bullet hole **5,585.00**
- 32-1/2" l, 18-1/2" h, copper and zinc, full-bodied, weathered silvered paint, traces of gold gilt, no stand, minor

dents, repaired bullet holes 2,470.00
37-1/2" l, 63" h, running, copper, flattened full body with verdigris surface, traces of gilt, raised on cast iron directionals, copper sphere, pyramidal roof mount, repair to knee, dents 7,050.00
41-1/2" l, 21" h, running, copper head, hollow molded full body, no stand, gilt wear, minor dent 4,115.00

Horse and jockey, 31-1/2" l, 22-3/4" h, copper, old yellow sizing surface, no stand, minor dents on ears and jockey's head 9,400.00

Horse and rider, molded sheet iron, hollow body, orig mustard painted surface, wear, cracks 6,465.00

Quill pen, 36-1/2" l, 23-1/2" h, iron and copper, spire and sphere finial with weathered regilded surface, attributed to L. W. Cushing & Sons, Waltham, MA, late 19th C, repaired, minor imperfections 2,570.00

Plow, 38-1/4" l, 13-1/2" h, iron and bronze, old surface, no stand 3,415.00

Pointing hand, 23" l, 35-1/4" h, sheet iron and wood, two wood finials on iron shaft, hand and sunburst sheet iron motif, no stand, imperfections.................. 2,235.00

Rooster, standing on directional arrow, gilded sheet copper, American, 75 percent original gilt intact, had been painted, normal bend, small 22-caliber bullet hole in tail, 34" l, 31" h, **$1,600**. Photo courtesy of Cowan's Historic Americana Auctions.

Rooster, 18-1/2" h, copper, old verdigris and partial light green overpaint, steel mount with ball finials, cast directionals, lower feathers missing from arrow 475.00

Schooner, 39" l, 23-3/8" h, wooden, hull painted red and black, cream colored sail, wire rigging, America, 20th C, wooden stand, wear 275.00

Sloop, gaff-rigged, molded copper, verdigris surface, America, early 20th C, no stand..................................... 4,415.00

Stag, leaping
20" l, 19" h, molded copper, zinc antlers, old gilt surface, black metal stand, America, 19th C 8,225.00
21-1/2" l, 17-3/4" h, molded copper, old regilded surface, mounted on wooden stand..................... 5,290.00

Steer, 29-3/8" l, 20" h, zinc head, copper body, old painted surface, traces of gilt, no stain, wear, minor dents 6,475.00

Eagle, America, 19th C, gilded copper, spreadwing figure with cast zinc head and feet, mounted on sphere, two additional copper spheres and cast iron directionals, no stand, gilt wear, minor dent on one wing, 20" h, **$1,530**. Photo courtesy of Skinner, Inc.

Rooster, Hamburg, molded copper, attributed to L.W. Cushing & Sons, Waltham, Massachusetts, late 19th C, flattened full-body figure, verdigris patina with traces of gilt, repairs, bullet holes, dents, 29" l, 28" h, **$25,850**. Photo courtesy of Skinner, Inc.

Whirligig

Band leader, 9" w, 2-1/2" d, 20" h, polychrome carved pine, copper hat, bowtie and buttons, glass eyes, attributed to WI, late 19th C, stand, some paint wear............................... 10,925.00

Bicycle rider, 19" l, 4-1/2" d, 21" h, painted wood and sheet metal, man with metal wide brimmed hat, red body, high wheel green bicycle activated by blades in wheel, America, early 20th C 3,450.00

Flying fish, 17" l, 13-1/2" d, 5-1/2" h, carved and silver painted fish decoy, added tin wings and tail fin, rubber wheels, weathered surface, attributed to Minnesota, mid-20th C, with stand 250.00

Whirligig, Dutch mill, wood, gray and black paint, weathered surface, 16-1/2" h, **$175**.

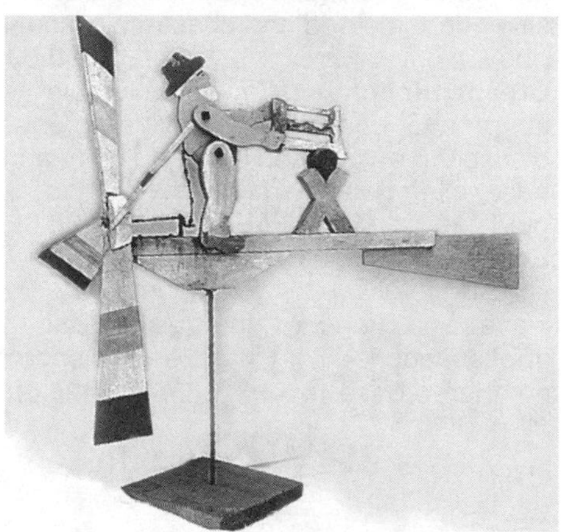

Whirligig, man sawing log, wood, red, white, and blue, c1930, 25-1/4" l, 24-3/4" h, **$150**.

Soldier, 9-5/8" w, 13" h, painted wood, black, gray, and white, wooden stand, wear.. 355.00

Trotting horse, tin propeller, horse with articulated legs, painted white, weathered surface, metal stand, 28-1/2" l, 21-1/2" w, 28-1/4" h........ 375.00

Webb, Thomas & Sons

History: Thomas Webb & Sons was established in 1837 in Stourbridge, England. The company probably is best known for its very beautiful English cameo glass. However, many other types of colored art glass were produced, including enameled, iridescent, heavily ornamented, and cased.

For more information, see Warman's Glass, 4th edition.

Bowl

5-3/4" d, 4-1/2" h, avocado green, sapphire blue stripes, mica flakes, crystal applied fancy drippings on sides, applied crystal rigaree around top edge, applied clear feet, clear berry pontil **235.00**

12" d, 3" h, ruffled, blue ext., cased white int., sgd "Thomas Webb & Sons" **350.00**

Candle holder, 3" h, paperweight type, suspended bubbles, cut shoulder band, sgd "Thos. Webb, England," early 20th C **60.00**

Cologne bottle, 6" h, cameo, spherical, clear frosted body, overlaid white and red, carved blossoms, buds, leafy stems, and butterfly, linear pattern, hallmarked silver dec, molded and chased blossoms dec **3,200.00**

Cream pitcher, 3-1/4" h, sepia to pale tan ground, heavy gold burnished prunus blossoms, butterfly on back, gold rim and base, clear glass handle with brushed gold **385.00**

Ewer, 9" h, 4" d, satin, deep green shading to off-white, gold enameled leaves and branches, three naturalistic applies, applied ivory handle, long spout, numbered base **425.00**

Fairy lamp, blue shade with bird and branch decoration, clear Clarke's Cricklite insert, square blue satin base, 6-1/2" h, **$1,500**. Photo courtesy of Woody Auctions.

Figure, 3" l, 1-1/2" h, pig, solid Burmese body, pink tint to hind quarters, curly tail, four feet, ears, and snout, Webb **750.00**

Flask, 11-5/8" h, fish shape, lemon yellow glass overlaid in white, wheel carved features, sterling silver fish tail screw lid, cameo carved "Rd. 15711," lid imp "Sterling," hairline and cameo loss at mouth **9,500.00**

Lamp, 3-1/4" h, 4-1/4" h, satin background, cameo cut rose shading to white sprig of cameo, three applied camphor feet, stamped "Thomas Webb and Sons" **1,265.00**

Perfume bottle

4-1/4" h, undulating body, yellow overlaid in white, cut and carved as swimming dolphin, inscribed registry mark, "Rd. 18100," rim and cap missing **4,950.00**

9" l, lay-down type, three-dimensional swan head, cameo carved in white over cranberry, orig metal top, orig presentation box marked "MAPPIN & WEBB SILVERSMITH TO THE QUEEN" **14,950.00**

Rose bowl

3" h, 3-3/4" d, Burmese, salmon shading to pink, dec with branch of pine cones, rim ground **200.00**

3-1/4" h, Burmese, salmon shading to pale yellow, amethyst flower leafy stem....................................... **260.00**

Vase

4-1/4" h, 7" d, cased glass, pink fish scale cameo cutting, gold gilt rim and underwater scene **865.00**

5" h, cameo, white florals and tendrils dec, citron green ground **600.00**

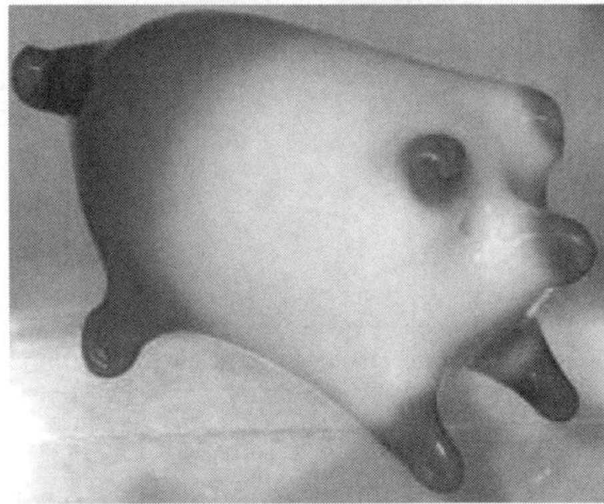

Whimsy, figural pig, lemon-yellow Burmese, shiny finish, curly tail, pink blushed ears, snout, and feet, 3" l, 1-1/2" h, **$750**. Photo courtesy of Clarence and Betty Maier.

5" h, 6" w, 18" circumference, shaded blue, sky blue to pale white cream, applied crystal edge, enameled gold and yellow dec of flowers, leaves, and buds, full butterfly, entire surface acid-cut in basketweave design **425.00**

5-7/8" h, cameo, raised rim, oval form, pale amber overlaid in white and blue glass, cameo etched dianthus blossoms and foliage, applied elbow-shaped arms cameo-etched in bamboo motif extending to rim, based sgd "Thomas Webb & Sons, Gem Cameo"............ **9,500.00**

7" h, MOP satin, purple shading to black air trapped body, gold trailing branches, two applied gold handles, registration numbers in gold **3,680.00**

7" h, 5" w, satin, basketweave mother of pearl, bulbous base shading from deep blue to pale blue, creamy lining **750.00**

Sweetmeats jar, ivory body, molded trailing branches, traces of red paint, silver-plated bale handle and lid with spoon opening, molded signature in banner "Thomas Webb & Sons," 3-3/4" d, 3" h, plus handle, **$425**. Photo courtesy of Garth's Auctions, Inc.

7-1/2" h, peachblow, dark rich pink fading to light pink, creamy white int., gold and pink floral dec, insects, and butterfly, Webb, minor wear to gold **450.00**

Vase, peachblow, raised rim of rounded bowl of opal glass cased to shaded peach, gilt flowering vines, two insects, signed"TIFFANY & CO. PARIS EXHIBITION 1889 THOMAS WEBB & SONS," 4-1/8" h, **$560**. Photo courtesy of Skinner, Inc.

8-3/4" h, cased satin, shading from pale yellow to deep caramel, black and gold morning glories dec, registration numbers on base **250.00**

9" h, crystal ground, overlaid in blue, cameo-cut tulips, overall crystal stippling effect, sgd "Webb" in cameo **665.00**

10" h, 4" w, satin, pulled down edges, deep rose shading to pink, creamy

lining, ruffled top, dome foot, pr 550.00

10-1/2" h, 4" w, bulbous, gold floral prunus blossoms, leaves, branches, pine needles, and insect, satin ground shaded brown to gold, creamy white lining, Jules Barbe dec 450.00

WEDGEWOOD

History: In 1754, Josiah Wedgwood and Thomas Whieldon of Fenton Vivian, Staffordshire, England, became partners in a pottery enterprise. Their products included marbled, agate, tortoiseshell, green glaze, and Egyptian black wares. In 1759, Wedgwood opened his own pottery at the Ivy House works, Burslem. In 1764, he moved to the Brick House (Bell Works) at Burslem. The pottery concentrated on utilitarian pieces.

For more information, see Warman's English & Continental Pottery & Porcelain, 3rd edition.

Between 1766 and 1769, Wedgwood built the famous works at Etruria. Among the most-renowned products of this plant were the Empress Catherina of Russia dinner service (1774) and the Portland Vase (1790s). The firm also made caneware, unglazed earthenwares (drabwares), piecrust wares, variegated and marbled wares, black basalt (developed in 1768), Queen's or creamware, and Jasperware (perfected in 1774).

Bone china was produced under the direction of Josiah Wedgwood II between 1812 and 1822 and revived in 1878. Moonlight luster was made from 1805 to 1815. Fairyland luster began in 1920. All luster production ended in 1932.

A museum was established at the Etruria pottery in 1906. When Wedgwood moved to its modern plant at Barlaston, North Staffordshire, the museum was expanded.

Additional Listings: Majolica.

Agate ware

Candle vase, cov, pr, 9-1/2" h, cream-colored foliate handle and swags, on stepped white biscuit terra cotta plinths, variegated brown, iron red, buff and cream clays, imp marks, c1775, restorations, rim chips 2,500.00

Carrara, figure group, "The Interpretation," modeled by William Beattie, Joseph before the Pharaoh, unmarked, c1860, 19" h, **$3,525**. Photo courtesy of Skinner, Inc.

Crocus pot, pierced cov, 6-1/2" h, four bulb reservoirs, allover surface agate in browns, tans and iron red to pearl glazed ground, traces of gilding, imp upper-lower case mark, late 18th C, slight chip to one reservoir rim, restored hairline 1,880.00

Garniture, 9-3/4" h, 11-3/8" h, three pcs, cream-colored scroll handles, foliate swags and sibyl finials on covers, white biscuit terra cotta plinths, brown, buff, iron red and cream clay bodies, imp marks, c1775, two with socle restored, two with restored rim chips, cover chips restored 4,750.00

Vase, cov, 8-3/4" h, cream-colored Bacchus head handles, drapery swag border, socle dec with variegated brown, buff and blue clays, square white biscuit terra cotta plinth, imp Wedgwood and Bentley mark, c1770, restored rim chips to cup, restored cover, plinth chip 2,850.00

Dragon Lustre, bowl, pattern Z4829, mottled blue exterior with dragon, mother-of-pearl interior with Chinese landscape cartouches to cell border, center dragons, printed mark, c1920, diameter is 9-1/8", **$650**. Photo courtesy of Skinner, Inc.

Artist designed

Bowl

4" d, Norman Wilson design, glazed black and white agate body, imp marks, mid-20th C 300.00

4" d, Norman Wilson design, matte brown/gray ext., mottled blue int., imp marks, mid-20th C 385.00

6-1/2" d, Keith Murray design, black basalt, simple engine turned rim band, printed and imp mark, c1940 .... 1,100.00

7" d, Elwyn Jones design, bone china, circular form with flaring rim, brown, green and blue glazes, printed mark and artist signed and dated 1973 .... 1,200.00

Inkstand, Keith Murray design, 10-1/8" l, rect form pen tray with shallow wells and central cov box supporting two inkpots, matte green ground, imp and printed marks, c1936, slight chip under cover's rim 590.00

Jug, 8" h, Keith Murray design, celadon slip, cream-colored ground, imp and printed marks, c1940 .... 210.00

Vase, Keith Murray design

6" h, globular, engine turned banding, imp and printed marks, c1935 .... 650.00

7-1/4" h, straw glaze, horizontally turned body, printed mark, c1940 .... 765.00

9-1/4" h, engine turned banding on matte blue ground, printed mark, c1935 .... 940.00

10" h, vertical turnings, scalloped rim, imp and printed mark, c1930 .... 530.00

Basalt

Bowl

6-3/4" l, oval, scrolled foliate molded handles, arabesque floral relief design on stippled ground, imp lower case mark, late 18th C 1,175.00

Moonlight Lustre, potpourri urn, mottled purple luster and orange enamel glaze, insert disc lid, impressed mark, c1810, cover missing, foot-rim chip, staining, surface flakes to glaze, 12-3/4" h, **$400**. Photo courtesy of Skinner, Inc.

9-1/4" d, rosso antico upturned loop handles, applied palmette band, imp mark, early 19th C 600.00

Bust, library type, mounted on waisted circular socle

7-3/4" h, Aristotle, imp title and lower case mark, late 18th C, restored chip to side of shoulder 600.00

7-3/4" h, Socrates, imp title and mark, late 18th C, restored to side of shoulder 600.00

Basalt, teapot, 8-1/2" h, **$320**.

Cabaret set, 6" h coffeepot, 3-1/8" h cov teapot; cov sugar bowl, 3-7/8" d waste bowl, tea cup and saucer, 16-3/4" d oval tray, iron red enamel trim lines, polychromed and gilded floral designs, imp marks, mid-19th C **1,880.00**

Candlesticks, pr

7-3/4" h, polychrome decorated floral designs, imp mark, mid-19th C **1,120.00**

10-1/2" h, seated Egyptian sphinx, wings supporting candle sconce, mounted on raised rectangular plinth, imp mark, 19th C, restorations, chips.................................. **3,000.00**

10-7/8" h, female figures representing Juno and Ceres, each holding cornucopia-form sconce, mounted on fluted drums and square plinths, gilded and bronzed, imp marks, c1880, restored sconces, plinths drilled as lamps **2,350.00**

11" h, Triton, male figure holding cornucopia-form sconce, imp marks, late 18th/early 19th C, possibly married, foot rim chips **3,825.00**

Center bowl, 12" d, Encaustic dec, iron red and white enamel decorated bands of laurel and berries above an Etruscan pattern, imp mark, early 19th C, restored to rim and handle **4,700.00**

Crater urn, cov, 6" h, pierced lid, hand-painted floral sprays, imp mark, mid-19th C, missing insert lid.................. **1,410.00**

Crocus pot, stand, 9" l oval shape hedgehog, pierced body; 10" l lobed oval stand with steep sides, imp marks, 19th C **1,650.00**

Ewer, 14-1/2" h, leaf molded spout, tall scrolled handle, applied foliage and laurel band, raised Wedgwood and Bentley wafer mark, c1775, handle restored, relief loss to acanthus leaves near socle................................. **2,750.00**

Figure, 6-3/8" h, King Charles the First, modeled as cavalier standing by his spaniel, circular plinth, incised title, imp mark, c1910................................. **500.00**

Inkstand, 7" l, oil lamp form, attached to oval tray, applied rosso antico foliate decoration, insert inkpot, imp mark, c1820, restored nozzle................ **360.00**

Jasper, cache pot, green, floral garland around rim, body decorated with leaf and grape motif swags emanating from lions' heads, cartouches featuring classical figures, imp marks on bottom, "WEDGWOOD Made in England 5 W 71," 5" d, 4-1/2" h, **$115**. Photo courtesy of Alderfer Auction Co.

Jug, cov, 9-1/4" h, vertical engine turned borders on both sides of central relief band of Bacchanalian boys, sibyl finial, loop handle terminating at satyr's mask, silver mounts, imp mark, late 18th C **2,115.00**

Jug, open, 7-1/2" h, all-over decorated with vertical engine-turning, loop handle terminating at satyr mask, silver mounted, imp mark, late 18th C **1,650.00**

Model, 5-1/8" l, Reclining Boy, after Della Robbia, modeled with head up, hand in pointing gesture, imp mark, mid-19th C, shallow foot rim chips.................. **600.00**

Plaque, self-framed

6-1/4" l, Claudius, oval shape, incised title below portrait, imp mark, late 18th C, set in modern frame **1,765.00**

6-1/4" l, Vesputian, oval shape, incised title below portrait, imp mark, late 18th C, set in modern frame **1,300.00**

Portrait medallion

3-1/2" l, Dr. Boerhaave, oval, imp upper-lower case mark, c1790, rim nicks, set in brass and leather bound frame **650.00**

4-5/8" l, Gyrus, self-framed oval shape, imp title and Wedgwood and Bentley mark, c1779 .... **450.00**

Portrait plaque, 6-5/8" l, Elizabeth I, oval, fluted and laurel banded frame, self-framed, unmarked, c1779......... **3,650.00**

Rum pot, cov

8-3/8" h, bail handle, body with relief of Bacchanalian boys above band of vertical engine-turning, cover with sibyl finial centering radiating engine turning, molded foliate border, imp mark, late 18th C, restoration at tip of spout **1,550.00**

10-1/2" h, bail handle, encaustic dec, iron red and white enamel decorated with running anthemion band on shoulder, "Antique" pattern on body, sibyl finial, imp mark, c1800, restored spout **9,695.00**

Tankard

4-1/4" h, molded body with wide central band of oak leaves on dimpled ground, imp Wedgwood and Bentley mark, c1778 .... **1,765.00**

4-7/8" h, wide molded band of oak leaves to a stippled ground, silver mounts, imp mark, late 18th C **1,100.00**

5" h, relief figures depicting "Bringing Home the Game," center vertical engine-turning, silver mounts, imp lower case mark, late 18th C **2,350.00**

Teapot, cov, 7-1/4" h, applied rosso antico acanthus and bell flowers on body, applied acanthus and foliage on cov, imp mark, early 19th C, rim nick.......... **900.00**

Vase, cov, 13" h, central self-framed medallion with classical subject, sphinx-head handles, raised Wedgwood and Bentley wafer mark, c1775, cover missing, slight nicks to shoulder rim, numerous chips to plinth **1,000.00**

Vase, 16-1/2" h, vertical engine turned body, lion's-head handles terminating at mask heads, shoulder with laurel band, imp Wedgwood and Bentley mark, c1775, rim plinth chip................ **5,875.00**

Bone china

Celery dish, gilt diamond border, printed mark, foot rim, light gilt war **175.00**

Coffee set, 8-1/2" h cov coffee pot, 3-3/4" cream jug, 5-1/4" h cov sugar bowl, Persian Ponies pattern, designed by Victor Skellern, printed marks, c1935 .... **1,765.00**

Service plate, 10-5/8" d, each with hp floral center, scrolled foliate gilding to wide border, pale green ground printed marks, 20th C, price for set of 12 .... **980.00**

Tea set, Liberty Ware, 5-1/2" h silver shaped cov teapot, 6-1/2" h creamer, cov sugar, six cups and saucers, 7-3/4" d cake plate, gilt trim line and printed flag ensemble polychrome dec, c1917 .... **1,265.00**

Vase, 10" h, white glazed, shell form, bowl mounted atop coral stem, raised circular plinth, printed mark, late 19th C **500.00**

Caneware, Game pie dish and underplate, recumbent cow finial, floral scrollwork ground, shell-shaped handles, 6" dish, 7-1/4" shell scrollwork underplate, unmarked, early 19th C, horns chipped, tiny flake on lid, **$340**. Photo courtesy of Cowan's Historic Americana Auctions.

Caneware

Bamboo vase, 10" h, four bamboo cane form spills encaustic decorated in shades of blue, naturalistic encrusted freeform base washed in green, imp mark, late 18th C, restored chips **7,950.00**

Bowl

7" d, applied gray/green drab relief of ferns and stars, imp mark, early 19th C **890.00**

10-7/8" d, smear glazed, applied white fruiting grapevine border, imp mark, 19th C **470.00**

Coffee cup and saucer, 5" d saucer, cup with relief of boys at play, lower body and saucer with fluted vertical engine turned band, upper-lower case mark, late 18th C **470.00**

Coffeepot, cov, 7-3/4" h, cylindrical, engine turned basket weave body and cover, sibyl finial, imp mark, c1880, slight spout nick **1,150.00**

Cream jug, 2-1/2" h, bamboo molded body and strap handle, encaustic dec, in shades of blue and white, imp upper-lower case mark, late 18th C, slight enamel rim flake **1,300.00**

Hot water pot, cov, 8-1/2" h, Egyptian, applied chocolate brown relief with a band of hieroglyphs above a meander border on pot, hieroglyphs surrounding a crocodile finial on cov, imp mark, early 19th C **3,825.00**

Inkpot, 2-1/8" h, globular form, loop handles, engine turned body, imp mark, late 18th C **825.00**

Jug, 7" h, classical relief with scenes of Domestic Employment above vertical engine turned band, imp mark, early 19th C, cov missing **1,000.00**

Mug

3-3/8" h, applied gray/green fern and star relief, imp mark, late 18th C **890.00**

3-1/2" h, barrel form, relief boys at play, vertical engine turned band, white glazed rim and int., upper-lower case mark, late 18th C **1,550.00**

Pie dish, cov, 13-1/2" l, oval, removable "crust" rim, applied and molded acanthus leaves dec radiating from cover handle, ornamental decoration to rim and crust, imp mark, late 18th C **1,530.00**

Plate, 8-1/8" d, blue enamel Greek key border, white glazed centers, imp marks, c1800, price for pr **1,645.00**

Teapot, cov

4" h, smear glazed, applied green foliate relief, imp mark, 19th C, faint star line to base **600.00**

5-3/8" h, silver form, octagonal, applied chocolate brown relief of classical females within beaded oval framed cartouches, trophy drops borders, oak leaves on cov, imp mark, late 18th C, restored to spout cover with chip to internal stop and shallow rim flakes **590.00**

Teapot, cov, stand, 6-1/2" h, beehive form, imp mark, early 19th C, slight hairline to handle, rim chips to cover **1,300.00**

Carrara

Bust

19-3/4" h, Lord Zetland, titled, mounted on waisted circular socle, reverse imp with registry date, c1868, "Proof" and factory mark, stain spots, socle chip repaired, filed firing lines on back **1,000.00**

15-1/2" h, Byron, modeled by E.W. Wyon, mounted on waisted circular socle, imp title, sculptor and factory marks, c1855......................... **900.00**

Figure, 20-1/4" h, Venus Victrix, seminude figure modeled standing on freeform base, inscribed title, imp mark, mid-19th C, shallow chip and nick to base **1,450.00**

Vase, cov, 7-1/2" h, trophy relief between floral festoons terminating at ram's heads, foliate borders, bronzed and gilt, imp and printed marks, c1900, cover restored **1,495.00**

Fairyland Lustre, vase, square, scene of city with large tree in the foreground and bridge with figures in front of the city, concealed figures of fairies and animals at base of tree, other two sides show stylized trees, partially concealing stairway to city, opalescent luster glaze on outside, blue wash interior with band of butterflies decoration, 5-1/2" square top, 7-3/4" h, **$6,100**. Photo courtesy of James D. Julia, Inc.

Cream ware

Bowl

7-1/2" d, scalloped edge, cut-out design, imp "Wedgwood" **600.00**

8-1/8" l, reticulated, molded fiddleback ladle, imp "Wedgwood," stains, edge chip................... **160.00**

Plate, 9-1/8" d, scenic, little girl and mother buying buns from the Bun Man, back titled "Buns!, Buns!, Buns!," 1863 mark and artist sgd "Lessore"...... **335.00**

Vase, 6" h, molded grape vines and foliage, painted band of strawberries, mid-19th C.................................. **250.00**

Diceware

Incense burner, 5-1/4" h, three-color jasper dip, double-handled bowl atop three paw feet set on drum shape, pale lilac ground engine turned dicing to white body applied with green quatrefoils, white foliate band at foot, imp mark, late 18th C, rim and foot rim chip repaired, faint firing lines to the surface of the drum **9,400.00**

Tea set, three-color jasper dip, 3-7/8" h cov teapot, 3" h cream jug, 4" h cov sugar, black ground with applied white vinework framing engine turned dicing with yellow quatrefoils, imp marks, 19th C **7,975.00**

Vase, cov

8-3/4" h, three-color dip, scrolled white handles, light blue dip body with applied white relief of dancing hours below drapery swags, green quatrefoils to shoulder, socle and cover, lower body with engine turned dicing, imp mark, 20th C, replacement brass finial, slight relief loss to one quatrefoil at shoulder **2,000.00**

11-1/2" h, three color jasper dip, applied white classical relief and foliate borders on black ground, yellow quatrefoils to engine turned dicing, imp mark, 19th C, restored **1,410.00**

Drabware

Bowl, 7" d, wide leaf design to ext., imp mark, c1820................................ **650.00**

Candlesticks, pr, glazed, columnar, sq plinth, gilt trim lines, imp mark, c1840, chips to plinths, one with slight chip and line to sconce rim **420.00**

Coffee biggin, 6-3/4" h, smear glazed, applied white floral bands, fitted with two insert strainers, imp mark, mid-19th C, finial ground................................ **600.00**

Compote, ftd, 10-1/4" l, 5-5/8" h, glazed, oval, upturned loop handles, enamel bird and floral dec, gilt trim lines, imp mark, c1830, faint rim line **400.00**

Inkstand dish, 9-1/4" l, glazed, leaf molded tray fitted with three attached pots, two with covers, gilt trim lines, imp mark, c1830................................ **715.00**

Teapot, cov, 5-1/8" h, applied blue fern and star relief, imp mark, c1830... **650.00**

Jasper, cheese stand and cover, blue, classical white frieze, 19th C, lid handle reglued, 7-1/2" x 10-1/2", **$435**. Photo courtesy of David Rago Auctions, Inc.

Jasper

Barber bottle, 11" h, three colors, green ground, white relief and lilac ground medallions, bacchus head reliefs to shoulder, imp mark, mid-19th C, cover insert damaged **2,100.00**

Biscuit jar

5-1/8" h, three-color dip, central dark blue ground with applied white classical relief, bordered in bands of light blue, silver plated rim, handle, and cov, imp mark, late 19th C **415.00**

5-1/4" h, dark blue dip, applied white birds in relief below laurel and berry banded border, silver plated rim, handle, and cov, imp mark, early 20th C.................................. **635.00**

5-1/4" h, lilac dip, applied white relief of fox hunting scene, silver plated rim, handle, and cov, imp mark, early 20th C.................................. **550.00**

5-1/4" h, three-color dip, green ground, applied vertical bands of white scrolls, yellow trellis, silver plated rim, handle, and cov, imp mark, c1882 .... **815.00**

5-1/2" h, lilac dip, applied classical figures, silver plated rim, handle, and cov, imp mark, late 19th C, light crazing to ground.................. **375.00**

5-1/2" h, yellow dip, applied black relief of fruiting grapevine festoons terminating at lion masks and rings, silver plated rim, cov, and handle, imp mark, c1930 .... **690.00**

5-3/4" h, three-color dip, central black ground with applied white classical relief, bordered in bands of yellow, silver plated rim, cov, and handle, imp mark, 19th C, shoulder nicks **800.00**

5-7/8" h, black dip, applied white classical relief, silver plated rim, handle, foot rim, and cov, imp mark, 19th C................................... **630.00**

6" h, pale lilac dip, applied white classical relief, silver plated rim, handle, and cov, imp mark, c1900 .... **375.00**

6" h, three-color dip, central dark blue ground with applied white classical relief, bordered in bands of light blue, silver plated rim, handle, and cov, imp mark, late 19th C **435.00**

6" h, three-color dip, dark blue ground with oval light blue medallions, applied white relief of classical figures on horseback between trophies and foliate borders, silver plated rim, handle, and cov, lion finial, imp mark, 19th C **1,265.00**

7-3/4" h, crimson dip, applied white classical relief on jar, oak leaves radiating from an acorn finial on lid, imp mark, c1920 .... **2,300.00**

Jasper, plate, blue, white classical decoration, **$95**. Photo courtesy of Wiederseim Associates, Inc.

Bough pot, cov

6-1/8" h, pale blue dip, sq, pierced disc lid, paneled sides with applied white classical relief bordered with flowering pots and stiff leaves, imp mark, late 18th C, chips **1,100.00**

6-3/8" h, solid pale blue, sq, arched and recessed panels applied with white relief figures representing four seasons, framed with foliage, pierced insert lids, imp mark, late 18th C, nicks and restorations, price for pr.................................. **4,460.00**

Bowl, 8-7/8" d, solid pale blue, lapidary polished int., ext. with applied white relief of Bacchanalian boys between festoons of fruiting grapevines, foliate borders, ftd, imp mark, c1785, slight relief loss at foot rim.. **7,050.00**

Box, cov, 5" d, crimson dip, circular, applied white classical relief centering floral banded border on cover, base with sunflowers, imp mark, c1920 .... **1,650.00**

Brooch, 3" l, dark blue, oval, applied white classical relief depicting "Poor Maria," cut steel mount, no visible mark, c1800, adapted from one-half a buckle **600.00**

Buckle frame, 3-1/8" l, dark blue dip, oval medallion with polished edge, applied white classical relief depicting Cupid Unmasked, framed in cut steel and faceted beadwork, imp mark, late 18th C, rust.. **600.00**

Butter tub, cov, 3-1/4" h, solid light blue, cylindrical, applied white foliate borders, imp mark, late 18th C, foot rim nick **1,000.00**

Candlesticks, pr

8" h, dark blue dip, cylindrical, applied white wreathed laurel, imp mark, early 19th C, rim damage to one nozzle............................ **560.00**

9-1/4" h, solid white, standing figures of Flora and Pomona supporting lilac jasper dip cornucopia-form candleholders, standing on circular lilac socles and sq plinths, imp date letters and mark, c1868, missing candle spikes, plinth rim nicks **3,820.00**

Cane, 2" d x 1-1/4" h pale blue and white porcelain knob handle, 1-1/4" sterling silver disk set on top with inscription "Baptist Church Warrington, Presented to Mrs. Margurette Morris, on Placing Foundation Stone, Dec, 12, 1912," Chester hallmarks for 1912, handle sides dec with white raised classical figures, name appears when knob is unscrewed, finely figured snakewood shaft, 2/3" silver collar, 1-1/4" horn ferrule, 34-1/4" l, c1912 .... **1,570.00**

Chamberstick, 2-3/4" h, crimson dip, applied white classical relief and foliate borders, imp mark, c1920, slight rim flake

to nozzle, bubbles to glaze on side 2,000.00
Chess figure, 2-3/8" h, solid blue, pawn modeled as warrior bearing sword and shield, circular plinth base, imp mark, late 18th C, chip to shield 300.00
Coffee cann, 4-5/8" d saucer, lilac dip, applied white foliate relief, can with lapidary polished int., late 18th C 1,300.00

Jasper, sugar caster, cobalt blue ground, ram's heads with floral swags over panels of classical figures in varying scenes, sterling silver rim, pierced lid of sterling silver with finial, both sterling portions with hallmarks for Chester, England, imp mark on bottom, 7-3/8" h, **$350**. Photo courtesy of Alderfer Auction Co.

Custard cup, cov, 2-1/2" h, blue dip, cylindrical form with applied white lattice relief and twisted loop handle, piercing to cover, imp mark, late 18th C, handle restored 360.00
Figure, 7" h, solid white, Hebe, mounted on cylindrical solid light blue jasper drum base with applied white floral festoons terminating at ram's heads, base with imp upper-lower case mark, 18th C, figure restored, base chips restored 3,290.00
Jardinière, 7-1/4" h, olive green dip, applied white relief figures of muses below fruiting grapevine festoons terminating at lion masks and rings, imp mark, c1920 .... 420.00
Jug
- 3-7/8" h, crimson dip, barrel shape, applied white classical Muses between foliate frames and vine borders, trophy beneath spout, imp mark, c1920 .... 825.00
- 4" h, crimson dip, applied white classical relief below fruiting grapevine border, imp mark, c1920, mark partially removed 1,000.00
- 6-1/4" h, crimson dip, rope twist handle, applied white classical relief with fruiting grapevine border, imp mark, c1920 .... 2,000.00
- 7-1/2" h, solid white, oenochoe shape, (ewer form) loop handle terminating at satyr mask, imp mark, early 19th C, rim nicks, line near base of handle 500.00

Mantel luster, 13-1/2" h, drum shaped base, dark blue dip, applied white classical relief, cut glass bobeches and prisms, early 19th C, electrified, chips to glass and rims, relief loss, price for pr 920.00
Mantle plaque, 7" x 18-1/4", green dip, rect, applied white relief of scrolling acanthus leaves within banded key border, imp mark, late 18th C, chip to banded border, set in modern gilded and ebonized wood frame 25,850.00
Match box, cov, 3-3/4" l, yellow dip, rect, applied white classical relief, imp mark, late 19th/early 20th C 550.00
Match holder, 2-3/8" h, crimson dip, cylindrical, applied white classical relief, imp mark, c1920, relief loss 490.00

Jasper, biscuit jar, covered, applied black relief of Muses below fruiting grapevine festoons terminating in lion masks with rings, grapevine border to foot, silver-plated rim, handle and cover, impressed mark, c1930, 5-3/4" h, **$800**. Photo courtesy of Skinner Auctioneers and Appraisers.

Medallion
- 2-5/8" l, five-color dip, applied white classical relief on lilac ground, framed in blue. applied yellow foliage, outer green frame, imp mark, late 18th/early 19th C 890.00
- 3-1/4" l, solid dark blue dip blue, oval, applied white relief depiction of "Io kissed by Jupiter disguised as wind," imp Wedgwood and Bentley mark, c1780, slight rim nick to front edge, shallow rim flakes to back edge 1,175.00
- 3-1/4" l, solid blue, oval, applied white relief depicting "Fame," imp Wedgwood and Bentley mark, c1775, surface blemish 500.00
- 3-1/4" l, solid blue, oval, applied white relief of classical female with sacrifice, imp Wedgwood and Bentley mark, c1780, shallow surface and back edge rim flakes 500.00

Mustard pot, 3" h, yellow dip, applied black fruiting grapevine festoons terminating at lion masks and rings, silver plated cover, imp mark, c1930 .... 320.00
Necklace, 21" l, lilac dip, 21 assorted beads, each with applied relief, 14 teardrop-shaped with classical subjects, seven oval with stars and stiff leaves, unmarked, 19th C 920.00
Oil lamp, 5-7/8" l, black jasper dip, applied white laurel bands surrounding female mask center, imp mark, mid-19th C 1,150.00

Jasper, brooch, oval carved chalcedony, mother and child, yellow gold border, signed "Wedgwood," **$300**. Photo courtesy of Sloan's Auctioneers and Appraisers.

Plaque
- 4-1/2" x 17-1/2", green dip, rect, applied white relief "Offerings to Peace" and "Sacrifice to Peace," from designs by Lady Templetown, imp mark, late 19th C, set in ebonized wood frame, losses to frame 1,100.00
- 7-1/4" d, solid light blue, Eve, circular, applied white relief designed by Anna Zinkeisen, imp mark, c1924, faint firing lines, set in a modern frame 1,175.00
- 12" l, 6" h, rect, solid light blue, applied white Blind Man's Bluff in relief, foliate frame, imp mark, early 19th C 750.00
- 15" l, 4-1/2" h, solid green, applied white relief of horses, modeled by Rosemary Barnett, unmarked, c1965, giltwood frame 2,415.00
- 18-1/4" l, 6-1/8" h, solid light blue, applied white classical relief of boys at play and gathering fruit, imp mark, and oval "O," attributed to Bert Bentley, c1925 .... 1,265.00
- 19-1/2" l, 7" h, solid light blue, applied white Dancing Hours in relief, framed, marks not visible, 19th C, price for pr 4,600.00

Portland vase
- 4-7/8" h, olive green dip, applied white classical relief, imp mark, c1920 .... 920.00
- 6-1/4" h, crimson dip, applied white classical relief, imp mark, c1920 .... 3,110.00

6-7/8" h, dark blue dip, applied white classical relief, imp mark, c1900 .... 375.00

10" h, solid black, applied white classical relief, base with half length figure wearing Phrygian cap, imp mark, c1900 .... 2,530.00

10-1/4" h, dark blue dip, white classical figures in relief, base with half-length figure wearing Phrygian cap, imp mark, 19th C, foot rim chip 1,100.00

Portrait medallion, oval, applied white relief

3-1/4" l, lilac dip, Charles Daniel Solander, imp title and mark, c1790, set in ebonized wood frame 1,880.00

3-1/4" l, solid blue, Benjamin Franklin, imp mark, c1775, set in gilt metal frame 4,230.00

4" l, black dip, Maria I of Portugal, imp title and mark, c1787, set in elaborate gilt metal frame 2,475.00

4" l, dark blue dip, Thomas Byerley, modeled by William Theed, imp mark, c1810, set in ebonized wood frame 1,300.00

4" l, solid dark blue dip, George Washington, imp Wedgwood and Bentley mark, c1779 .... 2,475.00

4-1/8" l, light blue dip, Sir William Hamilton, imp title and mark, c1780, very slight rim nick to back edge 3,820.00

Salad set, 7-1/2" d bowl, dark blue dip, applied white classical relief, silver plated rim, 11" l silver plate fork and spoon servers with dark blue handles, applied foliate relief, late 19th C... 350.00

Salt, open, 2-7/8" d, solid light blue, applied white Dancing Hours in relief, imp marks, 19th C, one with rim chip, other with relief loss to figure, price for pr 750.00

Spill vase, 3" h, three-color dip, light blue ground, engine turned fluting below lilac ground medallions, applied white classical relief above floral festoons terminating at ram's heads, imp mark, mid-19th C 1,035.00

Sucrier, cov, 3-1/2" h, yellow dip, cylindrical, applied white classical relief, imp mark, 20th C 420.00

Sugar bowl, cov, crimson dip, applied white classical relief, imp mark, c1920, restored chip on cover collar and two areas of relief 290.00

Syrup jug, 6-1/4" h, dark blue dip, applied white birds in relief below oak leaf banded border, silver plated insert cov, imp mark, early 20th C............ 550.00

Tea bowl, 5-1/4" d saucer, lilac dip, applied white foliate relief, lapidary polished bowl int., imp mark, late 18th C 1,300.00

Tea canister, cov, 6-1/2" h, crimson dip, applied white classical relief below florets, imp mark, c1920............ 1,775.00

Teapot, cov, 4-1/4" h, yellow dip, applied black classical relief and foliate borders, imp mark, 20th C 500.00

Tea tray, 13-3/4" l, solid blue, oval, applied white arabesque floral border and sunflower center, imp mark, late 18th C, rim chip repair............ 600.00

Jasper, oil lamp and cover, dark blue dip, applied white classical relief, cover with figure group above scrolled leaves, lamp with stiff leaf border, impressed mark, c1800, chip to cover, 5-1/4" l, **$1,000**. Photo courtesy of Skinner Auctioneers and Appraisers.

Tobacco jar, cov

4-1/4" h, lilac dip, applied white classical figures between foliate frames, lion masks and rings, silver plated replacement cov, imp mark, c1870, nick to festoon............ 350.00

5-7/8" h, light blue dip, applied white relief of male figures smoking and foliage, match strikes and holder on cover, weight insert, imp mark, late 19th C, small rim and foot rim chips 750.00

9" h, light blue dip, applied white classical figures within foliate frames, lion masks and rings, candle sconce finial, imp, c1870, light staining to cov, foot rim chip, one ring of relief repaired, foot rim hairlines and nicks 260.00

Vase, cov

6-1/4" h, dark blue dip, flaring sides, applied white classical relief, pierced disc cov, imp mark, early 20th C 210.00

6-3/4" h, crimson dip, two handles, applied white classical relief, imp mark, c1920, cover restored 1,380.00

7" h, crimson dip, bottle form, applied white classical relief, imp mark, c1920 .... 2,185.00

9-1/4" h, dark blue dip, two handles, applied white classical and foliate relief, imp mark, early 20th C 435.00

9-1/2" h, three-color dip, solid light blue body, lilac ground oval medallions, white relief of classical subjects, drapery swags, and foliate borders, imp mark, late 19th C, rim chip to shoulder 1,610.00

10-1/2" h, dark blue dip, applied white classical relief, imp mark, late 19th C, slight rim chip 435.00

11-1/4" h, black dip, applied white relief of Muses centering floral festoon and foliate borders, imp mark, mid-19th C............ 2,100.00

13" h, green dip, applied white classical relief centering foliate banded borders, imp mark, 19th C, hairline to socle 1,175.00

Vase

3" h, three-color dip, green ground, applied lilac medallions, white portraits in relief between drapery swags, imp mark, 19th C, rim and foot rim chips............ 435.00

6-1/4" h, green dip, applied white trellis and floral dec, imp mark, mid-19th C, light staining to foot rim 920.00

6-1/2" h, solid black, applied white relief of column and lion mask framed panels with medallions above flowering festoons, imp mark, c1890, restored rim chip 520.00

Lusters

Bowl

Celtic ornament, 5" d, matte black designs on yellow ground ext., mother of pearl int., printed mark, c1920 .... 825.00

Miscellaneous, dinnerware set, cream colored, service for eight plus serving pieces, **$495**. Photo courtesy of Alderfer Auction Co.

Dragon Lustre, lobed body, dragons on mottled blue ext., mother of pearl int., phoenix surrounding central "Three Jewel" design, pattern Z4829, printed mark, c1920 .... **1,410.00**

Empire Lustre, 4-1/4" d, matte black ext. gilt dec Gothic circles, mottled orange int. with Celtic ornament to center, printed mark, c1920 .... **715.00**

Fairyland Lustre Empire, leapfrogging elves on black ext., mother of pearl int. with elves on branch, pattern Z4968, printed mark, c1920 .... **4,415.00**

Lahore Lustre Imperial, polychrome dec on black ground ext., animals and riders in procession on yellow ground int., printed mark, c1920, slight wear to int. glaze **3,290.00**

Coffeepot, cov, 5-1/2" h, Moonlight, imp mark, c1810, small chips to spout and cover **690.00**

Compote, Hummingbird Lustre, 10-3/4" d, mottled dark blue ext. hummingbirds surrounding bowl, flying geese to foot rim, mottled orange int. with flying geese border and hummingbird center, printed mark, c1920 .... **2,115.00**

Cup, 3" h, gilt dec vein design, mottled pink/purple ext., mother of pearl int., printed mark, c1920 .... **360.00**

Dish, 4-3/4" d, Dragon, Daisy Makeig Jones marks, Z4831, c1914-31 .... **675.00**

Fruit bowl, 8-1/8" d, mottled deep blue ext. with fruits, mottled orange int. with berries surrounding fruit center, pattern Z5457, printed mark, c1920 .... **1,100.00**

Lily tray, Fairyland Lustre, 9-1/4" d, ext. with green fish border on mother of pearl ground, black firbolgs, outlined in gilt on orange ground int., printed mark, c1920, rim chip **900.00**

Plaque, Fairyland Lustre, 4-3/4" x 10-5/8", rect, Picnic by a River design, pattern Z5158, printed mark, c1920 .... **7,650.00**

Potpourri urn, 12-3/4" h, Moonlight Lustre, mottled purple lustre and orange enamel glaze, insert disc lid, imp mark, c1810, cover missing, foot rim chip, staining, surface flakes to glaze **390.00**

Punch bowl, 11" d, Fairyland, Firbolgs, ruby ext., MOP Thumbelina int., printed mark and no., c1920 .... **3,600.00**

Teapot, cov, 3" h, Moonlight, drum form, imp mark, c1810, rim chips restored, nicks to spout rim **575.00**

Vase

Dragon Lustre, 5" h, blue irid ground, gold dec of dragons and birds, some wear to gold **300.00**

Fairyland Lustre Candlemas, 7-1/2" h, black ground panels within blue lustre frames, printed mark, c1920 .... **9,400.00**

Fairyland Lustre, 9" h, Argus Pheasant design, birds and flowers in shades of red and pink, orange ground patterned background, printed mark, c1920 .... **7,100.00**

Fairyland Lustre, 13-5/8" h, Pillar design pattern Z4968, printed mark, c1920 .... **11,165.00**

Fairyland Lustre Torches, 11" h, brightly glowing torches along stairway leading to temple, trees, vines, birds and fairies dec, bottom marked with gold Wedgwood urn, "WEDGWOOD MADE IN ENGLAND" **5,175.00**

Fish Lustre, 8-7/8" h, mottled blue ext. with polychrome and gilt dec fish surrounding body, pattern Z4920, printed mark, c1920 .... **1,880.00**

Wall pocket, 9-3/4" l, Moonlight Lustre, shell form, pierced insert grid, imp mark, c1810, hairline on back **850.00**

Marsden Art Ware

Vase

10-1/2" h, slip dec, powder blue ground with oranges among leafy branches, imp mark, c1890 .... **1,645.00**

12-3/4" h, bottle form, slip dec, floral and scrolled vine design, imp mark, c1885 .... **940.00**

Pearlware

Bough pot, cov

6" h, polychrome dec transfer print chrysanthemum pattern, pierced flat lid, imp marks, early 19th C, rim chips to one lid, other lid damaged, price for pr **560.00**

Miscellaneous, pitcher, green glaze, mottled grapes and grape leaves, "Made in England" mark, **$65**. Photo courtesy of Joseph P. Smalley, Jr., Auctioneer.

9-3/4" h, brown slip dec, rouletted border above applied drapery swags and fluting, imp mark, c1800, (hairline to pierced cover, rim chip repair, glaze loss to dome cover **600.00**

Candlesticks, pr, turquoise glaze, modeled as classical female holding cornucopia form base, supporting leafy sconce, imp mark, c1872, glaze wear, nicks to glaze surface **1,380.00**

Fruit basket, 10-5/8" one stand, oval, basketweave molded center, pierced gallery, green enamel trim, imp mark, early 19th C, some damage to strapping of basket, glaze wear on stand **320.00**

Platter, well and tree, gaudy cobalt blue and rust Chrysanthemum pattern, c1800, repaired **595.00**

Potpourri vase, pierced cov, blue ground, white relief floral swags, band above engine-turned fluting, imp mark, c1800, body restoration, married cover **230.00**

Tankard, 5" h, polychrome enamel dec, black transfer printed floral and foliate border, gilt trim lines and handle, imp mark, early 19th C **235.00**

Tea tray, 18-1/8" l, rect, cut corners, red/pink transfer printed border, c1886 .... **200.00**

Queen's Ware

Bowl, 13" l, oval, undecorated, central bail handle, imp mark, late 18th C, minor stain spots **775.00**

Breakfast tray, 11-1/2" l, quatrefoil shape, polychrome dec brown transfer print with Mr. Punch centering gathering of men, bowl in foreground titled "The Very Best of Physic," printed and imp mark, c1880 .... **950.00**

Candlesticks, pr, 10-3/4" h, octagonal concave base with acanthus leaf border below tapered fluting, bellied shaft with laurel leaf border near its base, imp mark, late 18th C, foot rim chip, one nozzle repaired **400.00**

Compote, 5-1/2" h, oval, upturned loop handles, enamel Ivy pattern borders, imp marks, late 18th C, price for pr **1,250.00**

Fruit basket and stand, 13-1/4" l handle to handle, oval, basket with openwork basketweave body, double entwined handles, stand with openwork border, imp mark, 18th C, nicks to handles, rim repair to stand **550.00**

Inkstand, 8" l, oval, molded bird's head handles, two insert pots with scrolled handles, green, iron red and black enamel foliate vine borders, imp mark, 19th C, stand with hairline to top surface, light flaking to enamel trim lines, both pots restored **600.00**

Jug, 10-1/2" h, black transfer print, titled "John Penrose Andrew & Co." below spout, prints of rabbit hunt and Farmer's Arms on sides, traces of gilt foliate dec, imp mark, c1770 .... **2,750.00**

Sardine box, cov, 8-1/4" l, attached tray, rect, polychrome, brown transfers of flowers and butterflies, fish finial, imp mark, glaze rim flakes, light staining, shallow rim chip **500.00**

Teapot, cov, 4-3/4" h, globular, leaf molded spout, double entwined handle, floral finial, enamel Oriental subjects dec attributed to David Rhodes, imp upper-lower case mark, c1770, slight glaze wear to spout lip, cover restored **1,175.00**

Toast rack, 7-1/4" l, rect, green enamel trim lines, imp mark, 19th C.......... **295.00**

Tureen, cover, stand and ladle, 10" h, circular, scrolled handles, green enamel edge and foliate design surrounding leaf-molded knop, imp mark, c1800, slight chips to stand rim, tureen foot **600.00**

Vase, 10-1/4" h, pierced trumpet shape, molded acanthus leaves below lattice panels framed with laurel, floral swags along top rim, clear glass insert, imp mark, late 19th/early 20th C **1,000.00**

Vase, cov, 15-1/2" h, gilded horn handles terminating at satyr masks, Emile Lessore dec, polychrome enamel landscapes with two females, single female on reverse, gilt trim, imp mark, c1860, finial reglued, repair to rim of socle, light gilt wear **1,650.00**

Veilleuse, 11-1/2" h, pierced cylindrical form pedestal, insert bowl, covered teapot with bail handle, imp mark, late 18th C, slight chip to cover rim, hairline to insert bowl rim **1,250.00**

Miscallenous, plate, Ben Franklin, embossed portrait medallion and laurel garland, back stamped "Univ of PA Bicentennial, 1740-1940, The Young Franklin, drawn by Roy F. Carson, '23, Wedgwood, Etruria, England," Boston importer's stamp, **$125**. Photo courtesy of Wiederseim Associates, Inc.

Rosso Antico

Bowl, 7-7/8" d, Egyptian, applied black basalt meander band above stylized foliate molded body, imp mark, early 19th C **1,300.00**

Club jug, 5-1/4" h, relief prunus dec, imp mark, 19th C **775.00**

Coffee can and saucer, 5-1/4" d saucer, applied relief bands of black basalt hieroglyphs, imp mark, late 19th C, restored rim chip to cup, slight chip to saucer rim.................................... **775.00**

Egyptian jug, 8" h, club form, black, iron red and white dec, sphinx on both sides of a bird in flight, imp mark, c1854 .... **1,765.00**

Oil lamp, cov, 5-1/4" l, applied black basalt relief with Zodiac signs, bordering central classical subject, imp mark, early 19th C, shallow chip to side of spout **815.00**

Teapot, cov, 4-5/8" h, applied white prunus dec, twig form handle and spout, imp mark, late 18th C, slight spout chips, staining at handle and spout..... **1,450.00**

Tea set, 8-3/8" l cov teapot (spout shortened), 5-1/8" l creamer, 5-3/4" l cov sugar, applied white stoneware prunus dec, oval form parapet shape, crabstock handles, imp marks, early 19th C **815.00**

Tray, 8-1/2" l, oval, Egyptian, applied black basalt hieroglyphs in relief, imp mark, early 19th C **1,100.00**

Vase, 5-7/8" h, black ground engine turned dicing, foliate and Greek key borders in relief, imp mark, late 18th C, foot rim nicks, missing disc lid **950.00**

Skeaping

Animal, imp mark, 20th C

Fallow deer, 7-1/4" h, cream colored glaze...................................... **440.00**

Pearlware, soup tureen, underplatter, molded shell edges, underglaze blue decoration Mared pattern, 13-1/4" l double-handled oval tureen, foot-rim chip; cover with restored finial; 12-3/4" l ladle; and oval 18" l underplatter, staining, glaze usage wear; impressed marks, late 18th C, **$2,820**. Photo courtesy of Skinner, Inc.

Kangaroo, 8-3/4" h, cane colored glaze...................................... **765.00**

Monkey, 6-3/4" h, cream colored glaze...................................... **360.00**

Polar bear, 7-1/4" h, white moonstone glaze, imp and printed marks, slight flake to corner of base **235.00**

Sea lion, 7-3/4" h, cream colored glaze...................................... **440.00**

Stoneware

Bowl

9-1/2" sq, Water lily pattern, blue transfer print, printed mark, c1840, glaze wear **420.00**

11-1/4" d, green glaze ground, black splatter design, inscribed artist signature and mark for Elwyn James, c1976 .... **1,300.00**

Nautilus shell bowl, stand, 8-1/2" h, white, England, oval, imp mark, early 19th C, slight rim nick.......................... **600.00**

Potpourri low bowl, cov, 9-1/4" d, white smear glaze, upturned loop handles, applied blue acanthus and quatrefoil relief to cover, fruiting grapevines surrounding bowl, imp mark, c1820, slight rim flake under cover rim **1,120.00**

Sauce tureen, cov, stand, 5-1/4" h, white smear glazed, shell shape, shell finial, imp mark, early 19th C **420.00**

Transferware, plate, blue, central portrait of George Washington, rim decorated with floral garland, inscription on reverse in tribute to Washington, stamped and imp marks on reverse indicate manufacture in 1907, 9-1/4" d, **$200**. Photo courtesy of Alderfer Auction Co.

Terra Cotta

Potpourri vase, pierced cov, 4" h, white beaded borders to fluting, iron red slip, imp upper-lower case mark, late 18th C, slight rim nicks.......................... **1,650.00**

Vase, 6" h, white, meander border above fluted cup and base, iron red slip, imp upper-lower case mark, late 18th C, restored rim chips **750.00**

Victoria Ware

Portrait vase, 7-5/8" h, color slip dec, portrait medallions in relief above laurel festoons, mounted on raised drum base with ram's heads and laurel festoons, imp mark, c1880............................... **1,100.00**

Vase, cov, 10-1/8" h, white relief of trophies within floral festoons terminating at ram's heads, and with various foliate borders, all to an dark blue ground decorated with gilt florets, imp mark, c1880.. **2,400.00**

Weller Pottery

History: In 1872, Samuel A. Weller opened a small factory in Fultonham, near Zanesville, Ohio. There he produced utilitarian stoneware, such as milk pans and sewer tile. In 1882, he moved his facilities to Zanesville. Then in 1890 Weller built a new plant in the Putnam section of Zanesville along the tracks of the Cincinnati and Muskingum Railway. Additions followed in 1892 and 1894.

In 1894, Weller entered into an agreement with William A. Long to purchase the Lonhuda Faience Company, which had developed an art pottery line under the guidance of Laura A. Fry, formerly of Rookwood. Long left in 1895, but Weller continued to produce Lonhuda under the new name "Louwelsa." Replacing Long as art director was Charles Babcock Upjohn. He, along with Jacques Sicard, Frederick Hurten Rhead, and Gazo Fudji, developed Weller's art pottery lines.

At the end of World War I, many prestige lines were discontinued and Weller concentrated on commercial wares. Rudolph Lorber joined the staff and designed lines such as Roma, Forest, and Knifewood. In 1920, Weller purchased the plant of the Zanesville Art Pottery and claimed to produce more pottery than anyone else in the country.

Art pottery enjoyed a revival when the Hudson Line was introduced in the early 1920s. The 1930s saw Coppertone and Graystone Garden ware added. However, the Depression forced the closing of the Putnam plant and one on Marietta Street in Zanesville. After World War II, inexpensive Japanese imports took over Weller's market. In 1947, Essex Wire Company of Detroit bought the controlling stock, but early in 1948, operations ceased.

Additional Listings: See *Warman's Americana & Collectibles* for more examples.

Candleholders, pair, Coppertone, turtle and lilypad, marked, 3-1/4" h, **$535**. Photo courtesy of David Rago Auctions, Inc.

Boudoir lamp base, Blue Louwelsa, painted clover blossoms, stamped Louwelsa Weller, 6-1/2" h pottery base, **$500**. Photo courtesy of David Rago Auctions.

Bowl

Coppertone, 9-3/4" d, 5-1/2" h, perched frog, half-kiln stamp, 1/8" firing line to rim **1,100.00**

Flemish, 8" d, 3-3/4" h, trees and birds on a wire dec, unmarked, 2" line from rim **90.00**

Matte Green, 7-1/2" d, 3-3/4" h, emb dragonflies, unmarked **535.00**

Bud vase, Woodcraft, 8-3/4" x 3-1/4", unmarked **420.00**

Candlesticks, pr

3-1/4" x 5", turtle and lilypad, Coppertone, marked **535.00**

9-3/8" h, round rim, sq pyramid form, reticulated arches near base, raised flowers and berries on vine, matted brown glaze, pink, blue, and highlights, one imp "Weller" on base, late 1920s **150.00**

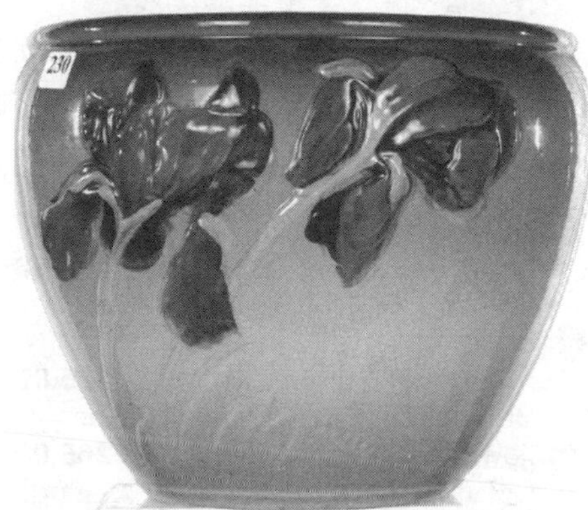

Jardiniére, gray, lavender iris decoration, signed, 8", **$100**. Photo courtesy of Woody Auctions.

Compote, Bonito, 4" h **65.00**

Console bowl, Sydonia, 17" x 6" **90.00**

Console set, Glendale, 15-1/2" d flaring center bowl, flower frog, pair of low candlesticks, bruise to flower frog, kiln mark **1,100.00**

Cornucopia, Wild Rose, peach and green **45.00**

Creamer, Jap Birdimal, 2-1/4" x 3-1/2", Dutch landscape in shades of blue, raised seal mark, restoration to handle **150.00**

Ewer, Barcelona Ware, orig label **250.00**

Figure, Muskota, 7-1/2" x 6", kneeling woman, stamped "WELLER" **370.00**

Garden ornament, swan, ivory glaze, 20" x 18", minor flakes **6,500.00**

Hair receiver, Jap Birdimal, 1-3/4" x 4", four tan, ivory, and black Viking ships on cobalt blue ground, dec by VH **525.00**

Jardinière

Aurelian, brown glaze, painted fruit, sgd "Frank Ferrell" **1,100.00**

Forest, 8"d **215.00**

Dish, Woodcraft, matching flower frog, 10" d, 2-1/2" h, **$275**. Photo courtesy of Joy Luke Auctions.

Jardinière and pedestal, Ardsley, panels of cattails and landscapes, one with blue bird, paint splatter on base, 13" d x 11" h jardinière, 8-1/2" x 19-1/2" h stand, **$1,870**. Photo courtesy of Alderfer Auction Co.

Matte Green, 11" x 12-1/4", emb elephant ear leaves, stamped "Weller," minor nicks **635.00**

Silvertone, 11" x 10-1/2", hydrangea dec, full kiln stamp, tight 2" line from rim **860.00**

Suevo, 7-1/4" x 9-1/4", incised band of stylized swirls on shoulder, terra cotta ground, unmarked **175.00**

Jug, Louwelsa, 6-1/2" x 5-3/4", spherical, painted blackberries and leaves, stamped mark **265.00**

Lamp base

5" d, 11-1/4" h, Forest, unmarked, 2" chip next to hole at base....... **460.00**

10" d, 13-1/4" h, Louwelsa, by Hattie Mitchell, gourd shape, painted yellow cherry blossoms, stamped "Weller Louwelsa," sgd "H. Mitchell" on body **460.00**

Mug

Dickensware, 5" x 3-3/4", by HR, squeezebag dec, inscription "A Chirping Cup is My Matin Song" in green, brown and white against powder blue ground, artist's initials, very minor abrasion to handle **385.00**

Jap Birdimal, 4" x 6-1/4", two handles, painted dark blue Viking ship on ivory ground, stamped "WELLER," tight 2" line from rim **95.00**

Pedestal, Baldin, 27" h, unmarked **490.00**

Pitcher, 8" h, emb foliage, c1930 .... **95.00**

Planter, Forest Tub, 4"................. **135.00**

Tobacco jar, cov, Creamware, 7-1/2" x 5-1/2", emb pipes and flowers, unmarked, int. firing lines **265.00**

Garden frog, Coppertone, seated frog, mouth spout, attached metal head sprinkler, unmarked, painted "7-," 1930s, hole in rear chipped, chips to rear feet, 10" h, **$1,880**. Photo courtesy of Skinner, Inc.

Planter, matte green, four loop handles, unmarked, interior rim 1/2" chip, nick, 8" d, 5-1/2" h, **$95**. Photo courtesy of David Rago Auctions, Inc.

Vase, Cornish corseted, blue, marked "Weller Pottery" in script, 4-1/4" d, 7-1/4" h, **$175**. Photo courtesy of David Rago Auctions, Inc.

Vase

Aurelian, 7-1/2" x 6", twisted, faceted, carnations dec, etched mark, several shallow scratches to body **365.00**

Vase, Hudson, two handles, painted by Sarah McLaughlin, blue and white irises on both sides, artist signedon body, 7" d, 16" h, **$4,600**. Photo courtesy of David Rago Auctions, Inc.

Baldin, 5-1/2" x 7", squat vase, stamped "WELLER," one leaf nicked **115.00**

Baldin, 10" x 9-1/4", emb apples, stamped mark **450.00**

Bonito, 6" x 5-1/4", bulbous, painted pink daises, script "Weller Pottery" mark **115.00**

Bulbous, 6" x 4-3/4", emb leaves, deep rose matte glaze, stamped mark **435.00**

Bulbous, 8" x 6-3/4", two handles, flowers, half-kiln stamp.......... **265.00**

Coppertone, 11-1/4" x 5-1/2", flaring, tall lilypad and trefoil dec, four frog heads around base, half-kiln stamp **4,025.00**

Vase, Dickensware, monk drinking ale, stamped X356/6, 4-1/4" d, 9" h, **$410**. Photo courtesy of David Rago Auctions.

Cornish, 7-1/4" x 4-1/4", corseted, blue, script mark "Weller Pottery" **200.00**

Dickensware, 4-3/4" x 6", pillow, etched monk, painted small green flowers, stamped mark, minor glaze inconsistency to rim and body **215.00**

Dickensware, 8-1/2", ovoid, decorated by JH, woman playing mandolin on crescent moon, stamped mark **500.00**

Eocean, 3-1/4" x 3", tapering, painted daisies, stamped mark **230.00**

Vase, faceted, smoth matte green glaze, unmarked, 3-3/4" d, 8-1/2" h, **$325**. Photo courtesy of David Rago Auctions.

Vase, Minerva, amber trees, brown background, Imp WELLER, 3/4" rim chip, small chip and nicks to base, 13-1/2" h, **$2,100**. Photo courtesy of David Rago Auctions.

Eocean, 7" x 2-1/2", tapering, painted berries and leaves on shaded green ground, circular stamp mark/Eocean **435.00**
Etna, 4-1/2" x 3-3/4", corseted, painted pink flowers, stamped "Weller Etna" **230.00**
Fleron, 8-1/4" x 5-1/4", bulbous, blue, mottled pink int., ink mark "Weller Ware/Hand Made" **175.00**
Hudson, 12" x 5-1/2", faceted, painted pink and white dogwood, edge nick, dark crazing lines **290.00**
Hudson, 16" x 7", two handles, painted by Sarah McLaughlin, blue and white irises on both sides, artist-signed on body **4,600.00**
Hudson Perfecto, 7-3/4" x 5-1/4", Hood dec, blue columbine on shaded pink and green ground, full kiln mark, artist sgd **815.00**
Kenova, 8-3/4" x 5", applied twisted stems and leaves, stamped "Weller," three tight hairlines from rim **265.00**
Louwelsa Poppy, 19-1/2" l, relief poppies painted in two shades of yellow, mahogany, caramel brown, and green ground, imp 1375/2 .... **1,100.00**
Malvern, 8" x 6-1/2", pillow, script mark **175.00**
Matte Green, 12-1/4" x 6-1/2", corseted, reticulated and emb poppy dec, unmarked, 1/8" edge glaze nick **2,100.00**
Sicard, 3-3/4" x 3", bulbous tapering, flowers and dots under nacreous purple, blue, green, and gold glaze, marked "Weller Sicard" **535.00**
Sicard, 5" x 3-1/2", tapering, falling leaves and wavy lines under nacreous purple, green, and yellow glaze, marked "WELLER SICARD," shallow scratches.................. **750.00**
Sicard, 10" x 3", mistletoe, script mark, pinhead sized fleck, shallow scratches to body **750.00**
Sicard, 10-1/2" x 6", pillow, spider mums dec under nacreous green, red, and orange glaze, script marked "WELLER"........................... **1,850.00**
Woodland, 9" h, emb apple dec, c1940, unmarked **90.00**

Vessel

Flemish, 5" x 6-1/4", basket shape, pink roses, unmarked............ **150.00**
Louwelsa, 3" x 5-1/2", squat, painted by A.S. with branches of wild roses, imp mark **265.00**

WHALING

History: Whaling items are a specialized part of nautical collecting. Provenance is of prime importance since collectors want assurances that their pieces are from a whaling voyage. Since ship's equipment seldom carries the ship's identification, some individuals have falsely attributed a whaling provenance to general nautical items. Know the dealer, auction house, or collector from whom you buy.

Billet head, 18-1/4" l, carved and painted wood, scrolling design, 19th C..... **920.00**
Block, carved whalebone, 19th C, pr
2-1/2" l **575.00**
3-1/4" l **1,095.00**
Blubber mincing knife, 36" l, two handles, orig wood scabbard, America, 19th C, wear, partial loss to scabbard **470.00**
Broadside, List of Shipping Owned in the District of New Bedford, Jan. 1, 1832, Employed in the Whale Fishery and Foreign Trade, lists vessels, tonnage, managing owners, New Bedford, 1832 .... **575.00**

Cane

35" l, whale ivory, baleen, and whalebone, 1" d x 2-1/4" l turned single-pc ivory handle, baleen and whale ivory separator, octo-shaped whalebone shaft tapers to smooth, eight baleen diamonds inlaid on each side, 1" brass and iron ferrule, sailor made, c1850............. **1,500.00**
36-1/2" l, 1-1/3" d x 2-1/4" turks-head knot handle, two thin baleen separators with thin silver separator, tapered whalebone shaft, 1" brass ferrule, attributed to America, c1850 .... **3,000.00**

Chart square, 29-7/8", brass and wood, inscribed "MST," 19th C **200.00**
Club, 11-7/8" l, whalebone, 19th C **950.00**
Cutting spade, 56-1/2" l, iron, orig wood handle, America, 19th C, rust pitting, wear **150.00**

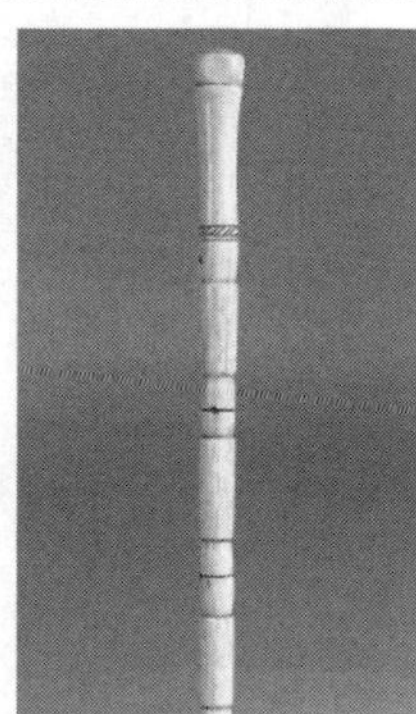

Walking stick, America, 19th C, the shaft made of sections of turned whalebone joined together with baleen pegs, mother-of-pearl button top, baleen tip, several age cracks, 34-1/2" l, **$1,300**. Photo courtesy of Skinner, Inc.

Dipper, 9-1/4" l, turned mahogany handle, ivory attachment, and coconut shell bowl with incised rosette, chain, and liner dec....................................... **550.00**

Whale's tooth, engraved portrait of gentleman and lighthouse, Lady Liberty holding globe and shield surmounted by vines, billowing flag, and angel on reverse, red and black decoration, inscribed "Warren," 19th C, 6-1/4" l, **$2,350**. Photo courtesy of Skinner Auctioneers and Appraisers.

Fid, 16" l, whalebone, 19th C, minor cracks.. **490.00**
Figure, 16-3/8" l, carved baleen, whale, whalebone inlaid eye, 19th C, repair to tail **865.00**
Harpoon, 7-1/2" l, hand forged...... **55.00**
Journal, whaling ship Arnold, sailed from New Bedford, MA, Captain Servant, four year journey.............................. **4,888.00**
Killing iron, 84" l, wood and iron, rope, shaft marked "A. J. Atwood," America, 19th C **325.00**
Lance, 55" l, iron, America, 19th C, rust, pitting... **200.00**
Marking gauge, 9-1/8" l, whalebone, 19th C **1,035.00**
Pan bone, 2-1/4" x 3-1/4", double sided engravings of three-masted ships under sail, 19th C, crack, gouges **375.00**

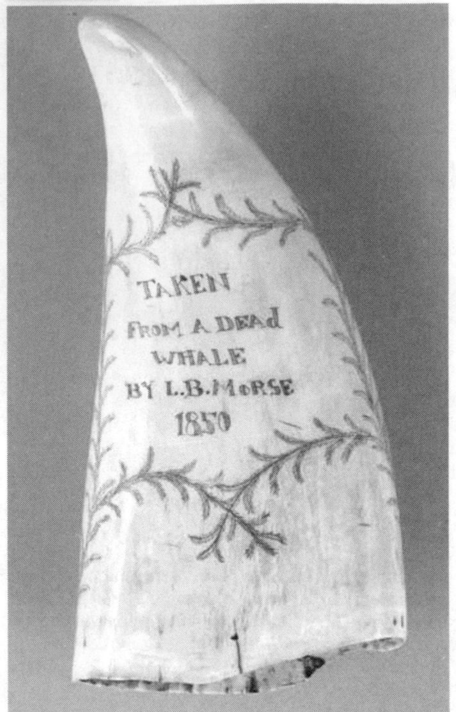

Whale's tooth, scrimshawed three-mastered schooner surrounded by fine vine patterns, reverse side is inscribed "TAKEN/FROM A DEAD/WHALE/ BY L.B. MORSE/1850," mellow patina, 2-3/4" w, 7" l, **$690**. Photo courtesy of James D. Julia Auctions.

Parceling tool, 5-7/8" l, whale ivory, crossbanded design, engraved "N. D. 1829," repair **175.00**

Print, lithograph with hand coloring

- 16" x 32-1/4", Sperm Whaling with Its Varieties, J. H. Bufford, lithographer and publisher, after Benjamin Russell, framed, minor abrasions, foxing, toning......................... **690.00**
- 21-1/2" x 32", Private Signals of the Whaling Vessels Belonging to the Port of New Bedford, Charles Taber & Co., identified in inscriptions in center of sheet, laid down on canvas, losses, tears, overall toning, scattered stains.................. **1,380.00**

Rubber, whalebone, 19th C......... **425.00**

Whaling gun with lance, unmarked, cal. 7/8", 20" part oct. bbl, wooden stock, 17" l iron lance, remains of wire wrap on tail, metal surfaces heavily pitted, very dark patina, wood badly damaged, shows numerous repairs with copper strap overlays, some wood filler, **$2,185**. Photo courtesy of James D. Julia Auctions.

Ship model, cased, seven carved men, three masts, seven small boats on sides, ship's name Alice Mandell New Bedford written on back of stern, alligatored old green, brown, and white paint, later case with small carved whale, plexiglass sides, 33" l, 26" h ship, 36-1/2" w, 15" d, 31" h case.. **2,500.00**

Toggle harpoon, 67" l, wood and iron, rope, America, 19th C **300.00**

WHIMSIES, GLASS

For more information, see Warman's English & Continental Pottery & Porcelain, 3rd edition.

History: During lunch or after completing their regular work schedule, glassworkers occasionally spent time creating unusual glass objects known as whimsies, e.g. candy-striped canes, darners, hats, paperweights, pipes, and witch balls. Whimsies were taken home and given as gifts to family and friends.

Because of their uniqueness and infinite variety, whimsies can rarely be attributed to a specific glass house or glassworker. Whimsies were created wherever glass was made, from New Jersey to Ohio and westward. Some have suggested that style and color can be used to pinpoint region or factory, but no one has yet developed an identification key that is adequate.

Glass canes are among the most collectible types of whimsies. These range in length from very short (under one foot) to 10 feet or more. They come in both hollow and solid form. Hollow canes can have a bulb-type handle or the rarer C- or L-shaped handle. Canes are found in many fascinating colors, with the candy striped being a regular favorite with collectors. Many canes are also filled with various colored powders, gold and white being the most common and silver being harder to find. Sometimes they were even used as candy containers.

Bracelet

- 2" to 3" d, Lutz type, clear, multicolored twists and spirals, gold **85.00**
- 3" d, solid glass, varied colored stripes.................................... **65.00**

Buttonhook

- 5" to 10" l, plain
  - Bottle green **35.00**
  - Colorless **25.00**
- 7" h, bottle green, elaborately twisted body, amber ends..................... **75.00**

Cane

- 35" h, colorless, rainbow threading **100.00**

Cane, colorless, cobalt blue, white, and maroon spirals, knob head, fire-polished tip, early to mid-19th C, 45" l, **$250**. Photo courtesy of Pacific Glass Auctions.

- 46-1/2" l, aqua, spiraled, mid-19th C **175.00**
- 48" l, cobalt blue, shepherd's crook handle **265.00**
- 60" l, bottle green, finely twisted, curved handle **150.00**

Darner

- 5" l, amber head, applied colorless handle **200.00**
- 7" l, white ground, blue Nailsea loopings................................ **165.00**
- Egg, 4-1/2" h, hollow, milk glass, various colored splotches **85.00**

Horn

- 8-1/2" l, French horn type, candy stripes.................................... **300.00**
- 20" l, trumpet type, red, white, yellow, purple, and green candy stripes **175.00**

Ladle, 10" l, hollow, gold powder filled, colored splotches, curved handles **70.00**

Pen, green, finely twisted applied bird finial.. **85.00**

Pipe

- 20" l, spatter, large bowl, English **250.00**
- 36" l, long twisted stem, small hollow bowl, aqua, America, c1900 .... **120.00**

Potichomanie ball, 12" d, blown, aqua, paper cut-outs of flowers, etc., matching 24" h stand, attributed to Lancaster NY **600.00**

Rolling pin

- 14" l, black or deep olive green, white dec, early Keene or Stoddard **150.00**
- 15" l, Nailsea type, cobalt blue ground, white loopings........... **175.00**

Top hat, 7" h, 15" d, colorless, folded rim, polished pontil................................ **75.00**

Whiskey Bottles, Early

History: The earliest American whiskey bottles were generic in shape and blown by pioneer glass makers in the 18th century. The Biningers (1820-1880s) were the first bottles specifically designed for whiskey. After the 1860s, distillers favored the cylindrical "fifth" design.

The first embossed brand-name bottle was the amber E. G. Booz Old Cabin Whiskey bottle which was issued in 1860. Many stories have been told about this classic bottle; unfortunately, most are not true. Research has proven that "booze" was a corruption of the words "bouse" and "boosy" from the 16th and 17th centuries. It was only a coincidence that the Philadelphia distributor also was named "Booz." This bottle has been reproduced extensively.

Prohibition (1920-1933) brought the legal whiskey industry to a standstill. Whiskey was marked "medicinal purposes only" and distributed by private distillers in unmarked or paper-labeled bottles.

The size and shape of whiskey bottles are standard. Colors are limited to amber, amethyst, clear, green, and cobalt blue (rare). Corks were the common closure in the early period, with the inside screw top being used between 1880 and 1910.

Bottles made prior to 1880 are the most desirable. When purchasing a bottle with a label, condition of that label is a critical factor. In the 1950s, distillers began to issue collectors' special-edition bottles to help increase sales.

Additional Listings: See *Warman's Americana & Collectibles* for a listing of Collectors' Special Edition Whiskey Bottles.

Bininger's Regular, 19 Broad St., New York, 1840-50, clock shape, deep gold amber, applied double-collared mouth, pontil scar, 5-7/8" h **300.00**

Bininger's Travelers Guide, A. M. Bininger & Co., No. 19 Broad St., NY, 1860-80, teardrop form, golden amber, applied double collared mouth, smooth base, 6-3/4" h **200.00**

C. A. Richards & Co., 99 Washington St., Boston, Mass, 1860-80, sq with beveled corners, yellow green, applied sloping collared mouth, smooth base, 9-1/2" h, 3/8" potstone................................ **550.00**

Caspers Whiskey, Made by Honest North Carolina People, 1870-90, cylindrical, paneled shoulder, cobalt blue, tooled sloping collared mouth with ring, smooth base, 11-3/4" h................. **325.00**

Chestnut Grove Whiskey, 1840-60, flattened chestnut form, applied handle, golden amber, applied mouth with ring, pontil scar, 9" h **110.00**

Spruance Stanley & Co., San Francisco, CA, 1869, amber, 6-1/2" h, **$30.**

Freeblown jug, applied handle, America, 1840-60

- 6-1/8" h, pear form, red amber, applied sloping collared mouth, pontil scar............................. **220.00**
- 8" h, cylindrical corseted form, golden amber, applied double collared mouth, pontil scar.... **350.00**
- 8" h, flattened chestnut, golden amber, applied mouth with ring, pontil scar, 8" h **475.00**

Griffith Hyatt & Co., Baltimore, 1840-80, globular, flattened label panels, applied handle, golden amber with olive tone, applied sq collared mouth, pontil scar, 7" h... **375.00**

Lancaster Glassworks, Lancaster, NY, 1860-80, barrel, puce amber, applied double collared mouth, smooth base, 9-5/8" h **180.00**

Old Continental Whiskey, yellow amber, 9-1/4" h **650.00**

Weeks Glass Works, Stoddard, NH, 1860-70, emb base, cylindrical, yellow amber with olive tone, applied sloping collared mouth with ring, smooth base, 11-1/2" h, retains cork and some int. residue.. **200.00**

White-Patterned Ironstone

History: White-patterned ironstone is a heavy earthenware, first patented under the name "Patent Ironstone China" in 1813 by Charles Mason, Staffordshire, England. Other English potters soon began copying this opaque, feldspathic, white china.

All-white ironstone dishes first became available in the American market in the early 1840s. The first patterns had simple Gothic lines similar to the shapes used in transfer wares. Pattern shapes, such as New York, Union, and Atlantic, were designed to appeal to the American housewife. Motifs, such as wheat, corn, oats, and poppies, were embossed on the pieces as the American prairie influenced design. Eventually, more than 200 shapes and patterns, with variations on finials and handles, were made.

White-patterned ironstone is identified by shape names and pattern names. Many potters only identified the shape in their catalogs. Pattern names usually refer to the decorative motif.

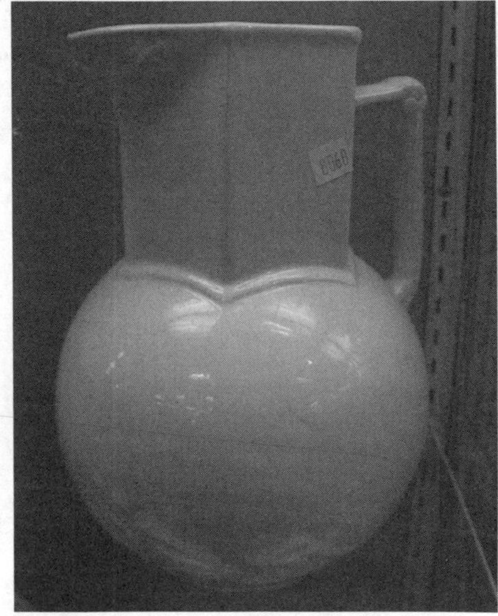

Pitcher, straight sided top, bulbous base, marked "Opaque Stone China, (crown) Trademark, Anthony Shaw & Son, England," **$125.**

Apple bowl, 9" d, pedestal base **270.00**

Bowl, 11" d, 3" h, flower chain border, marked, c1900, back chipped....... **25.00**

Butter dish, cov, Athens, Podmore Walker, c1857 .... **95.00**

Butter pat, 2-3/4" x 2-1/2", emb ridges along slanted sides, marked "Charles Meakin England, Royal Ironstone China" with coat of arms **20.00**

Cake stand, 10" d, short pedestal **395.00**

Chamber pot, 9" d, 15" h, emb scrolls **40.00**

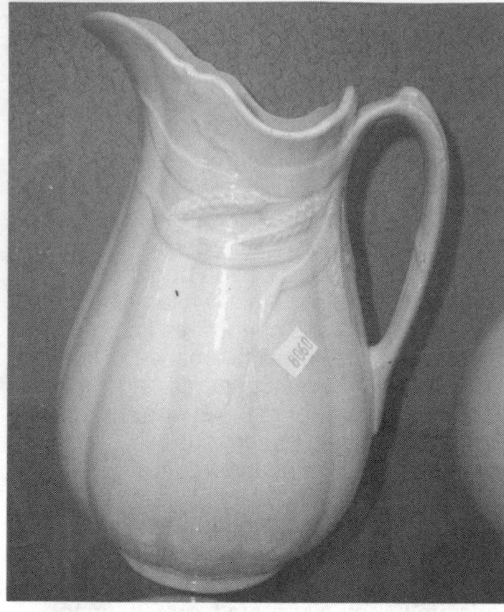

Pitcher, embossed corn and foliate at neck, marked "Royal Patent Ironstone, Turner, Goodard & Co." with lions and crown mark, **$225.**

Coffeepot, 9" w from spout to handle, 10" h, marked "Ironstone China Livesley Powell & Co.," spout chipped, hairline **175.00**
Compote, ftd, Taylor & Davis, 10" d, 6" h **220.00**
Creamer
Fig, Davenport **95.00**
Wheat in the Meadow, Powell & Bishop, 1870 .... **85.00**
Creamer and sugar, Scroll pattern, E. Walley, repaired finial, luster dec **170.00**
Cup and saucer
Acorn and Tiny Oak, Parkhurst **35.00**
Grape and Medallion, Challinor **40.00**
Laurel Wreath, handleless, set of 13, some chips **350.00**
Wheat, Brockhurst, handleless, luster dec **25.00**
Egg cup, 2-1/2" d, 3-3/4" h, raised grape and leaf dec **35.00**
Food mold, 7" l, 5-1/4" w, 3" h, raised ear of corn, c1880-90 .... **195.00**
Gravy boat
Bordered Fuchsia, Anthony Shaw **75.00**
Wheat & Blackberry, Meakin **65.00**
Milk pitcher, Leaf, marked "Royal Ironstone China, Alfred Meakin, England," 9" h **245.00**
Nappy, Prairie Flowers, Livesley & Powell **20.00**
Pitcher
Berlin Swirl, Mayer & Elliot **120.00**
Japan, Mason, c1915 .... **275.00**
Syndenhaum, T. & R. Boote **195.00**
Thomas Furnival, 9" w, 9-1/2" h **220.00**

Two pitchers, left: milk pitcher, Corn pattern, embossed rope around top, **$115**; right: water pitcher, plain top, paneled base, squared off handle, **$95**.

Plate
Ceres, Elsmore & Forster, 8-1/2" d **15.00**
Corn, Davenport, 10-1/2" d **20.00**
Fluted Pearl, Wedgwood, 9-1/2" d **15.00**
Gothic, Adams, 9-1/2" d **20.00**
Laurel Wreath, 10", set of 13 .... **325.00**
Prairie, Clemenston, Hanley, 6-5/8" d **15.00**
Scroll pattern, E. Walley, 8" d **55.00**
Wheat and Clover, Turner & Tomkinson **20.00**
Platter
Columbia, 20" x 15" **125.00**
Laurel Wreath, three graduated sizes **325.00**
Wheat, Meakin, 20-3/4" x 15-3/4" **95.00**
Punch bowl
Berry Cluster, J. Furnival **175.00**
Rosettes, handles, Thomas Furnival & Sons, c1851-90, 9-1/2" 3, 6" h **315.00**
Relish
Laurel Wreath, diamond shape **25.00**
Wheat, W. E. corn **30.00**
Salad plate, Laurel Wreath, set of eight **90.00**
Sauce tureen, cov
Columbia, underplate, Joseph Goodwin, 1855 .... **315.00**
Prize Bloom, T.J. & J. Mayer, Dale Hall Pottery **320.00**
Wheat & Blackberry, Clementson Bros. **275.00**
Shaving mug, 3-1/2" d, 3-3/4" h, emb, gold accents, marked "VPCO Admiral 21" **20.00**
Soap dish, Bordered Hyacinth, cov, insert, W. Baker & Co., 1860s **150.00**
Soup plate, Fig, Davenport, 9-1/2" d **25.00**
Sugar bowl, cov
Hyacinth, Wedgwood **145.00**
Fuchsia, Meakin **140.00**
Livesley Powell & Co., registry mark, 8" h, 6-1/2" w, gold accents **195.00**

Teapot, cov, T & R Boote, Burslem, registry mark for Nov. 26, 1879, 9-1/2" h **240.00**

Platter, embossed wheat border with gold trim, **$85.**

Toothbrush holder
Bell Flower, Burgess **50.00**

Sugar bowl with embossed leaves at handle, **$115**; Corn pattern creamer, **$135**; teapot, **$225**; both with embossed rope trim, marked "Elsmore Foster" with lion mark.

Cable and Ring, Cockson & Seddon **40.00**
Tureen, cov, underplate
Grape, matching ladle, chips **135.00**
Laurel Wreath, large **2,100.00**
Vegetable, cov
Blackberry **95.00**
Lily of the Valley, pear finial **110.00**
Vegetable, open, Laurel Wreath, pr **200.00**
Waste bowl, Laurel Wreath **45.00**

Willow Pattern China

History: Josiah Spode developed the first "traditional" willow pattern in 1810. The components, all motifs taken from Chinese export china, are a willow tree, "apple" tree, two pagodas, fence, two birds, and three figures crossing a bridge. The legend, in its many versions, is an English invention based on this scenic design.

By 1830, there were more than 200 makers of willow pattern china in England. The pattern has remained in continuous production. Some of the English firms that still produce it are Burleigh, Johnson Bros. (Wedgwood Group), Royal Doulton (continuing production of the Booths' pattern), and Wedgwood.

By the end of the 19th century, production of this pattern spread to France, Germany, Holland, Ireland, Sweden, and the United States. Buffalo Pottery made the first willow pattern in the United States beginning in 1902. Many other companies followed, developing willow variants using rubber-stamp simplified patterns, as well as overglaze decals. The largest American manufacturers of the traditional willow pattern were Royal China and Homer Laughlin, usually preferred because it is dated. Shenango pieces are the most desirable among restaurant-quality wares.

Japan began producing large quantities of willow pattern china in the early 20th century. Noritake began about 1902. Most Japanese pieces are porous earthenware with a dark blue pattern using the traditional willow design, usually with no inner border. Noritake did put the pattern on china bodies. Unusual forms include salt and pepper shakers, one-quarter pound butter dishes, and canisters. The most desirable Japanese willow is the fine quality NKT Co. ironstone with a copy of the old Booths pattern. Recent Japanese willow is a paler shade of blue on a porcelain body.

The most common dinnerware color is blue. However, pieces can also be found in black (with clear glaze or mustard-colored glaze by Royal Doulton), brown, green, mulberry, pink (red), and polychrome.

The popularity of the willow design has resulted in a large variety of willow-decorated products: candles, fabric, glass, graniteware, linens, needlepoint, plastic, tinware, stationery, watches, and wall coverings. All this material has collectible value.

Marks: Early pieces of Noritake have a Nippon "Royal Sometuke" mark. "Occupied Japan" may add a small percentage to the value of common tablewares. Pieces marked "Maruta" or "Moriyama" are especially valued.

Reproduction Alert: The Scio Pottery, Scio, Ohio, currently manufactures a willow pattern set sold in variety stores. The pieces have no marks or backstamps, and the transfer is of poor quality. The plates are flatter in shape than those of other manufacturers.

Note: Although colors other than blue are hard to find, there is less demand; thus, prices may not necessarily be higher priced.

Berry bowl, small
- Blue, Homer Laughlin Co. **6.50**
- Pink, marked "Japan" **5.00**

Bowl, 9" d, Mason **45.00**
Bread and butter plate, 6" d, Buffalo China Co. **9.00**

Set, assorted Japanese makers, grill plates, four sizes plates, cups, saucers, mugs, serving pieces, **$200**. Photo courtesy of Alderfer Auction Co.

Cake plate, Newport Pottery Ltd., England, SP base, c1920 .... **300.00**
Charger, 13" d **55.00**
Coffeepot, cov, 10" h, 3" h warmer stand **165.00**
Creamer, round handle, Royal China Co. **10.00**
Cup and saucer
- Buffalo China Co., handleleless, blue and white **25.00**
- Enoch Wedgwood, blue and white, 5-12" d **6.00**
- Homer Laughlin **10.00**
- Japan, pink and white, 3-5/8" d cup, 5-7/8" d saucer **20.00**
- Shenango **15.00**
- Tillson, marked "Trade Mark, Glove with Kang-He in center, Tillson Ware, Burslem, England," early 1900s, 3-1/2" d cup, 5-3/4" d saucer **80.00**

Platter, oval bowl, lidded sugar, cup and saucer, Japanese, **$95**. Photo courtesy of Joy Luke Auctions.

Dinner plate
- Allerton, 10" d **25.00**
- Buffalo Pottery, 9" d **20.00**
- Corean, mulberry and white, imp mark, c1850, 8-3/4" d **125.00**
- Davenport, c1820, blue and white, imp mark **175.00**
- Johnson Bros., 10" d **15.00**
- Royal China Co. **10.00**
- Tillson, blue and white, marked "Trade Mark, Glove with Kang-He in center, Tillson Ware, Burslem, England," early 1900s, 8" d **80.00**

Gravy boat, 5" x 6-1/2", Royal China Co. **25.00**
Grill plate, marked "Carr China St. Louis" **20.00**
Pie plate, 10" d **50.00**
Platter
- 11-3/4" l, oval, marked "Homer Laughlin Made in the USA" **15.00**
- 18-1/4" l, 14-1/2" w, 2-1/4" h, deep well, deep blue and white, Staffordshire, c1830 .... **350.00**

Salad plate, 7-1/2" d, blue and white, marked "Made in Japan" in banner under crown **10.00**
Saucer, 6" d, Buffalo China Co., deep blue and white **8.50**
Sugar, cov
- Allerton **65.00**
- Royal China Co., handleless **40.00**

Tea cup and saucer, scalloped, Allerton **45.00**
Tea plate, 6" d, stamped "Old Willow, England Ironstone Tableware Ltd., Staffordshire, England" **12.00**
Tea set, 5" h hexagonal teapot, creamer, cov sugar, tray, seven cups, six saucers, 20-3/4" d round tray with scalloped rim, gilt foo dog lid finials, gilt handles and rims, pattern registered January, 1879, printed at rim with quotation from Robert Burns' "Auld Lang Syne," Spode, late 19th C, retailed by Tiffany & Co., price for 17-pc set **950.00**
Wash bowl and pitcher, 7-1/2" h pitcher, 12" d bowl, Adderlys Ltd., Staffordshire, c1906, age crack in pitcher **375.00**

WOODENWARE

History: Many utilitarian household objects and farm implements were made of wood. Although they were subjected to heavy use, these implements were made of the strongest woods and well cared for by their owners. Today collectors and decorators treasure their worn lines and patina. Collectors often consider their hand-made wooden items as folk art, elevating what once might have been a common utilitarian item to a place of honor.

Bank, 4-1/2" w, 3-13/16" d, 3-5/8" h, rect, carved gardenia blossoms and leaves on top and sides, dark blue painted ground **525.00**
Barber pole, 30" l, painted red and white candy stripes, mounted on a full-length wrought iron wall bracket **460.00**

Bowl, burlwood, lid with trapezoidal handle, crack in bowl, 5" d, **$935**. Photo courtesy of Alderfer Auction Co.

Basket, 10-3/4" l, 5-3/4" h, carved freeform burl, America, 19th C **1,120.00**

Bird carrier, 14-1/2" w, 9" d, 10-1/4" h, pine, brown, red, and tan floral wallpaper, sliding door on one side with small center window, vertical wire cage inside with another hinged door, early redware feeding bowls inside, edge wear **350.00**

Bowl, burl

11-1/2" d, 4" h, ash, very good figure, old scrubbed surface, incised ring detail around base, ext. with raised rim, rim split **880.00**

12" d, 4-1/4" h, banded rim tapering to base, old surface, America, 19th C **635.00**

14-1/2" d, 4-3/4" h, ash, mellow brown surface inside and out, thinly turned, raised handle on either side of rim **3,300.00**

19-1/2" d, 6" h, ash, old refinishing, tight figure, cutout handles **2,750.00**

Bowl, cov, 7-3/4" d, 5-3/4" h, treen, mahogany, old red, pumpkin, and black painted line dec, ftd, turned handle at top **550.00**

Box, cov

5-1/4" d, 3-3/8" h, oval, bentwood, single finger construction with opposite directions on lid and base, iron tacks, old dark green paint shows lighter under lid, minor wear to paint **2,420.00**

5-3/4" w, 4" d, 1-3/4" h, book shape, spruce, inland bands, star, crescent boon, hearts, and leaves, one end with sliding lid, minor alligatoring to varnish, short age cracks **200.00**

6-3/8" w, 3" d, 1-7/8" h, book shape, Frisian carved, made from solid piece of wood, sliding lid, overall geometric carving, matching patterns on front and back, hearts and pinwheel on spine, good patina, int. with ivory paint, yellowed varnish, minor edge damage, few worm holes **220.00**

8-1/4" l, 5-1/4" w, 2-5/8" h, cherry, dovetailed, raised panel, sliding lid, divided int., old dark brown finish, glued splits **200.00**

Bucket, 11-1/2" d, 12-1/4" h, stave construction, wood bands, bentwood swing handle, layers of old red paint, some water damage on bottom **550.00**

Busk, 12" h, carved maple, engraved with Indian smoking pipe, chip-carved geometric compass designs, attributed to New England, early 19th C, stand **980.00**

Candlemold, 21-1/8" l, 6-1/2" d, 17-3/4" h, 14 pewter tubes, several sgd "W. Webb," pine framework with arched cutouts on ends, sq nail construction, three old steel wires for wicks **1,870.00**

Carrier, 12-1/2" d, 6-1/2" h plus bentwood swing handle, stave construction, two wide bentwood bands with laced seams, single board lid with lapped and nailed rim, handle attached with two wooden pegs, old refinishing **220.00**

Charger, 21-3/4" d, treenware, scribed dec, late 18th/early 19th C, minor imperfections **1,035.00**

Churn, 23" h, tapered sides, four wooden staves, steel band around base, orig green paint **315.00**

Cup

4" h, Treenware, small chalice, body carved with scrolling vines, silver-mounted lip dated 1785, inscription reads, "This cup was made of the mulberry tree planted by Shakepear (sic) in his garden at Stratford on Avon and the Maker offered to attest the Same on Oath to me ANTRIM July 1st, 1785," English **500.00**

5" h, Lehnware, Joseph Long Lehn, Lancaster County, PA, pale salmon ground, red stem, green and black trim, red rim with buds, red and yellow flowers with green leaves, yellow int., minor wear on foot **1,540.00**

Figure, bear, 30" h, Black Forest, nose partially missing **7,000.00**

Firkin

9" d base, 7" h, staved construction, four wooden bands, hand forged iron bail handle, wooden stopper, painted red, America, early 19th C, minor wear **265.00**

12" d, 12-1/2" h, staved construction, green lapped bands, swing handle fastened with pegs, painted red, "Cassia" inscribed in white letters, matching cover, America, mid-19th C, wear **530.00**

Flax wheel, 45" h, upright type, mixed hardwoods, four turned legs, single treadle, double flyers with bobbins, single wheel at top with turned spokes, few replacements **250.00**

Glove box, 13-1/2" l, sandalwood, lid and sides pierced carved with animals, deities, and flowers, supported by figures of ducks, India, 19th C **345.00**

Jar, cov

4-1/2" h, treen, Lehnware, Joseph Long Lehn, Lancaster County, PA, pale peach ground, green, yellow, brown, and black trim, black knob finial, red and green strawberries on lid, blue, white, and red pansy type flowers on body, bottom initialed "A.F.E.R. 8/7/58," few minor flakes **2,200.00**

Spoon, carved, seafarer's profile, polychrome decoration, **$45**. Photo courtesy of Joseph P. Smalley, Jr., Auctioneer

5" h, treen, Lehnware, Joseph Long Lehn, Lancaster County, PA, dusty rose ground, black trim, knob finial, green and red trim, red strawberries on lid, white, red, and green flowers on body, slight wear **1,650.00**

6" h, burl, urn shape, round foot, good figure and patina, traces of dark red **7,700.00**

8" d, 6-3/4" h, poplar, worn orig vinegar dec in red, brown, and green over mustard, raised turned rings around rim and base, domed lid, edge chip on lid, age split in base **770.00**

8-3/4" d, treen, attributed to Pease, poplar, slightly domed lid with incised rings, raised rings on body, turned foot, age splits on one side 450.00

Measuring device, carved and inlaid shoe-form, carved head of gentleman, ivory inlaid eyes, inlaid metal buckle, two ivory inlaid panels each dec with two engraved shoes, Holland, late 18th C, minor losses, wear, crack 920.00

Sugar bucket, marked "C. S. Hersey," 9-1/2" c, 9" h, **$295**.

Mortar and pestle, 6-1/4" d, 18-1/4" h, turned maple, acorn-shaped knop, three incised lines on cylindrical pestle, mortar with molded base, 19th C, cracks 90.00

Pantry box, 6-1/4" d, 2-1/4" h, round, painted black, top carved with central star within medallion and leafy border, cross hatch swags on side, int. lined with partial advertising lithographs, New England, mid-19th C, minor imperfections 715.00

Pewter rack, hanging, 35" w, 3-3/4" d, 29-3/4" h, oak, dark finish, two shelves, stylized lion finials on tops, wire nail construction, English 150.00

Picture frame

13-3/8" w, 15-1/2" h, stenciled and painted, rect, gold floral dec on black ground, remnants of paper label on reverse 375.00

19-5/16" w, 22" h, rect, reticulated scalloped edge, compass star corner rosettes, painted black, 19th C, finish alligatored 550.00

Pitcher, 6-1/2" h, curly maple, good patina, one pc handle, nose shaped finger rest under spout, some old rim damage 770.00

Quilt rack, folding

34-3/4" w, 64" h, two sections, pine, old natural finish, three cross pcs mortised into frame 95.00

108" w, 66" h, three sections, each fitted with three cross pcs mortised into frame, cast iron hinges, old putty colored paint 120.00

Trencher, hand carved, oval form, ends shaped to form handles, old black paint on exterior, minor shrinkage cracks, 23-1/2" l, 14" d, 4 1/4" h, **$185**. Photo courtesy of Alderfer Auction Co.

Saffron jar, 4-3/4" h, Lehnware, Joseph Long Lehn, Lancaster County, PA, urn shape, green ground on body, red stem, black, green, and yellow trim, lid with salmon ground, red and green strawberries with yellow, minor paint wear 1,870.00

Scoop, 9-3/4" l, carved, America, 19th C 210.00

Shelves, 30" w, 10" d, 37-3/4" h, walnut, orig dark finish, four graduated shelves with rounded edges, shaped corners, turned shelf supports and finials, scalloping and cut-outs on center backboard including pinwheel and medallion top, sq cut nail construction 600.00

Smoothing board, 5" w, 27" d, old dark blue paint, red tulip dec, carved horse handle, some paint wear, ear damage, age split...................................... 200.00

Snuff box, cov, 4-1/2" l, 1-7/8" w, 1-1/4" h, hand painted, black lacquer ground, oblong lid with husband rocking baby in cradle, wife in bed, surrounded by dog, cat, wood stove with kettle, gilt border, England, early 19th C, wear...... 2,235.00

Spice box, 9" d, 3-3/8" h, round box, lapped construction, eight small cylindrical cov wood containers, stenciled spice label on each, America, 19th C 250.00

Sugar bowl, cov, 8" d, 7-1/2" h, turned maple, acorn finial on flaring domed lid, bulbous body, flaring foot, old refinish, loss to inside rim.......................... 690.00

Sugar bucket, cov

13-1/2" h, orig dark green paint, faint signature "C. Wilder & Son, So. Hingham, Mass" on lid, tapering sides, lapped staves, copper tacks, arched bentwood handle, minor edge chips 550.00

15" h, orig blue paint, old hand plane marks, copper and steel tacks, arched bentwood handle, stenciled "E. F." on bottom, chips.......... 450.00

Toddy ladle, 14-1/4" l, carved, notched handle, round bowl, dark brown patina, America, early 19th C, wear......... 440.00

Tray, 22-3/4" l, 15" w, marquetry of mother elephant with two calves, one calf following the mother, other scratching back on palm tree, rayed sun shines above, second tree with bananas borders tray, lower left sgd "GALLE" in marquetry 2,550.00

Trencher, 23" l, 10-3/4" w, 3-1/4" h, rect, canted sides, rough hewn from pine, good patina 65.00

Wall pocket, Victorian, walnut, carved female head and leaves, 17" w, 22" h, **$195**. Photo courtesy of Joy Luke Auctions.

Trinket box, 8-7/8" w, Tunbridgeware, mid-19th C, rect, hinged lid with lifting handle and geometric inlay, sides inlaid to represent a brick manor house, metal trim on lid and base, metal ogee bracket feet, int. with three segments, hidden spring-loaded base drawer....... 4,465.00

Ventriloquist's head, 5-1/2" w, 5" d, 8-1/2" h, carved yellow pine, fixed eyes, spring-activated mouth with pull string, old patina, attributed to southern U.S., last quarter 19th C, mounted on later stand.. 1,150.00

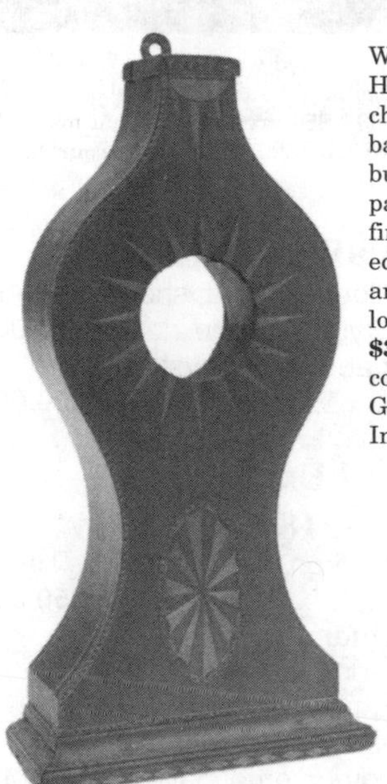

Watch hutch, Hepplewhite, cherry, inlaid banding, star-burst, and paterae, old finish, minor edge damage and veneer loss, 11-1/4" h, **$3,575**. Photo courtesy of Garth's Auction, Inc.

Wall pocket

Papers, fretwork back with train and boat, front pocket with carved "Papers," decorative edging, PA, late 19th C **295.00**

Victorian, Renaissance Revival, c1870, carved walnut, inlaid floral panel, mythological animals, 34" h **3,300.00**

Wash tub, 23-3/4" d, 16-1/2" h, painted pine, circular, pierced handle, stave and metal band construction, old red paint, America, late 19th C, wear, loose bands **260.00**

Panoramic view of Panama-Pacific International Exposition, San Francisco, 1915, period frame, **$75**. Photo courtesy of Dotta Auction Co., Inc.

WORLD'S FAIRS AND EXPOSITIONS

History: The Great Exhibition of 1851 in London marked the beginning of the World's Fair and Exposition movement. The fairs generally featured exhibitions from nations around the world displaying the best of their industrial and scientific achievements.

Many important technological advances have been introduced at world's fairs, including the airplane, telephone, and electric lights. Ice cream cones, hot dogs, and iced tea were first sold by vendors at fairs. Art movements often were closely connected to fairs, with the Paris Exhibition of 1900 generally considered to have assembled the best of the works of the Art Nouveau artists.

Tumbler, colorless, etched wreath and "World's Fair 1893," **$85**; milk glass tumbler, embossed "World's Fair 1893," **$50**; frosted glass hat marked "Columbia Exposition 1893," **$75**. Photo courtesy of Joy Luke Auctions.

Crystal Palace, NY, 1853

Dollar, so called, 1-3/4" d, shows seated Liberty and Crystal Palace **75.00**

Print, Currier and Ives, Crystal Palace **400.00**

Centennial Exposition, Philadelphia, 1876

Bank, still, cast iron, Independence Hall, 9" h x 7" w **350.00**

Candy container, Liberty bell, glass, pewter screw-on closure, marked "Centennial Exposition" on one side, "Proclaim Liberty Throughout All the Land" on the other, emb clapper on base, c1876.. **850.00**

Glass slipper, Gillinder

Clear....................................... **35.00**

Frosted **40.00**

Medal, wooden, Main Building, 3" d **60.00**

Scarf, 19" x 34", Memorial Hall, Art Gallery colorful **100.00**

New Orleans World's Industrial and Cotton Expo, 1885, program, cover stamped "April 1885" **45.00**

Columbian Exposition, 1893

Album, 5-3/4" x 9", hardcover, gold emb "World's Fair Album of Chicago 1893" **50.00**

Book, *History of the World's Fair Being A Complete Description of the World's Colombian Exposition from Inception*, Major Ben C. Truman, illus, 592 pgs **60.00**

Cup, 2-1/2" h, peachblow glass, double handles, ribbed, shading from pink to white, gilt dec "World's Fair-1893 Chicago," minor crack at handle **300.00**

Columbian Expo, 1893, jack-in-the-pulpit, vase, peachblow, raspberry shading to white glass with gold enameling "WORLD'S FAIR 1893," 7-1/2" h, **$750**. Photo courtesy of James D. Julia, Inc.

Medal, 1-1/2", brass luster finish white metal, bust portrait of Christopher Columbus on one side, other side "400th Anniversary of The Discovery of America," 1492-Oct-1892.............. **20.00**

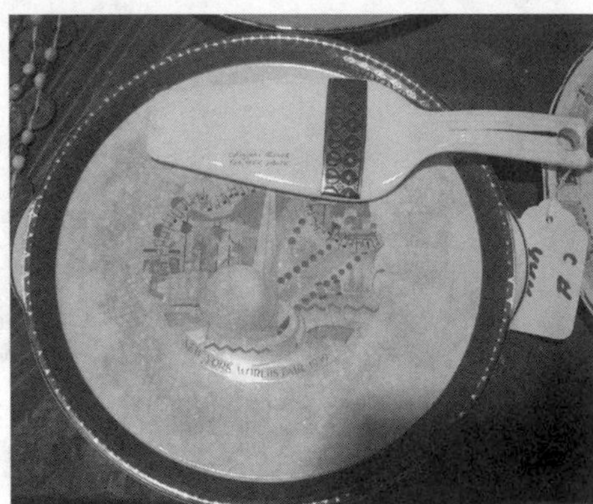

Cake plate and server, fair logo in center, gold border, tab handles, **$45**. Photo courtesy of Sky Hawk Auctions.

Mug, 4-3/4" h, salt glazed stoneware, imp, blue accents "World's Fair Chicago 1893" **165.00**

Photo booklet.............................. **25.00**

Souvenir spoon **25.00**

Ticket **30.00**

Pan American, 1901

Bookmark, 2-1/2" x 10-1/2", woven silk, McKinley portrait above image of Temple of Music **165.00**

Cigar case, hinged aluminum 2-1/2" x 5-1/2" **35.00**

Medallion, bright luster brass, profile of buffalo between "Souvenir" and "1901," reverse marked "Pan-American Exposition/May-November Buffalo, NY" **15.00**

Pinback button

Swifts Pig, multicolored plump pig seated in frying pan, tiny inscription "Pan-American Souvenir," black lettering "Swift's Premium Hams and Bacon-Swift & Co., U.S.A.".......**25.00**

Temple of Music, multicolored art view of building exterior **25.00**

Plate, frosted glass, three cats painted on dec, 7-1/2" d **35.00**

Pocket mirror, 2-1/16" h, Berry Brothers Varnish, black on cream, their building titled "Castle Copal" **60.00**

Columbian Expo, 1893, stevensgraph with five colors, showing Mrs. Potter Palmer, President of the Board of Lady Managers, graphic portrait of her and view of Woman's Building, mounted on original paper and produced by John Best & Co., Patterson, NJ, 10" x 2-1/2", **$100**. Photo courtesy of Sanford Alderfer Auction Company.

South Carolina Exposition, 1901

Pocket mirror, 2-1/8" h, bright gold paper label under celluloid, full-color center scene captioned "My Pal Met Her," green palm tree and white building background, black lady in elaborate red hat and dress holding matching fan arm-in-arm with dapper black man in tuxedo with top hat and cane, left shows grimacing black man in common clothes, 1901 copyright Baltimore Badge, text reads "South Carolina Inter-State & West Indian Exposition 1901,Charleston-1902" **150.00**

Automata, blue informed character, standing on orange platform with Trylon and Perisphere behind him. He was for sale at the October 2002 Atlantique City show for **$10,000**.

St. Louis, 1904

Match safe and cigar cutter, 2-3/4" w, 1-1/2" h, detailed drawing of Palace of Varied Industries on one side, picture of Gardens and Terraces of States on other, tarnished **150.00**

Plate, embossed potter at wheel, turquoise glaze, backstamp "Joint Exhibit of Capital and Labor, The American Pottery, New York World's Fair," **$25**. Photo courtesy of Sky Hawk Auctions.

Medal, silvered brass, 2-3/4" d **60.00**
Photo album, eight pgs, 15 orig photos **45.00**
Pinback button, KY home, multicolored exhibit building of Kentucky against upper half gold background, inscribed "Ky. Home World's Fair," bottom margin inscription "It's Part Mine" **25.00**
Plate, 7-1/4" d, scene in center, lacy border **25.00**
Souvenir mug, bronze, emb scene of Palace of Electricity, 6" h **115.00**
Souvenir plate, 7" d, Festival Hall, Cascade Gardens **55.00**
Tumbler, 4" high, copper plated base, metal, shows Louisiana Purchase Monument, Cascades, Union Station and Liberal Arts Bldg **35.00**

Chicago, 1933, mug, green glaze, molded figures "A Century of Progess - World's Fair Chicago 1933" nude female handle, minor chip in glaze near base, **$165**. Photo courtesy of Joy Luke Auctions.

Panama-Pacific, 1915

Bookmark, 5-1/2" h, red carnation at top, scene of black and white cows against green landscape, gray mountain peak, blue sky, full color illus of Carnation's Milk, marked "Souvenir of the Panama-Pacific Exposition, San Francisco, 1915" **45.00**
Pocket watch, official, silver plated, 2" d **300.00**
Postcard **5.00**

Sesquicentennial International Exposition,

Philadelphia, 1926

Poster, city hall, Lady Liberty, and flag image, 22" x 17" **518.00**

Century of Progress,

Chicago, 1933

Employee badge, round medallion with "A Century of Progress" around perimeter, "International Exposition Chicago 1933" and employee number below **55.00**
Menu, Walgreens **45.00**
Pinback button
- I Was There, red, white, and blue **20.00**
- New York Visitor, red, white, and blue **20.00**

Playing cards, full deck, showing views of the fair, all different, black and white **45.00**
Souvenir key, bright silver luster brass, sponsored by Master Lock Co., "Master Laminated Padlocks Sold All Over the World," opposite side with miniature form image of exhibit buildings and "World's Fair 1933," tiny horseshoe and four-leaf clover, inscribed "Keep Me For Good Luck" **28.00**
Tape measure, silver, blue, and white official logo, other side with black and white photo of Paris replica village exhibit **32.00**
Toy wagon, red, white wheels, decal of Transportation Bldg in middle approx 3-1/2" l **175.00**

Ashtray, New York, 1939, Art Deco, space for four cigarettes, blue and tan stylized fair logo showing Trylon and Perisphere. 5/8" x 2-1/2" x 3-1/2", **$25**. Photo courtesy of Hake's Americana & Collectibles.

Gaucho hat, Golden Gate International Expo, San Francisco, 1939, black, hand-painted text, top of rim with brown, blue, gray, and green silhouettes of buildings, Golden Gate Bridge, mountains, top of crown has fair building in white brown accents, brown and blue spotlights in background, bottom of crown has brown and yellow silhouettes of fair buildings and spotlight accents on back, yellow and brown attached cord, white painted text "Patent Applied For Sinbeck," crazing, 15-1/2" d, 3-1/2" h, **$45**. Photo courtesy of Hake's Americana & Collectibles.

Golden Gate, 1939

Bookmark, typical view, 4" l........... **20.00**
Match book, orig matches, pictures Pacifica.. **10.00**
Token, shows Sun Tower and Bridge, 1-1/8" d **15.00**

New York, 1939, busts, pair, white porcelain Art Deco heads of man and woman, green Lenox/USA stamps, 8-3/4" x 4", **$650**. Photo courtesy of David Rago Auctions.

New York, 1939

Bookmark, 3-3/4" l, diecut and silvered thin brass spear page marker and letter opener, applied metal disk with blue and dark orange accents on silver luster "New York Worlds Fair, 1939," plus images of Trylon and Perisphere **20.00**
Candy tin, miniature, by Bagatele, very colorful, 4-1/4" x 6-1/2" **65.00**
Folder, 6-1/4" x 12", printed paper, blue, white, and orange, one side with three images of Borden's Elsie, Trylon, and Perisphere, reverse with blue and white printing, pictorial family endorsement, recipe, and text relating to Borden's Chateau cheese, August 1939 publication date............................. **20.00**

Bracelet, 1934 Century of Progress, glossy silver metal, fair logo in symbol, six different links with detailed images of buildings including General Motors, Hall of Science, Sky Ride, Electrical, Blockhouse Fort Dearborn, Illinois Host Building, lightly tarnished, 5/8" w, 7" l, **$45**. Photo courtesy of Hake's Americana & Collectibles.

Pencil sharpener, bakelite........... **45.00**
Pin

Brass, formed as slightly concave seashell, soft white paint blending to soft blue, applied brass miniature Trylon and Perisphere, scroll style bottom margin......................... **65.00**

New York, 1939, clock, plastic Deco style case, art image of Trylon and Perisphere in front of General Electric Exhibit Building on face, 4" d, 4-1/4" h, **$475**. Photo courtesy of Hake's America & Collectibles.

Syroco, brown composition wood pin, formed in relief cloud formations above Trylon and Perisphere, landscaping trees on right and left, yellow, blue, and green accents, inscribed "New York World's Fair," tiny copyright and authorization, brass fastener **35.00**

Pinback button, 1-1/4" d, gold and blue cello, blue fabric ribbon inscribed in gold for May 1, 1939 event, Revolutionary War soldier behind inscription "New Haven Advertising Club, Inc./Vigilance," outer rim inscribed "New Haven Day-New York World's Fair" **125.00**
Pocketknife, 2" l steel knife based on each side by pearl-like plastic panels, one with tiny blue Trylon and Perisphere, plus inscription "New York World's Fair 1939," two steel blades................. **40.00**
Postcard, photo type...................... **6.00**
Ring, adjustable, silvered brass, inscribed "World's Fair" over "NY," flanked by numeral "19" on one left, "39" on right **25.00**
Souvenir spoon, 7" l, Theme Building on front, "Pat. Pend., Wm Rogers Mfg. Co." **25.00**

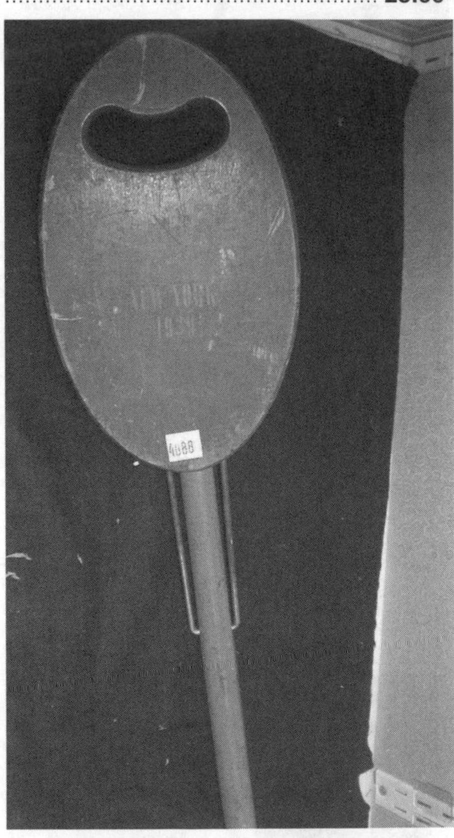

Seat, 1939 New York World's Fair, Yankee Snap Seat, oval wooden top painted blue, wooden standard painted orange, top marked "New York 1939," back labeled "Yankee Snap Seat, Patent Pending, New England Seat Co.," **$35**.

New York, 1964

Dime, circular plastic case with 1946 Eisenhower dime in center, reads "NY World's Fair, 1964-1965 Neutron Irradiated Dime," back reads "Atomic Energy Commission, United States of America," 2" d................................ **40.00**

Fork and spoon display, 11" l, mounted on wooden plaque, Unisphere decals on handles **45.00**
Hat, black felt, Unisphere emblem, white cord trim, feather, name "Richard" embroidered on front **25.00**
Lodge medallion, bronze luster finish, image of Unisphere and two exhibit buildings, brass hanger loop, inscribed "The Grand Lodge I.O.O.F. of the State of New York" **15.00**
Paperweight, panoramic scenes **40.00**
Postcard, 10 miniature pictures, 20 natural color reproductions, unused **20.00**
Souvenir book, Official Souvenir Book of the New York World's Fair, 1965 ..... **25.00**
Yo-yo **45.00**

Yard-Long Prints

History: In the early 1900s, many yard-long prints could be had for a few cents postage and a given number of wrappers or box tops. Others were premiums for renewing a subscription to a magazine or newspaper. A large number were advertising items created for a store or company and had calendars on the front or back. Many people believe that the only true yard-long print is 36 inches long and titled "A Yard of Kittens," etc. But lately collectors feel that any long and narrow print, horizontal or vertical, can be included in this category. It is a matter of personal opinion.

Values are listed for full-length prints in near-mint condition, nicely framed, and with original glass.

Reproduction Alert: Some prints are being reproduced. Know your dealer.

Note: Numbers in parentheses below indicate C. G. and J. M. Rhoden and W. D. and M. J. Keagy, *Those Wonderful Yard-Long Prints and More*, Book 1 (1989), Book 2 (1992), Book 3 (1995), book number and page on which the item is illustrated, e.g. (3-52) refers to Book 3, page 52.

Advisers: Charles G. and Joan M. Rhoden, and W. D. and M. J. Keagy.

Animals

A Yard of Kittens, sgd, Guy Bedford (Bk 1-50) **350.00**
Battle the Chicks, sgd Ben Austrian, c1920 (Bk 2-17) **300.00**
Cats and kittens on a see-saw, c1893, Art Interchange Co. (Bk 1-94) **300.00**
Down on the Congo, c1904, second in series of four (Bk 3-17) **450.00**
Piggies in Clover (Bk 3-25) **600.00**
Shallows Over Lily Pads, c1897, J. Hoover & Son, (Bk 2-107) **350.00**

Calendar, 1920, Selz Good Shoes, adv for E A. Mayne, General Merchandise, Sanborn, Iowa, signed Haskell Coffin (Bk 2-84), **$400**. Photo courtesy of Adivser Joan Rhoden.

Calendar

1904, Pabst Extract, different baby for each month (Bk 2-100) **400.00**
1910, Pabst Extract, lady in white hat and dress (Bk 1-14) **450.00**
1916-17, Pompein, Mary Pickford, split calendar on back (Bk 1-26) **400.00**
1918, Selz Good Shoes, ad for Hughes Clothing (Bk 2-83) **400.00**
1922, Pompeian, Honeymooning in Venice (Bk 1-32) **350.00**
1929, Selz Good Shoes, ad for Hughes Clothing (Bk 2-85) **400.00**

Children

A Shower of Roses, c1893, Art Interchange Co. (Bk 3-99) **400.00**
Butterfly Time, 1903, Maud Humphrey (Bk 2-104) **400.00**
Dutch Bitter Sweets, Dutch children playing with white goose (Bk 3-98) **450.00**
Yard of Youth, F. L. Martin (Bk 2-109) **350.00**

Flowers and fruits

Apple Blossoms, untitled (Bk 3-26) **250.00**

Framed yard long print of girl in red evening dress, holding opera glasses, 36" x 11-1/2", **$275**. Photo courtesy of Joy Luke Auctions.

Chrysanthemums, c1895, Paul DeLongpre (Bk 3-27) **300.00**
Roses and mixed flowers, 1900, supplement to Chicago Tribune (Bk 3-35) **300.00**
Water lilies with dragonfly, Fisher (Bk 2-68) **300.00**
Yard of cherries and flowers, LeRoy (Bk 2-70) **275.00**
Yard of violets (Bk 3-37) **275.00**

Long ladies

Alluring, Pompeian Art Panel, sgd, Bradshaw Krandall (Bk 2-99) **350.00**
A Sozodont Girl, Ready for the Opera, 1913, sgd, Rolf Armstrong (Bk 1-101) **425.00**
Barbara, 1912, sgd, C. Allan Gilbert (Bk 2-93) **325.00**
Cosmopolitan lady, 1914, sgd, Gregson (Bk 2-75) **400.00**
Hula Girl, sgd, Gene Pressler, girl on surfboard (Bk 1-94) **475.00**
ISNS, 1911, Frank J. Murck, college lad and lassie series (Bk 3-84) **375.00**
Mother and Child, 1913, National Stockman & Farmer Paper (Bk 3-54) **400.00**
Temptation Candy Girl, ad on box of chocolates (Bk 3-74) **425.00**
The Euthymol Girl, c1907, Parke, Davis & Co. (Bk 3-58) **400.00**

Yellowware

For more information, see Warman's American Pottery & Porcelain, 2nd edition.

History: Yellowware is a heavy earthenware which varies in color from a rich pumpkin to lighter shades, which are more tan than yellow. The weight and strength varies from piece to piece. Although plates, nappies, and custard cups are found, kitchen bowls and other cooking utensils are most prevalent.

The first American yellowware was produced at Bennington, Vermont. English yellowware has additional ingredients that make its body much harder. Derbyshire and Sharp's were foremost among the English manufacturers.

Baking dish, cov, oval, high gloss glaze, relief scale dec on rim and lid, applied handles, 19th C, hairlines, 15-1/2" w, 8-3/4" d, 5-1/2" h **90.00**

Bean pot, cov, 7-1/2" h, double handles, orig lid **115.00**

Bowl

3-3/4" d, lions heads dec **145.00**

Bowl, brown and cream striping, 9-1/2" d, 4-1/2" h, **$100**. Photo courtesy of Alderfer Auction Co.

10" d, 4-3/4" h, dark brown Rockingham glaze, int. stone pings, minor surface wear, repaired chip on ext. rim **25.00**

11" d, 5" h, dark brown Rockingham glaze, relief columns on outside, minor surface wear from use, in-the-making shallow stone pings on int **115.00**

11-1/2" d, 3-3/4" h, dark brown Rockingham glaze, relief columns on outside, flared rim, 1" hairline, surface chip **65.00**

Candlesticks, pr, 6" h, yellow and dark green mottle alkaline glaze, minor age crazing **875.00**

Canister, 4-3/4" d, 8" h, coral and dolphins dec, gilt accents **200.00**

Canning jar, relief draped design, some crazing to glaze, surface chips, **$125**. Photo courtesy of Vicki and Bruce Waasdorp.

Canning jar, 6-1/4" h, one qt, some staining from use **125.00**

Coffeepot, 10" h, matching lid, hanging game fish design, attributed to McNicol Burton Co., large chips in lid **125.00**

Colander, 8" d, 3-1/2" d, circles of pierced holes on bottom, ftd, relief drape design on ext., four tight hairlines **200.00**

Cream pitcher

2" h, black and two dark brown accent bands, base stamped in green "Incaware Shenango China New Castle PA USA," c1900 .... **25.00**

3" h, two brown accent bands surrounding imp tooled rim, overall applied mottled sand application, possibly English made for American market **100.00**

4-1/2" h, applied Rockingham glaze, relief leaf design at spout **90.00**

4-1/2" h, relief design of male profile in flowered frame **150.00**

Mug, band of cream and blue dec, hairline crack, chip in handle, 5" d, 4-1/2" h, **$125**. Photo courtesy of Alderfer Auction Co.

Custard cup, 2-1/2" h

Brown Rockingham glaze **35.00**

Plain **30.00**

Desk set, 7-1/2" l, 4-3/4" h, fruit and baskets dec, gilt accents, foot missing **85.00**

Dresser box, 3-3/4" d, floral garlands, gilt accents, lid missing **80.00**

Figure, 12" h, seated spaniel, open front feet design, attributed to Bennington factory, Rockingham glaze, c1850, few minor glaze flakes on base **275.00**

Flask, 7-3/4" h, book shape, Rockingham glaze, c1850, two unglazed spots on one side **275.00**

Foot warmer, 9" h, Rockingham glaze, relief scroll design at shoulder, c1850 .... **440.00**

Lamp base, 8-1/2" h, prominent rings, running brown and yellow/green glaze, partial lamp parts **115.00**

Measure, 5-3/4" h, 6-1/2"d, Spearpoint & Trellis **300.00**

Miniature, bowl, three bold white slip accent bands, 4-1/2" d, 2" h, Lot, **$150**.

Miniature

Bowl, 4-1/2" d, 2" h, three bold white slip accent bands, some use stains **145.00**

Coffeepot, 4-1/2" h, Rockingham glaze **375.00**

Mixing bowl

12" d, 5-3/4" h, blue and white accent bands, dark navy blue seaweed dec on white band, very tight age lines **350.00**

12-1/4" d, 6-1/2" h, relief swirl pattern, ftd **100.00**

Mug

3-1/2" h, applied dark brown Rockingham glaze, applied strap handle, unusual flared rim **100.00**

3-3/4" h, applied dark brown Rockingham glaze, applied strap handle **360.00**

Nappy

9-1/2" d, 2-3/4" h, brown Rockingham glaze, relief heart shaped ftd bottom, in-the-making int. small stone pings **85.00**

10-1/2" d, 3" h, brown Rockingham glaze, relief ribbed ftd bottom **75.00**

Pepper pot, 4-1/4" h, light blue stripes, two white bands, minor flake, Ohio **1,100.00**

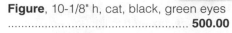

Pie funnel, 2-1/2" h, unmarked.... **125.00**

Pitcher, white mid band, applied strap handle, **$225**. Photo courtesy of Joseph P. Smalley, Jr., Auctioneer.

Pie plate

- 9-1/2" d, dark brown Rockingham glaze, 1" tight clay separation line that occurred in firing **75.00**
- 9-1/2" d, light brown Rockingham glaze, minor glaze crazing on bottom, surface chip **35.00**
- 9-3/4" d, dark brown Rockingham glaze, minor glaze wear **75.00**
- 10" d, dark brown Rockingham glaze, surface wear from use **50.00**
- 10-3/4" d, dark brown Rockingham glaze, very tight hairline **45.00**
- 11-1/2" d, light brown Rockingham glaze, glaze chips, tight hairline **30.00**

Pitcher

- 8" h, applied brown Rockingham glaze, relief petal and column design, ftd base, minor rim chip **90.00**
- 8" h, brown and greenish blue sponge dec at top and bottom, three light brown accent bands around center, old surface chips, stone ping **150.00**
- 8-1/4" h, applied brown Rockingham glaze, relief peacock and palm trees **100.00**

Platter, 12-1/2" x 9-1/2", light brown Rockingham glaze, glaze wear, surface scratching.................................... **200.00**

Rolling pin, 8" l, very minor glaze age crazing....................................... **470.00**

Soap dish, 6-1/2" d, 1-3/4" d, applied Rockingham glaze, mottled dec created by finger prints in wet glaze before firing, tight hairline **125.00**

Spittoon, 8" d, applied Rockingham glaze, overall relief vine pattern **30.00**

Sugar bowl, cov, 4-1/2" h, applied brown Rockingham glaze, relief ribbed design **75.00**

Rolling pin, wooden handle through central bore, 15" h, **$315**. Photo courtesy of Alderfer Auction Co.

Teapot, 5" h, applied brown/green sponged glaze, orig lid, small glaze flake **110.00**

Turk's head 7-1/2" d, 2-3/4" h...... **165.00**

Wash board, 5" w, 12" l, mottled Rockingham glaze, c1880, wooden frame with dry worn surface **615.00**

Wash bowl and pitcher, 9-1/2" d bowl, 7-3/4" h pitcher, brown and blue sponged dec, brown stripe on pitcher **335.00**

Wine glass, footed, Rockingham glaze, darker accents at rim, c1870, 4" h, **$275**.

Wine glass, 4" h, Rockingham glaze, darker accents at rim, c1870 .... **275.00**

Zane Pottery

History: In 1921, Adam Reed and Harry McClelland bought the Peters and Reed Pottery in Zanesville, Ohio. The firm continued production of garden wares and introduced several new art lines: Sheen, Powder Blue, Crystalline, and Drip. The factory was sold in 1941 to Lawton Gonder.

Bowl

- 5" d, brown and blue **45.00**
- 6-1/2" d, blue, marked "Zanesware" **35.00**

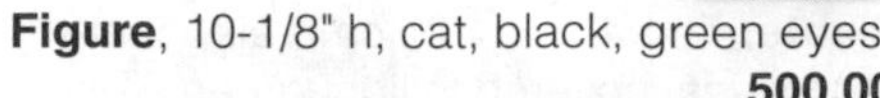

Figure, 10-1/8" h, cat, black, green eyes **500.00**

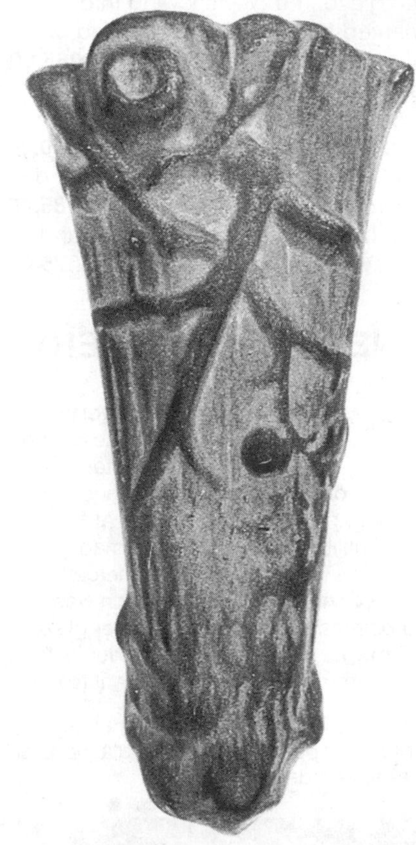

Wall pocket, Moss Aztec, 8-1/4" l, **$95**.

Jardinière, 34" h, green matte glaze, matching pedestal, artist sgd "Frank Ferreu" **375.00**

Jardiniére and pedestal base, green matte glaze, artist "Frank Ferreau," 34" h, **$375**.

Planter, 7-1/4" x 8-1/2", emb elephant ear leaves, covered in light green matte glaze, red clay showing through, unmarked, possibly Peters & Reed, 3" tight crack from rim **265.00**

Vase

5" h, green, cobalt blue drip glaze **30.00**

7" h, flowing medium green over dark forest green ground.................. **85.00**

8" h, ivory glaze, emb flowers and leaves...................................... **75.00**

ZANESVILLE POTTERY

LA MORO

History: Zanesville Art Pottery, one of several potteries located in Zanesville, Ohio, began production in 1900. At first, a line of utilitarian products was made; art pottery was introduced shortly thereafter. The major line was La Moro, which was hand painted and decorated under glaze. The firm was bought by S. A. Weller in 1920 and became known as Weller Plant No. 3.

Marks: The impressed block-print mark "La Moro" appears on the high-glazed and matte-glazed decorated ware.

Vase, baluster, speckled matte green glaze, unmarked, 12" h, **$230**. Photo courtesy of David Rago Auctions, Inc.

Bowl, 6-1/2" d, fluted edge, mottled blue glaze... **70.00**

Jardinière

7-1/8" h, 8-1/2" d, waisted cylindrical form, landscape scene, blue, green, and maroon matte glaze, c1908 .... **175.00**

8-1/4" h, ruffled rim, cream to light amber peony blossoms, shaded brown ground........................... **75.00**

Plate, 4-1/2" d, applied floral dec **25.00**

Vase, Standard Glaze, wild rose dec, marked "SO," factory-drilled, 4" d, 8-1/4" h, **$175**. Photo courtesy of David Rago Auctions, Inc.

Vase

8" h, pr, one pink, one green, both emb with single leaf, unmarked, green chipped........................ **150.00**

8-1/4" x 4", Standard Glaze, wild rose dec, marked "SO," factory-drilled **175.00**

12" h, baluster, speckled matte green glaze, unmarked **230.00**

ZSOLNAY POTTERY

History: Vilmos Zsolnay (1828-1900) assumed control of his brother's factory in Pécs, Hungary, in the mid-19th century. In 1899, Miklos, Vilmos's son, became manager. The firm still produces ceramic ware.

The early wares are highly ornamental, glazed, and have a cream-colored ground. Eosin glaze, a deep rich play of colors reminiscent of Tiffany's iridescent wares, received a gold medal at the 1900 Paris exhibition. Zsolnay Art Nouveau pieces show great creativity.

Marks: Originally, no trademark was used; but in 1878 the company began to use a blue mark depicting the five towers of the cathedral at Pécs. The initials "TJM" represent the names of Miklos's three children.

Bowl, 6-1/2" l, 2-1/2" h, sea shell shape, hp florals, gold highlights and edging, blue mark "Zsolnay Pecs," castle mark, "Patent," imp factory mark and numbers **160.00**

Cache pot, 13" d, young girls dance holding hands around stylized tree form, blue, pale silver, and pale lilac glazes **4,250.00**

Figure, dog, sitting, modern, **$90**. Photo courtesy of Jim and Susan Harran.

Candlesticks, pr, 6" x 5", two handles, mottled polychrome lustered glaze, medallion marks, 1" chip under rim **630.00**

Chalice, 6" h, 4 flower stems as handles attached to upper body, flowers and berries in relief as terminals, green and blue Eosin glazes, red int., form #5668, c1899, millennium factory mark, ext. rim chip repaired **1,650.00**

Coffee set, 8-1/2" h cov coffeepot, creamer, sugar, cake plate, six cups, saucers, and dessert plates, cobalt blue and gold trim, white ground **600.00**

Compote, 11" d, ribbed, four caryatids molded as angels supports, blue-green irid glaze.................................. **1,100.00**

Creamer, 6-1/2" l, fierce dragon handle **250.00**

Figure, nude woman standing with bathing urn and robe at her side, iridescent green-gold finish, marked "Zsolnay Hungary Hand Painted," 10-1/2", **$360**. Photo courtesy of Skinner, Inc.

Figure

Bears, pair, emerald green glaze, 7-1/2" l, 5" h **695.00**

Spaniel, artist sgd, 5" h **95.00**

Woman, 9-3/8" l, 4-3/4" w, 5-1/2" h, irid blue and green glaze, brown manufacturer's stamp "Zsolnay PECS Made in Hungary," repaired base chips....................................... **460.00**

Figure, musician, seated, traditional dress, earthenware, green and gold luster glaze, ovoid base with indistinct title/signature beside seat, Hungary, 20th C, 9" h, **$500**. Photo courtesy of Skinner, Inc.

Garden seat, 18-1/2" h, form #1105, c1882, wear to top surface, repairs to applied dec **1,850.00**

Jardinière, 16" l, ovoid, multicolored florals, protruding pierced roundels, cream ground, blue steep mark... **450.00**

Jug, 10-1/2" h, yellow glaze, worn gilt highlights, form #109, c1882........ **500.00**

Pitcher, 7-1/2" h, form #5064, red/maroon metallic Eosin ground, cream and pale brown flower dec, c1898, millennium factory mark **750.00**

Puzzle jug, 6-1/2" h, pierced roundels, irid dec, cream ground, castle mark, imp "Zsolnay" **195.00**

Figure, small girl feeding hen, iridescent green-gold glaze, gilt maker's stamps, Hungary, 20th C, 4-1/4" h, **$125**. Photo courtesy of Skinner, Inc.

Vase

3-3/4" h, all-over hp flower and leaf design, red, cream and gold-green metallic Eosin glazes, sgd "Flora Nici," dated Nov. 14, 1923 .... **1,200.00**

9" h, tapering reeded baluster, gold and cobalt blue irid finish....... **225.00**

9-1/4" h, quatrefoil rim, elongated neck, figure of woman wearing diaphanous dress seated on shoulder, irid gold, green and blue shaded glaze, irid stamped mark "Zsolnay PECS Made in Hungary" **460.00**

11" h, 5" d, classic shape, flaring rim, nacreous chartreuse glaze, stylized suns and flowers, gold stamp mark **495.00**

Vessel, 3-3/4", spherical, emb stylized leaves and trees, gold and green lustered glaze, c1970, stamped castle mark with Zsolnay Hungary **115.00**

Jug, earthenware, Japonesque, ovoid, short spout, dragon handle, mauve glazed ground, enamel decorated peonies, Hungary, late 19th C, 10-1/4" h, **$300**. Photo courtesy of Skinner, Inc.

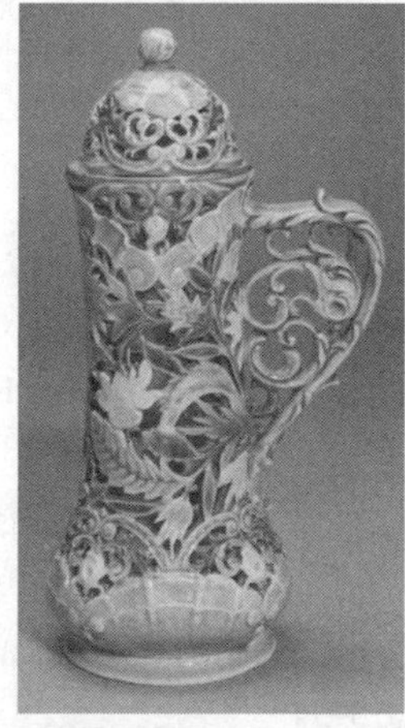

Pitcher, reticulated lid, handled cylindrical vessel, floral and foliate designs in gold, pink, blue, green, cream-colored glossy glaze, impressed and stamped marks, 12-1/2" h, crazing, **$600**. Photo courtesy of Skinner, Inc.

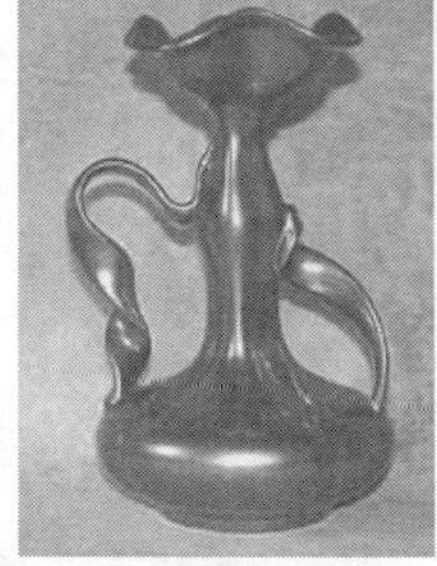

Vase, squat bulbous bowl, long neck, flared, ruffled rim, asymmetrical twisted handles, nacreous chartreuse glaze, gold printed stamp, 8-1/2" h, **$275**. Photo courtesy of Alderfer Auction Co.

Vase, classic shape, flaring rim, nacreous chartreuse glaze, stylized suns and flowers, gold stamp mark, 11" x 5", **$495**. Photo courtesy of David Rago Auctions.

Vessel, two-headed dragon, four legs, green, brown, gold, impressed mark, 7-3/4" h, 11-1/2" w, **$225**.

INDEX

D

E

F

G

P

Q

R

S

T

V

W

Y

Z

The Best of The Biggest and The Most Affordable Portable

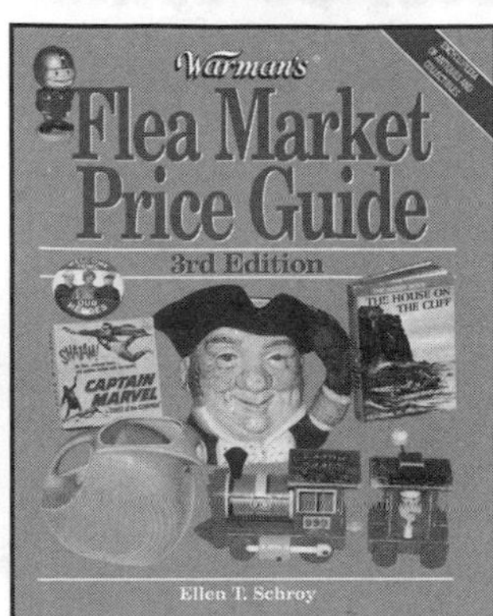

Warman's® Flea Market Price Guide
3rd Edition
by Ellen T. Schroy

Great deals lie ahead when you start your flea market adventures with this updated guide. Respected antiques author, Ellen Schroy, offers invaluable preparation tips, sound collecting advice, additional reference information, and completely updated pricing for today's hottest collectibles. Expanded coverage includes new categories such as Character Watches, Children's Records, Liberty Blue Dinnerware, Pet Equipment, and Lea Stein Jewelry.

Softcover • 8½ x 11 • 376 pages
800+ b&w photos • 8-page color section
Item# WFM3 • $21.99

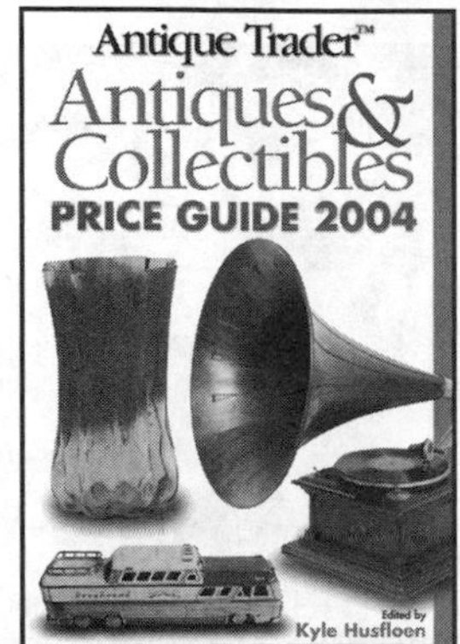

Antique Trader® Antiques & Collectibles Price Guide™ 2004
edited by Kyle Husfloen

You'll find more than 18,000 listings in this new, 20th edition. It includes coverage of 160 of the most popular collectibles categories, such as glass, furniture, breweriana, dolls, ceramics, and more. Confidently identify over 5,500 collectibles with this generously illustrated price guide. Use the thousands of photographs and detailed listings to identify and value just one single dusty piece, recovered from a dollar auction box, and this reliable guide will pay for itself!

Softcover • 6 x 9 • 1,168 pages
4,700 b&w photos • 16-page color section
Item# AT2004 • $17.99

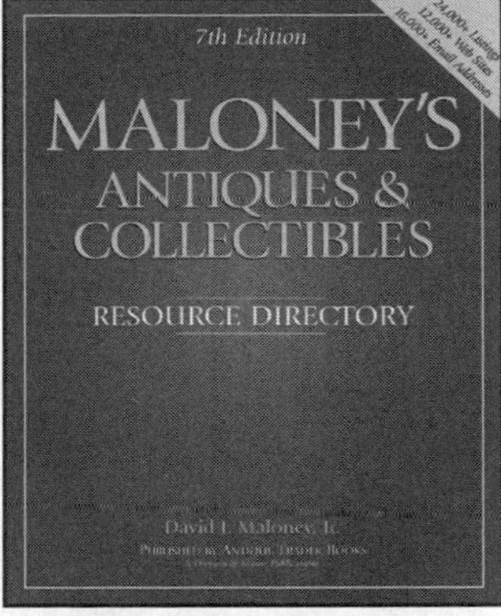

Maloney's Antiques & Collectibles Resource Directory, 7th Edition
by David J. Maloney Jr.

Where can I go to get parts for this? Find all the resource information you will need for buying, selling, researching, and enjoying antiques in one single reference-answers to questions such as where to go to match patterns. Now in its 7th edition, this comprehensive reference book boasts nearly 25,000 listings. Listings for collector clubs, specialty periodicals, dealers, collectors, experts, buyers, appraisers, parts suppliers, and much more.

Softcover • 8½ x 11
862 pages
Item# DMAL7 • $32.99

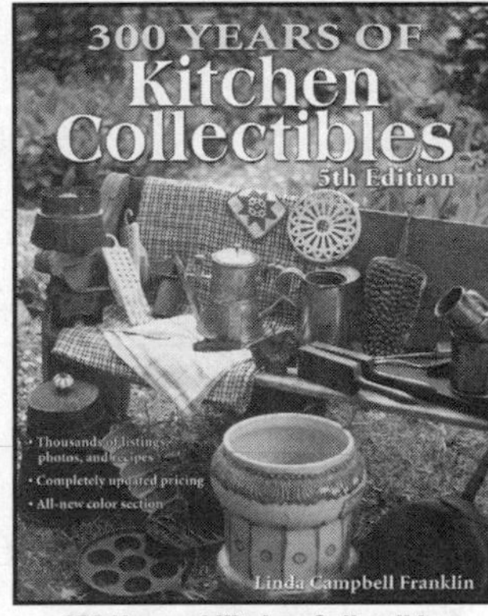

300 Years of Kitchen Collectibles
5th Edition
by Linda Campbell Franklin

Travel back to the kitchens of yesteryear with antique kitchen gadget expert Linda Campbell Franklin. You'll find listings for more than 7,000 items that dice, measure, filter, or whir in the kitchen, as well as classic recipes, helpful hints, and fascinating tidbits from trade catalogs and advertisements spanning three centuries. Features updated pricing, tips on collecting, buying and selling on the Internet, and more than 1,600 photos.

Softcover • 8½ x 11 • 896 pages
1,600+ photos & illus.
16-page color section
Item# KIT05 • $29.95

Antique Trader® Pottery & Porcelain Ceramics Price Guide
4th Edition
edited by Kyle Husfloen,
Contributing Editor Pat McPherson

No doubt you have an old pottery bowl or porcelain vase you'd love to learn more about. This comprehensive guide offers the perfect reference, with more than 4,000 pieces by dozens of makers described in detail. Hundreds of photos illustrate examples with every major type of ceramic from the 18th through the mid-20th century. Easy-to-use and packed with helpful tips.

Softcover • 6 x 9 • 784 pages
768 b&w photos • 16-page color section
Item# PPOR4 • $19.99

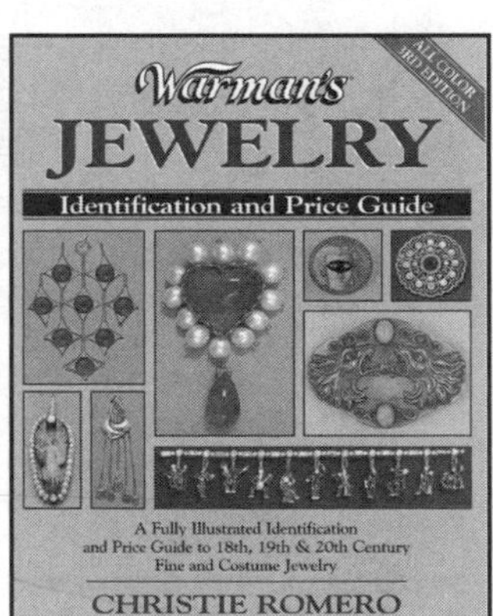

Warman's® Jewelry
3rd Edition
by Christie Romero

How old is it? Where was it made? Who made it? You'll find the answers to all the important questions regarding collectible jewelry in this fully revised, updated, full-color price and identification guide. With more than 1,000 listings of antique, period, and vintage collectible jewelry and 600 color photographs, this book is fascinating, informative, and valuable for anyone with an interest in jewelry.

Softcover • 8¼ x 10⅞
272 pages
600 color photos
Item# WJEW3 • $29.95

Looking for a portable and more affordable guide that you can take with you to shows, shops, auctions, or any other place your collecting takes you? Look no further! These convenient and "handy" 4½" x 5½" Warman's field guides are packed with 512 pages of photos and information on your favorite collectibles and are priced right at only $12.99 each. You'll have the information and images you need right at your fingertips-anywhere you go!

Warman's®
American Clocks Field Guide
Item# CLFG • $12.99

Warman's®
Antique Jewelry Field Guide
Item# ATFG • $12.95

Warman's®
Barbie® Doll Field Guide
Item# BDFG1 • $12.99

Warman's®
Bean Plush Field Guide
Item# BNSFG • $12.99

Warman's®
Depression Glass Field Guide
Item# DGPG1 • $12.95

Warman's®
Fishing Lures Field Guide
Item# FLFG1 • $12.99

Warman's®
Hummel Field Guide
Item# FGHUM • $12.99

Warman's®
Records Field Guide
Item# WRFG • $12.99

To order call **800-258-0929** **Offer ACB4**

Krause Publications, Offer ACB4
P.O. Box 5009, Iola WI 54945-5009
www.krausebooks.com

Please add $4.00 for the first book and $2.25 each additional for shipping & handling to U.S. addresses. Non-U.S. addresses please add $20.95 for the first book and $5.95 each additional.

Residents of CA, IA, IL, KS, NJ, PA, SD, TN, WI please add appropriate sales tax.

Warman's...Collectors Have Relied On Us for over 50 Years

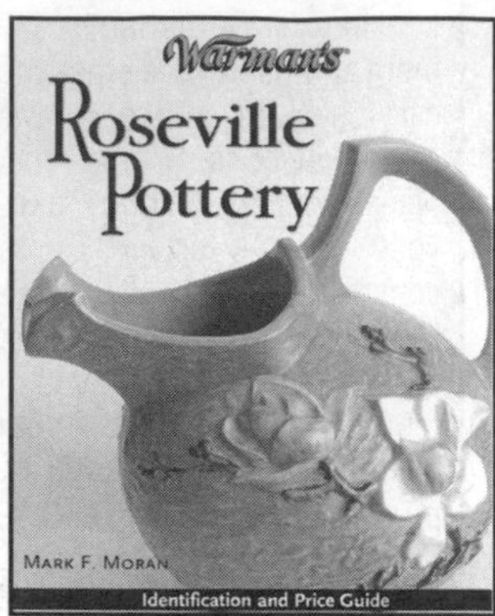

Warman's® Roseville Pottery
Identification and Price Guide
by Mark F. Moran

Captivating history, thorough condition reports, real-world prices, reproduction alerts-this sweeping guide is more than a standard price guide. Offering you the most accurate information, *Warman's® Roseville Pottery* includes detailed descriptions of the pieces listed, more than 1,200 color photographs displaying the brilliance of Roseville pottery, and true-to-life pricing reflecting the minor wear and damage of decades-old

Softcover • 8¼ x 10⅞ • 256 pages
1,200 color photos
Item# RVPT • $24.99

Warman's® Fiesta Ware
Identification & Price Guide
by Mark F. Moran

From the best of the old to the latest and greatest modern colors of the new, *Warman's® Fiesta Ware* provides comprehensive expert advice and up-to-date pricing for the line that lent distinction to the plainest table. With more than 1,000 eye-appealing photographs, this colorful story is well told by author Mark F. Moran.

Softcover • 8¼ x 10⅞
256 pages
1,200 color photos
Item# FWIP • $24.99

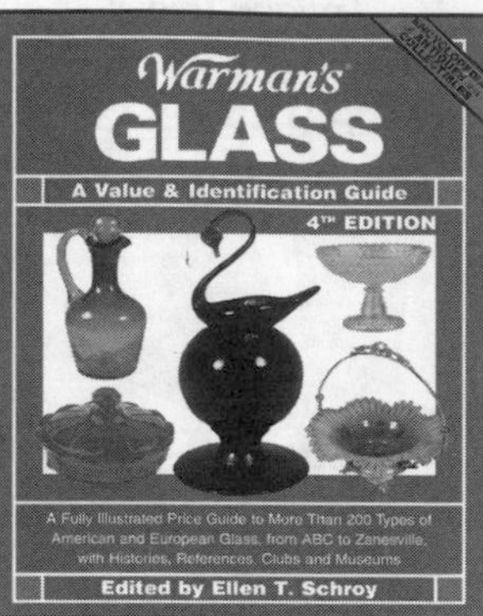

Warman's® Glass
A Value & Identification Guide, 4th Edition
edited by Ellen T. Schroy

This book is a great place to research that serving platter you've just inherited from your favorite aunt or those collectible Derby glasses your cousin thinks are worth a fortune. With the fourth edition of this best-selling guide, you'll find detailed descriptions and up-to-date prices for collectible glassware from more than 160 glass manufacturers. It covers American and European glass, including Carnival, Depression, Lalique, Pattern, Avon Dinnerware, Degenhart, Tiffany, and more.

Softcover • 8½ x 11 • 440 pages
200+ b&w photos • 8-page color section
Item# WGLA4 • $24.95

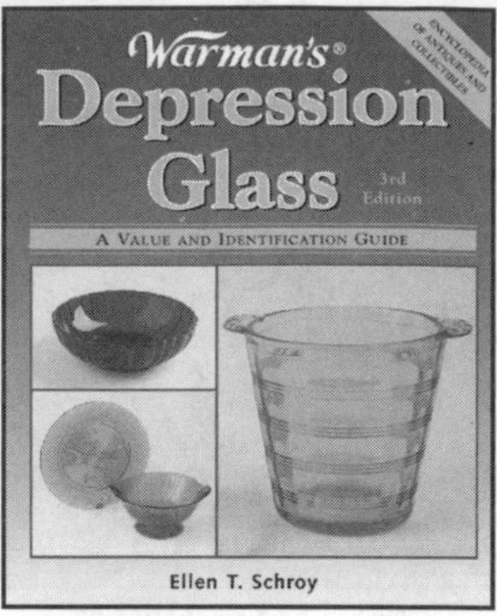

Warman's® Depression Glass
A Value and Identification Guide
3rd Edition
by Ellen T. Schroy

Discover how valuable Depression glass, once regarded as an inexpensive give-away, can be. Identify and value nearly 170 different Depression glass patterns with this completely updated 3rd edition. This comprehensive reference is expanded to include more than 10,000 current market values. Color photos and illustrations make identification of specific patterns, such as Cherryberry, Coin, Iris, Lorain, Sandwich, and Sierra easy.

Softcover • 8¼ x 10⅞ • 288 pages
170 patterns • 500 color photos
Item# WDG03 • $27.95

Warman's® Lalique
Identification and Price Guide
by Mark F. Moran

Complete with a biography of Rene Lalique, and an overview of his exquisite work, this book is the essential guide to Lalique glass. From the strikingly bold and original Art Nouveau and art deco styles of Rene Lalique, and those of Cristallerie Lalique after his death, this full-color guide presents the refined figurines, vases, and lamps as well as the clocks, ashtrays, and tableware and boudoir accessories complete with 350 large clear photographs of exquisite pieces and accurate up-to-date prices.

Softcover • 8¼ x 10⅞ • 176 pages
350 color photos
Item# WLALQ • $27.99

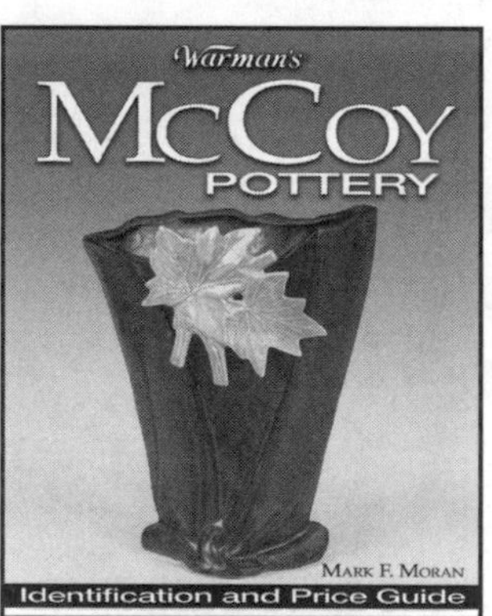

Warman's® McCoy Pottery
Identification and Price Guide
by Mark F. Moran

a wide variety of pieces produced since 1910 are all captured here in more than 1,500 color photographs lusciously illustrating one of the most cherished and popular pottery lines in American history. This new guide features an overview of what to look for, condition reports, and pricing information for these elaborately designed, attractively glazed decorative items, including jardinières, pedestals, and various other flower containers, umbrella stands, and sand jars.

Softcover • 8¼ x 10⅞ • 256 pages
1,200 color photos
Item# COYP • $24.99

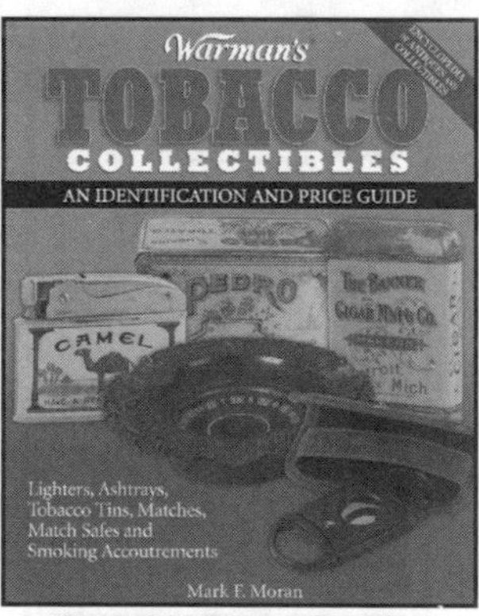

Warman's® Tobacco Collectibles
by Mark F. Moran

More than 3,000 tobacciana collectibles with more than 1,200 photos are listed and accurately priced in this new Warman's reference. Listings include prices for lighters, advertising, humidors, ashtrays, match safes, cigar cutters, pipes, cigarette cases, tobacco tins, strikers, match dispensers, snuff boxes, and much more. Find your pieces here and accurately value your collection or other items you're looking to buy or sell.

Softcover • 8½ x 11
352 pages
320 b&w photos
32-page color section
Item# WTC • $24.99

Warman's® Sterling Silver Flatware
Value & Identification Guide
by Mark F. Moran

Easily identify and accurately price thousands of sets of sterling silver flatware. Packed with photos and prices, this new reference lists sets from all major American manufacturers, as well as selected English and European manufacturers. You'll also receive information on prominent silversmiths, manufacturers, and patterns, with an overview of what to look for, condition reports, history, and descriptions.

Softcover • 8½ x 11 • 400 pages
1,200 b&w photos
16-page color section
Item# WSSF • $24.99

To order call **800-258-0929** **Offer ACB4**

Krause Publications, Offer ACB4
P.O. Box 5009, Iola WI 54945-5009
www.krausebooks.com

Please add $4.00 for the first book and $2.25 each additional for shipping & handling to U.S. addresses. Non-U.S. addresses please add $20.95 for the first book and $5.95 each additional.

Residents of CA, IA, IL, KS, NJ, PA, SD, TN, WI please add appropriate sales tax.